FORD TAURUS/MERCURY SABLE 1986-92 REPAIR MANUAL

Senior Vice President Ronald A. Hoxter

Publisher Kerry A. Freeman, S.A.E.
Editor-In-Chief Dean F. Morgantini, S.A.E.
Director of Manufacturing Mike D'Imperio
Production Manager W. Calvin Settle, Jr., S.A.E.
Senior Editor Richard J. Rivele, S.A.E.
Project Manager Martin J. Gunther
Editor Nick D'Andrea

CHILTON BOOK COMPANY
ONE OF THE ***DIVERSIFIED PUBLISHING COMPANIES,***
A PART OF ***CAPITAL CITIES/ABC, INC.***

Manufactured in USA

Chilton Way, Radnor, PA 19089
ISBN 0-8019-8251-0
Library of Congress Catalog Card No. 91-058817
1234567890 1098765432

Contents

Contents

SAFETY NOTICE

Proper service and repair procedures are vital to the safe, reliable operation of all motor vehicles, as well as the personal safety of those performing repairs. This manual outlines procedures for servicing and repairing vehicles using safe, effective methods. The procedures contain many NOTES, CAUTIONS and WARNINGS which should be followed along with standard safety procedures to eliminate the possibility of personal injury or improper service which could damage the vehicle or compromise its safety.

It is important to note that the repair procedures and techniques, tools and parts for servicing motor vehicles, as well as the skill and experience of the individual performing the work vary widely. It is not possible to anticipate all of the conceivable ways or conditions under which vehicles may be serviced, or to provide cautions as to all of the possible hazards that may result. Standard and accepted safety precautions and equipment should be used when handling toxic or flammable fluids, and safety goggles or other protection should be used during cutting, grinding, chiseling, prying, or any other process that can cause material removal or projectiles.

Some procedures require the use of tools specially designed for a specific purpose. Before substituting another tool or procedure, you must be completely satisfied that neither your personal safety, nor the performance of the vehicle will be endangered.

Although information in this manual is based on industry sources and is complete as possible at the time of publication, the possibility exists that some car manufacturers made later changes which could not be included here. While striving for total accuracy, Chilton Book Company cannot assume responsibility for any errors, changes or omissions that may occur in the compilation of this data.

PART NUMBERS

Part numbers listed in this reference are not recommendations by Chilton for any product by brand name. They are references that can be used with interchange manuals and aftermarket supplier catalogs to locate each brand supplier's discrete part number.

SPECIAL TOOLS

Special tools are recommended by the vehicle manufacturer to perform their specific job. Use has been kept to a minimum, but where absolutely necessary, they are referred to in the text by the part number of the tool manufacturer. These tools can be purchased, under the appropriate part number, from your Ford or Mercury dealer or regional distributor, or an equivalent tool can be purchased locally from a tool supplier or parts outlet. Before substituting any tool for the one recommended, read the SAFETY NOTICE at the top of this page.

ACKNOWLEDGMENTS

The Chilton Book Company expresses appreciation to Ford Motor Co.; Ford Parts and Service Division, Service Technical Communications Department, Dearborn, Michigan for their generous assistance.

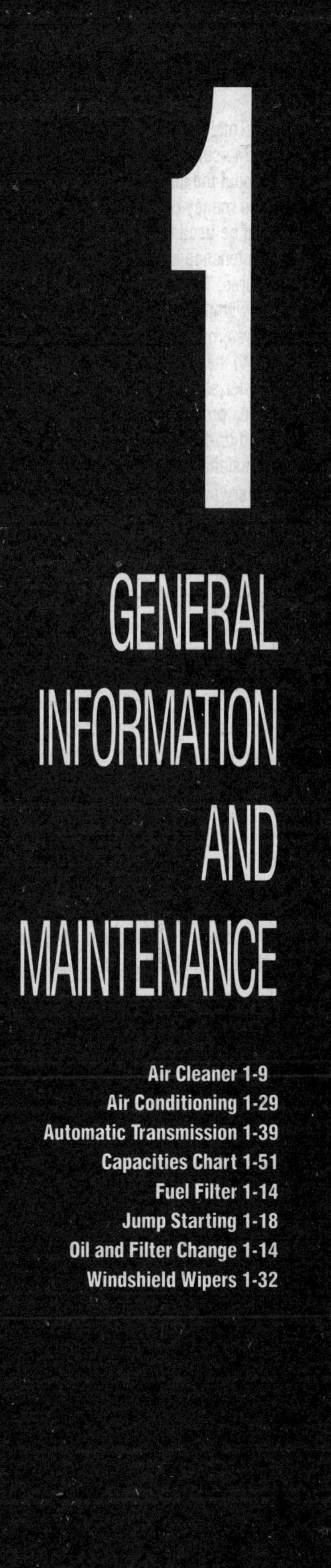

1 GENERAL INFORMATION AND MAINTENANCE

HOW TO USE THIS BOOK

Chilton's Total Car Care manual for Ford Taurus and Mercury Sable is intended to teach you more about the inner workings of your car and save you money on its upkeep. The first two Sections will be used the most, since they contain maintenance and tune-up information and procedures. The following Sections concern themselves with the more complex systems. Operating systems from engine through brakes are covered to the extent that we feel the average do-it-yourselfer should get involved as well as more complex procedures that will benefit both the advanced do-it-yourselfer mechanic as well as the professional.

A secondary purpose of this book is as a reference for owners who want to understand their car and/or their mechanics better. In this case, no tools at all are required.

Before attempting any repairs or service on your car, read through the entire procedure outlined in the appropriate Section. This will give you the overall view of what tools and supplies will be required. There is nothing more frustrating than having to walk to the bus stop on Monday morning because you were short one gasket on Sunday afternoon. So read ahead and plan ahead. Each operation should be approached logically and all procedures thoroughly understood before attempting any work. Some special tools that may be required can often be rented from local automotive jobbers or places specializing in renting tools and equipment. Check the yellow pages of your phone book.

All Sections contain adjustments, maintenance, removal and installation procedures, and overhaul procedures. When overhaul is not considered practical, we tell you how to remove the failed part and then how to install the new or rebuilt replacement. In this way, you at least save the labor costs. Backyard overhaul of some components is just not practical, but the removal and installation procedure is often simple and well within the capabilities of the average car owner.

Two basic mechanic's rules should be mentioned here. First, whenever the LEFT side of the car or engine is referred to, it is meant to specify the DRIVER'S side of the car. Conversely, the RIGHT side of the car means the PASSENGER'S side. Second, all screws and bolts are removed by turning counterclockwise, and tightened by turning clockwise, unless otherwise noted.

Safety is always the most important rule. Constantly be aware of the dangers involved in working on or around an automobile and take proper precautions to avoid the risk of personal injury or damage to the vehicle. See the section in this Section, Servicing Your Vehicle Safely, and the SAFETY NOTICE on the acknowledgment page before attempting any service procedures and pay attention to the instructions provided. There are 3 common mistakes in mechanical work:

1. Incorrect order of assembly, disassembly or adjustment. When taking something apart or putting it together, doing things in the wrong order usually just costs you extra time; however it CAN break something. Read the entire procedure before beginning disassembly. Do everything in the order in which the instructions say you should do it, even if you can't immediately see a reason for it. When you're taking apart something that is very intricate, you might want to draw a picture of how it looks when assembled at one point in order to make sure you get everything back in its proper position. We will supply exploded views whenever possible, but sometimes the job requires more attention to detail than an illustration provides. When making adjustments (especially tune-up adjustments), do them in order. One adjustment often affects another and you cannot expect satisfactory results unless each adjustment is made only when it cannot be changed by any other.

2. Overtorquing (or undertorquing) nuts and bolts. While it is more common for overtorquing to cause damage, undertorquing can cause a fastener to vibrate loose and cause serious damage, especially when dealing with aluminum parts. Pay attention to torque specifications and utilize a torque wrench in assembly. If a torque figure is not available remember that, if you are using the right tool to do the job, you will probably not have to strain yourself to get a fastener tight enough. The pitch of most threads is so slight that the tension you put on the wrench will be multiplied many times in actual force on what you are tightening. A good example of how critical torque is can be seen in the case of spark plug installation, especially where you are putting the plug into an aluminum cylinder head. Too little torque can fail to crush the gasket, causing leakage of combustion gases and consequent overheating of the plug and engine parts. Too much torque can damage the threads or distort the plug, which changes the spark gap at the electrode. Since more and more manufacturers are using aluminum in their engine and chassis parts to save weight, a torque wrench should be in any serious do-it-yourselfer's tool box.

There are many commercial chemical products available for ensuring that fasteners won't come loose, even if they are not torqued just right (a very common brand is Loctite®). If you're worried about getting something together tight enough to hold, but loose enough to avoid mechanical damage during assembly, one of these products might offer substantial insurance. Read the label on the package and make sure the product is compatible with the materials, fluids, etc. involved before choosing one.

3. Crossthreading. This occurs when a part such as a bolt is screwed into a nut or casting at the wrong angle and forced, causing the threads to become damaged. Crossthreading is more likely to occur if access is difficult. It helps to clean and lubricate fasteners, and to start threading with the part to be installed going straight in, using your fingers. If you encounter resistance, unscrew the part and start over again at a different angle until it can be inserted and turned several times without much effort. Keep in mind that many parts, especially spark plugs, use tapered threads so that gentle turning will automatically bring the part you're threading to the proper angle if you don't force it or resist a change in angle. Don't put a wrench on the part until it's been turned in a couple of times by hand. If you suddenly encounter resistance and the part has not seated fully, don't force it. Pull it back out and make sure it's clean and threading properly.

Always take your time and be patient; once you have some experience, working on your car will become an enjoyable hobby.

TOOLS AND EQUIPMENT

➧ SEE FIG. 1

Naturally, without the proper tools and equipment it is impossible to properly service your vehicle. It would be impossible to catalog each tool that you would need to perform each or every operation in this book. It would also be unwise for the amateur to rush out and buy an expensive set of tools an the theory that he may need one or more of them at sometime.

The best approach is to proceed slowly, gathering together a good quality set of those tools that are used most frequently. Don't be misled by the low cost of bargain tools. It is far better to spend a little more for better quality. Forged wrenches, 6- or 12-point sockets and fine tooth ratchets are by far preferable to their less expensive counterparts. As any good mechanic can tell you, there are few worse experiences than trying to work on a truck with bad tools. Your monetary savings will be far outweighed by frustration and mangled knuckles.

Certain tools, plus a basic ability to handle tools, are required to get started. A basic mechanics tool set, a torque wrench, and a Torx bits set. Torx bits are hexlobular drivers which fit both inside and outside on special Torx head fasteners used in various places on your vehicle.

Begin accumulating those tools that are used most frequently; those associated with routine maintenance and tune-up.

In addition to the normal assortment of screwdrivers and pliers you should have the following tools for routine maintenance jobs (your vehicle, depending on the model year, uses both SAE and metric fasteners):

1. SAE/Metric wrenches, sockets and combination open end/box end wrenches in sizes from 1/8 in. (3mm) to 3/4 in. (19mm); and a spark plug socket (13/16 in.) If possible, buy various length socket drive extensions. One break in this department is that the metric sockets available in the U.S. will all fit the ratchet handles and extensions you may already have (1/4 in., 3/8 in., and 1/2 in. drive).
2. Jackstands for support
3. Oil filter wrench
4. Oil filter spout for pouring oil
5. Grease gun for chassis lubrication
6. Hydrometer for checking the battery
7. A container for draining oil
8. Many rags for wiping up the inevitable mess.

In addition to the above items there are several others that are not absolutely necessary, but handy to have around. These include oil-dry (cat box litter works just as well and may be cheaper), a transmission funnel and the usual supply of lubricants, antifreeze and fluids, although these can be purchased as needed. This is a basic list for routine maintenance, but only your personal needs and desires can accurately determine your list of necessary tools.

The second list of tools is for tune-ups. While the tools involved here are slightly more sophisticated, they need not be outrageously expensive. There are several inexpensive tach/dwell meters on the market that are every bit as good for the average mechanic as a $100.00 professional model. Just be sure that it goes to at least 1,200–1,500 rpm on the tach scale and that it works on 4, 6 and 8 cylinder engines. A basic list of tune-up equipment could include:

1. Tach-dwell meter
2. Spark plug wrench
3. Timing light (a DC light that works from the vehicle's battery is best, although an AC light that plugs into 110V house current will suffice at some sacrifice in brightness)
4. Wire spark plug gauge/adjusting tools

In addition to these basic tools, there are several other tools and gauges you may find useful. These include:

1. A compression gauge. The screw-in type is slower to use, but eliminates the possibility of a faulty reading due to escaping pressure
2. A manifold vacuum gauge
3. A test light
4. An induction meter. This is used for determining whether or not there is current in a wire. These are handy for use if a wire is broken somewhere in a wiring harness.

Normally, the use of special factory tools is avoided for repair procedures, since these are not readily available for the do-it-yourself mechanic. When it is possible to perform the job with more commonly available tools, it will be pointed out, but occasionally, a special tool was designed to perform a specific function and should be used. Before substituting another tool, you should be convinced that neither your safety nor the performance of the vehicle will be compromised.

When a special tool is indicated, it will be referred to by the manufacturer's part number. Some special tools are available commercially from major tool manufacturers. Others for your car can be purchased from your Ford/Mercury dealer or from the Owatonna Tool Co., Owatonna, Minnesota 55060.

As a final note, you will probably find a torque wrench necessary for all but the most basic work. The beam type models are perfectly adequate, although the newer click (breakaway) type are more precise, and you don't have to crane your neck to see a torque reading in awkward situations. The breakaway torque wrenches are more expensive and should be recalibrated periodically.

Torque specification for each fastener will be given in the procedure in any case that a specific torque value is required. If no torque specifications are given, use the following values as a guide, based upon fastener size:

Bolts marked 6T

6mm bolt/nut — 5–7 ft. lbs.
8mm bolt/nut — 12–17 ft. lbs.
10mm bolt/nut — 23–34 ft. lbs.
12mm bolt/nut — 41–59 ft. lbs.
14mm bolt/nut — 56–76 ft. lbs.

Bolts marked 8T

6mm bolt/nut — 6–9 ft. lbs.
8mm bolt/nut — 13–20 ft. lbs.
10mm bolt/nut — 27–40 ft. lbs.
12mm bolt/nut — 46–69 ft. lbs.
14mm bolt/nut — 75–101 ft. lbs.

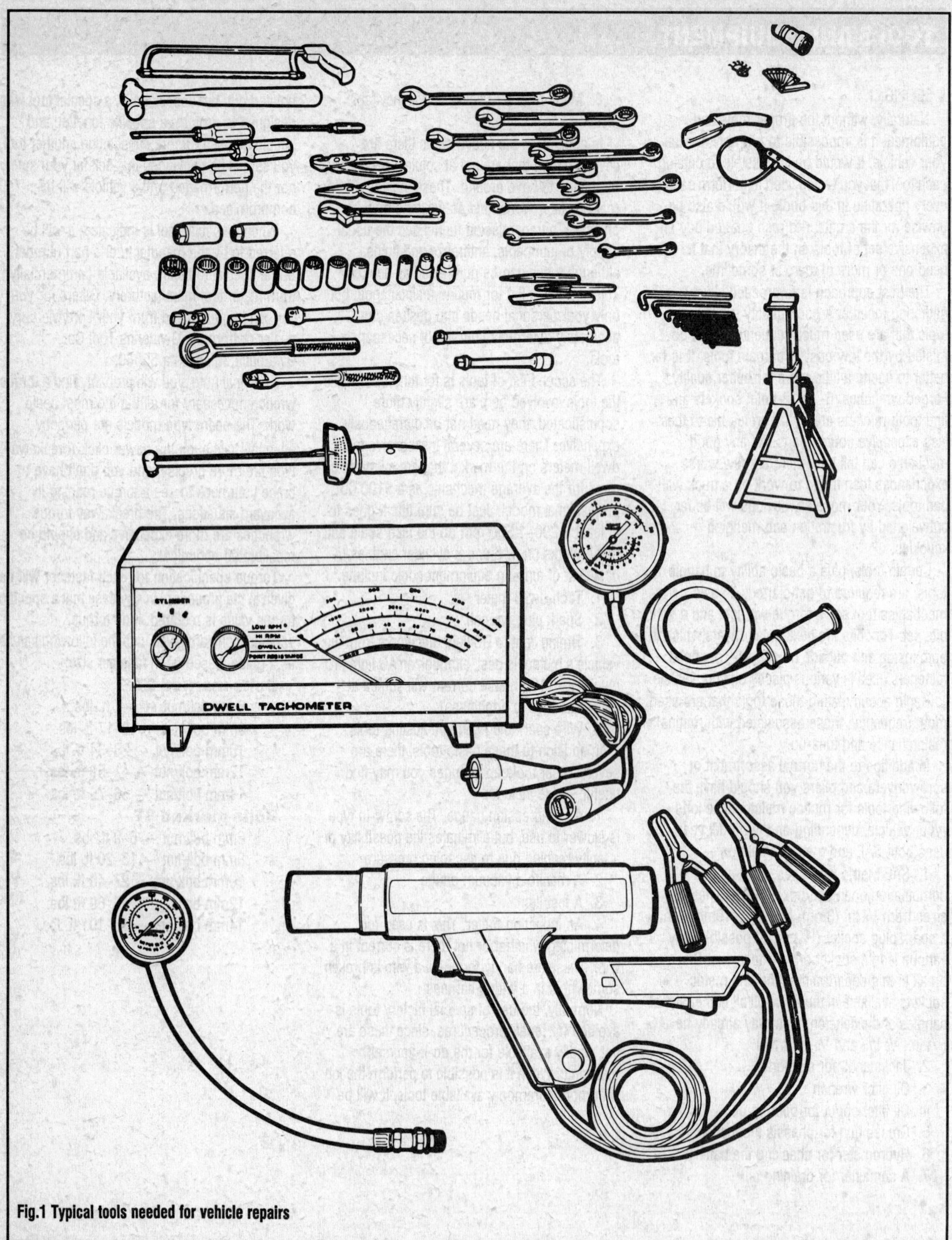

Fig.1 Typical tools needed for vehicle repairs

SERVICING YOUR VEHICLE SAFELY

It is virtually impossible to anticipate all of the hazards involved with automotive maintenance and service but care and common sense will prevent most accidents.

The rules of safety for mechanics range from "don't smoke around gasoline," to "use the proper tool for the job." The trick to avoid injuries is to develop safe work habits and take every possible precaution.

Do's

- Do keep a fire extinguisher and first aid kit within easy reach.
- Do wear safety glasses or goggles when cutting, drilling, grinding or prying. If you wear glasses for the sake of vision, then they should be made of hardened glass that can serve also as safety glasses, or wear safety goggles over your regular glasses.
- Do wear safety glasses whenever you work around the battery. Batteries contain sulphuric acid. In case of contact with the eyes or skin, flush the area with water or a mixture of water and baking soda and get medical attention immediately.
- Do use safety stands for any under-car service. Jacks are for raising vehicles; safety stands are for making sure the vehicle stays raised until you want it to come down. Whenever the vehicle is raised, block the wheels remaining on the ground and set the parking brake.
- Do use adequate ventilation when working with any chemicals. Asbestos dust resulting from brake lining wear can cause cancer.
- Do disconnect the negative battery cable when working on the electrical system. The primary ignition system can contain up to 40,000 volts.
- Do follow manufacturer's directions whenever working with potentially hazardous materials. Both brake fluid and antifreeze are poisonous if taken internally.
- Do properly maintain your tools. Loose hammerheads, mushroomed punches and chisels, frayed or poorly grounded electrical cords, excessively worn screwdriver, spread wrenches (open end), cracked sockets can cause accidents.
- Do use the proper size and type of tool for the job being done.
- Do when possible, pull on a wrench handle rather than push on it, and adjust your stance to prevent a fall.
- Do be sure that adjustable wrenches are tightly adjusted on the nut or bolt and pulled so that the face is on the side of the fixed jaw.
- Do select a wrench or socket that fits the nut or bolt. The wrench or socket should sit straight, not cocked.
- Do strike squarely with a hammer to avoid glancing blows.
- Do set the parking brake and block the drive wheels if the work requires that the engine is running.

Don'ts

- Don't run an engine in a garage or anywhere else without proper ventilation — EVER! Carbon monoxide is poisonous. It is absorbed by the body 400 times faster than oxygen. It takes a long time to leave the human body and you can build up a deadly supply of it in you system by simply breathing in a little every day. You may not realize you are slowly poisoning yourself. Always use power vents, windows, fans or open the garage doors.
- Don't work around moving parts while wearing a necktie or other loose clothing. Short sleeves are much safer than long, loose sleeves. Hard-toed shoes with neoprene soles protect your toes and give a better grip on slippery surfaces. Jewelry such as watches, fancy belt buckles, beads or body adornment of any kind is not safe working around a car. Long hair should be hidden under a hat or cap.
- Don't use pockets for tool boxes. A fall or bump can drive a screwdriver deep into you body. Even a wiping cloth hanging from the back pocket can wrap around a spinning shaft or fan.
- Don't smoke when working around gasoline, cleaning solvent or other flammable material.
- Don't smoke when working around the battery. When the battery is being charged, it gives off explosive hydrogen gas.
- Don't use gasoline to wash your hands. There are excellent soaps available. Gasoline may contain lead, and lead can enter the body through a cut, accumulating in the body until you are very ill. Gasoline also removes all the natural oils from the skin so that bone dry hands will suck up oil and grease.
- Don't service the air conditioning system unless you are equipped with the necessary tools and training. Do wear safety glasses, the refrigerant, is extremely cold and when exposed to the air, will instantly freeze any surface it comes in contact with, including your eyes. Although the refrigerant is normally nontoxic, it becomes a deadly poisonous gas in the presence of an open flame. One good whiff of the vapors from burning refrigerant can be fatal.

MODEL IDENTIFICATION

The vehicle model year identification can be confirmed by locating the 10th position of the VIN code and using the vehicle identification Chart.

SERIAL NUMBER IDENTIFICATION

Vehicle

The official vehicle identification (serial) number (used for title and registration purposes) is stamped on a metal tab fastened to the instrument panel and visible through the driver's side of the windshield from the outside. The vehicle identification (serial) number contains a 17 digit number. The number is used for warranty identification of the vehicle and indicates: manufacturer, type of restraint system, line, series, body type, engine, model year, and consecutive unit number.

VEHICLE IDENTIFICATION CHART

It is important for servicing and ordering parts to be certain of the vehicle and engine identification. The VIN (vehicle identification number) is a 17 digit number visible through the windshield on the driver's side of the dash and contains the vehicle and engine identification codes. The tenth digit indicates model year and the eighth digit indicates engine code. It can be interpreted as follows:

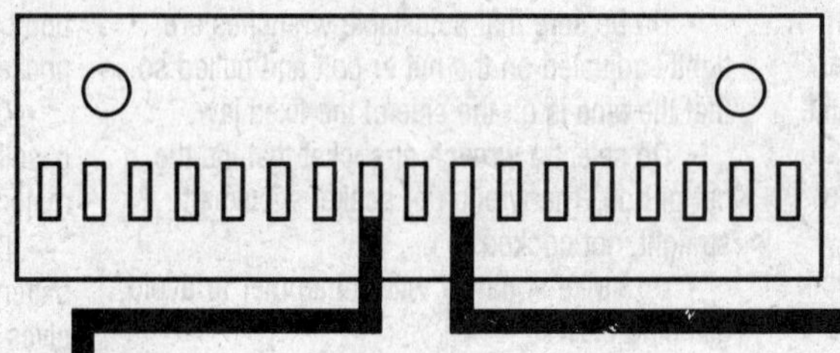

Engine Code						Model Year	
Code	**Liter**	**Cu. In. (cc)**	**Cyl.**	**Fuel Sys.**	**Eng. Mfg.**	**Code**	**Year**
D (86–90)	2.5	153	4	CEFI	FMCO	H	1986
D (1991)	2.5	153	4	SEFI	FMCO	I	1987
U (86–90)	3.0	182	6	EFI	FMCO	J	1988
U (91–92)	3.0	182	6	SEFI	FMCO	K	1989
Y	3.0	182	6	SEFI	Yamaha	L	1990
4 (88)	3.8	232	6	EFI	FMCO	M	1991
4 (89–92)	3.8	232	6	SEFI	FMCO	N	1992

CFI—Central fuel injection
EFI—Electronic fuel injection
SEFI—Sequential electronic fuel injection
FMCO—Ford Motor Company

Certification Label

➧ SEE FIG. 2

The Vehicle Certification Label is found on the left door lock face panel or door pillar. The upper half of the label contains the name of the manufacturer, month and year of manufacture, gross weight rating, gross axle weight, and the certification statements pertinent. The certification also repeats the VIN number and gives the color code and the accessories found on the car.

Engine

The vehicle engine identification can be located on the 8th position of the VIN code.

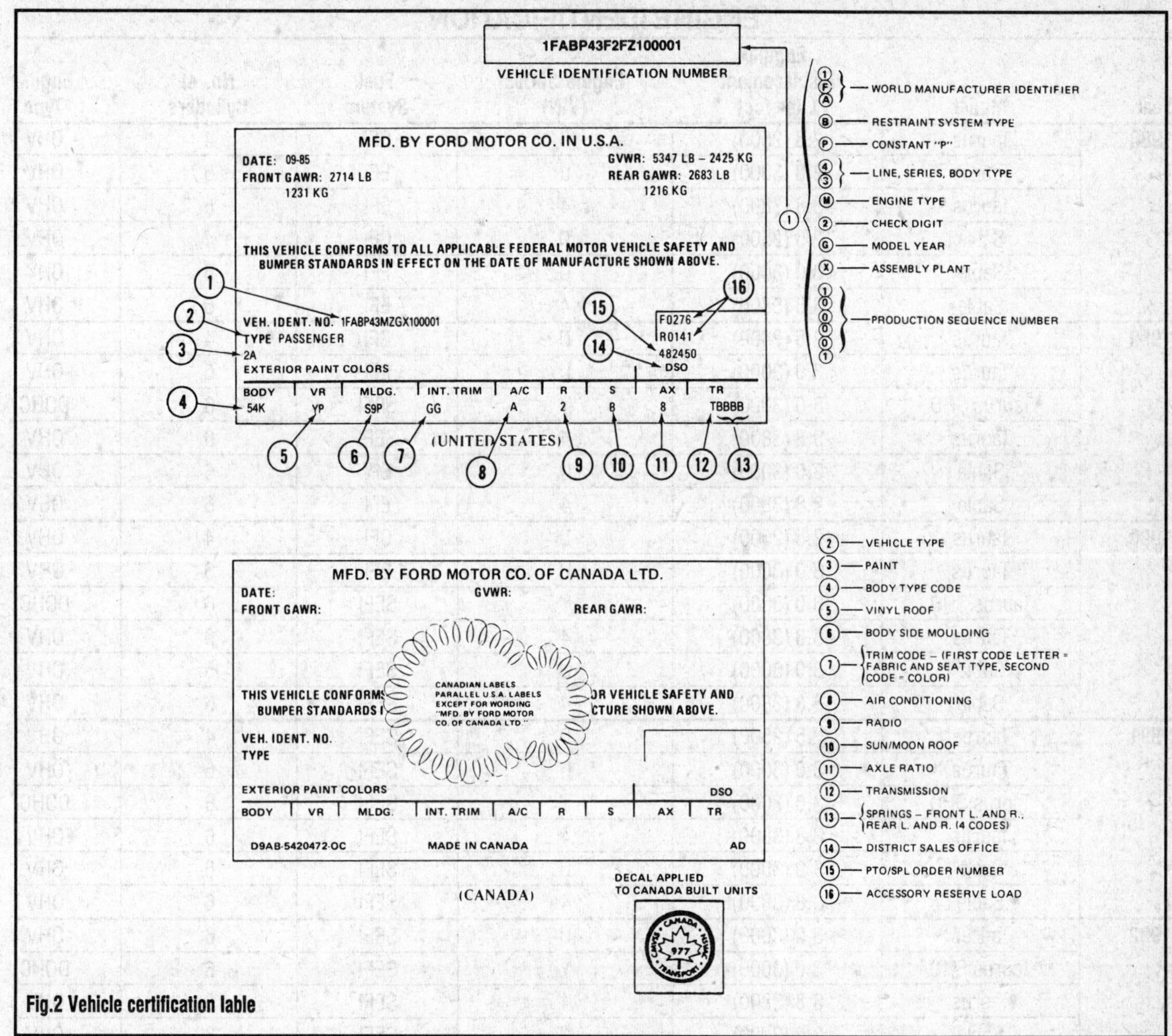

Fig.2 Vehicle certification lable

ENGINE IDENTIFICATION

Year	Model	Engine Displacement Liter (cc)	Engine Series (VIN)	Fuel System	No. of Cylinders	Engine Type
1986	Taurus	2.5 (2500)	D	CFI	4	OHV
	Taurus	3.0 (3000)	U	EFI	6	OHV
	Sable	2.5 (2500)	D	CFI	4	OHV
	Sable	3.0 (3000)	U	EFI	6	OHV
1987	Taurus	2.5 (2500)	D	CFI	4	OHV
	Taurus	3.0 (3000)	U	EFI	6	OHV
	Sable	2.5 (2500)	D	CFI	4	OHV
	Sable	3.0 (3000)	U	EFI	6	OHV

ENGINE IDENTIFICATION

Year	Model	Engine Displacement Liter (cc)	Engine Series (VIN)	Fuel System	No. of Cylinders	Engine Type
1988	Taurus	2.5 (2500)	D	CFI	4	OHV
	Taurus	3.0 (3000)	U	EFI	6	OHV
	Taurus	3.8 (3800)	4	EFI	6	OHV
	Sable	2.5 (2500)	D	CFI	4	OHV
	Sable	3.0 (3000)	U	EFI	6	OHV
	Sable	3.8 (3800)	4	EFI	6	OHV
1989	Taurus	2.5 (2500)	D	CFI	4	OHV
	Taurus	3.0 (3000)	U	EFI	6	OHV
	Taurus SHO	3.0 (3000)	Y	SEFI	6	DOHC
	Taurus	3.8 (3800)	4	SEFI	6	OHV
	Sable	3.0 (3000)	U	EFI	6	OHV
	Sable	3.8 (3800)	4	EFI	6	OHV
1990	Taurus	2.5 (2500)	D	CFI	4	OHV
	Taurus	3.0 (3000)	U	EFI	6	OHV
	Taurus SHO	3.0 (3000)	Y	SEFI	6	DOHC
	Taurus	3.8 (3800)	4	SEFI	6	OHV
	Sable	3.0 (3000)	U	SEFI	6	OHV
	Sable	3.8 (3800)	4	SEFI	6	OHV
1991	Taurus	2.5 (2500)	D	SEFI	4	OHV
	Taurus	3.0 (3000)	U	SEFI	6	OHV
	Taurus SHO	3.0 (3000)	Y	SEFI	6	DOHC
	Taurus	3.8 (3800)	4	SEFI	6	OHV
	Sable	3.0 (3000)	U	SEFI	6	OHV
	Sable	3.8 (3800)	4	SEFI	6	OHV
1992	Taurus	3.0 (3000)	U	SEFI	6	OHV
	Taurus SHO	3.0 (3000)	Y	SEFI	6	DOHC
	Taurus	3.8 (3800)	4	SEFI	6	OHV
	Sable	3.0 (3000)	U	SEFI	6	OHV
	Sable	3.8 (3800)	4	SEFI	6	OHV

Transaxle

➧ SEE FIG. 41–42

The transaxle code is located on the bottom edge of the Vehicle Certification Label for vehicles equipped with the manual transaxle. The identification tag for vehicles equipped with the ATX automatic transaxle is located under one of the valve body cover retaining bolts. The identification tag for vehicles equipped with the AXOD and AXOD-E automatic transaxles is located on top of the converter housing.

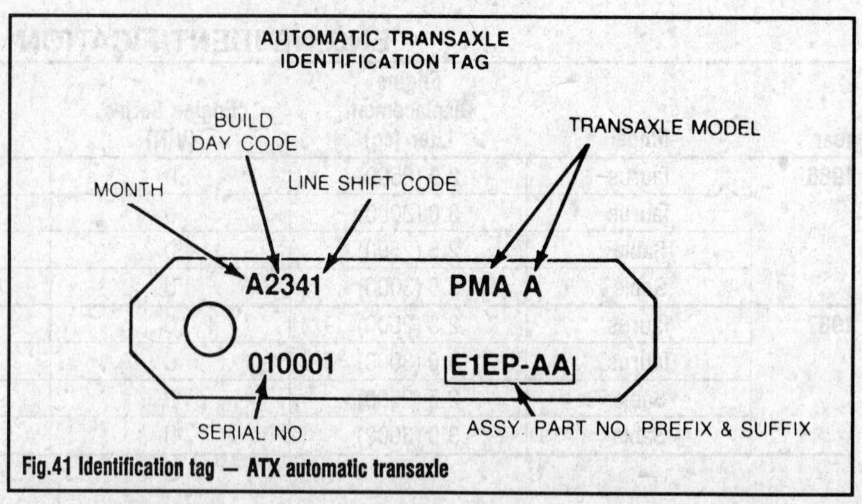

Fig.41 Identification tag — ATX automatic transaxle

Fig.42 Identification tag — AXOD and AXOD-E automatic transaxles

ROUTINE MAINTENANCE

Air Cleaner

➧ SEE FIG. 3–6

The air cleaner element should be replaced every 30 months or 30,000 miles. More frequent changes are necessary if the car is operated in dusty conditions.

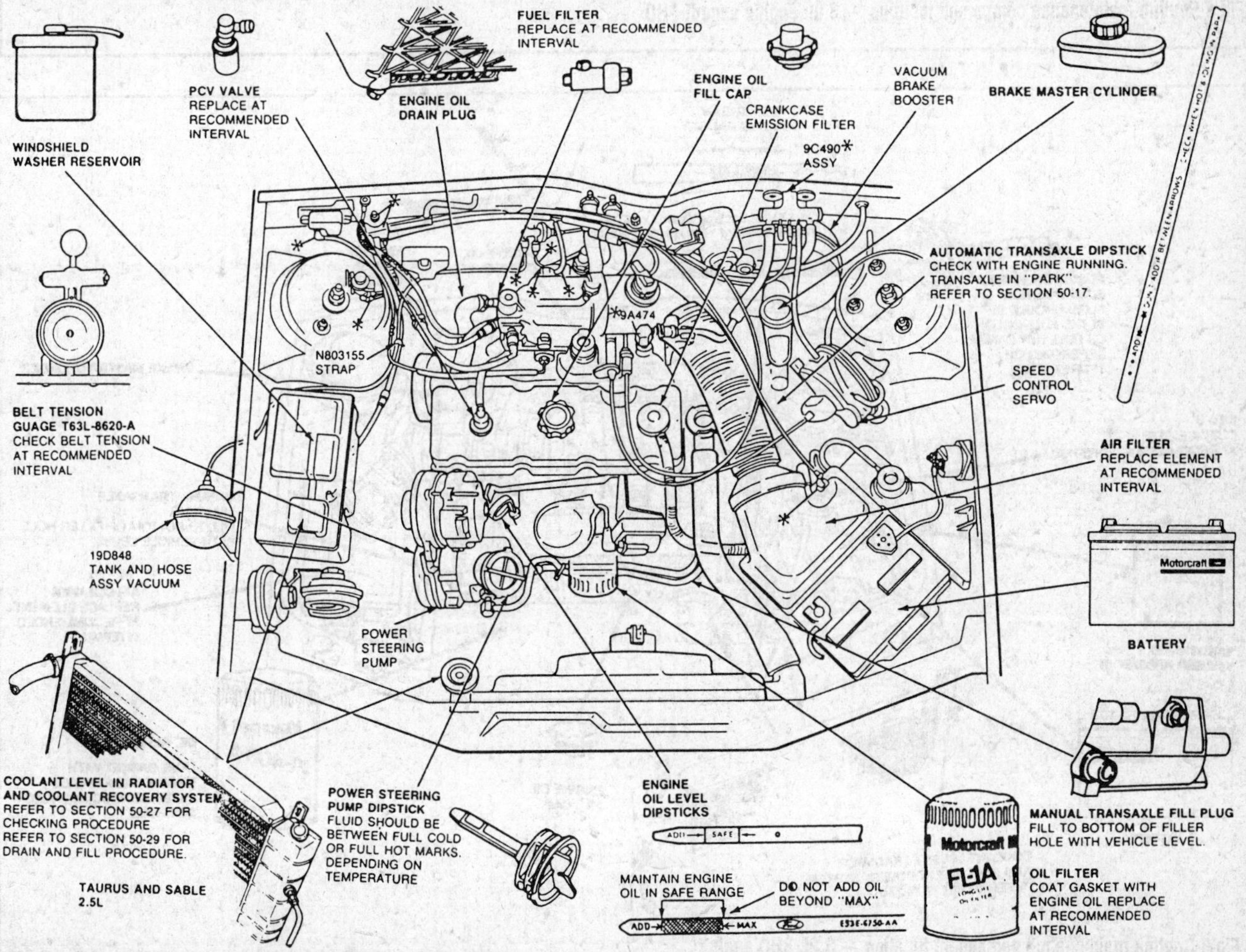

FUEL FILTER
REPLACE AT RECOMMENDED INTERVAL
PCV VALVE
REPLACE AT RECOMMENDED INTERVAL
ENGINE OIL DRAIN PLUG
ENGINE OIL FILL CAP
CRANKCASE EMISSION FILTER
9C490* ASSY
VACUUM BRAKE BOOSTER
BRAKE MASTER CYLINDER
WINDSHIELD WASHER RESERVOIR
AUTOMATIC TRANSAXLE DIPSTICK
CHECK WITH ENGINE RUNNING. TRANSAXLE IN "PARK". REFER TO SECTION 50-17.
*9A474
N803155 STRAP
SPEED CONTROL SERVO
BELT TENSION GUAGE T63L-8620-A
CHECK BELT TENSION AT RECOMMENDED INTERVAL
AIR FILTER
REPLACE ELEMENT AT RECOMMENDED INTERVAL
19D848 TANK AND HOSE ASSY VACUUM
Motorcraft
BATTERY
POWER STEERING PUMP
COOLANT LEVEL IN RADIATOR AND COOLANT RECOVERY SYSTEM
REFER TO SECTION 50-27 FOR CHECKING PROCEDURE
REFER TO SECTION 50-29 FOR DRAIN AND FILL PROCEDURE.
POWER STEERING PUMP DIPSTICK
FLUID SHOULD BE BETWEEN FULL COLD OR FULL HOT MARKS. DEPENDING ON TEMPERATURE
ENGINE OIL LEVEL DIPSTICKS
ADD SAFE
MAINTAIN ENGINE OIL IN SAFE RANGE
DO NOT ADD OIL BEYOND "MAX"
ADD MAX E93E-6750-AA
MANUAL TRANSAXLE FILL PLUG
FILL TO BOTTOM OF FILLER HOLE WITH VEHICLE LEVEL.
Motorcraft FL1A
OIL FILTER
COAT GASKET WITH ENGINE OIL REPLACE AT RECOMMENDED INTERVAL
TAURUS AND SABLE 2.5L

Fig.3 Routine maintenance component location — 2.5L engine

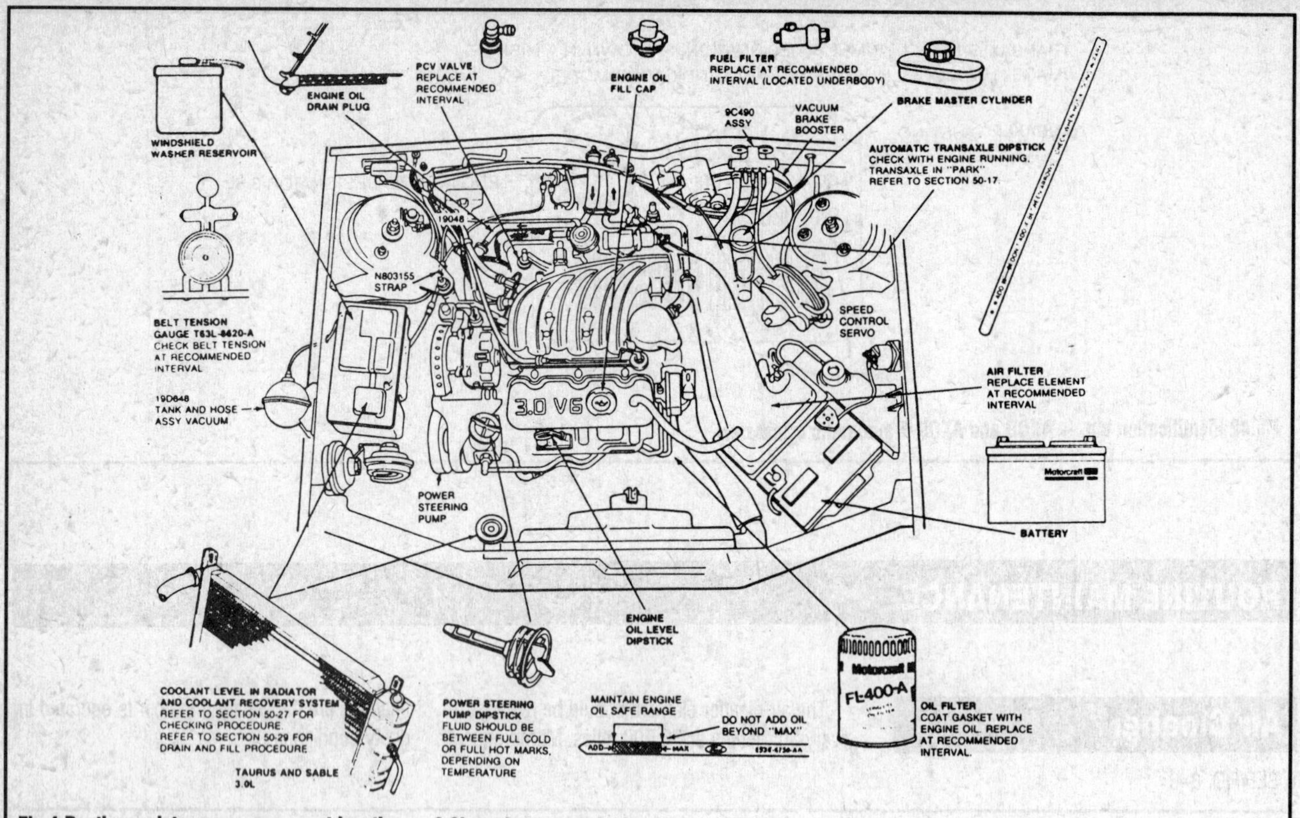

Fig.4 Routine maintenance component location – 3.0L engine except SHO

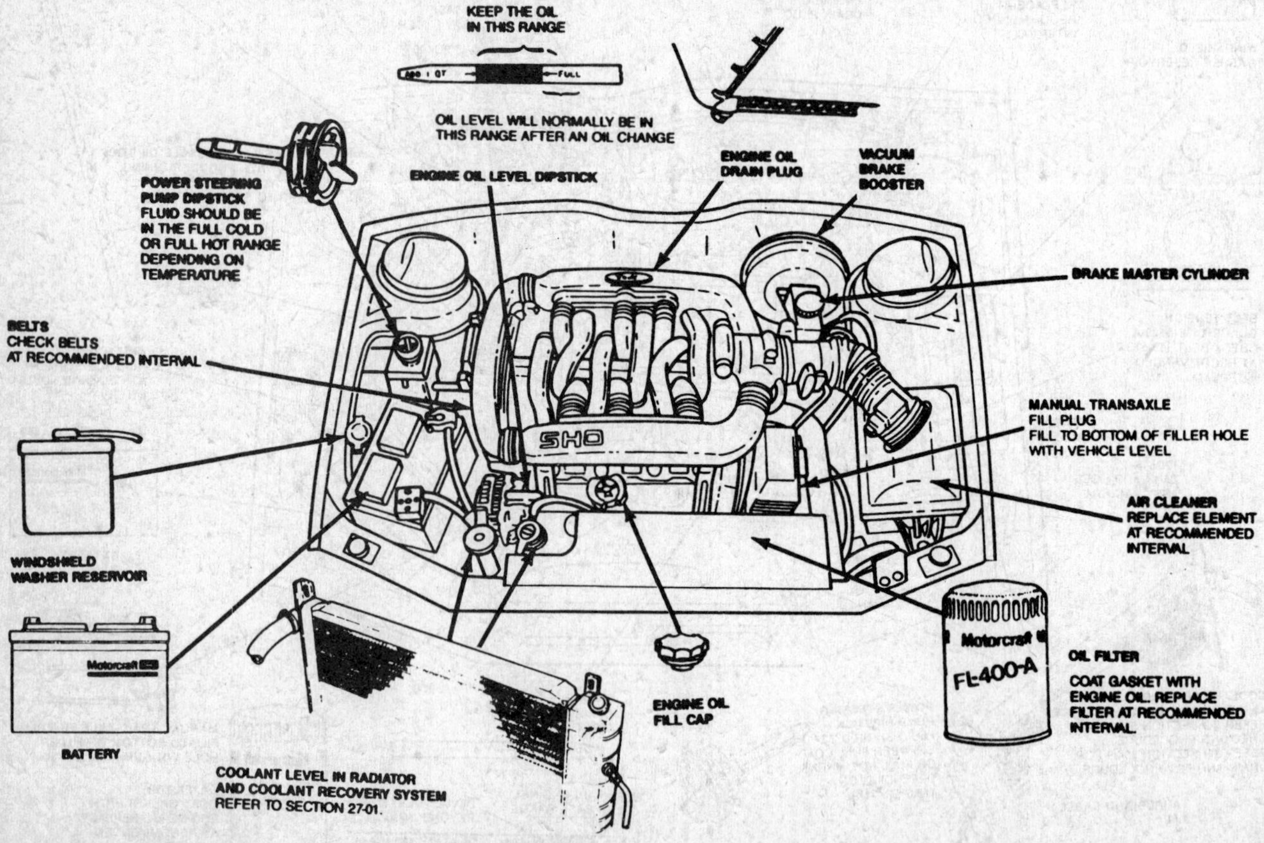

Fig.5 Routine maintenance component location – 3.0L SHO engine

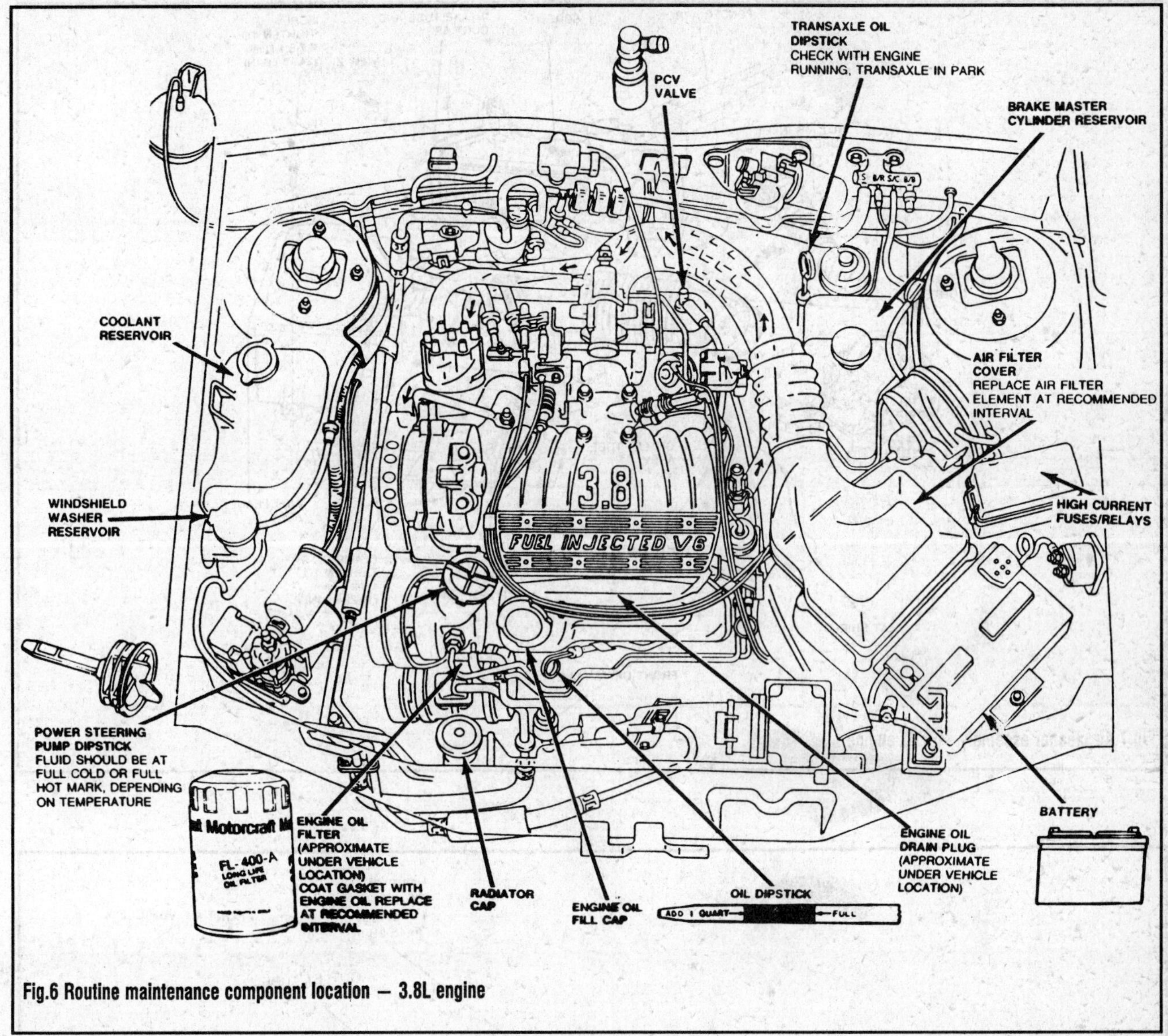

Fig.6 Routine maintenance component location — 3.8L engine

REMOVAL & INSTALLATION

➧ SEE FIG. 7–10

1. Loosen the air cleaner outlet tube clamp and disconnect the tube.
2. Disconnect the hot air tube (2.5L engine only), PCV inlet tube and the zip tube.
3. Disconnect the cold weather modulator vacuum hose at the temperature sensor (2.5L engine only).
4. Remove the air cleaner and cover retaining screws and the air cleaner assembly.
5. Inspect the inside surfaces of the cover for traces of dirt leakage past the cleaner element as a result of damaged seals, incorrect element or inadequate tightness of the cover retaining clips.
6. Remove the air cleaner element and clean the inside surfaces of the cleaner tray and cover.
7. Install a new air cleaner element, install the cover and assembly. Tighten the retaining clamp to 12–20 ft. lbs.
8. Reconnect all vacuum and air duct hoses and lines.
9. Start the engine and check for vacuum leaks around both ends of the tube from the air cleaner to the throttle body.

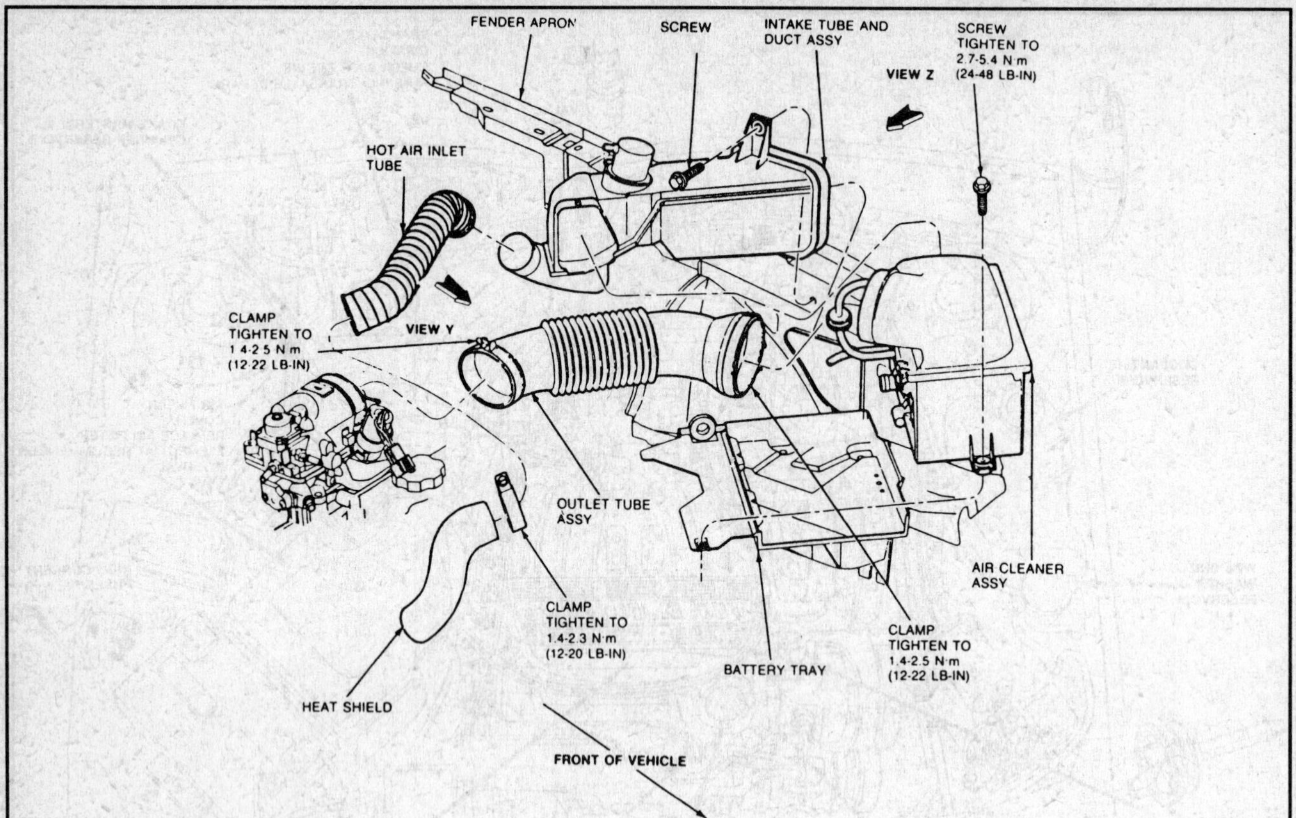

Fig.7 Air cleaner assembly — 2.5L engine

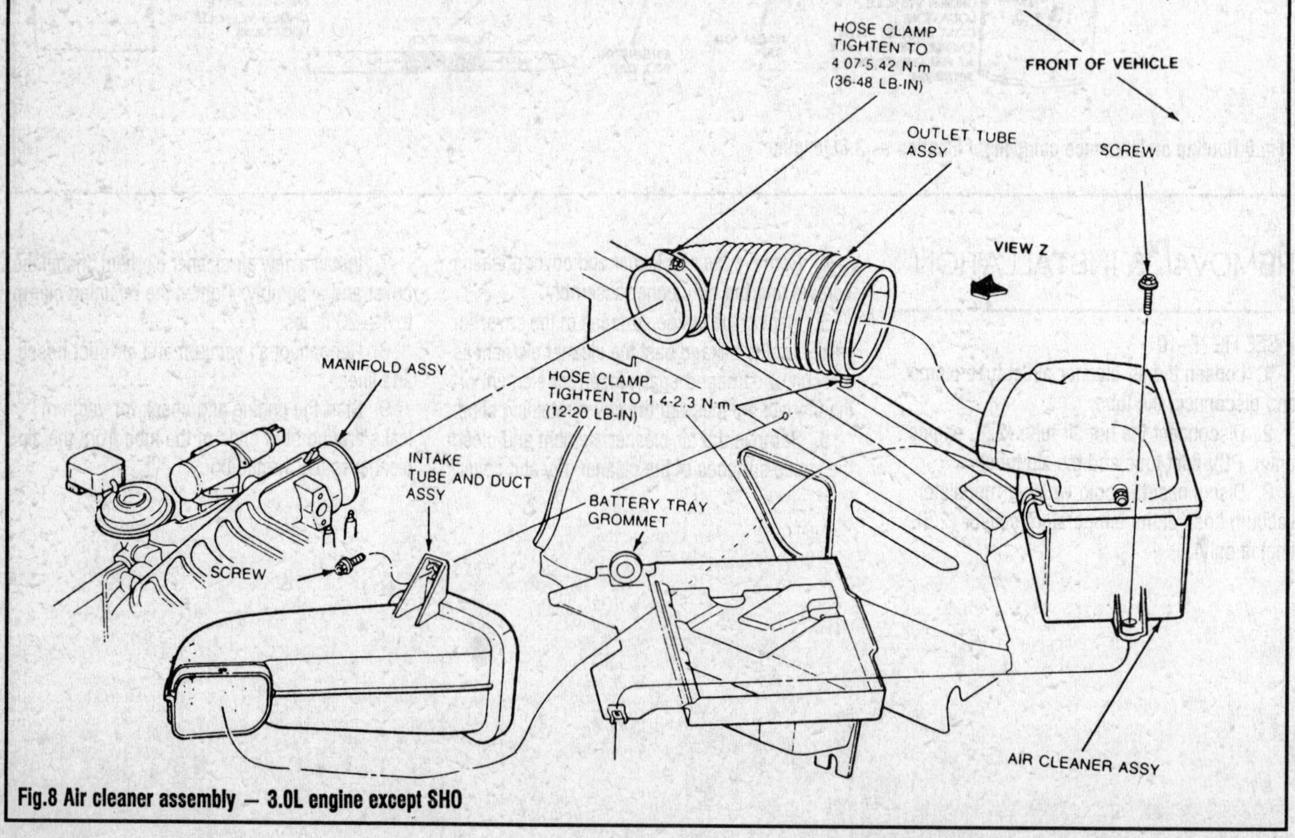

Fig.8 Air cleaner assembly — 3.0L engine except SHO

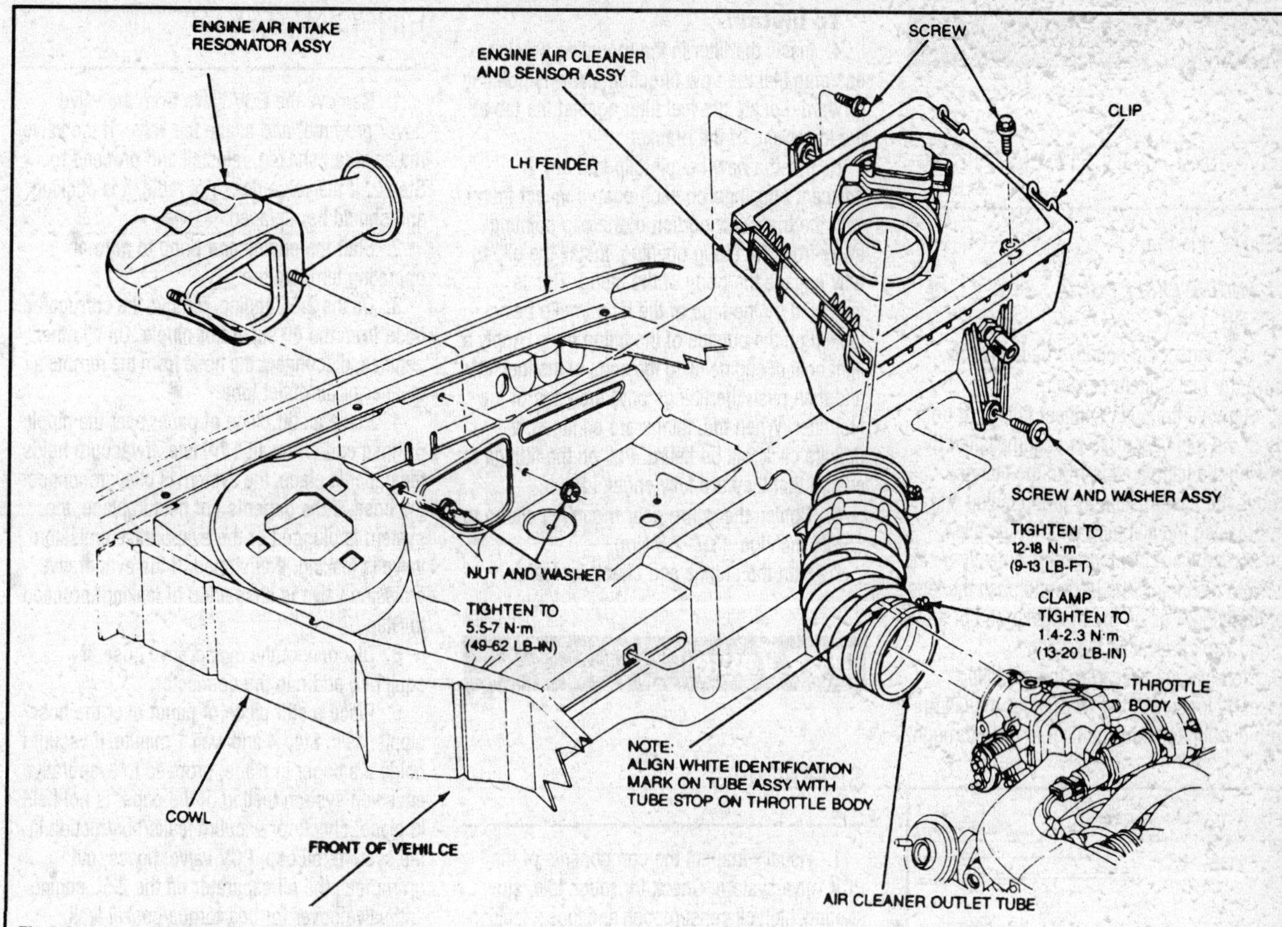

ENGINE AIR INTAKE RESONATOR ASSY
ENGINE AIR CLEANER AND SENSOR ASSY
SCREW
CLIP
LH FENDER
SCREW AND WASHER ASSY
TIGHTEN TO 12-18 N·m (9-13 LB-FT)
NUT AND WASHER
TIGHTEN TO 5.5-7 N·m (49-62 LB-IN)
CLAMP TIGHTEN TO 1.4-2.3 N·m (13-20 LB-IN)
THROTTLE BODY
NOTE: ALIGN WHITE IDENTIFICATION MARK ON TUBE ASSY WITH TUBE STOP ON THROTTLE BODY
COWL
FRONT OF VEHILCE
AIR CLEANER OUTLET TUBE

Fig.9 Air cleaner assembly — 3.0L SHO engine

SCREW
INLET TUBE AND DUCT ASSY
OUTLET TUBE ASSY
AIR CLEANER ASSY
SCREW
2 REQ'D TIGHTEN TO
(24-48 LB-IN)
CLAMP TIGHTEN TO
(12-22 LB-IN)
PCV HOSE ASSY
MANIFOLD ASSY FUEL CHARGER
BATTERY TRAY GROMMET
FRONT OF VEHICLE

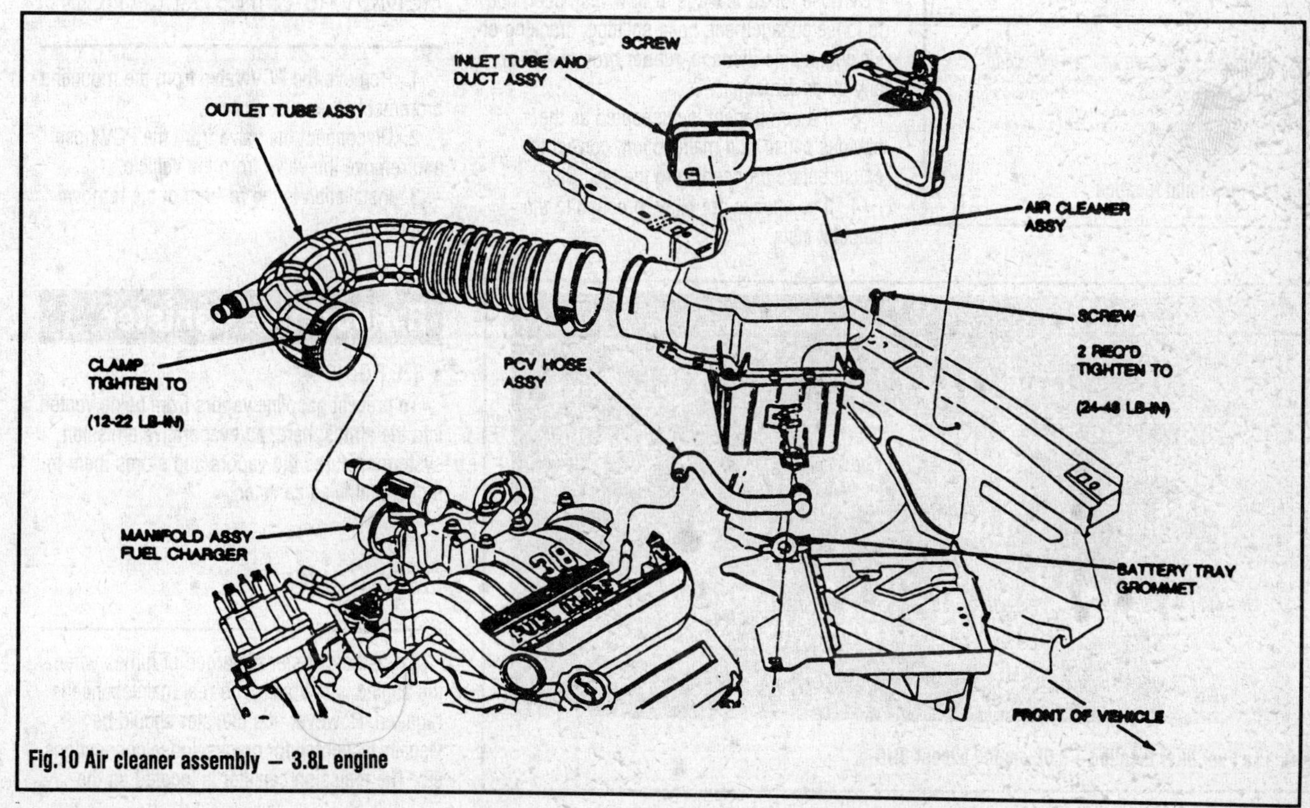

Fig.10 Air cleaner assembly — 3.8L engine

Fuel Filter

REMOVAL & INSTALLATION

➧ SEE FIG. 11–11a

3.0L ENGINE EXCEPT SHO

➧ SEE FIG. 17a

1. Disconnect the negative battery cable. Relieve the fuel system pressure.
2. Remove the push connect fittings at both ends of the fuel filter. This is accomplished by removing the hairpin clips from the fittings. Remove the hairpin clips by first bending and then breaking the shipping tabs on the clips. Then spread the 2 clip legs approximately 1/8 in. (3mm) to disengage the body and push the legs into the fitting. Pull on the triangular end of the clip and work it clear of the fitting.
3. Remove the filter from the mounting bracket by loosening the worm gear mounting clamp enough to allow the filter to pass through.

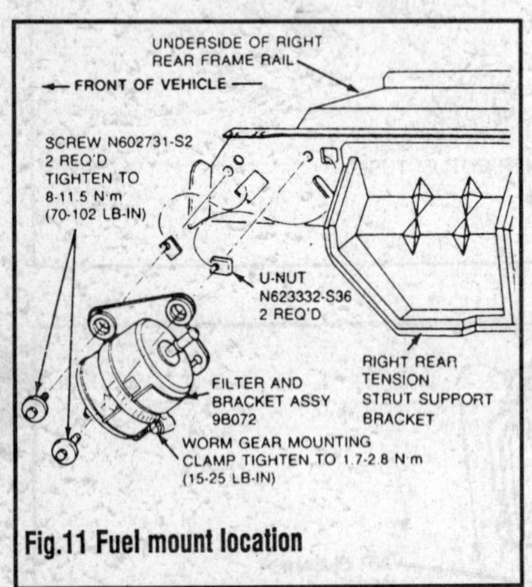

Fig.11 Fuel mount location

To Install:

4. Install the filter in the mounting bracket, ensuring that the flow direction arrow is pointing forward. Locate the fuel filter against the tab at the lower end of the bracket.
5. Insert a new hairpin clip into any 2 adjacent openings on each push connect fitting, with the triangular portion of the clip pointing away from the fitting opening. Install the clip to fully engage the body of the fitting. This is indicated by the legs of the hairpin clip being locked on the outside of the fitting body. Apply a light coat of engine oil to the ends of the fuel filter and then push the fittings onto the ends of the fuel filter. When the fittings are engaged, a definite click will be heard. Pull on the fittings to ensure that they are fully engaged.
6. Tighten the worm gear mounting clamp to 15–25 inch lbs. (1.7–2.8 Nm).
7. Start the engine and check for leaks.

FIG. 11a Fuel filter location—3.0L engine except SHO

PCV Valve

SERVICING

1. Visually inspect the components of the PCV valve system. Check for rough idle, slow starting, high oil consumption and loose, leaking, clogged or damaged hoses.
2. Check the fresh air supply hose and the PCV hose for air leakage or flow restriction due to loose engagement, hose splitting, cracking or kinking, nipple damage, rubber grommet fit or any other damage.
3. If a component is suspected as the obvious cause of a malfunction, correct the cause before proceeding to the next Step.
4. If all checks are okay, proceed to the pinpoint tests.

PINPOINT TESTS

1. Remove the PCV valve from the valve cover grommet and shake the valve. If the valve rattles when shaken, reinstall and proceed to Step 2. If the valve does not rattle, it is sticking and should be replaced.
2. Start the engine and bring to normal operating temperature.
3. On the 2.5L engine, remove the corrugated hose from the oil separator nipple. On all other engines, disconnect the hose from the remote air cleaner or air outlet tube.
4. Place a stiff piece of paper over the nipple or hose end and wait 1 minute. If vacuum holds the paper in place, the system is okay; reconnect the hose. If the paper is not held in place, the system is plugged or the evaporative emission valve is leaking, if equipped. If the evaporative emission valve is suspected of leaking, proceed to Step 5.
5. Disconnect the evaporative hose, if equipped and cap the connector.
6. Place a stiff piece of paper over the hose/nipple, as in Step 4 and wait 1 minute. If vacuum holds the paper in place, proceed to evaporative emission system testing. If the paper is not held in place, check for vacuum leaks/obstruction in the system: oil cap, PCV valve, hoses, cut grommets, the oil separator on the 2.5L engine and valve cover for bolt torque/gasket leak.

REMOVAL & INSTALLATION

1. Remove the PCV valve from the mounting grommet in the valve cover.
2. Disconnect the valve from the PCV hose and remove the valve from the vehicle.
3. Installation is the reverse of the removal procedure.

Evaporative Canister

➧ SEE FIG. 43–47

To prevent gasoline vapors from being vented into the atmosphere, an evaporative emission system captures the vapors and stores them in a charcoal filled canister.

SERVICING

Since the canister is purged of fumes when the engine is operating, no real maintenance is required. However, the canister should be visually inspected for cracks, loose connections, etc. The emission canister is located on the

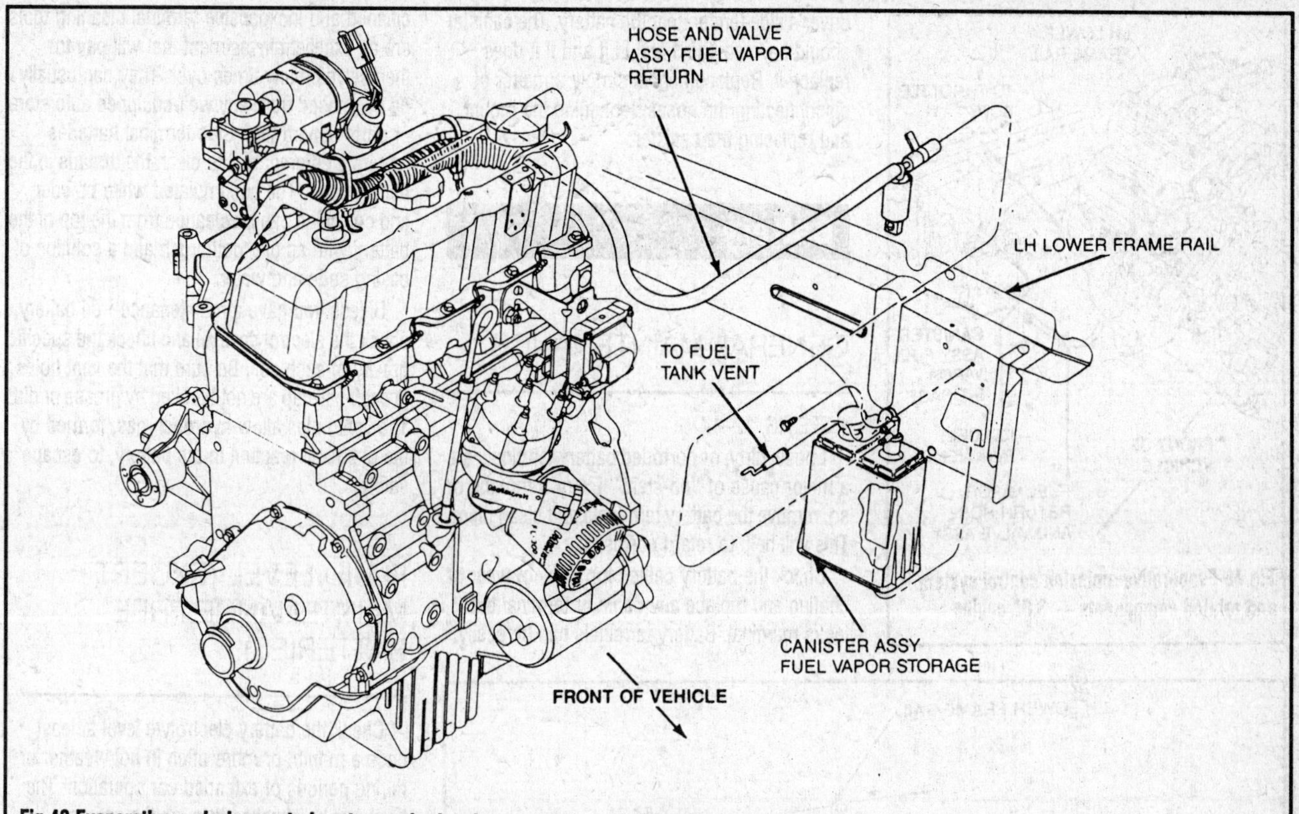

HOSE AND VALVE
ASSY FUEL VAPOR
RETURN
LH LOWER FRAME RAIL
TO FUEL
TANK VENT
CANISTER ASSY
FUEL VAPOR STORAGE
FRONT OF VEHICLE

Fig.43 Evaporative emission control system and related components — 2.5L engine

FRONT
CANISTER ASSY
FUEL VAPOR STORAGE
HEAD LAMP
OPENING
FUEL VAPOR
RETURN HOSE
ASSY
HOSE AND VALVE
ASSY FUEL VAPOR
RETURN
RADIATOR SUPPORT

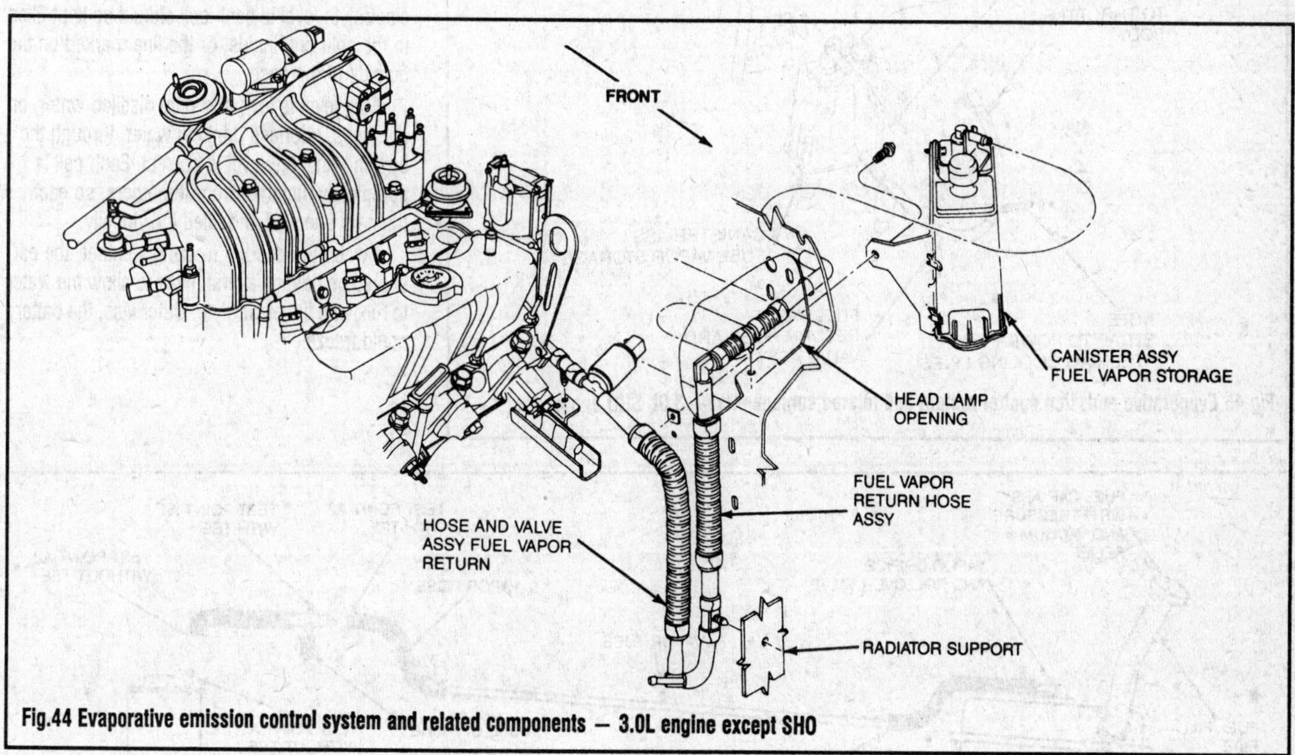

Fig.44 Evaporative emission control system and related components — 3.0L engine except SHO

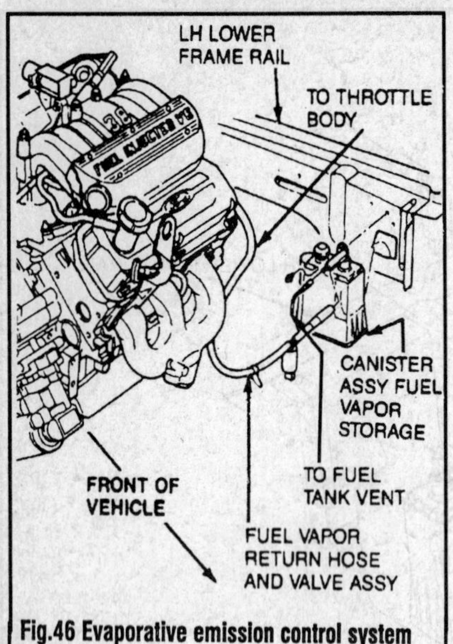

Fig.46 Evaporative emission control system and related components – 3.8L engine

driver's side fender near the battery. The canister should have no liquid fuel in it and if it does replace it. Replacement is simply a matter of disconnecting the hoses, loosening the mount and replacing the canister.

Battery

GENERAL MAINTENANCE

➧ SEE FIG. 12–14

Loose, dirty, or corroded battery terminals are a major cause of "no-start." Every 3 months or so, remove the battery terminals and clean them. This will help to retard corrosion.

Check the battery cables for signs of wear or chafing and replace any cable or terminal that looks marginal. Battery terminals can be easily cleaned and inexpensive terminal cleaning tools are an excellent investment that will pay for themselves many times over. They can usually be purchased from any well-equipped auto store or parts department. Side terminal batteries require a different tool to clean the threads in the battery case. The accumulated white powder and corrosion can be cleaned from the top of the battery with an old toothbrush and a solution of baking soda and water.

Unless you have a maintenance-free battery, check the electrolyte level and check the specific gravity of each cell. Be sure that the vent holes in each cell cap are not blocked by grease or dirt. The vent holes allow hydrogen gas, formed by the chemical reaction in the battery, to escape safely.

FLUID LEVEL (EXCEPT MAINTENANCE FREE BATTERIES)

Check the battery electrolyte level at least once a month, or more often in hot weather or during periods of extended car operation. The level can be checked through the case on translucent polypropylene batteries; the cell caps must be removed on other models. The electrolyte level in each cell should be kept filled to the split ring inside, or the line marked on the outside of the case.

If the level is low, add only distilled water, or colorless, odorless drinking water, through the opening until the level is correct. Each cell is completely separate from the others, so each must be checked and filled individually.

If water is added in freezing weather, the car should be driven several miles to allow the water to mix with the electrolyte. Otherwise, the battery could freeze.

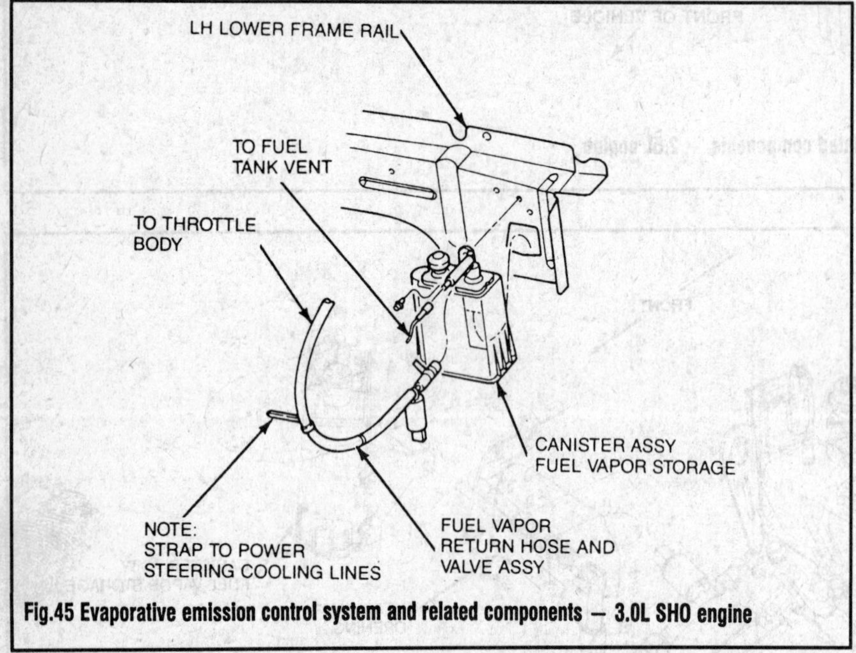

Fig.45 Evaporative emission control system and related components – 3.0L SHO engine

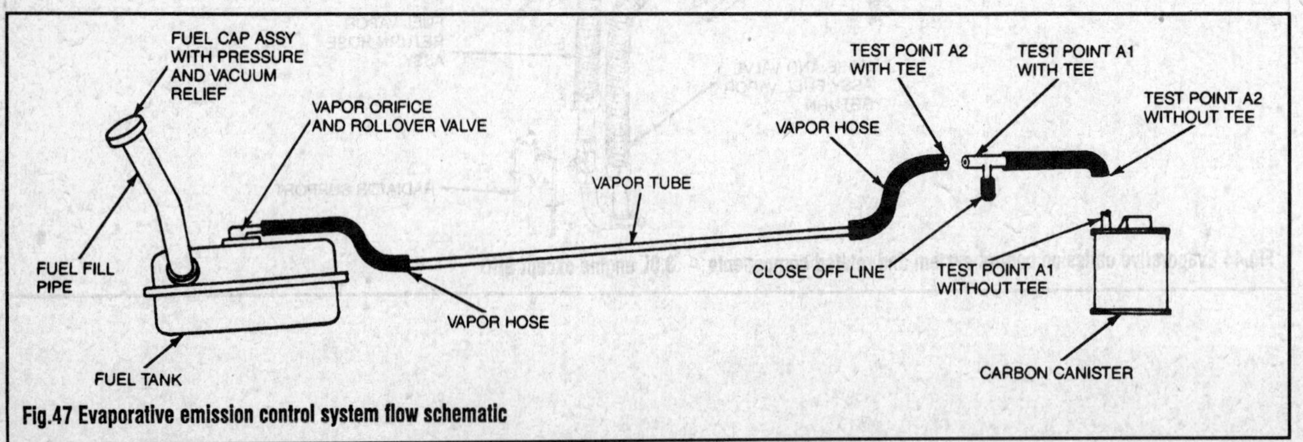

Fig.47 Evaporative emission control system flow schematic

Fig.12 Battery terminal cleaning

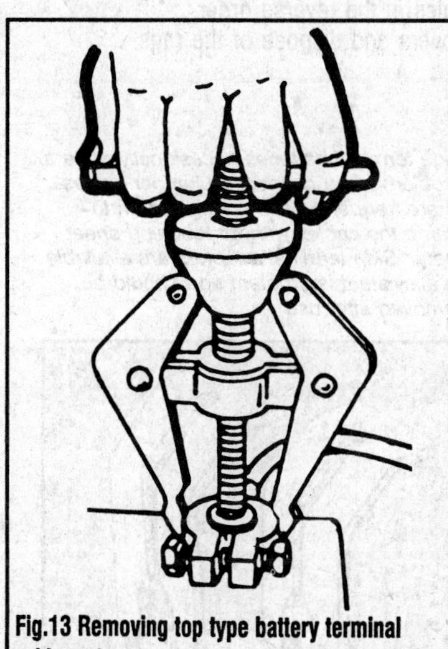
Fig.13 Removing top type battery terminal cable end

SPECIFIC GRAVITY (EXCEPT MAINTENANCE FREE BATTERIES)

At least once a year, check the specific gravity of the battery. It should be between 1.20 in.Hg and 1.26 in.Hg at room temperature.

The specific gravity can be check with the use of an hydrometer, an inexpensive instrument available from many sources, including auto parts stores. The hydrometer has a squeeze bulb at one end and a nozzle at the other. Battery electrolyte is sucked into the hydrometer until the float is lifted from its seat. The specific gravity is then read by noting the position of the float. Generally, if after charging, the specific gravity between any two cells varies more than 50 points (0.50), the battery is bad and should be replaced.

It is not possible to check the specific gravity in this manner on sealed (maintenance free) batteries. Instead, the indicator built into the top of the case must be relied on to display any signs of battery deterioration. If the indicator is dark, the battery can be assumed to be OK. If the indicator is light, the specific gravity is low, and the battery should be charged or replaced.

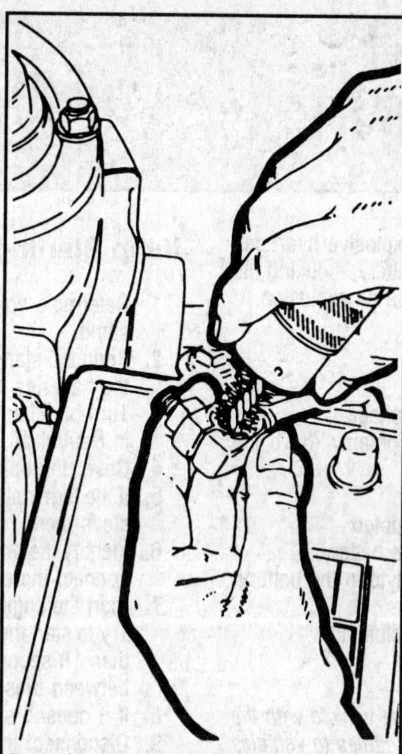
Fig.14 Cleaning top type battery terminal cable end

CABLES

Once every 6 months, the battery terminals and the cable clamps should be cleaned. Loosen the clamps and remove the cables, negative cable first. On batteries with posts on top, the use of a puller specially made for the purpose is recommended. Damage may occur to battery if proper terminal pullers are not used. These are inexpensive, and available in auto parts stores. Side terminal battery cables are secured with a bolt.

Clean the cable clamps and the battery terminal with a wire brush, until all corrosion, grease, etc. is removed and metal is shiny. It is especially important to clean the inside of the clamp thoroughly, since a small deposit of foreign material or oxidation there will prevent a sound electrical connection and inhibit either starting or charging. Special tools are available for cleaning these parts, one type of conventional batteries and another type for side terminal batteries.

Before installing the cable, loosen the battery holddown clamp or strap, remove the battery and check the battery tray. Clear it of any debris, and check it for soundness. Rust should be wire brushed away, and the metal given a coat of anti-rust paint. Before replacing the battery wash it with soap and water to remove any dirt. Replace the battery and tighten the holddown clamp or strap securely, but be careful not to overtighten, which will crack the battery case.

After the clamps and terminals are clean, reinstall the cables, negative cable last; do not hammer on the clamps to install. Tighten the clamps securely, but do not distort them. Give the clamps and terminals a thin external coat of grease after installation, to retard corrosion.

Check the cables at the same time that the terminals are cleaned. If the cable insulation is cracked or broken, or if the ends are frayed, the cable should be replace with a new cable of the same length and gauge.

➡ **Keep flame or sparks away from the battery; it gives off explosive hydrogen gas. Battery electrolyte contains sulphuric acid. If you should splash any on your skin or in your eyes, flush the affected areas with plenty of clear water; if it lands in your eyes, get medical help immediately.**

REPLACEMENT

The cold power rating of a battery measures battery starting performance and provides an approximate relationship between battery size and engine size. The cold power rating of a replacement battery should match or exceed your engine size in cubic inches.

JUMP STARTING A DEAD BATTERY

The chemical reaction in a battery produces explosive hydrogen gas. This is the safe way to jump start a dead battery, reducing the chances of an accidental spark that could cause an explosion.

Jump Starting Precautions

1. Be sure both batteries are of the same voltage.
2. Be sure both batteries are of the same polarity (have the same grounded terminal).
3. Be sure the vehicles are not touching.
4. Be sure the vent cap holes are not obstructed.
5. Do not smoke or allow sparks around the battery.
6. In cold weather, check for frozen electrolyte in the battery. Do not jump start a frozen battery.
7. Do not allow electrolyte on your skin or clothing.
8. Be sure the electrolyte is not frozen.

CAUTION: Make certin that the ignition key, in the vehicle with the dead battery, is in the OFF position. Connecting cables to vehicles with on-board computers will result in computer destruction if the key is not in the OFF position.

Jump Starting Procedure

1. Determine voltages of the two batteries; they must be the same.
2. Bring the starting vehicle close (they must not touch) so that the batteries can be reached easily.
3. Turn off all accessories and both engines. Put both vehicles in Neutral or Park and set the handbrake.
4. Cover the cell caps with a rag—do not cover terminals.
5. If the terminals on the run-down battery are heavily corroded, clean them.
6. Identify the positive and negative posts on both batteries and connect the cables in the order shown.
7. Start the engine of the starting vehicle and run it at fast idle. Try to start the car with the dead battery. Crank it for no more than 10 seconds at a time and let it cool for 20 seconds in between tries.
8. If it doesn't start in 3 tries, there is something else wrong.
9. Disconnect the cables in the reverse order.
10. Replace the cell covers and dispose of the rags.

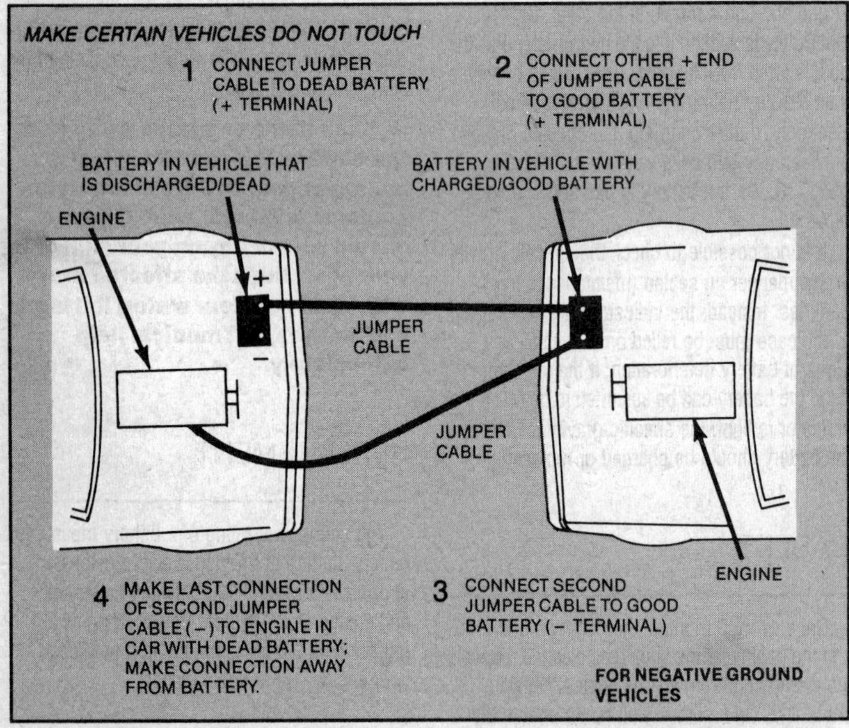
MAKE CERTAIN VEHICLES DO NOT TOUCH
1 CONNECT JUMPER CABLE TO DEAD BATTERY (+ TERMINAL)
2 CONNECT OTHER + END OF JUMPER CABLE TO GOOD BATTERY (+ TERMINAL)
BATTERY IN VEHICLE THAT IS DISCHARGED/DEAD
BATTERY IN VEHICLE WITH CHARGED/GOOD BATTERY
ENGINE
+
−
JUMPER CABLE
JUMPER CABLE
ENGINE
4 MAKE LAST CONNECTION OF SECOND JUMPER CABLE (−) TO ENGINE IN CAR WITH DEAD BATTERY; MAKE CONNECTION AWAY FROM BATTERY.
3 CONNECT SECOND JUMPER CABLE TO GOOD BATTERY (− TERMINAL)
FOR NEGATIVE GROUND VEHICLES

Side terminal batteries occasionally pose a problem when connecting jumper cables. There frequently isn't enough room to clamp the cables without touching sheet metal. Side terminal adaptors are available to alleviate this problem and should be removed after use

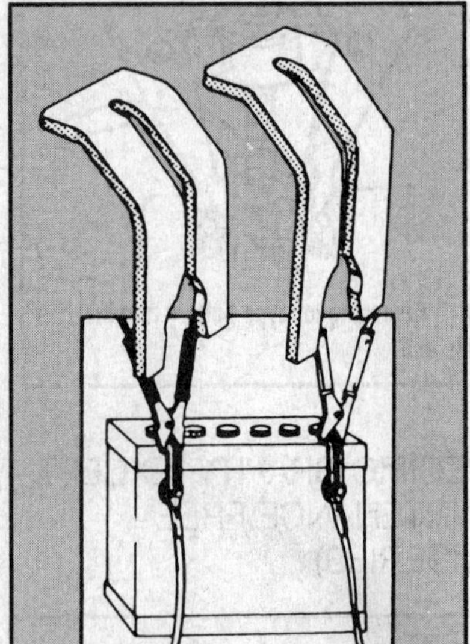

Belts

➧ SEE FIG. 15–17

All vehicles are equipped with V-ribbed belts. Replacement belts should be of the same type as originally installed. Loose belts will result in slippage and cause improper operation of the driven accessory, power steering, air conditioning, etc. Over-tightened belts will put a severe load on accessory bearings and will almost certainly cause them to self destruct.

INSPECTION

Inspect all drive belts for excessive wear, cracks, glazed condition and frayed or broken cords. Replace any drive belt showing the above condition(s).

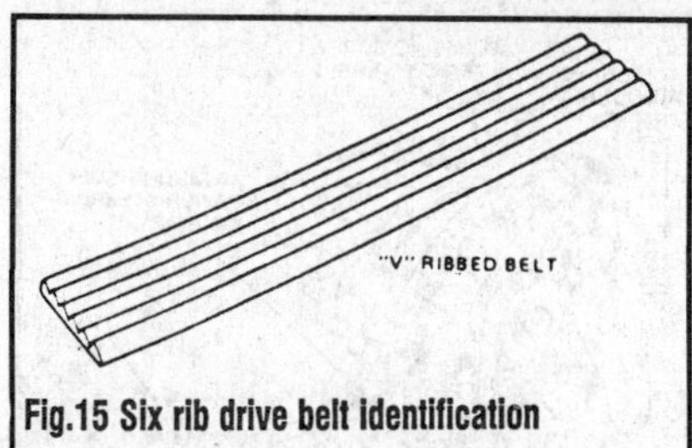

Fig.15 Six rib drive belt identification

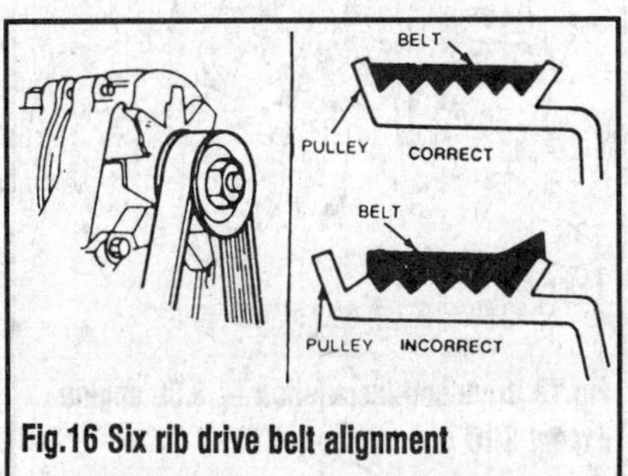

Fig.16 Six rib drive belt alignment

➡ **If a drive belt continually gets cut, the crankshaft pulley might have a sharp projection on it. Have the pulley replaced if this condition continues.**

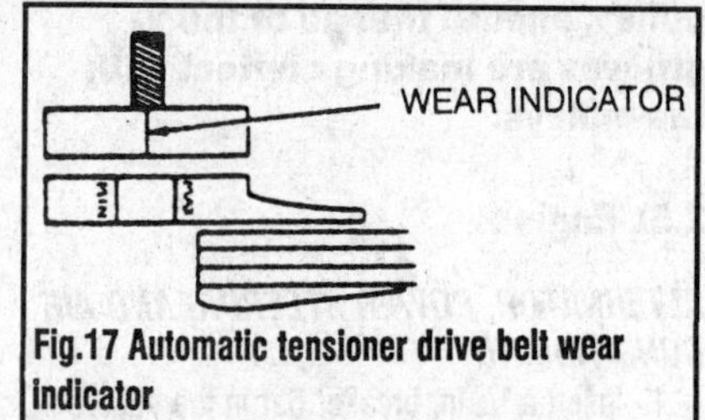

Fig.17 Automatic tensioner drive belt wear indicator

ADJUSTMENT

Alternator Belt

2.5L AND 3.8L ENGINES

The V-ribbed belts used on these engines, utilize an automatic belt tensioner which maintains the proper belt tension for the life of the belt. The automatic belt tensioner has a belt wear indicator mark and **MIN** and **MAX** marks. If the indicator mark is not between the **MIN** and **MAX** marks, the belt is worn or an incorrect belt is installed.

3.0L ENGINE EXCEPT SHO

➧ SEE FIG. 17a

1. Disconnect the negative battery cable.
2. Loosen the alternator adjustment and pivot bolts.
3. Apply tension to the belt using the adjusting screw.
4. Using a belt tension gauge, set the belt to the proper tension. The tension should be 150 lbs. for a new belt or 120 lbs. for a used belt, except for 1992 vehicles. On 1992 vehicles it should be 180–210 lbs. (82–95 kg) for a new belt and 140–160 lbs. (64–73 kg) for a used belt.
5. When the belt is properly tensioned, tighten the alternator adjustment bolt to 27 ft. lbs. (37 Nm).
6. Remove the tension gauge and run the engine for 5 minutes.
7. With the engine **OFF** and the belt tension gauge in place, check that the adjusting screw is in contact with the bracket before loosening the alternator adjustment bolt. Rotate the adjustment screw until the belt is tensioned to 120 lbs.
8. Tighten the alternator adjustment bolt to 27 ft. lbs. (37 Nm) and the pivot bolt to 43 ft. lbs. (58 Nm).

3.0L SHO ENGINE

1. Disconnect the negative battery cable.
2. Loosen the idler pulley nut.

FIG. 17a Alternator belt adjustment – 3.0L engine except SHO

3. Turn the adjusting bolt until the belt is adjusted properly.

➡ **Turning the wrench to the right tightens the belt adjustment and turning the wrench to the left loosens the belt tension.**

4. Tighten the idler pulley nut to 25–37 ft. lbs. (34–50 Nm) and check the belt tension.

REMOVAL & INSTALLATION

➧ SEE FIG. 18–21

➡ **When installing belts on the pulley, ensure that all of the V-grooves are making contact with the pulleys.**

2.5L Engine

ALTERNATOR, POWER STEERING AND AIR CONDITIONING

1. Insert a $1/2$ in. breaker bar in the square hole in the tensioner, rotate the tensioner counterclockwise and remove the belt from the pulleys.

➡ **Be careful when removing or installing belts that the tool doesn't slip!**

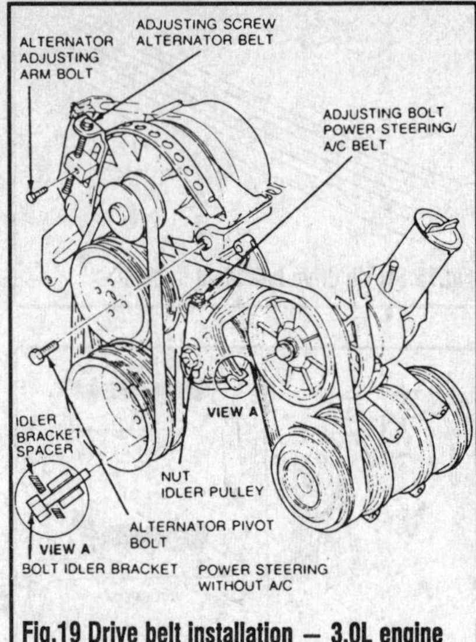

Fig.19 Drive belt installation — 3.0L engine except SHO

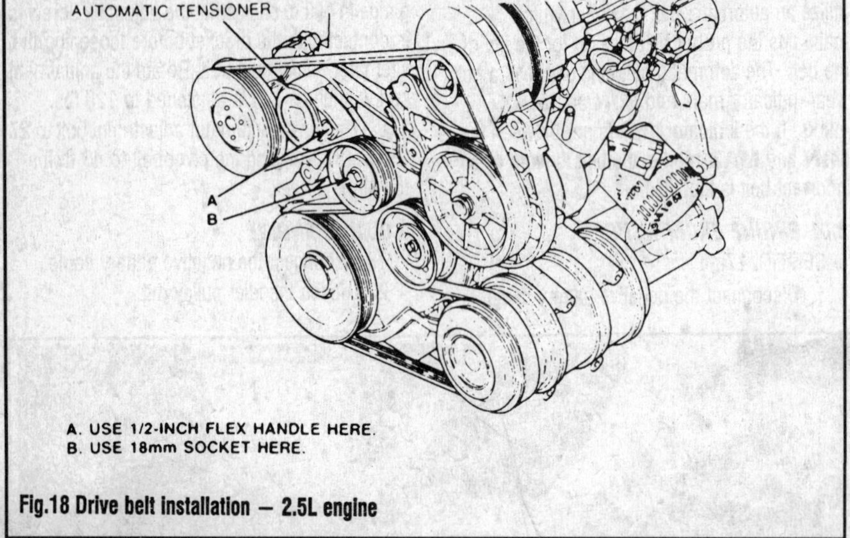

Fig.18 Drive belt installation — 2.5L engine

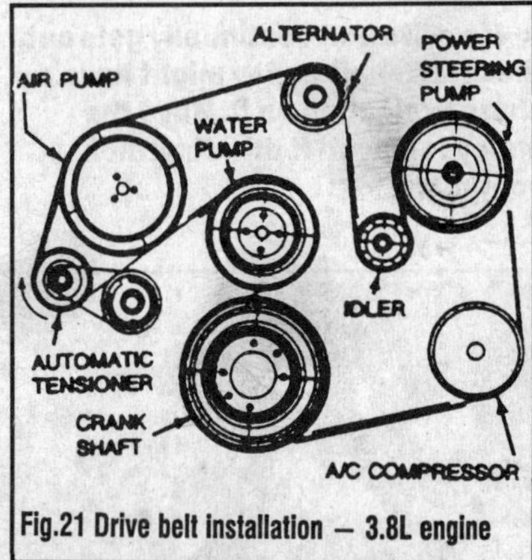

Fig.21 Drive belt installation — 3.8L engine

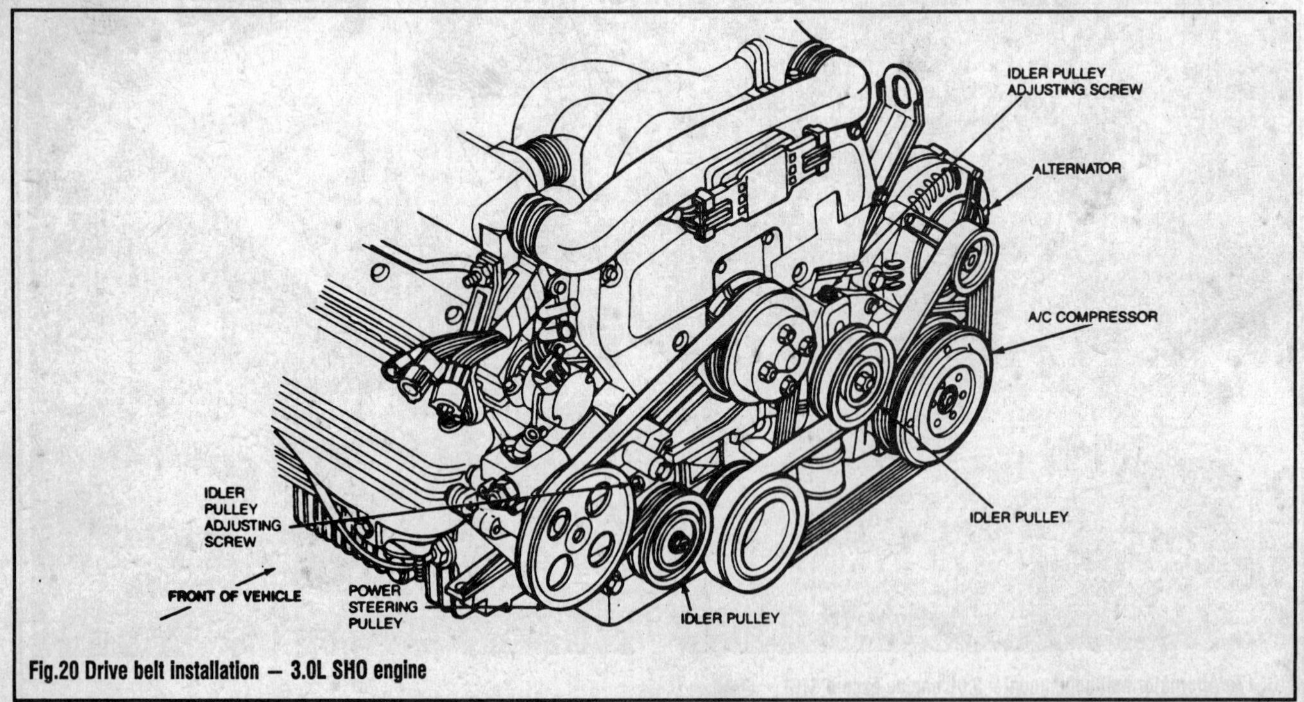

Fig.20 Drive belt installation — 3.0L SHO engine

HOW TO SPOT WORN V-BELTS

V–Belts are vital to efficient engine operation – they drive the fan, water pump and other accessories. They require little maintenance (occasional tightening) but they will not last forever. Slipping or failure of the V–belt will lead to overheating. If your V–belt looks like any of these, it should be replaced.

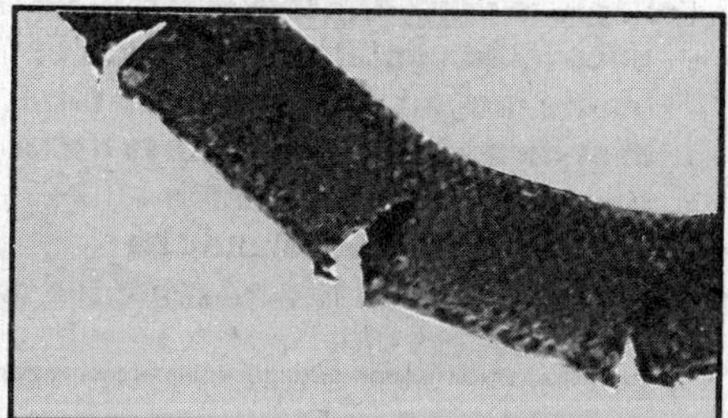

Cracking or Weathering

This belt has deep cracks, which cause it to flex. Too much flexing leads to heat build–up and premature failure. These cracks can be caused by using the belt on a pulley that is too small. Notched belts are available for small diameter pulleys.

Softening (Grease and Oil)

Oil and grease on a belt can cause the belt's rubber compounds to soften and separate from the reinforcing cords that hold the belt together. The belt will first slip, then finally fail altogether.

Glazing

Glazing is caused by a belt that is slipping. A slipping belt can cause a run-down battery, erratic power steering, overheating or poor accessory performance. The more the belt slips, the more glazing will be built up on the surface of the belt. The more the belt is glazed, the more it will slip. If the glazing is light, tighten the belt.

Worn Cover

The cover of this belt is worn off and is peeling away. The reinforcing cords will begin to wear and the belt will shortly break. When the belt cover wears in spots or has a rough jagged appearance, check the pulley grooves for roughness.

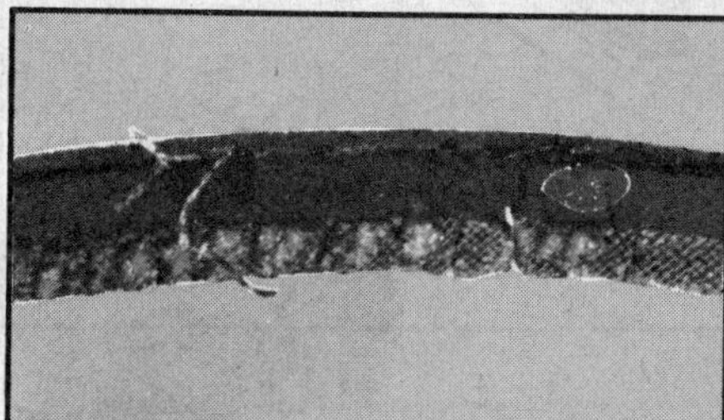

Separation

This belt is on the verge of breaking and leaving you stranded. The layers of the belt are separating and the reinforcing cords are exposed. It's just a matter of time before it breaks completely.

2. Install the belt over all pulleys except the alternator pulley.
3. Rotate the tensioner as described in Step 1 and install the belt over the alternator pulley. Check that all the V-grooves make proper contact with the pulleys.

3.0L Engine Except SHO

ALTERNATOR BELT WITHOUT AUTOMATIC TENSIONER

1. Loosen the adjusting arm and the pivot bolts.
2. Turn the alternator belt adjusting screw counterclockwise until the old belt can be removed. Remove the belt.
3. Install the new belt over the pulleys. Check that all the V-grooves make proper contact with the pulleys.
4. Adjust the belt tension.

3.0L SHO Engine

ALTERNATOR BELT

1. Loosen the nut in the center of the idler pulley.
2. Loosen the idler adjusting screw until the old belt can be removed and remove the belt.
3. Install the new belt over the pulleys in the proper contact with the pulleys.
4. Adjust the new belt to specifications as follows: Turn the idler pulley nut to the right to tighten the belt to a specification of 220–265 lbs. (100–120 kg) with a belt tension gauge. Torque the idler pulley nut to 25–37 ft. lbs. (34–50 Nm).

POWER STEERING AND AIR CONDITIONING BELT

1. Remove the alternator belt.
2. Loosen the nut on the tensioner pulley.
3. Turn the belt adjusting screw on the tensioner counterclockwise until the belt can be removed.
4. To install, position the new belt over the proper pulleys making sure the V-grooves are properly seated. Install the alternator belt. Adjust the power steering and air conditioning belt to a specification of 154–198 lbs. with a belt tension gauge. Adjust the alternator belt.

3.0L Engine Except SHO and 3.8L Engine

WITH AUTOMATIC TENSIONER

1. Insert a 1/2 in. breaker bar in the square hole in the tensioner.

➡ **On the 3.8L engine the tensioner has a 1/2 in. square hole cast into the rear of the tension arm directly behind the pulley. On the 3.0L engine the 1/2 in. square hole is cast into the spring housing on the front of the tensioner.**

2. Rotate the tensioner clockwise and remove the belt.
3. Installation is the reverse of the removal procedure.

Hoses

REMOVAL & INSTALLATION

➧ SEE FIG. 48–51 and 61–63

1. Open the hood and cover the fenders to protect them from scratches.
2. Disconnect the negative (−) battery cable at the battery.
3. Place a suitable drain pan under the radiator and drain the cooling system.

✻✻ CAUTION

Place a small hose on the end of the radiator petcock, this will direct the coolant into the drain pan. The engine must be cooled down before any hoses may be replaced. If engine is hot, let it cool down for at least an hour. When draining the coolant, keep in mind that cats and dogs are attracted by the ethylene glycol antifreeze, and are quite likely to drink any that is left in an uncovered container or in puddles on the ground. This will prove fatal in sufficient quantity. Always drain the coolant into a sealable container. Coolant should be reused unless it is contaminated or several years old.

4. After the radiator has drained, position the drain pan under the lower hose. Loosen the lower hose clamps, disconnect the hose from the water pump inlet pipe and allow to drain. Disconnect the other end of the hose from the radiator and remove the hose.
5. Loosen the clamps retaining the upper hose, disconnect and remove the hose.

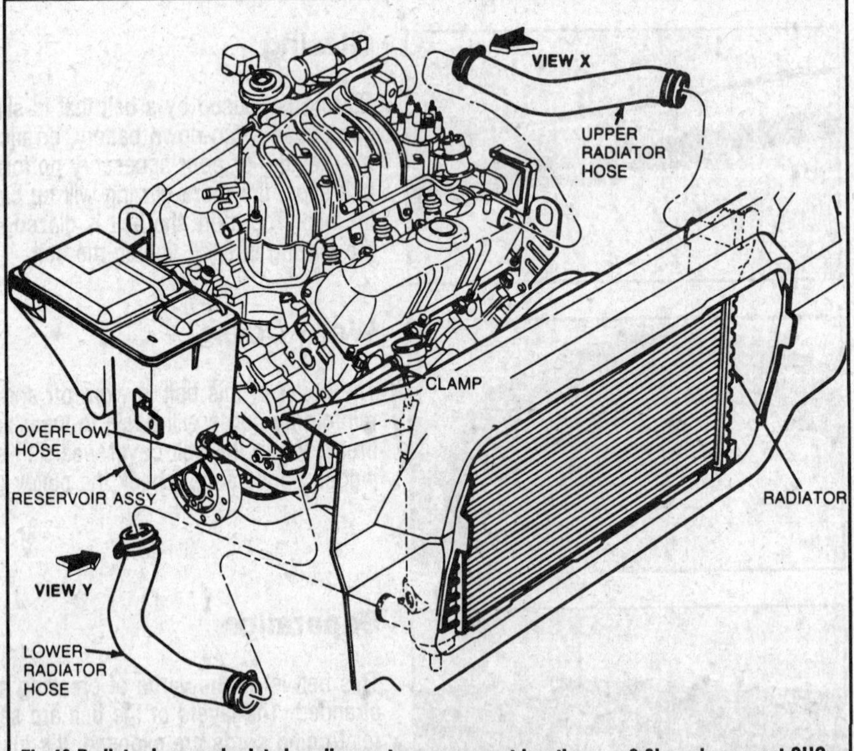

Fig.49 Radiator hose and related cooling system component locations — 3.0L engine except SHO

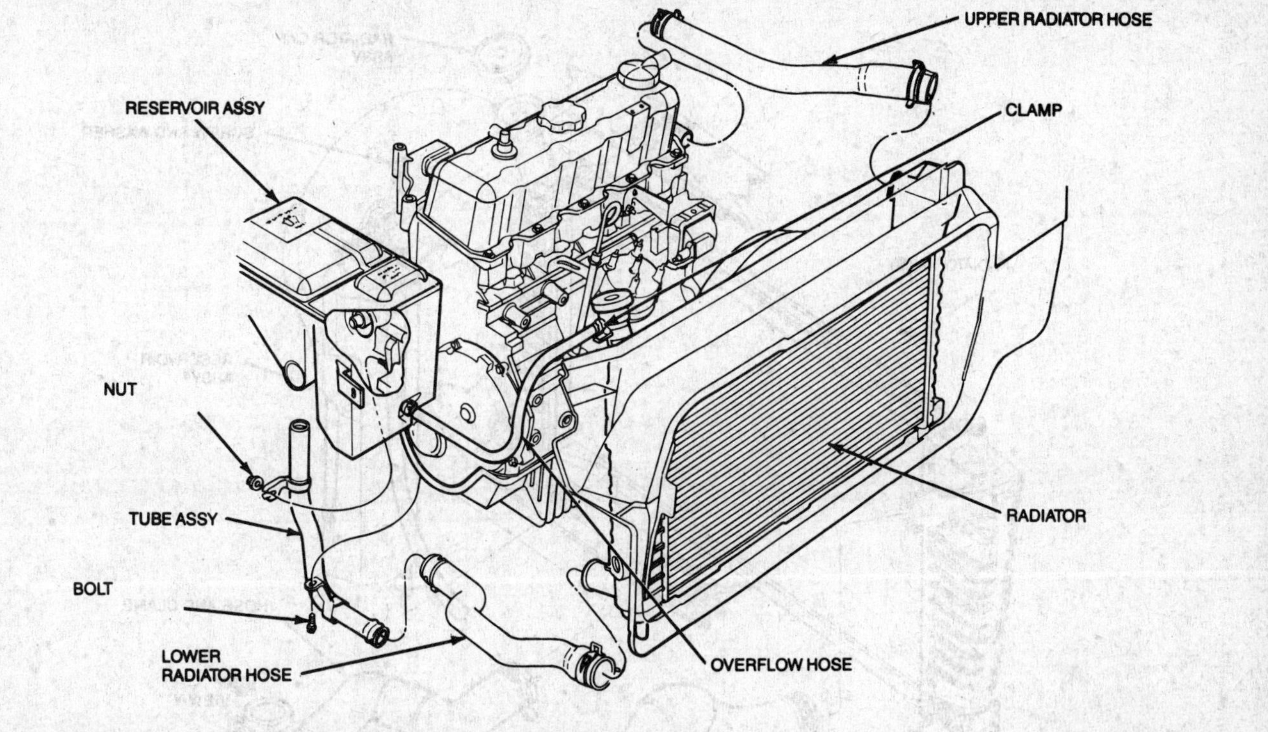

UPPER RADIATOR HOSE
RESERVOIR ASSY
CLAMP
NUT
TUBE ASSY
RADIATOR
BOLT
LOWER RADIATOR HOSE
OVERFLOW HOSE

Fig.48 Radiator hose and related cooling system component locations — 2.5L engine

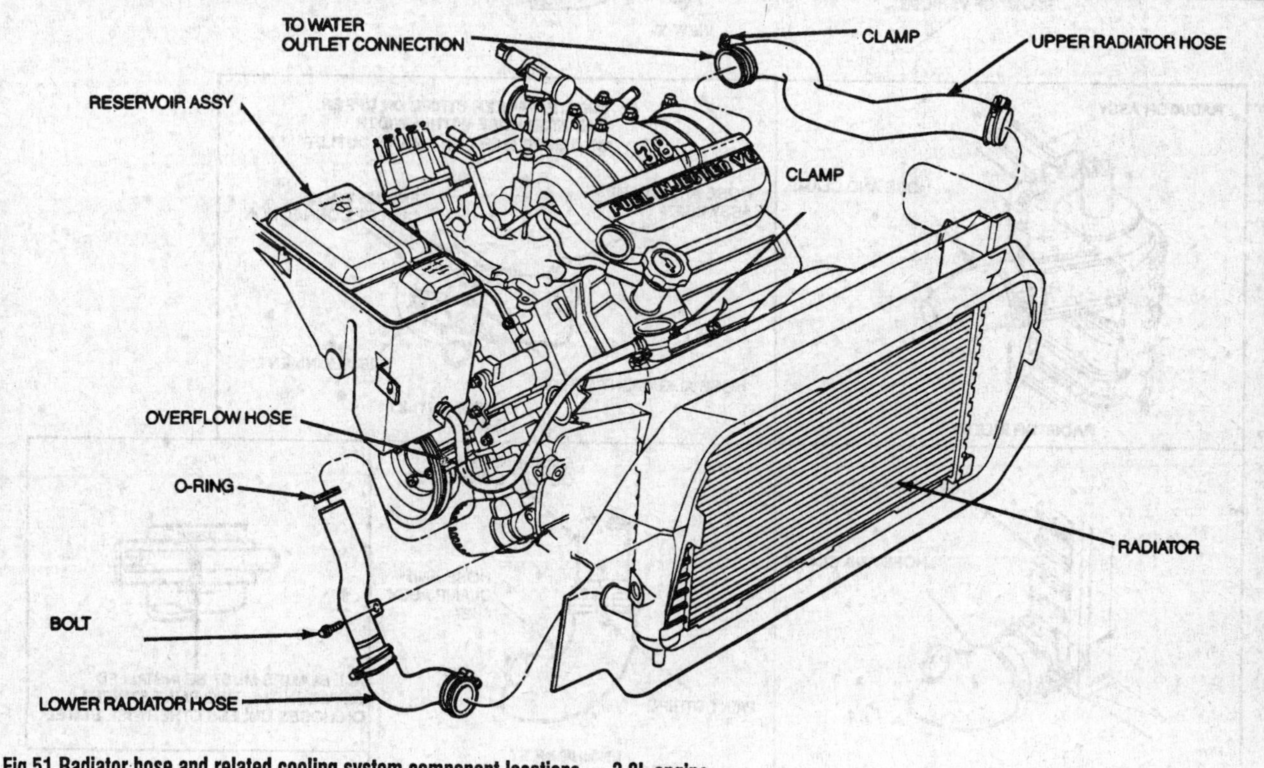

TO WATER OUTLET CONNECTION
CLAMP
UPPER RADIATOR HOSE
RESERVOIR ASSY
CLAMP
OVERFLOW HOSE
O-RING
RADIATOR
BOLT
LOWER RADIATOR HOSE

Fig.51 Radiator hose and related cooling system component locations — 3.8L engine

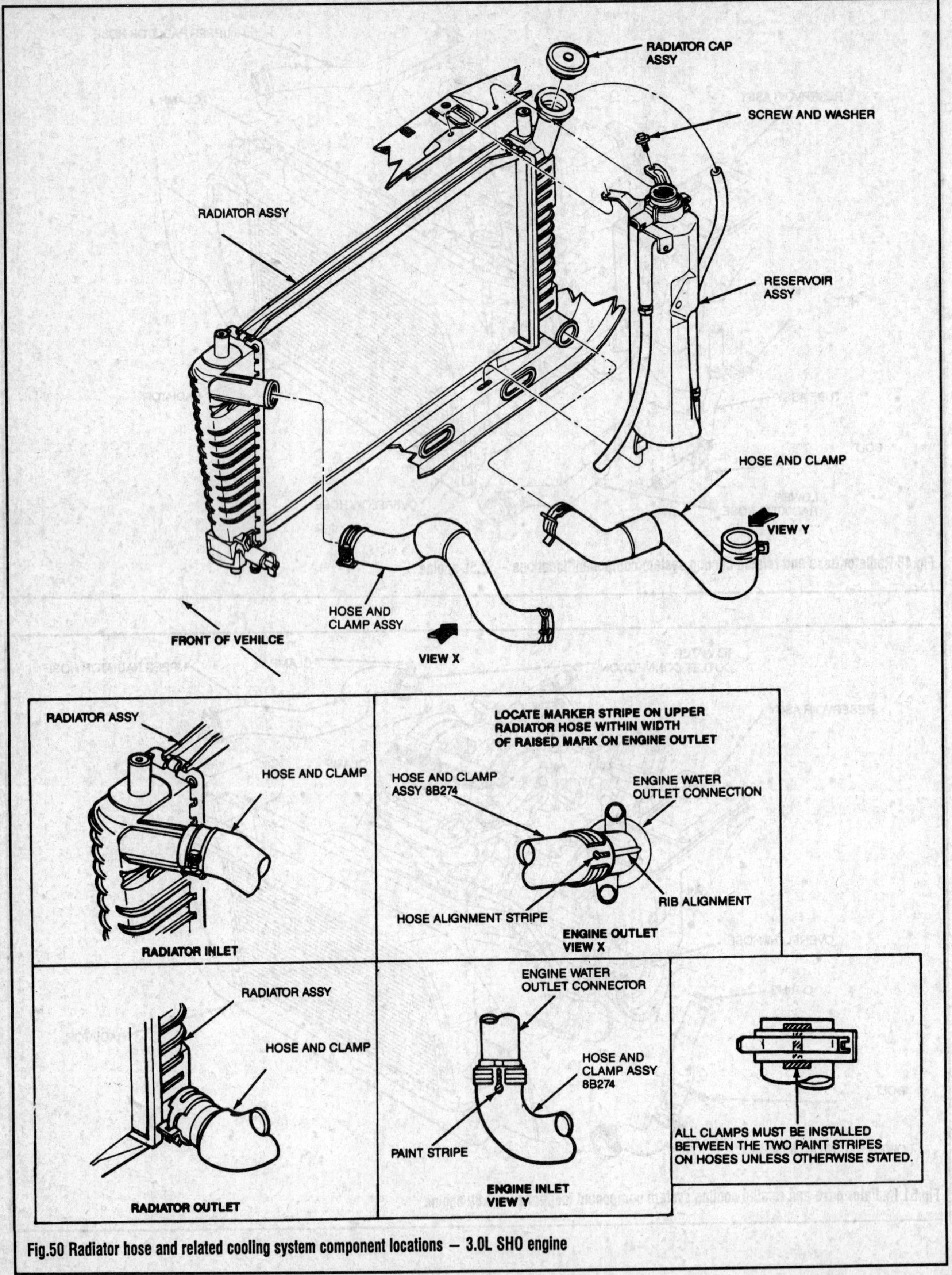

Fig.50 Radiator hose and related cooling system component locations — 3.0L SHO engine

1
2
3
4
5
6
ITEM DESCRIPTION
1. CLAMP
2. HEATER INLET HOSE
3. CRIMP
ITEM DESCRIPTION
4. HEATER WATER OUTLET TUBE ASSEMBLY
5. CLAMP
6. CLAMP

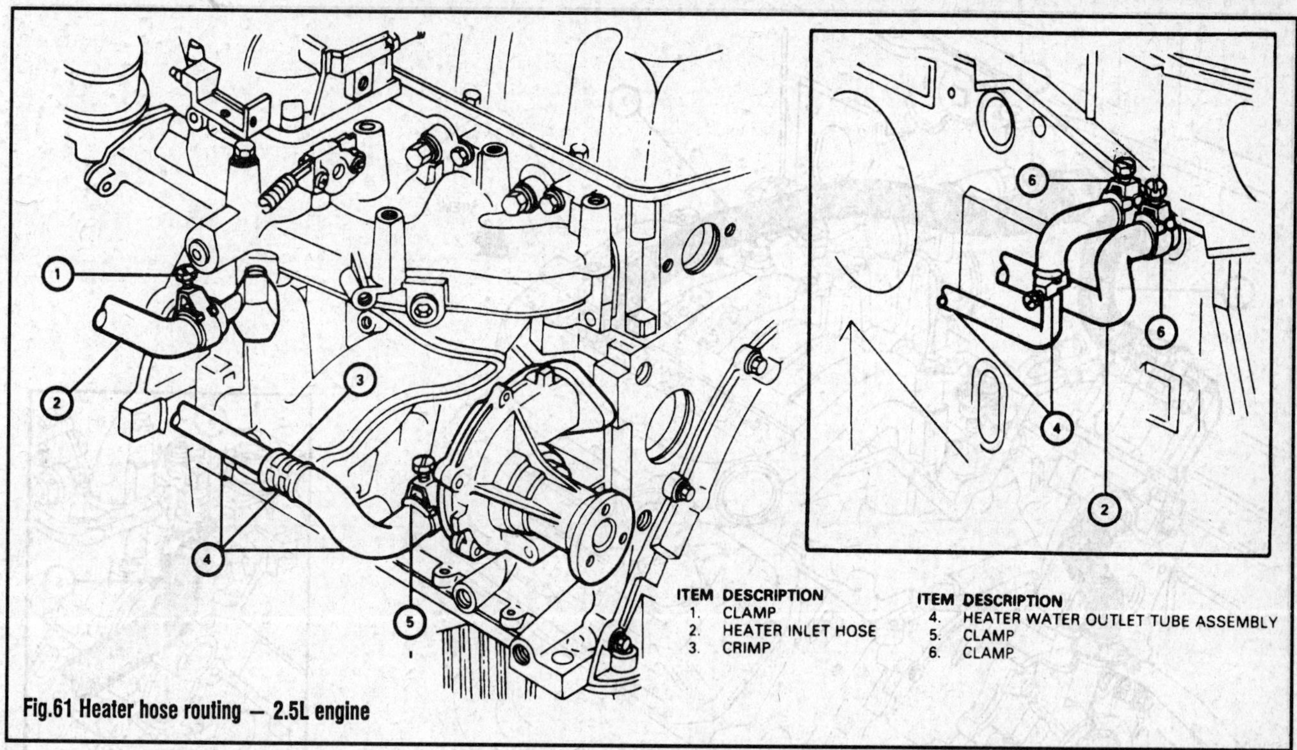

Fig.61 Heater hose routing — 2.5L engine

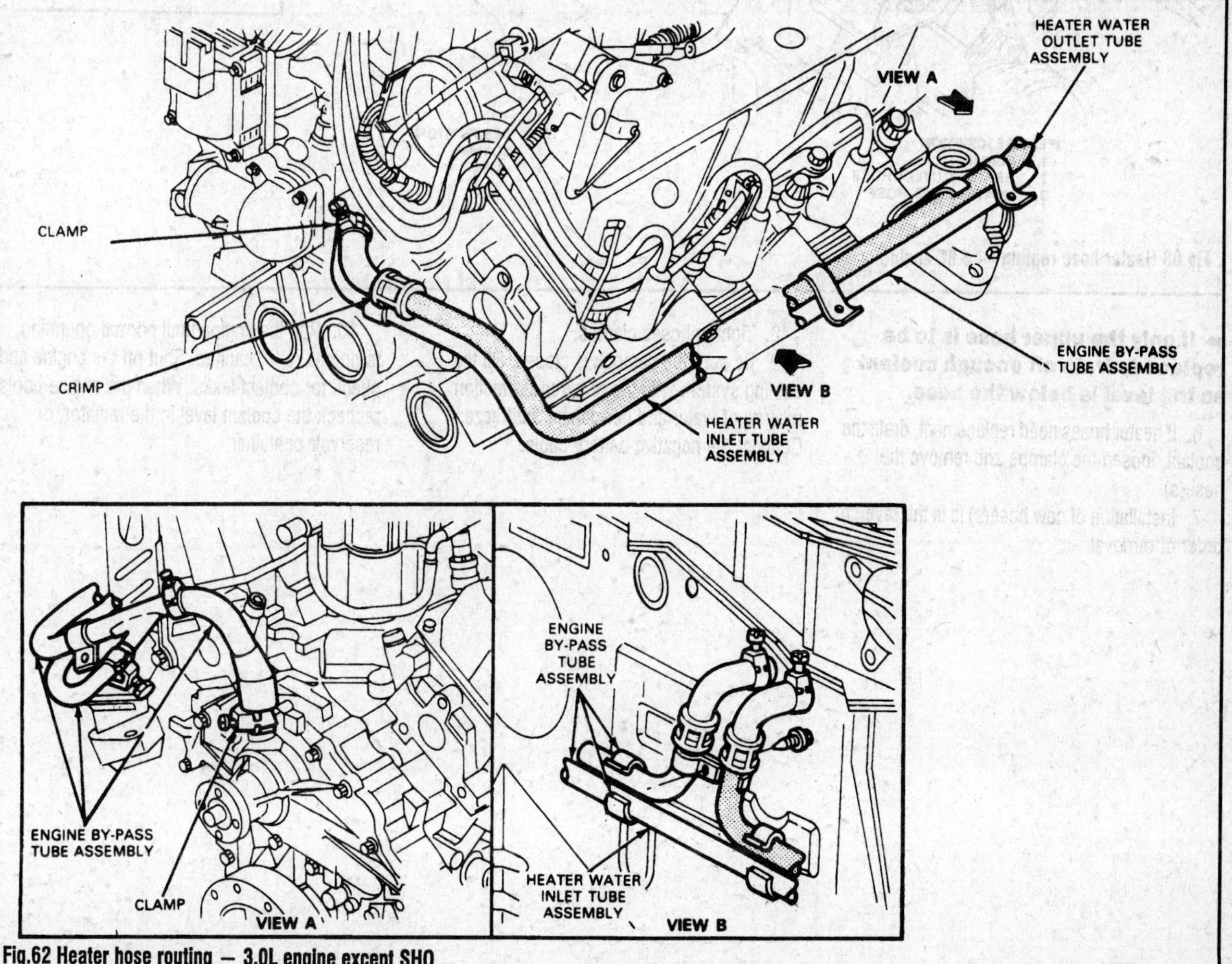

HEATER WATER
OUTLET TUBE
ASSEMBLY
VIEW A
CLAMP
ENGINE BY-PASS
TUBE ASSEMBLY
CRIMP
VIEW B
HEATER WATER
INLET TUBE
ASSEMBLY
ENGINE BY-PASS
TUBE ASSEMBLY
CLAMP
VIEW A
ENGINE
BY-PASS
TUBE
ASSEMBLY
HEATER WATER
INLET TUBE
ASSEMBLY
VIEW B

Fig.62 Heater hose routing — 3.0L engine except SHO

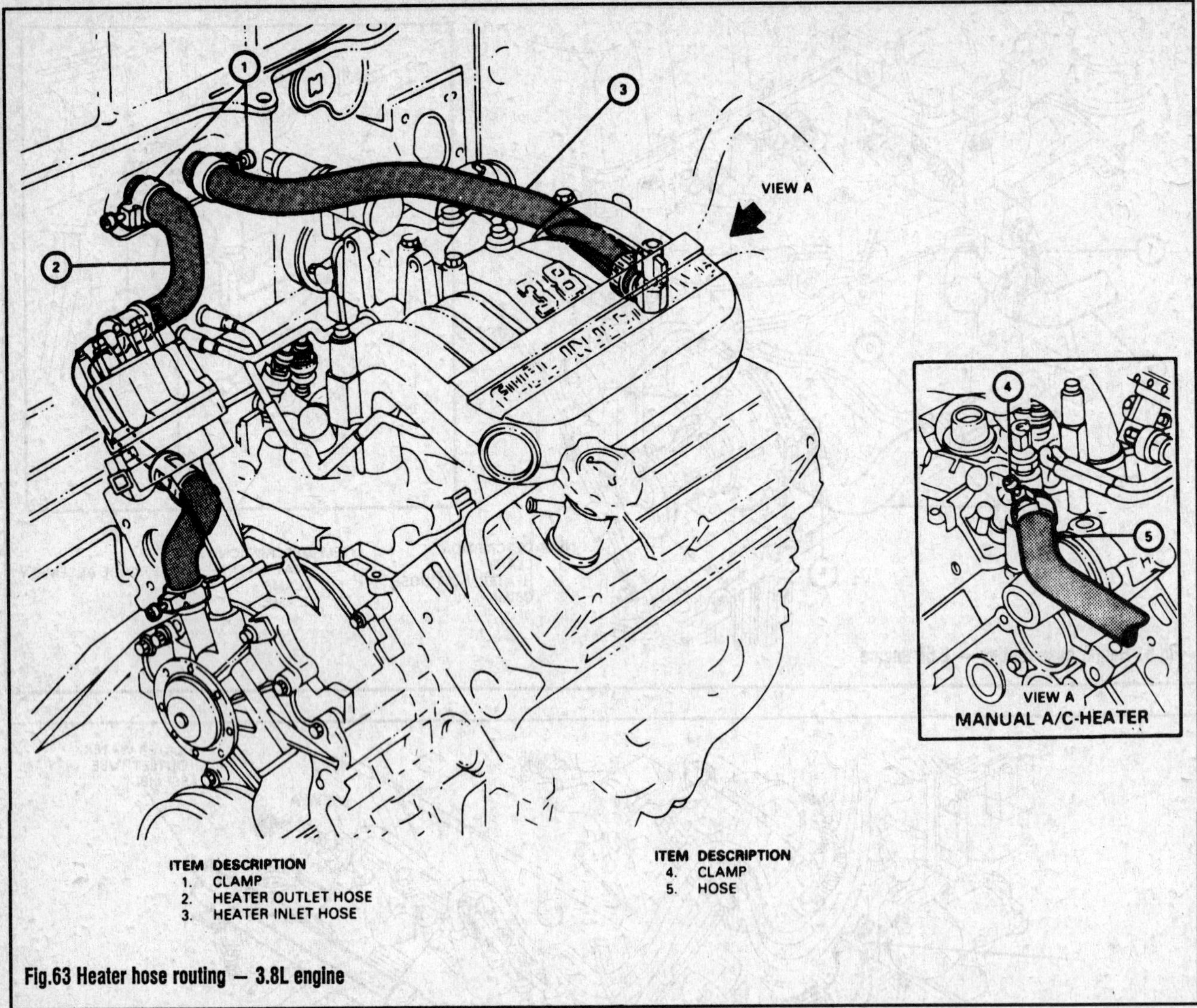

Fig.63 Heater hose routing — 3.8L engine

➡ **If only the upper hose is to be replaced, drain off enough coolant so the level is below the hose.**

6. If heater hoses need replacement, drain the coolant, loosen the clamps and remove the hose(s).
7. Installation of new hose(s) is in the reverse order of removal.
8. Tighten hoses clamps.
9. Be sure the petcock is closed. Fill the cooling system with the required protection mixture of water and permanent antifreeze. Connect the negative battery cable.
10. Run the engine until normal operating temperature is reached. Shut off the engine and check for coolant leaks. When the engine cools, recheck the coolant level in the radiator, or reservoir container.

HOW TO SPOT BAD HOSES

Both the upper and lower radiator hoses are called upon to perform difficult jobs in an inhospitable environment. They are subject to nearly 18 psi at under hood temperatures often over 280°F, and must circulate nearly 7500 gallons of coolant an hour—3 good reasons to have good hoses.

Swollen Hose

A good test for any hose is to feel it for soft or spongy spots. Frequently these will appear as swollen areas of the hose. The most likely cause is oil soaking. This hose could burst at any time, when hot or under pressure.

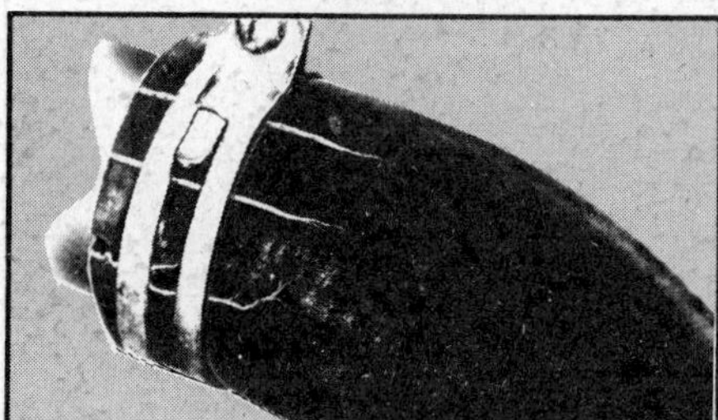

Cracked Hose

Cracked hoses can usually be seen but feel the hoses to be sure they have not hardened; a prime cause of cracking. This hose has cracked down to the reinforcing cords and could split at any of the cracks.

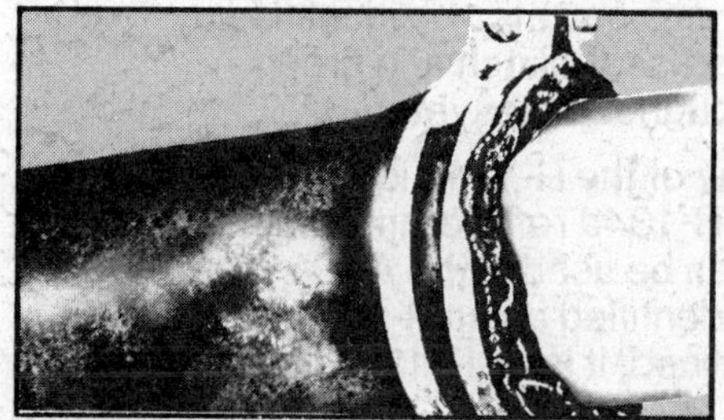

Frayed Hose End (Due to Weak Clamp)

Weakened clamps frequently are the cause of hose and cooling system failure. The connection between the pipe and hose has deteriorated enough to allow coolant to escape when the engine is hot.

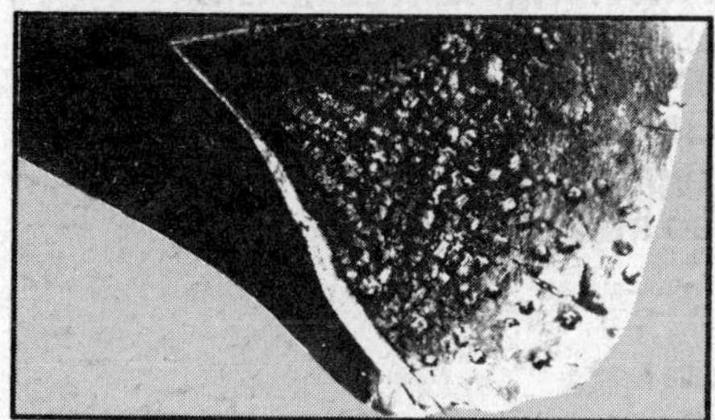

Debris in Cooling System

Debris, rust and scale in the cooling system can cause the inside of a hose to weaken. This can usually be felt on the outside of the hose as soft or thinner areas.

Air Conditioning

R-134a SYSTEMS

General Information

Some 1992 vehicles equipped with the 3.0L engine are using R-134a refrigerant rather than the conventional R-12 refrigerant. The new R-134a refrigerant is not harmful to the ozone layer of the atmosphere. The new refrigerant has many of the same properties as the old type of refrigerant and is similar in both form and function. These two refrigerants are not interchangeable with one another. Do not mix the two types of refrigerant, tools used in servicing the air conditioning system, or component replacement parts from the two air conditioning systems. Failure to follow these guidelines will result in damage to the vehicle air conditioning system and may also result in personal damage to the individual.

System Identification

➧ SEE FIG. 64

In order to determine which type of system your vehicle has an identification data plate is located on the major system components. If the system components have YELLOW R-134a non-cfc tags than the system requires R-134a refrigerant. These systems can also be identified by a gold colored air conditioning compressor clutch and green colored O-rings used through the system.

Identifying R-134a and R-12 Systems

In order to determine which type of A/C system a particular vehicle has, inspect the A/C system major components and refrigerant lines. If the system components have yellow R-134a NON-CFC tags as shown below, it is an R-134a system requiring the use of R-134a refrigerant.

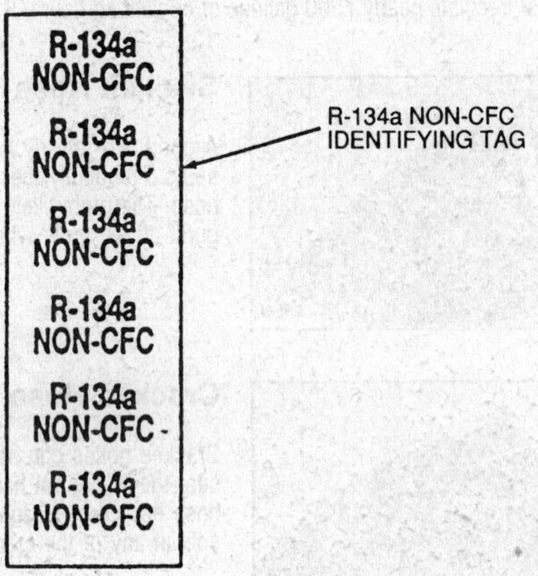

NOTE: R-134a A/C systems can also be identified by a gold colored A/C compressor clutch and green colored O-rings used throughout the system.

If the A/C system has any of the R-134a identifying characteristics outlined, R-134a refrigerant is the only type of refrigerant that can be used in the A/C system. If the A/C system is not identified as an R-134a system as previously outlined, it is an R-12 system requiring the use of R-12 refrigerant.

CAUTION: Do not add R-12 refrigerant to an A/C system that requires the use of R-134a refrigerant. Do not add R-134a refrigerant to an A/C system that requires the use of R-12 refrigerant. These two types of refrigerant should never be mixed. Doing so may cause damage to the A/C system.

Fig.64 R-134a identification tag and important data

GENERAL MAINTENANCE

➧ SEE FIG. 25

The most important aspect of air conditioning service is the maintenance of pure and adequate charge of refrigerant in the system. A refrigeration system cannot function properly if a significant percentage of the charge is lost. Leaks are common because the severe vibration encountered in an automobile can easily cause a sufficient cracking or loosening of the air conditioning fittings. As a result, the extreme operating pressures of the system force refrigerant out.

The problem can be understood by considering what happens to the system as it is operated with a continuous leak. Because the expansion valve regulates the flow of refrigerant to the evaporator, the level of refrigerant there is fairly constant. The receiver/drier stores any excess of refrigerant, and so a loss will first appear there as a reduction in the level of liquid. As this level nears the bottom of the vessel, some refrigerant vapor bubbles will begin to appear in the stream of liquid supplied to the expansion valve. This vapor decreases the capacity of the expansion valve very little as the valve opens to compensate for its presence. As the quantity of liquid in the condenser decreases, the operating pressure will drop there and throughout the high side of the system. As the refrigerant continues to be expelled, the pressure available to force the liquid through the expansion valve will continue to decrease, and,

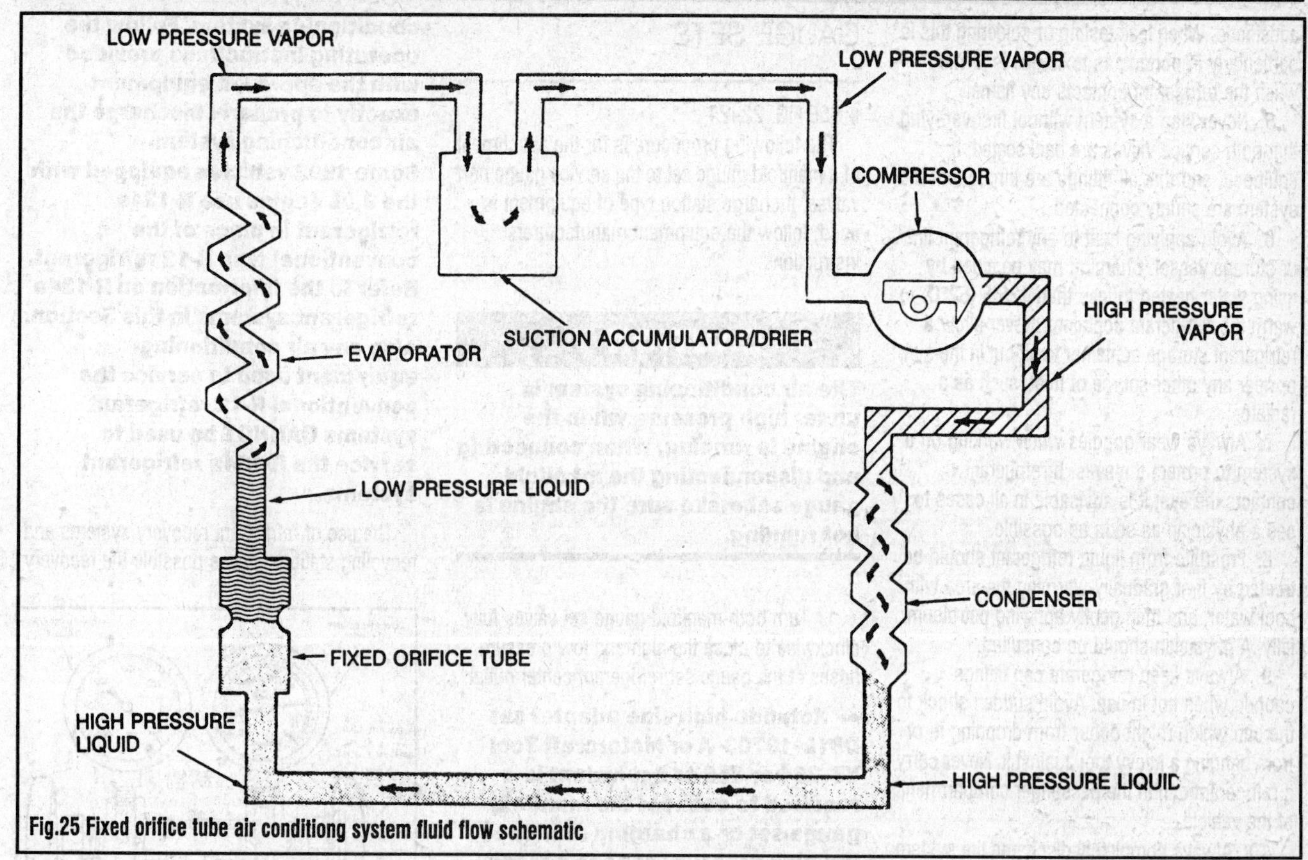

Fig.25 Fixed orifice tube air conditiong system fluid flow schematic

eventually, the valve's orifice will prove to be too much of a restriction for adequate flow even with the needle fully withdrawn.

At this point, low side pressure will start to drop, and severe reduction in cooling capacity, marked by freeze-up of the evaporator coil, will result. Eventually, the operating pressure of the evaporator will be lower than the pressure of the atmosphere surrounding it, and air will be drawn into the system wherever there are leaks in the low side.

Because all atmospheric air contains at least some moisture, water will enter the system and mix with the refrigerant and the oil. Trace amounts of moisture will cause sludging of the oil, and corrosion of the system. Saturation and clogging of the filter/drier, and freezing of the expansion valve orifice will eventually result. As air fills the system to a greater and greater extent, it will interfere more and more with the normal flows of refrigerant and heat.

A list of general precautions that should be observed while doing this follows:

1. Keep all tools as clean and dry as possible.
2. Thoroughly purge the service gauges and hoses of air and moisture before connecting them to the system. Keep them capped when not in use.
3. Thoroughly clean any refrigerant fitting before disconnecting it, in order to minimize the entrance of dirt into the system.
4. Plan any operation that requires opening the system beforehand in order to minimize the length of time it will be exposed to open air. Cap or seal the open ends to minimize the entrance of foreign material.
5. When adding oil, pour it through an extremely clean and dry tube or funnel. Keep the oil capped whenever possible. Do not use oil that has not been kept tightly sealed.
6. Use only the proper refrigerant. Purchase refrigerant intended for use in only automotive air conditioning system.
7. Completely evacuate any system that has been opened to replace a component, other than when isolating the compressor, or that has leaked sufficiently to draw in moisture and air. This requires evacuating air and moisture with a good vacuum pump for at least one hour.

If a system has been open for a considerable length of time it may be advisable to evacuate the system for up to 12 hours (overnight).

8. Use a wrench on both halves of a fitting that is to be disconnected, so as to avoid placing torque on any of the refrigerant lines.

SAFETY WARNINGS

Because of the importance of the necessary safety precautions that must be exercised when working with air conditioning systems and refrigerant, a recap of the safety precautions are outlined.

1. Avoid contact with a charged refrigeration system, even when working on another part of the air conditioning system or vehicle. If a heavy tool comes into contact with a section of copper tubing or a heat exchanger, it can easily cause the relatively soft material to rupture.
2. When it is necessary to apply force to a fitting which contains refrigerant, as when checking that all system couplings are securely tightened, use a wrench on both parts of the fitting involved, if possible. This will avoid putting torque on the refrigerant tubing. (It is advisable, when possible, to use tube or line wrenches when tightening these flare nut fittings.)
3. Do not attempt to discharge the system by merely loosening a fitting, or removing the service valve caps and cracking these valves. Precise control is possibly only when using the service gauges. Place a rag under the open end of the center charging hose while discharging the system to catch any drops of liquid that might escape. Wear protective gloves when connecting or disconnecting service gauge hoses.
4. Discharge the system using the proper discharge equipment, as high concentrations of the gas can exclude oxygen and act as an

anesthetic. When leak testing or soldering this is particularly important, as toxic gas is formed when the refrigerant contacts any flame.

5. Never start a system without first verifying that both service valves are backseated, if equipped, and that all fittings are throughout the system are snugly connected.

6. Avoid applying heat to any refrigerant line or storage vessel. Charging may be aided by using water heated to less than 125°F (52°C) to warm the refrigerant container. Never allow a refrigerant storage container to sit out in the sun, or near any other source of heat, such as a radiator.

7. Always wear goggles when working on a system to protect the eyes. If refrigerant contacts the eye, it is advisable in all cases to see a physician as soon as possible.

8. Frostbite from liquid refrigerant should be treated by first gradually warming the area with cool water, and then gently applying petroleum jelly. A physician should be consulted.

9. Always keep refrigerant can fittings capped when not in use. Avoid sudden shock to the can which might occur from dropping it, or from banging a heavy tool against it. Never carry a refrigerant can in the passenger compartment of the vehicle.

10. Always completely discharge the system before painting the vehicle (if the paint is to be baked on), or before welding anywhere near the refrigerant lines.

SYSTEM INSPECTION

It is possible to detect possible air conditioning system problems by a visual inspection. Check for a broken air conditioning belt, dirt blocking the condenser, disconnected wires, a loose compressor clutch and oily residue around the air conditioning hose fittings. Missing service gauge port caps may also cause a leak to be present.

REFRIGERANT LEVEL CHECKS

The only way to accurately check the refrigerant level to measure the system evaporator pressures with a manifold gauge set, although rapid on/off cycling of the compressor clutch indicates that the air conditioning system is low on refrigerant. The normal refrigerant capacity is 40 oz. ± 1 oz.

GAUGE SETS

➧ SEE FIG. 22–24

The following procedure is for the attachment of a manifold gauge set to the service gauge port valves. If charge station type of equipment is used, follow the equipment manufacturers instructions.

✲✲ CAUTION

The air conditioning system is under high pressure when the engine is running, When connecting and disconnecting the manifold gauge set make sure the engine is not running.

1. Turn both manifold gauge set valves fully clockwise to close the high and low pressure hoses at the gauge set refrigerant center outlet.

➡ Rotunda high side adapter set D81L–19703–A or Motorcraft Tool YT–354 or 355 or equivalent is required to connect the manifold gauge set or a charging station to the high pressure service access gauge port valve.

2. Remove the caps from the high and low pressure service gauge port valves.

3. If the manifold gauge set hoses do not have the valve depressing pins in them, install fitting adapters T71P–19703–S and –R containing the pins on the manifold gauge hoses.

4. Connect the high and low pressure refrigerant hoses to their respective service ports, making sure they are hooked up correctly and fully seated. Tighten the fittings by hand and make sure they are not cross-threaded. Remember that an adapter is necessary to connect the manifold gauge hose to the high pressure fitting.

DISCHARGING THE SYSTEM

➡ Air conditioning system R-12 refrigerant is a chloroflourocarbon which, when released into the atmosphere, can contribute to the depletion of the ozone layer in the upper atmosphere. Ozone filters out harmful radiation from the sun. If possible an approved recovery/ recycling machine that meets SAE standards should be employed when discharging the air conditioning system. Follow the operating instructions provided with the approved equipment exactly to properly discharge the air conditioning system.

Some 1992 vehicles equipped with the 3.0L engine use R-134a refrigerant in place of the conventional type R-12 refrigerant. Refer to the information on R-134a refrigerant systems in this Section. Also any air conditioning equipment used to service the conventional R-12 refrigerant systems CANNOT be used to service the R-134a refrigerant systems.

The use of refrigerant recovery systems and recycling stations makes possible the recovery

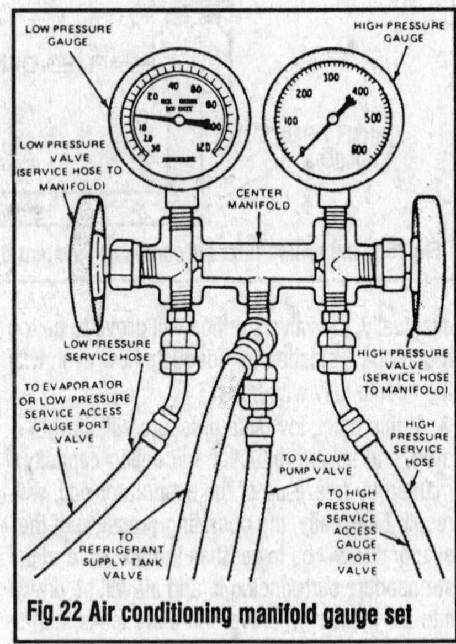

Fig.22 Air conditioning manifold gauge set

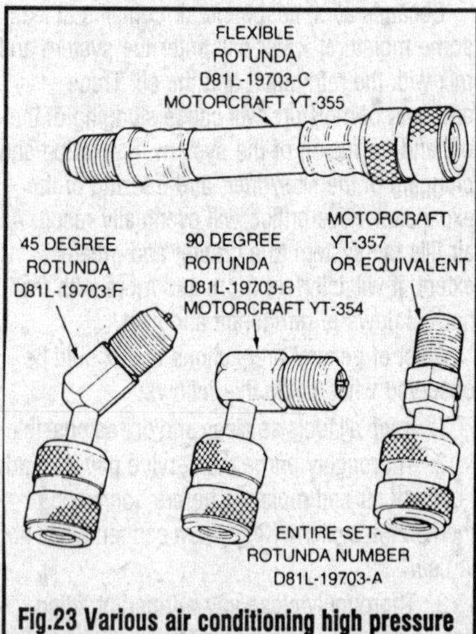

Fig.23 Various air conditioning high pressure gauge port adapter tools

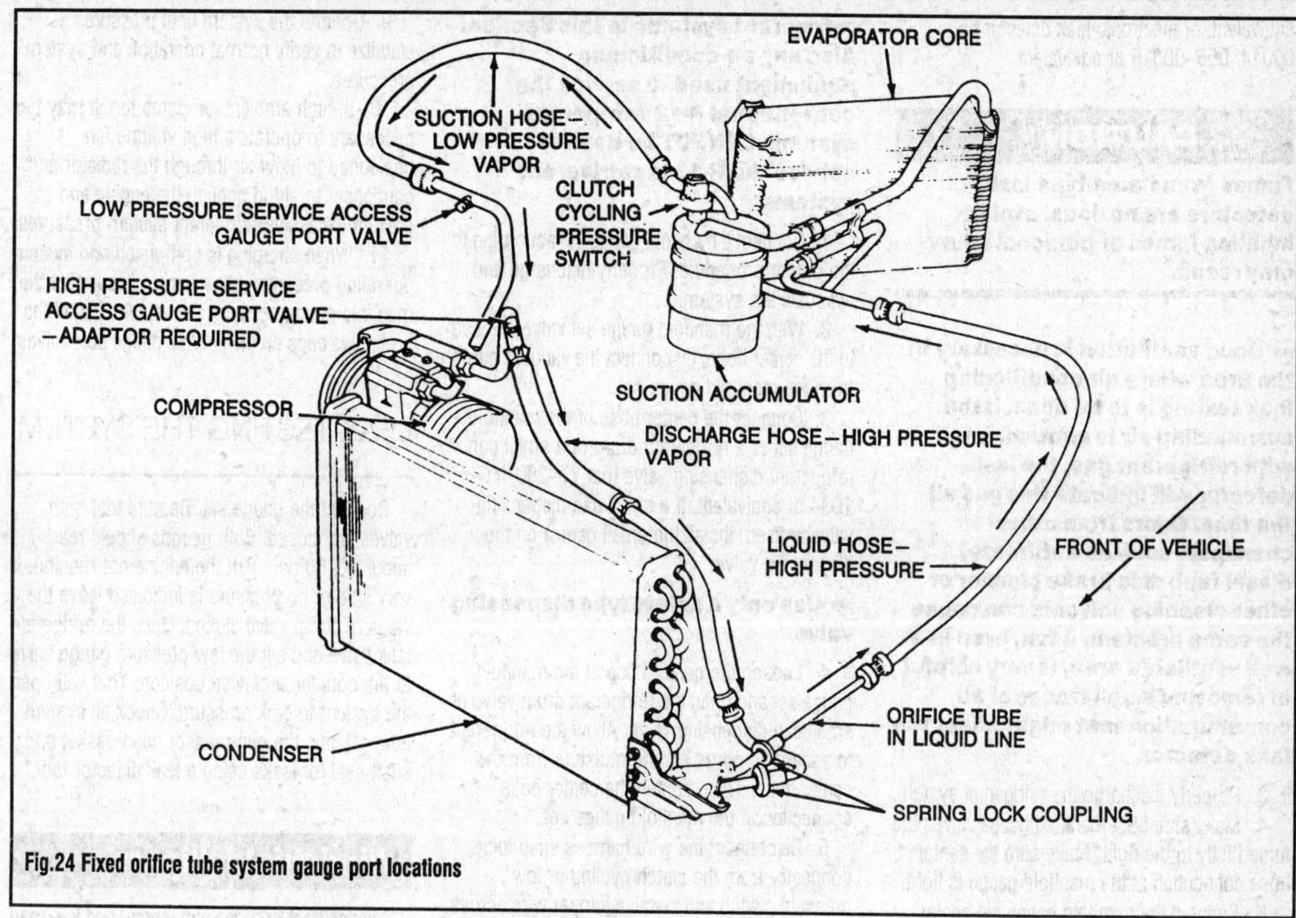

Fig.24 Fixed orifice tube system gauge port locations

and reuse of refrigerant after contaminants and moisture have been removed. If a recovery system or recycling station is used, the following general procedures should be observed, in addition to the operating instructions provided by the equipment manufacturer.

1. Connect the refrigerant recycling station hose(s) to the vehicle air conditioning service ports and the recovery station inlet fitting.

➡ **Hoses should have shut off devices or check valves within 12 in. (305mm) of the hose end to minimize the introduction of air into the recycling station and to minimize the amount of refrigerant released when the hose(s) is disconnected.**

2. Turn the power to the recycling station **ON** to start the recovery process. Allow the recycling station to pump the refrigerant from the system until the station pressure goes into a vacuum. On some stations the pump will be shut off automatically by a low pressure switch in the electrical system. On other units it may be necessary to manually turn off the pump.

3. Once the recycling station has evacuated the vehicle air conditioning system, close the station inlet valve, if equipped. Then switch **OFF** the electrical power.

4. Allow the vehicle air conditioning system to remain closed for about 2 minutes. Observe the system vacuum level as shown on the gauge. If the pressure does not rise, disconnect the recycling station hose(s).

5. If the system pressure rises, repeat Steps 2, 3 and 4 until the vacuum level remains stable for 2 minutes.

EVACUATING THE SYSTEM

➡ **Some 1992 vehicles equipped with the 3.0L engine use R-134a refrigerant in place of the conventional type R-12 refrigerant. Refer to the information on R-134a refrigerant systems in this Section. Also any air conditioning equipment used to service the conventional R-12 refrigerant systems CANNOT be used to service the R-134a refrigerant systems.**

1. Connect a manifold gauge set as follows:

a. Turn both manifold gauge set valves fully to the right, to close the high and low pressure hoses to the center manifold and hose.

b. Remove the caps from the high and low pressure service gauge port valves.

c. If the manifold gauge set hoses do not have valve depressing pins in them, install fitting adapters T71P–19703–S and R or equivalent, which have pins, on the low and high pressure hoses.

d. Connect the high and low pressure hoses, or adapters, to the respective high and low pressure service gauge port valves. High side adapter set D81L–19703–A or tool YT–354 or 355 or equivalent is required to connect a manifold gauge set or charging station to the high pressure gauge port valve.

➡ **Service tee fitting D87P–19703–A, which may be mounted on the clutch cycling pressure switch fitting, is available for use in the low pressure side of fixed orifice tube systems, to be used in place of the low pressure gauge port valve.**

2. Leak test all connections and components with flame-type leak detector 023–00006 or

equivalent, or electronic leak detector 055–00014, 055–00015 or equivalent.

:*: CAUTION

Fumes from flame-type leak detectors are noxious, avoid inhaling fumes or personal injury may result.

➡ **Good ventilation is necessary in the area where air conditioning leak testing is to be done. If the surrounding air is contaminated with refrigerant gas, the leak detector will indicate this gas all the time. Odors from other chemicals such as antifreeze, diesel fuel, disc brake cleaner or other cleaning solvents can cause the same problem. A fan, even in a well ventilated area, is very helpful in removing small traces of air contamination that might affect the leak detector.**

3. Properly discharge the refrigerant system.
4. Make sure both manifold gauge valves are turned fully to the right. Make sure the center hose connection at the manifold gauge is tight.
5. Connect the manifold gauge set center hose to a vacuum pump.
6. Open the manifold gauge set valves and start the vacuum pump.
7. Evacuate the system with the vacuum pump until the low pressure gauge reads at least 25 in. Hg or as close to 30 in. Hg as possible. Continue to operate the vacuum pump for 15 minutes. If a part of the system has been replaced, continue to operate the vacuum pump for another 20–30 minutes.
8. When evacuation of the system is complete, close the manifold gauge set valves and turn the vacuum pump **OFF**.
9. Observe the low pressure gauge for 5 minutes to ensure that system vacuum is held. If vacuum is held, charge the system. If vacuum is not held for 5 minutes, leak test the system, service the leaks and evacuate the system again.

CHARGING THE SYSTEM

➡ **Some 1992 vehicles equipped with the 3.0L engine use R-134a refrigerant in place of the conventional type R-12 refrigerant. Refer to the information on R-134a refrigerant systems in this Section. Also any air conditioning equipment used to service the conventional R-12 refrigerant systems CANNOT be used to service the R-134a refrigerant systems.**

1. Connect a manifold gauge set according to the proper procedure. Properly discharge and evacuate the system.
2. With the manifold gauge set valves closed to the center hose, disconnect the vacuum pump from the manifold gauge set.
3. Connect the center hose of the manifold gauge set to a refrigerant drum or a small can refrigerant dispensing valve tool YT–280, YT–1034 or equivalent. If a small can dispensing valve is used, install the small can(s) on the dispensing valve.

➡ **Use only a safety type dispensing valve.**

4. Loosen the center hose at the manifold gauge set and open the refrigerant drum valve or small can dispensing valve. Allow the refrigerant to escape to purge air and moisture from the center hose. Then, tighten the center hose connection at the manifold gauge set.
5. Disconnect the wire harness snap lock connector from the clutch cycling or low pressure switch and install a jumper wire across the 2 terminals of the connector.
6. Open the manifold gauge set low side valve to allow refrigerant to enter the system. Keep the refrigerant can in an upright position.

:*: CAUTION

Do not open the manifold gauge set high pressure (discharge) gauge valve when charging with a small container. Opening the valve can cause the small refrigerant container to explode, which can result in personal injury.

7. When no more refrigerant is being drawn into the system, start the engine and set the control assembly for MAX cold and HI blower to draw the remaining refrigerant into the system. If equipped, press the air conditioning switch. Continue to add refrigerant to the system until the specified weight of the refrigerant is in the system. Then close the manifold gauge set low pressure valve and the refrigerant supply valve.
8. Remove the jumper wire from the clutch cycling or low pressure switch snap lock connector. Connect the connector to the pressure switch.
9. Operate the system until pressures stabilize to verify normal operation and system pressures.
10. In high ambient temperatures, it may be necessary to operate a high volume fan positioned to blow air through the radiator and condenser to aid in cooling the engine and prevent excessive refrigerant system pressures.
11. When charging is completed and system operating pressures are normal, disconnect the manifold gauge set from the vehicle. Install the protective caps on the service gauge port valves.

LEAK TESTING THE SYSTEM

Connect the gauge set. Be sure that both valves are closed. Both gauges should read about 60–80 psi. with the engine not running. If very little or no pressure is indicated leave the vacuum pump valve closed. Open the refrigerant tank valve and set the low pressure gauge valve to the counterclockwise position. This will open the system to tank pressure. Check all system connections, the compressor head gasket and shaft seal for leaks using a leak detector tool.

Windshield Wipers

Intense heat from the sun, snow, and ice, road oils and the chemicals used in windshield washer solvent combine to deteriorate the rubber wiper refills. The refills should be replaced about twice a year or whenever the blades begin to streak or chatter.

REMOVAL & INSTALLATION

➧ SEE FIG. 26–27

Normally, if the wipers are not cleaning the windshield properly, only the refill has to be replaced. The blade and arm usually require replacement only in the event of damage. It is not necessary (except on new Tridon® refills) to remove the arm or the blade to replace the refill (rubber part), though you may have to position the arm higher on the glass. You can do this turning the ignition switch on and operating the wipers. When they are positioned where they are accessible, turn the ignition switch off.

There are several types of refills and your vehicle could have any kind, since aftermarket blades and arms may not use exactly the same type refill as the original equipment.

Most Anco® styles use a release button that is pushed down to allow the refill to slide out of the yoke jaws. The new refill slides in and locks in place.

Blade replacement

1. Cycle arm and blade assembly to a position on the windshield where removal of blade assembly can be performed without difficulty. Turn ignition key off at desired position.
2. To remove blade assembly from wiper arm, press on spring lock and pull blade assembly from pin (View A).
3. To install, push the blade assembly on the pin so that the spring lock engages the pin (View A). Be sure the blade assembly is securely attached to pin.

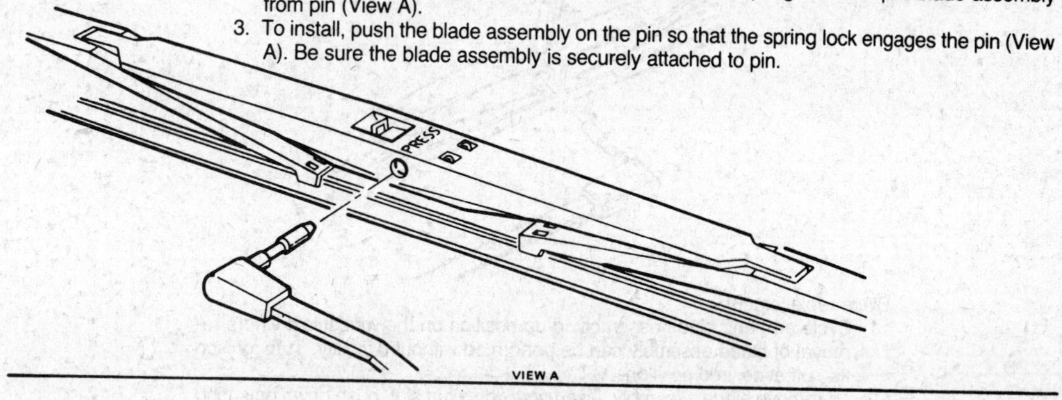

PRESS

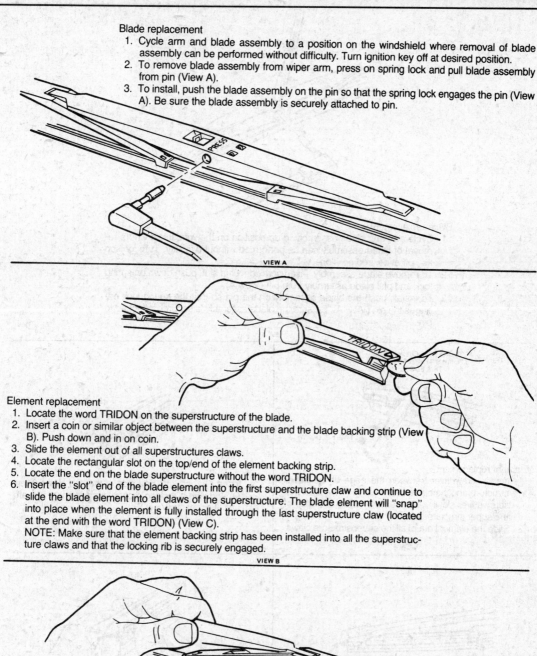

VIEW A

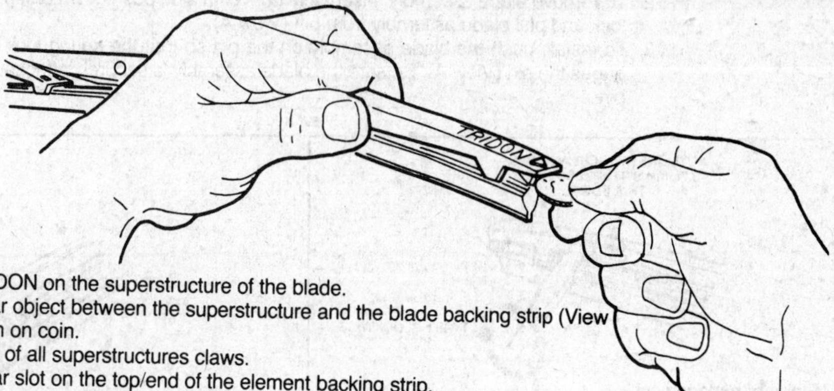

TRIDON

Element replacement

1. Locate the word TRIDON on the superstructure of the blade.
2. Insert a coin or similar object between the superstructure and the blade backing strip (View B). Push down and in on coin.
3. Slide the element out of all superstructures claws.
4. Locate the rectangular slot on the top/end of the element backing strip.
5. Locate the end on the blade superstructure without the word TRIDON.
6. Insert the "slot" end of the blade element into the first superstructure claw and continue to slide the blade element into all claws of the superstructure. The blade element will "snap" into place when the element is fully installed through the last superstructure claw (located at the end with the word TRIDON) (View C).

NOTE: Make sure that the element backing strip has been installed into all the superstructure claws and that the locking rib is securely engaged.

VIEW B

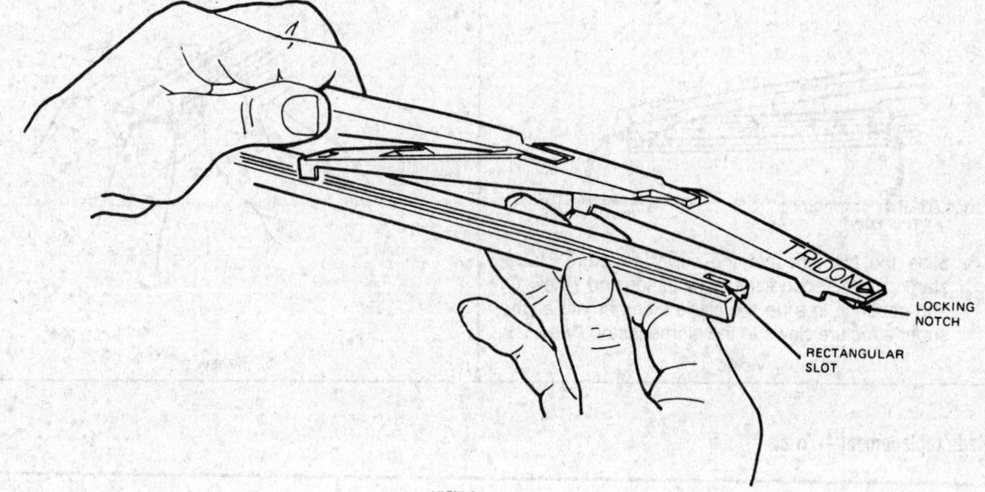

Fig.26 Wiper blade replacement — Tridon

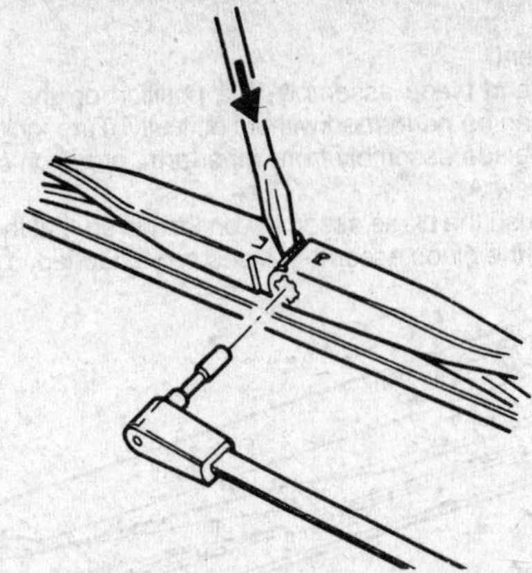

Blade replacement
1. Cycle arm and blade assembly to up position on the windshield where removal of blade assembly can be performed without difficulty. Turn ignition key off at desired position.
2. To remove blade assembly, insert screwdriver in slot, push down on spring lock and pull blade assembly from pin (View A).
3. To install, push the blade assembly on the pin so that the spring lock engages the pin (View A). Be sure the blade assembly is securely attached to pin.

VIEW A

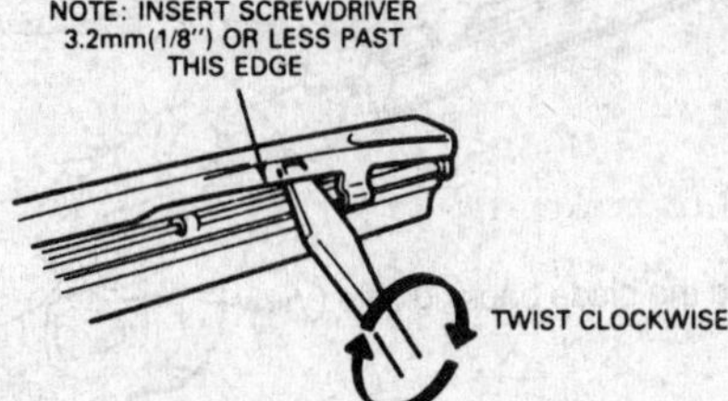

Element replacement
1. Insert screwdriver between the edge of the super structure and the blade backing drip (View B). Twist screwdriver slowly until element clears one side of the super structure claw.
2. Slide the element out of all the super structure claws.

VIEW B

4. Insert element into one side of the end claws (View D) and with a rocking motion push element upward until it snaps in (View E).

VIEW D

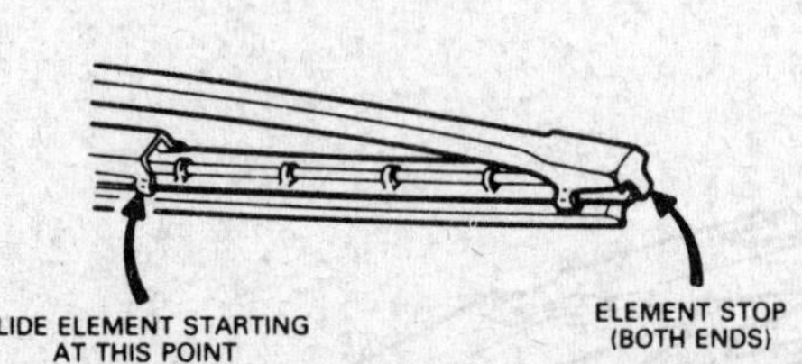

3. Slide the element into the super structure claws, starting with second set from either end (View C) and continue to slide the blade element into all the super structure claws to the element stop (View C).

VIEW C

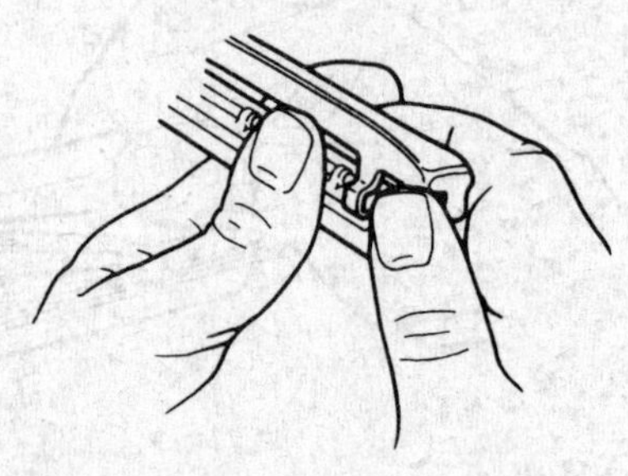

VIEW E

Fig.27 Wiper blade replacement – Trico

Some Trico® refills are removed by locating where the metal backing strip or the refill is wider. Insert a small pry bar type tool between the frame and metal backing strip. Press down to release the refill from the retaining tab.

Other Trico® blades are unlocked at one end by squeezing 2 metal tabs, and the refill is slid out of the frame jaws. When the new refill is installed, the tabs will click into place, locking the refill.

The polycarbonate type is held in place by a locking lever that is pushed downward out of the groove in the arm to free the refill. When the new refill is installed, it will lock in place automatically.

The Tridon® refill has a plastic backing strip with a notch about 1 in. (25mm) from the end. Hold the blade (frame) on a hard surface so that the frame is tightly bowed. Grip the tip of the backing strip and pull up while twisting counterclockwise. The backing strip will snap out of the retaining tab. Do this for the remaining tabs until the refill is free of the arm. The length of these refills is molded into the end and they should be replaced with identical types.

No matter which type of refill you use, be sure that all of the frame claws engage the refill. Before operating the wipers, be sure that no part of the metal frame is contacting the windshield.

Tires And Wheels

TIRE ROTATION

➧ SEE FIG. 30–30a

Tire wear can be equalized by switching the position of the tires about every 7,500 miles. Including a conventional spare in the rotation pattern can give up to 20% more tire life. Do not include the new SpaceSaver® temporary spare tires in the rotation pattern.

TIRE DESIGN

➧ SEE FIG. 28–29

All tires made since 1968 have 8 built-in tread wear indicator bars that show up as 1/2 in. (13mm) wide smooth bands across the tire when 1/16 in. (1.6mm) of tread remains. The appearance of tread wear indicators means that the tires should be replaced. In fact, many states have laws prohibiting the use of tires with less than 1/16 in. (1.6mm) of tread remains. The appearance of tread wear indicators means that the tires should be replace. In fact, many states have laws prohibiting the use of tires with less than 1/16 in. (1.6mm) tread. Tread thickness under 1/16 in. (1.6mm) is very dangerous on wet road conditions due to hydroplaning.

You can check you own tread depth with an inexpensive gauge or by using a Lincoln head penny. Slip the Lincoln penny into several tread grooves. If you can see the top of Lincoln's head in 2 adjacent grooves, the tires have less than 1/16 in. (1.6mm) tread left and should be replaced. You can measure snow tires in the same manner by using the tails side of the Lincoln penny. If you see the top of the Lincoln memorial, it's time to replace the snow tires.

➡ When you replace tires, never mix radial, bias-belted or bias type tires. Use only the tire sizes listed on the tire decal attached to your vehicle on the driver's side door post. Make sure that all tires are the same size, speed rating and load carrying capacity. Use only tire and wheel combinations as recommended on the tire decal or by your dealer. Failure to follow these precautions can adversely affect the safety and handling of your vehicle.

TIRE STORAGE

➧ SEE FIG. 52–53

Store the tires at proper inflation pressures if they are mounted on wheels. All tires should be kept in a cool, dry place. If they are stored in the garage or basement, do not let them stand on a concrete floor; set them on strips of wood.

TIRE INFLATION

Tire inflation is the most ignored item of auto maintenance. Gasoline mileage can drop as much as 0.8% for every 1 pound per square inch (psi) of under inflation.

Two items should be a permanent fixture in every glove compartment: a tire pressure gauge and a tread depth gauge. Check the tire air pressure (including the spare) regularly with a pocket type gauge. Kicking the tires won't tell

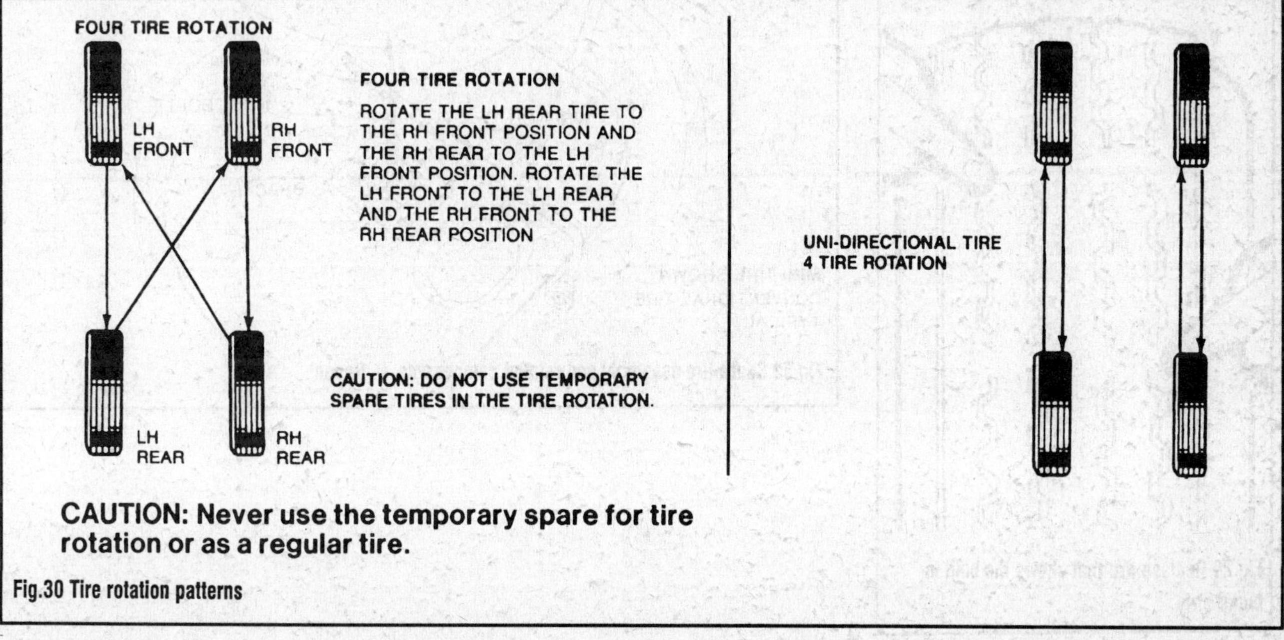
FOUR TIRE ROTATION
LH FRONT
RH FRONT
FOUR TIRE ROTATION
ROTATE THE LH REAR TIRE TO THE RH FRONT POSITION AND THE RH REAR TO THE LH FRONT POSITION. ROTATE THE LH FRONT TO THE LH REAR AND THE RH FRONT TO THE RH REAR POSITION
UNI-DIRECTIONAL TIRE 4 TIRE ROTATION
CAUTION: DO NOT USE TEMPORARY SPARE TIRES IN THE TIRE ROTATION.
LH REAR
RH REAR
CAUTION: Never use the temporary spare for tire rotation or as a regular tire.

Fig.30 Tire rotation patterns

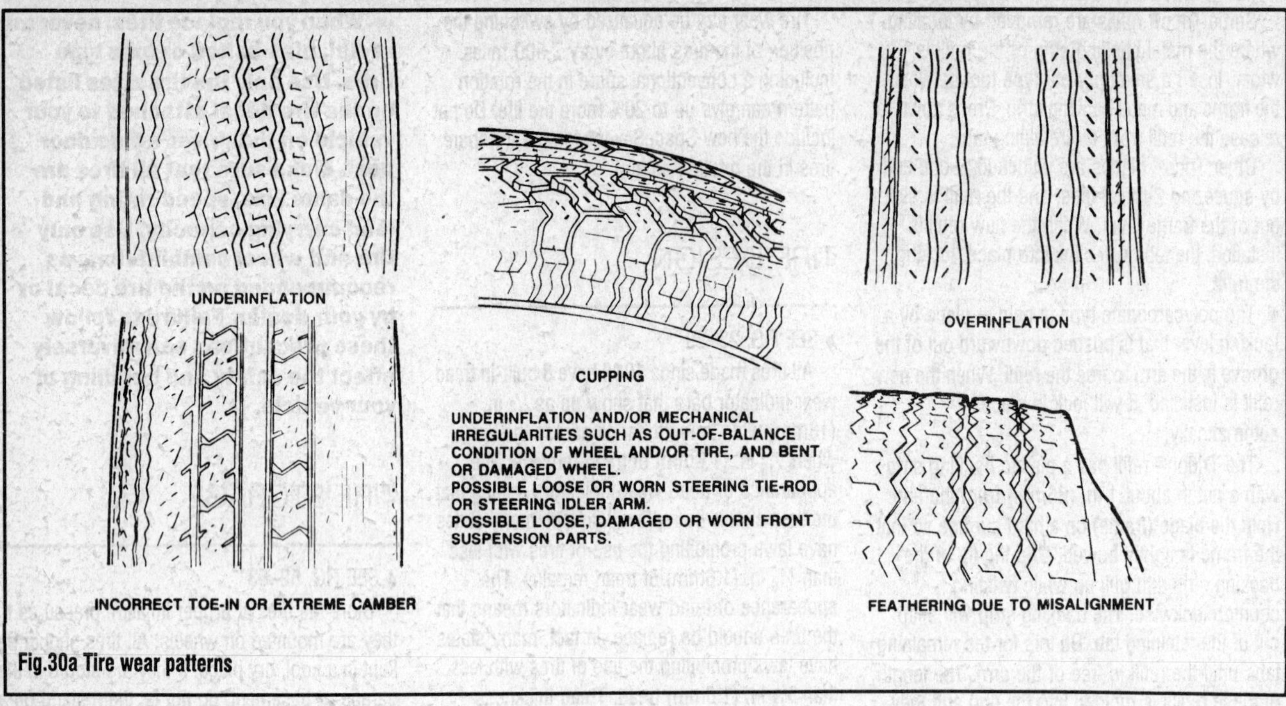

Fig.30a Tire wear patterns

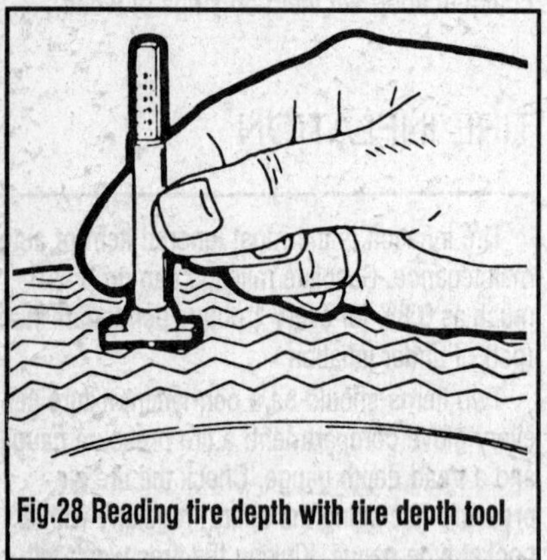
Fig.28 Reading tire depth with tire depth tool

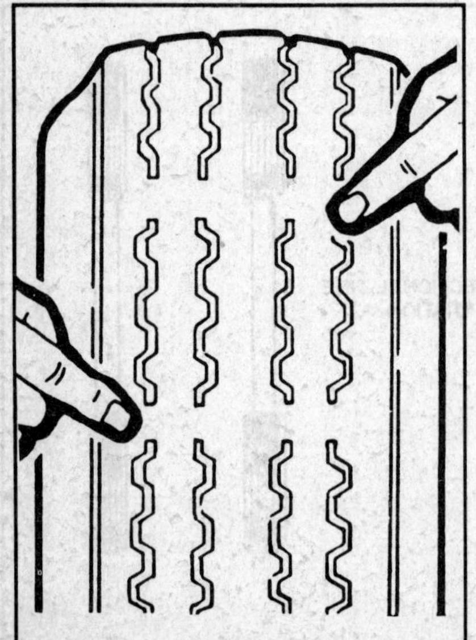
Fig.29 Replace tire that shows the built in bump strip

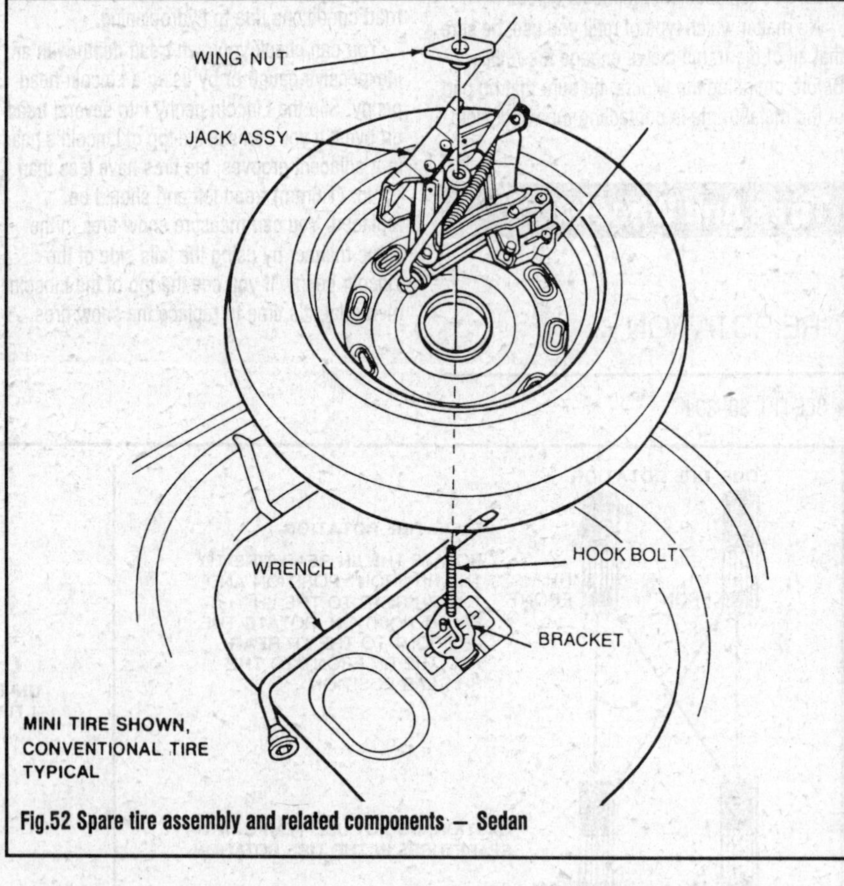

Fig.52 Spare tire assembly and related components — Sedan

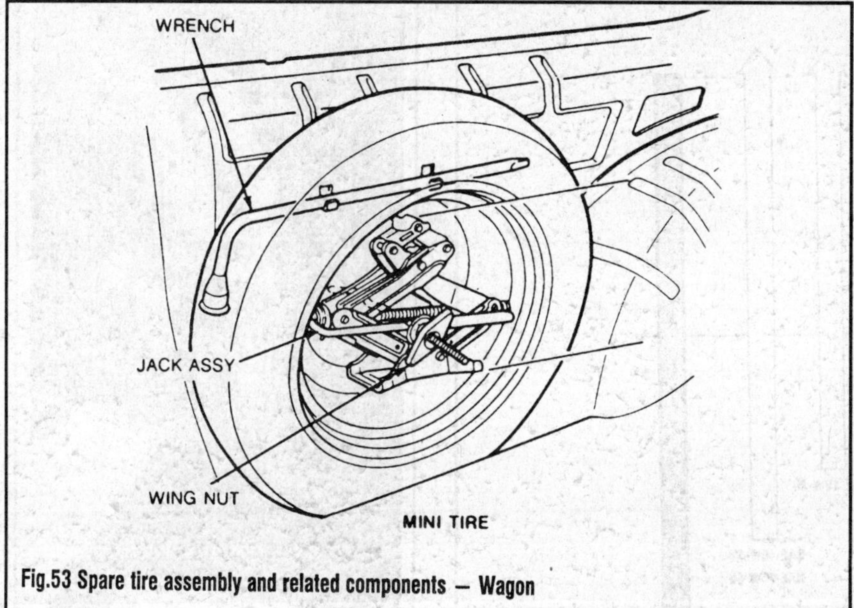

Fig.53 Spare tire assembly and related components — Wagon

you a thing, and the gauge on the service station air hose is notoriously inaccurate. Also, just looking at the tire does not indicate if it underinflated.

The tire pressures recommended for you car are usually found on a label attached to the door pillar or on the glove box inner cover or in the owner's manual. Ideally, inflation pressure should be checked when the tires are cool. When the air becomes heated it expands and the pressure increases. Every 10° rise (or drop) in temperature means a difference of 1 psi, which also explains why the tire appears to lose air on a very cold night. When it is impossible to check the tires cold, allow for pressure build-up due to heat. If the hot pressure exceeds the cold pressure by more than 15 psi, reduce your speed. Otherwise internal heat is created in the tire. When the heat approaches the temperature at which the tire was cured, during manufacture, the tread can separate from the body.

CAUTION

Never counteract excessive pressure build-up by bleeding off air pressure (letting some air out). This will only further raise the tire operating temperature.

Before starting a long trip with lots of luggage, you can add about 2–4 psi to the tires to make them run cooler, but never exceed the maximum inflation pressure on the side of the tire.

CARE OF SPECIAL WHEELS

To clean the wheels, wheel covers and wheel ornamentation use a mild soap solution and thoroughly rinse with clean water. Do not use steel wool, abrasive type cleaner or strong detergents containing high alkaline or caustic agents as damage to the protective coating and discoloration may result.

FLUIDS AND LUBRICANTS

Fuel And Engine Oil Recommendations

FUEL RECOMMENDATIONS

Unleaded gasoline having a Research Octane Number (RON) of 91, or an Antiknock Index of 87 is recommended for your car.

CAUTION

Leaded gasoline will quickly interfere the operation of the catalytic converter and just a few tankfuls of leaded gasoline will render the converter useless. This will cause the emission of much greater amounts of hydrocarbons and carbon monoxide from the exhaust system, void your warranty and cost a considerable amount of money for converter replacement.

OIL RECOMMENDATIONS

➧ SEE FIG. 31

Oil meeting API classification SG or SG/CC or SG/CD is recommended for use in your vehicle. Ford has filled your crankcase with SAE 5W-30 and recommends that you continue to use this as long as the outside temperatures don't exceed 100°F (38°C). There are other options however, see the viscosity to temperature chart in this section.

Engine

OIL LEVEL CHECK

➧ SEE FIG. 32–32b

It is a good idea to check the engine oil each time or at least every other time you fill your gas tank.

1. Be sure your car is on level ground. Shut off the engine and wait for a few minutes to allow the oil to drain back into the oil pan.
2. Remove the engine oil dipstick and wipe clean with a rag.
3. Reinsert the dipstick and push it down until it is fully seated in the tube.
4. Remove the stick and check the oil level shown. If the oil level is below the lower mark, add one quart.

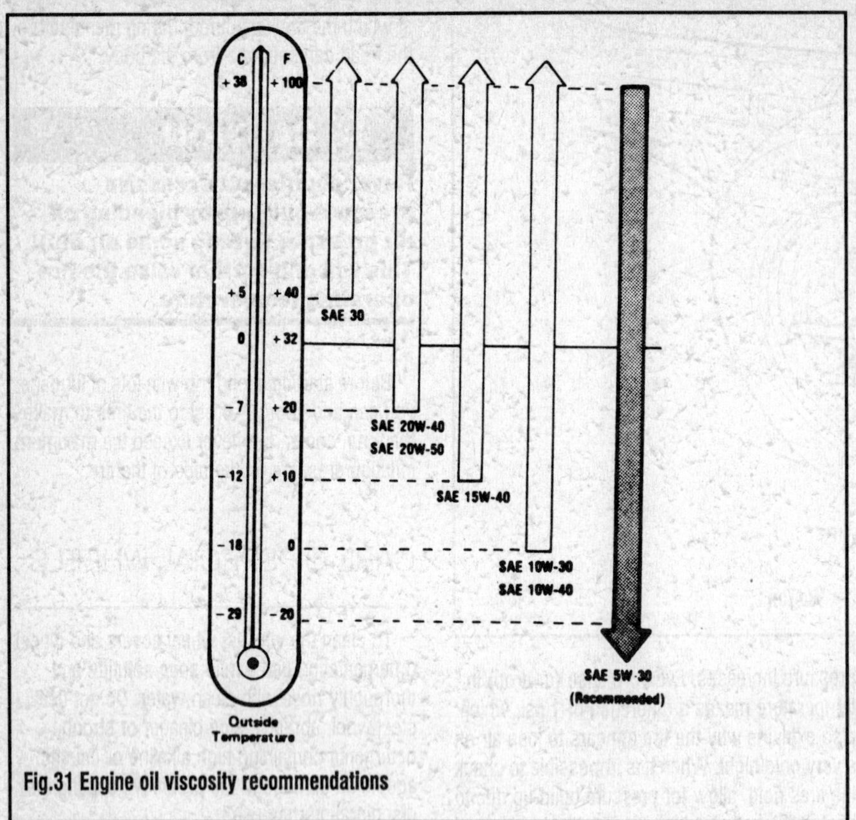

Fig.31 Engine oil viscosity recommendations

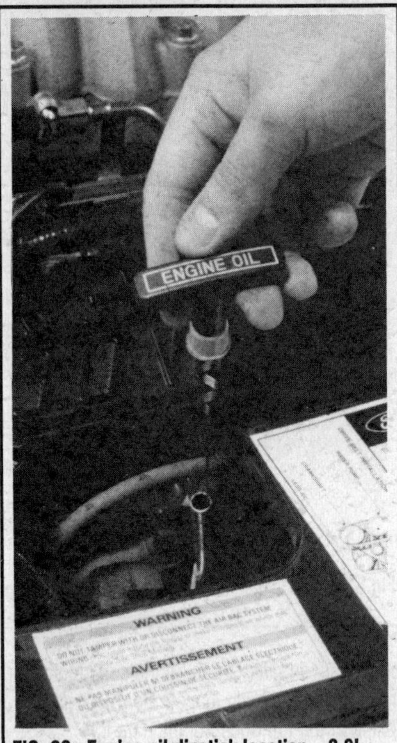

FIG. 32a Engine oil dipstick location – 3.0L engine except SHO

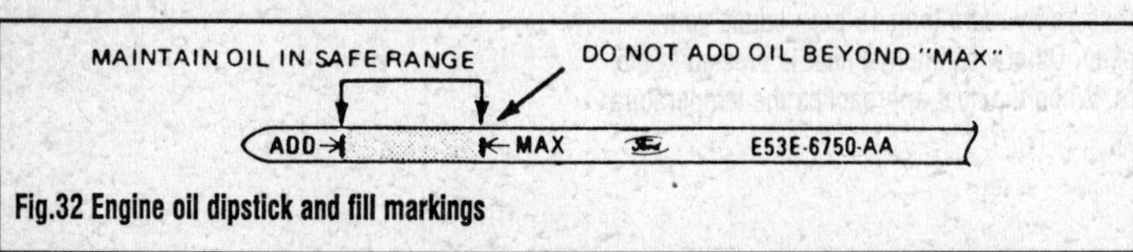

Fig.32 Engine oil dipstick and fill markings

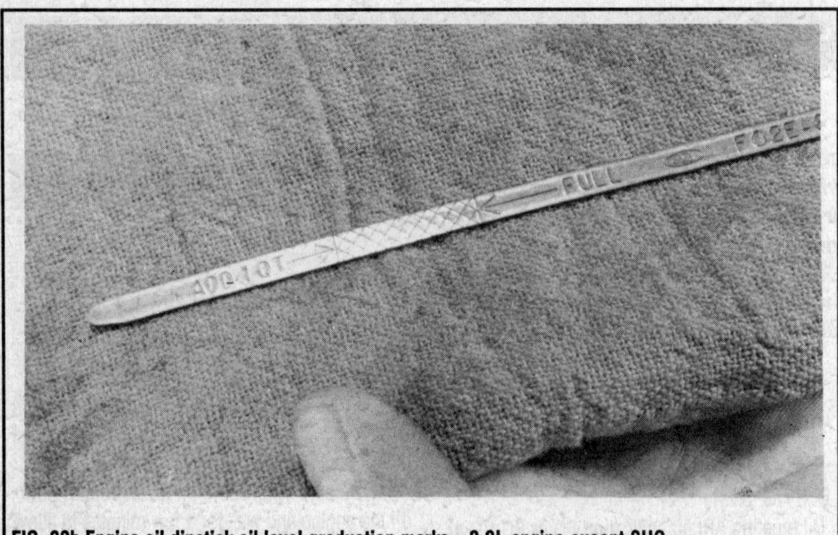

FIG. 32b Engine oil dipstick oil level graduation marks – 3.0L engine except SHO

5. If you wish, you may carefully fill the oil pan to the upper mark on the dipstick with less than a full quart. Do not, however, add a full quart when it would overfill the crankcase (level above the upper mark on the dipstick). The excess oil will generally be consumed at an excessive rate even if no damage to the engine seals occurs.

OIL AND FILTER CHANGE

➧ SEE FIG. 33–33a

Change the engine oil and oil filter every 3 months or3000 miles. If the car is used in severe service or dusty conditions, change the engine oil and oil filter more frequently. Following these recommended intervals will help keep you car engine in good condition. Dirty oil loses its lubricating qualities and can cause premature wear in your engine.

1. Make sure the engine is at normal operating temperature (this promotes complete draining of the old oil).
2. Apply the parking brake and block the wheels or raise and support the car evenly on jackstands.
3. Place a drain pan of about a gallon and a half capacity under the engine oil pan drain plug. Use the proper size box or socket wrench, loosen and remove the plug. Allow all the old oil to drain. Wipe the pan and the drain plug with a clean rag. Inspect the drain plug gasket, replace if necessary.
4. Reinstall and tighten the drain plug. DO NOT OVERTIGHTEN.
5. Move the drain pan under the engine oil filter. Use a strap wrench and loosen the oil filter (do not remove), allow the oil to drain. Unscrew the filter the rest of the way by hand. Use a rag, if necessary, to keep from burning your fingers. When the filter comes loose from the engine,

Fig.33 Lubricate oil filter filter with clean engine oil prior to installation

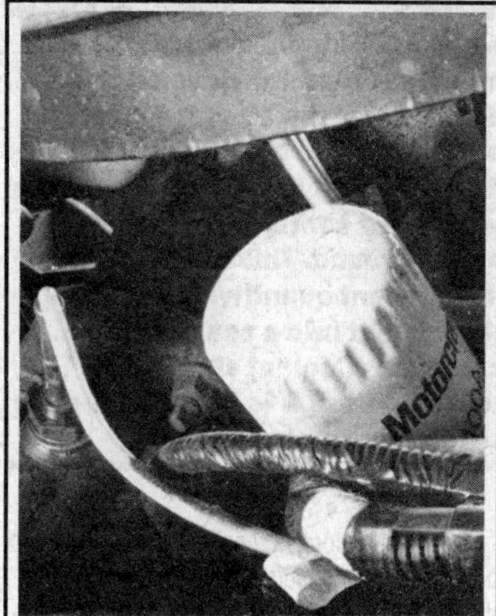
FIG. 33a Oil filter location—3.0L engine except SHO

turn the mounting base upward to avoid spilling the remaining oil.

6. Wipe the engine filter mount clean with a rag. Coat the rubber gasket on the new oil filter with clean engine oil, applying it with a finger. Carefully start the filter onto the threaded engine mount. Turn the filter until it touches the engine mounting surface. Tighten the filter, by hand, 1/2 turn more or as recommended by the filter manufacturer.

7. Lower the vehicle to the ground. Refill the crankcase to specification with the proper grade and type motor oil. Replace the filler cap and start the engine. Allow the engine to idle and check for oil leaks. Shut off the engine, wait for several minutes, then check the oil level with the dipstick. Oil level while drop as the filter fills up with oil, Add oil to the proper dipstick level.

Manual Transaxle

FLUID RECOMMENDATIONS AND LEVEL CHECK

Each time the engine oil is changed, the fluid level of the transaxle should be checked. The car must be resting on level ground or supported on jackstands (front and back) evenly. To check the fluid, remove the filler plug, located on the upper front (driver's side) of the transaxle with a 9/16 in. wrench.

The filler plug has a hex head, do not mistake any other bolts for the filler plug. Do not overfill the transaxle. The oil level should be even with the edge of the filler hole or within 1/4 in. (6mm) of the hole. If the oil is low, add Dexron®II or Mercon® automatic transmission fluid.

Automatic Transaxle

FLUID RECOMMENDATIONS AND LEVEL CHECK

➧ SEE FIG. 34–35a

A dipstick is provided in the engine compartment to check the level of the automatic transaxle. Check the lubrication and service charts in the beginning of this Section for dipstick location. Be sure the car is on level ground and that the car's engine and transaxle have reached normal operating temperatures. Start the engine, put the parking brake on the transaxle selector lever in the PARK position. Move the selector lever through all the positions and return to the PARK position. DO NOT TURN OFF THE ENGINE DURING THE FLUID LEVEL CHECK. Clean all dirt from the dipstick cap before removing the dipstick. Remove the dipstick and wipe clean. Reinsert the dipstick making sure it is fully seated. Pull the dipstick out of the tube and check the fluid level. The fluid level should be between the FULL and ADD marks.

If necessary, add enough fluid through the dipstick tube/filler to bring the level to the FULL mark on the dipstick. Use Dexron®II or Mercon® fluid in the ATX 3-speed transaxle, AXOD and AXOD-E overdrive transaxles.

Do not overfill. Can cause damage to transaxle. Make sure the dipstick is fully seated. If by chance you overfill the transaxle, Thread a small piece of rubber vacuum hose into the dipstick tube until it hits bottom. Using a large turkey baster or equivalent to pull the excess fluid out.

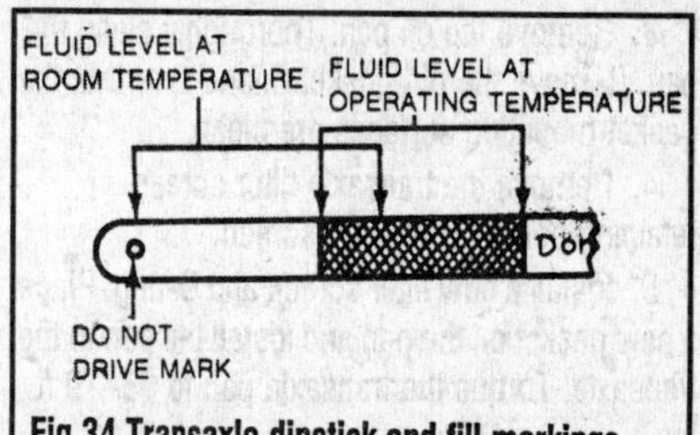

Fig.34 Transaxle dipstick and fill markings — ATX automatic transaxle

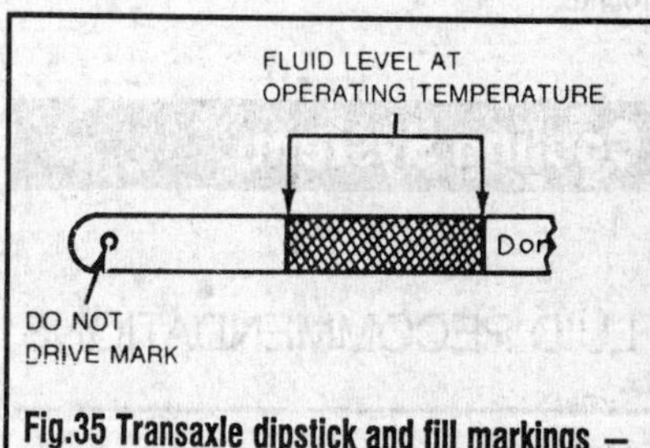

Fig.35 Transaxle dipstick and fill markings — AXOD and AXOD-E automatic transaxles

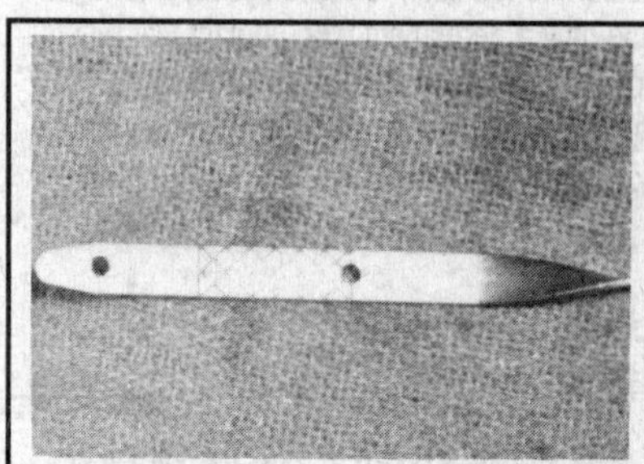
FIG. 35a Automatic transaxle dipstick fluid level graduation marks—3.0L engine except SHO

DRAIN AND REFILL

In normal service it should not be necessary or required to drain and refill the automatic transaxle. However, under severe operation or dusty conditions the fluid should be changed every 20 months or 20,000 miles.

1. Raise the car and safely support it on jackstands. If the pan is equipped with a drain plug, drain the fluid into a suitable container.

2. If the pan does not have a drain plug, place a suitable drain pan underneath the transaxle oil pan. Loosen the oil pan mounting bolts and allow the fluid to drain until it reaches the level of the pan flange. Remove the attaching bolts, leaving one end attached so that the pan will tip and the rest of the fluid will drain.

3. Remove the oil pan. Thoroughly clean the pan. Remove the old gasket. Make sure that the gasket mounting surfaces are clean.

4. Remove the transaxle filter screen retaining bolt. Remove the screen.

5. Install a new filter screen and O-ring. Place a new gasket on the pan and install the pan to the transaxle. Torque the transaxle pan to 15–19 ft. lbs.

6. Fill the transaxle to the correct level. Remove the jackstands and lower the car to the ground.

Cooling System

FLUID RECOMMENDATIONS

This engine has an aluminum cylinder head and requires a special unique corrosion inhibited coolant formulation to avoid radiator damage. Use only a permanent type coolant that meets Ford Specifications such as Ford Cooling System Fluid, Prestone® II or other approved coolants.

LEVEL CHECK

The cooling system of your car contains, among other items, a radiator and an expansion tank. When the engine is running heat is generated. The rise in temperature causes the coolant, in the radiator, to expand and builds up internal pressure. When a certain pressure is reached, a pressure relief valve in the radiator filler cap (pressure cap) is lifted from its seat and allows coolant to flow through the radiator filler neck, down a hose, and into the expansion reservoir.

When the system temperature and pressure are reduced in the radiator, the water in the expansion reservoir is siphoned back into the radiator.

DRAIN AND REFILL

➧ SEE FIG. 36

On systems without a coolant recovery tank, the engine coolant level should be maintained 1–2 in. (25–51mm) below the bottom of the radiator filler neck when the engine is at air temperature and 1 in. (25mm) below the bottom of the filler neck when the engine is hot.

On systems with a coolant recovery tank, maintain the coolant level at the level marks on the recovery bottle.

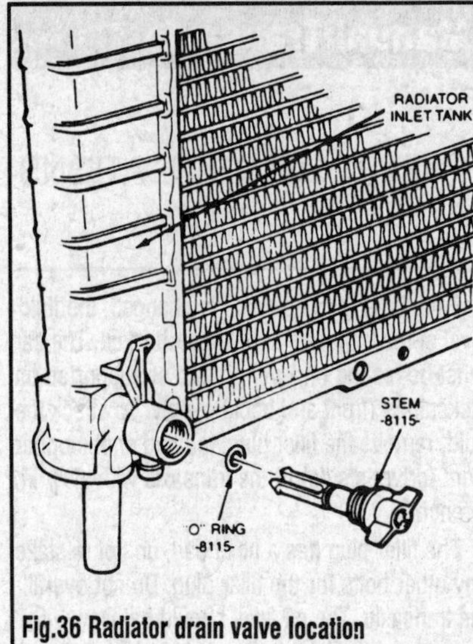

Fig.36 Radiator drain valve location

For best protection against freezing and overheating, maintain an approximate 50% water and 50% ethylene glycol antifreeze mixture in the cooling system. Do not mix different brands of antifreeze to avoid possible chemical damage to the cooling system.

Avoid using water that is known to have a high alkaline content or is very hard, except in emergency situations. Drain and flush the cooling system as soon as possible after using such water.

✱✱ CAUTION

Cover the radiator cap with a thick cloth before removing it from a radiator in a vehicle that is hot. Turn the cap counterclockwise slowly until pressure can be heard escaping. Allow all pressure to escape from the radiator before completely removing the radiator cap. It is best to allow the engine to cool if possible, before removing the radiator cap.

➡ Never add cold water to an overheated engine while the engine is not running.

After filling the radiator, run the engine until it reaches normal operating temperature, to make sure that the thermostat has opened and all the air is bled from the system.

✱✱ CAUTION

The cooling fan motor is controlled by a temperature switch. The fan may come on and run when the engine is off. It will continue to run until the correct temperature is reached. Take care not to get your fingers, etc. caught in the fan blades.

Draining Coolant

✱✱ CAUTION

When draining the coolant, keep in mind that cats and dogs are attracted by the ethylene glycol antifreeze, and are quite likely to drink any that is left in an uncovered container or in puddles on the ground. This will prove fatal in sufficient quantity. Always drain the coolant into a sealable container. Coolant should be reused unless it is contaminated or several years old.

To drain the coolant, connect a hose, 457mm long, with an inside diameter of 9.5mm, to the nipple on the drain valve located on the bottom left (driver side) of the radiator. With the engine cool, set the heater control to the maximum heat position, remove the radiator cap and open the drain valve or remove allen head plug ($\frac{3}{16}$ in.) allowing the coolant to drain into a container. When all of the coolant is drained, remove the 9.5mm hose and close the drain valve.

Replacing Coolant

If there is any evidence of rust or scaling in the cooling system, the system should be flushed thoroughly before refilling. With the engine OFF and COOL:

1. Using a funnel, add a 50 percent coolant and 50 percent water solution to the radiator.

2. Reinstall the radiator cap to the pressure relief position by installing the cap to the fully installed position and then backing off to the first stop.

3. Start and idle the engine until the upper radiator hose is warm.

4. Immediately shut off engine. Cautiously remove radiator cap and add water until the radiator is full. Reinstall radiator cap securely.

5. Add coolant to the ADD mark on the reservoir, then fill to the FULL HOT mark with water.

6. Check system for leaks and return the heater temperature control to normal position.

RADIATOR CAP INSPECTION

➧ SEE FIG. 37

Allow the engine to cool sufficiently before attempting to remove the radiator cap. Use a rag to cover the cap, then remove by pressing down and turning counterclockwise to the first stop. If any hissing is noted (indicating the release of pressure), wait until the hissing stops completely, then press down again and turn counterclockwise until the cap can be removed.

⁂ CAUTION

DO NOT attempt to remove the radiator cap while the engine is hot. Severe personal injury from steam burns can result.

Check the condition of the radiator cap gasket and seal inside of the cap. The radiator cap is designed to seal the cooling system under normal operating conditions which allows the build up of a certain amount of pressure (this pressure rating is stamped or printed on the cap). The pressure in the system raises the boiling point of the coolant to help prevent overheating. If the radiator cap does not seal, the boiling point of the coolant is lowered and overheating will occur. If the cap must be replaced, purchase the new cap according to the pressure rating which is specified for your vehicle.

Prior to installing the radiator cap, inspect and clean the filler neck. If you are reusing the old cap, clean it thoroughly with clear water. After turning the cap on, make sure the arrows align with the overflow hose.

FLUSHING AND CLEANING THE SYSTEM

1. Drain the cooling system. Drain the engine block. Refill the system with water at the radiator fill neck.
2. Allow the engine to idle for about 5 minutes. Turn the engine off. Drain the cooling system.
3. Repeat the above Steps until nearly clear water is drained from the radiator. Allow the remaining water to drain and then close the draincock.

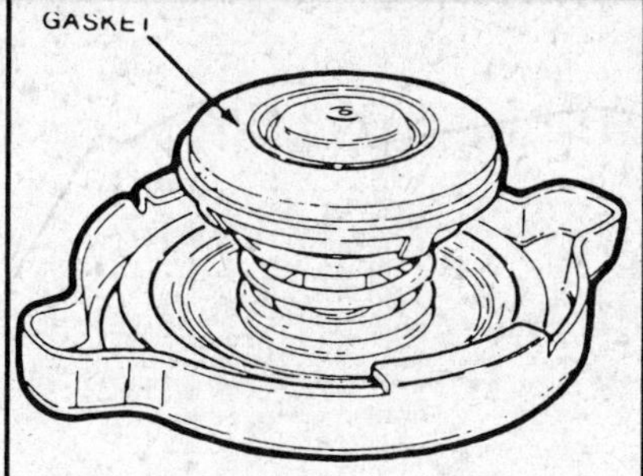

Fig.37 Check the radiator cap for defective gasket

4. Disconnect the overflow hose from the radiator filler neck connection. Remove the coolant recovery reservoir from the fender apron and empty the fluid.
5. Flush the reservoir with clean water. Reinstall the component.
6. Fill the radiator and cooling system with the proper grade and type antifreeze mixture.

Master Cylinder

FLUID RECOMMENDATIONS

When adding or refilling the master cylinder be sure to use H. D. brake fluid that meets or exceeds Ford Motor Company specification ESA-M6C25–A or Ford Motor Company part number C6AZ–19542–AA or BA.

LEVEL CHECK

The brake master cylinder is located under the hood, on the left side (drivers side) of firewall. Check the lubrication and service charts for location. Before removing the master cylinder reservoir cap, make sure the vehicle is resting on level ground and clean all the dirt away from the top of the master cylinder. Remove the master cylinder cap.

Some vehicles are equipped with Anti-lock brakes. To check the fluid level in the anti-lock master cylinder reservoir.

1. Turn ignition OFF.
2. Pump the brake pedal at least 20 times or until the pedal feel becomes hard, then turn ignition key to ON position.
3. Wait at least 60 seconds to be sure the fluid level is stabilized.
4. The fluid level should be at the MAX line as indicated on the side of the reservoir. If the level is low, remove the cap and add Heavy Duty Brake Fluid (Dot 3) until the MAX line is reached.

The level of the brake fluid should be at the **MAX** mark embossed on the translucent plastic reservoir of the master cylinder. If the level is less than half the volume of the reservoir, check the brake system for leaks. Leaks in the brake system most commonly occur at the rear wheel cylinders. or at the front calipers. Leaks at brake lines or the master cylinder can also be the cause of the loss of brake fluid.

The fluid level lowers due to normal brake shoe wear. After filling the master cylinder to the proper level with brake fluid (Type DOT 3), but before replacing the cap, fold the rubber diaphragm up into the cap, then replace the cap on the reservoir and snap the retaining clip back in place.

Power Steering Pump

➧ SEE FIG. 54–57a

FLUID RECOMMENDATIONS

Use premium power steering fluid Ford Motor Company E6AZ–19582–AA (ESW–M2C33–F) or equivalent.

LEVEL CHECK

Run the engine until it reaches normal operating temperature. While the engine is idling, turn the steering wheel all the way to the right and then left several times. Shut OFF the engine. Open the hood and remove the power steering pump dipstick located on the right side (passenger side) near the front of the engine. Wipe the dipstick clean and reinstall into the pump reservoir. Withdraw the dipstick and note the fluid level shown. The level must show in the hot full range on the dipstick. Add Ford power steering fluid, if necessary, but do not overfill. Remove any excess fluid with a suction bulb or equivalent.

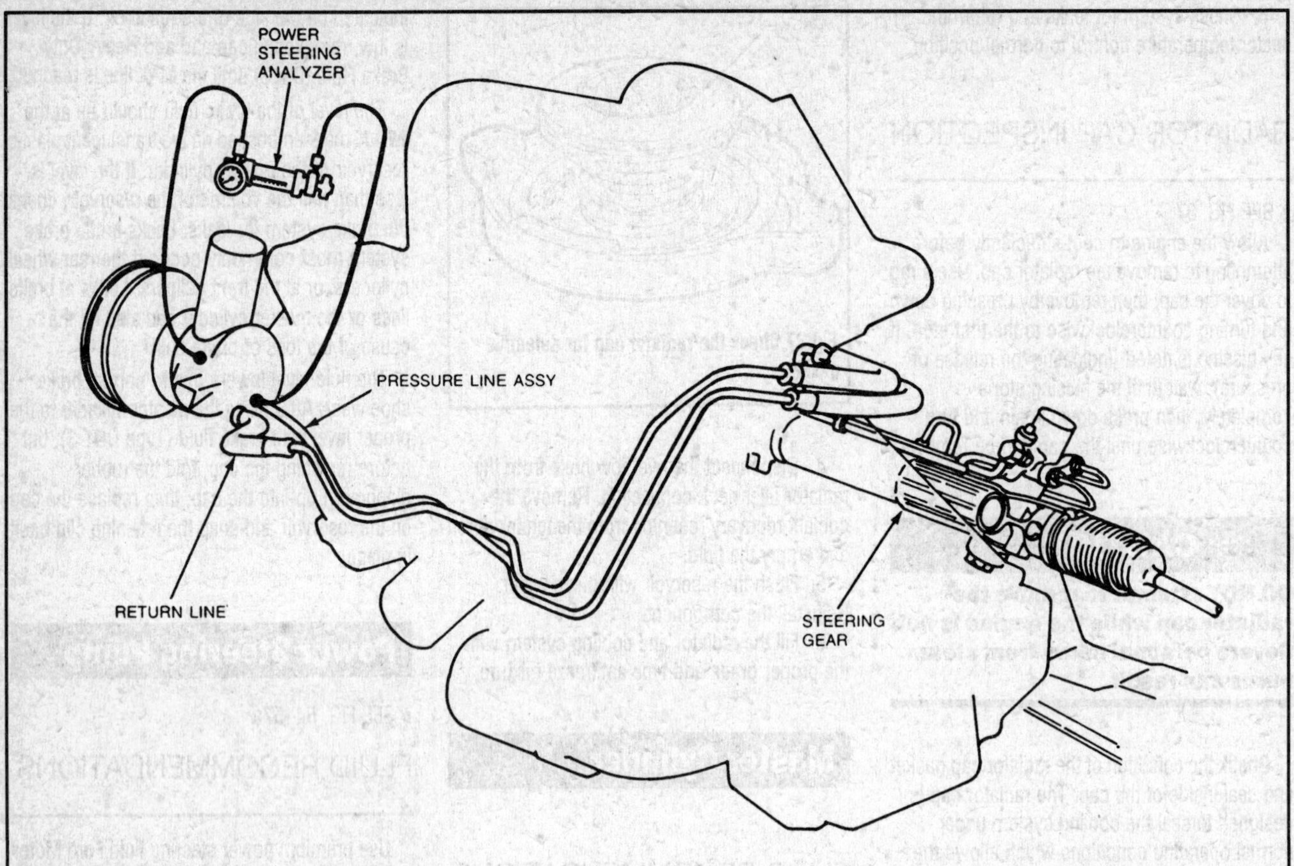

POWER STEERING ANALYZER
PRESSURE LINE ASSY
RETURN LINE
STEERING GEAR

Fig.54 Power steering system — except SHO engine

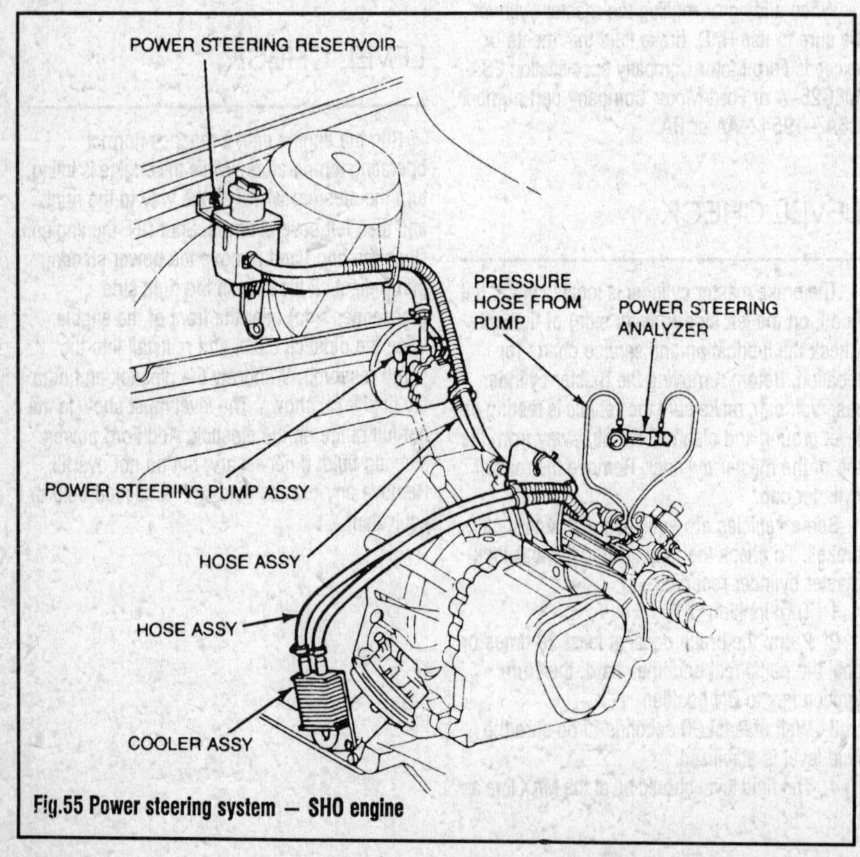

Fig.55 Power steering system — SHO engine

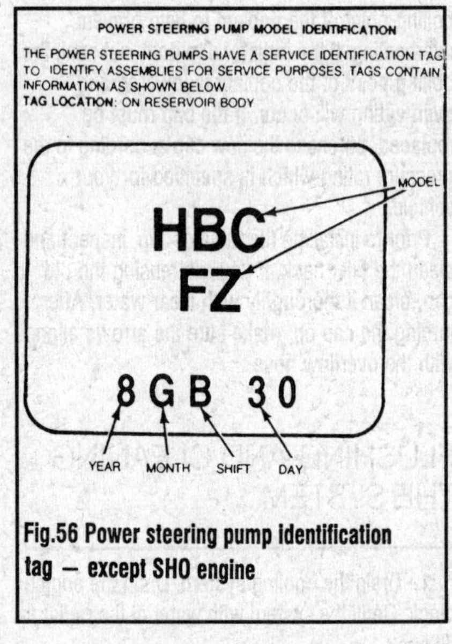

Fig.56 Power steering pump identification tag — except SHO engine

Power Steering Pump Model Identification
The Power Steering Pumps have a service identification tag to identify assemblies for service purposes. Tags contain the information shown.

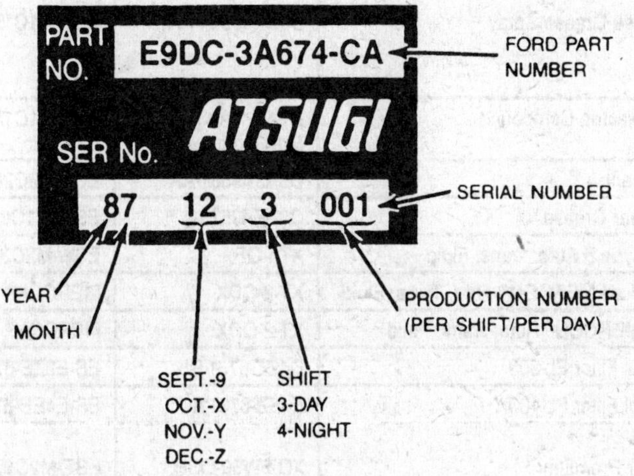

Fig.57 Power steering pump identification tag — SHO engine

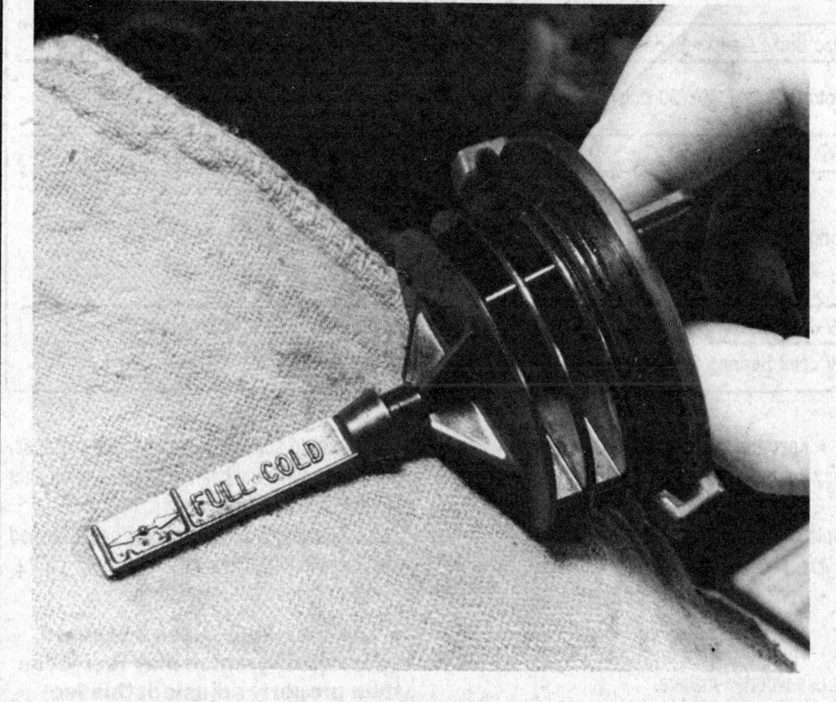

FIG. 57a Power steering pump dipstick fluid level graduation marks — 3.0L engine except SHO

Steering Rack

FLUID RECOMMENDATIONS

Use premium power steering fluid Ford Motor Company E6AZ–19582–AA (ESW–M2C33–F) or equivalent.

Body Maintenance

Regular body maintenance preserves the vehicles appearance during the life of the vehicle. When washing or waxing the exterior of the vehicle be sure to use products that meet or exceed Ford Motor Companies specifications. Replace all damaged weatherstrips as needed. Replace all chipped or cracked glass as needed. Drain holes are located under each rocker panel, quarter panel and door, these holes should be kept open to allow water to drain.

Wheel Bearings

⁂ CAUTION

When servicing the rear wheel bearings, brake shoes contain asbestos which has been determined to be a cancer causing agent. Never clean the brake surfaces with compressed air! Avoid inhaling any dust from any brake surface! When cleaning brake surfaces, use a commercially available brake cleaning fluid.

PACKING AND ADJUSTMENT

➡ Sodium-based grease is not compatible with lithium-based grease. Read the package labels and be careful not to mix the two types. If there is any doubt as to the type of grease used, completely clean the old grease from the bearing and hub before replacing.

LUBRICATION SPECIFICATIONS

Description	Part Name	Ford Part Number	Ford Specification
Door and Deck Lid Latches Hinges, Hinge Checks and Pivots Hood Latch and Auxiliary Catch Parking Brake Cable	Multi-Purpose Grease Spray	D7AZ-19584-AA	ESR-M1C159-A
Disc Brake Caliper Locating Pin and Insulator	Silicone Dielectric Compound	D7AZ-19A331-A Motorcraft WA-10	ESE-M1C171-A
Lock Cylinders	Lock Lubricant	D8AZ-19587-AA	ESB-M2C20-A
Steering Gear (Power)	Steering Gear Grease	C3AZ-19578-A	ESW-M1C87-A
Steering — Power (Pump Reservoir)	Motorcraft/Type F Auto. Trans. Fluid	XT-1-QF	ESW-M2C33-F
Transaxle AXODE (Automatic)	Motorcraft Ford MERCON® Auto. Trans. Fluid	XT-2-QDX	MERCON®
Transaxle (Manual)	Motorcraft MERCON® Auto. Trans. Fluid	XT-2-QDX	MERCON®
Oil Filter — 2.5L — Automatic Transaxle	Long-Life Oil Filter FL-300	D4ZZ-6731-B	ES-E3ZE-6714-CA
Engine Oil Filter 3.0L, 3.8L and 3.0L SHO	Long-Life Oil Filter FL-400A	E4FZ-6731-A	ES-E4EE-6714-AA
Engine Oil — Gasoline Engines	MOTORCRAFT: 5W30 Super Premium 10W30 Super Premium	XO-5W30-QSP XO-10W30-QSP	ESE-M2C153-E and API Category SG
Speedometer Cable	Speedometer Cable Lube	E6TZ-19581-A	ESF-M1C160-A
Engine Coolant	Premium Cooling System Fluid	E2FZ-19549-AA	ESE-M97B44-A
Brake Master Cylinder	H.D. Brake Fluid	C6AZ-19542-AA or BA	ESA-M6C25-A
Drum Brake Shoe Ledges	Disc Brake Caliper Slide Grease	D7AZ-19590-A	ESA-M1C172-A
Brake Master Cylinder Push Rod and Bushing Brake Pedal Pivot Bushing	Motorcraft SAE 10W30 Engine Oil	XO-10W30-QSP	ESE-M2C153-E
Tire Mounting Bead (of Tire)	Tire Mounting Lube	D9AZ-19583-A	ESA-M1B6-A
Clutch Cable Connection Transaxle End Clutch Release Lever — At Fingers (Both Sides and Fulcrum) Clutch Release Bearing Retainer	Long-Life Lubricant	XG-1-C	ESA-M1C75-B
Outboard CV Joints	CV Joint Bearing Grease	E2FZ-19590-B	ESP-M1C216-A
Inboard CV Joints	CV Joint Bearing Grease	E43Z-19590-A	ESP-M1C207-A

Before handling the bearings, there are a few things that you should remember to do and not to do.

Remember to DO the following:

• Remove all outside dirt from the housing before exposing the bearing.

• Treat a used bearing as gently as you would a new one.

• Work with clean tools in clean surroundings.

• Use clean, dry canvas gloves, or at least clean, dry hands.

• Clean solvents and flushing fluids are a must.

• Use clean paper when laying out the bearings to dry.

• Protect disassembled bearings from rust and dirt. Cover them up.

• Use clean rags to wipe bearings.

• Keep the bearings in oil-proof paper when they are to be stored or are not in use.

• Clean the inside of the housing before replacing the bearing.

Do NOT do the following:

• Don't work in dirty surroundings.

• Don't use dirty, chipped or damaged tools.

• Try not to work on wooden work benches or use wooden mallets.

• Don't handle bearings with dirty or moist hands.

• Do not use gasoline for cleaning; use a safe solvent.

• Do not spin-dry bearings with compressed air. They will be damaged.

• Do not spin dirty bearings.

• Avoid using cotton waste or dirty cloths to wipe bearings.

• Try not to scratch or nick bearing surfaces.

• Do not allow the bearing to come in contact with dirt or rust at any time.

The following procedure should be performed whenever the wheel is excessively loose on the spindle or it does not rotate freely.

➡ The rear wheel uses a tapered roller bearing which may feel loose when properly adjusted; this feel should be considered normal.

Adjustment

The following procedure applies only to 1986–89 vehicles. Adjustment is not possible on 1990–91 vehicles. This procedure should be performed whenever the wheel is excessively loose on the spindle or it does not rotate freely.

➡ **The rear wheel uses a tapered roller bearing which may feel loose when properly adjusted; this condition should be considered normal.**

1. Raise and support the rear of the vehicle until tires clear the floor.
2. Remove the wheel cover or the ornament and nut covers. Remove the hub grease cap.

➡ **If the vehicle is equipped with styled steel or aluminum wheels, the wheel/tire assembly must be removed to remove the dust cover.**

3. Remove the cotter pin and the nut retainer.
4. Back off the hub nut 1 full turn.
5. While rotating the hub/drum assembly, tighten the adjusting nut to 17–25 ft. lbs. (23–24 Nm). Back off the adjusting nut 1/2 turn, then retighten it to 24–28 inch lbs. (2.7–3.2 Nm).
6. Position the nut retainer over the adjusting nut so the slots are in line with cotter pin hole, without rotating the adjusting nut.
7. Install the cotter pin and bend the ends around the retainer flange.
8. Check the hub rotation. If the hub rotates freely, install the grease cap. If not, check the bearings for damage and replace, as necessary.
9. Install the wheel and tire assembly and the wheel cover, if necessary. Lower the vehicle.

REMOVAL & INSTALLATION

Drum Brakes

1986–89

➧ SEE FIG. 38

1. Raise the vehicle and support it safely. Remove the wheel from the hub and drum.
2. Remove the grease cap from the hub. Remove the cotter pin, nut retainer, adjusting nut and keyed flat washer from the spindle. Discard the cotter pin.
3. Pull the hub and drum assembly off of the spindle. Remove the outer bearing assembly.
4. Using seal remover tool 1175–AC or equivalent, remove and discard the grease seal. Remove the inner bearing assembly from the hub.
5. Wipe all lubricant from the spindle and inside of the hub. Cover the spindle with a clean cloth and vacuum all loose dust and dirt from the brake assembly. Carefully remove the cloth to prevent dirt from falling on the spindle.
6. Clean both bearing assemblies and cups using a suitable solvent. Inspect the bearing assemblies and cups for excessive wear, scratches, pits or other damage and replace as necessary.
7. If the cups are to be replaced, remove them with impact slide hammer T50T–100–A and bearing cup puller T77F–1102–A or equivalent.

To install:

8. If the inner and outer bearing cups were removed, install the replacement cups using driver handle T80T–4000–W and bearing cup replacers T73T–1217–A and T77F–1217–A or equivalent. Support the drum hub on a block of wood to prevent damage. Make sure the cups are properly seated in the hub.

➡ **Do not use the cone and roller assembly to install the cups. This will result in damage to the bearing cup and the cone and roller assembly.**

9. Make sure all of the spindle and bearing surfaces are clean.
10. Using a bearing packer, pack the bearing assemblies with a suitable wheel bearing grease. If a packer is not available, work in as much grease as possible between the rollers and cages. Grease the cup surfaces.

➡ **Allow all of the cleaning solvent to dry before repacking the bearings. Do not spin-dry the bearings with air pressure.**

11. Install the inner bearing cone and roller assembly in the inner cup. Apply a light film of grease to the lips of a new grease seal and install the seal with rear hub seal replacer T56T–4676–B or equivalent. Make sure the retainer flange is seated all around.
12. Apply a light film of grease on the spindle shaft bearing surfaces. Install the hub and drum assembly on the spindle. Keep the hub centered on the spindle to prevent damage to the grease seal and spindle threads.
13. Install the outer bearing assembly and the keyed flatwasher on the spindle. Install the adjusting nut and adjust the wheel bearings. Install a new cotter pin. Install the grease cap.
14. Install the wheel and tire assembly and lower the vehicle.

1990–92

➧ SEE FIG. 39

1. Raise the vehicle and support it safely.
2. Remove the wheel.
3. Remove the 2 pushnuts retaining the drum to the hub and remove the drum.
4. Remove the grease cap from the bearing and hub assembly and discard it.
5. Remove the hub retaining nut and remove the bearing and hub assembly from the spindle.
6. Install in the reverse order of removal. Use coil remover T89P–19623–FH or equivalent, to install the new grease cap. Tap on the tool to make sure the grease cap is fully seated. Tighten the hub retaining nut to 188–254 ft. lbs. (255–345 Nm).

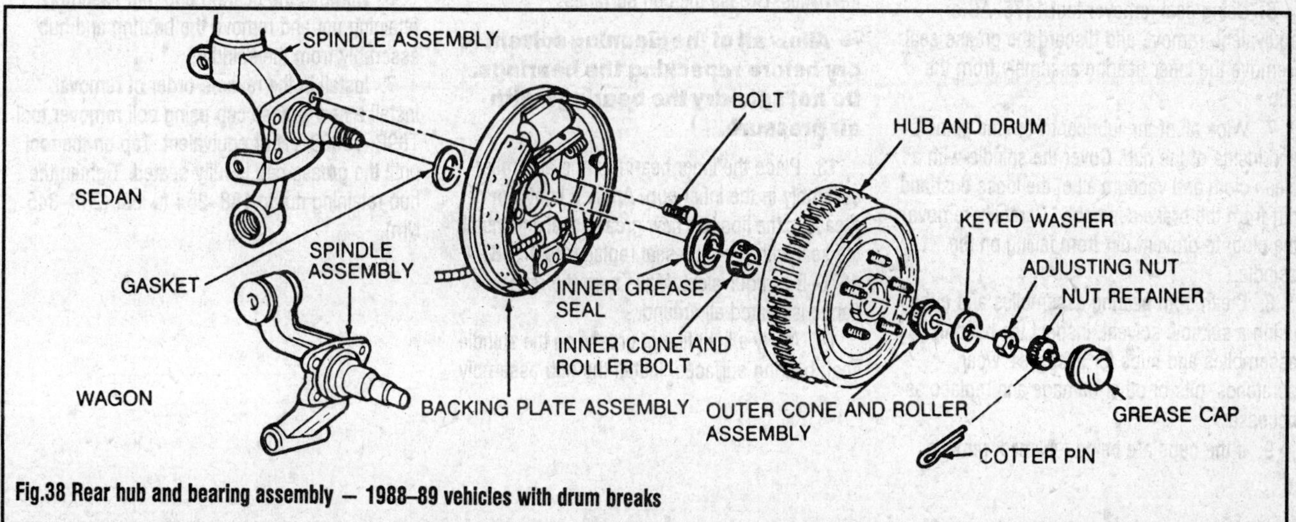

Fig.38 Rear hub and bearing assembly — 1988–89 vehicles with drum breaks

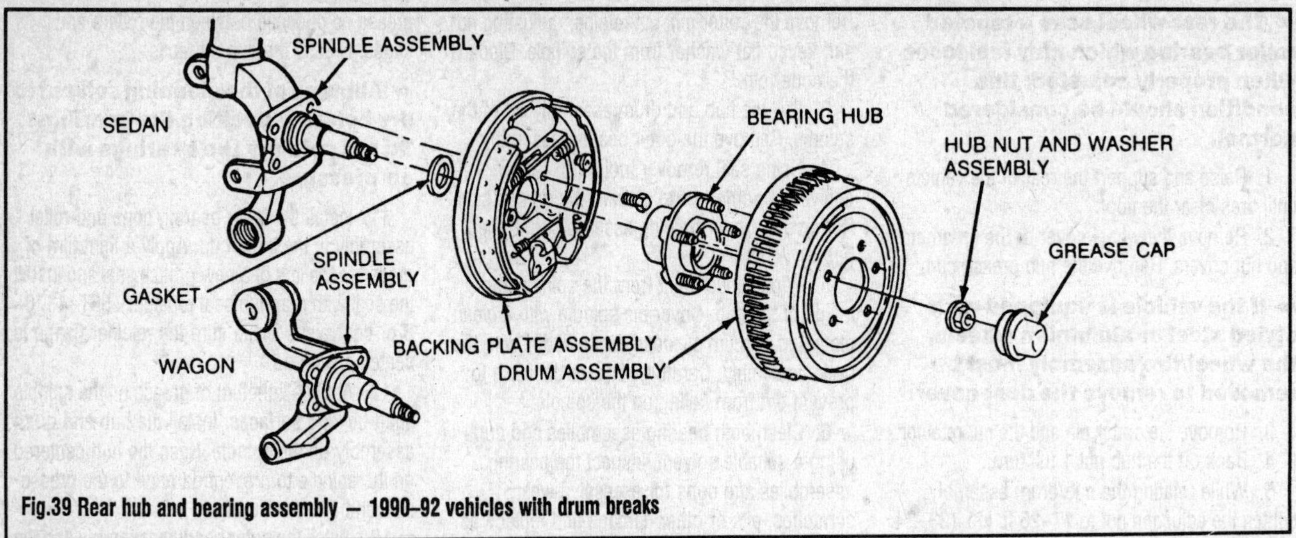

Fig.39 Rear hub and bearing assembly — 1990–92 vehicles with drum breaks

Disc Brakes

1986–89

1. Raise the vehicle and support it safely. Remove the tire and wheel assembly from the hub.
2. Remove the brake caliper by removing the 2 bolts that attach the caliper support to the cast iron brake adapter. Do not remove the caliper pins from the caliper assembly. Lift the caliper off of the rotor and support it with a length of wire. Do not allow the caliper assembly to hang from the brake hose.
3. Remove the rotor from the hub by pulling it off the hub bolts. If the rotor is difficult to remove, strike the rotor sharply between the studs with a rubber or plastic hammer.
4. Remove the grease cap from the hub. Remove the cotter pin, nut retainer, adjusting nut and keyed flat washer from the spindle. Discard the cotter pin.
5. Pull the hub assembly off of the spindle. Remove the outer bearing assembly.
6. Using seal remover tool 1175–AC or equivalent, remove and discard the grease seal. Remove the inner bearing assembly from the hub.
7. Wipe all of the lubricant from the spindle and inside of the hub. Cover the spindle with a clean cloth and vacuum all of the loose dust and dirt from the brake assembly. Carefully remove the cloth to prevent dirt from falling on the spindle.
8. Clean both bearing assemblies and cups using a suitable solvent. Inspect the bearing assemblies and cups for excessive wear, scratches, pits or other damage and replace as necessary.
9. If the cups are being replaced, remove them with impact slide hammer tool T50T–100–A and bearing cup puller tool T77F–1102–A or equivalent.

To install:

10. If the inner and outer bearing cups were removed, install the replacement cups using driver handle tool T80T–4000–W and bearing cup replacer tools T73F–1217–A and T77F–1217–B or equivalent. Support the hub on a block of wood to prevent damage. Make sure the cups are properly seated in the hub.

➡ Do not use the cone and roller assembly to install the cups. This will result in damage to the bearing cup and the cone and roller assembly.

11. Make sure all of the spindle and bearing surfaces are clean.
12. Pack the bearing assemblies with a suitable wheel bearing grease using a bearing packer. If a packer is not available, work in as much grease as possible between the rollers and the cages. Grease the cup surfaces.

➡ Allow all of the cleaning solvent to dry before repacking the bearings. Do not spin-dry the bearings with air pressure.

13. Place the inner bearing cone and roller assembly in the inner cup. Apply a light film of grease to the lips of a new grease seal and install the seal with rear hub seal replacer tool T56T–4676–B or equivalent. Make sure the retainer flange is seated all around.
14. Apply a light film of grease on the spindle shaft bearing surfaces. Install the hub assembly on the spindle. Keep the hub centered on the spindle to prevent damage to the grease seal and spindle threads.
15. Install the outer bearing assembly and keyed flat washer on the spindle. Install the adjusting nut and adjust the wheel bearings. Install a new cotter pin. Install the grease cap.
16. Install the disc brake rotor to the hub assembly. Install the disc brake caliper over the rotor.
17. Install the wheel and tire assembly and lower the vehicle.

1990–92

1. Raise the vehicle and support it safely.
2. Remove the wheel and tire assembly.
3. Remove the caliper assembly from the brake adapter. Support the caliper assembly with a length of wire.
4. Remove the push on nuts that retain the rotor to the hub and remove the rotor.
5. Remove the grease cap from the bearing and hub assembly and discard the grease cap.
6. Remove the bearing and hub assembly retaining nut and remove the bearing and hub assembly from the spindle.
7. Install in the reverse order of removal. Install a new grease cap using coil remover tool T89P–19623–FH or equivalent. Tap on the tool until the grease cap is fully seated. Tighten the hub retaining nut to 188–254 ft. lbs. (255–345 Nm).

TRAILER TOWING

General Recommendations

Towing a trailer puts additional load on your vehicles engine, drivetrain, brakes, tires and suspension. For your safety and the care of your car, make sure the trailer towing equipment is properly matched to the trailer. All towing equipment should be safely attached to the vehicle and of the proper weight class.

➡ Trailer towing should only be attempted with the 3.0L or 3.8L V6 engine!

The maximum trailer weight that your vehicle can tow is 1,000 lbs. gross trailer axle weight with a maximum tongue load of 100 lbs. and must abide to the following qualifications:

- Any model equipped with a AXOD or AXOD-E overdrive transaxle should be shifted to the "D" DRIVE position to avoid excessive shifting between the overdrive and third gears.
- Auxiliary oil coolers are recommended for the power steering system and the automatic transaxle during long distance towing (greater than 50 miles, towing in hilly terrain or frequent towing).
- Vehicle speed no higher than 55 mph is recommended while towing a trailer.

Towing Tips

Before starting on a trip, practice turning, stopping and backing up in an area away from other traffic (such as a deserted shopping center parking lot) to gain experience in handling the extra weight and length of the trailer. Take enough time to get the feel of the vehicle/trailer combination under a variety of situations.

Skillful backing requires practice. Back up slowly with an assistant acting as a guide and watching for obstructions. Use both rear view mirrors. Place your hand at the bottom of the steering wheel and move it in the direction you want the rear of the trailer to swing. Make small corrections, instead of exaggerated ones, as a slight movement of the steering wheel will result in a much larger movement of the rear of the trailer.

Allow considerable more room for stopping when a trailer is attached to the vehicle. Keep in mind, the car/trailer combination is a considerable increase in the weight that your car's brakes have to bring to a stop. If you have a manual brake controller, lead with the trailer brakes when approaching a stop. Trailer brakes are also handy for correcting side sway. So just touch them for a moment without using your vehicle brakes and the trailer should settle down and track straight again.

To assist in obtaining good handling with the car/trailer combination, it is important that the trailer tongue load be maintained at approximately 10–15% of the loaded trailer weight.

Check everything before starting out on the road, then stop after you've traveled about 50 miles and double-check the trailer hitch and electrical connections to make sure everything is still OK. Listen for sounds like chains dragging on the ground (indicating that a safety chain has come loose) and check your rear view mirrors frequently to make sure the trailer is still there and tracking properly. Check the trailer wheel lug nuts to make sure they're tight and never attempt to tow the trailer with a space saver spare installed on the car.

Remember that a car/trailer combination is more sensitive to cross winds and slow down when crossing bridges or wide open expanses in gusty wind conditions. Exceeding the speed limit while towing a trailer is not only illegal, it is foolhardy and invites disaster. A strong gust of wind can send a speeding car/trailer combination out of control.

Because the trailer wheels are closer than the towing vehicle wheels to the inside of a turn, drive slightly beyond the normal turning point when negotiating a sharp turn at a corner. Allow extra distance for passing other vehicles and downshift if necessary for better acceleration. Allow at least the equivalent of one vehicle and trailer length combined for each 10 mph of road speed.

Finally, remember to check the height of the loaded car/trailer, allowing for luggage racks, antenna, etc. mounted on the roof and take note of low bridges or parking garage clearances.

PUSHING AND TOWING

Vehicle Towing

➧ SEE FIG. 58–60

Whenever you are towing another vehicle, or being towed, make sure the strap or chain is sufficiently long and strong. Straps are recommended because they have more stretch then a chain. Attach the strap or chain securely at a point on the frame, shipping tie-down slots are provided on the front and rear of you car and should be used. Never attach a strap or chain to any steering or suspension part. Never try to start the vehicle when being towed, it might run into the back of the tow car. Do not allow too much slack in the tow line, the towed car could run over the line and damage to both cars could occur. If your car is being towed by a tow truck, the towing speed should be limited to 50 mph with the driving wheels off the ground. If it is necessary to tow the car with the drive wheels on the ground, speed should be limited to no more then 35 mph and the towing distance should not be greater than 50 miles. If towing distance is more than 50 miles the front of the car should be put on dollies.

➡ If the car is being towed with the front (drive) wheels on the ground, never allow the steering lock to keep the wheels straight, damage to the steering could occur. In general, don't do this! A new transaxle will cost you a lot more than a reasonable towing service. Remember the old saying, "you can pay me now, or you can pay me later".

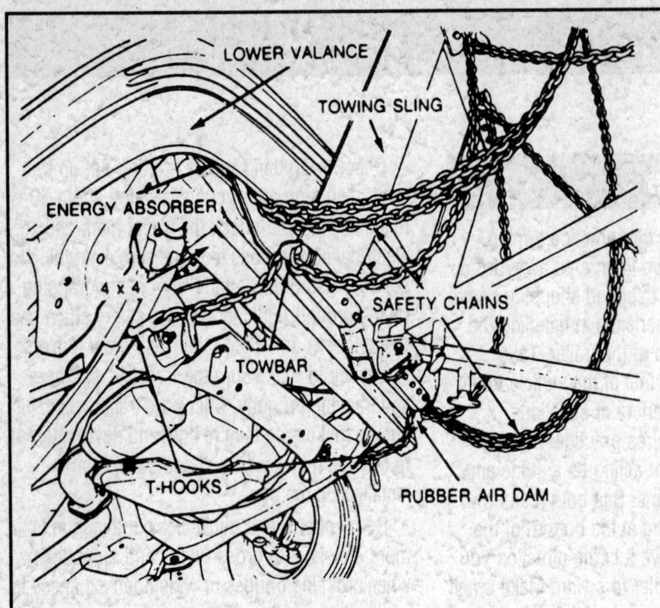

Fig.58 Proper vehicle tow hook up — front

CAUTION: Do not tow with J-Hooks under any circumstances. J-Hooks will damage driveshafts and control arms.

CAUTION: Placing towing chains on the transverse suspension arms will result in vehicle damage.

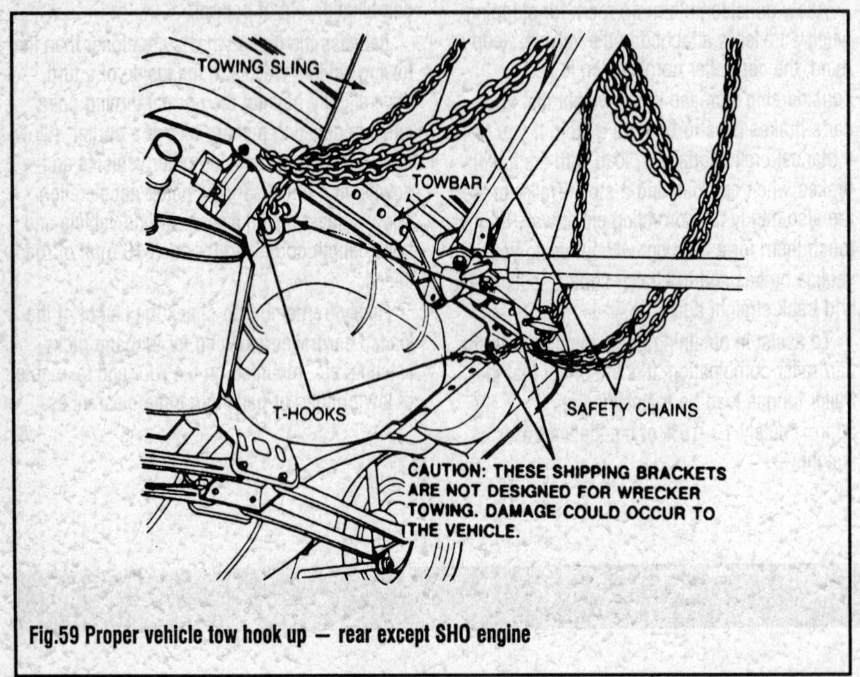

Fig.59 Proper vehicle tow hook up — rear except SHO engine

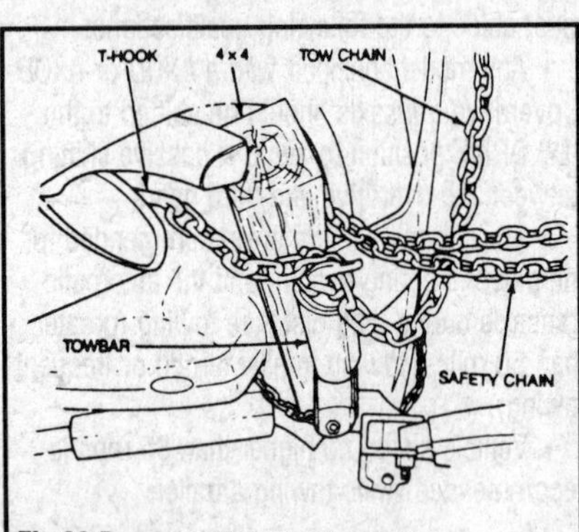

Fig.60 Proper vehicle tow hook up — rear SHO engine

Vehicle Pushing

Push starting is not recommended on cars with a catalytic converter. Gas accumulation in the converter will cause damage to the system. Also you can't push start a Taurus/Sable with an automatic transaxle anyway.

JACKING

The service jack that is provided with your vehicle is only intended to be used in an emergency for changing a flat tire. Never use this jack to hoist the vehicle for any other service. When servicing the vehicle use a floor jack. When using a floor jack, raise the front of the vehicle by positioning the floor jack under either the subframe or body side rail behind the engine support bracket. The rear may be lifted by positioning a floor jack under either rear suspension body bracket. Under no circumstances should the vehicle ever be lifted by the front or rear control arms, halfshafts or CV joints. Severe damage to the vehicle could result.

SCHEDULE A MAINTENANCE INFORMATION

Maintenance Schedules

CUSTOMER MAINTENANCE SCHEDULE A

Follow Maintenance Schedule A, if your driving habits MAINLY include one or more of the following conditions:

- Short trips of less than 16 km (10 miles) when outside temperatures remain below freezing.
- Operating during HOT WEATHER:
  — Driving in stop-and-go "rush hour" traffic.
- Towing a trailer, using a camper or car-top carrier.
- Operating in severe dust conditions.
- Extensive idling, such as police, taxi or door-to-door delivery service.

SERVICE INTERVAL Perform at the months or distances shown, whichever comes first. Miles x 1000	3	6	9	12	15	18	21	24	27	30	33	36	39	42	45	48	51	54	57	60
Kilometers x 1000	4.8	9.6	14.4	19.2	24	28.8	33.6	38.4	43.2	48	52.8	57.6	62.4	67.2	72	76.8	81.6	86.4	91.2	96
EMISSION CONTROL SERVICE																				
Replace Engine Oil and Oil Filter Every 3 Months OR	X	X	X	X	X	X	X	X	X	X	X	X	X	X	X	X	X	X	X	X
Spark Plugs 3.0L SHO Platinum Plugs																				X
2.5L, 3.0L, 3.8L										X										X
Inspect Accessory Drive Belt(s)										X										X
Replace Air Cleaner Filter ①										X										X
Replace Crankcase Filter Four Cylinder Engines Only ①										X										X
Replace Cam Belt and Adjust Valve Lash — 3.0L SHO																				X
Replace Engine Coolant Every 36 Months OR										X										X
Check Engine Coolant Protection, Hoses and Clamps	ANNUALLY																			
GENERAL MAINTENANCE																				
Inspect Exhaust Heat Shields										X										X
Change Automatic Transaxle Fluid (2.5L, 3.0L, 3.8L) ②										X										X
Inspect Disc Brake Pads and Rotors (Front) ③ (Front and Rear — SHO)										X										X
Inspect Brake Linings and Drums ③										X										X
Inspect Battery Fluid Level (SHO only) ④								X								X				
Inspect and Repack Rear Wheel Bearings										X										X
Rotate Tires		X					X					X					X			

① If operating in severe dust, more frequent intervals may be required — consult your dealer.

② Change automatic transaxle fluid if your driving habits frequently include one or more of the following conditions:
- Operation during HOT WEATHER (above 32°C (90°F)).
- Towing a trailer or using a car top carrier.
- Police, taxi or door-to-door delivery service.

③ If your driving includes continuous stop and go driving or driving in mountainous areas, more frequent intervals may be required.

X All items designated with an "X" must be performed in all states.

④ If operating in temperatures above 32°C (90°F) check more often.

SCHEDULE B MAINTENANCE INFORMATION

CUSTOMER MAINTENANCE SCHEDULE B

Follow this Schedule if, generally, you drive your vehicle on a daily basis for several miles and NONE OF THE UNIQUE DRIVING CONDITIONS SHOWN IN SCHEDULE A APPLY TO YOUR DRIVING HABITS.

SERVICE INTERVALS Perform at the months or distances shown, whichever comes first. Miles x 1000	7.5	15	22.5	30	37.5	45	52.5	60
Kilometers x 1000	12	24	36	48	60	72	84	96
EMISSIONS CONTROL SERVICE								
Replace Engine Oil and Oil Filter Every 6 Months OR	X	X	X	X	X	X	X	X
Replace Spark Plugs 2.5L, 3.8L				X				X
3.0L, 3.0L SHO Platinum Plugs								X
Replace Cam Belt and Adjust Valve Lash — 3.0L SHO								X
Replace Crankcase Filter — Four Cylinder Engine Only				X				X
Inspect Accessory Drive Belt(s)				X				X
Replace Air Cleaner Filter①				X				X
Replace Engine Coolant Every 36 Months OR				X				X
Check Engine Coolant Protection, Hoses and Clamps	ANNUALLY							
GENERAL MAINTENANCE								
Inspect Battery Fluid Level (SHO only) ③			X			X		
Check Exhaust Heat Shields				X				X
Inspect Disc Brake Pads and Rotors (Front) (Front and Rear — SHO) ②				X②				X②
Inspect Brake Linings and Drums (Rear)②				X②				X②
Rotate Tires	X		X		X		X	

① If operating in severe dust, more frequent intervals may be required. Consult your dealer.

② If your driving includes continuous stop-and-go driving or driving in mountainous areas, more frequent intervals may be required.

X All items designated with an "X" must be performed in all states.

③ If operating in temperatures above 32°C (90°F) check more often.

CAPACITIES

Year	Model	Engine VIN	Engine Displacement liter (cc)	Engine Crankcase with Filter	Transmission (pts.) 5-Spd	Transmission (pts.) Auto.	Drive Axle (pts.)	Fuel Tank (gal.)	Cooling System (qts.)
1986	Taurus	D	2.5 (2500)	5.0	6.2	16.6	①	②	8.3
	Taurus	U	3.0 (3000)	4.5	6.2	21.8	①	②	③
	Sable	D	2.5 (2500)	5.0	6.2	16.6	①	②	8.3
	Sable	U	3.0 (3000)	4.5	6.2	21.8	①	②	③
1987	Taurus	D	2.5 (2500)	5.0	6.2	16.6	①	②	8.3
	Taurus	U	3.0 (3000)	4.5	6.2	21.8	①	②	③
	Sable	D	2.5 (2500)	5.0	6.2	16.6	①	②	8.3
	Sable	U	3.0 (3000)	4.5	6.2	21.8	①	②	③
1988	Taurus	D	2.5 (2500)	5.0	6.2	16.6	①	②	8.3
	Taurus	U	3.0 (3000)	4.5	6.2	21.8	①	②	③
	Taurus	4	3.8 (3800)	5.0	—	26.2	①	②	12.1
	Sable	D	2.5 (2500)	5.0	6.2	16.6	①	②	8.3
	Sable	U	3.0 (3000)	4.5	6.2	21.8	①	②	③
	Sable	4	3.8 (3800)	5.0	—	26.2	①	②	12.1

CAPACITIES

Year	Model	Engine VIN	Engine Displacement liter (cc)	Engine Crankcase with Filter	Transmission (pts.) 5-Spd	Transmission (pts.) Auto.	Drive Axle (pts.)	Fuel Tank (gal.)	Cooling System (qts.)
1989	Taurus	D	2.5 (2500)	5.0	6.2	16.6	①	②	8.3
	Taurus	U	3.0 (3000)	4.5	6.2	21.8	①	②	③
	Taurus SHO	Y	3.0 (3000)	4.5	6.2	21.8	①	②	11.6
	Taurus	4	3.8 (3800)	5.0	—	26.2	①	②	12.1
	Sable	D	2.5 (2500)	5.0	6.2	16.6	①	②	8.3
	Sable	U	3.0 (3000)	4.5	6.2	21.8	①	②	③
	Sable	4	3.8 (3800)	5.0	—	26.2	①	②	12.1
1990	Taurus	D	2.5 (2500)	5.0	—	16.0	①	②	8.3
	Taurus	U	3.0 (3000)	4.5	—	25.6	①	②	③
	Taurus SHO	Y	3.0 (3000)	5.0	6.2	25.6	①	②	11.6
	Taurus	4	3.8 (3800)	4.5	—	25.6	①	②	12.1
	Sable	U	3.0 (3000)	4.5	—	25.6	①	②	③
	Sable	4	3.8 (3800)	4.5	—	25.6	①	②	12.1
1991	Taurus	D	2.5 (2500)	5.0	—	16.0	①	②	8.3
	Taurus	U	3.0 (3000)	4.5	—	25.6	①	②	③
	Taurus SHO	Y	3.0 (3000)	5.0	6.2	25.6	①	②	11.6
	Taurus	4	3.8 (3800)	4.5	—	25.6	①	②	12.1
	Sable	U	3.0 (3000)	4.5	—	25.6	①	②	③
	Sable	4	3.8 (3800)	4.5	—	25.6	①	②	12.1
1992	Taurus	U	3.0 (3000)	4.5	—	25.6	①	②	③
	Taurus SHO	Y	3.0 (3000)	5.0	6.2	25.6	①	②	11.6
	Taurus	4	3.8 (3800)	4.5	—	25.6	①	②	12.1
	Sable	U	3.0 (3000)	4.5	—	25.6	①	②	③
	Sable	4	3.8 (3800)	4.5	—	25.6	①	②	12.1

① Included in transaxle capacity
② Standard 16.0
Optional 18.6
③ Except Wagon with air conditinoing 11
Wagon with air conditioning 11.8

Troubleshooting Basic Air Conditioning Problems

Problem	Cause	Solution
There's little or no air coming from the vents (and you're sure it's on)	• The A/C fuse is blown • Broken or loose wires or connections • The on/off switch is defective	• Check and/or replace fuse • Check and/or repair connections • Replace switch
The air coming from the vents is not cool enough	• Windows and air vent wings open • The compressor belt is slipping • Heater is on • Condenser is clogged with debris • Refrigerant has escaped through a leak in the system • Receiver/drier is plugged	• Close windows and vent wings • Tighten or replace compressor belt • Shut heater off • Clean the condenser • Check system • Service system
The air has an odor	• Vacuum system is disrupted • Odor producing substances on the evaporator case • Condensation has collected in the bottom of the evaporator housing	• Have the system checked/repaired • Clean the evaporator case • Clean the evaporator housing drains
System is noisy or vibrating	• Compressor belt or mountings loose • Air in the system	• Tighten or replace belt; tighten mounting bolts • Have the system serviced
Sight glass condition		
Constant bubbles, foam or oil streaks	• Undercharged system	• Charge the system
Clear sight glass, but no cold air	• No refrigerant at all	• Check and charge the system
Clear sight glass, but air is cold	• System is OK	
Clouded with milky fluid	• Receiver drier is leaking dessicant	• Have system checked
Large difference in temperature of lines	• System undercharged	• Charge and leak test the system
Compressor noise	• Broken valves • Overcharged • Incorrect oil level • Piston slap • Broken rings • Drive belt pulley bolts are loose	• Replace the valve plate • Discharge, evacuate and install the correct charge • Isolate the compressor and check the oil level. Correct as necessary. • Replace the compressor • Replace the compressor • Tighten with the correct torque specification
Excessive vibration	• Incorrect belt tension • Clutch loose • Overcharged • Pulley is misaligned	• Adjust the belt tension • Tighten the clutch • Discharge, evacuate and install the correct charge • Align the pulley
Condensation dripping in the passenger compartment	• Drain hose plugged or improperly positioned • Insulation removed or improperly installed	• Clean the drain hose and check for proper installation • Replace the insulation on the expansion valve and hoses

Troubleshooting Basic Air Conditioning Problems (cont.)

Problem	Cause	Solution
Frozen evaporator coil	· Faulty thermostat · Thermostat capillary tube improperly installed · Thermostat not adjusted properly	· Replace the thermostat · Install the capillary tube correctly · Adjust the thermostat
Low side low—high side low	· System refrigerant is low · Expansion valve is restricted	· Evacuate, leak test and charge the system · Replace the expansion valve
Low side high—high side low	· Internal leak in the compressor—worn	· Remove the compressor cylinder head and inspect the compressor. Replace the valve plate assembly if necessary. If the compressor pistons, rings or
Low side high—high side low (cont.)	· Cylinder head gasket is leaking · Expansion valve is defective · Drive belt slipping	cylinders are excessively worn or scored replace the compressor · Install a replacement cylinder head gasket · Replace the expansion valve · Adjust the belt tension
Low side high—high side high	· Condenser fins obstructed · Air in the system · Expansion valve is defective · Loose or worn fan belts	· Clean the condenser fins · Evacuate, leak test and charge the system · Replace the expansion valve · Adjust or replace the belts as necessary
Low side low—high side high	· Expansion valve is defective · Restriction in the refrigerant hose	· Replace the expansion valve · Check the hose for kinks—replace if necessary
Low side low—high side high	· Restriction in the receiver/drier · Restriction in the condenser	· Replace the receiver/drier · Replace the condenser
Low side and high normal (inadequate cooling)	· Air in the system · Moisture in the system	· Evacuate, leak test and charge the system · Evacuate, leak test and charge the system

Troubleshooting Basic Wheel Problems

Problem	Cause	Solution
The car's front end vibrates at high speed	• The wheels are out of balance • Wheels are out of alignment	• Have wheels balanced • Have wheel alignment checked/adjusted
Car pulls to either side	• Wheels are out of alignment • Unequal tire pressure • Different size tires or wheels	• Have wheel alignment checked/adjusted • Check/adjust tire pressure • Change tires or wheels to same size
The car's wheel(s) wobbles	• Loose wheel lug nuts • Wheels out of balance • Damaged wheel • Wheels are out of alignment • Worn or damaged ball joint • Excessive play in the steering linkage (usually due to worn parts) • Defective shock absorber	• Tighten wheel lug nuts • Have tires balanced • Raise car and spin the wheel. If the wheel is bent, it should be replaced • Have wheel alignment checked/adjusted • Check ball joints • Check steering linkage • Check shock absorbers
Tires wear unevenly or prematurely	• Incorrect wheel size • Wheels are out of balance • Wheels are out of alignment	• Check if wheel and tire size are compatible • Have wheels balanced • Have wheel alignment checked/adjusted

Troubleshooting Basic Tire Problems

Problem	Cause	Solution
The car's front end vibrates at high speeds and the steering wheel shakes	• Wheels out of balance • Front end needs aligning	• Have wheels balanced • Have front end alignment checked
The car pulls to one side while cruising	• Unequal tire pressure (car will usually pull to the low side) • Mismatched tires • Front end needs aligning	• Check/adjust tire pressure • Be sure tires are of the same type and size • Have front end alignment checked
Abnormal, excessive or uneven tire wear See "How to Read Tire Wear"	• Infrequent tire rotation • Improper tire pressure • Sudden stops/starts or high speed on curves	• Rotate tires more frequently to equalize wear • Check/adjust pressure • Correct driving habits
Tire squeals	• Improper tire pressure • Front end needs aligning	• Check/adjust tire pressure • Have front end alignment checked

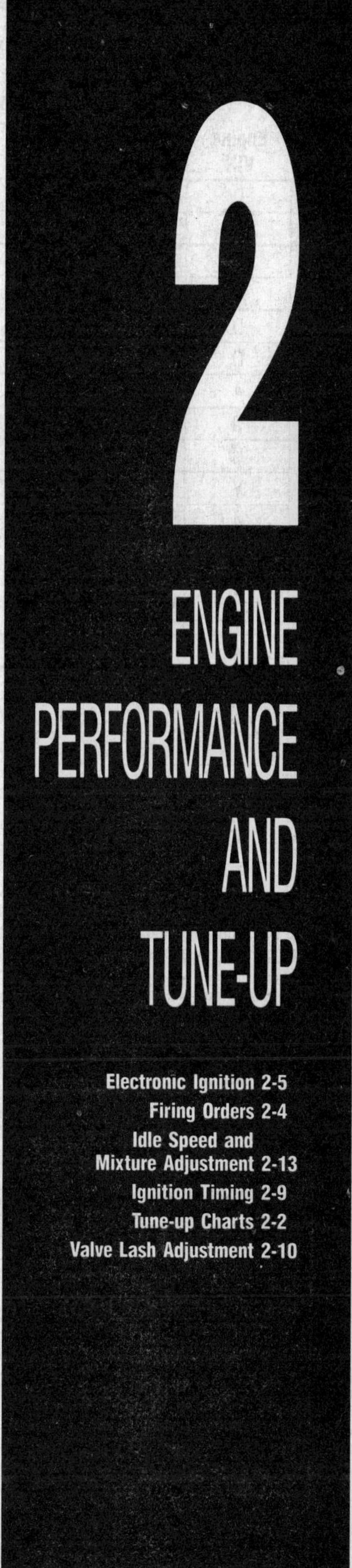

2 ENGINE PERFORMANCE AND TUNE-UP

GASOLINE ENGINE TUNE-UP SPECIFICATIONS

Year	Engine VIN	Engine Displacement liter (cc)	Spark Plugs Gap (in.)	Ignition Timing ① (deg.)		Fuel Pump (psi)	Idle Speed (rpm)		Valve Clearance	
				MT	AT		MT	AT	In.	Ex.
1986	D	2.5 (2500)	0.044	10	10	13–17	725	650	Hyd.	Hyd.
	U	3.0 (3000)	0.044	—	10	35–45	—	625	Hyd.	Hyd.
1987	D	2.5 (2500)	0.044	10	10	13–17	725	650	Hyd.	Hyd.
	U	3.0 (3000)	0.044	—	10	35–45	—	625	Hyd.	Hyd.
1988	D	2.5 (2500)	0.044	10	10	13–17	725	650	Hyd.	Hyd.
	U	3.0 (3000)	0.044	—	10	35–45	—	625	Hyd.	Hyd.
	4	3.8 (3800)	0.056	②	②	35–45	②	②	Hyd.	Hyd.
1989	D	2.5 (2500)	0.044	10	10	13–17	725	650	Hyd.	Hyd.
	U	3.0 (3000)	0.044	—	10	35–45	—	625	Hyd.	Hyd.
	Y	3.0 (3000)	0.044	10	—	36–39	800	—	0.008 ③	0.012 ③
	4	3.8 (3800)	0.054	②	②	35–45	②	②	Hyd.	Hyd.
1990	D	2.5 (2500)	0.044	—	②	13–17	—	②	Hyd.	Hyd.
	U	3.0 (3000)	0.044	—	②	35–45	—	②	Hyd.	Hyd.
	Y	3.0 (3000)	0.044	10	—	35–45	②	—	0.008 ③	0.012 ③
	4	3.8 (3800)	0.054	—	②	35–45	—	②	Hyd.	Hyd.
1991	D	2.5 (2500)	0.044	—	②	45–60	—	②	Hyd.	Hyd.
	U	3.0 (3000)	0.044	—	②	35–45	—	②	Hyd.	Hyd.
	Y	3.0 (3000)	0.044	10	—	35–45	②	—	0.008 ③	0.012 ③
	4	3.8 (3800)	0.054	—	②	35–45	—	②	Hyd.	Hyd.
1992	U	3.0 (3000)	0.044	—	②	35–45	—	②	Hyd.	Hyd.
	Y	3.0 (3000)	0.044	10	—	35–45	②	—	0.008 ③	0.012 ③
	4	3.8 (3800)	0.054	—	②	35–45	—	②	Hyd.	Hyd.

NOTE: The lowest cylinder pressure should be within 75% of the highest cylinder pressure reading. For example, if the highest cylinder is 134 psi, the lowest should be 101. Engine should be at normal operating temperature with throttle valve in the wide open position.

The underhood specifications sticker often reflects tune-up specifications changes in production. Sticker figures must be used if they disagree with those in this chart.

① BTDC—Before top dead center

② The Calibration levels vary from vehicle to vehicle. Refer to the Vehicle Emission Control information label for ignition timing and idle speed specifications.

③ Shim set bucket type valve lifter

TUNE-UP PROCEDURES

In order to extract the full measure of performance and economy from your engine it is essential that it be properly tuned at regular intervals. A regular tune-up will keep your vehicle's engine running smoothly and will prevent the annoying minor breakdowns and poor performance associated with an untuned engine.

A complete tune-up should be performed every 12,000 miles (19,300km) or twelve months, whichever comes first. This interval should be halved if the vehicle is operated under severe conditions, such as trailer towing, prolonged idling, continual stop and start driving, or if starting or running problems are noticed. It is assumed that the routine maintenance has been kept up, as this will have a decided effect on the results of a tune-up. All of the applicable steps of a tune-up should be followed in order, as the result is a cumulative one.

If the specifications on the tune-up sticker in the engine compartment disagree with the Tune-Up Specifications chart, the figures on the sticker must be used. The sticker often reflects changes made during the production run.

Spark Plugs

A typical spark plug consists of a metal shell surrounding a ceramic insulator. A metal electrode extends downward through the center of the insulator and protrudes a small distance. Located at the end of the plug and attached to the side of the outer metal shell is the side electrode. The side electrode bends in at a 90° angle so that its tip is even with, and parallel to, the tip of the center electrode. The distance between these two electrodes (measured in thousandths of an inch) is called the spark plug gap. The spark plug in no way produces a spark but merely provides a gap across which the current can arc. The coil produces anywhere from 20,000 to 40,000 volts which travels to the distributor where it is distributed through the spark plug wires to the spark plugs. The current passes along the center electrode and jumps the gap to the side electrode, and, in do doing, ignites the air/fuel mixture in the combustion chamber.

Spark plugs ignite the air and fuel mixture in the cylinder as the piston reaches the top of the compression stroke. The controlled explosion that results forces the piston down, turning the crankshaft and the rest of the drive train.

The average life of a spark plug is dependent on a number of factors: the mechanical condition of the engine; the type of engine; the type of fuel; driving conditions; and the driver.

When you remove the spark plugs, check their condition. They are a good indicator of the condition of the engine.

A small deposit of light tan or gray material on a spark plug that has been used for any period of time is to be considered normal.

The gap between the center electrode and the side or ground electrode can be expected to increase not more than 0.001 in. (0.025mm) every 1,000 miles (1,600km) under normal conditions.

When a spark plug is functioning normally or, more accurately, when the plug is installed in an engine that is functioning properly, the plugs can be taken out, cleaned, regapped, and reinstalled in the engine without doing the engine any harm.

When, and if, a plug fouls and beings to misfire, you will have to investigate, correct the cause of the fouling, and either clean or replace the plug.

Spark plug heat range is the ability of the plug to dissipate heat. The longer the insulator (or the farther it extends into the engine), the hotter the plug will operate; the shorter the insulator the cooler it will operate. A plug that absorbs little heat and remains too cool will quickly accumulate deposits of oil and carbon since it is not hot enough to burn them off. This leads to plug fouling and consequently to misfiring. A plug that absorbs too much heat will have no deposits, but, due to the excessive heat, the electrodes will burn away quickly and in some instances, preignition may result. Preignition takes place when plug tips get so hot that they glow sufficiently to ignite the fuel/air mixture before the actual spark occurs. This early ignition will usually cause a pinging during low speeds and heavy loads.

The general rule of thumb for choosing the correct heat range when picking a spark plug is: if most of your driving is long distance, high speed travel, use a colder plug; if most of your driving is stop and go, use a hotter plug. Original equipment plugs are compromise plugs, but most people never have occasion to change their plugs from the factory-recommended heat range.

Ford recommends that spark plugs be changed every 30,000 miles (48,300km) for the 2.5L, 3.0L, and 3.8L engines. The 3.0L SHO engine is equipped with Platinum spark plugs that have a recommended life of 60,000 miles (96,500km). Under severe driving conditions, those intervals should be halved (except 3.0L SHO). Severe driving conditions are:

1. Extended periods of idling or low speed operation, such as off-road or door-to-door delivery.
2. Driving short distances — less than 10 miles (16km) when the average temperature is below 10°F (–12°C) for 60 days or more.
3. Excessive dust or blowing dirt conditions.

REMOVAL & INSTALLATION

➧ SEE FIG. 1–2

A Set of spark plugs usually requires replacement every 30,000 miles (48,300km), — 60,000 miles (96,500km) for the 3.0L SHO engine — depending on your style of driving. In normal operation, plug gap increases about 0.025mm for every 1,000–2,500 miles (1600–4000km). As the gap increases, the plug's voltage requirement also increases. It requires greater voltage to jump the wider gap and about two to three times as much voltage to fire a plug at higher speeds than at idle.

The spark plugs used in your car require a deep spark plug socket for removal and installation. A special designed pair of plug wire removal pliers is also a good tool to have. The special pliers have cupped jaws that grip the plug wire boot and make the job of twisting and pulling the wire from the plug easier. Damage may occur to the spark plug wire if wire removal pliers are not used

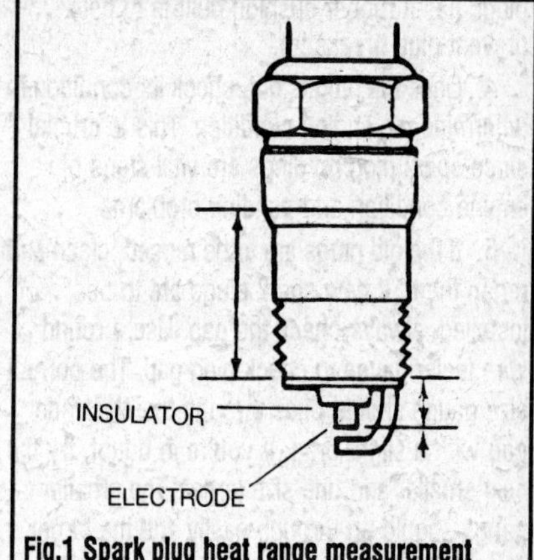

Fig.1 Spark plug heat range measurement location

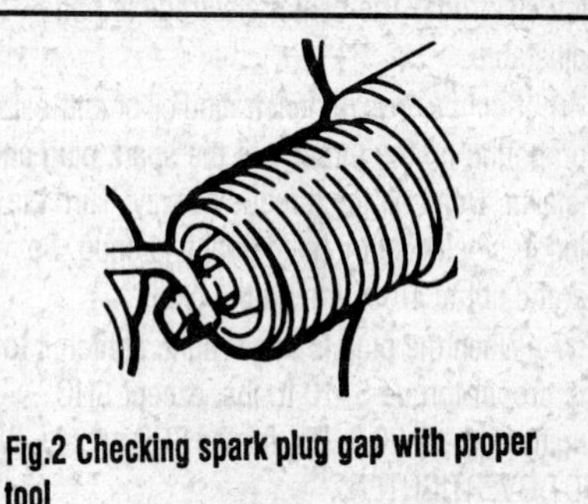
Fig.2 Checking spark plug gap with proper tool

➡ The original spark plug wires are marked for cylinder location. If replacement wires have been installed, be sure to tag them for proper location. It is a good idea to remove the wires one at a time, service the spark plug, reinstall the wire and move onto the next cylinder.

For easy access for servicing the spark plugs, remove the air cleaner assembly and air intake tube.

1. Twist the spark plug boot and gently pull it and the wire from the spark plug. This is where the special plug wire pliers come in handy.

➡ Never pull on the wire itself, damage to the inside conductor could occur.

2. The plug wire boot has a cover which shields the plug cavity (in the head) against dirt. After removing the wire, blow out the cavity with air or clean it out with a small brush so dirt will not fall into the engine when the spark plug is removed.
3. Remove the spark plug with a spark plug socket. Turn the socket counterclockwise to remove the plug. Be sure to hold the socket straight on the plug to avoid breaking the insulator (a deep socket designed for spark

plugs has a rubber cushion built-in to help prevent plug breakage).

4. Once the plug is out, check its condition to determine the engine condition. This is crucial since spark plug readings are vital signs of engine condition and pending problems.

5. If the old plugs are to be reused, clean and regap them. If new spark plugs are to be installed, always check the gap. Use a round wire feeler gauge to check plug gap. The correct size gauge should pass through the electrode gap with a slight drag. If you're in doubt, try the next smaller and one size larger. The smaller gauge should go through easily and the larger should not go through at all. If adjustment is necessary use the bending tool on the end of the gauge. When adjusting the gap, always bend the side electrode. The center electrode is non-adjustable.

6. Squirt a drop of penetrating oil or anti-seize compound on the threads of the spark plug and install it. Don't oil the threads heavily. Turn the plug in clockwise by hand until it is snug. Be careful not to cross thread the plug

7. When the plug is finger tight, tighten it to the proper torque 5–10 ft. lbs. except SHO engine and 16–20 ft. lbs. for the SHO engine. DO NOT OVERTIGHTEN.

8. Install the plug wire and boot firmly over the spark plug after coating the inside of the boot and terminal with a thin coat of dielectric compound (Motorcraft D7AZ19A331A or white lithium grease).

9. Proceed to the next spark plug.

Spark Plug Wires

Your car is equipped with a electronic ignition system which utilizes 8mm wires to conduct the hotter spark produced. The boots on these wires are designed to cover the spark plug cavities on the cylinder head.

Inspect the wires without removing them from the spark plugs, distributor cap or coil. Look for visible damage such as cuts, pinches, cracks or torn boots. Replace any wires that show damage. If the boot is damaged, it may be replaced by itself. It is not necessary to replace the complete wire just for the boot.

To replace the wire, grasp and twist the boot back and forth while pulling away from the spark plug. Use a special pliers if available.

➡ Always coat the terminals of any wire removed or replaced with a thin layer of dielectric compound.

When installing a wire be sure it is firmly mounted over or on the plug, distributor cap connector or coil terminal.

REMOVAL & INSTALLATION

1. Disconnect the negative battery cable.
2. Locate the plug wire. Tag it for reinstallation.
3. Before removing the plug wire from the distributor cap and the spark plug check and remove any retaining clamps.
4. Properly remove the spark plug wire using the proper tools, if required.
5. When reinstalling the spark plug wire be sure to route it exactly as it was removed.

FIRING ORDERS

➡ NOTE: To avoid confusion, remove and tag spark plug wires one at a time, for replacement

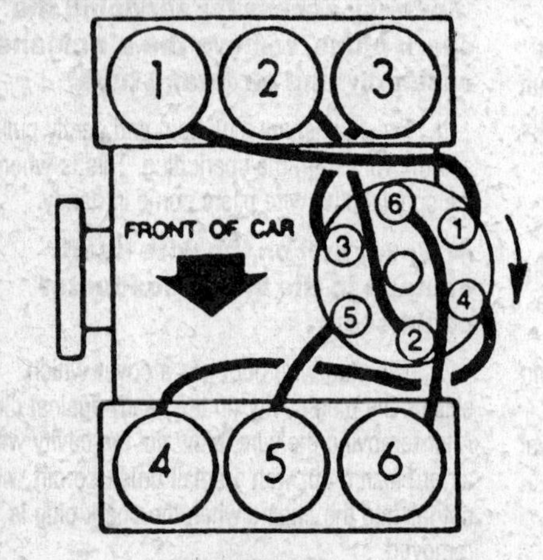

3.0LSHO Engine
Engine Firing Order: 1–4–2–5–3–6
Distributorless Ignition System

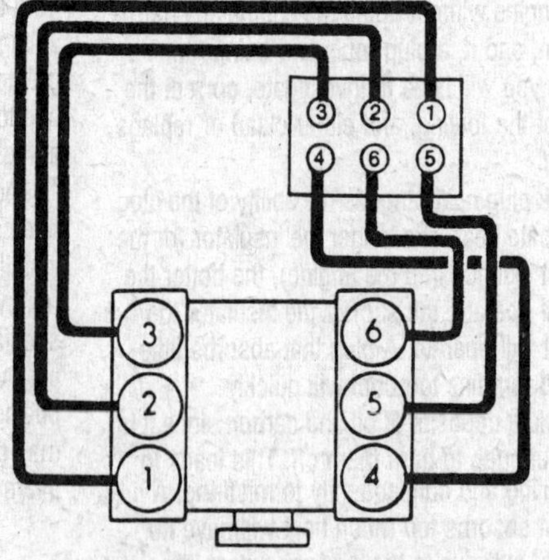

3.0LEngine
Engine Firing Order: 1–4–2–5–3–6
Distributor Rotation: Clockwise

1 2 3 4

FRONT

POSITION OF CAP ATTACHING SCREWS

2.5LEngine
Engine Firing Order: 1–3–4–2
Distributor Rotation: Clockwise

1 2 3

4 5 6

3.8LEngine
Engine Firing Order: 1–4–2–5–3–6
Distributor Rotation: Counterclockwise

ELECTRONIC IGNITION

Description And Operation

➧ SEE FIG. 7-8

Your car uses an electronic ignition system. The purpose of using an electronic ignition system is: To eliminate the deterioration of spark quality which occur in the breaker point ignition system as the breaker points wore. To extend maintenance intervals. To provide a more intense and reliable spark at every firing impulse in order to ignite the leaner gas mixtures necessary to control emissions.

The breaker points, point actuating cam and the condenser have been eliminated in the solid state distributor. They are replaced by an ignition module and a magnetic pulse-signal generator (pickup).

A Universal Distributor equipped with a TFI-IV system is used on all Taurus and Sable vehicles, except for the 3.0L SHO Taurus. TFI stands for Thick Film Integrated which incorporates a molded thermoplastic module mounted on the distributor base. TFI also uses an "E" coil which replaces the oil filled design used with earlier systems.

The Universal Distributor equipped with TFI-IV uses a vane switch stator assembly which replace the coil stator. The IV system incorporates provision for fixed octane adjustment and has no centrifugal or vacuum

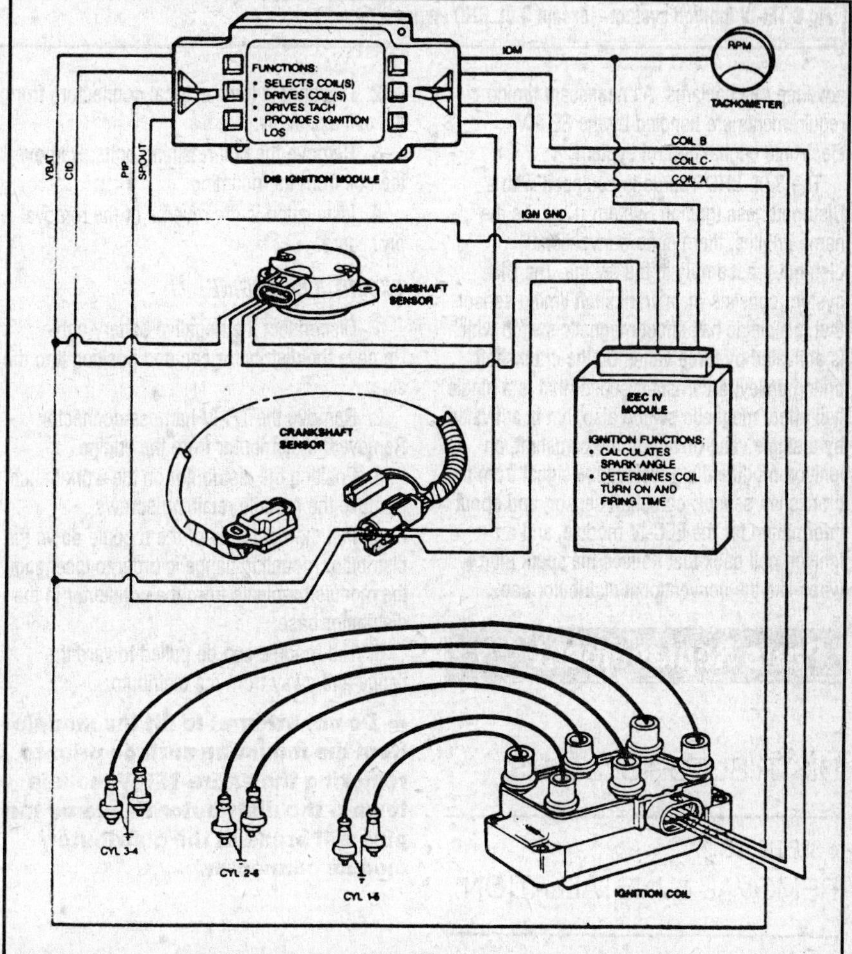

Fig.7 Distributorless ignition system and related components – 3.0L SHO engine

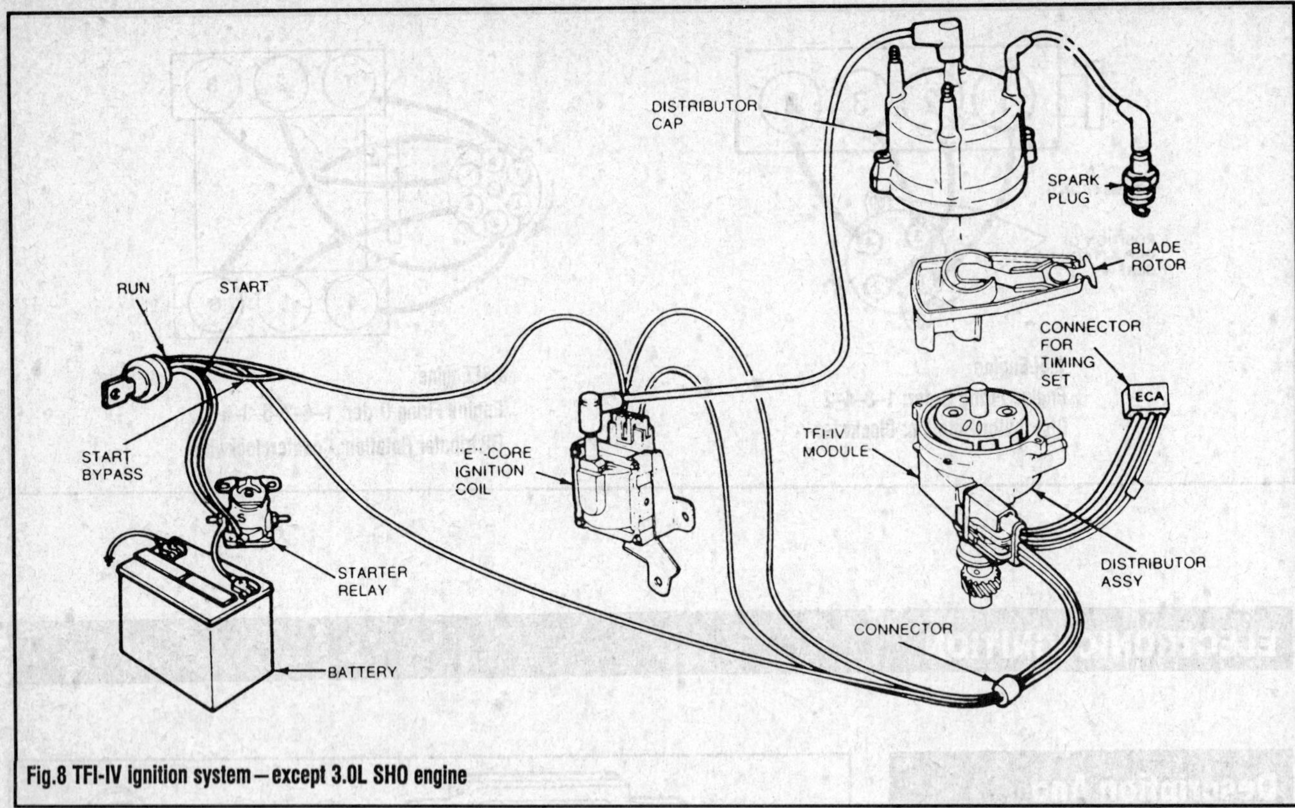

Fig.8 TFI-IV ignition system—except 3.0L SHO engine

advance mechanisms. All necessary timing requirements are handled by the EEC-IV electronic engine control system.

The 3.0L SHO Taurus is equipped with a Distributorless Ignition System (DIS). As the name implies, there is no conventional distributor assembly in the engine. The DIS system consists of: a crankshaft timing sensor that is a single hall effect magnetic switch which is activated by three vanes on the crankshaft timing pulley, a camshaft sensor that is a single hall effect magnetic switch also, but is activated by a single vane driven by the camshaft, an ignition module that receives the signal from the crankshaft sensor, camshaft sensor, and spout information for the EEC-IV module, and an ignition coil pack that houses the spark plug wires like the conventional distributor cap.

Parts Replacement

DISTRIBUTOR SYSTEMS

➧ SEE FIG. 26–27

REMOVAL & INSTALLATION

IGNITION COIL

1. Disconnect the negative battery cable.
2. Disconnect the electrical connectors from the coil assembly.
3. Remove the coil retaining bolts. Remove the coil from its mounting.
4. Installation is the reverse of the removal procedure.

EXCEPT 3.8L ENGINE

1. Disconnect the negative battery cable. Remove the distributor cap and position it to the side.
2. Remove the TFI-IV harness connector. Remove the distributor from the engine.
3. Position the distributor on the work bench. Remove the module retaining screws.
4. Pull the right side of the module down the distributor mounting flange in order to disengage the module terminals from the connector in the distributor base.
5. The module can be pulled toward the flange and away from the distributor.

➡ Do not attempt to lift the module from the mounting surface prior to removing the entire TFI-IV module toward the distributor flange as the pins will break at the distributor/ module connector.

6. Installation is the reverse of the removal procedure. Coat the metal base of the module with silicone compound approximately $\frac{1}{32}$ in. (0.8mm) thick prior to installing it.

3.8L ENGINE

1. Disconnect the negative battery cable
2. Remove the screws attaching the leaf screen and cowl dash extension panel in the area of the TFI module assembly. Remove the leaf screen.
3. Disconnect the harness connector from the module assembly. The connector latch is underneath the module shroud and must be pressed upward to unlatch it.
4. Remove the retaining nuts attaching the TFI/ heatsink assembly to the cowl dash extension panel.
5. Remove the TFI/Heat sink assembly. The assembly is mounted with the heatsink pointed down.
6. Remove the module retaining screws and remove the module from the heatsink. While holding the module connector shroud pull the seal off the other end of the module.
7. Installation is the reverse of the removal procedure. Coat the metal base of the module with silicone compound approximately $\frac{1}{32}$ in. (0.8mm) thick prior to installing it.

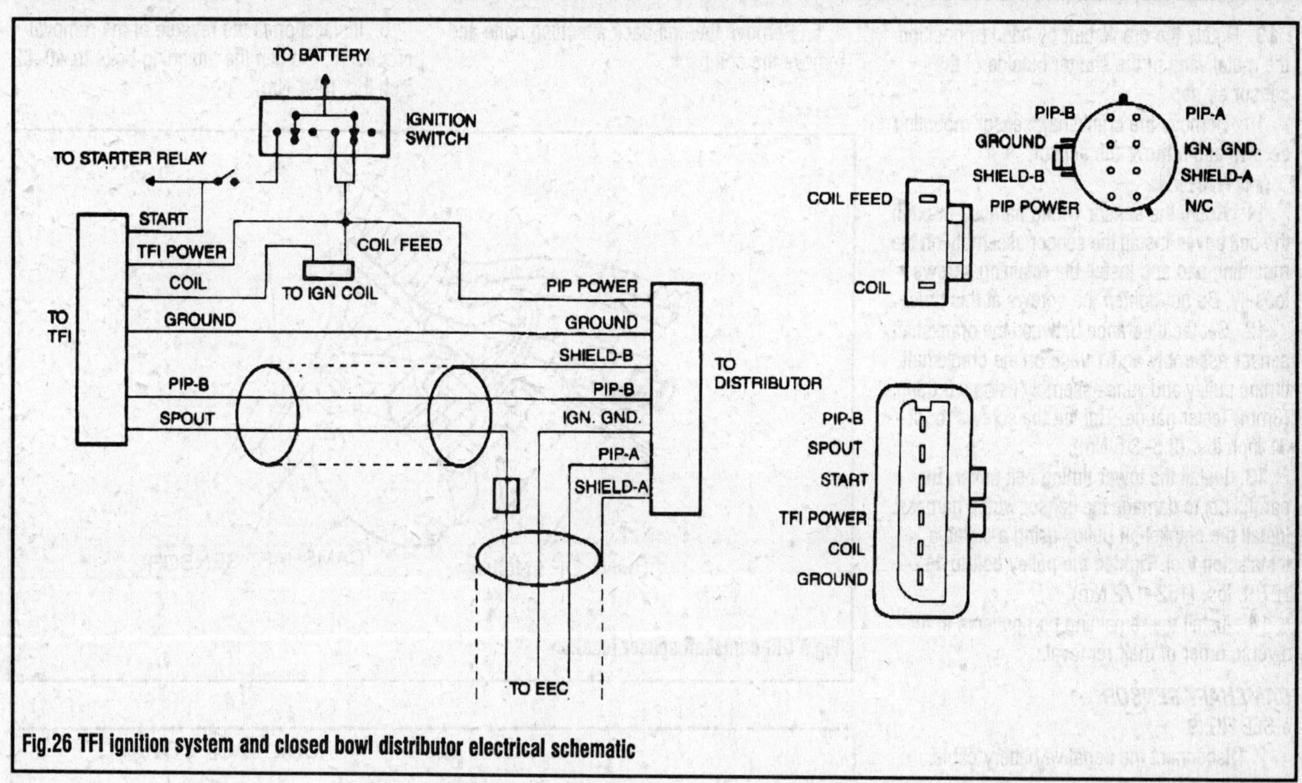

Fig.26 TFI ignition system and closed bowl distributor electrical schematic

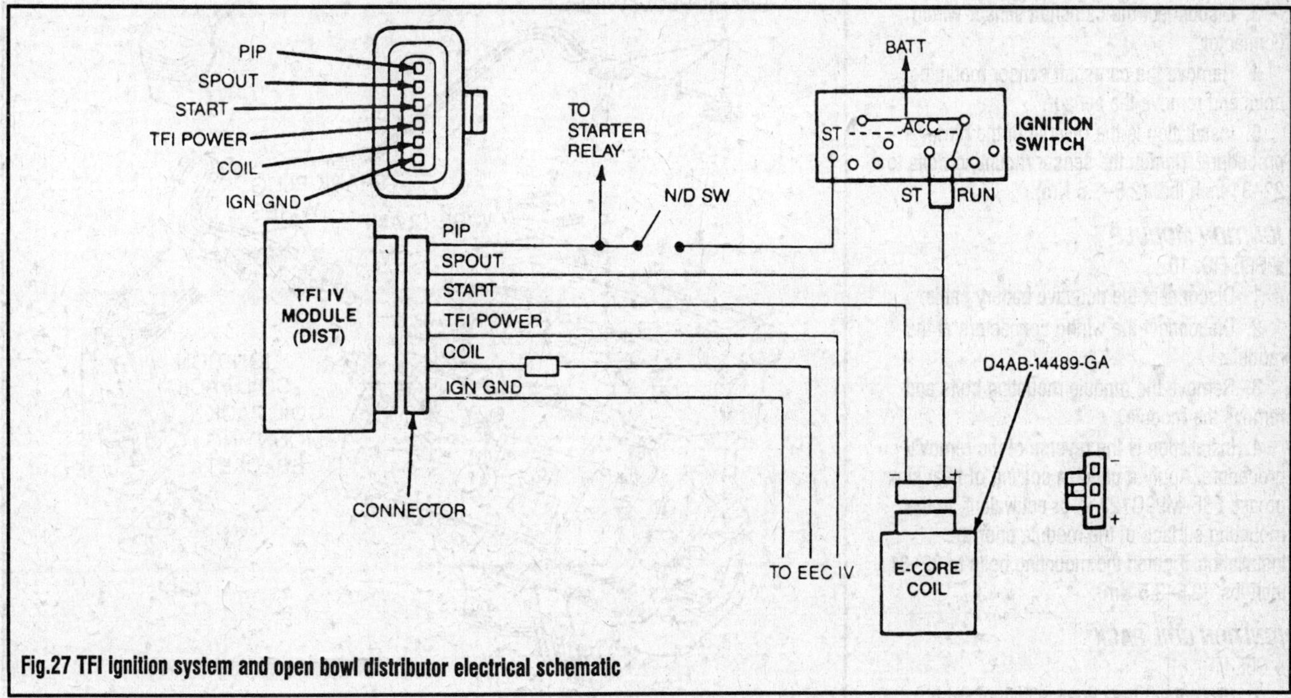

Fig.27 TFI ignition system and open bowl distributor electrical schematic

DISTRIBUTORLESS SYSTEMS

Removal and Installation

CRANKSHAFT SENSOR

1. Disconnect the negative battery cable.
2. Loosen the tensioner pulleys for the air conditioning compressor and power steering pump belts. Remove the belts from the crankshaft pulley.
3. Remove the upper timing belt cover.
4. Disconnect the sensor wiring harness at the connector and route the wiring harness through the belt cover.
5. Raise and safely support the vehicle.
6. Remove the right front wheel and tire assembly.
7. Remove the crankshaft pulley using a suitable puller.
8. Remove the lower timing belt cover.

9. Rotate the crankshaft by hand to position the metal vane of the shutter outside of the sensor air gap.

10. Remove the crankshaft sensor mounting screws and remove the sensor.

To install:

11. Route the sensor wiring harness through the belt cover. Install the sensor assembly on the mounting pad and install the retaining screws loosely. Do not tighten the screws at this time.

12. Set the clearance between the crankshaft sensor assembly and 1 vane on the crankshaft timing pulley and vane assembly using a 0.03 in. (8mm) feeler gauge. Tighten the screws to 22–31 inch lbs. (2.5–3.5 Nm).

13. Install the lower timing belt cover. Be careful not to damage the sensor wiring harness. Install the crankshaft pulley using a suitable installation tool. Tighten the pulley bolt to 112–127 ft. lbs. (152–172 Nm).

14. Install the remaining components in the reverse order of their removal.

CAMSHAFT SENSOR

➧ SEE FIG. 9

1. Disconnect the negative battery cable.
2. Remove the engine torque strut.
3. Disconnect the camshaft sensor wiring connector.
4. Remove the camshaft sensor mounting bolts and remove the sensor.
5. Installation is the reverse of the removal procedure. Tighten the sensor mounting bolts to 22–31 inch lbs. (2.5–3.5 Nm).

IGNITION MODULE

➧ SEE FIG. 10

1. Disconnect the negative battery cable.
2. Disconnect the wiring connectors at the module.
3. Remove the module mounting bolts and remove the module.
4. Installation is the reverse of the removal procedure. Apply a uniform coating of heat sink grease ESF–M99G123–A or equivalent, to the mounting surface of the module prior to installation. Tighten the mounting bolts to 22–31 inch lbs. (2.5–3.5 Nm).

IGNITION COIL PACK

➧ SEE FIG. 11

1. Disconnect the negative battery cable.
2. If equipped, remove the cover from the coil pack.
3. Disconnect the electrical connector from the coil pack.
4. Remove the spark plug wires by squeezing the locking tabs to release the coil boot retainers. Tag the wires and mark their position on the coil pack prior to removal.
5. Remove the coil pack attaching bolts and remove the coil pack.
6. Installation is the reverse of the removal procedure. Tighten the attaching bolts to 40–62 inch lbs. (5–7 Nm).

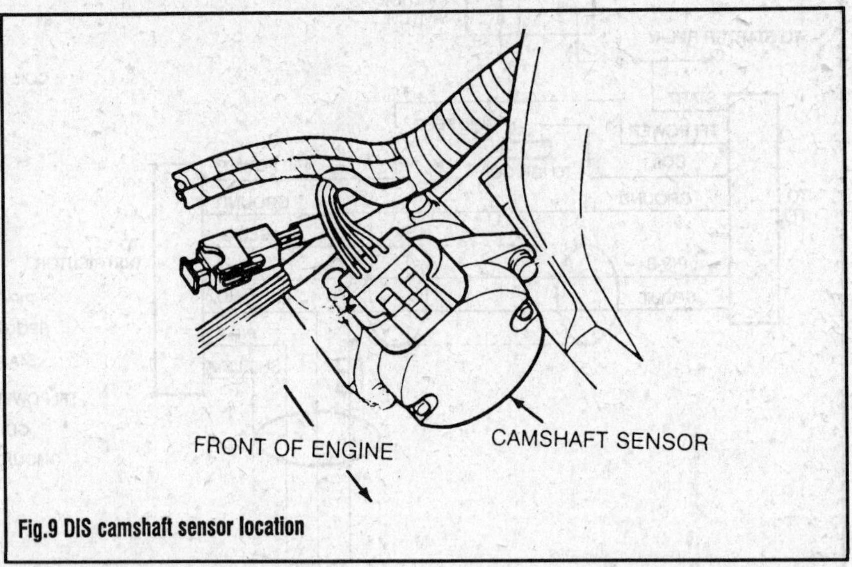

Fig.9 DIS camshaft sensor location

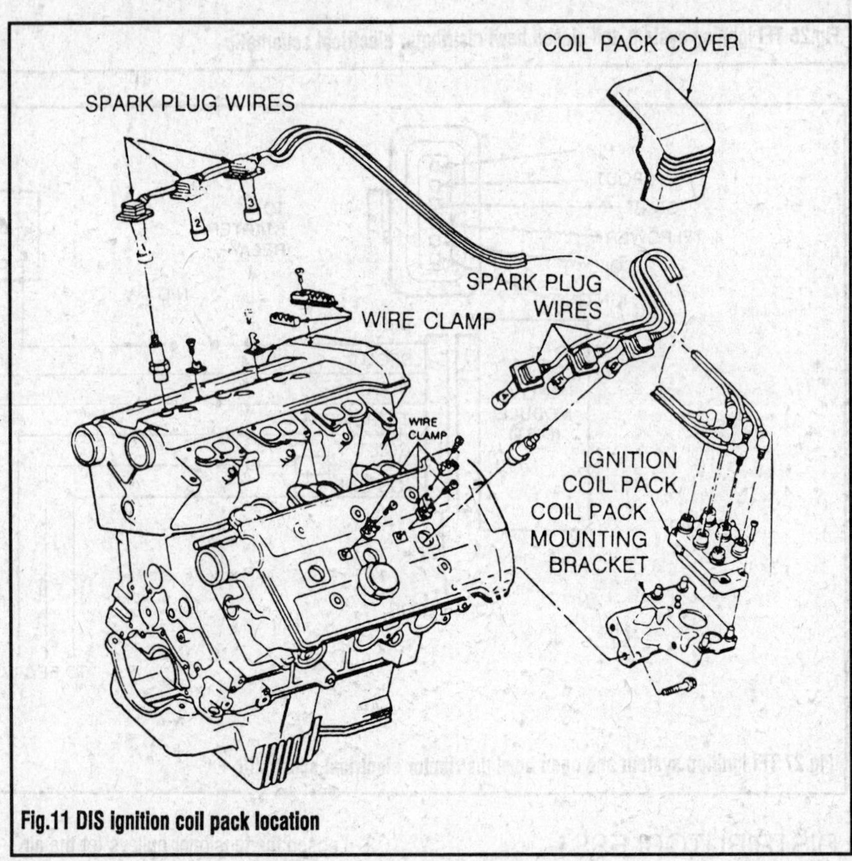

Fig.11 DIS ignition coil pack location

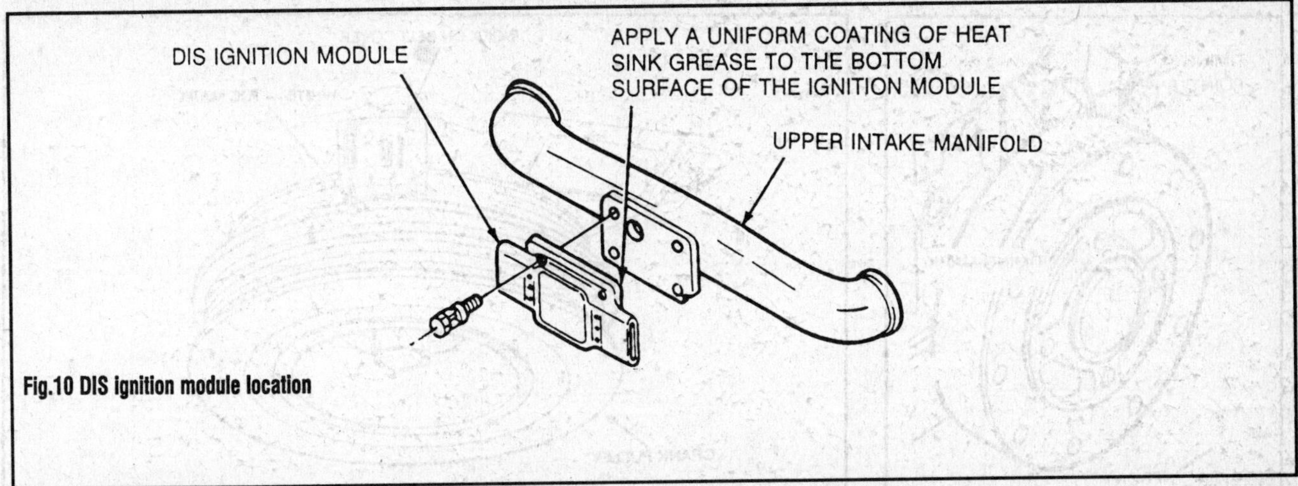

Fig.10 DIS ignition module location

IGNITION TIMING

ADJUSTMENT

Except 3.0L SHO Engine

The timing marks on the 2.5L engine are visible through a hole in the top of the transaxle case. The 3.0L and 3.8L engines have the timing marks on the crankshaft pulley and a timing pointer near the pulley.

1. Place the transaxle in the **P** or **N** position. Firmly apply the parking brake and block the wheels. The air conditioner and heater must be in the **OFF** position.
2. Open the hood, locate the timing marks and clean with a stiff brush or solvent. On vehicles with manual transaxle, it will be necessary to remove the cover plate which allows access to to the timing marks.
3. Using white chalk or paint, mark the specified timing mark and pointer.
4. Remove the inline spout connector or remove the shorting bar from the double wire spout connector. The spout connector is the center wire between the electronic control assembly (ECA) connector and the Thick Film Ignition (TFI) module.
5. Connect a suitable inductive type timing light to the No. 1 spark plug wire. Do not, puncture and ignition wire with any type of probing device.

➡ The high ignition coil charging currents generated in the EEC-IV ignition system may falsely trigger timing lights with capacitive or direct connect pickups. It is necessary that an inductive type timing light be used in this procedure.

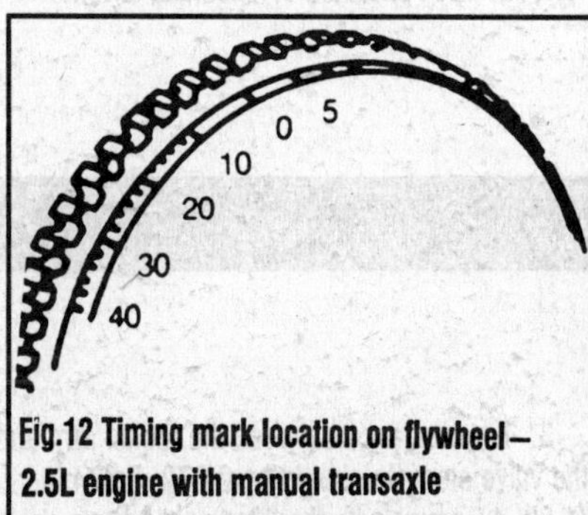

Fig.12 Timing mark location on flywheel—2.5L engine with manual transaxle

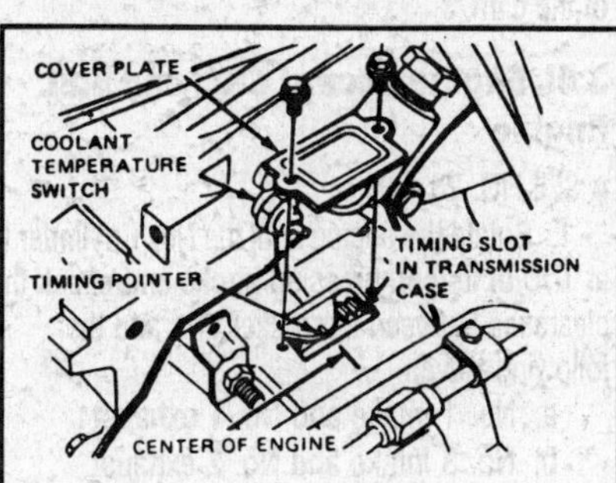

Fig.13 Timing mark location—2.5L engine with manual transaxle

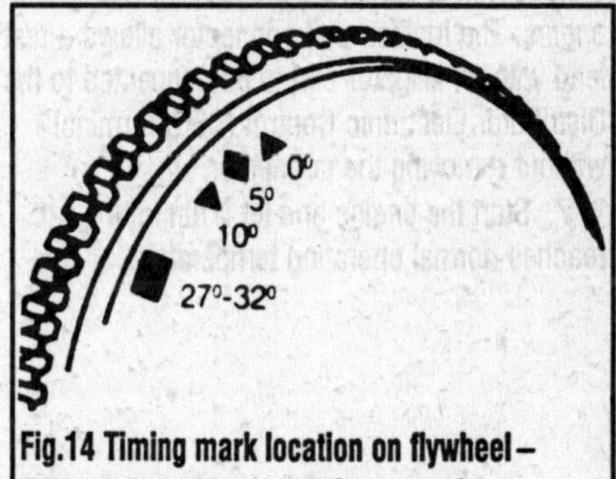

Fig.14 Timing mark location on flywheel—2.5L engine with automatic transaxle

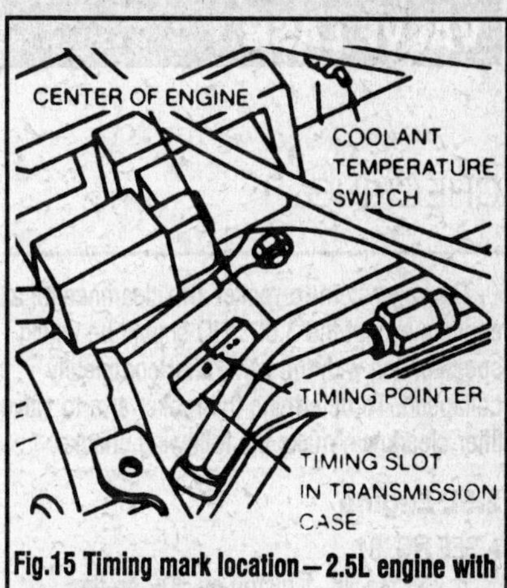

Fig.15 Timing mark location—2.5L engine with automatic transaxle

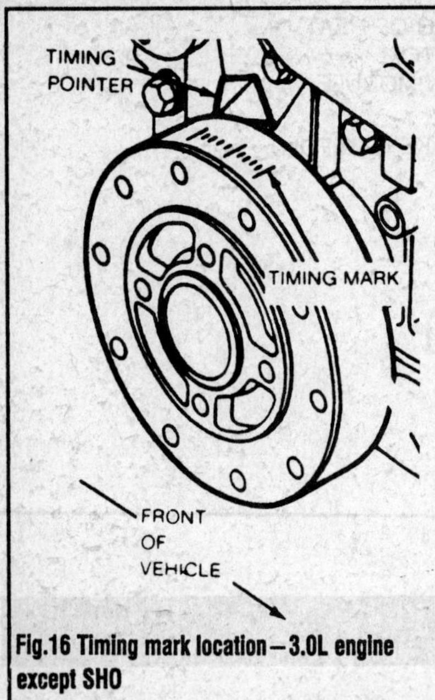

Fig.16 Timing mark location—3.0L engine except SHO

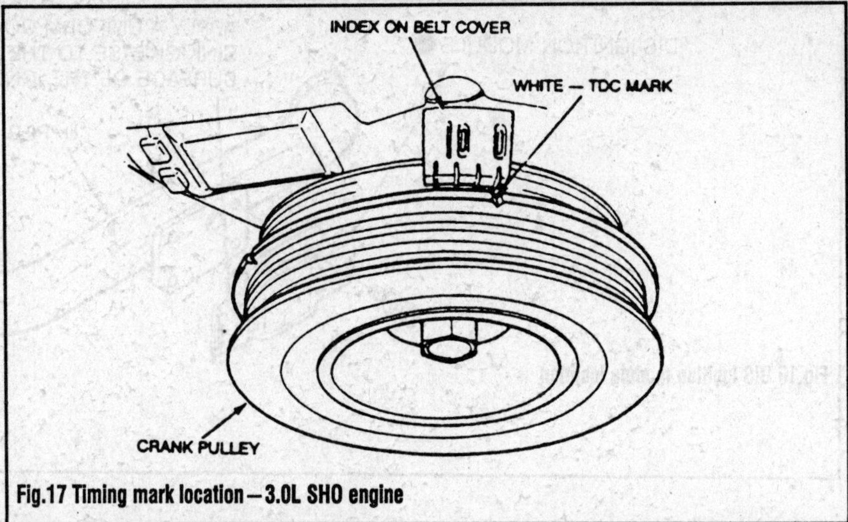

Fig.17 Timing mark location—3.0L SHO engine

6. Connect a suitable tachometer to the engine. The ignition coil connector allows a test lead with an alligator clip to be connected to the Distributor Electronic Control (DEC) terminal without removing the connector.

7. Start the engine and let it run until it reaches normal operating temperature.

➡ Only use the ignition key to start the vehicle. Do not use a remote starter, as disconnecting the start wire at the starter relay will cause the TFI module to revert to start mode timing, after the vehicle is started. Reconnecting the start wire after the vehicle is running will not correct the timing.

8. Check the engine idle rpm, if it is not within specifications, adjust as necessary. Idle speed is not adjustable on 1991–92 vehicles. After the rpm has been adjusted or checked, aim the timing light at the timing marks. If they are not aligned, loosen the distributor clamp bolt slightly and rotate the distributor body until the marks are aligned under timing light illumination.

9. Tighten the distributor clamp bolt and recheck the ignition timing. Readjust the idle speed as necessary. Shut the engine off, remove all test equipment, reconnect the inline spout connector to the distributor and, if necessary, reinstall the cover plate on the manual transaxle vehicles.

3.0L SHO Engine

The base ignition timing is set at 10° BTDC and is not adjustable.

VALVE LASH

CHECKING

The valve stem-to-rocker arm clearance for all engines except the 3.0L SHO should be within specification with the valve lifter completely collapsed. To determine the rocker arm to valve lifter clearance, make the following checks.

2.5L Engine

➧ SEE FIG. 31

1. Set the No. 1 piston on TDC on the compression stroke. The timing marks on the camshaft and crankshaft gears will be together. Check the clearance in No. 1 intake, No. 1 exhaust, No. 2 intake and No. 3 exhaust valves.

2. Rotate the crankshaft 1 complete turn, 180° for the camshaft gear. Check the clearance in No. 2 exhaust, No. 3 intake, No. 4 intake and No. 4 exhaust.

3. The clearance between the rocker arm and the valve stem tip should be 0.072–0.174 in. (1.80–4.34mm) with the lifter on the base circle of the cam.

3.0L Engine Except SHO and 3.8L Engine

➧ SEE FIG. 28–30

1. Rotate the engine until the No. 1 cylinder is at TDC of its compression stroke and check the clearance between the rocker arm and the following valves.
   a. No. 1 intake and No. 1 exhaust
   b. No. 3 intake and No. 2 exhaust
   c. No. 6 intake and No. 4 exhaust
2. Rotate the crankshaft 360° and check the clearance between the rocker arm and the following valves.
   a. No. 2 intake and No. 3 exhaust
   b. No. 4 intake and No. 5 exhaust
   c. No. 5 intake and No. 6 exhaust
3. The clearance should be 0.09–0.19 in. (2.3–4.8mm).

3.0L SHO Engine

1. Remove the valve cover.
2. Remove the intake manifold assembly.
3. Insert a feeler gauge under the cam lobe at a 90° angle to the camshaft. Clearance for the intake valves should be 0.006–0.010 in. (0.15–0.25mm). Clearance for the exhaust valves should be 0.010–0.014 in. (0.25–0.35mm).

➡ The cam lobes must be directed 90° or more away from the valve lifters.

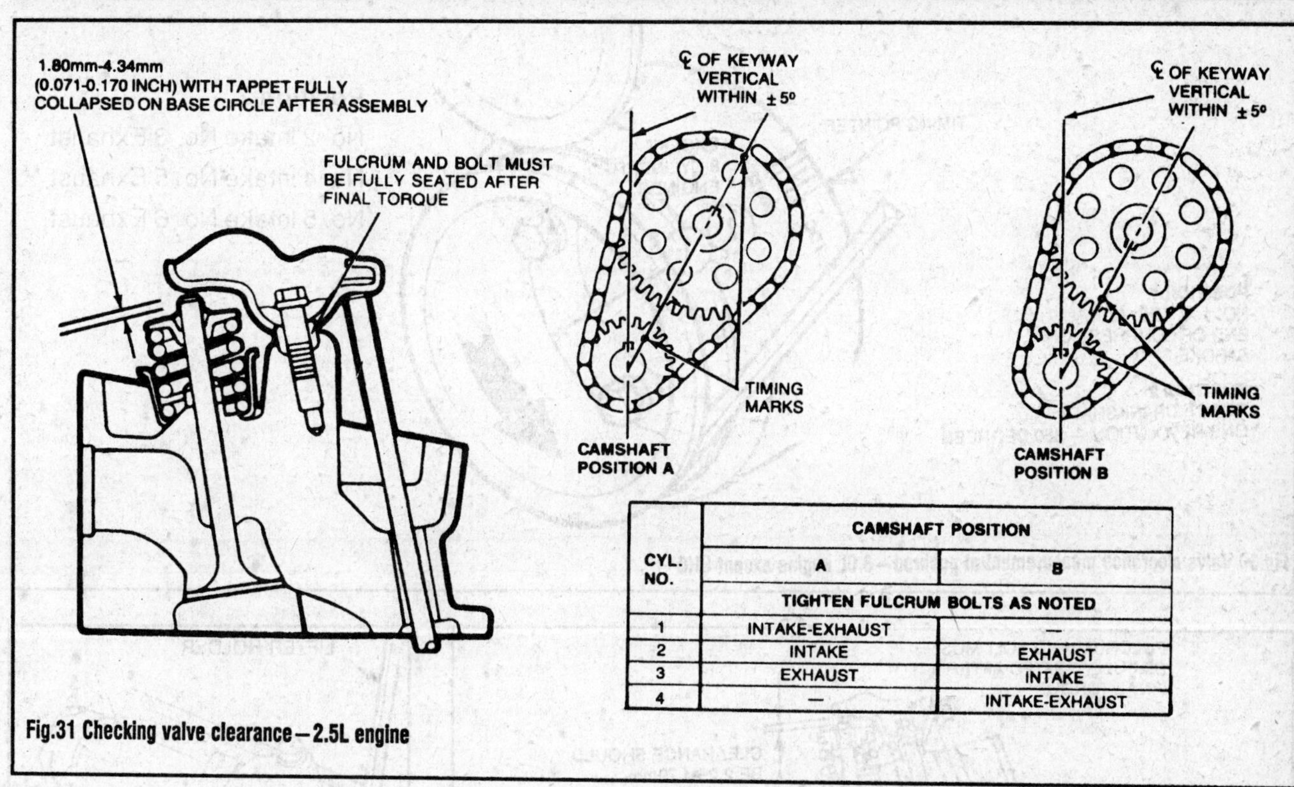

CYL. NO.	CAMSHAFT POSITION A	CAMSHAFT POSITION B
	TIGHTEN FULCRUM BOLTS AS NOTED	
1	INTAKE-EXHAUST	—
2	INTAKE	EXHAUST
3	EXHAUST	INTAKE
4	—	INTAKE-EXHAUST

Fig.31 Checking valve clearance – 2.5L engine

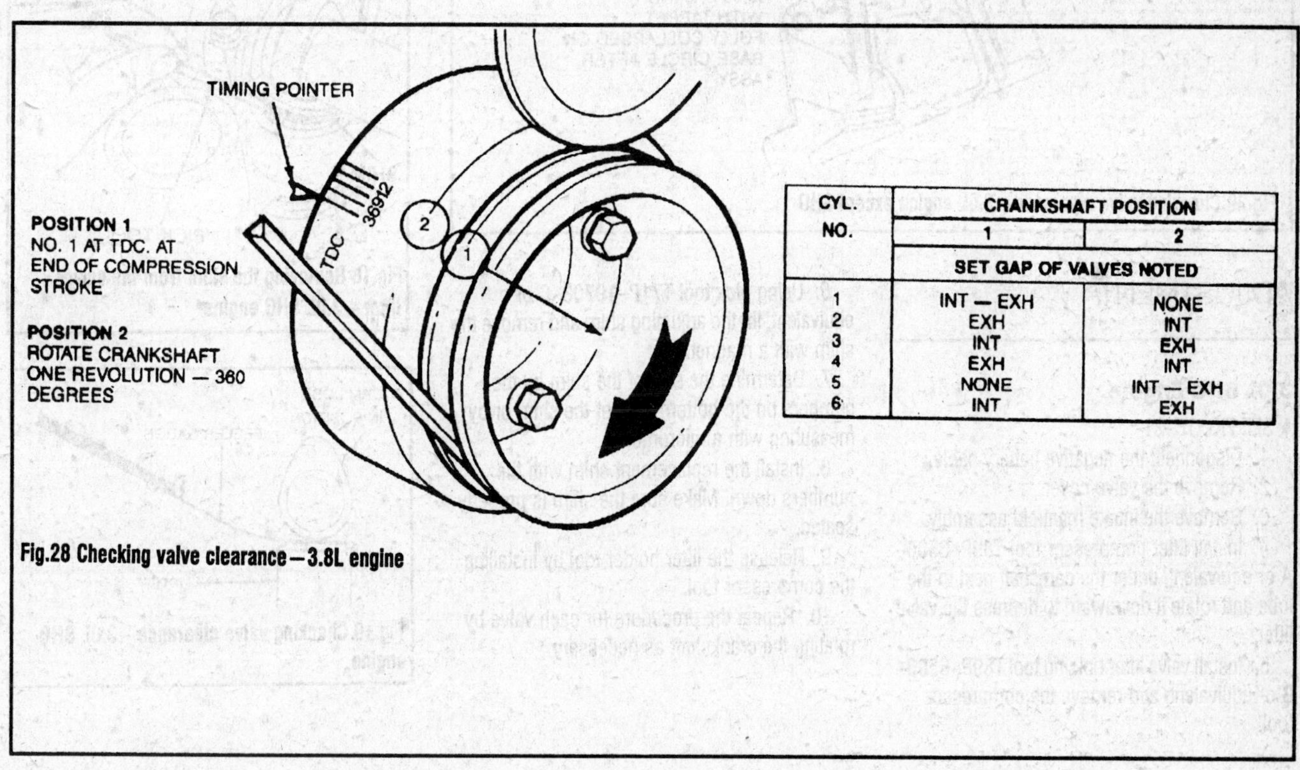

CYL. NO.	CRANKSHAFT POSITION 1	CRANKSHAFT POSITION 2
	SET GAP OF VALVES NOTED	
1	INT — EXH	NONE
2	EXH	INT
3	INT	EXH
4	EXH	INT
5	NONE	INT — EXH
6	INT	EXH

Fig.28 Checking valve clearance – 3.8L engine

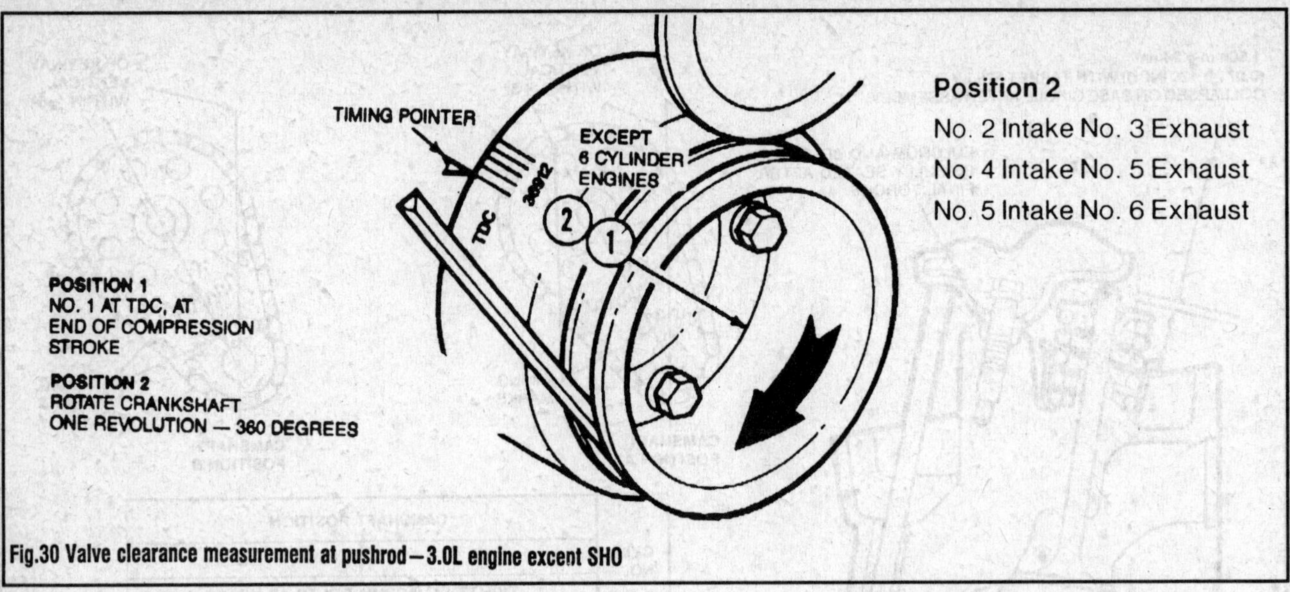

Fig.30 Valve clearance measurement at pushrod – 3.0L engine excent SHO

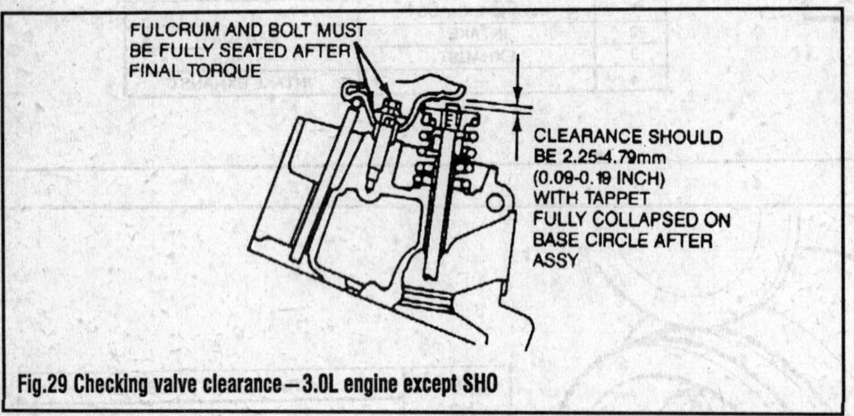

Fig.29 Checking valve clearance – 3.0L engine except SHO

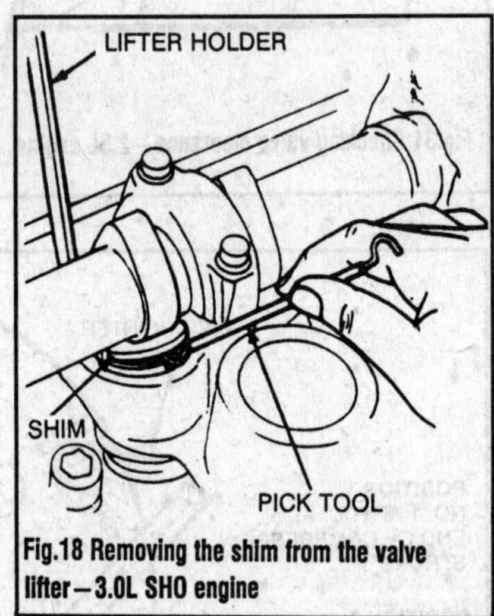

Fig.18 Removing the shim from the valve lifter – 3.0L SHO engine

ADJUSTMENT

3.0L SHO Engine

➧ SEE FIG. 18–21

1. Disconnect the negative battery cable.
2. Remove the valve cover.
3. Remove the intake manifold assembly.
4. Install lifter compressor tool T89P–6500–A or equivalent, under the camshaft next to the lobe and rotate it downward to depress the valve lifter.
5. Install valve lifter holding tool T89P–6500–B or equivalent, and remove the compressor tool.
6. Using pick tool T71P–19703–C or equivalent, lift the adjusting shim and remove the shim with a magnet.
7. Determine the size of the shim by the numbers on the bottom face of the shim or by measuring with a micrometer.
8. Install the replacement shim with the numbers down. Make sure the shim is properly seated.
9. Release the lifter holder tool by installing the compressor tool.
10. Repeat the procedure for each valve by rotating the crankshaft as necessary.

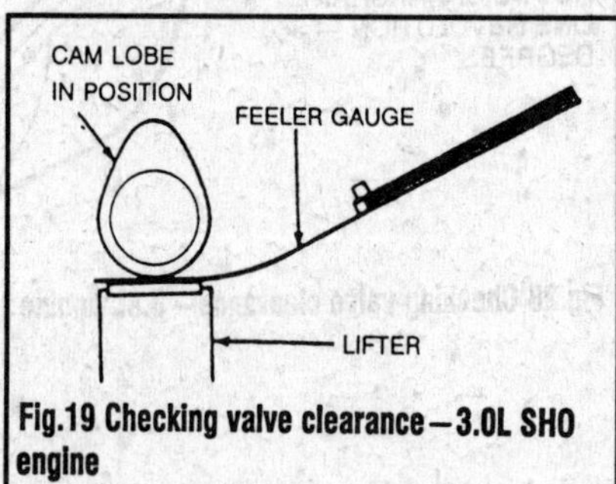

Fig.19 Checking valve clearance – 3.0L SHO engine

Fig.20 Valve lifter compressor tool—3.0L SHO engine

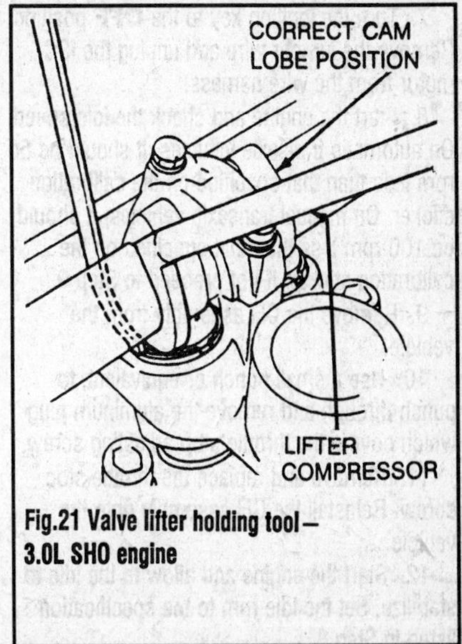

Fig.21 Valve lifter holding tool—3.0L SHO engine

IDLE SPEED AND MIXTURE ADJUSTMENT

Idle Speed

ADJUSTMENT

2.5L ENGINE

1986–90

➧ SEE FIG. 22–23

1. Apply the parking brake, block the drive wheels and place the vehicle in **P** or **N**.
2. Start the engine and let it run until it reaches normal operating temperature, then turn the engine **OFF**. Disconnect the negative battery cable for 5 minutes minimum, then reconnect it.
3. Start the engine and let it run at idle for 2 minutes. The idle rpm should now return to the specified idle speed. The Idle specifications can be found on the calibration sticker located under the hood. Now lightly step on and off the accelerator. The engine rpm should return to the specified idle speed. If the engine does not idle properly, proceed to Step 4.
4. Shut the engine **OFF** and remove the air cleaner. Locate the self-test connector and self-test input connector in the engine compartment.
5. Connect a jumper wire between the self-test input connector and the signal return pin, the top right terminal on the self-test connector.
6. Place the ignition key in the **RUN** position but do not start the engine. The ISC plunger will retract, so wait approximately 10–15 seconds until the ISC plunger is fully retracted.

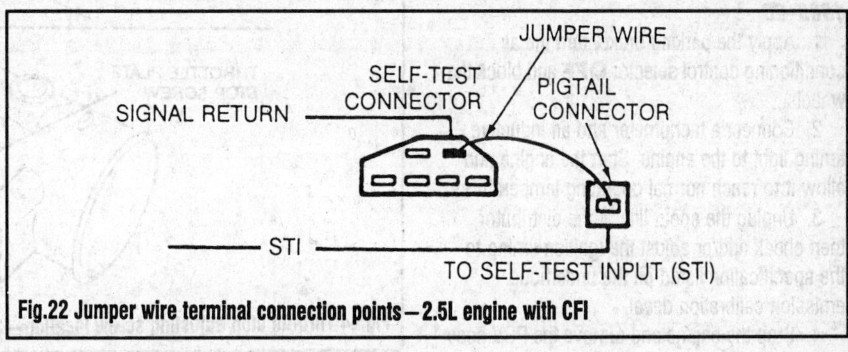

Fig.22 Jumper wire terminal connection points—2.5L engine with CFI

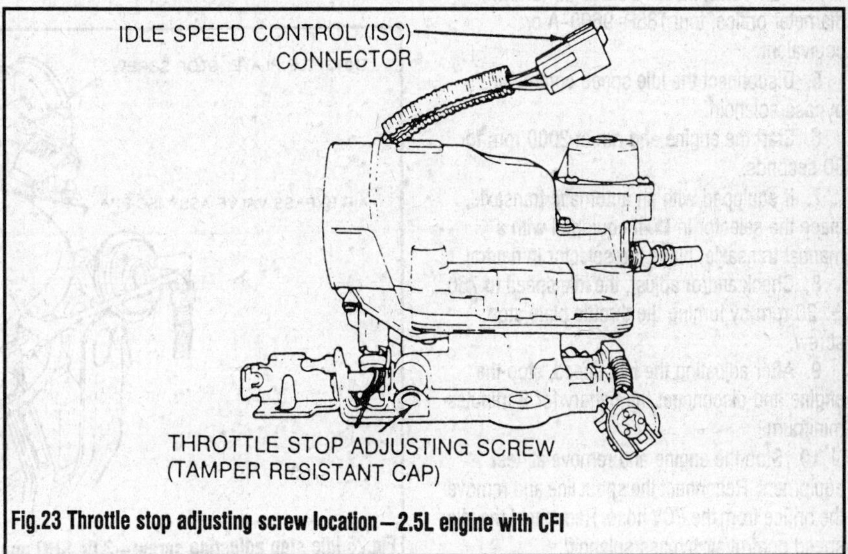

Fig.23 Throttle stop adjusting screw location—2.5L engine with CFI

7. Turn the ignition key to the **OFF** position. Remove the jumper wire and unplug the ISC motor from the wire harness.

8. Start the engine and check the idle speed. On automatic transaxle vehicles, it should be 50 rpm less than that specified on the calibration sticker. On manual transaxle vehicles, it should be 100 rpm less than that specified on the calibration sticker. If not proceed to Step 9.

9. Remove the CFI assembly from the vehicle.

10. Use a small punch or equivalent, to punch through and remove the aluminum plug which covers the throttle stop adjusting screw.

11. Remove and replace the throttle stop screw. Reinstall the CFI assembly onto the vehicle.

12. Start the engine and allow to the idle to stabilize. Set the idle rpm to the specification listed in Step 8.

13. Turn **OFF** the engine. Reconnect the ISC motor wire harness, remove all test equipment and reinstall the air cleaner assembly.

3.0L Engine Except SHO

1986–90

1. Apply the parking brake, turn the air conditioning control selector **OFF** and block the wheels.

2. Connect a tachometer and an inductive timing light to the engine. Start the engine and allow it to reach normal operating temperatures.

3. Unplug the spout line at the distributor, then check and/or adjust the ignition timing to the specification listed on the underhood emission calibration decal.

4. Stop the engine and remove the PCV hose at the PCV valve. Install a 0.200 in. (5mm) diameter orifice, tool T86P–9600–A or equivalent.

5. Disconnect the idle speed control/air bypass solenoid.

6. Start the engine and run at 2000 rpm for 30 seconds.

7. If equipped with an automatic transaxle, place the selector in **D**. If equipped with a manual transaxle, place the selector in neutral.

8. Check and/or adjust, the idle speed to 760 ± 20 rpm by turning the throttle plate stop screw.

9. After adjusting the idle speed, stop the engine and disconnect the battery for 5 minutes minimum.

10. Stop the engine and remove all test equipment. Reconnect the spout line and remove the orifice from the PCV hose. Reconnect the idle speed control/air bypass solenoid.

11. Make sure the throttle is not stuck in the bore and the linkage is not preventing the throttle from closing.

3.0L SHO Engine

1989–90

➧ SEE FIG. 24–25

1. Apply the parking brake, turn the air conditioning control selector **OFF** and block the wheels.

2. Connect a tachometer and an inductive timing light to the engine. Start the engine and allow it to reach normal operating temperatures.

3. Unplug the spout line at the distributor, then check and/or adjust the ignition timing to the specification listed on the underhood emission calibration decal.

4. Stop the engine and disconnect and plug the PCV hose at the intake manifold. Remove the CANP hose from the intake manifold and connect tool T89P–9600–AH or equivalent, between the PCV and CANP ports.

5. Disconnect the idle speed control/air bypass solenoid.

6. Start the engine and let it idle. Place the transaxle selector lever in **N**.

7. Check and/or adjust the idle speed to 800 ± 30 rpm by turning the throttle plate stop screw.

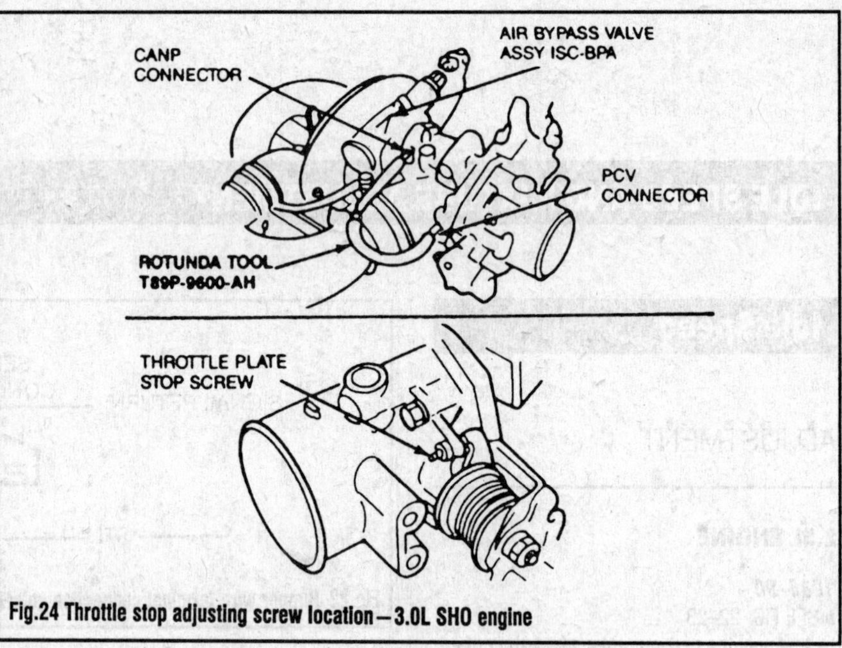

Fig.24 Throttle stop adjusting screw location – 3.0L SHO engine

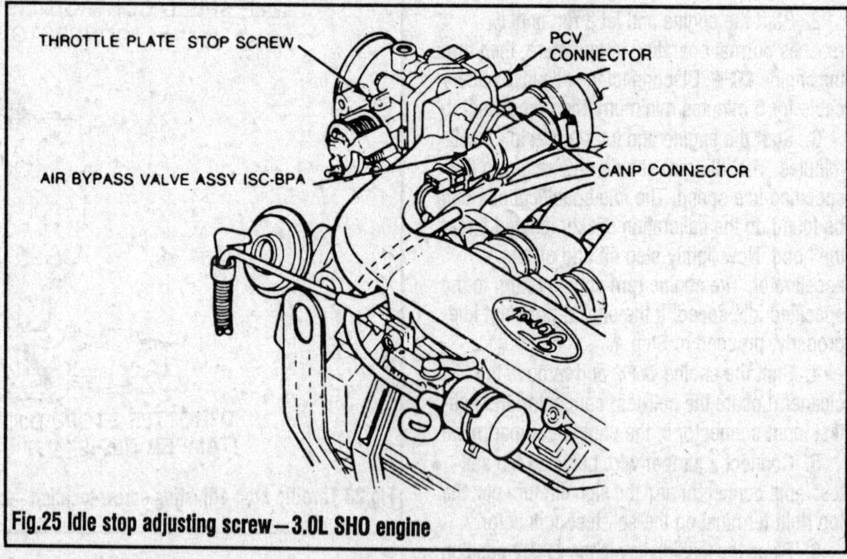

Fig.25 Idle stop adjusting screw – 3.0L SHO engine

8. Shut the engine off and repeat Steps 6–8.

9. Stop the engine and remove all test equipment. Remove tool T89P–9600–AH or equivalent, and unplug the PCV hose. Connect the PCV and CANP hoses. Reconnect the idle speed control/air bypass solenoid.

10. Make sure the throttle is not stuck in the bore and the linkage is not preventing the throttle from closing.

3.8L Engine

1988

1. Apply the parking brake, block the drive wheels and place the vehicle in **P** or **N**.

2. Start the engine and let it run until it reaches normal operating temperature, then turn the engine **OFF**. Connect a suitable tachometer.

3. Start the engine and run the engine at 2500 rpm for 30 seconds.

4. Allow the engine idle to stabilize.

5. Place the automatic transaxle in **D** or the manual transaxle in neutral.

6. Adjust the engine idle rpm to the specification shown on the vehicle emission control label by adjusting the throttle stop screw.

7. After the idle speed is within specification, repeat Steps 3–6 to ensure that the adjustment is correct.

8. Stop the engine. Disconnect all test equipment.

1988–90

1. Apply the parking brake, block the drive wheels and place the vehicle in **P**.

2. Start the engine and let it run until it reaches normal operating temperature, then turn the engine **OFF**.

3. Stop the engine and back out the throttle plate stop screw clear off the throttle lever pad.

4. Place a 0.010 in. (0.25mm) feeler gauge between the throttle plate stop screw and the throttle lever pad. Turn the screw in until contact is made, then turn it an additional $1^1/_2$ turns. Remove the feeler gauge.

5. Start the engine and let the idle stabilize for 2 minutes. Lightly depress and release the accelerator. Let the engine idle.

2.5L, 3.0L and 3.8L Engines

1991–92

The idle speed on these engines is preset at the factory and is not adjustable in the field. In the event that adjustment is necessary, STAR tester 007–00028 or equivalent, must be used.

Idle Mixture

ADJUSTMENT

Idle mixture is controlled by the electronic control unit. No adjustment is possible.

Diagnosis of Spark Plugs

Problem	Possible Cause	Correction
Brown to grayish-tan deposits and slight electrode wear.	• Normal wear.	• Clean, regap, reinstall.
Dry, fluffy black carbon deposits.	• Poor ignition output.	• Check distributor to coil connections.
Wet, oily deposits with very little electrode wear.	• "Break-in" of new or recently overhauled engine. • Excessive valve stem guide clearances. • Worn intake valve seals.	• Degrease, clean and reinstall the plugs. • Refer to Section 3. • Replace the seals.
Red, brown, yellow and white colored coatings on the insulator. Engine misses intermittently under severe operating conditions.	• By-products of combustion.	• Clean, regap, and reinstall. If heavily coated, replace.
Colored coatings heavily deposited on the portion of the plug projecting into the chamber and on the side facing the intake valve.	• Leaking seals if condition is found in only one or two cylinders.	• Check the seals. Replace if necessary. Clean, regap, and reinstall the plugs.
Shiny yellow glaze coating on the insulator.	• Melted by-products of combustion.	• Avoid sudden acceleration with wide-open throttle after long periods of low speed driving. Replace the plugs.
Burned or blistered insulator tips and badly eroded electrodes.	• Overheating.	• Check the cooling system. • Check for sticking heat riser valves. Refer to Section 1. • Lean air-fuel mixture. • Check the heat range of the plugs. May be too hot. • Check ignition timing. May be over-advanced. • Check the torque value of the plugs to ensure good plug-engine seat contact.
Broken or cracked insulator tips.	• Heat shock from sudden rise in tip temperature under severe operating conditions. Improper gapping of plugs.	• Replace the plugs. Gap correctly.

3
ENGINE
AND
ENGINE
OVERHAUL

Troubleshooting the Cooling System

Problem	Cause	Solution
High temperature gauge indication—overheating	• Coolant level low	• Replenish coolant
	• Fan belt loose	• Adjust fan belt tension
	• Radiator hose(s) collapsed	• Replace hose(s)
	• Radiator airflow blocked	• Remove restriction (bug screen, fog lamps, etc.)
	• Faulty radiator cap	• Replace radiator cap
	• Ignition timing incorrect	• Adjust ignition timing
	• Idle speed low	• Adjust idle speed
	• Air trapped in cooling system	• Purge air
	• Heavy traffic driving	• Operate at fast idle in neutral intermittently to cool engine
	• Incorrect cooling system component(s) installed	• Install proper component(s)
	• Faulty thermostat	• Replace thermostat
	• Water pump shaft broken or impeller loose	• Replace water pump
	• Radiator tubes clogged	• Flush radiator
	• Cooling system clogged	• Flush system
	• Casting flash in cooling passages	• Repair or replace as necessary. Flash may be visible by removing cooling system components or removing core plugs.
	• Brakes dragging	• Repair brakes
	• Excessive engine friction	• Repair engine
	• Antifreeze concentration over 68%	• Lower antifreeze concentration percentage
	• Missing air seals	• Replace air seals
	• Faulty gauge or sending unit	• Repair or replace faulty component
	• Loss of coolant flow caused by leakage or foaming	• Repair or replace leaking component, replace coolant
	• Viscous fan drive failed	• Replace unit
Low temperature indication—undercooling	• Thermostat stuck open	• Replace thermostat
	• Faulty gauge or sending unit	• Repair or replace faulty component
Coolant loss—boilover	• Overfilled cooling system	• Reduce coolant level to proper specification
	• Quick shutdown after hard (hot) run	• Allow engine to run at fast idle prior to shutdown
	• Air in system resulting in occasional "burping" of coolant	• Purge system
	• Insufficient antifreeze allowing coolant boiling point to be too low	• Add antifreeze to raise boiling point
	• Antifreeze deteriorated because of age or contamination	• Replace coolant
	• Leaks due to loose hose clamps, loose nuts, bolts, drain plugs, faulty hoses, or defective radiator	• Pressure test system to locate source of leak(s) then repair as necessary

Troubleshooting the Cooling System (cont.)

Problem	Cause	Solution
Coolant loss—boilover	• Faulty head gasket • Cracked head, manifold, or block • Faulty radiator cap	• Replace head gasket • Replace as necessary • Replace cap
Coolant entry into crankcase or cylinder(s)	• Faulty head gasket • Crack in head, manifold or block	• Replace head gasket • Replace as necessary
Coolant recovery system inoperative	• Coolant level low • Leak in system • Pressure cap not tight or seal missing, or leaking • Pressure cap defective • Overflow tube clogged or leaking • Recovery bottle vent restricted	• Replenish coolant to FULL mark • Pressure test to isolate leak and repair as necessary • Repair as necessary • Replace cap • Repair as necessary • Remove restriction
Noise	• Fan contacting shroud • Loose water pump impeller • Glazed fan belt • Loose fan belt • Rough surface on drive pulley • Water pump bearing worn • Belt alignment	• Reposition shroud and inspect engine mounts • Replace pump • Apply silicone or replace belt • Adjust fan belt tension • Replace pulley • Remove belt to isolate. Replace pump. • Check pulley alignment. Repair as necessary.
No coolant flow through heater core	• Restricted return inlet in water pump • Heater hose collapsed or restricted • Restricted heater core • Restricted outlet in thermostat housing • Intake manifold bypass hole in cylinder head restricted • Faulty heater control valve • Intake manifold coolant passage restricted	• Remove restriction • Remove restriction or replace hose • Remove restriction or replace core • Remove flash or restriction • Remove restriction • Replace valve • Remove restriction or replace intake manifold

NOTE: *Immediately after shutdown, the engine enters a condition known as heat soak. This is caused by the cooling system being inoperative while engine temperature is still high. If coolant temperature rises above boiling point, expansion and pressure may push some coolant out of the radiator overflow tube. If this does not occur frequently it is considered normal.*

ENGINE ELECTRICAL

Ignition Coil

TESTING

EEC-IV System

➧ SEE FIG. 1–2

1. At the center terminal on the distributor cap, follow the coil wire to the end. This is the ignition coil "E" type. Make sure transmission is in PARK and ignition is turned OFF.
2. Separate the wiring harness connector from the ignition module at the distributor. Inspect for dirt, corrosion and damage. Reconnect harness if no problem found.

➡ **Push connector tabs to separate.**

3. Attach a 12 volt DC test light between coil Tach terminal and engine ground. Crank engine, if the light flashes or lights continuous.
   a. Turn ignition switch OFF
   b. Disconnect ignition coil connector on top of the coil and inspect for dirt, corrosion and damage.
   c. Measure the ignition coil primary resistance, using an ohm Ω meter, from positive (+) to negative (–) terminal of ignition coil. Check coil diagram A for terminal location.
   d. The ohmmeter reading should be 0.3–1.0Ω. If the reading is less than 0.3Ω or greater than 1.0Ω, the ignition coil should be replaced.
   e. Measure the coil secondary resistance, using an ohmmeter, connect it to the negative (–) terminal and high voltage terminal.
   f. The resistance should be 6,500–11,500Ω with the ohm meter set on $\Omega \times 1000$. If the reading is less than 6,500Ω or greater than 11,500Ω, replace the coil.

REMOVAL & INSTALLATION

EEC-IV System

1. Disconnect the negative battery cable.
2. Disconnect the electrical connectors from the coil assembly.
3. Remove the coil retaining bolts. Remove the coil from its mounting.
4. Installation is the reverse of the removal procedure.

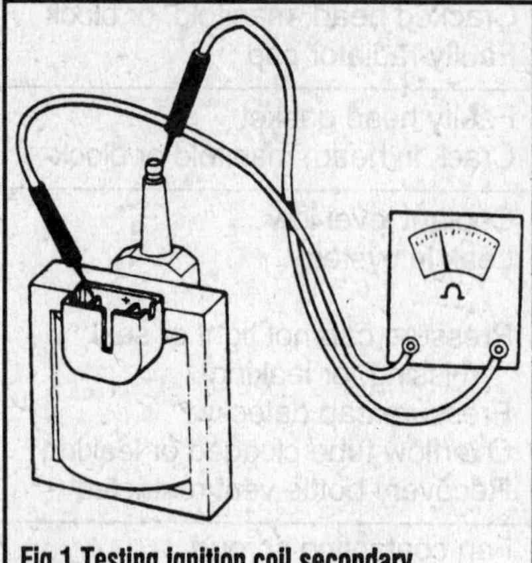

Fig.1 Testing ignition coil secondary resistance

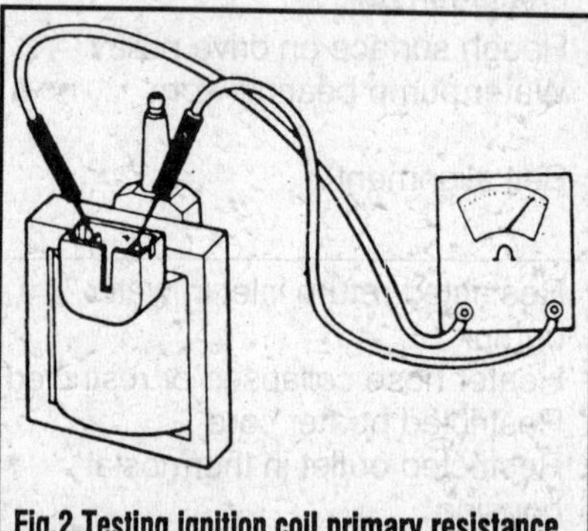

Fig.2 Testing ignition coil primary resistance

Thick Film Ignition Module

TESTING

➧ SEE FIG. 3–4

1. Make sure ignition is turned OFF.
2. Remove coil wire and ground it to car body.
3. Attach the negative (–) voltmeter lead to the distributor base.
4. Disconnect the pin in-line connector near the distributor and attach positive (+) voltmeter lead to the TFI module side of connector.
5. Turn the ignition to the ON position.
6. Bump the starter so that the engine rotates a small amount and stops. Record the voltage reading. (Allow sufficient time for the digital voltage reading to stabilize before taking measurement).
7. The voltage reading should be 70 percent of battery voltage.
8. If the voltage is less than 70 percent, remove the distributor from the engine to test the module and stator.
9. Remove the TFI module from the distributor by removing the two mounting screws. Be careful not to damage stator terminals when pulling module out of distributor.
10. Measure resistance between the TFI module by using an ohmmeter. Place one meter terminal on the ground terminal and place the second meter terminal on the PIP-IN terminal on the module. Check module testing diagram in this section for terminal location and ohm specifications.
11. After recording ohm resistances, if the readings are within specifications replace the stator assembly in the distributor. If the readings are NOT within specifications replace the module assembly.

REMOVAL & INSTALLATION

Except 3.8L Engine

1. Disconnect the negative battery cable. Remove the distributor cap and position it to the side.
2. Remove the TFI-IV harness connector. Remove the distributor from the engine.

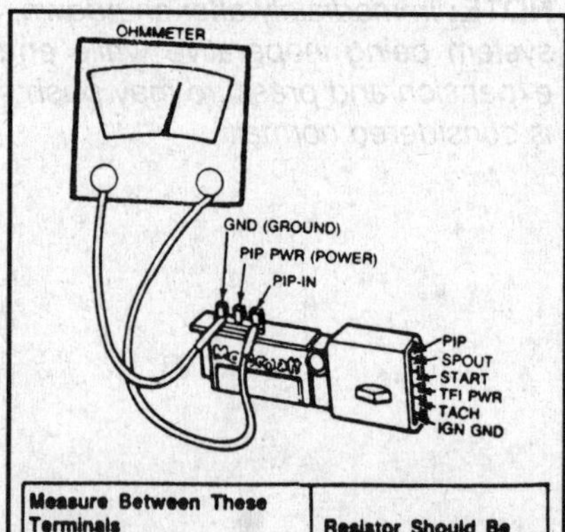

Measure Between These Terminals	Resistor Should Be
• GND - PIP In	Greater than 500 Ohms
• PIP PWR - PIP In	Less than 2K Ohms
• PIP PWR - TFI PWR	Less than 200 Ohms
• GND - IGN GND	Less than 2 Ohms
• PIP In - PIP	Less than 200 Ohms

Fig.3 Module testing locations

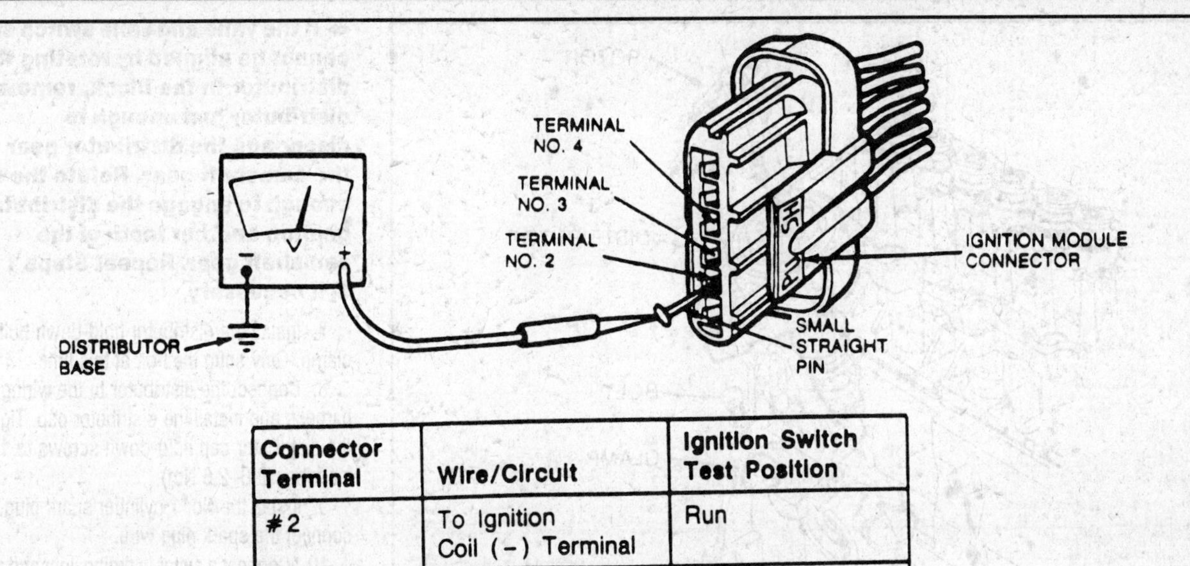

Connector Terminal	Wire/Circuit	Ignition Switch Test Position
#2	To Ignition Coil (−) Terminal	Run
#3	Run Circuit	Run and Start
#4	Start Circuit	Start

Fig.4 Wiring harness testing locations

3. Position the distributor on the work bench. Remove the module retaining screws.

4. Pull the right side of the module down the distributor mounting flange in order to disengage the module terminals from the connector in the distributor base.

5. The module can be pulled toward the flange and away from the distributor.

➡ **Do not attempt to lift the module from the mounting surface prior to removing the entire TFI-IV module toward the distributor flange as the pins will break at the distributor/module connector.**

6. Installation is the reverse of the removal procedure. Coat the metal base of the module with silicone compound approximately $\frac{1}{32}$ in. (0.8mm) thick prior to installing it.

3.8L Engine

1. Disconnect the negative battery cable

2. Remove the screws attaching the leaf screen and cowl dash extension panel in the area of the TFI module assembly. Remove the leaf screen.

3. Disconnect the harness connector from the module assembly. The connector latch is underneath the module shroud and must be pressed upward to unlatch it.

4. Remove the retaining nuts attaching the TFI/heatsink assembly to the cowl dash extension panel.

5. Remove the TFI/Heatsink assembly. The assembly is mounted with the heatsink pointed down.

6. Remove the module retaining screws and remove the module from the heatsink. While holding the module connector shroud pull the seal off the other end of the module.

7. Installation is the reverse of the removal procedure. Coat the metal base of the module with silicone compound approximately $\frac{1}{32}$ in. (0.8mm) thick prior to installing it.

Distributor

REMOVAL & INSTALLATION

➧ SEE FIG. 5–6

1. Disconnect the negative battery cable.

2. Disconnect the wiring connector from the distributor.

3. Remove distributor cap and position it and the attached wires aside, so as not to interfere with removing the distributor.

4. Mark the position of the rotor in relation to the distributor housing and mark the position of the distributor housing on the engine.

5. Remove the rotor.

6. Remove the distributor hold-down bolt and clamp and remove the distributor.

To install:

➡ **Before installation, inspect the distributor O-ring and drive gear for wear and/or damage. Rotate the distributor shaft to make sure it moves freely, without binding.**

TIMING NOT DISTURBED

1. Install the distributor, aligning the distributor housing and rotor with the marks that were made during the removal procedure.

2. Install the distributor hold-down bolt and clamp. Only snug the bolt at this time.

3. Connect the distributor to the wiring harness.

4. Install the rotor and the distributor cap. Make sure the ignition wires are securely connected to the distributor cap and spark plugs. Tighten the distributor cap screws to 18–23 inch lbs. (2.0–2.6 Nm).

5. Connect a suitable timing light and set the initial timing.

6. Tighten the distributor hold-down bolt to 17–25 ft. lbs. (23–34 Nm) on the 2.5L engine, 14–21 ft. lbs. (19–28 Nm) on the 3.0L engine or 20–29 ft. lbs. (27–40 Nm) on the 3.8L engine.

7. Recheck the initial timing and adjust if necessary.

TIMING DISTURBED

1. Disconnect the spark plug wire from the No. 1 cylinder spark plug and remove the spark plug.

2. Place a finger over the spark plug hole. Rotate the engine clockwise until compression is felt at the spark plug hole.

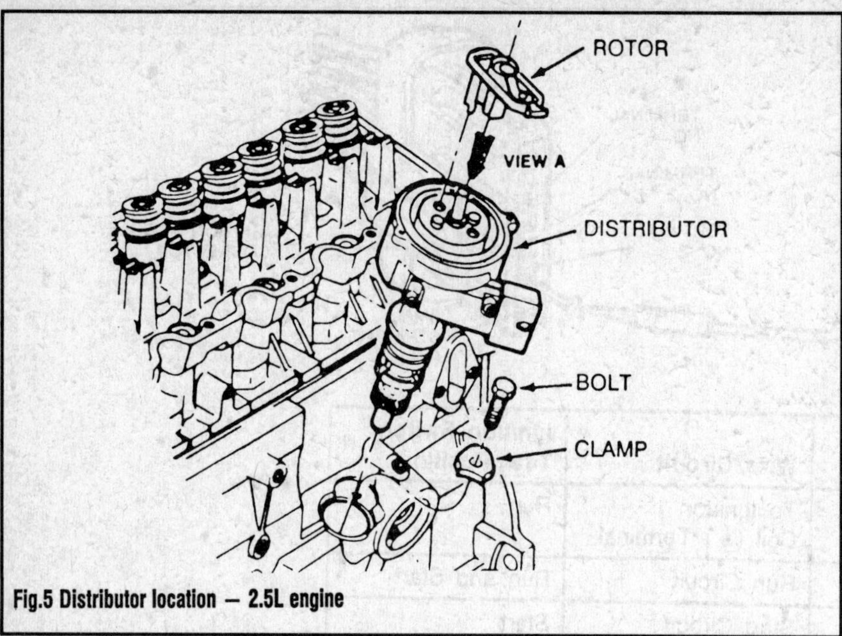

Fig.5 Distributor location — 2.5L engine

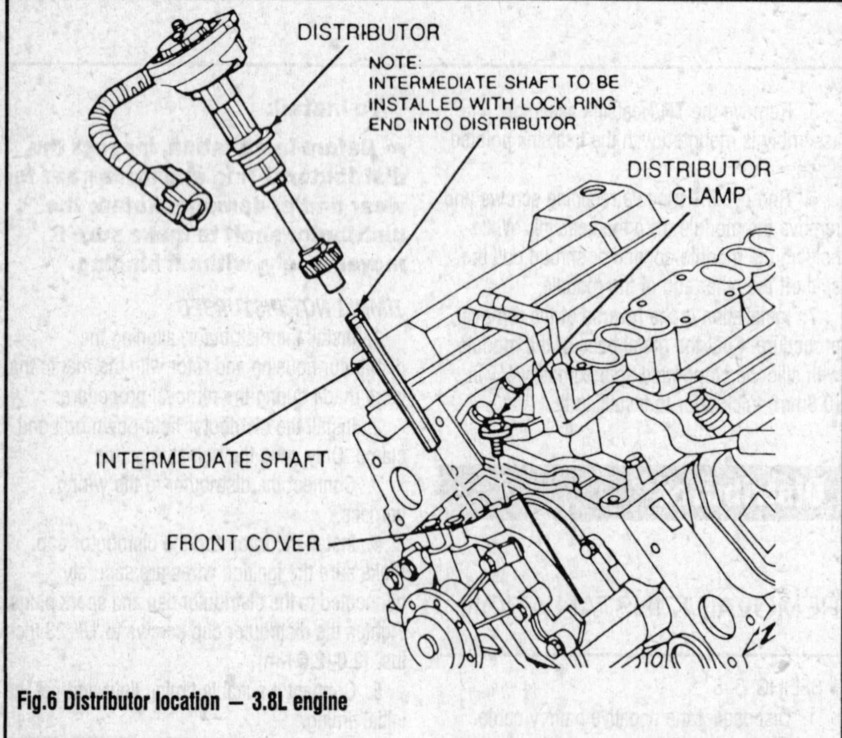

Fig.6 Distributor location — 3.8L engine

3. Align the timing pointer with the TDC mark on the crankshaft damper.

4. Install the rotor on the distributor shaft. Rotate the distributor shaft so the rotor tip is pointing to the distributor cap No. 1 spark plug tower position.

5. While installing the distributor, continue rotating the rotor slightly so the leading edge of the vane is centered in the vane switch stator assembly.

6. Rotate the distributor in the block to align the leading edge of the vane and vane switch stator assembly. Make sure the rotor is pointing to the distributor cap No. 1 spark plug tower position.

➡ **If the vane and vane switch stator cannot be aligned by rotating the distributor in the block, remove the distributor just enough to disengage the distributor gear from the camshaft gear. Rotate the rotor enough to engage the distributor gear on another tooth of the camshaft gear. Repeat Steps 1 and 2, if necessary.**

7. Install the distributor hold-down bolt and clamp. Only snug the bolt at this time.

8. Connect the distributor to the wiring harness and install the distributor cap. Tighten the distributor cap hold-down screws to 18–23 inch lbs. (2.0–2.6 Nm).

9. Install the No. 1 cylinder spark plug and connect the spark plug wire.

10. Connect a suitable timing light and set the initial timing.

11. Tighten the distributor hold-down bolt to 17–25 ft. lbs. (23–34 Nm) on the 2.5L engine, 14–21 ft. lbs. (19–28 Nm) on the 3.0L engine or 20–29 ft. lbs. (27–40 Nm) on the 3.8L engine.

12. Recheck the initial timing and adjust if necessary.

Distributorless Ignition

The 3.0L SHO engine is equipped with a Distributorless Ignition System (DIS) which consists of the following components:

- Crankshaft timing sensor
- Camshaft sensor
- DIS ignition module
- Ignition coil pack
- The spark angle portion of the EEC–IV module

REMOVAL & INSTALLATION

CRANKSHAFT TIMING SENSOR

➧ SEE FIG. 7

1. Disconnect the negative battery cable.

2. Loosen the tensioner pulleys for the air conditioning compressor and the power steering pump belts. Remove the belts from the crankshaft pulley.

3. Disconnect the DIS module and remove the intake manifold crossover tube.

4. Remove the upper timing belt cover.

5. Disconnect the sensor wiring harness at the connector and route the wiring harness through the belt cover.

6. Raise the vehicle and support it safely.

7. Remove the right front wheel and tire assembly.

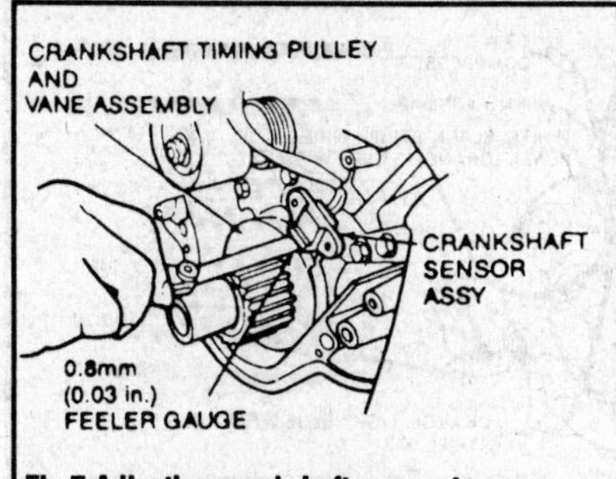

Fig.7 Adjusting crankshaft sensor to vane clearance — 3.0L SHO engine

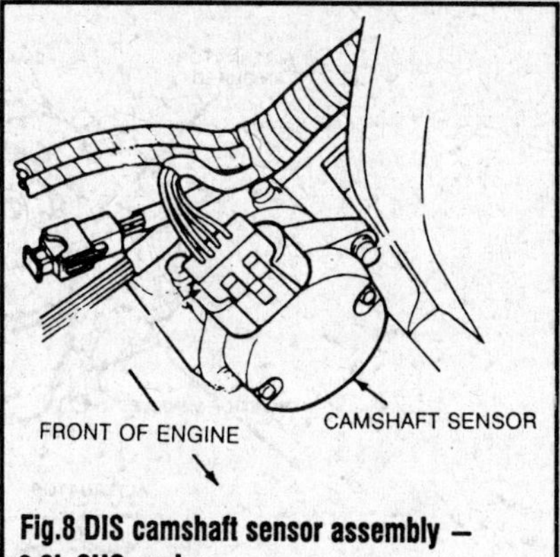

Fig.8 DIS camshaft sensor assembly — 3.0L SHO engine

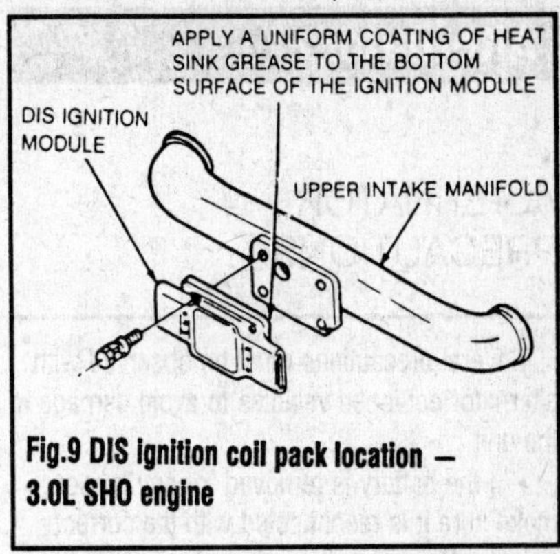

Fig.9 DIS ignition coil pack location — 3.0L SHO engine

8. Remove the crankshaft pulley using universal puller T67L–3600–A or equivalent.
9. Remove the center and lower timing belt covers.
10. Rotate the crankshaft by hand, to position the metal vane of the shutter outside of the sensor air gap.
11. Remove the crankshaft sensor mounting screws and remove the sensor.

To install:

12. Route the sensor wiring harness through the belt cover. Install the sensor assembly on the mounting pad and install but do not tighten, the retaining screws.
13. Use a 0.03 in. (0.76mm) feeler gauge to set the clearance between the crankshaft sensor assembly and 1 vane on the crankshaft timing pulley and vane assembly. Tighten the screws to 22–31 inch lbs. (2.5–3.5 Nm).

➡ **This is a critical torque. Overtightening can cause damage to the timing sensor.**

14. Install the lower timing belt cover. Install the crankshaft pulley using a suitable tool. Tighten the pulley bolt to 112–127 ft. lbs. (152–172 Nm).
15. Install the center timing belt cover.
16. Install the right front wheel and tire assembly. Lower the vehicle.
17. Route and connect the sensor wiring harness.
18. Install the upper timing belt cover.
19. Install the intake manifold crossover tube and connect the DIS module.
20. Install the air conditioning and power steering belts and adjust them to the proper tension.
21. Connect the negative battery cable.

CAMSHAFT SENSOR ASSEMBLY

➧ SEE FIG. 8

1. Disconnect the negative battery cable.
2. Remove the engine torque strut.
3. Remove the power steering belt and the pump pulley.
4. Disconnect the camshaft sensor wiring connector.
5. Remove the mounting bolts and remove the sensor.
6. To install, reverse the removal procedure. Tighten the mounting bolts to 22–31 inch lbs. (2.5–3.5 Nm).

DIS IGNITION MODULE

➧ SEE FIG. 10

1. Disconnect the negative battery cable.
2. Disconnect the wiring connectors at the module.
3. Remove the module mounting bolts and remove the module.
4. To install, reverse the removal procedure. Apply a uniform coating of heat sink grease to the mounting surface of the DIS module before it is installed. Tighten the mounting bolts to 22–31 inch lbs. (2.5–3.5 Nm).

IGNITION COIL PACK

➧ SEE FIG. 9

1. Disconnect the negative battery cable.
2. Remove the cover from the coil pack and disconnect the electrical connector.
3. Remove the spark plug wires by squeezing the locking tabs to release the coil boot retainers.
4. Remove the coil pack mounting screws and remove the coil pack.
5. To install, reverse the removal procedure. Tighten the mounting screws to 40–62 inch lbs. (4.5–7 Nm).

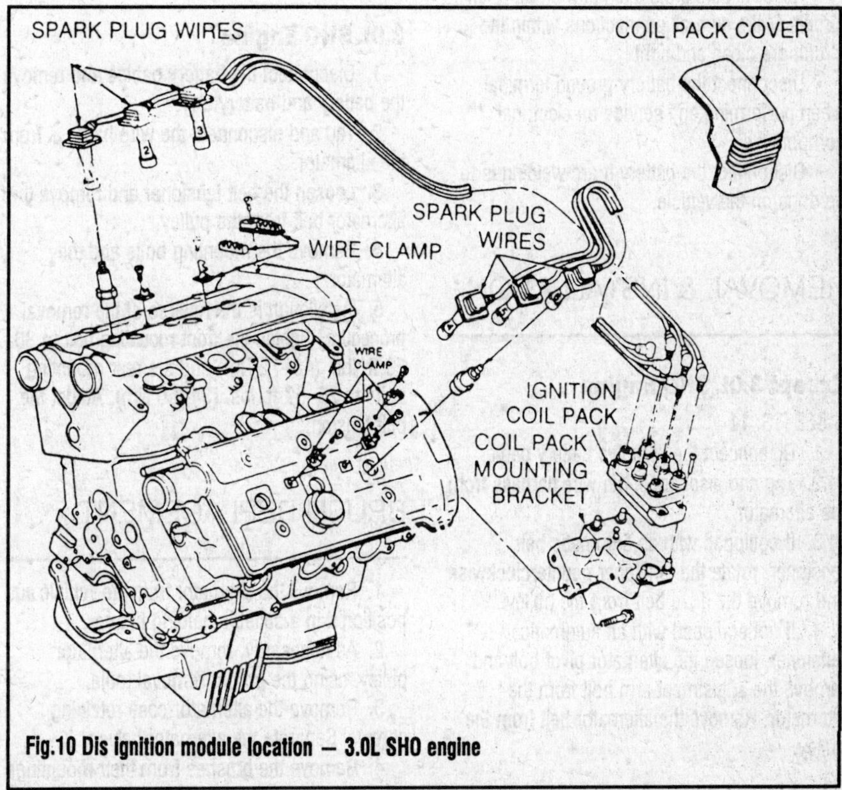

Fig.10 Dis ignition module location — 3.0L SHO engine

Alternator

ALTERNATOR PRECAUTIONS

Several precautions must be observed with alternator equipped vehicles to avoid damage to the unit.

- If the battery is removed for any reason, make sure it is reconnected with the correct polarity. Reversing the battery connections may result in damage to the one-way rectifiers.
- When utilizing a booster battery as a starting aid, always connect the positive to positive terminals and the negative terminal from the booster battery to a good engine ground on the vehicle being started.
- Never use a fast charger as a booster to start vehicles.
- Disconnect the battery cables when charging the battery with a fast charger.
- Never attempt to polarize the alternator.
- Do not use test lights of more than 12 volts when checking diode continuity.
- Do not short across or ground any of the alternator terminals.
- The polarity of the battery, alternator and regulator must be matched and considered before making any electrical connections within the system.
- Never separate the alternator on an open circuit. Make sure all connections within the circuit are clean and tight.
- Disconnect the battery ground terminal when performing any service on electrical components.
- Disconnect the battery if arc welding is to be done on the vehicle.

REMOVAL & INSTALLATION

Except 3.0L SHO Engine

➧ SEE FIG. 11

1. Disconnect the negative battery cable.
2. Tag and disconnect the wire harness from the alternator.
3. If equipped with an automatic belt tensioner, rotate the tensioner counterclockwise and remove the drive belt from the pulley.
4. If not equipped with an automatic tensioner, loosen the alternator pivot bolt and remove the adjustment arm bolt from the alternator. Remove the alternator belt from the pulley.

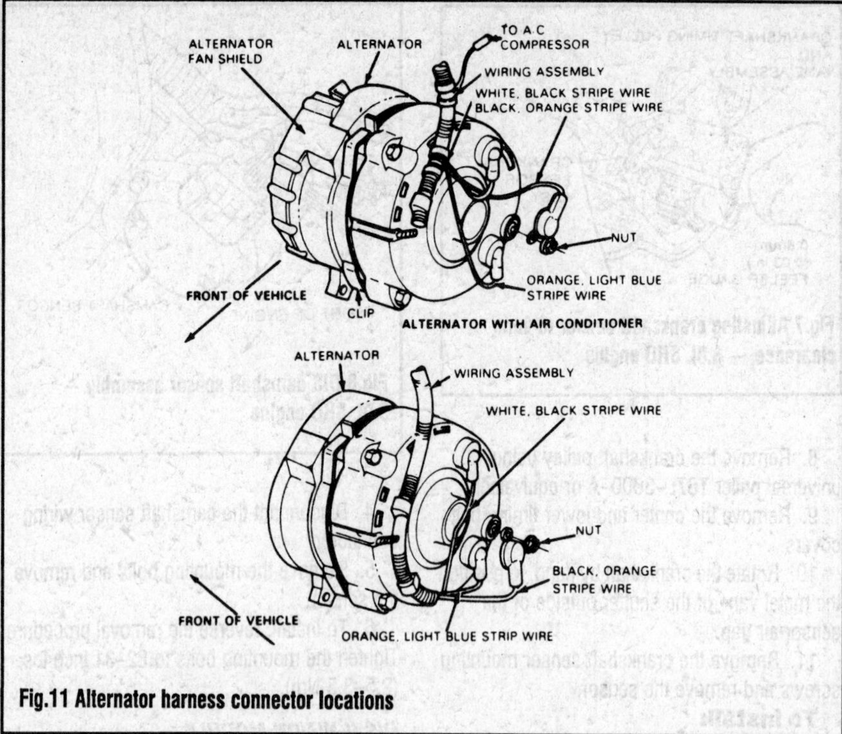

Fig.11 Alternator harness connector locations

5. Remove the alternator mounting bolts or the pivot bolt, as required, and remove the alternator.
6. Installation is the reverse of the removal procedure. Torque the adjusting arm bolt to 15-22 ft. lbs. and the pivot bolt to 40-45 ft. lbs.
7. Adjust the belt tension, if not equipped with an automatic belt tensioner.

3.0L SHO Engine

1. Disconnect the battery cables and remove the battery and battery tray.
2. Tag and disconnect the wire harness from the alternator.
3. Loosen the belt tensioner and remove the alternator belt from the pulley.
4. Remove the mounting bolts and the alternator.
5. Installation is the reverse of the removal procedure. Tighten the front mounting bolt to 36–53 ft. lbs. (48–72 Nm) and the rear mounting bolts to 25–37 ft. lbs. (34–50 Nm). Adjust the belt tension.

BRUSH REPLACEMENT

1. Remove the alternator from the vehicle and position it in a suitable holding fixture.
2. As necessary, remove the alternator pulley, using the proper removal tools.
3. Remove the alternator case retaining screws. Separate the alternator halves.
4. Remove the brushes from their mountings inside the alternator.

To Install:

5. Carefully position the new brushes inside the alternator case, using the proper brush retainer tool.
6. Assemble the alternator case halves together. Install the alternator pulley, if removed.
7. Install the alternator on the vehicle.

Voltage Regulator

ADJUSTMENT

The electronic voltage regulator is calibrated and preset by the manufacturer. No adjustment is required or possible.

REMOVAL & INSTALLATION

➧ SEE FIG. 12

1. Disconnect the negative battery cable.
2. Disconnect the electrical connectors from the wiring harness.
3. Remove the regulator mounting screws and the regulator.
4. Installation is the reverse of the removal procedure.
5. Connect the negative battery cable. Test the system for proper voltage regulation.

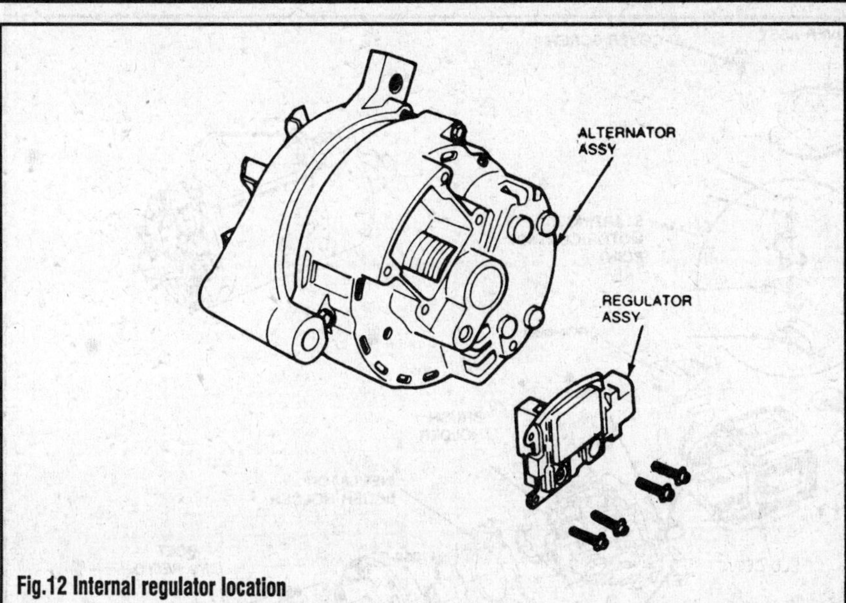

Fig.12 Internal regulator location

Battery

REMOVAL & INSTALLATION

➧ SEE FIG. 13

1. Disconnect the negative battery cable. Disconnect the positive battery cable.
2. Remove the battery holddown bracket retaining bolt. Remove the holddown bracket.
3. Carefully lift the battery from its mounting.
4. Installation is the reverse of the removal procedure.

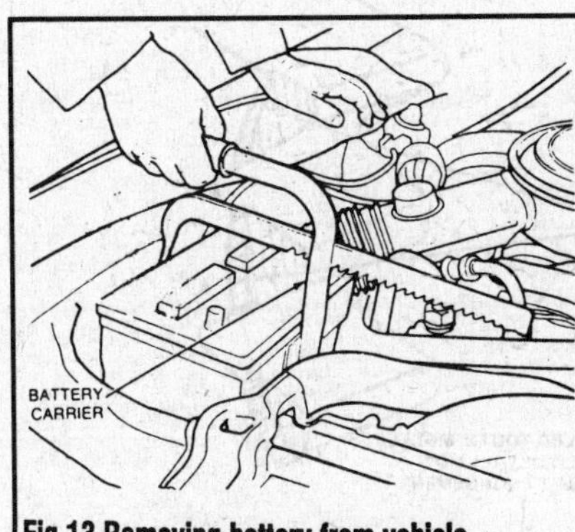

Fig.13 Removing battery from vehicle

Starter

REMOVAL & INSTALLATION

➧ SEE FIG. 14

1. Disconnect the negative battery cable and the cable connection at the starter.

➡ **On 1992 vehicles, when the battery has been disconnected and reconnected, some abnormal drive symptoms may occur while the EEC processor relearns its adaptive strategy. The vehicle may need to be driven ten miles or more to relearn the strategy.**

2. Raise and support the vehicle safely.
3. Remove the cable support and ground cable connection from the upper starter stud bolt, if necessary.
4. If equipped, remove the starter brace from the cylinder block and the starter.
5. Remove the starter-to-bell housing bolts and remove the starter.
6. Installation is the reverse of the removal procedure.

OVERHAUL

Brush Replacement

1. Remove the starter from the vehicle. Position the assembly in a suitable holding fixture.
2. Remove the top cover by taking out the retaining screw. Loosen and remove the two through bolts (long bolts that run the length of the starter). Remove the starter drive end housing and the starter drive plunger lever return spring.
3. Remove the starter drive plunger lever pivot pin and lever, and remove the armature. Remove the brush end plate.
4. Remove the ground brush retaining screws from the frame and remove the brushes.
5. Cut the insulated brush leads from the field coils, as close to the field connection point as possible.
6. Clean and inspect the starter motor. Check the exploded view of the starter motor in this section.
7. Replace the brush end plate if the insulator between the field brush holder and the end plate is cracked or broken.
8. Position the new insulated field brushes lead on the field coil connections. Position and crimp the clip provided with the brushes to hold the brush lead to the connection. Solder the lead, clip, and connection together using a resin core solder. Use a 300W soldering iron.
9. Install the ground brush leads to the frame with the retaining screws.
10. Clean the armature with special armature paper or very fine emory paper.
11. Position the brush end plate to the starter frame, with the end plate boss in the frame slot.
12. Install the armature in the starter frame.
13. Install the starter drive gear plunger lever to the frame and starter drive assembly, and install the pivot pin.
14. Partially fill the drive end housing bearing bore with grease (approximately 1/4 full). Position the return spring on the plunger lever, and the drive end housing to the starter frame. Install the through-bolts and tighten to specified torque (55-75 inch lbs.). Be sure that the stop ring retainer is seated properly in the drive end housing.
15. Install the armature brushes in the brush holders. Center the brush springs on the brushes.
16. Position the plunger lever cover and brush cover band, with its gasket, on the starter. Tighten the band retaining screw.

STARTER DRIVE REPLACEMENT

➧ SEE FIG. 15

1. Remove the starter from the engine.

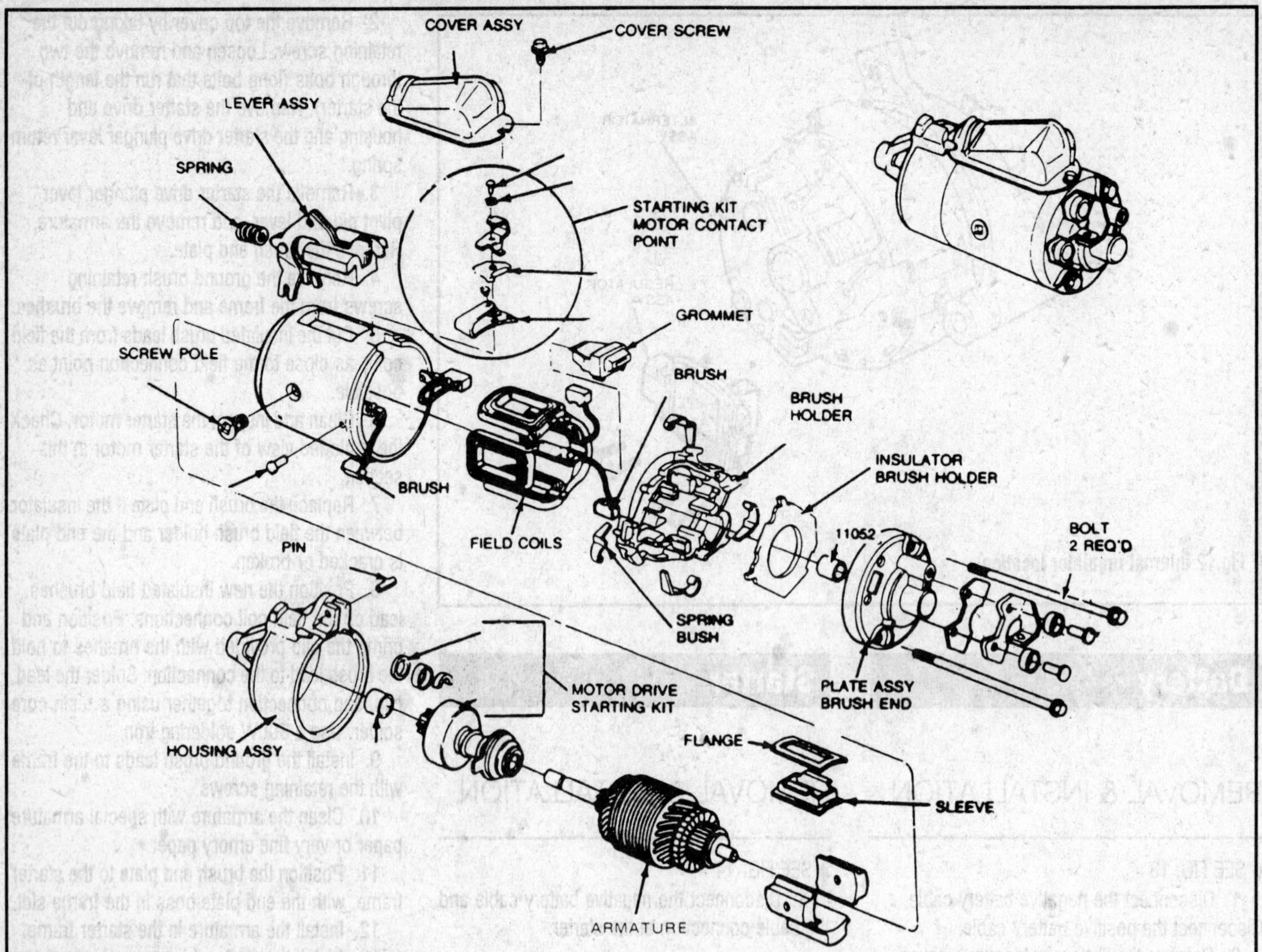

COVER ASSY
COVER SCREW
LEVER ASSY
SPRING
STARTING KIT
MOTOR CONTACT
POINT
GROMMET
SCREW POLE
BRUSH
BRUSH
HOLDER
INSULATOR
BRUSH HOLDER
BRUSH
FIELD COILS
PIN
11052
BOLT
2 REQ'D
SPRING
BUSH
MOTOR DRIVE
STARTING KIT
PLATE ASSY
BRUSH END
HOUSING ASSY
FLANGE
SLEEVE
ARMATURE

Fig.14 Starter motor assembly — exploded view

MILLED CONDITION.
EXCESSIVE WEAR ON
2 OR 3 TEETH
MILLED TOOTH. METAL
BUILD-UP WILL NOT
PERMIT ENGAGEMENT
NORMAL WEAR PATTERN
SMALL WEAR PATTERN
MILLED GEARS

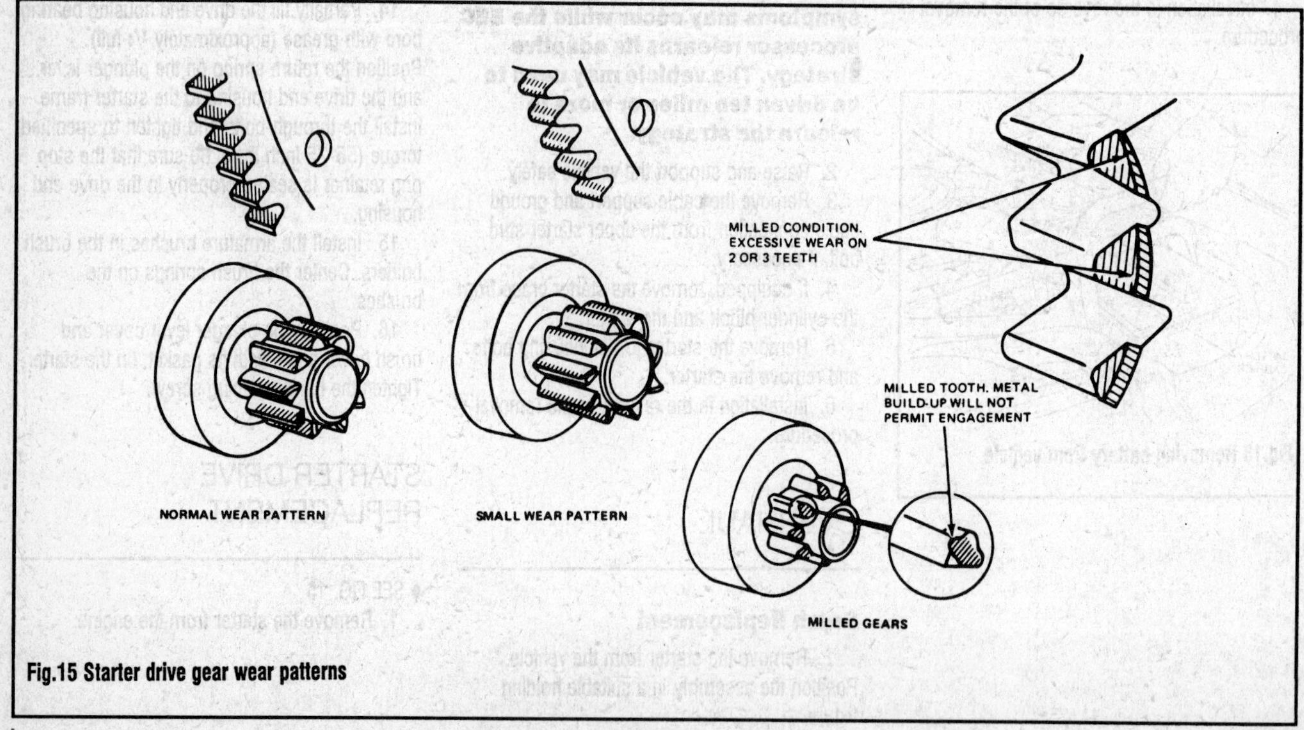

Fig.15 Starter drive gear wear patterns

2. Remove the starter drive plunger lever cover.

3. Loosen the through-bolts just enough to allow removal of the drive end housing and the starter drive plunger lever return spring.

4. Remove the pivot pin which attaches the starter drive plunger lever to the starter frame and remove the lever.

5. Remove the stop ring retainer and stop ring from the armature shaft.

6. Remove the starter drive from the armature shaft.

7. Inspect the teeth on the starter drive. If they are excessively worn, inspect the teeth on the ring gear of the flywheel. If the teeth on the flywheel are excessively worn, the flywheel ring gear should be replaced.

8. Apply a thin coat of white grease to the armature shaft, in the area in which the starter drive operates.

9. Install the starter drive on the armature shaft and install a new stopring.

10. Position the starter drive plunger lever on the starter frame and install the pivot pin. Make sure the plunger lever is properly engaged with the starter drive.

11. Install a new stop ring retainer on the armature shaft.

12. Fill the drive end housing bearing 1/4 full with grease.

13. Position the starter drive plunger lever return spring and the drive end housing to the starter frame.

14. Tighten the starter through-bolts to 55-75 inch lbs.

15. Install the starter drive plunger lever cover and the brush cover band on the starter.

16. Install the starter.

Sending Units and Sensors

** CAUTION

When draining the coolant, keep in mind that cats and dogs are attracted by the ethylene glycol antifreeze, and are quite likely to drink any that is left in an uncovered container or in puddles on the ground. This will prove fatal in sufficient quantity. Always drain the coolant into a sealable container. Coolant should be reused unless it is contaminated or several years old.

REMOVAL & INSTALLATION

Coolant Temperature

1. Disconnect the negative battery cable. Drain the cooling system.

2. Disconnect and tag the coolant temperature sensor electrical connector.

3. Remove the necessary components to gain access to the sensor assembly.

4. Using the proper size wrench or socket and ratchet, remove the sensor from its mounting.

5. Installation is the reverse of the removal procedure. Be sure to use Teflon tape on the sensor threads.

Oil Pressure

➧ SEE FIG. 120–123

1. Disconnect the negative battery cable. On the 3.8L engine remove the washer solvent/ coolant recovery bottle. Release the drive belt tension and remove the idler pulley below the power steering pump.

2. Disconnect and tag the oil pressure sensor electrical connector.

3. Remove the necessary components to gain access to the sensor assembly.

4. Using the proper size wrench or socket and ratchet, remove the sensor from its mounting.

5. Installation is the reverse of the removal procedure. Be sure to use Teflon tape on the sensor threads.

Electric Fan Switch

1. Disconnect the negative battery cable. Drain the cooling system.

2. Disconnect and tag the electric fan switch electrical connector.

3. Remove the necessary components to gain access to the switch assembly.

4. Using the proper size wrench or socket and ratchet, remove the switch from its mounting.

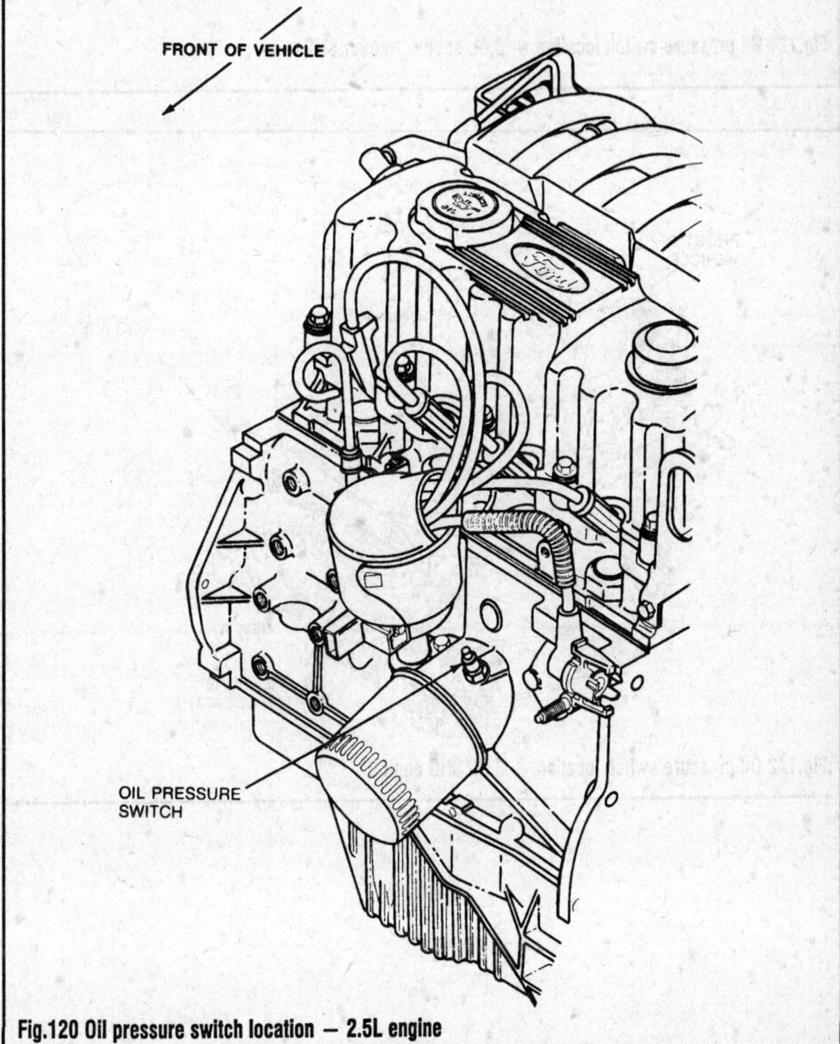

Fig.120 Oil pressure switch location — 2.5L engine

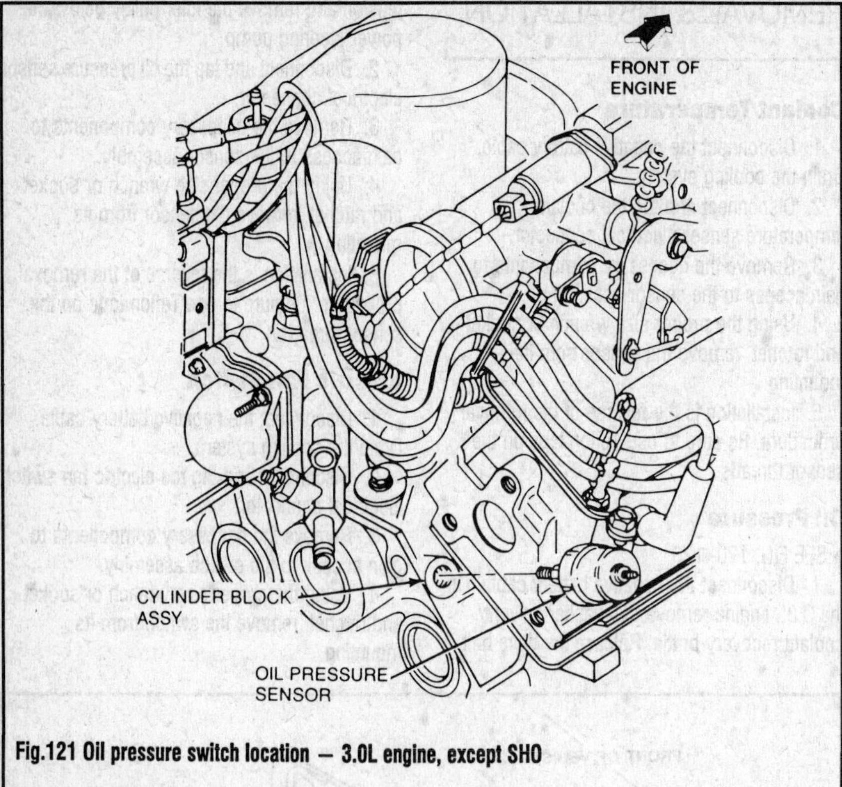

Fig.121 Oil pressure switch location — 3.0L engine, except SHO

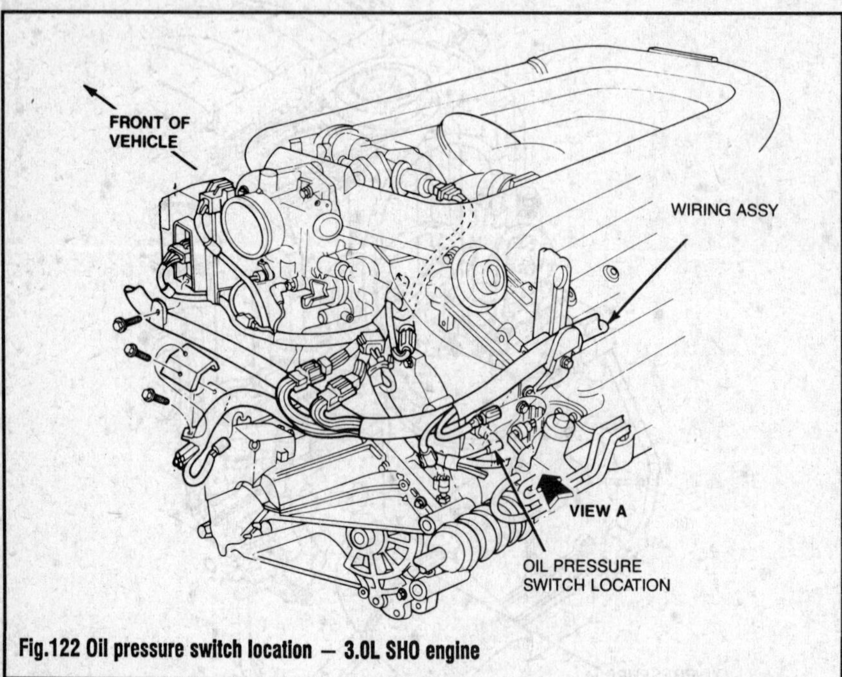

Fig.122 Oil pressure switch location — 3.0L SHO engine

5. Installation is the reverse of the removal procedure.

Oxygen Sensor

1. Disconnect the negative battery cable.
2. Disconnect and tag the oxygen sensor electric connector.
3. Using the proper size wrench or socket and ratchet, remove the sensor from its mounting.
4. Installation is the reverse of the removal procedure.

AIR TEMPERATURE SENSOR

The air temperature sensor in systems with vane air flow meters is used to measure the temperature of the incoming air and send the information to the ECU. In all other systems, the sensor provides the ECU with mixture, fuel and air temperature information.

The air temperature sensor is located in the meter in vane air flow meter systems. Otherwise it is located in the air cleaner assembly or in the side of the throttle body.

Without Vane Air Flow Meter

1. Disconnect the negative battery cable.
2. Disconnect the electrical connector from the air temperature sensor.
3. Remove the sensor.
4. Installation is the reverse of the removal procedure.

With Vane Air Flow Meter

The air temperature sensor is an integral component of the vane air flow meter. If the temperature sensor is defective, the vane air flow meter must be replaced.

ENGINE COOLANT TEMPERATURE SENSOR

The coolant temperature sensor detects the temperature of engine coolant and supplies the information to the ECU. The coolant temperature sensor is located on the cylinder head or on the intake manifold. The sensor signal is used to modify ignition timing, EGR flow and air/fuel ratio as a function of engine coolant temperature.

1. Disconnect the negative battery cable.
2. Drain the cooling system sufficiently to remove the sensor.
3. Disconnect the electrical connector from the temperature sensor.

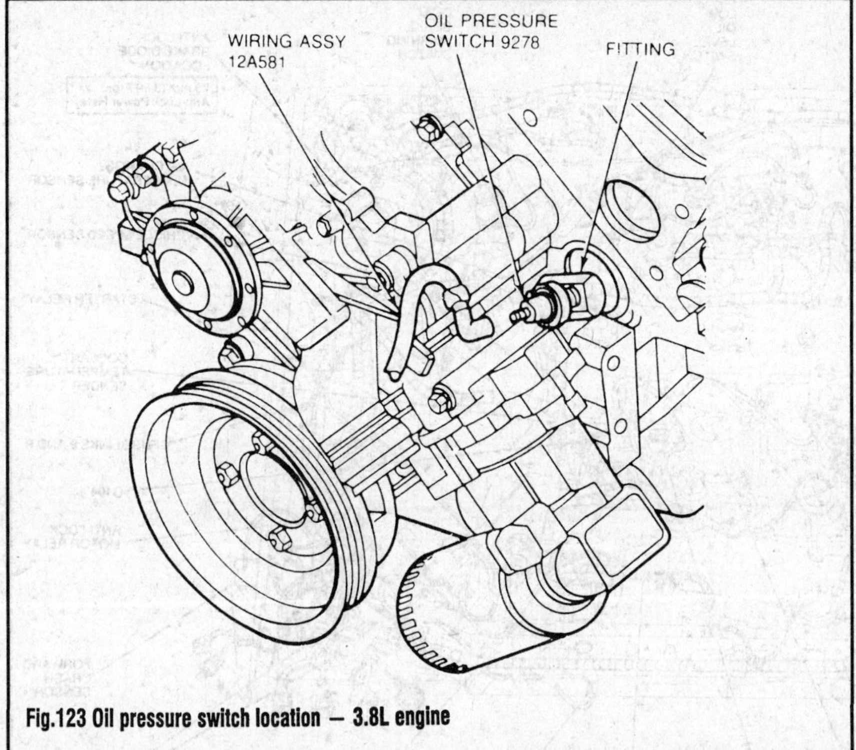

Fig.123 Oil pressure switch location — 3.8L engine

4. Remove the coolant temperature sensor.
5. Installation is the reverse of the removal procedure. Properly refill and bleed the cooling system.

EXHAUST GAS OXYGEN SENSOR

The oxygen sensor supplies the ECU with a signal which indicates a rich or lean condition during engine operation. This input information assists the ECU in determining the proper air/fuel ratio. The oxygen sensor is threaded into the exhaust manifold on all front wheel drive vehicles.

1. Disconnect the negative battery cable.
2. Disconnect the oxygen sensor connector.
3. Remove the sensor from the exhaust manifold.
4. Installation is the reverse of the removal procedure.

MANIFOLD ABSOLUTE PRESSURE SENSOR

The MAP sensor measures manifold vacuum using a frequency. This gives the ECU information on engine load. It is used as a barometric sensor for altitude compensation, updating the ECU during key ON, engine OFF and every wide-open throttle. The ECU uses the MAP sensor for spark advance, EGR flow and air/fuel ratio.

1. Disconnect the negative battery cable.
2. Disconnect the electrical connector and the vacuum line from the sensor.
3. Remove the sensor mounting bolts and remove the sensor.
4. Installation is the reverse of the removal procedure.

Relay, Sensor, Switch, Module and Computer Locations

➧ SEE FIG. 16–23

- **A/C Clutch Cycling Pressure Switch (except SHO engine)** — is at right the rear of engine compartment mounted on A/C accumulator.
- **A/C Clutch Cycling Pressure Switch (SHO engine)** — is at the right front of engine, mounted on A/C accumulator.
- **Air Bag Backup Power Supply** — is behind right instrument panel, right side of glove box.
- **Air Bag Diagnostic Module** — is behind center of instrument panel.
- **Air Bag Rear Sensor** — is inside left kick panel.
- **Air Charge Temperature Sensor (2.5L engine)** — is on the left rear of intake manifold.
- **Air Charge Temperature Sensor (3.0L engine)** — is on the top of engine.
- **Air Charge Temperature Sensor (SHO engine)** — is on the left side of engine, in air cleaner.
- **Alternator Output Control Relay** — is between right front inner fender and fender splash shield.
- **Ambient Temperature Sensor** — is at the left front of engine compartment on left side of radiator.
- **Anti-Lock Brake Control Module (except SHO engine)** — is at right fender apron.
- **Anti-Lock Brake Control Module (SHO engine)** — is at the lower left front of engine compartment.
- **Anti-Lock Brake Diode** — is on the left rear corner of engine compartment, taped to wiring harness

anti-Lock Motor Relay — is on the lower left front of engine compartment.

- **Anti-Lock Power Relay** — is at the left rear corner of engine compartment.
- **Anti-Lock Test Connector** — is at the left rear corner of engine compartment.
- **Autolamp Dual Coil Relay** — is behind center of instrument panel, mounted on brace.
- **AXOD Speed Sensor and Torque Converter Solenoid** — is at the lower left rear of engine.
- **Barometric Absolute Pressure (BAP) Sensor** — is on the right side of firewall.
- **Blower Motor Resistors** — is behind right side of instrument panel, inside heater plenum.
- **Brake Fluid Level Sensor** — is at the lower left front of engine compartment.
- **Brake Lamp Switch** — is behind left side instrument panel, on pedal support.
- **Cam Sensor** — is on the right side of engine.
- **Canister Purge Solenoid (2.5L, 3.0L and 3.8L engine)** — is on the left front side of engine.
- **Canister Purge Solenoid (2.5L, 3.0L and 3.8L engine)** — is on the left front side of engine.
- **Canister Purge Solenoid (SHO engine)** — is at the left side of radiator support.

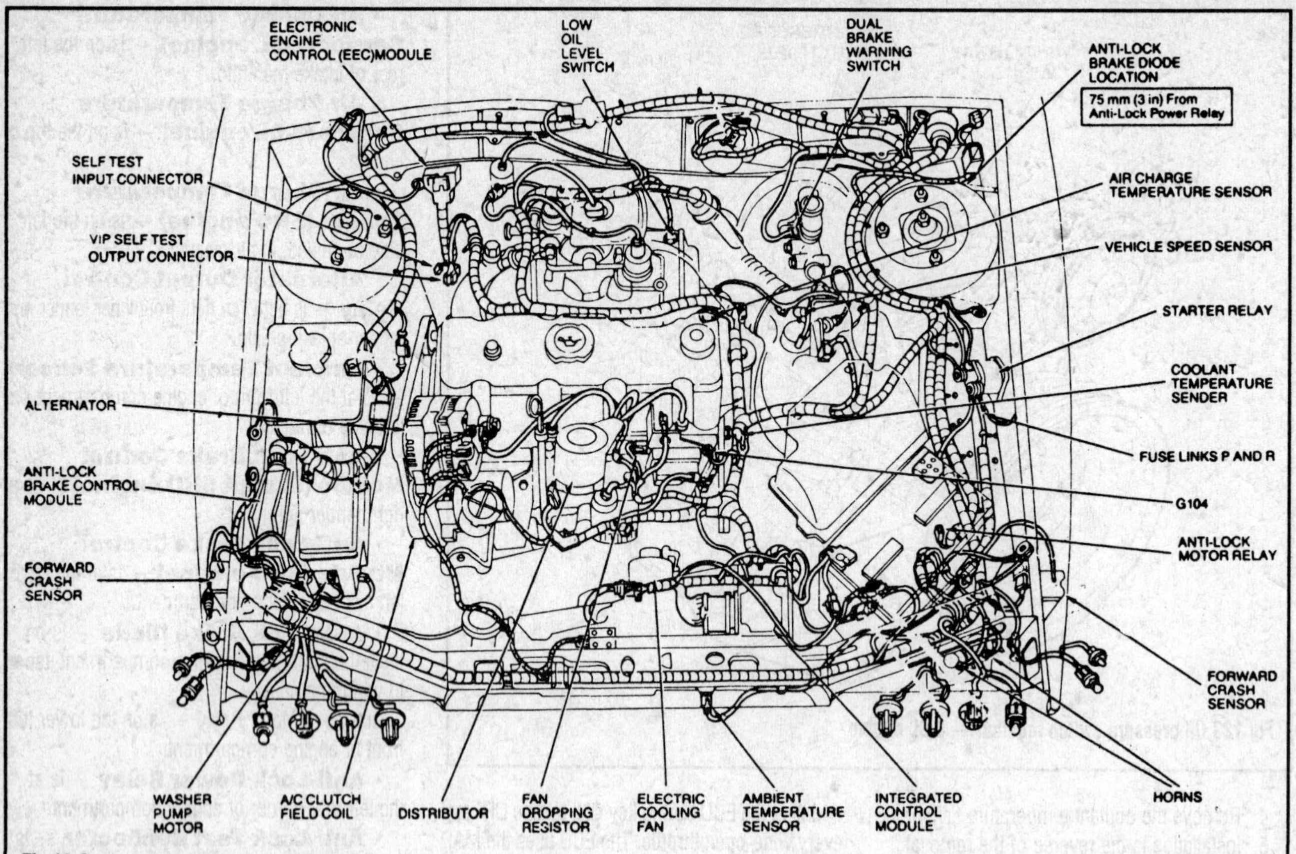

ELECTRONIC ENGINE CONTROL (EEC) MODULE
LOW OIL LEVEL SWITCH
DUAL BRAKE WARNING SWITCH
ANTI-LOCK BRAKE DIODE LOCATION
75 mm (3 in) From Anti-Lock Power Relay
SELF TEST INPUT CONNECTOR
AIR CHARGE TEMPERATURE SENSOR
VIP SELF TEST OUTPUT CONNECTOR
VEHICLE SPEED SENSOR
STARTER RELAY
COOLANT TEMPERATURE SENDER
ALTERNATOR
FUSE LINKS P AND R
ANTI-LOCK BRAKE CONTROL MODULE
G104
ANTI-LOCK MOTOR RELAY
FORWARD CRASH SENSOR
FORWARD CRASH SENSOR
HORNS
WASHER PUMP MOTOR
A/C CLUTCH FIELD COIL
DISTRIBUTOR
FAN DROPPING RESISTOR
ELECTRIC COOLING FAN
AMBIENT TEMPERATURE SENSOR
INTEGRATED CONTROL MODULE

Fig.16 Component locations — 2.5L engine

A/C CLUTCH CYCLING PRESSURE SWITCH
MANIFOLD ABSOLULTE PRESSURE (MAP) SENSOR
FUEL INJECTOR
IDLE SPEED CONTROL
PRESSURE FEEDBACK EGR SENSOR
WIPER MOTOR AND PARK SWITCH
ANTI-LOCK POWER RELAY
POWER STEERING PRESSURE SENSOR
FUSE LINKS B, C, D AND E
RADIO NOISE CAPACITOR
FUSE LINKS K, G AND F
IGNITION SUPPRESSION RESISTOR
ALTERNATOR OUTPUT CONTROL RELAY
VOLTAGE REGULATOR
LOW WASHER FLUID LEVEL SWITCH
TFI IGNITION MODULE
OIL PRESSURE SWITCH
CENTER LINE FORWARD CRASH SENSOR
SHORTING PLUG #1
IGNITION COIL

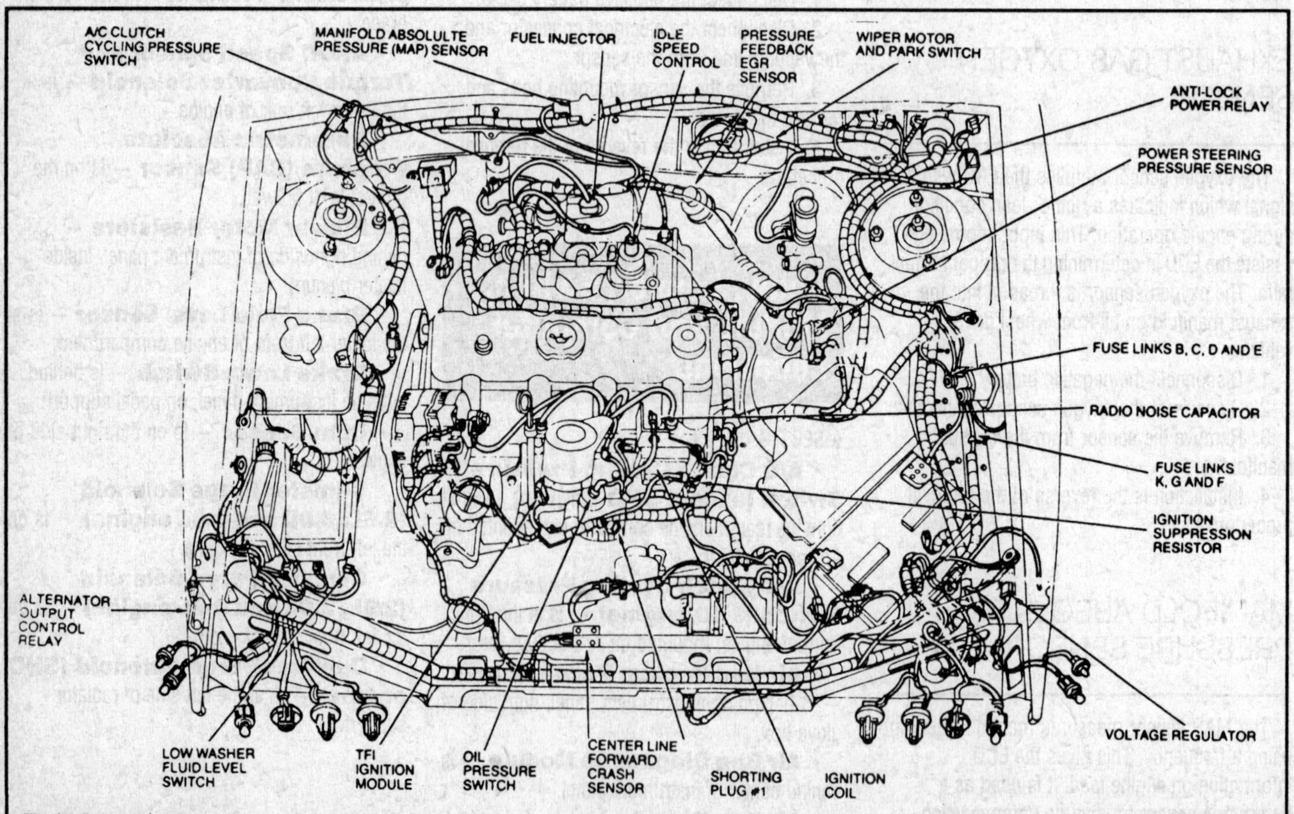

Fig.17 Component locations — 2.5L engine (continued)

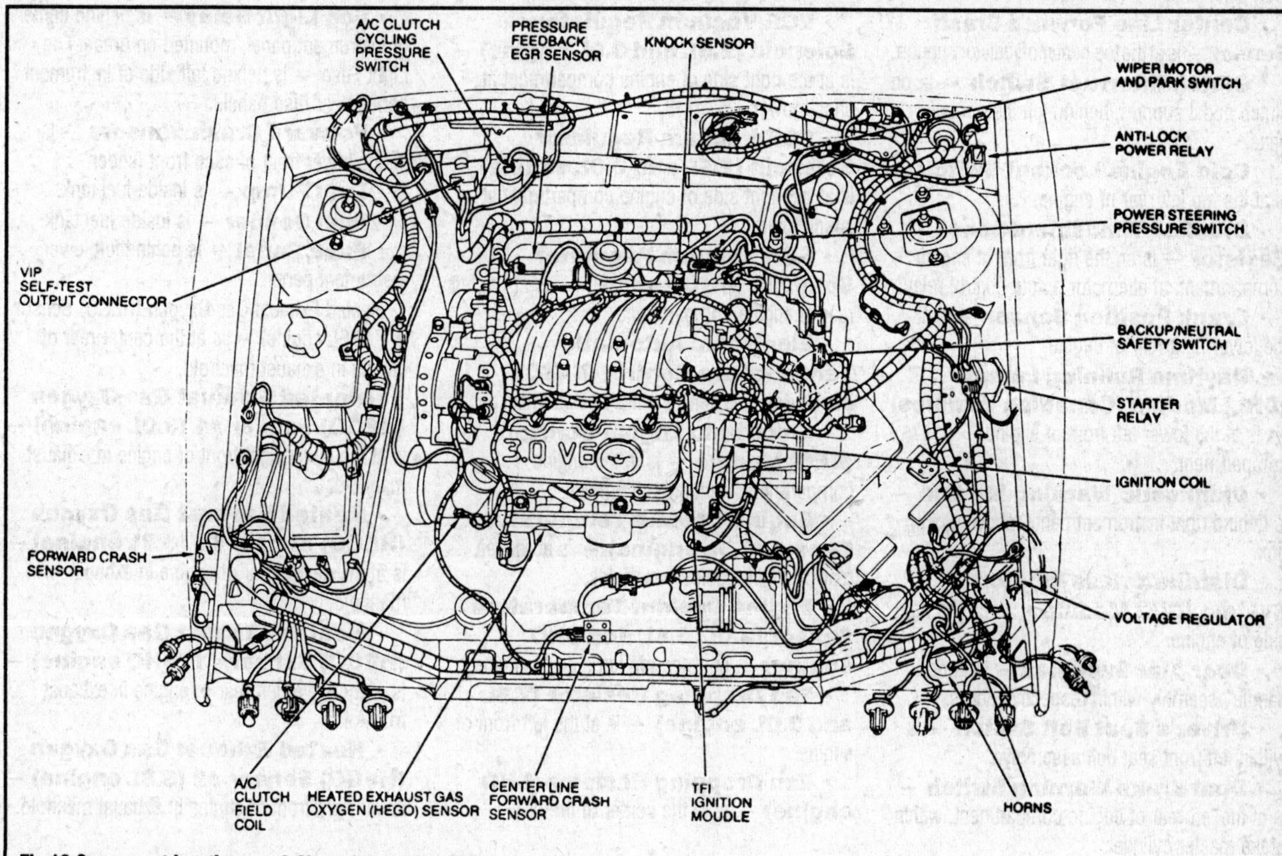

Fig.18 Component locations — 3.0L engine except SHO

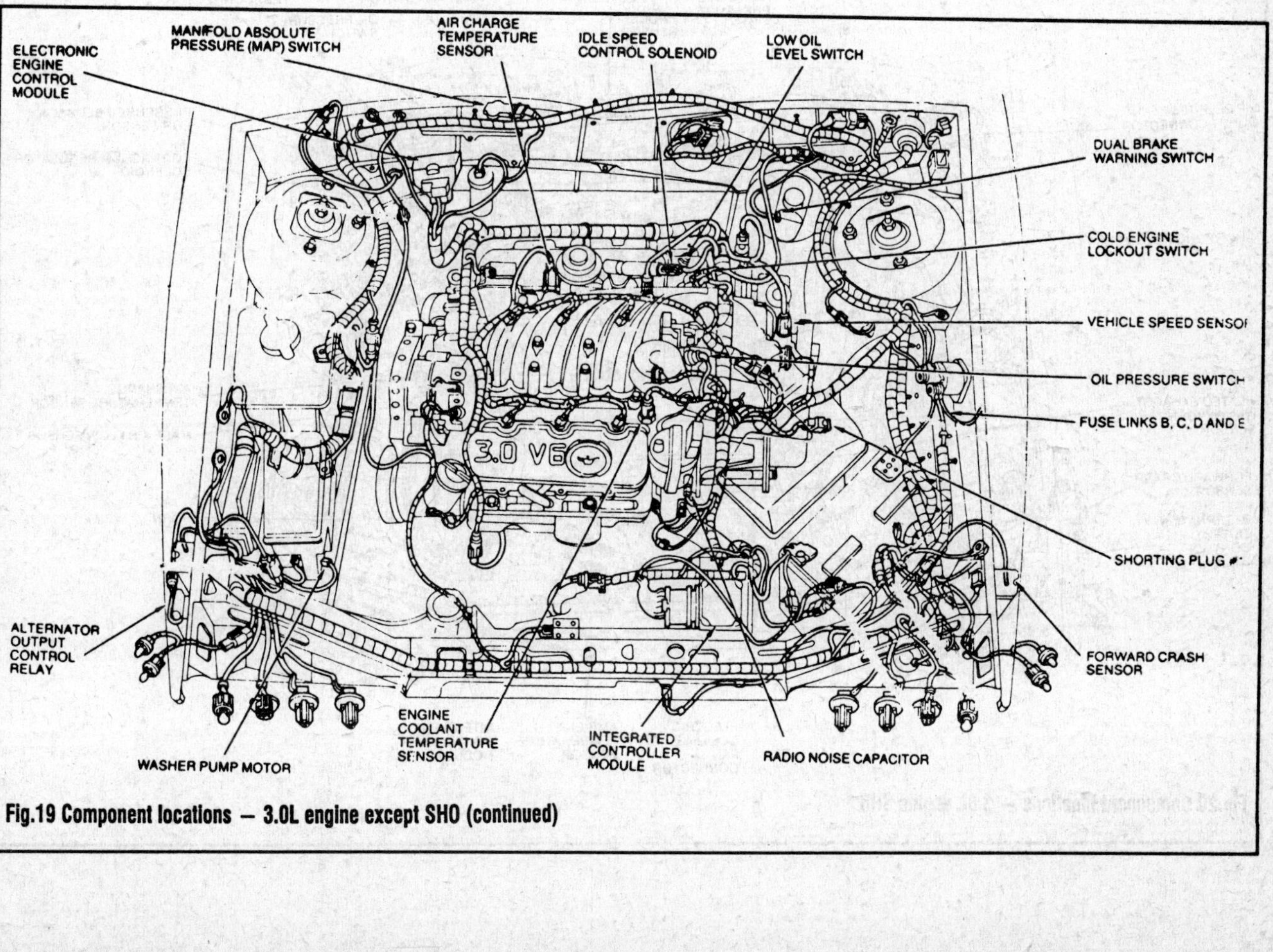

Fig.19 Component locations — 3.0L engine except SHO (continued)

• **Center Line Forward Crash Sensor** — is at the top center of radiator support.

• **Clutch Interrupt Switch** — is on clutch pedal support, behind left instrument panel.

• **Cold Engine Lockout Switch** — is at the top left rear of engine.

• **Cracked Windshield Sense Resistor** — is on the right front of engine compartment, at alternator output control relay.

• **Crank Position Sensor** — is at the lower right rear of engine.

• **Daytime Running Lamps (DRL) Module (Canadian vehicles)** — is at the lower left front of engine compartment.

• **Diagnostic Warning Module** — is behind right instrument panel, above glove box.

• **Distributorless Ignition System (DIS) Module** — is on the right side of engine.

• **Door Ajar Switches** — is at door handle assembly within respective doors.

• **Driver's Seat Belt Switch** — is within left front seat belt assembly.

• **Dual Brake Warning Switch** — is at the left rear of engine compartment, within brake master cylinder.

• **EGR Vacuum Regulator Solenoid (2.5L and 3.0L engine)** — is at the right side of engine compartment at shock tower.

• **EGR Vacuum Regulator Solenoid (2.5L and 3.0L engine)** — is at the right side of engine compartment at shock tower.

• **EGR Vacuum Regulator Solenoid (SHO engine)** — is at the left rear of engine compartment.

• **Electronic Automatic Temperature Control (EATC) Module** — is behind center of instrument panel.

• **Electronic Engine Control (EEC) Module** — is in the engine compartment, right side of firewall.

• **Engine Coolant Temperature Sensor (2.5L engine)** — is at the left rear of engine, below manifolds.

• **Engine Coolant Temperature Sensor (3.0L, 3.8L and SHO engine)** — is at the top left side of engine.

• **Fan Dropping Resistor (2.5L and 3.0L engine)** — is at the left front of engine.

• **Fan Dropping Resistor (SHO engine)** — is at the center of firewall.

• **Fog Light Relay** — is behind center of instrument panel, mounted on brace. Fog Light Fuse — is behind left side of instrument panel, near fuse panel.

• **Forward Crash Sensors** — is inside lower front of each front fender.

• **Fuel Pump** — is inside fuel tank.

• **Fuel Sender** — is inside fuel tank.

• **Fuse Panel** — is behind left lower instrument panel

Heated Exhaust Gas Oxygen (HEGO) Sensor #1 (2.5L engine) — is at the center rear of engine in exhaust manifold.

• **Heated Exhaust Gas Oxygen (HEGO) Sensor #1 (3.0L engine)** — is at the lower right front of engine in exhaust manifold.

• **Heated Exhaust Gas Oxygen (HEGO) Sensor #1 (3.8L engine)** — is at the center rear of engine in exhaust manifold.

• **Heated Exhaust Gas Oxygen (HEGO) Sensor #1 (SHO engine)** — is at the lower left rear of engine in exhaust manifold.

• **Heated Exhaust Gas Oxygen (HEGO) Sensor #2 (3.8L engine)** — lower right front of engine in exhaust manifold.

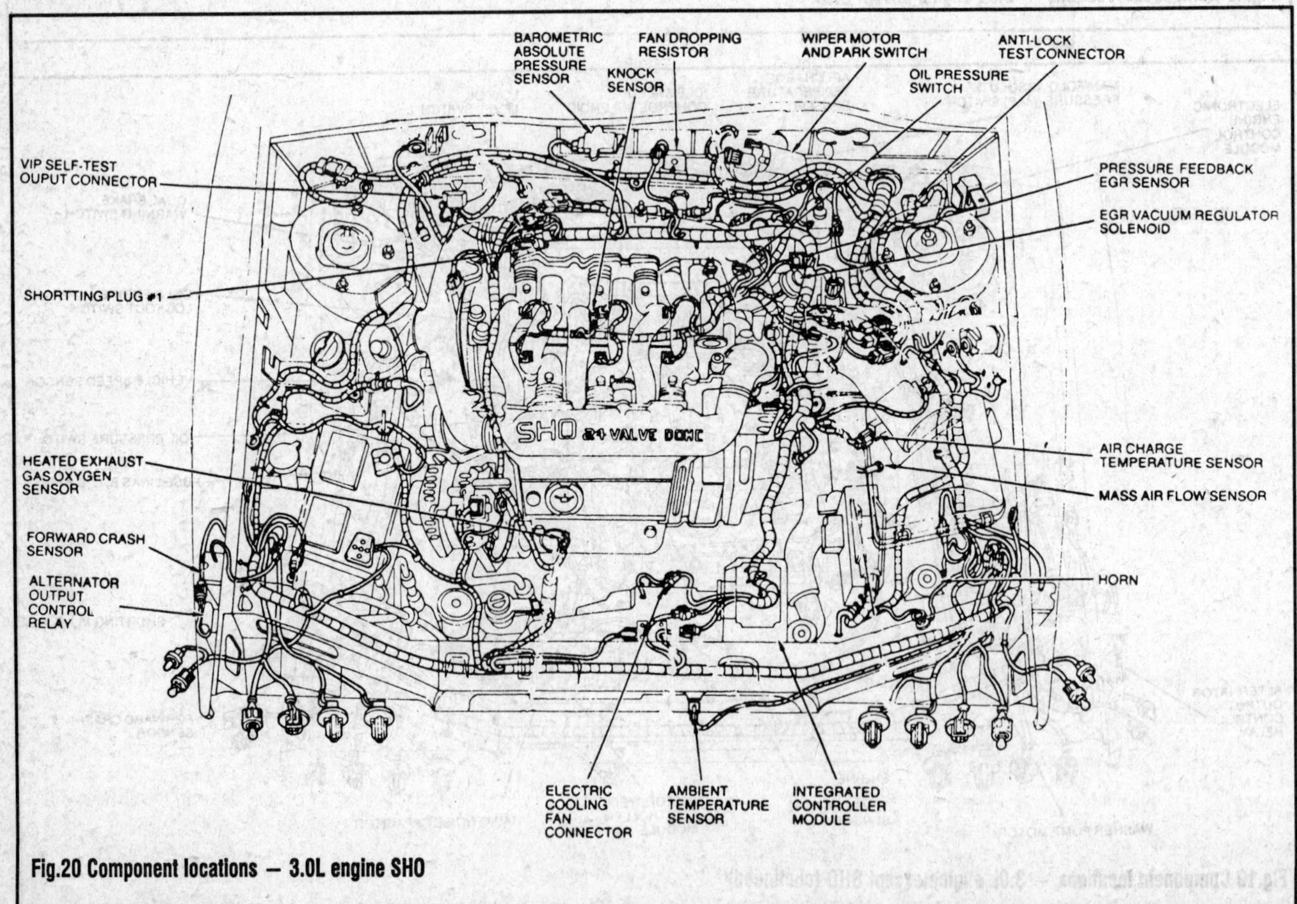

Fig.20 Component locations — 3.0L engine SHO

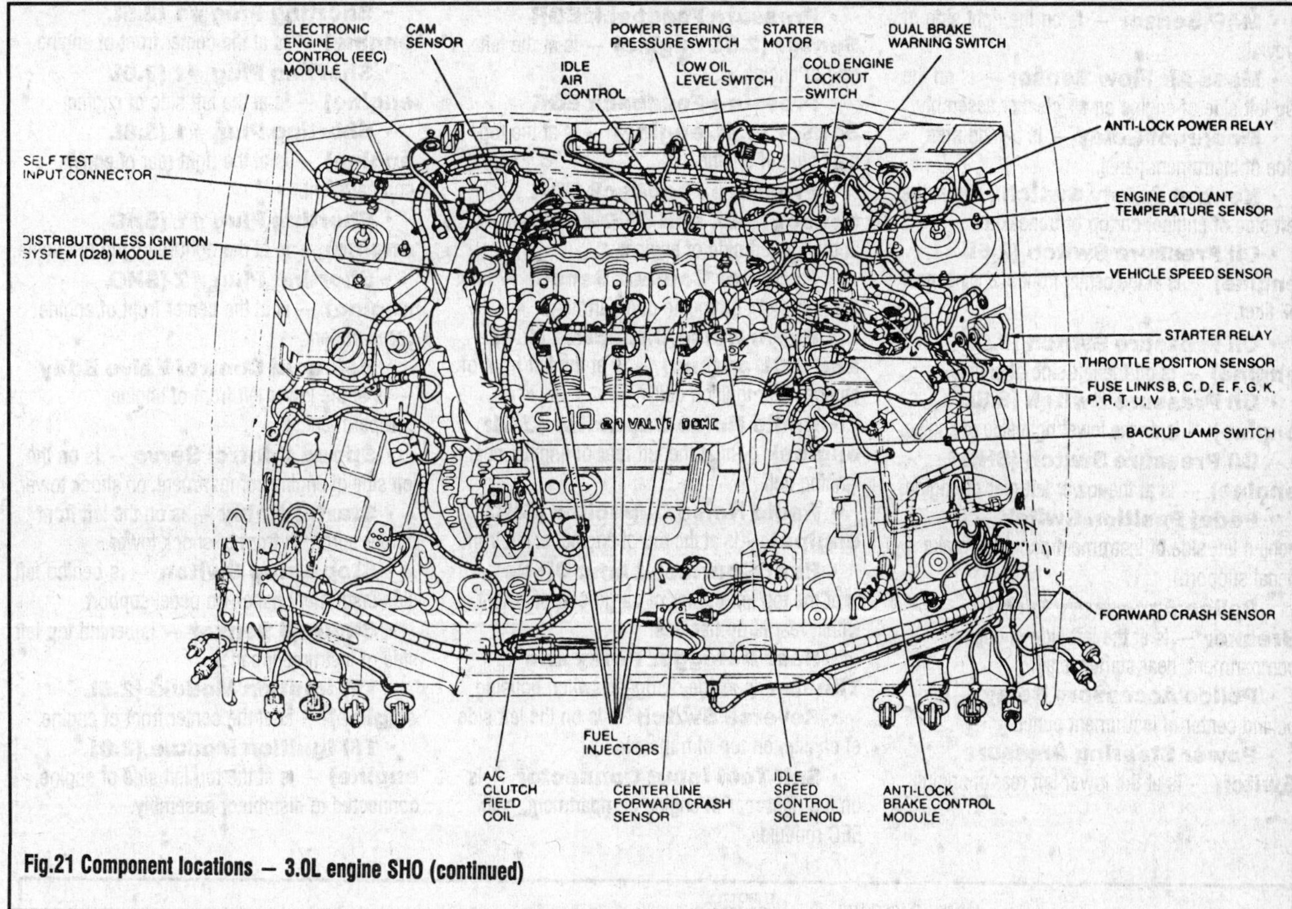

Fig.21 Component locations — 3.0L engine SHO (continued)

• **Heated Exhaust Gas Oxygen (HEGO) Sensor #2 (SHO engine)** — is at the lower right front of engine in exhaust manifold.

• **Heated Windshield Control Module** — is at the right side of steering column, behind instrument panel.

• **Heated Windshield Control Module** — is at the right side of steering column, behind instrument panel

Heated Windshield Test Connector — is at the left rear of engine compartment.

• **Horn Relay** — is behind center of instrument panel, mounted on brace.

• **Idle Air Control** — is at the top rear of engine.

• **Idle Speed Control (2.5L engine)** — is at the top rear of engine.

• **Ignition Suppressor Resistor (2.5L engine)** — is on the left front of engine, near ignition coil.

• **Ignition Suppressor Resistor (3.0L and 3.8L engine)** — is on the left side of engine, near ignition coil.

• **Illuminated Entry Module (Sedan)** — is behind rear seat, under left side of package tray.

• **Illuminated Entry Module (Wagon)** — is inside center of left rear quarter panel.

• **In Car Temperature Sensor** — is behind top right side of instrument panel.

• **Inertia Switch (Sedan)** — is inside front of left rear quarter panel.

• **Inertia Switch (Wagon)** — is inside center of rear quarter panel.

• **Integrated Control Module** — is at the front of engine compartment, on radiator support.

• **Interval Wiper/Washer Module** — is behind center of instrument panel, mounted on brace.

• **Key Warning Switch** — is contained within ignition switch.

• **Keyless Entry Module (Sedan)** — is behind rear seat, under left side of package tray.

• **Keyless Entry Module (Wagon)** — is inside center of left rear quarter panel.

• **Knock Sensor (except SHO engine)** — is at the center rear of engine.

• **Knock Sensor (SHO engine)** — is at the lower left front of engine on air cleaner assembly.

• **LCD Dimming Relay** — is behind center of instrument panel, mounted on brace.

• **Liftgate Ajar Switch** — is at the lower center of liftgate, part of latch assembly.

• **Liftgate Mercury Switch** — is inside top of liftgate.

• **Liftgate Release Relay** — is at the right rear corner of cargo area.

• **Liftgate Release Solenoid** — is in the bottom of liftgate.

• **Light Sensor/Amplifier** — is attached to underside of right side instrument panel.

• **Low Oil Level Relay** — is behind center of instrument panel, mounted on brace.

• **Low Oil Level Relay** — is behind center of instrument panel, mounted on brace.

• **Low Oil Level Switch (2.5L engine)** — is at the lower right rear of engine.

• **Low Oil Level Switch (3.0L, 3.8L and SHO engine)** — is at the lower center rear of engine.

• **Low Washer Fluid Level Switch** — is at the right front of engine compartment, within washer fluid reservoir.

• **Luggage Compartment Mercury Switch** — is at the left front corner of trunk lid, near hinge.

• **Manifold Absolute Pressure (MAP) Sensor** — is at the right side of firewall.

• **MAP Sensor** — is on the right side of firewall.

• **Mass Air Flow Sensor** — is on the top left side of engine on air cleaner assembly.

• **Moonroof Relay** — is behind right side of instrument panel.

• **Neutral Safety Switch** — is at the left side of engine, on top of transaxle.

• **Oil Pressure Switch (2.5L engine)** — is at the center front of engine, near oil filter.

• **Oil Pressure Switch (3.0L engine)** — is on the left side of engine.

• **Oil Pressure Switch (3.8L engine)** — is on the lower right side of engine.

• **Oil Pressure Switch (SHO engine)** — is at the lower left rear of engine.

• **Pedal Position Switch** — is behind left side of instrument panel, on brake pedal support.

• **Police Accessory Circuit Breaker** — is at the left side of engine compartment, near starter relay.

• **Police Accessory Relay** — is behind center of instrument panel.

• **Power Steering Pressure Switch** — is at the lower left rear of engine.

• **Pressure Feedback EGR Sensor (2.5L engine)** — is at the left rear of engine.

• **Pressure Feedback EGR Sensor (3.0L engine)** — is at the top right side of engine.

• **Pressure Feedback EGR Sensor (3.8L and SHO engine)** — is at the top left side of engine.

• **Radiator Coolant Sensor** — is at the right front of engine compartment.

• **Radio Noise Capacitor (2.5L and 3.0L engine)** — is at the left front of engine, near ignition coil.

• **Radio Noise Capacitor (3.8L engine)** — is at the left rear of engine, near ignition coil.

• **Radio Noise Capacitor (SHO engine)** — is at the top of engine, at left front.

• **Rear Courtesy Lamp Diode** — is at the top left corner of cargo compartment within rear lamp harness.

• **Rear Defogger Relay and Timer** — is inside defogger switch housing.

• **Reverse Switch** — is on the left side of engine, on top of transaxle.

• **Self Test Input Connector** — is on the right rear of engine compartment, near EEC module.

• **Shorting Plug #1 (2.5L engine)** — is at the center front of engine.

• **Shorting Plug #1 (3.0L engine)** — is at the left side of engine.

• **Shorting Plug #1 (3.8L engine)** — is at the right rear of engine compartment.

• **Shorting Plug #1 (SHO engine)** — is at the right rear side of engine.

• **Shorting Plug #2 (SHO engine)** — is at the center front of engine compartment.

• **Solenoid Control Valve Body** — is at the lower left front of engine compartment.

• **Speed Control Servo** — is on the left side of engine compartment, on shock tower.

• **Starter Relay** — is on the left front fender apron, in front of shock tower.

• **Stop Lamp Switch** — is behind left side instrument panel, on pedal support.

• **Sunload Sensor** — is behind top left side of instrument panel.

• **TFI Ignition Module (2.5L engine)** — is at the center front of engine.

• **TFI Ignition Module (3.0L engine)** — is at the top left side of engine, connected to distributor assembly.

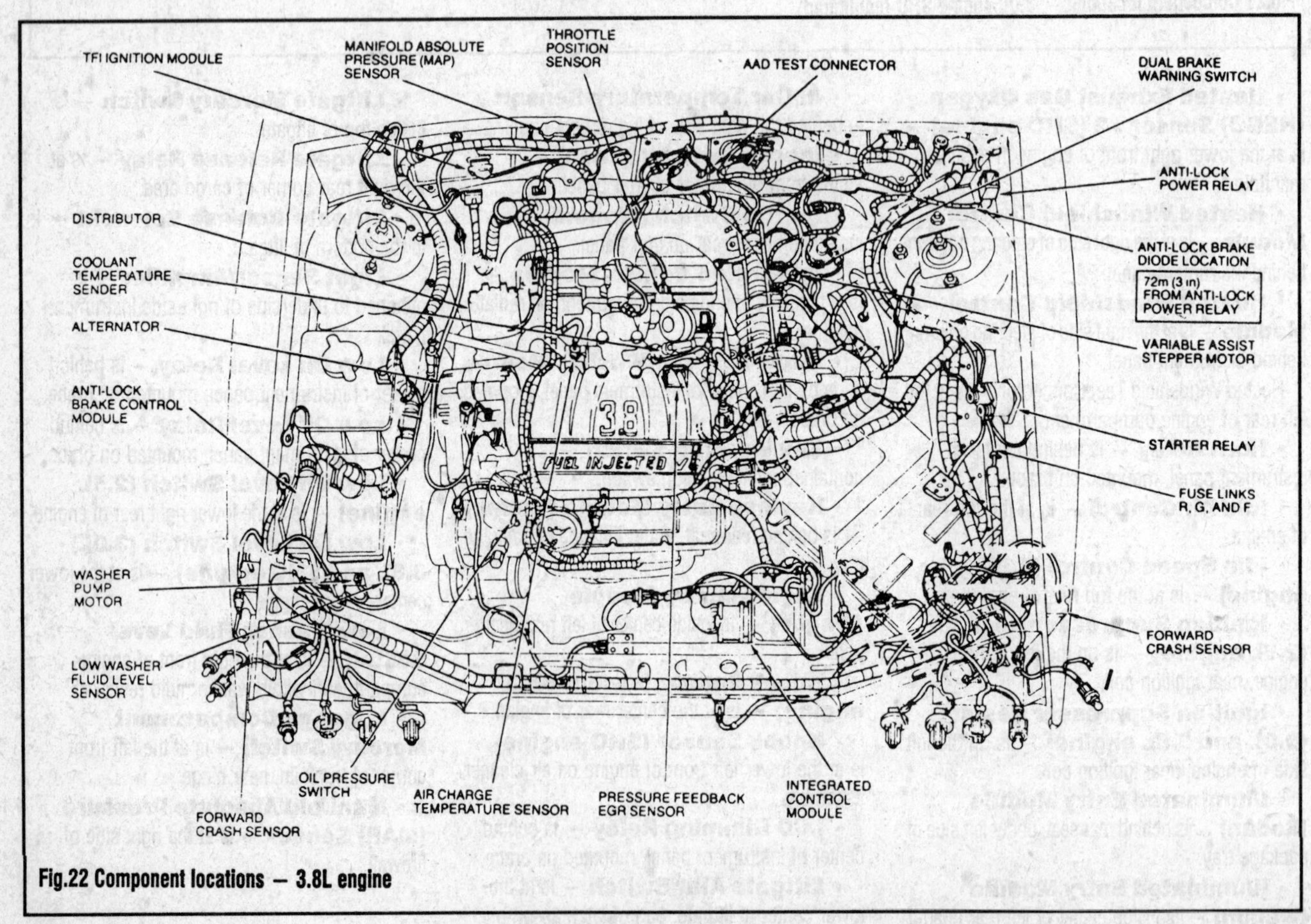

Fig.22 Component locations — 3.8L engine

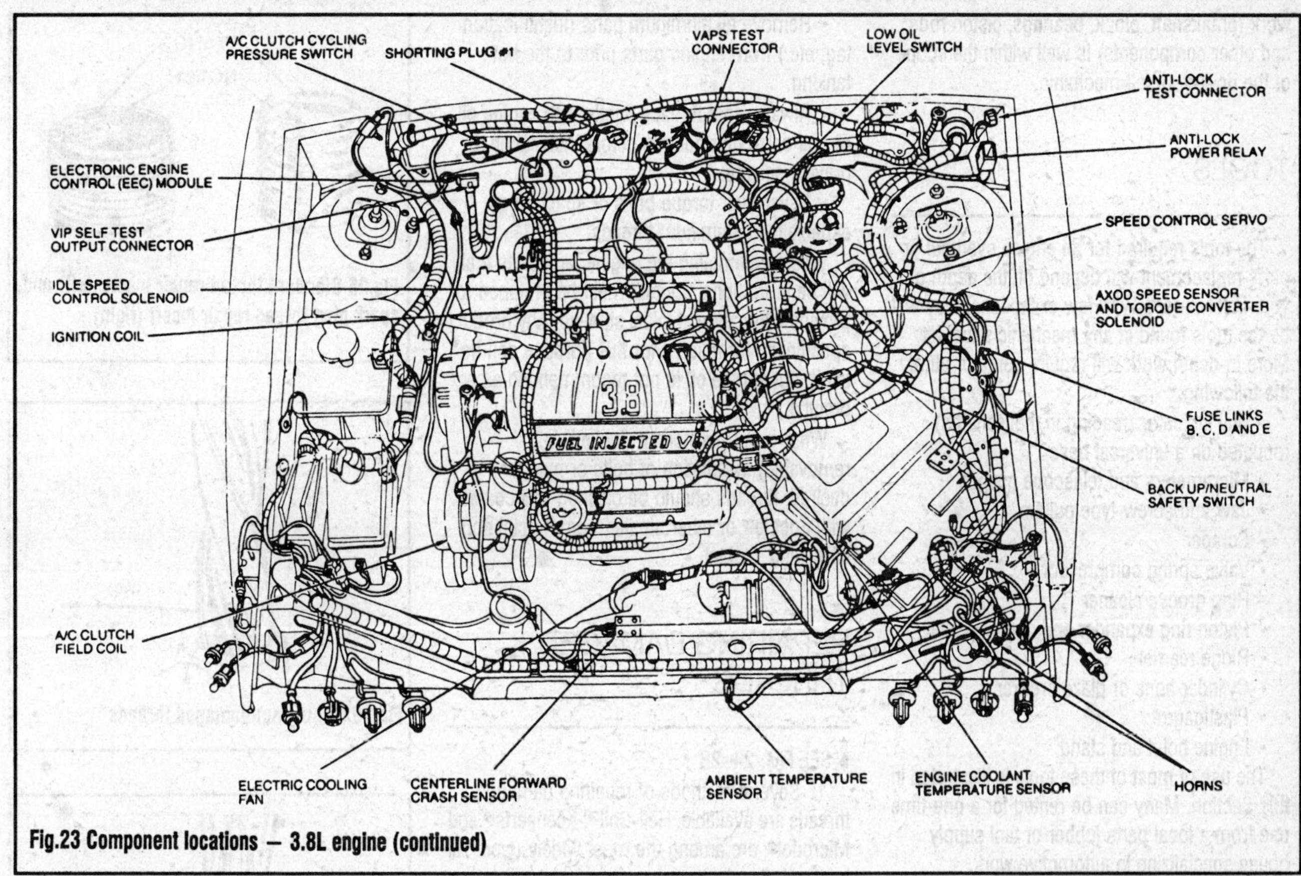

Fig.23 Component locations — 3.8L engine (continued)

- **TFI Ignition Module (3.8L engine)** — is on the right side of firewall.
- **Throttle Position Sensor (2.5L engine)** — is at the rear center of engine, on right side of injection assembly.
- **Throttle Position Sensor (3.0L engine)** — is on the top left side of engine.
- **Throttle Position Sensor (3.8L engine)** — is on the top center of engine.
- **Throttle Position Sensor (SHO engine)** — is on the top left side of engine compartment.
- **Trunk Release Solenoid** — is at the right rear of trunk lid, part of trunk latch assembly.
- **Variable Assist Power Steering (VAPS) Module** — is at the right side of steering column, behind instrument panel.
- **Variable Assist Power Steering (VAPS) Test Connector** — is at the left rear of engine compartment.
- **Variable Assist Stepper Motor** — is at the lower left rear of engine.
- **Vehicle Speed Sensor (2.5L engine)** — is on the left rear of transaxle.
- **Vehicle Speed Sensor (3.0L, 3.8L engine)** — is at the center rear of engine.
- **Vehicle Speed Sensor (SHO engine)** — is at the lower left rear of engine or mounted on transaxle.
- **VIP Self Test Output Connector** — is at the right rear of engine compartment, near EEC module.
- **Voltage Regulator** — is on the left front fender apron.
- **Warning Chime Module** — is behind lower left instrument panel.
- **Window Safety Relay** — is behind right kick panel.

ENGINE MECHANICAL

Engine Overhaul Tips

Most engine overhaul procedures are fairly standard. In addition to specific parts replacement procedures and complete specifications for each individual engine. This Section is also a guide to acceptable rebuilding procedures. Examples of standard rebuilding practice are shown and should be used along with specific details concerning your particular engine.

Competent and accurate machine shop services will insure maximum performance, reliability and engine life. In most instances, it is more profitable for the do-it-yourself mechanic to remove, clean and inspect the component, buy the necessary parts and deliver these to a shop for actual machine work.

On the other hand, much of the rebuilding

work (crankshaft, block, bearings, piston rods, and other components) is well within the scope of the do-it-yourself mechanic.

TOOLS

The tools required for an engine overhaul or parts replacement will depend on the depth of your involvement. With few exceptions, they will be the tools found in any mechanic's tool kit. More in-depth work will require some or all of the following:

- Dial indicator (reading in thousandths) mounted on a universal base
- Micrometers and telescope gauges
- Jaw and screw-type pullers
- Scraper
- Valve spring compressor
- Ring groove cleaner
- Piston ring expander and compressor
- Ridge reamer
- Cylinder hone or glaze breaker
- Plastigage®
- Engine hoist and stand

The use of most of these tools is illustrated in this Section. Many can be rented for a one-time use from a local parts jobber or tool supply house specializing in automotive work. Occasionally, the use of special tools is called for.

INSPECTION TECHNIQUES

Procedures and specifications are given in this Section for inspecting, cleaning and assessing the wear limits of most major components. Other procedures such as Magnaflux® and Zyglo® can be used to locate material flaws and stress cracks. Magnaflux® is a magnetic process applicable only to ferrous materials. The Zyglo® process coats the material with a fluorescent dye penetrant and can be used on any material. Checking for suspected surface cracks can be more readily made using spot check dye. The dye is sprayed onto the suspected area, wiped off and the area sprayed with a developer. Cracks will show up brightly.

OVERHAUL NOTES

Aluminum has become extremely popular for use in engines, due to its low weight. Observe the following precautions when handling aluminum parts:

- Never hot tank aluminum parts; the caustic hot-tank solution will dissolve the aluminum.
- Remove all aluminum parts (identification tag, etc.) from engine parts prior to the hot tanking.
- Always coat threads lightly with engine oil or anti-seize compounds before installation, to prevent seizure.
- Never over torque bolts or spark plugs, especially in aluminum threads.

When assembling the engine, any parts that will be in frictional contact must be prelubed to provide lubrication at initial start-up. Any product specifically formulated for this purpose can be used, but engine oil is not recommended as a prelube.

When semi-permanent (locked, but removable) installation of bolts or nuts is desired, threads should be cleaned and coated with Loctite® or other similar, commercial non-hardening sealant.

REPAIRING DAMAGED THREADS

➧ SEE FIG. 24–28

1. Several methods of repairing damaged threads are available. Heli-Coil®, Keenserts® and Microdot® are among the most widely used. All involve basically the same principle (drilling out stripped threads, tapping the hole and installing a prewound insert), making welding, plugging and oversize fasteners unnecessary.
2. Two types of thread repair inserts are usually supplied: a standard type for most Inch Coarse, Inch Fine, Metric Course and Metric Fine thread sizes and a spark lug type to fit most spark plug port sizes. Consult the individual manufacturer's catalog to determine exact applications.
3. Typical thread repair kits will contain a selection of prewound threaded inserts, a tap (corresponding to the outside diameter threads

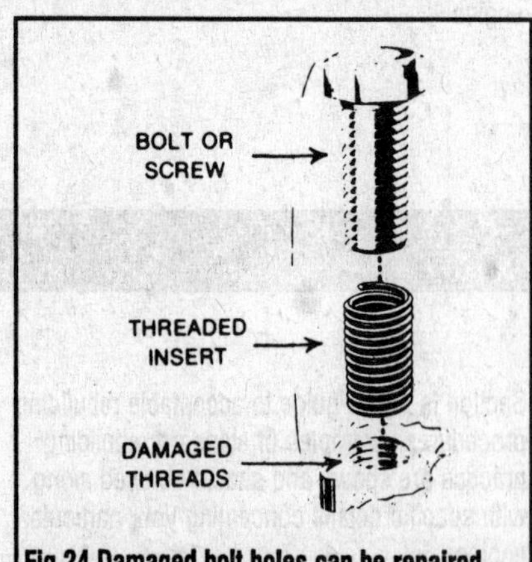

Fig.24 Damaged bolt holes can be repaired with thread repair inserts

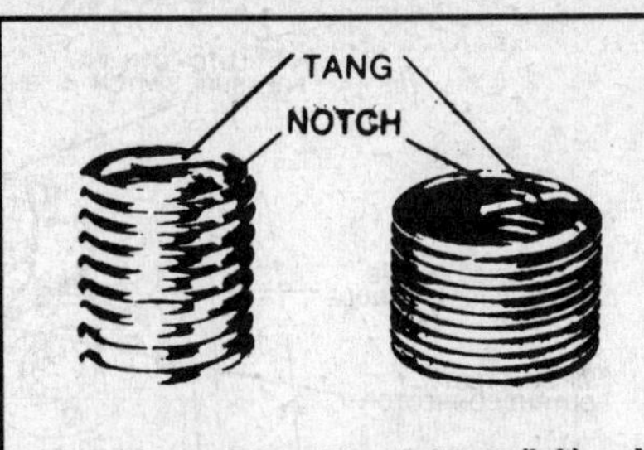

Fig.25 Standard thread repair insert (left) and spark plug thread repair insert (right)

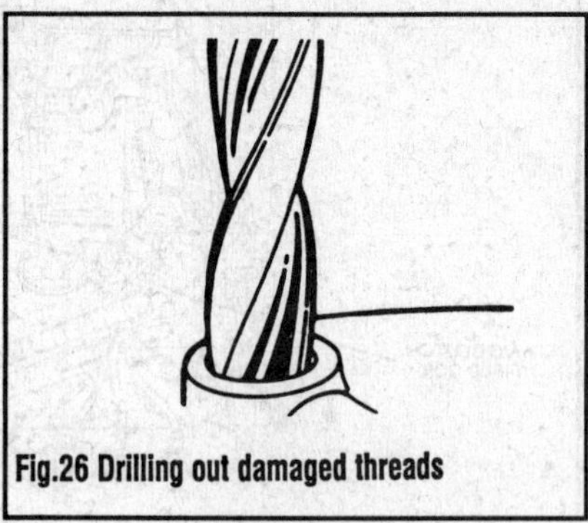

Fig.26 Drilling out damaged threads

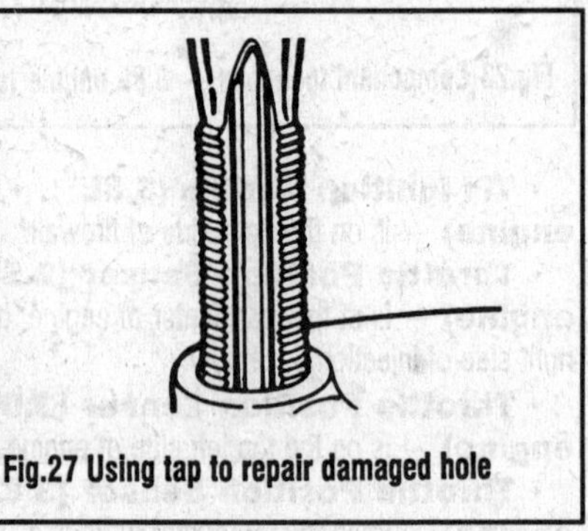

Fig.27 Using tap to repair damaged hole

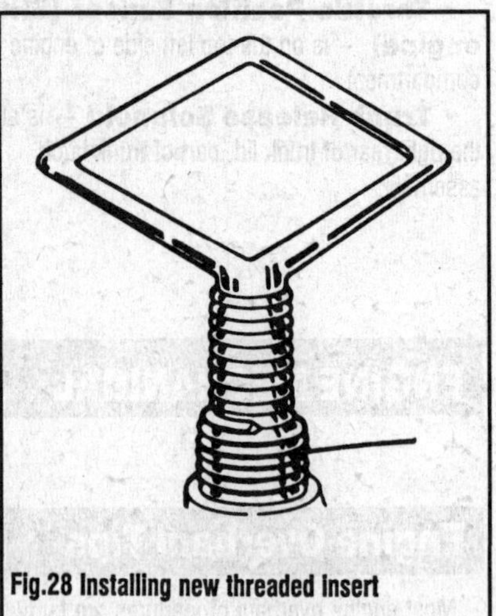

Fig.28 Installing new threaded insert

of the insert) and an installation tool. Spark plug inserts usually differ because they require a tap equipped with pilot threads and a combined reamer/tap section.

4. Most manufacturers also supply blister packed thread repair inserts separately in addition to a master kit containing a variety of taps and inserts plus installation tools.

5. Before attempting a repair to a threaded hole, remove any snapped, broken or damaged bolts or studs. Penetrating oil can be used to free frozen threads. The offending item can be removed with locking pliers or with a screw or stud extractor. After the hole is clear, the thread can be repaired.

GENERAL ENGINE SPECIFICATIONS

Year	Engine VIN	Engine Displacement liter (cc)	Fuel System Type	Net Horsepower @ rpm	Net Torque @ rpm (ft. lbs.)	Bore × Stroke (in.)	Com-pression Ratio	Oil Pressure @ rpm
1986	D	2.5 (2500)	CFI	80 @ 4600	130 @ 2800	3.70 × 3.60	9.7:1	55–70 @ 2000
	U	3.0 (3000)	EFI	140 @ 4800	160 @ 3000	3.50 × 3.10	9.3:1	55–70 @ 2000
1987	D	2.5 (2500)	CFI	80 @ 4600	130 @ 2800	3.70 × 3.60	9.7:1	55–70 @ 2000
	U	3.0 (3000)	EFI	140 @ 4800	160 @ 3000	3.50 × 3.10	9.3:1	55–70 @ 2000
1988	D	2.5 (2500)	CFI	88 @ 4600	130 @ 2800	3.70 × 3.60	9.7:1	55–70 @ 2000
	U	3.0 (3000)	EFI	140 @ 4800	160 @ 3000	3.50 × 3.10	9.3:1	55–70 @ 2000
	4	3.8 (3800)	EFI	140 @ 3800	215 @ 2200	3.81 × 3.39	9.0:1	40–60 @ 2000
1989	D	2.5 (2500)	CFI	88 @ 4600	130 @ 2800	3.70 × 3.60	9.7:1	55–70 @ 2000
	U	3.0 (3000)	EFI	140 @ 4800	160 @ 3000	3.50 × 3.10	9.3:1	55–70 @ 2000
	Y	3.0 (3000)	SEFI	220 @ 6200	200 @ 4800	3.50 × 3.15	9.8:1	13 @ 800
	4	3.8 (3800)	SEFI	140 @ 3800	215 @ 2200	3.81 × 3.39	9.0:1	40–60 @ 2000
1990	D	2.5 (2500)	CFI	90 @ 4400	130 @ 2800	3.70 × 3.60	9.7:1	55–70 @ 2000
	U	3.0 (3000)	EFI	140 @ 4800	160 @ 3000	3.50 × 3.10	9.3:1	40–60 @ 2500
	Y	3.0 (3000)	SEFI	220 @ 6200	200 @ 4800	3.50 × 3.15	9.8:1	13 @ 800
	4	3.8 (3800)	SEFI	140 @ 3800	215 @ 2200	3.81 × 3.39	9.0:1	40–60 @ 2500
1991	D	2.5 (2500)	SEFI	105 @ 4400	140 @ 2400	3.70 × 3.60	9.0:1	55–70 @ 2000
	U	3.0 (3000)	SEFI	140 @ 4800	160 @ 3000	3.50 × 3.10	9.3:1	40–60 @ 2500
	Y	3.0 (3000)	SEFI	220 @ 6200	200 @ 4800	3.50 × 3.15	9.8:1	13 @ 800
	4	3.8 (3800)	SEFI	140 @ 3800	215 @ 2200	3.81 × 3.39	9.0:1	40–60 @ 2500
1992	U	3.0 (3000)	SEFI	140 @ 4800	160 @ 3000	3.50 × 3.10	9.3:1	40–60 @ 2500
	Y	3.0 (3000)	SEFI	220 @ 6200	200 @ 4800	3.50 × 3.15	9.8:1	13 @ 800
	4	3.8 (3800)	SEFI	140 @ 3800	215 @ 2200	3.81 × 3.39	9.0:1	40–60 @ 2500

NOTE: Horsepower and torque are SAE net figures. They are measured at the rear of the transmission with all accessories installed and operating. Since the figures vary when a given engine is installed in different models, some are representative rather than exact.

CFI—Central fuel injection

EFI—Electronic fuel injection

SEFI—Sequential electronic fuel injection

VALVE SPECIFICATIONS

Year	Engine VIN	Engine Displacement liter (cc)	Seat Angle (deg.)	Face Angle (deg.)	Spring Test Pressure (lbs. @ in.)	Spring Installed Height (in.)	Stem-to-Guide Clearance (in.)		Stem Diameter (in.)	
							Intake	Exhaust	Intake	Exhaust
1986	D	2.5 (2500)	45	44	182 @ 1.13	1.49	0.0018	0.0023	0.3422	0.3418
	U	3.0 (3000)	45	44	185 @ 1.11	1.58	0.0010–0.0028	0.0015–0.0032	0.3126	0.3121
1987	D	2.5 (2500)	45	44	182 @ 1.13	1.49	0.0018	0.0023	0.3422	0.3418
	U	3.0 (3000)	45	44	185 @ 1.11	1.58	0.0010–0.0028	0.0015–0.0032	0.3126	0.3121
1988	D	2.5 (2500)	45	44	182 @ 1.13	1.49	0.0018	0.0023	0.3422	0.3418
	U	3.0 (3000)	45	44	185 @ 1.11	1.58	0.0010–0.0028	0.0015–0.0032	0.3126	0.3121
	4	3.8 (3800)	46	46	190 @ 1.28	1.70	0.0010–0.0028	0.0015–0.0033	0.3423–0.0033	0.3418–0.3410
1989	D	2.5 (2500)	45	44	182 @ 1.13	1.49	0.0018	0.0023	0.3422	0.3418
	U	3.0 (3000)	45	44	185 @ 1.11	1.58	0.0010–0.0028	0.0015–0.0032	0.3126	0.3121
	Y	3.0 (3000)	45	45.5	120.8 @ 1.19	1.52	0.0010–0.0023	0.0012–0.0025	0.2346–0.2352	0.2344–0.2350
	4	3.8 (3800)	46	46	220 @ 1.28	1.65	0.0010–0.0028	0.0015–0.0033	0.3423–0.3415	0.3418–0.3410
1990	D	2.5 (2500)	45	44	182 @ 1.13	1.49	0.0018	0.0023	0.3415–0.3422	0.3411–0.3418
	U	3.0 (3000)	45	44	180 @ 1.16	1.58	0.0010–0.0028	0.0015–0.0033	0.3134–0.3126	0.3129–0.3121
	Y	3.0 (3000)	45	45.5	120.8 @ 1.19	1.52	0.0010–0.0023	0.0012–0.0025	0.2346–0.2352	0.2344–0.2350
	4	3.8 (3800)	44.5	45.8	220 @ 1.18	1.65	0.0010–0.0028	0.0015–0.0033	0.3423–0.3415	0.3418–0.3410
1991	D	2.5 (2500)	45	44	182 @ 1.13	1.49	0.0018	0.0023	0.3415–0.3422	0.3411–0.3418
	U	3.0 (3000)	45	44	180 @ 1.16	1.58	0.0010–0.0028	0.0015–0.0033	0.3134–0.3126	0.3129–0.3121
	Y	3.0 (3000)	45	45.5	120.8 @ 1.19	1.52	0.0010–0.0023	0.0012–0.0025	0.2346–0.2352	0.2344–0.2350
	4	3.8 (3800)	44.5	45.8	220 @ 1.18	1.65	0.0010–0.0028	0.0015–0.0033	0.3423–0.3415	0.3418–0.3410
1992	U	3.0 (3000)	45	44	180 @ 1.16	1.58	0.0010–0.0028	0.0015–0.0033	0.3134–0.3126	0.3129–0.3121
	Y	3.0 (3000)	45	45.5	121 @ 1.19	1.52	0.0010–0.0023	0.0012–0.0025	0.2346–0.2352	0.2344–0.2350
	4	3.8 (3800)	44.5	45.8	220 @ 1.18	1.65	0.0010–0.0028	0.0015–0.0033	0.3423–0.3415	0.3418–0.3410

CAMSHAFT SPECIFICATIONS

All measurements given in inches.

Year	Engine VIN	Engine Displacement liter (cc)	Journal Diameter 1	2	3	4	5	Elevation In.	Ex.	Bearing Clearance	Camshaft End Play
1986	D	2.5 (2500)	2.006–2.008	2.006–2.008	2.006–2.008	2.006–2.008	2.006–2.008	0.249	0.239	0.001–0.003	0.009
	U	3.0 (3000)	2.007–2.008	2.007–2.008	2.007–2.008	2.007–2.008	2.007–2.008	0.260	0.260	0.001–0.003	0.005
1987	D	2.5 (2500)	2.006–2.008	2.006–2.008	2.006–2.008	2.006–2.008	2.006–2.008	0.249	0.239	0.001–0.003	0.009
	U	3.0 (3000)	2.007–2.008	2.007–2.008	2.007–2.008	2.007–2.008	2.007–2.008	0.260	0.260	0.001–0.003	0.005
1988	D	2.5 (2500)	2.006–2.008	2.006–2.008	2.006–2.008	2.006–2.008	2.006–2.008	0.249	0.239	0.001–0.003	0.009
	U	3.0 (3000)	2.007–2.008	2.007–2.008	2.007–2.008	2.007–2.008	2.007–2.008	0.260	0.260	0.001–0.003	0.005
	4	3.8 (3800)	2.050–2.052	2.050–2.052	2.050–2.052	2.050–2.052	2.050–2.052	0.240	0.241	0.001–0.003	①
1989	D	2.5 (2500)	2.006–2.008	2.006–2.008	2.006–2.008	2.006–2.008	2.006–2.008	0.249	0.239	0.001–0.003	0.009
	U	3.0 (3000)	2.007–2.008	2.007–2.008	2.007–2.008	2.007–2.008	2.007–2.008	0.260	0.260	0.001–0.003	0.001–0.005
	Y	3.0 (3000)	1.2189–1.2195	1.2189–1.2195	1.2189–1.2195	1.2189–1.2195	1.2189–1.2195	0.335	0.315	0.001–0.003	0.012
	4	3.8 (3800)	2.050–2.052	2.050–2.052	2.050–2.052	2.050–2.052	2.050–2.052	0.240	0.241	0.001–0.003	①
1990	D	2.5 (2500)	2.006–2.008	2.006–2.008	2.006–2.008	2.006–2.008	2.006–2.008	0.249	0.239	0.001–0.003	0.009
	U	3.0 (3000)	2.007–2.008	2.007–2.008	2.007–2.008	2.007–2.008	2.007–2.008	0.260	0.260	0.001–0.003	0.001–0.005
	Y	3.0 (3000)	1.2189–1.2195	1.2189–1.2195	1.2189–1.2195	1.2189–1.2195	1.2189–1.2195	0.335	0.315	0.001–0.003	0.012
	4	3.8 (3800)	2.050–2.052	2.050–2.052	2.050–2.052	2.050–2.052	2.050–2.052	0.245	0.259	0.001–0.003	①
1991	D	2.5 (2500)	2.006–2.008	2.006–2.008	2.006–2.008	2.006–2.008	2.006–2.008	0.249	0.241	0.001–0.003	0.009
	U	3.0 (3000)	2.007–2.008	2.007–2.008	2.007–2.008	2.007–2.008	2.007–2.008	0.260	0.260	0.001–0.003	0.001–0.005
	Y	3.0 (3000)	1.2189–1.2195	1.2189–1.2195	1.2189–1.2195	1.2189–1.2195	1.2189–1.2195	0.335	0.315	0.001–0.003	0.012
	4	3.8 (3800)	2.050–2.052	2.050–2.052	2.050–2.052	2.050–2.052	2.050–2.052	0.245	0.259	0.001–0.003	①
1992	U	3.0 (3000)	2.007–2.008	2.007–2.008	2.007–2.008	2.007–2.008	2.007–2.008	0.260	0.260	0.001–0.003	0.001–0.005
	Y	3.0 (3000)	1.2189–1.2195	1.2189–1.2195	1.2189–1.2195	1.2189–1.2195	1.2189–1.2195	0.335	0.315	0.001–0.003	0.012
	4	3.8 (3800)	2.050–2.052	2.050–2.052	2.050–2.052	2.050–2.052	2.050–2.052	0.245	0.259	0.001–0.003	①

① No endplay—camshaft retained by a spring

CRANKSHAFT AND CONNECTING ROD SPECIFICATIONS

All measurements are given in inches.

Year	Engine VIN	Engine Displacement liter (cc)	Crankshaft Main Brg. Journal Dia.	Crankshaft Main Brg. Oil Clearance	Crankshaft Shaft End-play	Crankshaft Thrust on No.	Connecting Rod Journal Diameter	Connecting Rod Oil Clearance	Connecting Rod Side Clearance
1986	D	2.5 (2500)	2.2489–2.2490	0.0008–0.0015	0.004–0.008	3	2.1232–2.1240	0.0008–0.0014	0.0035–0.0105
	U	3.0 (3000)	2.5190–2.5198	0.0010–0.0014	0.004–0.008	3	2.1253–2.1261	0.0010–0.0014	0.006–0.014
1987	D	2.5 (2500)	2.2489–2.2490	0.0008–0.0015	0.004–0.008	3	2.1232–2.1240	0.0008–0.0014	0.0035–0.0105
	U	3.0 (3000)	2.5190–2.5198	0.0010–0.0014	0.004–0.008	3	2.1253–2.1261	0.0010–0.0014	0.006–0.014
1988	D	2.5 (2500)	2.2489–2.2490	0.0008–0.0015	0.004–0.008	3	2.1232–2.1240	0.0008–0.0014	0.0035–0.0105
	U	3.0 (3000)	2.5190–2.5198	0.0010–0.0014	0.004–0.008	3	2.1253–2.1261	0.0010–0.0014	0.006–0.014
	4	3.8 (3800)	2.5190–2.5198	0.0010–0.0014	0.004–0.008	3	2.3103–2.3111	0.0010–0.0014	0.0047–0.0114
1989	D	2.5 (2500)	2.2489–2.2490	0.0008–0.0015	0.004–0.008	3	2.1232–2.1240	0.0008–0.0014	0.0035–0.0105
	U	3.0 (3000)	2.5190–2.5198	0.0010–0.0014	0.004–0.008	3	2.1253–2.1261	0.0010–0.0014	0.006–0.014
	Y	3.0 (3000)	2.5187–2.5197	0.0011–0.0022	0.0008–0.0087	3	2.0463–2.0472	0.0009–0.0022	0.0063–0.0123
	4	3.8 (3800)	2.5190–2.5198	0.0010–0.0014	0.004–0.008	3	2.3103–2.3111	0.0010–0.0014	0.0047–0.0114
1990	D	2.5 (2500)	2.2489–2.2490	0.0008–0.0015	0.004–0.008	3	2.1232–2.1240	0.0008–0.0014	0.0035–0.0105
	U	3.0 (3000)	2.5190–2.5198	0.0010–0.0014	0.004–0.008	3	2.1253–2.1261	0.0010–0.0014	0.006–0.014
	Y	3.0 (3000)	2.5187–2.5197	0.0011–0.0022	0.0008–0.0087	3	2.0463–2.0472	0.0009–0.0022	0.0063–0.0123
	4	3.8 (3800)	2.5190–2.5198	0.0010–0.0014	0.004–0.008	3	2.3103–2.3111	0.0010–0.0014	0.0047–0.0114
1991	D	2.5 (2500)	2.2489–2.2490	0.0008–0.0015	0.004–0.008	3	2.1232–2.1240	0.0008–0.0014	0.0035–0.0105
	U	3.0 (3000)	2.5190–2.5198	0.0010–0.0014	0.004–0.008	3	2.1253–2.1261	0.0010–0.0014	0.006–0.014
	Y	3.0 (3000)	2.5187–2.5197	0.0011–0.0022	0.0008–0.0087	3	2.0463–2.0472	0.0009–0.0022	0.0063–0.0123
	4	3.8 (3800)	2.5190–2.5198	0.0010–0.0014	0.004–0.008	3	2.3103–2.3111	0.0010–0.0014	0.0047–0.0114
1992	U	3.0 (3000)	2.5190–2.5198	0.0010–0.0014	0.004–0.008	3	2.1253–2.1261	0.0010–0.0014	0.006–0.014
	Y	3.0 (3000)	2.5187–2.5197	0.0011–0.0022	0.0008–0.0087	3	2.0463–2.0472	0.0009–0.0022	0.0063–0.0123
	4	3.8 (3800)	2.5190–2.5198	0.0010–0.0014	0.004–0.008	3	2.3103–2.3111	0.0010–0.0014	0.0047–0.0114

PISTON AND RING SPECIFICATIONS

All measurements are given in inches.

Year	Engine VIN	Engine Displacement liter (cc)	Piston Clearance	Ring Gap Top Compression	Ring Gap Bottom Compression	Ring Gap Oil Control	Ring Side Clearance Top Compression	Ring Side Clearance Bottom Compression	Ring Side Clearance Oil Control
1986	D	2.5 (2500)	0.0012–0.0022	0.0080–0.0160	0.0080–0.0160	0.0150–0.0550	0.0020–0.0040	0.0020–0.0040	Snug
	U	3.0 (3000)	0.0014–0.0022	0.0100–0.0200	0.0100–0.0200	0.0100–0.0490	0.0016–0.0037	0.0016–0.0037	Snug
1987	D	2.5 (2500)	0.0012–0.0022	0.0080–0.0160	0.0080–0.0160	0.0150–0.0550	0.0020–0.0040	0.0020–0.0040	Snug
	U	3.0 (3000)	0.0014–0.0022	0.0100–0.0200	0.0100–0.0200	0.0100–0.0490	0.0016–0.0037	0.0016–0.0037	Snug
1988	D	2.5 (2500)	0.0012–0.0022	0.0080–0.0160	0.0080–0.0160	0.0150–0.0550	0.0020–0.0040	0.0020–0.0040	Snug
	U	3.0 (3000)	0.0014–0.0022	0.0100–0.0200	0.0100–0.0200	0.0100–0.0490	0.0016–0.0037	0.0016–0.0037	Snug
	4	3.8 (3800)	0.0014–0.0032	0.0100–0.0200	0.0100–0.0200	0.0150–0.0583	0.0016–0.0037	0.0016–0.0037	Snug
1989	D	2.5 (2500)	0.0012–0.0022	0.0080–0.0160	0.0080–0.0160	0.0150–0.0550	0.0020–0.0040	0.0020–0.0040	Snug
	U	3.0 (3000)	0.0014–0.0022	0.0100–0.0200	0.0100–0.0200	0.0100–0.0490	0.0016–0.0037	0.0016–0.0037	Snug
	Y	3.0 (3000)	0.0012–0.0020	0.0120–0.0180	0.0120–0.0180	0.0080–0.0200	0.0008–0.0024	0.0006–0.0022	0.0024–0.0050
	4	3.8 (3800)	0.0014–0.0032	0.0110–0.0220	0.0100–0.0200	0.0150–0.0583	0.0016–0.0037	0.0016–0.0037	Snug
1990	D	2.5 (2500)	0.0012–0.0022	0.0080–0.0160	0.0080–0.0160	0.0150–0.0550	0.0020–0.0040	0.0020–0.0040	Snug
	U	3.0 (3000)	0.0014–0.0022	0.0100–0.0200	0.0100–0.0200	0.0100–0.0490	0.0016–0.0037	0.0016–0.0037	Snug
	Y	3.0 (3000)	0.0012–0.0020	0.0120–0.0180	0.0120–0.0180	0.0080–0.0200	0.0008–0.0024	0.0006–0.0022	0.0024–0.0059
	4	3.8 (3800)	0.0014–0.0032	0.0110–0.0220	0.0100–0.0200	0.0150–0.0583	0.0016–0.0034	0.0016–0.0034	Snug
1991	D	2.5 (2500)	0.0012–0.0022	0.0080–0.0160	0.0080–0.0160	0.0150–0.0550	0.0020–0.0040	0.0020–0.0040	Snug
	U	3.0 (3000)	0.0014–0.0022	0.0100–0.0200	0.0100–0.0200	0.0100–0.0490	0.0012–0.0031	0.0012–0.0031	Snug
	Y	3.0 (3000)	0.0012–0.0020	0.0120–0.0180	0.0120–0.0180	0.0080–0.0200	0.0008–0.0024	0.0006–0.0022	0.0024–0.0059
	4	3.8 (3800)	0.0014–0.0032	0.0110–0.0220	0.0100–0.0200	0.0150–0.0583	0.0016–0.0034	0.0016–0.0034	Snug
1992	U	3.0 (3000)	0.0014–0.0022	0.0100–0.0200	0.0100–0.0200	0.0100–0.0490	0.0012–0.0031	0.0012–0.0031	Snug
	Y	3.0 (3000)	0.0012–0.0020	0.0120–0.0180	0.0120–0.0180	0.0080–0.0200	0.0008–0.0024	0.0006–0.0022	0.0024–0.0059
	4	3.8 (3800)	0.0014–0.0032	0.0110–0.0220	0.0100–0.0200	0.0150–0.0583	0.0016–0.0034	0.0016–0.0034	Snug

TORQUE SPECIFICATIONS

All readings in ft. lbs.

Year	Engine VIN	Engine Displacement liter (cc)	Cylinder Head Bolts	Main Bearing Bolts	Rod Bearing Bolts	Crankshaft Damper Bolts	Flywheel Bolts	Manifold		Spark Plugs	Lug Nut
								Intake	Exhaust		
1986	D	2.5 (2500)	①	51–66	21–26	140–170	54–64	15–23	②	5–10	80–105
	U	3.0 (3000)	③	65–81	26	141–169	54–64	④	19	5–10	80–105
1987	D	2.5 (2500)	①	51–66	21–26	140–170	54–64	15–23	②	5–10	80–105
	U	3.0 (3000)	③	65–81	26	141–169	54–64	④	19	5–10	80–105
1988	D	2.5 (2500)	①	51–66	21–26	140–170	54–64	15–23	②	5–10	80–105
	U	3.0 (3000)	③	65–81	26	139–169	54–64	⑨	19	5–10	80–105
	4	3.8 (3800)	⑤	65–81	31–36	93–121	54–64	⑥	16–24	5–10	80–105
1989	D	2.5 (2500)	①	51–66	21–26	140–170	54–64	15–23	②	5–10	80–105
	U	3.0 (3000)	⑦	65–81	26	141–169	54–64	④	19	5–10	80–105
	Y	3.0 (3000)	⑩	⑪	⑫	112–127	⑬	12–17	26–38	16–20	80–105
	4	3.8 (3800)	⑤	65–81	31–36	93–121	54–64	⑥	16–24	5–10	80–105
1990	D	2.5 (2500)	①	51–66	21–26	140–170	54–64	15–23	②	5–10	80–105
	U	3.0 (3000)	⑦	63–69	26	107	54–64	⑨	19	5–10	80–105
	Y	3.0 (3000)	⑩	⑪	⑫	112–127	⑬	12–17	26–38	16–20	80–105
	4	3.8 (3800)	⑤	65–81	31–36	103–132	54–64	⑥	15–22	5–10	80–105
1991	D	2.5 (2500)	①	52–66	21–26	140–170	54–64	⑧	②	5–10	80–105
	U	3.0 (3000)	⑦	55–63	26	107	59	⑨	19	5–10	80–105
	Y	3.0 (3000)	⑩	⑪	⑫	113–126	⑬	11–17	26–38	17–19	80–105
	4	3.8 (3800)	⑭	65–81	31–36	103–132	54–64	⑥	15–22	5–10	80–105
1992	U	3.0 (3000)	⑦	55–63	26	107	59	⑨	19	6–10	80–105
	Y	3.0 (3000)	⑩	⑪	⑫	113–126	⑬	11–17	26–38	12–19	80–105
	4	3.8 (3800)	⑭	65–81	31–36	103–132	54–64	⑥	15–22	5–10	80–105

① Tighten in 2 steps: 52–59 ft. lbs. and then the final torque of 70–76 ft. lbs.

② Tighten in 2 steps:
Step 1: 5–7 ft. lbs.
Step 2: 20–30 ft. lbs.

③ Tighten in 2 steps: 48–54 ft. lbs. and then the final torque of 63–80 ft. lbs.

④ Tighten in 3 steps: 11, 18 and the final torque of 24 ft. lbs.

⑤ Tighten in 4 steps:
Step 1: 37 ft. lbs.
Step 2: 45 ft. lbs.
Step 3: 52 ft. lbs.
Step 4: 59 ft. lbs.
Back off all bolts 2–3 revolutions, then repeat steps 1–4.

⑥ Tighten in 3 steps:
Step 1: 7 ft. lbs.
Step 2: 15 ft. lbs.
Step 3: 24 ft. lbs.

⑦ Tighten in 2 steps:
Step 1: 37 ft. lbs.
Step 2: 68 ft. lbs.

⑧ Tighten in 2 steps:
Step 1: 5–7 ft. lbs.
Step 2: 15–22 ft. lbs.

⑨ Tighten in 2 steps:
Step 1: 11 ft. lbs.
Step 2: 21 ft. lbs.

⑩ Tighten in 2 steps:
Step 1: 37–50 ft. lbs.
Step 2: 62–68 ft. lbs.

⑪ Tighten in 2 steps:
Step 1: 34–50 ft. lbs.
Step 2: 58–65 ft. lbs.

⑫ Tighten in 2 steps:
Step 1: 22–26 ft. lbs.
Step 2: 33–36 ft. lbs.

⑬ Tighten in 2 steps:
Step 1: 29–43 ft. lbs.
Step 2: 51–58 ft. lbs.

⑭ A. Tighten in 4 steps:
Step 1: 37 ft. lbs.
Step 2: 45 ft. lbs.
Step 3: 52 ft. lbs.
Step 4: 59 ft. lbs.
B. In sequence, loosen each bolt 2–3 revolutions
C. Tighten long bolts to 11–18 ft. lbs., then an additional 85–105 degrees. Tighten short bolts to 11–18 ft. lbs., then an additional 65–85 degrees.

Engine

REMOVAL & INSTALLATION

CAUTION

When draining the coolant, keep in mind that cats and dogs are attracted by the ethylene glycol antifreeze, and are quite likely to drink any that is left in an uncovered container or in puddles on the ground. This will prove fatal in sufficient quantity. Always drain the coolant into a sealable container. Coolant should be reused unless it is contaminated or several years old.

The EPA warns that prolonged contact with used engine oil may cause a number of skin disorders, including cancer! You should make every effort to minimize your exposure to used engine oil. Protective gloves should be worn when changing the oil. Wash your hands and any other exposed skin areas as soon as possible after exposure to used engine oil. Soap and water, or waterless hand cleaner should be used.

2.5L Engine

➧ SEE FIG. 29–31

1. Disconnect the negative battery cable and relieve the fuel system pressure.
2. If equipped with automatic transaxle, remove the transaxle timing window cover and rotate the engine until the flywheel timing marker is aligned with the timing pointer.
3. Place a reference mark on the crankshaft pulley at the 12 o'clock position (TDC) then rotate the crankshaft pulley mark to the 6 o'clock postion (BTDC).
4. Mark the position of the hood hinges and remove the hood.
5. Remove the air cleaner assembly and drain the cooling system.
6. Disconnect the upper radiator hose at the engine.
7. Identify, tag and disconnect all electrical wiring and vacuum hoses as required.
8. Disconnect the crankcase ventilation hose at the valve cover and intake manifold.
9. Disconnect the fuel lines and heater hoses.
10. Disconnect the engine ground wire.
11. Disconnect the accelerator and throttle valve control cables at the throttle body.
12. Properly discharge the air conditioning system and remove the suction and discharge lines from the compressor, if equipped.
13. On manual transaxle equipped vehicles, remove the engine damper brace.
14. Remove the driver belt and water pump pulley.
15. Remove the air cleaner-to-canister hose.
16. Raise the vehicle and support safely.
17. Drain the engine oil and remove the oil filter.
18. Disconnect the starter cable and remove the starter motor.
19. On automatic transaxle equipped vehicles, remove the converter nuts and align the previously made reference mark as close to the 6 o'clock (BTDC) position as possible with the converter stud visible.

➡ **The flywheel timing marker must be in the 6 o'clock (BTDC) position for proper engine removal and installation.**

20. Remove the engine insulator nuts.
21. Disconnect the exhaust pipe from the manifold.
22. Disconnect the canister and halfshaft brackets from the engine.
23. Remove the lower engine-to-transaxle retaining bolts.
24. Disconnect the lower radiator hose.
25. Lower the vehicle and position a floor jack under the transaxle.
26. Disconnect the power steering lines from the pump.
27. Install engine lifting eyes tool D81L–

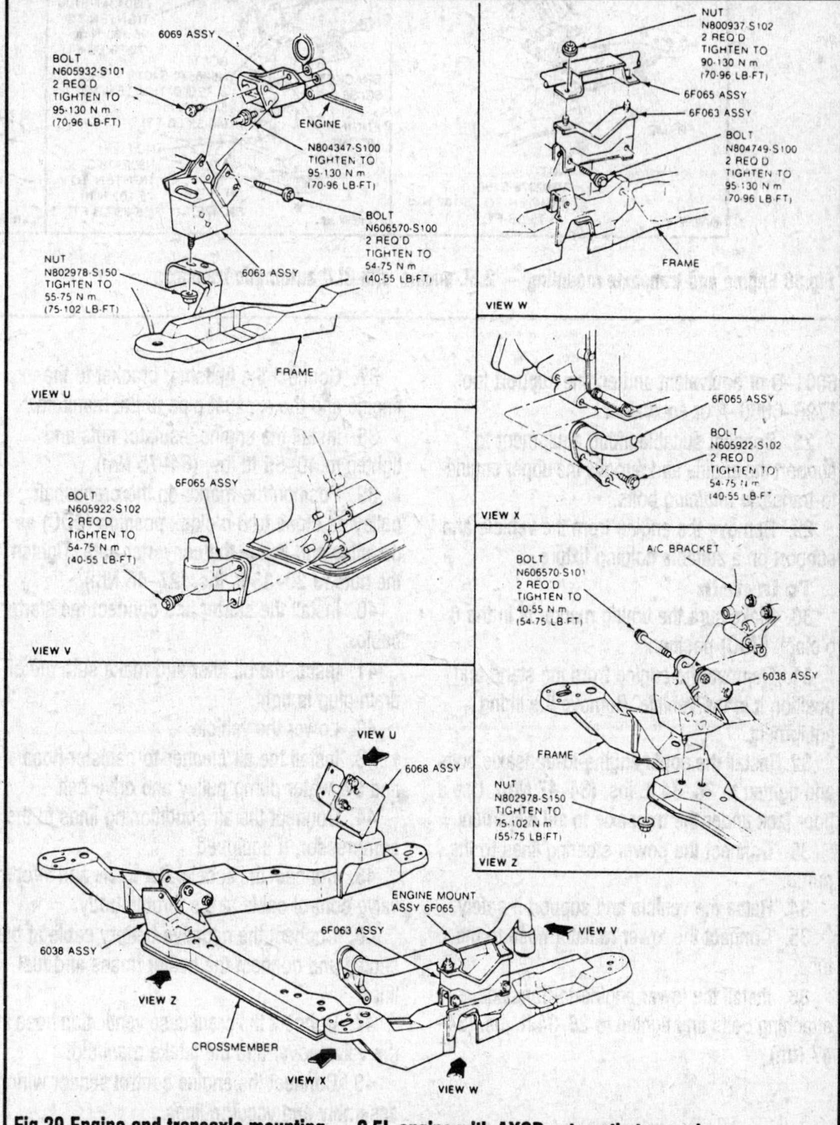

Fig.29 Engine and transaxle mounting – 2.5L engine with AXOD automatic transaxle

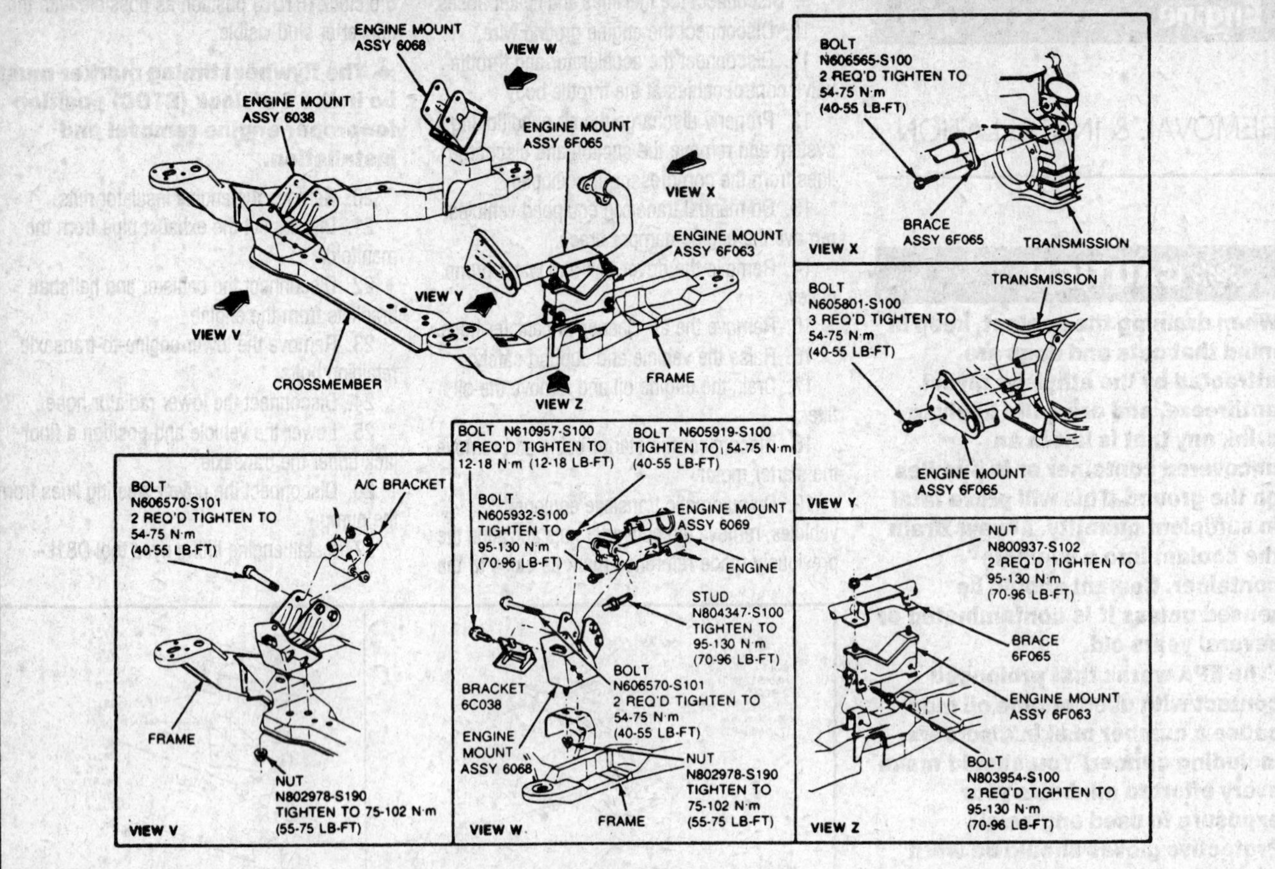

Fig.30 Engine and transaxle mounting — 2.5L engine with CLC automatic transaxle

6001–D or equivalent and engine support tool T79P–6000–A or equivalent.

28. Connect suitable lifting equipment to support the engine and remove the upper engine-to-transaxle retaining bolts.

29. Remove the engine from the vehicle and support on a suitable holding fixture.

To install:

30. Make sure the timing marker is in the 6 o'clock (BDC) position.

31. Remove the engine from the stand and position it in the vehicle. Remove the lifting equipment.

32. Install the upper engine-to-transaxle bolts and tighten to 26–34 ft. lbs. (34–47 Nm). Use a floor jack under the transaxle to aid alignment.

33. Connect the power steering lines to the pump.

34. Raise the vehicle and support it safely.

35. Connect the lower radiator hose to the tube.

36. Install the lower engine-to-transaxle attaching bolts and tighten to 26–34 ft. lbs. (34–47 Nm).

37. Connect the halfshaft bracket to the engine and the exhaust pipe to the manifold.

38. Install the engine insulator nuts and tighten to 40–55 ft. lbs. (54–75 Nm).

39. Position the marks on the crankshaft pulley as close to 6 o'clock position (BDC) as possible and install the converter nuts. Tighten the nuts to 20–33 ft. lbs. (27–46 Nm).

40. Install the starter and connect the starter cable.

41. Install the oil filter and make sure the oil drain plug is tight.

42. Lower the vehicle.

43. Install the air cleaner-to-canister hose and the water pump pulley and drive belt.

44. Connect the air conditioning lines to the compressor, if equipped.

45. Connect the accelerator cable and throttle valve control cable at the throttle body.

46. Connect the negative battery cable at the engine and connect the heater hoses and fuel lines.

47. Connect the crankcase ventilation hose at the valve cover and the intake manifold.

48. Connect the engine control sensor wiring assembly and vacuum lines.

49. Connect the upper radiator hose at the engine and install the air cleaner assembly.

50. Connect the negative battery cable.

51. Rotate the engine until the flywheel timing marker is aligned with the timing pointer. Install the timing window cover.

52. Connect the electrical connector at the inertia switch.

53. Fill the cooling system with the proper amount and type of coolant and fill the crankcase with the proper engine oil to the required level.

54. Install the hood.

55. Charge the air conditioning system, if equipped.

56. Check all fluid levels and start the vehicle. Check for leaks.

3.0L Engine

➧ SEE FIG. 32–35

1. Disconnect the battery cables and drain the cooling system. Mark the position of the hood on the hinges and remove the hood.

2. Evacuate the air conditioning system safely and properly. Relieve the fuel system pressure. Remove the air cleaner assembly. Remove the battery and the battery tray.

3. Remove the integrated relay controller, cooling fan and radiator with fan shroud.

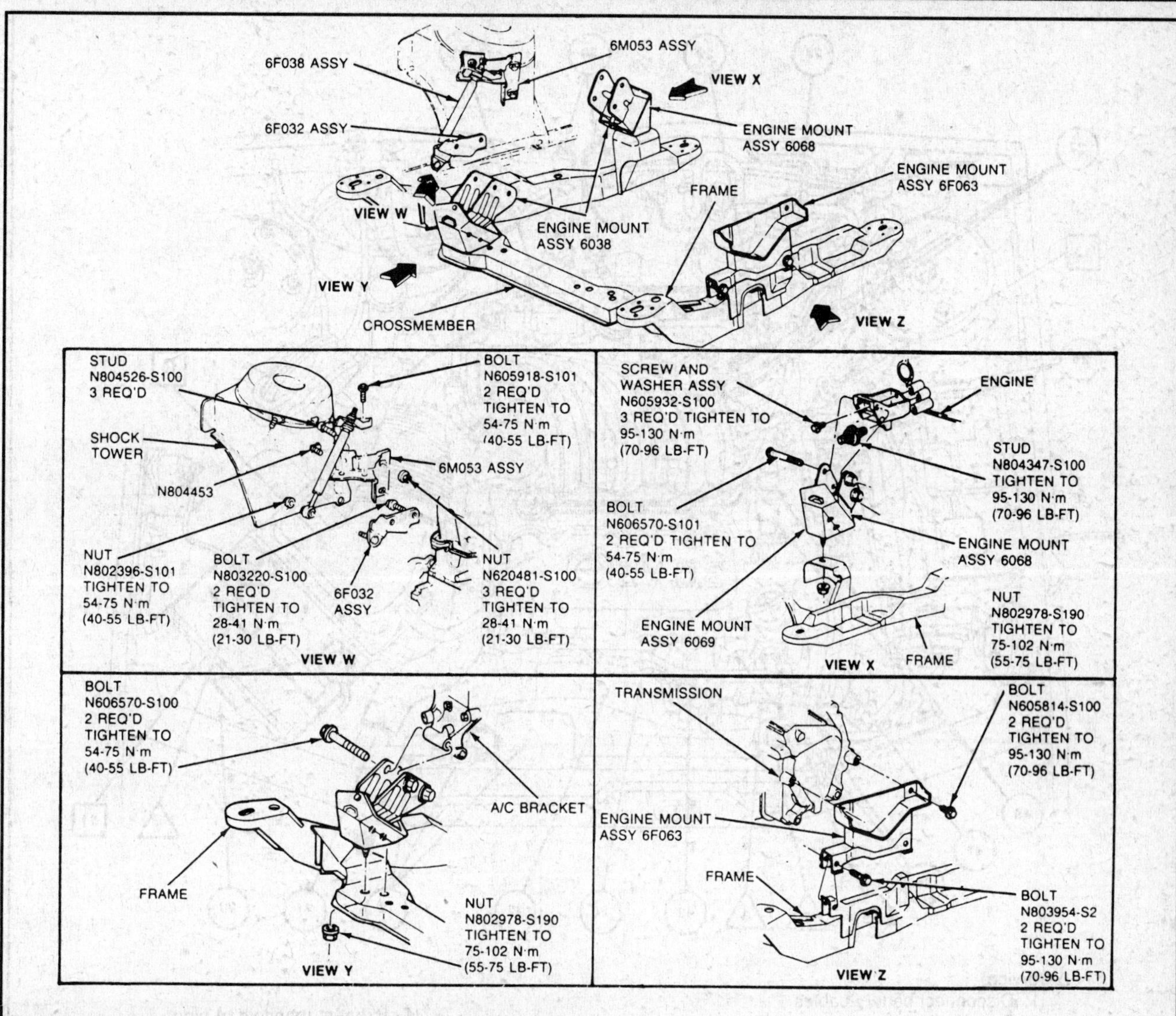

Fig.31 Engine and transaxle mounting — 2.5L engine with manual transaxle

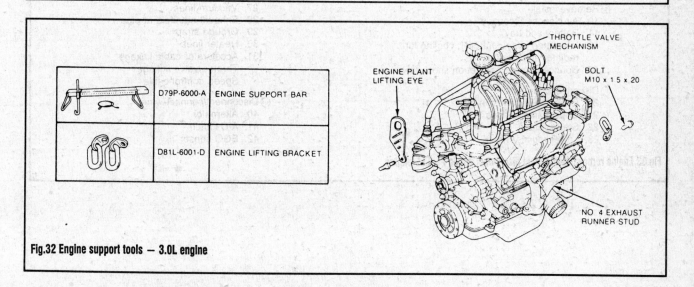

	D79P-6000-A	ENGINE SUPPORT BAR
	D81L-6001-D	ENGINE LIFTING BRACKET

THROTTLE VALVE MECHANISM

ENGINE PLANT LIFTING EYE

BOLT M10 x 1.5 x 20

NO. 4 EXHAUST RUNNER STUD

Fig.32 Engine support tools — 3.0L engine

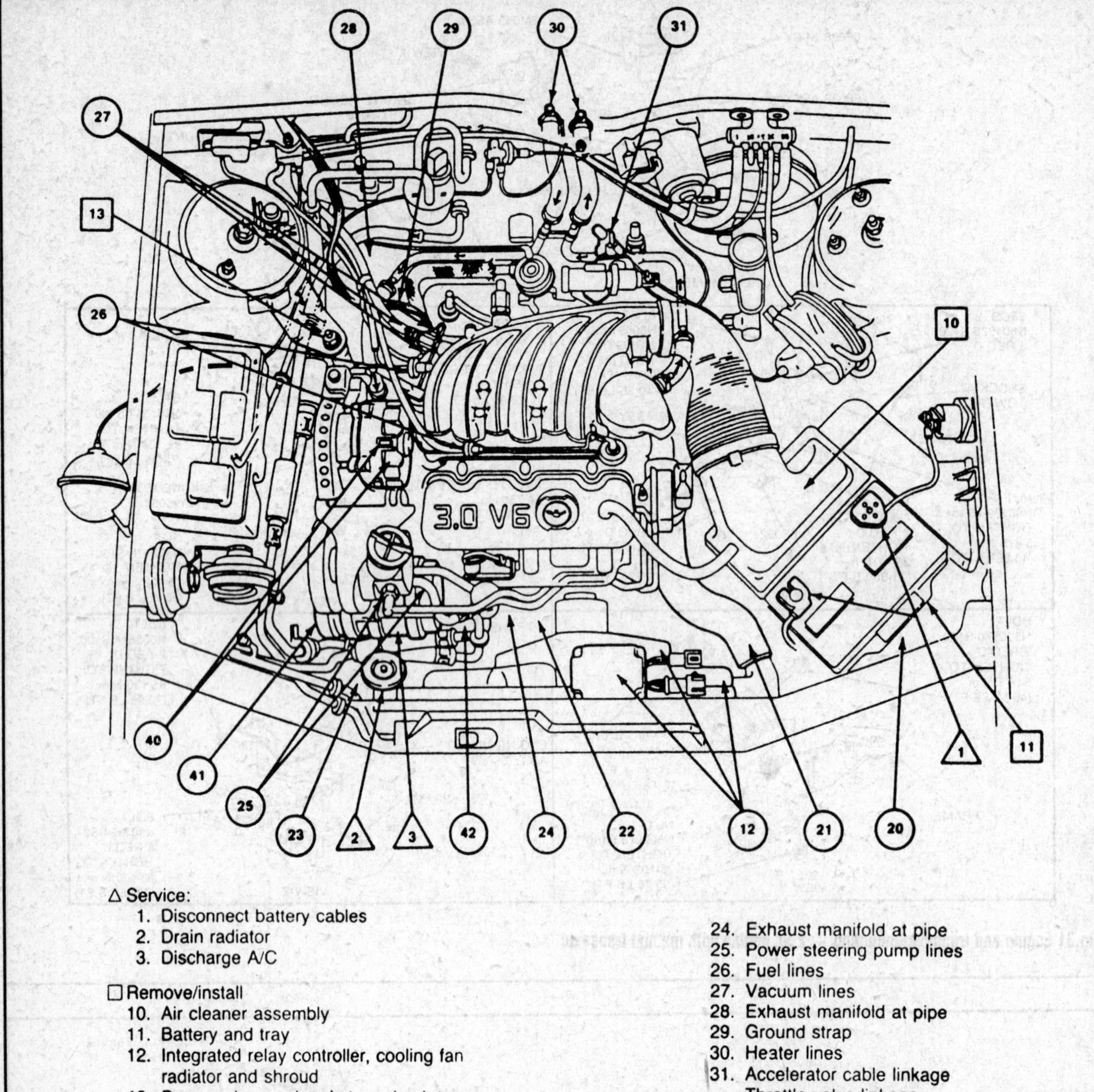

△ Service:
1. Disconnect battery cables
2. Drain radiator
3. Discharge A/C

□ Remove/install
10. Air cleaner assembly
11. Battery and tray
12. Integrated relay controller, cooling fan radiator and shroud
13. Bounce damper bracket on shock tower

○ Disconnect/connect:
20. Evaporative emission line
21. Upper radiator hose
22. Starter brace
23. Lower radiator hose
24. Exhaust manifold at pipe
25. Power steering pump lines
26. Fuel lines
27. Vacuum lines
28. Exhaust manifold at pipe
29. Ground strap
30. Heater lines
31. Accelerator cable linkage
    Throttle valve linkage
    Speed control cable

○ Disconnect/connect-wiring:
40. Alternator
41. A/C clutch
42. EGO sensor

Fig.33 Engine removal/component disconnect points — 3.0L engine

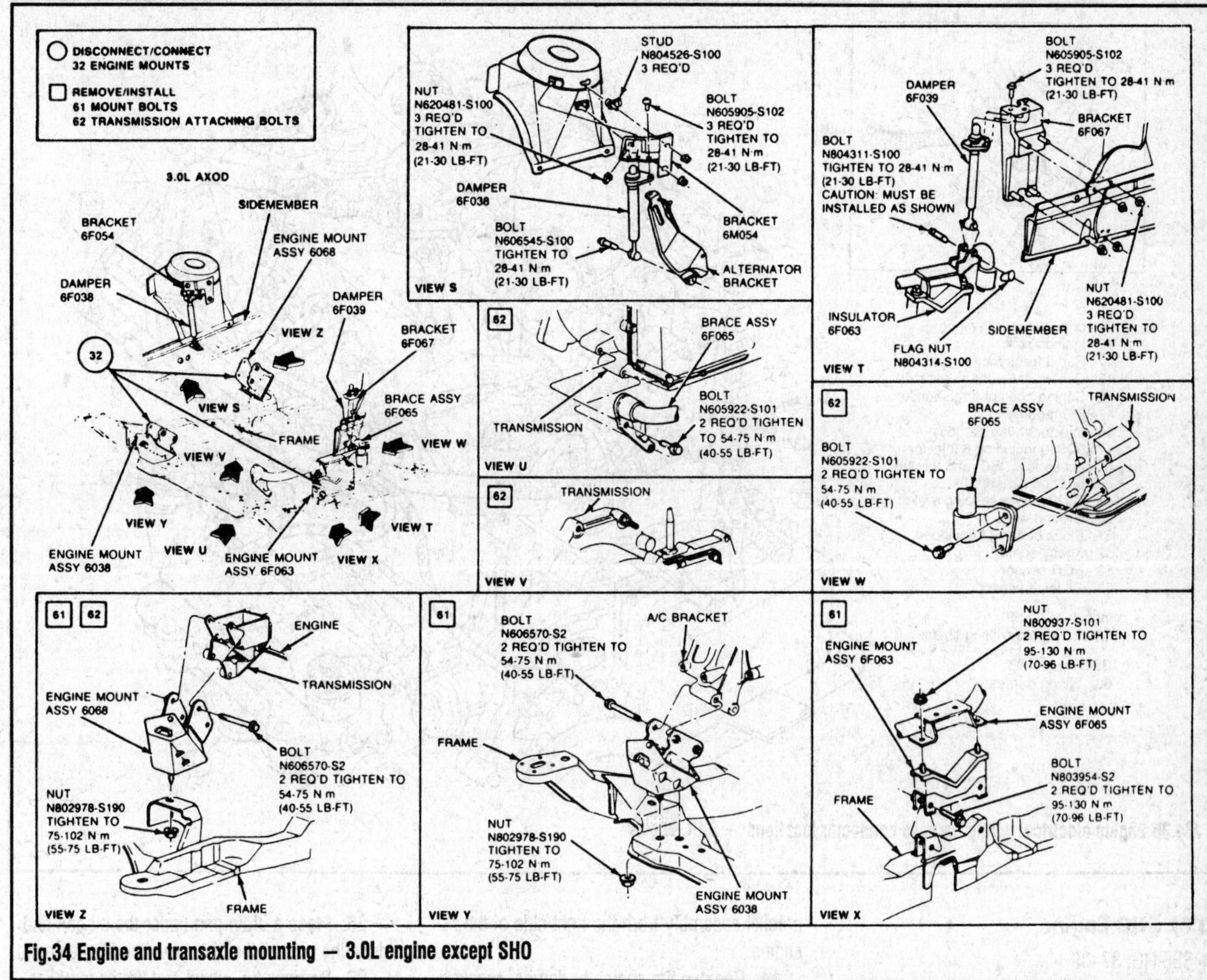

Fig.34 Engine and transaxle mounting — 3.0L engine except SHO

Remove the engine bounce damper bracket on the shock tower.

4. Remove the evaporative emission line, upper radiator hose, starter brace and lower radiator hose.

5. Remove the exhaust pipes from both exhaust manifolds. Remove and plug the power steering pump lines.

6. Remove the fuel lines and remove and tag all necessary vacuum lines.

7. Disconnect the ground strap, heater lines, accelerator cable linkage, throttle valve linkage and speed control cable.

8. Disconnect and label the following wiring connectors; alternator, air conditioning clutch, oxygen sensor, ignition coil, radio frequency suppressor, cooling fan voltage resistor, engine coolant temperature sensor, Thick film ignition module, injector wiring harness, ISC motor wire, throttle position sensor, oil pressure sending switch, ground wire, block heater, if equipped, knock sensor, EGR sensor and oil level sensor.

9. Raise the vehicle and support it safely. Remove the engine mount bolts and engine mounts. Remove the transaxle to engine mounting bolts and transaxle brace assembly.

10. Lower the vehicle. Install a suitable engine lifting plate onto the engine and use a suitable engine hoist to remove the engine from the vehicle. Remove the main wiring harness from the engine.

To install:

11. Install the main wiring harness on the engine. Position the engine in the vehicle and remove the engine lifting plate.

12. Raise the vehicle and support it safely. Install the engine mounts and bolts and tighten to 40–55 ft. lbs. (54–75 Nm). Install the transaxle brace assembly and tighten the bolts to 40–55 ft. lbs. (54–75 Nm).

13. Connect all wiring connectors according to their labels.

14. Connect the ground strap, heater lines, accelerator cable linkage, throttle valve linkage and speed control cables.

15. Connect the power steering pump lines.

16. Connect the exhaust pipes to the exhaust manifolds.

17. Connect the fuel lines and vacuum lines.

18. Install the evaporative emission line, upper radiator hose, starter brace and lower radiator hose.

19. Install the integrated relay controller, cooling fan and radiator with fan shroud. Install the engine bounce damper bracket on the shock tower.

20. Install the battery tray and the battery.

21. Install the air cleaner assembly and charge the air conditioning system.

22. Fill the cooling system with the proper type and quantity of coolant. Fill the crankcase with the correct type of motor oil to the required level.

23. Install the hood.

24. Connect the negative battery cable. Start the engine and check for leaks.

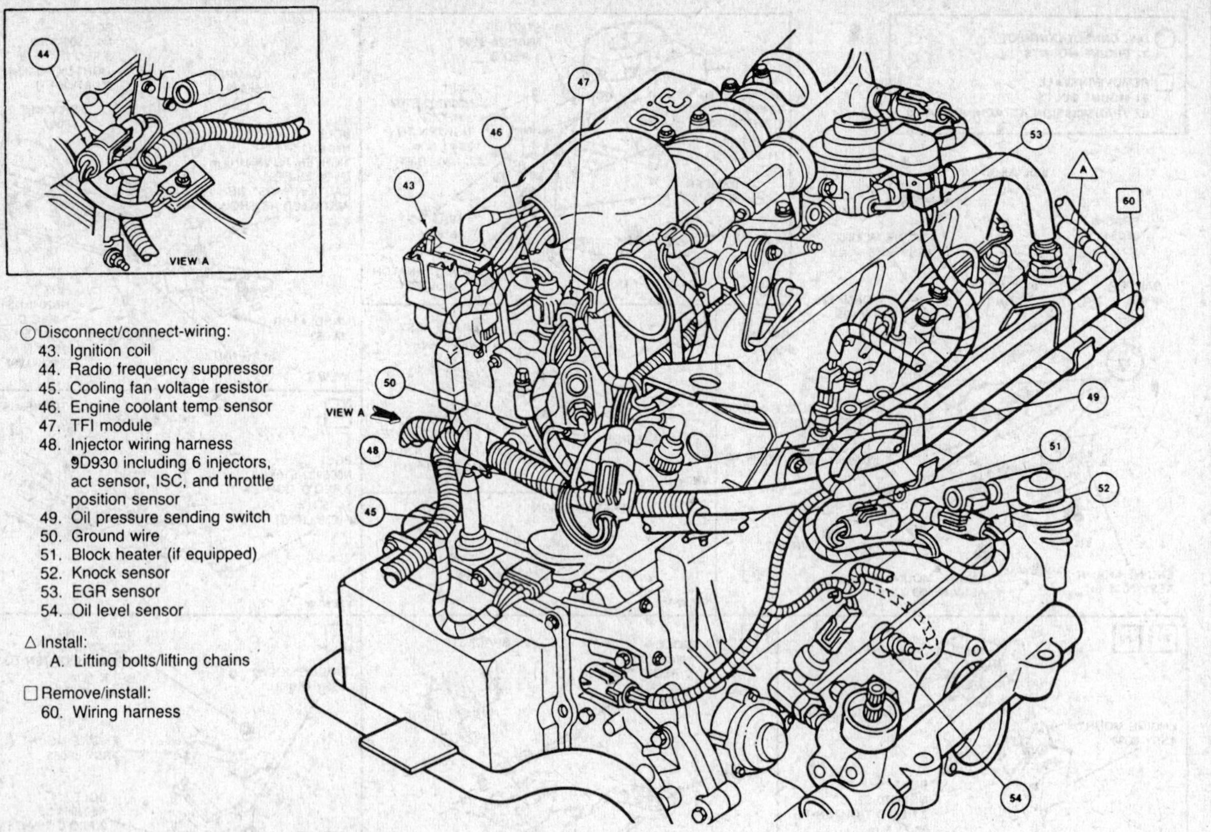

VIEW A

○ Disconnect/connect-wiring:
43. Ignition coil
44. Radio frequency suppressor
45. Cooling fan voltage resistor
46. Engine coolant temp sensor
47. TFI module
48. Injector wiring harness 9D930 including 6 injectors, act sensor, ISC, and throttle position sensor
49. Oil pressure sending switch
50. Ground wire
51. Block heater (if equipped)
52. Knock sensor
53. EGR sensor
54. Oil level sensor

△ Install:
A. Lifting bolts/lifting chains

□ Remove/install:
60. Wiring harness

Fig.35 Engine electrical wiring harness connector locations — 3.0L engine

3.0L SHO Engine

➧ SEE FIG. 37–39

1. Disconnect the battery cables and remove the battery and battery tray.
2. Drain the cooling system and relieve the fuel system pressure.
3. Disconnect the wiring connector retaining the under hood light, if equipped, mark the position of the hood hinges and remove the hood.
4. Remove the oil level indicator.
5. Disconnect the alternator and voltage regulator wiring assembly.
6. Remove the radiator upper sight shield.
7. Discharge the air conditioning system.
8. Remove the radiator coolant recovery reservoir assembly.
9. Remove the integrated relay controller, air cleaner hose assembly, upper radiator hose, electric fan and shroud assembly.
10. Remove the lower radiator hose and the radiator.
11. Disconnect the fuel inlet and return hose.
12. Remove the Barometric Air Pressure (BAP) sensor.
13. Remove the engine vibration damper and bracket assembly from the right side of the engine.
14. Remove the engine to damper bracket.
15. Remove the retaining bolt from the power steering reservoir and place the reservoir aside. Disconnect the hose to the power steering cooler at the pump.
16. Disconnect the throttle linkage and disconnect and tag the vacuum hoses.
17. Disconnect the heater hoses at the heater core.
18. Disconnect the electrical connectors from the harness on the rear of the engine.
19. Loosen the belt tensioner pulleys and remove the air conditioning compressor/ alternator belt and the steering pump belt. Remove the lower tensioner pulley.
20. Disconnect the cycling switch on the top of the suction accumulator/drier.
21. Disconnect the air conditioning line at the dash panel and remove the accumulator and bracket assembly.
22. Remove the alternator assembly.
23. Disconnect the air conditioning discharge hose and remove the air conditioning compressor and bracket assembly.
24. Raise the vehicle and support it safely.
25. Place a drain pan under the oil pan and drain the motor oil and remove the filter element.
26. Remove the wheel and tire assemblies. Disconnect the oil level sensor switch.
27. Disconnect the right lower ball joint, tie rod end and stabilizer bar.
28. Disconnect the center support bearing bracket and right-hand CV-joint from the transaxle.

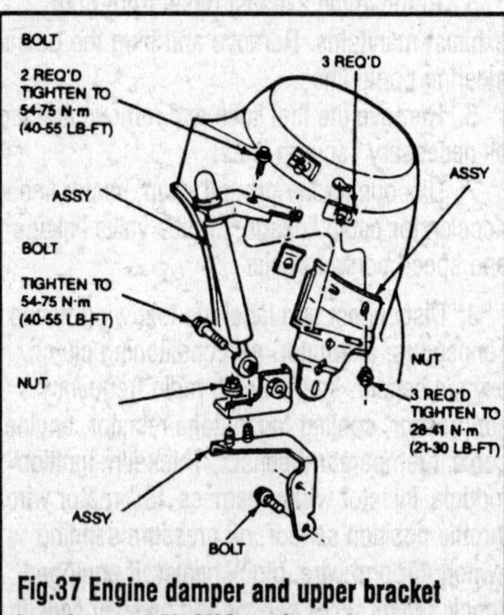

Fig.37 Engine damper and upper bracket location — 3.0L SHO engine

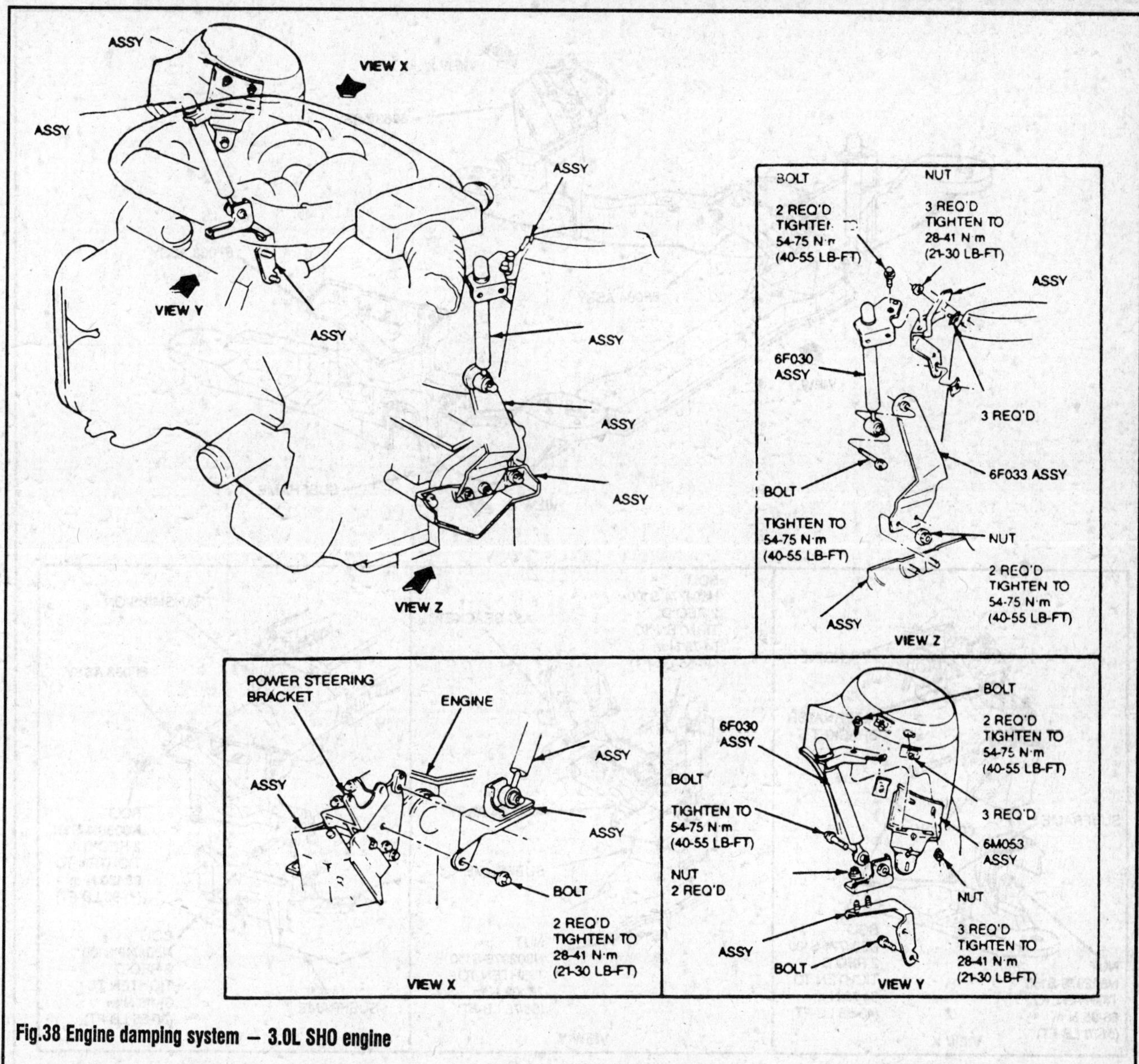

Fig.38 Engine damping system — 3.0L SHO engine

29. Disconnect the oxygen sensor assembly and the 4 exhaust catalyst to engine retaining bolts.
30. Remove the starter motor assembly.
31. Remove the lower transaxle to engine retaining bolts.
32. Remove the engine mount to sub-frame nuts.
33. Remove the crankshaft pulley assembly.
34. Lower the vehicle and remove the upper transaxle to engine retaining bolts.
35. Install engine lifting eyes.
36. Position a floor jack under the transaxle.
37. Position suitable engine lifting equipment, raise the transaxle assembly slightly and remove the engine from the vehicle.

To Install:

38. Position the engine assembly in the vehicle.
39. Install the upper transaxle to engine bolts and remove the floor jack and engine lifting equipment. Remove the engine lifting eyes.
40. Raise the vehicle and support it safely.
41. Install the crankshaft pulley assembly. Tighten the retaining bolt to 113–126 ft. lbs. (152–172 Nm).
42. Install the engine mount to sub-frame nuts and the lower transaxle to engine retaining bolts. Tighten the bolts to 25–35 ft. lbs. (34–47 Nm).
43. Install the starter motor assembly.
44. Install the 4 exhaust catalyst to engine retaining nuts and tighten them to 19–34 ft. lbs. (27–47 Nm). Apply anti-seize compound to the threads, then install the oxygen sensor assembly. Tighten to 27–33 ft. lbs. (37–45 Nm).
45. Connect the center support bearing bracket and install the right-hand CV-joint.
46. Connect the right lower ball joint, tie rod end and stabilizer bar.
47. Connect the oil level sensor and install the wheel and tire assemblies.
48. Install the oil filter. Install the oil drain plug and tighten to 15–24 ft. lbs. (20–33 Nm).
49. Lower the vehicle.
50. Install the air conditioning compressor and bracket assembly, tighten to 27–40 ft. lbs. (36–55 Nm) and connect the air conditioning discharge hose.
51. Install the alternator assembly and tighten to 36–53 ft. lbs. (48–72 Nm).
52. Install the accumulator and bracket assembly and connect the cycling switch to the top of the accumulator.
53. Install the lower belt tensioner. Install the

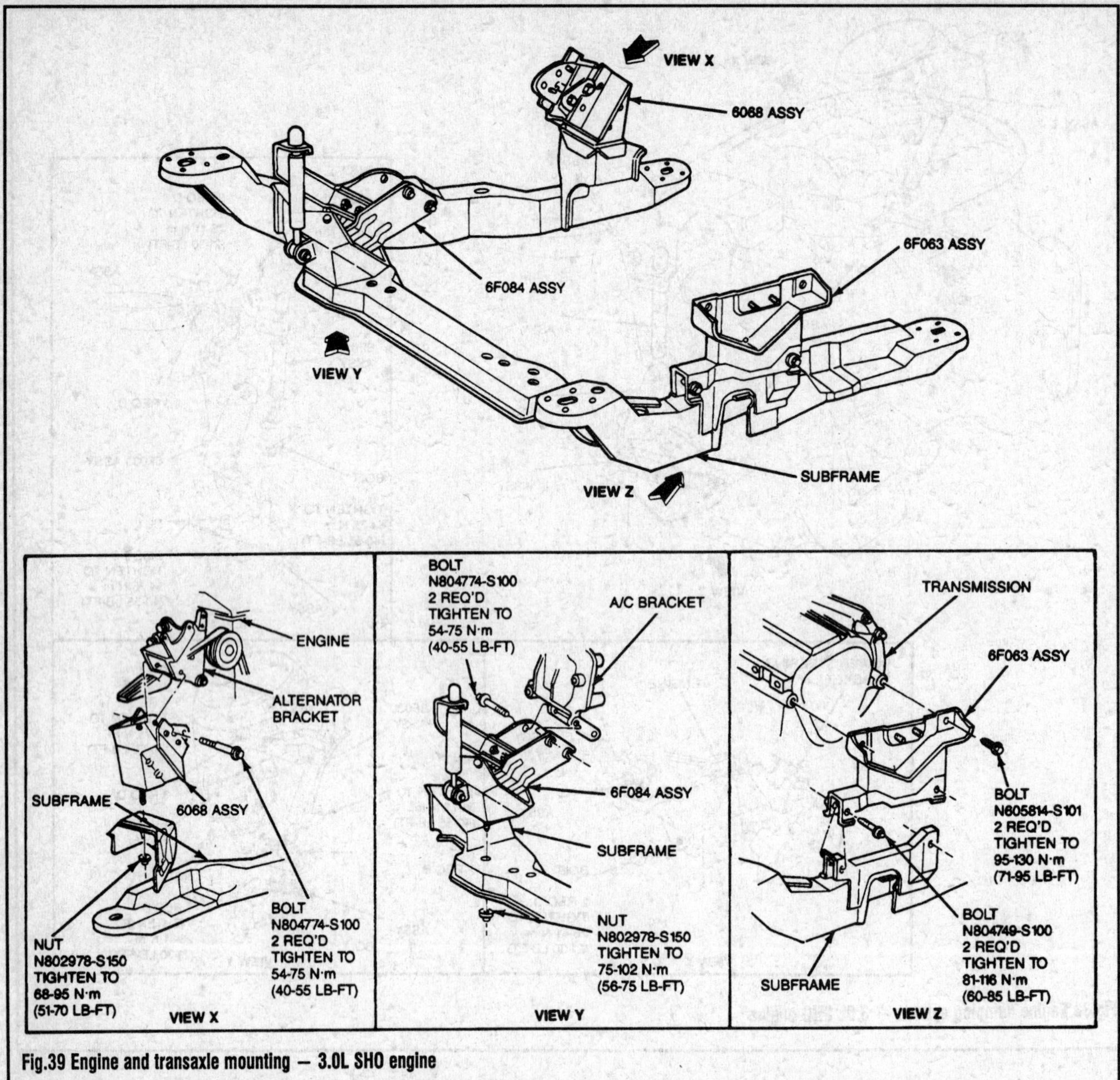

Fig.39 Engine and transaxle mounting — 3.0L SHO engine

power steering and air conditioning compressor/alternator belts and tighten the tensioner pulleys.

54. Connect the electrical connectors from the harness on the rear of the engine.
55. Connect the heater hoses, vacuum hoses and throttle linkage.
56. Connect the hose from the power steering cooler at the pump and install the power steering reservoir.
57. Install the damper bracket to the engine and install the engine vibration damper and bracket assembly to the right side of the engine.
58. Install the BAP sensor.
59. Connect the fuel inlet and return hoses.
60. Install the radiator assembly and the lower radiator hose.
61. Install the electric fan and shroud assembly, upper radiator hose, air cleaner hose, integrated relay controller, radiator coolant recovery reservoir and radiator upper sight shield.
62. Connect the alternator and voltage regulator wiring.
63. Install the oil level indicator tube.
64. Install the hood and connect the under hood light wiring, if equipped.
65. Install the battery tray and the battery.
66. Install the negative battery cable.
67. Fill the cooling system with the proper type and quantity of coolant and fill the crankcase with the proper type of motor oil to the required level.
68. Drain, evacuate, pressure test and recharge the air conditioning system.
69. Start the engine and check for leaks.

3.8L Engine

➧ SEE FIG. 36

1. Drain the cooling system and disconnect the battery ground cable. Properly relieve the fuel system pressure.
2. Disconnect the underhood light wiring connector. Mark position of hood hinges and remove hood.
3. Remove the oil level indicator tube.
4. Disconnect alternator to voltage regulator wiring assembly.
5. Remove the radiator upper sight shield. Remove the engine cooling fan motor relay retaining bolts and position cooling fan motor relay aside.
6. Remove the air cleaner assembly.

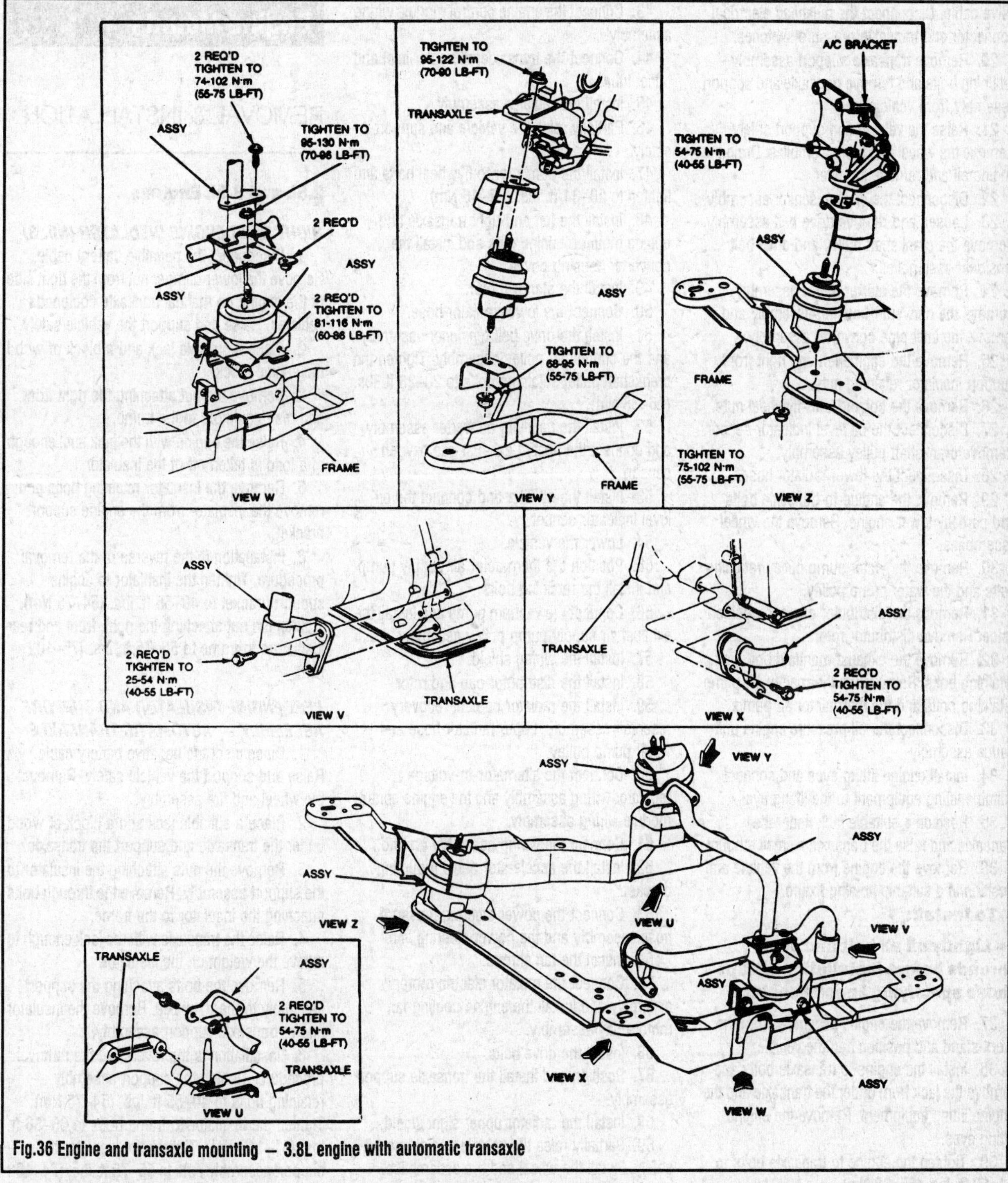

Fig.36 Engine and transaxle mounting — 3.8L engine with automatic transaxle

7. Disconnect the radiator electric fan and motor assembly. Remove fan shroud.
8. Remove upper radiator hose.
9. Disconnect the transaxle oil cooler inlet and outlet tubes and cover the openings to prevent the entry of dirt and grease. Disconnect the heater hoses.
10. Disconnect the power steering pressure hose assembly.
11. Disconnect the air conditioner compressor clutch wire assembly. Discharge the air conditioning system and disconnect the compressor-to-condenser line.
12. Remove the radiator coolant recovery reservoir assembly. Remove the wiring shield.
13. Remove accelerator cable mounting bracket.
14. Disconnect fuel inlet and return lines.
15. Disconnect power steering pump pressure and return tube brackets.
16. Disconnect the engine control sensor wiring assembly.
17. Identify, tag and disconnect all necessary vacuum hoses.
18. Disconnect the ground wire assembly. Remove the duct assembly.
19. Disconnect one end of the throttle control

valve cable. Disconnect the bulkhead electrical connector and transaxle pressure switches.

20. Remove transaxle support assembly retaining bolts and remove transaxle and support assembly from vehicle.

21. Raise the vehicle and support safely. Remove the wheel and tire assemblies. Drain the engine oil and remove the filter.

22. Disconnect the oxygen sensor assembly.

23. Loosen and remove drive belt assembly. Remove the crankshaft pulley and drive belt tensioner assemblies.

24. Remove the starter motor assembly. Remove the converter housing assembly and remove the inlet pipe converter assembly.

25. Remove the engine left and right front support insulator retaining nuts.

26. Remove the converter-to-flywheel nuts.

27. Disconnect the oil level indicator sensor. Remove crankshaft pulley assembly.

28. Disconnect the lower radiator hose.

29. Remove the engine-to-transaxle bolts and partially lower engine. Remove the wheel assemblies.

30. Remove the water pump pulley retaining bolts and the water pump pulley.

31. Remove the distributor cap and position aside. Remove distributor rotor.

32. Remove the exhaust manifold bolt lock retaining bolts. Remove the thermactor air pump retaining bolts and the thermactor air pump.

33. Disconnect the oil pressure engine unit gauge assembly.

34. Install engine lifting eyes and connect suitable lifting equipment to the lifting eyes.

35. Position a suitable jack under the transaxle and raise the transaxle a small amount.

36. Remove the engine from the vehicle and position in a suitable holding fixture.

To install:

➡ Lightly oil all bolt and stud threads before installation except those specifying special sealant.

37. Remove the engine assembly from the work stand and position it in the vehicle.

38. Install the engine to transaxle bolts and remove the jack from under the transaxle and the engine lifting equipment. Remove the engine lifting eyes.

39. Tighten the engine to transaxle bolts to 41–50 ft. lbs. (55–68 Nm).

40. Connect the oil pressure engine unit gauge assembly.

41. Install the air conditioning compressor and tighten the retaining bolts to 30–45 ft. lbs. (41–61 Nm). Connect the compressor to condenser discharge line and the compressor clutch wire assembly.

42. Connect the heater hoses, vacuum hoses and the fuel tube hose and return line hose.

43. Connect the engine control module wiring assembly.

44. Connect the transaxle oil cooler inlet and outlet tubes.

45. Install the radiator assembly.

46. Partially raise the vehicle and support it safely.

47. Install the converter to flywheel bolts and tighten to 20–34 ft. lbs. (27–46 Nm).

48. Install the left and right transaxle and engine mount retaining nuts and install the converter housing cover.

49. Install the starter motor.

50. Connect the lower radiator hose.

51. Install the drive belt tensioner assembly and the crankshaft pulley assembly. Tighten the crankshaft pulley retaining bolts to 20–28 ft. lbs. (26–38 Nm).

52. Install the catalytic converter assembly and connect the heated exhaust gas oxygen sensor.

53. Install the oil filter and connect the oil level indicator sensor.

54. Lower the vehicle.

55. Position the thermactor air supply pump and install the retaining bolts.

56. Connect the vacuum pump and install the exhaust air supply pump pulley assembly.

57. Install the wiring shield.

58. Install the distributor cap and rotor.

59. Install the radiator coolant recovery reservoir assembly, upper radiator hose and water pump pulley.

60. Connect the alternator-to-voltage regulator wiring assembly and the engine control module wiring assembly.

61. Connect the wiring assembly ground.

62. Install the accelerator cable mounting bracket.

63. Connect the power steering pressure hose assembly and the power steering line.

64. Install the fan shroud.

65. Connect the radiator electric motor assembly and install the engine cooling fan motor relay assembly.

66. Install the drive belts.

67. Position and install the transaxle support assembly.

68. Install the radiator upper sight shield.

69. Partially raise the vehicle and support it safely. Install the wheel and tire assemblies.

70. Install the hood and connect the negative battery cable.

71. Fill the cooling system with the proper type and quantity of coolant and fill the crankcase with the proper type of motor oil to the required level.

72. Drain, evacuate, pressure test and recharge the air conditioning system.

73. Start the engine and check for leaks.

Engine Mounts

REMOVAL & INSTALLATION

2.5L and 3.0L Engines

RIGHT REAR ENGINE INSULATOR (NO. 3)

1. Disconnect the negative battery cable. Remove the lower damper nut from the right side of the engine on manual transaxle equipped vehicles. Raise and support the vehicle safely.

2. Place a suitable jack and a block of wood the engine block.

3. Remove the nut attaching the right front and rear insulators to the frame.

4. Raise the engine with the jack until enough of a load is taken off of the insulator.

5. Remove the insulator retaining bolts and remove the insulator from the engine support bracket.

6. Installation is the reverse of the removal procedure. Tighten the insulator to engine support bracket to 40–55 ft. lbs. (54–75 Nm). Tighten the nut attaching the right, front and rear insulators to frame to 55–75 ft. lbs. (75–102 Nm).

LEFT ENGINE INSULATOR AND SUPPORT ASSEMBLY — AUTOMATIC TRANSAXLE

1. Disconnect the negative battery cable. Raise and support the vehicle safely. Remove the wheel and tire assembly.

2. Place a suitable jack and a block of wood under the transaxle and support the transaxle.

3. Remove the nuts attaching the insulator to the support assembly. Remove the through bolts attaching the insulator to the frame.

4. Raise the transaxle with the jack enough to relieve the weight on the insulator.

5. Remove the bolts attaching the support assembly to the transaxle. Remove the insulator and/or transaxle support assembly.

6. .Installation is the reverse of the removal procedure. Tighten the support assembly retaining bolts to 40–55 ft. lbs. (54–75 Nm). Tighten the insulator-to-frame bolts to 60–86 ft. lbs. (81–116 Nm). Tighten the insulator to support assembly nuts to 55–75 ft. lbs. (74–102 Nm).

LEFT ENGINE INSULATOR AND SUPPORT ASSEMBLY — MANUAL TRANSAXLE

1. Disconnect the negative battery cable. Raise and support the vehicle safely. Remove the tire and wheel assembly.

2. Place a jack and a block of wood under the transaxle and support the transaxle.

3. Remove the bolts attaching the insulator to the frame.

4. Raise the transaxle with the jack enough to relieve the weight on the insulator.

5. Remove the bolts attaching the insulator to the transaxle. Remove the insulator.

6. Installation is the reverse of the removal procedure. Tighten the insulator-to-transaxle bolts to 60–86 ft. lbs. (81–116 Nm). Tighten the insulator-to-frame bolts to 60–86 ft. lbs. (81–116 Nm).

RIGHT FRONT ENGINE INSULATOR (NO. 2)

1. Disconnect the negative battery cable. Remove the lower damper nut or bolt from the right side of the engine. Raise and support the vehicle safely.

2. Place a jack and a block of wood under the engine block.

3. Remove the nuts attaching the right front and rear insulators to the frame.

4. Raise the engine with the jack until enough of a load is taken off of the insulator.

5. Remove the bolt(s) and the insulator from the engine bracket.

6. Installation is the reverse of the removal procedure. Tighten the insulator-to-engine bracket bolt(s) to 40–55 ft. lbs. (54–75 Nm) on 2.5L engine or 71–95 ft. lbs. (90–130 Nm) on 3.0L engine. Tighten the nut attaching the right front and right rear insulators to frame to 55–75 ft. lbs. (75–102 Nm).

3.0L SHO Engine

RIGHT FRONT (NO. 2) AND RIGHT REAR (No. 3)

1. Remove the lower damper bolt from the right side of the engine.

2. Raise the vehicle and support it safely.

3. Place a jack and a wood block in a suitable place under the engine.

4. Remove the roll damper to engine retaining nuts and remove the roll damper.

5. Raise the engine enough to unload the insulator.

6. Remove the 2 through bolts and remove the insulators from the engine bracket.

7. Installation is the reverse of the removal procedure. Tighten the insulator-to-engine bracket bolts to 40–55 ft. lbs. (54–75 Nm). Tighten the insulator to frame nuts to 50–70 ft. lbs. (68–95 Nm). Tighten the roll damper retaining nuts to 40–55 ft. lbs. (54–75 Nm). Tighten the engine damper to engine bolt to 40–55 ft. lbs. (54–75 Nm).

LEFT ENGINE INSULATOR AND SUPPORT ASSEMBLY

1. Remove the bolt retaining the roll damper to the lower damper bracket and place the damper shaft aside.

2. Remove the backup light switch and the energy management bracket.

3. Raise the vehicle and support it with jackstands under the vehicle body, allowing the sub-frame to hang.

4. Remove the left tire and wheel assembly.

5. Place a jack and wood block under the transaxle.

6. Remove the nuts retaining the lower damper bracket to engine mount and the bolts retaining the insulator to the transaxle and sub-frame.

7. Raise the transaxle with the jack enough to unload the insulator.

8. Remove the insulator and lower damper bracket.

9. Installation is the reverse of the removal procedure. Tighten the damper bracket to insulator nuts to 40–55 ft. lbs. (54–75 Nm). Tighten the insulator to transaxle bolts to 70–95 ft. lbs. (95–130 Nm). Tighten the insulator to frame bolts to 60–85 ft. lbs. (81–116 Nm). Tighten the damper to damper bracket bolt to 40–55 ft. lbs. (54–75 Nm).

3.8L Engine

RIGHT FRONT ENGINE INSULATOR

1. Disconnect the negative battery cable. Remove the air conditioning compressor-to-engine mounting bracket mounting bolts and position the compressor to the side. Do not discharge the air conditioning system.

2. Raise the vehicle and support safely.

3. Remove nut attaching engine mount to air conditioning compressor bracket.

4. Temporarily attach the air conditioning compressor to the mounting bracket with the 2 lower bolts.

5. Position a jack and wood block in a convenient location under the engine block.

6. Remove the upper and lower nuts attaching the right front and left rear insulators to the frame.

7. Raise the engine with the jack enough to relieve the load on the insulator.

8. Remove insulator assembly. Remove heat shield from insulator.

9. Installation is the reverse of the removal procedure. Tighten the upper insulator stud retaining nut to 40–55 ft. lbs. (54–75 Nm) and the lower retaining nut to 50–70 ft. lbs. (68–95 Nm).

RIGHT REAR ENGINE INSULATOR (NO. 3)

1. Disconnect the negative battery cable and raise and support the vehicle safely.

2. Remove the nuts retaining the right front and right rear engine mounts to the frame.

3. Lower the vehicle.

4. Using suitable engine lifting equipment, raise the engine approximately 1 in. (25mm).

5. Loosen the retaining nut on the right rear (No. 3) mount and heat shield assembly.

6. Raise and support the vehicle safely.

7. Remove the insulator retaining nut and the insulator and heat shield assembly.

8. Installation is the reverse of the removal procedure. Tighten the top retaining nut on the insulator to 40–55 ft. lbs. (54–75 Nm). Tighten the retaining nuts on the right front and right rear engine mounts to 55–75 ft. lbs. (68–95 Nm).

LEFT ENGINE MOUNT AND SUPPORT ASSEMBLY

1. Raise the vehicle and support it safely.

2. Remove the tire and wheel assembly.

3. Place a jack and wood block under the transaxle and support the transaxle.

4. Remove the 2 bolts retaining the vertical restrictor assembly.

5. Remove the nut retaining the transaxle mount to the support assembly.

6. Remove the 2 through bolts retaining the transaxle mount to the frame.

7. Raise the transaxle with the jack enough to unload the mount.

8. Remove the bolts retaining the support assembly to the transaxle and remove the mount and/or transaxle support assembly.

9. Installation is the reverse of the removal procedure. Tighten the support assembly to transaxle bolts to 35 ft. lbs. (48 Nm). Tighten the mount to frame bolts to 60–86 ft. lbs. (81–116 Nm). Tighten the transaxle mount to support nut to 55–75 ft. lbs. (74–102 Nm). Tighten the 2 bolts retaining the vertical restrictor assembly to 40–55 ft. lbs. (54–75 Nm).

Rocker Arm Cover

REMOVAL & INSTALLATION

2.5L Engine

1. Disconnect the negative battery cable.

2. Remove the oil fill cap and rocker arm filter and set aside. Disconnect the PCV hose and set it aside.

3. Disconnect the throttle linkage cable from the top of the rocker arm cover. Disconnect the speed control cable from the top of the rocker arm cover, if equipped.

4. Remove the rocker arm cover bolts. Remove the rocker cover and gasket from the engine.

5. Installation is the reverse of the removal procedure. Be sure to use new gaskets or RTV sealant, as required.

3.0L Engine

➧ SEE FIG. 40

1. Disconnect the negative battery cable. Disconnect and tag the spark plug wires.
2. Remove the ignition wire/separator assembly from the rocker arm attaching bolt studs. If the left rocker arm cover is being removed, remove the oil fill cap, disconnect the air cleaner closure system hose and remove the fuel injector harness from the inboard rocker arm cover studs.
3. If the right rocker arm cover is being removed, remove the PCV valve, loosen the lower EGR tube, if equipped, retaining nut and rotate the tube aside, remove the throttle body and move the fuel injection harness aside.
4. Remove the rocker arm cover attaching screws and the covers and gaskets from the vehicle.
5. Installation is the reverse of the removal procedure. Be sure to use new gaskets or RTV sealant, as required.

3.0L SHO Engine

1. Disconnect the negative battery cable. Relieve the fuel system pressure.
2. Disconnect all vacuum lines and electrical connectors from the intake assembly. Remove the upper intake assembly.
3. Disconnect the spark plug wires. If the left cover is being removed, remove the oil fill cap and the coil pack plastic cover.
4. If the right cover is being removed, disconnect the fuel lines.
5. Remove the cylinder head cover retaining bolts and remove the cover.
6. Installation is the reverse of the removal procedure. Coat all bolt and stud threads with clean engine oil prior to installation. Torque the cover retaining bolts to 8-11 ft. lbs.

3.8L Engine

➧ SEE FIG. 41

1. Disconnect the negative battery cable.
2. Tag and disconnect the spark plug wires from the spark plugs.
3. If the left cover is being removed, remove the oil fill cap.
4. If the right cover is being removed, position the air cleaner assembly aside and remove the PCV valve.
5. Remove the rocker arm cover mounting bolts and remove the rocker arm cover.
6. Installation is the reverse of the removal procedure. Be sure to use new gaskets or RTV sealant, as required.

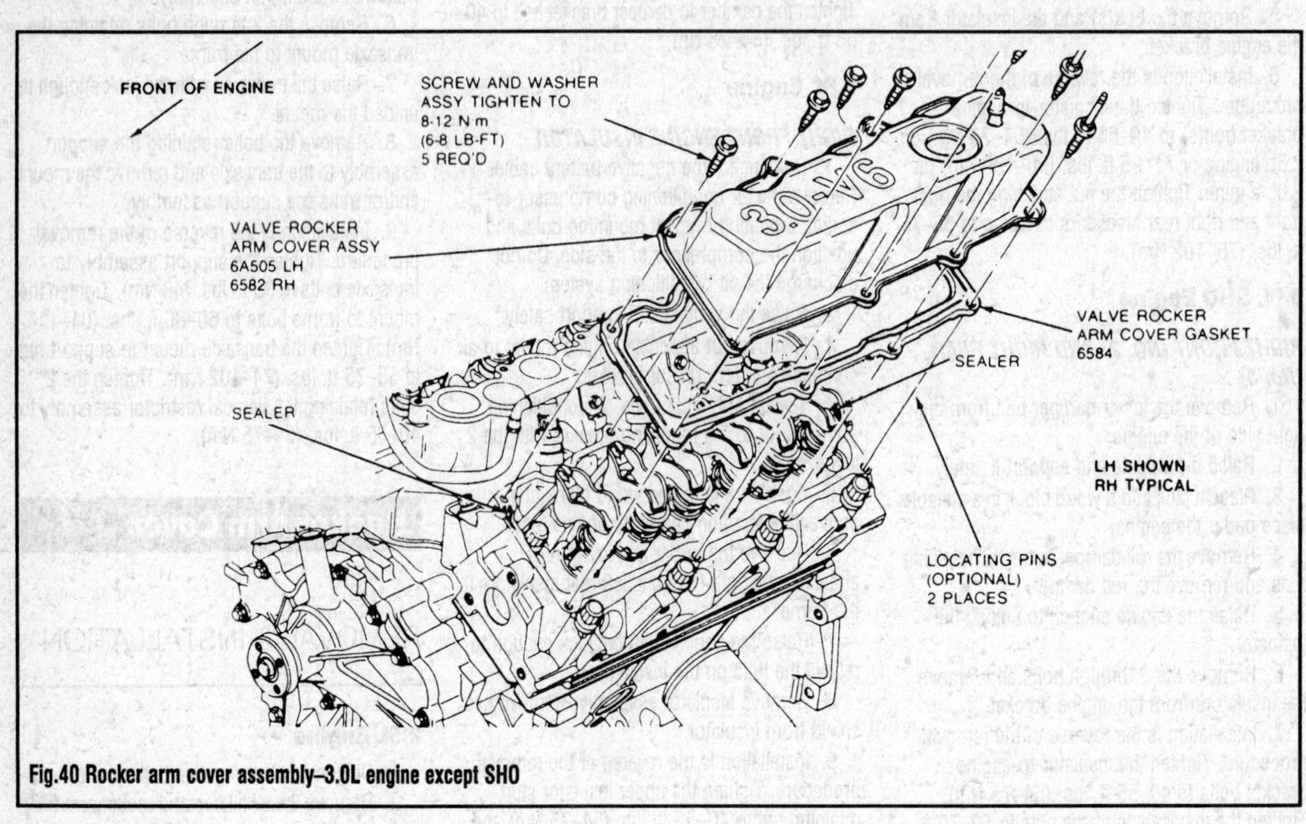

Fig.40 Rocker arm cover assembly–3.0L engine except SHO

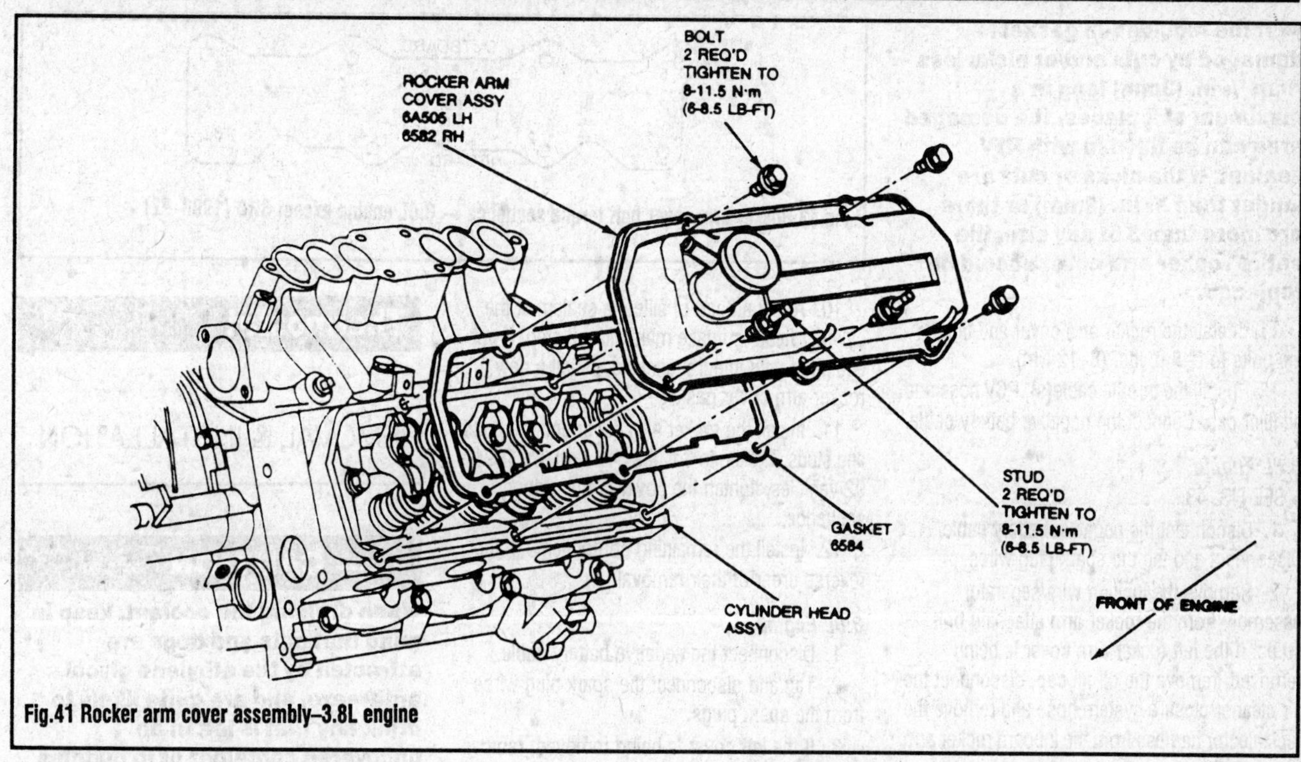

Fig.41 Rocker arm cover assembly–3.8L engine

Rocker Arms

REMOVAL & INSTALLATION

2.5L Engine

➧ SEE FIG. 42

1. Disconnect the negative battery cable.
2. Remove the oil fill cap and rocker arm filter and set aside. Disconnect the PCV hose and set it aside.
3. Disconnect the throttle linkage cable from the top of the rocker arm cover. Disconnect the speed control cable from the top of the rocker arm cover, if equipped.
4. Remove the rocker arm cover bolts. Remove the rocker cover and gasket from the engine.
5. Remove the rocker arm bolts, fulcrums, rocker arms and fulcrum washers. Keep all parts in order so they can be reinstalled to their original position.

To install:

6. Clean the cylinder head and rocker arm cover mating surfaces.
7. Coat the valve tips, rocker arm and fulcrum contact areas with Lubriplate® or equivalent.
8. For each valve, rotate the engine until the lifter is on the base circle of the cam (valve closed).
9. Install the rocker arm and components and tighten the rocker arm bolts in 2 steps, the first to 6–8 ft. lbs. (8–12 Nm) and the second torque to 20–26 ft. lbs. (28–35 Nm). Be sure the lifter is on the base circle of the cam for each rocker arm as it is installed. For the final tightening, the camshaft may be in any position. Check the valve lash.
10. Install a new rocker arm cover gasket, using suitable sealer, unless the cover is equipped with a moulded-in gasket, in which case no sealer should be used.

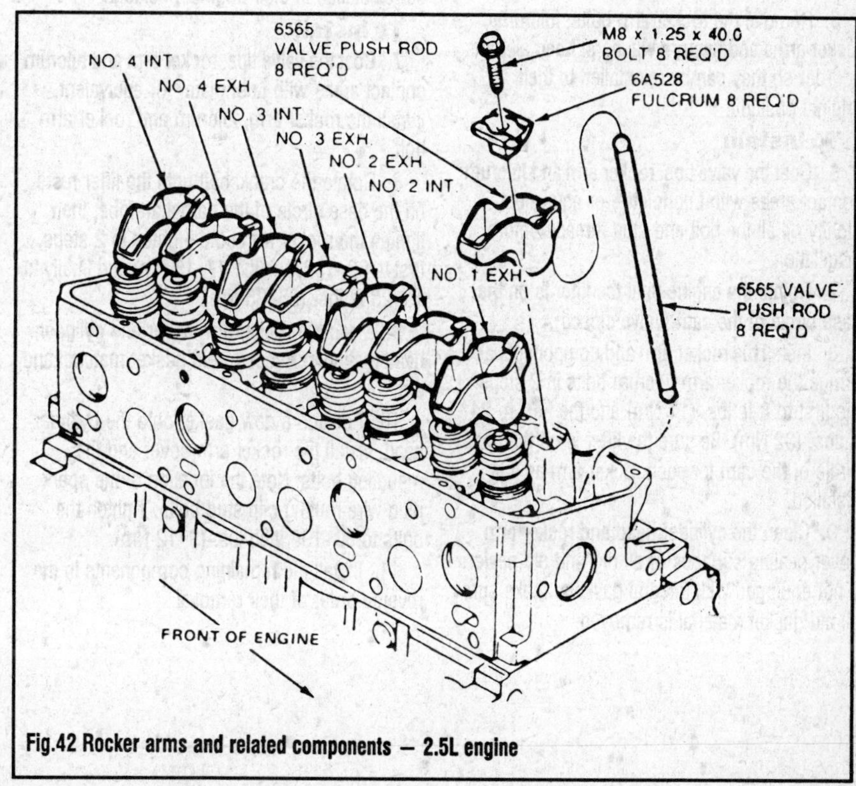

Fig.42 Rocker arms and related components — 2.5L engine

➡ **If the moulded-in gasket is damaged by cuts and/or nicks less than 1/8 in. (3mm) long in a maximum of 2 places, the damaged area can be filled in with RTV sealant. If the nicks or cuts are longer than 1/8 in. (3mm) or there are more than 3 of any size, the entire rocker arm cover should be replaced.**

11. Install the rocker arm cover and tighten the bolts to 6–8 ft. lbs. (8–12 Nm).

12. Install the throttle cable(s), PCV hose and oil filler cap. Connect the negative battery cable.

3.0L Engine

➧ SEE FIG. 43

1. Disconnect the negative battery cable. Disconnect and tag the spark plug wires.

2. Remove the ignition wire/separator assembly from the rocker arm attaching bolt studs. If the left rocker arm cover is being removed, remove the oil fill cap, disconnect the air cleaner closure system hose and remove the fuel injector harness from the inboard rocker arm cover studs.

3. If the right rocker arm cover is being removed, remove the PCV valve, loosen the lower EGR tube, if equipped, retaining nut and rotate the tube aside, remove the throttle body and move the fuel injection harness aside.

4. Remove the rocker arm cover attaching screws and the covers and gaskets from the vehicle.

5. Remove the rocker arm bolts, fulcrums, rocker arms and fulcrum washers. Keep all parts in order so they can be reinstalled to their original position.

To install:

6. Coat the valve tips, rocker arm and fulcrum contact areas with Lubriplate® or equivalent. Lightly oil all the bolt and stud threads before installation.

7. Rotate the engine until the lifter is on the base circle of the cam (valve closed).

8. Install the rocker arm and components and torque the rocker arm fulcrum bolts in 2 steps: the first to 8 ft. lbs. (11 Nm) and the final to 24 ft. lbs. (32 Nm). Be sure the lifter is on the base circle of the cam for each rocker arm as it is installed.

9. Clean the cylinder head and rocker arm cover sealing surfaces of all dirt and old sealer. If not equipped with integral gaskets, make sure all old gasket material is removed.

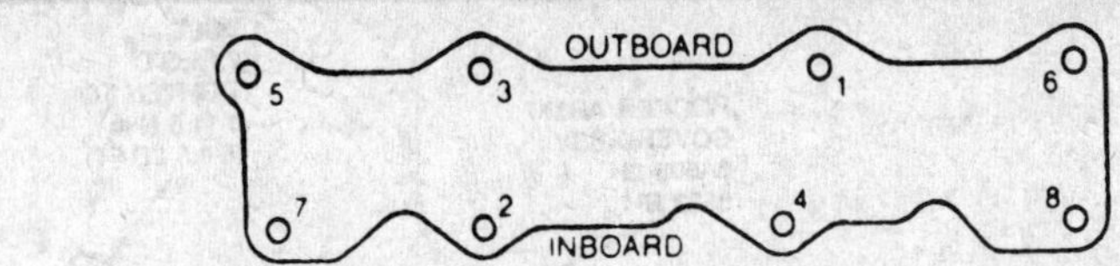

Fig.43 Rocker arm cover bolt torque sequence – 3.0L engine except SHO (1990–92)

10. Apply a bead of silicone sealant at the cylinder head to intake manifold rail step. If not equipped with integral gaskets, install a new rocker arm cover gasket.

11. Install the rocker arm cover and the bolts and studs. Tighten to 9 ft. lbs. (12 Nm). On 1991–92 vehicles, tighten the cover in the proper sequence.

12. Install the remaining components in the reverse order of their removal.

3.8L Engine

1. Disconnect the negative battery cable.

2. Tag and disconnect the spark plug wires from the spark plugs.

3. If the left cover is being removed, remove the oil fill cap.

4. If the right cover is being removed, position the air cleaner assembly aside and remove the PCV valve.

5. Remove the rocker arm cover mounting bolts and remove the rocker arm cover.

6. Remove the rocker arm bolt, fulcrum and rocker arm. Keep all parts in order so they can be reinstalled in their original positions.

To install:

7. Coat the valve tips, rocker arm and fulcrum contact areas with Lubriplate® or equivalent. Install the rocker arm, fulcrum and rocker arm bolt.

8. Rotate the crankshaft until the lifter rests on the base circle of the camshaft lobe, then tighten the rocker arm bolt. Tighten in 2 steps, first to 62–132 inch lbs. (7–15 Nm) and finally to 19–25 ft. lbs. (25–35 Nm).

9. Clean the rocker arm cover and cylinder head mating surfaces of old gasket material and dirt.

10. Position a new gasket onto the cylinder head. install the rocker arm cover and the mounting bolts. Note the location of the spark plug wire routing clip stud bolts. Tighten the bolts to 80–106 inch lbs. (9–12 Nm).

11. Install the remaining components in the reverse order of their removal.

Thermostat

REMOVAL & INSTALLATION

✻✻ CAUTION

When draining the coolant, keep in mind that cats and dogs are attracted by the ethylene glycol antifreeze, and are quite likely to drink any that is left in an uncovered container or in puddles on the ground. This will prove fatal in sufficient quantity. Always drain the coolant into a sealable container. Coolant should be reused unless it is contaminated or several years old.

2.5L Engine

➧ SEE FIG. 44

1. Disconnect the negative battery cable.

2. Position a suitable drain pan below the radiator. Remove the radiator cap and open the draincock. Drain the radiator to a corresponding level below the water outlet connection. Close the draincock.

3. Remove the vent plug from the water outlet connection.

4. Loosen the top hose clamp at the radiator, remove the water outlet connection retaining bolts, lift clear of the engine and remove the thermostat by pulling it out of the water outlet connection.

➡ **Do not pry the housing off.**

To install:

5. Make sure the water outlet connection and cylinder head mating surfaces are clean and free from gasket material. Make sure the water outlet connection pocket and air vent passage are clean and free from rust. Clean the vent plug and gasket.

6. Place the thermostat in position, fully inserted to compress the gasket and pressed

into the water outlet connection to secure. Install the water outlet connection to the cylinder head using a new gasket. Tighten the bolts to 12–18 ft. lbs. (16–24 Nm). Position the top hose to the radiator and tighten the clamps.

7. Refill the cooling system. Connect the negative battery cable. Start the engine and check for leaks. Check the coolant level and add as required.

3.0L Engine Except SHO

➧ SEE FIG. 45

1. Disconnect the negative battery cable.
2. Place a suitable drain pan under the radiator.
3. Remove the radiator cap and open the draincock. Drain the cooling system.
4. Remove the upper radiator hose from the thermostat housing.
5. Remove the 3 retaining bolts from the thermostat housing.
6. Remove the housing and the thermostat as an assembly.

To install:

7. Make sure all sealing surfaces are free of old gasket material.
8. Install the thermostat into the housing.
9. Position a new gasket onto the housing using the bolts as a holding device. Install the thermostat assembly and tighten the bolts to 9 ft. lbs. (12 Nm).
10. Install the upper radiator hose and tighten the clamp.
11. Fill and bleed the cooling system. Connect the negative battery cable, start the engine and check for coolant leaks. Check the coolant level and add as required.

3.0L SHO Engine

➧ SEE FIG. 47

1. Disconnect the negative battery cable.
2. Place a suitable drain pan below the radiator. Remove the radiator cap and open the draincock. Partially drain the cooling system and then close the draincock.
3. Remove the air cleaner tube.
4. Disconnect the hose from the water outlet tube.
5. Remove the 2 retaining nuts and remove the water outlet tube.
6. Remove the thermostat and seal from the water outlet housing.

To install:

7. Install the seal around the outer rim of the thermostat and install the thermostat into the water outlet housing. Align the jiggle valve of the thermostat with the upper bolt on the water outlet housing.
8. Install the water outlet tube. Tighten the 2 retaining nuts to 5–8 ft. lbs. (7–11 Nm).
9. Install the air cleaner tube.

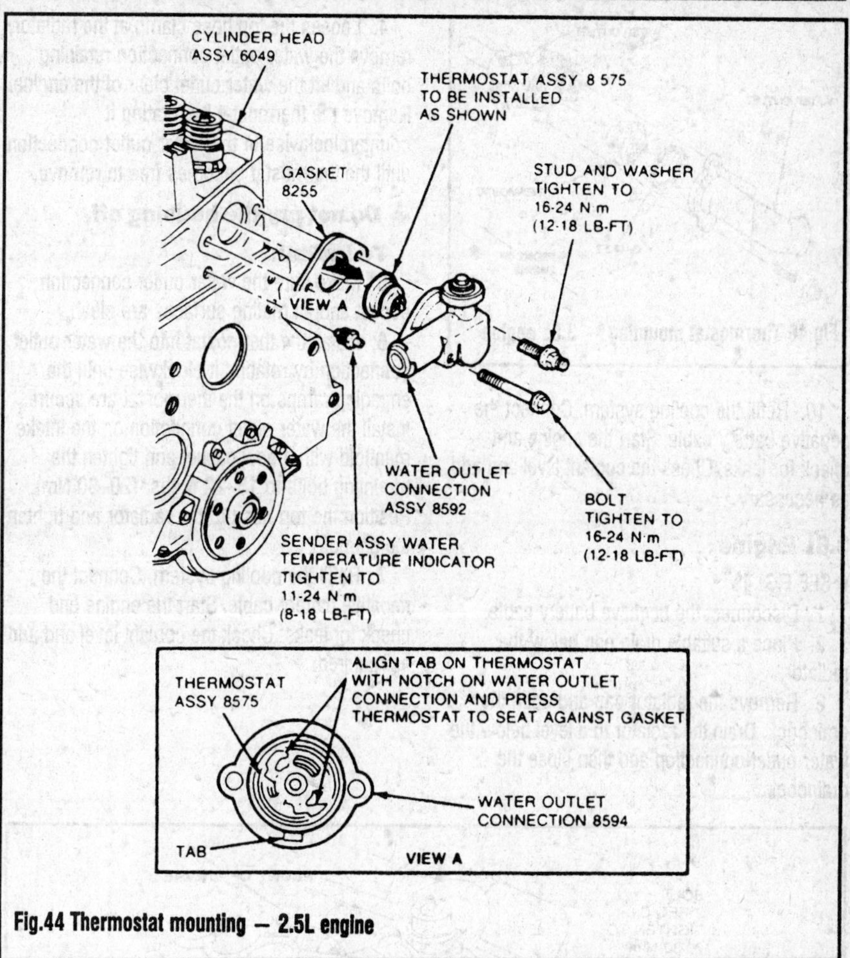

Fig.44 Thermostat mounting — 2.5L engine

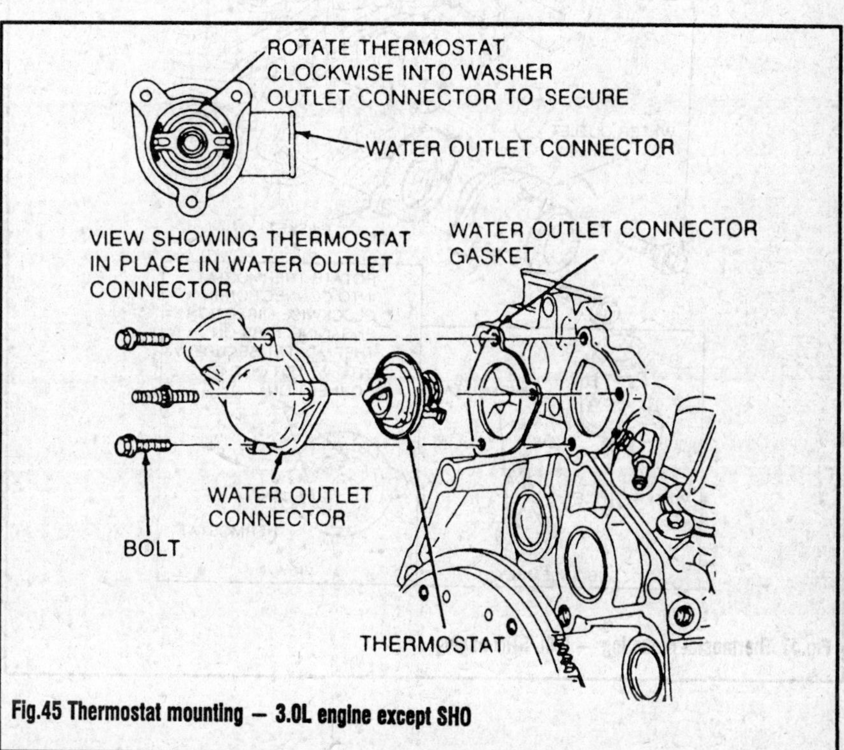

Fig.45 Thermostat mounting — 3.0L engine except SHO

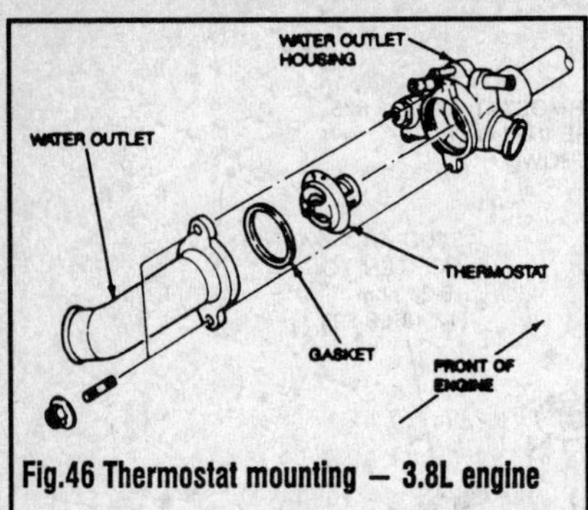

Fig.46 Thermostat mounting — 3.8L engine

10. Refill the cooling system. Connect the negative battery cable. Start the engine and check for leaks. Check the coolant level and add as necessary.

3.8L Engine

➧ SEE FIG. 46

1. Disconnect the negative battery cable.
2. Place a suitable drain pan below the radiator.
3. Remove the radiator cap and open the draincock. Drain the radiator to a level below the water outlet connection and then close the draincock.
4. Loosen the top hose clamp at the radiator, remove the water outlet connection retaining bolts and lift the water outlet clear of the engine. Remove the thermostat by rotating it counterclockwise in the water outlet connection until the thermostat becomes free to remove.

➡ Do not pry the housing off.

To Install:

5. Make sure the water outlet connection pocket and all mating surfaces are clean.
6. Install the thermostat into the water outlet connection by rotating it clockwise until the engaging ramps on the thermostat are secure. Install the water outlet connection on the intake manifold with a new gasket and tighten the mounting bolts to 15–22 ft. lbs. (20–30 Nm). Position the top hose to the radiator and tighten the clamps.
7. Refill the cooling system. Connect the negative battery cable. Start the engine and check for leaks. Check the coolant level and add as required.

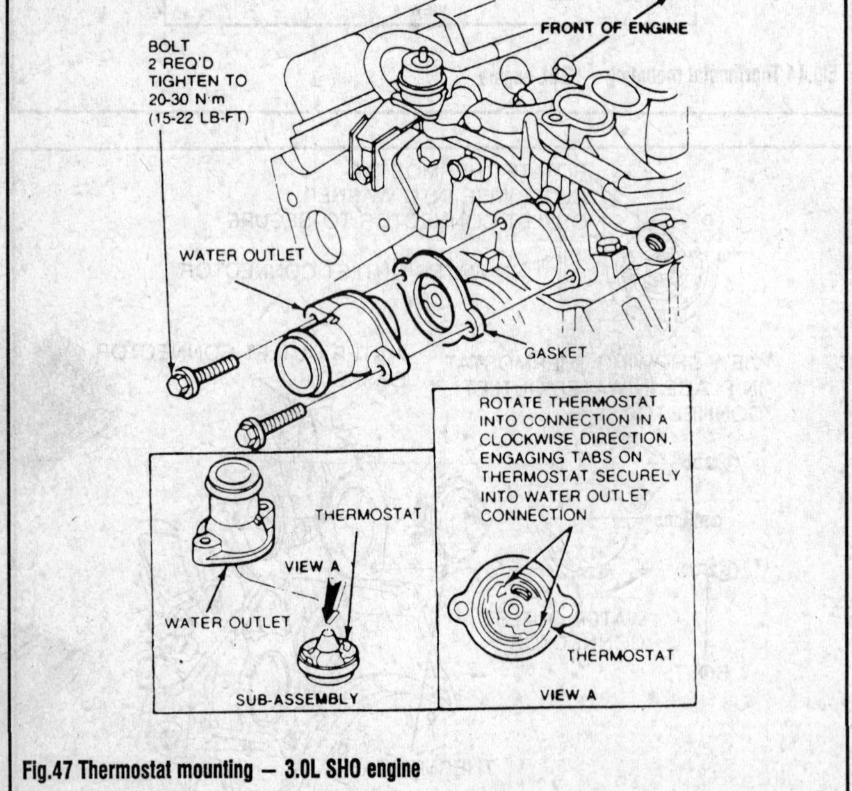

Fig.47 Thermostat mounting — 3.0L SHO engine

Cooling System Bleeding

✲✲ CAUTION

When draining the coolant, keep in mind that cats and dogs are attracted by the ethylene glycol antifreeze, and are quite likely to drink any that is left in an uncovered container or in puddles on the ground. This will prove fatal in sufficient quantity. Always drain the coolant into a sealable container. Coolant should be reused unless it is contaminated or several years old.

When the entire cooling system is drained, the following procedure should be used to ensure a complete fill.

1. Install the block drain plug, if removed and close the draincock. With the engine off, add anti-freeze to the radiator to a level of 50 percent of the total cooling system capacity. Then add water until it reaches the radiator filler neck seat.

➡ On 2.5L engine, remove the vent plug on the water connection outlet. The vent plug must be removed before the radiator is filled or the engine may not fill completely. Do not turn the plastic cap under the vent plug or the gasket may be damaged. Do not try to add coolant through the vent plug hole. Install the vent plug after filling the radiator and before starting the engine.

2. Install the radiator cap to the first notch to keep spillage to a minimum.
3. Start the engine and let it idle until the upper radiator hose is warm. This indicates that the thermostat is open and coolant is flowing through the entire system.
4. Carefully remove the radiator cap and top off the radiator with water. Install the cap on the radiator securely.
5. Fill the coolant recovery reservoir to the FULL COLD mark with anti-freeze, then add water to the FULL HOT mark. This will ensure that a proper mixture is in the coolant recovery bottle.
6. Check for leaks at the draincock, block plug and at the vent plug on 2.5L engine.

Intake Manifold

REMOVAL & INSTALLATION

CAUTION

When draining the coolant, keep in mind that cats and dogs are attracted by the ethylene glycol antifreeze, and are quite likely to drink any that is left in an uncovered container or in puddles on the ground. This will prove fatal in sufficient quantity. Always drain the coolant into a sealable container. Coolant should be reused unless it is contaminated or several years old.

2.5L Engine

➧ SEE FIG. 48

1. Open and secure the hood.
2. Disconnect the negative battery cable. Properly relieve the fuel system pressure.
3. Drain the cooling system.
4. Remove accelerator cable and the cruise control cable, if equipped.
5. Remove air cleaner assembly and heat stove tube at heat shield.
6. Remove required vacuum lines and electrical connections.
7. As required on vehicles before 1990, disconnect the thermactor check valve hose at the tube assembly and remove the bracket to EGR valve attaching nuts.
8. Disconnect the fuel supply and return lines.
9. As required on vehicles before 1990, disconnect the water inlet tube at the intake manifold. On 1991–92 vehicles, remove the exhaust manifold heat shroud assembly.
10. Disconnect EGR tube at EGR valve.
11. Remove the intake manifold retaining bolts. Remove the intake manifold. Remove the gasket and clean the gasket contact surfaces.

To install:

12. Install intake manifold with gasket and retaining bolts. Tighten the retaining bolts to 15–22 ft. lbs. (20–30 Nm) in the proper sequence.
13. As required on vehicles before 1990, connect water inlet tube at intake manifold, connect thermactor check valve hose at tube assembly and install bracket to EGR valve attaching nuts.
14. Connect EGR tube to EGR valve.
15. Connect the fuel supply and return lines.
16. Install vacuum lines and connect electrical connectors.
17. On 1991–92 vehicles, install the heat shroud.
18. Install air cleaner assembly and heat stove tube.
19. Install accelerator cable and cruise control cable, if equipped.
20. Connect negative battery cable and fill the cooling system.
21. Start engine and check for leaks.

3.0L Except SHO Engine

➧ SEE FIG. 49–50

1. Disconnect the negative battery cable and drain the engine cooling system. Relieve the fuel system pressure.
2. Loosen the hose clamp attaching the flex hose to the throttle body. Remove the air cleaner flex hose.
3. Identify, tag and disconnect and all vacuum connections to the throttle body.

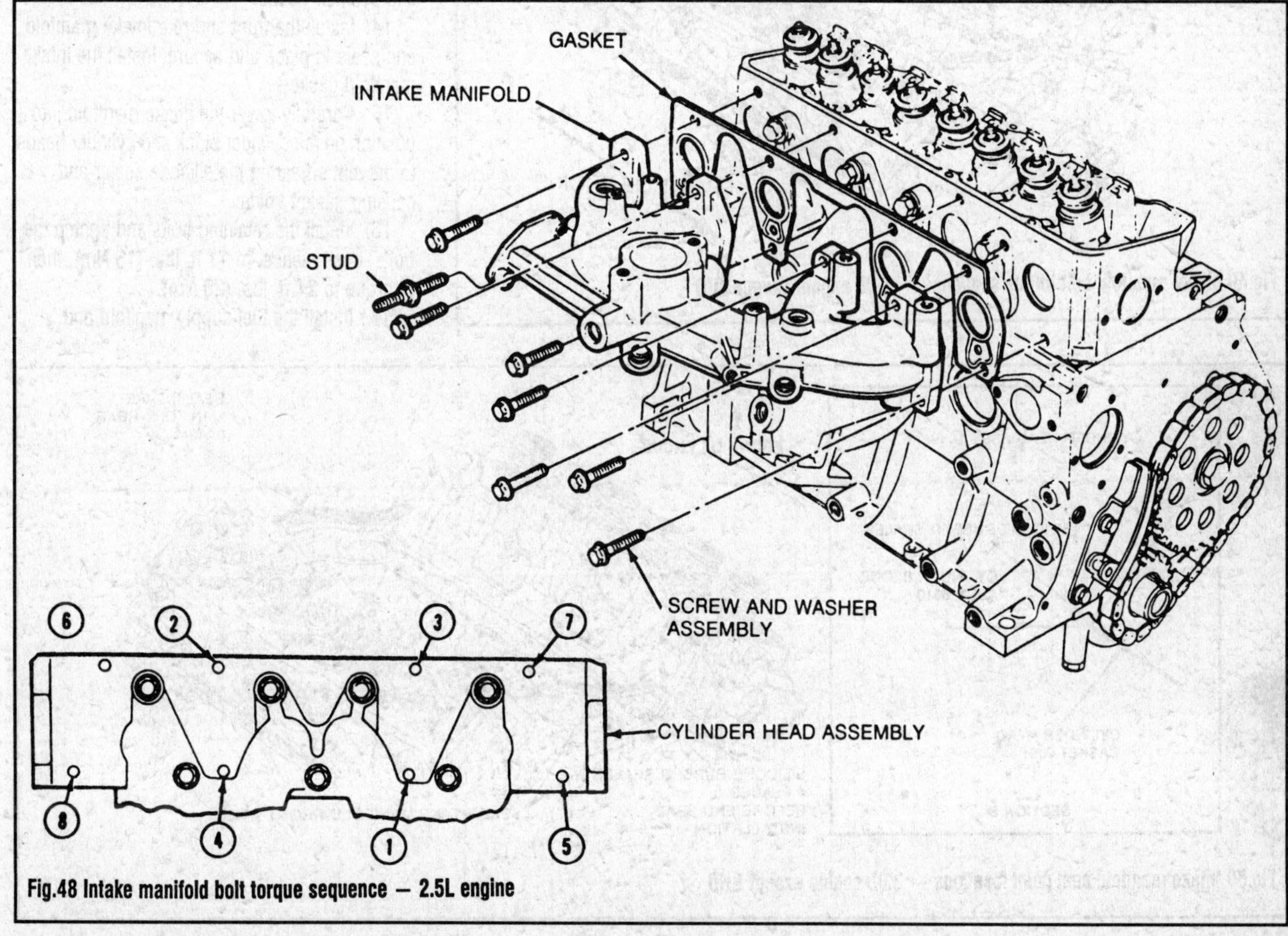

Fig.48 Intake manifold bolt torque sequence — 2.5L engine

4. Loosen the lower EGR tube nut and rotate the tube away from the valve. Disconnect the throttle and TV cable from the throttle linkage.

5. Disconnect the throttle position sensor, air charge temperature sensor and idle speed control electrical connectors.

6. Disconnect the PCV hose and disconnect the alternator support brace. Remove the throttle body retaining bolts and the throttle body.

7. Disconnect the fuel lines. Remove the fuel injection wiring harness from the engine. Remove the fuel supply manifold and injectors.

8. Disconnect and tag the spark plug wires and remove the rocker arm covers.

9. Disconnect the upper radiator hose and heater hoses. Mark the position of the distributor housing and rotor and remove the distributor assembly.

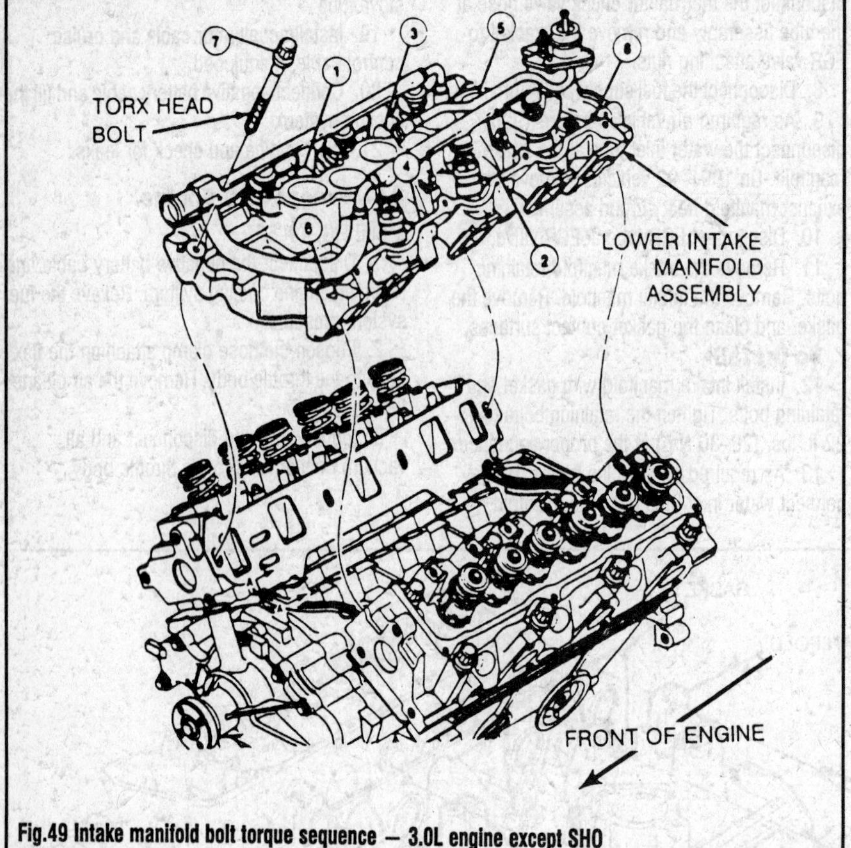

Fig.49 Intake manifold bolt torque sequence — 3.0L engine except SHO

10. Disconnect the engine coolant temperature sensor and temperature sending unit connector. Loosen the intake valve retaining bolt from cylinder No. 3 and rotate the rocker arm from the retainer and remove the pushrod.

11. Remove the intake manifold attaching bolts. Use a suitable prybar to loosen the intake manifold. Remove the manifold and old gaskets and seals.

To install:

➡ Lightly oil all the attaching bolts and stud threads before installation. When using a silicone rubber sealer, assembly must occur within 15 minutes after the sealer has been applied. After this time, the sealer may start to set-up and its sealing quality may be reduced. In high temperature/humidity conditions, the sealant will start to set up in approximately 5 minutes.

12. The intake manifold, cylinder head and cylinder block mating surfaces should be clean and free of old silicone rubber sealer. Use a suitable solvent to clean these surfaces.

13. Apply a suitable silicone rubber sealer to the intersection of the cylinder block end rails and cylinder heads.

14. Install the front and rear intake manifold end seals in place and secure. Install the intake manifold gaskets.

15. Carefully lower the intake manifold into position on the cylinder block and cylinder heads to prevent smearing the silicone sealer and causing gasket voids.

16. Install the retaining bolts and tighten the bolts, in sequence, to 11 ft. lbs. (15 Nm), then retorque to 21 ft. lbs. (28 Nm).

17. Install the fuel supply manifold and

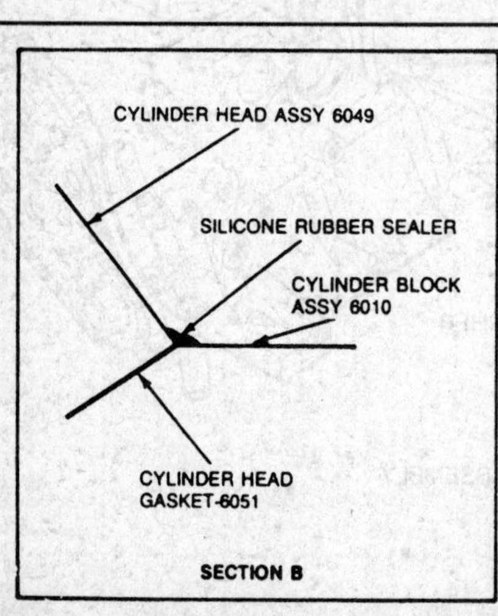

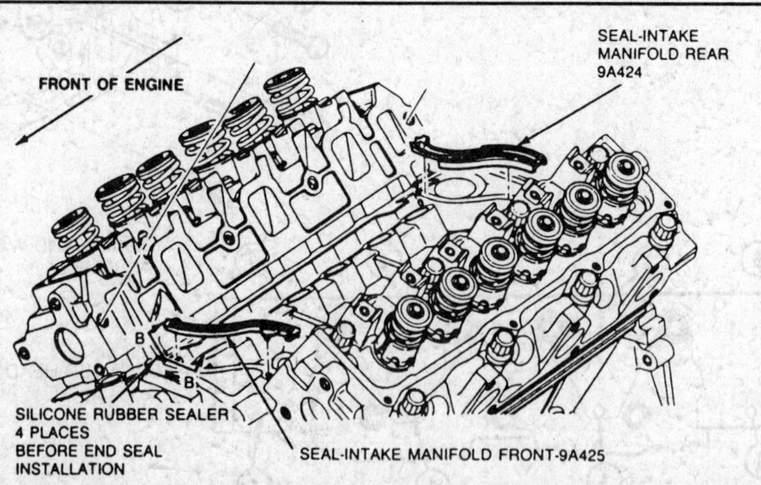

Fig.50 Intake manifold seal point locations — 3.0L engine except SHO

injectors. Apply lubricant to the injector holes in the intake manifold and fuel supply manifold prior to injector installation. Install the fuel supply manifold retaining bolts and tighten to 7 ft. lbs. (10 Nm).

18. Install the thermostat housing and a new gasket, if removed. Tighten the retaining bolts to 9 ft. lbs. (12 Nm).

19. Install the No. 3 cylinder intake valve pushrod. Apply Lubriplate® or equivalent to the pushrod and valve stem prior to installation. Position the lifter on the base circle of the camshaft and tighten the rocker arm bolt in 2 steps, first to 8 ft. lbs. (11 Nm) and then to 24 ft. lbs. (32 Nm).

20. Install the rocker arm covers. Install the fuel injector harness and attach to the injectors.

21. Install the throttle body with new gaskets.

22. Connect the PCV line at the PCV valve. Connect all necessary electrical connections and vacuum lines.

23. Connect the EGR tube and the fuel lines.

24. Install the distributor assembly, aligning the marks that were made during the removal procedure.

25. Install the coil and bracket. Install the upper radiator and heater hose.

26. Install and connect the air cleaner assembly and outlet tube. Fill the cooling system.

27. Reconnect the negative battery cable, start the engine and check for coolant, fuel and oil leaks.

28. Check and if necessary, adjust the engine idle speed, transaxle throttle linkage and speed control.

3.0L SHO Engine

➧ SEE FIG. 51

1. Disconnect the negative battery cable. Properly relieve the fuel system pressure.

2. Partially drain the engine cooling system.

3. Disconnect all electrical connectors and vacuum lines from the intake assembly.

4. Remove the air cleaner tube.

5. Disconnect the coolant lines and cables from the throttle body.

6. Remove the bolts retaining the upper intake brackets.

7. Loosen the lower bolts and remove the brackets.

8. Remove the bolts retaining the intake to the cylinder heads.

9. Remove the intake assembly and the gaskets.

10. Installation is the reverse of the removal procedure.

11. Lightly oil the attaching bolts and stud threads before installation.

➡ The intake gasket is reusable.

12. Install the retaining bolts and tighten to 11–17 ft. lbs. (15–23 Nm).

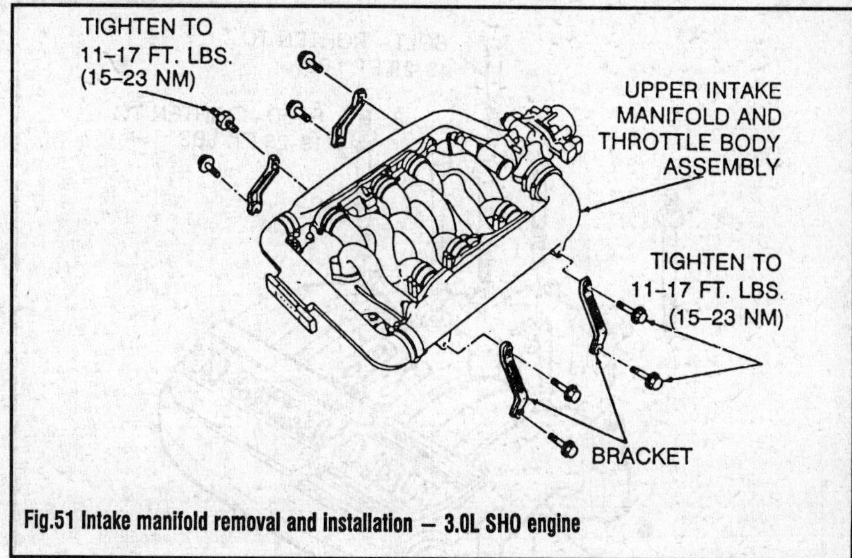

Fig.51 Intake manifold removal and installation — 3.0L SHO engine

3.8L Engine

➧ SEE FIG. 52

1. Disconnect the negative battery cable. Drain the cooling system.

2. Properly relieve the fuel system pressure. Remove the air cleaner assembly including air intake duct and heat tube.

3. Disconnect the accelerator cable at throttle body assembly. Disconnect speed control cable, if equipped.

4. Disconnect the transaxle linkage at the upper intake manifold.

5. Remove the attaching bolts from accelerator cable mounting bracket and position cables aside.

6. Disconnect the thermactor air supply hose at the check valve.

7. Disconnect the flexible fuel lines from steel lines over rocker arm cover.

8. Disconnect the fuel lines at injector fuel rail assembly.

9. Disconnect the radiator hose at thermostat housing connection.

10. Disconnect the coolant bypass hose at manifold connection.

11. Disconnect the heater tube at the intake manifold. Remove the heater tube support bracket attaching nut. Remove the heater hose at rear of heater tube. Loosen hose clamp at heater elbow and remove heater tube with hose attached. Remove heater tube with fuel lines attached and set the assembly aside.

12. Disconnect vacuum lines at fuel rail assembly and intake manifold.

13. Identify, tag and disconnect all necessary electrical connectors.

14. If equipped with air conditioning, remove the air compressor support bracket.

15. Disconnect the PCV lines. One is located on upper intake manifold. The second is located at the left rocker cover and the lower intake stud.

16. Remove the throttle body assembly and remove the EGR valve assembly from the upper manifold.

17. Remove the attaching nut and remove wiring retainer bracket located at the left front of the intake manifold and set aside with the spark plug wires.

18. Remove the upper intake manifold attaching bolts/studs. Remove the upper intake manifold.

19. Remove the injectors with fuel rail assembly.

20. Remove the heater water outlet hose.

21. Remove the lower intake manifold attaching bolts/stud and remove the lower intake manifold. Remove the manifold side gaskets and end seals. Discard and replace with new.

➡ The manifold is sealed at each end with RTV-type sealer. To break the seal, it may be necessary to pry on the front of the manifold with a small or medium pry bar. If it is necessary to pry on the manifold, use care to prevent damage to the machined surfaces.

To install:

22. Lightly oil all attaching bolt and stud threads before installation.

➡ When using silicone rubber sealer, assembly must occur within 15 minutes after sealer application. After this time, the sealer may start to set-up and its sealing effectiveness may be reduced. The lower intake manifold, cylinder head and cylinder block mating surfaces should be clean and free of oil gasketing material. Use a suitable solvent to clean these surfaces.

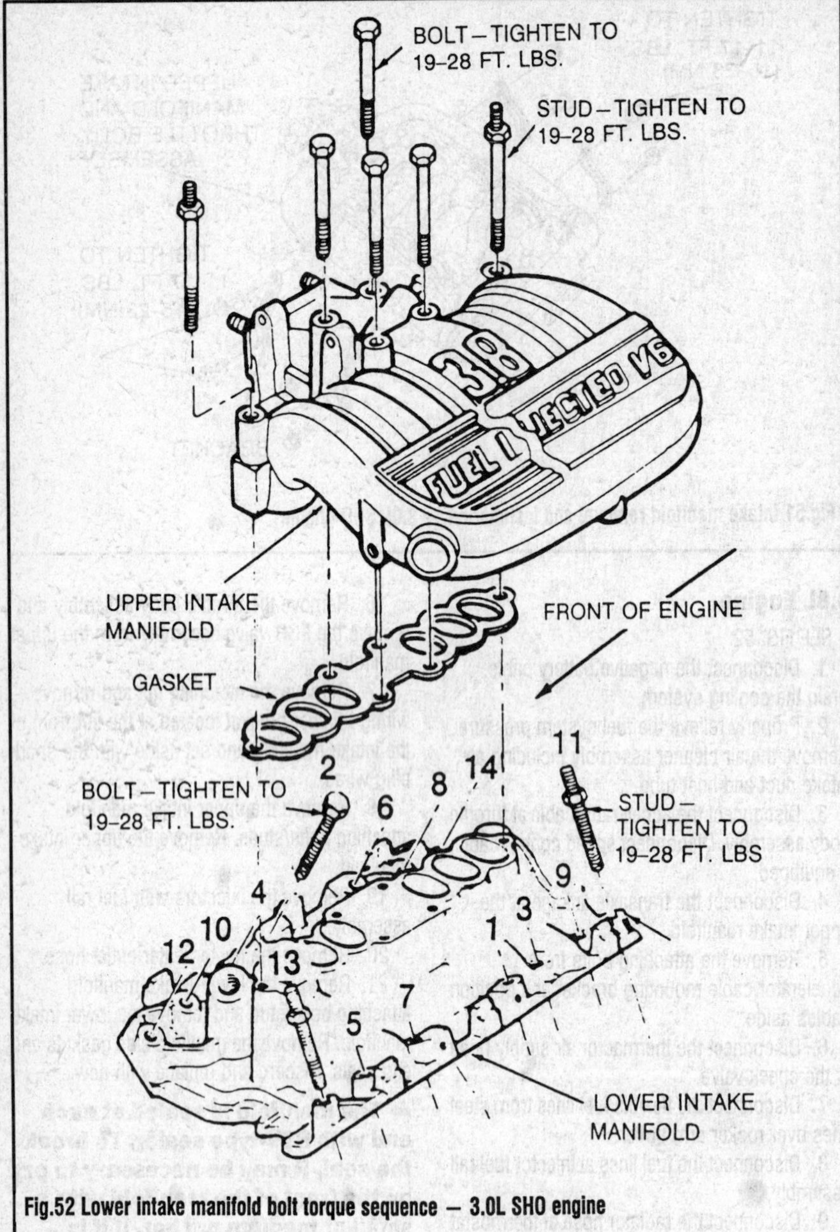

Fig.52 Lower intake manifold bolt torque sequence – 3.0L SHO engine

23. Apply a bead of contact adhesive to each cylinder head mating surface. Press the new intake manifold gaskets into place, using locating pins as necessary to aid in assembly alignment.

24. Apply a 1/8 in. (3mm) bead of silicone sealer at each corner where the cylinder head joins the cylinder block.

25. Install the front and rear intake manifold end seals.

26. Carefully lower the intake manifold into position on cylinder block and cylinder heads. Use locating pins as necessary to guide the manifold.

27. Install the retaining bolts and stud bolts in their original locations. Torque the retaining bolts in numerical sequence to the following specifications in 3 steps.

a. Step 1—8 ft. lbs. (10 Nm)
b. Step 2—15 ft. lbs. (20 Nm)
c. Step 3—24 ft. lbs. (32 Nm)

28. Connect the rear PCV line to upper intake tube and install the front PCV tube so the mounting bracket sits over the lower intake stud.

29. Install the injectors and fuel rail assembly. Tighten the screws to 6–8 ft. lbs. (8–11 Nm).

30. Position the upper intake gasket and manifold on top of the lower intake. Use locating pins to secure position of gasket between manifolds.

31. Install bolts and studs in their original locations. Tighten the 4 center bolts, then tighten the end bolts. Repeat Step 27.

32. Install the EGR valve assembly on the manifold. Tighten the attaching bolt to 15–22 ft. lbs. (20–30 Nm).

33. Install the throttle body. Cross-tighten the retaining nuts to 15–22 ft. lbs. (20–30 Nm).

34. Connect the rear PCV line at PCV valve and upper intake manifold connections. If equipped with air conditioning, install the compressor support bracket. Tighten attaching fasteners to 15–22 ft. lbs. (20–30 Nm).

35. Connect all electrical connectors and vacuum hoses.

36. Connect the heater tube hose to the heater elbow. Position the heater tube support bracket and tighten attaching nut to 15–22 ft. lbs. (20–30 Nm). Connect the heater hose to the rear of the heater tube and tighten hose clamp.

37. Connect coolant bypass and upper radiator hoses and secure with hose clamps.

38. Connect the fuel line(s) at injector fuel rail assembly and connect the flexible fuel lines to steel lines.

39. Position the accelerator cable mounting bracket and install and tighten attaching bolts to 15–22 ft. lbs. (20–30 Nm).

40. Connect the speed control cable, if equipped. Connect the transaxle linkage at upper intake manifold.

41. Fill the cooling system to the proper level.

42. Start the engine and check for coolant or fuel leaks.

43. Check and, if necessary, adjust engine idle speed, transaxle throttle linkage and speed control.

44. Install the air cleaner assembly and air intake duct.

Exhaust Manifold

REMOVAL & INSTALLATION

CAUTION

When draining the coolant, keep in mind that cats and dogs are attracted by the ethylene glycol antifreeze, and are quite likely to drink any that is left in an

uncovered container or in puddles on the ground. This will prove fatal in sufficient quantity. Always drain the coolant into a sealable container. Coolant should be reused unless it is contaminated or several years old.

2.5L Engine

➧ SEE FIG. 53

1. Open and secure the hood.
2. Disconnect the negative battery cable.
3. Drain the cooling system.
4. Remove the accelerator cable and the cruise control cable, if equipped.
5. Remove air cleaner assembly and heat stove tube at heat shield.
6. Identify, tag and disconnect all necessary vacuum lines and electrical connections.
7. Disconnect the exhaust pipe-to-exhaust manifold retaining nuts.
8. Remove exhaust manifold heat shroud. Disconnect the oxygen sensor wire at the connector.
9. Disconnect the fuel supply and return lines.
10. As required on vehicles before 1990, disconnect the thermactor check valve hose at tube assembly, remove bracket-to-EGR valve attaching nuts and disconnect water inlet tube at intake manifold.
11. Disconnect EGR tube from the EGR valve.
12. Remove the intake manifold.
13. Remove the exhaust manifold retaining nuts. Remove the exhaust manifold from the vehicle.

To install:

14. Position exhaust manifold to the cylinder head using guide bolts in holes 2 and 3.
15. Install the remaining attaching bolts.
16. Tighten the attaching bolts until snug, then remove guide bolts and install attaching bolts in holes 2 and 3.
17. Tighten all exhaust manifold bolts to specification using the following tightening procedure: torque retaining bolts, in sequence, to 5–7 ft. lbs. (7–10 Nm), then retorque, in sequence, to 20–30 ft. lbs. (27–41 Nm).
18. Install the intake manifold gasket and bolts. Tighten the intake manifold retaining bolts to 15–23 ft. lbs. (20–30 Nm).
19. As required on vehicles before 1990, connect the water inlet tube at intake manifold, connect thermactor check valve hose at tube assembly and install bracket to EGR valve attaching nuts.
20. Connect the oxygen sensor wire.
21. Connect the EGR tube to EGR valve.
22. Install exhaust manifold studs.
23. Connect exhaust pipe to exhaust manifold.
24. Install vacuum lines and electrical connectors.
25. Install air cleaner assembly and heat stove tube.
26. Install accelerator cable and cruise control cable, if equipped.
27. Connect the negative battery cable.
28. Fill the cooling system.
29. Start engine and check for leaks.

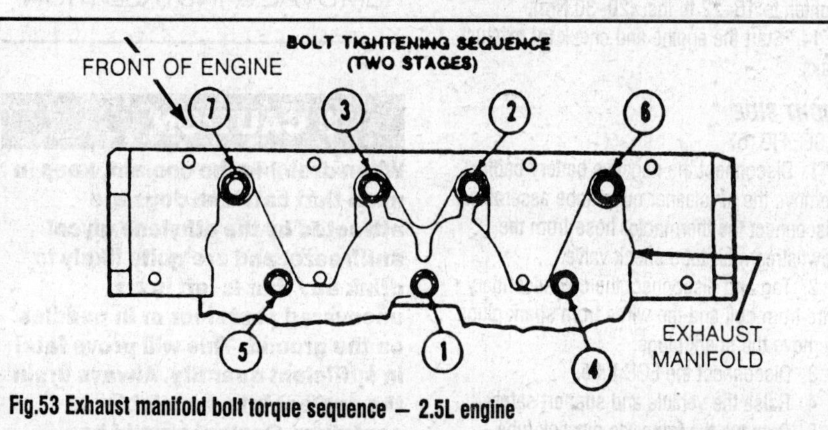

Fig.53 Exhaust manifold bolt torque sequence — 2.5L engine

3.0L Engine

LEFT SIDE

➧ SEE FIG. 54

1. Disconnect the negative battery cable. Remove the oil level indicator support bracket.
2. On 1986–89 vehicles, remove the power steering pump pressure and return hoses.
3. Raise and safely support the vehicle. Remove the manifold-to-exhaust pipe retaining nuts.
4. Lower the vehicle. Remove the exhaust manifold attaching bolts and the manifold.
5. Installation is the reverse of the removal procedure. Clean all mating surfaces and lightly oil all bolt and stud threads prior to installation. Tighten the exhaust manifold retaining bolts to 19 ft. lbs. (25 Nm) and tighten the exhaust pipe attaching nuts to 30 ft. lbs. (41 Nm).

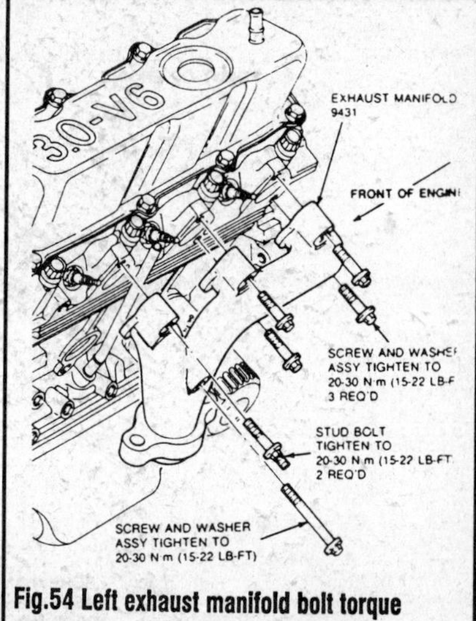

Fig.54 Left exhaust manifold bolt torque sequence — 3.0L engine except SHO

RIGHT SIDE

➧ SEE FIG. 55

1. Disconnect the negative battery cable. Remove the heater hose support bracket.
2. Disconnect and plug the heater hoses. Remove the EGR tube from the exhaust manifold. Use a back-up wrench on the lower adapter.
3. Raise the vehicle and support it safely. Remove the manifold-to-exhaust pipe attaching nuts and remove the pipe from the manifold.
4. Lower the vehicle. Remove the exhaust manifold attaching bolts and remove the exhaust manifold from the vehicle.
5. Installation is the reverse of the removal procedure. Clean all mating surfaces and lightly oil all bolt and stud threads prior to installation. Tighten the exhaust manifold retaining bolts to 19 ft. lbs. (25 Nm) and tighten the exhaust pipe attaching nuts to 30 ft. lbs. (41 Nm). Tighten the EGR tube to the exhaust manifold to 31 ft. lbs. (42 Nm).

3.0L SHO Engine

LEFT SIDE

1. Disconnect the negative battery cable.
2. Remove the oil level indicator tube support bracket.
3. Remove the power steering pump pressure and return hoses.
4. Remove the manifold to exhaust pipe attaching nuts.
5. Remove the heat shield retaining bolts.
6. Remove the exhaust manifold retaining nuts and manifold.
7. Installation is the reverse of the removal procedure. Clean all mating surfaces and lightly oil all bolt and stud threads before installation. Tighten the manifold retaining nuts to 26–38 ft.

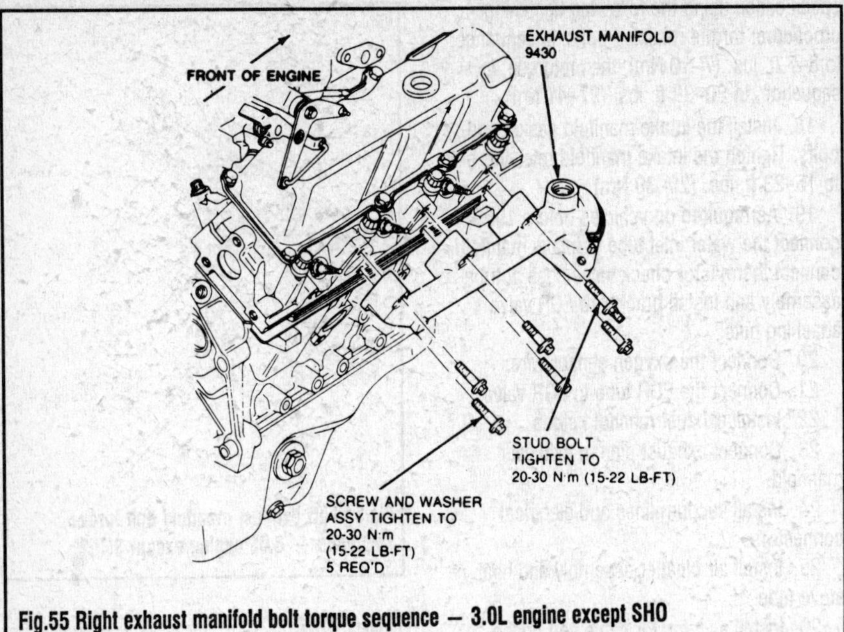

Fig.55 Right exhaust manifold bolt torque sequence — 3.0L engine except SHO

lbs. (35–52 Nm), the heat shield retaining bolts to 11–17 ft. lbs. (15–23 Nm) and the exhaust pipe to manifold nuts to 16–24 ft. lbs. (21–32 Nm).

RIGHT SIDE

1. Disconnect the negative battery cable.
2. Remove the right cylinder head.
3. Remove the heat shield retaining bolts.
4. Remove the exhaust manifold retaining nuts and manifold.
5. Installation is the reverse of the removal procedure. Clean all mating surfaces and lightly oil all bolt and stud threads prior to installation. Tighten the manifold retaining nuts to 26–38 ft. lbs. (35–52 Nm). Tighten the heat shield retaining bolts to 11–17 ft. lbs. (15–23 Nm).

3.8L Engine

LEFT SIDE

➧ SEE FIG. 56

1. Disconnect the negative battery cable. Remove the oil level dipstick tube support bracket.
2. Tag and disconnect the spark plug wires.
3. Raise the vehicle and support safely.
4. Remove the manifold-to-exhuast pipe attaching nuts.
5. Lower the vehicle.
6. Remove the exhaust manifold retaining bolts and remove the manifold from vehicle.

To install:

7. Lightly oil all bolt and stud threads before installation. Clean the mating surfaces on the exhaust manifold, cylinder head and exhaust pipe.
8. Position the exhaust manifold on the cylinder head. Install the lower front bolt hole on No. 5 cylinder as a pilot bolt.
9. Install the remaining manifold retaining bolts. Tighten the bolts 15–22 ft. lbs. (20–30 Nm).

➡ A slight warpage in the exhaust manifold may cause a misalignment between the bolt holes in the head and the manifold. Elongate the holes in the exhaust manifold as necessary to correct the misalignment, if apparent. Do not elongate the pilot hole, the lower front bolt on No. 5 cylinder.

10. Raise the vehicle and support safely.
11. Connect the exhaust pipe to the manifold. Tighten the attaching nuts to 16–24 ft. lbs. (21–32 Nm).
12. Lower the vehicle.
13. Connect the spark plug wires. Install dipstick tube support bracket attaching nut. Tighten to 15–22 ft. lbs. (20–30 Nm).
14. Start the engine and check for exhaust leaks.

RIGHT SIDE

➧ SEE FIG. 57

1. Disconnect the negative battery cable. Remove the air cleaner outlet tube assembly. Disconnect the thermactor hose from the downstream air tube check valve.
2. Tag and disconnect the coil secondary wire from coil and the wires from spark plugs. Remove the spark plugs.
3. Disconnect the EGR tube.
4. Raise the vehicle and support safely.
5. Remove the transaxle dipstick tube. Remove the thermactor air tube by cutting the tube clamp at the underbody catalyst fitting with a suitable cutting tool.
6. Remove the manifold-to-exhaust pipe attaching nuts.
7. Lower the vehicle.
8. Remove the exhaust manifold retaining bolts and the exhaust manifold.

To install:

9. Lightly oil all bolt and stud threads before installation. Clean the mating surfaces on exhaust manifold cylinder head and exhaust pipe.
10. Position the inner half of the heat shroud, if equipped, and exhaust manifold on cylinder head. Start 2 attaching bolts to align the manifold with the cylinder head. Install the remaining retaining bolts and tighten to 15–22 ft. lbs. (20–30 Nm).
11. Raise the vehicle and support safely.
12. Connect the exhaust pipe to manifold. Tighten the attaching nuts to 16–24 ft. lbs. (21–32 Nm). Position the thermactor hose to the downstream air tube and clamp tube to the underbody catalyst fitting.
13. Install the transaxle dipstick tube and lower vehicle.
14. Install the outer heat shroud and tighten the retaining screws to 50–70 inch lbs. (5–8 Nm).
15. Install the spark plugs. Connect the wires to their respective spark plugs and connect coil secondary wire to coil.
16. Connect the EGR tube. Connect the thermactor hose to the downstream air tube and secure with clamp. Install the air cleaner outlet tube assembly.
17. Start the engine and check for exhaust leaks.

Radiator

REMOVAL & INSTALLATION

CAUTION

When draining the coolant, keep in mind that cats and dogs are attracted by the ethylene glycol antifreeze, and are quite likely to drink any that is left in an uncovered container or in puddles on the ground. This will prove fatal in sufficient quantity. Always drain the coolant into a sealable container. Coolant should be

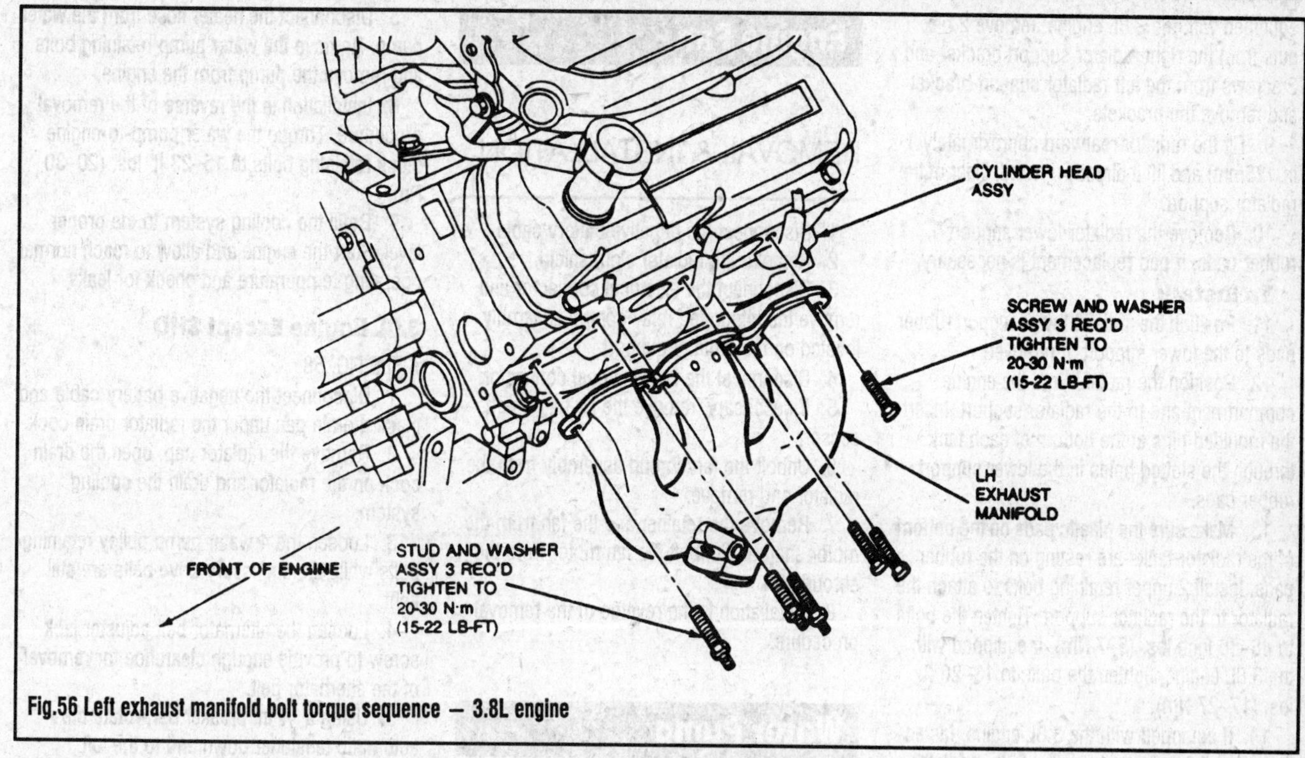

Fig.56 Left exhaust manifold bolt torque sequence — 3.8L engine

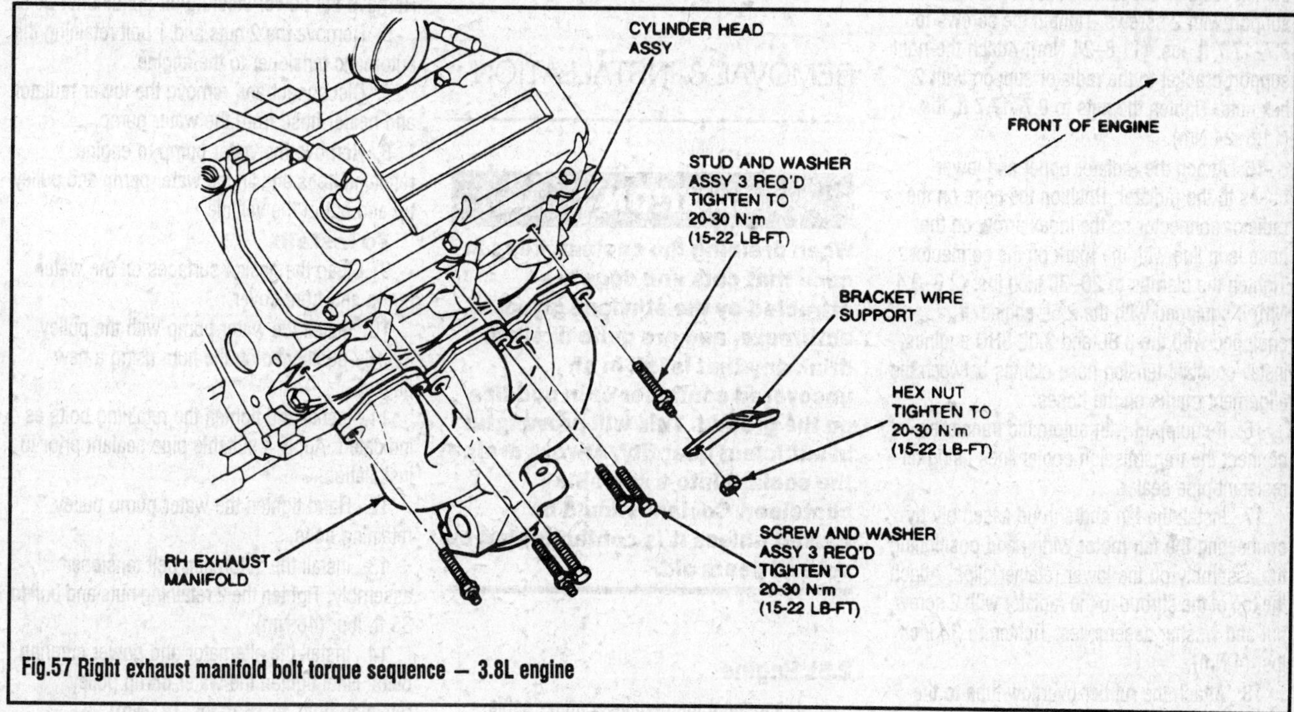

Fig.57 Right exhaust manifold bolt torque sequence — 3.8L engine

reused unless it is contaminated or several years old.

1. Disconnect the negative battery cable.
2. Drain the cooling system by removing the radiator cap and opening the draincock located at the lower rear corner of the radiator inlet tank.
3. Remove the rubber overflow tube from the coolant recovery bottle and detach it from the radiator. On Taurus SHO, disconnect the tube from the radiator and remove the recovery bottle.
4. Remove 2 upper shroud retaining screws and lift the shroud out of the lower retaining clips.
5. Disconnect the electric cooling fan motor wires and remove the fan and shroud assembly.
6. Loosen the upper and lower hose clamps at the radiator and remove the hoses from the radiator connectors.
7. If equipped with an automatic transaxle, disconnect the transmission oil cooling lines from the radiator fittings using disconnect tool T82L–9500–AH or equivalent.
8. If equipped with 3.0L and SHO engines, remove 2 radiator upper retaining screws. If

equipped with the 3.8L engine, remove 2 hex nuts from the right radiator support bracket and 2 screws from the left radiator support bracket and remove the brackets.

9. Tilt the radiator rearward approximately 1 in. (25mm) and lift it directly upward, clear of the radiator support.

10. Remove the radiator lower support rubber pads, if pad replacement is necessary.

To install:

11. Position the radiator lower support rubber pads to the lower support, if removed.

12. Position the radiator into the engine compartment and to the radiator support. Insert the moulded pins at the bottom of each tank through the slotted holes in the lower support rubber pads.

13. Make sure the plastic pads on the bottom of the radiator tanks are resting on the rubber pads. Install 2 upper retaining bolts to attach the radiator to the radiator support. Tighten the bolts to 46–60 inch lbs. (5–7 Nm). If equipped with the 3.8L engine, tighten the bolts to 13–20 ft. lbs. (17–27 Nm).

14. If equipped with the 3.8L engine, fasten the left radiator support bracket to the radiator support with 2 screws. Tighten the screws to 8.7–17.7 ft. lbs. (11.8–24 Nm). Attach the right support bracket to the radiator support with 2 hex nuts. Tighten the nuts to 8.7–17.7 ft. lbs. (11.8–24 Nm).

15. Attach the radiator upper and lower hoses to the radiator. Position the hose on the radiator connector so the index arrow on the hose is in line with the mark on the connector. Tighten the clamps to 20–30 inch lbs. (2.3–3.4 Nm) if equipped with the 2.5L engine. If equipped with the 3.8L and 3.0L SHO engines, install constant tension hose clamps between the alignment marks on the hoses.

16. If equipped with automatic transaxles, connect the transmission cooler lines using oil resistant pipe sealer.

17. Install the fan and shroud assembly by connecting the fan motor wiring and positioning the assembly on the lower retainer clips. Attach the top of the shroud to the radiator with 2 screw, nut and washer assemblies. Tighten to 35 inch lbs. (4 Nm).

18. Attach the rubber overflow tube to the radiator filler neck overflow nipple and coolant recovery bottle. On Taurus SHO, install the coolant recovery bottle and connect the overflow hose.

19. Refill the cooling system. If the coolant is being replaced, refill with a 50/50 mixture of water and anti-freeze. Connect the negative battery cable. Operate the engine for 15 minutes and check for leaks. Check the coolant level and add, as required.

Engine Fan

REMOVAL & INSTALLATION

1. Disconnect the negative battery cable.
2. Remove the radiator sight shield.
3. Disconnect the electrical connector and remove the integrated relay control assembly located on the radiator support.
4. Disconnect the fan electrical connector.
5. If necessary, remove the air bag crash sensor.
6. Unbolt the fan/shroud assembly from the radiator and remove.
7. Remove the retainer and the fan from the motor shaft and unbolt the fan motor from the shroud.
8. Installation is the reverse of the removal procedure.

Water Pump

REMOVAL & INSTALLATION

CAUTION

When draining the coolant, keep in mind that cats and dogs are attracted by the ethylene glycol antifreeze, and are quite likely to drink any that is left in an uncovered container or in puddles on the ground. This will prove fatal in sufficient quantity. Always drain the coolant into a sealable container. Coolant should be reused unless it is contaminated or several years old.

2.5L Engine

1. Disconnect the negative battery cable.
2. Remove the radiator cap and position a drain pan under the bottom radiator hose.
3. Raise and support the vehicle safely. Remove the lower radiator hose from the radiator and drain the coolant into the drain pan.
4. Remove the water pump inlet tube. Loosen the belt tensioner by inserting a 1/2 in. flex handle in the square hole of the tensioner and rotate the tensioner counterclockwise and remove the belt from the pulleys.
5. Disconnect the heater hose from the water pump. Remove the water pump retaining bolts and remove the pump from the engine.
6. Installation is the reverse of the removal procedure. Torque the water pump-to-engine block retaining bolts to 15–23 ft. lbs. (20–30 Nm).
7. Refill the cooling system to the proper level. Start the engine and allow to reach normal operating temperature and check for leaks.

3.0L Engine Except SHO

➧ SEE FIG. 58

1. Disconnect the negative battery cable and place a drain pan under the radiator drain cock.
2. Remove the radiator cap, open the drain cock on the radiator and drain the cooling system.
3. Loosen the 4 water pump pulley retaining bolts while the accessory drive belts are still tight.
4. Loosen the alternator belt adjuster jack screw to provide enough clearance for removal of the alternator belt.
5. Using a 1/2 in. breaker bar, rotate the automatic tensioner down and to the left. Remove the power steering/air conditioner belt.
6. Remove the 2 nuts and 1 bolt retaining the automatic tensioner to the engine.
7. Disconnect and remove the lower radiator and heater hose from the water pump.
8. Remove the water pump to engine retaining bolts and lift the water pump and pulley up and out of the vehicle.

To install:

9. Clean the gasket surfaces on the water pump and front cover.
10. Install the water pump with the pulley loosely positioned on the hub, using a new gasket.
11. Install and tighten the retaining bolts as indicated. Apply a suitable pipe sealant prior to installation.
12. Hand tighten the water pump pulley retaining bolts.
13. Install the automatic belt tensioner assembly. Tighten the 2 retaining nuts and bolt to 35 ft. lbs. (48 Nm).
14. Install the alternator and power steering belts. Final tighten the water pump pulley retaining bolts to 16 ft. lbs. (21 Nm).
15. Install the lower radiator and heater hoses. Fill and bleed the cooling system with the appropriate quantity and coolant type.
16. Connect the negative battery cable. Start the engine and check for leaks.

3.0L SHO Engine

1. Disconnect the battery cables and remove the battery and the battery tray.

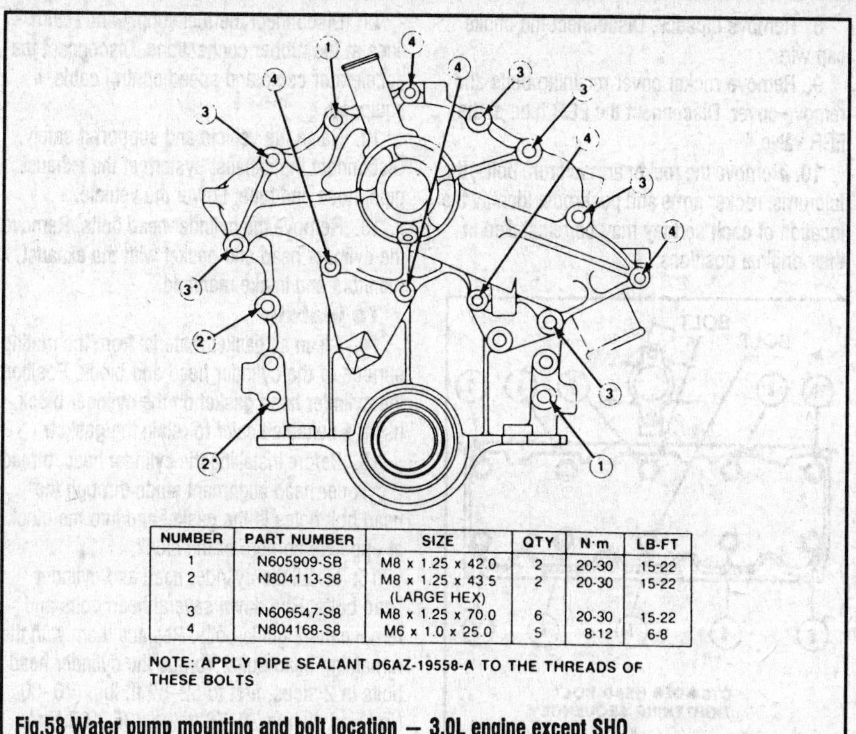

NUMBER	PART NUMBER	SIZE	QTY	N·m	LB-FT
1	N605909-SB	M8 x 1.25 x 42.0	2	20-30	15-22
2	N804113-S8	M8 x 1.25 x 43.5 (LARGE HEX)	2	20-30	15-22
3	N606547-S8	M8 x 1.25 x 70.0	6	20-30	15-22
4	N804168-S8	M6 x 1.0 x 25.0	5	8-12	6-8

NOTE: APPLY PIPE SEALANT D6AZ-19558-A TO THE THREADS OF THESE BOLTS

Fig.58 Water pump mounting and bolt location — 3.0L engine except SHO

2. Drain the cooling system and remove the accessory drive belts.
3. Remove the bolts retaining the air conditioning and alternator idler pulley and bracket assembly.
4. Disconnect the electrical connector from the ignition module and ground strap.
5. Loosen the clamps on the upper intake connector tube, remove the retaining bolts and remove the connector tube.
6. Raise and safely support the vehicle. Remove the right wheel and tire assembly.
7. Remove the splash shield.
8. Remove the upper timing belt cover, crankshaft pulley and lower timing belt cover.
9. Remove the bolts from the center timing belt cover and position it aside.
10. Remove the water pump attaching bolts and remove the water pump.
11. To install, reverse the removal procedure. Tighten the water pump bolts to 12–16 ft. lbs. (15–23 Nm). Tighten the crankshaft pulley bolt to 113–126 ft. lbs. (152–172 Nm).

3.8L Engine

➧ SEE FIG. 59

1. Disconnect the negative battery cable. Drain the cooling system.
2. Remove the lower nut on both right engine mounts. Raise and safely support the engine.
3. Loosen the accessory drive belt idler. Remove the drive belt and water pump pulley.
4. Remove the air suspension pump, if equipped.
5. Remove the power steering pump mounting bracket attaching bolts. Leaving hoses connected, place pump/bracket assembly aside in a position to prevent fluid from leaking out.
6. If equipped with air conditioning, remove the compressor front support bracket.
7. Leave the compressor in place, if removed.
8. Disconnect coolant bypass and heater hoses at the water pump.
9. Remove the water pump-to-engine block attaching bolts and remove the pump from the vehicle. Discard the gasket and replace with new.

To Install:

10. Lightly oil all bolt and stud threads before installation except those that require sealant. Thoroughly clean the water pump and front cover gasket contact surfaces.
11. Apply a coating of contact adhesive to both surfaces of the new gasket. Position a new gasket on water pump sealing surface.
12. Position water pump on the front cover and install attaching bolts.
13. Tighten the attaching bolts to 15–22 ft. lbs.
14. Connect the cooling bypass hose, heater hose and radiator lower hose to water pump and tighten the clamps.
15. If equipped with air conditioning, install compressor front support bracket.

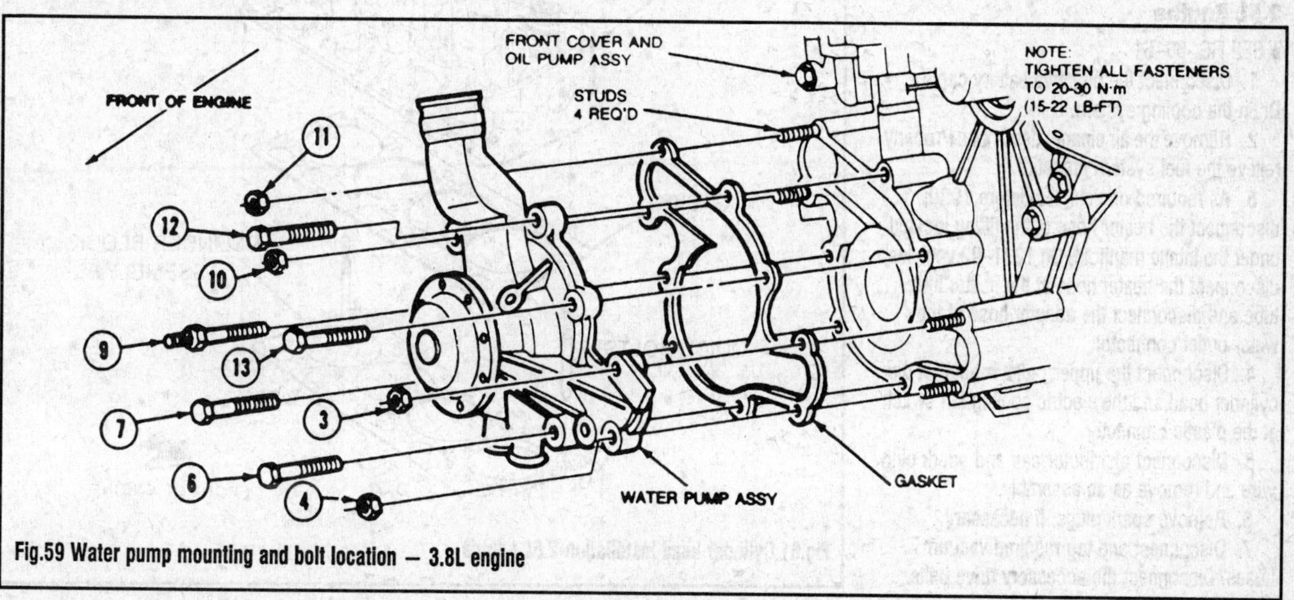

Fig.59 Water pump mounting and bolt location — 3.8L engine

16. Install the air suspension pump, if equipped.
17. Position the accessory drive belt over the pulleys.
18. Install the water pump pulley, fan/clutch assembly and fan shroud. Cross-tighten fan/clutch assembly attaching bolts to 12–18 ft. lbs.
19. Position accessory drive belt over pump pulley and adjust drive belt tension.
20. Lower the engine.
21. Install and tighten the lower right engine mount nuts.
22. Fill cooling system to the proper level.
23. Start engine and check for coolant leaks.

Cylinder Head

REMOVAL & INSTALLATION

CAUTION

When draining the coolant, keep in mind that cats and dogs are attracted by the ethylene glycol antifreeze, and are quite likely to drink any that is left in an uncovered container or in puddles on the ground. This will prove fatal in sufficient quantity. Always drain the coolant into a sealable container. Coolant should be reused unless it is contaminated or several years old.

2.5L Engine

SEE FIG. 60–61

1. Disconnect the negative battery cable. Drain the cooling system.
2. Remove the air cleaner assembly. Properly relieve the fuel system pressure.
3. As required on vehicles before 1990, disconnect the heater hose at the fitting located under the intake manifold. On 1991–92 vehicles, disconnect the heater hose at the heater inlet tube and disconnect the adapter hose at the water outlet connector.
4. Disconnect the upper radiator hose at the cylinder head and the electric cooling fan switch at the plastic connector.
5. Disconnect distributor cap and spark plug wire and remove as an assembly.
6. Remove spark plugs, if necessary.
7. Disconnect and tag required vacuum hoses. Disconnect the accessory drive belts.
8. Remove dipstick. Disconnect the choke cap wire.
9. Remove rocker cover retaining bolts and remove cover. Disconnect the EGR tube at the EGR valve.
10. Remove the rocker arm fulcrum bolts, the fulcrums, rocker arms and pushrods. Identify the location of each so they may be reinstalled in their original positions.

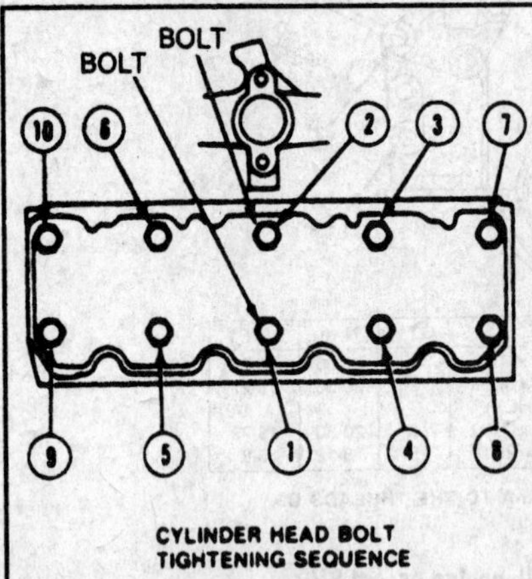

Fig.60 Cylinder head bolt torque sequence — 2.5L engine

11. Disconnect the fuel supply and return lines at the rubber connections. Disconnect the accelerator cable and speed control cable, if equipped.
12. Raise the vehicle and support it safely. Disconnect the exhaust system at the exhaust pipe, hose and tube. Lower the vehicle.
13. Remove the cylinder head bolts. Remove the cylinder head and gasket with the exhaust manifold and intake manifold.

To install:

14. Clean all gasket material from the mating surface of the cylinder head and block. Position the cylinder head gasket on the cylinder block, using a suitable sealer to retain the gasket.
15. Before installing the cylinder head, thread 2 cylinder head alignment studs through the head bolt holes in the gasket and into the block at opposite corners of the block.
16. Install the cylinder head and cylinder head bolts. Run down several head bolts and remove the 2 guide bolts. Replace them with the remaining head bolts. Torque the cylinder head bolts in 2 steps, first to 52–59 ft. lbs. (70–80 Nm) and then to 70–76 ft. lbs. (95–103 Nm).
17. Raise and support the vehicle safely. Connect the exhaust system at the exhaust pipe and hose to metal tube.

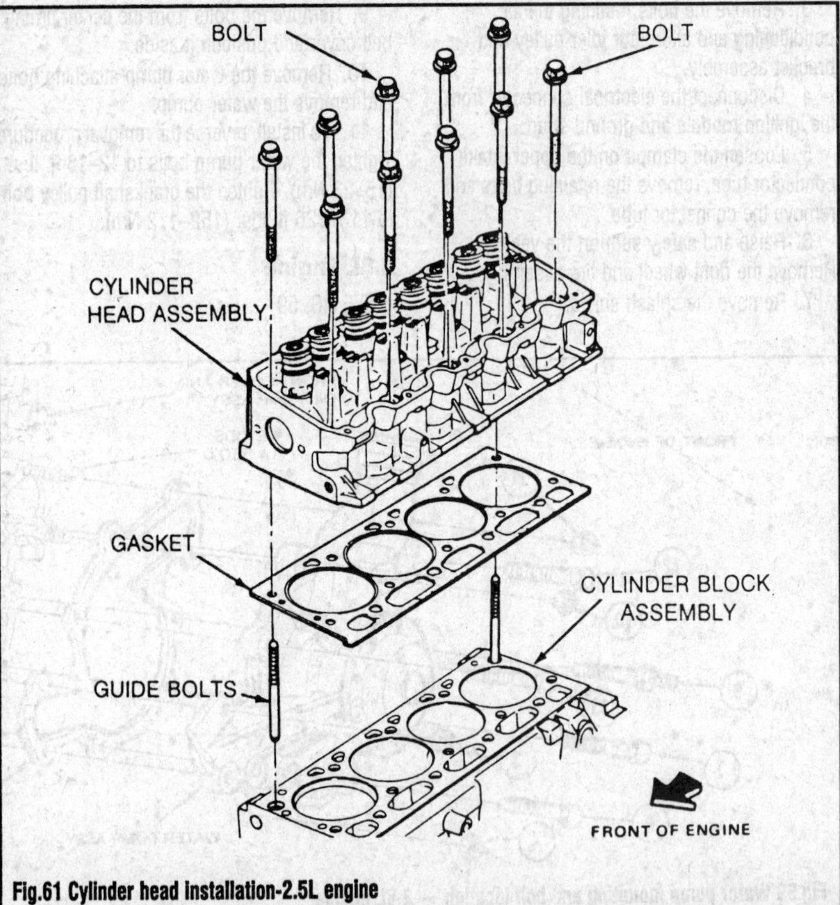

Fig.61 Cylinder head installation-2.5L engine

18. Lower the vehicle. Install the thermactor pump drive belt, if equipped. Connect the accelerator cable and speed control cable, if equipped.

19. Connect the fuel supply and return lines. Connect the choke cap wire, if equipped.

20. Install the pushrods, rocker arms, fulcrums and fulcrum bolts in their original positions. Install the rocker arm cover.

21. Connect the EGR tube at the EGR valve. Install the distributor cap and spark plug wires as an assembly. Install the spark plugs, if removed.

22. Connect all accessory drive belts.

23. Connect the required vacuum hoses. Install the air cleaner assembly. Connect the electric cooling fan switch at the connector.

24. Connect the upper radiator hose and the heater hose. Fill the cooling system. Connect the negative battery cable.

25. Start the engine and check for leaks. After the engine has reached normal operating temperature, check and if necessary add coolant.

3.0L Except SHO Engine

➧ SEE FIG. 62

1. Disconnect the negative battery cable. Properly relieve the fuel system pressure. Drain the cooling system. Remove the air cleaner assembly.

2. Loosen the accessory drive belt idler pulley, remove the drive belt.

3. If the left cylinder head is being removed, perform the following:

a. Disconnect the alternator electrical connectors.

b. Rotate the tensioner clockwise and remove the accessory drive belt.

c. Remove the automatic belt tensioner assembly.

d. Remove the alternator.

e. Remove the power steering mounting bracket retaining bolts. Leave the hoses connected and place the pump aside in a position to prevent fluid from leaking out.

f. Remove the engine oil dipstick tube from the exhaust manifold.

4. If the right head is being removed, perform the following:

a. Remove the alternator belt tensioner bracket.

b. Remove the heater supply tube retaining brackets from the exhaust manifold.

c. Remove the vehicle speed sensor cable retaining bolt and the EGR vacuum regulator sensor and bracket.

5. Remove the exhaust manifolds from both heads. Remove the PCV and the rocker arm covers. Loosen the rocker arm fulcrum attaching bolts enough to allow the rocker arm to be lifted off the pushrod and rotated to one side.

6. Remove the pushrods. Be sure to identify and label the position of each pushrod. The rods should be installed in their original position during reassembly.

7. Remove the intake manifold.

8. Remove the cylinder head attaching bolts and remove the cylinder heads from the engine. Remove and discard the old cylinder head gaskets.

To Install:

9. Lightly oil all bolt and stud bolt threads before installation. Clean the cylinder head, intake manifold, rocker arm cover and cylinder head gasket contact surfaces. If the cylinder head was removed for a cylinder head gasket replacement, check the flatness of the cylinder head and block gasket surfaces.

➡ If the flat surface of the cylinder head is warped, do not plane or grind off more than 0.010 in. (0.25mm). If the head is machined past its resurface limit, the head will have to be replaced with a new one.

10. Position new head gaskets on the cylinder block using the dowels in the engine block for alignment. If the dowels are damaged, they must be replaced.

11. Position the cylinder head on the cylinder block. Tighten the cylinder head attaching bolts in 2 steps following the proper torque sequence. The first step is 37 ft. lbs. (50 Nm) and the second step is 68 ft. lbs. (92 Nm).

➡ When cylinder head attaching bolts have been tightened using the above procedure, it is not necessary to retighten the bolts after extended engine operation. The bolts can be rechecked for tightness if desired.

12. Install the intake manifold. Connect the coolant temperature sending unit connectors.

13. Dip each pushrod end in oil conditioner or

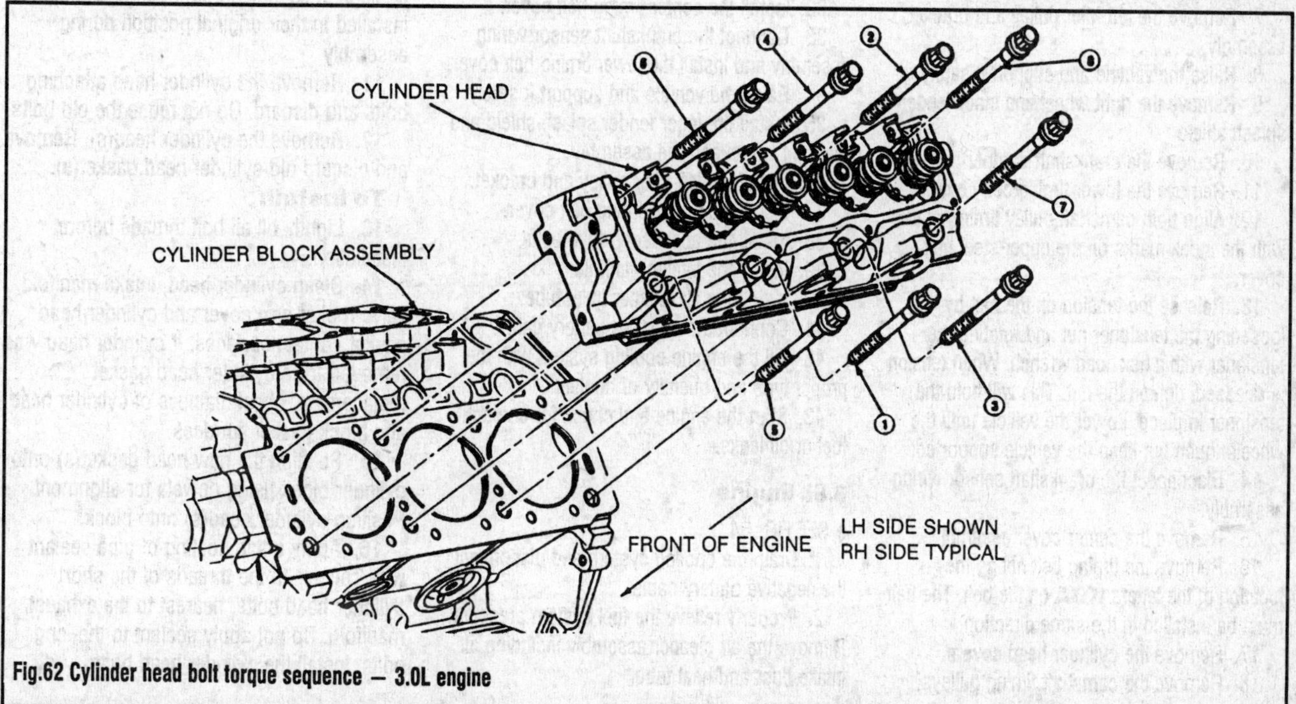

Fig.62 Cylinder head bolt torque sequence — 3.0L engine

heavy engine oil. Install the pushrods in their original position.

14. Before installation, coat the valve tips, rocker arm and fulcrum contact areas with Lubriplate® or equivalent. Lightly oil all the bolt and stud threads before installation.

15. Rotate the engine until the lifter is on the base circle of the cam (valve closed).

16. Install the rocker arm and components and torque the rocker arm fulcrum bolts to 24 ft. lbs. (32 Nm). Be sure the lifter is on the base circle of the cam for each rocker arm as it is installed.

➡ **The fulcrums must be fully seated in the cylinder head and the pushrods must be seated in the rocker arm sockets prior to the final tightening.**

17. Install the exhaust manifolds, the oil dipstick tube. Install the remaining components by reversing the removal procedure.

18. Start the engine and check for leaks.

19. Check and if necessary, adjust the transaxle throttle linkage and speed control. Install the air cleaner outlet tube duct.

3.0L SHO Engine

➧ SEE FIG. 63

1. Disconnect the negative battery cable.
2. Drain the cooling system. Properly relieve the fuel system pressure.
3. Remove the air cleaner outlet tube.
4. Remove the intake manifold.
5. Loosen the accessory drive belt idlers and remove the drive belts.
6. Remove the upper timing belt cover.
7. Remove the left idler pulley and bracket assembly.
8. Raise the vehicle and support it safely.
9. Remove the right wheel and inner fender splash shield.
10. Remove the crankshaft damper pulley.
11. Remove the lower timing belt cover.
12. Align both camshaft pulley timing marks with the index marks on the upper steel belt cover.
13. Release the tension on the belt by loosening the tensioner nut and rotating the tensioner with a hex head wrench. When tension is released, tighten the nut. This will hold the tensioner in place. Lower the vehicle until the wheels touch but keep the vehicle supported.
14. Disconnect the crankshaft sensor wiring assembly.
15. Remove the center cover assembly.
16. Remove the timing belt noting the location of the letters **KOA** on the belt. The belt must be installed in the same direction.
17. Remove the cylinder head covers.
18. Remove the camshaft timing pulleys.
19. Remove the upper rear and the center rear timing belt covers.
20. If the left cylinder head is being removed, remove the DIS coil bracket and the oil dipstick tube. If the right cylinder head is being removed, remove the coolant outlet hose.
21. Remove the exhaust manifold on the left cylinder head. On the right cylinder head the exhaust manifold must be removed with the head.
22. Remove the cylinder head to block retaining bolts.
23. Remove the cylinder head.

To install:

➡ **Lightly oil all bolt and stud bolt threads before installation except those specifying special sealant.**

24. Clean the cylinder head and engine block mating surfaces of all gasket material.
25. Position the cylinder head and gasket on the engine block and align with the dowel pins.
26. Install the cylinder head bolts and tighten, in sequence, in 2 steps, the first to 37–50 ft. lbs. (49–69 Nm) and finally to 62–68 ft. lbs. (83–93 Nm).
27. When installing the left cylinder head, install the exhaust manifold, DIS coil bracket and oil dipstick tube. When installing the right cylinder head, install the coolant outlet hose and connect the exhaust catalyst.
28. Install the upper rear and center rear timing belt covers.
29. Install the camshaft pulleys in the timed position.
30. Install the cylinder head covers.
31. Install and adjust the timing belt.
32. Install the center timing belt cover.
33. Connect the crankshaft sensor wiring assembly and install the lower timing belt cover.
34. Raise the vehicle and support it safely.
35. Install the inner fender splash shield and the right wheel and tire assembly.
36. Install the left idler pulley and bracket.
37. Install the upper timing belt cover.
38. Install the accessory drive belts.
39. Install the intake manifold.
40. Install the air cleaner oulet tube.
41. Connect the negative battery cable.
42. Fill the engine cooling system with the proper type and quantity of coolant.
43. Start the engine and check for coolant, fuel or oil leaks.

3.8L Engine

➧ SEE FIG. 64

1. Drain the cooling system and disconnect the negative battery cable.
2. Properly relieve the fuel system pressure. Remove the air cleaner assembly including air intake duct and heat tube.
3. Loosen the accessory drive belt idler and remove the drive belt.
4. If the right head is being removed, proceed to Step 5. If the left cylinder head is being removed, perform the following:
   a. Remove the oil fill cap.
   b. Remove the power steering pump. Leave the hoses connected and place the pump/bracket assembly aside in a position to prevent fluid from leaking out.
   c. If equipped with air conditioning, remove mounting bracket attaching bolts. Leaving the hoses connected, position the compressor aside.
   d. Remove the alternator and bracket.
5. If the right cylinder head is being removed, perform the following:
   a. Disconnect the thermactor air control valve or bypass valve hose assembly at the air pump.
   b. Disconnect the thermactor tube support bracket from the rear of cylinder head.
   c. Remove accessory drive idler.
   d. Remove the thermactor pump pulley and thermactor pump.
   e. Remove the PCV valve.
6. Remove the upper intake manifold.
7. Remove the valve rocker arm cover attaching screws.
8. Remove the injector fuel rail assembly.
9. Remove the lower intake manifold and the exhaust manifold(s).
10. Loosen the rocker arm fulcrum attaching bolts enough to allow rocker arm to be lifted off the pushrod and rotate to one side. Remove the pushrods. Identify and label the position of each pushrod. Pushrods should be installed in their original position during assembly.
11. Remove the cylinder head attaching bolts and discard. Do not reuse the old bolts.
12. Remove the cylinder head(s). Remove and discard old cylinder head gasket(s).

To install:

13. Lightly oil all bolt threads before installation.
14. Clean cylinder head, intake manifold, valve rocker arm cover and cylinder head gasket contact surfaces. If cylinder head was removed for a cylinder head gasket replacement, check flatness of cylinder head and block gasket surfaces.
15. Position the new head gasket(s) onto cylinder block using dowels for alignment. Position cylinder head(s) onto block.
16. Apply a thin coating of pipe sealant with Teflon® to the threads of the short cylinder head bolts, nearest to the exhaust manifold. Do not apply sealant to the long bolts. Install the cylinder head bolts.

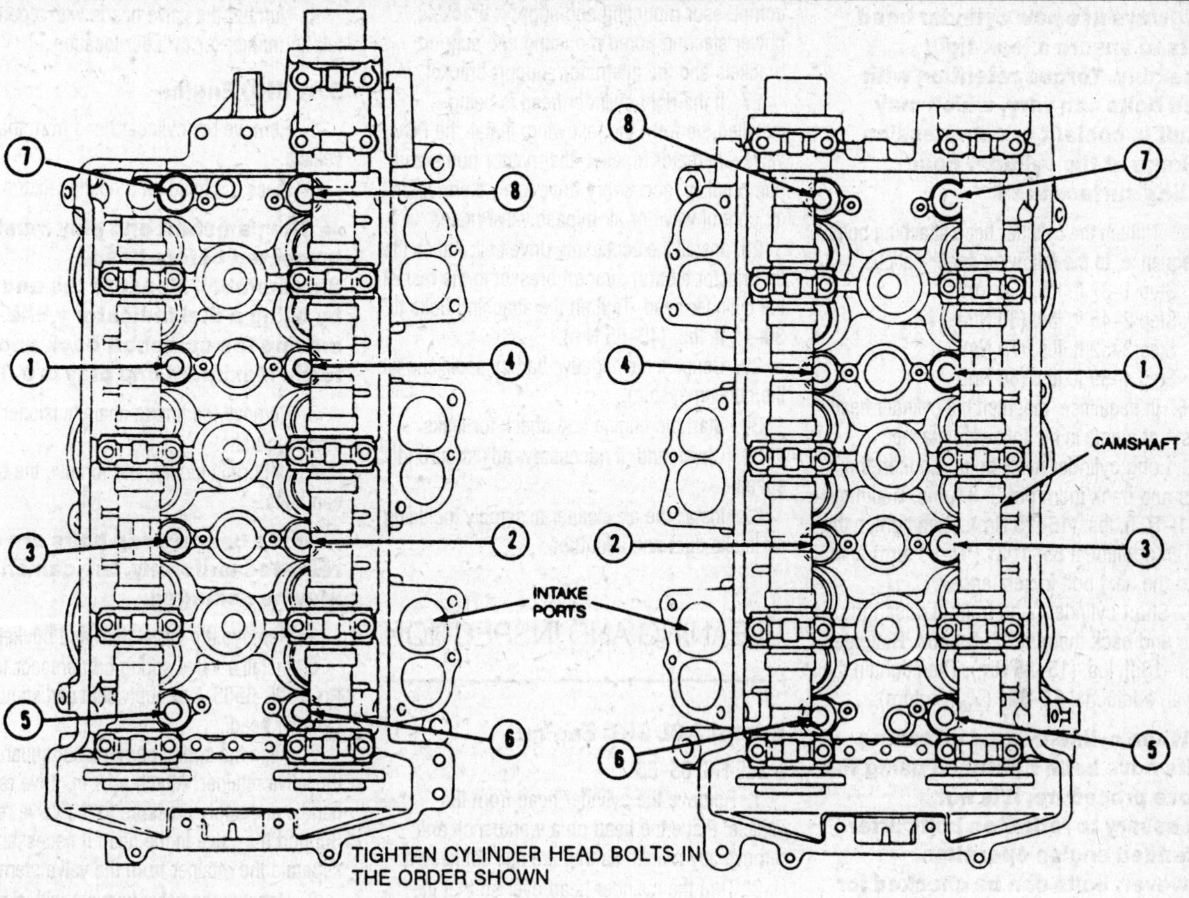

TIGHTEN CYLINDER HEAD BOLTS IN THE ORDER SHOWN

Fig.63 Cylinder head bolt torque sequence — 3.0L SHO engine

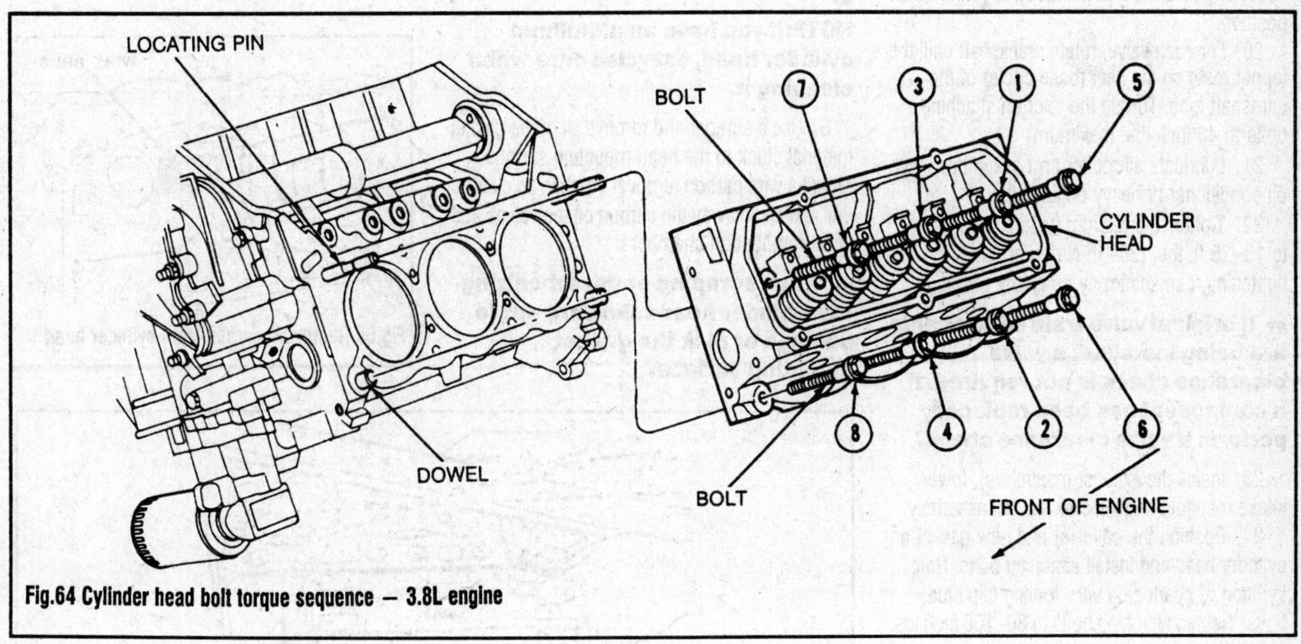

Fig.64 Cylinder head bolt torque sequence — 3.8L engine

➡ **Always use new cylinder head bolts to ensure a leak-tight assembly. Torque retention with used bolts can vary, which may result in coolant or compression leakage at the cylinder head mating surface area.**

17. Tighten the cylinder head attaching bolts, in sequence, to the following specifications:
 Step 1–37 ft. lbs. (50 Nm)
 Step 2–45 ft. lbs. (60 Nm)
 Step 3–52 ft. lbs. (70 Nm)
 Step 4–59 ft. lbs. (80 Nm)

18. In sequence, retighten the cylinder head bolts 1 at a time in the following manner:

a. Long cylinder head bolts: Loosen the bolts and back them out 2–3 turns. Retighten to 11–18 ft. lbs. (15–25 Nm). Then tighten the bolt an additional 85–105° (1/4–1/3 turn) and go to the next bolt in sequence.

b. Short cylinder head bolts: Loosen the bolts and back them out 2–3 turns. Retighten to 11–18 ft. lbs. (15–25 Nm). Then tighten the bolt an additional 65–85° (3/16–1/4 turn).

➡ **When cylinder head attaching bolts have been tightened using the above procedure, it is not necessary to retighten bolts after extended engine operation. However, bolts can be checked for tightness if desired.**

19. Dip each pushrod end in oil conditioner or heavy engine oil. Install pushrods in their original position.

20. For each valve, rotate crankshaft until the tappet rests on the heel (base circle) of the camshaft lobe. Torque the fulcrum attaching bolts to 43 inch lbs. maximum.

21. Lubricate all rocker arm assemblies with oil conditioner or heavy engine oil.

22. Tighten the fulcrum bolts a second time to 19–25 ft. lbs. (25–35 Nm). For final tightening, camshaft may be in any position.

➡ **If original valve train components are being installed, a valve clearance check is not required. If a component has been replaced, perform a valve clearance check.**

23. Install the exhaust manifold(s), lower intake manifold and injector fuel rail assembly.

24. Position the cover(s) and new gasket on cylinder head and install attaching bolts. Note location of spark plug wire routing clip stud bolts. Tighten attaching bolts to 80–106 inch lbs. (9–12 Nm).

25. Install the upper intake manifold and connect the secondary wires to the spark plugs.

26. If the left cylinder head is being installed, perform the following: install oil fill cap, compressor mounting and support brackets, power steering pump mounting and support brackets and the alternator/support bracket.

27. If the right cylinder head is being installed, perform the following: install the PCV valve, alternator bracket, thermactor pump and pump pulley, accessory drive idler, thermactor air control valve or air bypass valve hose.

28. Install the accessory drive belt. Attach the thermactor tube(s) support bracket to the rear of the cylinder head. Tighten the attaching bolts to 30–40 ft. lbs. (40–55 Nm).

29. Connect the negative battery cable and fill the cooling system.

30. Start the engine and check for leaks.

31. Check and, if necessary, adjust curb idle speed.

32. Install the air cleaner assembly including air intake duct and heat tube.

CLEANING AND INSPECTION

Except 3.0L SHO Engine

➧ SEE FIG. 65–66

1. Remove the cylinder head from the vehicle. Place the head on a workbench and remove any manifolds that are still connected.

2. Turn the cylinder head over so that the mounting surface is facing up and support evenly on wooden blocks.

➡

NOTE:If you have an aluminum cylinder head, exercise care when cleaning it.

3. Use a scraper and remove all of the gasket material stuck to the head mounting surface. Mount a wire carbon removal brush in an electric drill and clean away the carbon on the valves and head combustion chambers.

➡ **When scraping or decarbonizing the cylinder head take care not to damage or nick the gasket mounting surface.**

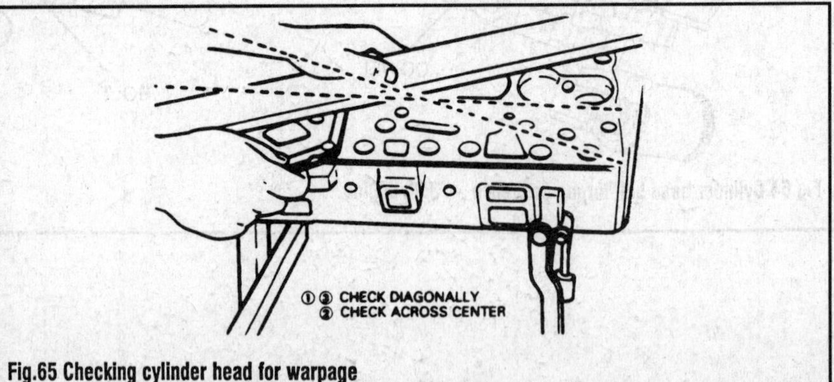

Fig.65 Checking cylinder head for warpage

4. Number the valve heads with a permanent felt-tip marker for cylinder location.

3.0L SHO Engine

1. Remove the cylinder head from the vehicle.

2. Place the head on a holding fixture.

➡ **The camshaft end play must be inspected before head disassembly. Measure the end play by using a dial indicator while moving the camshaft back and forth. Maximum end play is 0.3mm.**

3. Remove the timing chain tensioner attaching bolts.

4. Uniformly loosen and remove the bearing cap bolts.

➡ **If the bearing cap bolts are not removed uniformly, the camshaft may be damaged.**

5. Remove the valve shim and bucket.

6. Install a valve spring compressor tool part No. T89P-6565-A or equivalent and stand on the cylinder head.

7. Align the spring compressor squarely over the valve retainer. Attach a 1/2 in. drive ratchet handle and apply pressure to the valve retainer. Support the valve in the head if necessary to separate the retainer from the valve stem.

8. Remove the valve keepers with a magnet and remove the valve.

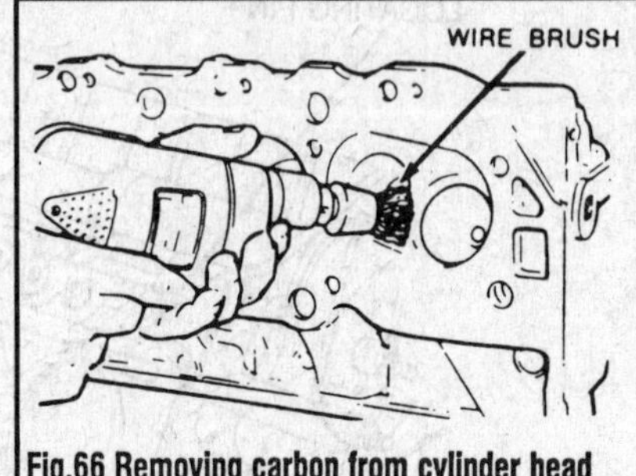

Fig.66 Removing carbon from cylinder head

RESURFACING

If the cylinder head is warped resurfacing by a machine shop is required. Place a straightedge across the gasket surface of the head. Using feeler gauges, determine the clearance at the center and along the length between the head and straightedge. Measure clearance at the center and along the lengths of both diagonals. If warpage exceeds 0.076mm in a 152mm span, or 0.15mm over the total length the cylinder head must be resurfaced.

Valves and Springs

REMOVAL & INSTALLATION

➧ SEE FIG. 68–72

1. Block the head on its side, or install a pair of head-holding brackets made especially for valve removal.
2. Use a socket slightly larger than the valve stem and keepers, place the socket over the valve stem and gently hit the socket with a plastic hammer to break loose any varnish buildup.
3. Remove the valve keepers, retainer, spring shield and valve spring using a valve spring compressor (the locking C-clamp type is the easiest kind to use).
4. Put the parts in a separate container numbered for the cylinder being worked on. Do not mix them with other parts removed.
5. Remove and discard the valve stem oil seal, a new seal will be used at assembly time.
6. Remove the valve from the cylinder head and place, in order, through numbered holes punched in a stiff piece of cardboard or wooden valve holding stick.

➡ The exhaust valve stems, on some engines, are equipped with small metal caps. Take care not to lose the caps. Make sure to reinstall them at assembly time. Replace any caps that are worn.

7. Use an electric drill and rotary wire brush to clean the intake and exhaust valve ports, combustion chamber and valve seats. In some cases, the carbon will need to be chipped away. Use a blunt pointed drift for carbon chipping, be careful around the valve seat areas.
8. Use a wire valve guide cleaning brush and safe solvent to clean the valve guides.
9. Clean the valves with a revolving wire brush. Heavy carbon deposits may be removed with the blunt drift.

➡ When using a wire brush to clean carbon from the valve ports, valves etc., be sure that the deposits are actually removed, rather than burnished.

10. Wash and clean all valve spring, keepers, retaining caps etc., in safe solvent.
11. Clean the head with a brush and some safe solvent and wipe dry.
12. Check the head for cracks. Cracks in the cylinder head usually start around an exhaust valve seat because it is the hottest part of the combustion chamber. If a crack is suspected but cannot be detected visually have the area checked with dye penetrant or other method by a machine shop.
13. After all cylinder head parts are reasonably clean, check the valve stem-to-guide clearance. If a dial indicator is not on hand, a visual inspection can give you a fairly good idea if the guide, valve stem or both are worn.
14. Insert the valve into the guide until slightly away from the valve seat. Wiggle the valve sideways. A small amount of wobble is normal, excessive wobble means a worn guide or valve stem. If a dial indicator is on hand, mount the indicator so that the stem of the valve is at 90° to the valve stem, as close to the valve guide as possible. Move the valve off the seat, and measure the valve guide-to-stem clearance by rocking the stem back and forth to actuate the dial indicator. Measure the valve stem using a micrometer and compare to specifications to determine whether stem or guide wear is causing excessive clearance.
15. The valve guide, if worn, must be repaired before the valve seats can be resurfaced. Ford supplies valves with oversize stems to fit valve guides that are reamed to oversize for repair. The machine shop will be able to handle the guide reaming for you. In some cases, if the guide is not too badly worn, knurling may be all that is required.
16. Reface, or have the valves and valve seats refaced. The valve seats should be a true 45° angle for the 2.5L and 3.0L engines, and 44.5° angle for the 3.8L engine. Remove only enough material to clean up any pits or grooves. Be sure the valve seat is not too wide or narrow. Use a 60° grinding wheel to remove material from the bottom of the seat for raising and a 30° grinding wheel to remove material from the top of the seat to narrow.
17. After the valves are refaced by machine, hand lap them to the valve seat. Clean the grinding compound off and check the position of face-to-seat contact. Contact should be close to the center of the valve face. If contact is close to the top edge of the valve, narrow the seat; if too close to the bottom edge, raise the seat.
18. Valves should be refaced to a true angle of 44° for the 2.5L and 3.0L engines, and 45.8° for the 3.8L engine. Remove only enough metal to clean up the valve face or to correct runout. If the edge of the valve head, after machining, is 0.8mm or less replace the valve. The tip of the valve stem should also be dressed on the valve grinding machine, however, do not remove more than 0.25mm.

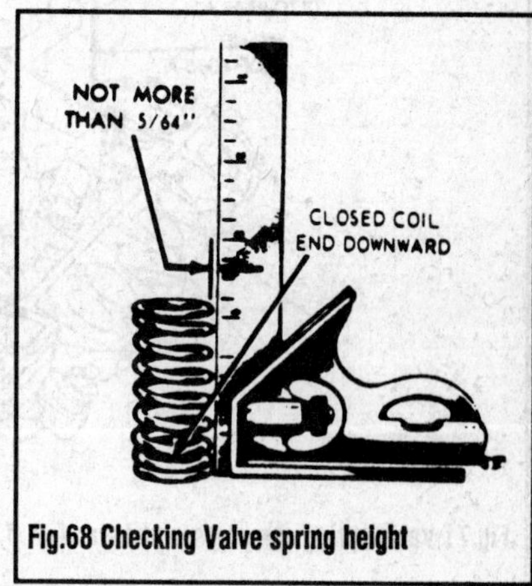

Fig.68 Checking Valve spring height

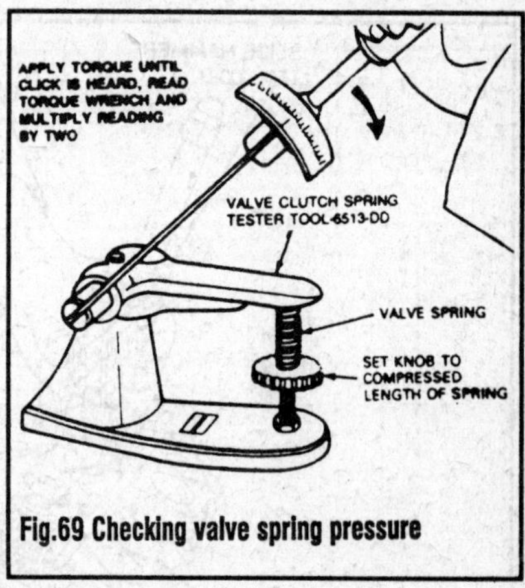

Fig.69 Checking valve spring pressure

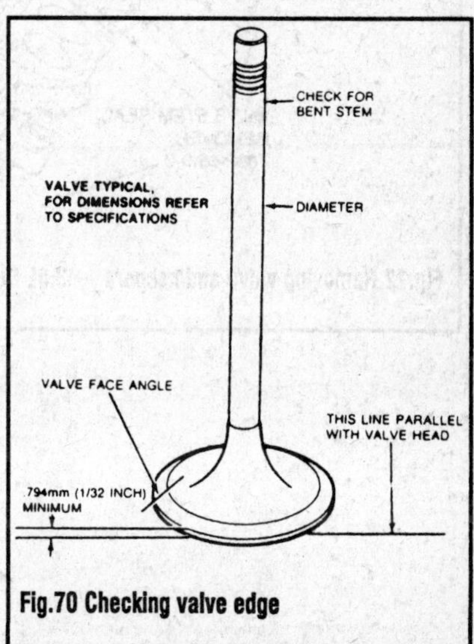

Fig.70 Checking valve edge

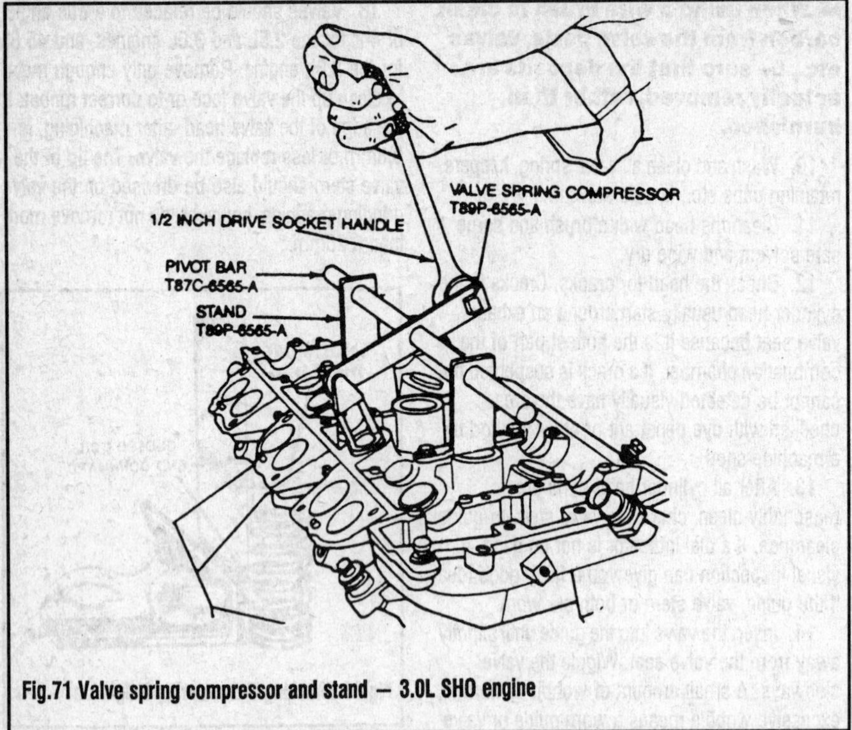

Fig.71 Valve spring compressor and stand — 3.0L SHO engine

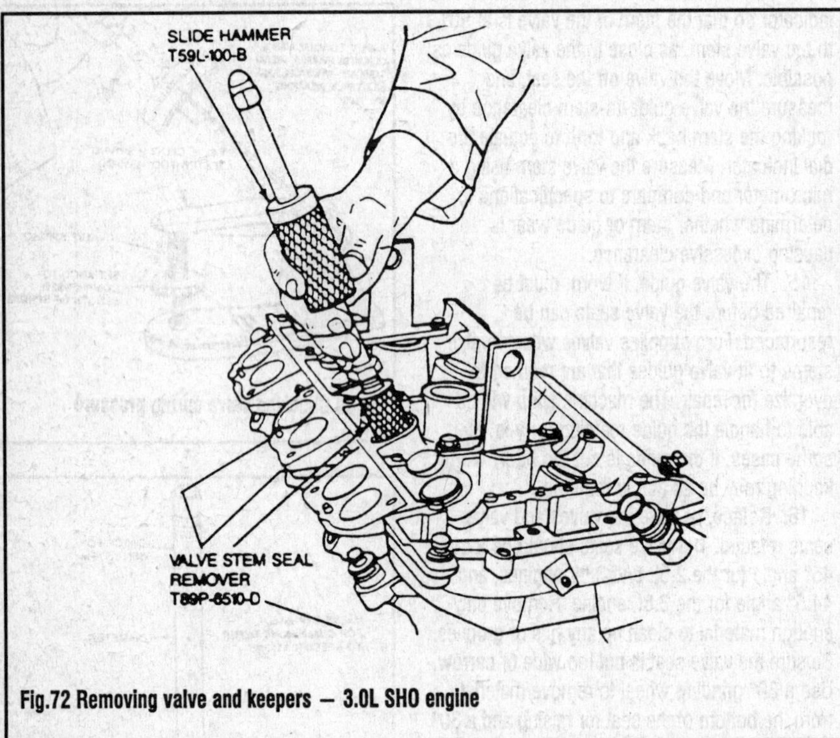

Fig.72 Removing valve and keepers — 3.0L SHO engine

19. After all valve and valve seats have been machined, check the remaining valve train parts (springs, retainers, keepers, etc.) for wear. Check the valve springs for straightness and tension.

20. Reassemble the head in the reverse order of disassembly using new valve guide seals and lubricating the valve stems. Check the valve spring installed height, shim or replace as necessary.

Valve Stem Seals

REPLACEMENT

Most engines are equipped with a positive valve stem seal using a Teflon® insert. Teflon® seals are available for other engines but usually require valve guide machining, consult your automotive machine shop for advice on having positive valve stem oil seals installed.

When installing valve stem oil seals, ensure that a small amount of oil is able to pass the seal to lubricate the valve stems and guide walls; otherwise, excessive wear will occur.

Head Off Vehicle

➧ SEE FIG. 67

1. Remove the cylinder head from the vehicle. Position the assembly in a cylinder head holding fixture.
2. Using the proper valve stem seal removal tool, remove the valve keepers from the valve stem. Remove and discard the old valve stem seal.
3. As required, remove the valve from the cylinder head. Be sure to keep the valves in the proper order for reassembly.
4. Continue this process for the remaining valves.
5. Installation is the reverse of the removal procedure.

Head On Vehicle

1. Disconnect the negative battery cable. Remove the valve cover.
2. Remove the spark plug from the cylinder that you are working on.
3. Position the engine so that both the intake and exhaust valves are closed.
4. Screw the proper tool into the spark plug hole. Attach an air line to the tool and pressurize the cylinder with low pressure compressed air, just enough to hold the valves in the closed position.

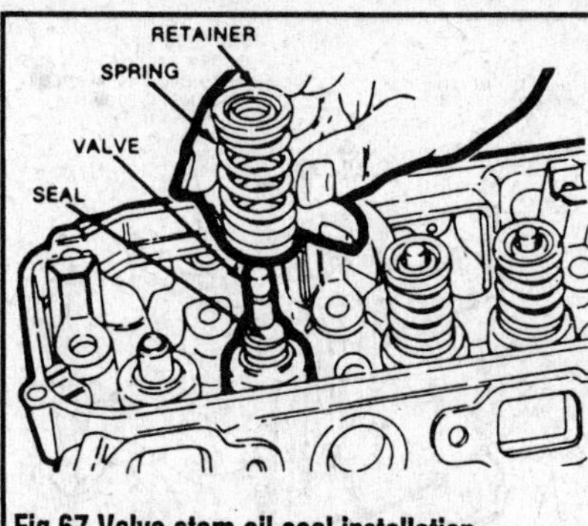

Fig.67 Valve stem oil seal installation

➡ **Failure to properly compress air into the cylinder will result in the valve falling into the cylinder bore which will necessitate disassembling the engine to retrieve them.**

5. Using the proper valve stem seal removal tool, remove the valve keepers from the valve stem. Remove and discard the old valve seal.
6. Installation is the reverse of the removal procedure.

Valve Seats

If a valve seat is damaged or burnt and cannot be serviced by refacing, it may be possible to have the seat machined and an insert installed. Consult the automotive machine shop for their advice.

➡ **The aluminum heads on some engines are equipped with inserts.**

Valve Guides

Worn valve guides can, in most cases, be reamed to accept a valve with an oversized stem. Valve guides that are not excessively worn or distorted may, in some cases, be knurled rather than reamed. However, if the valve stem is worn reaming for an oversized valve stem is the answer since a new valve would be required.

Knurling is a process in which metal is displaced and raised, thereby reducing clearance. Knurling also produces excellent oil control. The possibility of knurling instead of reaming the valve guides should be discussed with a machinist.

Valve Lifters

REMOVAL & INSTALLATION

⁂ CAUTION

When draining the coolant, keep in mind that cats and dogs are attracted by the ethylene glycol antifreeze, and are quite likely to drink any that is left in an uncovered container or in puddles on the ground. This will prove fatal in sufficient quantity. Always drain the coolant into a sealable container. Coolant should be reused unless it is contaminated or several years old. The EPA warns that prolonged contact with used engine oil may cause a number of skin disorders, including cancer! You should make every used engine oil. Protective gloves should be worn when changing the oil. Wash your hands and any other exposed skin areas as soon as possible after exposure to used engine oil. Soap and water, or waterless hand cleaner should be used.

2.5L Engine

1. Disconnect the negative battery cable. Remove the cylinder head.
2. Using a magnet, remove the lifters. Identify, tag and place the lifters in a rack so they can be installed in the original positions.
3. If the lifters are stuck in their bores by excessive varnish or gum, it may be necessary to use a hydraulic lifter puller tool to remove the lifters. Rotate the lifters back and forth to loosen any gum and varnish which may have formed. Keep the assemblies intact until the are to be cleaned.
4. Install the lifters through the pushrod openings with a magnet.
5. Install the cylinder head and related parts.

3.0L Engine Except SHO

1. Disconnect the negative battery cable.
2. Drain the cooling system and relieve the fuel system pressure.
3. Disconnect the fuel lines from the fuel supply manifold and remove the throttle body.
4. Disconnect the spark plug wires from the spark plugs. Remove the ignition wire/separator assembly from the rocker cover retaining studs.
5. Mark the position of the distributor housing and rotor and remove the distributor.
6. Remove the rocker arm covers. Loosen the No. 3 intake valve rocker arm retaining bolt to allow the rocker arm to be rotated to 1 side.
7. Remove the intake manifold assembly.
8. Loosen the rocker arm fulcrum retaining bolt enough to allow the rocker arm to be lifted off the pushrod and rotated to 1 side.
9. Remove the pushrod(s). If more than 1 is removed, identify each pushrods location. The pushrods should be installed in their original position during reassembly.
10. On 1992 engines equipped with roller lifters, loosen the two roller lifter guide plate retaining bolts. Remove the guide plate retainer assembly from the lifter valley. Remove the lifter guide plate from the lifter by lifting straight up. To remove, grasp the lifter and pull it in line with the bore.
11. Remove the lifter(s) using a magnet, as required.

➡ **If the lifter(s) are stuck in the bore(s) due to excessive varnish or gum deposits, it may be necessary to use a claw-type tool to aid removal. Rotate the lifter back and forth to loosen it from the gum or varnish that may have formed on the lifter.**

To install:

11. Clean all gasket mating surfaces. Place a rag in the lifter valley to catch any stray gasket material.
12. Lubricate each lifter and bore with heavy engine oil. Install the lifter in the bore, checking for free fit.
13. If equipped with roller lifters align the lifter flat to the lifter guide plate. Install the plate with the word UP and or button visible. Install the guide retainer assembly over the guide plates. Tighten the bolts to 8–10 ft. lbs.
14. Install the intake manifold and new gaskets. Dip each pushrod end in oil conditioner and install in it's original position.
15. For each valve, rotate the crankshaft until the lifter rests on the base circle of the camshaft lobe. Position the rocker arms over the pushrod and valve. Tighten the retaining bolt to 8 ft. lbs. (11 Nm) to initially seat the fulcrum into the cylinder head and onto the pushrod. Final tighten the bolt to 24 ft. lbs. (32 Nm).
16. Install the rocker arm covers and the distributor.

17. Install the throttle body and connect the fuel lines to the fuel supply manifold. Install the safety clips.

18. Install the coolant hoses. Fill and bleed the cooling system. Drain and change the crankcase oil.

19. Connect the air cleaner hoses to the throttle body and rocker cover.

20. Connect the negative battery cable, start the engine and check for leaks. Check the ignition timing.

3.8L Engine

1. Disconnect the negative battery cable. Disconnect the secondary ignition wires at the spark plugs.

2. Remove the plug wire routing clips from mounting studs on the rocker arm cover attaching bolts. Lay plug wires with routing clips toward the front of engine.

3. Remove the upper intake manifold, rocker arm covers and lower intake manifold.

4. Sufficiently loosen each rocker arm fulcrum attaching bolt to allow the rocker arm to be lifted off the pushrod and rotated to one side.

5. Remove the pushrods. The location of each pushrod should be identified and labeled. When engine is assembled, each rod should be installed in its original position.

6. If equipped with roller lifters, remove the 2 tappet guide plate retainers and 6 guide plates.

7. Remove the lifters using a magnet. The location of each lifters should be identified and labeled. When engine is assembled, each lifter should be installed in its original position.

➡ If lifters are stuck in bores due to excessive varnish or gum deposits, it may be necessary to use a hydraulic lifter puller tool to aid removal. When using a remover tool, rotate lifter back and forth to loosen it from gum or varnish that may have formed on the lifter.

To install:

8. Lightly oil all bolt and stud threads before installation. Using solvent, clean the cylinder head and valve rocker arm cover sealing surfaces.

9. Lubricate each lifter and bore with oil conditioner or heavy engine oil.

10. Install each lifter in bore from which it was removed. If a new tappet(s) is being installed, check new lifter for a free fit in bore.

11. If equipped with roller lifters, align the flats on the sides of the lifters and install the 6 guide plates between the adjacent lifters. Make sure the word "up" and/or button is showing. Install the 3 guide plate retainers and tighten the 4 bolts to 6–10 ft. lbs. (8–14 Nm).

12. Dip each pushrod end in oil conditioner or heavy engine oil. Install pushrods in their original positions.

13. For each valve, rotate crankshaft until lifter rests onto heel (base circle) of camshaft lobe. Position rocker arms over pushrods and install the fulcrums. Initially tighten the fulcrum attaching bolts to 44 inch lbs. maximum.

14. Lubricate all rocker arm assemblies with suitable heavy engine oil.

15. Finally tighten the fulcrum bolts to 19–25 ft. lbs. (25–35 Nm). For the final tightening, the camshaft may be in any position.

➡ Fulcrums must be fully seated in the cylinder head and pushrods must be seated in rocker arm sockets prior to the final tightening.

16. Complete the installation of the lower intake manifold, valve rocker arm covers and the upper intake manifold by reversing the removal procedure.

17. Install the plug wire routing clips and connect wires to the spark plugs.

18. Start the engine and check for oil or coolant leaks.

Oil Pan

REMOVAL & INSTALLATION

CAUTION

The EPA warns that prolonged contact with used engine oil may cause a number of skin disorders, including cancer! You should make every effort to minimize your exposure to used engine oil. Protective gloves should be worn when changing the oil. Wash your hands and any other exposed skin areas as soon as possible after exposure to used engine oil. Soap and water, or waterless hand cleaner should be used.

2.5L Engine

➧ SEE FIG. 73

1. Disconnect the negative battery cable. Raise the vehicle and support safely.

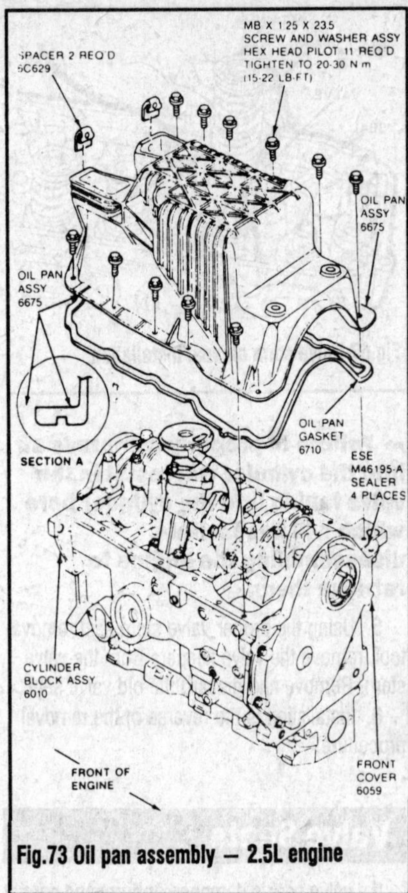

Fig.73 Oil pan assembly — 2.5L engine

2. Drain the crankcase and drain the cooling system by removing the lower radiator hose.

3. Remove the roll restrictor on manual transaxle equipped vehicles.

4. Disconnect the starter cable and remove the starter.

5. Disconnect the exhaust pipe from oil pan.

6. Remove the engine coolant tube located from the lower radiator hose, water pump and at the tabs on the oil pan. Position air conditioner line off to the side. Remove the retaining bolts and remove the oil pan.

To install:

7. Clean both mating surfaces of oil pan and cylinder block making certain all traces of RTV sealant are removed.

8. Remove and clean oil pump pick-up tube and screen assembly. After cleaning, install tube and screen assembly.

9. Fill the oil pan groove with RTV sealer; the bead should be approximately 1/8 in. (3mm) above the surface of the pan rail. Immediately (within 5 minutes) install the oil pan.

10. Install and tighten the 2 oil pan-to-transaxle bolts to 30–39 ft. lbs. (40–50 Nm) to align the pan with the transaxle then back off 1/2 turn.

11. Tighten the pan flange bolts to 6–8 ft. lbs. (8–12 Nm).

12. Tighten the 2 oil pan-to-transaxle bolts to 30–39 ft. lbs. (40–50 Nm).

13. Install the remaining components in the reverse order of their removal.

14. Fill the crankcase and cooling system to the proper level.

15. Start the engine and inspect for leaks.

3.0L Except SHO Engine

➧ SEE FIG. 74

1. Disconnect the negative battery cable and remove the oil level dipstick.

2. Raise the vehicle and support safely. If equipped with a low level sensor, remove the retainer clip at the sensor. Remove the electrical connector from the sensor.

3. Drain the crankcase. Remove the starter motor and disconnect the electrical connector from the oxygen sensor.

4. Remove the catalyst and pipe assembly. Remove the lower engine/flywheel dust cover from the torque converter housing.

5. Remove the oil pan attaching bolts and slowly remove the oil pan from the engine block. Remove the oil pan gasket.

To install:

6. Clean the gasket surfaces on the cylinder block and oil pan. Apply a $^{3}/_{16}$ in. (5mm) bead of silicone sealer to the junction of the rear main bearing cap and cylinder block junction of the front cover assembly and cylinder block.

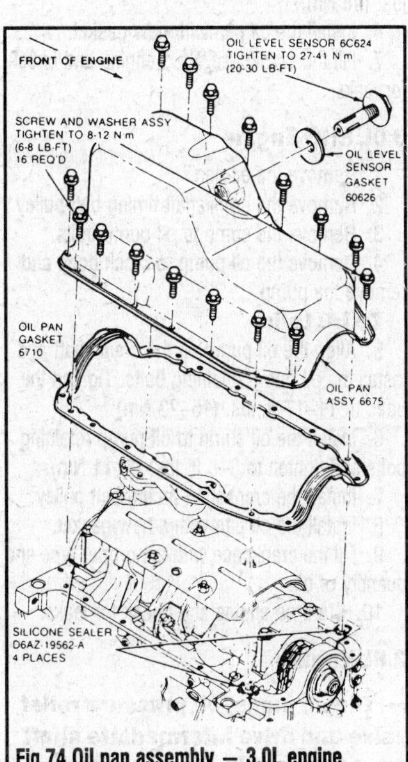

Fig.74 Oil pan assembly — 3.0L engine except SHO

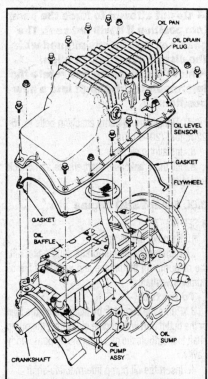

➡ When using a silicone sealer, the assembly process should occur within 15 minutes after the sealer has been applied. After this time, the sealer may start to set-up and its sealing effectiveness may be affected.

7. Position the oil pan gasket over the oil pan and secure the gasket with a suitable sealer contact adhesive.

8. Position the oil pan on the engine block and install the oil pan attaching bolts. Torque the bolts to 8 ft. lbs. (10 Nm).

9. Install the lower engine/flywheel dust cover to the torque converter housing. Install the catalyst and pipe assembly. Connect the oxygen sensor connector.

10. Install the starter motor. Install the low oil level sensor connector to the sensor and install the retainer clip. Lower the vehicle and replace the oil level dipstick.

11. Connect the negative battery cable. Fill the crankcase. Start the engine and check for oil and exhaust leaks.

3.0L SHO Engine

➧ SEE FIG. 76

1. Disconnect the negative battery cable.

2. Remove the oil level dipstick.

3. Remove the accessory drive belts.

4. Remove the timing belt.

Fig.75 Oil pan assembly — 3.8L engine

5. Raise the vehicle and support it safely.

6. If equipped with a low oil level sensor, remove the retainer clip and the electrical connector from the sensor.

7. Drain the engine oil.

8. Remove the starter motor.

9. Disconnect the oxygen sensors.

10. Remove the catalyst and pipe assembly.

11. Remove the lower flywheel dust cover from the converter housing.

12. Remove the oil pan attaching bolts and the oil pan.

To install:

13. Clean the gasket surfaces of the cylinder block and the oil pan.

14. Position the oil pan gasket on the oil pan and secure with silicone sealer.

15. Position the oil pan and tighten the retaining bolts to 11–17 ft. lbs. (15–23 Nm).

16. Install the lower flywheel dust cover to the converter housing.

17. Install the catalyst and pipe assembly and connect the oxygen sensors.

18. Install the starter and connect the low oil level sensor connector to the sensor. Install the retainer clip.

19. Lower the vehicle and install the accessory drive belts.

20. Replace the oil level dipstick and connect the negative battery cable.

21. Fill the crankcase with the proper type and quantity of oil. Start the vehicle and check for leaks.

3.8L Engine

➧ SEE FIG. 75

1. Disconnect the negative battery cable.

2. Raise the vehicle and support safely.

3. Drain the crankcase and remove the oil filter element.

4. Remove the converter assembly, starter motor and converter housing cover.

5. Remove the retaining bolts and remove the oil pan.

To install:

6. Clean the gasket surfaces on cylinder block, oil pan and oil pickup tube.

7. Trial fit oil pan to cylinder block. Ensure enough clearance has been provided to allow oil pan to be installed without sealant being scraped off when pan is positioned under engine.

8. Apply a bead of silicone sealer to the oil pan flange. Also apply a bead of sealer to the front cover/cylinder block joint and fill the grooves on both sides of the rear main seal cap.

➡ When using silicone rubber sealer, assembly must occur within 15 minutes after sealer application. After this time, the sealer may start to harden and its sealing effectiveness may be reduced.

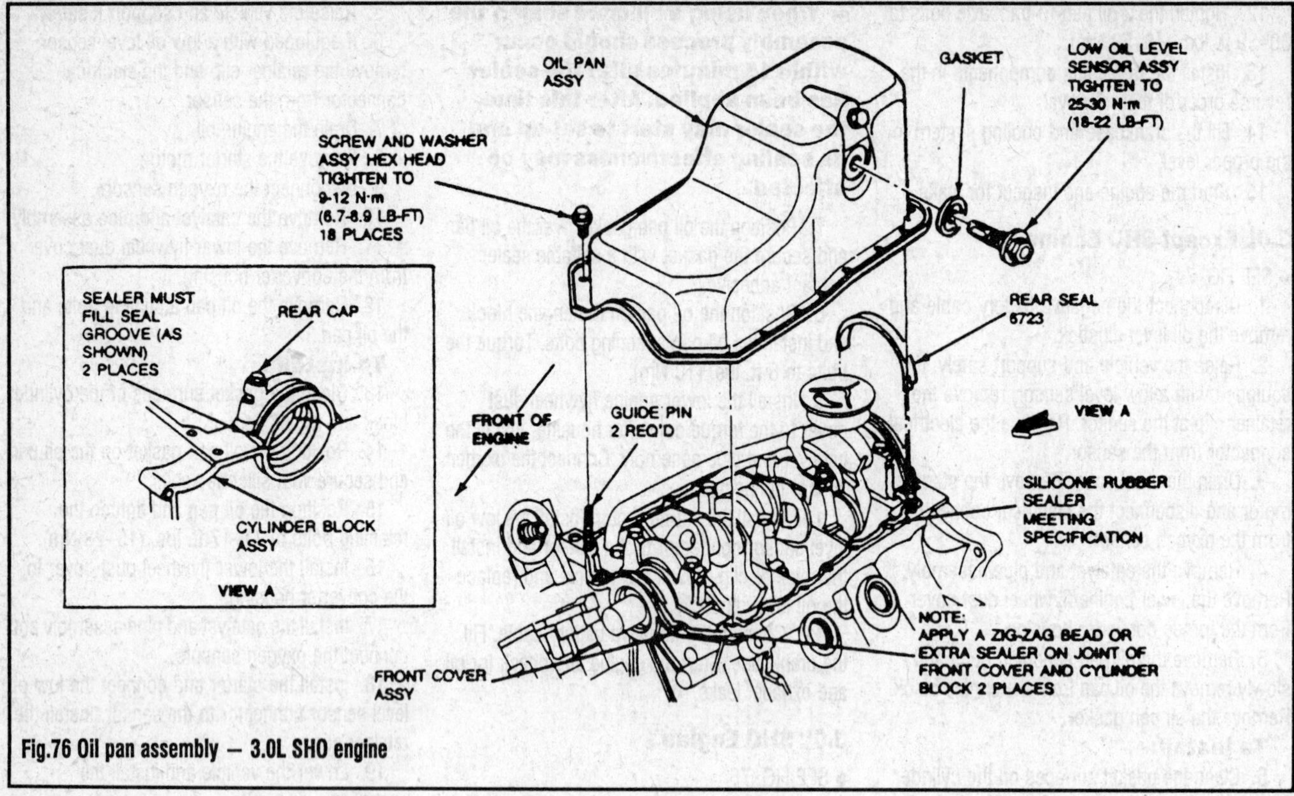

Fig.76 Oil pan assembly — 3.0L SHO engine

9. Install the oil pan and secure to the block with the attaching screws. Tighten the screws to 7–9 ft. lbs. (9–12 Nm).
10. Install a new oil filter element. Install the converter housing cover and starter motor.
11. Install the converter assembly and lower the vehicle.
12. Fill the crankcase and connect the negative battery cable.
13. Start the engine and check for leaks.

Oil Pump

REMOVAL & INSTALLATION

2.5L Engine

1. Remove the oil pan.
2. Remove oil pump attaching bolts and remove oil pump and intermediate driveshaft.

To install:

3. Prime oil pump by filling inlet port with engine oil. Rotate pump shaft until oil flows from outlet port.
4. If screen and cover assembly have been removed, replace gasket. Clean screen and reinstall screen and cover assembly and tighten attaching bolts.
5. Position intermediate driveshaft into distributor socket.
6. Insert intermediate driveshaft into oil pump. Install pump and shaft as an assembly.

➡ Do not attempt to force the pump into position if it will not seat. The shaft hex may be mis-aligned with the distributor shaft. To align, remove the oil pump and rotate the intermediate driveshaft into a new position.

7. Tighten the oil pump attaching bolts to 15–22 ft. lbs. (20–30 Nm).
8. Install the oil pan.
9. Fill the crankcase. Start engine and check for leaks.

3.0L Except SHO Engine

➧ SEE FIG. 77

1. Remove the oil pan.
2. Remove the oil pump attaching bolts. Lift the oil pump off the engine and withdraw the oil pump driveshaft.

To install:

3. Prime the oil pump by filling either the inlet or the outlet port with engine oil. Rotate the pump shaft to distribute the oil within the oil pump body cavity.
4. Insert the oil pump intermediate shaft assembly into the hex drive hole in the oil pump assembly until the retainer "clicks" into place. Place the oil pump in the proper position with a new gasket and install the retaining bolt.
5. Torque the oil pump retaining bolt to 35 ft. lbs. (48 Nm).
6. Install the oil pan with new gasket.
7. Fill the crankcase. Start engine and check for leaks.

3.0L SHO Engine

1. Remove the oil pan.
2. Remove the crankshaft timing belt pulley.
3. Remove the sump to oil pump bolts.
4. Remove the oil pump to block bolts and remove the pump.

To install:

5. Align the oil pump on the crankshaft and install the oil pump retaining bolts. Tighten the bolts to 11–17 ft. lbs. (15–23 Nm).
6. Install the oil sump to oil pump retaining bolts and tighten to 6–8 ft. lbs. (7–11 Nm).
7. Install the crankshaft timing belt pulley.
8. Install the oil pan with a new gasket.
9. Fill the crankcase with the proper type and quantity of oil.
10. Start the engine and check for leaks.

3.8L Engine

➡ The oil pump, oil pressure relief valve and drive intermediate shaft are contained in the front cover assembly.

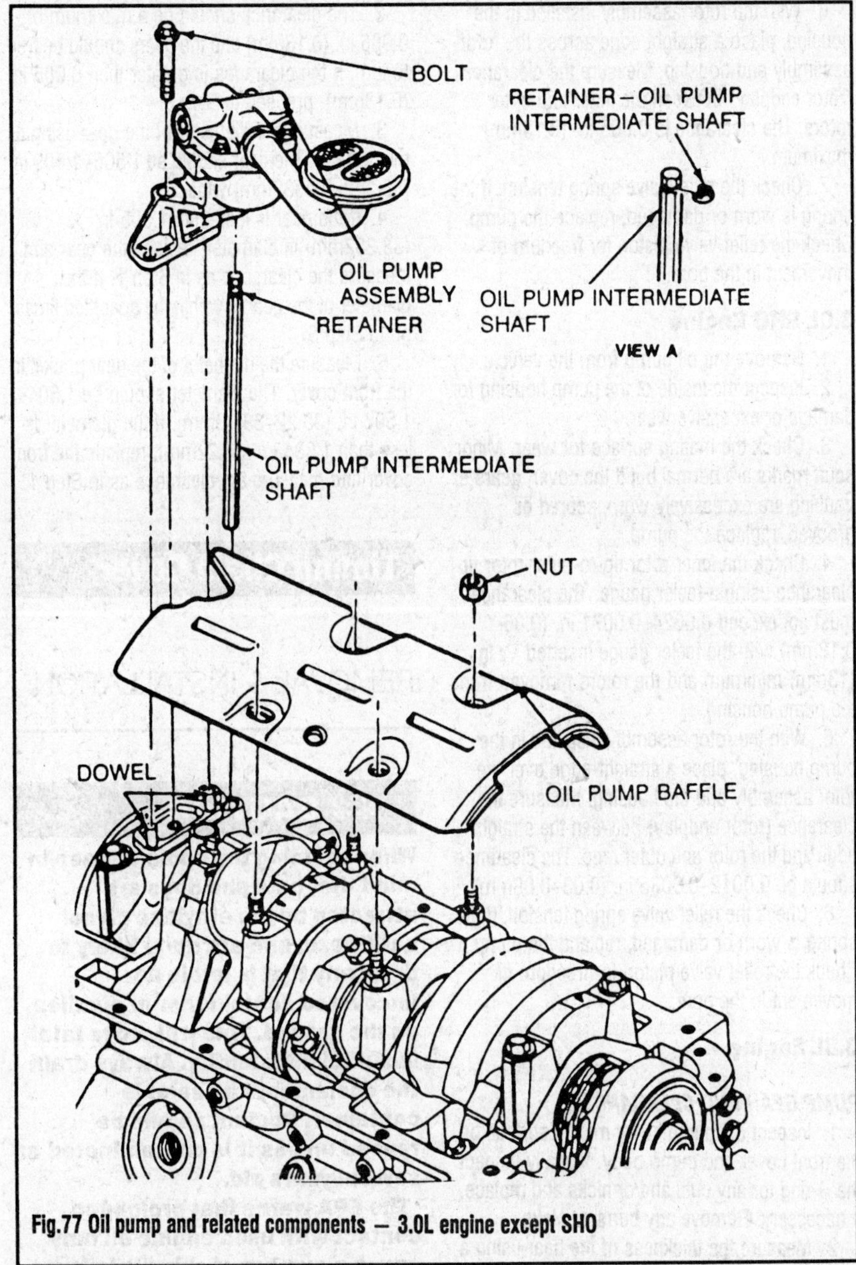

Fig.77 Oil pump and related components — 3.0L engine except SHO

1. Disconnect the negative battery cable. Drain the cooling system and crankcase.
2. Remove the air cleaner assembly and air intake duct.
3. Loosen the accessory drive belt idler. Remove the belt and water pump pulley.
4. Remove the power steering pump mounting bracket attaching bolts. Leaving the hoses connected, place the pump/bracket assembly in a position that will prevent the loss of power steering fluid.
5. If equipped with air conditioning, remove the compressor front support bracket. Leave the compressor in place.
6. Disconnect coolant bypass and heater hoses at the water pump. Disconnect radiator upper hose at thermostat housing.
7. Disconnect the coil wire from distributor cap and remove cap with secondary wires attached. Remove the distributor hold-down clamp and lift distributor out of the front cover.
8. Raise the vehicle and support safely.
9. Remove the crankshaft damper and pulley.

➡ **If the crankshaft pulley and vibration damper have to be separated, mark the damper and pulley so they may be reassembled in the same relative position. This is important as the damper and pulley are initially balanced as a unit. If the crankshaft damper is being replaced, check if the original damper has balance pins installed. If so, new balance pins (E0SZ-6A328-A or equivalent) must be installed on the new damper in the same position as the original damper. The crankshaft pulley must also be installed in original installation position.**

10. Remove the oil filter, disconnect the radiator lower hose at the water pump and remove the oil pan.
11. Lower the vehicle.
12. Remove the front cover.

➡ **Do not overlook the cover attaching bolt located behind the oil filter adapter. The front cover will break if pried upon if all attaching bolts are not removed.**

13. Remove the oil pump cover attaching bolts and remove the cover. Lift the pump gears off the front cover pocket. Remove the cover gasket and replace with new.

To install:

14. Clean the front cover oil pump gasket contact surface. Place a straight edge across the oil pump cover mounting surface and check for wear or warpage using a feeler gauge. If the surface is out of flat by more than 0.0016 in. (0.04mm), replace the cover.
15. Lightly pack the gear pocket with petroleum jelly or coat all pump gear surfaces with oil conditioner.
16. Install the gears in the pocket. Make certain the petroleum jelly fills the gap between the gears and the pocket.
17. Position the oil pump cover gasket and install the oil pump cover. Tighten the oil pump cover retaining bolts to 18–22 ft. lbs. (25–30 Nm).
18. Clean the gasket surfaces of the front cover and cylinder block.
19. Position a new gasket and the front cover on the cylinder block.
20. Install the front cover attaching bolts. Apply Loctite® or equivalent, to the threads of the bolt installed below the oil filter housing prior to installation. This bolt is to be installed and tightened last. Tighten all bolts to 15–22 ft. lbs. (20–30 Nm).
21. Raise the vehicle and support safely.

22. Install the oil pan. Connect the radiator lower hose. Install a new oil filter.
23. Coat the crankshaft damper sealing surface with clean engine oil.
24. Position the crankshaft pulley key in the crankshaft keyway.
25. Install the damper with damper washer and attaching bolt. Tighten the bolt to 104–132 ft. lbs. (140–180 Nm).
26. Install the crankshaft pulley and tighten the attaching bolts 19–28 ft. lbs. (26–28 Nm).
27. Lower the vehicle.
28. Connect the coolant bypass hose.
29. Install the distributor with rotor pointing at No. 1 distributor cap tower. Install the distributor cap and coil wire.
30. Connect the radiator upper hose at thermostat housing.
31. Connect the heater hose.
32. If equipped with air conditioning, install compressor and mounting brackets.
33. Install the power steering pump and mounting brackets.
34. Position the accessory drive belt over the pulleys.
35. Install the water pump pulley. Position the accessory drive belt over water pump pulley and tighten the belt.
36. Connect battery ground cable. Fill the crankcase and cooling system to the proper level.
37. Start the engine and check for leaks.
38. Check the ignition timing and curb idle speed, adjust as required.
39. Install the air cleaner assembly and air intake duct.

INSPECTION AND OVERHAUL

2.5L and 3.0L Engines

1. Remove the oil pump from the vehicle.
2. Inspect the inside of the pump housing for damage or excessive wear.
3. Check the mating surface for wear. Minor scuff marks are normal but if the cover, gears or housing are excessively worn, scored or grooved, replace the pump.
4. Inspect the rotor for nicks, burrs, or score marks. Remove minor imperfections with an oil stone.
5. Measure the inner-to-outer rotor tip clearance. The clearance must not exceed 0.012 in. (0.30mm) with a feeler gauge inserted 1/2 in. (13mm) minimum with the rotors removed from the pump housing.
6. With the rotor assembly installed in the housing, place a straight edge across the rotor assembly and housing. Measure the clearance (rotor endplay) between the inner and outer rotors. The clearance is 0.005 in. (0.13mm) maximum.
7. Check the relief valve spring tension. If the spring is worn or damaged, replace the pump. Check the relief valve piston for freedom of movement in the bore.

3.0L SHO Engine

1. Remove the oil pump from the vehicle.
2. Inspect the inside of the pump housing for damage or excessive wear.
3. Check the mating surface for wear. Minor scuff marks are normal but if the cover, gears or housing are excessively worn, scored or grooved, replace the pump.
4. Check the inner rotor tip-to-outer rotor tip clearance using a feeler gauge. The clearance must not exceed 0.0024–0.0071 in. (0.06–0.18mm) with the feeler gauge inserted 1/2 in. (13mm) minimum and the rotors removed from the pump housing.
5. With the rotor assembly installed in the pump housing, place a straight-edge over the rotor assembly and the housing. Measure the clearance (rotor endplay) between the straight-edge and the rotor and outer race. The clearance should be 0.0012–0.0035 in. (0.03–0.09mm).
6. Check the relief valve spring tension. If the spring is worn or damaged, replace the pump. Check the relief valve piston for freedom of movement in the bore.

3.8L Engine

PUMP GEAR END CLEARANCE

1. Inspect the pump cover mating surface on the front cover and pump body. Visually inspect the O-ring for any cuts and/or nicks and replace, if necessary. Remove any burrs or nicks.
2. Measure the thickness of the hear using a micrometer. The gear should measure 1.19–1.20 in. (30.455–30.480mm) thick.
3. If the gear is less than the specified minimum thickness, replace the gear. If the gear thickness is within specification, it may be necessary to replace the pump body. If the gear thickness is within the specified limits, proceed to Step 4.
4. Measure the depth of the gear pocket in the oil pump body. The depth should be 1.200–1.202 in. (30.49–30.54mm).
5. If the depth is more than 1.202 in. (30.54mm), replace the oil pump body.

PUMP GEAR SIDE CLEARANCE

1. Measure the side clearance by inserting a feeler gauge between the gear tooth and the side wall of the gear pocket.
2. The clearance should be a maximum of 0.005 in. (0.13mm) and the gears should be free to turn. If the clearance is greater than 0.005 in. (0.13mm), proceed to Step 3.
3. Measure the diameter of the gear using a micrometer. The gear should be 1.505–1.509 in. (38.252–38.332mm) wide.
4. If the gear is less than 1.505 in. (38.252mm) in diameter, replace the gear and measure the clearance as in Step 1. If the diameter of the gear is within the specified limits, go to Step 5.
5. Measure the diameter of the gear pocket in the front cover. The diameter should be 1.504–1.507 in. (38.22–38.30mm). If the diameter is less than 1.504 in. (38.22mm), replace the front cover and measure the clearance as in Step 1.

Timing Chain Cover

REMOVAL & INSTALLATION

**** CAUTION**

When draining the coolant, keep in mind that cats and dogs are attracted by the ethylene glycol antifreeze, and are quite likely to drink any that is left in an uncovered container or in puddles on the ground. This will prove fatal in sufficient quantity. Always drain the coolant into a sealable container. Coolant should be reused unless it is contaminated or several years old.

The EPA warns that prolonged contact with used engine oil may cause a number of skin disorders, including cancer! You should make every effort to minimize your exposure to used engine oil. Protective gloves should be worn when changing the oil. Wash your hands and any other exposed skin areas as soon as possible after exposure to used engine oil. Soap and water, or waterless hand cleaner should be used.

2.5L Engine

➧ SEE FIG. 78

1. Disconnect the negative battery cable.
2. Remove the engine and transaxle assembly from the vehicle and position in a

suitable holding fixture. Remove the dipstick.

3. Remove accessory drive pulley, if equipped. Remove the crankshaft pulley attaching bolt and washer and remove pulley.

4. Remove front cover attaching bolts from front cover. Pry the top of the front cover away from the block.

5. Remove the oil pan.

6. Clean all dirt and old gasket material from all mating surfaces.

To install:

7. Clean and inspect all parts before installation. Clean the oil pan, cylinder block and front cover of gasket material and dirt.

8. Apply oil resistant sealer to a new front cover gasket and position gasket into front cover.

9. Remove the front cover oil seal and position the front cover on the engine.

10. Position front cover alignment tool T84P–6019–C or equivalent, onto the end of the crankshaft, ensuring the crank key is aligned with the keyway in the tool. Bolt the front cover to the engine and tighten the bolts to 6–8 ft. lbs. (10–12 Nm). Remove the front cover alignment tool.

11. Install a new front cover oil seal using a suitable seal installer. Lubricate the hub of the crankshaft pulley with polyethylene grease to prevent damage to the seal during installation and initial engine start. Install crankshaft pulley.

12. Install the oil pan.

13. Install the accessory drive pulley, if equipped.

14. Install crankshaft pulley attaching bolt and washer. Tighten to 140–170 ft. lbs. (190–230 Nm).

15. Install the engine and transaxle assembly in the vehicle. Connect the negative battery cable.

3.0L Engine Except SHO

➧ SEE FIG. 79

1. Disconnect the negative battery cable.

2. Loosen the 4 water pump pulley bolts while the water pump drive belt is in place.

3. Loosen the alternator belt-adjuster jackscrew to provide enough slack in the alternator drive belt for removal.

4. Using a $^1/_2$ in. drive breaker bar, rotate the automatic belt tensioner down and to the left to remove the water pump drive belt.

5. Drain the cooling system.

6. Remove the lower radiator hose and the heater hose from the water pump.

7. Remove the crankshaft pulley and damper.

8. Drain and remove the oil pan.

9. Remove the retaining bolts from the timing cover to the block and remove the timing cover.

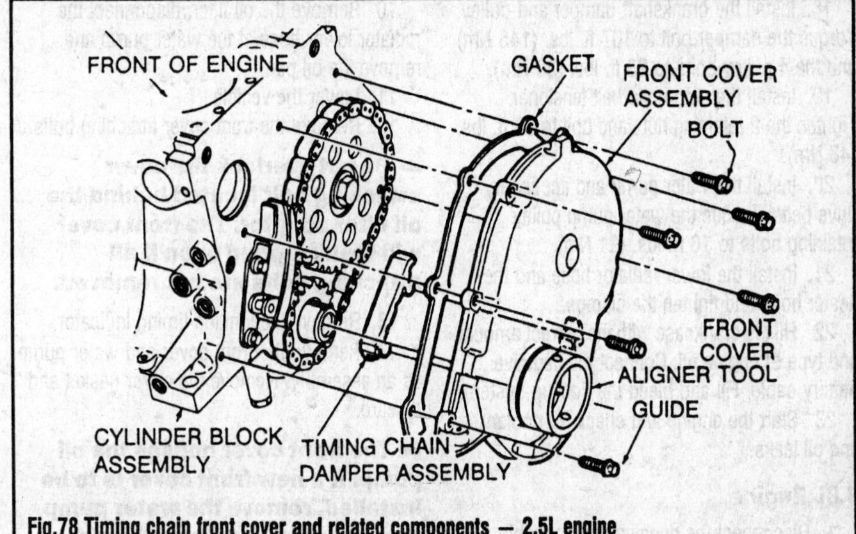

Fig.78 Timing chain front cover and related components — 2.5L engine

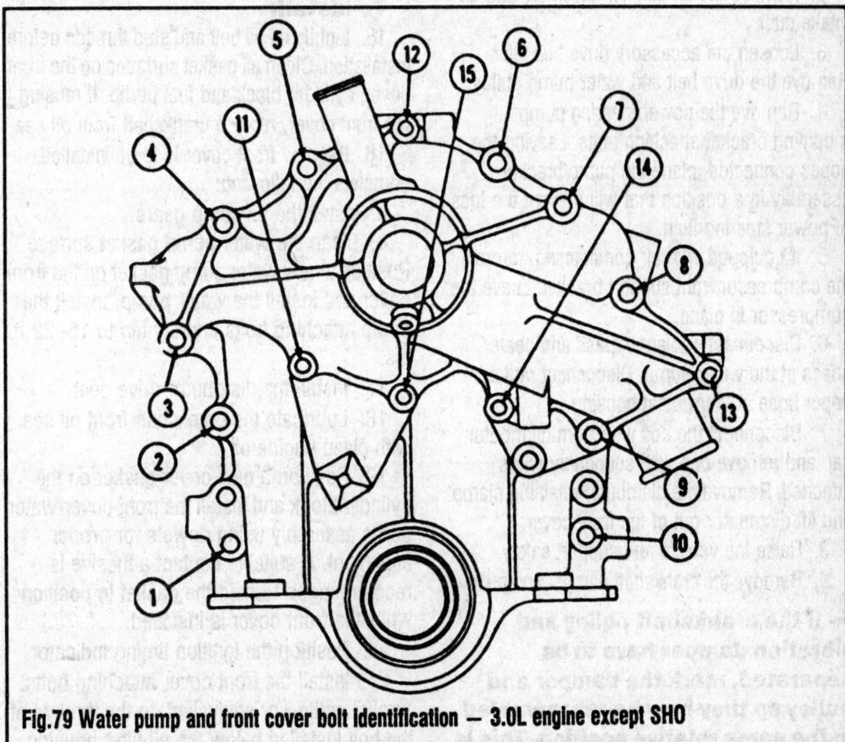

Fig.79 Water pump and front cover bolt identification — 3.0L engine except SHO

➧ **The timing cover and water pump may be removed as an assembly by not removing bolts 11–15.**

To install:

10. Lightly oil all bolt and stud threads except those specifying special sealant.

11. Clean all old gasket material and sealer from the timing cover, oil pan and cylinder block.

12. Inspect the timing cover seal for wear or damage and replace if necessary.

13. Align a new timing cover gasket over the cylinder block dowels.

14. Install the timing cover/water pump assembly onto the cylinder block with the water pump pulley loosely attached to the water pump hub.

15. Apply pipe sealant to bolt numbers 1, 2 and 3 and hand start them along with the rest of the cover retaining bolts. Tighten bolts 1–10 to 19 ft. lbs. (25 Nm) and 11–15 to 7 ft. lbs. (10 Nm).

16. Install the oil pan and tighten the retaining bolts to 9 ft. lbs. (12 Nm).

17. Hand tighten the water pump pulley retaining bolts.

18. Install the crankshaft damper and pulley. Torque the damper bolt to 107 ft. lbs. (145 Nm) and the 4 pulley bolts to 26 ft. lbs. (35 Nm).
19. Install the automatic belt tensioner. Tighten the 2 retaining nuts and bolt to 35 ft. lbs. (48 Nm).
20. Install the water pump and accessory drive belts. Torque the water pump pulley retaining bolts to 16 ft. lbs. (21 Nm).
21. Install the lower radiator hose and the heater hose and tighten the clamps.
22. Fill the crankcase with the correct amount and type of engine oil. Connect the negative battery cable. Fill and bleed the cooling system.
23. Start the engine and check for coolant and oil leaks.

3.8L Engine

1. Disconnect the negative battery cable. Drain the cooling system and crankcase.
2. Remove the air cleaner assembly and air intake duct.
3. Loosen the accessory drive belt idler. Remove the drive belt and water pump pulley.
4. Remove the power steering pump mounting bracket attaching bolts. Leaving the hoses connected, place the pump/bracket assembly in a position that will prevent the loss of power steering fluid.
5. If equipped with air conditioning, remove the compressor front support bracket. Leave the compressor in place.
6. Disconnect coolant bypass and heater hoses at the water pump. Disconnect radiator upper hose at thermostat housing.
7. Disconnect the coil wire from distributor cap and remove cap with secondary wires attached. Remove the distributor retaining clamp and lift distributor out of the front cover.
8. Raise the vehicle and support safely.
9. Remove the crankshaft damper and pulley.

➡ If the crankshaft pulley and vibration damper have to be separated, mark the damper and pulley so they may be reassembled in the same relative position. This is important as the damper and pulley are initially balanced as a unit. If the crankshaft damper is being replaced, check if the original damper has balance pins installed. If so, new balance pins (E0SZ-6A328-A or equivalent) must be installed on the new damper in the same position as the original damper. The crankshaft pulley must also be installed in the original installation position.

10. Remove the oil filter, disconnect the radiator lower hose at the water pump and remove the oil pan.
11. Lower the vehicle.
12. Remove the front cover attaching bolts.

➡ Do not overlook the cover attaching bolt located behind the oil filter adapter. The front cover will break if pried upon if all attaching bolts are not removed.

13. Remove the ignition timing indicator.
14. Remove the front cover and water pump as an assembly. Remove the cover gasket and discard.

➡ The front cover houses the oil pump. If a new front cover is to be installed, remove the water pump and oil pump from the old front cover.

To install:

15. Lightly oil all bolt and stud threads before installation. Clean all gasket surfaces on the front cover, cylinder block and fuel pump. If reusing the front cover, replace crankshaft front oil seal.
16. If a new front cover is to be installed, complete the following:
    a. Install the oil pump gears.
    b. Clean the water pump gasket surface. Position a new water pump gasket on the front cover and install the water pump. Install the pump attaching bolts and tighten to 15–22 ft. lbs.
17. Install the distributor drive gear.
18. Lubricate the crankshaft front oil seal with clean engine oil.
19. Position a new cover gasket on the cylinder block and install the front cover/water pump assembly using dowels for proper alignment. A suitable contact adhesive is recommended to hold the gasket in position while the front cover is installed.
20. Position the ignition timing indicator.
21. Install the front cover attaching bolts. Apply Loctite® or equivalent, to the threads of the bolt installed below the oil filter housing prior to installation. This bolt is to be installed and tightened last. Tighten all bolts to 15–22 ft. lbs. (20–30 Nm).
22. Raise the vehicle and support safely.
23. Install the oil pan. Connect the radiator lower hose. Install a new oil filter.
24. Coat the crankshaft damper sealing surface with clean engine oil.
25. Position the crankshaft pulley key in the crankshaft keyway.
26. Install the damper with damper washer and attaching bolt. Tighten the bolt to 104–132 ft. lbs. (140–180 Nm).
27. Install the crankshaft pulley and tighten the attaching bolts 19–28 ft. lbs. (26–28 Nm).
28. Lower the vehicle.
29. Connect the coolant bypass hose.
30. Install the distributor with rotor pointing at No. 1 distributor cap tower. Install the distributor cap and coil wire.
31. Connect the radiator upper hose at thermostat housing.
32. Connect the heater hose.
33. If equipped with air conditioning, install compressor and mounting brackets.
34. Install the power steering pump and mounting brackets.
35. Position the accessory drive belt over the pulleys.
36. Install the water pump pulley. Position the accessory drive belt over water pump pulley and tighten the belt.
37. Connect battery ground cable. Fill the crankcase and cooling system to the proper level.
38. Start the engine and check for leaks.
39. Check the ignition timing and curb idle speed, adjust as required.
40. Install the air cleaner assembly and air intake duct.

Timing Chain Cover Oil Seal

REPLACEMENT

2.5L Engine

➡ The removal and installation of the front cover oil seal on these engines can only be accomplished with the engine removed from the vehicle.

1. Remove the engine from the vehicle and position in a suitable holding fixture.
2. Remove the bolt and washer at the crankshaft pulley.
3. Remove the crankshaft pulley.
4. Remove the front cover oil seal.
5. Coat a new seal with grease. Install and drive the seal until it is fully seated. Check the seal after installation to be sure the spring is properly positioned in the seal.

6. Install the crankshaft pulley, attaching bolt and washer. Tighten the crankshaft pulley bolt to 140–170 ft. lbs. (190–230 Nm).

3.0L Engine Except SHO

1. Disconnect the negative battery cable and remove the accessory drive belts.
2. Raise the vehicle and support safely. Remove the right front wheel and tire assembly.
3. Remove the pulley-to-damper attaching bolts and remove the crankshaft pulley.
4. Remove the crankshaft damper retaining bolt and washer. Remove the damper from the crankshaft using a damper removal tool.
5. Pry the seal from the timing cover with a suitable tool and be careful not to damage the front cover and crankshaft.

To install:

➡ **Before installation, inspect the front cover and shaft seal surface of the crankshaft damper for damage, nicks, burrs or other roughness which may cause the new seal to fail. Service or replace components as necessary.**

6. Lubricate the seal lip with clean engine oil and install the seal using a seal installer tool.
7. Coat the crankshaft damper sealing surface with clean engine oil. Apply RTV to the keyway of the damper prior to installation. Install the damper using a damper seal installer tool. Install the damper retaining bolt and washer. Tighten to 107 ft. lbs. (145 Nm).
8. Position the crankshaft pulley and install the attaching bolts. Tighten the attaching bolts to 26 ft. lbs. (35 Nm).
9. Install the right front wheel and tire assembly and lower the vehicle.
10. Position the drive belt over the crankshaft pulley. Check the drive belt for proper routing and engagement in the pulleys.
11. Reconnect the negative battery cable and start the engine and check for oil leaks.

3.8L Engine

1. Disconnect the negative battery cable.
2. Loosen the accessory drive belt idler.
3. Raise the vehicle and support safely.
4. Disengage the accessory drive belt and remove crankshaft pulley.
5. Remove the crankshaft damper using a suitable removal tool.
6. Remove the seal from the front cover with a suitable prying tool. Use care to prevent damage to front cover and crankshaft.

To install:

➡ **Inspect the front cover and crankshaft damper for damage, nicks, burrs or other roughness which may cause the seal to fail. Service or replace components as necessary.**

7. Lubricate the seal lip with clean engine oil and install the seal using suitable seal installer.
8. Lubricate the seal surface on the damper with clean engine oil. Install damper and pulley assembly. Install the damper attaching bolt and tighten to 103–132 ft. lbs. (140–180 Nm).
9. Position the crankshaft pulley and install the retaining bolts. Tighten to 19–28 ft. lbs. (26–38 Nm).
10. Position accessory drive belt over crankshaft pulley.
11. Lower the vehicle.
12. Check accessory drive belt for proper routing and engagement in the pulleys. Adjust the drive belt tension.
13. Connect the negative battery cable. Start the engine and check for leaks.

Timing Chain And Sprockets

REMOVAL & INSTALLATION

CAUTION

When draining the coolant, keep in mind that cats and dogs are attracted by the ethylene glycol antifreeze, and are quite likely to drink any that is left in an uncovered container or in puddles on the ground. This will prove fatal in sufficient quantity. Always drain the coolant into a sealable container. Coolant should be reused unless it is contaminated or several years old.

The EPA warns that prolonged contact with used engine oil may cause a number of skin disorders, including cancer! You should make every effort to minimize your exposure to used engine oil. Protective gloves should be worn when changing the oil. Wash your hands and any other exposed skin areas as soon as possible after exposure to used engine oil. Soap and water, or waterless hand cleaner should be used.

2.5L Engine

➧ SEE FIG. 80

1. Remove the engine and transaxle from the vehicle as an assembly and position in a suitable holding fixture. Remove the dipstick.
2. Remove accessory drive pulley, if equipped, Remove the crankshaft pulley attaching bolt and washer and remove pulley.
3. Remove front cover attaching bolts from front cover. Pry the top of the front cover away from the block.
4. Clean any gasket material from the surfaces.
5. Check timing chain and sprockets for excessive wear. If the timing chain and sprockets are worn, replace with new.
6. Check timing chain tensioner blade for wear depth. If the wear depth exceeds specification, replace tensioner.
7. Turn engine over until the timing marks are aligned. Remove camshaft sprocket attaching bolt and washer. Slide both sprockets and timing chain forward and remove as an assembly.
8. If equipped, check timing chain vibration damper for excessive wear. Replace if necessary; the damper is located inside the front cover.
9. Remove the oil pan.

To install:

10. Clean and inspect all parts before installation. Clean the oil pan, cylinder block and front cover of gasket material and dirt.
11. Slide both sprockets and timing chain onto the camshaft and crankshaft with timing marks aligned. Install camshaft bolt and washer and tighten to 41–56 ft. lbs. (55–75 Nm). Oil timing chain, sprockets and tensioner after installation with clean engine oil.
12. Apply oil resistant sealer to a new front cover gasket and position gasket into front cover.
13. Remove the front cover oil seal and position the front cover on the engine.
14. Position front cover alignment tool T84P–6019–C or equivalent, onto the end of the crankshaft, ensuring the crank key is aligned with the keyway in the tool. Bolt the front cover to the engine and tighten the bolts to 6–8 ft. lbs. (8–12 Nm). Remove the front cover alignment tool.
15. Install a new front cover oil seal using a suitable seal installer. Lubricate the hub of the crankshaft pulley with polyethylene grease to prevent damage to the seal during installation and initial engine start. Install crankshaft pulley.
16. Install the oil pan.

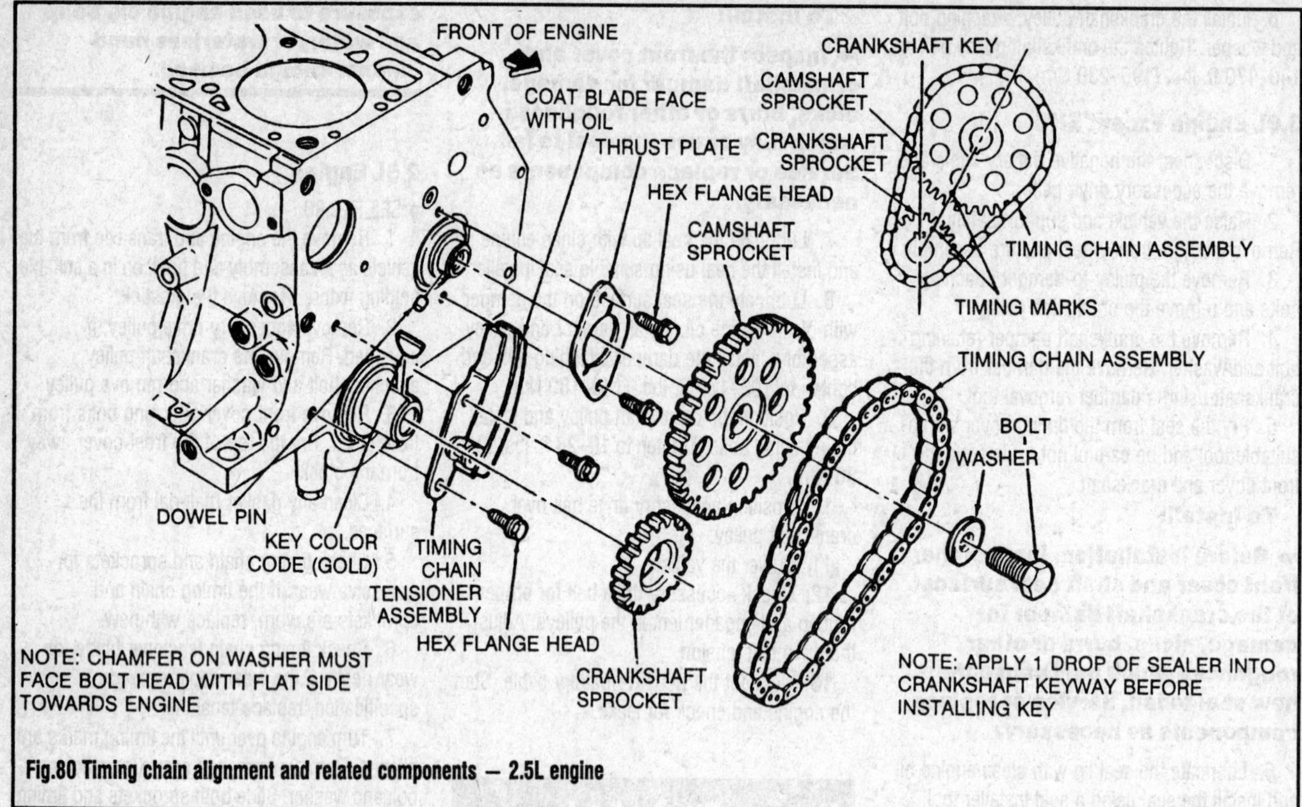

Fig.80 Timing chain alignment and related components — 2.5L engine

17. Install the accessory drive pulley, if equipped.

18. Install crankshaft pulley attaching bolt and washer. Tighten to 140–170 ft. lbs. (190–230 Nm).

19. Remove engine from work stand and install in vehicle.

3.0L Engine Except SHO

➧ SEE FIG. 88

1. Disconnect the negative battery cable. Drain the cooling system and crankcase. Remove the crankshaft pulley and front cover assemblies.

2. Rotate the crankshaft until the No. 1 piston is at the TDC on its compression stroke and the timing marks are aligned.

3. Remove the camshaft sprocket attaching bolt and washer. Slide both sprockets and timing chain forward and remove as an assembly.

4. Check the timing chain and sprockets for excessive wear. Replace if necessary.

To install:

➡ Before installation, clean and inspect all parts. Clean the gasket material and dirt from the oil pan, cylinder block and front cover.

5. Slide both sprockets and timing chain onto the camshaft and crankshaft with the timing marks aligned. Install the camshaft bolt and washer and torque to 46 ft. lbs. (63 Nm). Apply clean engine oil to the timing chain and sprockets after installation.

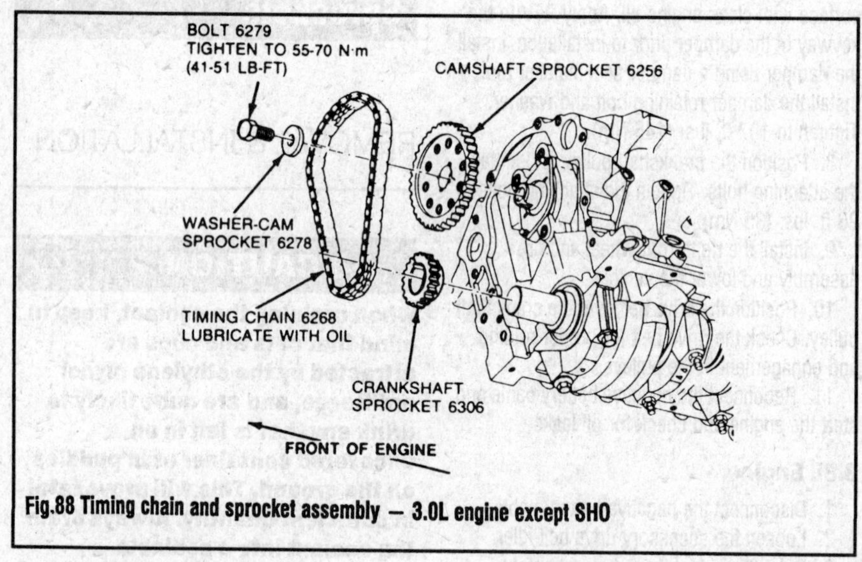

Fig.88 Timing chain and sprocket assembly — 3.0L engine except SHO

➡ The camshaft bolt has a drilled oil passage in it for timing chain lubrication. If the bolt is damaged, do not replace it with a standard bolt.

6. Install the timing cover and the crankshaft pulley and damper. Tighten the crankshaft damper bolt to 107 ft. lbs. (145 Nm) and the pulley bolts to 26 ft. lbs. (35 Nm).

7. Fill the crankcase with the proper type and quantity of oil and the cooling system with coolant. Connect the negative battery cable.

3.8L Engine

➧ SEE FIG. 81

1. Disconnect the negative battery cable. Drain the cooling system and crankcase.
2. Remove the air cleaner assembly and air intake duct.
3. Loosen the accessory drive belt idler. Remove the drive belt and water pump pulley.
4. Remove the power steering pump mounting bracket attaching bolts. Leaving the hoses connected, place the pump/bracket assembly in a position that will prevent the loss of power steering fluid.
5. If equipped with air conditioning, remove the compressor front support bracket. Leave the compressor in place.
6. Disconnect coolant bypass and heater hoses at the water pump. Disconnect radiator upper hose at thermostat housing.
7. Disconnect the coil wire from distributor cap and remove cap with secondary wires attached. Remove the distributor retaining clamp and lift distributor out of the front cover.
8. Raise the vehicle and support safely.
9. Remove the crankshaft damper and pulley.

➡ If the crankshaft pulley and vibration damper have to be separated, mark the damper and pulley so they may be reassembled in the same relative position. This is important as the damper and pulley are initially balanced as a unit. If the crankshaft damper is being replaced, check if the original damper has balance pins installed. If so, new balance pins (E0SZ-6A328-A or equivalent) must be installed on the new damper in the same position as the original damper. The crankshaft pulley must also be installed in original installation position.

10. Remove the oil filter, disconnect the radiator lower hose at the water pump and remove the oil pan.
11. Lower the vehicle.
12. Remove the front cover attaching bolts.

➡ Do not overlook the cover attaching bolt located behind the oil filter adapter. The front cover will break if pried upon if all attaching bolts are not removed.

13. Remove the ignition timing indicator.
14. Remove the front cover and water pump as an assembly. Remove the cover gasket and discard.
15. Remove the camshaft bolt and washer from end of the camshaft. Remove the distributor drive gear.
16. Remove the camshaft sprocket, crankshaft sprocket and timing chain.
17. Remove the chain tensioner assembly from the front of the cylinder block. This is accomplished by pulling back on the ratcheting mechanism and installing a pin through the hole in the bracket to relieve tension.

➡ The front cover houses the oil pump. If a new front cover is to be installed, remove the water pump and oil pump from the old front cover.

To install:

18. Lightly oil all bolt and stud threads before installation. Clean all gasket surfaces on the front cover, cylinder block and fuel pump. If reusing the front cover, replace crankshaft front oil seal.
19. If a new front cover is to be installed, complete the following:
    a. Install the oil pump gears.
    b. Clean the water pump gasket surface. Position a new water pump gasket on the front cover and install water pump. Install the pump attaching bolts and tighten to 15–22 ft. lbs.
20. Rotate the crankshaft as necessary to position piston No. 1 at TDC and the crankshaft keyway at the 12 o' clock position.
21. Install the tensioner assembly. Make sure the ratcheting mechanism is in the retracted position with the pin pointing outward from the hole in the bracket assembly. Tighten the retaining bolts to 6–10 ft. lbs. (8–14 Nm).
22. Lubricate timing chain with clean engine oil. Install the camshaft sprocket, crankshaft sprocket and timing chain.
23. Remove the pin from the tensioner assembly. Make certain the timing marks are positioned across from each other.
24. Install the distributor drive gear.
25. Install the washer and bolt at end of camshaft and tighten to 30–37 ft. lbs. (40–50 Nm).
26. Lubricate the crankshaft front oil seal with clean engine oil.
27. Position a new cover gasket on the cylinder block and install the front cover/water pump assembly using dowels for proper alignment. A suitable contact adhesive is recommended to hold the gasket in position while the front cover is installed.
28. Position the ignition timing indicator.
29. Install the front cover attaching bolts. Apply Loctite® or equivalent, to the threads of the bolt installed below the oil filter housing prior to installation. This bolt is to be installed and tightened last. Tighten all bolts to 15–22 ft. lbs. (20–30 Nm).
30. Raise the vehicle and support safely.
31. Install the oil pan. Connect the radiator lower hose. Install a new oil filter.
32. Coat the crankshaft damper sealing surface with clean engine oil.
33. Position the crankshaft pulley key in the crankshaft keyway.
34. Install the damper with damper washer and attaching bolt. Tighten the bolt to 104–132 ft. lbs. (140–180 Nm).
35. Install the crankshaft pulley and tighten the attaching bolts 19–28 ft. lbs. (26–28 Nm).
36. Lower the vehicle.
37. Connect the coolant bypass hose.
38. Install the distributor with rotor pointing at No. 1 distributor cap tower. Install the distributor cap and coil wire.
39. Connect the radiator upper hose at thermostat housing.
40. Connect the heater hose.
41. If equipped with air conditioning, install compressor and mounting brackets.
42. Install the power steering pump and mounting brackets.
43. Position the accessory drive belt over the pulleys.

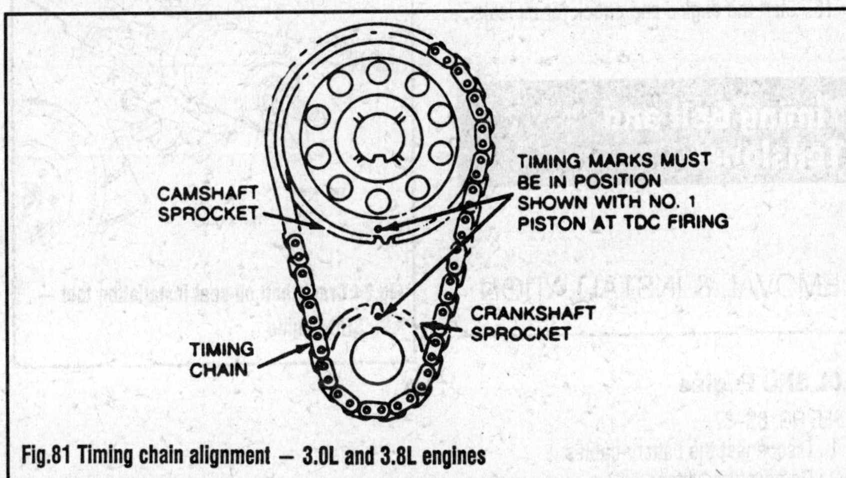

Fig.81 Timing chain alignment — 3.0L and 3.8L engines

44. Install the water pump pulley. Position the accessory drive belt over water pump pulley and tighten the belt.
45. Connect battery ground cable. Fill the crankcase and cooling system to the proper level.
46. Start the engine and check for leaks.
47. Check the ignition timing and curb idle speed, adjust as required.
48. Install the air cleaner assembly and air intake duct.

Timing Belt Cover

REMOVAL & INSTALLATION

3.0L SHO Engine

➧ SEE FIG. 83

1. The front cover on the 3.0L SHO engine is made up of 3 sections. Disconnect the battery cables and remove the battery. Remove the right engine roll damper.
2. Disconnect the wiring to the ignition module. Remove the intake manifold crossover tube bolts, loosen the crossover tube clamps and remove the crossover tube.
3. Loosen the alternator/air conditioner belt tensioner pulley and relieve the tension on the belt by backing out the adjustment screw. Remove the belt.
4. Loosen the water pump/power steering belt tensioner pulley and relieve the tension on the belt by backing out the adjustment screw. Remove the belt.
5. Remove the alternator/air conditioner belt tensioner pulley and bracket assembly. Remove the water pump/power steering belt tensioner pulley only.
6. Remove the upper timing belt cover.
7. Disconnect the crankshaft sensor connectors.
8. Raise and safely support the vehicle. Remove the right front wheel and tire assembly.
9. Loosen the fender splash shield and move aside. Remove the crankshaft damper using a suitable puller.
10. Remove the center and lower timing belt covers.
11. Installation is the reverse of the removal procedure. Tighten the timing belt cover retaining bolts to 60–90 inch lbs. (7–11 Nm) and the crankshaft damper bolt to 113–126 ft. lbs. (152–172 Nm).

Timing Belt Cover Oil Seal

REPLACEMENT

3.0L SHO Engine

➧ SEE FIG. 84

1. Loosen the accessory drive belts.
2. Raise the vehicle and support it safely.
3. Remove the right front wheel.
4. Remove the damper attaching bolt and the accessory drive belts from the crankshaft damper.
5. Using a suitable puller, remove the crankshaft damper from the crankshaft.
6. Remove the timing belt.
7. Remove the crankshaft timing gear using a suitable puller.

➡ Be careful not to damage the crankshaft sensor or shutter.

8. Remove the crankshaft front oil seal using a suitable puller.

To install:

9. Inspect the front cover and shaft seal surface of the crankshaft damper for damage, nicks, burrs or other roughness which may cause the new seal to fail. Repair or replace as necessary.
10. Using suitable tools, install a new crankshaft front oil seal and the crankshaft timing gear.
11. Install the timing belt.
12. Install the crankshaft damper using a suitable tool. Tighten the damper attaching bolt to 113–126 ft. lbs. (152–172 Nm).
13. Install the accessory drive belts.
14. Lower the vehicle.
15. Start the engine and check for oil leaks.

Timing Belt and Tensioner

REMOVAL & INSTALLATION

3.0L SHO Engine

➧ SEE FIG. 82–87

1. Disconnect the battery cables.
2. Remove the battery.

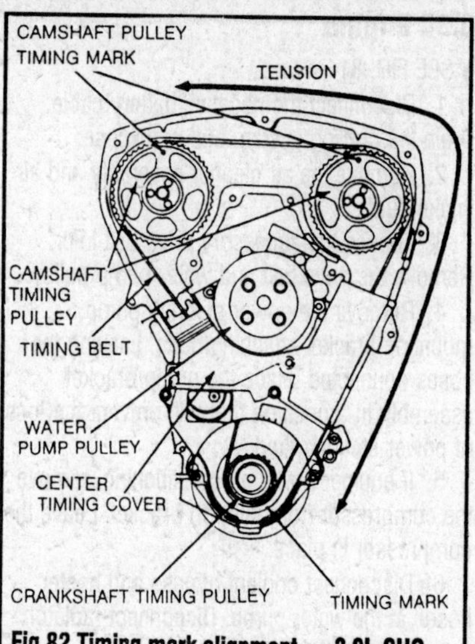

Fig.82 Timing mark alignment — 3.0L SHO engine

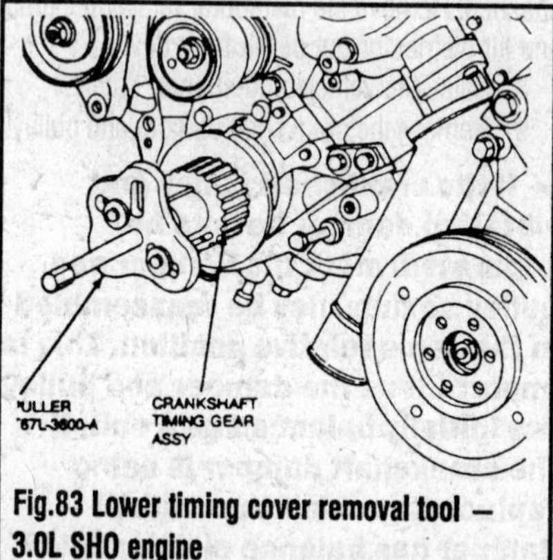

Fig.83 Lower timing cover removal tool — 3.0L SHO engine

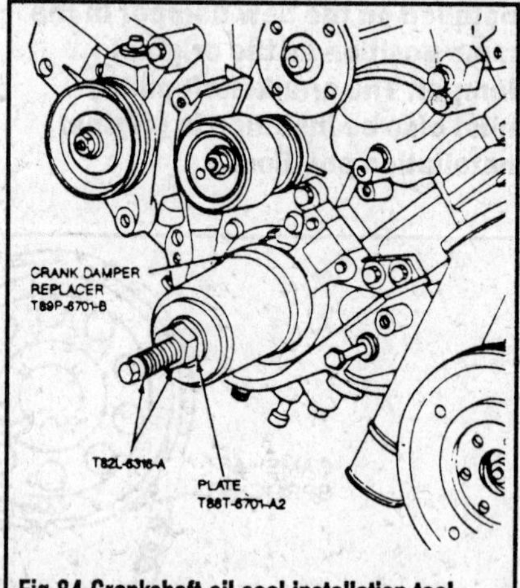

Fig.84 Crankshaft oil seal installation tool — 3.0L SHO engine

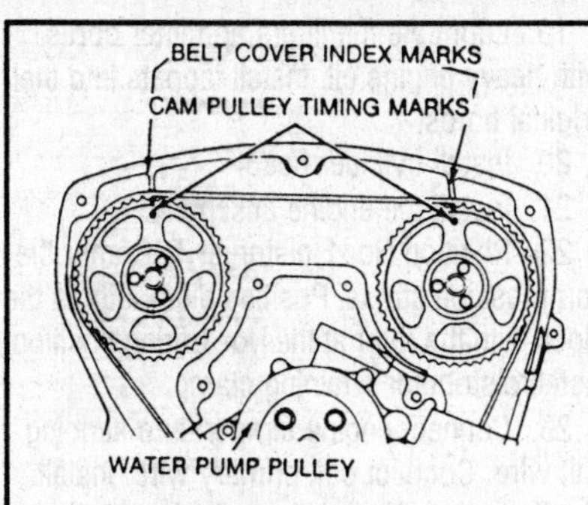

Fig.85 Camshaft pulley to belt cover index marks — 3.0L SHO engine

Fig.86 Crankshaft damper to lower timing cover index mark alignment — 3.0L SHO engine

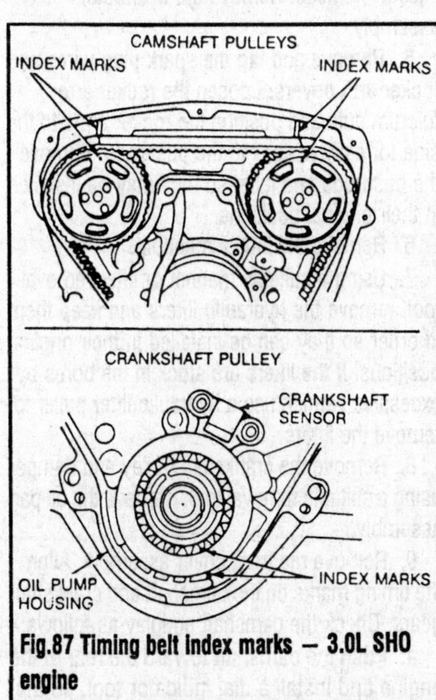

Fig.87 Timing belt index marks — 3.0L SHO engine

3. Remove the right engine roll damper.
4. Disconnect the wiring to the ignition module.
5. Remove the intake manifold crossover tube bolts. Loosen the intake manifold tube hose clamps. Remove the intake manifold crossover tube.
6. Loosen the alternator/air conditioning belt tensioner pulley and relieve the tension on the belt by backing out the adjustment screw. Remove the alternator/air conditioning belt.
7. Loosen the water pump/power steering belt tensioner pulley and relieve the tension on the belt by backing out the adjustment screw. Remove the water pump/power steering belt.
8. Remove the alternator/air conditioning belt tensioner pulley and bracket assembly.
9. Remove the water pump/power steering belt tensioner pulley only.
10. Remove the upper timing belt cover.
11. Disconnect the crankshaft sensor connectors.
12. Place the gear selector in **N**.
13. Set the engine to the TDC on No. 1 cylinder position. Make sure the white mark on the crankshaft damper aligns with the **O** degree index mark on the lower timing belt cover and that the marks on the intake camshaft pulleys align with the index marks on the metal timing belt cover.
14. Raise the vehicle and support safely.
15. Remove the right front wheel and tire assembly.
16. Loosen the fender splash shield and place it aside.
17. Using a suitable puller, remove the crankshaft damper.
18. Remove the lower timing belt cover.
19. Remove the center timing belt cover and disconnect the crankshaft sensor wire and grommet from the slot in the cover and the stud on the water pump.
20. Loosen the timing belt tensioner, rotate the pulley 180° (1/2 turn) clockwise and tighten the tensioner nut to hold the pulley in the unload position.
21. Lower the vehicle and remove the timing belt.

To install:

➡ Before installing the timing belt, inspect it for cracks, wear or other damage and replace, if necessary. Do not allow the timing belt to come into contact with gasoline, oil, water, coolant or steam. Do not twist or turn the belt inside out.

22. Make sure the engine is at TDC on the No. 1 cylinder. Check that the camshaft pulley marks line up with the index marks on the upper steel belt cover and that the crankshaft pulley aligns with the index mark on the oil pump housing. The timing belt has 3 yellow lines. Each line aligns with the index marks.
23. Install the timing belt over the crankshaft and camshaft pulleys. The lettering on the belt **KOA** should be readable from the rear of the engine; top of the lettering to the front of the engine. Make sure the yellow lines are aligned with the index marks on the pulleys.
24. Release the tensioner locknut and leave the nut loose.
25. Raise the vehicle and support safely.
26. Install the center timing belt cover. Make sure the crankshaft sensor wiring and grommet are installed and routed properly. Tighten the mounting bolts to 60–90 inch lbs. (7–11 Nm).
27. Install the lower timing belt cover. Tighten the bolts to 60–90 inch lbs. (7–11 Nm).
28. Using a suitable tool, install the crankshaft damper. Tighten the damper attaching bolt to 113–126 ft. lbs. (152–172 Nm).
29. Rotate the crankshaft 2 revolutions in the clockwise direction until the yellow mark on the damper aligns with the 0° mark on the lower timing belt cover.
30. Remove the plastic door in the lower timing belt cover. Tighten the tensioner locknut to 25–37 ft. lbs. (33–51 Nm) and install the plastic door.
31. Rotate the crankshaft 60° (3/5 turn) more in the clockwise direction until the white mark on the damper aligns with the 0° mark on the lower timing belt cover.
32. Lower the vehicle.
33. Make sure the index marks on the camshaft pulleys align with the marks on the rear metal timing belt cover.
34. Route the crankshaft sensor wiring and connect with the engine wiring harness.
35. Install the upper timing belt cover. Tighten the bolts to 60–90 inch lbs. (7–11 Nm).
36. Install the water pump/power steering tensioner pulley. Tighten the nut to 11–17 ft. lbs. (15–23 Nm).
37. Install the alternator/air conditioning tensioner pulley and bracket assembly. Tighten the bolts to 11–17 ft. lbs. (15–23 Nm).
38. Install the water pump/power steering and alternator/air conditioning belts and set the tension. Tighten the idler pulley nut to 25–36 ft. lbs. (34–50 Nm).
39. Install the intake manifold crossover tube. Tighten the bolts to 11–17 ft. lbs. (15–23 Nm).
40. Install the engine roll damper and the battery.
41. Connect the battery cables.
42. Raise the vehicle and support safely.
43. Install the splash shield and the right front wheel and tire assembly.
44. Lower the vehicle.

Timing Sprockets

REMOVAL & INSTALLATION

3.0L SHO Engine

➧ SEE FIG. 90

1. Disconnect the negative battery cable.
2. Remove the timing belt.
3. Remove the camshaft and crankshaft timing belt sprockets.
4. Install in the reverse order of removal. Tighten the camshaft timing belt sprocket bolts to 15–18 ft. lbs. (21–25 Nm) and the crankshaft pulley bolt to 113–126 ft. lbs. (152–172 Nm).

Camshaft

REMOVAL & INSTALLATION

✻✻ CAUTION

When draining the coolant, keep in mind that cats and dogs are attracted by the ethylene glycol antifreeze, and are quite likely to drink any that is left in an uncovered container or in puddles on the ground. This will prove fatal in sufficient quantity. Always drain the coolant into a sealable container. Coolant should be reused unless it is contaminated or several years old.

2.5L Engine

1. Drain the cooling system and the crankcase. Relieve the fuel system pressure.
2. Remove the engine from the vehicle and position in a suitable holding fixture. Remove the engine oil dipstick.
3. Remove necessary drive belts and pulleys.
4. Remove cylinder head.
5. Using a magnet, remove the hydraulic lifters and label them so they can be installed in their original positions. If the tappets are stuck in the bores by excessive varnish, etc., use a suitable claw-type puller to remove the tappets.
6. Loosen and remove the drive belt, fan and pulley and crankshaft pulley.
7. Remove the oil pan.

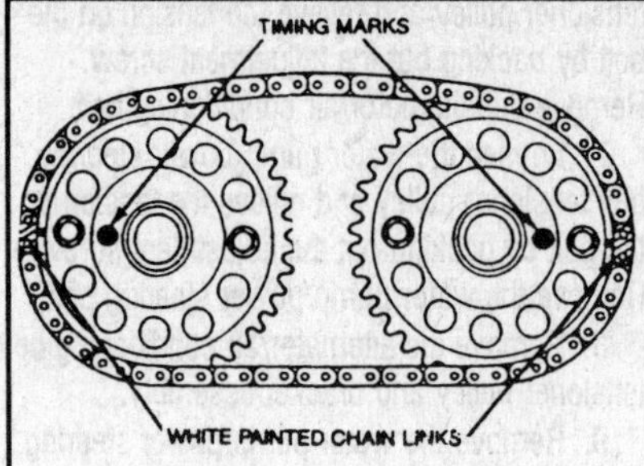

Fig.90 Camshaft sprocket timing marks — 3.0L SHO engine

8. Remove the cylinder front cover and gasket.
9. Check the camshaft endplay as follows:
   a. Push the camshaft toward the rear of the engine and install a dial indicator tool, so the indicator point is on the camshaft sprocket attaching screw.
   b. Zero the dial indicator. Position a small prybar or equivalent, between the camshaft sprocket or gear and block.
   c. Pull the camshaft forward and release it. Compare the dial indicator reading with the camshaft endplay specification of 0.009 in. (0.23mm).
   d. If the camshaft endplay is over the amount specified, replace the thrust plate.
10. Remove the timing chain, sprockets and timing chain tensioner.
11. Remove camshaft thrust plate. Carefully remove the camshaft by pulling it toward the front of the engine. Use caution to avoid damaging bearings, journals and lobes.

To install:

12. Clean and inspect all parts before installation.
13. Lubricate camshaft lobes and journals with heavy engine oil. Carefully slide the camshaft through the bearings in the cylinder block.
14. Install the thrust plate. Tighten attaching bolts to 6–9 ft. lbs. (8–12 Nm).
15. Install the timing chain, sprockets and timing chain tensioner.
16. Install the cylinder front cover and crankshaft pulley.
17. Clean the oil pump inlet tube screen, oil pan and cylinder block gasket surfaces. Prime oil pump by filling the inlet opening with oil and rotate the pump shaft until oil emerges from the outlet tube. Install oil pump, oil pump inlet tube screen and oil pan.
18. Install the accessory drive belts and pulleys.
19. Lubricate the lifters and lifter bores with heavy engine oil. Install tappets into their original bores.
20. Install cylinder head.
21. Install the engine assembly.
22. Position No. 1 piston at TDC after the compression stroke. Position distributor in the block with the rotor at the No. 1 firing position. Install distributor retaining clamp.
23. Connect engine temperature sending unit wire. Connect coil primary wire. Install distributor cap. Connect spark plug wires and the coil high tension lead.
24. Fill the cooling system and crankcase to the proper levels. Connect the negative battery cable.
25. Start the engine. Check and adjust ignition timing. Check for leaks.

3.0L Except SHO Engine

➧ SEE FIG. 89

1. Drain the cooling system and crankcase. Relieve the fuel system pressure.
2. Remove the engine from the vehicle and position in a suitable holding fixture.
3. Remove the accessory drive components from the front of the engine.
4. Remove the throttle body and the fuel injector harness. Remove the distributor assembly.
5. Remove and tag the spark plug wires and rocker arm covers. Loosen the rocker arm fulcrum nuts and position the rocker arms to the side for easy access to the pushrods. Remove the pushrods and label so they may be installed in their original positions.
6. Remove the intake manifold.
7. Using a suitable magnet or lifter removal tool, remove the hydraulic lifters and keep them in order so they can be installed in their original positions. If the lifters are stuck in the bores by excessive varnish use a hydraulic lifter puller to remove the lifters.
8. Remove the crankshaft pulley and damper using a suitable removal tool. Remove the oil pan assembly.
9. Remove the front cover assembly. Align the timing marks on the camshaft and crankshaft gears. Check the camshaft endplay as follows:
   a. Push the camshaft toward the rear of the engine and install a dial indicator tool, so the indicator point is on the camshaft sprocket attaching screw.
   b. Zero the dial indicator. Position a small prybar or equivalent, between the camshaft sprocket or gear and block.
   c. Pull the camshaft forward and release it. Compare the dial indicator reading with the camshaft endplay service limit specification of 0.005 in. (0.13mm).

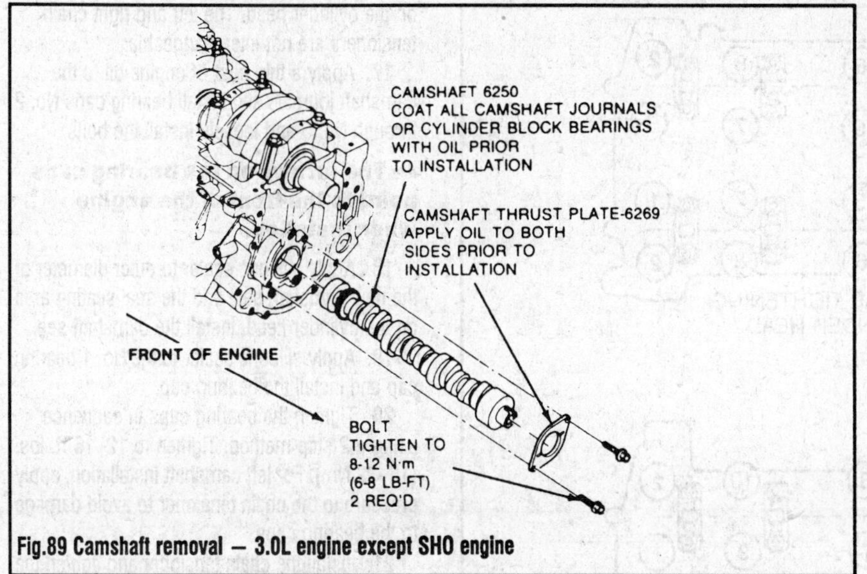

Fig.89 Camshaft removal — 3.0L engine except SHO engine

d. If the camshaft endplay is over the amount specified, replace the thrust plate.

10. Remove the timing chain and sprockets.

11. Remove the camshaft thrust plate. Carefully remove the camshaft by pulling it toward the front of the engine. Remove it slowly to avoid damaging the bearings, journals and lobes.

To Install:

12. Clean and inspect all parts before installation.

13. Lubricate camshaft lobes and journals with heavy engine oil. Carefully insert the camshaft through the bearings in the cylinder block.

14. Install the thrust plate. Tighten the retaining bolts to 7 ft. lbs. (10 Nm).

15. Install the timing chain and sprockets. Check the camshaft sprocket bolt for blockage of drilled oil passages prior to installation and clean, if necessary.

16. Install the front timing cover and crankshaft damper and pulley.

17. Lubricate the lifters and lifter bores with a heavy engine oil. Install the lifters into their original bores.

18. Install the intake manifold assembly.

19. Lubricate the pushrods and rocker arms with heavy engine oil. Install the pushrods and rocker arms into their original positions. Rotate the crankshaft to set each lifter on its base circle, then tighten the rocker arm bolt. Tighten the rocker arm bolts to 24 ft. lbs. (32 Nm).

20. Install the oil pan and the rocker covers.

21. Install the fuel injector harness and the throttle body. Install the distributor and connect the spark plug wires to the spark plugs.

22. Install the accessory drive components and install the engine assembly.

23. Connect the negative battery cable. Start the engine and check for leaks. Check

3.0L SHO Engine

➧ SEE FIG. 91–95

1. Disconnect the negative battery cable. Properly relieve the fuel system pressure.
2. Set the engine on TDC on No. 1 cylinder.
3. Remove the intake manifold assembly.
4. Remove the timing cover and belt.
5. Remove the cylinder head covers.
6. Remove the camshaft pulleys, noting the location of the dowel pins.
7. Remove the upper rear timing belt cover.
8. Uniformly loosen the camshaft bearing caps.

➡ **If the camshaft bearing caps are not uniformly loosened, camshaft damage may result.**

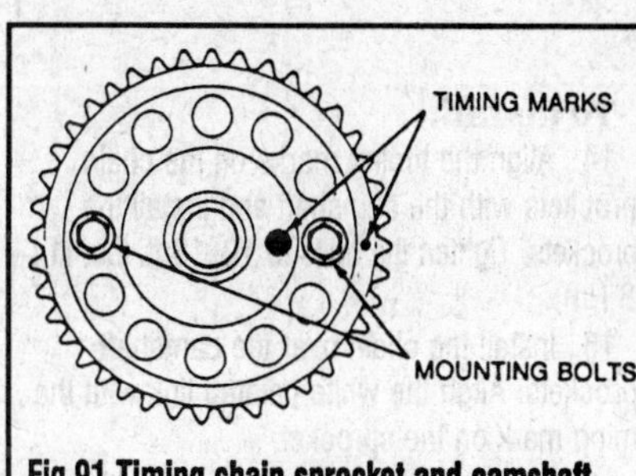

Fig.91 Timing chain sprocket and camshaft alignment — 3.0L SHO engine

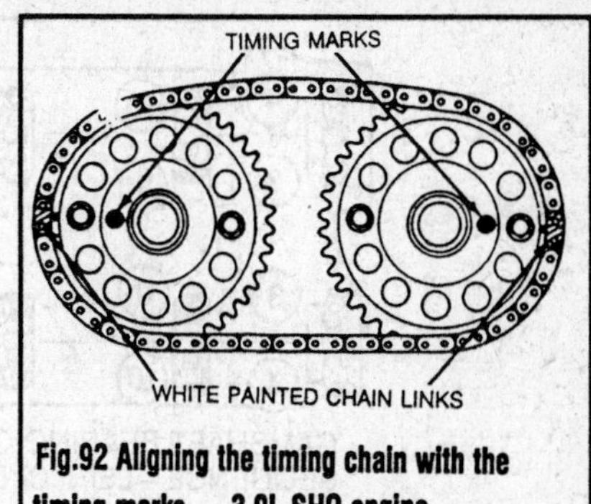

Fig.92 Aligning the timing chain with the timing marks — 3.0L SHO engine

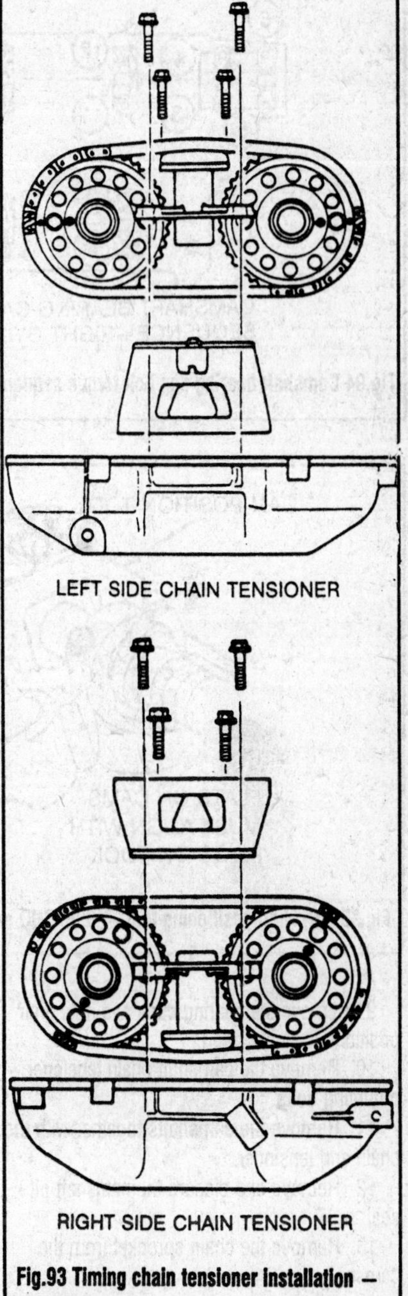

Fig.93 Timing chain tensioner installation — 3.0L SHO engine

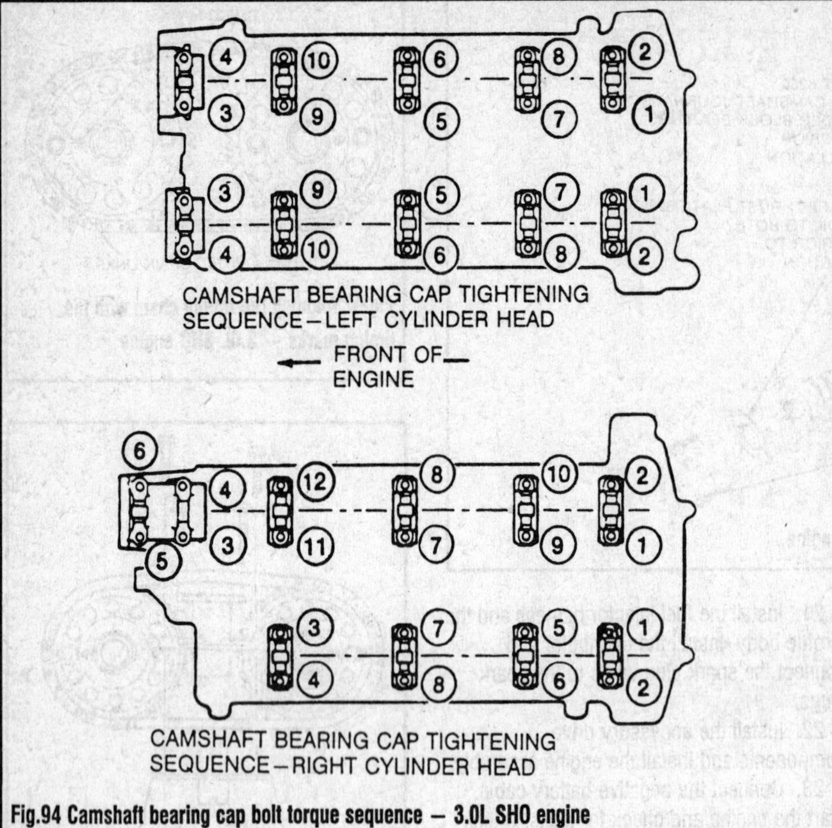

Fig.94 Camshaft bearing cap bolt torque sequence – 3.0L SHO engine

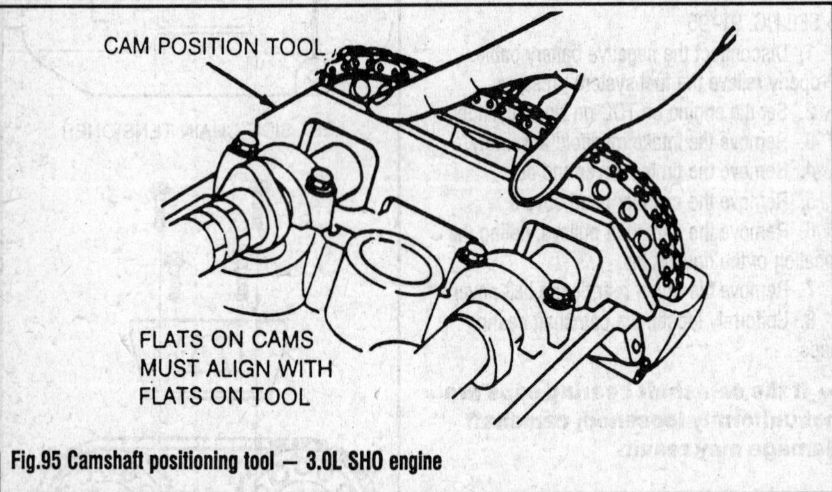

Fig.95 Camshaft positioning tool – 3.0L SHO engine

9. Remove the bearing caps and note their positions for installation.
10. Remove the camshaft chain tensioner mounting bolts.
11. Remove the camshafts together with the chain and tensioner.
12. Remove and discard the camshaft oil seal.
13. Remove the chain sprocket from the camshaft.

To install:

14. Align the timing marks on the chain sprockets with the camshaft and install the sprockets. Tighten the bolts to 10–13 ft. lbs. (14–18 Nm).
15. Install the chain over the camshaft sprockets. Align the white painted link with the timing mark on the sprocket.
16. Rotate the camshafts 60° ($\frac{3}{5}$ turn) counterclockwise. Set the chain tensioner between the sprockets and install the camshafts on the cylinder head. The left and right chain tensioners are not interchangeable.
17. Apply a thin coat of engine oil to the camshaft journals and install bearing caps No. 2 through No. 5 and loosely install the bolts.

➡ The arrows on the bearing caps point to the front of the engine when installed.

18. Apply silicone sealer to outer diameter of the new camshaft seal and the seal seating area on the cylinder head. Install the camshaft seal.
19. Apply silicone sealer to the No. 1 bearing cap and install the bearing cap.
20. Tighten the bearing caps in sequence using a 2 step method. Tighten to 12–16 ft. lbs. (16–22 Nm). For left camshaft installation, apply pressure to the chain tensioner to avoid damage to the bearing caps.
21. Install the chain tensioner and tighten the bolts to 11–14 ft. lbs. (15–19 Nm). Rotate the camshafts 60° ($\frac{3}{5}$ turn) clockwise and check for proper alignment of the timing marks. Marks on the camshaft sprockets should align with the cylinder head cover mating surface.
22. Install the camshaft positioning tool T89P–6256–C or equivalent, on the camshafts to check for correct positioning. The flats on the tool should align with the flats on the camshaft. If the tool does not fit and/or timing marks will not line up, repeat the procedure from Step 14.
23. Install the timing belt rear cover and tighten the bolts to 70 inch lbs. (8.8 Nm).
24. Install the camshaft pulleys and tighten the bolts to 15–18 ft. lbs. (21–25 Nm).
25. Install the timing belt and cover.
26. Install the cylinder head covers and tighten the bolts to 8–11 ft. lbs. (10–16 Nm).
27. Install the intake manifold assembly.

3.8L Engine

1. Disconnect the negative battery cable.
2. Properly relieve the fuel system pressure.
3. Drain the cooling system and crankcase.
4. Remove the engine from the vehicle and position in a suitable holding fixture.
5. Remove the intake manifold.
6. Remove the rocker arm covers, rocker arms, pushrods and lifters.
7. Remove the oil pan.
8. Remove the front cover and timing chain.
9. Remove the thrust plate. Remove the camshaft through the front of the engine, being careful not to damage bearing surfaces.

To install:

10. Lightly oil all attaching bolts and stud threads before installation. Lubricate the cam lobes, thrust plate and bearing surfaces with a suitable heavy engine oil.
11. Install the camshaft being careful not to damage bearing surfaces while sliding into

position. Install the thrust plate and tighten the bolts to 6–10 ft. lbs. (8–14 Nm).

12. Install the front cover and timing chain.
13. Install the oil pan.
14. Install the lifters.
15. Install the upper and lower intake manifolds.
16. Install the engine assembly.
17. Fill the cooling system and crankcase to the proper level and connect the negative battery cable.
18. Start the engine. Check and adjust the ignition timing and engine idle speed as necessary. Check for leaks.

INSPECTION

1. Remove the camshaft from the engine.
2. Check each lobe for excessive wear, flatness, pitting or other physical damage. Replace the camshaft as required.
3. Using a micrometer measure the lobes, if not within specification, replace the camshaft.
4. If replacing the camshaft be sure to check and replace the valve lifters.

Balance Shaft

REMOVAL & INSTALLATION

CAUTION

When draining the coolant, keep in mind that cats and dogs are attracted by the ethylene glycol antifreeze, and are quite likely to drink any that is left in an uncovered container or in puddles on the ground. This will prove fatal in sufficient quantity. Always drain the coolant into a sealable container. Coolant should be reused unless it is contaminated or several years old.

The EPA warns that prolonged contact with used engine oil may cause a number of skin disorders, including cancer! You should make every effort to minimize your exposure to used engine oil. Protective gloves should be worn when changing the oil. Wash your hands and any other exposed skin areas as soon as possible after exposure to used engine oil. Soap and water, or waterless hand cleaner should be used.

3.8L Engine

SEE FIG. 96

1. Remove the engine from the vehicle.
2. Remove the intake manifolds.
3. Remove the oil pan.
4. Remove the front cover and timing chain and camshaft sprocket.
5. Remove the balance shaft drive gear and spacer.
6. Remove the balance shaft gear, thrust plate and shaft assembly.

To install:

7. Thoroughly coat the balance shaft bearings in the block with engine oil.
8. Install the balance shaft gear.
9. Install the balance shaft, thrust plate and gear and tighten the retaining bolts to 6–10 ft. lbs. (8–14 Nm).
10. Install the timing chain and camshaft sprocket.
11. Install the oil pan.
12. Install the timing cover.
13. Install the intake manifolds.
14. Install the engine in the vehicle.

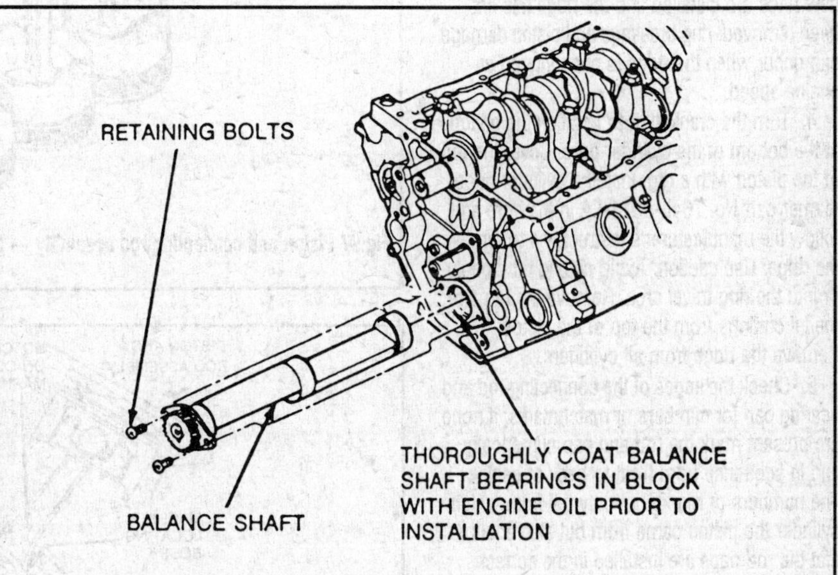
RETAINING BOLTS
THOROUGHLY COAT BALANCE SHAFT BEARINGS IN BLOCK WITH ENGINE OIL PRIOR TO INSTALLATION
BALANCE SHAFT

Fig.96 Balancer shaft assembly and related components — 3.8L engine

Piston and Connecting Rods

REMOVAL & INSTALLATION

CAUTION

When draining the coolant, keep in mind that cats and dogs are attracted by the ethylene glycol antifreeze, and are quite likely to drink any that is left in an uncovered container or in puddles on the ground. This will prove fatal in sufficient quantity. Always drain the coolant into a sealable container. Coolant should be reused unless it is contaminated or several years old.

The EPA warns that prolonged contact with used engine oil may cause a number of skin disorders, including cancer! You should make every effort to minimize your

exposure to used engine oil. Protective gloves should be worn when changing the oil. Wash your hands and any other exposed skin areas as soon as possible after exposure to used engine oil. Soap and water, or waterless hand cleaner should be used.

➧ SEE FIG. 97–100

1. Although, in most cases, the pistons and connecting rods can be removed from the engine (after the cylinder head and oil pan are removed) while the engine is still in the car, it is far easier to remove the engine from the car. If removing pistons with the engine still installed, disconnect the radiator hoses, automatic transmission cooler lines and radiator shroud. Unbolt front mounts before jacking up the engine. Block the engine in position with wooden blocks between the mounts.
2. Remove the engine from the car. Remove cylinder head(s), oil pan and front cover (if necessary).
3. Because the top piston ring does not travel to the very top of the cylinder bore, a ridge is built up between the end of the travel and the top of the cylinder. Pushing the piston and connecting rod assembly past the ridge is difficult and may cause damage to the piston. If new rings are installed and the ridge has not been removed, ring breakage and piston damage can occur when the ridge is encountered at engine speed.
4. Turn the crankshaft to position the piston at the bottom of the cylinder bore. Cover the top of the piston with a rag. Install a cylinder ridge reamer part No. T64L-6011-EA in the bore and follow the manufacturer's instructions to remove the ridge. Use caution. Avoid cutting too deeply or into the ring travel area. Remove the rag and medal cuttings from the top of the piston. Remove the ridge from all cylinders.
5. Check the edges of the connecting rod and bearing cap for numbers or matchmarks, if none are present mark the rod and cap numerically and in sequence from front to back of engine. The numbers or marks not only tell from which cylinder the piston came from but also ensures that the rod caps are installed in the correct matching position.
6. Turn the crankshaft until the connecting rod is at the bottom of the travel. Remove the two attaching nuts and the bearing cap. Take two pieces of rubber tubing and cover the rod bolts to prevent crank or cylinder scoring. Use a wooden hammer handle to help push the piston and rod up and out of the cylinder. Reinstall the rod cap in proper position. Remove all pistons and connecting rods. Inspect cylinder walls and

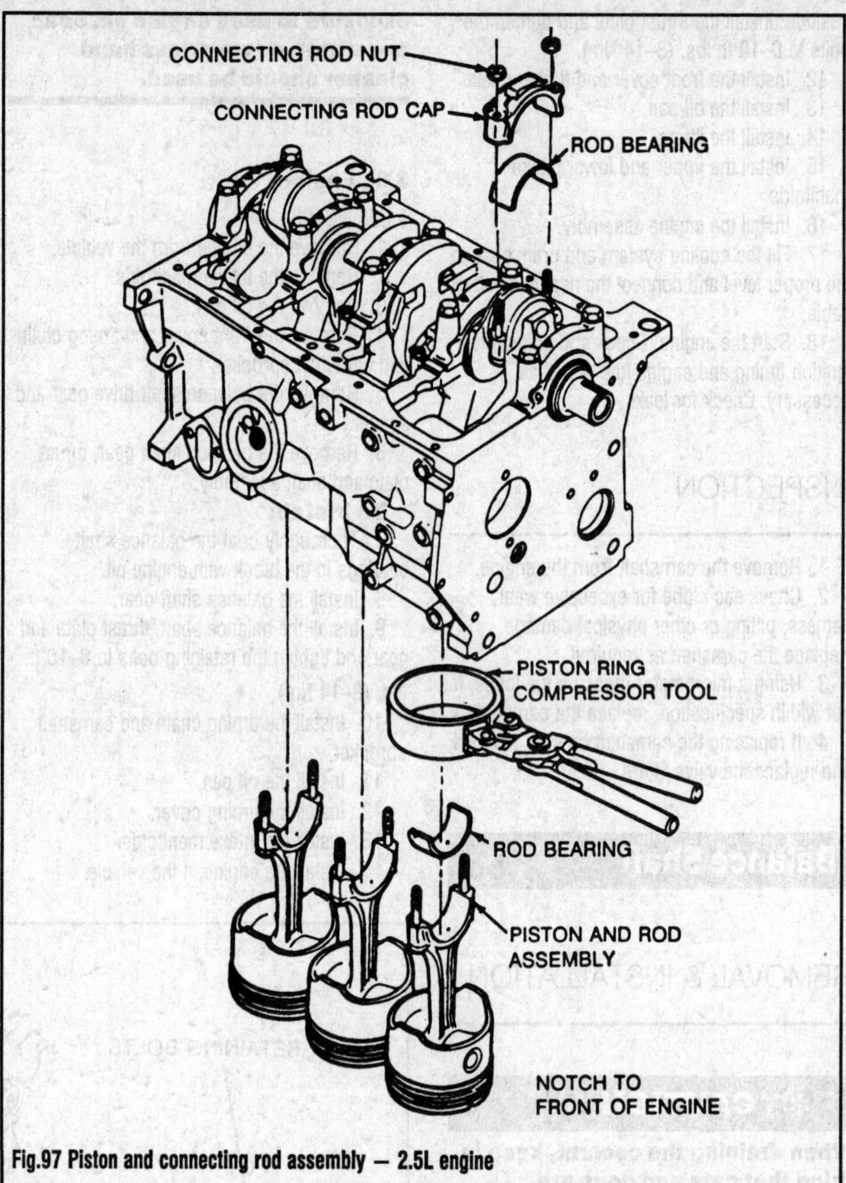

Fig.97 Piston and connecting rod assembly — 2.5L engine

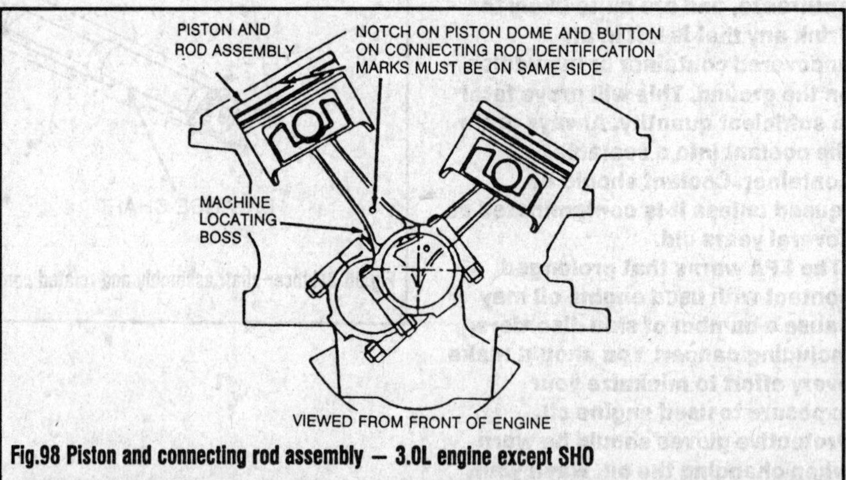

Fig.98 Piston and connecting rod assembly — 3.0L engine except SHO

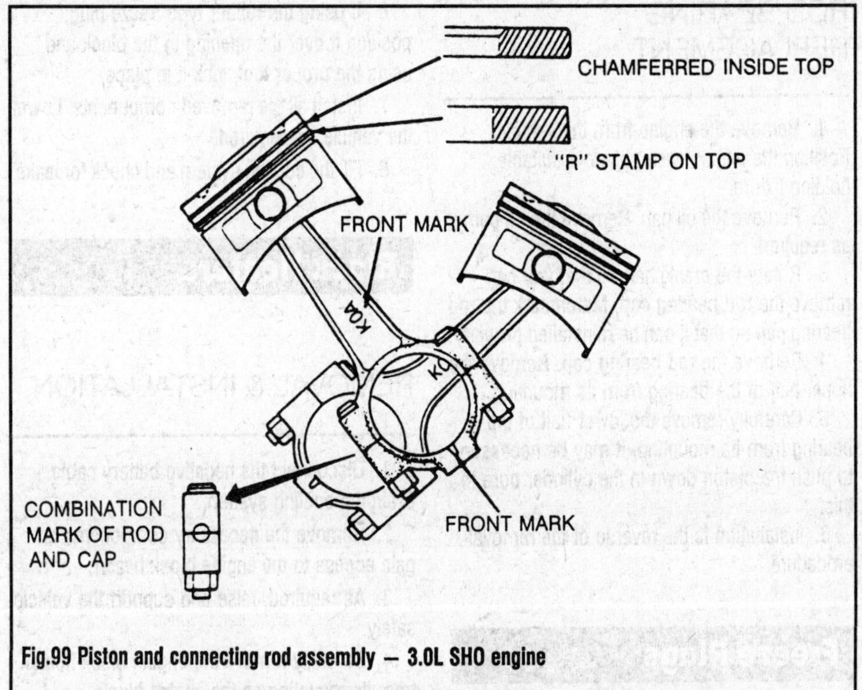

Fig.99 Piston and connecting rod assembly — 3.0L SHO engine

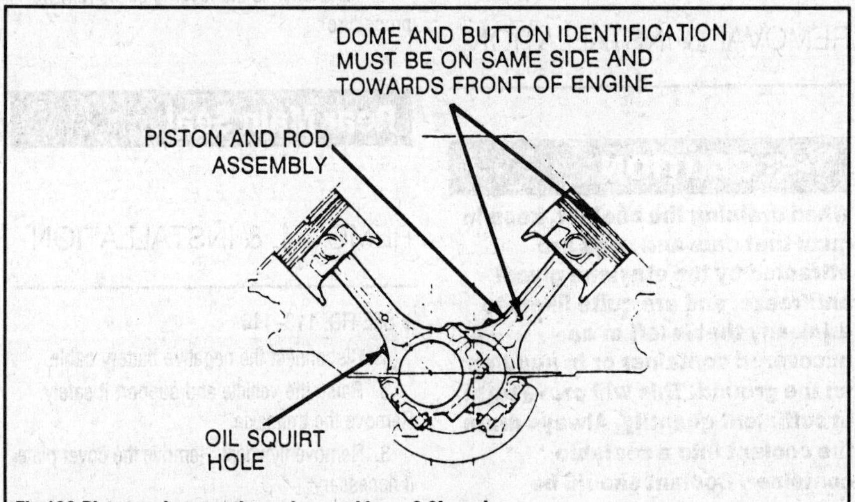

Fig.100 Piston and connecting rod assembly — 3.8L engine

deglaze or hone using a cylinder hone set part No. T73L-6011-A or equivalent.

To install:

7. Lubricate each piston, rod bearing, and cylinder wall with heavy weight engine oil.
8. Take the bearing nuts and cap off connecting rod. Install rubber hoses over the connecting rod bolts to protect the block and crankshaft journal.
9. Install a ring compressor over the piston, position piston with the mark toward front of engine and carefully install.
10. Position the connecting rod with bearing insert over the crank journal. Install the rod cap with bearing in proper position. Secure with rod nuts and torque to the proper specifications. Install all of the rod and piston assemblies.

CLEANING AND INSPECTION

1. Use a piston ring expander and remove the rings from the piston.
2. Clean the ring grooves using piston ring groove cleaner part No. D81L-6002-D or equivalent. Exercise care to avoid cutting too deeply.
3. Clean all varnish and carbon from the piston with a safe solvent. Do not use a wire brush or caustic solution on the pistons.
4. Inspect the pistons for scuffing, scoring, cracks, pitting or excessive ring groove wear. If wear is evident, the piston must be replaced.
5. Have the piston and connecting rod assembly checked by a machine shop for correct alignment, piston pin wear and piston diameter. If the piston has collapsed it will have to be replace or knurled to restore original diameter. Connecting rod bushing replacement, piston pin fitting and piston changing can be handled by the machine shop.

CYLINDER BORE

Check the cylinder bore for wear using a telescope gauge and a micrometer, measure the cylinder bore diameter perpendicular to the piston pin at a point 63.5mm below the top of the engine block. Measure the piston skirt perpendicular to the piston pin. The difference between the two measurements is the piston clearance. If the clearance is within specifications, finish honing or glaze breaking is all that is required. If clearance is excessive a slightly oversize piston may be required. If greatly oversize, the engine will have to be bored and oversized pistons installed.

PISTON RING REPLACEMENT

➧ SEE FIG. 101

1. Take the new piston rings and compress them, one at a time into the cylinder that they will be used in. Press the ring about 25mm below the top of the cylinder block using an inverted piston.
2. Use a feeler gauge and measure the distance between the ends of the ring. This is called measuring the ring end gap. Compare the reading to the one called for in the specifications table. If the measurement is too small, when the engine heats up the ring ends will butt together and cause damage. File the ends of the ring with a fine file to obtain necessary clearance.

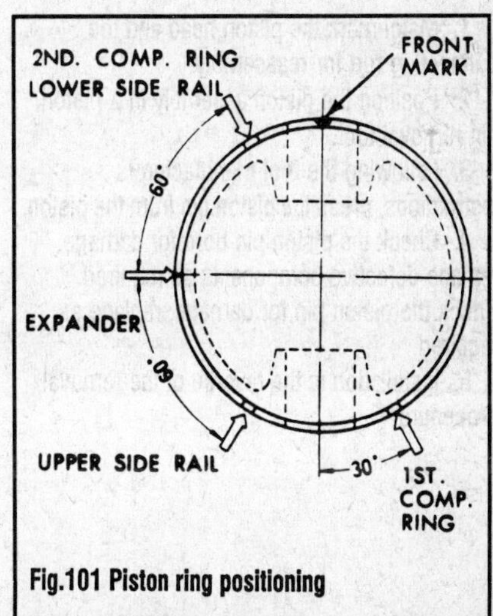

Fig.101 Piston ring positioning

➡ **If inadequate ring end gap is utilized, ring breakage will result.**

3. Inspect the ring grooves on the piston for excessive wear or taper. If necessary, have the grooves recut for use with a standard ring and spacer. The machine shop can handle the job for you.

4. Check the ring grooves by rolling the new piston ring around the groove to check for burrs or carbon deposits. If any are found, remove with a fine file. Hold the ring in the groove and measure side clearance with a feeler gauge. If the clearance is excessive, spacer(s) will have to be added.

➡ **Always add spacers above the piston ring.**

5. Install the ring on the piston, lower oil ring first. Use a ring installing tool (piston ring expander) on the compression rings. Consult the instruction sheet that comes with the rings to be sure they are installed with the correct side up. A mark on the ring usually faces upward.

6. When installing oil rings, first, install the expanding ring in the groove. Hold the ends of the ring butted together (they must not overlap) and install the bottom rail (scraper) with the end about 25mm away from the butted end of the control ring. Install the top rail about 25mm away from the butted end of the control but on the opposite side from the lower rail. Be careful not to scrap the piston when installing oil control rings.

7. Install the two compression rings. The lower ring first.

8. Consult the illustration for ring positioning, arrange the rings as shown, install a ring compressor and insert the piston and rod assembly into the engine.

PISTON PIN REPLACEMENT

1. Matchmark the piston head and the connecting rod for reassembly.

2. Position the piston assembly in a piston pin removal tool.

3. Following the tool manufacturers instructions, press the piston pin from the piston.

4. Check the piston pin bore for damage, replace defective components as required. Check the piston pin for damage, replace as required.

5. Installation is the reverse of the removal procedure.

ROD BEARING REPLACEMENT

1. Remove the engine from the vehicle. Position the engine assembly in a suitable holding fixture.

2. Remove the oil pan. Remove the oil pump, as required.

3. Rotate the crankshaft so that you can remove the rod bearing cap. Matchmark the rod bearing cap so that it can be reinstalled properly.

4. Remove the rod bearing cap. Remove the upper half of the bearing from its mounting.

5. Carefully remove the lower half of the bearing from its mounting. It may be necessary to push the piston down in the cylinder bore to this.

6. Installation is the reverse of the removal procedure.

Freeze Plugs

REMOVAL & INSTALLATION

⁂ CAUTION

When draining the coolant, keep in mind that cats and dogs are attracted by the ethylene glycol antifreeze, and are quite likely to drink any that is left in an uncovered container or in puddles on the ground. This will prove fatal in sufficient quantity. Always drain the coolant into a sealable container. Coolant should be reused unless it is contaminated or several years old.

1. Disconnect the negative battery cable. Drain the cooling system.

2. Remove the necessary components to gain access to the freeze plug that requires service.

3. As required, raise and support the vehicle safely.

4. Using the proper freeze plug removal tool remove and discard the old freeze plug.

To install:

5. If using a new metal freeze plug, position it over the opening in the block. Lightly tap it in place until it sits flush with the bore in the block.

6. If using the rubber type freeze plug, position it over the opening in the block and using the proper tool, lock it in place.

7. Install all the removed components. Lower the vehicle, as required.

8. Fill the cooling system and check for leaks.

Block Heaters

REMOVAL & INSTALLATION

1. Disconnect the negative battery cable. Drain the cooling system.

2. Remove the necessary components to gain access to the engine block heater.

3. As required, raise and support the vehicle safely.

4. Carefully remove the engine block heater from its mounting on the engine block.

5. Installation is the reverse of the removal procedure.

Rear Main Seal

REMOVAL & INSTALLATION

➧ SEE FIG. 113–116

1. Disconnect the negative battery cable.

2. Raise the vehicle and support it safely. Remove the transaxle.

3. Remove flywheel. Remove the cover plate, if necessary.

4. With a suitable tool, remove the oil seal.

➡ **Use caution to avoid damaging the oil seal surface.**

To install:

5. Inspect the crankshaft seal area for any damage which may cause the seal to leak. If damage is evident, service or replace the crankshaft as necessary.

6. Coat the crankshaft seal area and the seal lip with engine oil.

7. Using a seal installer tool, install the seal. Tighten the 2 bolts of the seal installer tool evenly so the seal is straight and seats without misalignment.

8. Install the flywheel. Tighten attaching bolts to 54–64 ft. lbs. (73–87 Nm) on all except the

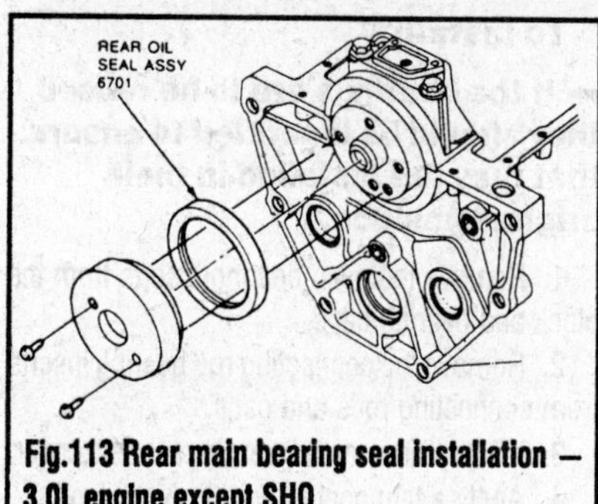

Fig.113 Rear main bearing seal installation — 3.0L engine except SHO

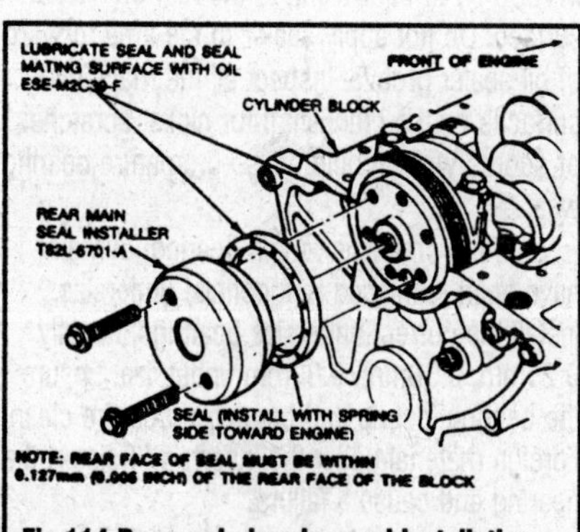

Fig.114 Rear main bearing seal installation — 3.8L engine

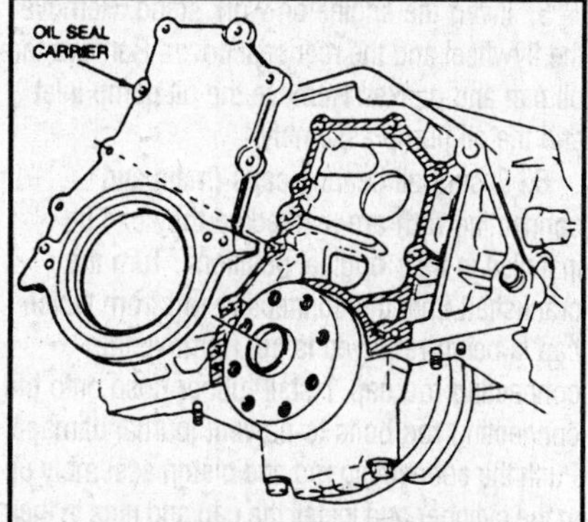

Fig.115 Rear main bearing seal and seal carrier installation — 3.0L SHO engine

3.0L SHO engine. On the 3.0L SHO engine, tighten the bolts to 51–58 ft. lbs. (69–78 Nm).

9. Install rear cover plate, if necessary.

10. Install the transaxle and connect the negative battery cable.

Crankshaft and Main Bearings

REMOVAL & INSTALLATION

✲✲ CAUTION

When draining the coolant, keep in mind that cats and dogs are attracted by the ethylene glycol antifreeze, and are quite likely to drink any that is left in an uncovered container or in puddles on the ground. This will prove fatal in sufficient quantity. Always drain the coolant into a sealable container. Coolant should be reused unless it is contaminated or several years old.

The EPA warns that prolonged contact with used engine oil may cause a number of skin disorders,

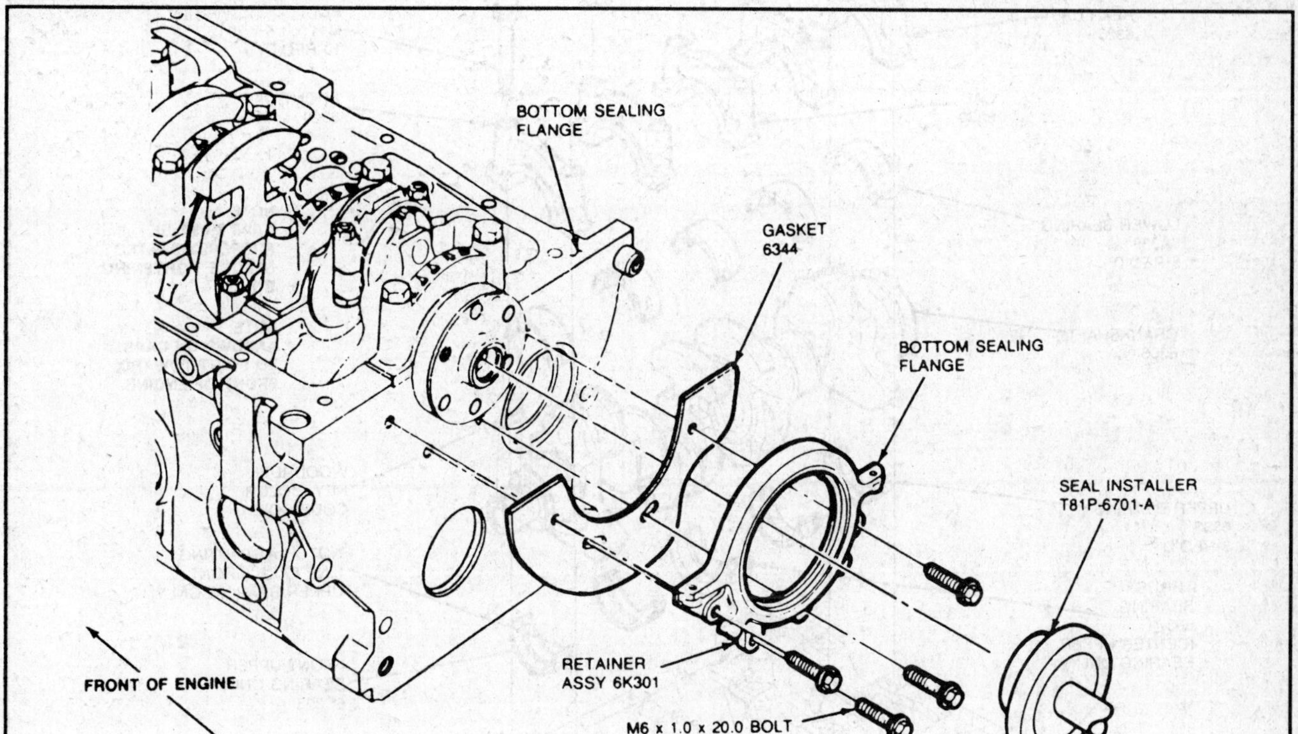

Fig.116 Rear main bearing seal installation — 2.5L engine

including cancer! You should make every effort to minimize your exposure to used engine oil. Protective gloves should be worn when changing the oil. Wash your hands and any other exposed skin areas as soon as possible after exposure to used engine oil. Soap and water, or waterless hand cleaner should be used.

2.5L Engine

➧ SEE FIG. 102

1. With the engine removed from the vehicle and placed on a work stand, remove the oil level dipstick.
2. Remove the accessory drive pulley, if so equipped. Remove the crankshaft pulley attaching bolts and washer.
3. Remove the cylinder front cover and the air conditioning idler pulley assembly, if so equipped. Remove cover assembly.
4. Check the timing chain deflection. Remove the timing chain and sprockets.
5. Invert the engine on work stand. Remove the flywheel and the rear seal cover. Remove the oil pan and gasket. Remove the oil pump inlet and the oil pump assembly.
6. Ensure all bearing caps (main and connecting rod) are marked so they can be installed in their original positions. Turn the crankshaft until the connecting rod from which cap is being removed is up. Remove the connecting rod cap. Install rubber hose onto the connecting rod bolts to prevent journal damage. Push the connecting rod and piston assembly up in the cylinder and install the cap and nuts in their original positions. Repeat the procedure for the remaining connecting rod assemblies.
7. Remove the main bearing caps.
8. Carefully lift crankshaft out of block so upper thrust bearing surfaces are not damaged. Reinstall the main bearing caps on the block.

➡ **Handle the crankshaft with care to avoid possible fracture or damage to the finished surfaces.**

To install:

➡ **If the bearings are to be reused they should be identified to ensure that they are installed in their original position.**

1. Remove the main bearing inserts from the block and bearing caps.
2. Remove the connecting rod bearing inserts from connecting rods and caps.
3. Install a new rear oil seal in rear seal cover.
4. Apply a thin coat of Ford Polyethylene Grease D0AZ-19584-A (ESR-M1C159-A or ESB-M1C93-A) or equivalent, to the rear crankshaft surface. Do not apply sealer to the area forward of oil sealer groove. Inspect all the machined surfaces on the crankshaft for nicks, scratches or scores which could cause premature bearing wear.
5. If the crankshaft main bearing journals have been refinished to a definite undersize, install the correct undersize bearings, usually 0.25mm, 0.50mm, 0.80mm undersize. Ensure the bearing inserts and bearing bores are clean. Foreign material under the inserts will distort the bearing and cause a failure.

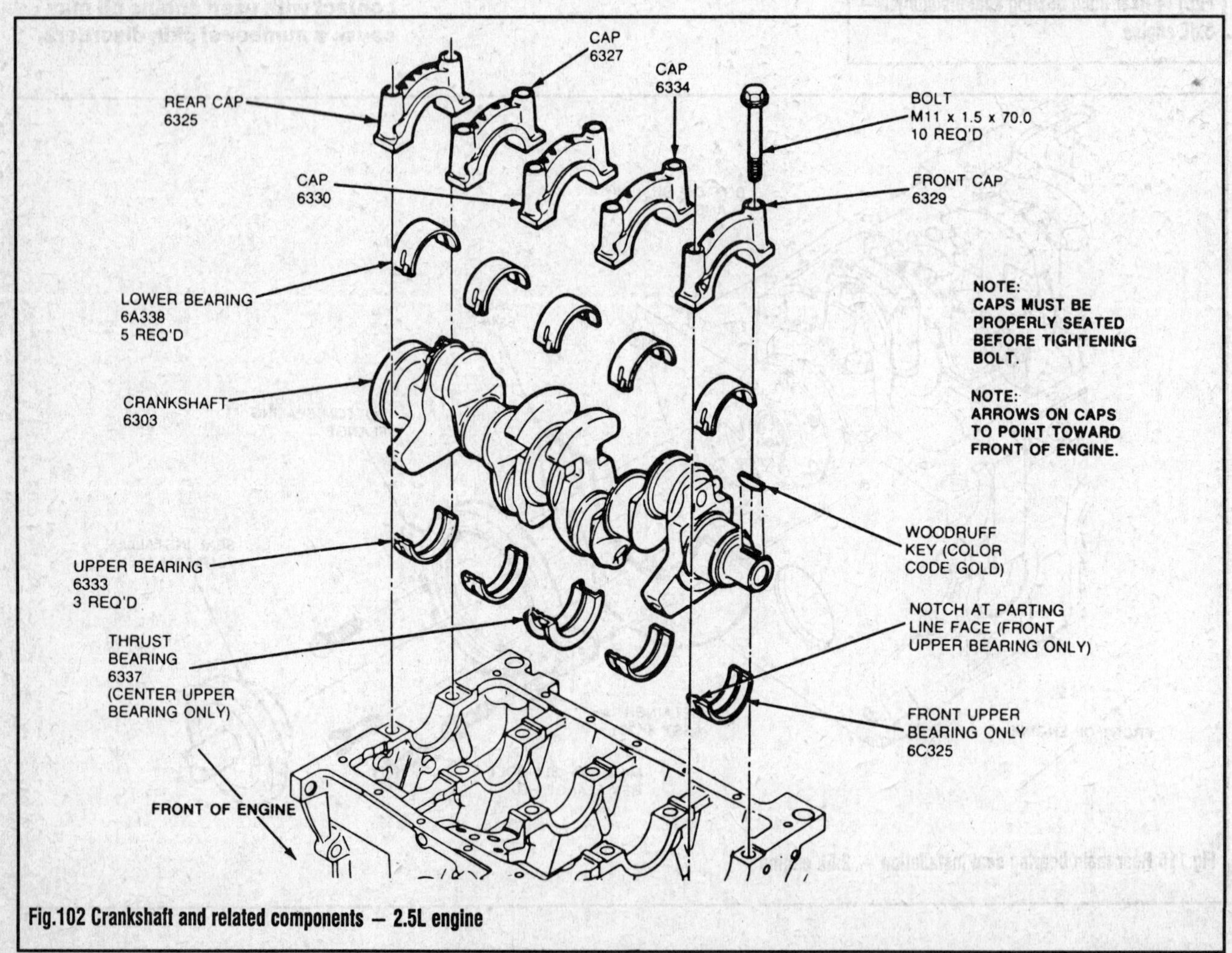

Fig.102 Crankshaft and related components — 2.5L engine

6. Place the upper main bearing inserts in position in the bores with the tang fitted in the slot provided.

➡ **Lubricate the bearing surfaces with Oil Conditioner part No. D9AZ-19579-CF or equivalent. Conditioner is needed for lubrication at initial start up.**

7. Install the lower main bearings inserts in the bearing caps.

8. Carefully lower the crankshaft into place.

9. Check the clearance of each main bearing. Select fit the bearings for proper clearance.

10. After the bearings have been fitted, apply a light coat of oil conditioner to journals and bearings. Install all the bearing caps and torque to proper specifications.

➡ **The main bearing cap must be installed in their original positions.**

11. Align the upper thrust bearing.

12. Check the crankshaft end play, using a dial indicator mounted on the front of the engine.

13. If the end play exceeds specification, replace the upper thrust bearing. If the end play is less than the specification, inspect the thrust bearing faces for damage, dirt or improper alignment. Install the thrust bearing and align the faces. Check the end play.

14. Install the new bearing inserts in the connecting rods and caps. Install rubber hoses on the rod bolts to prevent crankshaft journal damage. Check the clearance of each bearing using a piece of Plastigage®.

15. If the bearing clearances are to specification, apply a light coat of Oil Conditioner part No. D9AZ-19579-CF to the journals and bearings.

16. Turn the crankshaft throw to the bottom of the stroke. Push the piston all the way down until the rod bearings seat on the crankshaft journal.

17. Install the connecting rod cap and nuts. Torque the nuts to specifications

18. After the piston and connecting rod assemblies have been installed, check all the connecting-rod-crankshaft journal clearances using a piece of Plastigage®.

19. Turn the engine on the work stand so the front end is up. Install the timing chain, sprockets, timing chain tensioner, front cover, oil seal and the crankshaft pulley.

20. Clean the oil pan, oil pump and the oil pump screen assembly.

21. Prime the oil pump by filling the inlet opening with oil and rotating the pump shaft until oil emerges from the outlet opening. Install the oil pump. Install the oil pan.

22. Position the flywheel on the crankshaft. Apply Pipe Sealant with Teflon D8AZ-19554-A (ESG-M4G194-A and ESR-M18P7-A) or equivalent oil resistant sealer to the flywheel attaching bolts. Torque to specification.

➡ **On the flywheel, if equipped with manual transmission, locate clutch disc and install pressure plate.**

23. Turn the engine on the work stand so the engine is in the normal upright position. Install the oil level dipstick. Install the accessory drive pulley, if so equipped. Install and adjust the drive belt and the accessory belts to specification.

24. Remove the engine from work stand. Install the engine in the vehicle.

3.0L Engine

♦ SEE FIG. 103–107

1. With the engine removed from the vehicle and placed on a workstand, loosen the idler pulley and the alternator belt adjusting bolt.

2. Remove the oil pan and gasket.

3. Remove the front cover assembly.

4. Check the timing chain deflection. Remove the timing chain and sprockets.

5. Invert the engine on the workstand. Remove the flywheel. Remove the oil pump inlet and the oil pump assembly.

6. Ensure all bearing caps (main and connecting rod) are marked so that they can be installed in their original positions. Turn the crankshaft until the connecting rod from which the cap is being removed is up. Remove the connecting rod cap. Push the connecting rod and piston assembly up in the cylinder. Repeat the procedure for the remaining connecting rod assemblies.

7. Remove the main bearing caps.

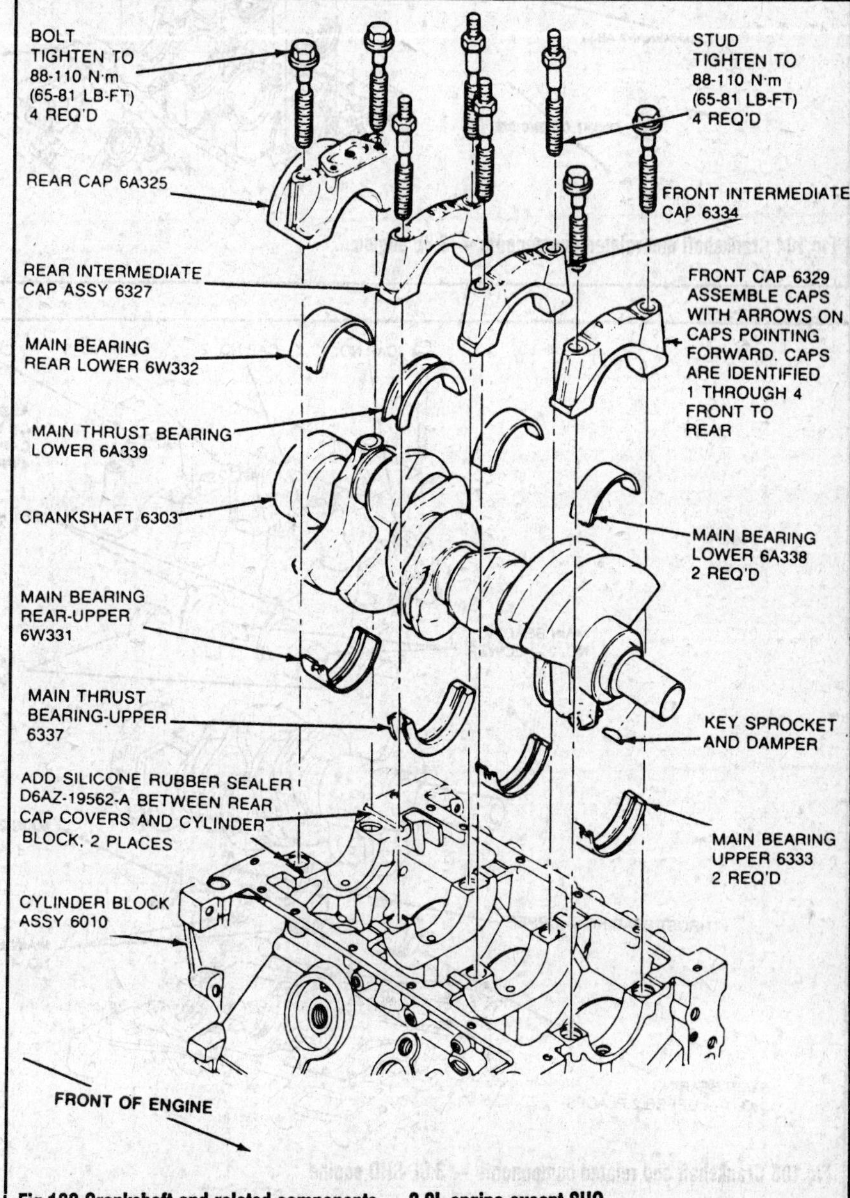

Fig.103 Crankshaft and related components — 3.0L engine except SHO

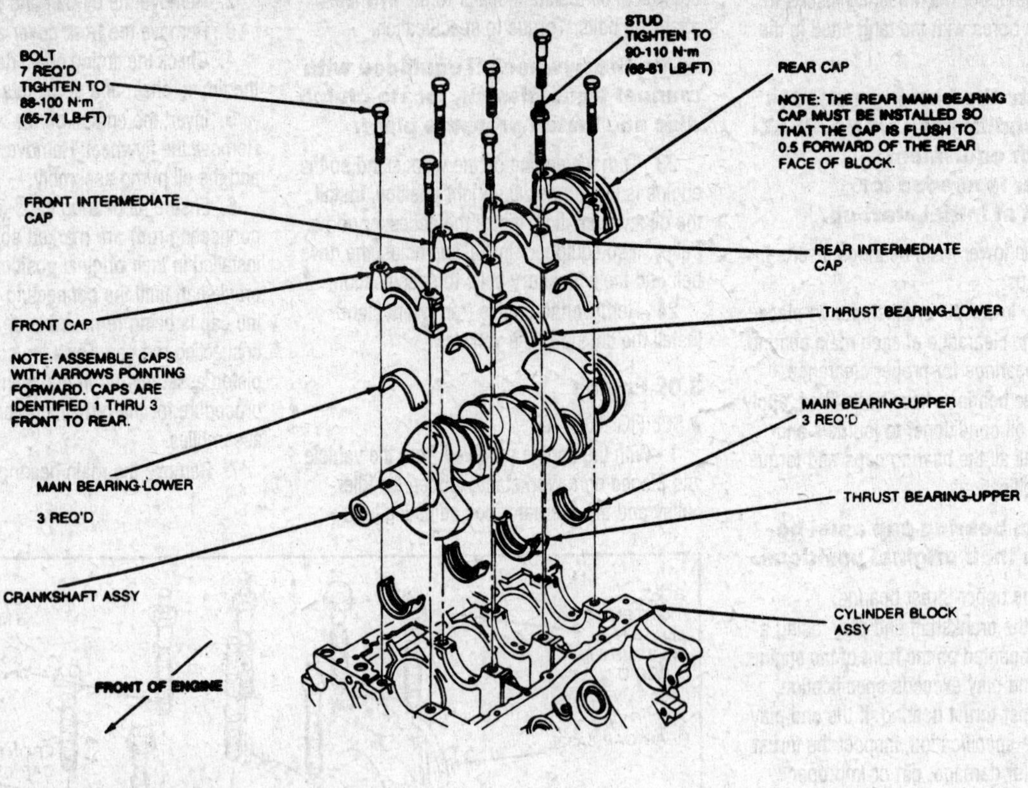

Fig.104 Crankshaft and related components — 3.8L engine

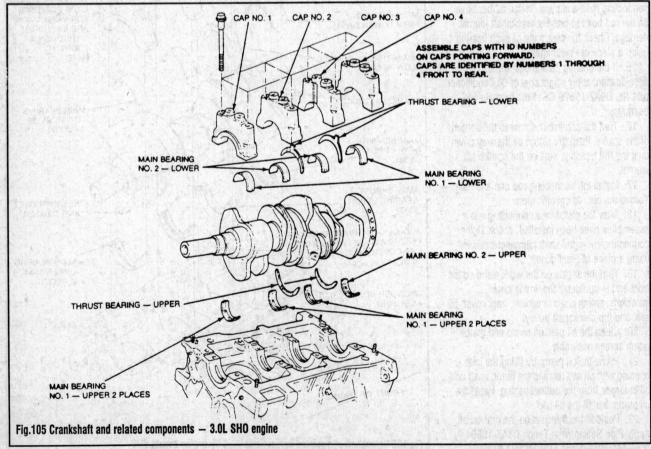

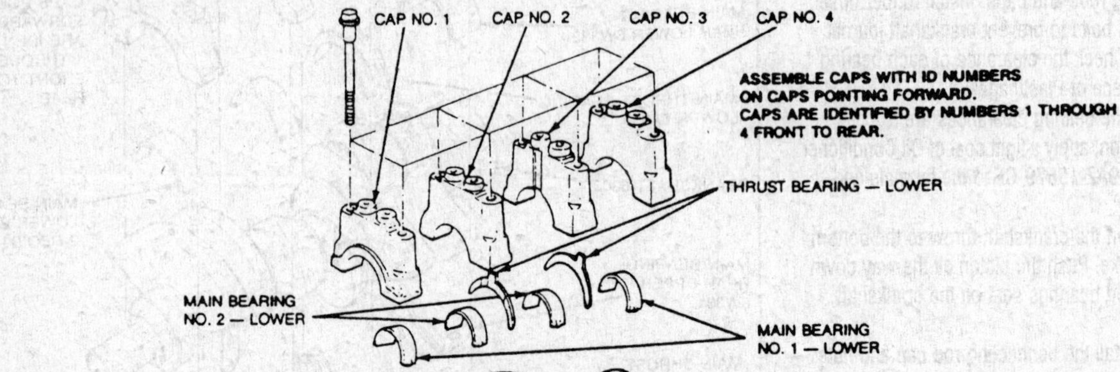

Fig.105 Crankshaft and related components — 3.0L SHO engine

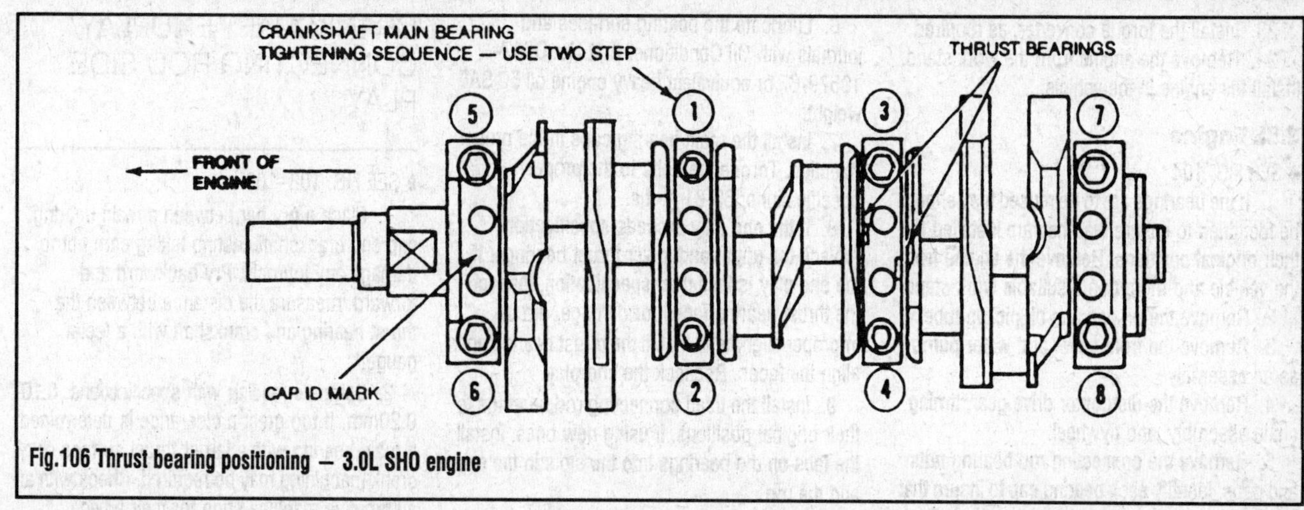

Fig.106 Thrust bearing positioning — 3.0L SHO engine

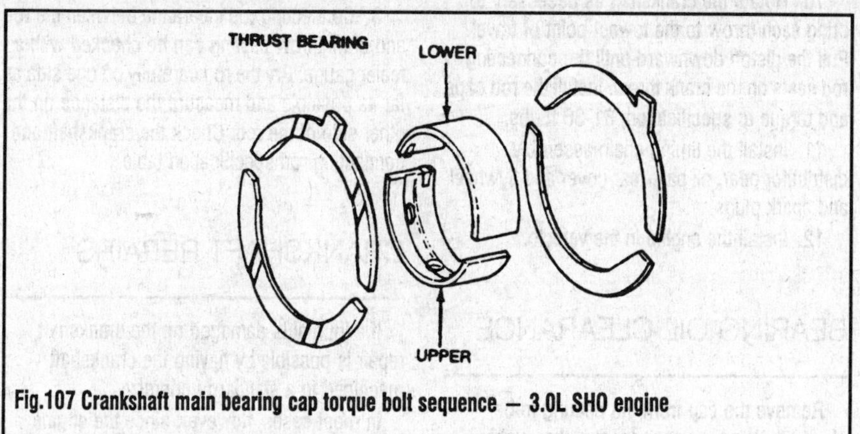

Fig.107 Crankshaft main bearing cap torque bolt sequence — 3.0L SHO engine

8. Carefully lift the crankshaft out of the block so that the upper thrust bearing surfaces are not damaged.

To install:

➡ **If the bearings are to be reused they should be identified to ensure that they are installed in their original positions.**

1. Remove the main bearing inserts from the block and bearing caps.
2. Remove the connecting rod bearing inserts from the connecting rods and caps.
3. Inspect all the machined surfaces on the crankshaft for nicks, scratches, scores, etc., which could cause premature bearing wear.
4. If the crankshaft main bearing journals have been refinished to a definite undersize, install the correct undersize bearings, usually in 0.25mm, 0.50mm, 0.80mm undersize.

➡ **Ensure the bearing inserts and the bearing bores are clean. Foreign material under the inserts will distort the bearing and cause a failure.**

5. Place the upper main bearing inserts in position in the bores with the tang fitted in the slot provided.
6. Install the lower main bearing inserts in the bearing caps.
7. Carefully lower the crankshaft into place.
8. Check the clearance of each main bearing. Select fit the bearings for proper clearance.
9. After the bearings have been fitted, apply a light coat of Oil Conditioner part No. D9AZ-19578-CO or heavy engine oil, SAE 50 weight, to the journals bearings and rear seal surface. Install all the bearing caps. Apply RTV to the gap between the rear main bearing and the block. Take care to keep RTV from the parting surfaces between the block and the cap.

➡ **Ensure the main bearing caps are installed in their original positions and orientation.**

10. Lubricate the journal with oil conditioner or heavy engine oil 50 SAE weight. Install the thrust bearing cap with the bolts finger-tight. Pry the crankshaft forward against the thrust surface of the upper half of the bearing. Hold the crankshaft cap to the rear. This will align the thrust surfaces of both halves of the bearing to be positioned properly. Retain the forward pressure on the crankshaft. Tighten the cap bolts to 65-81 ft. lbs.
11. Check the crankshaft end play with a dial indicator mounted on the front of the engine.
12. If the end play exceeds specification, replace the upper and lower thrust bearings. If the end play is less than specification, inspect the thrust bearing faces for damage, dirt or improper alignment. Install the thrust bearing and align the faces. Recheck the end play.
13. Install the new bearing inserts in the connecting rods and caps. Check the clearance of each bearing by using a piece of Plastigage®.
14. If the bearing clearances are to specification, apply a light coat of Oil Conditioner part No. D9AZ-19579-C or heavy engine oil, SAE 50 weight, to the journals and bearings.
15. Turn the crankshaft throw to the bottom of the stroke. Push the piston all the way down until the rod bearings seat on the crankshaft journal.
16. Install the connecting rod cap.
17. After the piston and connecting rod assemblies have been installed, check all the connecting rod crankshaft journal clearances using a piece of Plastigage®.
18. Turn the engine on the work stand so that the front end is up. Install the timing chain, sprockets, front cover, new oil seal and crankshaft pulley. Turn the engine on the work stand so that the rear end is up. Install the rear oil seal.
19. Clean the oil pan, oil pump and the oil pump screen assembly.
20. Prime the oil pump by filling the inlet opening with oil and rotating the pump shaft until the oil emerges from the outlet opening. Install the oil pump, baffle and oil pan.
21. Position the flywheel on the crankshaft. Tighten to 54-64 ft lbs.
22. Turn the engine on work stand so that the engine is in the normal upright position. Install the accessory drive pulley. Install and adjust the accessory drive belts to specification.

23. Install the torque converter, as required.

24. Remove the engine from the work stand. Install the engine in the vehicle.

3.8L Engine

➧ SEE FIG. 104

1. If the bearings are to be reused they should be identified to ensure that they are installed in their original positions. Remove the engine from the vehicle and mount on a suitable work stand.

2. Remove the oil pan and oil pickup tube.

3. Remove the front cover and water pump as an assembly.

4. Remove the distributor drive gear, timing chain assembly, and flywheel.

5. Remove the connecting rod bearing nuts and caps. Identify each bearing cap to insure that they are installed in their original positions. Push the pistons up into the cylinder and put pieces of rubber hose on the connecting rod bolts so the crankshaft journals do not get damaged.

6. Inspect all the machined surfaces on the crankshaft for nicks, scratches, scores, etc., which could cause premature bearing wear.

➡ Because the engine crankshaft incorporates deep rolling of the main journal fillets, journal refinishing is limited to 0.25mm undersize. Further refinishing may result in fatigue failure of the crankshaft.

Ensure the bearing inserts and the bearing bores are clean. Foreign material under the inserts will distort the bearing and cause a failure.

7. Remove the main bearing caps and identify each bearing cap to insure that they are installed in their original positions.

8. Carefully lift the crankshaft out of the block to prevent damage to bearing surfaces.

To install:

1. Make sure all crankshaft bearing journals and bearing caps are clean. Contaminants under a bearing will cause distortion. Contaminants on the bearing surface will cause damage to the bearing journals.

2. If the crankshaft journals have been refinished to a definite undersize, make sure the proper undersize is being used.

3. Install the used main bearings to their original positions. If using new ones, install the tabs on the bearings into the slots in the cap and the block.

4. Carefully lower crankshaft into position in the cylinder block. Be careful not to damage the thrust bearing surfaces.

5. Apply a 3mm bead of Silicone Sealer part No. D6AZ-19562-A or equivalent to the rear main bearing cap-to-cylinder block parting line.

6. Lubricate the bearing surfaces and journals with Oil Conditioner part No. D9AZ-19579-CF or equivalent heavy engine oil 50 SAE weight.

7. Install the main bearing caps in the proper direction. Torque the bolts to the proper specifications, 65-81 ft. lbs.

8. If the end play exceeds specification, replace the upper and lower thrust bearings. If the end play is less than specification, inspect the thrust bearing faces for damage, dirt or improper alignment. Install the thrust bearing and align the faces. Recheck the end play.

9. Install the used connecting rod bearings to their original positions. If using new ones, install the tabs on the bearings into the slots in the cap and the rod.

10. Rotate the crankshaft as necessary to bring each throw to the lowest point of travel. Pull the piston downward until the connecting rod seats on the crank throw. Install the rod caps and torque to specification, 31-36 ft. lbs.

11. Install the timing chain assembly, distributor gear, oil pan, rear cover and flywheel, and spark plugs.

12. Install the engine in the vehicle.

BEARING OIL CLEARANCE

Remove the cap from the bearing to be checked. Using a clean, dry rag, thoroughly clean all oil from the crankshaft journal and bearing insert.

➡ Plastigage® is soluble in oil, therefore, oil on the journal or bearing could result in erroneous readings.

Place a piece of Plastigage® along the full width of the bearing insert, reinstall cap, and torque to specifications.

Remove the bearing cap, and determine bearing clearance by comparing width of the bearing insert, reinstall cap, and torque to specifications.

➡ Do not rotate crankshaft with Plastigage® installed. If the bearing insert and journal appear intact, and are within tolerances, no further main bearing service is required. If the bearing or journal appear defective, cause of failure should be determined before replacement.

CRANKSHAFT ENDPLAY/ CONNECTING ROD SIDE PLAY

➧ SEE FIG. 108–109

1. Place a pry bar between a main bearing cap and crankshaft casting taking care not to damage any journals. Pry backward and forward, measure the distance between the thrust bearing and crankshaft with a feeler gauge.

2. Compare reading with specifications, 0.10-0.20mm. If too great a clearance is determined, a main bearing with a larger thrust surface or crank machining may be required. Check with an automotive machine shop for their advice.

3. Connecting rod clearance between the rod and crankthrow casting can be checked with a feeler gauge. Pry the rod carefully on one side as far as possible and measure the distance on the other side of the rod. Check the crankshaft and connecting rod specification table.

CRANKSHAFT REPAIRS

If a journal is damaged on the crankshaft, repair is possible by having the crankshaft machined to a standard undersize.

In most cases, however, since the engine must be removed from the car and disassembled, some thought should be given to replacing the damaged crankshaft with a reground shaft kit. A reground crankshaft kit contains the necessary main and rod bearings for installation. The shaft has been ground and polished to undersize specifications and will usually hold up well if installed correctly.

Flywheel/Flexplate

REMOVAL & INSTALLATION

➧ SEE FIG. 110–112

1. Remove the transaxle from the vehicle.

2. Remove the flywheel/flexplate attaching bolts and the flywheel.

3. The rear cover plate can be removed (manual transmission only).

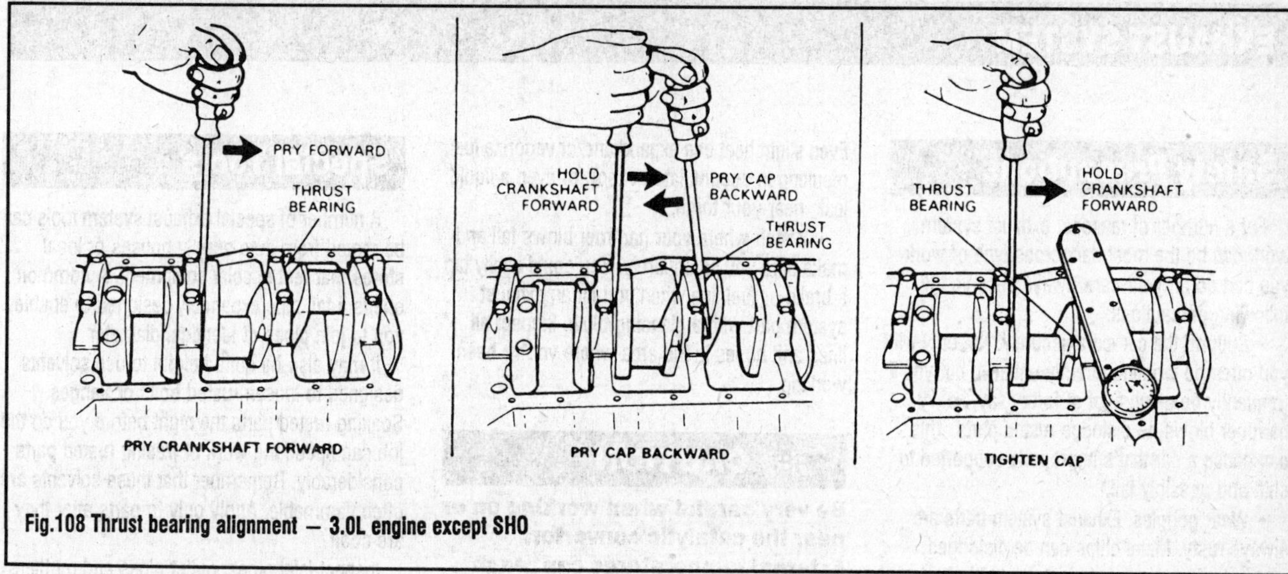

Fig.108 Thrust bearing alignment — 3.0L engine except SHO

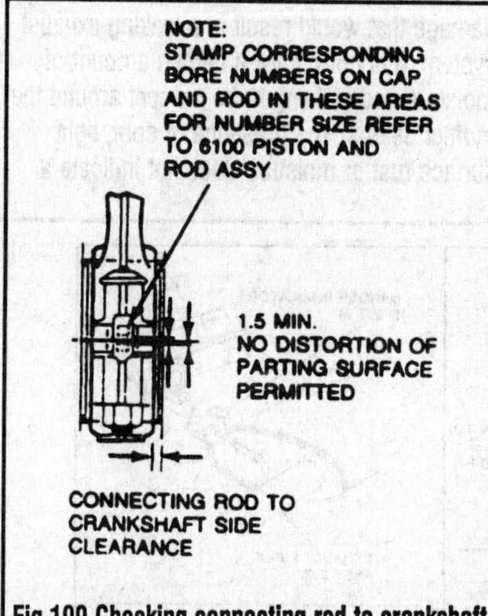

Fig.109 Checking connecting rod to crankshaft side clearance

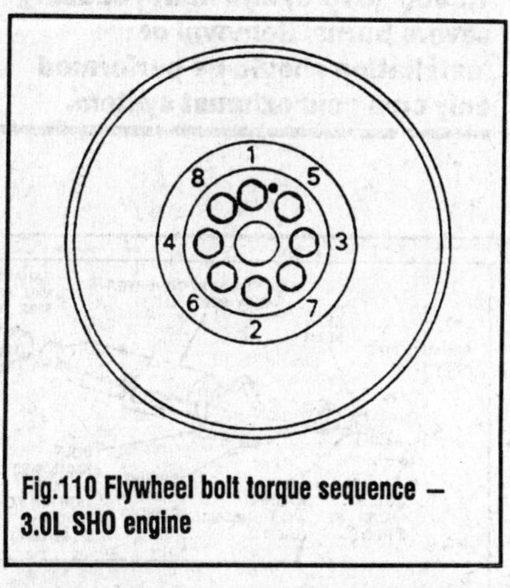

Fig.110 Flywheel bolt torque sequence — 3.0L SHO engine

To install:

➡ **All major rotating components including the flexplate/flywheel are individually balance to zero. Engine assembly balancing is not required. Balance weights should not be installed on new flywheels.**

1. Install the rear cover plate, if removed.
2. Position the flywheel on the crankshaft and install the attaching bolts. Tighten the attaching bolts to 54-64 ft. lbs., using the standard cross-tightening sequence.

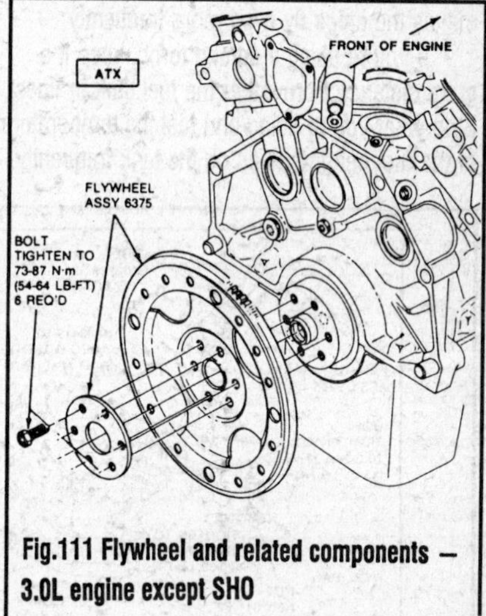

Fig.111 Flywheel and related components — 3.0L engine except SHO

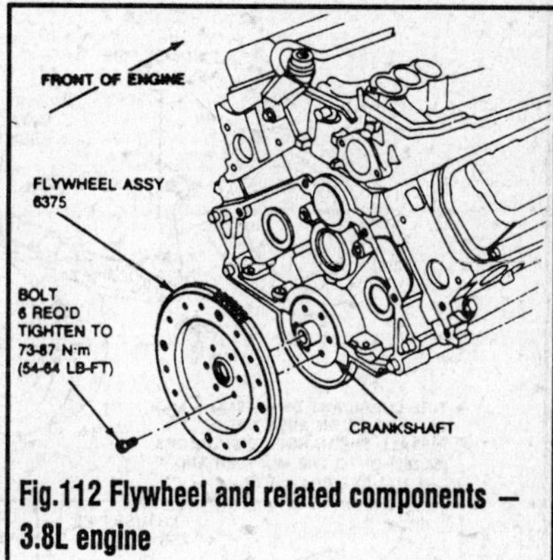

Fig.112 Flywheel and related components — 3.8L engine

EXHAUST SYSTEM

Safety Precautions

For a number of reasons, exhaust system work can be the most dangerous type of work you can do on your car. Always observe the following precautions:

• Support the car extra securely. Not only will you often be working directly under it, but you'll frequently be using a lot of force, say, heavy hammer blows, to dislodge rusted parts. This can cause a car that's improperly supported to shift and possibly fall.

• Wear goggles. Exhaust system parts are always rusty. Metal chips can be dislodged, even when you're only turning rusted bolts. Attempting to pry pipes apart with a chisel makes the chips fly even more frequently.

• If you're using a cutting torch, keep it a great distance from either the fuel tank or lines. Stop what you're doing and feel the temperature of the fuel bearing pipes on the tank frequently. Even slight heat can expand and/or vaporize fuel, resulting in accumulated vapor, or even a liquid leak, near your torch.

• Watch where your hammer blows fall and make sure you hit squarely. You could easily tap a brake or fuel line when you hit an exhaust system part with a glancing blow. Inspect all lines and hoses in the area where you've been working.

✻✻ CAUTION

Be very careful when working on or near the catalytic converter. External temperatures can reach 1,500°F (816°C) and more, causing severe burns. Removal or installation should be performed only on a cold exhaust system.

Special Tools

A number of special exhaust system tools can be rented from auto supply houses or local stores that rent special equipment. A common one is a tail pipe expander, designed to enable you to join pipes of identical diameter.

It may also be quite helpful to use solvents designed to loosen rusted bolts or flanges. Soaking rusted parts the night before you do the job can speed the work of freeing rusted parts considerably. Remember that these solvents are often flammable. Apply only to parts after they are cool!

Inspect inlet pipes, outlet pipes and mufflers for cracked joints, broken welds and corrosion damage that would result in a leaking exhaust system. It is normal for a certain amount of moisture and staining to be present around the muffler seams. The presence of soot, light surface rust or moisture does not indicate a

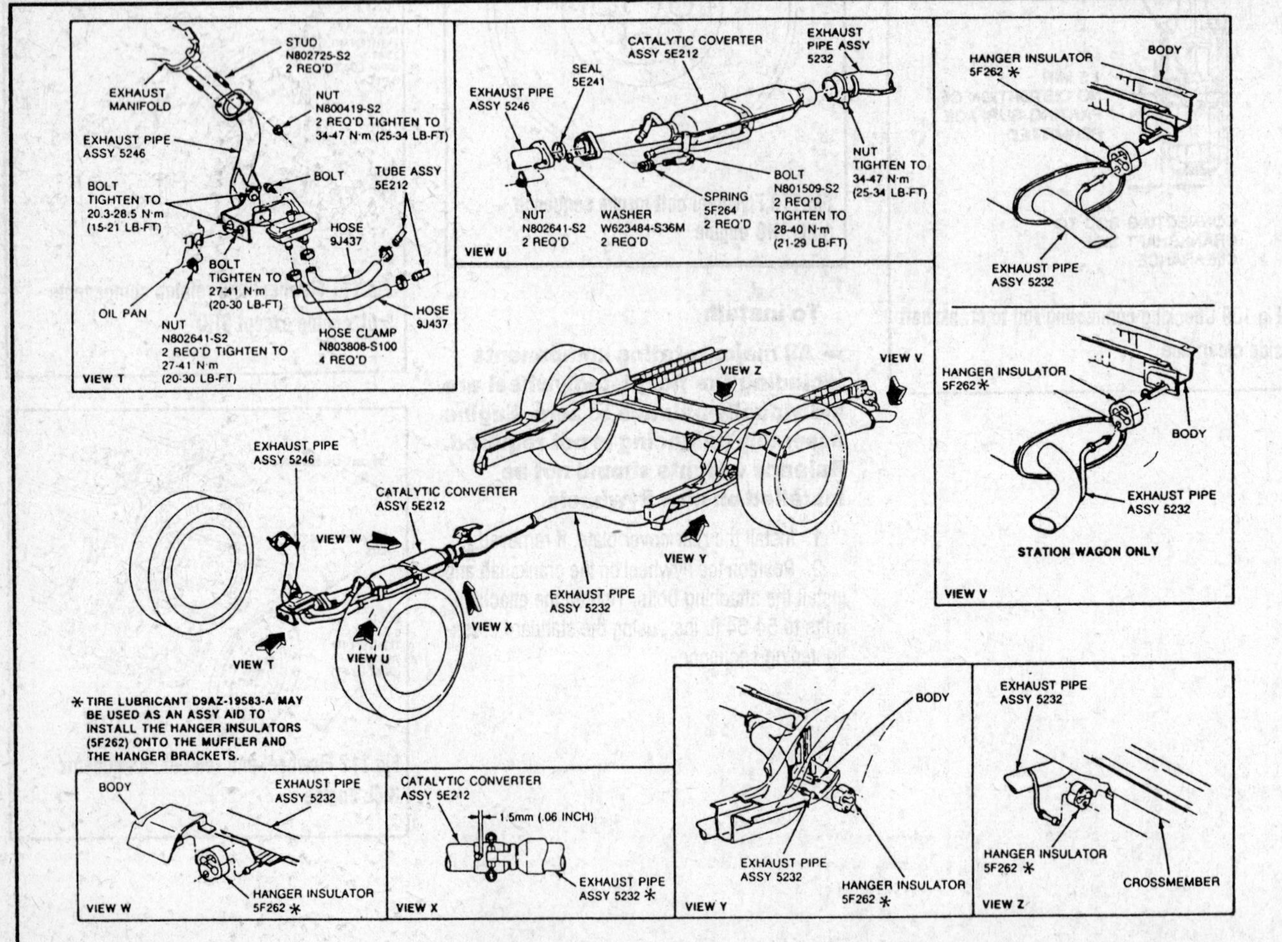

Fig.117 Exhaust system and related components — 2.5L engine

faulty muffler. Inspect the clamps, brackets and insulators for cracks and stripped or badly corroded bolt threads. When flat joints are loosened and/or disconnected to replace a shield pipe or muffler, replace the bolts and flange nuts if there is reasonable doubt that its service life is limited.

The exhaust system, including brush shields, must be free of leaks, binding, grounding and excessive vibrations. These conditions are usually caused by loose or broken flange bolts, shields, brackets or pipes. If any of these conditions exist, check the exhaust system components and alignment. Align or replace as necessary. Brush shields are positioned on the underside of the catalytic converter and should be free from bends which would bring any part of the shield in contact with the catalytic converter or muffler. The shield should also be clear of any combustible material such as dried grass or leaves.

Coat all of the exhaust connections and bolt threads with anti-seize compound to prevent corrosion from making the next disassembly difficult.

Muffler

REMOVAL & INSTALLATION

➧ SEE FIG. 117–119

1. Raise and support the vehicle safely.
2. Remove the retaining clamps that support the muffler to its mounting under the car.
3. Using the proper tools separate the muffler from the exhaust pipes.
4. Carefully slide the muffler forward, to remove it from the rear exhaust pipe. Slide the muffler backward to remove it from the other exhaust pipe. Lower the muffler to the ground.
5. Installation is the reverse of the removal procedure. Be sure to use new retaining clamps.
6. Lower the vehicle. Start the engine and check for leaks.

Catalytic Converter

REMOVAL & INSTALLATION

1. Raise the vehicle and support the vehicle safely. As required, remove the transmission to converter support brace.
2. Remove the front catalytic converter flange fasteners at the flex joint and discard the flex joint gasket, remove the rear U-bolt connection.
3. Separate the catalytic converter inlet and outlet connections. Remove the converter.
4. Installation is the reverse of the removal procedure. Be sure to use new retaining clamps.
5. Lower the vehicle. Start the engine and check for leaks.

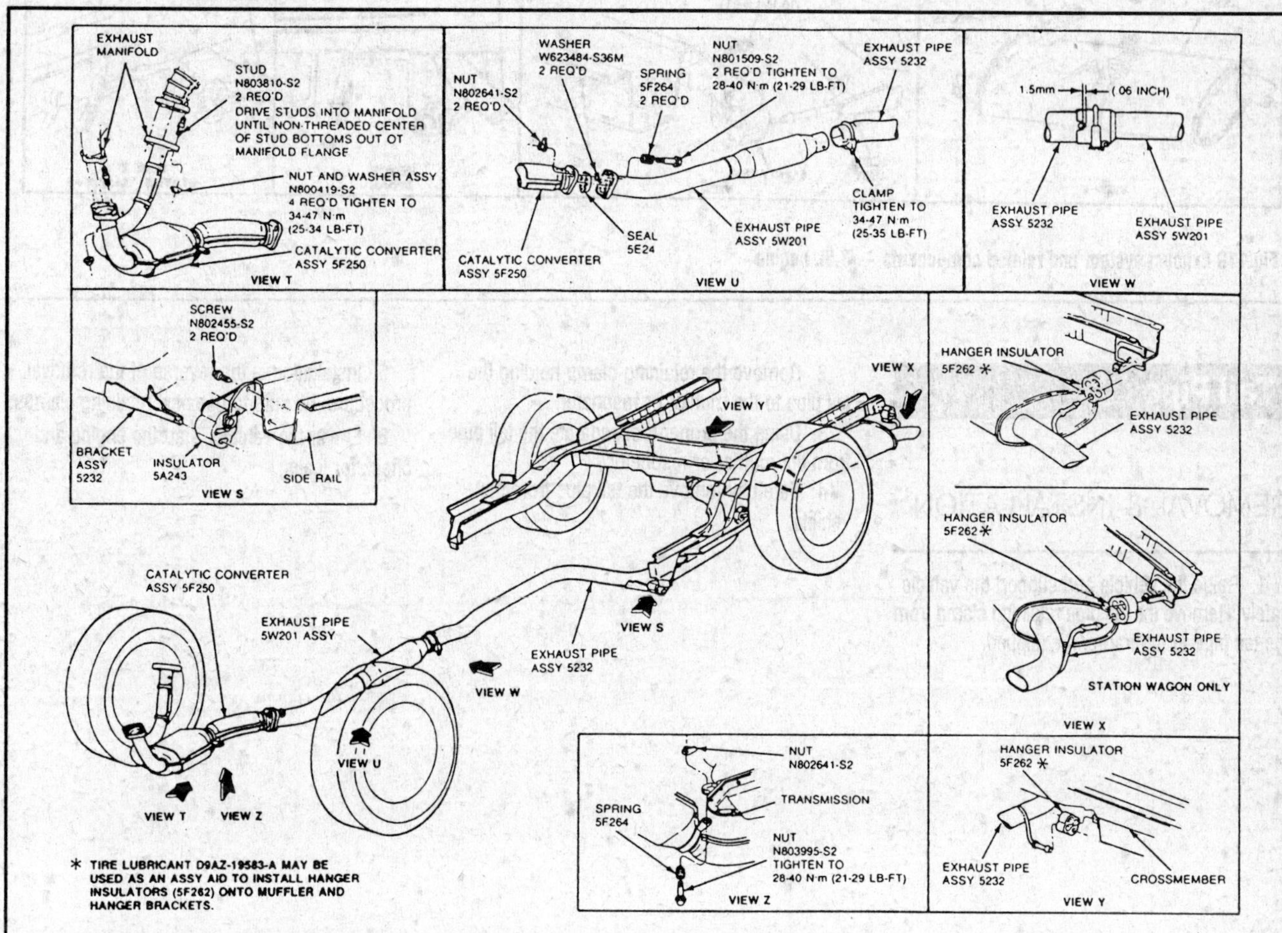

Fig.118 Exhaust system and related components — 3.0L engine

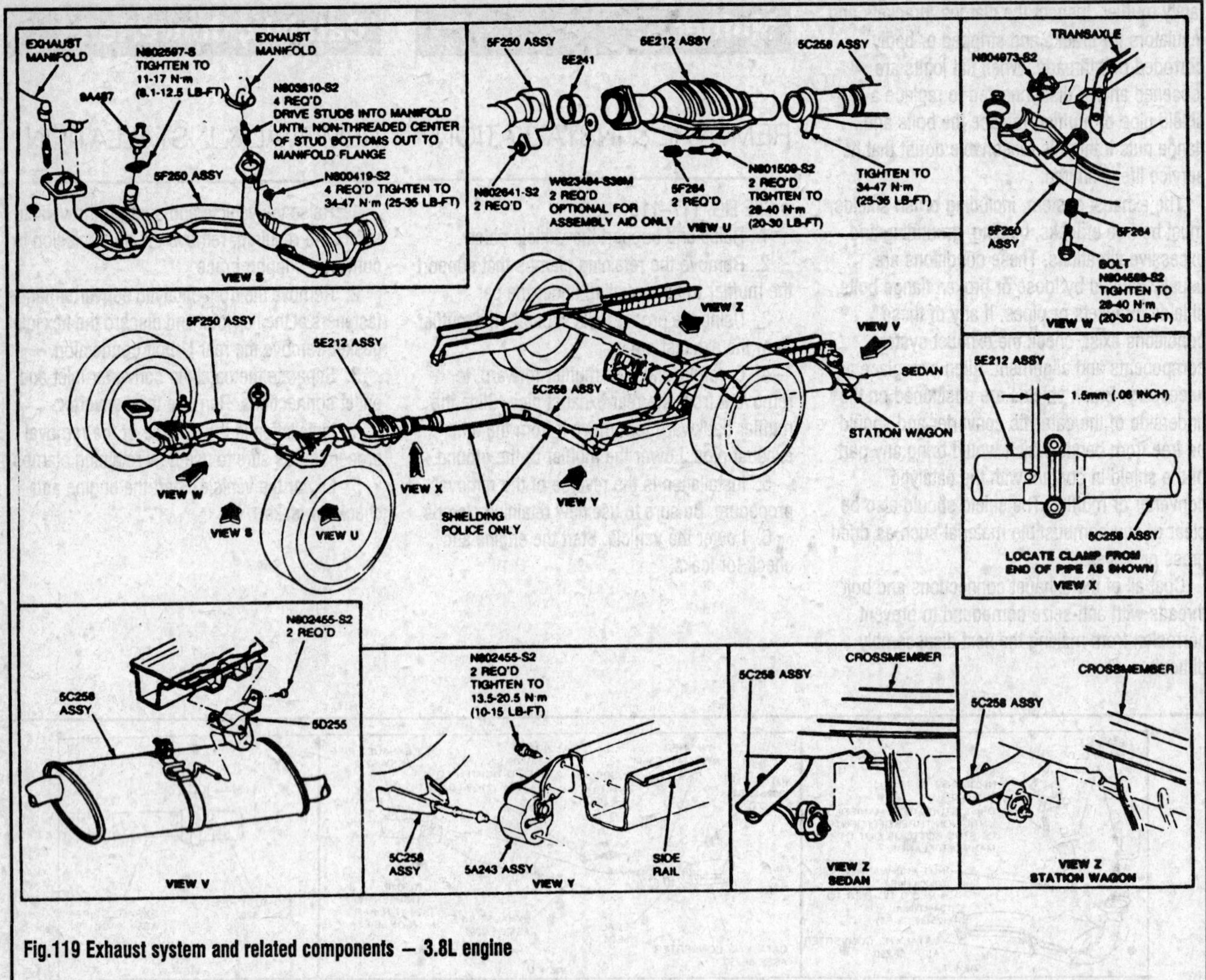

Fig.119 Exhaust system and related components — 3.8L engine

Tail Pipe

REMOVAL & INSTALLATION

1. Raise the vehicle and support the vehicle safely. Remove the tail pipe retaining clamp from the tail pipe to the frame, if equipped.
2. Remove the retaining clamp holding the tail pipe to the muffler or resonator.
3. Using the proper tool separate the tail pipe from the muffler or resonator.
4. Carefully remove the tail pipe from the vehicle.
5. Installation is the reverse of the removal procedure. Be sure to use new retaining clamps.
6. Lower the vehicle. Start the engine and check for leaks.

TORQUE SPECIFICATIONS

Component	U.S.	Metric
Alternator		
Except 3.0L SHO Engine		
Adjusting arm bolt	15-22 ft. lbs.	20–30 Nm
Pivot bolt	40-45 ft. lbs.	54–61 Nm
3.0L SHO Engine		
Front mounting bolt	36–53 ft. lbs.	48–72 Nm
Rear mounting bolts	25–37 ft. lbs.	34–50 Nm
Balance Shaft		
3.8L Engine	6–10 ft. lbs.	8–14 Nm
Coil pack mounting screws	40–62 inch lbs.	4.5–7 Nm
Connecting rod caps	31-36 ft. lbs.	42–49 Nm
Crankshaft sensor assembly screws	22–31 inch lbs.	2.5–3.5 Nm
Cylinder Head		
2.5L Engine		
2 steps:		
first	52–59 ft. lbs.	70–80 Nm
second	70–76 ft. lbs.	95–103 Nm
3.0L Except SHO Engine		
2 steps:		
first	37 ft. lbs.	50 Nm
second	68 ft. lbs.	92 Nm
3.0L SHO Engine		
2 steps:		
first	37–50 ft. lbs.	49–69 Nm
second	62–68 ft. lbs.	83–93 Nm
3.8L Engine		
4 steps:		
Step 1	37 ft. lbs.	50 Nm
Step 2	45 ft. lbs.	60 Nm
Step 3	52 ft. lbs.	70 Nm
Step 4	59 ft. lbs.	80 Nm
See text for retorque sequence		
Distributor cap screws	to 18–23 inch lbs.	2.0–2.6 Nm
Distributor hold-down bolt		
2.5L engine	17–25 ft. lbs.	23–34 Nm
3.0L engine	14–21 ft. lbs.	19–28 Nm
3.8L engine	20–29 ft. lbs.	27–40 Nm
Engine Installation		
2.5L Engine		
Upper engine-to-transaxle bolts	26–34 ft. lbs.	34–47 Nm
Lower engine-to-transaxle attaching bolts	26–34 ft. lbs.	34–47 Nm
Engine insulator nuts	40–55 ft. lbs.	54–75 Nm
3.0L Engine		
Engine mount bolts	40–55 ft. lbs.	54–75 Nm
Transaxle brace assembly bolts	40–55 ft. lbs.	54–75 Nm
3.0L SHO Engine		
Engine mount to sub-frame nuts	25–35 ft. lbs.	34–47 Nm
Lower transaxle to engine retaining bolts	25–35 ft. lbs.	34–47 Nm
3.8L Engine		
Engine to transaxle bolts	41–50 ft. lbs.	55–68 Nm

TORQUE SPECIFICATIONS

Component	U.S.	Metric
Engine Mounts		
2.5L and 3.0L Engines		
RIGHT REAR ENGINE INSULATOR (NO. 3		
Insulator to engine support bracket	40–55 ft. lbs.	54–75 Nm
Right, front and rear insulators to frame	55–75 ft. lbs.	75–102 Nm
LEFT ENGINE INSULATOR AND SUPPORT ASSEMBLY – AUTOMATIC TRANSAXLE		
Support assembly bolts	40–55 ft. lbs.	54–75 Nm
Insulator-to-frame bolts	60–86 ft. lbs.	81–116 Nm
Insulator to support assembly nuts	55–75 ft. lbs.	74–102 Nm
LEFT ENGINE INSULATOR AND SUPPORT ASSEMBLY – MANUAL TRANSAXLE		
Insulator-to-transaxle bolts	60–86 ft. lbs.	81–116 Nm
Insulator-to-frame bolts	60–86 ft. lbs.	81–116 Nm
RIGHT FRONT ENGINE INSULATOR (NO. 2		
Insulator-to-engine bracket bolt(s)		
2.5L engine	40–55 ft. lbs.	54–75 Nm
3.0L engine	71–95 ft. lbs.	90–130 Nm
Right front insulators to frame	55–75 ft. lbs.	75–102 Nm
Right rear insulators to frame	55–75 ft. lbs.	75–102 Nm
3.0L SHO Engine		
RIGHT FRONT (NO. 2 AND RIGHT REAR (No. 3		
Insulator-to-engine bracket bolts	40–55 ft. lbs.	54–75 Nm
Insulator to frame nuts	50–70 ft. lbs.	68–95 Nm
Roll damper retaining nuts	40–55 ft. lbs.	54–75 Nm
Engine damper to engine bolt	40–55 ft. lbs.	54–75 Nm
LEFT ENGINE INSULATOR AND SUPPORT ASSEMBLY		
Damper bracket to insulator nuts	40–55 ft. lbs.	54–75 Nm
Insulator to transaxle bolts	70–95 ft. lbs.	95–130 Nm
Insulator to frame bolts	60–85 ft. lbs.	81–116 Nm
Damper to damper bracket bolt	40–55 ft. lbs.	54–75 Nm
3.8L Engine		
RIGHT FRONT ENGINE INSULATOR		
Upper insulator stud retaining nut	40–55 ft. lbs.	54–75 Nm
Lower retaining nut	50–70 ft. lbs.	68–95 Nm
RIGHT REAR ENGINE INSULATOR (NO. 3)		
Top retaining nut on the insulator	40–55 ft. lbs.	54–75 Nm
Right front engine mounts	55–75 ft. lbs.	68–95 Nm
Right rear engine mounts	55–75 ft. lbs.	68–95 Nm
LEFT ENGINE MOUNT AND SUPPORT ASSEMBLY		
Support assembly to transaxle bolts	35 ft. lbs.	48 Nm
Mount to frame bolts	60–86 ft. lbs.	81–116 Nm
Mount to support nut	55–75 ft. lbs.	74–102 Nm
Vertical restrictor assembly	40–55 ft. lbs.	54–75 Nm
Exhaust Manifold		
2.5L Engine		
2 steps		
first	5–7 ft. lbs.	7–10 Nm
second	20–30 ft. lbs.	27–41 Nm
3.0L Engine	19 ft. lbs.	25 Nm
3.0L SHO Engine	26–38 ft. lbs.	35–52 Nm
3.8L Engine	15–22 ft. lbs.	20–30 Nm

TORQUE SPECIFICATIONS

Component	U.S.	Metric
Flywheel		
All except the 3.0L SHO	54–64 ft. lbs.	73–87 Nm
3.0L SHO engine	51–58 ft. lbs.	69–78 Nm
Intake Manifold		
2.5L Engine	15–22 ft. lbs.	20–30 Nm
3.0L Except SHO Engine		
2 steps:		
first	11 ft. lbs.	15 Nm
second	21 ft. lbs.	28 Nm
3.0L SHO Engine	11–17 ft. lbs.	15–23 Nm
3.8L Engine		
3 steps		
first	1–8 ft. lbs.	10 Nm
second	2–15 ft. lbs.	20 Nm
third	24 ft. lbs.	32 Nm
Main Bearings	65-81 ft. lbs.	88–110 Nm
Oil Pan		
2.5L Engine		
Pan flange bolts	6–8 ft. lbs.	8–12 Nm
Pan-to-transaxle bolts	30–39 ft. lbs.	40–50 Nm
3.0L Except SHO Engine	8 ft. lbs.	10 Nm
3.0L SHO Engine	11–17 ft. lbs.	15–23 Nm
3.8L Engine	7–9 ft. lbs.	9–12 Nm
Oil Pump		
2.5L Engine	15–22 ft. lbs.	20–30 Nm
3.0L Except SHO Engine	35 ft. lbs.	48 Nm
3.0L SHO Engine	11–17 ft. lbs.	15–23 Nm
3.8L Engine pump cover retaining bolts	18–22 ft. lbs.	25–30 Nm
Radiator		
Radiator to the radiator support bolts		
Exc. 3.8L	46–60 inch lbs.	5–7 Nm.
3.8L	13–20 ft. lbs.	17–27 Nm
Rocker Arm Cover Bolts	8-11 ft. lbs.	11–15 Nm
Rocker Arms		
2.5L Engine		
2 steps:		
first	6–8 ft. lbs.	8–12 Nm
second	20–26 ft. lbs.	28–35 Nm
3.0L Engine		
2 steps:		
first	8 ft. lbs.	11 Nm
second	24 ft. lbs.	32 Nm
3.8L Engine		
2 steps		
first	62–132 inch lbs.	7–15 Nm
second	19–25 ft. lbs.	25–35 Nm

TORQUE SPECIFICATIONS

Component	U.S.	Metric
Thermostat Housing		
2.5L Engine	12–18 ft. lbs.	16–24 Nm
3.0L Engine Except SHO	9 ft. lbs.	12 Nm
3.0L SHO Engine	5–8 ft. lbs.	7–11 Nm
3.8L Engine	15–22 ft. lbs.	20–30 Nm
Timing Belt Cover		
3.0L SHO Engine		
Timing belt cover retaining bolts	60–90 inch lbs.	7–11 Nm
Crankshaft damper bolt	113–126 ft. lbs.	152–172 Nm
Timing belt tensioner locknut	25–37 ft. lbs.	33–51 Nm
Camshaft sprocket bolts	15–18 ft. lbs.	21–25 Nm
Timing Chain And Sprockets		
2.5L Engine		
Camshaft bolt	41–56 ft. lbs.	55–75 Nm
Crankshaft pulley bolt	140–170 ft. lbs.	190–230 Nm
3.0L Engine Except SHO		
Camshaft bolt	46 ft. lbs.	63 Nm
Crankshaft damper bolt	107 ft. lbs.	145 Nm
Crankshaft pulley bolts	26 ft. lbs.	35 Nm
3.8L Engine		
Camshaft bolt	30–37 ft. lbs.	40–50 Nm
Crankshaft damper bolt	104–132 ft. lbs.	140–180 Nm
Timing Chain Cover		
2.5L Engine	6–8 ft. lbs.	
3.0L Engine Except SHO		
Bolts 1–10	19 ft. lbs.	25 Nm
Bolts 11–15	7 ft. lbs.	10 Nm
3.8L Engine	15–22 ft. lbs.	20–30 Nm
Valve Lifters		
3.0L		
Roller lifter guide retainer assembly	to 8–10 ft. lbs.	11–14 Nm
Water Pump		
2.5L	15–23 ft. lbs.	20–30 Nm
3.0L	12–16 ft. lbs.	15–23 Nm
3.8L	15–22 ft. lbs.	20–20 Nm

Troubleshooting Basic Charging System Problems

Problem	Cause	Solution
Noisy alternator	• Loose mountings • Loose drive pulley • Worn bearings • Brush noise • Internal circuits shorted (High pitched whine)	• Tighten mounting bolts • Tighten pulley • Replace alternator • Replace alternator • Replace alternator
Squeal when starting engine or accelerating	• Glazed or loose belt	• Replace or adjust belt
Indicator light remains on or ammeter indicates discharge (engine running)	• Broken fan belt • Broken or disconnected wires • Internal alternator problems • Defective voltage regulator	• Install belt • Repair or connect wiring • Replace alternator • Replace voltage regulator
Car light bulbs continually burn out—battery needs water continually	• Alternator/regulator overcharging	• Replace voltage regulator/alternator
Car lights flare on acceleration	• Battery low • Internal alternator/regulator problems	• Charge or replace battery • Replace alternator/regulator
Low voltage output (alternator light flickers continually or ammeter needle wanders)	• Loose or worn belt • Dirty or corroded connections • Internal alternator/regulator problems	• Replace or adjust belt • Clean or replace connections • Replace alternator or regulator

Troubleshooting Engine Mechanical Problems

Problem	Cause	Solution
External oil leaks	• Fuel pump gasket broken or improperly seated • Cylinder head cover RTV sealant broken or improperly seated • Oil filler cap leaking or missing	• Replace gasket • Replace sealant; inspect cylinder head cover sealant flange and cylinder head sealant surface for distortion and cracks • Replace cap

Troubleshooting Engine Mechanical Problems (cont.)

Problem	Cause	Solution
External oil leaks	• Oil filter gasket broken or improperly seated	• Replace oil filter
	• Oil pan side gasket broken, improperly seated or opening in RTV sealant	• Replace gasket or repair opening in sealant; inspect oil pan gasket flange for distortion
	• Oil pan front oil seal broken or improperly seated	• Replace seal; inspect timing case cover and oil pan seal flange for distortion
	• Oil pan rear oil seal broken or improperly seated	• Replace seal; inspect oil pan rear oil seal flange; inspect rear main bearing cap for cracks, plugged oil return channels, or distortion in seal groove
	• Timing case cover oil seal broken or improperly seated	• Replace seal
	• Excess oil pressure because of restricted PCV valve	• Replace PCV valve
	• Oil pan drain plug loose or has stripped threads	• Repair as necessary and tighten
	• Rear oil gallery plug loose	• Use appropriate sealant on gallery plug and tighten
	• Rear camshaft plug loose or improperly seated	• Seat camshaft plug or replace and seal, as necessary
	• Distributor base gasket damaged	• Replace gasket
Excessive oil consumption	• Oil level too high	• Drain oil to specified level
	• Oil with wrong viscosity being used	• Replace with specified oil
	• PCV valve stuck closed	• Replace PCV valve
	• Valve stem oil deflectors (or seals) are damaged, missing, or incorrect type	• Replace valve stem oil deflectors
	• Valve stems or valve guides worn	• Measure stem-to-guide clearance and repair as necessary
	• Poorly fitted or missing valve cover baffles	• Replace valve cover
	• Piston rings broken or missing	• Replace broken or missing rings
	• Scuffed piston	• Replace piston
	• Incorrect piston ring gap	• Measure ring gap, repair as necessary
	• Piston rings sticking or excessively loose in grooves	• Measure ring side clearance, repair as necessary
	• Compression rings installed upside down	• Repair as necessary
	• Cylinder walls worn, scored, or glazed	• Repair as necessary

Troubleshooting Engine Mechanical Problems (cont.)

Problem	Cause	Solution
	• Piston ring gaps not properly staggered	• Repair as necessary
	• Excessive main or connecting rod bearing clearance	• Measure bearing clearance, repair as necessary
No oil pressure	• Low oil level	• Add oil to correct level
	• Oil pressure gauge, warning lamp or sending unit inaccurate	• Replace oil pressure gauge or warning lamp
	• Oil pump malfunction	• Replace oil pump
	• Oil pressure relief valve sticking	• Remove and inspect oil pressure relief valve assembly
	• Oil passages on pressure side of pump obstructed	• Inspect oil passages for obstruction
	• Oil pickup screen or tube obstructed	• Inspect oil pickup for obstruction
	• Loose oil inlet tube	• Tighten or seal inlet tube
Low oil pressure	• Low oil level	• Add oil to correct level
	• Inaccurate gauge, warning lamp or sending unit	• Replace oil pressure gauge or warning lamp
	• Oil excessively thin because of dilution, poor quality, or improper grade	• Drain and refill crankcase with recommended oil
	• Excessive oil temperature	• Correct cause of overheating engine
	• Oil pressure relief spring weak or sticking	• Remove and inspect oil pressure relief valve assembly
	• Oil inlet tube and screen assembly has restriction or air leak	• Remove and inspect oil inlet tube and screen assembly. (Fill inlet tube with lacquer thinner to locate leaks.)
	• Excessive oil pump clearance	• Measure clearances
	• Excessive main, rod, or camshaft bearing clearance	• Measure bearing clearances, repair as necessary
High oil pressure	• Improper oil viscosity	• Drain and refill crankcase with correct viscosity oil
	• Oil pressure gauge or sending unit inaccurate	• Replace oil pressure gauge
	• Oil pressure relief valve sticking closed	• Remove and inspect oil pressure relief valve assembly
Main bearing noise	• Insufficient oil supply	• Inspect for low oil level and low oil pressure
	• Main bearing clearance excessive	• Measure main bearing clearance, repair as necessary
	• Bearing insert missing	• Replace missing insert
	• Crankshaft end play excessive	• Measure end play, repair as necessary
	• Improperly tightened main bearing cap bolts	• Tighten bolts with specified torque
	• Loose flywheel or drive plate	• Tighten flywheel or drive plate attaching bolts
	• Loose or damaged vibration damper	• Repair as necessary

Troubleshooting Engine Mechanical Problems (cont.)

Problem	Cause	Solution
Connecting rod bearing noise	• Insufficient oil supply	• Inspect for low oil level and low oil pressure
	• Carbon build-up on piston	• Remove carbon from piston crown
	• Bearing clearance excessive or bearing missing	• Measure clearance, repair as necessary
	• Crankshaft connecting rod journal out-of-round	• Measure journal dimensions, repair or replace as necessary
	• Misaligned connecting rod or cap	• Repair as necessary
	• Connecting rod bolts tightened improperly	• Tighten bolts with specified torque
Piston noise	• Piston-to-cylinder wall clearance excessive (scuffed piston)	• Measure clearance and examine piston
	• Cylinder walls excessively tapered or out-of-round	• Measure cylinder wall dimensions, rebore cylinder
	• Piston ring broken	• Replace all rings on piston
	• Loose or seized piston pin	• Measure piston-to-pin clearance, repair as necessary
	• Connecting rods misaligned	• Measure rod alignment, straighten or replace
	• Piston ring side clearance excessively loose or tight	• Measure ring side clearance, repair as necessary
	• Carbon build-up on piston is excessive	• Remove carbon from piston
Valve actuating component noise	• Insufficient oil supply	• Check for: (a) Low oil level (b) Low oil pressure (c) Plugged push rods (d) Wrong hydraulic tappets (e) Restricted oil gallery (f) Excessive tappet to bore clearance
	• Push rods worn or bent	• Replace worn or bent push rods
	• Rocker arms or pivots worn	• Replace worn rocker arms or pivots
	• Foreign objects or chips in hydraulic tappets	• Clean tappets
	• Excessive tappet leak-down	• Replace valve tappet
	• Tappet face worn	• Replace tappet; inspect corresponding cam lobe for wear
	• Broken or cocked valve springs	• Properly seat cocked springs; replace broken springs
	• Stem-to-guide clearance excessive	• Measure stem-to-guide clearance, repair as required
	• Valve bent	• Replace valve
	• Loose rocker arms	• Tighten bolts with specified torque
	• Valve seat runout excessive	• Regrind valve seat/valves
	• Missing valve lock	• Install valve lock
	• Push rod rubbing or contacting cylinder head	• Remove cylinder head and remove obstruction in head
	• Excessive engine oil (four-cylinder engine)	• Correct oil level

Troubleshooting the Cooling System

Problem	Cause	Solution
High temperature gauge indication—overheating	• Coolant level low	• Replenish coolant
	• Fan belt loose	• Adjust fan belt tension
	• Radiator hose(s) collapsed	• Replace hose(s)
	• Radiator airflow blocked	• Remove restriction (bug screen, fog lamps, etc.)
	• Faulty radiator cap	• Replace radiator cap
	• Ignition timing incorrect	• Adjust ignition timing
	• Idle speed low	• Adjust idle speed
	• Air trapped in cooling system	• Purge air
	• Heavy traffic driving	• Operate at fast idle in neutral intermittently to cool engine
	• Incorrect cooling system component(s) installed	• Install proper component(s)
	• Faulty thermostat	• Replace thermostat
	• Water pump shaft broken or impeller loose	• Replace water pump
	• Radiator tubes clogged	• Flush radiator
	• Cooling system clogged	• Flush system
	• Casting flash in cooling passages	• Repair or replace as necessary. Flash may be visible by removing cooling system components or removing core plugs.
	• Brakes dragging	• Repair brakes
	• Excessive engine friction	• Repair engine
	• Antifreeze concentration over 68%	• Lower antifreeze concentration percentage
	• Missing air seals	• Replace air seals
	• Faulty gauge or sending unit	• Repair or replace faulty component
	• Loss of coolant flow caused by leakage or foaming	• Repair or replace leaking component, replace coolant
	• Viscous fan drive failed	• Replace unit
Low temperature indication—undercooling	• Thermostat stuck open	• Replace thermostat
	• Faulty gauge or sending unit	• Repair or replace faulty component
Coolant loss—boilover	• Overfilled cooling system	• Reduce coolant level to proper specification
	• Quick shutdown after hard (hot) run	• Allow engine to run at fast idle prior to shutdown
	• Air in system resulting in occasional "burping" of coolant	• Purge system
	• Insufficient antifreeze allowing coolant boiling point to be too low	• Add antifreeze to raise boiling point
	• Antifreeze deteriorated because of age or contamination	• Replace coolant
	• Leaks due to loose hose clamps, loose nuts, bolts, drain plugs, faulty hoses, or defective radiator	• Pressure test system to locate source of leak(s) then repair as necessary

Troubleshooting the Cooling System (cont.)

Problem	Cause	Solution
Coolant loss—boilover	• Faulty head gasket • Cracked head, manifold, or block • Faulty radiator cap	• Replace head gasket • Replace as necessary • Replace cap
Coolant entry into crankcase or cylinder(s)	• Faulty head gasket • Crack in head, manifold or block	• Replace head gasket • Replace as necessary
Coolant recovery system inoperative	• Coolant level low • Leak in system • Pressure cap not tight or seal missing, or leaking • Pressure cap defective • Overflow tube clogged or leaking • Recovery bottle vent restricted	• Replenish coolant to FULL mark • Pressure test to isolate leak and repair as necessary • Repair as necessary • Replace cap • Repair as necessary • Remove restriction
Noise	• Fan contacting shroud • Loose water pump impeller • Glazed fan belt • Loose fan belt • Rough surface on drive pulley • Water pump bearing worn • Belt alignment	• Reposition shroud and inspect engine mounts • Replace pump • Apply silicone or replace belt • Adjust fan belt tension • Replace pulley • Remove belt to isolate. Replace pump. • Check pulley alignment. Repair as necessary.
No coolant flow through heater core	• Restricted return inlet in water pump • Heater hose collapsed or restricted • Restricted heater core • Restricted outlet in thermostat housing • Intake manifold bypass hole in cylinder head restricted • Faulty heater control valve • Intake manifold coolant passage restricted	• Remove restriction • Remove restriction or replace hose • Remove restriction or replace core • Remove flash or restriction • Remove restriction • Replace valve • Remove restriction or replace intake manifold

NOTE: *Immediately after shutdown, the engine enters a condition known as heat soak. This is caused by the cooling system being inoperative while engine temperature is still high. If coolant temperature rises above boiling point, expansion and pressure may push some coolant out of the radiator overflow tube. If this does not occur frequently it is considered normal.*

Troubleshooting the Serpentine Drive Belt

Problem	Cause	Solution
Tension sheeting fabric failure (woven fabric on outside circumference of belt has cracked or separated from body of belt)	• Grooved or backside idler pulley diameters are less than minimum recommended • Tension sheeting contacting (rubbing) stationary object • Excessive heat causing woven fabric to age • Tension sheeting splice has fractured	• Replace pulley(s) not conforming to specification • Correct rubbing condition • Replace belt • Replace belt
Noise (objectional squeal, squeak, or rumble is heard or felt while drive belt is in operation)	• Belt slippage • Bearing noise • Belt misalignment • Belt-to-pulley mismatch • Driven component inducing vibration • System resonant frequency inducing vibration	• Adjust belt • Locate and repair • Align belt/pulley(s) • Install correct belt • Locate defective driven component and repair • Vary belt tension within specifications. Replace belt.
Rib chunking (one or more ribs has separated from belt body)	• Foreign objects imbedded in pulley grooves • Installation damage • Drive loads in excess of design specifications • Insufficient internal belt adhesion	• Remove foreign objects from pulley grooves • Replace belt • Adjust belt tension • Replace belt
Rib or belt wear (belt ribs contact bottom of pulley grooves)	• Pulley(s) misaligned • Mismatch of belt and pulley groove widths • Abrasive environment • Rusted pulley(s) • Sharp or jagged pulley groove tips • Rubber deteriorated	• Align pulley(s) • Replace belt • Replace belt • Clean rust from pulley(s) • Replace pulley • Replace belt
Longitudinal belt cracking (cracks between two ribs)	• Belt has mistracked from pulley groove • Pulley groove tip has worn away rubber-to-tensile member	• Replace belt • Replace belt
Belt slips	• Belt slipping because of insufficient tension • Belt or pulley subjected to substance (belt dressing, oil, ethylene glycol) that has reduced friction • Driven component bearing failure • Belt glazed and hardened from heat and excessive slippage	• Adjust tension • Replace belt and clean pulleys • Replace faulty component bearing • Replace belt
"Groove jumping" (belt does not maintain correct position on pulley, or turns over and/or runs off pulleys)	• Insufficient belt tension • Pulley(s) not within design tolerance • Foreign object(s) in grooves	• Adjust belt tension • Replace pulley(s) • Remove foreign objects from grooves

Troubleshooting the Serpentine Drive Belt (cont.)

Problem	Cause	Solution
"Groove jumping" (belt does not maintain correct position on pulley, or turns over and/or runs off pulleys)	• Excessive belt speed • Pulley misalignment • Belt-to-pulley profile mismatched • Belt cordline is distorted	• Avoid excessive engine acceleration • Align pulley(s) • Install correct belt • Replace belt
Belt broken (Note: identify and correct problem before replacement belt is installed)	• Excessive tension • Tensile members damaged during belt installation • Belt turnover • Severe pulley misalignment • Bracket, pulley, or bearing failure	• Replace belt and adjust tension to specification • Replace belt • Replace belt • Align pulley(s) • Replace defective component and belt
Cord edge failure (tensile member exposed at edges of belt or separated from belt body)	• Excessive tension • Drive pulley misalignment • Belt contacting stationary object • Pulley irregularities • Improper pulley construction • Insufficient adhesion between tensile member and rubber matrix	• Adjust belt tension • Align pulley • Correct as necessary • Replace pulley • Replace pulley • Replace belt and adjust tension to specifications
Sporadic rib cracking (multiple cracks in belt ribs at random intervals)	• Ribbed pulley(s) diameter less than minimum specification • Backside bend flat pulley(s) diameter less than minimum • Excessive heat condition causing rubber to harden • Excessive belt thickness • Belt overcured • Excessive tension	• Replace pulley(s) • Replace pulley(s) • Correct heat condition as necessary • Replace belt • Replace belt • Adjust belt tension

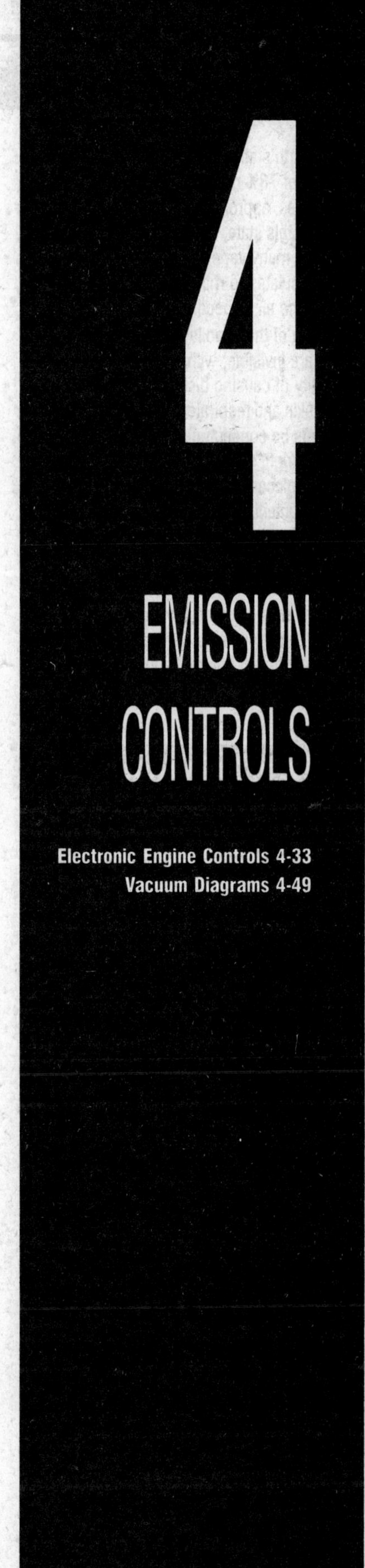

4 EMISSION CONTROLS

AIR POLLUTION

The earth's atmosphere, at or near sea level, consists of 78% nitrogen, 21% oxygen and 1% other gases, approximately. If it were possible to remain in this state, 100% clean air would result. However, many varied causes allow other gases and particulates to mix with the clean air, causing the air to become unclean or polluted.

Certain of these pollutants are visible while others are invisible, with each having the capability of causing distress to the eyes, ears, throat, skin and respiratory system. Should these pollutants be concentrated in a specific area and under the right conditions, death could result due to the displacement or chemical change of the oxygen content in the air. These pollutants can cause much damage to the environment and to the many man made objects that are exposed to the elements.

To better understand the causes of air pollution, the pollutants can be categorized into 3 separate types, natural, industrial and automotive.

Natural Pollutants

Natural pollution has been present on earth before man appeared and is still a factor to be considered when discussing air pollution, although it causes only a small percentage of the present overall pollution problem existing in our country. It is the direct result of decaying organic matter, wind born smoke and particulates from such natural events as plains and forest fires (ignited by heat or lightning), volcanic ash, sand and dust which can spread over a large area of the countryside.

Such a phenomenon of natural pollution has been recent volcanic eruptions, with the resulting plume of smoke, steam and volcanic ash blotting out the sun's rays as it spreads and rises higher into the atmosphere, where the upper air currents catch and carry the smoke and ash, while condensing the steam back into water vapor. As the water vapor, smoke and ash traveled on their journey, the smoke dissipates into the atmosphere while the ash and moisture settle back to earth in a trail hundred of miles long. In many cases, lives are lost and millions of dollars of property damage result, and ironically, man can only stand by and watch it happen.

Industrial Pollution

Industrial pollution is caused primarily by industrial processes, the burning of coal, oil and natural gas, which in turn produces smoke and fumes. Because the burning fuels contain much sulfur, the principal ingredients of smoke and fumes are sulfur dioxide (SO_2) and particulate matter. This type of pollutant occurs most severely during still, damp and cool weather, such as at night. Even in its less severe form, this pollutant is not confined to just cities. Because of air movements, the pollutants move for miles over the surrounding countryside, leaving in its path a barren and unhealthy environment for all living things.

Working with Federal, State and Local mandated rules, regulations and by carefully monitoring the emissions, industries have greatly reduced the amount of pollutant emitted from their industrial sources, striving to obtain an acceptable level. Because of the mandated industrial emission clean up, many land areas and streams in and around the cities that were formerly barren of vegetation and life, have now begun to move back in the direction of nature's intended balance.

Automotive Pollutants

The third major source of air pollution is the automotive emissions. The emissions from the internal combustion engine were not an appreciable problem years ago because of the small number of registered vehicles and the nation's small highway system. However, during the early 1950's, the trend of the American people was to move from the cities to the surrounding suburbs. This caused an immediate problem in the transportation areas because the majority of the suburbs were not afforded mass transit conveniences. This lack of transportation created an attractive market for the automobile manufacturers, which resulted in a dramatic increase in the number of vehicles produced and sold, along with a marked increase in highway construction between cities and the suburbs. Multi-vehicle families emerged with much emphasis placed on the individual vehicle per family member. As the increase in vehicle ownership and usage occurred, so did the pollutant levels in and around the cities, as the suburbanites drove daily to their businesses and employment in the city and its fringe area, returning at the end of the day to their homes in the suburbs.

It was noted that a fog and smoke type haze was being formed and at times, remained in suspension over the cities and did not quickly dissipate. At first this "smog", derived from the words "smoke" and "fog", was thought to result from industrial pollution but it was determined that the automobile emissions were largely to blame. It was discovered that as normal automobile emissions were exposed to sunlight for a period of time, complex chemical reactions would take place.

It was found the smog was a photo chemical layer and was developed when certain oxides of nitrogen (NOx) and unburned hydrocarbons (HC) from the automobile emissions were exposed to sunlight and was more severe when the smog would remain stagnant over an area in which a warm layer of air would settle over the top of a cooler air mass at ground level, trapping and holding the automobile emissions, instead of the emissions being dispersed and diluted through normal air flows. This type of air stagnation was given the name "Temperature Inversion".

Temperature Inversion

In normal weather situations, the surface air is warmed by the heat radiating from the earth's surface and the sun's rays and will rise upward, into the atmosphere, to be cooled through a convection type heat expands with the cooler upper air. As the warm air rises, the surface pollutants are carried upward and dissipated into the atmosphere.

When a temperature inversion occurs, we find the higher air is no longer cooler but warmer than the surface air, causing the cooler surface air to become trapped and unable to move. This warm air blanket can extend from above ground level to a few hundred or even a few thousand feet into the air. As the surface air is trapped, so are the pollutants, causing a severe smog condition. Should this stagnant air mass extend to a few thousand feet high, enough air movement with the inversion takes place to allow the smog layer to rise above ground level but the pollutants still cannot dissipate. This inversion can remain for days over an area, with only the smog level rising or lowering from ground level to a few hundred feet high. Meanwhile, the pollutant levels increases, causing eye irritation, respirator problems, reduced visibility, plant damage and in some cases, cancer type diseases.

This inversion phenomenon was first noted in the Los Angeles, California area. The city lies in a basin type of terrain and during certain weather conditions, a cold air mass is held in the basin while a warmer air mass covers it like a lid.

Because this type of condition was first documented as prevalent in the Los Angeles area, this type of smog was named Los Angeles Smog, although it occurs in other areas where a large concentration of automobiles are used and the air remains stagnant for any length of time.

Internal Combustion Engine Pollutants

Consider the internal combustion engine as a machine in which raw materials must be placed so a finished product comes out. As in any machine operation, a certain amount of wasted material is formed. When we relate this to the internal combustion engine, we find that by putting in air and fuel, we obtain power from this mixture during the combustion process to drive the vehicle. The by-product or waste of this power is, in part, heat and exhaust gases with which we must concern ourselves.

HEAT TRANSFER

The heat from the combustion process can rise to over 4000°F (2204°C). The dissipation of this heat is controlled by a ram air effect, the use of cooling fans to cause air flow and having a liquid coolant solution surrounding the combustion area and transferring the heat of combustion through the cylinder walls and into the coolant. The coolant is then directed to a thin-finned, multi-tubed radiator, from which the excess heat is transferred to the outside air by 1 or all of the 3 heat transfer methods, conduction, convection or radiation.

The cooling of the combustion area is an important part in the control of exhaust emissions. To understand the behavior of the combustion and transfer of its heat, consider the air/fuel charge. It is ignited and the flame front burns progressively across the combustion chamber until the burning charge reaches the cylinder walls. Some of the fuel in contact with the walls is not hot enough to burn, thereby snuffing out or Quenching the combustion process. This leaves unburned fuel in the combustion chamber. This unburned fuel is then forced out of the cylinder along with the exhaust gases and into the exhaust system.

Many attempts have been made to minimize the amount of unburned fuel in the combustion chambers due to the snuffing out or "Quenching", by increasing the coolant temperature and lessening the contact area of the coolant around the combustion area. Design limitations within the combustion chambers prevent the complete burning of the air/fuel charge, so a certain amount of the unburned fuel is still expelled into the exhaust system, regardless of modifications to the engine.

EXHAUST EMISSIONS

Composition Of The Exhaust Gases

The exhaust gases emitted into the atmosphere are a combination of burned and unburned fuel. To understand the exhaust emission and its composition review some basic chemistry.

When the air/fuel mixture is introduced into the engine, we are mixing air, composed of nitrogen (78%), oxygen (21%) and other gases (1%) with the fuel, which is 100% hydrocarbons (HC), in a semi-controlled ratio. As the combustion process is accomplished, power is produced to move the vehicle while the heat of combustion is transferred to the cooling system. The exhaust gases are then composed of nitrogen, a diatomic gas (N_2), the same as was introduced in the engine, carbon dioxide (CO2), the same gas that is used in beverage carbonation and water vapor (H_2O). The nitrogen (N_2), for the most part passes through the engine unchanged, while the oxygen (O_2) reacts (burns) with the hydrocarbons (HC) and produces the carbon dioxide (CO_2) and the water vapors (H_2O). If this chemical process would be the only process to take place, the exhaust emissions would be harmless. However, during the combustion process, other pollutants are formed and are considered dangerous. These pollutants are carbon monoxide (CO), hydrocarbons (HC), oxides of nitrogen (NOx) oxides of sulfur (SOx) and engine particulates.

Lead (Pb), is considered 1 of the particulates and is present in the exhaust gases whenever leaded fuels are used. Lead (Pb) does not dissipate easily. Levels can be high along roadways when it is emitted from vehicles and can pose a health threat. Since the increased usage of unleaded gasoline and the phasing out of leaded gasoline for fuel, this pollutant is gradually diminishing. While not considered a major threat lead is still considered a dangerous pollutant.

HYDROCARBONS

Hydrocarbons (HC) are essentially unburned fuel that have not been successfully burned during the combustion process or have escaped into the atmosphere through fuel evaporation. The main sources of incomplete combustion are rich air/fuel mixtures, low engine temperatures and improper spark timing. The main sources of hydrocarbon emission through fuel evaporation come from the vehicle's fuel tank and carburetor bowl.

To reduce combustion hydrocarbon emission, engine modifications were made to minimize dead space and surface area in the combustion chamber. In addition the air/fuel mixture was made more lean through improved carburetion, fuel injection and by the addition of external controls to aid in further combustion of the hydrocarbons outside the engine. Two such methods were the addition of an air injection system, to inject fresh air into the exhaust manifolds and the installation of a catalytic converter, a unit that is able to burn traces of hydrocarbons without affecting the internal combustion process or fuel economy.

To control hydrocarbon emissions through fuel evaporation, modifications were made to the fuel tank and carburetor bowl to allow storage of the fuel vapors during periods of engine shut-down, and at specific times during engine operation, to purge and burn these same vapors by blending them with the air/fuel mixture.

CARBON MONOXIDE

Carbon monoxide is formed when not enough oxygen is present during the combustion process to convert carbon (C) to carbon dioxide (CO_2). An increase in the carbon monoxide (CO) emission is normally accompanied by an increase in the hydrocarbon (HC) emission because of the lack of oxygen to completely burn all of the fuel mixture.

Carbon monoxide (CO) also increases the rate at which the photo chemical smog is formed by speeding up the conversion of nitric oxide (NO) to nitrogen dioxide (NO_2). To accomplish this, carbon monoxide (CO) combines with oxygen (O_2) and nitrogen dioxide (NO_2) to produce carbon dioxide (CO_2) and nitrogen dioxide (NO_2). ($CO + O_2 + NO = CO_2 + NO_2$).

The dangers of carbon monoxide, which is an odorless, colorless toxic gas are many. When carbon monoxide is inhaled into the lungs and passed into the blood stream, oxygen is replaced by the carbon monoxide in the red blood cells, causing a reduction in the amount of oxygen being supplied to the many parts of the body. This lack of oxygen causes headaches, lack of coordination, reduced mental alertness and should the carbon monoxide concentration be high enough, death could result.

NITROGEN

Normally, nitrogen is an inert gas. When heated to approximately 2500°F (1371°C) through the combustion process, this gas becomes active and causes an increase in the nitric oxide (NOx) emission.

Oxides of nitrogen (NOx) are composed of approximately 97–98% nitric oxide (NO2). Nitric oxide is a colorless gas but when it is passed into the atmosphere, it combines with oxygen and forms nitrogen dioxide (NO2). The nitrogen dioxide then combines with chemically active hydrocarbons (HC) and when in the presence of sunlight, causes the formation of photo chemical smog.

OZONE

To further complicate matters, some of the nitrogen dioxide (NO_2) is broken apart by the sunlight to form nitric oxide and oxygen. (NO_2 + sunlight = NO + O). This single atom of oxygen then combines with diatomic (meaning 2 atoms) oxygen (O_2) to form ozone (O_3). Ozone is 1 of the smells associated with smog. It has a pungent and offensive odor, irritates the eyes and lung tissues, affects the growth of plant life and causes rapid deterioration of rubber products. Ozone can be formed by sunlight as well as electrical discharge into the air.

The most common discharge area on the automobile engine is the secondary ignition electrical system, especially when inferior quality spark plug cables are used. As the surge of high voltage is routed through the secondary cable, the circuit builds up an electrical field around the wire, acting upon the oxygen in the surrounding air to form the ozone. The faint glow along the cable with the engine running that may be visible on a dark night, is called the "corona discharge." It is the result of the electrical field passing from a high along the cable, to a low in the surrounding air, which forms the ozone gas. The combination of corona and ozone has been a major cause of cable deterioration. Recently, different types and better quality insulating materials have lengthened the life of the electrical cables.

Although ozone at ground level can be harmful, ozone is beneficial to the earth's inhabitants. By having a concentrated ozone layer called the 'ozonosphere', between 10 and 20 miles (16–32km) up in the atmosphere much of the ultra violet radiation from the sun's rays are absorbed and screened. If this ozone layer were not present, much of the earth's surface would be burned, dried and unfit for human life.

There is much discussion concerning the ozone layer and its density. A feeling exists that this protective layer of ozone is slowly diminishing and corrective action must be directed to this problem. Much experimenting is presently being conducted to determine if a problem exists and if so, the short and long term effects of the problem and how it can be remedied.

OXIDES OF SULFUR

Oxides of sulfur (SOx) were initially ignored in the exhaust system emissions, since the sulfur content of gasoline as a fuel is less than $1/_{10}$ of 1%. Because of this small amount, it was felt that it contributed very little to the overall pollution problem. However, because of the difficulty in solving the sulfur emissions in industrial pollutions and the introduction of catalytic converter to the automobile exhaust systems, a change was mandated. The automobile exhaust system, when equipped with a catalytic converter, changes the sulfur dioxide (SO_2) into the sulfur trioxide (SO_3).

When this combines with water vapors (H_2O), a sulfuric acid mist (H_2SO_4) is formed and is a very difficult pollutant to handle and is extremely corrosive. This sulfuric acid mist that is formed, is the same mist that rises from the vents of an automobile storage battery when an active chemical reaction takes place within the battery cells.

When a large concentration of vehicles equipped with catalytic converters are operating in an area, this acid mist will rise and be distributed over a large ground area causing land, plant, crop, paints and building damage.

PARTICULATE MATTER

A certain amount of particulate matter is present in the burning of any fuel, with carbon constituting the largest percentage of the particulates. In gasoline, the remaining percentage of particulates is the burned remains of the various other compounds used in its manufacture. When a gasoline engine is in good internal condition, the particulate emissions are low but as the engine wears internally, the particulate emissions increase. By visually inspecting the tail pipe emissions, a determination can be made as to where an engine defect may exist. An engine with light gray smoke emitting from the tail pipe normally indicates an increase in the oil consumption through burning due to internal engine wear. Black smoke would indicate a defective fuel delivery system, causing the engine to operate in a rich mode. Regardless of the color of the smoke, the internal part of the engine or the fuel delivery system should be repaired to a "like new" condition to prevent excess particulate emissions.

Diesel and turbine engines emit a darkened plume of smoke from the exhaust system because of the type of fuel used. Emission control regulations are mandated for this type of emission and more stringent measures are being used to prevent excess emission of the particulate matter. Electronic components are being introduced to control the injection of the fuel at precisely the proper time of piston travel, to achieve the optimum in fuel ignition and fuel usage. Other particulate after-burning components are being tested to achieve a cleaner particular emission.

Good grades of engine lubricating oils should be used, meeting the manufacturers specification. "Cut-rate" oils can contribute to the particulate emission problem because of their low "flash" or ignition temperature point. Such oils burn prematurely during the combustion process causing emissions of particulate matter.

The cooling system is an important factor in the reduction of particulate matter. With the cooling system operating at a temperature specified by the manufacturer, the optimum of combustion will occur. The cooling system must be maintained in the same manner as the engine oiling system, as each system is required to perform properly in order for the engine to operate efficiently for a long time.

Other Automobile Emission Sources

Before emission controls were mandated on the internal combustion engines, other sources of engine pollutants were discovered, along with the exhaust emission. It was determined the engine combustion exhaust produced 60% of the total emission pollutants, fuel evaporation from the fuel tank and carburetor vents produced 20%, with the another 20% being produced through the crankcase as a by-product of the combustion process.

CRANKCASE EMISSIONS

Crankcase emissions are made up of water, acids, unburned fuel, oil fumes and particulates. The emissions are classified as hydrocarbons (HC) and are formed by the small amount of unburned, compressed air/fuel mixture entering the crankcase from the combustion area during the compression and power strokes, between the cylinder walls and piston rings. The head of the compression and combustion help to form the remaining crankcase emissions.

Since the first engines, crankcase emissions were allowed to go into the air through a road draft tube, mounted on the lower side of the engine block. Fresh air came in through an open oil filler cap or breather. The air passed through the crankcase mixing with blow-by gases. The motion of the vehicle and the air blowing past the open end of the road draft tube caused a low pressure area at the end of the tube. Crankcase emissions were simply drawn out of the road draft tube into the air.

To control the crankcase emission, the road draft tube was deleted. A hose and/or tubing was routed from the crankcase to the intake manifold so the blow-by emission could be burned with the air/fuel mixture. However, it was found that intake manifold vacuum, used to draw the crankcase emissions into the manifold, would vary in strength at the wrong time and not allow the proper emission flow. A regulating type valve was needed to control the flow of air through the crankcase.

Testing, showed the removal of the blow-by gases from the crankcase as quickly as possible, was most important to the longevity of the engine. Should large accumulations of blow-by gases remain and condense, dilution of the engine oil would occur to form water, soots, resins, acids and lead salts, resulting in the formation of sludge and varnishes. This condensation of the blow-by gases occur more frequently on vehicles used in numerous starting and stopping conditions, excessive idling and when the engine is not allowed to attain normal operating temperature through short runs. The crankcase purge control or PCV system will be described in detail later in this section.

FUEL EVAPORATIVE EMISSIONS

Gasoline fuel is a major source of pollution, before and after it is burned in the automobile engine. From the time the fuel is refined, stored, pumped and transported, again stored until it is pumped into the fuel tank of the vehicle, the gasoline gives off unburned hydrocarbons (HC) into the atmosphere. Through redesigning of the storage areas and venting systems, the pollution factor has been diminished but not eliminated, from the refinery standpoint. However, the automobile still remained the primary source of vaporized, unburned hydrocarbon (HC) emissions.

Fuel pumped form an underground storage tank is cool but when exposed to a warner ambient temperature, will expand. Before controls were mandated, an owner would fill the fuel tank with fuel from an underground storage tank and park the vehicle for some time in warm area, such as a parking lot. As the fuel would warm, it would expand and should no provisions or area be provided for the expansion, the fuel would spill out the filler neck and onto the ground, causing hydrocarbon (HC) pollution and creating a severe fire hazard. To correct this condition, the vehicle manufacturers added overflow plumbing and/or gasoline tanks with built in expansion areas or domes.

However, this did not control the fuel vapor emission from the fuel tank and the carburetor bowl. It was determined that most of the fuel evaporation occurred when the vehicle was stationary and the engine not operating. Most vehicles carry 5–25 gallons (19–95 liters) of gasoline. Should a large concentration of vehicles be parked in one area, such as a large parking lot, excessive fuel vapor emissions would take place, increasing as the temperature increases.

To prevent the vapor emission from escaping into the atmosphere, the fuel system is designed to trap the fuel vapors while the vehicle is stationary, by sealing the fuel system from the atmosphere. A storage system is used to collect and hold the fuel vapors from the carburetor and the fuel tank when the engine is not operating. When the engine is started, the storage system is then purged of the fuel vapors, which are drawn into the engine and burned with the air/fuel mixture.

The components of the fuel evaporative system will be described in detail later in this section.

EMISSION CONTROLS

Crankcase Ventilation System

OPERATION

The PCV valve system is used on all vehicles. The PCV valve system vents harmful combustion blow-by fumes from the engine crankcase into the engine air intake for burning with the fuel and air mixture. The PCV valve limits the fresh air intake to suit the engine demand and also serves to prevent combustion backfiring into the crankcase. The PCV valve system maximizes oil cleanliness by venting moisture and corrosive fumes from the crankcase.

On some engine applications, the PCV valve system is connected with the evaporative emission system. Do not remove the PCV valve system from the engine, as doing so will adversely affect fuel economy and engine ventilation with resultant shortening of engine life.

The components used in the PCV valve system consist of the PCV valve, the rubber mounting grommet in the valve cover, the nipple in the air intake system and the necessary connecting hoses.

The PCV valve controls the amount of blow-by vapors pulled into the intake manifold from the crankcase. It also acts as a one-way check valve that prevents air from entering the crankcase in the opposite direction.

SERVICE

System Inspection

➧ SEE FIG. 1–2

1. Visually inspect the components of the PCV valve system. Check for rough idle, slow starting, high oil consumption and loose, leaking, clogged or damaged hoses.
2. Check the fresh air supply hose and the PCV hose for air leakage or flow restriction due to loose engagement, hose splitting, cracking or kinking, nipple damage, rubber grommet fit or any other damage.
3. If a component is suspected as the obvious cause of a malfunction, correct the cause before proceeding to the next Step.

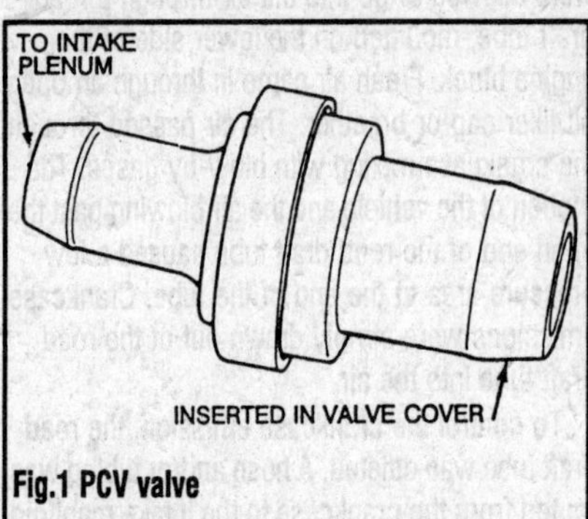

Fig.1 PCV valve

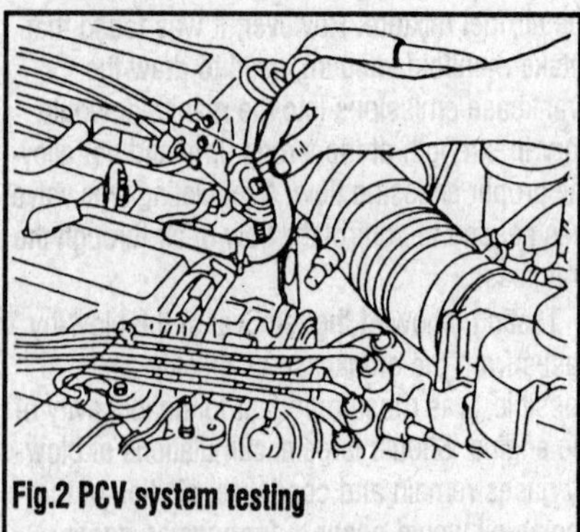

Fig.2 PCV system testing

4. If all checks are okay, proceed to the pinpoint tests.

Pinpoint Tests

1. Remove the PCV valve from the valve cover grommet and shake the valve. If the valve rattles when shaken, reinstall and proceed to Step 2. If the valve does not rattle, it is sticking and should be replaced.
2. Start the engine and bring to normal operating temperature.
3. On the 2.5L engine, remove the corrugated hose from the oil separator nipple. On all other engines, disconnect the hose from the remote air cleaner or air outlet tube.
4. Place a stiff piece of paper over the nipple or hose end and wait 1 minute. If vacuum holds the paper in place, the system is okay; reconnect the hose. If the paper is not held in place, the system is plugged or the evaporative emission valve is leaking, if equipped. If the evaporative emission valve is suspected of leaking, proceed to Step 5.
5. Disconnect the evaporative hose, if equipped and cap the connector.
6. Place a stiff piece of paper over the hose/nipple, as in Step 4 and wait 1 minute. If vacuum holds the paper in place, proceed to evaporative emission system testing. If the paper is not held in place, check for vacuum leaks/obstruction in the system: oil cap, PCV valve, hoses, cut grommets, the oil separator on the 2.5L engine and valve cover for bolt torque/gasket leak.

REMOVAL & INSTALLATION

1. Remove the PCV valve from the mounting grommet in the valve cover.
2. Disconnect the valve from the PCV hose and remove the valve from the vehicle.
3. Installation is the reverse of the removal procedure.

Evaporative Emission Controls

➧ SEE FIG. 3

The evaporative emission control system prevents the escape of fuel vapors to the atmosphere under hot soak and engine off conditions by storing the vapors in a carbon canister. Then, with the engine warm and running, the system controls the purging of stored vapors from the canister to the engine, where they are efficiently burned.

Evaporative emission control components consist of the carbon canister, purge valve(s), vapor valve, rollover vent valve, check valve and the necessary lines. All vehicles may not share all components.

SYSTEM INSPECTION

1. Visually inspect the components of the evaporative emission system. Check for the following, as applicable:
   a. Discharged battery.
   b. Damaged connectors.
   c. Damaged insulation.
   d. Malfunctioning ECU.
   e. Damaged air flow meter or speed sensor.
   f. Inoperative solenoids.
   g. Fuel odor or leakage.
   h. Damaged vacuum or fuel vapor lines.
   i. Loose or poor line connections.
   j. Poor driveability during engine warm-up.
2. Check the wiring and connectors for the

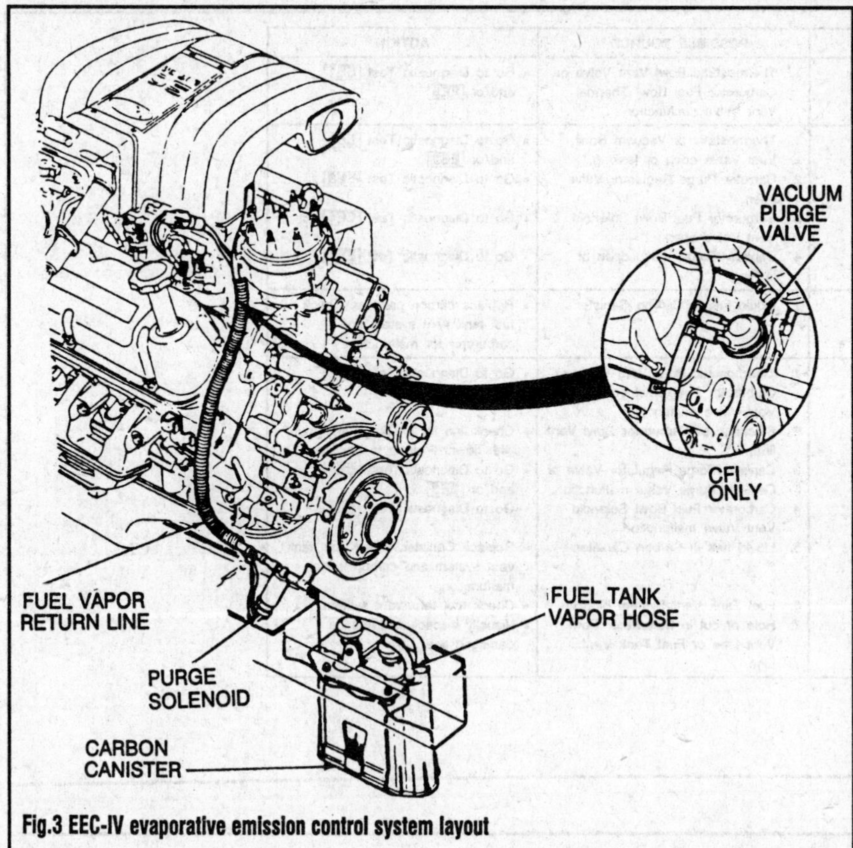

Fig.3 EEC-IV evaporative emission control system layout

solenoids, vane air flow meter, speed sensor and ECU, as applicable, for looseness, corrosion, damage or other problems. This must be done with the engine fully warmed up so as to activate the purging controls.

3. Check the fuel tank, fuel vapor lines, vacuum lines and connections for looseness, pinching, leakage, damage or other obvious cause for malfunction.

4. If fuel line, vacuum line or orifice blockage is suspected as the obvious cause of an observed malfunction, correct the cause before proceeding further.

CARBON CANISTER

The carbon canister contains vapor absorbent material to facilitate the storage of fuel vapors. Fuel vapors flow from the fuel tank to the canister, where they are stored until purged to the engine for burning.

Adjustment

There are no moving parts and nothing to wear in the canister. Check for loose, missing, cracked or broken connections and parts. There should be no liquid in the canister.

Removal and Installation

1. Disconnect the vapor hoses from the carbon canister.
2. Remove the canister mounting bolts and remove the canister.
3. Installation is the reverse of the removal procedure.

PURGE VALVES

The purge valves control the flow of fuel vapor from the carbon canister to the engine. Purge valves are either vacuum or electrically controlled. When electrically controlled, a purge valve is known as a purge solenoid. A vehicle may be equipped with a vacuum purge valve or purge solenoid or a combination of the two. Purging occurs when the engine is at operating temperature and off idle.

Removal and Installation

1. Disconnect the negative battery cable.
2. Disconnect the vacuum hose or the electrical connector from the purge valve.
3. Disconnect the vapor hoses and remove the purge valve from the vehicle.
4. Installation is the reverse of the removal procedure.

VAPOR VALVE

The vapor valve is located on or near the fuel tank. It's function is to prevent fuel from flooding the carbon canister. The vapor valve incorporates the rollover valve. In the event of a vehicle rollover, the valve blocks the vapor line automatically to prevent fuel leakage.

Removal and Installation

➧ SEE FIG. 4

1. Disconnect the negative battery cable.
2. Raise and safely support the vehicle. Remove the fuel tank to gain access to the vapor valve.
3. Disconnect the vapor hoses from the vapor valve.
4. Remove the vapor valve mounting screws and the vapor valve from the underside of the vehicle or remove the vapor valve from the fuel tank, as necessary.
5. Installation is the reverse of the removal procedure.

CHECK VALVE

The check valve is located in the fuel filler cap or on the underside of the vehicle. It's function is to protect the fuel tank from heat build-up rupture and cool-down collapse by allowing air to pass in or out of the tank to equalize pressure. On cool-down, air enters either at the carbon canister vent or at the check valve.

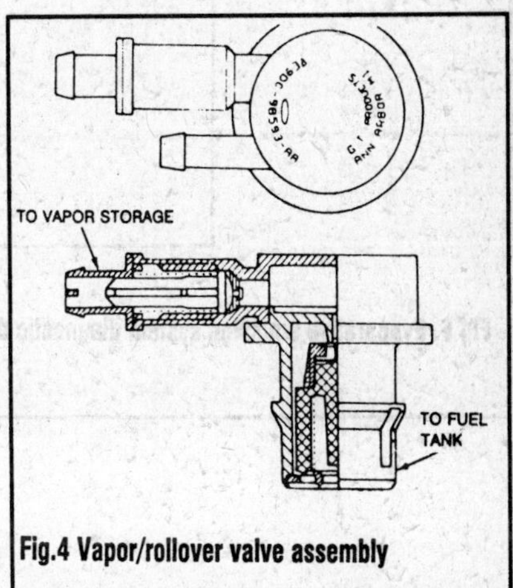

Fig.4 Vapor/rollover valve assembly

CONDITION	POSSIBLE SOURCE *	ACTION
• Cranks Normally But Slow to Start	1. Thermostatic Bowl Vent Valve or Carburetor Fuel Bowl Thermal Vent Valve malfunction.	• Go to Diagnostic Test EE1 and/or EE5.
• Rough Idle	1. Thermostatic or Vacuum Bowl Vent Valve open or leaking. 2. Canister Purge Regulator Valve open. 3. Carburetor Fuel Bowl Solenoid Vent Valve open. 4. Canister Purge Valve open or leaking.	• Go to Diagnostic Test EE1 and/or EE2. • Go to Diagnostic Test EE3. • Go to Diagnostic Test EE4. • Go to Diagnostic Test EE3.
• Surge at Steady Speed	1. Liquid fuel in Carbon Canister.	• Replace carbon canister. Check fuel tank vent system and carburetor for malfunction.
• Gas Smell	1. Thermostatic Bowl Vent Valve or Carburetor Fuel Bowl Thermal Vent Valve malfunction. 2. Blockage of Carburetor Bowl Vent line. 3. Canister Purge Regulator Valve or Canister Purge Valve malfunction. 4. Carburetor Fuel Bowl Solenoid Vent Valve malfunction. 5. Liquid fuel in Carbon Canister. 6. Fuel Tank Vent System blocked. 7. Hole or cut in Carburetor Bowl Vent Line or Fuel Tank Vent Line.	• Go to Diagnostic Test EE1 and/or EE5. • Check line for blockage and route with downhill slope to canister. • Go to Diagnostic Test EE6 and/or EE3. • Go to Diagnostic Test EE4. • Replace Canister. Check fuel tank vent system and carburetor for malfunction. • Check fuel tank vent system. • Visually inspect and replace damaged line.

Fig.5. Evaporative emission system diagnostic data

DIAGNOSTIC TEST NUMBER	SOURCE COMPONENT	DIAGNOSTIC ACTION
EE1	Thermostatic Bowl Vent Valve	• At a temperature of 120°F or more, the Vacuum Vent Valve should flow air between carburator port and canister port when no vacuum is applied to vacuum signal nipple. It should not flow air with a vacuum applied at the vacuum signal nipple At a temperature of 90°F or less, the valve should not flow air or be very restrictive to airflow. *Vacuum/Thermostatic Bowl Vent Valve*

Fig.6. Evaporative emission system diagnostic data

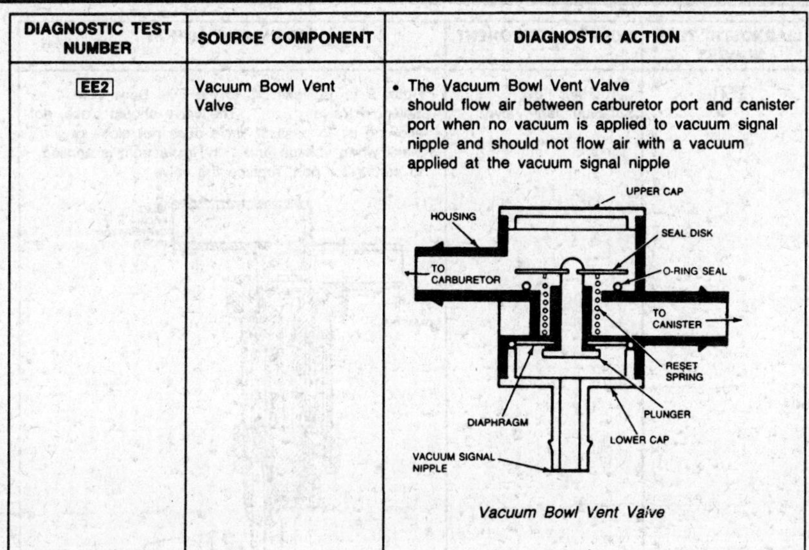

DIAGNOSTIC TEST NUMBER	SOURCE COMPONENT	DIAGNOSTIC ACTION
EE2	Vacuum Bowl Vent Valve	• The Vacuum Bowl Vent Valve should flow air between carburetor port and canister port when no vacuum is applied to vacuum signal nipple and should not flow air with a vacuum applied at the vacuum signal nipple

Vacuum Bowl Vent Valve

Fig.7. Evaporative emission system diagnostic data

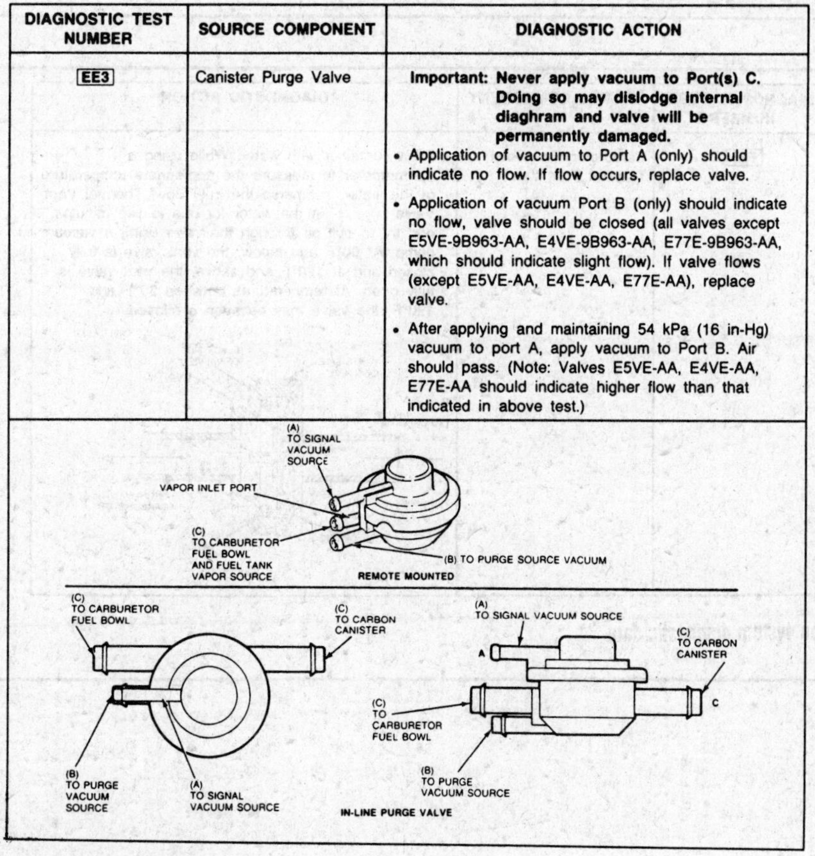

DIAGNOSTIC TEST NUMBER	SOURCE COMPONENT	DIAGNOSTIC ACTION
EE3	Canister Purge Valve	**Important: Never apply vacuum to Port(s) C. Doing so may dislodge internal diaghram and valve will be permanently damaged.** • Application of vacuum to Port A (only) should indicate no flow. If flow occurs, replace valve. • Application of vacuum Port B (only) should indicate no flow, valve should be closed (all valves except E5VE-9B963-AA, E4VE-9B963-AA, E77E-9B963-AA, which should indicate slight flow). If valve flows (except E5VE-AA, E4VE-AA, E77E-AA), replace valve. • After applying and maintaining 54 kPa (16 in-Hg) vacuum to port A, apply vacuum to Port B. Air should pass. (Note: Valves E5VE-AA, E4VE-AA, E77E-AA should indicate higher flow than that indicated in above test.)

Fig.8. Evaporative emission system diagnostic data

DIAGNOSTIC TEST NUMBER	SOURCE COMPONENT	DIAGNOSTIC ACTION
EE4	Carburetor Fuel Solenoid Vent Valve	• Apply 9 to 14 volts DC to the Fuel Bowl Vent Solenoid Valve The valve should close, not allowing air to pass. If valve does not close or leaks when voltage and 1 in-Hg vacuum is applied to carburetor port, replace the valve

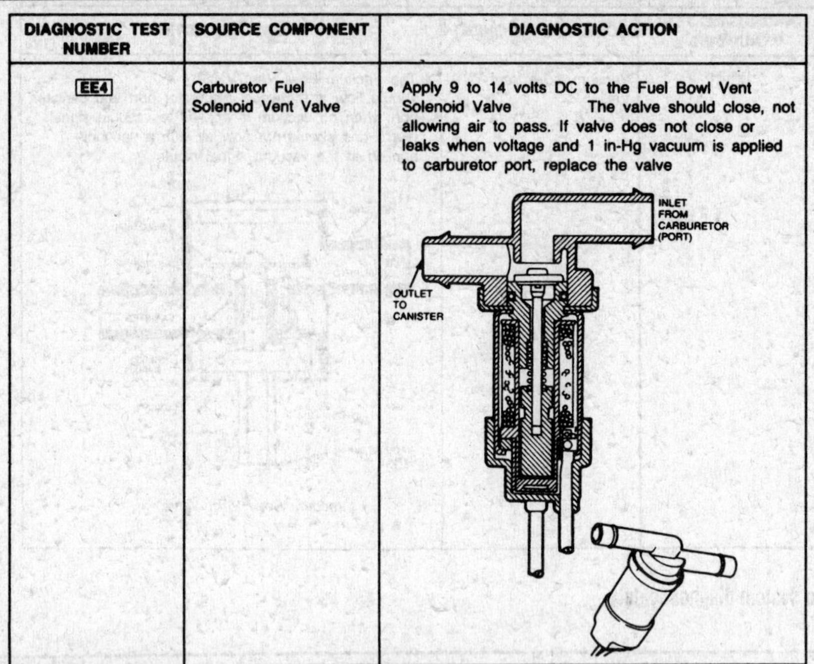

Fig.9. Evaporative emission system diagnostic data

DIAGNOSTIC TEST NUMBER	SOURCE COMPONENT	DIAGNOSTIC ACTION
EE5	Carburetor Fuel Bowl Thermal Vent Valve	• Fill a container with water. While using a thermometer to measure the appropriate temperature of the water, submerse the Fuel Bowl Thermal Vent Valve in the water for one to two minutes and try to pull air through the valve using a vacuum pump. At 90°F and below, the vent valve is fully closed and at 120°F and above, the vent valve is fully open. At temperatures between 90°F and 120°F, the valve may be open or closed

WHITE SIDE OF VALVE
BLACK SIDE OF VALVE
BI-METAL
TO CANISTER
FROM CARBURETOR
SPRING
SEAL

Fig.10. Evaporative emission system diagnostic data

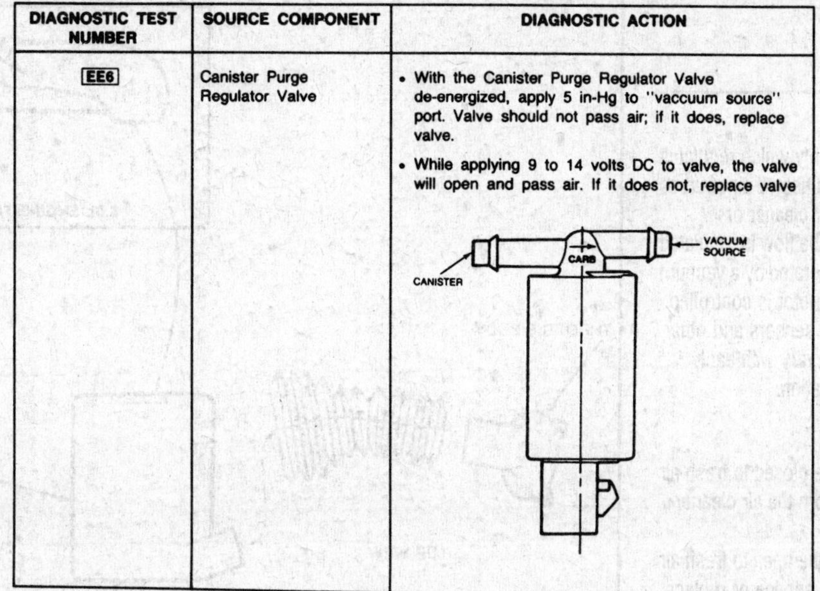

DIAGNOSTIC TEST NUMBER	SOURCE COMPONENT	DIAGNOSTIC ACTION
EE6	Canister Purge Regulator Valve	• With the Canister Purge Regulator Valve de-energized, apply 5 in-Hg to "vacuum source" port. Valve should not pass air; if it does, replace valve. • While applying 9 to 14 volts DC to valve, the valve will open and pass air. If it does not, replace valve

Fig.11. Evaporative emission system diagnostic data

Exhaust Emission Control system

The exhaust emission control system begins at the air intake and ends at the tailpipe. All vehicles are equipped with the following systems or components to manage exhaust emission control: thermostatic air inlet system, Thermactor air injection system, pulse air injection system, exhaust gas recirculation system and exhaust catalyst. All vehicles do not share all systems or all components.

THERMOSTATIC AIR INLET SYSTEM

➧ SEE FIG. 12

The thermostatic air inlet system is used on is used on vehicles equipped with the 2.5L engine. The thermostatic air inlet system regulates the air inlet temperature by drawing air in from a cool air source as well as heated air from a heat shroud which is mounted on the exhaust manifold. The system consists of the following components: duct and valve assembly, heat shroud, bimetal sensor, cold weather modulator, vacuum delay valve and the necessary vacuum lines and air ducts. All vehicles do not share all components.

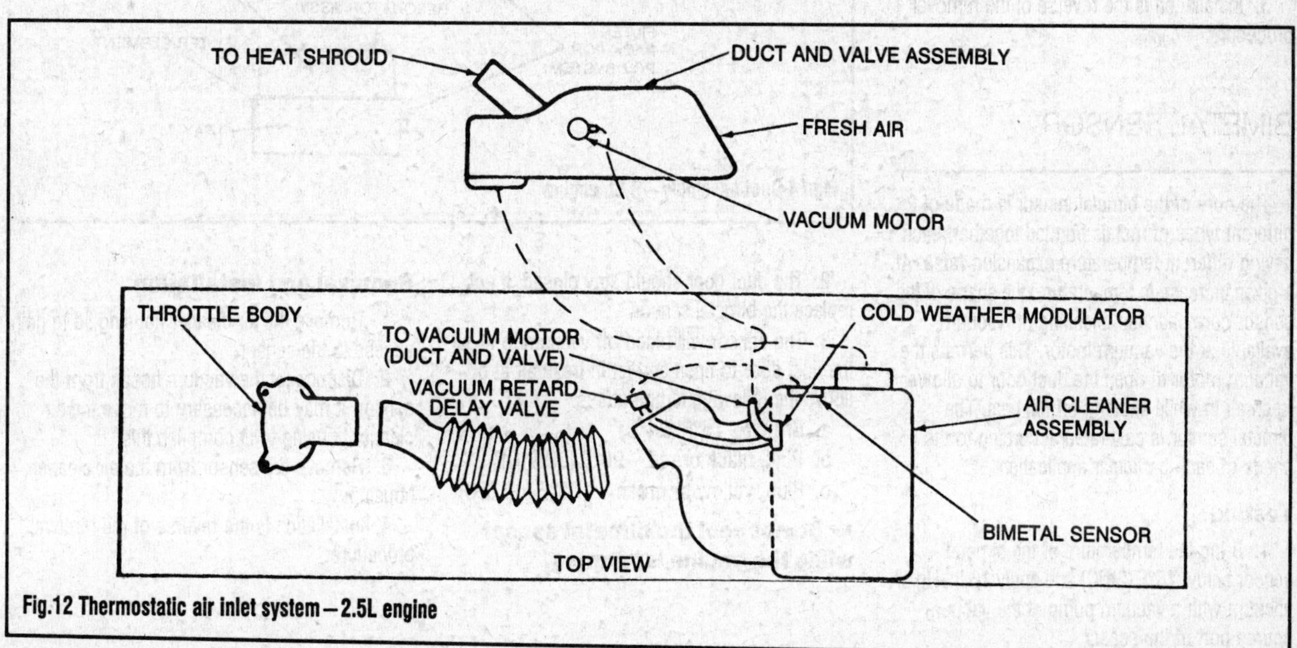

Fig.12 Thermostatic air inlet system — 2.5L engine

DUCT AND VALVE ASSEMBLY

➧ SEE FIG. 13–14

The duct and valve assembly which regulates the air flow from the cool and heated air sources is located either inside the air cleaner or mounted on the air cleaner. The flow is regulated by means of a door that is operated by a vacuum motor. The operation of the motor is controlled by delay valves, temperature sensors and other vacuum control systems. All vary with each application and engine calibration.

Testing

1. If the duct door is in the closed to fresh air position, remove the hose from the air cleaner vacuum motor.
2. The door should go to the open to fresh air position. If it sticks or binds, service or replace, as required.
3. If the door is in the open to fresh air position, check the door by applying 8 in. Hg or greater of vacuum to the vacuum motor.
4. The door should move freely to the closed to fresh air position. If it binds or sticks, service or replace, as required.

➡ Make sure the vacuum motor is functional before changing the duct and valve assembly.

Removal and Installation

1. Disconnect the vacuum hose from the vacuum motor.
2. Separate the vacuum motor from the vacuum operated door and remove the vacuum motor.
3. Installation is the reverse of the removal procedure.

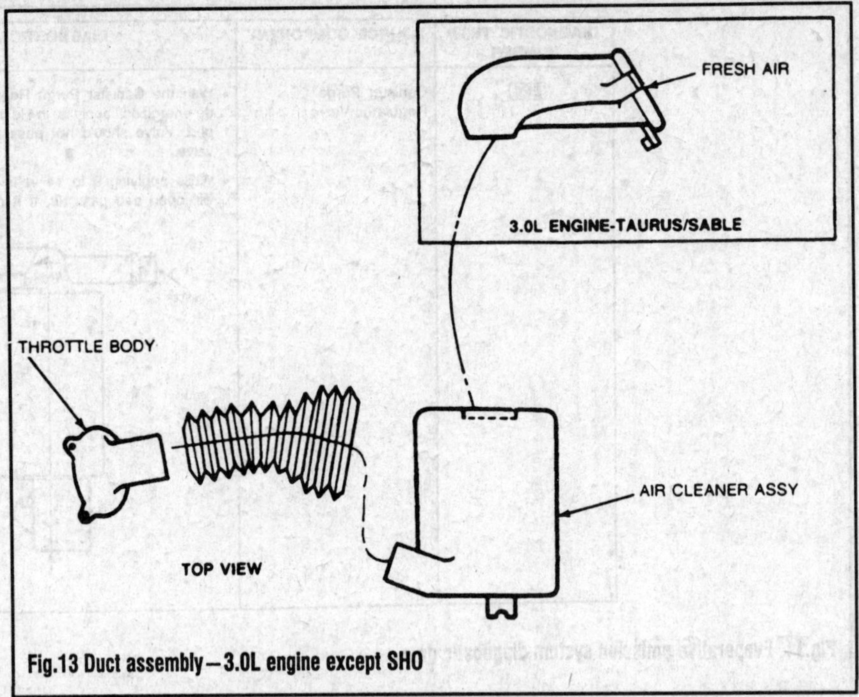

Fig.13 Duct assembly—3.0L engine except SHO

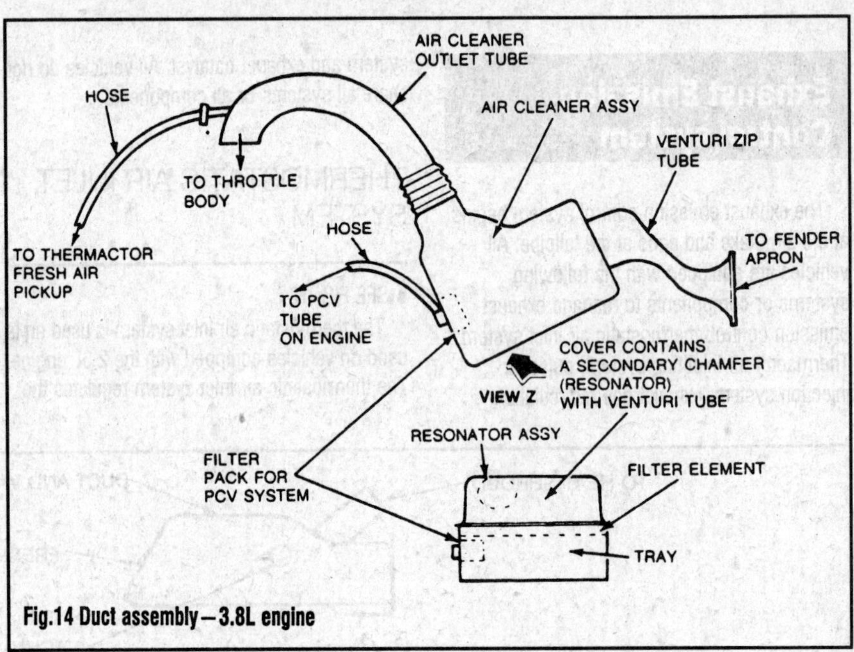

Fig.14 Duct assembly—3.8L engine

BIMETAL SENSOR

The core of the bimetal sensor is made of 2 different types of metals bonded together, each having different temperature expansion rates. At a given increase in temperature, the shape of the sensor core changes, bleeding off vacuum available at the vacuum motor. This permits the vacuum motor to open the duct door to allow fresh air in while shutting off full heat. The bimetal sensor is calibrated according to the needs of each particular application.

Testing

1. Bring the temperature of the bimetal sensor below 75°F (24°C) and apply 16 in. Hg of vacuum with a vacuum pump at the vacuum source port of the sensor.
2. The duct door should stay closed. If not, replace the bimetal sensor.
3. The sensor will bleed off vacuum to allow the duct door to open and let in fresh air at or above the following temperatures:
   a. Brown—75°F (24°C)
   b. Pink, black or red—90°F (32.2°C)
   c. Blue, yellow or green—105°F (40.6°C)

➡ Do not cool the bimetal sensor while the engine is running.

Removal and Installation

1. Remove the air cleaner housing lid to gain access to the sensor.
2. Disconnect the vacuum hoses from the sensor. It may be necessary to move the air cleaner housing to accomplish this.
3. Remove the sensor from the air cleaner housing.
4. Installation is the reverse of the removal procedure.

COLD WEATHER MODULATOR

The cold weather modulator is used in addition to the bimetal sensor to control the inlet air temperature. The modulator traps vacuum in the system, so the door will not switch to cold air when the vacuum drops during acceleration. The cold weather modulator only works when the outside air is cold.

Testing

A 16 in. Hg vacuum applied to the motor side of the modulator holds or leaks as follows:

Black—holds below 20°F (-6.7°C) and leaks above 35°F (1.7°C)

Blue—holds below 40°F (4.4°C) and leaks above 55°F (12.8°C)

Green—holds below 50°F (10°C) and leaks above 76°F (24.4°C)

Yellow—holds above 65°F (18.3°C) and leaks below 50°F (10°C)

Removal and Installation

1. Remove the air cleaner housing lid to gain access to the modulator.
2. Disconnect the vacuum hoses from the modulator. It may be necessary to move the air cleaner housing to accomplish this.
3. Remove the modulator from the air cleaner housing.
4. Installation is the reverse of the removal procedure.

VACUUM DELAY VALVE

The vacuum delay valve is used for the gradual release of vacuum to the vacuum motor.

Testing

1. Connect a hand vacuum pump to the vacuum delay valve.
2. Valves with 1 side black or white and the other side colored are good if vacuum can be built up in 1 direction but not the other direction and if that built up vacuum can be seen to slowly decrease.
3. Valves with both sides the same color are good if vacuum can be built up in both directions before visibly decreasing.

➡ Be careful in order to prevent oil or dirt from getting into the valve.

Removal and Installation

1. Disconnect the vacuum hoses from the delay valve and remove the valve.
2. Installation is the reverse of the removal procedure.

CONDITION	POSSIBLE SOURCE	ACTION
Cranks normally but slow to start.	1. Air filter restricted	• Go to Diagnostic Test IA4.
Hesitates or stalls on acceleration.	1. Vacuum motor inoperative 2. Air cleaner duct and valve door not operating properly 3. CWM inoperative 4. Bimetal sensor inoperative	• Go to Diagnostic Test IA2. • Go to Diagnostic Test IA5. • Go to Diagnostic Test IA1. • Go to Diagnostic Test IA3.
Lack of power.	1. Vacuum motor inoperative 2. Air cleaner duct and valve door not operating properly 3. CWM inoperative 4. Bimetal sensor inoperative 5. Air filter element restricted 6. Collapsed air inlet and outlet tubes	• Go to Diagnostic Test IA2. • Go to Diagnostic Test IA5. • Go to Diagnostic Test IA1. • Go to Diagnostic Test IA3. • Go to Diagnostic Test IA4. • Service or replace.
Poor fuel economy.	1. Air cleaner duct and valve door stuck in "hot air" position 2. CWM inoperative 3. Bimetal sensor inoperative 4. Air filter element restricted	• Go to Diagnostic Test IA5. • Go to Diagnostic Test IA1. • Go to Diagnostic Test IA3. • Go to Diagnostic Test IA4.

Fig.15. Thermostatic air inlet system diagnostic data

CONDITION	POSSIBLE SOURCE	ACTION
High oil consumption.	1. Air intake system sealing integrity 2. Air filter element sealing	• Check hoses that connect the air cleaner to the engine (check for holes or cracks) and ensure clamps are to proper torque. • Check the air filter gasket sealing area and the clean side of the air cleaner housing for excessive dirt. Replace components as required.
Spark knocking.	1. Air cleaner duct and valve door stuck in hot air position 2. CWM inoperative 3. Bimetal sensor inoperative	• Go to Diagnostic Test IA5. • Go to Diagnostic Test IA1. • Go to Diagnostic Test IA3.
Air Induction Noise.	1. Loose air intake tube, outlet tubes, or air cleaner cover 2. Intake or outlet tube cracks or holes	• Connect or tighten screw(s) as necessary. • Service or replace.
Engine Failure or Reduced Performance.	1. Unfiltered air from air outlet tubes, air cleaner cover, idle by-pass hose or crankcase ventilation hose	• Connect or tighten screws. Service as necessary.

Fig.16. Thermostatic air inlet system diagnostic data

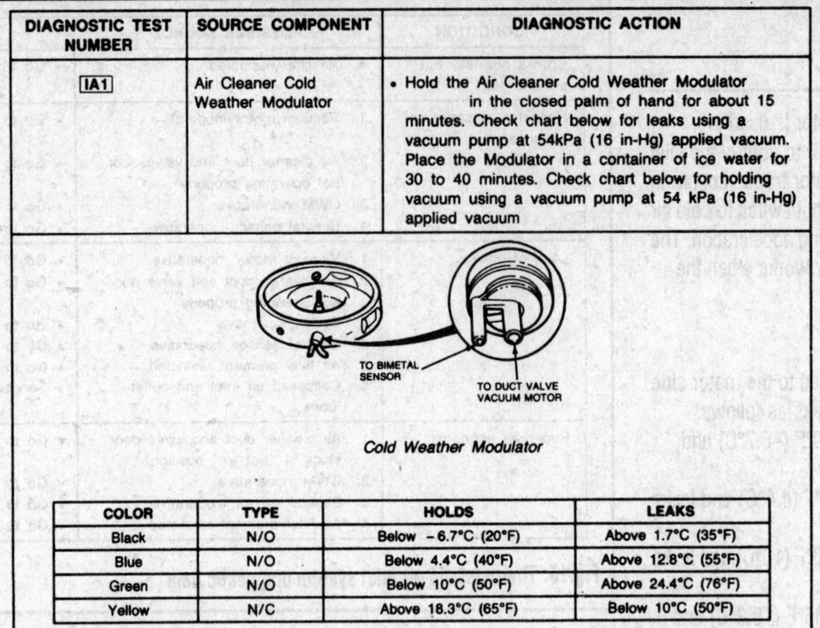

DIAGNOSTIC TEST NUMBER	SOURCE COMPONENT	DIAGNOSTIC ACTION
IA1	Air Cleaner Cold Weather Modulator	• Hold the Air Cleaner Cold Weather Modulator in the closed palm of hand for about 15 minutes. Check chart below for leaks using a vacuum pump at 54kPa (16 in-Hg) applied vacuum. Place the Modulator in a container of ice water for 30 to 40 minutes. Check chart below for holding vacuum using a vacuum pump at 54 kPa (16 in-Hg) applied vacuum

Cold Weather Modulator

COLOR	TYPE	HOLDS	LEAKS
Black	N/O	Below −6.7°C (20°F)	Above 1.7°C (35°F)
Blue	N/O	Below 4.4°C (40°F)	Above 12.8°C (55°F)
Green	N/O	Below 10°C (50°F)	Above 24.4°C (76°F)
Yellow	N/C	Above 18.3°C (65°F)	Below 10°C (50°F)

Fig.17. Thermostatic air inlet system diagnostic data

DIAGNOSTIC TEST NUMBER	SOURCE COMPONENT	DIAGNOSTIC ACTION
IA2	Air Cleaner Vacuum Motor	• When a vacuum of 27 kPa (8 in-Hg) or greater is applied to the vacuum motor, the door stem should pull up and stay as long as vacuum is applied to the vacuum motor *Air Cleaner Vacuum Motor*

Fig.18. Thermostatic air inlet system diagnostic data

DIAGNOSTIC TEST NUMBER	SOURCE COMPONENT	DIAGNOSTIC ACTION
IA3	Air Cleaner Temperature Sensor (Bimetal Sensor)	• Bring the temperature of the Air Cleaner Temperature Sensor below 24°C (75°F) and apply 27 kPa (8 in-Hg) of vacuum with a vacuum pump at the vacuum source port of the sensor. Does the duct door stay closed? If not, replace the sensor BIMETAL SENSOR / VACUUM MOTOR / FULL FRESH AIR / FRESH AIR IN / FULL HEAT / HEATED AIR IN / TO VACUUM SOURCE / TO DUCT VALVE MOTOR OR CWM *Air Cleaner Temperature Sensor* • The sensor will bleed off vacuum to allow the duct door to open and let in fresh air at or above the following temperatures: Brown — 24°C (75°F) Pink, black or red — 32.2°C (90°F) Blue, yellow or green — 40.6°C (105°F) **CAUTION** Do not cool bimetal sensor while the engine is running. If refrigerant R-12 is drawn into the intake system while the engine is running, poisonous phosgene gas will be exhausted into the test area. Perform this test only in a well-ventilated area.

Fig.19. Thermostatic air inlet system diagnostic data

DIAGNOSTIC TEST NUMBER	SOURCE COMPONENT	DIAGNOSTIC ACTION
IA4	Air Cleaner Filter Element	• Remove the Air Cleaner Filter Element from the Air Cleaner Assembly. Inspect for heavy contamination. If the filter cannot be cleaned by shaking and applying vacuum, replace the filter element.
IA5	Air Cleaner Duct and Valve System	• If the duct door is in the closed to fresh air position, remove the hose from the Air Cleaner Vacuum Motor. The door should go to the open to fresh air position. If it sticks or binds, service or replace as required. If the door is in the open to fresh air position, check the door by applying vacuum of 27 kPa (8 in-Hg) or greater to the Air Cleaner Vacuum Motor. The door should move freely to the closed to fresh air position. If it binds or sticks, service or replace as required. **NOTE: Make sure the Vacuum Motor is functional before changing the Duct and Valve System.** VACUUM MOTOR / FRESH AIR IN / FRESH AIR OPEN / FULL HEAT / HEATED AIR IN / FRESH AIR CLOSED

Fig.20. Thermostatic air inlet system diagnostic data

Thermactor Air Injection System

SEE FIG. 21

A conventional Thermactor air injection system is used on some vehicles equipped with the 3.8L engine. The system reduces the hydrocarbon and carbon monoxide content of the exhaust gases by continuing the combustion of unburned gases after they leave the combustion chamber. This is done by injecting fresh air into the hot exhaust stream leaving the exhaust ports or into the catalyst. At this point, the fresh air mixes with hot exhaust gases to promote further oxidation of both the hydrocarbons and carbon monoxide, thereby reducing their concentration and converting some of them into harmless carbon dioxide and water. During highway cruising and WOT operation, the Thermactor air is dumped to atmosphere to prevent overheating in the exhaust system.

A typical air injection system consists of an air supply pump and filter, air bypass valve, check valves, air manifold, air hoses and air control valve.

AIR SUPPLY PUMP

SEE FIG. 22

The air supply pump is a belt-driven, positive displacement, vane-type pump that provides air for the Thermactor system. It is available in 19 and 22 cu. in. (311.35 and 360.5cc) sizes, either of which may be driven with different pulley ratios for different applications. Pumps receive air from a remote silencer filter on the rear side of the engine air cleaner attached to the pumps' air inlet nipple or through an impeller-type centrifugal filter fan.

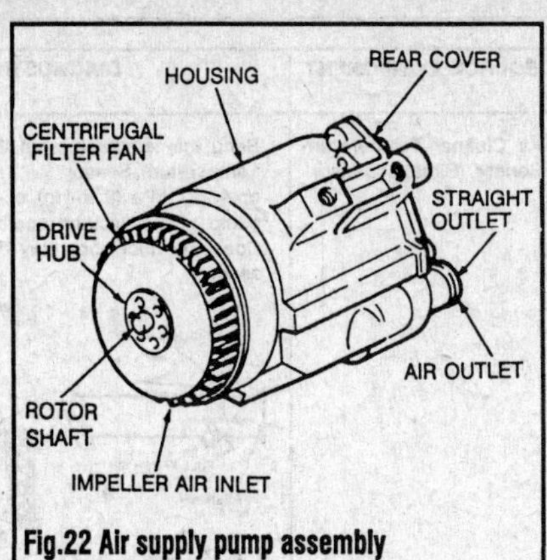

Fig.22 Air supply pump assembly

Testing

1. Check belt tension and adjust if needed.

➡ **Do not pry on the pump to adjust the belt. The aluminum housing is likely to collapse.**

2. Disconnect the air supply hose from the bypass control valve.
3. The pump is operating properly if airflow is felt at the pump outlet and the flow increases as engine speed increases.

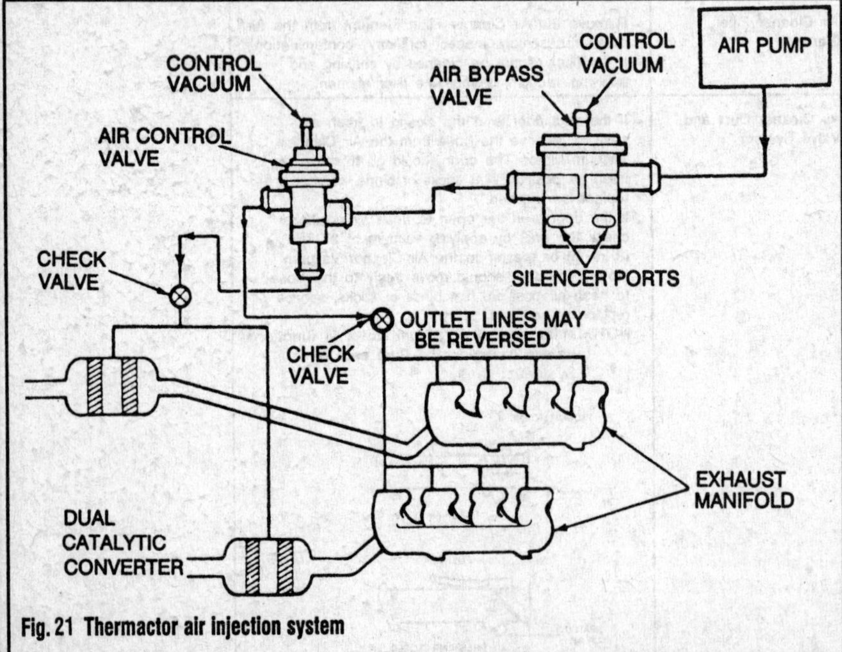

Fig. 21 Thermactor air injection system

Removal and Installation

1. Disconnect the negative battery cable.
2. Remove the drive belt from the air pump pulley.
3. Disconnect the air hose(s) from the air pump.
4. Remove the mounting bolts and, if necessary, the mounting brackets.
5. Remove the air pump from the vehicle.
6. Installation is the reverse of the removal procedure.

AIR BYPASS VALVE

SEE FIG. 23

The air bypass valve supplies air to the exhaust system with medium and high applied vacuum signals when the engine is at normal operating temperature. With low or no vacuum applied, the pumped air is dumped through the silencer ports of the valve or through the dump port.

Testing

1. Disconnect the air supply hose at the valve outlet.
2. Remove the vacuum line to check that a vacuum signal is present at the vacuum nipple. There must be a vacuum present at the nipple before proceeding.
3. With the engine at 1500 rpm and the vacuum line connected to the vacuum nipple, air pump supply air should be heard and felt at the air bypass valve outlet.
4. With the engine at 1500 rpm, disconnect the vacuum line. Air at the outlet should be significantly decreased or shut off. Air pump supply air should be heard or felt at the silencer ports or at the dump port.
5. If the air bypass valve does not successfully complete these tests, check the air pump. If the air pump is operating properly, replace the air bypass valve.

Removal and Installation

1. Disconnect the negative battery cable.
2. Disconnect the air inlet and outlet hoses and the vacuum hose from the bypass valve.
3. Remove the bypass valve from the vehicle.
4. Installation is the reverse of the removal procedure.

CHECK VALVE

SEE FIG. 24

The air check valve is a 1-way valve that allows Thermactor air to pass into the exhaust

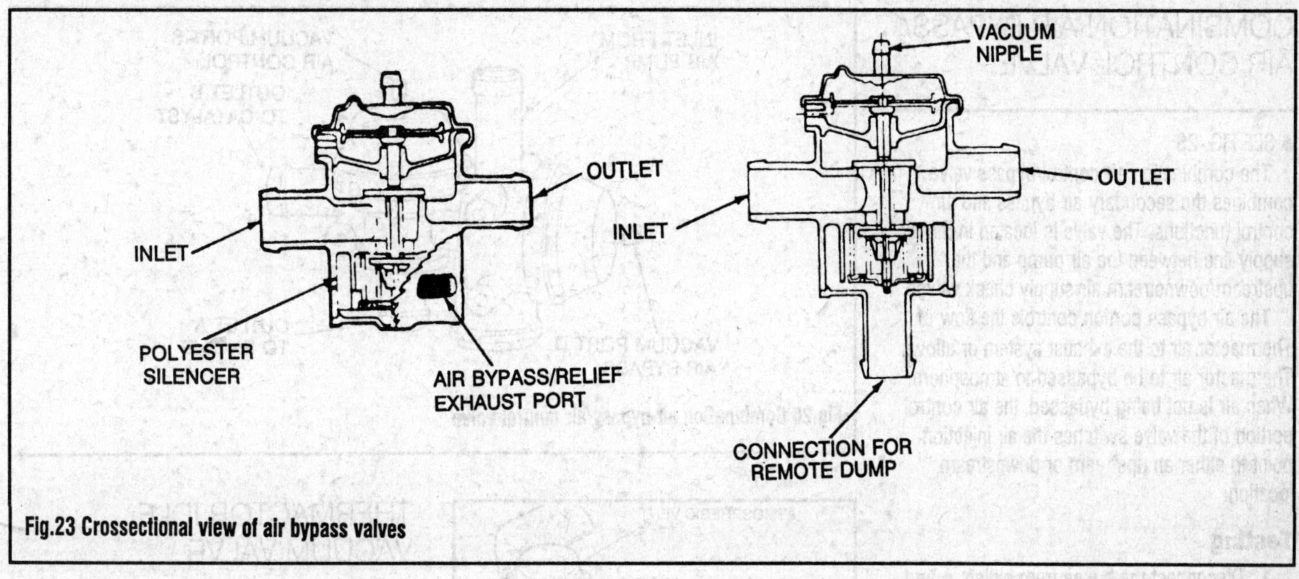

Fig.23 Crossectional view of air bypass valves

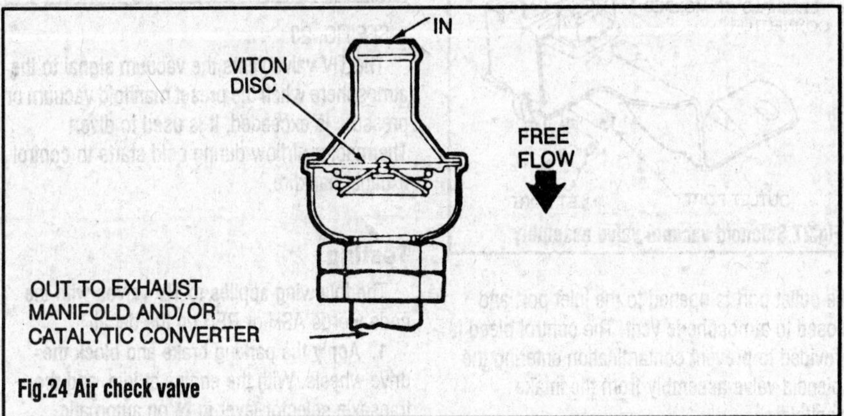

Fig.24 Air check valve

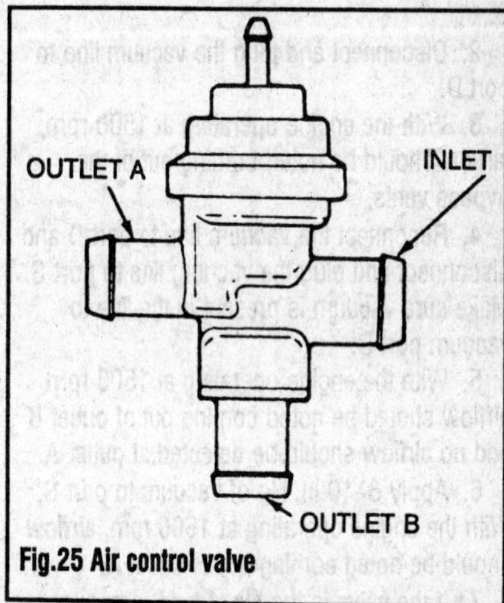

Fig.25 Air control valve

system while preventing exhaust gases from passing in the opposite direction.

Testing

1. Visually inspect the Thermactor system hoses, tubes, control valve(s) and check valve(s) for leaks that may be due to the backflow of exhaust gas. If holes are found and/ or traces of exhaust gas products are evident, the check valve may be suspect.
2. Check valves should allow free flow of air in the incoming direction only. The valves should check or block, the free flow of exhaust gas in the opposite direction.
3. Replace the valve if air does not flow as indicated or if exhaust gas backflows in the opposite direction.

Removal and Installation

1. Disconnect the negative battery cable.
2. Disconnect the input hose from the check valve.
3. Remove the check valve from the connecting tube.
4. Installation is the reverse of the removal procedure.

AIR SUPPLY CONTROL VALVE

➧ SEE FIG. 25

The air supply control valve directs air pump output to the exhaust manifold or downstream to the catalyst system depending upon the engine control strategy. It may also be used to dump air to the air cleaner or dump silencer.

Testing

1. Verify that airflow is being supplied to the valve inlet by disconnecting the air supply hose at the inlet and verifying the presence of airflow with the engine at 1500 rpm. Reconnect the air supply hose to the valve inlet.
2. Disconnect the air supply hose at outlets A and B.
3. Remove the vacuum line at the vacuum nipple.
4. Accelerate the engine to 1500 rpm. Airflow should be heard and felt at outlet B with little or no airflow at outlet A.
5. With the engine at 1500 rpm, connect a direct vacuum line from any manifold vacuum fitting to the air control valve vacuum nipple. Airflow should be heard and felt at outlet A with little or no airflow at outlet B.
6. If airflow is noted in Steps 4 and 5, the valve is okay. Reinstall the clamps and hoses. If the valve does not pass Step 4 and/or 5, replace the valve.

Removal and Installation

1. Disconnect the negative battery cable.
2. Disconnect the air hoses and the vacuum line from the air control valve.
3. Remove the air control valve from the vehicle.
4. Installation is the reverse of the removal procedure.

COMBINATION AIR BYPASS/ AIR CONTROL VALVE

SEE FIG. 26

The combination air control/bypass valve combines the secondary air bypass and air control functions. The valve is located in the air supply line between the air pump and the upstream/downstream air supply check valves.

The air bypass portion controls the flow of Thermactor air to the exhaust system or allows Thermactor air to be bypassed to atmosphere. When air is not being bypassed, the air control portion of the valve switches the air injection point to either an upstream or downstream location.

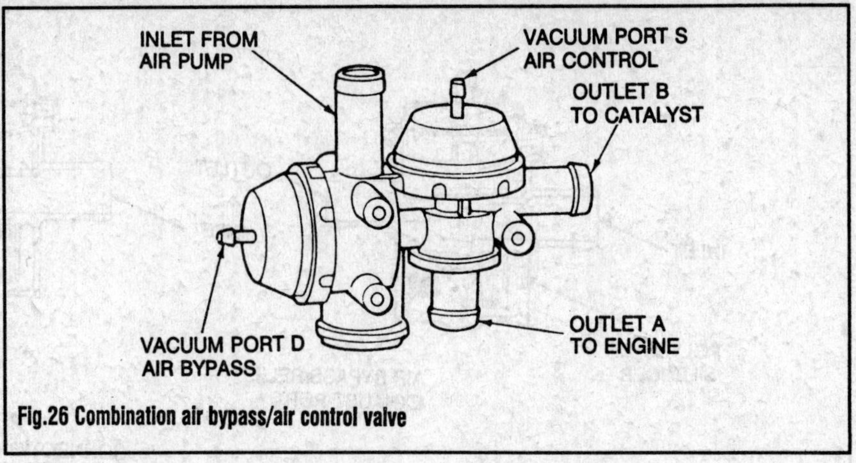

Fig.26 Combination air bypass/air control valve

Testing

1. Disconnect the hoses from outlets A and B.
2. Disconnect and plug the vacuum line to port D.
3. With the engine operating at 1500 rpm, airflow should be noted coming out of the bypass vents.
4. Reconnect the vacuum line to port D and disconnect and plug the vacuum line to port S. Make sure vacuum is present in the line to vacuum port D.
5. With the engine operating at 1500 rpm, airflow should be noted coming out of outlet B and no airflow should be detected at outlet A.
6. Apply 8–10 in. Hg of vacuum to port S. With the engine operating at 1500 rpm, airflow should be noted coming out of outlet A.
7. If the valve is the bleed type, some lesser amount of air will flow from outlet A or B and the main discharge will change when vacuum is applied to port S.

Removal and Installation

1. Disconnect the negative battery cable.
2. Disconnect the air hoses and vacuum lines from the valve.
3. Remove the valve from the vehicle.
4. Installation is the reverse of the removal procedure.

SOLENOID VACUUM VALVE ASSEMBLY

SEE FIG. 27

The normally closed solenoid valve assembly consists of 2 vacuum ports with an atmospheric vent. The valve assembly can be with or without control bleed. The outlet port of the valve is opened to atmospheric vent and closed to the inlet port when de-energized. When energized, the outlet port is opened to the inlet port and closed to atmospheric vent. The control bleed is provided to prevent contamination entering the solenoid valve assembly from the intake manifold.

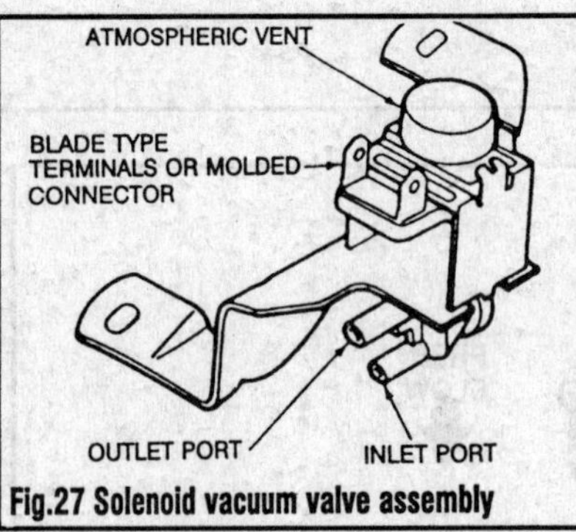

Fig.27 Solenoid vacuum valve assembly

Testing

1. The ports should flow air when the solenoid is energized.
2. Check the resistance at the solenoid terminals with an ohmmeter. The resistance should be 51–108Ω.
3. If the resistance is not as specified, replace the solenoid.

➡ The valve can be expected to have a very small leakage rate when energized or de-energized. This leakage is not measurable in the field and is not detrimental to valve function.

Removal and Installation

1. Disconnect the negative battery cable.
2. Disconnect the electrical connector and the vacuum lines from the solenoid valve.
3. Remove the mounting bolts and remove the solenoid valve.
4. Installation is the reverse of the removal procedure.

THERMACTOR IDLE VACUUM VALVE

SEE FIG. 28

The TIV valve vents the vacuum signal to the atmosphere when the preset manifold vacuum or pressure is exceeded. It is used to divert Thermactor airflow during cold starts to control exhaust backfire.

Testing

The following applies to TIV valves with the code words ASH or RED on the decal.

1. Apply the parking brake and block the drive wheels. With the engine at idle, and the transaxle selector lever in **N** on automatic transaxle equipped vehicles or neutral on manual transaxle equipped vehicles, apply vacuum to the small nipple and place fingers over the TIV valve atmospheric vent holes. If no vacuum is sensed, the TIV is damaged and must be replaced.
2. With the engine still idling and the transaxle selector lever remaining in **N** or neutral, apply 1.5–3.0 in. Hg of vacuum to the large nipple of

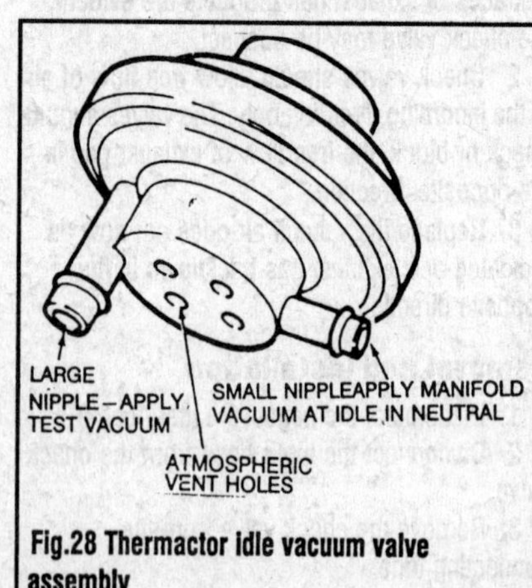

Fig.28 Thermactor idle vacuum valve assembly

the ASH TIV valve or 3.5–4.5 in. Hg of vacuum to the large nipple of the RED TIV valve from a test source. If vacuum is still sensed when placing fingers over the vent holes, the TIV is damaged and must be replaced.

3. If the TIV valve meets both requirements, disconnect the TIV valve small nipple from the manifold vacuum and the TIV valve large nipple from the test vacuum. Reconnect the TIV valve to the original hoses or connectors.

Removal and Installation

1. Disconnect the negative battery cable.
2. Disconnect the vacuum lines from the TIV valve and remove the valve from the vehicle.
3. Installation is the reverse of the removal procedure.

SYMPTOM	POSSIBLE SOURCE	ACTION
• Backfire (Exhaust)	• Air bypass valve malfunction • Air control valve malfunction • Combination air bypass/control valve malfunction • Thermactor solenoid valve malfunction • Thermactor idle vacuum valve malfunction • Exhaust manifolds or pipes loose	• Perform bypass valve diagnosis • Perform air control valve diagnosis • Perform combination valve diagnosis • Perform solenoid diagnosis • Perform TIV diagnosis • Inspect and tighten nuts or bolts to specification.
• Surge at Steady Speed	• Air control valve malfunction • Combination air bypass/control valve malfunction • Thermactor solenoid malfunction	• Perform control valve diagnosis • Perform combination valve diagnosis • Perform solenoid diagnosis
• Engine Noise - (Hiss) • Engine Noise - (Rap, Roar)	• Thermactor hose leaks or disconnect • Thermactor hose or valves leak exhaust	• Visual inspection of hoses and connections • Visual inspection of hoses and valves. Perform air check valve diagnosis
• Poor Fuel Economy	• Air control valve malfunction • Combination air bypass/control valve malfunction • Thermactor solenoid valve malfunction • Disconnected vacuum or electrical connections for thermactor components	• Perform air control valve diagnosis • Perform combination valve diagnosis • Perform solenoid diagnosis • Visual inspection
• Exhaust Smoke (White)	• Disconnected vacuum or electrical connections for thermactor components • Air bypass valve malfunction • Air control valve malfunction • Combination air bypass/control valve malfunction • Thermactor solenoid valve malfunction	• Visual inspection • Perform bypass valve diagnosis • Perform air control valve diagnosis • Perform combination valve diagnosis • Perform solenoid diagnosis
• State Emission Test Failure	• Disconnected vacuum or electrical connections for thermactor components • Air bypass valve malfunction • Air control valve malfunction • Combination air bypass/control valve malfunction • Thermactor solenoid valve malfunction	• Visual inspection • Perform bypass valve diagnosis • Perform air control valve diagnosis • Perform combination valve diagnosis • Perform solenoid diagnosis
• Rolling Idle	• Thermactor solenoid valve malfunction • Disconnected vacuum or electrical connections for thermactor components • Air bypass valve malfunction • Air control valve malfunction • Combination air bypass/control valve malfunction	• Perform solenoid diagnosis • Visual inspection • Perform bypass valve diagnosis • Perform air control valve diagnosis • Perform combination valve diagnosis

Air injection system diagnostic data

THERMACTOR SYSTEM NOISE TEST

CAUTION

Do not use a pry bar to move the air pump for belt adjustment.

NOTE: The thermactor system is not completely noiseless. Under normal conditions, noise rises in pitch as engine speed increases. To determine if noise is the fault of the air injection system, disconnect the belt drive (only after verifying that belt tension is correct), and operate the engine. If the noise disappears, proceed with the following diagnosis.

Diagnosis

SYMPTOM	POSSIBLE SOURCE	ACTION
• Excessive Belt Noise	• Loose belt.	• Tighten to specification **CAUTION: Do not use a pry bar to move air pump.**
	• Seized pump.	• Replace pump.
	• Loose pulley.	• Replace pulley and/or pump if damaged. Tighten bolts to 13.6-17.0 N·m (120-150 lb-in).
	• Loose or broken mounting brackets or bolts.	• Replace parts as required and tighten bolts to specification.
• Excessive Mechanical Noise, Chirps, Squeaks, Clicks or Ticks	• Overtightened mounting bolt.	• Tighten to 34 N·m (25 lb-ft).
	• Overtightened drive belt.	• Same as loose belt.
	• Excessive flash on the air pump adjusting arm boss.	• Remove flash from the boss.
	• Distorted adjusting arm.	• Replace adjusting arm.
	• Pump or pulley mounting fasteners loose.	• Tighten fasteners to specifications.
• Excessive Thermactor System Noise (Putt-Putt, Whirling or Hissing)	• Leak in hose.	• Locate source of leak using soap solution and replace hoses as necessary.
	• Loose, pinched or kinked hose.	• Reassemble, straighten or replace hose and clamps as required.
	• Hose touching other engine parts.	• Adjust hose to prevent contact with other engine parts.
	• Bypass valve inoperative.	• Test the valve.
	• Check valve inoperative.	• Test the valve.
	• Restricted or bent pump outlet fitting.	• Inspect fitting and remove any flash blocking the air passage way. Replace bent fittings.
	• Air dumping through bypass valve (at idle only).	• On many vehicles, the thermactor system has been designed to dump air at idle to prevent overheating the catalyst. This condition is normal. Determine that the noise persists at higher speeds before proceeding.
	• Air dump through bypass valve (decel and cruise).	• On many vehicles, the thermactor air is dumped in the air cleaner or in remote silencer. Make sure hoses are connected and not cracked.
	• Air pump resonator leaking or blocked.	• Check resonator for hole or restricted inlet/outlet tubes.
• Excessive Pump Noise (Chirps, Squeaks and Ticks)	• Worn or damaged pump.	• Check the thermactor system for wear or damage and make necessary corrections.
• Engine noise-(Rap or Roar)	• Hose disconnected.	• Audible and visual inspection to assure all hoses are connected.
• State Emissions Test Failure	• Restricted hose.	• Inspect hoses for crimped and/or kinked hoses.
	• Plugged pulse air silencer.	• Remove inlet hose and inspect silencer inlet for dirt and foreign material. Clean or replace silencer as appropriate.
	• Pulse air valve malfunction, leaking or restricted.	• Perform pulse air check valve diagnosis.
	• Pulse air control valve malfunction.	• Perform pulse air control valve diagnosis.

Air injection system diagnostic data

Pulse Air Injection System

➧ SEE FIG. 32

The pulse air injection system is used on some vehicles equipped with the 2.5L engine.

The pulse air injection system does not use an air pump. The system uses natural pulses present in the exhaust system to pull air into the catalyst through pulse air valves. The pulse air valve is connected to the catalyst with a long tube and to the air cleaner and silencer with hoses.

PULSE AIR VALVE

The pulse air control valve is normally closed. Without a vacuum signal from the solenoid, the flow of air is blocked.

TESTING

➧ SEE FIG. 33

1. Visually inspect the system hoses, tubes, control valve(s) and check valve(s) for leaks that may be due to backflow of exhaust gas. If holes are found and/or traces of exhaust gas products are evident, the check valve may be suspect.
2. The valve should allow free flow of air in 1 direction only. The valve should check or block, the free flow of exhaust gas in the opposite direction.
3. Replace the valve if air does not flow as indicated or if exhaust gas backflows in the wrong direction.
4. Remove the inlet hose.
5. Apply the parking brake and block the drive wheels. With the engine at normal operating temperature and idling and the transaxle selector lever in **N** on automatic transaxle equipped vehicles or neutral on manual transaxle equipped vehicles, air should be drawn into the valve.
6. Remove the vacuum line and air flow should stop.
7. If these conditions are met, the valve is operating properly.
8. If these conditions are not met, verify that vacuum is present at the valve. Check the solenoid valve if vacuum is not present.
9. If vacuum is present but no air flows, check the pulse air check valve, silencer filter and air cleaner for blocked or restricted passages.
10. If vacuum is present and no blocked or restricted passages are found, replace the valve.

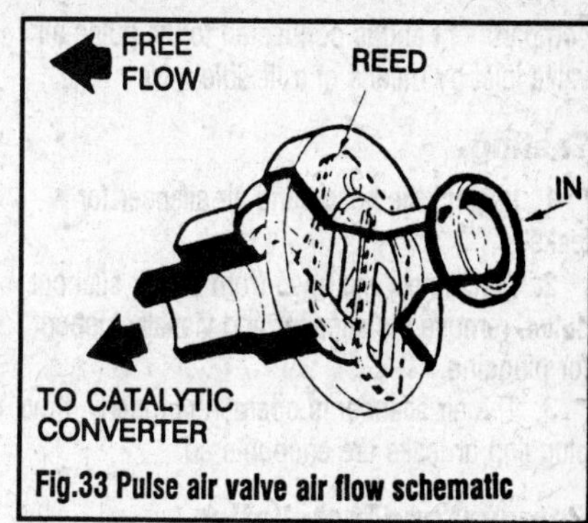

Fig.33 Pulse air valve air flow schematic

Removal and Installation

1. Disconnect the negative battery cable.
2. Disconnect the air hose(s) from the pulse air valve.
3. Disconnect the vacuum line, if necessary.
4. Remove the pulse air valve.
5. Installation is the reverse of the removal procedure.

AIR SILENCER/FILTER

The air silencer is a combustion silencer and filter for the pulse air system. The air silencer is mounted in a convenient position in the engine

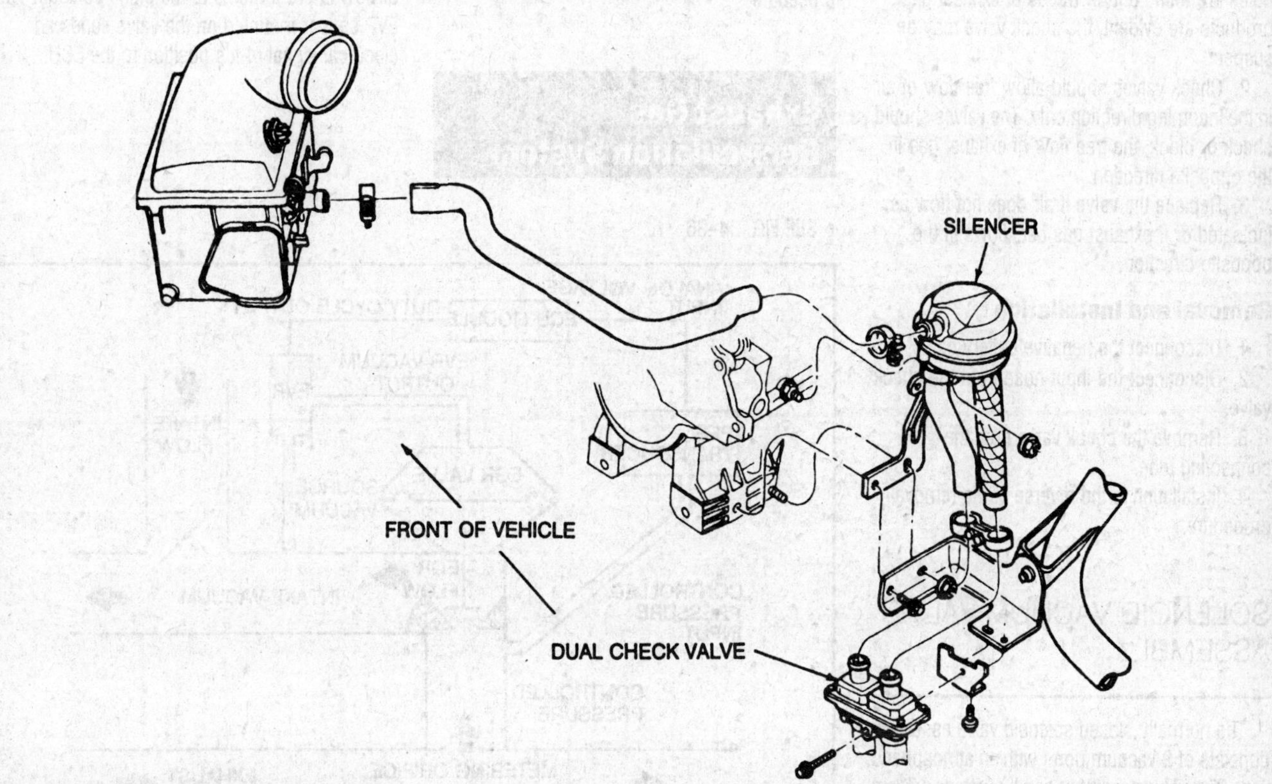

Fig.32 Pulse air injection system—2.5L engine

compartment and is connected to the pulse air valve inlet by means of a flexible hose.

Testing

1. Inspect the hoses and air silencer for leaks.
2. Disconnect the hose from the air silencer outlet, remove the silencer and visually inspect for plugging.
3. The air silencer is operating properly, if no plugging or leaks are encountered.

Removal and Installation

1. Disconnect the negative battery cable.
2. Disconnect the hose from the silencer and remove the silencer.
3. Installation is the reverse of the removal procedure.

CHECK VALVE

The air check valve is a 1-way valve that allows air to pass into the exhaust system while preventing exhaust gases from passing in the opposite direction.

Testing

1. Visually inspect the system hoses, tubes, control valve(s) and check valve(s) for leaks that may be due to the backflow of exhaust gas. If holes are found and/or traces of exhaust gas products are evident, the check valve may be suspect.
2. Check valves should allow free flow of air in the incoming direction only. The valves should check or block, the free flow of exhaust gas in the opposite direction.
3. Replace the valve if air does not flow as indicated or if exhaust gas backflows in the opposite direction.

Removal and Installation

1. Disconnect the negative battery cable.
2. Disconnect the input hose from the check valve.
3. Remove the check valve from the connecting tube.
4. Installation is the reverse of the removal procedure.

SOLENOID VACUUM VALVE ASSEMBLY

The normally closed solenoid valve assembly consists of 2 vacuum ports with an atmospheric vent. The valve assembly can be with or without control bleed. The outlet port of the valve is opened to atmospheric vent and closed to the inlet port when de-energized. When energized, the outlet port is opened to the inlet port and closed to atmospheric vent. The control bleed is provided to prevent contamination entering the solenoid valve assembly from the intake manifold.

Testing

1. The ports should flow air when the solenoid is energized.
2. Check the resistance at the solenoid terminals with an ohmmeter. The resistance should be 51–108Ω.
3. If the resistance is not as specified, replace the solenoid.

➡ **The valve can be expected to have a very small leakage rate when energized or de-energized. This leakage is not measurable in the field and is not detrimental to valve function.**

Removal and Installation

1. Disconnect the negative battery cable.
2. Disconnect the electrical connector and the vacuum lines from the solenoid valve.
3. Remove the mounting bolts and remove the solenoid valve.
4. Installation is the reverse of the removal procedure.

Exhaust Gas Recirculation System

➧ SEE FIG. 34–36

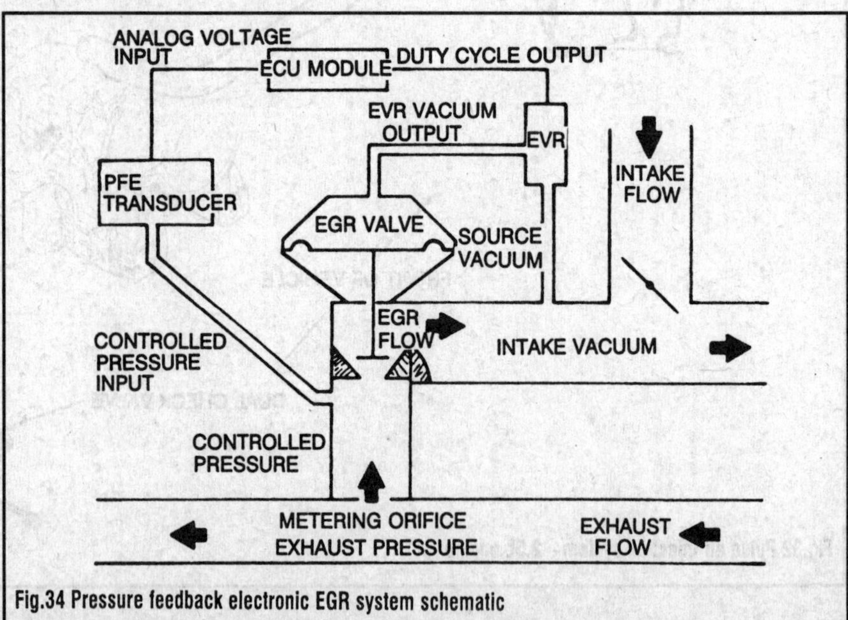

Fig.34 Pressure feedback electronic EGR system schematic

The Exhaust Gas Recirculation (EGR) system is designed to reintroduce exhaust gas into the combustion cycle, thereby lowering combustion temperatures and reducing the formation of nitrous oxide. There are a few different EGR systems used on front wheel drive vehicles.

The most commonly used system is the Pressure Feedback Electronic (PFE) system. The PFE is a subsonic closed loop EGR system that controls EGR flow rate by monitoring the pressure drop across a remotely located sharp-edged orifice. The system uses a pressure transducer as the feedback device and controlled pressure is varied by valve modulation using vacuum output of the EGR Vacuum Regulator (EVR) solenoid. With the PFE system, the EGR valve only serves as a pressure regulator rather than a flow metering device.

The Electronic EGR valve (EEGR) system is used on some vehicles equipped with the 2.5L engine. An electronic EGR valve is required in EEC systems where EGR flow is controlled according to computer demands by means of an EGR Valve Position (EVP) sensor attached to the valve. The valve is operated by a vacuum signal from the electronic vacuum regulator which actuates the valve diaphragm. As supply vacuum overcomes the spring load, the diaphragm is actuated. This lifts the pintle off of it's seat allowing exhaust gas to recirculate. The amount of flow is proportional to the pintle position. The EVP sensor mounted on the valve sends an electrical signal of it's position to the ECU.

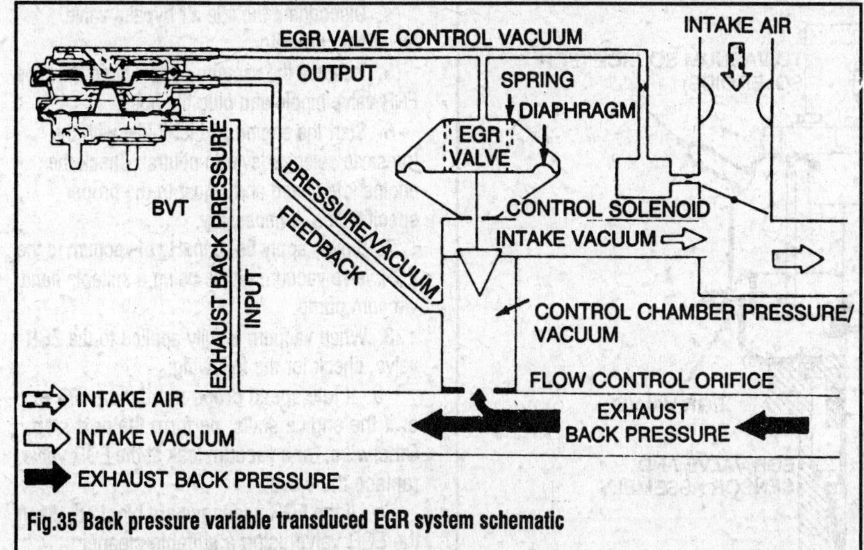

Fig.35 Back pressure variable transduced EGR system schematic

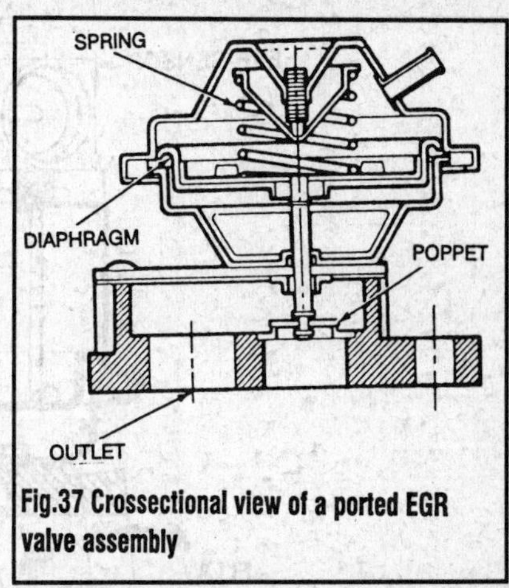

Fig.37 Crossectional view of a ported EGR valve assembly

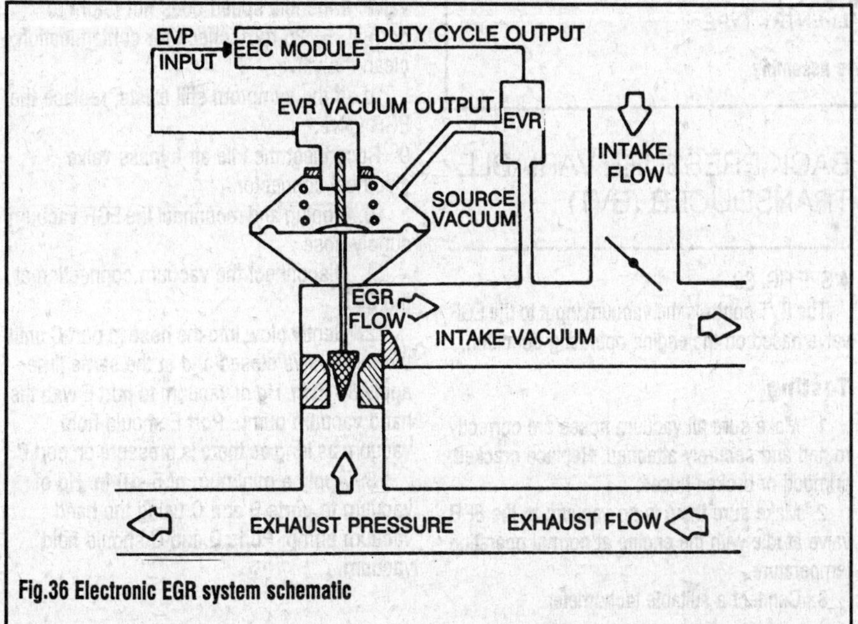

Fig.36 Electronic EGR system schematic

PORTED EGR VALVE

➧ SEE FIG. 37

This is the most common form of EGR valve. The ported EGR valve is operated by a vacuum signal which actuates the valve diaphragm. As the vacuum increases sufficiently to overcome the power spring, the valve is opened allowing EGR flow. The vacuum to the EGR valve is controlled using devices such as the EVR or the BVT, depending on system application.

Removal and Installation

1. Disconnect the negative battery cable.
2. Disconnect the vacuum line from the EGR valve.
3. Remove the mounting bolts and remove the EGR valve.
4. Installation is the reverse of the removal procedure. Be sure to remove all old gasket material before installation. Use a new gasket during installation.

ELECTRONIC EGR (EEGR) VALVE

➧ SEE FIG. 38

The electronic EGR valve is similar to the ported EGR valve. It is also vacuum operated, lifting the pintle off of it's seat to allow exhaust gas to recirculate when the vacuum signal is strong enough. The difference lies in the EVP sensor which is mounted on top of the electronic EGR valve. The electronic EGR valve assembly is not serviceable. The EVP sensor and the EGR valve must be serviced separately.

Removal and Installation

1. Disconnect the negative battery cable.
2. Disconnect the vacuum line from the EGR valve and the connector from the EVP sensor.
3. Remove the mounting bolts and remove the EGR valve.
4. Remove the EVP sensor from the EGR valve.
5. Installation is the reverse of the removal procedure. Be sure to remove all old gasket material before installation. Use a new gasket during installation.

PRESSURE FEEDBACK ELECTRONIC (PFE) EGR TRANSDUCER

The PFE EGR transducer converts a varying exhaust pressure signal into a proportional analog voltage which is digitized by the ECU. The ECU uses the signal received from the PFE transducer to complete the optimum EGR flow.

Removal and Installation

1. Disconnect the negative battery cable.
2. Disconnect the electrical connector and the exhaust pressure line from the transducer.
3. Remove the transducer.
4. Installation is the reverse of the removal procedure.

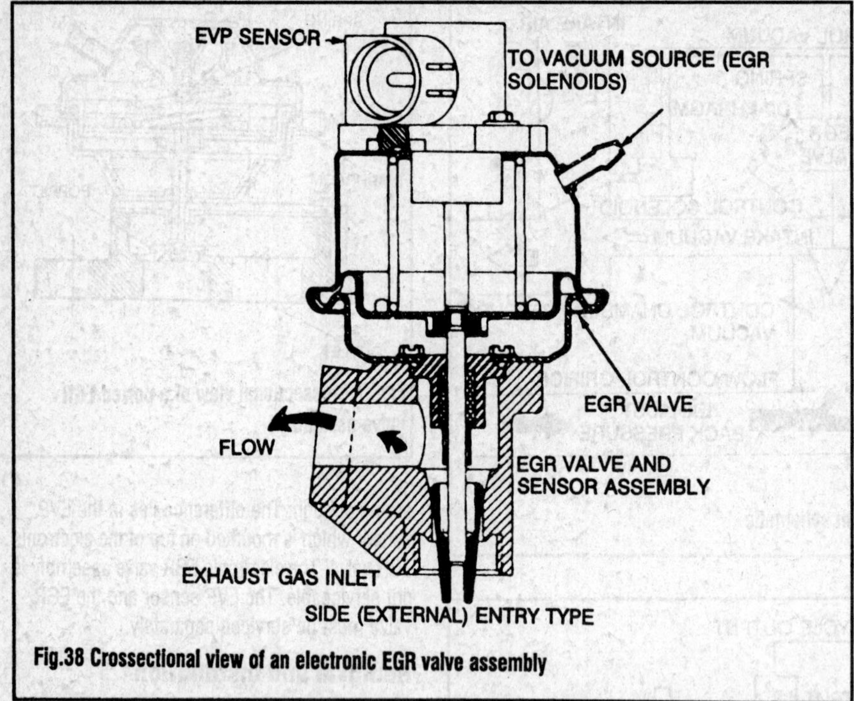

Fig.38 Crossectional view of an electronic EGR valve assembly

4. Disconnect the idle air bypass valve electrical connector.
5. Remove the vacuum supply hose from the EGR valve nipple and plug the hose.
6. Start the engine and let it idle with the transaxle selector lever in neutral. Check the engine idle speed and adjust to the proper specification, if necessary.
7. Slowly apply 5–10 in. Hg of vacuum to the EGR valve vacuum nipple using a suitable hand vacuum pump.
8. When vacuum is fully applied to the EGR valve, check for the following:
   a. If idle speed drops more than 100 rpm or if the engine stalls, perform the next step. Otherwise, for a vacuum leak at the EGR valve, replace the valve.
   b. If the EGR passages are blocked, clean the EGR valve using a suitable cleaner.
   c. Remove the vacuum from the EGR valve. If the idle speed does not return to normal, ± 25 rpm, check for contamination; clean the valve.
   d. If the symptom still exists, replace the EGR valve.
9. Reconnect the idle air bypass valve electrical connector.
10. Unplug and reconnect the EGR vacuum supply hose.
11. Disconnect the vacuum connection at the BVT.
12. Gently blow into the hose to port C until the relief valve closes and at the same time apply 5–10 in. Hg of vacuum to port E with the hand vacuum pump. Port E should hold vacuum as long as there is pressure on port C.
13. Apply a minimum of 5–10 in. Hg of vacuum to ports B and C using the hand vacuum pump. Ports B and C should hold vacuum.

EGR VALVE POSITION (EVP) SENSOR

The EVP sensor provides the ECU with a signal indicating the position of the EGR valve.

Removal and Installation

1. Disconnect the negative battery cable.
2. Disconnect the electrical connector from the sensor.
3. Remove the sensor mounting nuts and remove the sensor from the EGR valve.
4. Installation is the reverse of the removal procedure.

BACK PRESSURE VARIABLE TRANSDUCER (BVT)

➧ SEE FIG. 39

The BVT controls the vacuum input to the EGR valve based on the engine operating condition.

Testing

1. Make sure all vacuum hoses are correctly routed and securely attached. Replace cracked, crimped or broken hoses.
2. Make sure there is no vacuum to the EGR valve at idle with the engine at normal operating temperature.
3. Connect a suitable tachometer.

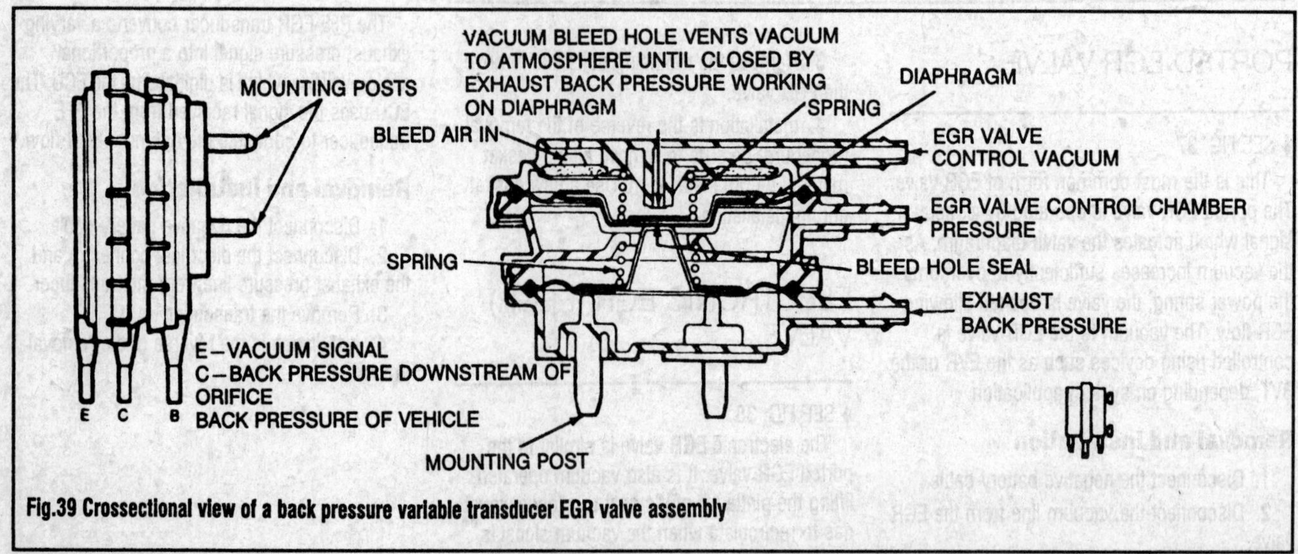

Fig.39 Crossectional view of a back pressure variable transducer EGR valve assembly

14. Replace the BVT if any of the ports do not hold vacuum.

15. Reconnect the vacuum at the BVT.

16. If neither the EGR valve nor the BVT were replaced, the system is okay.

Removal and Installation

1. Disconnect the negative battery cable.
2. Disconnect the vacuum lines from the BVT.
3. Remove the BVT from it's mounting position and remove it from the vehicle.
4. Installation is the reverse of the removal procedure.

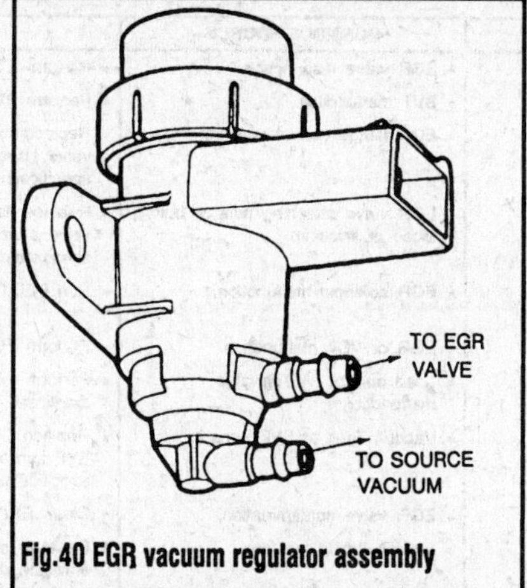

Fig.40 EGR vacuum regulator assembly

EGR VACUUM REGULATOR (EVR)

SEE FIG. 40

The EVR is an electromagnetic device which controls vacuum output to the EGR valve. The EVR replaces the EGR solenoid vacuum vent valve assembly. An electric current in the coil induces a magnetic field in the armature. The magnetic field pulls the disk closed, closing the vent and increasing the vacuum level. The vacuum source is either manifold or vacuum. As the duty cycle is increased, an increased vacuum signal goes to the EGR valve.

Removal and Installation

1. Disconnect the negative battery cable.
2. Disconnect the electrical connector and the vacuum lines from the regulator.
3. Remove the regulator mounting bolts and remove the regulator.
4. Installation is the reverse of the removal procedure.

SYMPTOM	POSSIBLE SOURCE	ACTION
• Rough Idle Cold	• EGR valve malfunction.	• Run EEC-IV Quick Test.
	• BVT malfunction.	• Perform BVT diagnosis.
	• EGR flange gasket leaking.	• Replace flange gasket and tighten valve attaching nuts or bolts to specification.
	• EGR valve attaching nuts or bolts loose or missing.	• Replace flange gasket and tighten valve attaching nuts or bolts to specification.
	• EGR or VCV malfunction.	• Perform EGR or VCV diagnosis.
	• Load control (WOT) valve malfunction.	• Perform load control (WOT) valve diagnosis.
	• Vacuum leak at EVP sensor.	• Replace O-ring seal and tighten EVP sensor attaching nuts to specification.
	• EGR valve contamination.	• Clean EGR valve.
	• Curb idle speed too high or low.	• Reset
• Rough Idle Hot	• EGR valve malfunction.	• Run EEC-IV Quick Test.
	• BVT malfunction.	• Perform BVT diagnosis.
	• EGR flange gasket leaking.	• Replace flange gasket and tighten valve attaching nuts or bolts to specification.
	• EGR valve attaching nuts or bolts loose or missing.	• Replace flange gasket and tighten valve attaching nuts or bolts to specification.
	• Load control (WOT) valve malfunction.	• Perform load control (WOT) valve diagnosis.
	• Vacuum leak at EVP sensor.	• Replace O-ring seal and tighten EVP sensor attaching nuts to specification.
	• EGR valve contamination.	• Clean EGR valve.
	• Curb idle speed too high or low.	• Reset

EGR system general diagnostic data

SYMPTOM	POSSIBLE SOURCE	ACTION
• Rough Running, Surge, Hesitation, Poor Part Throttle Performance —Cold	• EGR valve malfunction.	• Perform EGR valve diagnosis.
	• BVT malfunction.	• Perform BVT diagnosis.
	• EGR flange gasket leaking.	• Replace flange gasket and tighten valve attaching nuts or bolts to specification.
	• EGR valve attaching nuts or bolts loose or missing.	• Replace flange gasket and tighten valve attaching nuts or bolts to specification.
	• EGR solenoid malfunction.	• Run EEC-IV Quick Test.
	• EGR or VCV malfunction.	• Perform EGR or VCV diagnosis.
	• Load control (WOT) valve malfunction.	• Perform load control (WOT) valve diagnosis.
	• Vacuum leak at EVP sensor.	• Replace O-ring seal and tighten EVP sensor attaching nuts to specification.
	• EGR valve contamination.	• Clean EGR valve.
	• Ignition timing too low.	• Reset to specification shown on emission decal.
• Rough Running, Surge, Hesitation, Poor Part Throttle Performance —Hot	• EGR valve malfunction.	• Perform EGR valve diagnosis.
	• BVT malfunction.	• Perform BVT diagnosis.
	• EGR flange gasket leaking.	• Replace flange gasket and tighten valve attaching nuts or bolts to specification.
	• EGR valve attaching nuts or bolts loose or missing.	• Replace flange gasket and tighten valve attaching nuts or bolts to specification.
	• EGR or VCV malfunction.	• Perform EGR or VCV diagnosis.
	• EGR valve contamination.	• Clean EGR valve and if necessary, replace EGR valve.
	• Load control (WOT) valve malfunction.	• Perform load control (WOT) valve diagnosis.
	• Vacuum leak at EVP sensor.	• Replace O-ring seal and tighten EVP sensor attaching nuts to specification.
	• Insufficient exhaust back pressure to activate valve.	• Check exhaust system for leaks.
	• Ignition timing too low.	• Reset to specification shown on emission decal.
• Engine Stalls On Deceleration — Hot and Cold	• EGR valve malfunction.	• Perform EGR valve diagnosis.
	• BVT malfunction.	• Perform BVT functional test.
	• EGR flange gasket leaking.	• Replace flange gasket and tighten valve attaching nuts or bolts to specification.
	• EGR valve attaching nuts or bolts loose or missing.	• Replace flange gasket and tighten valve attaching nuts or bolts to specification.
	• EGR solenoid malfunction.	• Run EEC-IV Quick Test.
	• EGR or VCV malfunction.	• Perform EGR or VCV diagnosis.
	• EGR valve contamination.	• Clean EGR valve and if necessary, replace EGR valve.
	• Load control (WOT) valve malfunction.	• Perform load control (WOT) valve diagnosis.
	• Curb idle speed too low.	• Reset
	• Ignition timing too low.	• Reset to specification shown on emission decal.

EGR system general diagnostic data

SYMPTOM	POSSIBLE SOURCE	ACTION
• Engine Spark Knock or Ping	• EGR malfunction.	• Perform EGR valve diagnosis.
	• BVT malfunction.	• Perform BVT diagnosis.
	• EGR flange gasket leaking.	• Replace flange gasket and tighten valve attaching nuts or bolts to specification.
	• EGR valve attaching nuts or bolts loose or missing.	• Replace flange gasket and tighten valve attaching nuts or bolts to specification.
	• EGR solenoid malfunction.	• Run EEC-IV Quick Test.
	• EGR or VCV malfunction.	• Perform EGR or VCV diagnosis.
	• Blocked or restricted passages in valve or spacer.	• Clean passages in EGR spacer and EGR valve.
	• Vacuum leak at EVP sensor.	• Replace O-ring seal and tighten EVP sensor attaching nuts to specification.
	• Insufficient exhaust back pressure to actuate valve.	• Check exhaust system for leaks.
	• Ignition timing too high.	• Reset to specification shown on emission decal.
• Engine Stalls At Idle — Cold	• EGR valve malfunction.	• Perform EGR valve diagnosis.
	• BVT malfunction.	• Perform BVT diagnosis.
	• EGR flange gasket leaking.	• Replace flange gasket and tighten valve attaching nuts or bolts to specification.
	• EGR valve attaching nuts or bolts loose or missing.	• Replace flange gasket and tighten valve attaching nuts or bolts to specification.
	• EGR solenoid malfunction.	• Run EEC-IV Quick Test.
	• EGR or PVS malfunction.	• Perform EGR or PVS diagnosis.
	• EGR valve contamination.	• Clean EGR valve.
	• Load control (WOT) valve malfunction.	• Perform load control (WOT) valve diagnosis.
	• Curb idle speed too low.	• Reset
	• Ignition timing too low.	• Reset to specification shown on emission decal.
• Engine Stalls At Idle — Hot	• EGR valve malfunction.	• Perform EGR valve diagnosis.
	• BVT malfunction.	• Perform BVT diagnosis.
	• EGR flange gasket leaking.	• Replace flange gasket and tighten valve attaching nuts or bolts to specification.
	• EGR valve attaching nuts or bolts loose or missing.	• Replace flange gasket and tighten valve attaching nuts or bolts to specification.
	• EGR valve contamination.	• Clean EGR valve and if necessary, replace EGR valve.
	• Load control (WOT) valve malfunction.	• Perform load control (WOT) valve diagnosis.
	• Vacuum leak at EVP sensor.	• Replace O-ring seal and tighten EVP sensor attaching nuts to specification.
	• EGR solenoid malfunction.	• Run EEC-IV Quick Test.
	• Curb idle speed too high or low.	• Reset
	• Ignition timing too low.	• Reset to specification shown on emission decal.
• Low Power at Wide-Open Throttle	• EGR valve malfunction.	• Perform EGR valve diagnosis.
	• BVT malfunction.	• Perform BVT diagnosis.
	• EGR flange gasket leaking.	• Replace flange gasket and tighten valve attaching nuts or bolts to specification.
	• EGR valve attaching nuts or bolts loose or missing.	• Replace flange gasket and tighten valve attaching nuts or bolts to specification.
	• Load control (WOT) valve malfunction.	• Perform load control (WOT) valve diagnosis.
	• EGR solenoid malfunction.	• Run EEC-IV Quick Test.
	• Ignition timing too low.	• Reset to specification shown on emission decal.

EGR system general diagnostic data

SYMPTOM	POSSIBLE SOURCE	ACTION
• Engine Starts But Will Not Run —Engine Hard To Start Or Will Not Start	• EGR valve malfunction.	• Perform EGR valve diagnosis.
	• BVT malfunction.	• Perform BVT diagnosis.
	• EGR flange gasket leaking.	• Replace flange gasket and tighten valve attaching nuts or bolts to specification.
	• EGR valve attaching nuts or bolts loose or missing.	• Replace flange gasket and tighten valve attaching nuts or bolts to specification.
	• EGR solenoid malfunction.	• Run EEC-IV Quick Test.
	• EGR or VCV malfunction.	• Perform EGR or VCV diagnosis,
	• EGR valve contamination.	• Clean EGR valve.
	• Vacuum leak at EVP sensor.	• Replace O-ring seal and tighten EVP sensor attaching nuts to specification.
• Poor Fuel Economy	• EGR valve malfunction.	• Perform EGR valve diagnosis.
	• BVT malfunction.	• Perform BVT diagnosis.
	• EGR flange gasket leaking.	• Replace flange gasket and tighten valve attaching nuts or bolts to specification.
	• EGR valve attaching nuts or bolts loose or missing.	• Replace flange gasket and tighten attaching nuts or bolts to specification.
	• EGR solenoid malfunction.	• Run EEC-IV Quick Test.
	• EGR or PVS malfunction.	• Perform EGR or PVS diagnosis.
	• Blocked or restricted EGR passages in valve or spacer.	• Clean passages in EGR spacer and replace EGR valve.
	• Load control (WOT) valve malfunction.	• Perform load control (WOT) valve diagnosis.
	• Vacuum leak at EVP sensor.	• Replace O-ring seal and tighten EVP sensor attaching nuts to specification.
	• Insufficient exhaust back pressure to activate valve.	• Check exhaust system for leaks.
	• Ignition timing too low.	• Reset to specification shown on emission decal.

EGR system general diagnostic data

TEST STEP	RESULT ▶	ACTION TO TAKE
PEV1 CHECK SYSTEM INTEGRITY		
• Check vacuum hoses and connections for looseness, pinching, leakage, splitting, blockage and proper routing. • Inspect EGR valve for loose attaching bolts or damaged flange gasket. • **Does system appear to be in good condition and vacuum hoses properly routed?**	Yes ▶ No ▶	GO to **PEV2** SERVICE EGR system as required. RE-EVALUATE symptom.
PEV2 CHECK EGR VACUUM AT IDLE		
• Run engine until normal operating temperature is reached. • With engine running at idle, disconnect EGR vacuum supply at the EGR valve and check for a vacuum signal. **NOTE: The EVR solenoid has a constant internal leak. You may notice a small vacuum signal. This signal should be less than 1.0 in-Hg at idle.** • **Is EGR vacuum signal less than 1.0 in-Hg at idle?**	Yes ▶ No ▶	GO to **PEV3**. RECONNECT EGR vacuum hose. INSPECT EVR solenoid for leakage. RUN EEC-IV Quick Test

Fig.47. Pressure feedback electronic EGR system diagnostic data

TEST STEP	RESULT ▶	ACTION TO TAKE
PEV3 CHECK EGR VALVE FUNCTION		
• Install a tachometer • Disconnect the Idle Air Bypass Valve electrical connector • Remove and plug the vacuum supply hose from the EGR valve nipple. • Start engine, idle with transmission in NEUTRAL, and observe idle speed. If necessary, adjust idle speed • Slowly apply 5-10 inches of vacuum to the EGR valve nipple using a hand vacuum pump • **Does idle speed drop more than 100 rpm with vacuum applied and return to normal (± 25 rpm) after the vacuum is removed?**	Yes ▶ NO ▶	The EGR system is OK. UNPLUG and RECONNECT the EGR valve vacuum supply hose. RECONNECT the idle air bypass valve connector. INSPECT the EGR valve for blockage or contamination. CLEAN the valve INSPECT valve for vacuum leakage. REPLACE if necessary.

Fig.48. Pressure feedback electronic EGR system diagnostic data

TEST STEP	RESULT ▶	ACTION TO TAKE
EEGR1 **CHECK SYSTEM INTEGRITY**		
• Check vacuum hoses and connections for looseness, pinching, leakage, splitting, blockage, and proper routing. • Inspect EGR valve for loose attaching bolts or damaged flange gasket. • **Does system appear to be in good condition and vacuum hoses properly routed?**	Yes ▶ NO ▶	GO to **EEGR2**. SERVICE EGR system as required. RE-EVALUATE symptom.
EEGR2 **CHECK EGR VACUUM AT IDLE**		
• Run engine until normal operating temperature is reached. • With engine running at idle, disconnect EGR vacuum supply at the EGR valve and check for a vacuum signal. **NOTE: The EVR solenoid has a constant internal leak. You may notice a small vacuum signal. This signal should be less than 1.0 in-Hg at idle.** • **Is EGR vacuum signal less than 1.0 in-Hg at idle?**	Yes ▶ No ▶	GO to **EEGR3** RECONNECT EGR vacuum hose. INSPECT EVR solenoid for leakage. RUN EEC-IV Quick Test

Fig.49. Electronic EGR system diagnostic data

TEST STEP	RESULT	▶	ACTION TO TAKE
EEGR3 CHECK EGR VALVE FUNCTION			
• Install a tachometer • Disconnect the Idle Air Bypass Valve electrical connector • Remove and plug the vacuum supply hose from the EGR valve nipple. • Start engine, idle with transmission in NEUTRAL, and observe idle speed. If necessary, adjust idle speed • Slowly apply 5-10 inches of vacuum to the EGR valve nipple using a hand vacuum pump • **Does idle speed drop more than 100 rpm with vacuum applied and return to normal (± 25 rpm) after the vacuum is removed?**	Yes	▶	The EGR system is OK. UNPLUG and RECONNECT the EGR valve vacuum supply hose. RECONNECT the idle air bypass valve connector. If you were sent here from EEC Pinpoint Tests for EVP/EGR code, then REPLACE EVP sensor.
	No	▶	INSPECT the EGR valve for blockage or contamination. CLEAN the valve INSPECT valve for vacuum leakage. REPLACE if necessary.

Fig.50. Electronic EGR system diagnostic data

Catalytic Converters

➧ SEE FIG. 51

Engine exhaust consists mainly of Nitrogen (N_2), however, it also contains Carbon Monoxide (CO), Carbon Dioxide (CO_2), Water Vapor (H_2O), Oxygen (O_2), Nitrogen Oxides (NOx) and Hydrogen, as well as various, unburned Hydrocarbons (HC). Three of these exhaust components, CO, NOx and HC, are major air pollutants, so their emission to the atmosphere has to be controlled.

The catalytic converter, mounted in the engine exhaust stream, plays a major role in the emission control system. The converter works as a gas reactor and it's catalytic function is to speed up the heat producing chemical reaction between the exhaust gas components in order to reduce the air pollutants in the engine exhaust. The catalyst material, contained inside the converter, is made of a ceramic substrate that is coated with a high surface area alumina and impregnated with catalytically active, precious metals.

CATALYTIC CONVERTER

All vehicles use a 3-way catalyst and some also use this in conjunction with a conventional oxidation catalyst. The conventional oxidation catalyst, containing Platinum (Pt) and Palladium (Pd), is effective for catalyzing the oxidation reactions of HC and CO. The 3-way catalyst, containing Platinum (Pt) and Rhodium (RH) or Palladium (Pd) and Rhodium (RH), is not only effective for catalyzing the oxidation reactions of HC and CO, but it also catalyzes the reduction of NOx.

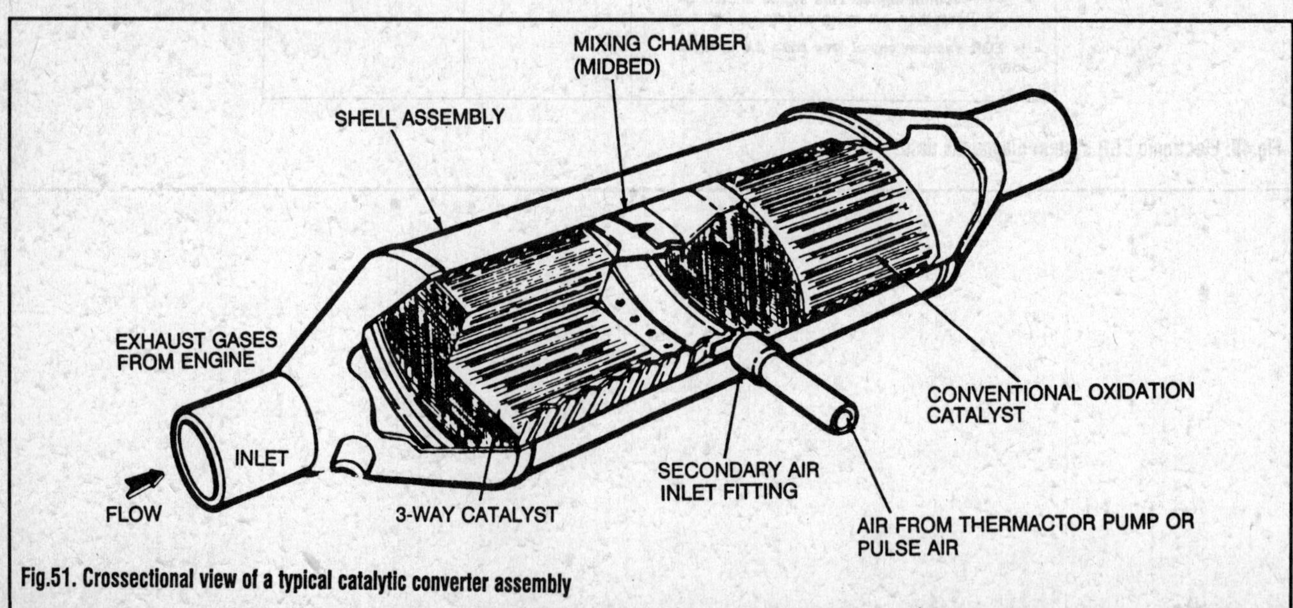

Fig.51. Crossectional view of a typical catalytic converter assembly

The catalytic converter assembly consists of a structured shell containing a monolithic substrate—a ceramic, honeycomb construction. In order to maintain the converter's exhaust oxygen content at a high level to obtain the maximum oxidation for producing the heated chemical reaction, the oxidation catalyst usually requires the use of a secondary air source. This is provided by the pulse air or Thermactor air injection systems.

The catalytic converter is protected by several devices that block out the air supply from the air injection system when the engine is laboring under 1 or more of the following conditions:

- Cold engine operation with rich choke mixture.
- Abnormally high engine coolant temperatures above 225°F (107°C), which may result from a condition such as an extended, hot idle on a hot day.
- Wide-open throttle.
- Engine deceleration.
- Extended idle operation.

TEST STEP	RESULT ▶	ACTION TO TAKE
B0 VISUAL INSPECTION		
• Visually inspect exhaust system. • **Is exhaust system visually OK?**	Yes ▶	GO to B1 .
	No ▶	REPLACE any collapsed exhaust components. If problem is not corrected, GO to B1 .
B1 VACUUM TEST		
• Attach vacuum gauge to intake manifold vacuum source. • Hook up tachometer. • Observe the vacuum gauge needle while performing the following: — Start engine and gradually increase the engine RPM to 2000 with the transmission in NEUTRAL. **NOTE: — The vacuum gauge reading may be normal when the engine is first started and idled. However, excessive restriction in the exhaust system will cause the vacuum gauge needle to drop to a low point even while the engine is idled.** • Decrease engine speed to base idle RPM. • **Did manifold vacuum reach above 16 inches of mercury with the engine RPM at 2000?**	Yes ▶	No restriction in the exhaust system.
	No ▶	GO to B2 .

Fig.52. Catalyst and exhaust system diagnostic data

TEST STEP	RESULT ▶	ACTION TO TAKE
B4 VACUUM TEST — CATALYTIC CONVERTER(S) ON/MUFFLER(S) OFF		
• Turn engine Off. • Reconnect exhaust system at exhaust manifold(s). • Disconnect muffler(s). • Repeat vacuum test. • **Is the manifold vacuum above 16 inches of mercury?**	Yes ▶ No ▶	REPLACE muffler(s). REPLACE catalytic converter and inspect muffler to be sure converter debris has not entered muffler.
B5 EXHAUST MANIFOLD RESTRICTED		
• Remove the exhaust manifold(s). Inspect the ports for casting flash by dropping a length of chain into each port. **NOTE: Do not use a wire or lamp to check ports. The restriction may be large enough for them to pass through but small enough to cause excessive back pressure at high engine rpm.** • **Is a restriction present?**	Yes ▶ No	REMOVE casting flash. If flash cannot be removed, REPLACE exhaust manifold(s).

Fig.54. Catalyst and exhaust system diagnostic data

TEST STEP	RESULT ▶	ACTION TO TAKE
B2 VACUUM TEST — RATE OF VACUUM GAUGE NEEDLE RETURN MOVEMENT		
• Vacuum gauge attached to intake manifold vacuum source. • Tachometer installed. • Increase the engine speed gradually from base idle RPM to 2000 RPM with the transmission in NEUTRAL. • Observe the RATE of speed of the vacuum gauge needle as it falls and rises, while maintaining the increased engine RPM. **NOTES:** — **On a non-restricted system, the vacuum gauge needle will drop to zero and then quickly return to the normal setting without delay.** — **On a restricted system, as the engine RPM is increased to 2000, the vacuum gauge needle will slowly drop to zero. As the increased RPM is maintained, the needle will slowly rise to normal.** — **The RATE of speed at which the vacuum gauge needle returns to the normal setting is much slower on a restricted system than on a non-restricted system.** • Decrease engine speed to base idle RPM. • **Is RATE of speed that the vacuum gauge needle returns to the normal setting much slower than that of a non-restricted system?**	Yes ▶ No ▶	GO to B3. No restriction in the exhaust system.
B3 VACUUM TEST — EXHAUST DISCONNECTED		
• Turn engine Off. • Disconnect exhaust system at exhaust manifold(s). • Repeat vacuum test. • **Is manifold vacuum above 16 inches of mercury?**	Yes ▶ No ▶	GO to B4. GO to B5.

Fig.53. Catalyst and exhaust system diagnostic data

Service Interval Reminder Lights

RESETTING

Every 5000 or 7,500 miles (approximately, depending on engine application) the word SERVICE will appear on the electronic display for the first 1.5 miles to remind the driver that is time for the regular vehicle service interval maintenance (i.e. oil change).

To reset the service interval reminder light for another interval proceed as follows. With the engine running, press the ODO SEL and TRIP RESET buttons. Hold the buttons down until the SERVICE light disappears from the display and 3 audible beeps are heard to verify that the service reminder has been reset.

Oxygen Sensor

➧ SEE FIG. 60–61

The oxygen sensor supplies the ECU with a signal which indicates a rich or lean condition during engine operation. This input information assists the ECU in determining the proper air/fuel ratio. The oxygen sensor is threaded into the exhaust manifold on all vehicles.

TESTING

Except Engines Equipped With MAF Sensor

1. Disconnect the oxygen sensor from the vehicle harness.
2. Connect a voltmeter between the HEGO signal terminal of the oxygen sensor connector and the negative battery terminal.

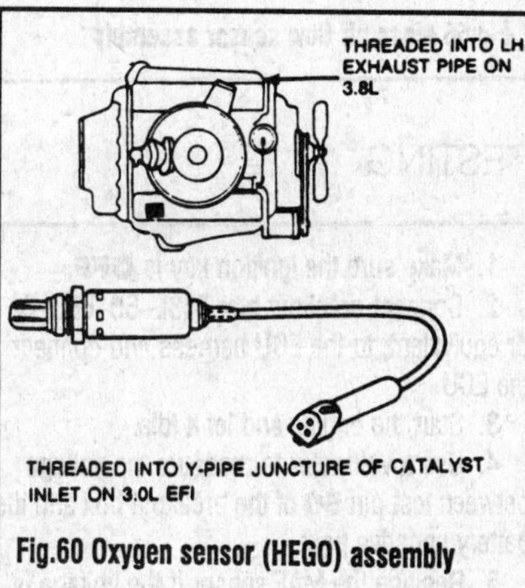

Fig.60 Oxygen sensor (HEGO) assembly

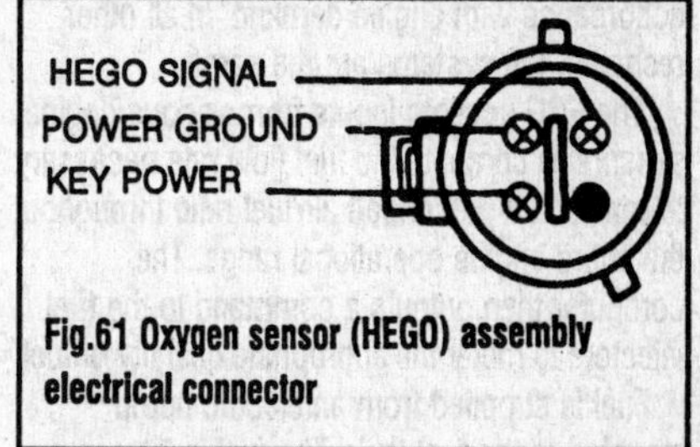

Fig.61 Oxygen sensor (HEGO) assembly electrical connector

3. Disconnect and plug the vacuum line at the MAP sensor and set the voltmeter on the 20 volt scale.
4. Apply 10–14 in. Hg of vacuum to the MAP sensor.
5. Start the engine and run it at approximately 2000 rpm for 2 minutes.
6. If the voltmeter does not indicate greater than 0.5 volts within 2 minutes, replace the sensor.

REMOVAL & INSTALLATION

1. Disconnect the negative battery cable.
2. Disconnect the oxygen sensor connector.
3. Remove the sensor from the exhaust manifold.
4. Installation is the reverse of the removal procedure.

ELECTRONIC ENGINE CONTROLS

General Information

All vehicles are equipped with fuel injection. Three different fuel injection systems are used, Central Fuel Injection (CFI), Electronic Fuel Injection (EFI) and Sequential Electronic Fuel Injection (SEFI).

CENTRAL FUEL INJECTION

The CFI system is a single-point, pulse time modulated injection system. Fuel is metered into the air intake stream according to engine demands by a single solenoid injection valve, mounted in a throttle body on the intake manifold.

Fuel is supplied from the fuel tank by an electric fuel pump mounted in the fuel tank. The fuel is filtered and sent to the fuel charging assembly injector fuel cavity and then to the pressure regulator where the fuel delivery pressure is maintained at the specified value. A single injector nozzle is mounted vertically above the throttle plate and connected in series with the fuel pressure regulator. Excess fuel supplied by the pump but not needed by the engine, is returned to the fuel tank by a fuel return line.

The fuel charging assembly mounts to the intake manifold. It provides packaging of the 5 major components which perform the fuel and air metering function to the engine: air control components, fuel injector nozzle. fuel pressure regulator, idle speed control motor and throttle position sensor.

The CFI system is controlled by the ECU, which is located under the instrument panel. The ECU receives inputs from sensors such as the temperature sensor, HEGO and MAP sensors in order to determine the proper air/fuel mixture for specific operating conditions.

ELECTRONIC AND SEQUENTIAL ELECTRONIC FUEL INJECTION

Both EFI and SEFI are multi-point, pulse time, speed density control systems. The difference between the 2 lies in the method of fuel metering. In the EFI system, fuel is metered into the intake air stream in accordance with engine demand. In the SEFI system, fuel is metered into each intake port in sequence with the engine firing order, in accordance with engine demand. In all other respects, the systems are the same.

The ECU accepts inputs from various engine sensors to compute the fuel flow rate necessary to maintain a prescribed air/fuel ratio throughout the entire engine operational range. The computer then outputs a command to the fuel injectors to meter the appropriate quantity of fuel.

Fuel is supplied from an electric pump mounted in the fuel tank. The fuel is filtered and delivered to the fuel charging manifold assembly. The fuel charging manifold assembly incorporates electrically actuated fuel injectors directly above each of the engine's intake ports. The injectors, when energized, spray a metered quantity of fuel into the intake air stream.

A constant fuel pressure drop is maintained across the injector nozzles by a pressure regulator. The regulator is connected in series with the fuel injectors and is positioned downstream from them. Excess fuel supplied by the pump, but not required by the engine, passes through the regulator and returns to the fuel tank through a fuel return line.

In the EFI system, the fuel injectors are energized in groups, while in the SEFI system, each injector is energized once every other crankshaft revolution, in sequence with the engine firing order. The period of time the injectors are energized is controlled by the ECU. Air entering the engine is measured by speed, pressure and temperature sensors. The resultant airflow information and input from various other engine sensors is used to compute the required fuel flow rate necessary to maintain a prescribed air/fuel ratio for the given engine operation. The computer determines the needed injector pulse width and outputs a command to the injector to meter the exact quantity of fuel.

Mass Air Flow Sensor

➧ SEE FIG. 56

The Mass Air Flow (MAF) sensor directly measures the mass of the air flowing into the engine. The sensor output is an analog signal ranging from about 0.5–5.0 volts. The signal is used by the ECU to calculate the injector pulse width. The sensing element is a thin platinum wire wound on a ceramic bobbin and coated with glass. This "hot wire" is maintained at 200°C above the ambient temperature as measured by a constant "cold wire". The MAF sensor is located in the outlet side of the air cleaner lid assembly.

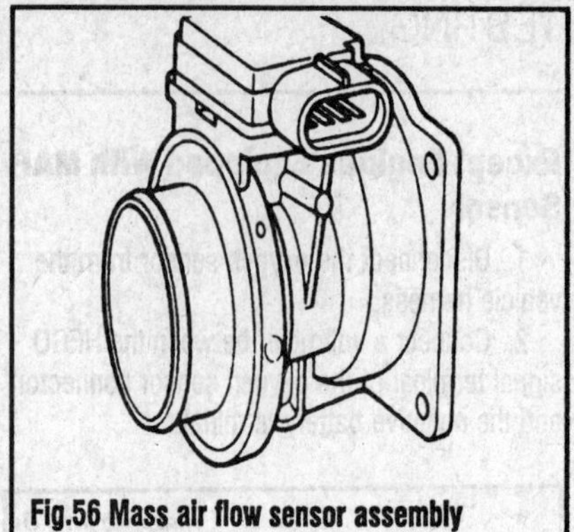

Fig.56 Mass air flow sensor assembly

TESTING

1. Make sure the ignition key is **OFF**.
2. Connect breakout box T83L–50–EEC–IV or equivalent, to the ECU harness and connect the ECU.
3. Start the engine and let it idle.
4. Use a voltmeter to measure the voltage between test pin **50** of the breakout box and the battery negative post.
5. Replace the MAF sensor if the voltage is not 0.36–1.50 volts.

REMOVAL & INSTALLATION

1. Disconnect the negative battery cable.
2. Remove the air intake tube.
3. Disconnect the MAF sensor electrical connector.
4. Remove the sensor attaching screws and remove the sensor.

➡ Inspect the MAF sensor-to-air cleaner lid gasket for any signs of deterioration. Replace the gasket, as necessary. If scraping is necessary, be careful not to damage the air cleaner lid or the MAF sensor gasket surfaces.

5. Installation is the reverse of the removal procedure.

Air Bypass Valve

➧ SEE FIG. 59

The idle air bypass valve is used to control engine idle speed and is operated by the ECU or in response to engine coolant temperature change, depending upon vehicle application. The valve allows air to flow into the intake air stream to control cold engine fast idle, no touch start, dashpot, over temperature idle boost and engine idle load correction. The air bypass valve is used on all EFI and SEFI systems. The air bypass valve is located on the throttle body housing.

TESTING

1. Make sure the ignition key is **OFF**.
2. Disconnect the air bypass valve.
3. Use an ohmmeter to measure the resistance between the terminals of the valve solenoid.

➡ Due to the diode in the solenoid, place the ohmmeter positive lead on the VPWR pin and the negative lead on the ISC pin.

4. If the resistance is not 7–13Ω, replace the air bypass valve.

ISC Motor

➧ SEE FIG. 57

The ISC motor controls idle speed by moving the throttle lever. It regulates airflow to maintain the desired engine rpm for both warm and cold engine idles. An idle tracking switch, integral to the motor, is utilized to determine when the throttle lever has contacted it, thereby signalling the need to control engine rpm. The motor extends or retracts a linear shaft through a gear reduction system. The motor direction is determined by the polarity of the applied voltage. The ISC motor is used in the CFI system.

TESTING

➧ SEE FIG. 58

1. Connect breakout box T83L–50–EEC–IV or equivalent, to the ECU wiring harness.
2. Use a jumper wire to connect the positive circuit of the ISC motor, test pin **21**, to the positive battery terminal and connect another jumper wire between the negative circuit of the motor, test pin **41**, to battery ground for 4 seconds.
3. Reverse the jumper wires, connecting the positive circuit of the ISC motor to battery ground and the negative circuit to battery positive for 4 seconds.
4. The ISC motor shaft should extend to greater than 2 in. (51mm) and retract to less than 1.75 in. (44.5mm) from the mounting bracket. If it does not, replace the ISC motor.

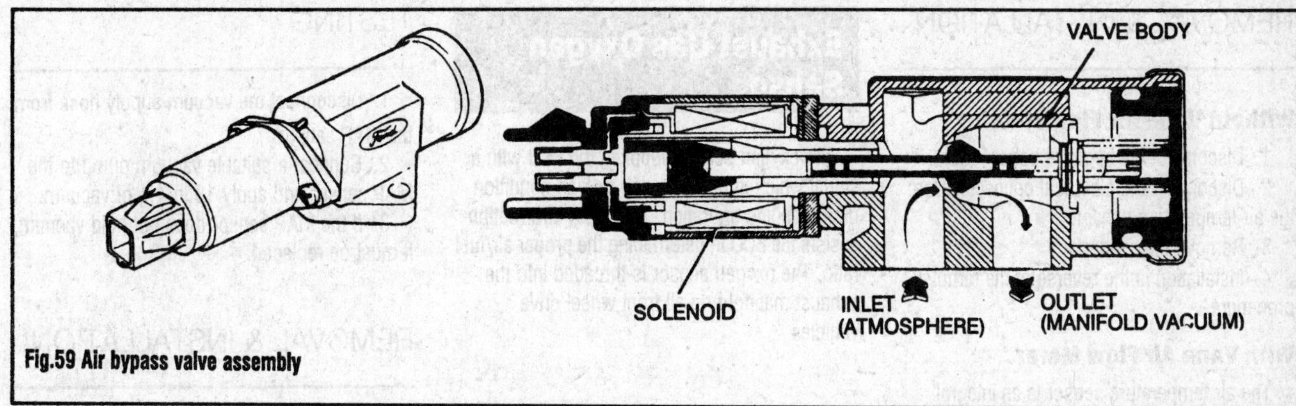

Fig.59 Air bypass valve assembly

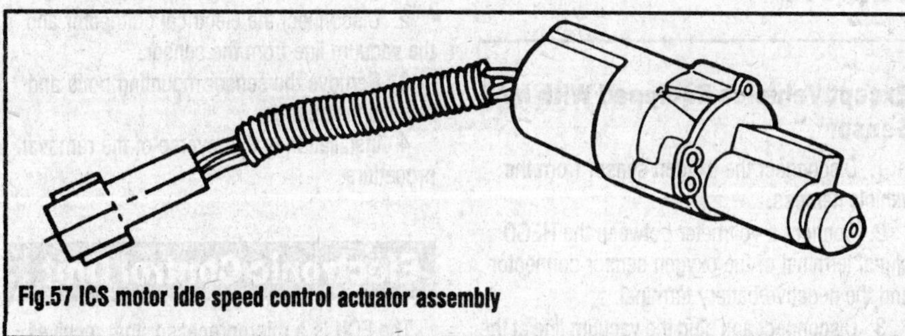
Fig.57 ICS motor idle speed control actuator assembly

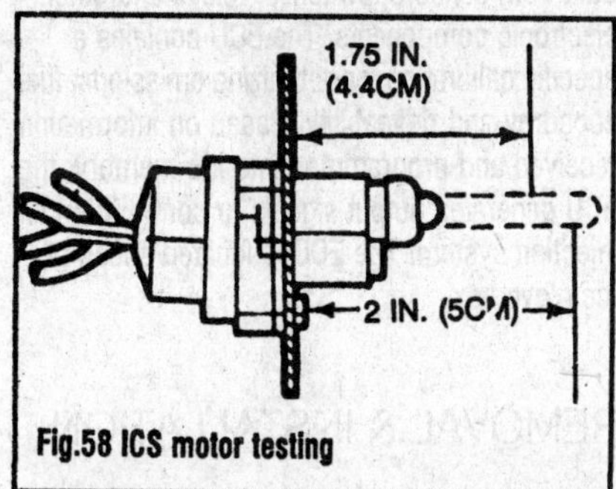

Fig.58 ICS motor testing

REMOVAL & INSTALLATION

1. Disconnect the negative battery cable.
2. Disconnect the electrical connector from the ISC motor.
3. Remove the ISC motor mounting screws and remove the ISC motor.
4. Installation is the reverse of the removal procedure.

Throttle Position Sensor

The sensor is mounted to the throttle shaft and is used to supply a voltage output change proportional to the change in the throttle position. The TP sensor is used by the ECU to determine engine operation mode: closed throttle, part throttle and wide-open throttle. The proper fuel mixture, spark and EGR will be output only when the operation mode has been determined correctly.

REMOVAL & INSTALLATION

1. Disconnect the negative battery cable.
2. Disconnect the electrical connector from the TP sensor.
3. Remove the TP sensor mounting screws and remove the TP sensor.
4. Installation is the reverse of the removal procedure.
5. Adjust the sensor, if necessary.

Air Temperature Sensor

➧ SEE FIG. 55

The air temperature sensor in systems with vane air flow meters is used to measure the temperature of the incoming air and send the information to the ECU. In all other systems, the sensor provides the ECU with mixture, fuel and air temperature information.

The air temperature sensor is located in the meter in vane air flow meter systems. Otherwise it is located in the air cleaner assembly or in the side of the throttle body.

TESTING

Without Vane Air Flow Meter

1. Disconnect the temperature sensor.

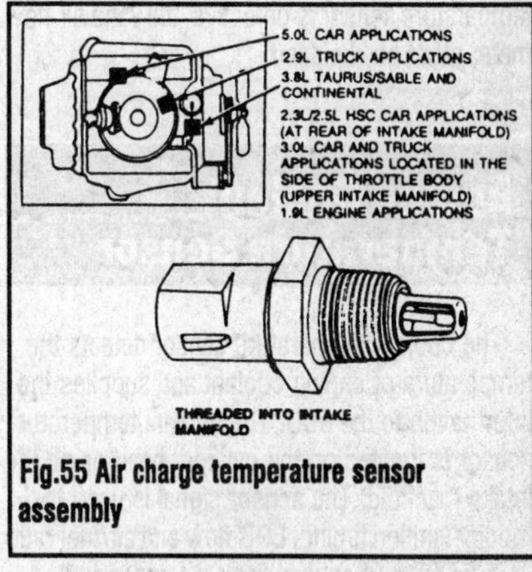

Fig.55 Air charge temperature sensor assembly

2. Connect an ohmmeter between the sensor terminals and set the ohmmeter scale on 200,000Ω.
3. Measure the resistance with the engine off and cool and with the engine running and warmed up. Compare the resistance values obtained with the chart.
4. Replace the sensor if the readings are incorrect.

With Vane Air Flow Meter

1. Disconnect the vane air flow meter connector.
2. Access the sensor in the meter.
3. Monitor the temperature near the sensor.

➡ **If using a hot air gun to heat the sensor, be careful not to melt any plastic or rubber components.**

4. Measure the resistance between the meter **VAT** terminal and the meter **SIGRTN** terminal and record.
5. Compare the resistance readings with the chart. If the readings are incorrect, replace the sensor.

REMOVAL & INSTALLATION

Without Vane Air Flow Meter

1. Disconnect the negative battery cable.
2. Disconnect the electrical connector from the air temperature sensor.
3. Remove the sensor.
4. Installation is the reverse of the removal procedure.

With Vane Air Flow Meter

The air temperature sensor is an integral component of the vane air flow meter. If the temperature sensor is defective, the vane air flow meter must be replaced.

Engine Coolant Temperature Sensor

The coolant temperature sensor detects the temperature of engine coolant and supplies the information to the ECU. The coolant temperature sensor is located on the cylinder head or on the intake manifold. The sensor signal is used to modify ignition timing, EGR flow and air/fuel ratio as a function of engine coolant temperature.

TESTING

1. Disconnect the temperature sensor.
2. Connect an ohmmeter between the sensor terminals and set the ohmmeter scale on 200,000Ω.
3. Measure the resistance with the engine off and cool and with the engine running and warmed up. Compare the resistance values obtained with the chart.
4. Replace the sensor if the readings are incorrect.

REMOVAL & INSTALLATION

1. Disconnect the negative battery cable.
2. Drain the cooling system sufficiently to remove the sensor.
3. Disconnect the electrical connector from the temperature sensor.
4. Remove the coolant temperature sensor.
5. Installation is the reverse of the removal procedure. Properly refill and bleed the cooling system.

Exhaust Gas Oxygen Sensor

The oxygen sensor supplies the ECU with a signal which indicates a rich or lean condition during engine operation. This input information assists the ECU in determining the proper air/fuel ratio. The oxygen sensor is threaded into the exhaust manifold on all front wheel drive vehicles.

TESTING

Except Vehicles Equipped With MAF Sensor

1. Disconnect the oxygen sensor from the vehicle harness.
2. Connect a voltmeter between the HEGO signal terminal of the oxygen sensor connector and the negative battery terminal.
3. Disconnect and plug the vacuum line at the MAP sensor and set the voltmeter on the 20 volt scale.
4. Apply 10–14 in. Hg of vacuum to the MAP sensor.
5. Start the engine and run it at approximately 2000 rpm for 2 minutes.
6. If the voltmeter does not indicate greater than 0.5 volts within 2 minutes, replace the sensor.

REMOVAL & INSTALLATION

1. Disconnect the negative battery cable.
2. Disconnect the oxygen sensor connector.
3. Remove the sensor from the exhaust manifold.
4. Installation is the reverse of the removal procedure.

Manifold Absolute Pressure Sensor (MAP)

The MAP sensor measures manifold vacuum using a frequency. This gives the ECU information on engine load. It is used as a barometric sensor for altitude compensation, updating the ECU during key ON, engine OFF and every wide-open throttle. The ECU uses the MAP sensor for spark advance, EGR flow and air/fuel ratio.

TESTING

1. Disconnect the vacuum supply hose from the MAP sensor.
2. Connect a suitable vacuum pump to the MAP sensor and apply 18 in. Hg of vacuum.
3. If the MAP sensor does not hold vacuum, it must be replaced.

REMOVAL & INSTALLATION

1. Disconnect the negative battery cable.
2. Disconnect the electrical connector and the vacuum line from the sensor.
3. Remove the sensor mounting bolts and remove the sensor.
4. Installation is the reverse of the removal procedure.

Electronic Control Unit

The ECU is a microprocessor that receives data from sensors, switches, relays and other electronic components. The ECU contains a specific calibration for optimizing emissions, fuel economy and driveability. Based on information received and programmed into it's memory, the ECU generates output signals to control the fuel injection system. The ECU is located ahead of the glove box.

REMOVAL & INSTALLATION

1. Disconnect the negative battery cable.
2. Remove the glove box or kick panel, as necessary.
3. Disconnect the electrical connector from the ECU.
4. Remove the mounting bolts and remove the ECU.
5. Installation is the reverse of the removal procedure.

Diagnosis And Testing

GENERAL INFORMATION

➧ SEE FIG. 62–66

All vehicles have self-diagnostic capabilities. Malfunctions in the engine control system are found through the Self-Test procedure. Vehicles using the EEC-IV system use a Self-Test divided into 3 specialized tests: Key On Engine Off Self-Test, Engine Running Self-Test and Continuous Self-Test. The Self-Test is not a conclusive test by itself, but is used as a part of a functional Quick Test diagnostic procedure. The ECU stores the Self-Test program in it's permanent memory. When activated, it checks the EEC-IV system by testing it's memory integrity and processing capability and verifies that various sensors and actuators are connected and operating properly. The Key On Engine Off and Engine Running Self-Tests are functional tests which only detect faults present at the time of the Self-Test. Continuous Self-Test is an ongoing test that stores fault information in Keep Alive Memory (KAM) for retrieval at a later time.

Fault information is communicated through the Self-Test service codes. These service codes are 2-digit or 3-digit numbers representing the results of the Self-Test. The service codes are transmitted on the Self-Test output line found in the vehicle Self-Test connector. They are in the form of timed pulses and are read on a voltmeter, STAR or SUPER STAR II tester and the malfunction indicator light.

Vehicle Preparation and Equipment Hook-up

VEHICLE PREPARATION

1. Apply the parking brake, place the transaxle shift lever firmly into **P** on automatic transaxle or neutral on manual transaxles and block the drive wheels.

2. Turn all electrical loads—radio, lights, blower fan, etc. **OFF**.

USING THE STAR OR SUPER STAR II TESTER

➡ The STAR tester cannot be used to read 3-digit service codes. If the STAR tester is used on a 3-digit service code application, the display will be blank. The SUPER STAR II tester must be used to read 3-digit service codes.

After hooking up the STAR tester and turning on it's power switch, the tester will run a display check and the numerals **88** will begin to flash in the display window. A steady **00** will then appear, indicating that the STAR tester is ready. To receive service codes, press the button on the front of the STAR tester. The button will latch down and a colon will appear in the display window in front of the **00** numerals. The colon must be displayed to receive the service codes.

If it is desired to clear the display window during the Self-Test, turn **OFF** the vehicle's engine, press the tester's button once to unlatch it, then press the button again to latch down the button.

Connect the STAR or SUPER STAR II tester as follows:

1. Turn the ignition key **OFF**.

2. Connect the color coded adapter cable to the STAR tester.

3. Connect the adapter cable leads to the proper Self-Test connectors.

4. Ground the adapter cable for vehicles using the SUPER STAR II tester.

5. Slide the SUPER STAR II tester switch to the MECS or EEC-IV position, according to the vehicle system.

USING THE ANALOG VOLTMETER

Service codes will be represented by pulsing or sweeping movements of the voltmeter's needle across the dial face of the voltmeter. Therefore, a single digit number of 3 will be reported by 3 needle sweeps. However, a service code is represented by a 2-digit or 3-digit number, such as 23. As a result, the Self-Test service code of 23 will appear on the

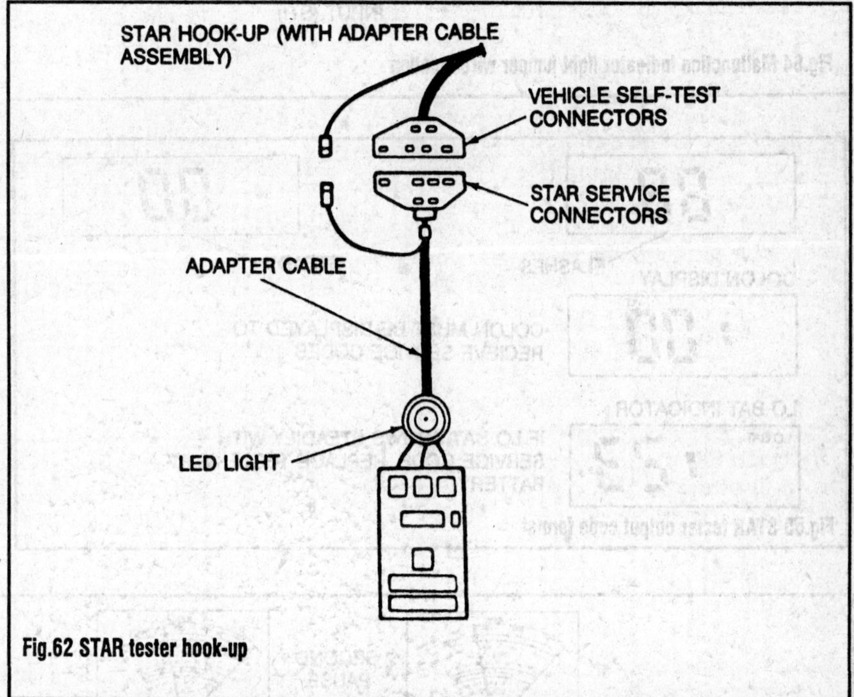

Fig.62 STAR tester hook-up

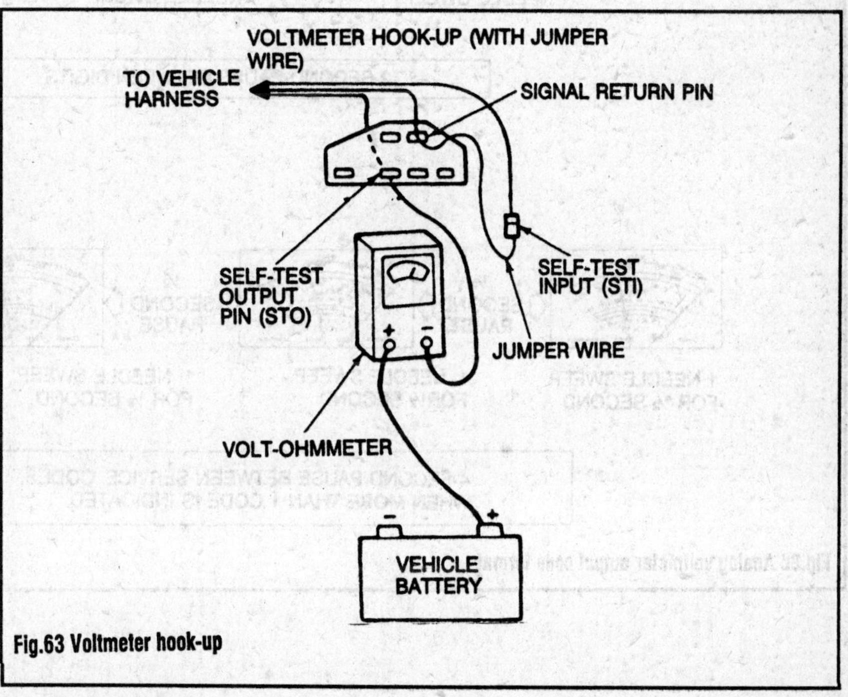

Fig.63 Voltmeter hook-up

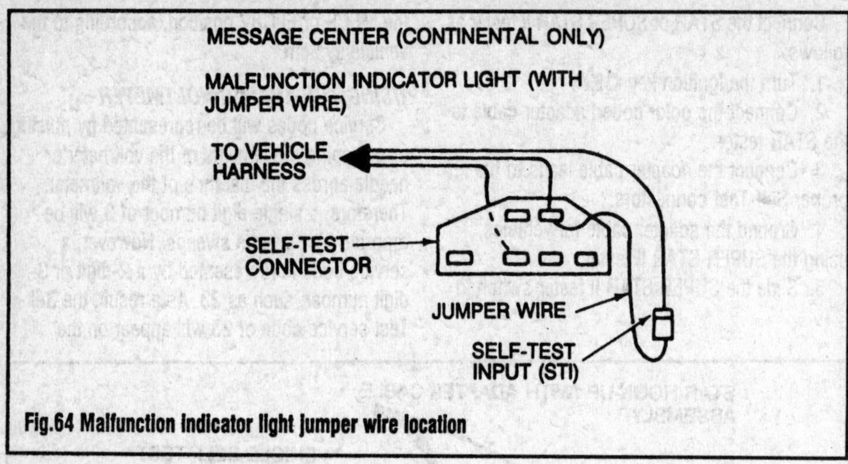

Fig.64 Malfunction indicator light jumper wire location

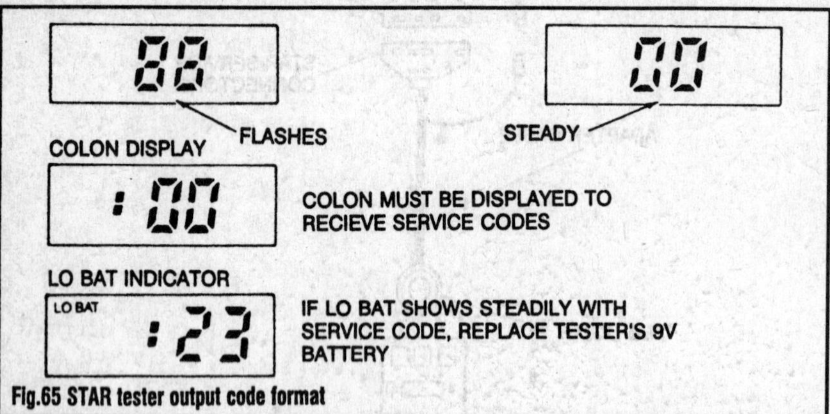

Fig.65 STAR tester output code format

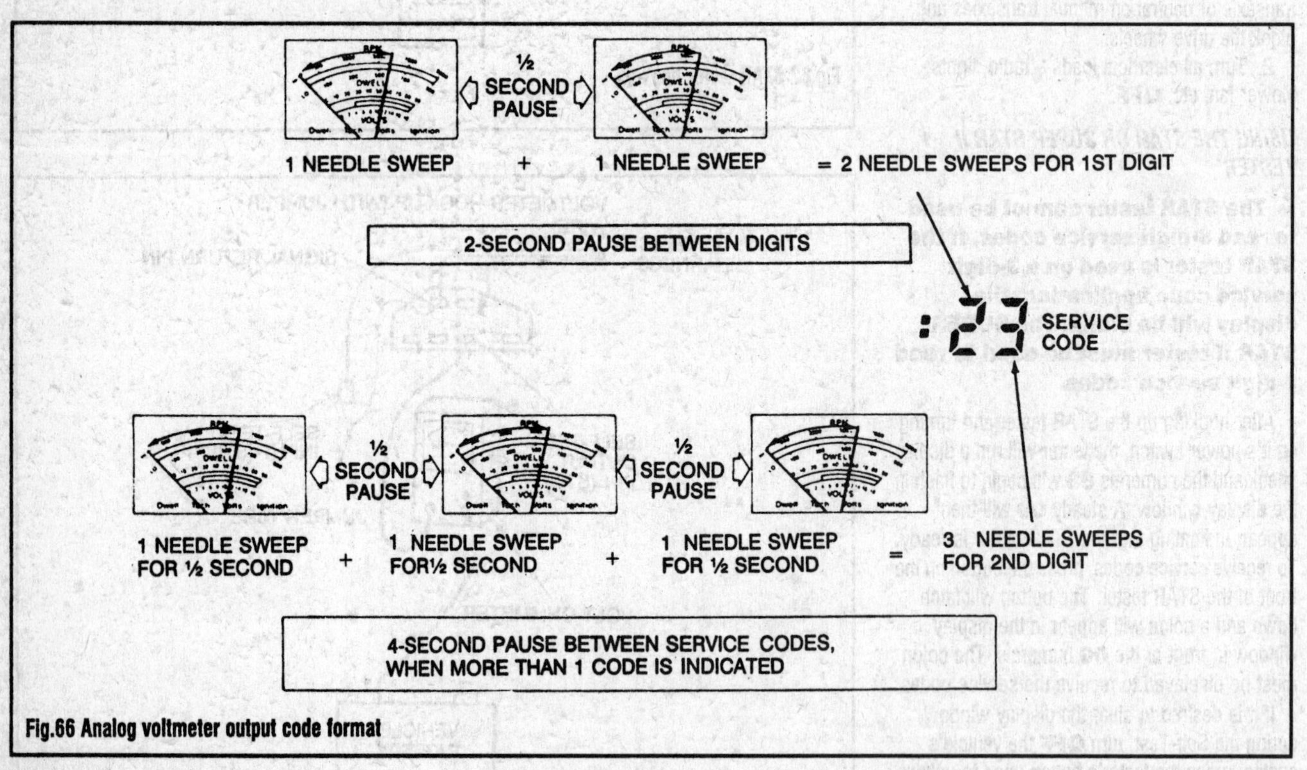

Fig.66 Analog voltmeter output code format

voltmeter as 2 needle sweeps, then after a 2 second pause, the needle will sweep 3 times.

Connect the analog voltmeter as follows:

1. Turn the ignition key **OFF**.
2. Set the voltmeter on a DC voltage range to read from 0–20 volts.
3. On all EEC-IV vehicles, connect the voltmeter from the battery positive post to the Self-Test output pin of the large Self-Test connector. On all others Connect the positive voltmeter lead to the EEC STO line and the negative lead to engine ground and jumper the EEC STI to ground.

USING THE INDICATOR LIGHT

During the Self-Test a service code is reported by the malfunction indicator light. It will represent itself as a flash on the CHECK ENGINE or SERVICE ENGINE SOON light on the dash panel. A single digit number of 3 will be reported by 3 flashes. However, a service code is represented by a 2-digit or 3-digit number, such as 23. As a result, the Self-Test service code of 23 will appear on the MIL light as 2 flashes, then, after a 2 second pause, the light will flash 3 times.

Key On Engine Off Self-Test

Start the engine and let it run until it reaches normal operating temperature. Turn the engine **OFF** and activate the Self-Test.

1. If using the STAR tester, proceed as follows:

a. Latch the center button in the down position.

b. Place the ignition key in the **ON** position.

c. Record all service codes displayed.

2. If using the SUPER STAR II tester, proceed as follows:

a. Latch the center button in the **TEST** position.

b. Turn the ignition key **ON**.

c. Turn the tester **ON**, the tester will sound and **888** will be displayed for 2 seconds.

d. Unlatch and relatch the center test button. After all codes are received, unlatch the center button to review all codes retained in tester memory.

➡ **The SUPER STAR II tester has a mode switch. The tester will only display 3-digit service codes in fast code mode. If slow code mode is used on 3-digit service code applications, the display will be blank.**

3. If using the analog voltmeter jumper the STI to the SIG RTN at the Self-Test connectors and turn the ignition key and the voltmeter **ON**. Observe the needle for any code indications and record.

4. If using the malfunction indicator light connect the jumper wire from STI to the SIG RTN at the Self-Test connectors and turn the ignition switch **ON**. Service codes will be flashed on the MIL light.

Engine Running Self-Test

1. Deactivate the Self-Test.

2. Start and run the engine at 2000 rpm for 2 minutes.

3. Turn the engine **OFF** and wait 10 seconds.

4. Activate the Self-Test.

5. Start the engine.

6. Record all service codes displayed.

➡ **Engine identification codes are issued at the beginning of the Engine Running Self-Test and are 1-digit numbers represented by the number of pulses sent out. The engine identification code is equal to $^1/_2$ the number of engine cylinders. Two pulses equals 4 cylinders. The identification codes are used to verify that the proper processor is installed and that the Self-Test has been entered.**

Clearing Continuous Memory Codes

➡ **Do not disconnect the battery to clear continuous memory codes. This will erase the Keep Alive Memory (KAM) information which may cause a driveability concern.**

1. Run the Key On Engine Off Self-Test.

2. When the service codes begin to be displayed, deactivate the Self-Test as follows:

a. STAR tester: unlatch the center button to the UP position.

b. Analog voltmeter, MIL, Continental message center: remove the jumper wire from between the Self-Test Input (STI) connector and the signal return pin of the Self-Test connector.

c. The continuous memory codes will be erased from the ECU memory.

Trouble Codes	Quick Test Mode	Car Engines				
		2.5L CLC CFI	2.5L MTX CFI	3.0L EFI	3.0L SHO SEFI	3.8L SEFI
11—System pass	O/R/C	X	X	X	X	X
12—Rpm unable to reach upper test limit	R	X	X	X	X	X
13—Rpm unable to reach lower test limit	R	X	X	X	X	X
13—DC motor did not move	O	X	X	—	—	—
13—DC motor did follow dashpot	O	X	X	—	—	—
14—PIP circuit failure	C	X	X	X	X	X
15—ROM test failure	O	X	X	X	X	X
15—Power interrupted to keep alive memory	C	X	X	X	X	X
16—Rpm above self-test limit, set too high	R	X	X	—	—	—
16—Rpm too low to perform test	R	—	—	—	—	—
17—Rpm below self-test limit, set too low	R	X	X	—	—	—
18—Loss of tach input to ECU, spout grounded	C	X	X	X	X	X
18—Spout circuit open	R	X	X	X	X	X
19—Erratic rpm during test or rpm too low	R	—	—	—	—	—
19—Failure of EEC power supply	O	—	—	X	—	X
19—CID sensor input failed	C	—	—	—	X	—
21—ECT sensor input out of test range	O/R	X	X	X	X	X
22—BP sensor input out of test range	O/R/C	—	—	—	②	—
22—MAP sensor input out of test range	O/R/C	X	X	X	—	X
23—TP sensor input out of test range	O/R	①	①	X	X	X
24—ACT sensor input out of test range	O/R	X	X	X	X	X
24—VAT sensor input out of test range	O/R	—	—	—	—	—
25—KS sensor not detected during test	R	—	—	X	X	—
26—VAF sensor input out of test range	O/R	—	—	—	—	—
26—MAF sensor input out of test range	O/R	—	—	—	X	—
26—TOT sensor input out of test range	O/R	—	—	—	—	—
28—VAT sensor input out of test range	O/R	—	—	—	—	—
28—Loss of primary tach, right side	C	—	—	—	—	—
29—Insufficient input from vehicle speed sensor	C	X	X	X	X	
31—PFE circuit below minimum voltage	O/R/C	—	—	X	X	X
31—EVP circuit below minimum voltage	O/R/C	X	X	—	—	—
32—EGR valve not seated	R/C	—	—	X	X	X
32—EVP voltage below closed limit	O/R/C	X	X	—	—	—
33—EGR valve not opening	R/C	X	X	X	X	X
33—EVP not closing in limits	R	—	—	—	—	—
34—Insufficient EGR flow	R	—	—	—	—	—
34—Defective PFE sensor	O	—	—	X	X	X
34—Excessive exhaust back pressure	R/C	—	—	X	X	X
34—EVP voltage above closed limit	O/R/C	X	X	—	—	—
35—EVP circuit above maximum voltage	O/R/C	X	X	—	—	—
35—PFE circuit above maximum voltage	O/R/C	—	—	X	X	X
35—Rpm too low for EGR test	R	—	—	—	—	—
38—Idle track switch circuit open	C	X	X	—	—	—
39—AXOD by-pass clutch not applying properly	C	—	—	X	—	X
41—EGO/HEGO circuit shows system lean	R	X	X	X	③	⑤
41—No EGO/HEGO switching detected, system lean	C	X	X	X	⑤	⑤
42—EGO/HEGO shows system rich	R	X	X	X	⑤	⑤
42—No EGO/HEGO switching detected, system rich	C	—	—	—	—	—

Trouble Codes	Quick Test Mode	Car Engines				
		2.5L CLC CFI	2.5L MTX CFI	3.0L EFI	3.0L SHO SEFI	3.8L SEFI
43—EGO/HEGO lean at wide open throttle	C	—	—	—	—	—
44—Thermactor air system inoperative (cyl. 1–4)	R	—	—	—	—	—
45—DIS coil Pack 3 circuit failure	C	—	—	—	X	—
45—Thermactor air upstream during self test	R	—	—	—	—	—
46—DIS coil Pack 1 circuit failure	C	—	—	—	X	—
46—Thermactor air not bypassed during self-test	R	—	—	—	—	—
47—Airflow at base idle	R	—	—	—	—	—
47—4x4 switch is closed	O	—	—	—	—	—
48—Airflow high at base idle	R	—	—	—	—	—
48—DIS coil Pack 2 circuit failure	C	—	—	—	X	—
48—Loss of secondary tach, left side	C	—	—	—	—	—
49—1-2 shift error	C	—	—	—	—	—
49—Spout signal defaulted to 10 degrees BTDC	C	—	—	—	X	—
51—ECT sensor input exceeds test max.	O/C	X	X	X	X	X
52—PSPS circuit open	O	X	X	X	X	X
52—PSPS always open or always closed	R	X	X	X	X	X
53—TP sensor input exceeds test maximum	O/C	X	X	X	X	X
54—ACT sensor input exceeds test maximum	O/C	X	X	X	X	X
54—VAT sensor input exceeds test maximium	O/C	—	—	—	—	—
55—Key power input to processor is open	R	X	X	—	—	—
56—VAF sensor input exceeds test maximum	O/C	—	—	—	—	—
56—MAF sensor input exceeds test maximum	O/C	—	—	—	X	—
56—TOT sensor input exceeds test maximum	O/C	—	—	—	—	—
57—AXOD neutral pressure switch failed open	C	—	—	X	—	X
58—VAT sensor input exceeds test maximum	O/C	—	—	—	—	—
58—Idle tracking switch circuit closed	R	X	X	—	—	X
58—Idle tracking switch circuit open	O	X	X	—	—	—
59—AXOD 4/3 pressure switch failed open	C	—	—	—	X	—
59—Low speed fuel pump circuit failure	O/C	—	—	X	—	X
59—AXOD 4/3 pressure switch failed closed	O	—	—	—	—	X
59—2-3 shift error	C	—	—	—	—	—
61—ECT test sensor input below test minimum	O/C	X	X	X	X	X
62—AXOD 4/3 or 3/2 pressure switch failed closed	O	—	—	X	—	—
63—Converter clutch failure	C	—	—	—	—	—
63—TP sensor below test minimum	O/C	X	X	X	X	X
64—ACT sensor input below test minimum	O/C	X	X	X	X	X
64—VAT sensor input below test minimum	O/C	—	—	—	—	—
65—Failed to enter closed loop mode	C	—	—	—	—	—
65—Overdrive cancel switch not changing state	R	—	—	—	—	—
66—VAF sensor input below test minimum	O/C	—	—	—	—	—
66—MAF sensor input below test minimum	C	—	—	—	X	—
66—TOT sensor input below test minimum	O/C	—	—	—	—	—
67—Neutral drive switch open, A/C input high	O	X	③	X	④	⑦
67—Clutch switch circuit failure	C	X	X	—	—	—
67—AXOD neutral pressure switch failed closed	O	—	—	—	—	X
67—MLP sensor out of range, A/C input high	O/C	—	—	—	—	—
68—VAT sensor input below test minimum	O/C	—	—	—	—	—

Trouble Codes	Quick Test Mode	Car Engines 2.5L CLC CFI	2.5L MTX CFI	3.0L EFI	3.0L SHO SEFI	3.8L SEFI
68—Idle tracking switch circuit open	R	X	X	—	—	—
68—Idle tracking switch closed	O	X	X	—	—	—
68—AXOD temperature switch failed open	O/R/C	—	—	—	—	X
69—AXOD 3/4 pressure switch failed open	C	—	—	X	—	X
69—AXOD 3/2 pressure switch failed closed	O	—	—	—	—	X
69—3-4 shift error	C	—	—	—	—	—
70—EEC-IV data transmission link failed	C	—	—	—	—	X
71—Software re-initialization detected	C	—	—	—	—	—
71—Idle tracking switch closed on pre-position	C	X	X	—	—	—
71—Cluster control assembly circuit failed	C	—	—	—	—	X
72—Power interrupt detected	C	X	X	—	—	—
72—Insufficient BP change during test	R	—	—	—	X	—
72—Insufficient MAP output change during test	R	—	—	X	—	—
72—Message center control circuit failed	C	—	—	—	—	X
73—Insufficient TP output change during test	R	—	—	X	X	—
73—Insufficient TP change	O	X	X	—	—	—
74—Brake on/off circuit open, not on during test	R	X	X	X	X	X
75—Brake on/off circuit closed, always high	R	—	—	—	—	—
76—Insufficient VAF output change during test	R	—	—	—	—	—
77—Wide open throttle not sensed during test	R	—	—	X	X	—
79—A/C on during self test	O	—	—	—	X	X
81—Insufficient IAS output during test	O	—	—	—	X	—
81—Air management 2 circuit failure	O	—	—	—	—	—
82—Supercharger bypass circuit failure	O	—	—	—	—	—
82—Air management 1 circuit failure	O	—	—	—	—	—
83—EGRC solenoid circuit failure	O	—	—	—	—	—
83—High speed electro drive fan circuit failure	O	X	X	X	—	X
83—Low speed fuel pump relay circuit open	O/C	—	—	—	X	—
84—EGR VAC regulator circuit failure	O	X	X	X	X	X
84—EGRV solenoid circuit failure	O	—	—	—	—	—
85—Adaptive lean limit reached	C	—	—	—	—	—
85—Canister purge circuit failure	O	X	X	X	X	X
86—Adaptive rich limit reached	C	—	—	—	—	—
86—3-4 shift solenoid circuit failure	O	—	—	—	—	—
87—Fuel pump primary circuit failure	O/C	X	X	X	X	X
88—Electro drive fan circuit failure	O	X	X	X	X	X
88—Loss of dual plug input control	C	—	—	—	—	—
89—Clutch converter overdrive circuit failure	O	—	—	—	—	—
89—AXOD lock-up solenoid circuit failure	O	—	—	X	—	X
91—HEGO sensor circuit shows system lean	R	—	—	—	⑥	⑥

① Occurs also in continuous memory (C)
② Occurs only in key on, engine off (O) or continuous memory (C)
③ A/C input high only
④ Neutral pressure switch open
⑤ Right side HEGO
⑥ Left side HEGO
⑦ N–D switch only (no A/C signal)

ENGINE (Liters) / FUEL SYSTEM Service Codes	Quick Test Mode	2.5L FLC CFI	3.0L EFI	3.0L SHO SEFI	3.8L AXOD SEFI
11—System pass	O/R/C	✓	✓	✓	✓
12—Rpm unable to reach upper test limit	R	✓	✓	✓	✓
13—DC motor movement not detected	O	✓			
13—Rpm unable to achieve lower test limit	R	✓	✓		✓
13—DC motor did follow dashpot	C	✓			
14—PIP circuit failure	C	✓	✓	✓	✓
15—ECA read only memory test failed	O	✓	✓	✓	✓
15—ECA keep alive memory test failed	C	✓	✓	✓	✓
16—Idle rpm high with ISC off	R	✓			
16—Idle too low to perform EGO test	R				
17—Idle rpm low with ISC off	R	✓			
18—SPOUT circuit open or spark angle word failure	R	✓		✓	✓
18—IDM circuit failure or SPOUT circuit grounded	C	✓		✓	✓
19—Failure in ECA internal voltage	O	✓	✓	✓	✓
19—CID circuit failure	C		✓		
19—Rpm dropped too low in ISC off test	R				
19—Rpm for EGR test not achieved	R				
21—ECT out of self-test range	O/R	✓	✓	✓	✓
22—BP sensor out of self-test range	O/C			✓	
22—BP or MAP out of self-test range	O/R/C	✓	✓	✓	✓
23—TP out of self-test range	O/R		✓	✓	✓
23—TP out of self-test range	O/R/C	✓			
24—ACT sensor out of self-test range	O/R	✓	✓	✓	✓
25—Knock not sensed during dynamic test	R			✓	✓
26—VAF/MAF out of self-test range	O/R		✓	✓	
28—VAT out of self-test range	O/R		✓		
29—Insufficient input from vehicle speed sensor	C	✓	✓	✓	✓
31—PFE, EVP or EVR circuit below minimum voltage	O/R/C	✓	✓	✓	✓
32—EPT circuit voltage low (PFE)	R/C	✓	✓	✓	✓
32—EVP voltage below closed limit	O/R/C	✓			
32—EGR not controlling	R				
33—EGR valve opening not detected	R/C	✓	✓	✓	✓
33—EGR not closing fully	R				
34—Defective PFE sensor or voltage out of range	O		✓	✓	✓
34—EPT sensor voltage high (PFE)	R/C		✓	✓	✓
34—EVP voltage above closed limit	O/R/C	✓			
34—EGR opening not detected	R				
35—PFE or EVP circuit above maximum voltage	O/R/C	✓	✓	✓	✓
35—Rpm too low to perform EGR test	R				
38—Idle tracking switch circuit open	C	✓			
39—AXOD lock up failed	C		✓		
41—HEGO sensor circuit indicates system lean	R	✓	✓	✓ ④	✓ ②
41—No HEGO switching detected	R	✓	✓	✓ ④	✓ ②
42—HEGO sensor circuit indicates system rich	R	✓	✓	✓ ④	✓ ②
42—No HEGO switching detected—reads rich	C				
43—HEGO lean at wide open throttle	C				
44—Thermactor air system inoperative—ride side	R				
45—Thermactor air upstream during self-test	R			✓	
45—Coil 1 primary circuit failure	C				
46—Thermactor air not bypassed during self-test	R			✓	
46—Coil 2 primary circuit failure	C			✓	
47—Measured airflow low at base idle	R				
48—Coil 3 primary circuit failure	C			✓	
48—Measured airflow high at base idle	R				
49—SPOUT signal defaulted to 10°BTDC or SPOUT open	C			✓	
51—ECT/ACT reads −40°F or circuit open	O/C	✓	✓	✓	✓
52—Power steering pressure switch circuit open	O	✓	✓	✓	✓
52—Power steering pressure switch always open or closed	R	✓	✓	✓	✓

Service Codes / ENGINE (Liters) / FUEL SYSTEM	Quick Test Mode	2.5L FLC CFI	3.0L EFI	3.0L SHO SEFI	3.8L AXOD SEFI
53—TP circuit above maximum voltage	O/C	✓	✓	✓	✓
54—ACT sensor circuit open	O/C	✓	✓	✓	✓
55—Keypower circuit open	R	✓			
56—VAF or MAF circuit above maximum voltage	O/C			✓	
56—MAF circuit above maximum voltage	O/R/C				
57—Octane adjust service pin in use	O				
57—AXOD neutral pressure switch circuit failed open	C		✓		✓
58—Idle tracking switch circuit open	O	✓			
58—Idle tracking switch closed/circuit grounded	R	✓			
58—VAT reads −40°F or circuit open	O/C	✓			
59—Idle adjust service pin in use	O				
59—AXOD 4/3 pressure switch circuit failed open	C		✓		✓
59—Low speed fuel pump circuit open—Battery to ECA	O/C			✓	
59—AXOD 4/3 pressure switch failed closed	O				✓
61—ECT reads 254°F or circuit grounded	O/C	✓	✓	✓	✓
62—AXOD 4/3 or 3/2 pressure switch circuit grounded	O		✓		
63—TP circuit below minimum voltage	O/C	✓	✓	✓	✓
64—ACT sensor input below test minimum or grounded	O/C	✓	✓	✓	✓
65—Never went to closed loop fuel control	C				
66—MAF sensor input below minimum voltage	C			✓	
66—VAF sensor below minimum voltage	O/C				
66—MAF circuit below minimum voltage	R/C				
67—Neutral/drive switch open or A/C on	O	✓	✓	✓	✓
67—Clutch switch circuit failure	C	✓			
67—Neutral/drive switch open or A/C on	O/R				
68—Idle tracking switch closed or circuit grounded	O	✓			
68—Idle tracking switch circuit open	R	✓			
68—AXOD transmission temperature switch failed open	O/R/C				✓
68—VAT reads 254°F or circuit grounded	O/C				
69—AXOD 3/2 pressure switch circuit failed closed	O				
69—AXOD 3/4 pressure switch circiut failed open	C		✓		✓
70—ECA DATA communications link circuit failure	C				✓
71—Software re-initialization detected	C				
71—Idle tracking switch shorted to ground	C	✓			
71—Cluster control assembly circuit failed	C				✓
72—Insufficient MAF/MAP change during dynamic test	R		✓	✓	
72—Power interrupt or re-initialization detected	C	✓			
72—Message center control assembly circuit failed	C				✓
73—Insufficient throttle position change	O	✓			
73—Insufficient TP change during dynamic test	R		✓	✓	
74—Brake on/off switch failure or not actuated	R	✓	✓	✓	✓
75—Brake on/off switch circuit closed or ECA input open	R				
76—Insufficient VAF change during dynamic test	R				
77—No WOT seen in self-test or operator error	R		✓	✓	
79—A/C or defrost on during self-test	O			✓	✓

Service Codes	ENGINE (Liters) FUEL SYSTEM	Quick Test Mode	2.5L FLC CFI	3.0L EFI	3.0L SHO SEFI	3.8L AXOD SEFI
81—IAS circuit failure		0			✓	
81—Air management 2 circuit failure		0				
82—Air management 1 circuit failure		0				
82—Supercharger bypass circuit failure		0				
83—High speed electro drive fan circuit failure		0	✓	✓		✓
83—Low speed fuel pump circuit failure		0/C			✓	
84—EGR vacuum solenoid circuit failure		0	✓	✓	✓	✓
84—EGR vacuum regulator circuit failure		0/R				
85—Canister purge circuit failure		0/R				
85—Canister purge solenoid circuit failure		0	✓	✓	✓	✓
85—Adaptive fuel lean limit reached		C				
86—3-4 shift solenoid circuit failure		0				
86—Adaptive fuel rich limit reached		C				
87—Fuel pump primary circuit failure		0/C	✓	✓		✓
87—Fuel pump primary circuit failure		0/C/R				
87—Fuel pump primary circuit failure		0				
88—Electro drive fan circuit failure		0	✓	✓	✓	✓
89—Converter clutch override circuit failure		0				
89—Lock-up solenoid circuit failure		0		✓		✓
91—HEGO sensor indicates system lean		R			✓①	✓③
91—No HEGO switching detected		C			✓①	✓③
92—HEGO sensor indicates system rich		R			✓①	✓③
93—TP sensor input low at maximum motor travel		0	✓			
94—Thermactor air system inoperative-left side		R				
95—Fuel pump secondary circuit failure—ECA to ground		0/C	✓	✓		✓
96—Fuel pump secondary circuit failure—Battery to ECA		0/C	✓	✓		✓
96—High speed fuel pump circuit open		0/C			✓	
98—Hard fault present		R		✓	✓	✓
99—EEC has not learned to control idle: ignore codes 12 & 13		R	✓			

No Codes: Cannot begin self-test or cannot transmit codes
Codes Not Listed: Do not apply to vehicle being tested
0—Key on, engine off test
R—Key on, engine running test
C—Continuous memory
① Front HEGO
② Right HEGO
③ Left HEGO
④ Rear HEGO

Service Codes / ENGINE (Liters) / FUEL SYSTEM	Quick Test Mode	2.5L AXODE SEFI	3.0L EFI	3.0L AXODE SEFI	3.8L AXODE SEFI
111—System pass	O/R/C	✓	✓	✓	✓
112—ACT sensor circuit grounded or reads 254°F	O/C	✓	✓	✓	✓
112—ACT sensor circuit grounded	O/R				
113—ACT sensor circuit open	O/R				
113—ACT sensor circuit open or reads –40°F	O/C	✓	✓	✓	✓
114—ACT outside test limits during KOEO or KOER tests	O/R	✓	✓	✓	✓
116—ECT outside test limits during KOEO or KOER tests	O/R	✓	✓	✓	✓
117—ECT sensor circuit grounded	O/C	✓	✓	✓	✓
118—ECT sensor circiut above maximum voltage or reads –40°F	O/C			✓	
118—ECT sensor circuit open	O/C	✓	✓		✓
121—Closed throttle voltage higher or lower than expected	O/R/C	✓	✓	✓	✓
122—TP sensor circuit below minimum voltage	O/C	✓	✓	✓	✓
123—TP sensor above maximum voltage	O/C	✓	✓	✓	✓
124—TP sensor voltage higher than expected, in range	C	✓		✓	✓
125—TP sensor voltage lower than expected in range	C	✓		✓	✓
126—BP or MAP sensor higher or lower than expected	O/R/C		✓		
129—Insufficient MAF change during Dynamic Response test	R	✓	✓	✓	✓
136—HEGO shows system always lean (front)	R			✓	✓
136—HEGO shows sytem always lean (left)	R				
137—HEGO shows system always rich (front)	R			✓	✓
137—HEGO shows system always rich (left)	R				
139—No HEGO switching (front)	C			✓	✓
139—No HEGO switching (left)	C				
144—No HEGO switching (rear)	C			✓	✓
144—No HEGO switching (right)	C				
144—No HEGO switching	C		✓		
144—No HEGO switching detected	C	✓			
157—MAF sensor circiut below minimum voltage	C	✓		✓	✓
158—MAF sensor circuit above maximum voltage	O/C	✓		✓	✓
158—MAF sensor circuit above maximum voltage	O/R/C				
159—MAF higher or lower than expected during KOEO and KOER test	O/R	✓		✓	✓
167—Insufficient TP change during Dynamic Response test	R	✓	✓	✓	✓
171—Fuel system at adaptive limit, HEGO unable to switch	C	✓			
171—Fuel system at adaptive limit, HEGO unable to switch (right)	C				
171—No HEGO switching; system at adaptive limit (rear)	C				
172—HEGO shows system always lean (rear)	R/C		✓	✓	✓
172—No HEGO switching seen; indicates lean	R/C	✓			
172—No HEGO switching seen; indicates lean (right)	R/C				
173—HEGO shows system always rich (rear)	R/C		✓	✓	✓
173—No HEGO switching seen; indicates rich	R/C	✓			
173—No HEGO switching seen; indicates rich (right)	R/C				
174—HEGO switching time is slow (right)	C				
175—No HEGO switching; system at adaptive limit (front)	C		✓	✓	✓
175—No HEGO switching; system at adaptive limit (left)	C				
176—HEGO shows system alway lean (front)	C		✓	✓	✓
176—HEGO shows system always lean (left)	C	✓	✓		
177—HEGO shows system always rich (front)	C		✓	✓	✓
177—HEGO shows system always rich (left)	C				
178—HEGO switching time is slow (left)	C				
179—Fuel at lean adaptive limit at part throttle; system rich	C	✓			
179—System at lean adaptive limit at part throttle; system rich (rear)	C		✓	✓	✓
179—System at lean adaptive limit at part throttle; system rich (right)	C				

Service Codes / ENGINE (Liters) / FUEL SYSTEM	Quick Test Mode	2.5L AXODE SEFI	3.0L EFI	3.0L AXODE SEFI	3.8L AXODE SEFI
181—Fuel at rich adaptive limit at part throttle; system lean	C	✓			
181—System at rich adaptive limit at part throttle; system lean (rear)	C		✓	✓	✓
181—System at rich adaptive limit at part throttle, system lean (right)	C				
182—Fuel at lean adaptive limit at idle; system rich	C	✓			
182—System at lean adaptive limit at idle; system rich (rear)	C		✓	✓	✓
182—System at lean adaptive limit at idle; system rich (right)	C				
183—Fuel at rich adaptive limit at idle; system lean	C	✓			
183—System at rich adaptive limit at idle; system lean (rear)	C		✓	✓	✓
184—MAF higher than expected	C	✓		✓	✓
185—MAF lower than expected	C	✓		✓	✓
186—Injector pulse width higher than expected	C	✓		✓	✓
187—Injector pulse width lower than expected	C	✓		✓	✓
188—System at lean adaptive limit at part throttle; system rich (front)	C		✓	✓	
188—System at lean adaptive limit at part throttle; system rich (left)	C				
189—System at rich adaptive limit at part throttle, system lean (front)	C		✓	✓	✓
189—System at rich adaptive limit at part throttle, system lean (left)	C				
191—System at lean adaptive limit at idle; system rich (front)	C		✓	✓	✓
191—System at lean adaptive limit at idle; system rich (left)	C				
192—System at rich adaptive limit at idle; system lean (front)	C		✓	✓	✓
192—System at rich adaptive limit at idle; system lean (left)	C				
211—PIP circuit fauilt	C	✓	✓	✓	✓
212—Loss of IDM input to ECA or SPOUT circuit grounded	C	✓	✓	✓	✓
213—SPOUT circuit open	R	✓	✓	✓	✓
214—Cylinder identification circuit faiulre	C	✓		✓	✓
215—EEC processor detected Coil 1 primary circuit failure	C				
216—EEC processor detected Coil 2 primary circuit failure	C				
218—Loss of IDM signal, left side	C				
219—Spark timing defaulted to 10°BTDC or SPOUT circ. open	C				
222—Loss of IDM signal, right side					
223—Loss of dual plug inhibit control	C	✓			
224—Erratic IDM input to processor	C	✓			
225—Knock not sensed during Dynamic Response test	R	✓			
311—Thermactor air system inoperative (right)	R				
313—Thermactor air not bypassed during self-test	R				
314—Thermactor air system inoperative (left)	R				
326—PFE or DPFE circuit voltage lower than expected	R/C	✓	✓	✓	✓
327—EVP or DPFE circuit below minimum voltage	O/R/C	✓	✓	✓	✓
328—EGR closed voltage lower than expected	O/R/C				
332—Insufficient EGR flow detected	R/C	✓	✓	✓	✓
334—EGR closed voltage higher than expected	O/R/C				
335—PFE or DPFE sensor voltage out of self-test range	O	✓	✓	✓	✓
336—PFE sensor voltage higher than expected	R/C	✓	✓	✓	✓
337—EVP or DPFE circiut above maximum voltage	O/R/C	✓	✓	✓	✓
341—Octane adjust service pin in use	O				
411—Cannot control rpm during KOER low rpm check	R	✓	✓	✓	✓
412—Cannot control rpm during KOER high rpm check	R	✓	✓	✓	✓
452—Insufficient input from vehicle speed sensor	C	✓	✓	✓	✓
511—EEC processor ROM test failed	O	✓	✓	✓	✓
512—EEC processor Keep Alive Memory test failed	O	✓			
512—EEC processor Keep Alive Memory test failed	C		✓	✓	✓
513—Failure in EEC processor internal voltage	O	✓	✓	✓	✓
519—Power steering pressure switch circuit open	O	✓	✓	✓	✓

Service Codes	ENGINE (Liters) FUEL SYSTEM	Quick Test Mode	2.5L AXODE SEFI	3.0L EFI	3.0L AXODE SEFI	3.8L AXODE SEFI
519—Power steering pressure switch did not change state		R	✓	✓	✓	✓
522—Vehicle not in Park or Neutral during KOEO test		O	✓		✓	✓
525—Vehicle in gear or A/C on during self-test		O		✓		
528—Clutch switch circuit failure		C		✓		
536—Brake On/Off circuit failure/not actuated during KOER test		R/C	✓		✓	✓
538—Insufficient rpm change during KOER Dynamic Response test		R	✓	✓	✓	✓
539—A/C on or Defroster on during KOEO test		O				
542—Fuel pump secondary circuit failure: ECA to ground		O/C	✓	✓	✓	✓
543—Fuel pump secondary circuit failure: Batt to ECA		O/C	✓	✓	✓	✓
552—Air management 1 circuit failure		O				
556—Fuel pump primary circuit failure		O/C	✓	✓	✓	✓
558—EGR vacuum regulator circuit failure		O	✓	✓	✓	✓
563—High speed electro-drive fan circuit failure		O	✓	✓	✓	✓
564—Electro-drive fan circuit failure		O	✓	✓	✓	✓
565—Canister purge circuit failure		O	✓	✓	✓	✓
566—3-4 shift solenoid circuit failure		O				
621—Shift solenoid 1 circuit failure		O	✓		✓	✓
622—Shift solenoid 2 circuit failure		O	✓		✓	✓
624—EPC solenoid or driver circuit failure		O/C	✓		✓	✓
625—EPC driver open in ECA		O	✓		✓	✓
628—Lock-up solenoid failure; excesive clutch slippage		C	✓		✓	✓
629—Converter clutch control circuit failure		O	✓			
629—Lock-up solenoid failure		o			✓	✓
634—MLP sensor voltage out of self-test range		C	✓		✓	✓
636—TOT sensor voltage out of self-test range		O/R	✓		✓	✓
637—TOT sensor circuit above maximum voltage		O/C	✓		✓	✓
638—TOT sensor circuit below mamimum voltage		O/C	✓		✓	✓
639—Insufficient input from turbine speed sensor		R/C	✓		✓	✓
641—Shift solenoid 3 circuit failure		O	✓		✓	✓
645—Incorrect gear ratio obtained for 1st gear		C	✓		✓	✓
646—Incorrect gear ratio obtained for 2nd gear		C	✓		✓	✓
647—Incorrect gear ratio obtained for 3rd gear		C	✓		✓	✓
648—Incorrect gear ratio obtained for 4th gear		C	✓		✓	✓
649—EPC range failure		C	✓		✓	✓
651—EPC circuit failure		C	✓		✓	✓
998—Hard fault present		R	✓	✓	✓	✓

Codes Not Listed: Do not apply to vehicle being tested
No Codes: Cannot begin self-test or cannot transmit codes
O—Key on, engine off test
R—Key on, engine running test
C—Continuous memory

2.5L ENGINE VACUUM SCHEMATIC – 1986–87 TAURUS AND SABLE

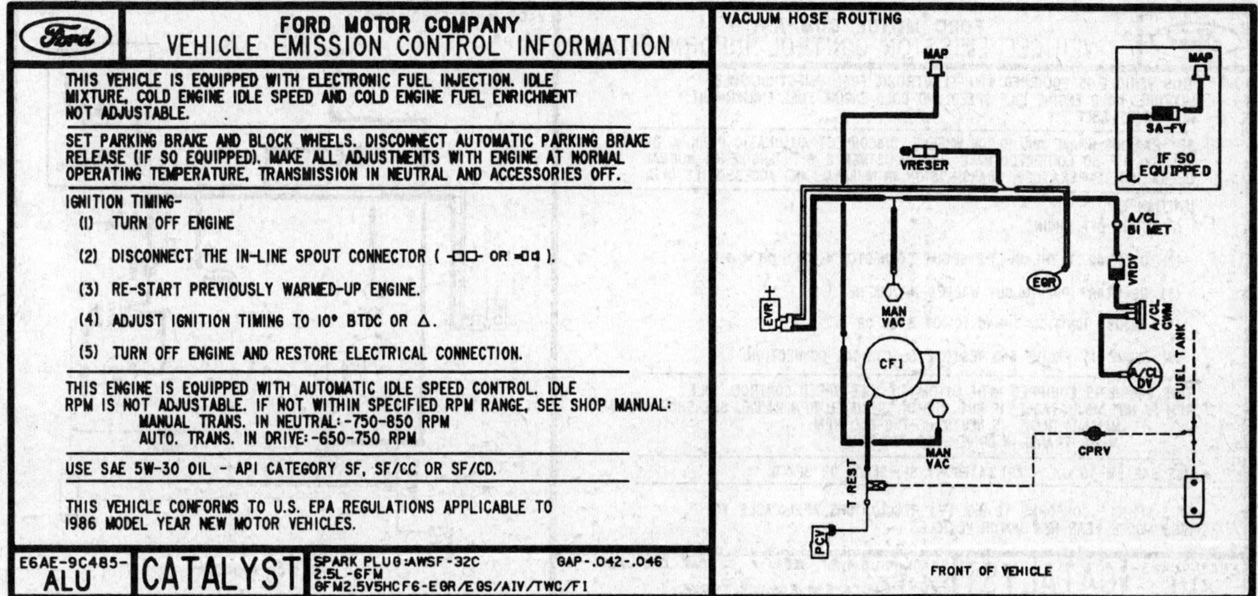

FORD MOTOR COMPANY
VEHICLE EMISSION CONTROL INFORMATION

THIS VEHICLE IS EQUIPPED WITH ELECTRONIC FUEL INJECTION. IDLE MIXTURE, COLD ENGINE IDLE SPEED AND COLD ENGINE FUEL ENRICHMENT NOT ADJUSTABLE.

SET PARKING BRAKE AND BLOCK WHEELS. DISCONNECT AUTOMATIC PARKING BRAKE RELEASE (IF SO EQUIPPED). MAKE ALL ADJUSTMENTS WITH ENGINE AT NORMAL OPERATING TEMPERATURE, TRANSMISSION IN NEUTRAL AND ACCESSORIES OFF.

IGNITION TIMING–
(1) TURN OFF ENGINE
(2) DISCONNECT THE IN-LINE SPOUT CONNECTOR (-□□- OR =□◁).
(3) RE-START PREVIOUSLY WARMED-UP ENGINE.
(4) ADJUST IGNITION TIMING TO 10° BTDC OR Δ.
(5) TURN OFF ENGINE AND RESTORE ELECTRICAL CONNECTION.

THIS ENGINE IS EQUIPPED WITH AUTOMATIC IDLE SPEED CONTROL. IDLE RPM IS NOT ADJUSTABLE. IF NOT WITHIN SPECIFIED RPM RANGE, SEE SHOP MANUAL:
MANUAL TRANS. IN NEUTRAL: -750-850 RPM
AUTO. TRANS. IN DRIVE: -650-750 RPM

USE SAE 5W-30 OIL - API CATEGORY SF, SF/CC OR SF/CD.

THIS VEHICLE CONFORMS TO U.S. EPA REGULATIONS APPLICABLE TO 1986 MODEL YEAR NEW MOTOR VEHICLES.

E6AE-9C485-ALU | CATALYST | SPARK PLUG: AWSF-32C GAP-.042-.046 2.5L-6FM 6FM2.5V5HCF6-EGR/EGS/AIV/TWC/FI

2.5L ENGINE VACUUM SCHEMATIC – 1986–87 TAURUS AND SABLE

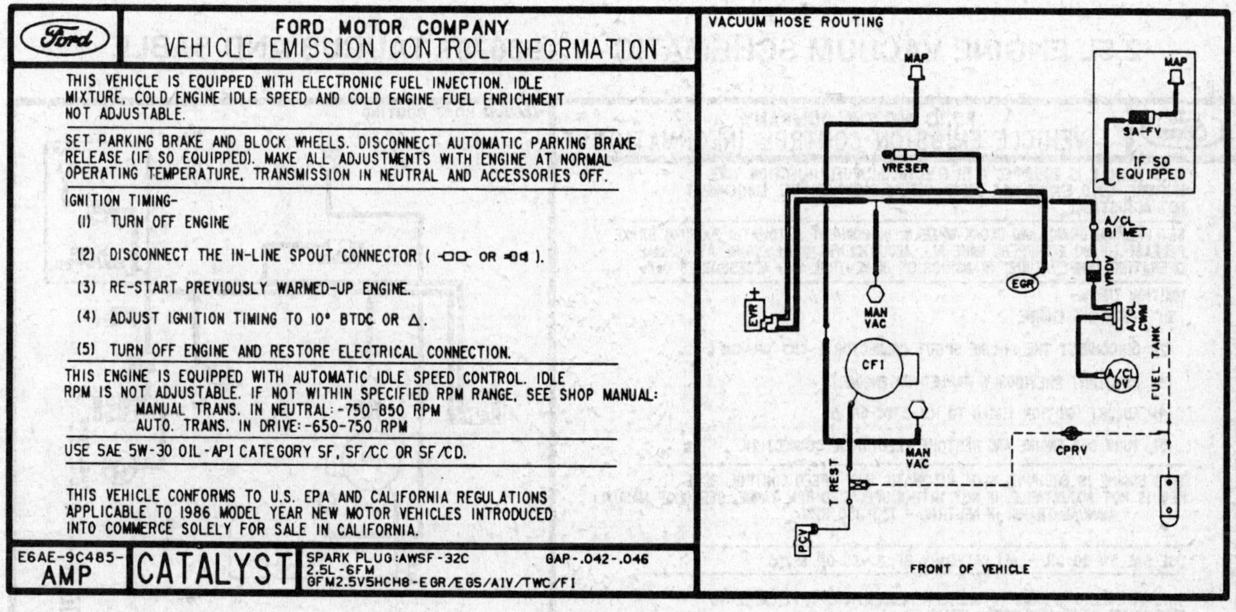

FORD MOTOR COMPANY
VEHICLE EMISSION CONTROL INFORMATION

THIS VEHICLE IS EQUIPPED WITH ELECTRONIC FUEL INJECTION. IDLE MIXTURE, COLD ENGINE IDLE SPEED AND COLD ENGINE FUEL ENRICHMENT NOT ADJUSTABLE.

SET PARKING BRAKE AND BLOCK WHEELS. DISCONNECT AUTOMATIC PARKING BRAKE RELEASE (IF SO EQUIPPED). MAKE ALL ADJUSTMENTS WITH ENGINE AT NORMAL OPERATING TEMPERATURE, TRANSMISSION IN NEUTRAL AND ACCESSORIES OFF.

IGNITION TIMING–
(1) TURN OFF ENGINE
(2) DISCONNECT THE IN-LINE SPOUT CONNECTOR (-□□- OR =□◁).
(3) RE-START PREVIOUSLY WARMED-UP ENGINE.
(4) ADJUST IGNITION TIMING TO 10° BTDC OR Δ.
(5) TURN OFF ENGINE AND RESTORE ELECTRICAL CONNECTION.

THIS ENGINE IS EQUIPPED WITH AUTOMATIC IDLE SPEED CONTROL. IDLE RPM IS NOT ADJUSTABLE. IF NOT WITHIN SPECIFIED RPM RANGE, SEE SHOP MANUAL:
MANUAL TRANS. IN NEUTRAL: -750-850 RPM
AUTO. TRANS. IN DRIVE: -650-750 RPM

USE SAE 5W-30 OIL-API CATEGORY SF, SF/CC OR SF/CD.

THIS VEHICLE CONFORMS TO U.S. EPA AND CALIFORNIA REGULATIONS APPLICABLE TO 1986 MODEL YEAR NEW MOTOR VEHICLES INTRODUCED INTO COMMERCE SOLELY FOR SALE IN CALIFORNIA.

E6AE-9C485-AMP | CATALYST | SPARK PLUG: AWSF-32C GAP-.042-.046 2.5L-6FM 6FM2.5V5HCH8-EGR/EGS/AIV/TWC/FI

2.5L ENGINE VACUUM SCHEMATIC – 1986–87 TAURUS AND SABLE

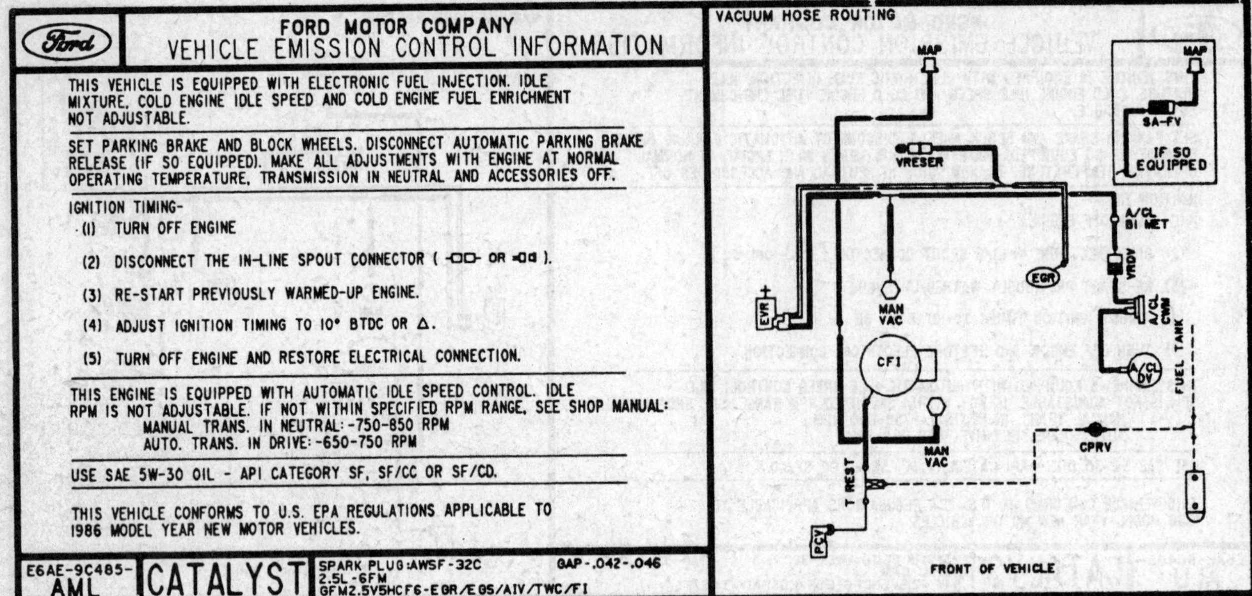

Ford

FORD MOTOR COMPANY
VEHICLE EMISSION CONTROL INFORMATION

THIS VEHICLE IS EQUIPPED WITH ELECTRONIC FUEL INJECTION. IDLE MIXTURE, COLD ENGINE IDLE SPEED AND COLD ENGINE FUEL ENRICHMENT NOT ADJUSTABLE.

SET PARKING BRAKE AND BLOCK WHEELS. DISCONNECT AUTOMATIC PARKING BRAKE RELEASE (IF SO EQUIPPED). MAKE ALL ADJUSTMENTS WITH ENGINE AT NORMAL OPERATING TEMPERATURE, TRANSMISSION IN NEUTRAL AND ACCESSORIES OFF.

IGNITION TIMING-
(1) TURN OFF ENGINE
(2) DISCONNECT THE IN-LINE SPOUT CONNECTOR (-□□- OR =□□).
(3) RE-START PREVIOUSLY WARMED-UP ENGINE.
(4) ADJUST IGNITION TIMING TO 10° BTDC OR Δ.
(5) TURN OFF ENGINE AND RESTORE ELECTRICAL CONNECTION.

THIS ENGINE IS EQUIPPED WITH AUTOMATIC IDLE SPEED CONTROL. IDLE RPM IS NOT ADJUSTABLE. IF NOT WITHIN SPECIFIED RPM RANGE, SEE SHOP MANUAL:
MANUAL TRANS. IN NEUTRAL:-750-850 RPM
AUTO. TRANS. IN DRIVE:-650-750 RPM

USE SAE 5W-30 OIL - API CATEGORY SF, SF/CC OR SF/CD.

THIS VEHICLE CONFORMS TO U.S. EPA REGULATIONS APPLICABLE TO 1986 MODEL YEAR NEW MOTOR VEHICLES.

E6AE-9C485-AML | CATALYST | SPARK PLUG:AWSF-32C GAP-.042-.046 2.5L-6FM GFM2.5V5HCF6-EGR/EGS/AIV/TWC/FI

2.5L ENGINE VACUUM SCHEMATIC – 1986–87 TAURUS AND SABLE

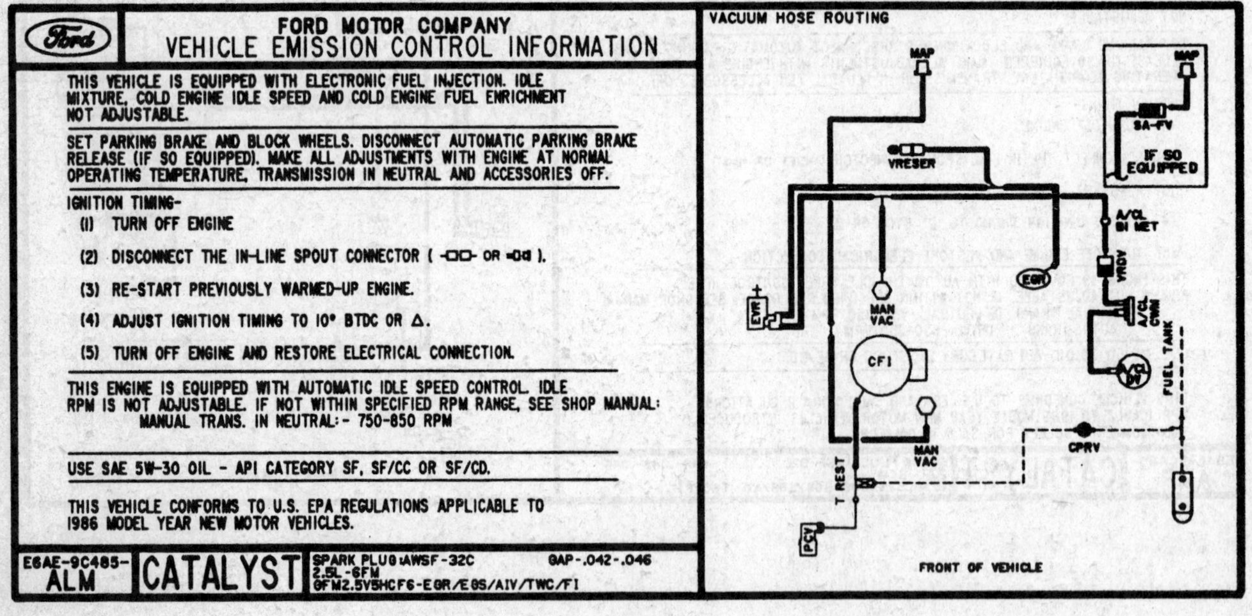

Ford

FORD MOTOR COMPANY
VEHICLE EMISSION CONTROL INFORMATION

THIS VEHICLE IS EQUIPPED WITH ELECTRONIC FUEL INJECTION. IDLE MIXTURE, COLD ENGINE IDLE SPEED AND COLD ENGINE FUEL ENRICHMENT NOT ADJUSTABLE.

SET PARKING BRAKE AND BLOCK WHEELS. DISCONNECT AUTOMATIC PARKING BRAKE RELEASE (IF SO EQUIPPED). MAKE ALL ADJUSTMENTS WITH ENGINE AT NORMAL OPERATING TEMPERATURE, TRANSMISSION IN NEUTRAL AND ACCESSORIES OFF.

IGNITION TIMING-
(1) TURN OFF ENGINE
(2) DISCONNECT THE IN-LINE SPOUT CONNECTOR (-□□- OR =□□).
(3) RE-START PREVIOUSLY WARMED-UP ENGINE.
(4) ADJUST IGNITION TIMING TO 10° BTDC OR Δ.
(5) TURN OFF ENGINE AND RESTORE ELECTRICAL CONNECTION.

THIS ENGINE IS EQUIPPED WITH AUTOMATIC IDLE SPEED CONTROL. IDLE RPM IS NOT ADJUSTABLE. IF NOT WITHIN SPECIFIED RPM RANGE, SEE SHOP MANUAL:
MANUAL TRANS. IN NEUTRAL:- 750-850 RPM

USE SAE 5W-30 OIL - API CATEGORY SF, SF/CC OR SF/CD.

THIS VEHICLE CONFORMS TO U.S. EPA REGULATIONS APPLICABLE TO 1986 MODEL YEAR NEW MOTOR VEHICLES.

E6AE-9C485-ALM | CATALYST | SPARK PLUG:AWSF-32C GAP-.042-.046 2.5L-6FM GFM2.5V5HCF6-EGR/EGS/AIV/TWC/FI

2.5L ENGINE VACUUM SCHEMATIC – 1986–87 TAURUS AND SABLE

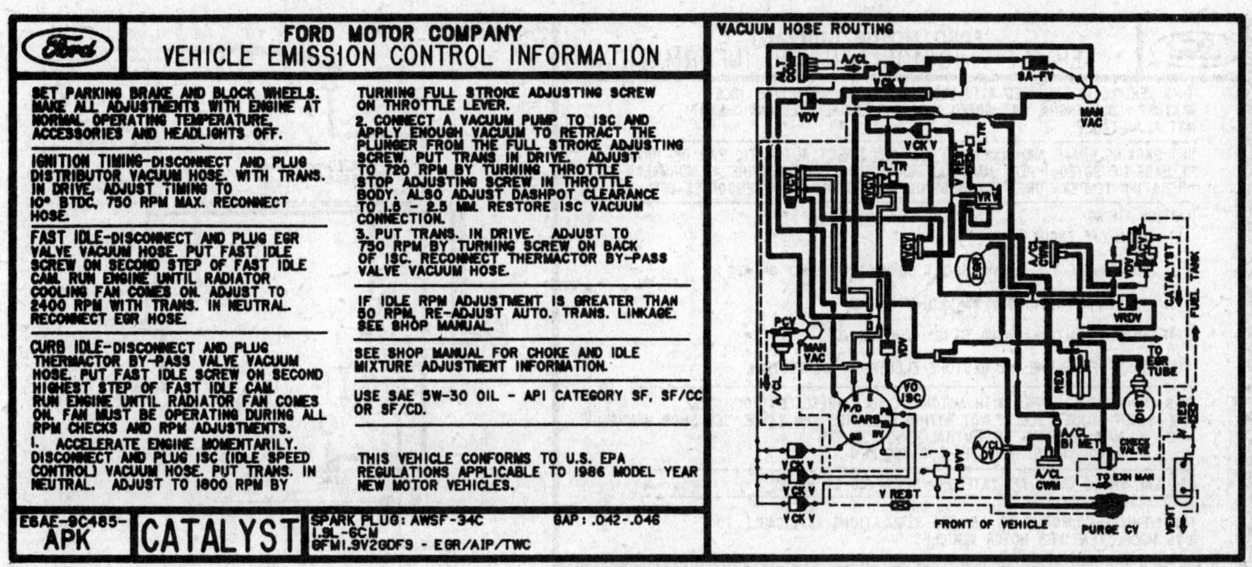

FORD MOTOR COMPANY
VEHICLE EMISSION CONTROL INFORMATION

SET PARKING BRAKE AND BLOCK WHEELS. MAKE ALL ADJUSTMENTS WITH ENGINE AT NORMAL OPERATING TEMPERATURE, ACCESSORIES AND HEADLIGHTS OFF.

IGNITION TIMING–DISCONNECT AND PLUG DISTRIBUTOR VACUUM HOSE. WITH TRANS. IN DRIVE, ADJUST TIMING TO 10° BTDC, 750 RPM MAX. RECONNECT HOSE.

FAST IDLE–DISCONNECT AND PLUG EGR VALVE VACUUM HOSE. PUT FAST IDLE SCREW ON SECOND STEP OF FAST IDLE CAM. RUN ENGINE UNTIL RADIATOR COOLING FAN COMES ON. ADJUST TO 2400 RPM WITH TRANS. IN NEUTRAL. RECONNECT EGR HOSE.

CURB IDLE–DISCONNECT AND PLUG THERMACTOR BY-PASS VALVE VACUUM HOSE. PUT FAST IDLE SCREW ON SECOND HIGHEST STEP OF FAST IDLE CAM. RUN ENGINE UNTIL RADIATOR FAN COMES ON. FAN MUST BE OPERATING DURING ALL RPM CHECKS AND RPM ADJUSTMENTS.
1. ACCELERATE ENGINE MOMENTARILY. DISCONNECT AND PLUG ISC (IDLE SPEED CONTROL) VACUUM HOSE. PUT TRANS. IN NEUTRAL. ADJUST TO 1800 RPM BY TURNING FULL STROKE ADJUSTING SCREW ON THROTTLE LEVER.
2. CONNECT A VACUUM PUMP TO ISC AND APPLY ENOUGH VACUUM TO RETRACT THE PLUNGER FROM THE FULL STROKE ADJUSTING SCREW. PUT TRANS IN DRIVE. ADJUST TO 720 RPM BY TURNING THROTTLE STOP ADJUSTING SCREW IN THROTTLE BODY. ALSO ADJUST DASHPOT CLEARANCE TO 1.5 – 2.5 MM. RESTORE ISC VACUUM CONNECTION.
3. PUT TRANS. IN DRIVE. ADJUST TO 750 RPM BY TURNING SCREW ON BACK OF ISC. RECONNECT THERMACTOR BY-PASS VALVE VACUUM HOSE.

IF IDLE RPM ADJUSTMENT IS GREATER THAN 50 RPM, RE-ADJUST AUTO. TRANS. LINKAGE. SEE SHOP MANUAL.

SEE SHOP MANUAL FOR CHOKE AND IDLE MIXTURE ADJUSTMENT INFORMATION.

USE SAE 5W-30 OIL – API CATEGORY SF, SF/CC OR SF/CD.

THIS VEHICLE CONFORMS TO U.S. EPA REGULATIONS APPLICABLE TO 1986 MODEL YEAR NEW MOTOR VEHICLES.

E6AE-9C485-APK | CATALYST | SPARK PLUG: AWSF-34C GAP: .042-.046 | 1.9L-6CM | 6FM1.9V2GDF9 - EGR/AIP/TWC

2.5L ENGINE VACUUM SCHEMATIC – 1986–87 TAURUS AND SABLE

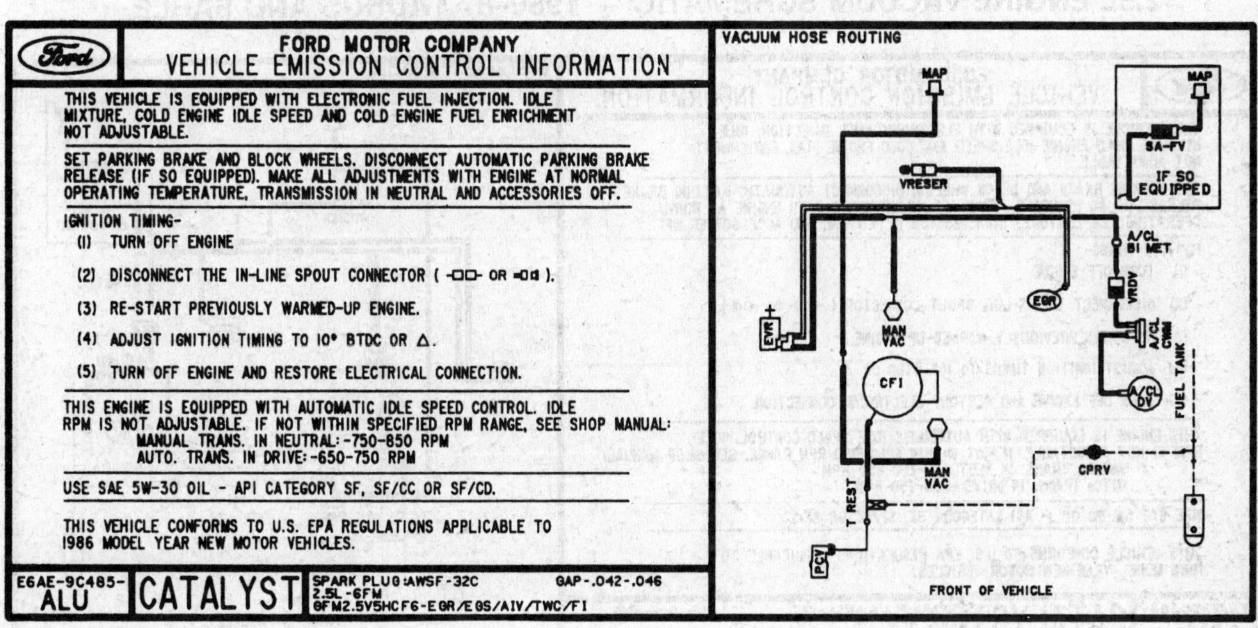

FORD MOTOR COMPANY
VEHICLE EMISSION CONTROL INFORMATION

THIS VEHICLE IS EQUIPPED WITH ELECTRONIC FUEL INJECTION. IDLE MIXTURE, COLD ENGINE IDLE SPEED AND COLD ENGINE FUEL ENRICHMENT NOT ADJUSTABLE.

SET PARKING BRAKE AND BLOCK WHEELS. DISCONNECT AUTOMATIC PARKING BRAKE RELEASE (IF SO EQUIPPED). MAKE ALL ADJUSTMENTS WITH ENGINE AT NORMAL OPERATING TEMPERATURE, TRANSMISSION IN NEUTRAL AND ACCESSORIES OFF.

IGNITION TIMING–
(1) TURN OFF ENGINE
(2) DISCONNECT THE IN-LINE SPOUT CONNECTOR (-□□- OR ▭□).
(3) RE-START PREVIOUSLY WARMED-UP ENGINE.
(4) ADJUST IGNITION TIMING TO 10° BTDC OR △.
(5) TURN OFF ENGINE AND RESTORE ELECTRICAL CONNECTION.

THIS ENGINE IS EQUIPPED WITH AUTOMATIC IDLE SPEED CONTROL. IDLE RPM IS NOT ADJUSTABLE. IF NOT WITHIN SPECIFIED RPM RANGE, SEE SHOP MANUAL:
MANUAL TRANS. IN NEUTRAL:-750-850 RPM
AUTO. TRANS. IN DRIVE:-650-750 RPM

USE SAE 5W-30 OIL – API CATEGORY SF, SF/CC OR SF/CD.

THIS VEHICLE CONFORMS TO U.S. EPA REGULATIONS APPLICABLE TO 1986 MODEL YEAR NEW MOTOR VEHICLES.

E6AE-9C485-ALU | CATALYST | SPARK PLUG:AWSF-32C GAP-.042-.046 | 2.5L-6FM | 6FM2.5V5HCF6-EGR/EGS/AIV/TWC/FI

2.5L ENGINE VACUUM SCHEMATIC – 1986–87 TAURUS AND SABLE

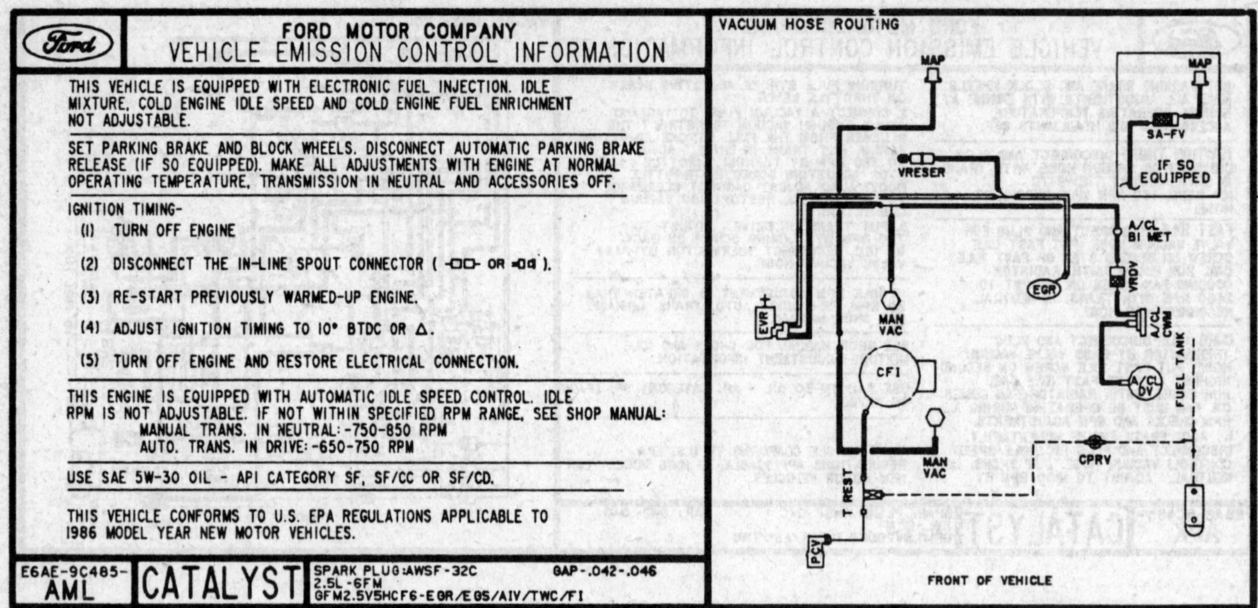
Ford

FORD MOTOR COMPANY
VEHICLE EMISSION CONTROL INFORMATION

THIS VEHICLE IS EQUIPPED WITH ELECTRONIC FUEL INJECTION. IDLE MIXTURE, COLD ENGINE IDLE SPEED AND COLD ENGINE FUEL ENRICHMENT NOT ADJUSTABLE.

SET PARKING BRAKE AND BLOCK WHEELS. DISCONNECT AUTOMATIC PARKING BRAKE RELEASE (IF SO EQUIPPED). MAKE ALL ADJUSTMENTS WITH ENGINE AT NORMAL OPERATING TEMPERATURE, TRANSMISSION IN NEUTRAL AND ACCESSORIES OFF.

IGNITION TIMING-
(1) TURN OFF ENGINE
(2) DISCONNECT THE IN-LINE SPOUT CONNECTOR (-□□- OR =□□).
(3) RE-START PREVIOUSLY WARMED-UP ENGINE.
(4) ADJUST IGNITION TIMING TO 10° BTDC OR Δ.
(5) TURN OFF ENGINE AND RESTORE ELECTRICAL CONNECTION.

THIS ENGINE IS EQUIPPED WITH AUTOMATIC IDLE SPEED CONTROL. IDLE RPM IS NOT ADJUSTABLE. IF NOT WITHIN SPECIFIED RPM RANGE, SEE SHOP MANUAL:
MANUAL TRANS. IN NEUTRAL:-750-850 RPM
AUTO. TRANS. IN DRIVE:-650-750 RPM

USE SAE 5W-30 OIL - API CATEGORY SF, SF/CC OR SF/CD.

THIS VEHICLE CONFORMS TO U.S. EPA REGULATIONS APPLICABLE TO 1986 MODEL YEAR NEW MOTOR VEHICLES.

E6AE-9C485-AML | CATALYST | SPARK PLUG:AWSF-32C GAP-.042-.046 2.5L-6FM GFM2.5V5HCF6-EGR/EGS/AIV/TWC/FI

2.5L ENGINE VACUUM SCHEMATIC – 1986–87 TAURUS AND SABLE

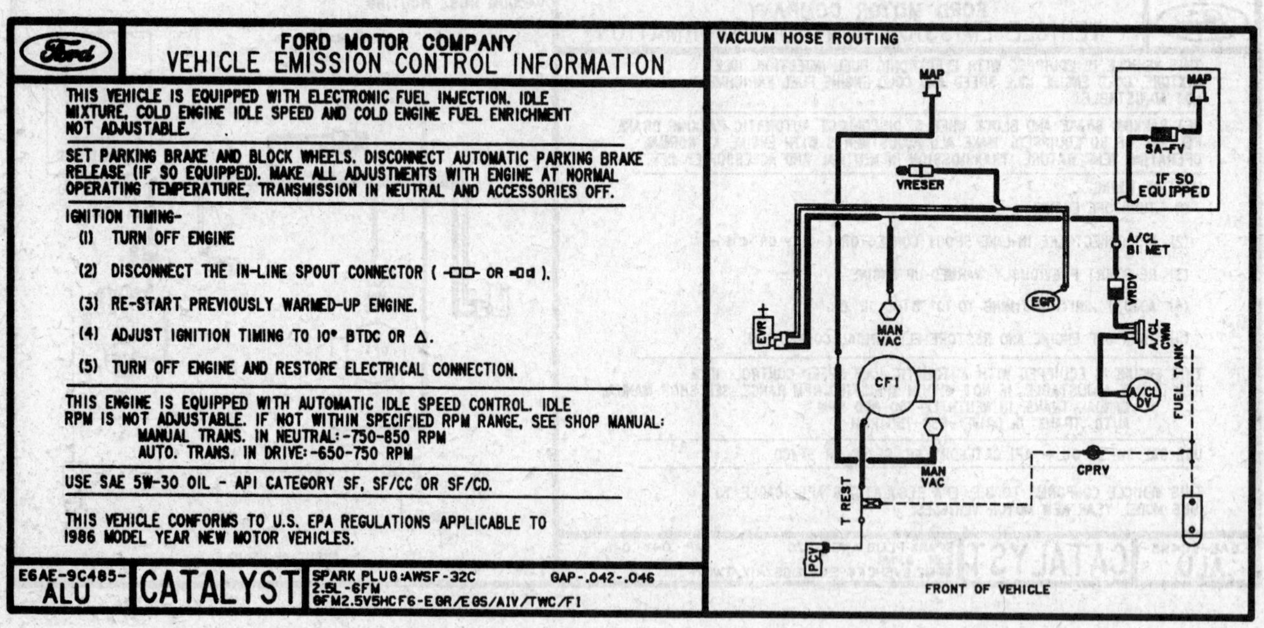
Ford

FORD MOTOR COMPANY
VEHICLE EMISSION CONTROL INFORMATION

THIS VEHICLE IS EQUIPPED WITH ELECTRONIC FUEL INJECTION. IDLE MIXTURE, COLD ENGINE IDLE SPEED AND COLD ENGINE FUEL ENRICHMENT NOT ADJUSTABLE.

SET PARKING BRAKE AND BLOCK WHEELS. DISCONNECT AUTOMATIC PARKING BRAKE RELEASE (IF SO EQUIPPED). MAKE ALL ADJUSTMENTS WITH ENGINE AT NORMAL OPERATING TEMPERATURE, TRANSMISSION IN NEUTRAL AND ACCESSORIES OFF.

IGNITION TIMING-
(1) TURN OFF ENGINE
(2) DISCONNECT THE IN-LINE SPOUT CONNECTOR (-□□- OR =□□).
(3) RE-START PREVIOUSLY WARMED-UP ENGINE.
(4) ADJUST IGNITION TIMING TO 10° BTDC OR Δ.
(5) TURN OFF ENGINE AND RESTORE ELECTRICAL CONNECTION.

THIS ENGINE IS EQUIPPED WITH AUTOMATIC IDLE SPEED CONTROL. IDLE RPM IS NOT ADJUSTABLE. IF NOT WITHIN SPECIFIED RPM RANGE, SEE SHOP MANUAL:
MANUAL TRANS. IN NEUTRAL:-750-850 RPM
AUTO. TRANS. IN DRIVE:-650-750 RPM

USE SAE 5W-30 OIL - API CATEGORY SF, SF/CC OR SF/CD.

THIS VEHICLE CONFORMS TO U.S. EPA REGULATIONS APPLICABLE TO 1986 MODEL YEAR NEW MOTOR VEHICLES.

E6AE-9C485-ALU | CATALYST | SPARK PLUG:AWSF-32C GAP-.042-.046 2.5L-6FM GFM2.5V5HCF6-EGR/EGS/AIV/TWC/FI

2.5L ENGINE VACUUM SCHEMATIC – 1986–87 TAURUS AND SABLE

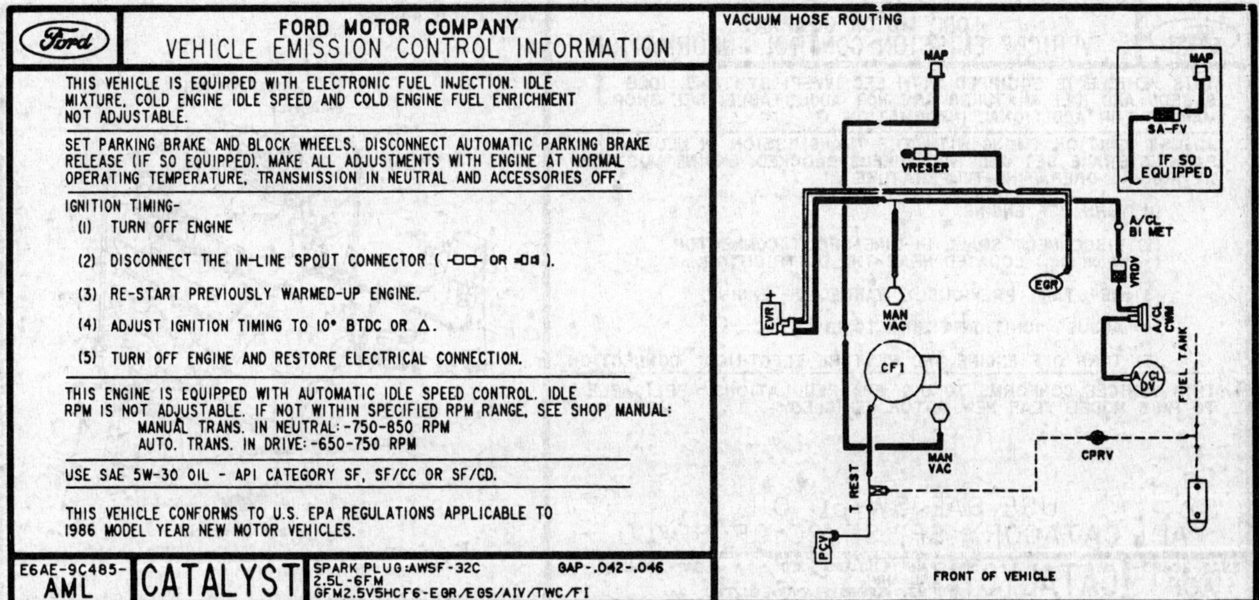

2.5L ENGINE VACUUM SCHEMATIC – 1986–87 TAURUS AND SABLE

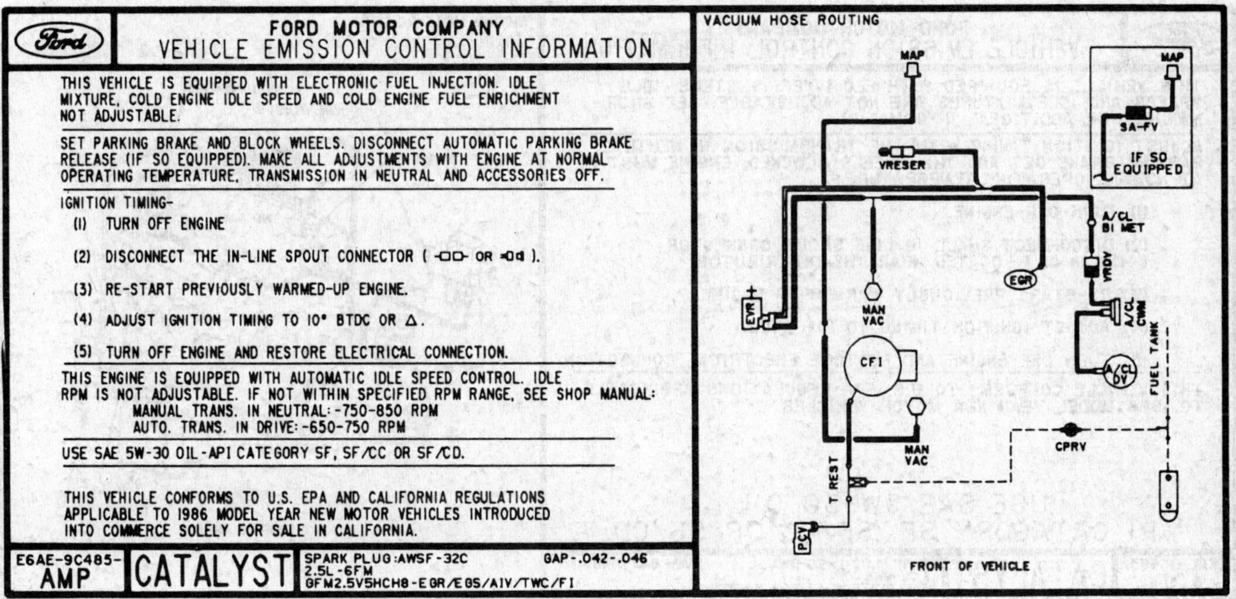

3.0L ENGINE VACUUM SCHEMATIC – 1986–87 TAURUS AND SABLE

FORD MOTOR COMPANY
VEHICLE EMISSION CONTROL INFORMATION

THIS VEHICLE IS EQUIPPED WITH EEC IV/EFI SYSTEMS. IDLE SPEEDS AND IDLE MIXTURES ARE NOT ADJUSTABLE. SEE SHOP MANUAL FOR ADDITIONAL INFORMATION.

ADJUST IGNITION TIMING WITH THE TRANSMISSION IN NEUTRAL, PARKING BRAKE SET AND THE WHEELS BLOCKED. ENGINE MUST BE AT NORMAL OPERATING TEMPERATURE.

(1) TURN OFF ENGINE.

(2) DISCONNECT SMALL IN-LINE SPOUT CONNECTOR (-□□- OR =□□) LOCATED NEAR THE DISTRIBUTOR.

(3) RE-START PREVIOUSLY WARMED-UP ENGINE.

(4) ADJUST IGNITION TIMING TO 10° BTDC.

(5) TURN OFF ENGINE AND RESTORE ELECTRICAL CONNECTION.

THIS VEHICLE CONFORMS TO U.S. EPA REGULATIONS APPLICABLE TO 1986 MODEL YEAR NEW MOTOR VEHICLES.

USE SAE 5W-30 OIL
API CATAGORY SF, SF/CC OR SF/CD.

E6AE-9C485-ACF | CATALYST | SPARK PLUG:AWSF-32C GAP-.042-.046 3.0L-6HW GFM3.0V5FEG5-FI/EGR/EGS/TWC

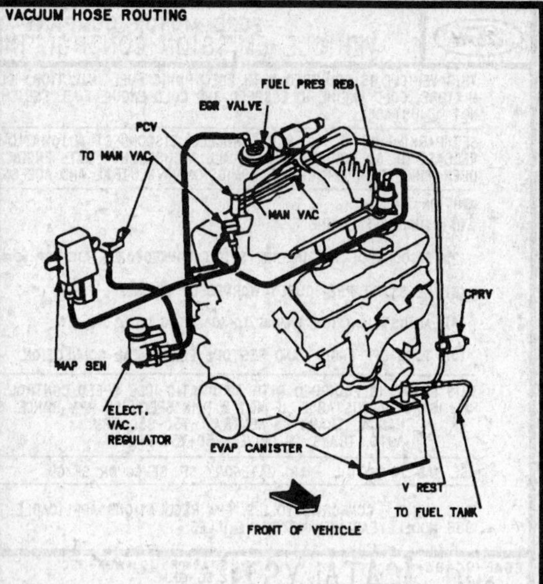

3.0L ENGINE VACUUM SCHEMATIC – 1986–87 TAURUS AND SABLE

FORD MOTOR COMPANY
VEHICLE EMISSION CONTROL INFORMATION

THIS VEHICLE IS EQUIPPED WITH EEC IV/EFI SYSTEMS. IDLE SPEEDS AND IDLE MIXTURES ARE NOT ADJUSTABLE. SEE SHOP MANUAL FOR ADDITIONAL INFORMATION.

ADJUST IGNITION TIMING WITH THE TRANSMISSION IN NEUTRAL, PARKING BRAKE SET AND THE WHEELS BLOCKED. ENGINE MUST BE AT NORMAL OPERATING TEMPERATURE.

(1) TURN OFF ENGINE.

(2) DISCONNECT SMALL IN-LINE SPOUT CONNECTOR (-□□- OR =□□) LOCATED NEAR THE DISTRIBUTOR.

(3) RE-START PREVIOUSLY WARMED-UP ENGINE.

(4) ADJUST IGNITION TIMING TO 10° BTDC.

(5) TURN OFF ENGINE AND RESTORE ELECTRICAL CONNECTION.

THIS VEHICLE CONFORMS TO U.S. EPA REGULATIONS APPLICABLE TO 1986 MODEL YEAR NEW MOTOR VEHICLES.

USE SAE 5W-30 OIL
API CATAGORY SF, SF/CC OR SF/CD.

E6AE-9C485-ACF | CATALYST | SPARK PLUG:AWSF-32C GAP-.042-.046 3.0L-6HW GFM3.0V5FEG5-FI/EGR/EGS/TWC

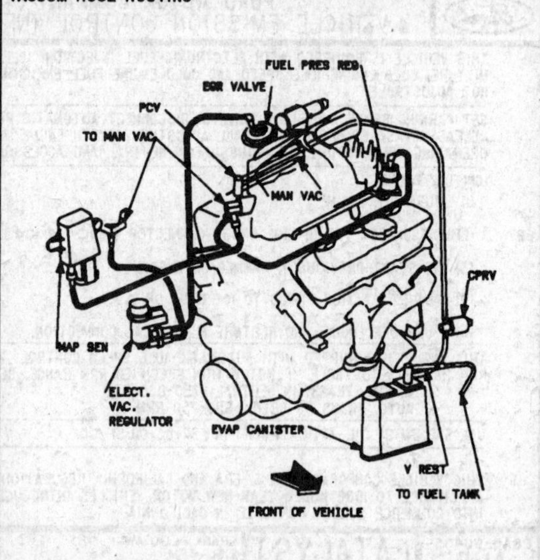

3.0L ENGINE VACUUM SCHEMATIC – 1986–87 TAURUS AND SABLE

FORD MOTOR COMPANY
VEHICLE EMISSION CONTROL INFORMATION

THIS VEHICLE IS EQUIPPED WITH EEC IV/EFI SYSTEMS. IDLE SPEEDS AND IDLE MIXTURES ARE NOT ADJUSTABLE. SEE SHOP MANUAL FOR ADDITIONAL INFORMATION.

ADJUST IGNITION TIMING WITH THE TRANSMISSION IN NEUTRAL, PARKING BRAKE SET AND THE WHEELS BLOCKED. ENGINE MUST BE AT NORMAL OPERATING TEMPERATURE.

(1) TURN OFF ENGINE.

(2) DISCONNECT SMALL IN-LINE SPOUT CONNECTOR (-□□- OR =□◁) LOCATED NEAR THE DISTRIBUTOR.

(3) RE-START PREVIOUSLY WARMED-UP ENGINE.

(4) ADJUST IGNITION TIMING TO 10° BTDC.

(5) TURN OFF ENGINE AND RESTORE ELECTRICAL CONNECTION.

THIS VEHICLE CONFORMS TO U.S. EPA REGULATIONS APPLICABLE TO 1986 MODEL YEAR NEW MOTOR VEHICLES.

USE SAE 5W-30 OIL
API CATAGORY SF, SF/CC OR SF/CD.

VACUUM HOSE ROUTING

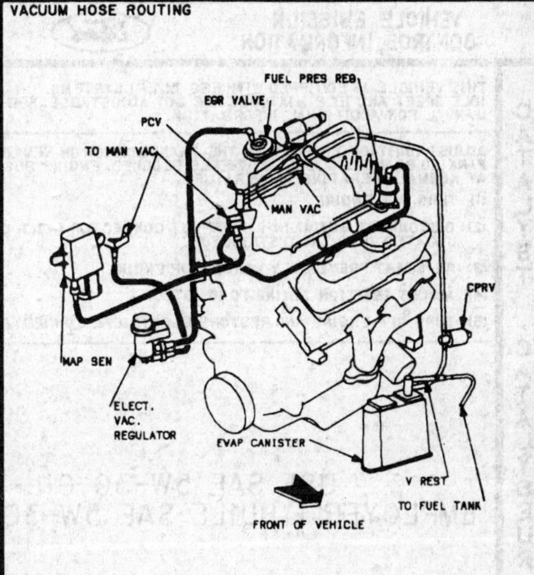

E6AE-9C485-
ACF

CATALYST

SPARK PLUG: AWSF-32C GAP-.042-.046
3.0L-6HM
GFM3.0V5FEG5-FI/EGR/EGS/TWC

3.0L ENGINE VACUUM SCHEMATIC – 1986–87 TAURUS AND SABLE

VEHICLE EMISSION CONTROL INFORMATION

FORD MOTOR COMPANY

CONTRÔLE DES ÉMISSIONS DU VÉHICULE

CATALYST

THIS VEHICLE IS EQUIPPED WITH EEC IV/EFI SYSTEMS. IDLE SPEED AND IDLE MIXTURES ARE NOT ADJUSTABLE. SEE SHOP MANUAL FOR ADDITIONAL INFORMATION.

ADJUST IGNITION TIMING WITH THE TRANSMISSION IN NEUTRAL, PARKING BRAKE SET AND THE WHEELS BLOCKED. ENGINE MUST BE AT NORMAL OPERATING TEMPERATURE.

(1) TURN OFF ENGINE.

(2) DISCONNECT SMALL IN-LINE SPOUT CONNECTOR (-□□- OR =□◁) LOCATED NEAR THE DISTRIBUTOR.

(3) RE-START PREVIOUSLY WARMED-UP ENGINE.

(4) ADJUST IGNITION TIMING TO 10° BTDC.

(5) TURN OFF ENGINE AND RESTORE ELECTRICAL CONNECTION.

CE VÉHICULE EST MUNI DES SYSTÈMES EEC IV ET EFI.* LE RÉGIME DE RALENTI ET LE MÉLANGE DE RALENTI NE SONT PAS RÉGLABLES. POUR DE PLUS AMPLES DÉTAILS, CONSULTEZ LE MANUEL DE RÉPARATION.

POUR LE CALAGE DE L'ALLUMAGE, PLACEZ LE LEVIER DE VITESSE EN POSITION "N". SERREZ LE FREIN DE STATIONNEMENT ET BLOQUEZ LES ROUES. LE MOTEUR DOIT ÊTRE NORMALEMENT CHAUD.

(1) ARRÊTEZ LE MOTEUR.

(2) DÉBRANCHEZ LE PETIT CONNECTEUR (-□□- OR =□◁) (DU CIRCUIT DE DÉCLENCHEMENT DE L'ETINCELLE) MONTÉ À MÊME LE FIL PRÈS DE L'ALLUMEUR.

(3) REDÉMARREZ LE MOTEUR PRÉALABLEMENT RÉCHAUFFÉ.

(4) CALEZ L'ALLUMAGE À 10° AVPMH.

(5) ARRÊTEZ LE MOTEUR ET REBRANCHEZ LE CONNECTEUR.

* EEC IV = COMMANDE ÉLECTRONIQUE DU MOTEUR, VERSION IV
EFI = INJECTION ÉLECTRONIQUE

CATALYSEUR

USE SAE 5W-30 OIL-API CATEGORY SF, SF/CC OR SF/CD.
EMPLOYER L'HUILE SAE 5W-30, CLASSIFICATION API: SF, SF/CC OU SF/CD.

E6AE-9C485-
ACH

3.0 L SPARK PLUG/BOUGIES AWSF-32C GAP/ÉLECTRODES .042–.046

3.0L ENGINE VACUUM SCHEMATIC — 1986–87 TAURUS AND SABLE

VEHICLE EMISSION CONTROL INFORMATION — Ford — **FORD MOTOR COMPANY** — **CONTRÔLE DES ÉMISSIONS DU VÉHICULE**

CATALYST / CATALYSEUR

THIS VEHICLE IS EQUIPPED WITH EEC IV/EFI SYSTEMS. IDLE SPEED AND IDLE MIXTURES ARE NOT ADJUSTABLE. SEE SHOP MANUAL FOR ADDITIONAL INFORMATION.

ADJUST IGNITION TIMING WITH THE TRANSMISSION IN NEUTRAL, PARKING BRAKE SET AND THE WHEELS BLOCKED. ENGINE MUST BE AT NORMAL OPERATING TEMPERATURE.

(1) TURN OFF ENGINE.

(2) DISCONNECT SMALL IN-LINE SPOUT CONNECTOR (-□□- OR =□◁) LOCATED NEAR THE DISTRIBUTOR.

(3) RE-START PREVIOUSLY WARMED-UP ENGINE.

(4) ADJUST IGNITION TIMING TO 10° BTDC.

(5) TURN OFF ENGINE AND RESTORE ELECTRICAL CONNECTION.

CE VÉHICULE EST MUNI DES SYSTÈMES EEC IV ET EFI.* LE RÉGIME DE RALENTI ET LE MÉLANGE DE RALENTI NE SONT PAS RÉGLABLES. POUR DE PLUS AMPLES DÉTAILS, CONSULTEZ LE MANUEL DE RÉPARATION.

POUR LE CALAGE DE L'ALLUMAGE, PLACEZ LE LEVIER DE VITESSE EN POSITION "N", SERREZ LE FREIN DE STATIONNEMENT ET BLOQUEZ LES ROUES. LE MOTEUR DOIT ÊTRE NORMALEMENT CHAUD.

(1) ARRÊTEZ LE MOTEUR.

(2) DÉBRANCHEZ LE PETIT CONNECTEUR (-□□- OR =□◁) (DU CIRCUIT DE DÉCLENCHEMENT DE L'ETINCELLE) MONTÉ À MÊME LE FIL PRÈS DE L'ALLUMEUR.

(3) REDÉMARREZ LE MOTEUR PRÉALABLEMENT RÉCHAUFFÉ.

(4) CALEZ L'ALLUMAGE À 10° AVPMH.

(5) ARRÊTEZ LE MOTEUR ET REBRANCHEZ LE CONNECTEUR.

* EEC IV = COMMANDE ÉLECTRONIQUE DU MOTEUR, VERSION IV
EFI = INJECTION ÉLECTRONIQUE

USE SAE 5W-30 OIL-API CATEGORY SF, SF/CC OR SF/CD.
EMPLOYER L'HUILE SAE 5W-30, CLASSIFICATION API: SF, SF/CC OU SF/CD.

E6AE-9C485-ACH | 3.0 L | SPARK PLUG/BOUGIES AWSF-32C | GAP/ÉLECTRODES .042-.046

3.0L ENGINE VACUUM SCHEMATIC — 1986–87 TAURUS AND SABLE

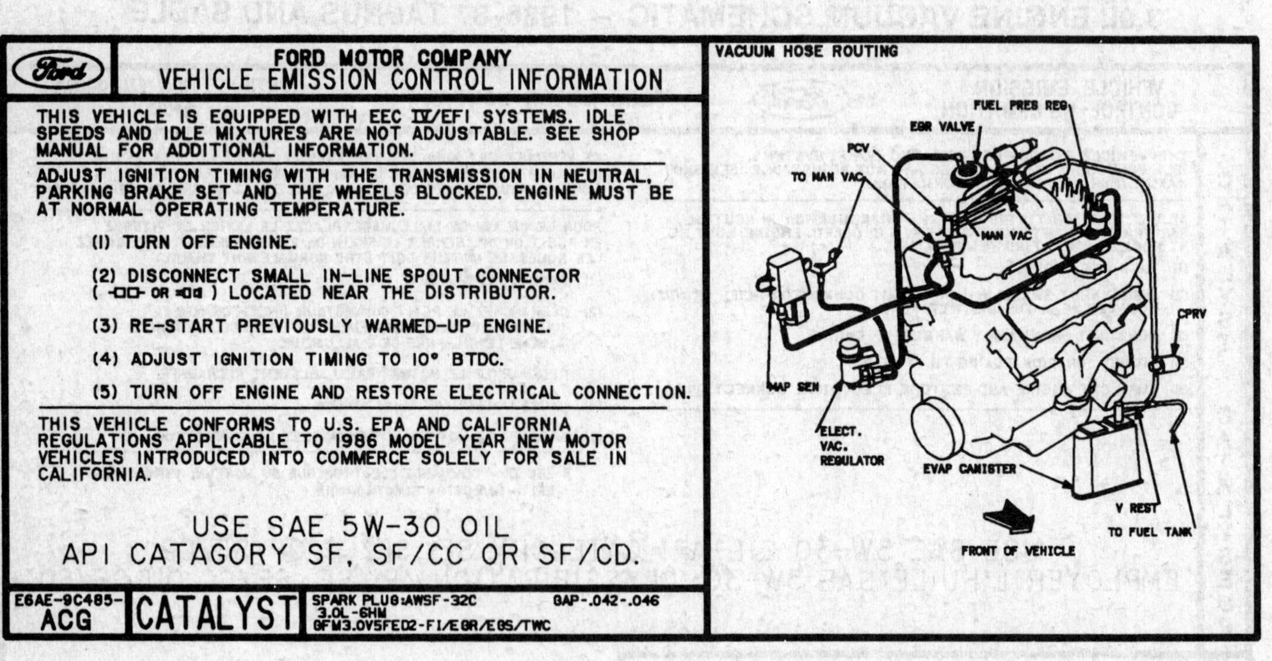
Ford — FORD MOTOR COMPANY
VEHICLE EMISSION CONTROL INFORMATION

THIS VEHICLE IS EQUIPPED WITH EEC IV/EFI SYSTEMS. IDLE SPEEDS AND IDLE MIXTURES ARE NOT ADJUSTABLE. SEE SHOP MANUAL FOR ADDITIONAL INFORMATION.

ADJUST IGNITION TIMING WITH THE TRANSMISSION IN NEUTRAL, PARKING BRAKE SET AND THE WHEELS BLOCKED. ENGINE MUST BE AT NORMAL OPERATING TEMPERATURE.

(1) TURN OFF ENGINE.

(2) DISCONNECT SMALL IN-LINE SPOUT CONNECTOR (-□□- OR =□◁) LOCATED NEAR THE DISTRIBUTOR.

(3) RE-START PREVIOUSLY WARMED-UP ENGINE.

(4) ADJUST IGNITION TIMING TO 10° BTDC.

(5) TURN OFF ENGINE AND RESTORE ELECTRICAL CONNECTION.

THIS VEHICLE CONFORMS TO U.S. EPA AND CALIFORNIA REGULATIONS APPLICABLE TO 1986 MODEL YEAR NEW MOTOR VEHICLES INTRODUCED INTO COMMERCE SOLELY FOR SALE IN CALIFORNIA.

USE SAE 5W-30 OIL
API CATAGORY SF, SF/CC OR SF/CD.

E6AE-9C485-ACG | CATALYST | SPARK PLUG:AWSF-32C GAP-.042-.046 3.0L-6HM GFM3.0V5FED2-FI/EGR/EGS/TWC

VACUUM HOSE ROUTING

3.0L ENGINE VACUUM SCHEMATIC – 1986–87 TAURUS AND SABLE

Ford

FORD MOTOR COMPANY
VEHICLE EMISSION CONTROL INFORMATION

THIS VEHICLE IS EQUIPPED WITH EEC IV/EFI SYSTEMS. IDLE SPEEDS AND IDLE MIXTURES ARE NOT ADJUSTABLE. SEE SHOP MANUAL FOR ADDITIONAL INFORMATION.

ADJUST IGNITION TIMING WITH THE TRANSMISSION IN NEUTRAL, PARKING BRAKE SET AND THE WHEELS BLOCKED. ENGINE MUST BE AT NORMAL OPERATING TEMPERATURE.

(1) TURN OFF ENGINE.

(2) DISCONNECT SMALL IN-LINE SPOUT CONNECTOR (-□□- OR =□◁) LOCATED NEAR THE DISTRIBUTOR.

(3) RE-START PREVIOUSLY WARMED-UP ENGINE.

(4) ADJUST IGNITION TIMING TO 10° BTDC.

(5) TURN OFF ENGINE AND RESTORE ELECTRICAL CONNECTION.

THIS VEHICLE CONFORMS TO U.S. EPA AND CALIFORNIA REGULATIONS APPLICABLE TO 1986 MODEL YEAR NEW MOTOR VEHICLES INTRODUCED INTO COMMERCE SOLELY FOR SALE IN CALIFORNIA.

USE SAE 5W-30 OIL
API CATAGORY SF, SF/CC OR SF/CD.

E6AE-9C485-ACG | CATALYST | SPARK PLUG:AWSF-32C GAP-.042-.046
3.0L-6HM
6FM3.0V5FED2-FI/EGR/EGS/TWC

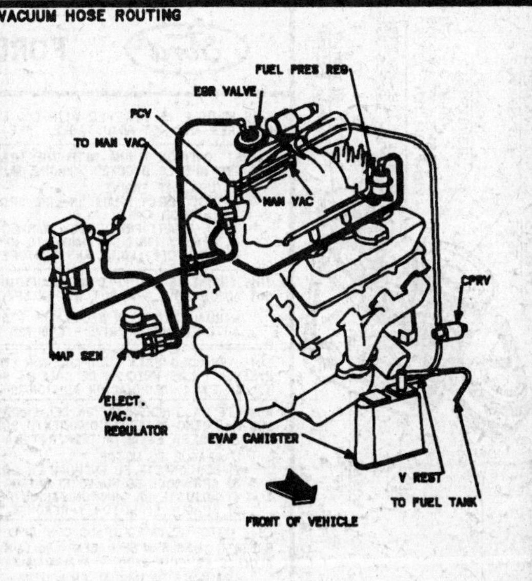

3.0L ENGINE VACUUM SCHEMATIC – 1986–87 TAURUS AND SABLE

Ford

FORD MOTOR COMPANY
VEHICLE EMISSION CONTROL INFORMATION

THIS VEHICLE IS EQUIPPED WITH EEC IV/EFI SYSTEMS. IDLE SPEEDS AND IDLE MIXTURES ARE NOT ADJUSTABLE. SEE SHOP MANUAL FOR ADDITIONAL INFORMATION.

ADJUST IGNITION TIMING WITH THE TRANSMISSION IN NEUTRAL, PARKING BRAKE SET AND THE WHEELS BLOCKED. ENGINE MUST BE AT NORMAL OPERATING TEMPERATURE.

(1) TURN OFF ENGINE.

(2) DISCONNECT SMALL IN-LINE SPOUT CONNECTOR (-□□- OR =□◁) LOCATED NEAR THE DISTRIBUTOR.

(3) RE-START PREVIOUSLY WARMED-UP ENGINE.

(4) ADJUST IGNITION TIMING TO 10° BTDC.

(5) TURN OFF ENGINE AND RESTORE ELECTRICAL CONNECTION.

THIS VEHICLE CONFORMS TO U.S. EPA AND CALIFORNIA REGULATIONS APPLICABLE TO 1986 MODEL YEAR NEW MOTOR VEHICLES INTRODUCED INTO COMMERCE SOLELY FOR SALE IN CALIFORNIA.

USE SAE 5W-30 OIL
API CATAGORY SF, SF/CC OR SF/CD.

E6AE-9C485-ACG | CATALYST | SPARK PLUG:AWSF-32C GAP-.042-.046
3.0L-6HM
6FM3.0V5FED2-FI/EGR/EGS/TWC

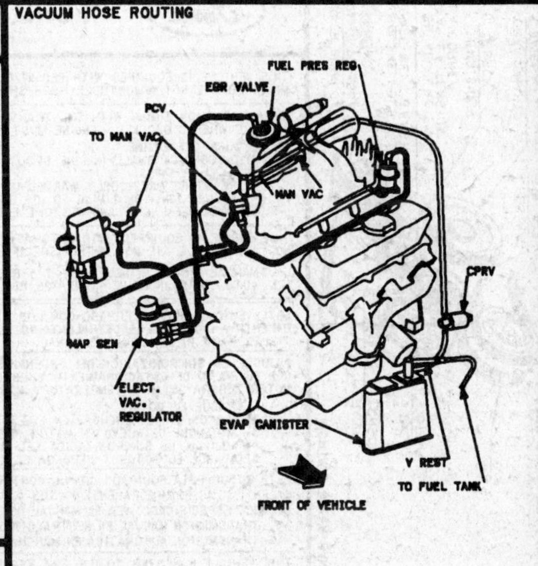

2.5L ENGINE VACUUM SCHEMATIC — 1986–87 TAURUS AND SABLE

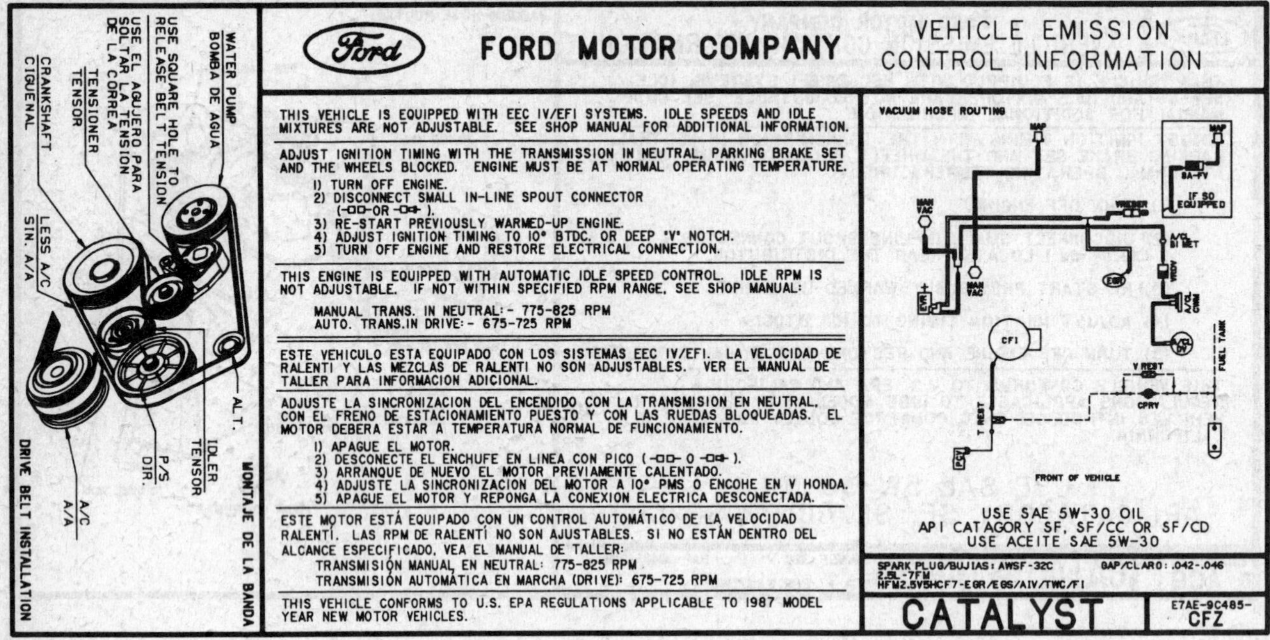

DRIVE BELT INSTALLATION
MONTAJE DE LA BANDA

WATER PUMP
BOMBA DE AGUA
USE SQUARE HOLE TO RELEASE BELT TENSION
USE EL AGUJERO PARA SOLTAR LA TENSION DE LA CORREA
TENSIONER
TENSOR
CRANKSHAFT
CIGUENAL
LESS A/C
SIN. A/A
ALT.
IDLER
TENSOR
P/S
DIR.
A/C
A/A

Ford — FORD MOTOR COMPANY — VEHICLE EMISSION CONTROL INFORMATION

THIS VEHICLE IS EQUIPPED WITH EEC IV/EFI SYSTEMS. IDLE SPEEDS AND IDLE MIXTURES ARE NOT ADJUSTABLE. SEE SHOP MANUAL FOR ADDITIONAL INFORMATION.

ADJUST IGNITION TIMING WITH THE TRANSMISSION IN NEUTRAL, PARKING BRAKE SET AND THE WHEELS BLOCKED. ENGINE MUST BE AT NORMAL OPERATING TEMPERATURE.
1) TURN OFF ENGINE.
2) DISCONNECT SMALL IN-LINE SPOUT CONNECTOR (-□□- OR -□□-).
3) RE-START PREVIOUSLY WARMED-UP ENGINE.
4) ADJUST IGNITION TIMING TO 10° BTDC. OR DEEP "V" NOTCH.
5) TURN OFF ENGINE AND RESTORE ELECTRICAL CONNECTION.

THIS ENGINE IS EQUIPPED WITH AUTOMATIC IDLE SPEED CONTROL. IDLE RPM IS NOT ADJUSTABLE. IF NOT WITHIN SPECIFIED RPM RANGE, SEE SHOP MANUAL:
MANUAL TRANS. IN NEUTRAL: - 775-825 RPM
AUTO. TRANS.IN DRIVE: - 675-725 RPM

ESTE VEHICULO ESTA EQUIPADO CON LOS SISTEMAS EEC IV/EFI. LA VELOCIDAD DE RALENTI Y LAS MEZCLAS DE RALENTI NO SON ADJUSTABLES. VER EL MANUAL DE TALLER PARA INFORMACION ADICIONAL.

ADJUSTE LA SINCRONIZACION DEL ENCENDIDO CON LA TRANSMISION EN NEUTRAL, CON EL FRENO DE ESTACIONAMIENTO PUESTO Y CON LAS RUEDAS BLOQUEADAS. EL MOTOR DEBERA ESTAR A TEMPERATURA NORMAL DE FUNCIONAMIENTO.
1) APAGUE EL MOTOR.
2) DESCONECTE EL ENCHUFE EN LINEA CON PICO (-□□- O -□□-).
3) ARRANQUE DE NUEVO EL MOTOR PREVIAMENTE CALENTADO.
4) ADJUSTE LA SINCRONIZACION DEL MOTOR A 10° PMS O ENCOHE EN V HONDA.
5) APAGUE EL MOTOR Y REPONGA LA CONEXION ELECTRICA DESCONECTADA.

ESTE MOTOR ESTÁ EQUIPADO CON UN CONTROL AUTOMÁTICO DE LA VELOCIDAD RALENTÍ. LAS RPM DE RALENTÍ NO SON AJUSTABLES. SI NO ESTÁN DENTRO DEL ALCANCE ESPECIFICADO, VEA EL MANUAL DE TALLER:
TRANSMISIÓN MANUAL EN NEUTRAL: 775-825 RPM
TRANSMISIÓN AUTOMÁTICA EN MARCHA (DRIVE): 675-725 RPM

THIS VEHICLE CONFORMS TO U.S. EPA REGULATIONS APPLICABLE TO 1987 MODEL YEAR NEW MOTOR VEHICLES.

VACUUM HOSE ROUTING
MAP
SA-FV
IF SO EQUIPPED
MAN VAC
WEBER
A/CL BI MET
EGR
CFI
V REST
CPRV
T REST
FUEL TANK
FRONT OF VEHICLE

USE SAE 5W-30 OIL
API CATAGORY SF, SF/CC OR SF/CD
USE ACEITE SAE 5W-30

SPARK PLUG/BUJIAS: AWSF-32C GAP/CLARO: .042-.046
2.5L-7FM
HFM2.5V5HCF7-EGR/EGS/AIV/TWC/FI

CATALYST

E7AE-9C485-CFZ

2.5L ENGINE VACUUM SCHEMATIC — 1986–87 TAURUS AND SABLE

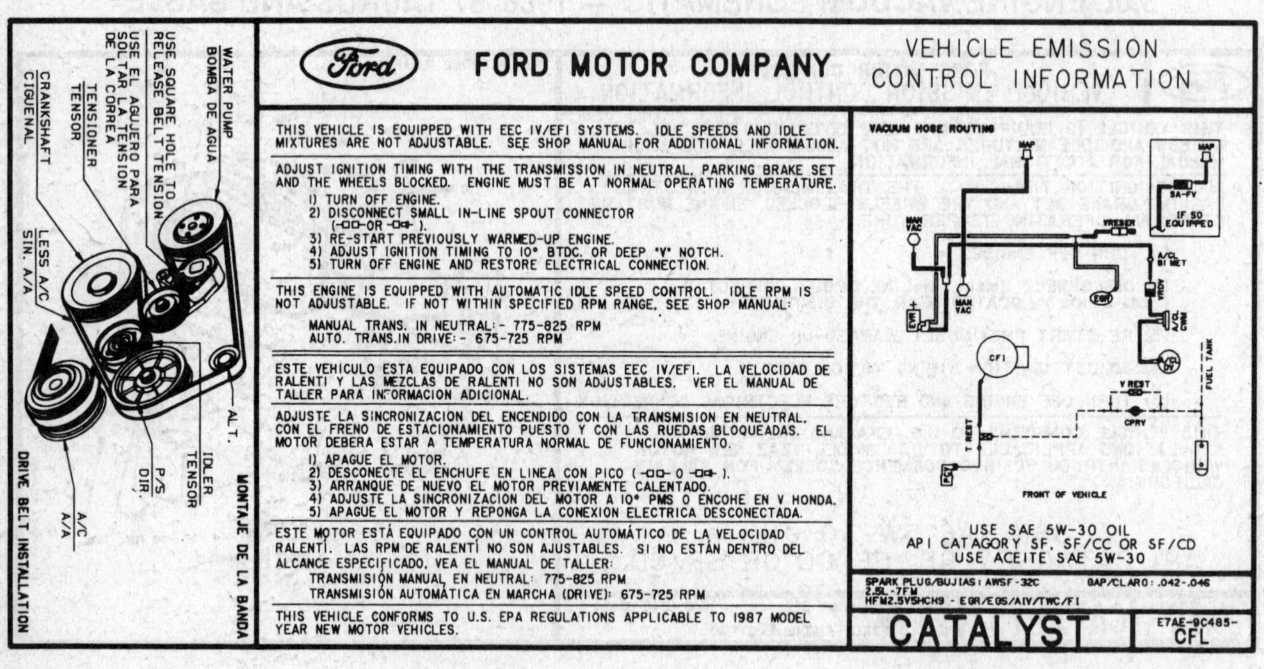

DRIVE BELT INSTALLATION
MONTAJE DE LA BANDA

WATER PUMP
BOMBA DE AGUA
USE SQUARE HOLE TO RELEASE BELT TENSION
USE EL AGUJERO PARA SOLTAR LA TENSION DE LA CORREA
TENSIONER
TENSOR
CRANKSHAFT
CIGUENAL
LESS A/C
SIN. A/A
ALT.
IDLER
TENSOR
P/S
DIR.
A/C
A/A

Ford — FORD MOTOR COMPANY — VEHICLE EMISSION CONTROL INFORMATION

THIS VEHICLE IS EQUIPPED WITH EEC IV/EFI SYSTEMS. IDLE SPEEDS AND IDLE MIXTURES ARE NOT ADJUSTABLE. SEE SHOP MANUAL FOR ADDITIONAL INFORMATION.

ADJUST IGNITION TIMING WITH THE TRANSMISSION IN NEUTRAL, PARKING BRAKE SET AND THE WHEELS BLOCKED. ENGINE MUST BE AT NORMAL OPERATING TEMPERATURE.
1) TURN OFF ENGINE.
2) DISCONNECT SMALL IN-LINE SPOUT CONNECTOR (-□□- OR -□□-).
3) RE-START PREVIOUSLY WARMED-UP ENGINE.
4) ADJUST IGNITION TIMING TO 10° BTDC. OR DEEP "V" NOTCH.
5) TURN OFF ENGINE AND RESTORE ELECTRICAL CONNECTION.

THIS ENGINE IS EQUIPPED WITH AUTOMATIC IDLE SPEED CONTROL. IDLE RPM IS NOT ADJUSTABLE. IF NOT WITHIN SPECIFIED RPM RANGE, SEE SHOP MANUAL:
MANUAL TRANS. IN NEUTRAL: - 775-825 RPM
AUTO. TRANS.IN DRIVE: - 675-725 RPM

ESTE VEHICULO ESTA EQUIPADO CON LOS SISTEMAS EEC IV/EFI. LA VELOCIDAD DE RALENTI Y LAS MEZCLAS DE RALENTI NO SON ADJUSTABLES. VER EL MANUAL DE TALLER PARA INFORMACION ADICIONAL.

ADJUSTE LA SINCRONIZACION DEL ENCENDIDO CON LA TRANSMISION EN NEUTRAL, CON EL FRENO DE ESTACIONAMIENTO PUESTO Y CON LAS RUEDAS BLOQUEADAS. EL MOTOR DEBERA ESTAR A TEMPERATURA NORMAL DE FUNCIONAMIENTO.
1) APAGUE EL MOTOR.
2) DESCONECTE EL ENCHUFE EN LINEA CON PICO (-□□- O -□□-).
3) ARRANQUE DE NUEVO EL MOTOR PREVIAMENTE CALENTADO.
4) ADJUSTE LA SINCRONIZACION DEL MOTOR A 10° PMS O ENCOHE EN V HONDA.
5) APAGUE EL MOTOR Y REPONGA LA CONEXION ELECTRICA DESCONECTADA.

ESTE MOTOR ESTÁ EQUIPADO CON UN CONTROL AUTOMÁTICO DE LA VELOCIDAD RALENTÍ. LAS RPM DE RALENTÍ NO SON AJUSTABLES. SI NO ESTÁN DENTRO DEL ALCANCE ESPECIFICADO, VEA EL MANUAL DE TALLER:
TRANSMISIÓN MANUAL EN NEUTRAL: 775-825 RPM
TRANSMISIÓN AUTOMÁTICA EN MARCHA (DRIVE): 675-725 RPM

THIS VEHICLE CONFORMS TO U.S. EPA REGULATIONS APPLICABLE TO 1987 MODEL YEAR NEW MOTOR VEHICLES.

VACUUM HOSE ROUTING
MAP
SA-FV
IF SO EQUIPPED
MAN VAC
VREBER
A/CL BI MET
EGR
CFI
V REST
CPRV
T REST
FUEL TANK
FRONT OF VEHICLE

USE SAE 5W-30 OIL
API CATAGORY SF, SF/CC OR SF/CD
USE ACEITE SAE 5W-30

SPARK PLUG/BUJIAS: AWSF-32C GAP/CLARO: .042-.046
2.5L-7FM
HFM2.5V5HCH9 - EGR/EGS/AIV/TWC/FI

CATALYST

E7AE-9C485-CFL

2.5L ENGINE VACUUM SCHEMATIC – 1986–87 TAURUS AND SABLE

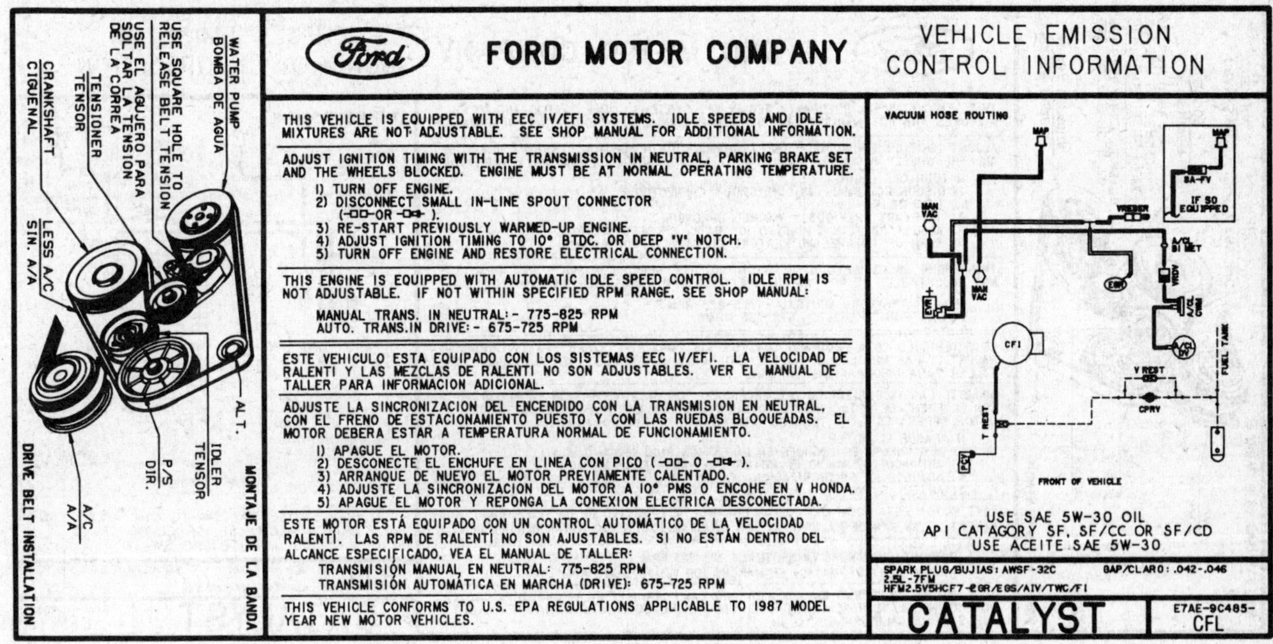

WATER PUMP
BOMBA DE AGUA
USE SQUARE HOLE TO RELEASE BELT TENSION
USE EL AGUJERO PARA SOLTAR LA TENSION DE LA CORREA
TENSIONER
TENSOR
CRANKSHAFT
CIGUENAL
LESS A/C
SIN. A/A
ALT.
IDLER
TENSOR
P/S
DIR.
A/C
A/A
DRIVE BELT INSTALLATION
MONTAJE DE LA BANDA

FORD MOTOR COMPANY
VEHICLE EMISSION CONTROL INFORMATION

THIS VEHICLE IS EQUIPPED WITH EEC IV/EFI SYSTEMS. IDLE SPEEDS AND IDLE MIXTURES ARE NOT ADJUSTABLE. SEE SHOP MANUAL FOR ADDITIONAL INFORMATION.

ADJUST IGNITION TIMING WITH THE TRANSMISSION IN NEUTRAL, PARKING BRAKE SET AND THE WHEELS BLOCKED. ENGINE MUST BE AT NORMAL OPERATING TEMPERATURE.

1) TURN OFF ENGINE.
2) DISCONNECT SMALL IN-LINE SPOUT CONNECTOR (-□□- OR -□◁-).
3) RE-START PREVIOUSLY WARMED-UP ENGINE.
4) ADJUST IGNITION TIMING TO 10° BTDC. OR DEEP 'V' NOTCH.
5) TURN OFF ENGINE AND RESTORE ELECTRICAL CONNECTION.

THIS ENGINE IS EQUIPPED WITH AUTOMATIC IDLE SPEED CONTROL. IDLE RPM IS NOT ADJUSTABLE. IF NOT WITHIN SPECIFIED RPM RANGE, SEE SHOP MANUAL:

MANUAL TRANS. IN NEUTRAL:- 775-825 RPM
AUTO. TRANS.IN DRIVE:- 675-725 RPM

ESTE VEHICULO ESTA EQUIPADO CON LOS SISTEMAS EEC IV/EFI. LA VELOCIDAD DE RALENTI Y LAS MEZCLAS DE RALENTI NO SON ADJUSTABLES. VER EL MANUAL DE TALLER PARA INFORMACION ADICIONAL.

ADJUSTE LA SINCRONIZACION DEL ENCENDIDO CON LA TRANSMISION EN NEUTRAL, CON EL FRENO DE ESTACIONAMIENTO PUESTO Y CON LAS RUEDAS BLOQUEADAS. EL MOTOR DEBERA ESTAR A TEMPERATURA NORMAL DE FUNCIONAMIENTO.

1) APAGUE EL MOTOR.
2) DESCONECTE EL ENCHUFE EN LINEA CON PICO (-□□- O -□◁-).
3) ARRANQUE DE NUEVO EL MOTOR PREVIAMENTE CALENTADO.
4) ADJUSTE LA SINCRONIZACION DEL MOTOR A 10° PMS O ENCOHE EN V HONDA.
5) APAGUE EL MOTOR Y REPONGA LA CONEXION ELECTRICA DESCONECTADA.

ESTE MOTOR ESTÁ EQUIPADO CON UN CONTROL AUTOMÁTICO DE LA VELOCIDAD RALENTÍ. LAS RPM DE RALENTÍ NO SON AJUSTABLES. SI NO ESTÁN DENTRO DEL ALCANCE ESPECIFICADO, VEA EL MANUAL DE TALLER:

TRANSMISIÓN MANUAL EN NEUTRAL: 775-825 RPM
TRANSMISIÓN AUTOMÁTICA EN MARCHA (DRIVE): 675-725 RPM

THIS VEHICLE CONFORMS TO U.S. EPA REGULATIONS APPLICABLE TO 1987 MODEL YEAR NEW MOTOR VEHICLES.

USE SAE 5W-30 OIL
API CATAGORY SF, SF/CC OR SF/CD
USE ACEITE SAE 5W-30

SPARK PLUG/BUJIAS: AWSF-32C GAP/CLARO: .042-.046
2.5L-7FM
HFM2.5V5HCF7-EGR/EGS/AIV/TWC/FI

CATALYST

E7AE-9C485-CFL

2.5L ENGINE VACUUM SCHEMATIC – 1986–87 TAURUS AND SABLE

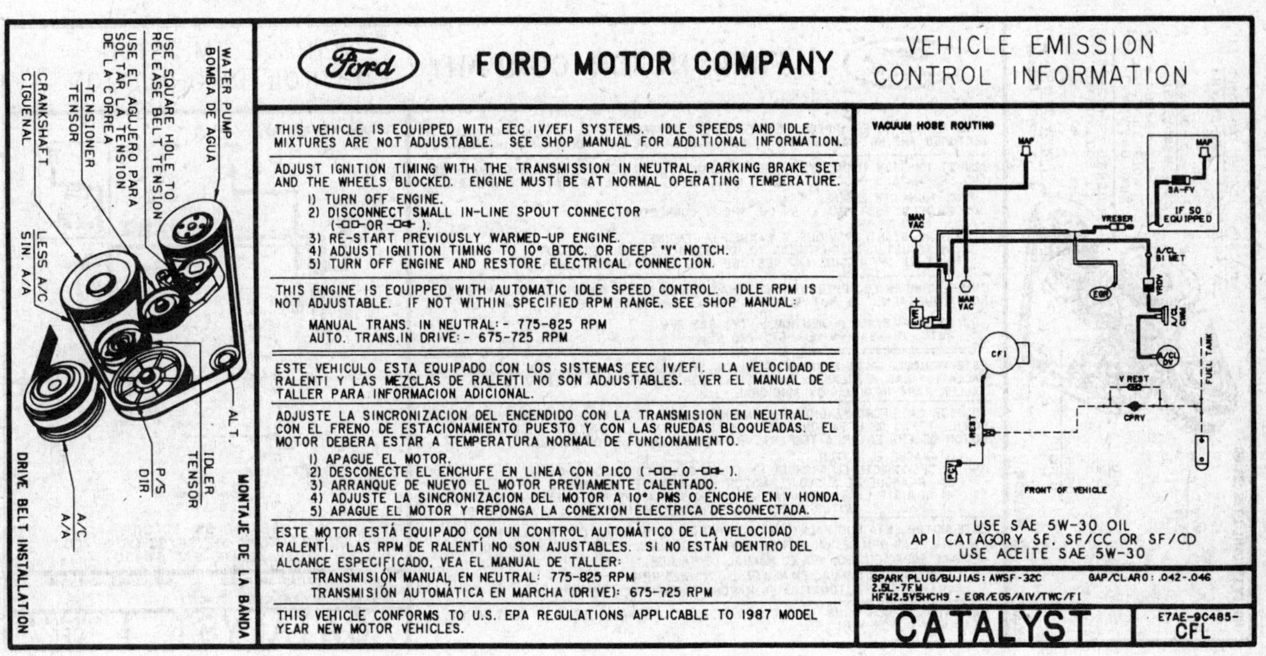

WATER PUMP
BOMBA DE AGUA
USE SQUARE HOLE TO RELEASE BELT TENSION
USE EL AGUJERO PARA SOLTAR LA TENSION DE LA CORREA
TENSIONER
TENSOR
CRANKSHAFT
CIGUENAL
LESS A/C
SIN. A/A
ALT.
IDLER
TENSOR
P/S
DIR.
A/C
A/A
DRIVE BELT INSTALLATION
MONTAJE DE LA BANDA

FORD MOTOR COMPANY
VEHICLE EMISSION CONTROL INFORMATION

THIS VEHICLE IS EQUIPPED WITH EEC IV/EFI SYSTEMS. IDLE SPEEDS AND IDLE MIXTURES ARE NOT ADJUSTABLE. SEE SHOP MANUAL FOR ADDITIONAL INFORMATION.

ADJUST IGNITION TIMING WITH THE TRANSMISSION IN NEUTRAL, PARKING BRAKE SET AND THE WHEELS BLOCKED. ENGINE MUST BE AT NORMAL OPERATING TEMPERATURE.

1) TURN OFF ENGINE.
2) DISCONNECT SMALL IN-LINE SPOUT CONNECTOR (-□□- OR -□◁-).
3) RE-START PREVIOUSLY WARMED-UP ENGINE.
4) ADJUST IGNITION TIMING TO 10° BTDC. OR DEEP 'V' NOTCH.
5) TURN OFF ENGINE AND RESTORE ELECTRICAL CONNECTION.

THIS ENGINE IS EQUIPPED WITH AUTOMATIC IDLE SPEED CONTROL. IDLE RPM IS NOT ADJUSTABLE. IF NOT WITHIN SPECIFIED RPM RANGE, SEE SHOP MANUAL:

MANUAL TRANS. IN NEUTRAL:- 775-825 RPM
AUTO. TRANS.IN DRIVE:- 675-725 RPM

ESTE VEHICULO ESTA EQUIPADO CON LOS SISTEMAS EEC IV/EFI. LA VELOCIDAD DE RALENTI Y LAS MEZCLAS DE RALENTI NO SON ADJUSTABLES. VER EL MANUAL DE TALLER PARA INFORMACION ADICIONAL.

ADJUSTE LA SINCRONIZACION DEL ENCENDIDO CON LA TRANSMISION EN NEUTRAL, CON EL FRENO DE ESTACIONAMIENTO PUESTO Y CON LAS RUEDAS BLOQUEADAS. EL MOTOR DEBERA ESTAR A TEMPERATURA NORMAL DE FUNCIONAMIENTO.

1) APAGUE EL MOTOR.
2) DESCONECTE EL ENCHUFE EN LINEA CON PICO (-□□- O -□◁-).
3) ARRANQUE DE NUEVO EL MOTOR PREVIAMENTE CALENTADO.
4) ADJUSTE LA SINCRONIZACION DEL MOTOR A 10° PMS O ENCOHE EN V HONDA.
5) APAGUE EL MOTOR Y REPONGA LA CONEXION ELECTRICA DESCONECTADA.

ESTE MOTOR ESTÁ EQUIPADO CON UN CONTROL AUTOMÁTICO DE LA VELOCIDAD RALENTÍ. LAS RPM DE RALENTÍ NO SON AJUSTABLES. SI NO ESTÁN DENTRO DEL ALCANCE ESPECIFICADO, VEA EL MANUAL DE TALLER:

TRANSMISIÓN MANUAL EN NEUTRAL: 775-825 RPM
TRANSMISIÓN AUTOMÁTICA EN MARCHA (DRIVE): 675-725 RPM

THIS VEHICLE CONFORMS TO U.S. EPA REGULATIONS APPLICABLE TO 1987 MODEL YEAR NEW MOTOR VEHICLES.

USE SAE 5W-30 OIL
API CATAGORY SF, SF/CC OR SF/CD
USE ACEITE SAE 5W-30

SPARK PLUG/BUJIAS: AWSF-32C GAP/CLARO: .042-.046
2.5L-7FM
HFM2.5V5HCH9 - EGR/EGS/AIV/TWC/FI

CATALYST

E7AE-9C485-CFL

2.5L ENGINE VACUUM SCHEMATIC — 1986–87 TAURUS AND SABLE

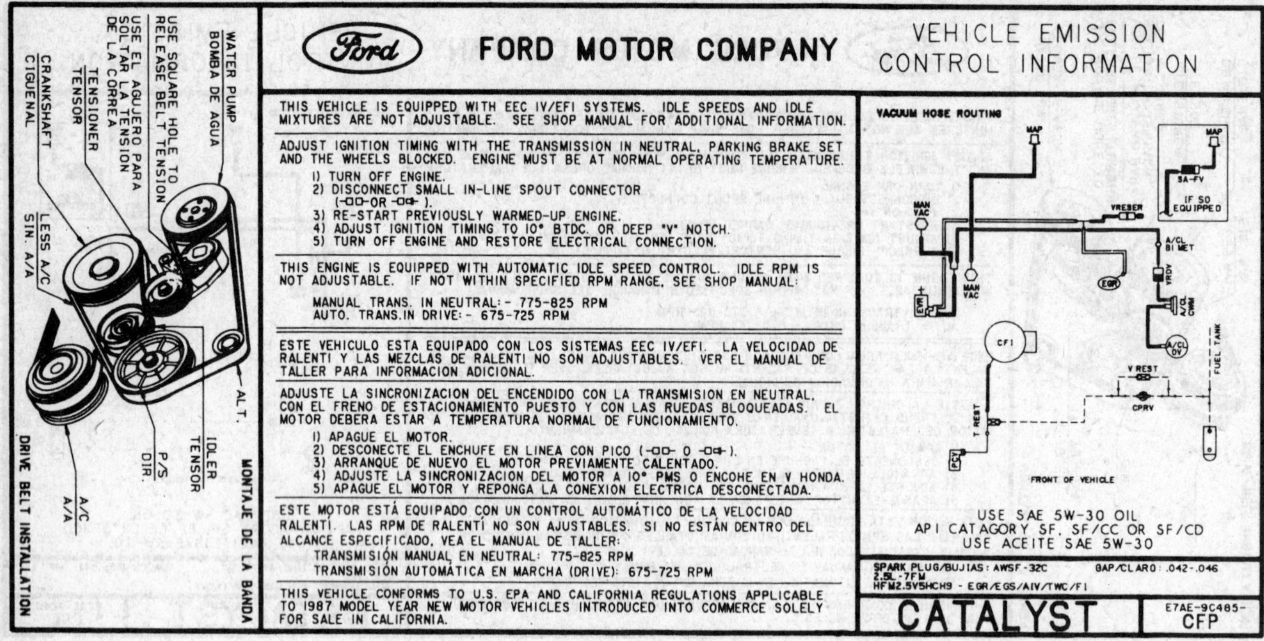

FORD MOTOR COMPANY

VEHICLE EMISSION CONTROL INFORMATION

THIS VEHICLE IS EQUIPPED WITH EEC IV/EFI SYSTEMS. IDLE SPEEDS AND IDLE MIXTURES ARE NOT ADJUSTABLE. SEE SHOP MANUAL FOR ADDITIONAL INFORMATION.

ADJUST IGNITION TIMING WITH THE TRANSMISSION IN NEUTRAL, PARKING BRAKE SET AND THE WHEELS BLOCKED. ENGINE MUST BE AT NORMAL OPERATING TEMPERATURE.

1) TURN OFF ENGINE.
2) DISCONNECT SMALL IN-LINE SPOUT CONNECTOR (-◻◻-OR -◻◻-).
3) RE-START PREVIOUSLY WARMED-UP ENGINE.
4) ADJUST IGNITION TIMING TO 10° BTDC. OR DEEP "V" NOTCH.
5) TURN OFF ENGINE AND RESTORE ELECTRICAL CONNECTION.

THIS ENGINE IS EQUIPPED WITH AUTOMATIC IDLE SPEED CONTROL. IDLE RPM IS NOT ADJUSTABLE. IF NOT WITHIN SPECIFIED RPM RANGE, SEE SHOP MANUAL:

MANUAL TRANS. IN NEUTRAL: - 775-825 RPM
AUTO. TRANS. IN DRIVE: - 675-725 RPM

ESTE VEHICULO ESTA EQUIPADO CON LOS SISTEMAS EEC IV/EFI. LA VELOCIDAD DE RALENTI Y LAS MEZCLAS DE RALENTI NO SON ADJUSTABLES. VER EL MANUAL DE TALLER PARA INFORMACION ADICIONAL.

ADJUSTE LA SINCRONIZACION DEL ENCENDIDO CON LA TRANSMISION EN NEUTRAL, CON EL FRENO DE ESTACIONAMIENTO PUESTO Y CON LAS RUEDAS BLOQUEADAS. EL MOTOR DEBERA ESTAR A TEMPERATURA NORMAL DE FUNCIONAMIENTO.

1) APAGUE EL MOTOR.
2) DESCONECTE EL ENCHUFE EN LINEA CON PICO (-◻◻- O -◻◻-).
3) ARRANQUE DE NUEVO EL MOTOR PREVIAMENTE CALENTADO.
4) ADJUSTE LA SINCRONIZACION DEL MOTOR A 10° PMS O ENCOHE EN V HONDA.
5) APAGUE EL MOTOR Y REPONGA LA CONEXION ELECTRICA DESCONECTADA.

ESTE MOTOR ESTÁ EQUIPADO CON UN CONTROL AUTOMÁTICO DE LA VELOCIDAD RALENTÍ. LAS RPM DE RALENTÍ NO SON AJUSTABLES. SI NO ESTÁN DENTRO DEL ALCANCE ESPECIFICADO, VEA EL MANUAL DE TALLER:
TRANSMISIÓN MANUAL EN NEUTRAL: 775-825 RPM
TRANSMISIÓN AUTOMÁTICA EN MARCHA (DRIVE): 675-725 RPM

THIS VEHICLE CONFORMS TO U.S. EPA AND CALIFORNIA REGULATIONS APPLICABLE TO 1987 MODEL YEAR NEW MOTOR VEHICLES INTRODUCED INTO COMMERCE SOLELY FOR SALE IN CALIFORNIA.

USE SAE 5W-30 OIL
API CATAGORY SF, SF/CC OR SF/CD
USE ACEITE SAE 5W-30

SPARK PLUG/BUJIAS: AWSF-32C GAP/CLARO: .042-.046
2.5L-7FM
HFM2.5V5HCH9 - EGR/EGS/AIV/TWC/FI

CATALYST

E7AE-9C485-CFP

2.5L ENGINE VACUUM SCHEMATIC — 1986–87 TAURUS AND SABLE

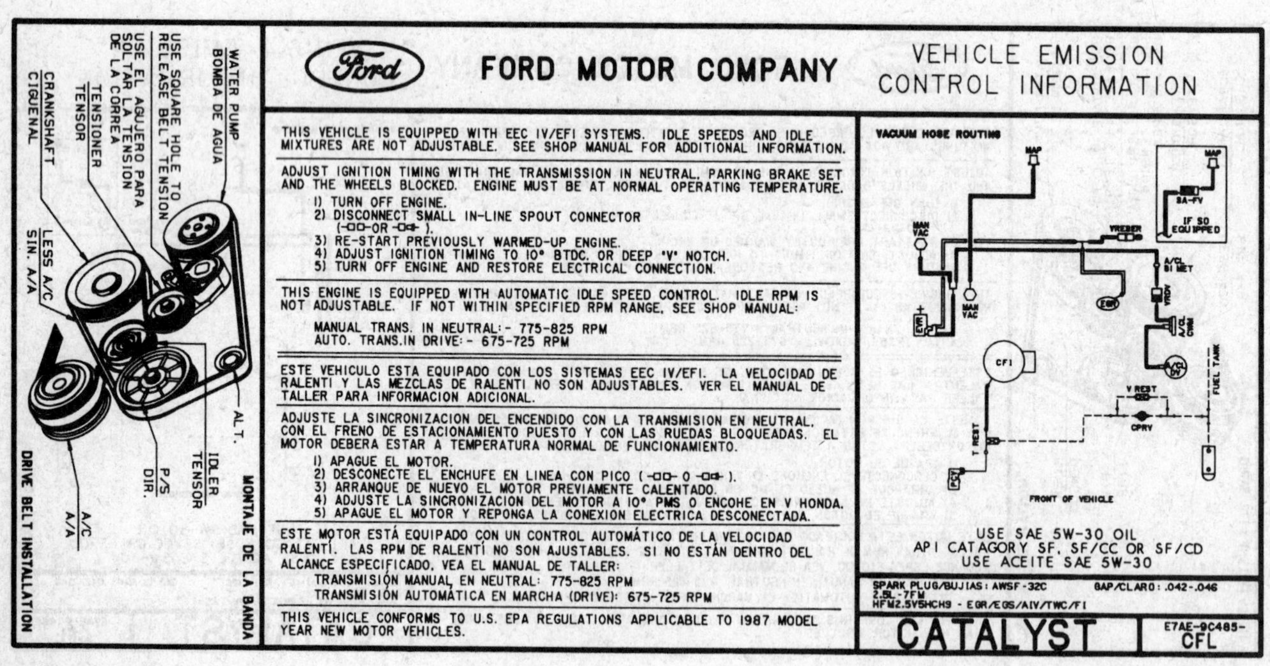

FORD MOTOR COMPANY

VEHICLE EMISSION CONTROL INFORMATION

THIS VEHICLE IS EQUIPPED WITH EEC IV/EFI SYSTEMS. IDLE SPEEDS AND IDLE MIXTURES ARE NOT ADJUSTABLE. SEE SHOP MANUAL FOR ADDITIONAL INFORMATION.

ADJUST IGNITION TIMING WITH THE TRANSMISSION IN NEUTRAL, PARKING BRAKE SET AND THE WHEELS BLOCKED. ENGINE MUST BE AT NORMAL OPERATING TEMPERATURE.

1) TURN OFF ENGINE.
2) DISCONNECT SMALL IN-LINE SPOUT CONNECTOR (-◻◻-OR -◻◻-).
3) RE-START PREVIOUSLY WARMED-UP ENGINE.
4) ADJUST IGNITION TIMING TO 10° BTDC. OR DEEP "V" NOTCH.
5) TURN OFF ENGINE AND RESTORE ELECTRICAL CONNECTION.

THIS ENGINE IS EQUIPPED WITH AUTOMATIC IDLE SPEED CONTROL. IDLE RPM IS NOT ADJUSTABLE. IF NOT WITHIN SPECIFIED RPM RANGE, SEE SHOP MANUAL:

MANUAL TRANS. IN NEUTRAL: - 775-825 RPM
AUTO. TRANS. IN DRIVE: - 675-725 RPM

ESTE VEHICULO ESTA EQUIPADO CON LOS SISTEMAS EEC IV/EFI. LA VELOCIDAD DE RALENTI Y LAS MEZCLAS DE RALENTI NO SON ADJUSTABLES. VER EL MANUAL DE TALLER PARA INFORMACION ADICIONAL.

ADJUSTE LA SINCRONIZACION DEL ENCENDIDO CON LA TRANSMISION EN NEUTRAL, CON EL FRENO DE ESTACIONAMIENTO PUESTO Y CON LAS RUEDAS BLOQUEADAS. EL MOTOR DEBERA ESTAR A TEMPERATURA NORMAL DE FUNCIONAMIENTO.

1) APAGUE EL MOTOR.
2) DESCONECTE EL ENCHUFE EN LINEA CON PICO (-◻◻- O -◻◻-).
3) ARRANQUE DE NUEVO EL MOTOR PREVIAMENTE CALENTADO.
4) ADJUSTE LA SINCRONIZACION DEL MOTOR A 10° PMS O ENCOHE EN V HONDA.
5) APAGUE EL MOTOR Y REPONGA LA CONEXION ELECTRICA DESCONECTADA.

ESTE MOTOR ESTÁ EQUIPADO CON UN CONTROL AUTOMÁTICO DE LA VELOCIDAD RALENTÍ. LAS RPM DE RALENTÍ NO SON AJUSTABLES. SI NO ESTÁN DENTRO DEL ALCANCE ESPECIFICADO, VEA EL MANUAL DE TALLER:
TRANSMISIÓN MANUAL EN NEUTRAL: 775-825 RPM
TRANSMISIÓN AUTOMÁTICA EN MARCHA (DRIVE): 675-725 RPM

THIS VEHICLE CONFORMS TO U.S. EPA REGULATIONS APPLICABLE TO 1987 MODEL YEAR NEW MOTOR VEHICLES.

USE SAE 5W-30 OIL
API CATAGORY SF, SF/CC OR SF/CD
USE ACEITE SAE 5W-30

SPARK PLUG/BUJIAS: AWSF-32C GAP/CLARO: .042-.046
2.5L-7FM
HFM2.5V5HCH9 - EGR/EGS/AIV/TWC/FI

CATALYST

E7AE-9C485-CFL

2.5L ENGINE VACUUM SCHEMATIC – 1986–87 TAURUS AND SABLE

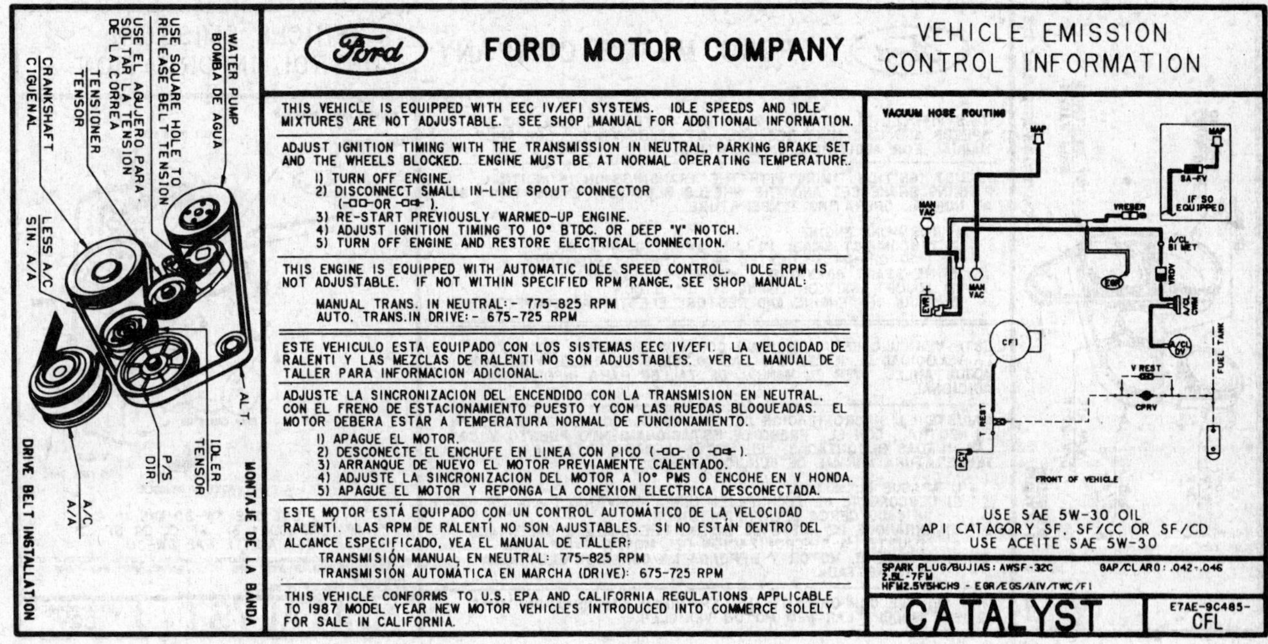

FORD MOTOR COMPANY

VEHICLE EMISSION CONTROL INFORMATION

THIS VEHICLE IS EQUIPPED WITH EEC IV/EFI SYSTEMS. IDLE SPEEDS AND IDLE MIXTURES ARE NOT ADJUSTABLE. SEE SHOP MANUAL FOR ADDITIONAL INFORMATION.

ADJUST IGNITION TIMING WITH THE TRANSMISSION IN NEUTRAL, PARKING BRAKE SET AND THE WHEELS BLOCKED. ENGINE MUST BE AT NORMAL OPERATING TEMPERATURE.

1) TURN OFF ENGINE.
2) DISCONNECT SMALL IN-LINE SPOUT CONNECTOR (-□□- OR -□⊲-).
3) RE-START PREVIOUSLY WARMED-UP ENGINE.
4) ADJUST IGNITION TIMING TO 10° BTDC. OR DEEP "V" NOTCH.
5) TURN OFF ENGINE AND RESTORE ELECTRICAL CONNECTION.

THIS ENGINE IS EQUIPPED WITH AUTOMATIC IDLE SPEED CONTROL. IDLE RPM IS NOT ADJUSTABLE. IF NOT WITHIN SPECIFIED RPM RANGE, SEE SHOP MANUAL:

MANUAL TRANS. IN NEUTRAL:- 775-825 RPM
AUTO. TRANS. IN DRIVE:- 675-725 RPM

ESTE VEHICULO ESTA EQUIPADO CON LOS SISTEMAS EEC IV/EFI. LA VELOCIDAD DE RALENTI Y LAS MEZCLAS DE RALENTI NO SON ADJUSTABLES. VER EL MANUAL DE TALLER PARA INFORMACION ADICIONAL.

ADJUSTE LA SINCRONIZACION DEL ENCENDIDO CON LA TRANSMISION EN NEUTRAL, CON EL FRENO DE ESTACIONAMIENTO PUESTO Y CON LAS RUEDAS BLOQUEADAS. EL MOTOR DEBERA ESTAR A TEMPERATURA NORMAL DE FUNCIONAMIENTO.

1) APAGUE EL MOTOR.
2) DESCONECTE EL ENCHUFE EN LINEA CON PICO (-□□- O -□⊲-).
3) ARRANQUE DE NUEVO EL MOTOR PREVIAMENTE CALENTADO.
4) ADJUSTE LA SINCRONIZACION DEL MOTOR A 10° PMS O ENCOHE EN V HONDA.
5) APAGUE EL MOTOR Y REPONGA LA CONEXION ELECTRICA DESCONECTADA.

ESTE MOTOR ESTÁ EQUIPADO CON UN CONTROL AUTOMÁTICO DE LA VELOCIDAD RALENTÍ. LAS RPM DE RALENTÍ NO SON AJUSTABLES. SI NO ESTÁN DENTRO DEL ALCANCE ESPECIFICADO, VEA EL MANUAL DE TALLER:

TRANSMISIÓN MANUAL EN NEUTRAL: 775-825 RPM
TRANSMISIÓN AUTOMÁTICA EN MARCHA (DRIVE): 675-725 RPM

THIS VEHICLE CONFORMS TO U.S. EPA AND CALIFORNIA REGULATIONS APPLICABLE TO 1987 MODEL YEAR NEW MOTOR VEHICLES INTRODUCED INTO COMMERCE SOLELY FOR SALE IN CALIFORNIA.

USE SAE 5W-30 OIL
API CATAGORY SF, SF/CC OR SF/CD
USE ACEITE SAE 5W-30

SPARK PLUG/BUJIAS: AWSF-32C GAP/CLARO: .042-.046
2.5L-7FM
HFM2.5V5HCH9 - EGR/EGS/AIV/TWC/FI

CATALYST

E7AE-9C485-CFL

3.0L ENGINE VACUUM SCHEMATIC – 1986–87 TAURUS AND SABLE

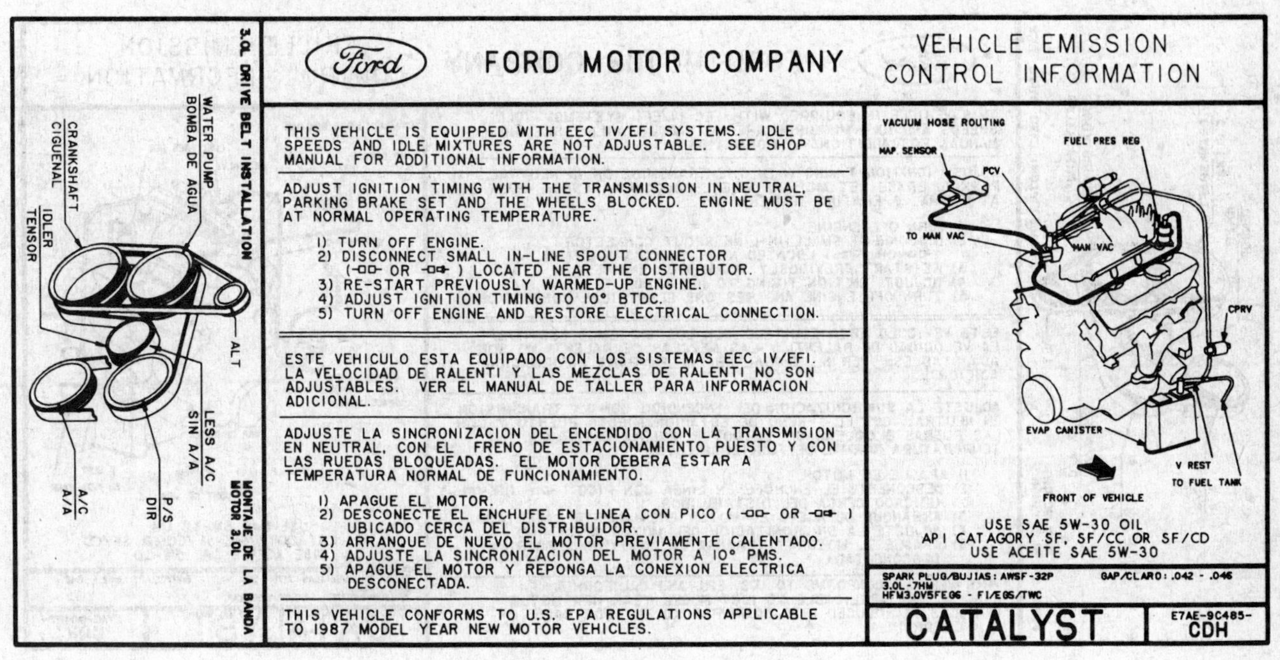

FORD MOTOR COMPANY

VEHICLE EMISSION CONTROL INFORMATION

THIS VEHICLE IS EQUIPPED WITH EEC IV/EFI SYSTEMS. IDLE SPEEDS AND IDLE MIXTURES ARE NOT ADJUSTABLE. SEE SHOP MANUAL FOR ADDITIONAL INFORMATION.

ADJUST IGNITION TIMING WITH THE TRANSMISSION IN NEUTRAL, PARKING BRAKE SET AND THE WHEELS BLOCKED. ENGINE MUST BE AT NORMAL OPERATING TEMPERATURE.

1) TURN OFF ENGINE.
2) DISCONNECT SMALL IN-LINE SPOUT CONNECTOR (-□□- OR -□⊲-) LOCATED NEAR THE DISTRIBUTOR.
3) RE-START PREVIOUSLY WARMED-UP ENGINE.
4) ADJUST IGNITION TIMING TO 10° BTDC.
5) TURN OFF ENGINE AND RESTORE ELECTRICAL CONNECTION.

ESTE VEHICULO ESTA EQUIPADO CON LOS SISTEMAS EEC IV/EFI. LA VELOCIDAD DE RALENTI Y LAS MEZCLAS DE RALENTI NO SON ADJUSTABLES. VER EL MANUAL DE TALLER PARA INFORMACION ADICIONAL.

ADJUSTE LA SINCRONIZACION DEL ENCENDIDO CON LA TRANSMISION EN NEUTRAL, CON EL FRENO DE ESTACIONAMIENTO PUESTO Y CON LAS RUEDAS BLOQUEADAS. EL MOTOR DEBERA ESTAR A TEMPERATURA NORMAL DE FUNCIONAMIENTO.

1) APAGUE EL MOTOR.
2) DESCONECTE EL ENCHUFE EN LINEA CON PICO (-□□- OR -□⊲-) UBICADO CERCA DEL DISTRIBUIDOR.
3) ARRANQUE DE NUEVO EL MOTOR PREVIAMENTE CALENTADO.
4) ADJUSTE LA SINCRONIZACION DEL MOTOR A 10° PMS.
5) APAGUE EL MOTOR Y REPONGA LA CONEXION ELECTRICA DESCONECTADA.

THIS VEHICLE CONFORMS TO U.S. EPA REGULATIONS APPLICABLE TO 1987 MODEL YEAR NEW MOTOR VEHICLES.

USE SAE 5W-30 OIL
API CATAGORY SF, SF/CC OR SF/CD
USE ACEITE SAE 5W-30

SPARK PLUG/BUJIAS: AWSF-32P GAP/CLARO: .042 - .046
3.0L-7HM
HFM3.0V5FEG6 - FI/EGS/TWC

CATALYST

E7AE-9C485-CDH

3.0L ENGINE VACUUM SCHEMATIC – 1986–87 TAURUS AND SABLE

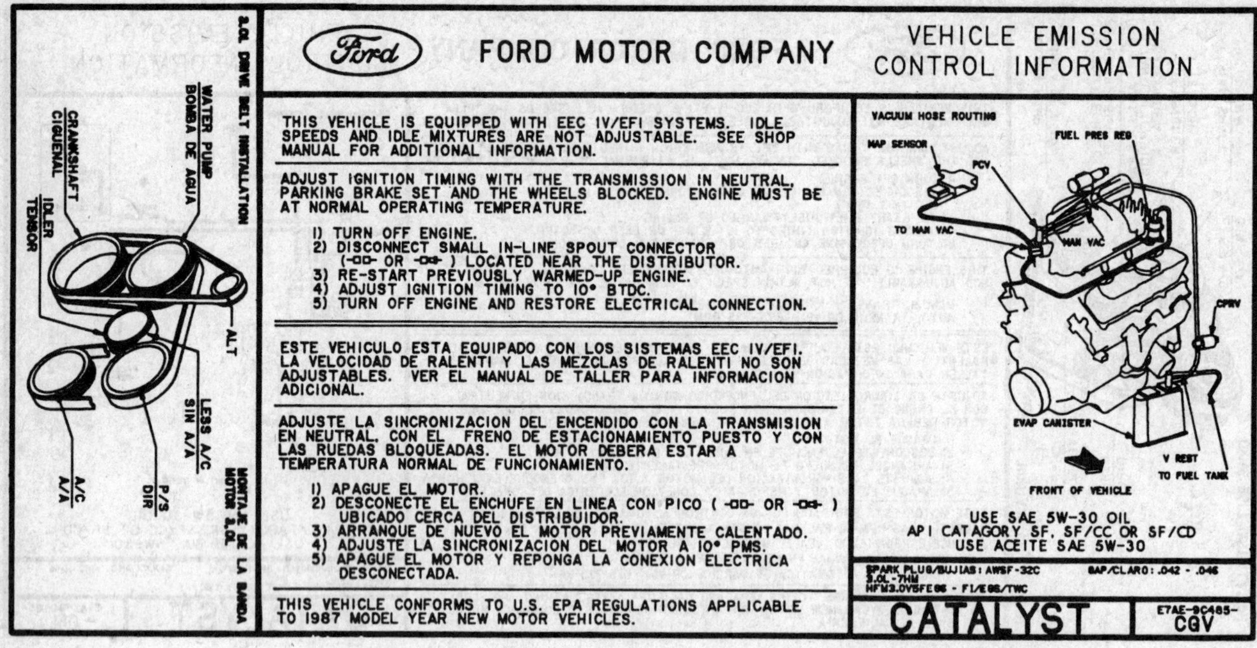

3.0L ENGINE VACUUM SCHEMATIC – 1986–87 TAURUS AND SABLE

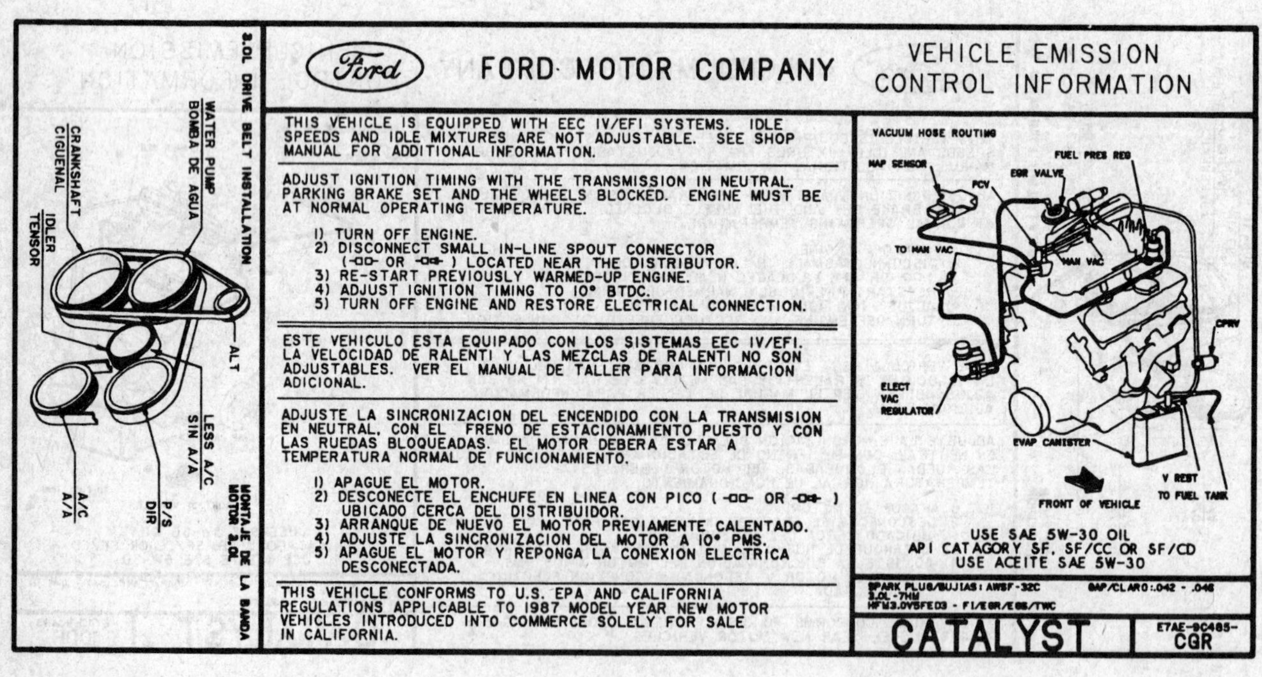

3.0L ENGINE VACUUM SCHEMATIC – 1986–87 TAURUS AND SABLE

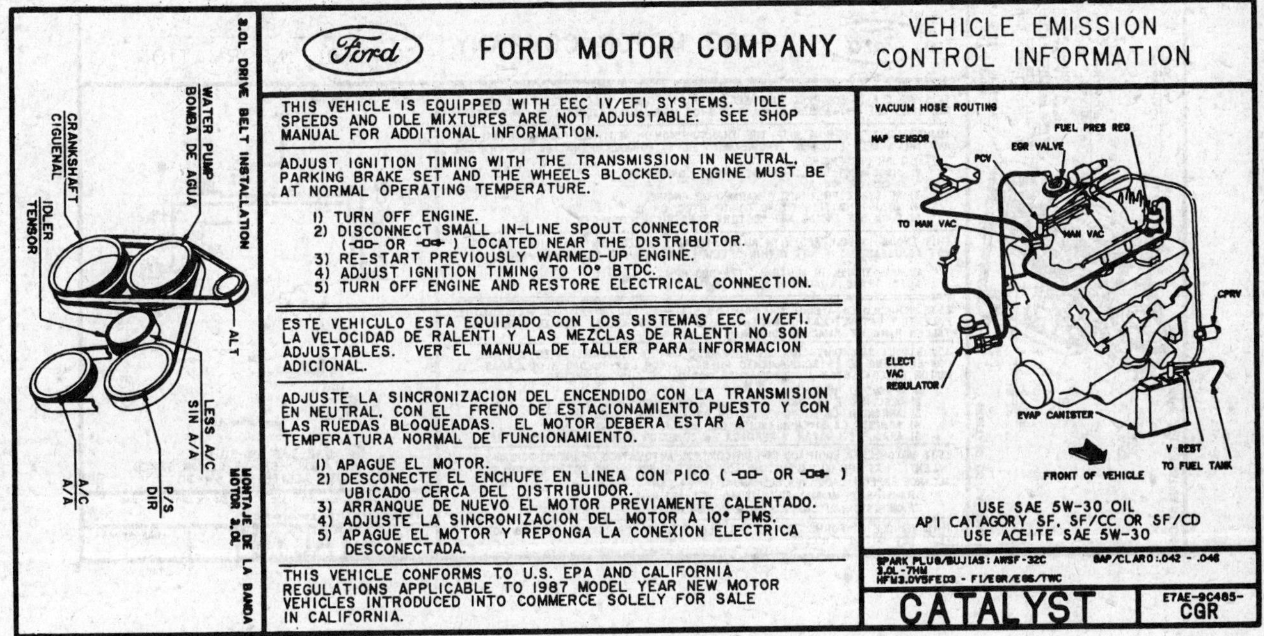

FORD MOTOR COMPANY

VEHICLE EMISSION CONTROL INFORMATION

THIS VEHICLE IS EQUIPPED WITH EEC IV/EFI SYSTEMS. IDLE SPEEDS AND IDLE MIXTURES ARE NOT ADJUSTABLE. SEE SHOP MANUAL FOR ADDITIONAL INFORMATION.

ADJUST IGNITION TIMING WITH THE TRANSMISSION IN NEUTRAL, PARKING BRAKE SET AND THE WHEELS BLOCKED. ENGINE MUST BE AT NORMAL OPERATING TEMPERATURE.

1) TURN OFF ENGINE.
2) DISCONNECT SMALL IN-LINE SPOUT CONNECTOR (-□□- OR -□◁-) LOCATED NEAR THE DISTRIBUTOR.
3) RE-START PREVIOUSLY WARMED-UP ENGINE.
4) ADJUST IGNITION TIMING TO 10° BTDC.
5) TURN OFF ENGINE AND RESTORE ELECTRICAL CONNECTION.

ESTE VEHICULO ESTA EQUIPADO CON LOS SISTEMAS EEC IV/EFI. LA VELOCIDAD DE RALENTI Y LAS MEZCLAS DE RALENTI NO SON ADJUSTABLES. VER EL MANUAL DE TALLER PARA INFORMACION ADICIONAL.

ADJUSTE LA SINCRONIZACION DEL ENCENDIDO CON LA TRANSMISION EN NEUTRAL, CON EL FRENO DE ESTACIONAMIENTO PUESTO Y CON LAS RUEDAS BLOQUEADAS. EL MOTOR DEBERA ESTAR A TEMPERATURA NORMAL DE FUNCIONAMIENTO.

1) APAGUE EL MOTOR.
2) DESCONECTE EL ENCHUFE EN LINEA CON PICO (-□□- OR -□◁-) UBICADO CERCA DEL DISTRIBUIDOR.
3) ARRANQUE DE NUEVO EL MOTOR PREVIAMENTE CALENTADO.
4) ADJUSTE LA SINCRONIZACION DEL MOTOR A 10° PMS.
5) APAGUE EL MOTOR Y REPONGA LA CONEXION ELECTRICA DESCONECTADA.

THIS VEHICLE CONFORMS TO U.S. EPA AND CALIFORNIA REGULATIONS APPLICABLE TO 1987 MODEL YEAR NEW MOTOR VEHICLES INTRODUCED INTO COMMERCE SOLELY FOR SALE IN CALIFORNIA.

USE SAE 5W-30 OIL
API CATAGORY SF, SF/CC OR SF/CD
USE ACEITE SAE 5W-30

SPARK PLUG/BUJIAS: AWSF-32C GAP/CLARO:.042 - .046
3.0L-7HM
HFM3.0V5FED3 - FI/EGR/EGS/TWC

CATALYST

E7AE-9C485-CGR

2.5L ENGINE VACUUM SCHEMATIC – 1988 TAURUS AND SABLE

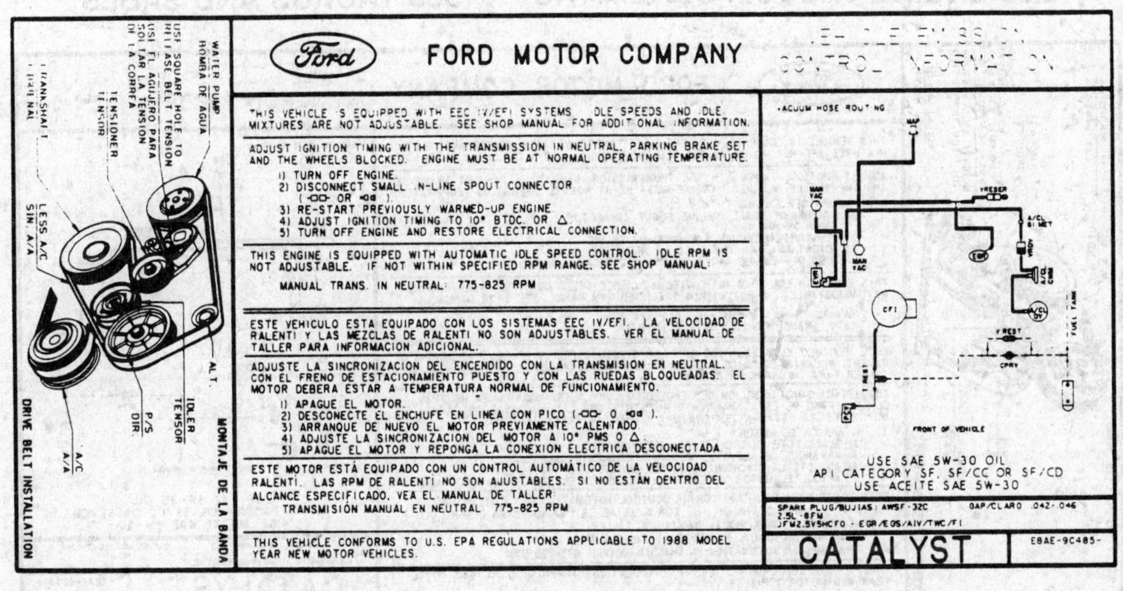

FORD MOTOR COMPANY

VEHICLE EMISSION CONTROL INFORMATION

THIS VEHICLE IS EQUIPPED WITH EEC IV/EFI SYSTEMS. IDLE SPEEDS AND IDLE MIXTURES ARE NOT ADJUSTABLE. SEE SHOP MANUAL FOR ADDITIONAL INFORMATION.

ADJUST IGNITION TIMING WITH THE TRANSMISSION IN NEUTRAL, PARKING BRAKE SET AND THE WHEELS BLOCKED. ENGINE MUST BE AT NORMAL OPERATING TEMPERATURE.

1) TURN OFF ENGINE.
2) DISCONNECT SMALL IN-LINE SPOUT CONNECTOR (-□□- OR ◁□).
3) RE-START PREVIOUSLY WARMED-UP ENGINE.
4) ADJUST IGNITION TIMING TO 10° BTDC. OR △.
5) TURN OFF ENGINE AND RESTORE ELECTRICAL CONNECTION.

THIS ENGINE IS EQUIPPED WITH AUTOMATIC IDLE SPEED CONTROL. IDLE RPM IS NOT ADJUSTABLE. IF NOT WITHIN SPECIFIED RPM RANGE, SEE SHOP MANUAL:

MANUAL TRANS. IN NEUTRAL: 775-825 RPM

ESTE VEHICULO ESTA EQUIPADO CON LOS SISTEMAS EEC IV/EFI. LA VELOCIDAD DE RALENTI Y LAS MEZCLAS DE RALENTI NO SON ADJUSTABLES. VER EL MANUAL DE TALLER PARA INFORMACION ADICIONAL.

ADJUSTE LA SINCRONIZACION DEL ENCENDIDO CON LA TRANSMISION EN NEUTRAL, CON EL FRENO DE ESTACIONAMIENTO PUESTO Y CON LAS RUEDAS BLOQUEADAS. EL MOTOR DEBERA ESTAR A TEMPERATURA NORMAL DE FUNCIONAMIENTO.

1) APAGUE EL MOTOR.
2) DESCONECTE EL ENCHUFE EN LINEA CON PICO (-□□- O ◁□).
3) ARRANQUE DE NUEVO EL MOTOR PREVIAMENTE CALENTADO.
4) ADJUSTE LA SINCRONIZACION DEL MOTOR A 10° PMS O △.
5) APAGUE EL MOTOR Y REPONGA LA CONEXION ELECTRICA DESCONECTADA.

ESTE MOTOR ESTÁ EQUIPADO CON UN CONTROL AUTOMÁTICO DE LA VELOCIDAD RALENTI. LAS RPM DE RALENTI NO SON AJUSTABLES. SI NO ESTÁN DENTRO DEL ALCANCE ESPECIFICADO, VEA EL MANUAL DE TALLER:

TRANSMISIÓN MANUAL EN NEUTRAL 775-825 RPM

THIS VEHICLE CONFORMS TO U.S. EPA REGULATIONS APPLICABLE TO 1988 MODEL YEAR NEW MOTOR VEHICLES.

USE SAE 5W-30 OIL
API CATEGORY SF, SF/CC OR SF/CD
USE ACEITE SAE 5W-30

SPARK PLUG/BUJIAS: AWSF-32C GAP/CLARO .042-.046
2.5L-8FM
JFM2.5V5HCFO - EGR/EGS/AIV/TWC/FI

CATALYST

E8AE-9C485-

2.5L ENGINE VACUUM SCHEMATIC – 1988 TAURUS AND SABLE

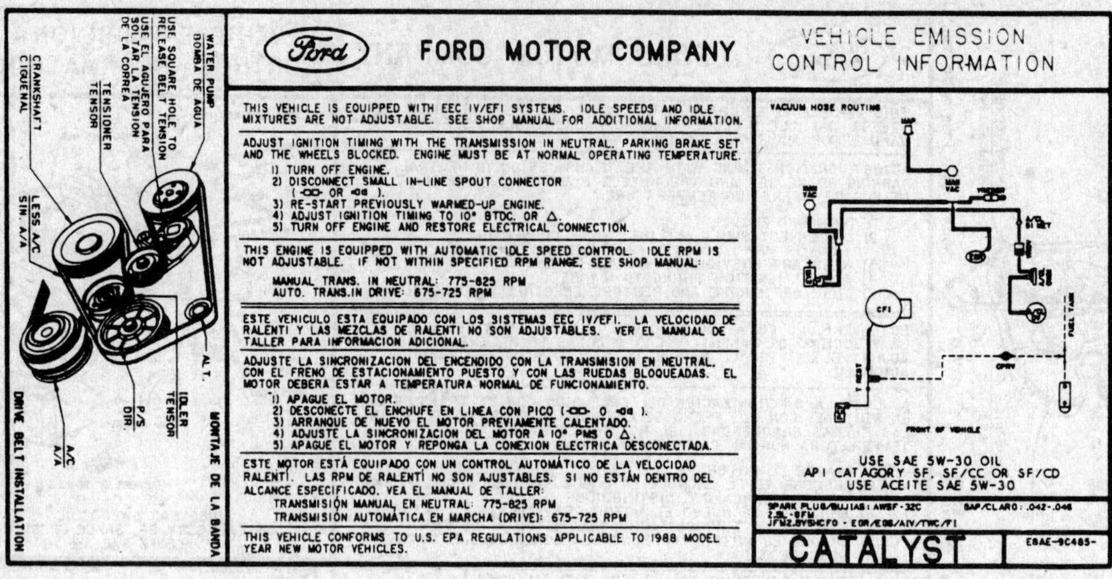

2.5L ENGINE VACUUM SCHEMATIC – 1988 TAURUS AND SABLE

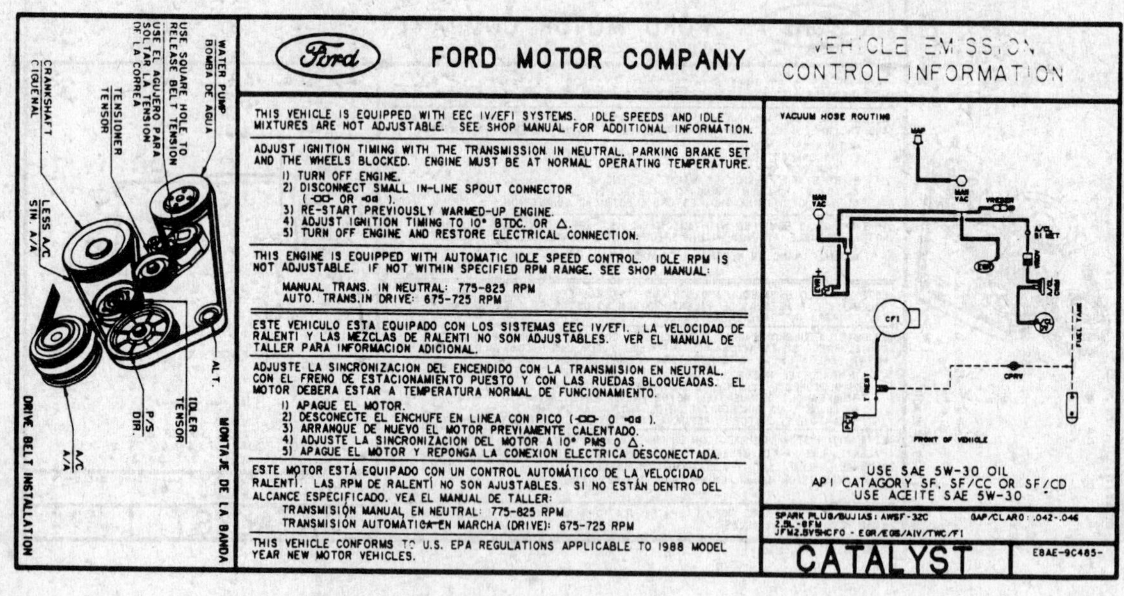

2.5L ENGINE VACUUM SCHEMATIC — 1988 TAURUS AND SABLE

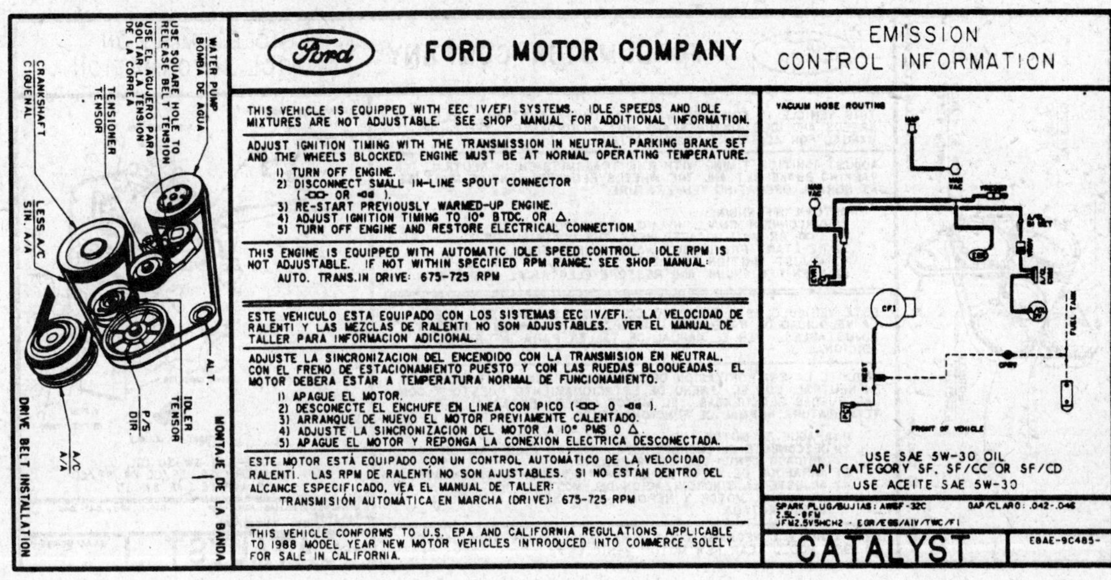

2.5L ENGINE VACUUM SCHEMATIC — 1988 TAURUS AND SABLE

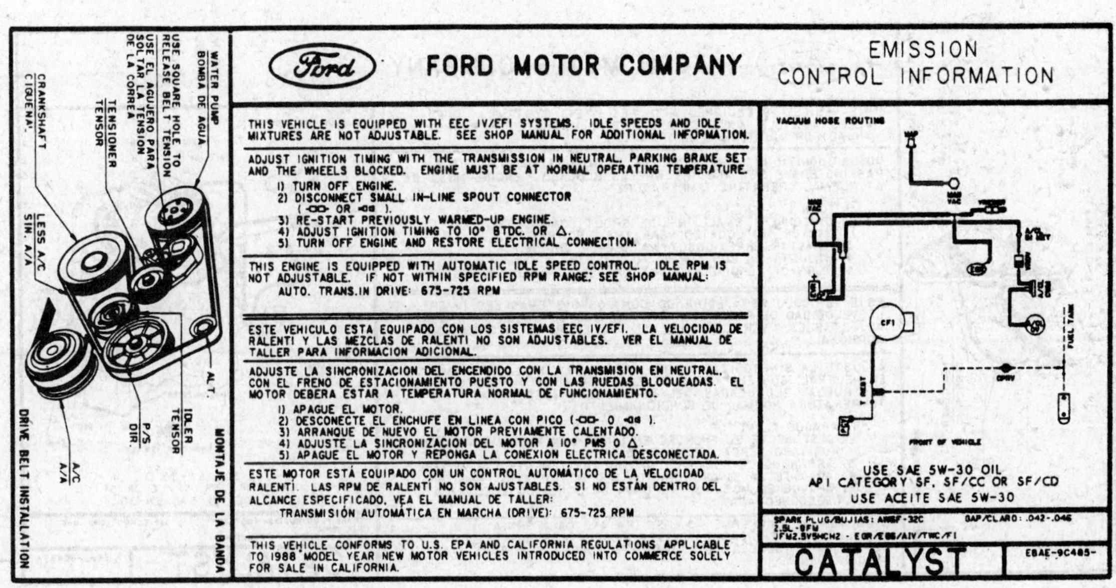

3.0L ENGINE VACUUM SCHEMATIC – 1988 TAURUS AND SABLE

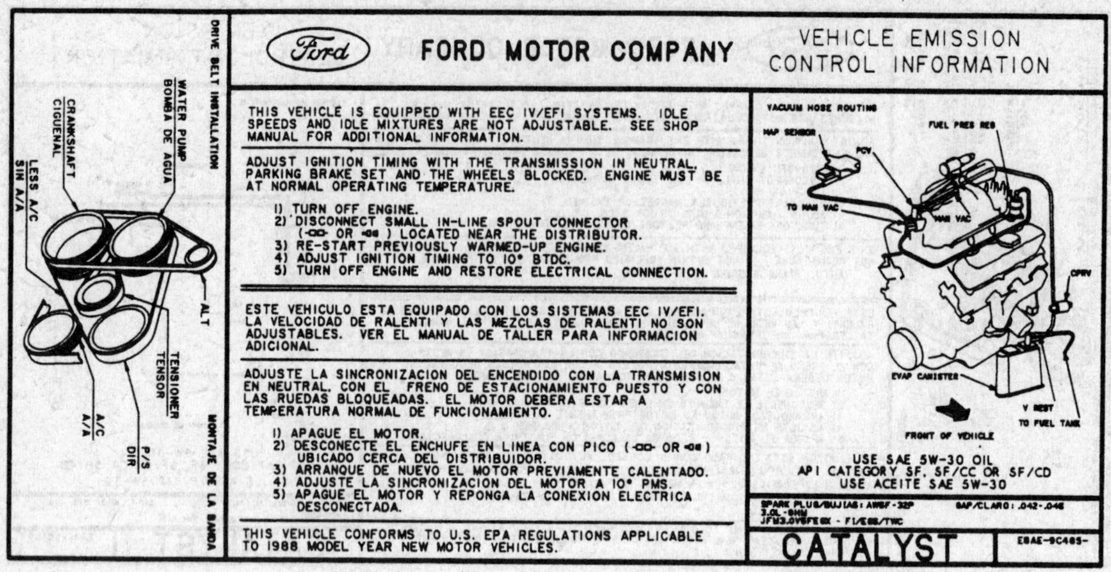

3.0L ENGINE VACUUM SCHEMATIC – 1988 TAURUS AND SABLE

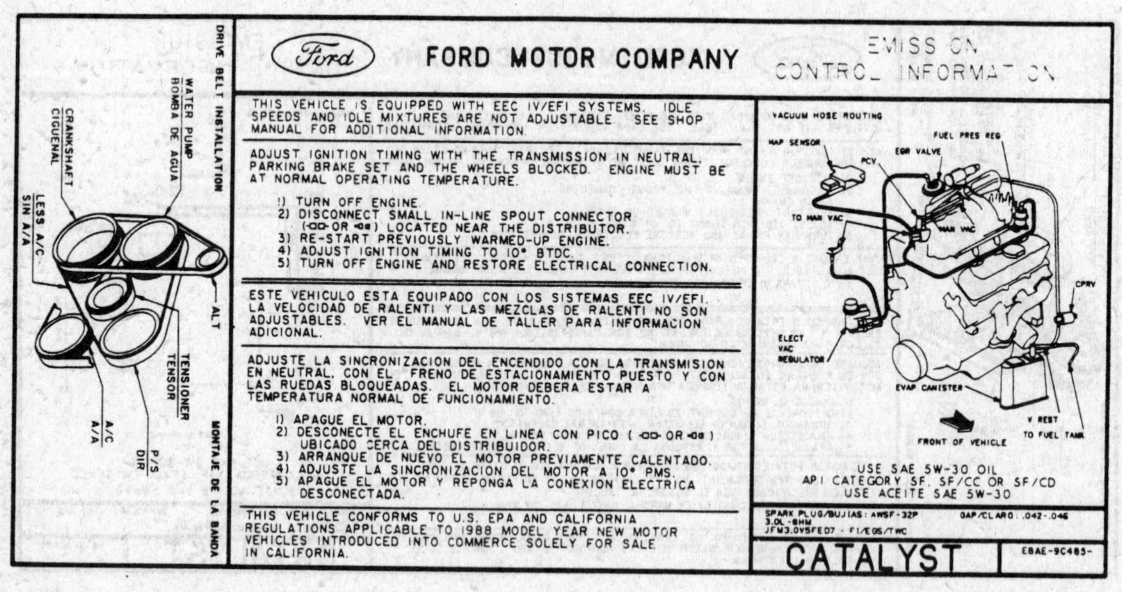

3.8L ENGINE VACUUM SCHEMATIC – 1988 TAURUS AND SABLE

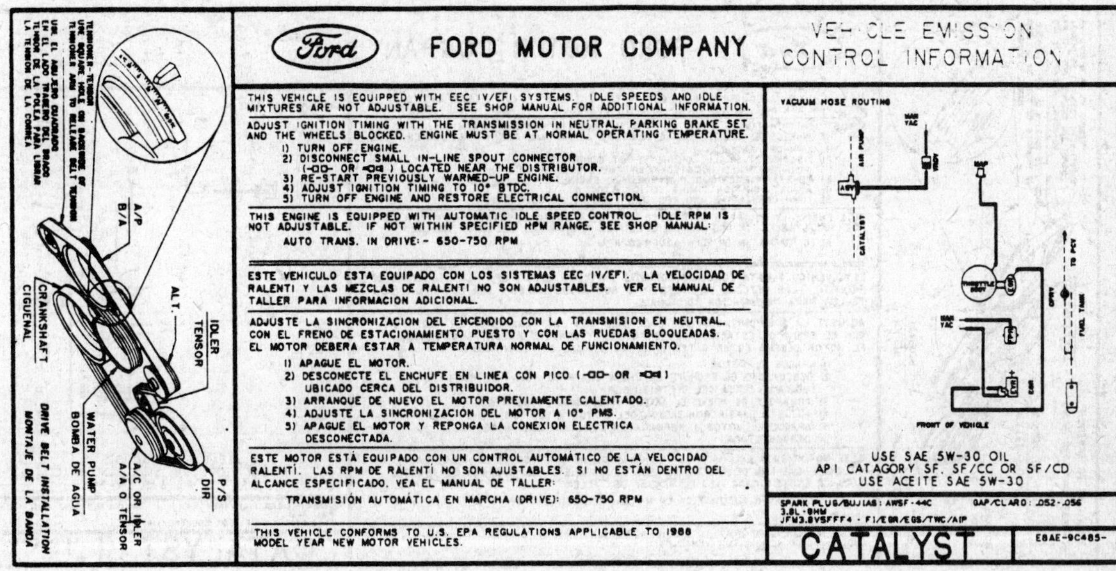

3.8L ENGINE VACUUM SCHEMATIC – 1988 TAURUS AND SABLE

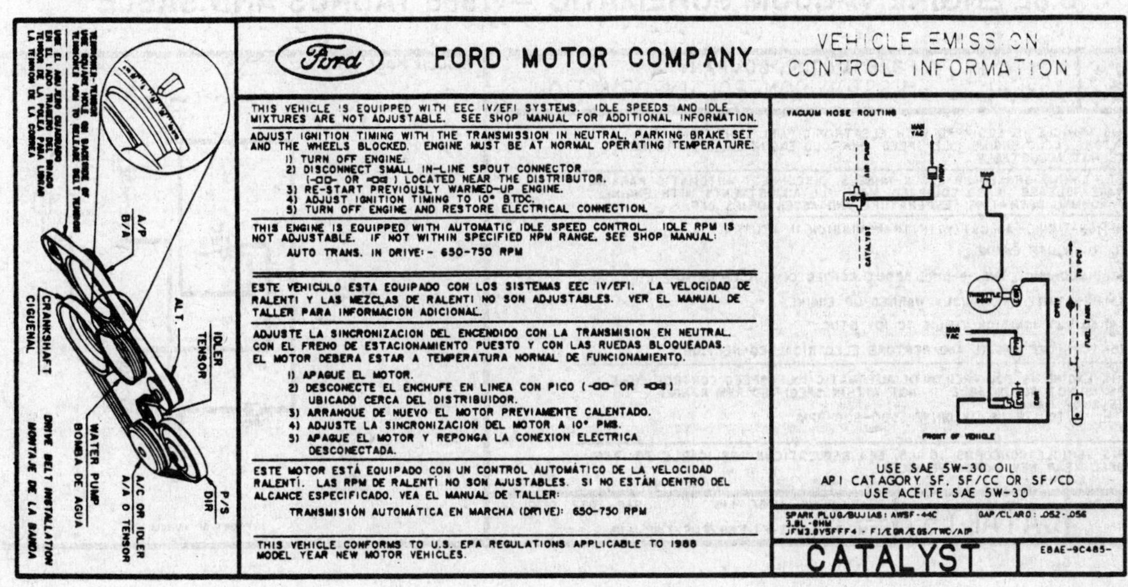

3.8L ENGINE VACUUM SCHEMATIC — 1988 TAURUS AND SABLE

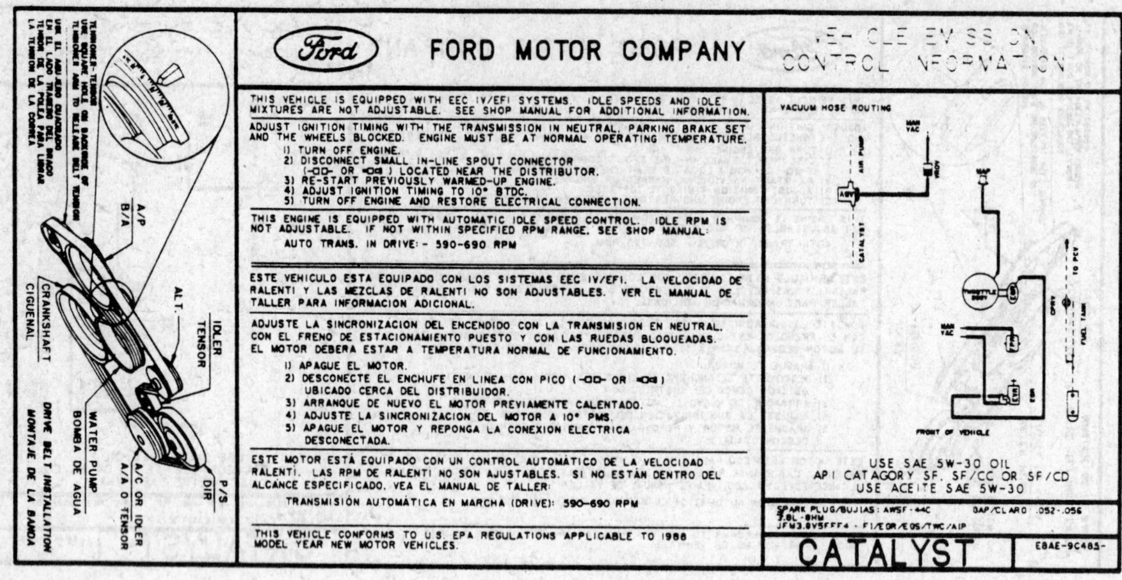

3.8L ENGINE VACUUM SCHEMATIC — 1988 TAURUS AND SABLE

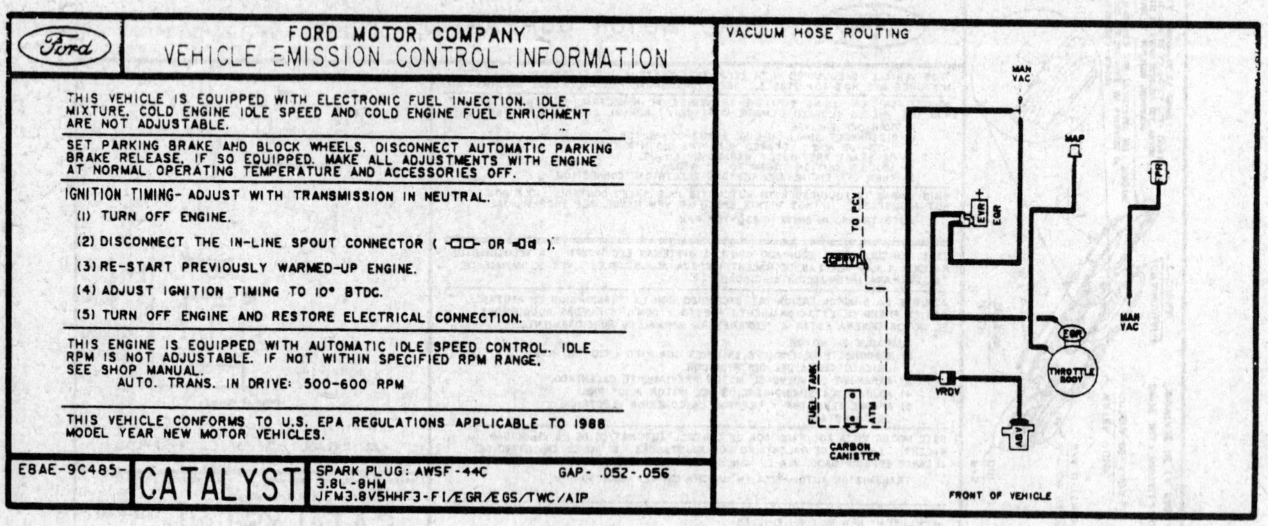

3.8L ENGINE VACUUM SCHEMATIC – 1988 TAURUS AND SABLE

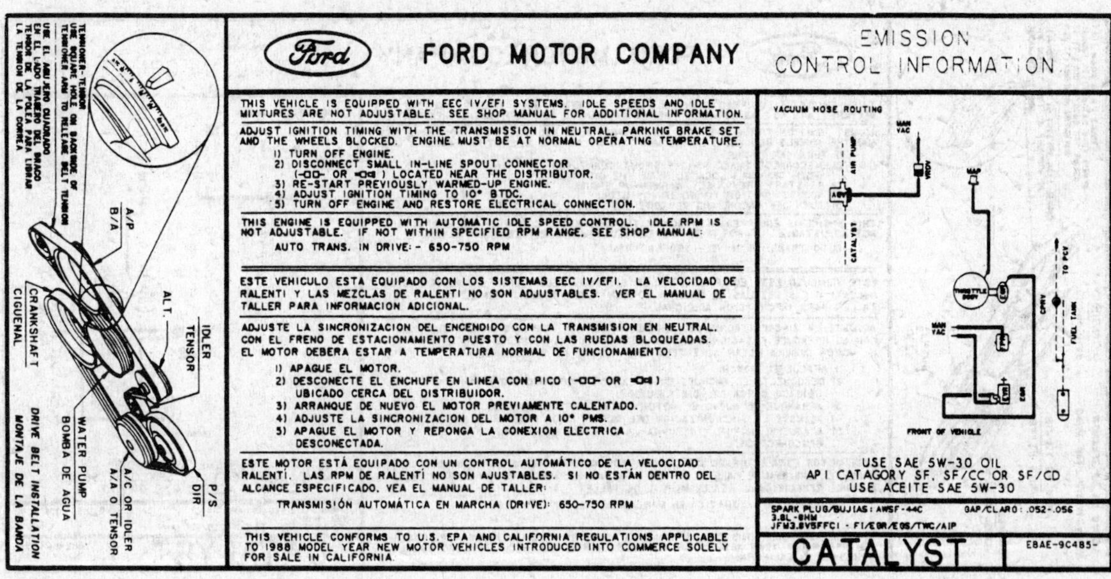

3.8L ENGINE VACUUM SCHEMATIC – 1988 TAURUS AND SABLE

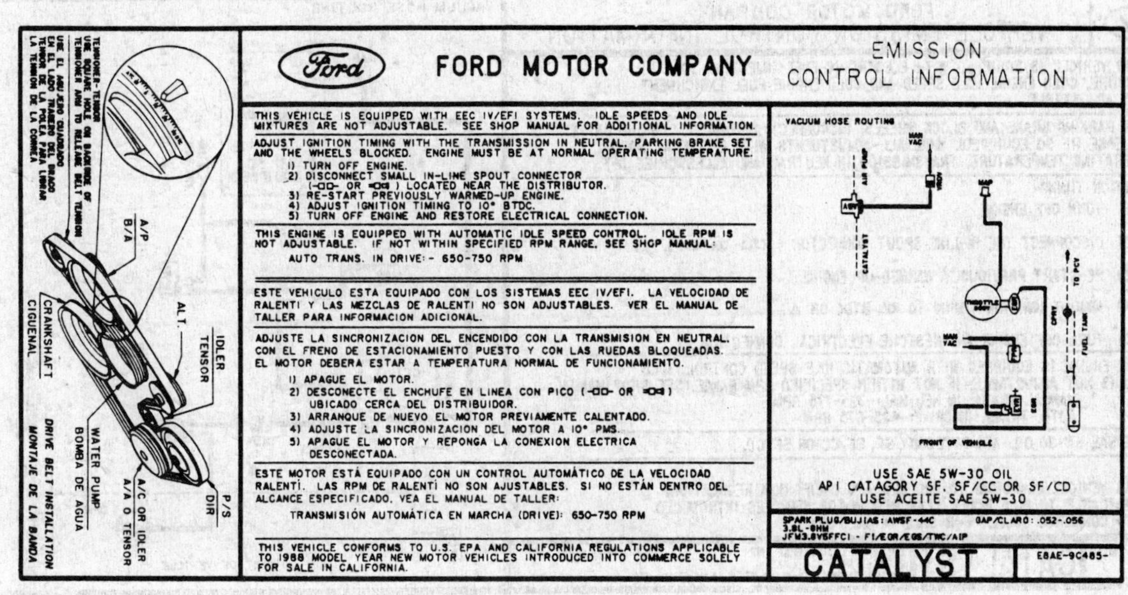

3.8L ENGINE VACUUM SCHEMATIC – 1988 TAURUS AND SABLE

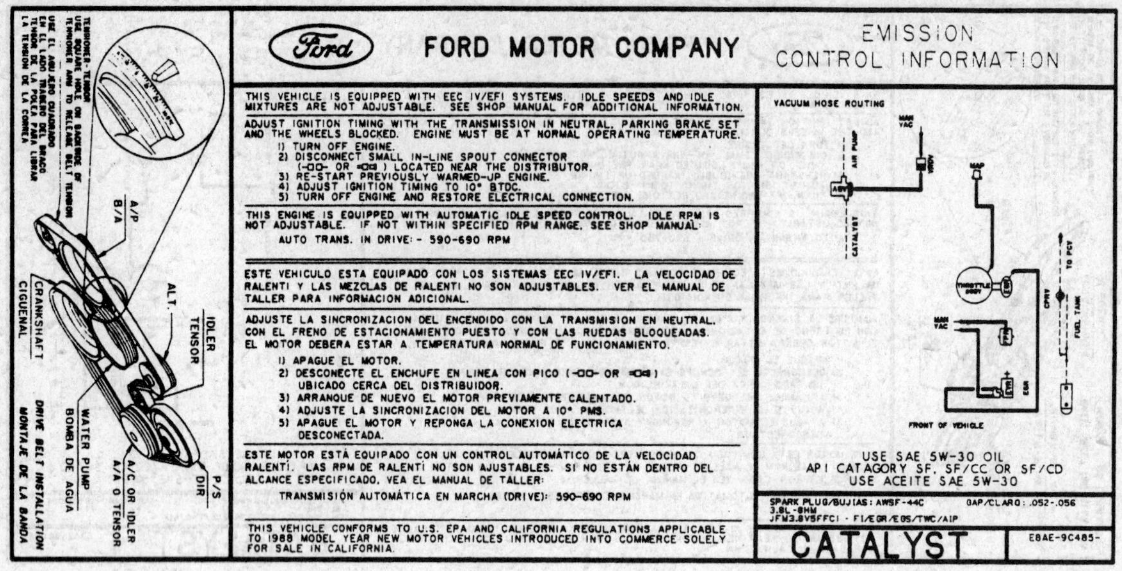

FORD MOTOR COMPANY

EMISSION CONTROL INFORMATION

THIS VEHICLE IS EQUIPPED WITH EEC IV/EFI SYSTEMS. IDLE SPEEDS AND IDLE MIXTURES ARE NOT ADJUSTABLE. SEE SHOP MANUAL FOR ADDITIONAL INFORMATION.

ADJUST IGNITION TIMING WITH THE TRANSMISSION IN NEUTRAL, PARKING BRAKE SET AND THE WHEELS BLOCKED. ENGINE MUST BE AT NORMAL OPERATING TEMPERATURE.

1) TURN OFF ENGINE.
2) DISCONNECT SMALL IN-LINE SPOUT CONNECTOR (-◻◻- OR =◻◅) LOCATED NEAR THE DISTRIBUTOR.
3) RE-START PREVIOUSLY WARMED-UP ENGINE.
4) ADJUST IGNITION TIMING TO 10° BTDC.
5) TURN OFF ENGINE AND RESTORE ELECTRICAL CONNECTION.

THIS ENGINE IS EQUIPPED WITH AUTOMATIC IDLE SPEED CONTROL. IDLE RPM IS NOT ADJUSTABLE. IF NOT WITHIN SPECIFIED RPM RANGE, SEE SHOP MANUAL:

AUTO TRANS. IN DRIVE: - 590-690 RPM

ESTE VEHICULO ESTA EQUIPADO CON LOS SISTEMAS EEC IV/EFI. LA VELOCIDAD DE RALENTI Y LAS MEZCLAS DE RALENTI NO SON ADJUSTABLES. VER EL MANUAL DE TALLER PARA INFORMACION ADICIONAL.

ADJUSTE LA SINCRONIZACION DEL ENCENDIDO CON LA TRANSMISION EN NEUTRAL. CON EL FRENO DE ESTACIONAMIENTO PUESTO Y CON LAS RUEDAS BLOQUEADAS. EL MOTOR DEBERA ESTAR A TEMPERATURA NORMAL DE FUNCIONAMIENTO.

1) APAGUE EL MOTOR.
2) DESCONECTE EL ENCHUFE EN LINEA CON PICO (-◻◻- OR =◻◅) UBICADO CERCA DEL DISTRIBUIDOR.
3) ARRANQUE DE NUEVO EL MOTOR PREVIAMENTE CALENTADO.
4) ADJUSTE LA SINCRONIZACION DEL MOTOR A 10° PMS.
5) APAGUE EL MOTOR Y REPONGA LA CONEXION ELECTRICA DESCONECTADA.

ESTE MOTOR ESTÁ EQUIPADO CON UN CONTROL AUTOMÁTICO DE LA VELOCIDAD RALENTÍ. LAS RPM DE RALENTÍ NO SON AJUSTABLES. SI NO ESTÁN DENTRO DEL ALCANCE ESPECIFICADO, VEA EL MANUAL DE TALLER:

TRANSMISIÓN AUTOMÁTICA EN MARCHA (DRIVE): 590-690 RPM

THIS VEHICLE CONFORMS TO U.S. EPA AND CALIFORNIA REGULATIONS APPLICABLE TO 1988 MODEL YEAR NEW MOTOR VEHICLES INTRODUCED INTO COMMERCE SOLELY FOR SALE IN CALIFORNIA.

USE SAE 5W-30 OIL
API CATAGORY SF, SF/CC OR SF/CD
USE ACEITE SAE 5W-30

SPARK PLUG/BUJIAS: AWSF-44C GAP/CLARO: .052-.056
3.8L-8HM
JFM3.8V5FFC1 - FI/EGR/EGS/TWC/AIP

CATALYST

E8AE-9C485-

3.8L ENGINE VACUUM SCHEMATIC – 1988 TAURUS AND SABLE

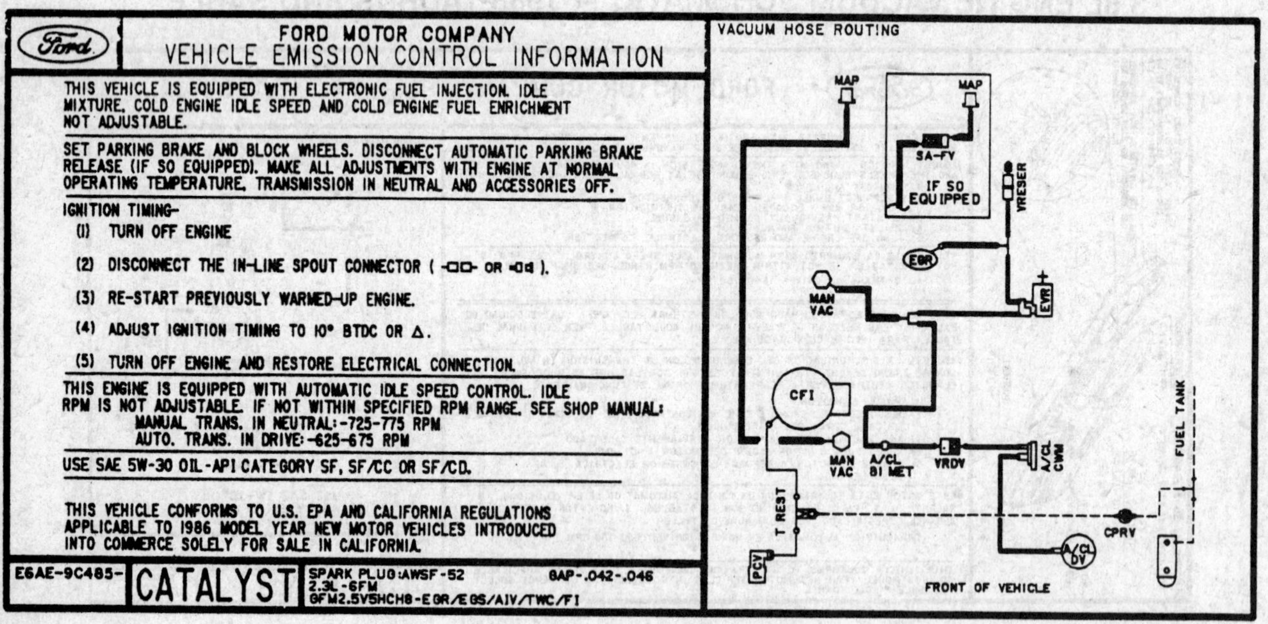

FORD MOTOR COMPANY
VEHICLE EMISSION CONTROL INFORMATION

THIS VEHICLE IS EQUIPPED WITH ELECTRONIC FUEL INJECTION. IDLE MIXTURE, COLD ENGINE IDLE SPEED AND COLD ENGINE FUEL ENRICHMENT NOT ADJUSTABLE.

SET PARKING BRAKE AND BLOCK WHEELS. DISCONNECT AUTOMATIC PARKING BRAKE RELEASE (IF SO EQUIPPED). MAKE ALL ADJUSTMENTS WITH ENGINE AT NORMAL OPERATING TEMPERATURE, TRANSMISSION IN NEUTRAL AND ACCESSORIES OFF.

IGNITION TIMING–

(1) TURN OFF ENGINE
(2) DISCONNECT THE IN-LINE SPOUT CONNECTOR (-◻◻- OR =◻◅).
(3) RE-START PREVIOUSLY WARMED-UP ENGINE.
(4) ADJUST IGNITION TIMING TO 10° BTDC OR △.
(5) TURN OFF ENGINE AND RESTORE ELECTRICAL CONNECTION.

THIS ENGINE IS EQUIPPED WITH AUTOMATIC IDLE SPEED CONTROL. IDLE RPM IS NOT ADJUSTABLE. IF NOT WITHIN SPECIFIED RPM RANGE, SEE SHOP MANUAL:
MANUAL TRANS. IN NEUTRAL:-725-775 RPM
AUTO. TRANS. IN DRIVE:-625-675 RPM

USE SAE 5W-30 OIL-API CATEGORY SF, SF/CC OR SF/CD.

THIS VEHICLE CONFORMS TO U.S. EPA AND CALIFORNIA REGULATIONS APPLICABLE TO 1986 MODEL YEAR NEW MOTOR VEHICLES INTRODUCED INTO COMMERCE SOLELY FOR SALE IN CALIFORNIA.

E6AE-9C485- CATALYST

SPARK PLUG:AWSF-52 GAP-.042-.046
2.3L-6FM
GFM2.5V5HCH8-EGR/EGS/AIV/TWC/FI

3.8L ENGINE VACUUM SCHEMATIC — 1988 TAURUS AND SABLE

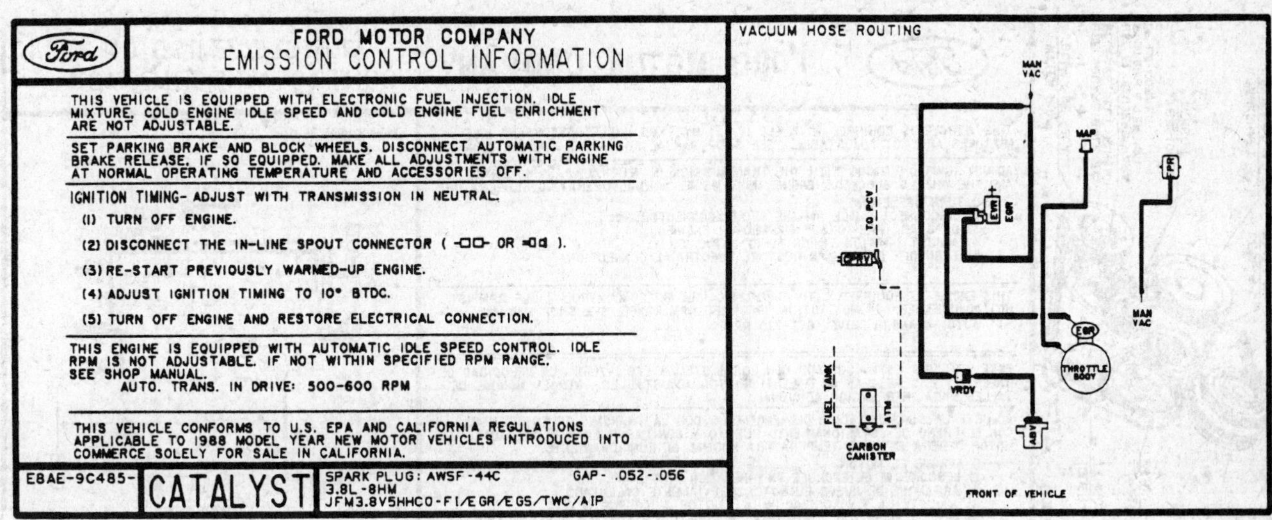

Ford

FORD MOTOR COMPANY
EMISSION CONTROL INFORMATION

THIS VEHICLE IS EQUIPPED WITH ELECTRONIC FUEL INJECTION. IDLE MIXTURE, COLD ENGINE IDLE SPEED AND COLD ENGINE FUEL ENRICHMENT ARE NOT ADJUSTABLE.

SET PARKING BRAKE AND BLOCK WHEELS. DISCONNECT AUTOMATIC PARKING BRAKE RELEASE, IF SO EQUIPPED. MAKE ALL ADJUSTMENTS WITH ENGINE AT NORMAL OPERATING TEMPERATURE AND ACCESSORIES OFF.

IGNITION TIMING- ADJUST WITH TRANSMISSION IN NEUTRAL.

(1) TURN OFF ENGINE.

(2) DISCONNECT THE IN-LINE SPOUT CONNECTOR (-□□- OR =□□).

(3) RE-START PREVIOUSLY WARMED-UP ENGINE.

(4) ADJUST IGNITION TIMING TO 10° BTDC.

(5) TURN OFF ENGINE AND RESTORE ELECTRICAL CONNECTION.

THIS ENGINE IS EQUIPPED WITH AUTOMATIC IDLE SPEED CONTROL. IDLE RPM IS NOT ADJUSTABLE. IF NOT WITHIN SPECIFIED RPM RANGE, SEE SHOP MANUAL.
AUTO. TRANS. IN DRIVE: 500-600 RPM

THIS VEHICLE CONFORMS TO U.S. EPA AND CALIFORNIA REGULATIONS APPLICABLE TO 1988 MODEL YEAR NEW MOTOR VEHICLES INTRODUCED INTO COMMERCE SOLELY FOR SALE IN CALIFORNIA.

E8AE-9C485- CATALYST SPARK PLUG: AWSF-44C GAP- .052-.056
3.8L-8HM
JFM3.8V5HHC0-FI/EGR/EGS/TWC/AIP

VACUUM HOSE ROUTING

2.5L ENGINE VACUUM SCHEMATIC — 1989 TAURUS AND SABLE

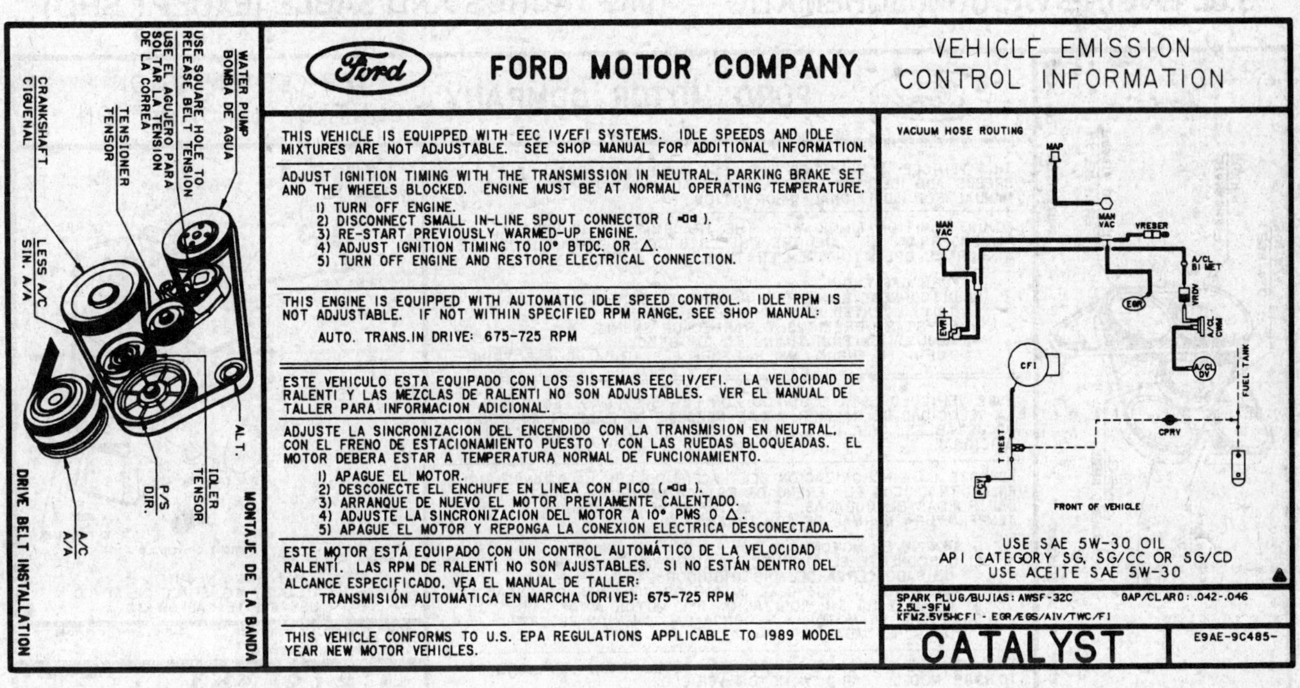

Ford

FORD MOTOR COMPANY

VEHICLE EMISSION CONTROL INFORMATION

THIS VEHICLE IS EQUIPPED WITH EEC IV/EFI SYSTEMS. IDLE SPEEDS AND IDLE MIXTURES ARE NOT ADJUSTABLE. SEE SHOP MANUAL FOR ADDITIONAL INFORMATION.

ADJUST IGNITION TIMING WITH THE TRANSMISSION IN NEUTRAL, PARKING BRAKE SET AND THE WHEELS BLOCKED. ENGINE MUST BE AT NORMAL OPERATING TEMPERATURE.

1) TURN OFF ENGINE.
2) DISCONNECT SMALL IN-LINE SPOUT CONNECTOR (=□□).
3) RE-START PREVIOUSLY WARMED-UP ENGINE.
4) ADJUST IGNITION TIMING TO 10° BTDC. OR △.
5) TURN OFF ENGINE AND RESTORE ELECTRICAL CONNECTION.

THIS ENGINE IS EQUIPPED WITH AUTOMATIC IDLE SPEED CONTROL. IDLE RPM IS NOT ADJUSTABLE. IF NOT WITHIN SPECIFIED RPM RANGE, SEE SHOP MANUAL:

AUTO. TRANS.IN DRIVE: 675-725 RPM

ESTE VEHICULO ESTA EQUIPADO CON LOS SISTEMAS EEC IV/EFI. LA VELOCIDAD DE RALENTI Y LAS MEZCLAS DE RALENTI NO SON ADJUSTABLES. VER EL MANUAL DE TALLER PARA INFORMACION ADICIONAL.

ADJUSTE LA SINCRONIZACION DEL ENCENDIDO CON LA TRANSMISION EN NEUTRAL, CON EL FRENO DE ESTACIONAMIENTO PUESTO Y CON LAS RUEDAS BLOQUEADAS. EL MOTOR DEBERA ESTAR A TEMPERATURA NORMAL DE FUNCIONAMIENTO.

1) APAGUE EL MOTOR.
2) DESCONECTE EL ENCHUFE EN LINEA CON PICO (=□□).
3) ARRANQUE DE NUEVO EL MOTOR PREVIAMENTE CALENTADO.
4) ADJUSTE LA SINCRONIZACION DEL MOTOR A 10° PMS 0 △.
5) APAGUE EL MOTOR Y REPONGA LA CONEXION ELECTRICA DESCONECTADA.

ESTE MOTOR ESTÁ EQUIPADO CON UN CONTROL AUTOMÁTICO DE LA VELOCIDAD RALENTÍ. LAS RPM DE RALENTÍ NO SON AJUSTABLES. SI NO ESTÁN DENTRO DEL ALCANCE ESPECIFICADO, VEA EL MANUAL DE TALLER:
TRANSMISIÓN AUTOMÁTICA EN MARCHA (DRIVE): 675-725 RPM

THIS VEHICLE CONFORMS TO U.S. EPA REGULATIONS APPLICABLE TO 1989 MODEL YEAR NEW MOTOR VEHICLES.

VACUUM HOSE ROUTING

USE SAE 5W-30 OIL
API CATEGORY SG, SG/CC OR SG/CD
USE ACEITE SAE 5W-30

SPARK PLUG/BUJIAS: AWSF-32C GAP/CLARO: .042-.046
2.5L-9FM
KFM2.5V5HCFI - EGR/EGS/AIV/TWC/FI

CATALYST E9AE-9C485-

2.5L ENGINE VACUUM SCHEMATIC — 1989 TAURUS AND SABLE

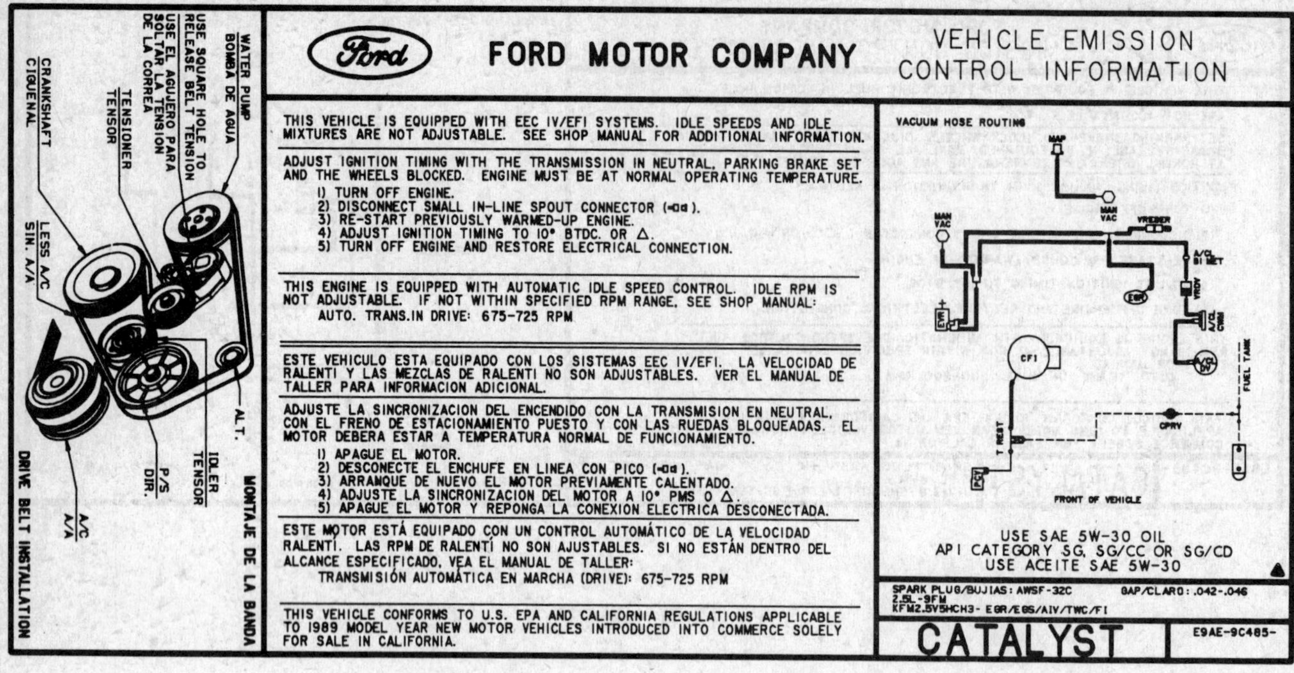

FORD MOTOR COMPANY

VEHICLE EMISSION CONTROL INFORMATION

THIS VEHICLE IS EQUIPPED WITH EEC IV/EFI SYSTEMS. IDLE SPEEDS AND IDLE MIXTURES ARE NOT ADJUSTABLE. SEE SHOP MANUAL FOR ADDITIONAL INFORMATION.

ADJUST IGNITION TIMING WITH THE TRANSMISSION IN NEUTRAL, PARKING BRAKE SET AND THE WHEELS BLOCKED. ENGINE MUST BE AT NORMAL OPERATING TEMPERATURE.

1) TURN OFF ENGINE.
2) DISCONNECT SMALL IN-LINE SPOUT CONNECTOR.
3) RE-START PREVIOUSLY WARMED-UP ENGINE.
4) ADJUST IGNITION TIMING TO 10° BTDC. OR △.
5) TURN OFF ENGINE AND RESTORE ELECTRICAL CONNECTION.

THIS ENGINE IS EQUIPPED WITH AUTOMATIC IDLE SPEED CONTROL. IDLE RPM IS NOT ADJUSTABLE. IF NOT WITHIN SPECIFIED RPM RANGE, SEE SHOP MANUAL:
AUTO. TRANS.IN DRIVE: 675-725 RPM

ESTE VEHICULO ESTA EQUIPADO CON LOS SISTEMAS EEC IV/EFI. LA VELOCIDAD DE RALENTI Y LAS MEZCLAS DE RALENTI NO SON ADJUSTABLES. VER EL MANUAL DE TALLER PARA INFORMACION ADICIONAL.

ADJUSTE LA SINCRONIZACION DEL ENCENDIDO CON LA TRANSMISION EN NEUTRAL, CON EL FRENO DE ESTACIONAMIENTO PUESTO Y CON LAS RUEDAS BLOQUEADAS. EL MOTOR DEBERA ESTAR A TEMPERATURA NORMAL DE FUNCIONAMIENTO.

1) APAGUE EL MOTOR.
2) DESCONECTE EL ENCHUFE EN LINEA CON PICO.
3) ARRANQUE DE NUEVO EL MOTOR PREVIAMENTE CALENTADO.
4) ADJUSTE LA SINCRONIZACION DEL MOTOR A 10° PMS O △.
5) APAGUE EL MOTOR Y REPONGA LA CONEXION ELECTRICA DESCONECTADA.

ESTE MOTOR ESTÁ EQUIPADO CON UN CONTROL AUTOMÁTICO DE LA VELOCIDAD RALENTÍ. LAS RPM DE RALENTÍ NO SON AJUSTABLES. SI NO ESTÁN DENTRO DEL ALCANCE ESPECIFICADO, VEA EL MANUAL DE TALLER:
TRANSMISIÓN AUTOMÁTICA EN MARCHA (DRIVE): 675-725 RPM

THIS VEHICLE CONFORMS TO U.S. EPA AND CALIFORNIA REGULATIONS APPLICABLE TO 1989 MODEL YEAR NEW MOTOR VEHICLES INTRODUCED INTO COMMERCE SOLELY FOR SALE IN CALIFORNIA.

USE SAE 5W-30 OIL
API CATEGORY SG, SG/CC OR SG/CD
USE ACEITE SAE 5W-30

SPARK PLUG/BUJIAS: AWSF-32C GAP/CLARO: .042-.046
2.5L-9FM
KFM2.5V5HCH3- EGR/EGS/AIV/TWC/FI

CATALYST

E9AE-9C485-

3.0L ENGINE VACUUM SCHEMATIC — 1989 TAURUS AND SABLE (EXCEPT SHO)

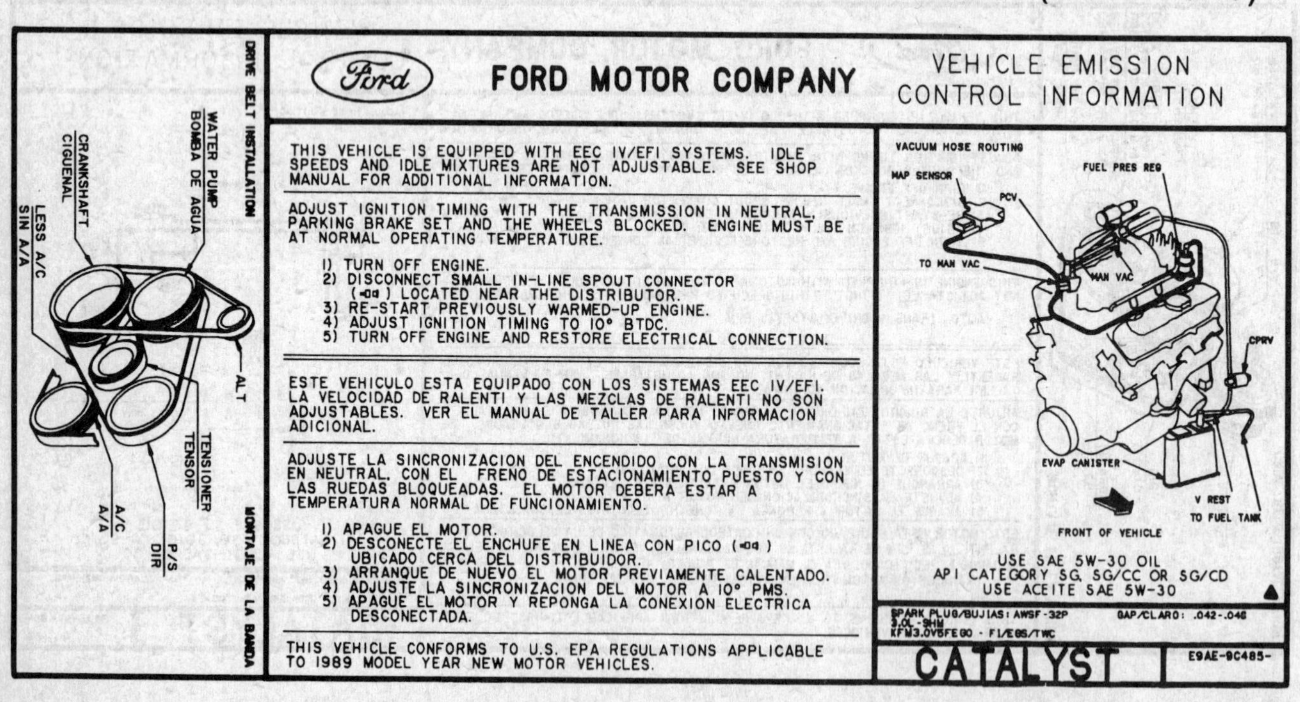

FORD MOTOR COMPANY

VEHICLE EMISSION CONTROL INFORMATION

THIS VEHICLE IS EQUIPPED WITH EEC IV/EFI SYSTEMS. IDLE SPEEDS AND IDLE MIXTURES ARE NOT ADJUSTABLE. SEE SHOP MANUAL FOR ADDITIONAL INFORMATION.

ADJUST IGNITION TIMING WITH THE TRANSMISSION IN NEUTRAL, PARKING BRAKE SET AND THE WHEELS BLOCKED. ENGINE MUST BE AT NORMAL OPERATING TEMPERATURE.

1) TURN OFF ENGINE.
2) DISCONNECT SMALL IN-LINE SPOUT CONNECTOR LOCATED NEAR THE DISTRIBUTOR.
3) RE-START PREVIOUSLY WARMED-UP ENGINE.
4) ADJUST IGNITION TIMING TO 10° BTDC.
5) TURN OFF ENGINE AND RESTORE ELECTRICAL CONNECTION.

ESTE VEHICULO ESTA EQUIPADO CON LOS SISTEMAS EEC IV/EFI. LA VELOCIDAD DE RALENTI Y LAS MEZCLAS DE RALENTI NO SON ADJUSTABLES. VER EL MANUAL DE TALLER PARA INFORMACION ADICIONAL.

ADJUSTE LA SINCRONIZACION DEL ENCENDIDO CON LA TRANSMISION EN NEUTRAL, CON EL FRENO DE ESTACIONAMIENTO PUESTO Y CON LAS RUEDAS BLOQUEADAS. EL MOTOR DEBERA ESTAR A TEMPERATURA NORMAL DE FUNCIONAMIENTO.

1) APAGUE EL MOTOR.
2) DESCONECTE EL ENCHUFE EN LINEA CON PICO UBICADO CERCA DEL DISTRIBUIDOR.
3) ARRANQUE DE NUEVO EL MOTOR PREVIAMENTE CALENTADO.
4) ADJUSTE LA SINCRONIZACION DEL MOTOR A 10° PMS.
5) APAGUE EL MOTOR Y REPONGA LA CONEXION ELECTRICA DESCONECTADA.

THIS VEHICLE CONFORMS TO U.S. EPA REGULATIONS APPLICABLE TO 1989 MODEL YEAR NEW MOTOR VEHICLES.

USE SAE 5W-30 OIL
API CATEGORY SG, SG/CC OR SG/CD
USE ACEITE SAE 5W-30

SPARK PLUG/BUJIAS: AWSF-32P GAP/CLARO: .042-.046
3.0L-9HM
KFM3.0V5FEG0 - FI/EGS/TWC

CATALYST

E9AE-9C485-

3.0L ENGINE VACUUM SCHEMATIC — 1989 TAURUS AND SABLE

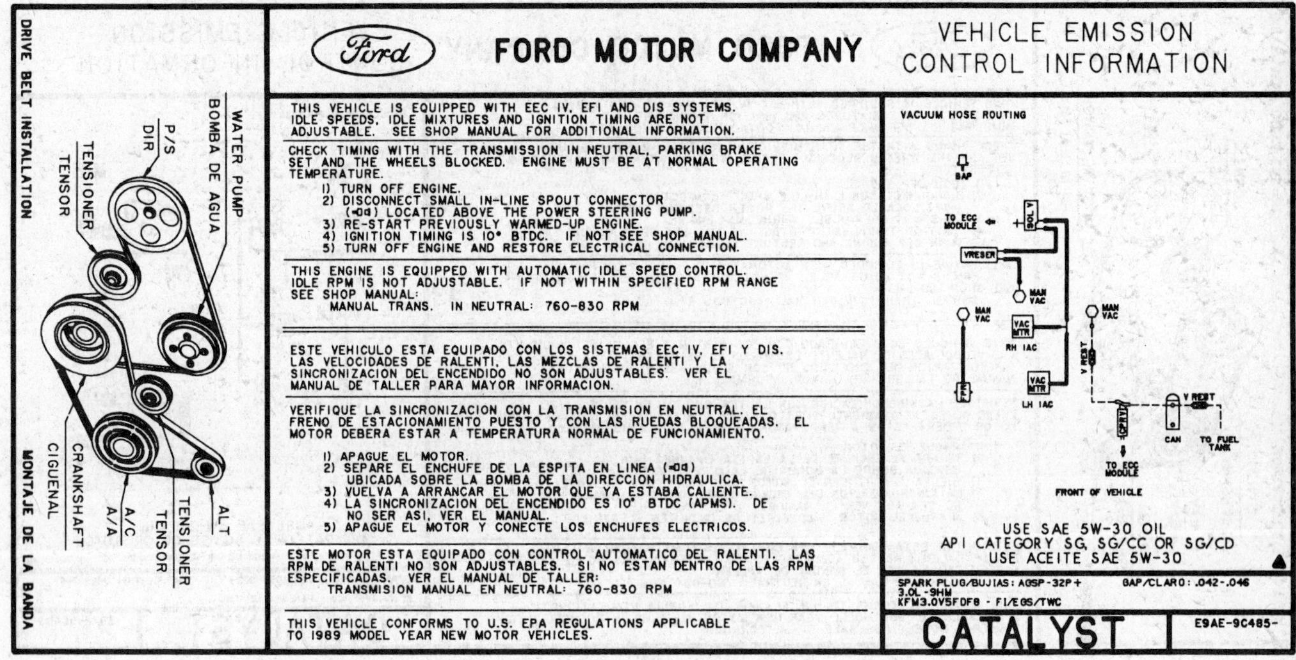

FORD MOTOR COMPANY

VEHICLE EMISSION CONTROL INFORMATION

THIS VEHICLE IS EQUIPPED WITH EEC IV, EFI AND DIS SYSTEMS. IDLE SPEEDS, IDLE MIXTURES AND IGNITION TIMING ARE NOT ADJUSTABLE. SEE SHOP MANUAL FOR ADDITIONAL INFORMATION.

CHECK TIMING WITH THE TRANSMISSION IN NEUTRAL, PARKING BRAKE SET AND THE WHEELS BLOCKED. ENGINE MUST BE AT NORMAL OPERATING TEMPERATURE.

1) TURN OFF ENGINE.
2) DISCONNECT SMALL IN-LINE SPOUT CONNECTOR (⊸⊲) LOCATED ABOVE THE POWER STEERING PUMP.
3) RE-START PREVIOUSLY WARMED-UP ENGINE.
4) IGNITION TIMING IS 10° BTDC. IF NOT SEE SHOP MANUAL.
5) TURN OFF ENGINE AND RESTORE ELECTRICAL CONNECTION.

THIS ENGINE IS EQUIPPED WITH AUTOMATIC IDLE SPEED CONTROL. IDLE RPM IS NOT ADJUSTABLE. IF NOT WITHIN SPECIFIED RPM RANGE SEE SHOP MANUAL:
MANUAL TRANS. IN NEUTRAL: 760-830 RPM

ESTE VEHICULO ESTA EQUIPADO CON LOS SISTEMAS EEC IV, EFI Y DIS. LAS VELOCIDADES DE RALENTI, LAS MEZCLAS DE RALENTI Y LA SINCRONIZACION DEL ENCENDIDO NO SON ADJUSTABLES. VER EL MANUAL DE TALLER PARA MAYOR INFORMACION.

VERIFIQUE LA SINCRONIZACION CON LA TRANSMISION EN NEUTRAL, EL FRENO DE ESTACIONAMIENTO PUESTO Y CON LAS RUEDAS BLOQUEADAS. EL MOTOR DEBERA ESTAR A TEMPERATURA NORMAL DE FUNCIONAMIENTO.

1) APAGUE EL MOTOR.
2) SEPARE EL ENCHUFE DE LA ESPITA EN LINEA (⊸⊲) UBICADA SOBRE LA BOMBA DE LA DIRECCION HIDRAULICA.
3) VUELVA A ARRANCAR EL MOTOR QUE YA ESTABA CALIENTE.
4) LA SINCRONIZACION DEL ENCENDIDO ES 10° BTDC (APMS). DE NO SER ASI, VER EL MANUAL.
5) APAGUE EL MOTOR Y CONECTE LOS ENCHUFES ELECTRICOS.

ESTE MOTOR ESTA EQUIPADO CON CONTROL AUTOMATICO DEL RALENTI. LAS RPM DE RALENTI NO SON ADJUSTABLES. SI NO ESTAN DENTRO DE LAS RPM ESPECIFICADAS, VER EL MANUAL DE TALLER:
TRANSMISION MANUAL EN NEUTRAL: 760-830 RPM

THIS VEHICLE CONFORMS TO U.S. EPA REGULATIONS APPLICABLE TO 1989 MODEL YEAR NEW MOTOR VEHICLES.

VACUUM HOSE ROUTING

USE SAE 5W-30 OIL
API CATEGORY SG, SG/CC OR SG/CD
USE ACEITE SAE 5W-30

SPARK PLUG/BUJIAS: AGSP-32P+ GAP/CLARO: .042-.046
3.0L-9HM
KFM3.0V5FDF8 - FI/EGS/TWC

CATALYST E9AE-9C485-

3.0L ENGINE VACUUM SCHEMATIC — 1989 TAURUS AND SABLE

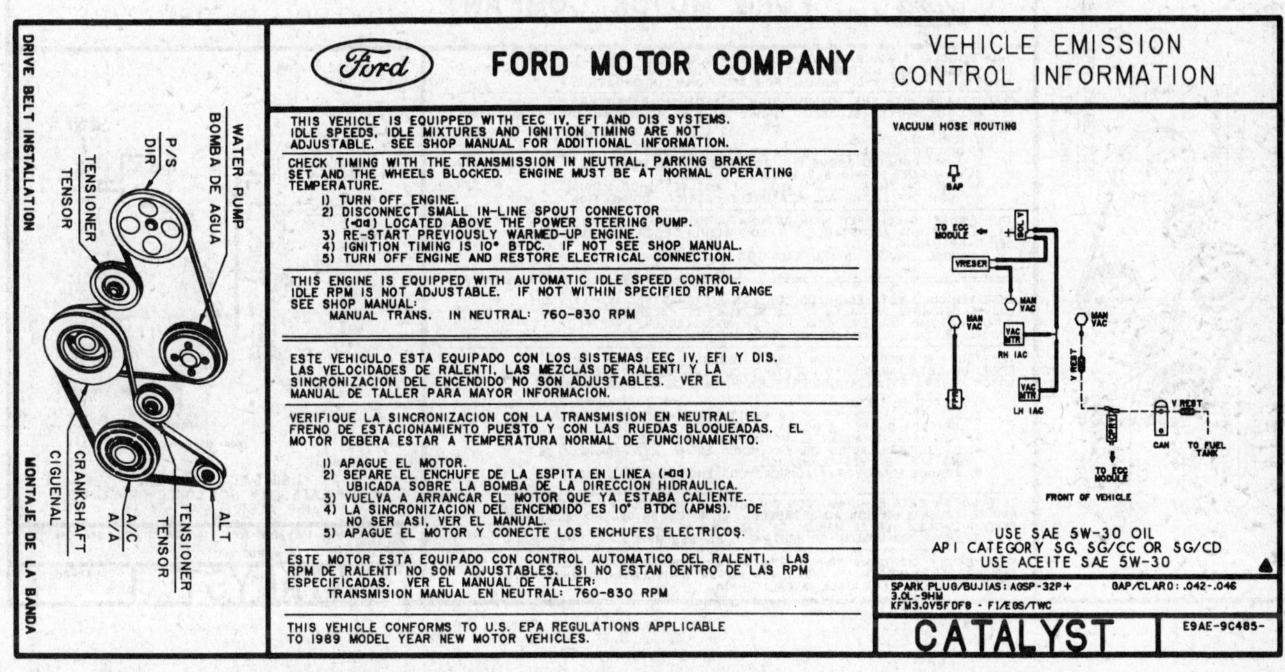

FORD MOTOR COMPANY

VEHICLE EMISSION CONTROL INFORMATION

THIS VEHICLE IS EQUIPPED WITH EEC IV, EFI AND DIS SYSTEMS. IDLE SPEEDS, IDLE MIXTURES AND IGNITION TIMING ARE NOT ADJUSTABLE. SEE SHOP MANUAL FOR ADDITIONAL INFORMATION.

CHECK TIMING WITH THE TRANSMISSION IN NEUTRAL, PARKING BRAKE SET AND THE WHEELS BLOCKED. ENGINE MUST BE AT NORMAL OPERATING TEMPERATURE.

1) TURN OFF ENGINE.
2) DISCONNECT SMALL IN-LINE SPOUT CONNECTOR (⊸⊲) LOCATED ABOVE THE POWER STEERING PUMP.
3) RE-START PREVIOUSLY WARMED-UP ENGINE.
4) IGNITION TIMING IS 10° BTDC. IF NOT SEE SHOP MANUAL.
5) TURN OFF ENGINE AND RESTORE ELECTRICAL CONNECTION.

THIS ENGINE IS EQUIPPED WITH AUTOMATIC IDLE SPEED CONTROL. IDLE RPM IS NOT ADJUSTABLE. IF NOT WITHIN SPECIFIED RPM RANGE SEE SHOP MANUAL:
MANUAL TRANS. IN NEUTRAL: 760-830 RPM

ESTE VEHICULO ESTA EQUIPADO CON LOS SISTEMAS EEC IV, EFI Y DIS. LAS VELOCIDADES DE RALENTI, LAS MEZCLAS DE RALENTI Y LA SINCRONIZACION DEL ENCENDIDO NO SON ADJUSTABLES. VER EL MANUAL DE TALLER PARA MAYOR INFORMACION.

VERIFIQUE LA SINCRONIZACION CON LA TRANSMISION EN NEUTRAL, EL FRENO DE ESTACIONAMIENTO PUESTO Y CON LAS RUEDAS BLOQUEADAS. EL MOTOR DEBERA ESTAR A TEMPERATURA NORMAL DE FUNCIONAMIENTO.

1) APAGUE EL MOTOR.
2) SEPARE EL ENCHUFE DE LA ESPITA EN LINEA (⊸⊲) UBICADA SOBRE LA BOMBA DE LA DIRECCION HIDRAULICA.
3) VUELVA A ARRANCAR EL MOTOR QUE YA ESTABA CALIENTE.
4) LA SINCRONIZACION DEL ENCENDIDO ES 10° BTDC (APMS). DE NO SER ASI, VER EL MANUAL.
5) APAGUE EL MOTOR Y CONECTE LOS ENCHUFES ELECTRICOS.

ESTE MOTOR ESTA EQUIPADO CON CONTROL AUTOMATICO DEL RALENTI. LAS RPM DE RALENTI NO SON ADJUSTABLES. SI NO ESTAN DENTRO DE LAS RPM ESPECIFICADAS, VER EL MANUAL DE TALLER:
TRANSMISION MANUAL EN NEUTRAL: 760-830 RPM

THIS VEHICLE CONFORMS TO U.S. EPA REGULATIONS APPLICABLE TO 1989 MODEL YEAR NEW MOTOR VEHICLES.

VACUUM HOSE ROUTING

USE SAE 5W-30 OIL
API CATEGORY SG, SG/CC OR SG/CD
USE ACEITE SAE 5W-30

SPARK PLUG/BUJIAS: AGSP-32P+ GAP/CLARO: .042-.046
3.0L-9HM
KFM3.0V5FDF8 - FI/EGS/TWC

CATALYST E9AE-9C485-

3.0L ENGINE VACUUM SCHEMATIC — 1989 TAURUS AND SABLE

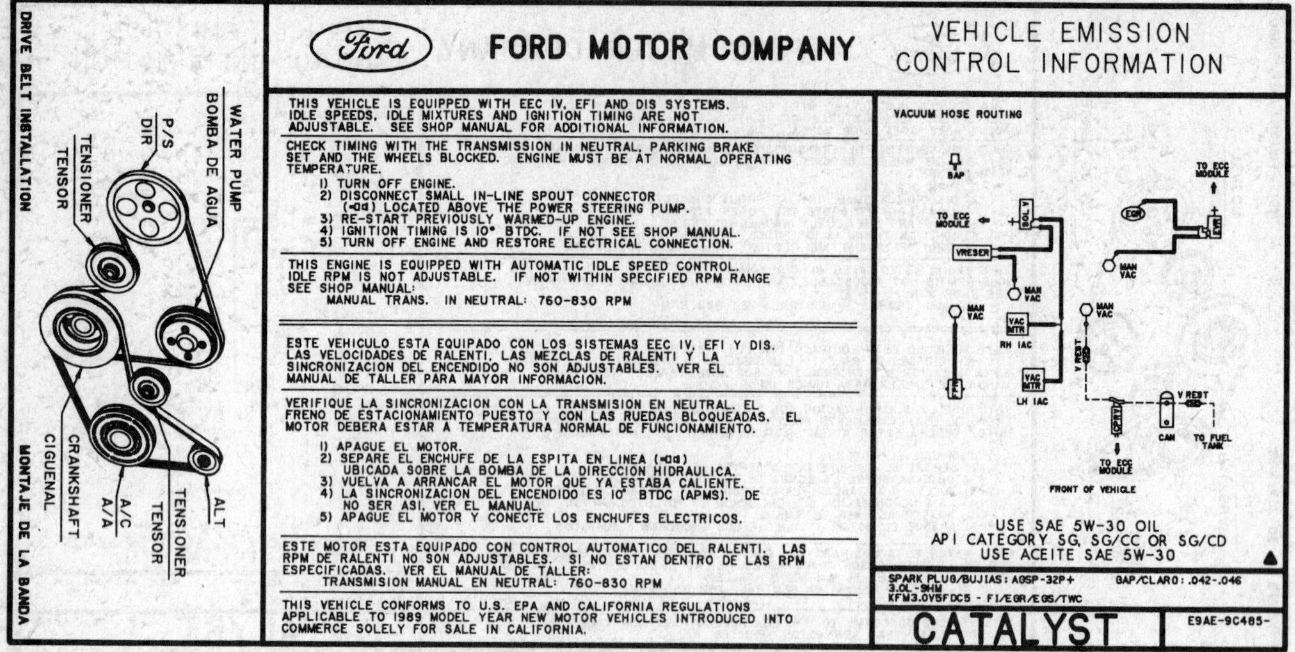

3.0L ENGINE VACUUM SCHEMATIC — 1989 TAURUS AND SABLE

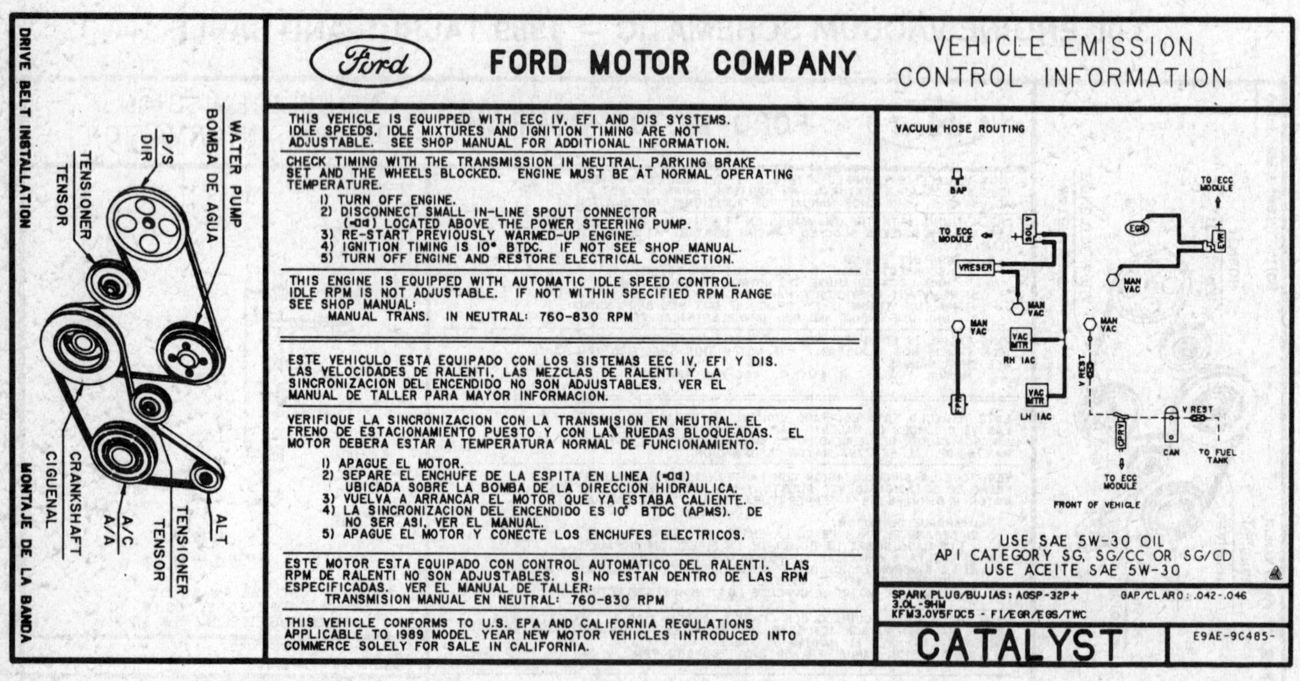
DRIVE BELT INSTALLATION
WATER PUMP
BOMBA DE AGUA
P/S
DIR
TENSIONER
TENSOR
ALT
TENSIONER
TENSOR
A/C
A/A
CRANKSHAFT
CIGUENAL
MONTAJE DE LA BANDA
Ford
FORD MOTOR COMPANY
VEHICLE EMISSION CONTROL INFORMATION
THIS VEHICLE IS EQUIPPED WITH EEC IV, EFI AND DIS SYSTEMS. IDLE SPEEDS, IDLE MIXTURES AND IGNITION TIMING ARE NOT ADJUSTABLE. SEE SHOP MANUAL FOR ADDITIONAL INFORMATION.
CHECK TIMING WITH THE TRANSMISSION IN NEUTRAL, PARKING BRAKE SET AND THE WHEELS BLOCKED. ENGINE MUST BE AT NORMAL OPERATING TEMPERATURE.
1) TURN OFF ENGINE.
2) DISCONNECT SMALL IN-LINE SPOUT CONNECTOR (⊲⊲) LOCATED ABOVE THE POWER STEERING PUMP.
3) RE-START PREVIOUSLY WARMED-UP ENGINE.
4) IGNITION TIMING IS 10° BTDC. IF NOT SEE SHOP MANUAL.
5) TURN OFF ENGINE AND RESTORE ELECTRICAL CONNECTION.
THIS ENGINE IS EQUIPPED WITH AUTOMATIC IDLE SPEED CONTROL. IDLE RPM IS NOT ADJUSTABLE. IF NOT WITHIN SPECIFIED RPM RANGE SEE SHOP MANUAL:
MANUAL TRANS. IN NEUTRAL: 760-830 RPM
ESTE VEHICULO ESTA EQUIPADO CON LOS SISTEMAS EEC IV, EFI Y DIS. LAS VELOCIDADES DE RALENTI, LAS MEZCLAS DE RALENTI Y LA SINCRONIZACION DEL ENCENDIDO NO SON ADJUSTABLES. VER EL MANUAL DE TALLER PARA MAYOR INFORMACION.
VERIFIQUE LA SINCRONIZACION CON LA TRANSMISION EN NEUTRAL, EL FRENO DE ESTACIONAMIENTO PUESTO Y CON LAS RUEDAS BLOQUEADAS. EL MOTOR DEBERA ESTAR A TEMPERATURA NORMAL DE FUNCIONAMIENTO.
1) APAGUE EL MOTOR.
2) SEPARE EL ENCHUFE DE LA ESPITA EN LINEA (⊲⊲) UBICADA SOBRE LA BOMBA DE LA DIRECCION HIDRAULICA.
3) VUELVA A ARRANCAR EL MOTOR QUE YA ESTABA CALIENTE.
4) LA SINCRONIZACION DEL ENCENDIDO ES 10° BTDC (APMS). DE NO SER ASI, VER EL MANUAL.
5) APAGUE EL MOTOR Y CONECTE LOS ENCHUFES ELECTRICOS.
ESTE MOTOR ESTA EQUIPADO CON CONTROL AUTOMATICO DEL RALENTI. LAS RPM DE RALENTI NO SON ADJUSTABLES. SI NO ESTAN DENTRO DE LAS RPM ESPECIFICADAS, VER EL MANUAL DE TALLER:
TRANSMISION MANUAL EN NEUTRAL: 760-830 RPM
THIS VEHICLE CONFORMS TO U.S. EPA AND CALIFORNIA REGULATIONS APPLICABLE TO 1989 MODEL YEAR NEW MOTOR VEHICLES INTRODUCED INTO COMMERCE SOLELY FOR SALE IN CALIFORNIA.
VACUUM HOSE ROUTING
BAP
TO ECC MODULE
SOL V
EGR
EVR
VRESER
MAN VAC
MAN VAC
MAN VAC
MAN VAC
VAC MTR
RH IAC
VAC MTR
LH IAC
V REST
V REST
CAN
TO FUEL TANK
CPRV
TO ECC MODULE
FRONT OF VEHICLE
USE SAE 5W-30 OIL
API CATEGORY SG, SG/CC OR SG/CD
USE ACEITE SAE 5W-30
SPARK PLUG/BUJIAS: AGSP-32P+
GAP/CLARO: .042-.046
3.0L-9HW
KFM3.0V5FDC5 - FI/EGR/EGS/TWC
CATALYST
E9AE-9C485-

3.0L ENGINE VACUUM SCHEMATIC — 1989 TAURUS AND SABLE (EXCEPT SHO)

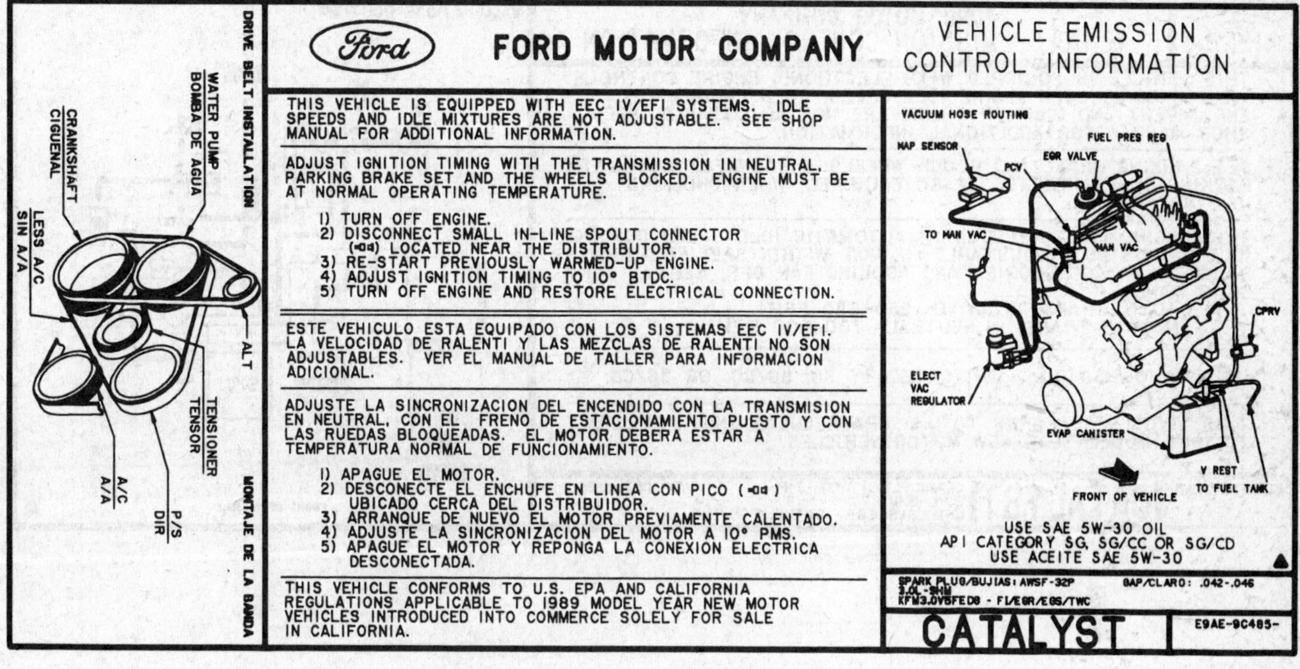

3.0L ENGINE VACUUM SCHEMATIC — 1989 TAURUS AND SABLE (EXCEPT SHO)

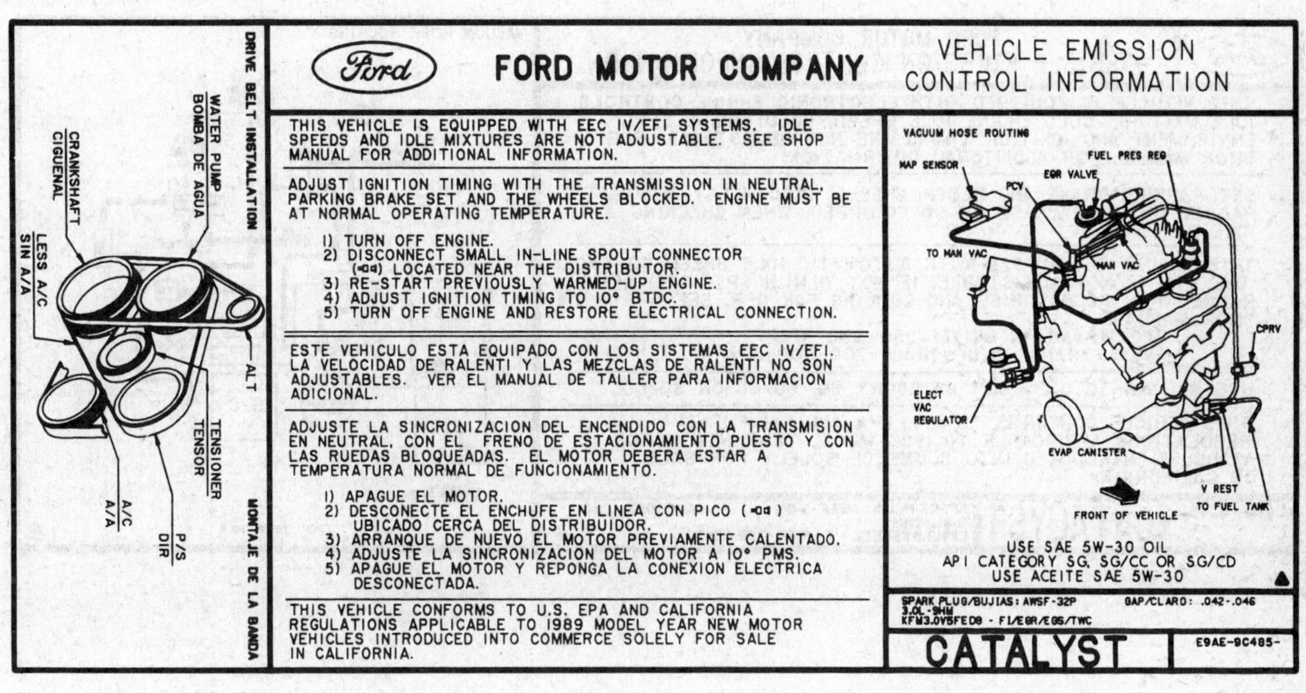

3.8L ENGINE VACUUM SCHEMATIC – 1989 TAURUS AND SABLE

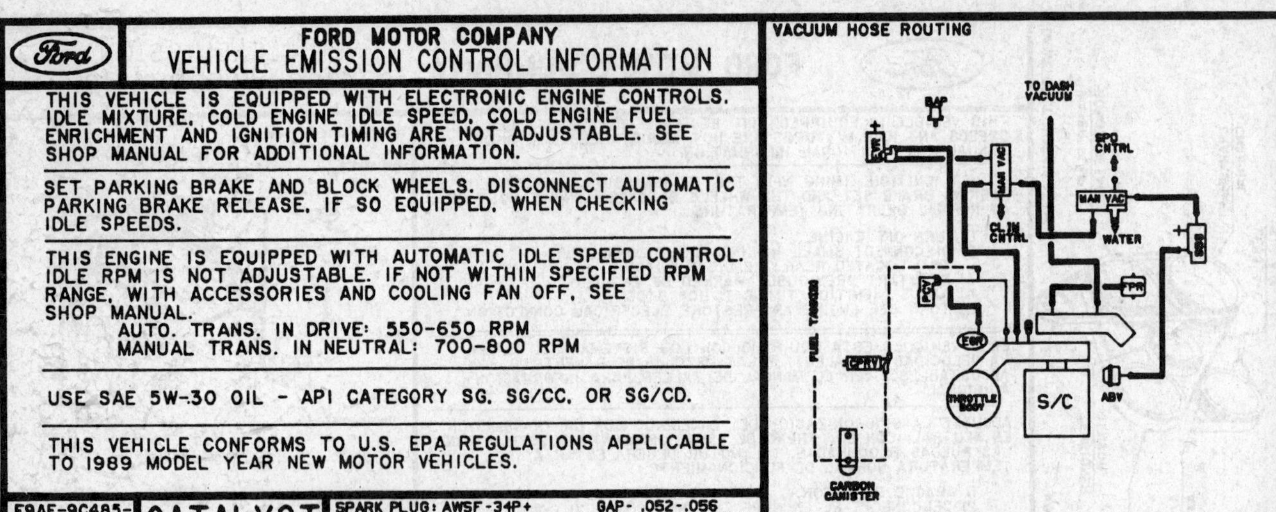

FORD MOTOR COMPANY
VEHICLE EMISSION CONTROL INFORMATION

THIS VEHICLE IS EQUIPPED WITH ELECTRONIC ENGINE CONTROLS. IDLE MIXTURE, COLD ENGINE IDLE SPEED, COLD ENGINE FUEL ENRICHMENT AND IGNITION TIMING ARE NOT ADJUSTABLE. SEE SHOP MANUAL FOR ADDITIONAL INFORMATION.

SET PARKING BRAKE AND BLOCK WHEELS. DISCONNECT AUTOMATIC PARKING BRAKE RELEASE, IF SO EQUIPPED, WHEN CHECKING IDLE SPEEDS.

THIS ENGINE IS EQUIPPED WITH AUTOMATIC IDLE SPEED CONTROL. IDLE RPM IS NOT ADJUSTABLE. IF NOT WITHIN SPECIFIED RPM RANGE, WITH ACCESSORIES AND COOLING FAN OFF, SEE SHOP MANUAL.
AUTO. TRANS. IN DRIVE: 550-650 RPM
MANUAL TRANS. IN NEUTRAL: 700-800 RPM

USE SAE 5W-30 OIL - API CATEGORY SG, SG/CC, OR SG/CD.

THIS VEHICLE CONFORMS TO U.S. EPA REGULATIONS APPLICABLE TO 1989 MODEL YEAR NEW MOTOR VEHICLES.

E9AE-9C485- CATALYST SPARK PLUG: AWSF-34P+ GAP- .052-.056
3.8L-9HM
KFM3.8V5FEG4 - FI/EGR/EGS/TWC

3.8L ENGINE VACUUM SCHEMATIC – 1989 TAURUS AND SABLE

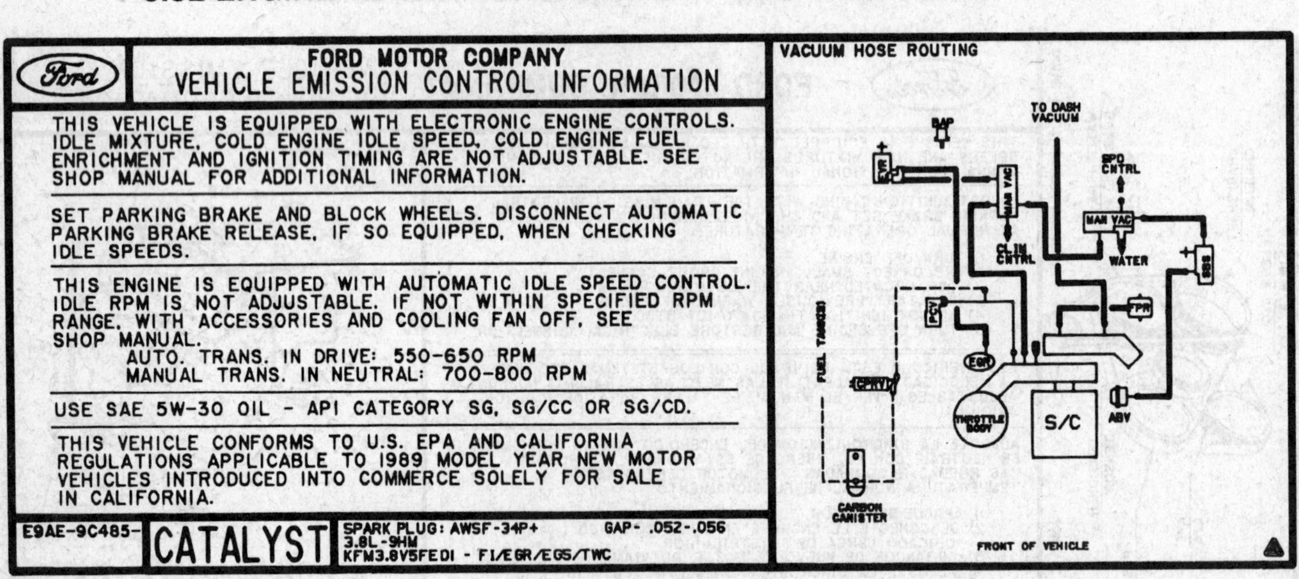

FORD MOTOR COMPANY
VEHICLE EMISSION CONTROL INFORMATION

THIS VEHICLE IS EQUIPPED WITH ELECTRONIC ENGINE CONTROLS. IDLE MIXTURE, COLD ENGINE IDLE SPEED, COLD ENGINE FUEL ENRICHMENT AND IGNITION TIMING ARE NOT ADJUSTABLE. SEE SHOP MANUAL FOR ADDITIONAL INFORMATION.

SET PARKING BRAKE AND BLOCK WHEELS. DISCONNECT AUTOMATIC PARKING BRAKE RELEASE, IF SO EQUIPPED, WHEN CHECKING IDLE SPEEDS.

THIS ENGINE IS EQUIPPED WITH AUTOMATIC IDLE SPEED CONTROL. IDLE RPM IS NOT ADJUSTABLE. IF NOT WITHIN SPECIFIED RPM RANGE, WITH ACCESSORIES AND COOLING FAN OFF, SEE SHOP MANUAL.
AUTO. TRANS. IN DRIVE: 550-650 RPM
MANUAL TRANS. IN NEUTRAL: 700-800 RPM

USE SAE 5W-30 OIL - API CATEGORY SG, SG/CC OR SG/CD.

THIS VEHICLE CONFORMS TO U.S. EPA AND CALIFORNIA REGULATIONS APPLICABLE TO 1989 MODEL YEAR NEW MOTOR VEHICLES INTRODUCED INTO COMMERCE SOLELY FOR SALE IN CALIFORNIA.

E9AE-9C485- CATALYST SPARK PLUG: AWSF-34P+ GAP- .052-.056
3.8L-9HM
KFM3.8V5FEDI - FI/EGR/EGS/TWC

3.8L ENGINE VACUUM SCHEMATIC – 1989 TAURUS AND SABLE

FORD MOTOR COMPANY
VEHICLE EMISSION CONTROL INFORMATION

THIS VEHICLE IS EQUIPPED WITH ELECTRONIC ENGINE CONTROLS. IDLE MIXTURE, COLD ENGINE IDLE SPEED, COLD ENGINE FUEL ENRICHMENT AND IGNITION TIMING ARE NOT ADJUSTABLE. SEE SHOP MANUAL FOR ADDITIONAL INFORMATION.

SET PARKING BRAKE AND BLOCK WHEELS. DISCONNECT AUTOMATIC PARKING BRAKE RELEASE, IF SO EQUIPPED, WHEN CHECKING IDLE SPEEDS.

THIS ENGINE IS EQUIPPED WITH AUTOMATIC IDLE SPEED CONTROL. IDLE RPM IS NOT ADJUSTABLE. IF NOT WITHIN SPECIFIED RPM RANGE, WITH ACCESSORIES AND COOLING FAN OFF, SEE SHOP MANUAL.
AUTO. TRANS. IN DRIVE: 550-650 RPM
MANUAL TRANS. IN NEUTRAL: 700-800 RPM

USE SAE 5W-30 OIL - API CATEGORY SG, SG/CC, OR SG/CD.

THIS VEHICLE CONFORMS TO U.S. EPA REGULATIONS APPLICABLE TO 1989 MODEL YEAR NEW MOTOR VEHICLES.

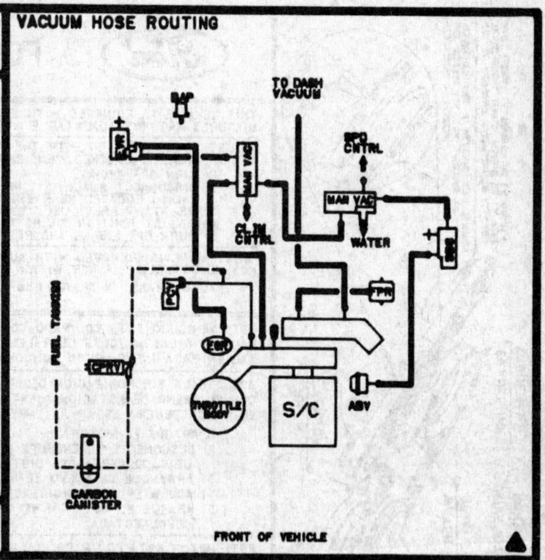

E9AE-9C485- | CATALYST | SPARK PLUG: AWSF-34P+ GAP- .052-.056
3.8L-9HM
KFM3.8V5FEG4 - FI/EGR/EGS/TWC

3.8L ENGINE VACUUM SCHEMATIC – 1989 TAURUS AND SABLE

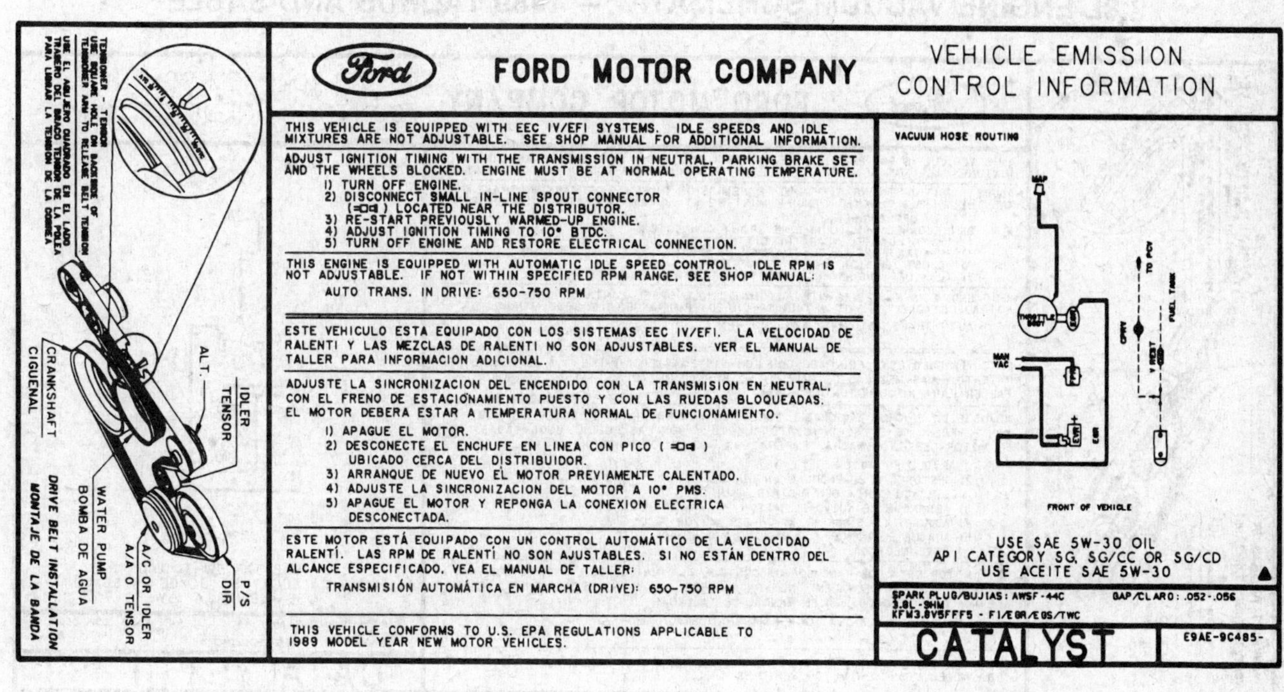

FORD MOTOR COMPANY
VEHICLE EMISSION CONTROL INFORMATION

THIS VEHICLE IS EQUIPPED WITH EEC IV/EFI SYSTEMS. IDLE SPEEDS AND IDLE MIXTURES ARE NOT ADJUSTABLE. SEE SHOP MANUAL FOR ADDITIONAL INFORMATION.

ADJUST IGNITION TIMING WITH THE TRANSMISSION IN NEUTRAL, PARKING BRAKE SET AND THE WHEELS BLOCKED. ENGINE MUST BE AT NORMAL OPERATING TEMPERATURE.
1) TURN OFF ENGINE.
2) DISCONNECT SMALL IN-LINE SPOUT CONNECTOR (=◻◅) LOCATED NEAR THE DISTRIBUTOR.
3) RE-START PREVIOUSLY WARMED-UP ENGINE.
4) ADJUST IGNITION TIMING TO 10° BTDC.
5) TURN OFF ENGINE AND RESTORE ELECTRICAL CONNECTION.

THIS ENGINE IS EQUIPPED WITH AUTOMATIC IDLE SPEED CONTROL. IDLE RPM IS NOT ADJUSTABLE. IF NOT WITHIN SPECIFIED RPM RANGE, SEE SHOP MANUAL:
AUTO TRANS. IN DRIVE: 650-750 RPM

ESTE VEHICULO ESTA EQUIPADO CON LOS SISTEMAS EEC IV/EFI. LA VELOCIDAD DE RALENTI Y LAS MEZCLAS DE RALENTI NO SON ADJUSTABLES. VER EL MANUAL DE TALLER PARA INFORMACION ADICIONAL.

ADJUSTE LA SINCRONIZACION DEL ENCENDIDO CON LA TRANSMISION EN NEUTRAL, CON EL FRENO DE ESTACIONAMIENTO PUESTO Y CON LAS RUEDAS BLOQUEADAS. EL MOTOR DEBERA ESTAR A TEMPERATURA NORMAL DE FUNCIONAMIENTO.
1) APAGUE EL MOTOR.
2) DESCONECTE EL ENCHUFE EN LINEA CON PICO (=◻◅) UBICADO CERCA DEL DISTRIBUIDOR.
3) ARRANQUE DE NUEVO EL MOTOR PREVIAMENTE CALENTADO.
4) ADJUSTE LA SINCRONIZACION DEL MOTOR A 10° PMS.
5) APAGUE EL MOTOR Y REPONGA LA CONEXION ELECTRICA DESCONECTADA.

ESTE MOTOR ESTÁ EQUIPADO CON UN CONTROL AUTOMÁTICO DE LA VELOCIDAD RALENTÍ. LAS RPM DE RALENTÍ NO SON AJUSTABLES. SI NO ESTÁN DENTRO DEL ALCANCE ESPECIFICADO, VEA EL MANUAL DE TALLER:
TRANSMISIÓN AUTOMÁTICA EN MARCHA (DRIVE): 650-750 RPM

THIS VEHICLE CONFORMS TO U.S. EPA REGULATIONS APPLICABLE TO 1989 MODEL YEAR NEW MOTOR VEHICLES.

VACUUM HOSE ROUTING

MAP
TO PCV
FUEL TANK
THROTTLE BODY
MAN VAC
EGR
FRONT OF VEHICLE

USE SAE 5W-30 OIL
API CATEGORY SG, SG/CC OR SG/CD
USE ACEITE SAE 5W-30

SPARK PLUG/BUJIAS: AWSF-44C GAP/CLARO: .052-.056
3.8L-9HM
KFM3.8V5FFF5 - FI/EGR/EGS/TWC

CATALYST | E9AE-9C485-

IDLER TENSOR
ALT.
CRANKSHAFT CIGUENAL
WATER PUMP BOMBA DE AGUA
A/C OR IDLER A/A O TENSOR
P/S DIR
DRIVE BELT INSTALLATION
MONTAJE DE LA BANDA

3.8L ENGINE VACUUM SCHEMATIC – 1989 TAURUS AND SABLE

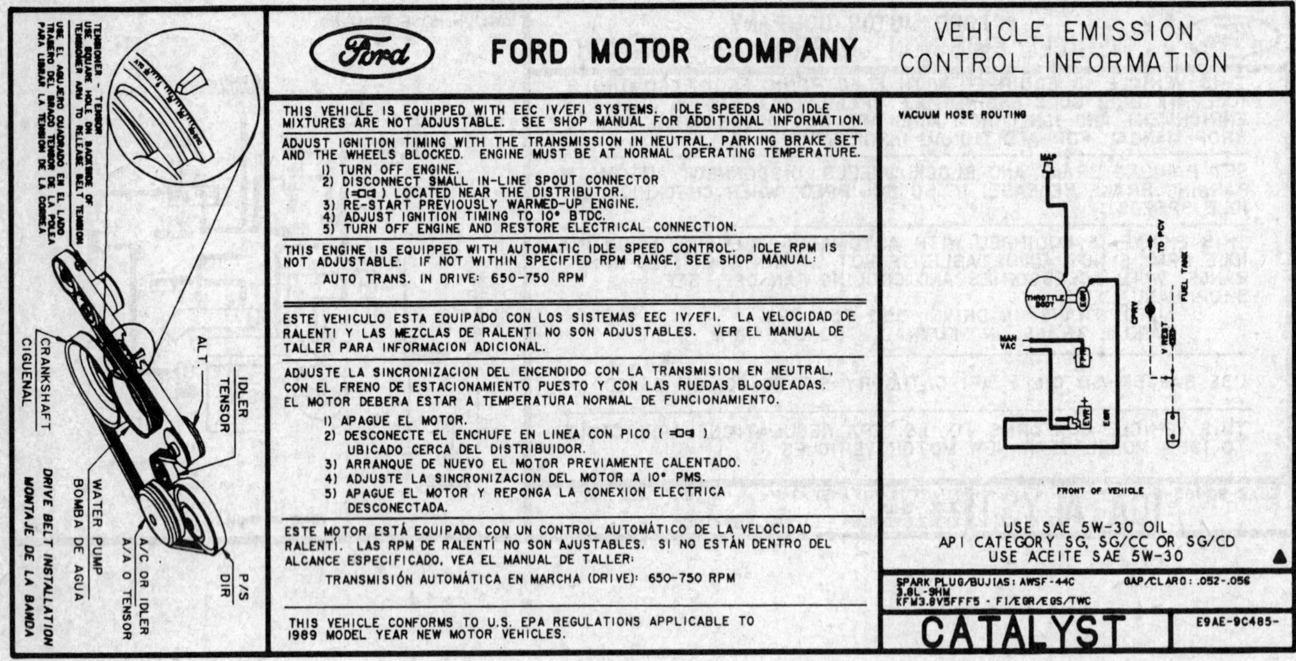

3.8L ENGINE VACUUM SCHEMATIC – 1989 TAURUS AND SABLE

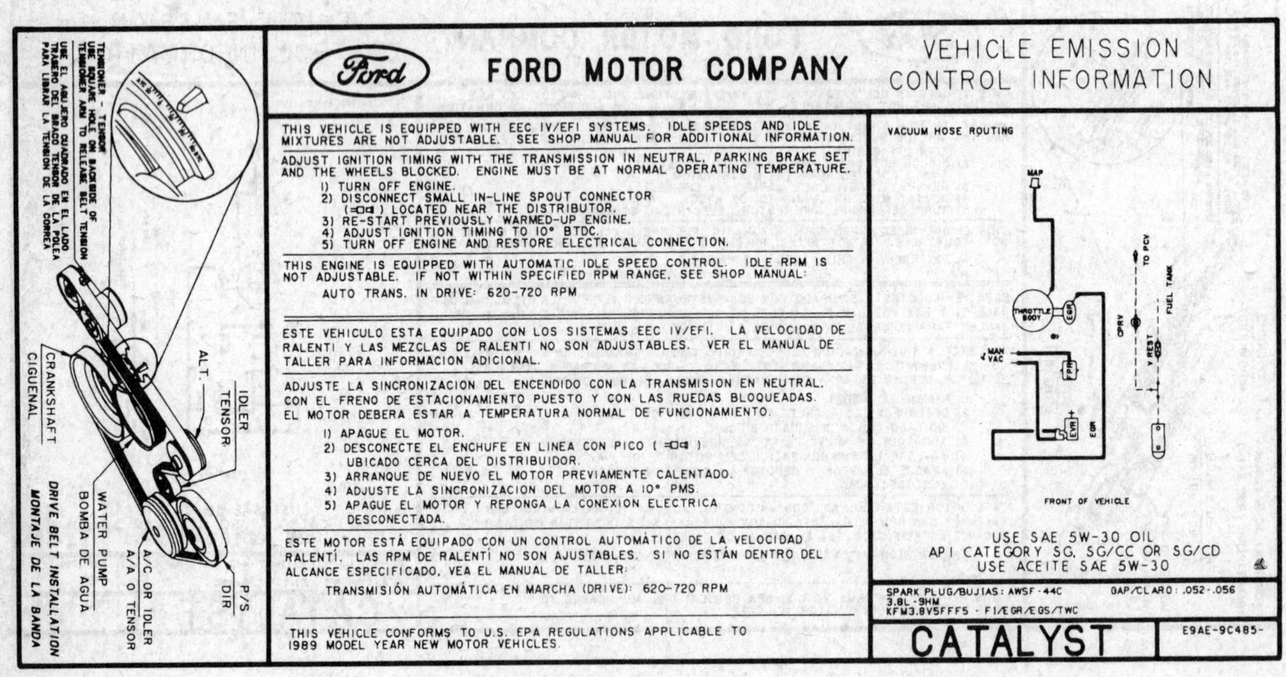

3.8L ENGINE VACUUM SCHEMATIC — 1989 TAURUS AND SABLE

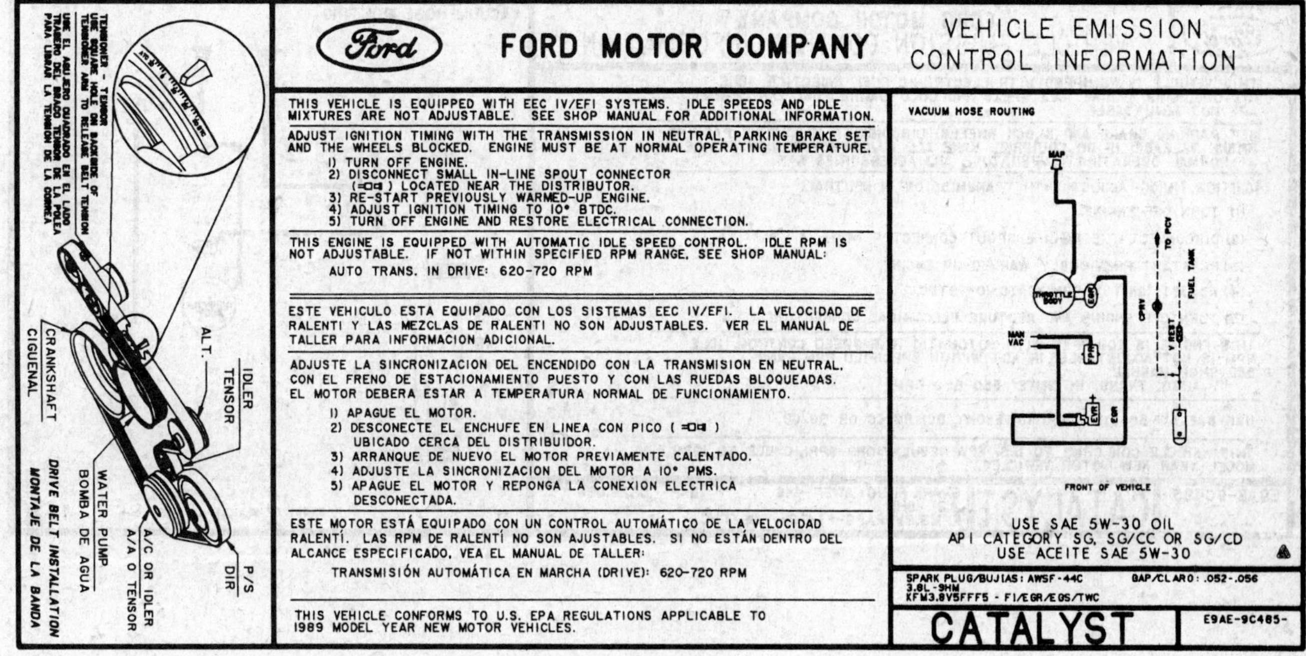

Ford — FORD MOTOR COMPANY — VEHICLE EMISSION CONTROL INFORMATION

THIS VEHICLE IS EQUIPPED WITH EEC IV/EFI SYSTEMS. IDLE SPEEDS AND IDLE MIXTURES ARE NOT ADJUSTABLE. SEE SHOP MANUAL FOR ADDITIONAL INFORMATION.

ADJUST IGNITION TIMING WITH THE TRANSMISSION IN NEUTRAL, PARKING BRAKE SET AND THE WHEELS BLOCKED. ENGINE MUST BE AT NORMAL OPERATING TEMPERATURE.

1) TURN OFF ENGINE.
2) DISCONNECT SMALL IN-LINE SPOUT CONNECTOR (=◻◅) LOCATED NEAR THE DISTRIBUTOR.
3) RE-START PREVIOUSLY WARMED-UP ENGINE.
4) ADJUST IGNITION TIMING TO 10° BTDC.
5) TURN OFF ENGINE AND RESTORE ELECTRICAL CONNECTION.

THIS ENGINE IS EQUIPPED WITH AUTOMATIC IDLE SPEED CONTROL. IDLE RPM IS NOT ADJUSTABLE. IF NOT WITHIN SPECIFIED RPM RANGE, SEE SHOP MANUAL:

AUTO TRANS. IN DRIVE: 620-720 RPM

ESTE VEHICULO ESTA EQUIPADO CON LOS SISTEMAS EEC IV/EFI. LA VELOCIDAD DE RALENTI Y LAS MEZCLAS DE RALENTI NO SON ADJUSTABLES. VER EL MANUAL DE TALLER PARA INFORMACION ADICIONAL.

ADJUSTE LA SINCRONIZACION DEL ENCENDIDO CON LA TRANSMISION EN NEUTRAL, CON EL FRENO DE ESTACIONAMIENTO PUESTO Y CON LAS RUEDAS BLOQUEADAS. EL MOTOR DEBERA ESTAR A TEMPERATURA NORMAL DE FUNCIONAMIENTO.

1) APAGUE EL MOTOR.
2) DESCONECTE EL ENCHUFE EN LINEA CON PICO (=◻◅) UBICADO CERCA DEL DISTRIBUIDOR.
3) ARRANQUE DE NUEVO EL MOTOR PREVIAMENTE CALENTADO.
4) ADJUSTE LA SINCRONIZACION DEL MOTOR A 10° PMS.
5) APAGUE EL MOTOR Y REPONGA LA CONEXION ELECTRICA DESCONECTADA.

ESTE MOTOR ESTÁ EQUIPADO CON UN CONTROL AUTOMÁTICO DE LA VELOCIDAD RALENTÍ. LAS RPM DE RALENTÍ NO SON AJUSTABLES. SI NO ESTÁN DENTRO DEL ALCANCE ESPECIFICADO, VEA EL MANUAL DE TALLER:

TRANSMISIÓN AUTOMÁTICA EN MARCHA (DRIVE): 620-720 RPM

THIS VEHICLE CONFORMS TO U.S. EPA REGULATIONS APPLICABLE TO 1989 MODEL YEAR NEW MOTOR VEHICLES.

USE SAE 5W-30 OIL
API CATEGORY SG, SG/CC OR SG/CD
USE ACEITE SAE 5W-30

SPARK PLUG/BUJIAS: AWSF-44C GAP/CLARO: .052-.056
3.8L-9HM
KFM3.8V5FFF5 - FI/EGR/EGS/TWC

CATALYST — E9AE-9C485-

3.8L ENGINE VACUUM SCHEMATIC — 1989 TAURUS AND SABLE

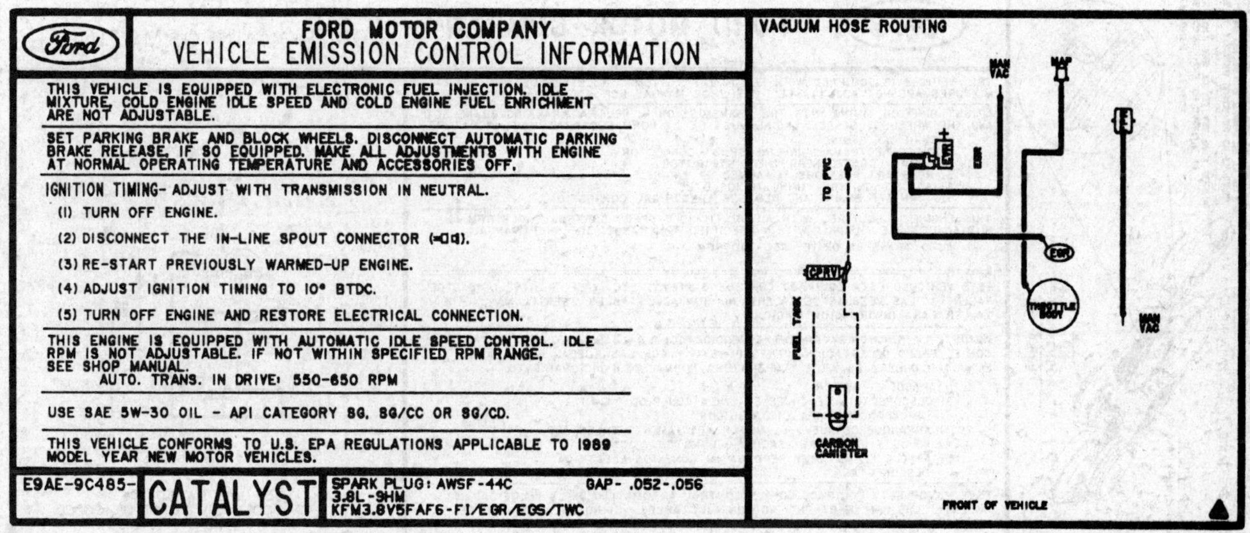

Ford — FORD MOTOR COMPANY — VEHICLE EMISSION CONTROL INFORMATION

THIS VEHICLE IS EQUIPPED WITH ELECTRONIC FUEL INJECTION. IDLE MIXTURE, COLD ENGINE IDLE SPEED AND COLD ENGINE FUEL ENRICHMENT ARE NOT ADJUSTABLE.

SET PARKING BRAKE AND BLOCK WHEELS. DISCONNECT AUTOMATIC PARKING BRAKE RELEASE, IF SO EQUIPPED. MAKE ALL ADJUSTMENTS WITH ENGINE AT NORMAL OPERATING TEMPERATURE AND ACCESSORIES OFF.

IGNITION TIMING- ADJUST WITH TRANSMISSION IN NEUTRAL.

(1) TURN OFF ENGINE.
(2) DISCONNECT THE IN-LINE SPOUT CONNECTOR (=◻◅).
(3) RE-START PREVIOUSLY WARMED-UP ENGINE.
(4) ADJUST IGNITION TIMING TO 10° BTDC.
(5) TURN OFF ENGINE AND RESTORE ELECTRICAL CONNECTION.

THIS ENGINE IS EQUIPPED WITH AUTOMATIC IDLE SPEED CONTROL. IDLE RPM IS NOT ADJUSTABLE. IF NOT WITHIN SPECIFIED RPM RANGE, SEE SHOP MANUAL.

AUTO. TRANS. IN DRIVE: 550-650 RPM

USE SAE 5W-30 OIL - API CATEGORY SG, SG/CC OR SG/CD.

THIS VEHICLE CONFORMS TO U.S. EPA REGULATIONS APPLICABLE TO 1989 MODEL YEAR NEW MOTOR VEHICLES.

E9AE-9C485- CATALYST SPARK PLUG: AWSF-44C GAP- .052-.056
3.8L-9HM
KFM3.8V5FAF6-FI/EGR/EGS/TWC

3.8L ENGINE VACUUM SCHEMATIC – 1989 TAURUS AND SABLE

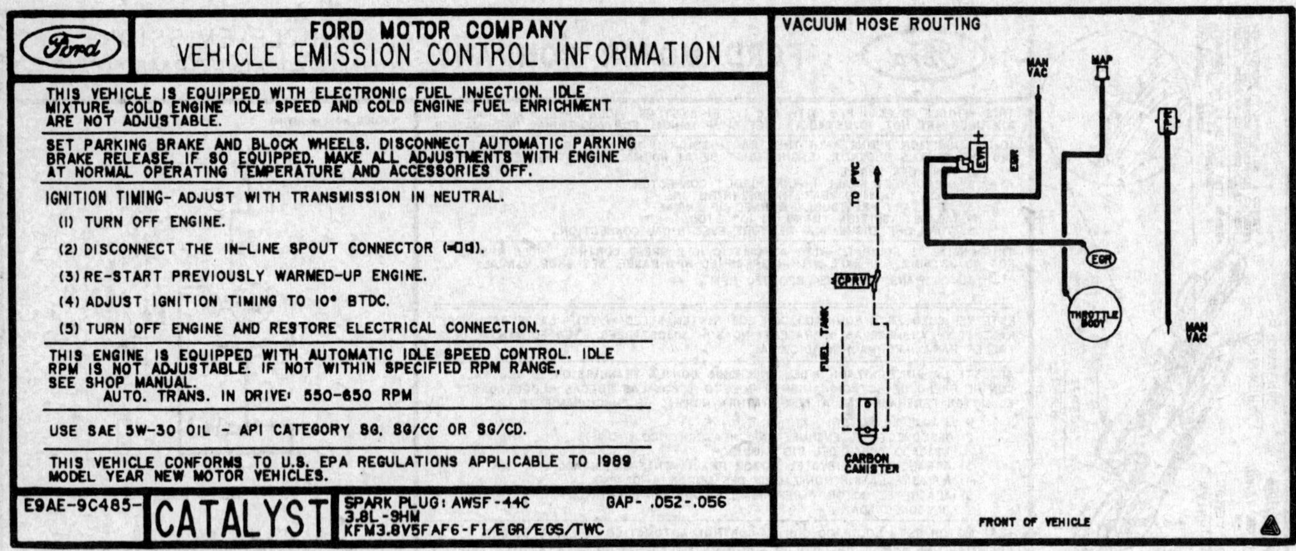

FORD MOTOR COMPANY
VEHICLE EMISSION CONTROL INFORMATION

THIS VEHICLE IS EQUIPPED WITH ELECTRONIC FUEL INJECTION. IDLE MIXTURE, COLD ENGINE IDLE SPEED AND COLD ENGINE FUEL ENRICHMENT ARE NOT ADJUSTABLE.

SET PARKING BRAKE AND BLOCK WHEELS. DISCONNECT AUTOMATIC PARKING BRAKE RELEASE, IF SO EQUIPPED. MAKE ALL ADJUSTMENTS WITH ENGINE AT NORMAL OPERATING TEMPERATURE AND ACCESSORIES OFF.

IGNITION TIMING- ADJUST WITH TRANSMISSION IN NEUTRAL.

(1) TURN OFF ENGINE.

(2) DISCONNECT THE IN-LINE SPOUT CONNECTOR (=⊐⊲).

(3) RE-START PREVIOUSLY WARMED-UP ENGINE.

(4) ADJUST IGNITION TIMING TO 10° BTDC.

(5) TURN OFF ENGINE AND RESTORE ELECTRICAL CONNECTION.

THIS ENGINE IS EQUIPPED WITH AUTOMATIC IDLE SPEED CONTROL. IDLE RPM IS NOT ADJUSTABLE. IF NOT WITHIN SPECIFIED RPM RANGE, SEE SHOP MANUAL.
AUTO. TRANS. IN DRIVE: 550-650 RPM

USE SAE 5W-30 OIL - API CATEGORY SG, SG/CC OR SG/CD.

THIS VEHICLE CONFORMS TO U.S. EPA REGULATIONS APPLICABLE TO 1989 MODEL YEAR NEW MOTOR VEHICLES.

E9AE-9C485- CATALYST SPARK PLUG: AWSF-44C GAP- .052-.056
3.8L-9HM
KFM3.8V5FAF6-FI/EGR/EGS/TWC

3.8L ENGINE VACUUM SCHEMATIC – 1989 TAURUS AND SABLE

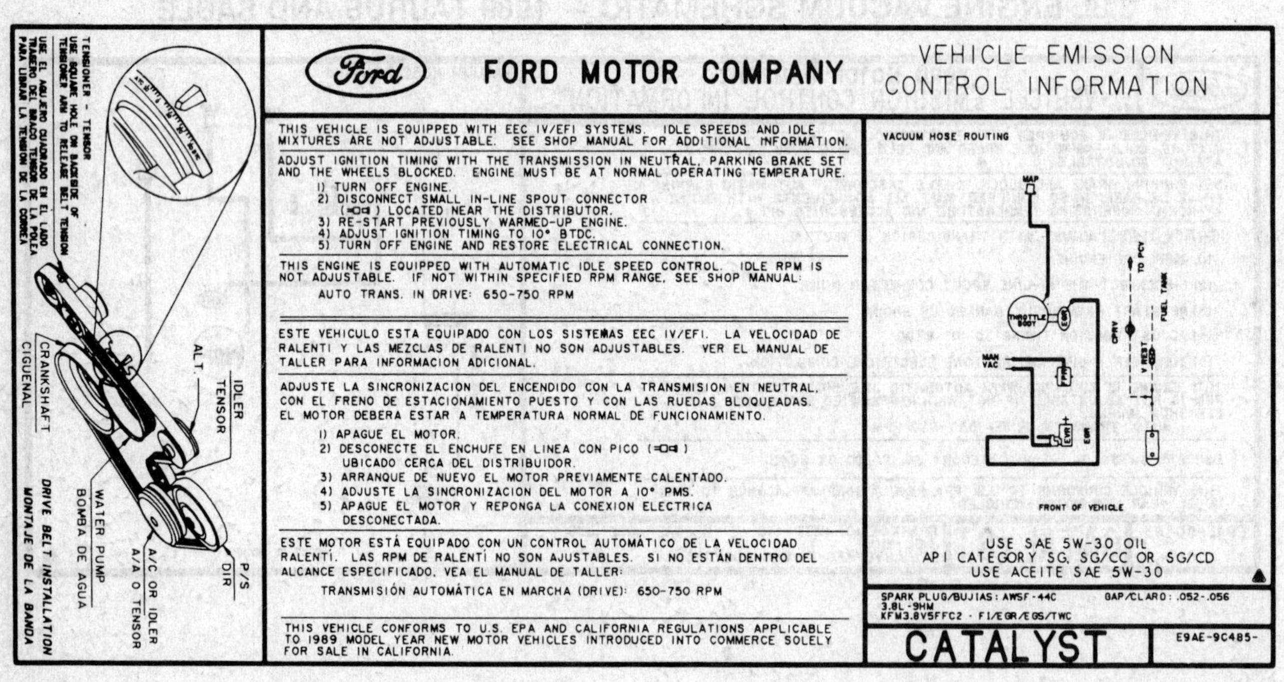

FORD MOTOR COMPANY
VEHICLE EMISSION CONTROL INFORMATION

THIS VEHICLE IS EQUIPPED WITH EEC IV/EFI SYSTEMS. IDLE SPEEDS AND IDLE MIXTURES ARE NOT ADJUSTABLE. SEE SHOP MANUAL FOR ADDITIONAL INFORMATION.

ADJUST IGNITION TIMING WITH THE TRANSMISSION IN NEUTRAL, PARKING BRAKE SET AND THE WHEELS BLOCKED. ENGINE MUST BE AT NORMAL OPERATING TEMPERATURE.
1) TURN OFF ENGINE.
2) DISCONNECT SMALL IN-LINE SPOUT CONNECTOR (=⊐⊲) LOCATED NEAR THE DISTRIBUTOR.
3) RE-START PREVIOUSLY WARMED-UP ENGINE.
4) ADJUST IGNITION TIMING TO 10° BTDC.
5) TURN OFF ENGINE AND RESTORE ELECTRICAL CONNECTION.

THIS ENGINE IS EQUIPPED WITH AUTOMATIC IDLE SPEED CONTROL. IDLE RPM IS NOT ADJUSTABLE. IF NOT WITHIN SPECIFIED RPM RANGE, SEE SHOP MANUAL:
AUTO TRANS. IN DRIVE: 650-750 RPM

ESTE VEHICULO ESTA EQUIPADO CON LOS SISTEMAS EEC IV/EFI. LA VELOCIDAD DE RALENTI Y LAS MEZCLAS DE RALENTI NO SON ADJUSTABLES. VER EL MANUAL DE TALLER PARA INFORMACION ADICIONAL.

ADJUSTE LA SINCRONIZACION DEL ENCENDIDO CON LA TRANSMISION EN NEUTRAL, CON EL FRENO DE ESTACIONAMIENTO PUESTO Y CON LAS RUEDAS BLOQUEADAS. EL MOTOR DEBERA ESTAR A TEMPERATURA NORMAL DE FUNCIONAMIENTO.
1) APAGUE EL MOTOR.
2) DESCONECTE EL ENCHUFE EN LINEA CON PICO (=⊐⊲) UBICADO CERCA DEL DISTRIBUIDOR.
3) ARRANQUE DE NUEVO EL MOTOR PREVIAMENTE CALENTADO.
4) ADJUSTE LA SINCRONIZACION DEL MOTOR A 10° PMS.
5) APAGUE EL MOTOR Y REPONGA LA CONEXION ELECTRICA DESCONECTADA.

ESTE MOTOR ESTÁ EQUIPADO CON UN CONTROL AUTOMÁTICO DE LA VELOCIDAD RALENTÍ. LAS RPM DE RALENTÍ NO SON AJUSTABLES. SI NO ESTÁN DENTRO DEL ALCANCE ESPECIFICADO, VEA EL MANUAL DE TALLER:
TRANSMISIÓN AUTOMÁTICA EN MARCHA (DRIVE): 650-750 RPM

THIS VEHICLE CONFORMS TO U.S. EPA AND CALIFORNIA REGULATIONS APPLICABLE TO 1989 MODEL YEAR NEW MOTOR VEHICLES INTRODUCED INTO COMMERCE SOLELY FOR SALE IN CALIFORNIA.

USE SAE 5W-30 OIL
API CATEGORY SG, SG/CC OR SG/CD
USE ACEITE SAE 5W-30

SPARK PLUG/BUJIAS: AWSF-44C GAP/CLARO: .052-.056
3.8L-9HM
KFM3.8V5FFC2 - FI/EGR/EGS/TWC

CATALYST E9AE-9C485-

3.8L ENGINE VACUUM SCHEMATIC — 1989 TAURUS AND SABLE

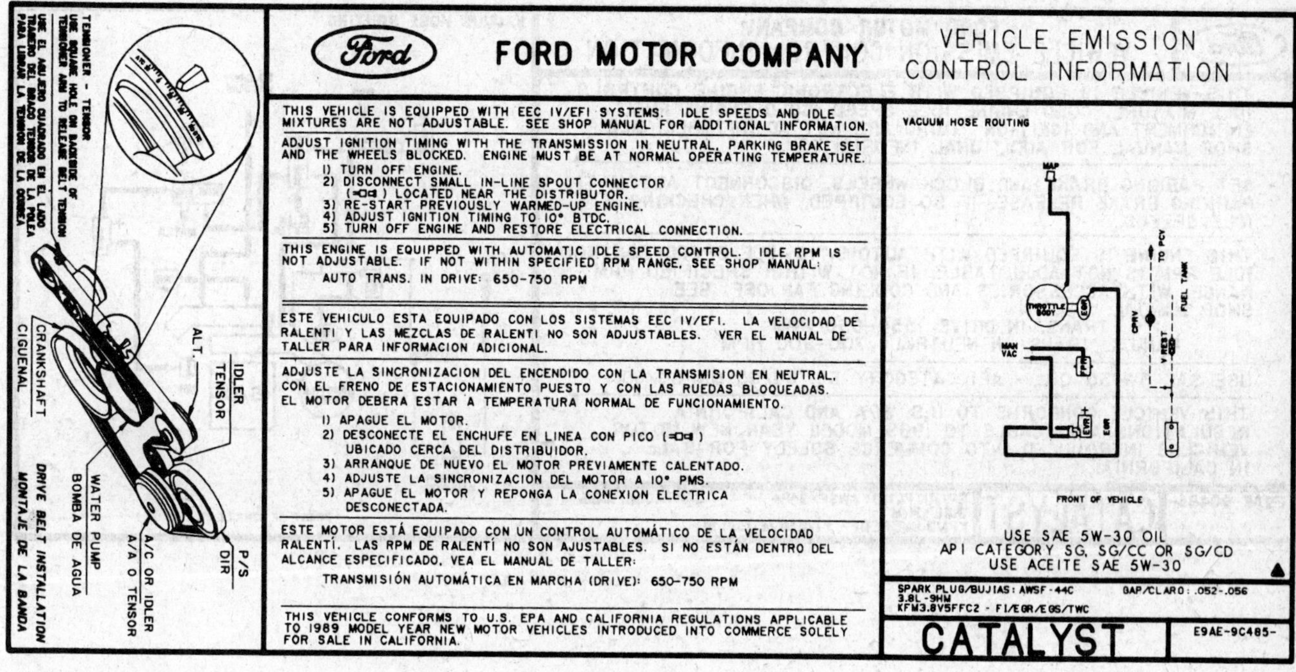

3.8L ENGINE VACUUM SCHEMATIC — 1989 TAURUS AND SABLE

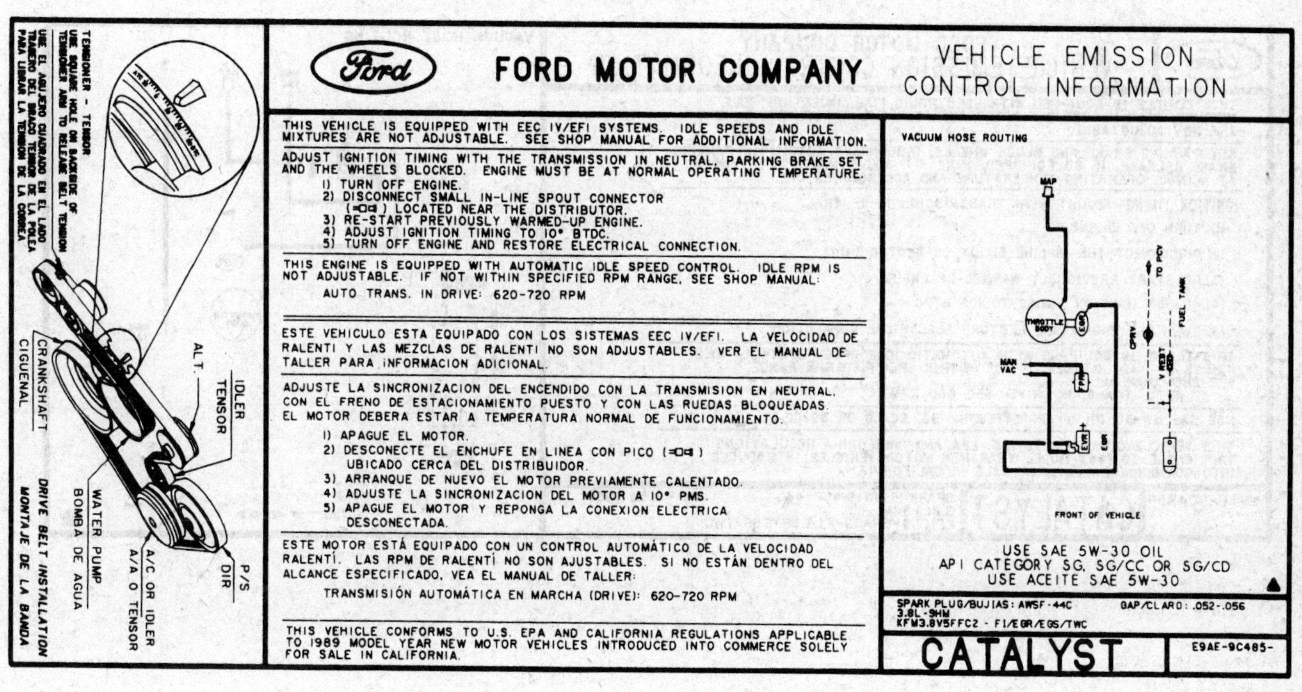

3.8L ENGINE VACUUM SCHEMATIC — 1989 TAURUS AND SABLE

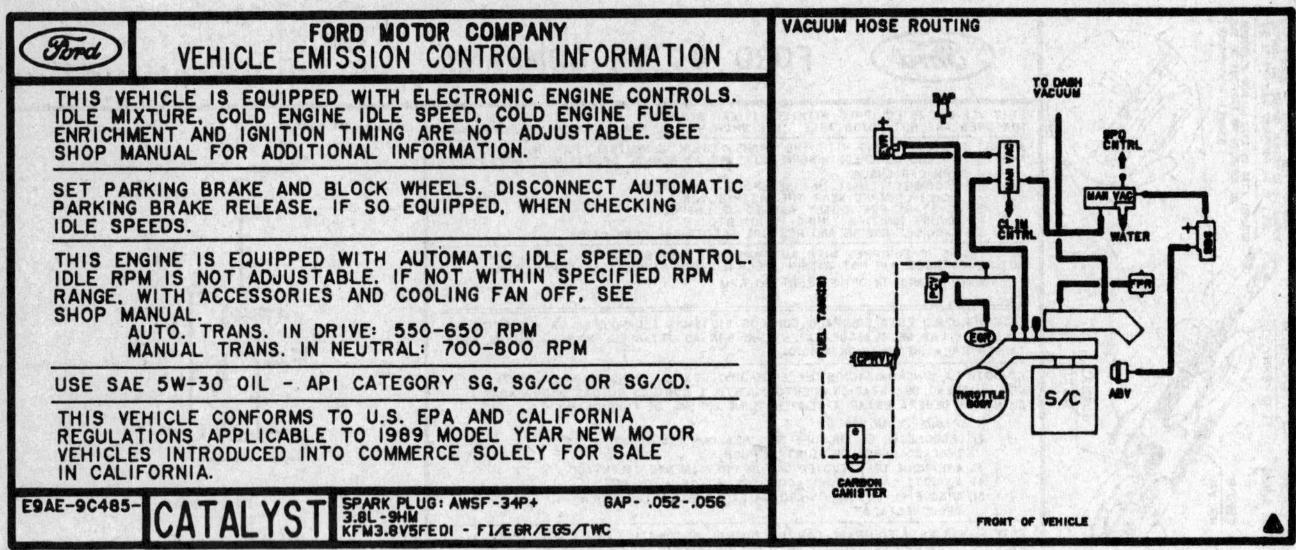

Ford

FORD MOTOR COMPANY
VEHICLE EMISSION CONTROL INFORMATION

THIS VEHICLE IS EQUIPPED WITH ELECTRONIC ENGINE CONTROLS. IDLE MIXTURE, COLD ENGINE IDLE SPEED, COLD ENGINE FUEL ENRICHMENT AND IGNITION TIMING ARE NOT ADJUSTABLE. SEE SHOP MANUAL FOR ADDITIONAL INFORMATION.

SET PARKING BRAKE AND BLOCK WHEELS. DISCONNECT AUTOMATIC PARKING BRAKE RELEASE, IF SO EQUIPPED, WHEN CHECKING IDLE SPEEDS.

THIS ENGINE IS EQUIPPED WITH AUTOMATIC IDLE SPEED CONTROL. IDLE RPM IS NOT ADJUSTABLE. IF NOT WITHIN SPECIFIED RPM RANGE, WITH ACCESSORIES AND COOLING FAN OFF, SEE SHOP MANUAL.
AUTO. TRANS. IN DRIVE: 550-650 RPM
MANUAL TRANS. IN NEUTRAL: 700-800 RPM

USE SAE 5W-30 OIL - API CATEGORY SG, SG/CC OR SG/CD.

THIS VEHICLE CONFORMS TO U.S. EPA AND CALIFORNIA REGULATIONS APPLICABLE TO 1989 MODEL YEAR NEW MOTOR VEHICLES INTRODUCED INTO COMMERCE SOLELY FOR SALE IN CALIFORNIA.

E9AE-9C485- CATALYST
SPARK PLUG: AWSF-34P+ GAP- .052-.056
3.8L-9HM
KFM3.8V5FED1 - FI/EGR/EGS/TWC

3.8L ENGINE VACUUM SCHEMATIC — 1989 TAURUS AND SABLE

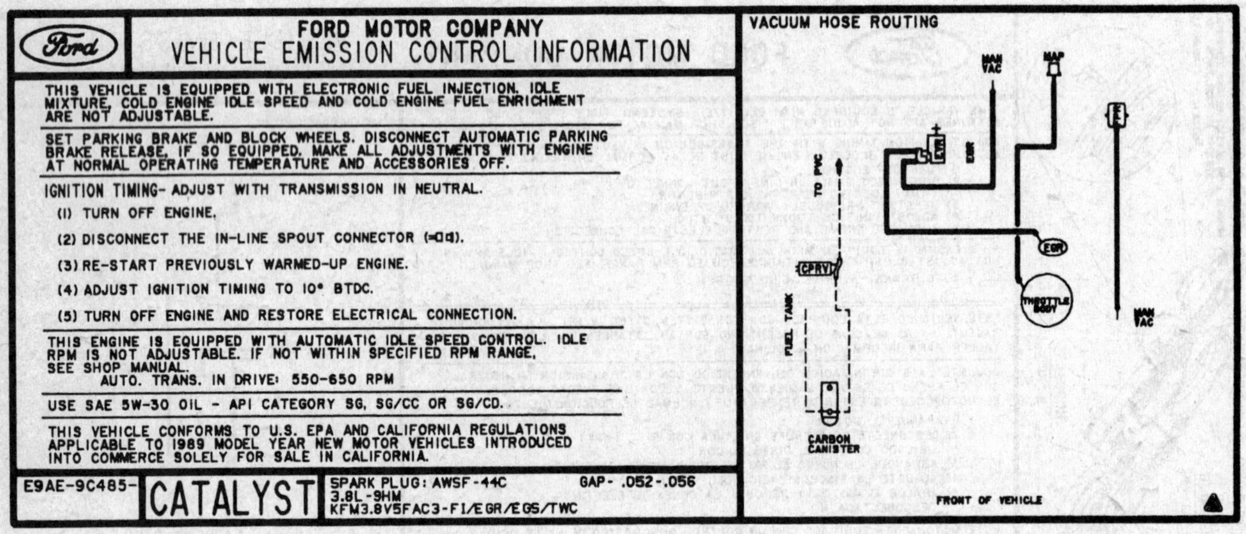

Ford

FORD MOTOR COMPANY
VEHICLE EMISSION CONTROL INFORMATION

THIS VEHICLE IS EQUIPPED WITH ELECTRONIC FUEL INJECTION. IDLE MIXTURE, COLD ENGINE IDLE SPEED AND COLD ENGINE FUEL ENRICHMENT ARE NOT ADJUSTABLE.

SET PARKING BRAKE AND BLOCK WHEELS. DISCONNECT AUTOMATIC PARKING BRAKE RELEASE, IF SO EQUIPPED. MAKE ALL ADJUSTMENTS WITH ENGINE AT NORMAL OPERATING TEMPERATURE AND ACCESSORIES OFF.

IGNITION TIMING- ADJUST WITH TRANSMISSION IN NEUTRAL.
(1) TURN OFF ENGINE.
(2) DISCONNECT THE IN-LINE SPOUT CONNECTOR (=□◁).
(3) RE-START PREVIOUSLY WARMED-UP ENGINE.
(4) ADJUST IGNITION TIMING TO 10° BTDC.
(5) TURN OFF ENGINE AND RESTORE ELECTRICAL CONNECTION.

THIS ENGINE IS EQUIPPED WITH AUTOMATIC IDLE SPEED CONTROL. IDLE RPM IS NOT ADJUSTABLE. IF NOT WITHIN SPECIFIED RPM RANGE, SEE SHOP MANUAL.
AUTO. TRANS. IN DRIVE: 550-650 RPM

USE SAE 5W-30 OIL - API CATEGORY SG, SG/CC OR SG/CD.

THIS VEHICLE CONFORMS TO U.S. EPA AND CALIFORNIA REGULATIONS APPLICABLE TO 1989 MODEL YEAR NEW MOTOR VEHICLES INTRODUCED INTO COMMERCE SOLELY FOR SALE IN CALIFORNIA.

E9AE-9C485- CATALYST
SPARK PLUG: AWSF-44C GAP- .052-.056
3.8L-9HM
KFM3.8V5FAC3-FI/EGR/EGS/TWC

3.8L ENGINE VACUUM SCHEMATIC — 1989 TAURUS AND SABLE

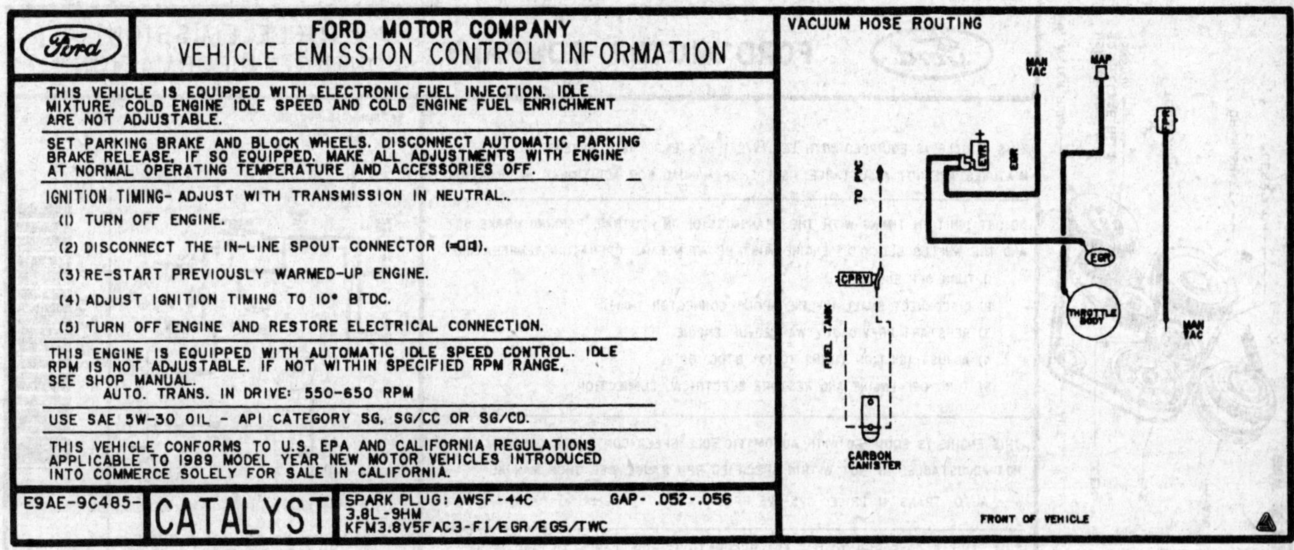

FORD MOTOR COMPANY
VEHICLE EMISSION CONTROL INFORMATION

THIS VEHICLE IS EQUIPPED WITH ELECTRONIC FUEL INJECTION. IDLE MIXTURE, COLD ENGINE IDLE SPEED AND COLD ENGINE FUEL ENRICHMENT ARE NOT ADJUSTABLE.

SET PARKING BRAKE AND BLOCK WHEELS. DISCONNECT AUTOMATIC PARKING BRAKE RELEASE, IF SO EQUIPPED. MAKE ALL ADJUSTMENTS WITH ENGINE AT NORMAL OPERATING TEMPERATURE AND ACCESSORIES OFF.

IGNITION TIMING- ADJUST WITH TRANSMISSION IN NEUTRAL.

(1) TURN OFF ENGINE.

(2) DISCONNECT THE IN-LINE SPOUT CONNECTOR (=◻◻).

(3) RE-START PREVIOUSLY WARMED-UP ENGINE.

(4) ADJUST IGNITION TIMING TO 10° BTDC.

(5) TURN OFF ENGINE AND RESTORE ELECTRICAL CONNECTION.

THIS ENGINE IS EQUIPPED WITH AUTOMATIC IDLE SPEED CONTROL. IDLE RPM IS NOT ADJUSTABLE. IF NOT WITHIN SPECIFIED RPM RANGE, SEE SHOP MANUAL.
AUTO. TRANS. IN DRIVE: 550-650 RPM

USE SAE 5W-30 OIL - API CATEGORY SG, SG/CC OR SG/CD.

THIS VEHICLE CONFORMS TO U.S. EPA AND CALIFORNIA REGULATIONS APPLICABLE TO 1989 MODEL YEAR NEW MOTOR VEHICLES INTRODUCED INTO COMMERCE SOLELY FOR SALE IN CALIFORNIA.

E9AE-9C485- CATALYST SPARK PLUG: AWSF-44C GAP- .052-.056
3.8L-9HM
KFM3.8V5FAC3-FI/EGR/EGS/TWC

VACUUM HOSE ROUTING

2.5L ENGINE VACUUM SCHEMATIC — 1990 TAURUS AND SABLE

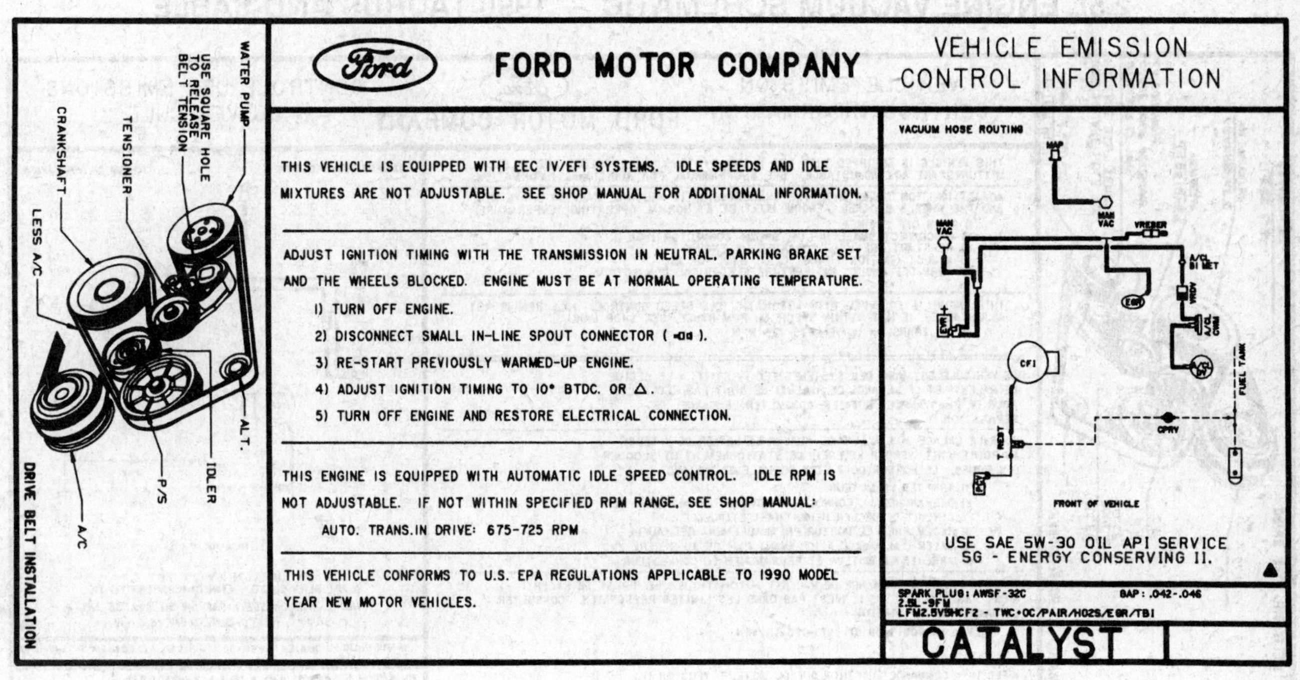

FORD MOTOR COMPANY
VEHICLE EMISSION CONTROL INFORMATION

THIS VEHICLE IS EQUIPPED WITH EEC IV/EFI SYSTEMS. IDLE SPEEDS AND IDLE MIXTURES ARE NOT ADJUSTABLE. SEE SHOP MANUAL FOR ADDITIONAL INFORMATION.

ADJUST IGNITION TIMING WITH THE TRANSMISSION IN NEUTRAL, PARKING BRAKE SET AND THE WHEELS BLOCKED. ENGINE MUST BE AT NORMAL OPERATING TEMPERATURE.

1) TURN OFF ENGINE.
2) DISCONNECT SMALL IN-LINE SPOUT CONNECTOR (=◻◻).
3) RE-START PREVIOUSLY WARMED-UP ENGINE.
4) ADJUST IGNITION TIMING TO 10° BTDC. OR △.
5) TURN OFF ENGINE AND RESTORE ELECTRICAL CONNECTION.

THIS ENGINE IS EQUIPPED WITH AUTOMATIC IDLE SPEED CONTROL. IDLE RPM IS NOT ADJUSTABLE. IF NOT WITHIN SPECIFIED RPM RANGE, SEE SHOP MANUAL:
AUTO. TRANS. IN DRIVE: 675-725 RPM

THIS VEHICLE CONFORMS TO U.S. EPA REGULATIONS APPLICABLE TO 1990 MODEL YEAR NEW MOTOR VEHICLES.

VACUUM HOSE ROUTING

USE SAE 5W-30 OIL API SERVICE SG - ENERGY CONSERVING II.

SPARK PLUG: AWSF-32C GAP: .042-.046
2.5L-9FM
LFM2.5V5HCF2 - TWC+OC/PAIR/HO2S/EGR/TBI

CATALYST

2.5L ENGINE VACUUM SCHEMATIC — 1990 TAURUS AND SABLE

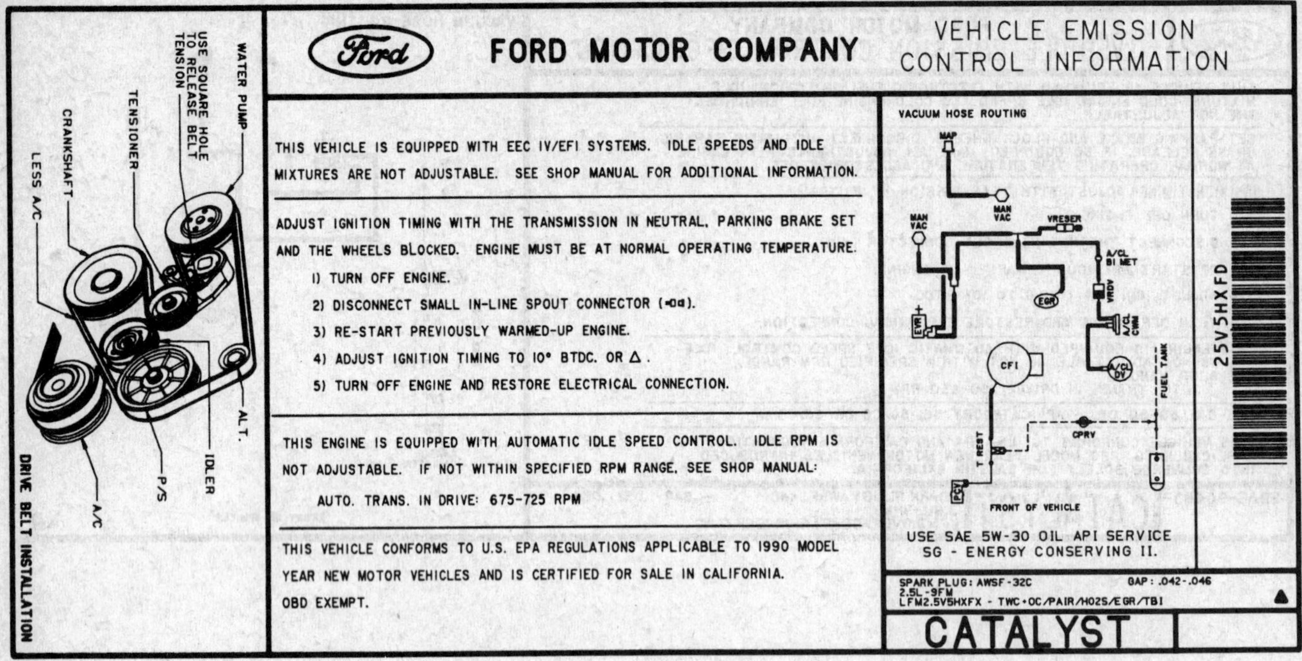

2.5L ENGINE VACUUM SCHEMATIC — 1990 TAURUS AND SABLE

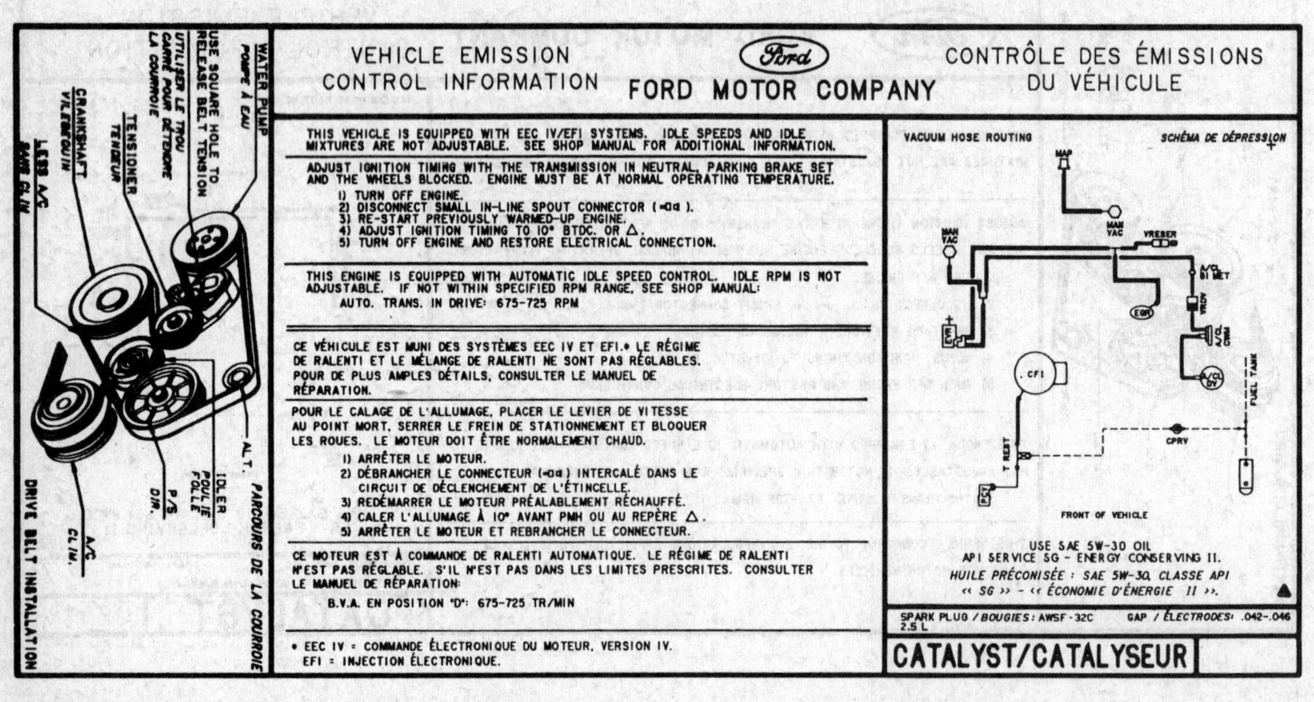

3.0L ENGINE VACUUM SCHEMATIC — 1990 TAURUS AND SABLE

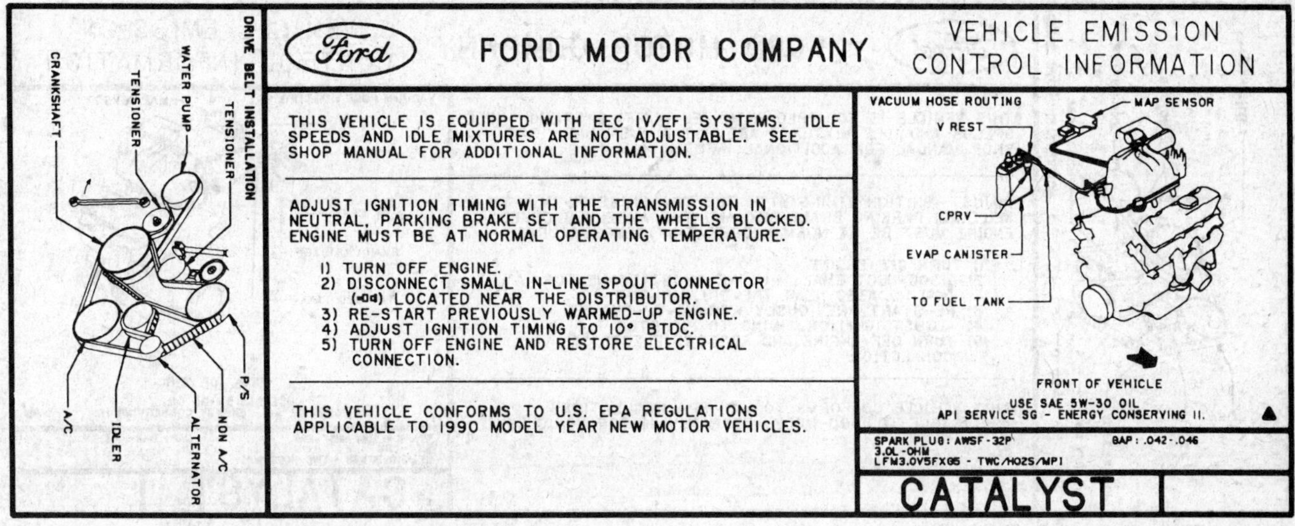

3.0L ENGINE VACUUM SCHEMATIC — 1990 TAURUS AND SABLE

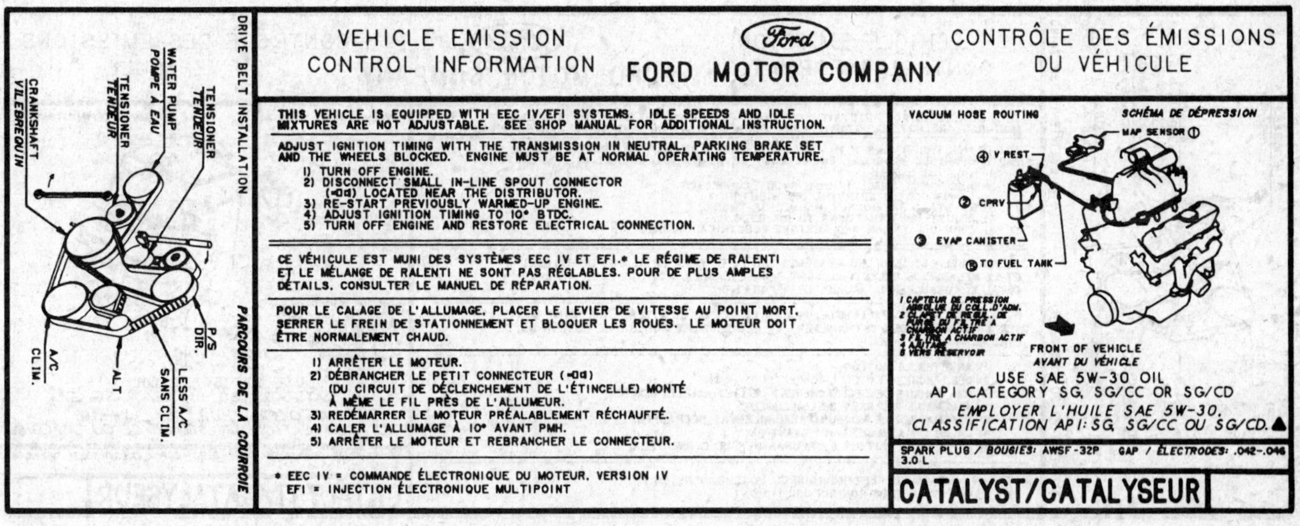

3.0L ENGINE VACUUM SCHEMATIC — 1990 TAURUS AND SABLE

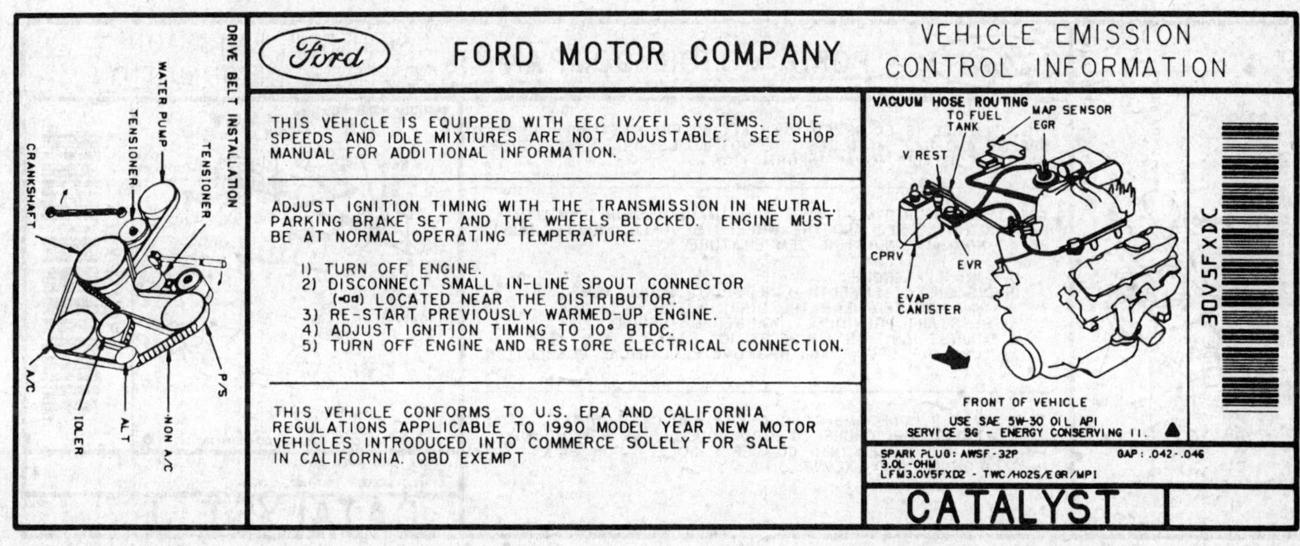

3.0L ENGINE VACUUM SCHEMATIC — 1990 TAURUS AND SABLE

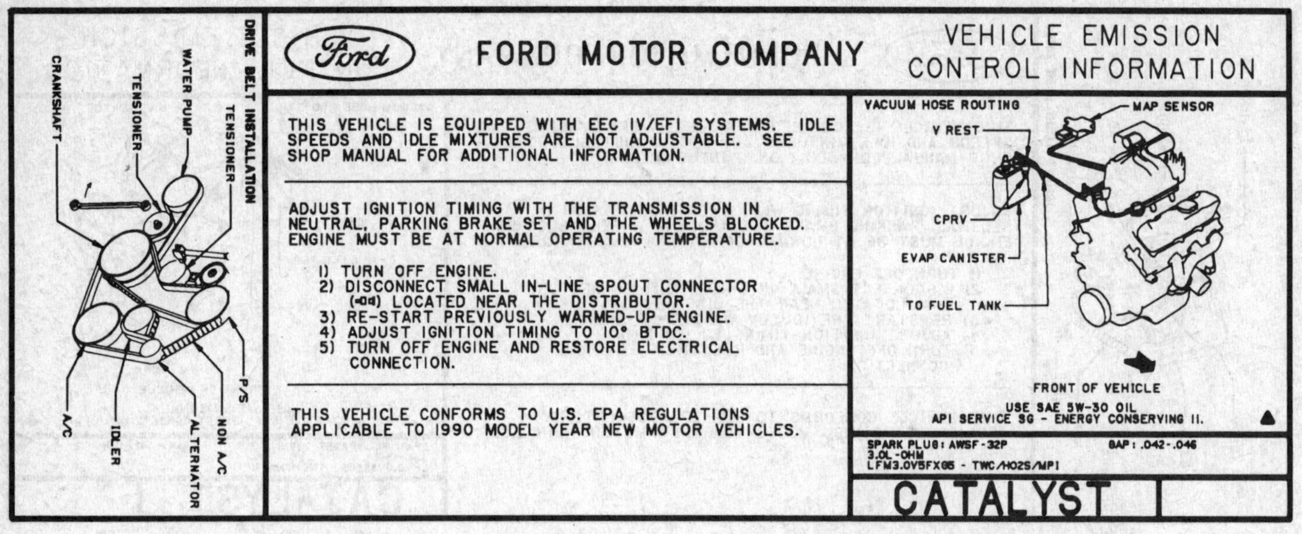

3.0L ENGINE VACUUM SCHEMATIC — 1990 TAURUS AND SABLE

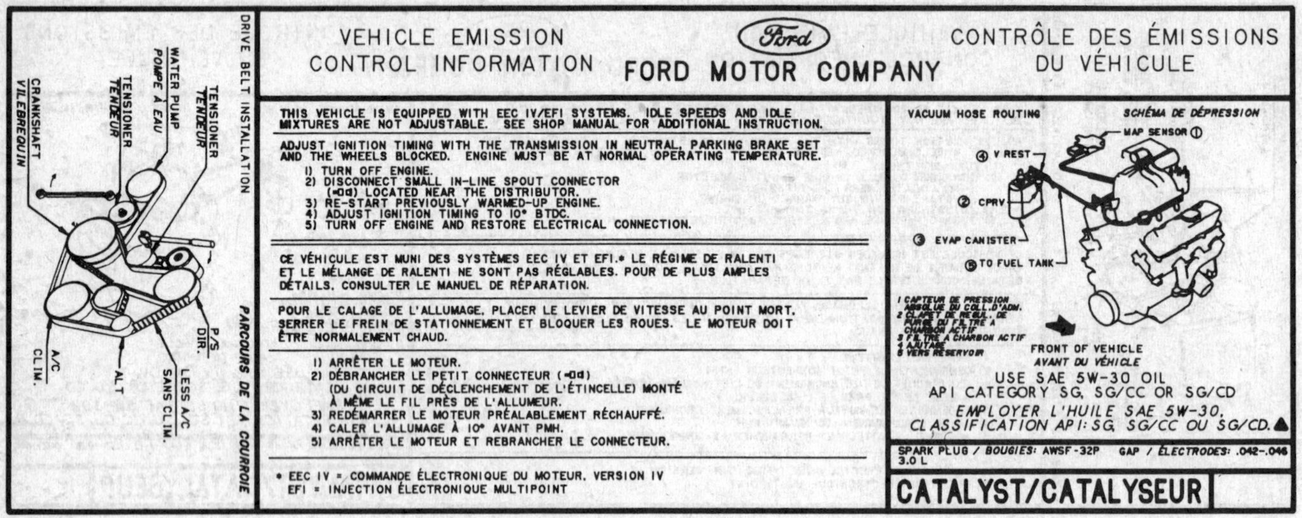

3.0L ENGINE VACUUM SCHEMATIC — 1990 TAURUS AND SABLE

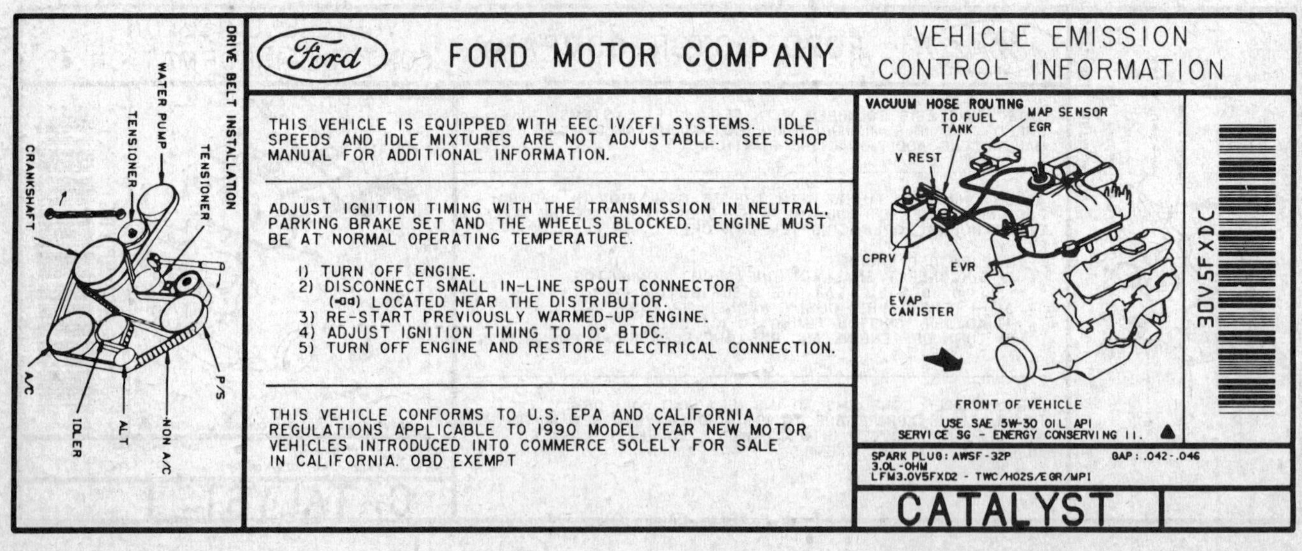

3.0L ENGINE VACUUM SCHEMATIC – 1990 TAURUS AND SABLE (EXCEPT SHO)

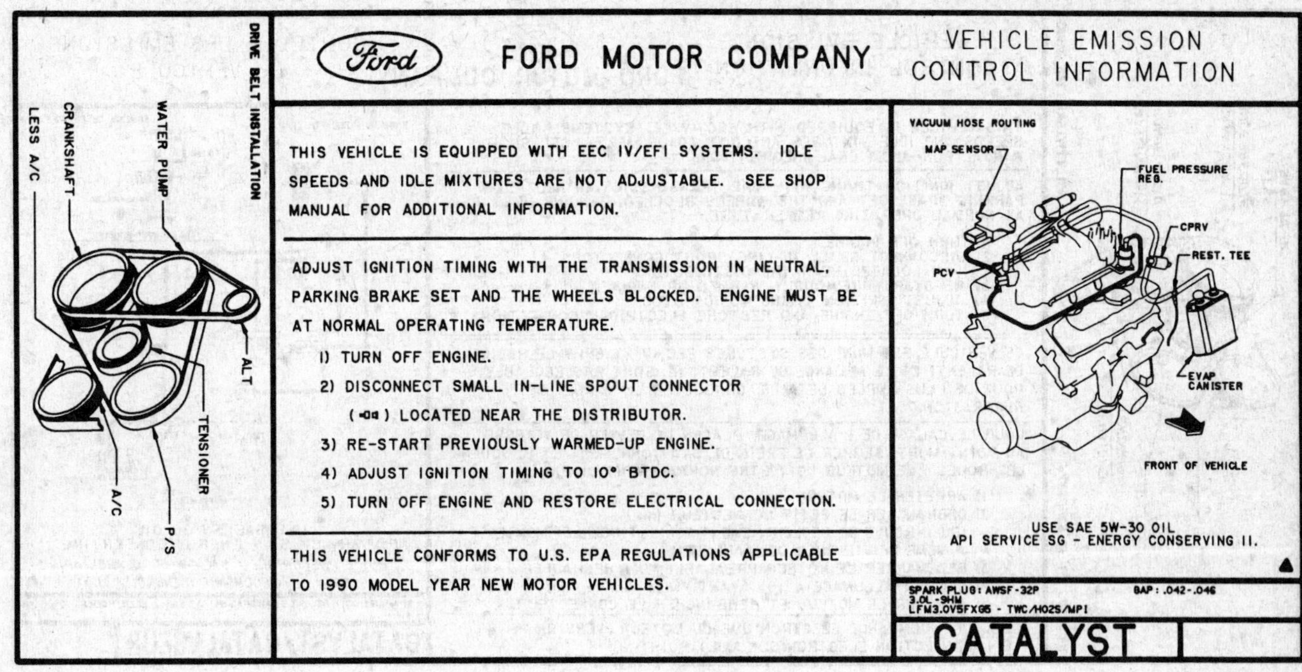

3.0L ENGINE VACUUM SCHEMATIC – 1990 TAURUS AND SABLE (EXCEPT SHO)

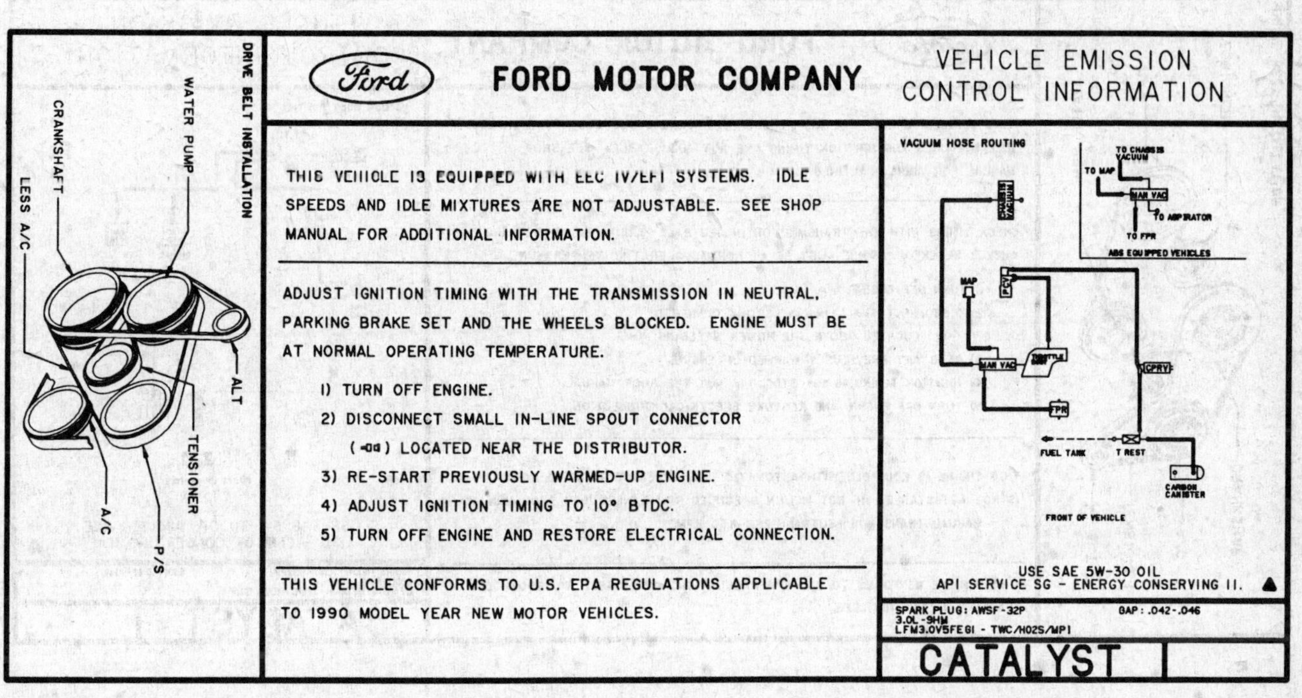

3.0L ENGINE VACUUM SCHEMATIC – 1990 TAURUS AND SABLE (EXCEPT SHO)

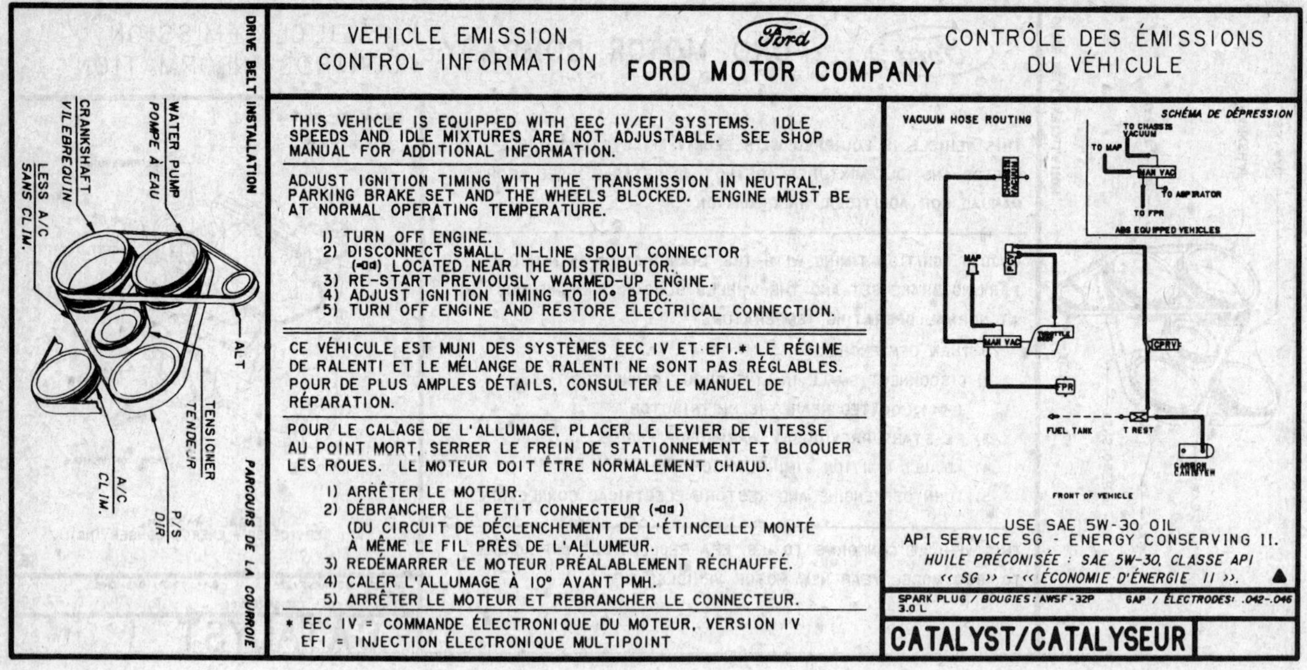

VEHICLE EMISSION CONTROL INFORMATION — FORD MOTOR COMPANY — CONTRÔLE DES ÉMISSIONS DU VÉHICULE

THIS VEHICLE IS EQUIPPED WITH EEC IV/EFI SYSTEMS. IDLE SPEEDS AND IDLE MIXTURES ARE NOT ADJUSTABLE. SEE SHOP MANUAL FOR ADDITIONAL INFORMATION.

ADJUST IGNITION TIMING WITH THE TRANSMISSION IN NEUTRAL, PARKING BRAKE SET AND THE WHEELS BLOCKED. ENGINE MUST BE AT NORMAL OPERATING TEMPERATURE.

1) TURN OFF ENGINE.
2) DISCONNECT SMALL IN-LINE SPOUT CONNECTOR (▭◻) LOCATED NEAR THE DISTRIBUTOR.
3) RE-START PREVIOUSLY WARMED-UP ENGINE.
4) ADJUST IGNITION TIMING TO 10° BTDC.
5) TURN OFF ENGINE AND RESTORE ELECTRICAL CONNECTION.

CE VÉHICULE EST MUNI DES SYSTÈMES EEC IV ET EFI.* LE RÉGIME DE RALENTI ET LE MÉLANGE DE RALENTI NE SONT PAS RÉGLABLES. POUR DE PLUS AMPLES DÉTAILS, CONSULTER LE MANUEL DE RÉPARATION.

POUR LE CALAGE DE L'ALLUMAGE, PLACER LE LEVIER DE VITESSE AU POINT MORT, SERRER LE FREIN DE STATIONNEMENT ET BLOQUER LES ROUES. LE MOTEUR DOIT ÊTRE NORMALEMENT CHAUD.

1) ARRÊTER LE MOTEUR.
2) DÉBRANCHER LE PETIT CONNECTEUR (▭◻) (DU CIRCUIT DE DÉCLENCHEMENT DE L'ÉTINCELLE) MONTÉ À MÊME LE FIL PRÈS DE L'ALLUMEUR.
3) REDÉMARRER LE MOTEUR PRÉALABLEMENT RÉCHAUFFÉ.
4) CALER L'ALLUMAGE À 10° AVANT PMH.
5) ARRÊTER LE MOTEUR ET REBRANCHER LE CONNECTEUR.

* EEC IV = COMMANDE ÉLECTRONIQUE DU MOTEUR, VERSION IV
EFI = INJECTION ÉLECTRONIQUE MULTIPOINT

USE SAE 5W-30 OIL
API SERVICE SG - ENERGY CONSERVING II.
HUILE PRÉCONISÉE : SAE 5W-30, CLASSE API « SG » - « ÉCONOMIE D'ÉNERGIE II ».

SPARK PLUG / BOUGIES: AWSF-32P GAP / ÉLECTRODES: .042-.046
3.0 L

CATALYST/CATALYSEUR

3.0L ENGINE VACUUM SCHEMATIC – 1990 TAURUS AND SABLE

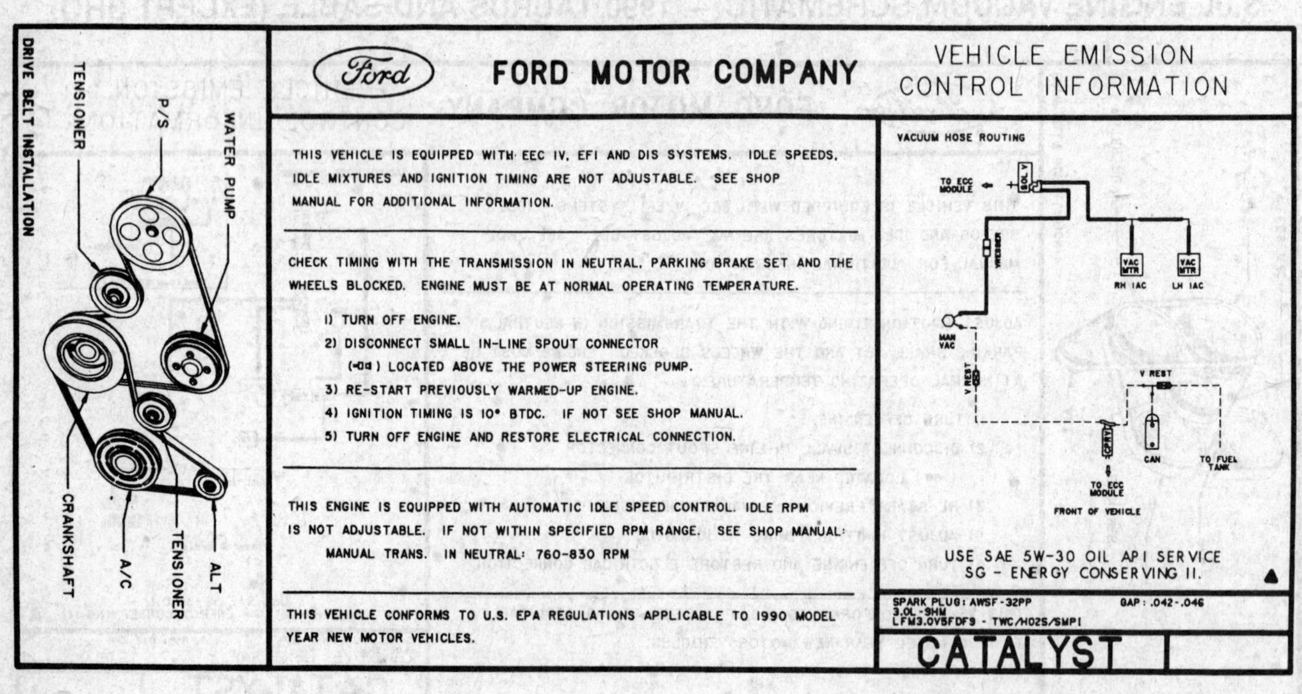

FORD MOTOR COMPANY — VEHICLE EMISSION CONTROL INFORMATION

THIS VEHICLE IS EQUIPPED WITH EEC IV, EFI AND DIS SYSTEMS. IDLE SPEEDS, IDLE MIXTURES AND IGNITION TIMING ARE NOT ADJUSTABLE. SEE SHOP MANUAL FOR ADDITIONAL INFORMATION.

CHECK TIMING WITH THE TRANSMISSION IN NEUTRAL, PARKING BRAKE SET AND THE WHEELS BLOCKED. ENGINE MUST BE AT NORMAL OPERATING TEMPERATURE.

1) TURN OFF ENGINE.
2) DISCONNECT SMALL IN-LINE SPOUT CONNECTOR (▭◻) LOCATED ABOVE THE POWER STEERING PUMP.
3) RE-START PREVIOUSLY WARMED-UP ENGINE.
4) IGNITION TIMING IS 10° BTDC. IF NOT SEE SHOP MANUAL.
5) TURN OFF ENGINE AND RESTORE ELECTRICAL CONNECTION.

THIS ENGINE IS EQUIPPED WITH AUTOMATIC IDLE SPEED CONTROL. IDLE RPM IS NOT ADJUSTABLE. IF NOT WITHIN SPECIFIED RPM RANGE, SEE SHOP MANUAL:
MANUAL TRANS. IN NEUTRAL: 760-830 RPM

THIS VEHICLE CONFORMS TO U.S. EPA REGULATIONS APPLICABLE TO 1990 MODEL YEAR NEW MOTOR VEHICLES.

USE SAE 5W-30 OIL API SERVICE SG - ENERGY CONSERVING II.

SPARK PLUG: AWSF-32PP GAP: .042-.046
3.0L-9HM
LFM3.0V5FDF9 - TWC/HO2S/SMPI

CATALYST

3.0L ENGINE VACUUM SCHEMATIC – 1990 TAURUS AND SABLE

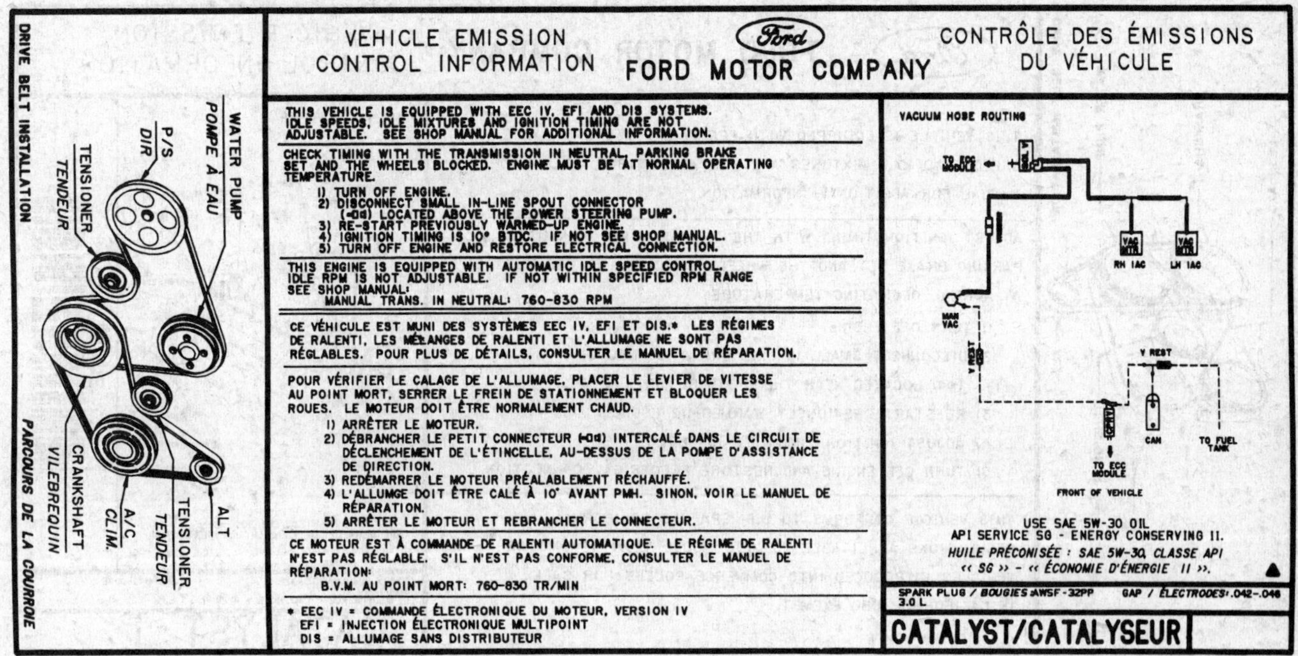

VEHICLE EMISSION CONTROL INFORMATION — Ford — FORD MOTOR COMPANY — CONTRÔLE DES ÉMISSIONS DU VÉHICULE

THIS VEHICLE IS EQUIPPED WITH EEC IV, EFI AND DIS SYSTEMS. IDLE SPEEDS, IDLE MIXTURES AND IGNITION TIMING ARE NOT ADJUSTABLE. SEE SHOP MANUAL FOR ADDITIONAL INFORMATION.

CHECK TIMING WITH THE TRANSMISSION IN NEUTRAL, PARKING BRAKE SET AND THE WHEELS BLOCKED. ENGINE MUST BE AT NORMAL OPERATING TEMPERATURE.

1) TURN OFF ENGINE.
2) DISCONNECT SMALL IN-LINE SPOUT CONNECTOR (⊸◘) LOCATED ABOVE THE POWER STEERING PUMP.
3) RE-START PREVIOUSLY WARMED-UP ENGINE.
4) IGNITION TIMING IS 10° BTDC. IF NOT SEE SHOP MANUAL.
5) TURN OFF ENGINE AND RESTORE ELECTRICAL CONNECTION.

THIS ENGINE IS EQUIPPED WITH AUTOMATIC IDLE SPEED CONTROL. IDLE RPM IS NOT ADJUSTABLE. IF NOT WITHIN SPECIFIED RPM RANGE SEE SHOP MANUAL:
MANUAL TRANS. IN NEUTRAL: 760-830 RPM

CE VÉHICULE EST MUNI DES SYSTÈMES EEC IV, EFI ET DIS.* LES RÉGIMES DE RALENTI, LES MÉLANGES DE RALENTI ET L'ALLUMAGE NE SONT PAS RÉGLABLES. POUR PLUS DE DÉTAILS, CONSULTER LE MANUEL DE RÉPARATION.

POUR VÉRIFIER LE CALAGE DE L'ALLUMAGE, PLACER LE LEVIER DE VITESSE AU POINT MORT, SERRER LE FREIN DE STATIONNEMENT ET BLOQUER LES ROUES. LE MOTEUR DOIT ÊTRE NORMALEMENT CHAUD.

1) ARRÊTER LE MOTEUR.
2) DÉBRANCHER LE PETIT CONNECTEUR (⊸◘) INTERCALÉ DANS LE CIRCUIT DE DÉCLENCHEMENT DE L'ÉTINCELLE, AU-DESSUS DE LA POMPE D'ASSISTANCE DE DIRECTION.
3) REDÉMARRER LE MOTEUR PRÉALABLEMENT RÉCHAUFFÉ.
4) L'ALLUMGE DOIT ÊTRE CALÉ À 10° AVANT PMH. SINON, VOIR LE MANUEL DE RÉPARATION.
5) ARRÊTER LE MOTEUR ET REBRANCHER LE CONNECTEUR.

CE MOTEUR EST À COMMANDE DE RALENTI AUTOMATIQUE. LE RÉGIME DE RALENTI N'EST PAS RÉGLABLE. S'IL N'EST PAS CONFORME, CONSULTER LE MANUEL DE RÉPARATION:
B.V.M. AU POINT MORT: 760-830 TR/MIN

* EEC IV = COMMANDE ÉLECTRONIQUE DU MOTEUR, VERSION IV
EFI = INJECTION ÉLECTRONIQUE MULTIPOINT
DIS = ALLUMAGE SANS DISTRIBUTEUR

USE SAE 5W-30 OIL API SERVICE SG - ENERGY CONSERVING II.
HUILE PRÉCONISÉE : SAE 5W-30, CLASSE API « SG » - « ÉCONOMIE D'ÉNERGIE II ».

SPARK PLUG / BOUGIES: AWSF-32PP GAP / ÉLECTRODES: .042-.046
3.0 L

CATALYST/CATALYSEUR

3.0L ENGINE VACUUM SCHEMATIC – 1990 TAURUS AND SABLE

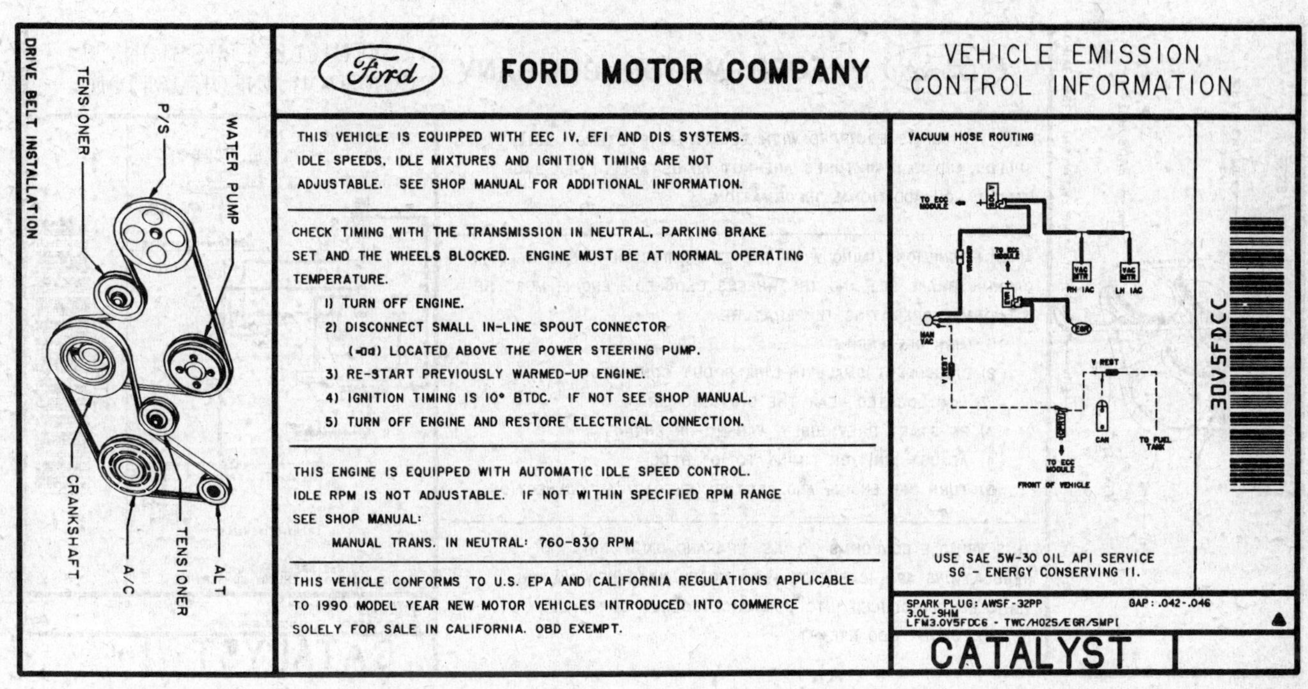

Ford — FORD MOTOR COMPANY — VEHICLE EMISSION CONTROL INFORMATION

THIS VEHICLE IS EQUIPPED WITH EEC IV, EFI AND DIS SYSTEMS. IDLE SPEEDS, IDLE MIXTURES AND IGNITION TIMING ARE NOT ADJUSTABLE. SEE SHOP MANUAL FOR ADDITIONAL INFORMATION.

CHECK TIMING WITH THE TRANSMISSION IN NEUTRAL, PARKING BRAKE SET AND THE WHEELS BLOCKED. ENGINE MUST BE AT NORMAL OPERATING TEMPERATURE.

1) TURN OFF ENGINE.
2) DISCONNECT SMALL IN-LINE SPOUT CONNECTOR (⊸◘) LOCATED ABOVE THE POWER STEERING PUMP.
3) RE-START PREVIOUSLY WARMED-UP ENGINE.
4) IGNITION TIMING IS 10° BTDC. IF NOT SEE SHOP MANUAL.
5) TURN OFF ENGINE AND RESTORE ELECTRICAL CONNECTION.

THIS ENGINE IS EQUIPPED WITH AUTOMATIC IDLE SPEED CONTROL. IDLE RPM IS NOT ADJUSTABLE. IF NOT WITHIN SPECIFIED RPM RANGE SEE SHOP MANUAL:
MANUAL TRANS. IN NEUTRAL: 760-830 RPM

THIS VEHICLE CONFORMS TO U.S. EPA AND CALIFORNIA REGULATIONS APPLICABLE TO 1990 MODEL YEAR NEW MOTOR VEHICLES INTRODUCED INTO COMMERCE SOLELY FOR SALE IN CALIFORNIA. OBD EXEMPT.

USE SAE 5W-30 OIL API SERVICE SG - ENERGY CONSERVING II.

SPARK PLUG: AWSF-32PP GAP: .042-.046
3.0L-9HM
LFM3.0V5FDC6 - TWC/HO2S/EGR/SMPI

CATALYST

3.0L ENGINE VACUUM SCHEMATIC — 1990 TAURUS AND SABLE

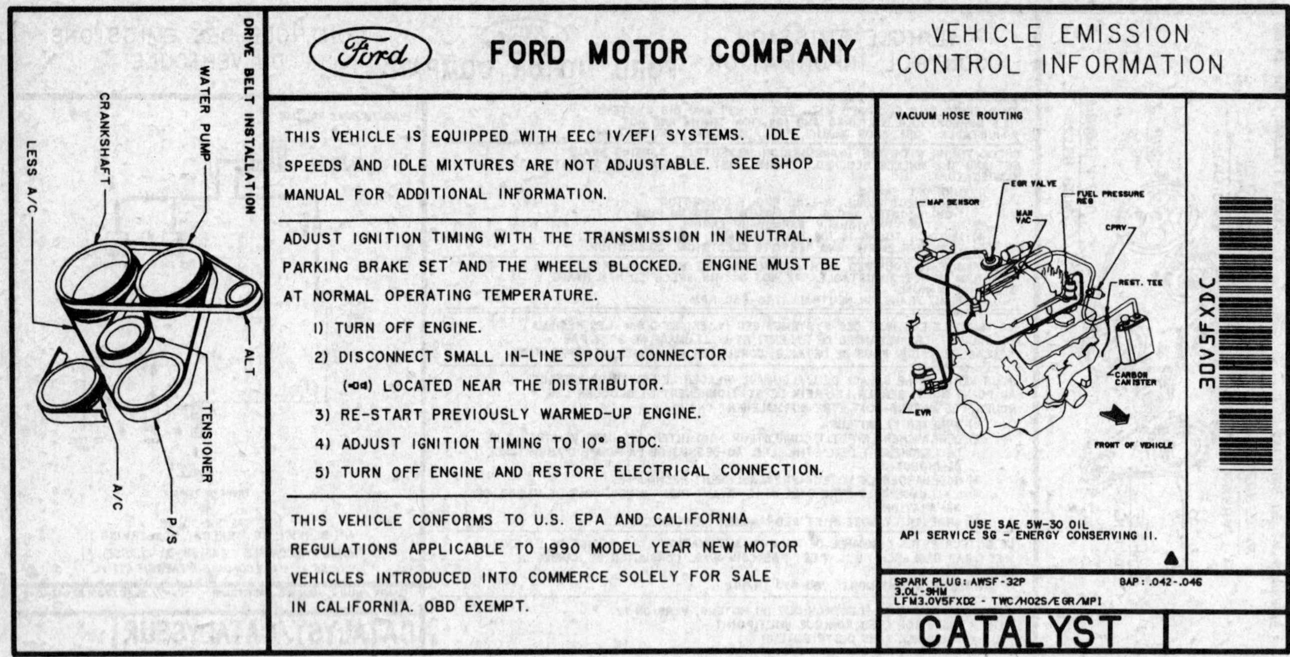

3.0L ENGINE VACUUM SCHEMATIC — 1990 TAURUS AND SABLE

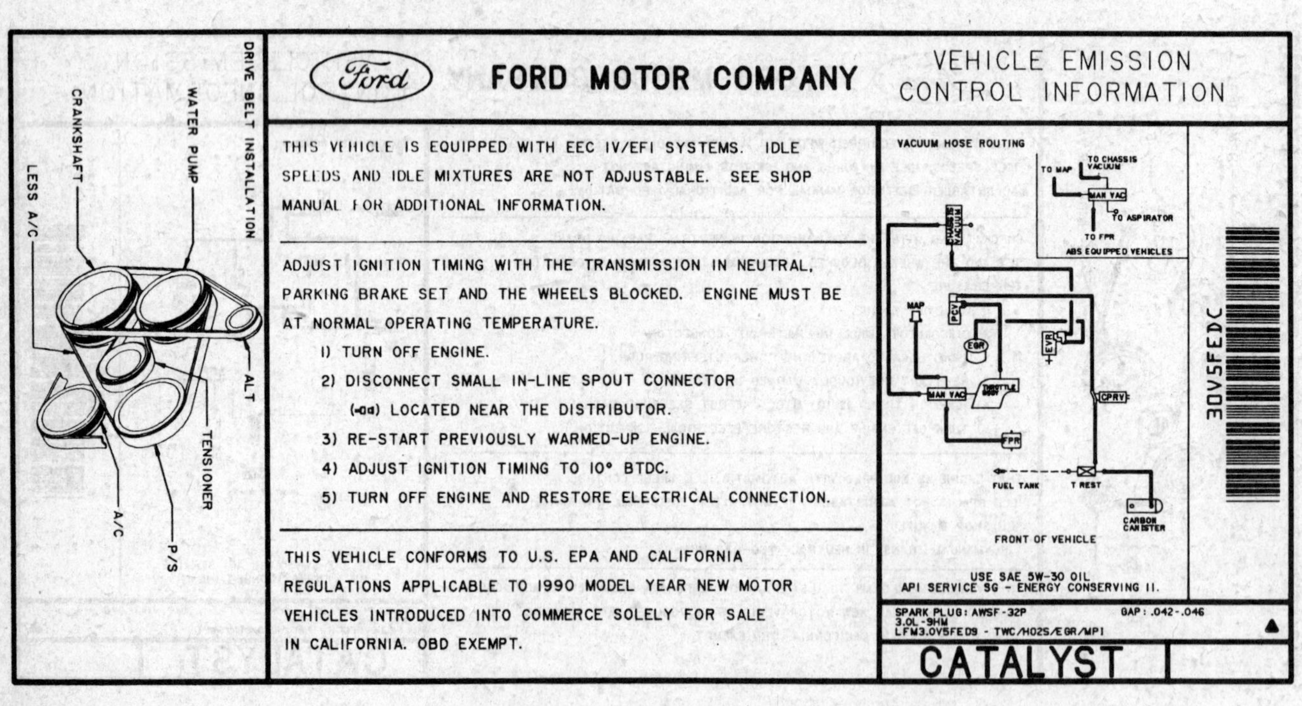

3.8L ENGINE VACUUM SCHEMATIC – 1990 TAURUS AND SABLE

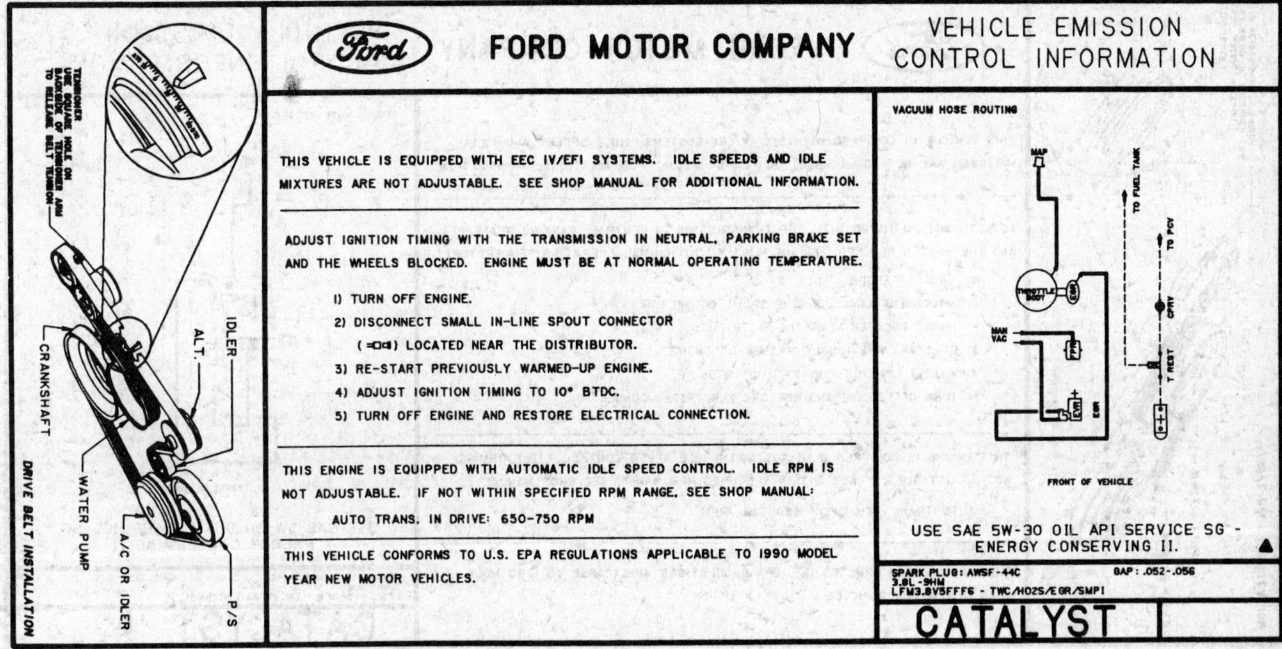

FORD MOTOR COMPANY

VEHICLE EMISSION CONTROL INFORMATION

THIS VEHICLE IS EQUIPPED WITH EEC IV/EFI SYSTEMS. IDLE SPEEDS AND IDLE MIXTURES ARE NOT ADJUSTABLE. SEE SHOP MANUAL FOR ADDITIONAL INFORMATION.

ADJUST IGNITION TIMING WITH THE TRANSMISSION IN NEUTRAL, PARKING BRAKE SET AND THE WHEELS BLOCKED. ENGINE MUST BE AT NORMAL OPERATING TEMPERATURE.

1) TURN OFF ENGINE.
2) DISCONNECT SMALL IN-LINE SPOUT CONNECTOR (=□⊐) LOCATED NEAR THE DISTRIBUTOR.
3) RE-START PREVIOUSLY WARMED-UP ENGINE.
4) ADJUST IGNITION TIMING TO 10° BTDC.
5) TURN OFF ENGINE AND RESTORE ELECTRICAL CONNECTION.

THIS ENGINE IS EQUIPPED WITH AUTOMATIC IDLE SPEED CONTROL. IDLE RPM IS NOT ADJUSTABLE. IF NOT WITHIN SPECIFIED RPM RANGE, SEE SHOP MANUAL:

AUTO TRANS. IN DRIVE: 650-750 RPM

THIS VEHICLE CONFORMS TO U.S. EPA REGULATIONS APPLICABLE TO 1990 MODEL YEAR NEW MOTOR VEHICLES.

USE SAE 5W-30 OIL API SERVICE SG - ENERGY CONSERVING II.

SPARK PLUG: AWSF-44C GAP: .052-.056
3.8L-9HM
LFM3.8V5FFF6 - TWC/HO2S/EGR/SMPI

CATALYST

3.8L ENGINE VACUUM SCHEMATIC – 1990 TAURUS AND SABLE

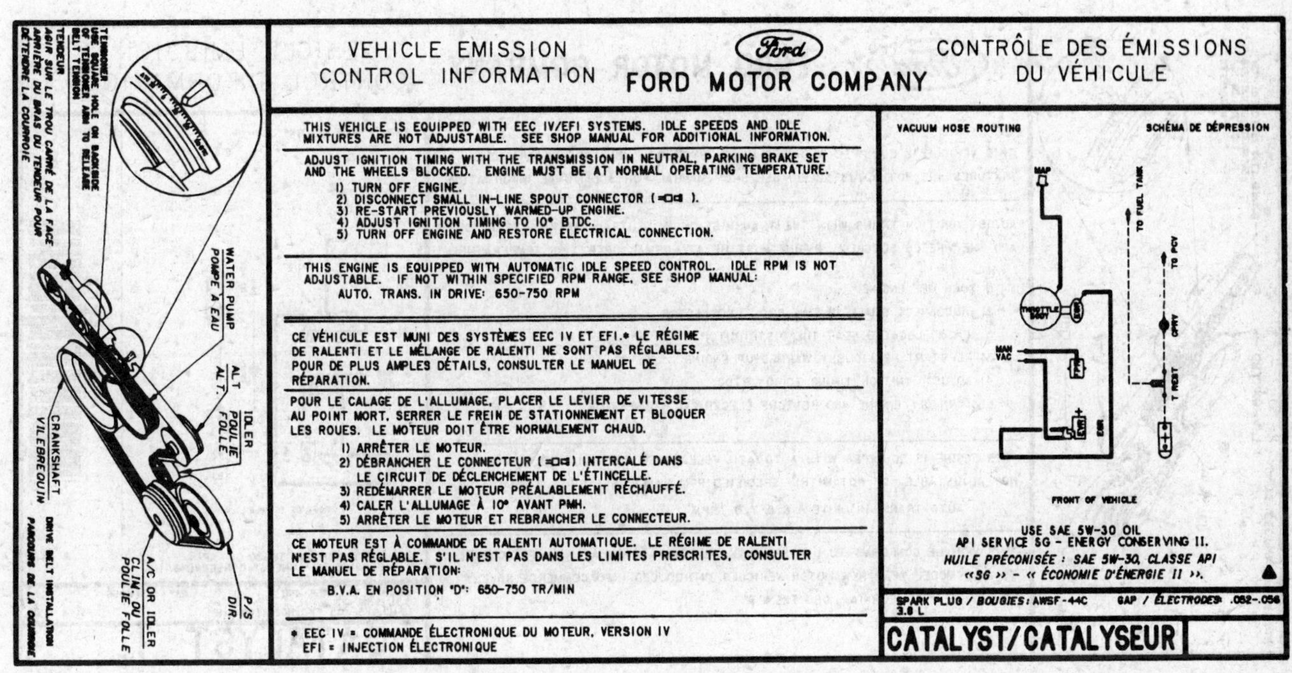

VEHICLE EMISSION CONTROL INFORMATION

FORD MOTOR COMPANY

CONTRÔLE DES ÉMISSIONS DU VÉHICULE

THIS VEHICLE IS EQUIPPED WITH EEC IV/EFI SYSTEMS. IDLE SPEEDS AND IDLE MIXTURES ARE NOT ADJUSTABLE. SEE SHOP MANUAL FOR ADDITIONAL INFORMATION.

ADJUST IGNITION TIMING WITH THE TRANSMISSION IN NEUTRAL, PARKING BRAKE SET AND THE WHEELS BLOCKED. ENGINE MUST BE AT NORMAL OPERATING TEMPERATURE.

1) TURN OFF ENGINE.
2) DISCONNECT SMALL IN-LINE SPOUT CONNECTOR (=□⊐).
3) RE-START PREVIOUSLY WARMED-UP ENGINE.
4) ADJUST IGNITION TIMING TO 10° BTDC.
5) TURN OFF ENGINE AND RESTORE ELECTRICAL CONNECTION.

THIS ENGINE IS EQUIPPED WITH AUTOMATIC IDLE SPEED CONTROL. IDLE RPM IS NOT ADJUSTABLE. IF NOT WITHIN SPECIFIED RPM RANGE, SEE SHOP MANUAL:

AUTO. TRANS. IN DRIVE: 650-750 RPM

CE VÉHICULE EST MUNI DES SYSTÈMES EEC IV ET EFI.* LE RÉGIME DE RALENTI ET LE MÉLANGE DE RALENTI NE SONT PAS RÉGLABLES. POUR DE PLUS AMPLES DÉTAILS, CONSULTER LE MANUEL DE RÉPARATION.

POUR LE CALAGE DE L'ALLUMAGE, PLACER LE LEVIER DE VITESSE AU POINT MORT, SERRER LE FREIN DE STATIONNEMENT ET BLOQUER LES ROUES. LE MOTEUR DOIT ÊTRE NORMALEMENT CHAUD.

1) ARRÊTER LE MOTEUR.
2) DÉBRANCHER LE CONNECTEUR (=□⊐) INTERCALÉ DANS LE CIRCUIT DE DÉCLENCHEMENT DE L'ÉTINCELLE.
3) REDÉMARRER LE MOTEUR PRÉALABLEMENT RÉCHAUFFÉ.
4) CALER L'ALLUMAGE À 10° AVANT PMH.
5) ARRÊTER LE MOTEUR ET REBRANCHER LE CONNECTEUR.

CE MOTEUR EST À COMMANDE DE RALENTI AUTOMATIQUE. LE RÉGIME DE RALENTI N'EST PAS RÉGLABLE. S'IL N'EST PAS DANS LES LIMITES PRESCRITES, CONSULTER LE MANUEL DE RÉPARATION:

B.V.A. EN POSITION "D": 650-750 TR/MIN

* EEC IV = COMMANDE ÉLECTRONIQUE DU MOTEUR, VERSION IV
EFI = INJECTION ÉLECTRONIQUE

USE SAE 5W-30 OIL
API SERVICE SG - ENERGY CONSERVING II.
HUILE PRÉCONISÉE : SAE 5W-30, CLASSE API «SG» - «ÉCONOMIE D'ÉNERGIE II».

SPARK PLUG / *BOUGIES*: AWSF-44C GAP / *ÉLECTRODES*: .052-.056
3.8 L

CATALYST/CATALYSEUR

3.8L ENGINE VACUUM SCHEMATIC – 1990 TAURUS AND SABLE

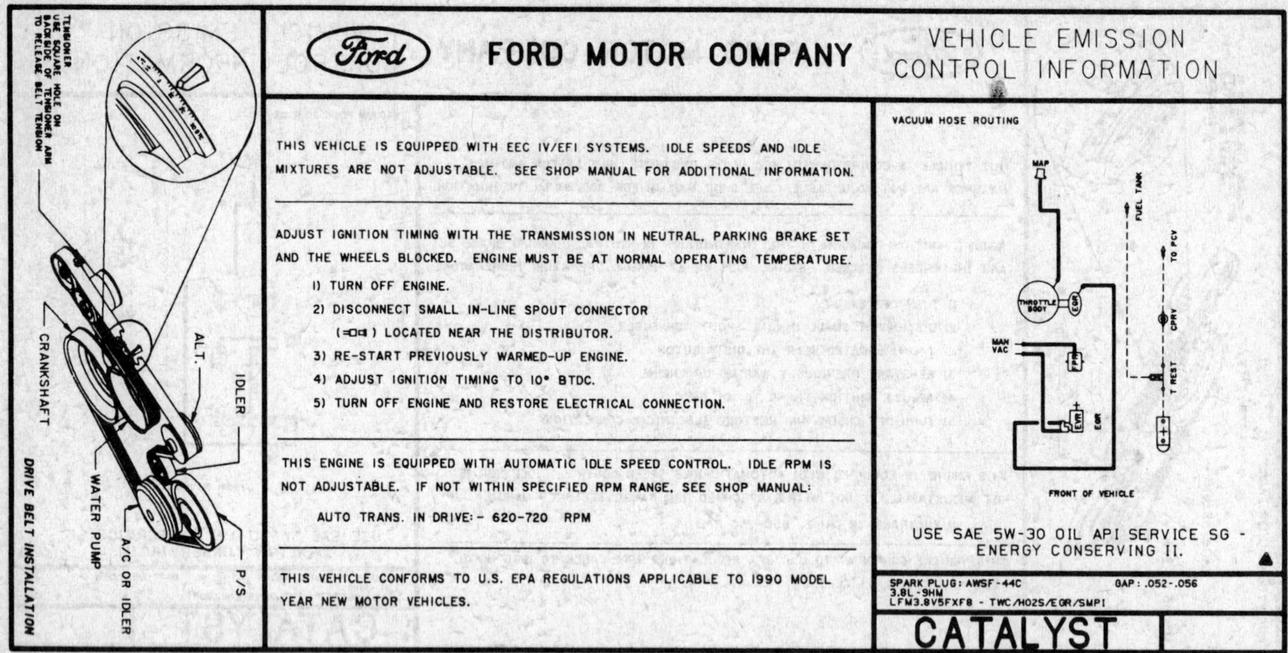

3.8L ENGINE VACUUM SCHEMATIC – 1990 TAURUS AND SABLE

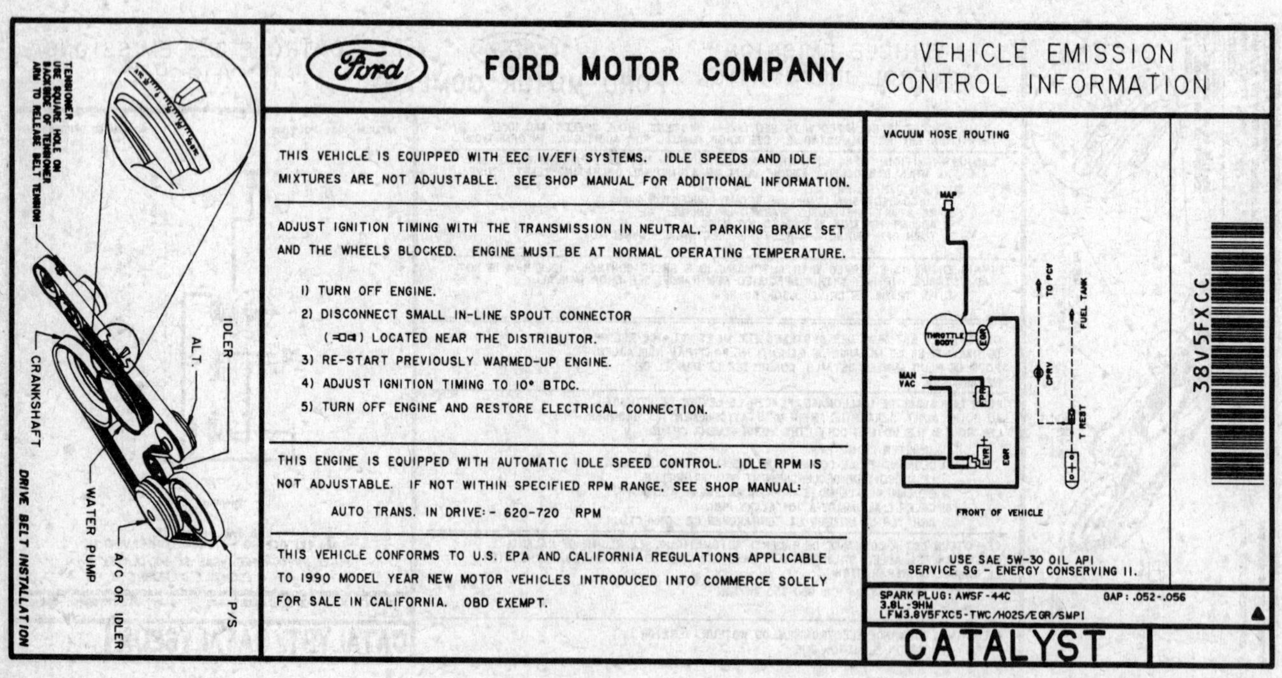

3.8L ENGINE VACUUM SCHEMATIC – 1990 TAURUS AND SABLE

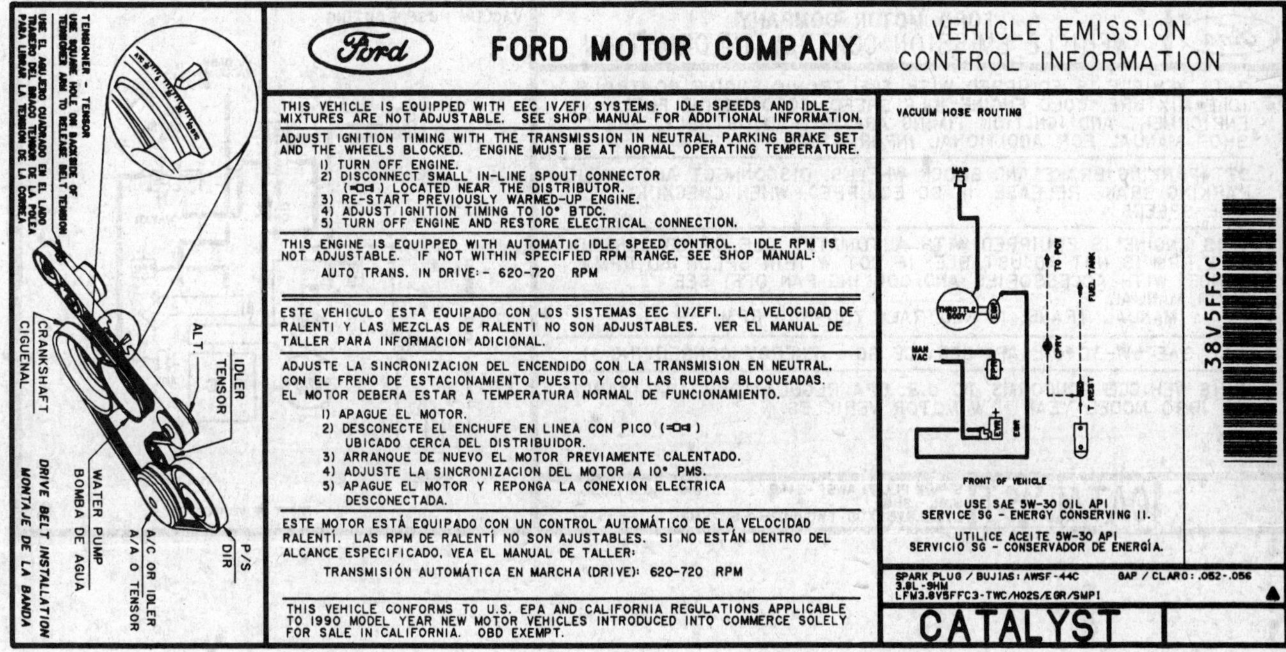

3.8L ENGINE VACUUM SCHEMATIC – 1990 TAURUS AND SABLE

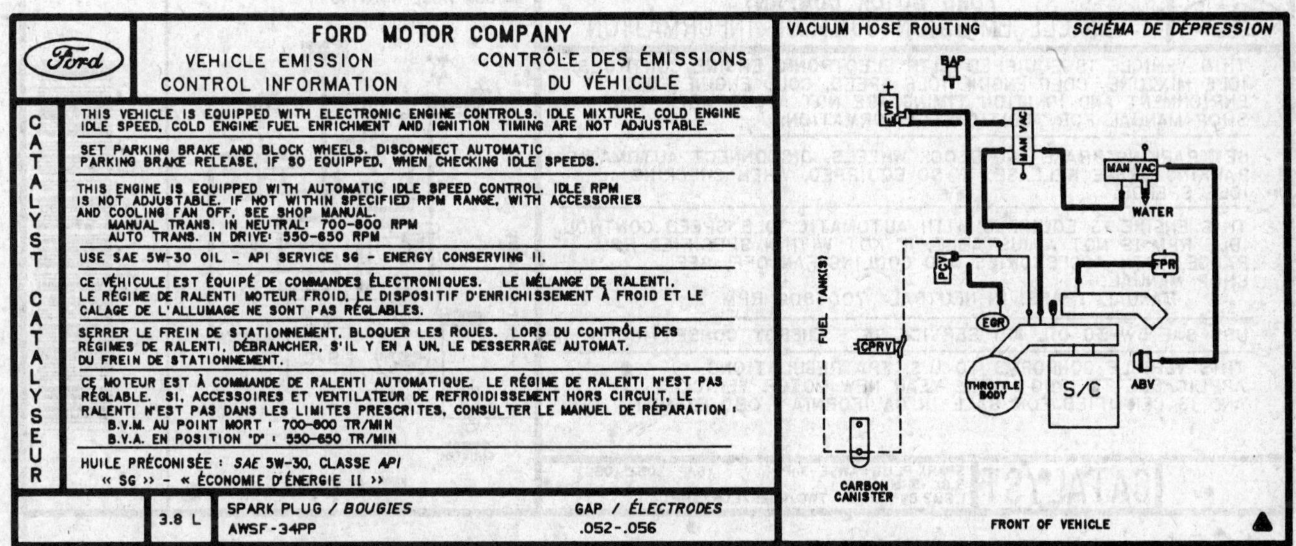

3.8L ENGINE VACUUM SCHEMATIC – 1990 TAURUS AND SABLE

FORD MOTOR COMPANY
VEHICLE EMISSION CONTROL INFORMATION

THIS VEHICLE IS EQUIPPED WITH ELECTRONIC ENGINE CONTROLS. IDLE MIXTURE, COLD ENGINE IDLE SPEED, COLD ENGINE FUEL ENRICHMENT AND IGNITION TIMING ARE NOT ADJUSTABLE. SEE SHOP MANUAL FOR ADDITIONAL INFORMATION.

SET PARKING BRAKE AND BLOCK WHEELS. DISCONNECT AUTOMATIC PARKING BRAKE RELEASE, IF SO EQUIPPED, WHEN CHECKING IDLE SPEEDS.

THIS ENGINE IS EQUIPPED WITH AUTOMATIC IDLE SPEED CONTROL. IDLE RPM IS NOT ADJUSTABLE. IF NOT WITHIN SPECIFIED RPM RANGE, WITH ACCESSORIES AND COOLING FAN OFF, SEE SHOP MANUAL.
MANUAL TRANS. IN NEUTRAL: 700-800 RPM

USE SAE 5W-30 OIL API SERVICE SG - ENERGY CONSERVING II.

THIS VEHICLE CONFORMS TO U.S. EPA REGULATIONS APPLICABLE TO 1990 MODEL YEAR NEW MOTOR VEHICLES.

CATALYST

SPARK PLUG: AWSF-34PP GAP- .052-.056
3.8L-9HM
LFM3.8V5FXG9-TWC/HO2S/EGR/SMPI

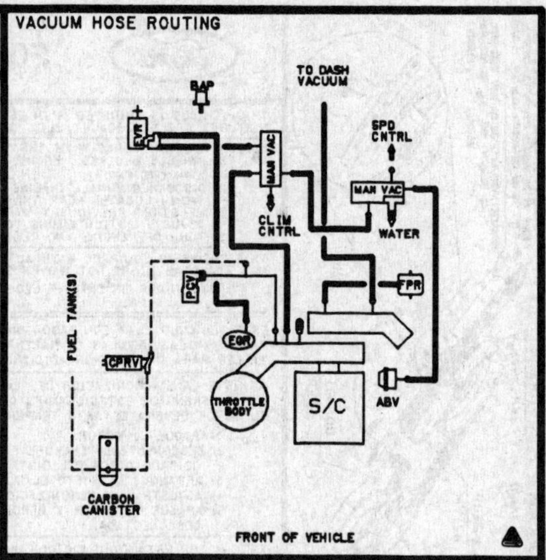

3.8L ENGINE VACUUM SCHEMATIC – 1990 TAURUS AND SABLE

FORD MOTOR COMPANY
VEHICLE EMISSION CONTROL INFORMATION

THIS VEHICLE IS EQUIPPED WITH ELECTRONIC ENGINE CONTROLS. IDLE MIXTURE, COLD ENGINE IDLE SPEED, COLD ENGINE FUEL ENRICHMENT AND IGNITION TIMING ARE NOT ADJUSTABLE. SEE SHOP MANUAL FOR ADDITIONAL INFORMATION.

SET PARKING BRAKE AND BLOCK WHEELS. DISCONNECT AUTOMATIC PARKING BRAKE RELEASE, IF SO EQUIPPED, WHEN CHECKING IDLE SPEEDS.

THIS ENGINE IS EQUIPPED WITH AUTOMATIC IDLE SPEED CONTROL. IDLE RPM IS NOT ADJUSTABLE. IF NOT WITHIN SPECIFIED RPM RANGE, WITH ACCESSORIES AND COOLING FAN OFF, SEE SHOP MANUAL.
MANUAL TRANS. IN NEUTRAL: 700-800 RPM

USE SAE 5W-30 OIL API SERVICE SG - ENERGY CONSERVING II.

THIS VEHICLE CONFORMS TO U.S. EPA REGULATIONS APPLICABLE TO 1990 MODEL YEAR NEW MOTOR VEHICLES AND IS CERTIFIED FOR SALE IN CALIFORNIA. OBD EXEMPT.

CATALYST

SPARK PLUG: AWSF-34PP GAP- .052-.056
3.8L-9HM
LFM3.8V5FXG9 - TWC/HO2S/EGR/SMPI

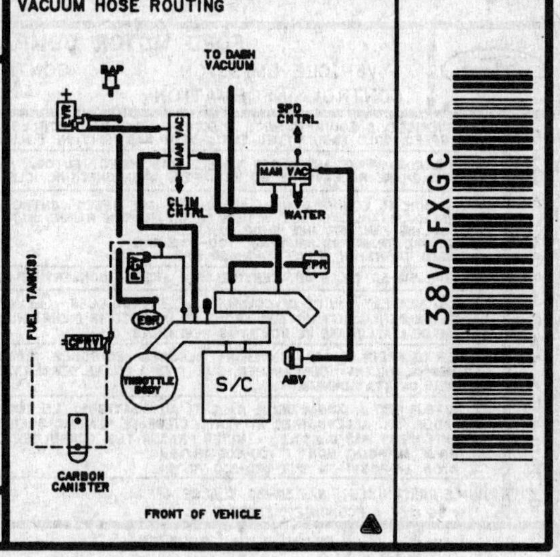

38V5FXGC

3.8L ENGINE VACUUM SCHEMATIC – 1990 TAURUS AND SABLE

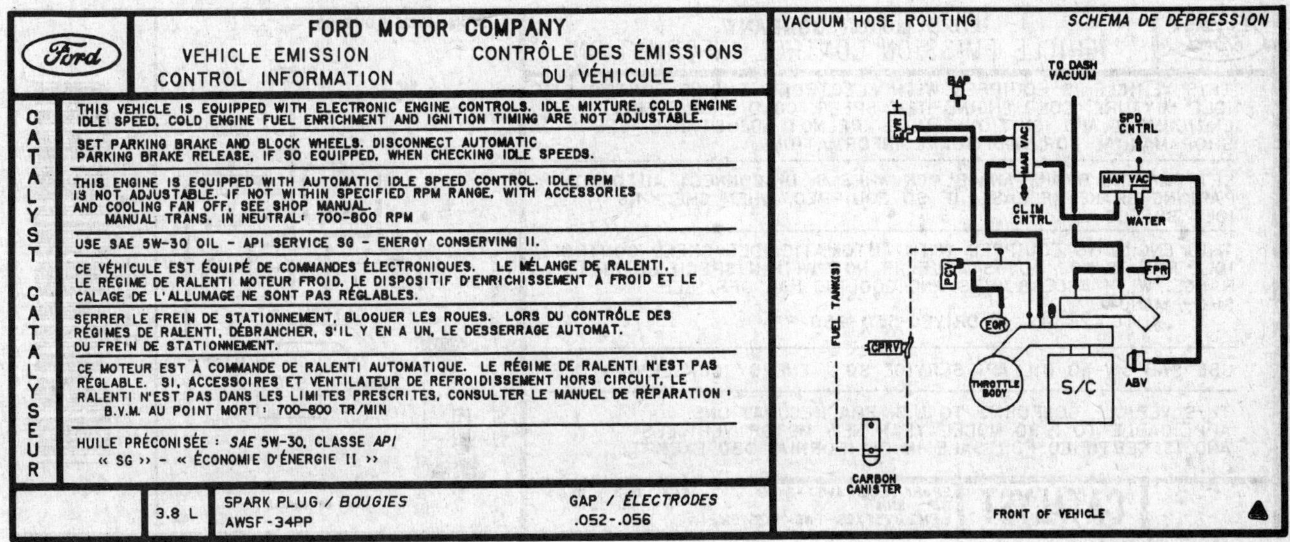

FORD MOTOR COMPANY

VEHICLE EMISSION CONTROL INFORMATION — CONTRÔLE DES ÉMISSIONS DU VÉHICULE

CATALYST / CATALYSEUR

THIS VEHICLE IS EQUIPPED WITH ELECTRONIC ENGINE CONTROLS. IDLE MIXTURE, COLD ENGINE IDLE SPEED, COLD ENGINE FUEL ENRICHMENT AND IGNITION TIMING ARE NOT ADJUSTABLE.

SET PARKING BRAKE AND BLOCK WHEELS. DISCONNECT AUTOMATIC PARKING BRAKE RELEASE, IF SO EQUIPPED, WHEN CHECKING IDLE SPEEDS.

THIS ENGINE IS EQUIPPED WITH AUTOMATIC IDLE SPEED CONTROL. IDLE RPM IS NOT ADJUSTABLE. IF NOT WITHIN SPECIFIED RPM RANGE, WITH ACCESSORIES AND COOLING FAN OFF, SEE SHOP MANUAL.
MANUAL TRANS. IN NEUTRAL: 700-800 RPM

USE SAE 5W-30 OIL - API SERVICE SG - ENERGY CONSERVING II.

CE VÉHICULE EST ÉQUIPÉ DE COMMANDES ÉLECTRONIQUES. LE MÉLANGE DE RALENTI, LE RÉGIME DE RALENTI MOTEUR FROID, LE DISPOSITIF D'ENRICHISSEMENT À FROID ET LE CALAGE DE L'ALLUMAGE NE SONT PAS RÉGLABLES.

SERRER LE FREIN DE STATIONNEMENT, BLOQUER LES ROUES. LORS DU CONTRÔLE DES RÉGIMES DE RALENTI, DÉBRANCHER, S'IL Y EN A UN, LE DESSERRAGE AUTOMAT. DU FREIN DE STATIONNEMENT.

CE MOTEUR EST À COMMANDE DE RALENTI AUTOMATIQUE. LE RÉGIME DE RALENTI N'EST PAS RÉGLABLE. SI, ACCESSOIRES ET VENTILATEUR DE REFROIDISSEMENT HORS CIRCUIT, LE RALENTI N'EST PAS DANS LES LIMITES PRESCRITES, CONSULTER LE MANUEL DE RÉPARATION :
B.V.M. AU POINT MORT : 700-800 TR/MIN

HUILE PRÉCONISÉE : *SAE* 5W-30, CLASSE *API* « SG » - « ÉCONOMIE D'ÉNERGIE II »

	SPARK PLUG / *BOUGIES*	GAP / *ÉLECTRODES*
3.8 L	AWSF-34PP	.052-.056

VACUUM HOSE ROUTING — *SCHEMA DE DÉPRESSION*

3.8L ENGINE VACUUM SCHEMATIC – 1990 TAURUS AND SABLE

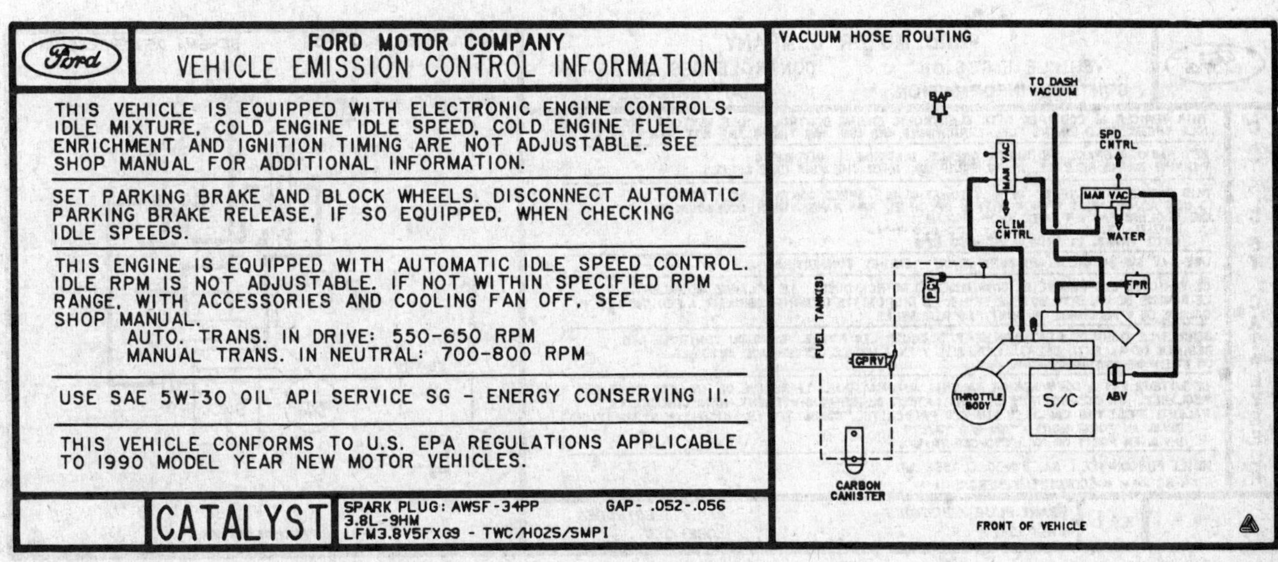

FORD MOTOR COMPANY

VEHICLE EMISSION CONTROL INFORMATION

THIS VEHICLE IS EQUIPPED WITH ELECTRONIC ENGINE CONTROLS. IDLE MIXTURE, COLD ENGINE IDLE SPEED, COLD ENGINE FUEL ENRICHMENT AND IGNITION TIMING ARE NOT ADJUSTABLE. SEE SHOP MANUAL FOR ADDITIONAL INFORMATION.

SET PARKING BRAKE AND BLOCK WHEELS. DISCONNECT AUTOMATIC PARKING BRAKE RELEASE, IF SO EQUIPPED, WHEN CHECKING IDLE SPEEDS.

THIS ENGINE IS EQUIPPED WITH AUTOMATIC IDLE SPEED CONTROL. IDLE RPM IS NOT ADJUSTABLE. IF NOT WITHIN SPECIFIED RPM RANGE, WITH ACCESSORIES AND COOLING FAN OFF, SEE SHOP MANUAL.
AUTO. TRANS. IN DRIVE: 550-650 RPM
MANUAL TRANS. IN NEUTRAL: 700-800 RPM

USE SAE 5W-30 OIL API SERVICE SG - ENERGY CONSERVING II.

THIS VEHICLE CONFORMS TO U.S. EPA REGULATIONS APPLICABLE TO 1990 MODEL YEAR NEW MOTOR VEHICLES.

CATALYST

SPARK PLUG: AWSF-34PP GAP- .052-.056
3.8L-9HM
LFM3.8V5FXG9 - TWC/HO2S/SMPI

VACUUM HOSE ROUTING

3.8L ENGINE VACUUM SCHEMATIC – 1990 TAURUS AND SABLE

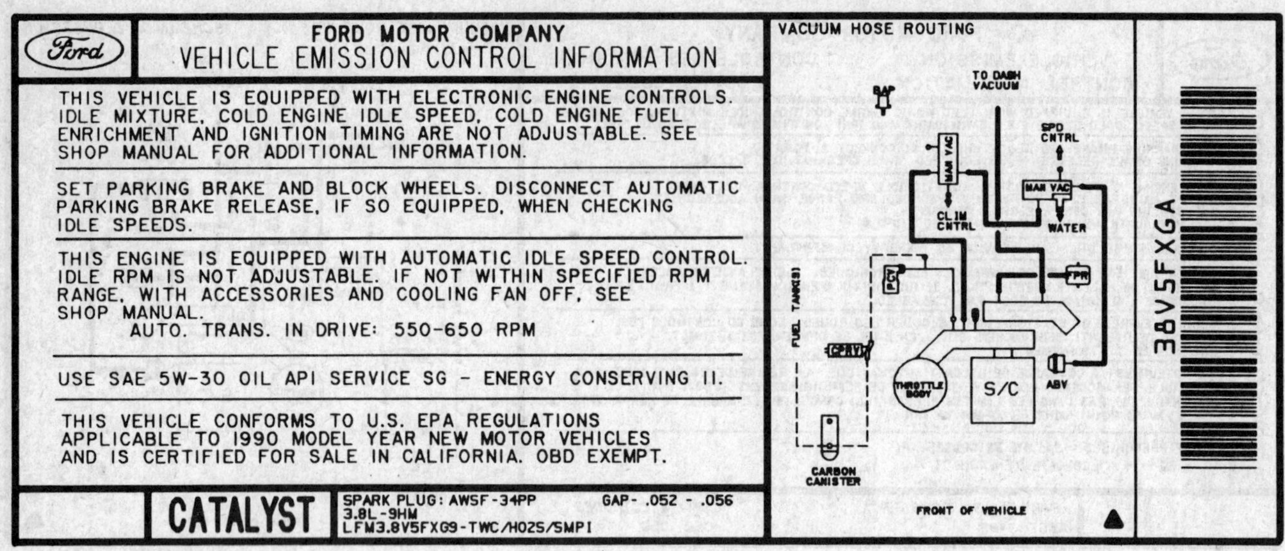

Ford

FORD MOTOR COMPANY
VEHICLE EMISSION CONTROL INFORMATION

THIS VEHICLE IS EQUIPPED WITH ELECTRONIC ENGINE CONTROLS. IDLE MIXTURE, COLD ENGINE IDLE SPEED, COLD ENGINE FUEL ENRICHMENT AND IGNITION TIMING ARE NOT ADJUSTABLE. SEE SHOP MANUAL FOR ADDITIONAL INFORMATION.

SET PARKING BRAKE AND BLOCK WHEELS. DISCONNECT AUTOMATIC PARKING BRAKE RELEASE, IF SO EQUIPPED, WHEN CHECKING IDLE SPEEDS.

THIS ENGINE IS EQUIPPED WITH AUTOMATIC IDLE SPEED CONTROL. IDLE RPM IS NOT ADJUSTABLE. IF NOT WITHIN SPECIFIED RPM RANGE, WITH ACCESSORIES AND COOLING FAN OFF, SEE SHOP MANUAL.
AUTO. TRANS. IN DRIVE: 550-650 RPM

USE SAE 5W-30 OIL API SERVICE SG – ENERGY CONSERVING II.

THIS VEHICLE CONFORMS TO U.S. EPA REGULATIONS APPLICABLE TO 1990 MODEL YEAR NEW MOTOR VEHICLES AND IS CERTIFIED FOR SALE IN CALIFORNIA. OBD EXEMPT.

CATALYST

SPARK PLUG: AWSF-34PP GAP- .052 - .056
3.8L-9HM
LFM3.8V5FXG9-TWC/HO2S/SMPI

VACUUM HOSE ROUTING

3.8L ENGINE VACUUM SCHEMATIC – 1990 TAURUS AND SABLE

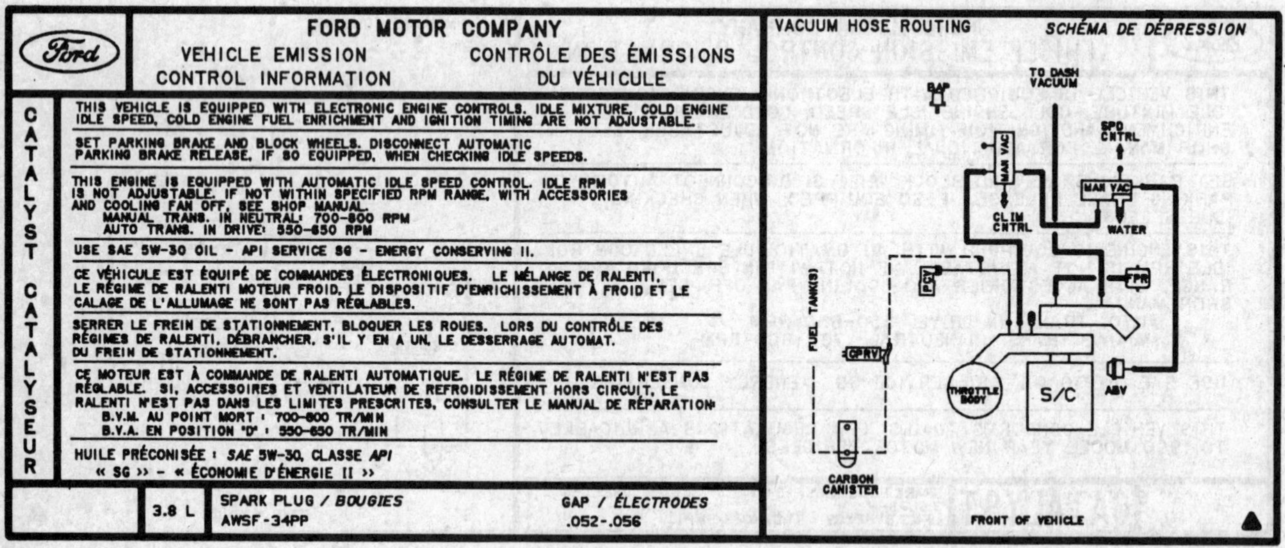

Ford

FORD MOTOR COMPANY
VEHICLE EMISSION CONTROL INFORMATION — CONTRÔLE DES ÉMISSIONS DU VÉHICULE

CATALYST CATALYSEUR

THIS VEHICLE IS EQUIPPED WITH ELECTRONIC ENGINE CONTROLS. IDLE MIXTURE, COLD ENGINE IDLE SPEED, COLD ENGINE FUEL ENRICHMENT AND IGNITION TIMING ARE NOT ADJUSTABLE.

SET PARKING BRAKE AND BLOCK WHEELS. DISCONNECT AUTOMATIC PARKING BRAKE RELEASE, IF SO EQUIPPED, WHEN CHECKING IDLE SPEEDS.

THIS ENGINE IS EQUIPPED WITH AUTOMATIC IDLE SPEED CONTROL. IDLE RPM IS NOT ADJUSTABLE. IF NOT WITHIN SPECIFIED RPM RANGE, WITH ACCESSORIES AND COOLING FAN OFF, SEE SHOP MANUAL.
MANUAL TRANS. IN NEUTRAL: 700-800 RPM
AUTO TRANS. IN DRIVE: 550-650 RPM

USE SAE 5W-30 OIL - API SERVICE SG - ENERGY CONSERVING II.

CE VÉHICULE EST ÉQUIPÉ DE COMMANDES ÉLECTRONIQUES. LE MÉLANGE DE RALENTI, LE RÉGIME DE RALENTI MOTEUR FROID, LE DISPOSITIF D'ENRICHISSEMENT À FROID ET LE CALAGE DE L'ALLUMAGE NE SONT PAS RÉGLABLES.

SERRER LE FREIN DE STATIONNEMENT, BLOQUER LES ROUES. LORS DU CONTRÔLE DES RÉGIMES DE RALENTI, DÉBRANCHER, S'IL Y EN A UN, LE DESSERRAGE AUTOMAT. DU FREIN DE STATIONNEMENT.

CE MOTEUR EST À COMMANDE DE RALENTI AUTOMATIQUE. LE RÉGIME DE RALENTI N'EST PAS RÉGLABLE. SI, ACCESSOIRES ET VENTILATEUR DE REFROIDISSEMENT HORS CIRCUIT, LE RALENTI N'EST PAS DANS LES LIMITES PRESCRITES, CONSULTER LE MANUAL DE RÉPARATION:
B.V.M. AU POINT MORT : 700-800 TR/MIN
B.V.A. EN POSITION "D" : 550-650 TR/MIN

HUILE PRÉCONISÉE : *SAE* 5W-30, CLASSE *API* « SG » – « ÉCONOMIE D'ÉNERGIE II »

3.8 L — SPARK PLUG / *BOUGIES* AWSF-34PP — GAP / *ÉLECTRODES* .052-.056

VACUUM HOSE ROUTING — *SCHÉMA DE DÉPRESSION*

3.8L ENGINE VACUUM SCHEMATIC — 1990 TAURUS AND SABLE

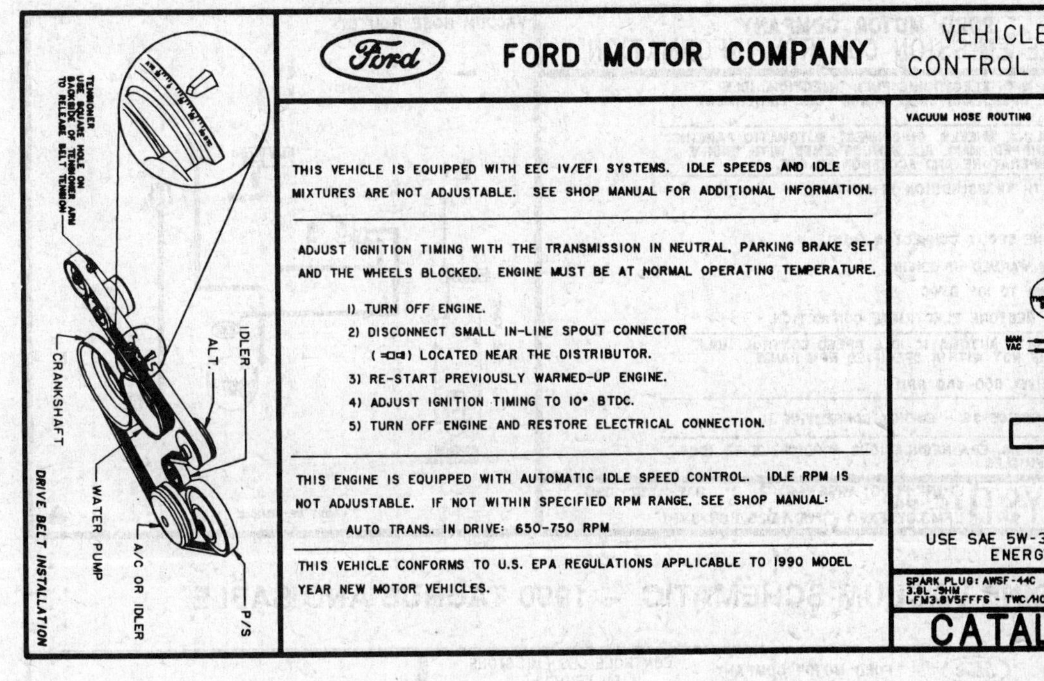

3.8L ENGINE VACUUM SCHEMATIC — 1990 TAURUS AND SABLE

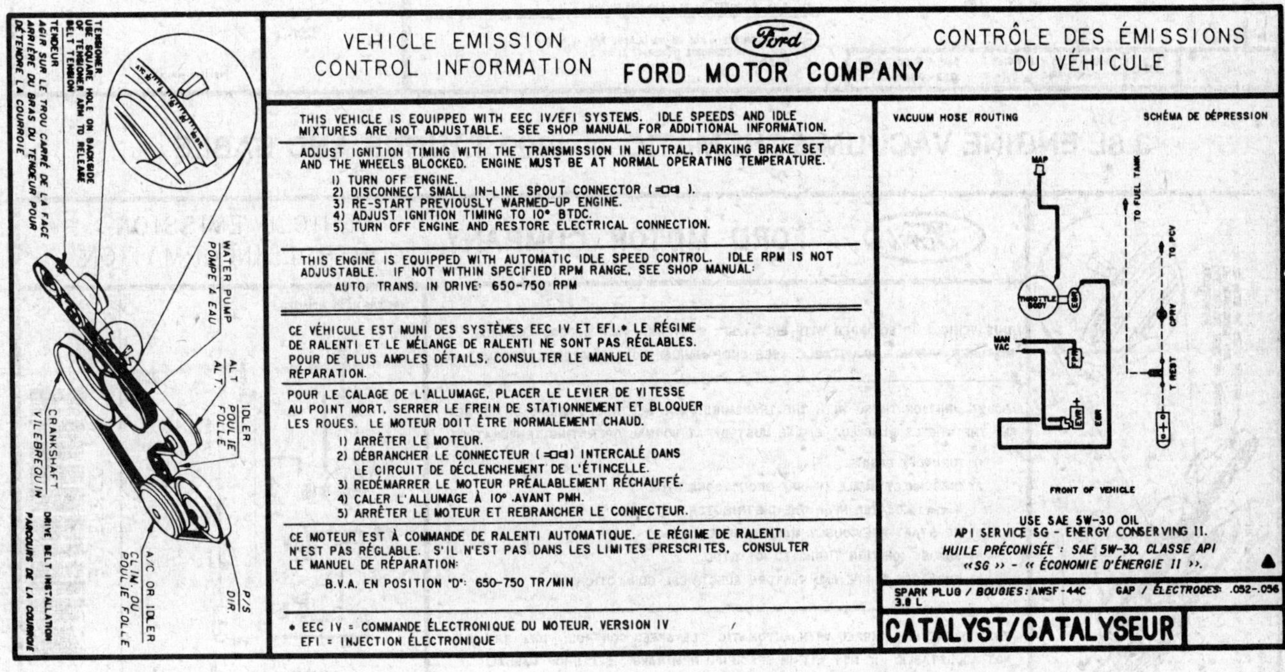

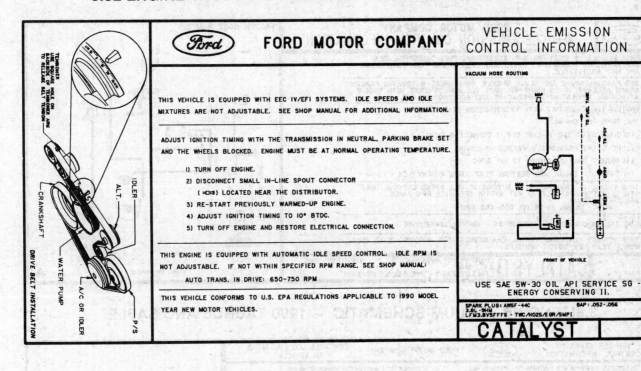

3.8L ENGINE VACUUM SCHEMATIC — 1990 TAURUS AND SABLE

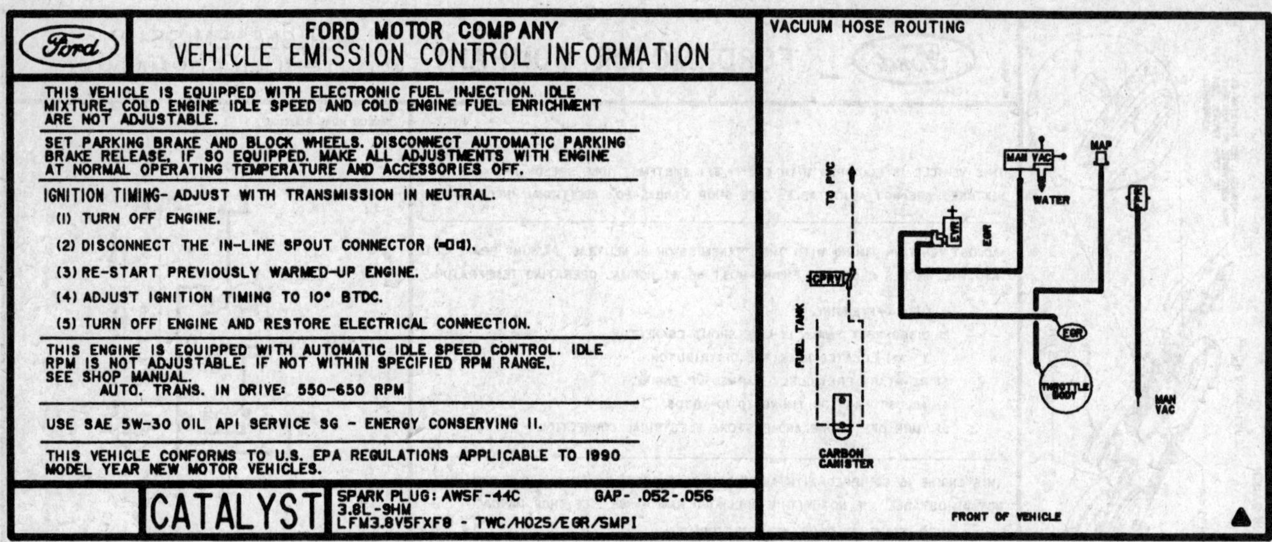

FORD MOTOR COMPANY
VEHICLE EMISSION CONTROL INFORMATION

THIS VEHICLE IS EQUIPPED WITH ELECTRONIC FUEL INJECTION. IDLE MIXTURE, COLD ENGINE IDLE SPEED AND COLD ENGINE FUEL ENRICHMENT ARE NOT ADJUSTABLE.

SET PARKING BRAKE AND BLOCK WHEELS. DISCONNECT AUTOMATIC PARKING BRAKE RELEASE, IF SO EQUIPPED. MAKE ALL ADJUSTMENTS WITH ENGINE AT NORMAL OPERATING TEMPERATURE AND ACCESSORIES OFF.

IGNITION TIMING- ADJUST WITH TRANSMISSION IN NEUTRAL.

(1) TURN OFF ENGINE.
(2) DISCONNECT THE IN-LINE SPOUT CONNECTOR (=◻◁).
(3) RE-START PREVIOUSLY WARMED-UP ENGINE.
(4) ADJUST IGNITION TIMING TO 10° BTDC.
(5) TURN OFF ENGINE AND RESTORE ELECTRICAL CONNECTION.

THIS ENGINE IS EQUIPPED WITH AUTOMATIC IDLE SPEED CONTROL. IDLE RPM IS NOT ADJUSTABLE. IF NOT WITHIN SPECIFIED RPM RANGE, SEE SHOP MANUAL.
AUTO. TRANS. IN DRIVE: 550-650 RPM

USE SAE 5W-30 OIL API SERVICE SG - ENERGY CONSERVING II.

THIS VEHICLE CONFORMS TO U.S. EPA REGULATIONS APPLICABLE TO 1990 MODEL YEAR NEW MOTOR VEHICLES.

CATALYST
SPARK PLUG: AWSF-44C GAP- .052-.056
3.8L-9HM
LFM3.8V5FXF8 - TWC/HO2S/EGR/SMPI

3.8L ENGINE VACUUM SCHEMATIC — 1990 TAURUS AND SABLE

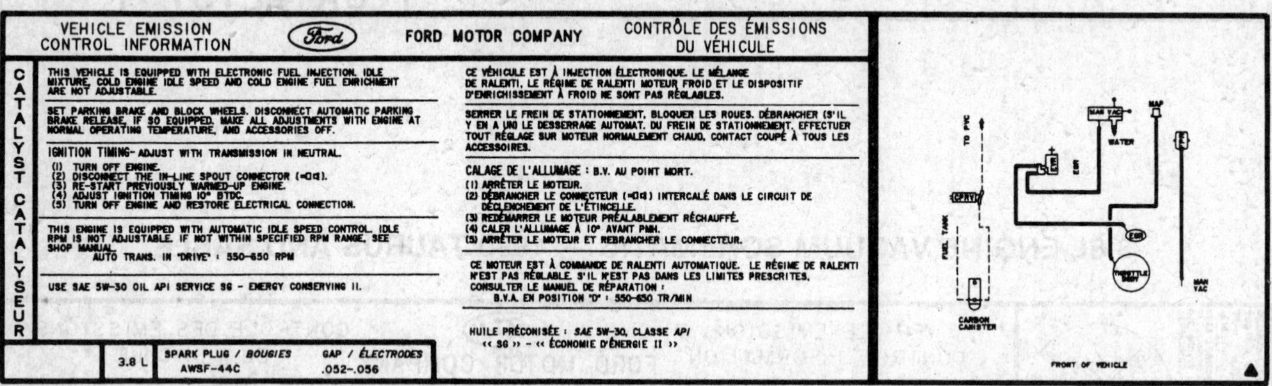

VEHICLE EMISSION CONTROL INFORMATION — FORD MOTOR COMPANY — CONTRÔLE DES ÉMISSIONS DU VÉHICULE

CATALYST CATALYSEUR

THIS VEHICLE IS EQUIPPED WITH ELECTRONIC FUEL INJECTION. IDLE MIXTURE, COLD ENGINE IDLE SPEED AND COLD ENGINE FUEL ENRICHMENT ARE NOT ADJUSTABLE.

SET PARKING BRAKE AND BLOCK WHEELS. DISCONNECT AUTOMATIC PARKING BRAKE RELEASE, IF SO EQUIPPED. MAKE ALL ADJUSTMENTS WITH ENGINE AT NORMAL OPERATING TEMPERATURE, AND ACCESSORIES OFF.

IGNITION TIMING- ADJUST WITH TRANSMISSION IN NEUTRAL.
(1) TURN OFF ENGINE.
(2) DISCONNECT THE IN-LINE SPOUT CONNECTOR (=◻◁).
(3) RE-START PREVIOUSLY WARMED-UP ENGINE.
(4) ADJUST IGNITION TIMING 10° BTDC.
(5) TURN OFF ENGINE AND RESTORE ELECTRICAL CONNECTION.

THIS ENGINE IS EQUIPPED WITH AUTOMATIC IDLE SPEED CONTROL. IDLE RPM IS NOT ADJUSTABLE. IF NOT WITHIN SPECIFIED RPM RANGE, SEE SHOP MANUAL.
AUTO TRANS. IN "DRIVE" : 550-650 RPM

USE SAE 5W-30 OIL API SERVICE SG - ENERGY CONSERVING II.

CE VÉHICULE EST À INJECTION ÉLECTRONIQUE. LE MÉLANGE DE RALENTI, LE RÉGIME DE RALENTI MOTEUR FROID ET LE DISPOSITIF D'ENRICHISSEMENT À FROID NE SONT PAS RÉGLABLES.

SERRER LE FREIN DE STATIONNEMENT, BLOQUER LES ROUES. DÉBRANCHER (S'IL Y EN A UN) LE DESSERRAGE AUTOMAT. DU FREIN DE STATIONNEMENT. EFFECTUER TOUT RÉGLAGE SUR MOTEUR NORMALEMENT CHAUD, CONTACT COUPÉ À TOUS LES ACCESSOIRES.

CALAGE DE L'ALLUMAGE : B.V. AU POINT MORT.
(1) ARRÊTER LE MOTEUR.
(2) DÉBRANCHER LE CONNECTEUR (=◻◁) INTERCALÉ DANS LE CIRCUIT DE DÉCLENCHEMENT DE L'ÉTINCELLE.
(3) REDÉMARRER LE MOTEUR PRÉALABLEMENT RÉCHAUFFÉ.
(4) CALER L'ALLUMAGE À 10° AVANT PMH.
(5) ARRÊTER LE MOTEUR ET REBRANCHER LE CONNECTEUR.

CE MOTEUR EST À COMMANDE DE RALENTI AUTOMATIQUE. LE RÉGIME DE RALENTI N'EST PAS RÉGLABLE. S'IL N'EST PAS DANS LES LIMITES PRESCRITES, CONSULTER LE MANUEL DE RÉPARATION :
B.V.A. EN POSITION "D" : 550-650 TR/MIN

HUILE PRÉCONISÉE : *SAE* 5W-30, CLASSE *API* « SG » - « ÉCONOMIE D'ÉNERGIE II »

	SPARK PLUG / *BOUGIES*	GAP / *ÉLECTRODES*
3.8 L	AWSF-44C	.052-.056

3.8L ENGINE VACUUM SCHEMATIC — 1990 TAURUS AND SABLE

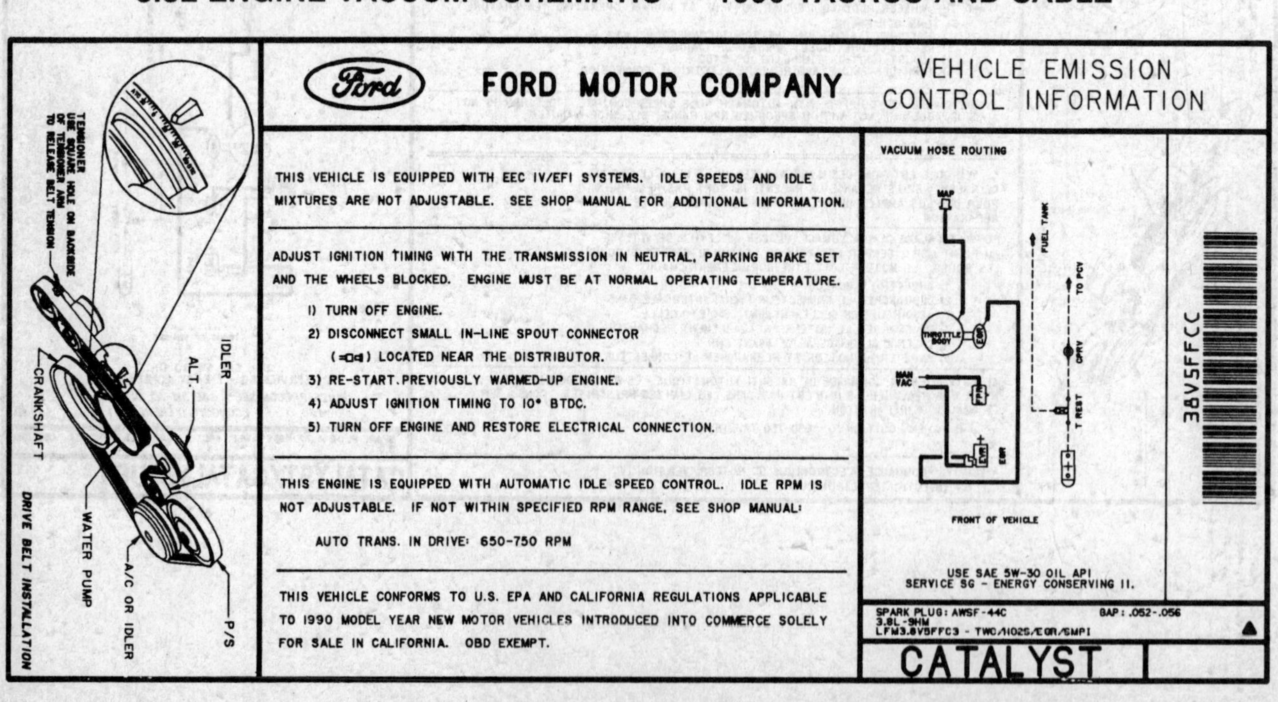

FORD MOTOR COMPANY
VEHICLE EMISSION CONTROL INFORMATION

THIS VEHICLE IS EQUIPPED WITH EEC IV/EFI SYSTEMS. IDLE SPEEDS AND IDLE MIXTURES ARE NOT ADJUSTABLE. SEE SHOP MANUAL FOR ADDITIONAL INFORMATION.

ADJUST IGNITION TIMING WITH THE TRANSMISSION IN NEUTRAL, PARKING BRAKE SET AND THE WHEELS BLOCKED. ENGINE MUST BE AT NORMAL OPERATING TEMPERATURE.

1) TURN OFF ENGINE.
2) DISCONNECT SMALL IN-LINE SPOUT CONNECTOR (=◻◁) LOCATED NEAR THE DISTRIBUTOR.
3) RE-START PREVIOUSLY WARMED-UP ENGINE.
4) ADJUST IGNITION TIMING TO 10° BTDC.
5) TURN OFF ENGINE AND RESTORE ELECTRICAL CONNECTION.

THIS ENGINE IS EQUIPPED WITH AUTOMATIC IDLE SPEED CONTROL. IDLE RPM IS NOT ADJUSTABLE. IF NOT WITHIN SPECIFIED RPM RANGE, SEE SHOP MANUAL:

AUTO TRANS. IN DRIVE: 650-750 RPM

THIS VEHICLE CONFORMS TO U.S. EPA AND CALIFORNIA REGULATIONS APPLICABLE TO 1990 MODEL YEAR NEW MOTOR VEHICLES INTRODUCED INTO COMMERCE SOLELY FOR SALE IN CALIFORNIA. OBD EXEMPT.

USE SAE 5W-30 OIL API SERVICE SG - ENERGY CONSERVING II.

SPARK PLUG: AWSF-44C GAP: .052-.056
3.8L-9HM
LFM3.8V5FFC3 - TWC/HO2S/EGR/SMPI

CATALYST

3.8L ENGINE VACUUM SCHEMATIC – 1990 TAURUS AND SABLE

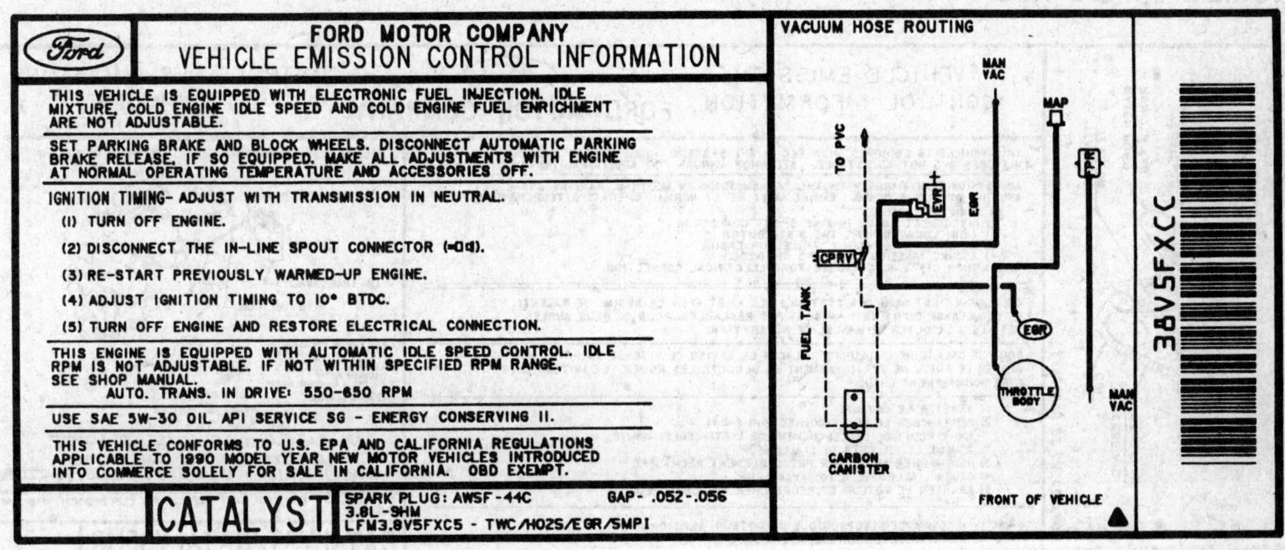

3.0L ENGINE VACUUM SCHEMATIC – 1991 TAURUS AND SABLE WITH CALIBRATION NUMBER 1-10T-R00

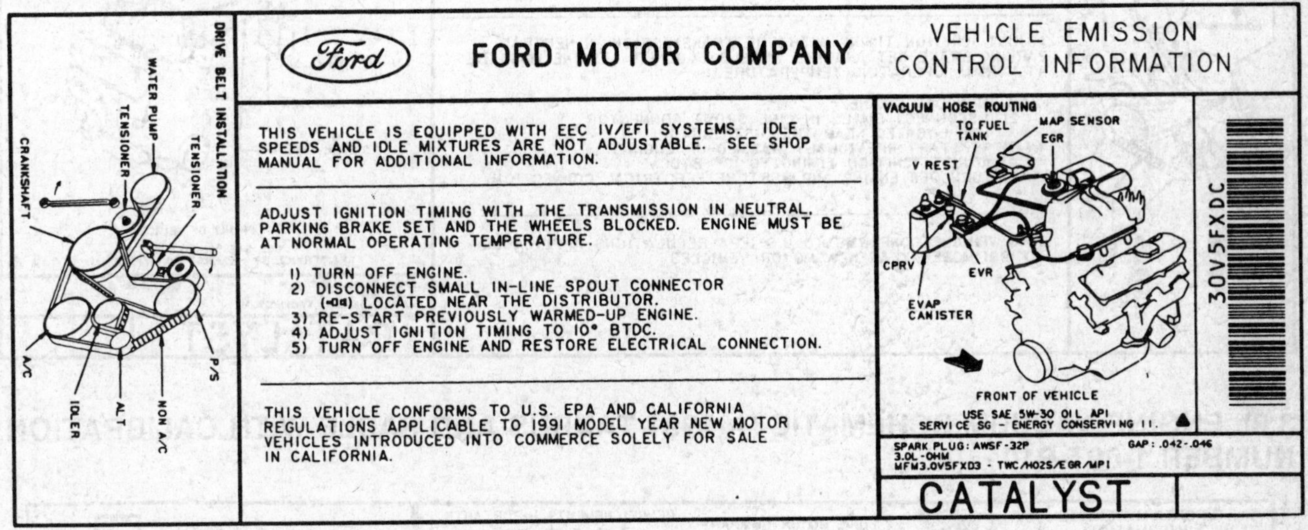

3.0L ENGINE VACUUM SCHEMATIC – 1991 TAURUS AND SABLE WITH CALIBRATION NUMBER 1-10B-R00

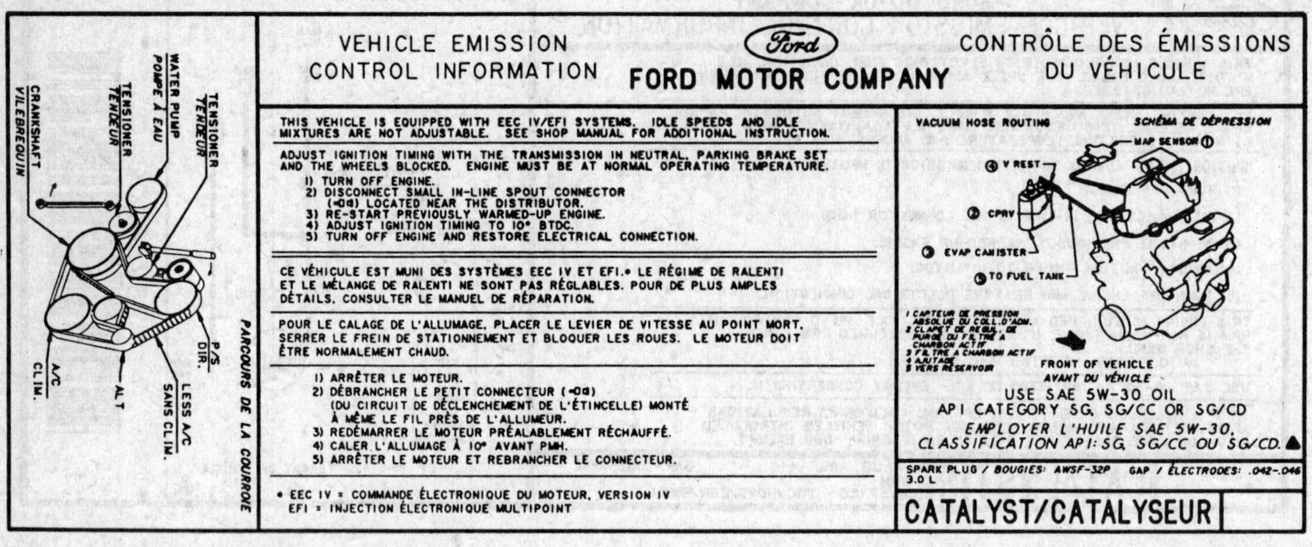

3.0L ENGINE VACUUM SCHEMATIC – 1991 TAURUS AND SABLE WITH CALIBRATION NUMBER 1-10B-R00

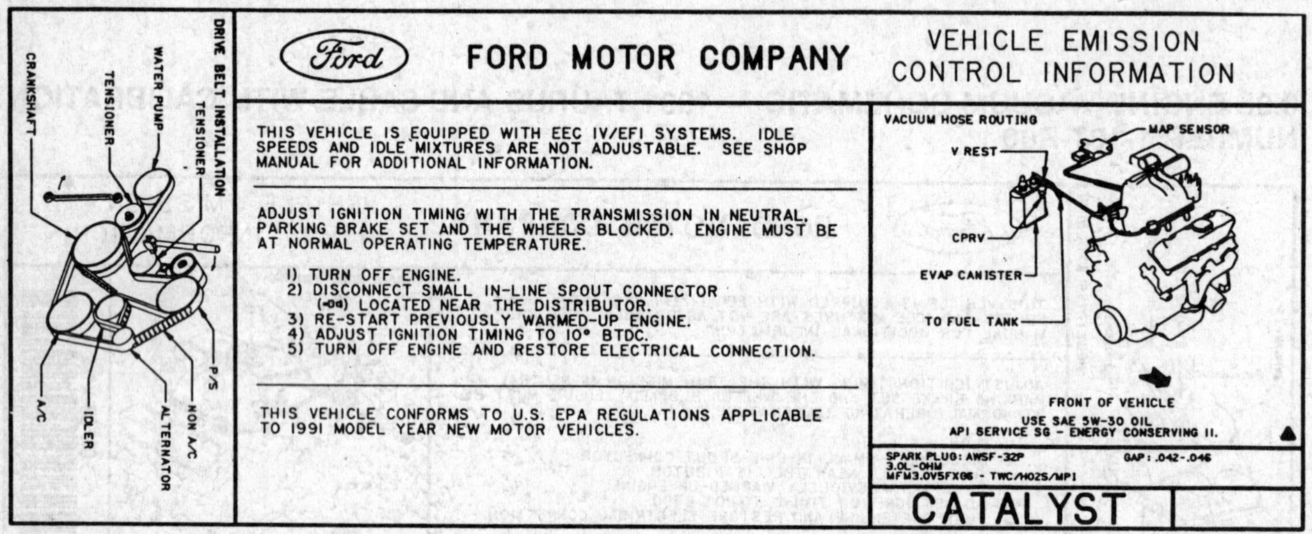

3.0L ENGINE VACUUM SCHEMATIC – 1991 TAURUS AND SABLE WITH CALIBRATION NUMBER 1-09T-R10

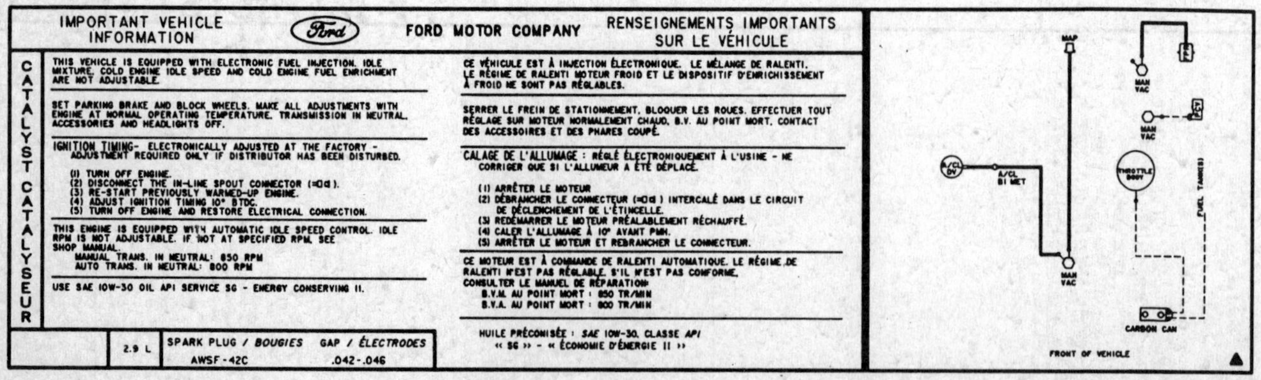

3.0L ENGINE VACUUM SCHEMATIC – 1991 TAURUS AND SABLE WITH CALIBRATION NUMBER 0-09P-R00

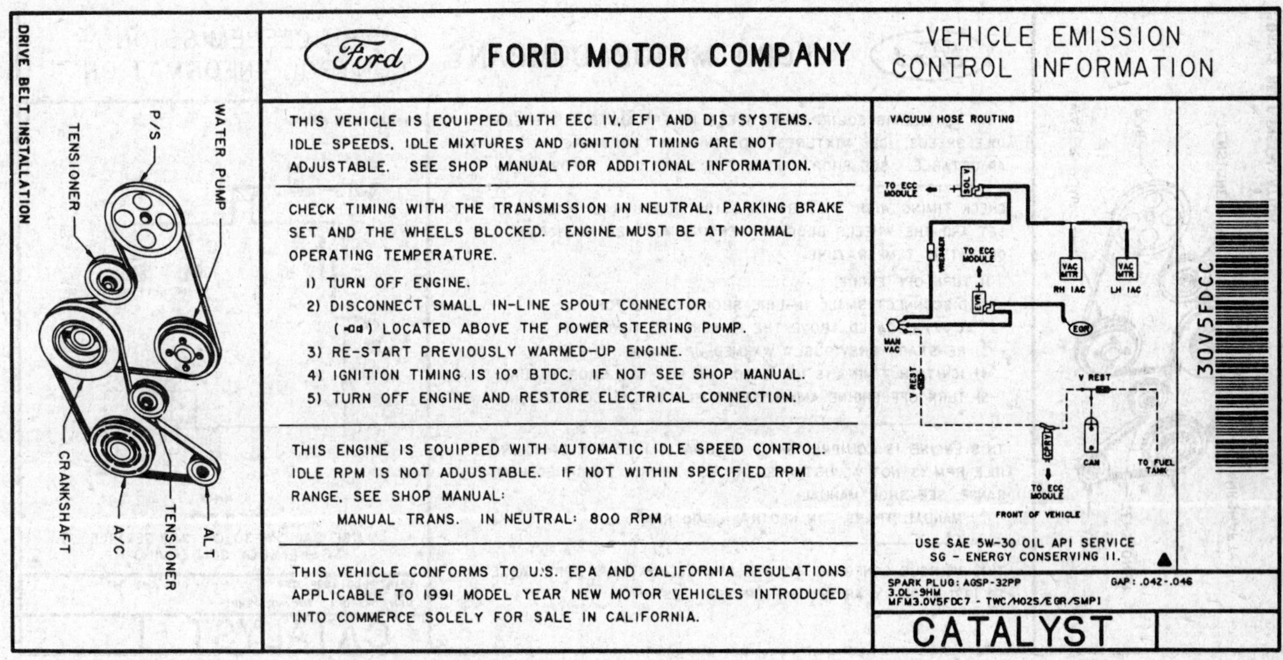

3.0L ENGINE VACUUM SCHEMATIC – 1991 TAURUS AND SABLE WITH CALIBRATION NUMBER 0-09P-R00

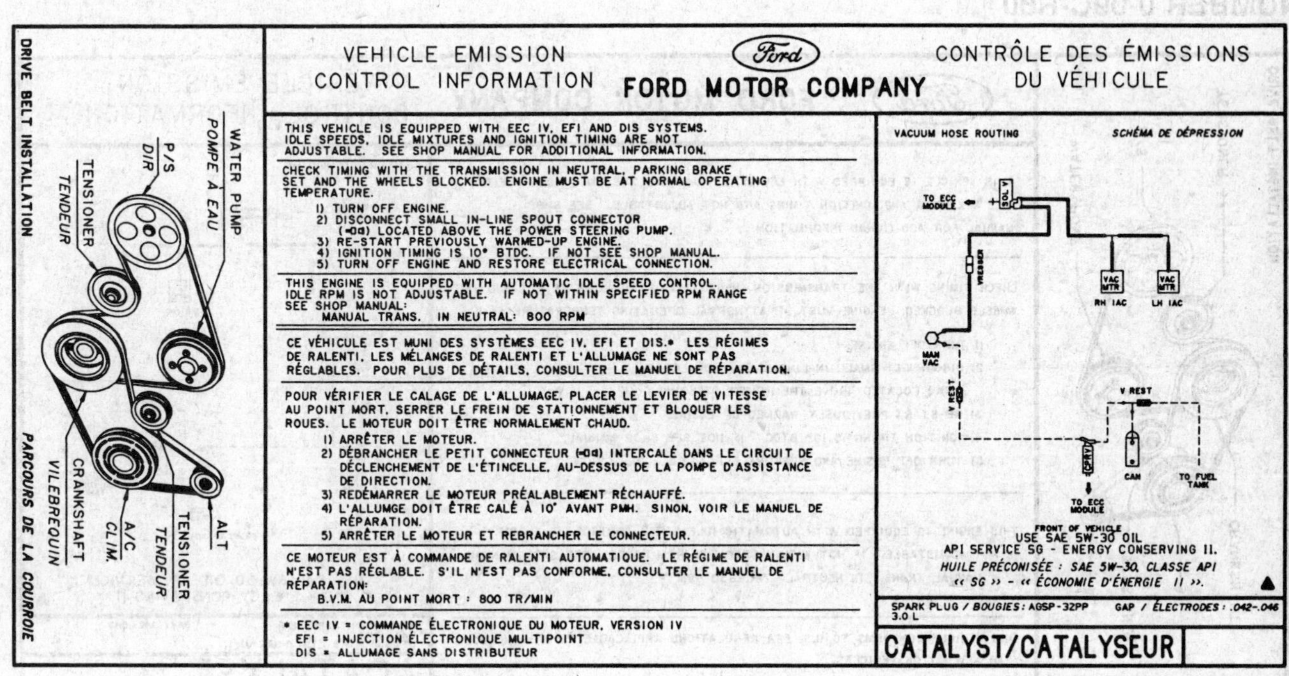

3.0L ENGINE VACUUM SCHEMATIC – 1991 TAURUS AND SABLE WITH CALIBRATION NUMBER 0-09C-R00

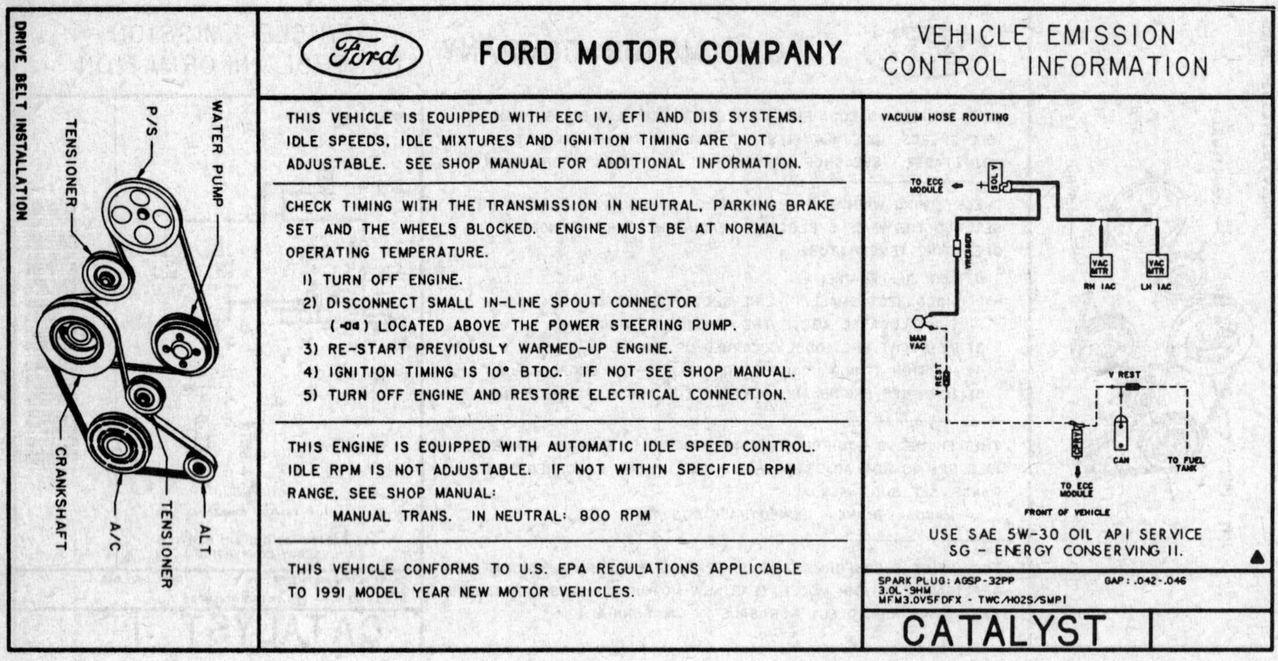

3.0L ENGINE VACUUM SCHEMATIC – 1991 TAURUS AND SABLE WITH CALIBRATION NUMBER 0-09C-R00

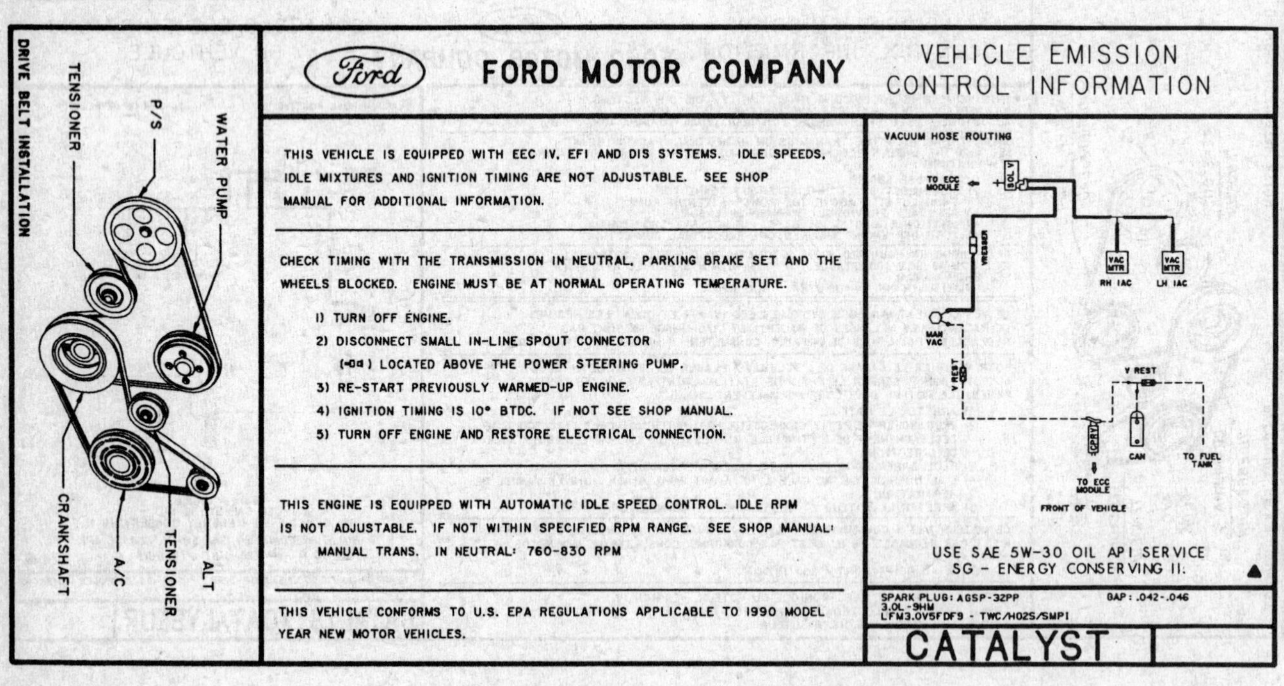

3.0L ENGINE VACUUM SCHEMATIC – 1991 TAURUS AND SABLE WITH CALIBRATION NUMBER 0-09C-R00

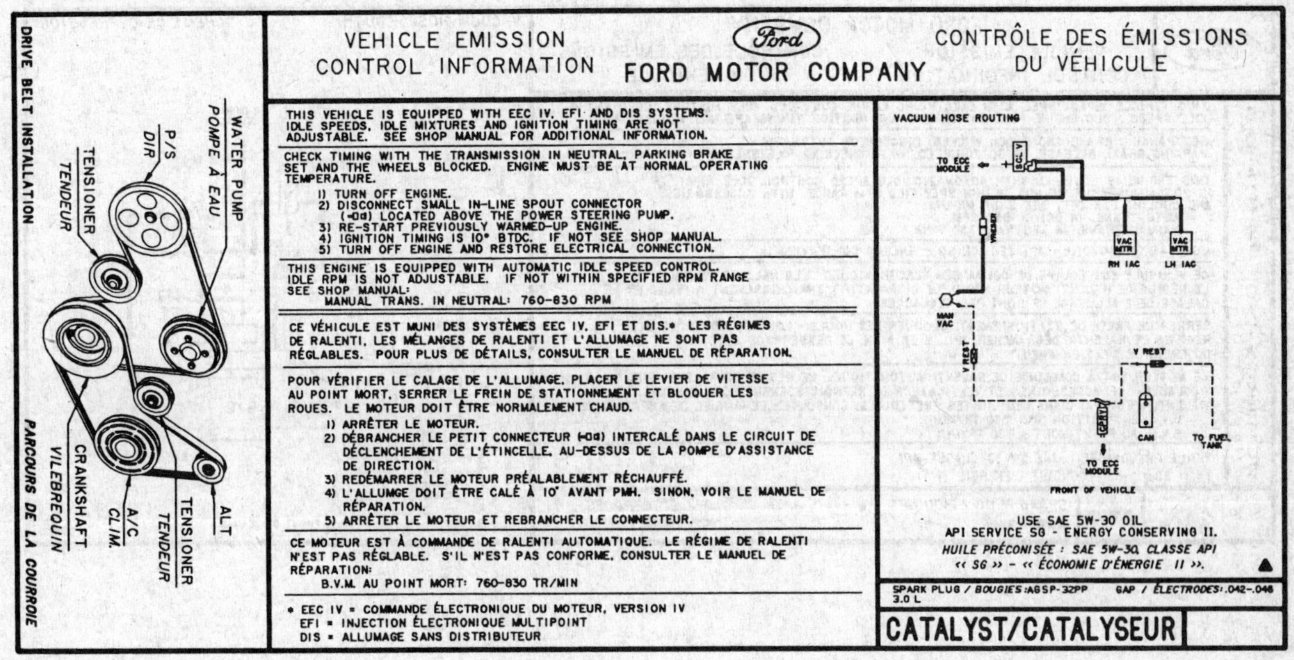

VEHICLE EMISSION CONTROL INFORMATION

FORD MOTOR COMPANY

CONTRÔLE DES ÉMISSIONS DU VÉHICULE

THIS VEHICLE IS EQUIPPED WITH EEC IV, EFI AND DIS SYSTEMS. IDLE SPEEDS, IDLE MIXTURES AND IGNITION TIMING ARE NOT ADJUSTABLE. SEE SHOP MANUAL FOR ADDITIONAL INFORMATION.

CHECK TIMING WITH THE TRANSMISSION IN NEUTRAL, PARKING BRAKE SET AND THE WHEELS BLOCKED. ENGINE MUST BE AT NORMAL OPERATING TEMPERATURE.

1) TURN OFF ENGINE.
2) DISCONNECT SMALL IN-LINE SPOUT CONNECTOR (-□◘) LOCATED ABOVE THE POWER STEERING PUMP.
3) RE-START PREVIOUSLY WARMED-UP ENGINE.
4) IGNITION TIMING IS 10° BTDC. IF NOT SEE SHOP MANUAL.
5) TURN OFF ENGINE AND RESTORE ELECTRICAL CONNECTION.

THIS ENGINE IS EQUIPPED WITH AUTOMATIC IDLE SPEED CONTROL. IDLE RPM IS NOT ADJUSTABLE. IF NOT WITHIN SPECIFIED RPM RANGE SEE SHOP MANUAL:
MANUAL TRANS. IN NEUTRAL: 760-830 RPM

CE VÉHICULE EST MUNI DES SYSTÈMES EEC IV, EFI ET DIS.* LES RÉGIMES DE RALENTI, LES MÉLANGES DE RALENTI ET L'ALLUMAGE NE SONT PAS RÉGLABLES. POUR PLUS DE DÉTAILS, CONSULTER LE MANUEL DE RÉPARATION.

POUR VÉRIFIER LE CALAGE DE L'ALLUMAGE, PLACER LE LEVIER DE VITESSE AU POINT MORT, SERRER LE FREIN DE STATIONNEMENT ET BLOQUER LES ROUES. LE MOTEUR DOIT ÊTRE NORMALEMENT CHAUD.

1) ARRÊTER LE MOTEUR.
2) DÉBRANCHER LE PETIT CONNECTEUR (-□◘) INTERCALÉ DANS LE CIRCUIT DE DÉCLENCHEMENT DE L'ÉTINCELLE, AU-DESSUS DE LA POMPE D'ASSISTANCE DE DIRECTION.
3) REDÉMARRER LE MOTEUR PRÉALABLEMENT RÉCHAUFFÉ.
4) L'ALLUMGE DOIT ÊTRE CALÉ À 10° AVANT PMH. SINON, VOIR LE MANUEL DE RÉPARATION.
5) ARRÊTER LE MOTEUR ET REBRANCHER LE CONNECTEUR.

CE MOTEUR EST À COMMANDE DE RALENTI AUTOMATIQUE. LE RÉGIME DE RALENTI N'EST PAS RÉGLABLE. S'IL N'EST PAS CONFORME, CONSULTER LE MANUEL DE RÉPARATION:
B.V.M. AU POINT MORT: 760-830 TR/MIN

* EEC IV = COMMANDE ÉLECTRONIQUE DU MOTEUR, VERSION IV
EFI = INJECTION ÉLECTRONIQUE MULTIPOINT
DIS = ALLUMAGE SANS DISTRIBUTEUR

USE SAE 5W-30 OIL
API SERVICE SG - ENERGY CONSERVING II.
HUILE PRÉCONISÉE : SAE 5W-30, CLASSE API « SG » - « ÉCONOMIE D'ÉNERGIE II ».

SPARK PLUG / *BOUGIES*: AGSP-32PP GAP / *ÉLECTRODES*: .042-.046
3.0 L

CATALYST/CATALYSEUR

3.8L ENGINE VACUUM SCHEMATIC – 1991 TAURUS AND SABLE WITH CALIBRATION NUMBER 1-15A-R00

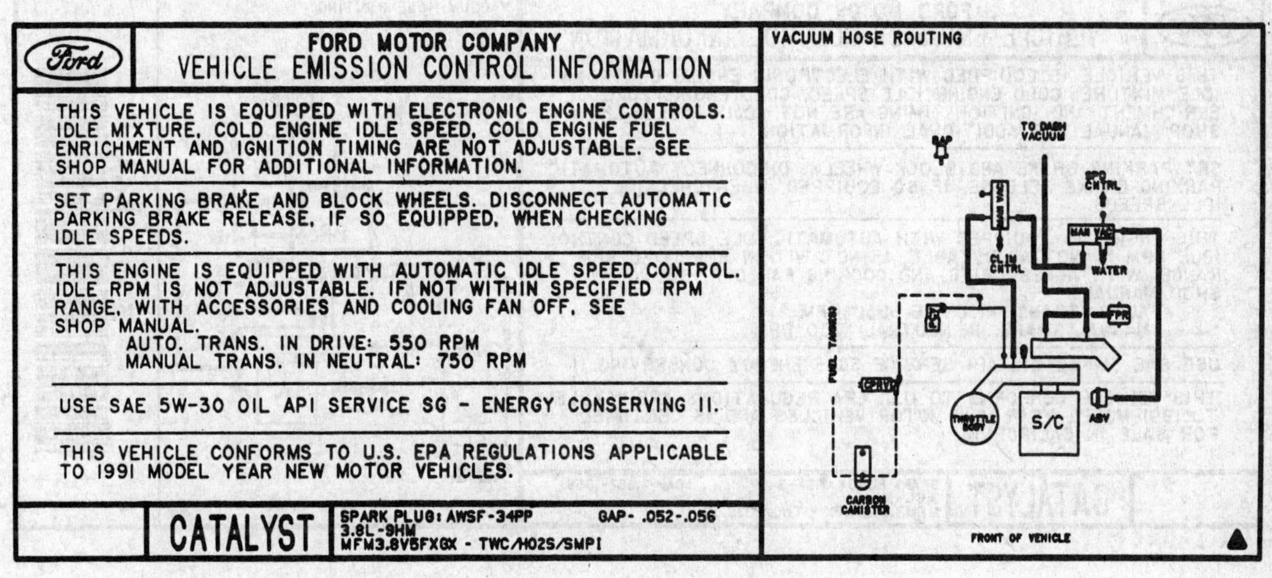

FORD MOTOR COMPANY
VEHICLE EMISSION CONTROL INFORMATION

THIS VEHICLE IS EQUIPPED WITH ELECTRONIC ENGINE CONTROLS. IDLE MIXTURE, COLD ENGINE IDLE SPEED, COLD ENGINE FUEL ENRICHMENT AND IGNITION TIMING ARE NOT ADJUSTABLE. SEE SHOP MANUAL FOR ADDITIONAL INFORMATION.

SET PARKING BRAKE AND BLOCK WHEELS. DISCONNECT AUTOMATIC PARKING BRAKE RELEASE, IF SO EQUIPPED, WHEN CHECKING IDLE SPEEDS.

THIS ENGINE IS EQUIPPED WITH AUTOMATIC IDLE SPEED CONTROL. IDLE RPM IS NOT ADJUSTABLE. IF NOT WITHIN SPECIFIED RPM RANGE, WITH ACCESSORIES AND COOLING FAN OFF, SEE SHOP MANUAL.
AUTO. TRANS. IN DRIVE: 550 RPM
MANUAL TRANS. IN NEUTRAL: 750 RPM

USE SAE 5W-30 OIL API SERVICE SG - ENERGY CONSERVING II.

THIS VEHICLE CONFORMS TO U.S. EPA REGULATIONS APPLICABLE TO 1991 MODEL YEAR NEW MOTOR VEHICLES.

CATALYST

SPARK PLUG: AWSF-34PP GAP- .052-.056
3.8L-9HM
MFM3.8V5FXGX - TWC/HO2S/SMPI

3.8L ENGINE VACUUM SCHEMATIC – 1991 TAURUS AND SABLE WITH CALIBRATION NUMBER 1-15A-R00

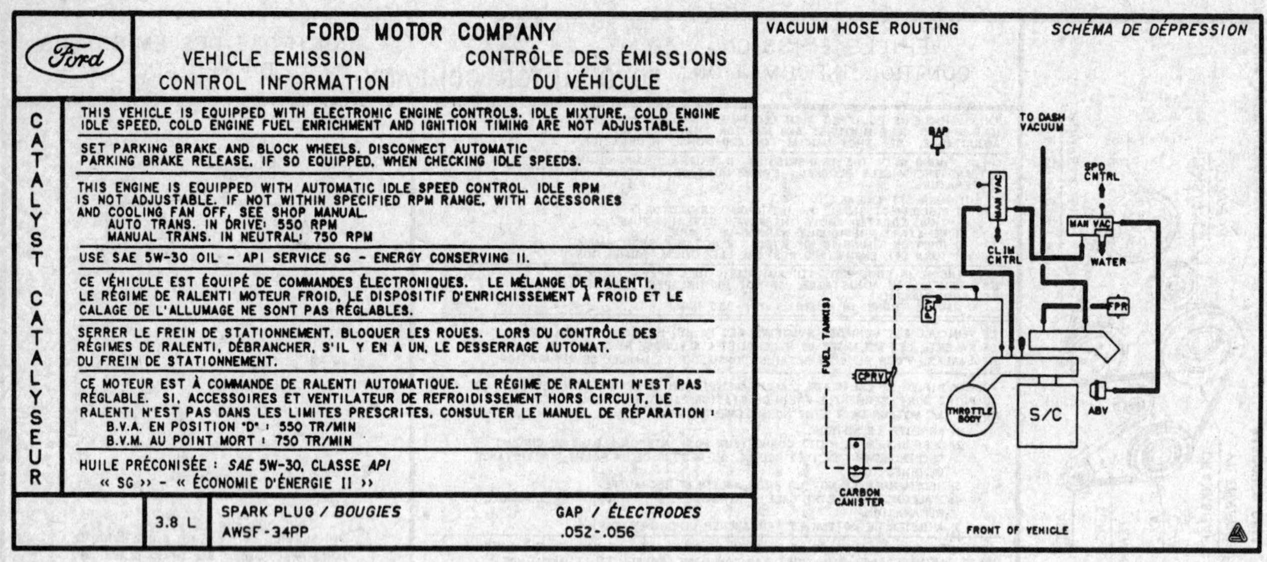

Ford

FORD MOTOR COMPANY
VEHICLE EMISSION CONTROL INFORMATION — CONTRÔLE DES ÉMISSIONS DU VÉHICULE

CATALYST — CATALYSEUR

THIS VEHICLE IS EQUIPPED WITH ELECTRONIC ENGINE CONTROLS. IDLE MIXTURE, COLD ENGINE IDLE SPEED, COLD ENGINE FUEL ENRICHMENT AND IGNITION TIMING ARE NOT ADJUSTABLE.

SET PARKING BRAKE AND BLOCK WHEELS. DISCONNECT AUTOMATIC PARKING BRAKE RELEASE, IF SO EQUIPPED, WHEN CHECKING IDLE SPEEDS.

THIS ENGINE IS EQUIPPED WITH AUTOMATIC IDLE SPEED CONTROL. IDLE RPM IS NOT ADJUSTABLE. IF NOT WITHIN SPECIFIED RPM RANGE, WITH ACCESSORIES AND COOLING FAN OFF, SEE SHOP MANUAL.
AUTO TRANS. IN DRIVE: 550 RPM
MANUAL TRANS. IN NEUTRAL: 750 RPM

USE SAE 5W-30 OIL - API SERVICE SG - ENERGY CONSERVING II.

CE VÉHICULE EST ÉQUIPÉ DE COMMANDES ÉLECTRONIQUES. LE MÉLANGE DE RALENTI, LE RÉGIME DE RALENTI MOTEUR FROID, LE DISPOSITIF D'ENRICHISSEMENT À FROID ET LE CALAGE DE L'ALLUMAGE NE SONT PAS RÉGLABLES.

SERRER LE FREIN DE STATIONNEMENT, BLOQUER LES ROUES. LORS DU CONTRÔLE DES RÉGIMES DE RALENTI, DÉBRANCHER, S'IL Y EN A UN, LE DESSERRAGE AUTOMAT. DU FREIN DE STATIONNEMENT.

CE MOTEUR EST À COMMANDE DE RALENTI AUTOMATIQUE. LE RÉGIME DE RALENTI N'EST PAS RÉGLABLE. SI, ACCESSOIRES ET VENTILATEUR DE REFROIDISSEMENT HORS CIRCUIT, LE RALENTI N'EST PAS DANS LES LIMITES PRESCRITES, CONSULTER LE MANUEL DE RÉPARATION :
B.V.A. EN POSITION "D" : 550 TR/MIN
B.V.M. AU POINT MORT : 750 TR/MIN

HUILE PRÉCONISÉE : *SAE* 5W-30, CLASSE *API* « SG » - « ÉCONOMIE D'ÉNERGIE II »

3.8 L	SPARK PLUG / *BOUGIES* AWSF-34PP	GAP / *ÉLECTRODES* .052-.056

VACUUM HOSE ROUTING — *SCHÉMA DE DÉPRESSION*

3.8L ENGINE VACUUM SCHEMATIC – 1991 TAURUS AND SABLE WITH CALIBRATION NUMBER 1-15A-R00

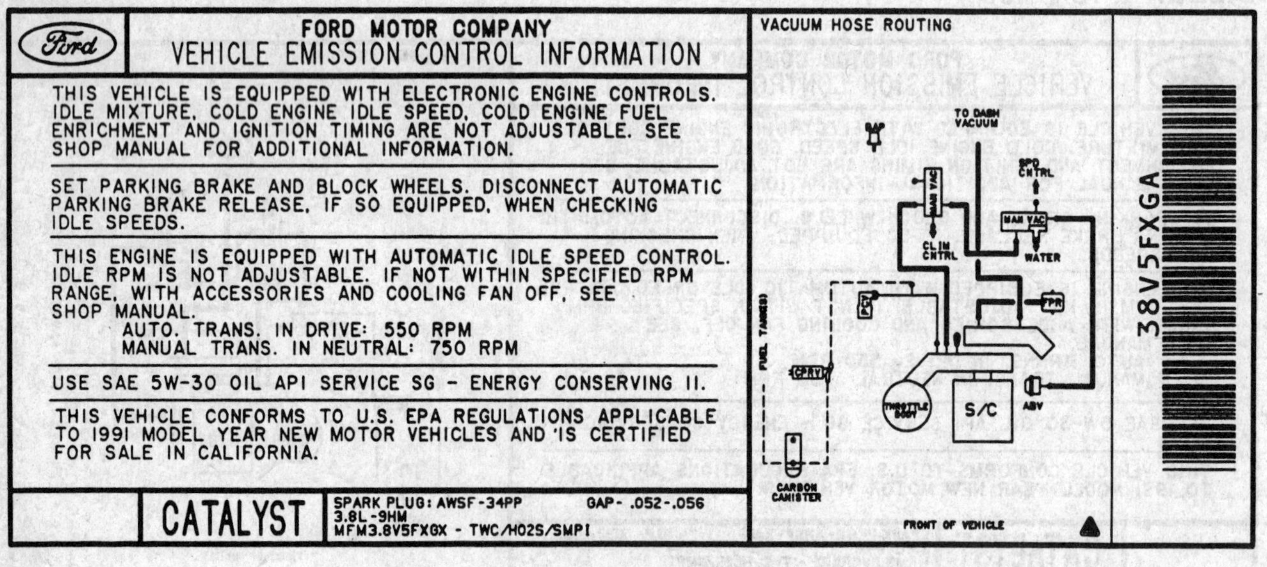

Ford

FORD MOTOR COMPANY
VEHICLE EMISSION CONTROL INFORMATION

THIS VEHICLE IS EQUIPPED WITH ELECTRONIC ENGINE CONTROLS. IDLE MIXTURE, COLD ENGINE IDLE SPEED, COLD ENGINE FUEL ENRICHMENT AND IGNITION TIMING ARE NOT ADJUSTABLE. SEE SHOP MANUAL FOR ADDITIONAL INFORMATION.

SET PARKING BRAKE AND BLOCK WHEELS. DISCONNECT AUTOMATIC PARKING BRAKE RELEASE, IF SO EQUIPPED, WHEN CHECKING IDLE SPEEDS.

THIS ENGINE IS EQUIPPED WITH AUTOMATIC IDLE SPEED CONTROL. IDLE RPM IS NOT ADJUSTABLE. IF NOT WITHIN SPECIFIED RPM RANGE, WITH ACCESSORIES AND COOLING FAN OFF, SEE SHOP MANUAL.
AUTO. TRANS. IN DRIVE: 550 RPM
MANUAL TRANS. IN NEUTRAL: 750 RPM

USE SAE 5W-30 OIL API SERVICE SG - ENERGY CONSERVING II.

THIS VEHICLE CONFORMS TO U.S. EPA REGULATIONS APPLICABLE TO 1991 MODEL YEAR NEW MOTOR VEHICLES AND IS CERTIFIED FOR SALE IN CALIFORNIA.

CATALYST — SPARK PLUG: AWSF-34PP GAP- .052-.056
3.8L-9HM
MFM3.8V5FXGX - TWC/HO2S/SMPI

VACUUM HOSE ROUTING

3.8L ENGINE VACUUM SCHEMATIC – 1991 TAURUS AND SABLE WITH CALIBRATION NUMBER 1-15A-R11

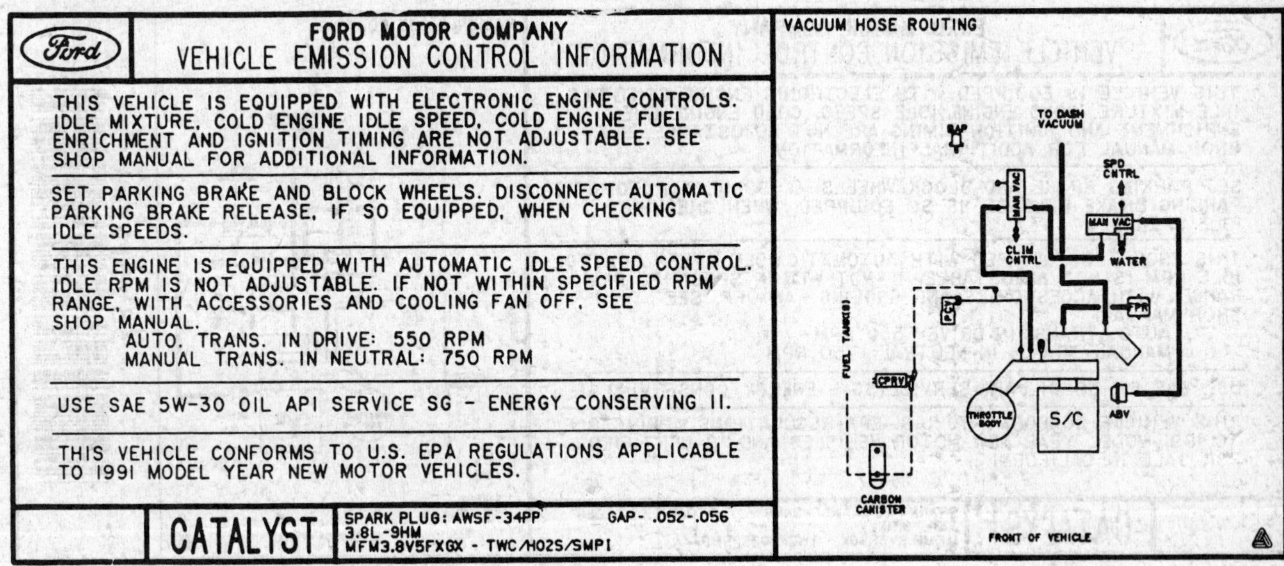

Ford

FORD MOTOR COMPANY
VEHICLE EMISSION CONTROL INFORMATION

THIS VEHICLE IS EQUIPPED WITH ELECTRONIC ENGINE CONTROLS. IDLE MIXTURE, COLD ENGINE IDLE SPEED, COLD ENGINE FUEL ENRICHMENT AND IGNITION TIMING ARE NOT ADJUSTABLE. SEE SHOP MANUAL FOR ADDITIONAL INFORMATION.

SET PARKING BRAKE AND BLOCK WHEELS. DISCONNECT AUTOMATIC PARKING BRAKE RELEASE, IF SO EQUIPPED, WHEN CHECKING IDLE SPEEDS.

THIS ENGINE IS EQUIPPED WITH AUTOMATIC IDLE SPEED CONTROL. IDLE RPM IS NOT ADJUSTABLE. IF NOT WITHIN SPECIFIED RPM RANGE, WITH ACCESSORIES AND COOLING FAN OFF, SEE SHOP MANUAL.
AUTO. TRANS. IN DRIVE: 550 RPM
MANUAL TRANS. IN NEUTRAL: 750 RPM

USE SAE 5W-30 OIL API SERVICE SG - ENERGY CONSERVING II.

THIS VEHICLE CONFORMS TO U.S. EPA REGULATIONS APPLICABLE TO 1991 MODEL YEAR NEW MOTOR VEHICLES.

CATALYST

SPARK PLUG: AWSF-34PP GAP- .052-.056
3.8L-9HM
MFM3.8V5FXGX - TWC/HO2S/SMPI

3.8L ENGINE VACUUM SCHEMATIC – 1991 TAURUS AND SABLE WITH CALIBRATION NUMBER 1-15A-R11

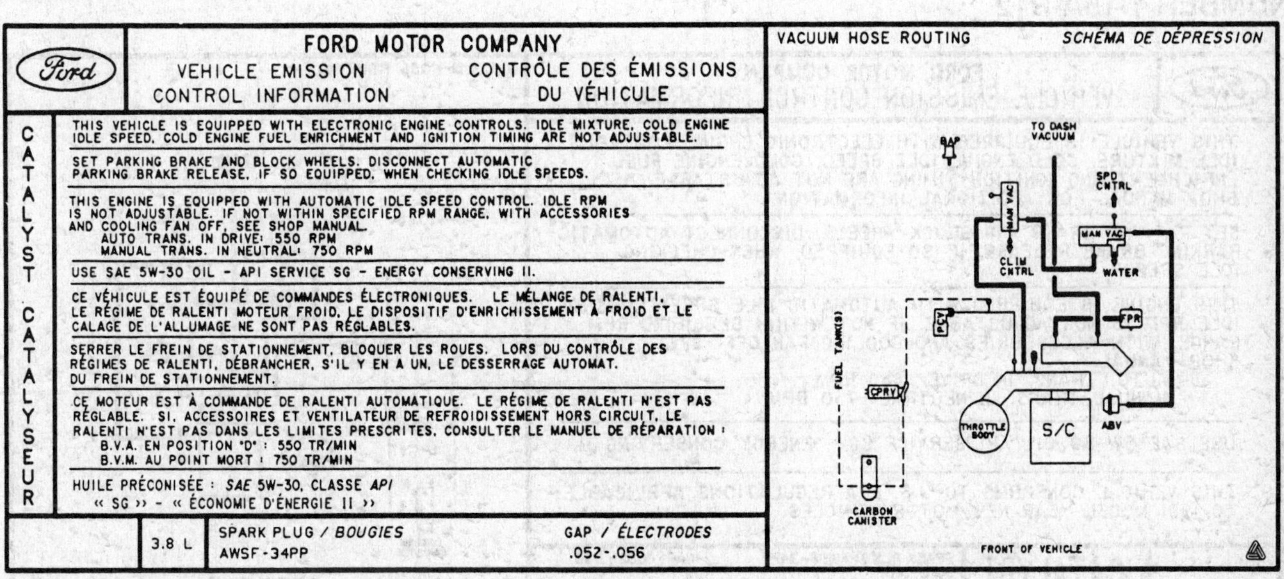

Ford

FORD MOTOR COMPANY
VEHICLE EMISSION CONTROL INFORMATION — CONTRÔLE DES ÉMISSIONS DU VÉHICULE

CATALYST CATALYSEUR

THIS VEHICLE IS EQUIPPED WITH ELECTRONIC ENGINE CONTROLS. IDLE MIXTURE, COLD ENGINE IDLE SPEED, COLD ENGINE FUEL ENRICHMENT AND IGNITION TIMING ARE NOT ADJUSTABLE.

SET PARKING BRAKE AND BLOCK WHEELS. DISCONNECT AUTOMATIC PARKING BRAKE RELEASE, IF SO EQUIPPED, WHEN CHECKING IDLE SPEEDS.

THIS ENGINE IS EQUIPPED WITH AUTOMATIC IDLE SPEED CONTROL. IDLE RPM IS NOT ADJUSTABLE. IF NOT WITHIN SPECIFIED RPM RANGE, WITH ACCESSORIES AND COOLING FAN OFF, SEE SHOP MANUAL.
AUTO TRANS. IN DRIVE: 550 RPM
MANUAL TRANS. IN NEUTRAL: 750 RPM

USE SAE 5W-30 OIL - API SERVICE SG - ENERGY CONSERVING II.

CE VÉHICULE EST ÉQUIPÉ DE COMMANDES ÉLECTRONIQUES. LE MÉLANGE DE RALENTI, LE RÉGIME DE RALENTI MOTEUR FROID, LE DISPOSITIF D'ENRICHISSEMENT À FROID ET LE CALAGE DE L'ALLUMAGE NE SONT PAS RÉGLABLES.

SERRER LE FREIN DE STATIONNEMENT, BLOQUER LES ROUES. LORS DU CONTRÔLE DES RÉGIMES DE RALENTI, DÉBRANCHER, S'IL Y EN A UN, LE DESSERRAGE AUTOMAT. DU FREIN DE STATIONNEMENT.

CE MOTEUR EST À COMMANDE DE RALENTI AUTOMATIQUE. LE RÉGIME DE RALENTI N'EST PAS RÉGLABLE. SI, ACCESSOIRES ET VENTILATEUR DE REFROIDISSEMENT HORS CIRCUIT, LE RALENTI N'EST PAS DANS LES LIMITES PRESCRITES, CONSULTER LE MANUEL DE RÉPARATION :
B.V.A. EN POSITION "D" : 550 TR/MIN
B.V.M. AU POINT MORT : 750 TR/MIN

HUILE PRÉCONISÉE : *SAE* 5W-30, CLASSE *API* « SG » - « ÉCONOMIE D'ÉNERGIE II »

3.8 L	SPARK PLUG / *BOUGIES* AWSF-34PP	GAP / *ÉLECTRODES* .052-.056

3.8L ENGINE VACUUM SCHEMATIC – 1991 TAURUS AND SABLE WITH CALIBRATION NUMBER 1-15A-R11

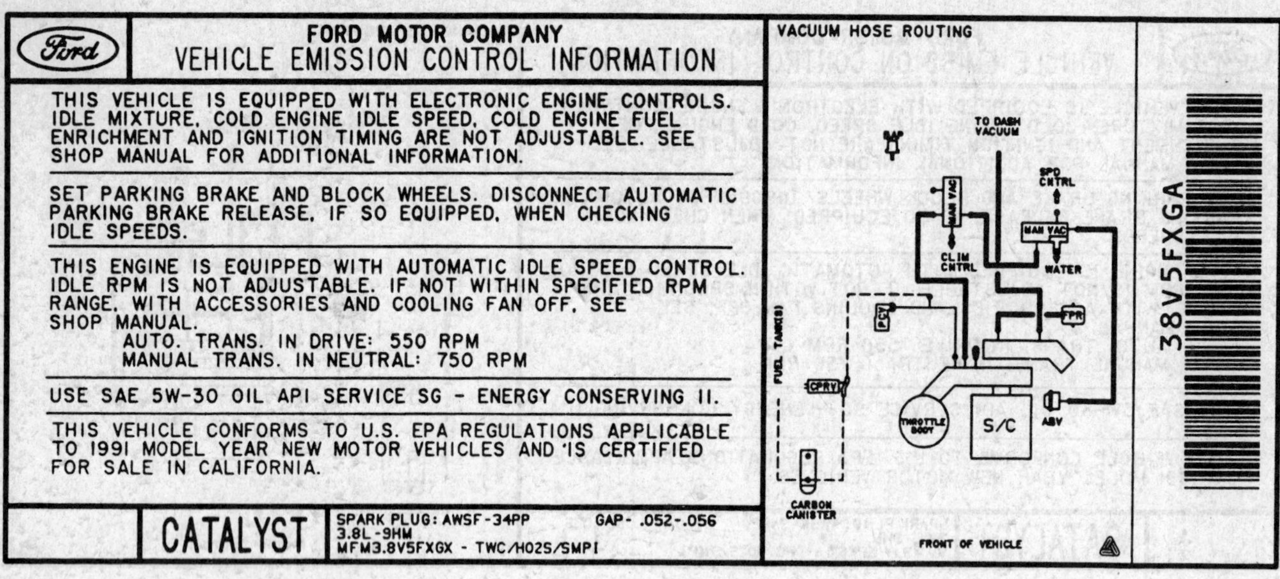

3.8L ENGINE VACUUM SCHEMATIC – 1991 TAURUS AND SABLE WITH CALIBRATION NUMBER 1-15A-R12

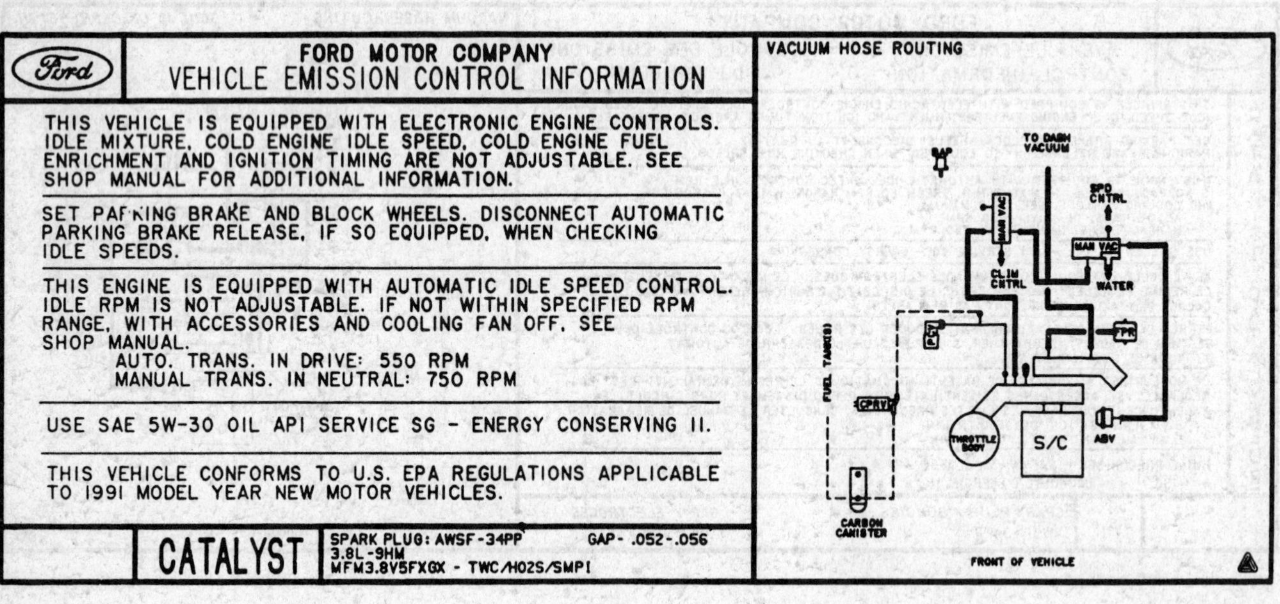

3.8L ENGINE VACUUM SCHEMATIC – 1992 TAURUS AND SABLE WITH CALIBRATION NUMBER 2-16A-R12

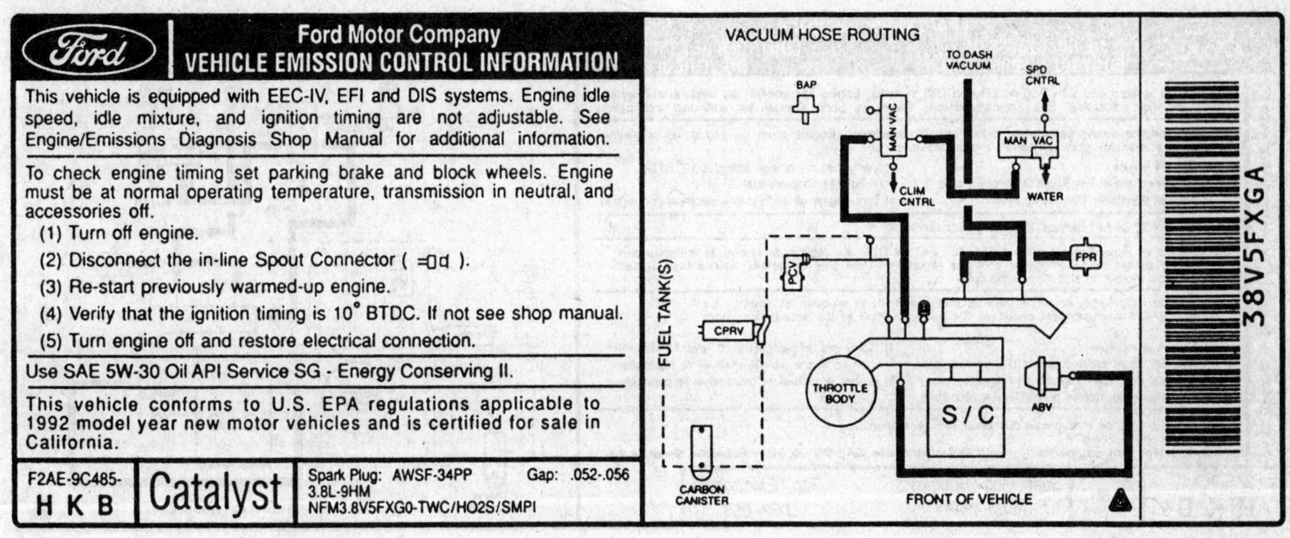

Ford Motor Company
VEHICLE EMISSION CONTROL INFORMATION

This vehicle is equipped with EEC-IV, EFI and DIS systems. Engine idle speed, idle mixture, and ignition timing are not adjustable. See Engine/Emissions Diagnosis Shop Manual for additional information.

To check engine timing set parking brake and block wheels. Engine must be at normal operating temperature, transmission in neutral, and accessories off.

(1) Turn off engine.
(2) Disconnect the in-line Spout Connector (=▯◁).
(3) Re-start previously warmed-up engine.
(4) Verify that the ignition timing is 10° BTDC. If not see shop manual.
(5) Turn engine off and restore electrical connection.

Use SAE 5W-30 Oil API Service SG - Energy Conserving II.

This vehicle conforms to U.S. EPA regulations applicable to 1992 model year new motor vehicles and is certified for sale in California.

F2AE-9C485-
H K B

Catalyst

Spark Plug: AWSF-34PP Gap: .052-.056
3.8L-9HM
NFM3.8V5FXG0-TWC/HO2S/SMPI

3.8L ENGINE VACUUM SCHEMATIC – 1992 TAURUS AND SABLE WITH CALIBRATION NUMBER 2-16A-R12

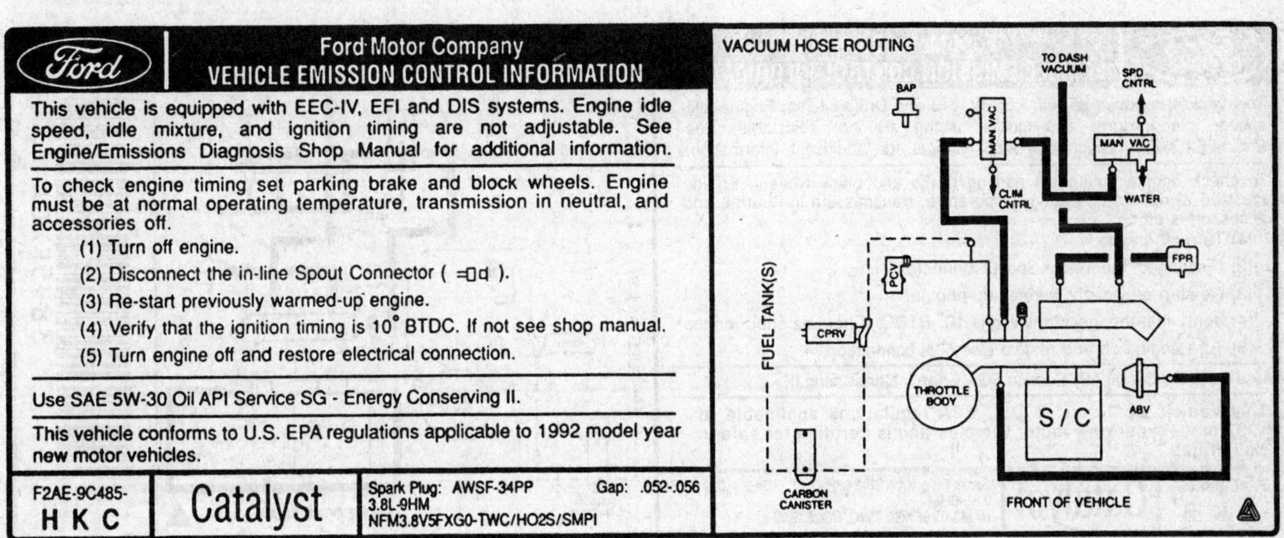

Ford Motor Company
VEHICLE EMISSION CONTROL INFORMATION

This vehicle is equipped with EEC-IV, EFI and DIS systems. Engine idle speed, idle mixture, and ignition timing are not adjustable. See Engine/Emissions Diagnosis Shop Manual for additional information.

To check engine timing set parking brake and block wheels. Engine must be at normal operating temperature, transmission in neutral, and accessories off.

(1) Turn off engine.
(2) Disconnect the in-line Spout Connector (=▯◁).
(3) Re-start previously warmed-up engine.
(4) Verify that the ignition timing is 10° BTDC. If not see shop manual.
(5) Turn engine off and restore electrical connection.

Use SAE 5W-30 Oil API Service SG - Energy Conserving II.

This vehicle conforms to U.S. EPA regulations applicable to 1992 model year new motor vehicles.

F2AE-9C485-
H K C

Catalyst

Spark Plug: AWSF-34PP Gap: .052-.056
3.8L-9HM
NFM3.8V5FXG0-TWC/HO2S/SMPI

3.8L ENGINE VACUUM SCHEMATIC – 1992 TAURUS AND SABLE WITH CALIBRATION NUMBER 2-16A-R12

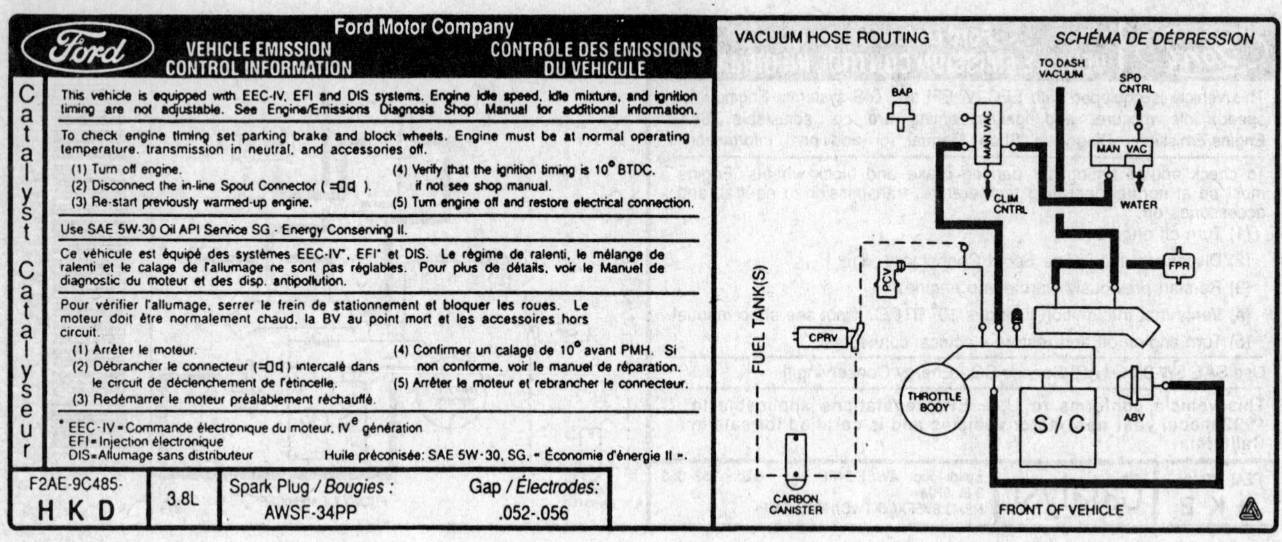

Ford Motor Company
Ford
VEHICLE EMISSION CONTROL INFORMATION
CONTRÔLE DES ÉMISSIONS DU VÉHICULE

Catalyst Catalyseur

This vehicle is equipped with EEC-IV, EFI and DIS systems. Engine idle speed, idle mixture, and ignition timing are not adjustable. See Engine/Emissions Diagnosis Shop Manual for additional information.

To check engine timing set parking brake and block wheels. Engine must be at normal operating temperature, transmission in neutral, and accessories off.

(1) Turn off engine.
(2) Disconnect the in-line Spout Connector (=▯ᑫ).
(3) Re-start previously warmed-up engine.
(4) Verify that the ignition timing is 10° BTDC. If not see shop manual.
(5) Turn engine off and restore electrical connection.

Use SAE 5W-30 Oil API Service SG - Energy Conserving II.

Ce véhicule est équipé des systèmes EEC-IV*, EFI* et DIS. Le régime de ralenti, le mélange de ralenti et le calage de l'allumage ne sont pas réglables. Pour plus de détails, voir le Manuel de diagnostic du moteur et des disp. antipollution.

Pour vérifier l'allumage, serrer le frein de stationnement et bloquer les roues. Le moteur doit être normalement chaud, la BV au point mort et les accessoires hors circuit.

(1) Arrêter le moteur.
(2) Débrancher le connecteur (=▯ᑫ) intercalé dans le circuit de déclenchement de l'étincelle.
(3) Redémarrer le moteur préalablement réchauffé.
(4) Confirmer un calage de 10° avant PMH. Si non conforme, voir le manuel de réparation.
(5) Arrêter le moteur et rebrancher le connecteur.

* EEC-IV = Commande électronique du moteur, IVe génération
EFI = Injection électronique
DIS = Allumage sans distributeur

Huile préconisée: SAE 5W-30, SG, « Économie d'énergie II ».

F2AE-9C485- HKD	3.8L	Spark Plug / *Bougies :* AWSF-34PP	Gap / *Électrodes:* .052-.056

3.8L ENGINE VACUUM SCHEMATIC – 1992 TAURUS AND SABLE WITH CALIBRATION NUMBER 2-15A-R10

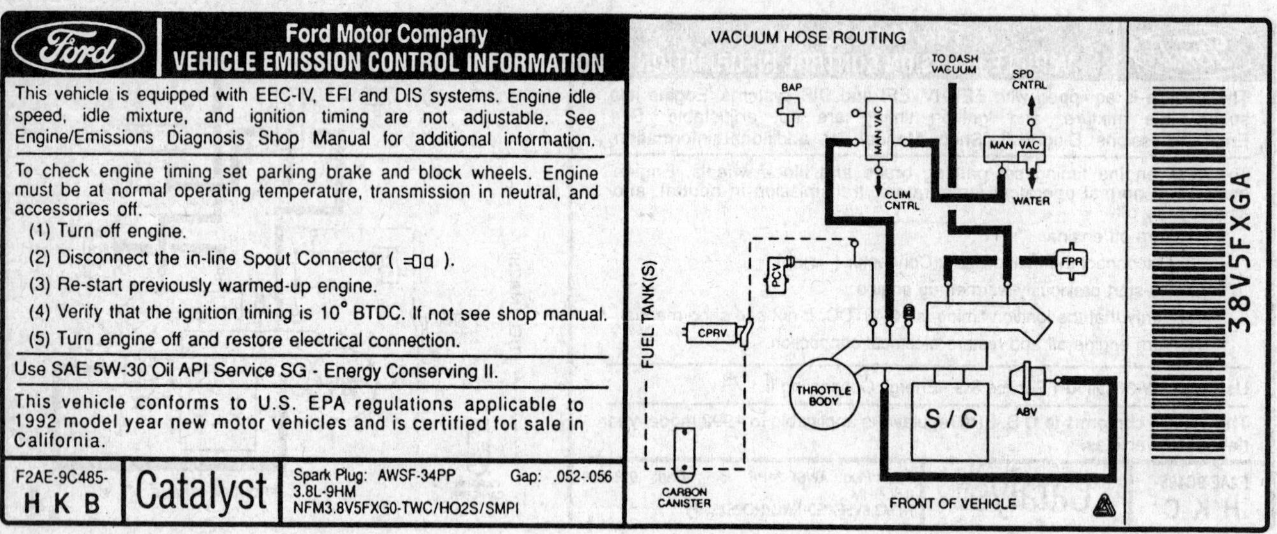

Ford Motor Company
Ford
VEHICLE EMISSION CONTROL INFORMATION

This vehicle is equipped with EEC-IV, EFI and DIS systems. Engine idle speed, idle mixture, and ignition timing are not adjustable. See Engine/Emissions Diagnosis Shop Manual for additional information.

To check engine timing set parking brake and block wheels. Engine must be at normal operating temperature, transmission in neutral, and accessories off.

(1) Turn off engine.
(2) Disconnect the in-line Spout Connector (=▯ᑫ).
(3) Re-start previously warmed-up engine.
(4) Verify that the ignition timing is 10° BTDC. If not see shop manual.
(5) Turn engine off and restore electrical connection.

Use SAE 5W-30 Oil API Service SG - Energy Conserving II.

This vehicle conforms to U.S. EPA regulations applicable to 1992 model year new motor vehicles and is certified for sale in California.

F2AE-9C485- HKB	Catalyst	Spark Plug: AWSF-34PP 3.8L-9HM NFM3.8V5FXG0-TWC/HO2S/SMPI	Gap: .052-.056

bracket by loosening the worm gear mounting clamp enough to allow the filter to pass through.

To install:

4. Install the filter in the mounting bracket, ensuring that the flow direction arrow is pointing forward. Locate the fuel filter against the tab at the lower end of the bracket.
5. Insert a new hairpin clip into any 2 adjacent openings on each push connect fitting, with the triangular portion of the clip pointing away from the fitting opening. Install the clip to fully engage the body of the fitting. This is indicated by the legs of the hairpin clip being locked on the outside of the fitting body. Apply a light coat of engine oil to the ends of the fuel filter and then push the fittings onto the ends of the fuel filter. When the fittings are engaged, a definite click will be heard. Pull on the fittings to ensure that they are fully engaged.
6. Tighten the worm gear mounting clamp to 15–25 inch lbs. (1.7–2.8 Nm).
7. Start the engine and check for leaks.

Electric Fuel Pump

REMOVAL & INSTALLATION

➧ SEE FIG. 5–6

1. Disconnect the negative battery cable.
2. Relieve the fuel system pressure.
3. Remove the fuel tank from the vehicle and place it on a work bench. Remove any dirt around the fuel pump attaching flange.
4. Turn the fuel pump locking ring counterclockwise and remove the lock ring.
5. Remove the fuel pump from the fuel tank and discard the flange gasket.

To install:

6. Clean the fuel pump mounting flange and fuel tank mounting surface and seal ring groove.
7. Put a light coating of grease on the new seal gasket to hold it in place during assembly and install it in the fuel ring groove.
8. Install the fuel pump and sender assembly. Make sure the locating keys are in the keyways and the seal gasket remains in place.
9. Hold the assembly in place and install the lock ring making sure all locking tabs are under the tank lock ring tabs. Tighten the lock ring by turning it clockwise until it is up against the stops.
10. Install the fuel tank.
11. Fill the tank with a minimum of 10 gallons of fuel and check for leaks.
12. Connect a suitable fuel pressure gauge. Turn the ignition switch to the **ON** position 5–10 times, leaving it on for 3 seconds at a time, until the pressure gauge reads at least 30 psi. Check for leaks at the fittings.
13. Remove the pressure gauge, start the engine and recheck for leaks.

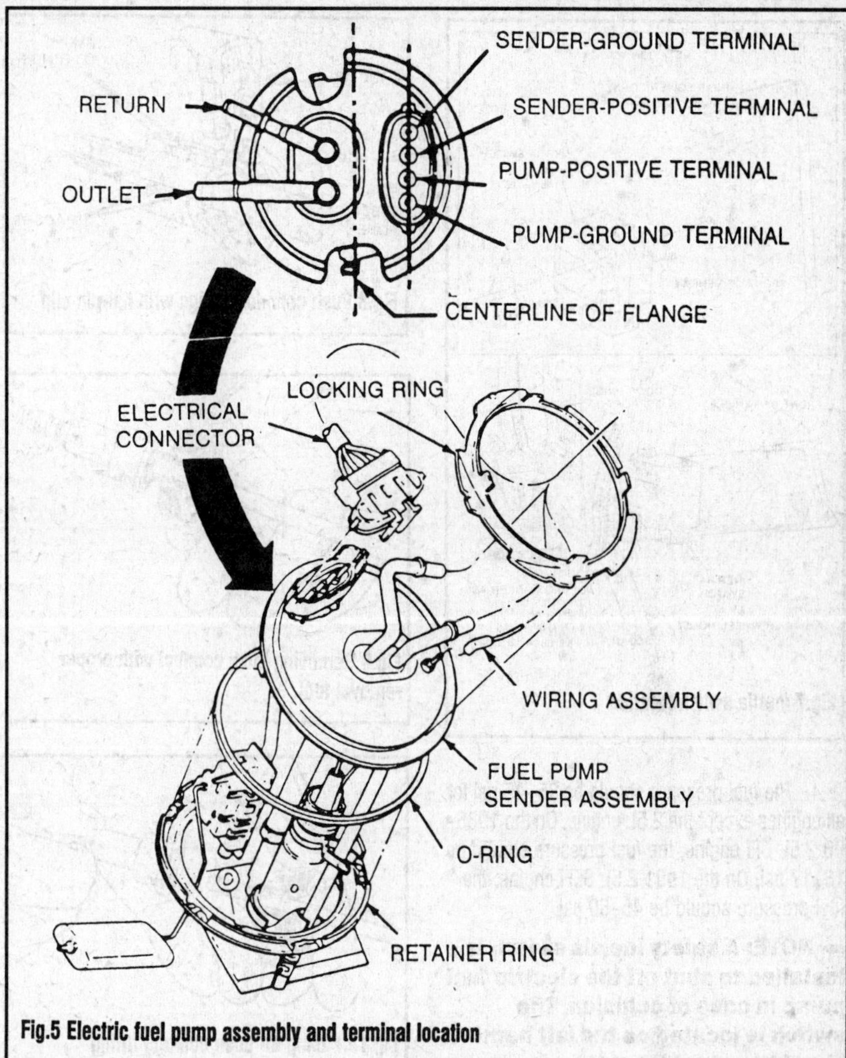

Fig.5 Electric fuel pump assembly and terminal location

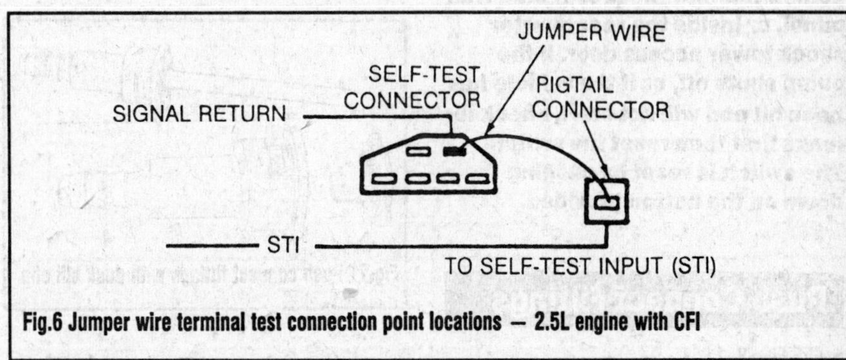

Fig.6 Jumper wire terminal test connection point locations — 2.5L engine with CFI

TESTING

➧ SEE FIG. 7

1. Ground the fuel pump lead of the self-test connector through a jumper wire at the FP lead.
2. Connect a suitable fuel pressure tester to the fuel pump outlet.
3. Turn the ignition key to the **RUN** position to operate the fuel pump.

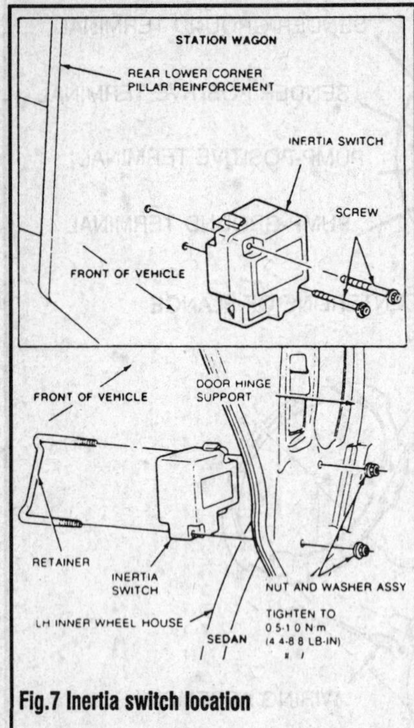

Fig.7 Inertia switch location

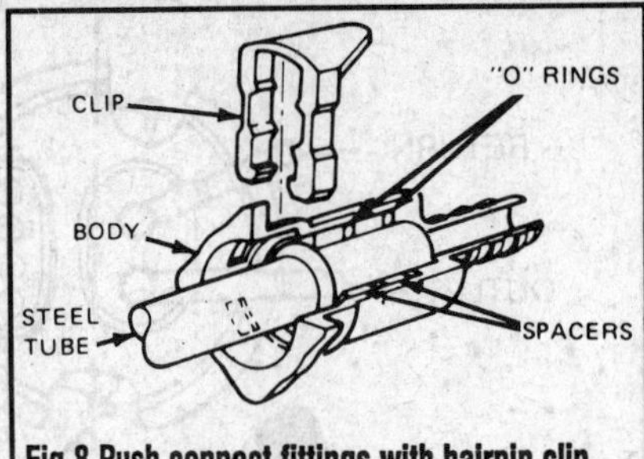

Fig.8 Push connect fittings with hairpin clip

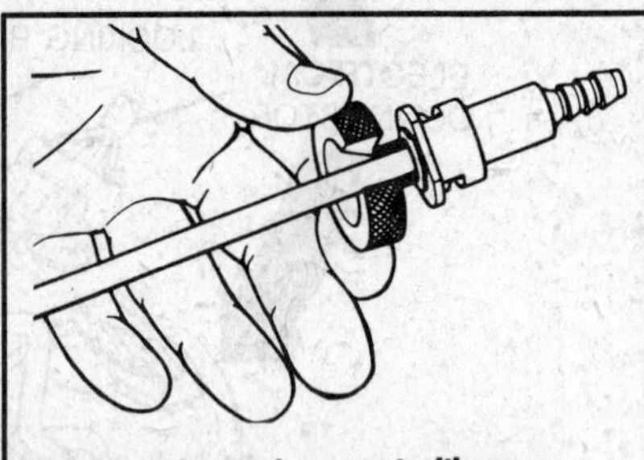
Fig.9 Removing push connect with proper removal tool

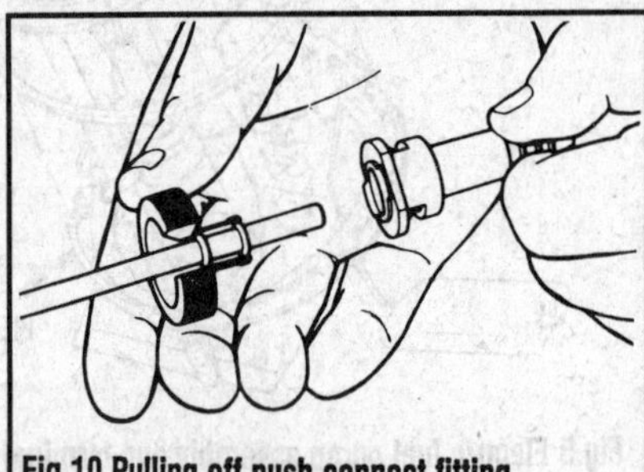
Fig.10 Pulling off push connect fitting

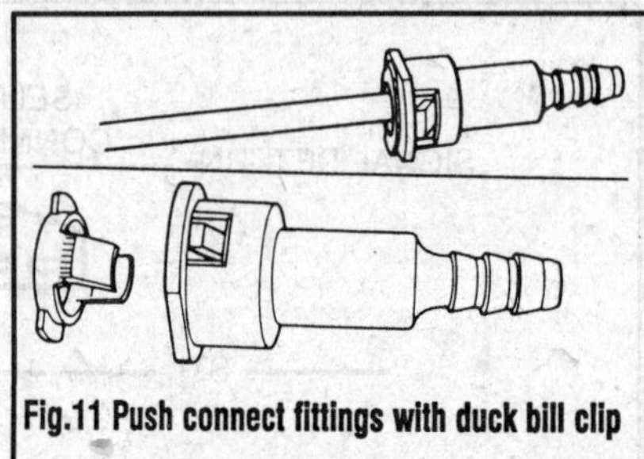
Fig.11 Push connect fittings with duck bill clip

4. The fuel pressure should be 35–45 psi for all engines except the 2.5L engine. On the 1986–90 2.5L CFI engine, the fuel pressure should be 13–17 psi. On the 1991 2.5L SEFI engine, the fuel pressure should be 45–60 psi.

➡ NOTE: A safety inertia switch is installed to shut off the electric fuel pump in case of collision. The switch is located on the left hand side (driver's side) of the car, behind the rear most seat side trim panel, or inside the rear quarter shock tower access door. If the pump shuts off, or if the vehicle has been hit and will not start, check for leaks first then reset the switch. The switch is reset by pushing down on the button provided.

Push Connect Fittings

➧ SEE FIG. 8–11

Push connect fittings are designed with two different retaining clips. The fittings used with 8mm diameter tubing use a hairpin clip. The fittings used with 6mm and 12.7mm diameter tubing use a "duck bill" clip. Each type of fitting requires different procedures for service.

Push connect fitting disassembly must be accomplished prior to fuel component removal (filter, pump, etc.) except for the fuel tank where removal is necessary for access to the push connects.

REMOVAL & INSTALLATION

$^{5}/_{16}$ in. Fittings (Hairpin Clip)

1. Inspect the internal portion of the fitting for dirt accumulation. If more than a light coating of dust is present, clean the fitting before disassembly.

2. Remove the hairpin type clip from the fitting. This is done (using hands only) by spreading the two clip legs about 3mm each to disengage the body and pushing the legs into the fitting. Complete removal is accomplished by lightly pulling from the triangular end of the clip and working it clear of the tube and fitting.

➡ Do not use any tools.

3. Grasp the fitting and hose assembly and pull in an axial direction to remove the fitting from the steel tube. Adhesion between sealing surfaces may occur. A slight twist of the fitting may be required to break this adhesion and permit effortless removal.

4. When the fitting is removed from the tube end, inspect clip to ensure it has not been damaged. If damaged, replace the clip. If undamaged, immediately reinstall the clip, insert the clip into any two adjacent openings with the triangular portion pointing away from the fitting opening. Install the clip to fully engage the body (legs of hairpin clip locked on outside of body). Piloting with an index finger is necessary.

5. Before installing the fitting on the tube, wipe the tube end with a clean cloth. Inspect the inside of the fitting to ensure it is free of dirt and/or obstructions.

6. To reinstall the fitting onto the tube, lubricate the sealing O-rings with clean engine oil, align the fitting and tube axially and push the fitting onto the tube end. When the fitting is engaged, a definite click will be heard. Pull on the fitting to ensure it is fully engaged.

$^{1}/_{2}$ in. and $^{1}/_{4}$ in. Fittings (Duck Bill Clip)

The fitting consists of a body, spacers, O-rings and a duck bill retaining clip. The clip maintains the fitting to the steel tube juncture. When disassembly is required for service, one of the two following methods are to be followed:

$^{1}/_{4}$ in. FITTINGS

To disengage the tube from the fitting, align the slot on the push connect disassembly Tool T82L-9500-AH or equivalent with either tab on the clip (90° from slots on side of fitting) and insert the tool. This disengages the duck bill from the tube. Holding the tool and the tube with one hand, pull fitting away from the tube.

➡ Only moderate effort is required if the tube has been properly disengaged. Use hands only. After disassembly, inspect and clean the tube sealing surface. Also inspect the inside of the fitting for damage to the retaining clip. If the retaining clip appears to be damaged, replace it. Some fuel tubes have a secondary bead which aligns with

the outer surface of the clip. These beads can make tool insertion difficult. If there is extreme difficulty, use the disassembly method following.

1/2 in. FITTING AND ALTERNATE METHOD FOR 1/4 in. FITTING

This method of disassembly disengages the retaining clip from the fitting body.

Use a pair of narrow pliers, (6 in. [153mm] locking pliers are ideal). The pliers must have a jaw width of 5mm or less.

Align the jaws of the pliers with the openings in the side of the fitting case and compress the portion of the retaining clip that engages the fitting case. This disengages the retaining clip from the case (often one side of the clip will disengage before the other. It is necessary to disengage the clip from both openings). Pull the fitting off the tube.

➡ **Only moderate effort is required if the retaining clip has been properly disengaged. Use hands only.**

The retaining clip will remain on the tube. Disengage the clip from the tube bead and remove. Replace the retaining clip if it appears to be damaged.

➡ **Slight ovality of the ring of the clip will usually occur. If there are no visible cracks and the ring will pinch back to its circular configuration, it is not damaged. If there is any doubt, replace the clip.**

Install the clip into the body by inserting one of the retaining clip serrated edges on the duck bill portion into one of the window openings. Push on the other side until the clip snaps into place. Lubricate the O-rings with clean engine oil and slide the fuel line back into the clip.

Fuel Charging Assembly

REMOVAL & INSTALLATION

CFI Injection

1986–90

1. Disconnect the negative battery cable. Remove the air cleaner.
2. Release pressure from the fuel system at the diagnostic (pressure relief) valve on the fuel charging assembly by carefully depressing the pin and discharging fuel into the throttle body.
3. Disconnect the throttle cable and transmission throttle valve lever.
4. Disconnect fuel, vacuum and electrical connections.

➡ **Either the multi or single ten pin connectors may be used on the system. To disconnect electrical ten pin connectors, push in or squeeze on the right side lower locking tab while pulling up on the connection. Multi connectors disconnect by pulling apart. The ISC (Idle Speed Control) connector tab must be moved out while pulling apart.**

5. Remove fuel charging assembly retaining nuts, then, remove fuel charging assembly.
6. Remove mounting gasket from intake manifold. Always use a new gasket for installation.

To install:

1. Clean gasket mounting surfaces of spacer and fuel charging assembly.
2. Place spacer between two new gaskets and place spacer and gaskets on the intake manifold. Position the charging assembly on the spacer and gasket.
3. Secure fuel charging assembly with attaching nuts.

➡ **To prevent leakage, distortion or damage to the fuel charging assembly body flange, snug the nuts; then, alternately tighten each nut in a criss-cross pattern. Tighten to 10 ft. lbs.**

4. Connect the fuel line, electrical connectors, throttle cable and all emission lines.
5. Start the engine, check for leaks. Adjust engine idle speed if necessary. Refer to the Engine/Emission Control Decal for idle speed specifications.

1991

1. Disconnect the negative battery cable. Properly relieve fuel system pressure. Disconnect the air bypass connector from the EEC-IV harness. Disconnect the spring lock coupling. Remove the engine air cleaner outlet tube.
2. Disconnect and remove the accelerator and speed control cables from the accelerator mounting bracket and the throttle lever.
3. Disconnect the top manifold vacuum fitting by disconnecting the rear vacuum line to dash panel vacuum tee, the vacuum line at the intake manifold, the MAP sensor vacuum line and the fuel pressure regulator vacuum line.
4. Disconnect the PCV system hoses. Disconnect the EGR vacuum line at the EGR valve.
5. Disconnect the EGR tube from the upper intake manifold by supporting the connector while loosening the compression nut.
6. Disconnect the upper support manifold bracket by removing only the top bolt. Leave the bottom bolts attached.
7. Disconnect the electrical connectors at the main engine harness.
8. Remove the fuel supply and return lines. Remove the eight manifold retaining bolts.
9. Disconnect the lower support manifold bracket by removing only the top bolt. Leave the bottom bolts attached.
10. Remove the manifold along with the wiring harness and gasket.

To install:

11. Clean and inspect the mounting surfaces. Install a new gasket.
12. Install the manifold assembly and finger tighten the retaining bolts at this time.
13. Install the fuel return line. Tighten the manifold retaining bolts to 15–22 ft. lbs.
14. Connect the upper and lower manifold support brackets. Torque the retaining bolts to 15–22 ft. lbs.
15. Install the EGR tube. Install the PCV system. Connect the rear manifold connections.
16. Connect the accelerator and speed control linkages. Connect the electrical wiring harness.
17. Connect the fuel supply line. Connect the fuel return line. Install the spring lock coupling.
18. Use the EEC-IV self test connector to check that the EEC-IV sensor is functioning properly.
19. Start the engine and check for fuel leaks. Adjust the idle speed, as required.

EFI Injection

EXCEPT 3.8L ENGINE

➧ SEE FIG. 12

1. With the ignition OFF, disconnect the negative (–) battery cable.
2. Remove the fuel cap and release the pressure at the pressure relief valve on the fuel rail assembly using a Fuel Pressure Gauge part No. T80L-9974-B.
3. Disconnect electrical connectors at air bypass valve, throttle position sensor, EGR sensor and air charge temperature sensor (ACT).
4. Disconnect the fuel supply and return lines using a Fuel Line Disconnect Tool part No. D87L-9280-A or equivalent.
5. Disconnect the wiring connectors from the fuel injectors.
6. Remove snow/ice shield to expose throttle linkage. Disconnect throttle cable from ball stud.
7. Remove the engine air cleaner outlet tube between air cleaner and air throttle body by loosening the two clamps.

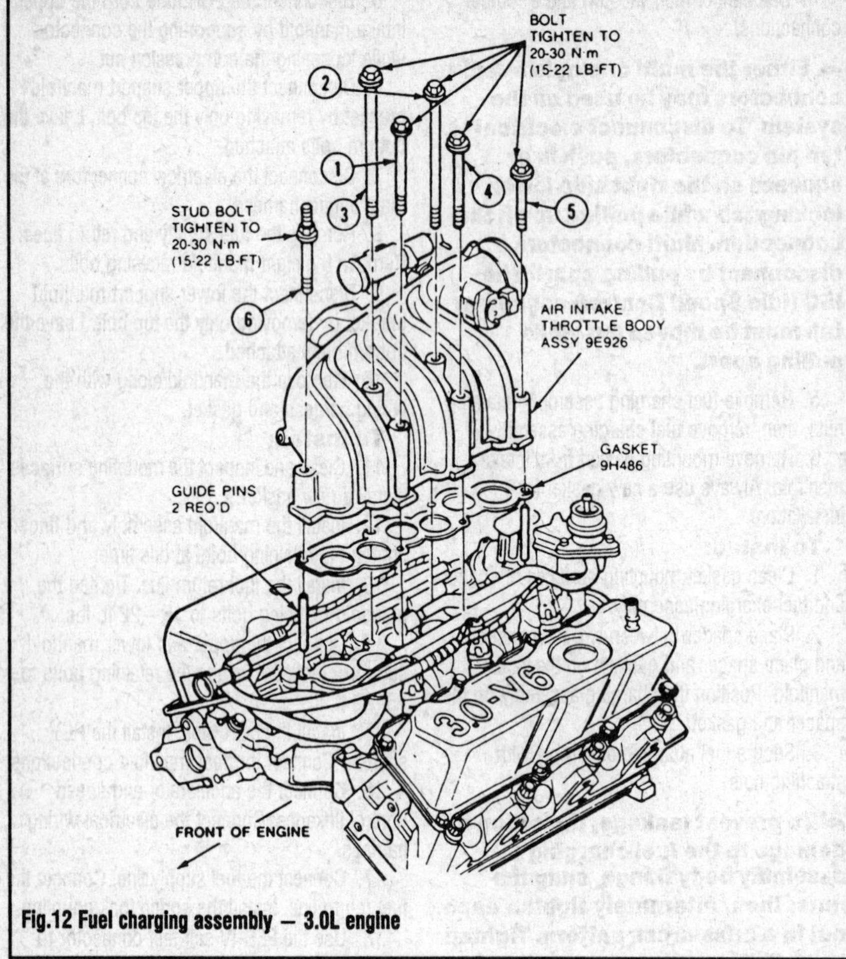

Fig.12 Fuel charging assembly — 3.0L engine

8. Disconnect and remove the accelerator and speed control cables, if so equipped, from the throttle lever.

9. Remove the transaxle TV (throttle valve) linkage from the throttle lever (automatic only).

10. Loosen bolt which retains A/C line at the upper rear of the upper manifold and disengage retainer.

11. Remove the six retaining bolts and lift air intake throttle body assembly from the lower intake manifold assembly.

12. Clean and inspect mounting faces of the lower and upper intake manifold.

To install:

1. Position new gasket on lower intake mounting face. The use of alignment studs may be helpful.

2. Install upper intake manifold and throttle body assembly to lower manifold making sure gasket remains in place (if alignment studs aren't used). Align EGR tube in valve.

3. Install six upper intake manifold retaining bolts. Tighten to 15-22 ft. lbs. in sequence as shown in the fuel charging assembly diagram in this section.

4. Engage A/C line retainer cup and tighten bolt to specification.

5. Tighten EGR tube and flare fitting. Tighten lower retainer nut at the exhaust manifold.

6. Install canister purge line to fitting.

7. Connect PCV vacuum hose to bottom of upper manifold and PCV closure hose to throttle body.

8. Connect vacuum lines to vacuum tree, EGR valve, and fuel pressure regulator.

9. Connect throttle cable to throttle body and install snow/ice shield.

10. Connect electrical connector at air bypass valve, TPS sensor, EGR sensor, and ACT sensor.

11. Install the fuel cap, start the engine and idle, and check for vacuum, fuel, or coolant leaks.

12. The transaxle TV (throttle valve) linkage has to be readjusted after the fuel charging assembly has been serviced:

a. With the ignition key OFF and shift selector in PARK.

b. Reset the automatic transaxle TV linkage by holding the ratchet in the released position and pushing the cable fitting toward the accelerator control bracket.

c. At the throttle body, reset the TV cable by rotating the throttle linkage to wide-open throttle position by hand and release.

➡ **If lower intake manifold was removed, fill and bleed the cooling system.**

3.8L ENGINE

➧ SEE FIG. 13

1. Disconnect the battery negative (–) cable.
2. Drain cooling system
3. Remove the fuel cap at the tank.
4. Release the fuel pressure by attaching a Fuel Pressure Gauge part No. T80L-9974-B or equivalent to the pressure relief valve on the fuel rail assembly.
5. Disconnect the electrical connectors at the air bypass valve, throttle position sensor, and EGR position sensor.
6. Disconnect the throttle linkage at the throttle ball and transaxle linkage from the throttle body.
7. Position the throttle and speed control linkage out of the way.
8. Disconnect the upper intake manifold vacuum fittings at the vacuum tree.
9. Remove the six upper intake manifold retaining bolts.
10. Remove the upper intake and throttle body assembly from the lower intake.

To install:

1. Clean and inspect the mounting surfaces of the upper and lower intake manifolds. Be careful not to damage the mounting surfaces.

2. Install the new gasket and upper intake into position using the alignment studs. If alignment studs are not used, make sure the gasket stays in place.

3. Install the six manifold retaining bolts and torque to 20-28 ft. lbs.

4. Install the canister purge lines, PCV hose, and vacuum lines to the vacuum tree.

5. Install the throttle and speed control, if so equipped, to the upper intake manifold. Connect the TV cable to the throttle body.

6. The transaxle TV (throttle valve) linkage has to be readjusted after the fuel charging assembly has been serviced

a. With the ignition key OFF and shift selector in PARK

b. Reset the automatic transaxle TV linkage by holding the ratchet in the released position and pushing the cable fitting toward the accelerator control bracket.

c. At the throttle body, reset the TV cable by rotating the throttle linkage to wide-open throttle position by hand and release.

7. Refill the engine with coolant. Start the

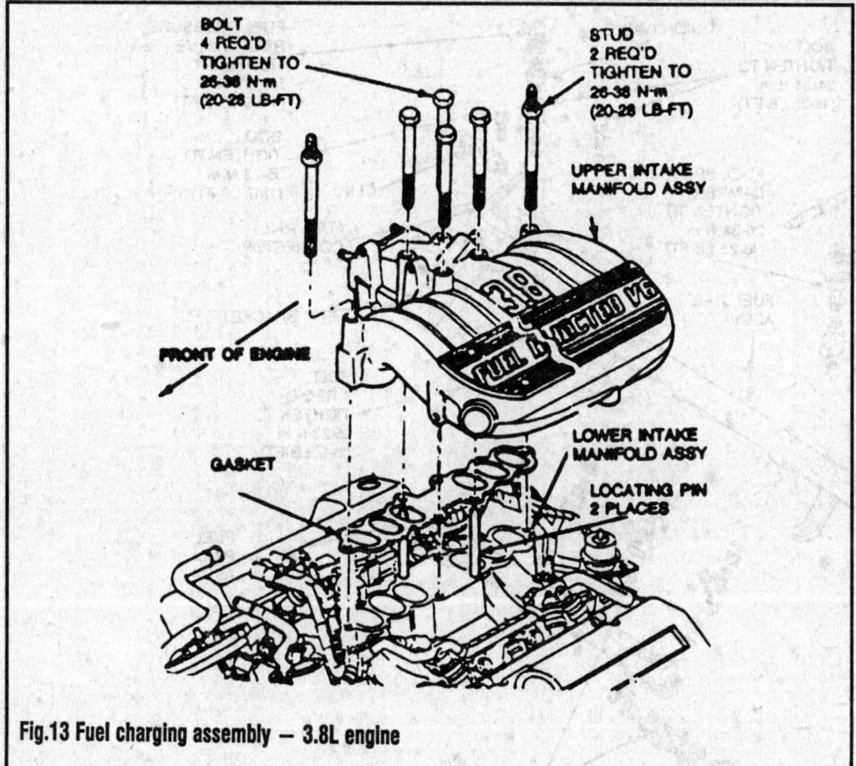

Fig.13 Fuel charging assembly — 3.8L engine

engine and check for fuel, vacuum, and coolant leaks.

SEFI Injection

➧ SEE FIG. 14–15

➡ The fuel charging assembly consists of the air throttle body, and the upper and lower intake manifolds. Prior to service or removal of the fuel charging assembly, the following procedures must be taken.

a. Open the hood and install protective fender covers.

b. Disconnect the negative (–) battery cable.

c. Remove the fuel cap at the tank.

d. Release the fuel pressure from the fuel system. Depressurize the fuel system by connecting a Fuel Pressure Gauge part No. T80L-9974-B or equivalent to the pressure relief valve on the fuel rail assembly.

1. Remove the intake air boot from the throttle body and airflow sensor and disconnect the throttle cable.
2. Disconnect the vacuum and electrical connectors from the throttle body.
3. Disconnect the coolant bypass hoses at the throttle body.

⁂ CAUTION

The cooling system may be under pressure. Release the pressure at the radiator cap before removing the hoses. Also, allow the engine to cool down before performing any service.

4. Disconnect the EGR pipe from the EGR valve, if so equipped.
5. Remove the eight bolts at the intake manifold support brackets and remove the brackets.
6. Remove the bolt retaining the coolant hose bracket and disconnect the PCV hoses, if so equipped.
7. Remove the intake and throttle body assembly.

To install:

1. Clean and inspect the manifold mounting surfaces.
2. Position new intake manifold gaskets and

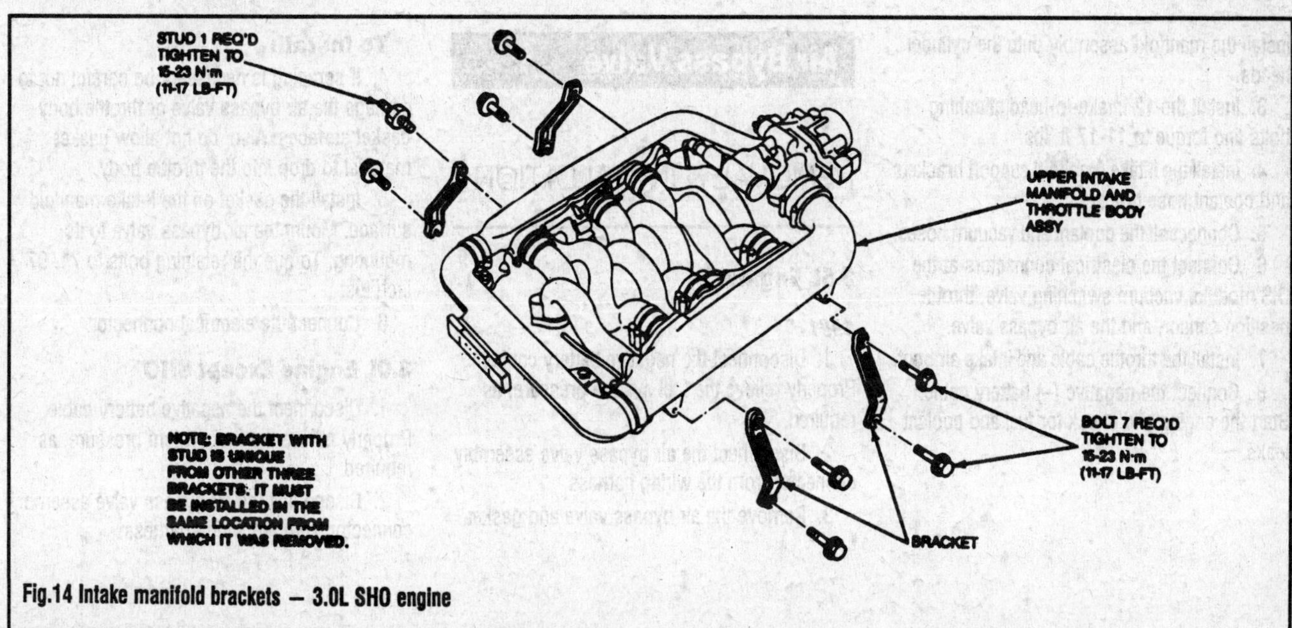

Fig.14 Intake manifold brackets — 3.0L SHO engine

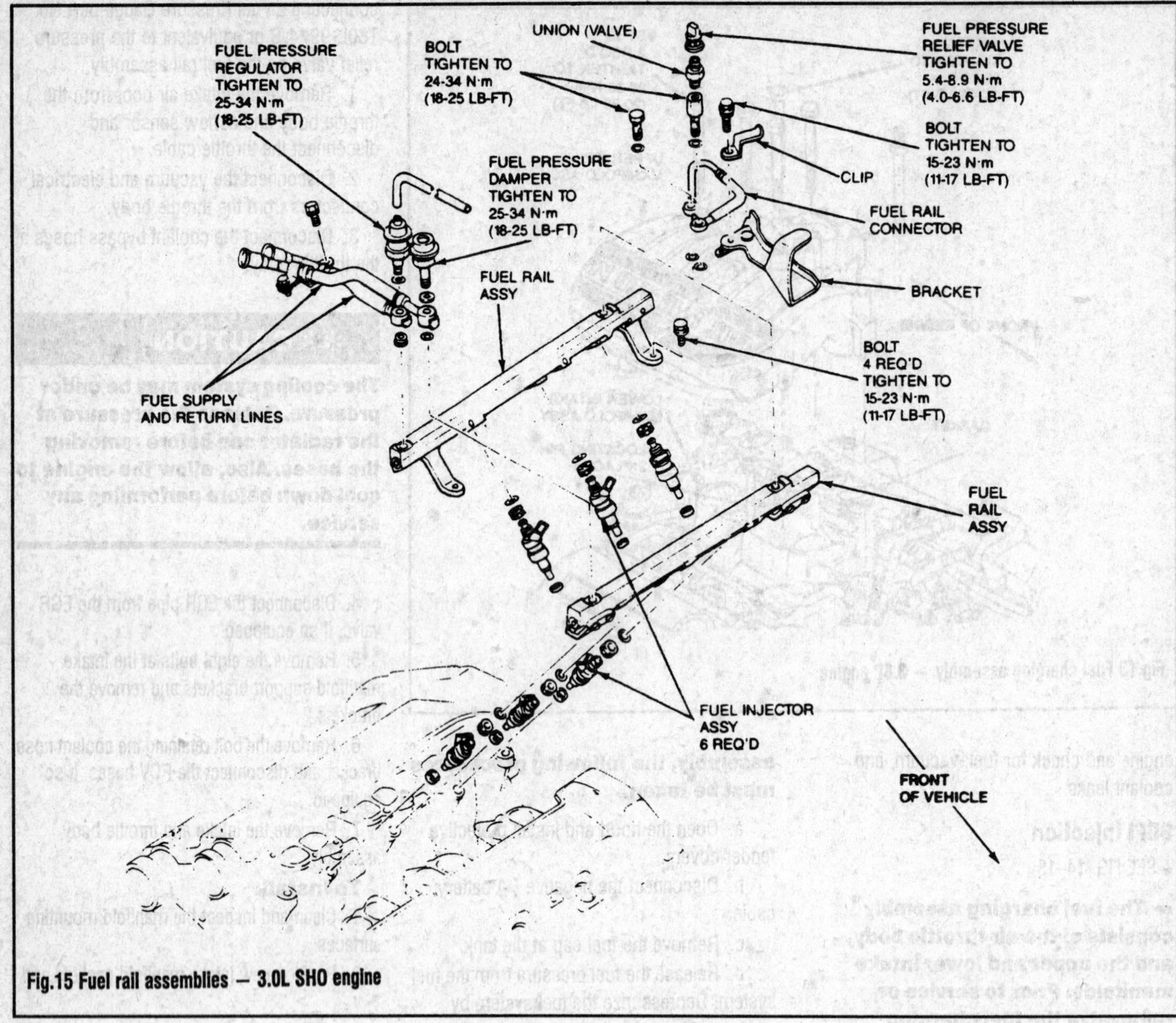

Fig.15 Fuel rail assemblies — 3.0L SHO engine

install the manifold assembly onto the cylinder heads.

3. Install the 12 intake-to-head attaching bolts and torque to 11-17 ft. lbs.

4. Install the intake manifold support brackets and coolant hose bracket.

5. Connect all the coolant and vacuum hoses.

6. Connect the electrical connectors at the DIS module, vacuum switching valve, throttle position sensor, and the air bypass valve.

7. Install the throttle cable and intake air boot.

8. Connect the negative (−) battery cable. Start the engine and check for fuel and coolant leaks.

Air Bypass Valve

REMOVAL & INSTALLATION

2.5L Engine

1991

1. Disconnect the negative battery cable. Properly relieve the fuel system pressure, as required.

2. Disconnect the air bypass valve assembly connector from the wiring harness.

3. Remove the air bypass valve and gasket.

To Install:

4. If scraping is necessary be careful not to damage the air bypass valve or throttle body gasket surfaces. Also, do not allow gasket material to drop into the throttle body.

5. Install the gasket on the intake manifold surface. Mount the air bypass valve to its mounting. Torque the retaining bolts to 71–97 inch lbs.

6. Connect the electrical connector.

3.0L Engine Except SHO

1. Disconnect the negative battery cable. Properly relieve the fuel system pressure, as required.

2. Disconnect the air bypass valve assembly connector from the wiring harness.

3. Remove the air bypass valve retaining bolts. Remove the valve and gasket.

To install:

4. If scraping is necessary be careful not to damage the air bypass valve or throttle body gasket surfaces. Also, do not allow gasket material to drop into the throttle body.

5. Install the gasket on the intake manifold surface. Mount the air bypass valve to its mounting. Torque the retaining bolts to 84 inch lbs.

6. Connect the electrical connector.

3.0L SHO Engine

1. Disconnect the negative battery cable. Properly relieve the fuel system pressure, as required.

2. Disconnect the air bypass valve assembly connector from the wiring harness.

3. Remove the air bypass valve retaining bolts. Remove the top retaining bolt first and swing the valve upward to provide working clearance in order to remove the lower retaining bolt. Remove the valve and gasket.

To install:

4. If scraping is necessary be careful not to damage the air bypass valve or throttle body gasket surfaces. Also, do not allow gasket material to drop into the throttle body.

5. Install the gasket on the intake manifold surface. Mount the air bypass valve to its mounting. Torque the retaining bolts to 63–97 inch lbs.

6. Connect the electrical connector.

3.8L Engine

1. Disconnect the negative battery cable. Properly relieve the fuel system pressure, as required.

2. Disconnect the air bypass valve assembly connector from the wiring harness.

3. Remove the air bypass valve retaining bolts. Remove the valve and gasket.

To install:

4. If scraping is necessary be careful not to damage the air bypass valve or throttle body gasket surfaces. Also, do not allow gasket material to drop into the throttle body.

5. Install the gasket on the intake manifold surface. Mount the air bypass valve to its mounting. Torque the retaining bolts to 87 inch lbs.

6. Connect the electrical connector.

Air Intake/Throttle Body Assembly

REMOVAL & INSTALLATION

➧ SEE FIG. 22–24

2.5L Engine

1986–90

Refer to the above figures for disassembly and assembly information. To remove the TPS sensor and the ISC motor proceed as follows.

1. Remove the throttle position sensor retaining screws. Remove the throttle position sensor from the throttle body.

2. Remove the idle speed control motor retaining screws. Remove the idle speed control motor from the throttle body assembly.

3. Installation is the reverse of the removal procedure.

4. Position the TPS sensor with the connector facing up toward the main body. Rotate the assembly in the counterclockwise position only and align the screw holes. Failure to properly install this sensor will result in excessive idle speeds.

1991

1. Disconnect the negative battery cable. Remove the air cleaner assembly.

2. Remove the throttle valve body retaining bolts. Be sure that the TPS electrical connector has been disconnected from the wiring harness.

3. Disconnect the air cleaner outlet tube. Disconnect the air bypass hose.

4. Disconnect the throttle control cable. If equipped with speed control, disconnect the speed control cable. If equipped with automatic transaxle, disconnect the TV control rod.

5. Disconnect and remove the throttle bracket. Separate the throttle body from the upper intake manifold.

6. Remove and discard the gasket between the throttle body and upper intake manifold. If scraping is necessary be careful not to damage the air bypass valve or throttle body gasket surfaces. Also, do not allow gasket material to drop into the throttle body.

To install:

7. Install the upper throttle body gasket on the two studs of the upper intake manifold.

8. Retain the throttle body to the intake manifold with the attaching bolts. Torque the bolts to 12–15 ft. lbs.

9. Install the throttle body bracket. Connect the TPS electrical connector. Connect the engine air cleaner outlet tube.

10. Connect the throttle control cable, speed control cable and transaxle TV control rod, as required.

3.0L Engine Except SHO

1. Disconnect the negative battery cable. Loosen the air cleaner duct hose retaining clamps and remove the hose.

2. Remove the idle speed control solenoid shield. Disconnect the throttle and TV cable from the throttle body linkage.

3. Mark the location and remove the vacuum hoses from the vacuum tee.

4. Loosen the EGR tube nuts, if equipped at the EGR valve and exhaust manifold fitting. Remove or rotate the tube to the side.

5. Remove the PCV valve hose from under the throttle body. Disconnect the electrical connectors for the ACT, ISC and TPS sensors.

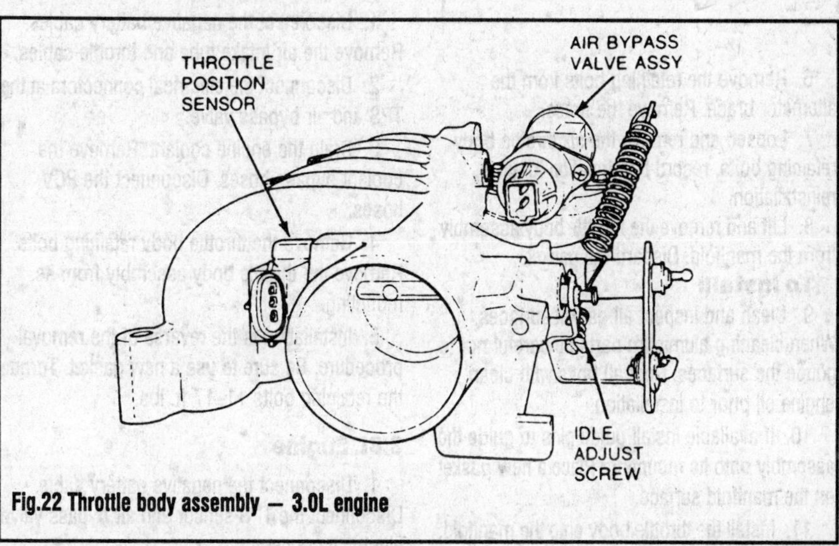

Fig.22 Throttle body assembly — 3.0L engine

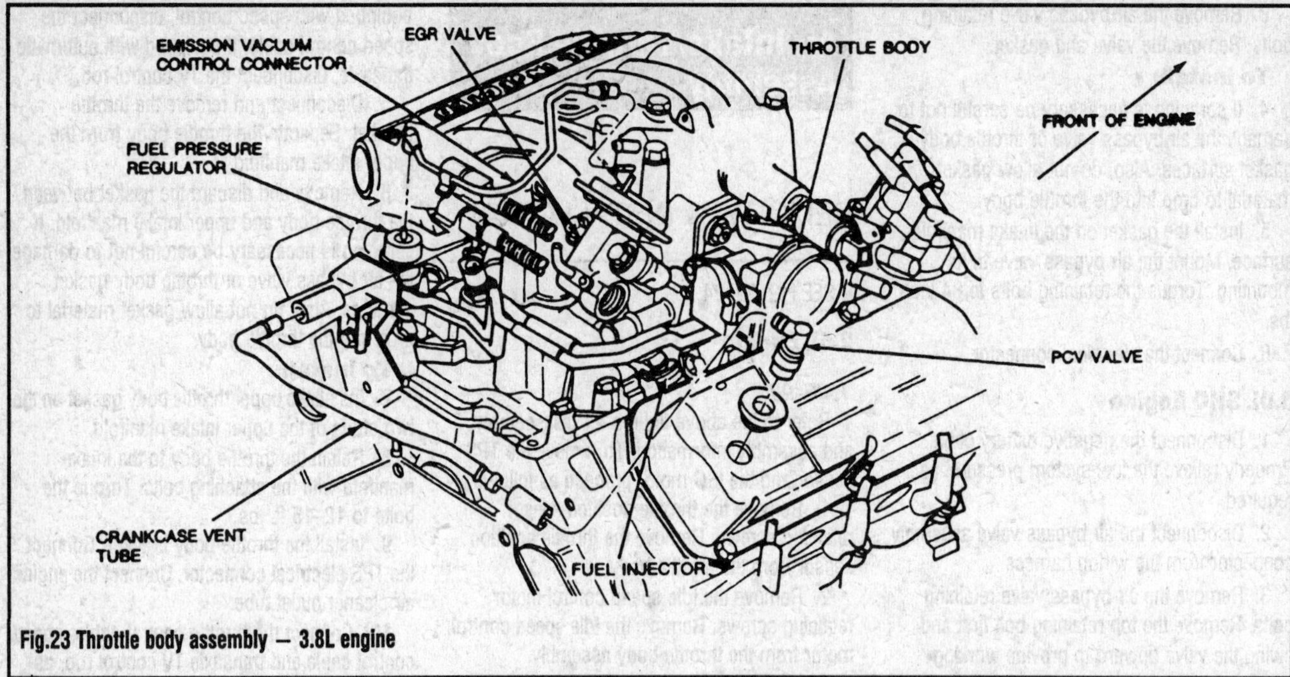

Fig.23 Throttle body assembly — 3.8L engine

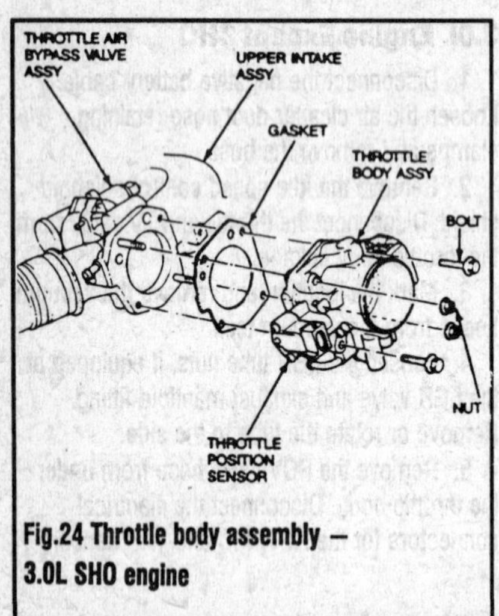

Fig.24 Throttle body assembly — 3.0L SHO engine

6. Remove the retaining bolts from the alternator brace. Remove the brace.

7. Loosen and remove the six throttle body retaining bolts, record bolt location to air in reinstallation.

8. Lift and remove the throttle body assembly from the manifold. Discard the gasket.

To install:

9. Clean and inspect all gasket surfaces. When cleaning aluminum parts be careful not to gouge the surfaces. Coat all bolts with clean engine oil prior to installation.

10. If available install guide pins to guide the assembly onto its mounting. Place a new gasket on the manifold surface.

11. Install the throttle body onto the manifold. Torque the retaining bolts to 19 ft. lbs.

12. Install the alternator brace. Connect the PCV hose. Install the EGR tube to the EGR valve.

13. Connect the vacuum hoses. Connect the required electrical connectors to there proper locations.

14. Connect the throttle cable, speed control cable and TV cable, as required. Connect the air cleaner assembly to its mounting.

15. Connect the negative battery cable. Start the engine and check for vacuum leaks.

16. Check and adjust the engine idle speed as necessary. Adjust the transaxle TV cable. Install the idle speed control solenoid shield. Torque the retaining bolts to 13 inch lb.

3.0L SHO Engine

1. Disconnect the negative battery cables. Remove the air intake tube and throttle cables.

2. Disconnect the electrical connectors at the TPS and air bypass valve.

3. Drain the engine coolant. Remove the coolant bypass hoses. Disconnect the PCV hoses.

4. Remove the throttle body retaining bolts. Remove the throttle body assembly from its mounting.

5. Installation is the reverse of the removal procedure. Be sure to use a new gasket. Torque the retaining bolts 11–17 ft. lbs.

3.8L Engine

1. Disconnect the negative battery cable. Disconnect the TPS sensor and air bypass valve electrical connectors.

2. Remove the four throttle body retaining bolts. Remove the throttle body assembly.

3. Remove and discard the gasket. If scraping is necessary be careful not to damage the air bypass valve or throttle body gasket surfaces. Also, do not allow gasket material to drop into the throttle body.

4. Installation is the reverse of the removal procedure. Be sure to use a new gasket. Torque the retaining bolts to 19 ft. lbs.

Pressure Relief Valve

REMOVAL & INSTALLATION

CFI Engine

1. If the fuel charging assembly is mounted to the engine, remove the fuel tank gas cap.

2. Properly release the fuel system pressure, using the proper tools.

3. Using the proper wrench, remove the pressure relief valve from the fuel injection manifold.

4. Installation is the reverse of the removal procedure. Tighten the valve 4–6 inch lbs.

EFI Engine

1. If the fuel charging assembly is mounted to the engine, remove the fuel tank gas cap.

2. Properly release the fuel system pressure, using the proper tools.

3. Using the proper wrench, remove the pressure relief valve from the fuel injection manifold.

4. Installation is the reverse of the removal procedure. Tighten the valve 5.5 inch lbs.

Fuel Injector

REMOVAL & INSTALLATION

2.5L Engine

1986–90

➧ SEE FIG. 16

1. Disconnect the negative battery cable.
2. Relieve the fuel system pressure.
3. Remove the fuel injector retaining screw and retainer.
4. Remove the injector and lower O-ring. Discard the O-ring.

To install:

5. Lubricate a new lower O-ring and the injector seat area with clean engine oil; do not use transmission fluid. Install the lower O-ring on the injector.

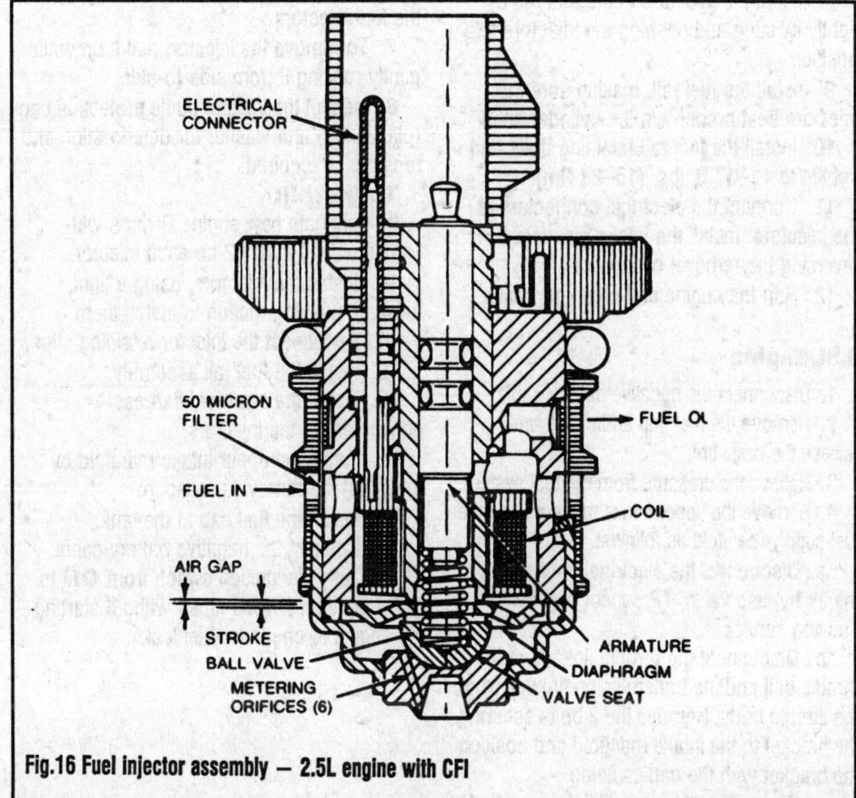

Fig.16 Fuel injector assembly — 2.5L engine with CFI

6. Lubricate the upper O-ring and install the injector by centering and applying a steady downward pressure with a slight rotational force.
7. Install the injector retainer and retaining screw. Tighten the screw to 18–22 inch lbs. (2.0–2.5 Nm).

1991

1. Disconnect the negative battery cable.
2. Relieve the fuel pressure in the system.
3. Disconnect the engine air cleaner outlet tube from the air intake throttle body and the TP sensor from the wiring harness.
4. Disconnect the vacuum lines from the upper manifold and disconnect the EGR tube at the manifold connection.
5. Disconnect the air bypass valve connector, remove the accelerator and, if equipped, speed control cables and remove the manifold upper support bracket top bolt.
6. Remove the fuel supply manifold shield and the 4 upper manifold retaining bolts and 1 retaining shoulder stud.
7. Remove the upper manifold assembly and gasket and set it aside.
8. Disconnect the fuel supply and return lines and the vacuum line at the pressure regulator.
9. Disconnect the fuel injector wiring harness and disconnect the connectors from the injectors.
10. Remove the fuel supply manifold retaining bolts and remove the fuel supply manifold.
11. Grasping the injector body, pull up while gently rocking the injector from side-to-side.
12. Inspect the injector O-rings, the injector plastic hat and washer for signs of deterioration. Replace as necessary. If the hat is missing, look for it in the intake manifold.

To install:

13. Before installation, lubricate new O-rings with light engine oil and install on the injectors prior to installation.
14. Install the injectors.
15. Install the fuel supply manifold. Tighten the fuel supply manifold retaining bolts and the upper intake manifold retaining bolts to 15–22 ft. lbs. (20–30 Nm).
16. Install the fuel injector wiring harness. Connect the fuel supply and return lines and the vacuum line at the pressure regulator.
17. Connect the fuel supply manifold shield and the 4 upper manifold retaining bolts and 1 retaining shoulder stud.
18. Connect the air bypass valve connector, accelerator and, if equipped, speed control cables.
19. Connect the vacuum lines from the upper manifold and connect the EGR tube at the manifold connection.
20. Connect the engine air cleaner outlet tube to the air intake throttle body and the TP sensor to the wiring harness.
21. Connect the battery cable. Start the engine and check for leaks, correct as required.

3.0L Engine Except SHO

➧ SEE FIG. 18

1. Disconnect the negative battery cable.
2. Relieve the fuel system pressure. Remove the air intake throttle body.
3. On the 1992 engine, the distributor must be raised to allow the crossover tube to clear the distributor housing and lower intake manifold assembly.
4. Disconnect the fuel supply and fuel return lines.
5. Disconnect the wiring harness from the injectors.
6. Disconnect the vacuum line from the fuel pressure regulator valve.
7. Remove the 4 fuel injector manifold retaining bolts.
8. Carefully disengage the fuel rail assembly from the fuel injectors by lifting and gently rocking the rail.
9. Remove the injectors by lifting while gently rocking from side to side.

To install:

10. Lubricate new O-rings with engine oil and install 2 on each injector.

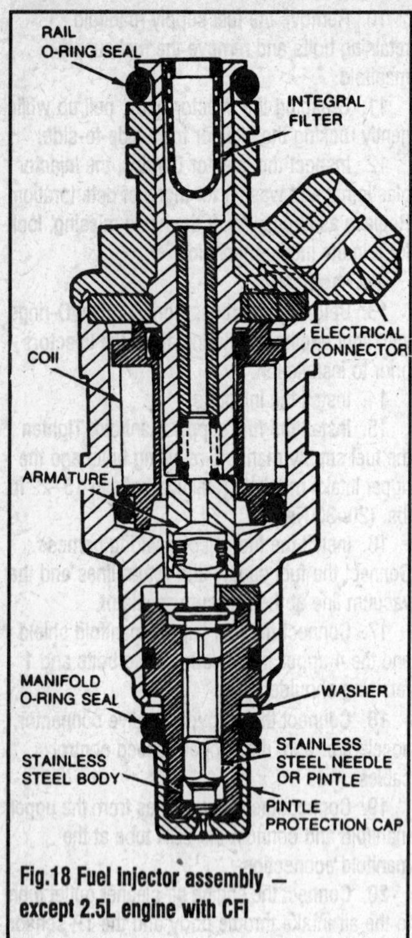

Fig.18 Fuel injector assembly — except 2.5L engine with CFI

11. Make sure the injector cups are clean and undamaged.

12. Install the injectors in the fuel rail using a light twisting-pushing motion.

13. Carefully install the rail assembly and injectors into the lower intake manifold, 1 side at a time. Make sure the O-rings are seated by pushing down on the fuel rail.

14. While holding the fuel rail assembly in place, install the 2 retaining bolts and tighten to 7 ft. lbs. (10 Nm).

15. Connect the fuel supply and fuel return lines.

16. Before connecting the fuel injector harness, turn the ignition switch to the **ON** position. This will pressurize the fuel system.

17. Using a clean paper towel. check for leaks where the injector connects to the fuel rail.

18. Install the air intake throttle body and connect the vacuum line to the fuel pressure regulator valve.

19. Connect the fuel injector harness, start the engine and let it idle for 2 minutes.

20. Using a clean paper towel, check for leaks where the injector is installed into the intake manifold.

3.0L SHO Engine

➧ SEE FIG. 25

1. Disconnect the negative battery cable.
2. Relieve the fuel system pressure.
3. Remove the intake manifold as follows:
   a. Drain the cooling system.
   b. Remove the intake air tube from the throttle body and MAF sensor. Disconnect the throttle cables.
   c. Disconnect the electrical connectors at the TP sensor, air bypass valve, vacuum switching valve and DIS module.
   d. Disconnect the coolant bypass hoses and vacuum lines.
   e. Disconnect the EGR pipe from the EGR valve.
   f. Remove the 8 bolts at the intake manifold support brackets and remove the brackets.
   g. Remove the bolt retaining the coolant hose bracket and disconnect the PCV hoses.
   h. Remove the 12 manifold retaining bolts and remove the intake manifold and throttle body assembly.
4. Disconnect the electrical connectors at the fuel injectors.
5. Remove the fuel rail retaining bolts.
6. Raise and slightly rotate the fuel rail assembly and remove the injectors.

To install:

7. Lubricate new O-rings with engine oil and install them on the fuel injectors.
8. Install the injectors in the fuel rail by lightly twisting and pushing the injectors into position.
9. Install the fuel rail, making sure the injectors seat properly in the cylinder head.
10. Install the fuel rail retaining bolts and tighten to 11–17 ft. lbs. (15–23 Nm).
11. Connect the electrical connectors at the injectors. Install the intake manifold by reversing the removal procedure.
12. Run the engine and check for leaks.

3.8L Engine

1. Disconnect the negative battery cable.
2. Remove the fuel cap at the tank and release the pressure.
3. Relieve the pressure from the fuel system.
4. Remove the upper intake manifold and the fuel supply manifold as follows:
   a. Disconnect the electrical connectors at the air bypass valve, TP sensor and EGR position sensor.
   b. Disconnect the throttle linkage at the throttle ball and the transmission linkage from the throttle body. Remove the 2 bolts securing the bracket to the intake manifold and position the bracket with the cables aside.
   c. Disconnect the upper intake manifold vacuum fitting connections by disconnecting all vacuum lines to the vacuum tree, EGR valve and pressure regulator.
   d. Disconnect the PCV hose and remove the nut retaining the EGR transducer to the upper intake manifold.
   e. Loosen the EGR tube at the exhaust manifold and disconnect at the EGR valve.
   f. Remove 2 bolts retaining the EGR valve to the upper intake manifold and remove the EGR valve and EGR transducer as an assembly.
   g. Remove the 2 canister purge lines from the fittings on the throttle body and remove the 6 upper intake manifold retaining bolts.
   h. Remove 2 retaining bolts on the front and rear edges of the upper intake manifold where the manifold support brackets are located.
   i. Remove the nut retaining the alternator bracket to the upper intake manifold and the 2 bolts retaining the alternator bracket to the water pump and alternator.
   j. Remove the upper intake manifold and throttle body as an assembly.
   k. Disconnect the fuel supply and return lines from the fuel rail assembly.
   l. Remove the fuel rail assembly retaining bolts, carefully disengage the fuel rail from the fuel injectors and remove the fuel rail.
5. Remove the injector retaining clips.
6. Remove the electrical connectors from the fuel injectors.
7. To remove the injector, pull it up while gently rocking it from side-to-side.
8. Inspect the injector pintle protection cap (plastic hat) and washer for deterioration and replace, as required.

To install:

9. Lubricate new engine O-rings with engine oil and install 2 on each injector.
10. Install the injectors, using a light, twisting, pushing motion to install them.
11. Reconnect the injector retaining clips.
12. Install the fuel rail assembly.
13. Install the electrical harness connectors to the injectors.
14. Install the upper intake manifold by reversing the removal procedure.
15. Install the fuel cap at the tank.
16. Connect the negative battery cable.
17. Turn the ignition switch from **ON** to **OFF** position several times without starting the engine to check for fuel leaks.

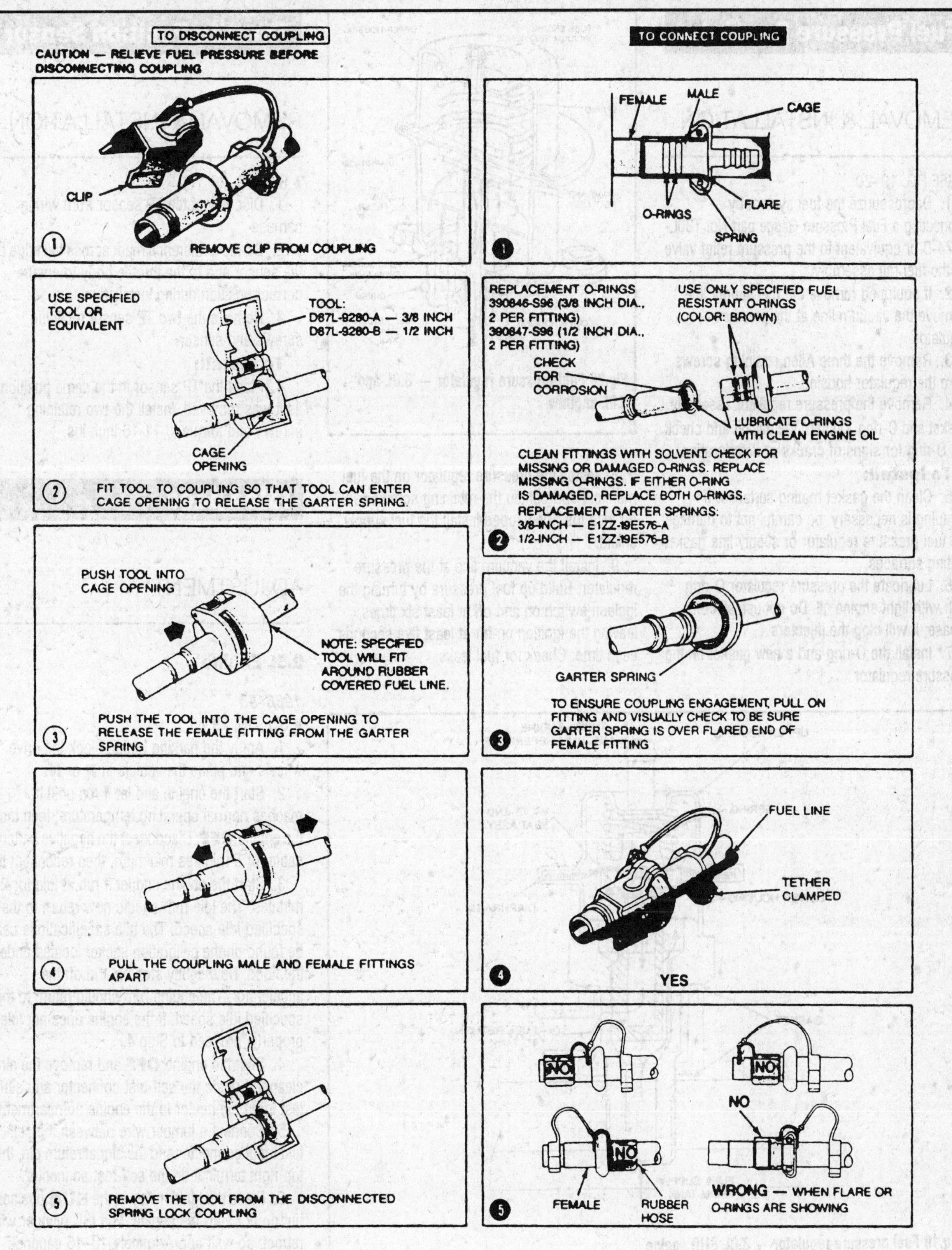

TO DISCONNECT COUPLING
CAUTION — RELIEVE FUEL PRESSURE BEFORE DISCONNECTING COUPLING
CLIP
1 REMOVE CLIP FROM COUPLING
USE SPECIFIED TOOL OR EQUIVALENT
TOOL:
D87L-9280-A — 3/8 INCH
D87L-9280-B — 1/2 INCH
CAGE OPENING
2 FIT TOOL TO COUPLING SO THAT TOOL CAN ENTER CAGE OPENING TO RELEASE THE GARTER SPRING.
PUSH TOOL INTO CAGE OPENING
NOTE: SPECIFIED TOOL WILL FIT AROUND RUBBER COVERED FUEL LINE.
3 PUSH THE TOOL INTO THE CAGE OPENING TO RELEASE THE FEMALE FITTING FROM THE GARTER SPRING
4 PULL THE COUPLING MALE AND FEMALE FITTINGS APART
5 REMOVE THE TOOL FROM THE DISCONNECTED SPRING LOCK COUPLING
TO CONNECT COUPLING
FEMALE
MALE
CAGE
FLARE
O-RINGS
SPRING
1
REPLACEMENT O-RINGS
390846-S96 (3/8 INCH DIA., 2 PER FITTING)
390847-S96 (1/2 INCH DIA., 2 PER FITTING)
USE ONLY SPECIFIED FUEL RESISTANT O-RINGS (COLOR: BROWN)
CHECK FOR CORROSION
LUBRICATE O-RINGS WITH CLEAN ENGINE OIL
CLEAN FITTINGS WITH SOLVENT. CHECK FOR MISSING OR DAMAGED O-RINGS. REPLACE MISSING O-RINGS. IF EITHER O-RING IS DAMAGED, REPLACE BOTH O-RINGS.
REPLACEMENT GARTER SPRINGS:
3/8-INCH — E1ZZ-19E576-A
2 1/2-INCH — E1ZZ-19E576-B
GARTER SPRING
3 TO ENSURE COUPLING ENGAGEMENT, PULL ON FITTING AND VISUALLY CHECK TO BE SURE GARTER SPRING IS OVER FLARED END OF FEMALE FITTING
FUEL LINE
TETHER CLAMPED
4 YES
NO
NO
NO
NO
FEMALE
RUBBER HOSE
5 WRONG — WHEN FLARE OR O-RINGS ARE SHOWING

Fig.25 Fuel line disconnect points — 3.0L SHO engine

Fuel Pressure Regulator

REMOVAL & INSTALLATION

➧ SEE FIG. 19–20

1. Depressurize the fuel system by connecting a Fuel Pressure Gauge part No. T80L-9974-B or equivalent to the pressure relief valve on the fuel rail assembly.
2. If equipped remove the fuel supply line. Remove the vacuum line at the pressure regulator.
3. Remove the three Allen retaining screws from the regulator housing.
4. Remove the pressure regulator assembly, gasket and O-ring. Discard the gasket and check the O-ring for signs of cracks or deterioration.

To install:

5. Clean the gasket mating surfaces. If scraping is necessary, be careful not to damage the fuel pressure regulator or supply line gasket mating surfaces.
6. Lubricate the pressure regulator O-ring with with light engine oil. Do not use silicone grease; it will clog the injectors.
7. Install the O-ring and a new gasket on the pressure regulator.

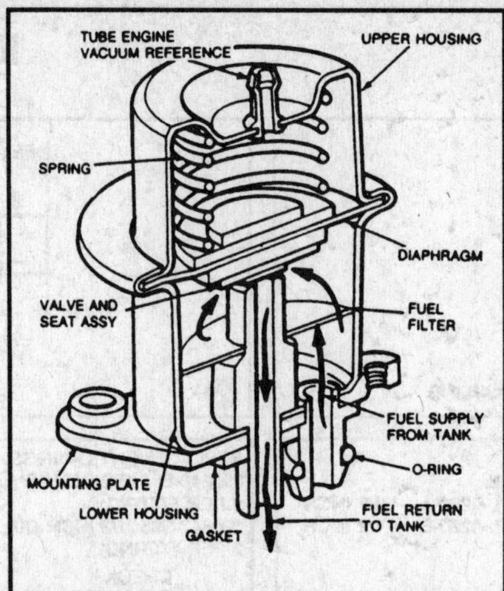

Fig.20 Fuel pressure regulator — 3.0L and 3.8L engines

8. Install the pressure regulator on the fuel manifold and tighten the retaining screws to 27-40 inch lbs. If equipped install the fuel supply shield.
9. Install the vacuum line at the pressure regulator. Build up fuel pressure by turning the ignition switch on and off at least six times, leaving the ignition on for at least five seconds each time. Check for fuel leaks.

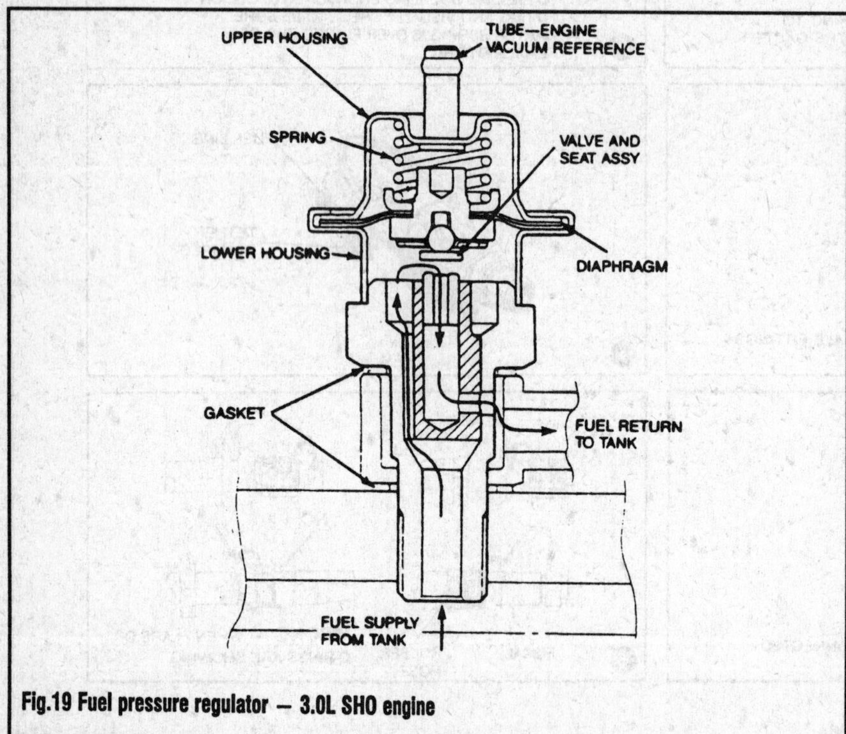

Fig.19 Fuel pressure regulator — 3.0L SHO engine

Throttle Position Sensor

REMOVAL & INSTALLATION

➧ SEE FIG. 26

1. Disconnect the TP sensor from wiring harness
2. Scribe a reference mark across the edge of the sensor and to the throttle body to ensure correct position during installation.
3. Remove the two TP sensor retaining screws and sensor.

To install:

4. Place the TP sensor in the same position as it was removed. Install the two retaining screws and torque to 11-16 inch lbs.

Idle Speed

ADJUSTMENT

2.5L Engine

1986–90

➧ SEE FIG. 29

1. Apply the parking brake, block the drive wheels and place the vehicle in **P** or **N**.
2. Start the engine and let it run until it reaches normal operating temperature, then turn the engine **OFF**. Disconnect the negative battery cable for 5 minutes minimum, then reconnect it.
3. Start the engine and let it run at idle for 2 minutes. The idle rpm should now return to the specified idle speed. The idle specifications can be found on the calibration sticker located under the hood. Now lightly step on and off the accelerator. The engine rpm should return to the specified idle speed. If the engine does not idle properly, proceed to Step 4.
4. Shut the engine **OFF** and remove the air cleaner. Locate the self-test connector and self-test input connector in the engine compartment.
5. Connect a jumper wire between the self-test input connector and the signal return pin, the top right terminal on the self-test connector.
6. Place the ignition key in the **RUN** position but do not start the engine. The ISC plunger will retract, so wait approximately 10–15 seconds until the ISC plunger is fully retracted.
7. Turn the ignition key to the **OFF** position. Remove the jumper wire and unplug the ISC motor from the wire harness.

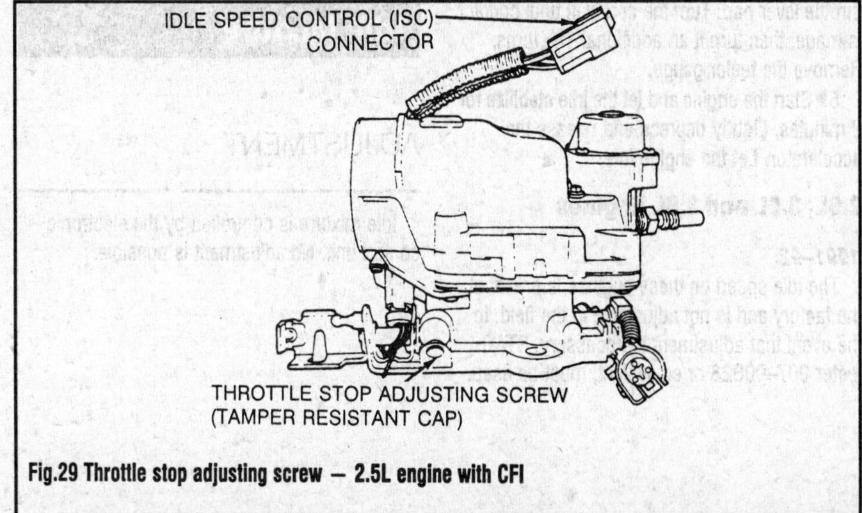

Fig.29 Throttle stop adjusting screw — 2.5L engine with CFI

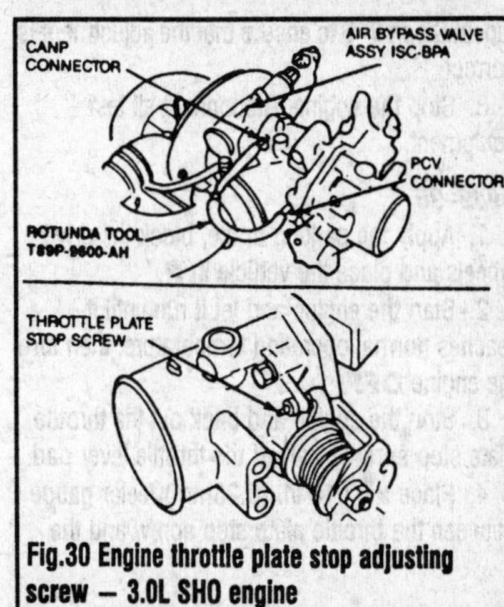

Fig.30 Engine throttle plate stop adjusting screw — 3.0L SHO engine

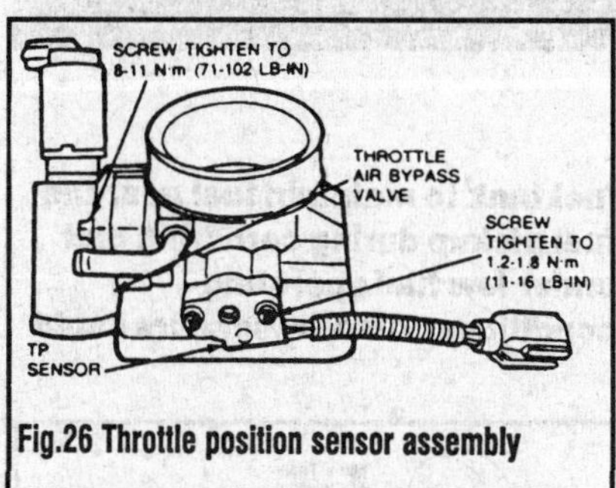

Fig.26 Throttle position sensor assembly

8. Start the engine and check the idle speed. On automatic transaxle vehicles, it should be 50 rpm less than that specified on the calibration sticker. On manual transaxle vehicles, it should be 100 rpm less than that specified on the calibration sticker. If not proceed to Step 9.

9. Remove the CFI assembly from the vehicle.

10. Use a small punch or equivalent, to punch through and remove the aluminum plug which covers the throttle stop adjusting screw.

11. Remove and replace the throttle stop screw. Reinstall the CFI assembly onto the vehicle.

12. Start the engine and allow to the idle to stabilize. Set the idle rpm to the specification listed in Step 8.

13. Turn **OFF** the engine. Reconnect the ISC motor wire harness, remove all test equipment and reinstall the air cleaner assembly.

3.0L Engine Except SHO

1986–90

1. Apply the parking brake, turn the air conditioning control selector **OFF** and block the wheels.

2. Connect a tachometer and an inductive timing light to the engine. Start the engine and allow it to reach normal operating temperatures.

3. Unplug the spout line at the distributor, then check and/or adjust the ignition timing to the specification listed on the underhood emission calibration decal.

4. Stop the engine and remove the PCV hose at the PCV valve. Install a 0.200 in. (5mm) diameter orifice, tool T86P–9600–A or equivalent.

5. Disconnect the idle speed control/air bypass solenoid.

6. Start the engine and run at 2000 rpm for 30 seconds.

7. If equipped with an automatic transaxle, place the selector in **D**. If equipped with a manual transaxle, place the selector in neutral.

8. Check and/or adjust, the idle speed to 760 ± 20 rpm by turning the throttle plate stop screw.

9. After adjusting the idle speed, stop the engine and disconnect the battery for 5 minutes minimum.

10. Stop the engine and remove all test equipment. Reconnect the spout line and remove the orifice from the PCV hose. Reconnect the idle speed control/air bypass solenoid.

11. Make sure the throttle is not stuck in the bore and the linkage is not preventing the throttle from closing.

3.0L SHO Engine

1989–90

➧ SEE FIG. 30

1. Apply the parking brake, turn the air conditioning control selector **OFF** and block the wheels.

2. Connect a tachometer and an inductive timing light to the engine. Start the engine and allow it to reach normal operating temperatures.

3. Unplug the spout line at the distributor, then check and/or adjust the ignition timing to the specification listed on the underhood emission calibration decal.

4. Stop the engine and disconnect and plug the PCV hose at the intake manifold. Remove the CANP hose from the intake manifold and connect tool T89P–9600–AH or equivalent, between the PCV and CANP ports.

5. Disconnect the idle speed control/air bypass solenoid.

6. Start the engine and let it idle. Place the transaxle selector lever in **N**.

7. Check and/or adjust the idle speed to 800 ± 30 rpm by turning the throttle plate stop screw.

8. Shut the engine off and repeat Steps 6–8.

9. Stop the engine and remove all test equipment. Remove tool T89P–9600–AH or equivalent, and unplug the PCV hose. Connect the PCV and CANP hoses. Reconnect the idle speed control/air bypass solenoid.

10. Make sure the throttle is not stuck in the bore and the linkage is not preventing the throttle from closing.

3.8L Engine

1988

1. Apply the parking brake, block the drive wheels and place the vehicle in **P** or **N**.

2. Start the engine and let it run until it reaches normal operating temperature, then turn the engine **OFF**. Connect a suitable tachometer.

3. Start the engine and run the engine at 2500 rpm for 30 seconds.

4. Allow the engine idle to stabilize.

5. Place the automatic transaxle in **D** or the manual transaxle in neutral.

6. Adjust the engine idle rpm to the specification shown on the vehicle emission control label by adjusting the throttle stop screw.

7. After the idle speed is within specification,

repeat Steps 3–6 to ensure that the adjustment is correct.

8. Stop the engine. Disconnect all test equipment.

1989–90

1. Apply the parking brake, block the drive wheels and place the vehicle in **P**.

2. Start the engine and let it run until it reaches normal operating temperature, then turn the engine **OFF**.

3. Stop the engine and back out the throttle plate stop screw clear off the throttle lever pad.

4. Place a 0.010 in. (0.25mm) feeler gauge between the throttle plate stop screw and the throttle lever pad. Turn the screw in until contact is made, then turn it an additional 1½ turns. Remove the feeler gauge.

5. Start the engine and let the idle stabilize for 2 minutes. Lightly depress and release the accelerator. Let the engine idle.

2.5L, 3.0L and 3.8L Engines

1991–92

The idle speed on these engines is preset at the factory and is not adjustable in the field. In the event that adjustment is necessary, STAR tester 007–00028 or equivalent, must be used.

Idle Mixture

ADJUSTMENT

Idle mixture is controlled by the electronic control unit. No adjustment is possible.

FUEL TANK

REMOVAL & INSTALLATION

➧ SEE FIG. 27–28

1. Disconnect the negative battery cable.

2. Relieve the fuel system pressure.

3. Siphon or pump the fuel from the fuel tank, through the filler neck, into a suitable container.

➡ **There are reservoirs inside the fuel tank to maintain fuel near the fuel pickup during cornering and under low fuel operating conditions. These reservoirs could**

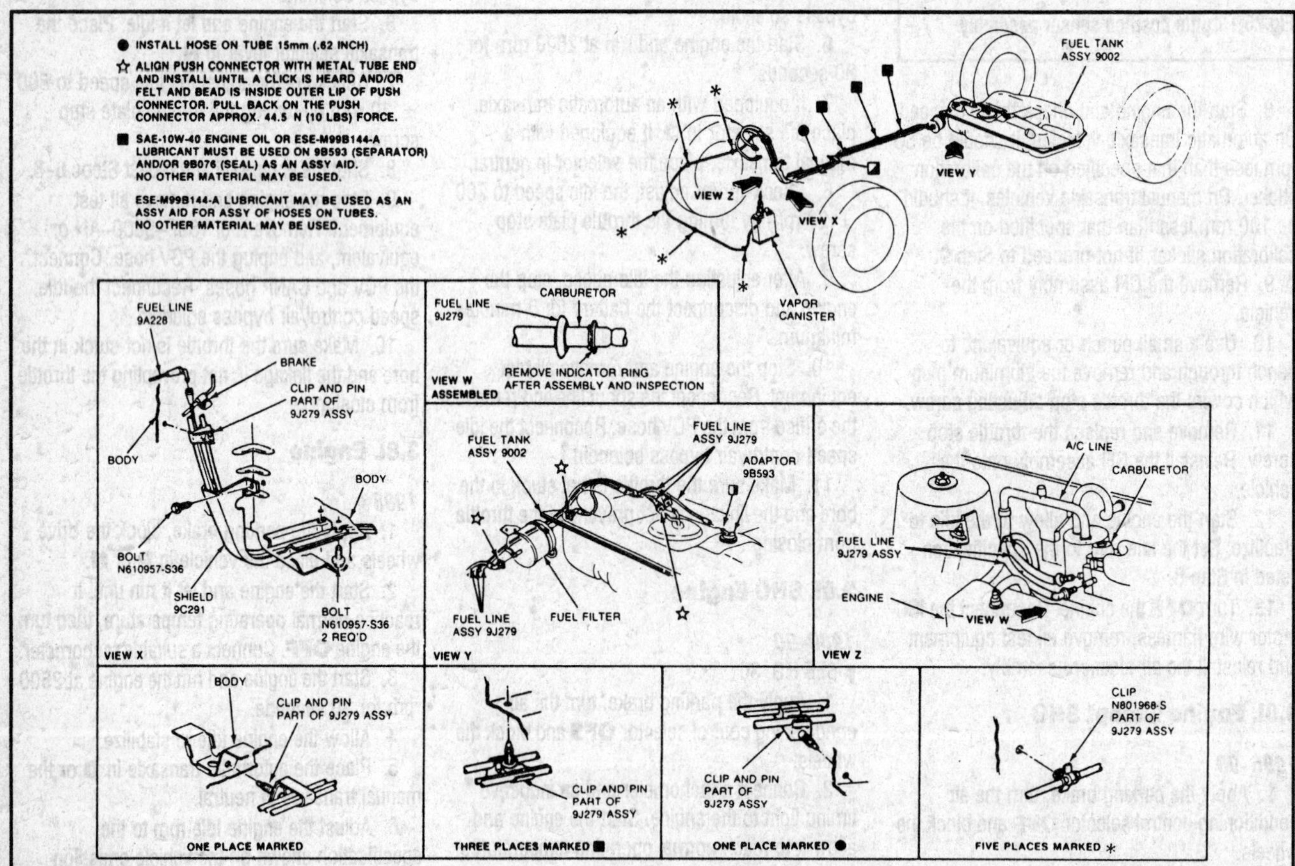

Fig.27 Fuel tank, lines and related components

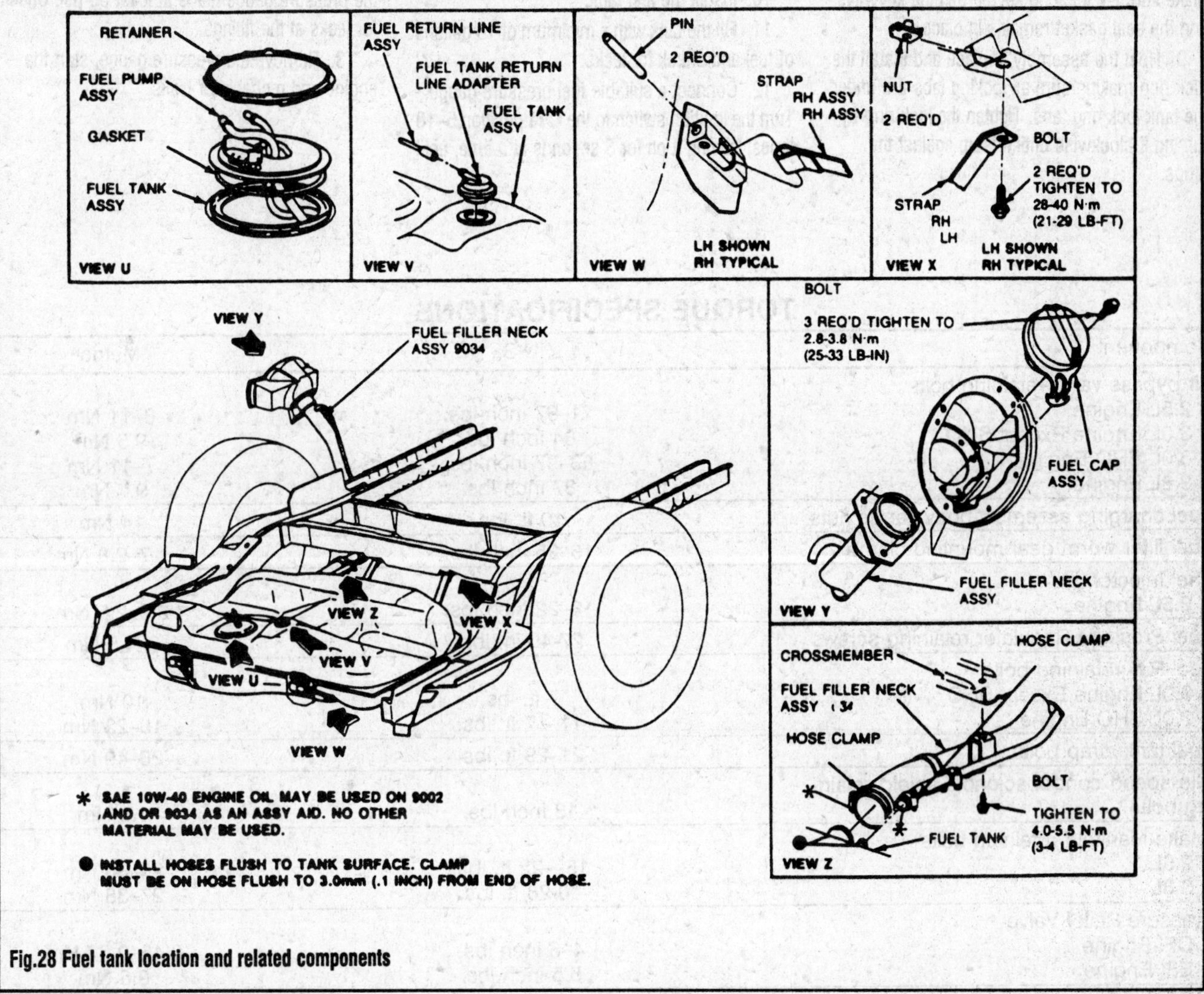

Fig.28 Fuel tank location and related components

block siphon tubes or hoses from reaching the bottom of the tank. A few repeated attempts using different hose orientations can overcome this situation.

4. Raise and safely support the vehicle.
5. Loosen the filler pipe and vent hose clamps at the tank and remove the hoses from the tank.
6. Place a safety support under the fuel tank and remove the bolts from the rear of the fuel tank straps. The straps are hinged at the front and will swing aside.
7. Partially remove the tank. Remove the hairpin clips from the push connect fitting and disconnect the fuel lines. Disconnect the electrical connector from the fuel sender/pump assembly.
8. Remove the fuel tank.

To install:

9. Raise the fuel tank into position. Connect the fuel lines and the electrical connector.
10. Bring the fuel tank straps around the tank and start the retaining bolt. Align the tank as far forward in the vehicle as possible while securing the retaining bolts.

➡ **If equipped with a heat shield, make sure it is installed with the straps and positioned correctly on the tank.**

11. Check the hoses and wiring mounted on the tank top, to make sure they are correctly routed and will not be pinched between the tank and the body.
12. Tighten the fuel tank strap retaining bolts to 21–29 ft. lbs. (28–40 Nm).
13. Install the fuel filler hoses and tighten the clamps. Refill the fuel tank.
14. Check all connections for leaks. Connect the negative battery cable.

SENDING UNIT REPLACEMENT

1. Disconnect the negative battery cable.
2. Relieve the fuel system pressure.
3. Remove the fuel tank from the vehicle and place it on a work bench. Remove any dirt around the fuel pump attaching flange.
4. Turn the fuel pump locking ring counterclockwise and remove the lock ring.
5. Remove the fuel pump from the fuel tank and discard the flange gasket.

To install:

6. Clean the fuel pump mounting flange and fuel tank mounting surface and seal ring groove.
7. Put a light coating of grease on the new seal gasket to hold it in place during assembly and install it in the fuel ring groove.
8. Install the fuel pump and sender assembly.

Make sure the locating keys are in the keyways and the seal gasket remains in place.

9. Hold the assembly in place and install the lock ring making sure all locking tabs are under the tank lock ring tabs. Tighten the lock ring by turning it clockwise until it is up against the stops.

10. Install the fuel tank.

11. Fill the tank with a minimum of 10 gallons of fuel and check for leaks.

12. Connect a suitable fuel pressure gauge. Turn the ignition switch to the **ON** position 5–10 times, leaving it on for 3 seconds at a time, until the pressure gauge reads at least 30 psi. Check for leaks at the fittings.

13. Remove the pressure gauge, start the engine and recheck for leaks.

TORQUE SPECIFICATIONS

Component	U.S.	Metric
Air bypass valve retaining bolts		
2.5L Engine	71–97 inch lbs.	8–11 Nm
3.0L Engine Except SHO	84 inch lbs.	9.5 Nm
3.0L SHO Engine	63–97 inch lbs.	7–11 Nm
3.8L Engine	87 inch lbs.	9.7 Nm
Fuel charging assembly body flange nuts	10 ft. lbs.	14 Nm
Fuel filter worm gear mounting clamp	15–25 inch lbs.	1.7–2.8 Nm
Fuel Injector		
2.5L Engine	18–22 inch lbs.	2.0–2.5 Nm
Fuel Pressure Regulator retaining screws	27-40 in. lbs.	3–4.5 Nm
Fuel Rail retaining bolts		
3.0L Engine Except SHO	7 ft. lbs.	10 Nm
3.0L SHO Engine	11–17 ft. lbs.	15–23 Nm
Fuel tank strap bolts	21–29 ft. lbs.	28–40 Nm
Idle speed control solenoid shield retaining bolts	13 inch lbs.	1.5 Nm
Intake Manifold retaining bolts		
2.5L	15 – 22 ft. lbs.	20–30 Nm
3.8L	20-28 ft. lbs.	27–38 Nm
Pressure Relief Valve		
CFI Engine	4–6 inch lbs.	0.45–0.67 Nm
EFI Engine	5.5 inch lbs.	0.6 Nm
Throttle body to the intake manifold bolts		
2.5L	12–15 ft. lbs.	16–20 Nm
3.0L Except SHO	19 ft. lbs.	26 Nm
3.0L SHO	11–17 ft. lbs.	15–23 Nm
3.8L	19 ft. lbs.	26 Nm
TP sensor retaining screws	11-16 in. lbs.	1.2–1.8 Nm
Upper and lower manifold support brackets	15–22 ft. lbs.	20–30 Nm

6 CHASSIS ELECTRICAL

HEATER

Blower Motor

SEE FIG. 7

REMOVAL & INSTALLATION

1. Disconnect the negative battery cable.
2. Open the glove compartment door, release the door retainers and lower the door.
3. Remove the screw attaching the recirculation duct support bracket to the instrument panel cowl.
4. Remove the vacuum connection to the recirculation door vacuum motor. Remove the screws attaching the recirculation duct to the heater assembly.
5. Remove the recirculation duct from the heater assembly, lowering the duct from between the instrument panel and the heater case.
6. Disconnect the blower motor electrical lead. Remove the blower motor wheel clip and remove the blower motor wheel.
7. Remove the blower motor mounting plate screws and remove the blower motor from the evaporator case.
8. Complete the installation of the blower motor by reversing the removal procedure.

Blower Motor Resistor

REMOVAL & INSTALLATION

1. Disconnect the negative battery cable.
2. Open the glove compartment door and release the glove compartment retainers so that the glove compartment hangs down.
3. Disconnect the wire harness connector from the resistor assembly.
4. Remove the 2 resistor attaching screws and remove the resistor from the evaporator case.

To install:

5. Position the resistor assembly in the evaporator case opening and install 2 attaching screws. Do not apply sealer to the resistor assembly mounting surface.
6. Connect the wire harness connector to the resistor.
7. Connect the negative battery cable, check the operation of the blower motor and close the glove compartment door.

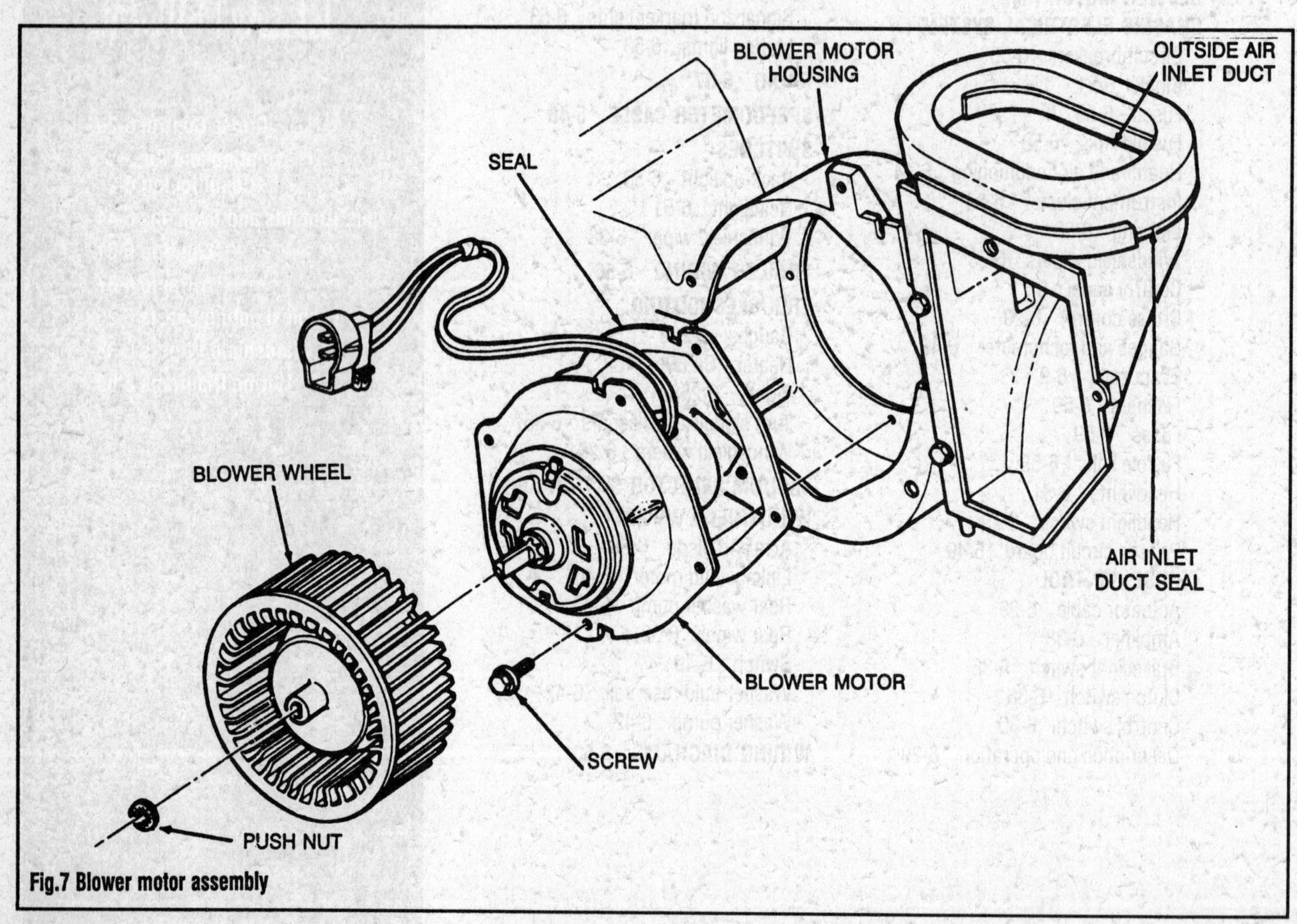

Fig.7 Blower motor assembly

Heater Core

REMOVAL & INSTALLATION

SEE FIG. 8–10

CAUTION

When draining the coolant, keep in mind that cats and dogs are attracted by the ethylene glycol antifreeze, and are quite likely to drink any that is left in an uncovered container or in puddles on the ground. This will prove fatal in sufficient quantity. Always drain the coolant into a sealable container. Coolant should be reused unless it is contaminated or several years old.

Without Air Conditioning

1. Disconnect the negative battery cable.
2. Remove the instrument panel on 1986–89 vehicles as follows:
   a. Remove the 4 screws retaining the steering column opening cover and remove the cover.
   b. Remove the sound insulator under the glove compartment by removing the 2 push nuts securing the insulator to the studs on the climate control case.
   c. Remove the steering column trim shrouds and disconnect all electrical connections from the steering column switches.
   d. Remove the 4 screws at the steering column bracket to remove the steering column.
   e. Remove the screws retaining the lower left and radio finish panels and remove the panels by snapping out.
   f. Remove the cluster opening finish panel retaining screws. On Taurus remove 1 jam nut behind the headlight switch and 1 screw behind the clock or clock cover. Remove the finish panel by rocking the upper edge toward the driver.
   g. Disconnect the speedometer cable by reaching up under the instrument panel and pressing on the flat surface of the plastic connector. The panel can be removed with the cluster installed.
   h. Release the glove compartment assembly by depressing the side of the glove compartment bin and swinging the door/bin down.
   i. Using the steering column, cluster and glove compartment openings and by reaching under the instrument panel, tag and disconnect all electrical connections, vacuum hoses, heater control cables and the radio antenna cable.
   j. Disconnect all underhood electrical connectors of the main wire loom. Disengage the rubber grommet from the dash panel and push the wire and connectors into the instrument panel area.
   k. Remove the right and left speaker opening covers by snapping out.
   l. Remove the 2 lower instrument panel-to-cowl side retaining screws from the right and left side. Remove the 1 instrument panel brace retaining screw from under the radio area. On Sable, remove the defroster grille by snapping out.
   m. Remove the 3 instrument panel upper retaining screws and remove the instrument panel.
3. Remove the instrument panel on 1990–92 vehicles as follows:
   a. Position the front wheels in the straight-ahead position.
   b. Remove the ignition lock cylinder and, if equipped, remove the tilt lever.
   c. Remove the steering column trim shrouds. Disconnect all electrical connections from the steering column switches.
   d. Remove the 4 bolts and opening cover and the 2 bolts and reinforcement from under the steering column.
   e. Disengage the insulator retainer and remove the insulator. Remove the 4 nuts and reinforcement from under the steering column.

   ➡ **Do not rotate the steering column shaft.**

   f. Remove the 4 nuts retaining the steering column to the instrument panel, disconnect the shift indicator cable and lower the column on the front seat. Install the lock cylinder to make sure the steering column shaft does not turn.
   g. Remove 1 bolt at the steering column opening attaching the instrument panel to the brace. Remove 1 instrument panel brace retaining bolt from under the radio area.
   h. Remove the sound insulator under the glove compartment by removing the 2 push nuts that secure the insulator to the studs on the climate control case.
   i. Disconnect the wires of the main wire loom in the engine compartment. Disengage the rubber grommet from the dash panel, then feed the wiring through the hole in the dash panel into the passenger compartment.
   j. Remove the right and left cowl side trim panels. Disconnect the wires from the instrument panel at the right and left cowl sides.
   k. Remove 1 screw each from the left and right side retaining the instrument panel. Pull up to unsnap the right and left speaker opening covers and remove.
   l. Release the glove compartment assembly by depressing the side of the glove compartment bin and swinging the door/bin down.
   m. Using the steering column and glove compartment openings and by reaching under the instrument panel, tag and disconnect all electrical connections, vacuum hoses, heater control cables, speedometer cable and radio antenna cable.
   n. Close the glove compartment door, support the panel and remove the 3 screws attaching the top of the instrument panel to the cowl top and disconnect any remaining wires. Remove the panel from the vehicle.
4. Drain the coolant from the radiator.
5. Disconnect and plug the heater hoses at the heater core. Plug the heater core tubes.
6. Disconnect the vacuum supply hose from the inline vacuum check valve in the engine compartment. Remove the screw holding the instrument panel shake brace to the heater case and remove the shake brace.
7. Remove the floor register and rear floor ducts from the bottom of the heater case. Remove the 3 nuts attaching the heater case to the dash panel in the engine compartment.
8. Remove the 2 screws attaching the brackets to the cowl top panel. Pull the heater case assembly away from the dash panel and remove from the vehicle.
9. Remove the vacuum source line from the heater core tube seal and remove the seal from the heater core tubes.
10. Remove the 4 heater core access cover attaching screws and remove the access cover from the heater case. Lift the heater core and seals from the heater case.

To install:

11. Transfer the 3 foam core seals to the new heater core. Install the heater core and seals into the heater case.
12. Position the heater case access cover on the case and install the 4 screws.
13. Install the seal on the heater core tubes and install the vacuum source line through the seal.
14. Position the heater case assembly to the dash panel and cowl top panel at the air inlet opening. Install the 2 screws to attach the support brackets to the cowl top panel.

15. Install the 3 nuts in the engine compartment to attach the heater case to the dash panel. Install the floor register and rear floor ducts on the bottom of the heater case.

16. Install the instrument panel shake brace and screw to the heater case. Install the instrument panel by reversing the removal procedure.

17. Connect the heater hoses to the heater core. Connect the black vacuum supply hose to the vacuum check valve in the engine compartment.

18. Fill the radiator and bleed the cooling system.

19. Connect the negative battery cable and check the system for proper operation.

With Air Conditioning

➡ **It is necessary to remove the evaporator case in order to remove the heater core. Whenever an evaporator case is removed, it will be necessary to replace the suction accumulator/drier.**

1. Disconnect the negative battery cable.
2. Remove the instrument panel on 1986–89 vehicles as follows:
   a. Remove the 4 screws retaining the steering column opening cover and remove the cover.
   b. Remove the sound insulator under the glove compartment by removing the 2 push nuts securing the insulator to the studs on the climate control case.

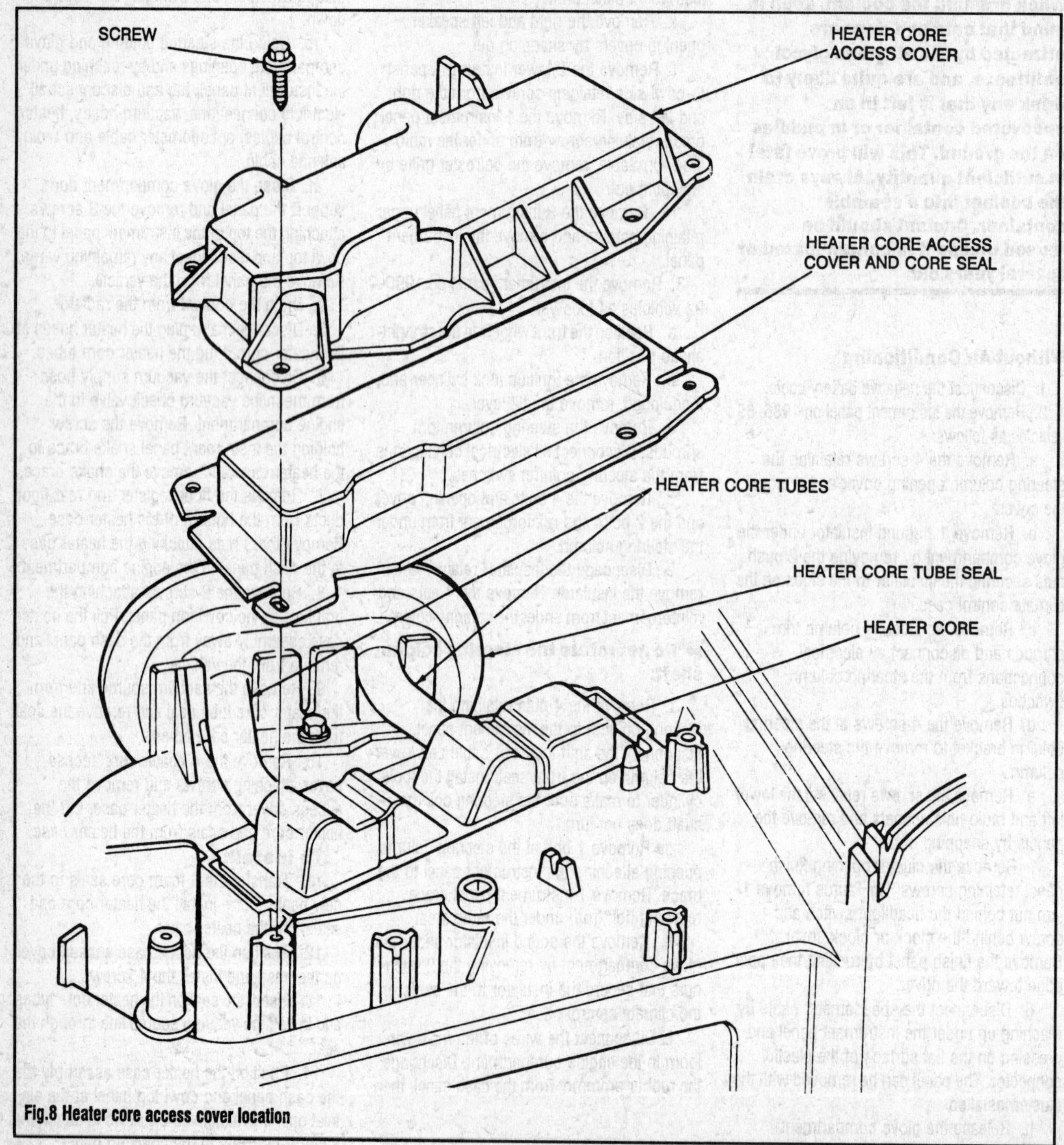

Fig.8 Heater core access cover location

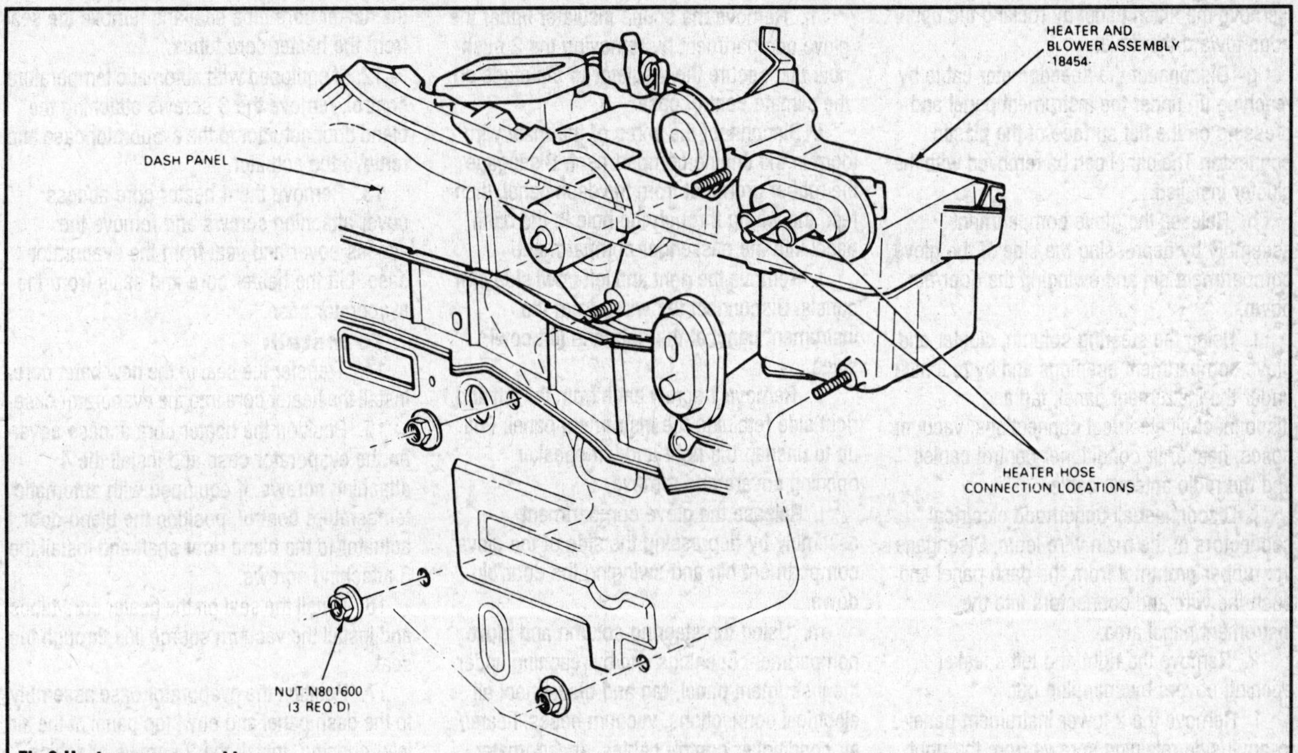

HEATER AND BLOWER ASSEMBLY -18454-

DASH PANEL

HEATER HOSE CONNECTION LOCATIONS

NUT-N801600 (3 REQ'D)

Fig.9 Heater case assembly

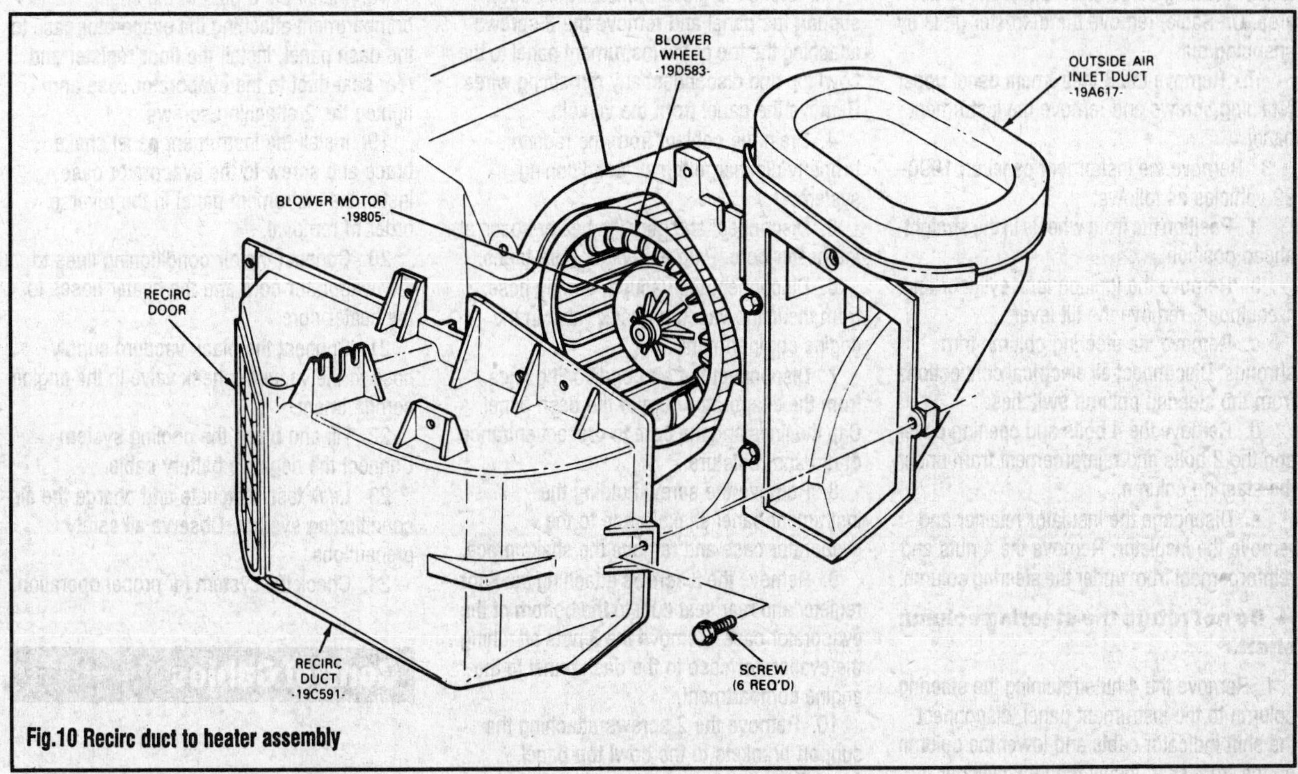

Fig.10 Recirc duct to heater assembly

c. Remove the steering column trim shrouds and disconnect all electrical connections from the steering column switches.

d. Remove the 4 screws at the steering column bracket to remove the steering column.

e. Remove the screws retaining the lower left and radio finish panels and remove the panels by snapping out.

f. Remove the cluster opening finish panel retaining screws. On Taurus remove 1 jam nut behind the headlight switch and 1 screw behind the clock or clock cover.

Remove the finish panel by rocking the upper edge toward the driver.

g. Disconnect the speedometer cable by reaching up under the instrument panel and pressing on the flat surface of the plastic connector. The panel can be removed with the cluster installed.

h. Release the glove compartment assembly by depressing the side of the glove compartment bin and swinging the door/bin down.

i. Using the steering column, cluster and glove compartment openings and by reaching under the instrument panel, tag and disconnect all electrical connections, vacuum hoses, heater/air conditioner control cables and the radio antenna cable.

j. Disconnect all underhood electrical connectors of the main wire loom. Disengage the rubber grommet from the dash panel and push the wire and connectors into the instrument panel area.

k. Remove the right and left speaker opening covers by snapping out.

l. Remove the 2 lower instrument panel-to-cowl side retaining screws from the right and left side. Remove the 1 instrument panel brace retaining screw from under the radio area. On Sable, remove the defroster grille by snapping out.

m. Remove the 3 instrument panel upper retaining screws and remove the instrument panel.

3. Remove the instrument panel on 1990–92 vehicles as follows:

a. Position the front wheels in the straight-ahead position.

b. Remove the ignition lock cylinder and, if equipped, remove the tilt lever.

c. Remove the steering column trim shrouds. Disconnect all electrical connections from the steering column switches.

d. Remove the 4 bolts and opening cover and the 2 bolts and reinforcement from under the steering column.

e. Disengage the insulator retainer and remove the insulator. Remove the 4 nuts and reinforcement from under the steering column.

➡ **Do not rotate the steering column shaft.**

f. Remove the 4 nuts retaining the steering column to the instrument panel, disconnect the shift indicator cable and lower the column on the front seat. Install the lock cylinder to make sure the steering column shaft does not turn.

g. Remove 1 bolt at the steering column opening attaching the instrument panel to the brace. Remove 1 instrument panel brace retaining bolt from under the radio area.

h. Remove the sound insulator under the glove compartment by removing the 2 push nuts that secure the insulator to the studs on the climate control case.

i. Disconnect the wires of the main wire loom in the engine compartment. Disengage the rubber grommet from the dash panel, then feed the wiring through the hole in the dash panel into the passenger compartment.

j. Remove the right and left cowl side trim panels. Disconnect the wires from the instrument panel at the right and left cowl sides.

k. Remove 1 screw each from the left and right side retaining the instrument panel. Pull up to unsnap the right and left speaker opening covers and remove.

l. Release the glove compartment assembly by depressing the side of the glove compartment bin and swinging the door/bin down.

m. Using the steering column and glove compartment openings and by reaching under the instrument panel, tag and disconnect all electrical connections, vacuum hoses, heater/air conditioner control cables, speedometer cable and radio antenna cable.

n. Close the glove compartment door, support the panel and remove the 3 screws attaching the top of the instrument panel to the cowl top and disconnect any remaining wires. Remove the panel from the vehicle.

4. Drain the coolant from the radiator. Properly discharge the air conditioning system.

5. Disconnect and plug the heater hoses at the heater core. Plug the heater core tubes.

6. Disconnect the vacuum supply hose from the inline vacuum check valve in the engine compartment.

7. Disconnect the air conditioning lines from the evaporator core at the dash panel. Cap the lines and the core to prevent entrance of dirt and moisture.

8. Remove the screw holding the instrument panel shake brace to the evaporator case and remove the shake brace.

9. Remove the 2 screws attaching the floor register and rear seat duct to the bottom of the evaporator case. Remove the 3 nuts attaching the evaporator case to the dash panel in the engine compartment.

10. Remove the 2 screws attaching the support brackets to the cowl top panel. Carefully pull the evaporator assembly away from the dash panel and remove the evaporator case from the vehicle.

11. Remove the vacuum source line from the heater core tube seal and remove the seal from the heater core tubes.

12. If equipped with automatic temperature control, remove the 3 screws attaching the blend door actuator to the evaporator case and remove the actuator.

13. Remove the 4 heater core access cover attaching screws and remove the access cover and seal from the evaporator case. Lift the heater core and seals from the evaporator case.

To install:

14. Transfer the seal to the new hater core. Install the heater core into the evaporator case.

15. Position the heater core access cover on the evaporator case and install the 4 attaching screws. If equipped with automatic temperature control, position the blend door actuator to the blend door shaft and install the 3 attaching screws.

16. Install the seal on the heater core tubes and install the vacuum source line through the seal.

17. Position the evaporator case assembly to the dash panel and cowl top panel at the air inlet opening. Install the 2 screws attaching the support brackets to the cowl top panel.

18. Install the 3 nuts in the engine compartment attaching the evaporator case to the dash panel. Install the floor register and rear seat duct to the evaporator case and tighten the 2 attaching screws.

19. Install the instrument panel shake brace and screw to the evaporator case. Install the instrument panel in the reverse order of removal.

20. Connect the air conditioning lines to the evaporator core and the heater hoses to the heater core.

21. Connect the black vacuum supply hose to the vacuum check valve in the engine compartment.

22. Fill and bleed the cooling system. Connect the negative battery cable.

23. Leak test, evacuate and charge the air conditioning system. Observe all safety precautions.

24. Check the system for proper operation.

Control Cables

REMOVAL & INSTALLATION

➧ SEE FIG. 11

1. Disconnect the negative battery cable.

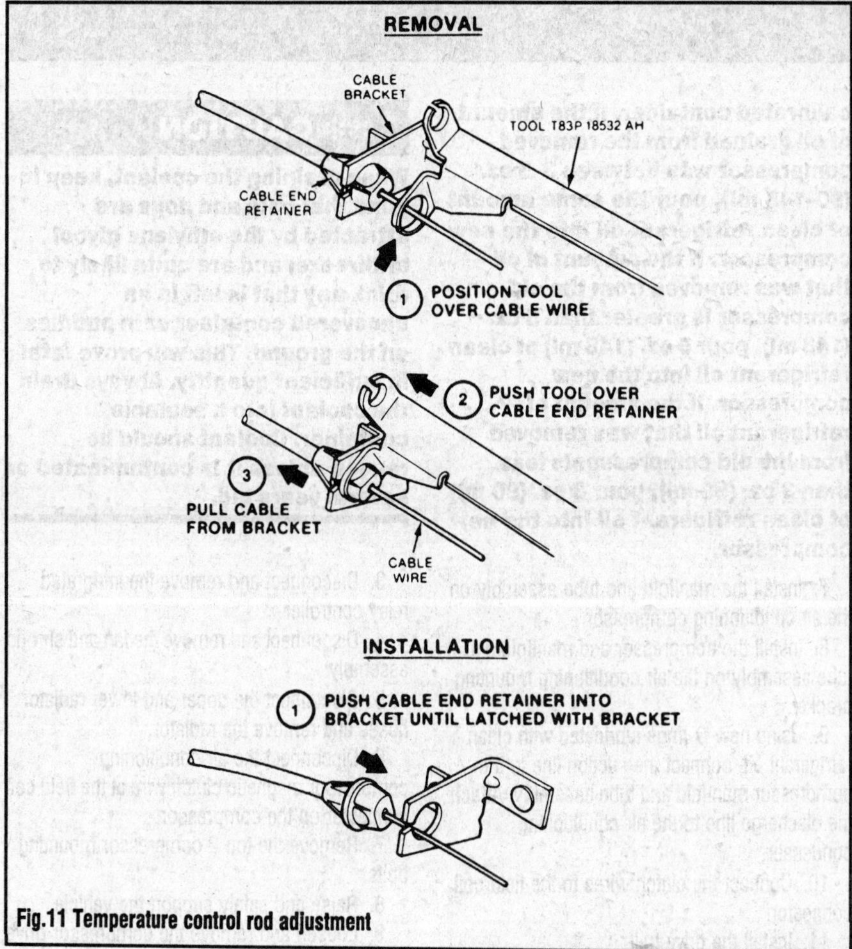
REMOVAL
CABLE BRACKET
TOOL T83P 18532 AH
CABLE END RETAINER
1 POSITION TOOL OVER CABLE WIRE
2 PUSH TOOL OVER CABLE END RETAINER
3
PULL CABLE FROM BRACKET
CABLE WIRE
INSTALLATION
1 PUSH CABLE END RETAINER INTO BRACKET UNTIL LATCHED WITH BRACKET

Fig.11 Temperature control rod adjustment

2. Remove the instrument cluster opening finish panel.
3. Rotate the temperature control knob to the COOL position.
4. Disconnect the control knob cable housing end retainer from the heater case bracket using the proper tool.
5. Disconnect the cable wire from the temperature door crank arm, using the proper tool.
6. Remove the retaining screws that retain the control assembly to the instrument panel. Pull the control assembly away from its mounting.
7. Disconnect the cable housing end retainer from the control assembly and the cable wire from the temperature control lever arm.
8. Remove the cable assembly from the vehicle.
9. Installation is the reverse of the removal procedure.

Control Panel

REMOVAL & INSTALLATION

1. Disconnect the negative battery cable.
2. Remove the instrument panel finish applique.
3. Remove the 4 screws attaching the control assembly to the instrument panel.
4. Pull the control assembly from the instrument panel opening and disconnect the wire connectors from the control assembly.
5. Disconnect the vacuum harness and temperature control cable from the control assembly. Discard the used pushnut from the vacuum harness.

To install:

6. Connect the temperature cable to the control assembly.
7. Connect the wire connectors and vacuum harness to the control assembly using new pushnuts.

➡ Push on the vacuum harness retaining nuts. Do not attempt to screw them onto the post.

8. Position the control assembly to the instrument panel opening and install 4 attaching screws.
9. Install the instrument panel finish applique.
10. Connect the negative battery cable and check the system for proper operation.

Blower Switch

REMOVAL & INSTALLATION

1. Disconnect the negative battery cable.
2. Remove the control assembly from the instrument panel. Remove the switch knob.
3. Remove the screw from the switch and its mounting. Disconnect the switch electrical connector.
4. Installation is the reverse of the removal procedure.

Vacuum Selector Switch

REMOVAL & INSTALLATION

1. Disconnect the negative battery cable.
2. Remove the control assembly from the instrument panel. Remove the knob from the function selector shaft.
3. Remove the screw from the switch and its mounting. Remove the switch.
4. Installation is the reverse of the removal procedure. Before installation rotate the function selector shaft to the OFF position.

AIR CONDITIONER

➡ **Refer to SECTION 1 for air conditioning system discharging information.**

Compressor

REMOVAL & INSTALLATION

Except 3.8L Engine

➡ **Whenever a compressor is replaced, it will be necessary to replace the suction accumulator/ drier.**

1. Disconnect the negative battery cable and properly discharge the system.
2. Disconnect the compressor clutch wires at the field coil connector on the compressor.
3. Loosen the drive belt and disconnect the hose assemblies from the condenser and suction line.
4. Remove the mounting bolts and remove the compressor and manifold and tube assembly from the vehicle as a unit. The assembly will not clear the sub-frame and radio support if an attempt is made to remove the unit from the bottom. It must be removed from the top.
5. Remove the manifold and tube assembly as an on-bench operation.
6. If the compressor is to be replaced, remove the clutch and field coil assembly.

To install:

➡ **New service replacement FS-6 compressors contain 10 oz. (300 ml) of refrigerant oil. Before replacement compressor installation, drain 4 oz. (120 ml) of refrigerant oil from the compressor. This will maintain the total system oil charge within the specified limits. New service replacement 10P15F compressors contain 8 oz. (240 ml) of refrigerant oil and new service replacement FX-15 compressors contain 7 oz. (207 ml) of refrigerant oil. Prior to installing either type replacement compressor, drain the refrigerant oil from the removed compressor into a calibrated container. Then, drain the refrigerant oil from the new compressor into a clean calibrated container. If the amount of oil drained from the removed compressor was between 3–5 oz. (90–148 ml), pour the same amount of clean refrigerant oil into the new compressor. If the amount of oil that was removed from the old compressor is greater than 5 oz. (148 ml), pour 5 oz. (148 ml) of clean refrigerant oil into the new compressor. If the amount of refrigerant oil that was removed from the old compressor is less than 3 oz. (90 ml), pour 3 oz. (90 ml) of clean refrigerant oil into the new compressor.**

7. Install the manifold and tube assembly on the air conditioning compressor.
8. Install the compressor and manifold and tube assembly on the air conditioning mounting bracket.
9. Using new O-rings lubricated with clean refrigerant oil, connect the suction line to the compressor manifold and tube assembly. Attach the discharge line to the air conditioning condenser.
10. Connect the clutch wires to the field coil connector.
11. Install the drive belt.
12. Leak test, evacuate and charge the system according to the proper procedure. Observe all safety precautions.
13. Check the system for proper operation.

3.8L Engine

➧ SEE FIG. 12

➡ **Whenever a compressor is replaced, it will be necessary to replace the suction accumulator/ drier.**

1. Disconnect the negative battery cable and properly discharge the air conditioning system.
2. Position a suitable clean drain pan under the radiator and drain the coolant.

✲✲ CAUTION

When draining the coolant, keep in mind that cats and dogs are attracted by the ethylene glycol antifreeze, and are quite likely to drink any that is left in an uncovered container or in puddles on the ground. This will prove fatal in sufficient quantity. Always drain the coolant into a sealable container. Coolant should be reused unless it is contaminated or several years old.

3. Disconnect and remove the integrated relay controller.
4. Disconnect and remove the fan and shroud assembly.
5. Disconnect the upper and lower radiator hoses and remove the radiator.
6. Disconnect the air conditioning compressor magnetic clutch wire at the field coil connector on the compressor.
7. Remove the top 2 compressor mounting bolts.
8. Raise and safely support the vehicle.
9. Loosen and remove the compressor drive belt.
10. Disconnect the HEGO sensor wire connector and remove the air conditioning muffler supporting strap bolt from the sub-frame.
11. Disconnect the air conditioning system hose from the condenser and suction accumulator/drier using the spring-lock coupling tool or equivalent. Immediately install protective caps on the open lines.
12. Remove the bottom 2 compressor mounting bolts. Make sure the compressor is properly supported as the bolts are removed.
13. Remove the compressor, manifold and tube assemblies from the vehicle as a unit. The assembly can be removed from the bottom using care not to scrape against the condenser.
14. Remove the manifold and tube assemblies from the compressor.
15. If the compressor is to be replaced, remove the clutch and field coil assembly.

To install:

➡ **A new service replacement 10P15C compressor contains 8 oz. (240 ml) of refrigerant oil. Before installing a new compressor, drain**

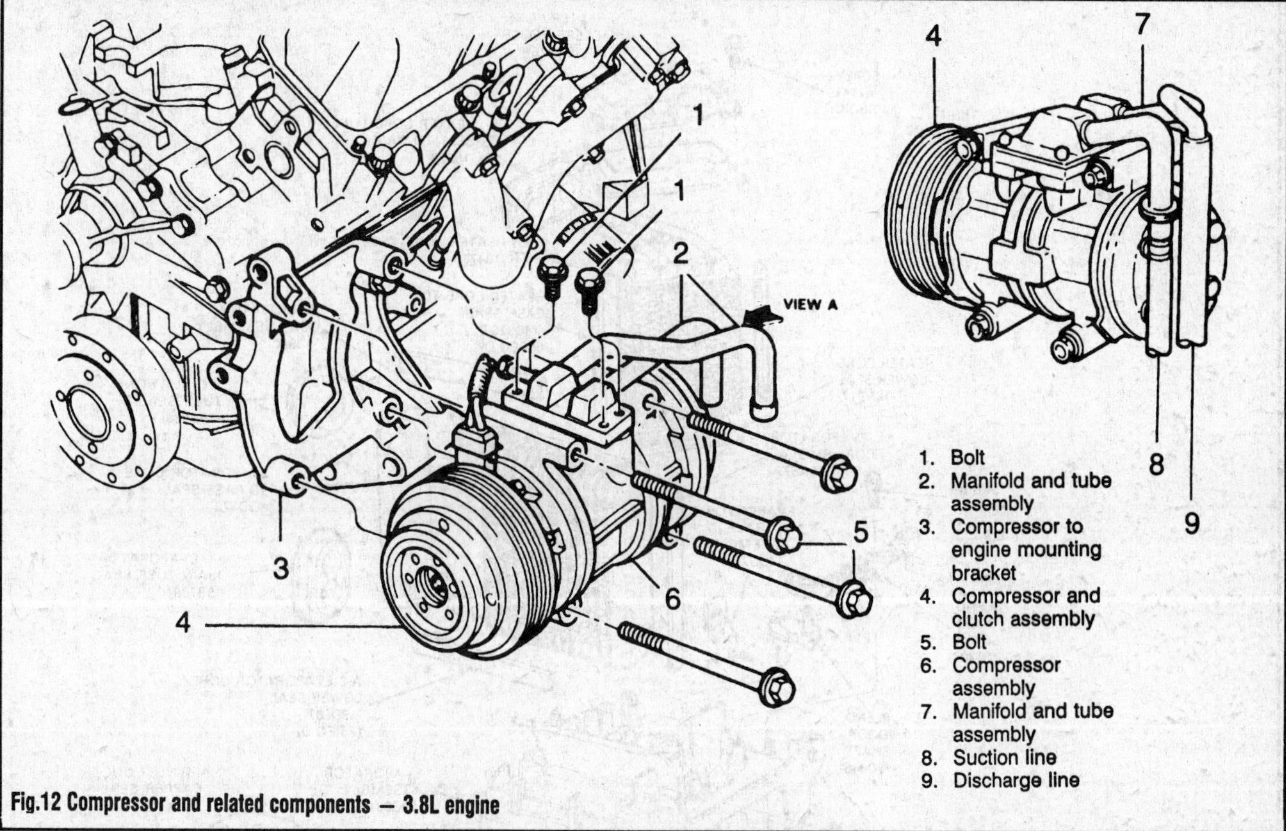

Fig.12 Compressor and related components — 3.8L engine

4 oz. (120 ml) of refrigerant oil from the compressor. This will maintain total system oil charge within specified limits.

16. Using new O-rings, lubricated with clean refrigerant oil, install the manifold and tube assemblies onto the new compressor.

17. Install the compressor, manifold and tube assemblies onto the compressor mounting bracket.

18. Using new O-rings lubricated with clean refrigerant oil, connect the suction line to the compressor and manifold assembly.

19. Using new O-rings lubricated with clean refrigerant oil, connect the discharge line to the compressor and manifold assembly.

20. Install the muffler support onto the sub-frame and connect the HEGO sensor wire connector.

21. Install the compressor drive belt and lower the vehicle.

22. Install the radiator and connect the radiator hoses.

23. Install the fan and shroud assembly and connect the integrated relay connector.

24. Connect the negative battery cable and fill the radiator with the coolant that was saved.

25. Leak test, evacuate and charge the system according to the proper procedure. Check the system for proper operation.

Condenser

➡ Refer to SECTION 1 for air conditioning system discharging information.

REMOVAL & INSTALLATION

➡ Whenever a condenser is replaced, it will be necessary to replace the suction accumulator/ drier.

1. Disconnect the negative battery cable and properly discharge the refrigerant from the air conditioning system. Observe all safety precautions.

2. Disconnect the 2 refrigerant lines at the fittings on the right side of the radiator. Perform the spring-lock coupling disconnect procedure.

3. Remove the 4 bolts attaching the condenser to the radiator support and remove the condenser from the vehicle.

To Install:

4. Add 1 oz. (30 ml) of clean refrigerant oil to a new replacement condenser.

5. Position the condenser assembly to the radiator support brackets and install the attaching bolts.

6. Connect the refrigerant lines to the condenser assembly. Perform the spring-lock coupling connection procedure.

7. Leak test, evacuate and charge the refrigerant system following the proper procedures. Observe all safety precautions.

Evaporator Core

➡ Refer to SECTION 1 for air conditioning system discharging information.

REMOVAL & INSTALLATION

➧ SEE FIG. 1–6

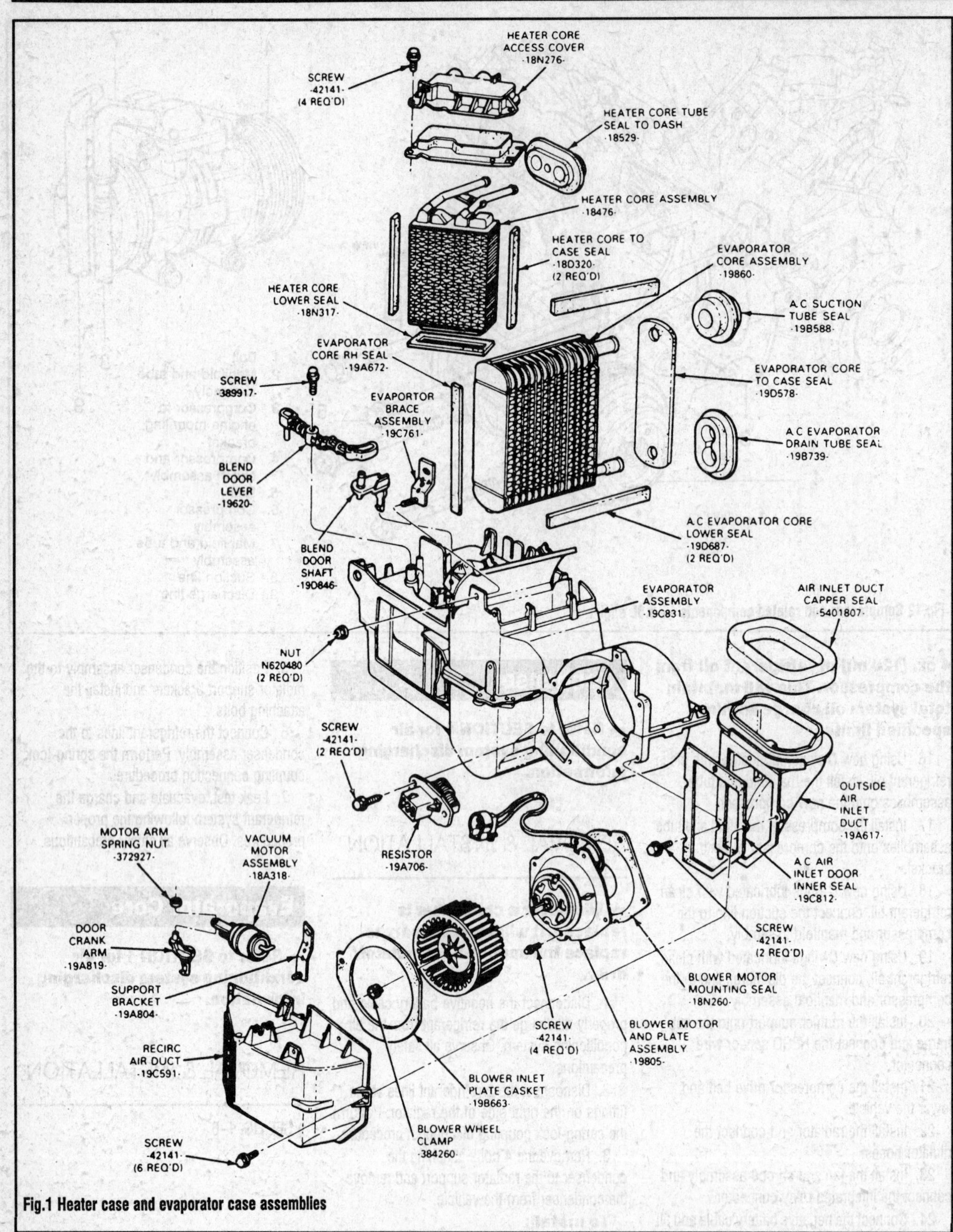
HEATER CORE ACCESS COVER -18N276-
SCREW -42141- (4 REQ'D)
HEATER CORE TUBE SEAL TO DASH -18529-
HEATER CORE ASSEMBLY -18476-
HEATER CORE TO CASE SEAL -18D320- (2 REQ'D)
EVAPORATOR CORE ASSEMBLY -19860-
HEATER CORE LOWER SEAL -18N317-
A/C SUCTION TUBE SEAL -19B588-
EVAPORATOR CORE RH SEAL -19A672-
EVAPORATOR CORE TO CASE SEAL -19D578-
SCREW -389917-
EVAPORTOR BRACE ASSEMBLY -19C761-
A/C EVAPORATOR DRAIN TUBE SEAL -19B739-
BLEND DOOR LEVER -19620-
A/C EVAPORATOR CORE LOWER SEAL -19D687- (2 REQ'D)
BLEND DOOR SHAFT -19D846-
EVAPORATOR ASSEMBLY -19C831-
AIR INLET DUCT CAPPER SEAL -5401807-
NUT N620480 (2 REQ'D)
SCREW -42141- (2 REQ'D)
OUTSIDE AIR INLET DUCT -19A617-
MOTOR ARM SPRING NUT -372927-
VACUUM MOTOR ASSEMBLY -18A318-
RESISTOR -19A706-
A/C AIR INLET DOOR INNER SEAL -19C812-
SCREW -42141- (2 REQ'D)
DOOR CRANK ARM -19A819-
BLOWER MOTOR MOUNTING SEAL -18N260-
SUPPORT BRACKET -19A804-
SCREW -42141- (4 REQ'D)
BLOWER MOTOR AND PLATE ASSEMBLY -19805-
RECIRC AIR DUCT -19C591-
BLOWER INLET PLATE GASKET -19B663-
BLOWER WHEEL CLAMP -384260-
SCREW -42141- (6 REQ'D)

Fig.1 Heater case and evaporator case assemblies

✱✱ CAUTION

When draining the coolant, keep in mind that cats and dogs are attracted by the ethylene glycol antifreeze, and are quite likely to drink any that is left in an uncovered container or in puddles on the ground. This will prove fatal in sufficient quantity. Always drain the coolant into a sealable container. Coolant should be reused unless it is contaminated or several years old.

➡ Whenever an evaporator is removed, it will be necessary to replace the accumulator/drier.

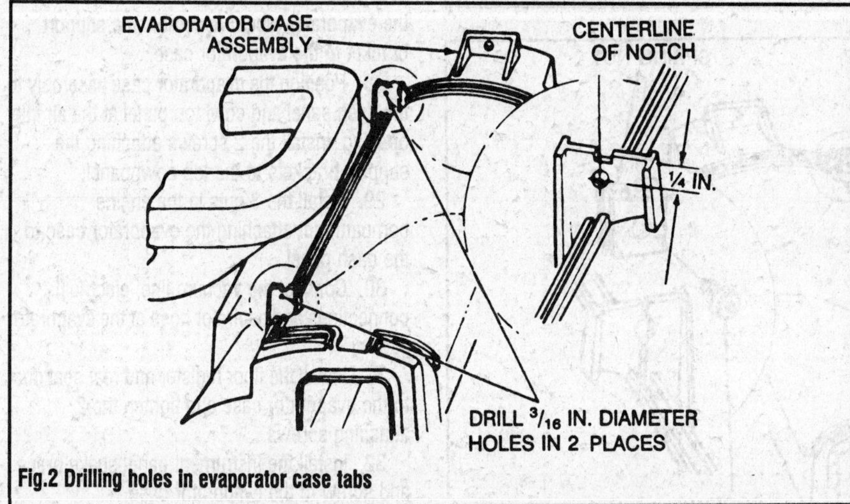

Fig.2 Drilling holes in evaporator case tabs

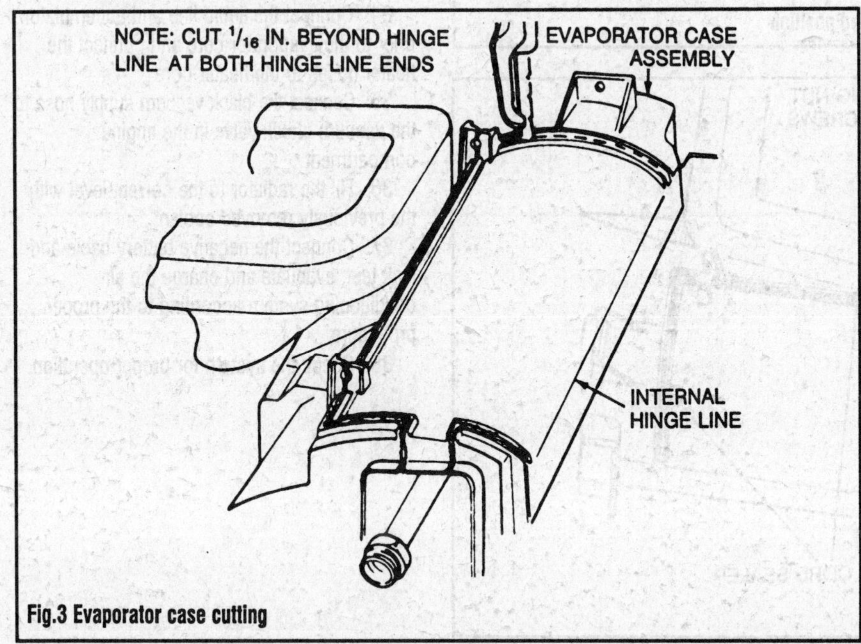

Fig.3 Evaporator case cutting

1. Disconnect the negative battery cable.
2. Drain the coolant from the radiator into a clean container.
3. Properly discharge the refrigerant from the air conditioning system.
4. Disconnect the heater hoses from the heater core. Plug the heater core tubes.
5. Disconnect the vacuum supply hose from the in-line vacuum check valve in the engine compartment.
6. Disconnect the liquid line and the accumulator from the evaporator core at the dash panel. Cap the refrigerant lines and evaporator core to prevent entrance of dirt and moisture.
7. Remove the instrument panel and place it on the front seat.
8. Remove the screw holding the instrument panel shake brace to the evaporator case and remove the instrument panel shake brace.
9. Remove the 2 screws attaching the floor register and rear seat duct to the bottom of the evaporator case.
10. Disconnect the vacuum line, electrical connections and aspirator hose from the evaporator case.
11. Remove the 3 nuts attaching the evaporator case to the dash panel in the engine compartment. Remove the 2 screws attaching the support brackets to the cowl top panel.
12. Carefully pull the evaporator assembly away from the dash panel and remove the evaporator case from the vehicle.
13. Disconnect and remove the vacuum harness.
14. Remove the 6 screws attaching the recirculation duct and remove the duct from the evaporator case.
15. Remove the 2 screws from the air inlet duct and remove the duct from the evaporator case.
16. Remove the support bracket from the evaporator case.
17. If equipped with automatic temperature control, remove the screws holding the electronic connector bracket to the recirculation duct and remove the blend door actuator and cold engine lock out switch, which is held on by spring tension at the outermost heater core tube.
18. Remove the molded seals from the evaporator core tubes.
19. Drill a $^{3}/_{16}$ in. (4.75mm) hole in both upright tabs on top of the evaporator case.
20. Using a suitable tool, cut the top of the evaporator case between the raised outline. Fold the cutout cover back from the opening and lift the evaporator core from the case.

To install:

➡ Add 3 oz. (90 ml) of clean refrigerant oil to a new replacement evaporator core to maintain total system refrigerant oil requirements.

21. Transfer the foam core seals to the new evaporator core.
22. Position the evaporator core in the case and close the cutout cover.
23. Install a spring nut on each of the 2 upright tabs with 2 holes drilled in the front flange. Make sure the holes in the spring nuts are aligned with the $^{3}/_{16}$ in. (4.75mm) holes drilled in

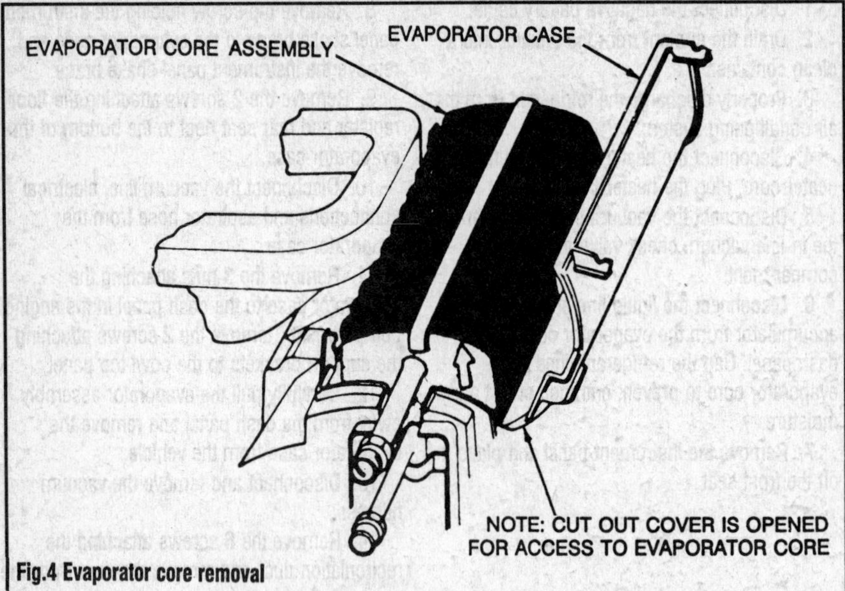

Fig.4 Evaporator core removal

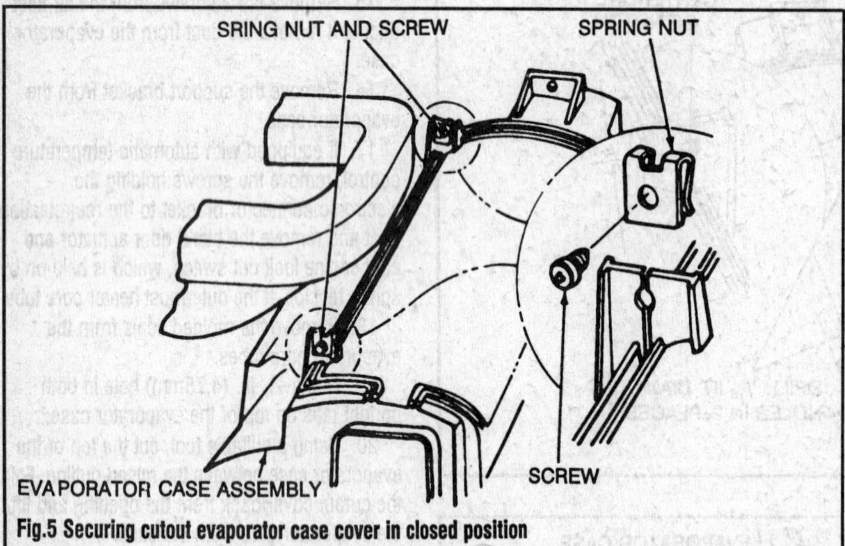

Fig.5 Securing cutout evaporator case cover in closed position

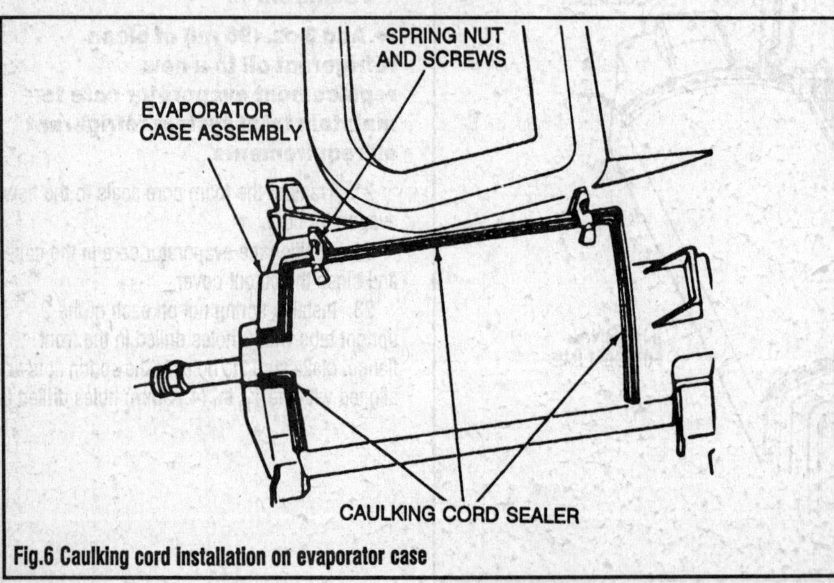

Fig.6 Caulking cord installation on evaporator case

the tab and flange. Install and tighten the screw in each spring nut to secure the cutout cover in the closed position.

24. Install caulking cord to seal the evaporator case against leakage along the cut line.

25. Install the air inlet duct to the evaporator case and tighten the 2 screws. Install the recirculation duct to the evaporator case and tighten 6 screws.

26. If equipped with automatic temperature control, install the electrical connector bracket to the recirculation duct, install the speed controller connector to the bracket and attach the blend door actuator to the evaporator case. Install the electrical connector to the bracket. Attach the cold engine lock out switch by snapping the spring clip in place on the outermost heater core tube.

27. Install the vacuum harness to the evaporator case and install the foam seals over the evaporator tubes. Assemble the support bracket to the evaporator case.

28. Position the evaporator case assembly to the dash panel and cowl top panel at the air inlet opening. Install the 2 screws attaching the support brackets to the top cowl panel.

29. Install the 3 nuts in the engine compartment attaching the evaporator case to the dash panel.

30. Connect the vacuum line, electrical connections and aspirator hose at the evaporator case.

31. Install the floor register and rear seat duct to the evaporator case and tighten the 2 attaching screws.

32. Install the instrument panel shake brace and screw to the evaporator case.

33. Install the instrument panel.

34. Connect the liquid line and accumulator/drier to the evaporator core and connect the heater hoses to the heater core.

35. Connect the black vacuum supply hose to the vacuum check valve in the engine compartment.

36. Fill the radiator to the correct level with the previously removed coolant.

37. Connect the negative battery cable and leak test, evacuate and charge the air conditioning system according to the proper procedure.

38. Check the system for proper operation.

Control Panel

REMOVAL & INSTALLATION

Manual Control Head

➧ SEE FIG. 13

1. Disconnect the negative battery cable.
2. Remove the instrument panel finish applique.
3. Remove the 4 screws attaching the control assembly to the instrument panel.
4. Pull the control assembly from the instrument panel opening and disconnect the wire connectors from the control assembly.
5. Disconnect the vacuum harness and temperature control cable from the control assembly. Discard the used pushnut from the vacuum harness.

To install:

6. Connect the temperature cable to the control assembly.
7. Connect the wire connectors and vacuum harness to the control assembly using new pushnuts.

➡ Push on the vacuum harness retaining nuts. Do not attempt to screw them onto the post.

8. Position the control assembly to the instrument panel opening and install 4 attaching screws.
9. Install the instrument panel finish applique.
10. Connect the negative battery cable and check the system for proper operation.

Electronic Control Head

➧ SEE FIG. 14

1. Disconnect the negative battery cable.
2. Perform the following:

   a. Pull out the lower left and lower right instrument panel snap-on finish panel inserts. Remove the 8 screws retaining the upper finish panel.

   b. Pull the lower edge of the upper finish panel away from the instrument panel. It is best to grasp the finish panel from the lower left corner and pull the panel away by walking the hands around the panel in a clockwise direction.

3. Remove the 4 Torx® head screws

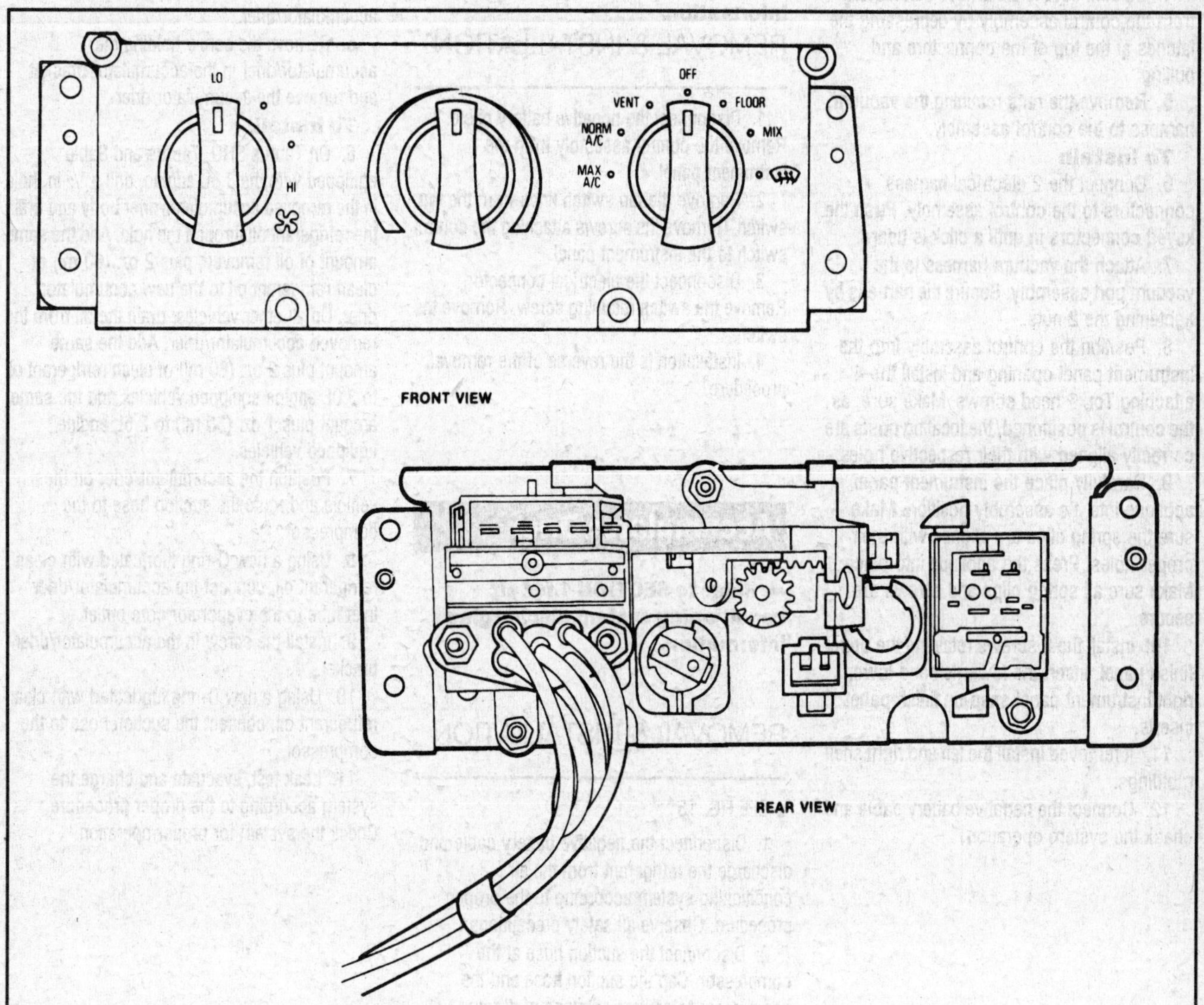

Fig.13 Control head assembly — manual air conditioning

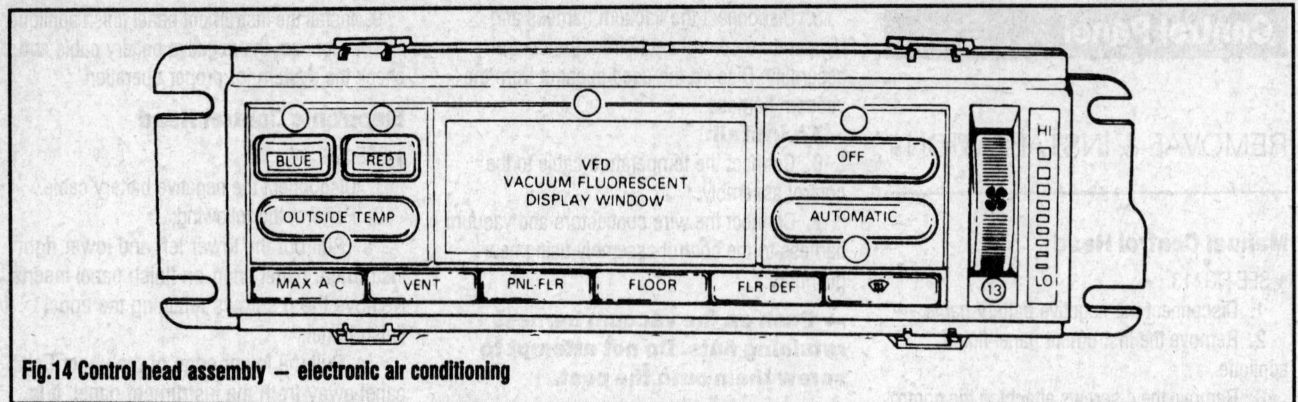

Fig.14 Control head assembly — electronic air conditioning

retaining the control assembly. Pull the control assembly away from the instrument panel into a position which provides access to the rear connections.

4. Disconnect the 2 harness connectors from the control assembly by depressing the latches at the top of the connectors and pulling.

5. Remove the nuts retaining the vacuum harness to the control assembly.

To install:

6. Connect the 2 electrical harness connectors to the control assembly. Push the keyed connectors in until a click is heard.

7. Attach the vacuum harness to the vacuum port assembly. Secure the harness by tightening the 2 nuts.

8. Position the control assembly into the instrument panel opening and install the 4 attaching Torx® head screws. Make sure, as the control is positioned, the locating posts are correctly aligned with their respective holes.

9. Carefully place the instrument panel applique into it's assembly position. Make sure the spring clips are aligned with their proper holes. Press the applique into place. Make sure all spring clips and screws are secure.

10. Install the 8 screws retaining the upper finish panel. Insert the lower left and lower right instrument panel snap-on finish panel inserts.

11. If removed install the left and right shelf moldings.

12. Connect the negative battery cable and check the system operation.

Blower Switch

➡ Refer to SECTION 1 for air conditioning system discharging information.

REMOVAL & INSTALLATION

1. Disconnect the negative battery cable. Remove the control assembly from the instrument panel.

2. Remove the fan switch knob from the fan switch. Remove the screws attaching the control switch to the instrument panel.

3. Disconnect the electrical connector. Remove the switch retaining screw. Remove the switch.

4. Installation is the reverse of the removal procedure.

Accumulator/Drier

➡ Refer to SECTION 1 for air conditioning system discharging information.

REMOVAL & INSTALLATION

➧ SEE FIG. 15

1. Disconnect the negative battery cable and discharge the refrigerant from the air conditioning system according to the proper procedure. Observe all safety precautions.

2. Disconnect the suction hose at the compressor. Cap the suction hose and the compressor to prevent entrance of dirt and moisture.

3. Disconnect the accumulator/drier inlet tube from the evaporator core outlet. Perform the spring-lock coupling disconnect procedure.

4. Disconnect the wire harness connector from the pressure switch on top of the accumulator/drier.

5. Remove the screw holding the accumulator/drier in the accumulator bracket and remove the accumulator/drier.

To install:

6. On Taurus SHO, Taurus and Sable equipped with the 3.8L engine, drill a $1/2$ in. hole in the removed accumulator/drier body and drain the refrigerant oil through the hole. Add the same amount of oil removed, plus 2 oz. (60 ml) of clean refrigerant oil to the new accumulator/drier. On all other vehicles, drain the oil from the removed accumulator/drier. Add the same amount plus 2 oz. (60 ml) of clean refrigerant oil to 3.0L engine equipped vehicles and the same amount plus 1 oz. (30 ml) to 2.5L engine equipped vehicles.

7. Position the accumulator/drier on the vehicle and route the suction hose to the compressor.

8. Using a new O-ring lubricated with clean refrigerant oil, connect the accumulator/drier inlet tube to the evaporator core outlet.

9. Install the screw in the accumulator/drier bracket.

10. Using a new O-ring lubricated with clean refrigerant oil, connect the suction hose to the compressor.

11. Leak test, evacuate and charge the system according to the proper procedure. Check the system for proper operation.

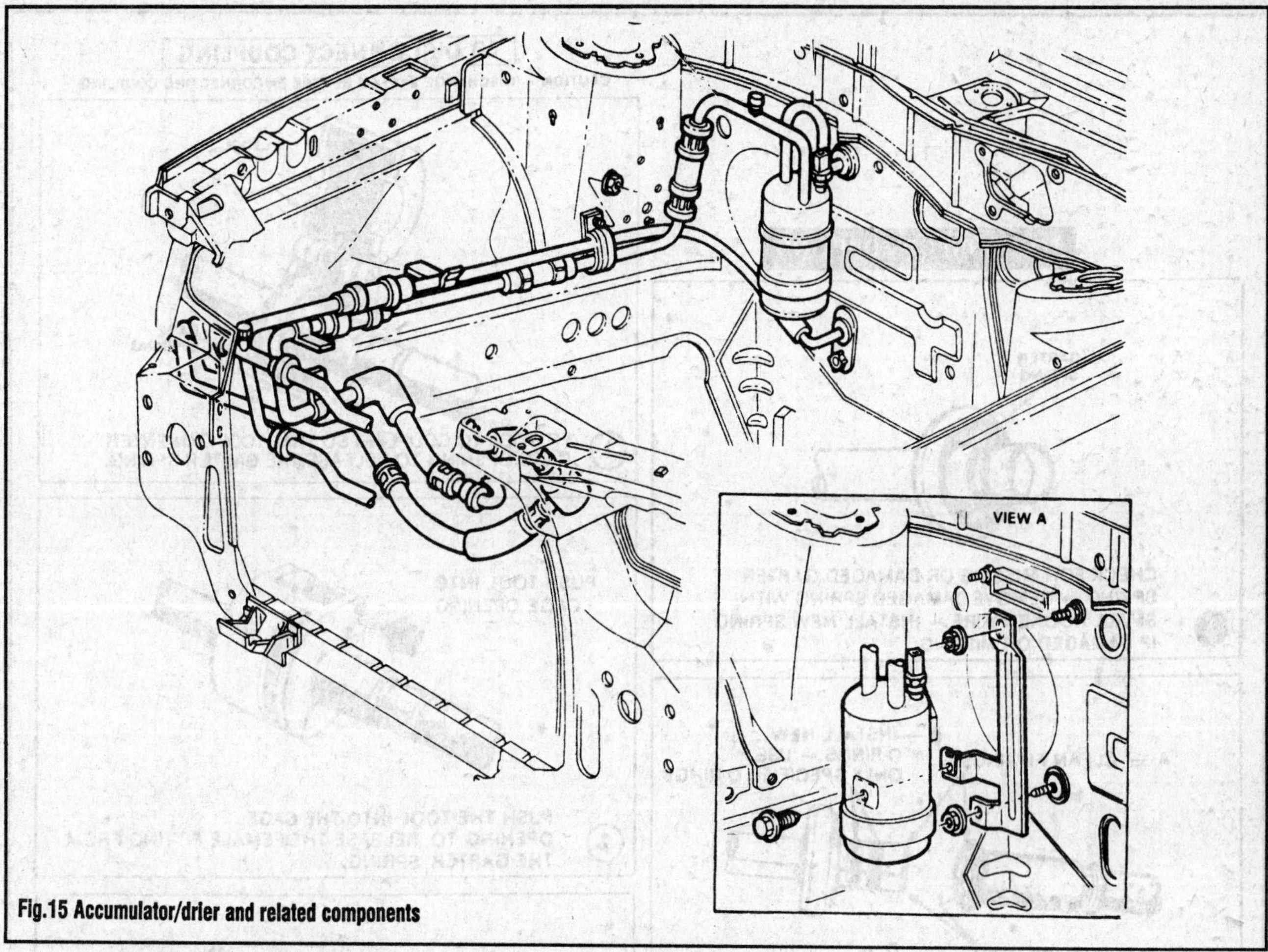

Fig.15 Accumulator/drier and related components

Refrigerant Lines

➡ **Refer to SECTION 1 for air conditioning system discharging information.**

REMOVAL & INSTALLATION

➧ SEE FIG. 16

➡ **Whenever a refrigerant line is replaced it will be necessary to replace the suction accumulator/drier.**

1. Disconnect the negative battery cable. Properly discharge the air conditioning system.
2. Disconnect and remove the defective refrigerant line.
3. Install the new refrigerant line using new O-rings lubricated with the proper type refrigerant oil.
4. Properly recharge the refrigerant system.

Control Cables

REMOVAL & INSTALLATION

1. Remove the control assembly from the instrument panel.
2. Disconnect the cable retainer and wire from the control assembly.
3. Disconnect the temperature cable from the plenum temperature blend door crank arm and cable mounting bracket.

To install:

4. Check to make sure the self-adjusting clip is at least 1 in. (25.4mm) from the end loop of the control cable.
5. Route the cable behind the instrument panel and connect the control cable to the mounting bracket on the plenum.
6. Install the self-adjusting clip on the temperature blend door crank arm.
7. Snap the cable housing into place at the control assembly. Connect the "S" bend end of the control cable to the temperature lever arm on the control assembly.
8. Install the control assembly into the instrument panel.

ADJUSTMENT

The temperature control cable is self-adjusting when the temperature selector knob is rotated to it's fully clockwise (red) position, as marked on the face of the control assembly. A preset adjustment should be made before attempting to perform the self-adjustment operation, to prevent kinking the control wire. The preset adjustment can be performed either with the cable installed in the vehicle or before cable installation.

Before Cable Installation

1. Insert the end of a suitable tool in the end loop of the temperature control cable.
2. Slide the self-adjusting clip down the control wire, away from the loop, approximately 1 in. (25.4mm).
3. Install the cable assembly.
4. Rotate the temperature selector knob to

TO CONNECT COUPLING

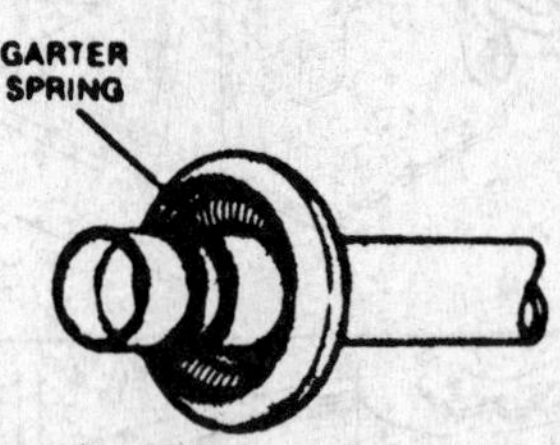
GARTER SPRING

1 CHECK FOR MISSING OR DAMAGED GARTER SPRING — REMOVE DAMAGED SPRING WITH SMALL HOOKED WIRE — INSTALL NEW SPRING IF DAMAGED OR MISSING.

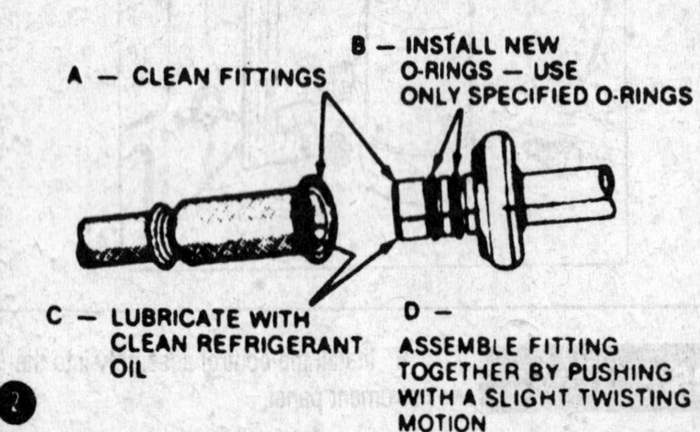
A — CLEAN FITTINGS
B — INSTALL NEW O-RINGS — USE ONLY SPECIFIED O-RINGS
C — LUBRICATE WITH CLEAN REFRIGERANT OIL
D — ASSEMBLE FITTING TOGETHER BY PUSHING WITH A SLIGHT TWISTING MOTION

2

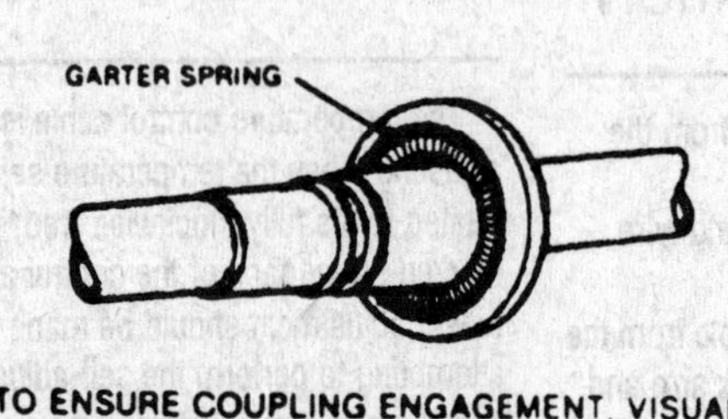
GARTER SPRING

3 TO ENSURE COUPLING ENGAGEMENT, VISUALLY CHECK TO BE SURE GARTER SPRING IS OVER FLARED END OF FEMALE FITTING.

TO DISCONNECT COUPLING

CAUTION — DISCHARGE SYSTEM BEFORE DISCONNECTING COUPLING

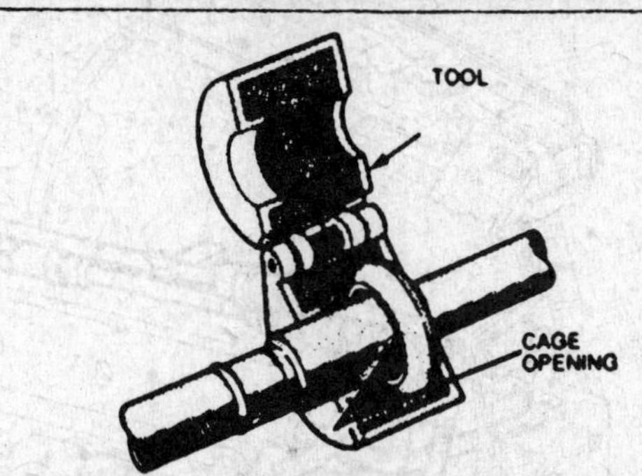
TOOL
CAGE OPENING

1 FIT TOOL TO COUPLING SO THAT TOOL CAN ENTER CAGE OPENING TO RELEASE THE GARTER SPRING.

PUSH TOOL INTO CAGE OPENING

2 PUSH THE TOOL INTO THE CAGE OPENING TO RELEASE THE FEMALE FITTING FROM THE GARTER SPRING.

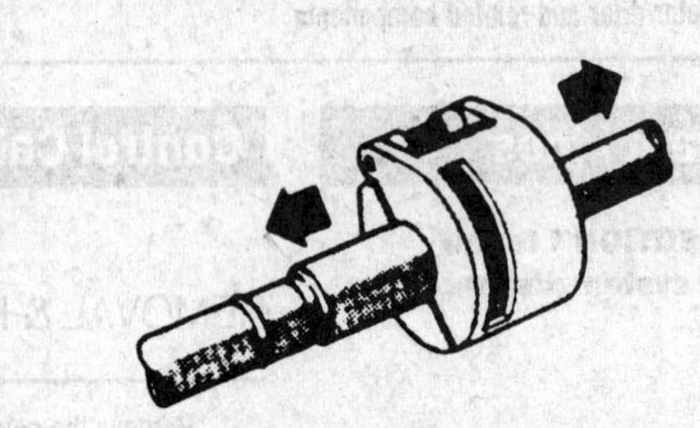

3 PULL THE COUPLING MALE AND FEMALE FITTINGS APART.

4 REMOVE THE TOOL FROM THE DISCONNECTED SPRING LOCK COUPLING.

Fig.16 Refrigerant line uncoupling tool and procedure

the clockwise (red) position marked on the control assembly face to position the self-adjusting clip.

5. Check for proper control operation.

After Cable Installation

1. Move the selector knob clockwise to the **COOL** position.

2. Hold the crank arm firmly in position and insert a suitable tool into the wire loop. Pull the cable wire through the self-adjusting clip until there is a space of approximately 1 in. (25.4mm) between the clip and the wire end loop.

3. Rotate the selector knob clockwise to allow positioning of the self-adjusting clip.

4. Check for proper control operation.

Vacuum Selector Valve

➡ **Refer to SECTION 1 for air conditioning system discharging information.**

REMOVAL & INSTALLATION

1. Disconnect the negative battery cable.

2. Remove the control assembly from the instrument panel. Remove the knob from the function selector shaft.

3. Remove the screw from the switch and its mounting. Remove the switch.

4. Installation is the reverse of the removal procedure. Before installation rotate the function selector shaft to the OFF position.

Cycling Clutch Switch

➡ **Refer to SECTION 1 for air conditioning system discharging information.**

REMOVAL & INSTALLATION

➧ SEE FIG. 20

1. Disconnect the negative battery cable. As required, properly discharge the air conditioning system.

2. Disconnect the wire harness connector from the pressure switch. Remove the switch.

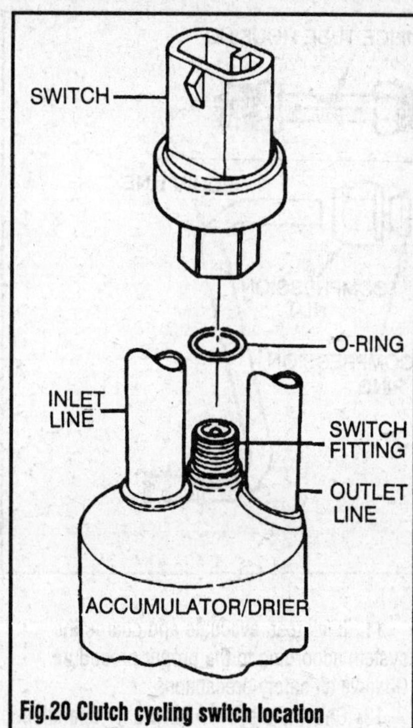

Fig.20 Clutch cycling switch location

3. Installation is the reverse of the removal procedure. Be sure to use a new O-ring. Check the new switch for pressure leaks. Check the system for proper operation.

Orifice Tube

➡ **Refer to SECTION 1 for air conditioning system discharging information.**

REMOVAL & INSTALLATION

➧ SEE FIG. 17–19

➡ **Fixed orifice tube replacement kits are available to replace the fixed orifice tube, if it should be defective. Although it is recommended that if the fixed orifice tube is found to be defective the complete liquid line should be replaced.**

The fixed orifice tube should be replaced whenever a compressor is replaced. If high pressure reads extremely high and low pressure is almost a vacuum, the fixed orifice is plugged and must be replaced.

REMOVAL & INSTALLATION

Liquid Line

➡ **Whenever a refrigerant line is replaced, it will be necessary to replace the accumulator/drier.**

1. Disconnect the negative battery cable. Properly discharge the refrigerant from the air conditioning system. Observe all safety precautions.

2. Disconnect and remove the refrigerant line using a wrench on each side of the tube O-fittings. If the refrigerant line has a spring-lock coupling, disconnect according to the spring-lock coupling disconnect procedure.

To install:

3. Route the new refrigerant line with the protective caps installed.

4. Connect the new refrigerant line into the system using new O-rings lubricated with clean refrigerant oil. Use 2 wrenches when tightening tube O-fittings or perform the spring-lock coupling connect procedure, as necessary.

5. Leak test, evacuate and charge the refrigerant system according to the proper procedure. Observe all safety precautions.

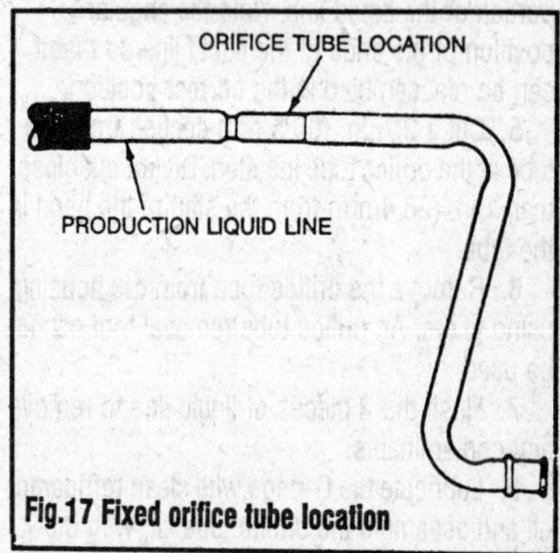

Fig.17 Fixed orifice tube location

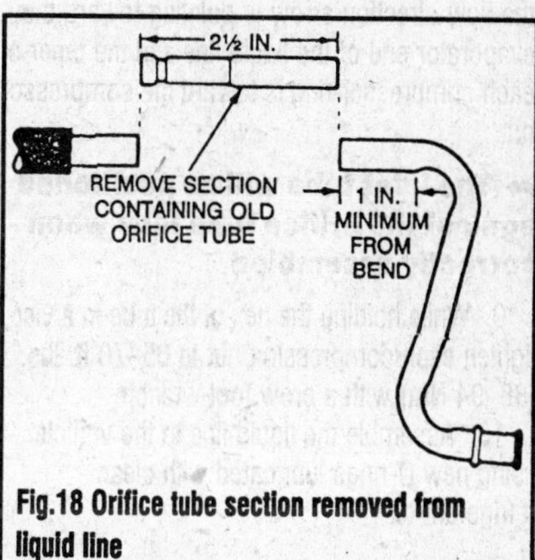

Fig.18 Orifice tube section removed from liquid line

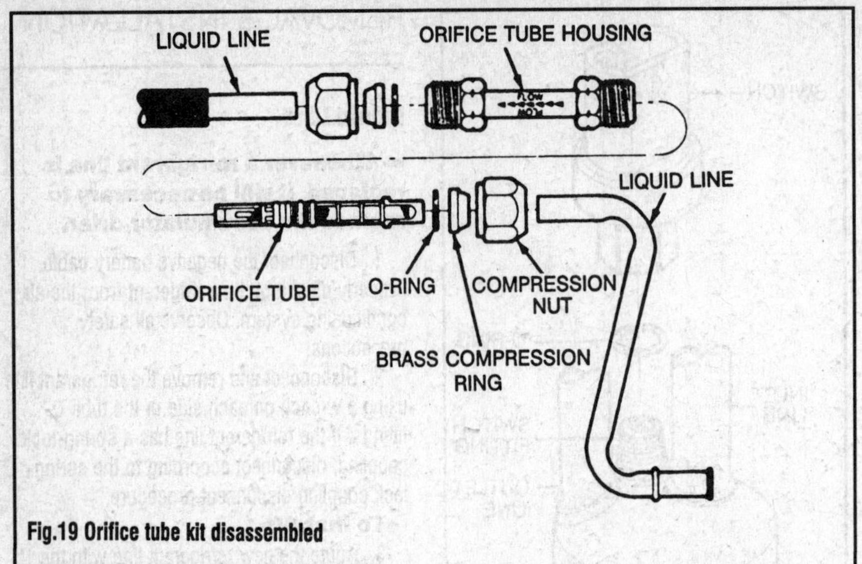

Fig.19 Orifice tube kit disassembled

Fixed Orifice Tube Replacement Kit

1. Disconnect the negative battery cable.
2. Discharge the refrigerant from the air conditioning system according to the proper procedure.
3. Remove the liquid line from the vehicle.
4. Locate the orifice tube by 3 indented notches or a circular depression in the metal portion of the liquid line. Note the angular position of the ends of the liquid line so that it can be reassembled in the correct position.
5. Cut a 2½ in. (63.5mm) section from the tube at the orifice tube location. Do not cut closer than 1 in. (25.4mm) from the start of the bend in the tube.
6. Remove the orifice tube from the housing using pliers. An orifice tube removal tool cannot be used.
7. Flush the 2 pieces of liquid line to remove any contaminants.
8. Lubricate the O-rings with clean refrigerant oil and assemble the orifice tube kit, with the orifice tube installed, to the liquid line. Make sure the flow direction arrow is pointing toward the evaporator end of the liquid line and the taper of each compressor ring is toward the compressor nut.

➡ The inlet tube will be positioned against the orifice tube tabs when correctly assembled.

9. While holding the hex of the tube in a vise, tighten each compression nut to 65–70 ft. lbs. (88–94 Nm) with a crow foot wrench.
10. Assemble the liquid line to the vehicle using new O-rings lubricated with clean refrigerant oil.
11. Leak test, evacuate and charge the system according to the proper procedure. Observe all safety precautions.
12. Check the system for proper operation.

Cold Engine Lockout Switch

OPERATION

The cold engine lock out switch is used in the automatic temperature control systems. It prevents the air conditioning compressor from running when the engine is cold. The switch is located in the heater core inlet tube in the engine compartment.

REMOVAL & INSTALLATION

➧ SEE FIG. 21

1. Disconnect the negative battery cable.
2. Disconnect the 2 wire connector from the switch.
3. Partially drain the coolant from the radiator.

CAUTION

When draining the coolant, keep in mind that cats and dogs are attracted by the ethylene glycol antifreeze, and are quite likely to drink any that is left in an uncovered container or in puddles on the ground. This will prove fatal in sufficient quantity. Always drain the coolant into a sealable container. Coolant should be reused unless it is contaminated or several years old.

4. Remove the threaded switch from the heater tube.

To install:

5. Apply sealer to the switch threads and install it into the fitting in the heater tube. Tighten to 8–14 ft. lbs. (11–19 Nm).
6. Attach the electrical connector to the top of the switch.
7. Refill the radiator with the removed coolant to the proper level.
8. Connect the negative battery cable.

Ambient Temperature Sensor

OPERATION

The ambient temperature sensor is used in the automatic temperature control systems. It contains a thermistor which measures the temperature of the outside air. The sensor is located in front of the condenser on the left side of the vehicle.

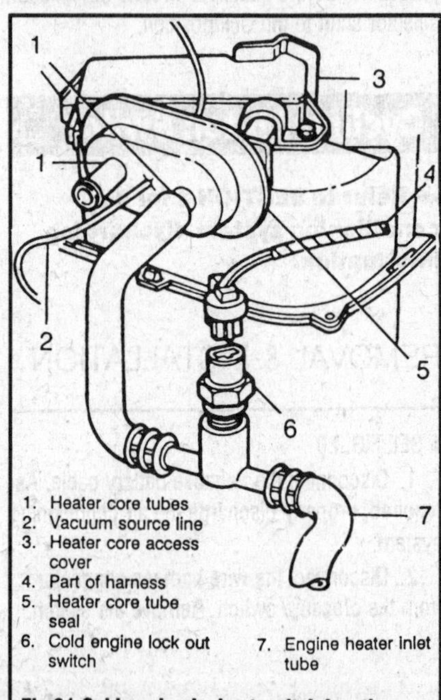

Fig.21 Cold engine lockout switch location

REMOVAL & INSTALLATION

1. Disconnect the negative battery cable.
2. Remove the ambient sensor mounting nut and remove the sensor.
3. Disconnect the electrical connector from the ambient sensor.

To install:

4. Connect the electrical connector to the ambient sensor.
5. Position the ambient sensor and install the mounting nut. Tighten to 55–65 inch lbs. (6.2–7.3 Nm).
6. Connect the negative battery cable and check the system for proper operation.

In Vehicle Temperature Sensor

OPERATION

The in-vehicle temperature sensor is used in the automatic temperature control systems. It contains a thermistor which measures the temperature of the air inside the passenger compartment. The sensor is located behind the instrument panel above the glove compartment.

REMOVAL & INSTALLATION

➧ SEE FIG. 22

1. Disconnect the negative battery cable.
2. Disengage the glove compartment door stops and allow the door to hang by the hinge.
3. Working through the glove compartment opening, unclip the sensor from the retainer by squeezing the side tabs.
4. Pull the sensor down into the glove compartment, then disconnect the electrical connector and aspirator flex hose from the sensor.

To install:

5. Connect the electrical connector and aspirator flex hose to the sensor.
6. Working through the glove compartment opening, attach the sensor to the retaining clip.
7. Engage the glove compartment door stops and close the door.
8. Connect the negative battery cable.

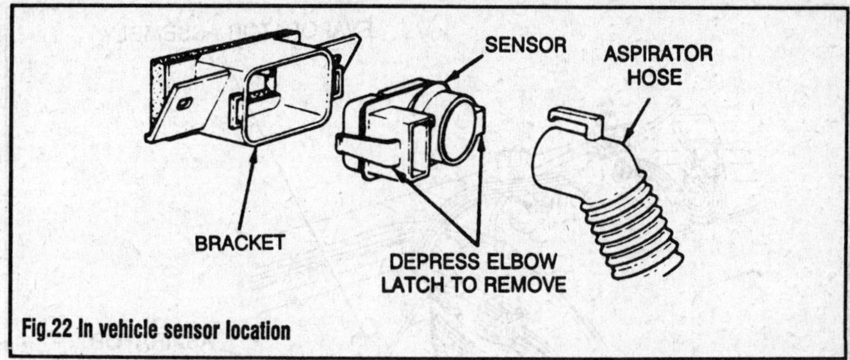

Fig.22 In vehicle sensor location

Sunload Sensor

OPERATION

The sunload sensor is used in the automatic temperature control systems. It contains a photovoltaic (sensitive to sunlight) diode that provides input to the system microcomputer. The sensor is located in the left radio speaker grille assembly except on 1992 vehicles it is located on the right side upper outer finish panel.

REMOVAL & INSTALLATION

1. Disconnect the negative battery cable.
2. Remove the left-hand speaker grille assembly, except 1992 vehicles. On 1992 vehicles remove the right side upper outer finish panel.
3. Remove the sunload sensor assembly from the 2 mounting studs and disconnect the electrical connector.

To install:

4. Connect the electrical connector to the sunload sensor.
5. Install the sensor to the speaker grille by pushing the sensor firmly over the 2 mounting studs.
6. Install the left-hand speaker grille assembly, except 1992 vehicles. On 1992 vehicles install the right side upper outer finish panel.
7. Install the negative battery cable.

Blower Speed Controller

OPERATION

The blower speed controller is used with automatic temperature control. It converts the base current received from the electronic control assembly into high current, variable ground feed to the blower motor. The blower fan speed is therefore infinitely variable. The blower speed controller is located in the evaporator case, upstream of the evaporator core.

REMOVAL & INSTALLATION

➧ SEE FIG. 23

1. Disconnect the negative battery cable.
2. Disengage the glove compartment door stops and allow the door to hang by the hinge.
3. Working through the glove compartment opening, disconnect the electrical snap-lock connector and aspirator hose at the blower motor controller. Also, disconnect the snap-lock connector from it's mounting bracket.
4. Remove the 2 screws attaching the blower controller to the evaporator case and remove the controller. Do not touch the fins of the controller until it has had a sufficient time to cool.

To install:

5. Position the blower controller on the evaporator case and install the 2 attaching screws.
6. Connect the wire connector and aspirator hose to the blower controller. Install the connector on the mounting bracket.
7. Close the glove compartment door, connect the negative battery cable and check the system for proper operation.

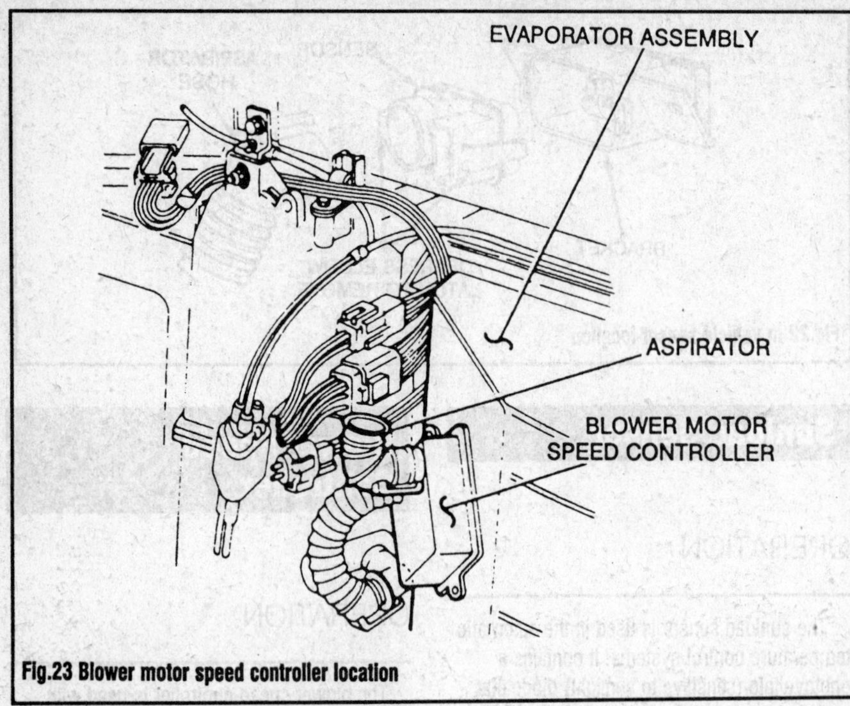

Fig.23 Blower motor speed controller location

Temperature Blend Door Actuator

OPERATION

The temperature blend door actuator is used on vehicles equipped with automatic temperature control. The actuator controls blend door movement on command from the control assembly. The blend door actuator is located on top of the evaporator assembly.

REMOVAL & INSTALLATION

1. Disconnect the negative battery cable.
2. Loosen the instrument panel and pull back from the cowl.
3. Remove the blend door actuator electrical connector and plastic clamp from the bracket on the evaporator case. Remove the 3 actuator attaching screws.
4. Lift the actuator vertically for a distance of approximately 1/2 in. (12mm) to disengage it from the bracket and blend door shaft. Pull the actuator back toward the passenger compartment.

➡ The mounting bracket remains in place on the evaporator case.

To install:

5. Insert the blend door actuator horizontally over the actuator bracket on the evaporator case.
6. Insert the actuator shaft into the blend door. Manually moving the door will help engage the shaft.
7. Attach the actuator bracket with the 3 attaching screws.
8. Attach the actuator electrical connector and plastic clamp to the bracket on the evaporator case.
9. Install the instrument panel and connect the negative battery cable.

➡ After replacement of the blend door actuator, the system must be recalibrated for proper operation. To recalibrate, disconnect the positive battery cable from the battery, wait 30 seconds and reconnect the battery cable. Calibration will be performed automatically when the automatic temperature control electronic control assembly is energized.

Recirculate/Fresh Air Selector Door Actuator Motor

OPERATION

The recirculate/fresh air selector door actuator motor is used on vehicles equipped with automatic temperature control. The motor controls the position of the door which allows fresh air or recirculated air, or a combination of the two, into the vehicle. The motor is mounted on the recirculate/fresh air duct.

REMOVAL & INSTALLATION

1. Lower the glove compartment door to provide access to the recirculation duct assembly.
2. Disconnect the vacuum hose from the end of the vacuum motor and the motor arm retainer from the door crank arm.
3. Remove the 2 nuts retaining the vacuum motor to the recirculation duct and remove the motor.

To install:

4. Position the vacuum motor to the fresh air/recirculate door crank arm, position the motor to the recirculation duct and install the 2 retaining nuts.
5. Install the retainer on the door crank arm.
6. Connect the white vacuum hose to the vacuum motor and check the operation of the vacuum motor.
7. Close the glove compartment door.

Function Control Actuator Motor

OPERATION

The function control actuator motor is used on vehicles equipped with automatic temperature control. The motor controls the door which directs the flow of air to the defroster ducts, instrument panel ducts or floor ducts. Two motors are used to perform the control function and they are both located on the plenum.

REMOVAL & INSTALLATION

Panel/Floor Door Vacuum Motor

1. Disconnect the negative battery cable.
2. Remove the instrument panel.
3. Depress the tabs and disconnect the vacuum motor arm from the door shaft.
4. Remove the 2 screws retaining the vacuum motor to the mounting bracket.
5. Remove the vacuum motor from the mounting bracket and disconnect the vacuum hose.

To install:

6. Position the vacuum motor on the mounting bracket and door shaft.
7. Install the 2 screws attaching the vacuum motor to the mounting bracket.
8. Connect the vacuum hose to the vacuum motor and check the operation of the motor.
9. Install the instrument panel and connect the negative battery cable.

Panel/Defrost Door Vacuum Motor

1. Disconnect the negative battery cable.
2. Remove the instrument panel.
3. Remove the panel-defrost door vacuum motor arm to door shaft.
4. Remove the 2 nuts retaining the vacuum motor to the mounting bracket.
5. Remove the vacuum motor from the mounting bracket and disconnect the vacuum hose.

To install:

6. Position the vacuum motor to the mounting bracket and door shaft.
7. Install the 2 nuts attaching the vacuum motor to the mounting bracket and connect the vacuum hose. Check the operation of the motor.
8. Install the instrument panel and connect the negative battery cable.

AIR CONDITIONING SYSTEM DIAGNOSIS

Automatic Temperature Control System

➧ SEE FIG. 24–37

DIAGNOSTIC PROCEDURE

1. Perform the Self Diagnostic Test. Record all error codes displayed during the test.
2. If error codes appear during the Self Diagnostic Test, follow the diagnostic procedures indicated in the Error Code Key.
3. If a malfunction exists but no error code appears during the Self Diagnostic Test, perform the Functional Test.

SELF DIAGNOSTIC TEST

The control assembly will detect electrical malfunctions occurring during the self test.

1. Make sure the coolant temperature is at least 120°F (49°C).
2. To display error codes, push the OFF and FLOOR buttons simultaneously and then the AUTOMATIC button within 2 seconds. The test may run as long as 20 seconds, during which time the display will be blank. If the display is blank for more than 20 seconds, consult the No Error Code Found Diagnosis and Testing chart.
3. The Self Diagnostic Test can be initiated at any time with the resulting error codes being displayed. Normal operation of the system stops when the Self Diagnostic Test is activated. To exit the self test and restart the system, push the COOLER button. The self test should be deactivated before powering the system down.

FUNCTIONAL TEST

The Functional Test is designed to catch those system failures that the self test is unable to test.

1. Make sure the engine is cold.
2. The in-vehicle temperature should be greater than 50°F (10°C) for proper evaluation of system response.
3. Follow the instructions in each step of the Functional Test.

VACUUM SYSTEM DIAGNOSIS

To test the automatic temperature control vacuum system, start the engine and depress the function buttons slowly from 1 position to another. A momentary hiss should be heard as each button is depressed from 1 position to another, indicating that vacuum is available at the control assembly. A continuous hiss at the control assembly indicates a major leak somewhere in the system. It does not necessarily indicate that the leak is at the control assembly.

If a momentary hiss cannot be heard as each function button is depressed from 1 position to another, check for a kinked, pinched or disconnected vacuum supply hose. Also, inspect the check valve between the vacuum intake manifold and the vacuum reservoir to ensure it is working properly.

If a momentary hiss can be heard as each function button is depressed from 1 position to another, vacuum is available at the control assembly. Cycle the function buttons through each position with the blower on HI and check the location(s) of the discharge air. The airflow schematic and vacuum control chart shows the vacuum motors applied for each function selection along with an airflow diagram of the system. The airflow diagram shows the position of each door when vacuum is applied and their no-vacuum position. With this chart, airflow for each position of the control assembly can be determined. If a vacuum motor fails to operate, the motor can readily be found because the airflow will be incorrect.

If a vacuum motor is inoperative, check the operation of the motor with a vacuum tester. If the vacuum motor operates properly, the vacuum hose is probably kinked, pinched, disconnected or has a leak.

If the function system functions normally at idle, but goes to defrost during acceleration, a small leak exists in the system. The leak can best be located by shutting **OFF** the engine and using a gauge to check for vacuum loss while selectively blocking off vacuum hoses.

ATC CONTROL ERROR CODE KEY

ERROR CODE KEY

Error Code	Detected Condition	Troubleshooting/Repair Procedure
01	Replace control head	
02	Blend door problem	• Refer to Blend Door Actuator Diagnosis
03	In-car temp sensor open or short	• Refer to In-Car Temp Sensor Diagnosis
04	Ambient temp sensor open or short	• Refer to Ambient Temp Sensor Diagnosis
05	Sunload sensor short	• Refer to Sunload Sensor Diagnosis
888	Testing complete — no test failure (all segments on)	• Refer to EATC System Functional Check

	TEST STEP	RESULT	ACTION TO TAKE
1	Turn ignition switch to the RUN position. Press the AUTO button. Set control at 90°F setting.	Control powers up	GO to 2.
		Control does not light	REFER to Diagnosis When Self-Test And Functional Test Indicate No Errors Found.
2	Verify that the blower does not come on. (Engine coolant temp. < 120°F)	Blower off	GO to 3.
		Blower on	REFER to CELO Inoperative.
3	Ensure that engine is warm (coolant temp. > 120°F). Set control at 75 setting.	Blower on	GO to 4.
		Blower off	REFER to Blower Speed Controller Diagnosis-No Blower.
4	Rotate blower thumbwheel fully down.	Blower goes to low blower	GO to 5.
			CHECK battery voltage. If voltage is below 10 volts, refer to Charging System Diagnosis.
		Blower does not go to low blower	REFER to Blower Speed Controller Diagnosis.
5	Rotate blower thumbwheel fully up.	Blower goes to high blower	GO to 6.
		Blower does not go to high blower	REFER to Blower Speed Controller Diagnosis.
6	Press the DEFROST button.	Verify that air is discharged from defroster nozzle with small bleed through the side window demistors. Verify that the outside air/recirc door is in the outside air position.	GO to 7.
		Air is not discharged through the defroster or side window demistors.	REFER to Vacuum System Diagnosis.

ATC FUNCTIONAL TEST

	TEST STEP	RESULT	ACTION TO TAKE
7	Press the FLOOR button.	Verify that the air is discharged through the floor ducts.	GO to 8.
		Air is not discharged through the floor ducts.	REFER to Vacuum System Diagnosis.
8	Press the VENT button.	Verify that the air is discharged through the panel ducts.	GO to 9.
		Air is not discharged through the panel ducts.	REFER to Vacuum System Diagnosis.
9	Make sure that the ambient temperature is greater than 40°F. Press the MAX A/C button.	Verify that the outside air/recirc door is in the recirc position.	GO to 10.
		Outside air/Recirc door is not in the recirc position.	REFER to Vacuum System Diagnosis.
10	Press the VENT button.	Verify that the VENT display is lit. Verify that the clutch is off.	GO to 11.
		A/C clutch is still on.	REFER to Clutch Does Not Disengage When In OFF Diagnosis.
11	Press the MAX A/C button again.	Verify that the MAX A/C display is lit and that the clutch is on.	GO to 12.
		A/C clutch is off.	REFER to No Clutch Operation Diagnosis.
12	Press the AUTO button.	Verify that the AUTO display is lit.	REFER to Diagnosis When Self-Test And Functional Test Indicate No Errors Found.

ATC NO ERROR CODE FOUND DIAGNOSIS AND TESTING

CONDITION	POSSIBLE SOURCE	ACTION
• Cool Discharge Air When System is Set to Auto/90°F	• Heater system malfunction. • Blend door not in max. heat.	• REFER to heater system operating principles • CHECK position of blend door. • CHECK coolant level. • CHECK shaft attachment. • TEST per Blend Door Actuator Diagnosis (assume 2 was displayed in the Self-Test).
• Warm Discharge Air in Auto/60°F	• Clutch circuit malfunction. • Check refrigerant. • Blend door not in max. A/C position. • Outside/Recirc door not in recirc.	• TEST clutch circuit per No Clutch Operation Diagnosis. • REFER to Section 36-32. • CHECK position of blend door. • CHECK shaft attachment. • TEST per Blend Door Actuator Diagnosis (assume 2 was displayed in the Self-Test). • TEST per Vacuum System Diagnosis.
• Cool Air in 85°F, Max. Heat in 90°F • Heat in 65°F Max. Cool in 60°F	• Sensor shorted. • Sensor open.	• TROUBLESHOOT according to Sensor Diagnosis. • TROUBLESHOOT according to Sensor Diagnosis.
• No Blower	• Damaged CELO switch/wiring. • Damaged blower controller. • Damaged control head. • Damaged blower motor. • Damaged wiring.	• TEST per No Blower Section of Blower Speed Controller.
• High Blower Only	• Damaged control head. • Damaged blower controller. • Damaged wiring.	• TEST per High Blower Only Section of Blower Speed Controller.
• Clutch is On in Off Mode	• Damaged control head. • Damaged wiring or interface components.	• TEST according to "Clutch does not Disengage when in OFF mode".

CONDITION	POSSIBLE SOURCE	ACTION
• Control Assembly Digits and VFD Do Not Light Up Blower Off	• Fuse. • Ignition Circuit No. 298 open. • Ignition Circuit No. 797 open. • Ground Circuit No. 57A open. • Damaged control head.	• Replace fuse. • Check Circuit No. 298. • Check Circuit No. 797. • Check Circuit No. 57A. • Change control assembly.
• Cold Air is Delivered During Heating when Engine is Cold.	• Damaged wiring. • Damaged or inoperative engine temperature switch.	• Place system at 90°F/Auto. With ignition off, (ignition must be off when grounding Circuit No. 244 for valid results) ground Circuit No. 244 at engine temp. switch. Start vehicle. If blower is off, replace cold engine lockout (CELO). If blower is on, check wiring. If OK, replace control assembly. • Replace engine temperature switch.
• Temperature Set Point Does Not Repeat After Turning Off Ignition	• Circuit No. 797 not connected to control head. • Damaged or inoperative control assembly.	• Remove control assembly connector. With ignition off, check for 12 volts at Pin 12 (Driver's side connector VA). • If no voltage, check fuse/wiring. If voltage, replace control head.
• Control Head Temperature Display Will Not Switch From Fahrenheit To Centigrade When the E/M Trip Computer Button is Pushed	• Damaged or inoperative wiring, trip minder or control head.	• **CAUTION: ACCIDENTAL SHORTING OF THE WRONG PIN COULD DESTROY THE CONTROL HEAD.** Short Pin 20 of connector VA (Circuit No. 506) to ground. Turn on ignition. If the display does not switch from F to C, Circuit No. 506 is open at the control assembly and the control assembly is damaged. Otherwise check the wiring and the trip minder.
• System Does Not Control Temperature	• Sensor hose not connected to aspirator or sensor. • Aspirator not secured to evaporator case. • Sensor seal(s) missing or not installed properly. • Aspirator or sensor hose blocked with foreign material or kinked. • Damaged aspirator hose.	• Inspect and service. • Inspect and service. • Inspect and service. • Inspect and service. • Inspect and service.
• EATC Control Head Turns On and Off Erratically. No Control of System.	• Damaged charging system. EATC will not function with too low or too high battery voltage.	• Check battery voltage. If battery voltage is less than 10 volts or greater than 16 volts, refer to charging system diagnosis. Do not replace EATC control head.

ATC IN VEHICLE TEMPERATURE SENSOR DIAGNOSIS AND TESTING

CONDITION	POSSIBLE SOURCE	ACTION
• Self-Diagnostics Error Code 03 (Warm Air Discharge at 65°F or Cool Air Discharge at 85°F)	1. Sensor open or shorted.	• Disconnect wire harness connector at sensor. Measure resistance across sensor terminals and compare with Sensor Resistance Table below. • If resistance is out of specifications shown in Table, replace sensor. If sensor is okay, go to Step 2.
	2. Wire harness open or shorted.	• Disconnect battery cables. Disconnect wire harness connector from sensor and disconnect both connectors from control head. • Check for continuity and for possible shorting between the two wires (pin 2 and pin 17). Repair if necessary. Reconnect wire harness and battery cables.

SENSOR RESISTANCE TABLE

APPROXIMATE TEMPERATURE	SENSOR RESISTANCE ACCEPTABLE RANGE
10°C to 20°C (50°F to 68°F)	37K to 58K ohms
20°C to 30°C (68°F to 86°F)	24K to 37K ohms
30°C to 40°C (86°F to 104°F)	16K to 24K ohms

ATC AMBIENT SENSOR DIAGNOSIS AND TESTING

CONDITION	POSSIBLE SOURCE	ACTION
• Self-Diagnostics Error Code 04 and Outside Temperature Display is Reading −40°F or 140°F (Warm Air Discharge at 65°F or Cool Air Discharge at 85°F)	1. Sensor open or shorted.	• Disconnect battery cables (this is necessary to reset outside temperature display memory). Disconnect the wire harness connector at sensor. Measure resistance across sensor terminal and compare with Sensor Resistance Table in In-Car Temperature Sensor Diagnosis Chart. • If resistance is out of specifications shown in Sensor Resistance Table, replace sensor. If sensor is okay, go to Step 2. Reconnect battery cables. NOTE: Install sensor and electrical connections before battery is reconnected.
• Intermittent Heating and Cooling. Outside Temperature Display Sometimes Inaccurate	2. Sensor wire harness open or shorted.	• Disconnect battery cables. Disconnect wire harness connector from sensor and disconnect both connectors from the control head. • Inspect for crimped terminals. • Check for continuity and for possible shorting between the two wires (pins 1 and 2). Service if necessary. Reconnect wire harness and battery cables.

ATC AMBIENT SENSOR DIAGNOSIS AND TESTING

CONDITION	POSSIBLE SOURCE	ACTION
• Self-Diagnostics Error Code 05	1. Sensor shorted.	• Disconnect battery cables. Disconnect wire harness connector at sensor and disconnect both connectors from control head.* Check for continuity and for possible shorting between the two wires (pin 3 and pin 16). Repeat if necessary. Reconnect battery cables.

* NOTE: Check the sensor for a short using an ohmmeter. Since the sensor is a Photodiode, there should be some unspecified resistance across the terminals dependent upon the available light in the area. The only test that should be made is for a short circuit (zero resistance). If resistance is zero ohms, replace the sensor.

ATC NO CLUTCH DIAGNOSIS AND TESTING

	TEST STEP	RESULT	ACTION TO TAKE
A	Jump the LB/PK and LG/P wires Pin 26 and Pin 25 of driver side connector VA.	Clutch engages ▶	REPLACE control assembly.
		Clutch does not engage ▶	(Damaged wiring, integrated controller or EEC-IV module, damaged pressure switch.)
		15A fuse blows ▶	Clutch is shorted. CHECK diode in wiring harness across clutch in particular. Service short, then test to see if the control head will turn the clutch off and on. If not, replace control assembly.

ATC CLUTCH DOES NOT ENGAGE IN "OFF" POSITION DIAGNOSIS AND TESTING

	TEST STEP	RESULT	▶	ACTION TO TAKE
A	Disconnect connector VA (driver's side) from control assembly.	Clutch disengages	▶	CHANGE control assembly.
		Clutch stays on	▶	(Faulty wiring, faulty integrated controller or EEC-IV module, faulty pressure switch.)

ATC NO BLOWER, IGNITION IN "RUN", AUTO FUNCTION AT 90° DIAGNOSIS AND TESTING

	TEST STEP (CELO TEST)	RESULT	▶	ACTION TO TAKE
A	Change temp. setting to 60° Auto.	Blower On	▶	GO to B.
		No blower	▶	GO to C.
B	Disconnect cold engine lockout (CELO) switch and change temp. to 90° setting Auto.	Blower On	▶	Faulty CELO switch.
		No blower	▶	CELO wire grounded.
C	Connect voltmeter between BSC ignition Pin 3 and ground Pin 4.	0 volts	▶	CHECK V ignition circuit fuse, continuity in wiring.
		More than 10 volts	▶	GO to D.
D	Connect voltmeter between BSC input Pin 2 and ground Pin 4.	Fluctuating voltage less than 3 volts	▶	GO to E.
		More than 3 volts	▶	GO to F.
E	Connect voltmeter between BSC output Pin 1 and ground Pin 4.	Less than 1 volt	▶	Damaged motor, B+ feed to motor.
		More than 1 volt	▶	REPLACE BSC.
F	Connect voltmeter between control head Pin 23 and Pin 24.	More than 3 volts	▶	REPLACE control assembly.
		Less than 3 volts	▶	CHECK circuit continuity.

ATC BLOWER HIGH, NO AUTO FUNCTION, THUMBWHEEL TO LOW POSITION DIAGNOSIS AND TESTING

	TEST STEP (Voltmeter Connections)	RESULT	ACTION TO TAKE
A	Disconnect HBR and BSC electronic connections.	Blower in high	Faulty blower motor or blower wire circuit.
		Blower OFF	GO to B.
B	Reconnect BSC and connect voltmeter between BSC input Pin 2 and ground Pin 4 (auto function). Rotate blower switch from high to low blower.	Less than 7 volts fluctuating	REPLACE control assembly.
		More than 7 volts fluctuating	REPLACE BSC.

ATC BLOWER OPERATES BUT DOES NOT VARY DIAGNOSIS AND TESTING

	TEST STEP (Voltmeter Connection)	RESULT	ACTION TO TAKE
A	Connect voltmeter between BSC input Pin 2 and ground Pin 4 (Auto mode). Rotate blower switch from min. to max. then back to min.	Voltage fluctuation from below 7 volts to above 7 volts then back below 7 volts	GO to B.
		No change in voltage	Replace control head assy.
B	Connect voltmeter between BSC output Pin 1 and ground Pin 4 (Auto mode). Rotate blower switch from min. to max.	Voltage changes from less than 1 volt to 7 volts	Faulty blower motor, or B+ feed to motor.
		No change in voltage	Replace BSC.

ATC COLD ENGINE LOCKOUT INOPERATIVE DIAGNOSIS AND TESTING

	TEST STEP	RESULT	ACTION TO TAKE
A	Cold engine (engine coolant temp. below 120°) control set at auto 90°.	Blower on ▶	CHECK coolant and retest. If blower turns on again with a cold engine, REPLACE CELO.
		Blower off ▶	CELO OK.

ATC BLEND DOOR ACTUATOR DIAGNOSIS AND TESTING

	TEST STEP	RESULT	ACTION TO TAKE
	Letters in parentheses indicate (wire color, circuit no.). See Fig. 11 for wiring schematic and connector pin diagrams.		
A	Check error code during EATC functional test.	02 Any other number ▶	GO to B. REVIEW error code key
B	Disconnect both connectors from EATC control head and drive actuator in both directions using any 9-12 volt battery. The following pins can be jumped to utilize the vehicle battery. Insure the ignition is in the RUN position. All pins are located on the LEFT connector (E6DB-14489-VA). Trial 1: Pin 24 (BK, 57) to Pin 22 (DB/LG, 249) Trial 2: Pin 24 (BK, 57) to Pin 21 (0,250)	Actuator drives both directions ▶ Actuator does not drive both directions ▶	GO to C. GO to F.
C	Reconnect control head and test according to EATC functional test.	Test successful Test fails ▶	Done GO to D.
D	Disconnect both connectors from EATC control assembly. Measure resistance as shown below at the control assembly connector with the connector disconnected. All pins are located on the RIGHT connector (E6DB-14489-UA). Pin 15 (LG/O, 243) to Pin 6 (O/BK, 776) 5000-7000 ohms Pin 5 (O/W, 351) to Pin 6 (O/BK, 776) 300-7300 ohms Pin 5 (O/W, 351) to Pin 15 (LG/O, 243) 300-7300 ohms	All resistances OK ▶ Any resistance not OK ▶	GO to E. GO to F.
E	Change control head and test according to EATC functional test.	Test successful Test fails ▶	Done GO to A.
F	Check vehicle wiring harness and connector continuity as shown below. Disconnect connectors from both control assembly and blend door actuator. Blend door actuator connector is accessible through glove compartment. PIN — COLOR/CIRCUIT — FUNCTION 1 (DB/LG, 249) Motor CCW 2 (LG/O, 243) Feedback Pot. (−) 3 (O/W, 351) Feedback Pot. (Wiper) 4 (O/BK, 776) Feedback Pot. (+) 5 (O, 250) Motor CW 6 (BK, 57) Ground 7 — No Connection 8 (LB/PK, 295) Voltage In Reconnect all three connectors at end of this test.	Continuity bad ▶ Continuity good ▶	GO to H. GO to G.
G	Change blend door actuator and test according to EATC functional test.	Test successful Test fails ▶	Done GO to A.
H	Fix/replace wiring harness, connect and test according to EATC functional test.	Test successful Test fails ▶	Done GO to A.

CRUISE CONTROL

General Description And Operation

The Integrated Vehicle Speed Control (IVSC) system consists of operator controls, servo (throttle actuator), stoplamp switch, speed sensor (not required for vehicle with electronic cluster), horn relay, vacuum dump valve, vacuum reservoir (called an aspirator on some models), check valve(s), wiring and hoses for vacuum. The vacuum reservoir or aspirator provides an additional vacuum signal when the engine is under heavy load to improve speed control performance. In the IVSC system, speed control amplifier assembly function has been integrated into the EEC-IV Electronic Control Assembly (ECA). The servo assembly is mounted in the engine compartment (on Mark VII, left hand hinge pillar) and is connected to the throttle linkage with an actuator cable. The servo is connected to the vacuum reservoir (aspirator) and to manifold vacuum through the check valve. The speed control sensor is located on the transmission or transaxle.

For the system to be activated, the engine must be running and the vehicle must be greater than a predetermined speed (25 mph (40 km/h) — IVSC except 2.5L engine, 35 mph (56 km/h) — 2.5L engine and 30 mph (48 km/h) for all others). Under these conditions, the system is activated and is ready to accept a set speed signal by pressing the ON switch in the steering wheel. Then, the operator must depress and release the SET ACCEL switch. This will result in the current speed being maintained until a new speed is set by the operator, the brake pedal is depressed, the clutch pedal is depressed or the OFF switch is depressed.

To decrease the set speed, the vehicle speed may by reduced by applying the brake or clutch pedal and then resetting the speed using the foregoing method or by depressing the COAST switch. When the vehicle has slowed to the desired speed, the COAST switch is released and the new speed is set automatically. If the vehicle speed is reduced below a predetermined speed (25 mph (40 km/h) — IVSC except 2.5L engine, 35 mph (56 km/h) — 2.5L engine and 30 mph (48 km/h) for all others), the operator must manually increase the speed and reset the system.

To increase the set speed, the vehicle set speed may be manually increased at any time by depressing the accelerator until the higher speed is reached and stabilized, then depressing and releasing the SET ACCEL button. Speed may also be increased by depressing the SET ACCEL switch button, at speeds over a predetermined speed (25 mph (40 km/h) — IVSC except 2.5L engine, 35 mph (56 km/h) — 2.5L engine and 30 mph (48 km/h) for all others), and holding it in that position. The vehicle will then automatically increase speed. When the desired rate of speed is attained and the button is released, that new set speed will be maintained.

The speed control system may be deactivated by depressing the brake or clutch pedal. To resume the set speed prior to deactivation, the RESUME switch is depressed and prior set speed may be re-established. The RESUME switch is hinged on the side closest to the SET ACCEL switch. Therefore, it should be depressed on the side farthest from the SET ACCEL switch. The resume feature will not function if the system is deactivated with the OFF switch, or if the vehicle speed has been reduced to below a predetermined speed (25 mph (40 km/h) — IVSC except 2.5L engine, 35 mph (56 km/h) — 2.5L engine and 30 mph (48 km/h) for all others). In addition, when the ignition switch is turned **OFF**, the speed control memory is erased and the resume feature will not function.

Actuator Cable

REMOVAL & INSTALLATION

➧ SEE FIG. 38–41

1. Remove the servo assembly.
2. Attach the new actuator cable assembly to the servo.
3. Install the complete assembly.

ADJUSTMENT

1. Remove speed control cable retaining clip.
2. Push speed control cable through adjuster until a slight tension is felt.
3. Insert the cable retaining clip and snap into place.

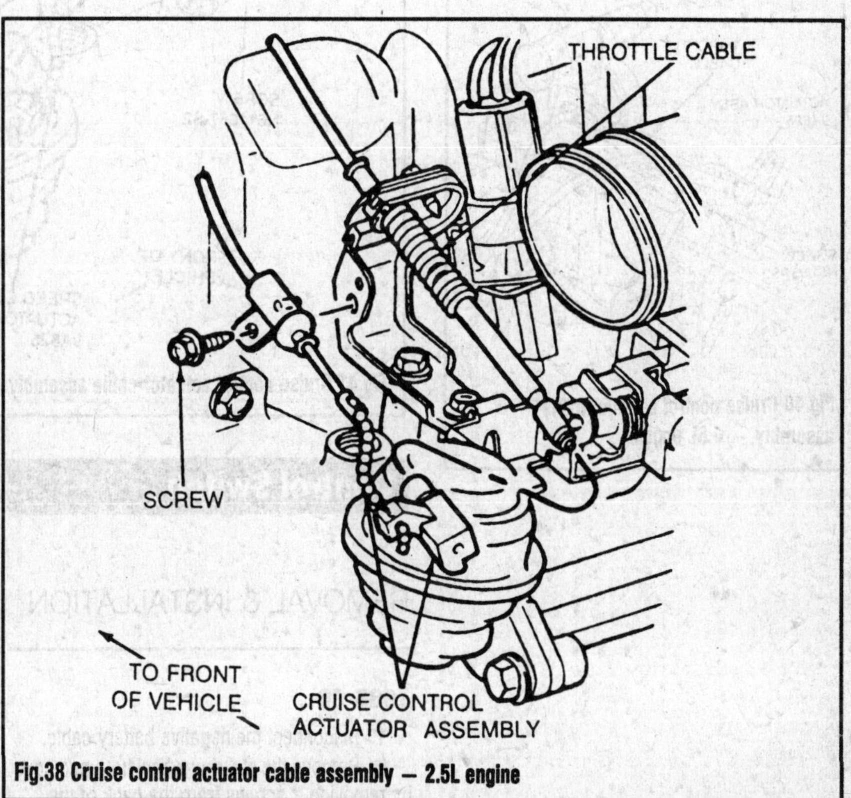

Fig.38 Cruise control actuator cable assembly — 2.5L engine

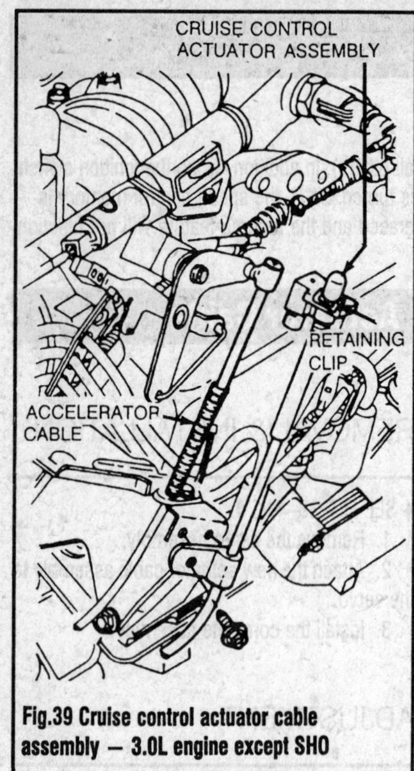

Fig.39 Cruise control actuator cable assembly — 3.0L engine except SHO

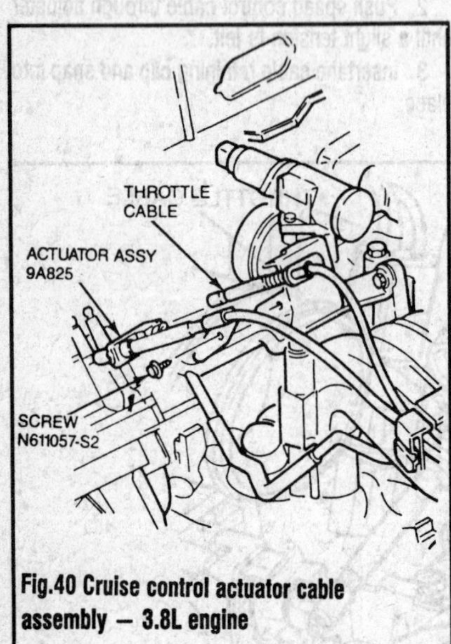

Fig.40 Cruise control actuator cable assembly — 3.8L engine

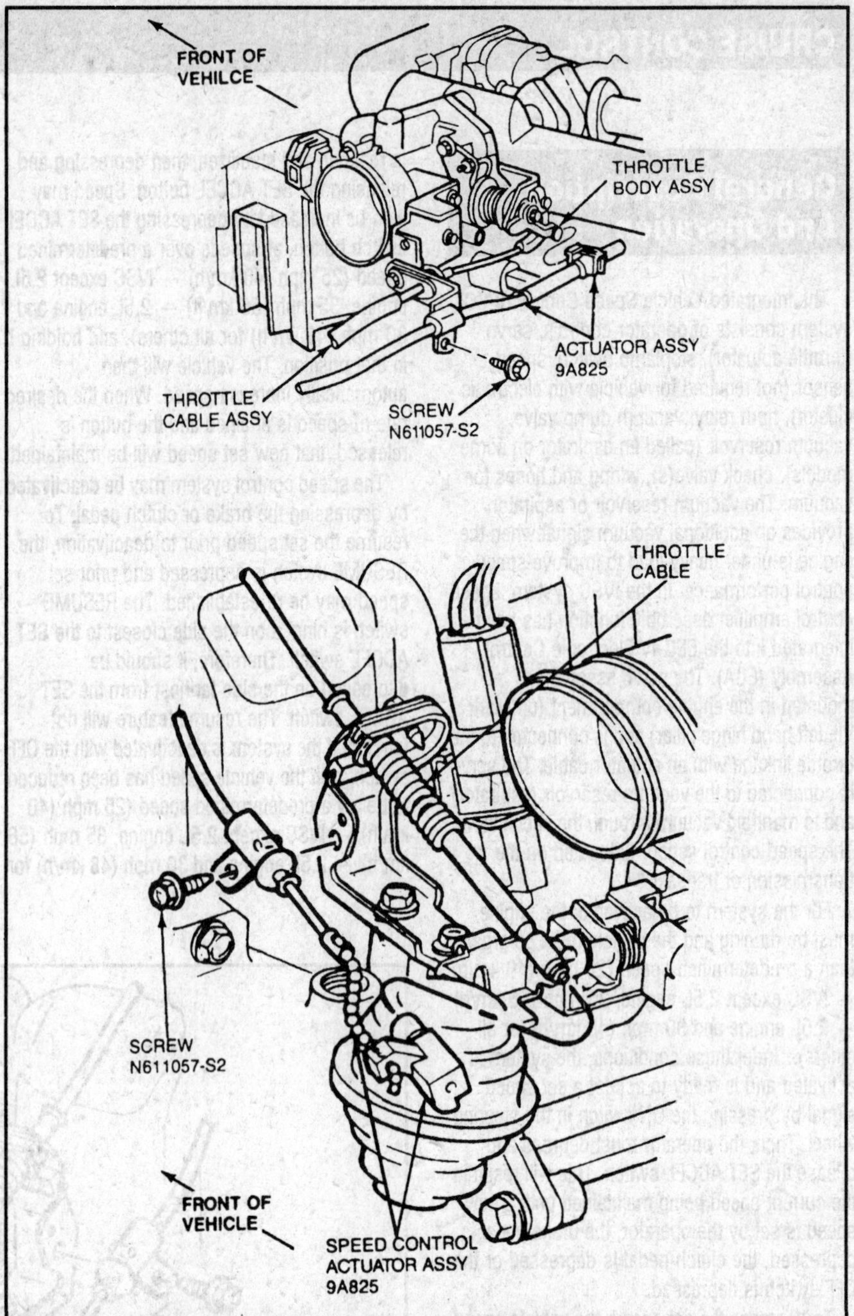

Fig.41 Cruise control actuator cable assembly — 3.0L SHO engine

Control Switch

REMOVAL & INSTALLATION

1986–90

1. Disconnect the negative battery cable.
2. Remove the steering wheel horn pad cover by removing 2 screws from the back of the steering wheel.
3. Disconnect the wiring connector from the slip ring terminal.
4. Remove the speed control switch assembly from the horn pad cover by removing the 2 attaching screws from each switch.

To install:

5. Install the control switches into the horn pad cover. Attach each switch with 2 screws.
6. Attach the control switch connector to the terminal on the slip ring.
7. Install the steering wheel horn pad cover. Snap latching hook in at the 12 o'clock position. Attach with 2 screws.

1990–92

CAUTION

Some vehicles are equipped with an inflatable restraint or air bag system. The air bag system must be disabled before performing service on or around the air bag or instrument panel components or wiring. Failure to follow safety and disabling procedures could result in possible air bag deployment, personal injury or un-necessary air bag system repairs.

1. Disconnect the negative battery cable and air bag back up power supply.
2. Remove the 4 nuts retaining the air bag module to the steering wheel.
3. Disconnect the air bag electrical connector from the clockspring contact connector.
4. Remove the air bag module from the steering wheel. Place the module on the work bench with the trim cover facing upward.
5. Remove the horn buttons from the steering wheel and disconnect the electrical connectors.
6. Remove the screws from the speed control switch assemblies.
7. Disconnect the speed control switches from the wiring harness and remove the switches.

To install:

8. Position the switches onto the steering wheel and install the retaining screws.
9. Connect the wiring harness to the horn buttons and install the horn buttons.
10. Connect the speed control switches. Ensure the wires are positioned so that not interference is encountered when installing the air bag module.
11. Position the air bag module on the steering wheel so that the clockspring contact connector can be connected to the air bag module.
12. Install the air bag module on the steering wheel and install the 4 nuts behind the steering wheel.
13. Connect negative battery cable and the air bag back up power supply.

TESTING

1. Check to see that main fuse and stop lamp fuse are good. If so, disconnect 6-way connector at amplifier assembly.
2. Connect a voltmeter between light blue/black wire and ground. Depress ON button and check for battery voltage.
3. Connect an ohmmeter between light blue/black wire and ground.
4. Rotate steering wheel through its full range and make the following checks:
   a. Depress OFF button and check for a reading between 0–1Ω.
   b. Depress SET/ACCEL button and check for a reading between 714–646Ω.
   c. Depress COAST button and check for a reading between 126–114Ω.
   d. Depress RESUME button and check for a reading between 2090–2310Ω.
5. If the resistance values are not as indicated, but ohmmeter fluctuates, remove the steering wheel and clean brushes and slip ring surface. Apply slip ring grease E1AZ–19590–A or equivalent, equally on ring, approximately 0.02 in. (0.5mm) thick.
6. If the resistance values are greater than those specified above, check switch assemblies and ground circuit.
7. Reconnect the 6–way connector at amplifier.

Ground Brush

REMOVAL & INSTALLATION

1986–89

1. Disconnect the negative battery cable.
2. Remove the steering wheel hub horn pad cover by removing the 2 screws from the back of the steering wheel.
3. Remove and discard the steering wheel attaching bolt.
4. Remove the steering wheel from the upper shaft by grasping the rim of the steering wheel and pulling it off. Do not use a steering wheel puller.
5. Remove the tilt lever, if so equipped.
6. Remove the ignition lock cylinder and steering column lower trim shroud.
7. Separate the speed control brush wire harness at the connector and remove the wire harness retainers from the steering column.
8. Remove the screw securing the brush assembly to the upper steering column.

To install:

9. Position the brush assembly housing on the upper steering column and secure with 1 screw.
10. Install the wire harness into the steering column with the attached retainers. Connect the harness to the main wiring harness.
11. Attach the lower trim shroud to the upper shroud with 3 retaining screws.
12. Install the ignition lock cylinder and tilt lever, if equipped.
13. Position the steering wheel on the end of the steering wheel shaft. Align the index mark on the wheel with the index mark on the shaft.
14. Install a new steering wheel bolt. Tighten to 23–33 ft. lbs. (31–45 Nm).
15. Install the steering wheel horn pad.

1990–92

1. Set the steering wheel in the straight ahead position.
2. Disconnect the negative battery cable.
3. Remove the 4 nut and washer assemblies retaining the air bag module to the steering wheel.
4. Disconnect the air bag electrical connector from the clockspring contact connector.
5. Remove the air bag module from the steering wheel.

CAUTION

Place the air bag module on the bench with the trim cover facing up to prevent personal injury in the event of accidental deployment of the air bag.

6. Disconnect the speed control switches and horn switches from the contact assembly.
7. Remove the steering wheel retaining bolt.
8. Remove the steering wheel using a suitable puller.
9. If equipped, remove the tilt lever.
10. Remove the lower trim panel and lower steering column shroud.
11. Disconnect the contact assembly wiring harness.
12. Apply 2 pieces of tape across the contact assembly stator and rotor to prevent accidental rotation.
13. Remove the 3 contact assembly retaining screws and lift the contact assembly off the steering column shaft.
14. Disconnect the speed control brush wiring harness at the connector and remove the wiring harness retainers from the steering column.
15. Remove the screw retaining brush assembly to the upper steering column. Remove the brush and harness assembly.

To install:

16. Position the brush assembly wire on the

upper steering column and install the retaining screw. Tighten to 18–26 inch lbs. (2–3 Nm).

17. Install the wiring harness retainer into the steering column and connect the harness to the main wiring.

18. Align the contact assembly to the column shaft and mounting bosses and slide the contact assembly onto the shaft.

19. Install the 3 screws that retain the contact assembly and tighten to 18–26 inch lbs. (2–3 Nm). Remove the tape from the contact assembly.

20. Route the contact assembly harness down the column and connect to the main wiring harness.

➡ If installing a new contact assembly, remove the lock mechanism.

21. Install the steering column shroud.

22. Install the lower trim panel.

23. If equipped, install the tilt lever.

24. Position the steering wheel on the steering shaft and install a new steering wheel retaining bolt. Tighten to 23–33 ft. lbs. (31–45 Nm).

25. Connect the speed control and horn switches to the contact assembly.

26. Position the air bag module on the steering wheel so that the clockspring contact connector can be connected to the air bag module.

27. Install the air bag module on the steering wheel and install the 4 nut and washer assemblies.

28. Connect negative battery cable.

Speed Sensor

REMOVAL & INSTALLATION

➧ SEE FIG. 49–50

1. Raise and safely support the vehicle. Remove the mounting clip.

2. On 1992 vehicles equipped with an automatic transaxle remove the Y-pipe and HEGO sensors from the exhaust system. Remove the speed sensor exhaust heat shield.

3. Loosen the retaining nut holding the sensor in the transaxle. Remove the driven gear with the sensor from the transaxle.

4. Disconnect the electrical connector from the speed sensor.

5. Disconnect the speedometer cable by pulling it out of the speed sensor.

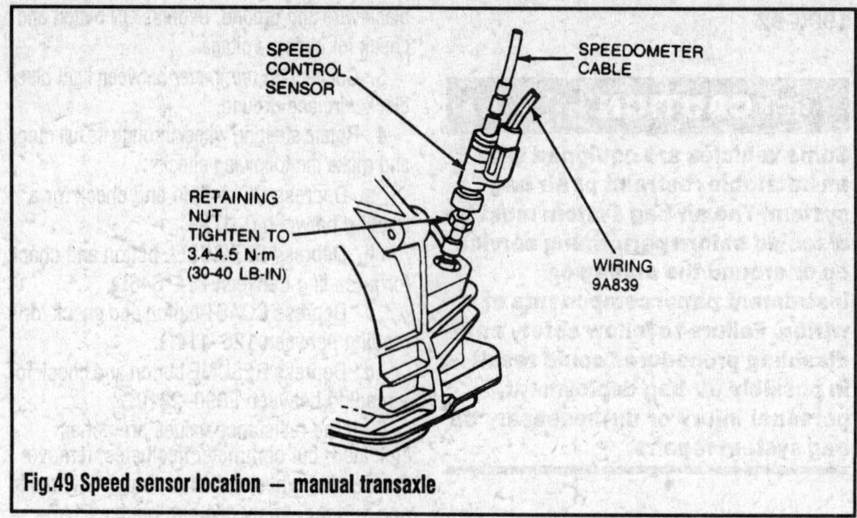

Fig.49 Speed sensor location — manual transaxle

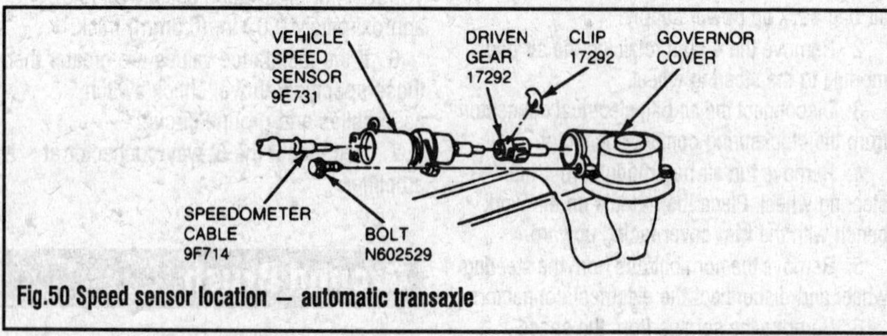

Fig.50 Speed sensor location — automatic transaxle

➡ Do not attempt to remove the spring retainer clip with the speedometer cable in the sensor.

To install:

6. Position the driven gear to the speed sensor. Install the gear retainer.

7. Connect the electrical connector.

8. Ensure the internal O-ring is properly seated in the sensor housing. Snap the speedometer cable into the sensor housing.

9. Insert the sensor assembly into the transaxle housing. Tighten the retaining nut. Install the retaining clip.

10. On 1992 vehicles equipped with an automatic transaxle install the Y-pipe and HEGO sensors to the exhaust system. Install the speed sensor exhaust heat shield.

11. Lower the vehicle.

TESTING

Without Electronic Instrument Cluster

1. Disconnect connector at speed sensor and connect an ohmmeter between wire connector terminals and speed sensor end. Reading should be 200–300Ω.

➡ A reading of 0Ω indicates a shorted coil and the speed sensor should be replaced. A maximum reading indicates an open coil and speed sensor should be replaced.

2. If the ohmmeter reading is between 200–300Ω, and speedometer operates properly within needle waver, speed sensor is probably functioning properly.

3. If available, a known good quality speed sensor can also be substituted in place of existing sensor to check for proper operation.

With Electronic Instrument Cluster

➡ Because AC and DC voltage measurements are required in the diagnosis of the speed control system on vehicles equipped with an electronic instrument cluster, a special diagnostic tool, Fluke 8022A or equivalent should be used. Do not perform speed senor test on vehicles with electronic speedometer.

1. Raise and safely support the vehicle drive wheels.

2. Bring vehicle speed to approximately 30 mph (48 km/h).

3. Connect an AC voltmeter to dark green/white wire and ground.

4. Back probe the amplifier connector. Voltmeter should read about 6–24 volts. If not, check speed sensor and related wiring. Repair and/or replace as necessary.

5. Lower the vehicle.

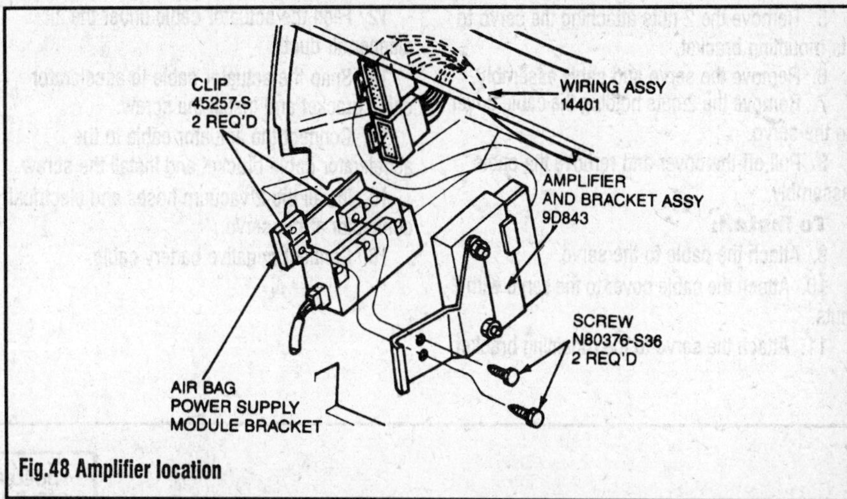

Fig.48 Amplifier location

Amplifier

REMOVAL & INSTALLATION

On Integrated Vehicle Speed Control (IVSC) equipped vehicles, the amplifier assembly has been incorporated into the EEC-IV system Electronic Control Assembly (ECA).

Non-IVSC Vehicles

➧ SEE FIG. 48

1. Disconnect the negative battery cable.
2. Remove the amplifier assembly mounting hardware.
3. Remove the 2 amplifier assembly electrical connectors.
4. Remove the amplifier assembly.

To install:

5. Place the amplifier assembly into position and connect the electrical connectors.
6. Install the amplifier assembly mounting hardware.
7. Connect negative battery cable.

TESTING

➡ Do not use a test lamp to perform the amplifier tests as excessive current draw will damage electronic components inside the amplifier. Use a voltmeter of 5000 ohm/volt rating or higher.

ON Circuit

1. With ignition in **RUN**, connect a voltmeter between white/pink wire and black wire (ground) in the 6-way connector at the amplifier. Voltmeter should read battery voltage.

2. Connect the voltmeter between light blue/black wire and black wire (ground) in the 6-way connector at the amplifier. Voltmeter should read battery voltage only when ON switch in steering wheel is depressed and held. If voltage is not present, perform control switch test.

3. Release ON button, voltmeter should read about 7.8 volts, this indicates that ON circuit is engaged. If voltmeter reads 0.0, check for a bad ground at amplifier.

4. If there is no ground at amplifier, check system ground connections and wiring. Also check fuse.

5. If available, substitute a known good amplifier and check for proper circuit operation.

Brake Circuit

1. Connect an ohmmeter between red/light green wire on 6-way connector and ground. Resistance should be less than 5Ω.

2. If resistance is greater than indicated, check for improper wiring, burned out stop lamp lights or clutch malfunction, if equipped.

OFF Circuit

1. With ignition in **RUN**, connect voltmeter between light blue/black wire of 6-way amplifier connector and ground. Depress OFF switch on steering wheel. Voltage on light blue/black wire should drop to 0 which indicates that ON circuit is not energized.

2. If voltage does not drop to 0, perform the control switch test. If control switch checks out good, install a good amplifier and recheck OFF circuit.

SET/ACCEL Circuit

1. With ignition in **RUN**, connect voltmeter between light blue/black of 6-way amplifier connector and black wire (ground). Depress and hold SET/ACCEL button on steering wheel. Voltmeter should read about 4.5 volts.

2. Rotate steering wheel back and forth and watch voltmeter for fluctuations.

3. If voltage varies more than 0.5 volts, perform control switch test.

COAST Circuit

1. With ignition in **RUN**, connect voltmeter between light blue/black of 6-way amplifier connector and ground. Depress and hold COAST button on steering wheel. Voltmeter should read about 1.5 volts.

2. If circuit checks out good, perform servo assembly test. If servo test checks out good, install a new amplifier and repeat tests. Do not substitute amplifier until after performing servo assembly test.

RESUME Circuit

1. With ignition in **RUN**, connect voltmeter between light blue/black of 6-way amplifier connector and ground. Depress and hold RESUME button on steering wheel. Voltmeter should read about 6.5 volts.

2. If circuit checks out good, perform servo assembly test. If servo test checks out good, install a new amplifier and repeat tests. Do not substitute amplifier until after performing servo assembly test.

Servo

REMOVAL & INSTALLATION

➧ SEE FIG. 42–45

1. Disconnect the negative battery cable.
2. Remove the screw and disconnect the speed control actuator cable from the accelerator cable bracket.
3. Disconnect the speed control actuator cable with the adjuster from the accelerator cable.
4. Remove the 2 vacuum hoses and electrical connector from the servo assembly.

5. Remove the 2 nuts attaching the servo to its mounting bracket.
6. Remove the servo and cable assembly.
7. Remove the 2 nuts holding the cable cover to the servo.
8. Pull off the cover and remove the cable assembly.

To Install:

9. Attach the cable to the servo.
10. Attach the cable cover to the servo with 2 nuts.
11. Attach the servo to the mounting bracket.
12. Feed the actuator cable under the air cleaner air duct.
13. Snap the actuator cable to accelerator cable bracket and install the screw.
14. Connect the actuator cable to the accelerator cable bracket and install the screw.
15. Install the 2 vacuum hoses and electrical connector at the servo.
16. Connect negative battery cable.

TESTING

1. Disconnect 8-way amplifier connector. At connector, connect an ohmmeter between orange/yellow wire and grey/black wire. Resistance should be 40–125Ω.
2. Connect an ohmmeter between orange/yellow wire and white/pink wire. Resistance should be 60–190Ω.
3. Connect an ohmmeter between pink/light blue wire and brown/light green wire. Resistance should be 40,000–60,000Ω.

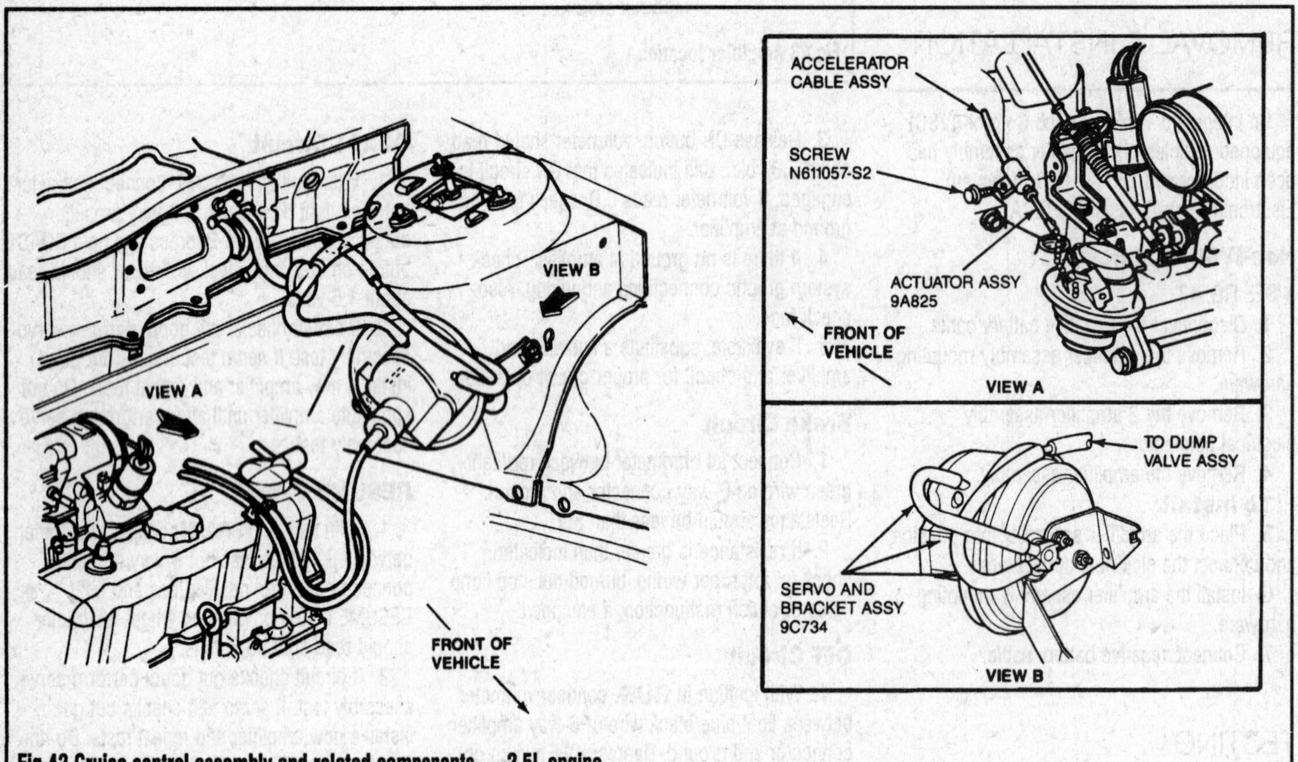

Fig.42 Cruise control assembly and related components – 2.5L engine

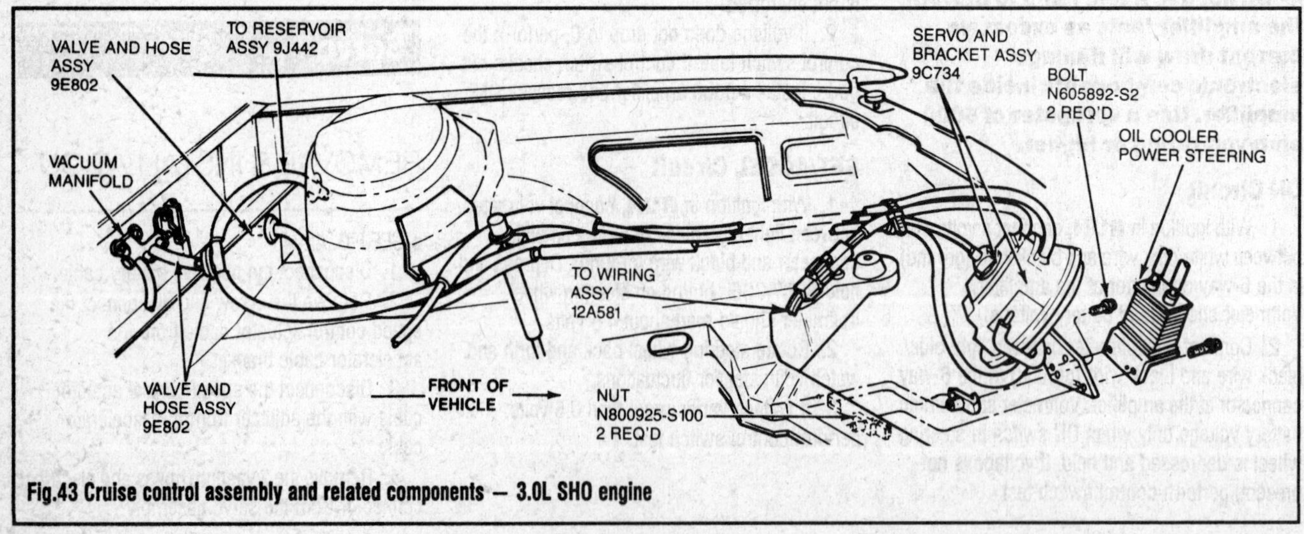

Fig.43 Cruise control assembly and related components – 3.0L SHO engine

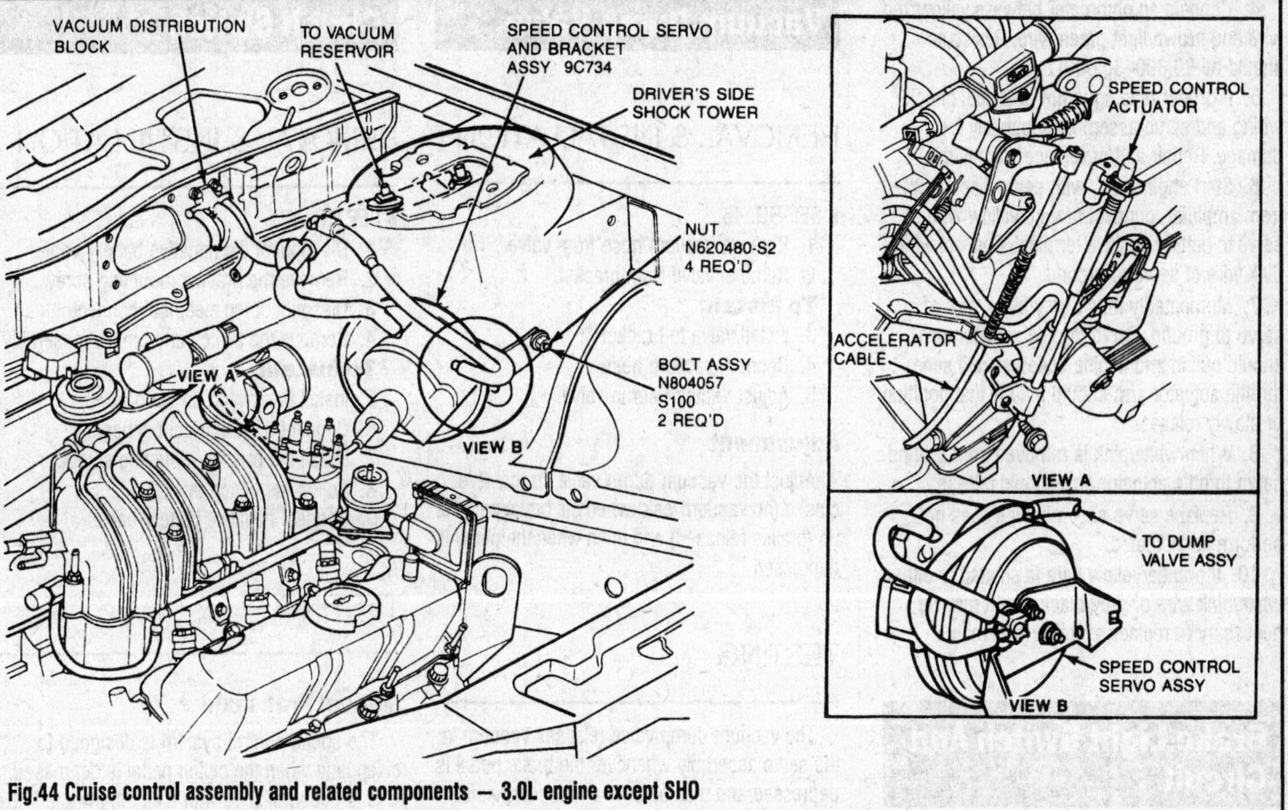

Fig.44 Cruise control assembly and related components — 3.0L engine except SHO

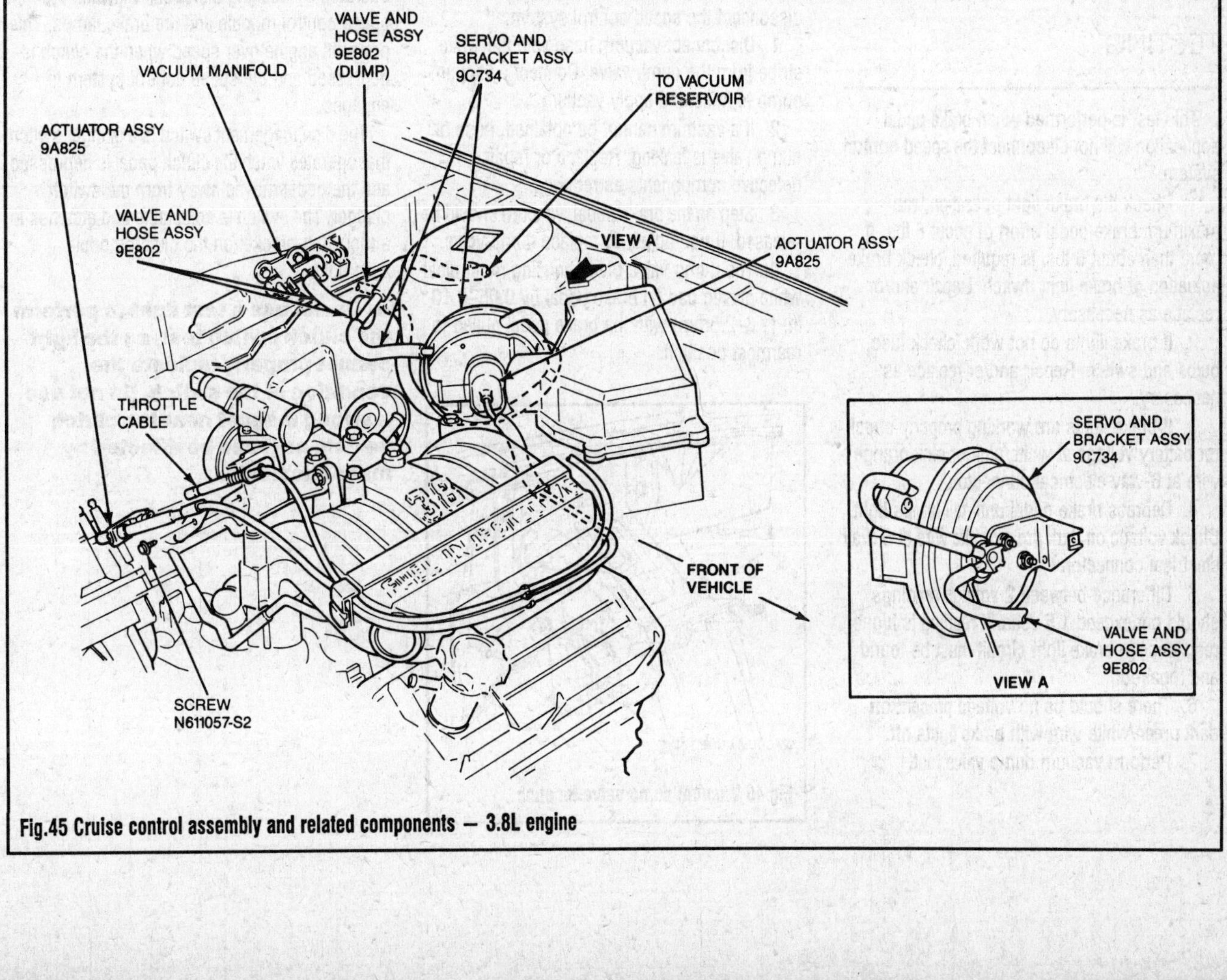

Fig.45 Cruise control assembly and related components — 3.8L engine

4. Connect an ohmmeter between yellow/red wire and brown/light green wire. Resistance should be 20,000–30,000Ω.
5. If proper reading is not obtained, check wiring and servo assembly separately for damage. Repair and/or replace as required.
6. Start engine and, with servo disconnected from amplifier, connect orange/yellow wire of servo to battery positive terminal. Connect white/pink wire of servo to ground.
7. Momentarily touch grey/black wire of servo to ground. Servo throttle actuator arm should pull in and engine speed should servo throttle actuator arm should hold in that position or slowly release.
8. When white/pink is removed from ground servo throttle actuator arm should release.
9. Replace servo assembly if it does not perform as indicated.
10. If orange/yellow wire is shorted to either white/pink wire or grey/black wire it may be necessary to replace amplifier assembly.

Brake Light Switch And Circuit

TESTING

This test is performed when brake pedal application will not disconnect the speed control system.

1. Check the brake light operation with maximum brake pedal effort of about 6 lbs. If more than about 6 lbs. is required, check brake actuation of brake light switch. Repair and/or replace as necessary.
2. If brake lights do not work, check fuse, bulbs and switch. Repair and/or replace as necessary.
3. If brake lights are working properly check for battery voltage at white/pink or pink/orange wire at 6-way electrical connector.
4. Depress brake pedal until tail lamps light. Check voltage on dark green/white wire at 6-way electrical connector.
5. Difference between 2 voltage readings should not exceed 1.5 volts. If reading is higher, resistance in brake light circuit must be found and repaired.
6. There should be no voltage present on dark green/white wire with brake lights off.
7. Perform vacuum dump valve test.

Vacuum Dump Valve

REMOVAL & INSTALLATION

➧ SEE FIG. 46

1. Remove vacuum hose from valve.
2. Remove valve from bracket.

To Install:

3. Install valve to bracket.
4. Connect vacuum hose.
5. Adjust vacuum dump valve.

Adjustment

Adjust the vacuum dump valve so that it is closed (no vacuum leak) when the brake pedal is up (brakes released) and open when the pedal is depressed.

TESTING

The vacuum dump valve releases vacuum in the servo assembly whenever the brake pedal is depressed and thus acts as a redundant safety feature. The vacuum dump valve should be checked whenever brake application does not disconnect the speed control system.

1. Disconnect vacuum hose with the white stripe from the dump valve. Connect a vacuum pump to hose and apply vacuum.
2. If a vacuum cannot be obtained, hose or dump valve is leaking. Replace or repair defective components as required.
3. Step on the brake pedal, vacuum should be released. If not, adjust or replace dump valve.
4. The dump valve black housing must clear white plastic pad on brake pedal by 0.05–0.10 in. (1.3–2.5mm) with the brake pedal pulled to rearmost position.

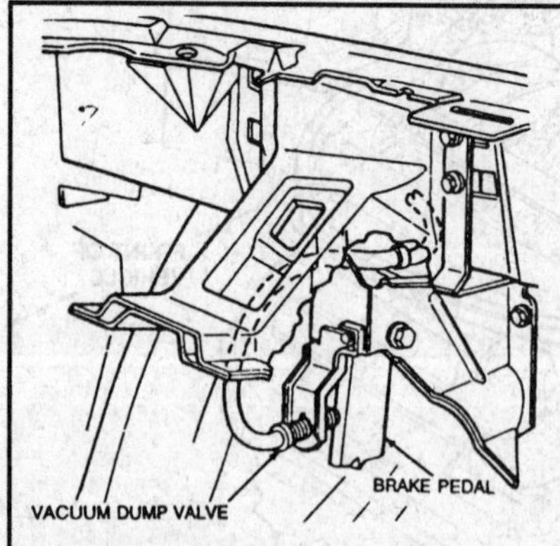

Fig.46 Vacuum dump valve location

Clutch Switch

REMOVAL & INSTALLATION

➧ SEE FIG. 47

1. Disconnect the negative battery cable.
2. Remove the bracket mounting screw.
3. Disconnect the electrical connector.
4. Remove the switch and bracket assembly.

To Install:

5. Install the switch on the bracket.
6. Connect the electrical connector.
7. Install the bracket mounting screw.
8. Adjust the clutch switch.
9. Connect negative battery cable.

TESTING

Manual Transaxle

The speed control system is designed to disengage when the clutch pedal is depressed. This is accomplished with a clutch switch. The speed control system disengage function is operated by opening the circuit between the speed control module and the brake lamps. This prevents engine over speed when the clutch is depressed and the speed control system is engaged.

The disengagement switch is a plunger switch that operates when the clutch pedal is depressed and the pedal moves away from the switch plunger. The switch is adjustable and attaches to a mounting bracket on the clutch module assembly.

➡ Do not use a test light to perform the clutch switch test, as the light cannot properly indicate the condition of the switch. Do not use a strong magnet near the clutch switch, as it can be affected by magnetic fields.

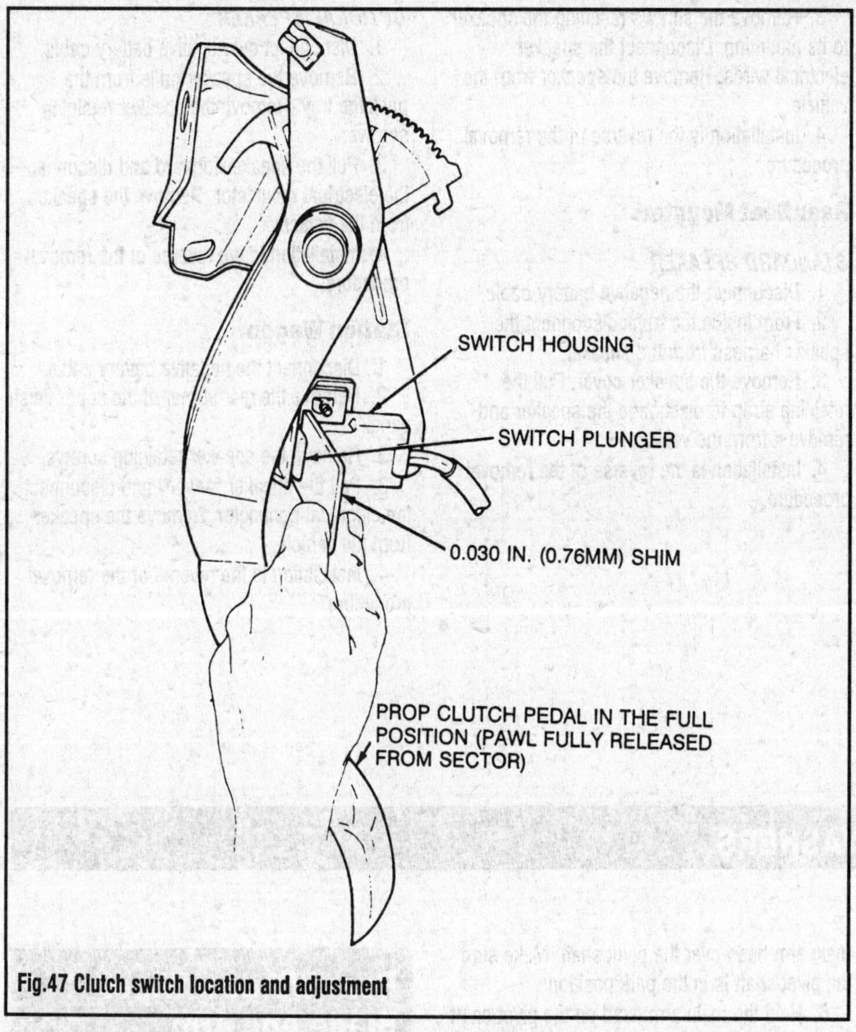

Fig.47 Clutch switch location and adjustment

1. Disconnect clutch pigtail connector from speed control harness connector. Connect an ohmmeter to 2 switch connector terminals.
2. With the clutch pedal in full up position, resistance should be less than 5Ω.
3. With clutch pedal depressed, circuit should be open.
4. If switch does not perform as indicated, it must be replaced.

Automatic Transaxle

Vehicles equipped with automatic transmission use a shorting plug instead of a clutch switch. Make sure the plug is installed and has good contact.

ENTERTAINMENT SYSTEMS

Radio Receiver/Tape Player

REMOVAL & INSTALLATION

1986–89

1. Disconnect the negative (–) battery cable.
2. Remove the trim panel-to-center instrument panel.
3. Remove the radio/bracket-to-instrument panel screws.
4. Push the radio toward the front, then raise the rear of the radio slightly so that the rear support bracket clears the clip in the instrument panel. Slowly, pull the radio from the instrument panel.
5. Disconnect the electrical connectors and the antenna cable from the radio.
6. Installation is the reverse of the removal procedures. Torque the radio/bracket-to-instrument panel screws to 14–16 inch lbs. Test the radio for operation.

Radio Receiver/CD Player

REMOVAL & INSTALLATION

1990–92

1. Disconnect the negative battery cable.
2. Install radio removal tool T87P–19061–A into the radio assembly face plate. Push the tool in about 1 in. (25mm) in order to release the retaining clips.

➡ Do not use excessive force when installing the special tool as this will cause damage to the retaining clips.

3. Apply a light spreading force to the tool and pull the assembly from the dash.
4. Disconnect the electrical connectors and the antenna wire from the assembly and remove it from the vehicle.
5. Installation is the reverse of the removal procedure.

Speakers

REMOVAL & INSTALLATION

Door Mounted

1. Disconnect the negative battery cable.
2. Remove the inner door panel trim panel.
3. Remove the screws retaining the speaker to its mounting. Disconnect the speaker electrical wires. Remove the speaker from the vehicle.
4. Installation is the reverse of the removal procedure.

Rear Seat Mounted

STANDARD SPEAKER

1. Disconnect the negative battery cable.
2. From inside the trunk disconnect the speaker harness from the speaker.
3. Remove the speaker cover. Pull the retaining strap to disengage the speaker and remove it from the vehicle.
4. Installation is the reverse of the removal procedure.

OPTIONAL SPEAKER

1. Disconnect the negative battery cable.
2. Remove the speaker grille from the package tray. Remove the speaker retaining screws.
3. Pull the speaker forward and disconnect the electrical connector. Remove the speaker from the vehicle.
4. Installation is the reverse of the removal procedure.

Station Wagon

1. Disconnect the negative battery cable.
2. Remove the rear corner of the upper finish panel.
3. Remove the speaker retaining screws.
3. Pull the speaker forward and disconnect the electrical connector. Remove the speaker from the vehicle.
4. Installation is the reverse of the removal procedure.

WINDSHIELD WIPERS AND WASHERS

Windshield Wiper Blade And Arm

REMOVAL & INSTALLATION

➧ SEE FIG. 51

1. Turn the ignition switch to the ACC position. Turn the wiper switch ON. Allow the motor to move the pivot shafts 3 or 4 cycles, then turn off the switch.
2. This operation will place the pivot shafts in the PARK position. Turn the ignition switch to the OFF position. Disconnect the negative battery cable.
3. Raise the blade end of the arm off the windshield and move the slide latch away from the pivot shaft.
4. The wiper arm should not be unlocked and can now be pulled off of the pivot shaft.

To install:

5. Position the auxiliary arm (if so equipped) over the pivot pin, hold it down and push the main arm head over the pivot shaft. Make sure the pivot shaft is in the park position.
6. Hold the main arm head on the pivot shaft while raising the blade end of the wiper arm and push the slide latch into the lock under the pivot shaft. Lower the blade to the windshield.

➡ If the blade does not touch the windshield, the slide latch is not completely in place.

ADJUSTMENT

➧ SEE FIG. 54

1. With the arm and blade assemblies removed from the pivot shafts turn on the wiper switch and allow the motor to move the pivot shaft three or four cycles, and then turn off the wiper switch. This will place the pivot shafts in the park position.
2. Install the arm and blade assemblies on the pivot shafts to the correct distance between the windshield lower molding or weatherstrip and the blade saddle centerline.

Rear Window Wiper Blade And Arm

REMOVAL & INSTALLATION

➧ SEE FIG. 52–53

1. Raise the arm away from the glass. Insert a 0.062 in. (1.6mm) pin into the holes in the retainer arm.
2. Allow the arm to move toward the glass to relieve arm spring tension. Lift the arm assembly off of the pivot shaft.
3. To install push the main arm head over the pivot shaft. Be sure that the pivot shaft is in the park position.
4. Hold the main arm head on the pivot shaft while raising the blade end of the wiper arm and remove the 0.062 in. (1.6mm) pin.
5. Lower the blade to the glass.

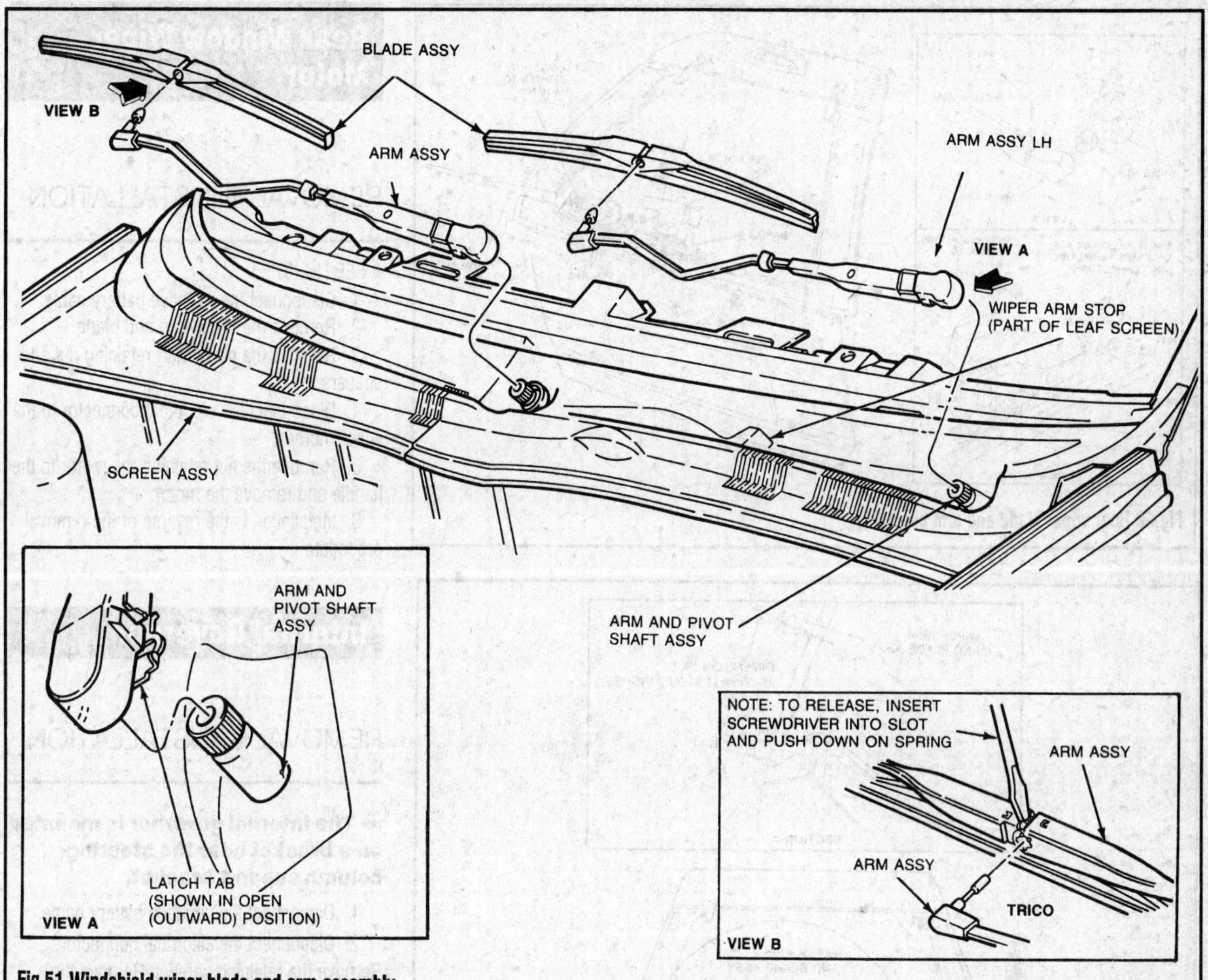

Fig.51 Windshield wiper blade and arm assembly

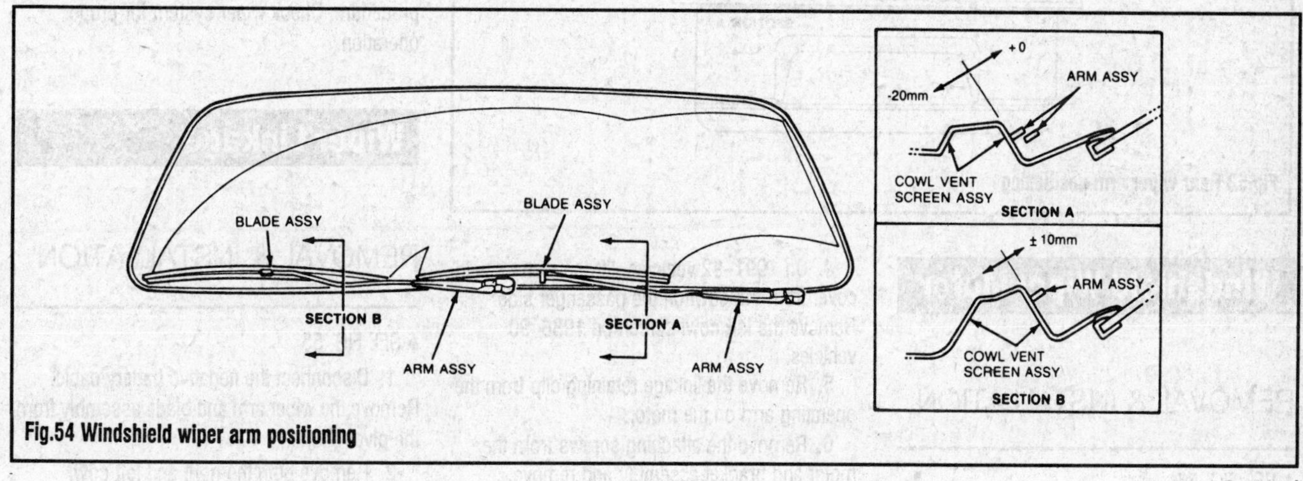

Fig.54 Windshield wiper arm positioning

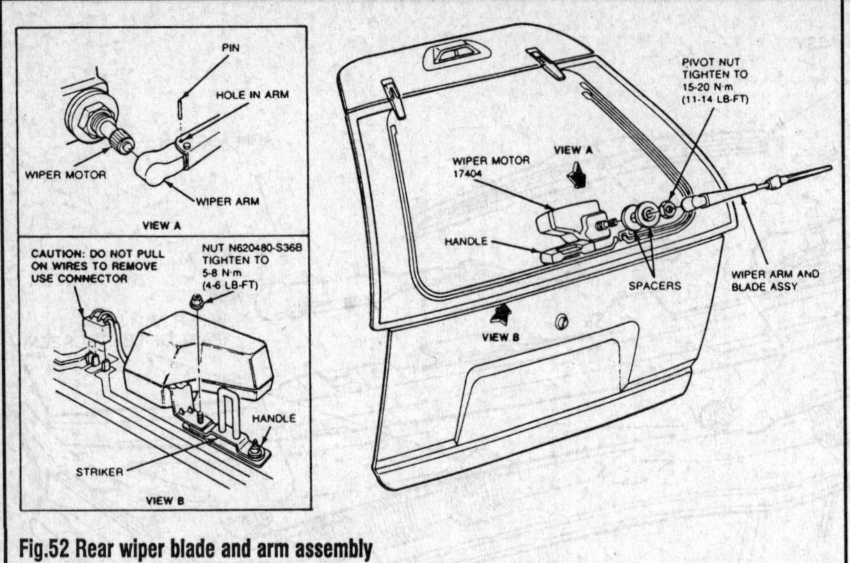

Fig.52 Rear wiper blade and arm assembly

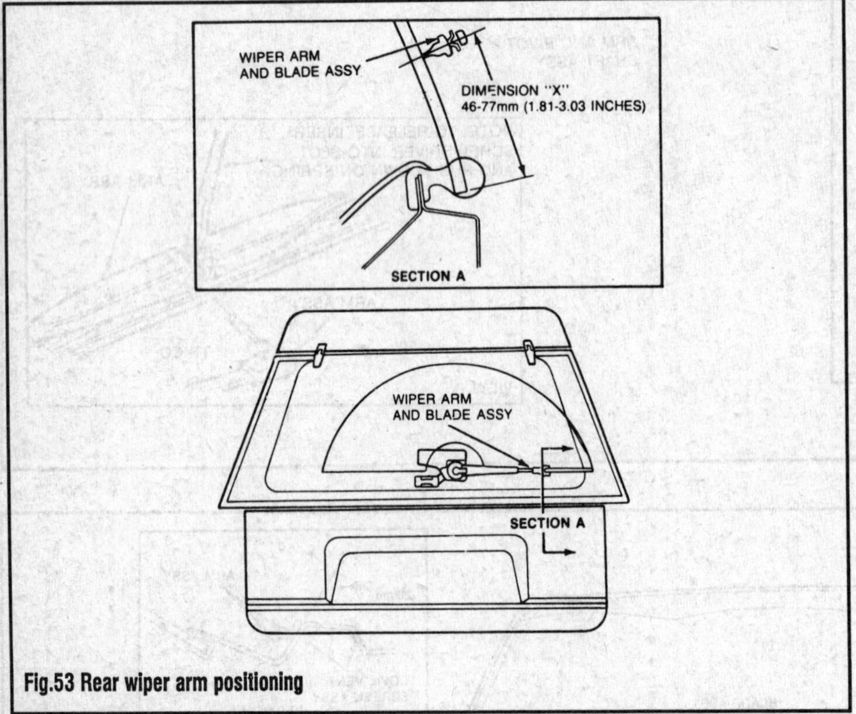

Fig.53 Rear wiper arm positioning

Windshield Wiper Motor

REMOVAL & INSTALLATION

➧ SEE FIG. 56

1. Disconnect the negative battery cable.
2. Disconnect the power lead from the motor.
3. Remove the left wiper arm.
4. On 1991–92 vehicles, lift the water shield cover from the cowl on the passenger side. Remove the left cowl screen on 1986–90 vehicles.
5. Remove the linkage retaining clip from the operating arm on the motor.
6. Remove the attaching screws from the motor and bracket assembly and remove.
7. Installation is the reverse of the removal procedure.

Rear Window Wiper Motor

REMOVAL & INSTALLATION

➧ SEE FIG. 57

1. Disconnect the negative battery cable.
2. Remove the wiper arm and blade.
3. Remove the pivot shaft retaining nut and spacers.
4. Disconnect the electrical connector to the wiper motor.
5. Remove the nut retaining the motor to the handle and remove the motor.
6. Installation is the reverse of the removal procedure.

Internal Governor

REMOVAL & INSTALLATION

➡ The internal governor is mounted on a bracket near the steering column support bracket.

1. Disconnect the negative battery cable.
2. Disconnect the electrical connector. Remove the retaining screws. Remove the component from the vehicle.
3. Installation is the reverse of the removal procedure. Check wiper system for proper operation.

Wiper Linkage

REMOVAL & INSTALLATION

➧ SEE FIG. 55

1. Disconnect the negative battery cable. Remove the wiper arm and blade assembly from the pivot shafts.
2. Remove both the right and left cowl screens. Disconnect the linkage drive arm from the motor crank pin after removing the clip.
3. Remove the screws retaining the pivot

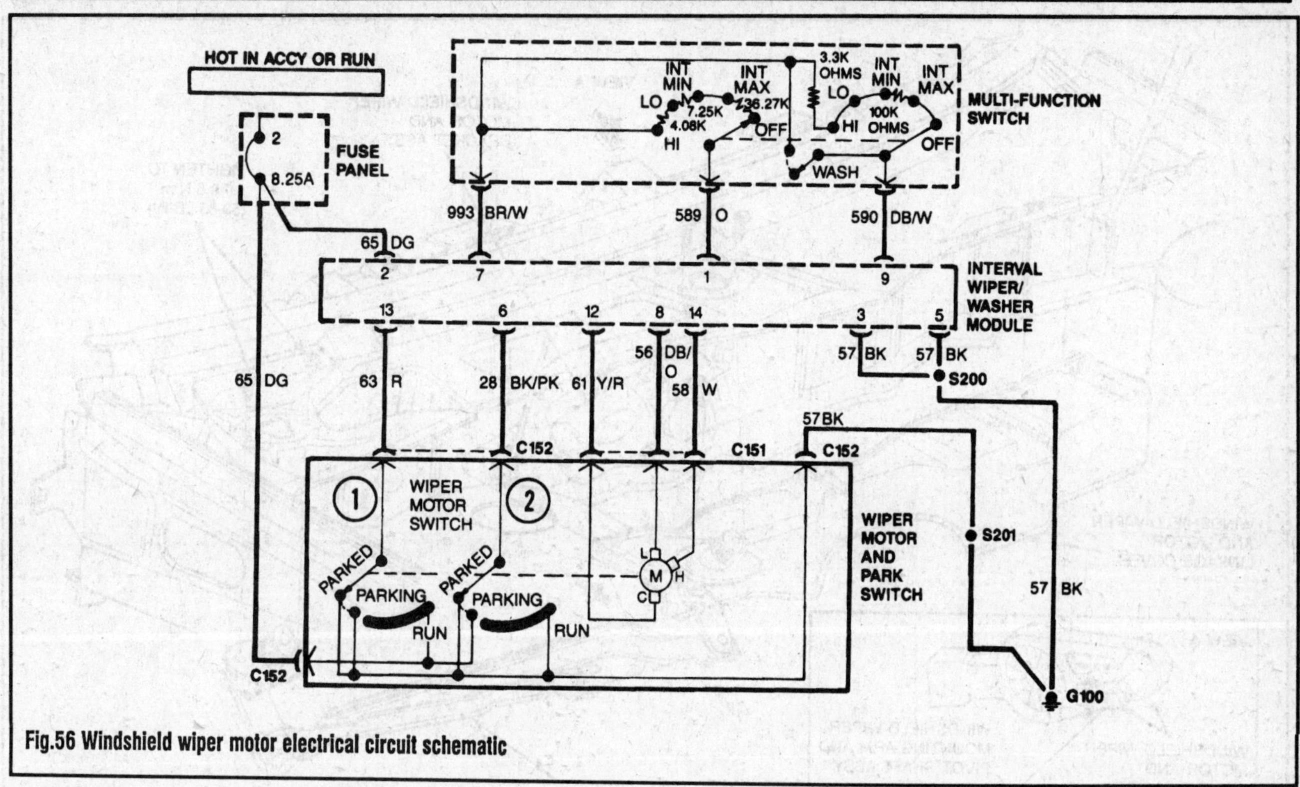

Fig.56 Windshield wiper motor electrical circuit schematic

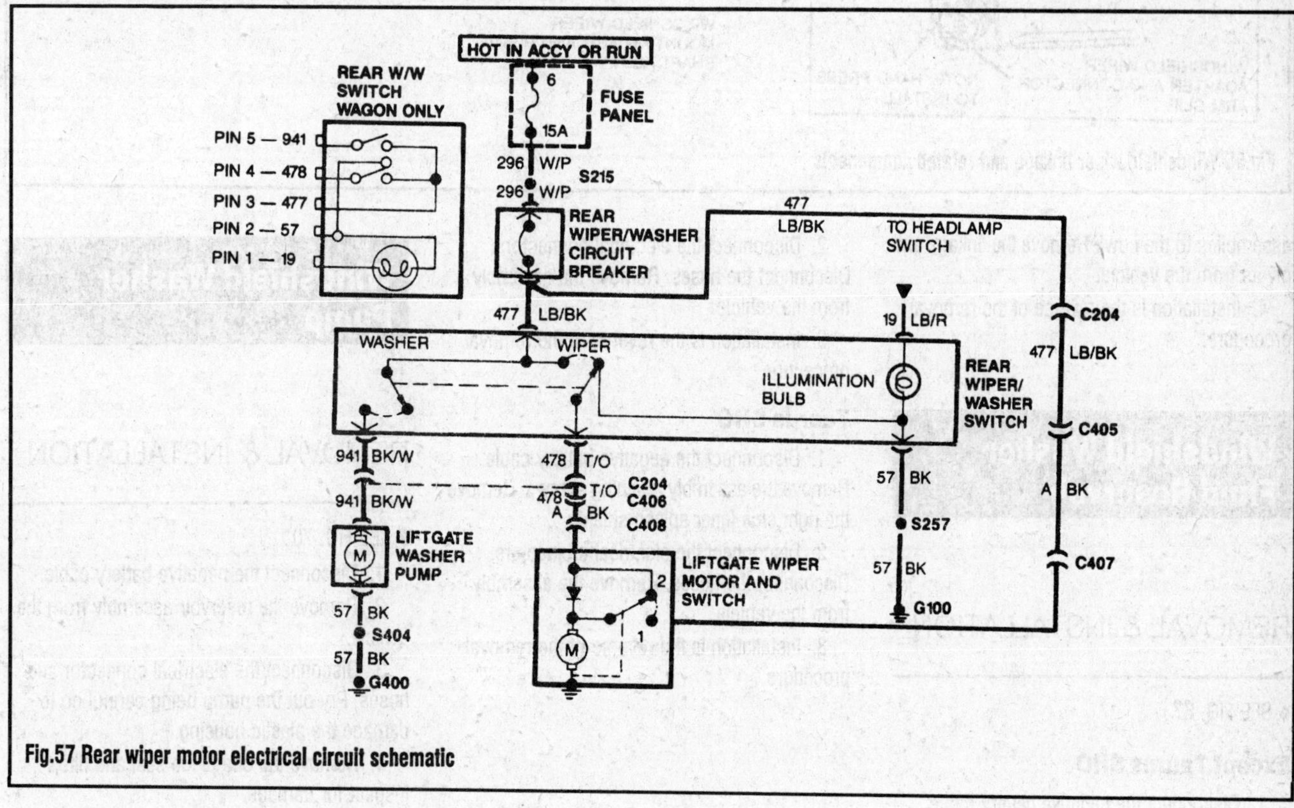

Fig.57 Rear wiper motor electrical circuit schematic

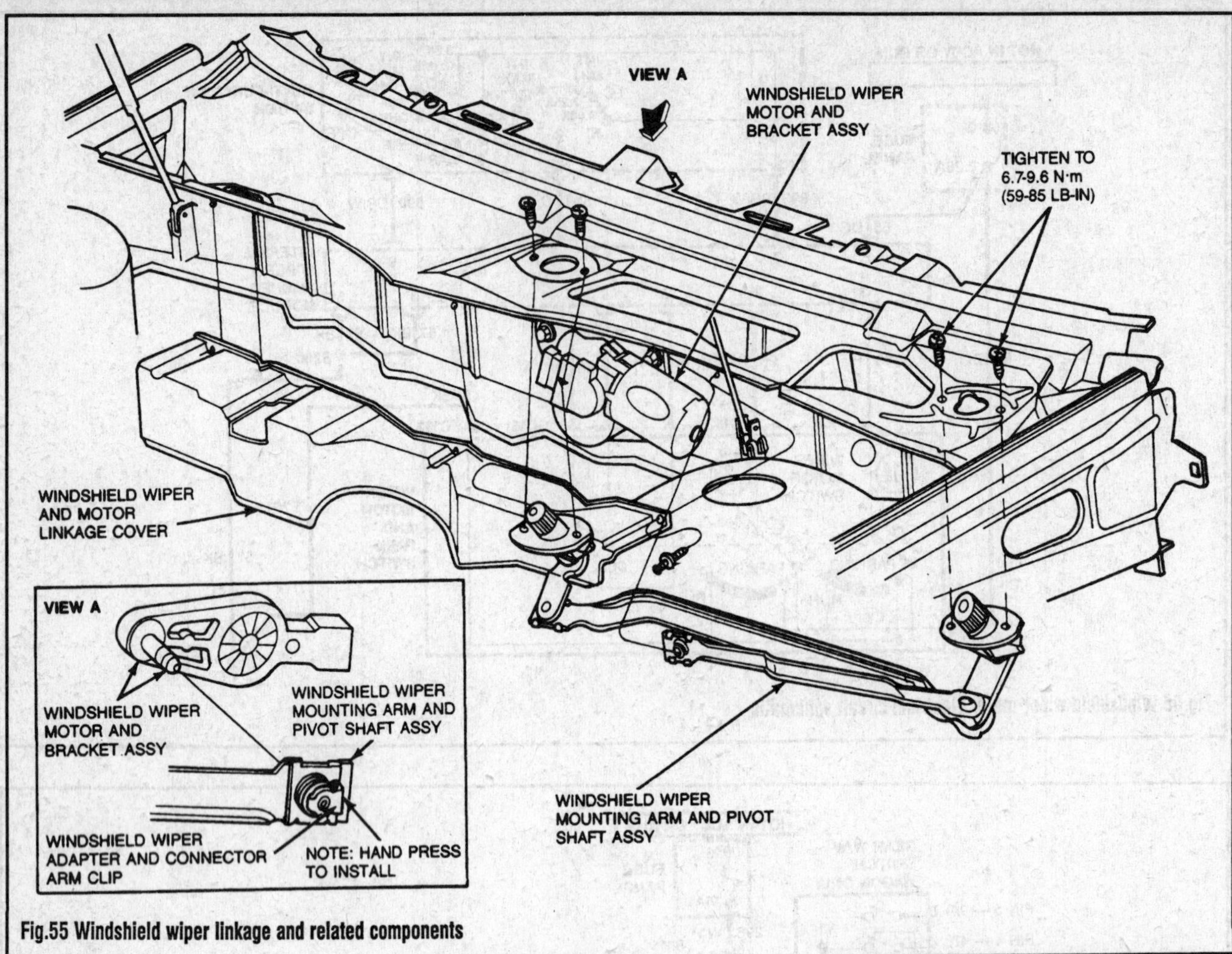

Fig.55 Windshield wiper linkage and related components

assemblies to the cowl. Remove the linkage and pivots from the vehicle.

4. Installation is the reverse of the removal procedure.

Windshield Washer Fluid Reservoir

REMOVAL & INSTALLATION

➧ SEE FIG. 67

Except Taurus SHO

1. Disconnect the negative battery cable. Remove the assembly retaining screw.

2. Disconnect the electrical connectors. Disconnect the hoses. Remove the assembly from the vehicle.

3. Installation is the reverse of the removal procedure.

Taurus SHO

1. Disconnect the negative battery cable. Remove the assembly retaining screws. Remove the right side inner splash shield.

2. Disconnect the electrical connectors. Disconnect the hoses. Remove the assembly from the vehicle.

3. Installation is the reverse of the removal procedure.

Windshield Washer Pump

REMOVAL & INSTALLATION

➧ SEE FIG. 70

1. Disconnect the negative battery cable.

2. Remove the reservoir assembly from the vehicle.

3. Disconnect the electrical connector and hoses. Pry out the pump being careful no to damage the plastic housing.

4. Remove the one piece seal and filter. Inspect for damage.

5. Installation is the reverse of the removal procedure. Do not operate the pump until fluid has been added to the reservoir.

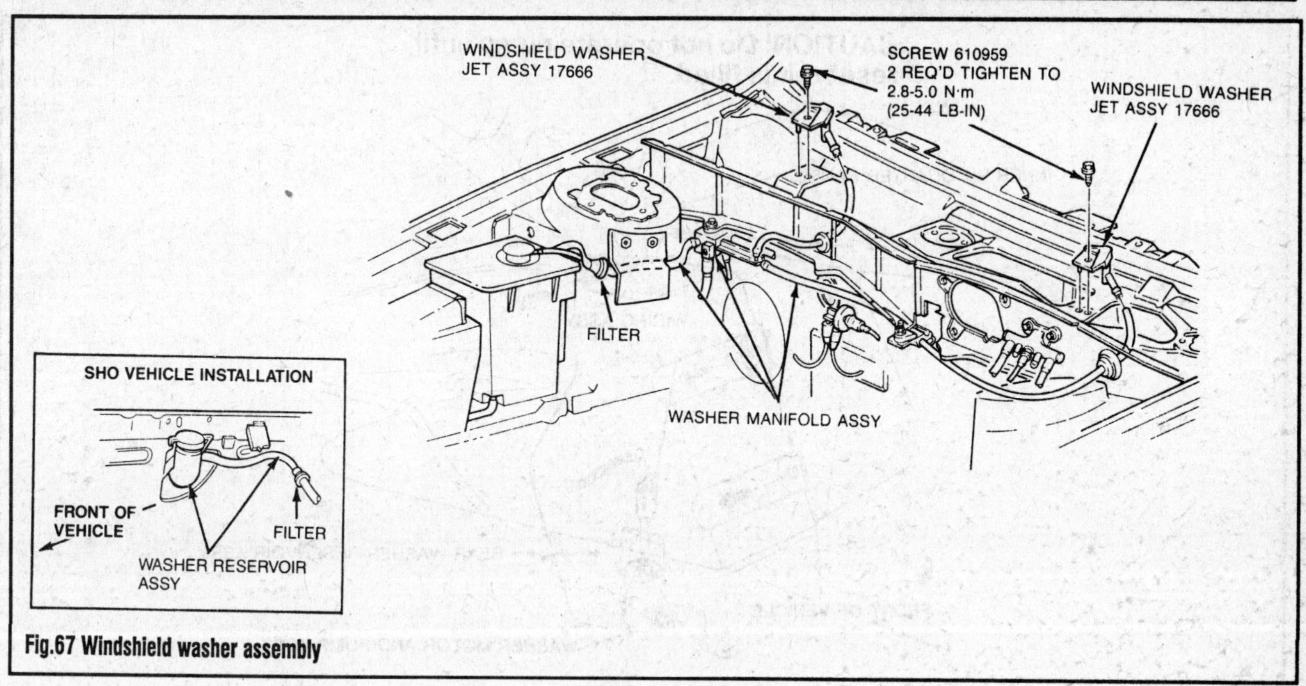

Fig.67 Windshield washer assembly

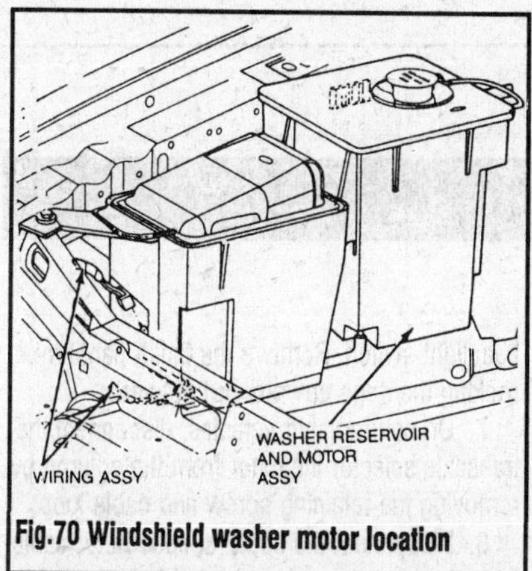

Fig.70 Windshield washer motor location

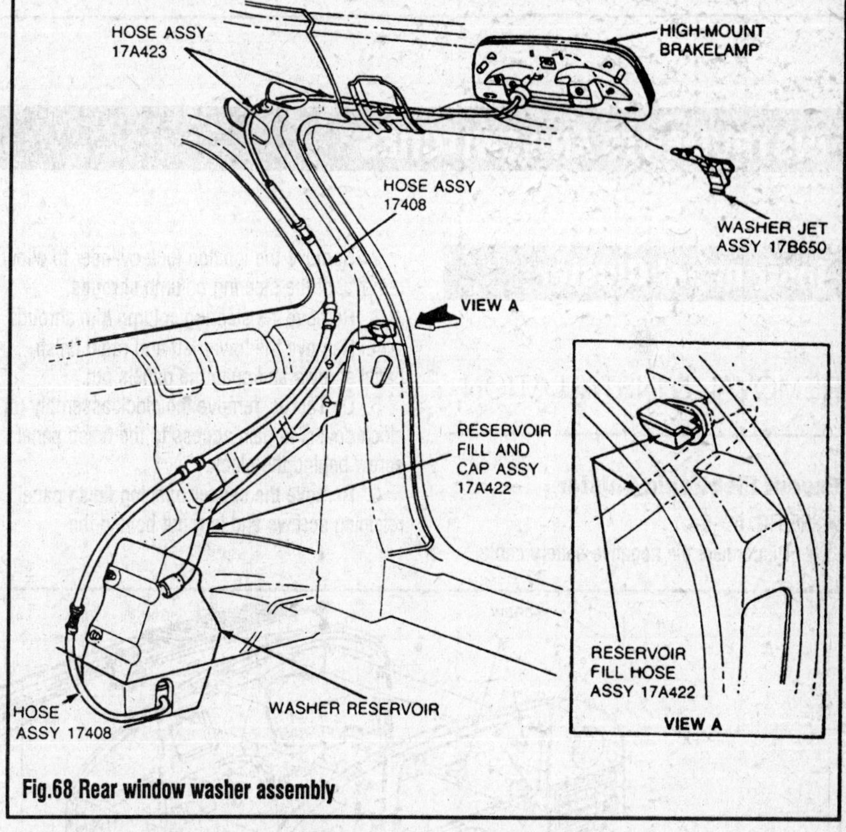

Fig.68 Rear window washer assembly

Rear Window Washer Pump And Fluid Reservoir

REMOVAL & INSTALLATION

➧ SEE FIG. 68–69

1. Disconnect the negative battery cable. Remove the right quarter trim panel.
2. Disconnect the electrical connectors. Disconnect and plug the hoses.
3. Remove the reservoir retaining screws. Remove the reservoir from the vehicle.
4. Pry out the pump being careful no to damage the plastic housing.
5. Remove the one piece seal and filter. Inspect for damage.
6. Installation is the reverse of the removal procedure.

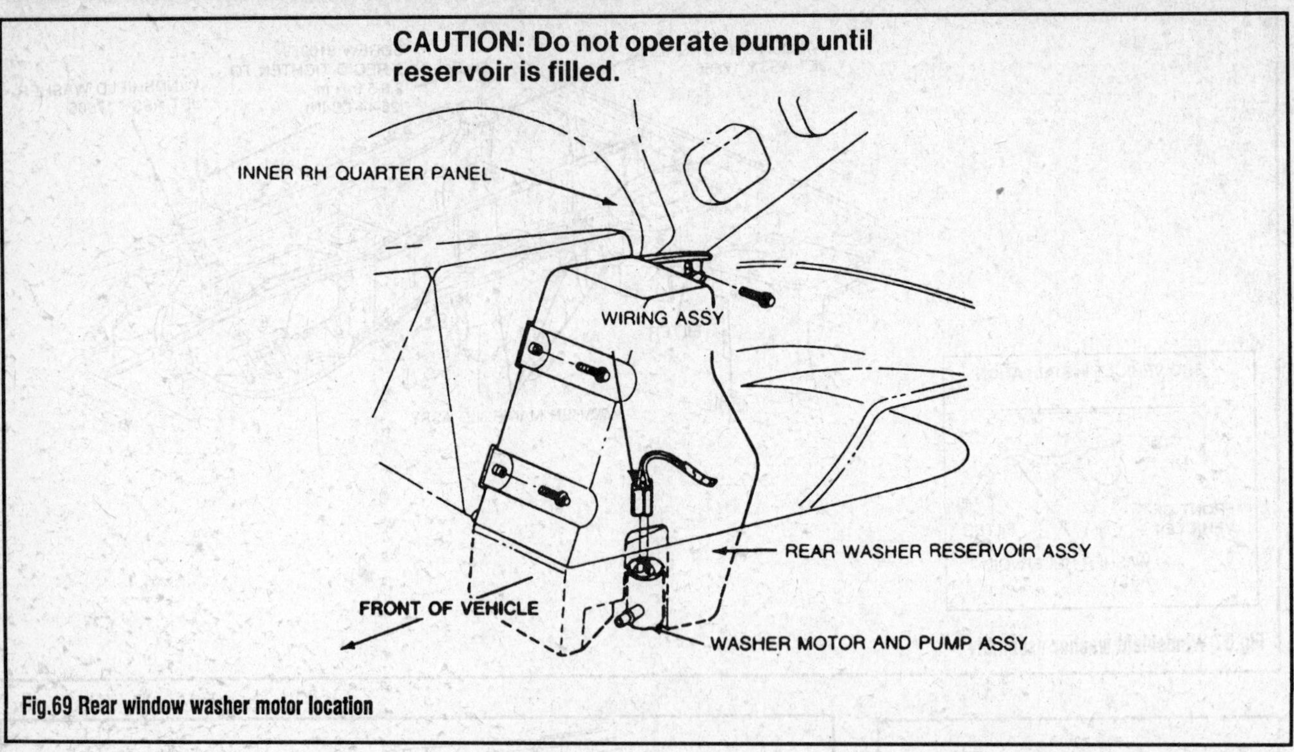

Fig.69 Rear window washer motor location

INSTRUMENTS AND SWITCHES

Instrument Cluster

REMOVAL & INSTALLATION

Except Electronic Cluster

➧ SEE FIG. 58–64

1. Disconnect the negative battery cable.
2. Remove the ignition lock cylinder to allow removal of the steering column shrouds.
3. Remove the steering column trim shrouds.
4. Remove the lower left and radio finish panel screws and snap the panels out.
5. On Taurus, remove the clock assembly (or clock cover) to gain access to the finish panel screw behind the clock.
6. Remove the cluster opening finish panel retaining screws and jam nut behind the headlight switch. Remove the finish panel by rocking the edge upward and outward.
7. On column shift vehicles, disconnect the transaxle selector indicator from the column by removing the retaining screw and cable loop.
8. Disconnect the upper speedometer cable from the lower speedometer cable in the engine compartment.
9. Remove the 4 cluster-to-instrument panel retaining screws and pull the cluster assembly forward.

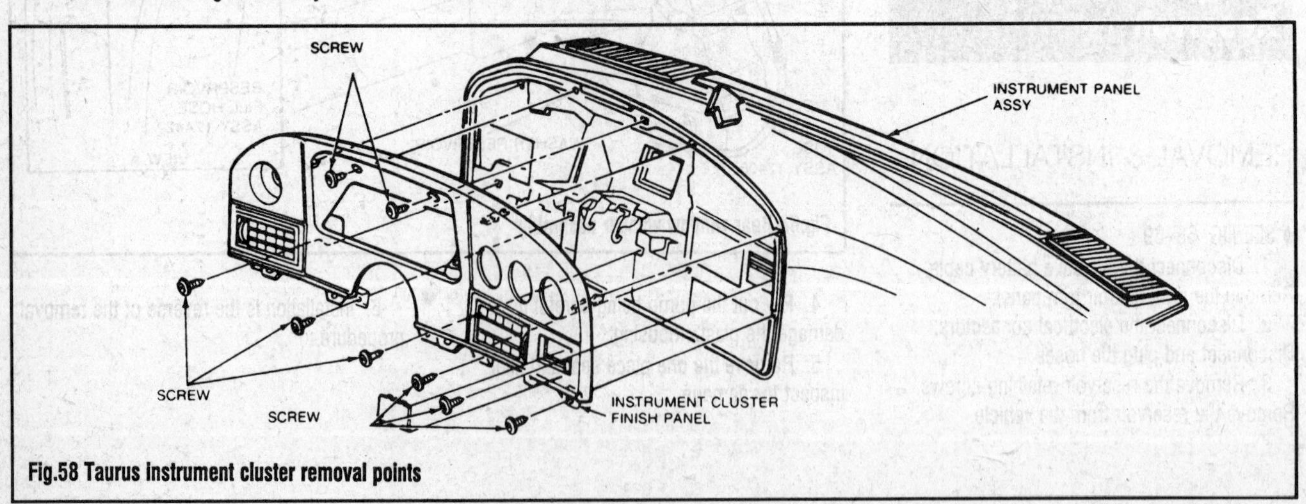

Fig.58 Taurus instrument cluster removal points

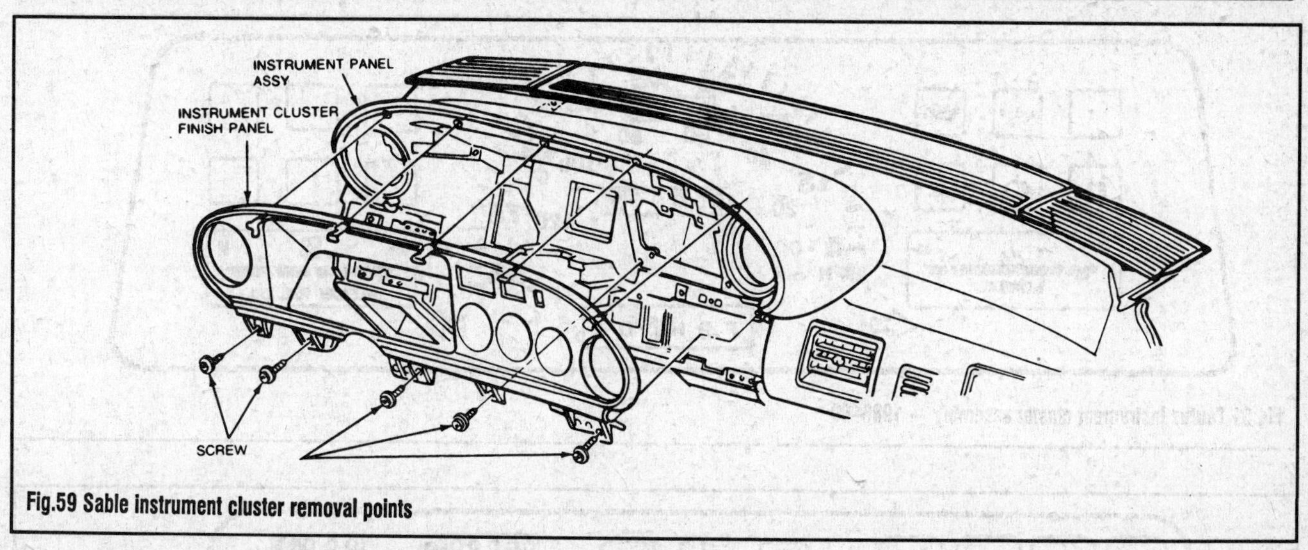

Fig.59 Sable instrument cluster removal points

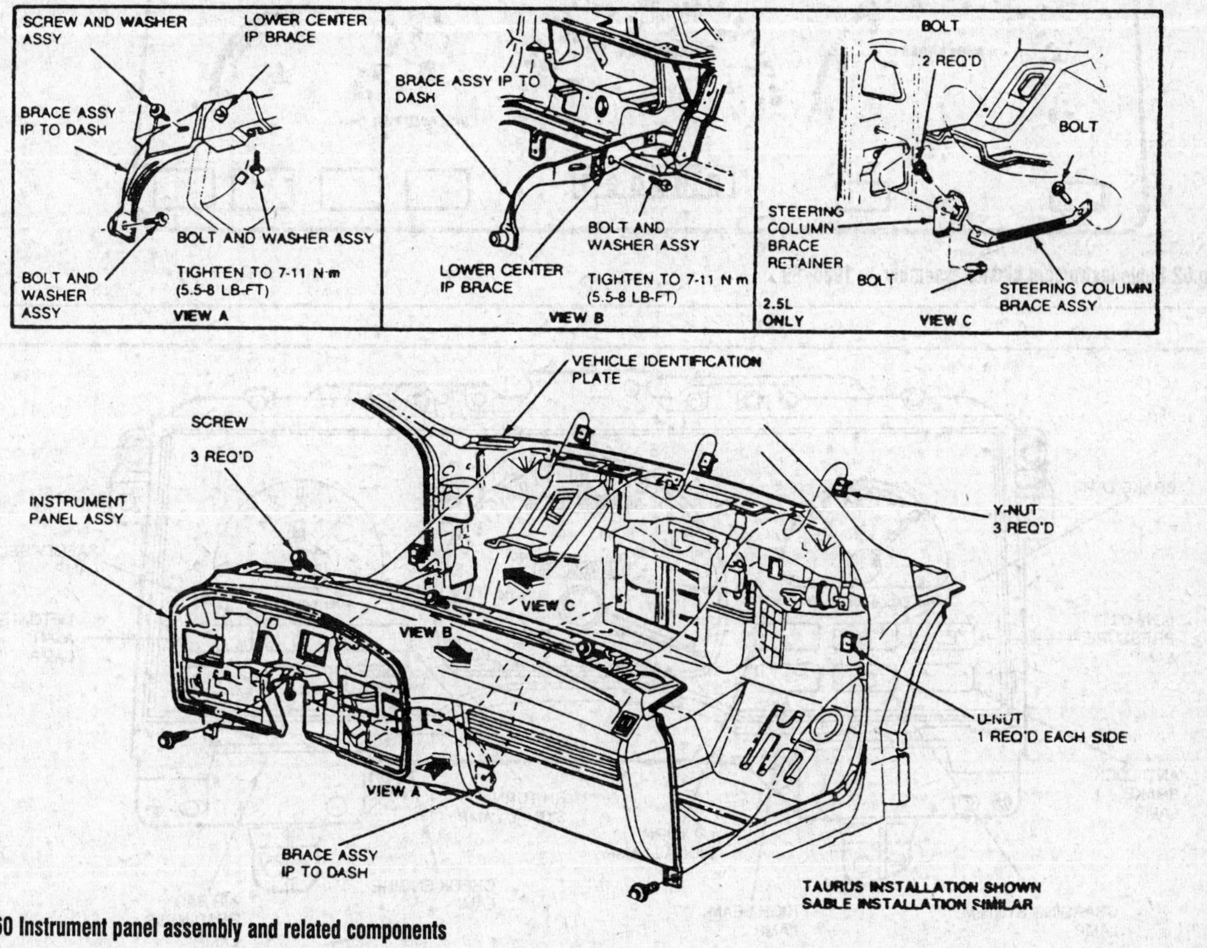

Fig.60 Instrument panel assembly and related components

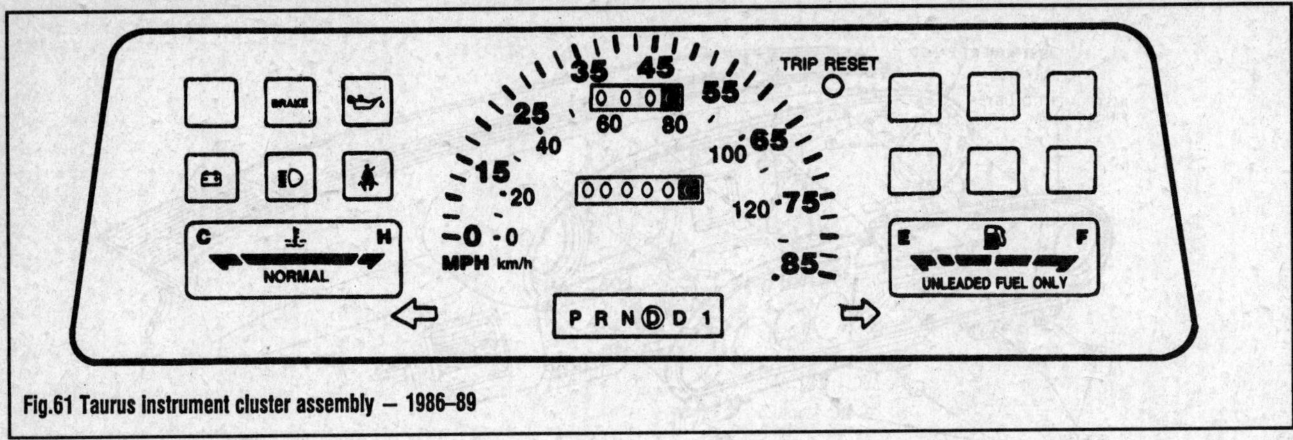

Fig.61 Taurus instrument cluster assembly — 1986–89

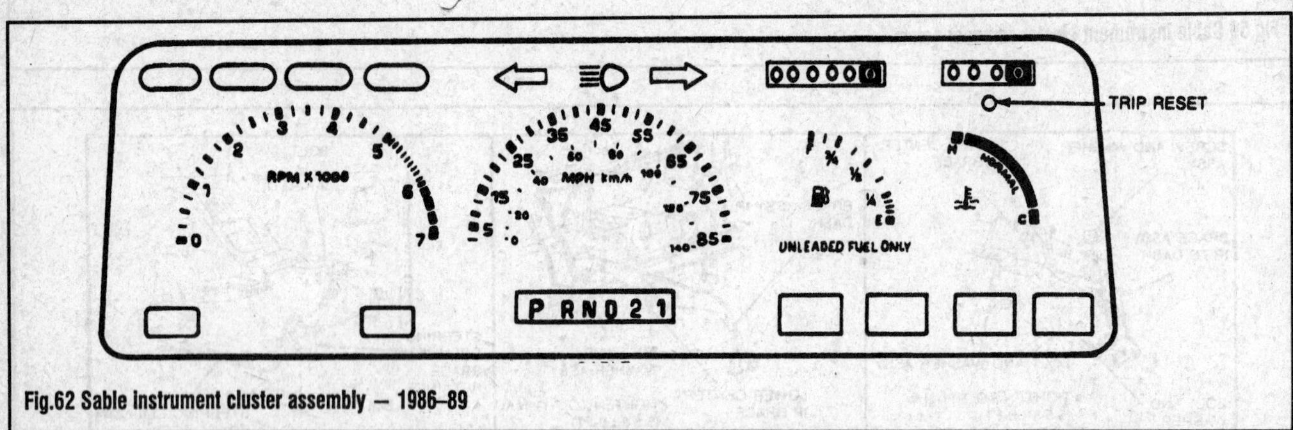

Fig.62 Sable instrument cluster assembly — 1986–89

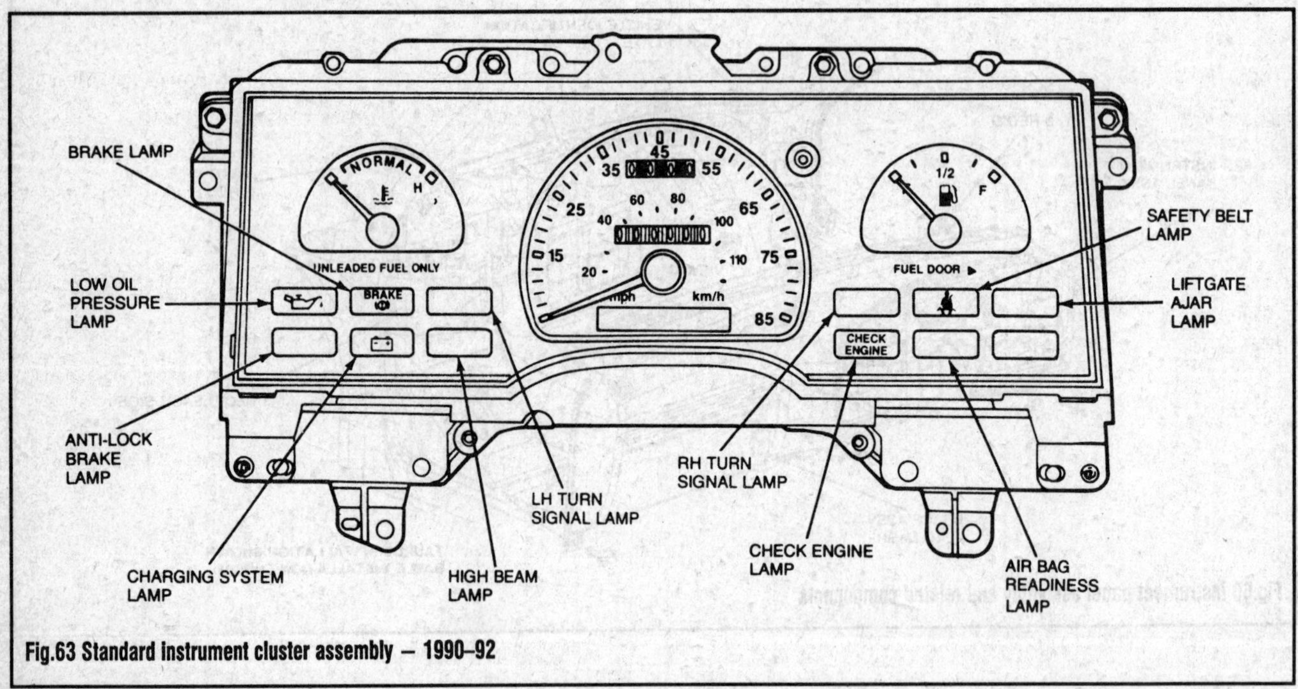

Fig.63 Standard instrument cluster assembly — 1990–92

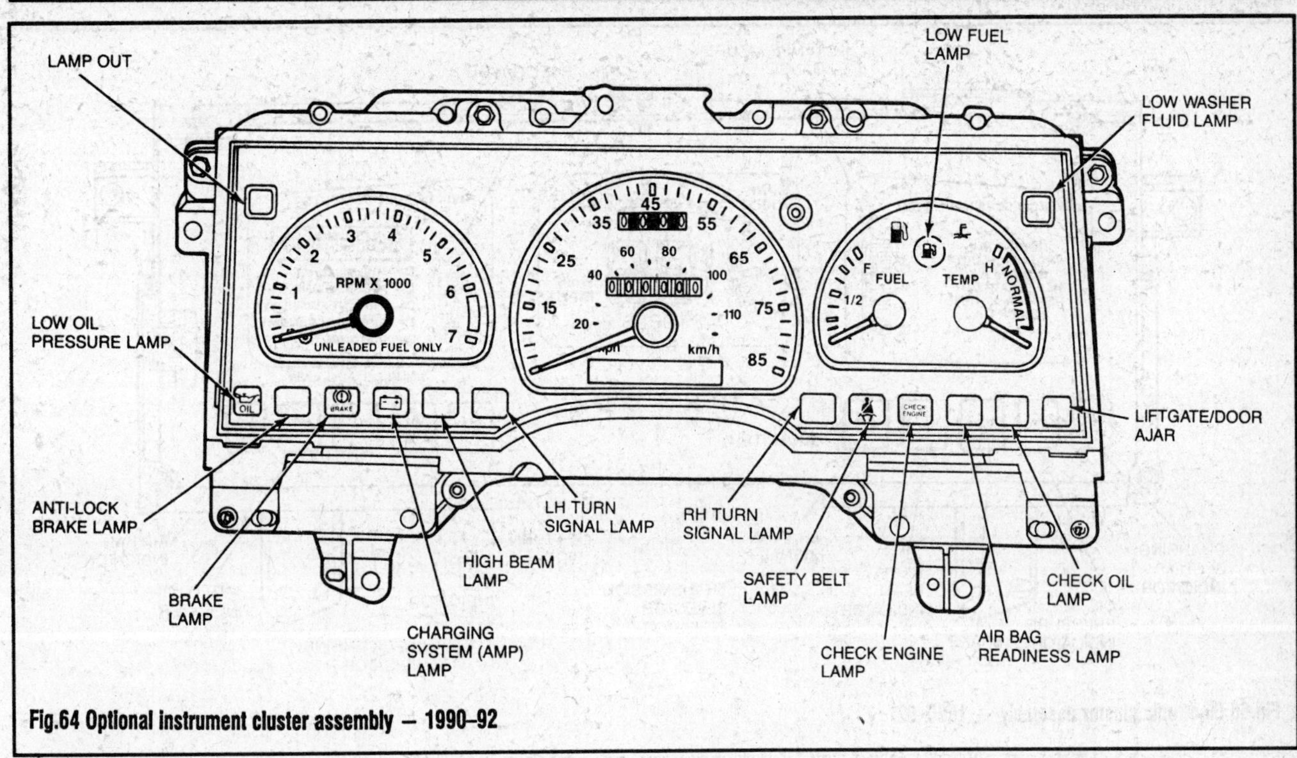

Fig.64 Optional instrument cluster assembly — 1990–92

10. Disconnect the cluster electrical connector and speedometer cable. Press the cable latch to disengage the cable from the speedometer head while pulling the cable away from the cluster. Remove the cluster.

To Install:

11. Position the cluster in front of the cluster opening.
12. Connect the speedometer cable and electrical connectors.
13. Install the cluster and the 4 cluster-to-instrument panel retaining screws.
14. Connect the upper speedometer cable to the lower speedometer cable in the engine compartment.
15. On column shift vehicles, connect the transaxle selector indicator.
16. Install the cluster opening finish panel.
17. On Taurus vehicles, install the clock assembly or clock cover.
18. Install the lower left and radio finish panels.
19. Install the steering column trim shrouds.
20. Install the ignition lock cylinder and connect the negative battery cable.

Electronic Cluster

➧ SEE FIG. 65–66

1. Disconnect the negative battery cable.
2. Remove the lower trim covers.
3. Remove the steering column cover and disconnect the shift indicator cable from the cluster by removing the retaining screws.
4. Disconnect the switch module and remove the cluster trim panel.
5. Remove the cluster mounting screws and pull the bottom of the cluster toward the steering wheel.

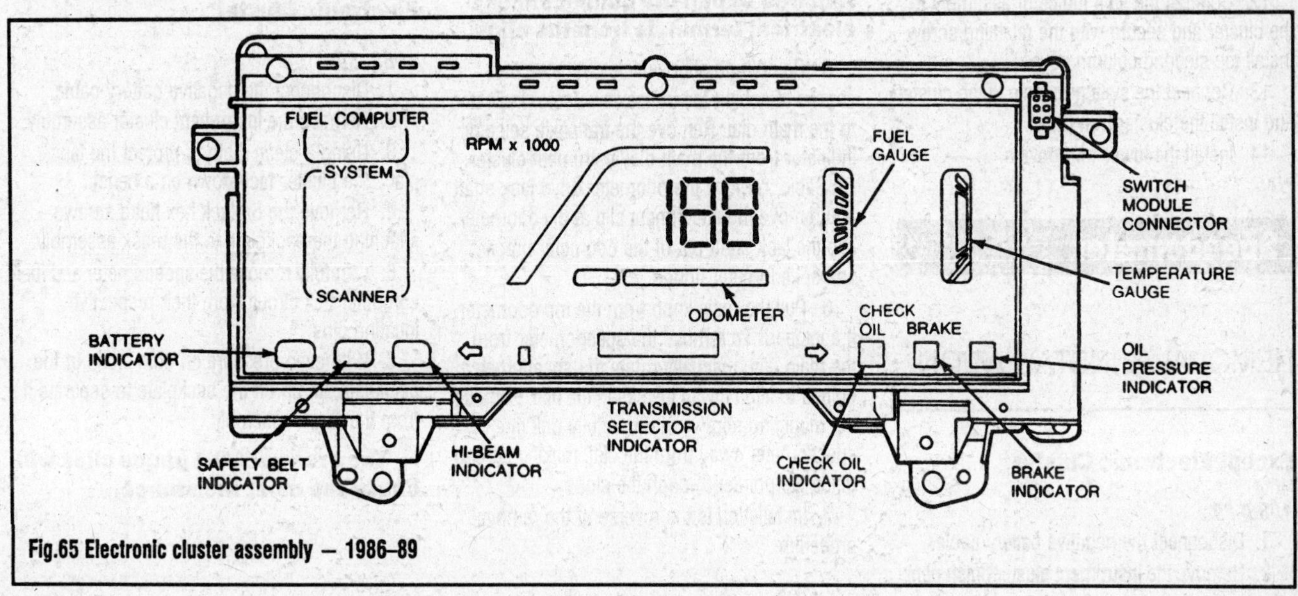

Fig.65 Electronic cluster assembly — 1986–89

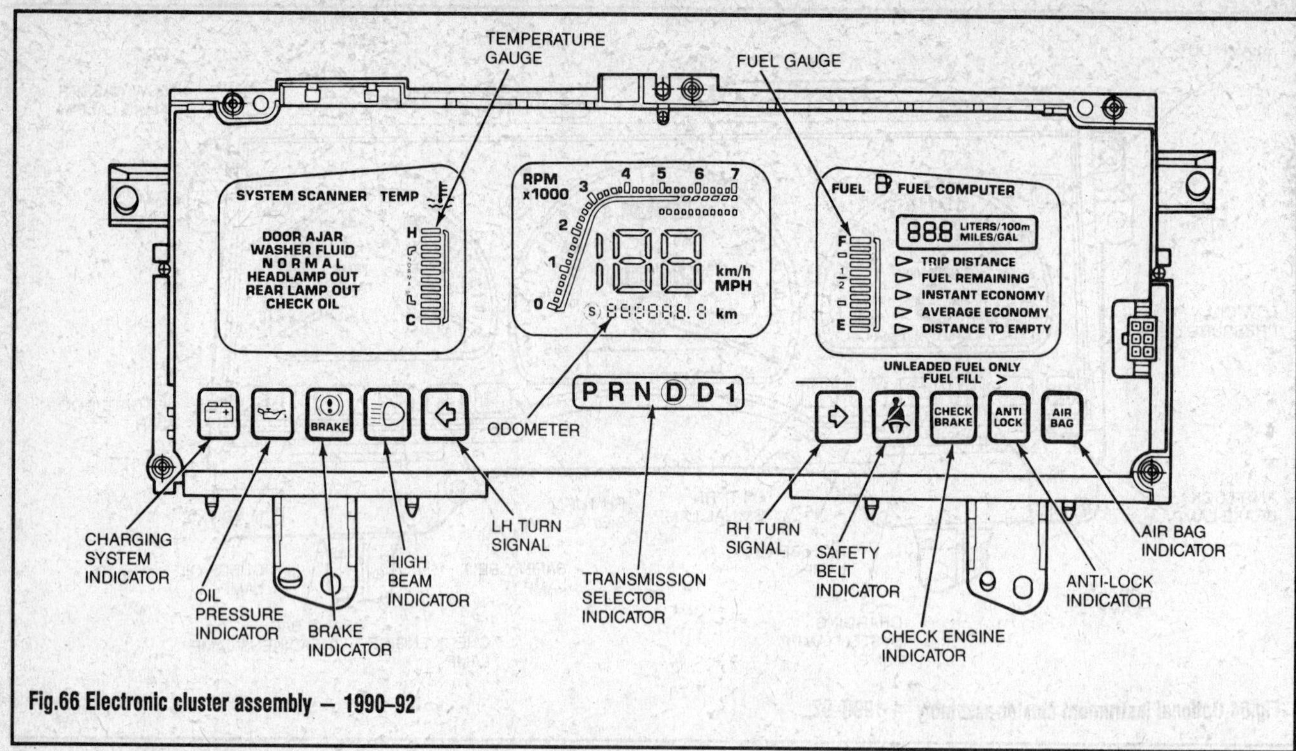

Fig.66 Electronic cluster assembly — 1990–92

6. Reach behind and under the cluster, disconnect the 3 electrical connectors.

7. Swing the bottom of the cluster out to clear the top of the cluster from the crash pad and remove.

To Install:

8. Insert the top of the cluster under the crash pad, leaving the bottom out.

9. Connect the 3 connectors.

10. Properly seat the cluster and install the retaining screws.

11. Connect the battery ground cable and check the cluster for proper operation.

12. Connect the shift indicator assembly to the cluster and secure with the retaining screw. Install the steering column cover.

13. Connect the switch module to the cluster and install the cluster trim panel.

14. Install the lower trim covers.

Speedometer

REMOVAL & INSTALLATION

Except Electronic Cluster

1986–89

1. Disconnect the negative battery cable.

2. Remove the instrument cluster finish panel retaining screws and remove the finish panel. On Sable, remove the lower trim panel attaching screws and the trim panel.

3. Remove the mask-and-lens mounting screws and remove the mask and lens. On Sable, remove the lower floodlight bulb and socket assemblies.

4. Remove the entire dial assembly from the instrument cluster by carefully pulling it away from the cluster backplate.

➡ The speedometer, tachometer and gauges are mounted to the main dial and some effort may be required to pull the quick-connect electrical terminals from the clips.

5. On column shift vehicles, remove the screws attaching the transaxle selector indicator to the main dial. Remove the transaxle selector indicator from the main dial/instrument cluster. On Sable, remove the odometer drive jack shaft and remove the attachment clip at the odometer, slip the jack shaft out of the odometer bracket and speedometer bridge.

6. Pull the reset knob from the trip odometer, if equipped. To remove the speedometer from the main dial, manually rotate the speedometer pointer to align it with the slot in the dial. Remove the mounting screws and carefully pull the speedometer away from the dial, making sure to guide the pointer through the slot.

7. Installation is the reverse of the removal procedure.

1990–92

1. Disconnect the negative battery cable.

2. Remove the instrument cluster.

3. Remove the 8 mask and lens mounting screws. Remove the mask and lens.

4. Remove the 2 screws attaching the transaxle selector indicator or the filler bezel to the speedometer and remove the indicator or filler bezel from the cluster.

5. Lift the speedometer from the instrument cluster.

6. Installation is the reverse of the removal procedure.

Electronic Cluster

1988–89

1. Disconnect the negative battery cable.

2. Remove the instrument cluster assembly.

3. Using a clean cloth to protect the lens, place the cluster face down on a bench.

4. Remove the 5 black hex head screws attaching the backplate to the mask assembly.

5. Carefully remove the speedometer and fuel computer flex circuit from their respective locating pins.

6. With even pressure on both sides of the backplate, lift up on the backplate to separate it from the mask assembly.

➡ The area near the gauge clips will cause the most resistance.

7. Turn the cluster assembly over and disconnect the switch connector from the mask assembly by squeezing in on the retaining clips and pushing the connector through the hole in the mask.

8. Remove the 4 screws attaching the speedometer to the mask assembly.

9. Installation is the reverse of the removal procedure.

1990–92

The speedometer is part of a single electronic instrument cluster module and cannot be removed separately.

Gauges And Tachometer

REMOVAL & INSTALLATION

Except Electronic Cluster

1. Disconnect the negative battery cable. Remove the instrument cluster.

2. Remove the mask and lens retaining screws. Remove the mask and lens.

3. Remove the screws that retain the transaxle selector indicator or filler bezel to the speedometer. Remove the indicator or filler bezel from the cluster.

4. Pull the speedometer from the instrument cluster. Pull the gauge or the tachometer from its mounting.

5. Installation is the reverse of the removal procedure.

Speedometer Core

REMOVAL & INSTALLATION

1. Disconnect the negative battery cable.

2. Disconnect the speedometer cable from the speedometer head. Pull the speedometer core out of the upper end of the casing.

3. Install a new core in the casing.

Printed Circuit Board

REMOVAL & INSTALLATION

1. Disconnect the negative battery cable. Remove the instrument cluster from the vehicle.

2. Remove the low fuel warning assembly, if equipped.

3. Remove all bulb and socket assemblies. Remove the speedometer and gauges.

4. Remove the retaining clips. Do not over bend the retaining clips as they may break.

5. After the clips are removed remove the printer circuit from its mounting.

6. Installation is the reverse of the removal procedure. When the clips are installed an audible click will be heard.

Windshield Wiper Switch

REMOVAL & INSTALLATION

The front wiper switch is a function of the combination switch refer to the proper Section for detailed information.

Rear Window Wiper Switch

REMOVAL & INSTALLATION

1986–89

1. Disconnect the negative battery cable.

2. Remove the 4 cluster opening finish panel retaining screws. Remove the finish panel by rocking the upper edge toward the driver.

3. Disconnect the wiring connector from the rear wiper switch.

4. Remove the wiper switch from the instrument panel. On Sable, the switch is retained with 2 screws.

5. Installation is the reverse of the removal procedure.

1990–92

1. Disconnect the negative battery cable.

2. Remove the cluster opening finish panel as follows:

a. Engage the parking brake.

b. Remove the ignition lock cylinder.

c. If equipped with a tilt column, tilt the column to the full down position and remove the tilt lever.

d. Remove the 4 bolts and the opening cover from under the steering column.

e. Remove the steering column trim shrouds. Disconnect all electrical connections from the combination switch.

f. Remove the 2 screws retaining the combination switch and remove the switch.

g. Pull the gear shift lever to the full down position.

h. Remove the 4 cluster opening finish panel retaining screws and the light switch knob and retaining nut.

i. Remove the finish panel by pulling it toward the driver to unsnap the snap-in retainers and disconnect the wiring from the switches, clock and warning lights.

3. Remove the washer switch from the cluster opening finish panel.

To Install:

4. Push the rear washer switch into the cluster finish panel until it snaps into place.

5. Install the cluster opening finish panel in the reverse order of removal.

6. Connect the negative battery cable.

Headlight Switch

REMOVAL & INSTALLATION

1986–89 Taurus

➧ SEE FIG. 82

1. Disconnect the negative battery cable.

2. Remove the bezel retaining nut and remove the bezel.

3. Remove the instrument cluster finish panel.

4. Remove the 2 screws retaining the headlight switch, pull the switch out of the instrument panel and disconnect the electrical connector.

5. Installation is the reverse of the removal procedure.

1988–89 Sable

➧ SEE FIG. 83

1. Disconnect the negative battery cable.

2. Remove the lower left finish panel.

3. Remove the 2 screws retaining the headlight switch to the finish panel, disconnect the electrical connector and remove the switch.

4. Installation is the reverse of the removal procedure.

1990–92 Taurus and Sable

1. Disconnect the negative battery cable.

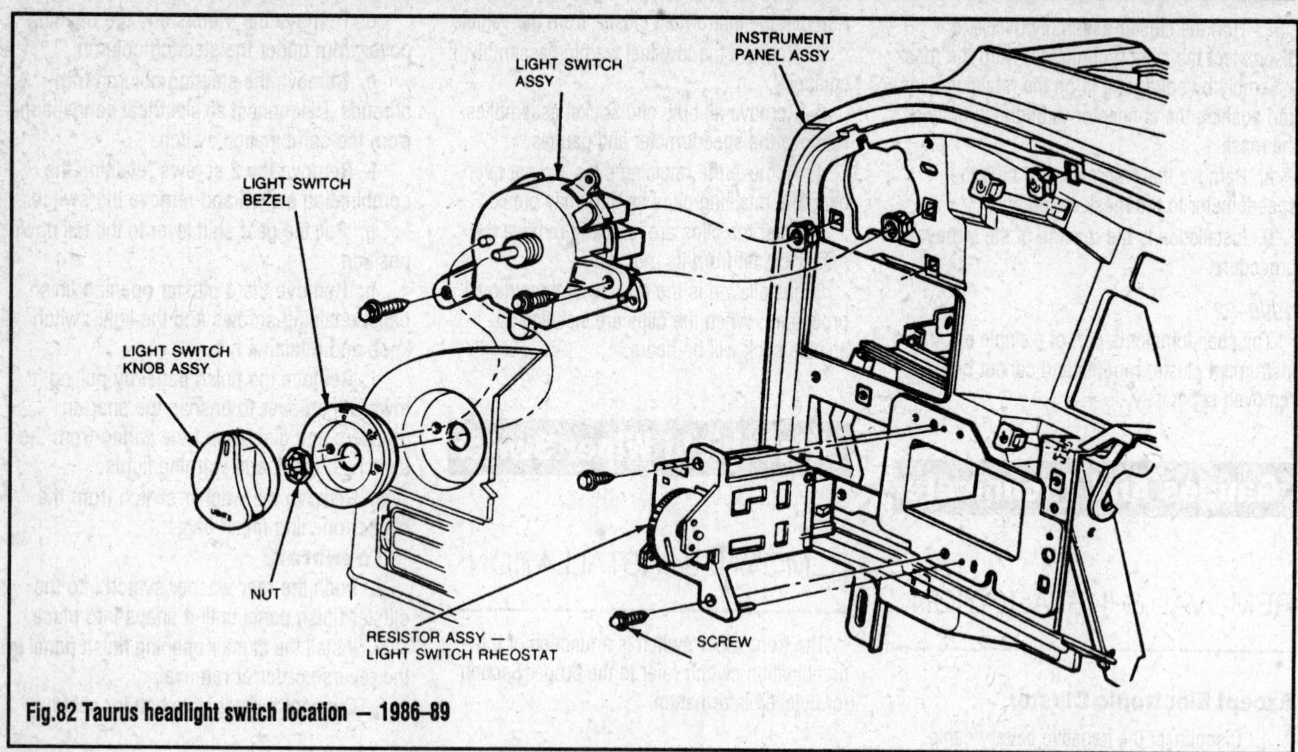

Fig.82 Taurus headlight switch location — 1986–89

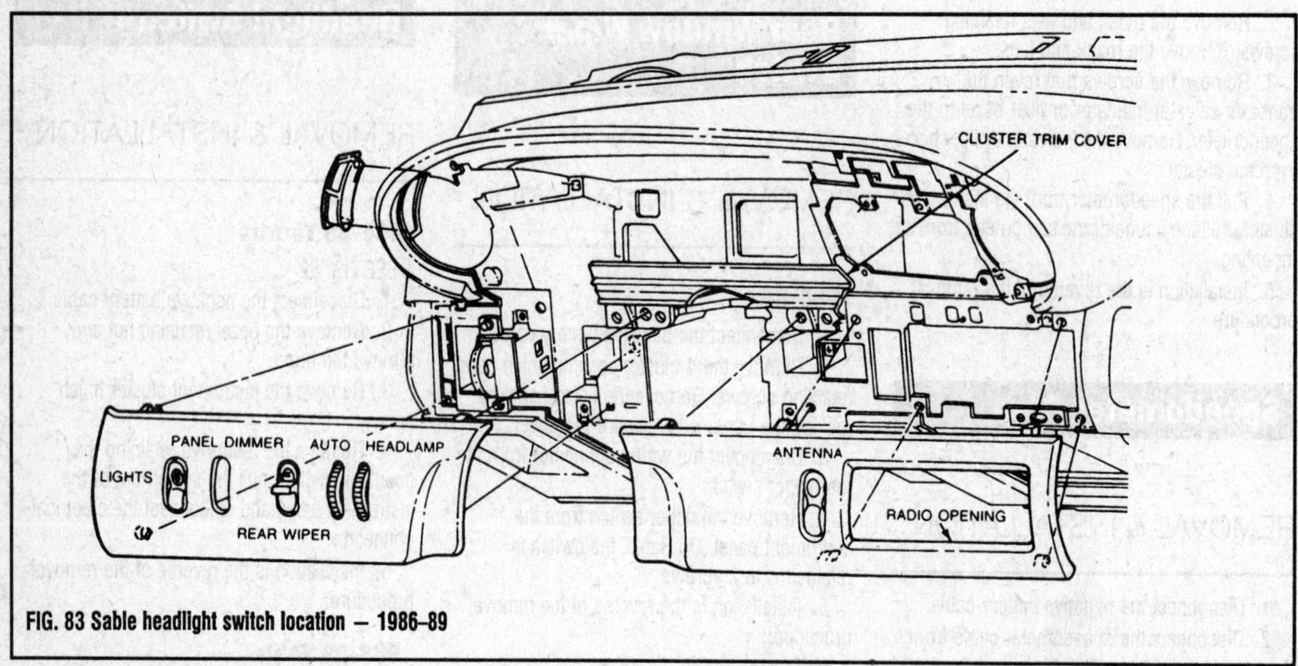

FIG. 83 Sable headlight switch location — 1986–89

2. Pull off the headlight switch knob and remove the retaining nut.

3. Remove the instrument cluster finish panel as follows:

a. Apply the parking brake.

b. Remove the ignition lock cylinder.

c. If equipped with a tilt column, tilt the column to the most downward position and remove the tilt lever.

d. Remove the 4 bolts and opening cover from under the steering column.

e. Remove the steering column trim shrouds. Disconnect all electrical connections from the steering column combination switch.

f. Remove the 2 screws retaining the combination switch and remove the switch.

g. Pull the gear shift lever to the full down position.

h. Remove the 4 cluster opening finish panel retaining screws. Remove the finish panel by pulling it toward the driver to unsnap the snap-in retainers and disconnect the wiring from the switches, clock and warning lights.

4. Remove the 2 screws retaining the headlight switch, pull the switch out of the instrument panel and disconnect the electrical connector.

5. Installation is the reverse of the removal procedure.

Clock

REMOVAL & INSTALLATION

➧ SEE FIG. 71

1. Using a 90° bent scriber, dental pick or similar hardened tool, insert the bent end of the tool into the slot at the bottom center of the clock.
2. Gently pull the scriber tool outward until the bottom clock retaining spring releases.
3. Grasp the clock and pull it outward to remove.
4. Disconnect the electrical connector.
5. To install connect the electrical connector and snap the clock back into position.

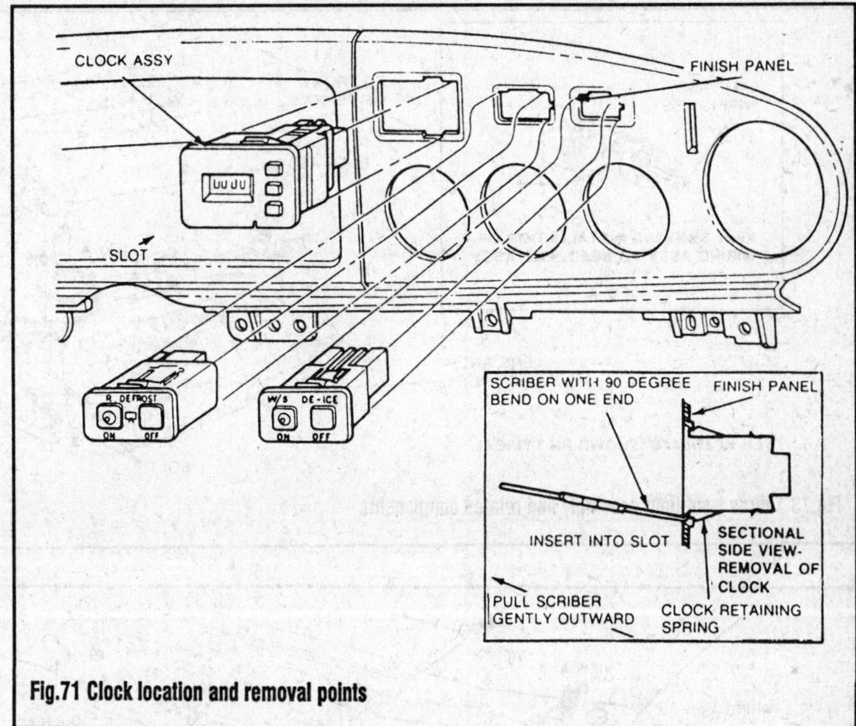

Fig.71 Clock location and removal points

LIGHTING

Headlights

REMOVAL & INSTALLATION

➧ SEE FIG. 72–74

Bulb Replacement

CAUTION

The replaceable Halogen headlamp bulb contains gas under pressure. The bulb may shatter if the glass envelope is scratched or the bulb is dropped. Handle the bulb carefully. Grasp the bulb ONLY by its plastic base. Avoid touching the glass envelope because the finger prints from your hand may cause the bulb to burst when turned on. Keep the bulb out of the reach of children.

1. Check to see that the headlight switch is in the OFF position.
2. Raise the hood and locate the bulb installed in the rear of the headlight body.
3. Remove the electrical connector from the bulb by grasping the wires firmly and snapping the connector rearward.
4. Remove the bulb retaining ring by rotating it counterclockwise (when viewed from the rear) about 1/8 of a turn, then slide the ring off the plastic base.

➡ Keep the bulb retaining ring, it will be reused with the new bulb.

5. Carefully remove the headlight bulb from its socket in the reflector by gently pulling it straight backward out of the socket. DO NOT rotate the bulb during removal.

To install:

6. With the flat side of the plastic base of the bulb facing upward, insert the glass envelope of the bulb into the socket. Turn the base slightly to the left or right, if necessary to align the grooves in the forward part of the plastic base with the corresponding locating tabs inside the socket. When the grooves are aligned, push the bulb firmly into the socket until the mounting flange on the base contacts the rear face of the socket.
7. Slip the bulb retaining ring over the rear of the plastic base against the mounting flange. Lock the ring into the socket by rotating the ring counterclockwise. A stop will be felt when the retaining ring is fully engaged.
8. Push the electrical connector into the rear of the plastic until it snaps and locks into position.
9. Turn the headlights on and check for proper operation.

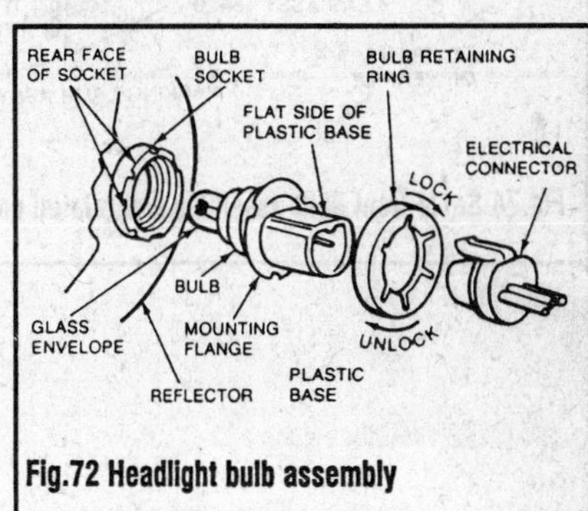

Fig.72 Headlight bulb assembly

LAMP ASSY
WIRING ASSY
VIEW SHOWING INSTALLATION OF
WIRING ASSY TO HEADLAMP ASSY
VIEW A
TO FRONT
OF VEHICLE
BULB ASSY
WIRING ASSY
SPRING NUT
VIEW A
SCREW
NUT
LENS AND
BODY ASSY
LAMP ASSY
LH HEADLAMP SHOWN RH TYPICAL
BOLT

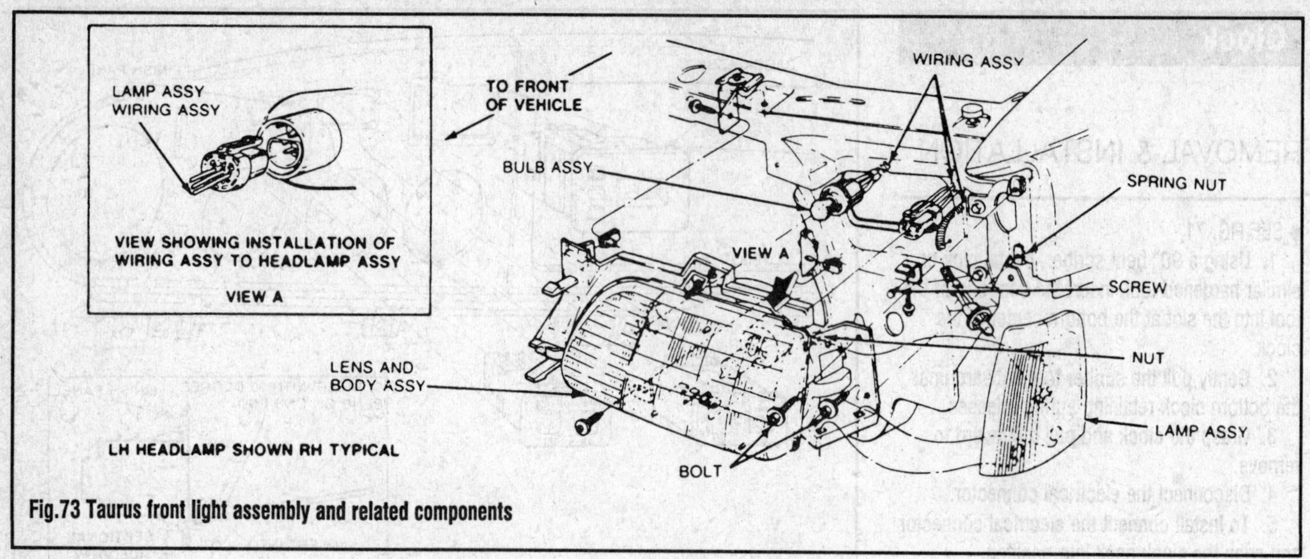

Fig.73 Taurus front light assembly and related components

VIEW B
VIEW A
WIRING ASSY
SCREW
BULB ASSY
NUT
RADIATOR
SUPPORT
WIRING ASSY
LAMP ASSY (PARKING INNER)
VIEW C
NUT
HEADLAMP HOUSING
MOUNTING BRACKET
NUT
BULB ASSY
NUT
NUT
RADIATOR SUPPORT UPPER
LENS AND
BODY ASSY
INSTALLATION OF BRACKET TO
RADIATOR SUPPORT
VIEW B
HOUSING LOWER MOUNTING
BRACKET HEADLAMP
SCREW
NUT
SCREW
CORNERING LAMP
LENS ASSY 15A201
HEADLAMP ASSY
TO FRONT
OF VEHICLE
PARKING LAMP ASSY
INSTALLATION OF HEADLAMPS
TO UPPER BRACKET
VIEW A
INSTALLATION OF HEADLAMPS TO
LOWER BRACKET
VIEW C

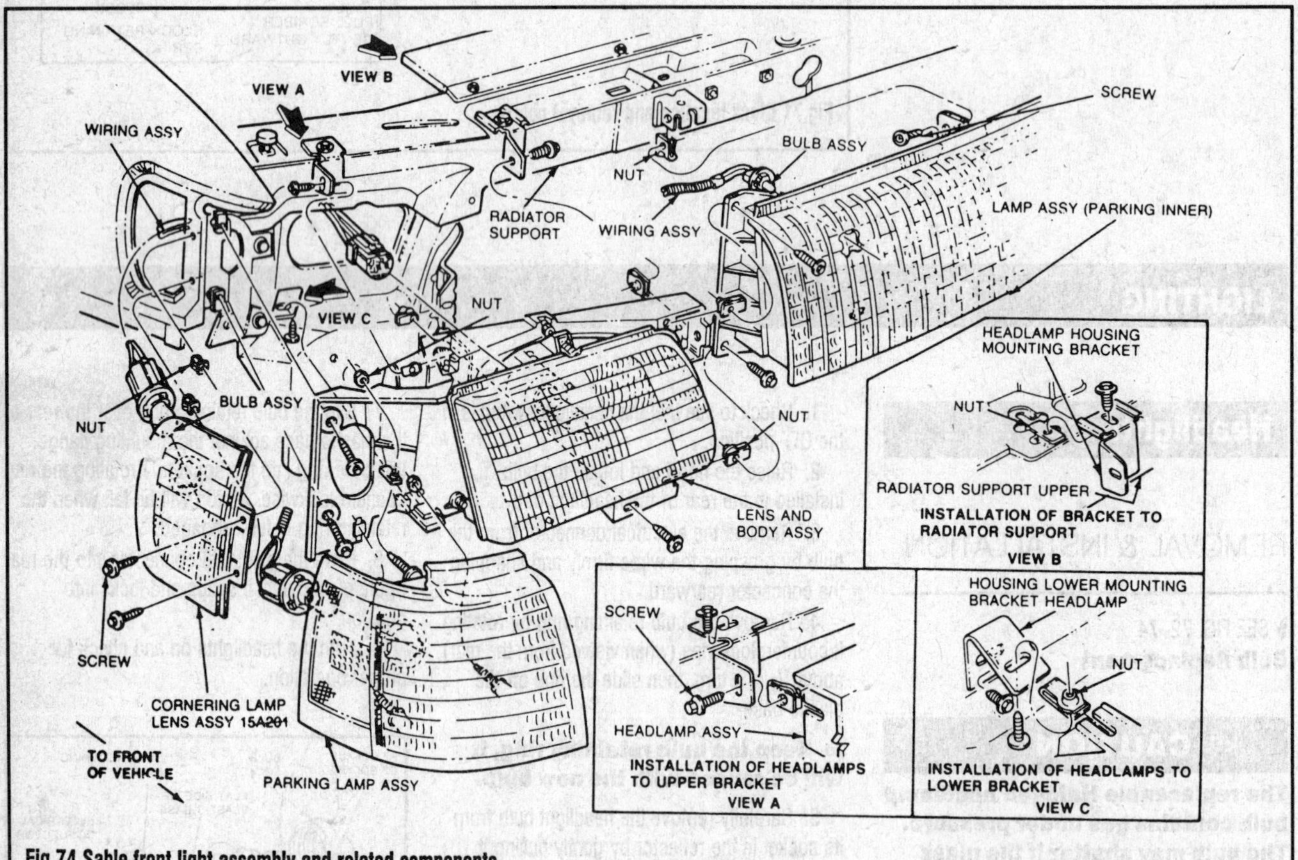

Fig.74 Sable front light assembly and related components

AIMING

All adjustments should be made with at least a half tank of gas in the fuel tank, an empty trunk except for the spare tire and jack and the correct tire pressures.

Special equipment is used to properly aim the front headlights.

Signal And Marker Lights

REMOVAL & INSTALLATION

Parking/Front Turn Signal Light Combination

The parking and turn signal lights share the same dual filament bulb.

TAURUS

1. Using the access hole in the radiator support, rotate the bulb socket counterclockwise to disengage it from the light housing and remove the bulb.
2. To install reverse the removal procedure. Rotate the bulb socket clockwise to engage the socket into the housing.

SABLE

1. Remove the two screws attaching the parking lamp assembly and pull it forward.
2. Remove the bulb socket by twisting and then remove the bulb.
3. Install the bulb in the socket, and install the socket in the lamp assembly by twisting.
4. Position the parking lamp in place and install the screws.

Side Marker Lights

TAURUS

1. Remove one nut and washer from the attaching stud at the top of the lamp assembly.
2. Rotate the top outboard until the stud tip has cleared the slot in the housing.
3. Lift the lamp to clear the two lower tabs (on the headlamp) from the headlamp housing.
4. Remove the bulb socket by twisting it counterclockwise and pull the bulb from the socket.

To Install:

5. Install the bulb into the socket, and install the socket by twisting it counterclockwise.
6. Position the lamp in place by lowering the two tabs on the lamp into the two slots on the headlamp housing.
7. Rotate the lamp inboard to allow the stud to enter the upper slot in the housing.
8. Install the nut and washer to the attaching stud, and secure them.

Cornering Lights

SABLE

1. Remove the two screws attaching the parking lamp assembly and pull it forward.
2. Remove the bulb socket by twisting and then remove the bulb.
3. Remove the two screws attaching the cornering lamp assembly and lift it out.
4. Remove the bulb by twisting it counterclockwise.

To Install:

5. Install the bulb, and install the socket by turning it clockwise.
6. Position the cornering light back in place, and install the two screws.
7. Install the parking lamp bulb in the socket, and install the socket in the lamp assembly by twisting.
8. Position the parking lamp in place and install the screws.

1990–92 TAURUS

1. Disconnect the negative battery cable.
2. Remove the cornering lamp retaining nuts. Lift the cornering lamp from its mounting.
3. Remove the bulb and socket assembly. Remove the cornering lamp from the vehicle.
4. Installation is the reverse of the removal procedure.

Auxiliary Headlight Assembly

TAURUS SHO

1. Disconnect the negative battery cable. Remove the headlight assembly.
2. Remove the two screws attaching the auxiliary headlight to the headlight assembly.
3. Installation is the reverse of the removal procedure.

Rear Turn Signal/Brake Lights

➧ SEE FIG. 75–77

1. Bulbs can be serviced from the inside of the luggage compartment by removing the luggage compartment rear trim panel, if so equipped.
2. Remove the socket(s) from the lamp body and replace the bulb(s).
3. Install the socket(s) in the lamp body and install the trim panel.

High Mount Brake Light

1. Disconnect the negative battery cable.
2. On the sedan remove the two covers and screws that retain the lamp assembly to the retainer.

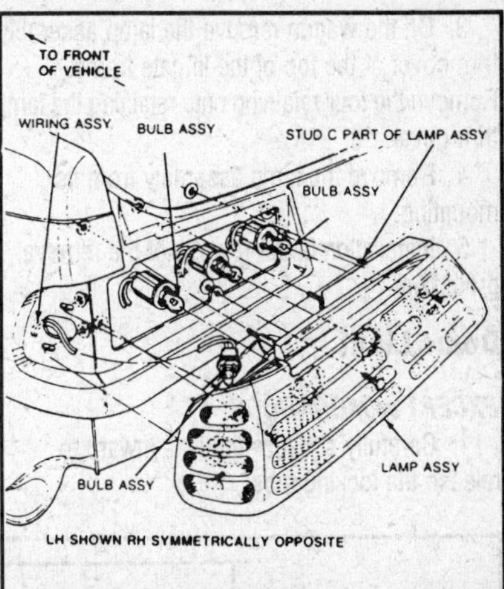

Fig.75 Taurus rear light assembly and related components – except wagon

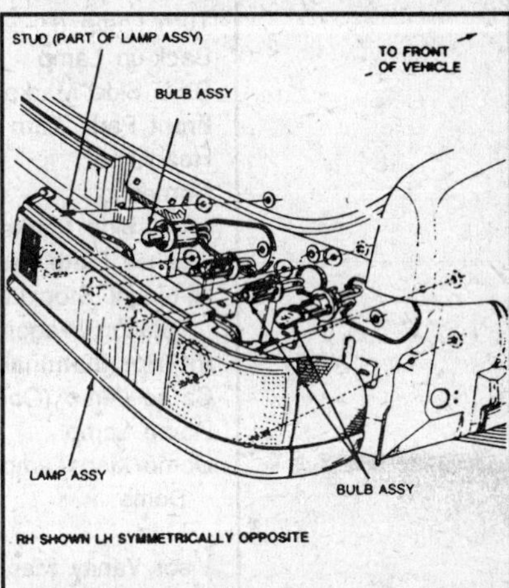

Fig.76 Sable rear light assembly and related components – except wagon

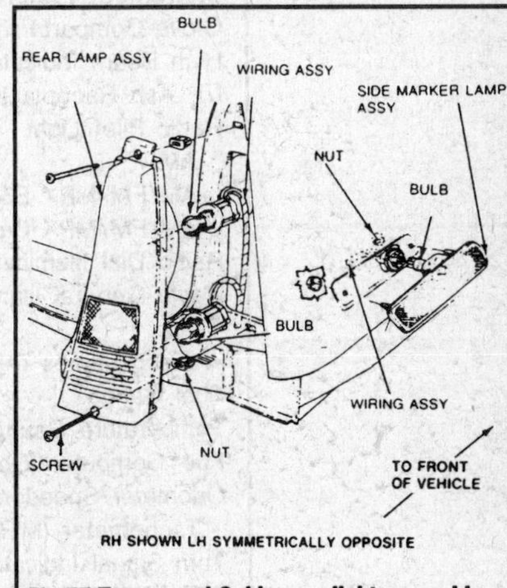

Fig.77 Taurus and Sable rear light assembly and related components – wagon

3. On the wagon remove the lamp assembly trim cover at the top of the liftgate frame. Remove the four retaining nuts retaining the lamp trim cover.

4. Remove the lamp assembly from its mounting.

5. Installation is the reverse of the removal procedure.

Dome Light

EXCEPT w/MOONROOF

1. Carefully squeeze the lens inward to release the locking tabs.

2. Remove the lens from the lamp body. Replace the defective bulb.

3. Installation is the reverse of the removal procedure.

WITH MOONROOF

1. Use a thin bladed tool and carefully pry out and unsnap the lens.

2. Replace the defective bulb.

3. Installation is the reverse of the removal procedure.

License Plate Lights

1. Remove the two lamp body plastic retaining rivets.

2. Remove the lamp assembly.

3. Remove the socket and bulb assembly from the rear of the lamp assembly. Replace the defective bulb.

4. Installation is the reverse of the removal procedure.

Function	Number of Bulbs	Trade Number
Exterior Illumination		
Tail Lamp, Stop Lamp, Turn Lamp (Lo-Series)	2	1157
Tail Lamp, Stop Lamp, (Hi-Series)	2	1157
Turn Lamp (Hi-Series)	2	1156
Back-up Lamp	2	1156
Rear Side Marker Lamp	2	194
Front Park, Turn Lamp	2	2357
Headlamp	2	9004
Cornering	2	1156
Front Side Marker Lamp	2	194
License Plate Lamp	2	194
Hi-Mount Stop Lamp (Sedan)	2	912
(Station Wagon)	2	921
Interior Illumination		
Cargo Lamp (Opt.)	1	906
Dome Lamp	1	906
Dome/Map Lamp (Opt.)		
Dome	1	912
Map	2	105
Visor Vanity Map (Opt.)	4	168
Door Courtesy Lamp	2	194
Engine Compartment Lamp	1	168
Floor Console	1	168
Luggage Compartment Lamp	1	906
Instrument Panel Illumination		
Glove Compartment	1	194
High Beam Indicator	1	194
I/P Ash Receptacle Lamp	1	1892
Radio Pilot Light		
AM	1	37
AM/FM/MPX ESR	6	7152
AM/FM/MPX Cassette ESR	6	7152
Radio Dial Illumination	1	936
Radio General Illumination	6	7152
Clock	1	ENW-2
Warning Lamps (All)	1 each	194
Fuel Gauge	2	194
Temperature Gauge	2	194
Fuel Computer (Opt.)	1	882
Odometer/Speedometer/ Tachometer (MT5 Models Only)	2	882
Turn Signal Indicator	2	194
"PRNDL" Bulb	1	194
Heater or Heater-A/C (Opt.)	2	161
Automatic Climate Control (Opt.)	5	37

Light bulb usage information — 1986–87

Fog/Driving Lights

REMOVAL & INSTALLATION

1. Disconnect the negative battery cable.

2. From inside the front fascia remove the two nuts, retaining springs and lamp mounting brackets.

3. Disconnect the electrical connector. Slide the fog lamp assembly off its mounting studs and remove it from the vehicle.

4. Installation is the reverse of the removal procedure.

Function	Number of Bulbs	Trade Number
Exterior Illumination		
Tail Lamp, Stop Lamp, Turn Lamp (Lo-Series)	2	2458
Tail Lamp, Stop Lamp, (Hi-Series)	2	2458
Tail Lamp, Stop Lamp, Turn Lamp (Wagons)	2	2458
Turn Lamp (Hi-Series)	2	1156
Back-up Lamp	2	2456
Rear Side Marker Lamp	2	194
Front Park, Turn Lamp	2	2458
Headlamp	2	9004
Cornering	2	2456
Front Side Marker Lamp	2	194
License Plate Lamp	2	194
Hi-Mount Stop Lamp (Sedan)	2	912
(Station Wagon)	2	921
Interior Illumination		
Cargo Lamp (Opt.)	1	562
Cargo Lamp (Wagon)	2	214-2
Dome Lamp	1	562
Dome/Map Lamp (Opt.)		
Dome	1	563
Map	2	561
Visor Vanity Map (Opt.)	4	74-194
Door Courtesy Lamp	2	168
Engine Compartment Lamp	1	906
Floor Console	1	906
Luggage Compartment Lamp	1	906
Instrument Panel Illumination		
Glove Compartment	1	194
High Beam Indicator	1	194
I/P Ash Receptacle Lamp	1	194
Radio Pilot Light		
AM	1	37
AM/FM/MPX Search	6	7152
AM/FM/MPX Cassette EPC	6	7152
Radio Stereo Light	1	936
Clock	1	ENW-2
Warning Lamps (All)	1 each	194
Fuel Gauge	2	194
Temperature Gauge	2	194
Fuel Computer (Opt.)	1	882
Odometer/Speedometer/ Tachometer (MT5 Models Only)	2	882
Turn Signal Indicator	2	194
"PRNDL" Bulb	1	194
Heater or Heater-A/C (Opt.)	2	161
Automatic Climate Control (Opt.)	5	37

Light bulb usage information — 1988–92

TRAILER WIRING

Wiring the car for towing is fairly easy. There are a number of good wiring kits available and these should be used, rather than trying to design your own. All trailers will need brake lights and turn signals as well as tail lights and side marker lights. Most states require extra marker lights for overly wide trailers. Also, most states have recently required back-up lights for trailers, and most trailer manufacturers have been building trailers with back-up lights for several years.

Additionally, some Class I, most Class II and just about all Class III trailers will have electric brakes.

Add to this number an accessories wire, to operate trailer internal equipment or to charge the trailer's battery, and you can have as many as seven wires in the harness.

Determine the equipment on your trailer and buy the wiring kit necessary. The kit will contain all the wires needed, plus a plug adapter set which included the female plug, mounted on the bumper or hitch, and the male plug, wired into, or plugged into the trailer harness.

When installing the kit, follow the manufacturer's instructions. The color coding of the wires is standard throughout the industry.

One point to note: some vehicles, have separate turn signals. On most vehicles, the brake lights and rear turn signals operate with the same bulb. For those vehicles with separate turn signals, you can purchase an isolation unit so that the brake lights won't blink whenever the turn signals are operated, or, you can go to your local electronics supply house and buy four diodes to wire in series with the brake and turn signal bulbs. Diodes will isolate the brake and turn signals. The choice is yours. The isolation units are simple and quick to install, but far more expensive than the diodes. The diodes, however, require more work to install properly, since they require the cutting of each bulb's wire and soldering in place of the diode.

One final point, the best kits are those with a spring loaded cover on the vehicle mounted socket. This cover prevents dirt and moisture from corroding the terminals. Never let the vehicle socket hang loosely; always mount it securely to the bumper or hitch.

CIRCUIT PROTECTION

Fuses

➧ SEE FIG. 78–79

REPLACEMENT

All vehicles have a fuse panel located under the left side of the instrument panel.

Fuses are a one-time circuit protection. If a circuit is overloaded or shorts, the fuse will blow thus protecting the circuit. A fuse will continue to blow until the circuit is repaired.

Fusible Links

➧ SEE FIG. 80

REPLACEMENT

Fusible links are used to prevent major wire harness damage in the event of a short circuit or an overload condition in the wiring circuits that are normally not fused, due to carrying high amperage loads or because of their locations within the wiring harness. Each fusible link is of a fixed value for a specific electrical load and should a fusible link fail, the cause of the failure must be determined and repaired prior to installing a new fusible link of the same value. Please be advised that the color coding of replacement fusible links may vary from the production color coding that is outlined in the text that follows.

Taurus and Sable

Gray 12 Gauge Wire — located in left side of engine compartment at starter relay; used to protect battery to alternator circuit on all except 3.0L SHO engine.

Green 14 Gauge Wire — located in left side of engine compartment at starter relay; used to protect battery to alternator circuit if with 3.0L SHO engine.

Green 14 Gauge Wire — located in left side of engine compartment at starter relay; used to protect anti-lock brake system power relay circuit.

Black 16 Gauge Wire — located on the left shock tower; used to protect the battery feed to headlight switch and fuse panel circuits.

Black 16 Gauge Wire — located on the left shock tower; used to protect the battery feed to ignition switch and fuse panel circuits.

Black 16 Gauge Wire — located in left side of engine compartment at starter relay; used to protect rear window defrost circuit on 1986–90 vehicles and 1991–92 2.5L engine vehicles.

Brown 18 Gauge Wire — located in left side of engine compartment at starter relay; used to protect rear window defrost circuit on 1991–92 vehicles, except 2.5L engine.

Brown 18 Gauge Wire — located in right front of engine compartment at alternator output control relay; used to protect the alternator output control relay to heated windshield circuit.

Blue 20 Gauge Wire — located on the left shock tower; used to protect the ignition coil, ignition module and cooling fan controller circuits.

Blue 20 Gauge Wire — located in left rear of engine compartment; used to protect ignition switch to anti-lock brake system circuit.

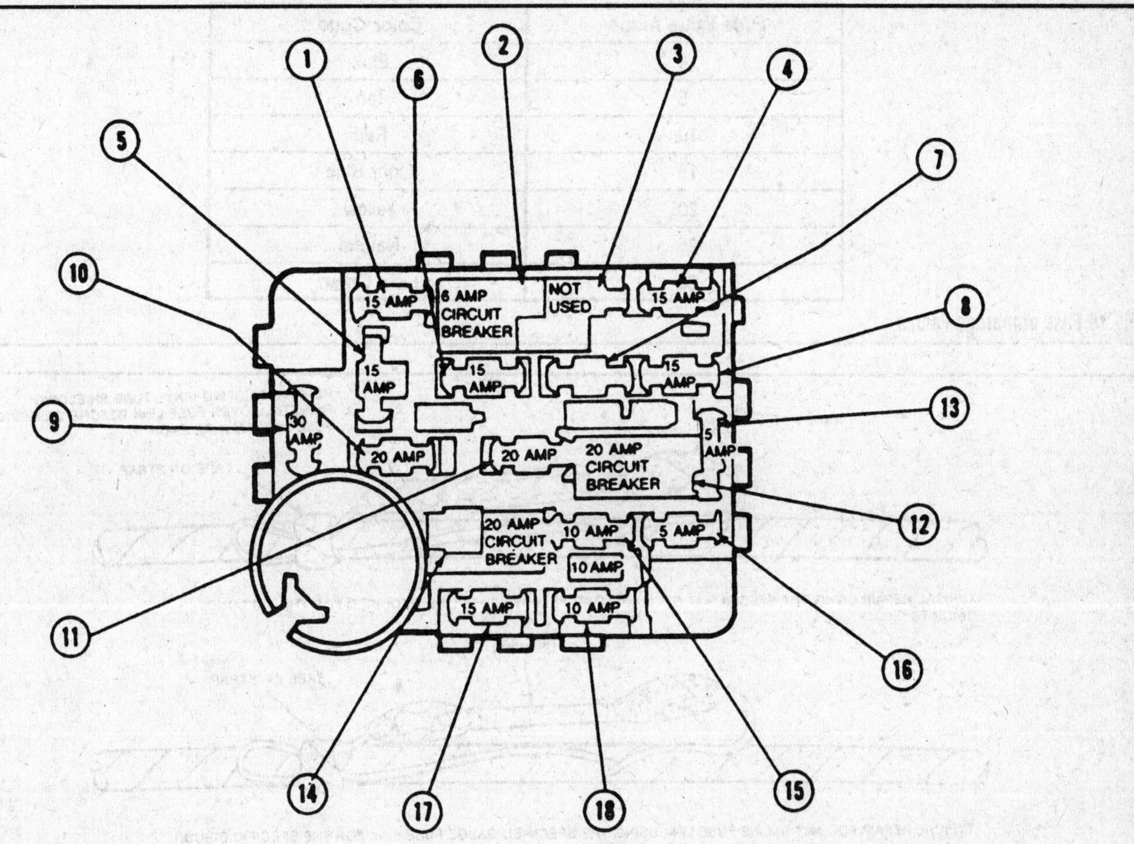

CAVITY NUMBER	CIRCUIT PROTECTED
1	HI-MOUNT STOPLAMP, STOPLAMPS, FRONT AND REAR TURN SIGNALS, INSTRUMENT PANEL TURN INDICATOR LAMPS
2	WINDSHIELD WIPER MOTOR, INTERMITTENT WIPER MODULE, WINDSHIELD WASHER MOTOR
3	NOT USED
4	FRONT PARK, SIDE MARKER AND TAIL LAMPS, "HEADLAMPS-ON" WARNING BUZZER/CHIME, FRONT LASER LAMP (SABLE).
5	ELECTRONIC CLUSTER, HEATED BACKLIGHT SWITCH, ELECTRONIC FLASHER, BACKUP LAMPS, HEATED E G O , ILLUMINATED/KEYLESS ENTRY MODULE
6	REAR WINDOW WIPER AND WASHER MOTORS (WAGONS), DIAGNOSTIC WARNING LAMP MODULE, WARNING CHIME, HEADLAMP SWITCH ILLUMINATION (SABLE), CLOCK ILLUMINATION, RADIO ILLUMINATION, EATC CONTROL ILLUMINATION, POWER WINDOW RELAY
7	NOT USED
8	CLOCK, RADIO MEMORY, GLOVE COMPT. LAMP, LUGGAGE COMPT. LAMP, INST. PANEL COURTESY LAMPS, INTERIOR LAMPS, ILLUMINATED/KEYLESS ENTRY MODULE, POWER MIRRORS

CAVITY NUMBER	CIRCUIT PROTECTED
9	BLOWER MOTOR, BLOWER SPEED CONTROLLER (EATC)
10	FLASH-TO-PASS, HIGH BEAM HEADLAMPS AND INDICATOR LAMP
11	RADIO, PREMIUM SOUND AMPLIFIER, POWER ANTENNA MOTOR
12	CIGAR LIGHTERS, HORN RELAY, HORNS
13	CLUSTER ILLUMINATION, RADIO DISPLAY, ASH TRAY ILLUM., EATC CONTROL DISPLAY, HEATED BACKLIGHT SWITCH ILLUM., HEATED WINDSHIELD SWITCH ILLUM., REAR WIPER SWITCH ILLUM., HEADLAMP SWITCH ILLUM., CLOCK DISPLAY, P R N D L ILLUMINATION
14	NOT USED
15	LICENSE LAMPS, SIDE MARKER AND TAIL LAMPS
16	ELECTRONIC CLUSTER EATC CONTROL SWITCH
17	EATC COMPRESSOR CLUTCH, EATC BLEND DOOR ACTUATOR, A/C COMPRESSOR CLUTCH
18	AUTOLAMP MODULE, CLUSTER WARNING LAMPS, LOW OIL LEVEL RELAY, BUZZER/CHIME

Fig.78 Fuse locations

Fuse Value Amps	Color Code
4	Pink
5	Tan
10	Red
15	Light Blue
20	Yellow
25	Natural
30	Light Green

Fig.79 Fuse amperage values

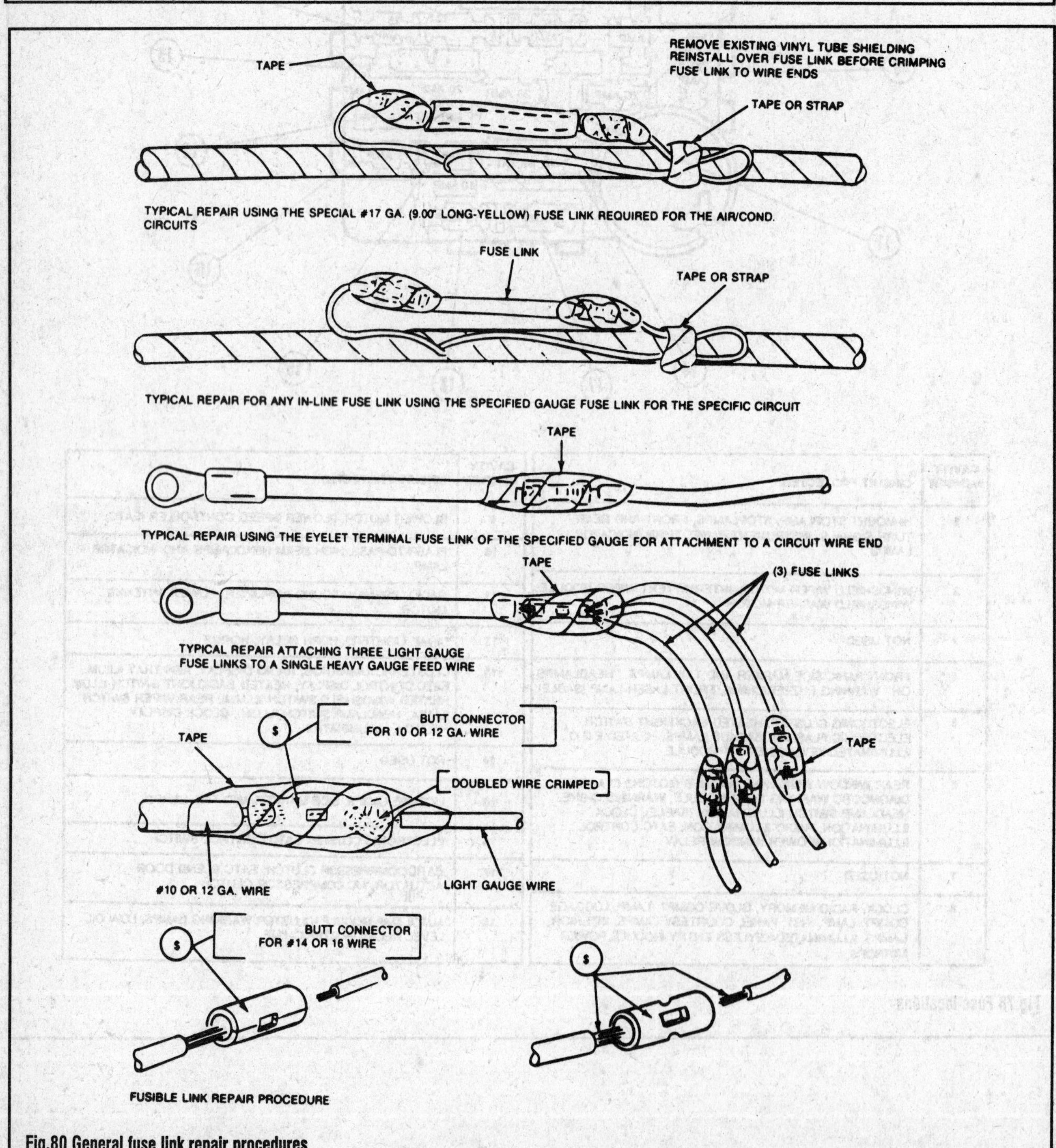

Fig.80 General fuse link repair procedures

Circuit Breakers

REPLACEMENT

Circuit breakers protect electrical circuits by interrupting the current flow. A circuit breaker conducts current through an arm made of 2 types of metal bonded together. If the arm starts to carry too much current, it heats up. As 1 metal expands faster than the other the arm bends, opening the contacts and interrupting the current flow.

Taurus and Sable

Station Wagon Rear Window/ Washer — One 4.5 amp circuit breaker located on the instrument panel brace, on the left side of the steering column on Taurus or on the left instrument panel end panel on Sable.

Windshield Wipers and Washer Pump — One 6 amp circuit breaker located on the fuse panel, on 1988 vehicles.

Windshield Wipers and Washer Pump — One 8.25 amp circuit breaker located on the fuse panel, on 1989–92 vehicles.

Cigar Lighters, Horn Relay and Horns — One 20 amp circuit breaker located on the fuse panel.

Power Windows, Power Locks and Power Seats — One 20 amp circuit breaker located near the starter relay, on 1986–89 vehicles.

Power Windows, Power Locks and Power Seats — One 20 amp circuit breaker located on the fuse panel, on 1990–92 vehicles.

Headlights — One 22 amp circuit breaker incorporated in the headlight switch.

Relays

REPLACEMENT

Various relays are used in conjunction with the vehicle's electrical components. If a relay should fail it must be replaced with one of equal value

Taurus and Sable

Alternator Output Control Relay — located between the right front inner fender and fender splash shield, if with 3.0L or 3.8L engines and heated windshield.

Anti-lock Motor Relay — located in lower left front of engine compartment, if with anti-lock brakes.

Anti-lock Power Relay — located in left rear corner of engine compartment, if with anti-lock brakes.

Autolite Dual Coil Relay — located behind the center of the instrument panel on the instrument panel brace, if with automatic headlights.

Fog Light Relay — located behind the center of the instrument panel on the instrument panel brace.

Horn Relay — located behind the center of the instrument panel on the instrument panel brace.

LCD Dimming Relay — located behind the center of the instrument panel on the instrument panel brace, if with automatic headlights.

Low Oil Level Relay — located behind the center of the instrument panel on the instrument panel brace.

Moonroof Relay — located behind the right side of the instrument panel.

Police Accessory Relay — located behind the center of the instrument panel.

Starter Relay — located on the left fender apron, in front of the strut tower.

Window Safety Relay — located behind the right side of the instrument panel.

Computers

LOCATION

Electronic Engine Control Module — located on the passenger side of the firewall.

Anti-lock Brake Control Module — located at the front of the engine compartment next to the passenger side fender, except on Taurus SHO where it is located at the front of the engine compartment on the driver's side.

Automatic Temperature Control Module — located behind the center of the instrument panel.

Heated Windshield Control Module — located behind the left side of the instrument panel, to the right of the steering column.

Integrated Control Module — located at the front of the engine compartment, on the upper radiator support.

Air Bag Diagnostic Module — located behind the right side of the instrument panel, above the glove box.

Flashers

REPLACEMENT

An electronic combination turn signal and emergency warning flasher is attached to the lower left instrument panel reinforcement above the fuse panel.

The turn signal unit is located on the LH side of the instrument panel. The combination turn signal and hazard flasher can be removed by pressing the plastic retaining clip and pulling straight rearward. One phillips® head screw has to be removed from the retaining bracket.

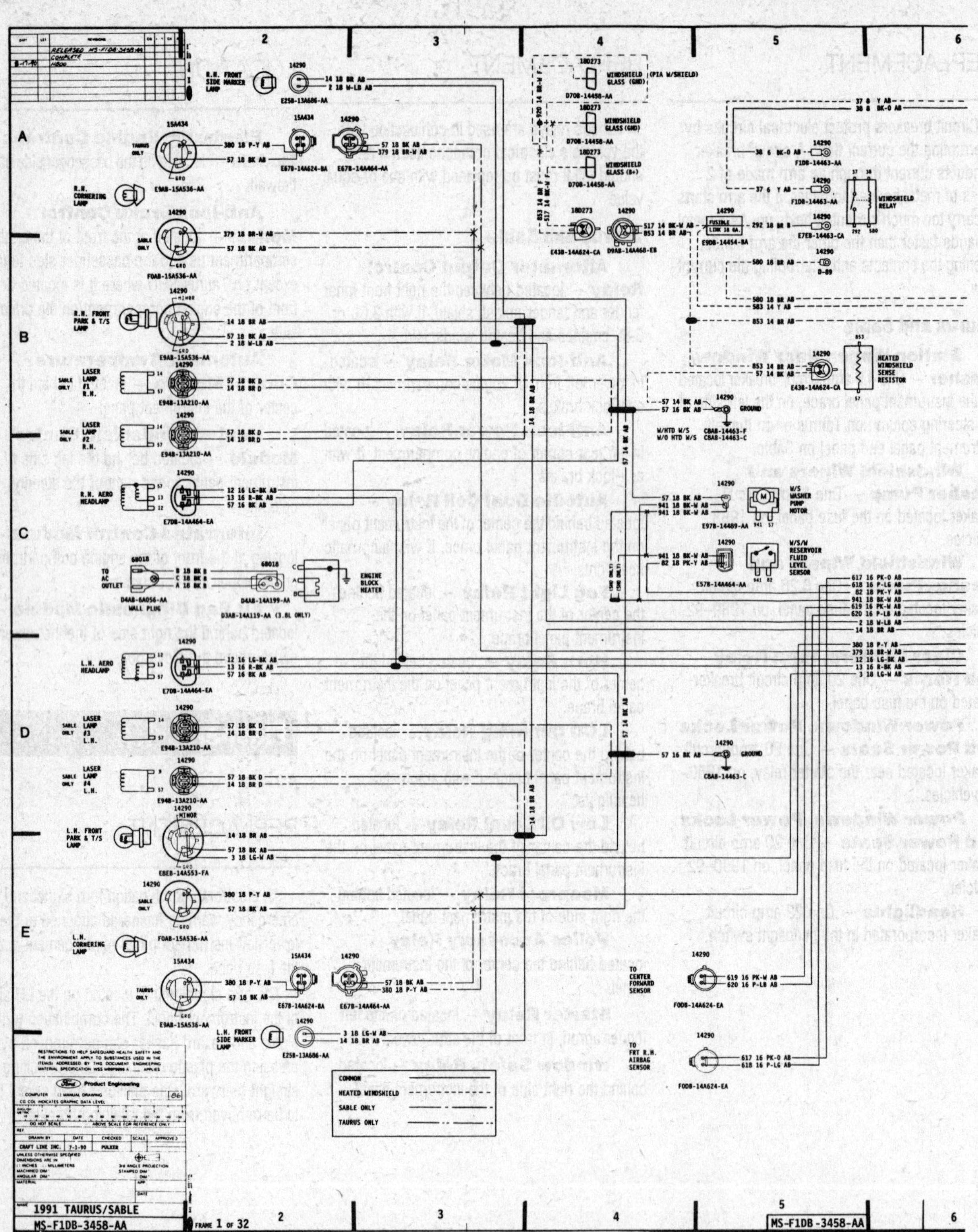

Taurus and Sable electrical schematics — 1991

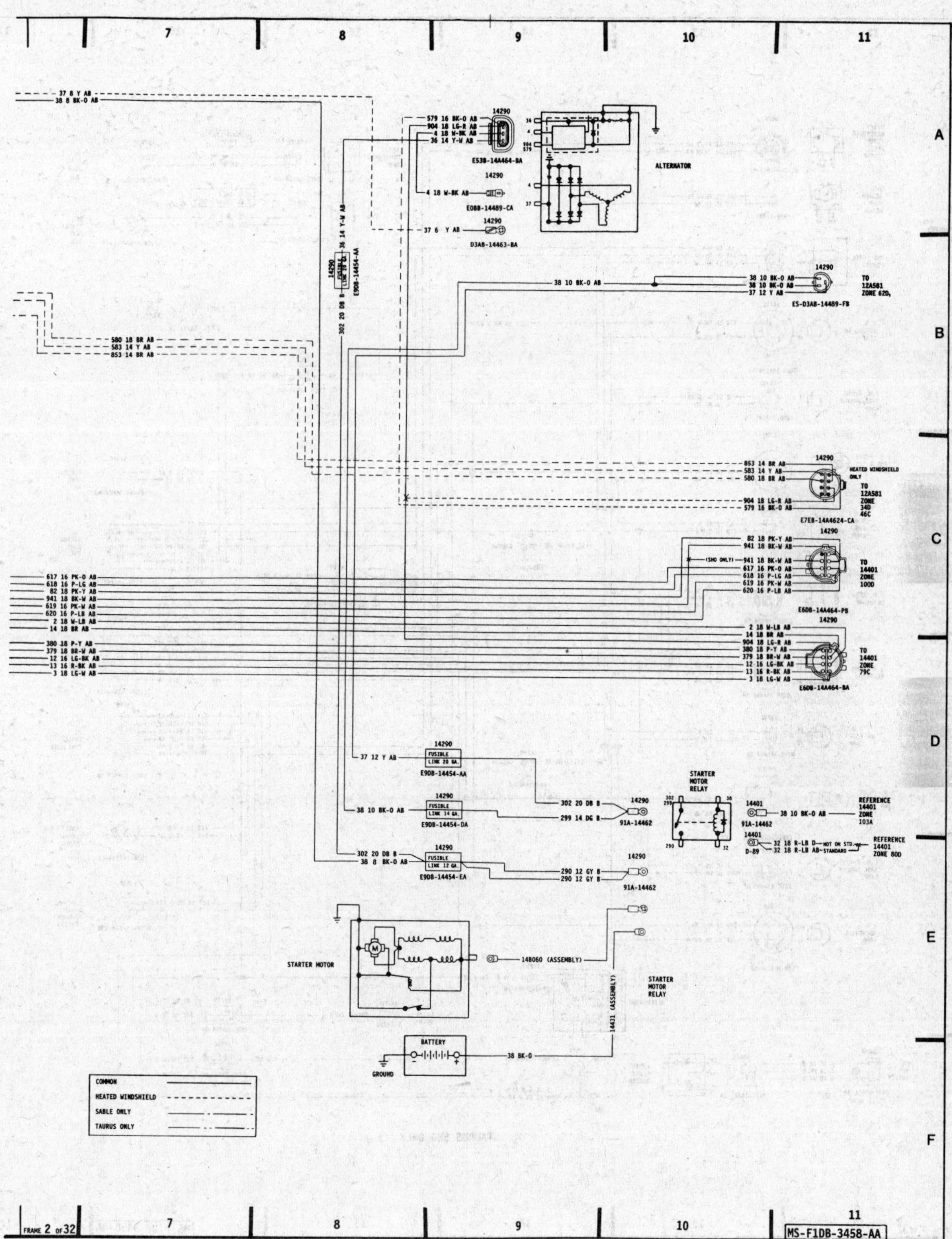

Taurus and Sable electrical schematics — 1991

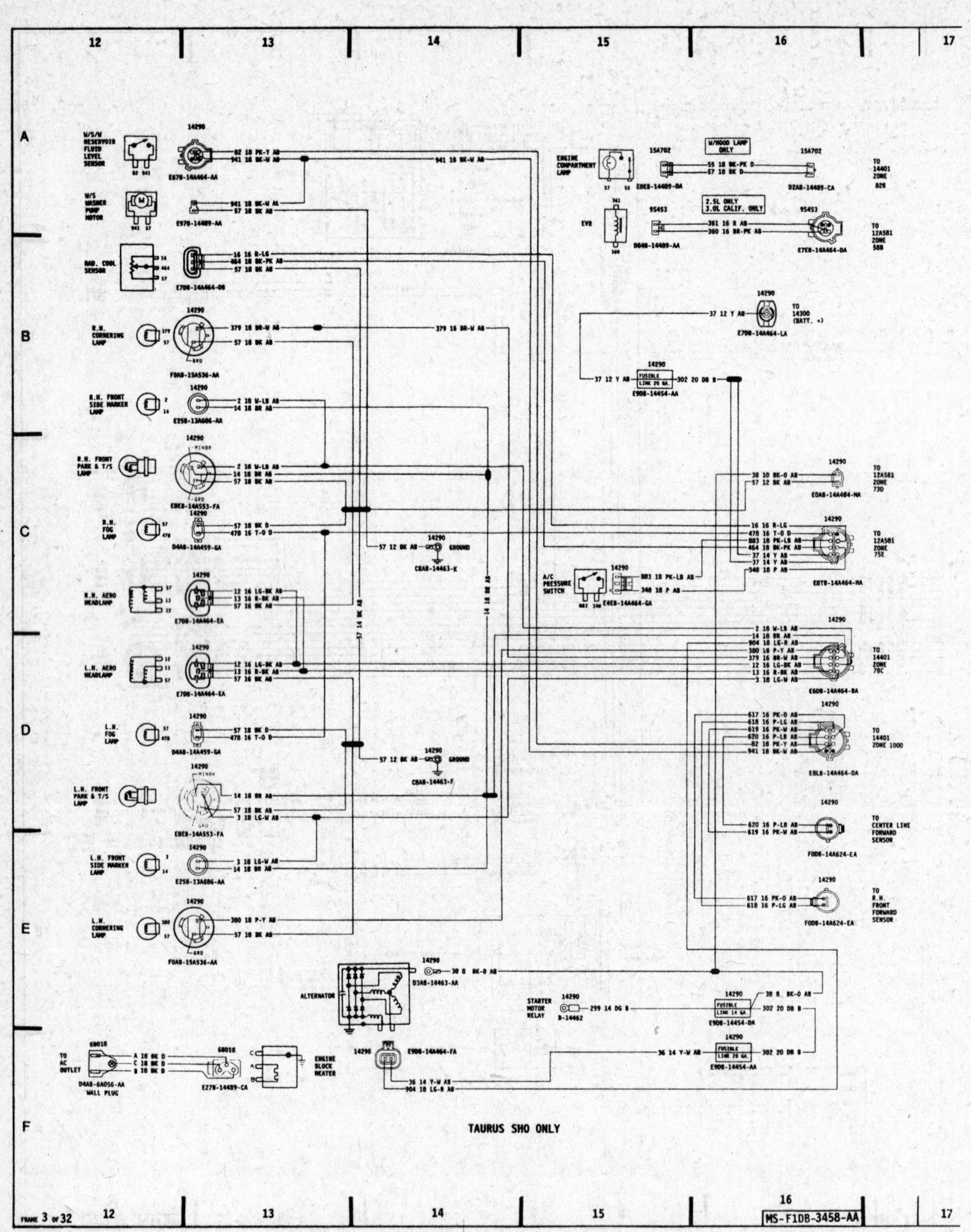
12
13
14
15
16
17
A
B
C
D
E
F
W/S/W RESERVOIR FLUID LEVEL SENSOR
W/S WASHER PUMP MOTOR
RAD. COOL SENSOR
R.H. CORNERING LAMP
R.H. FRONT SIDE MARKER LAMP
R.H. FRONT PARK & T/S LAMP
R.H. FOG LAMP
R.H. AERO HEADLAMP
L.H. AERO HEADLAMP
L.H. FOG LAMP
L.H. FRONT PARK & T/S LAMP
L.H. FRONT SIDE MARKER LAMP
L.H. CORNERING LAMP
ENGINE COMPARTMENT LAMP
W/HOOD LAMP ONLY
EVR
2.5L ONLY 3.0L CALIF. ONLY
A/C PRESSURE SWITCH
ALTERNATOR
STARTER MOTOR RELAY
ENGINE BLOCK HEATER
TO AC OUTLET
WALL PLUG
TO CENTER LINE FORWARD SENSOR
TO R.H. FRONT FORWARD SENSOR
GROUND
TAURUS SHO ONLY
FRAME 3 OF 32
MS-F1DB-3458-AA

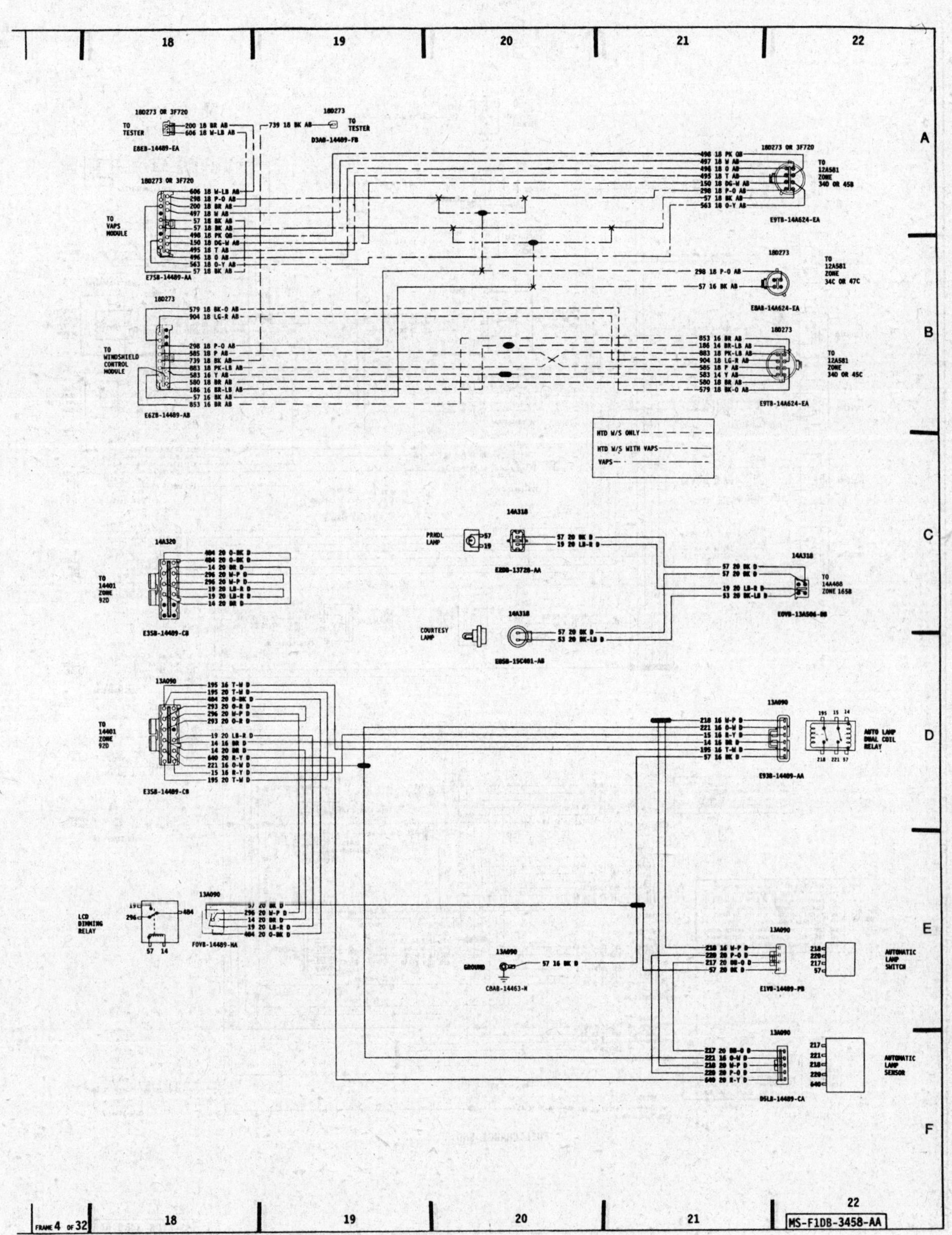

Taurus and Sable electrical schematics — 1991

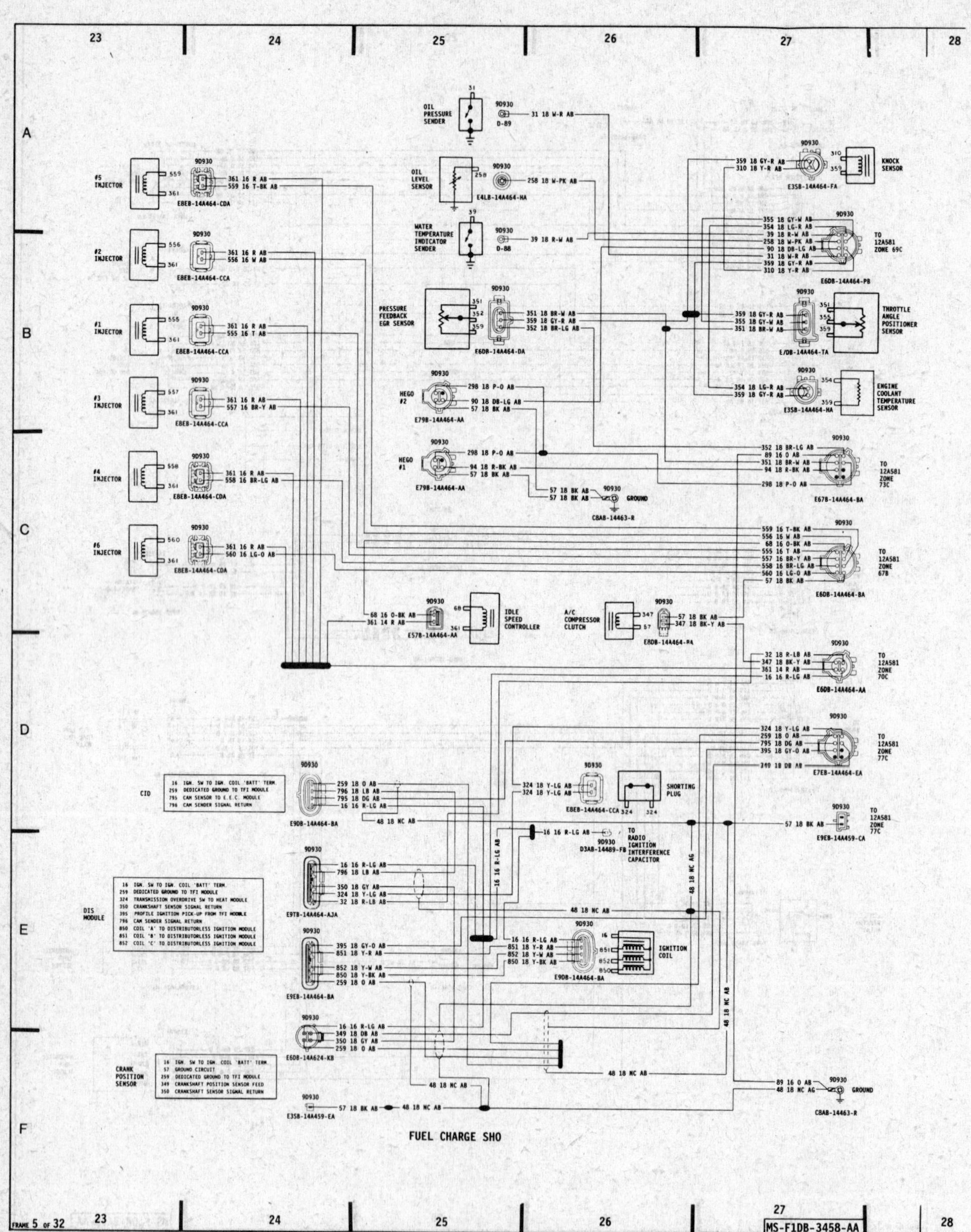

Taurus and Sable electrical schematics — 1991

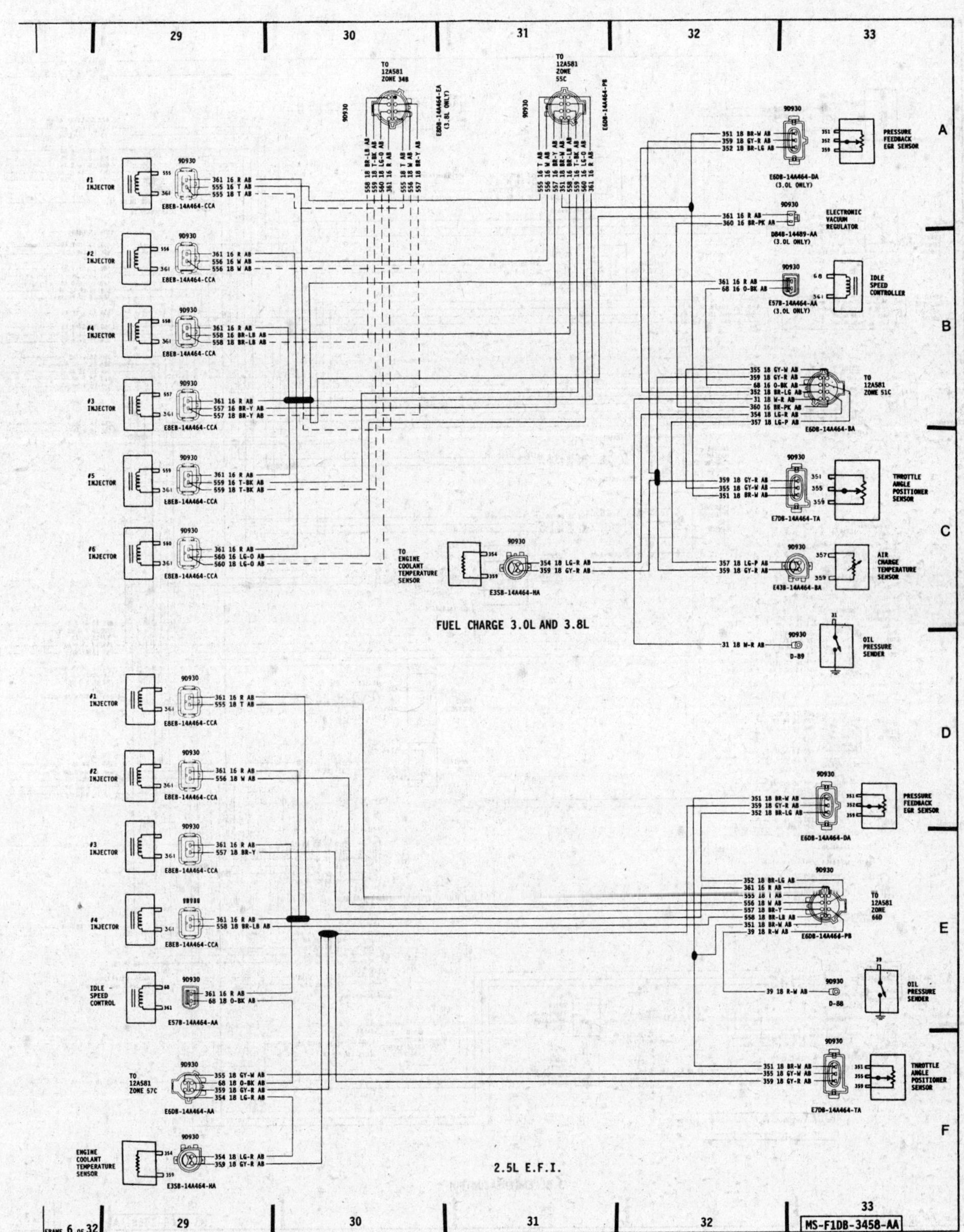

Taurus and Sable electrical schematics — 1991

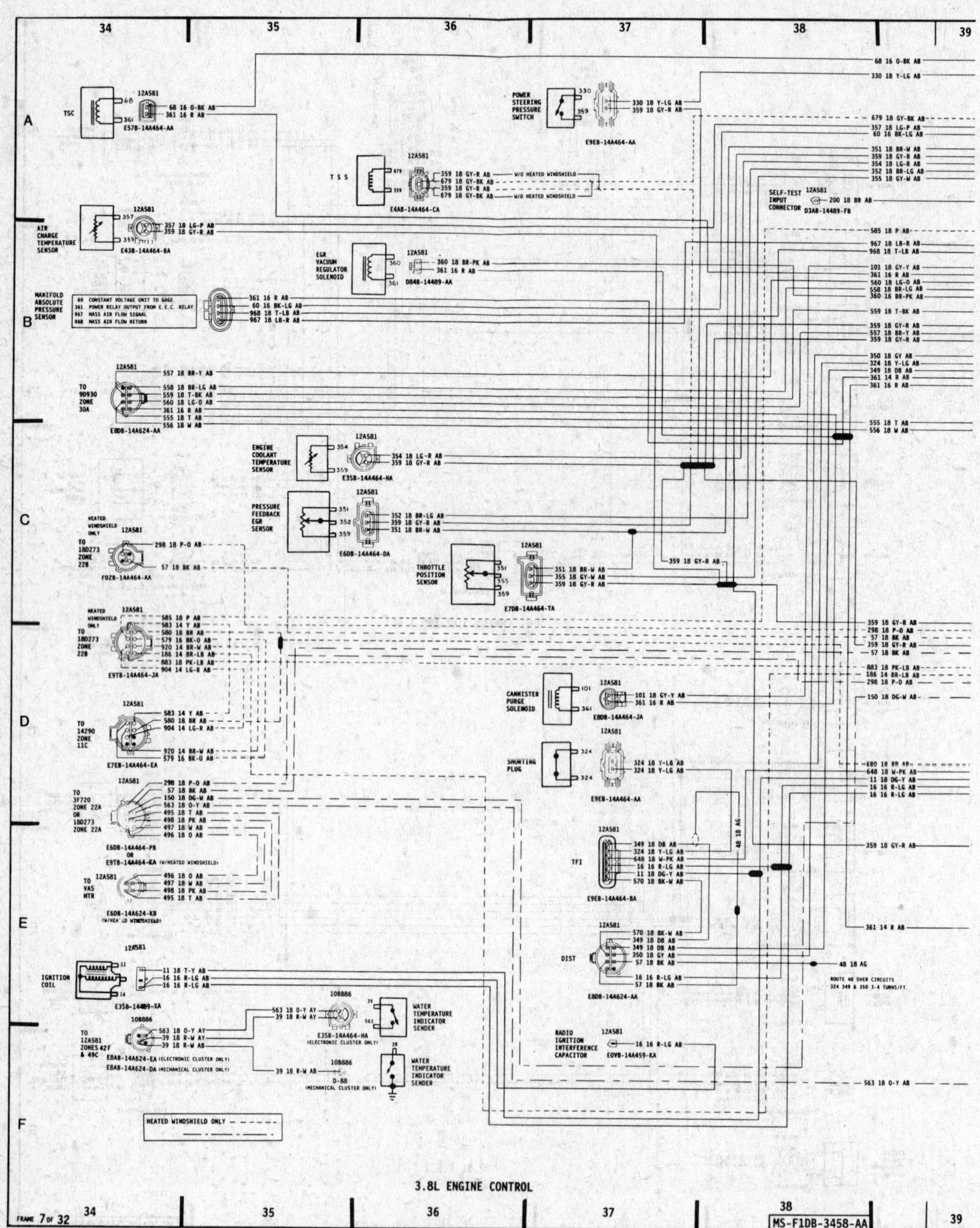
3.8L ENGINE CONTROL
FRAME 7 OF 32
MS-F1DB-3458-AA

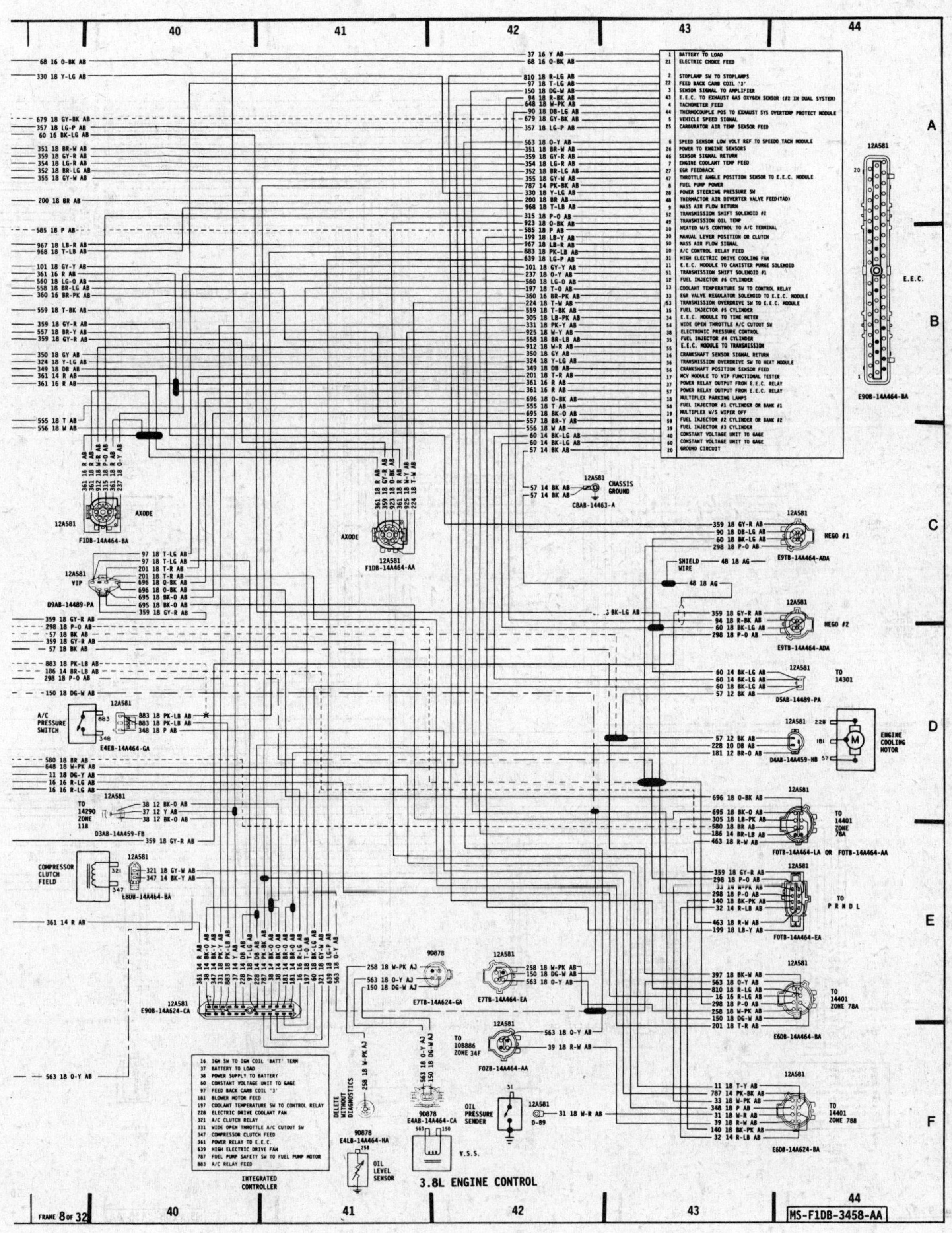

Taurus and Sable electrical schematics — 1991

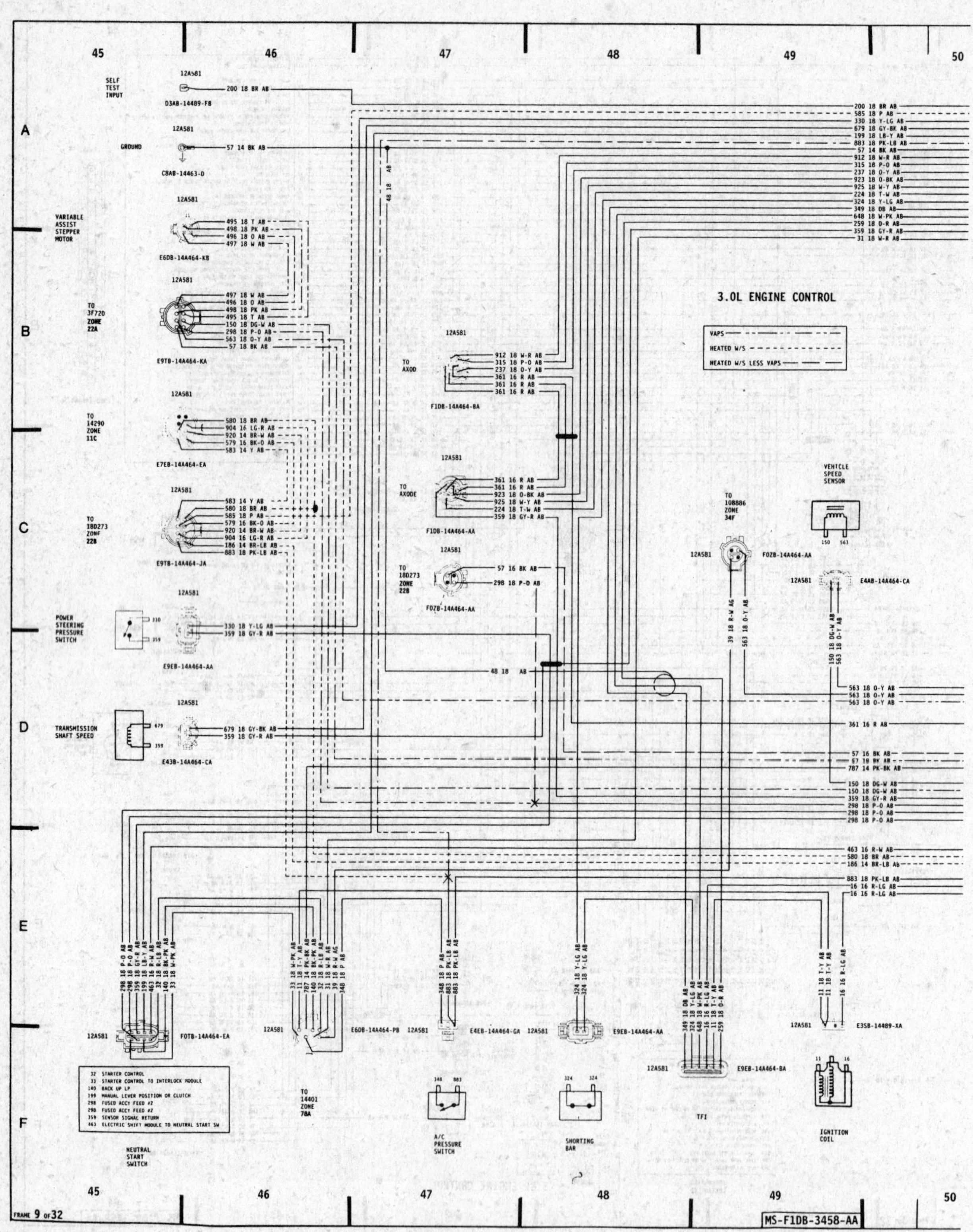

Taurus and Sable electrical schematics – 1991

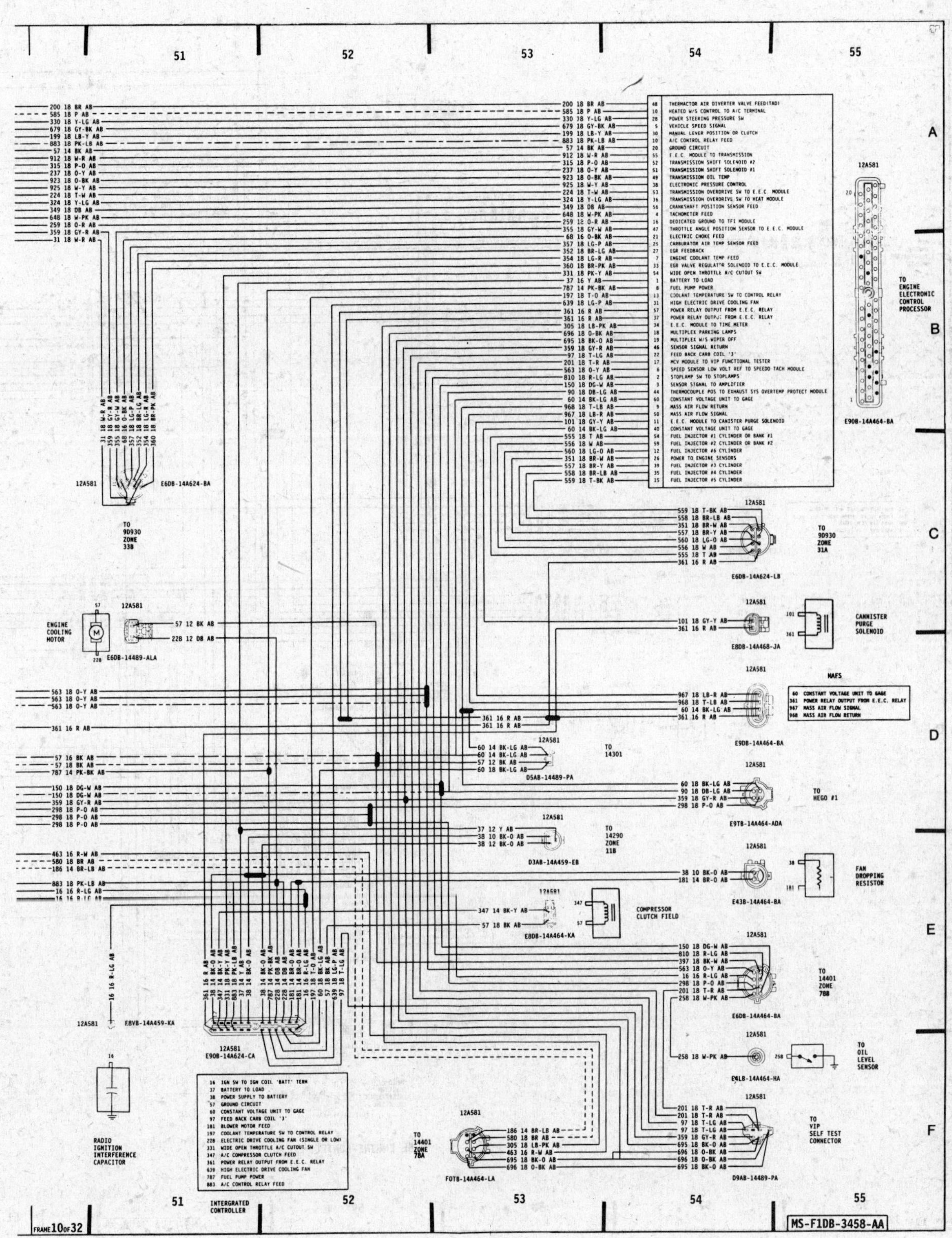

Taurus and Sable electrical schematics – 1991

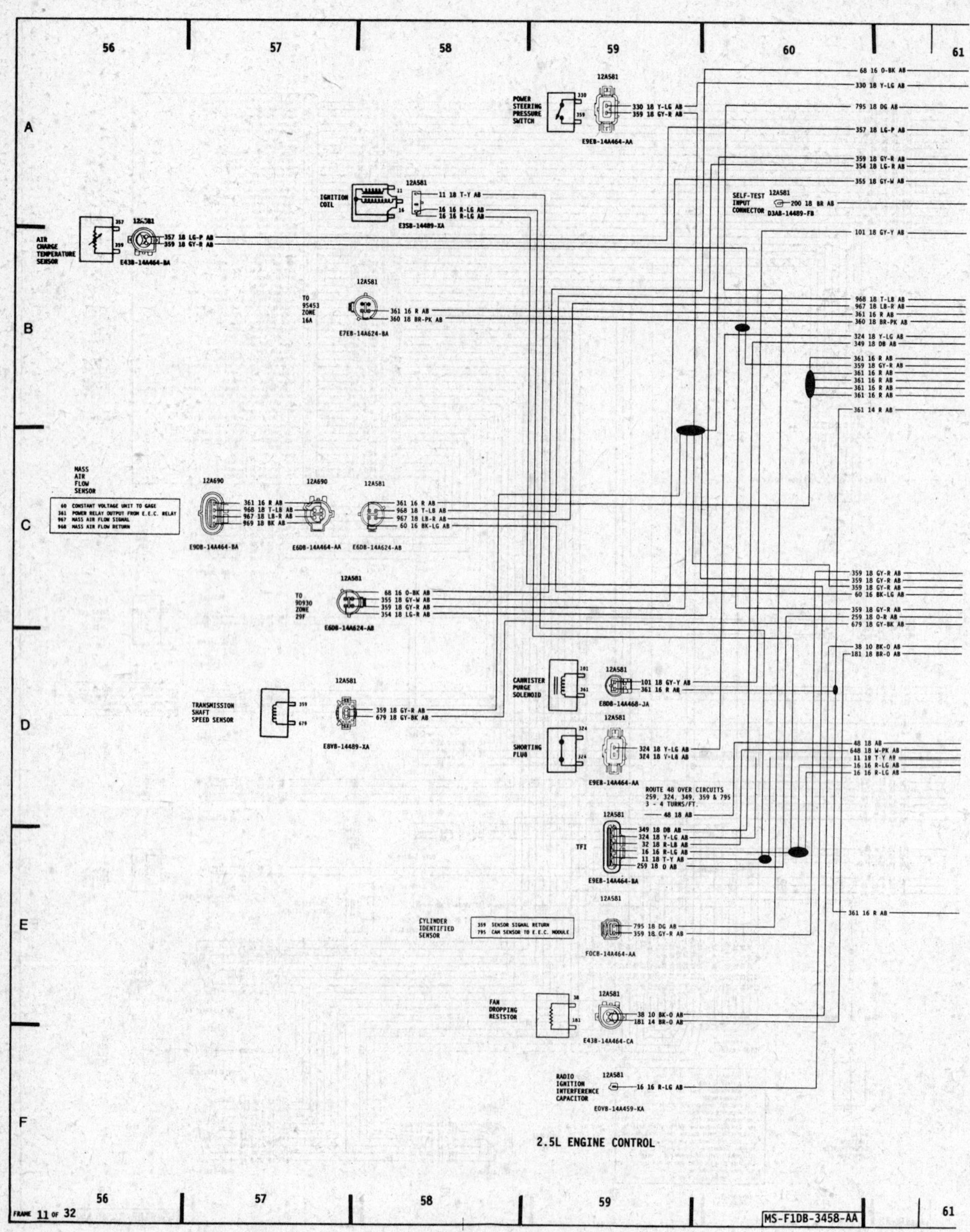

Taurus and Sable electrical schematics — 1991

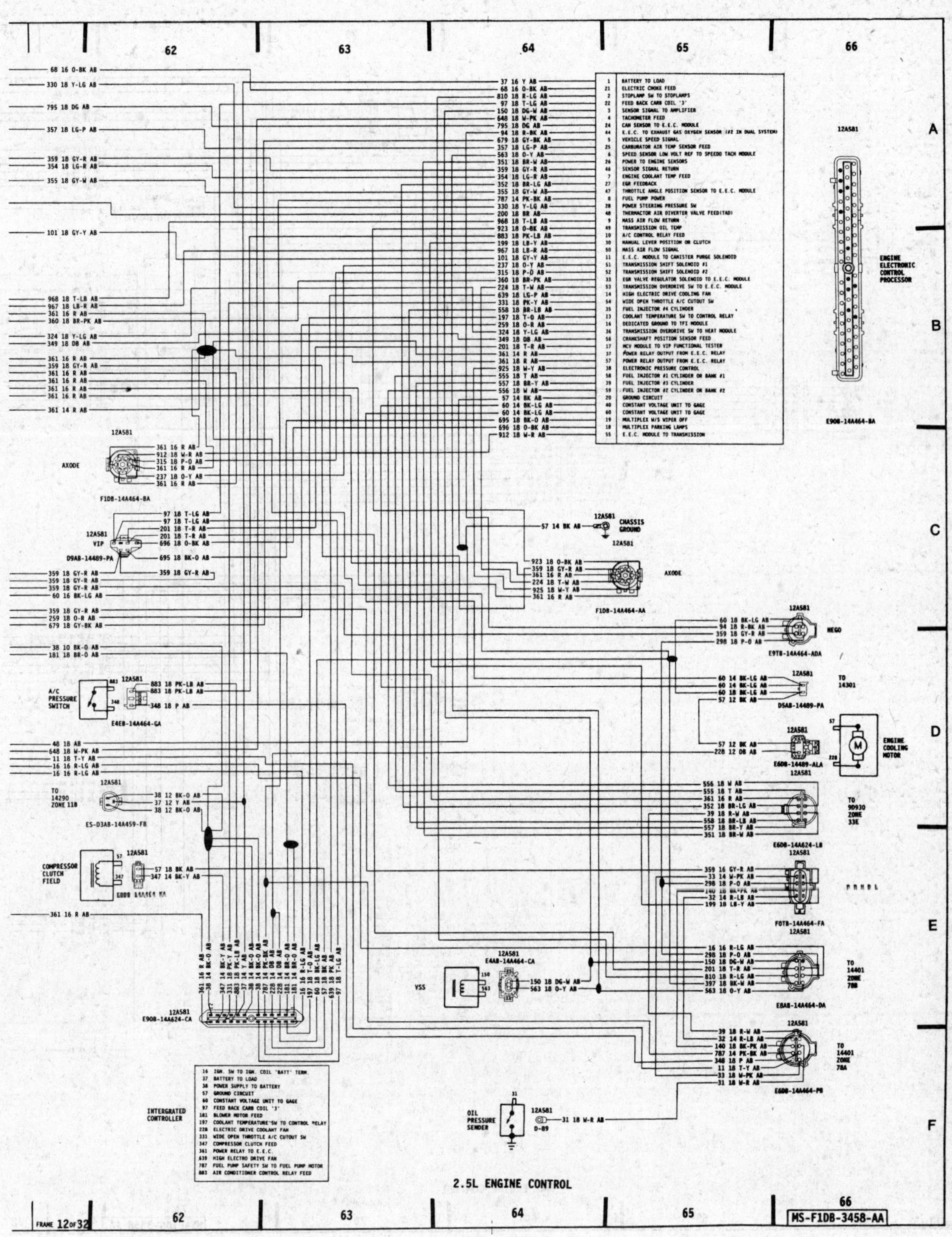

ENGINE ELECTRONIC CONTROL PROCESSOR
E9OB-14A464-BA
AXODE
F1DB-14A464-BA
VIP
D9AB-14489-PA
CHASSIS GROUND
A/C PRESSURE SWITCH
E4EB-14A464-GA
NEGO
E9TB-14A464-ADA
D5AB-14489-PA
ENGINE COOLING MOTOR
E6DB-14489-ALA
COMPRESSOR CLUTCH FIELD
YSS
E4AB-14A464-CA
E9OB-14A624-CA
INTERGRATED CONTROLLER
OIL PRESSURE SENDER
2.5L ENGINE CONTROL
MS-F1DB-3458-AA

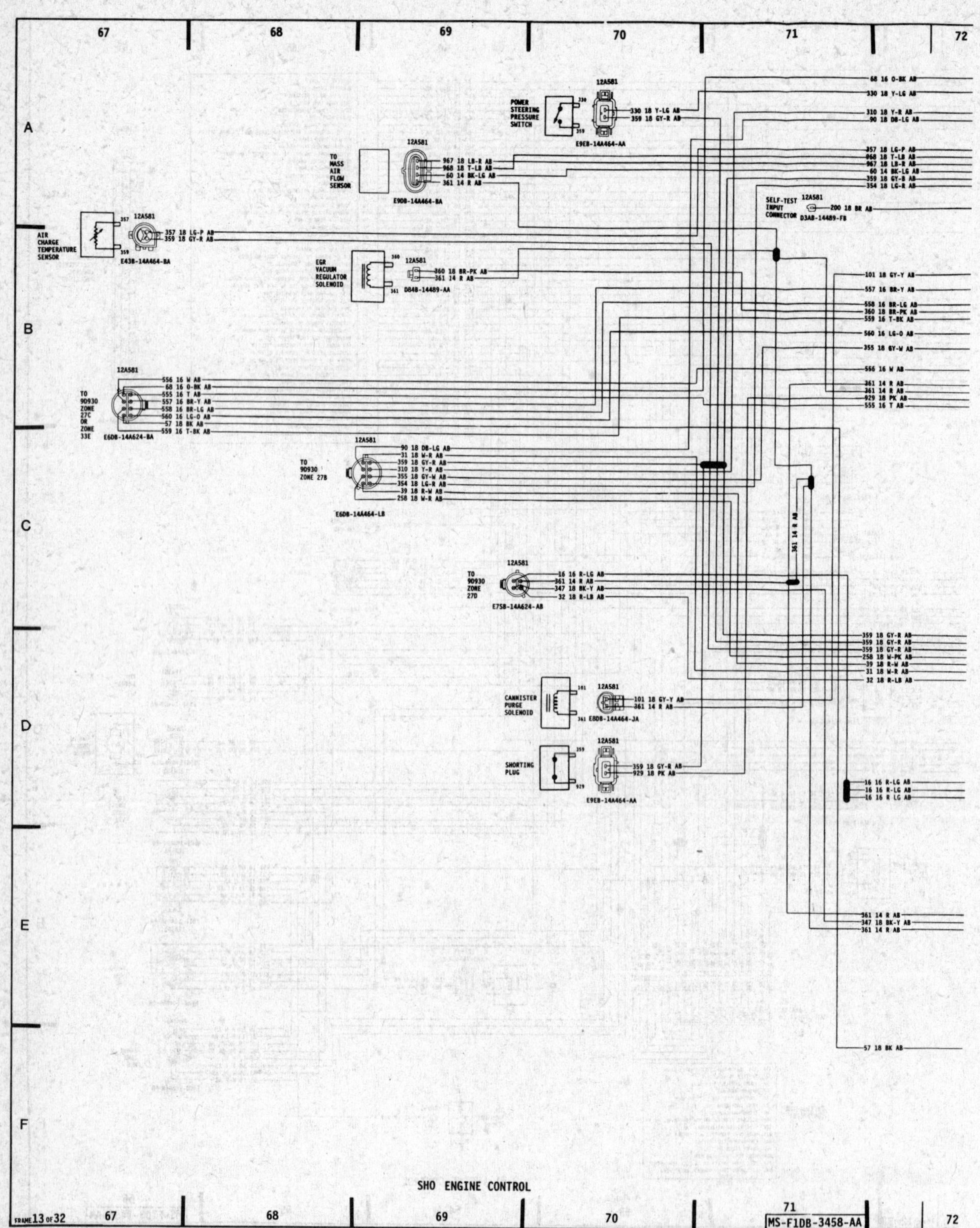

Taurus and Sable electrical schematics – 1991

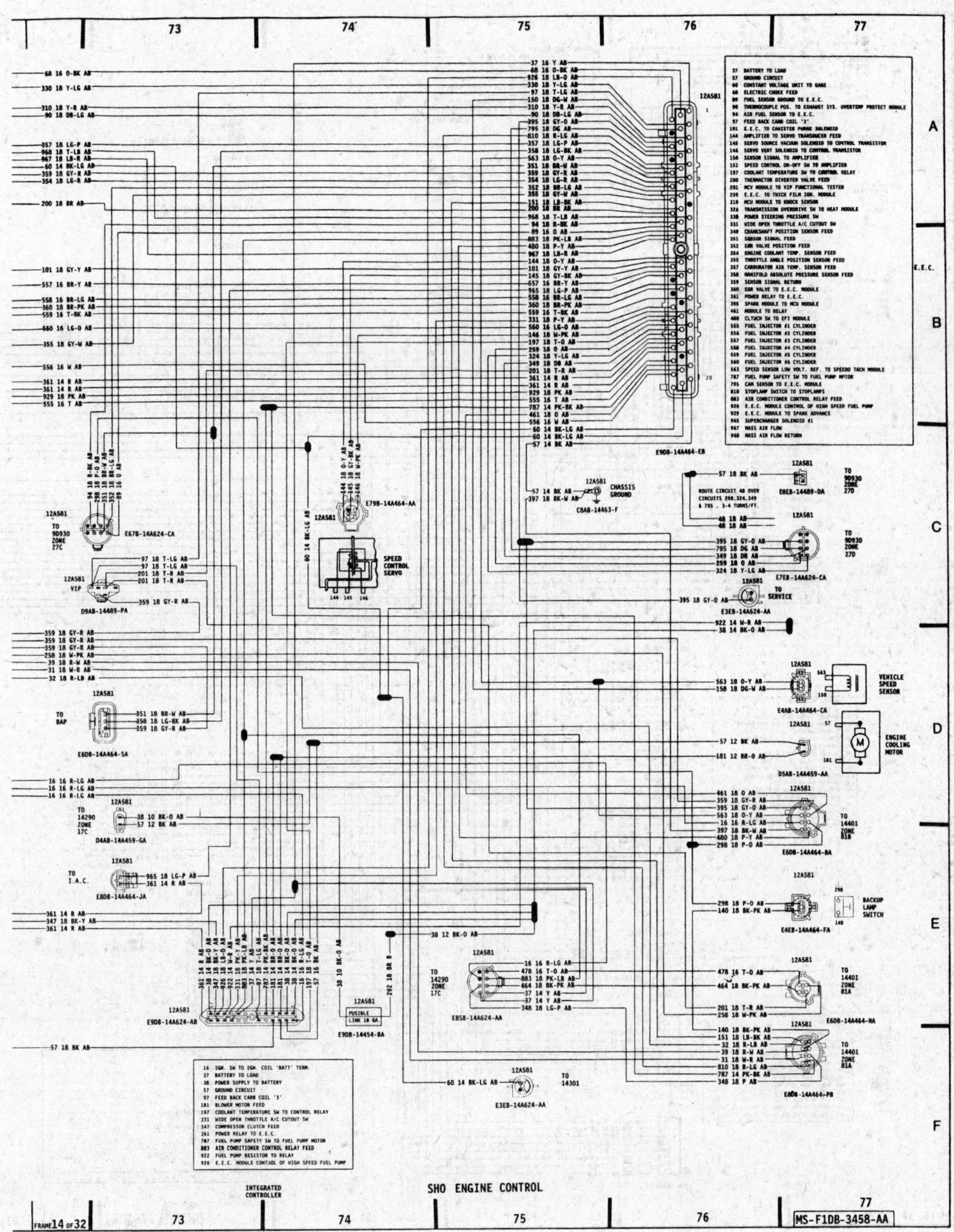

Taurus and Sable electrical schematics — 1991

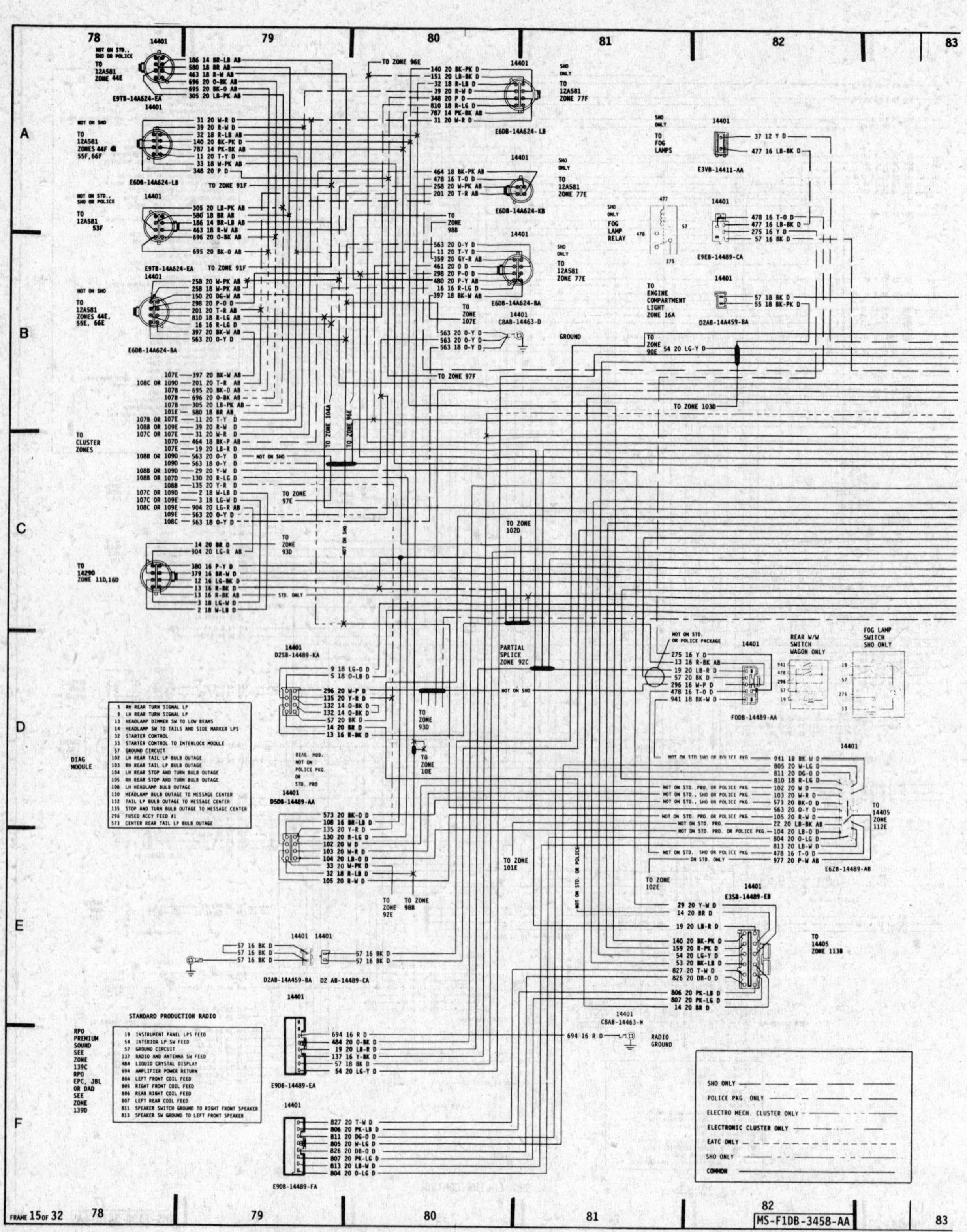

Taurus and Sable electrical schematics – 1991

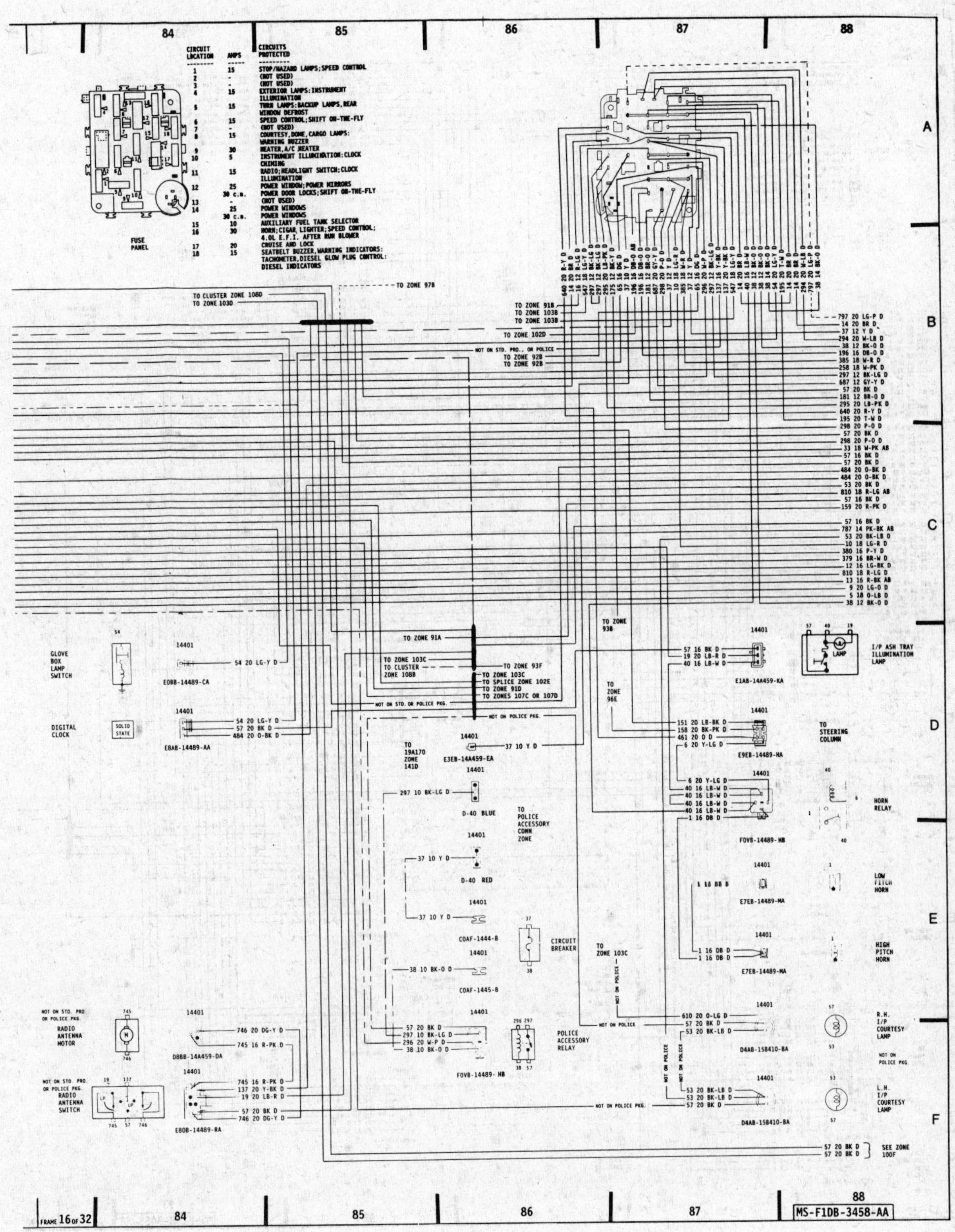

Taurus and Sable electrical schematics — 1991

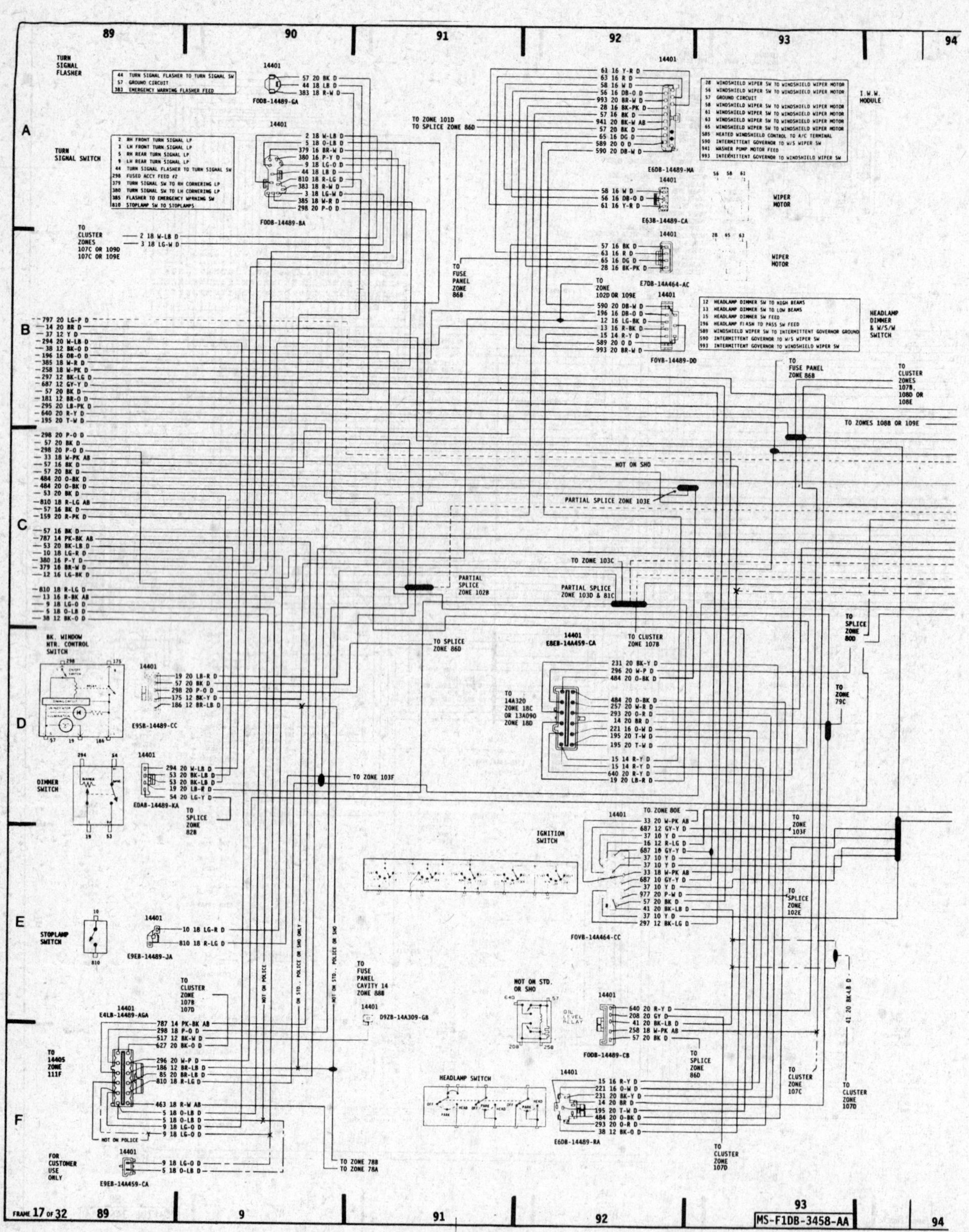

Taurus and Sable electrical schematics – 1991

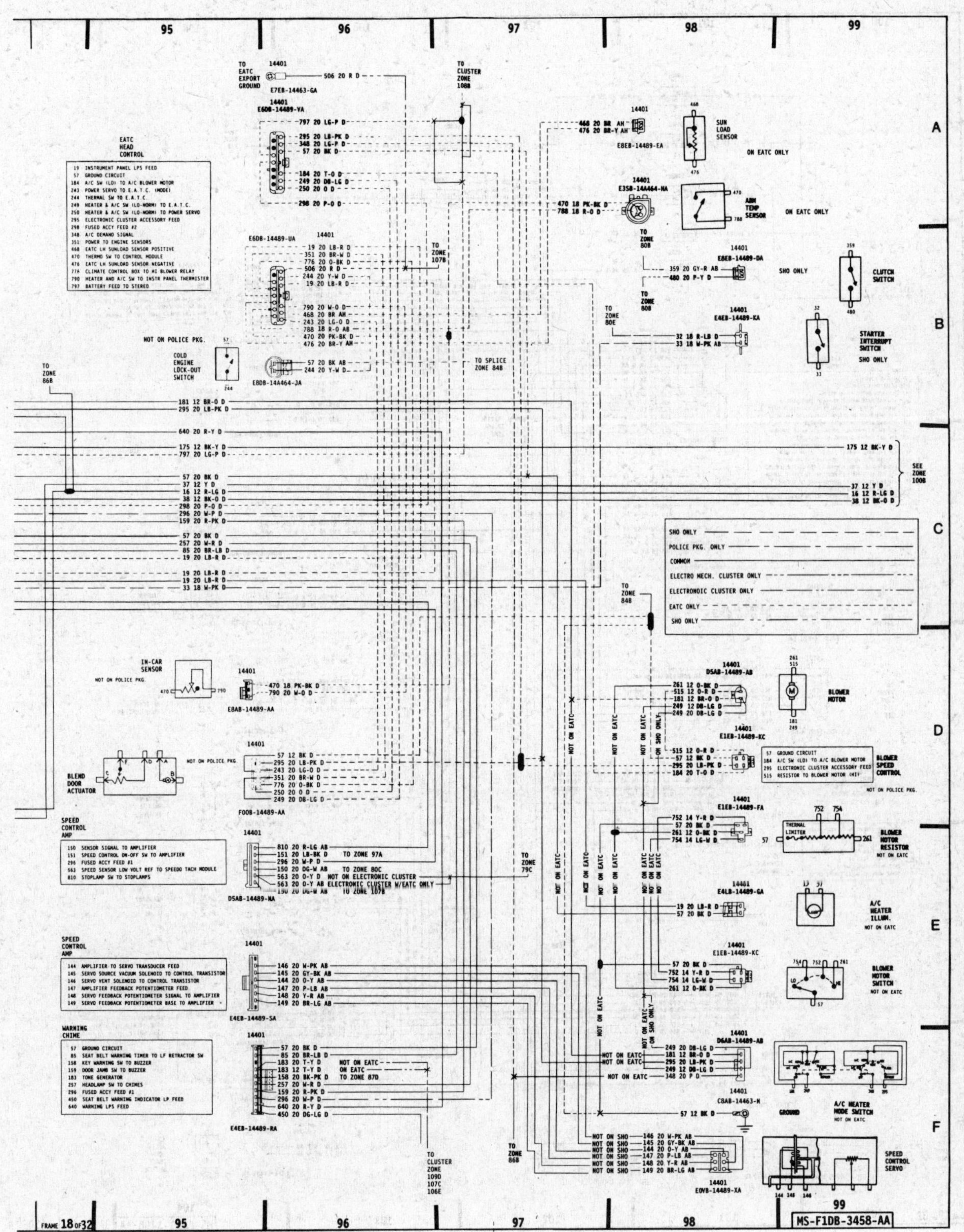

Taurus and Sable electrical schematics — 1991

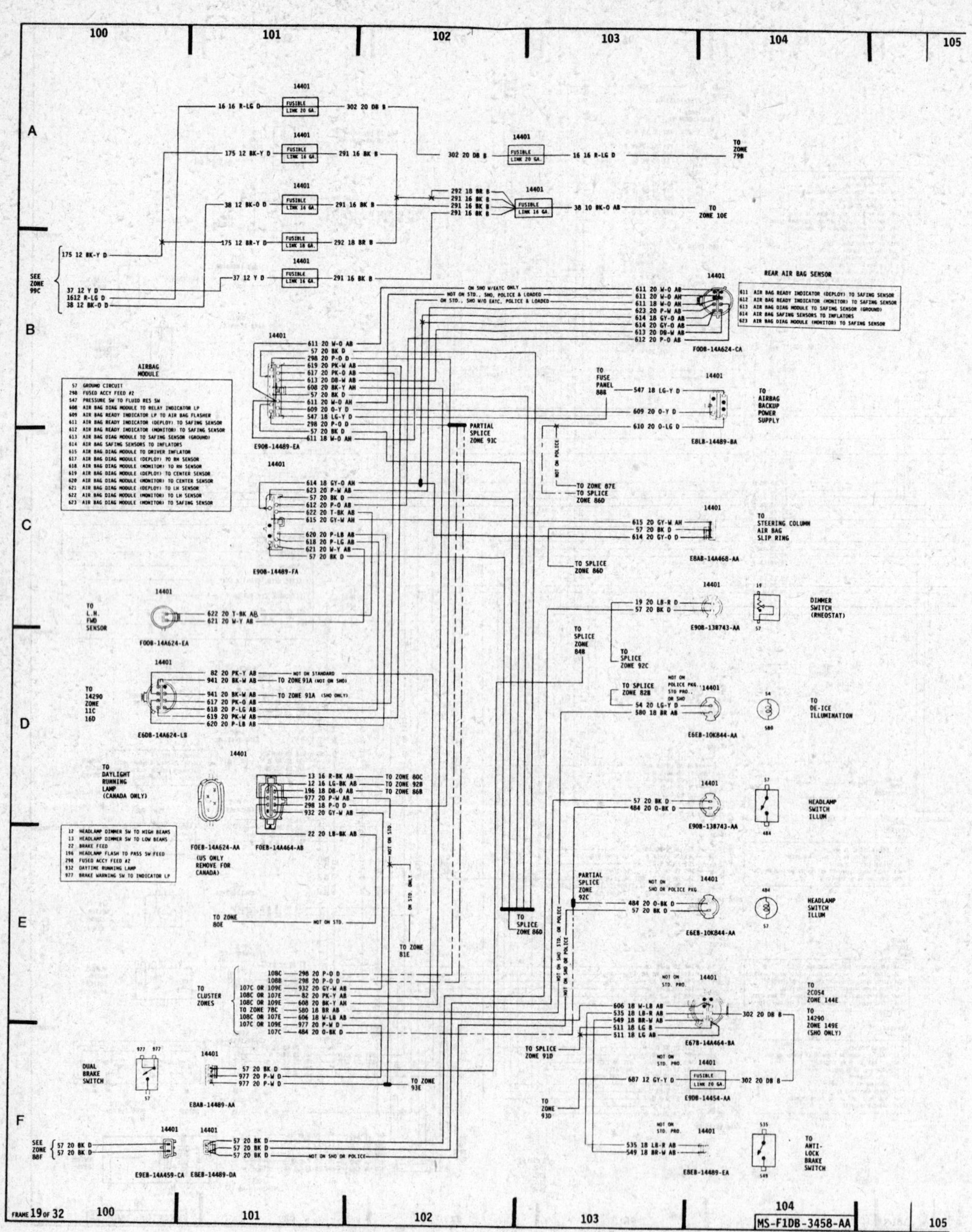

100
101
102
103
104
105
A
B
C
D
E
F
14401
FUSIBLE LINK 20 GA.
FUSIBLE LINK 16 GA.
FUSIBLE LINK 18 GA.
16 16 R-LG D
302 20 DB B
175 12 BK-Y D
291 16 BK B
38 12 BK-O D
175 12 BR-Y D
292 18 BR B
37 12 Y D
38 10 BK-O AB
TO ZONE 79B
TO ZONE 10E
SEE ZONE 99C
1612 R-LG D
38 12 BK-O D
REAR AIR BAG SENSOR
ON SHO W/EATC ONLY
NOT ON STD., SHO, POLICE & LOADED
ON STD., SHO W/O EATC, POLICE & LOADED
611 AIR BAG READY INDICATOR (DEPLOY) TO SAFING SENSOR
612 AIR BAG READY INDICATOR (MONITOR) TO SAFING SENSOR
613 AIR BAG DIAG MODULE TO SAFING SENSOR (GROUND)
614 AIR BAG SAFING SENSORS TO INFLATORS
623 AIR BAG DIAG MODULE (MONITOR) TO SAFING SENSOR
F0DB-14A624-CA
AIRBAG MODULE
57 GROUND CIRCUIT
298 FUSED ACCY FEED #2
547 PRESSURE SW TO FLUID RES SW
608 AIR BAG DIAG MODULE TO RELAY INDICATOR LP
609 AIR BAG READY INDICATOR LP TO AIR BAG FLASHER
611 AIR BAG READY INDICATOR (DEPLOY) TO SAFING SENSOR
612 AIR BAG READY INDICATOR (MONITOR) TO SAFING SENSOR
613 AIR BAG DIAG MODULE TO SAFING SENSOR (GROUND)
614 AIR BAG SAFING SENSORS TO INFLATORS
615 AIR BAG DIAG MODULE TO DRIVER INFLATOR
617 AIR BAG DIAG MODULE (DEPLOY) TO RH SENSOR
618 AIR BAG DIAG MODULE (MONITOR) TO RH SENSOR
619 AIR BAG DIAG MODULE (DEPLOY) TO CENTER SENSOR
620 AIR BAG DIAG MODULE (MONITOR) TO CENTER SENSOR
621 AIR BAG DIAG MODULE (DEPLOY) TO LH SENSOR
622 AIR BAG DIAG MODULE (MONITOR) TO LH SENSOR
623 AIR BAG DIAG MODULE (MONITOR) TO SAFING SENSOR
E90B-14489-EA
E90B-14489-FA
TO FUSE PANEL 88B
TO AIRBAG BACKUP POWER SUPPLY
E8LB-14489-BA
PARTIAL SPLICE ZONE 91C
NOT ON POLICE
TO ZONE 87E
TO SPLICE ZONE 86D
TO STEERING COLUMN AIR BAG SLIP RING
E8AB-14A468-AA
TO SPLICE ZONE 86D
TO L.H. FWD SENSOR
F0DB-14A624-EA
DIMMER SWITCH (RHEOSTAT)
E90B-13B743-AA
TO SPLICE ZONE 84B
TO SPLICE ZONE 92C
TO 14290 ZONE 11C 16D
NOT ON STANDARD
TO ZONE 91A (NOT ON SHO)
TO ZONE 91A (SHO ONLY)
E6DB-14A624-LB
TO SPLICE ZONE 82B
NOT ON POLICE PKG. STD PRO. OR SHO
TO DE-ICE ILLUMINATION
E6EB-10K844-AA
TO DAYLIGHT RUNNING LAMP (CANADA ONLY)
TO ZONE 80C
TO ZONE 92B
TO ZONE 86B
12 HEADLAMP DIMMER SW TO HIGH BEAMS
13 HEADLAMP DIMMER SW TO LOW BEAMS
22 BRAKE FEED
196 HEADLAMP FLASH TO PASS SW FEED
298 FUSED ACCY FEED #2
932 DAYTIME RUNNING LAMP
977 BRAKE WARNING SW TO INDICATOR LP
F0EB-14A624-AA
(US ONLY REMOVE FOR CANADA)
F0EB-14A464-AB
NOT ON STD.
ON STD ONLY
HEADLAMP SWITCH ILLUM
E90B-13B743-AA
PARTIAL SPLICE ZONE 92C
NOT ON SHO OR POLICE PKG
E6EB-10K844-AA
TO ZONE 80E
TO SPLICE ZONE 86D
TO ZONE 81E
TO CLUSTER ZONES
NOT ON STD. PRO
TO 2C054 ZONE 144E
TO 14290 ZONE 149E (SHO ONLY)
E67B-14A464-BA
TO SPLICE ZONE 91D
DUAL BRAKE SWITCH
E8AB-14489-AA
TO ZONE 93E
NOT ON STD. PRO
E9DB-14454-AA
TO ZONE 93D
TO ANTI-LOCK BRAKE SWITCH
E8EB-14489-EA
SEE ZONE 88F
NOT ON SHO OR POLICE
E9EB-14A459-CA
E8EB-14489-DA
FRAME 19 OF 32
MS-F1DB-3458-AA

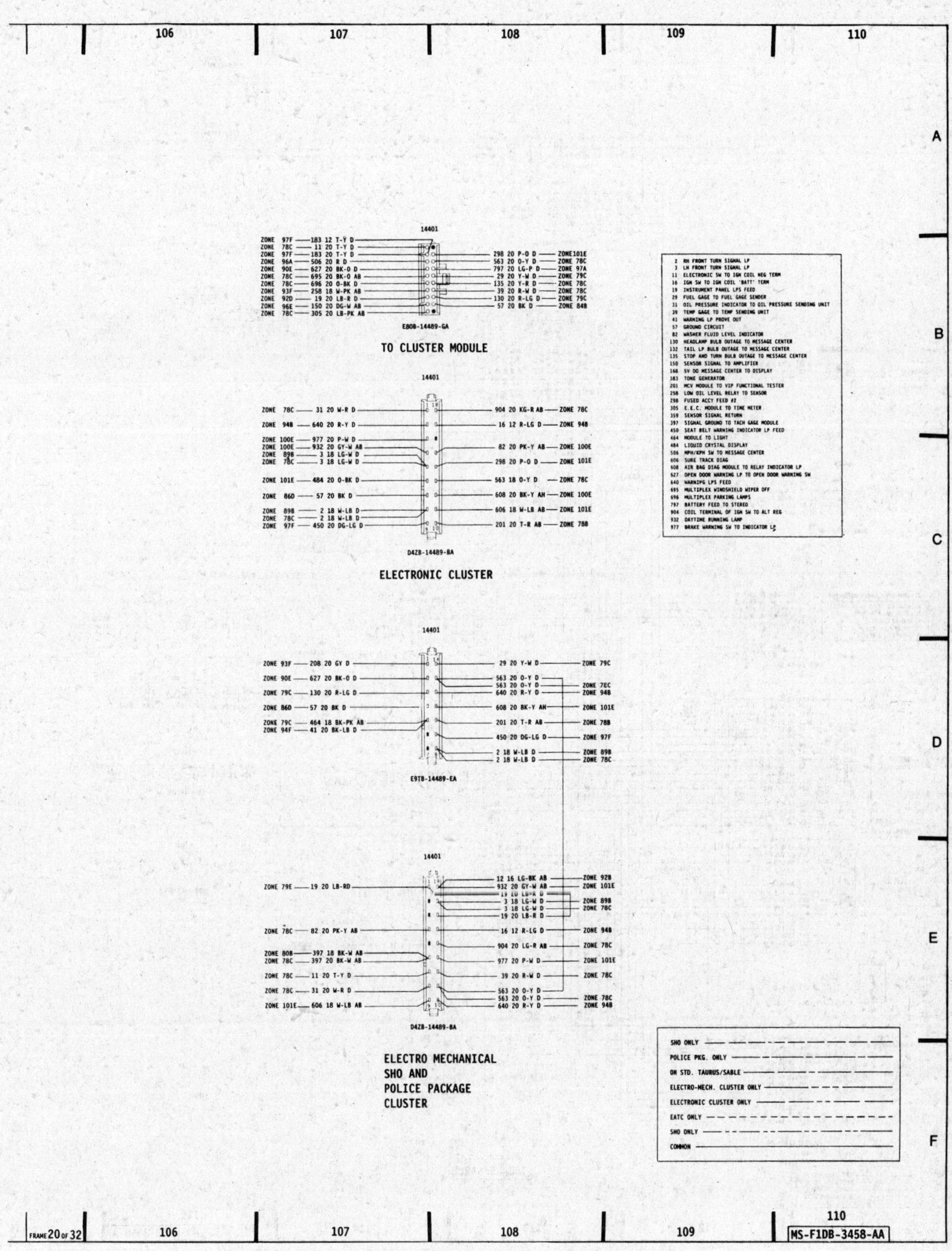

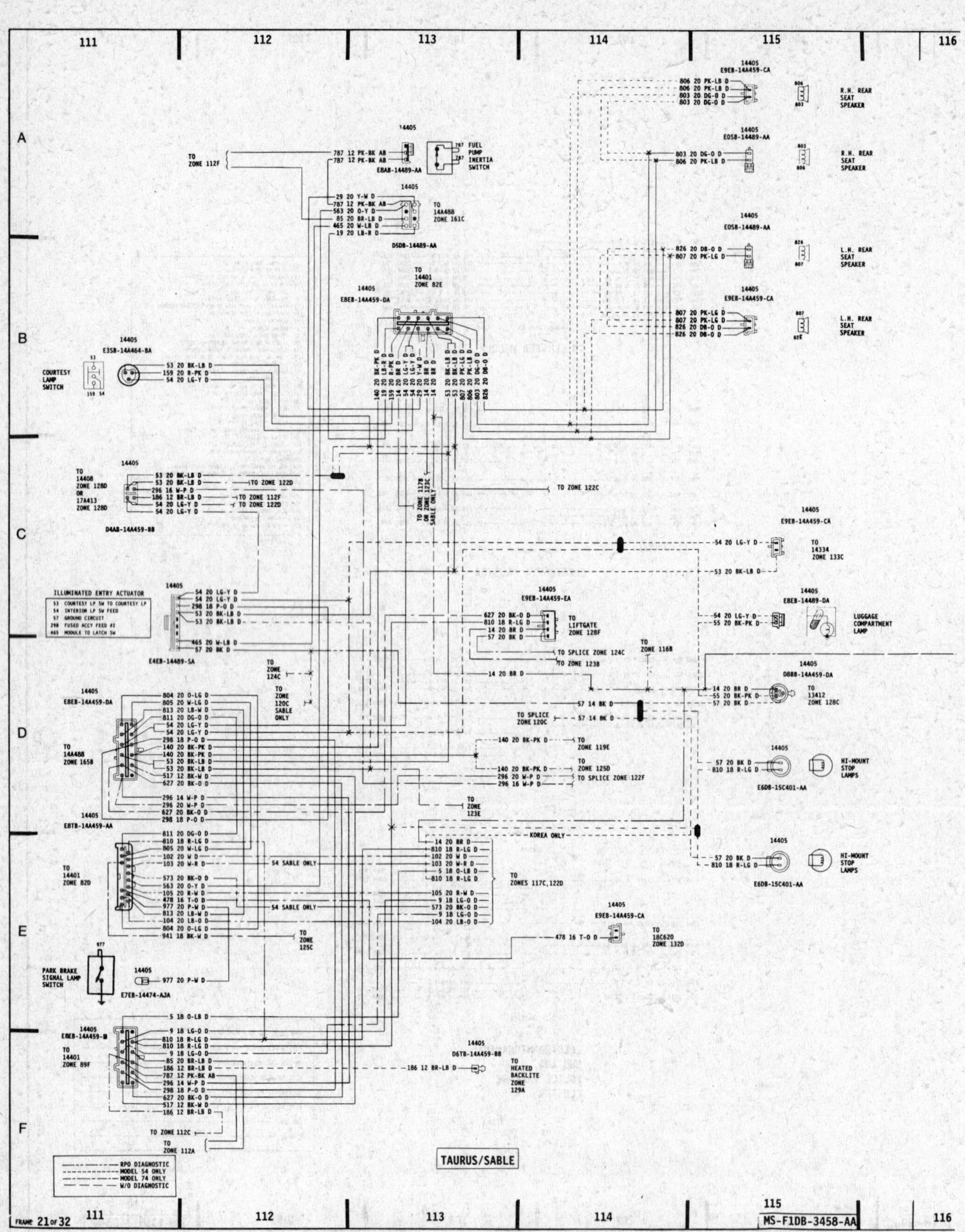

Taurus and Sable electrical schematics — 1991

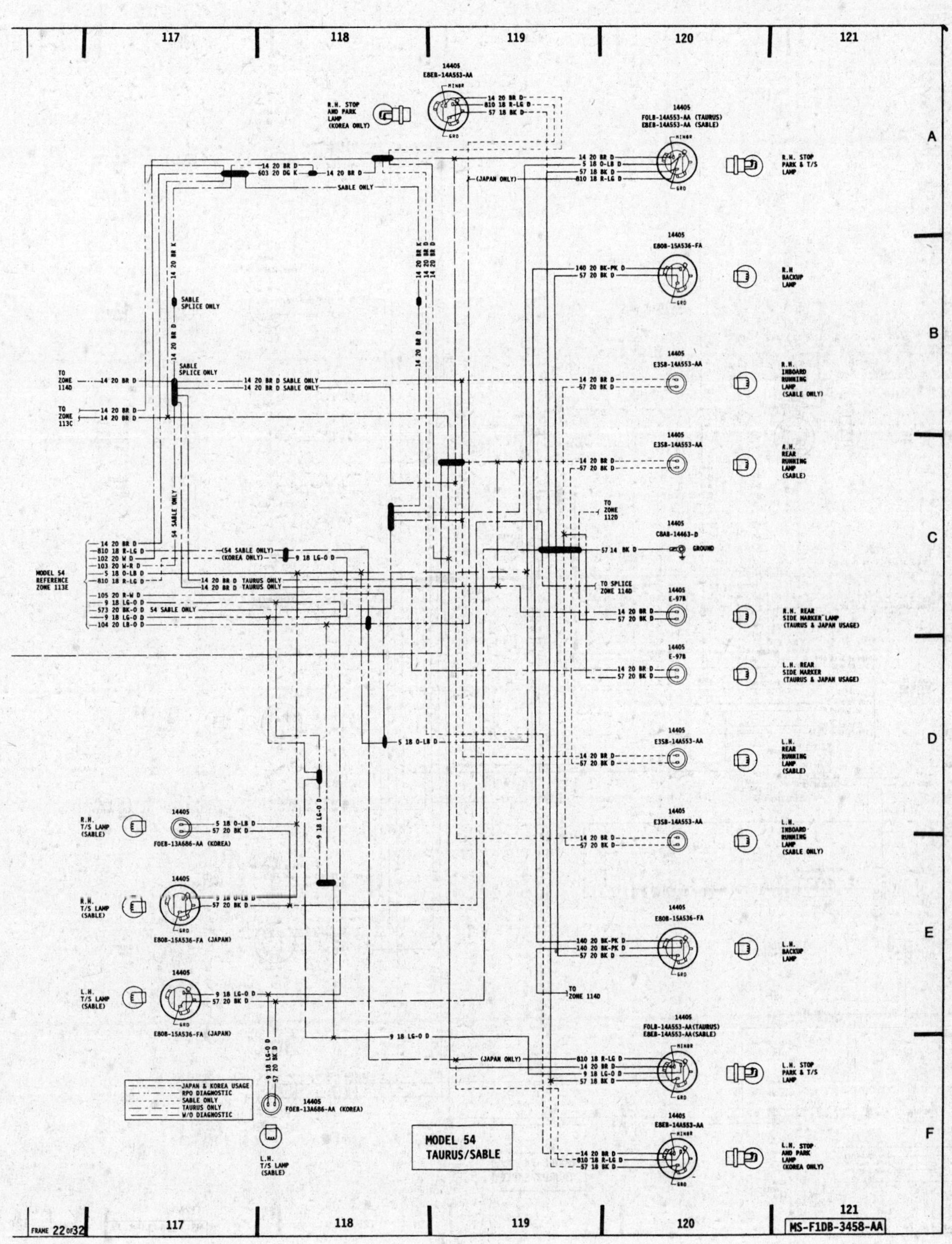

Taurus and Sable electrical schematics – 1991

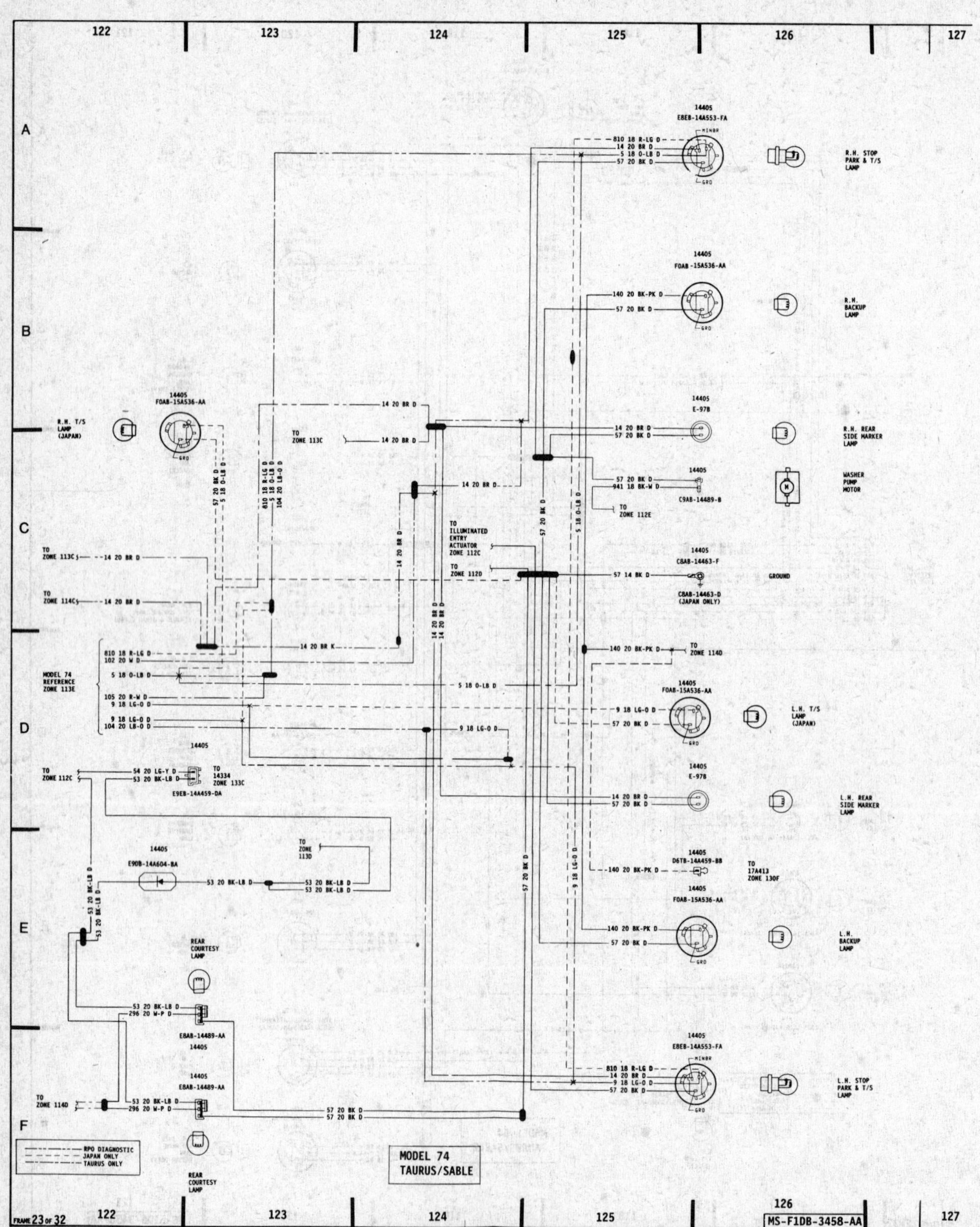

Taurus and Sable electrical schematics — 1991

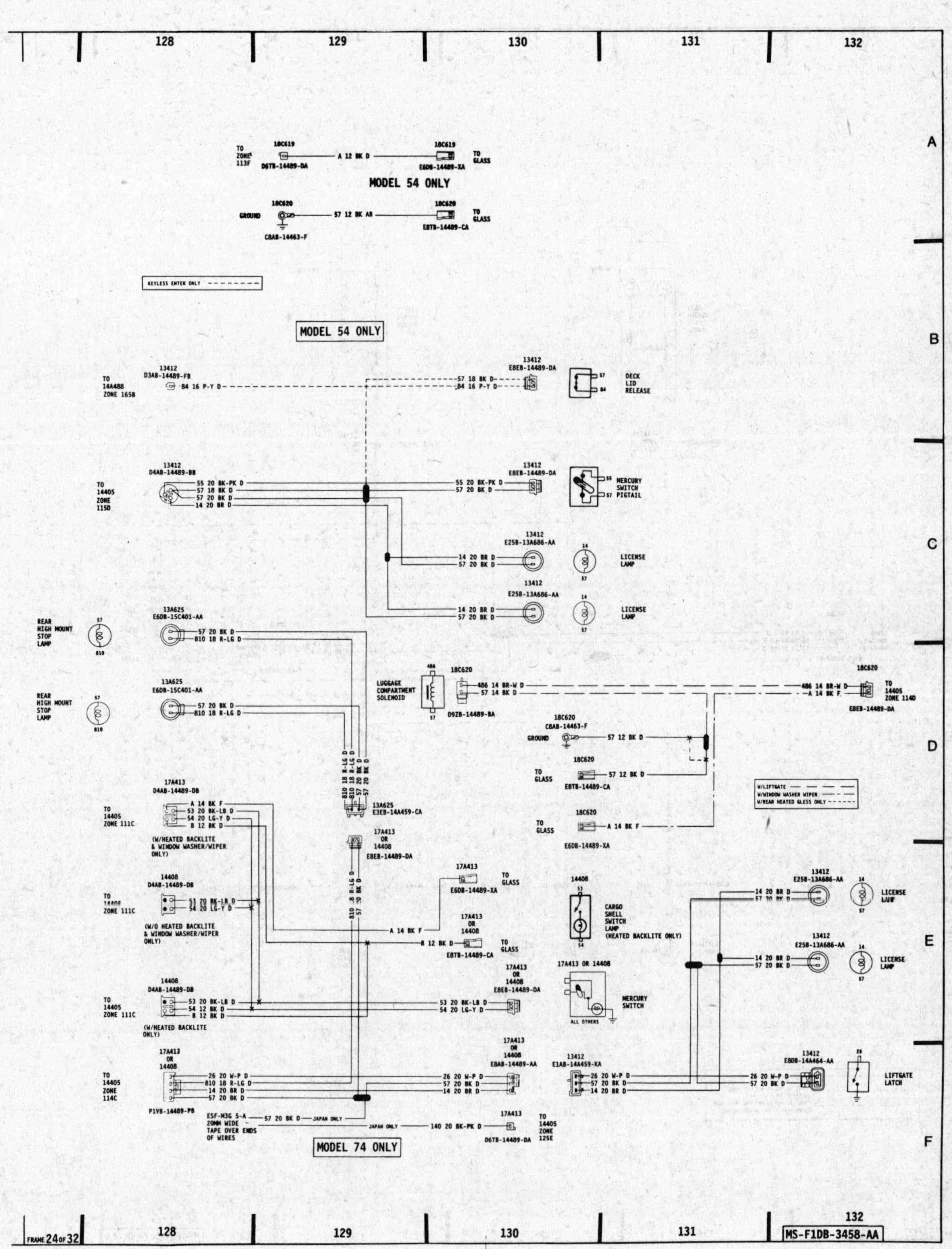

Taurus and Sable electrical schematics – 1991

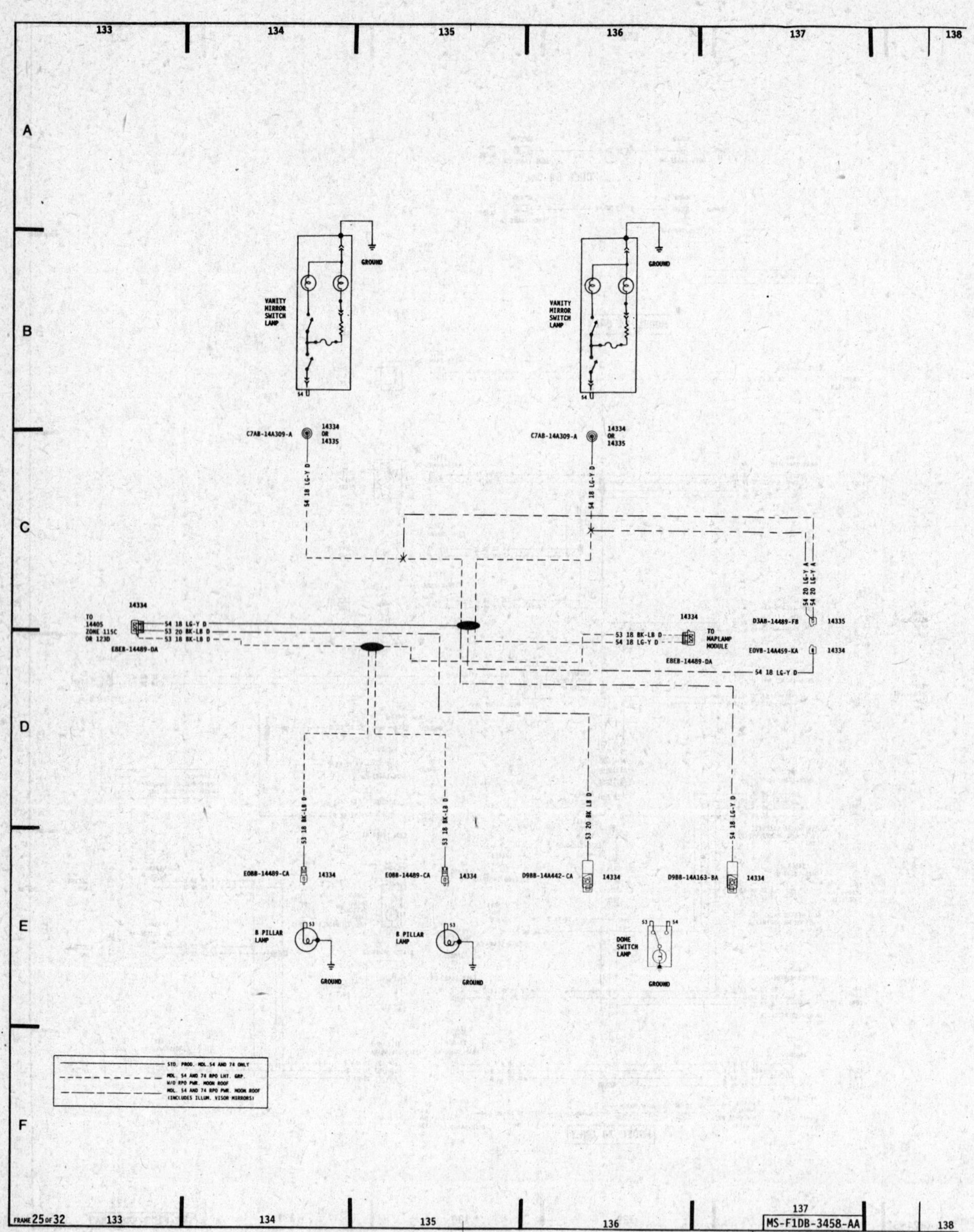

Taurus and Sable electrical schematics — 1991

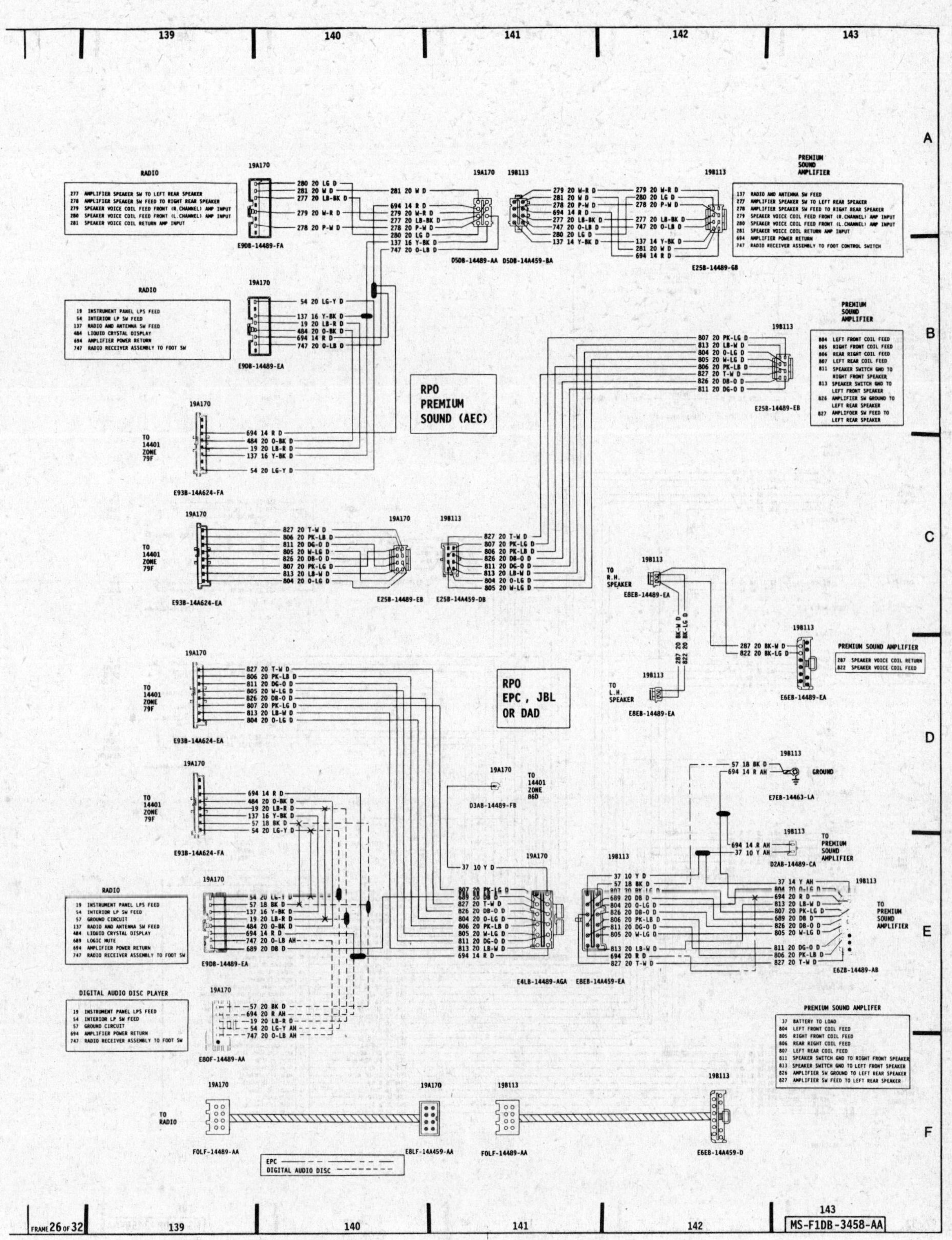

Taurus and Sable electrical schematics – 1991

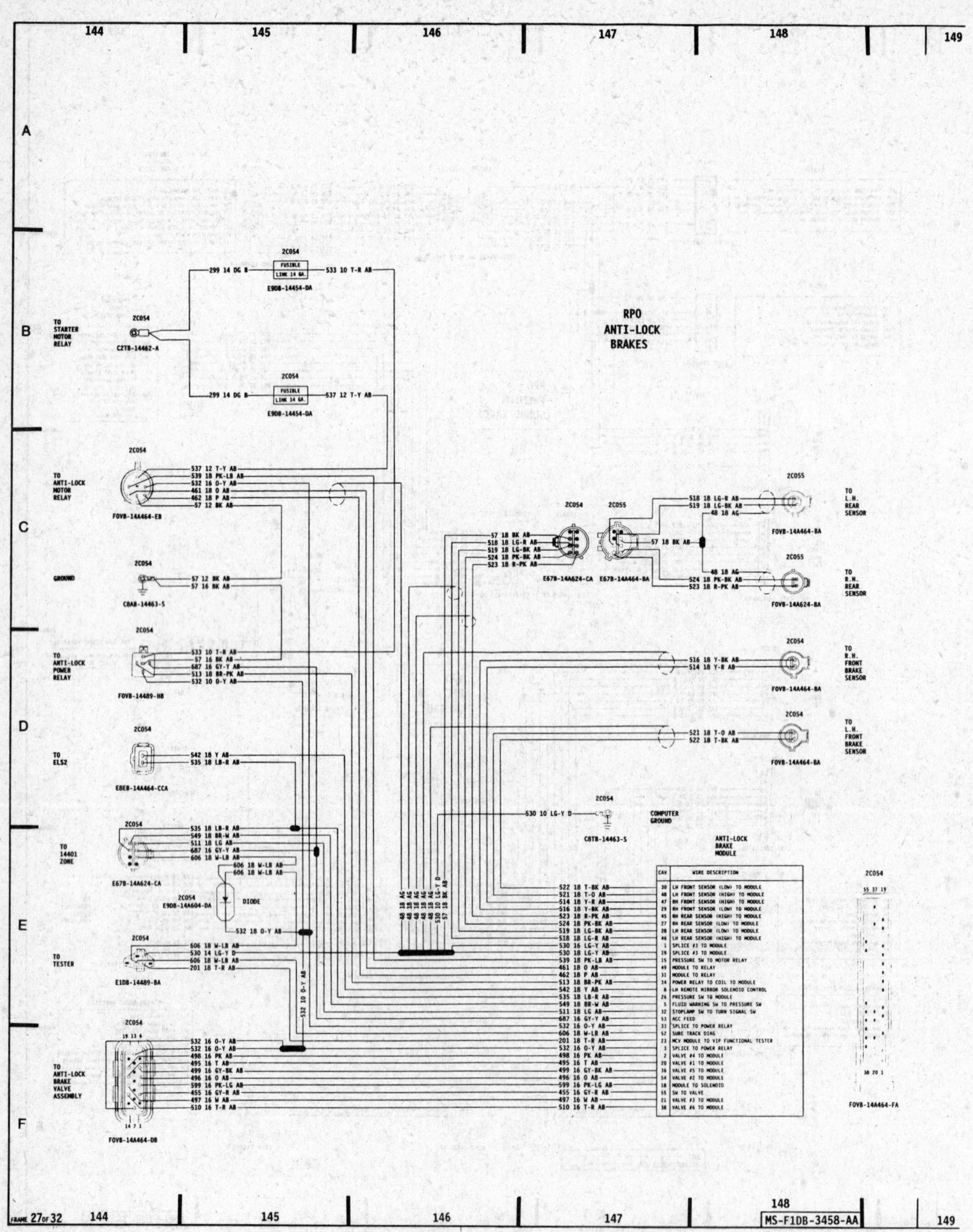

Taurus and Sable electrical schematics – 1991

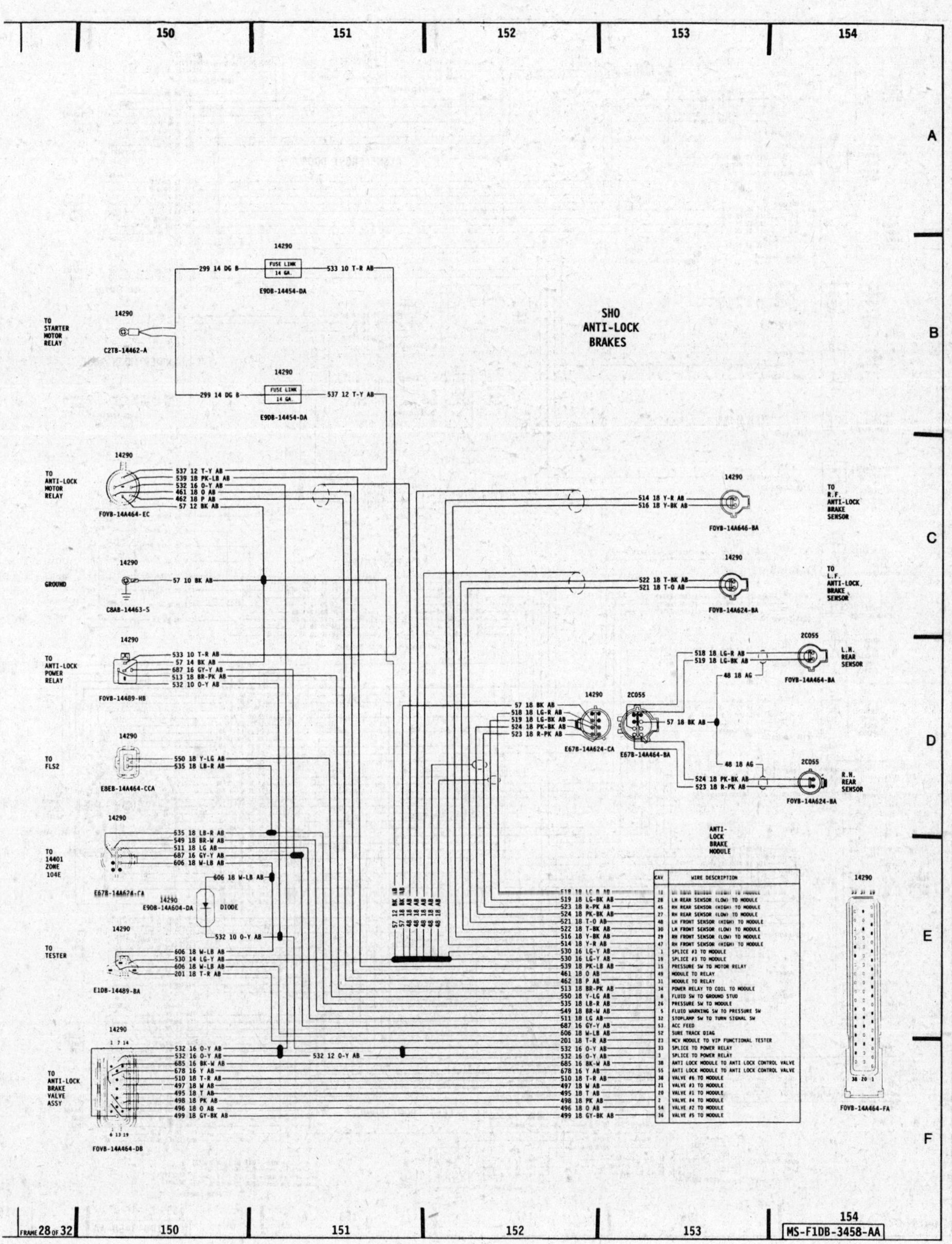

Taurus and Sable electrical schematics — 1991

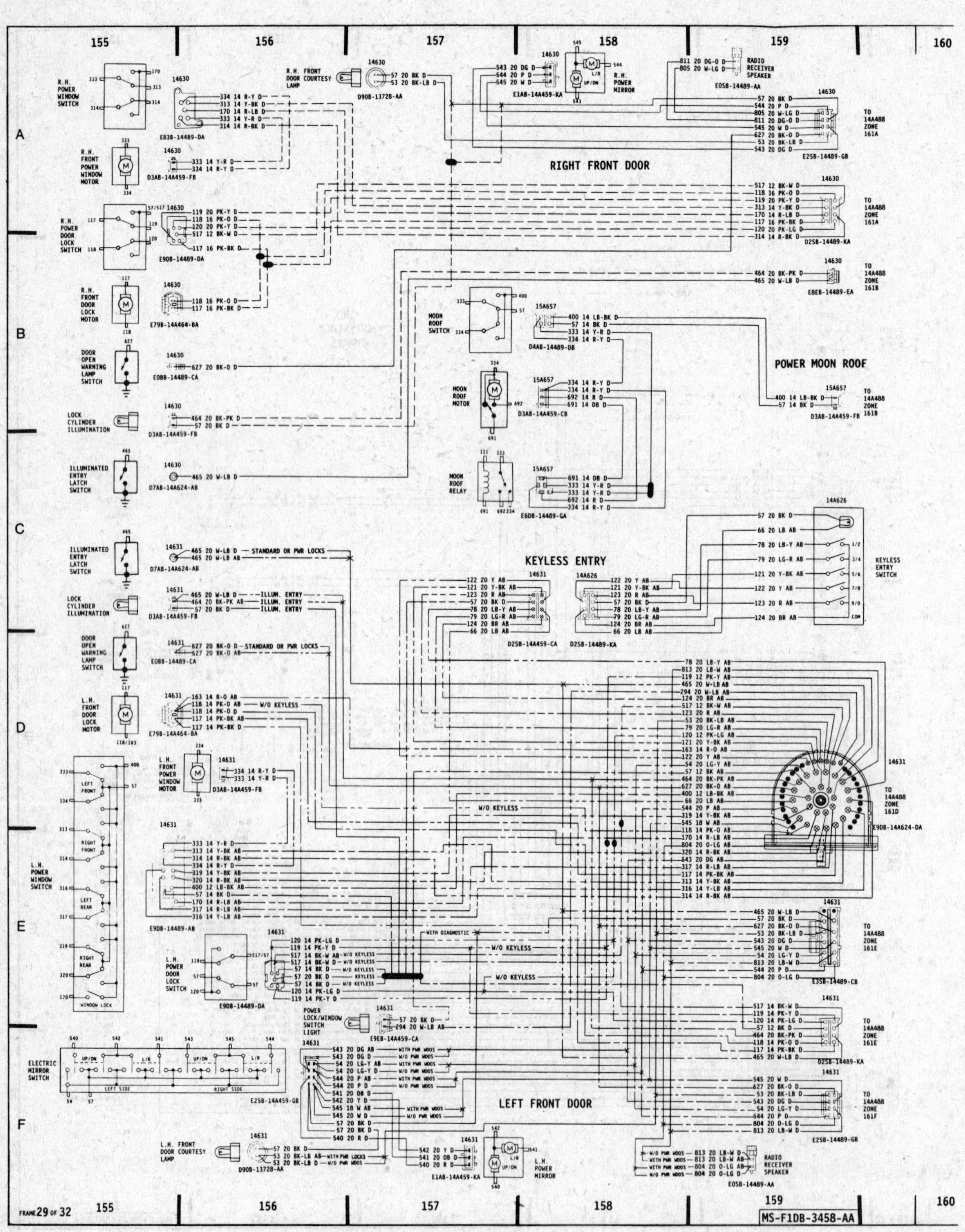

Taurus and Sable electrical schematics – 1991

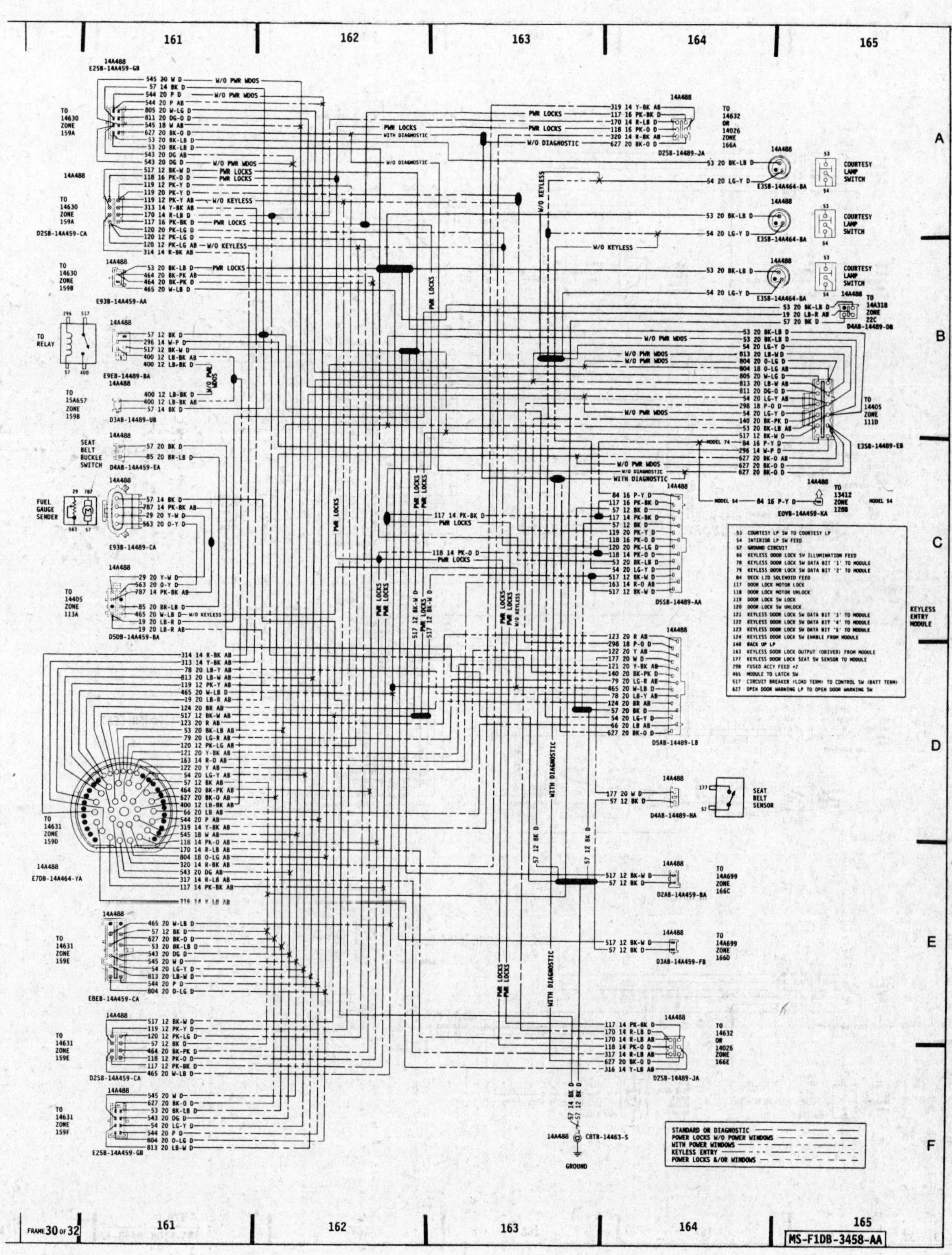

Taurus and Sable electrical schematics — 1991

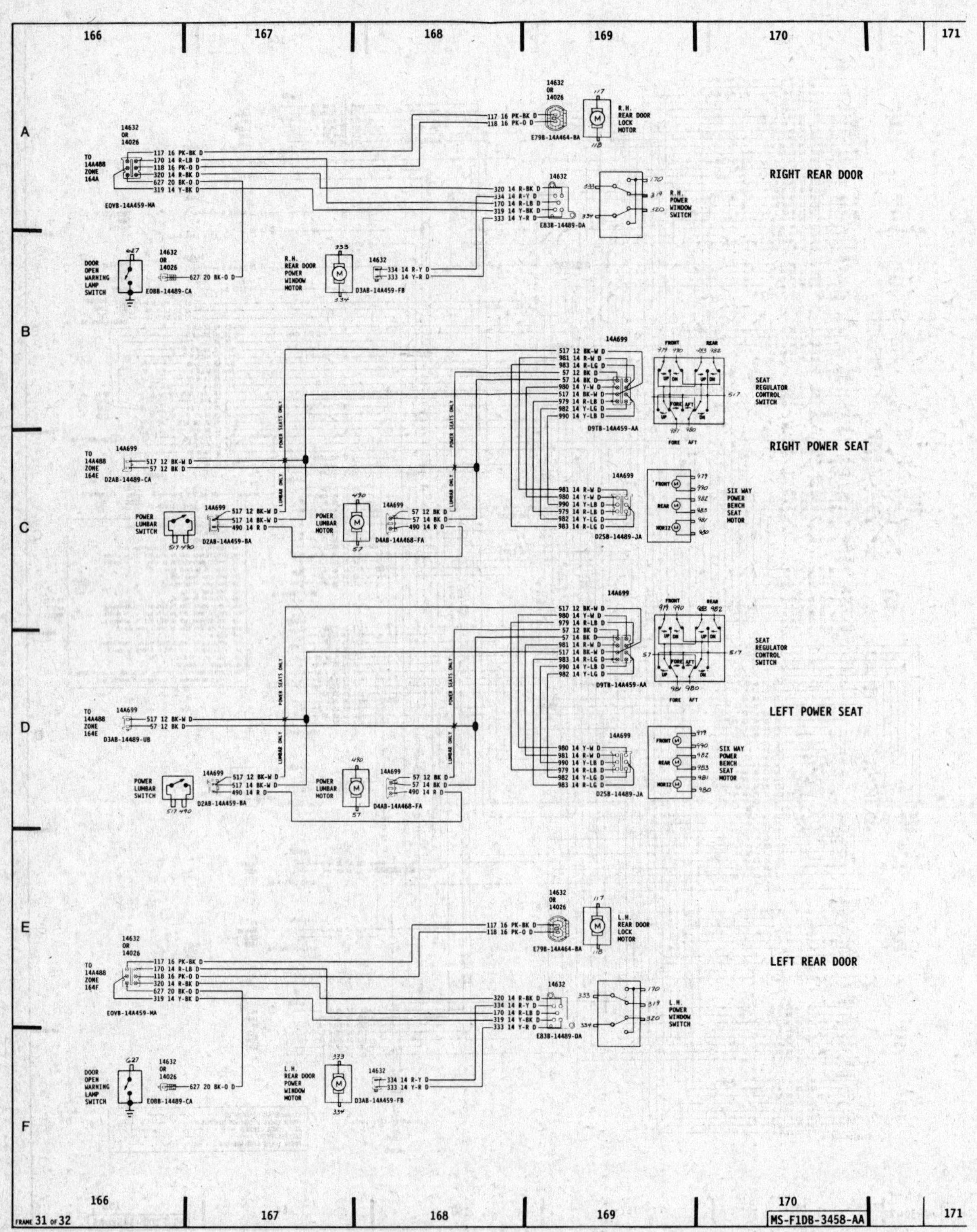
166
167
168
169
170
171
RIGHT REAR DOOR
RIGHT POWER SEAT
LEFT POWER SEAT
LEFT REAR DOOR
R.H. REAR DOOR LOCK MOTOR
R.H. POWER WINDOW SWITCH
DOOR OPEN WARNING LAMP SWITCH
R.H. REAR DOOR POWER WINDOW MOTOR
SEAT REGULATOR CONTROL SWITCH
SIX WAY POWER BENCH SEAT MOTOR
POWER LUMBAR SWITCH
POWER LUMBAR MOTOR
L.H. REAR DOOR LOCK MOTOR
L.H. POWER WINDOW SWITCH
L.H. REAR DOOR POWER WINDOW MOTOR
FRAME 31 OF 32
MS-F1DB-3458-AA

172 173 174 175 176

A

B

C

D

E

F

FRAME 32 OF 32 172 173 174 175 176

MS-F1DB-3458-AA

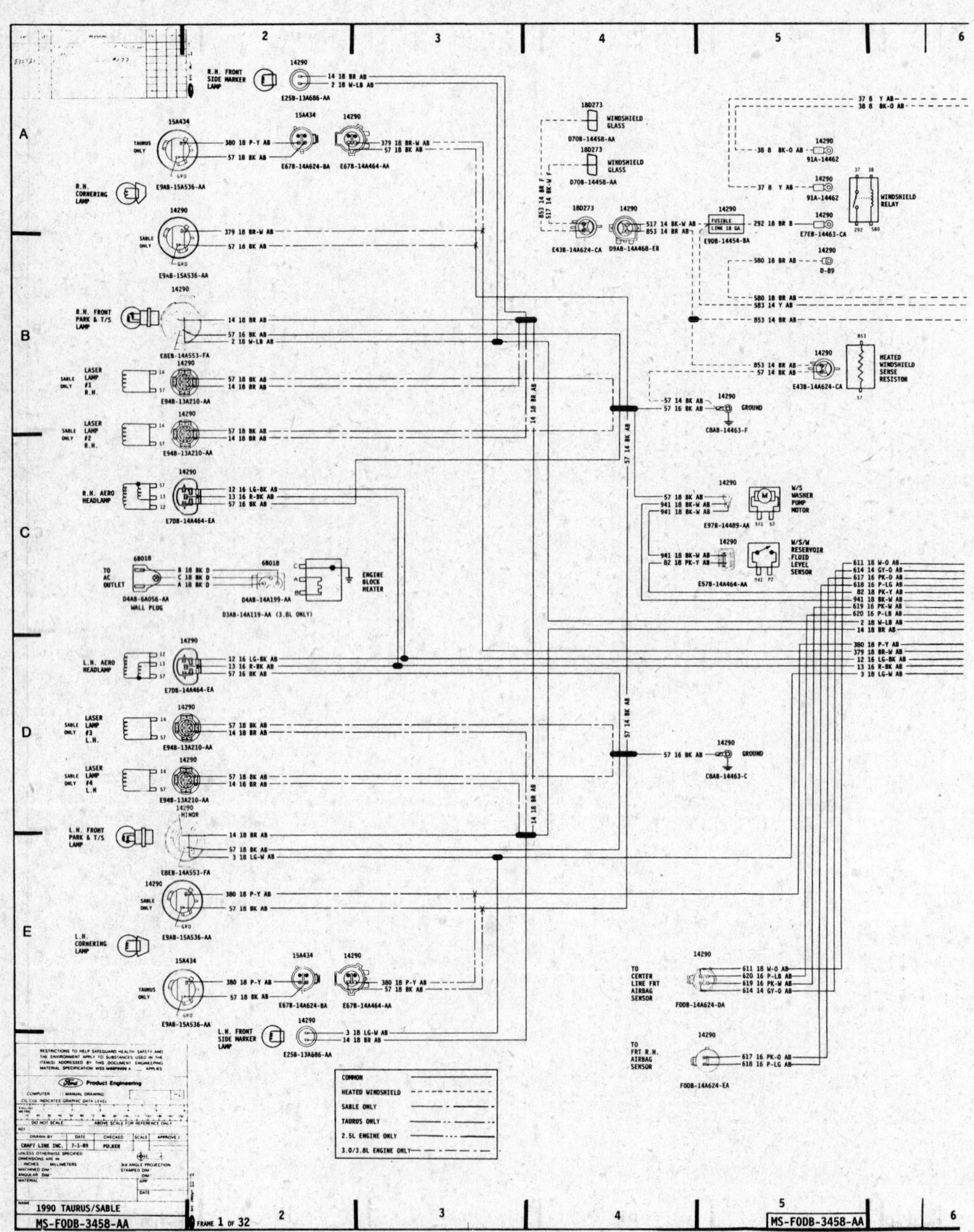

Taurus and Sable electrical schematics — 1990

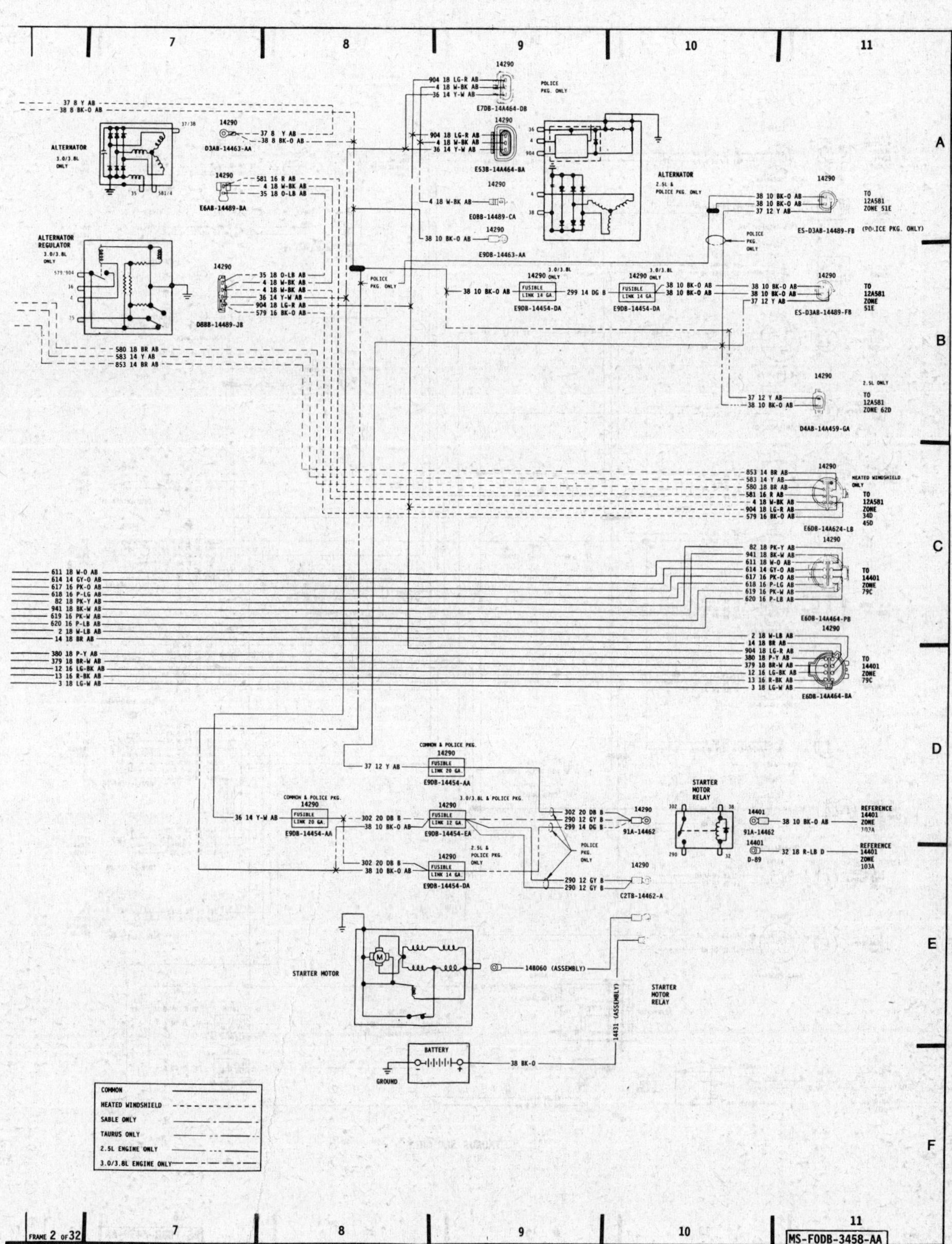

Taurus and Sable electrical schematics – 1990

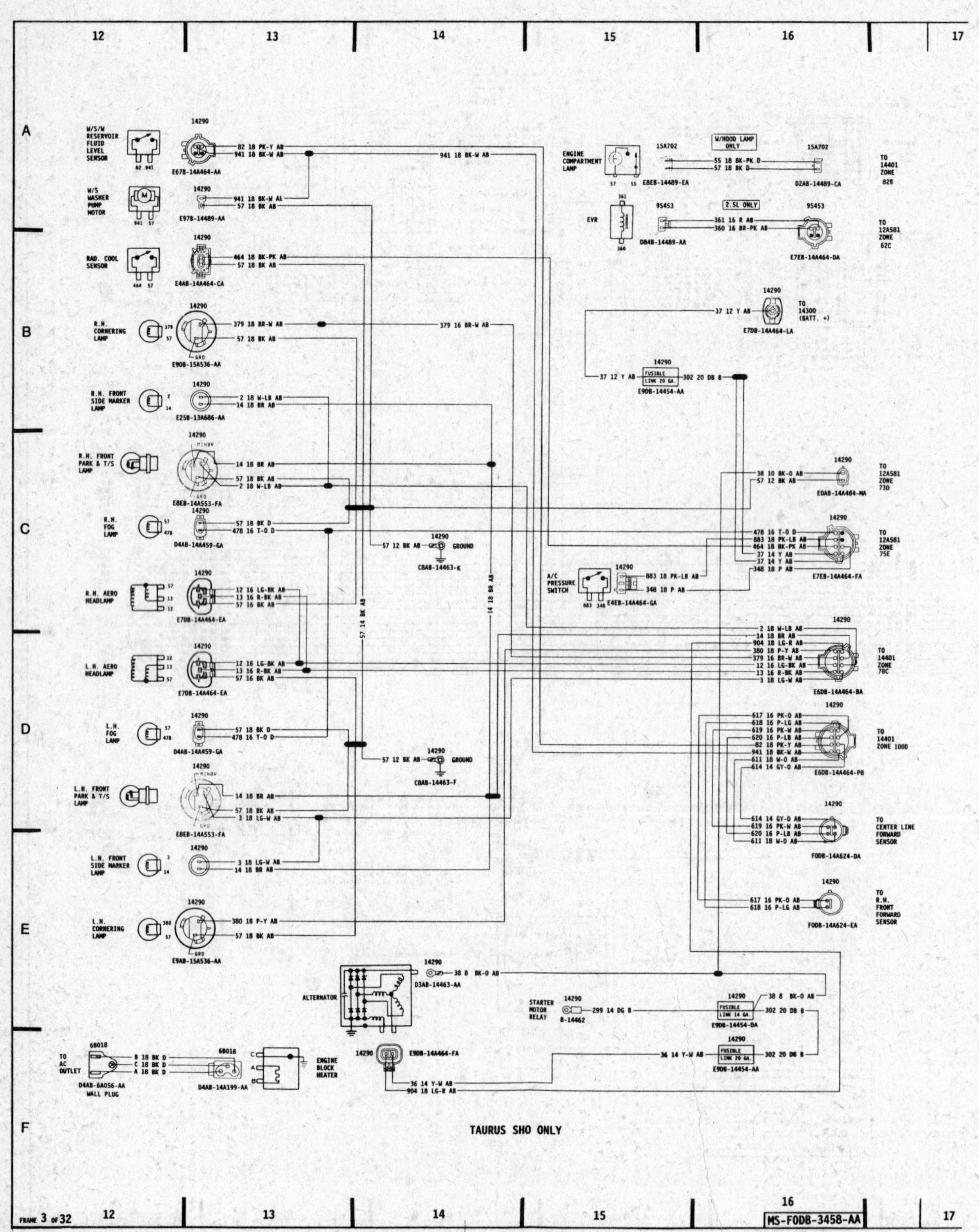

Taurus and Sable electrical schematics — 1990

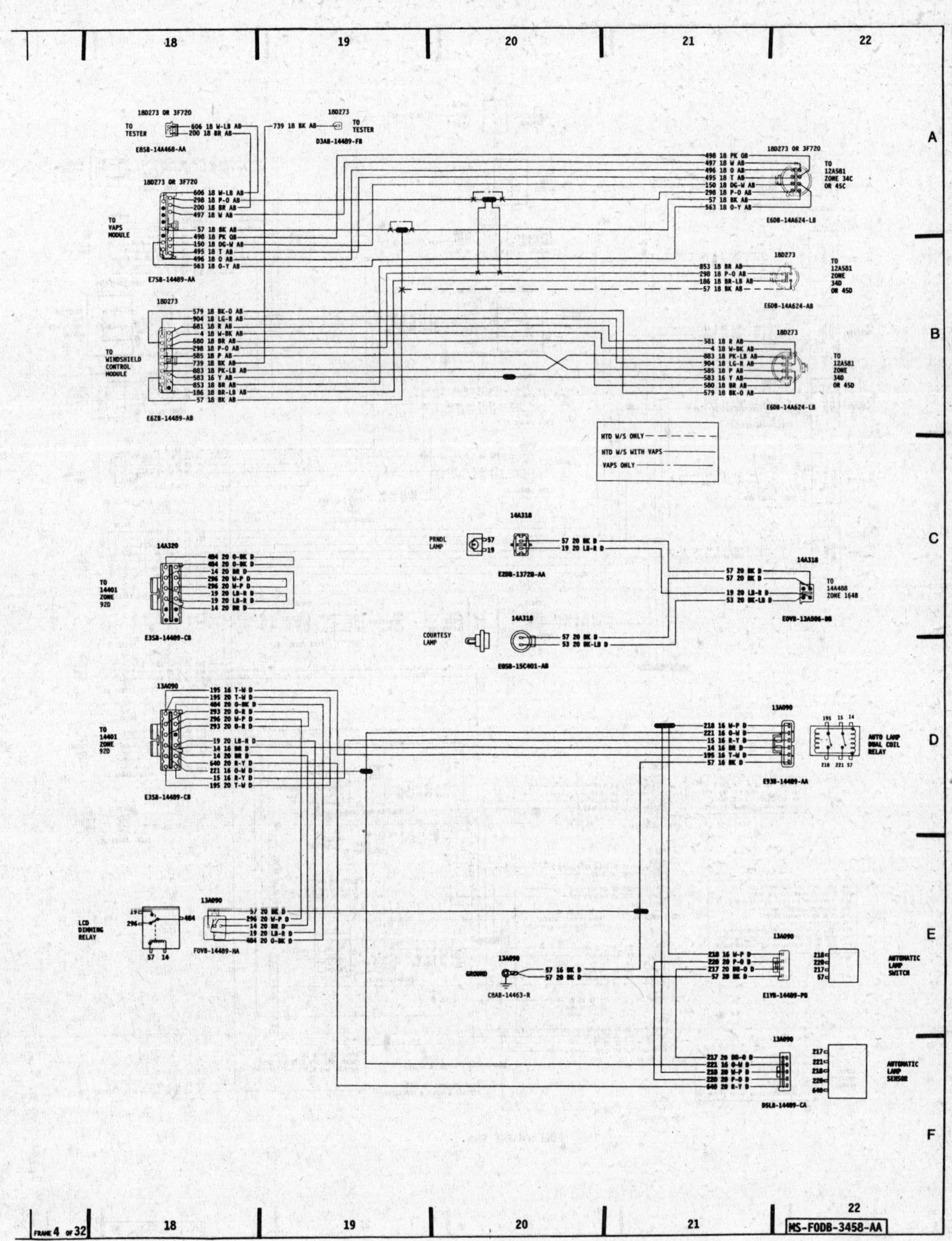

Taurus and Sable electrical schematics — 1990

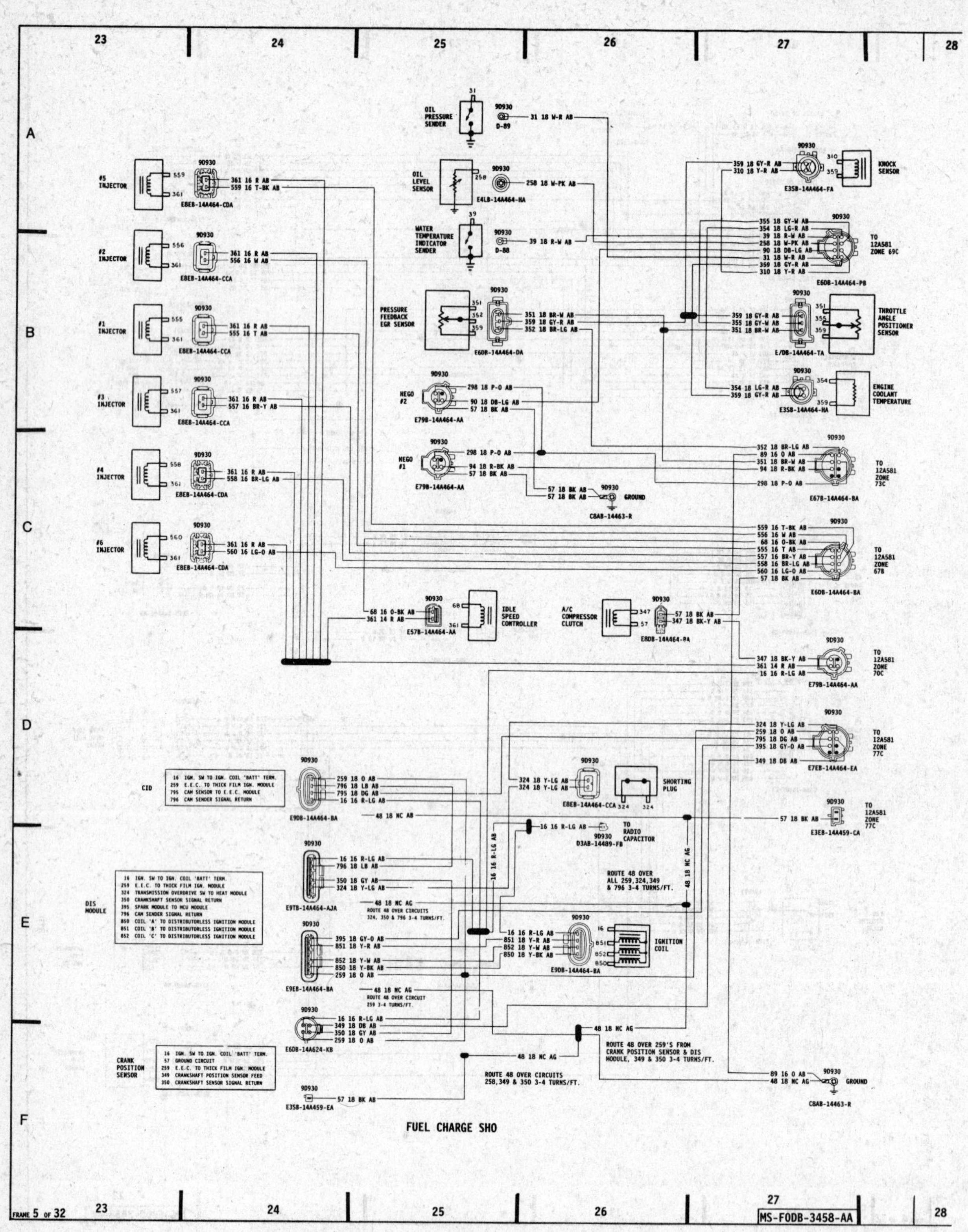

Taurus and Sable electrical schematics — 1990

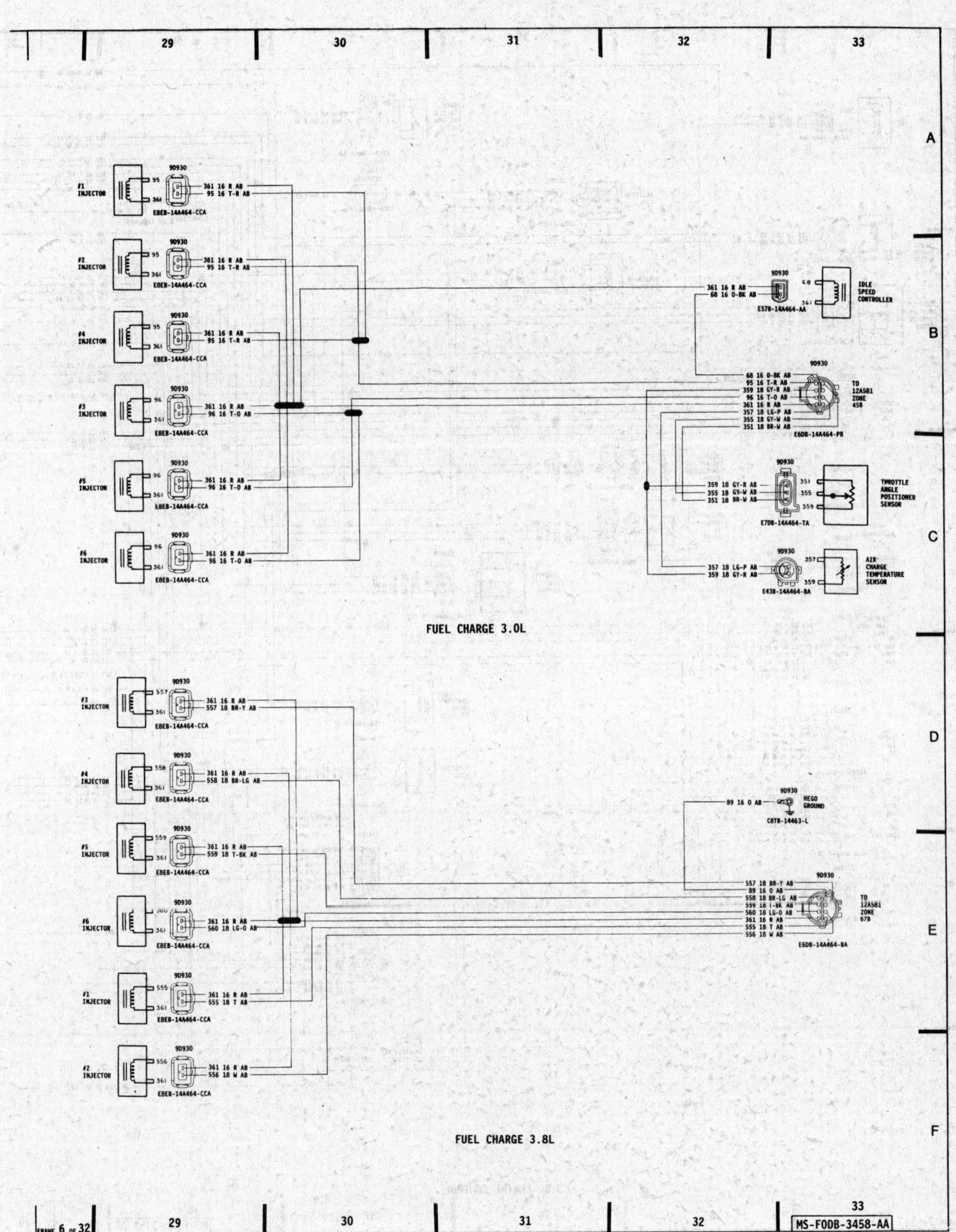
29
30
31
32
33
A
B
C
D
E
F
#1 INJECTOR
#2 INJECTOR
#4 INJECTOR
#3 INJECTOR
#5 INJECTOR
#6 INJECTOR
IDLE SPEED CONTROLLER
THROTTLE ANGLE POSITIONER SENSOR
AIR CHARGE TEMPERATURE SENSOR
FUEL CHARGE 3.0L
HEGO GROUND
FUEL CHARGE 3.8L
FRAME 6 OF 32
MS-F0DB-3458-AA

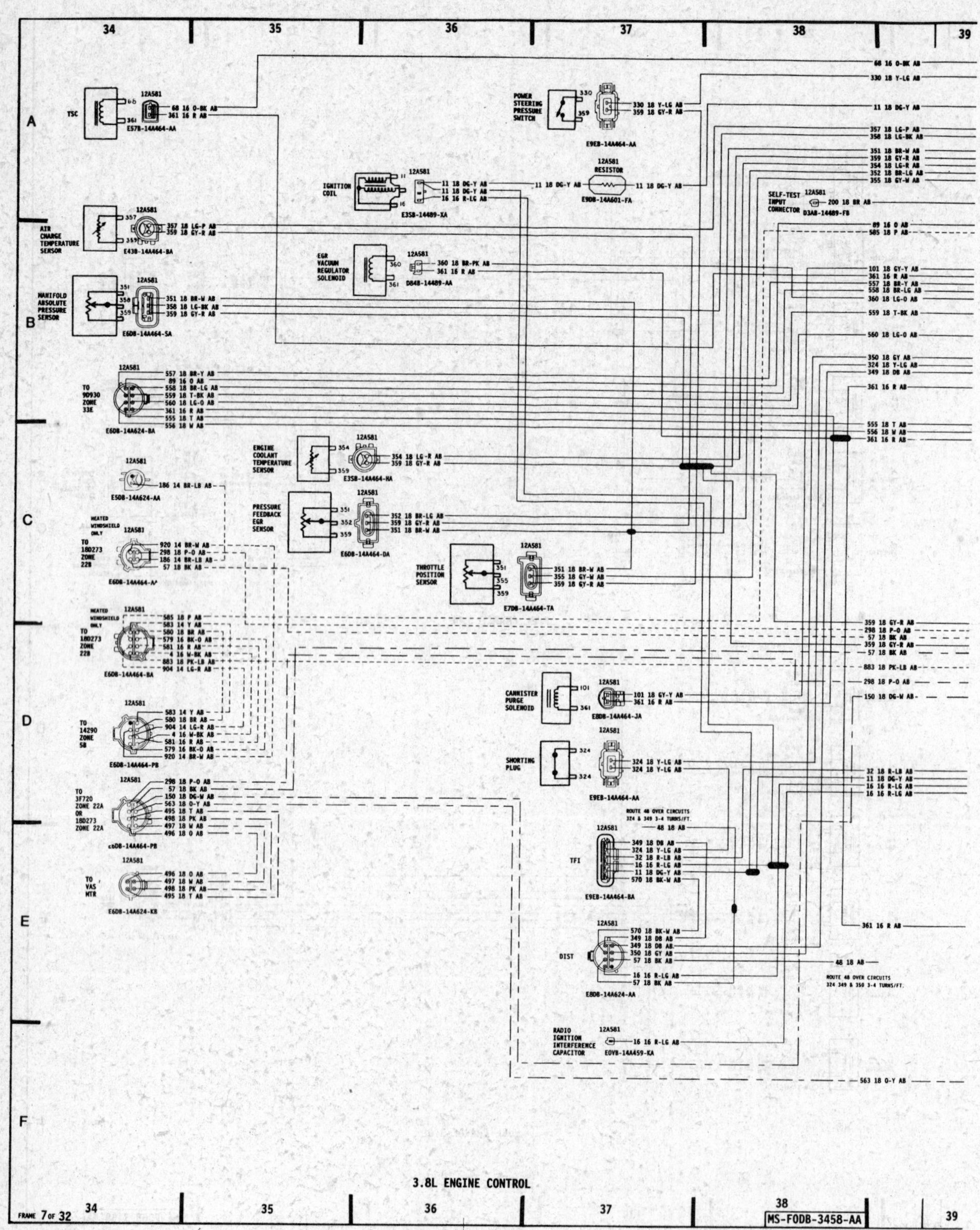

Taurus and Sable electrical schematics — 1990

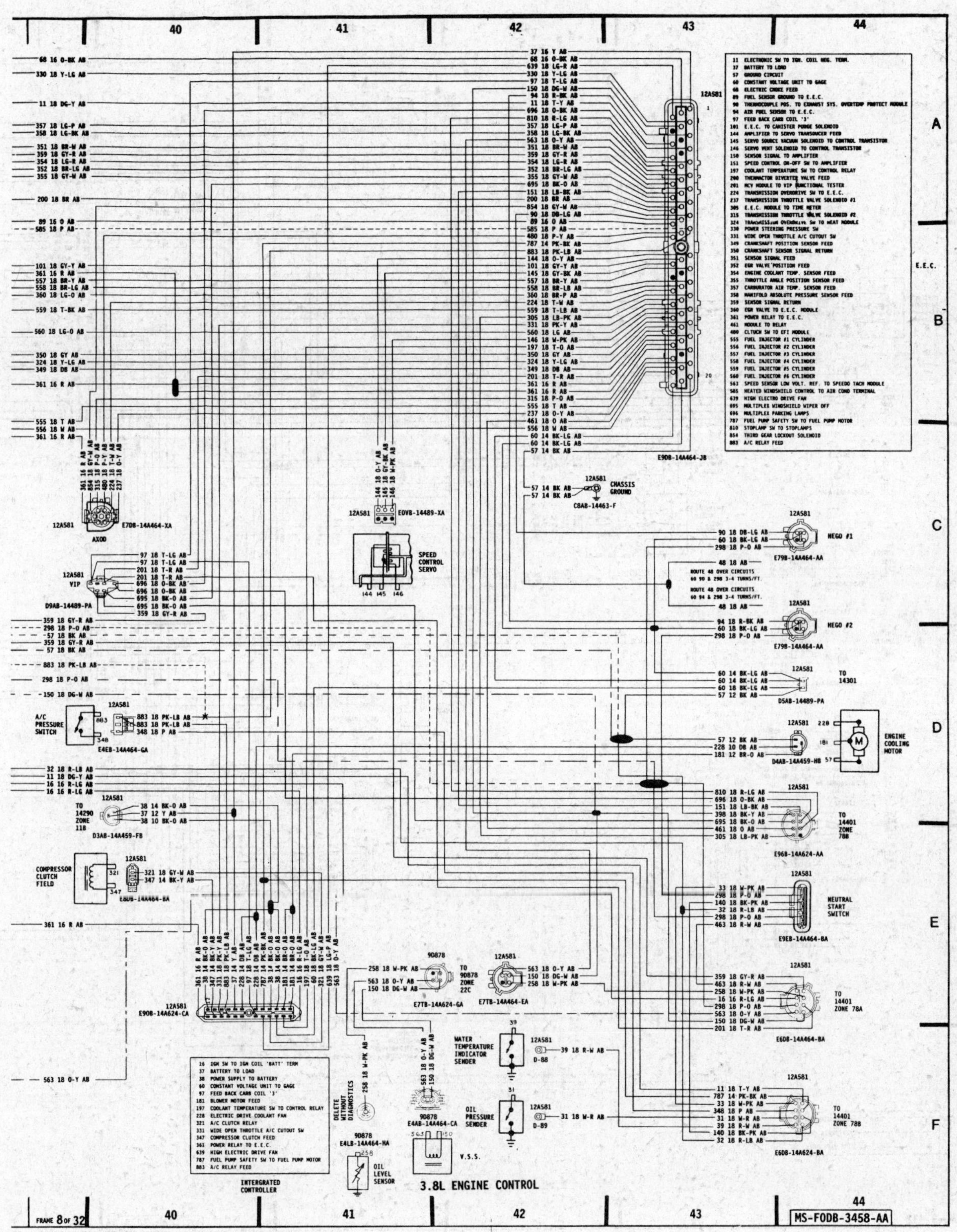

Taurus and Sable electrical schematics — 1990

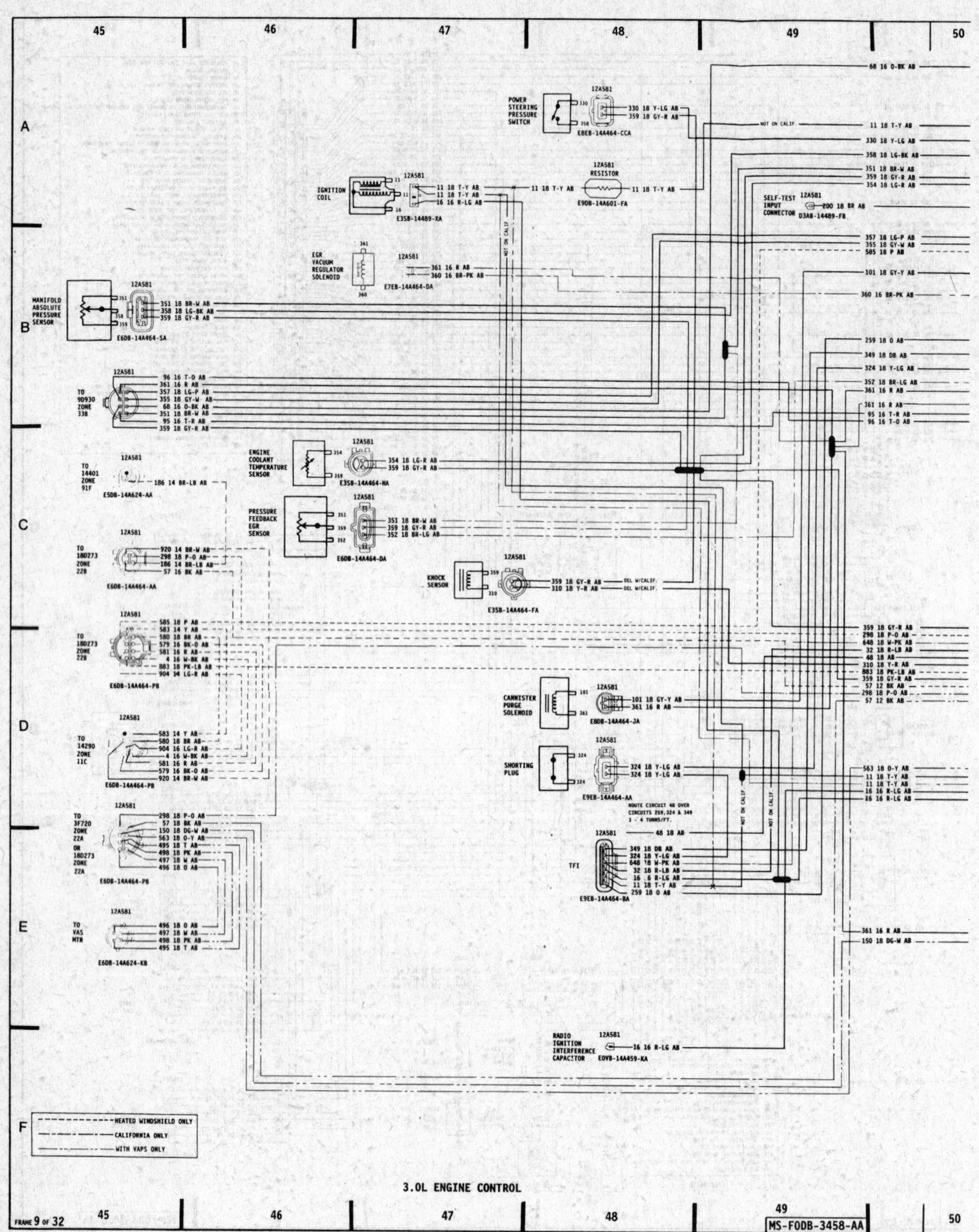

Taurus and Sable electrical schematics — 1990

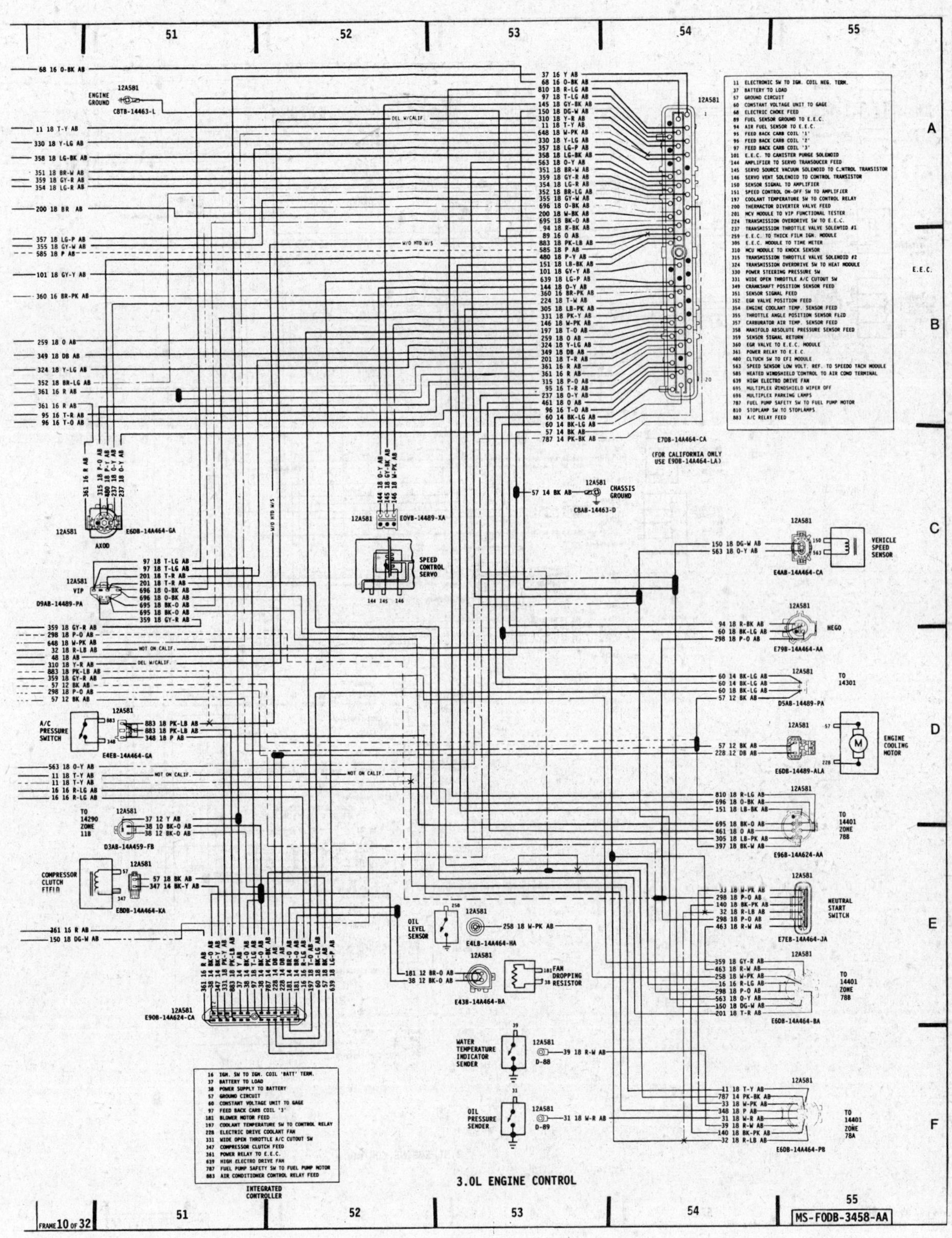
3.0L ENGINE CONTROL
E.E.C.
AXOD
VIP
SPEED CONTROL SERVO
CHASSIS GROUND
ENGINE GROUND
VEHICLE SPEED SENSOR
HEGO
ENGINE COOLING MOTOR
NEUTRAL START SWITCH
A/C PRESSURE SWITCH
COMPRESSOR CLUTCH FIELD
OIL LEVEL SENSOR
FAN DROPPING RESISTOR
WATER TEMPERATURE INDICATOR SENDER
OIL PRESSURE SENDER
INTEGRATED CONTROLLER
(FOR CALIFORNIA ONLY USE E90B-14A464-LA)
MS-F0DB-3458-AA
FRAME 10 OF 32

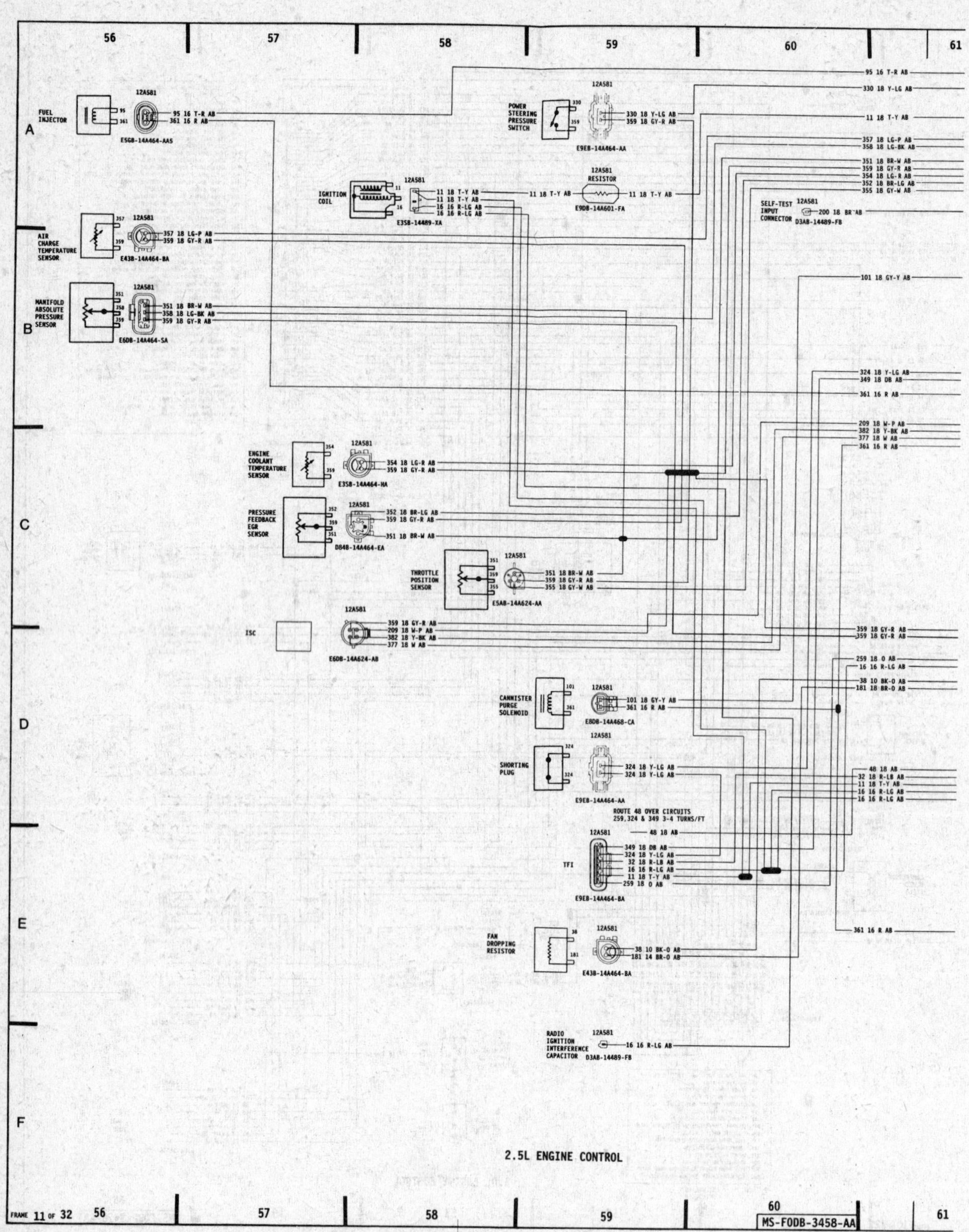

Taurus and Sable electrical schematics — 1990

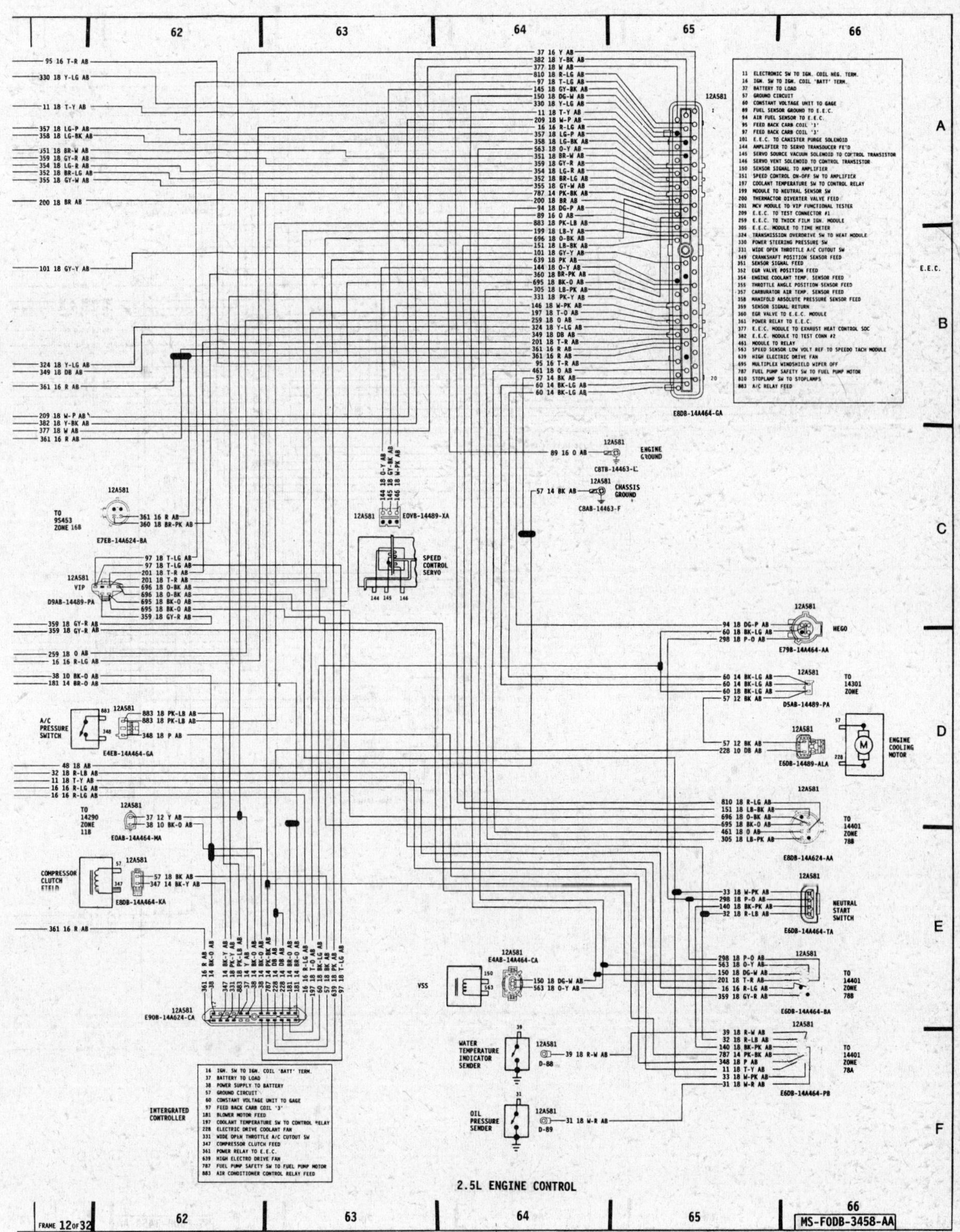
2.5L ENGINE CONTROL
MS-F0DB-3458-AA
FRAME 12 OF 32
HEGO
ENGINE COOLING MOTOR
NEUTRAL START SWITCH
VSS
WATER TEMPERATURE INDICATOR SENDER
OIL PRESSURE SENDER
INTERGRATED CONTROLLER
SPEED CONTROL SERVO
A/C PRESSURE SWITCH
COMPRESSOR CLUTCH FIELD
ENGINE GROUND
CHASSIS GROUND
E.E.C.

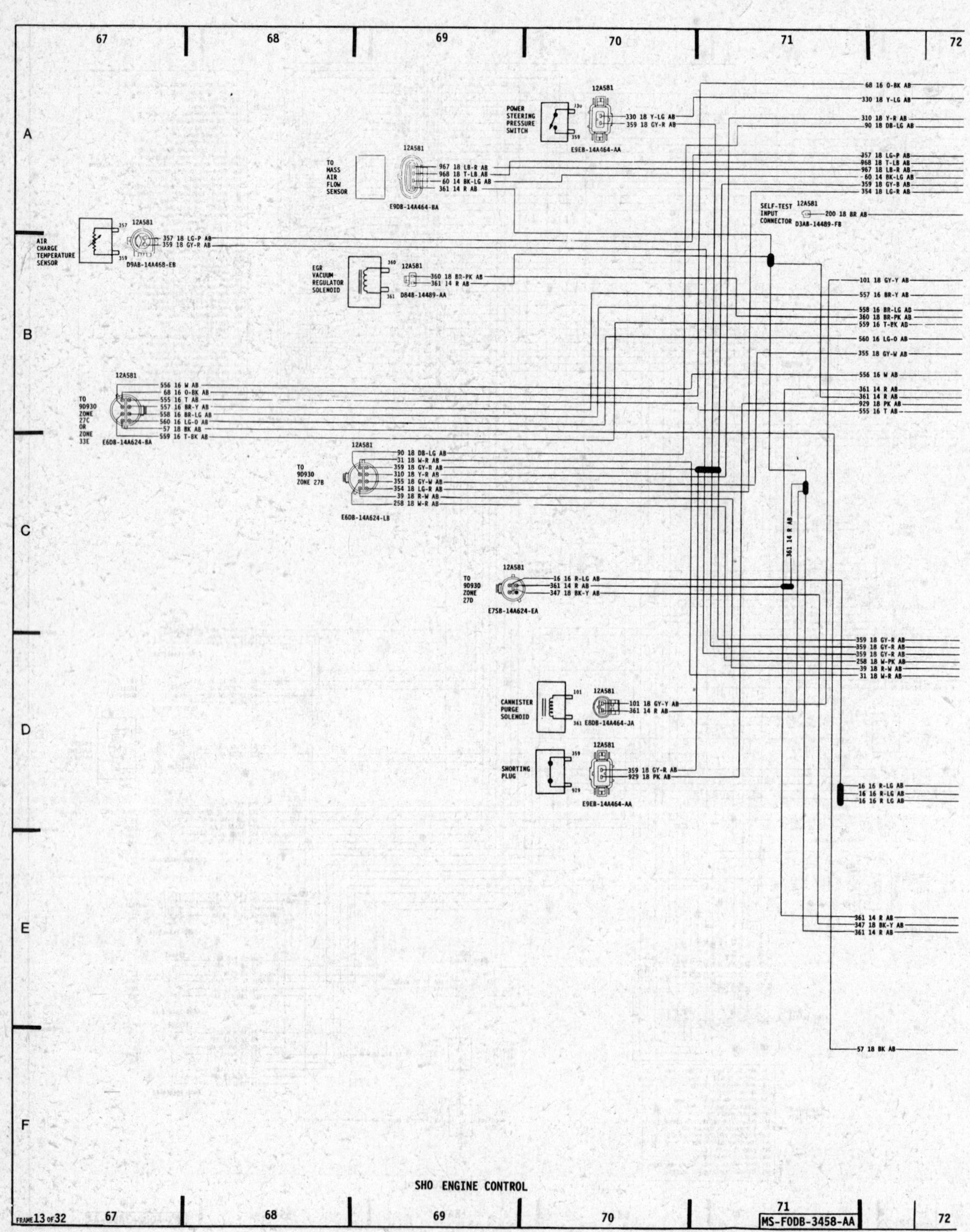
POWER STEERING PRESSURE SWITCH
TO MASS AIR FLOW SENSOR
AIR CHARGE TEMPERATURE SENSOR
EGR VACUUM REGULATOR SOLENOID
SELF-TEST INPUT CONNECTOR
CANNISTER PURGE SOLENOID
SHORTING PLUG
SHO ENGINE CONTROL
MS-F0DB-3458-AA

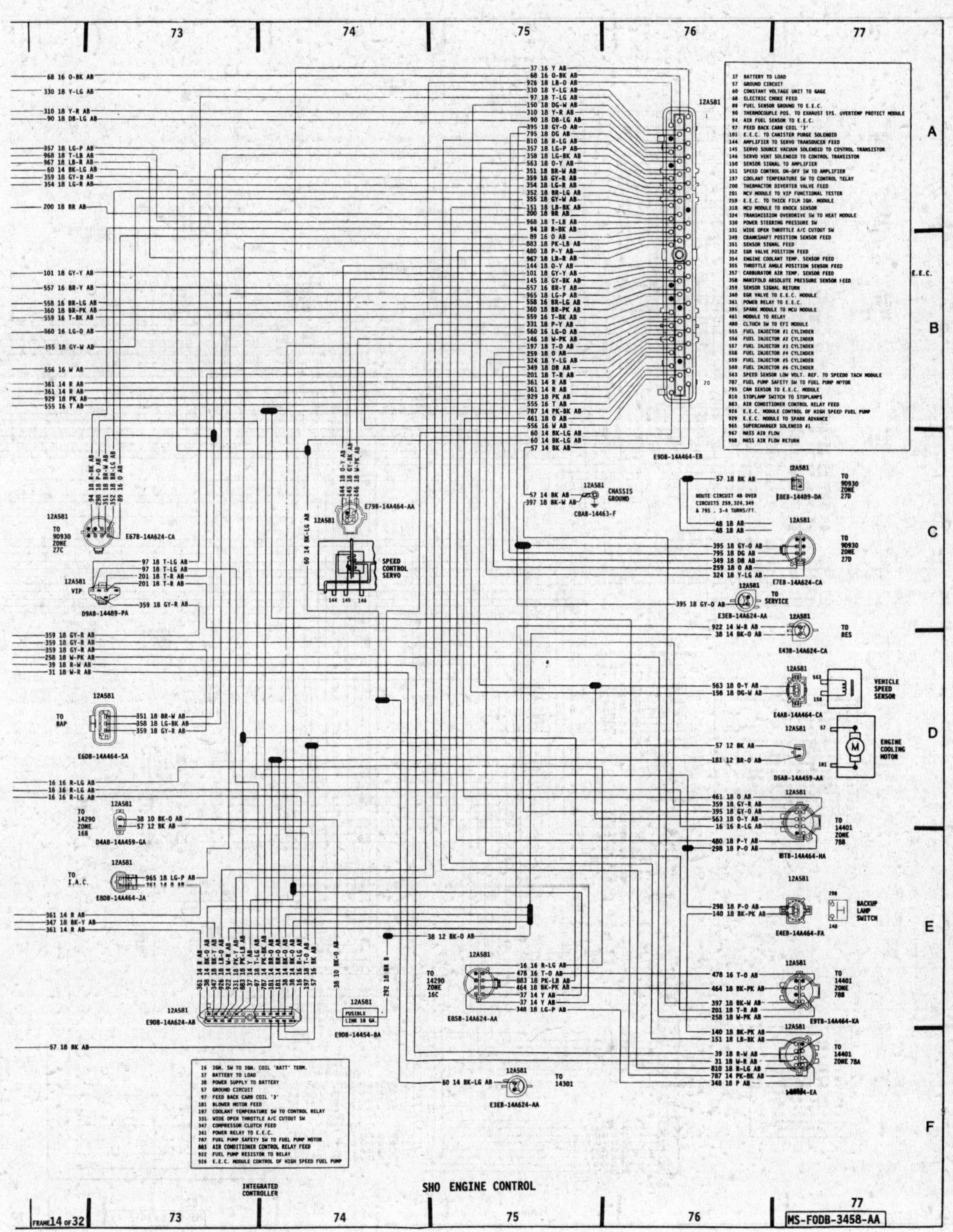

Taurus and Sable electrical schematics — 1990

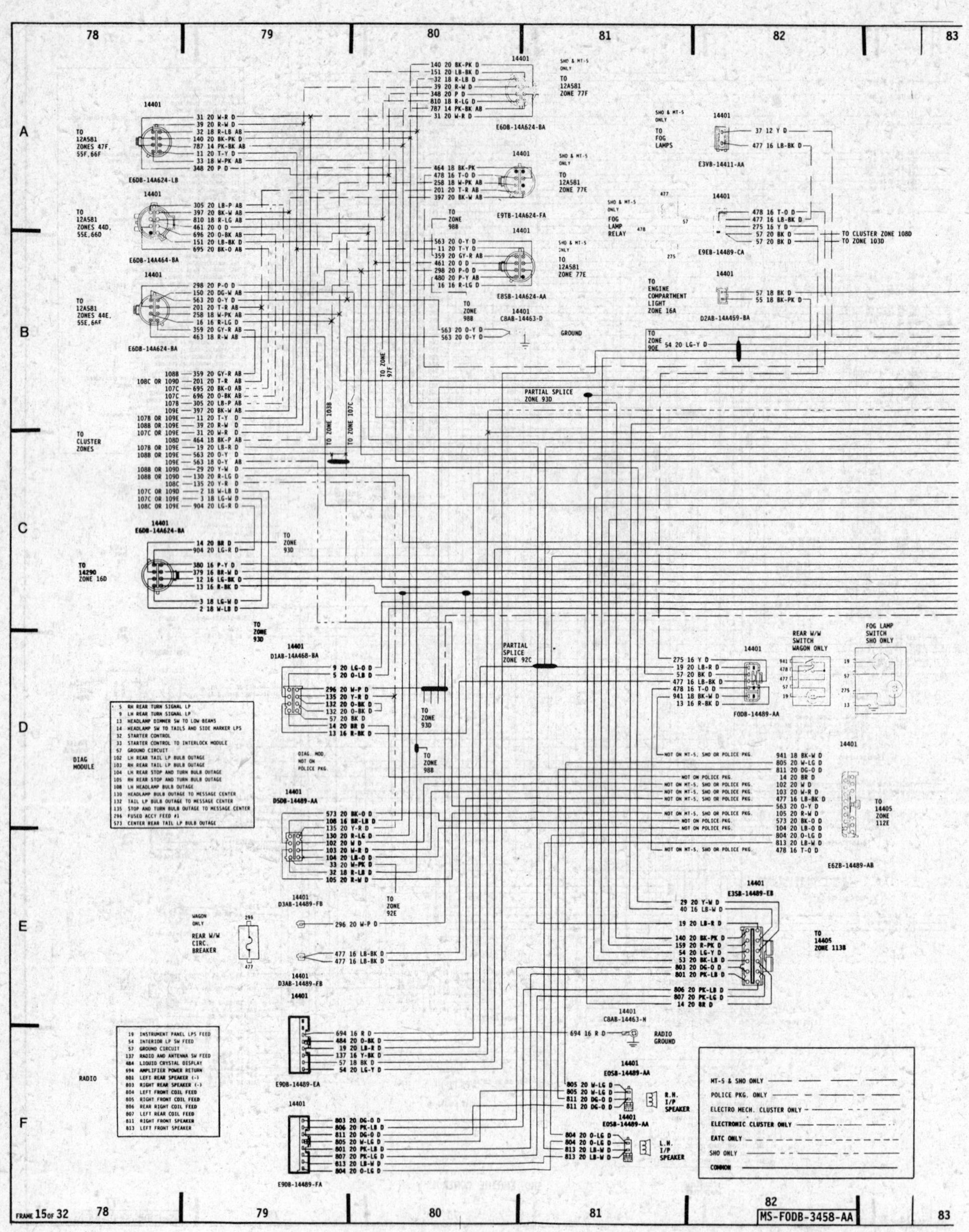

Taurus and Sable electrical schematics – 1990

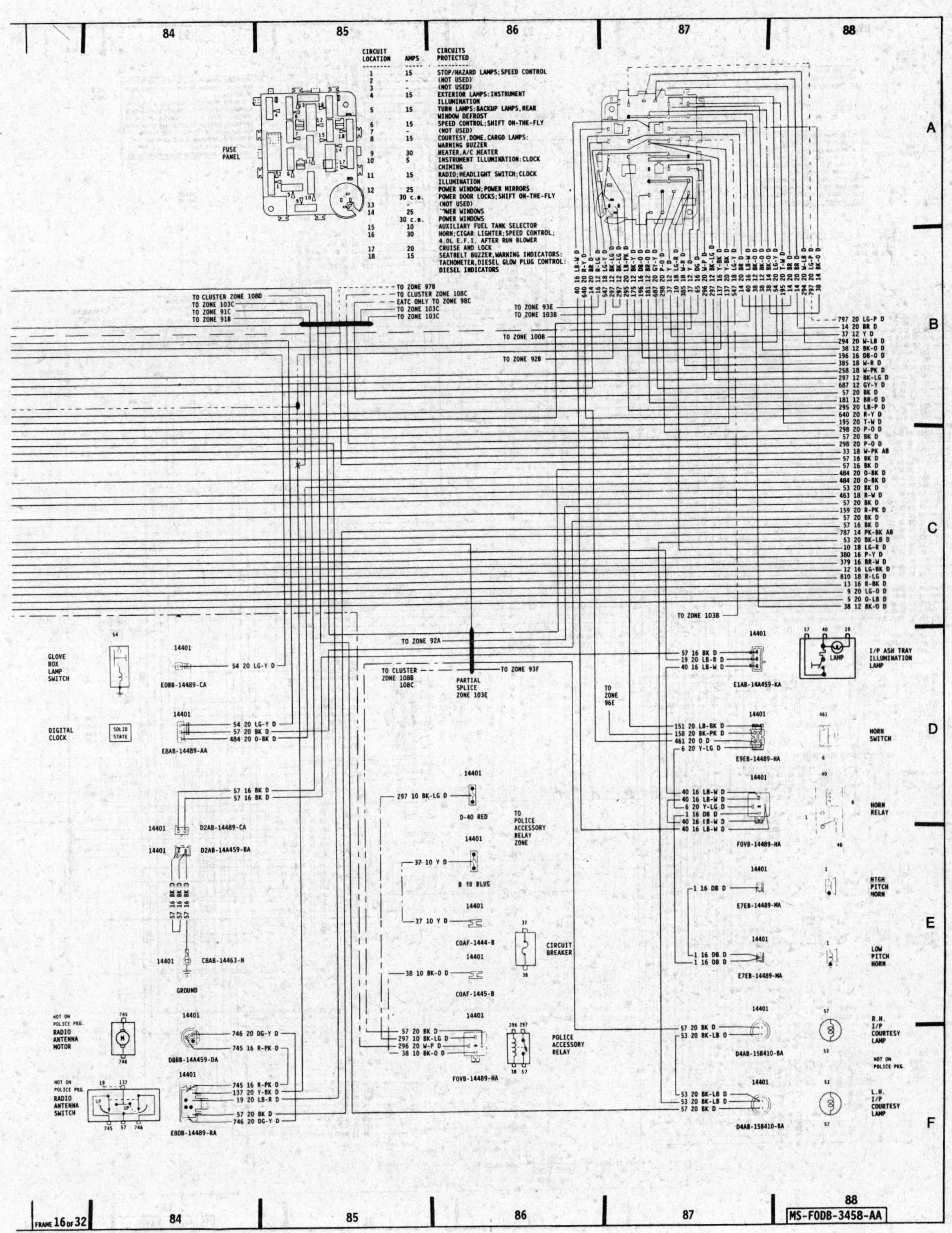

Taurus and Sable electrical schematics — 1990

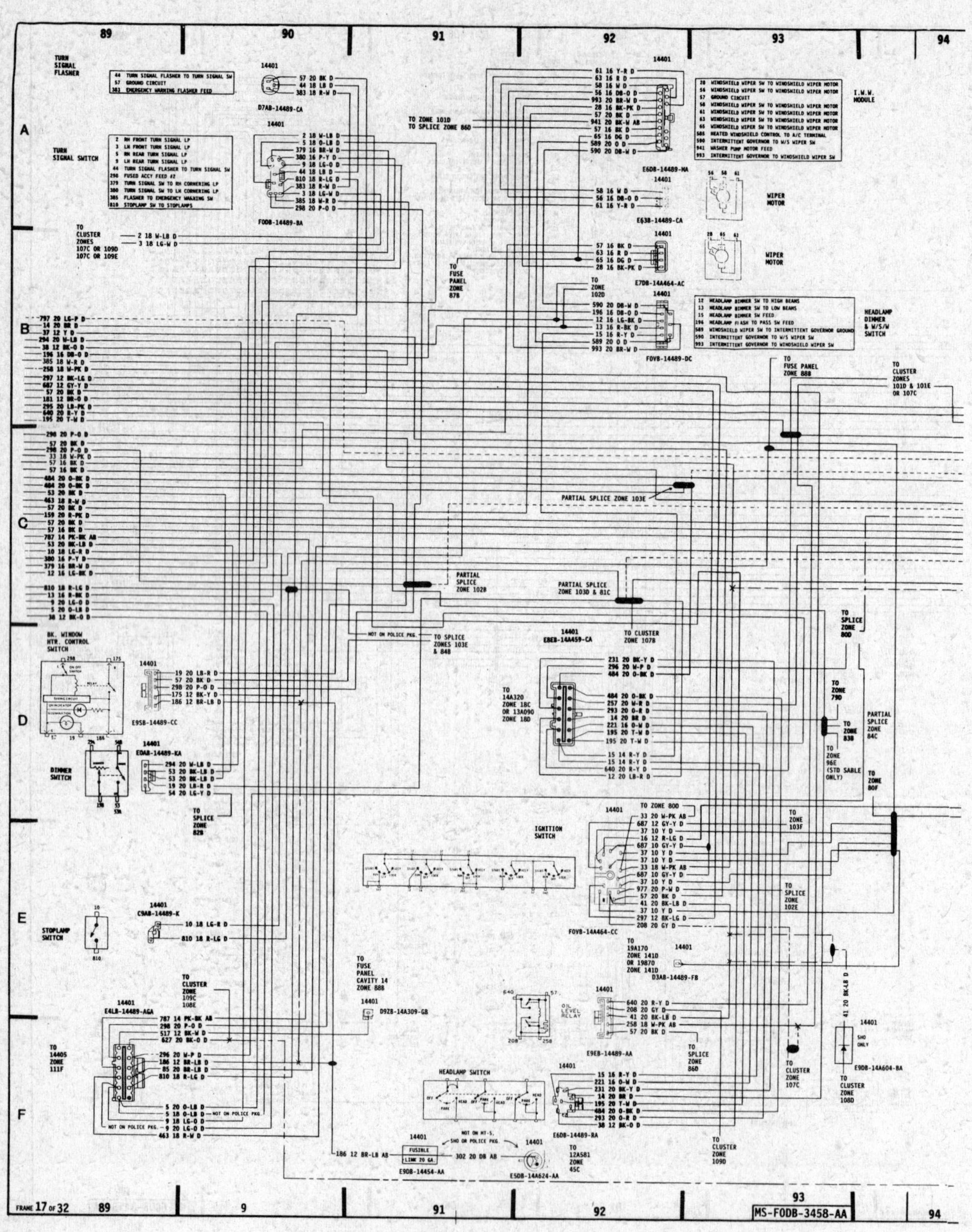

Taurus and Sable electrical schematics — 1990

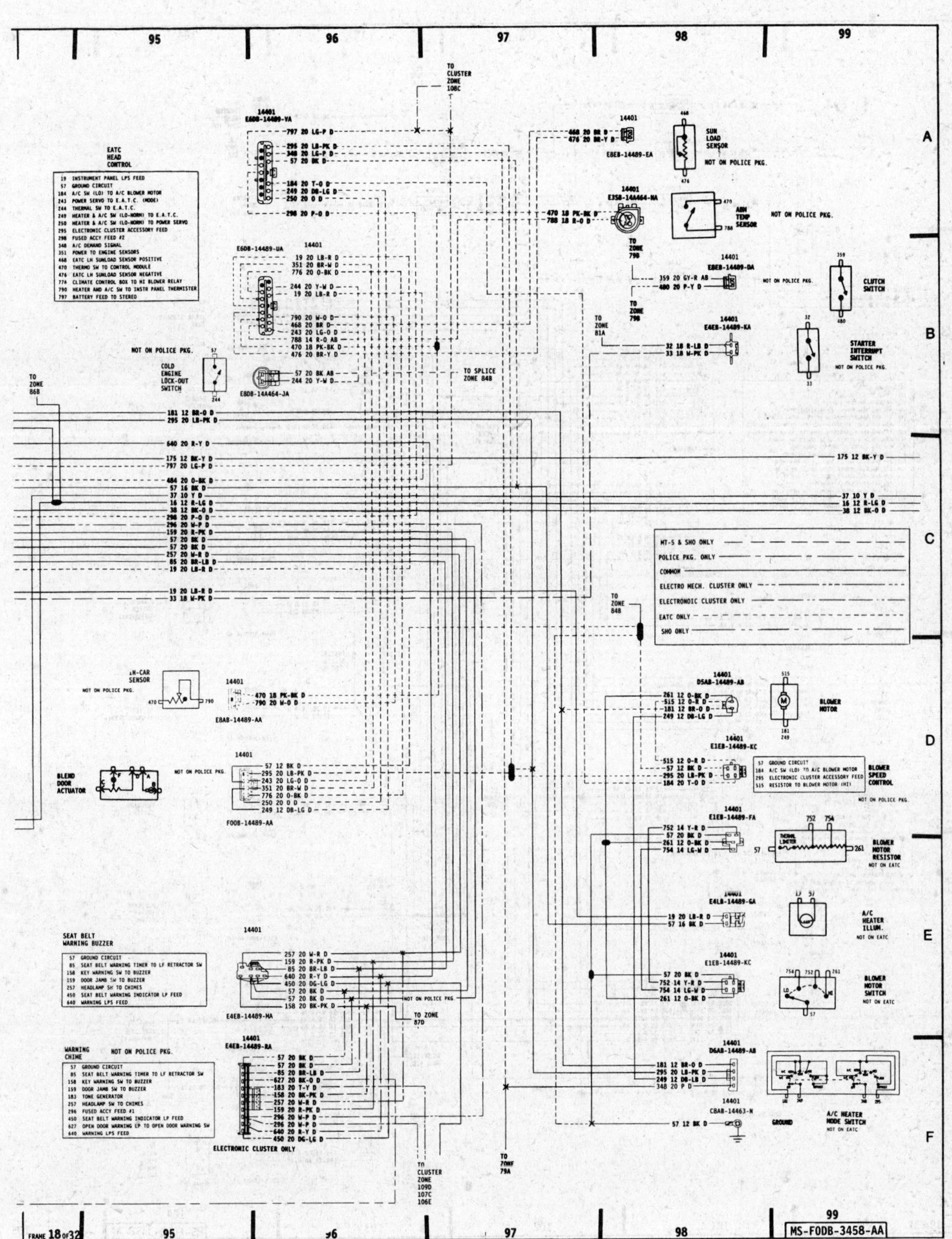

Taurus and Sable electrical schematics – 1990

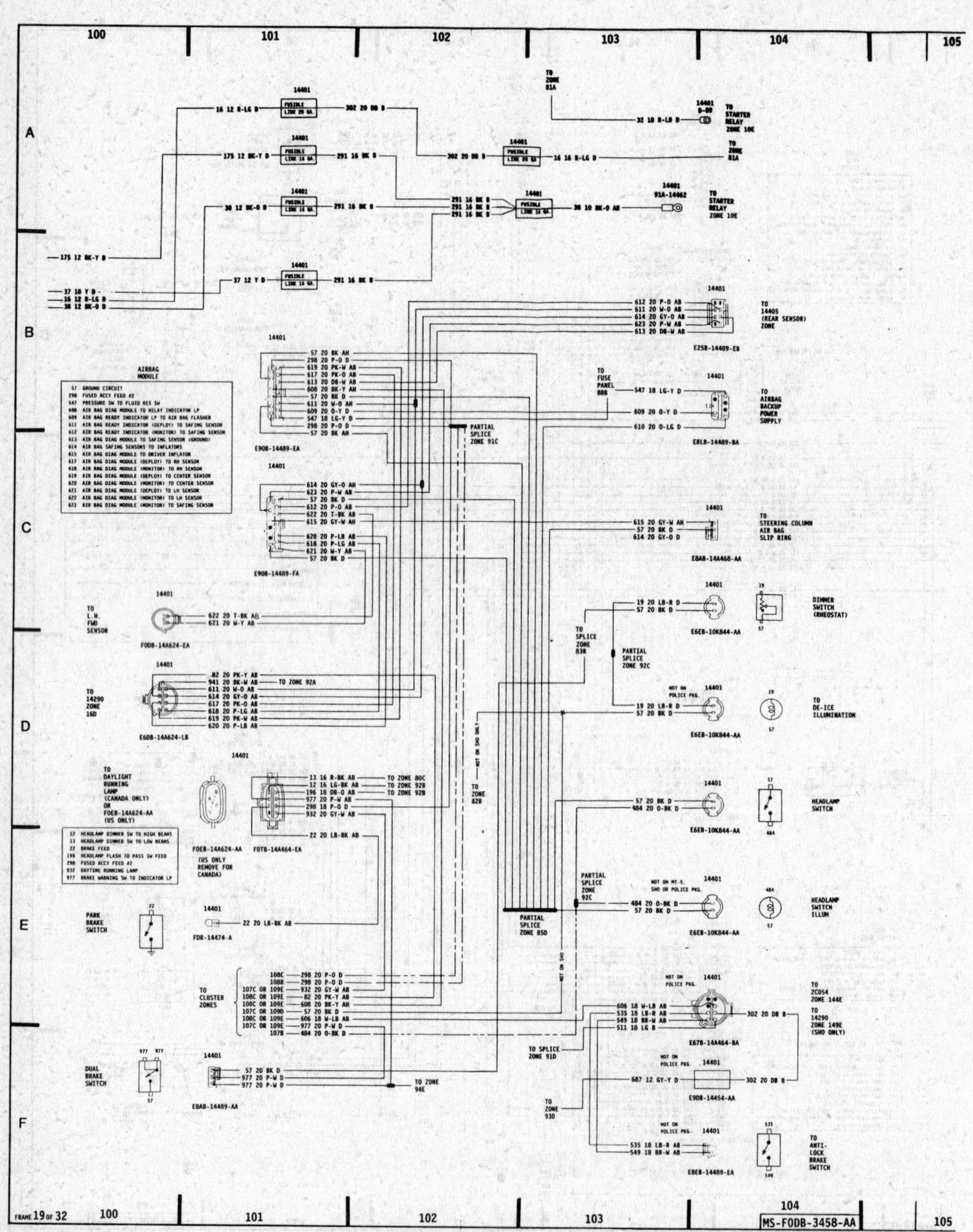

Taurus and Sable electrical schematics — 1990

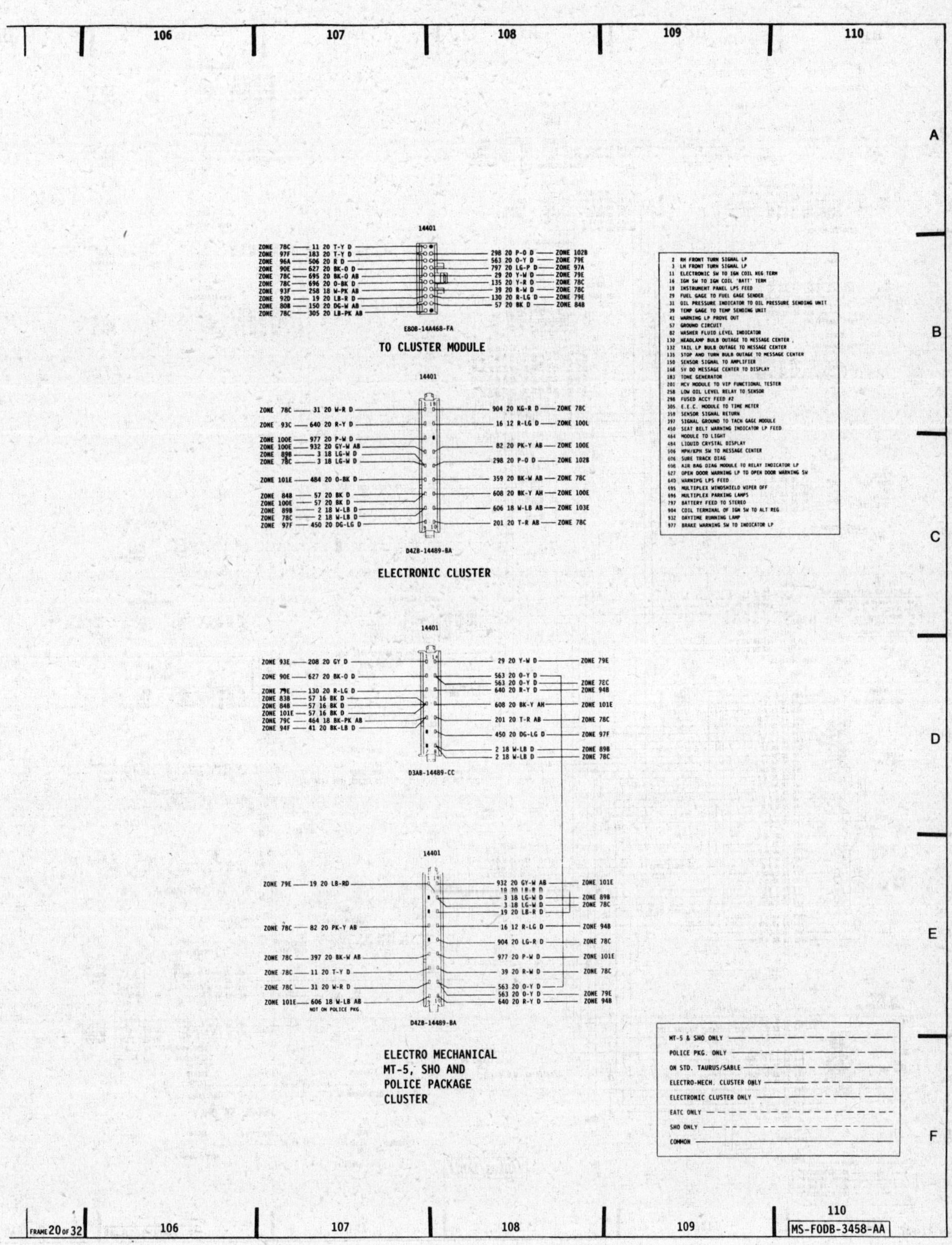
106
107
108
109
110
A
B
C
D
E
F
14401
E8OB-14A468-FA
TO CLUSTER MODULE
14401
D4ZB-14489-BA
ELECTRONIC CLUSTER
14401
D3AB-14489-CC
14401
D4ZB-14489-BA
ELECTRO MECHANICAL
MT-5, SHO AND
POLICE PACKAGE
CLUSTER
2 RH FRONT TURN SIGNAL LP
3 LH FRONT TURN SIGNAL LP
11 ELECTRONIC SW TO IGN COIL NEG TERM
16 IGN SW TO IGN COIL 'BATT' TERM
19 INSTRUMENT PANEL LPS FEED
29 FUEL GAGE TO FUEL GAGE SENDER
31 OIL PRESSURE INDICATOR TO OIL PRESSURE SENDING UNIT
39 TEMP GAGE TO TEMP SENDING UNIT
41 WARNING LP PROVE OUT
57 GROUND CIRCUIT
82 WASHER FLUID LEVEL INDICATOR
130 HEADLAMP BULB OUTAGE TO MESSAGE CENTER
132 TAIL LP BULB OUTAGE TO MESSAGE CENTER
135 STOP AND TURN BULB OUTAGE TO MESSAGE CENTER
150 SENSOR SIGNAL TO AMPLIFIER
168 5V DO MESSAGE CENTER TO DISPLAY
183 TONE GENERATOR
201 MCV MODULE TO VIP FUNCTIONAL TESTER
258 LOW OIL LEVEL RELAY TO SENSOR
298 FUSED ACCY FEED #2
305 E.E.C. MODULE TO TIME METER
359 SENSOR SIGNAL RETURN
397 SIGNAL GROUND TO TACH GAGE MODULE
450 SEAT BELT WARNING INDICATOR LP FEED
464 MODULE TO LIGHT
484 LIQUID CRYSTAL DISPLAY
506 MPH/KPH SW TO MESSAGE CENTER
606 SURE TRACK DIAG
608 AIR BAG DIAG MODULE TO RELAY INDICATOR LP
627 OPEN DOOR WARNING LP TO OPEN DOOR WARNING SW
640 WARNIPG LPS FEED
695 MULTIPLEX WINDSHIELD WIPER OFF
696 MULTIPLEX PARKING LAMPS
797 BATTERY FEED TO STEREO
904 COIL TERMINAL OF IGN SW TO ALT REG
932 DAYTIME RUNNING LAMP
977 BRAKE WARNING SW TO INDICATOR LP
MT-5 & SHO ONLY
POLICE PKG. ONLY
ON STD. TAURUS/SABLE
ELECTRO-MECH. CLUSTER ONLY
ELECTRONIC CLUSTER ONLY
EATC ONLY
SHO ONLY
COMMON
FRAME 20 OF 32
MS-FODB-3458-AA

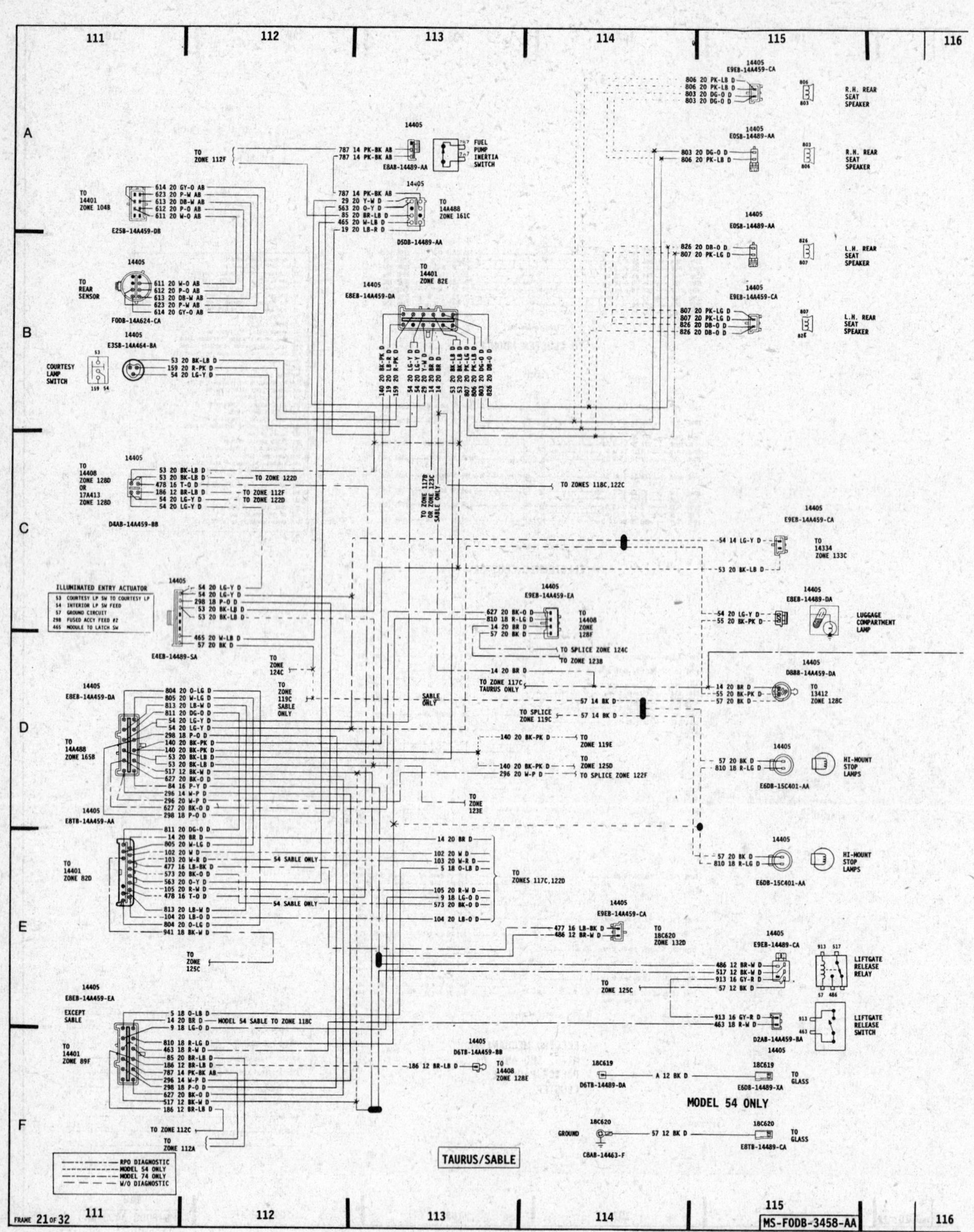

Taurus and Sable electrical schematics – 1990

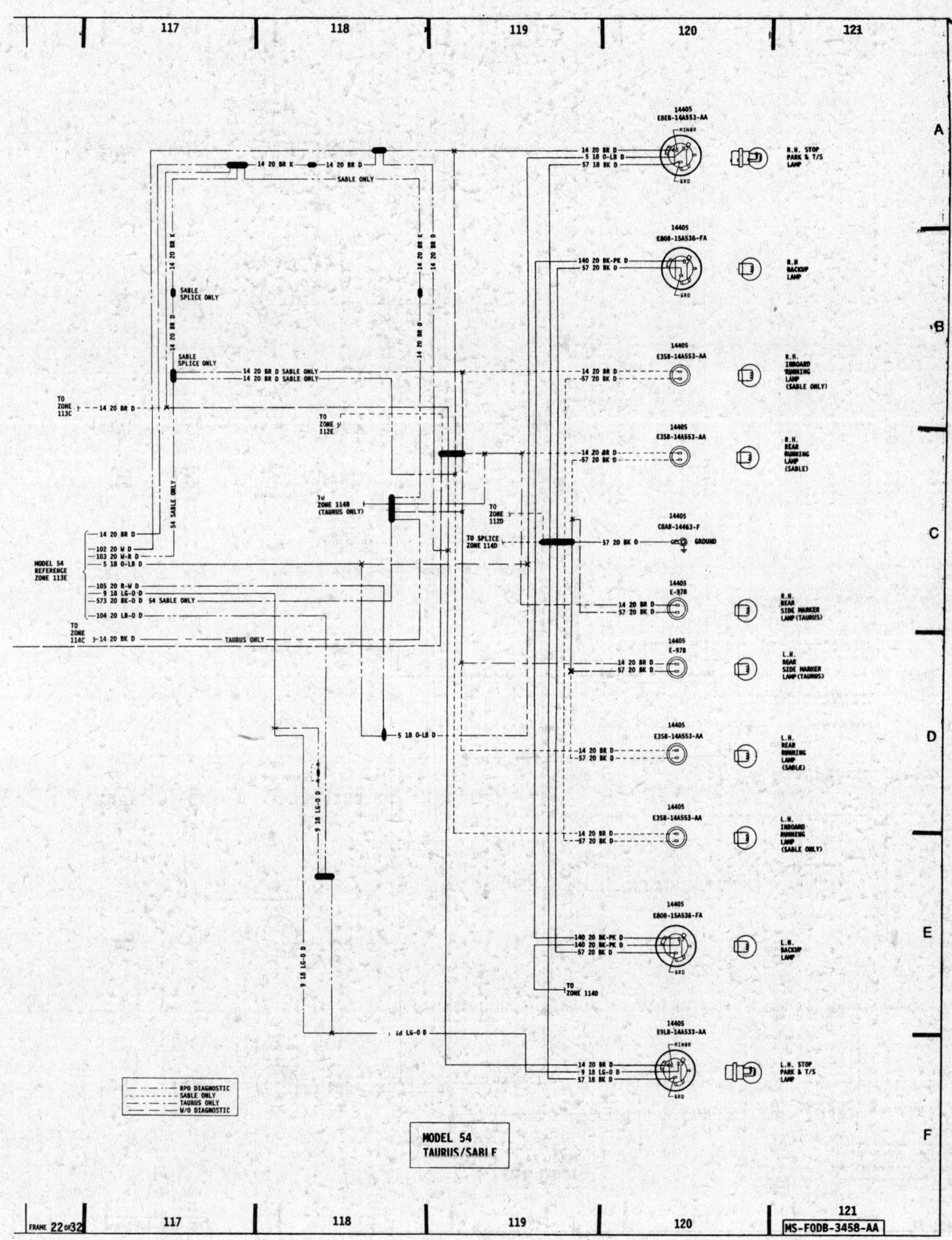

Taurus and Sable electrical schematics — 1990

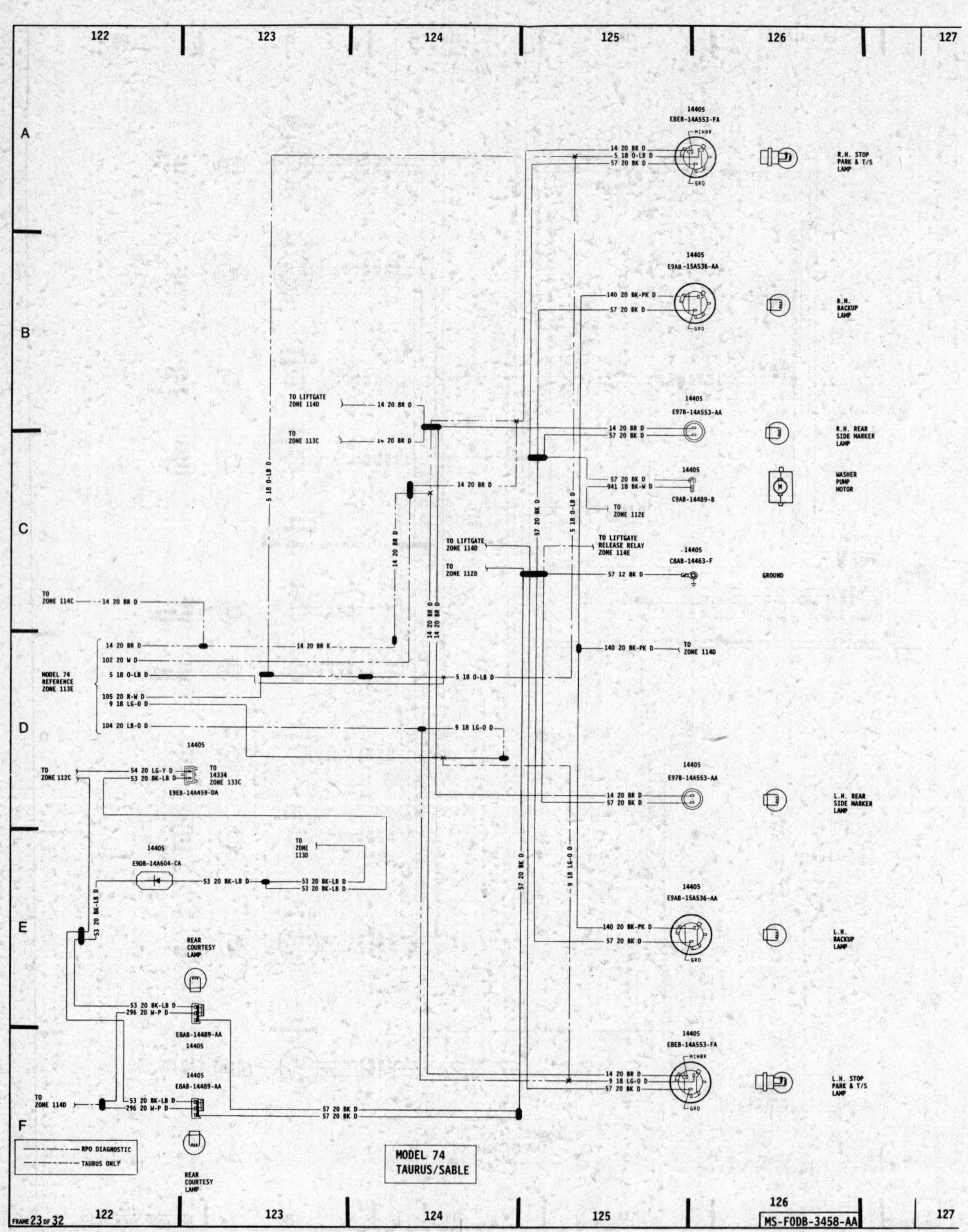

Taurus and Sable electrical schematics — 1990

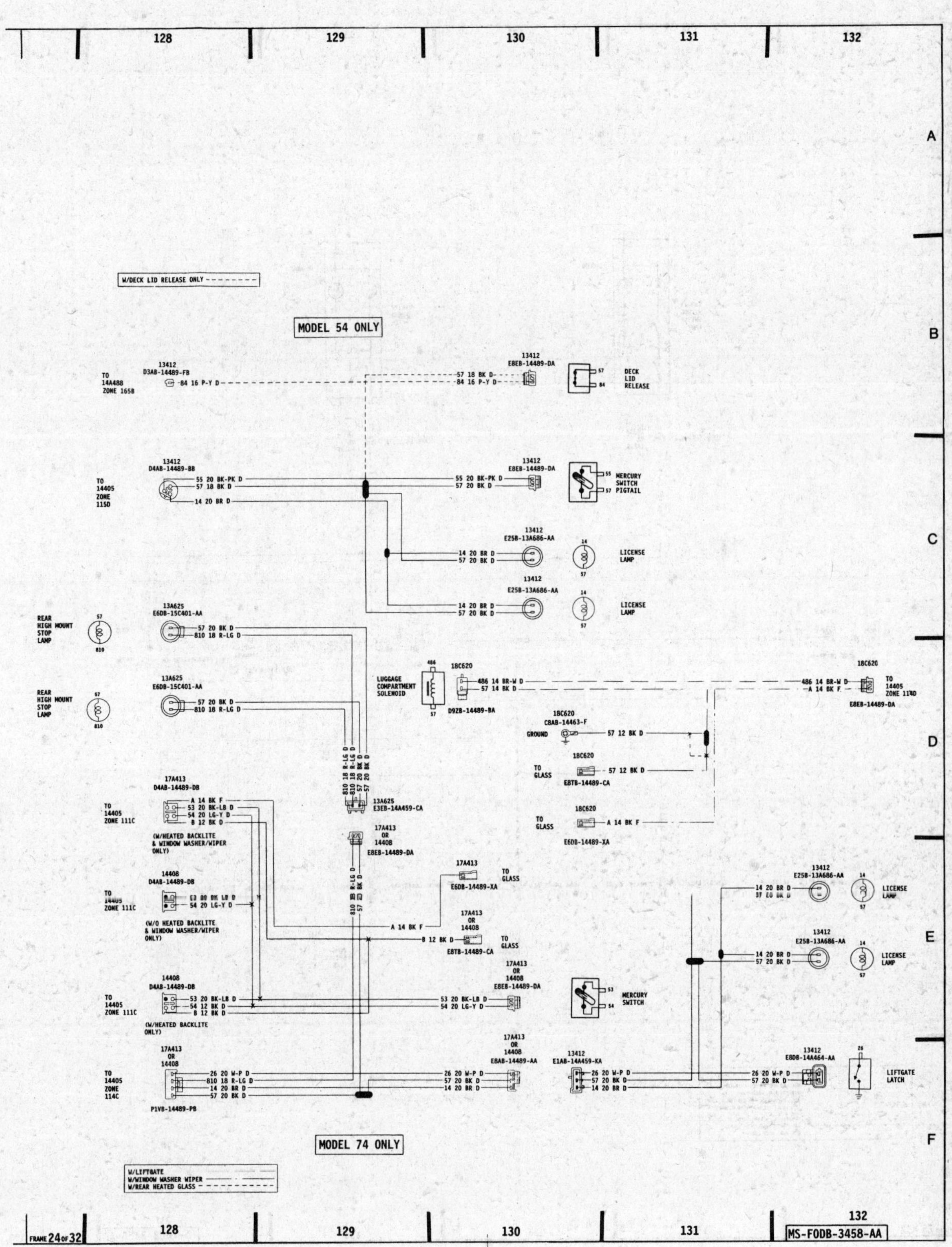

Taurus and Sable electrical schematics — 1990

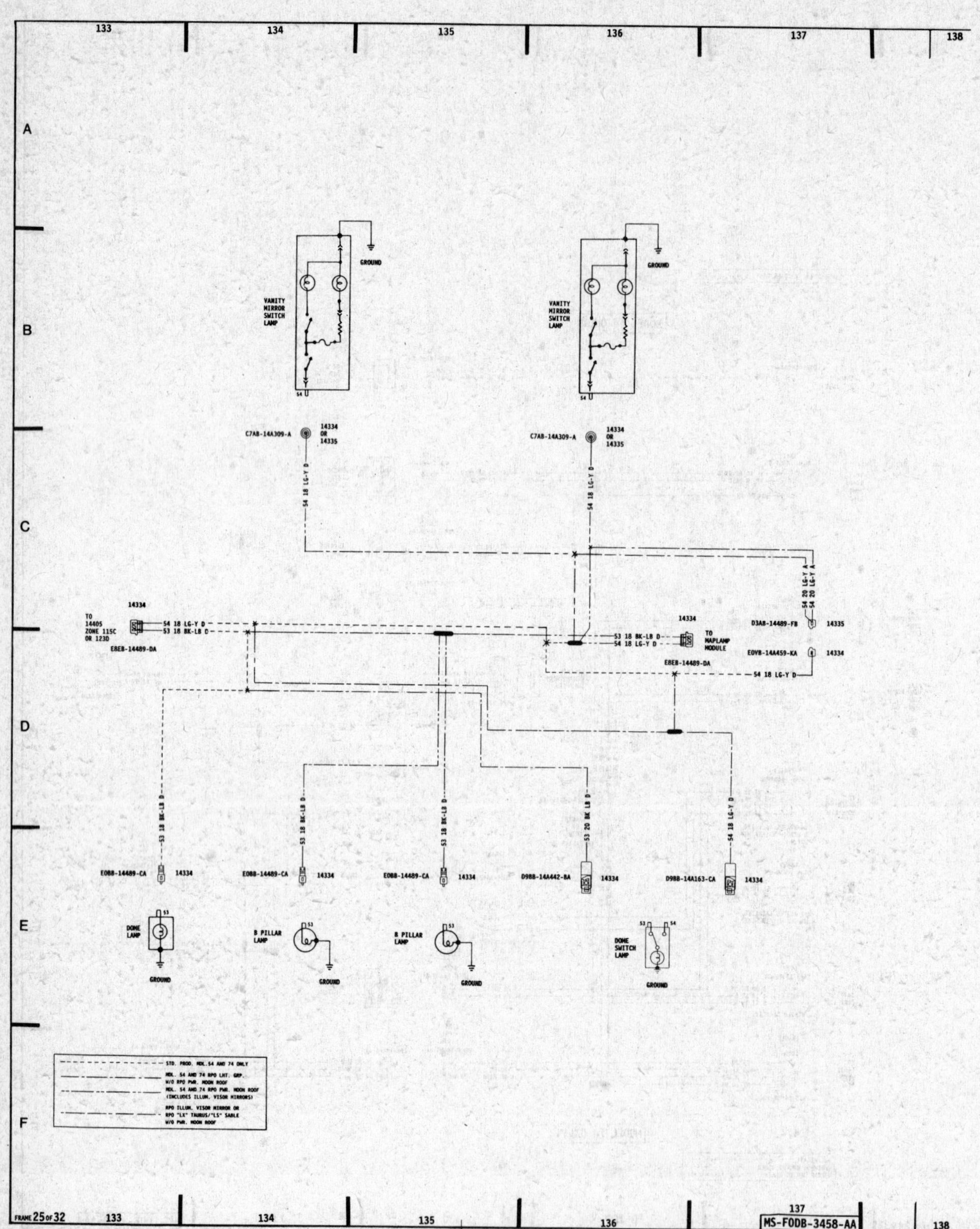

Taurus and Sable electrical schematics — 1990

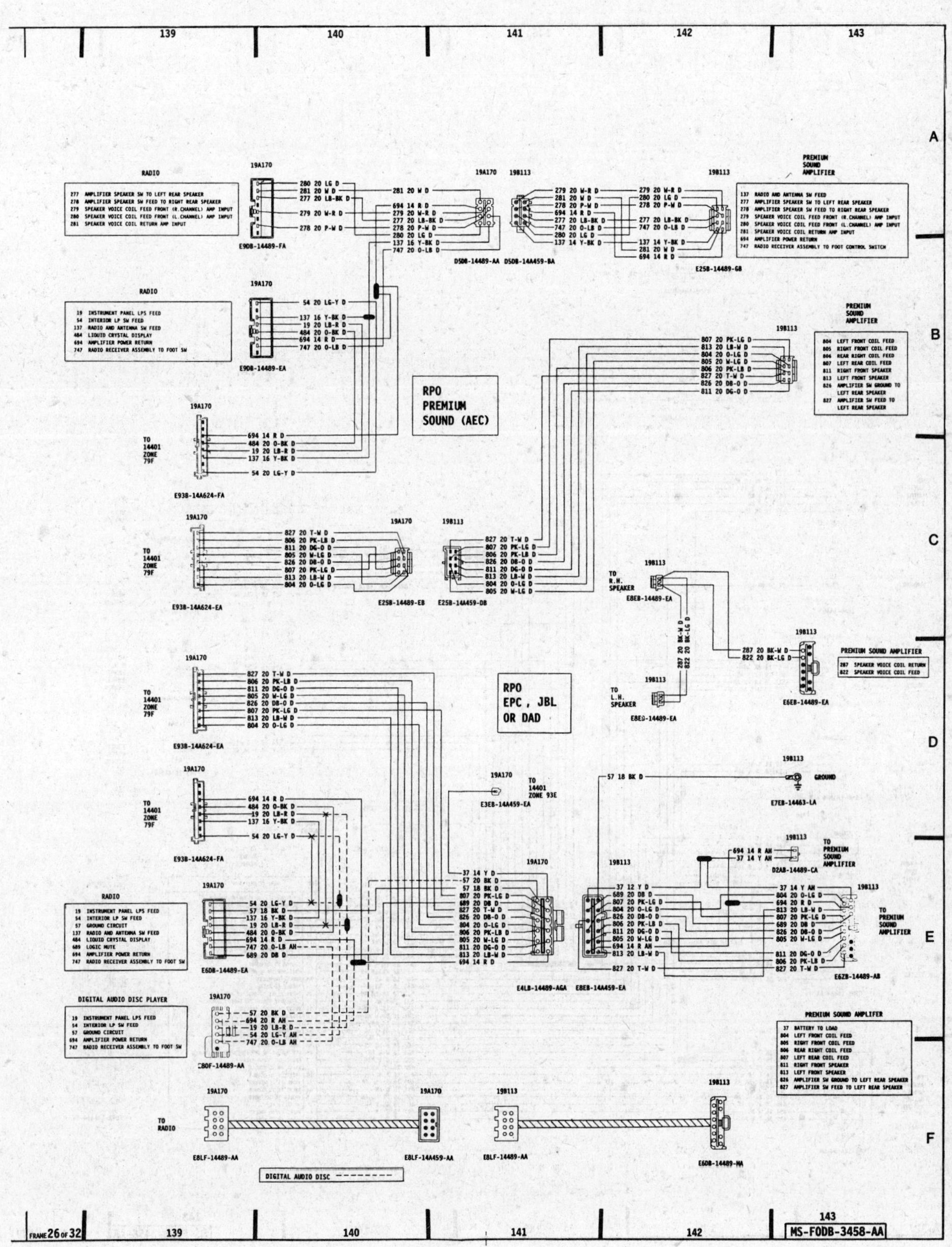
139
140
141
142
143
A
B
C
D
E
F
RADIO
PREMIUM SOUND AMPLIFIER
RPO PREMIUM SOUND (AEC)
RPO EPC, JBL OR DAD
TO R.H. SPEAKER
TO L.H. SPEAKER
PREMIUM SOUND AMPLIFIER
GROUND
TO PREMIUM SOUND AMPLIFIER
DIGITAL AUDIO DISC PLAYER
TO RADIO
DIGITAL AUDIO DISC
FRAME 26 OF 32
MS-F0DB-3458-AA

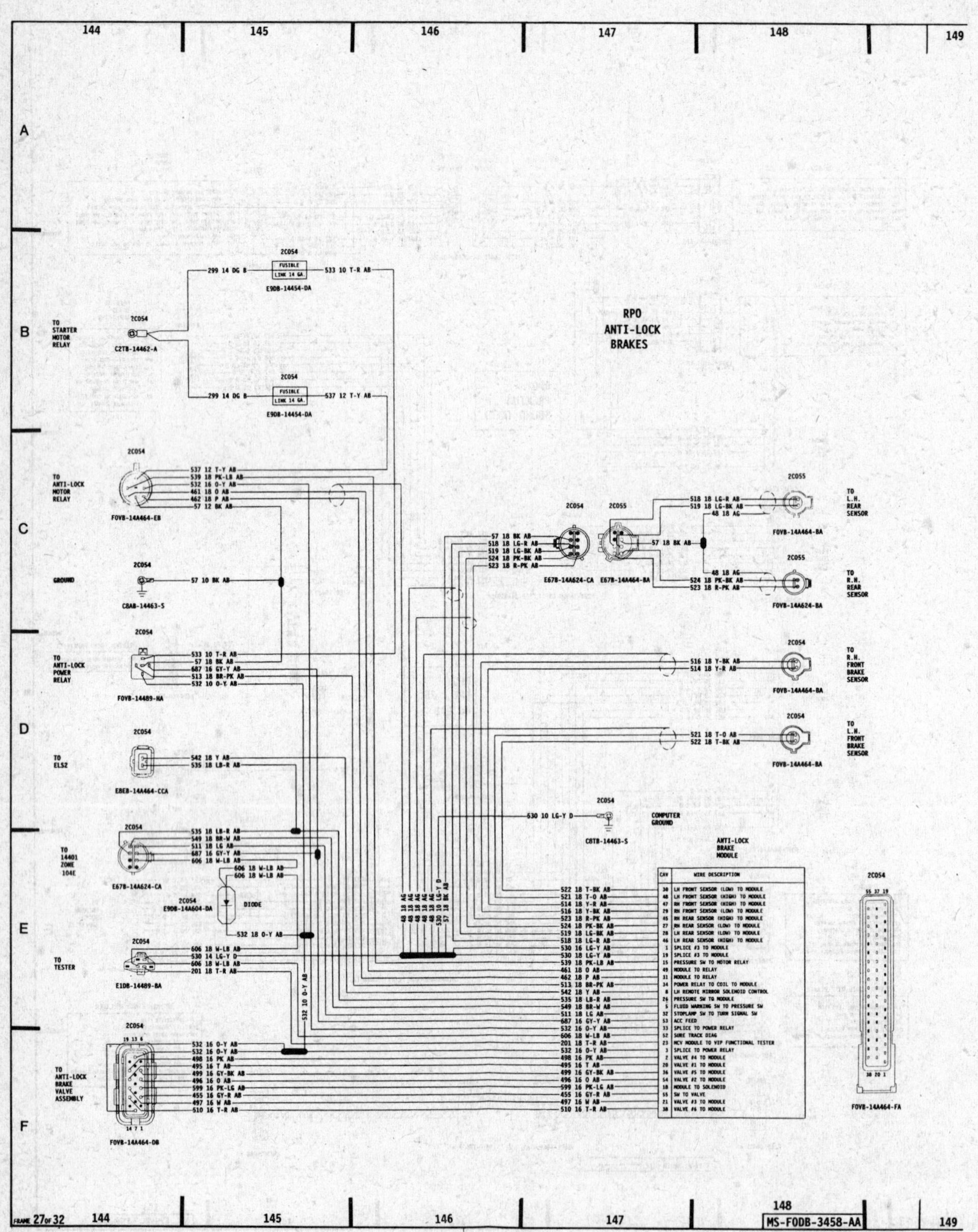
144
145
146
147
148
149
A
B
C
D
E
F
RPO
ANTI-LOCK
BRAKES
TO STARTER MOTOR RELAY
TO ANTI-LOCK MOTOR RELAY
GROUND
TO ANTI-LOCK POWER RELAY
TO ELS2
TO 14401 ZONE 104E
TO TESTER
TO ANTI-LOCK BRAKE VALVE ASSEMBLY
TO L.H. REAR SENSOR
TO R.H. REAR SENSOR
TO R.H. FRONT BRAKE SENSOR
TO L.H. FRONT BRAKE SENSOR
COMPUTER GROUND
ANTI-LOCK BRAKE MODULE
DIODE
FRAME 27 OF 32
MS-F0DB-3458-AA

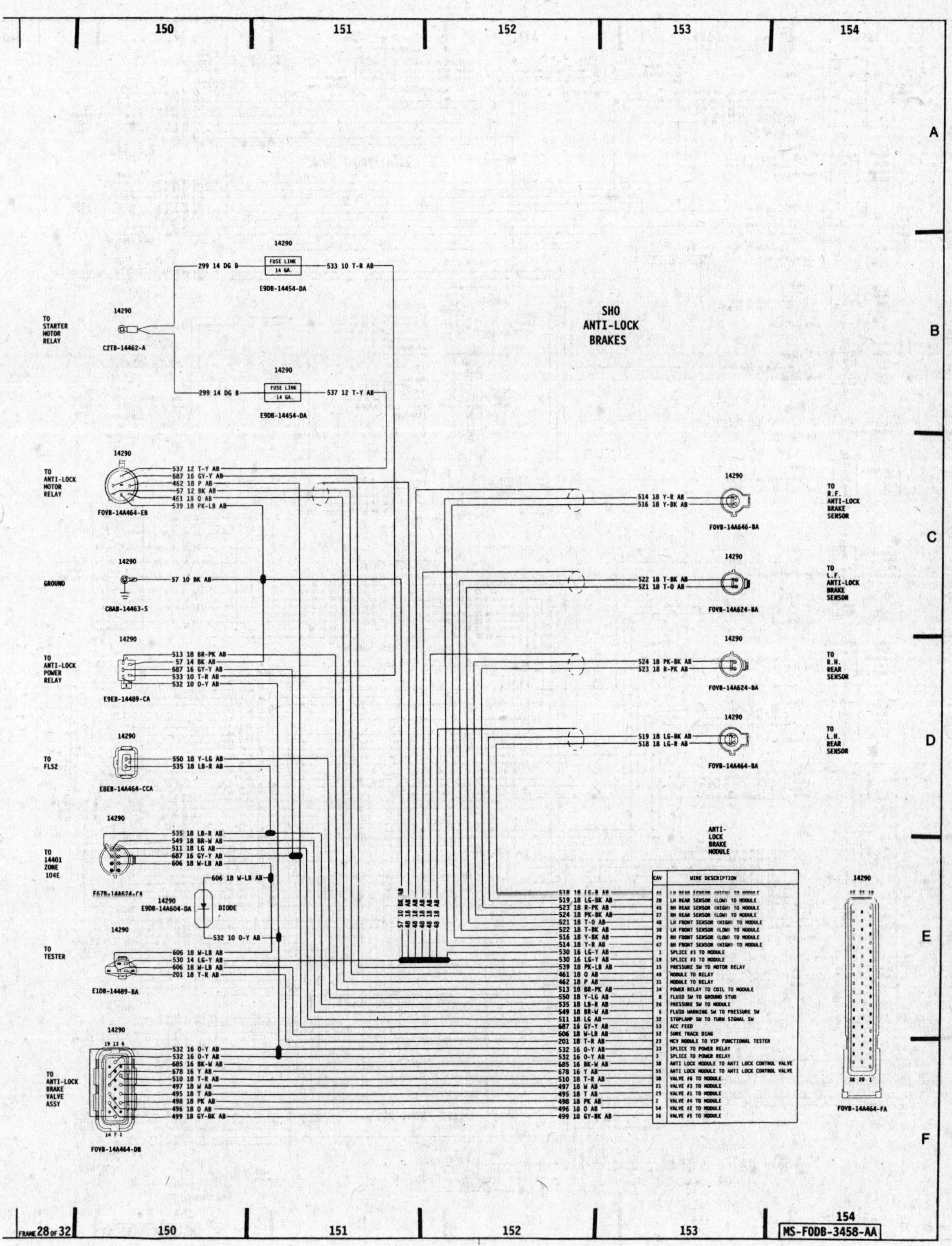

Taurus and Sable electrical schematics — 1990

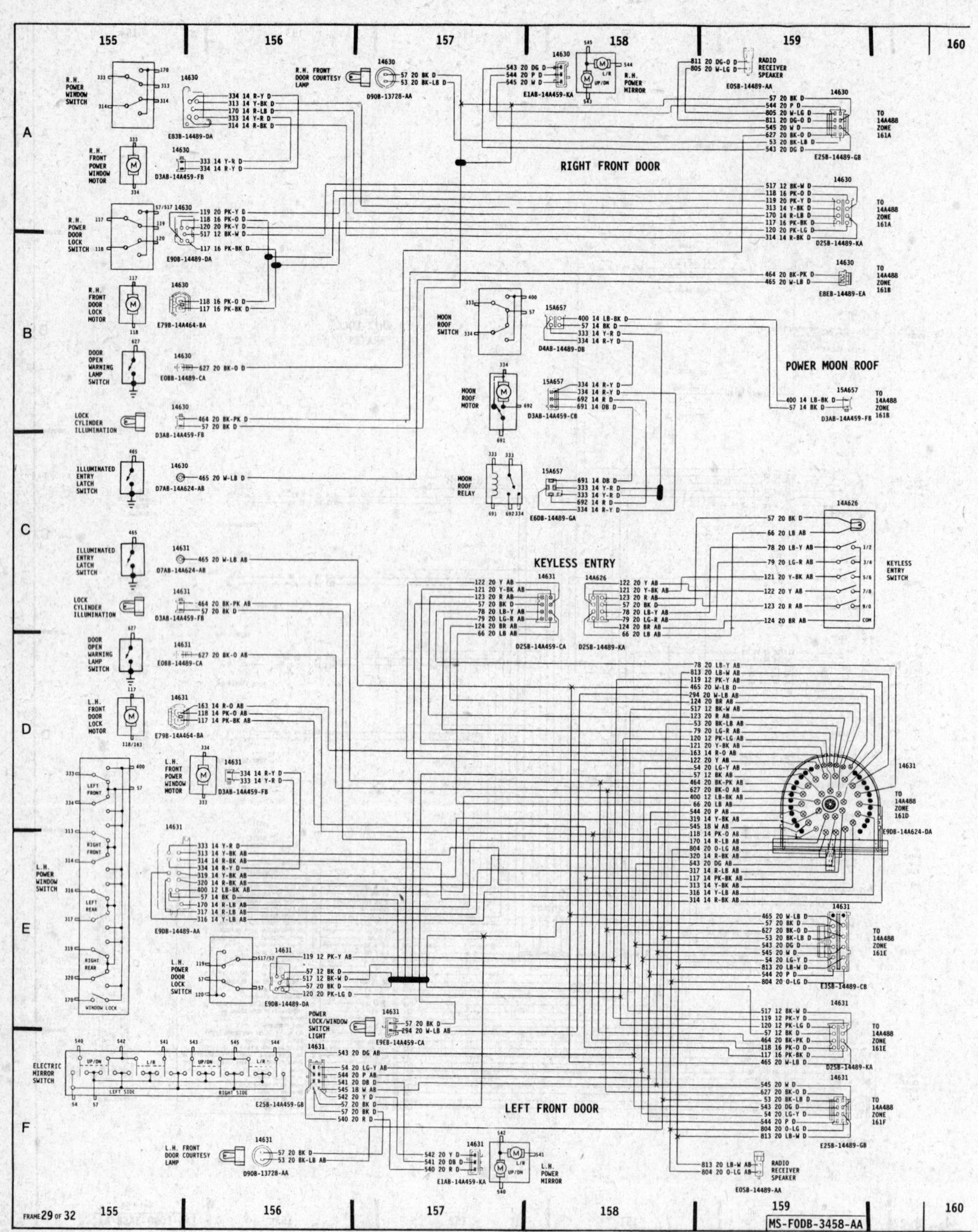

Taurus and Sable electrical schematics — 1990

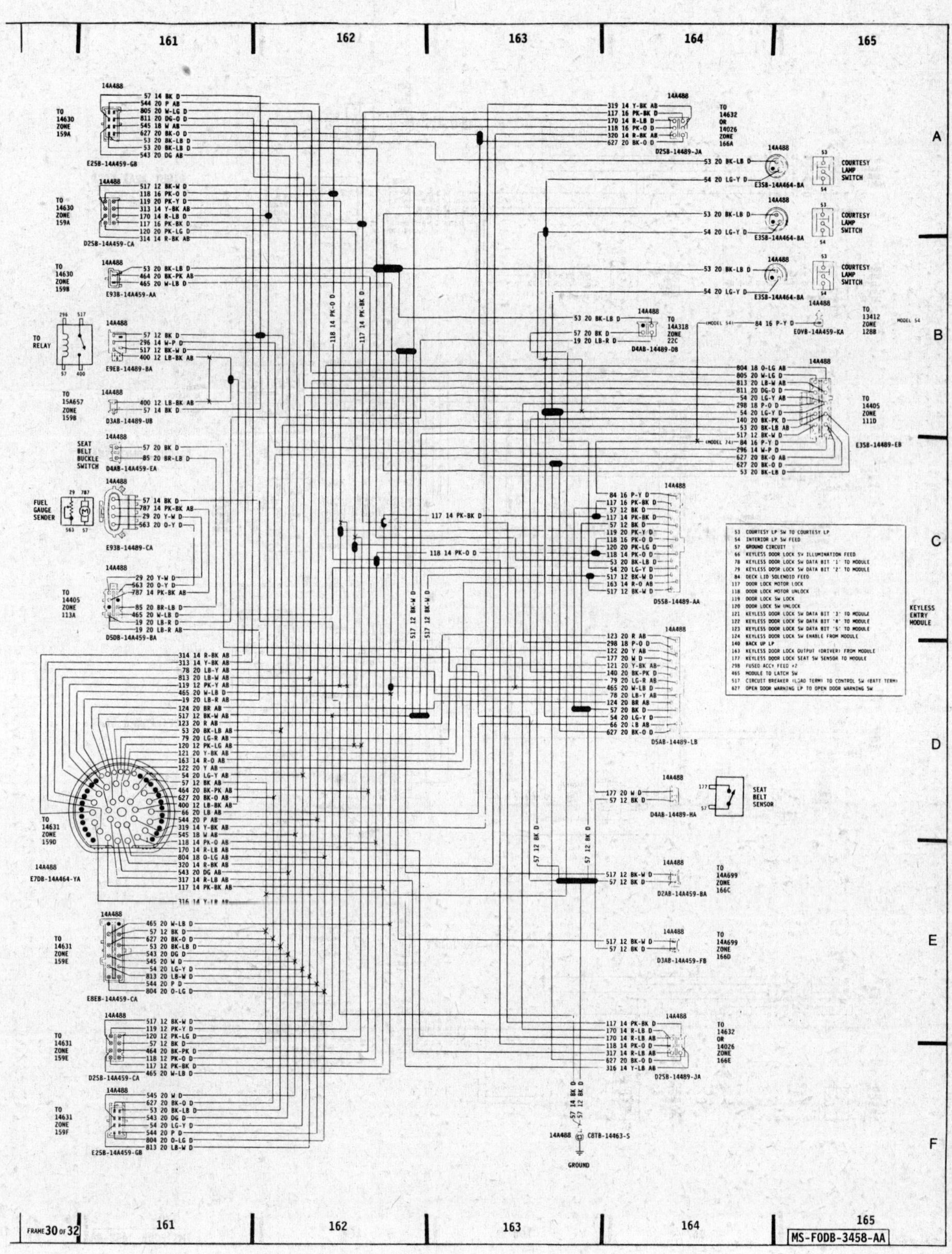

Taurus and Sable electrical schematics — 1990

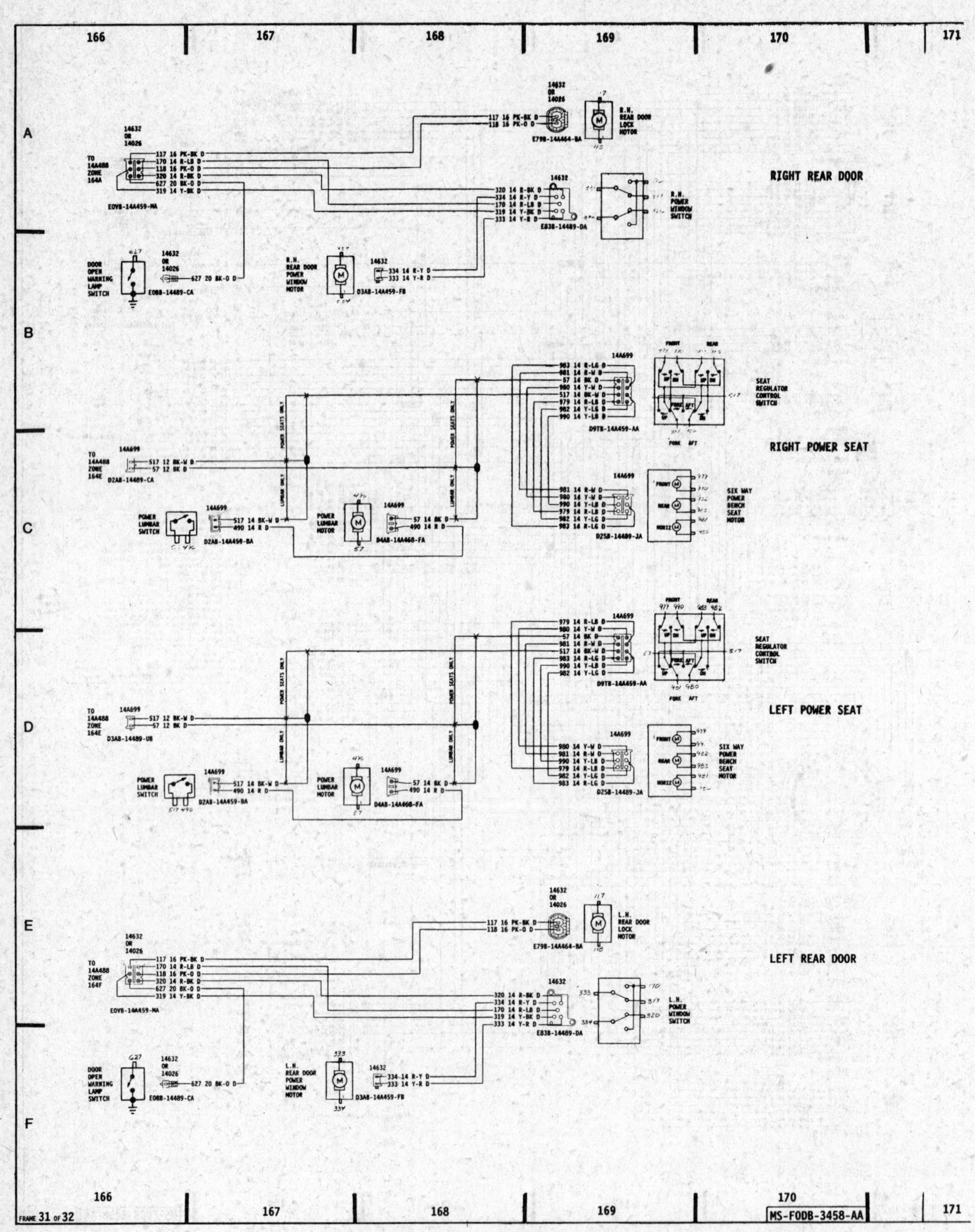

Taurus and Sable electrical schematics — 1990

172
173
174
175
176
A
B
C
D
E
F
FRAME 32 OF 32
MS-F0DB-3458-AA

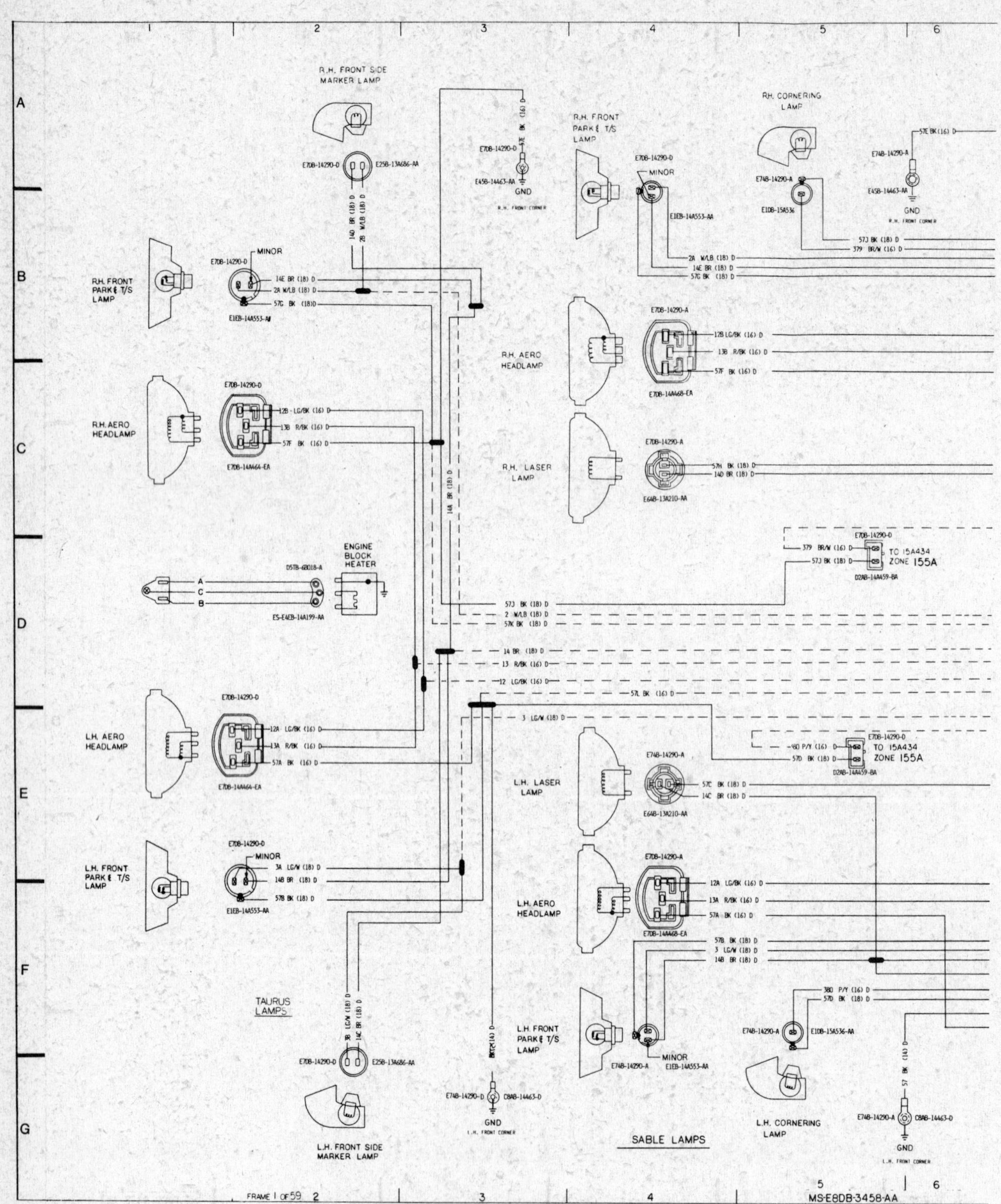

Taurus and Sable electrical schematics — 1988

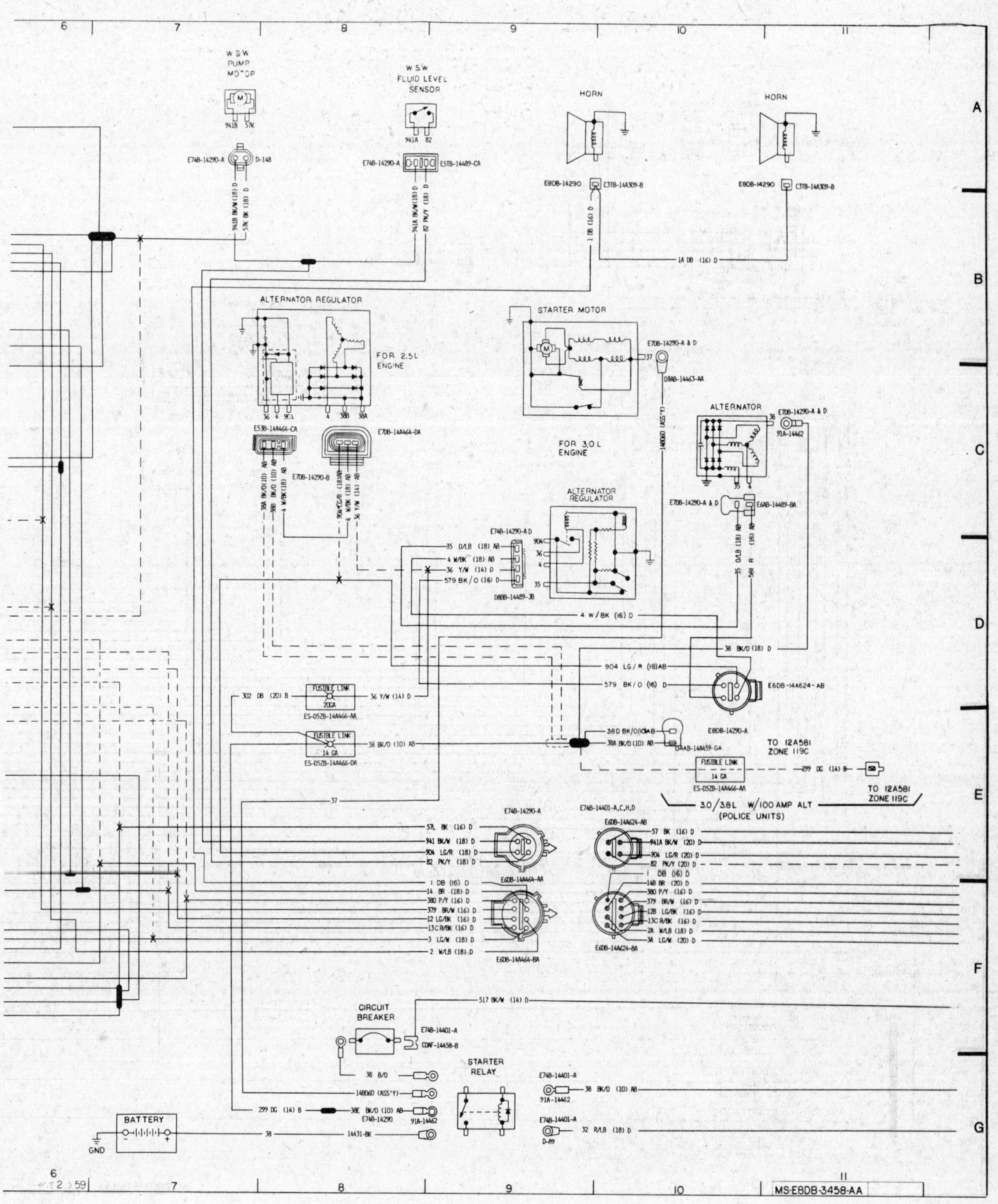

Taurus and Sable electrical schematics – 1988

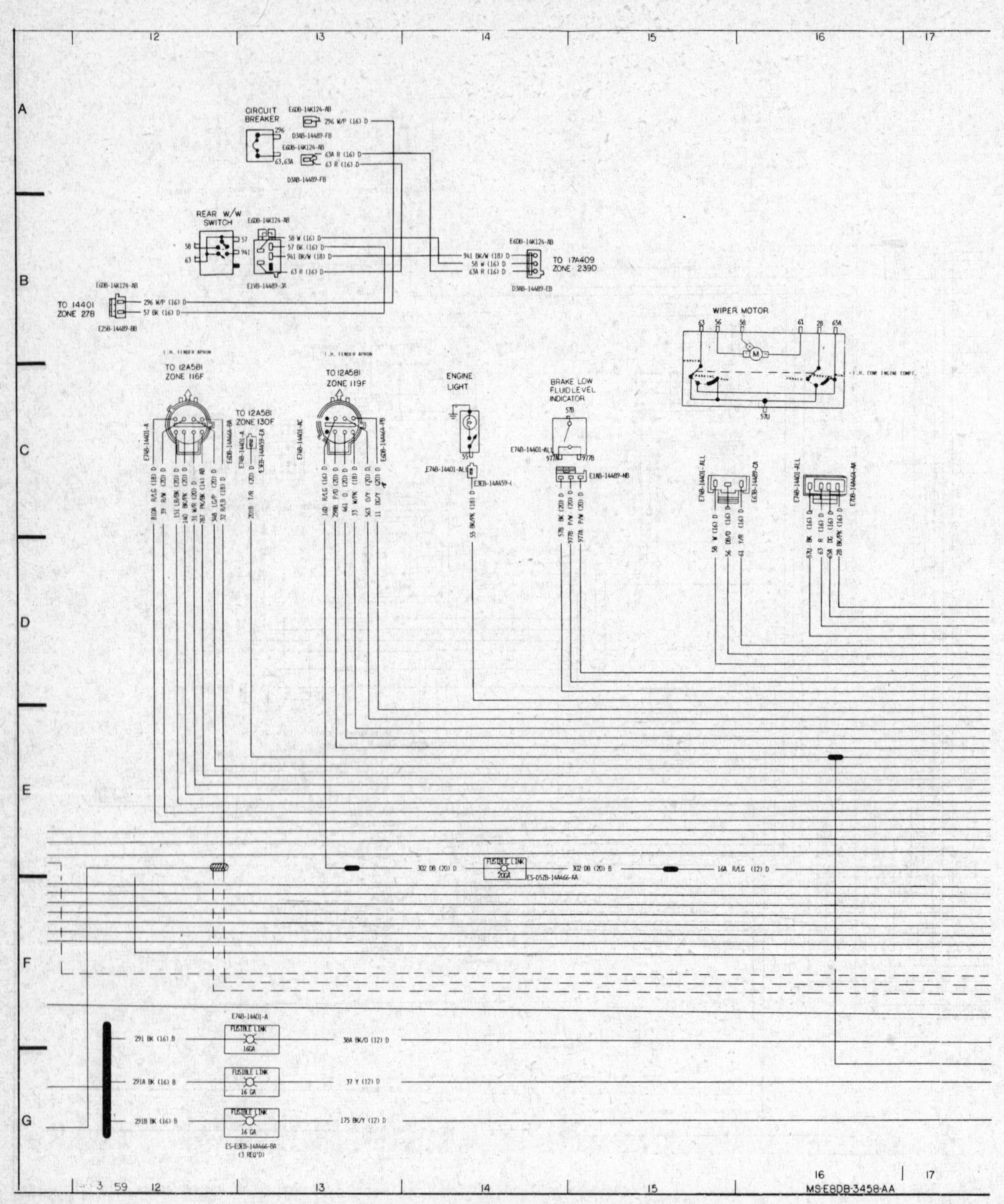

Taurus and Sable electrical schematics — 1988

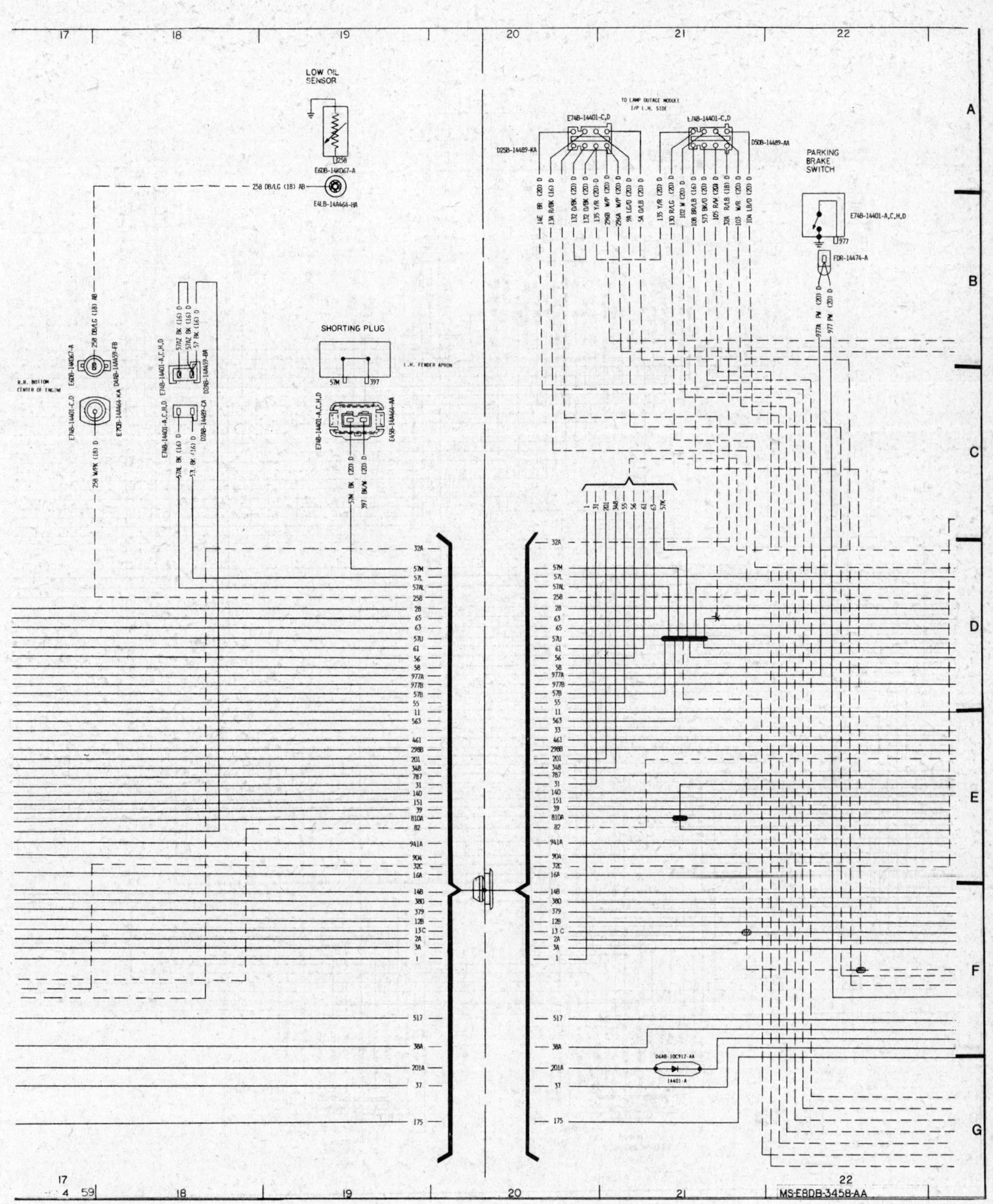

Taurus and Sable electrical schematics — 1988

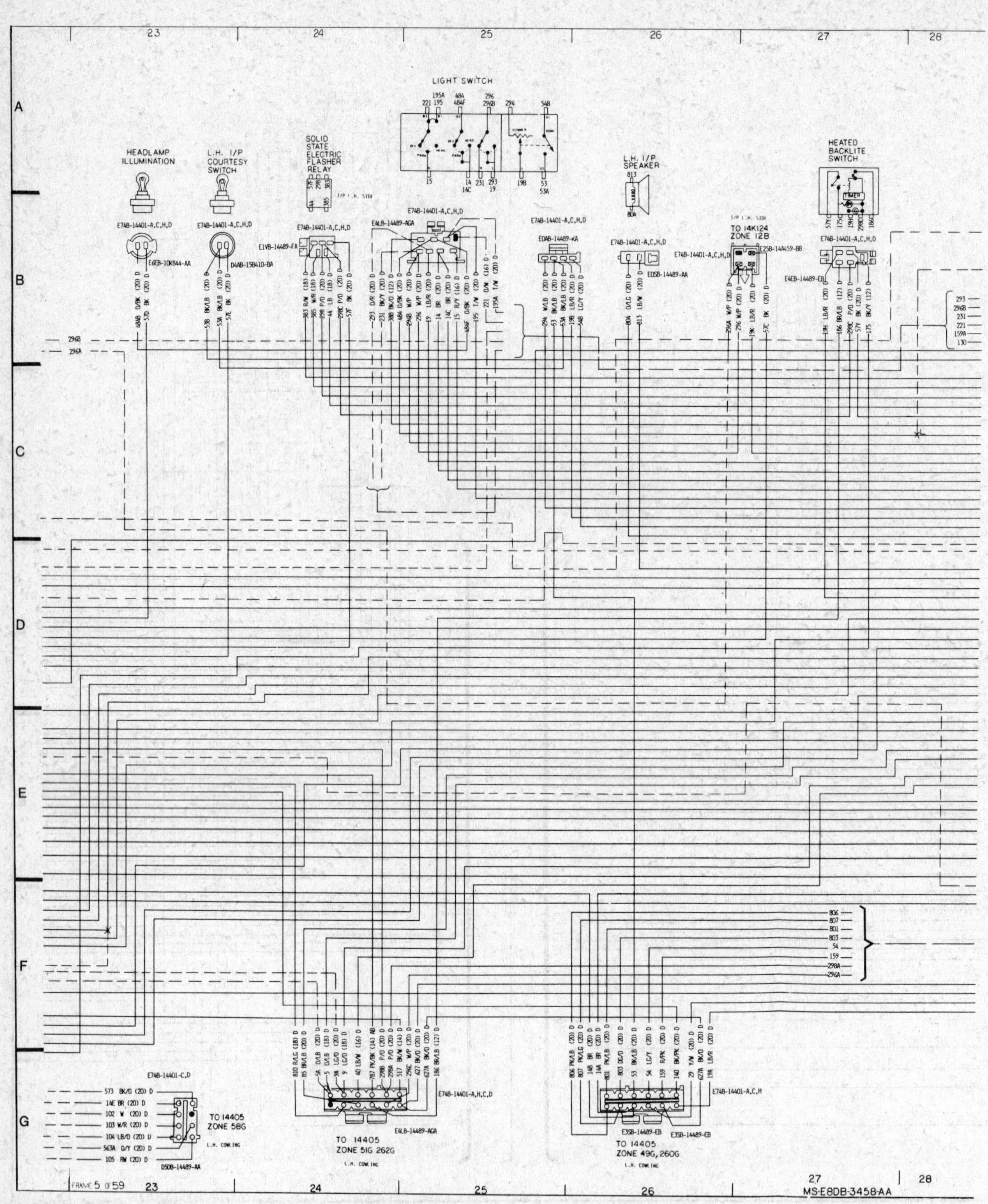

Taurus and Sable electrical schematics – 1988

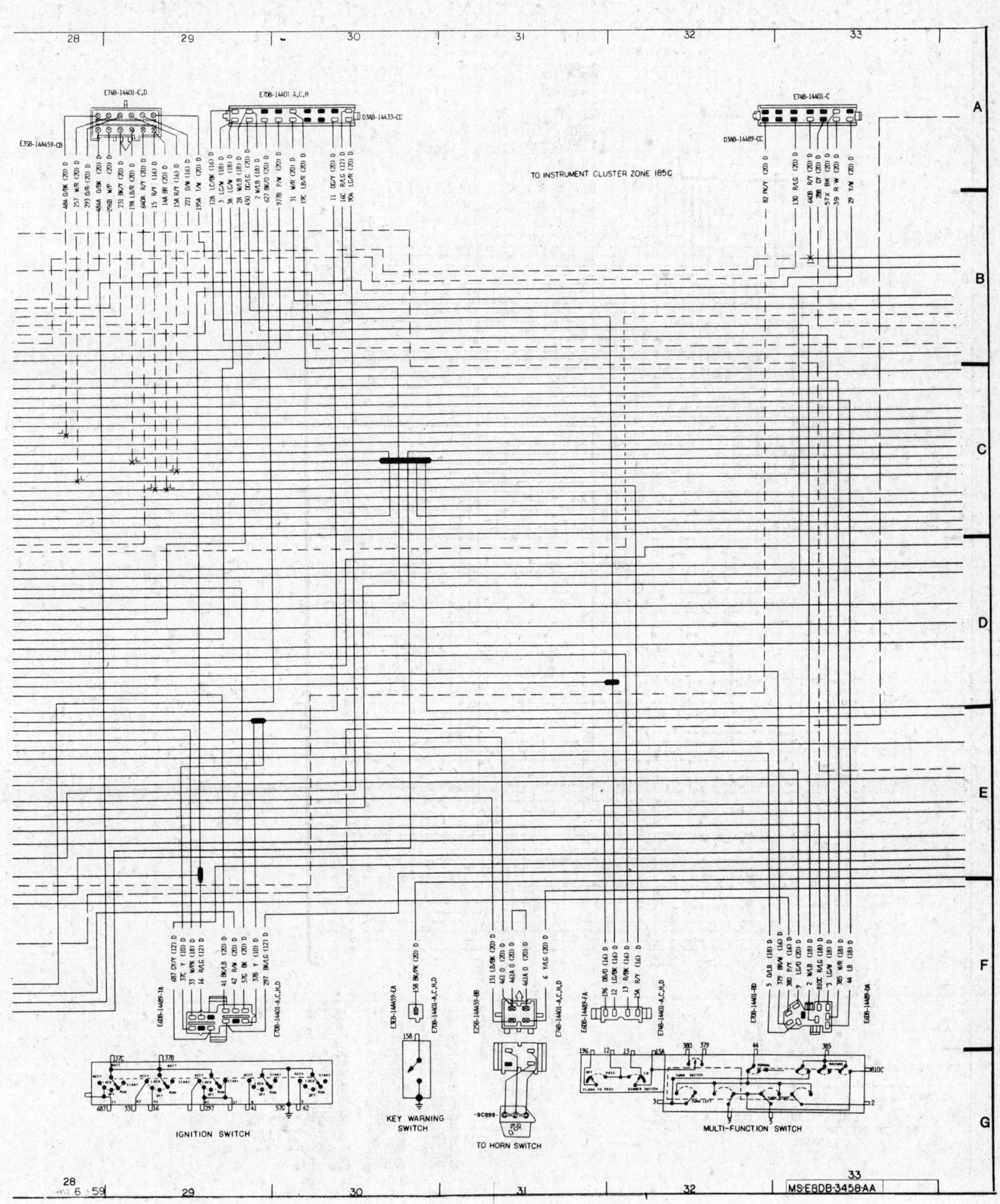

Taurus and Sable electrical schematics — 1988

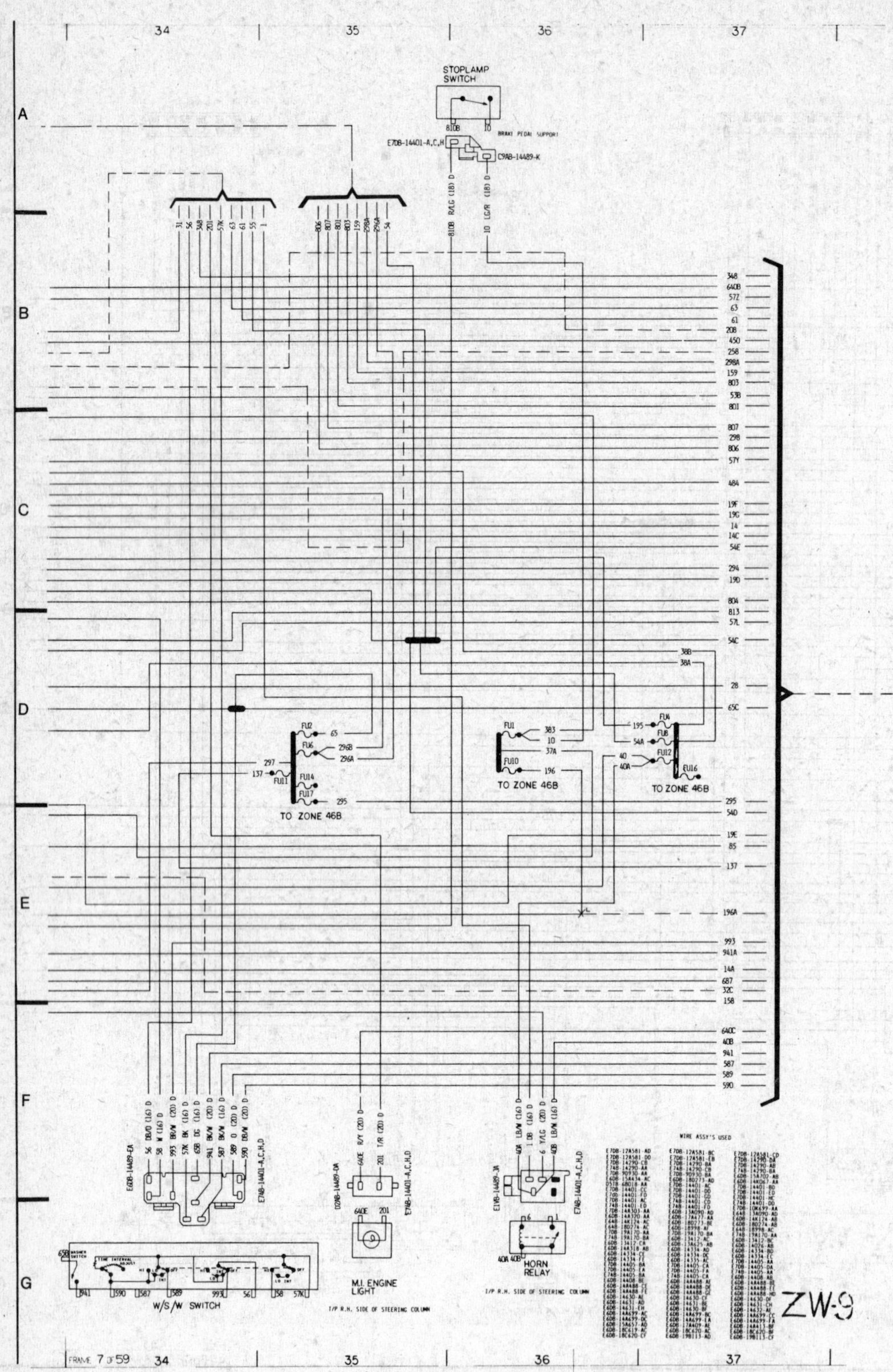

Taurus and Sable electrical schematics – 1988

A

B

C

D

E

F

G

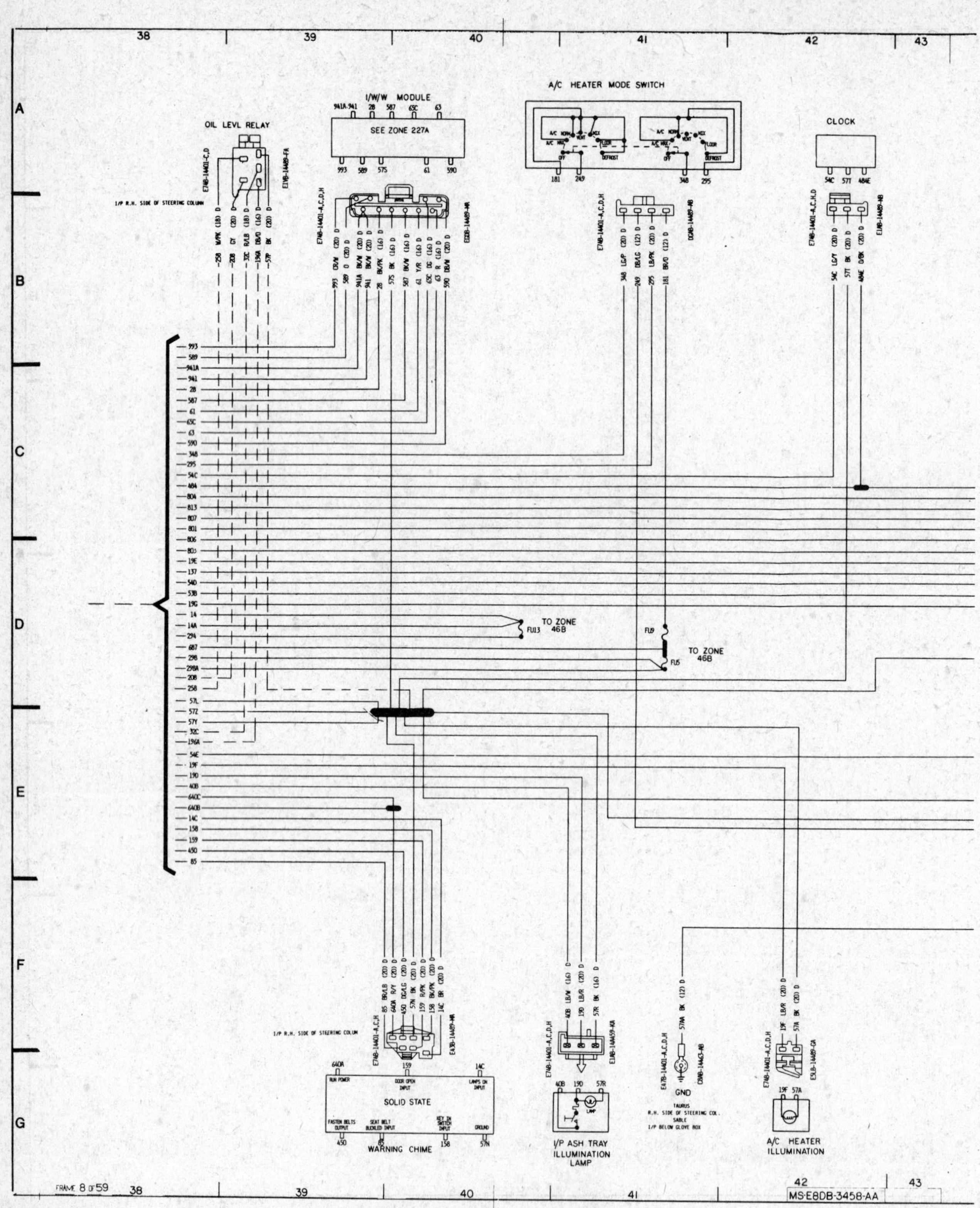

Taurus and Sable electrical schematics — 1988

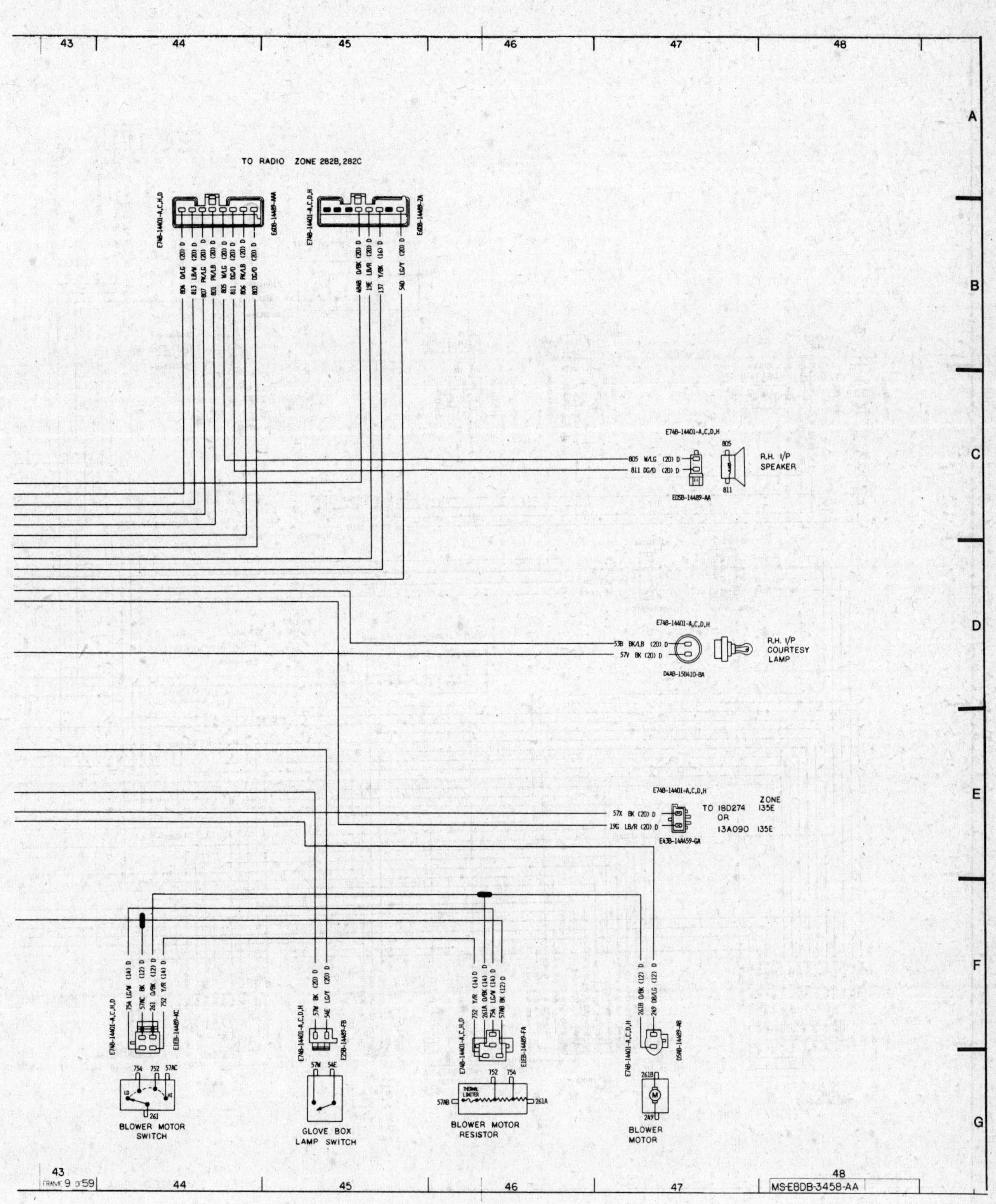

Taurus and Sable electrical schematics — 1988

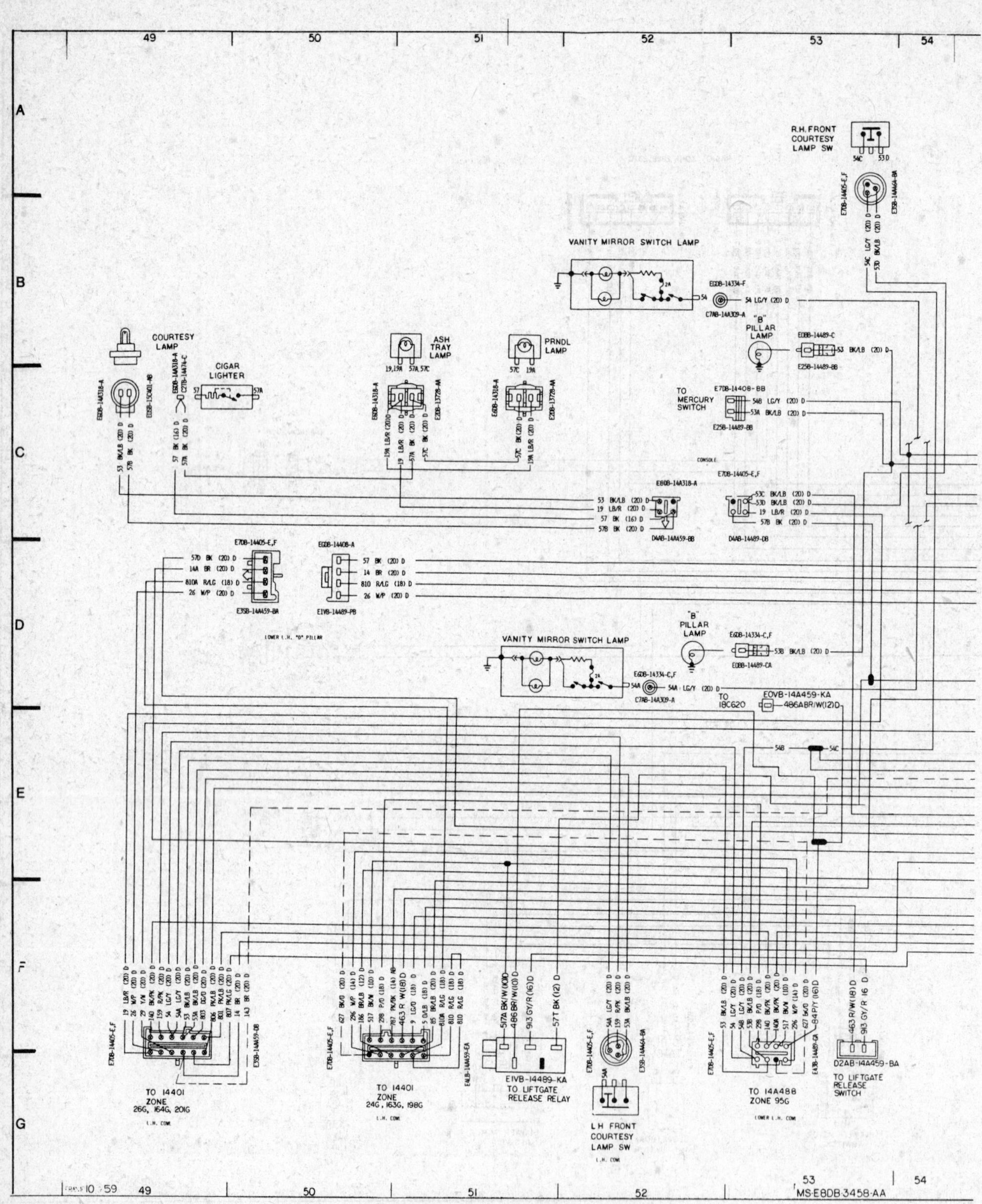

Taurus and Sable electrical schematics — 1988

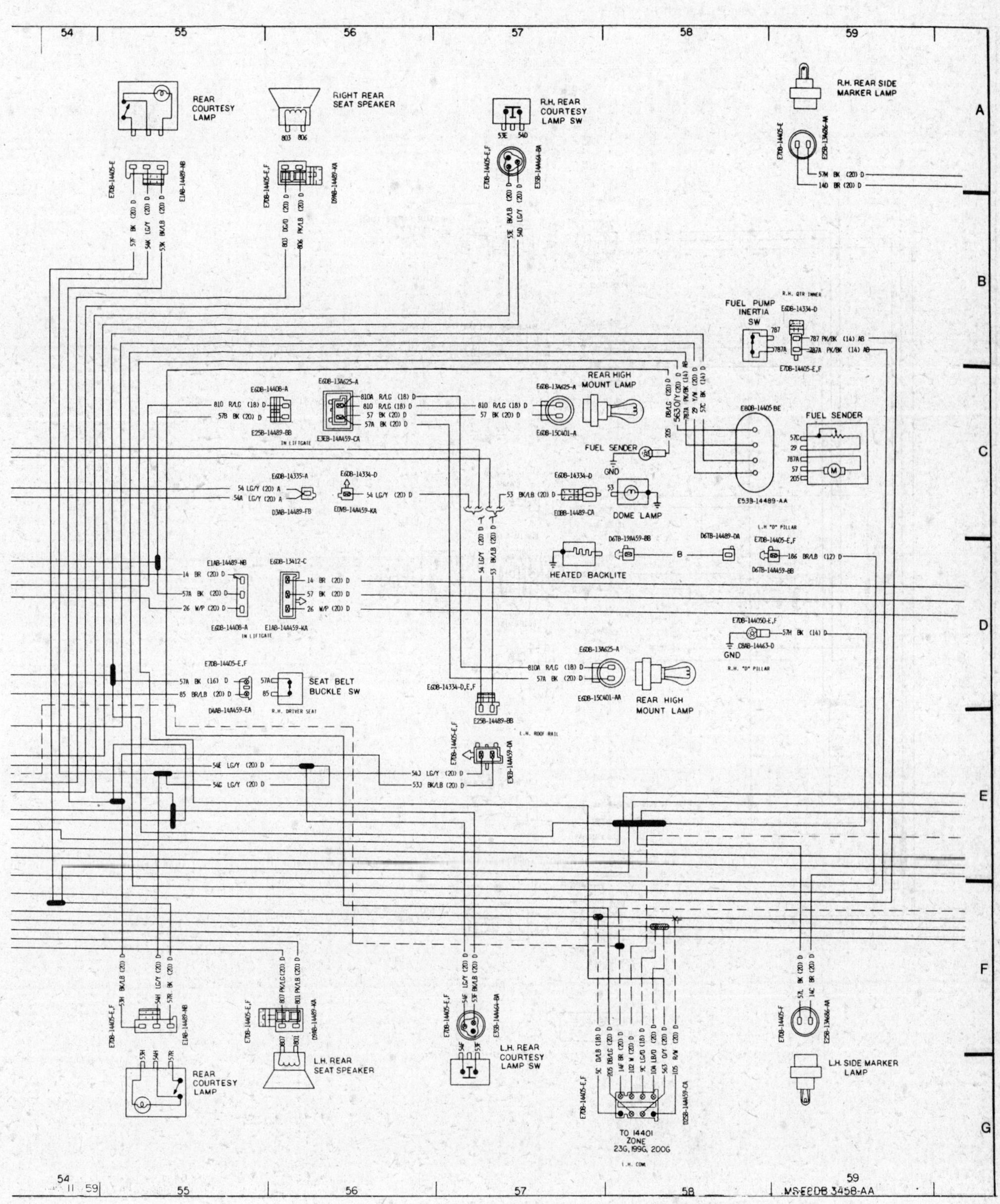

Taurus and Sable electrical schematics – 1988

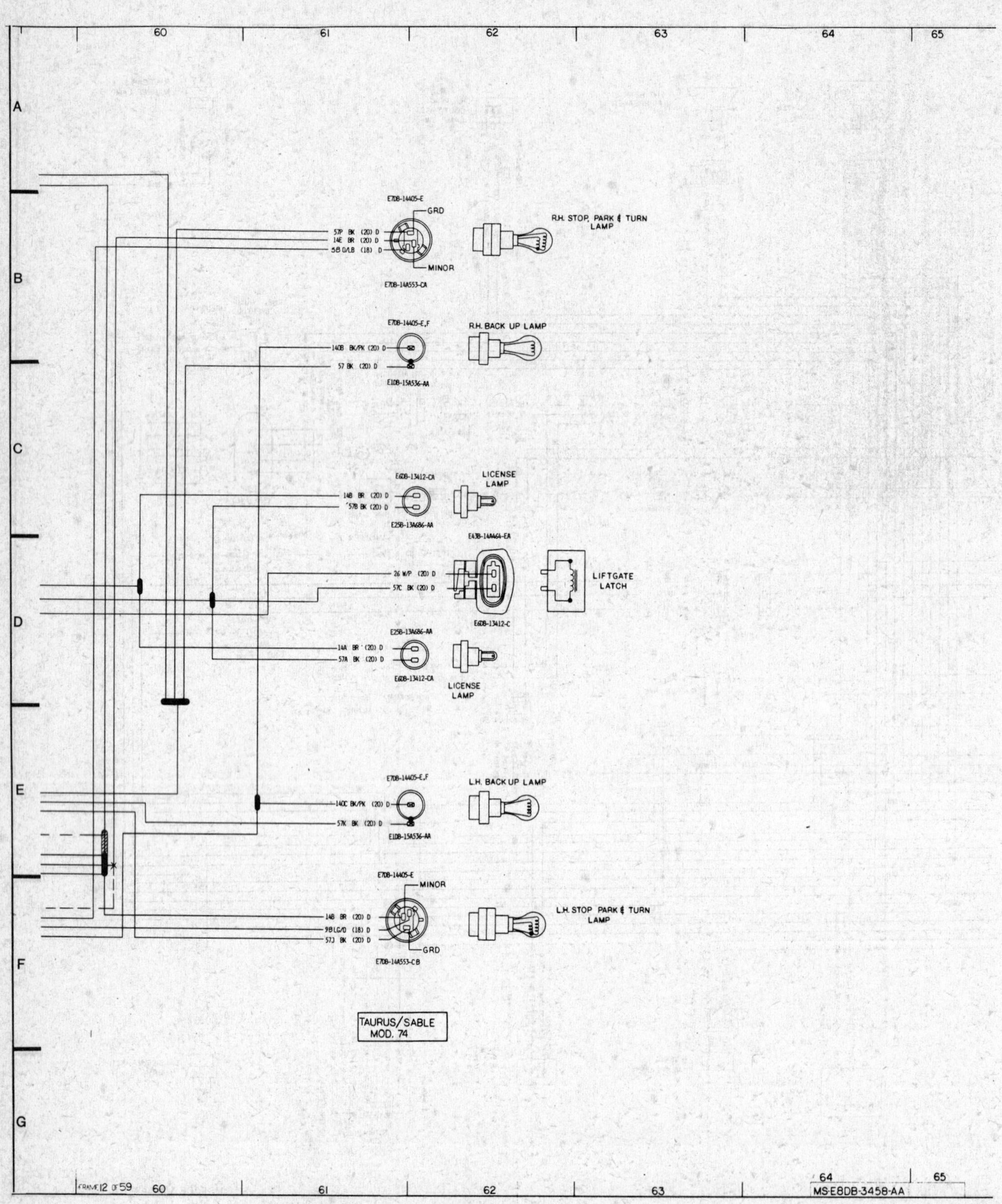

Taurus and Sable electrical schematics — 1988

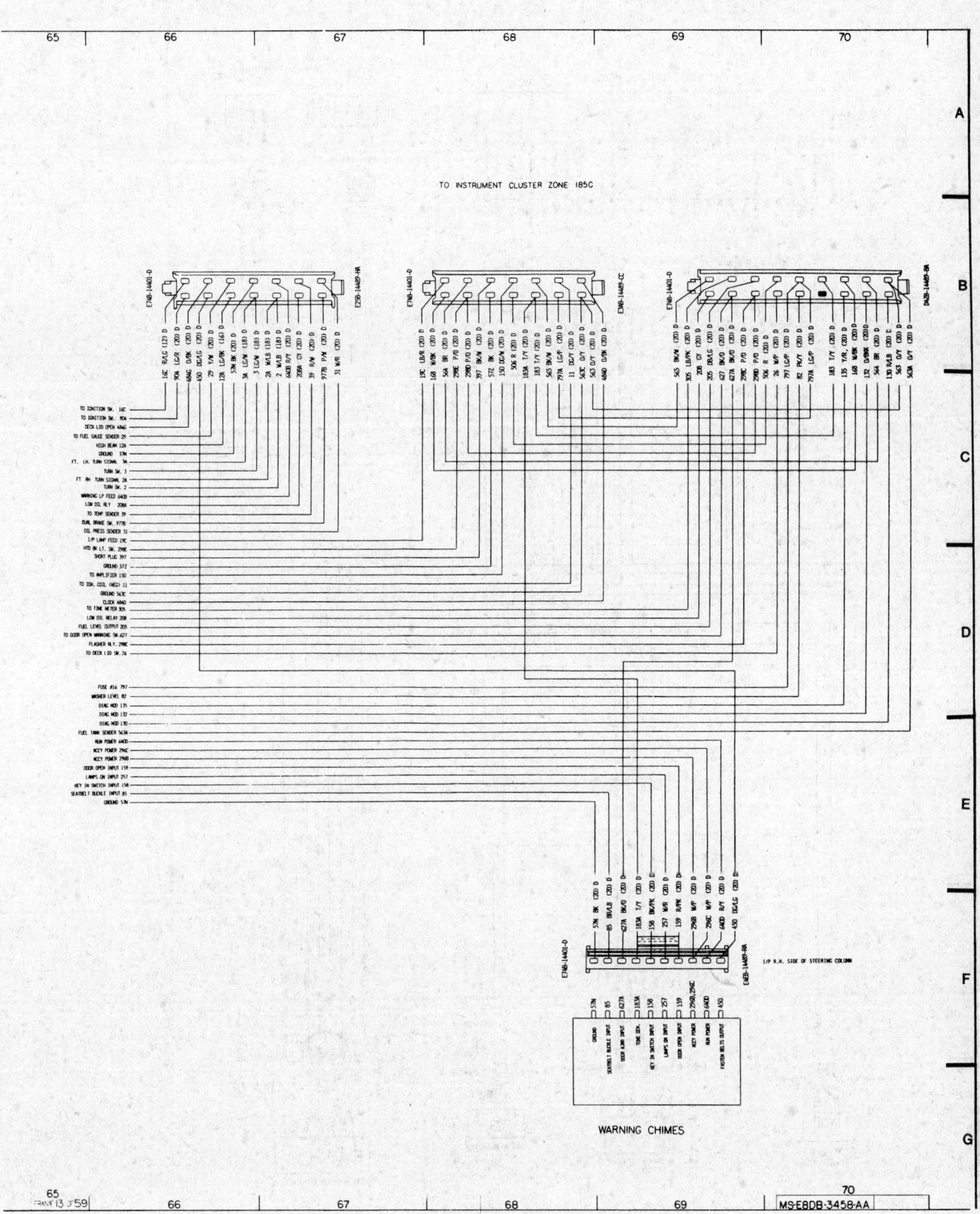

Taurus and Sable electrical schematics – 1988

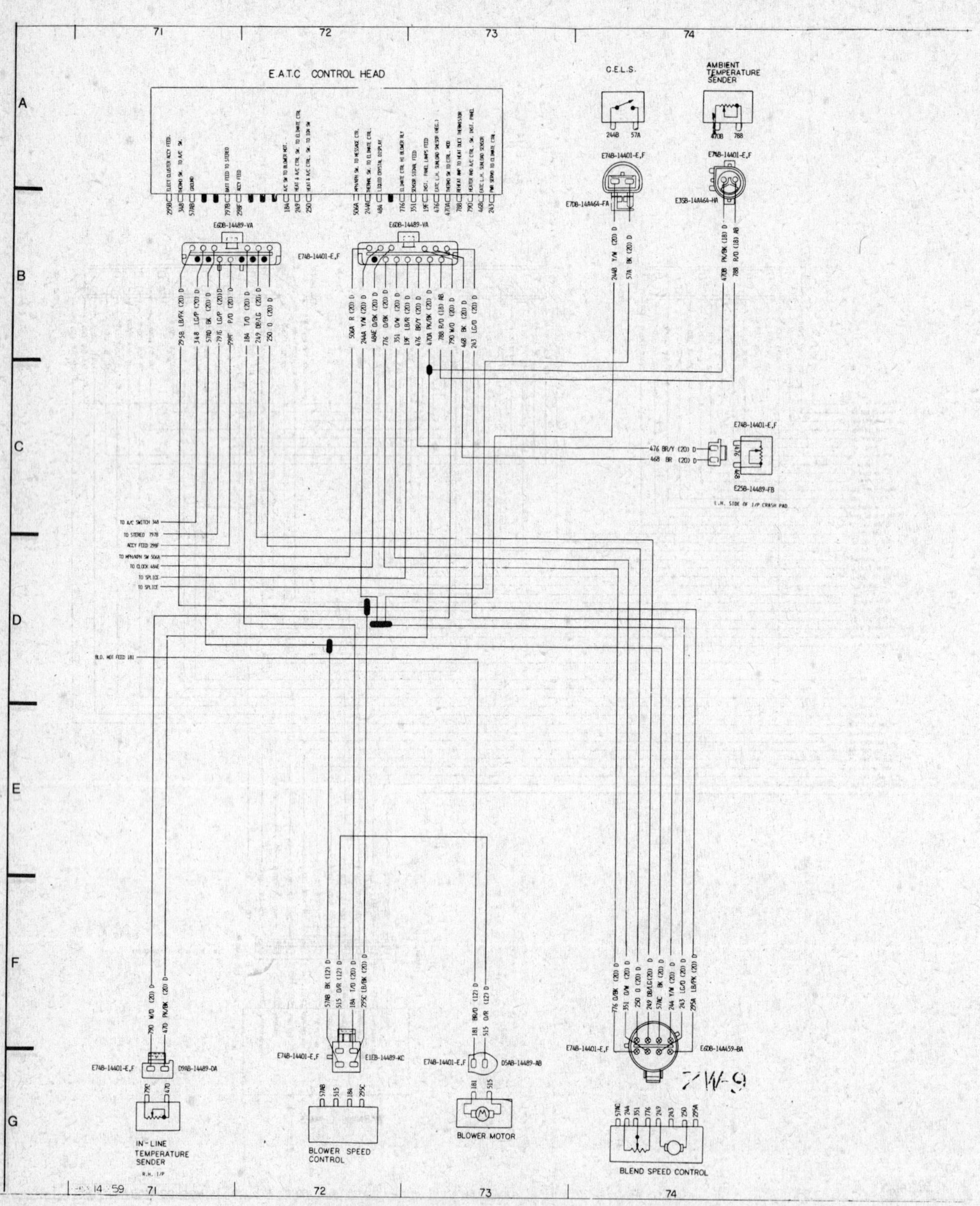

Taurus and Sable electrical schematics – 1988

A

B

C

D

E

F

G

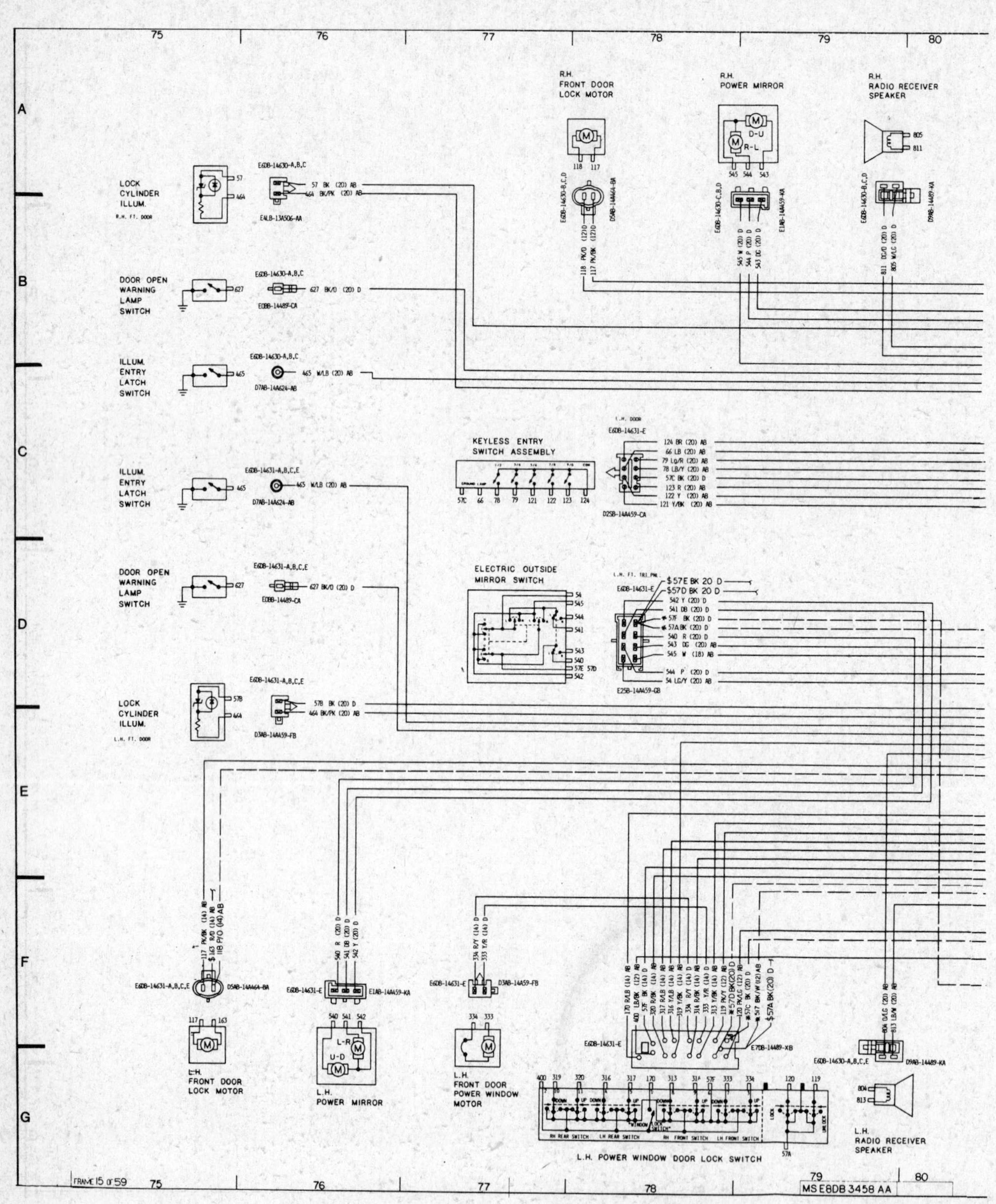

R.H. FRONT DOOR LOCK MOTOR
R.H. POWER MIRROR
R.H. RADIO RECEIVER SPEAKER
LOCK CYLINDER ILLUM.
DOOR OPEN WARNING LAMP SWITCH
ILLUM. ENTRY LATCH SWITCH
KEYLESS ENTRY SWITCH ASSEMBLY
ELECTRIC OUTSIDE MIRROR SWITCH
L.H. FRONT DOOR LOCK MOTOR
L.H. POWER MIRROR
L.H. FRONT DOOR POWER WINDOW MOTOR
L.H. POWER WINDOW DOOR LOCK SWITCH
L.H. RADIO RECEIVER SPEAKER
FRAME 15 OF 59
MS E8DB 3458 AA

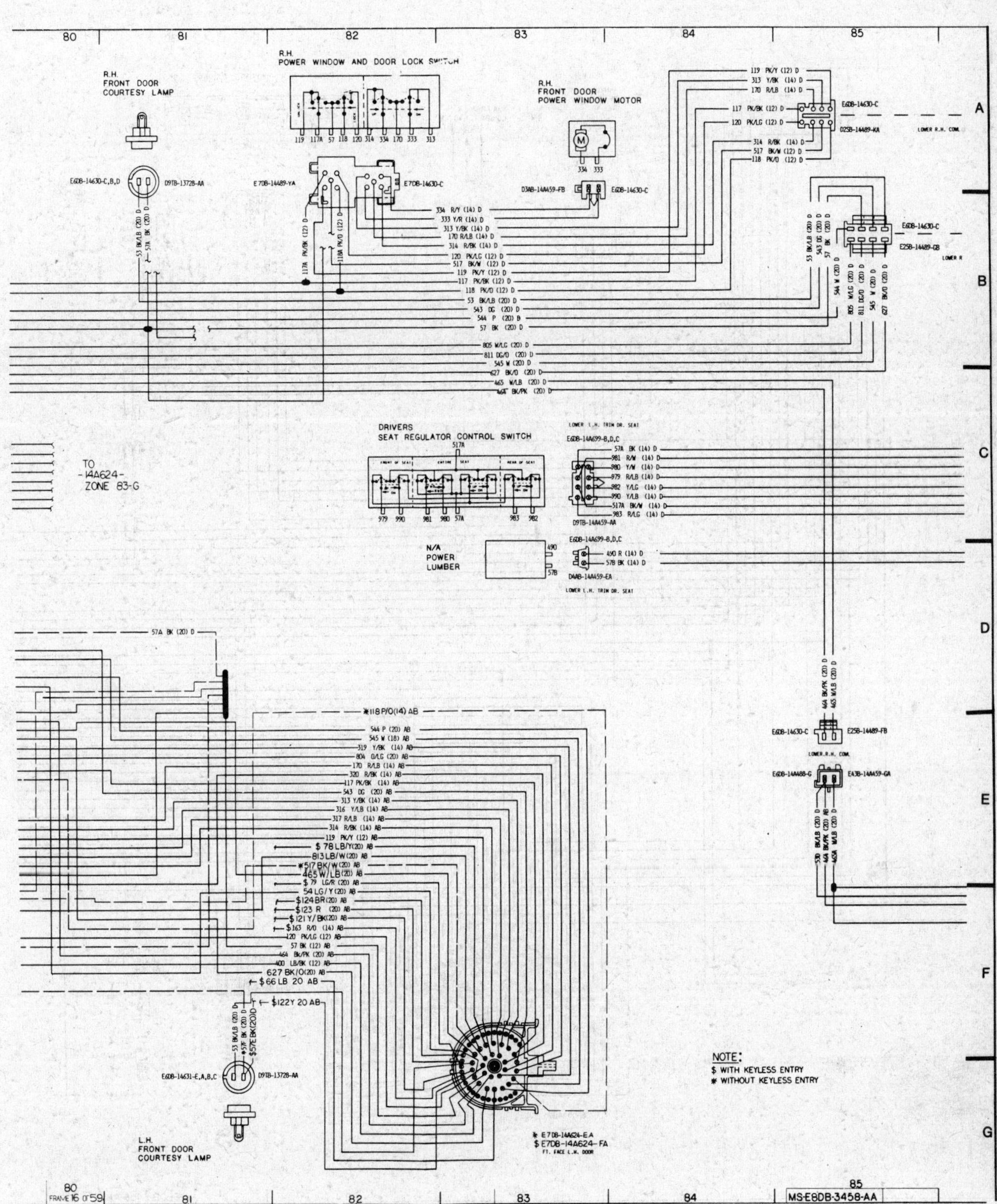

Taurus and Sable electrical schematics — 1988

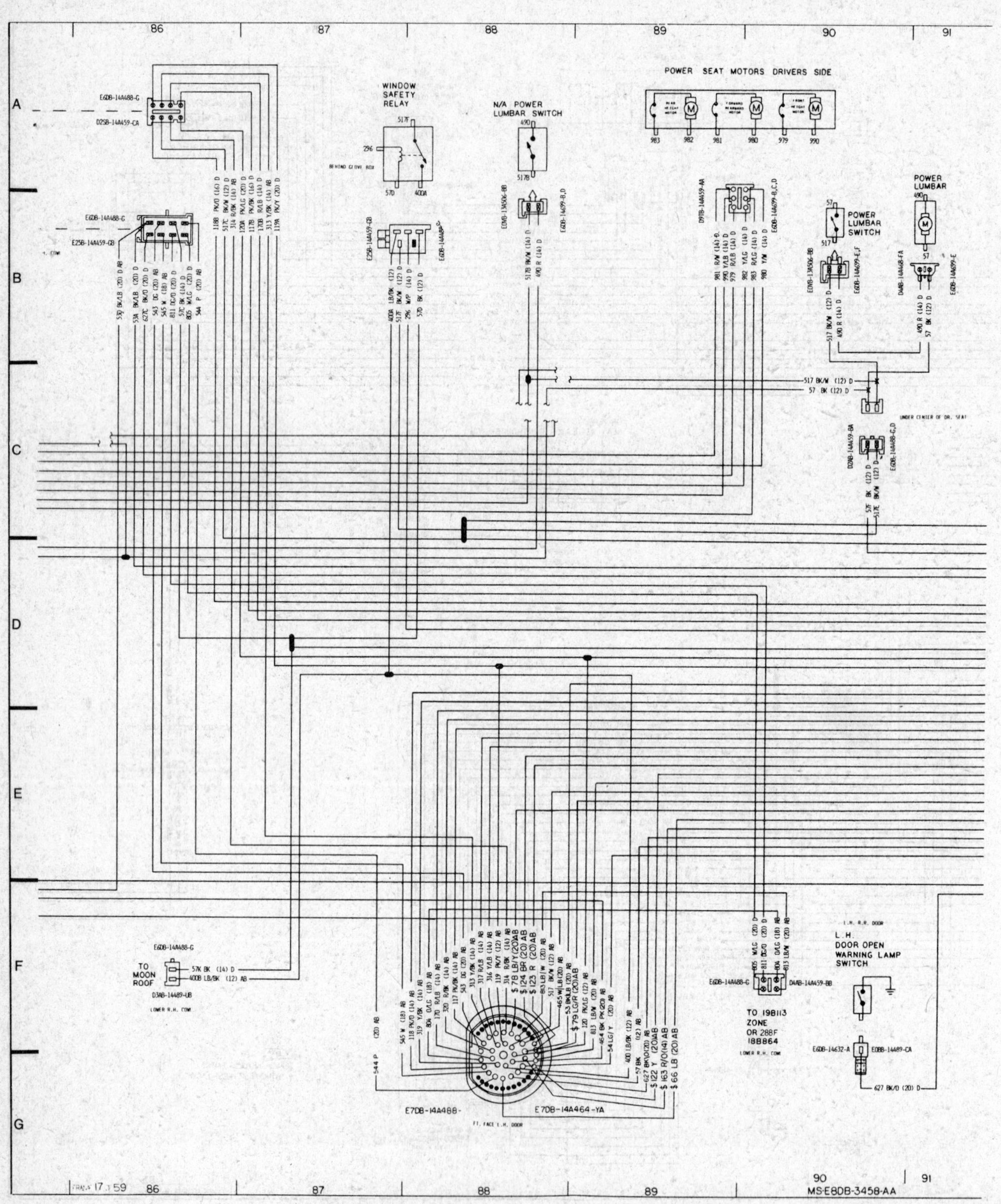

Taurus and Sable electrical schematics — 1988

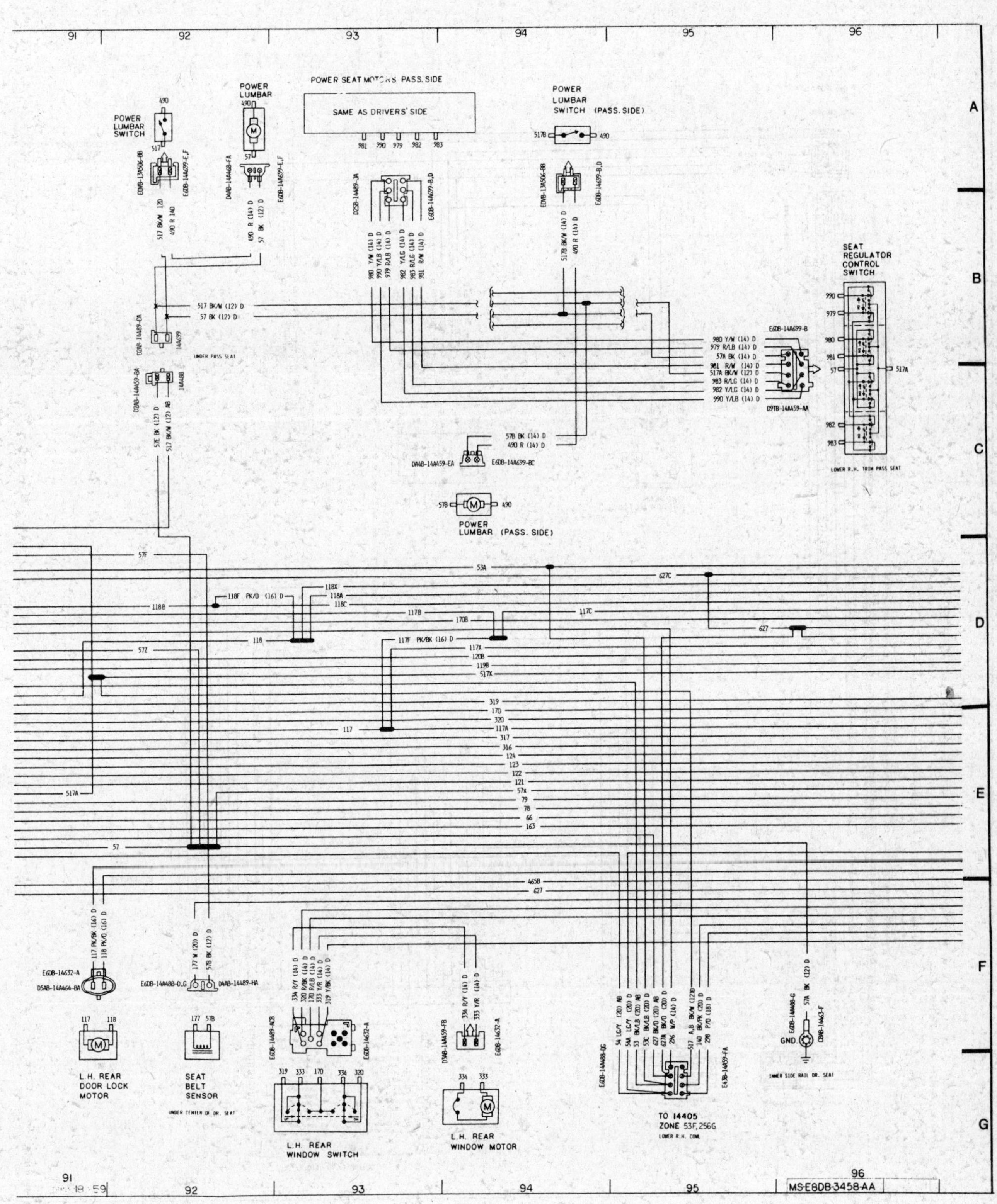

Taurus and Sable electrical schematics — 1988

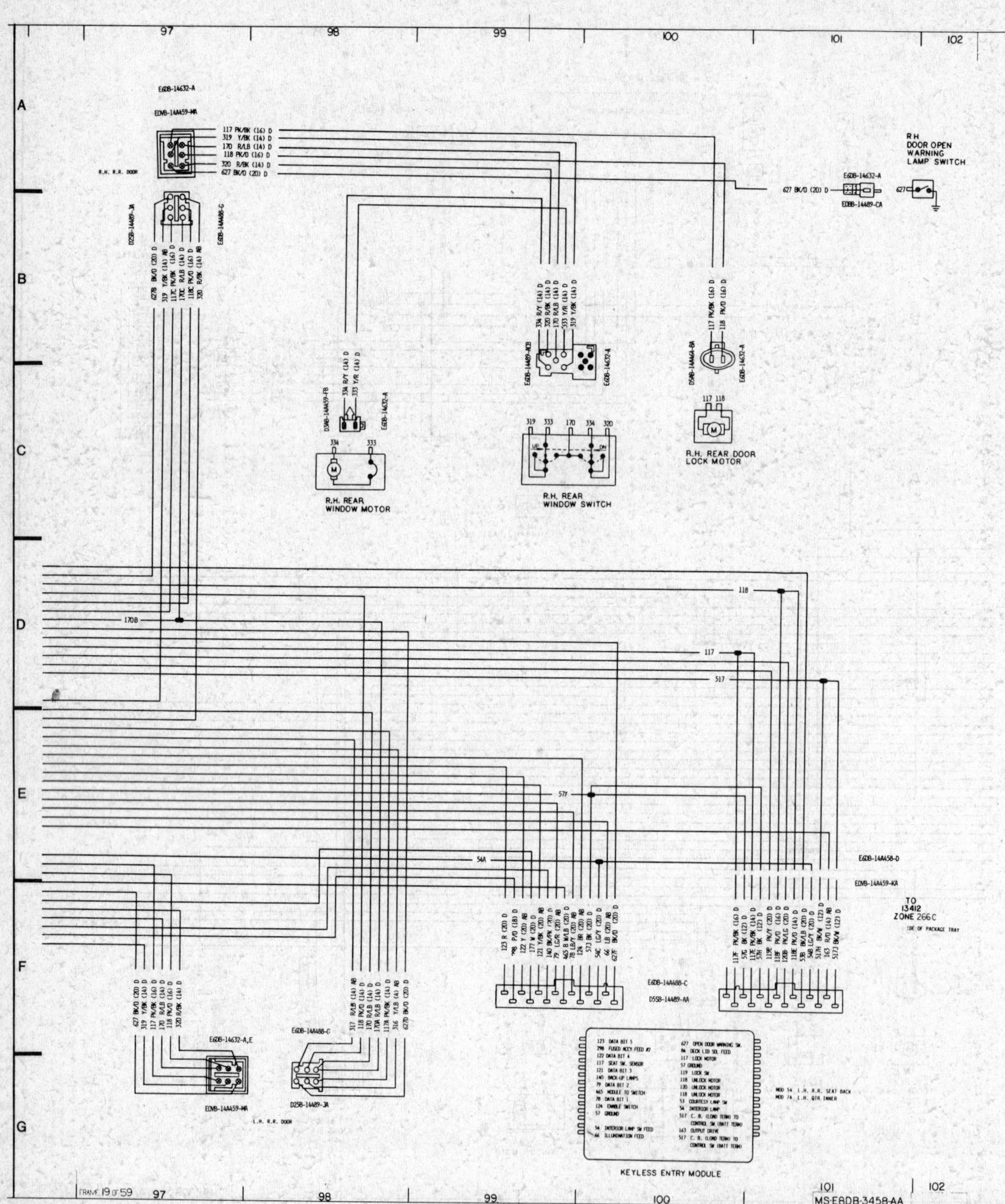
RH
DOOR OPEN
WARNING
LAMP SWITCH
R.H. REAR
WINDOW MOTOR
R.H. REAR
WINDOW SWITCH
R.H. REAR DOOR
LOCK MOTOR
KEYLESS ENTRY MODULE
TO
13412
ZONE 266C
MS-E8DB-3458-AA

102 103 104 105 106 107

A

B

C

D

E

F

ZONES 102 THROUGH 112
CONTAIN NO INFORMATION

G

102 FRAME 20 OF 59 103 104 105 106 107

MS-E8DB-3458-AA

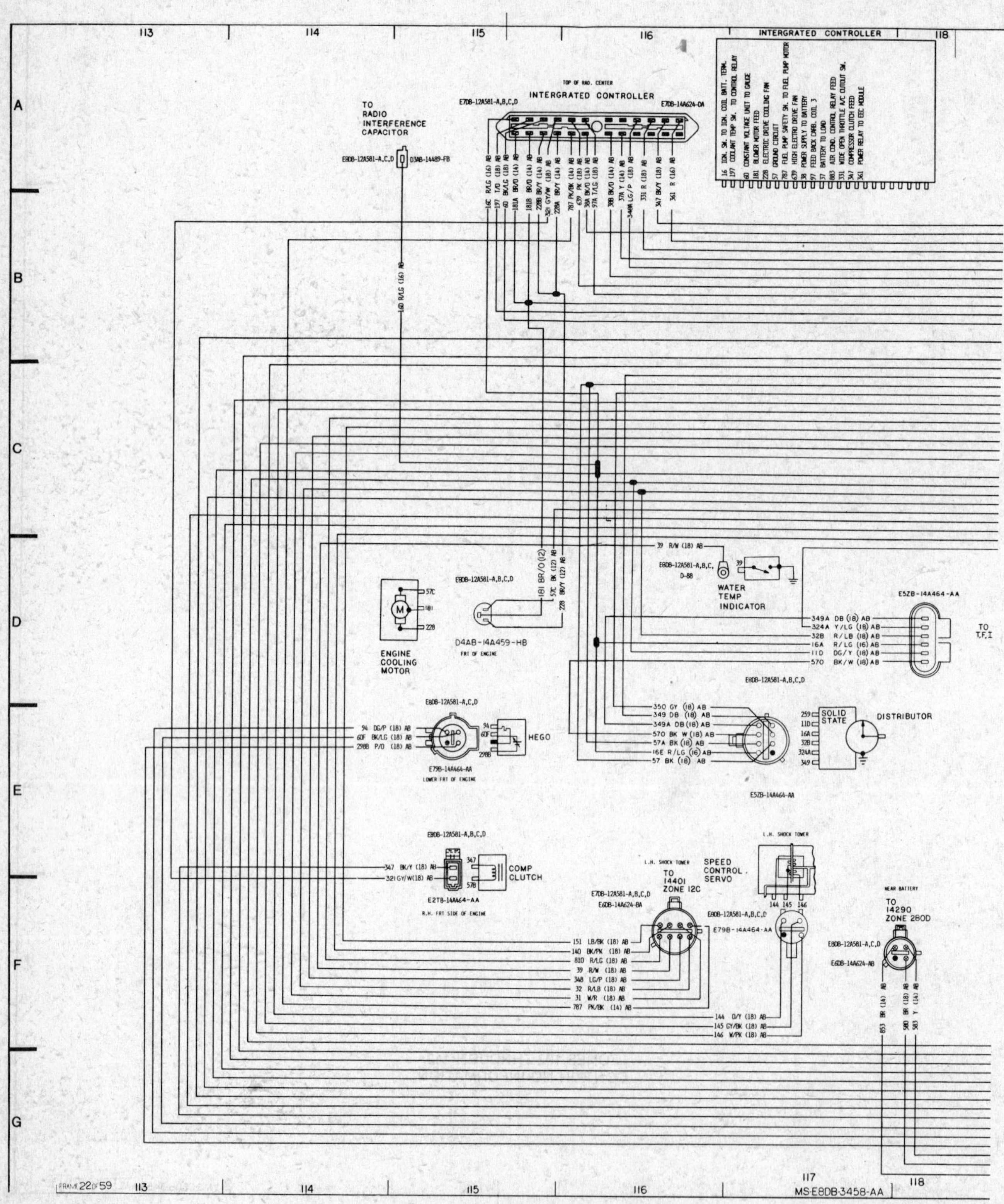
INTERGRATED CONTROLLER
16 IGN. SW. TO IGN. COIL BATT. TERM.
197 COOLANT TEMP SW. TO CONTROL RELAY
60 CONSTANT VOLTAGE UNIT TO GAUGE
181 BLOWER MOTOR FEED
228 ELECTRIC DRIVE COOLING FAN
57 GROUND CIRCUIT
787 FUEL PUMP SAFETY SW. TO FUEL PUMP MOTOR
639 HIGH ELECTRO DRIVE FAN
38 POWER SUPPLY TO BATTERY
97 FEED BACK CARB. COIL 3
37 BATTERY TO LOAD
883 AIR COND. CONTROL RELAY FEED
331 WIDE OPEN THROTTLE A/C CUTOUT SW.
347 COMPRESSOR CLUTCH FEED
361 POWER RELAY TO EEC MODULE
TOP OF RAD. CENTER
INTERGRATED CONTROLLER
TO RADIO INTERFERENCE CAPACITOR
WATER TEMP INDICATOR
ENGINE COOLING MOTOR
D4AB-14A459-HB
HEGO
SOLID STATE
DISTRIBUTOR
TO T.F.I
COMP CLUTCH
SPEED CONTROL SERVO
TO 14401 ZONE 12C
TO 14290 ZONE 280D
MS-E8DB-3458-AA

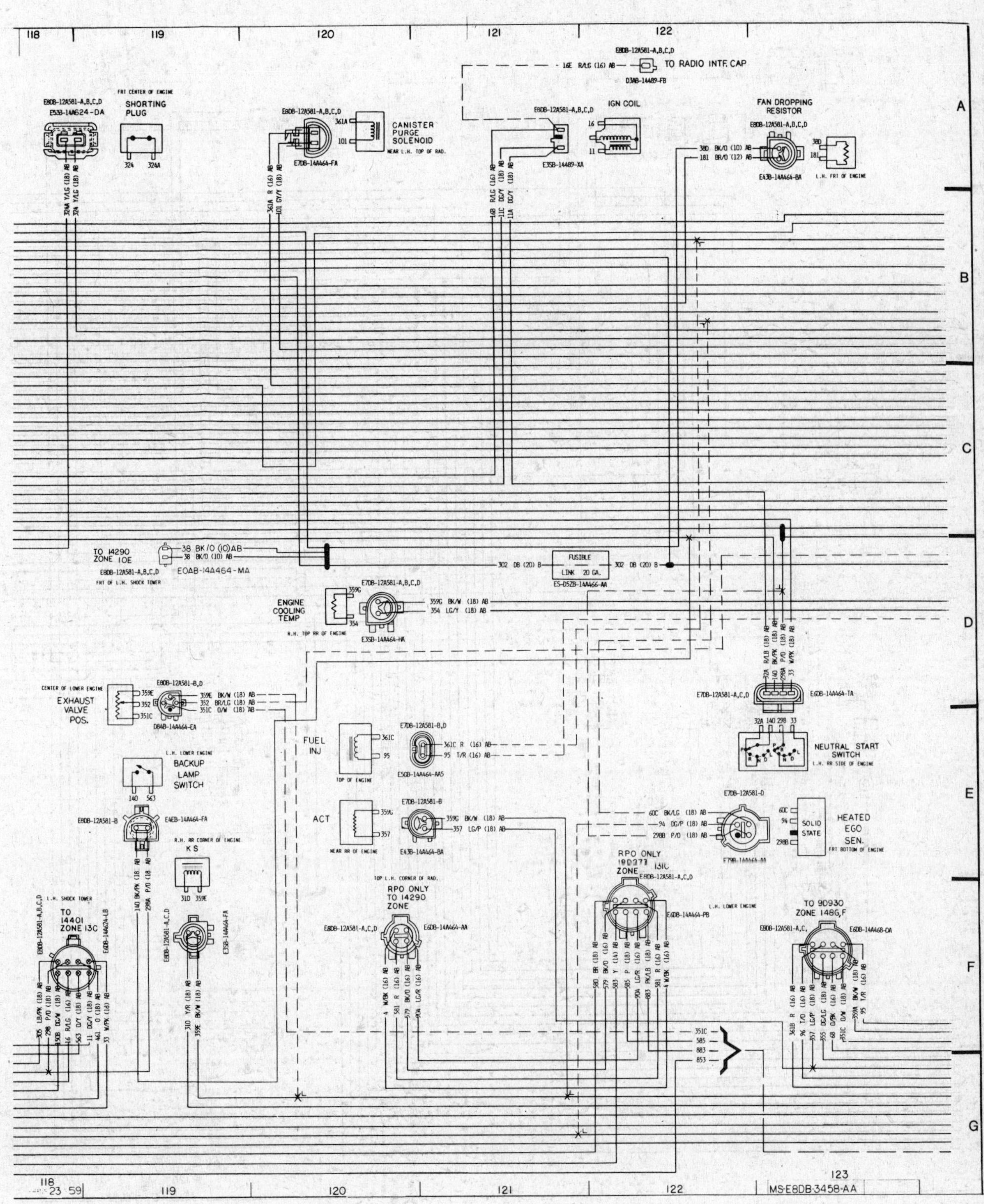

Taurus and Sable electrical schematics — 1988

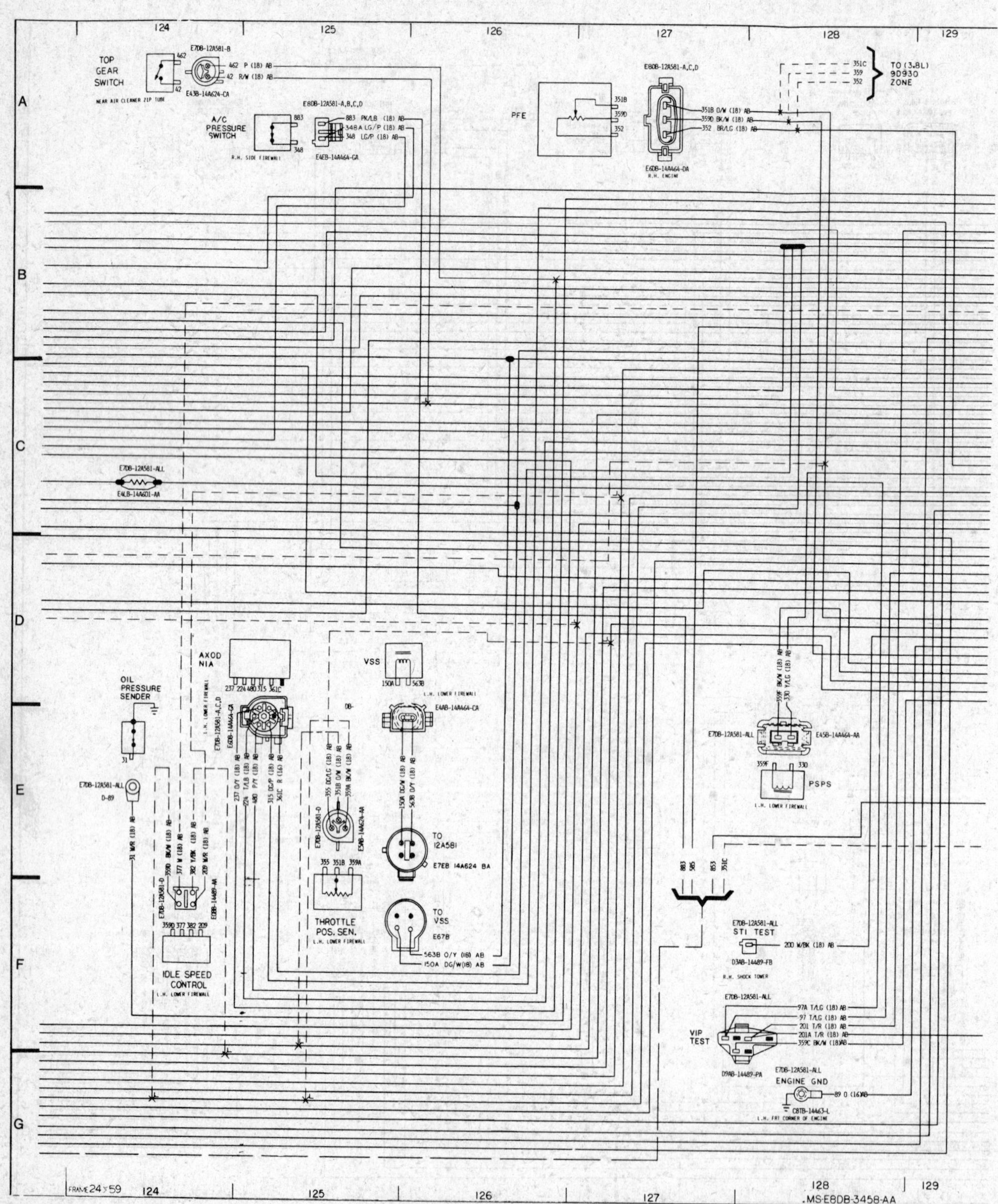

Taurus and Sable electrical schematics – 1988

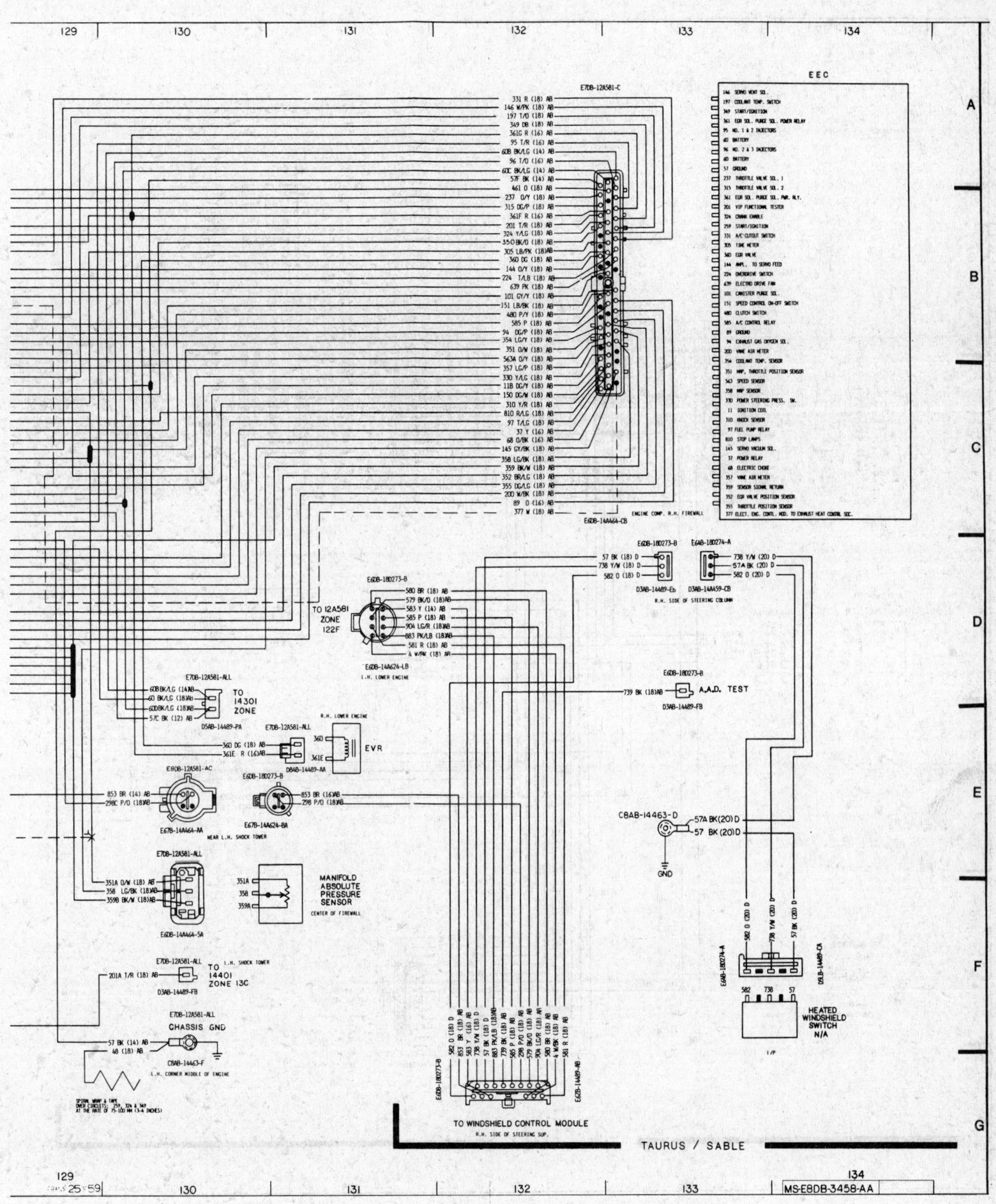

Taurus and Sable electrical schematics — 1988

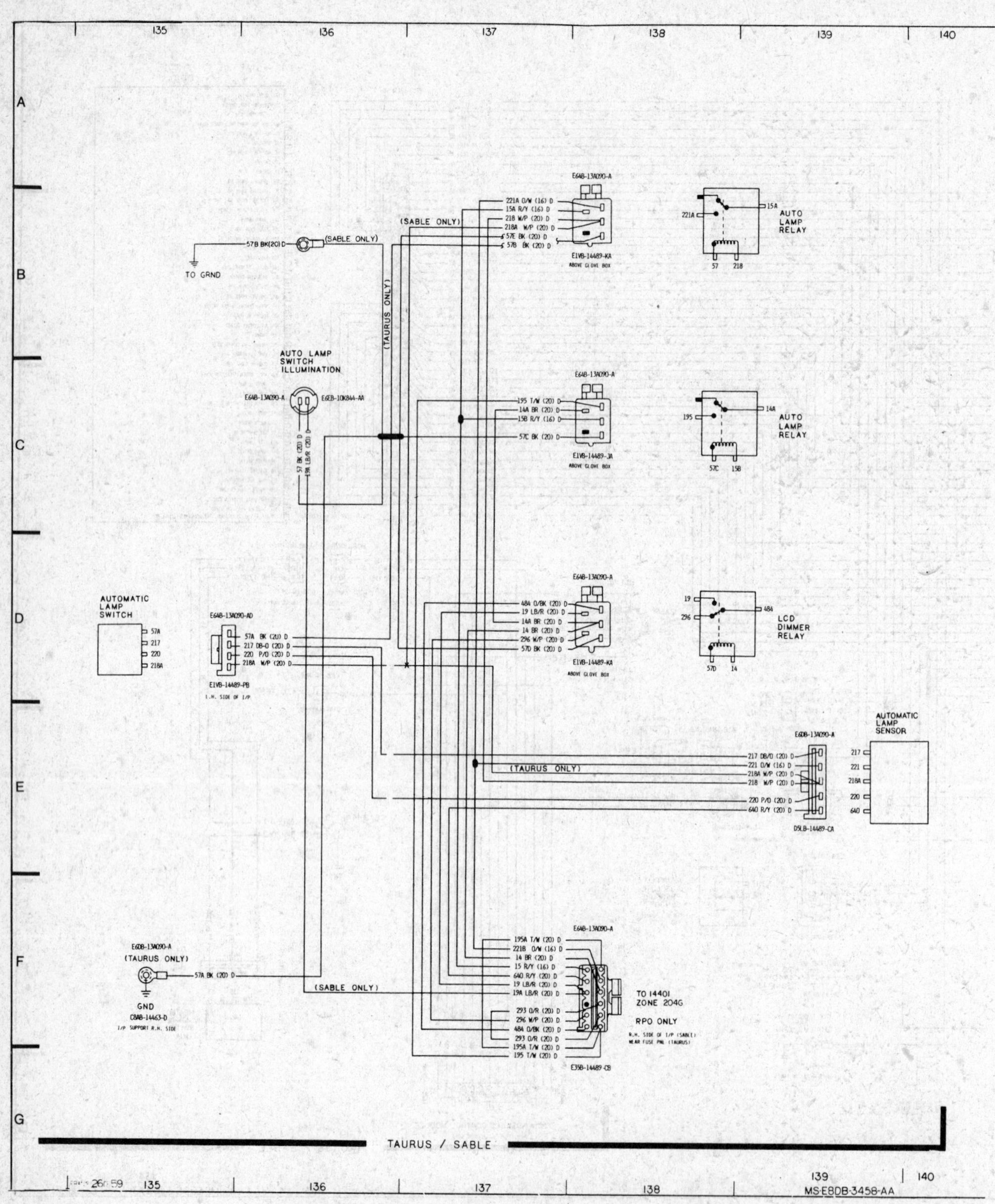

Taurus and Sable electrical schematics – 1988

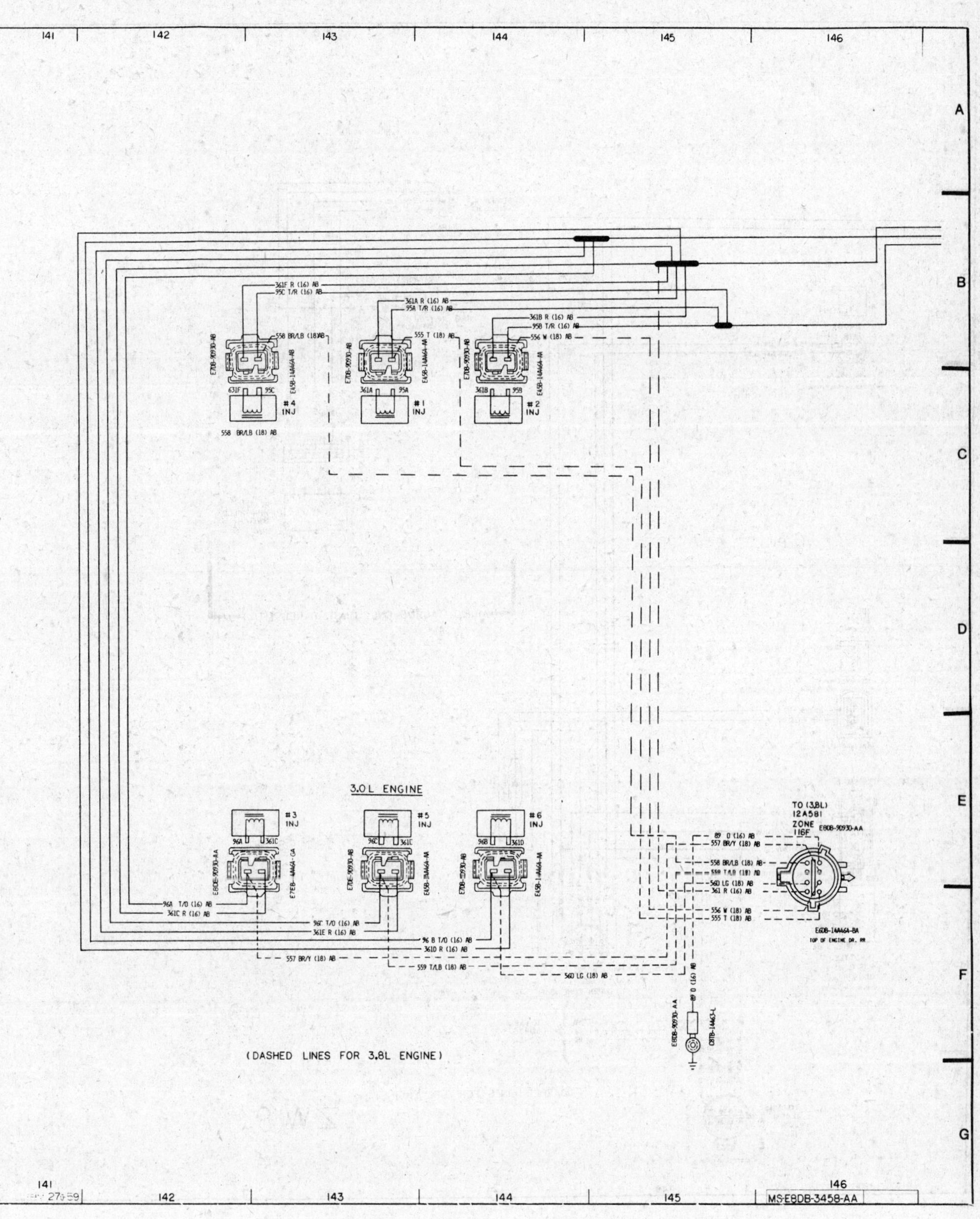
141
142
143
144
145
146
A
B
C
D
E
F
G
#4 INJ
#1 INJ
#2 INJ
#3 INJ
#5 INJ
#6 INJ
3.0L ENGINE
TO (3.8L) 12A581 ZONE 116F
(DASHED LINES FOR 3.8L ENGINE)
MS-E8DB-3458-AA

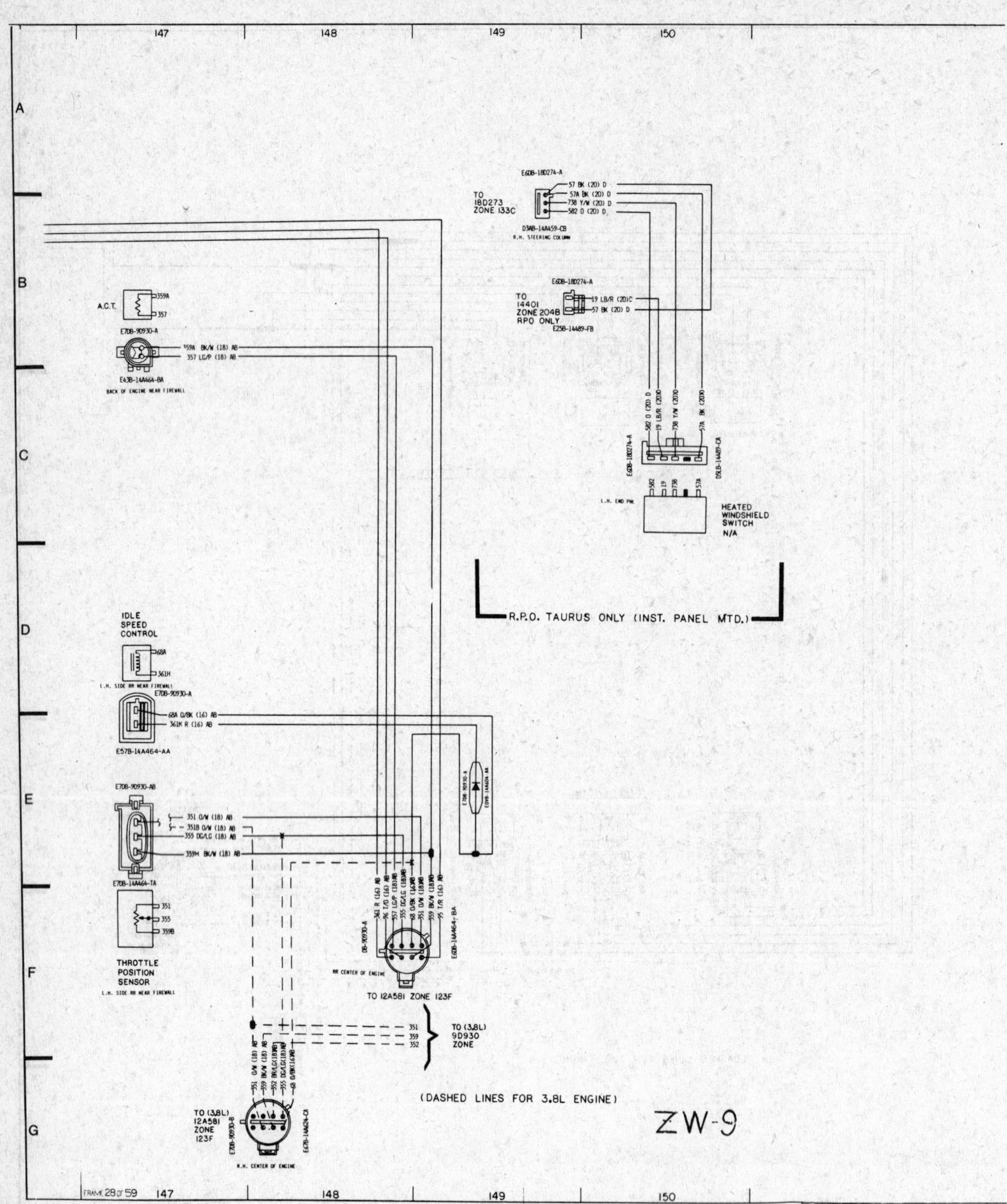

147
148
149
150
A
B
C
D
E
F
G
TO 18D273 ZONE 133C
TO 14401 ZONE 204B RPO ONLY
A.C.T.
HEATED WINDSHIELD SWITCH N/A
R.P.O. TAURUS ONLY (INST. PANEL MTD.)
IDLE SPEED CONTROL
THROTTLE POSITION SENSOR
TO 12A581 ZONE 123F
TO (3.8L) 9D930 ZONE
(DASHED LINES FOR 3.8L ENGINE)
TO (3.8L) 12A581 ZONE 123F
ZW-9
FRAME 28 OF 59

A

B

C

D

E

F

G

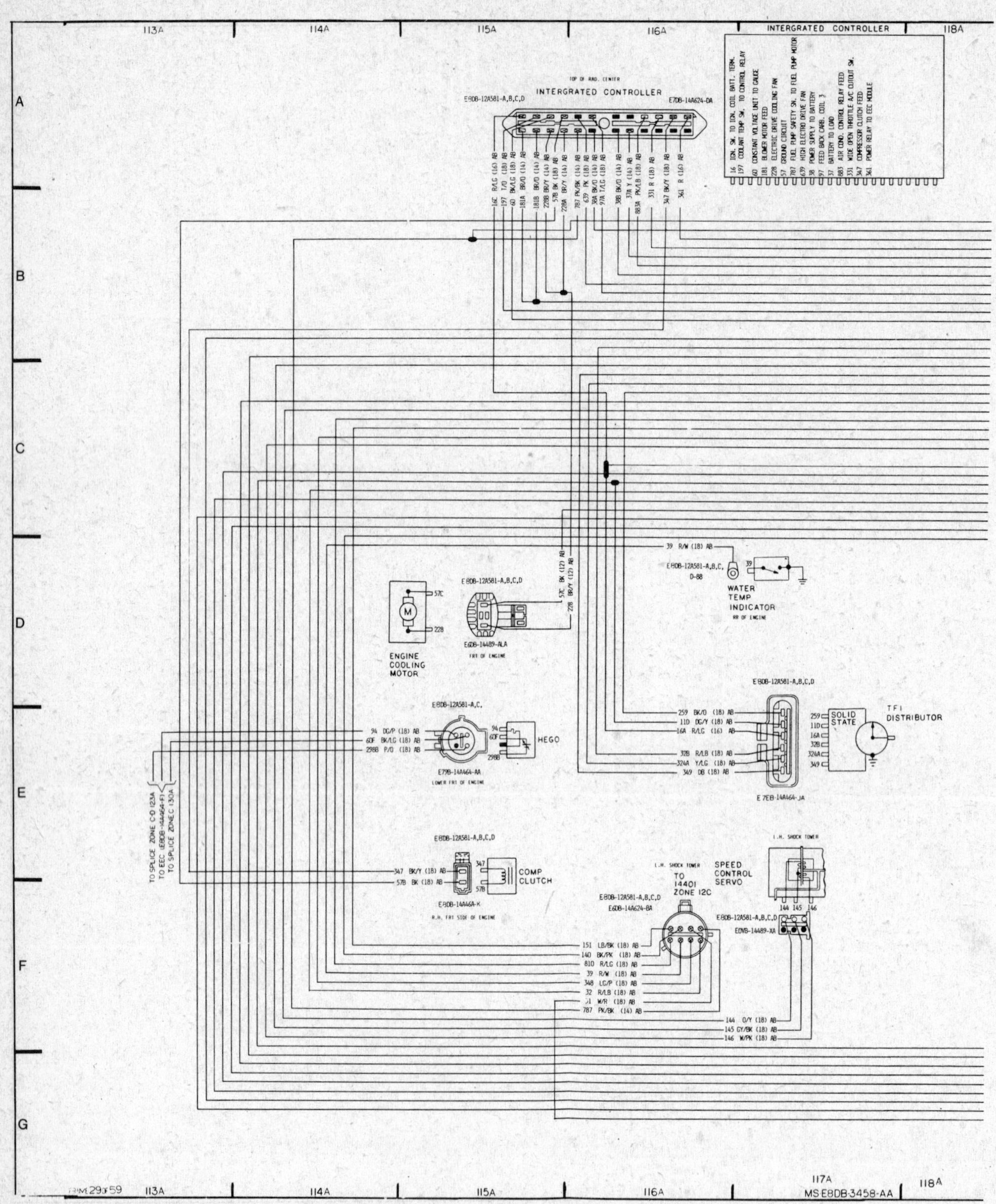

Taurus and Sable electrical schematics — 1988

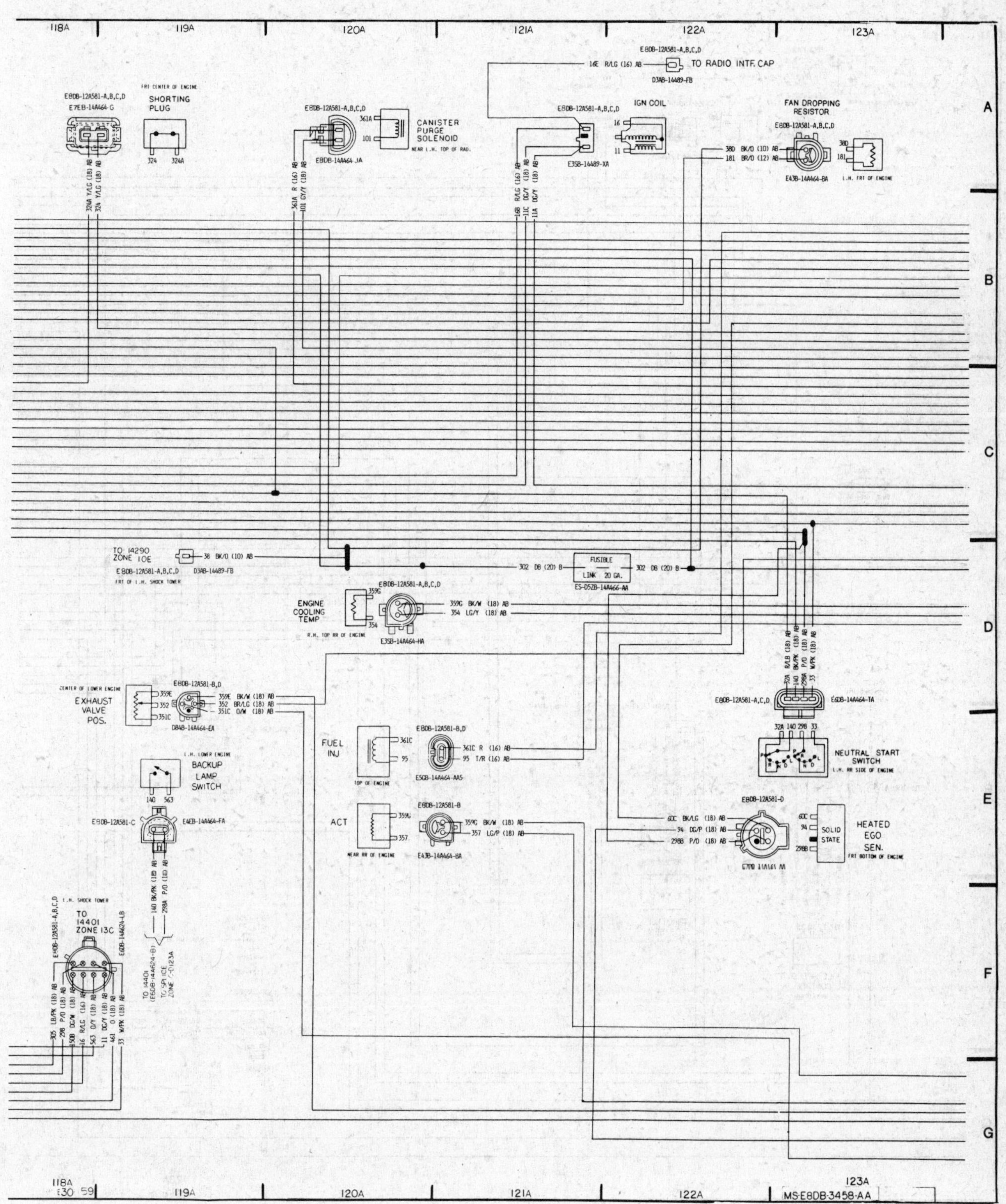

Taurus and Sable electrical schematics — 1988

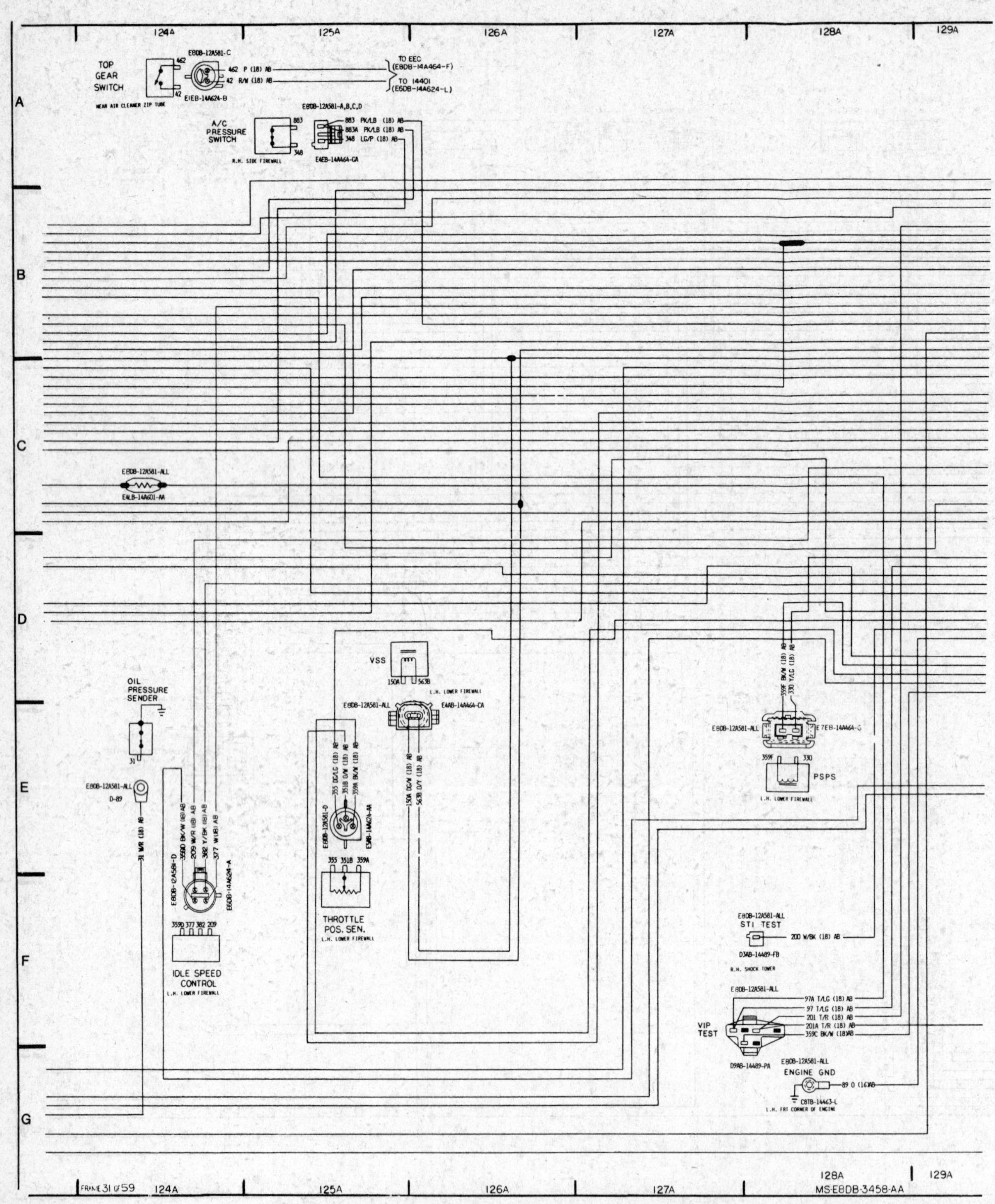

Taurus and Sable electrical schematics — 1988

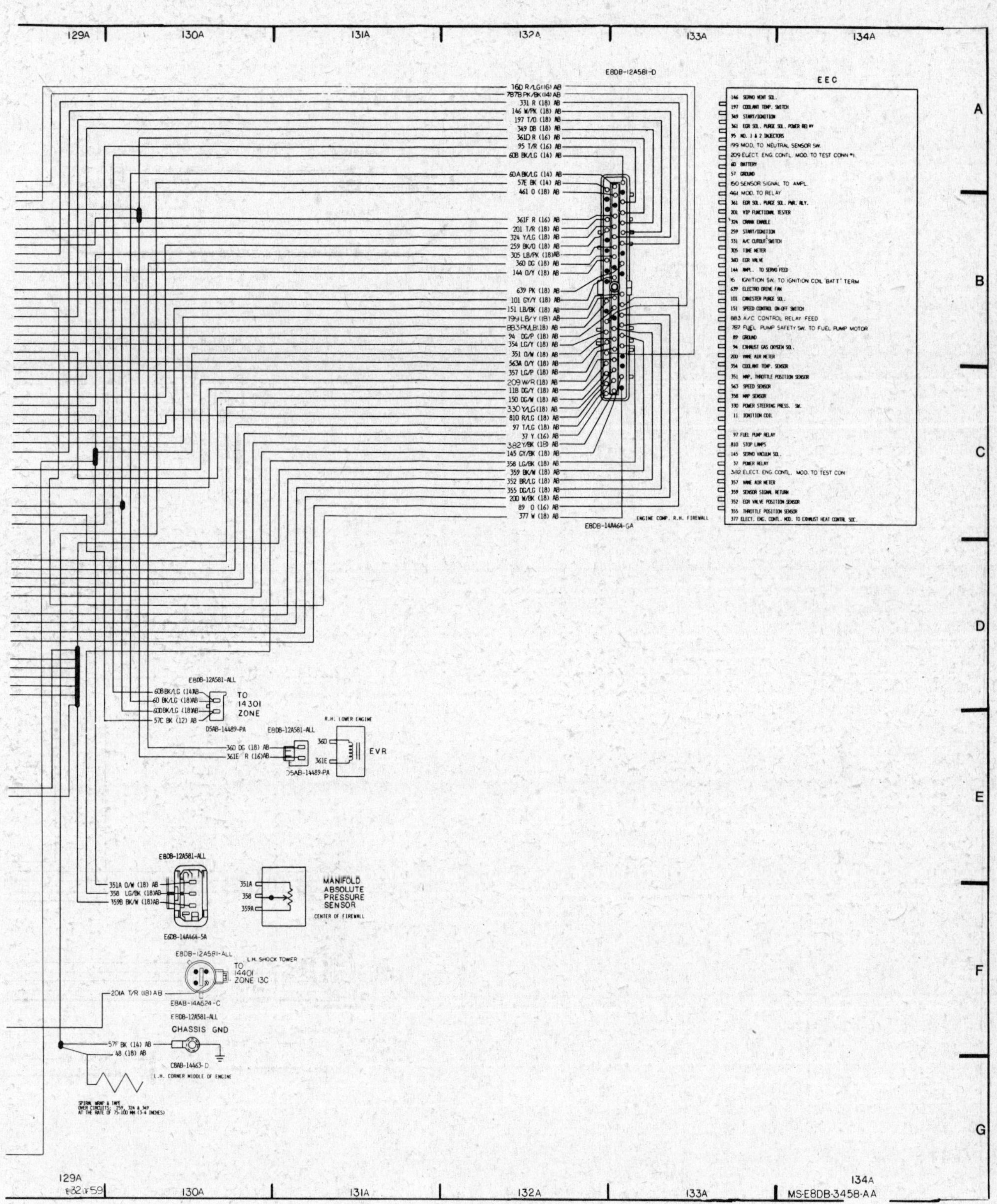

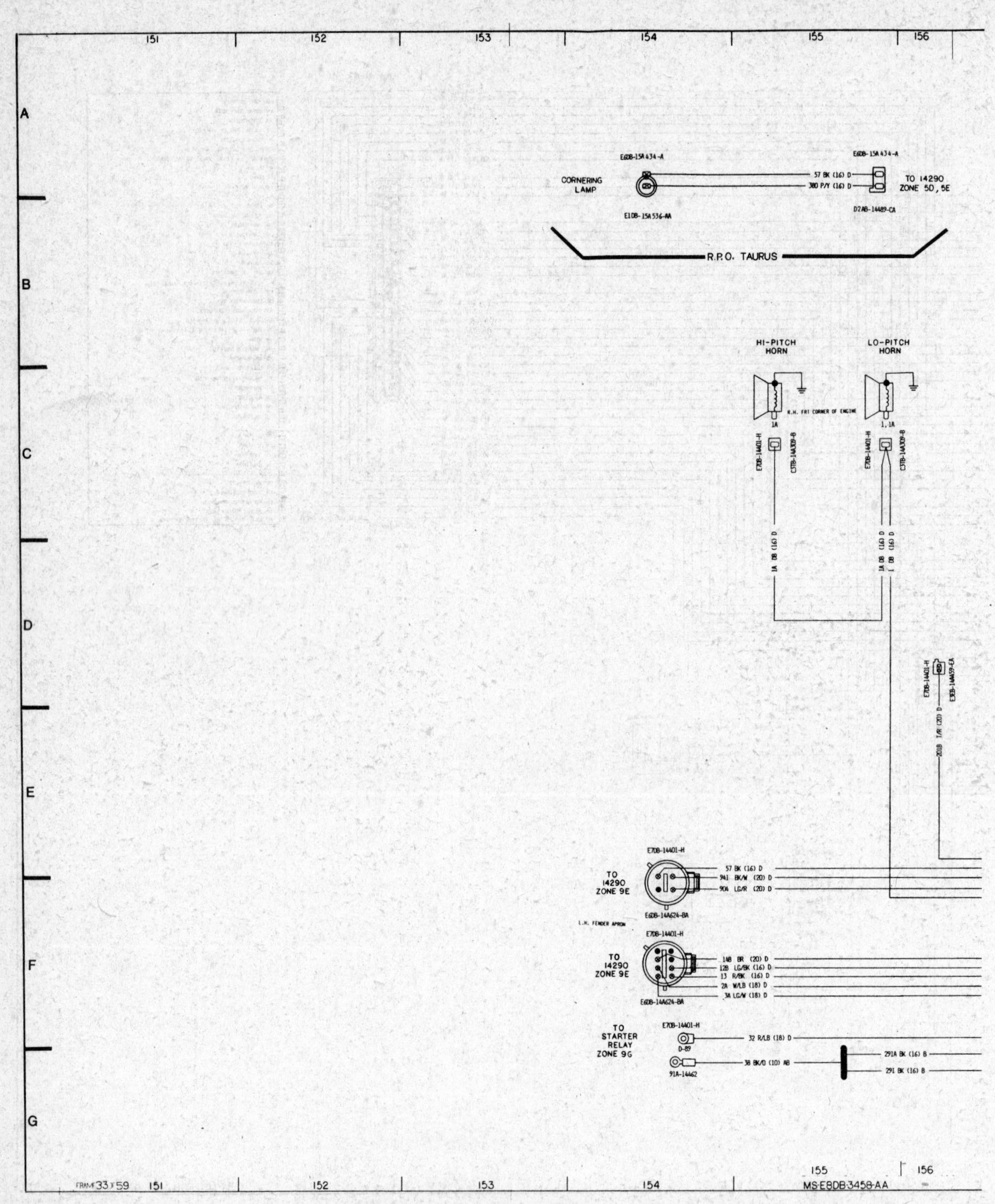

Taurus and Sable electrical schematics — 1988

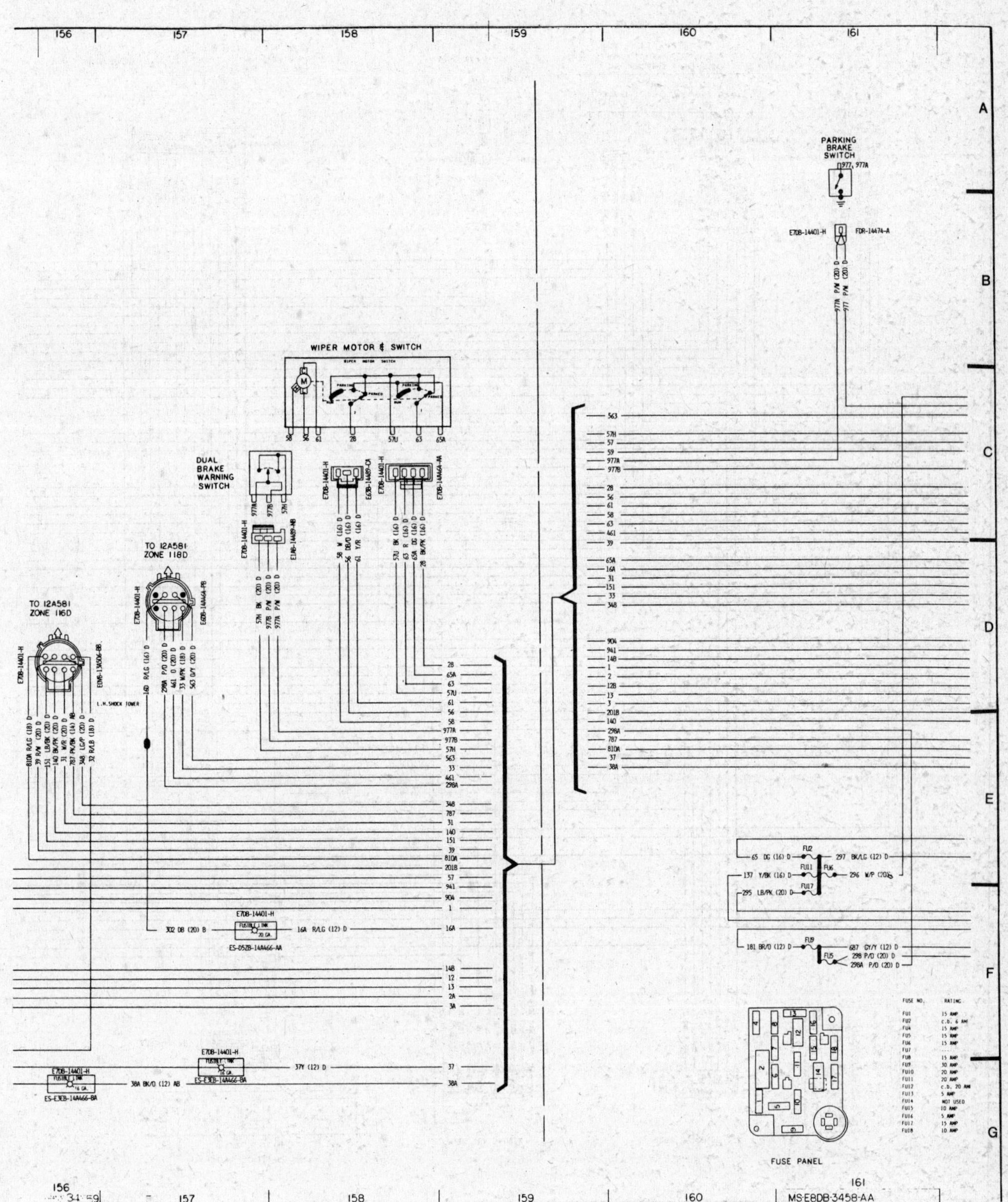

Taurus and Sable electrical schematics – 1988

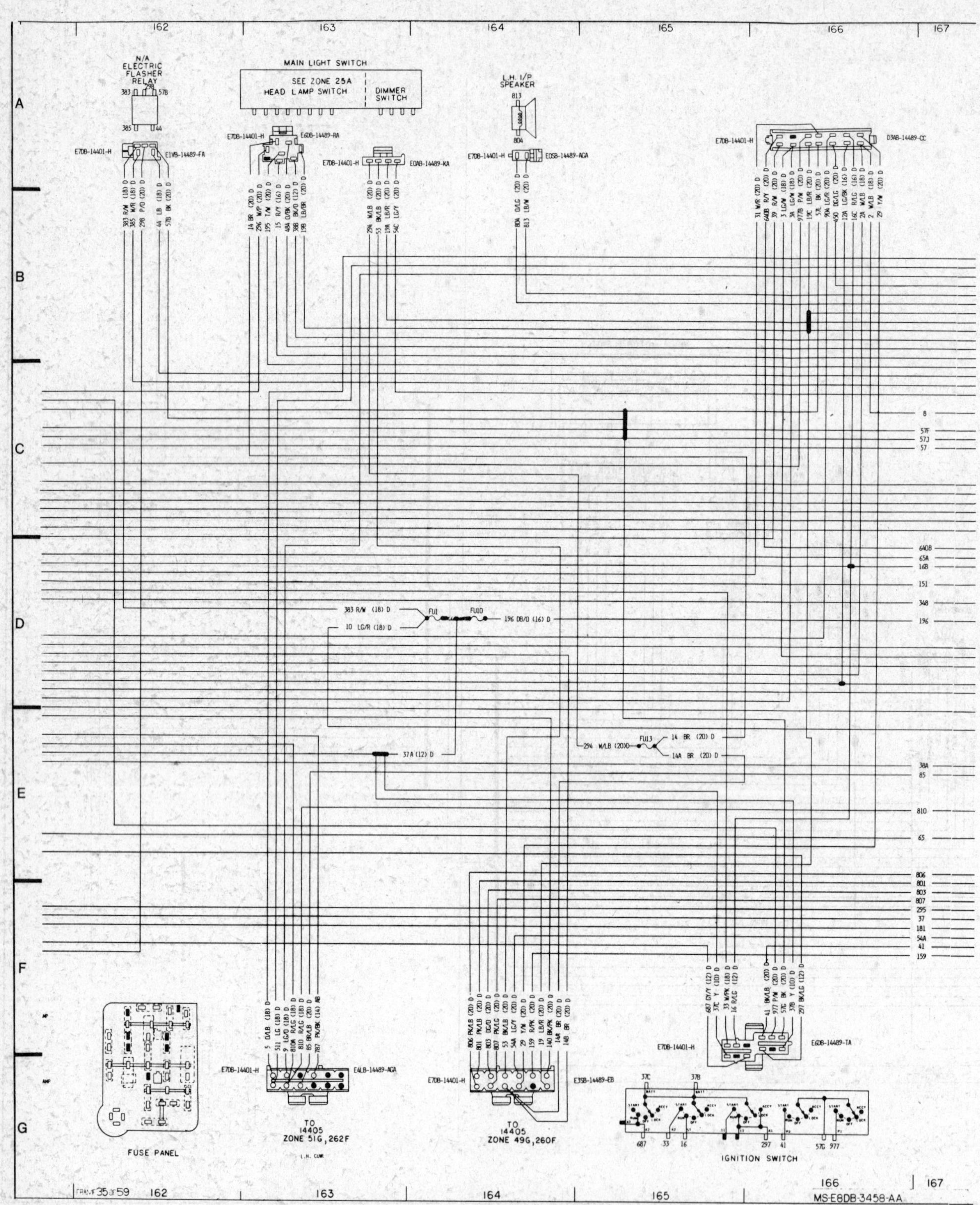

Taurus and Sable electrical schematics – 1988

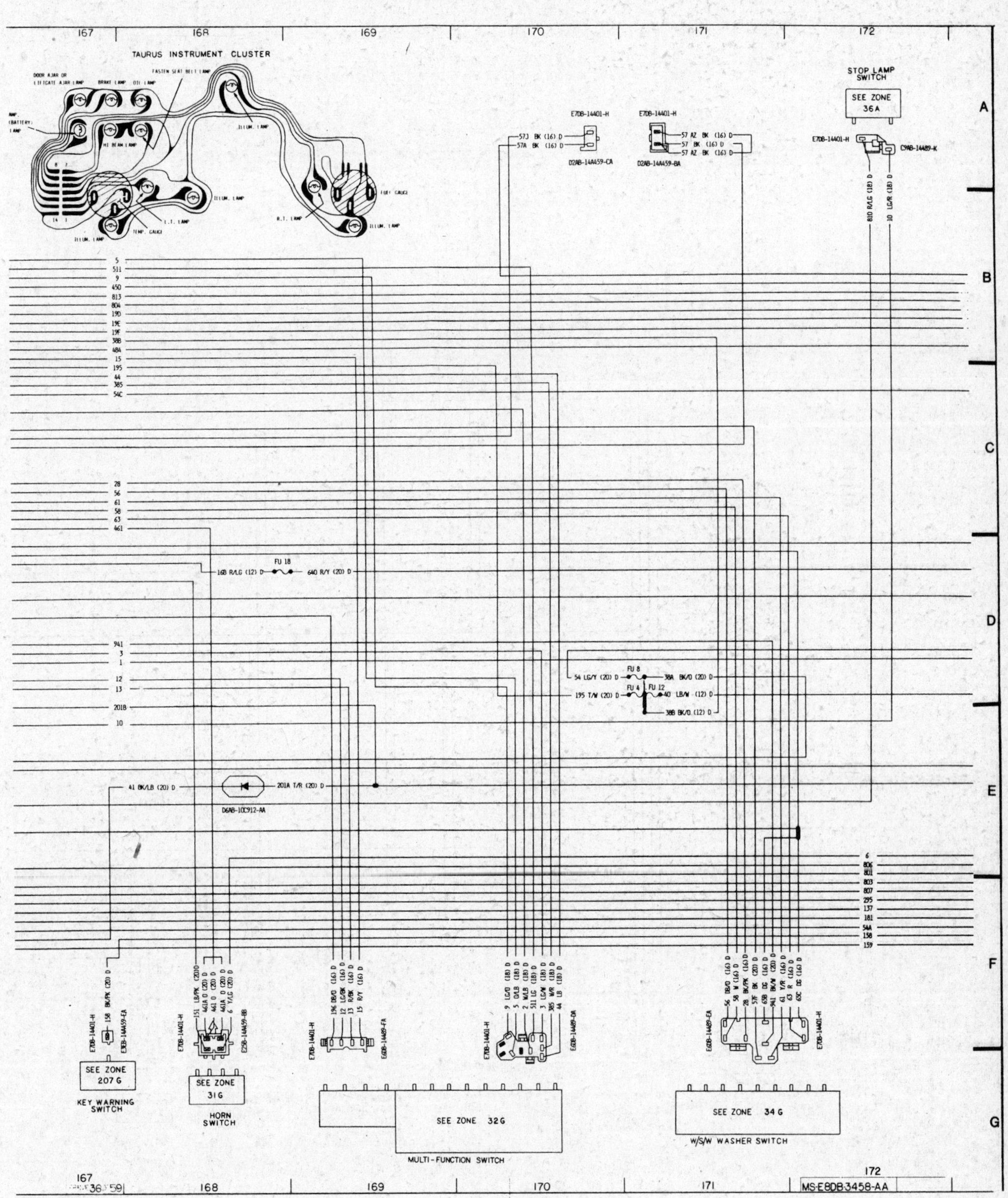

Taurus and Sable electrical schematics — 1988

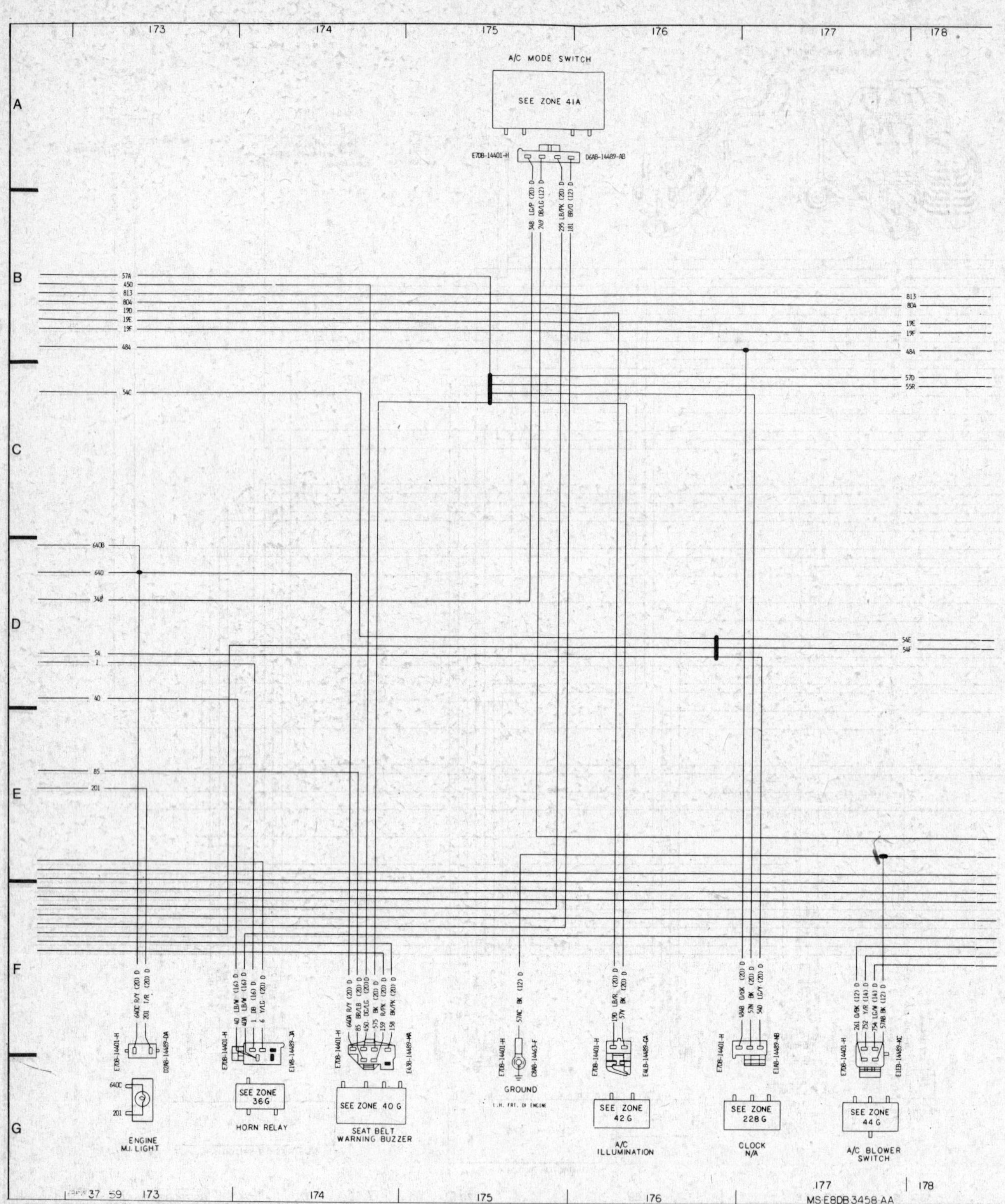

Taurus and Sable electrical schematics – 1988

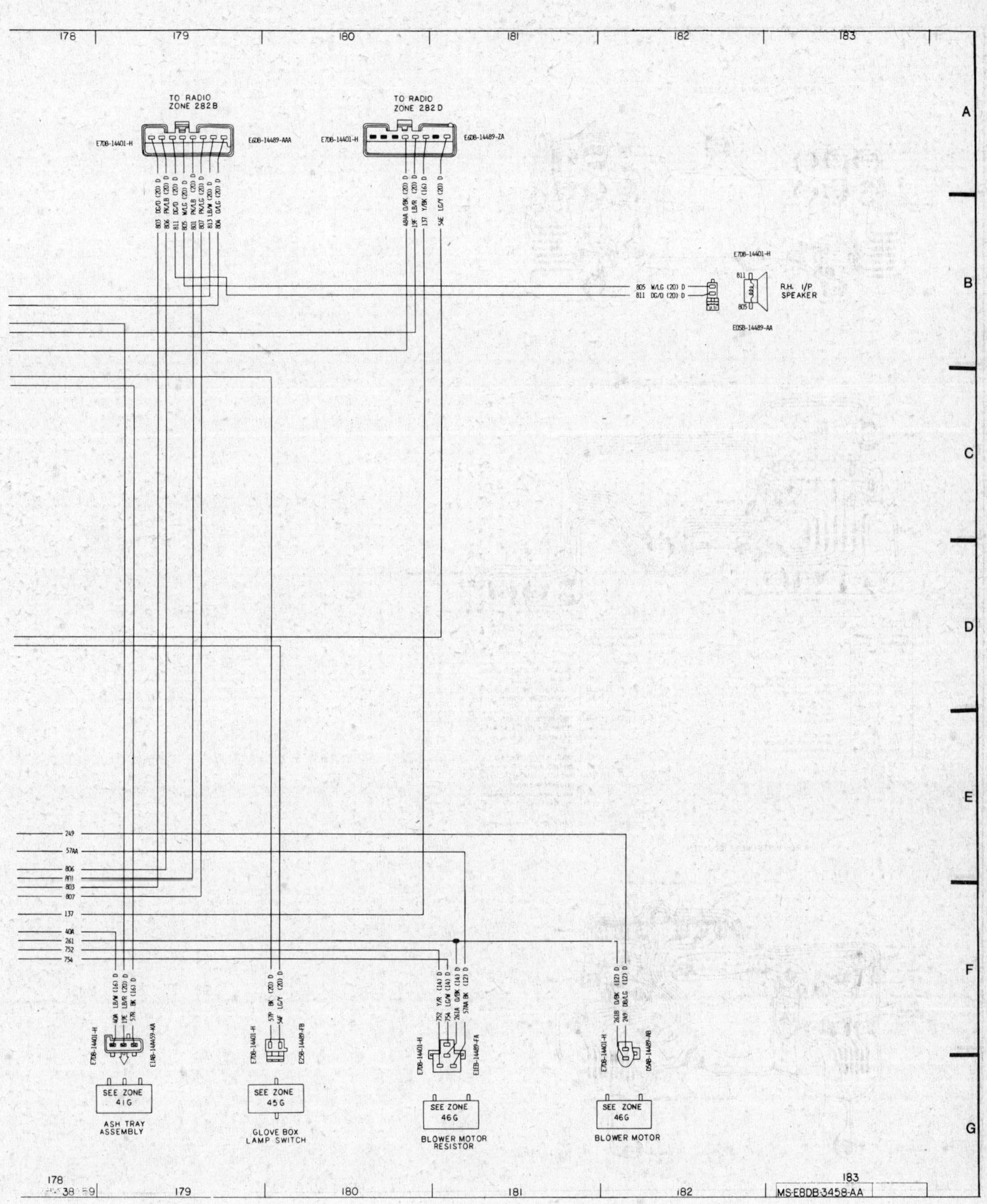

Taurus and Sable electrical schematics – 1988

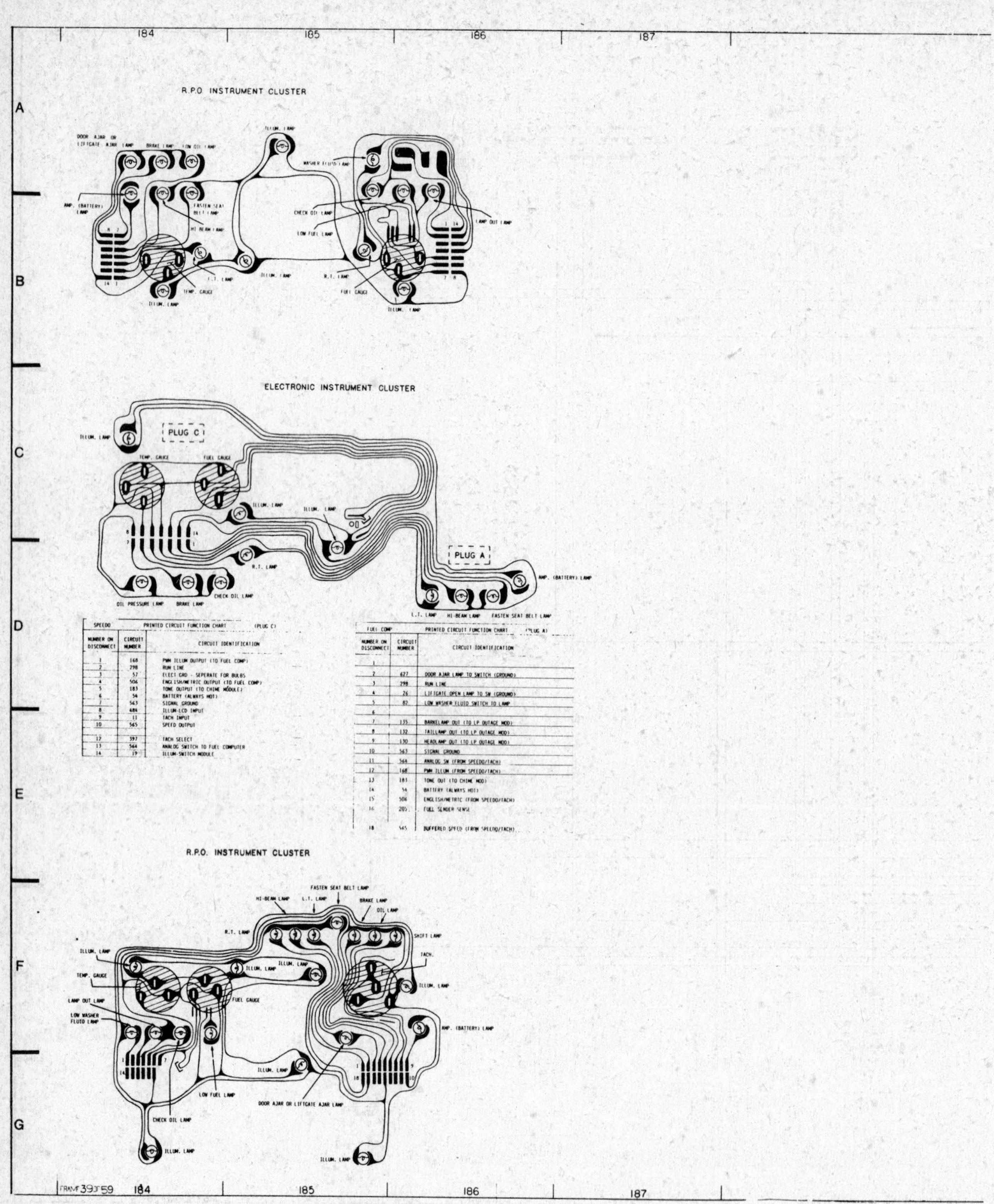

SPEEDO	PRINTED CIRCUIT FUNCTION CHART	(PLUG C)
NUMBER ON DISCONNECT	CIRCUIT NUMBER	CIRCUIT IDENTIFICATION
1	168	PWM ILLUM OUTPUT (TO FUEL COMP)
2	298	RUN LINE
3	57	ELECT GRD - SEPERATE FOR BULBS
4	506	ENGLISH/METRIC OUTPUT (TO FUEL COMP)
5	183	TONE OUTPUT (TO CHIME MODULE)
6	54	BATTERY (ALWAYS HOT)
7	563	SIGNAL GROUND
8	484	ILLUM-LCD INPUT
9	11	TACH INPUT
10	565	SPEED OUTPUT
12	397	TACH SELECT
13	564	ANALOG SWITCH TO FUEL COMPUTER
14	19	ILLUM-SWITCH MODULE

FUEL COMP	PRINTED CIRCUIT FUNCTION CHART	(PLUG A)
NUMBER ON DISCONNECT	CIRCUIT NUMBER	CIRCUIT IDENTIFICATION
1		
2	627	DOOR AJAR LAMP TO SWITCH (GROUND)
3	298	RUN LINE
4	26	LIFTGATE OPEN LAMP TO SW (GROUND)
5	82	LOW WASHER FLUID SWITCH TO LAMP
6		
7	135	BARKELAMP OUT (TO LP OUTAGE MOD)
8	132	TAILLAMP OUT (TO LP OUTAGE MOD)
9	130	HEADLAMP OUT (TO LP OUTAGE MOD)
10	563	SIGNAL GROUND
11	564	ANALOG SW (FROM SPEEDO/TACH)
12	168	PWM ILLUM (FROM SPEEDO/TACH)
13	183	TONE OUT (TO CHIME MOD)
14	54	BATTERY (ALWAYS HOT)
15	506	ENGLISH/METRIC (FROM SPEEDO/TACH)
16	205	FUEL SENDER SENSE
18	565	BUFFERED SPEED (FROM SPEEDO/TACH)

Taurus and Sable electrical schematics — 1988

A

B

C

D

E

F

G

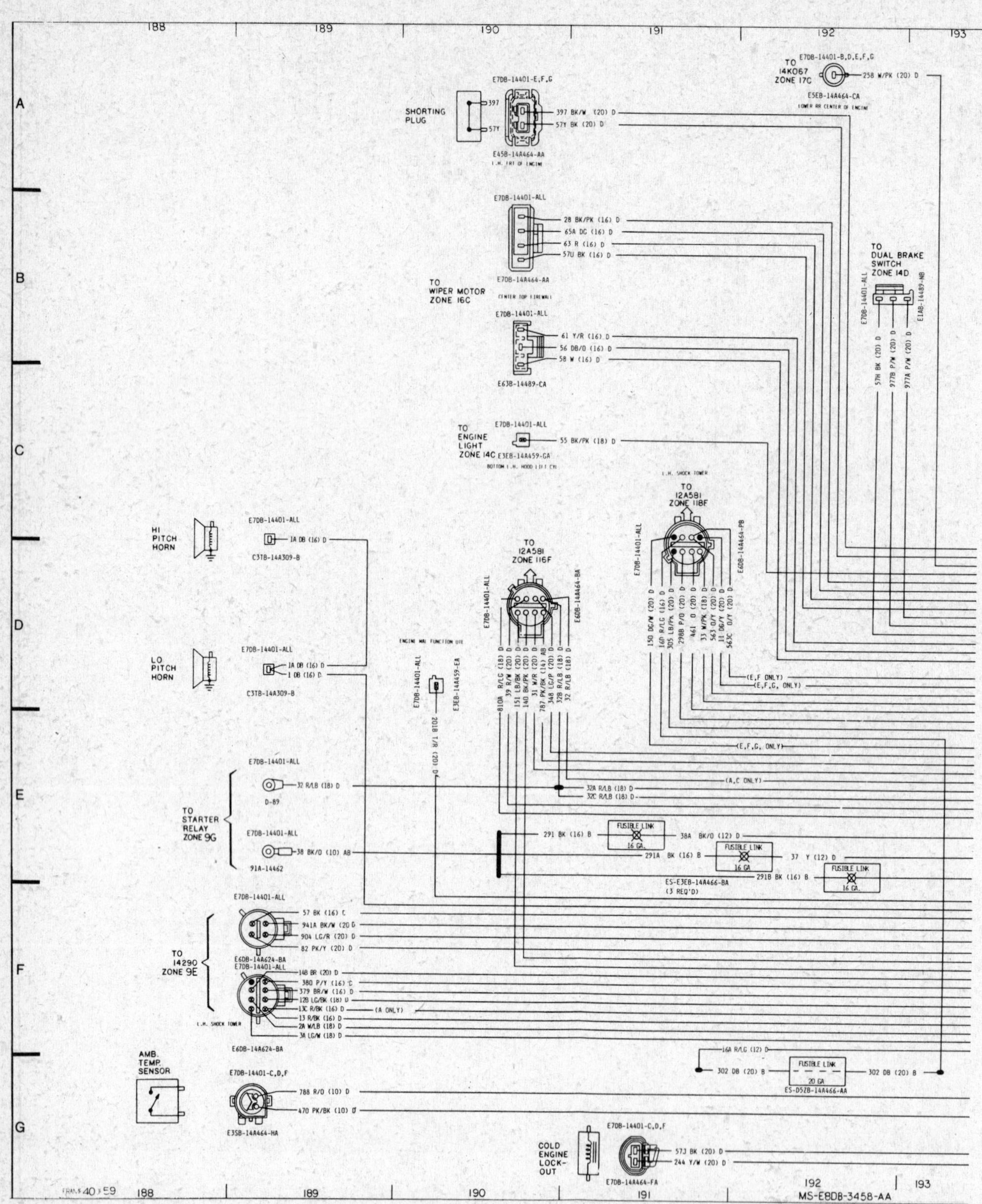

Taurus and Sable electrical schematics — 1988

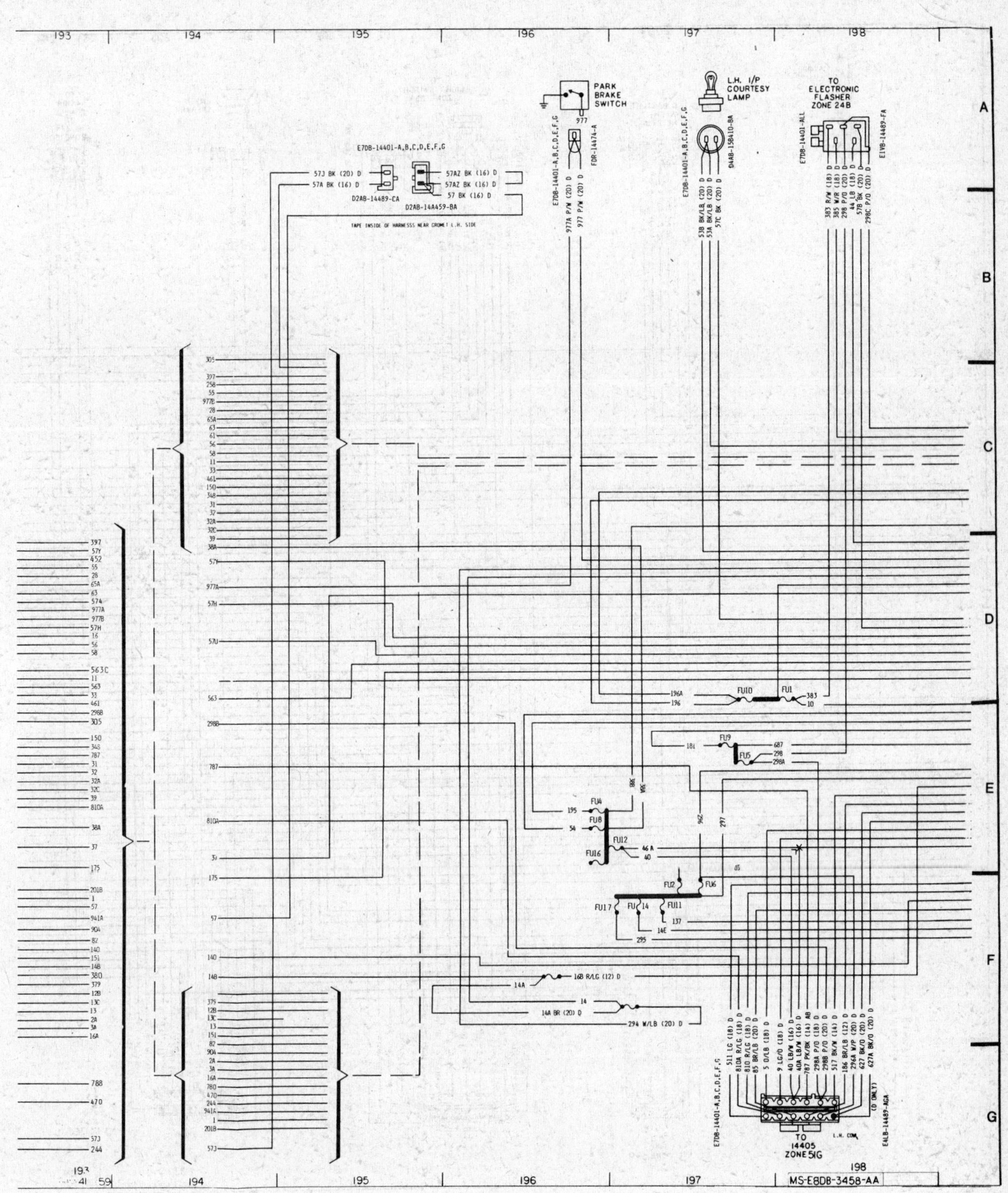

Taurus and Sable electrical schematics — 1988

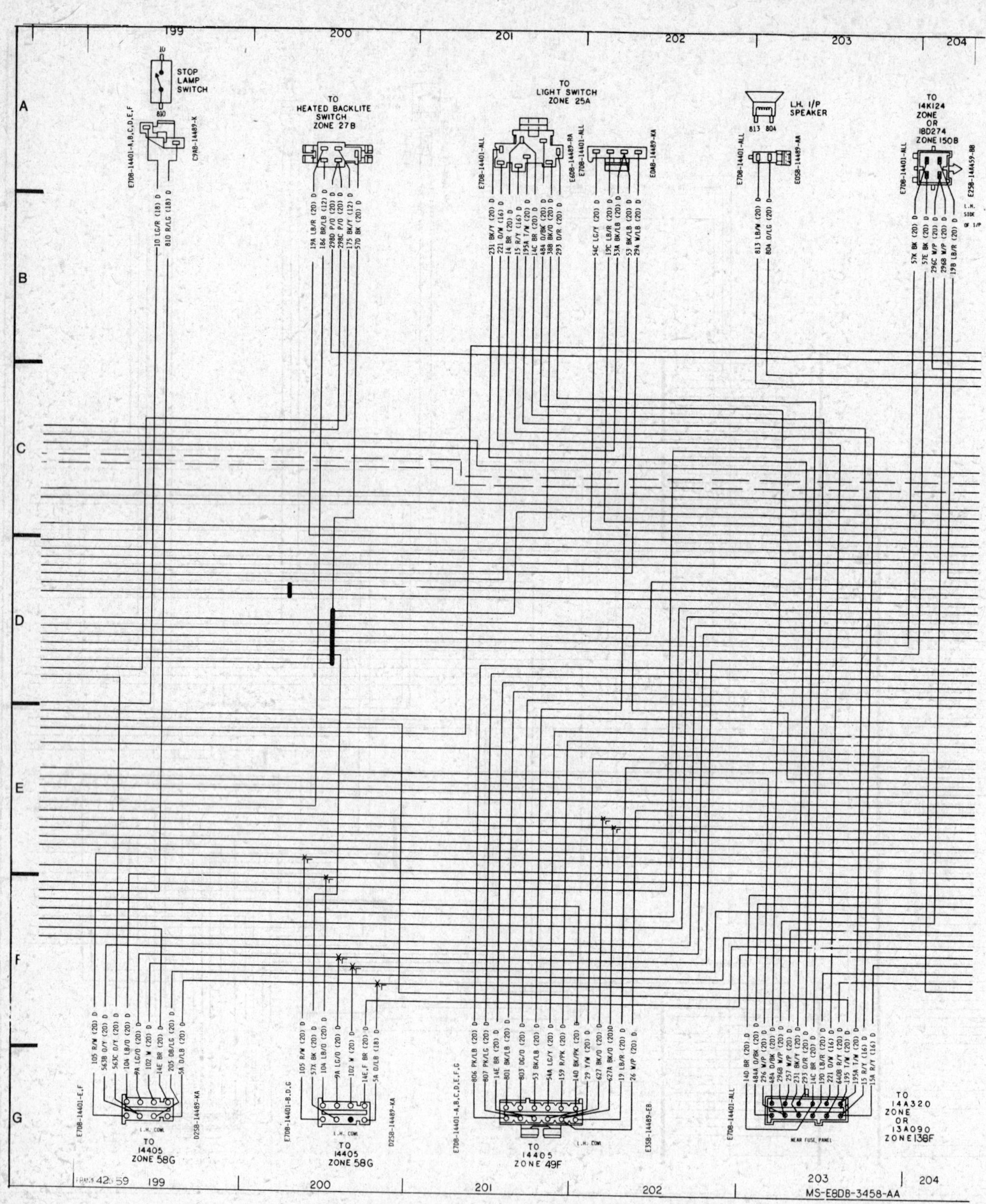

Taurus and Sable electrical schematics — 1988

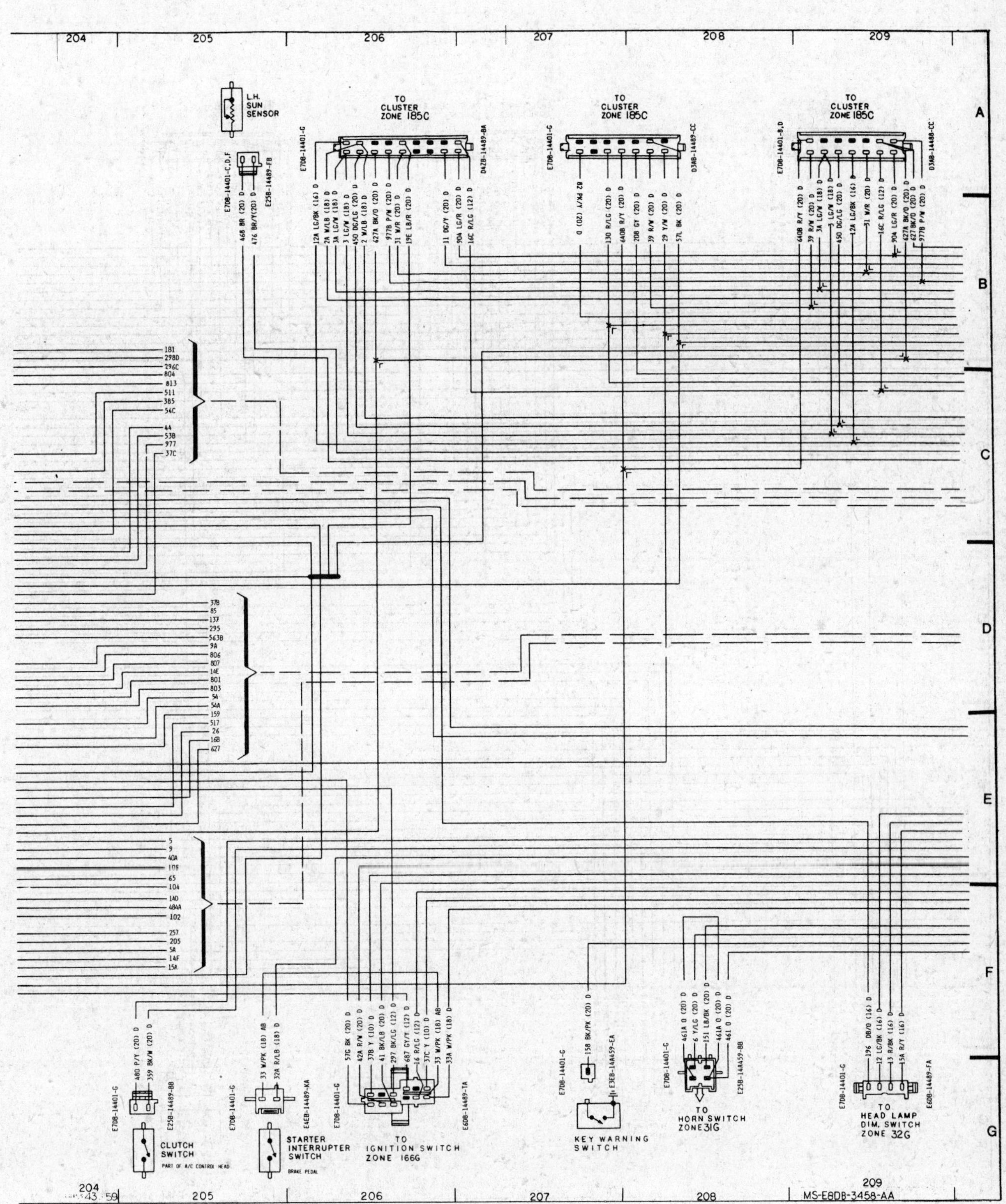

Taurus and Sable electrical schematics — 1988

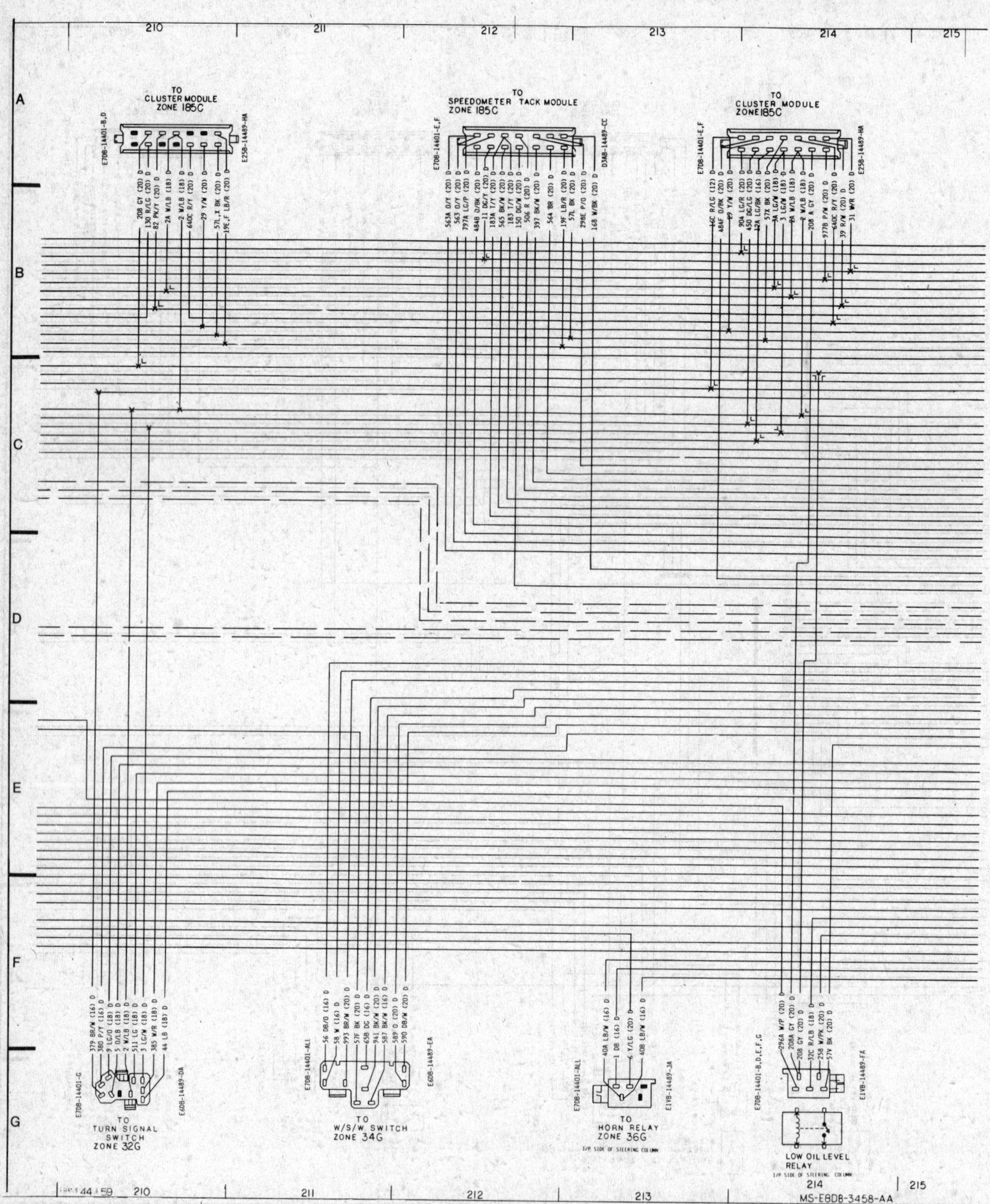

Taurus and Sable electrical schematics — 1988

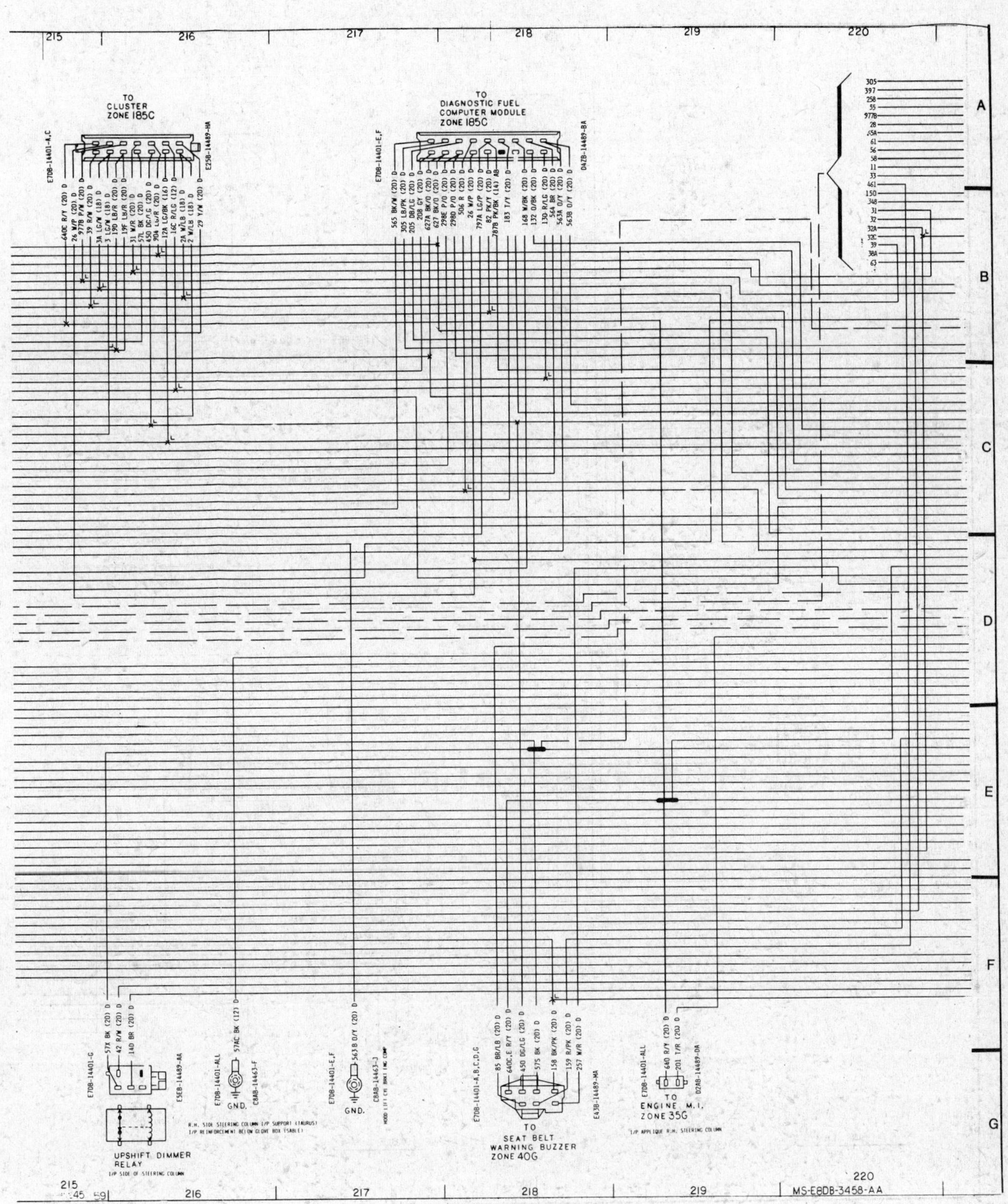

Taurus and Sable electrical schematics – 1988

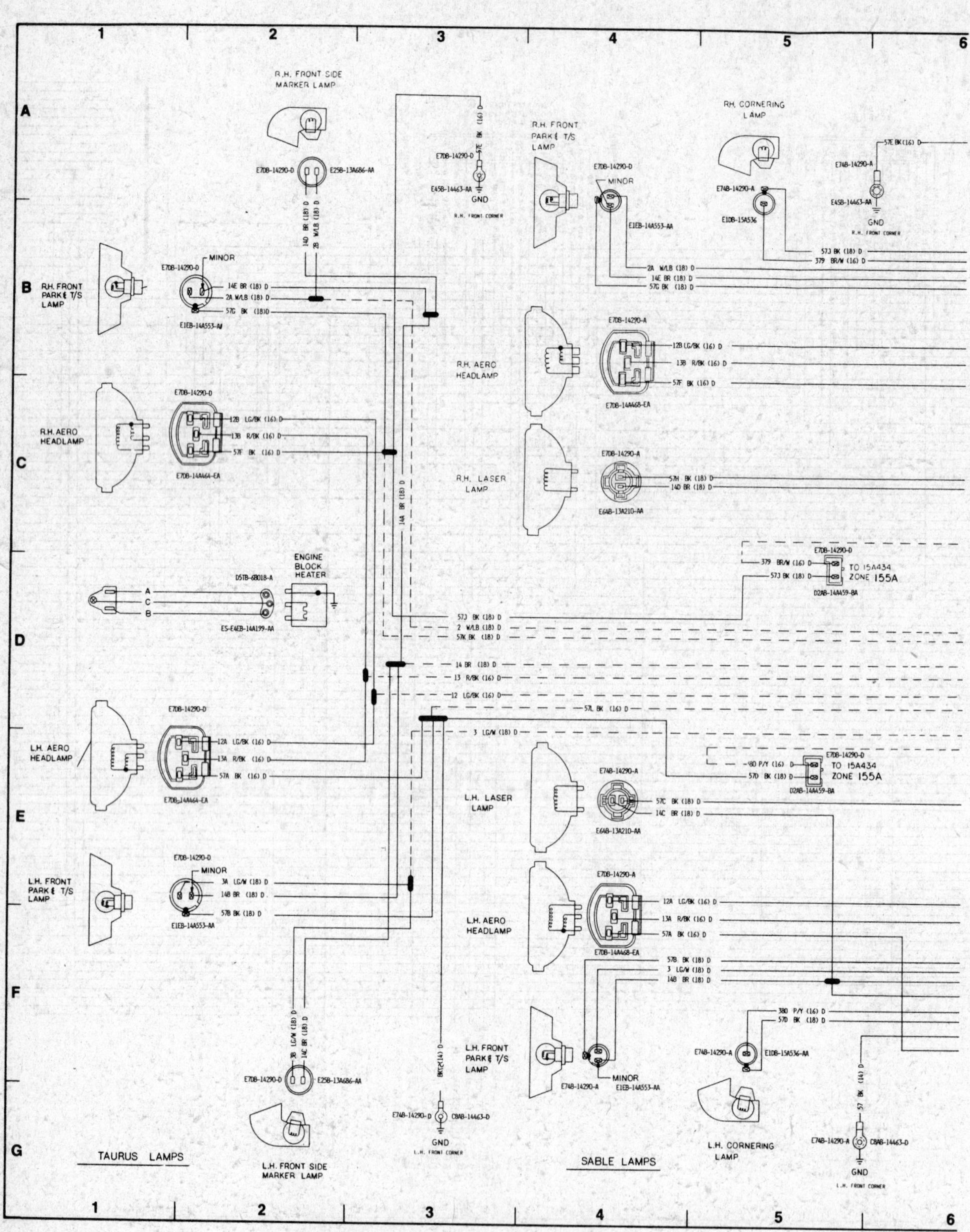

Taurus and Sable electrical schematics – 1986–87

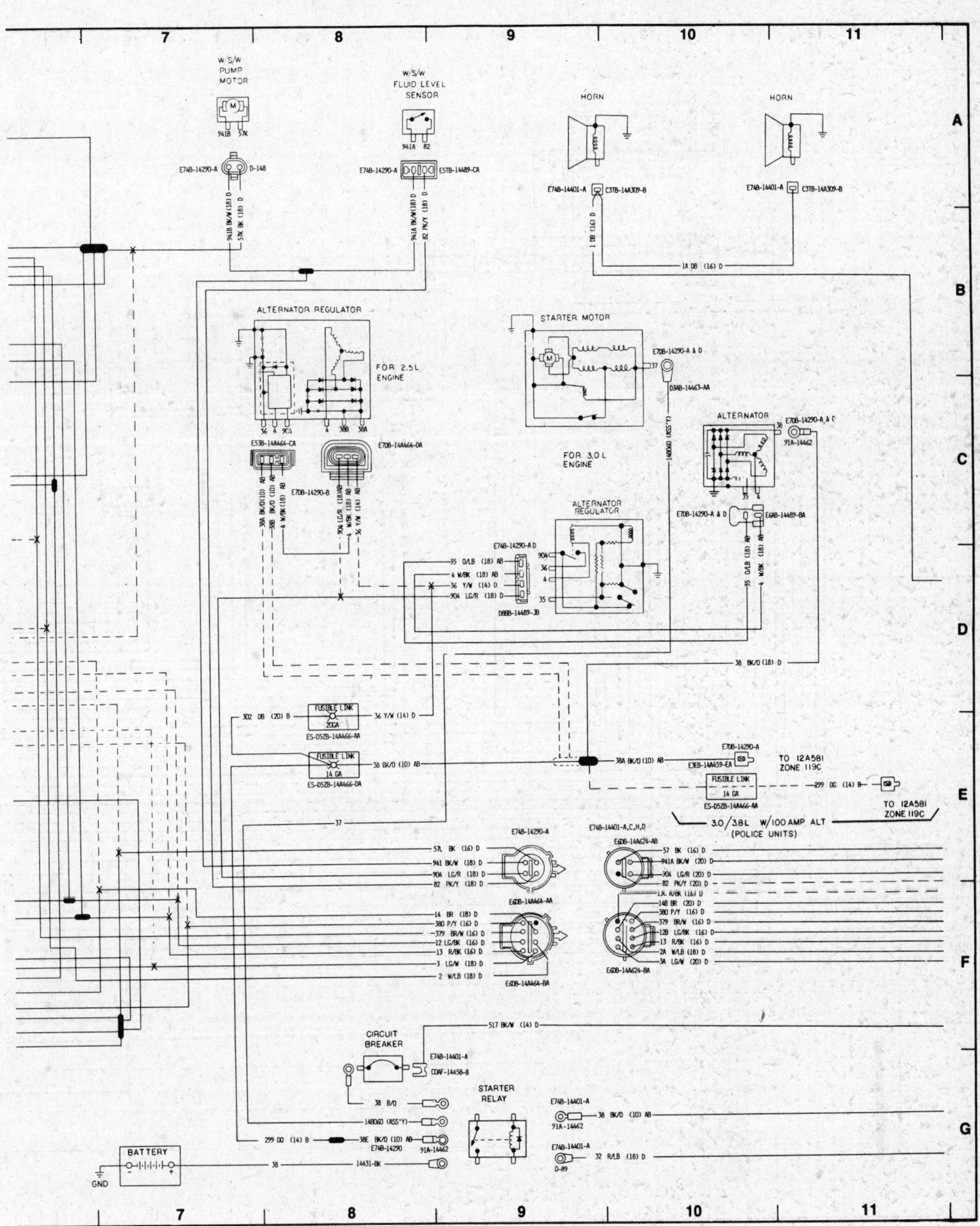

Taurus and Sable electrical schematics — 1986–87

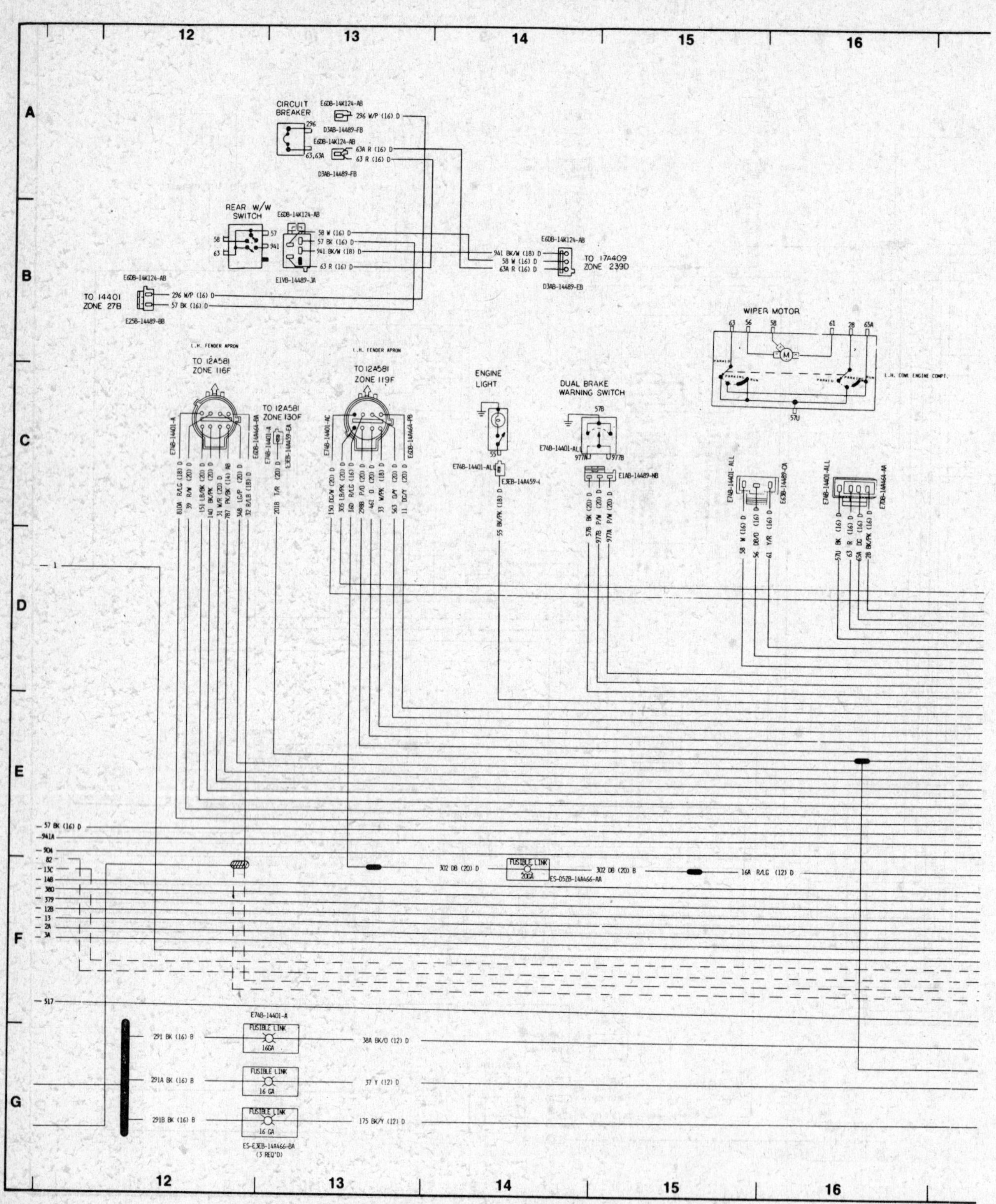

Taurus and Sable electrical schematics – 1986–87

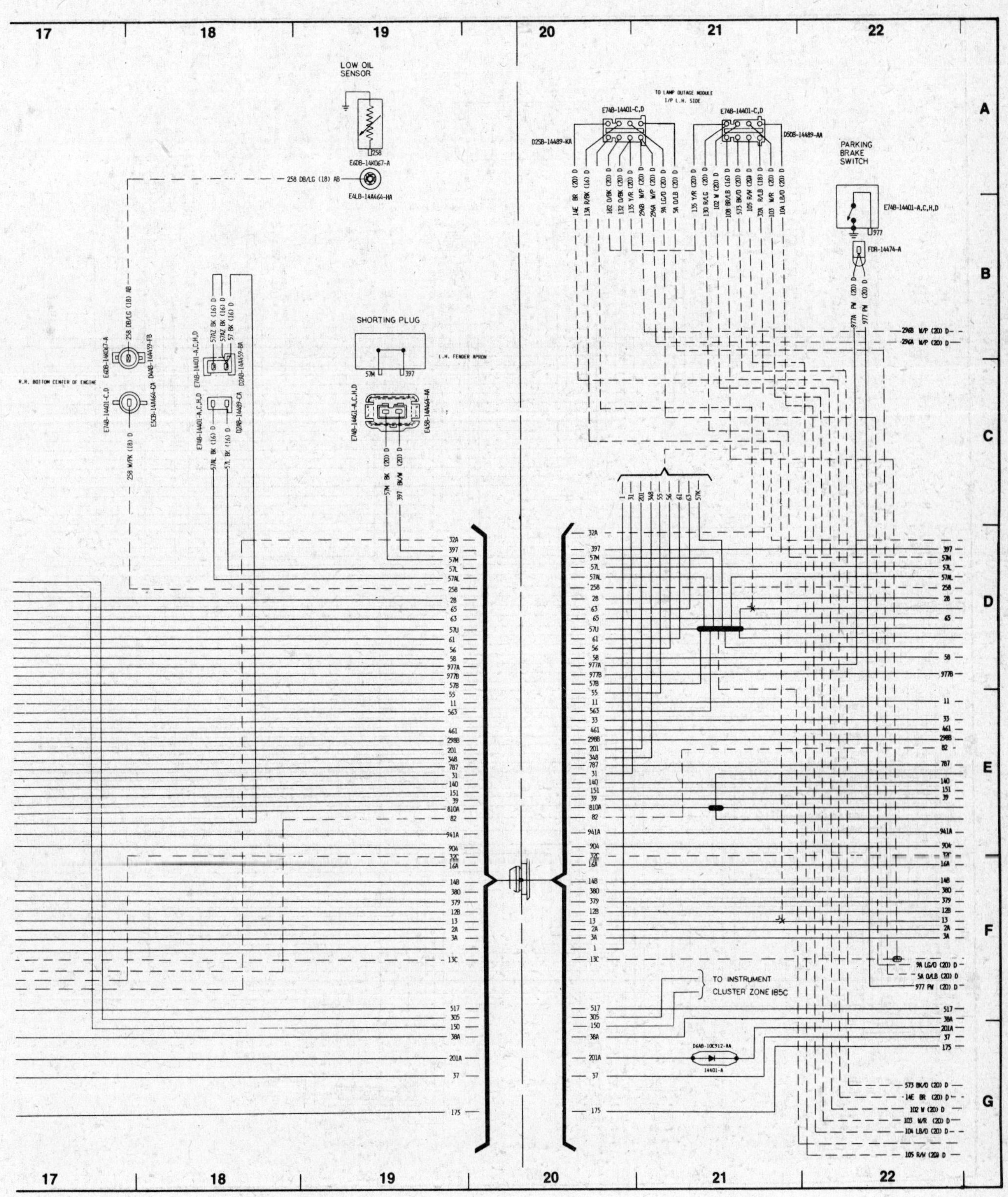

Taurus and Sable electrical schematics — 1986–87

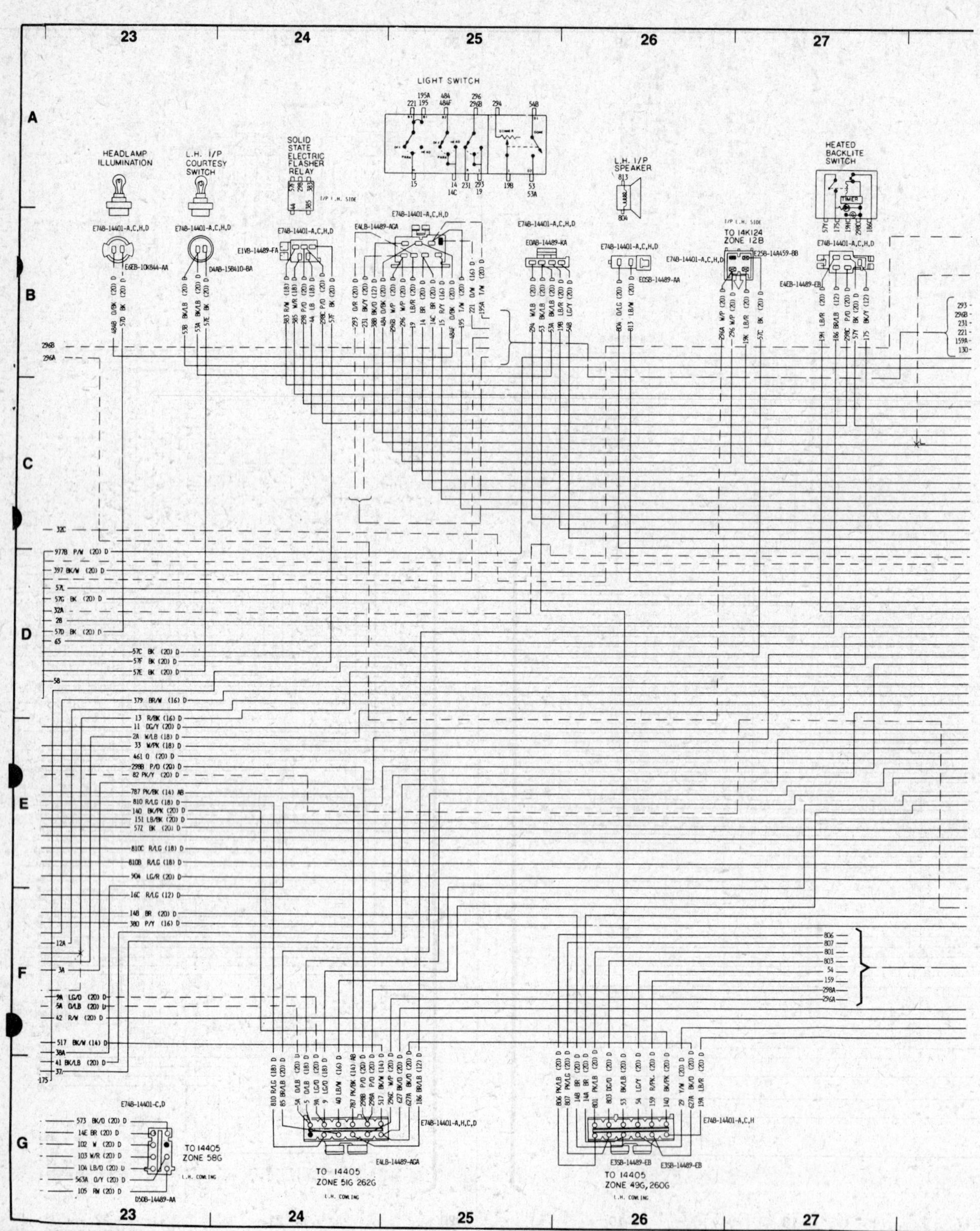

Taurus and Sable electrical schematics – 1986–87

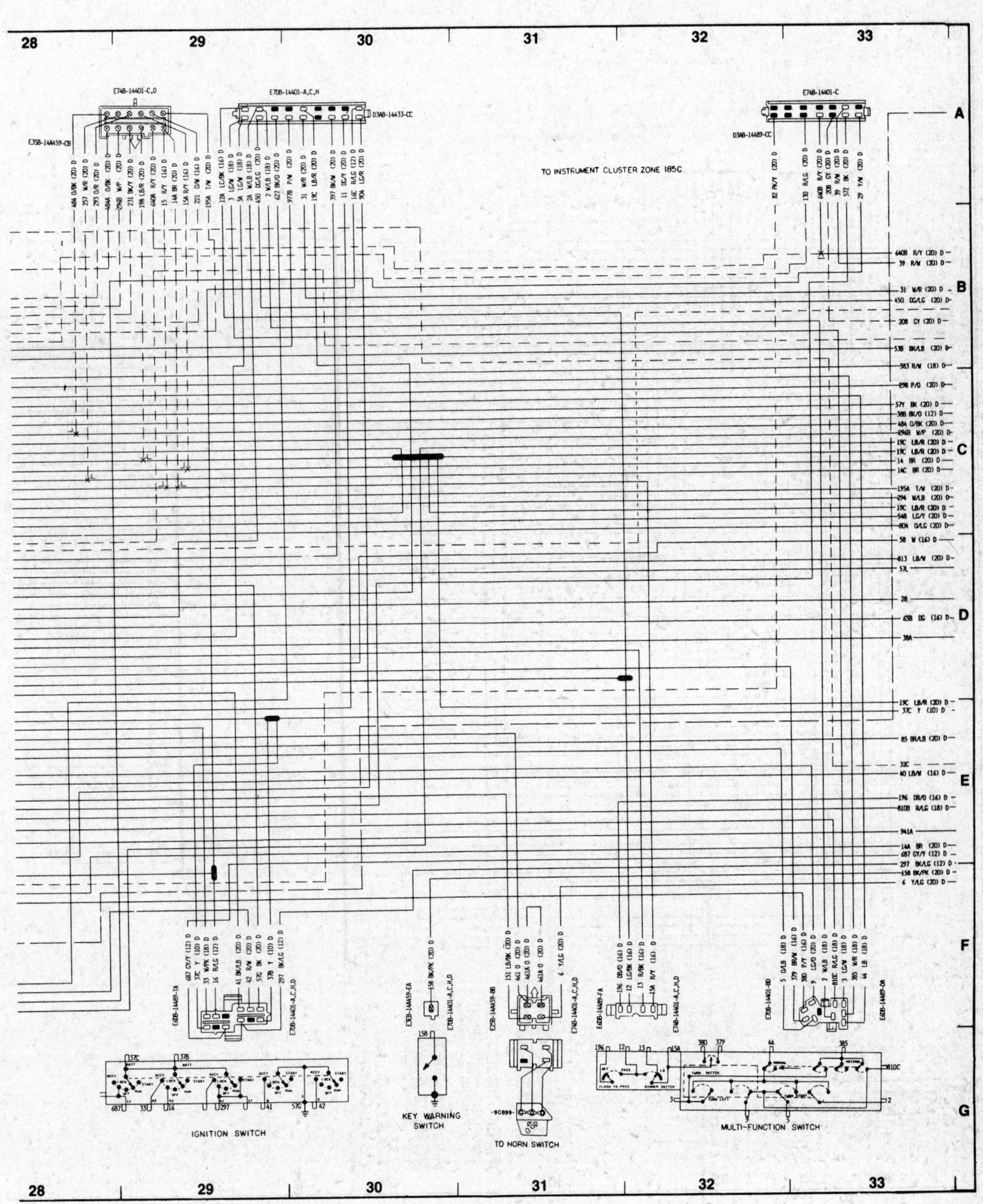

Taurus and Sable electrical schematics – 1986–87

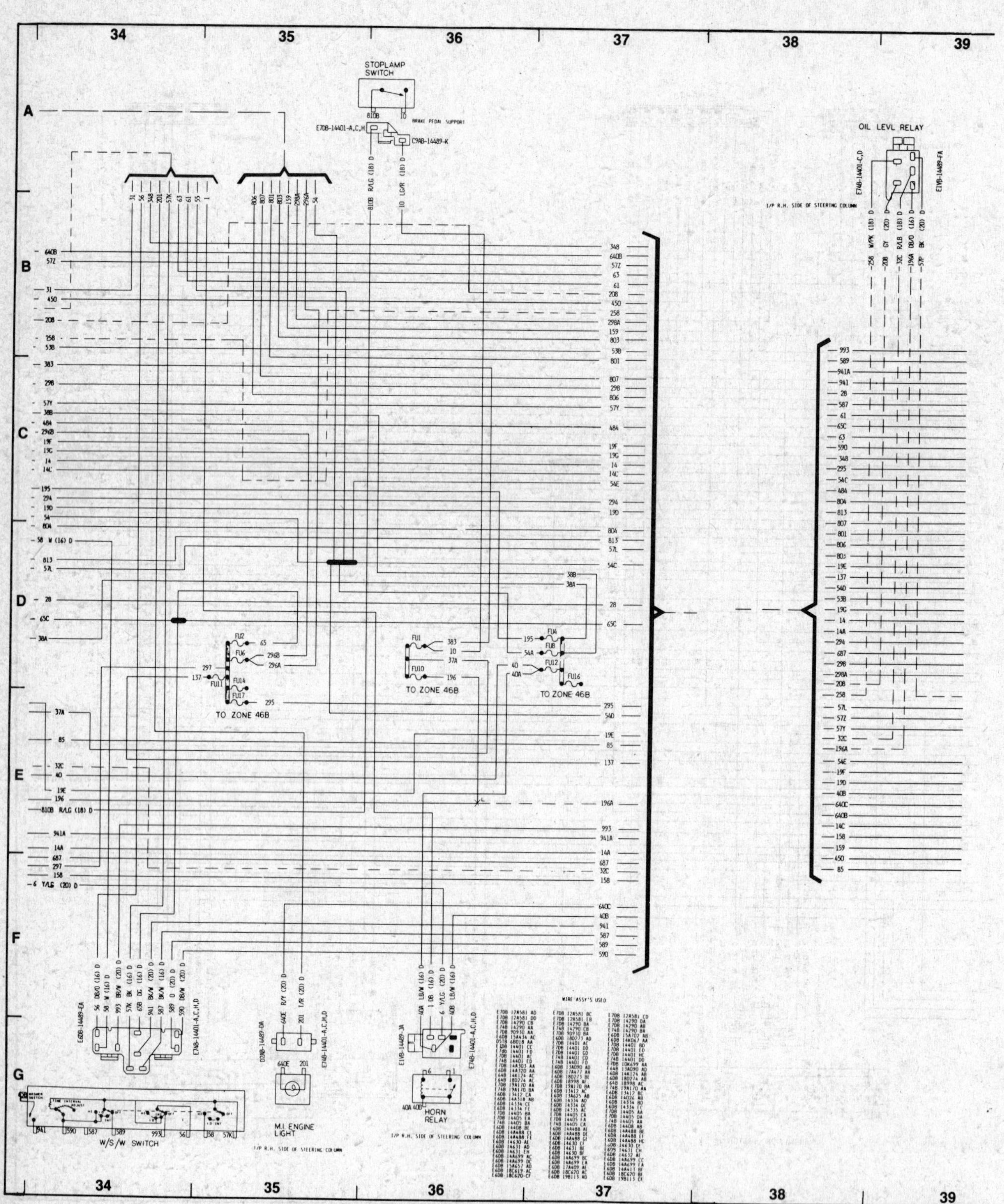

Taurus and Sable electrical schematics — 1986–87

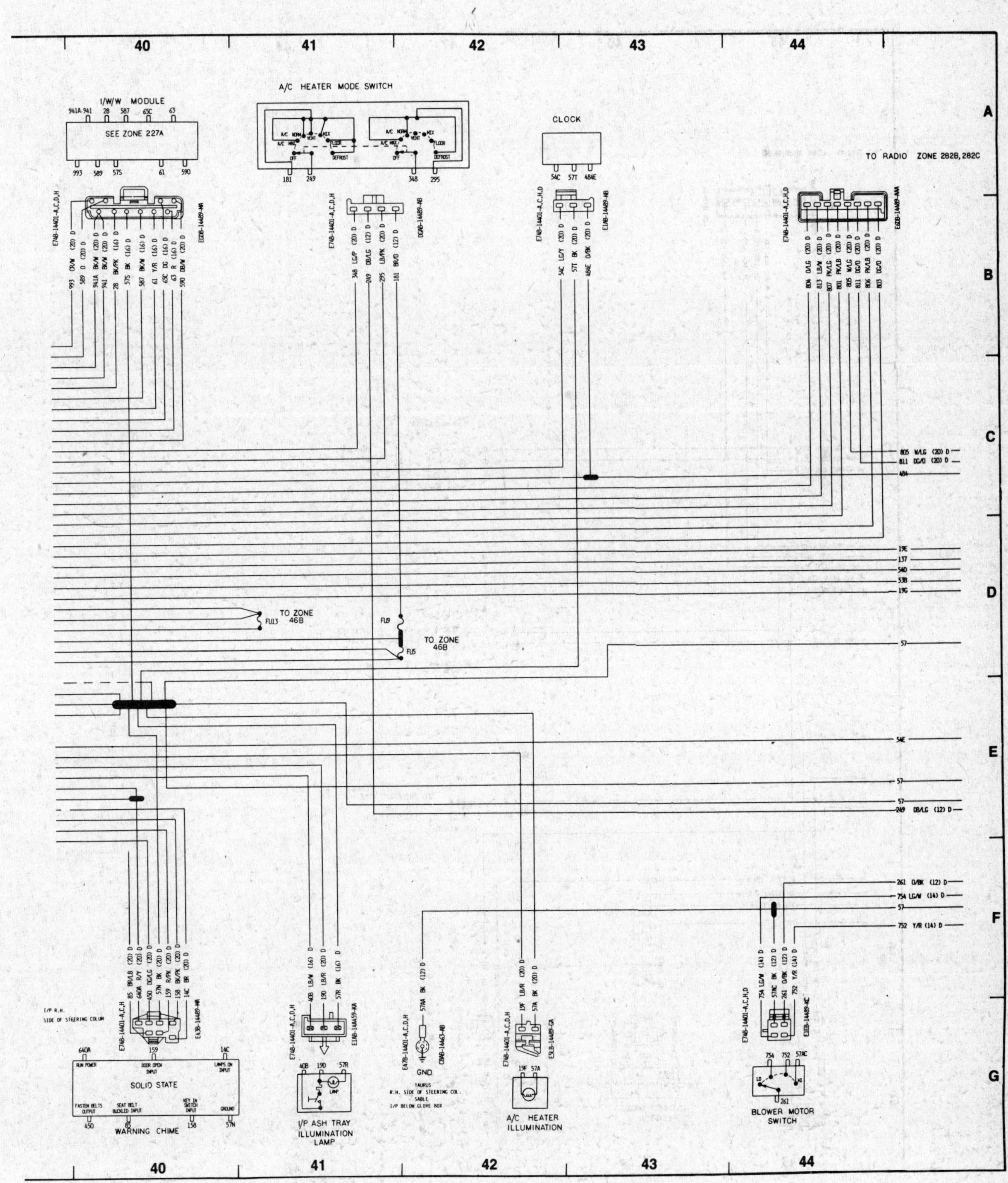

Taurus and Sable electrical schematics — 1986–87

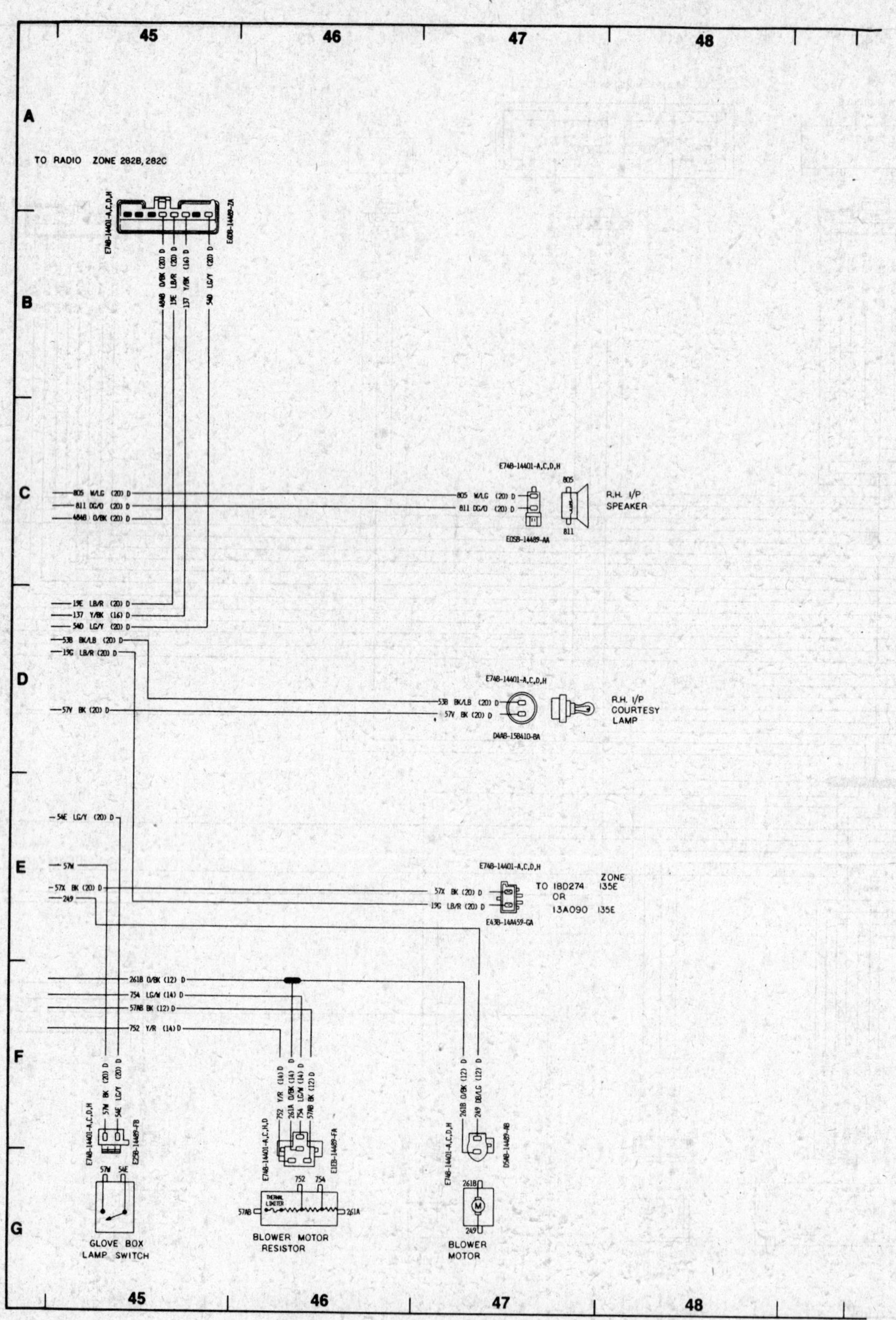

Taurus and Sable electrical schematics – 1986–87

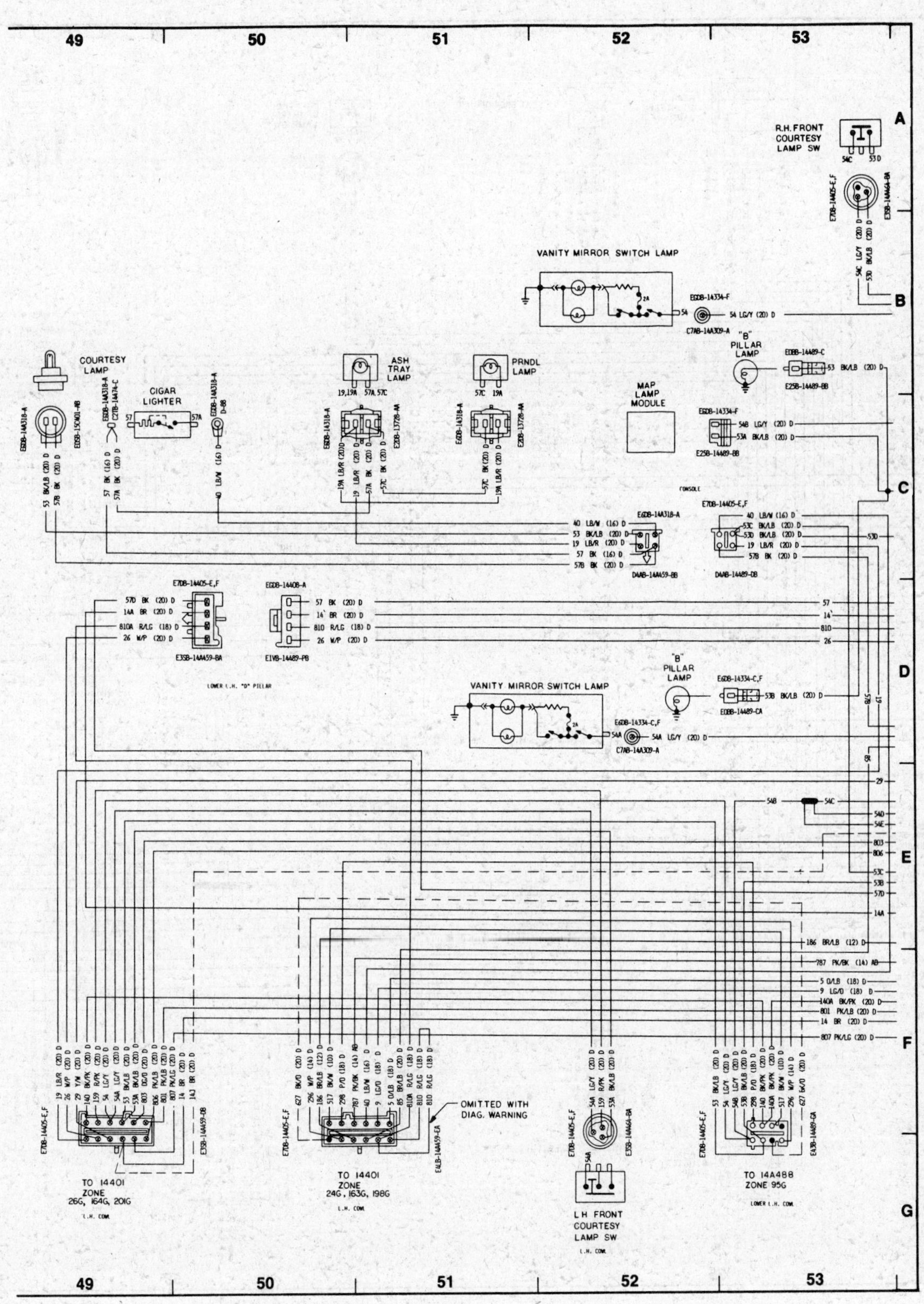

Taurus and Sable electrical schematics — 1986–87

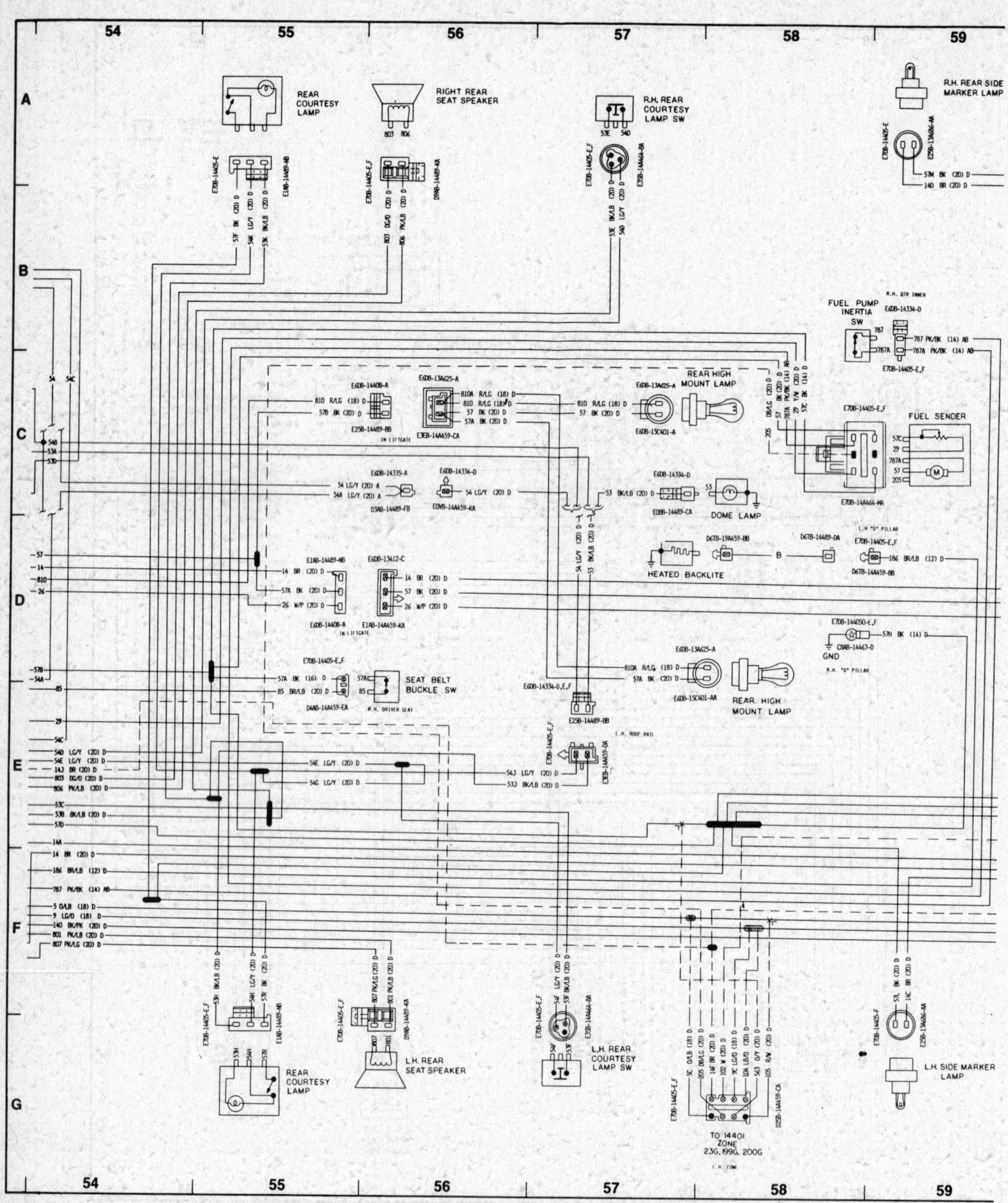

Taurus and Sable electrical schematics – 1986–87

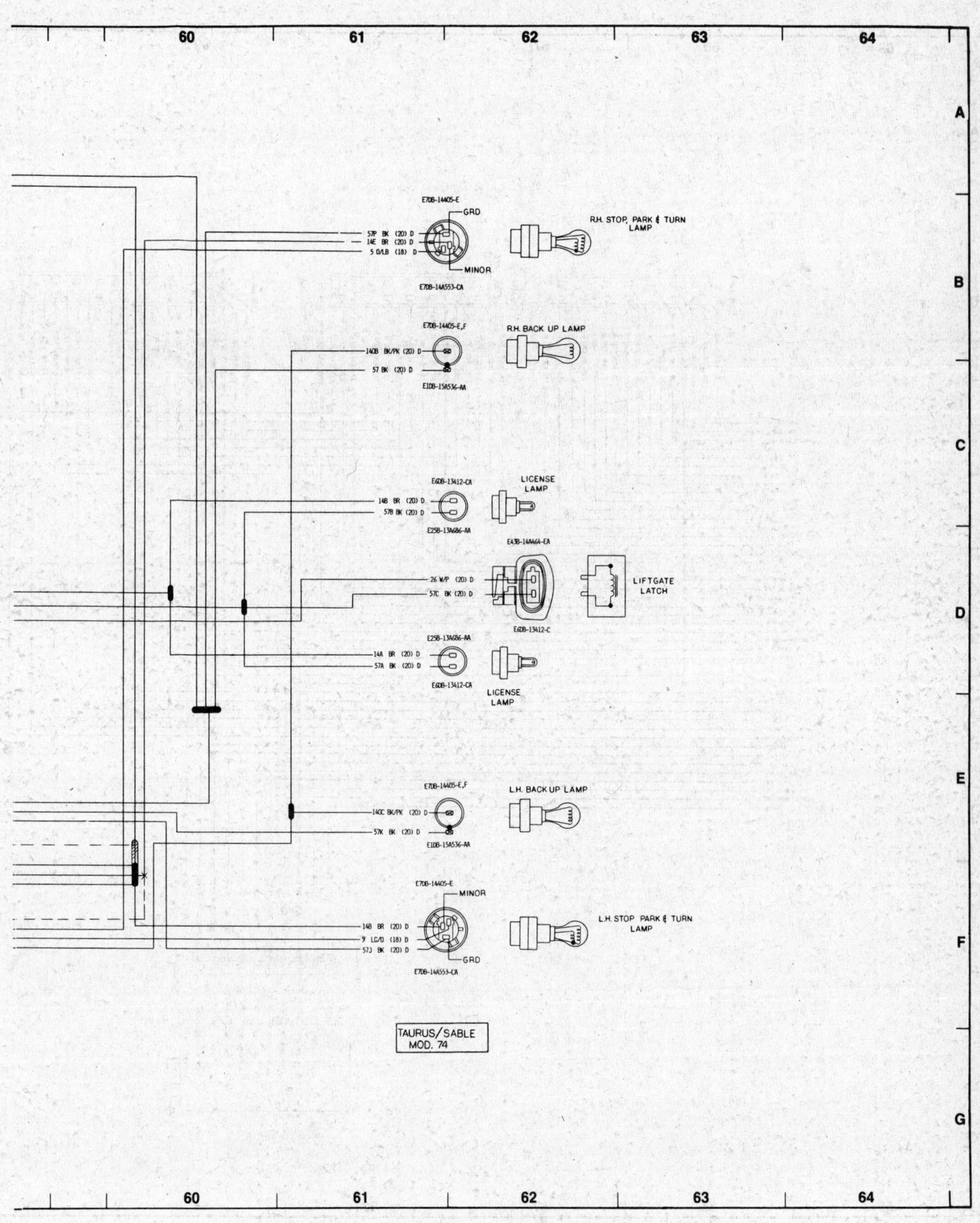

Taurus and Sable electrical schematics — 1986–87

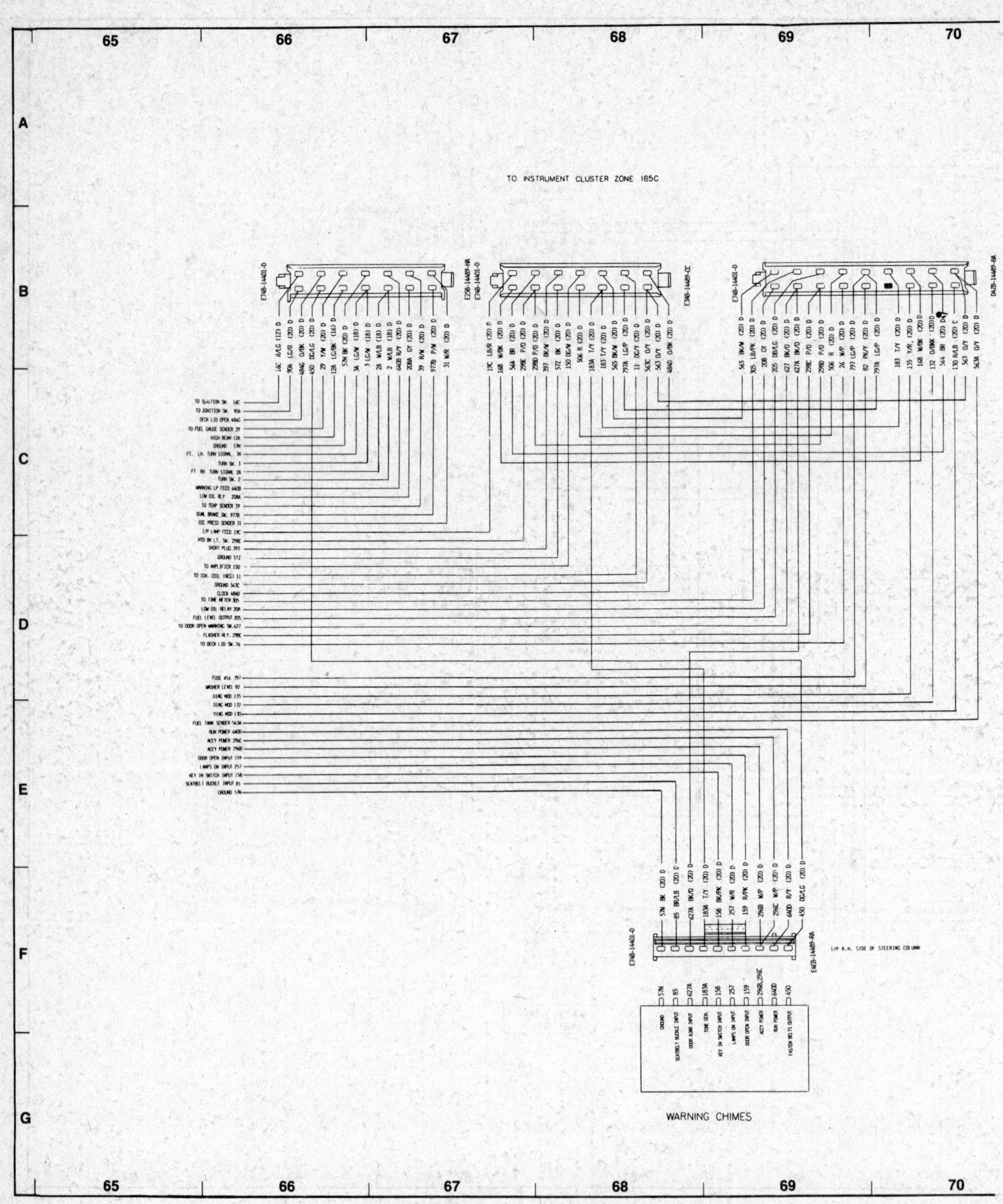

Taurus and Sable electrical schematics — 1986–87

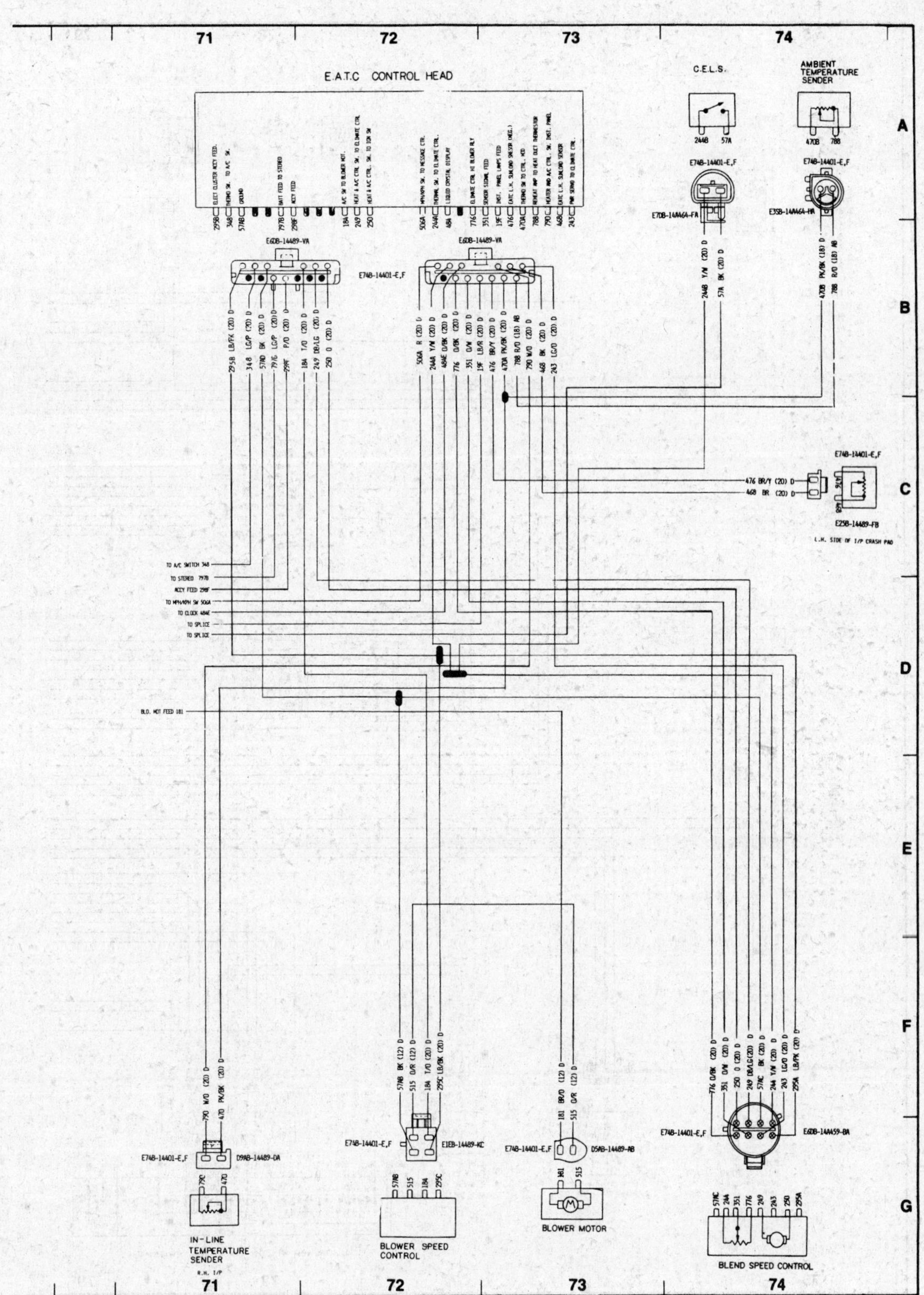

Taurus and Sable electrical schematics – 1986–87

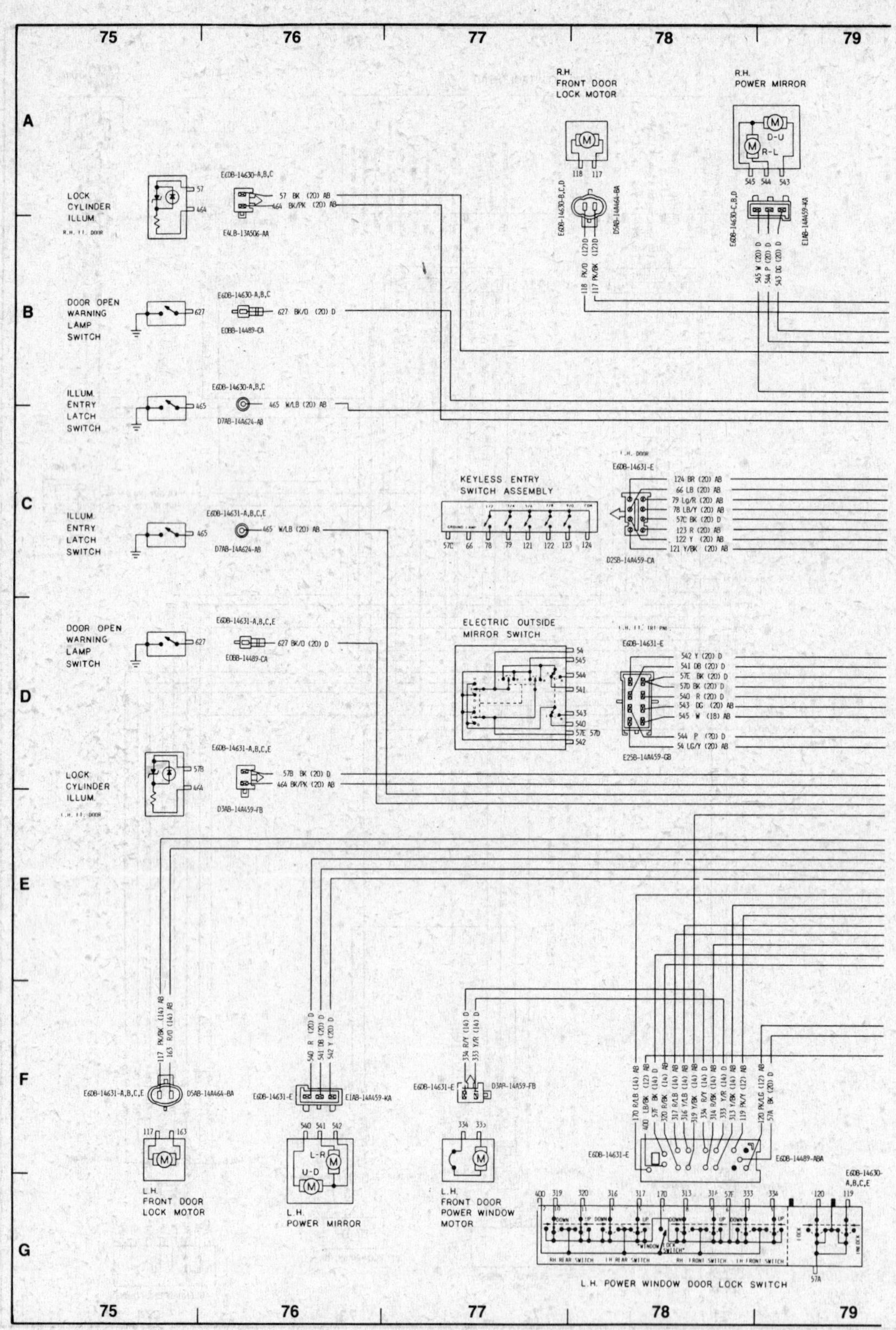

Taurus and Sable electrical schematics – 1986–87

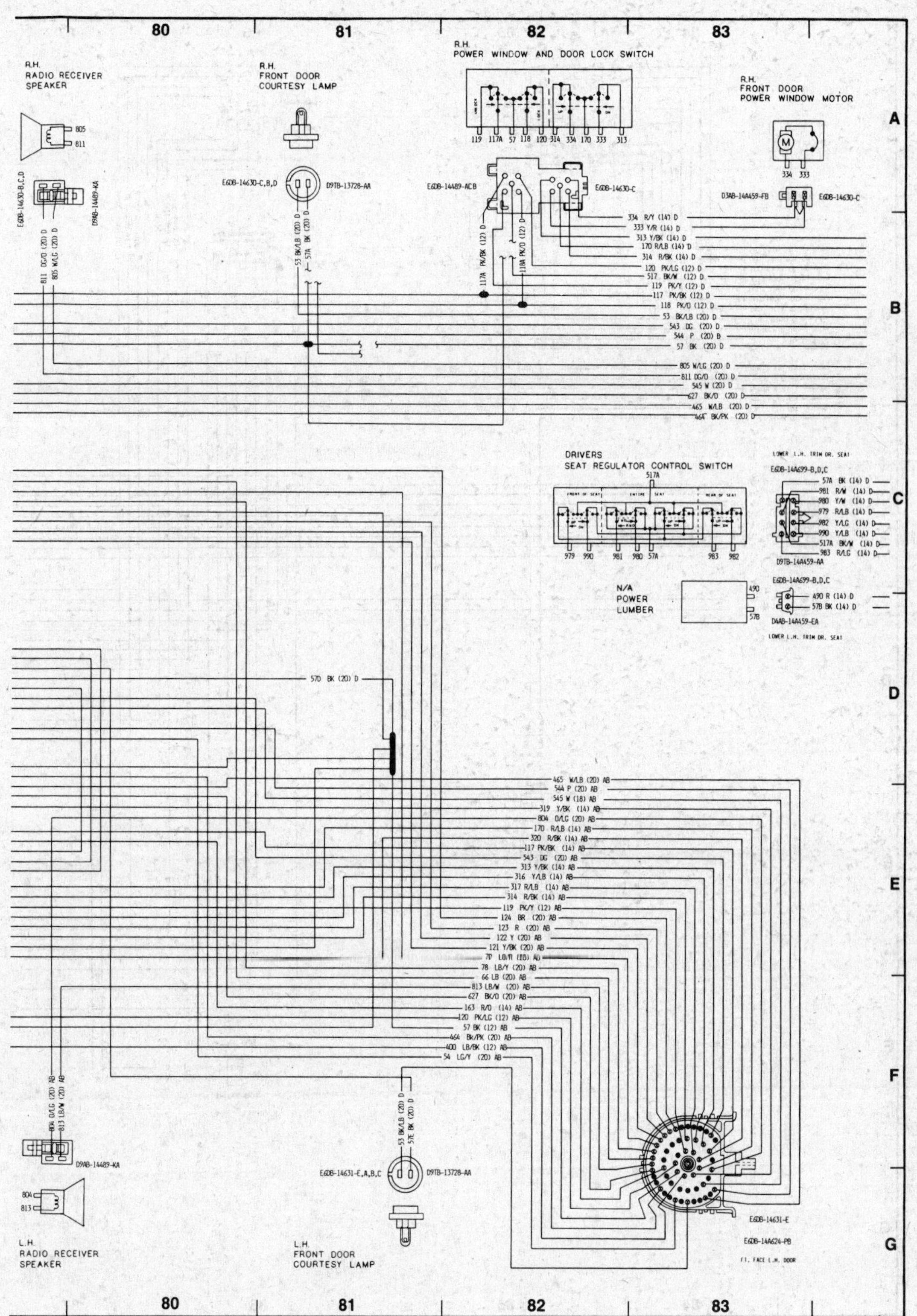

Taurus and Sable electrical schematics — 1986-87

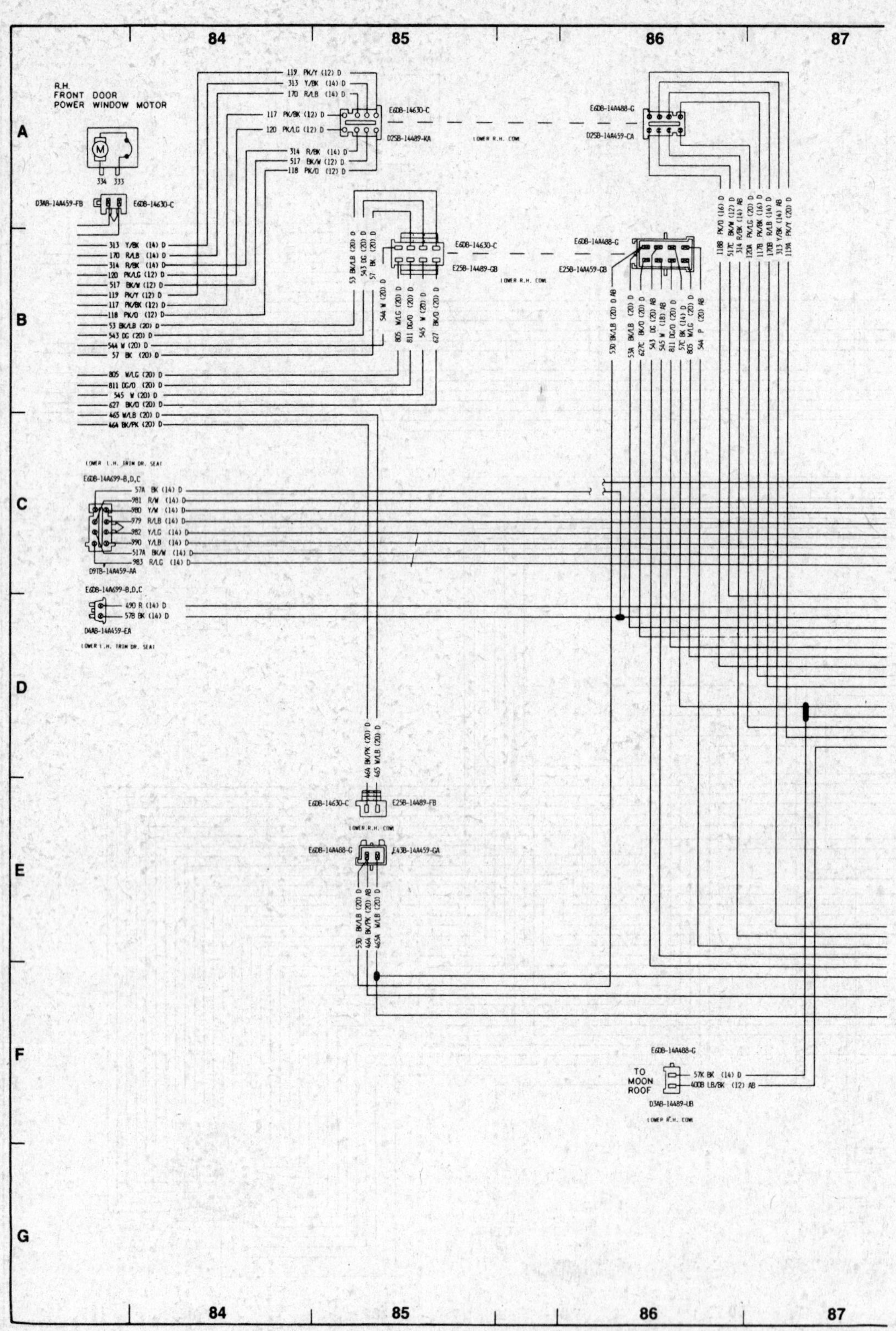

Taurus and Sable electrical schematics – 1986–87

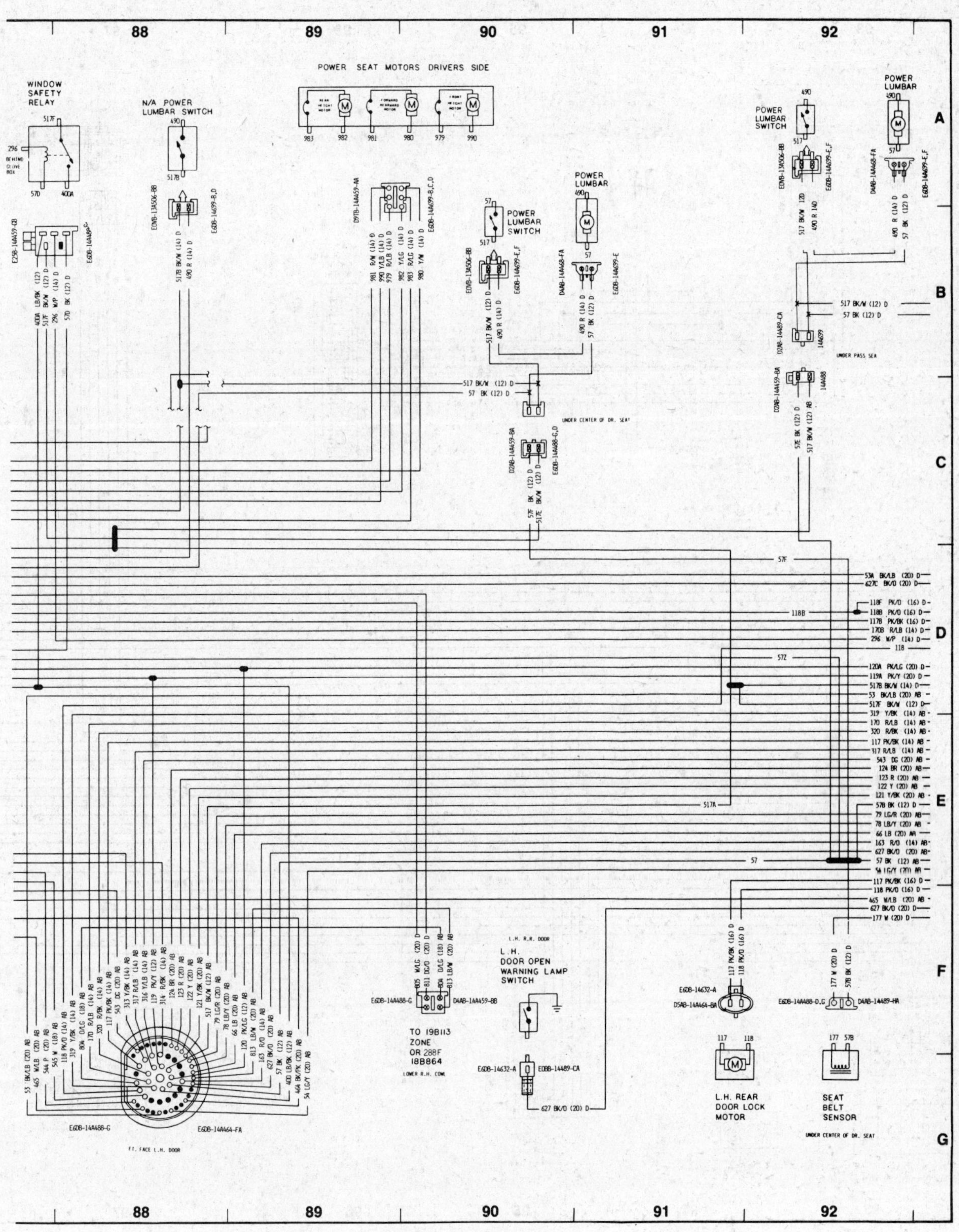

Taurus and Sable electrical schematics – 1986–87

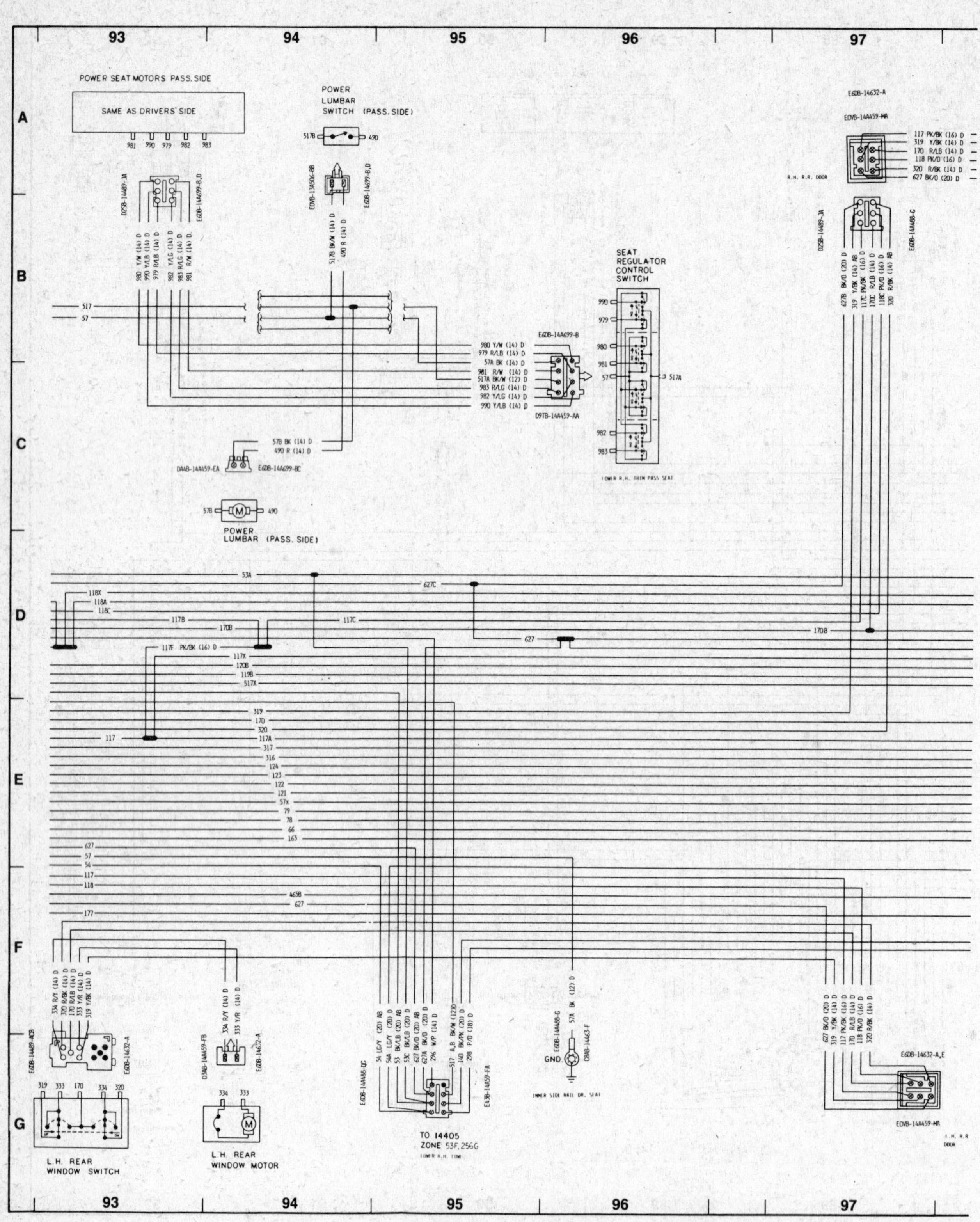

Taurus and Sable electrical schematics – 1986–87

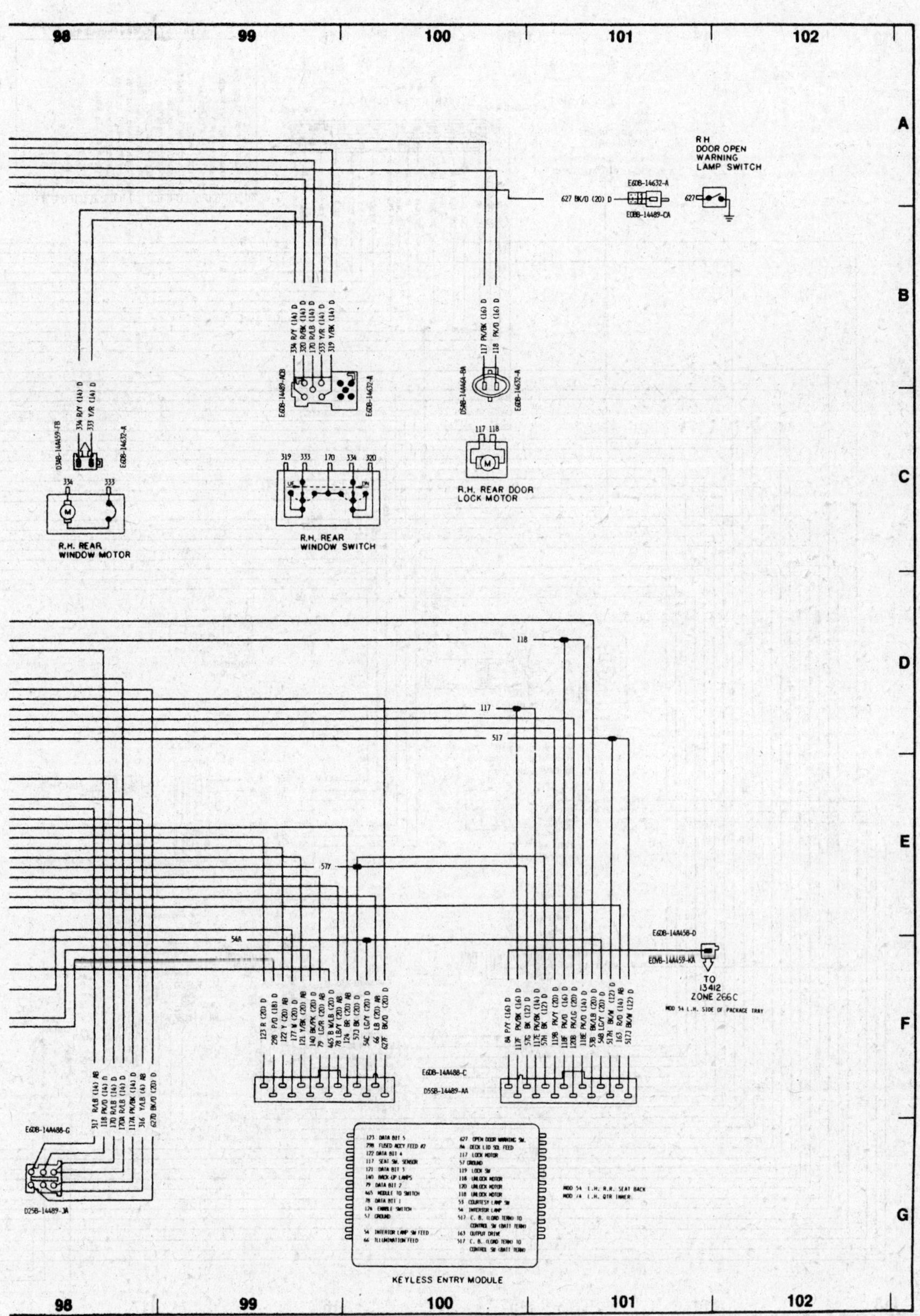

Taurus and Sable electrical schematics — 1986–87

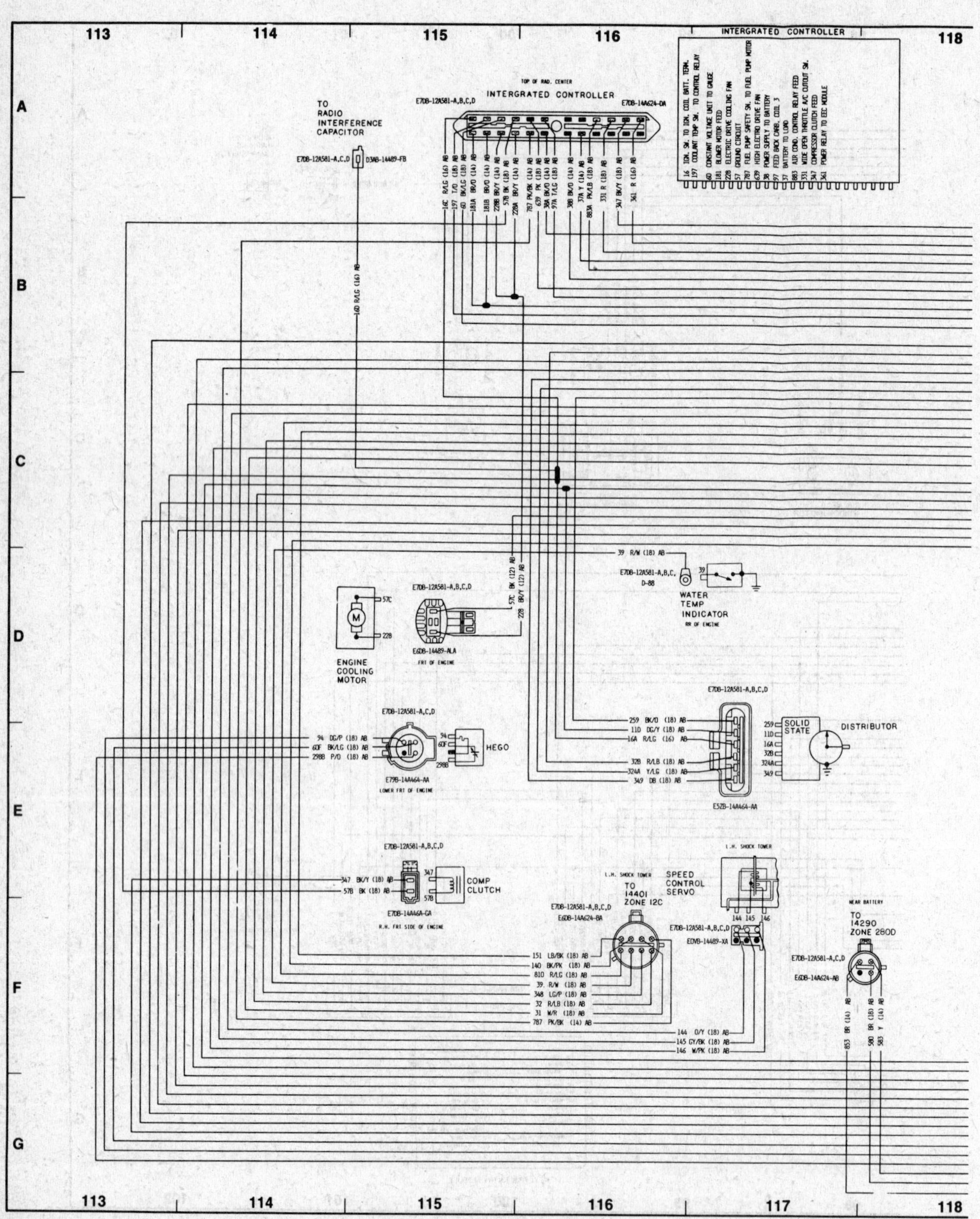

Taurus and Sable electrical schematics — 1986–87

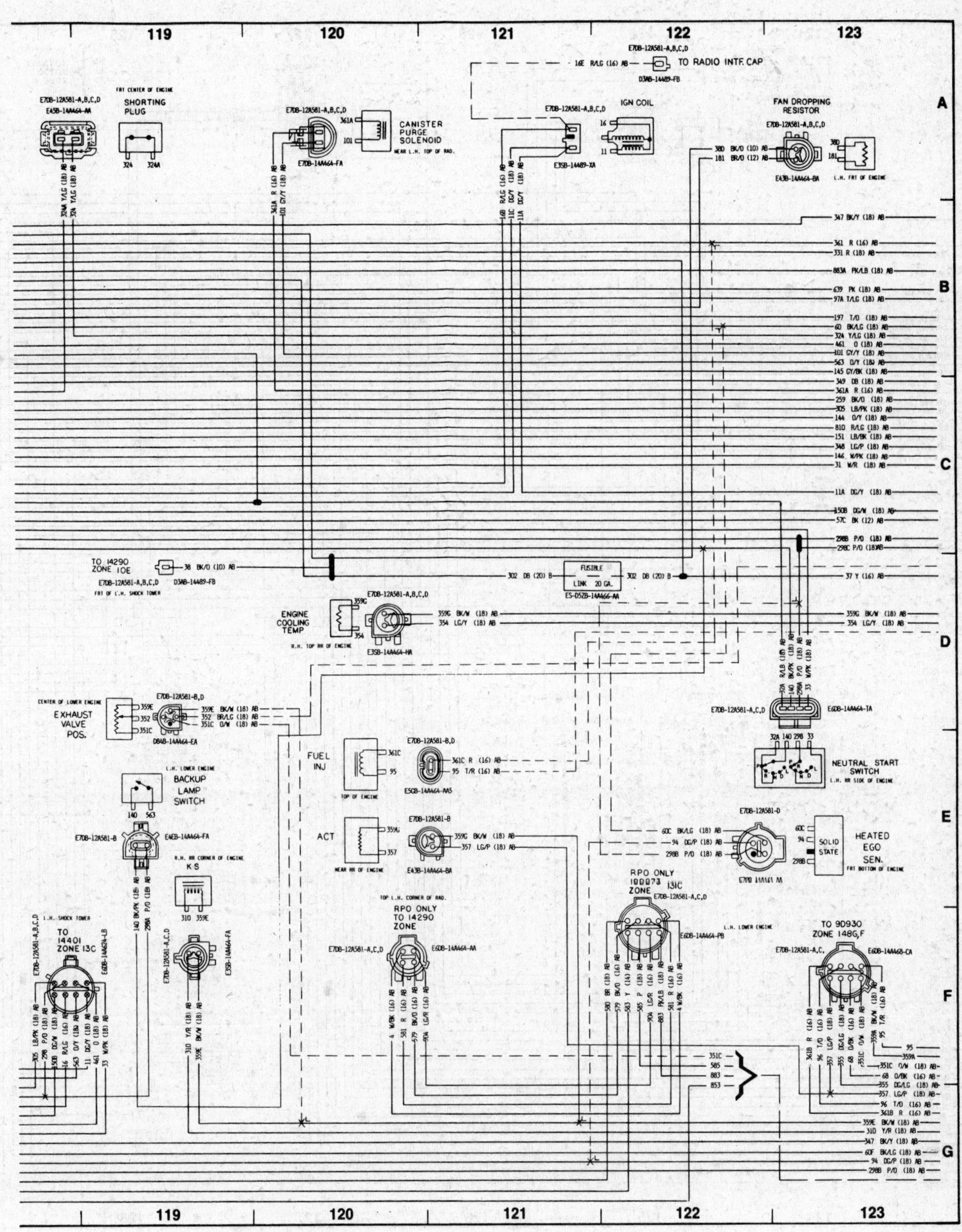

Taurus and Sable electrical schematics — 1986–87

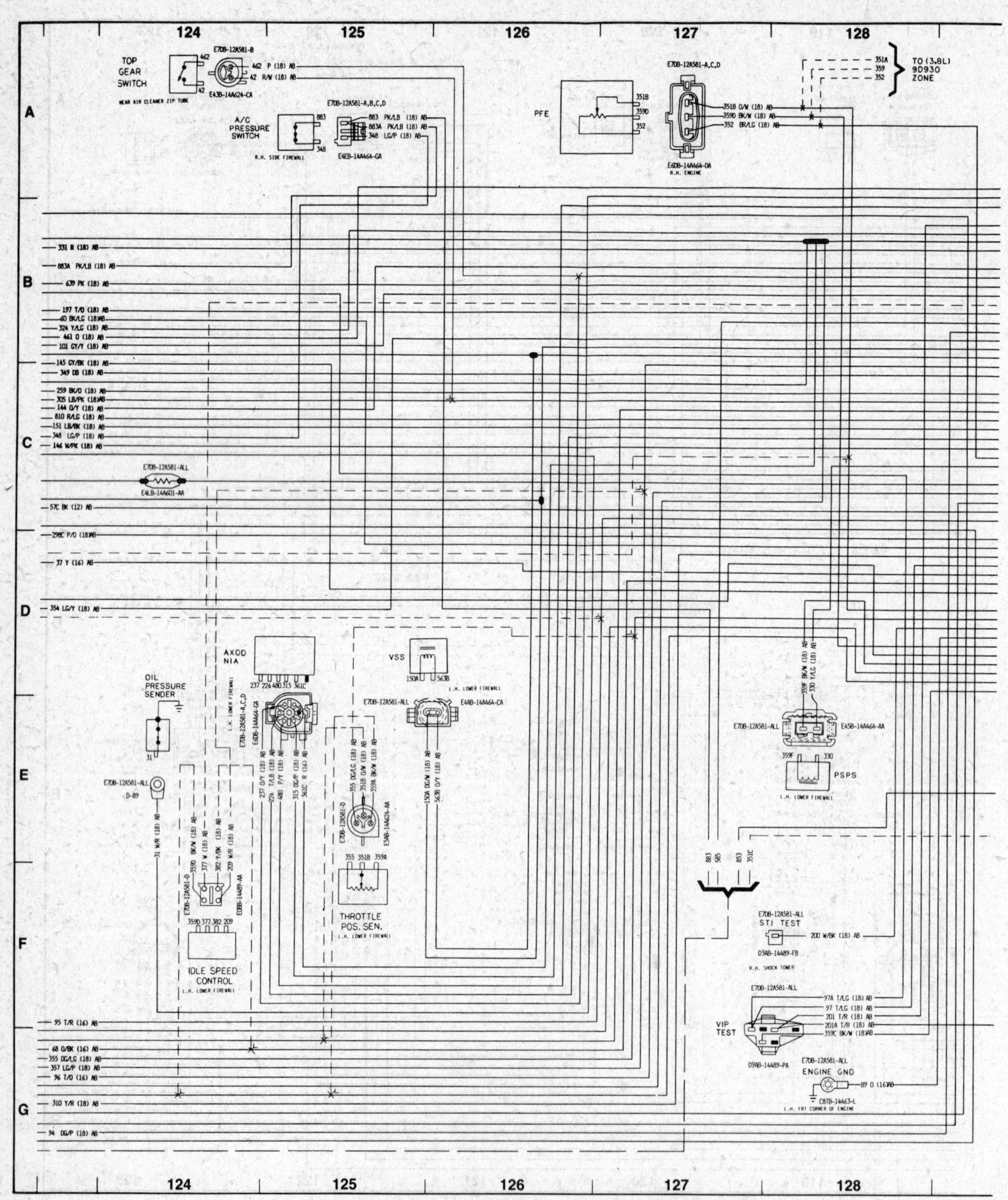

Taurus and Sable electrical schematics — 1986–87

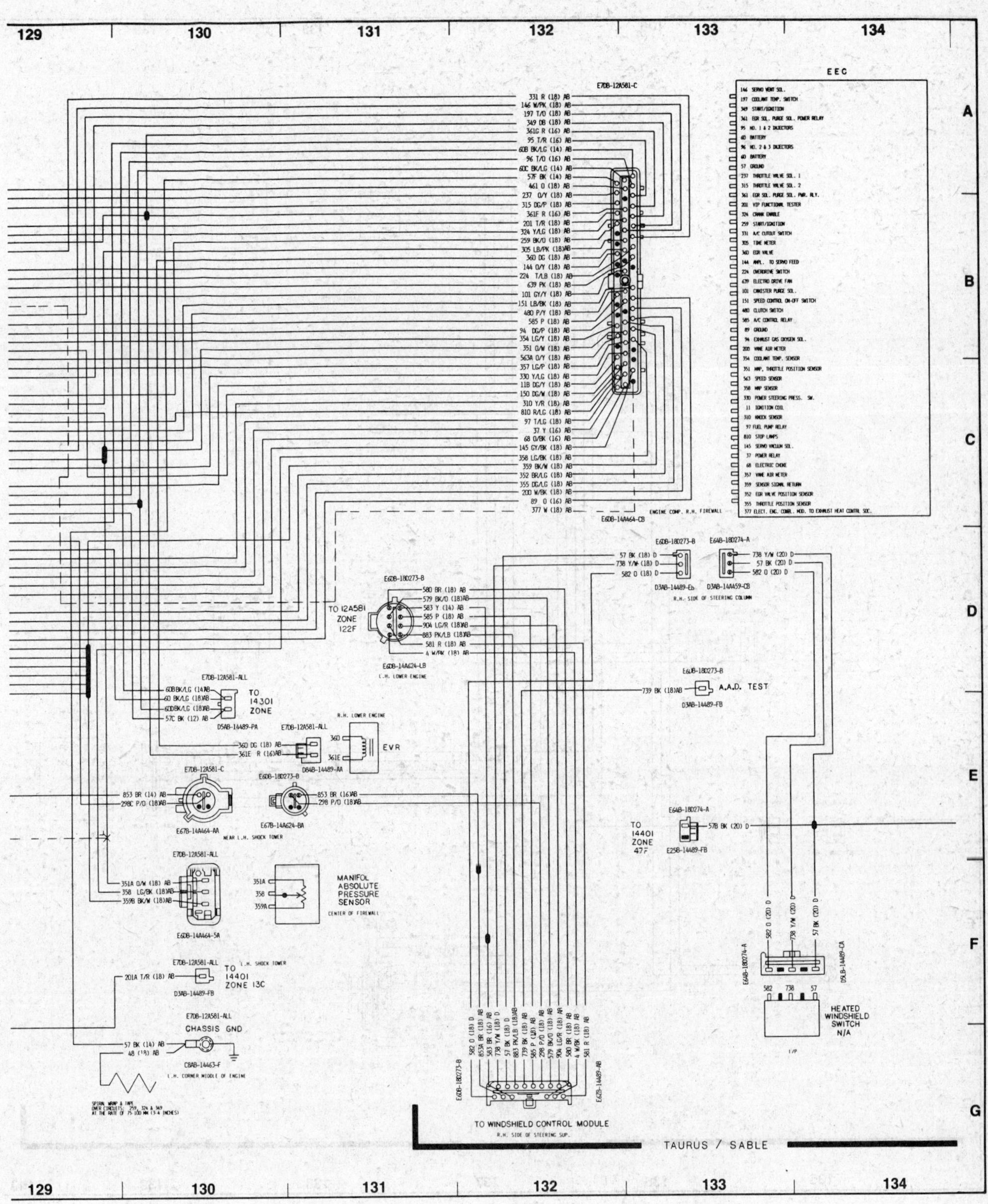

Taurus and Sable electrical schematics — 1986–87

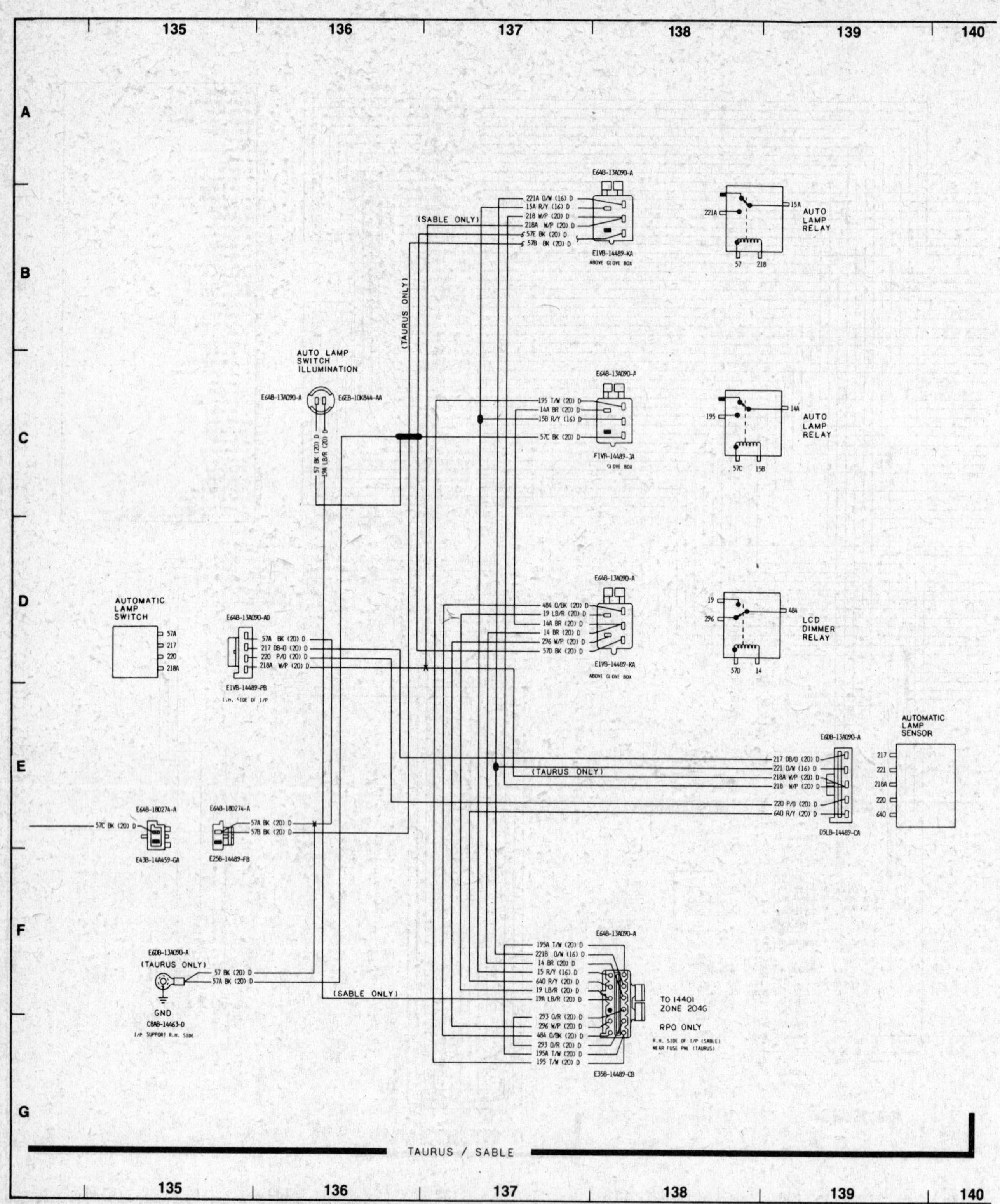

Taurus and Sable electrical schematics – 1986–87

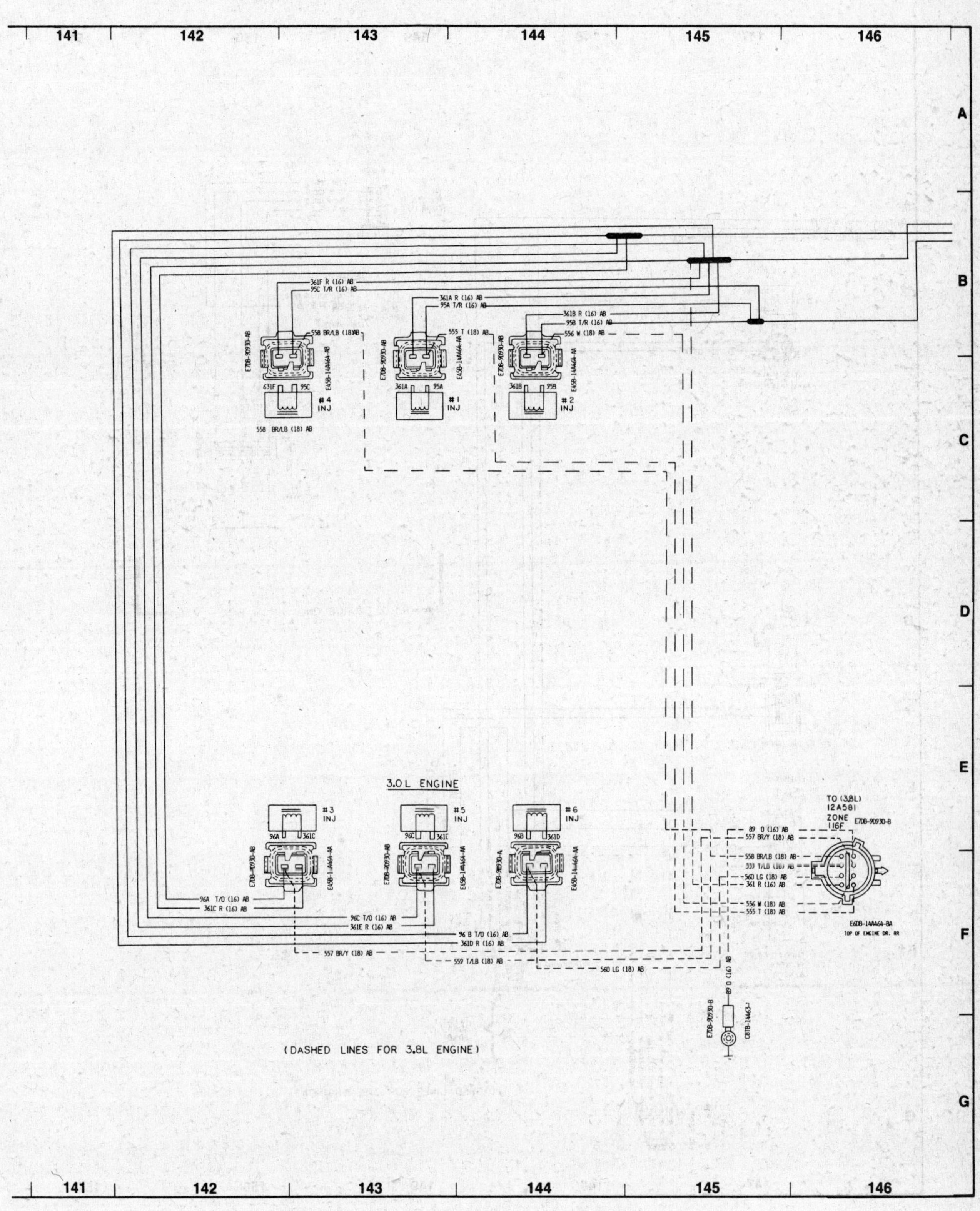

Taurus and Sable electrical schematics – 1986–87

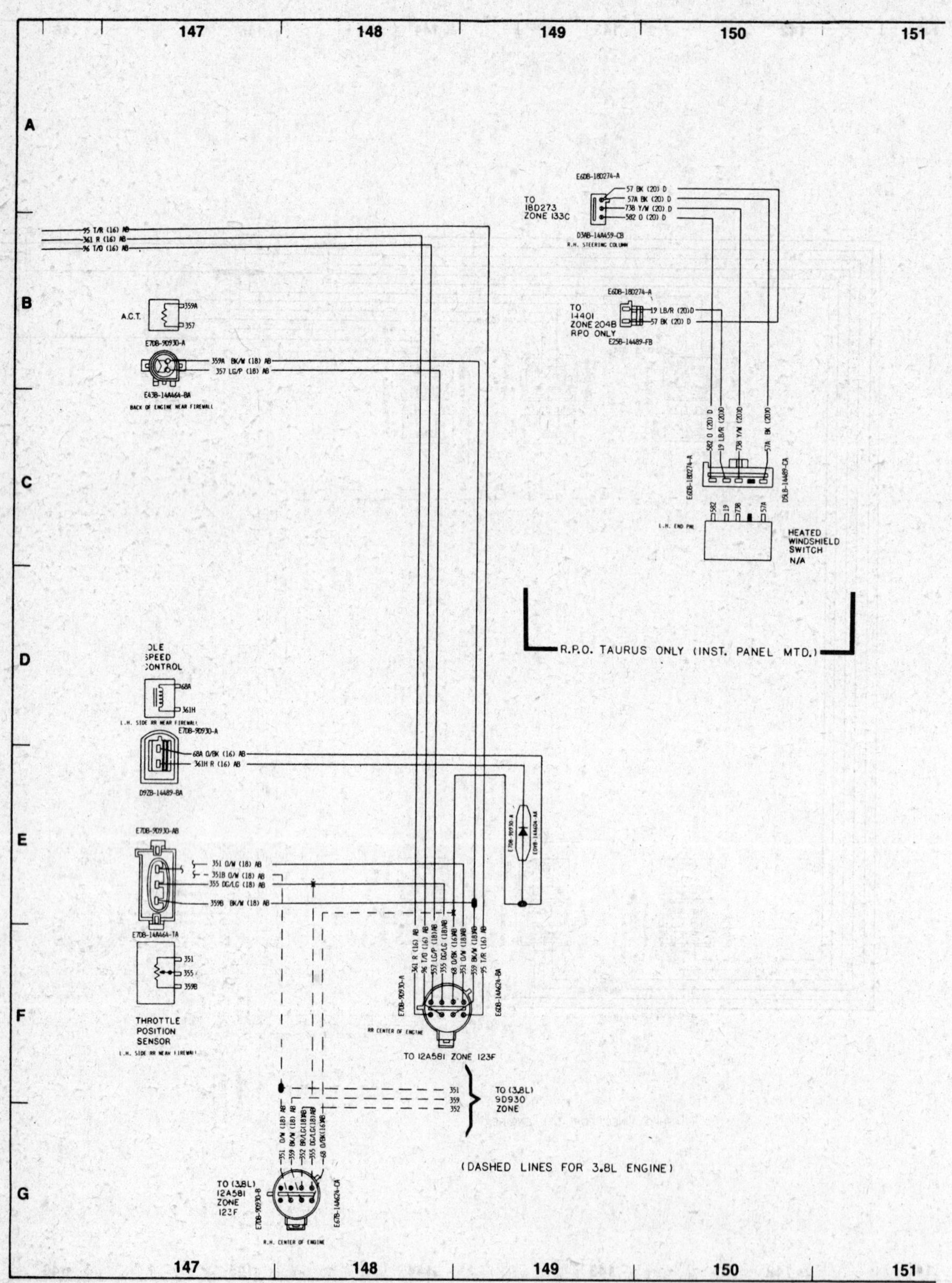

147
148
149
150
151
A
B
C
D
E
F
G
95 T/R (16) AB
361 R (16) AB
96 T/O (16) AB
TO
18D273
ZONE 133C
A.C.T.
359A
357
359A BK/W (18) AB
357 LG/P (18) AB
TO
14401
ZONE 204B
RPO ONLY
19 LB/R (20) D
57 BK (20) D
HEATED
WINDSHIELD
SWITCH
N/A
R.P.O. TAURUS ONLY (INST. PANEL MTD.)
68A O/BK (16) AB
361H R (16) AB
351 O/W (18) AB
351B O/W (18) AB
355 DG/LG (18) AB
359B BK/W (18) AB
THROTTLE
POSITION
SENSOR
TO 12A581 ZONE 123F
351
359
352
TO (3.8L)
9D930
ZONE
(DASHED LINES FOR 3.8L ENGINE)
TO (3.8L)
12A581
ZONE
123F

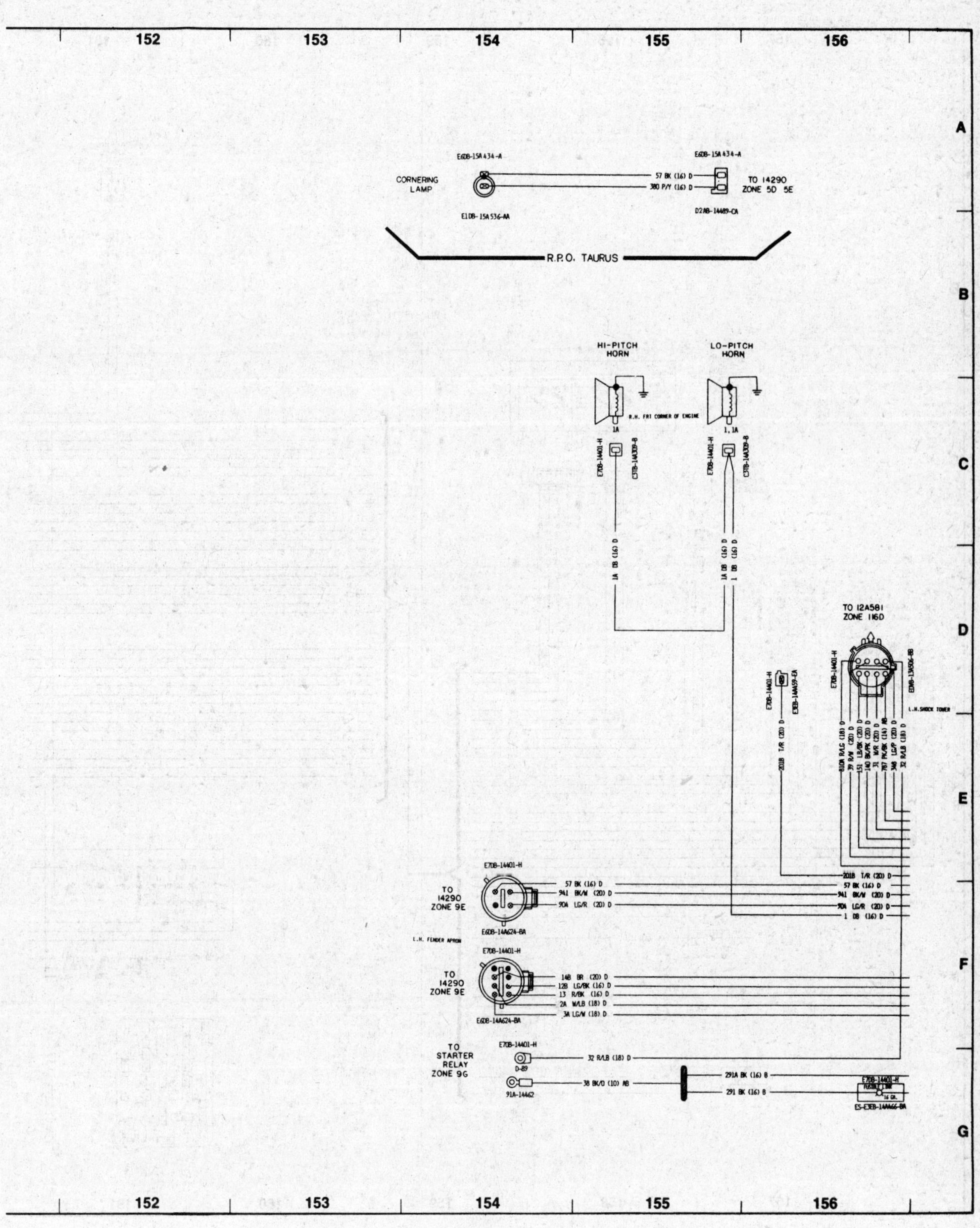
152
153
154
155
156
A
B
C
D
E
F
G
CORNERING LAMP
TO 14290 ZONE 5D 5E
R.P.O. TAURUS
HI-PITCH HORN
LO-PITCH HORN
TO 12A581 ZONE 11GD
TO 14290 ZONE 9E
TO 14290 ZONE 9E
TO STARTER RELAY ZONE 9G

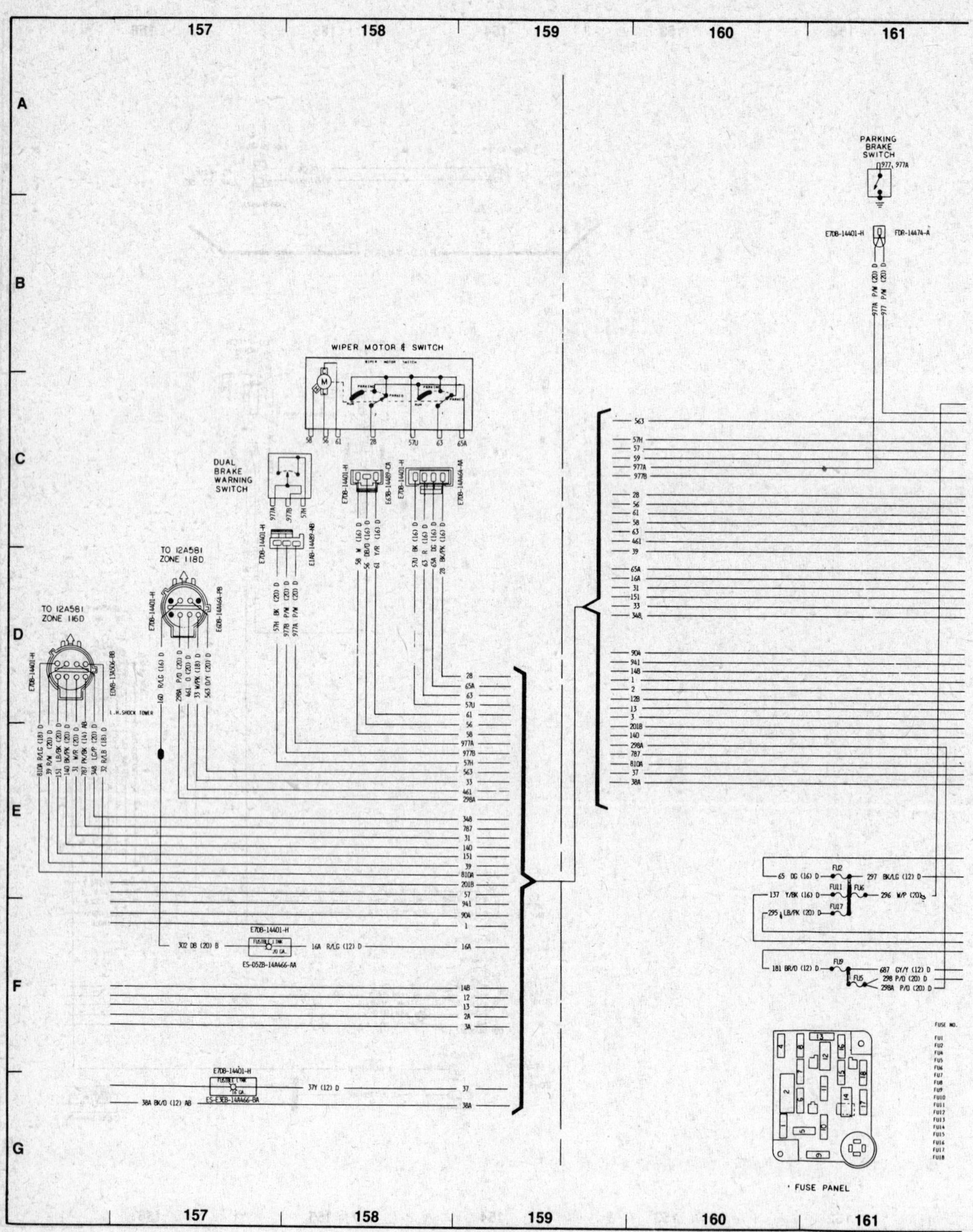

Taurus and Sable electrical schematics – 1986–87

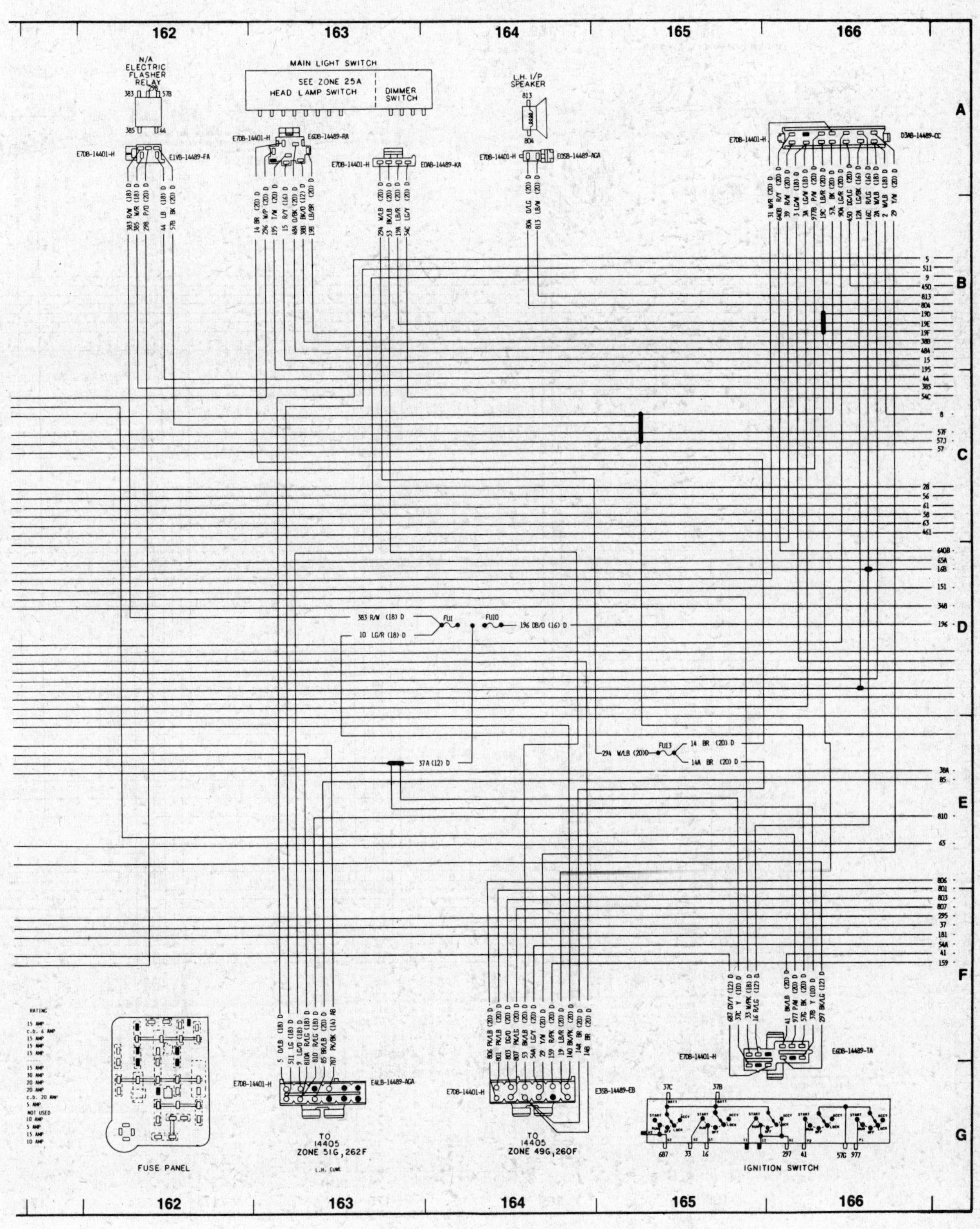

Taurus and Sable electrical schematics — 1986–87

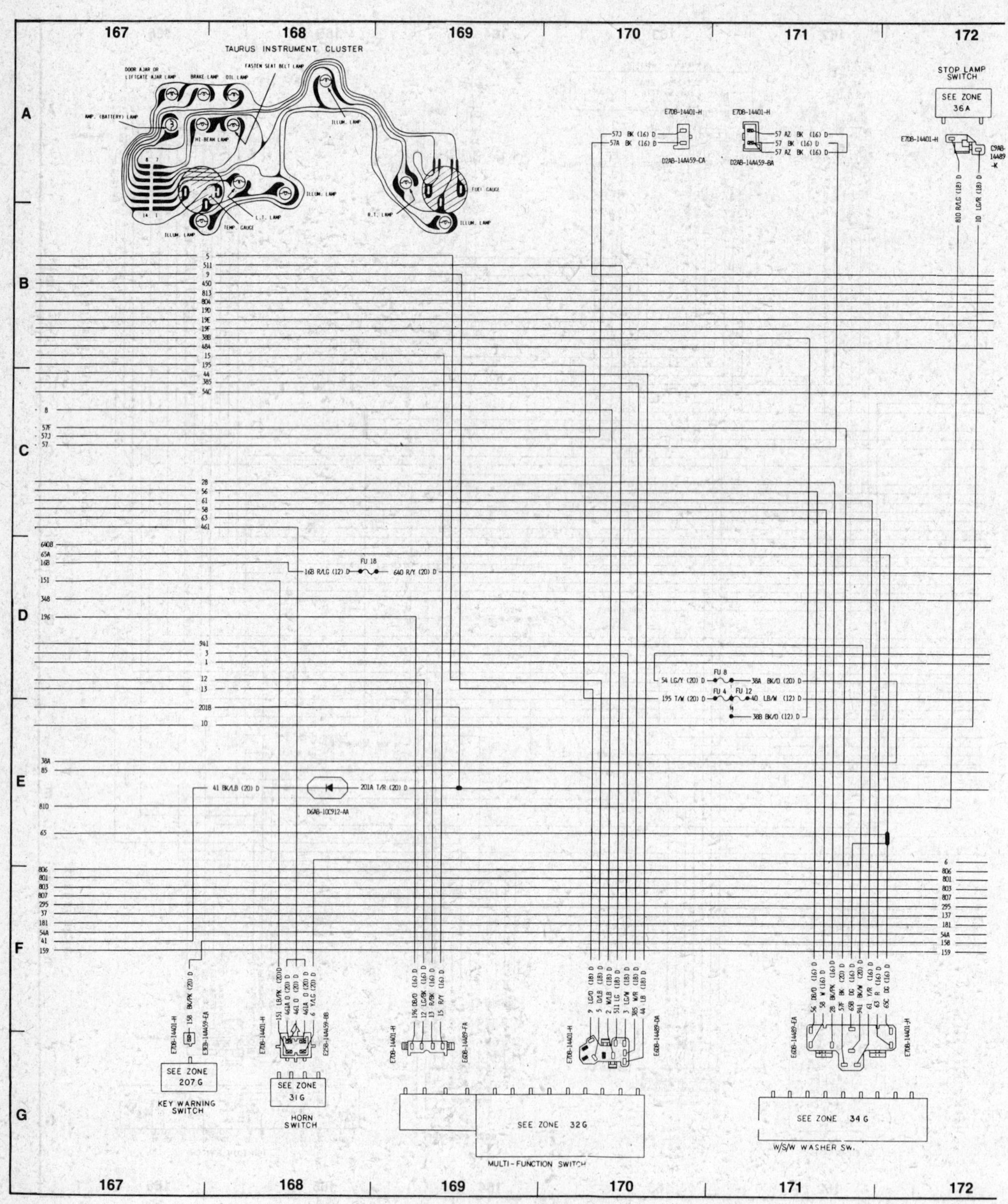

Taurus and Sable electrical schematics – 1986–87

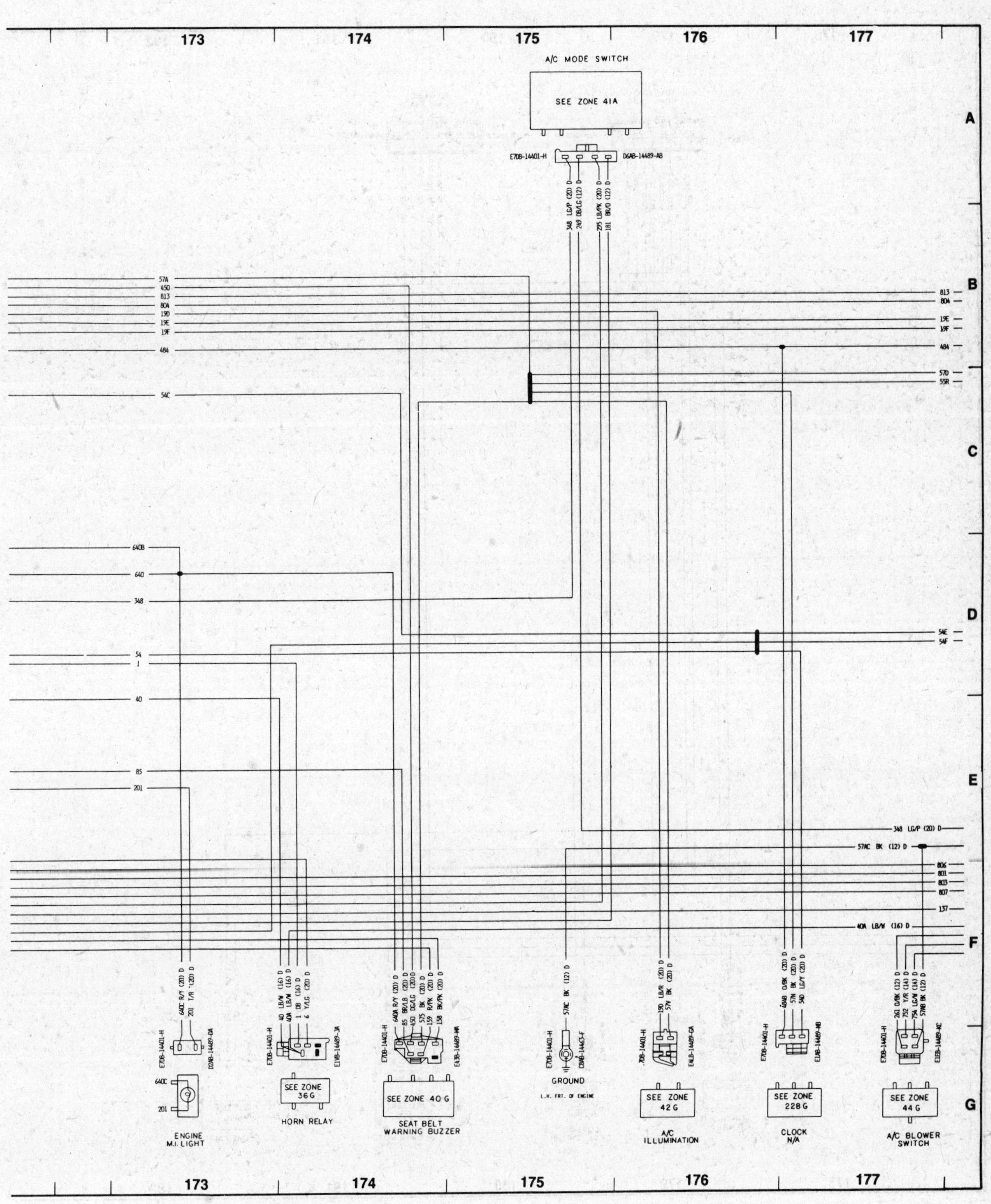

Taurus and Sable electrical schematics — 1986–87

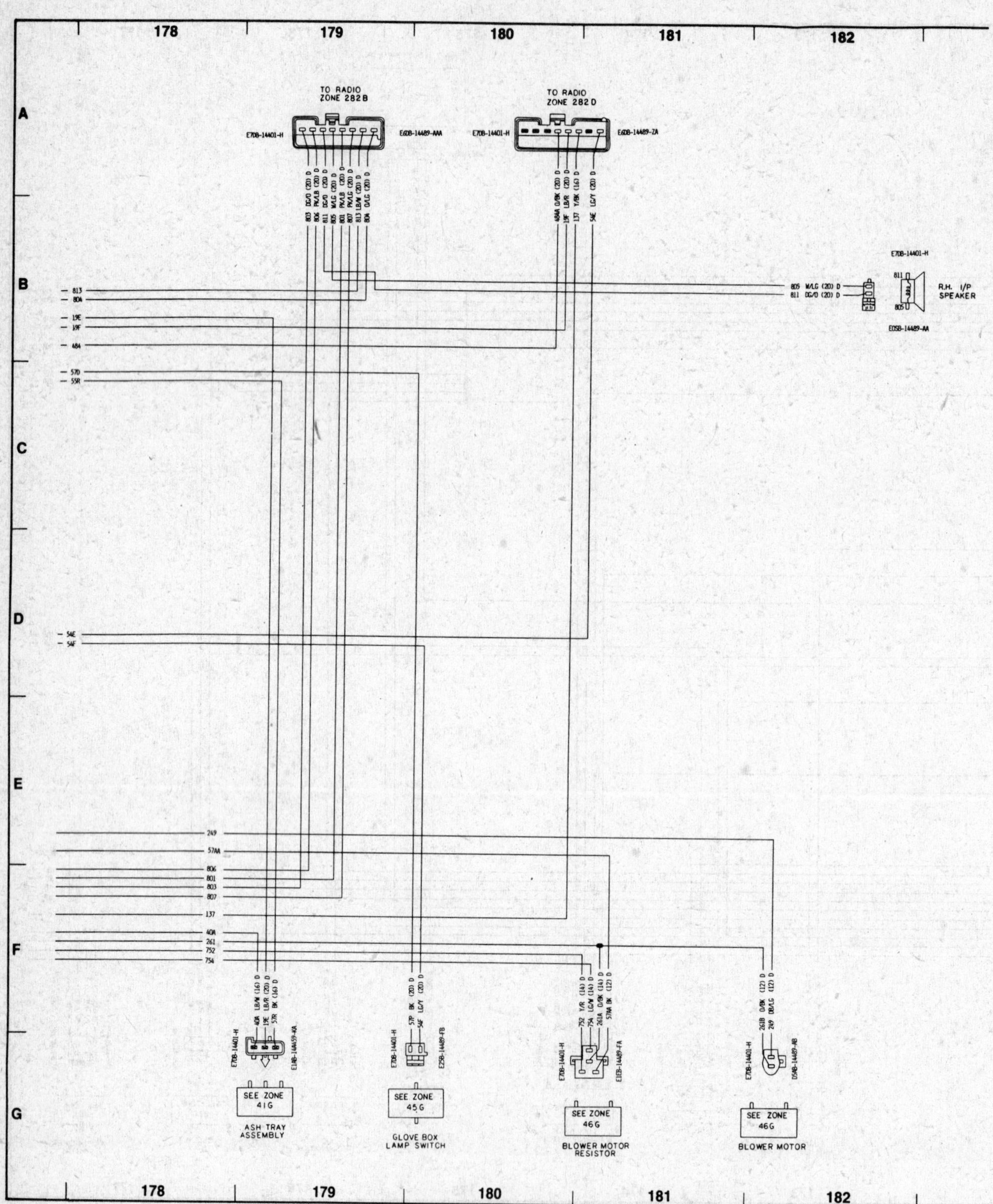

Taurus and Sable electrical schematics – 1986–87

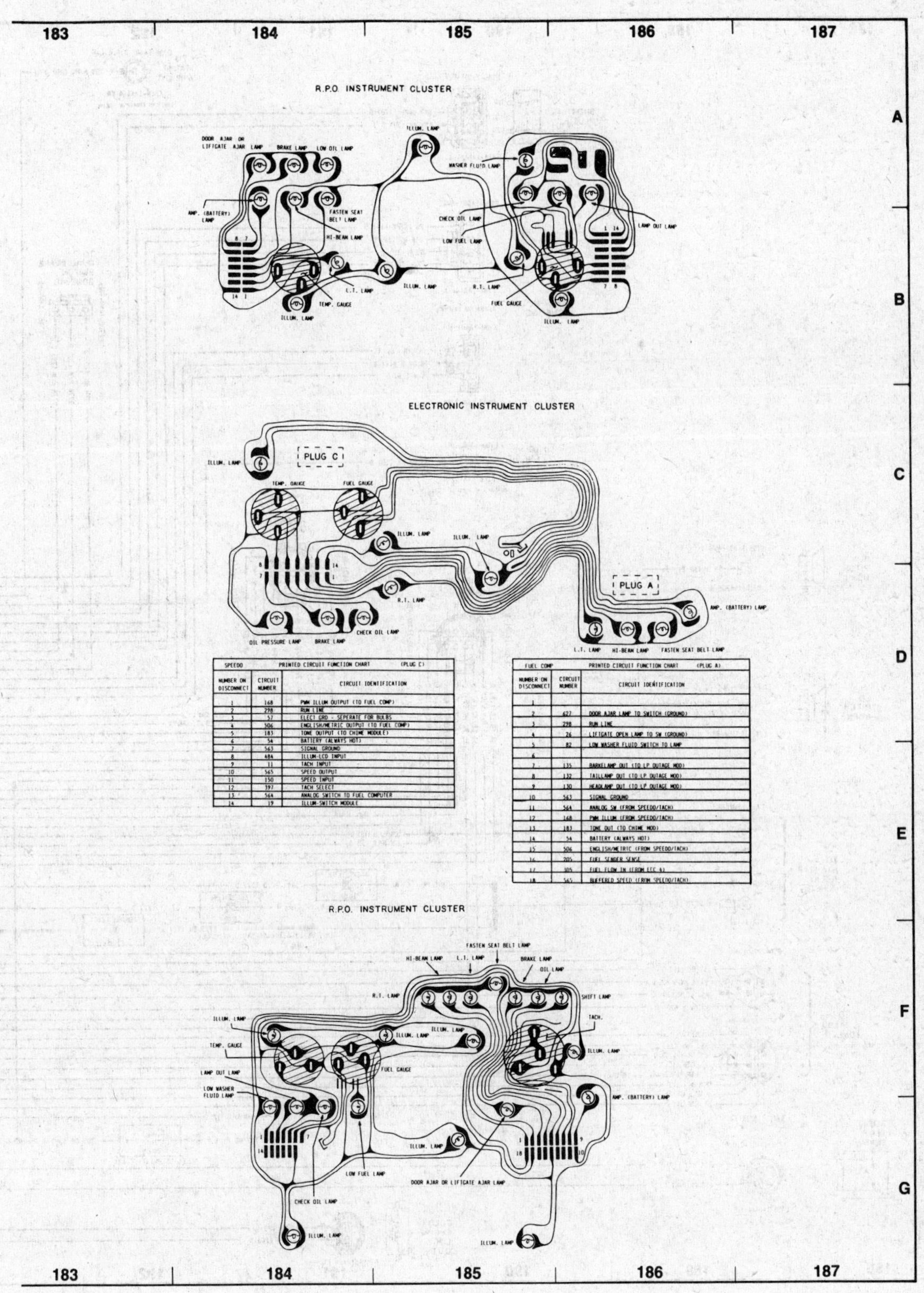

SPEEDO	PRINTED CIRCUIT FUNCTION CHART (PLUG C)	
NUMBER ON DISCONNECT	CIRCUIT NUMBER	CIRCUIT IDENTIFICATION
1	168	PWM ILLUM OUTPUT (TO FUEL COMP)
2	298	RUN LINE
3	57	ELECT GRD - SEPERATE FOR BULBS
4	506	ENGLISH/METRIC OUTPUT (TO FUEL COMP)
5	183	TONE OUTPUT (TO CHIME MODULE)
6	54	BATTERY (ALWAYS HOT)
7	563	SIGNAL GROUND
8	484	ILLUM-LCD INPUT
9	11	TACH INPUT
10	565	SPEED OUTPUT
11	150	SPEED INPUT
12	397	TACH SELECT
13	564	ANALOG SWITCH TO FUEL COMPUTER
14	19	ILLUM-SWITCH MODULE

FUEL COMP	PRINTED CIRCUIT FUNCTION CHART (PLUG A)	
NUMBER ON DISCONNECT	CIRCUIT NUMBER	CIRCUIT IDENTIFICATION
1		
2	627	DOOR AJAR LAMP TO SWITCH (GROUND)
3	298	RUN LINE
4	26	LIFTGATE OPEN LAMP TO SW (GROUND)
5	82	LOW WASHER FLUID SWITCH TO LAMP
6		
7	135	BARKELAMP OUT (TO LP OUTAGE MOD)
8	132	TAILLAMP OUT (TO LP OUTAGE MOD)
9	130	HEADLAMP OUT (TO LP OUTAGE MOD)
10	563	SIGNAL GROUND
11	564	ANALOG SW (FROM SPEEDO/TACH)
12	168	PWM ILLUM (FROM SPEEDO/TACH)
13	183	TONE OUT (TO CHIME MOD)
14	54	BATTERY (ALWAYS HOT)
15	506	ENGLISH/METRIC (FROM SPEEDO/TACH)
16	205	FUEL SENDER SENSE
17	305	FUEL FLOW IN (FROM EEC 4)
18	565	BUFFERED SPEED (FROM SPEEDO/TACH)

Taurus and Sable electrical schematics – 1986–87

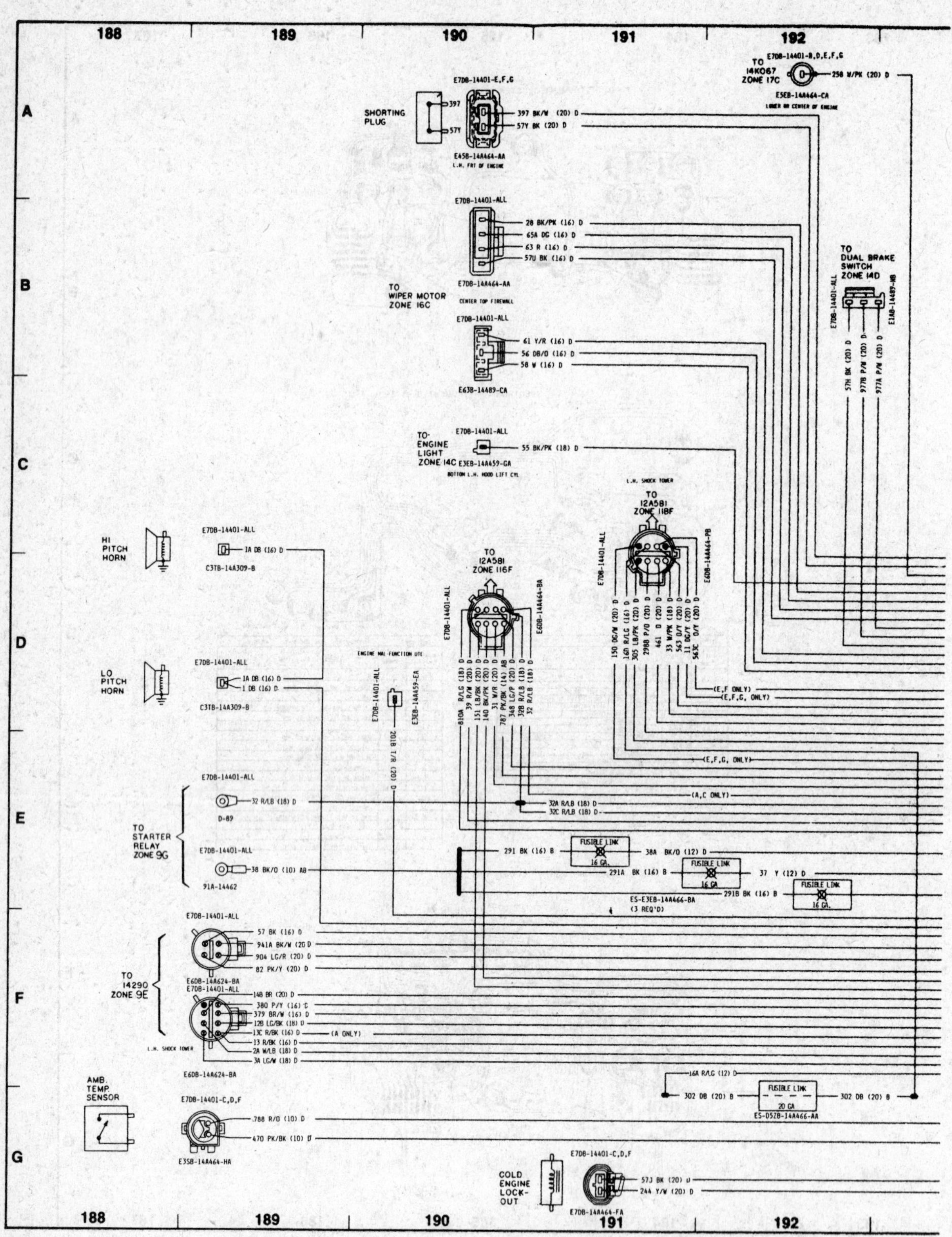

Taurus and Sable electrical schematics — 1986–87

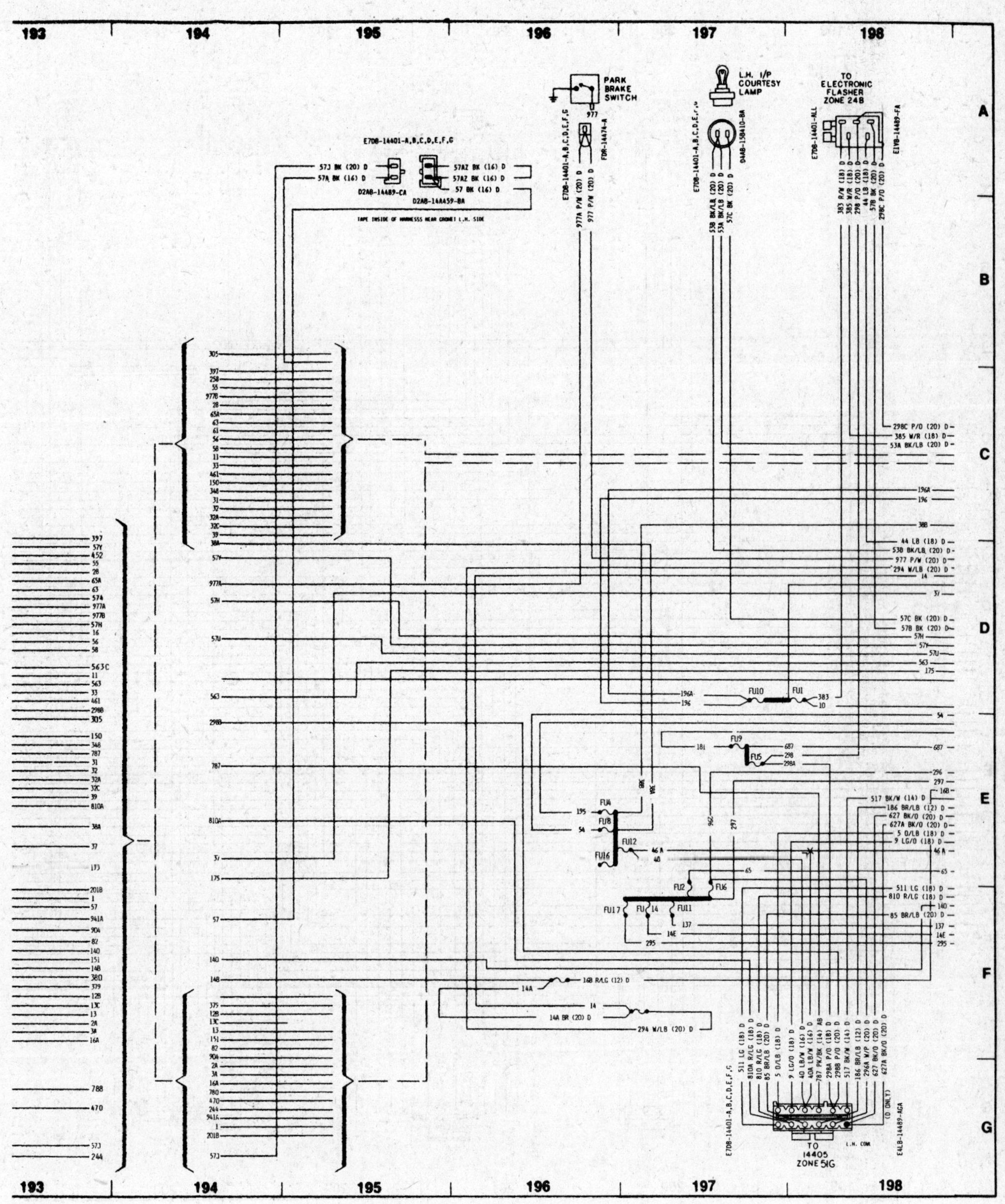

Taurus and Sable electrical schematics – 1986–87

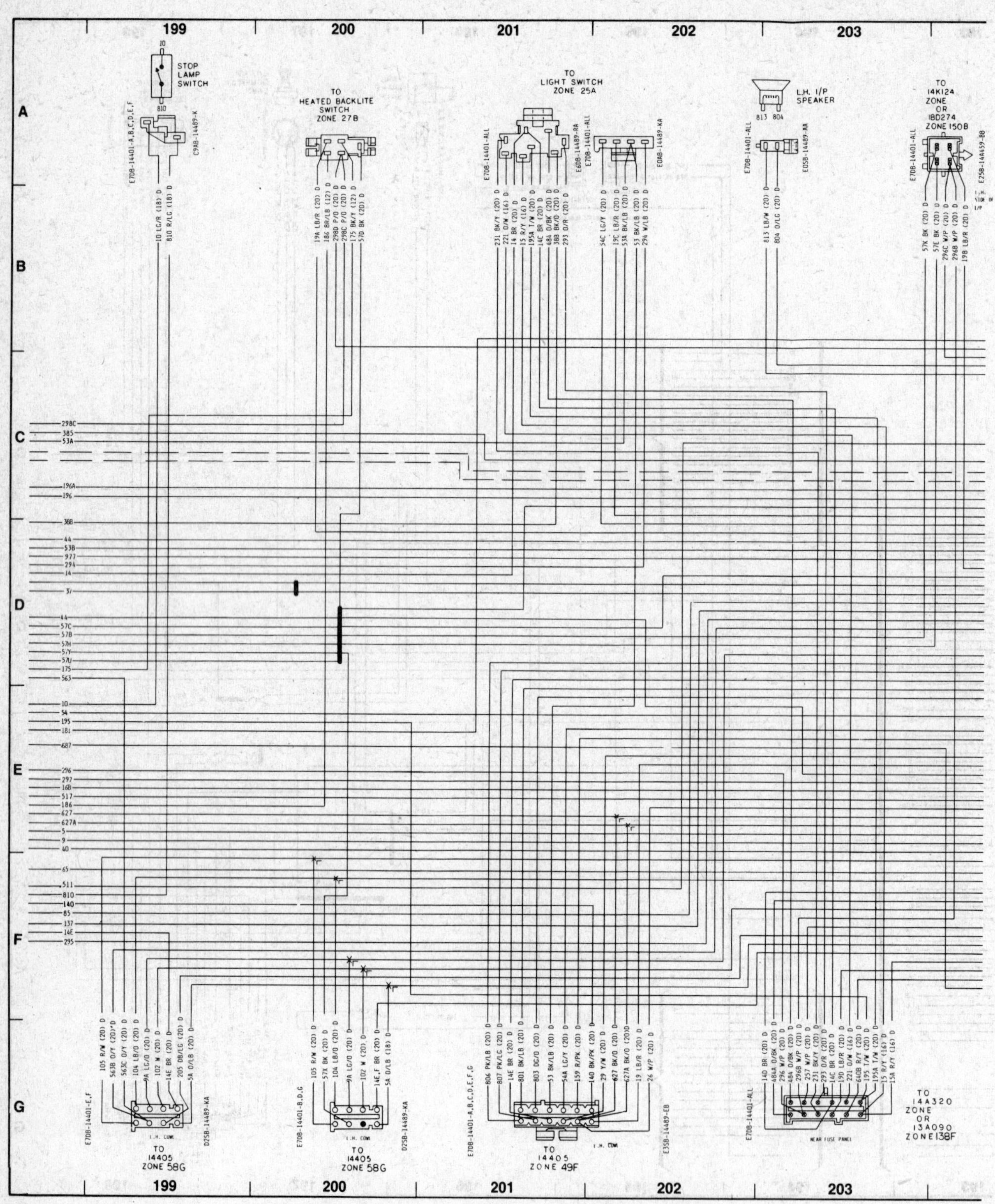

Taurus and Sable electrical schematics – 1986–87

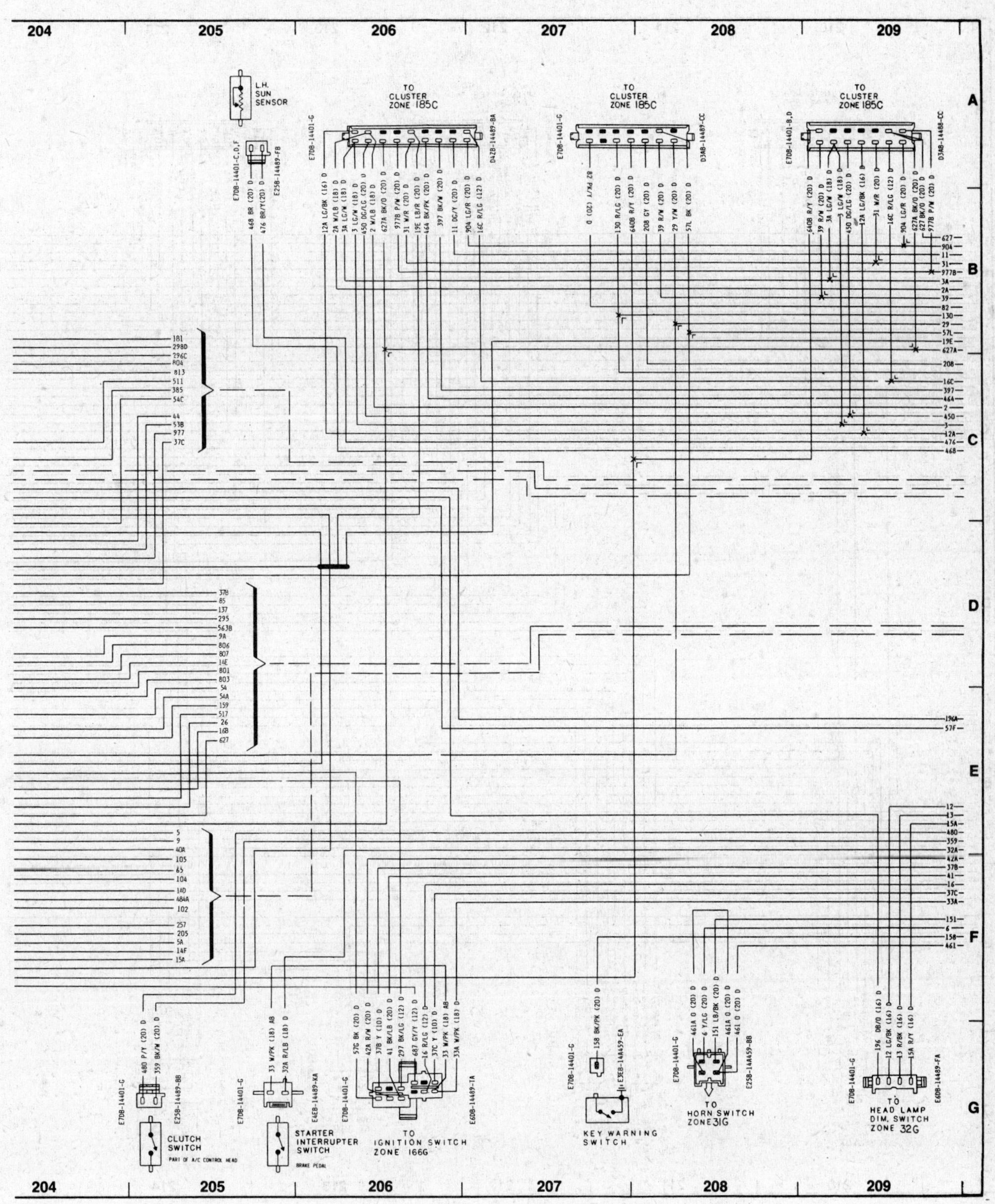

Taurus and Sable electrical schematics – 1986–87

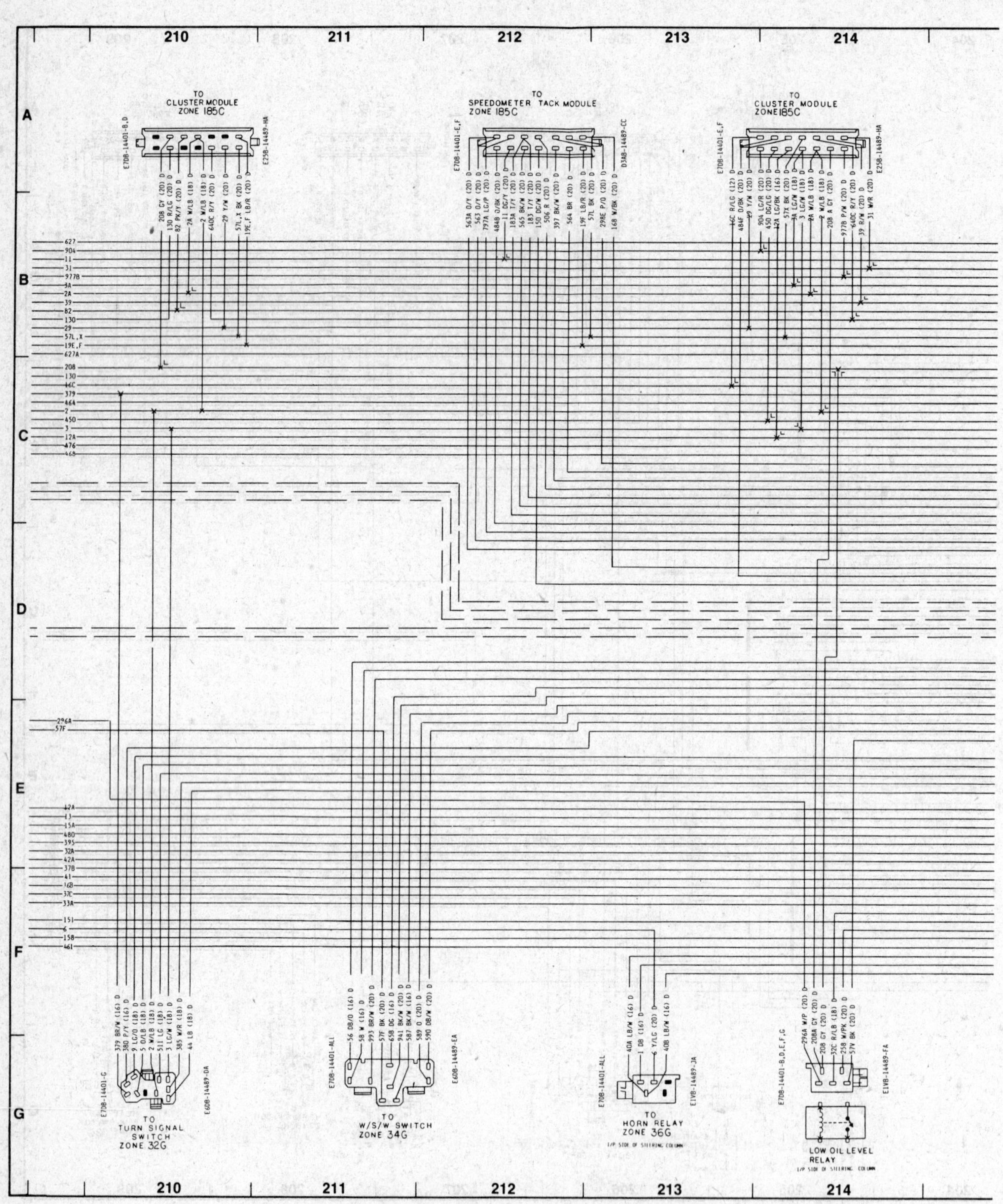

Taurus and Sable electrical schematics – 1986–87

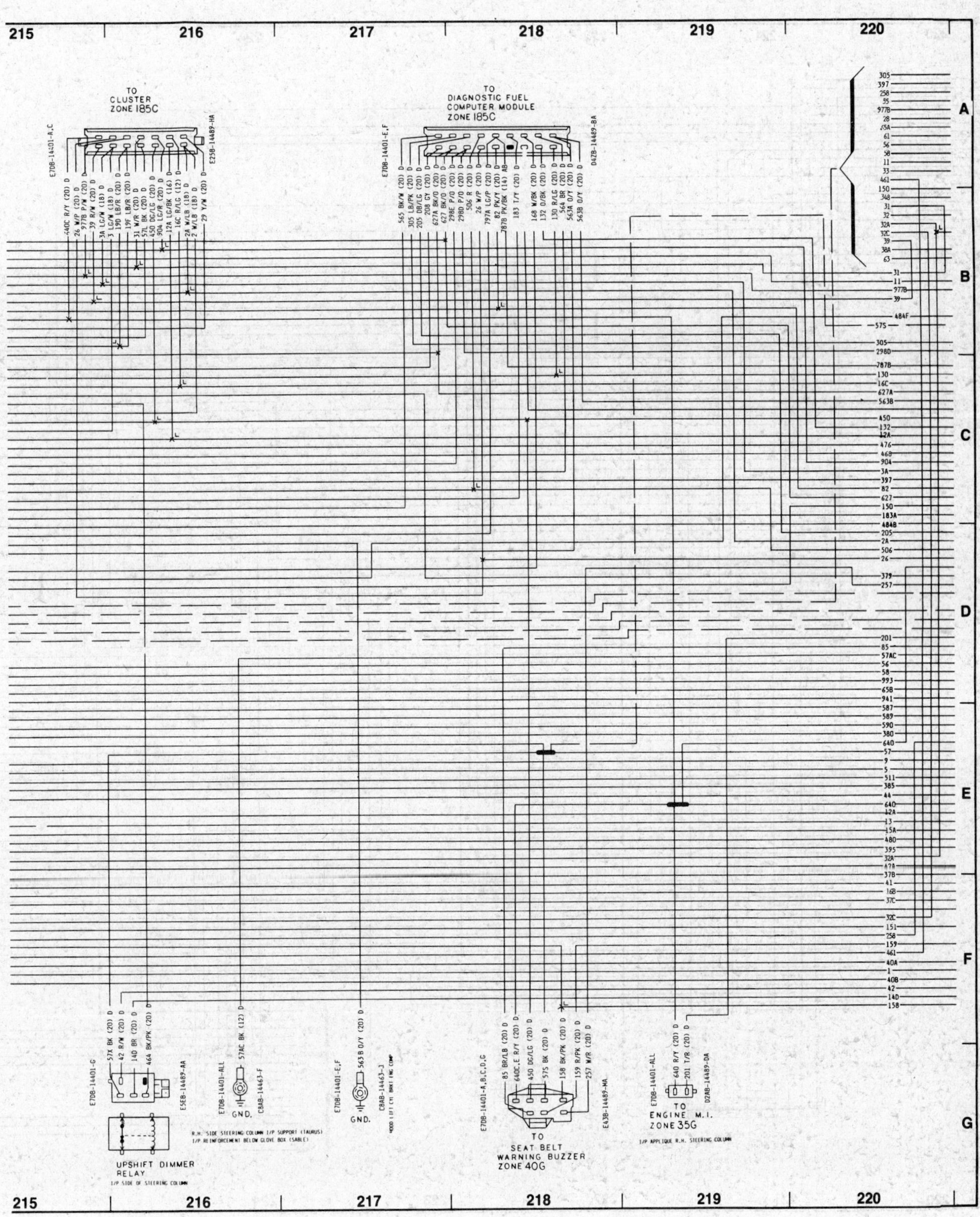

Taurus and Sable electrical schematics – 1986–87

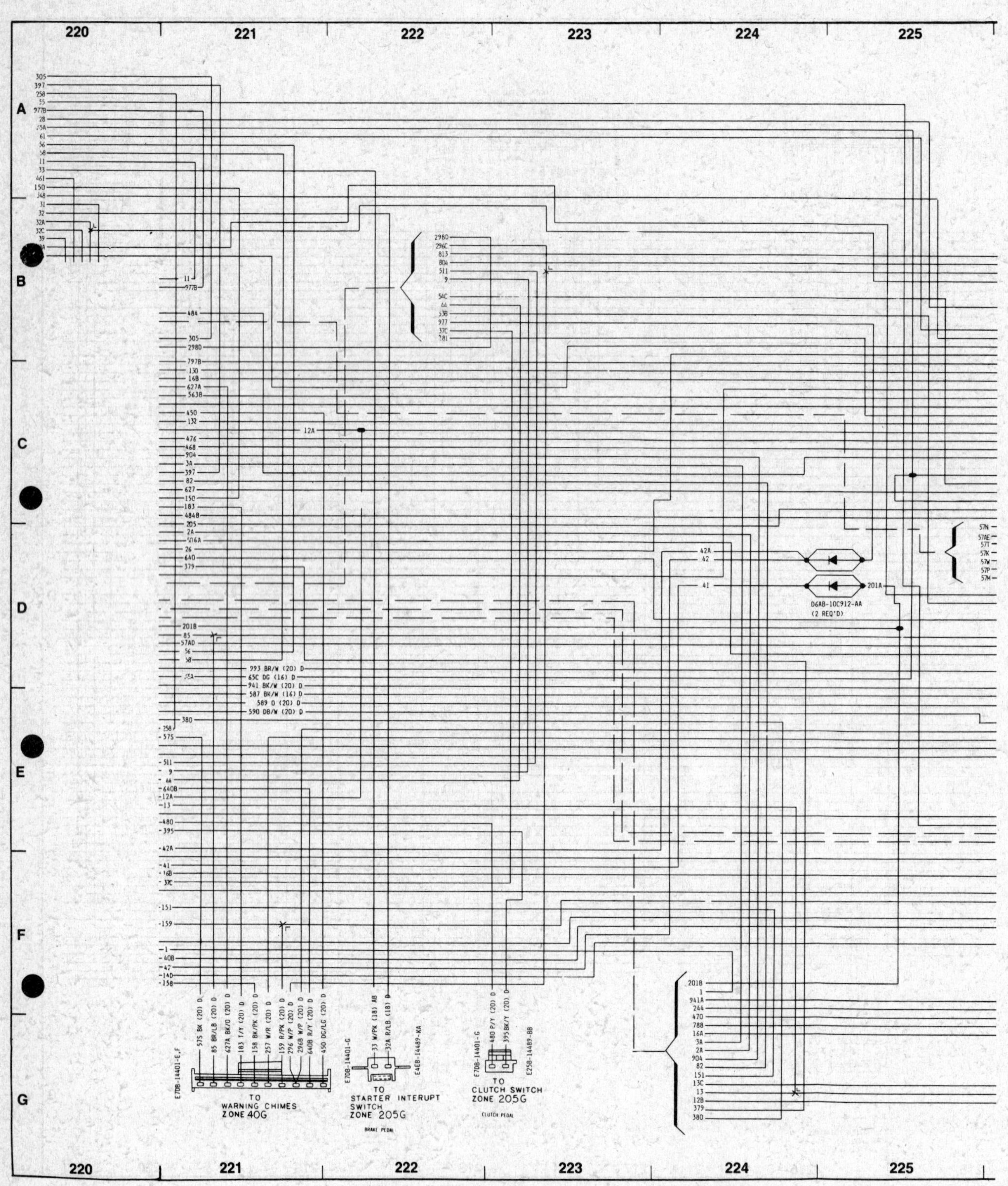

Taurus and Sable electrical schematics – 1986–87

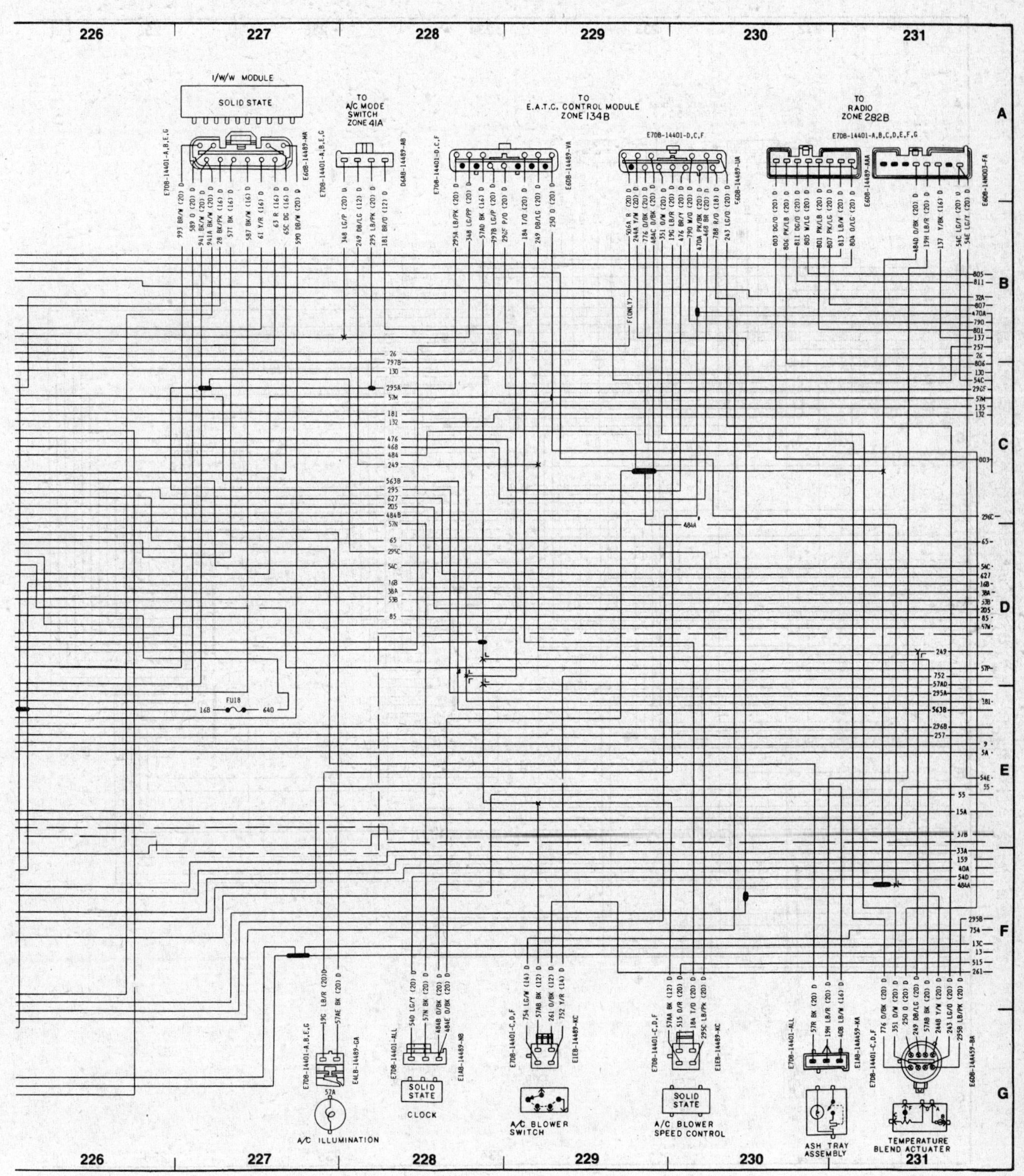

Taurus and Sable electrical schematics – 1986–87

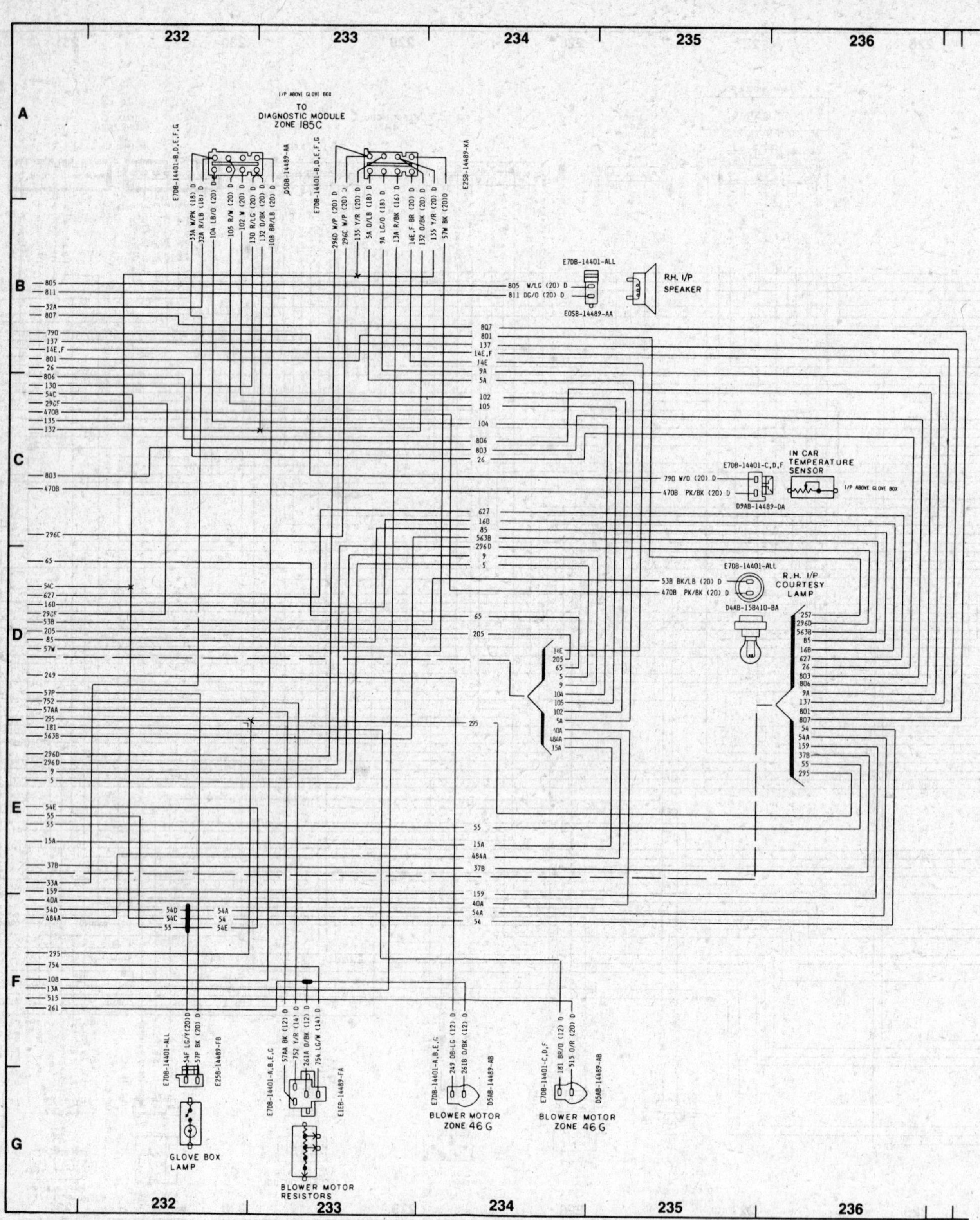

Taurus and Sable electrical schematics — 1986-87

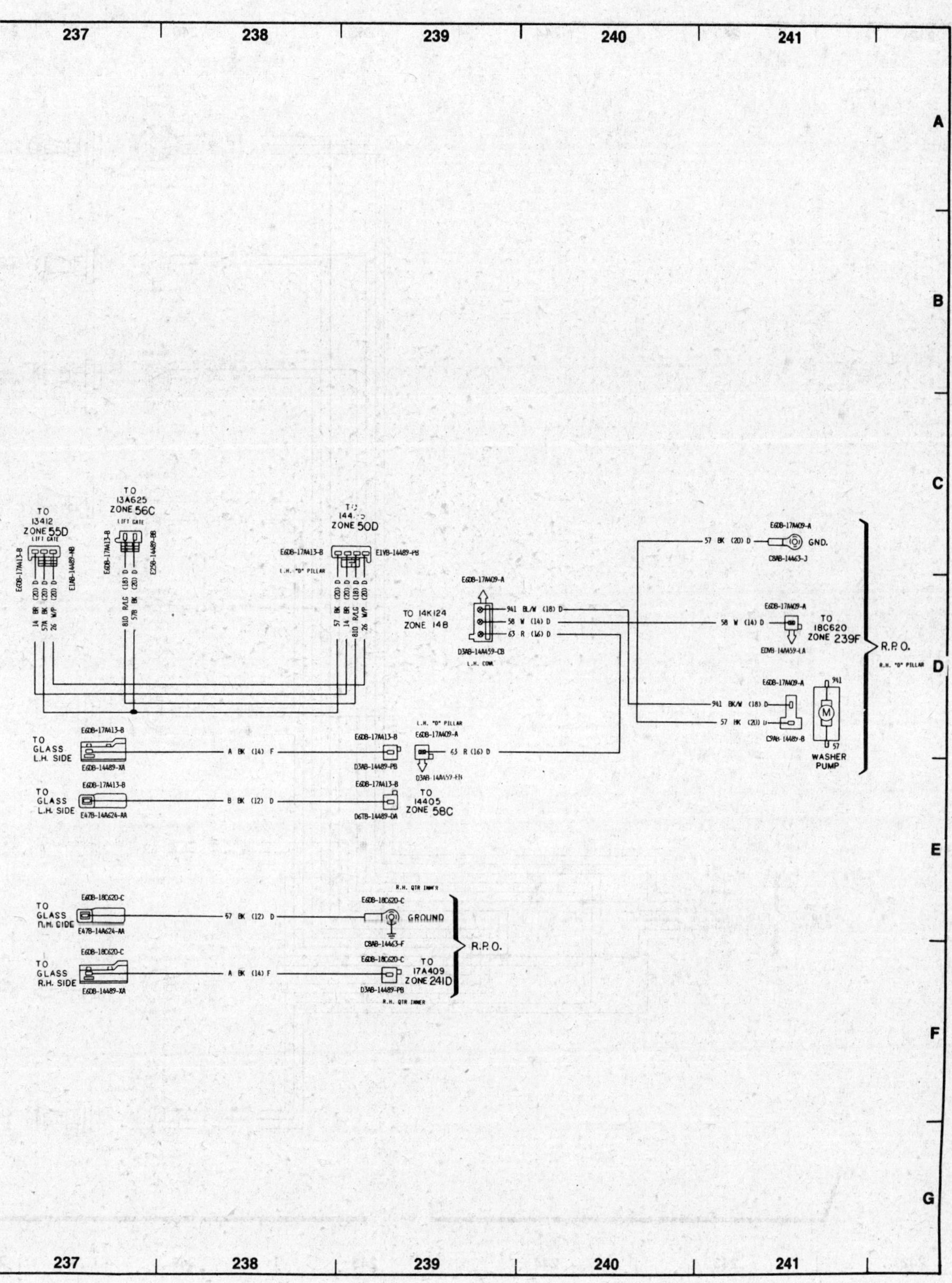
237
238
239
240
241
A
B
C
D
E
F
G
TO 13412 ZONE 55D
TO 13A625 ZONE 56C
ZONE 50D
TO 14K124 ZONE 14B
GND.
TO 18C620 ZONE 239F
R.P.O.
WASHER PUMP
TO GLASS L.H. SIDE
TO GLASS L.H. SIDE
TO 14405 ZONE 58C
TO GLASS R.H. SIDE
GROUND
R.P.O.
TO GLASS R.H. SIDE
TO 17A409 ZONE 241D

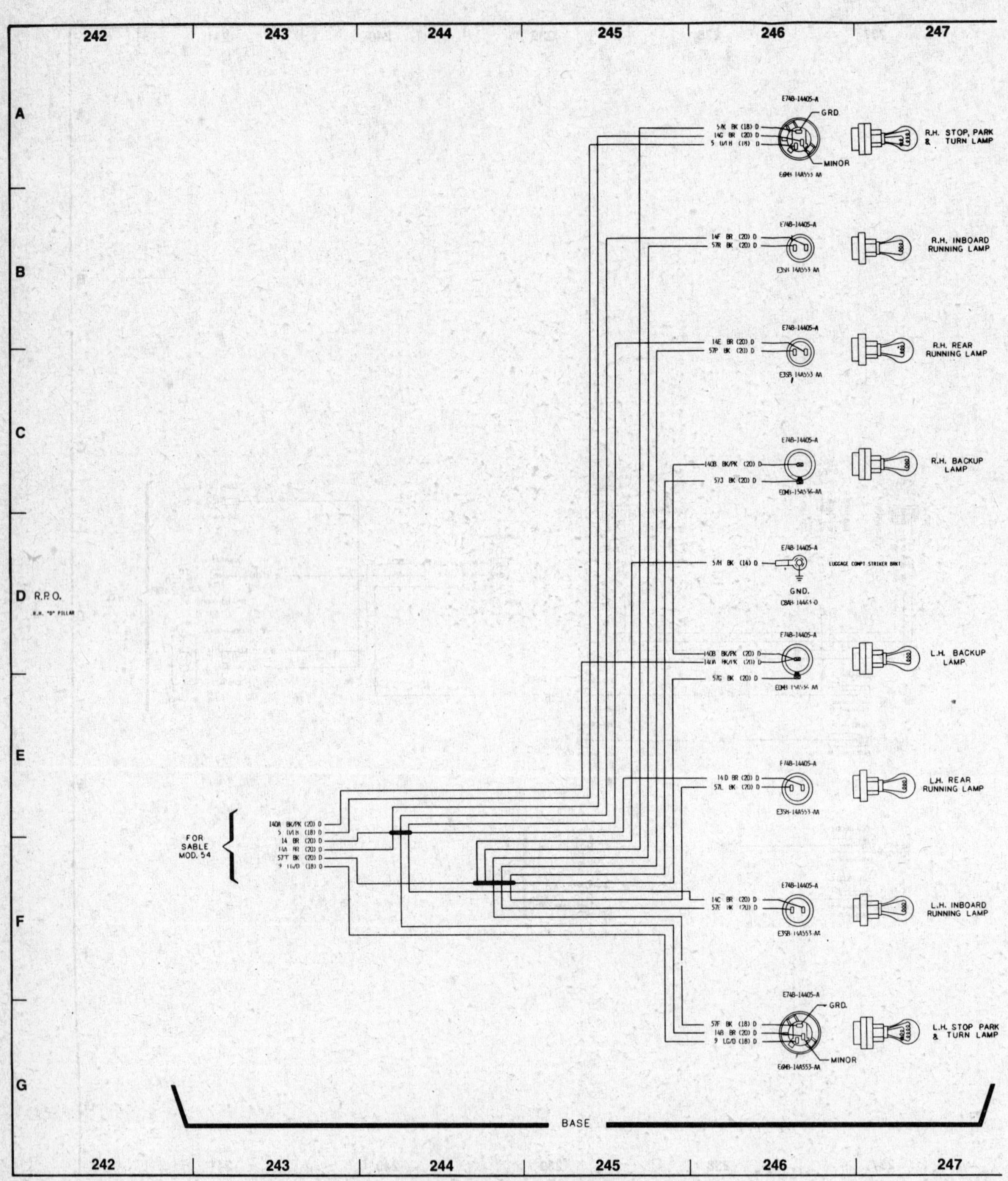

Taurus and Sable electrical schematics — 1986–87

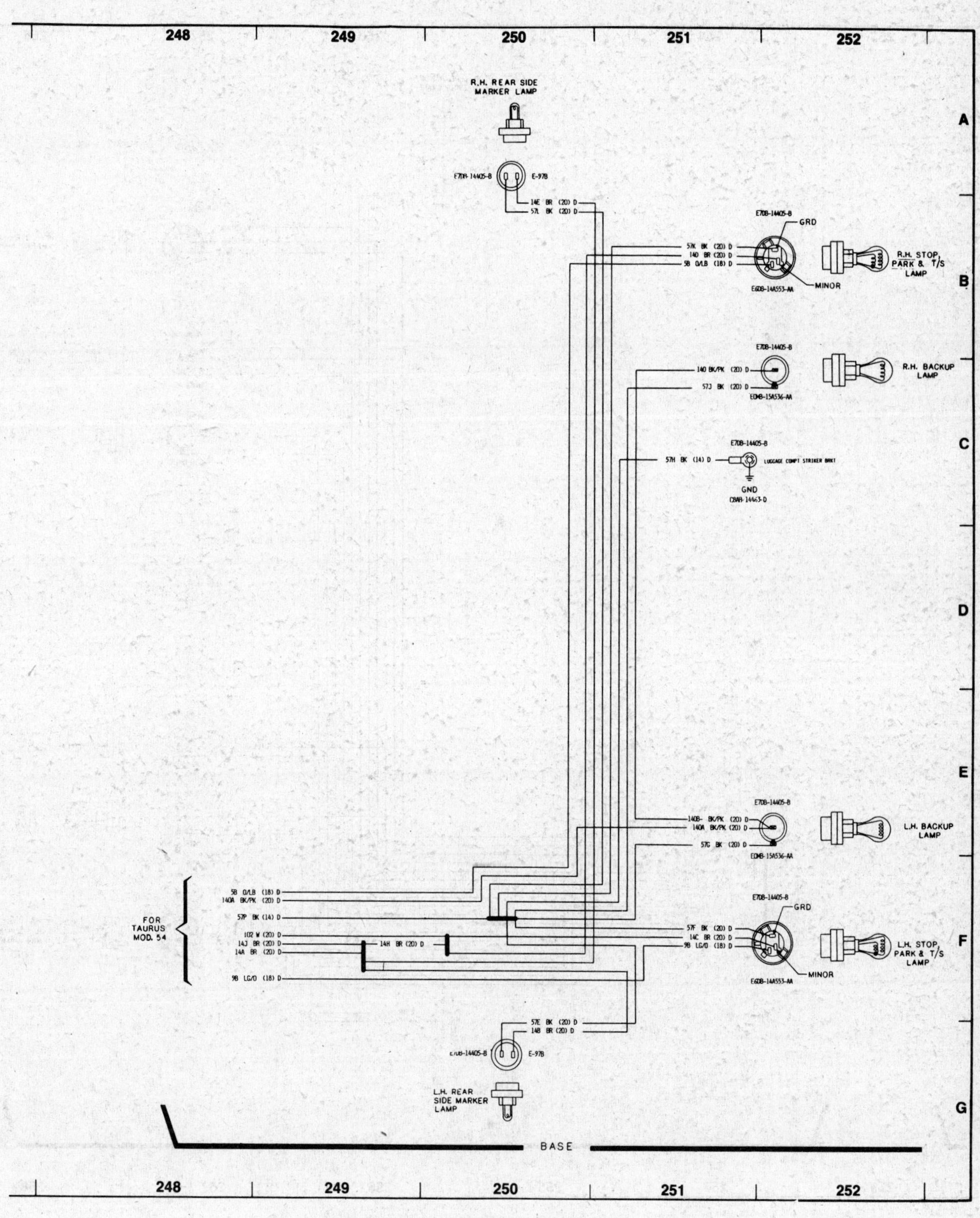

Taurus and Sable electrical schematics – 1986–87

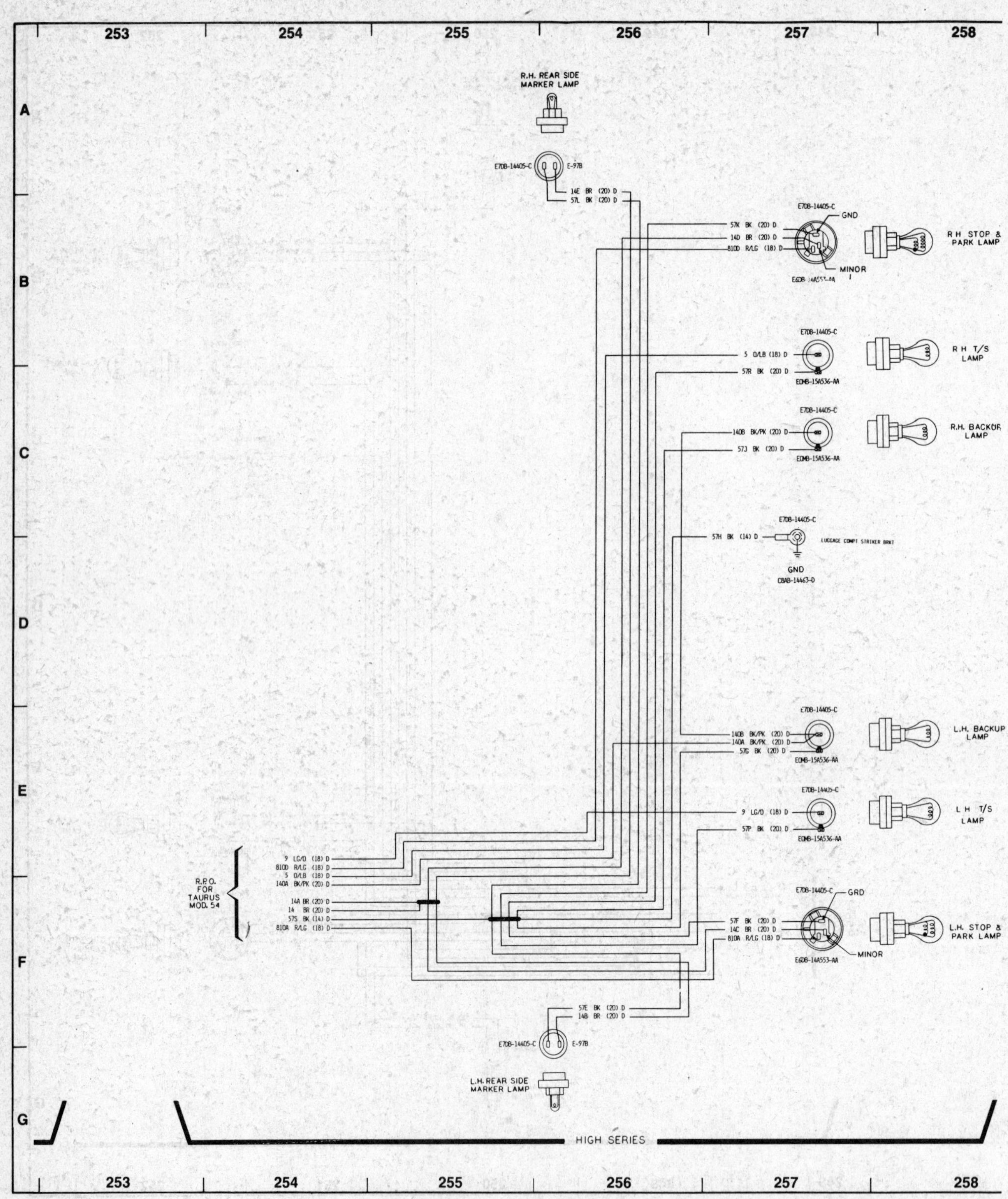

Taurus and Sable electrical schematics — 1986–87

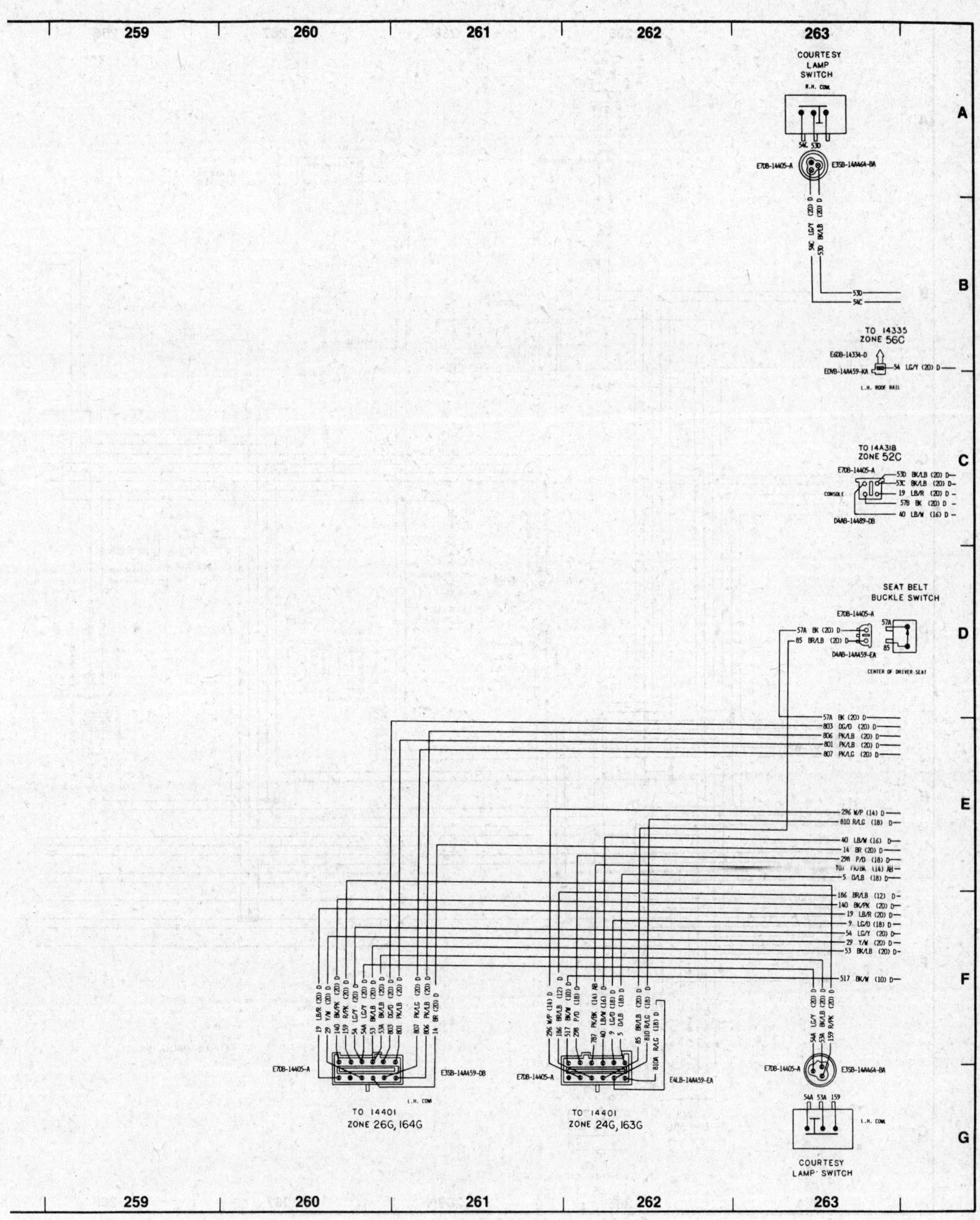

Taurus and Sable electrical schematics – 1986–87

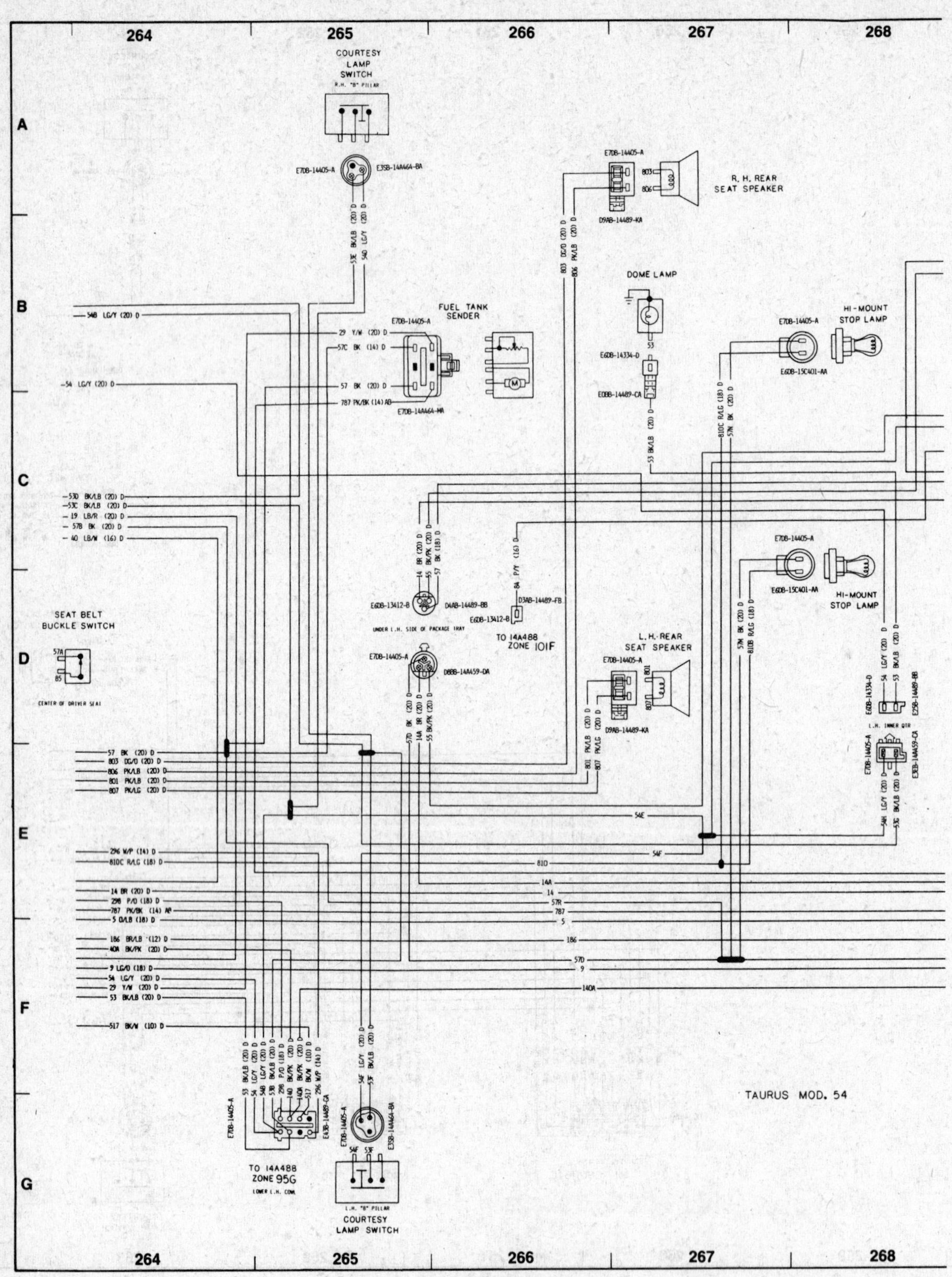

Taurus and Sable electrical schematics — 1986–87

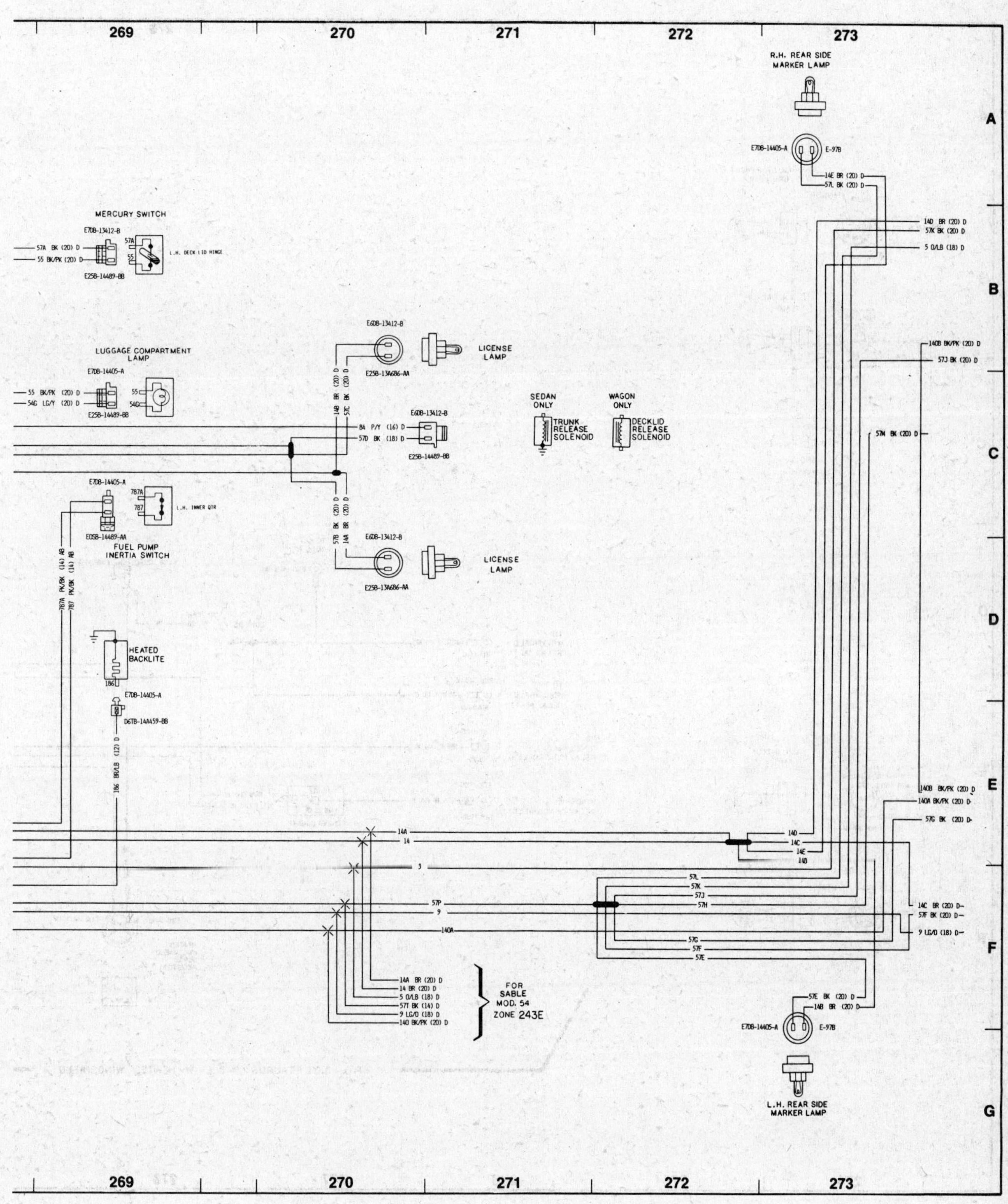

Taurus and Sable electrical schematics – 1986-87

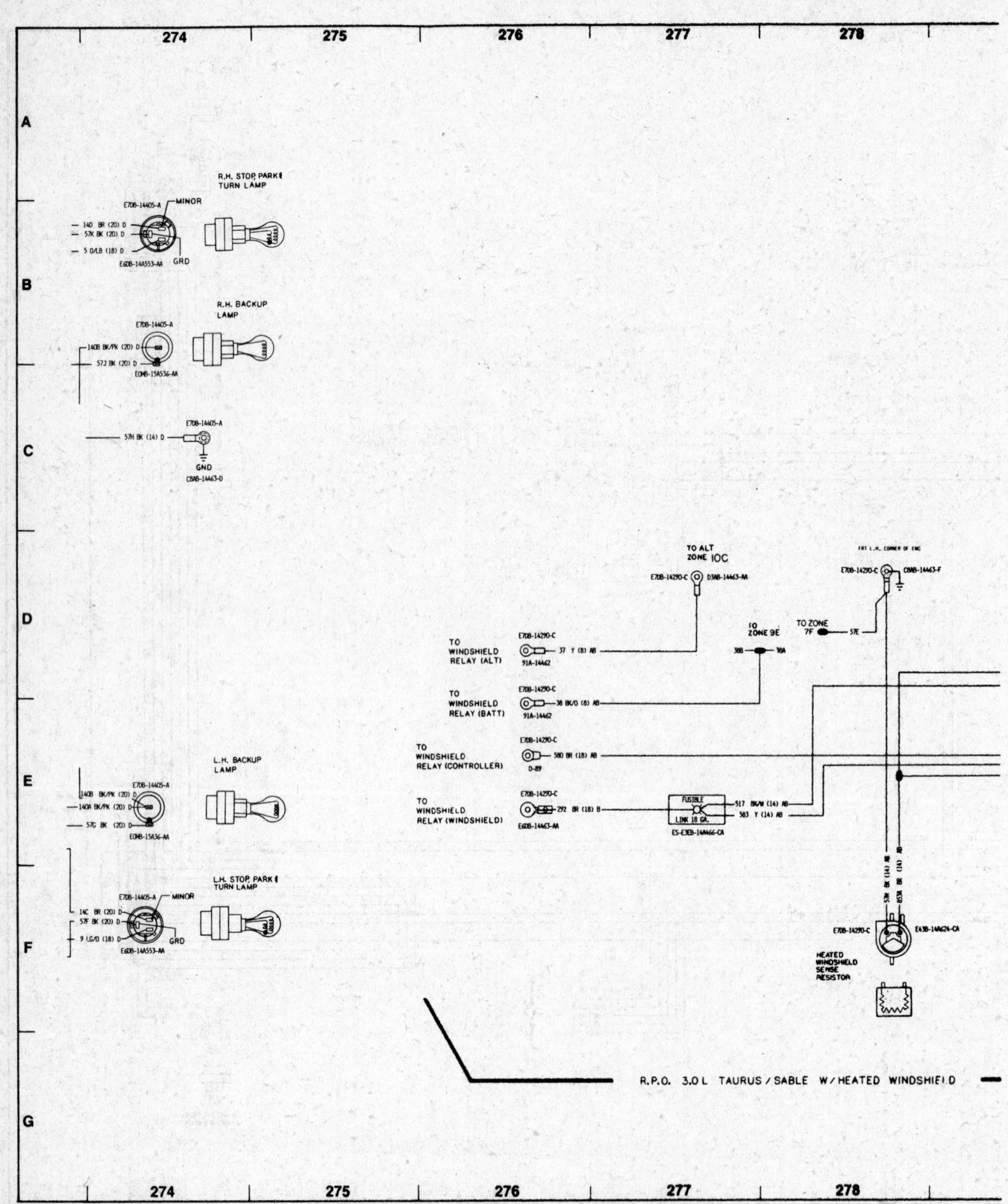

Taurus and Sable electrical schematics — 1986-87

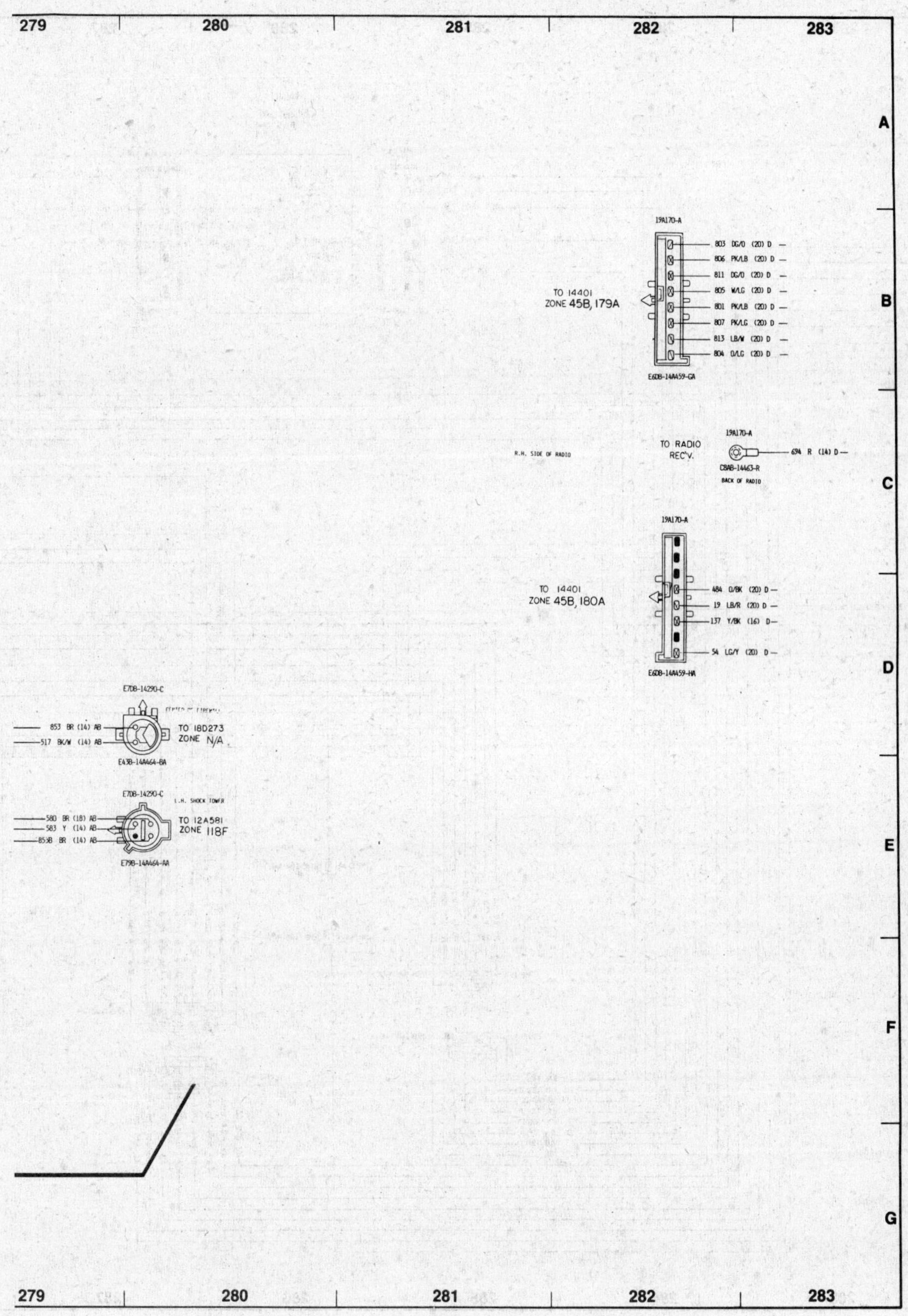

Taurus and Sable electrical schematics — 1986–87

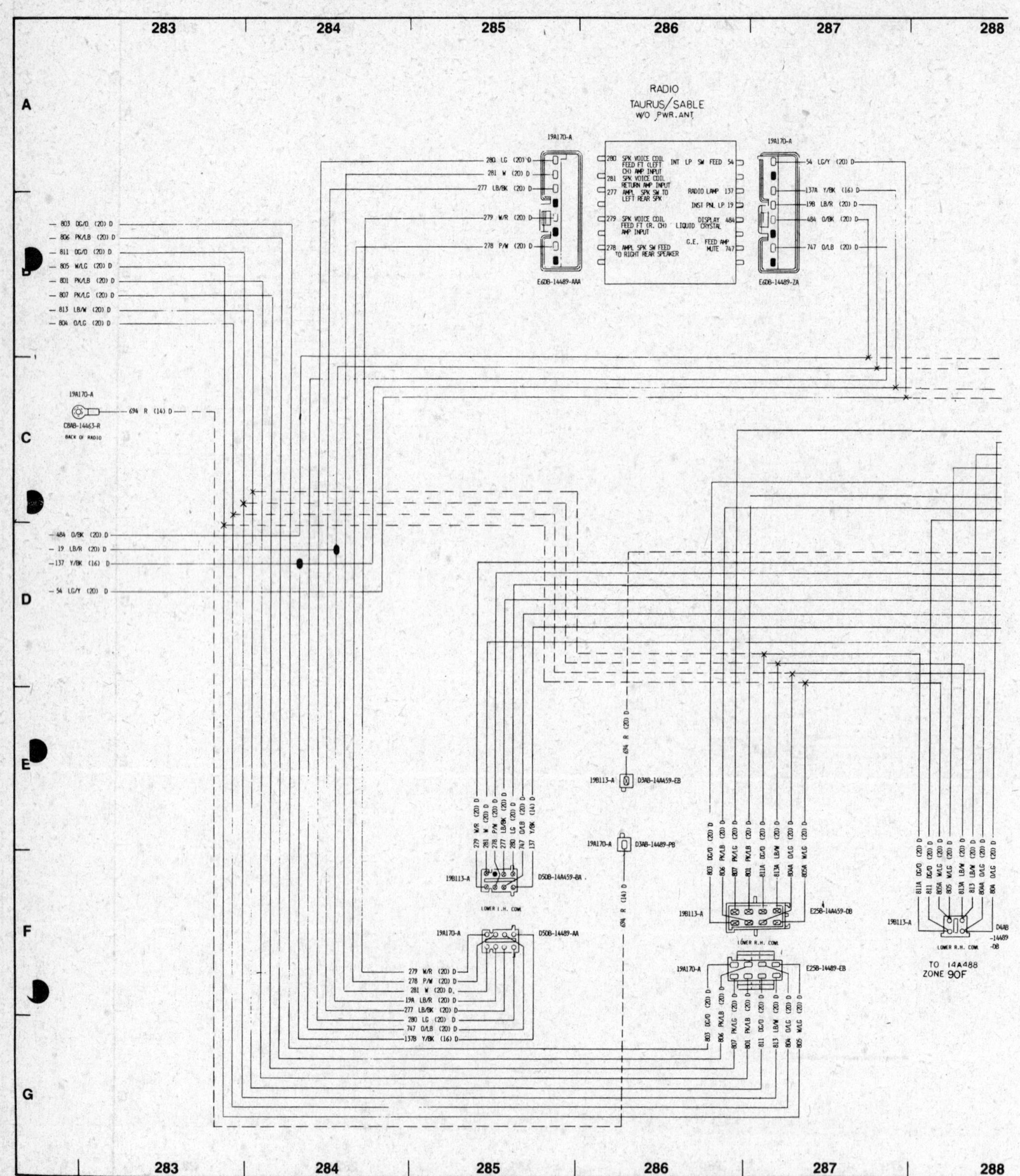
283
284
285
286
287
288
A
B
C
D
E
F
G
RADIO
TAURUS/SABLE
W/O PWR. ANT
19A170-A
E6DB-14489-AAA
E6DB-14489-ZA
SPK VOICE COIL FEED FT (LEFT CH) AMP INPUT
SPK VOICE COIL RETURN AMP INPUT
AMPL SPK SW TO LEFT REAR SPK
SPK VOICE COIL FEED FT (R. CH) AMP INPUT
AMPL SPK SW FEED TO RIGHT REAR SPEAKER
INT LP SW FEED 54
RADIO LAMP 137
INST PNL LP 19
DISPLAY 484
LIQUID CRYSTAL
G.E. FEED AMP MUTE 747
C8AB-14463-R
BACK OF RADIO
694 R (14) D
19B113-A
D3AB-14A459-EB
D3AB-14489-PB
D5DB-14A459-BA
LOWER L.H. COWL
D5DB-14489-AA
E25B-14A459-DB
LOWER R.H. COWL
E25B-14489-EB
TO 14A488
ZONE 90F

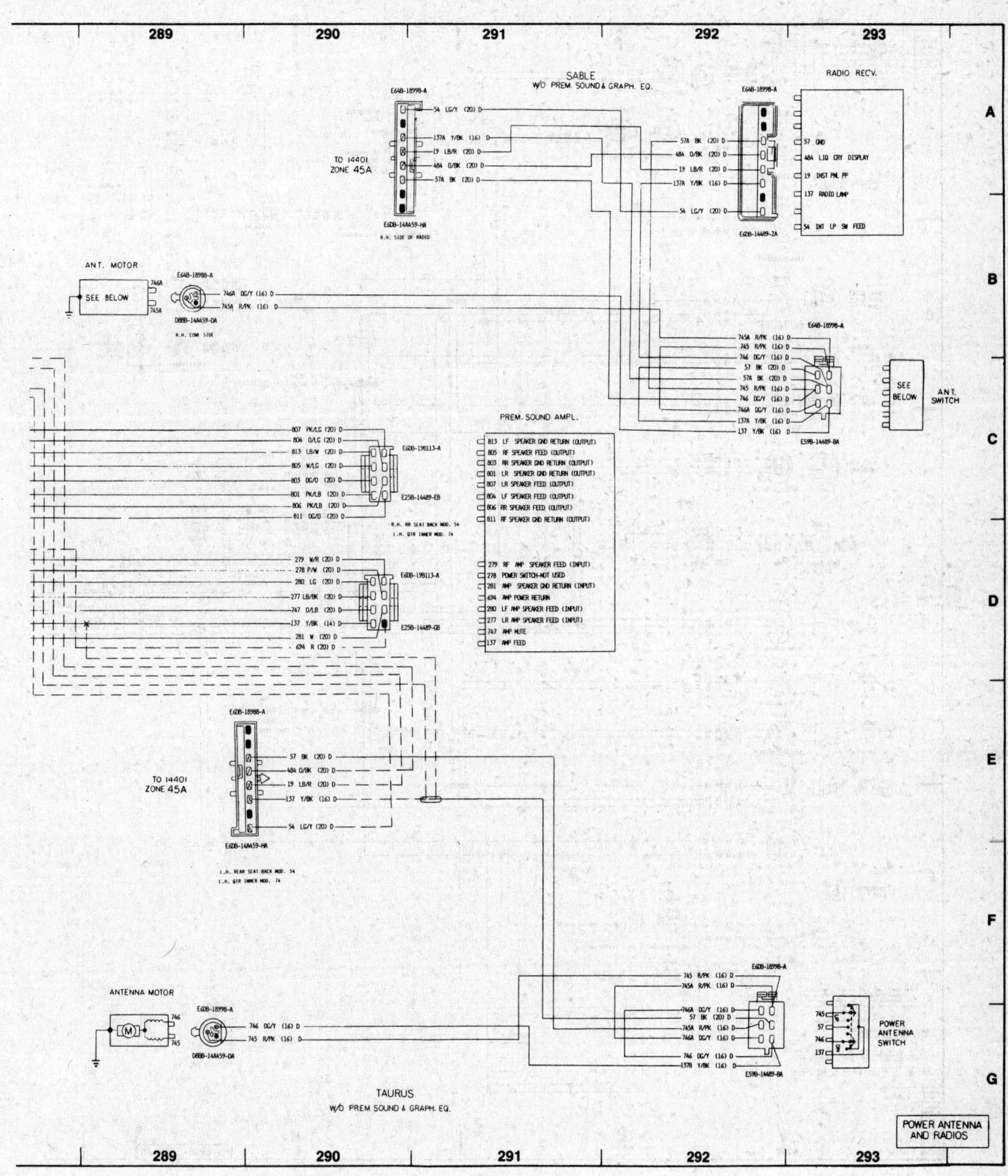

Taurus and Sable electrical schematics – 1986–87

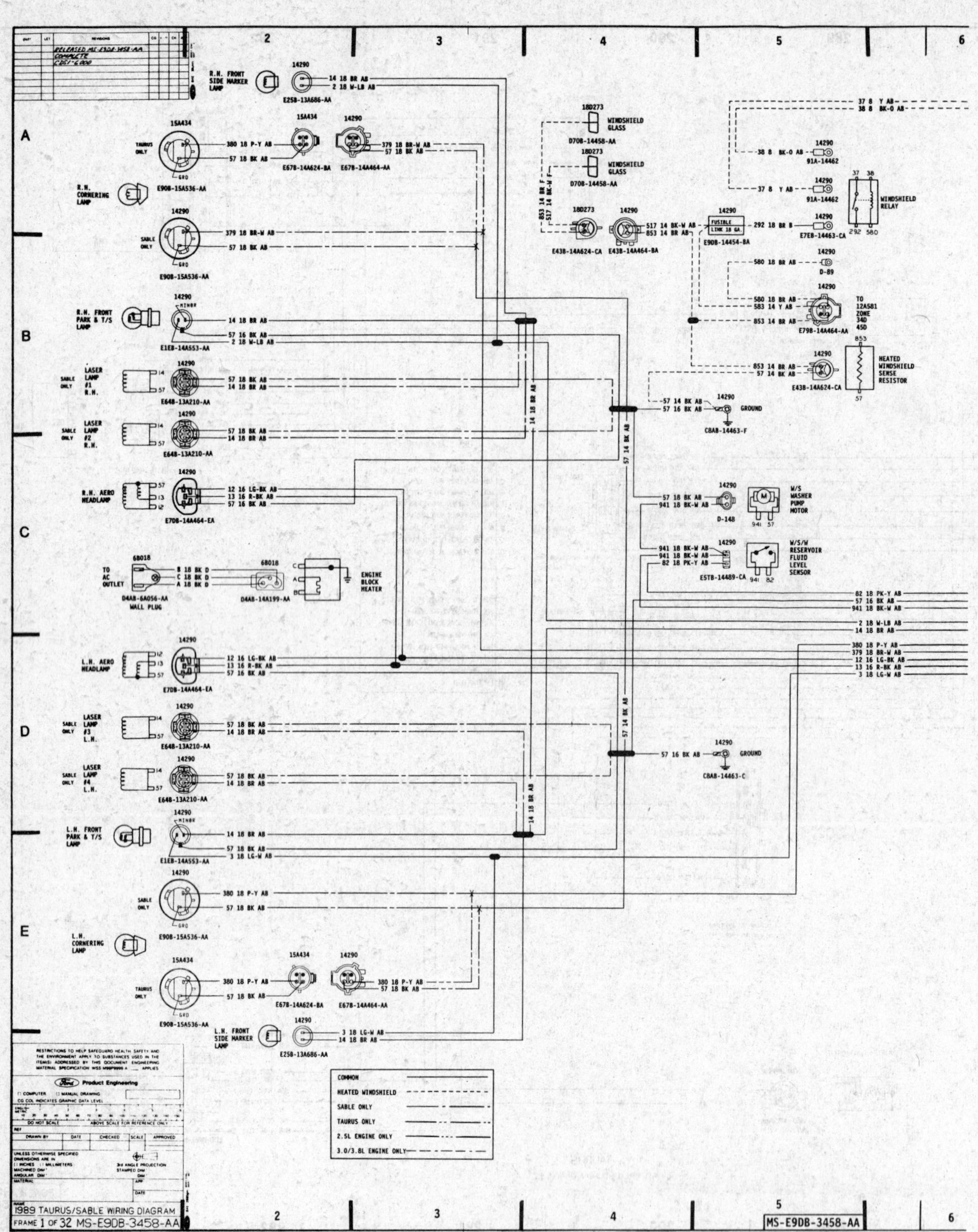

Taurus and Sable electrical schematics — 1989

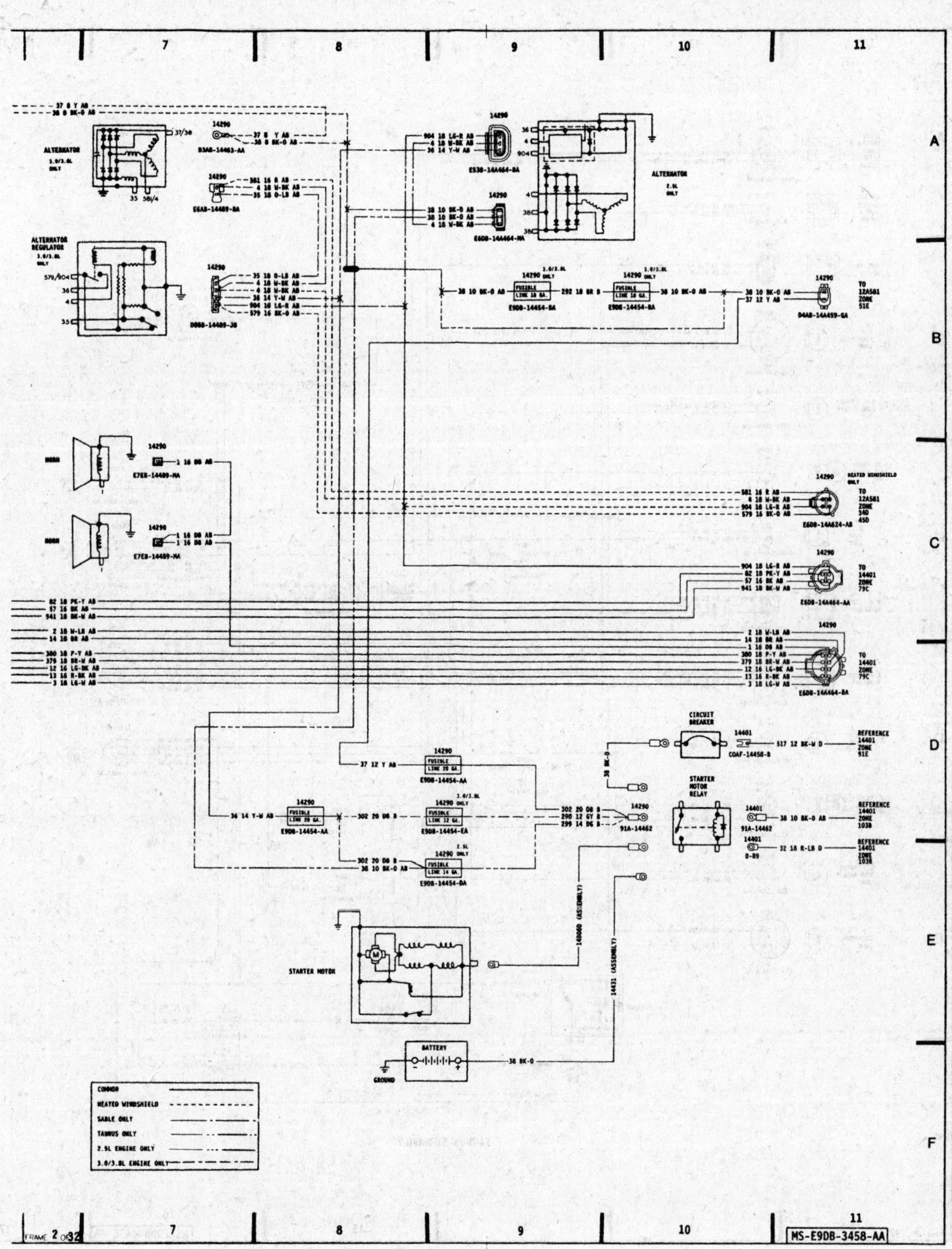

Taurus and Sable electrical schematics — 1989

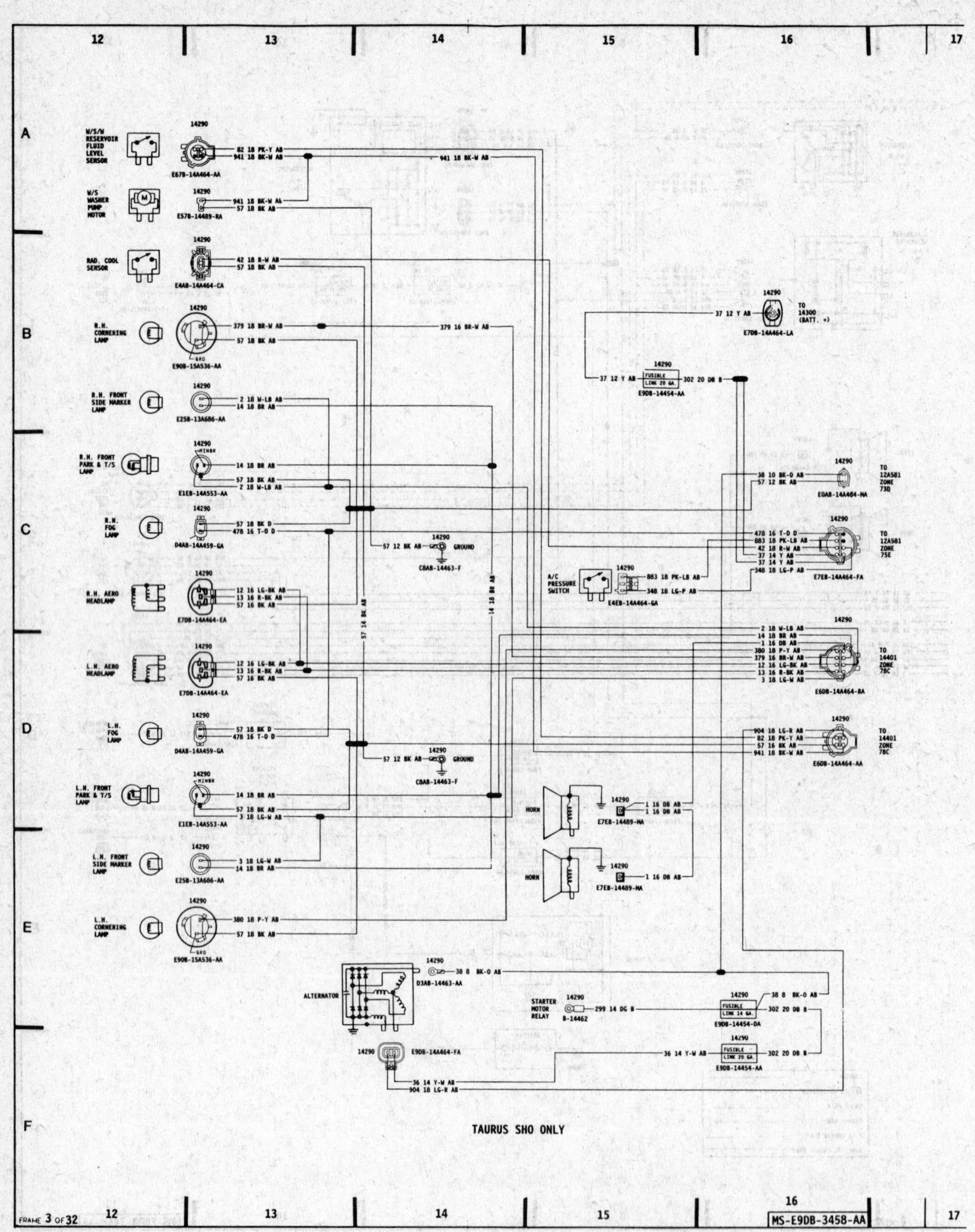

Taurus and Sable electrical schematics — 1989

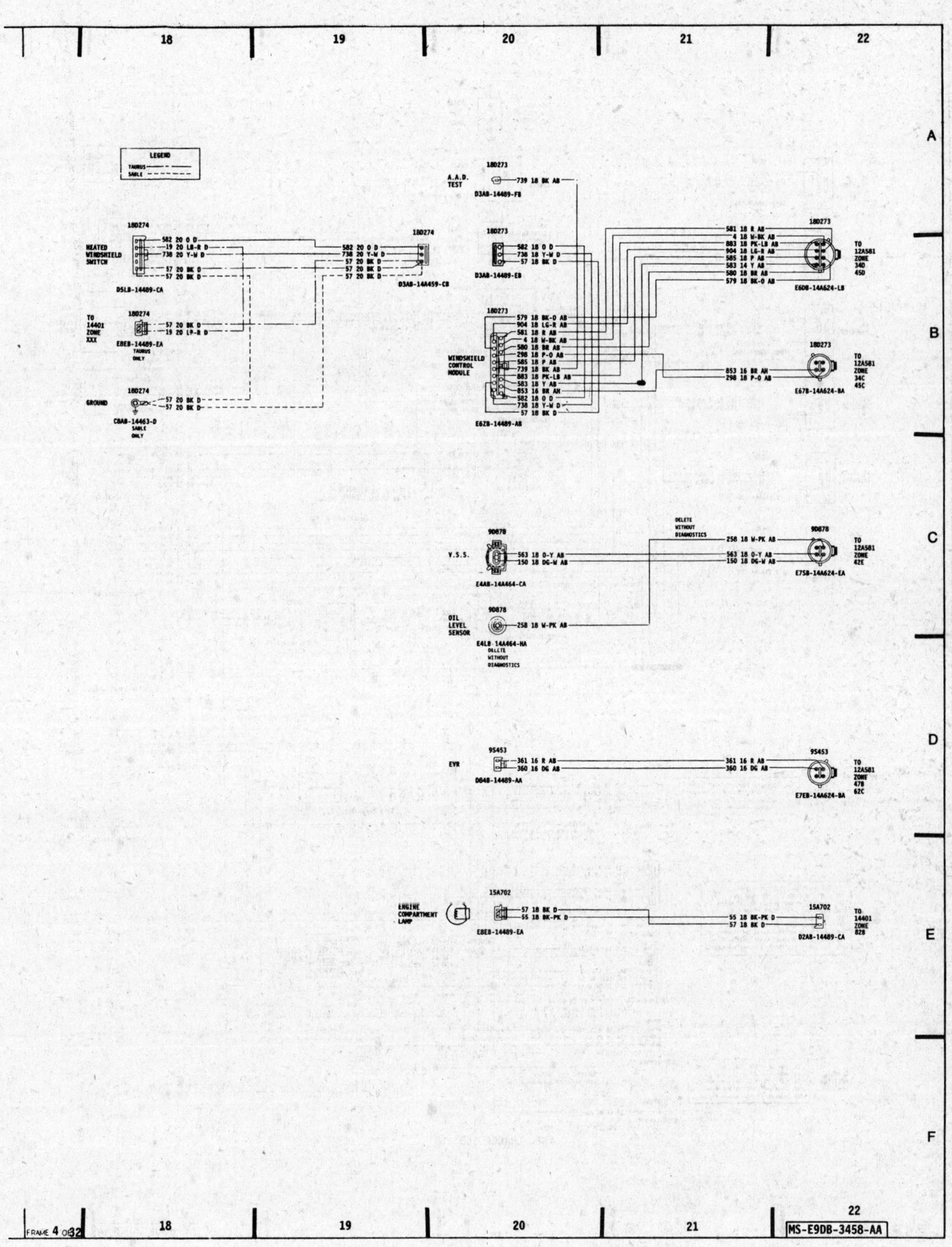

Taurus and Sable electrical schematics — 1989

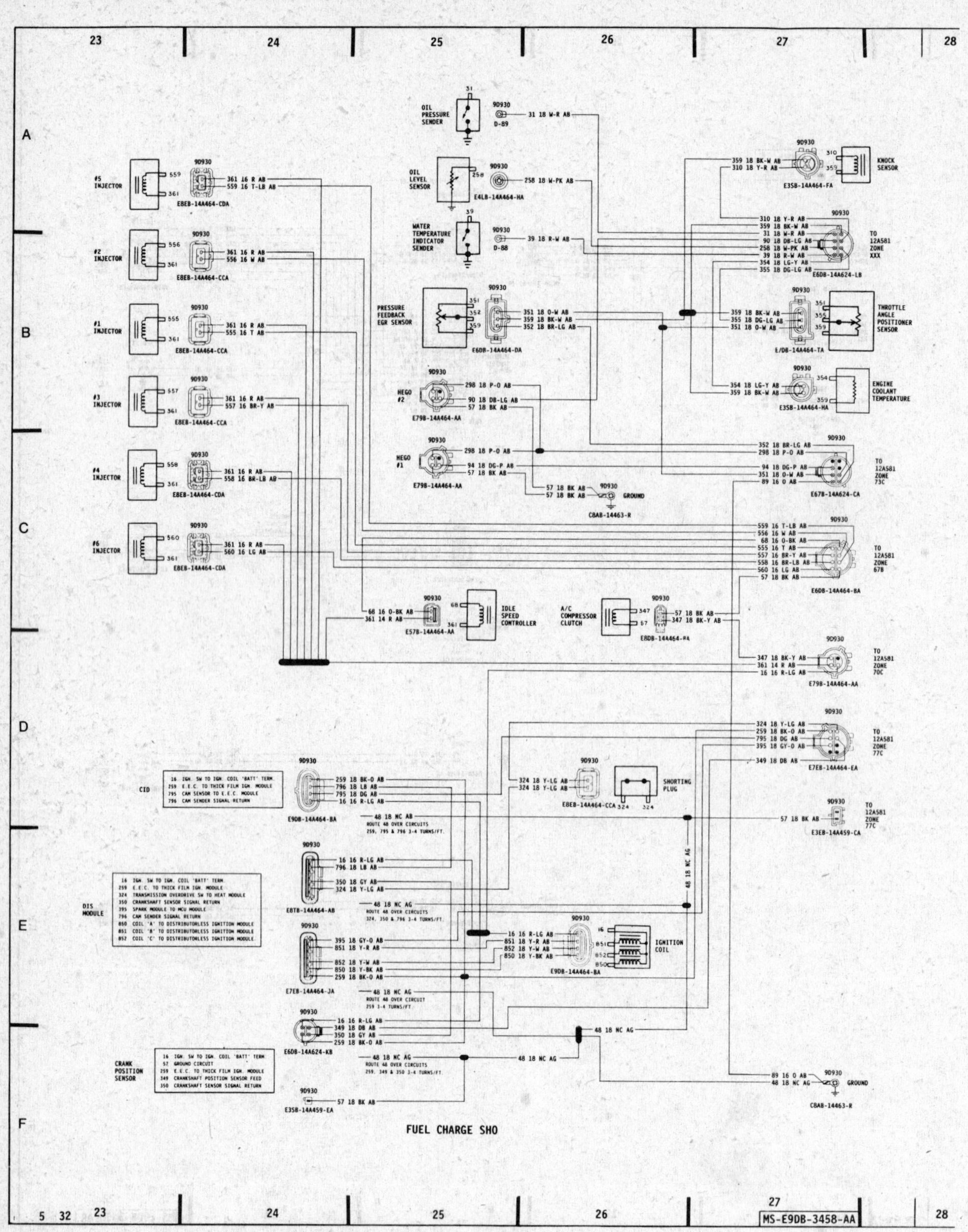

Taurus and Sable electrical schematics — 1989

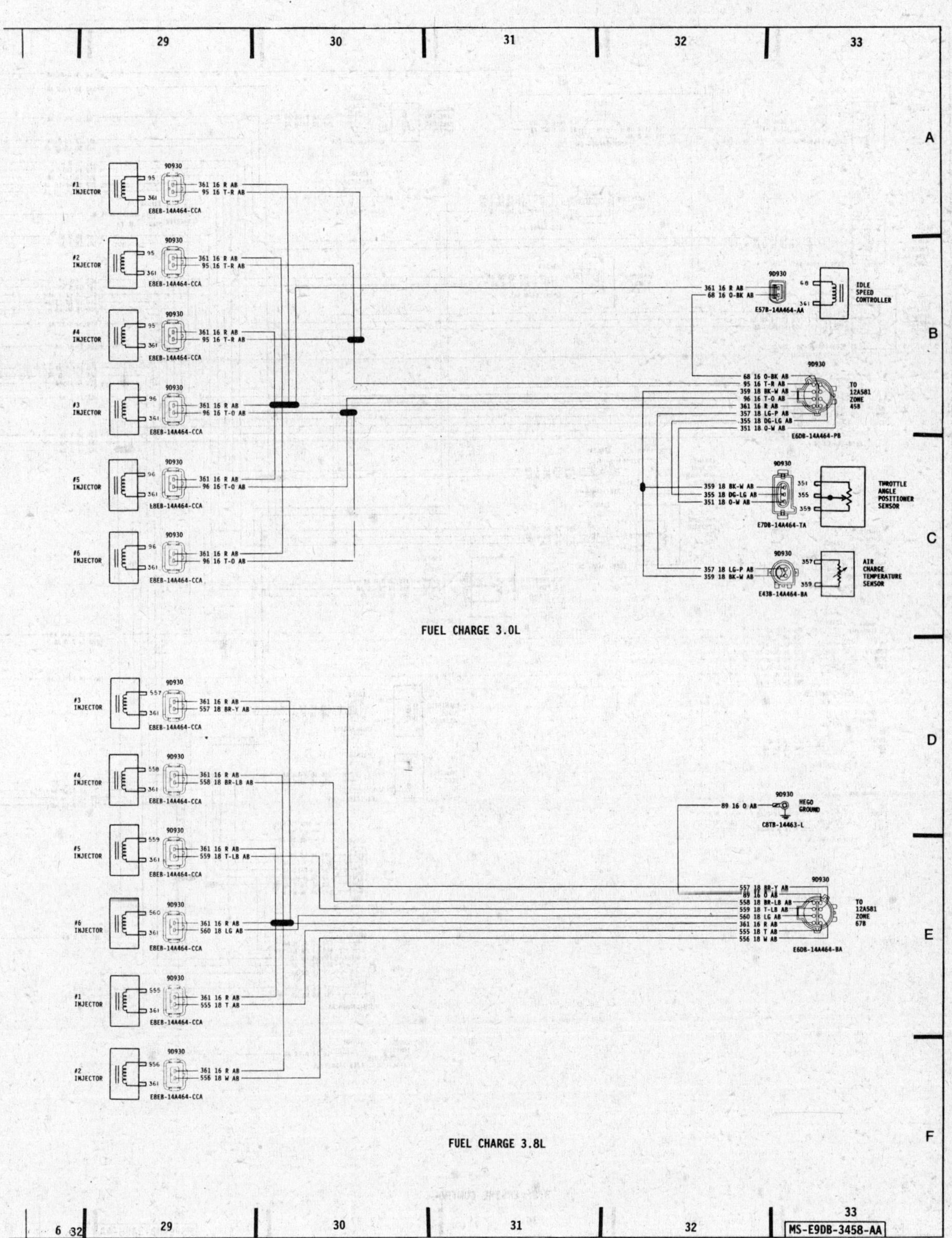
FUEL CHARGE 3.0L
FUEL CHARGE 3.8L
MS-E9DB-3458-AA

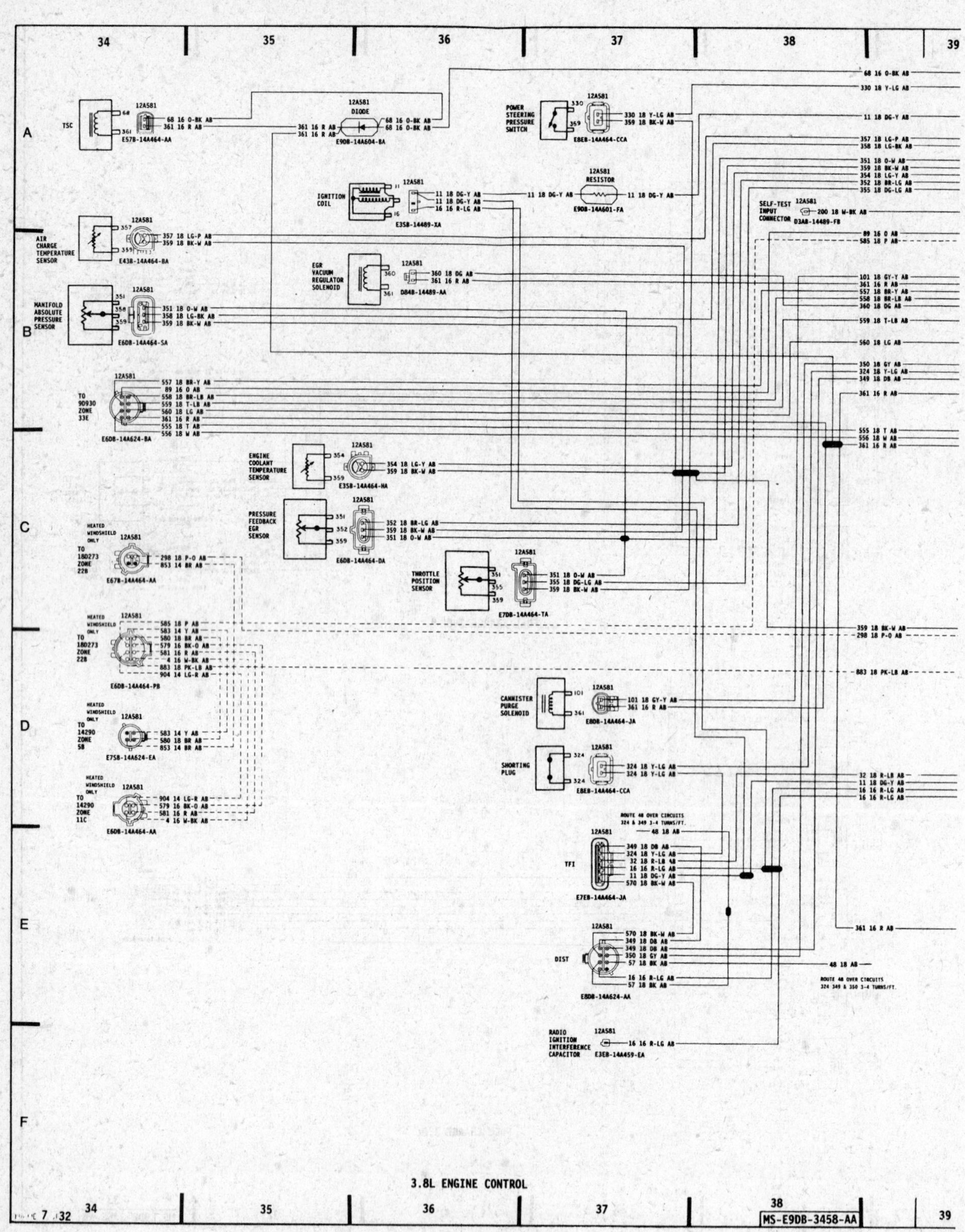
3.8L ENGINE CONTROL
MS-E9DB-3458-AA

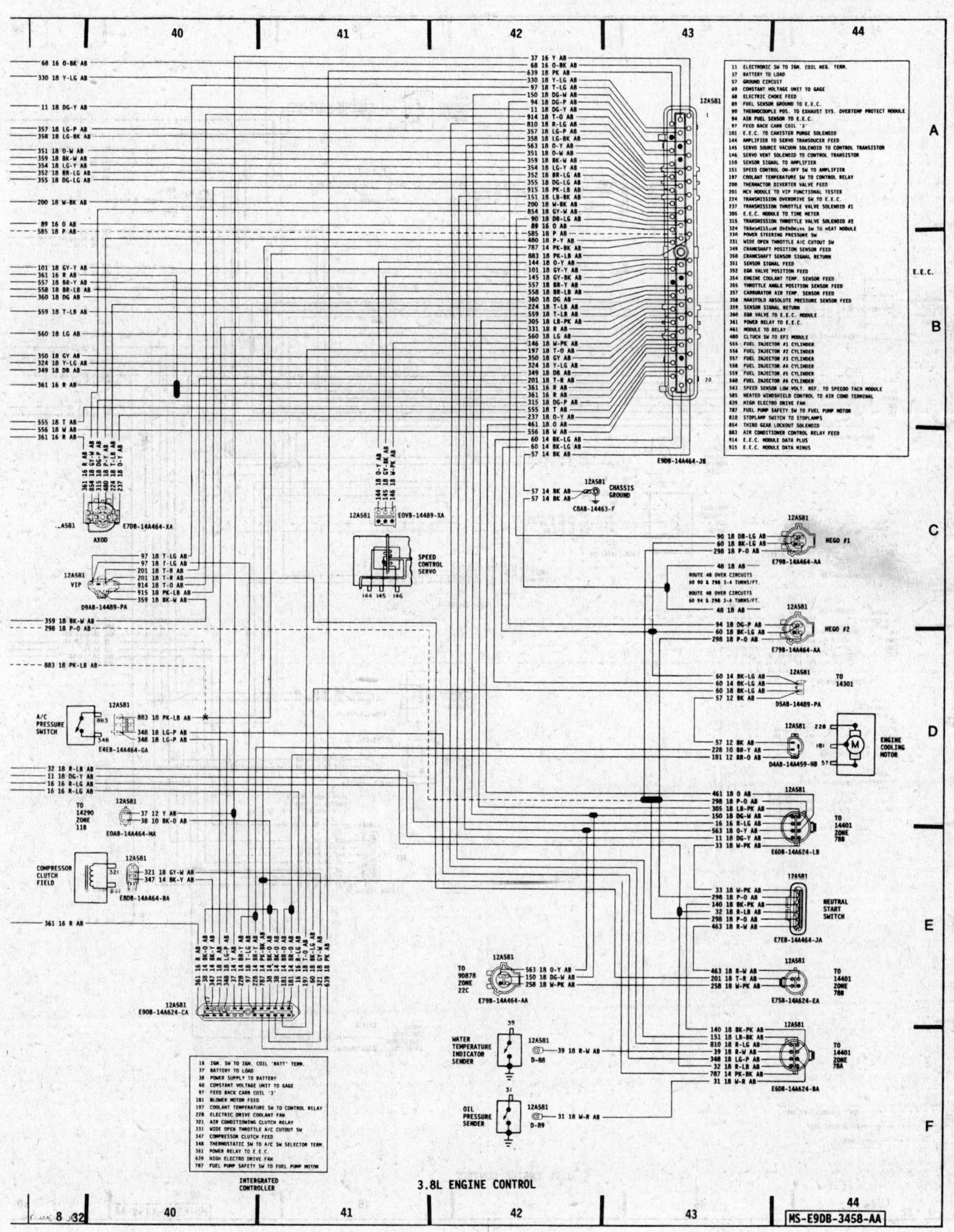

Taurus and Sable electrical schematics – 1989

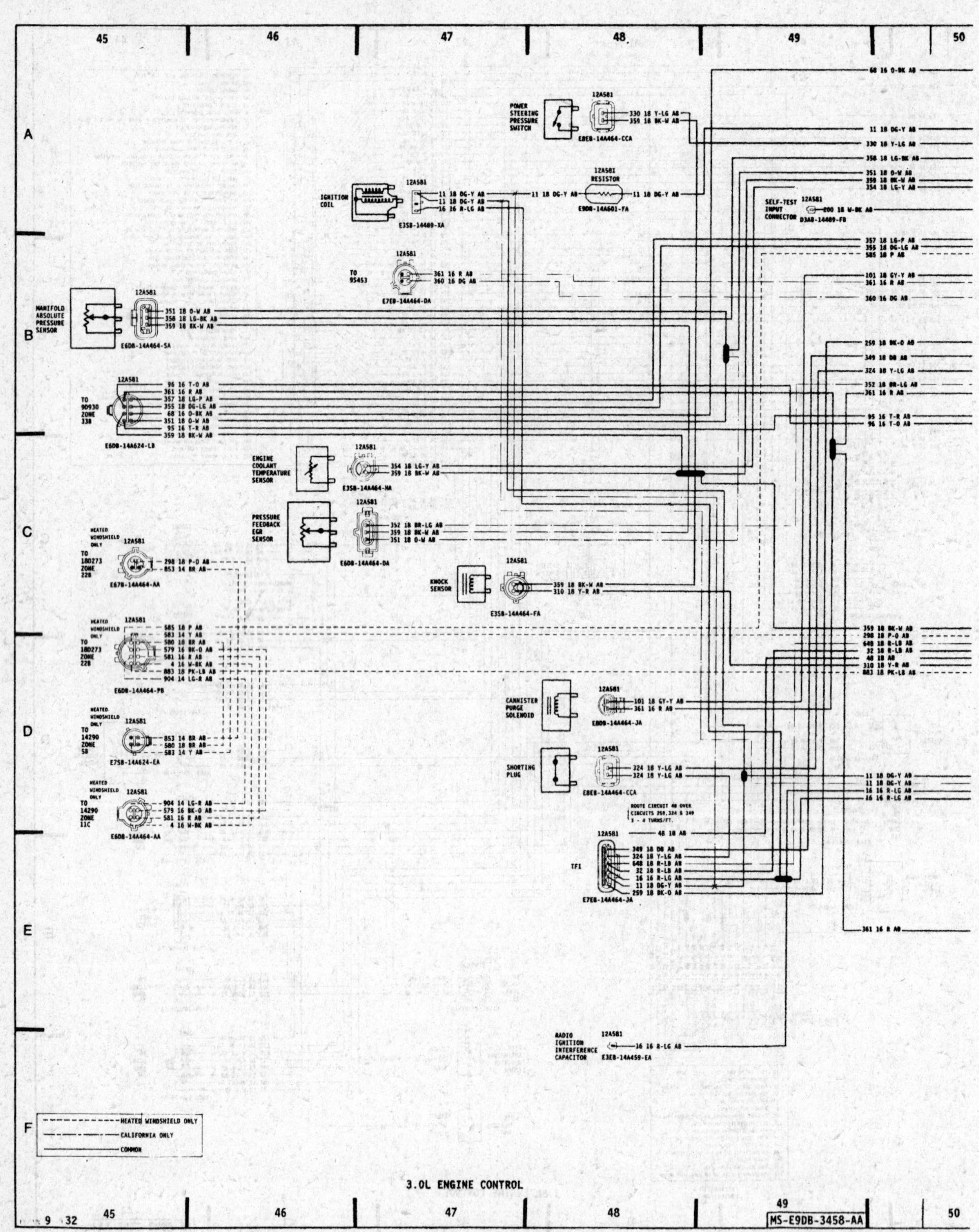

Taurus and Sable electrical schematics – 1989

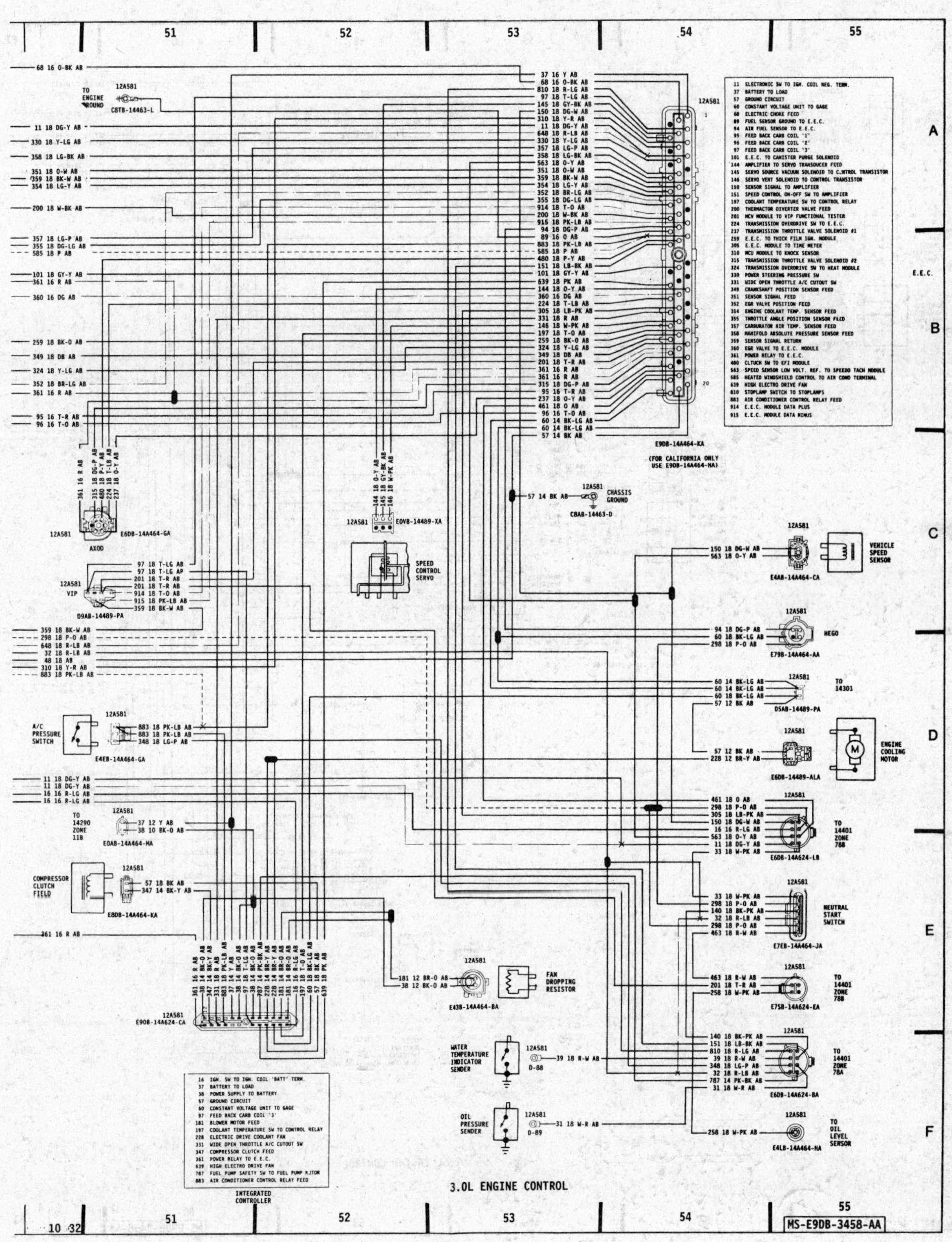

Taurus and Sable electrical schematics — 1989

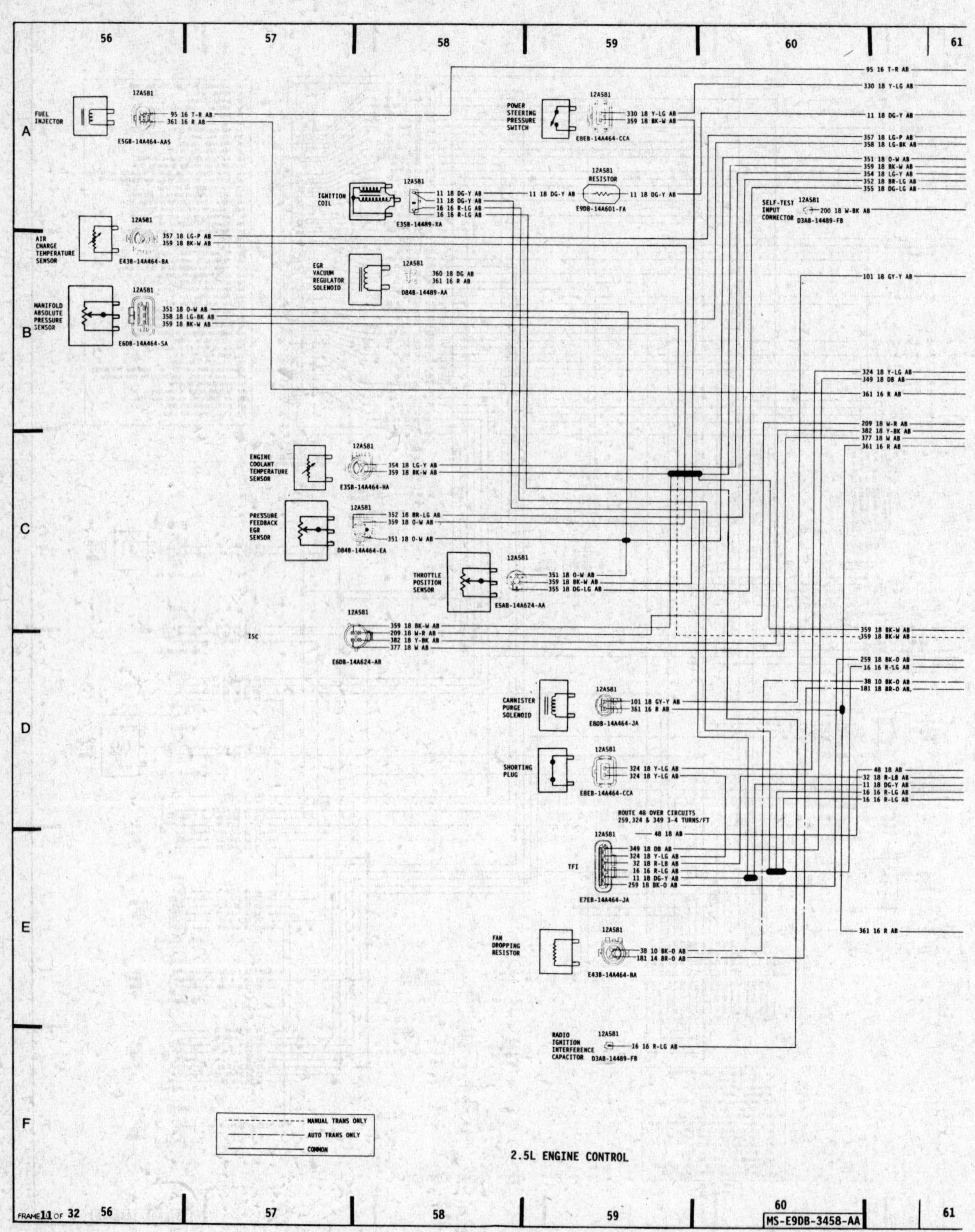

Taurus and Sable electrical schematics – 1989

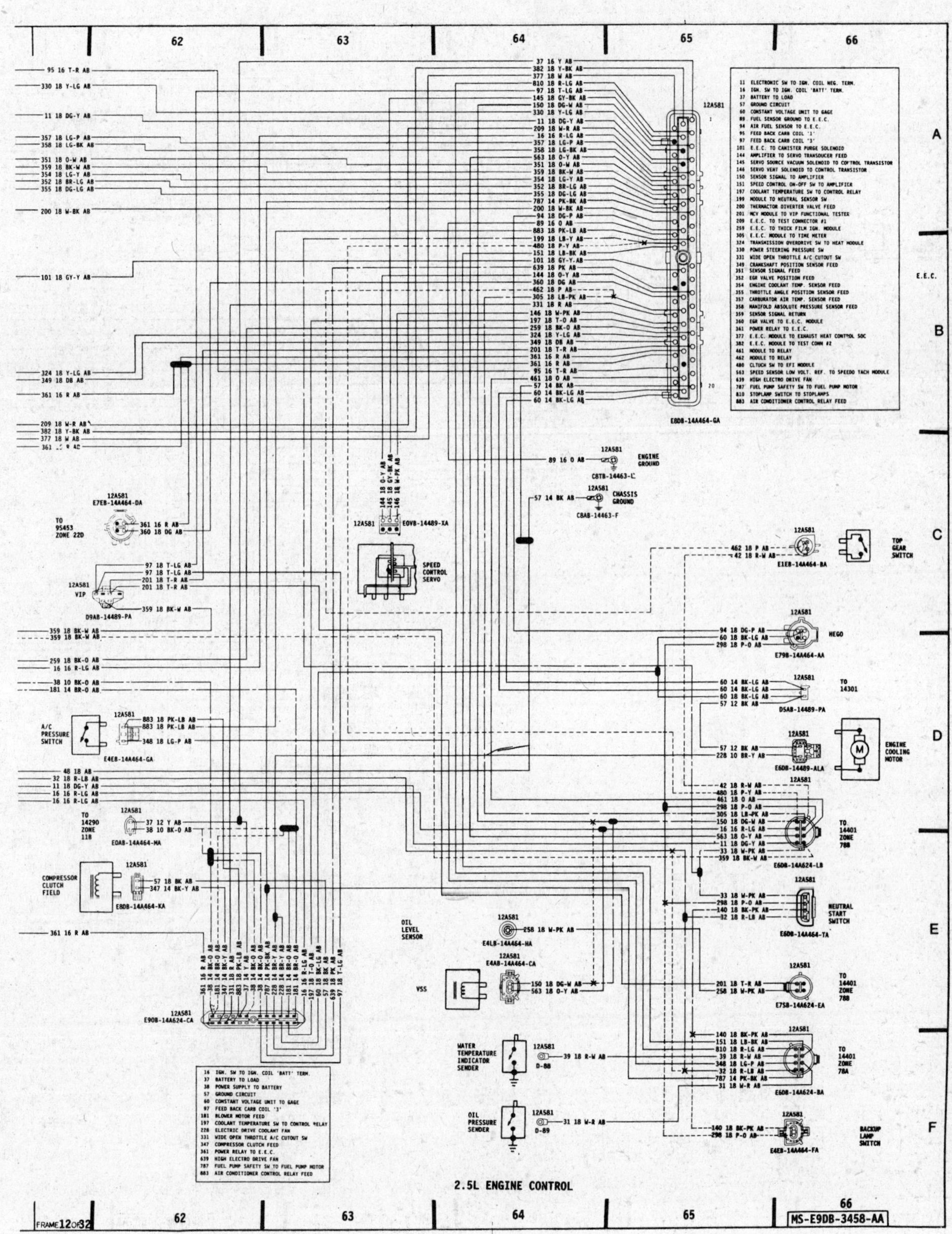

Taurus and Sable electrical schematics — 1989

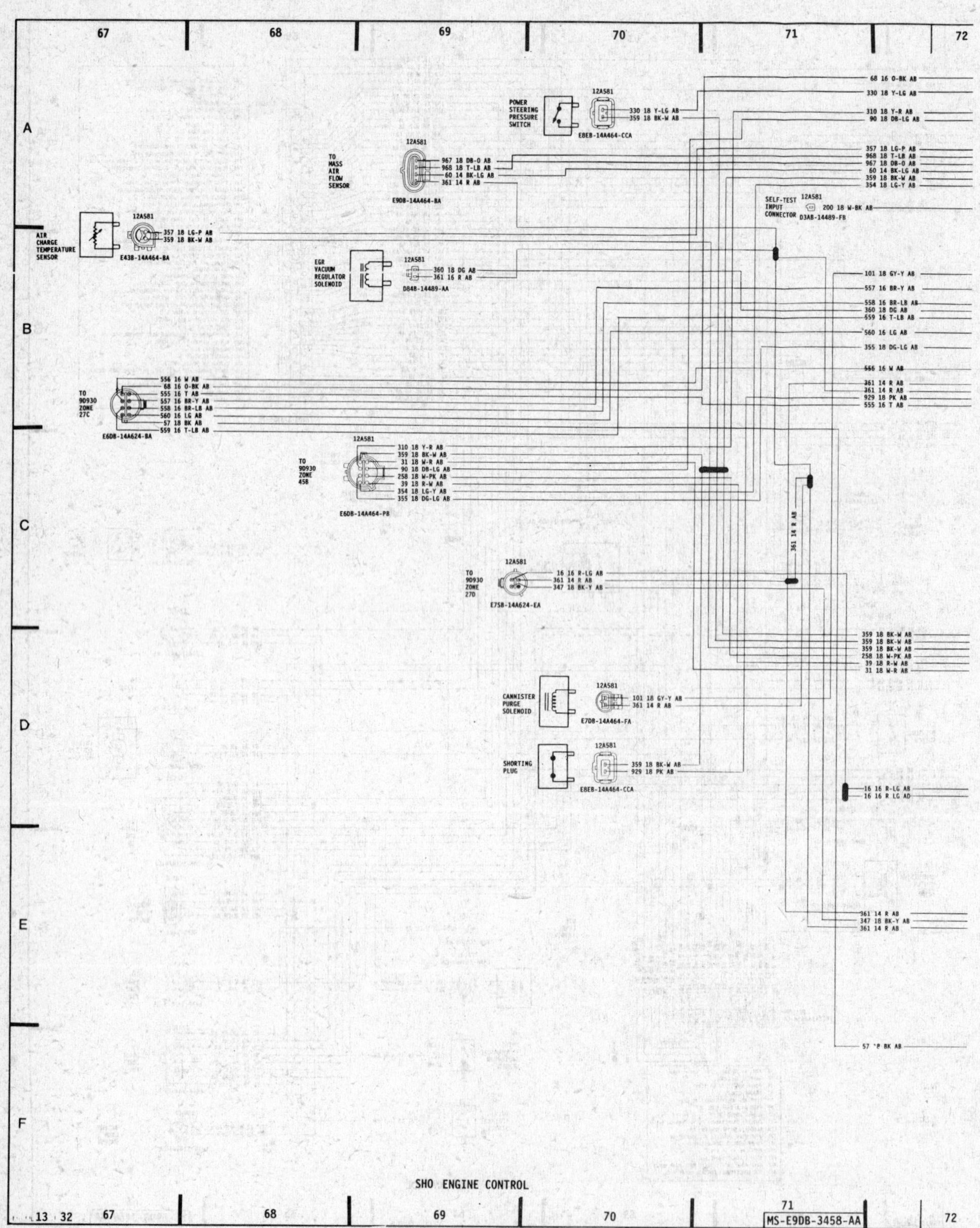
POWER STEERING PRESSURE SWITCH
TO MASS AIR FLOW SENSOR
AIR CHARGE TEMPERATURE SENSOR
EGR VACUUM REGULATOR SOLENOID
SELF-TEST INPUT CONNECTOR
TO 90930 ZONE 27C
TO 90930 ZONE 45B
TO 90930 ZONE 27D
CANNISTER PURGE SOLENOID
SHORTING PLUG
SHO ENGINE CONTROL
MS-E9DB-3458-AA

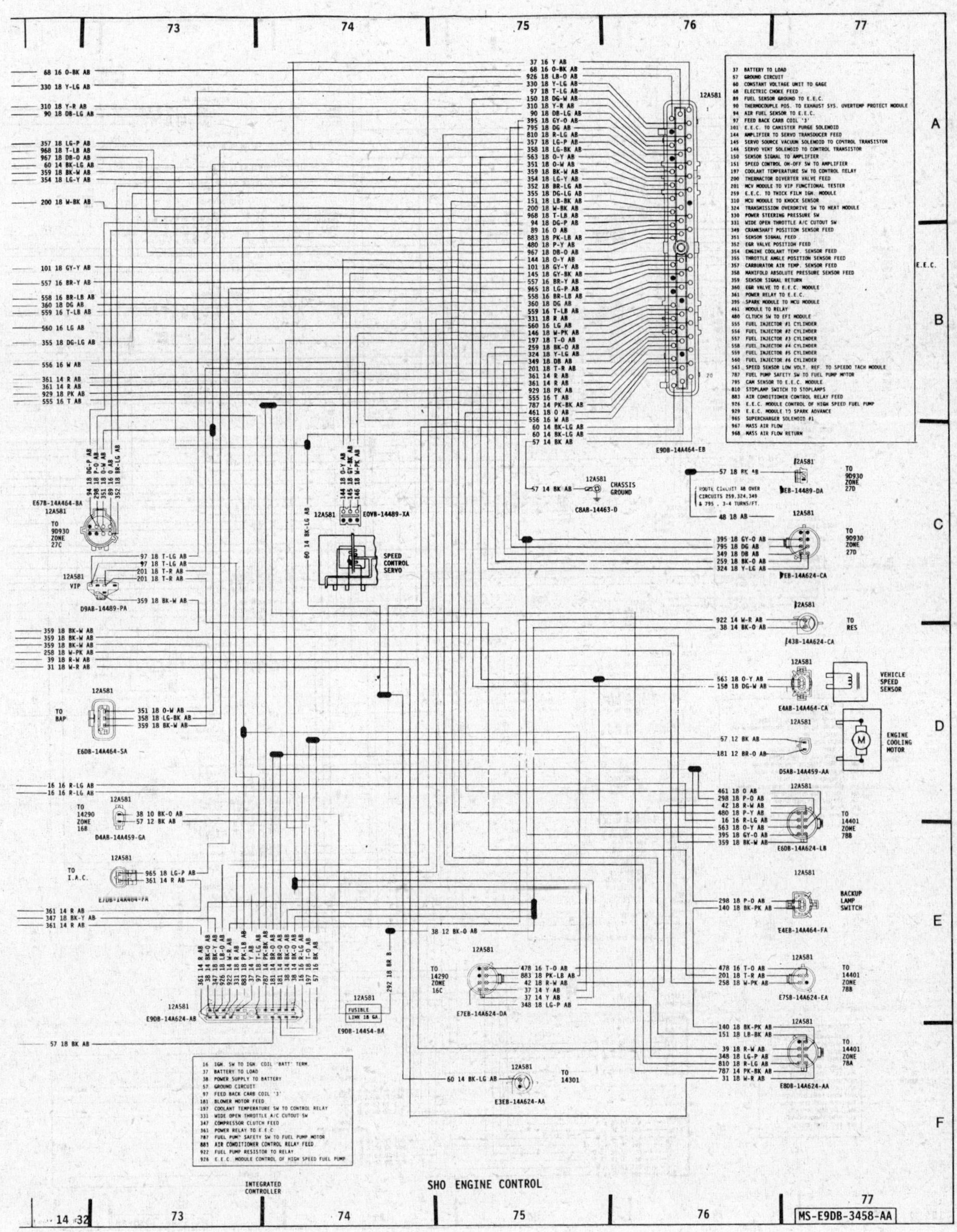

Taurus and Sable electrical schematics — 1989

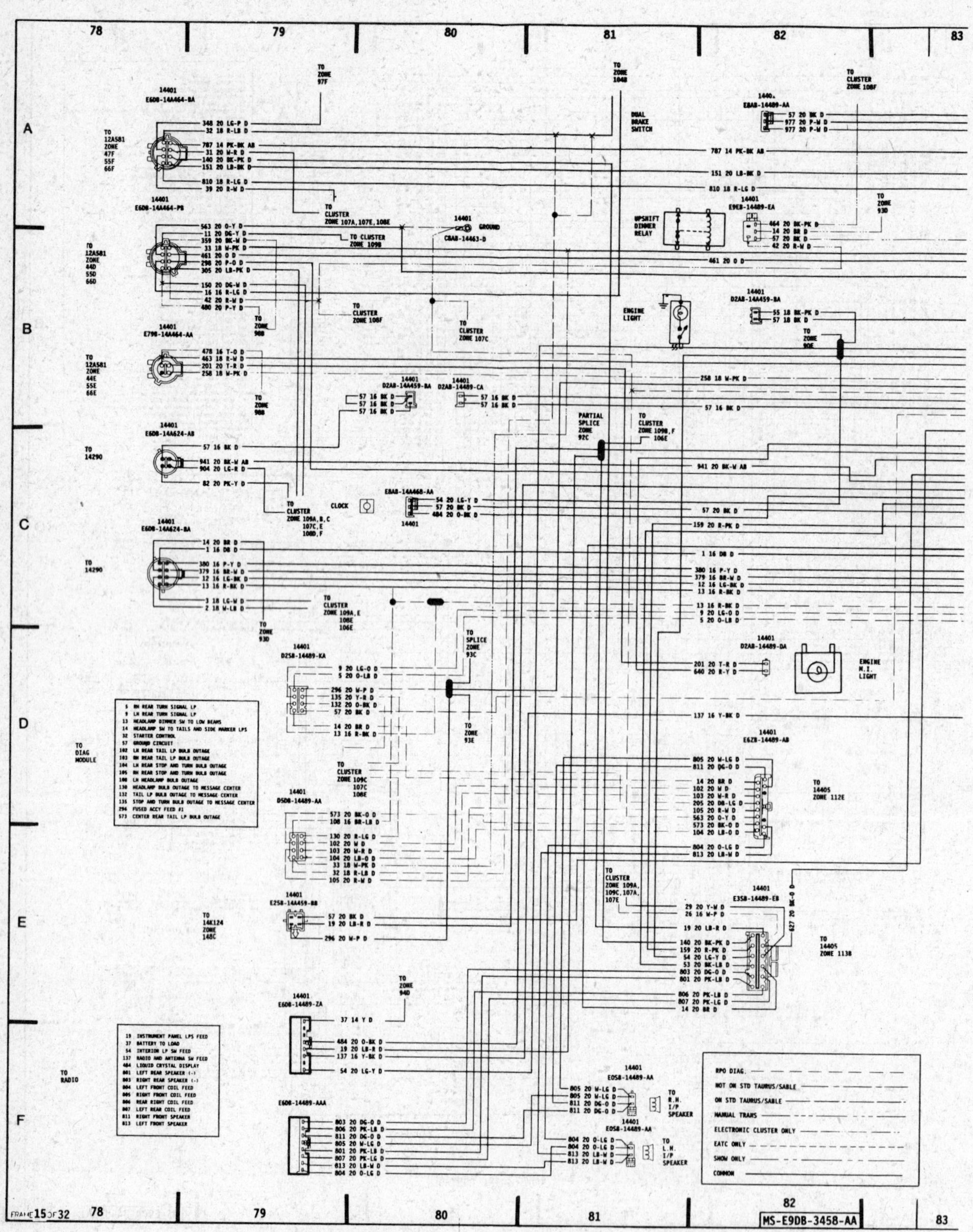

Taurus and Sable electrical schematics – 1989

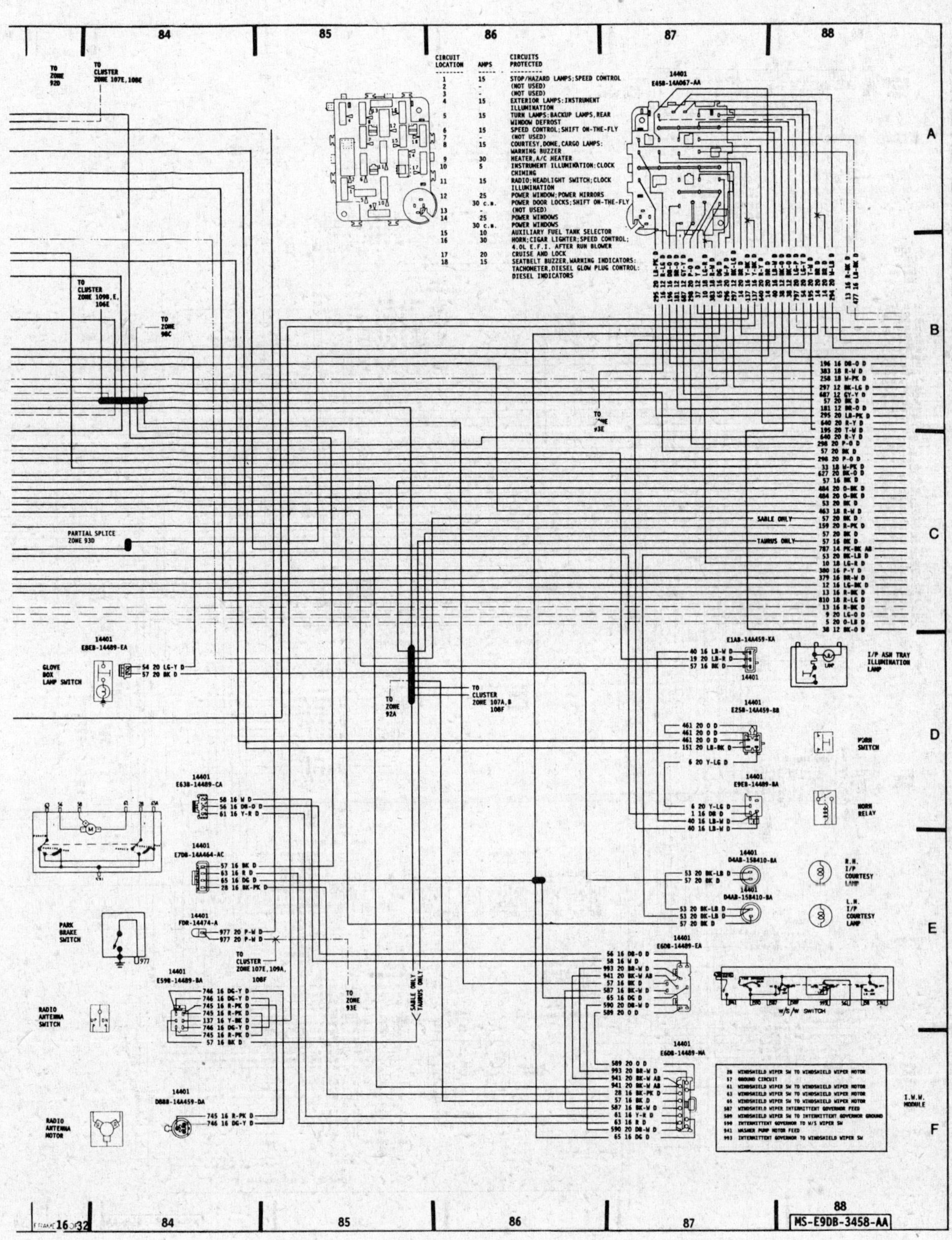

Taurus and Sable electrical schematics — 1989

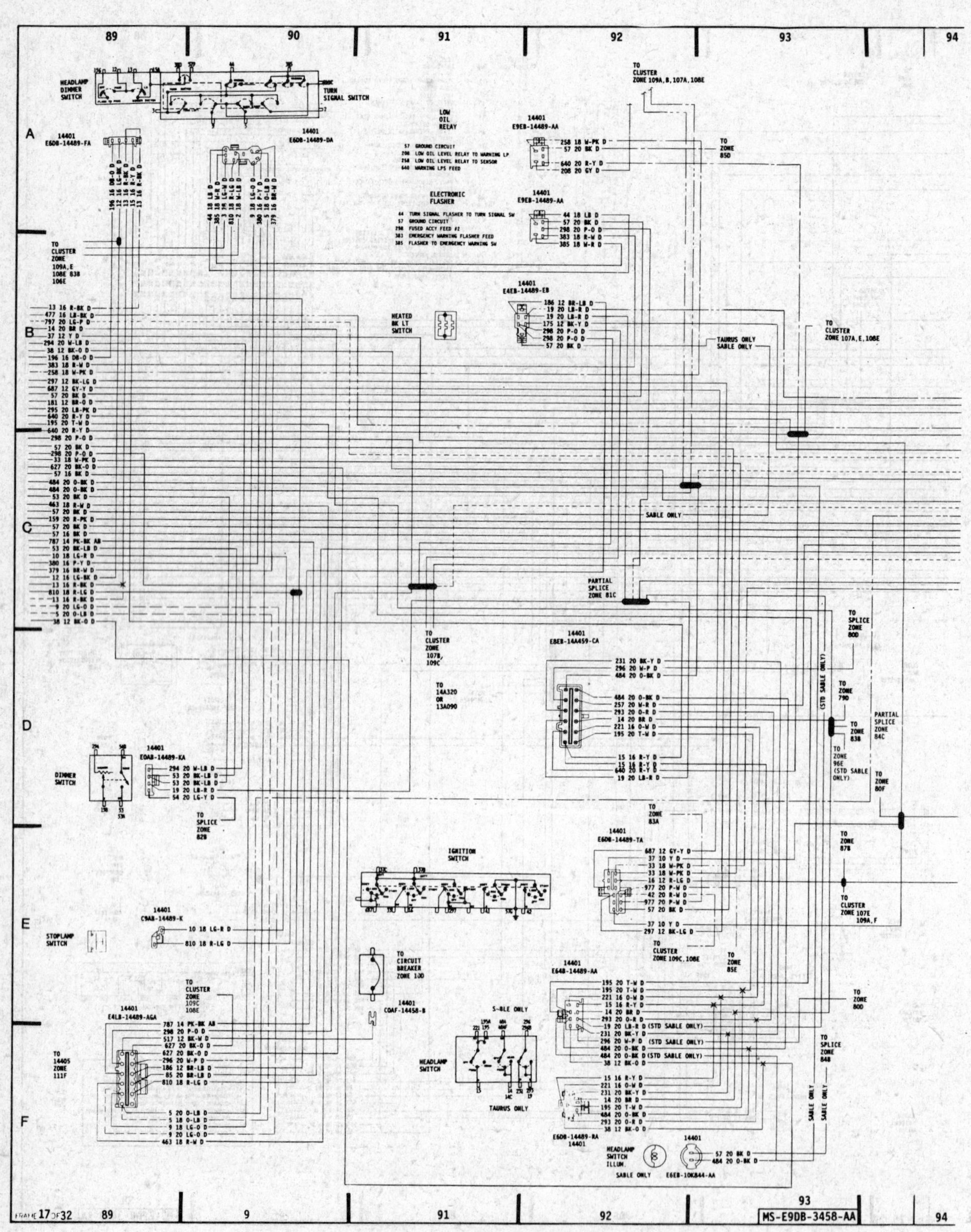

Taurus and Sable electrical schematics — 1989

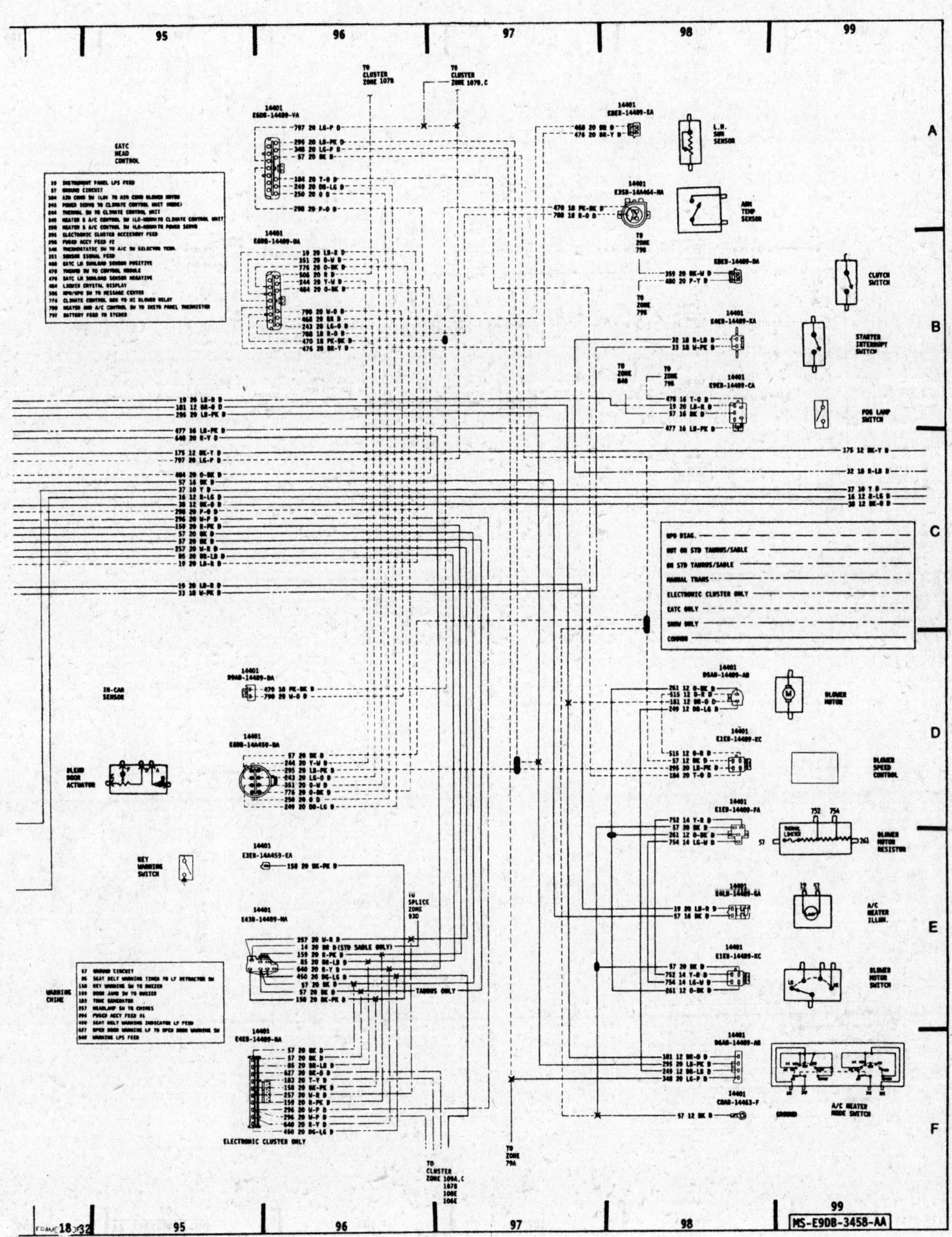

Taurus and Sable electrical schematics — 1989

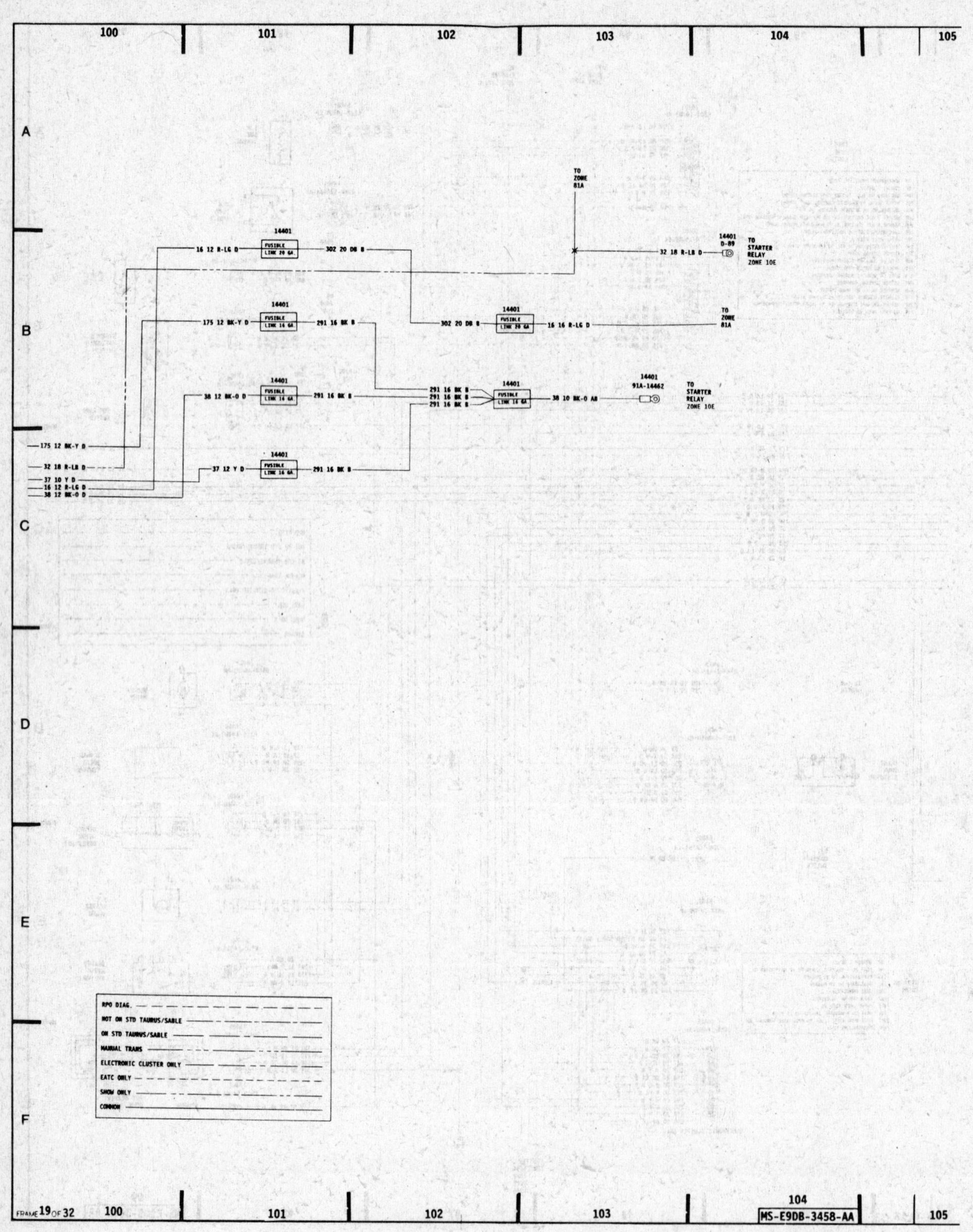

Taurus and Sable electrical schematics — 1989

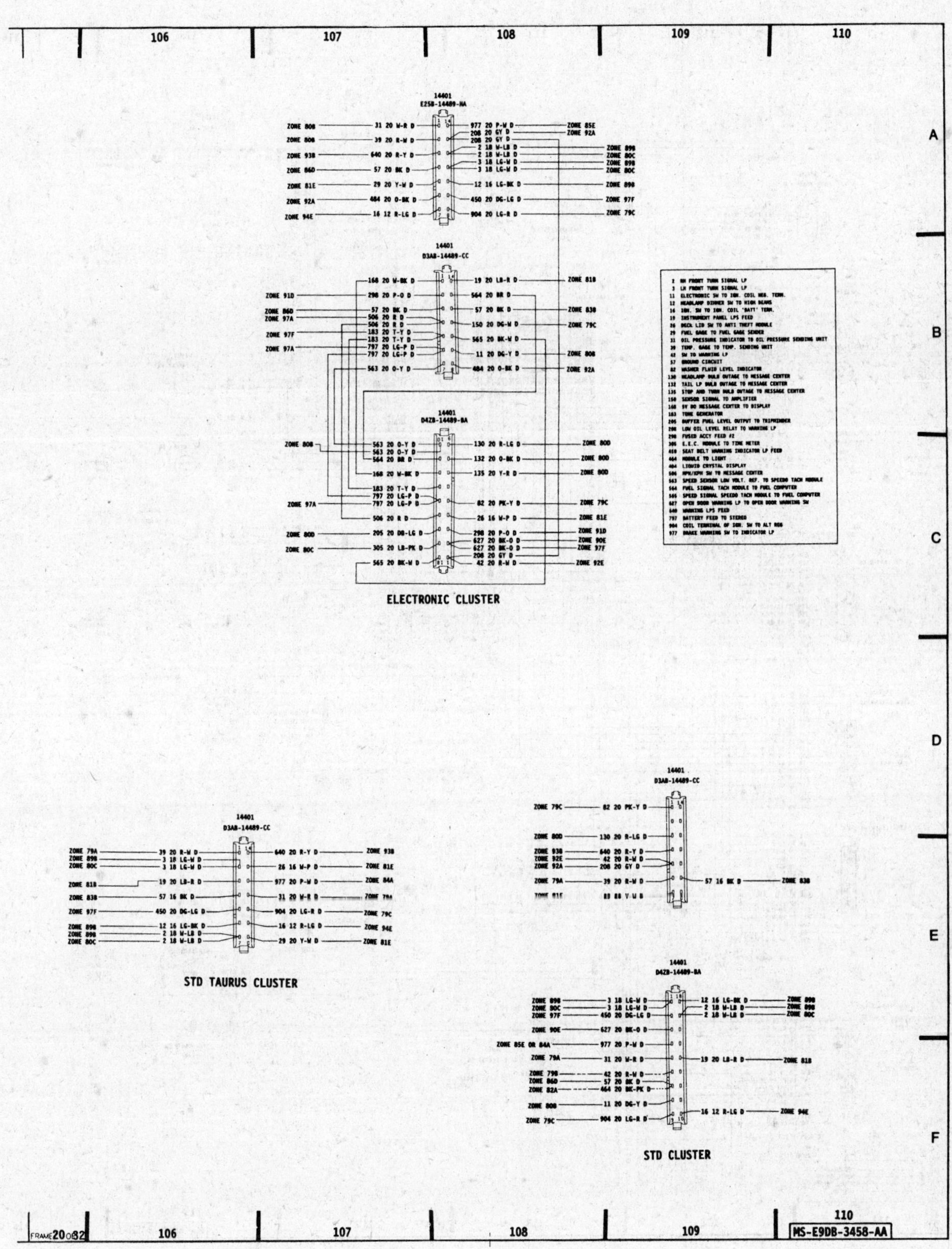
106
107
108
109
110
A
B
C
D
E
F
14401
E25B-14489-HA
14401
D3AB-14489-CC
14401
D4ZB-14489-BA
ELECTRONIC CLUSTER
2 RH FRONT TURN SIGNAL LP
3 LH FRONT TURN SIGNAL LP
11 ELECTRONIC SW TO IGN. COIL NEG. TERM.
12 HEADLAMP DIMMER SW TO HIGH BEAMS
16 IGN. SW TO IGN. COIL 'BATT' TERM.
19 INSTRUMENT PANEL LPS FEED
26 DECK LID SW TO ANTI THEFT MODULE
29 FUEL GAGE TO FUEL GAGE SENDER
31 OIL PRESSURE INDICATOR TO OIL PRESSURE SENDING UNIT
39 TEMP. GAGE TO TEMP. SENDING UNIT
42 SW TO WARNING LP
57 GROUND CIRCUIT
82 WASHER FLUID LEVEL INDICATOR
130 HEADLAMP BULB OUTAGE TO MESSAGE CENTER
132 TAIL LP BULB OUTAGE TO MESSAGE CENTER
135 STOP AND TURN BULB OUTAGE TO MESSAGE CENTER
150 SENSOR SIGNAL TO AMPLIFIER
160 5V DC MESSAGE CENTER TO DISPLAY
183 TONE GENERATOR
205 BUFFER FUEL LEVEL OUTPUT TO TRIPMINDER
208 LOW OIL LEVEL RELAY TO WARNING LP
298 FUSED ACCY FEED #2
305 E.E.C. MODULE TO TIME METER
450 SEAT BELT WARNING INDICATOR LP FEED
464 MODULE TO LIGHT
484 LIQUID CRYSTAL DISPLAY
506 MPH/KPH SW TO MESSAGE CENTER
563 SPEED SENSOR LOW VOLT. REF. TO SPEEDO TACH MODULE
564 FUEL SIGNAL TACH MODULE TO FUEL COMPUTER
565 SPEED SIGNAL SPEEDO TACH MODULE TO FUEL COMPUTER
627 OPEN DOOR WARNING LP TO OPEN DOOR WARNING SW
640 WARNING LPS FEED
797 BATTERY FEED TO STEREO
904 COIL TERMINAL OF IGN. SW TO ALT REG
977 BRAKE WARNING SW TO INDICATOR LP
14401
D3AB-14489-CC
STD TAURUS CLUSTER
14401
D3AB-14489-CC
14401
D4ZB-14489-BA
STD CLUSTER
FRAME 20032
MS-E9DB-3458-AA

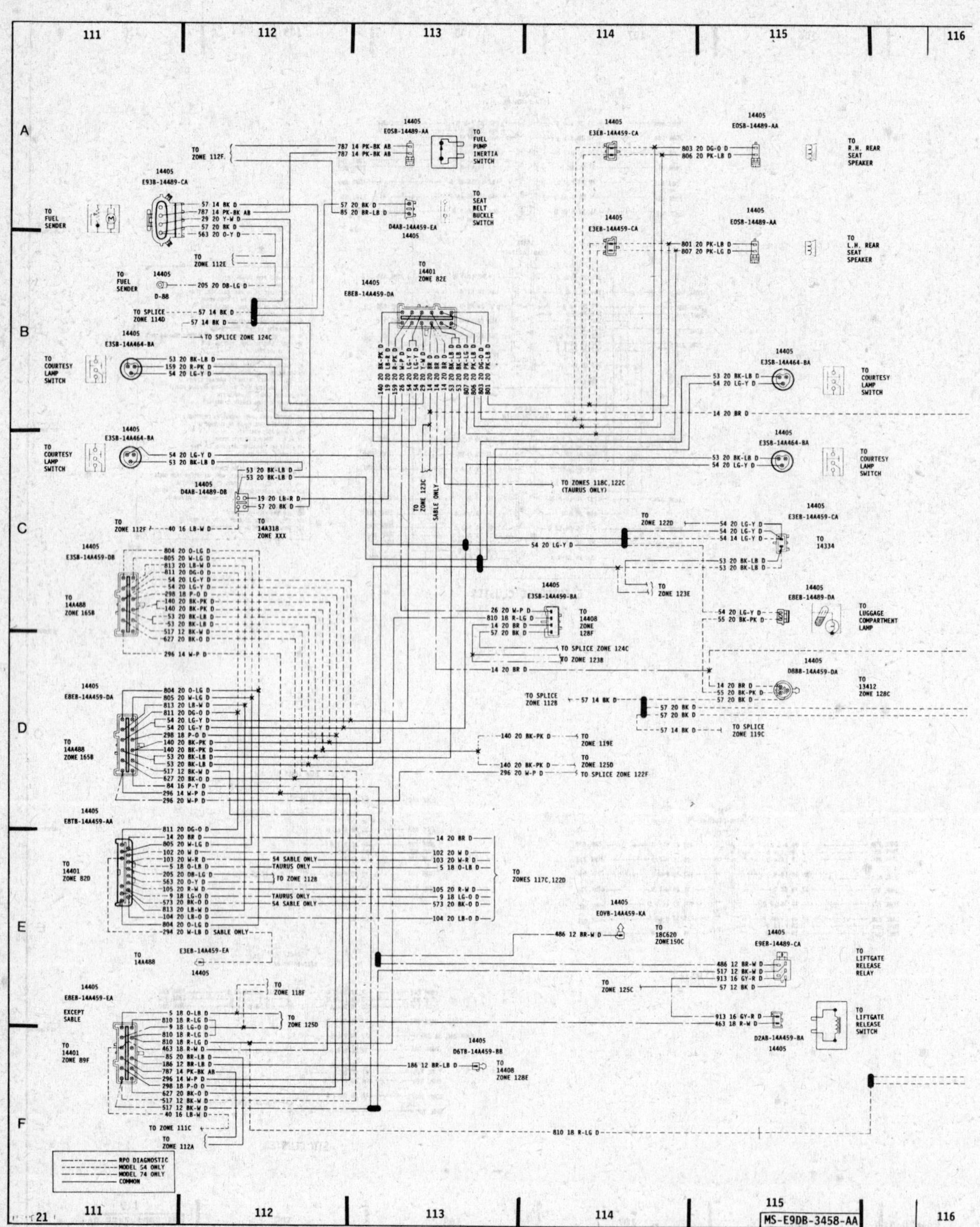

Taurus and Sable electrical schematics — 1989

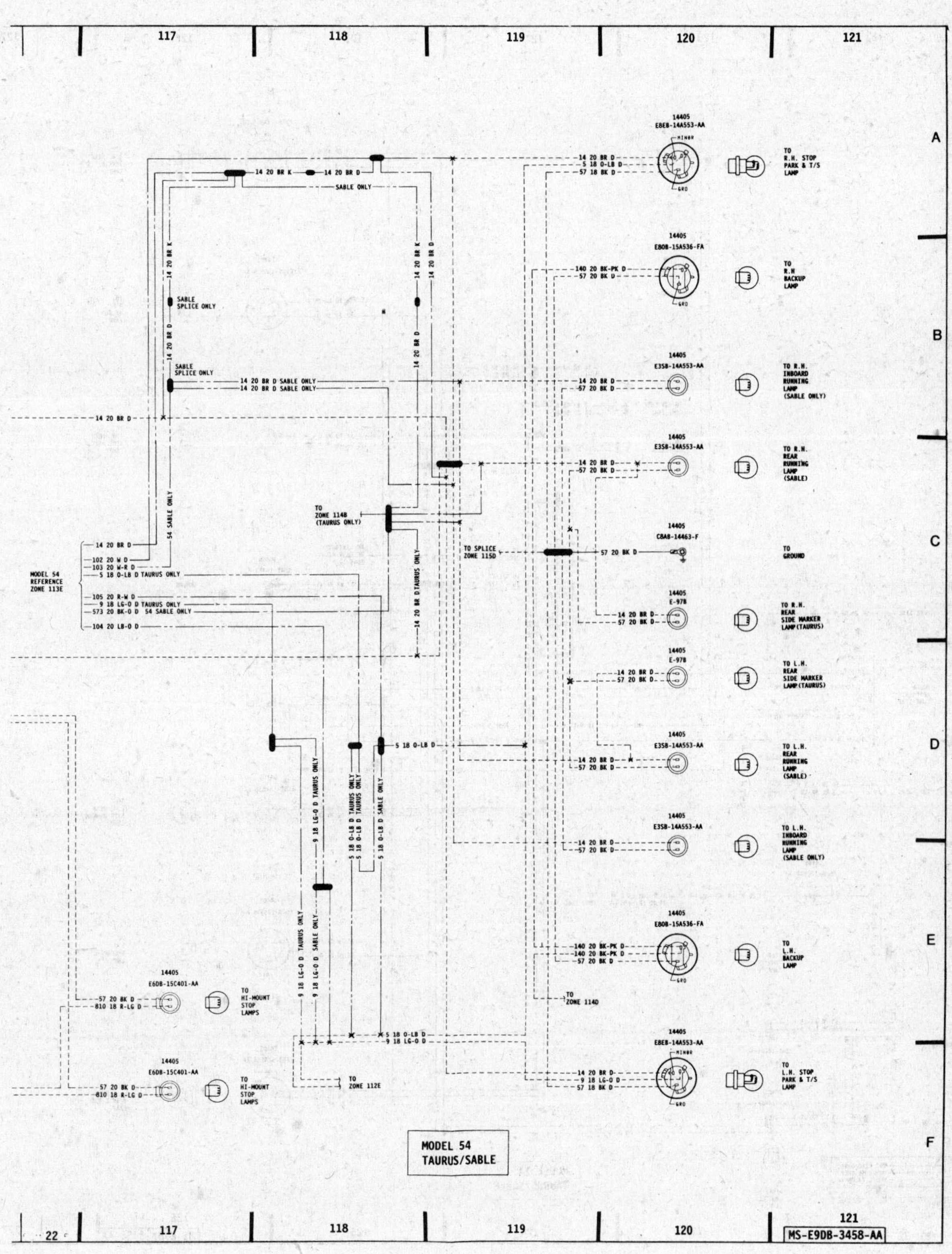

Taurus and Sable electrical schematics — 1989

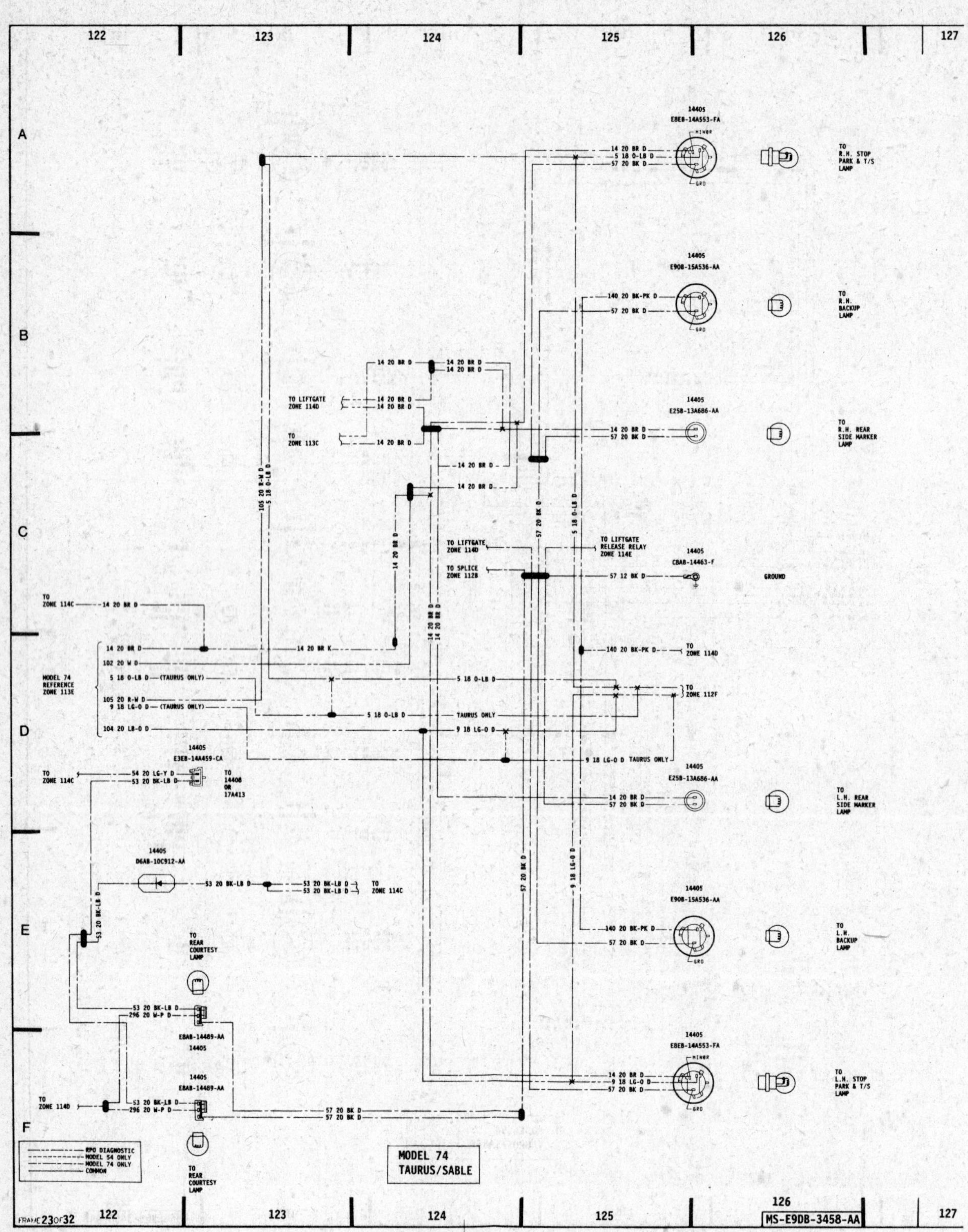

Taurus and Sable electrical schematics – 1989

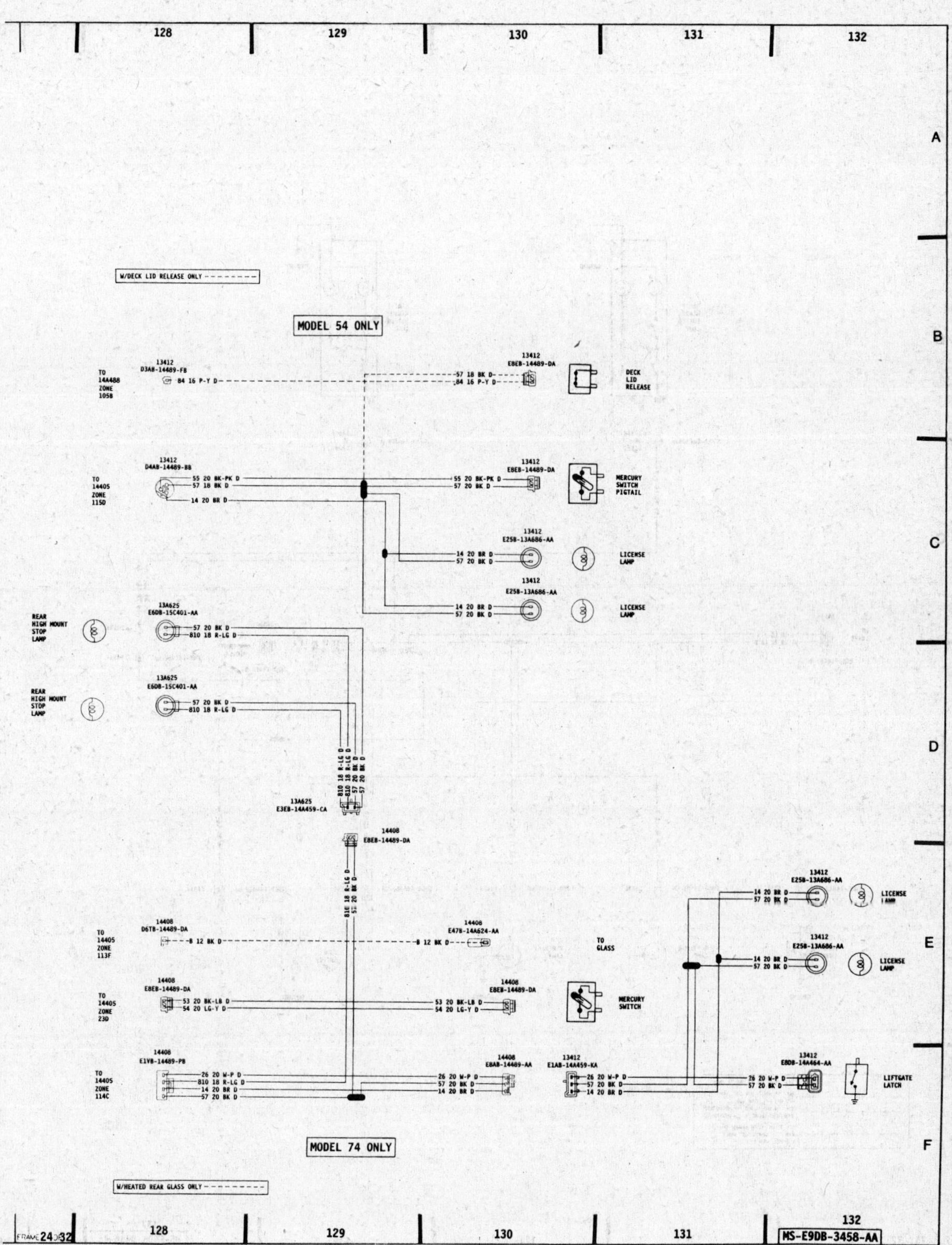

Taurus and Sable electrical schematics – 1989

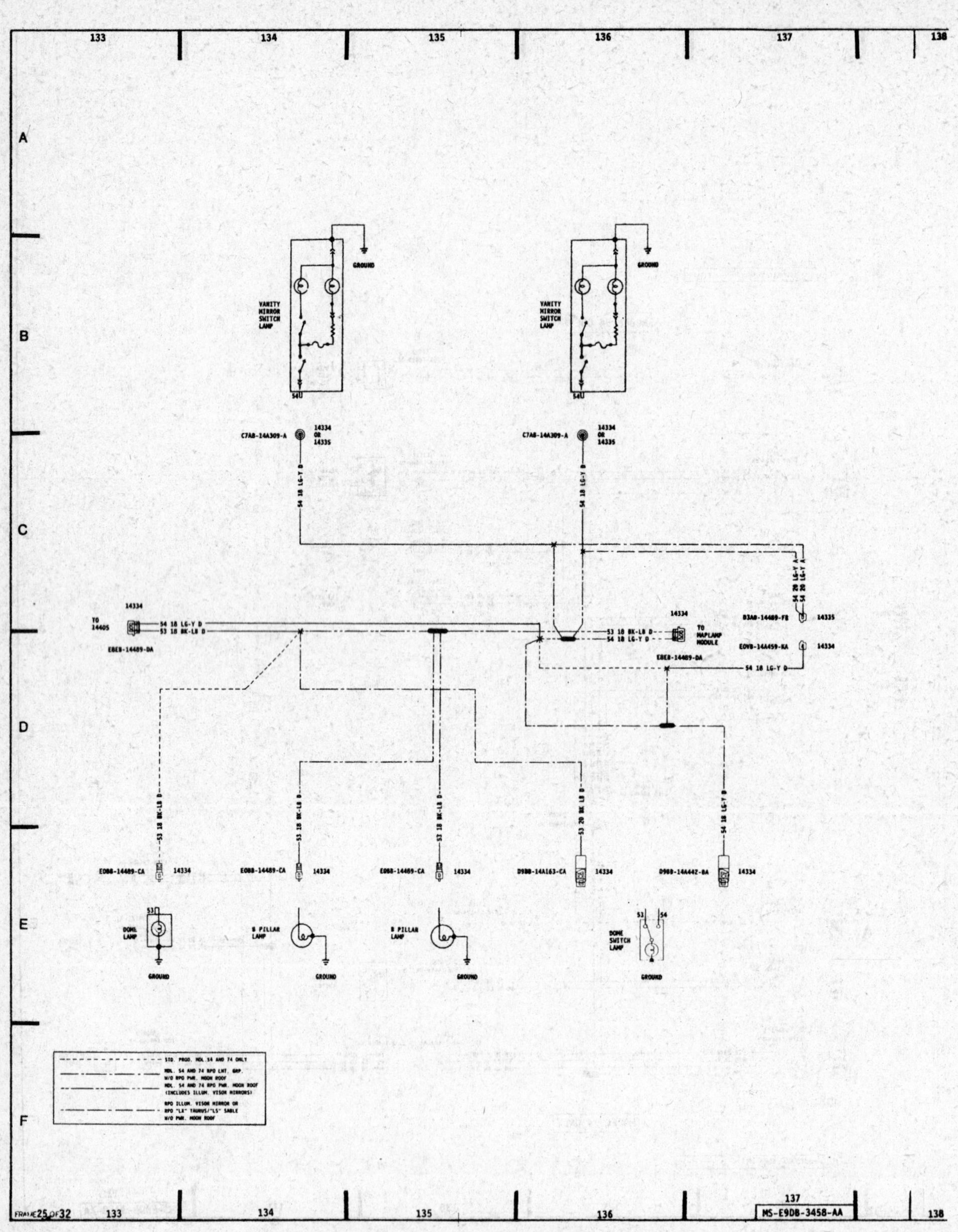

Taurus and Sable electrical schematics — 1989

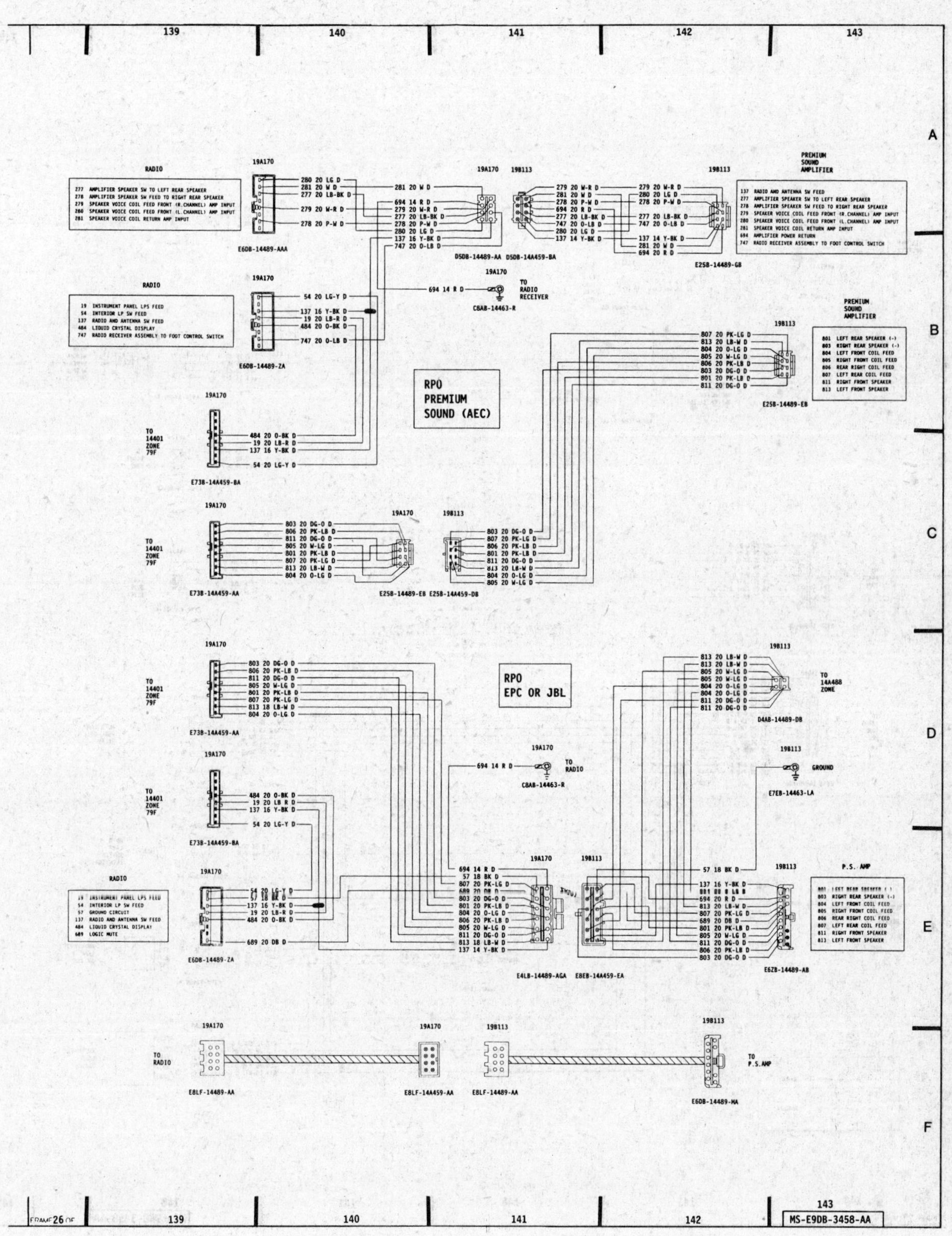

Taurus and Sable electrical schematics — 1989

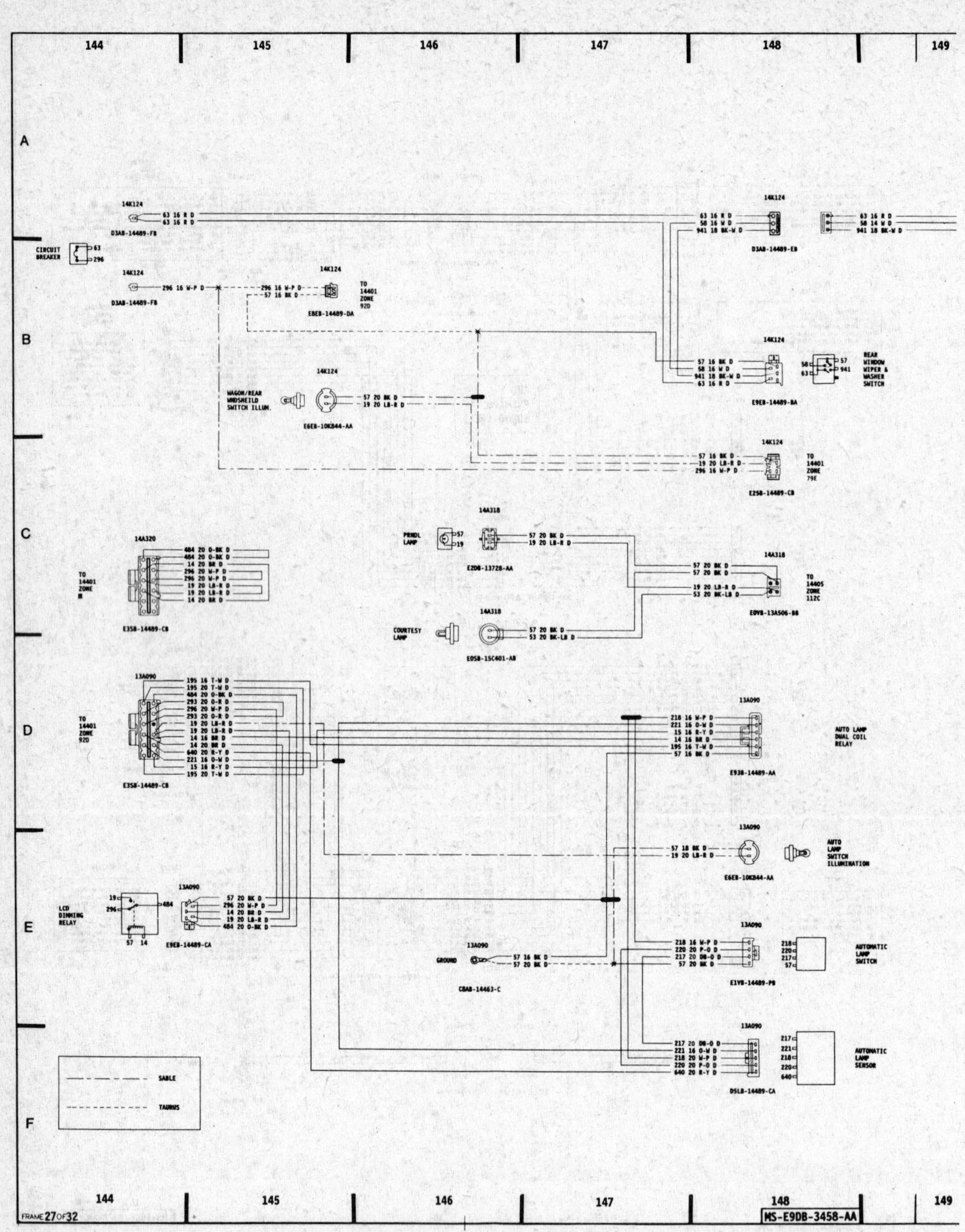

Taurus and Sable electrical schematics — 1989

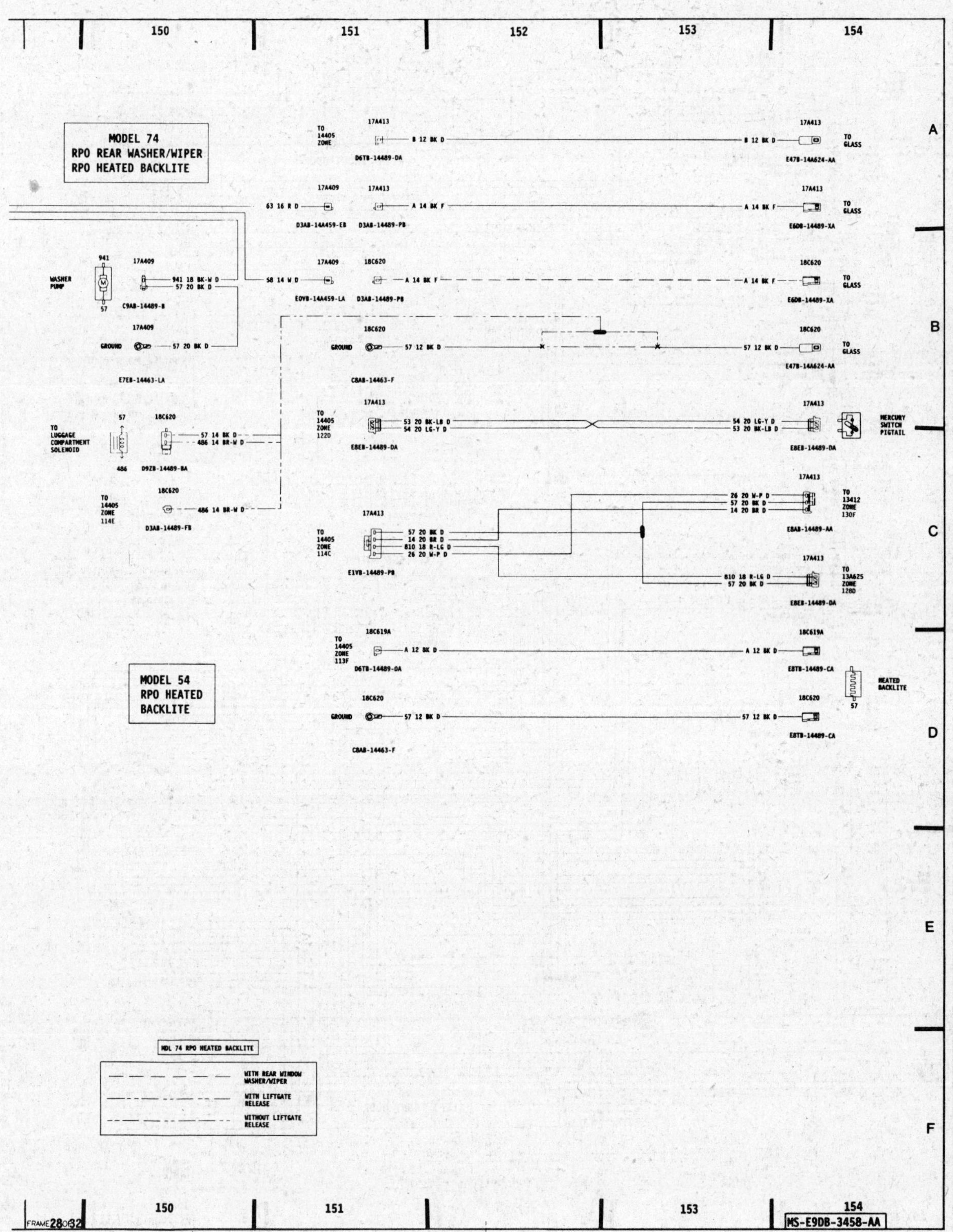
MODEL 74
RPO REAR WASHER/WIPER
RPO HEATED BACKLITE
MODEL 54
RPO HEATED
BACKLITE
WASHER PUMP
TO LUGGAGE COMPARTMENT SOLENOID
MERCURY SWITCH PIGTAIL
HEATED BACKLITE
TO GLASS
GROUND
MDL 74 RPO HEATED BACKLITE
WITH REAR WINDOW WASHER/WIPER
WITH LIFTGATE RELEASE
WITHOUT LIFTGATE RELEASE
MS-E9DB-3458-AA

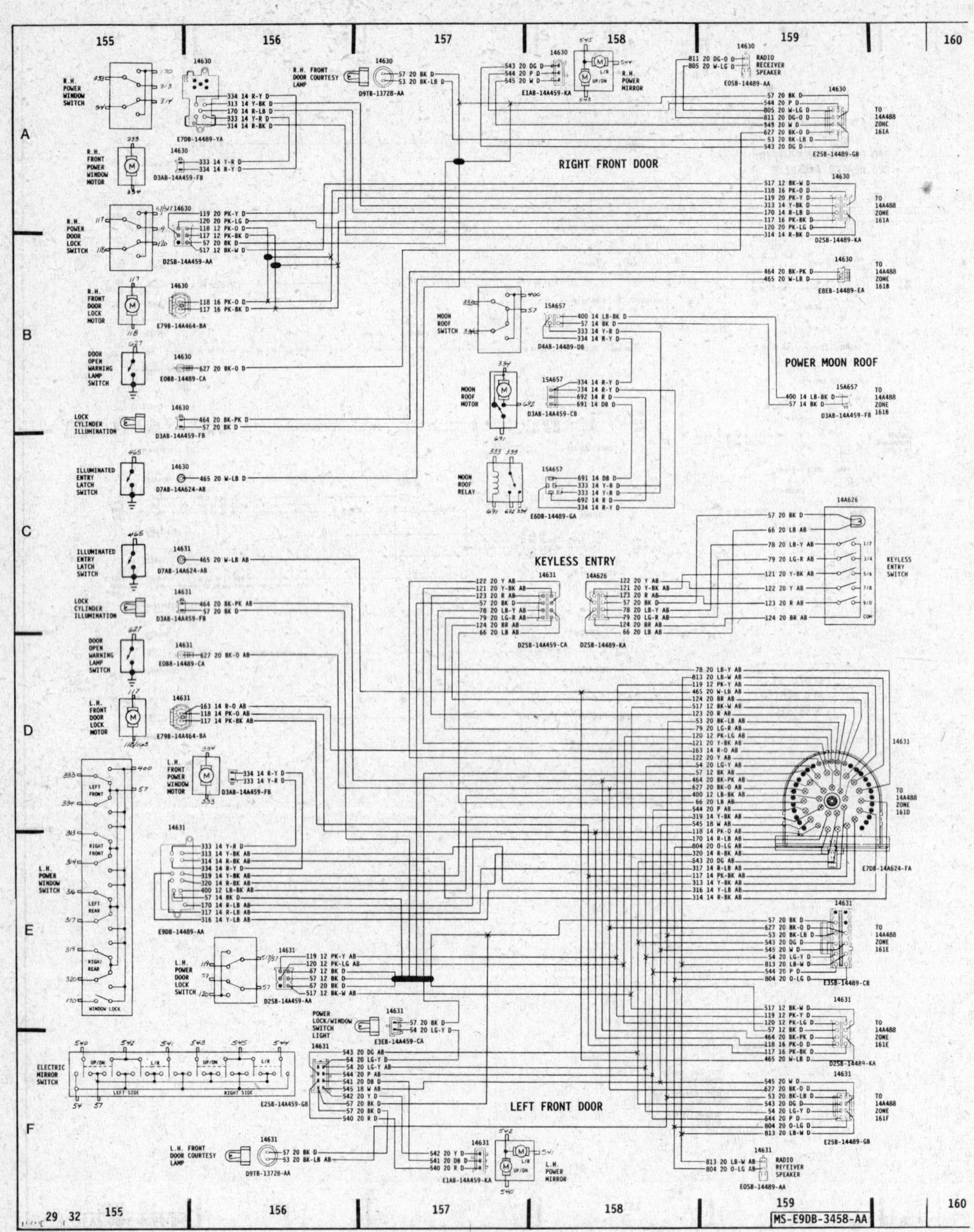

Taurus and Sable electrical schematics – 1989

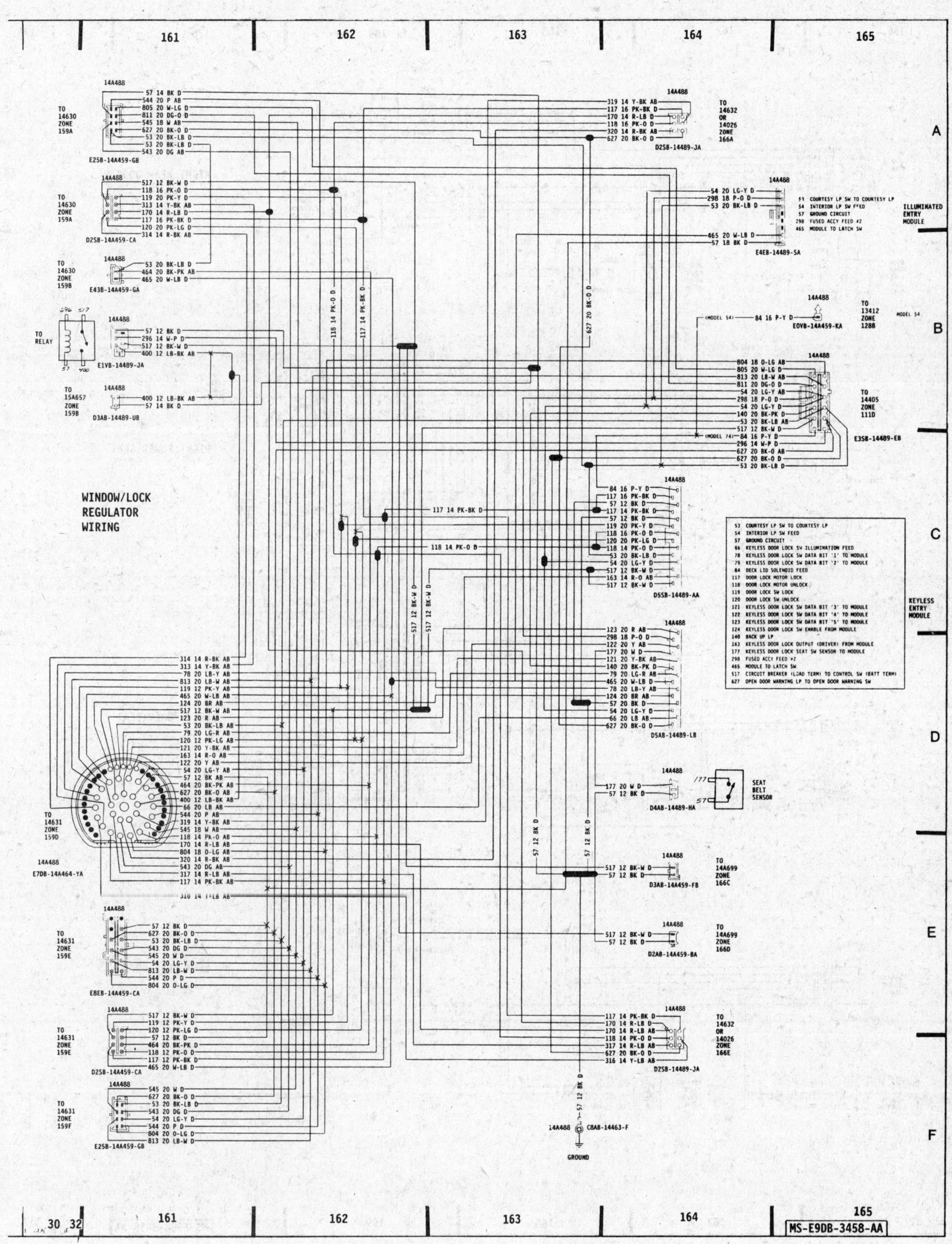

Taurus and Sable electrical schematics — 1989

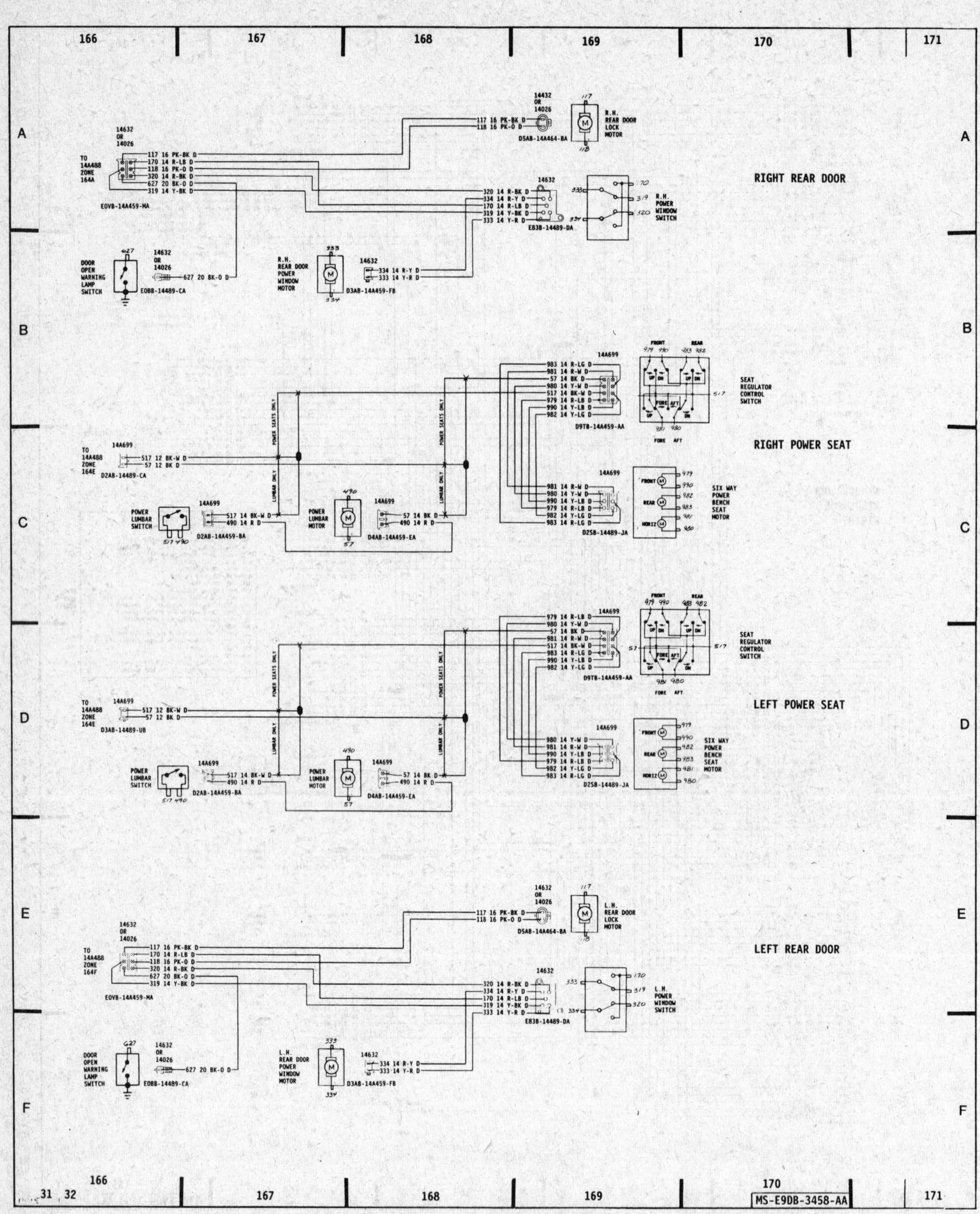

Taurus and Sable electrical schematics — 1989

Troubleshooting Basic Turn Signal and Flasher Problems

Most problems in the turn signals or flasher system can be reduced to defective flashers or bulbs, which are easily replaced. Occasionally, problems in the turn signals are traced to the switch in the steering column, which will require professional service.

F = Front R = Rear ● = Lights off ○ = Lights on

Problem		Solution
Turn signals light, but do not flash	F F R R	• Replace the flasher
No turn signals light on either side	F F R R	• Check the fuse. Replace if defective. • Check the flasher by substitution • Check for open circuit, short circuit or poor ground
Both turn signals on one side don't work	F F R R	• Check for bad bulbs • Check for bad ground in both housings
One turn signal light on one side doesn't work	F F R R	• Check and/or replace bulb • Check for corrosion in socket. Clean contacts. • Check for poor ground at socket
Turn signal flashes too fast or too slow	F F R R	• Check any bulb on the side flashing too fast. A heavy-duty bulb is probably installed in place of a regular bulb. • Check the bulb flashing too slow. A standard bulb was probably installed in place of a heavy-duty bulb. • Check for loose connections or corrosion at the bulb socket
Indicator lights don't work in either direction		• Check if the turn signals are working • Check the dash indicator lights • Check the flasher by substitution

Troubleshooting Basic Turn Signal and Flasher Problems

Most problems in the turn signals or flasher system can be reduced to defective flashers or bulbs, which are easily replaced. Occasionally, problems in the turn signals are traced to the switch in the steering column, which will require professional service.

F = Front R = Rear ● = Lights off ○ = Lights on

Problem	Solution
One indicator light doesn't light	• On systems with 1 dash indicator: See if the lights work on the same side. Often the filaments have been reversed in systems combining stoplights with taillights and turn signals. Check the flasher by substitution • On systems with 2 indicators: Check the bulbs on the same side Check the indicator light bulb Check the flasher by substitution

Troubleshooting Basic Lighting Problems

Problem	Cause	Solution
Lights		
One or more lights don't work, but others do	• Defective bulb(s) • Blown fuse(s) • Dirty fuse clips or light sockets • Poor ground circuit	• Replace bulb(s) • Replace fuse(s) • Clean connections • Run ground wire from light socket housing to car frame
Lights burn out quickly	• Incorrect voltage regulator setting or defective regulator • Poor battery/alternator connections	• Replace voltage regulator • Check battery/alternator connections
Lights go dim	• Low/discharged battery • Alternator not charging • Corroded sockets or connections • Low voltage output	• Check battery • Check drive belt tension; repair or replace alternator • Clean bulb and socket contacts and connections • Replace voltage regulator
Lights flicker	• Loose connection • Poor ground • Circuit breaker operating (short circuit)	• Tighten all connections • Run ground wire from light housing to car frame • Check connections and look for bare wires
Lights "flare"—Some flare is normal on acceleration—if excessive, see "Lights Burn Out Quickly"	• High voltage setting	• Replace voltage regulator

Troubleshooting Basic Lighting Problems

Problem	Cause	Solution
Lights		
Lights glare—approaching drivers are blinded	• Lights adjusted too high • Rear springs or shocks sagging • Rear tires soft	• Have headlights aimed • Check rear springs/shocks • Check/correct rear tire pressure
Turn Signals		
Turn signals don't work in either direction	• Blown fuse • Defective flasher • Loose connection	• Replace fuse • Replace flasher • Check/tighten all connections
Right (or left) turn signal only won't work	• Bulb burned out • Right (or left) indicator bulb burned out • Short circuit	• Replace bulb • Check/replace indicator bulb • Check/repair wiring
Flasher rate too slow or too fast	• Incorrect wattage bulb • Incorrect flasher	• Flasher bulb • Replace flasher (use a variable load flasher if you pull a trailer)
Indicator lights do not flash (burn steadily)	• Burned out bulb • Defective flasher	• Replace bulb • Replace flasher
Indicator lights do not light at all	• Burned out indicator bulb • Defective flasher	• Replace indicator bulb • Replace flasher

Troubleshooting Basic Dash Gauge Problems

Problem	Cause	Solution
Coolant Temperature Gauge		
Gauge reads erratically or not at all	• Loose or dirty connections • Defective sending unit • Defective gauge	• Clean/tighten connections • Bi-metal gauge: remove the wire from the sending unit. Ground the wire for an instant. If the gauge registers, replace the sending unit. • Magnetic gauge: disconnect the wire at the sending unit. With ignition ON gauge should register COLD. Ground the wire; gauge should register HOT.
Ammeter Gauge—Turn Headlights ON (do not start engine). Note reaction		
Ammeter shows charge Ammeter shows discharge Ammeter does not move	• Connections reversed on gauge • Ammeter is OK • Loose connections or faulty wiring • Defective gauge	• Reinstall connections • Nothing • Check/correct wiring • Replace gauge

Troubleshooting Basic Dash Gauge Problems

Problem	Cause	Solution
Warning Lights		
Light(s) do not come on when ignition is ON, but engine is not started	• Defective bulb • Defective wire	• Replace bulb • Check wire from light to sending unit
	• Defective sending unit	• Disconnect the wire from the sending unit and ground it. Replace the sending unit if the light comes on with the ignition ON.
Light comes on with engine running	• Problem in individual system • Defective sending unit	• Check system • Check sending unit (see above)

Troubleshooting the Heater

Problem	Cause	Solution
Blower motor will not turn at any speed	• Blown fuse • Loose connection • Defective ground • Faulty switch • Faulty motor • Faulty resistor	• Replace fuse • Inspect and tighten • Clean and tighten • Replace switch • Replace motor • Replace resistor
Blower motor turns at one speed only	• Faulty switch • Faulty resistor	• Replace switch • Replace resistor
Blower motor turns but does not circulate air	• Intake blocked • Fan not secured to the motor shaft	• Clean intake • Tighten security
Heater will not heat	• Coolant does not reach proper temperature • Heater core blocked internally • Heater core air-bound • Blend-air door not in proper position	• Check and replace thermostat if necessary • Flush or replace core if necessary • Purge air from core • Adjust cable
Heater will not defrost	• Control cable adjustment incorrect • Defroster hose damaged	• Adjust control cable • Replace defroster hose

Troubleshooting Basic Windshield Wiper Problems

Problem	Cause	Solution
Electric Wipers		
Wipers do not operate— Wiper motor heats up or hums	• Internal motor defect • Bent or damaged linkage • Arms improperly installed on linking pivots	• Replace motor • Repair or replace linkage • Position linkage in park and reinstall wiper arms
Electric Wipers		
Wipers do not operate— No current to motor	• Fuse or circuit breaker blown • Loose, open or broken wiring • Defective switch • Defective or corroded terminals • No ground circuit for motor or switch	• Replace fuse or circuit breaker • Repair wiring and connections • Replace switch • Replace or clean terminals • Repair ground circuits
Wipers do not operate— Motor runs	• Linkage disconnected or broken	• Connect wiper linkage or replace broken linkage
Vacuum Wipers		
Wipers do not operate	• Control switch or cable inoperative • Loss of engine vacuum to wiper motor (broken hoses, low engine vacuum, defective vacuum/fuel pump) • Linkage broken or disconnected • Defective wiper motor	• Repair or replace switch or cable • Check vacuum lines, engine vacuum and fuel pump • Repair linkage • Replace wiper motor
Wipers stop on engine acceleration	• Leaking vacuum hoses • Dry windshield • Oversize wiper blades • Defective vacuum/fuel pump	• Repair or replace hoses • Wet windshield with washers • Replace with proper size wiper blades • Replace pump

Troubleshooting Basic Dash Gauge Problems

Problem	Cause	Solution
Oil Pressure Gauge		
Gauge does not register or is inaccurate	• On mechanical gauge, Bourdon tube may be bent or kinked	• Check tube for kinks or bends preventing oil from reaching the gauge
	• Low oil pressure	• Remove sending unit. Idle the engine briefly. If no oil flows from sending unit hole, problem is in engine.
	• Defective gauge	• Remove the wire from the sending unit and ground it for an instant with the ignition ON. A good gauge will go to the top of the scale.
	• Defective wiring	• Check the wiring to the gauge. If it's OK and the gauge doesn't register when grounded, replace the gauge.
	• Defective sending unit	• If the wiring is OK and the gauge functions when grounded, replace the sending unit
All Gauges		
All gauges do not operate	• Blown fuse	• Replace fuse
	• Defective instrument regulator	• Replace instrument voltage regulator
All gauges read low or erratically	• Defective or dirty instrument voltage regulator	• Clean contacts or replace
All gauges pegged	• Loss of ground between instrument voltage regulator and car	• Check ground
	• Defective instrument regulator	• Replace regulator

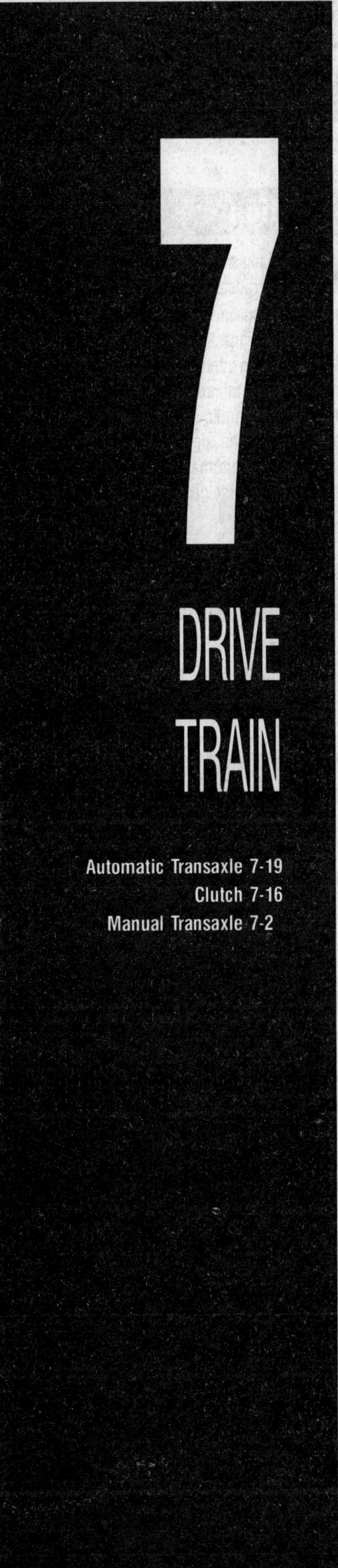

7 DRIVE TRAIN

MANUAL TRANSAXLE

Identification

Your Taurus/Sable uses a front wheel drive transmission called a transaxle.

A 5-speed fully synchronized manual transaxle is available on the 2.5L and 3.0L SHO Taurus/Sable models. An internally gated shift mechanism and a single rail shift linkage eliminate the need for periodic shift linkage adjustments. The MTX transaxle is designed to use Type F or Dexron®II automatic transmission fluid as a lubricant. Never use gear oil (GL) in the place of Type F or Dexron®II.

Adjustments

The manual shift mechanism and cables incorporate no adjustable features, therefore adjustments are neither possible or necessary.

Shift Linkage

REMOVAL & INSTALLATION

1. Disconnect the negative battery cable. Remove the console, shift knob and boot.
2. Fold the carpet back from the dash panel to expose the shift cables and cable sealing grom- mets.
3. Remove the rear seat heating duct. Loosen the two screws and remove the cable bracket.
4. Pull the cable sealing grommets loose from the floorpan and dash panel.
5. Raise and support the vehicle safely.
6. Remove the two retaining screws that retain the cables to the bracket assembly.
7. Pry the cable sockets off the clamp assembly pivot balls and slide the cable insulators out of the bracket slots.
8. Loosen the two bolts retaining the bracket assembly to the transaxle case. Remove the bracket assembly.
9. Lower the vehicle. From inside the vehicle pull the shift cables through the sheet metal holes and remove them from the vehicle.

To Install:

10. From inside the vehicle push the shift cables through the sheet metal holes. The crossover cable goes through the dash panel hole and the selector cable goes through the tunnel hole.
11. Seat the cable grommets in the sheet metal holes. Install the cable bracket. Torque the retaining screws to 17–22 inch lbs.
12. Make sure the crossover cable is secured under the hook on the bracket. A white alignment mark on the cable will assist in where to clip the cable under the hook.
13. Install the rear seat heat duct. Fold back the carpet over the cables.
14. Install the shifter, shift knob, boot and console.
15. Raise and support the vehicle safely. Install the clamp assembly onto the transaxle input shift shaft. Torque the retaining nut to 6–10 ft. lbs.
16. Install the bracket assembly to the transaxle case. Torque the M12 retaining bolt to 22–35 ft. lbs. and the M10 bolt to 16–24 ft. lbs.
17. Feed the shift cables into the slots of the bracket assembly. Retain the cables with two retainers and four bolts. Tighten the bolts 6–10 ft. lbs.
18. Snap the crossover cable socket onto the clamp assembly pivot ball. Position the selector cable rod end with the yellow painted side down. Snap the rod end onto the clamp assembly post.

Shift Handle

REMOVAL & INSTALLATION

1. Disconnect the negative battery cable. Remove the leather wrapped knob, by rotating the knob counterclockwise.
2. Remove the console trim surrounding the shift boot in order to expose the four screws which connect the boot to the top of the console. Slide the boot assembly off the shift lever.
3. Remove the console to expose the shifter assembly. Remove the four bolts retaining the shifter to the floorpan.
4. Pry the two clips holding the shift cables to control assembly and pry the cable sockets off the control assembly pivot balls.
5. Do not bend or kink the cable core rods.

To Install:

6. Feed the loose ends of the cables into the control assembly slots. A green painted mark on the shifter and crossover cable will aid in proper alignment.
7. Attach the control assembly to the floorpan J-nuts with four bolts. Torque the bolts to 49–70 inch lbs.
8. Seat the cable insulators into the shifter slots. Install new U-clips. Snap the cable sockets onto the shifter pivot balls. Install the console.
9. Slide the boot assembly over the shift lever. Attach it to the console and tighten the retaining screws to 14–21 inch lbs.
10. Attach the shift knob to the shift lever.

Back-Up Light Switch

REMOVAL & INSTALLATION

➧ SEE FIG. 1–2

1. The back-up lamp switch is located on the top left side of the transaxle.
2. Disconnect the negative (–) battery cable.
3. Disconnect the switch electrical connector.
4. Using a 22mm wrench, remove the switch.

To Install:

5. Apply Pipe Sealant with Teflon® part No. D8AZ–19554–A or equivalent to the threads of the switch. Turn the switch into the transaxle case clockwise and torque to 14–18 ft. lbs, and connect the electrical connector.
6. There is no adjustment needed on the back-up lamp switch.

Transaxle

REMOVAL & INSTALLATION

1986–88

1. Disconnect the negative battery cable. Wedge a wood block approximately 7 in. (178mm) long under the clutch pedal to hold the pedal up slightly beyond its normal position. Grasp the clutch cable and pull forward, disconnecting it from the clutch release shaft

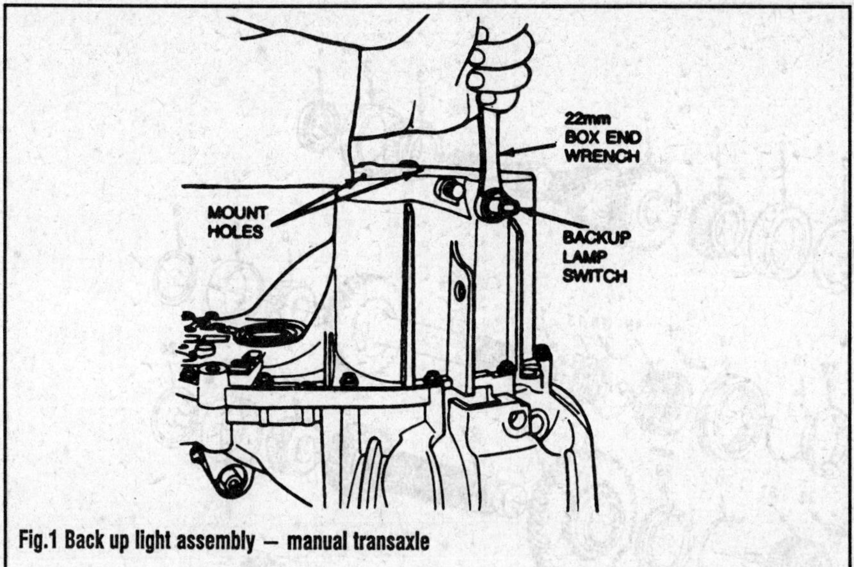

Fig.1 Back up light assembly — manual transaxle

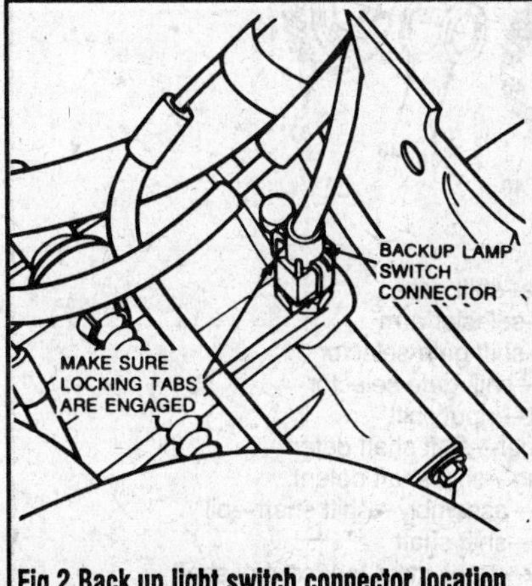

Fig.2 Back up light switch connector location — automatic transaxle

assembly. Remove the clutch casing from the rib on the top surface of the transaxle case.

2. Remove the 2 top transaxle-to-engine mounting bolts.

3. Raise the vehicle and support safely.

4. Remove the nut and bolt that secures the lower control arm ball joint to the steering knuckle assembly. Discard the nut and bolt. Repeat this procedure on the opposite side.

5. Using a large prybar, pry the lower control arm away from the knuckle.

➡ **Exercise care not to damage or cut the ball joint boot. Prybar must not contact the lower arm.**

6. Using a large prybar, pry the left inboard CV-joint assembly from the transaxle.

➡ **Plug the seal opening to prevent lubricant leakage.**

7. Remove the inboard CV-joint from the transaxle by grasping the left-hand steering knuckle and swinging the knuckle and halfshaft outward from the transaxle.If the CV-joint assembly cannot be pried from the transaxle, insert differential rotator tool T81P–4026–A or equivalent, through the left side and tap the joint out. Tool can be used from either side of transaxle.

8. Wire the halfshaft assembly in a near level position to prevent damage to the assembly during the remaining operations. Repeat this procedure on the opposite side.

9. Disengage the locking tabs and remove the backup light switch connector from the transaxle backup light switch.

10. Remove the starter stud bolts.

11. Remove the shift mechanism to shift shaft attaching nut and bolt and control selector indicator switch arm. Remove from the shift shaft.

12. Remove the bolts attaching the shift cable and bracket assembly to the transaxle.

13. Remove the speedometer cable from the transaxle.

14. Remove the stiffener brace attaching bolts from the lower position of the clutch housing.

15. Remove the sub-frame.

16. Position a suitable jack under the transaxle.

17. Lower the transaxle support jack.

18. Remove the lower engine to transaxle attaching bolts.

19. Remove the transaxle from the rear face of the engine and lower it from the vehicle.

To Install:

20. Raise the transaxle into position with the support jack. Engage the input shaft spline into the clutch disc and work the transaxle onto the dowel sleeves. Make sure the transaxle assembly is flush with the rear face of the engine prior to installation of the attaching bolts.

21. Install the lower engine to transaxle attaching bolts and tighten them to 28–31 ft. lbs. (38–42 Nm).

22. Install the speedometer cable.

23. Install the 10M and 12M bolts attaching the the shift cable and bracket to the transaxle. Tighten the 10M bolt to 16–22 ft. lbs. (22–30 Nm) and the 12M bolt to 22–35 ft. lbs. (31–48 Nm).

24. Install the bolt attaching the shift mechanism-to-shift shaft and tighten to 7–10 ft. lbs. (9–13 Nm).

25. Install the 2 bolts that attach the stiffener brace to the lower portion of the clutch housing and tighten to 15–21 ft. lbs. (21–28 Nm).

26. Install the starter stud bolts and tighten to 30–40 ft. lbs. (41–54 Nm).

27. Install the backup light switch connector to the transaxle switch.

28. Remove the seal plugs and install the inner CV-joints into the transaxle.

29. Install the center bearing to the bracket on the right side halfshaft.

➡ **New circlips are required on both inner CV-joints prior to installation. Make sure both CV-joints are seated in the transaxle.**

30. Attach the sub-frame and the lower ball joint to the steering knuckle. Insert a new service pinch bolt and a new nut. Tighten the nut to 37–44 ft. lbs. (50–60 Nm) but do not tighten the bolt.

31. Fill the transaxle with the proper type and quantity of transmission fluid.

32. Install the top transaxle to engine mounting bolts and tighten to 28–31 ft. lbs. (38–42 Nm).

33. Connect the clutch cable to the clutch release shaft assembly.

34. Remove the wood block from under the clutch pedal. Prior to starting the engine, set the hand brake and pump the clutch pedal a minimum of 2 times to ensure proper clutch adjustment.

1989-92

➧ SEE FIG. 3–4

1. Disconnect the negative battery cable.

2. Wedge a 7 in. (178mm) block of wood under the clutch pedal to hold the pedal up beyond it's normal position.

3. Remove the air cleaner hose.

4. Grasp the clutch cable and pull it forward, disconnecting it from the clutch release shaft assembly.

5. Disconnect the clutch cable casing from the rib on top of the transaxle case.

6. Install engine lifting eyes.

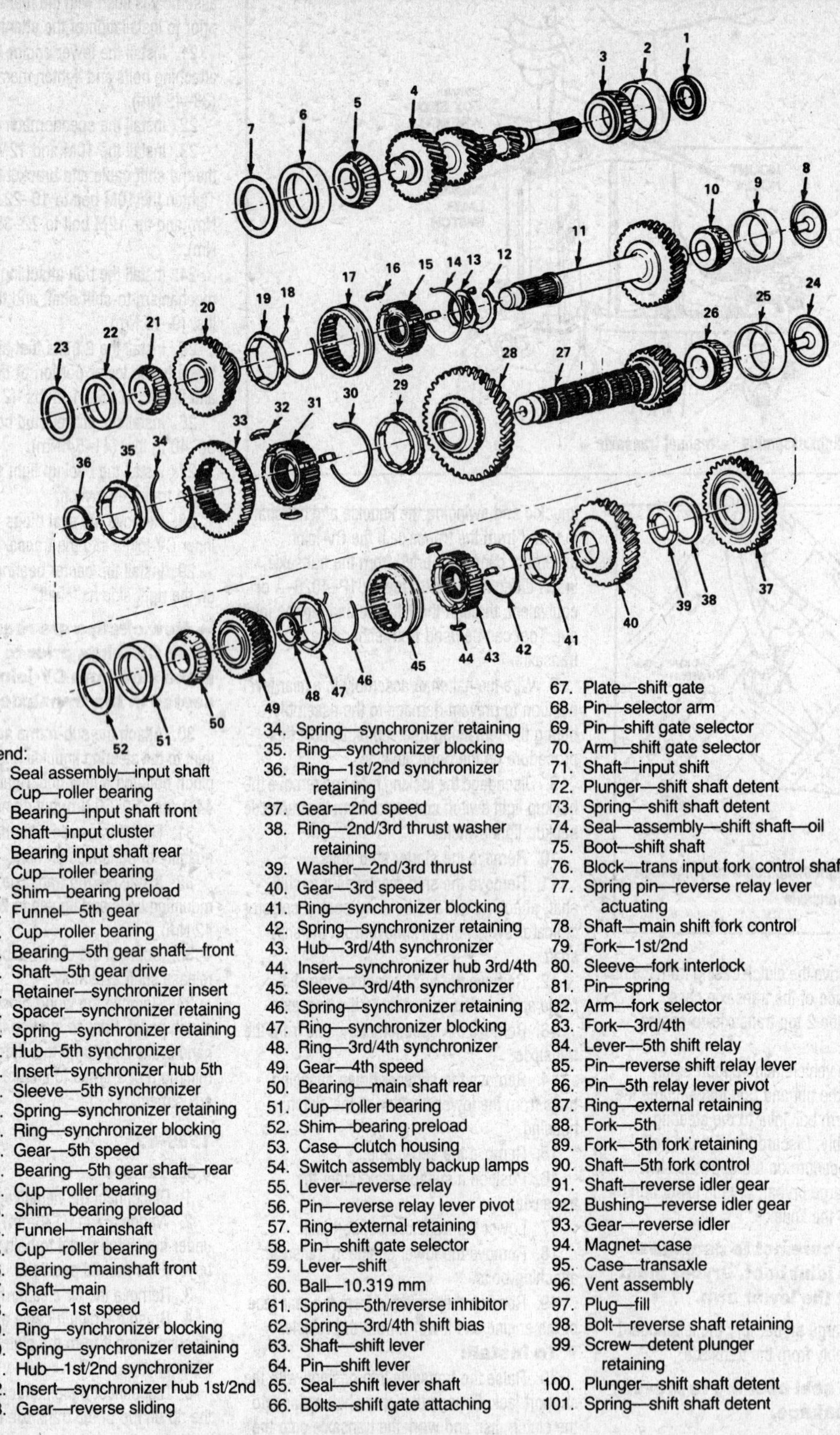
Legend:
1. Seal assembly—input shaft
2. Cup—roller bearing
3. Bearing—input shaft front
4. Shaft—input cluster
5. Bearing input shaft rear
6. Cup—roller bearing
7. Shim—bearing preload
8. Funnel—5th gear
9. Cup—roller bearing
10. Bearing—5th gear shaft—front
11. Shaft—5th gear drive
12. Retainer—synchronizer insert
13. Spacer—synchronizer retaining
14. Spring—synchronizer retaining
15. Hub—5th synchronizer
16. Insert—synchronizer hub 5th
17. Sleeve—5th synchronizer
18. Spring—synchronizer retaining
19. Ring—synchronizer blocking
20. Gear—5th speed
21. Bearing—5th gear shaft—rear
22. Cup—roller bearing
23. Shim—bearing preload
24. Funnel—mainshaft
25. Cup—roller bearing
26. Bearing—mainshaft front
27. Shaft—main
28. Gear—1st speed
29. Ring—synchronizer blocking
30. Spring—synchronizer retaining
31. Hub—1st/2nd synchronizer
32. Insert—synchronizer hub 1st/2nd
33. Gear—reverse sliding
34. Spring—synchronizer retaining
35. Ring—synchronizer blocking
36. Ring—1st/2nd synchronizer retaining
37. Gear—2nd speed
38. Ring—2nd/3rd thrust washer retaining
39. Washer—2nd/3rd thrust
40. Gear—3rd speed
41. Ring—synchronizer blocking
42. Spring—synchronizer retaining
43. Hub—3rd/4th synchronizer
44. Insert—synchronizer hub 3rd/4th
45. Sleeve—3rd/4th synchronizer
46. Spring—synchronizer retaining
47. Ring—synchronizer blocking
48. Ring—3rd/4th synchronizer
49. Gear—4th speed
50. Bearing—main shaft rear
51. Cup—roller bearing
52. Shim—bearing preload
53. Case—clutch housing
54. Switch assembly backup lamps
55. Lever—reverse relay
56. Pin—reverse relay lever pivot
57. Ring—external retaining
58. Pin—shift gate selector
59. Lever—shift
60. Ball—10.319 mm
61. Spring—5th/reverse inhibitor
62. Spring—3rd/4th shift bias
63. Shaft—shift lever
64. Pin—shift lever
65. Seal—shift lever shaft
66. Bolts—shift gate attaching
67. Plate—shift gate
68. Pin—selector arm
69. Pin—shift gate selector
70. Arm—shift gate selector
71. Shaft—input shift
72. Plunger—shift shaft detent
73. Spring—shift shaft detent
74. Seal—assembly—shift shaft—oil
75. Boot—shift shaft
76. Block—trans input fork control shaft
77. Spring pin—reverse relay lever actuating
78. Shaft—main shift fork control
79. Fork—1st/2nd
80. Sleeve—fork interlock
81. Pin—spring
82. Arm—fork selector
83. Fork—3rd/4th
84. Lever—5th shift relay
85. Pin—reverse shift relay lever
86. Pin—5th relay lever pivot
87. Ring—external retaining
88. Fork—5th
89. Fork—5th fork retaining
90. Shaft—5th fork control
91. Shaft—reverse idler gear
92. Bushing—reverse idler gear
93. Gear—reverse idler
94. Magnet—case
95. Case—transaxle
96. Vent assembly
97. Plug—fill
98. Bolt—reverse shaft retaining
99. Screw—detent plunger retaining
100. Plunger—shift shaft detent
101. Spring—shift shaft detent

Fig.3 Manual transaxle gear set – exploded view

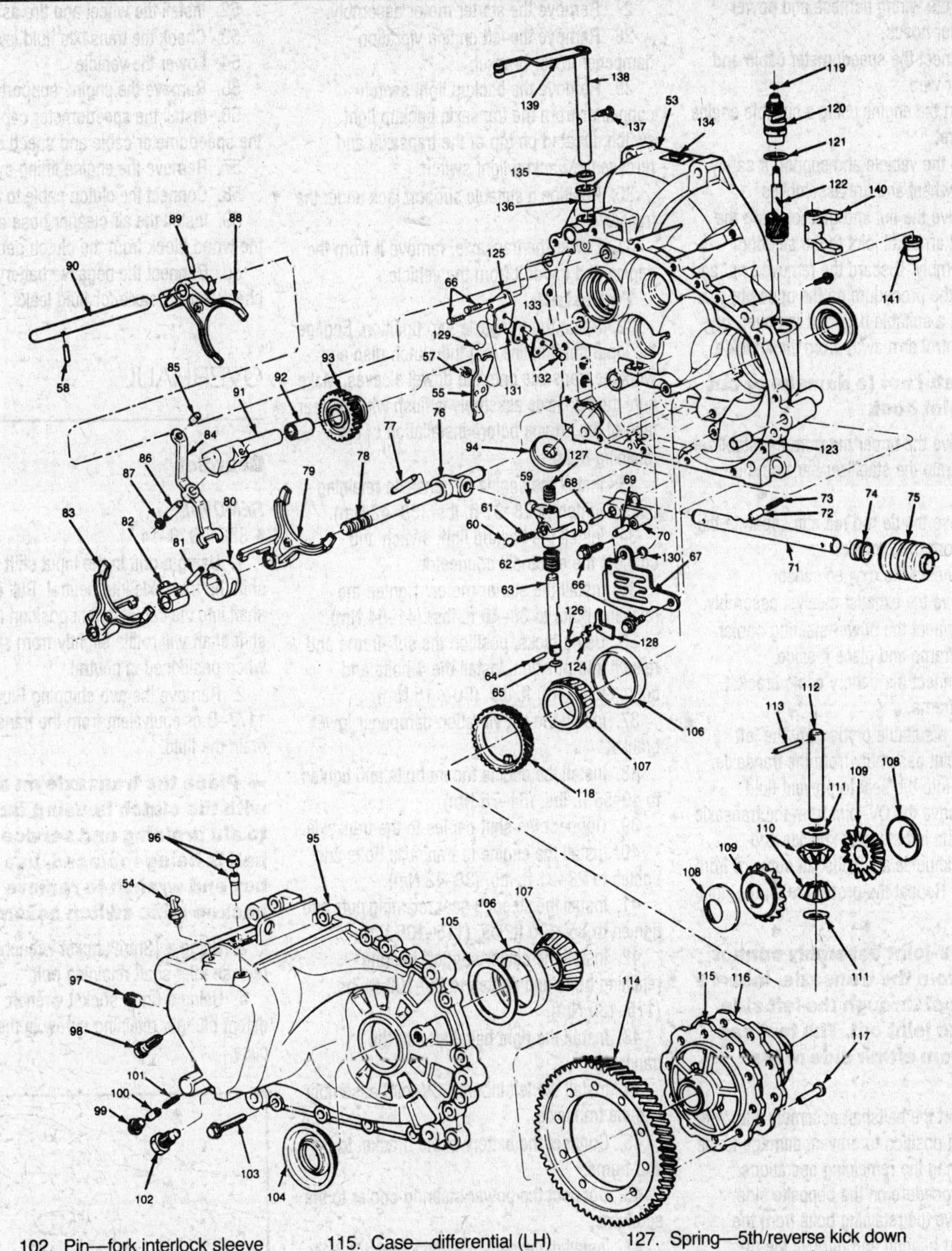

102. Pin—fork interlock sleeve retaining
103. Botl—transaxle case
104. Seal assembly (LH) differential
105. Shim differential bearing preload
106. Cup—differential bearing
107. Bearing assembly—differential
108. Washer—side gear thrust
109. Gear—side
110. Gear—pinion
111. Washer—pinion gear thrust
112. Shaft—pinion gear
113. Pin—pinion gear shaft retaining
114. Gear—final drive
115. Case—differential (LH)
116. Case—differential (RH)
117. Rivet—case and drive gear attaching
118. Gear—speedo drive
119. Seal—5.16mm x 1.6 O-ring
120. Retainer—speedo gear
121. Seal—speedo retainer-to-case
122. Gear—speedo driven
123. Dowel—case-to-clutch housing
124. Spring—shift gate pawl
125. Bracket—reverse shift relay lever support
126. Pin—reverse lockout pawl pivot
127. Spring—5th/reverse kick down
128. Pawl—shift gate plate
129. Ball
130. C—clip
131. Ball 8.731mm
132. Spring—trans reverse shift relay lever
133. Spring—trans reverse shift relay lever ret
134. Plug—trans timing window
135. Washer—flat (felt)
136. Bushing—clutch release shaft—upper
137. Pin—clutch release lever
138. Shaft—clutch release
139. Lever—clutch release

Fig.4 Manual transaxle — exploded view

7. Tie up the wiring harness and power steering cooler hoses.

8. Disconnect the speedometer cable and speed sensor wire.

9. Support the engine using a suitable engine support fixture.

10. Raise the vehicle and support it safely. Remove the wheel and tire assemblies.

11. Remove the nut and bolt retaining the lower control arm ball joint to the steering knuckle assembly. Discard the removed nut and bolt. Repeat the procedure on the opposite side.

12. Using a suitable halfshaft remover, pry the lower control arm away from the knuckle.

➡ Be careful not to damage or cut the ball joint boot.

13. Remove the upper nut from the stabilizer bar and separate the stabilizer bar from the knuckle.

14. Remove the tie rod nut and separate the tie rod end from the knuckle.

15. Disconnect the oxygen sensor.

16. Remove the exhaust catalyst assembly.

17. Disconnect the power steering cooler from the subframe and place it aside.

18. Disconnect the battery cable bracket from the subframe.

19. Using a suitable prybar, pry the left inboard CV-joint assembly from the transaxle. Install a plug into the seal to prevent fluid leakage. Remove the CV-joint from the transaxle by grasping the left steering knuckle and swinging the knuckle and halfshaft outward from the transaxle. Repeat the procedure on the right side.

➡ If the CV-joint assembly cannot be pried from the transaxle, insert a suitable tool through the left side and tap the joint out. The tool can be used from either side of the transaxle.

20. Support the halfshaft assembly with wire in a near level position to prevent damage to the assembly during the remaining operations. Repeat the procedure on the opposite side.

21. Remove the retaining bolts from the center support bearing and remove the right halfshaft from the transaxle.

22. Remove the 2 steering gear retaining nuts from the sub-frame. Support the steering gear by wiring up the tie rod ends to the coil springs.

23. Remove the transaxle to engine retaining bolts.

24. Disconnect the 2 shift cables from the transaxle.

25. Remove the engine mount bolts.

26. Position jacks under the body mount positions and remove the 4 bolts, lower the subframe and position it aside.

27. Remove the starter motor assembly.

28. Remove the left engine vibration dampener lower bracket.

29. Remove the backup light switch connector from the transaxle backup light switch, located on top of the transaxle and remove the backup light switch.

30. Position a suitable support jack under the transaxle.

31. Lower the transaxle, remove it from the engine and lower it from the vehicle.

To install:

32. Raise the transaxle into position. Engage the input shaft spline into the clutch disc and work the transaxle onto the dowel sleeves. Make sure the transaxle assembly is flush with the rear face of the engine before installation of the retaining bolts.

33. Install the engine to transaxle retaining bolts. Tighten to 28–31 ft. lbs. (38–42 Nm).

34. Install the backup light switch and connect the electrical connector.

35. Install the starter motor. Tighten the retaining bolts to 30–40 ft. lbs. (41–54 Nm).

36. Using jacks, position the sub-frame and raise it into position. Install the 4 bolts and tighten to 65–85 ft. lbs. (90–115 Nm).

37. Install the left vibration dampener lower bracket.

38. Install the engine mount bolts and tighten to 40–55 ft. lbs. (54–75 Nm).

39. Connect the shift cables to the transaxle.

40. Install the engine to transaxle bolts and tighten to 28–31 ft. lbs. (38–42 Nm).

41. Install the steering gear retaining nuts and tighten to 85–100 ft. lbs. (115–135 Nm).

42. Install the center support bearing retaining bolts and tighten to 85–100 ft. lbs. (115–135 Nm).

43. Install the right halfshaft into the transaxle.

44. Install the left inboard CV-joint assembly into the transaxle.

45. Connect the battery cable bracket to the sub-frame.

46. Connect the power steering cooler to the subframe.

47. Install the exhaust catalyst retaining bolts and tighten to 25–34 ft. lbs. (34–47 Nm).

48. Connect the oxygen sensor.

49. Install the tie rod in the knuckle and the tie rod retaining nut. Tighten to 35–47 ft. lbs. (47–64 Nm).

50. Position the stabilizer bar to the knuckle and install the nut.

51. Install the lower control arm ball joint to steering knuckle assembly. Install and tighten a new retaining nut and bolt to 37–44 ft. lbs. (50–60 Nm).

52. Install the wheel and tire assemblies.

53. Check the transaxle fluid level.

54. Lower the vehicle.

55. Remove the engine support tool.

56. Install the speedometer cable. Connect the speedometer cable and speed sensor wire.

57. Remove the engine lifting eyes.

58. Connect the clutch cable to the transaxle.

59. Install the air cleaner hose and remove the wood block from the clutch pedal.

60. Connect the negative battery cable and check the transaxle for fluid leaks.

OVERHAUL

Gear Set

REMOVAL

➧ SEE FIG. 6–14

1. Using a drift in the input shift shaft hole, shift the transaxle into neutral. Pull or push the shaft into the center detent position (neutral). The shift shaft will rotate slightly from side-to-side when positioned in neutral.

2. Remove the two shipping Plugs T81P–1177–B or equivalent from the transaxle and drain the fluid.

➡ Place the transaxle on a bench with the clutch housing face down to aid draining and service. If case half is being replaced, use a 22mm box end wrench to remove the backup lamp switch assembly.

3. Using a 13mm socket wrench, remove the reverse idler shaft retaining bolt.

4. Using a 8mm socket wrench, loosen the detent plunger retaining screw in the transaxle case.

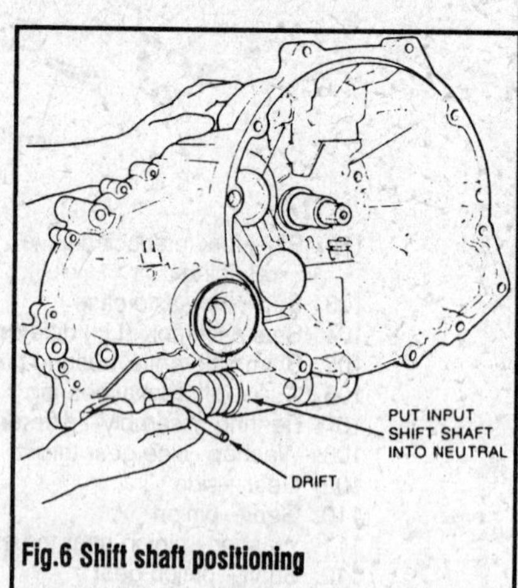

Fig.6 Shift shaft positioning

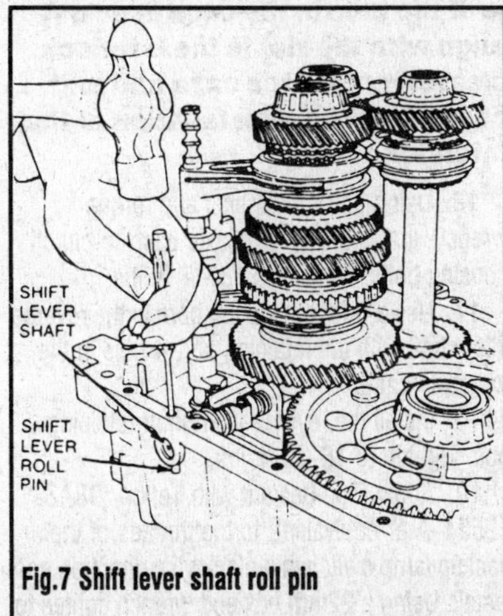

Fig.7 Shift lever shaft roll pin

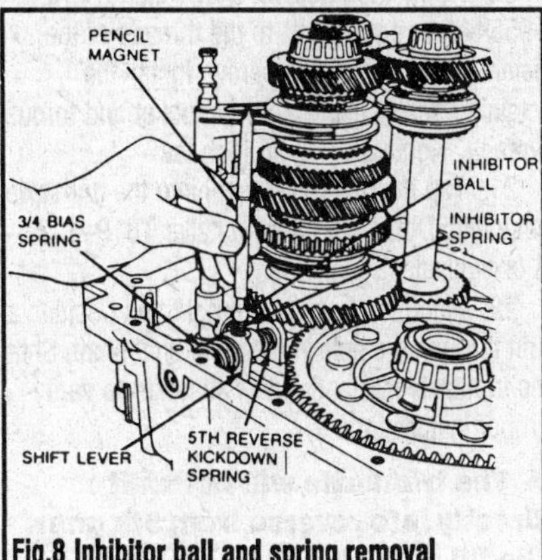

Fig.8 Inhibitor ball and spring removal

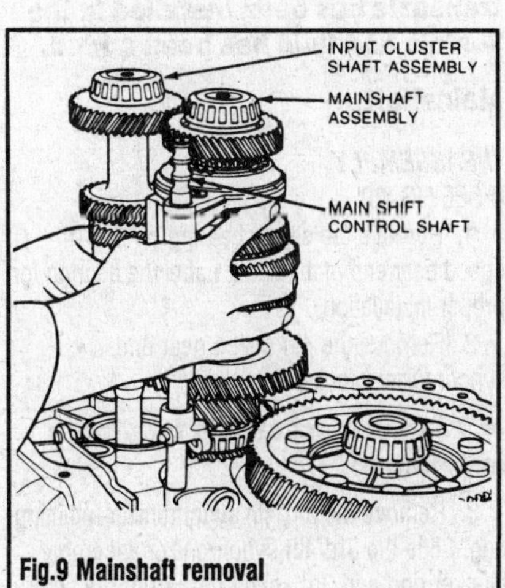

Fig.9 Mainshaft removal

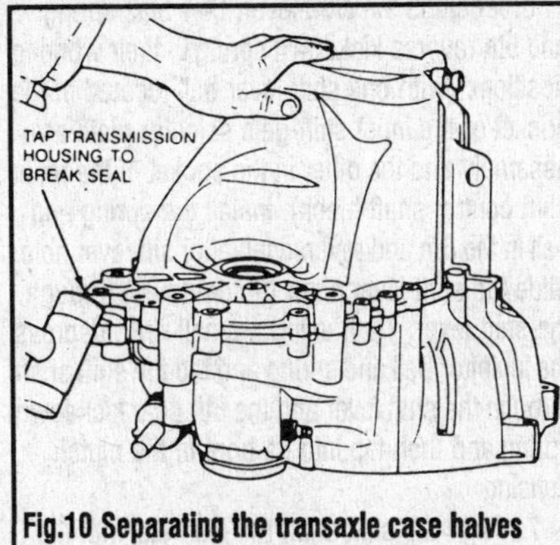

Fig.10 Separating the transaxle case halves

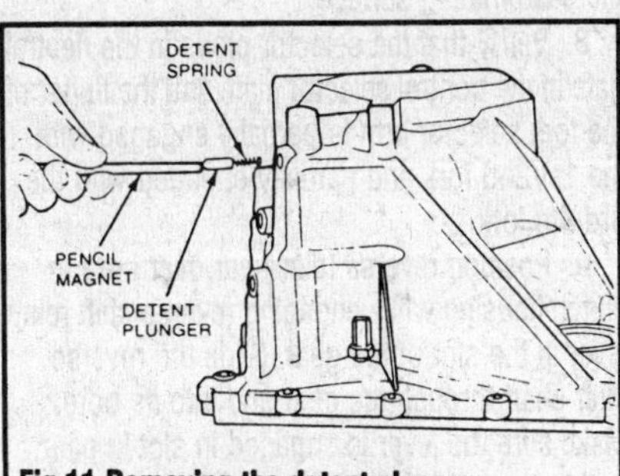

Fig.11 Removing the detent plunger

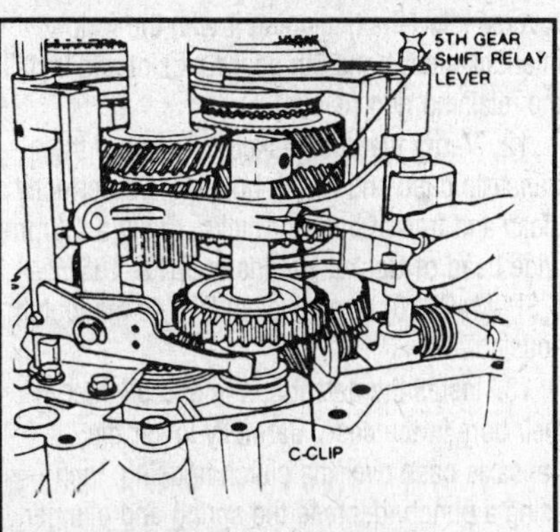

Fig.12 Shift relay rod lever removal

Fig.13 Reverse idler shaft and gear removal

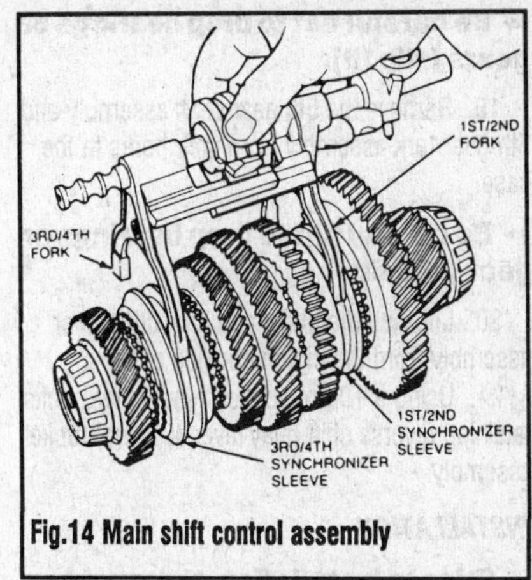

Fig.14 Main shift control assembly

5. Using a 13mm wrench, remove the shift fork interlock sleeve retaining pin.

6. Using a $^3/_8$ in. extension bar and ratchet, remove the fill plug.

7. Using a 10mm socket wrench, remove the 15 clutch housing-to-transaxle case attaching bolts.

8. Using a plastic tipped hammer, tap the transaxle case to break the seal between the case halves.

9. Separate the case halves.

➡ Do not insert pry bars or screwdrivers between the case halves. Be careful not to drop the bearing cup or shims from the transaxle case housing.

10. Remove the detent plunger retaining screw. Then, using a pencil magnet, remove the detent spring and the detent plunger.

11. Remove the case magnet.

12. Using a small prybar, remove the C-clip retaining ring from the 5th relay lever pivot pin. Remove the 5th gear shift relay lever.

13. Lift the reverse idler shaft and reverse idler gear from the case.

14. Using a 4mm punch, drive the roll pin from the shift lever shaft.

15. Using a small prybar, gently pry on the shaft lever shaft so that the hole in the shaft is exposed.

➡ Be careful not to damage the main shaft gear teeth or pedestal when prying with the prybar.

16. Hold a rag over the hole in the lever to prevent the ball and the 5th inhibitor spring from shooting out and remove the shift lever shaft.

17. Remove the inhibitor ball and spring from the hole in the shift lever using a pencil magnet. Then, remove the shift lever, 5th/reverse kickdown spring, and 3–4 bias spring.

18. Remove the main shaft assembly, input cluster shaft assembly and the main shift control shaft assembly as one unit.

➡ **Be careful not to drop bearings or gears (slip fit).**

19. Remove the 5th gear shaft assembly and 5th gear fork assembly from their bores in the case.

➡ **Be careful not to drop bearings or gear (slip fit).**

20. Lift the differential and final drive gear assembly from the clutch housing case.

21. Using a 10mm socket, remove two bolts retaining reverse shift relay lever support bracket assembly.

INSTALLATION

➡ **Prior to installation, thoroughly clean all parts and inspect their condition. Lightly oil the bores with Type F or Dexron®II transmission fluid or equivalent.**

1. Using a 10mm socket, install reverse relay lever support bracket assembly to the case with two bolts. Tighten bolts to 72–84 inch lbs.

2. Place the differential and the final drive gear assembly into the clutch housing case. Align the differential gears for later installation of the halfshafts.

3. Install the 5th gear shaft assembly and the fork shaft assembly in the case.

➡ **Be careful not to damage the 5th gear shaft oil funnel.**

4. Position the main shift control shaft assembly so that the shift forks engage their respective slots in the synchronizer sleeves on the main shaft assembly.

5. Bring the main shaft assembly into mesh with the input Cluster shaft assembly. Holding the three shafts (input cluster shaft, main shaft and the main shift control shaft) in their respective working positions, lower them into their bores in the clutch housing case as one unit.

➡ **When performing this operation care must be taken to avoid movement of the 3rd/4th synchronizer sleeve. This could result in over travel of the synchronizing sleeve to hub, allowing inserts to pop out of position.**
Be careful not to damage the input shaft oil seal or main shaft oil funnel.

6. Position the shift lever, 3–4 bias spring and 5th/reverse kickdown spring in their working positions (with one shift lever ball located in the socket of the input shift gate selector plate arm assembly and the other in the socket of the main shift control shaft block). Install the spring and ball in the 5th and reverse inhibitor sift lever hole. Slide the shift lever shaft (notch down) through the shift lever. Then using a small drift, depress the inhibitor ball and spring and tap the shift shaft through the shift lever and the 5th gear kickdown spring and then tap into its bore in the clutch housing.

7. Align the shift shaft roll pin hole with the case bore and tap the roll pin in slightly below the case mating surface.

8. Verify that the selector pin is in the neutral gate of the control selector plate and the finger of the fork selector arm is partially engaged with the 1st/2nd fork and partially engaged with the 3rd/4th fork.

9. Position reverse idler gear over bore in clutch housing while engaging reverse shift relay lever in the slot of the gear. Slide the reverse idler shaft through the gear and into its bore. Make sure the lever is engaged in slot in gear.

10. Install the magnet in its pocket in the clutch housing case.

11. Install the 5th shift relay lever onto the reverse idler shaft, aligning it with the fork interlock sleeve and 5th gear fork slot and install the retaining ring (C-clip).

12. Verify that the gasket surfaces of the transaxle case and clutch housing are perfectly clean and free of burrs or nicks. Apply a 1.5mm wide bead of Gasket Eliminator E1FZ–19562–A (ESP–M4G228) or equivalent RTV to the clutch housing.

13. Install the detent spring and plunger in their bore in the case. Carefully lower the transaxle case over the clutch housing, then using a punch, depress the spring and plunger. Gently move the transaxle case until the shift control shaft, main shaft, input cluster shaft and 5th gear shaft align with their respective bores in the transaxle case.

14. Gently slide the transaxle case over the dowels and flush onto the clutch housing case. Make sure that the case does not bind on the magnet.

15. Apply Pipe Sealant with Teflon D8AZ–19554–A or equivalent to the threads of the interlock sleeve retaining pin, in a clockwise direction. Use a drift to align the slot in the interlock sleeve with the hole in the transaxle case and install the retaining pin. Using a 13mm socket tighten to 12–15 ft. lbs.

➡ **If the hole in the case does not align with the slot in the interlock sleeve, remove the case half and check for proper installation of the interlock sleeve.**

16. Using a 10mm socket and torque wrench, install the 15 transaxle case-to-clutch housing bolts. Tighten to 13–17 ft. lbs.

17. Use a drift to align the bore in the reverse idler shaft with the retaining screw hole in the transaxle case.

18. Install the reverse idler shaft retaining bolt. Tighten to 16–20 ft. lbs.

19. Apply Pipe Sealant with Teflon (D8AZ–19554–A or equivalent) to the threads of the backup lamp switch in a clockwise direction and install. Using a 22mm box end wrench tighten to 12–15 ft. lbs.

20. Apply Pipe Sealant with Teflon (D8AZ–19554–A or equivalent) to the threads of the detent plunger retaining screw. Install the retaining screw using a 8mm socket and torque wrench. Tighten to 72–96 inch lbs.

21. Tap the differential seal into the transaxle case with Differential Seal Installer T81P–1177–A or equivalent.

22. Place the transaxle upright and position a drift through the hole in the input shift shaft. Shift the transaxle into and out of all gears to verify proper installation.

➡ **The transaxle will not shift directly into reverse from 5th gear. The fill plug should be attached to the transaxle and installed after the transaxle has been installed in the vehicle and fluid has been added.**

Mainshaft

DISASSEMBLY

➧ SEE FIG. 20

1. Remove the slip fit bearing on the 4th speed gear end of the shaft. Label the bearing for proper installation.

2. Remove the 4th speed gear and synchronizer blocker ring.

➡ **Tag the blocker ring for proper installation.**

3. Remove the 3rd/4th synchronizer retaining ring. Slide the 3rd/4th synchronizer assembly, blocker ring and 3rd speed gear from the shaft.

➡ **Tag the blocker ring from proper installation.**

4. Remove the 2nd/3rd thrust washer retaining ring and the two piece thrust washer.

5. Remove the 2nd speed gear and its blocker ring.

➡ **Tag the blocker ring for proper installation.**

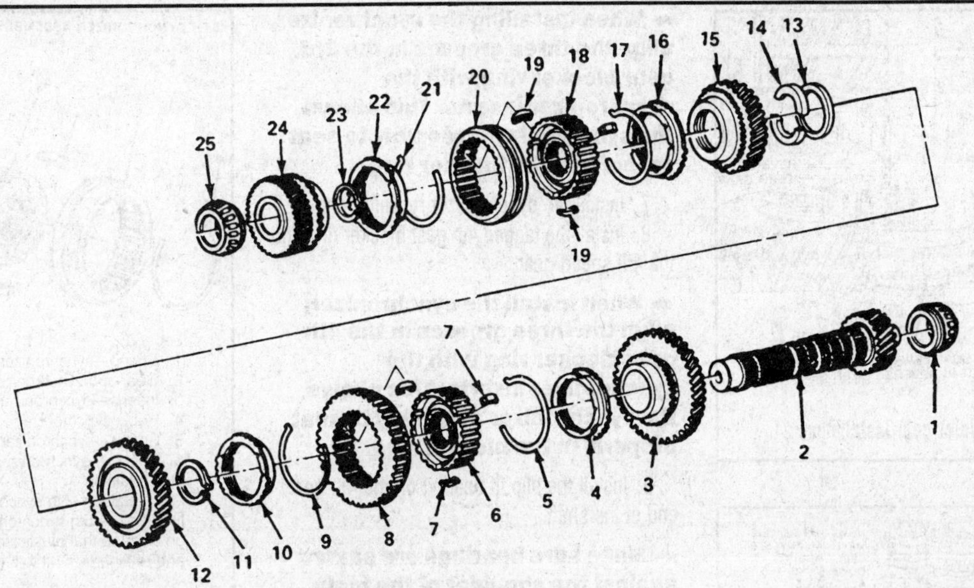

Legend
1. Bearing—mainshaft front
2. Shaft—main
3. Gear—1st speed
4. Ring—synchro blocker
5. Spring—synchronizer
6. Hub—1st/2nd synchro
7. Insert—synchro hub 1st/2nd
8. Gear—reverse sliding
9. Spring—synchronizer
10. Ring—synchro blocker
11. Ring—1st/2nd synchro retaining
12. Gear—2nd speed
13. Ring—2nd/3rd thrust washer retaining
14. Washer—2nd/3rd gear thrust
15. Gear—3rd speed
16. Ring—synchro blocker
17. Spring—synchronizer
18. Hub—3rd/4th synchro
19. Insert—synchro hub 3rd/4th
20. Sleeve—3rd/4th synchro
21. Spring—synchronizer
22. Ring—synchro retaining
23. Ring—retaining
24. Gear—4th speed
25. Bearing—mainshaft rear

Fig.20 Mainshaft assembly — exploded view

6. Remove the 1st/2nd synchronizer retaining ring. Slide the 1st/2nd synchronizer assembly, blocker ring and 1st speed gear off the shaft.

➡ **Tag the blocker ring for proper installation.**

7. Remove the tapered roller bearing from the pinion end of the main shaft using a socket or extension and Pinion Bearing Cone Remover part No. D79L–4621–A or equivalent and an arbor press. Label the bearing.

➡ **This bearing does not have to be removed to disassemble the main shaft only to replace if damaged.**

ASSEMBLY

➧ SEE FIG. 15–19

1. Prior to assembly of the main shaft, thoroughly clean all parts and inspect their condition. Lightly oil the gear bores and other parts with Type F or DEXRON®II transmission fluid. Install the bearing on the pinion end of the shaft using a 27mm socket and an arbor press.

2. Slide the 1st speed gear and tagged blocker ring onto the main shaft. slide the 1st/2nd synchronizer assembly into place, making sure the shift fork groove on the reverse sliding gear faces the 1st speed gear.

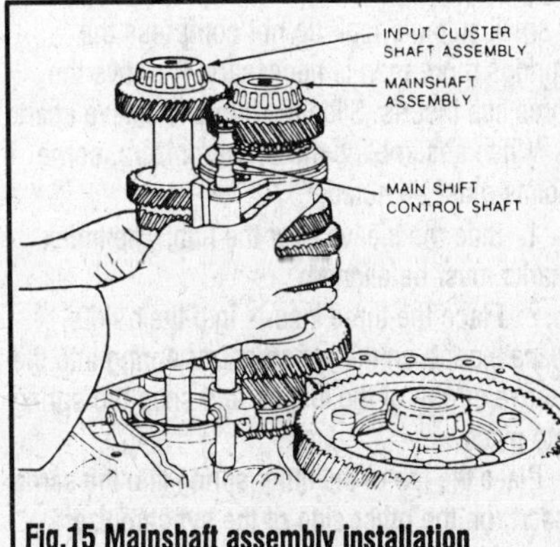

Fig.15 Mainshaft assembly installation

➡ **When installing the synchronizer, align the three grooves in the 1st gear blocker ring with the synchronizer inserts. This allows the synchronizer assembly to seat properly in the blocker ring.**

3. Install the synchronizer retaining ring.

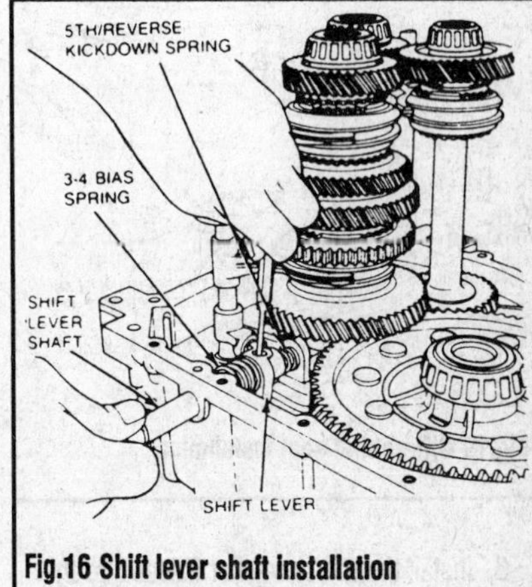

Fig.16 Shift lever shaft installation

4. Install the tagged 2nd speed blocker ring and the 2nd speed gear.

➡ **When install the synchronizer, align the three grooves in the 2nd gear blocker ring with the synchronizer inserts. This allows the synchronizer assembly to seat properly in the blocker ring.**

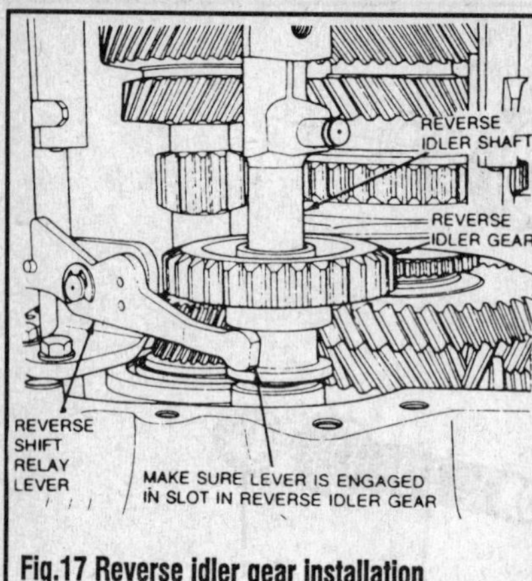

Fig.17 Reverse idler gear installation

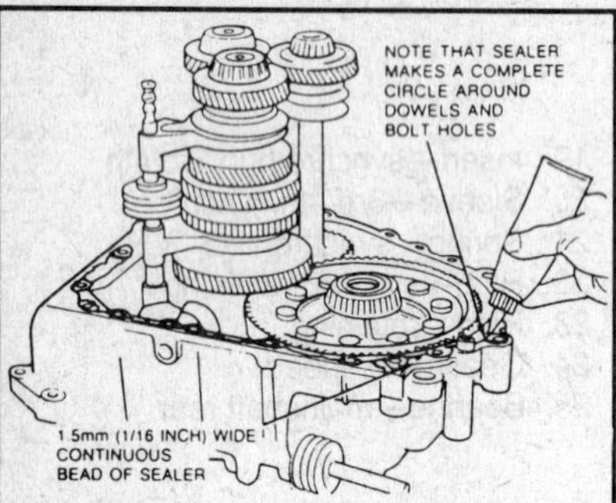

Fig.18 Sealing the transaxle halves with RTV sealant

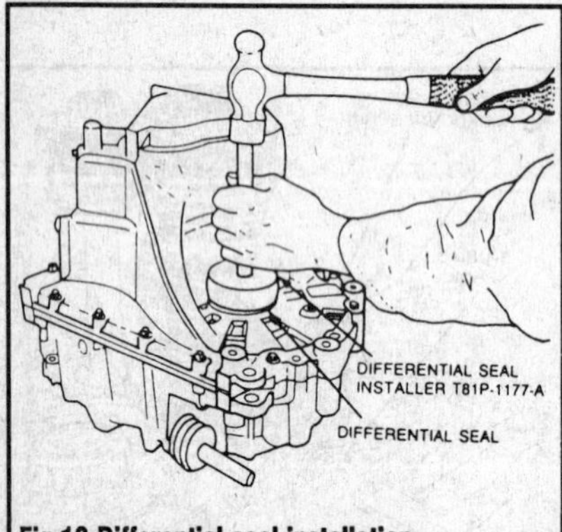

Fig.19 Differential seal installation

5. Install the thrust washer halves into the groove on the main shaft and then the retaining ring around the thrust washer halves.

6. Slide the 3rd speed gear onto the shaft followed by the tagged 3rd gear synchronizer blocker ring and the 3rd/4th gear synchronizer assembly.

➡ When installing the synchronizer, align the three grooves in the 3rd gear blocker ring with the synchronizer inserts. This allows the synchronizer assembly to seat properly in the blocker ring.

7. Install the synchronizer retaining ring.

8. Install the tagged 4th gear blocker ring and the 4th speed gear.

➡ When install the synchronizer, align the three grooves in the 4th gear blocker ring with the synchronizer inserts. This allows the synchronizer assembly to seat properly in the blocker ring.

9. Install the slip fit bearing on the 4th gear end of the shaft.

➡ Make sure bearings are seated against the shoulder of the main shaft. Make sure bearings are placed on the proper end, as labeled during disassembly. Rotate each gear on the shaft to check for binding or roughness. Make sure that the synchronizer sleeves are in the neutral position.

Synchronizer

DISASSEMBLY AND ASSEMBLY

➧ SEE FIG. 21–22

Prior to disassembly note position of index marks. To disassemble the synchronizer assembly, remove the synchronizer springs with a small suitable tool. do not compress the springs more than is necessary. Remove the three hub inserts. Slide the hub and sleeve apart.

When assembling the synchronizers, some points must be noted:

1. Side the sleeve over the hub. The index marks must be aligned.
2. Place the three inserts into their slots. Place the tab on the synchronizer spring into the groove of one of the inserts and snap the spring into place.

Place the tab of the other spring into the same insert (on the other side of the synchronizer assembly) and rotate the spring in the opposite direction and snap into place.

➡ When assembling synchronizers, notice that the sleeve and the hub have an extremely close fit and must be held square to prevent jamming. (Do not force the sleeve onto the hub).

5TH Gear Shaft

DISASSEMBLY

➧ SEE FIG. 23

1. Remove the slip fit bearing from the 5th gear end of the shaft and label it for proper installation.
2. Remove the 5th gear and blocking ring.
3. Remove the 5th gear synchronizer assembly.
4. Remove the press fit bearing from the pinion end of the shaft, using Pinion Bearing Cone Remover D79L–4621–A or equivalent.

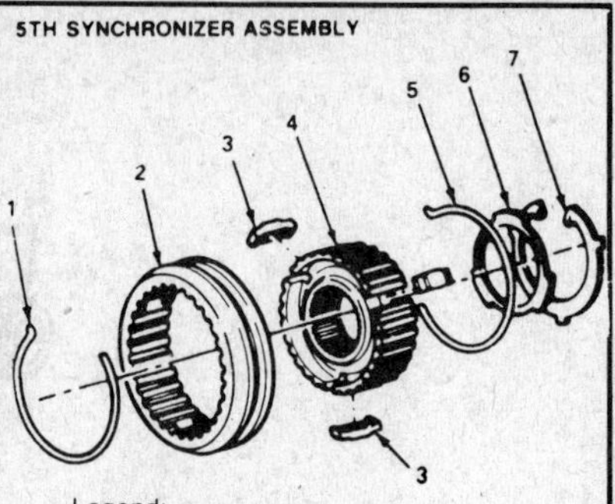

Fig.21 5th gear synchronizer assembly — exploded view

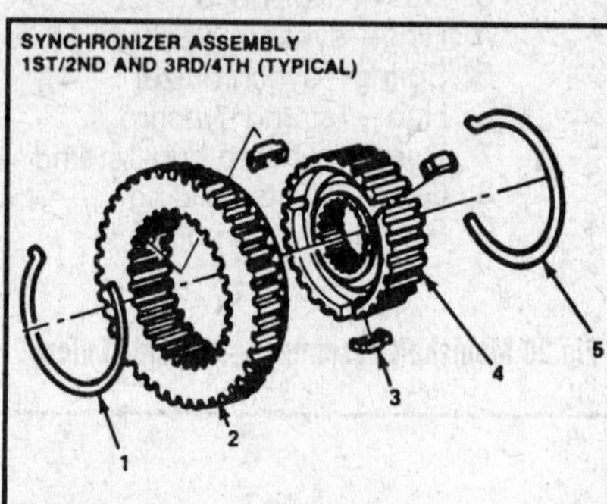

Fig.22 1st/2nd and 3rd/4th gear synchronizer assembly — exploded view

ASSEMBLY

➡ Prior to assembly, thoroughly clean all parts and inspect their condition. Lightly oil the gear bore with either Type F or DEXRON®II transmission fluid.

1. Press the bearing onto the pinion gear end of the 5th gear shaft.

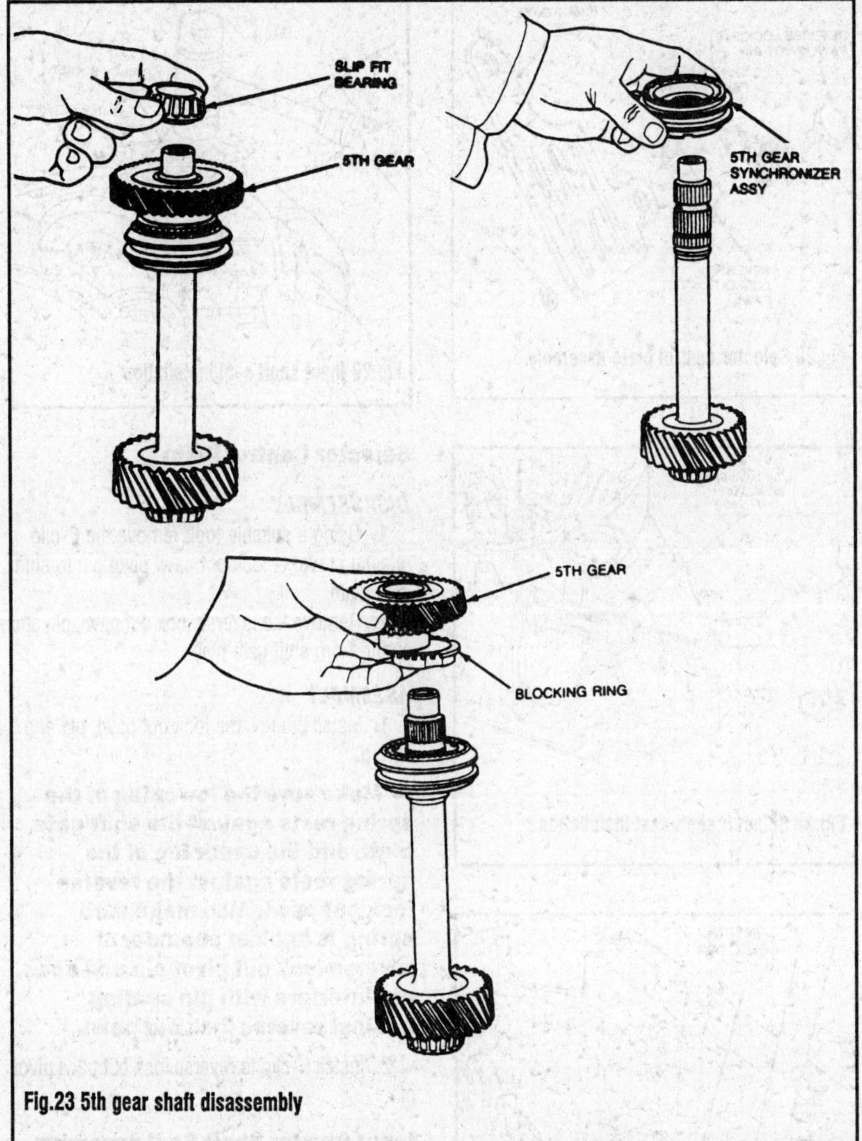

Fig.23 5th gear shaft disassembly

2. Install the 5th synchronizer assembly with the plastic insert retainer facing the pinion gear.

3. Install the 5th gear and blocking ring.

4. Install the slip fit bearing on the 5th gear end of the shaft.

Clutch Housing

DISASSEMBLY

1. Using a 10mm socket wrench, remove the two control selector plate attaching bolts and remove the plate from the case.

2. With the input shift shaft in the center detent position, using a drift, drive the spring pin through the selector plate arm assembly and through the input shift shaft into the recess in the clutch housing case.

3. Remove the shift shaft boot. Using a drift, rotate the input shift shaft 90°, depressing the detent notches inside the housing and pull input shift shaft out. Remove the input shift shaft selector plate arm assembly and the spring pin.

4. Using a pencil magnet, remove the input shift shaft detent plunger and spring and label for proper installation.

5. Using Sector Shaft Seal Tool part No. T77F–7288–A and Impact Slide Hammer T50T–100–A or equivalent, remove the transaxle input shift shaft oil seal assembly.

ASSEMBLY

➡ Prior to assembly, thoroughly clean all parts and inspect their condition. Lightly oil all parts and inspect their condition. Lightly oil all parts and bore with Type F or DEXRON®II transmission fluid.

1. Grease the seal lip of the new shift shaft oil seal. Using Sector Shaft Seal Tool part No. T77F–7288–A and Impact Slide Hammer T50T0100–A or equivalent, install a new shift shaft oil seal assembly.

2. Install the input shift shaft detent spring and plunger in the clutch housing case.

3. Using a small drift, force the spring and plunger down into its bore while sliding the input shift shaft into its bore and over the plunger.

➡ Be careful not to cut the shift shaft oil seal when inserting the shaft.

4. Install the selector plate arm in its working position and slide the shaft through the selector plate arm. Align the hole in the selector plate arm with the hole in the shaft and install the roll pin. Install the input shift shaft boot.

➡ Be sure notches in the shift shaft face the detent plunger.

5. Install the control selector plate. Using a 10mm socket wrench, tighten the attaching bolts to 72–96 inch lbs., (pin in selector arm must ride in cut-out of gate in the selector plate). Move input shift shaft through the selector plate positions to make sure everything works properly.

Main Shift Control Shaft

DISASSEMBLY

➧ SEE FIG. 25

1. Rotate the 3rd/4th shift fork on the shaft until the notch in the fork is located over the interlock sleeve. Rotate the 1st/2nd shift fork on the shaft until the notch in the fork is located over the shift fork selector arm finger. With the forks in position, slide 3rd/4th and interlock sleeve off the shaft.

2. Using a 5mm punch, remove the selector arm retaining pin.

3. Remove the shift fork selector arm and 1st/2nd shift fork from the shaft.

4. Using a 5mm punch, remove the fork control block retaining pin. Remove the fork control block from the shift control shaft.

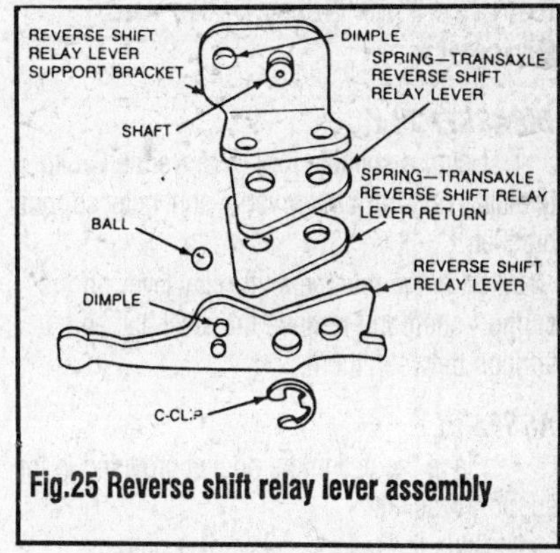

Fig.25 Reverse shift relay lever assembly

ASSEMBLY

➡ **Prior to assembly of the main shaft control shaft, thoroughly clean all parts and inspect their condition. Lightly oil all parts with Type F or DEXRON®II transmission fluid.**

1. Slide the fork control block onto the shift control shaft. Align the hole in the block with the hole in the shaft and install the fork CONTROL block pin using a 5mm punch.

➡ **With the pin installed in control block, off-set must point towards end of shaft.**

2. Install the 1st/2nd shift fork and the selector arm on the shaft.

➡ **The 1st/2nd shift fork is thinner than the 3rd/4th shift fork.**

3. Align the hold in the shift fork selector arm with the hold in the shaft and install the retaining pin.
4. Position the slot in the 1st/2nd fork over the fork selector arm finger. Slide the 3rd/4th fork and interlock sleeve onto the main shift control shaft. Align the slot in the interlock sleeve with the spline on the shift fork selector arm and slide the sleeve and 3rd/4th fork into position.

➡ **When assembled, the forks should be aligned.**

5th Gear Shift Control

DISASSEMBLY

▸ SEE FIG. 26–29

1. Using a 5mm punch, remove the roll pin.
2. Slide the fork from the shaft.

ASSEMBLY

1. Holding the shaft with the hole on the left, install the 5th gear shift fork so that the protruding arm is pointing toward the long end of the shaft.
2. Install the roll pin.

Reverse Shift Relay Lever and Bracket

DISASSEMBLY

1. Using a suitable tool, remove the C-clip retaining ring from the reverse shift relay support bracket.
2. Slide the reverse shift relay lever off the support shaft and remove the steel ball and springs between them.

ASSEMBLY

1. Place the ball in the pocket provided in the support bracket.
2. Slide the reverse relay lever onto the support bracket pin.

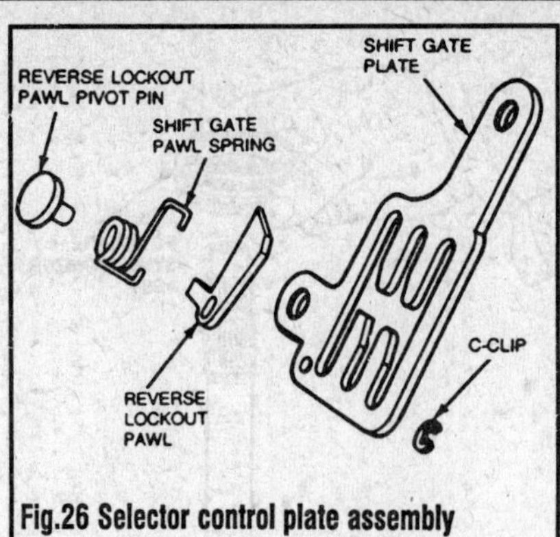

Fig.26 Selector control plate assembly

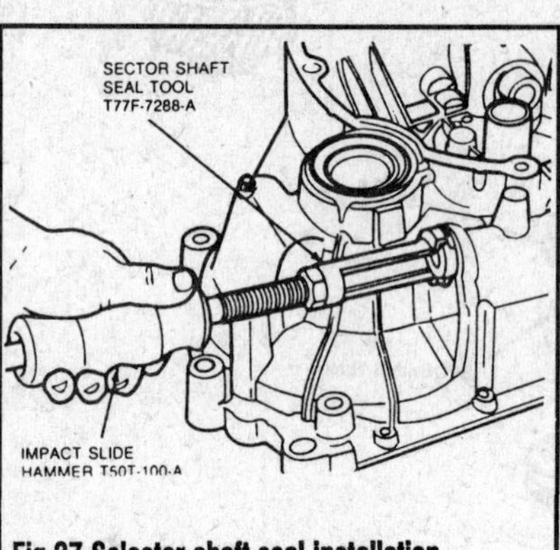

Fig.27 Selector shaft seal installation

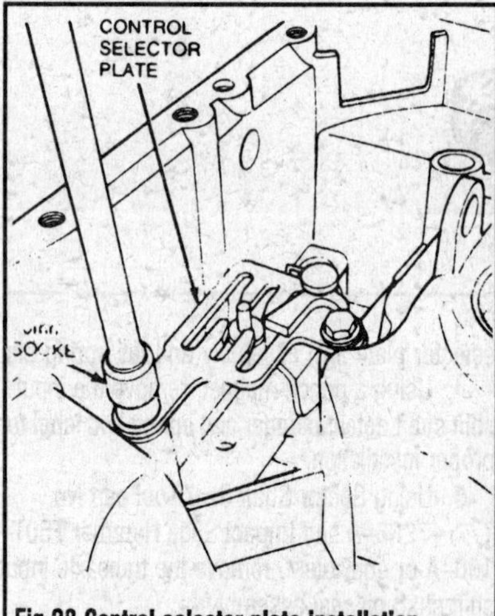

Fig.28 Control selector plate installation

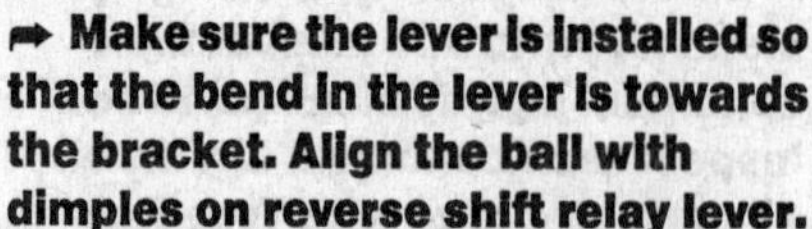
➡ **Make sure the lever is installed so that the bend in the lever is towards the bracket. Align the ball with dimples on reverse shift relay lever.**

3. Install C-clip onto reverse shift lever support bracket shaft to retain reverse shift relay lever.

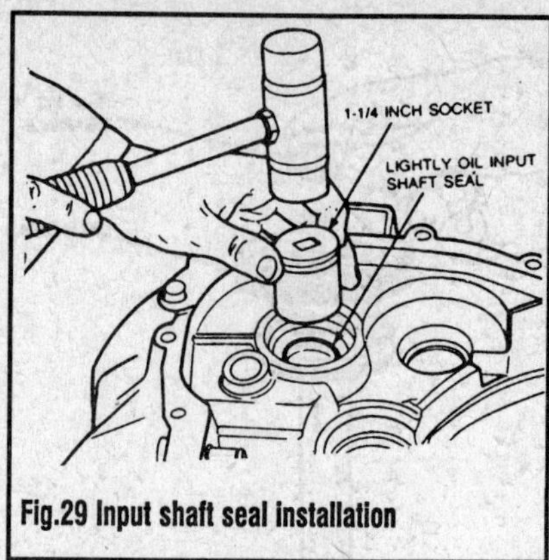

Fig.29 Input shaft seal installation

Selector Control Plate

DISASSEMBLY

1. Using a suitable tool, remove the C-clip retaining reverse lock out pawl pivot pin to shift gate plate.
2. Remove the reverse lock out pawl, pin and spring from shift gate plate.

ASSEMBLY

1. Install the reverse lock out pawl, pin and spring.

➡ **Make sure the lower leg of the spring rests against the shift gate plate and the upper leg of the spring rests against the reverse lock out pawl. Also make sure spring is against shoulder of reverse lock out pivot pin and does not interfere with pin seating against reverse lock out pawl.**

2. Install C-clip to reverse lock out pawl pivot pin.

Input Cluster Shaft Seal Assembly

REMOVAL

1. Using Input Shaft Seal Remover T77F-7050–A or equivalent and a hammer, remove the input shaft seal, working from outside the case.
2. Position the remover against the seal by placing it in the slot cut in the case.

INSTALLATION

To install, lightly oil the input shaft seal and using a 32mm socket and hammer, tap into place.

Input Cluster Shaft Bearings

REMOVAL

➡ **Inspect the bearings and replace them only if worn or damaged.**

Remove the bearing cone and roller assemblies using Pinion Bearing Cone Remover/Installer part No. D79L–4621–A or equivalent and an arbor press. Label bearings for proper installation.

INSTALLATION

➡ Prior to installation of the bearings, thoroughly clean the bearing and inspect their condition. Lightly oil the bearings with Type F or DEXRON®II transmission fluid.

Using Pinion Bearing Cone Remover/Installer part No. D79L–4621–A or equivalent and an arbor press, install the bearing on the shaft. Make sure the bearings are pressed on the proper end as labeled during disassembly.

Speedometer Drive Gear

REMOVAL

1. Using a 7mm socket, remove the retaining screw from the speedometer driven gear retainer assembly.
2. Using a suitable tool, pry on the speedometer retainer to remove both the speedometer gear and retainer assembly from the clutch housing case bore.

INSTALLATION

➡ Prior to install, clean all speedometer gear parts and the retainer's bore in the case. Inspect all parts.

1. Lightly grease the (25mm x 2.6mm) O-ring seal on the speedometer driven gear retainer.
2. Align the relief in the retainer with the attaching screw bore and using a 21mm deep-well socket, tap the assembly into its bore.
3. Using a 7mm socket and torque wrench, tighten the retaining screw to 12–24 inch lbs.

Speedometer Drive Gear

DISASSEMBLY AND ASSEMBLY

1. Carefully remove the O-ring seal from the stem end of the speedometer driven gear.
2. Slide the speedometer driven gear from the retainer.
3. Carefully remove the O-ring seal from its groove in the retainer.

➡ Prior to assembly of the speedometer driven gear, clean all parts thoroughly. Inspect all parts and replace if damaged. Lightly grease the O-ring on the retainer.

4. To assembly the speedometer driven gear, reverse Steps 1, 2, and 3.

Halfshafts

When removing both the left and right halfshafts, install suitable shipping plugs to prevent dislocation of the differential side gears. Should the gears become misaligned, the differential will have to be removed from the transaxle to re-align the side gears.

REMOVAL & INSTALLATION

➧ SEE FIG. 30–34

1. Disconnect the negative battery cable. Remove the wheel cover/hub cover from the wheel and tire assembly and loosen the wheel nuts.
2. Raise the vehicle and support safely. Remove the wheel assembly, remove the hub nut and washer. Discard the old hub nut. Remove the nut from the ball joint to steering knuckle attaching bolts.
3. Drive the bolt out of the steering knuckle using a punch and hammer. Discard this bolt and nut after removal.
4. If equipped with anti-lock brakes, remove the anti-lock brake sensor and position aside. If equipped with air suspension, remove the height sensor bracket retaining bolt and wire sensor bracket to inner fender. Position the sensor link aside.
5. Separate the ball joint from the steering knuckle using a suitable prybar. Position the end of the prybar outside of the bushing pocket to avoid damage to the bushing. Use care to prevent damage to the ball joint boot. Remove the stabilizer bar link at the stabilizer bar.
6. To remove the right halfshaft perform the following:
   a. Remove the bolts attaching the bearing support to the bracket. Slide the link shaft out of the transaxle. Support the end of the shaft by suspending it from a convenient underbody component with a piece of wire. Do not allow the shaft to hang unsupported, damage to the outboard CV-joint may occur.
   b. Separate the outboard CV-joint from the hub using front hub remover tool T81P–1104–C or equivalent and metric adapter tools T83–P–1104–BH, T86P–1104–AI and T81P–1104–A or equivalent.

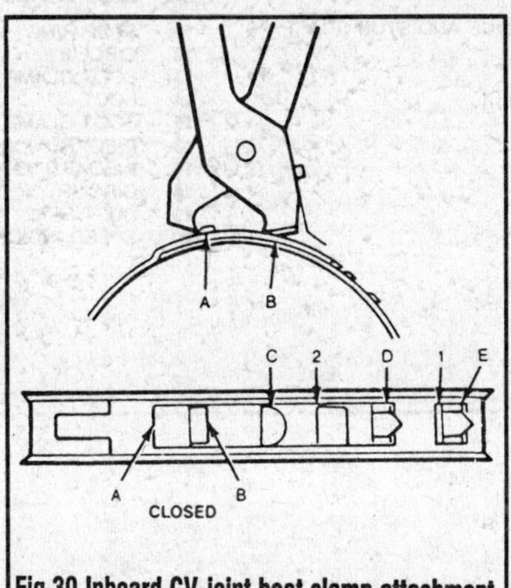

Fig.30 Inboard CV-joint boot clamp attachment

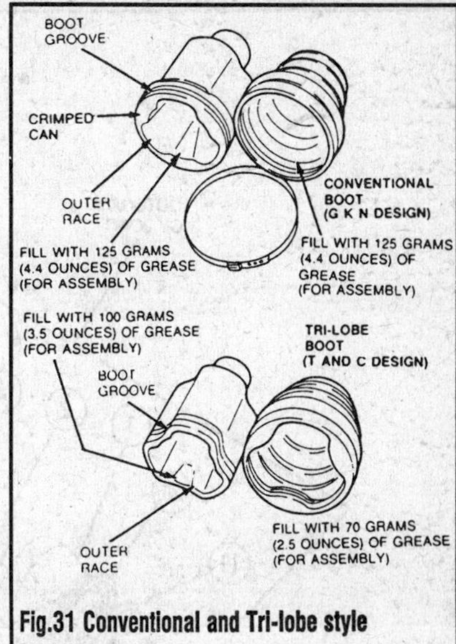

Fig.31 Conventional and Tri-lobe style CV-joints

➡ Never use a hammer to separate the outboard CV-joint stub shaft from the hub. Damage to the CV-joint threads and internal components may result. The right side link shaft and halfshaft assembly is removed as a complete unit.

7. To remove the left halfshaft perform the following:
   a. Install the CV-joint puller tool T86P–3514–A1 or equivalent, between CV-joint and transaxle case. Turn the steering hub and/or wire strut assembly aside.
   b. Screw extension tool T86P–3514–A2 or equivalent, into the CV-joint puller and hand tighten. Screw an impact slide hammer onto the extension and remove the CV-joint.
   c. Support the end of the shaft by suspending it from a convenient underbody component with a piece of wire. Do not allow the shaft to hang un-supported, damage to the outboard CV-joint may occur.
   d. Separate the outboard CV-joint from the hub using front hub remover tool T81P–1104–C or equivalent and metric adapter tools

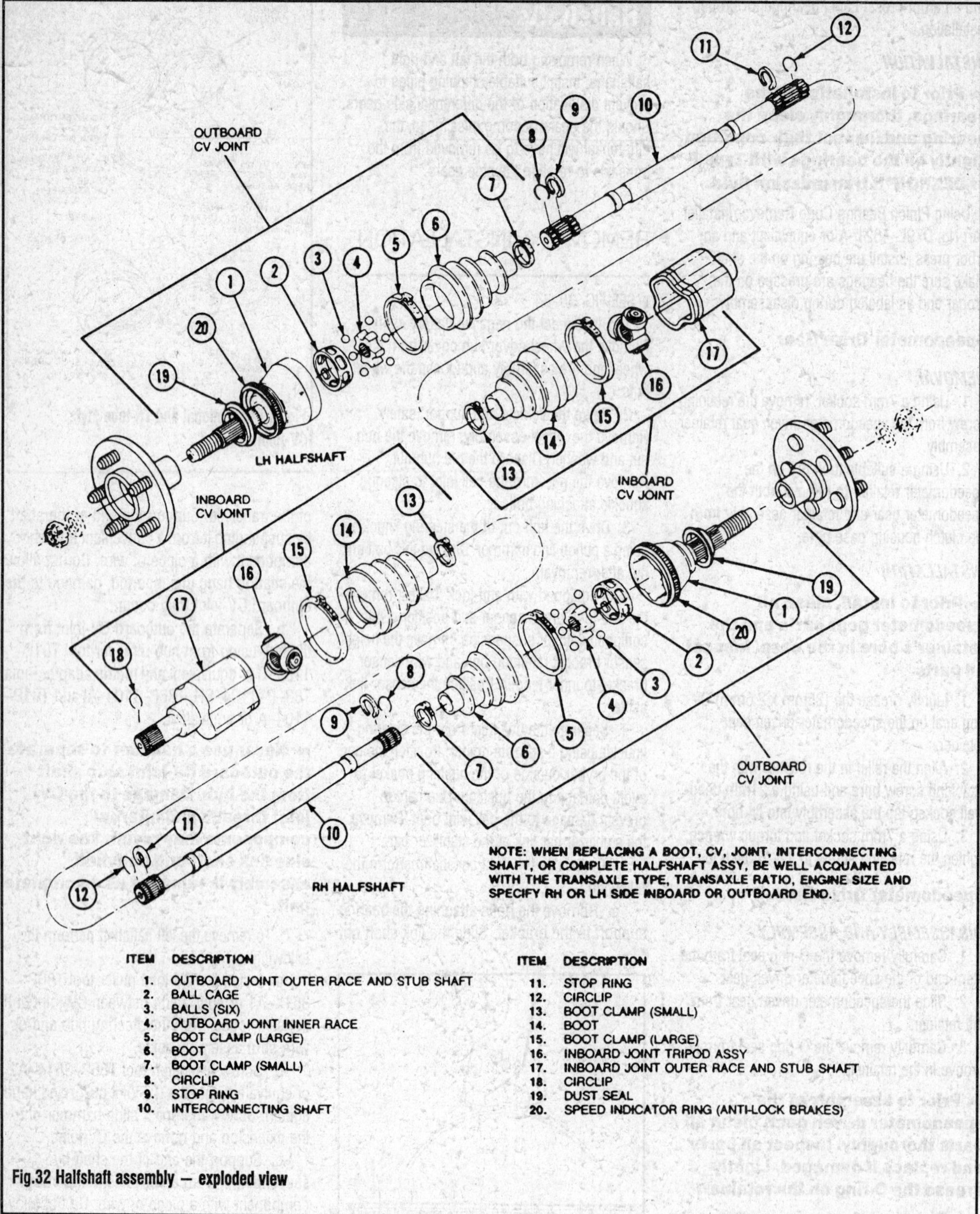
OUTBOARD CV JOINT
LH HALFSHAFT
INBOARD CV JOINT
INBOARD CV JOINT
OUTBOARD CV JOINT
RH HALFSHAFT
NOTE: WHEN REPLACING A BOOT, CV, JOINT, INTERCONNECTING SHAFT, OR COMPLETE HALFSHAFT ASSY, BE WELL ACQUAINTED WITH THE TRANSAXLE TYPE, TRANSAXLE RATIO, ENGINE SIZE AND SPECIFY RH OR LH SIDE INBOARD OR OUTBOARD END.
ITEM DESCRIPTION
1. OUTBOARD JOINT OUTER RACE AND STUB SHAFT
2. BALL CAGE
3. BALLS (SIX)
4. OUTBOARD JOINT INNER RACE
5. BOOT CLAMP (LARGE)
6. BOOT
7. BOOT CLAMP (SMALL)
8. CIRCLIP
9. STOP RING
10. INTERCONNECTING SHAFT
ITEM DESCRIPTION
11. STOP RING
12. CIRCLIP
13. BOOT CLAMP (SMALL)
14. BOOT
15. BOOT CLAMP (LARGE)
16. INBOARD JOINT TRIPOD ASSY
17. INBOARD JOINT OUTER RACE AND STUB SHAFT
18. CIRCLIP
19. DUST SEAL
20. SPEED INDICATOR RING (ANTI-LOCK BRAKES)

Fig.32 Halfshaft assembly — exploded view

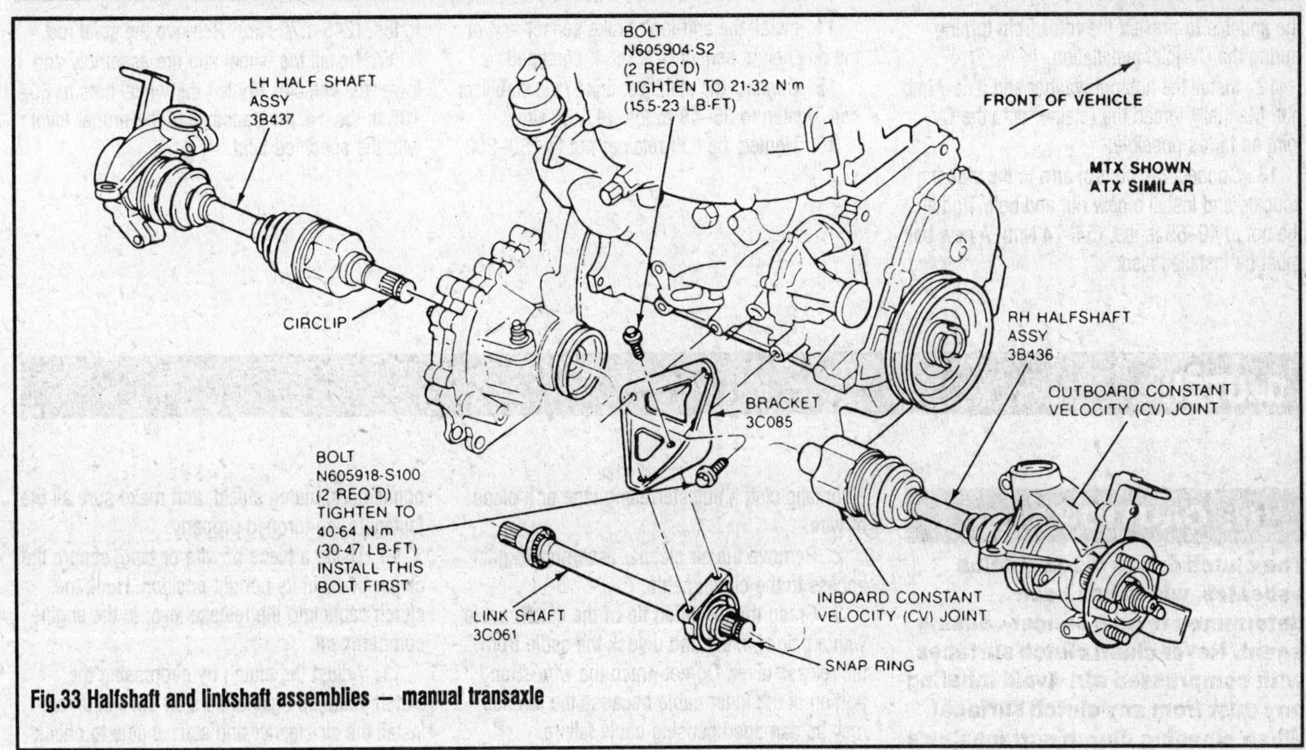

Fig.33 Halfshaft and linkshaft assemblies — manual transaxle

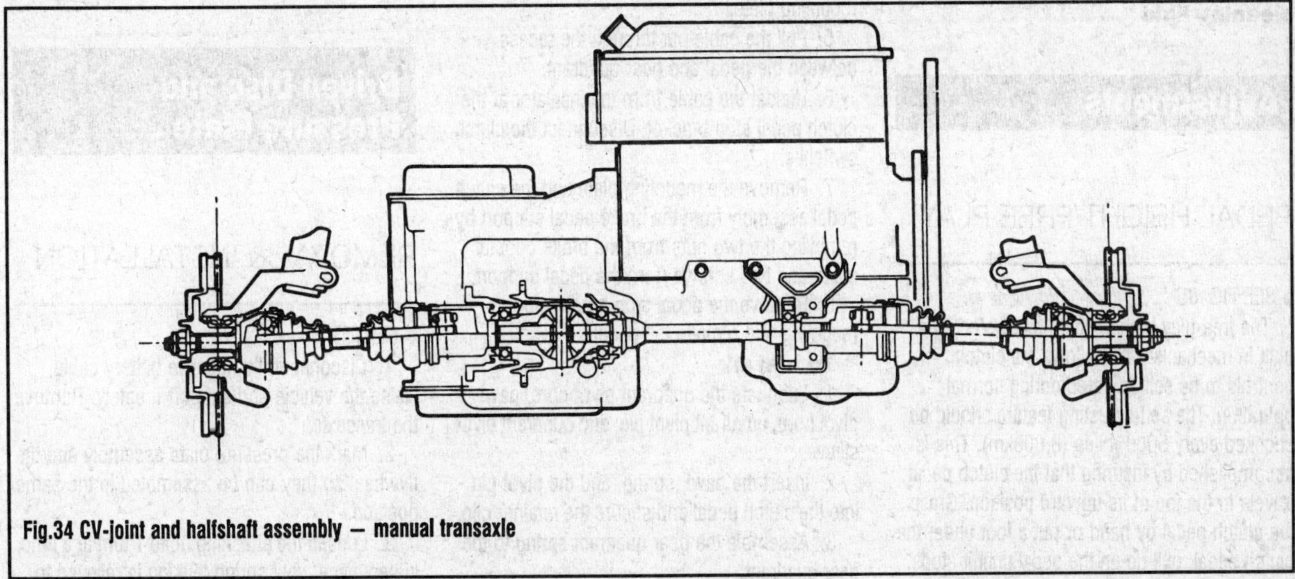
Fig.34 CV-joint and halfshaft assembly — manual transaxle

T83–P–1104–BH, T86P–1104–AI and T81P–1104–A or equivalent.

e. Remove the halfshaft assembly from the vehicle.

To install:

8. Install a new circlip on the inboard CV-joint stub shaft and/or link shaft. The outboard CV-joint does not have a circlip. When installing the circlip, start one end in the groove and work the circlip over the stub shaft end into the groove. This will avoid over expanding the circlip.

➡ The circlip must not be re-used. A new circlip must be installed each time the inboard CV-joint is installed into the transaxle differential.

9. Carefully align the splines of the inboard CV-joint stub shaft with the splines in the differential. Exerting some force, push the CV-joint into the differential until the circlip is felt to seat in the differential side gear. Use care to prevent damage to the differential oil seal. If equipped, torque the link shaft bearing to 16–23 ft. lbs.

➡ A non-metallic mallet may be used to aid in seating the circlip into the differential side gear groove. If a mallet is necessary, tap only on the outboard CV-joint stub shaft.

10. Carefully align the splines of the outboard CV-joint stub shaft with the splines in the hub and push the shaft into the hub as far as possible.

11. Temporarily fasten the rotor to the hub with washers and 2 wheel lug nuts. Insert a steel rod into the rotor and rotate clockwise to contact

the knuckle to prevent the rotor from turning during the CV-joint installation.

12. Install the hub nut washer and a new hub nut. Manually thread the retainer onto the CV-joint as far as possible.

13. Connect the control arm to the steering knuckle and install a new nut and bolt. Tighten the nut to 40–55 ft. lbs. (54–74 Nm). A new bolt must be installed also.

14. Install the anti-lock brake sensor and/or the ride height sensor bracket, if equipped.

15. Connect the stabilizer link to the stabilizer bar. Tighten to 35–48 ft. lbs. (47–65 Nm).

16. Tighten the hub retainer nut to 180–200 ft. lbs. (245–270 Nm). Remove the steel rod.

17. Install the wheel and tire assembly and lower the vehicle. Tighten the wheel nuts to 80–105 ft. lbs. Fill the transaxle to the proper level with the specified fluid.

CLUTCH

**** CAUTION**

The clutch driven disc contains asbestos, which has been determined to be a cancer causing agent. Never clean clutch surfaces with compressed air! Avoid inhaling any dust from any clutch surface! When cleaning clutch surfaces, use a commercially available brake cleaning fluid

Adjustments

PEDAL HEIGHT/FREE PLAY

➧ SEE FIG. 35

The free-play in the clutch is adjusted by a built in mechanism that allows the clutch controls to be self-adjusted during normal operation. The self-adjusting feature should be checked every 5000 miles (8,000km). This is accomplished by insuring that the clutch pedal travels to the top of its upward position. Grasp the clutch pedal by hand or put a foot under the clutch pedal; pull up on the pedal until it stops. Very little effort is required (about 10 lbs.). During the application of upward pressure, a click may be heard which means an adjustment was necessary and has been accomplished.

Clutch Pedal

REMOVAL & INSTALLATION

➧ SEE FIG. 36

1. Prop the clutch pedal up to disengage the automatic clutch adjuster using tape or a piece of wire.

2. Remove the air cleaner assembly to gain access to the clutch cable.

3. Grasp the extended tip of the clutch cable with a pair of pliers and unlock the cable from the release lever. Do not grasp the wire strand portion of the inner cable because the strands may be damaged causing cable failure.

4. Position the clutch shield away from the mounting plate.

5. Pull the cable out through the recess between the pedal and gear quadrant.

6. Unseat the cable from the insulator at the clutch pedal stop bracket. Disconnect the clutch switches.

7. Remove the mounting plate and the clutch pedal assembly from the brake pedal support by removing the two nuts from the brake booster studs and two screws from the pedal support.

8. Remove the pedal stop bracket-to-mounting and remove the pedal.

To install:

1. Lubricate the quadrant pivot bore, pawl pivot bore, quadrant pivot pin, and quadrant pivot sleeve.

2. Insert the pawl, spring, and the pivot pin into the clutch pedal and secure the retainer clip.

3. Assemble the gear quadrant spring to the gear quadrant.

4. Install the two bushings and pivot sleeve into clutch pedal.

5. Place the bolt through the pivot sleeve and torque to 25–30 ft. lbs.

6. Position the assembly on the mounting plate and install the three nuts, torque to 15–25 ft. lbs.

7. Secure the clutch pedal assembly and mounting plate to the brake booster studs and brake pedal support.

8. Pull the clutch cable through the insulator and gear quadrant. Hook the cable into the gear quadrant.

9. Install the clutch switch electrical connectors, clutch shield, and make sure all the fasteners are torqued properly.

10. Using a piece of wire or tape, secure the clutch pedal in its upright position. Hook the clutch cable into the release lever in the engine compartment.

11. Adjust the clutch by depressing the clutch pedal up against its stop several times. Install the air cleaner and start engine to check clutch operation.

Driven Disc and Pressure Plate

REMOVAL & INSTALLATION

➧ SEE FIG. 38

1. Disconnect the negative battery cable. Raise the vehicle and support it safely. Remove the transaxle.

2. Mark the pressure plate assembly and the flywheel so they can be assembled in the same position.

3. Loosen the attaching bolts 1 turn at a time, in sequence, until spring tension is relieved to prevent pressure plate cover distortion.

4. Support the pressure plate and remove the bolts. Remove the pressure plate and clutch disc from the flywheel.

5. Inspect the flywheel, clutch disc, pressure plate, throwout bearing and the clutch fork for wear. Replace parts as required. If the flywheel shows any signs of overheating (blue discoloration) or if it is badly grooved or scored, it should be refaced or replaced.

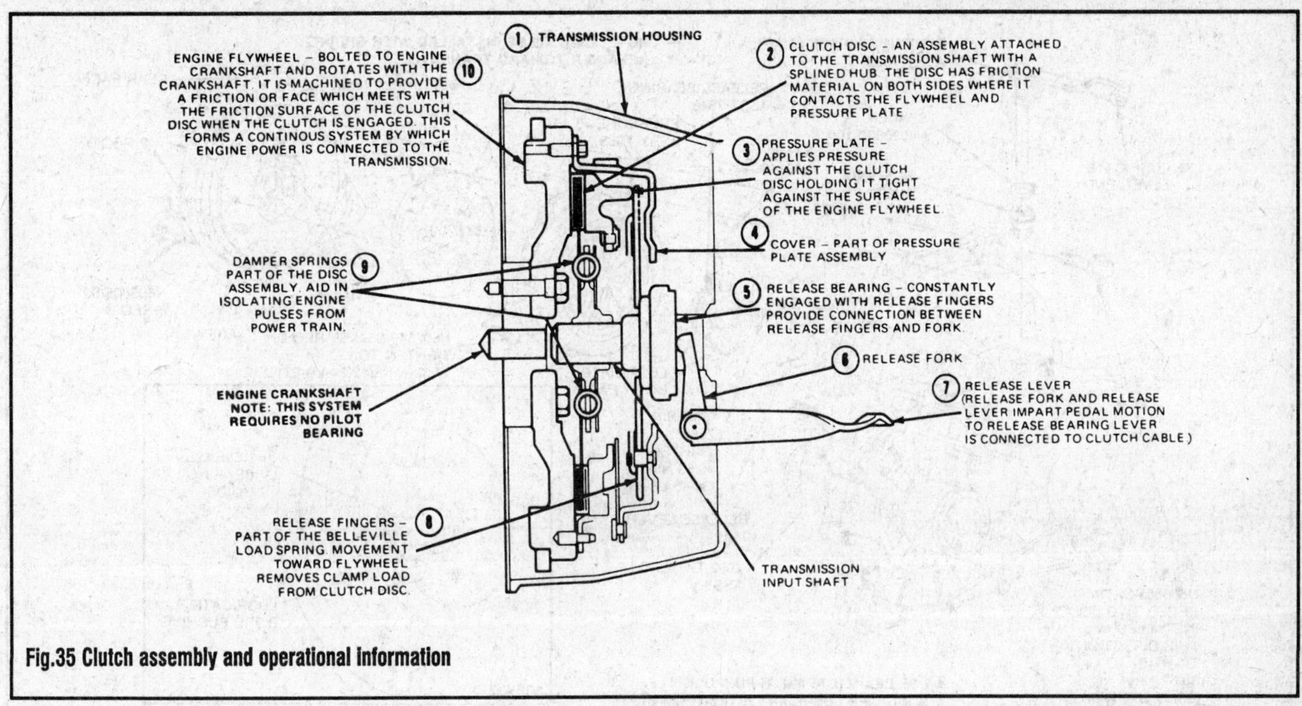

Fig.35 Clutch assembly and operational information

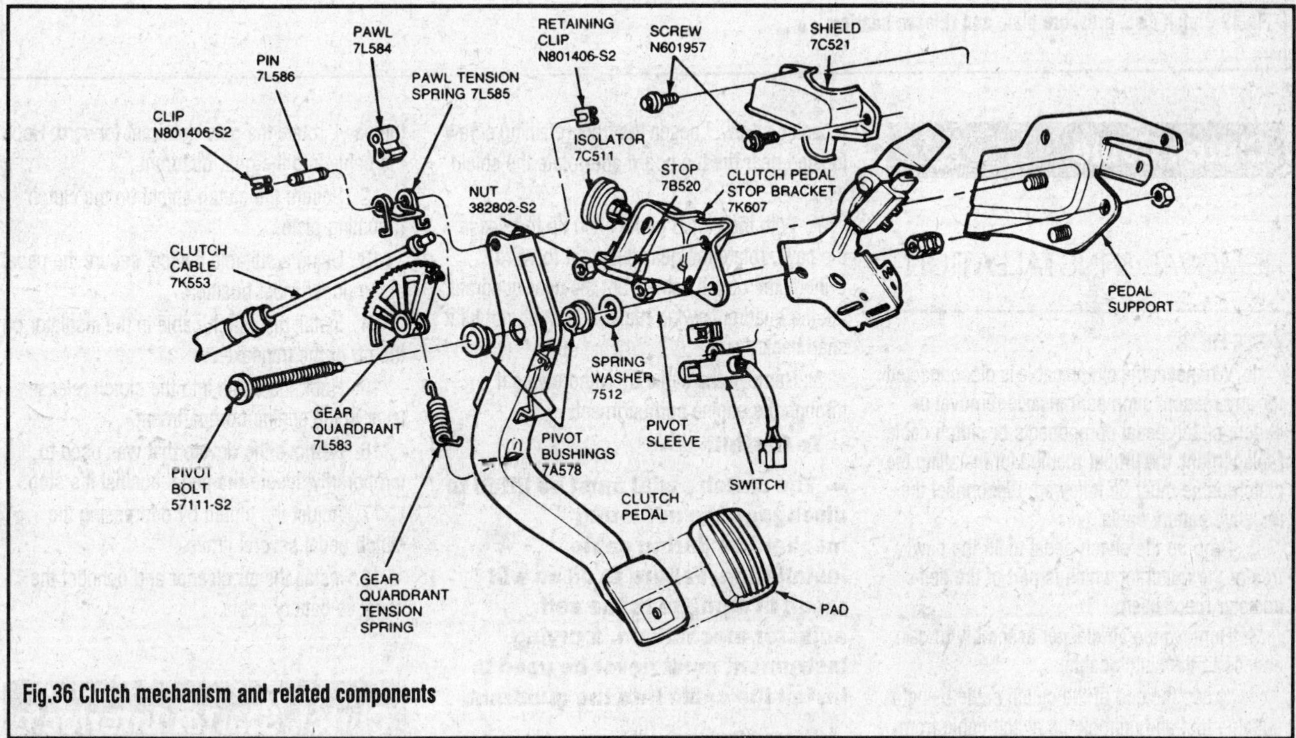

Fig.36 Clutch mechanism and related components

To install:

6. Install the flywheel, if removed. Tighten attaching bolts to 54–64 ft. lbs. (73–87 Nm) on all except the 3.0L SHO engine. On the 3.0L SHO engine, tighten the bolts to 51–58 ft. lbs. (69–78 Nm).

7. Clean the pressure plate and flywheel surfaces thoroughly. Place the clutch disc and pressure plate into the installed position. Align the marks made during the removal procedure if components are being reused. Support the clutch disc and pressure plate with a suitable dummy shaft or clutch aligning tool.

8. Install the pressure plate-to-flywheel bolts. Tighten them gradually in a cross pattern to 12–24 ft. lbs. (17–32 Nm). Remove the alignment tool.

9. Lubricate the release bearing and install it in the fork.

10. Install the transaxle and connect the negative battery cable.

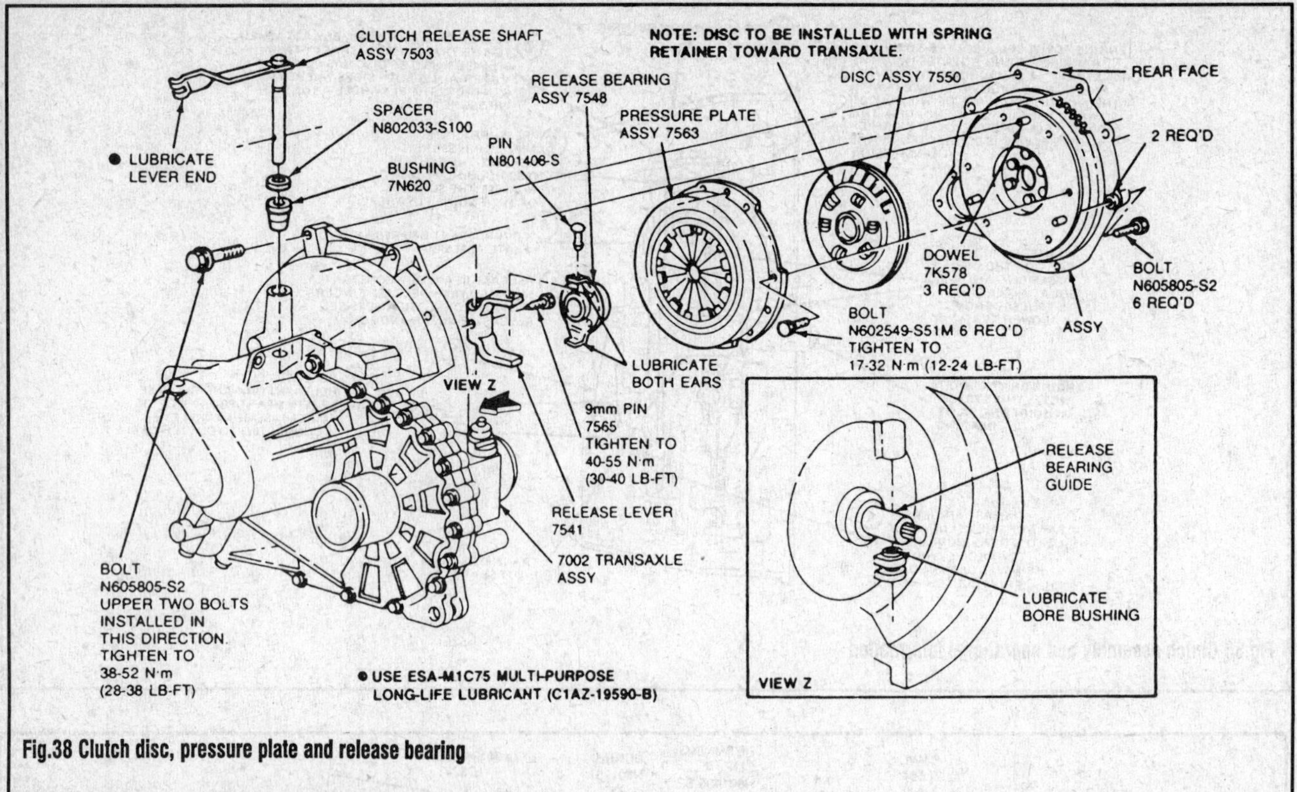

Fig.38 Clutch disc, pressure plate and release bearing

Clutch Cable

REMOVAL & INSTALLATION

➧ SEE FIG. 37

1. Whenever the clutch cable is disconnected for any reason, such as transaxle removal or clutch, clutch pedal components or clutch cable replacement, the proper method for installing the clutch cable must be followed. Disconnect the negative battery cable.
2. Prop up the clutch pedal to lift the pawl free of the quadrant which is part of the self-adjuster mechanism.
3. Remove the air cleaner assembly to gain access to the clutch cable.
4. Grasp the end of the clutch cable using a suitable tool and unhook the clutch cable from the clutch bearing release lever.

➡ Do not grasp the wire strand portion of the inner cable since this might cut the wires and result in cable failure.

5. Disconnect the cable from the insulator that is located on the rib of the transaxle.
6. Position the clutch shield away from the mounting plate bracket by removing the rear retaining screw. Loosen the front retaining screw located near the toe board and rotate the shield aside.
7. With the clutch pedal lifted up to release the pawl, rotate the gear quadrant forward. Unhook the clutch cable from the gear quadrant. Let the quadrant swing rearward but do not let it snap back.
8. Remove the cable by withdrawing it through the engine compartment.

To install:

➡ The clutch pedal must be lifted to disengage the adjusting mechanism during cable installation. Failure to do so will result in damage to the self adjuster mechanism. A prying instrument must never be used to install the cable into the quadrant.

9. Insert the clutch cable assembly from the engine or passenger compartment through the dash panel and dash panel grommet. Make sure the cable is routed inboard of the brake lines and not trapped at the spring tower by the brake lines.
10. Push the clutch cable through the insulator on the stop bracket and through the recess between the pedal and the gear quadrant.
11. With the clutch pedal lifted up to release the pawl, rotate the gear quadrant forward. Hook the cable into the gear quadrant.
12. Secure the clutch shield on the clutch mounting plate.
13. Using a suitable device, secure the pedal in the upper most position.
14. Install the clutch cable in the insulator on the rib of the transaxle.
15. Hook the cable into the clutch release lever in the engine compartment.
16. Remove the device that was used to temporarily secure the pedal against it's stop.
17. Adjust the clutch by depressing the clutch pedal several times.
18. Install the air cleaner and connect the negative battery cable.

Clutch/Starter Interlock Switch

REMOVAL & INSTALLATION

1. Disconnect the negative battery cable. Disconnect the electrical connector.

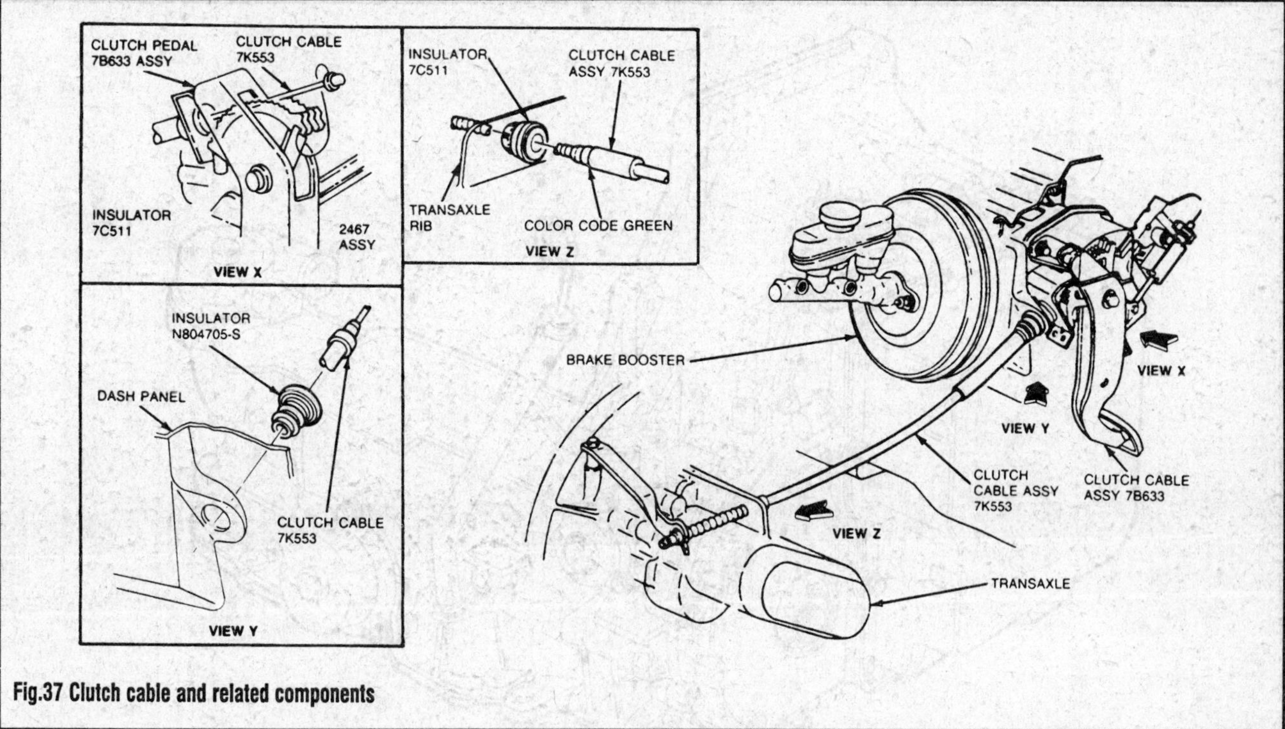

Fig.37 Clutch cable and related components

2. Remove the clutch/starter interlock retaining screw and hairpin clip. Remove the component from the vehicle.

3. Installation is the reverse of the removal procedure.

4. Always install the switch with the self adjusting clip about 1 in. (25mm) from the end of the rod. Be sure that the clutch pedal is in the full up position or the switch will be improperly adjusted.

AUTOMATIC TRANSAXLE

Identification

➧ SEE FIG. 39

Two automatic transaxle units are available, the ATX (automatic transaxle) model which is used with the 2.5L engine, and the AXOD (automatic transaxle overdrive) which is used with the 3.0L and 3.8L engine. Beginning in 1991 some vehicles were equipped with the AXOD-E transaxle which is basically the same as the AXOD with the addition of electronic transaxle controls.

The ATX automatic transaxle is a 3-speed unit. A unique feature is a patented split path torque converter. The engine torque in second and third gears is divided, so that part of the engine torque is transmitted hydrokinetically through the torque converter, and part is transmitted mechanically by direct connection of the engine and transaxle. In the third gear, 93% of the torque is transmitted mechanically, making the ATX highly efficient. Torque splitting is accomplished through a splitter gear set. A conventional compound gear set is also used.

Only one band is used in the ATX. In service fluid additions, or fluid changes may be made with **Motorcraft Type H** automatic transmission fluid.

The AXOD and the AXOD-E automatic transaxle is a 4-speed unit. This unit has two planetary gear sets and a combination planetary/differential gear set. Four multiple plate clutches, two band assemblies, and two one-way clutches act together for proper operation of the planetary gear sets.

A lockup torque converter is coupled to the engine crankshaft and transmits engine power to the gear train by means of a drive link assembly (chain) that connects the drive and the driven sprockets. The application of the converter clutch is controlled through an electronic control integrated in the on-board EEC-IV system computer. These controls, along with the hydraulic controls in the valve body, operate a piston plate clutch in the torque converter to provide improved fuel economy by eliminating converter slip when applied.

In service fluid additions, or fluid changes may be made with **Motorcraft Type H** automatic transmission fluid.

The AXOD-E uses a turbine speed sensor in conjunction with a vehicle electronic control system. These components send operational signals to the EEC-IV microprocessor.

Fluid Pan

REMOVAL & INSTALLATION

In normal service it should not be necessary or required to drain and refill the automatic transaxle. However, under severe operation or

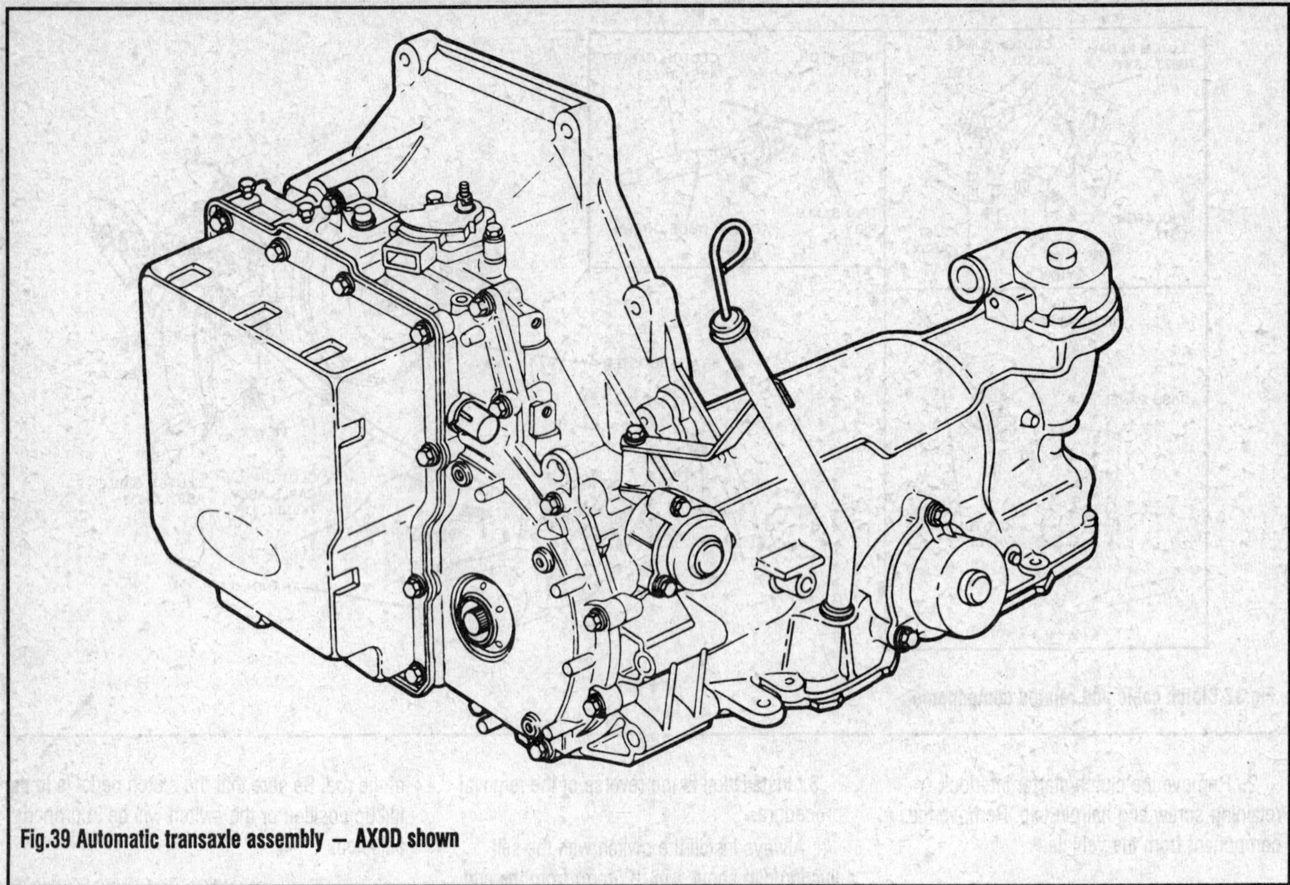
Fig.39 Automatic transaxle assembly — AXOD shown

dusty conditions the fluid should be changed every 20 months or 20,000 miles.

1. Raise the car and safely support it on jackstands. If the pan is equipped with a drain plug, drain the fluid into a suitable container.

2. If the pan does not have a drain plug, place a suitable drain pan underneath the transaxle oil pan. Loosen the oil pan mounting bolts and allow the fluid to drain until it reaches the level of the pan flange. Remove the attaching bolts, leaving one end attached so that the pan will tip and the rest of the fluid will drain.

3. Remove the oil pan. Thoroughly clean the pan. Remove the old gasket. Make sure that the gasket mounting surfaces are clean.

4. Remove the transaxle filter screen retaining bolt. Remove the screen.

5. Install a new filter screen and O-ring. Place a new gasket on the pan and install the pan to the transaxle. Torque the transaxle pan to 15–19 ft. lbs.

6. Fill the transaxle to the correct level. Remove the jackstands and lower the car to the ground.

Adjustments

SHIFT CABLE

AXOD and AXOD-E Transaxle

1. Position the selector lever in the **OD** position against the rearward stop. The shift lever must be held in the rearward position using a constant force of 3 lbs. (1.4 Kg) while the linkage is being adjusted.

2. Loosen the manual lever-to-control cable retaining nut.

3. Move the transaxle manual lever to the **OD** position, second detent from the most rearward position.

4. Tighten the retaining nut to 11–19 ft. lbs. (14–27 Nm).

5. Check the operation of the transaxle in each selector lever position. Make sure the park and neutral start switch are functioning properly.

ATX Transaxle

1. Position the selector lever in the **D** position against the drive stop. The shift lever must be held in the **D** position while the linkage is being adjusted.

2. Loosen the transaxle manual lever-to-control cable adjustment trunnion bolt.

3. Move the transaxle manual lever to the **D** position, second detent from the most rearward position.

4. Tighten the adjustment trunnion bolt to 12–20 ft. lbs. (16–27 Nm).

5. Check the operation of the transaxle in each selector lever position. Make sure the neutral start switch functions properly in **P** and **N** and the back-up lights are on in **R**.

THROTTLE CABLE

➡ Transaxle downshift control is controlled through the throttle position switch on 1991–92 vehicles equipped with the electronic automatic overdrive transaxle.

1986–90 3.0L and 3.8L Engines

The Throttle Valve (TV) cable normally does not need adjustment. The cable should be adjusted only if one of the following components is removed for service or replacement:

- Main control assembly
- Throttle valve cable
- Throttle valve cable engine mounting bracket
- Throttle control lever link or lever assembly
- Engine throttle body
- Transaxle assembly

1. Connect the TV cable eye to the transaxle throttle control lever link and attach the cable boot to the chain cover.

2. If equipped with the 3.0L engine, with the TV cable mounted in the engine bracket, make sure the threaded shank is fully retracted. To retract the shank, pull up on the spring rest with the index fingers and wiggle the top of the thread shank while pressing the shank through the spring with the thumbs.

3. If equipped with the 3.8L engine, the TV cable must be unclipped from the right intake manifold clip. To retract the shank, span the crack between the two 180 degree segments of the adjuster spring rest with a suitable tool. Compress the spring by pushing the rod toward the throttle body with the right hand. While the spring is compressed, push the threaded shank toward the spring with the index and middle fingers of the left hand. Do not pull on the cable sheath.

4. Attach the end of the TV cable to the throttle body.

5. If equipped with the 3.8L engine, rotate the throttle body primary lever by hand, the lever to which the TV-driving nail head is attached, to the wide-open-throttle position. The white adjuster shank must be seen to advance. If not, look for cable sheath/foam hang-up on engine/body components. Attach the TV cable into the top position of the right intake manifold clip.

➡ **The threaded shank must show movement or "ratchet" out of the grip jaws. If there is no movement, inspect the TV cable system for broken or disconnected components and repeat the procedure.**

THROTTLE VALVE CONTROL LINKAGE

ATX Transaxle

➧ SEE FIG. 40

The Throttle Valve (TV) Control Linkage System consists of a lever on the throttle body of the injection unit, linkage shaft assembly, mounting bracket assembly, control rod

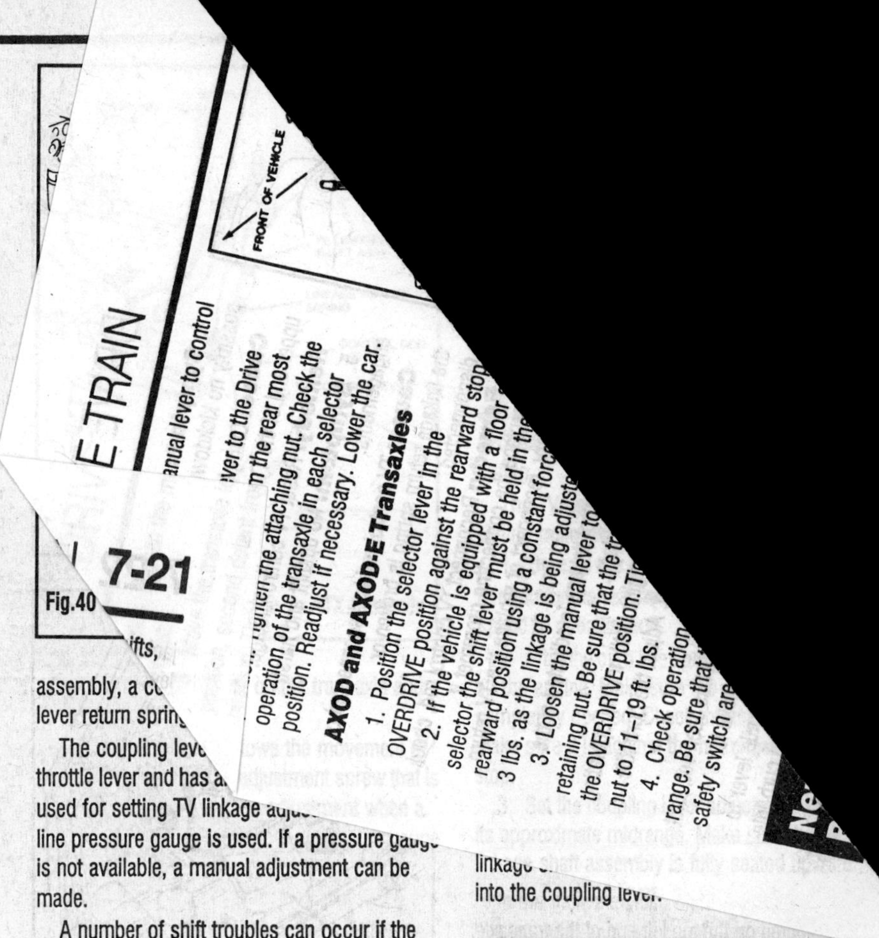

Fig.40

…ifts, assembly, a co… lever return spring…

The coupling leve… throttle lever and has a… used for setting TV linkage adju… line pressure gauge is used. If a pressure gauge is not available, a manual adjustment can be made.

A number of shift troubles can occur if the throttle valve linkage is not in adjustment. Some are:

1. **Symptom:** Excessively early and/or soft upshift with or without slip-bump feel. No forced downshift (kickdown) function at appropriate speeds.

Cause: TV control linkage is set too short.

Remedy: Adjust linkage.

2. **Symptom:** Extremely delayed or harsh upshifts and harsh idle engagement.

Cause: TV control linkage is set too long.

Remedy: Adjust linkage.

3. **Symptom:** Harsh idle engagement after the engine is warmed up. Shift clunk when throttle is backed off after full or heavy throttle acceleration. Harsh coasting downshifts (automatic 3–2, 2–1 shift in D range). Delayed upshift at light acceleration.

Cause: Interference due to hoses, wires, etc. prevents return of TV control rod or TV linkage shaft. Excessive friction caused by binding grommets prevents the TV control linkage to return to its proper location.

Remedy: Correct the interference area, check for bent or twisted rods, levers. or damaged grommets. Repair or replace whatever is necessary. Check and adjust linkage is necessary.

… linkage … into the coupling lever.

⁂ CAUTION

If adjustment of the linkage is necessary, allow the EGR valve to cool so you won't get burned.

4. To adjust, loosen the bolt on the sliding block on the TV control rod a minimum of one turn. Clean any dirt or corrosion from the control rod, free-up the trunnion block so that it will slide freely on the control rod.

5. Rotate the transaxle TV control lever up using a finger and light force, to insure that the TV control lever is against its internal stop. With reducing the pressure on the control lever, tighten the bolt on the trunnion block.

6. Check the throttle lever to be sure it is still against the hot idle stop. If not, repeat the adjustment steps.

TRANSAXLE CONTROL LEVER

ATX Transaxle

1. Position the selector lever in DRIVE against the rear stop.

2. Raise the car and support it safely on

... shift
... of about
... ed.
... control cable
... ansaxle lever is in
... ghten the retaining
... of the transaxle in each
... he park switch and neutral
... working properly.

...utral Safety Switch/ ...ack-Up Light Switch

The neutral start and backup switch are one unit mounted on the top left end of the transaxle. The neutral start portion of the switch allows electrical current to travel to the ignition system when the shift selector is in park or neutral only. The vehicle will not start when the selector is in any other gear. The backup portion operates the rear backup lamps when selector is in the reverse gear.

REMOVAL & INSTALLATION

➧ SEE FIG. 41

1. Place the shift selector in the Park position and apply the emergency brake.
2. Disconnect the negative (–) battery cable.
3. Disconnect the neutral start switch electrical connector and remove the shift control lever on top of the switch.
4. Remove the two neutral switch attaching bolts and remove the switch.
5. Installation is the reverse of the removal procedure.

ADJUSTMENT

➧ SEE FIG. 42

1. Loosely install the two switch attaching bolts and washers, insert a No. 43 drill bit through the hole provided in the switch.
2. Torque the two attaching bolts to 84–108 inch lbs.
3. Check the neutral start switch for proper operation.

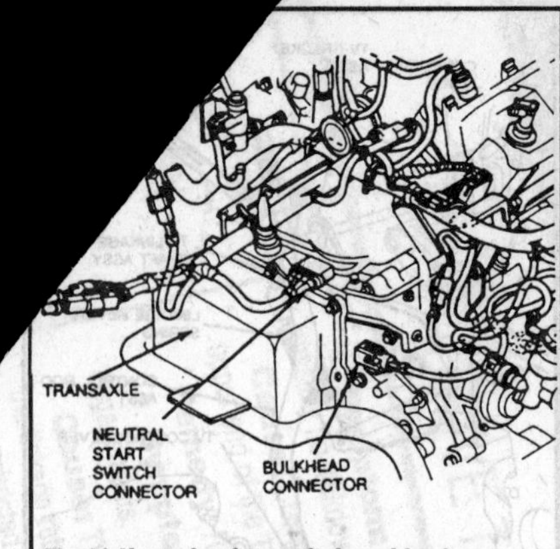

Fig.41 Neutral safety switch and back up switch location – automatic transaxle

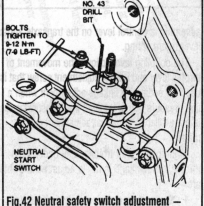

NO. 43 DRILL BIT
BOLTS TIGHTEN TO 9-12 N·m (7-9 LB-FT)
NEUTRAL START SWITCH

Fig.42 Neutral safety switch adjustment – automatic transaxle

Shift Lever Cable

REMOVAL AND INSTALLATION

➧ SEE FIG. 43

1. Remove the shift knob, locknut, console, bezel assembly, control cable clip and cable retaining pin.
2. Disengage the rubber grommet from the floor pan by pushing it into the engine compartment.
3. Raise the car and safely support it on jackstands.
4. Remove the retaining nut and control cable assembly from the transaxle lever.
5. Remove the control cable bracket bolts. Pull the cable through the floor.
6. To install the cable, feed the round end through the floor board. Press the rubber grommet into its mounting hole.
7. Position the control cable assembly in the selector lever housing and install the spring clip.
8. Install the bushing and control cable assembly on the selector lever and housing assembly shaft and secure it with the retaining pin.
9. Install the bezel assembly, console, locknut and shift knob.
10. Position the selector lever in the Drive position. The selector lever must be held in this position while attaching the other end of the control cable.
11. Position the control cable bracket on the retainer bracket and secure the tow mounting bolts.
12. Shift the control lever into the second detent from full rearward (Drive position).
13. Place the cable end on the transaxle lever stud. Align the flats on the stud with the slot in the cable. Make sure the transaxle selector lever has not moved from the second detent position and tighten the retaining nut.
14. Lower the car to the ground. Check the operation of the transaxle selector in all positions. Make sure the neutral safety switch is operating properly. The engine should start only in park or neutral position.

Transaxle

REMOVAL & INSTALLATION

1986–90

EXCEPT TAURUS WITH 2.5L ENGINE

1. Disconnect the negative battery cable. Raise and support the vehicle safely. Remove the air cleaner assembly.
2. Remove the bolt retaining the shift cable and bracket assembly to the transaxle.

➡ Hold the bracket with a prybar in the slot to prevent the bracket from moving.

3. Remove the shift cable bracket bolts and bracket from the transaxle. Disconnect the electrical connector from the neutral safety switch.
4. Disconnect the electrical bulkhead connector from the rear of the transaxle. Remove the dipstick. If with 3.8L engines, remove the throttle valve cable cover. Unsnap the throttle valve cable from the throttle body lever. Remove the throttle valve cable from the transaxle case.

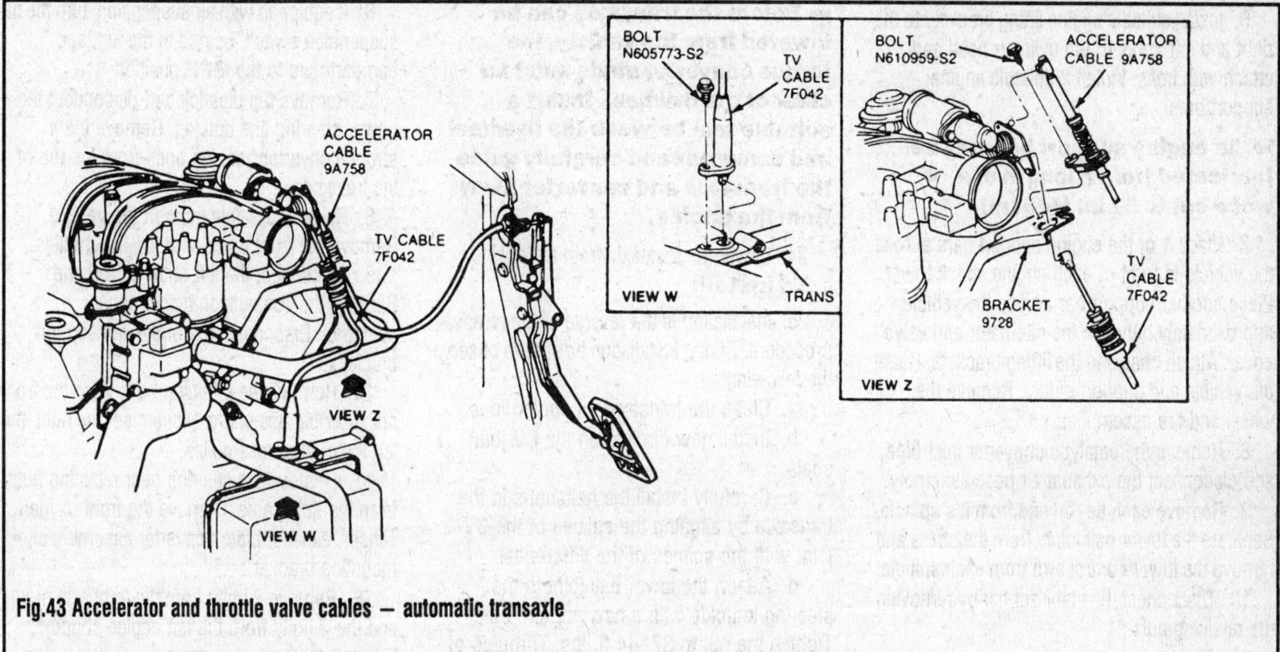

Fig.43 Accelerator and throttle valve cables — automatic transaxle

5. Carefully pull up on the throttle valve cable and disconnect the throttle valve cable from the TV link.

➡ **Pulling to hard on the throttle valve may bend the internal TV bracket.**

6. Install engine lifting brackets.
7. Disconnect the power steering pump pressure and return line bracket.
8. Remove the converter housing bolts from the top of the transaxle.
9. Install a suitable engine support fixture.
10. Raise the vehicle and support it safely.
11. Remove both front wheels. Remove the left outer tie rod end.
12. Remove the lower ball joint attaching nuts and bolts. Remove the lower ball joints and remove the lower control arms from each spindle. Remove stabilizer bar bolts.
13. Remove the nuts securing the steering rack to the sub-frame.
14. If equipped with 3.8L engine, disconnect the oxygen sensor electrical connection and remove the exhaust pipe, converter assembly and mounting bracket.
15. Remove the two 15mm bolts from the transaxle mount. Remove the four 15mm bolts from the left engine support and remove the bracket.
16. Position the sub-frame removal tool.
17. Remove the steering gear from the subframe and secure to the rear of the engine compartment. Remove the sub-frame.
18. Remove the dust cover and the starter assembly.
19. Rotate the engine by the crankshaft pulley bolt to align the torque converter bolts with the starter drive hole. Remove the torque converter-to-flywheel retaining nuts.
20. Remove the transaxle cooler line retaining clips. Disconnect the transaxle cooler lines.
21. Remove the engine to transaxle retaining bolts.
22. Remove the speedometer sensor heat shield.
23. Remove the vehicle speed sensor from the transaxle.

➡ **Vehicles with electronic instrument clusters do not use a speedometer cable.**

24. Position the transaxle jack. Remove the halfshafts.
25. Remove the last 2 torque converter housing bolts.
26. Separate the transaxle from the engine and carefully lower the transaxle from the vehicle.

To install:

27. Installation is the reverse of the removal procedure. During installation be sure to observe the following:
    a. Clean the transaxle oil cooler lines.
    b. Install new circlips on the CV-joint seals.
    c. Carefully install the halfshafts in the transaxle by aligning the splines of the CV-joint with the splines of the differential.
    d. Attach the lower ball joint to the steering knuckle with a new nut and bolt. Tighten the nut to 37–44 ft. lbs.
    e. When installing the transaxle to the engine, verify that the converter-to-transaxle engagement is maintained. Prevent the converter from moving forward and disengaging during installation.
    f. Adjust the TV and manual linkages. Check the transaxle fluid level.
    g. Tighten the following bolts to the torque specifications listed:
    - Transaxle-to-engine bolts: 41–50 ft. lbs. (55–68 Nm)
    - Control arm-to-knuckle bolts: 36–44 ft. lbs. (50–60 Nm)
    - Stabilizer U-clamp-to-bracket bolts: 60–70 ft. lbs. (81–95 Nm)
    - Tie rod-to-knuckle nut: 23–35 ft. lbs. (31–47 Nm)
    - Starter-to-transaxle bolts: 30–40 ft. lbs. (41–54 Nm)
    - Converter-to-flywheel bolts: 23–39 ft. lbs. (31–53 Nm)
    - Insulator-to-bracket bolts: 55–70 ft. lbs. (75–90 Nm)

TAURUS WITH 2.5L ENGINE

1. Disconnect the negative battery cable and remove the air cleaner assembly.
2. Position the engine control wiring harness away from the transaxle converter housing.
3. Disconnect the TV linkage and manual lever cable at the respective levers. Failure to disconnect the linkage during transaxle removal and allowing the transaxle to hang will fracture the throttle valve cam shaft joint, which is located under the transaxle cover.
4. Remove the power steering hose brackets.
5. Remove the upper transaxle-to-engine attaching bolts.

6. Install suitable engine lifting brackets to the right and left areas of the cylinder head and attach with bolts. Install 2 suitable engine support bars.

➡ **An engine support bar may be fabricated from a length of 4×4 wood cut to 57 in. (145cm).**

7. Place 1 of the engine support bars across the vehicle in front of each engine shock tower. Place another support bar across the vehicle approximately between the alternator and valve cover. Attach chains to the lifting brackets. Raise the vehicle and support safely. Remove the wheel and tire assemblies.

8. Remove the catalytic converter inlet pipe and disconnect the exhaust air hose assembly.

9. Remove each tie rod end from it's spindle. Separate the lower ball joints from the struts and remove the lower control arm from each spindle.

10. Disconnect the stabilizer bar by removing the retaining nuts.

11. Disconnect and remove the rack and pinion and auxiliary cooler from the sub-frame. Position the rack and pinion away from the subframe and secure with wire.

12. Remove the right front axle support and bearing assembly retaining bolts.

13. Remove the halfshaft and link shaft assembly out of the right side of the transaxle.

14. Disengage the left halfshaft from the differential side gear. Pull the halfshaft from the transaxle.

➡ **Support and secure the halfshaft from an underbody component with a length of wire. Do not allow the halfshafts to hang unsupported.**

15. Plug the seal holes.

16. Remove the front support insulator and position the left front splash shield aside.

17. Properly support the sub-frame and lower the vehicle onto the sub-frame support. Remove the sub-frame and disconnect the neutral start switch wire assembly.

18. Raise the vehicle after the sub-frame is removed. Disconnect the speedometer cable.

19. Disconnect and remove the shift cable from the transaxle.

20. Disconnect the oil cooler lines and remove the starter.

21. Remove the dust cover from the torque converter housing and remove the torque converter-to-flywheel housing nuts.

22. Position a suitable transaxle jack under the transaxle.

23. Remove the remaining transaxle-to-engine attaching bolts.

➡ **Before the transaxle can be lowered from the vehicle, the torque converter studs must be clear of the flywheel. Insert a suitable tool between the flywheel and converter and carefully guide the transaxle and converter away from the engine.**

24. Lower the transaxle from the engine.

To install:

25. Installation is the reverse of the removal procedure. During installation be sure to observe the following:

a. Clean the transaxle oil cooler lines.

b. Install new circlips on the CV-joint seals.

c. Carefully install the halfshafts in the transaxle by aligning the splines of the CV-joint with the splines of the differential.

d. Attach the lower ball joint to the steering knuckle with a new nut and bolt. Tighten the nut to 37–44 ft. lbs. Torquing of the bolt is not required.

e. When installing the transaxle to the engine, verify that the converter-to-transaxle engagement is maintained. Prevent the converter from moving forward and disengaging during installation.

f. Adjust the TV and manual linkages. Check the transaxle fluid level.

g. Tighten the following bolts to the torque specifications listed:

- Transaxle-to-engine bolts: 25–33 ft. lbs. (34–45 Nm)
- Control arm-to-knuckle bolts: 36–44 ft. lbs. (50–60 Nm)
- Stabilizer U-clamp-to-bracket bolts: 60–70 ft. lbs. (81–95 Nm)
- Tie rod-to-knuckle nut: 23–35 ft. lbs. (31–47 Nm)
- Starter-to-transaxle bolts: 30–40 ft. lbs. (41–54 Nm)
- Converter-to-flywheel bolts: 23–39 ft. lbs. (31–53 Nm)
- Insulator-to-bracket bolts: 55–70 ft. lbs. (75–90 Nm)

1991-92

1. Disconnect the battery cables and remove the battery and battery tray.

2. Remove the air cleaner assembly, hoses and tubes.

3. Disconnect the electrical connectors from the engine and remove the bolt retaining the main wiring harness bracket.

4. Remove the shift lever. Remove the EGR bracket and throttle body bracket retaining bolts and install engine lifting eyes.

5. Secure the wiring harness aside and remove the radiator sight shield. Position a suitable engine support fixture.

6. If equipped with air suspension, turn the air suspension switch located in the luggage compartment to the **OFF** position.

7. Remove the dipstick and disconnect the power steering line bracket. Remove the 4 torque converter housing bolts from the top of the transaxle.

8. Raise and safely support the vehicle. Remove the front wheel and tire assemblies.

9. Disconnect the left outer tie rod end. Remove the suspension height sensor, if equipped. Disconnect the brake line support brackets.

10. Remove the retaining bolts from the front stabilizer bar assembly. Disconnect the right and left lower arm assemblies.

11. Remove the steering gear retaining nuts from the sub-frame. Remove the front oxygen sensor, exhaust pipe, converter assembly and mounting bracket.

12. Remove 2 bolts from the transaxle mount and the 4 bolts from the left engine support. Remove the engine support.

13. Position a suitable sub-frame removal tool. Remove the steering gear from the subframe and secure to the rear of the engine compartment. Remove the sub-frame-to-body bolts and lower the sub-frame.

14. Remove the starter and the dust cover.

15. Rotate the engine at the crankshaft pulley to align the torque converter bolts with the starter drive hole. Remove the 4 torque converter-to-flywheel retaining nuts.

16. Disconnect the transaxle cooler lines. Remove the engine-to-transaxle retaining bolts.

17. Remove the speedometer sensor heat shield. Remove the vehicle speed sensor from the transaxle.

➡ **Vehicles with electronic instrument clusters do not use a speedometer cable.**

18. Position a suitable transaxle jack. Remove the halfshafts.

19. Remove the last 2 torque converter housing bolts, carefully separate the transaxle from the engine and lower out of the vehicle.

20. Installation is the reverse of the removal procedure. During installation be sure to observe the following:

a. Clean the transaxle oil cooler lines.

b. Install new circlips on the CV-joint seals.

c. Carefully install the halfshafts in the transaxle by aligning the splines of the CV-joint with the splines of the differential.

d. Attach the lower ball joint to the steering knuckle with a new nut and bolt. Tighten the nut to 37–44 ft. lbs.

e. When installing the transaxle to the

engine, verify that the converter-to-transaxle engagement is maintained. Prevent the converter from moving forward and disengaging during installation.

f. Adjust the TV and manual linkages. Check the transaxle fluid level.

g. Tighten the following bolts to the torque specifications listed:

- Transaxle-to-engine bolts: 41–50 ft. lbs. (55–68 Nm)
- Control arm-to-knuckle bolts: 36–44 ft. lbs. (50–60 Nm)
- Stabilizer U-clamp-to-bracket bolts: 60–70 ft. lbs. (81–95 Nm)
- Tie rod-to-knuckle nut: 23–35 ft. lbs. (31–47 Nm)
- Starter-to-transaxle bolts: 30–40 ft. lbs. (41–54 Nm)
- Converter-to-flywheel bolts: 23–39 ft. lbs. (31–53 Nm)
- Insulator-to-bracket bolts: 55–70 ft. lbs. (75–90 Nm)

Halfshafts

When removing both the left and right halfshafts, install suitable shipping plugs to prevent dislocation of the differential side gears. Should the gears become misaligned, the differential will have to be removed from the transaxle to re-align the side gears.

➡ Due to the automatic transaxle case configuration, the right halfshaft assembly must be removed first. Differential Rotator T81P–4026–A or equivalent, is then inserted into the transaxle to drive the left inboard CV-joint assembly from the transaxle. If only the left halfshaft assembly is to be removed for service, remove only the right halfshaft assembly from the transaxle. After removal, support it with a length of wire. Then drive the left halfshaft assembly from the transaxle.

REMOVAL & INSTALLATION

➧ SEE FIG. 52–55

1. Disconnect the negative battery cable. Remove the wheel cover/hub cover from the wheel and tire assembly and loosen the wheel nuts.

2. Raise the vehicle and support safely. Remove the wheel assembly, remove the hub nut and washer. Discard the old hub nut. Remove the nut from the ball joint to steering knuckle attaching bolts.

3. Drive the bolt out of the steering knuckle using a punch and hammer. Discard this bolt and nut after removal.

4. If equipped with anti-lock brakes, remove the anti-lock brake sensor and position aside. If equipped with air suspension, remove the height sensor bracket retaining bolt and wire sensor bracket to inner fender. Position the sensor link aside.

5. Separate the ball joint from the steering knuckle using a suitable prybar. Position the end of the prybar outside of the bushing pocket to avoid damage to the bushing. Use care to prevent damage to the ball joint boot. Remove the stabilizer bar link at the stabilizer bar.

6. The following removal procedure applies to the right side halfshaft/link shaft for the 1986–90 2.5L engine Taurus. For all other automatic transaxles, proceed to Step 7:

a. Remove the bolts attaching the bearing support to the bracket. Slide the link shaft out of the transaxle. Support the end of the shaft by suspending it from a convenient underbody component with a piece of wire. Do not allow the shaft to hang unsupported, damage to the outboard CV-joint may occur.

b. Separate the outboard CV-joint from the hub using front hub remover tool T81P–1104–C or equivalent and metric adapter tools T83–P–1104–BH, T86P–1104–AI and T81P–1104–A or equivalent.

➡ Never use a hammer to separate the outboard CV-joint stub shaft from the hub. Damage to the CV-joint threads and internal components may result. The right side link shaft and halfshaft assembly is removed as a complete unit.

7. The following removal procedure applies to the right and left side halfshafts for the automatic transaxle, except 1986–90 2.5L engine Taurus.

a. Install the CV-joint puller tool T86P–3514–A1 or equivalent, between CV-joint and transaxle case. Turn the steering hub and/or wire strut assembly aside.

b. Screw extension tool T86P–3514–A2 or equivalent, into the CV-joint puller and hand tighten. Screw an impact slide hammer onto the extension and remove the CV-joint.

c. Support the end of the shaft by suspending it from a convenient underbody component with a piece of wire. Do not allow the shaft to hang un-supported, damage to the outboard CV-joint may occur.

d. Separate the outboard CV-joint from the hub using front hub remover tool T81P–1104–C or equivalent and metric adapter tools T83–P–1104–BH, T86P–1104–AI and T81P–1104–A or equivalent.

e. Remove the halfshaft assembly from the vehicle.

8. The following removal procedure applies to the left side halfshaft for the 1986–90 Taurus with 2.5L engine automatic transaxle:

➡ Due to the automatic transaxle case configuration, the right halfshaft assembly must be removed first. Differential rotator tool T81P–4026–A or equivalent, is then inserted into the transaxle to drive the left inboard CV-joint assembly from the transaxle. If only the left halfshaft assembly is to be removed for service, remove the right halfshaft assembly from the transaxle first. After removal, support it with a length of wire. Then drive the left halfshaft assembly from the transaxle.

a. Support the end of the shaft by suspending it from a convenient underbody component with a piece of wire. Do not allow the shaft to hang unsupported as damage to the outboard CV-joint may occur.

b. Separate the outboard CV-joint from the hub front hub remover tool T81P–1104–C or equivalent and metric adapter tools T83–P–1104–BH, T86P–1104–AI and T81P–1104–A or equivalent.

c. Remove the halfshaft assembly from the vehicle.

To install:

9. Install a new circlip on the inboard CV-joint stub shaft and/or link shaft. The outboard CV-joint does not have a circlip. When installing the circlip, start one end in the groove and work the circlip over the stub shaft end into the groove. This will avoid over expanding the circlip.

➡ The circlip must not be re-used. A new circlip must be installed each time the inboard CV-joint is installed into the transaxle differential.

10. Carefully align the splines of the inboard CV-joint stub shaft with the splines in the differential. Exerting some force, push the CV-joint into the differential until the circlip is felt to seat in the differential side gear. Use care to prevent damage to the differential oil seal. If equipped, torque the link shaft bearing to 16–23 ft. lbs.

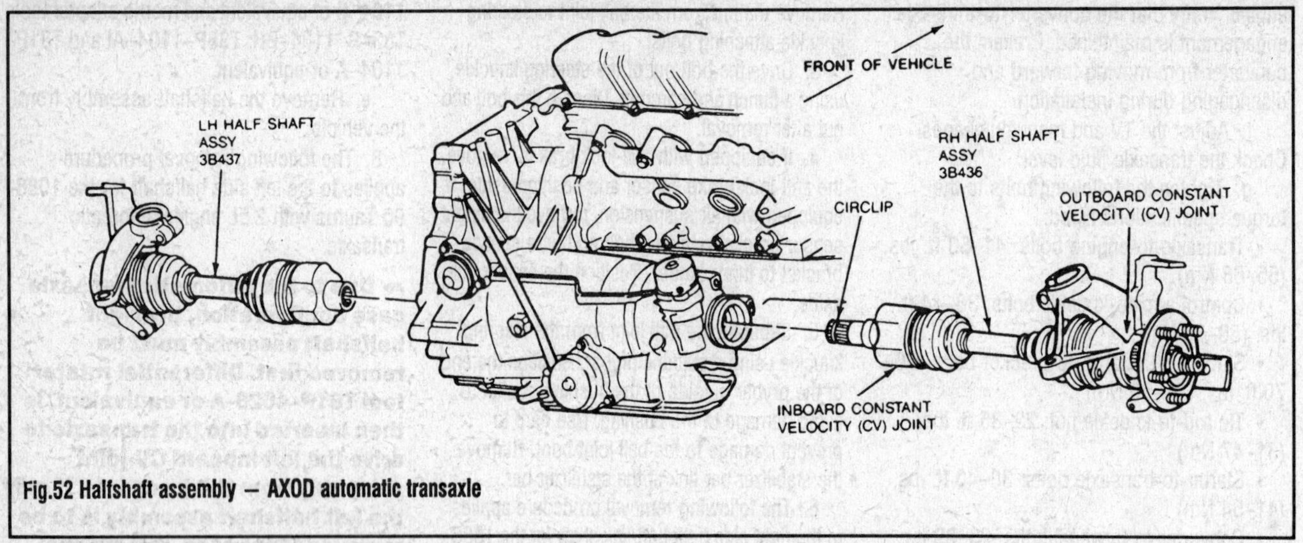
FRONT OF VEHICLE
LH HALF SHAFT ASSY 3B437
RH HALF SHAFT ASSY 3B436
CIRCLIP
OUTBOARD CONSTANT VELOCITY (CV) JOINT
INBOARD CONSTANT VELOCITY (CV) JOINT

Fig.52 Halfshaft assembly — AXOD automatic transaxle

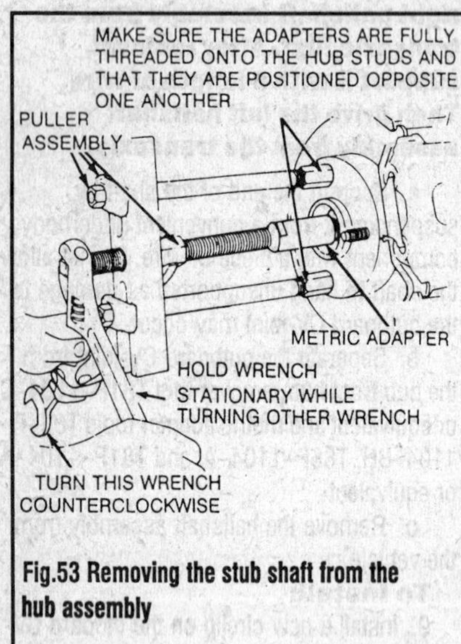
MAKE SURE THE ADAPTERS ARE FULLY THREADED ONTO THE HUB STUDS AND THAT THEY ARE POSITIONED OPPOSITE ONE ANOTHER
PULLER ASSEMBLY
METRIC ADAPTER
HOLD WRENCH STATIONARY WHILE TURNING OTHER WRENCH
TURN THIS WRENCH COUNTERCLOCKWISE

Fig.53 Removing the stub shaft from the hub assembly

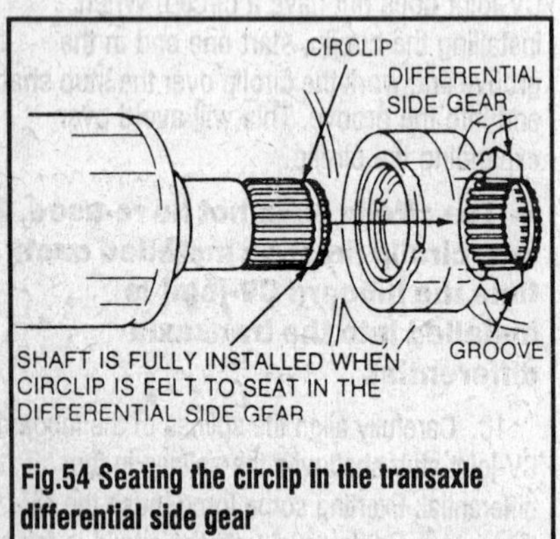
CIRCLIP
DIFFERENTIAL SIDE GEAR
GROOVE
SHAFT IS FULLY INSTALLED WHEN CIRCLIP IS FELT TO SEAT IN THE DIFFERENTIAL SIDE GEAR

Fig.54 Seating the circlip in the transaxle differential side gear

➡ **A non-metallic mallet may be used to aid in seating the circlip into the differential side gear groove. If a mallet is necessary, tap only on the outboard CV-joint stub shaft.**

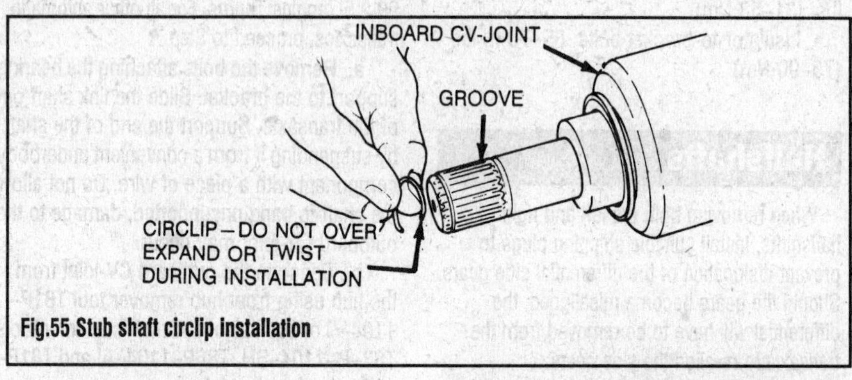
INBOARD CV-JOINT
GROOVE
CIRCLIP—DO NOT OVER EXPAND OR TWIST DURING INSTALLATION

Fig.55 Stub shaft circlip installation

11. Carefully align the splines of the outboard CV-joint stub shaft with the splines in the hub and push the shaft into the hub as far as possible.

12. Temporarily fasten the rotor to the hub with washers and 2 wheel lug nuts. Insert a steel rod into the rotor and rotate clockwise to contact the knuckle to prevent the rotor from turning during the CV-joint installation.

13. Install the hub nut washer and a new hub nut. Manually thread the retainer onto the CV-joint as far as possible.

14. Connect the control arm to the steering knuckle and install a new nut and bolt. Tighten the nut to 40–55 ft. lbs. (54–74 Nm). A new bolt must be installed also.

15. Install the anti-lock brake sensor and/or the ride height sensor bracket, if equipped.

16. Connect the stabilizer link to the stabilizer bar. Tighten to 35–48 ft. lbs. (47–65 Nm).

17. Tighten the hub retainer nut to 180–200 ft. lbs. (245–270 Nm). Remove the steel rod.

18. Install the wheel and tire assembly and lower the vehicle. Tighten the wheel nuts to 80–105 ft. lbs. Fill the transaxle to the proper level with the specified fluid.

CV-Boot

REMOVAL & INSTALLATION

Outboard CV-Joint Boot

➧ SEE FIG. 44–49

1. Disconnect the negative battery cable. Raise and safely support the vehicle.

2. Remove the halfshaft assembly from the vehicle.

3. Clamp the halfshaft in a vise that is equipped with soft jaw covers. Do not allow the vise jaws to contact the boot or boot clamp.

4. Cut the large boot clamp with a pair of side cutters and peel the clamp away from the boot. Roll the boot back over the shaft after the clamp has been removed.

5. Clamp the interconnecting shaft in a soft jawed vise with the CV-joint pointing downward so the inner bearing race is exposed.

6. Use a brass drift and hammer, give a sharp tap to the inner bearing race to dislodge the internal snapring and separate the CV-joint from the interconnecting shaft. Take care to secure

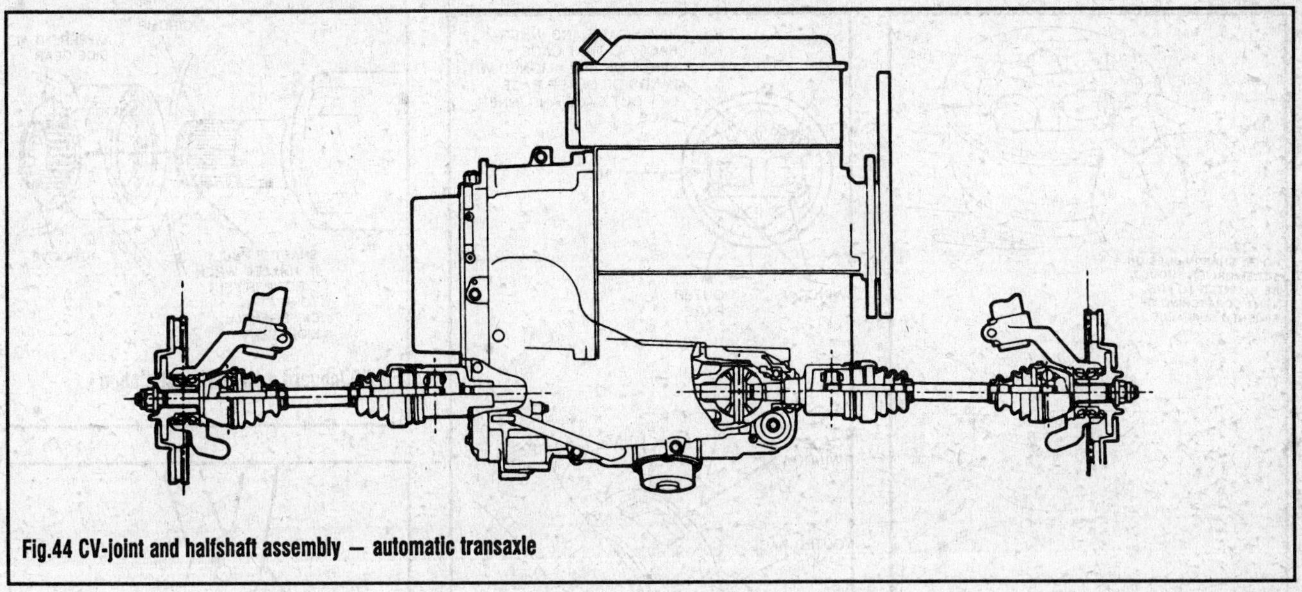

Fig.44 CV-joint and halfshaft assembly — automatic transaxle

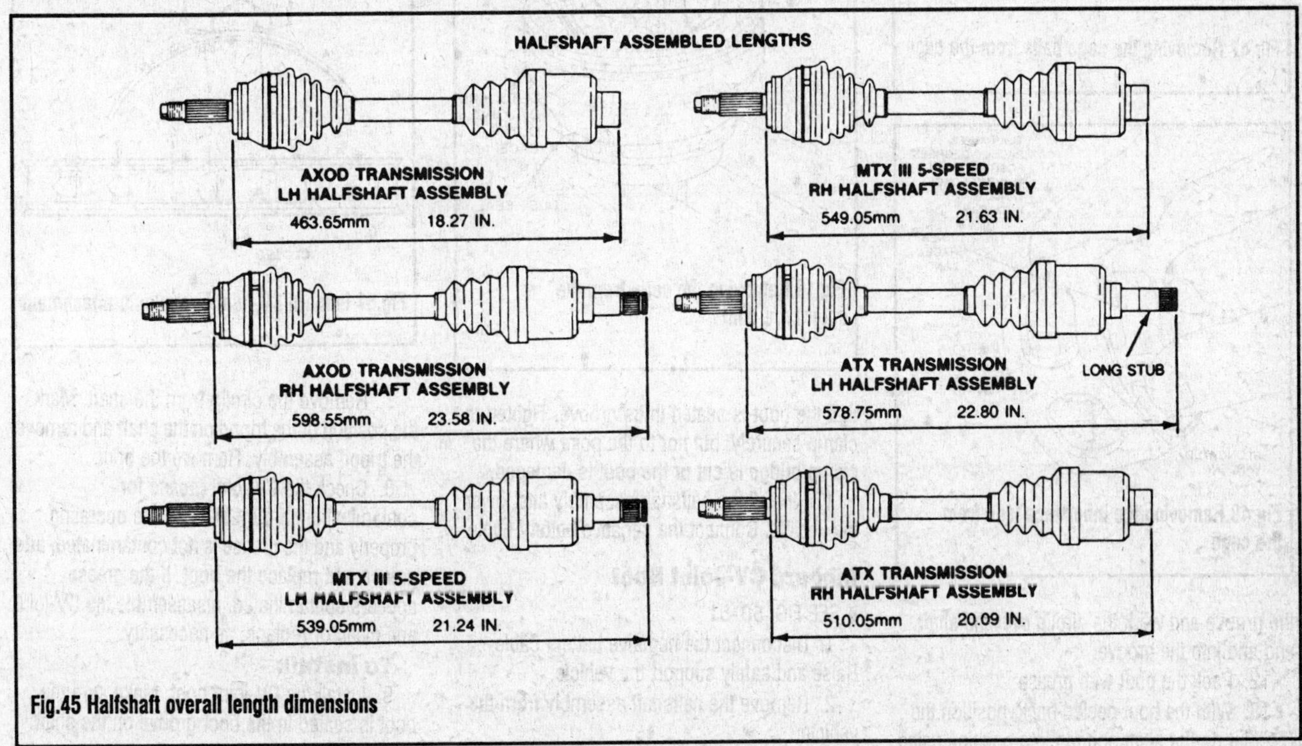

Fig.45 Halfshaft overall length dimensions

the CV-joint so it does not drop after separation. Remove the clamp and boot from the shaft.

7. Remove and discard the circlip at the end of the interconnecting shaft. The stop ring, located just below the circlip should be removed and replaced only if damaged or worn.

To Install:

8. Clean the joint and repack with fresh grease. Do not reuse the old grease Install a new boot or reinstall the old boot with a new clamp.

9. The left and right interconnecting shafts are different, depending on year and vehicle application. The outboard end of the shaft is shorter from the end of the shaft to the end of the boot groove than the inboard end. Take a measurement to insure correct installation.

10. Install the new boot. Make sure the boot is seated in the mounting groove and secure it in position with a new clamp. Tighten the clamp securely, but not to the point where the clamp bridge is cut or the boot is damaged.

11. Clean the interconnecting shaft splines and install a new circlip and stop ring if removed. To install the circlip correctly, start one end in

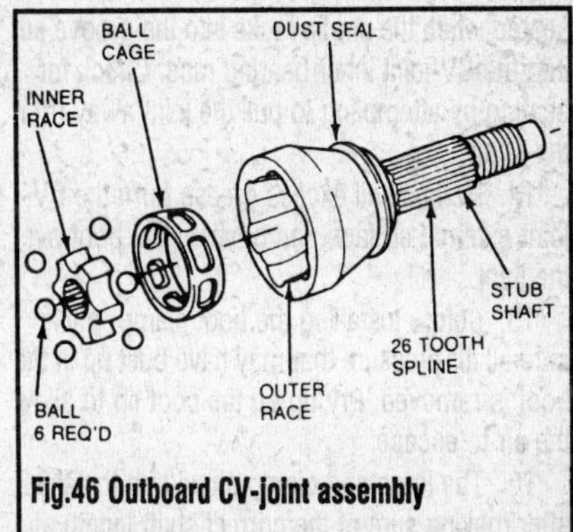

Fig.46 Outboard CV-joint assembly

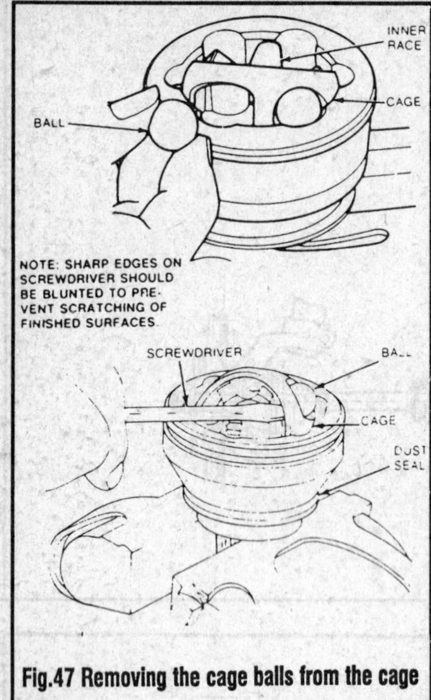

Fig.47 Removing the cage balls from the cage

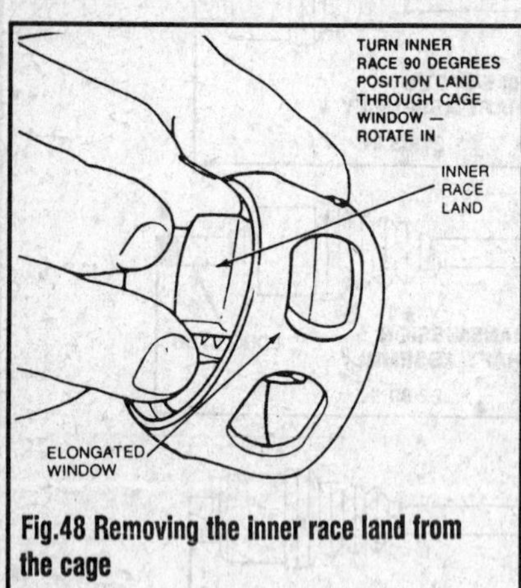

Fig.48 Removing the inner race land from the cage

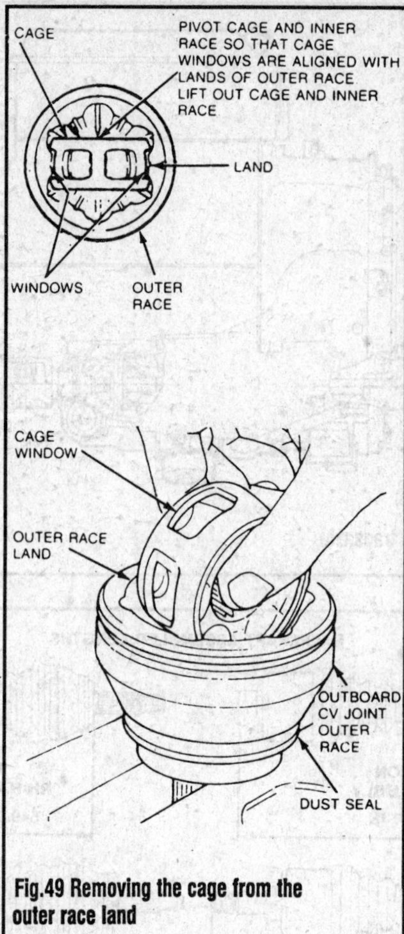

Fig.49 Removing the cage from the outer race land

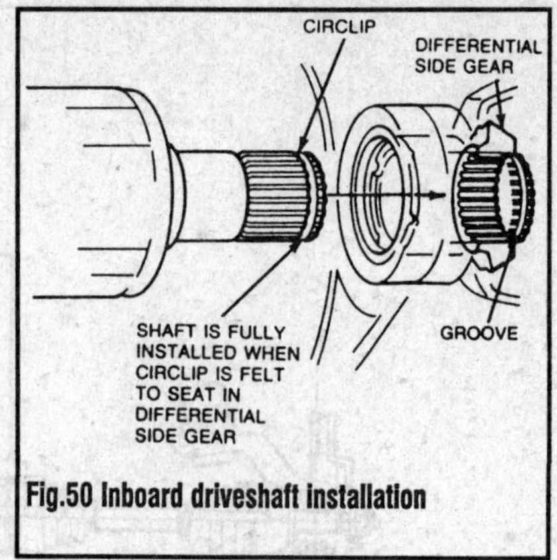

Fig.50 Inboard driveshaft installation

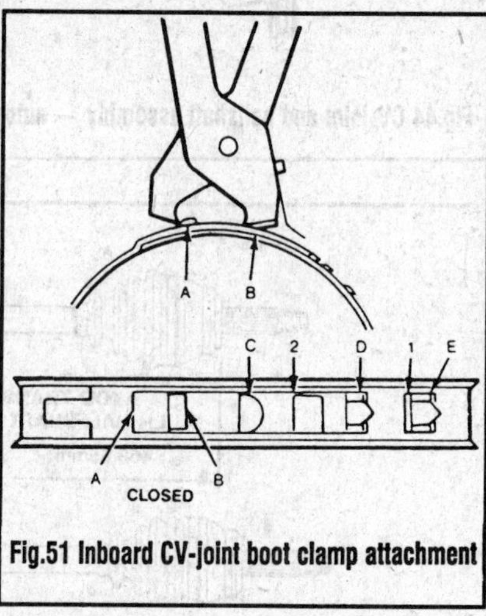

Fig.51 Inboard CV-joint boot clamp attachment

the groove and work the circlip over the shaft end and into the groove.

12. Pack the boot with grease.

13. With the boot peeled back, position the CV-joint on the shaft and tap into position using a plastic tipped hammer. The CV-joint is fully seated when the circlip locks into the groove cut into the CV-joint inner bearing race. Check for seating by attempting to pull the joint away from the shaft.

14. Remove all excess grease form the CV-joint external surface and position the boot over the joint.

15. Before installing the boot clamp, make sure all air pressure that may have built up in the boot is removed. Pry up on the boot lip to allow the air to escape.

16. The large end clamp should be installed after making sure of the correct shaft length and that the boot is seated in its groove. Tighten the clamp securely, but not to the point where the clamp bridge is cut or the boot is damaged.

17. Install the halfshaft assembly and lower the vehicle. Connect the negative battery cable.

Inboard CV-Joint Boot

➧ SEE FIG. 50–51

1. Disconnect the negative battery cable. Raise and safely support the vehicle.

2. Remove the halfshaft assembly from the vehicle.

3. Clamp the halfshaft in a vise that is equipped with soft jaw covers. Do not allow the vise jaws to contact the boot or boot clamp.

4. Cut and remove both boot clamps and slide the boot back on the shaft. Remove the clamp by engaging the pincer jaws of boot clamp pliers D87P–1090–A or equivalent, in the closing hooks on the clamp and draw together. Disengage the windows and locking hooks and remove the clamp.

5. Mark the position of the outer race in relation to the shaft and remove the outer race.

6. Move the stop ring back on the shaft using snapring pliers. Move the tripod assembly back on the shaft to allow access to the circlip.

7. Remove the circlip from the shaft. Mark the position of the tripod on the shaft and remove the tripod assembly. Remove the boot.

8. Check the CV-joint grease for contamination. If the CV-joints are operating properly and the grease is not contaminated, add grease and replace the boot. If the grease appears contaminated, disassemble the CV-joint and clean or replace, as necessary.

To Install:

9. Install the CV-joint boot. Make sure the boot is seated in the boot groove on the shaft. Tighten the clamp using crimping pliers, but do not tighten to the point where the clamp bridge is cut or the boot is damaged.

10. Install the tripod assembly with chamfered side toward the stop ring. If the tripod is being reused, align the marks that were made during the removal procedure.

11. Install a new circlip. Compress the circlip and slide the tripod assembly forward over the circlip to expose the stop ring groove.

12. Move the stop ring into the groove using snapring pliers, making sure it is fully seated in the groove.

13. Fill the CV-joint outer race and CV-boot

with grease. Install the outer race over the tripod assembly, aligning the marks made during the removal procedure.

14. Remove all excess grease from the CV-joint external surfaces and mating boot surface. Position the boot over the CV-joint making sure the boot is seated in the groove. Move the CV-joint in and out, as necessary, to adjust the length to the following specifications:

- Automatic transaxle left halfshaft, except 1986–90 2.5L engine Taurus — 18.27 in. (464mm)
- Automatic transaxle right halfshaft, except 1986–90 2.5L engine Taurus — 23.58 in. (599mm)
- Automatic transaxle left halfshaft, 1986–90 2.5L engine Taurus — 22.80 in. (579mm)
- Automatic transaxle right halfshaft, 1986–90 2.5L engine Taurus — 20.09 in. (510mm)
- Manual transaxle left halfshaft — 21.24 in. (539.5mm)
- Manual transaxle right halfshaft — 21.63 in. (549.5mm)

15. Before installing the boot clamp, make sure any air pressure that may have built up in the boot is relieved. Insert a small prybar between the boot and outer race to allow the trapped air to escape. Release the air only after adjusting the length dimension.

16. Seat the boot in the groove and clamp in position using crimping pliers D87P–1098–A or equivalent. Install the clamp as follows:

a. With the boot seated in the groove, place the clamp over the boot.

b. Engage hook C in the window.

c. Place the pincer jaws of the crimping pliers in closing hooks A and B.

d. Secure the clamp by drawing the closing hooks together. When windows 1 and 2 are above locking hooks D and E, the spring tab will press the windows over the locking hooks and engage the clamp.

17. Install the halfshaft and lower the vehicle. Connect the negative battery cable.

Troubleshooting the Manual Transmission

Problem	Cause	Solution
Transmission shifts hard	• Clutch adjustment incorrect	• Adjust clutch
	• Clutch linkage or cable binding	• Lubricate or repair as necessary
	• Shift rail binding	• Check for mispositioned selector arm roll pin, loose cover bolts, worn shift rail bores, worn shift rail, distorted oil seal, or extension housing not aligned with case. Repair as necessary.
	• Internal bind in transmission caused by shift forks, selector plates, or synchronizer assemblies	• Remove, dissemble and inspect transmission. Replace worn or damaged components as necessary.
	• Clutch housing misalignment	• Check runout at rear face of clutch housing
	• Incorrect lubricant	• Drain and refill transmission
	• Block rings and/or cone seats worn	• Blocking ring to gear clutch tooth face clearance must be 0.030 inch or greater. If clearance is correct it may still be necessary to inspect blocking rings and cone seats for excessive wear. Repair as necessary.
Gear clash when shifting from one gear to another	• Clutch adjustment incorrect	• Adjust clutch
	• Clutch linkage or cable binding	• Lubricate or repair as necessary
	• Clutch housing misalignment	• Check runout at rear of clutch housing
	• Lubricant level low or incorrect lubricant	• Drain and refill transmission and check for lubricant leaks if level was low. Repair as necessary.
	• Gearshift components, or synchronizer assemblies worn or damaged	• Remove, disassemble and inspect transmission. Replace worn or damaged components as necessary.
Transmission noisy	• Lubricant level low or incorrect lubricant	• Drain and refill transmission. If lubricant level was low, check for leaks and repair as necessary.
	• Clutch housing-to-engine, or transmission-to-clutch housing bolts loose	• Check and correct bolt torque as necessary
	• Dirt, chips, foreign material in transmission	• Drain, flush, and refill transmission
	• Gearshift mechanism, transmission gears, or bearing components worn or damaged	• Remove, disassemble and inspect transmission. Replace worn or damaged components as necessary.
	• Clutch housing misalignment	• Check runout at rear face of clutch housing

Troubleshooting the Manual Transmission

Problem	Cause	Solution
Jumps out of gear	• Clutch housing misalignment	• Check runout at rear face of clutch housing
	• Gearshift lever loose	• Check lever for worn fork. Tighten loose attaching bolts.
	• Offset lever nylon insert worn or lever attaching nut loose	• Remove gearshift lever and check for loose offset lever nut or worn insert. Repair or replace as necessary.
	• Gearshift mechanism, shift forks, selector plates, interlock plate, selector arm, shift rail, detent plugs, springs or shift cover worn or damaged	• Remove, disassemble and inspect transmission cover assembly. Replace worn or damaged components as necessary.
	• Clutch shaft or roller bearings worn or damaged	• Replace clutch shaft or roller bearings as necessary
Jumps out of gear (cont.)	• Gear teeth worn or tapered, synchronizer assemblies worn or damaged, excessive end play caused by worn thrust washers or output shaft gears	• Remove, disassemble, and inspect transmission. Replace worn or damaged components as necessary.
	• Pilot bushing worn	• Replace pilot bushing
Will not shift into one gear	• Gearshift selector plates, interlock plate, or selector arm, worn, damaged, or incorrectly assembled	• Remove, disassemble, and inspect transmission cover assembly. Repair or replace components as necessary.
	• Shift rail detent plunger worn, spring broken, or plug loose	• Tighten plug or replace worn or damaged components as necessary
	• Gearshift lever worn or damaged	• Replace gearshift lever
	• Synchronizer sleeves or hubs, damaged or worn	• Remove, disassemble and inspect transmission. Replace worn or damaged components.
Locked in one gear—cannot be shifted out	• Shift rail(s) worn or broken, shifter fork bent, setscrew loose, center detent plug missing or worn	• Inspect and replace worn or damaged parts
	• Broken gear teeth on countershaft gear, clutch shaft, or reverse idler gear	• Inspect and replace damaged part
	Gearshift lever broken or worn, shift mechanism in cover incorrectly assembled or broken, worn damaged gear train components	• Disassemble transmission. Replace damaged parts or assemble correctly.

Troubleshooting Basic Clutch Problems

Problem	Cause
Excessive clutch noise	Throwout bearing noises are more audible at the lower end of pedal travel. The usual causes are: • Riding the clutch • Too little pedal free-play • Lack of bearing lubrication A bad clutch shaft pilot bearing will make a high pitched squeal, when the clutch is disengaged and the transmission is in gear or within the first 2″ of pedal travel. The bearing must be replaced. Noise from the clutch linkage is a clicking or snapping that can be heard or felt as the pedal is moved completely up or down. This usually requires lubrication. Transmitted engine noises are amplified by the clutch housing and heard in the passenger compartment. They are usually the result of insufficient pedal free-play and can be changed by manipulating the clutch pedal.
Clutch slips (the car does not move as it should when the clutch is engaged)	This is usually most noticeable when pulling away from a standing start. A severe test is to start the engine, apply the brakes, shift into high gear and SLOWLY release the clutch pedal. A healthy clutch will stall the engine. If it slips it may be due to: • A worn pressure plate or clutch plate • Oil soaked clutch plate • Insufficient pedal free-play
Clutch drags or fails to release	The clutch disc and some transmission gears spin briefly after clutch disengagement. Under normal conditions in average temperatures, 3 seconds is maximum spin-time. Failure to release properly can be caused by: • Too light transmission lubricant or low lubricant level • Improperly adjusted clutch linkage
Low clutch life	Low clutch life is usually a result of poor driving habits or heavy duty use. Riding the clutch, pulling heavy loads, holding the car on a grade with the clutch instead of the brakes and rapid clutch engagement all contribute to low clutch life.

Troubleshooting Basic Automatic Transmission Problems

Problem	Cause	Solution
Fluid leakage	• Defective pan gasket • Loose filler tube • Loose extension housing to transmission case • Converter housing area leakage	• Replace gasket or tighten pan bolts • Tighten tube nut • Tighten bolts • Have transmission checked professionally
Fluid flows out the oil filler tube	• High fluid level • Breather vent clogged • Clogged oil filter or screen • Internal fluid leakage	• Check and correct fluid level • Open breather vent • Replace filter or clean screen (change fluid also) • Have transmission checked professionally
Transmission overheats (this is usually accompanied by a strong burned odor to the fluid)	• Low fluid level • Fluid cooler lines clogged • Heavy pulling or hauling with insufficient cooling • Faulty oil pump, internal slippage	• Check and correct fluid level • Drain and refill transmission. If this doesn't cure the problem, have cooler lines cleared or replaced. • Install a transmission oil cooler • Have transmission checked professionally
Buzzing or whining noise	• Low fluid level • Defective torque converter, scored gears	• Check and correct fluid level • Have transmission checked professionally
No forward or reverse gears or slippage in one or more gears	• Low fluid level • Defective vacuum or linkage controls, internal clutch or band failure	• Check and correct fluid level • Have unit checked professionally
Delayed or erratic shift	• Low fluid level • Broken vacuum lines • Internal malfunction	• Check and correct fluid level • Repair or replace lines • Have transmission checked professionally

Lockup Torque Converter Service Diagnosis

Problem	Cause	Solution
No lockup	• Faulty oil pump • Sticking governor valve • Valve body malfunction (a) Stuck switch valve (b) Stuck lockup valve (c) Stuck fail-safe valve • Failed locking clutch • Leaking turbine hub seal • Faulty input shaft or seal ring	• Replace oil pump • Repair or replace as necessary • Repair or replace valve body or its internal components as necessary • Replace torque converter • Replace torque converter • Repair or replace as necessary
Will not unlock	• Sticking governor valve • Valve body malfunction (a) Stuck switch valve (b) Stuck lockup valve (c) Stuck fail-safe valve	• Repair or replace as necessary • Repair or replace valve body or its internal components as necessary
Stays locked up at too low a speed in direct	• Sticking governor valve • Valve body malfunction (a) Stuck switch valve (b) Stuck lockup valve (c) Stuck fail-safe valve	• Repair or replace as necessary • Repair or replace valve body or its internal components as necessary
Locks up or drags in low or second	• Faulty oil pump • Valve body malfunction (a) Stuck switch valve (b) Stuck fail-safe valve	• Replace oil pump • Repair or replace valve body or its internal components as necessary
Sluggish or stalls in reverse	• Faulty oil pump • Plugged cooler, cooler lines or fittings • Valve body malfunction (a) Stuck switch valve (b) Faulty input shaft or seal ring	• Replace oil pump as necessary • Flush or replace cooler and flush lines and fittings • Repair or replace valve body or its internal components as necessary
Loud chatter during lockup engagement (cold)	• Faulty torque converter • Failed locking clutch • Leaking turbine hub seal	• Replace torque converter • Replace torque converter • Replace torque converter

Lockup Torque Converter Service Diagnosis

Problem	Cause	Solution
Vibration or shudder during lockup engagement	• Faulty oil pump	• Repair or replace oil pump as necessary
	• Valve body malfunction	• Repair or replace valve body or its internal components as necessary
	• Faulty torque converter • Engine needs tune-up	• Replace torque converter • Tune engine
Vibration after lockup engagement	• Faulty torque converter • Exhaust system strikes underbody • Engine needs tune-up • Throttle linkage misadjusted	• Replace torque converter • Align exhaust system • Tune engine • Adjust throttle linkage
Vibration when revved in neutral	• Torque converter out of balance	• Replace torque converter
Overheating: oil blows out of dip stick tube or pump seal	• Plugged cooler, cooler lines or fittings • Stuck switch valve	• Flush or replace cooler and flush lines and fittings • Repair switch valve in valve body or replace valve body
Shudder after lockup engagement	• Faulty oil pump • Plugged cooler, cooler lines or fittings • Valve body malfunction	• Replace oil pump • Flush or replace cooler and flush lines and fittings • Repair or replace valve body or its internal components as necessary
	• Faulty torque converter • Fail locking clutch • Exhaust system strikes underbody • Engine needs tune-up • Throttle linkage misadjusted	• Replace torque converter • Replace torque converter • Align exhaust system • Tune engine • Adjust throttle linkage

Transmission Fluid Indications

The appearance and odor of the transmission fluid can give valuable clues to the overall condition of the transmission. Always note the appearance of the fluid when you check the fluid level or change the fluid. Rub a small amount of fluid between your fingers to feel for grit and smell the fluid on the dipstick.

If the fluid appears:	It indicates:
Clear and red colored	• Normal operation
Discolored (extremely dark red or brownish) or smells burned	• Band or clutch pack failure, usually caused by an overheated transmission. Hauling very heavy loads with insufficient power or failure to change the fluid, often result in overheating. Do not confuse this appearance with newer fluids that have a darker red color and a strong odor (though not a burned odor).
Foamy or aerated (light in color and full of bubbles)	• The level is too high (gear train is churning oil) • An internal air leak (air is mixing with the fluid). Have the transmission checked professionally.
Solid residue in the fluid	• Defective bands, clutch pack or bearings. Bits of band material or metal abrasives are clinging to the dipstick. Have the transmission checked professionally.
Varnish coating on the dipstick	• The transmission fluid is overheating

8

SUSPENSION AND STEERING

WHEELS

Wheels

REMOVAL & INSTALLATION

➧ SEE FIG.56

1. Position the vehicle on a level surface. Apply the emergency brake.
2. If equipped with automatic transaxle be sure that the selector lever is in the PARK position.
3. If equipped with manual transaxle be sure that the selector lever is gear.
4. Remove the hub cap from the wheel and tire assembly.
5. Using the proper size lug nut wrench, loosen but do not remove the lug nuts from the wheel and tire assembly.
6. Raise and properly support the vehicle. Loosen and remove the lug nuts from the wheel and tire assembly.
7. Remove the wheel and tire assembly from its mounting.

To Install:

8. Install the tire and wheel assembly to the brake rotor or drum.
9. Install the lug nuts finger tight. Lower the vehicle to the ground.
10. Torque the lug nuts to specification using the proper tool. Install the hub cap.

INSPECTION

Replace wheels if they are bent, dented, heavily rusted, have air leaks, elongated bolt holes or excessive lateral and radial runout.

Also inspect wheel lug nuts and be sure that they are torqued to specification.

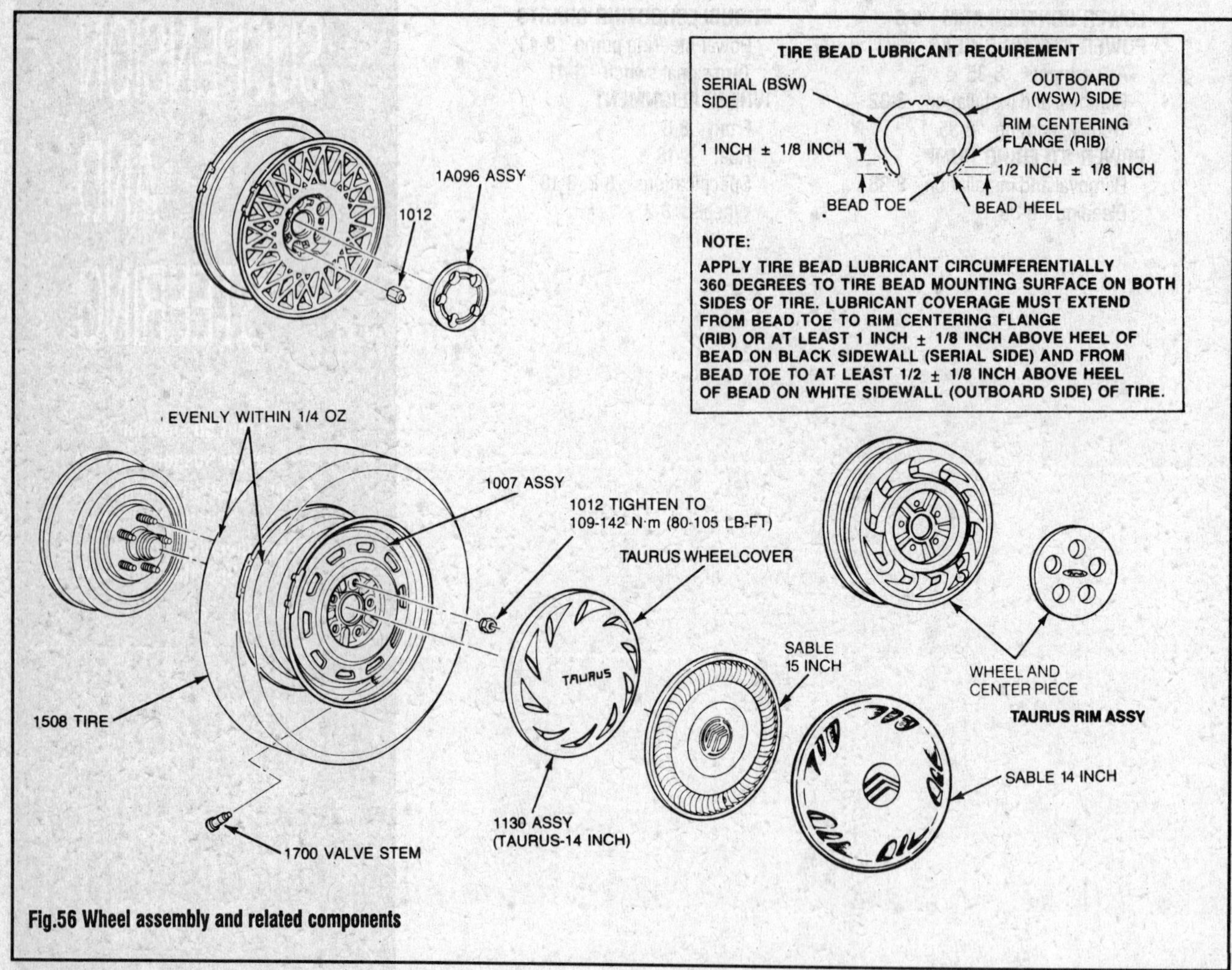

Fig.56 Wheel assembly and related components

FRONT SUSPENSION

MacPherson Struts

REMOVAL & INSTALLATION

➧ SEE FIG. 1–3

1. Place the ignition switch in the **OFF** position and the steering column in the **UNLOCKED** position.
2. Remove the hub nut. Loosen the 3 top mount-to-shock tower nuts; do not remove the nuts at this time.
3. Raise and support the vehicle safely.

➡ **When raising the vehicle, do not lift by using the lower control arms.**

4. Remove the tire and wheel assembly. Remove the brake caliper, supporting it on a wire. Remove the rotor.
5. At the tie rod end, remove the cotter pin and the castle nut. Discard the cotter pin and nut and replace with new.
6. Using tie rod end remover tool 3290–D and the tie rod remover adapter tool T81P–3504–W or equivalents, separate the tie rod from the steering knuckle.

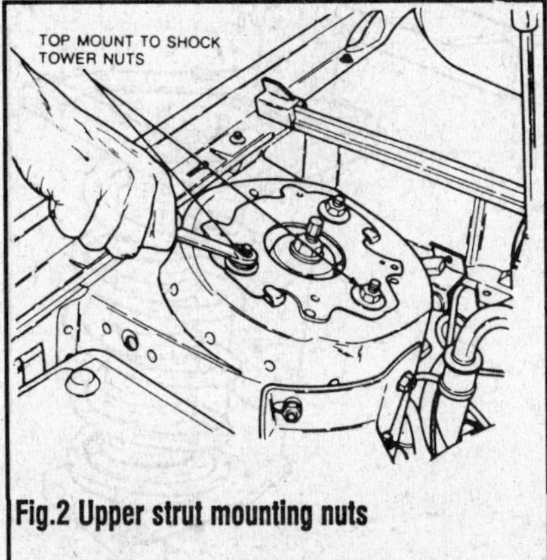

Fig.2 Upper strut mounting nuts

7. Remove the stabilizer bar link nut and the link from the strut.
8. Remove the lower arm-to-steering knuckle pinch bolt and nut; it may be necessary to use a drift punch to remove the bolt. Using a suitable tool, spread the knuckle-to-lower arm pinch joint and remove the lower arm from the steering knuckle. Discard the pinch nut/bolt and replace with new.
9. Remove the halfshaft from the hub and support it on a wire.

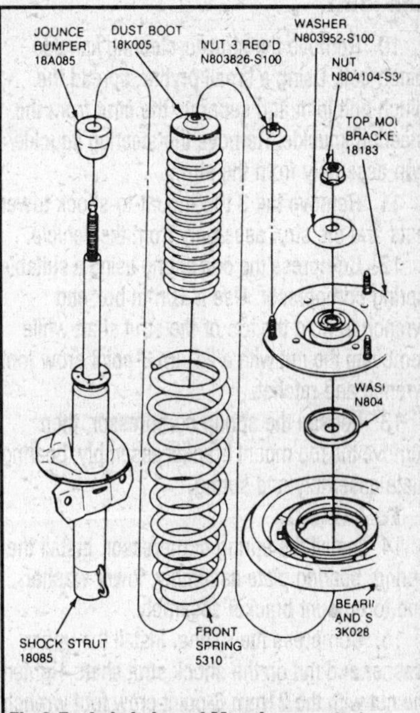

Fig.3 Exploded view of Macpherson strut assembly

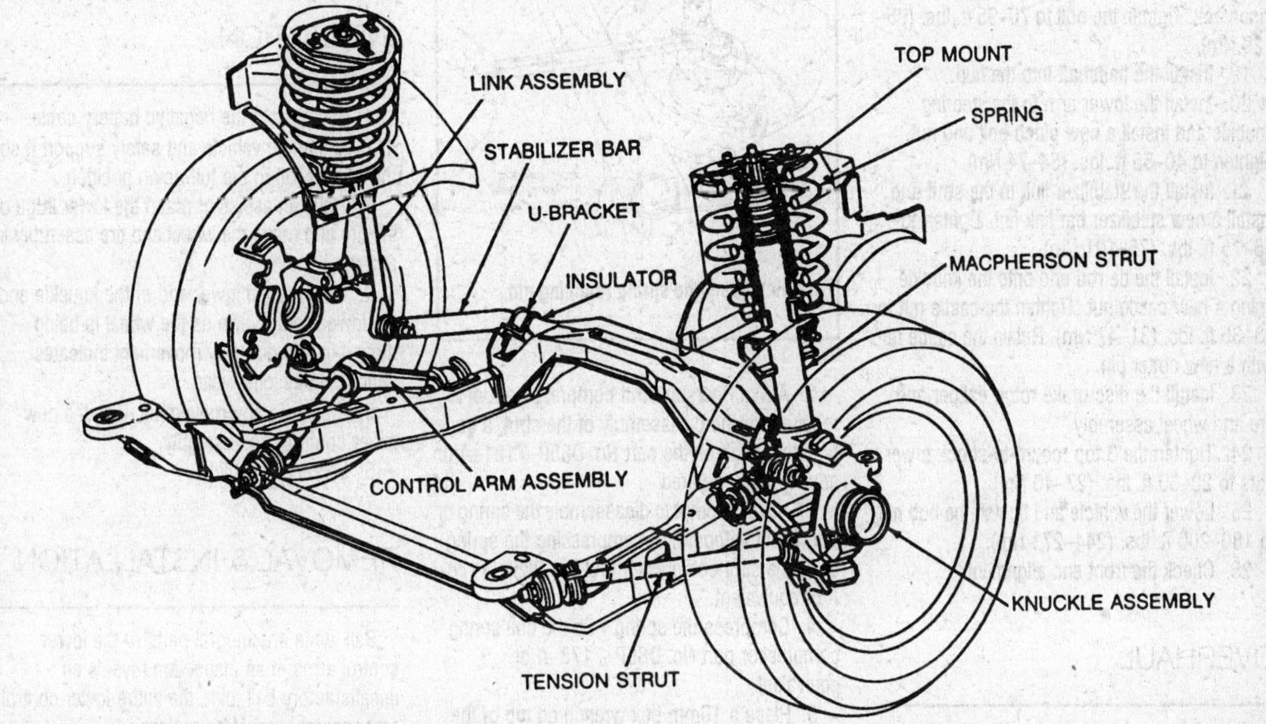

Fig.1 Front suspension and related components

➡ When removing the halfshaft, do not allow it to move outward as the internal parts of the tripod CV-joint could separate, causing failure of the joint.

10. Remove the strut-to-steering knuckle pinch bolt. Using a small prybar, spread the pinch bolt joint and separate the strut from the steering knuckle. Remove the steering knuckle/hub assembly from the strut.

11. Remove the 3 top mount-to-shock tower nuts and the strut assembly from the vehicle.

12. Compress the coil spring using a suitable spring compressor. Use a 10mm box end wrench to hold the top of the strut shaft while removing the nut with a 21mm 6-point crow foot wrench and ratchet.

13. Loosen the spring compressor, then remove the top mount bracket assembly, bearing plate assembly and spring.

To install:

14. Install the spring compressor. Install the spring, bearing plate assembly, lower washer and top mount bracket assembly.

15. Compress the spring. Install the upper washer and nut on the shock strut shaft. Tighten the nut with the 21mm 6-point crow foot wrench and ratchet while holding the shaft with the 10mm box end wrench.

16. Install the strut assembly and the 3 top mount-to-shock tower nuts.

17. Install the steering knuckle and hub assembly to the strut.

18. Install a new strut-to-steering knuckle pinch bolt. Tighten the bolt to 70–95 ft. lbs. (95–129 Nm).

19. Install the halfshaft into the hub.

20. Install the lower arm to the steering knuckle and install a new pinch bolt and nut. Tighten to 40–55 ft. lbs. (54–74 Nm).

21. Install the stabilizer link to the strut and install a new stabilizer bar link nut. Tighten to 55–75 ft. lbs. (75–101 Nm).

22. Install the tie rod end onto the knuckle using a new castle nut. Tighten the castle nut to 23–35 ft. lbs. (31–47 Nm). Retain the castle nut with a new cotter pin.

23. Install the disc brake rotor, caliper and tire and wheel assembly.

24. Tighten the 3 top mount-to-shock tower nuts to 20–30 ft. lbs. (27–40 Nm).

25. Lower the vehicle and tighten the hub nut to 180–200 ft. lbs. (244–271 Nm).

26. Check the front end alignment.

OVERHAUL

➧ SEE FIG. 4–5

1. The following procedure is performed with the strut assembly removed from the car.

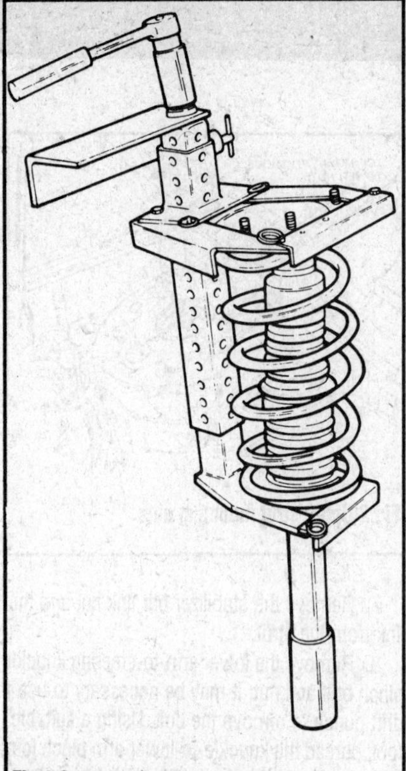

Fig.4 Compressing the coil spring using a strut spring compressor tool

CROW FOOT WRENCH

COIL SPRING COMPRESSOR D85P-7178-A

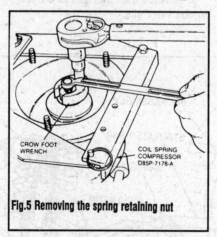

Fig.5 Removing the spring retaining nut

2. A MacPherson Strut compression tool is required for the disassembly of the strut, a cage type tool such as the part No. D85P–7181–A or equivalent is required.

3. Never attempt to disassemble the spring or top mount without first compressing the spring using the strut compressor tool No. D85P–7178–A or equivalent.

4. Compress the spring with the coil spring compressor part No. D85P–7178–A or equivalent.

5. Place a 10mm box wrench on top of the shock strut shaft and hold while removing the top shaft mounting nut with a 21mm 6-point crow foot wrench and ratchet.

➡ It is important that the mounting nut be turned and the rod held still to prevent fracture of the rod at the base of the hex.

6. Loosen the spring compressor tool, then remove the top mounting bracket assembly, bearing plate assembly and spring.

To assemble:

➡ Ensure that the correct assembly sequence and proper positioning of the bearing and seat assembly are followed. The bearing and seat assembly is press-fit onto the upper mount. The mount washers must be installed with orientation.

7. Install the spring compressor tool part No. D85P–7178–A or equivalent.

8. Install the spring, bearing plate assembly, lower washer and top mount bracket assembly.

9. Compress the spring with the coil spring compressor tool. Install the upper washer and nut on the shock strut shaft.

10. Place a 10mm box end wrench on the top of the shock strut shaft and hold while tightening the top shaft mounting nut with a 21mm 6-point crow foot wrench and a ratchet.

11. The strut assembly may now be installed in the vehicle.

Lower Ball Joint

INSPECTION

1. Disconnect the negative battery cable.

2. Raise the vehicle and safely support it so the wheels fall to the full-down position.

3. Have an assistant grasp the lower edge of the tire and move the wheel and tire assembly in and out.

4. Observe the lower end of the knuckle and the lower control arm as the wheel is being moved in and out. Any movement indicates abnormal ball joint wear.

5. If there is any movement, install a new lower control arm assembly.

6. Lower the vehicle.

REMOVAL & INSTALLATION

Ball joints are integral parts of the lower control arms. If an inspection reveals an unsatisfactory ball joint, the entire lower control arm assembly must be replaced.

Stabilizer Bar

REMOVAL & INSTALLATION

SEE FIG. 6

1. Raise and support the front of the vehicle on jackstands behind the subframe.

➡ Do not raise or support the vehicle on the front control arms.

2. Remove and discard the stabilizer bar link-to-stabilizer bar nut, the stabilizer bar link-to-strut nut and the link from the vehicle.
3. Remove the steering gear-to-subframe nuts and move the gear from the sub-frame.
4. Position another set of jackstands under the subframe and remove the rear subframe-to-frame bolts. Lower the subframe rear to gain access to the stabilizer bar brackets.
5. Remove the stabilizer bar U-bracket bolts and the stabilizer bar from the vehicle.

➡ When removing the stabilizer bar, replace the insulators and the U-bracket bolts with new ones.

To install:

6. To install, reverse the removal procedure. Tighten the bolts to the following torque specifications:
   - U-bracket-to-subframe 21–32 ft. lbs. (28–43 Nm)
   - Subframe-to-steering gear 85–100 ft. lbs. (115–135 Nm)
   - Stabilizer bar-to-stabilizer bar link 35–48 ft. lbs. (47–65 Nm)
   - Stabilizer bar-to-strut 55–75 ft. lbs. (75–101 Nm)
7. Prior to assembly, coat the inside diameter of the new insulators with No. E25Y–19553–A or equivalent lubricant. Do not use any mineral or petroleum base lubricants as they will cause deterioration of the rubber insulators.

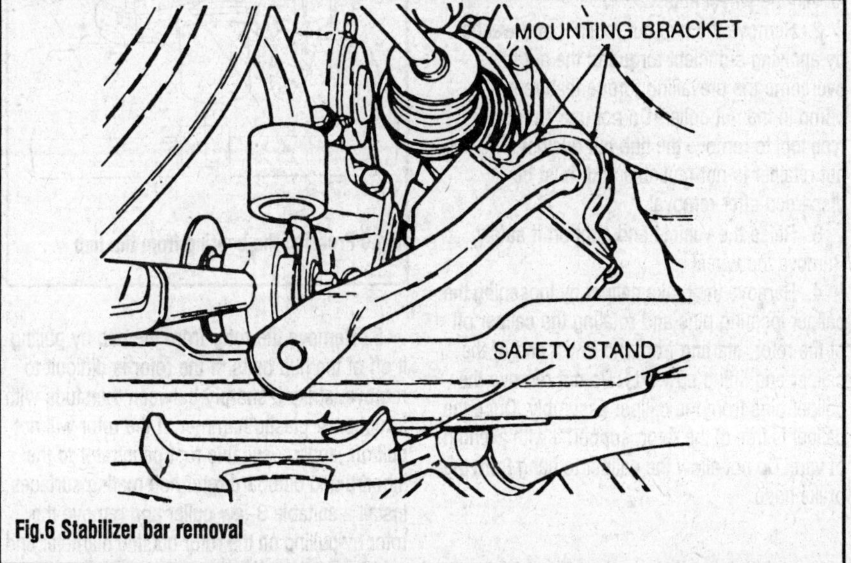

Fig.6 Stabilizer bar removal

Lower Control Arm

REMOVAL & INSTALLATION

1. Disconnect the negative battery cable.
2. Raise and support the front of the vehicle safely. Remove the wheel and tire assembly.
3. Position the steering column in the unlocked position.
4. Remove the tension strut-to-control arm nut and the dished washer.
5. Remove and discard the control arm-to-steering knuckle pinch bolt. Using a small prybar, spread the pinch joint and separate the control arm from the steering knuckle.

➡ When separating the control arm from the steering knuckle, do not use a hammer. Be careful not to damage the ball joint boot seal.

6. Remove the control arm-to-frame nut/bolt, then the control arm from the frame and the tension strut.

➡ Do not allow the halfshaft to move outward or the tripod CV-joint internal parts could separate, causing failure of the joint.

7. To install, use a new pinch nut/bolt and reverse the removal procedures. Tighten the bolts to the following torque specifications:
   - Control arm-to-frame 70–95 ft. lbs. (95–129 Nm)
   - Control arm-to-steering knuckle 40–55 ft. lbs. (54–74 Nm)
   - Tension strut-to-control arm 70–95 ft. lbs. (95–129 Nm)
   - Wheel lug nuts 80–105 ft. lbs. (109–142 Nm)
8. Check the front end alignment.

BUSHING REPLACEMENT

Inner Pivot Bushing

1. Remove the lower control arm from the vehicle.
2. Using bushing removal tools T86P–5493–A3 and T86P–5493–A2 and a C clamp assembly remove the old bushings from the control arm assembly.

To install:

3. Use the bushing removal tool and press new bushings in place on the lower control arm assembly.
4. Be sure that the bushing flange is at the front of the arm.
5. Install the lower control arm on the vehicle.
6. Check and adjust the front end alignment, as required.

Control Arm/Tension Strut Bushing

1. Remove the lower control arm from the vehicle.
2. Using bushing removal tools T86P–5493–A5 and T86P–5493–A and a C clamp assembly remove the old bushings from the control arm assembly. Be sure that the C clamp is positioned tightly in a bench vise.

To install:

3. Before install the new bushing saturate it in motor oil, this will aid in the installation process.
4. Use the bushing removal tool and install new bushings in place on the lower control arm assembly. Stop tightening the C clamp when the bushing pops in place.
5. Install the lower control arm on the vehicle.
6. Check and adjust the front end alignment, as required.

Tension Strut/Sub Frame Insulators

1. Remove the lower control arm from the vehicle.
2. Remove and discard the nut, washer and insulator from the front of the tension strut. Pull the strut rearward to remove it from the sub frame.
3. Remove and discard the insulator from the tension strut.

To install:

4. Install a new insulator on the tension strut end and insert it into the sub frame.

5. Install a new front insulator. Clean the tension strut threads. Install a new washer, and nut. Torque to 70–95 ft. lbs.

6. Install the lower control arm on the vehicle.

7. Check and adjust the front end alignment, as required.

Knuckle and Spindle

REMOVAL & INSTALLATION

1. Turn the ignition switch to the OFF position. Position the steering wheel in the unlocked position.

2. Remove the hub nut. Raise and support the vehicle safely. Remove the tire and wheel assembly.

3. Remove the cotter pin from the tie rod end stud and remove the slotted nut. Discard the cotter pin and nut.

4. Using a tie rod end removal tool remove the tie rod end from the knuckle.

5. Remove the stabilizer bar link assembly from the strut.

6. Remove the brake caliper and wire it aside in order to gain working clearance.

7. Loosen, but do not remove, the three top retaining nuts from the top of the shock tower.

8. Remove and discard the lower arm to steering knuckle pinch bolt and nut. Using the proper tool spread the knuckle to lower arm pinch joint apart. Remove the lower arm from the steering knuckle.

➡ Be sure that the steering column is in the unlocked position. Do not use a hammer to perform this operation. Use extreme care not to damage the boot seal.

9. Remove the shock absorber strut to steering knuckle pinch bolt.

➡ Do not allow the halfshaft to move outboard. Over extension of the CV joint could result in separation of internal parts, causing failure of the joint.

10. Press the halfshaft from the hub. Wire the halfshaft body to maintain a level position. If equipped, remove the rotor splash shield.

11. Remove the steering knuckle and hub assembly from the shock absorber strut.

12. Position the assembly on the work bench and remove the hub retainer ring and bearing.

To install:

13. Install the rotor splash shield using new rivets, if equipped.

14. Install the bearing, retainer ring and hub. If required, replace the seal on the outboard CV joint.

15. Install the steering knuckle onto the shock absorber strut. Loosely install a new pinch bolt in the knuckle to retain the strut.

16. Install the steering knuckle and hub onto the halfshaft.

17. Install the lower control arm to the knuckle. Be sure that the ball stud groove is properly positioned.

18. Install a new nut and bolt. Torque to 40–55 ft. lbs. Tighten the strut to knuckle pinch bolt to 70–95 ft. lbs.

19. Install the rotor and brake caliper. Torque the caliper retaining pins to 18–25 ft. lbs.

20. Position the tie rod into the knuckle, install a new slotted nut and tighten to 23–35 ft. lbs. If necessary advance the nut to the next slot.

21. Install the stabilizer link bar assembly. Torque to 75 ft. lbs. Install the tire and wheel assembly.

22. Lower the vehicle. Install the three top mount retaining bolts. Torque to 20–30 ft. lbs.

23. Tighten the hub nut to 180–200 ft. lbs.

24. Pump the brake pedal prior to moving the vehicle, in order to reposition the brake linings.

Front Hub and Bearing

REMOVAL & INSTALLATION

➧ SEE FIG. 7–13

1. Remove the wheelcover/hub cover and loosen the wheel nuts.

2. Remove the hub nut retainer and washer by applying sufficient torque to the nut to overcome the prevailing torque feature of the crimp in the nut collar. Do not use an impact-type tool to remove the hub nut retainer. The hub nut retainer is not reusable and must be discarded after removal.

3. Raise the vehicle and support it safely. Remove the wheel.

4. Remove the brake caliper by loosening the caliper locating pins and rotating the caliper off of the rotor, starting from the lower end of the caliper and lifting upwards. Do not remove the caliper pins from the caliper assembly. Once the caliper is free of the rotor, support it with a length of wire. Do not allow the caliper to hang from the brake hose.

METRIC ADAPTERS (12mm) MAKE SURE THE ADAPTERS ARE FULLY THREADED ONTO THE HUB STUDS AND ARE POSITIONED OPPOSITE THE OTHER ADAPTER
TWO STUD ADAPTER T86P-1104-A1
METRIC STUD ADAPTER T83P-1104-BH
PULLER T81P-1104-C ASSY AS SHOWN
METRIC ADAPTER T81P-1104-A
TURN THIS WRENCH COUNTERCLOCKWISE
HOLD WRENCH STATIONARY WHILE TURNING OTHER WRENCH

Fig.7 Removing the hub assembly

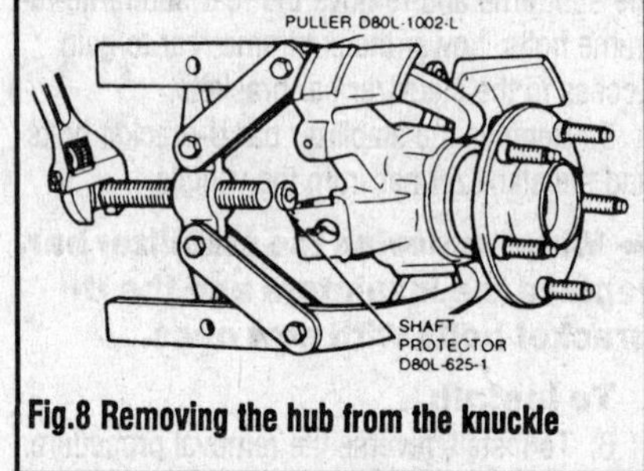

Fig.8 Removing the hub from the knuckle

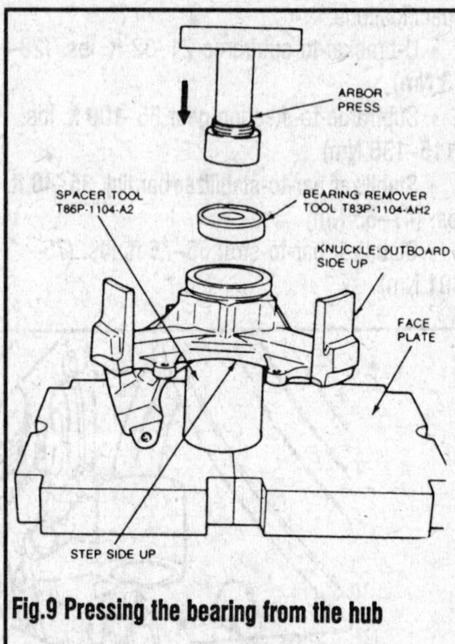

Fig.9 Pressing the bearing from the hub

5. Remove the rotor from the hub by pulling it off of the hub bolts. If the rotor is difficult to remove, strike it sharply between the studs with a rubber or plastic hammer. If the rotor will not pull off, apply a suitable rust penetrator to the inboard and outboard rotor hub mating surfaces. Install a suitable 3-jaw puller and remove the rotor by pulling on the rotor outside diameter and pushing on the hub center. If excessive force is

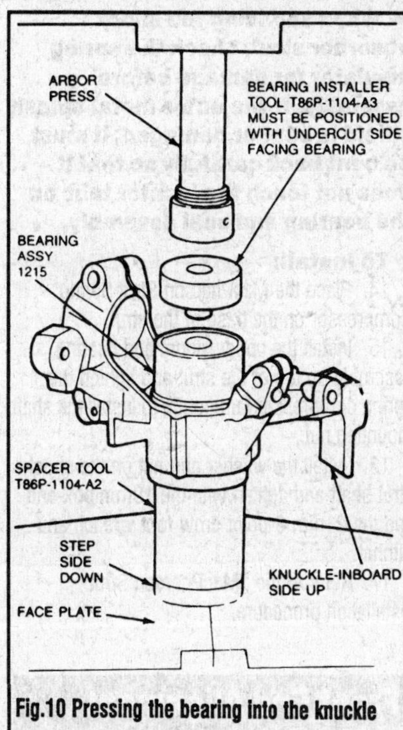

Fig.10 Pressing the bearing into the knuckle

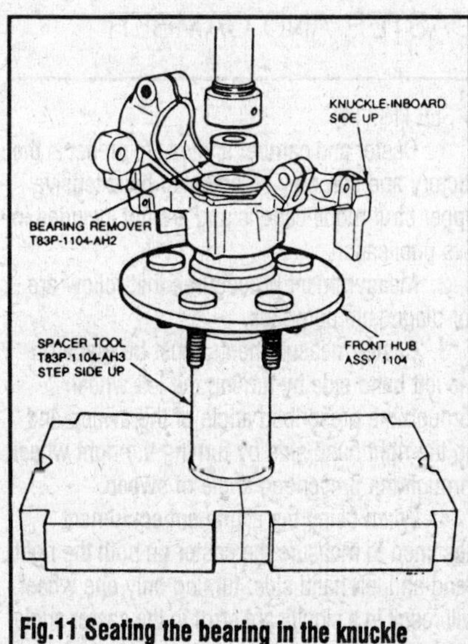

Fig.11 Seating the bearing in the knuckle

required to remove the rotor, check it for lateral runout prior to installation. Lateral runout must be checked with the nuts clamping the stamped hat section of the rotor.

6. Remove the rotor splash shield.

7. Disconnect the lower control arm and tie rod from the knuckle but leave the strut attached. Loosen the 2 strut top mount-to-apron nuts.

8. Install hub remover/installer adapter T81P–1104–A with front hub remover/installer T81P–1104–C and wheel bolt adapters T83P–1104–BH and 2 stud adapter T86P–1104–A1 or equivalent, and remove the hub, bearing and

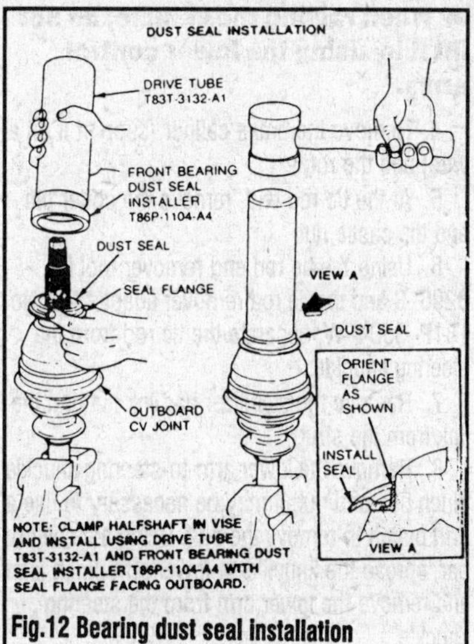

Fig.12 Bearing dust seal installation

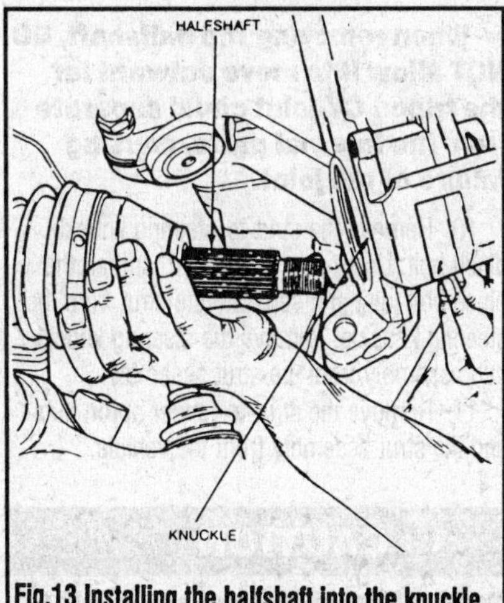

Fig.13 Installing the halfshaft into the knuckle

knuckle assembly by pushing out the CV-joint outer shaft until it is free of the assembly.

9. Support the knuckle with a length of wire, remove the strut bolt and slide the hub/bearing/knuckle assembly off of the strut. Remove the support wire and carry the hub/bearing/knuckle assembly to a bench.

10. Install front hub puller D80L–1002–L and shaft protector D80L–625–1 or equivalent, with the jaws of the puller on the knuckle bosses. Make sure the shaft protector is centered, clears the bearing inside diameter and rests on the end face of the hub journal. Remove the hub.

11. Remove the snapring that retains the bearing in the knuckle assembly and discard.

12. Using a suitable hydraulic press, place front bearing spacer T86P–1104–A2 or equivalent, on the press plate with the step side facing up and position the knuckle with the outboard side up on the spacer. Install front bearing remover T83P–1104–AH2 or equivalent, centered on the bearing inner race and press the bearing out of the knuckle and discard.

To install:

13. Remove all foreign material from the knuckle bearing bore and hub bearing journal to ensure correct seating of the new bearing.

➡ If the hub bearing journal is scored or damaged it must be replaced. The front wheel bearings are pregreased and sealed and require no scheduled maintenance. The bearings are preset and cannot be adjusted. If a bearing is disassembled for any reason, it must be replaced as a unit, as individual service seals, rollers and races are not available.

14. Place front bearing spacer T86P–1104–A2 or equivalent, with the step side down on the hydraulic press plate and position the knuckle with the outboard side down on the spacer. Position a new bearing in the inboard side of the knuckle. Install bearing installer T86P–1104–A3 or equivalent, with the undercut side facing the bearing, on the bearing outer race and press the bearing into the knuckle. Make sure the bearing seats completely against the shoulder of the knuckle bore.

➡ Bearing installer T86P–1104–A3 or equivalent, must be positioned as indicated above to prevent bearing damage during installation.

15. Install a new snapring (part of the bearing kit) in the knuckle groove.

16. Place front bearing spacer T86P–1104–A2 or equivalent, on the press plate and position the hub on the tool with the lugs facing downward. Position the knuckle assembly with the outboard side down on the hub barrel. Place bearing remover T83P–1104–AH2 or equivalent, flat side down, centered on the inner race of the bearing and press down on the tool until the bearing is fully seated onto the hub. Make sure the hub rotates freely in the knuckle after installation.

17. Prior to hub/bearing/knuckle installation, replace the bearing dust seal on the outboard CV-joint with a new seal from the bearing kit. Make sure the seal flange faces outboard toward the bearing. Use drive tube T83T–3132–A1 and front bearing dust seal installer T86P–1104–A4 or equivalent.

18. Suspend the hub/bearing/knuckle assembly on the vehicle with wire and attach the strut loosely to the knuckle. Lubricate the CV-joint stub shaft with SAE 30 weight motor oil and

insert the shaft into the hub splines as far as possible using hand pressure only. Make sure the splines are properly engaged.

19. Temporarily fasten the rotor to the hub with washers and 2 wheel lug nuts. Insert a suitable tool into the rotor diameter and rotate clockwise to contact the knuckle.

20. Install the hub nut washer and a new hub nut retainer. Rotate the nut clockwise to seat the CV-joint. Tighten the nut to 180–200 ft. lbs. (245–270 Nm). Remove the washers and lug nuts.

➡ **Do not use power or impact-type tools to tighten the hub nut.**

21. Install the remainder of the front suspension components and the rotor splash shield.

22. Install the disc brake rotor and caliper. Make sure the outer brake pad spring hook is seated under the upper arm of the knuckle.

23. Install the wheel and tighten the wheel nuts finger tight.

24. Lower the vehicle. Tighten the wheel nuts to 85–105 ft. lbs. (115–142 Nm). Install the wheelcover/hub cover.

Upper Mount and Bearing Assembly

REMOVAL & INSTALLATION

CAUTION

When servicing the front suspension, brake shoes contain asbestos which has been determined to be a cancer causing agent. Never clean the brake surfaces with compressed air! Avoid inhaling any dust from any brake surface! When cleaning brake surfaces, use a commercially available brake cleaning fluid.

1. Place the ignition switch to the OFF position and the steering column in the unlocked position.

2. Remove the hub nut. Loosen the strut-to-fender apron nuts; do not remove the nuts.

3. Raise and support the front of the vehicle on jackstands. Remove the wheels.

➡ **When raising the vehicle, do not lift it by using the lower control arms.**

4. Remove the brake caliper (support it on a wire) and the rotor.

5. At the tie rod end, remove the cotter pin and the castle nut.

6. Using the tie rod end remover tool No. 3290–C and the tie rod remover adapter tool No. T81P–3504–W, separate the tie rod from the steering knuckle.

7. Remove the stabilizer bar link nut and the link from the strut.

8. Remove the lower arm-to-steering knuckle pinch bolt and nut; it may be necessary to use a drift punch to remove the bolt. Using a small pry bar, spread the knuckle-to-lower arm pinch joint and remove the lower arm from the steering knuckle.

9. Remove the halfshaft from the hub and support it on a wire.

➡ **When removing the halfshaft, DO NOT allow it to move outward for the tripod CV-joint could separate from the internal parts, causing failure of the joint.**

10. Remove the strut-to-steering knuckle pinch bolt. Using a small pry bar, spread the pinch bolt joint and separate the strut from the steering knuckle. Remove the steering knuckle/hub assembly from the strut assembly.

11. Remove the strut-to-fender apron nuts and the strut assembly from the vehicle.

CAUTION

Never attempt to disassemble the spring or top mount without first compressing the spring using a Universal MacPherson Strut Spring Compressor D85P–7178–A or a Rotunda Spring Compressor 086–00029 or equivalent.

12. Place a 10mm box-end wrench on top of the shock strut shaft and hold while removing the top shaft mounting nut with a 21mm 6-point crow foot wrench and ratchet.

13. Loosen the MacPherson Strut Spring Compressor slowly. Remove the top mount bracket assembly, bearing plate, and spring.

➡ **When servicing the shock absorber strut, check the spring insulator for damage before assembly. If the outer metal splash shield is bent or damaged, it must be bent back carefully so that it does not touch the locator tabs on the bearing and seal assembly.**

To install:

14. Place the MacPherson Strut Spring Compressor on the base of the strut.

15. Install the upper mount and bearing assembly on top of the strut and tighten the spring compressor far enough to install the shaft mounting nut.

16. Install the washer and nut on the shock strut shaft and tighten with the 10mm box-end and the 21mm 6-point crow foot wrench and ratchet.

17. Refer to the "MacPherson Strut" installation procedure.

Front End Alignment

CASTER AND CAMBER

➧ SEE FIG. 14

1. Caster and camber angles are preset at the factory and can only be adjusted by extensive upper strut modifications and are not included in this publication.

2. Measurement procedures that follow are for diagnostic purposes.

3. Caster measurements must be made on the left hand side by turning the left wheel through the prescribed angle of the sweep and on the right hand side by turning the right wheel through the prescribed angle of sweep.

4. When using the alignment equipment designed to measure the caster on both the right hand and left hand side, turning only one wheel will result in a significant error in the caster angle for the opposite side.

TOE IN

The toe-in is controlled by adjusting the tie rod ends. To adjust the toe-in setting , loosen the tie rod jam nuts. Rotate the tie rod as required to adjust the toe-in into specifications. Once the toe-in is set, re-tighten the tie rod jam nuts.

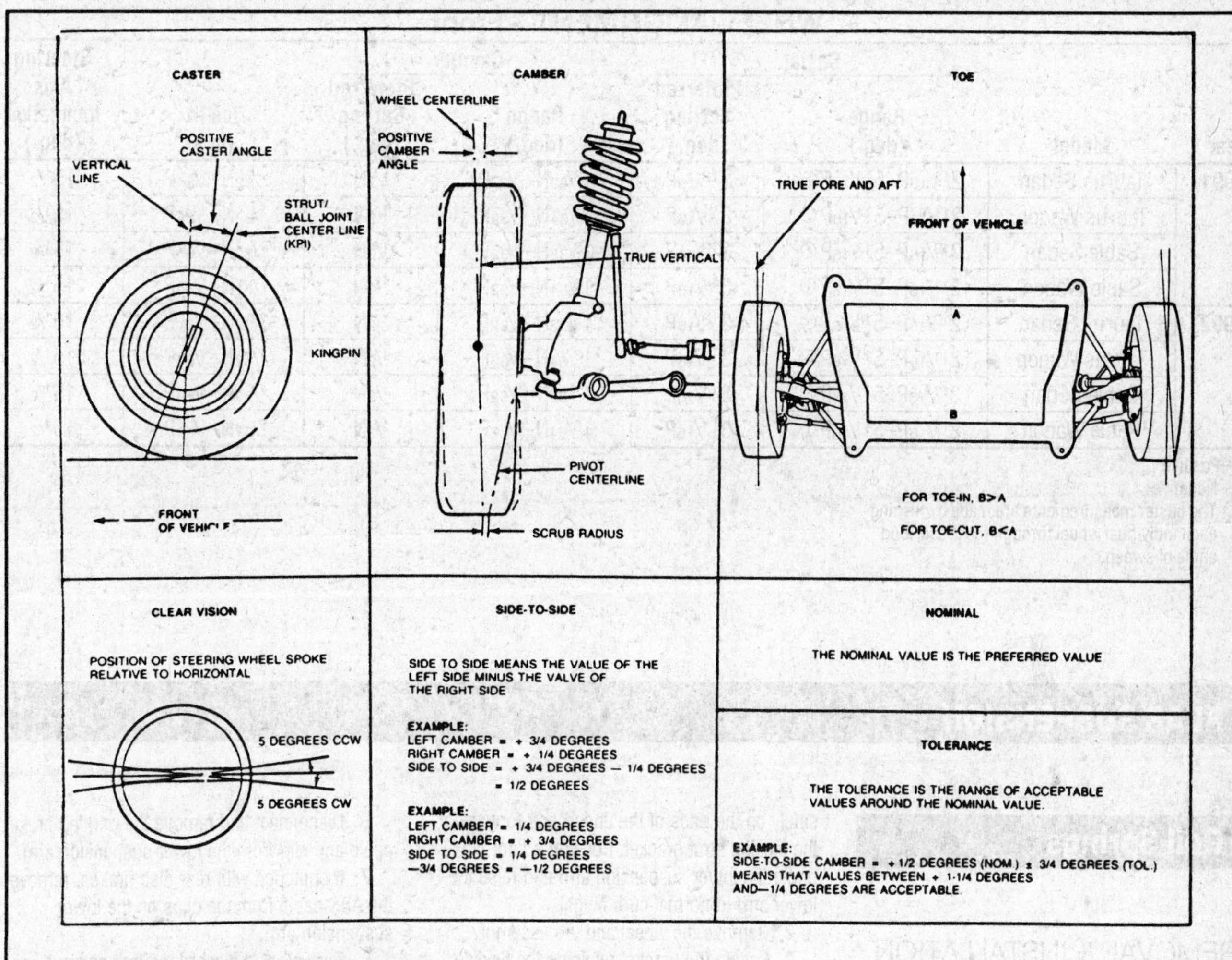

Fig.14 Front end wheel alignment reference points

WHEEL ALIGNMENT—Front

Year	Model	Caster Range (deg.)	Caster Preferred Setting (deg.)	Camber Range (deg.)	Camber Preferred Setting (deg.)	Toe-in (in.)	Steering Axis Inclination (deg.)
1986	Taurus	3P–6P ①	4P	1 3/32N–3/32P	1/2N	7/32–1/64	15 3/8
	Sable	3P–6P ①	4P	1 3/32N–3/32P	1/2N	7/32–1/64	15 3/8
1987	Taurus	3P–6P ①	4P	1 3/32N–3/32P	1/2N	7/32–1/64	15 3/8
	Sable	3P–6P ①	4P	1 3/32N–3/32P	1/2N	7/32–1/64	15 3/8
1988	Taurus	3P–6P ①	4P	1 3/32N–3/32P	1/2N	7/32–1/64	15 3/8
	Sable	3P–6P ①	4P	1 3/32N–3/32P	1/2N	7/32–1/64	15 3/8
1989	Taurus	3P–6P ①	4P	1 3/32N–3/32P	1/2N	7/32–1/64	15 3/8
	Sable	3P–6P ①	4P	1 3/32N–3/32P	1/2N	7/32–1/64	15 3/8
1990	Taurus Sedan	2 13/16P–5 13/16P ①	3 13/16P	1 3/32N–3/32P	1/2N	7/32N–1/64P	15 1/2
	Taurus Wagon	2 11/16P–5 11/16P ①	3 11/16P	1 3/32N–3/32P	1/2N	7/32N–1/64P	15 1/2
	Sable Sedan	2 13/16P–5 13/16P ①	3 13/16P	1 3/32N–3/32P	1/2N	7/32N–1/64P	15 1/2
	Sable Wagon	2 11/16P–5 11/16P ①	3 11/16P	1 3/64N–3/32P	1/2N	7/32N–1/64P	15 1/2

WHEEL ALIGNMENT—Front

Year	Model	Caster Range (deg.)	Caster Preferred Setting (deg.)	Camber Range (deg.)	Camber Preferred Setting (deg.)	Toe-in (in.)	Steering Axis Inclination (deg.)
1991	Taurus Sedan	$2\frac{13}{16}$P–$5\frac{13}{16}$P ①	$3\frac{13}{16}$P	$1\frac{3}{32}$N–$\frac{3}{32}$P	$\frac{1}{2}$N	$\frac{7}{32}$N–$\frac{1}{64}$P	$15\frac{1}{2}$
	Taurus Wagon	$2\frac{11}{16}$P–$5\frac{11}{16}$P ①	$3\frac{11}{16}$P	$1\frac{3}{64}$N–$\frac{3}{32}$P	$\frac{1}{2}$N	$\frac{7}{32}$N–$\frac{1}{64}$P	$15\frac{1}{2}$
	Sable Sedan	$2\frac{13}{16}$P–$5\frac{13}{16}$P ①	$3\frac{13}{16}$P	$1\frac{3}{32}$N–$\frac{3}{32}$P	$\frac{1}{2}$N	$\frac{7}{32}$N–$\frac{1}{64}$P	$15\frac{1}{2}$
	Sable Wagon	$2\frac{11}{16}$P–$5\frac{11}{16}$P ①	$3\frac{11}{16}$P	$1\frac{3}{64}$N–$\frac{3}{32}$P	$\frac{1}{2}$N	$\frac{7}{32}$N–$\frac{1}{64}$P	$15\frac{1}{2}$
1992	Taurus Sedan	$2\frac{13}{16}$P–$5\frac{13}{16}$P ①	$3\frac{13}{16}$P	$1\frac{3}{32}$N–$\frac{3}{32}$P	$\frac{1}{2}$N	$\frac{7}{32}$N–$\frac{1}{64}$P	$15\frac{1}{2}$
	Taurus Wagon	$2\frac{11}{16}$P–$5\frac{11}{16}$P ①	$3\frac{11}{16}$P	$1\frac{3}{64}$N–$\frac{3}{32}$P	$\frac{1}{2}$N	$\frac{7}{32}$N–$\frac{1}{64}$P	$15\frac{1}{2}$
	Sable Sedan	$2\frac{11}{16}$P–$5\frac{11}{16}$P ①	$3\frac{11}{16}$P	$1\frac{3}{32}$N–$\frac{3}{32}$P	$\frac{1}{2}$N	$\frac{7}{32}$N–$\frac{1}{64}$P	$15\frac{1}{2}$
	Sable Wagon	$2\frac{11}{16}$P–$5\frac{11}{16}$P ①	$3\frac{11}{16}$P	$1\frac{3}{64}$N–$\frac{3}{32}$P	$\frac{1}{2}$N	$\frac{7}{32}$N–$\frac{1}{64}$P	$15\frac{1}{2}$

P—Positive
N—Negative
① The caster measurements are made by turning each individual wheel through the prescribed angle of sweep.

REAR SUSPENSION

Coil Springs

REMOVAL & INSTALLATION

Wagon

➧ SEE FIG. 24–26

1. Raise the rear of the vehicle and support safely on the pads of the underbody forward of the tension strut bracket. Position a floor jack under the lower suspension arm and raise the lower arm to normal curb height.
2. Remove the wheel and tire assembly.
3. Locate the bracket retaining the flexible hose to the body. Remove the bracket retaining bolt and bracket from the body.
4. Remove the stabilizer bar U-bracket from the lower suspension arm.
5. Remove and discard the nuts attaching the shock absorber to the lower suspension arm.
6. Disconnect and remove the parking brake cable and clip from the lower suspension arm.
7. If equipped with rear disc brakes, remove the ABS cable from the clips on the lower suspension arm.
8. Remove and discard the bolt and nut attaching the tension strut to the lower suspension arm.
9. Suspend the spindle and upper suspension

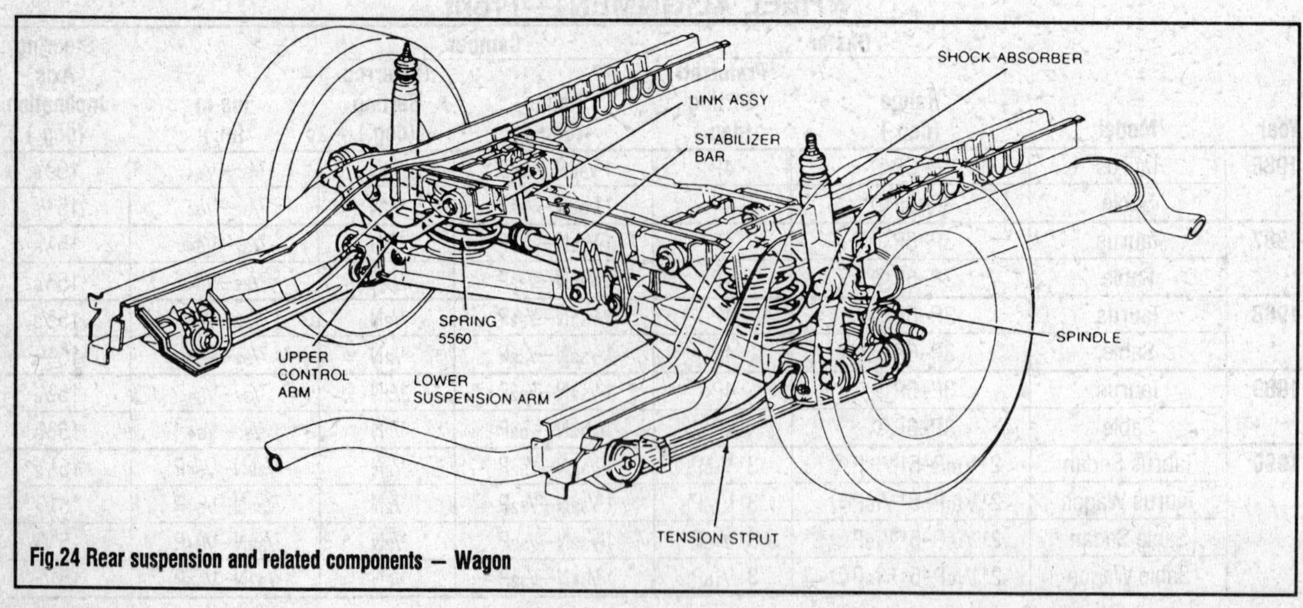

Fig.24 Rear suspension and related components — Wagon

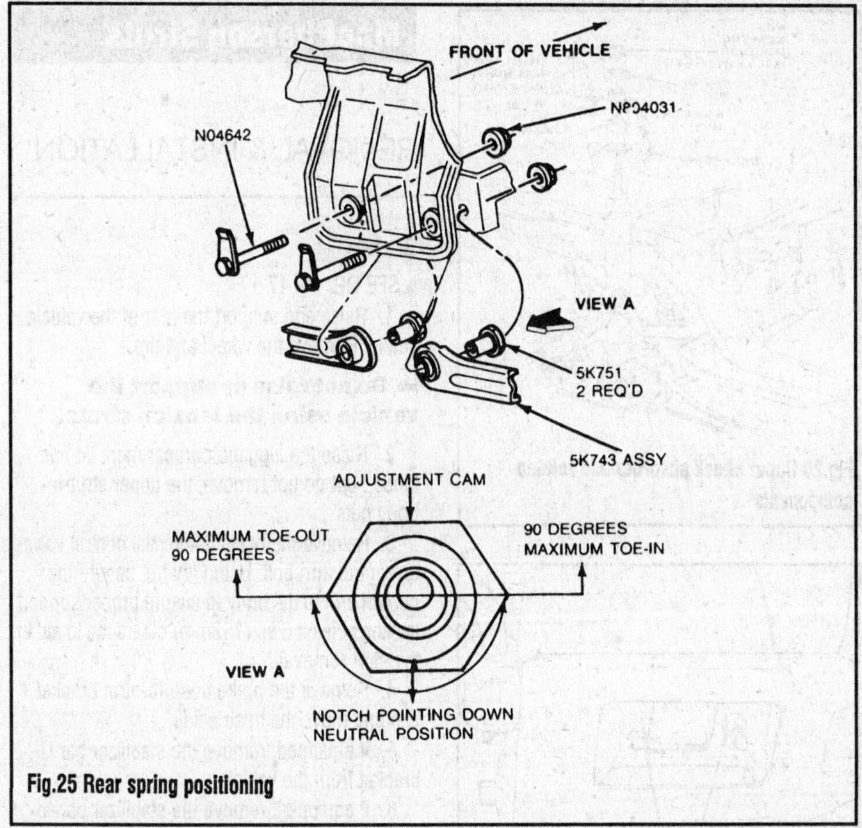

Fig.25 Rear spring positioning

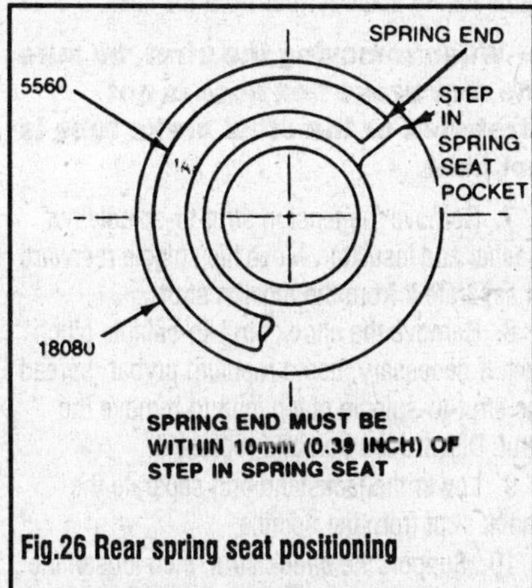

Fig.26 Rear spring seat positioning

arms from the body with a piece of wire to prevent them from dropping.

10. Remove the nut, bolt, washer and adjusting cam that retain the lower suspension arm to the spindle. Discard the nut, bolt and washer and replace with new. Set the cam aside.

11. With the floor jack, slowly lower the suspension arm until the spring, lower and upper insulators can be removed. Replace the spring and insulators as required.

To install:

12. Position the lower insulator on the lower suspension arm and press the insulator downward into place. Make certain the insulator is properly seated.

13. Position the upper insulator on top of the spring. Install the spring on the lower suspension arm. Make certain the spring is properly seated.

14. With the floor jack, slowly raise the suspension arm. Guide the upper spring insulator onto the upper spring underbody seat.

15. Position the spindle in the lower suspension arm with a new bolt, nut washer, and the existing cam. Install the bolt with the head of the bolt toward the front of the vehicle. Do not tighten the bolt at this time.

16. Remove the wire supporting the spindle and suspension arms.

17. Install the tension strut in the lower suspension arm using a new nut and bolt; do not tighten at this time.

18. Attach the parking brake cable and clip to the lower suspension arm.

19. If equipped with rear disc brakes, install the ABS cable into the clips on the lower suspension arm.

20. Position the shock absorber on the lower suspension arm and install 2 new nuts. Torque the nuts to 13–20 ft. lbs. (17–27 Nm).

21. Attach the stabilizer U-bracket to the lower suspension arm using a new bolt. Torque the bolt to 20–30 ft. lbs. (27–40 Nm).

22. Attach the flexible brake hose to the body and tighten the bolt to 8–12 ft. lbs. (11–16 Nm).

23. With the floor jack, raise the lower suspension to normal curb height. Torque the lower suspension arm to 40–55 ft. lbs. (54–74 Nm). Torque the bolt that attaches the tension strut to the body bracket to 40–55 ft. lbs. (54–74 Nm).

24. Install the wheel and tire assembly. Remove the floor jack and lower the vehicle.

25. Check the rear wheel alignment and adjust if necessary.

Shock Absorbers

REMOVAL & INSTALLATION

Wagon

SEE FIG. 17–21

1. Raise and support the vehicle safely.
2. Remove the wheel and tire assembly.
3. Position a jack stand under the lower suspension arm. Remove the 2 nuts retaining the shock absorber to the lower suspension arm.
4. From inside the vehicle, remove the rear compartment access panels.
5. Remove and discard the top shock absorber attaching nut using a crow's foot wrench and ratchet while holding the shock absorber shaft stationary with an open end wrench.

If the shock absorber is to be reused, do not grip the shaft with pliers or vise grips. Gripping the shaft in this manner will damage the shaft surface finish and will result in severe oil leakage.

6. Remove the rubber insulator from the shock and the shock from the vehicle.

The shocks are gas filled. It will require an effort to remove the shock from the lower arm.

To install:

7. Install a new washer and insulator on the upper shock absorber rod.
8. Maneuver the upper part of the shock absorber into the shock tower opening in the body. Push slowly on the lower part of the shock absorber until the mounting studs are aligned with the mounting holes in the lower suspension arm.
9. Install new lower attaching nuts but do not tighten at this time.
10. Install a new insulator, washer and nut on top of the shock absorber. Torque the nut to 19–27 ft. lbs. (26–37 Nm.).
11. Install the rear compartment access panel.

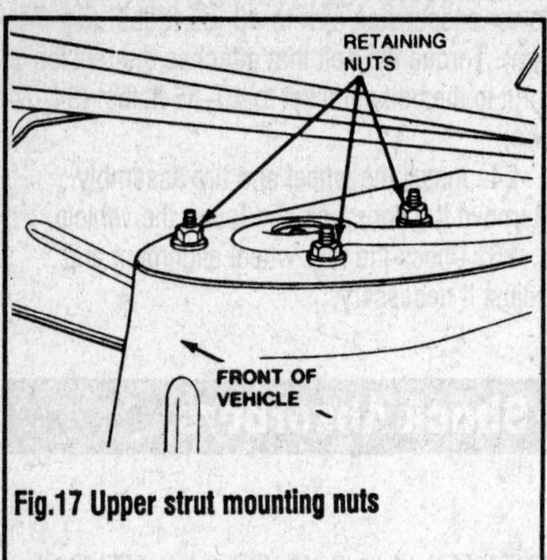

Fig.17 Upper strut mounting nuts

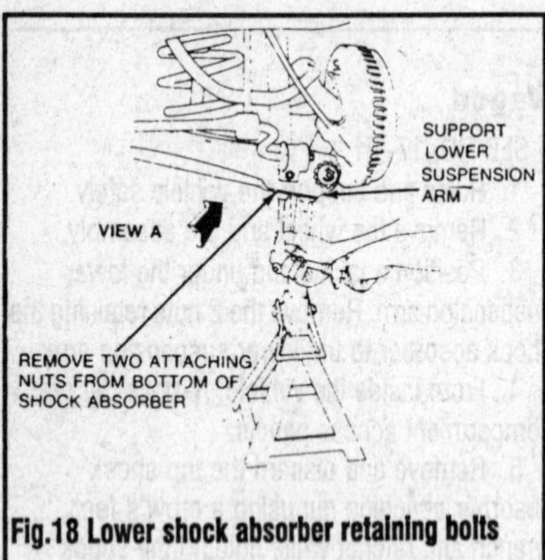

Fig.18 Lower shock absorber retaining bolts

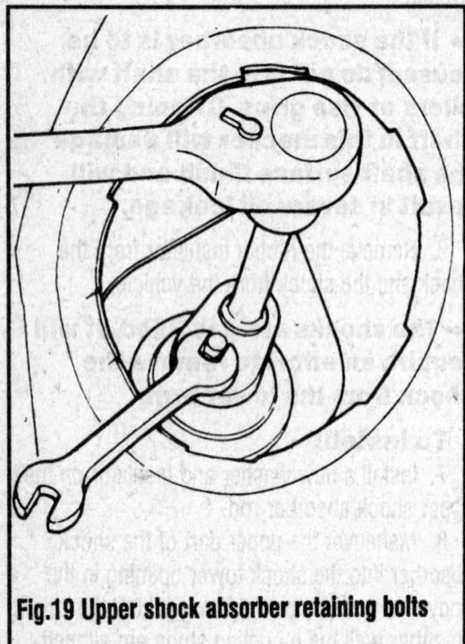
Fig.19 Upper shock absorber retaining bolts

12. Torque the 2 lower attaching nuts to 13–20 ft. lbs. (17–27 Nm).

13. Install the wheel and tire assembly. Remove the safety stand supporting the lower suspension arm and lower the vehicle.

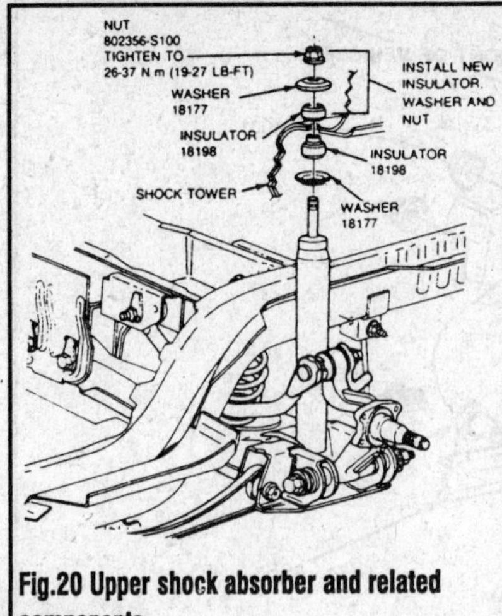

Fig.20 Upper shock absorber and related components

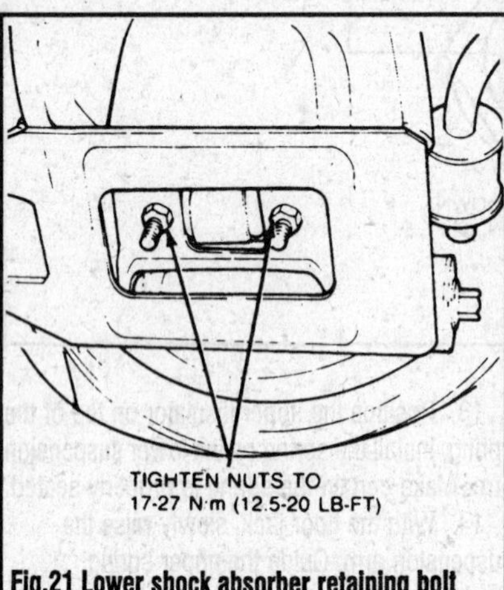

Fig.21 Lower shock absorber retaining bolt locations

TESTING

1. Visually inspect the shock absorber for signs of leakage.

2. If one shock absorber is leaking replace both shock absorbers.

3. Stand back and look at the vehicle if it sags on one end, check the shocks if defective replace them.

4. Bounce the vehicle up and down a few times it the vehicle bounces more that twice the shocks could be defective and require replacement.

MacPherson Struts

REMOVAL & INSTALLATION

Sedan

➧ SEE FIG. 16–17

1. Raise and support the rear of the vehicle safely. Remove the wheel and tire.

➡ Do not raise or support the vehicle using the tension struts.

2. Raise the luggage compartment lid and loosen but do not remove, the upper strut-to-body nuts.

3. Remove the brake differential control valve-to-control arm bolt. Using a wire, secure the control arm to the body to ensure proper support leaving at least 6 in. (152mm) clearance to aid in the strut removal.

4. Remove the brake hose-to-strut bracket clip and move the hose aside.

5. If equipped, remove the stabilizer bar U-bracket from the vehicle.

6. If equipped, remove the stabilizer bar-to-stabilizer link nut, washer and insulator, then separate the stabilizer bar from the link.

➡ When removing the strut, be sure the rear brake flex hose is not stretched or the steel brake tube is not bent.

7. Remove the tension strut-to-spindle nut, washer and insulator. Move the spindle rearward to separate it from the tension strut.

8. Remove the shock strut-to-spindle pinch bolt. If necessary, use a medium prybar, spread the strut-to-spindle pinch joint to remove the strut. Discard the bolt and replace it.

9. Lower the jackstand and separate the shock strut from the spindle.

10. Support the shock strut, then loosen the top strut-to-body nuts completely and remove the strut from the vehicle.

11. Remove the nut, washer and insulator attaching link to strut and remove link. Mark the location of the insulator to top mount, then compress the spring, using a suitable spring compressor.

12. Use a 10mm box end wrench to hold the top of the strut shaft while removing the nut with a 21mm 6-point crow foot wrench and ratchet. Loosen the spring compressor, then remove the top mount bracket assembly, spring insulator and spring.

To install:

13. Using the spring compressor, install the spring, spring insulator, bottom washer, if

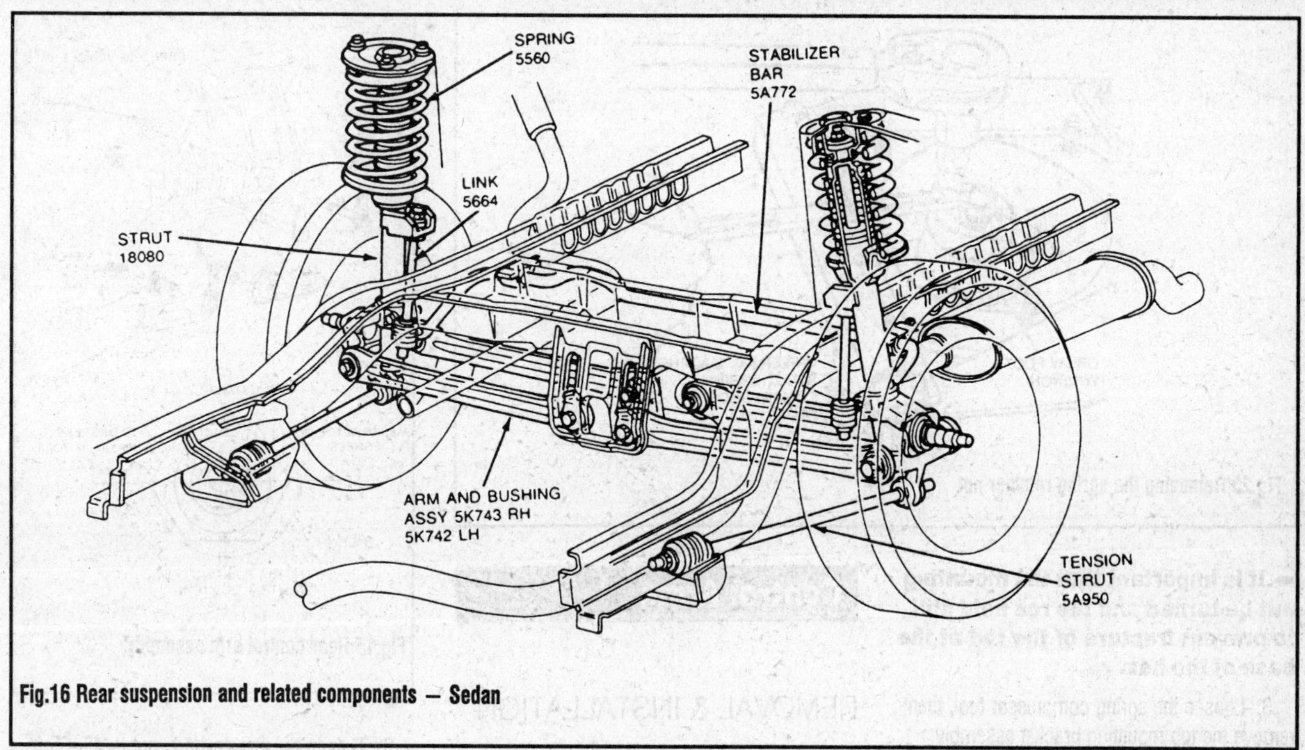

Fig.16 Rear suspension and related components — Sedan

equipped, top mount, upper washer and nut on the strut shaft. Make sure the spring is properly located in the upper and lower spring seats and the mount washers are positioned correctly.

14. Tighten the rod nut to 35–50 ft. lbs. (48–68 Nm). Use a 21mm crow foot wrench to turn the nut and a 10mm box end wrench to hold the shaft. Do not use pliers or vise grips.

15. Position the stabilizer bar link in the strut bracket. Install the insulator, washer and nut and tighten to 5–7 ft. lbs. (7–9.5 Nm).

16. Insert the 3 upper mount studs into the strut tower in the apron and hand start 3 new nuts. Do not tighten the nuts at this time.

17. Partially raise the vehicle.

18. Install the strut into the spindle pinch joint. Install a new pinch bolt into the spindle and through the strut bracket. Tighten the bolt to 50–70 ft. lbs. (68–95 Nm).

19. Move the spindle rearward and install the tension strut into the spindle. Install the insulator, washer and nut on the tension strut. Tighten the nut to 35–50 ft. lbs. (48–68 Nm).

20. Position the link into the stabilizer bar. Install the insulator, washer and nut on the link. Tighten to 5–7 ft. lbs. (7–9.5 Nm).

21. Position the stabilizer bar U-bracket on the body. Install the bolt and tighten to 25–37 ft. lbs. (34–50 Nm).

22. Install the brake hose to the strut bracket.

23. Install the brake control differential valve on the control arm and remove the retaining wire.

24. Install the top mount-to-body nuts and tighten to 19–26 ft. lbs. (26–35 Nm).

25. Install the wheel and tire assembly and lower the vehicle.

OVERHAUL

➧ SEE FIG. 22-23

The following procedure is performed with the strut assembly removed from the car. A MacPherson Strut compression tool is required for the disassembly of the strut, a cage type tool such as the No. D85P–7181 A or equivalent is required.

✻✻ CAUTION

Never attempt to disassemble the spring or top mount without first compressing the spring using the strut compressor tool No. D85P-7178-A or equivalent. If a strut spring compressor is not used, the assembly will fly apart by the force of the spring tension!

➡ Before compressing the spring, mark the location of the insulator to the top mount using a grease pencil.

1. Compress the spring with the coil spring compressor D85P–7178–A or equivalent.

2. Place a 10mm box wrench on top of the shock strut shaft and hold while removing the top shaft mounting nut with a 21mm 6-point crowfoot wrench and ratchet.

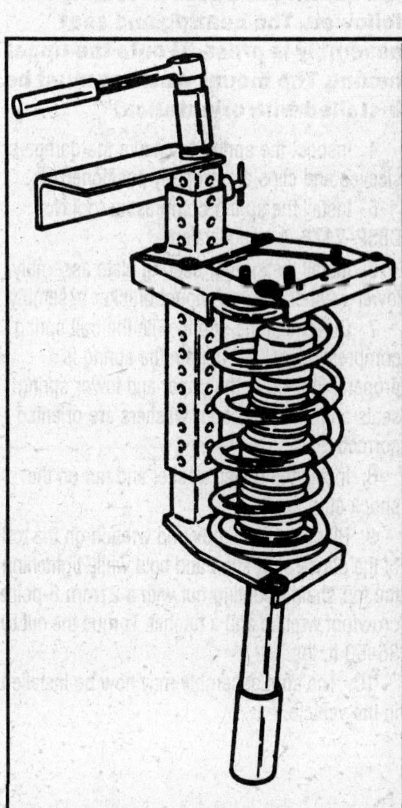

Fig.22 Compressing the strut using the proper tool

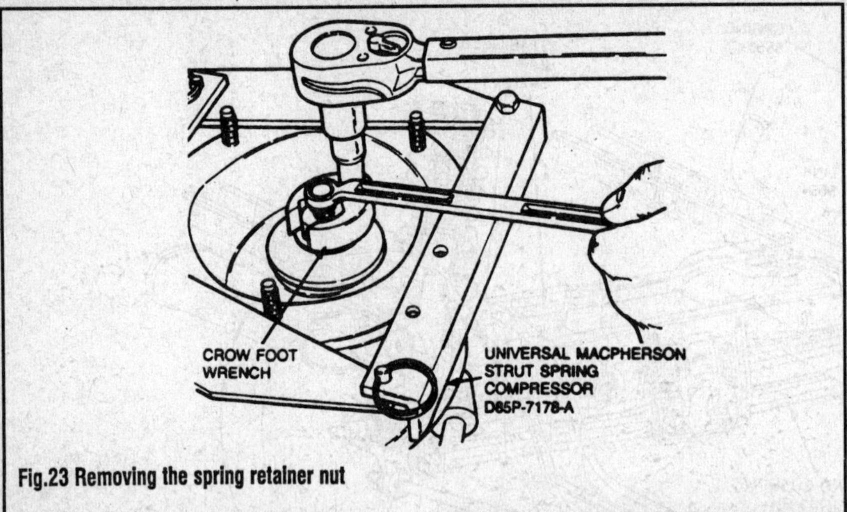

Fig.23 Removing the spring retainer nut

➡ It is important that the mounting nut be turned and the rod held still to prevent fracture of the rod at the base of the hex.

3. Loosen the spring compressor tool, then remove the top mounting bracket assembly, bearing plate assembly and spring.

To assemble:

➡ Ensure that the correct assembly sequence and proper positioning of the bearing and seat assembly are followed. The bearing and seat assembly is press-fit onto the upper mount. The mount washers must be installed with orientation.

4. Inspect the spring to ensure the dampers, sleeves and clips are properly positioned.
5. Install the spring compressor tool No. D85P-7178-A or equivalent.
6. Install the spring, bearing plate assembly, lower washer and top mount bracket assembly.
7. Compress the spring with the coil spring compressor tool. Be certain the spring is properly located in the upper and lower spring seats and that the mount washers are oriented correctly.
8. Install the upper washer and nut on the shock strut shaft.
9. Place a 10mm box end wrench on the top of the shock strut shaft and hold while tightening the top shaft mounting nut with a 21mm 6-point crowfoot wrench and a ratchet. Torque the nut to 35–50 ft. lbs.
10. The strut assembly may now be installed in the vehicle.

Control Arms

REMOVAL & INSTALLATION

Sedan

➧ SEE FIG. 15

1. Raise the vehicle and support it safely. Do not raise the vehicle by the tension strut.
2. Disconnect the brake proportioning valve from the left side front arm.
3. Disconnect the parking brake cable from the front arms.
4. Remove and discard the arm-to-spindle bolt, washer and nut.
5. Remove and discard the arm-to-body bolt and nut.
6. Remove the arm from the vehicle.

To install:

➡ When installing new control arms, the offset on all arms must face up. The arms are stamped "bottom" on the lower edge. The flange edge of the right side rear arm stamping must face the front of the vehicle. The other 3 must face the rear of the vehicle. The rear control arms have 2 adjustment cams that fit inside the bushings at the arm-to-body attachment. The cam is installed from the rear on the left arm and from the front on the right arm.

7. Position the arm and cam where required, at the center of the vehicle. Insert a new bolt and nut but do not tighten at this time.
8. Move the arm end up to the spindle and insert a new bolt, washer and nut. Tighten the nut to 42–57 ft. lbs. (57–77 Nm).

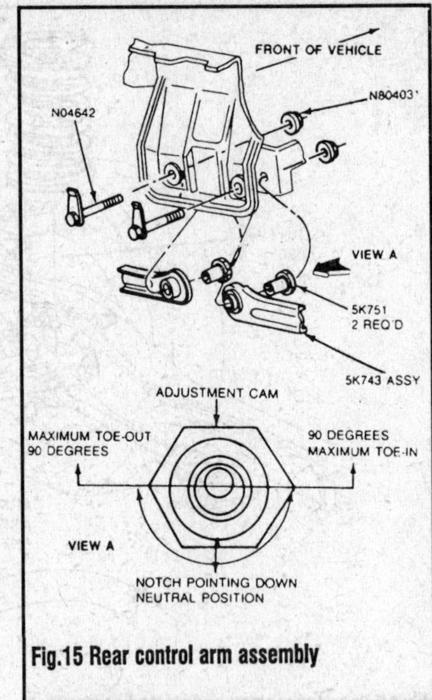

Fig.15 Rear control arm assembly

9. Tighten the arm-to-body nut to 45–65 ft. lbs. (61–88 Nm).
10. Attach the parking brake cable to the front arms and the brake proportioning valve to the left side front arm.
11. Lower the vehicle and check the alignment.

Wagon

UPPER ARM

1. Raise the vehicle and support it with wood blocks on jackstands so the suspension is at normal curb height.
2. Remove the wheel and tire assembly.
3. Remove the brake line flexible hose bracket from the body.
4. Loosen, but do not remove the nuts attaching the spindle to the upper and lower suspension arms.
5. Remove and discard the nuts and bolts attaching the front and rear upper suspension arms to the body brackets. Make sure the spindle does not fall outward.
6. Tilt the top of the spindle outward, letting it pivot on the lower suspension arm attaching bolt until the ends of the upper suspension arms are clear of the body bracket. Support the spindle with wire in this position.
7. Remove and discard the nut attaching the upper suspension arms to the spindle and remove the arms from the vehicle.

To install:

8. Install the upper suspension arms on the spindle and install a new nut but do not tighten the nut at this time.

9. Position the upper suspension arm ends to the body bracket and install new nuts and bolts. Tighten to 70–95 ft. lbs. (95–129 Nm). Remove the wire from the spindle.

10. Tighten the nut attaching the upper suspension arms to the spindle to 150–190 ft. lbs. (204–257 Nm). Tighten the nut attaching the lower suspension arm to the spindle to 40–55 ft. lbs. (54–74 Nm).

11. Install the brake line bracket to the body.

12. Install the wheel and tire assembly, remove the jackstand and wood block and lower the vehicle.

13. Check the rear wheel alignment.

LOWER ARM

1. Raise and support the vehicle safely on the lifting pads on the underbody forward of the tension strut body bracket.

2. Remove the wheel and tire assembly.

3. Place a floor jack under the lower suspension arm.

4. Remove the bracket retaining the flexible brake hose to the body.

5. Remove the stabilizer bar U-bracket from the lower suspension arm.

6. Remove and discard the nuts attaching the shock absorber to the lower suspension arm.

7. Remove the parking brake cable and clip from the lower suspension arm.

8. Remove and discard the bolt and nut attaching the tension strut to the lower suspension arm.

9. Support the spindle and upper suspension arms by wiring them to the body, to prevent them from dropping down.

10. Remove the nut, bolt, washer and adjusting cam retaining the lower suspension arm to the spindle. Discard the nut, bolt and washer.

11. Lower the suspension arm with the floor jack until the spring can be removed.

12. Remove and discard the bolt and nut attaching the lower suspension arm to the center body bracket and remove the arm.

To install:

13. Position the lower suspension arm-to-center body bracket and install but do not tighten a new bolt and nut with the bolt head toward the front of the vehicle.

14. Position the lower insulator on the lower suspension arm and press the insulator downward into place. Make sure the insulator is properly seated.

15. Position the upper insulator on top of the spring. Install the spring on the lower suspension arm, making sure the spring is properly seated.

16. Raise the suspension arm with the floor jack and guide the upper spring insulator onto the upper spring seat on the underbody.

17. Position the spindle in the lower suspension arm and install, but do not tighten, a new bolt, nut, washer and the existing cam, with the bolt head toward the front of the vehicle.

18. Remove the wire from the spindle and suspension arms.

19. Install the tension strut in the lower suspension arm using a new bolt and nut but do not tighten at this time.

20. Install the parking brake cable and clip to the lower suspension arm.

21. Position the shock absorber on the lower suspension arm and install 2 new nuts. Tighten the nuts to 13–20 ft. lbs. (17–27 Nm).

22. Install the stabilizer bar and U-bracket to the lower suspension arm using a new bolt. Tighten the bolt to 20–30 ft. lbs. (27–40 Nm).

23. Install the flexible brake hose bracket to the body. Tighten the bolt to 8–12 ft. lbs. (11–16 Nm).

24. Using the floor jack, raise the lower suspension arm to normal curb height.

- Lower suspension arm-to-body bracket nut: 40–55 ft. lbs.
- Lower suspension arm-to-spindle nut: 40–55 ft. lbs.
- Tension strut-to-body bracket bolt: 40–55 ft. lbs.

25. Install the wheel and tire assembly and lower the vehicle.

26. Check the rear wheel alignment.

Rear Wheel Bearings

REPLACEMENT

Drum Brakes

1986–89

➧ SEE FIG. 29–33

1. Raise the vehicle and support it safely. Remove the wheel from the hub and drum.

2. Remove the grease cap from the hub. Remove the cotter pin, nut retainer, adjusting nut and keyed flat washer from the spindle. Discard the cotter pin.

3. Pull the hub and drum assembly off of the spindle. Remove the outer bearing assembly.

4. Using seal remover tool 1175–AC or equivalent, remove and discard the grease seal. Remove the inner bearing assembly from the hub.

5. Wipe all lubricant from the spindle and inside of the hub. Cover the spindle with a clean cloth and vacuum all loose dust and dirt from the brake assembly. Carefully remove the cloth to prevent dirt from falling on the spindle.

6. Clean both bearing assemblies and cups using a suitable solvent. Inspect the bearing assemblies and cups for excessive wear, scratches, pits or other damage and replace as necessary.

7. If the cups are to be replaced, remove them with impact slide hammer T50T–100–A and bearing cup puller T77F–1102–A or equivalent.

To install:

8. If the inner and outer bearing cups were removed, install the replacement cups using driver handle T80T–4000–W and bearing cup replacers T73T–1217–A and T77F–1217–A or equivalent. Support the drum hub on a block of wood to prevent damage. Make sure the cups are properly seated in the hub.

➡ Do not use the cone and roller assembly to install the cups. This will result in damage to the bearing cup and the cone and roller assembly.

9. Make sure all of the spindle and bearing surfaces are clean.

10. Using a bearing packer, pack the bearing assemblies with a suitable wheel bearing grease. If a packer is not available, work in as much grease as possible between the rollers and cages. Grease the cup surfaces.

➡ Allow all of the cleaning solvent to dry before repacking the bearings. Do not spin-dry the bearings with air pressure.

11. Install the inner bearing cone and roller assembly in the inner cup. Apply a light film of grease to the lips of a new grease seal and install the seal with rear hub seal replacer T56T–4676–B or equivalent. Make sure the retainer flange is seated all around.

12. Apply a light film of grease on the spindle shaft bearing surfaces. Install the hub and drum assembly on the spindle. Keep the hub centered on the spindle to prevent damage to the grease seal and spindle threads.

13. Install the outer bearing assembly and the keyed flatwasher on the spindle. Install the adjusting nut and adjust the wheel bearings. Install a new cotter pin. Install the grease cap.

14. Install the wheel and tire assembly and lower the vehicle.

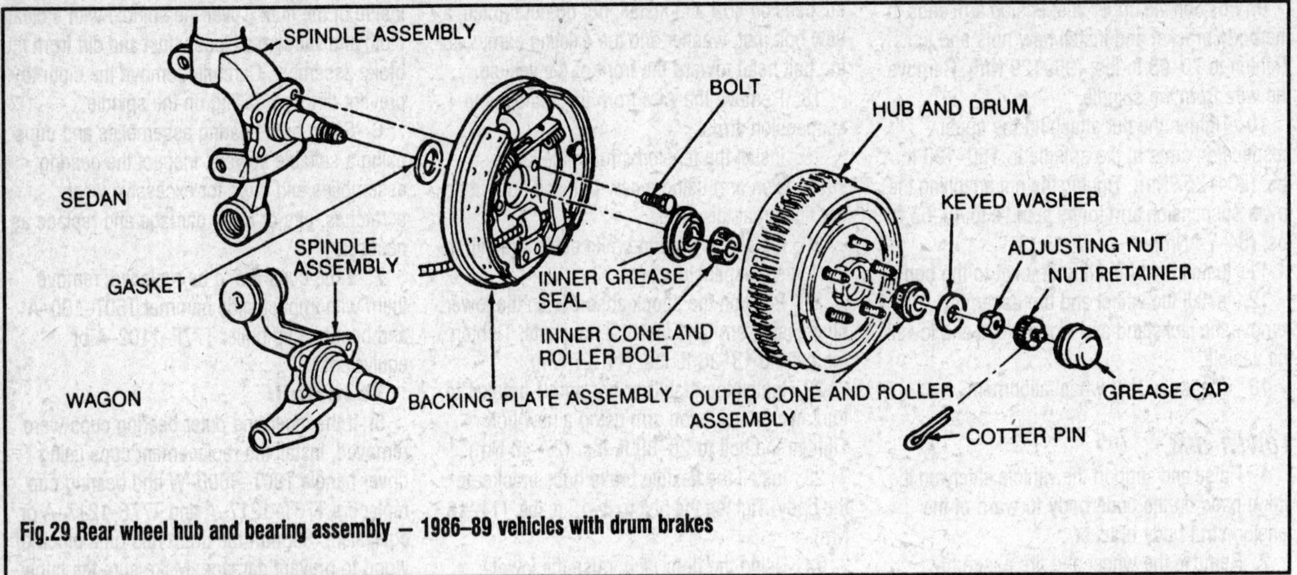

Fig.29 Rear wheel hub and bearing assembly — 1986–89 vehicles with drum brakes

Fig.30 Removing the bearing cups using a slide hammer

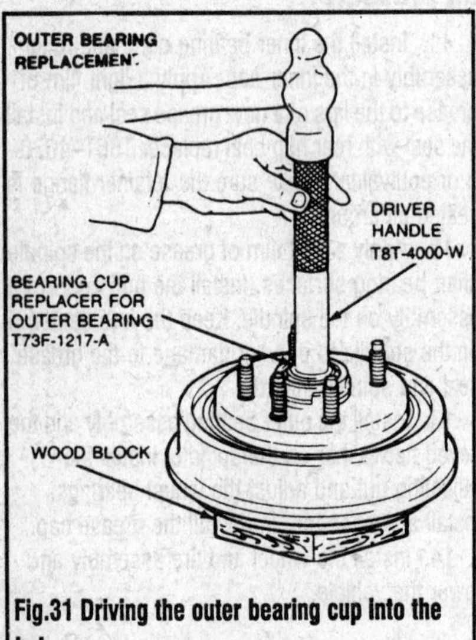

Fig.31 Driving the outer bearing cup into the hub

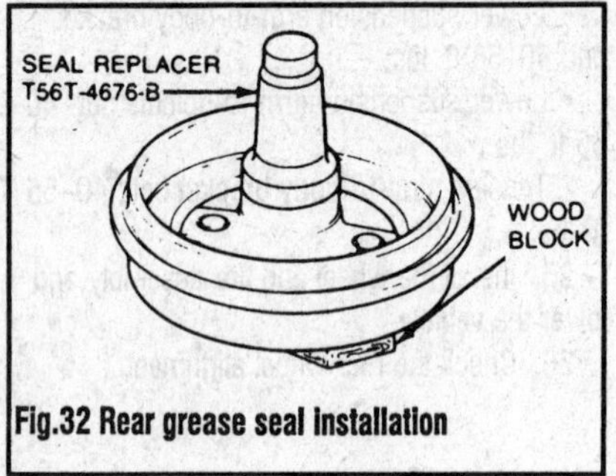

Fig.32 Rear grease seal installation

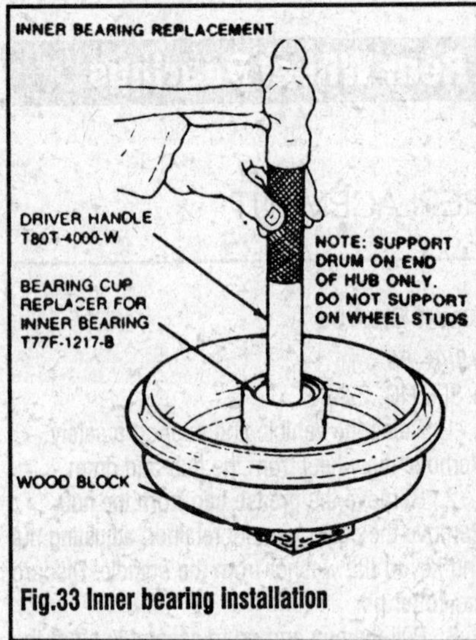

Fig.33 Inner bearing installation

1990–92

➧ SEE FIG. 27

1. Raise the vehicle and support it safely.
2. Remove the wheel.
3. Remove the 2 pushnuts retaining the drum to the hub and remove the drum.
4. Remove the grease cap from the bearing and hub assembly and discard it.
5. Remove the hub retaining nut and remove the bearing and hub assembly from the spindle.
6. Install in the reverse order of removal. Use coil remover T89P–19623–FH or equivalent, to install the new grease cap. Tap on the tool to make sure the grease cap is fully seated. Tighten the hub retaining nut to 188–254 ft. lbs. (255–345 Nm).

Disc Brakes

1986–89

1. Raise the vehicle and support it safely. Remove the tire and wheel assembly from the hub.
2. Remove the brake caliper by removing the 2 bolts that attach the caliper support to the cast iron brake adapter. Do not remove the caliper pins from the caliper assembly. Lift the caliper off of the rotor and support it with a length of wire. Do not allow the caliper assembly to hang from the brake hose.
3. Remove the rotor from the hub by pulling it off the hub bolts. If the rotor is difficult to remove, strike the rotor sharply between the studs with a rubber or plastic hammer.
4. Remove the grease cap from the hub. Remove the cotter pin, nut retainer, adjusting nut and keyed flat washer from the spindle. Discard the cotter pin.
5. Pull the hub assembly off of the spindle. Remove the outer bearing assembly.
6. Using seal remover tool 1175–AC or equivalent, remove and discard the grease seal. Remove the inner bearing assembly from the hub.
7. Wipe all of the lubricant from the spindle and inside of the hub. Cover the spindle with a clean cloth and vacuum all of the loose dust and dirt from the brake assembly. Carefully remove the cloth to prevent dirt from falling on the spindle.

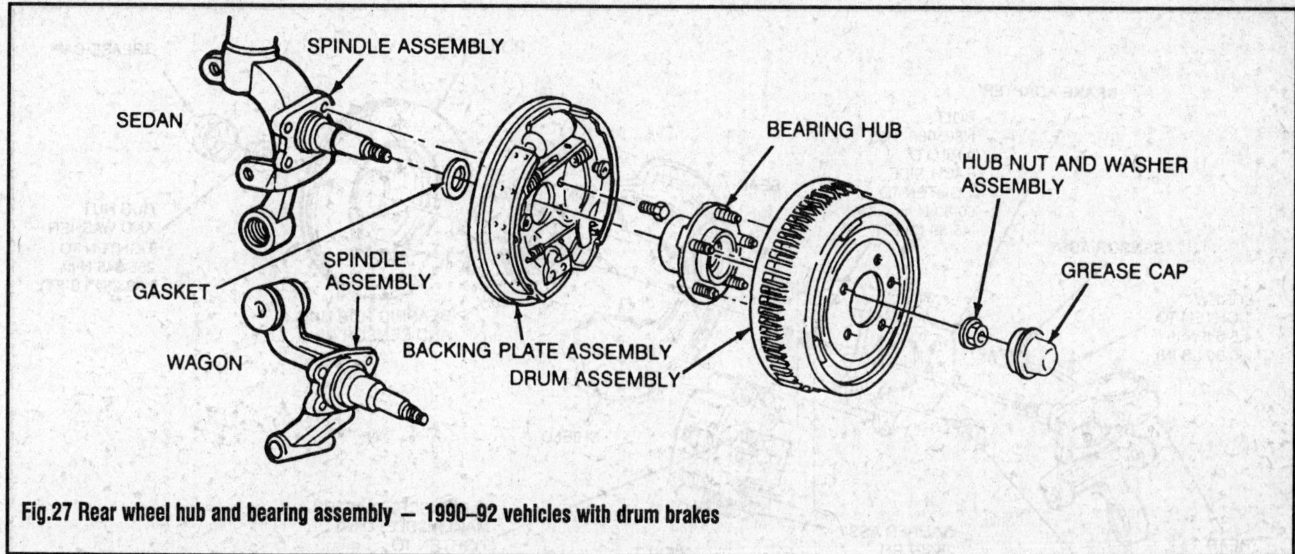

Fig.27 Rear wheel hub and bearing assembly — 1990–92 vehicles with drum brakes

8. Clean both bearing assemblies and cups using a suitable solvent. Inspect the bearing assemblies and cups for excessive wear, scratches, pits or other damage and replace as necessary.

9. If the cups are being replaced, remove them with impact slide hammer tool T50T–100–A and bearing cup puller tool T77F–1102–A or equivalent.

To install:

10. If the inner and outer bearing cups were removed, install the replacement cups using driver handle tool T80T–4000–W and bearing cup replacer tools T73F–1217–A and T77F–1217–B or equivalent. Support the hub on a block of wood to prevent damage. Make sure the cups are properly seated in the hub.

➡ Do not use the cone and roller assembly to install the cups. This will result in damage to the bearing cup and the cone and roller assembly.

11. Make sure all of the spindle and bearing surfaces are clean.

12. Pack the bearing assemblies with a suitable wheel bearing grease using a bearing packer. If a packer is not available, work in as much grease as possible between the rollers and the cages. Grease the cup surfaces.

➡ Allow all of the cleaning solvent to dry before repacking the bearings. Do not spin-dry the bearings with air pressure.

13. Place the inner bearing cone and roller assembly in the inner cup. Apply a light film of grease to the lips of a new grease seal and install the seal with rear hub seal replacer tool T56T–4676–B or equivalent. Make sure the retainer flange is seated all around.

14. Apply a light film of grease on the spindle shaft bearing surfaces. Install the hub assembly on the spindle. Keep the hub centered on the spindle to prevent damage to the grease seal and spindle threads.

15. Install the outer bearing assembly and keyed flat washer on the spindle. Install the adjusting nut and adjust the wheel bearings. Install a new cotter pin. Install the grease cap.

16. Install the disc brake rotor to the hub assembly. Install the disc brake caliper over the rotor.

17. Install the wheel and tire assembly and lower the vehicle.

1990–92

➧ SEE FIG. 55

1. Raise the vehicle and support it safely.

2. Remove the wheel and tire assembly.

3. Remove the caliper assembly from the brake adapter. Support the caliper assembly with a length of wire.

4. Remove the push on nuts that retain the rotor to the hub and remove the rotor.

5. Remove the grease cap from the bearing and hub assembly and discard the grease cap.

6. Remove the bearing and hub assembly retaining nut and remove the bearing and hub assembly from the spindle.

7. Install in the reverse order of removal. Install a new grease cap using coil remover tool T89P–19623–FH or equivalent. Tap on the tool until the grease cap is fully seated. Tighten the hub retaining nut to 188–254 ft. lbs. (255–345 Nm).

ADJUSTMENT

➧ SEE FIG. 28

The following procedure applies only to 1986–89 vehicles. Adjustment is not possible on 1990–92 vehicles. This procedure should be performed whenever the wheel is excessively loose on the spindle or it does not rotate freely.

➡ The rear wheel uses a tapered roller bearing which may feel loose when properly adjusted; this condition should be considered normal.

1. Raise and support the rear of the vehicle until tires clear the floor.

2. Remove the wheel cover or the ornament and nut covers. Remove the hub grease cap.

➡ If the vehicle is equipped with styled steel or aluminum wheels, the wheel/tire assembly must be removed to remove the dust cover.

3. Remove the cotter pin and the nut retainer.

4. Back off the hub nut 1 full turn.

5. While rotating the hub/drum assembly, tighten the adjusting nut to 17–25 ft. lbs. (23–24 Nm). Back off the adjusting nut $^1/_2$ turn, then retighten it to 24–28 inch lbs. (2.7–3.2 Nm).

6. Position the nut retainer over the adjusting nut so the slots are in line with cotter pin hole, without rotating the adjusting nut.

7. Install the cotter pin and bend the ends around the retainer flange.

8. Check the hub rotation. If the hub rotates freely, install the grease cap. If not, check the bearings for damage and replace, as necessary.

9. Install the wheel and tire assembly and the wheel cover, if necessary. Lower the vehicle.

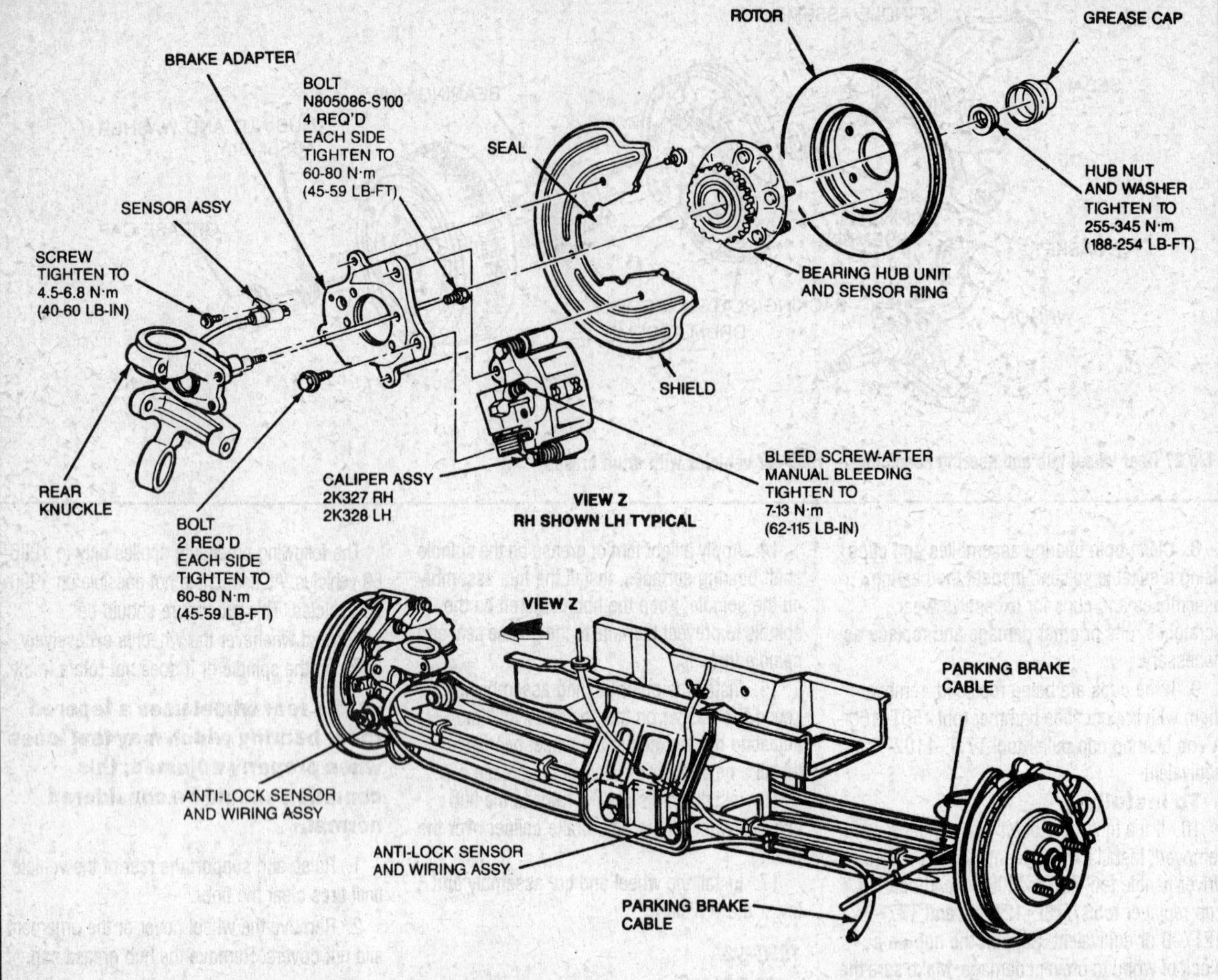

Fig.55 Rear wheel hub and bearing assembly — 1990–92 with disc brakes

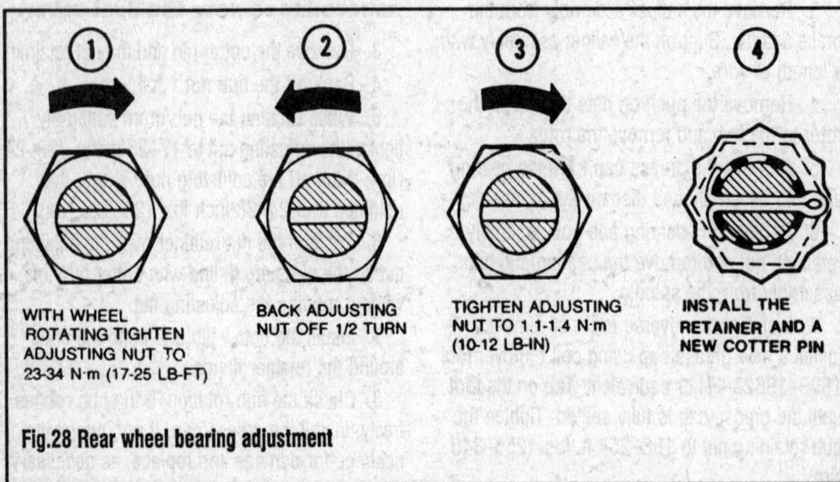

Fig.28 Rear wheel bearing adjustment

Rear Wheel Alignment

CASTER

Caster is pre set at the factory and not adjustable.

CAMBER

Camber is not adjustable on the Sedan. On the Wagon camber is adjustable but requires special equipment and procedures. If you suspect an alignment problem have it checked by a qualified repair shop.

TOE IN

➧ SEE FIGS. 73, 74

Rear toe is adjustable but requires special equipment and procedures. If you suspect an alignment problem have it checked by a qualified repair shop.

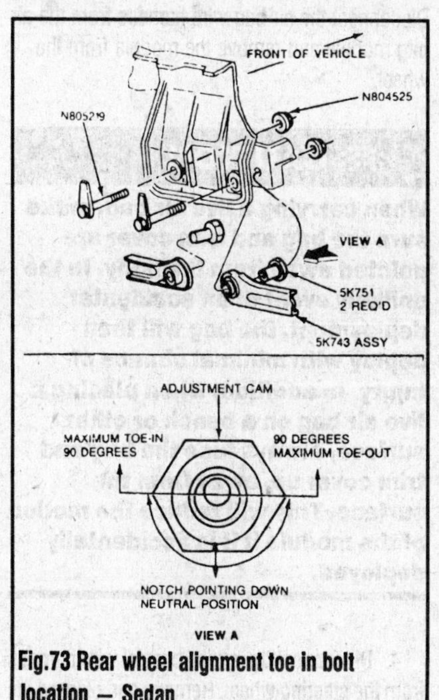

Fig.73 Rear wheel alignment toe in bolt location — Sedan

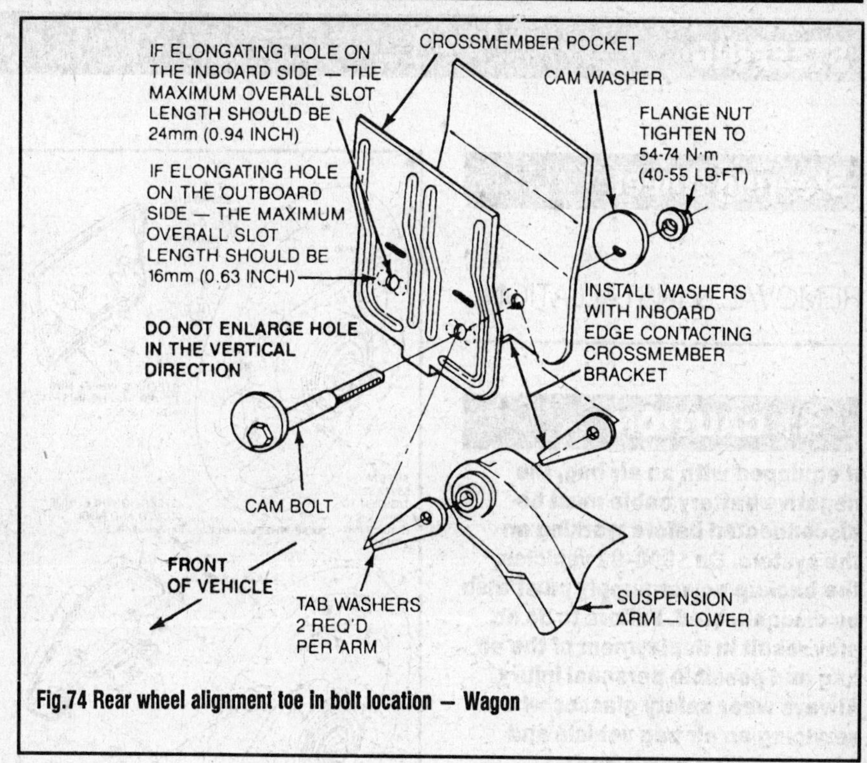

Fig.74 Rear wheel alignment toe in bolt location — Wagon

WHEEL ALIGNMENT—Rear

Year	Model	Caster Range (deg.)	Caster Preferred Setting (deg.)	Camber Range (deg.)	Camber Preferred Setting (deg.)	Toe-in (in.)	Steering Axis Inclination (deg.)
1986	Taurus	—	—	1⅝N–¼N	—	13/64N–19/64P ①	—
	Sable	—	—	1⅝N–¼N	—	13/64N–19/64P ①	—
1987	Taurus	—	—	1⅝N–¼N	—	13/64N–19/64P ①	—
	Sable	—	—	1⅝N–¼N	—	13/64N–19/64P ①	—
1988	Taurus	—	—	1⅝N–¼N	—	13/64N–19/64P ①	—
	Sable	—	—	1⅝N–¼N	—	13/64N–19/64P ①	—
1989	Taurus	—	—	1⅝N–¼N	—	13/64N–19/64P ①	—
	Sable	—	—	1⅝N–¼N	—	13/64N–19/64P ①	—
1990	Taurus	—	—	1⅝N–¼N	—	13/64N–19/64P ①	—
	Sable	—	—	1⅝N–¼N	—	13/64N–19/64P ①	—
1991	Taurus	—	—	1⅝N–¼N	—	13/64N–19/64P ①	—
	Sable	—	—	1⅝N–¼N	—	13/64N–19/64P ①	—
1992	Taurus	—	—	1⅝N–¼N	—	13/64N–19/64P ①	—
	Sable	—	—	1⅝N–¼N	—	13/64N–19/64P ①	—

① Individual sides

STEERING

Steering Wheel

REMOVAL & INSTALLATION

CAUTION

If equipped with an air bag, the negative battery cable must be disconnected before working on the system. On 1990–92 vehicles, the backup power supply must also be disconnected. Failure to do so may result in deployment of the air bag and possible personal injury. Always wear safety glasses when servicing an air bag vehicle and when handling an air bag.

1986–89

SEE FIG. 34

1. Disconnect the negative battery cable.
2. Remove the steering wheel horn pad cover by removing 2 screws from the back of the steering wheel. If equipped with cruise control, disconnect the connector from the slip ring terminal.
3. Remove and discard the steering wheel retaining bolt.
4. Remove the steering wheel from the upper shaft by grasping the rim of the steering wheel and pulling off. A steering wheel puller is not required.

To Install:

5. Position the steering wheel on the end of the shaft. Align the mark on the steering wheel with the mark on the shaft to ensure the straight-ahead steering wheel position corresponds to the straight-ahead position of the front wheels.

The combination switch lever must be in the middle position before installing the steering wheel or damage to the switch cam may result.

6. Install a new steering wheel retaining bolt and tighten to 23–33 ft. lbs. (31–45 Nm).
7. If equipped with cruise control, connect the connector to the slip ring terminal. Install the steering wheel horn pad cover with the 2 screws. Tighten to 5–10 inch lbs. (0.5–1.1 Nm).
8. Connect the negative battery cable.

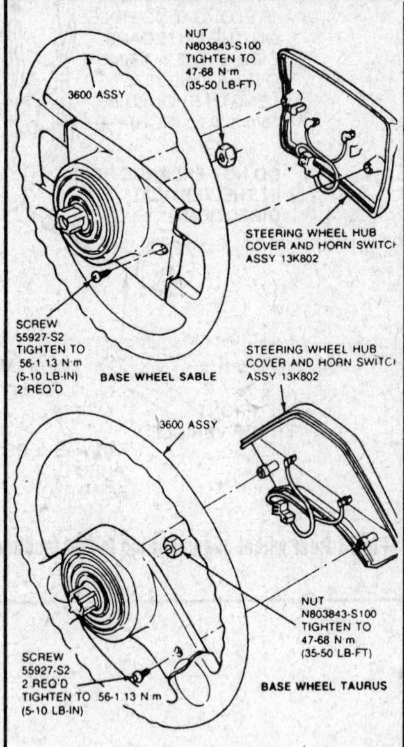

Fig.34 Steering wheel assemblies — 1986–89

1990–92

SEE FIG. 35–36

1. Center the front wheels in the straight-ahead position.
2. Disconnect the negative battery cable. Lower the glove compartment past it's stops and disconnect the air bag backup power supply..
3. Remove the 4 air bag module retaining nuts and lift the module from the wheel. Disconnect the air bag wire harness from the air bag module and remove the module from the wheel.

CAUTION

When carrying a live air bag, make sure the bag and trim cover are pointed away from the body. In the unlikely event of an accidental deployment, the bag will then deploy with minimal chance of injury. In addition, when placing a live air bag on a bench or other surface, always face the bag and trim cover up, away from the surface. This will reduce the motion of the module if it is accidentally deployed.

4. Disconnect the cruise control wire harness from the steering wheel. Remove and discard the steering wheel retaining bolt.
5. Install a suitable steering wheel puller and remove the steering wheel. Route the contact assembly wire harness through the steering wheel as the wheel is lifted off the shaft.

To Install:

6. Make sure the vehicle's front wheels are in the straight-ahead position.

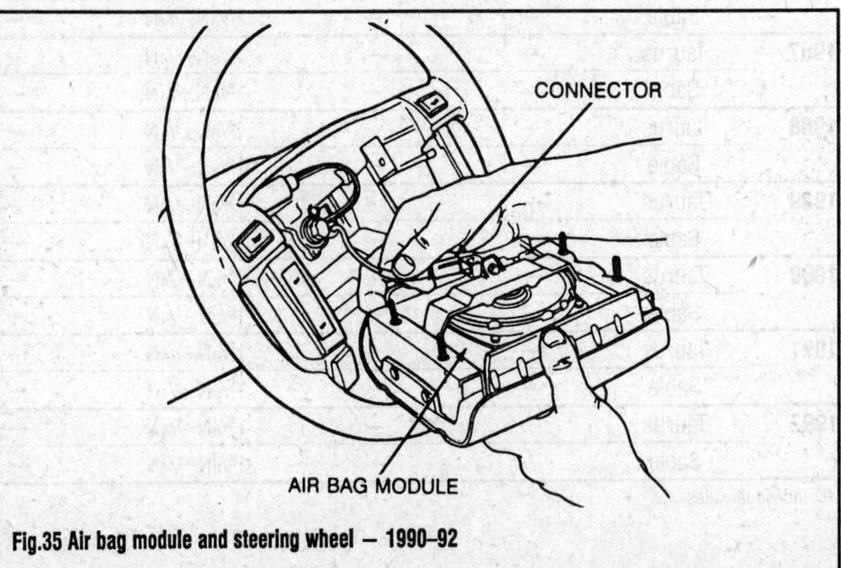

Fig.35 Air bag module and steering wheel — 1990–92

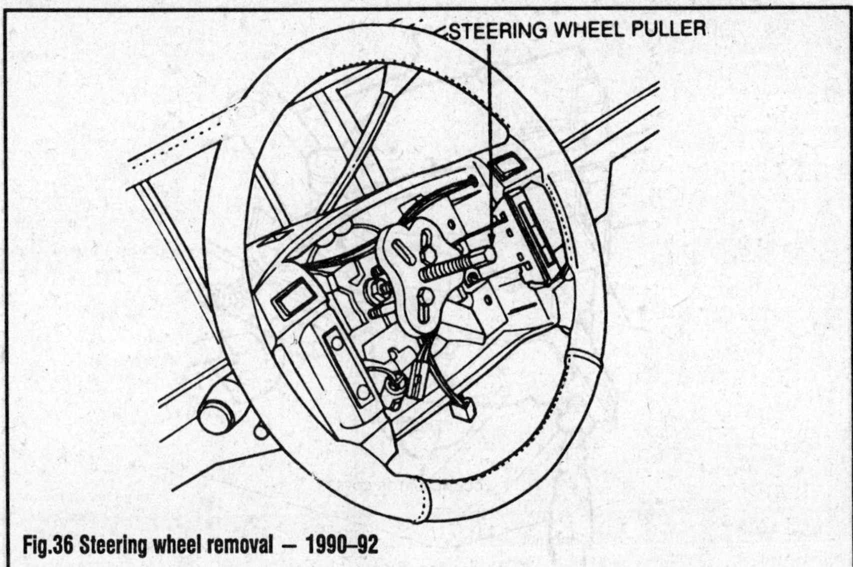

Fig.36 Steering wheel removal – 1990–92

7. Route the contact assembly wire harness through the steering wheel opening at the 3 o'clock position and install the steering wheel on the shaft. The steering wheel and shaft alignment marks should be aligned. Make sure the air bag contact wire is not pinched.

8. Install a new steering wheel retaining bolt and tighten to 23–33 ft. lbs. (31–48 Nm).

9. Connect the cruise control wire harness to the wheel and snap the connector assembly into the steering wheel clip. Make sure the wiring does not get trapped between the steering wheel and contact assembly.

10. Connect the air bag wire harness to the air bag module and install the module to the steering wheel. Tighten the module retaining nuts to 3–4 ft. lbs. (4–6 Nm).

11. Connect the air bag backup power supply and the negative battery cable. Verify the air bag warning indicator.

Combination Switch

The combination switch incorporates the turn signal, headlight dimmer, headlight flash-to-pass, hazard warning, cornering lights and windshield washer/wiper functions.

REMOVAL & INSTALLATION

➧ SEE FIG. 37–38

1. Disconnect the negative battery cable. If equipped with a tilt steering column, set the tilt column to its lowest position and remove the tilt lever by removing the Allen head retaining screw.

2. Remove the ignition lock cylinder. Remove the steering column shroud screws and remove the upper and lower shrouds.

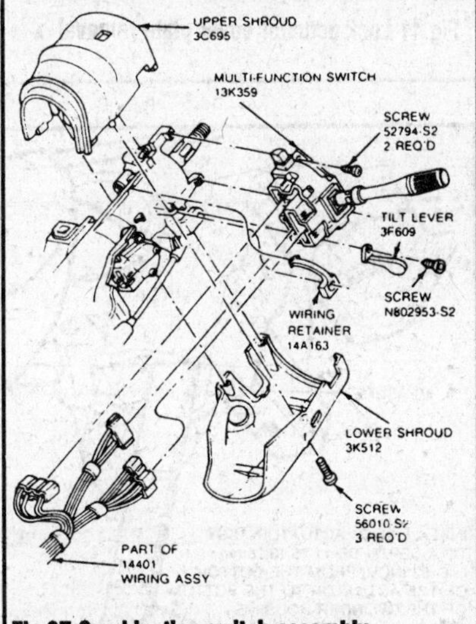

Fig.37 Combination switch assembly

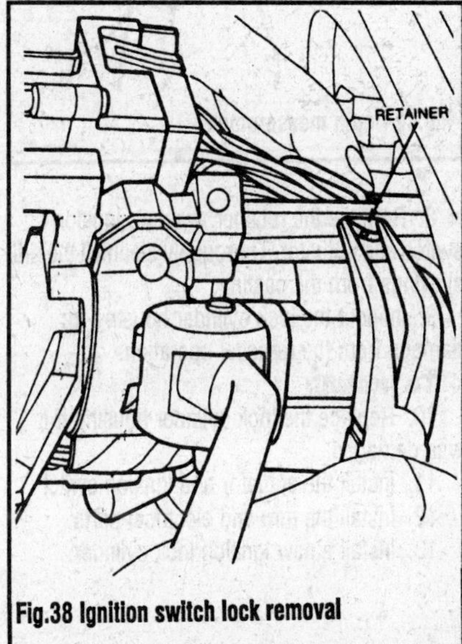

Fig.38 Ignition switch lock removal

3. Remove the wiring harness retainer and disconnect the 3 electrical connectors.

4. Remove the self tapping screws attaching the switch to the steering column and disengage the switch from the steering column casting.

To Install:

5. Align the turn signal switch mounting holes with the corresponding holes in the steering column and install self-tapping screws. Torque the screws to 17–26 inch lbs. (2–3 Nm).

6. Install the electrical connectors and install the wiring harness retainer.

7. Install the upper and lower steering column shroud and shroud retaining screws, torque the screws to 6–10 inch lbs. (0.7–1.1 Nm).

8. Install the ignition lock cylinder. Attach the tilt lever, if removed and torque the tilt lever Allen head retaining screw to 6–9 inch lbs. (0.7–1.0 Nm).

9. Connect the negative battery cable. Check the switch and the steering column for proper operation.

Ignition Lock Cylinder

REMOVAL & INSTALLATION

Functional Lock

The following procedure applies to vehicles that have functional lock cylinders. Lock cylinder keys are available for these vehicles or the lock cylinder key numbers are known and the proper key can be made.

1. Disconnect the negative battery cable.

2. Turn the lock cylinder key to the **RUN** position.

3. Using an 1/8 in. (3mm) diameter wire pin or a small drift, depress the lock cylinder retaining pin through the access hole, while pulling out on the lock cylinder to remove it from the column.

To Install:

4. Install the lock cylinder by turning it to the **RUN** position and depressing the retaining pin. Insert the lock cylinder into it's housing. Make sure the cylinder is fully seated and aligned in the interlocking washer before turning the key to the **OFF** position. This will permit the cylinder retaining pin to extend into the cylinder housing.

5. Rotate the lock cylinder using the lock cylinder key, to ensure correct mechanical operation in all positions.

6. Connect the negative battery cable.

Non-Functional Lock

The following procedure applies to vehicles in which the ignition lock is inoperative and the lock cylinder cannot be rotated due to a lost or broken lock cylinder key, unknown key number or a lock cylinder cap that has been damaged and/or broken to the extent that the lock cylinder cannot be rotated.

1986–90

➧ SEE FIG. 39–42

1. Disconnect the negative battery cable.
2. Remove the steering wheel.
3. Remove the 2 trim shroud halves by removing the 3 attaching screws.
4. Remove the electrical connector from the key warning switch.
5. Using an 1/8 in. (3mm) diameter drill, drill out the retaining pin, being careful not to drill deeper than 1/2 in. (13mm).
6. Place a suitable chisel at the base of the ignition lock cylinder cap and using a suitable hammer, strike the chisel with sharp blows to break the cap away from the lock cylinder.
7. Using a 3/8 in. (10mm) diameter drill, drill down the middle of the ignition key slot approximately 1 3/4 in. (44mm) until the lock cylinder breaks loose from the breakaway base of the lock cylinder. Remove the lock cylinder and drill shavings from the lock cylinder housing.

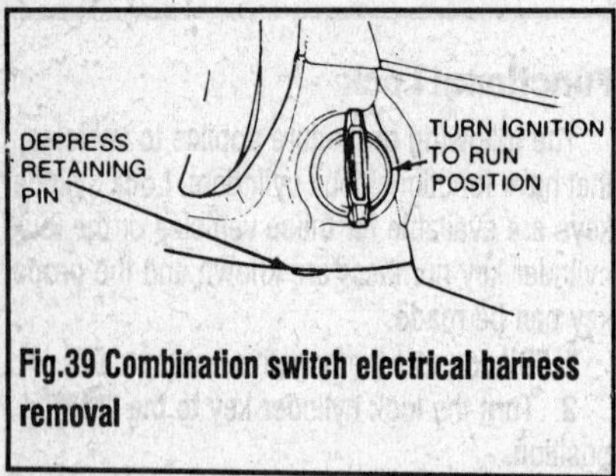

Fig.39 Combination switch electrical harness removal

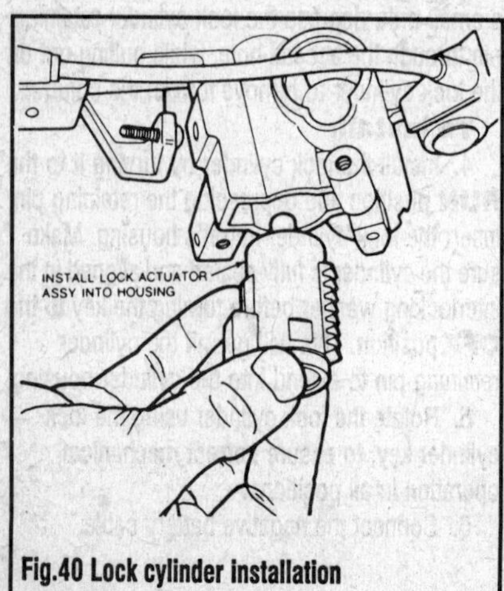

Fig.40 Lock cylinder installation

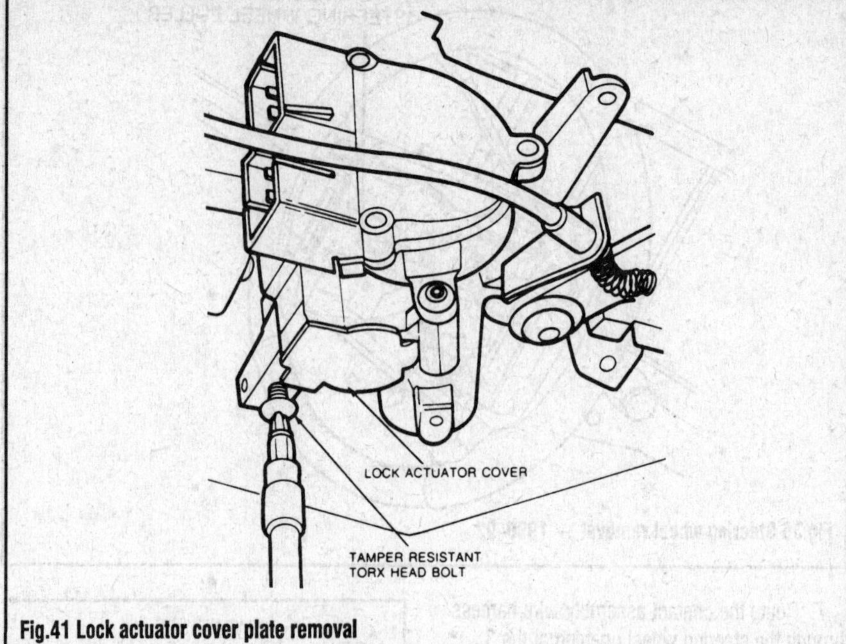

Fig.41 Lock actuator cover plate removal

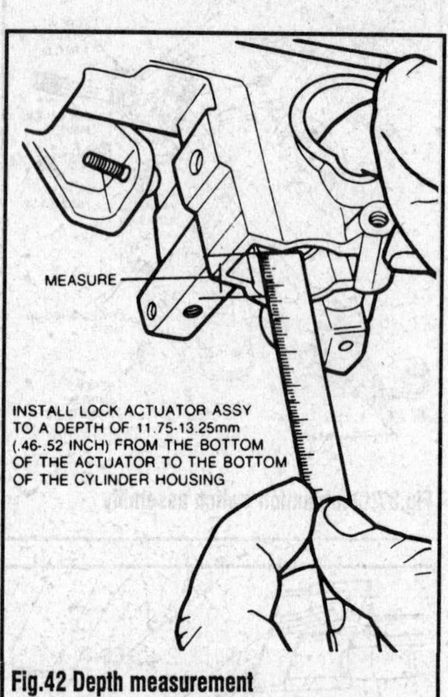

Fig.42 Depth measurement

8. Remove the retainer, washer, ignition switch and actuator. Thoroughly clean all the drill shavings from the casting.
9. Inspect the lock cylinder housing for damage from the removal operation.

To install:

10. Replace the lock cylinder housing if it was damaged.
11. Install the actuator and ignition switch.
12. Install the trim and electrical parts.
13. Install a new ignition lock cylinder.
14. Install the steering wheel.
15. Connect the negative battery cable.
16. Check the lock cylinder operation.

1991–92

1. Disconnect the negative battery cable.
2. Remove the steering wheel.
3. Using channel lock or vise grip pliers, twist the lock cylinder cap until it separates from the lock cylinder.
4. Using a 3/8 in. (10mm) diameter drill bit, drill down the middle of the ignition lock key slot approximately 1 3/4 in. (44mm) until the lock cylinder breaks loose from the breakaway base of the lock cylinder. Remove the lock cylinder and drill shavings from the lock cylinder housing.
5. Remove the retainer, washer, ignition switch and actuator. Thoroughly clean all drill shavings and other foreign materials from the casting.
6. Inspect the lock cylinder housing for damage from the removal operation. If the housing is damaged, it must be replaced.

To install:

7. Replace the lock cylinder housing, if damaged.
8. Install the actuator and ignition switch.
9. Install the trim and electrical parts.
10. Install the ignition lock cylinder.
11. Install the steering wheel.
12. Check the lock cylinder operation.

Ignition Switch

REMOVAL & INSTALLATION

1986-89

➧ SEE FIG. 43-44

1. Disconnect the negative battery cable.
2. Turn the ignition lock cylinder to the **RUN** position and depress the lock cylinder retaining pin through the access hole in the shroud with a 1/8 diameter punch.
3. Remove the lock cylinder. If equipped with tilt columns, remove the tilt release lever.
4. Remove the instrument panel lower cover and the steering column shroud.
5. Remove the 4 nuts attaching the steering column to the support bracket and lower the column.
6. Disconnect the ignition switch electrical connector.
7. Remove the lock actuator cover plate. The lock actuator assembly will slide freely out of the lock cylinder housing when the ignition switch is removed.
8. Remove the ignition switch and cover.

To Install:

9. Make sure the ignition switch is in the **RUN** position by rotating the driveshaft fully clockwise to the **START** position and releasing.
10. Install the lock actuator assembly to a depth of 0.46–0.52 in. (11.75–13.25mm) from the bottom of the actuator assembly to the bottom of the lock cylinder housing.
11. While holding the actuator assembly at the proper depth, install the ignition switch. Install the ignition switch cover and tighten the retaining bolts to 30–48 inch lbs. (3.4–5.4 Nm).
12. Install the lock cylinder. Rotate the ignition lock cylinder to the **LOCK** position and measure the depth of the actuator assembly as in Step 10. The actuator assembly must be 0.92–1.00 in. (23.5–25.5mm) inside the lock cylinder housing. If the depth measured does not meet specification, the actuator assembly must be removed and installed again.
13. Install the lock actuator cover plate and tighten the bolts to 30–48 inch lbs. (3.4–5.4 Nm).
14. Install the ignition switch electrical connector.
15. Connect the negative battery cable. Check the ignition switch for proper function in all positions, including **START** and **ACC**.
16. Check the column function as follows:
   a. With the column shift lever in the **P** position or with the floor shift key release button depressed and with the ignition lock cylinder in the **LOCK** position, make certain the steering column locks.
   b. Position the column shift lever in the **D** position or the floor shift key release button fully extended and rotate the cylinder lock to the **RUN** position. Continue to rotate the cylinder toward the **LOCK** position until it stops. In this position, make certain the engine and all electrical accessories are **OFF** and that the steering shaft does not lock.
   c. Turn the radio power button **ON**. Rotate the cylinder counterclockwise to the **ACC** position to verify that the radio is energized.
   d. Place the shift lever in **P** and rotate the cylinder clockwise to the **START** position to verify that the starter energizes.
17. Remove the ignition lock cylinder.
18. Align the steering column mounting holes with the support bracket, center the steering column in the instrument panel opening and install the 4 nuts. Tighten the nuts to 15–25 ft. lbs. (20–34 Nm).
19. Install the column trim shrouds and the instrument panel lower cover. Install the tilt release lever, if equipped.
20. Install the ignition lock cylinder.

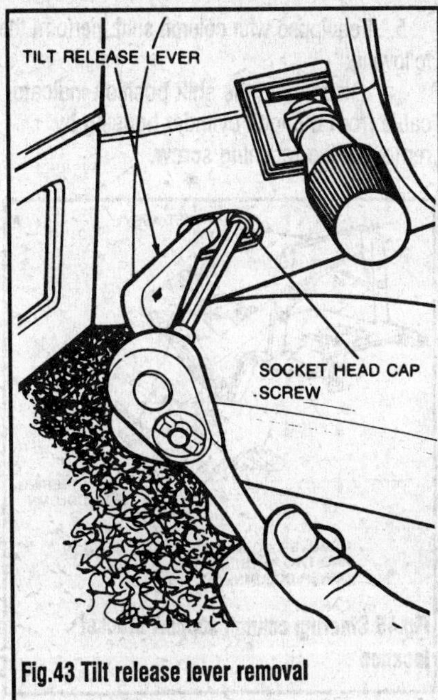
TILT RELEASE LEVER
SOCKET HEAD CAP SCREW
Fig.43 Tilt release lever removal

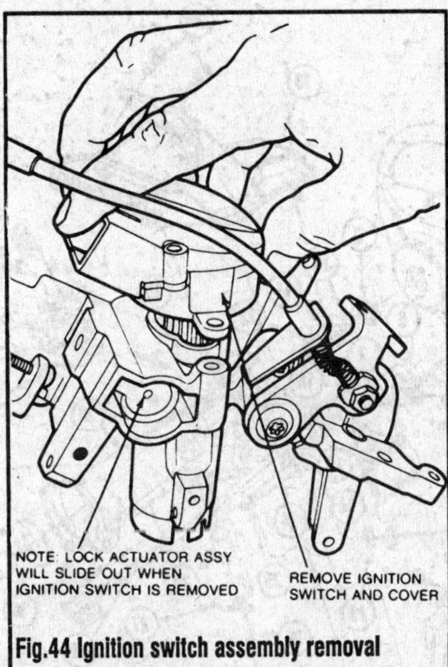
NOTE: LOCK ACTUATOR ASSY WILL SLIDE OUT WHEN IGNITION SWITCH IS REMOVED
REMOVE IGNITION SWITCH AND COVER
Fig.44 Ignition switch assembly removal

1990-92

1. Disconnect the negative battery cable.
2. Remove the steering column shroud by removing the self-tapping screws. Remove the tilt lever, if equipped.
3. Remove the instrument panel lower steering column cover.
4. Disconnect the ignition switch electrical connector.
5. Turn the ignition key lock cylinder to the **RUN** position.
6. Remove the 2 screws attaching the ignition switch and disengage the switch from the actuator pin.

To Install:

7. Adjust the ignition switch by sliding the carrier to the switch **RUN** position. A new replacement switch assembly will already be set in the **RUN** position.
8. Make sure the ignition key lock cylinder is in the **RUN** position. The **RUN** position is achieved by rotating the key lock cylinder approximately 90 degrees from the lock position.
9. Install the ignition switch into the actuator pin. It may be necessary to move the switch slightly back and forth to align the switch mounting holes with the column lock housing threaded holes.
10. Install the attaching screws and tighten to 50–69 inch lbs. (5.6–7.9 Nm).
11. Connect the electrical connector to the ignition switch.
12. Connect the negative battery cable.
13. Check the ignition switch for proper function, including **START** and **ACC** positions. Make sure the column is locked with the switch in the **LOCK** position.
14. Install the instrument panel lower steering column cover, the steering column trim shrouds and the tilt lever, if equipped.

Steering Column

REMOVAL & INSTALLATION

1986–89

➧ SEE FIG. 44–47

1. Disconnect the negative battery cable.
2. Remove the 4 self-tapping screws and remove the steering column cover from the lower portion of the instrument panel.
3. Remove the retaining screw and the tilt release lever. Remove the ignition lock cylinder.
4. Remove the 3 self-tapping screws from the bottom of the lower shroud and remove the steering column trim shrouds. Remove the steering wheel.

switch connector and remove the 2 self-

5. If equipped with column shift, perform the following:
   a. Disconnect the shift position indicator cable from the lock cylinder housing by removing the retaining screw.

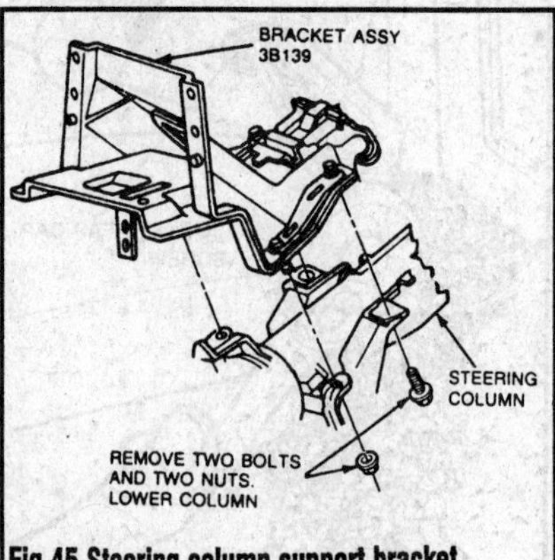

Fig.45 Steering column support bracket location

   b. Disconnect the shift position indicator cable from the shift socket.
   c. Remove the shift position indicator cable from the retaining hook on the bottom of the lock cylinder housing.
6. Using a punch, remove the shift lever-to-shift socket retaining pin and remove the shift lever.
7. Disconnect the cruise control/horn brush wiring connector from the main wiring harness.
8. Remove the combination switch wiring harness retainer from the lock cylinder housing by squeezing the end of the retainer and pushing out. Disconnect the combination tapping retaining screws. Remove the combination switch.
9. Disconnect the key warning buzzer switch wiring connector from the main wiring harness and disconnect the wiring connector from the ignition switch.

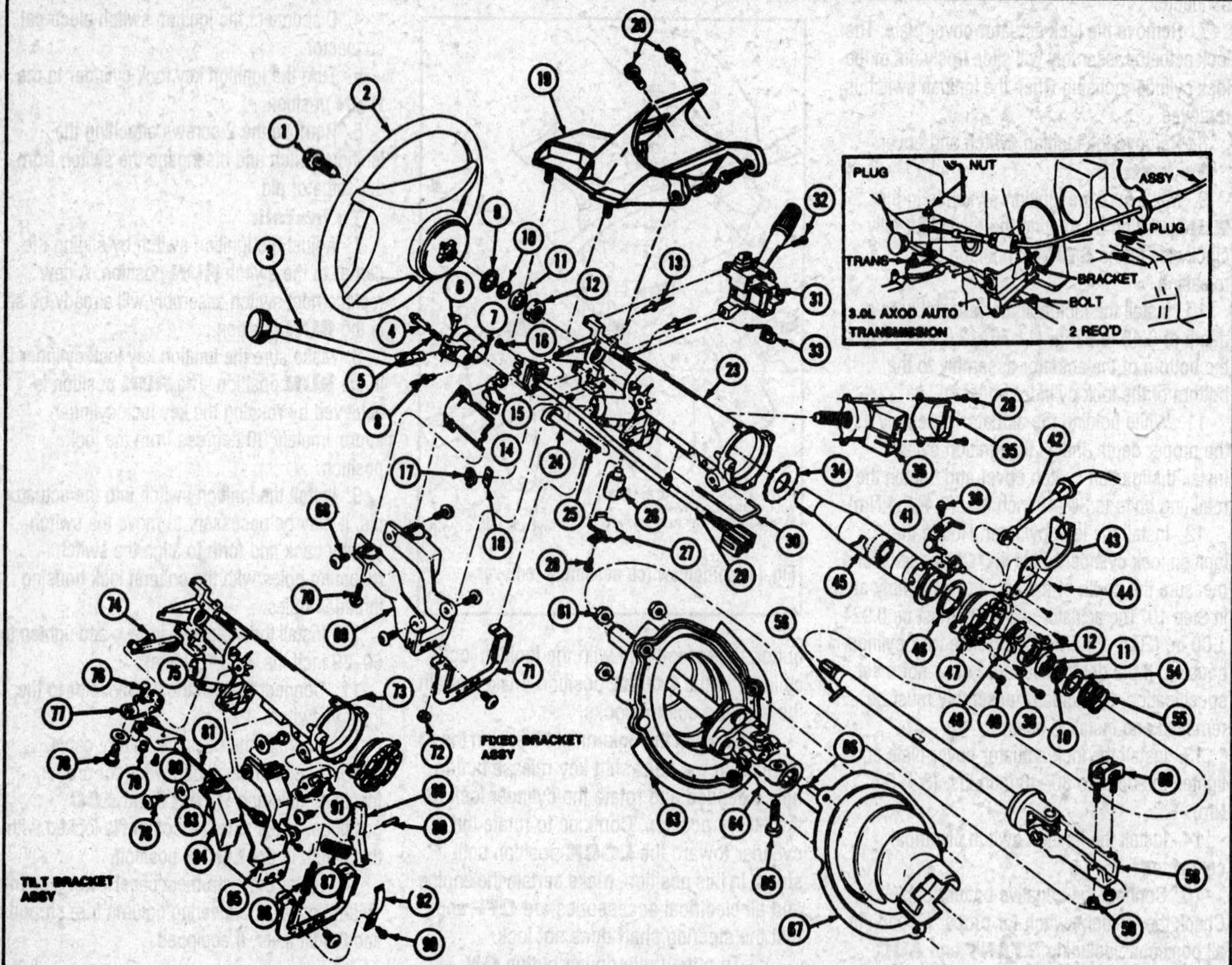

Fig.46 Steering column and related components — 1986–89

ITEM	PART NO.	DESCRIPTION	ITEM	PART NO.	DESCRIPTION
1	N805167	Bolt	45.	3K521	Tube and Bearing Assy.
2.	3600	Wheel	46.	3C708	Washer
3.	7202	Shift Lever	47.	3E738	Retainer
4.	7361	Plunger	48.	2B623	Parking Brake Rel. Switch
5.	7B071	Spring	49.	N804130	3 Screw Attach Retainer to Column
6.	7G357	Pin	54.	3D672	Spacer
7.	7228	Socket	55.	3C674	Spring
8.	380098	Rivet	56.	3E718	Pin
9.	3D640	Spacer	58.	3E729	Shaft Assy.
10.	3L539	Ring	59.	N620457	Nut — 2 Req'd.
11.	3517	Bearing Assy.	60.	3C088	Plate Assy.
12.	3518	Sleeve	61.	N804795-S2	Nut — 3 Req'd.
13.	3F643	Rivet Serviced	63.	3E735	Boot
*14.	3A673	Cover	64.		Intermediate Shaft
15.	3F643	Insert Serviced	65.	N803942	Bolt
16.	N804445-S2	Screw	66.		Steering Gear Input Shaft
17.	3F579	Retainer	67.	3E735	Boot
18.	3E700	Bearing	68.	N804086	Torx® Bolt — 5 Req'd. Also 2 Req'd.
19.		Not Used	69.	3E660	Fixed Bracket Assy.
20.	N805905	Bolt — 4 Req'd.	70.	N804140	Screw/Washer Assy. — 2 Req'd.
21.		Not Used	71.	3B632	Bracket
22.		Not Used	72.	N621939	Nut — 2 Req'd.
23.	3F643	Housing Assy.	73.	3F643	Pin Serviced
*24.	3F531	Key Release Knob	74.	N802953	Screw
*25.	3E696	Spring	75.	3F609	Handle Shank Assy.
26.	3E723	Actuator Assy.	76.	N804087	Bolt
27.	3E745	Actuator Cover	77.	3D544	Bracket
28.	N804089	Bolt — 3 Req'd.	78.	N804088	Bolt
29.	9C899	Brush Assy.	79.	N804084	Nut
*30.	3F528	Key Release Lever	80.	390345	Screw
31.	13K359	Turn Signal	81.	3F700	Bracket/Cable Assy.
32.	52794	Screw — 2 Req'd.	82.	3D655	Spring
33.	14A163	Wire Retainer	83.	N804085	Washer — 3 Req'd.
*34.	3K618	Bearing	84.	3E660	Tilt Bracket Assy.
35.		Not Used	85.	3D656	Bumper
36.	11572	Ignition Switch	86.	3D655	Spring
38.	N804444-S2	Screw — 3 Req'd.	87.	3D655	Spring
41.	2B624	Actuator	88.	3B662	Lever
42.	7E395	Cable	89.	N804090	Pin
43.	7E364	Bracket	90.	N804409	Screw — 7 Req'd.
44.	N805771	Screw — 2 Req'd.	91.	3F716	Locator

*Floor Shift only.

Fig.46a Steering column and related components — 1986–89 continued

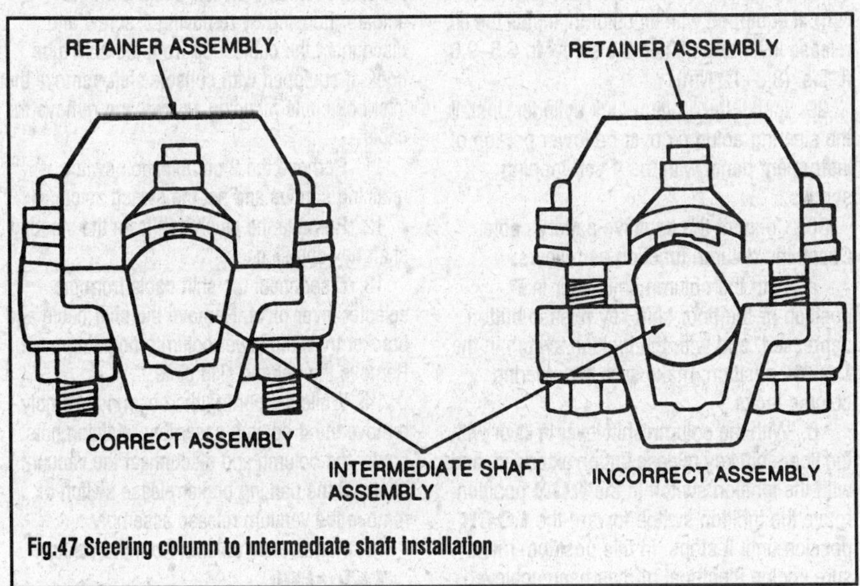

Fig.47 Steering column to intermediate shaft installation

10. Disconnect the steering shaft from the intermediate shaft by removing 2 nuts and 1 U-clamp. If equipped with an air bag, wire the lower end of the steering shaft to the column housing to prevent rotation of the steering shaft. Rotating the steering shaft could damage the air bag contact clockspring if the steering wheel is attached to the column.

11. If equipped with column shift, perform the following:

a. Remove the shift cable plastic terminal from the column selector lever pivot ball using a small prybar and prying between the plastic terminal and the selector lever. Be careful not to damage the cable during or after assembly.

b. Remove the shift cable bracket, with shift cable still attached, from the lock cylinder housing by removing the 2 retaining screws.

12. If equipped with an automatic parking brake release mechanism, remove the vacuum hoses from the parking brake release switch.

13. Remove the 2 nuts retaining the rear column assembly. Loosen the 2 nuts retaining

the front column assembly to the end of the studs, but do not remove at this time.

14. Use a downward force to disengage the column assembly push-on clips from the rear attachments. Remove the remaining 2 nuts.

➡ **When forcing downward, care should be taken to avoid damaging the safety slip-clips on the steering column.**

15. Carefully lower the steering column assembly and remove from the vehicle.

To install:

16. Raise the steering column assembly into position and align the 4 mounting holes over the 4 support bracket studs. Hand start the 4 retaining nuts.

17. Center the column assembly in the instrument panel opening and tighten the 4 nuts to 15–25 ft. lbs. (21–33 Nm).

18. If equipped with an automatic parking brake release mechanism, install the vacuum hoses on the parking brake release switch.

19. If equipped with column shift, perform the following:

a. Attach the cable shift bracket, with the shift cable attached, to the lock cylinder housing and tighten the retaining screws to 5–7 ft. lbs. (7–9 Nm).

b. Snap the transaxle shift cable terminal to the selector lever pivot ball on the steering column.

20. Apply a generous amount of grease to the V-shaped steering shaft yoke. Connect the steering shaft to the intermediate shaft with 1 U-clamp and 2 hex nuts. When installing the steering column to the intermediate shaft, connect the intermediate shaft to the steering column with the retainer assembly and 2 nuts.

➡ **Make sure the V-angle of the intermediate shaft fits correctly into the V-angle of the mating steering column yoke. If the V-angle is mis-aligned and the retainer is tightened, the retainer plate will be bent and then must be replaced.**

21. After correctly installing the steering column to the intermediate shaft, tighten the nuts to 15–25 ft. lbs. (21–33 Nm).

➡ **Tilt columns must be in the middle tilt position before the nuts are tightened.**

22. Connect the main wiring harness connector to the ignition switch and connect the key warning buzzer switch wiring connector to the main harness. Install the steering sensor wire connector to the sensor lead connector.

23. Install the combination switch and tighten the 2 self-tapping screws to 18–26 inch lbs. (2.0–2.9 Nm). Install the combination switch wiring harness retainer over the shroud mounting boss and snap it into the slot in the lock cylinder housing.

24. Connect the cruise control/horn brush wiring connector to the main wiring harness.

25. If equipped with column shift, install the shift position indicator cable into the retaining hook on the lock cylinder housing, connect the cable to the shift socket and loosely install the cable onto the lock cylinder housing with 1 screw. Adjust the shift position indicator cable as follows:

a. Place the shift lever in **D** on Taurus equipped with the 2.5L engine. On all others, place the shift lever in **OD**. A weight of 8 lbs. should be hung on the shift selector lever to make sure the lever is firmly against the **D** or **OD** drive detent.

b. Adjust the cable until the indicator pointer completely covers the **D** or **OD**, then tighten the screw to 18–30 inch lbs. (2.0–3.4 Nm).

c. Cycle the shift lever through all positions and check that the shift position indicator completely covers the proper letter or number in each position.

26. Install the shift lever into the shift lever socket and install a new shift lever retaining pin. Use care to avoid damaging the shift position indicator post on the shift socket.

27. Place the combination switch in the middle position and install the steering wheel.

28. Install the shrouds with the retaining screws. Tighten to 6–10 inch lbs. (0.7–1.1 Nm). If equipped with tilt column, install the tilt release lever and tighten the screw to 6.5–9.0 ft. lbs. (8.8–12 Nm).

29. Install the ignition lock cylinder. Install the steering column cover on lower portion of instrument panel with the 4 self-tapping screws.

30. Connect the negative battery cable. Check the column function as follows:

a. With the column shift lever in **P** position or the floor shift key release button depressed, and with the ignition switch in the **LOCK** position; make sure the steering column locks.

b. With the column shift lever in **D** or with the floor shift key release button extended, and with the ignition switch in the **RUN** position; rotate the ignition switch toward the **LOCK** position until it stops. In this position, make sure engine electrical off has been achieved and that the steering shaft does not lock.

c. On tilt columns, check column tilt travel through it's entire range to make sure there is no interference between the column and instrument panel.

d. Cycle the combination switch through all of it's functions.

1990–92

➧ SEE FIG. 57–60

1. Disconnect the negative battery cable. Lower the glove compartment past it's stops and disconnect the air bag backup power supply.

2. Remove the steering wheel.

3. Remove the left and right lower moldings from the instrument panel by pulling up and snapping out of the retainers.

4. Remove the instrument panel lower trim cover and the lower steering column shroud.

5. Disconnect the air bag clockspring contact assembly wire harness. Apply 2 strips of tape across the contact assembly stator and rotor to prevent accidental rotation. Remove the 3 contact assembly retaining screws and pull the contact assembly off the steering column shaft.

6. Remove the tilt lever by unscrewing it from the column.

7. Rotate the ignition lock cylinder to the **RUN** position. Using an 1/8 in. (3mm) drift, depress the lock cylinder retaining pin through the access hole and remove the lock cylinder.

8. Remove the 4 retaining screws from the lower shroud and remove the steering column shrouds.

9. Remove the 2 instrument panel reinforcement brace retaining bolts and remove the reinforcement.

10. If equipped with column shift, disconnect the shift position indicator cable from the actuator housing by removing 1 screw and disconnect the cable loop from the shift tube hook. If equipped with console shift, remove the interlock cable retaining screws and remove the cable.

11. Remove the 2 combination switch retaining screws and set the switch aside.

12. Remove the pinch bolt from the steering shaft flex coupling.

13. Disconnect the shift cable from the selector lever pivot. Remove the shift cable and bracket from the lower column mounting. Remove the column skid plate.

14. While supporting the column assembly, remove the 4 column assembly retaining nuts. Lower the column and disconnect the vacuum hoses at the parking brake release switch or remove the vacuum release assembly.

15. Remove the column from the vehicle.

To install:

16. Align the column lower universal joint to the lower shaft. Install 1 bolt and tighten to 29–41 ft. lbs. (40–56 Nm). Connect the parking brake release vacuum hoses.

17. Support the column assembly to the column support bracket. Install the 4 retaining nuts and tighten to 10–14 ft. lbs. (13–19 Nm).

18. Position the shift cable bracket, with the shift cable attached, to the lower 2 screws of the column. Tighten to 5–8 ft. lbs. (7–11 Nm). Snap the shift cable onto the shift selector pivot ball.

19. If equipped with automatic console shift, position the interlock cable and install the 2 retaining screws.

20. Position the combination switch and install the 2 retaining screws. Tighten to 18–26 inch lbs. (2–3 Nm). Connect all electrical connectors.

21. If equipped with column shift, attach the shift position indicator cable loop on the shift selector hook and install the cable bracket to the actuator housing. Install the retaining screw and tighten to 5–8 ft. lbs. (7–11 Nm).

22. Install the steering column skid plate and tighten the retaining nuts to 15–25 ft. lbs. (20–34 Nm).

23. Install the upper and lower column shrouds and the instrument panel reinforcement brace.

24. Install the lower instrument panel cover. Snap the right and left lower instrument panel moldings into place.

25. Install the lock cylinder assembly and the tilt lever.

26. Install the air bag clockspring contact assembly screws and tighten to 18–26 inch lbs. (2–3 Nm). Route the contact assembly down the column and connect to the wire harness.

➡ **If a new contact assembly is being installed, remove the plastic lock mechanism after the contact assembly is secured to the column.**

27. Install the steering wheel with a new bolt. Tighten to 23–33 ft. lbs. (31–48 Nm). Position the air bag module to the steering wheel. Install the 4 retaining nuts and tighten to 3–4 ft. lbs. (4–6 Nm).

28. Connect the air bag backup power supply and the negative battery cable. Verify the air bag warning indicator.

DISASSEMBLY

1986–89

1. Disconnect the negative battery cable. Remove the steering column assembly from the vehicle.

2. Disengage the speed control horn brush wiring from the lock cylinder housing, by removing the two wiring retainers from their holes.

3. Remove the speed control horn brush by first removing one hex head self tapping screw.

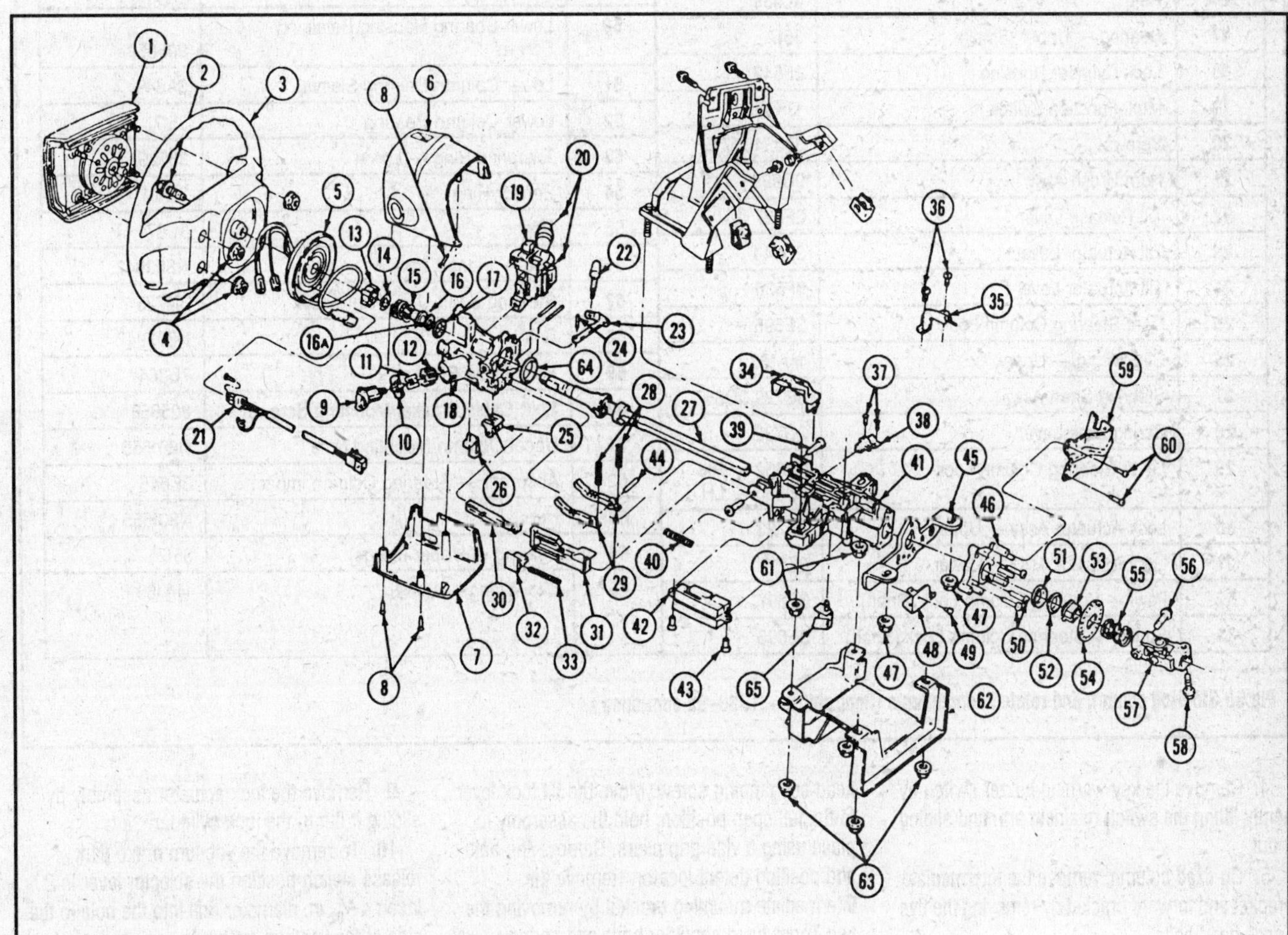

Fig.57 Steering column and related components (floor shift) — 1990–92

Item	Description	Part No.	Item	Description	Part No.
1	Air Bag Module	—	34	Shield	14A099
2	Steering Wheel Bolt	N804385-S100	35	Trans Control Selector Position Insert	7A216
3	Steering Wheel	—	36	Screws	N805858
4	Air Bag Module Retaining Nuts	—	37	Screws	390345-S36
5	Air Bag Clockspring Contact Assy	14A664	38	Parking Brake Vacuum Release Switch	2B623
6	Upper Column Shroud	3530	39	Tilt Pivot Screws	N805865
7	Lower Column Shroud	3533	40	Spring — Steering Column Position Lock	3D655
8	Shroud Retaining Screws	55929	41	Actuator Housing	3F723
9	Ignition Lock Cylinder Assy	11572	42	Ignition Switch	—
10	Retainer	3F579	43	Screws	N805858
11	Bearing	3E700	44	Pin — Pivot Lever	3F530
12	Gear — Steering Lock	3E717	45	Lower Column Bracket	3B632
13	Turn Signal Cancelling Cam	13318	46	Lower Bearing Housing Retainer	3E738
14	Snap Ring	3C610	47	Lower Column Mounting Nuts	N801555
15	Spring — Upper Bearing	3520	48	Bracket	14A206
16	Sleeve	3518	49	Screw	N804409
16A	Ring	3L539	50	Lower Bearing Housing Retaining Screws	805859
17	Bearing — Upper (Small)	3517	51	Lower Column Bearing Sleeve	3A649
18	Lock Cylinder Housing	3F642	52	Lower Column Bearing	3517
19	Multi-Function Switch	13K359	53	Tolerance Ring — Lower	36539
20	Screws	390345-S36	54	Sensor Ring	3C131
21	Horn Brush Assy	9C899	55	Spring	3C674
22	Tilt Release Lever	3F527	56	Bolt — Flange Yoke	N803942
23	Tilt Actuator Lever	3D544	57	Steering Shaft U — Joint Assy	3N725
24	Tilt Actuator Lever Pin	3F530	58	Bolt	N803942
25	Cam Steering Column Lock	3E695	59	Shift Cable Bracket	7E364
26	Clip Wiring — Upper	14A163	60	Shift Cable Bracket Mounting Screws	805858
27	Steering Shaft Assy	3E729 3D657	61	Upper Column Mounting Nuts	N801555
28	Spring Lock Lever	3C732	62	Absorber — Steering Column Impact	3E645
29	Lever Steering Column Lock	3B662 — RH 3D653 — LH	63	Nuts	N801555
30	Lock Actuator Assy — Upper	3E723	64	Bearing — Upper (Large)	3517
31	Lock Actuator Assy — Lower	3E715	65	Clip Wiring — Lower	14A163
32	Pawl — Steering Column Lock (Shaft)	3E691			
33	Spring — Steering Column Lock (Shaft)	3E696			

Fig.58 Steering column and related components (floor shift) — 1990–92 continued

4. Remove the key warning buzzer switch by gently lifting the switch retaining arm and sliding it out.

5. On fixed column, remove the intermediate bracket and forward bracket by removing the five Torx® head bolts.

6. On tilt column, remove the tilt position spring and detent position spring. Remove the forward bracket from the intermediate bracket by removing the one Torx® head bolt. Loosen the tilt release cable and the tilt release lever by removing the one Torx® head bolt and one Torx® head self tapping screw. Move the tilt lock lever to the full open position, hold the assembly in place using a vise grip pliers. Remove the bolt and position detent locator. Remove the intermediate mounting bracket by removing the two Torx® head shoulder bolts and spring washers.

7. Remove the ignition switch and cover by removing the two tamper resistant Torx® head bolts.

8. Remove the lock actuator cover by removing the one tamper resistant Torx® head bolt.

9. Remove the lock actuator assembly by sliding it out of the lock cylinder.

10. To remove the vacuum brake park release switch position the selector lever in D. Insert a $\frac{3}{32}$ in. diameter drill into the hole in the side of the vacuum switch in order to lock the assembly in place. Remove the switch actuator by removing one hex head self tapping screw. Remove the switch by removing two hex head self tapping screws.

11. To remove the steering shaft perform the following:

a. Make a tool from a piece of tubing — 1 in. (25mm) long × 2½ in. (63.5mm) in diameter.

b. Install the tool on the shaft. Align the tool over the shaft aligning slot which is over the steering shaft retainer pin.

c. Install the steering wheel bolt and washer. Tighten the bolt enough to relieve spring tension on the shaft retaining pin.

d. Using a $^{5}/_{32}$ in.(4mm) diameter drift punch, tap the retaining pin out of the steering shaft. Discard the pin.

e. Remove the steering wheel bolt, washer and tool. Remove the steering shaft retaining washer. Remove the upper alignment wedge from the steering shaft.

f. Slide the steering shaft from the lock cylinder housing and remove the lower alignment washer and preload spring.

13. If the vehicle is equipped with a column shift, perform the following:

a. Using a $^{5}/_{32}$ in. (4mm) diameter drift pin punch tap the retaining pin out of the shift socket and shift lever. Discard the pin and pin retainer.

b. Remove the shift lever from the shift socket. Rotate the shift socket fully in the counterclockwise direction.

c. Using a $^{3}/_{16}$ in. (5mm) drill, carefully drill out the pop rivet that attaches the shift tube socket to the shift tube.

d. Remove the lower bearing retainer by removing the three hex head bolts. Remove the bearing retainer and the shift tube preload washer from the shift tube.

e. Remove the shift tube. Remove the shift socket assembly. The shift tube is a tight fit. Effort is required in order to disengage the socket from the tube.

14. If the vehicle is equipped with a floor shift, perform the following:

a. Remove the key release actuating button by clamping a vise grip pliers around the button shank and against the button head. Sharply rap the pliers until the button is free. Discard the button.

b. Remove the return spring from the actuator and remove the actuator.

c. To remove the steering shaft center bearing from the lock cylinder insert a large diameter socket into the shift socket opening and attach it to a long extension which is inserted through the upper bearing opening in the housing.

d. Position a socket against the bearing and tap the extension until the bearing is free.

15. Remove the upper bearing from the housing by pushing it out from the rear.

16. Remove the lower bearing from the housing by pushing it out from the rear. Slip the bearing sleeves off the bearings.

To Install:

17. Install the metal bearing into the lock cylinder bore. Install the plastic bearing retainer into the lock cylinder bore. Slip the bearing sleeves over the upper and lower bearings.

18. Install the lower bearing and sleeve assembly into the lower bearing retainer.

19. Install the upper bearing and sleeve assembly into the lock cylinder housing.

20. If the vehicle is equipped with a floor shifter, perform the following:

a. Install the steering shaft center bearing into the lock cylinder housing. Insert a large diameter socket attached to a long extension into the lower opening in the housing. Place the socket against the bearing and gently tap the extension until the bearing is seated.

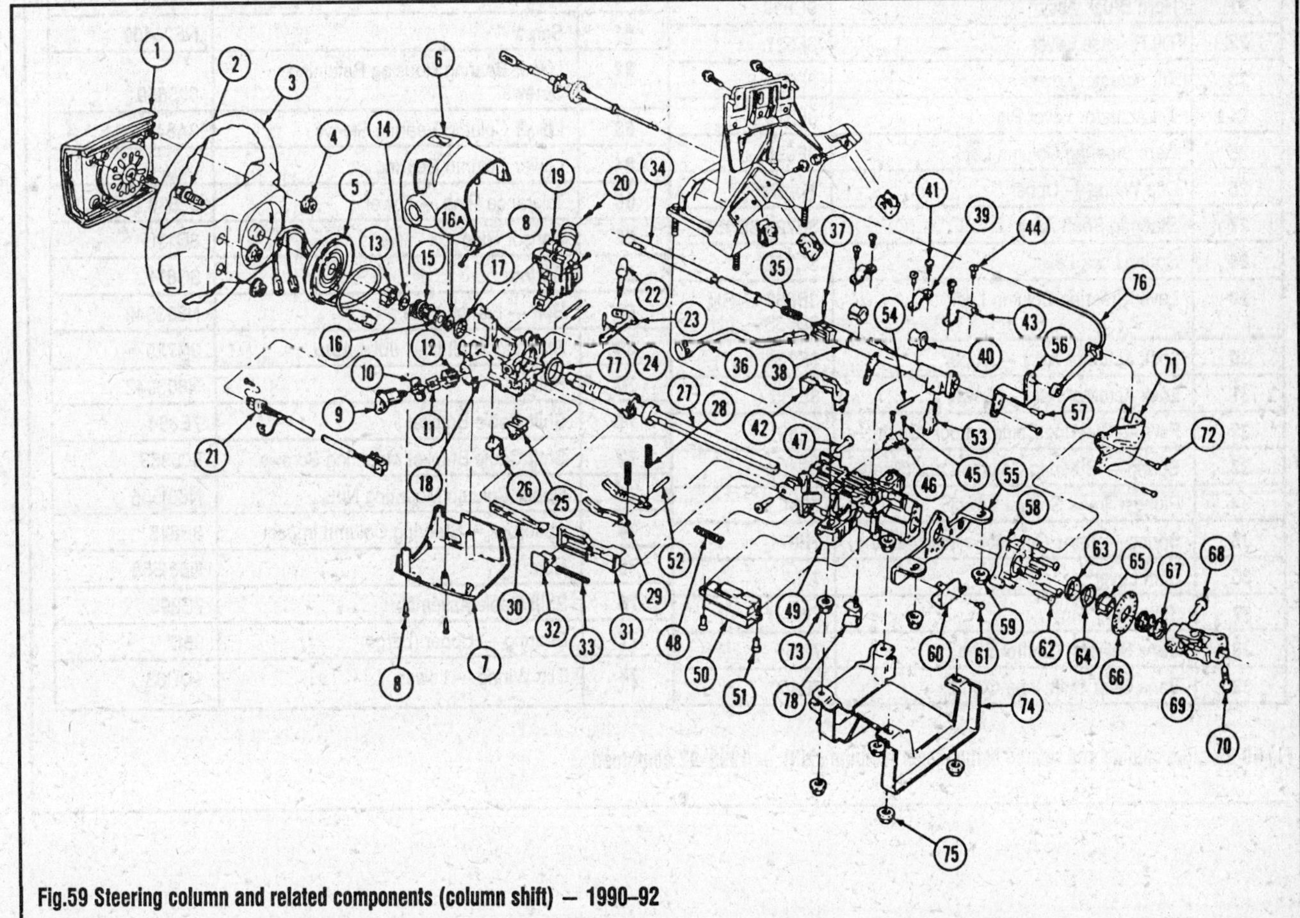

Fig.59 Steering column and related components (column shift) — 1990–92

Item	Description	Part No.
1	Air Bag Module	—
2	Steering Wheel Bolt	N804385-S100
3	Steering Wheel	—
4	Air Bag Module Retaining Nuts	—
5	Air Bag Clockspring Contact Assy	14A664
6	Upper Column Shroud	3530
7	Lower Column Shroud	3533
8	Shroud Retaining Screws	55929
9	Ignition Lock Cylinder Assy	11572
10	Retainer	3F579
11	Bearing	3E700
12	Gear — Steering Lock	3E717
13	Turn Signal Cancelling Cam	13318
14	Snap Ring	3C610
15	Spring — Upper Bearing	3520
16	Sleeve	3518
16A	Ring	3L539
17	Bearing — Upper (Small)	3517
18	Lock Cylinder Housing	3F642
19	Multi — Function Switch	13K359
20	Screws	390345-S36
21	Horn Brush Assy	9C899
22	Tilt Release Lever	3F527
23	Tilt Actuator Lever	3D544
24	Tilt Actuator Lever Pin	3F530
25	Cam Steering Column Lock	3E695
26	Clip Wiring — Upper	14A163
27	Steering Shaft Assy	3E729 3D657
28	Spring Lock Lever	3C732
29	Lever Steering Column Lock	3B662 — RH 3D653 — LH
30	Lock Actuator Assy — Upper	3E723
31	Lock Actuator Assy — Lower	3E715
32	Pawl — Steering Column Lock (Shaft)	3E691
33	Spring — Steering Column Lock (Shaft)	3E696
34	Plunger Trans Control Select	7361
35	Spring — Trans Control Selector Return	7B071
36	Shift Lever	7302
37	Shift Lever Pin	7W441
38	Trans Selector Control Tube	7215
39	Trans Gear Shift Tube Clamps	7E400
40	Bushings	7335
41	Screws	N805858
42	Shield	14A099
43	Trans Control Selector Position Insert	7A216
44	Screws	N805858
45	Screws	390345-S36
46	Parking Brake Vacuum Release Switch	2B623
47	Tilt Pivot Screws	N805865
48	Spring — Steering Column Position Lock	3D655
49	Actuator Housing	3F723
50	Ignition Switch	—
51	Screws	N805858
52	Pin — Pivot Lever	3F530
53	Pawl Steering Column Lock Shifter	3E691
54	Pin — Steering Column Lock Shifter	3B663
55	Lower Column Bracket	3B632
56	Trans Control Selector Lower Lever	7D282
57	Screws	805858
58	Lower Bearing Housing Retainer	3E738
59	Lower Column Mounting Nuts	N801555
60	Bracket	14A206
61	Screw	N804409
62	Lower Bearing Housing Retaining Screws	805859
63	Lower Column Bearing Sleeve	3A649
64	Lower Column Bearing	3517
65	Tolerance Ring — Lower	3L539
66	Sensor Ring	3C131
67	Spring	3C674
68	Bolt — Flange Yoke	N803942
69	Steering Shaft U — Joint Assy	3N725
70	Bolt	N803942
71	Shift Cable Bracket	7E364
72	Shift Cable Bracket Mounting Screws	805858
73	Upper Column Mounting Nuts	N801555
74	Absorber — Steering Column Impact	3E645
75	Nuts	N801555
76	Shift Cable Assembly	7E395
77	Bearing — Upper (Large)	3517
78	Clip Wiring — Lower	14A163

Fig.60 Steering column and related components (column shift) – 1990–92 continued

b. Install the key release actuator into the lock cylinder housing and install the return spring over the actuator.

c. Install a new key release actuating button over the actuator and apply pressure to the button head while supporting the actuator until the button snaps in place.

21. If the vehicle is equipped with a column shift perform the following:

a. Grease the lock cylinder housing bearing surface and install the shift socket.

b. Install the shift tube into the lock cylinder housing and into the shift socket assembly.

c. Grease the bearing surfaces on the shift tube and position the preload washer on the shift tube.

d. Grease the bearing surface on the lower retainer and install it on the lock cylinder housing. Hand tighten the three hex head bolts.

e. Rotate the shift socket fully to the counterclockwise direction and align the hole in the shift socket with the hole in the shift tube.

f. Using a $\frac{3}{16}$ in. (5mm) pop rivet, attach the shift socket to the shift tube.

g. Tighten the three hex head retaining bolts attaching the lower bearing retainer to the lock cylinder housing 42–60 inch lbs.

h. Grease the shift socket bearing surface and install the shift lever into the shift socket.

i. Attach the shift lever to shift socket with a new pin and pin retainer.

22. To install the steering shaft, perform the following:

a. Install the preload spring, washer and lower alignment wedge over the steering shaft and slide the steering shaft into the lock cylinder housing.

b. Install the upper alignment wedge and retaining washer over the steering shaft. Fabricate a tool from a piece of tubing — 1 in. (25mm) long × 2$\frac{1}{2}$ in. (63.5mm) in diameter.

c. Install the tool on the shaft aligning pin clearance slot which is over the shaft retaining pin hole.

d. Install the steering wheel bolt and washer. Tighten the bolt to compress the spring enough to provide adequate clearance to the shaft retaining pin hole.

e. Install the shaft retaining pin. Remove the steering wheel bolt, washer and tool.

23. To install the parking brake release vacuum switch perform the following:

a. Position the transaxle selector lever in the D detent. Install the vacuum switch. Tighten the retaining bolts 20–32 inch lbs.

b. Install the switch actuator to the lower shift arm. Tighten the retaining screw to 20–32 inch lbs.

c. Remove the drill from the hole in the side of the vacuum switch.

24. To install the ignition switch and the lock actuator perform the following:

a. Position the switch in the RUN position. Install the lock actuator assembly to a depth of 0.46–0.52 in. (11.6–13.2mm) from the bottom of the actuator assembly to the bottom of the lock cylinder housing.

b. While holding the actuator assembly in place, install the ignition switch assembly.

c. Install the ignition switch cover. Tighten the retaining screws to 30–48 inch lbs. Install the lock cylinder.

d. Rotate the ignition switch to the lock position and measure the depth of the actuator assembly. It must be 0.92–1.00 in. (23.3–25.4mm).

e. Install the lock actuator cover plate using a tamper resistant Torx® head screw. Torque to 30–48 inch lbs.

25. If equipped with a tilt column, perform the following:

a. Move the tilt lock lever on the intermediate mounting bracket to the full open position and clamp it in that position using a vise grip pliers.

b. Install the intermediate mounting bracket to the lock cylinder housing. Torque the retaining screws to 15–25 ft. lbs.

c. With the column positioned in the mid tilt position remove the vise grips. Install the position detent locator to the lock cylinder housing. Tighten the bolt to 30–60 inch lbs.

d. Install the forward mounting bracket to the intermediate bracket. Torque the retaining screws 12–20 ft. lbs.

e. Install the position detent spring and bolt. Finger tighten the bolt. Position the steering column in the mid tilt position.

f. Align the detent spring to the center notch in the detent locator. Tighten the bolt 6–10 ft. lbs. Install the tilt position spring.

g. Install the tilt release cable and tilt release lever to the lock cylinder housing. Torque the bolts to 15–25 ft. lbs. and the screw to 36–60 inch lbs.

h. Loosen the cable adjusting nut. Push the tilt release lever toward the lower end of the column until it reaches the stop on the cable bracket. Tighten the adjusting nut 30–60 inch lbs. while holding the lever in this position.

26. If equipped with a fixed column install the intermediate and forward mounting brackets to the lock cylinder housing. Tighten the retaining bolts 15–25 ft. lbs.

27. Install the key warning buzzer switch switch. Install the speed control/horn brush assembly. Torque the retaining screw to 18–30 inch lbs. Install the horn pad.

28. Install the steering column assembly in the vehicle.

1990–92

1. Disconnect the negative battery cable. Remove the steering wheel. Remove the steering column from the vehicle.

2. Remove the lower U-joint, spring, sensor ring and bushing.

3. Remove the turn signal canceling cam by pushing upward using a suitable tool. Note the direction of the flush surface.

4. Remove the ignition switch assembly. Remove the upper snapring and coil spring.

5. Remove the steel sleeve and ring. Remove the shift control assembly and shift control bracket, column shift vehicles.

6. Remove the shift cable bracket on column shift vehicles. Using a drift tap lock actuator cam pivot pin loose.

7. Remove the plastic bearing retainer from the lock cylinder bore. Remove the metal bearing from the lock cylinder bore. Remove the ignition lock gear.

8. Remove the two tilt pivot bolts. Use caution as the tilt spring will release when the bolts are removed. Remove the lock cylinder housing.

9. Remove the steering shaft from the column assembly. Remove the column lock actuator. Remove the lower bearing and mounting bracket.

10. Remove the tilt position lever arm pivot pin using a drift. Remove the lever lock arms and springs.

To install:

11. Install the steering shaft into the housing. Install the lower bearing and column mounting bracket. Tighten the screws to 5–8 ft. lbs.

12. Install the sensor ring, bushing, spring and flex coupling to the steering shaft. Tighten the pinch bolt to 29–41 ft. lbs.

13. Position the lock actuator assembly in the housing. Position the actuator cam in the lock housing and install the cam pivot pin. Be sure the pin is flush with the housing.

14. Install one tilt lever spring and arm into the housing. Install the outer lever spring and arm with the pivot pin. Tap the pin in place while driving out the drift.

15. Support the housing in a vise and drive the pin flush with the housing. Position the two nuts or spacers to hold the tilt lock arms away from the housing.

16. Position the tilt spring on the lock housing. With an assistant, install the lock housing and pivot bolts. Torque them to 14–20

ft. lbs. Lube the pivot bolts with grease before installation.

17. Install the steel sleeve and ring gear over the steering shaft and onto the upper bearing.

18. Install the spring and a new snapring on the top side of the spring using a 3/4 in. × 2 1/4 in. (19mm × 57mm) PVC pipe. Install the turn signal cancel cam, flush surface UP.

19. Install the ignition switch. Align the pin from the switch with the slot in the lock/column assembly. Position the slot in the assembly with the index mark on the casting. Torque the retaining screws 5–8 inch lbs.

20. Install the ignition lock gear. Coat the gear with grease before installation.

21. Install the metal bearing. Coat the metal bearing with grease before installation.

22. Install the plastic bearing retainer. Install the shift control tube assembly. Coat the bushings with grease prior to installation. Torque the retaining screws 5–8 ft. lbs.

23. Install the shift cable bracket on the lower column bearing assembly.

24. Install the steering column in the vehicle.

Steering Linkage

REMOVAL & INSTALLATION

Tie Rod Ends

1. Remove and discard the cotter pin and nut from the worn tie rod end ball stud.

2. Disconnect the tie rod end from the steering spindle, using tie rod remover tool 3290–D or equivalent.

3. Hold the tie rod end with a wrench and loosen the tie rod jam nut.

4. Note the depth to which the tie rod is located, then grip the tie rod with a pair of suitable pliers and remove the tie rod end assembly from the tie rod.

To Install:

5. Clean the tie rod threads. Thread the new tie rod end into the tie rod to the same depth as the removed tie rod end.

6. Place the tie rod end stud into the steering spindle. Make sure the front wheels are pointed straight-ahead before connecting the stud to the spindle.

7. Install a new nut on the tie rod end stud. Tighten the nut to 35 ft. lbs. (48 Nm) and continue tightening until the next castellation on the nut is aligned with the cotter pin hole in the stud. Install a new cotter pin.

8. Set the toe to specification. Tighten the jam nut to 35–50 ft. lbs. (47–68 Nm).

Power Steering Rack

ADJUSTMENTS

Integral Power Rack and Pinion Except 1990–92 Taurus LX and Sable with 3.8L Engine

RACK YOKE PLUG CLEARANCE

➡ **The rack yoke clearance adjustment is not a normal service adjustment. It is only required when the input shaft and valve assembly is removed.**

1. Remove the steering gear from the vehicle. Clean the exterior of the steering gear thoroughly.

2. Install the steering gear in a suitable holding fixture. Do not remove the external transfer tubes unless they are leaking or damaged. If these lines are removed, they must be replaced with new ones.

3. Drain the power steering fluid by rotating the input shaft lock-to-lock twice, using a suitable tool. Cover the ports on the valve housing with a shop cloth while draining the gear to avoid possible oil spray.

4. Insert an inch pound torque wrench with a maximum capacity of 60 inch lbs. (6.77 Nm) into pinion shaft torque adapter T74P–3504–R or equivalent. Position the adapter and wrench on the input shaft splines.

5. Loosen the yoke plug locknut and then the yoke plug.

6. With the rack at the center of travel, tighten the yoke plug to 45–50 inch lbs. (5–5.6 Nm). Clean the threads of the yoke plug prior to tightening to prevent a false reading.

7. Back off the yoke plug approximately 1/8 turn, 44 degrees minimum to 54 degrees maximum, until the torque required to initiate and sustain rotation of the input shaft is 7–18 inch lbs. (0.78–2.03 Nm).

8. Place a suitable wrench on the yoke plug locknut. While holding the yoke plug, tighten the locknut to 44–66 ft. lbs. (60–89 Nm). Do not allow the yoke plug to move while tightening or preload will be affected. Check the input shaft torque as in Step 7 after tightening the locknut.

9. Install the steering gear.

REMOVAL & INSTALLATION

Integral Power Rack and Pinion Except 1990–92 Taurus LX and Sable with 3.8L Engine

➧ SEE FIG. 48–49

1. Disconnect the negative battery cable. Working from inside the vehicle, remove the nuts retaining the steering shaft weather boot to the dash panel.

2. Remove the bolts retaining the intermediate shaft to the steering column shaft. Set the weather boot aside.

3. Remove the pinch bolt at the steering gear input shaft and remove the intermediate shaft. Raise the vehicle and support safely.

4. Remove the left front wheel and tire assembly. Remove the heat shield. Cut the bundling strap retaining the lines to the gear.

5. Remove the tie rod ends from the spindles. Place a drain pan under the vehicle and remove the hydraulic pressure and return lines from the steering gear.

➡ **The pressure and return lines are on the front of the housing. Do not confuse them with the transfer lines on the side of the valve.**

6. Remove the nuts from the gear mounting bolts. The bolts are pressed into the gear housing and should not be removed during gear removal.

7. Push the weather boot end into the vehicle and lift the gear out of the mounting holes. Rotate the gear so the input shaft will pass between the brake booster and the floor pan. Carefully start working the steering gear out through the left fender apron opening.

8. Rotate the input shaft so it clears the left fender apron opening and complete the removal of the steering gear. If the steering gear seems to be stuck, check the right tie rod to ensure the stud is not caught on anything.

To Install:

9. Install new plastic seals on the hydraulic line fittings.

10. Insert the steering gear through the left fender apron. Rotate the input shaft forward to completely clear the fender apron opening.

11. To allow the gear to pass between the brake booster and the floorpan, rotate the input shaft rearward. Align the steering gear bolts to the bolt holes. Install the mounting nuts and torque them to 85–100 ft. lbs. (115–135 Nm). Lower the vehicle.

12. From inside the engine compartment, install the hydraulic pressure and return lines. Tighten the pressure line to 20–25 ft. lbs. (28–33Nm) and the return line to 15–20 ft. lbs. (20–

28 Nm). Swivel movement of the lines is normal when the fittings are properly tightened.

13. Raise the vehicle and support safely. Secure the pressure and return lines to the transfer tube with the bundle strap. Install the heat shield.

14. Install the tie rod ends to spindles. Torque the castle nuts to 35 ft. lbs. (48 Nm) and if necessary, torque the nuts a little bit more to align the slot in the nut for the cotter pin. Install the cotter pin.

15. Install the left front wheel and tire assembly and lower the vehicle. Working from inside the vehicle, pull the weather boot end out of the vehicle and install it over the valve housing. Install the intermediate shaft to the steering gear input shaft. Install the the inner weather boot to the floor pan.

16. Install the intermediate shaft to the steering column shaft. Fill the power steering system.

17. Check the system for leaks and proper operation. Adjust the toe setting as necessary.

Variable Assist Power Steering (VAPS) 1990–92 Taurus LX and Sable with 3.8L Engine

➧ SEE FIG. 50

The Variable Assist Power Steering (VAPS) system used on these vehicles consists of a micro-processor based module, a power rack and pinion steering gear, an actuator valve assembly, hose assemblies and a high efficiency power steering pump.

1. Disconnect the negative battery cable. Remove the primary steering column boot attachments.

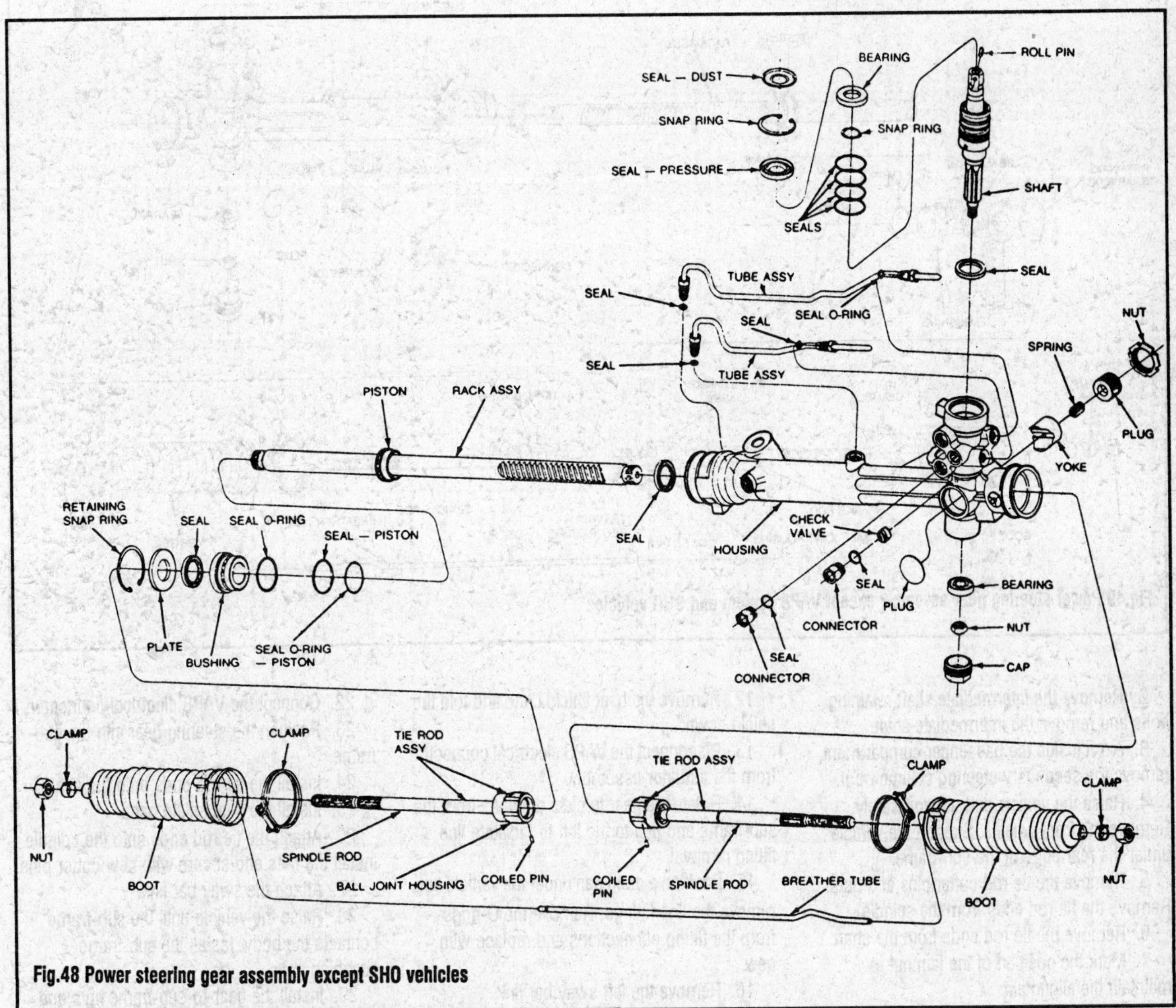

Fig.48 Power steering gear assembly except SHO vehicles

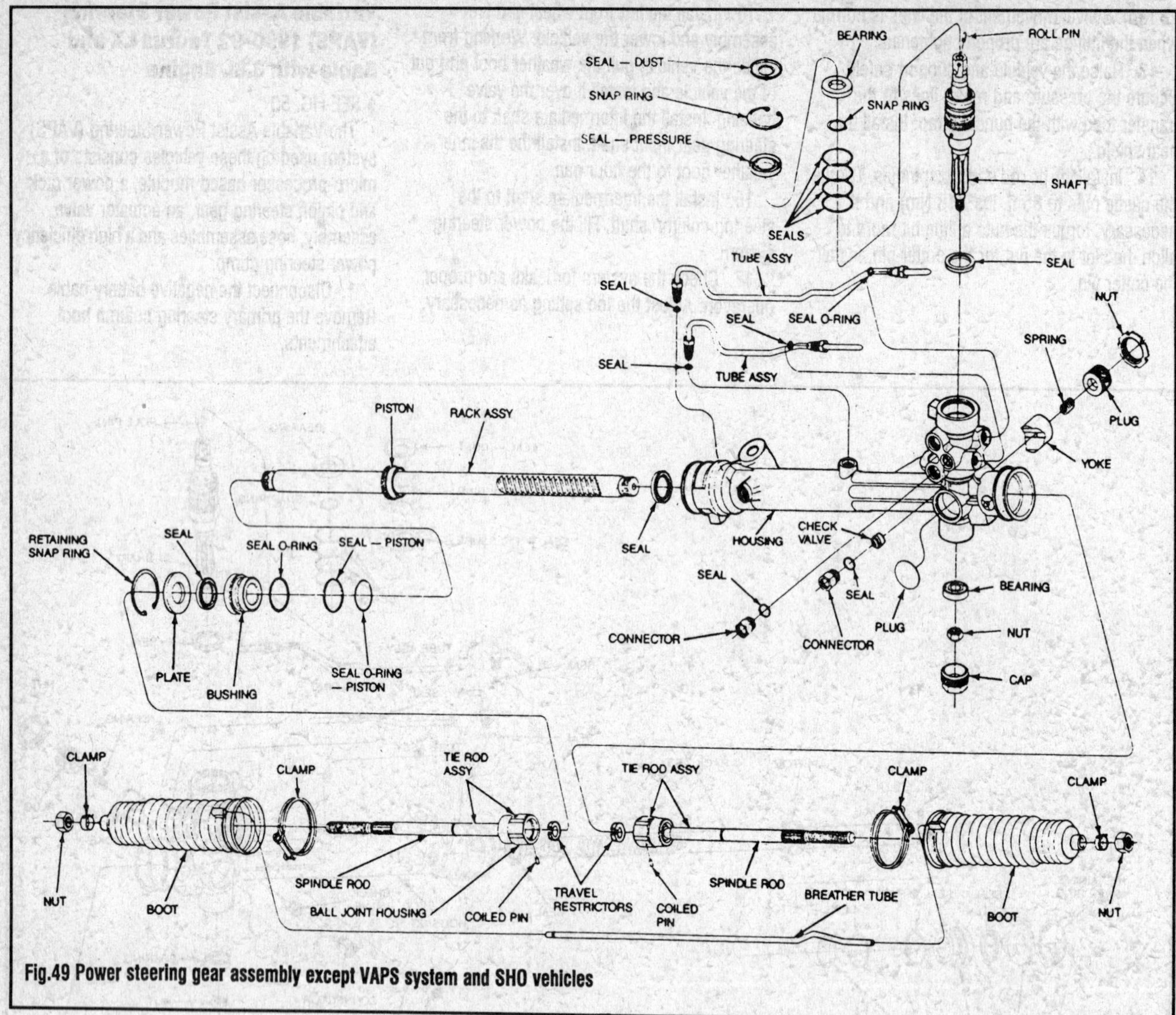

Fig.49 Power steering gear assembly except VAPS system and SHO vehicles

2. Remove the intermediate shaft retaining bolts and remove the intermediate shaft.
3. From inside the passenger compartment, remove the secondary steering column boot.
4. Raise the vehicle and support safely. Remove the front wheels. Support the vehicle under the rear edge of the sub-frame.
5. Remove the tie rod cotter pins and nuts. Remove the tie rod ends from the spindle.
6. Remove the tie rod ends from the shaft.
7. Mark the position of the jam nut to maintain the alignment.
8. Remove the nuts from the gear-to-sub-frame attaching bolts.
9. Remove the rear sub-frame-to-body attaching bolts.
10. Remove the exhaust pipe-to-catalytic converter attachment.
11. Lower the vehicle carefully until the subframe separates from the body; approximately 4 in. (102mm).
12. Remove the heat shield band and fold the shield down.
13. Disconnect the VAPS electrical connector from the actuator assembly.
14. Rotate the gear to clear the bolts from the sub-frame and pull to the left to facilitate line fitting removal.
15. Position a drain pan under the vehicle and remove the line fittings. Remove the O-rings from the fitting connections and replace with new.
16. Remove the left sway bar link.
17. Remove the steering gear assembly through the left wheel well.

To install:

18. Install new O-rings into the line fittings.
19. Place the gear attachment bolts in the gear housing.
20. Install the steering gear assembly through the left wheel well.
21. Connect and tighten the line fittings to the steering gear assembly.
22. Connect the VAPS electrical connector.
23. Position the steering gear into the sub-frame.
24. Install the tie rod ends onto the shaft.
25. Install the heat shield band.
26. Attach the tie rod ends onto the spindle. Install the nuts and secure with new cotter pins.
27. Attach the sway bar link.
28. Raise the vehicle until the sub-frame contacts the body. Install the sub-frame attaching bolts.
29. Install the gear-to-sub-frame nuts and torque to 85–100 ft. lbs. (115–135 Nm).
30. Attach the exhaust pipe to the catalytic converter.
31. Install the wheels and lower the vehicle.
32. Fill the power steering system.
33. Install the secondary steering column boot and attach the intermediate shaft to the steering gear. Tighten the bolt to 30–38 ft. lbs. (41–51 Nm).

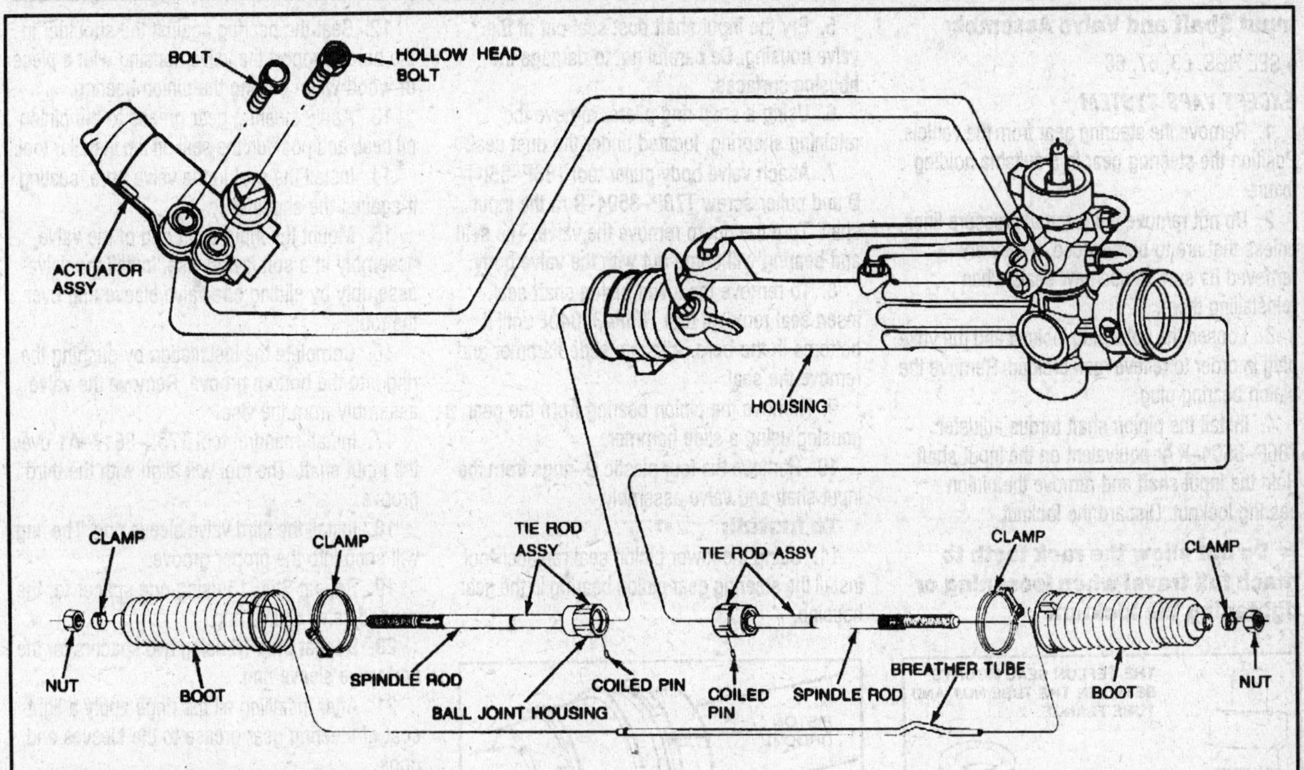

Fig.50 Power steering gear assembly VAPS system

34. Install the primary steering column boot and attach the intermediate shaft to the steering column.

35. Bleed the system and align the front end.

OVERHAUL

Tie Rod Bellows

➧ SEE FIG. 62

1. Remove the steering gear from the vehicle. Position the assembly in a suitable holding fixture. Remove the tie rod ends.

2. Remove the four clamps that retain the bellows to the gear housing and tie rods. Discard the clamps if damaged or corroded.

3. Remove the bellows along with the breather tube. Use care not to damage the bellows. For units equipped with rivets in place of coil springs perform Step 5.

4. Using locknut pin remover tool D81P–3504–N or equivalent, remove the coiled lock pins from the inner tie rod ball joints.

5. Using a sharp chisel, gently tap around the rivet head so that it lifts away from the ball joint. Use caution so that the center pin is not sheared off. Use side cutters to pry out the drive pin.

6. Position the rack so that several rack teeth are exposed. Hold the rack with an adjustable wrench on the end teeth only, while loosening the ball joint nuts with nut wrench T74P–3504–U or equivalent.

To install:

7. Position the rack so that several rack teeth are exposed. Hold the rack with an adjustable wrench on the end teeth.

8. Tighten each ball joint separately to 55–65 ft. lbs. Install new coil pins in the tie rod housing.

9. Clean the rack housing bore. Replenish any grease that may have been lost.

10. Apply steering gear grease to the groove in the rods where the bellows clamp to the tie rod. This allows for toe in adjustment without twisting the bellows.

11. Install the bellows and breather tube. Be sure that the tube is properly positioned.

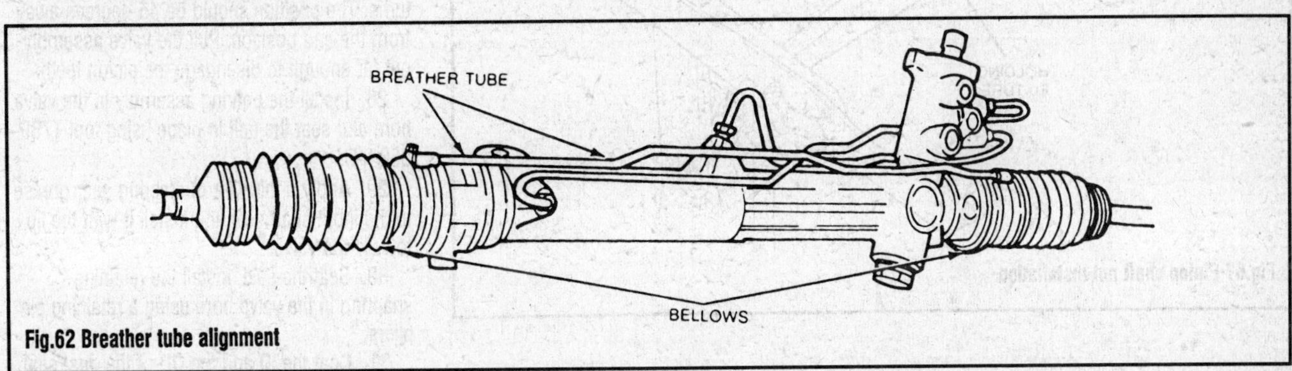

Fig.62 Breather tube alignment

Input Shaft and Valve Assembly

➧ SEE FIGS. 63, 67, 68

EXCEPT VAPS SYSTEM

1. Remove the steering gear from the vehicle. Position the steering gear in a suitable holding fixture.
2. Do not remove the external pressure lines, unless that are to be serviced. If they are removed be sure to use new seals when reinstalling them.
3. Loosen the yoke plug locknut and the yoke plug in order to relieve rack preload. Remove the pinion bearing plug.
4. Install the pinion shaft torque adjuster T86P–3504–K or equivalent on the input shaft. Hold the input shaft and remove the pinion bearing locknut. Discard the locknut.

➡ Do not allow the rack teeth to reach full travel when loosening or tightening the locknut.

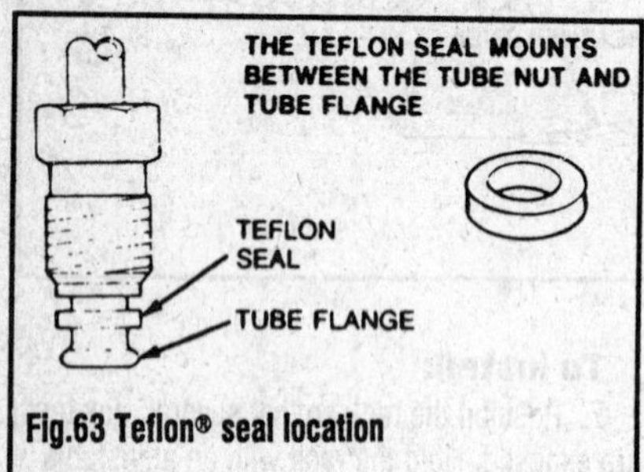

Fig.63 Teflon® seal location

5. Pry the input shaft dust seal out of the valve housing. Be careful not to damage the housing surfaces.
6. Using a snap ring pliers, remove the retaining snapring, located under the dust seal.
7. Attach valve body puller tool T86P–3504–D and puller screw T78P–3504–B to the input shaft. Turn the nut to remove the valve. The seal and bearing will come out with the valve body.
8. To remove the lower pinion shaft seal, insert seal removal tool T86P–35040F until it bottoms in the bore. Attach a slide hammer and remove the seal.
9. Remove the pinion bearing from the gear housing using a slide hammer.
10. Remove the four plastic O–rings from the input shaft and valve assembly.

To Install:

11. Using the lower pinion seal replacer tool, install the steering gear pinion bearing in the gear housing.

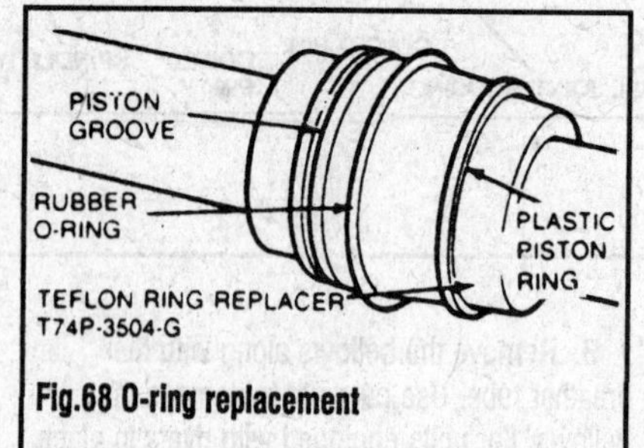

Fig.68 O-ring replacement

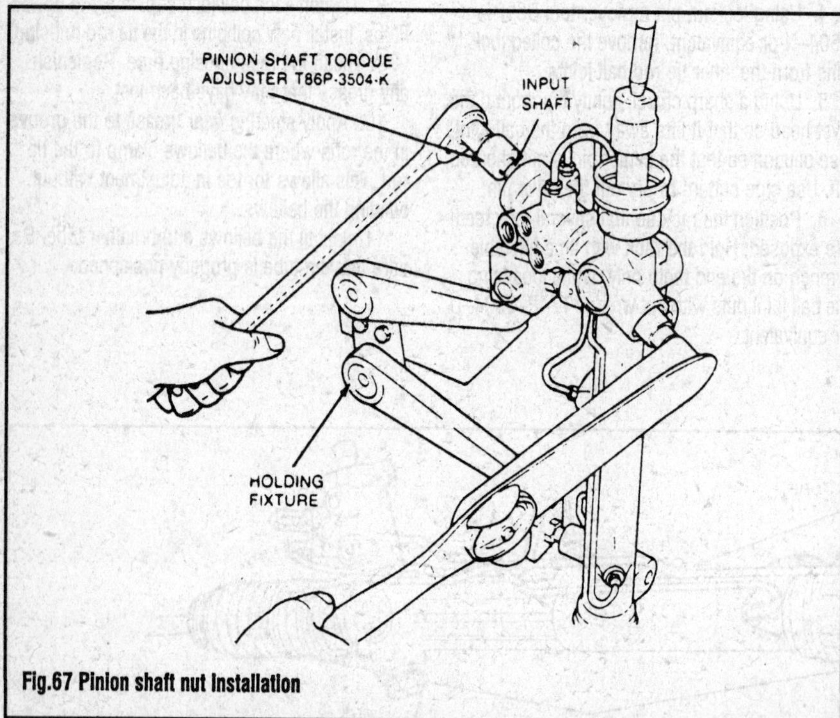

Fig.67 Pinion shaft nut installation

12. Seat the bearing against the shoulder in the bore. Support the valve housing with a piece of wood when seating the pinion bearing.
13. Apply steering gear grease to the pinion oil seal, and position the seal on the installer tool.
14. Install the seal in the valve bore, seating it against the shoulder.
15. Mount the input shaft end of the valve assembly in a soft jawed vise. Install the valve assembly by sliding one valve sleeve ring over the tool.
16. Complete the installation by pushing the ring into the bottom groove. Remove the valve assembly from the vise.
17. Install mandrel tool T75L–3517–A1 over the input shaft. The tool will align with the third groove.
18. Install the third valve sleeve ring. The ring will snap into the proper groove.
19. Repeat Step 18 using one spacer for the second valve sleeve ring.
20. Repeat Step 18 using two spacers for the first valve sleeve ring.
21. After installing all the rings apply a light coat of steering gear grease to the sleeves and rings.
22. Slowly install the sizing tube tool T75L–3517–A4 over the sleeve valve end of the input shaft onto the valve sleeve rings. Be sure that the rings are not being bent as the tube is slid over them.
23. Remove the sizing tube tool. Check the condition of the rings.
24. Center the rack in the housing so that equal amounts of rack shaft stick out of each end of the housing. Position the rack teeth so that they will mesh with the pinion.
25. Position the valve body insertion tool in the valve housing bore. Insert the valve assembly with the flats on the input shaft in alignment with the shaft body. If the pinion is off one tooth, it will be obvious, since one tooth equals 45 degrees.
26. Using pinion shaft torque adjuster tool T86P–3504–K count the total turns, stop to stop. It should be 2.5 turns.
27. From one stop back off half the total turns. The position should be 45 degrees away from the end position. Pull the valve assembly out far enough to disengage the pinion teeth.
28. Install the bearing assembly in the valve bore and seat the unit in place using tool T78P–3504–D.
29. Apply a thin film of steering gear grease to the input shaft seal and install it with the lip toward the valve.
30. Seat the seal. Install the retaining snapring in the valve bore using a retaining pin pliers.
31. Coat the ID and the OD of the dust seal and the input shaft with grease. Install the dust seal using the dust seal installer tool.

32. Install the nut on the pinion end of the valve assembly. Holding the input shaft with the pinion shaft torque adjuster tool, tighten the nut to 30–40 ft. lbs. The rack must be away from the stops during this operation.

33. Install the steering gear pinion bearing cap. Tighten the cap to 40–60 ft. lbs. Set the rack load preload.

Gear Housing, Rack Yoke Plug, Rack, Rack Bushing and Oil Seals

EXCEPT VAPS SYSTEM

SEE FIGS. 61, 66, 65, 69-72

1. Remove the steering gear from the vehicle. Position the assembly in a suitable holding fixture.
2. Remove the tie rod and socket assemblies from both ends of the rack, input shaft and valve assembly from the gear housing.
3. Remove the yoke plug and spring. The yoke cannot be removed at this time.
4. Working from the right hand side of the gear, push the rack in just far enough to facilitate removal of the snapring. Remove the snapring.
5. Slowly pull the rack out of the right hand side of the housing until the rack contacts the aluminum rack bushing.
6. Do not hammer on the rack until the bushing is withdrawn from the housing. Remove the rack from the housing.
7. To remove the rack oil seal, bottom oil seal removal tool T78P–3504–J into the housing. Using a slide hammer tool attached to the seal removal tool remove the seal from its mounting.
8. On the first attempt the nylon ring may pull out of the seal, leaving the seal in the gear. Repeat the procedure if this occurs.
9. Remove the plastic O-ring and rubber O-ring from the rack piston using O-ring removal tool T71P–19703–C or equivalent.

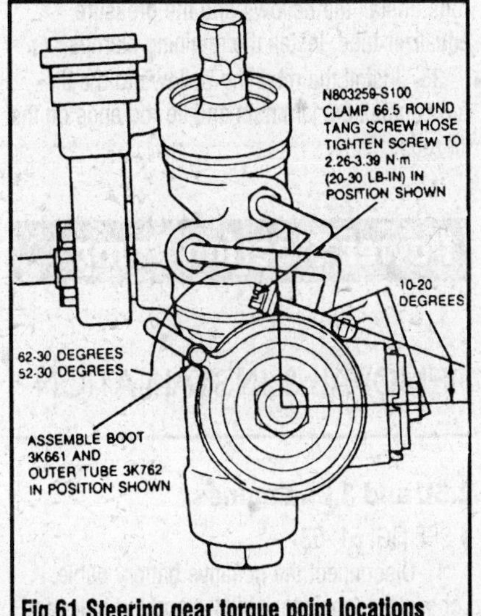

Fig.61 Steering gear torque point locations

10. Using the rack bushing tool T78P–3504–L remove the rack bushing seal. Remove the O-rings from the rack bushing.
11. Inspect the rack yoke while it is still in the gear housing. If it is in good condition, do not remove it. If it needs replacing remove it along with the expansion plug.

To install:

12. Slide Teflon ring replace tool T87P–3504–G over the plain end of the rack and up the piston.
13. Roll the rubber O-ring into the piston groove, then slide the plastic piston ring into the piston groove over the O-ring.
14. Remove the plastic insert from the rack seal. Save the insert. Install the rack seal protector over the rack teeth.
15. Install the seal with the lip facing toward the piston. Push the seal all the way against the piston. Remove the rack seal protector tool. Install the plastic insert in the rack seal.
16. Pack the rack teeth with steering gear lubricant. Apply a thin coat of steering gear lubricant to the yoke contact area on the back of the rack teeth.
17. Lubricate the piston seal and rack seal outside diameter with power steering fluid.
18. Install the sizing tool T78P–3504–M into the end of the gear housing. Be sure that the yoke is all the way in when installing the rack.
19. Install the rack, take care as not too scratch the housing piston bore. Carefully push

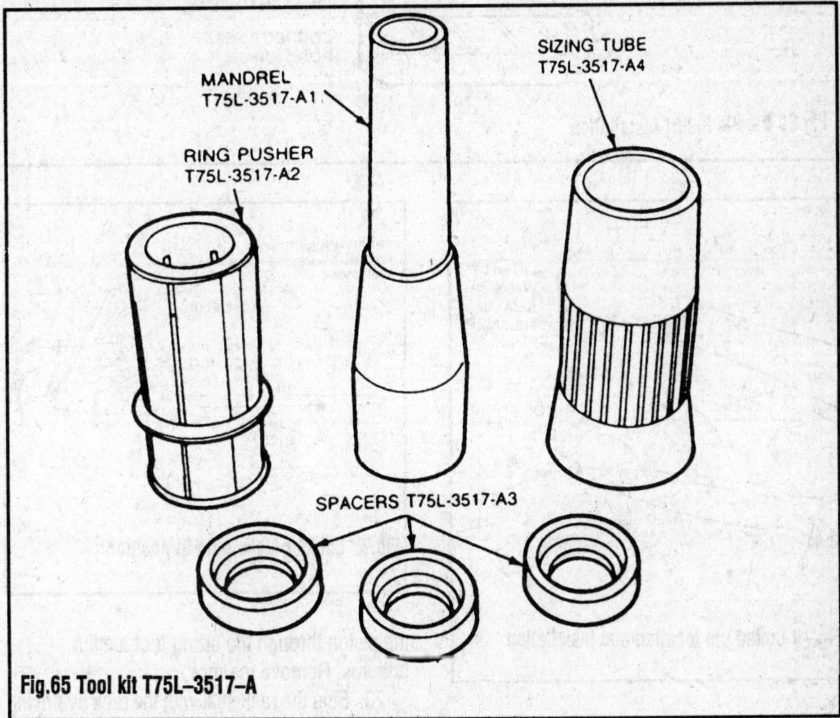

Fig.65 Tool kit T75L–3517–A

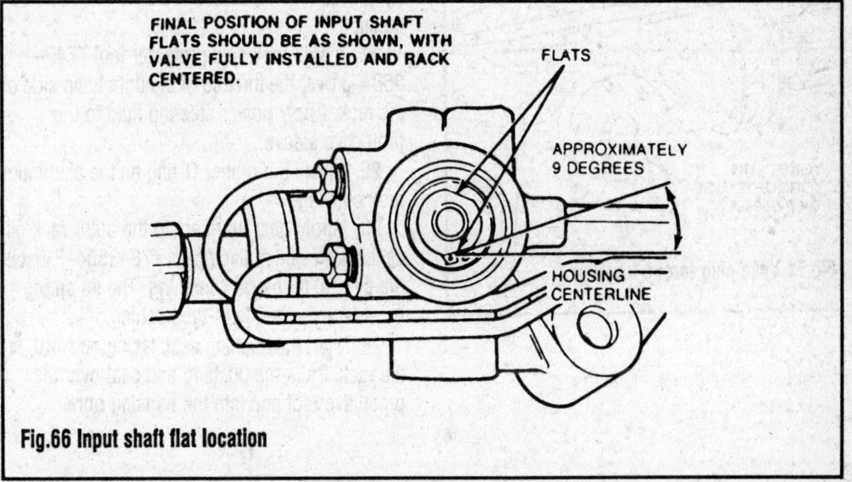

Fig.66 Input shaft flat location

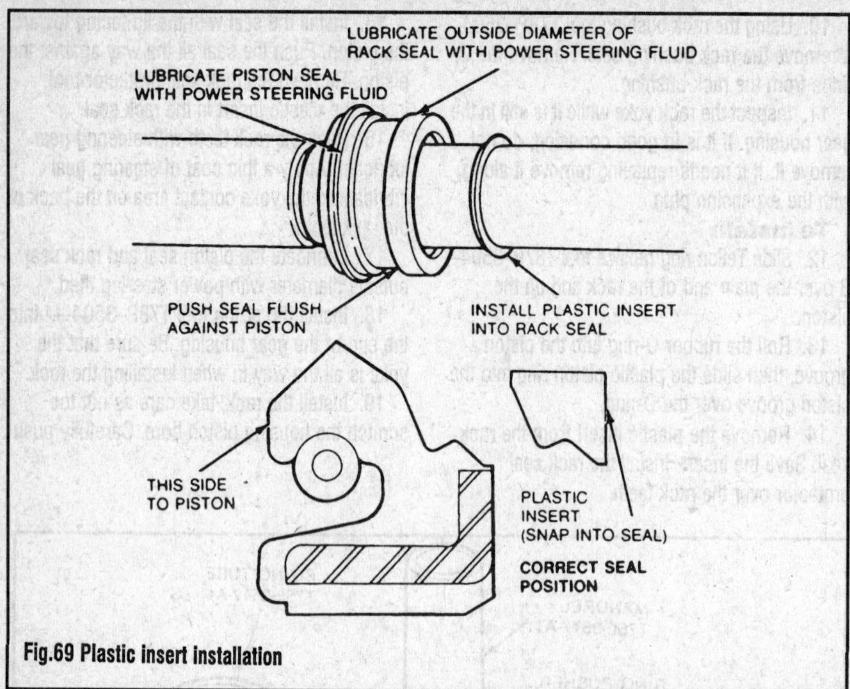

Fig.69 Plastic insert installation

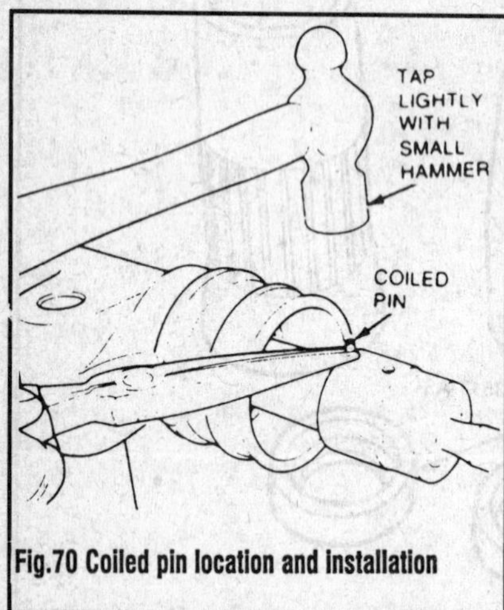

Fig.70 Coiled pin location and installation

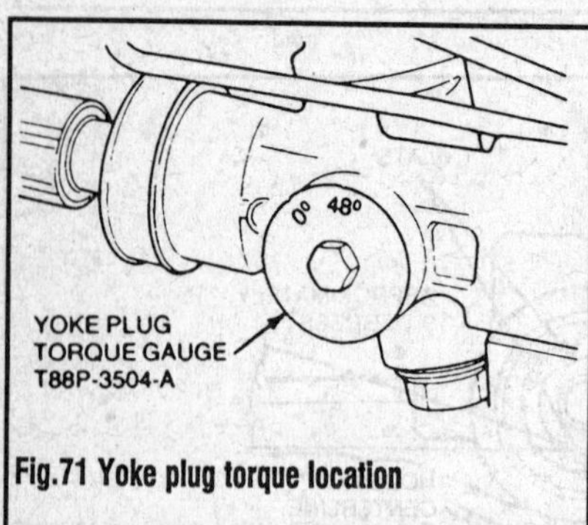

Fig.71 Yoke plug torque location

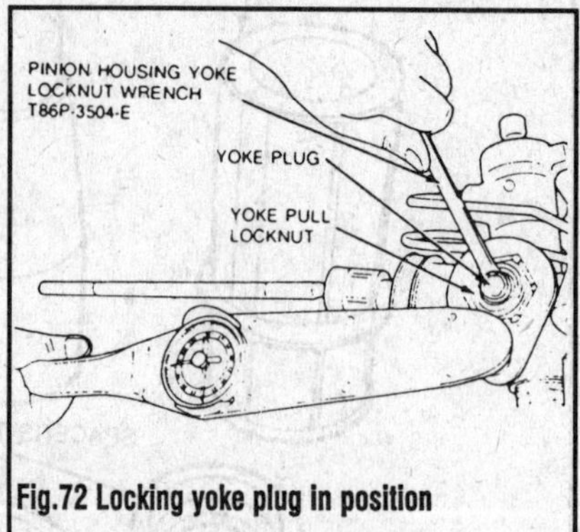

Fig.72 Locking yoke plug in position

the piston through the sizing tool, until it bottoms. Remove the tool.

20. Seat the rack seal with the rack by driving the end of the rack with a drift. Do not remove the rack. Move the rack so that it is in the centered position.

21. Install rack seal protector tool T74P–3504–J over the threads of the right hand side of the rack. Apply power steering fluid to the protective sleeve.

22. Install the rubber O-ring on the aluminum rack bushing.

23. Apply gear lubricant to the outer rack oil seal. Using seal replacer tool T78–3504–F install the oil seal in the rack bushing. The lip spring must face the inside of the bushing.

24. Start the bushing seal, facing outward, on the rack. Pass the bushing and seal over the protective tool and into the housing bore.

25. Place the end plate against the rack bushing. Using the sizing tool apply pressure to the end plate and rack bushing until the bushing seats in the gear housing. If the bushing will not seat tap it in place.

26. Install the rod assemblies. Tighten both the tie rod ball joint nuts at the same time to 55–65 ft. lbs. by holding one and turning the other.

27. Install the coiled pins in the ball joint nuts, tapping them in place until they are seated. Install the input shaft and the valve assembly.

28. If the yoke has not been removed do not support the gear on a wood surface at the yoke plug opening. Do not flatten the expansion plug until the flat portion is $^1/_2$ to $^3/_4$ of the total plug diameter. Do not flatten the plug completely or it will fall out.

29. Install the spring, plug and locknut. With the rack in the center of its travel, tighten the yoke plug 45–50 inch lbs.

30. Install the yoke plug torque gauge T88P–3504–A. Mark the location of the zero degree mark on the housing. Back off the adjuster so that the 48 degree mark lines up with the zero degree mark.

31. Using the pinion housing yoke locknut tool tighten the yoke locknut to 40–50 ft. lbs. Do not allow the yoke plug to move while tightening or preload will be affected. Check the input shaft torque after tightening the locknut.

32. If the external pressure lines were removed, they must be replaced with new service lines.

33. Fully extend the left end of the rack so that the rack teeth are exposed. Using 2 ounces of specified gear lubricant, pack rack teeth and pack any remaining grease into the left end of the gear housing. Return the rack to the center position.

34. Apply specified lubricant into the groove in the tie rods where the bellows clamp to the tie rods. Install the bellows and the pressure equalizer tube. Install the retaining clamps.

35. Install the retaining bellows to the tie rods. Install the jam nuts and tie rod ends on the tie rods.

Power Steering Pump

REMOVAL & INSTALLATION

2.5L and 3.8L Engines

➧ SEE FIG. 51–53

1. Disconnect the negative battery cable. Loosen the tensioner pulley attaching bolts and using the $^1/_2$ in. drive hole provided in the

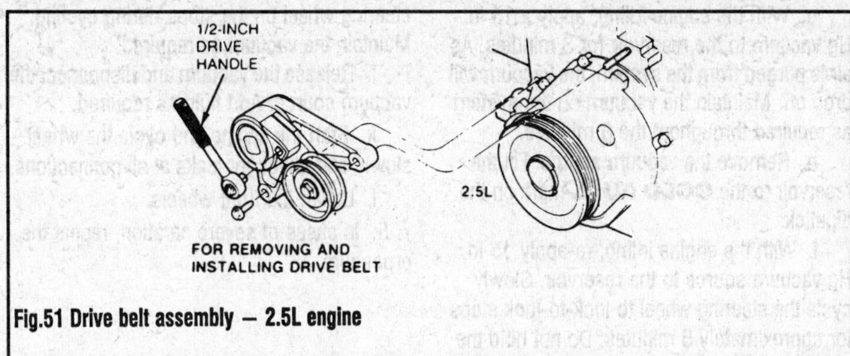

Fig.51 Drive belt assembly — 2.5L engine

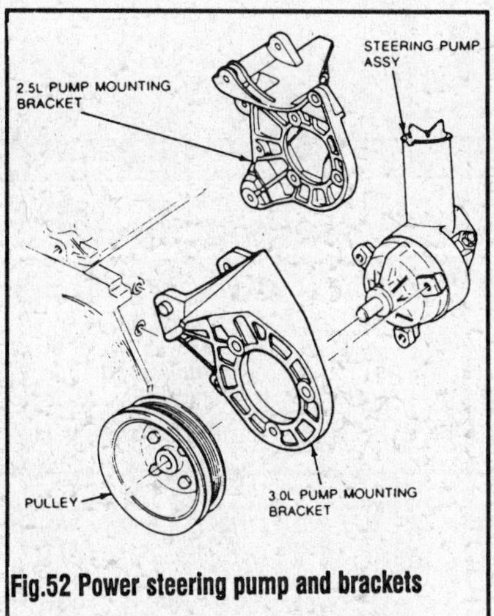

Fig.52 Power steering pump and brackets

tensioner pulley, rotate the tensioner pulley clockwise and remove the belt from the alternator and power steering pulley.

2. Position a drain pan under the power steering pump from underneath the vehicle. Disconnect the hydraulic pressure and return lines.

3. Remove the pulley from the pump shaft using hub puller T69L–10300–B or equivalent. Remove the bolts retaining pump to bracket and remove the power steering pump.

4. Installation is the reverse of the removal procedure. Fill the pump with fluid and check the system for proper operation.

➡ **To install the power steering pump pulley, use steering pump pulley replacer T65P–3A733–C or equivalent. When using this tool, the small diameter threads must be fully engaged in the pump shaft before pressing on the pulley. Hold the head screw and turn the nut to install the pulley. Install the pulley face flush with the pump shaft within ± 0.100 in. (0.25mm).**

3.0L Except SHO Engine

1. Disconnect the negative battery cable.

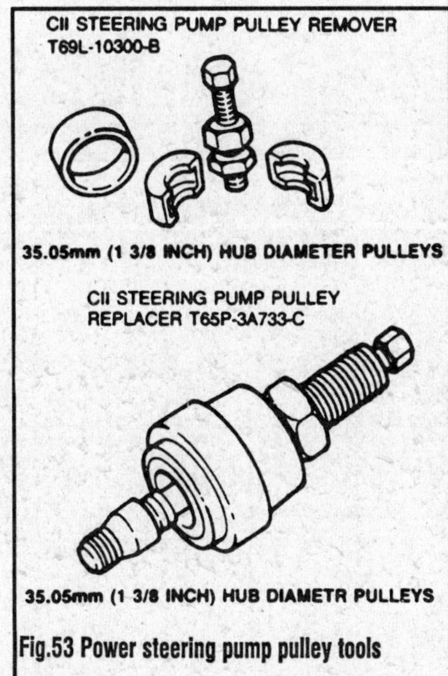

Fig.53 Power steering pump pulley tools

Loosen the idler pulley and remove the power steering belt.

2. Remove the radiator overflow bottle in order to gain access to the 3 screws attaching the pulleys to the pulley hub.

3. Matchmark both pulley to hub positions.

4. Remove the pulleys from the pulley hub.

5. Remove the return line from the pump. Be prepared to catch any spilled fluid in a suitable container.

6. Back off the pressure line attaching nut completely. The line will separate from the pump connection when the pump is removed.

7. Remove the pump mounting bolts and remove the pump.

8. Installation is the reverse of the removal procedure. Fill the pump with fluid and check for proper operation.

3.0L SHO Engine

➧ SEE FIG. 54

1. Disconnect the negative battery cable.

2. Remove the engine damper strut.

3. Remove the power steering belt.

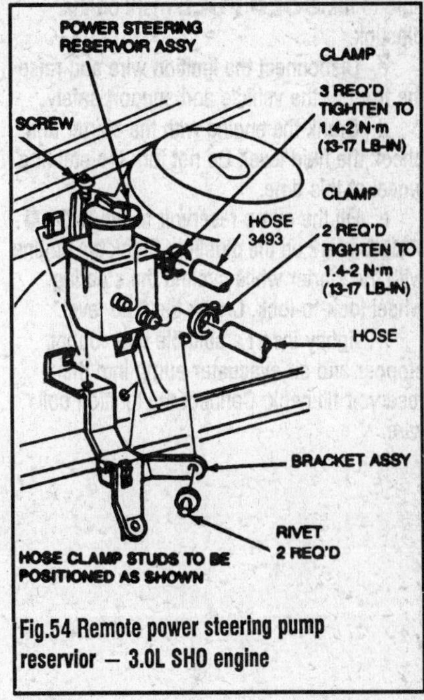

Fig.54 Remote power steering pump reservior — 3.0L SHO engine

4. Raise and support the vehicle safely.

5. Remove the right front wheel and tire assembly.

6. Position a jack under the engine and remove the right rear engine mount.

7. Remove the power steering pump pulley.

8. Place a drain pan under the pump and remove the pressure and return lines from the pump.

9. Remove the 4 pump retaining bolts and remove the pump.

10. Installation is the reverse of the removal procedure. Tighten the pump retaining bolts to 15–24 ft. lbs. (20–33 Nm).

BLEEDING

If air bubbles are present in the power steering fluid, bleed the system by performing the following:

1. Fill the reservoir to the proper level.

2. Operate the engine until the fluid reaches normal operating temperature of 165–175°F (74–79°C).

3. Turn the steering wheel all the way to the left then all the way to the right several times. Do not hold the steering wheel in the far left or far right position stops.

4. Check the fluid level and recheck the fluid for the presence of trapped air. If apparent that air is still in the system, fabricate or obtain a vacuum tester and purge the system as follows:

a. Remove the pump dipstick cap assembly.

b. Check and fill the pump reservoir with

fluid to the **COLD FULL** mark on the dipstick.

c. Disconnect the ignition wire and raise the front of the vehicle and support safely.

d. Crank the engine with the starter and check the fluid level. Do not turn the steering wheel at this time.

e. Fill the pump reservoir to the **COLD FULL** mark on the dipstick. Crank the engine with the starter while cycling the steering wheel lock-to-lock. Check the fluid level.

f. Tightly insert a suitable size rubber stopper and air evacuator pump into the reservoir fill neck. Connect the ignition coil wire.

g. With the engine idling, apply a 15 in. Hg vacuum to the reservoir for 3 minutes. As air is purged from the system, the vacuum will drop off. Maintain the vacuum on the system as required throughout the 3 minutes.

h. Remove the vacuum source. Fill the reservoir to the **COLD FULL** mark on the dipstick.

i. With the engine idling, re-apply 15 in. Hg vacuum source to the reservoir. Slowly cycle the steering wheel to lock-to-lock stops for approximately 5 minutes. Do not hold the steering wheel on the stops during cycling. Maintain the vacuum as required.

j. Release the vacuum and disconnect the vacuum source. Add fluid as required.

k. Start the engine and cycle the wheel slowly and check for leaks at all connections.

l. Lower the front wheels.

5. In cases of severe aeration, repeat the procedure.

Troubleshooting the Turn Signal Switch

Problem	Cause	Solution
Turn signal will not cancel	• Loose switch mounting screws • Switch or anchor bosses broken • Broken, missing or out of position detent, or cancelling spring	• Tighten screws • Replace switch • Reposition springs or replace switch as required
Turn signal difficult to operate	• Turn signal lever loose • Switch yoke broken or distorted • Loose or misplaced springs • Foreign parts and/or materials in switch • Switch mounted loosely	• Tighten mounting screws • Replace switch • Reposition springs or replace switch • Remove foreign parts and/or material • Tighten mounting screws
Turn signal will not indicate lane change	• Broken lane change pressure pad or spring hanger • Broken, missing or misplaced lane change spring • Jammed wires	• Replace switch • Replace or reposition as required • Loosen mounting screws, reposition wires and retighten screws
Turn signal will not stay in turn position	• Foreign material or loose parts impeding movement of switch yoke • Defective switch	• Remove material and/or parts • Replace switch
Hazard switch cannot be pulled out	• Foreign material between hazard support cancelling leg and yoke	• Remove foreign material. No foreign material impeding function of hazard switch—replace turn signal switch.
No turn signal lights	• Inoperative turn signal flasher • Defective or blown fuse • Loose chassis to column harness connector • Disconnect column to chassis connector. Connect new switch to chassis and operate switch by hand. If vehicle lights now operate normally, signal switch is inoperative • If vehicle lights do not operate, check chassis wiring for opens, grounds, etc.	• Replace turn signal flasher • Replace fuse • Connect securely • Replace signal switch • Repair chassis wiring as required

Troubleshooting the Turn Signal Switch (cont.)

Problem	Cause	Solution
Instrument panel turn indicator lights on but not flashing	• Burned out or damaged front or rear turn signal bulb	• Replace bulb
	• If vehicle lights do not operate, check light sockets for high resistance connections, the chassis wiring for opens, grounds, etc.	• Repair chassis wiring as required
	• Inoperative flasher	• Replace flasher
	• Loose chassis to column harness connection	• Connect securely
	• Inoperative turn signal switch	• Replace turn signal switch
	• To determine if turn signal switch is defective, substitute new switch into circuit and operate switch by hand. If the vehicle's lights operate normally, signal switch is inoperative.	• Replace turn signal switch
Stop light not on when turn indicated	• Loose column to chassis connection	• Connect securely
	• Disconnect column to chassis connector. Connect new switch into system without removing old.	• Replace signal switch
Stop light not on when turn indicated (cont.)	Operate switch by hand. If brake lights work with switch in the turn position, signal switch is defective.	
	• If brake lights do not work, check connector to stop light sockets for grounds, opens, etc.	• Repair connector to stop light circuits using service manual as guide
Turn indicator panel lights not flashing	• Burned out bulbs	• Replace bulbs
	• High resistance to ground at bulb socket	• Replace socket
	• Opens, ground in wiring harness from front turn signal bulb socket to indicator lights	• Locate and repair as required
Turn signal lights flash very slowly	• High resistance ground at light sockets	• Repair high resistance grounds at light sockets
	• Incorrect capacity turn signal flasher or bulb	• Replace turn signal flasher or bulb
	• If flashing rate is still extremely slow, check chassis wiring harness from the connector to light sockets for high resistance	• Locate and repair as required
	• Loose chassis to column harness connection	• Connect securely
	• Disconnect column to chassis connector. Connect new switch into system without removing old. Operate switch by hand. If flashing occurs at normal rate, the signal switch is defective.	• Replace turn signal switch

Troubleshooting the Turn Signal Switch (cont.)

Problem	Cause	Solution
Hazard signal lights will not flash—turn signal functions normally	• Blow fuse • Inoperative hazard warning flasher • Loose chassis-to-column harness connection • Disconnect column to chassis connector. Connect new switch into system without removing old. Depress the hazard warning lights. If they now work normally, turn signal switch is defective. • If lights do not flash, check wiring harness "K" lead for open between hazard flasher and connector. If open, fuse block is defective	• Replace fuse • Replace hazard warning flasher in fuse panel • Conect securely • Replace turn signal switch • Repair or replace brown wire or connector as required

Troubleshooting the Power Steering Pump

Problem	Cause	Solution
Chirp noise in steering pump	• Loose belt	• Adjust belt tension to specification
Belt squeal (particularly noticeable at full wheel travel and stand still parking)	• Loose belt	• Adjust belt tension to specification
Growl noise in steering pump	• Excessive back pressure in hoses or steering gear caused by restriction	• Locate restriction and correct. Replace part if necessary.
Growl noise in steering pump (particularly noticeable at stand still parking)	• Scored pressure plates, thrust plate or rotor • Extreme wear of cam ring	• Replace parts and flush system • Replace parts
Groan noise in steering pump	• Low oil level • Air in the oil. Poor pressure hose connection.	• Fill reservoir to proper level • Tighten connector to specified torque. Bleed system by operating steering from right to left—full turn.
Rattle noise in steering pump	• Vanes not installed properly • Vanes sticking in rotor slots	• Install properly • Free up by removing burrs, varnish, or dirt
Swish noise in steering pump	• Defective flow control valve	• Replace part
Whine noise in steering pump	• Pump shaft bearing scored	• Replace housing and shaft. Flush system.

Troubleshooting the Power Steering Pump (cont.)

Problem	Cause	Solution
Hard steering or lack of assist	• Loose pump belt • Low oil level in reservoir **NOTE:** Low oil level will also result in excessive pump noise • Steering gear to column misalignment • Lower coupling flange rubbing against steering gear adjuster plug • Tires not properly inflated	• Adjust belt tension to specification • Fill to proper level. If excessively low, check all lines and joints for evidence of external leakage. Tighten loose connectors. • Align steering column • Loosen pinch bolt and assemble properly • Inflate to recommended pressure
Foaming milky power steering fluid, low fluid level and possible low pressure	• Air in the fluid, and loss of fluid due to internal pump leakage causing overflow	• Check for leaks and correct. Bleed system. Extremely cold temperatures will cause system aeriation should the oil level be low. If oil level is correct and pump still foams, remove pump from vehicle and separate reservoir from body. Check welsh plug and body for cracks. If plug is loose or body is cracked, replace body.
Low pump pressure	• Flow control valve stuck or inoperative • Pressure plate not flat against cam ring	• Remove burrs or dirt or replace. Flush system. • Correct
Momentary increase in effort when turning wheel fast to right or left	• Low oil level in pump • Pump belt slipping • High internal leakage	• Add power steering fluid as required • Tighten or replace belt • Check pump pressure. (See pressure test)
Steering wheel surges or jerks when turning with engine running especially during parking	• Low oil level • Loose pump belt • Steering linkage hitting engine oil pan at full turn • Insufficient pump pressure	• Fill as required • Adjust tension to specification • Correct clearance • Check pump pressure. (See pressure test). Replace flow control valve if defective.
Steering wheel surges or jerks when turning with engine running especially during parking (cont.)	• Sticking flow control valve	• Inspect for varnish or damage, replace if necessary
Excessive wheel kickback or loose steering	• Air in system	• Add oil to pump reservoir and bleed by operating steering. Check hose connectors for proper torque and adjust as required.
Low pump pressure	• Extreme wear of cam ring • Scored pressure plate, thrust plate, or rotor • Vanes not installed properly • Vanes sticking in rotor slots • Cracked or broken thrust or pressure plate	• Replace parts. Flush system. • Replace parts. Flush system. • Install properly • Freeup by removing burrs, varnish, or dirt • Replace part

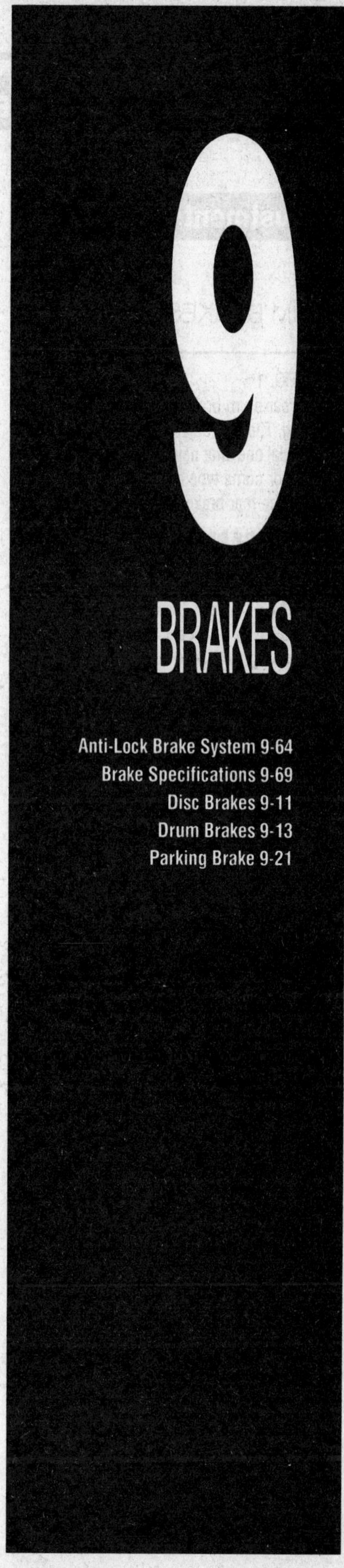

9
BRAKES
Anti-Lock Brake System 9-64
Brake Specifications 9-69
Disc Brakes 9-11
Drum Brakes 9-13
Parking Brake 9-21

BRAKE OPERATING SYSTEM

Adjustments

DRUM BRAKES

➧ SEE FIG. 1

The rear drum brakes, on your car, are self-adjusting. The only adjustment necessary should be an initial one after new brake shoes have been installed or some type of service work has been done on the rear brake system.

➡ After any brake service, obtain a firm brake pedal before moving the car. Adjusted brakes must not drag. The wheel must turn freely. Be sure the parking brake cables are not too tightly adjusted.

A special brake shoe gauge is necessary for making an accurate adjustment after installing new brake shoes. The special gauge measures both the drum diameter and the brake shoe setting.

Since no adjustment is necessary except when service work is done on the rear brakes, we will assume that the car is jacked up and safely supported by jackstands, and that the rear drums have been removed.

Measure and set the special brake gauge to the inside diameter of the brake drum. Lift the adjuster lever from the starwheel teeth. Turn the starwheel until the brake shoes are adjusted out to the shoe setting fingers of the brake gauge. Install the hub and drum.

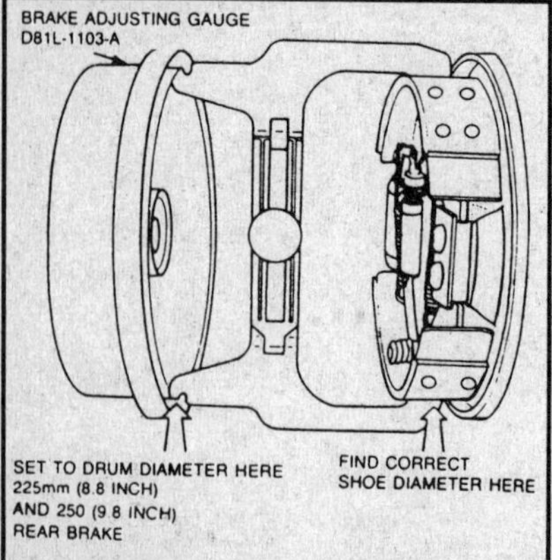

Fig.1 Measuring brake drum diameter for shoe adjustment

➡ Complete the adjustment by applying the brakes several times. After the brakes have been properly adjusted, check their operation by making several stops from varying forward speeds.

DISC BRAKES

Front disc brakes require no adjustment. Hydraulic pressure maintains the proper pad-to-disc contact at all times.

On vehicles equipped with rear disc brakes, the main difference is that the rear caliper houses the emergency brake actuator. The rear disc brakes are self-adjusting. Hydraulic pressure maintains the proper pad-to-disc at all times.

BRAKE PEDAL FREE HEIGHT

1. Insert a slender sharp pointed prod through the carpet and sound deadener to dash panel metal.
2. Measure the distance to the center on top of the brake pedal pad.
3. If the position of the pedal is not within specification, check the pedal for worn bushings, missing bushings and loose retaining bolts.
4. Repair defective components as required. Proper specification should be minimum 161mm (6.34 in.) pedal free height to maximum 180mm (7.09 in.) and maximum 59.4mm (2.34 in.) pedal travel.
5. If still not within specification check the brake pedal booster for proper adjustment.

Brake Light Switch

REMOVAL & INSTALLATION

The mechanical stoplight switch assembly is installed on the pin of the brake pedal arm, so it straddles the master cylinder pushrod.

1. Disconnect the negative battery cable.
2. Disconnect the wire harness at the connector from the switch.

➡ The locking tab must be lifted before the connector can be removed.

3. Remove the hairpin retainer and white nylon washer. Slide the stoplight switch and the pushrod away from the pedal. Remove the switch by sliding the switch up/down.

➡ Since the switch side plate nearest the brake pedal is slotted, it is not necessary to remove the brake master cylinder pushrod black bushing and 1 white spacer washer nearest the pedal arm from the brake pedal pin.

To install:

4. Position the switch so the U-shaped side is nearest the pedal and directly over/under the pin. The black bushing must be in position in the push rod eyelet with the washer face on the side away from the brake pedal arm.
5. Slide the switch up/down, trapping the master cylinder pushrod and black bushing between the switch side plates. Push the switch and pushrod assembly firmly towards the brake pedal arm. Assemble the outside white plastic washer to pin and install the hairpin retainer to trap the whole assembly.

➡ Do not substitute other types of pin retainer. Replace only with production hairpin retainer.

6. Connect the wire harness connector to the switch.
7. Check the stoplight switch for proper operation. Stoplights should illuminate with less than 6 lbs. applied to the brake pedal at the pad.

➡ The stoplight switch wire harness must have sufficient length to travel with the switch during full stroke at the pedal.

Brake Pedal

REMOVAL & INSTALLATION

1. Disconnect the negative battery cable. Disconnect the stoplight electrical connector.
2. Remove the pushrod retainer and nylon washer. Slide the stoplight switch outboard along the brake pedal pin just far enough for the outer hole of the switch frame to clear the pin.
3. Remove the switch by sliding it upward. Remove the black bushing from the pushrod.
4. Loosen the power brake booster retaining nuts at the pedal support. Slide the pushrod and

inner nylon washer off the pedal pin if the vehicle does not have speed control.

5. Remove the locknut and then remove the pivot bolt, brake pedal, pivot spacer and bushings from the pedal support. Remove the speed control adapter, if equipped by unlatching the locking tab.

To install:

6. Position the brake pedal in the pedal support. Install the pivot bolt and torque to 10–27 ft. lbs. Install the locknut.

7. Install the speed control adapter or the nylon washer. Install the stoplight switch.

8. Tighten the booster retaining nuts to 12–22 ft. lbs.

9. Connect the stoplight electrical wire. Check the stoplight adjustment. Check the pedal height and travel.

Master Cylinder

REMOVAL & INSTALLATION

1. Disconnect the negative battery cable.

2. Disconnect the brake lines from the primary and secondary outlet ports of the master cylinder and the pressure control valve.

3. Remove the nuts attaching the master cylinder to the brake booster assembly. Disconnect the brake warning light wire.

4. Slide the master cylinder forward and upward from the vehicle.

To install:

5. Before installation, bench bleed the new master cylinder as follows:

a. Mount the new master cylinder in a holding fixture. Be careful not to damage the housing.

b. Fill the master cylinder reservoir with brake fluid.

c. Using a suitable tool inserted into the booster pushrod cavity, push the master cylinder piston in slowly. Place a suitable container under the master cylinder to catch the fluid being expelled from the outlet ports.

d. Place a finger tightly over each outlet port and allow the master cylinder piston to return.

e. Repeat the procedure until clear fluid only is expelled from the master cylinder. Plug the outlet ports and remove the master cylinder from the holding fixture.

6. Mount the master cylinder on the booster. Attach the brake fluid lines to the master cylinder.

7. Install the brake warning light wire.

8. Bleed the system. Operate the brakes several times, then check for external hydraulic leaks.

OVERHAUL

1. Remove the master cylinder from the vehicle. Position the assembly in a suitable holding fixture. If mounting in a vise, clamp it to the vise by the flange to avoid damage to the bore or reservoir areas.

2. Remove the cap. Drain and properly discard all old brake fluid.

3. Depress the primary piston and remove the snapring from the retaining groove at the open end of the bore.

4. Remove the primary and secondary pistons from the master cylinder. If the secondary piston does not come out use low pressure compressed air to aid in removal.

5. Remove the reservoir assembly.

6. On wagon, remove the pressure control valves.

To assemble:

7. Clean all parts clean brake fluid. Inspect all seals on the pistons for damage and replace as required. Inspect the master cylinder body, replace if defective.

8. Install the secondary piston into the bore, spring end first. Install the primary piston into the bore, spring end first.

9. Install the pressure control valve on Wagon. Install the reservoir assembly.

10. Fill and bleed the master cylinder.

Power Brake Booster

REMOVAL & INSTALLATION

➧ SEE FIG. 2

1. Disconnect the battery ground cable and remove the brake lines from the master cylinder.

2. Disconnect the manifold vacuum hose and the warning indicator. Remove the retaining nuts and the master cylinder.

3. From under the instrument panel, remove the stoplight switch wiring connector from the switch. Remove the pushrod retainer and outer nylon washer from the brake pin, slide the stoplight switch along the brake pedal pin, far enough for the outer hole to clear the pin.

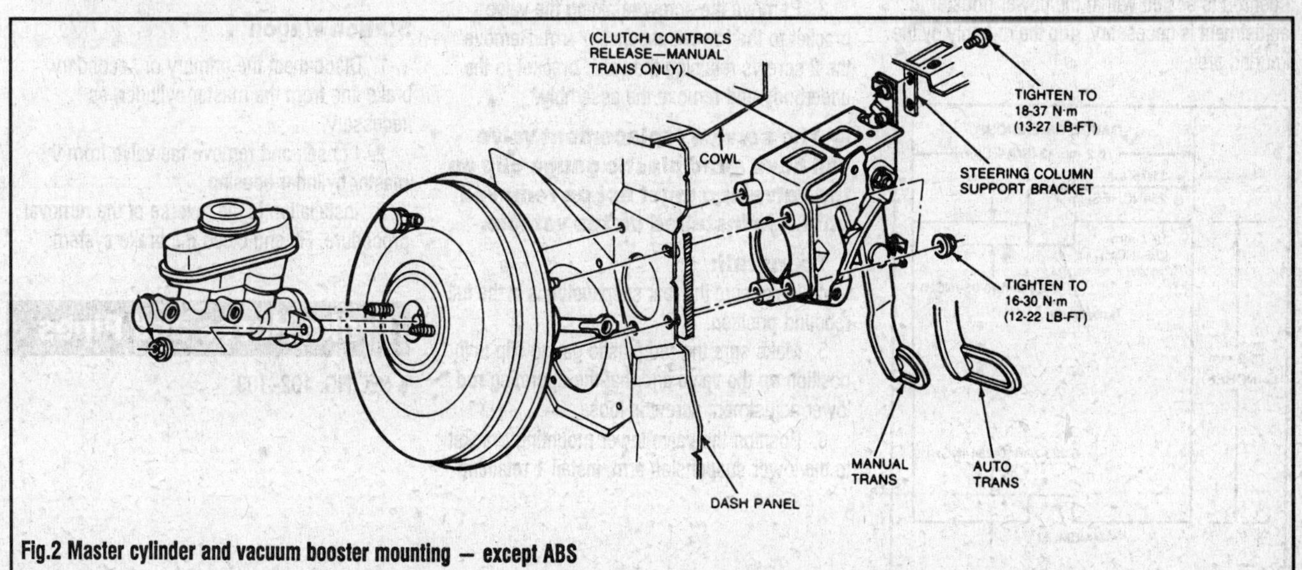

Fig.2 Master cylinder and vacuum booster mounting — except ABS

4. Remove the switch by sliding it upward. Remove the booster to dash panel retaining nuts. Slide the booster pushrod and pushrod bushing off the brake pedal pin.

5. Remove the screws and position the vacuum fitting at the dash panel aside. Position the wire harness aside. Remove the transaxle shift cable and bracket.

6. Move the booster forward until the booster studs clear the dash panel and remove the booster.

7. Installation is the reverse of the removal procedure. Bleed the brake system. Torque the master cylinder to brake booster retaining bolts to 13–25 ft. lbs. (18–34 Nm). Torque the brake booster to fire wall retaining nuts to 12–22 ft. lbs. (16–30 Nm). Torque the brake pedal pivot shaft nut to 10–20 fT. lbs. (14–27 Nm).

➡ **If equipped with speed control, the vacuum dump valve must be adjusted if the brake booster has been removed.**

ADJUSTMENT

➧ SEE FIG. 3–4

1. Without disconnecting the brake lines, disconnect the master cylinder and set it away from the booster power unit.

➡ **The master cylinder must be supported to prevent damaging the brake lines.**

2. With the engine running, check and adjust the pushrod length as shown in the illustration. A force of approximately 5 lbs. applied to the pushrod with the gauge will confirm that the pushrod is seated within the power booster. If adjustment is necessary, grip the rod only by the knurled area.

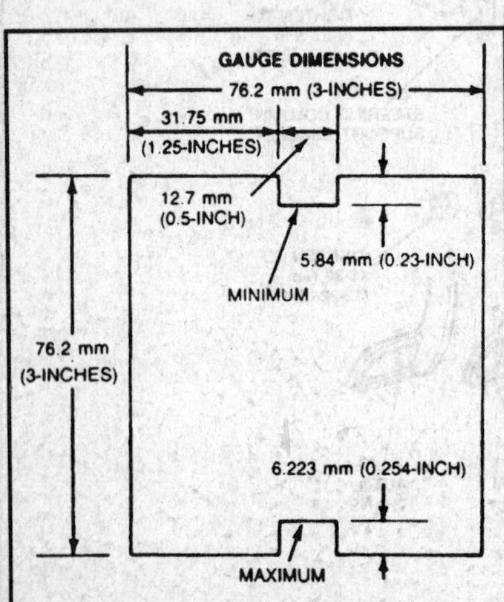

Fig.3 Power booster adjustment gauge

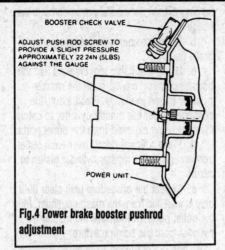

BOOSTER CHECK VALVE

ADJUST PUSH ROD SCREW TO PROVIDE A SLIGHT PRESSURE APPROXIMATELY 22 24N (5LBS) AGAINST THE GAUGE

POWER UNIT

Fig.4 Power brake booster pushrod adjustment

3. Install the master cylinder on the power booster. Gradually and alternately tighten the retaining nuts to 13–25 ft. lbs.

Proportioning Valve

REMOVAL & INSTALLATION

The valve for the sedan is mounted to the floorpan near the left rear wheel. The valve for the station wagon are screwed into the master cylinder.

Sedan

➧ SEE FIG. 5–6

1. Raise the vehicle and support it safely.

2. Disconnect the brake lines from the valve assembly and note their position.

3. Remove the screw retaining the valve bracket to the lower suspension arm. Remove the 2 screws retaining the valve bracket to the underbody and remove the assembly.

➡ **The service replacement valve will have a red plastic gauge clip on the valve and must not be removed until it is installed on the vehicle.**

To Install:

4. Make sure the rear suspension is in the full rebound position.

5. Make sure the red plastic gauge clip is in position on the valve and that the operating rod lower adjustment screw is loose.

6. Position the valve lower mounting bracket to the lower suspension arm. Install 1 retaining screw. Make sure the valve adjuster is resting on the lower bracket and tighten the set screw.

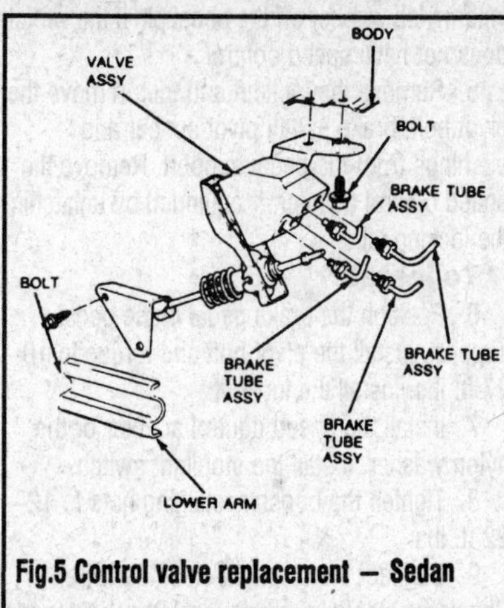

Fig.5 Control valve replacement — Sedan

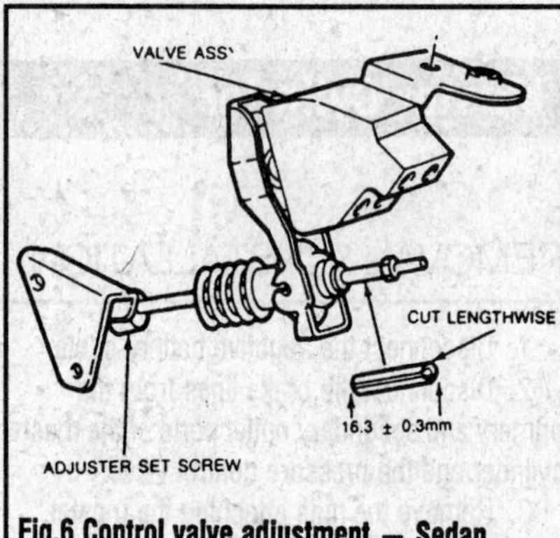

Fig.6 Control valve adjustment — Sedan

7. Connect the brake lines in the same position as removed. Bleed the rear brakes.

8. Remove the red plastic gauge clip and lower the vehicle.

Station Wagon

1. Disconnect the primary or secondary brake line from the master cylinder, as necessary.

2. Loosen and remove the valve from the master cylinder housing.

3. Installation is the reverse of the removal procedure. Fill and bleed the brake system.

Brake Hoses and Pipes

➧ SEE FIG. 102–103

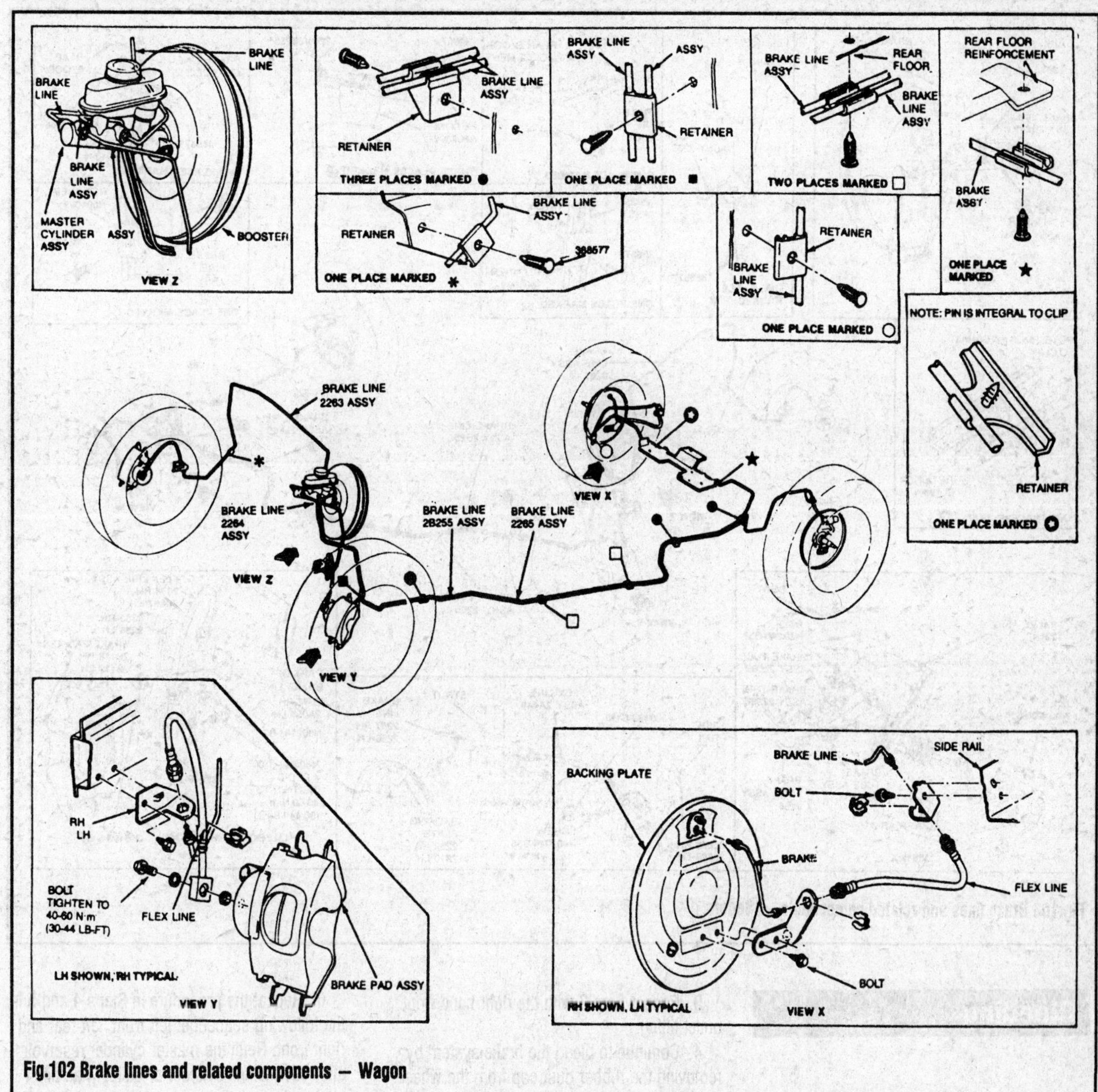

Fig.102 Brake lines and related components — Wagon

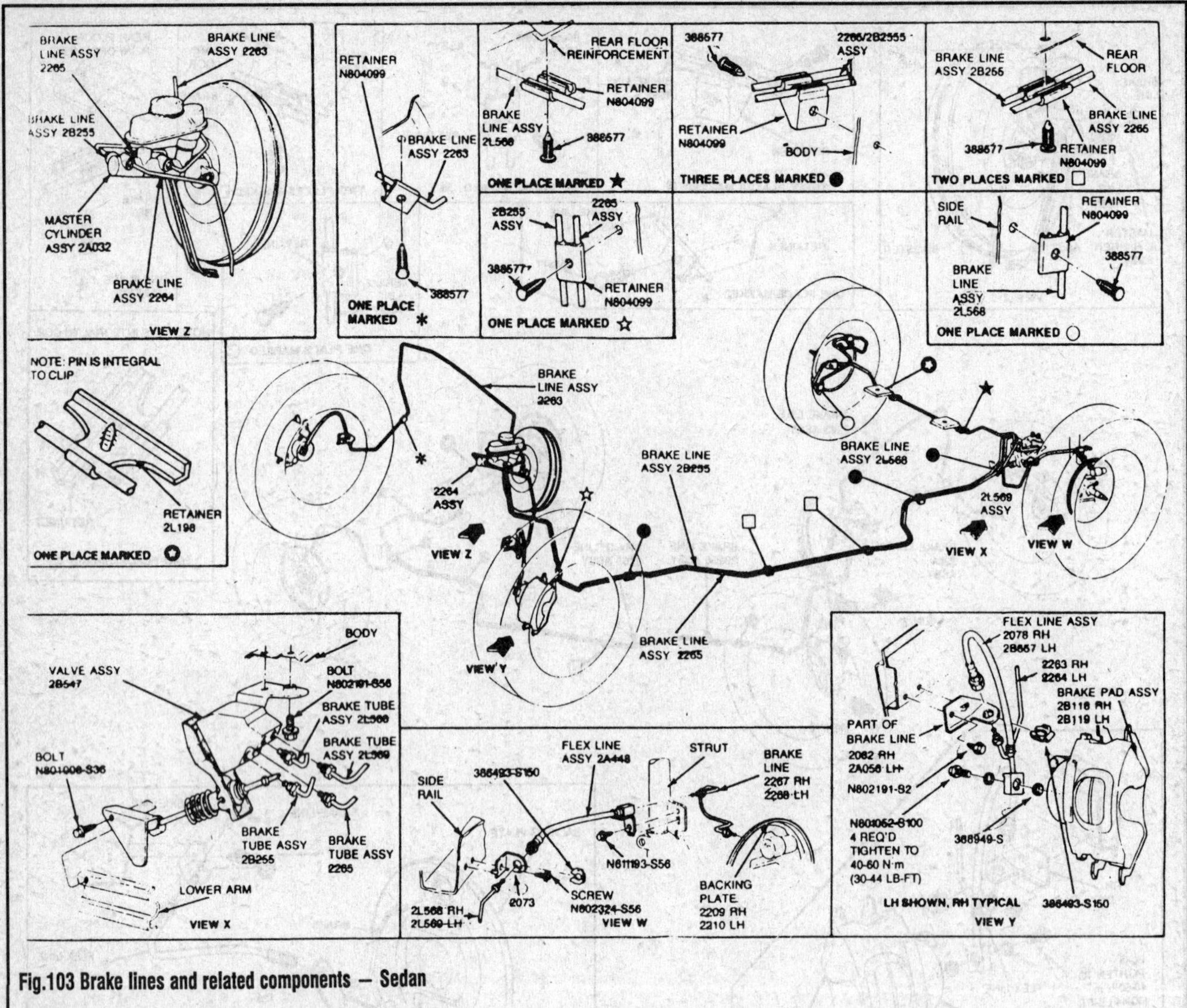

Fig.103 Brake lines and related components – Sedan

Bleeding

PROCEDURE

Except Pressure Bleeding

1. Clean all dirt from the master cylinder filler cap.

2. If the master cylinder is known or suspected to have air in the bore, it must be bled before any of the wheel cylinders or calipers. To bleed the master cylinder, loosen the upper secondary left front outlet fitting approximately 3/4 turn. Have an assistant depress the brake pedal slowly through it's full travel. Close the outlet fitting and let the pedal return slowly to the fully released position. Wait 5 seconds and then repeat the operation until all air bubbles disappear.

3. Repeat Step 2 with the right-hand front outlet fitting.

4. Continue to bleed the brake system by removing the rubber dust cap from the wheel cylinder bleeder fitting or caliper fitting at the right-hand rear of the vehicle. Place a suitable box wrench on the bleeder fitting and attach a rubber drain tube to the fitting. The end of the tube should fit snugly around the bleeder fitting. Submerge the other end of the tube in a container partially filled with clean brake fluid and loosen the fitting 3/4 turn.

5. Have an assistant push the brake pedal down slowly through it's full travel. Close the bleeder fitting and allow the pedal to slowly return to it's full release position. Wait 5 seconds and repeat the procedure until no bubbles appear at the submerged end of the bleeder tube. Secure the bleeder fitting and remove the bleeder tube. Install the rubber dust cap on the bleeder fitting.

6. Repeat the procedure in Steps 4 and 5 in the following sequence: left front, left rear and right front. Refill the master cylinder reservoir after each wheel cylinder or caliper has been bled and install the master cylinder cover and gasket. When brake bleeding is completed, the fluid level should be filled to the maximum level indicated on the reservoir.

7. Always make sure the disc brake pistons are returned to their normal positions by depressing the brake pedal several times until normal pedal travel is established. If the pedal feels spongy, repeat the bleeding procedure.

Pressure Bleeding

1. Clean all dirt from the reservoir filler cap area. Attach a suitable pressure bleeder to the reservoir cap opening.

2. Maintain 35 psi pressure on the system through the pressure bleeder.

3. Remove the dust cap from the right front caliper bleeder fitting. Attach a rubber drain tube to the fitting, making sure the tube fits snugly.

4. With the ignition switch in the **OFF** position and the brake pedal in the fully released position, open the bleeder fitting for 10 seconds at a time until an air-free stream of brake fluid flow is observed.

5. Repeat the procedure at the left front, right rear and left rear calipers, in that order.

6. Place the ignition switch in the **RUN** position and pump the brake pedal several times to complete the bleeding procedure and to fully charge the accumulator.

7. Turn the ignition switch to the **OFF** position and remove the pressure bleeder. Siphon off the excess fluid in the reservoir to adjust the level to the MAX mark with a fully charged accumulator.

Rear Brake Bleeding with a Fully Charged Accumulator

1. Remove the dust cap from the right rear caliper bleeder fitting. Attach a rubber drain tube to the fitting, making sure the tube fits snugly.

2. Turn the ignition switch to the **RUN** position. This will turn on the electric pump to charge the accumulator, as required.

3. Have an assistant hold the brake pedal in the applied position. Open the bleeder fitting for 10 seconds at a time until an air-free stream of brake fluid flow is observed.

CAUTION

To prevent possible injury, care must be used when opening the bleeder screws due to the high pressures available from a fully charged accumulator.

4. Repeat the procedure at the left rear caliper.

5. Pump the brake pedal several times to complete the bleeding procedure.

6. Adjust the fluid level in the reservoir to the MAX mark with a fully charged accumulator.

➡ If the pump motor is allowed to run continuously for approximately 20 minutes, a thermal safety switch inside the motor may shut the motor off to prevent it from overheating. If that happens, a 2-10 minute cool down period is typically required before normal operation can resume.

FRONT DISC BRAKES

CAUTION

Brake shoes contain asbestos, which has been determined to be a cancer causing agent. Never clean the brake surfaces with compressed air! Avoid inhaling any dust from and brake surface! When cleaning brake surfaces, use a commercially available brake cleaning fluid.

Brake Pads

REMOVAL & INSTALLATION

➧ SEE FIG. 7–9, 111–117

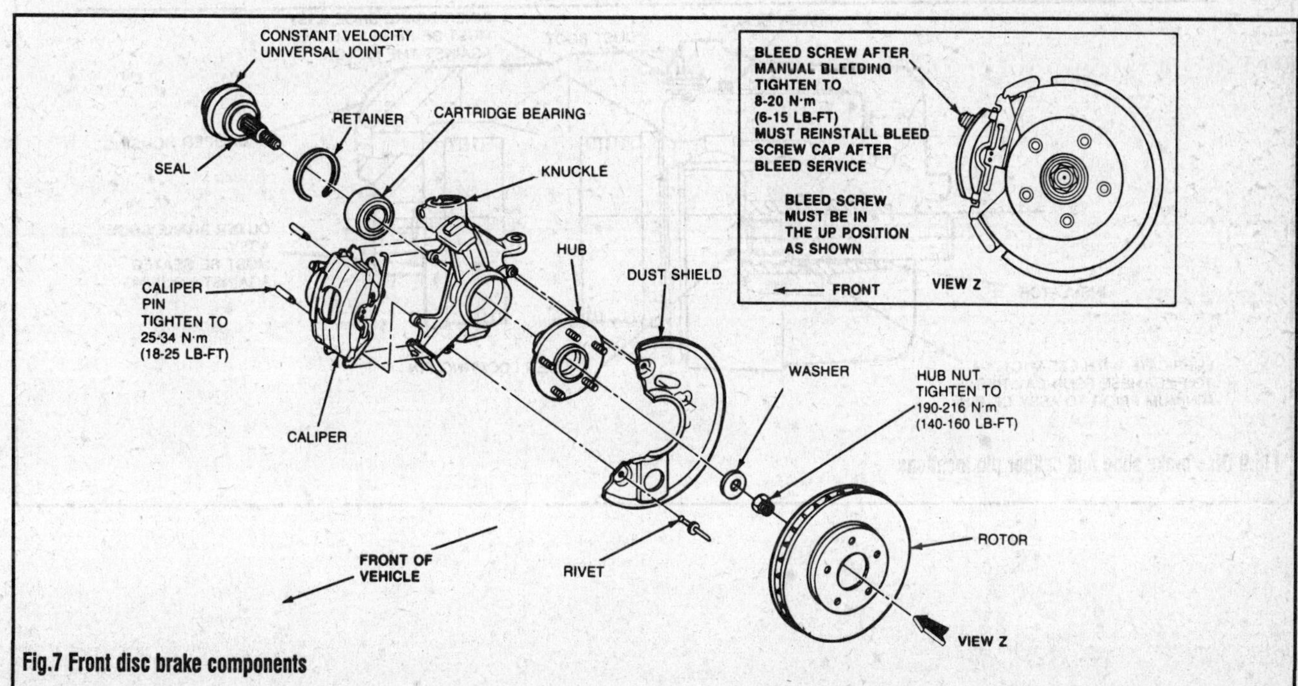

Fig.7 Front disc brake components

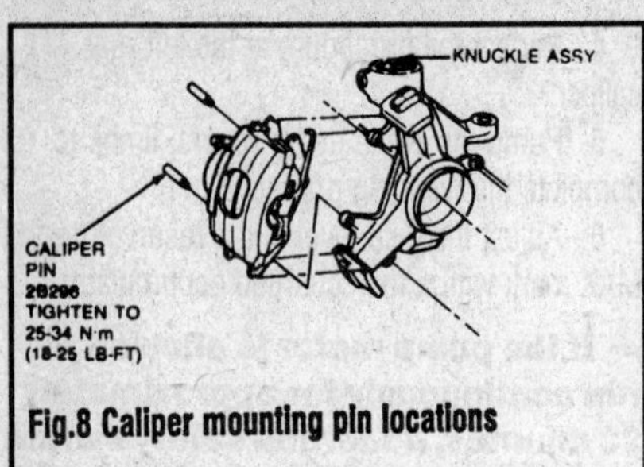

Fig.8 Caliper mounting pin locations

1. Remove the master cylinder cap and check the fluid level in the reservoir. Remove the brake fluid until the reservoir is half full. Discard the removed fluid.
2. Raise the vehicle and support it safely. Remove the wheel and tire assembly.
3. Remove the caliper locating pins. Lift the caliper assembly from the integral knuckle and anchor plate and rotor using a rotating motion. Suspend the caliper inside the fender housing with wire. Do not allow the caliper to hang from the brake hose.

➡ Do not pry directly against the plastic piston or damage will result.

4. Remove the inner and outer brake pads. Inspect the rotor braking surfaces for scoring and machine as necessary. Refer to the minimum rotor thickness specification when machining. If machining is not necessary, hand sand the glaze from the braking surfaces with medium grit sand paper.

To Install:

5. Use a 4 in. (102mm) C-clamp and a wood block $2^3/_4$ in. (70mm) × 1 in. (25mm) × $^3/_4$ in. (19mm) thick to seat the caliper piston in it's

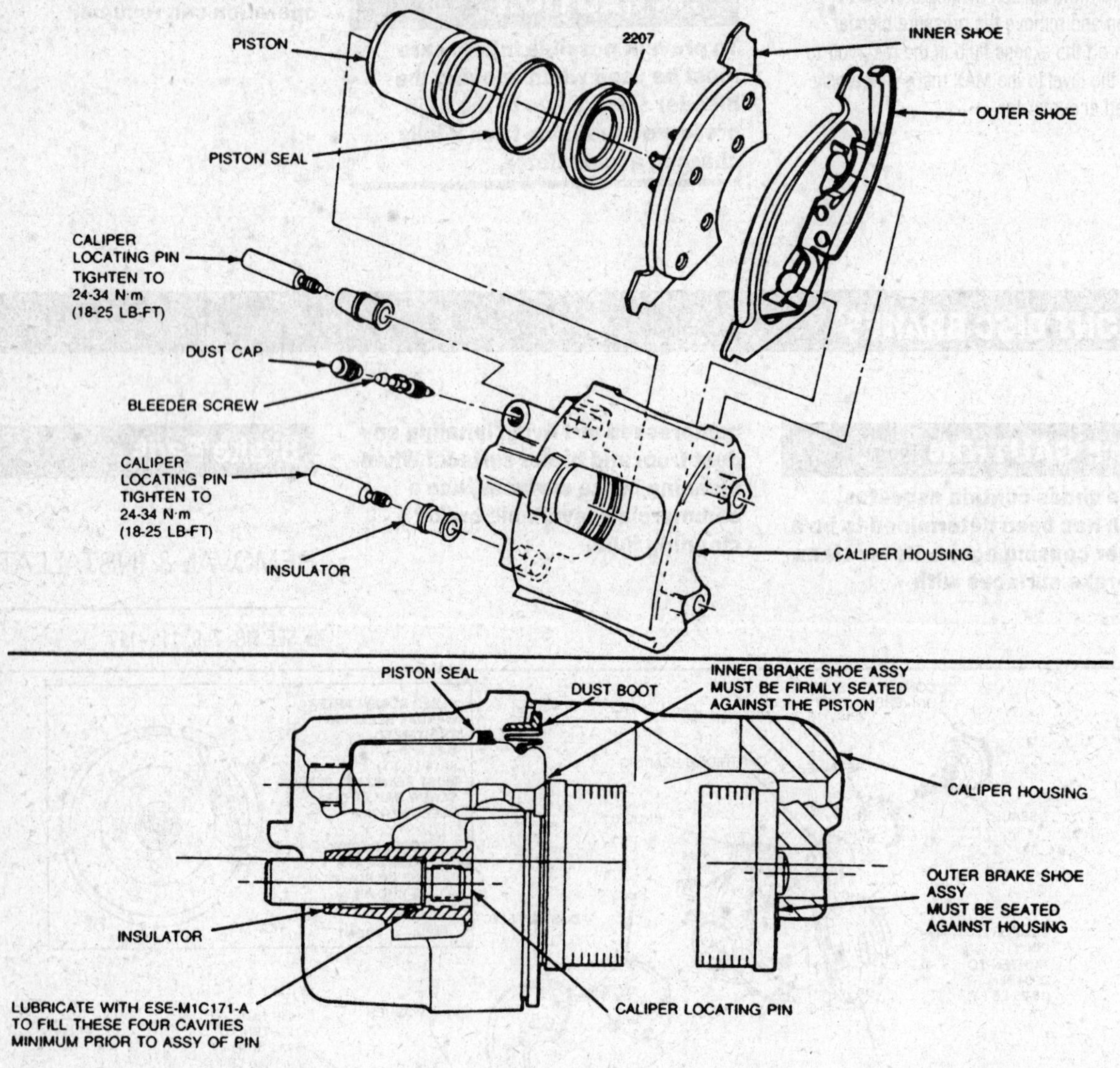

Fig.9 Disc brake shoe and caliper pin locations

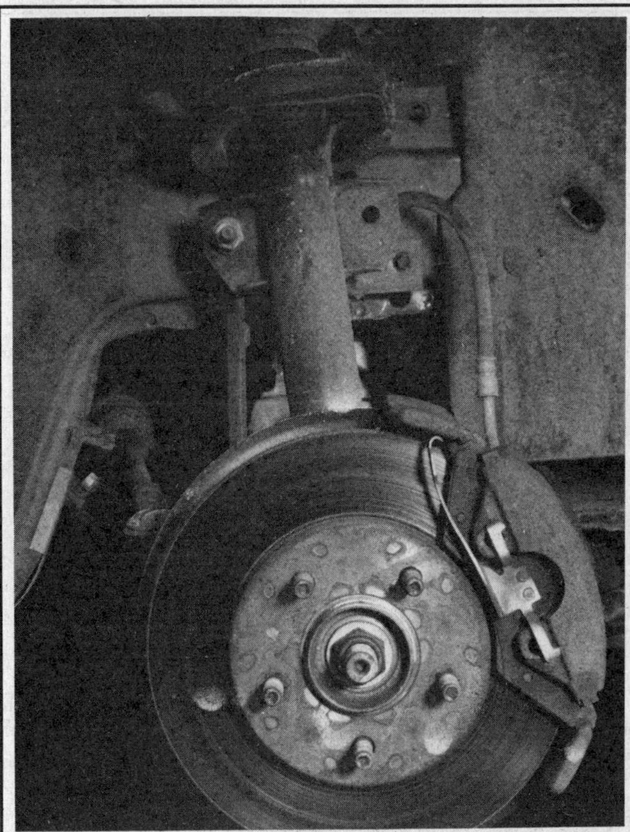
FIG. 111 Front disc brake and rotor assembly

FIG. 112 Spray caliper and disc brake pads with proper cleaning fluid

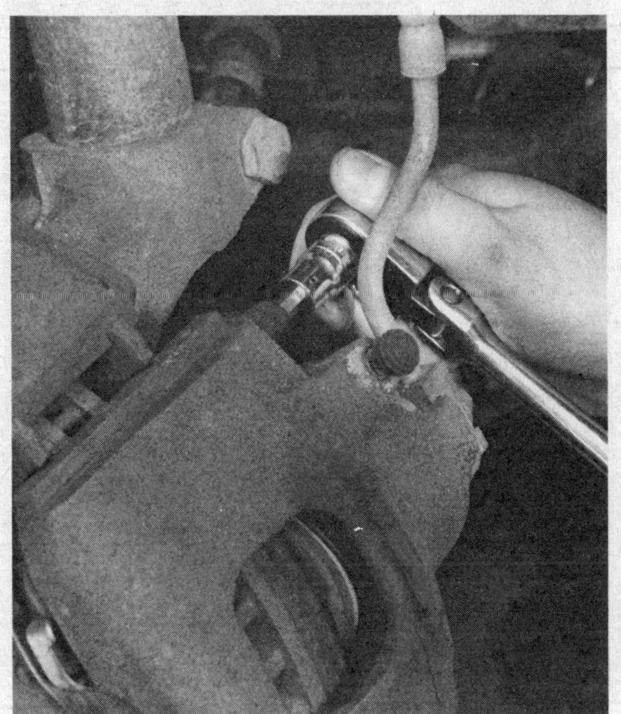
FIG. 113 Special Hex head bit retaining caliper to mounting

FIG. 114 Removing caliper holding pin from caliper

FIG. 115 Removing caliper and disc brake pads from rotor

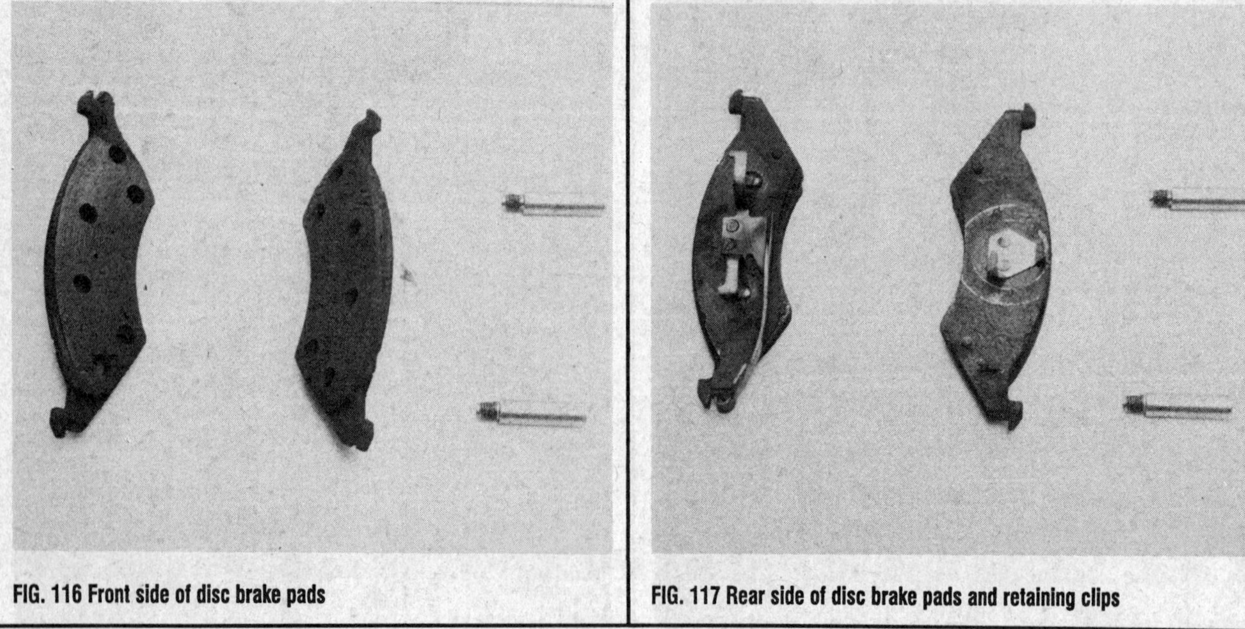

FIG. 116 Front side of disc brake pads

FIG. 117 Rear side of disc brake pads and retaining clips

bore. This must be done to provide clearance for the caliper assembly with the new brake pads to fit over the rotor during installation. Care must be taken during this procedure to prevent damage to the plastic piston. Do not allow metal or sharp objects to come into direct contact with the piston surface or damage will result.

6. Remove all rust buildup from the inside of the caliper legs. Install the inner pad in the caliper piston. Do not bend the pad clips during installation in the piston or distortion and rattles can occur. Install the outer pad. Make sure the clips are properly seated.

7. Install the caliper over the rotor and install the wheel. Lower the vehicle.

8. Pump the brake pedal prior to moving the vehicle to position the brake linings. Refill the master cylinder.

INSPECTION

1. Remove the pads from the caliper.

2. Check both the primary and secondary pad for excessive wear.

3. If only one pad is found to be defective, replace both of them not just the defective one.

Brake Caliper

REMOVAL & INSTALLATION

1. Raise and support the vehicle safely.

2. Remove the wheel and tire assembly. Mark the caliper to ensure that it is reinstalled on the correct knuckle.

3. Disconnect the flexible brake hose from the caliper. Remove the hollow retaining bolt that connects the hose fitting to the caliper. Remove the hose assembly from the caliper and plug the hose.

4. Remove the caliper locating pins.

5. Lift the caliper off of the rotor, integral knuckle and anchor plate using a rotating motion.

➡ **Do not pry directly against the plastic piston or damage to the piston will result.**

To install:

6. Retract the piston fully in the piston bore. Position the caliper assembly above the rotor with the anti-rattle spring under the upper arm of the knuckle. Install the caliper over the rotor with a rotating motion. Make sure the inner and outer shoes are properly positioned and the outer anti-rattle spring is properly positioned. Make sure the correct caliper assembly, as marked during removal, is installed on the correct knuckle. The caliper bleed screw should be positioned on top of the caliper when assembled on the vehicle.

7. Lubricate the locating pins and the inside of the insulators with silicone grease. Install the locating pins through the caliper insulators and hand start the threads into the knuckle attaching holes. Tighten the locating pins to 18–25 ft. lbs. (24–34 Nm).

8. Remove the plug and install the brake hose on the caliper with a new copper washer on each side of the fitting outlet. Insert the attaching bolt through the washers and fittings and tighten to 30–45 ft. lbs. (40–60 Nm).

9. Bleed the brake system, filling the master cylinder as required.

10. Install the wheel and lower the vehicle. Pump the brake pedal prior to moving the vehicle to position the brake linings.

OVERHAUL

➧ SEE FIG. 10

1. Remove the caliper assembly from knuckle and rotor. Do not use screwdriver or similar tool to pry piston back into cylinder bore. Use a C-clamp. Remove the outer shoe by pushing shoe to move the "buttons" from the caliper housing and slipping down caliper leg until clip is disengaged. Remove inner shoe by pulling it straight out of piston.

➡ **Inner shoe removal force may be as high as 10–20 lbs.**

2. If further disassembly is required to service the piston, disconnect the caliper from the hydraulic system, and blow the piston out using air pressure.

➡ **Do not use a screwdriver or any similar tool to pry the piston out of the bore. It will result in damage to the piston. Cushion the piston's impact against the caliper when blowing it out of the bore by placing rags between the piston and the caliper bridge.**

To assemble:

1. When assembling the caliper, examine the piston for surface irregularities or small chips and cracks. Replace the piston if damaged. Be sure to clean the foreign material from the piston surfaces and lubricate with brake fluid before inserting it into the caliper. Always install a new seal and dust boot.

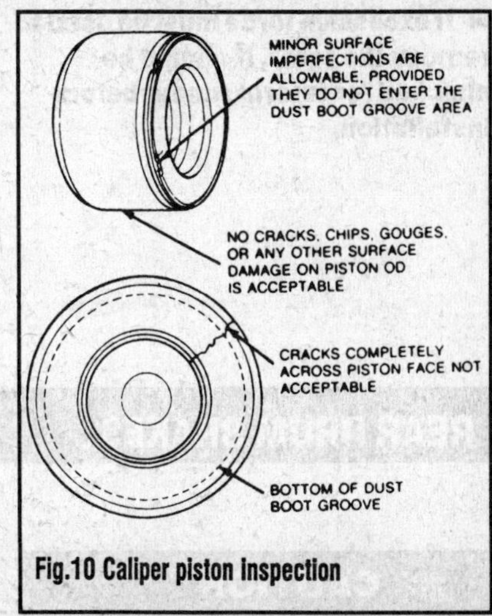
MINOR SURFACE IMPERFECTIONS ARE ALLOWABLE, PROVIDED THEY DO NOT ENTER THE DUST BOOT GROOVE AREA
NO CRACKS, CHIPS, GOUGES, OR ANY OTHER SURFACE DAMAGE ON PISTON OD IS ACCEPTABLE
CRACKS COMPLETELY ACROSS PISTON FACE NOT ACCEPTABLE
BOTTOM OF DUST BOOT GROOVE
Fig.10 Caliper piston inspection

2. When installing the piston back into bore, use a wood block or another flat stock, like an old shoe lining assembly, between C-clamp and piston. Do not apply C-clamp directly to the piston surface. This can result in damage to the piston. Be sure the piston is not cocked.

3. Be certain the dust boot is tight in boot groove on the piston and in the caliper.

4. To install the inner shoe with three-finger clip attached to the shoe into piston, grab each end of shoe, making it square with piston. Push firmly until the shoe clip snaps into the piston. Do not allow the shoe or the clip tangs to cock during installation.

Brake Rotor

REMOVAL & INSTALLATION

1. Raise the vehicle and support it safely.

2. Remove the wheel and tire assembly.

3. Remove the caliper assembly from the rotor. Position the caliper aside and support it with a length of wire. Do not allow the caliper to hang by the brake hose.

4. Remove the rotor from the hub assembly by pulling it off the hub studs. If additional force is required to remove the rotor, apply rust penetrator on the front and rear rotor/hub mating surfaces and then strike the rotor between the studs with a plastic hammer. If this does not work, attach a 3-jaw puller and remove the rotor.

➡ If excessive force must be used to remove the rotor, it should be checked for lateral runout before installation.

5. Check the rotor for scoring and/or other wear. Machine or replace, as necessary. If machining, observe the minimum thickness specification.

6. Install the rotor in the reverse order of removal.

INSPECTION

Using a micrometer measure the thickness of the rotor in four different places. If the rotor is not within specification either have it cut, if possible, or replace it.

REAR DRUM BRAKES

CAUTION

Brake shoes contain asbestos, which has been determined to be a cancer causing agent. Never clean the brake surfaces with compressed air! Avoid inhaling any dust from and brake surface! When cleaning brake surfaces, use a commercially available brake cleaning fluid.

Brake Drums

REMOVAL & INSTALLATION

1986–89

➧ SEE FIG. 103a

1. Raise and safely support the vehicle.
2. Remove the wheelcover and nut covers, as required. Remove the wheel and tire assembly.
3. Remove the grease cap from the hub. Remove the cotter pin, nut lock, adjusting nut and keyed flatwasher from the spindle. Remove the outer bearing and discard the cotter pin.
4. Remove the hub/drum assembly as a unit. Be careful not to damage the grease seal and inner bearing during removal.
5. Inspect the drum for scoring and/or other wear. Machine or replace, as necessary. If machining, observe the maximum permissible drum diameter specification.

To install:

6. Inspect and lubricate the bearings, as necessary. Replace the grease seal if any damage is visible.
7. Clean the spindle stem and apply a thin coat of wheel bearing grease.
8. Install the hub and drum assembly on the spindle. Install the outer bearing, keyed flat washer and adjusting nut. Tighten the nut finger-tight.
9. Adjust the wheel bearings. Install the nut retainer and a new cotter pin. Install the grease cap.
10. Install the wheel and tire assembly. Install the wheel cover and nut covers, as required. Lower the vehicle.

1990–92

1. Raise the vehicle and support it safely.
2. Remove the wheel cover.
3. Remove the lugnuts and the wheel and tire assembly.
4. Remove the 2 drum retaining nuts and the drum.

➡ If the drum will not come off, pry the rubber plug from the backing plate inspection hole. Remove the brake line-to-axle retention bracket. This will allow sufficient room to insert suitable brake tools through the inspection hole to disengage the adjusting lever and back off the adjusting screw.

5. Inspect the drum for scoring and/or other wear. Machine or replace, as necessary. If machining, observe the maximum permissible drum diameter specification.
6. Installation is the reverse of the removal procedure.

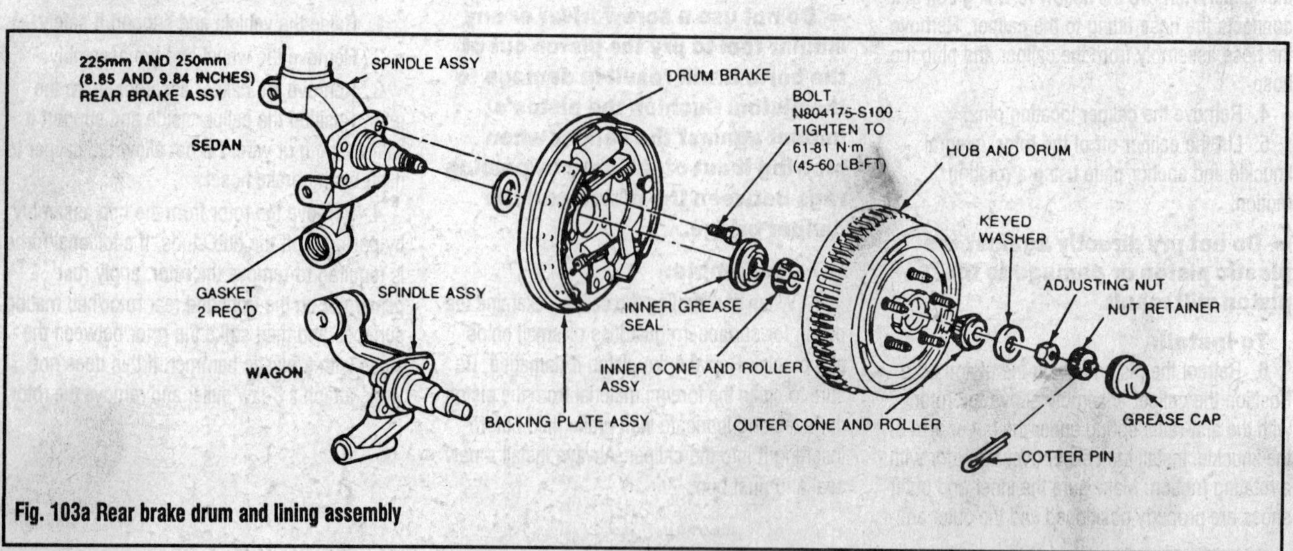

Fig. 103a Rear brake drum and lining assembly

INSPECTION

Inspect the brake drums for excessive wear. Using a brake drum inspection gauge tool D81L–1103–A measure the drum inside diameter. If the drum is not within specification it must be either cut or replaced. The maximum inside diameter of the drum is stamped on it. If this number exceeds the drum wear or the refinishing specification the drum must be replaced.

Brake Shoes

INSPECTION

Inspect the brake shoes for excessive lining wear or shoe damage. If the lining is worn below $\frac{1}{32}$ in. (0.8mm) replace both shoes. Replace lining that has become contaminated with brake fluid, oil or grease.

REMOVAL & INSTALLATION

SEE FIG. 11–14, 118–124

1. Raise the vehicle and support it safely.
2. Remove the wheel and tire assembly and the brake drum.
3. Remove the 2 shoe hold-down springs and pins.
4. Lift the brake shoes, springs and adjuster assembly off the backing plate and wheel cylinder assembly. When removing the

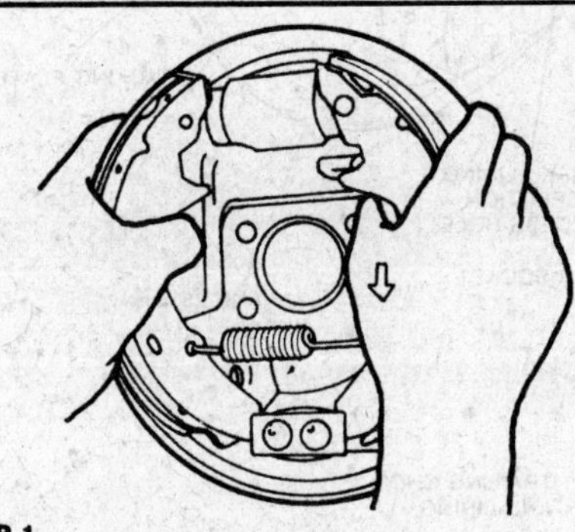

STEP 1

A. ASSEMBLE PARKING BRAKE CABLE TO TRAILING SHOE AND PARKING BRAKE LEVER.

B. INSTALL LOWER RETRACTING SPRING TO LEADING-TRAILING SHOES.

C. INSTALL THIS ASSY TO BACKING PLATE.

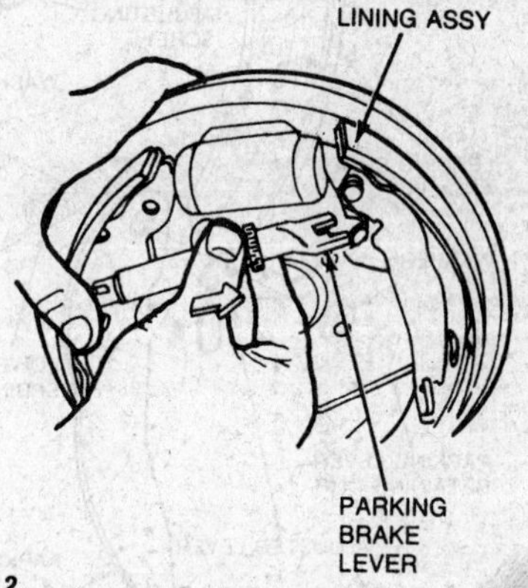

STEP 2

INSTALL ADJUSTER SCREW ASSY.

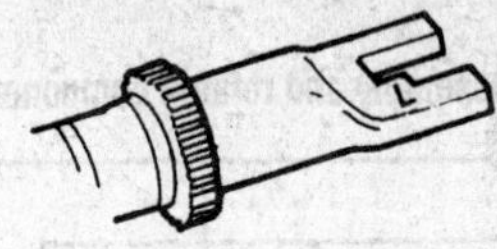

NOTE: SOCKET BLADE MARKED R AND L. INSTALL LETTER IN UPRIGHT POSITION TO ENSURE PROPER SLOT ENGAGEMENT TO PARKING BRAKE LEVER.

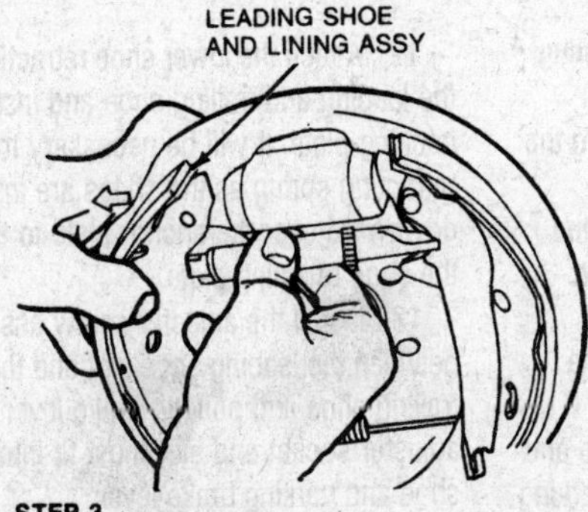

STEP 3

INSTALL ADJUSTER SCREW TO LEADING SHOE AND LINING ASSY.

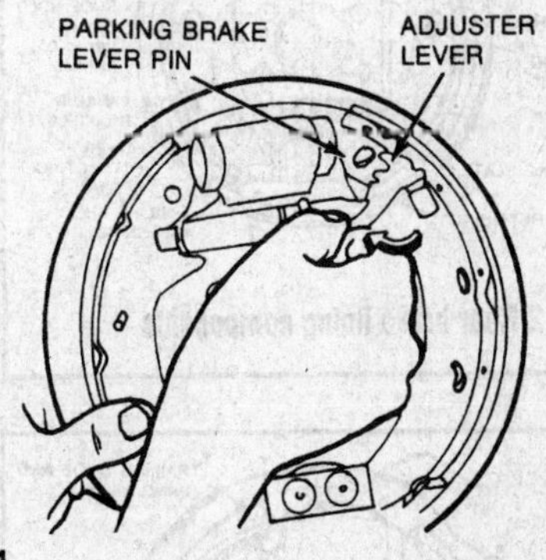

STEP 4

INSTALL THE ADJUSTER LEVER IN GROOVE OF PARKING BRAKE LEVER PIN.

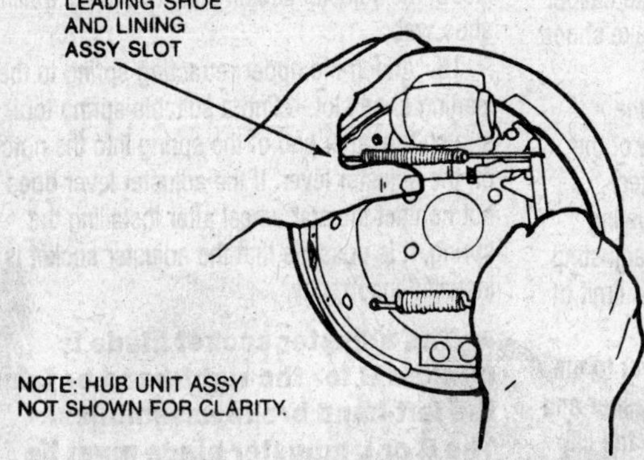

NOTE: HUB UNIT ASSY NOT SHOWN FOR CLARITY.

STEP 5

A. INTALL SHOE HOLD-DOWN SPRINGS AND PINS.

B. INSTALL UPPER RETRACTING SPRING TO LEADING SHOE SLOT- STRETCH SPRING TO INSTALL TO TRAILING SHOE. IF ADJUSTER LEVER DOES NOT CONTACT STAR WHEEL AFTER SPRING INSTALLATION CHECK ADJUSTER SOCKET INSTALLATION.

Fig.11 Drum brake replacement procedure

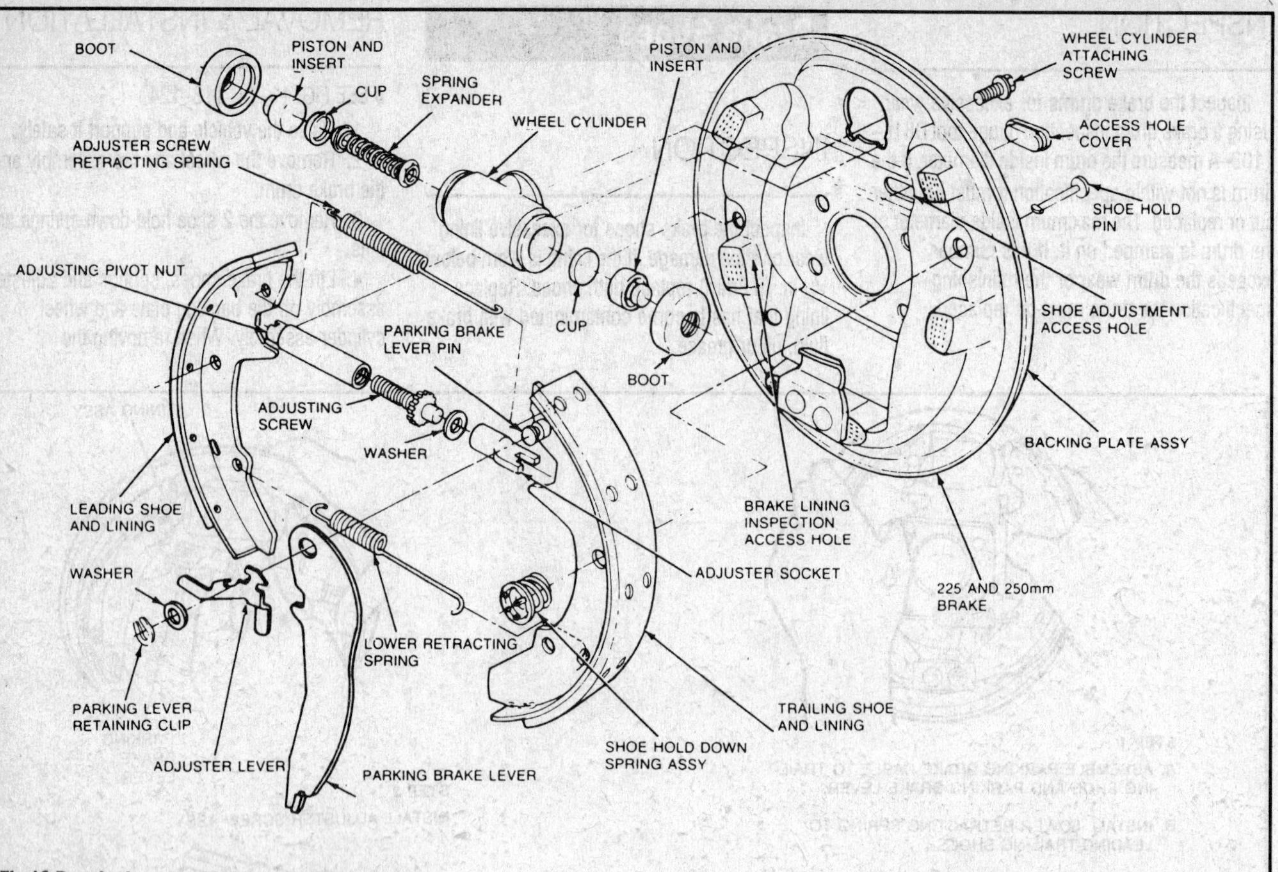

Fig.13 Rear brake assembly and related components

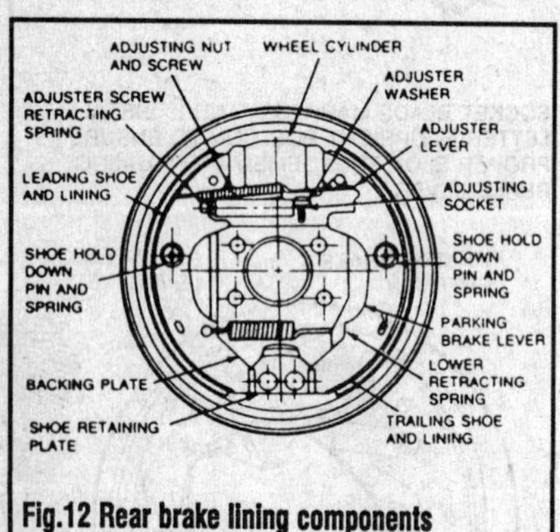

Fig.12 Rear brake lining components

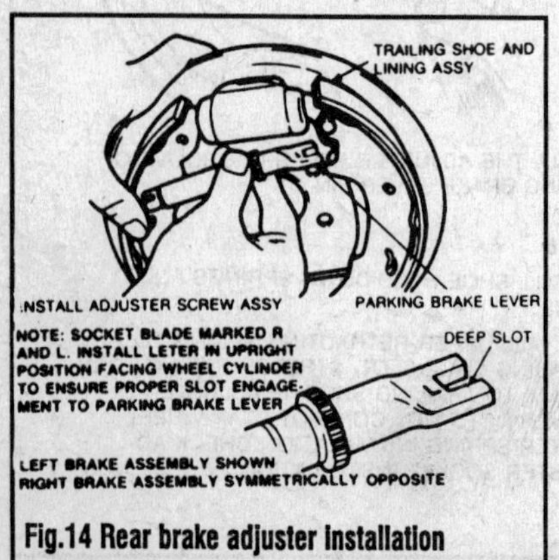

Fig.14 Rear brake adjuster installation

assembly, be careful not to bend the adjusting lever.

5. Remove the parking brake cable from the parking brake lever.

6. Remove the retracting springs from the lower brake attachments and upper shoe-to-adjusting lever attachment points. This will separate the brake shoes and disengage the adjuster mechanism.

7. Remove the horse shoe retaining clip and spring washer and slide the lever off the parking brake lever pin on the trailing shoe.

To Install:

8. Apply a light coating of disc brake caliper slide grease at the points where the brake shoes contact the backing plate.

9. Apply a thin coat of lubricant to the adjuster screw threads and socket end of the adjusting screw. Install the stainless steel washer over the socket end of the adjusting screw and install the socket. Turn the adjusting screw into the adjusting pivot nut to the limit of the threads and then back off 1/2 turn.

10. Assemble the parking brake lever to the trailing shoe by installing the spring washer and a new horse shoe retaining clip. Crimp the clip until it retains the lever to the shoe securely.

11. Attach the parking brake cable to the parking brake lever.

12. Attach the lower shoe retracting spring to the leading and trailing shoe and install to the backing plate. It will be necessary to stretch the retracting spring as the shoes are installed downward over the anchor plate to the inside of the shoe retaining plate.

13. Install the adjuster screw assembly between the leading shoe slot and the slot in the trailing shoe and parking brake lever. The adjuster socket end slot must fit into the trailing shoe and parking brake lever.

14. Assemble the adjuster lever in the groove located in the parking brake lever pin and into the slot of the adjuster socket that fits into the trailing shoe web.

15. Attach the upper retracting spring to the leading shoe slot. Using a suitable spring tool, stretch the other end of the spring into the notch on the adjuster lever. If the adjuster lever does not contact the star wheel after installing the spring, it is possible that the adjuster socket is installed incorrectly.

➡ The adjuster socket blade is marked R for the right-hand or L for the left-hand brake assemblies. The R or L adjuster blade must be installed with the letter R or L in the upright position, facing the wheel cylinder, on the correct side to

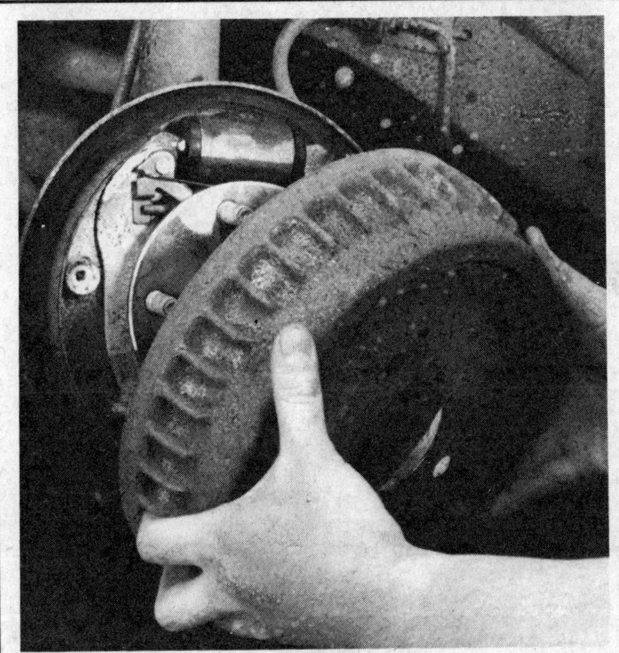

FIG. 118 Removing rear brake drum

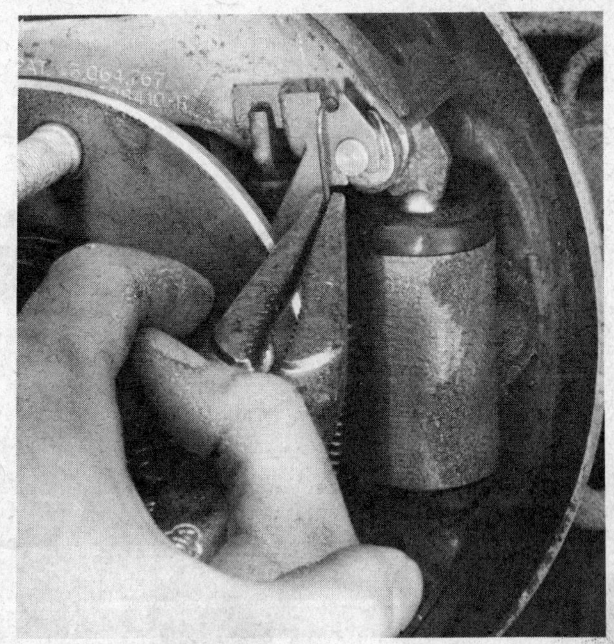

FIG. 119 Removing brake shoe holding spring

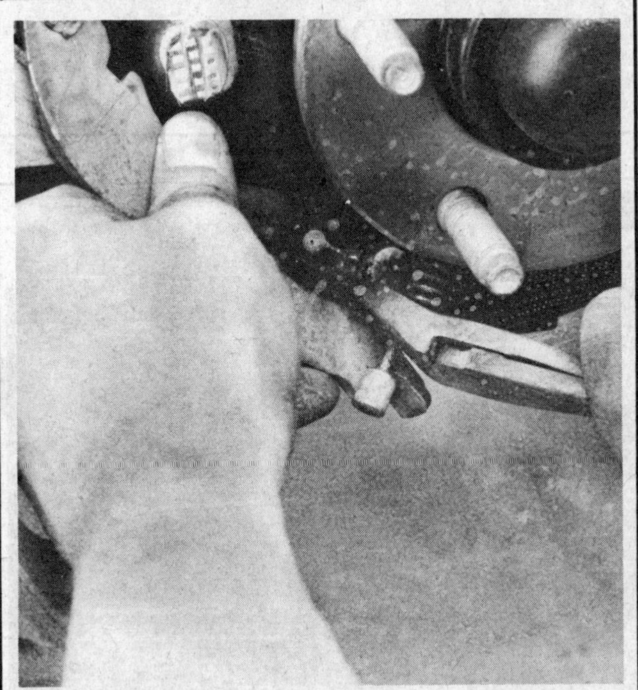

FIG. 120 Disconnecting emergency brake lever from mounting

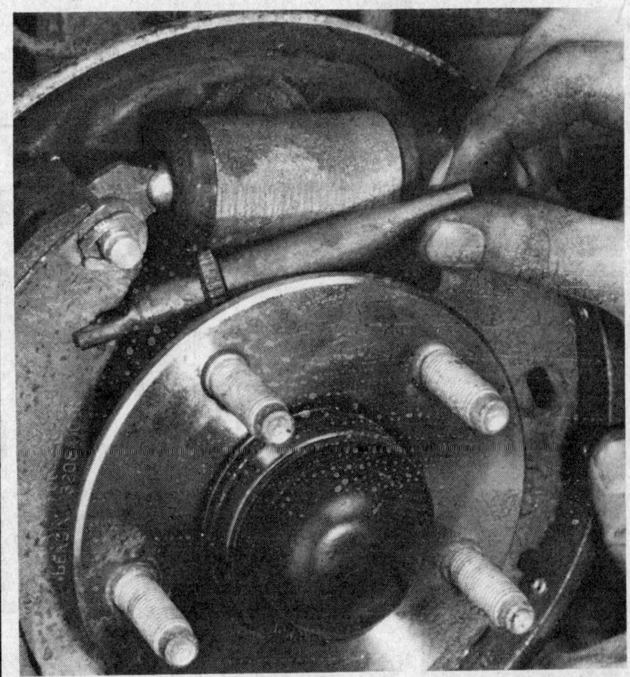

FIG. 121 Removing adjusting mechanism

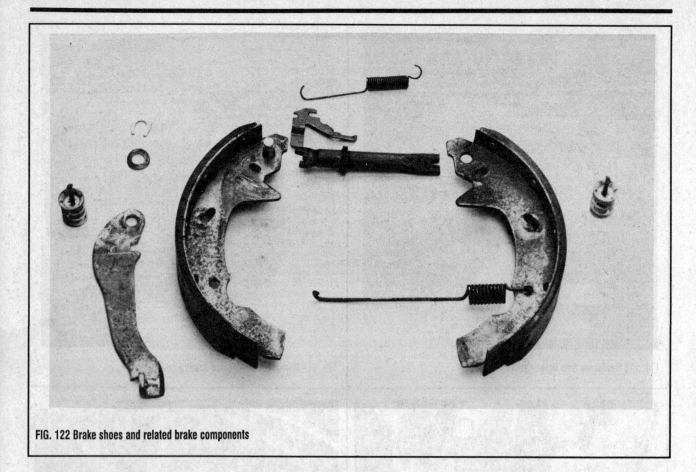

FIG. 122 Brake shoes and related brake components

FIG. 123 Grease contact points before reassembly

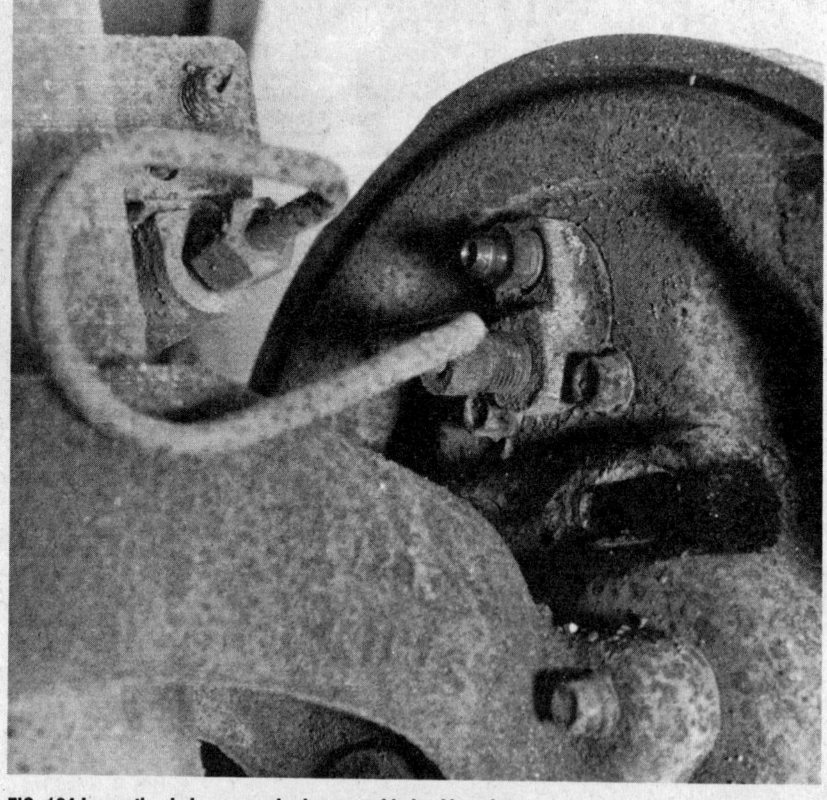

FIG. 124 Inspection hole on rear brake assembly backing plate

ensure that the deeper of the 2 slots in the adjuster sockets fits into the parking brake lever.

16. Adjust the brake shoes.
17. Install the brake drum and wheel and tire assembly. Lower the vehicle.

Wheel Cylinders

REMOVAL & INSTALLATION

1. Raise and support the vehicle safely.
2. Remove the wheel and tire assembly.
3. Remove the brake drum.
4. Remove the brake shoes, retainers and springs from the backing plate.
5. Disconnect and plug the brake line at the rear-side of the wheel cylinder.
6. Remove the wheel cylinder-to-backing plate bolts and remove the wheel cylinder.
7. To install, reverse the order of removal. Tighten the wheel cylinder-to-backing plate bolts to 8–10 ft. lbs. (10–14 Nm). Bleed the rear brake system.

OVERHAUL

➧ SEE FIG. 15

Wheel cylinders need not be rebuilt unless they are leaking or seized. To check the wheel cylinder for leakage, carefully pull the lower edge of the rubber end boot away from the cylinder. Excessive brake fluid in the boot or running out of the boot, when the edges are pulled away from the cylinder, denotes leakage. A certain (slight) amount of fluid in the boot is normal.

1. It is not necessary to remove the cylinder from the brake backing (mounting) plate to rebuild the cylinder, however removal makes the job easier.
2. Disengage and remove the rubber boots from both ends of the wheel cylinder. The piston should come out with the boot. If not, remove the piston by applying finger pressure inward on one piston, the piston on the opposite end should come out. Take care not to splash brake fluid all over yourself when the piston pops from the cylinder.
3. Remove the rubber cups, center expander and spring from the wheel cylinder. Remove the bleeder screw from the back of the cylinder.
4. Discard all rubber boots and cups. Wash the pistons and cylinder in denatured alcohol or clean brake fluid.
5. Inspect the pistons for scratches, scoring or other visible damage. Inspect the cylinder bore for score marks or rust. The cylinder may be honed (with a brake cylinder hone) if necessary. Do not hone more than 0.076mm beyond original diameter. If the scoring or pitting is deeper, replace the cylinder.
6. After honing the cylinder, wash again with alcohol or clean brake fluid. Check the bleeder screw hole to make sure it is opened. Wipe the cylinder bore with a clean cloth. Install the bleeder screw.
7. Never reuse the old rubber parts. Always use all of the parts supplied in the rebuilding kit.
8. Apply a light coat of brake fluid, or the special lubricant if supplied with the rebuilding kit, on the pistons, rubber cups and cylinder bore.
9. Insert the spring and expander assembly into the cylinder bore. Put the cups, facing in, and the pistons into the cylinder. Install the boots and fit the outer lips into the retaining grooves on the outer edges of the wheel cylinder.
10. Install the wheel cylinder onto the backing plate. Be sure that the inlet port (where the brake hose connects) is toward the rear of the car. Install the brake shoes, drum and wheel assembly. Adjust and bleed the brake system. Road test the car.

Brake Backing Plate

REMOVAL & INSTALLATION

1. Raise and support the vehicle safely. Remove the tire and wheel assembly.
2. Remove the brake drum. Remove the grease cap. Remove and discard the retaining nut.
3. Remove the bearing hub unit from the spindle. Disconnect the brake line.
4. Remove the brake shoes, adjuster assemblies, wheel cylinder and parking brake cable from the backing plate.
5. Remove the backing plate to spindle retaining bolts. Discard them.
6. Remove the backing plate and foam gasket.

To install:

7. Install the backing plate using a new foam gasket. Install the wheel cylinder. Connect the brake line.
8. Install the brake shoe assembly. Install the bearing and hub nut. Torque the nut to 188–254 ft. lbs.
9. Install a new grease cover. Install the brake drum. Adjust the brakes. Bleed the brake system. Check the parking brake cable adjustment.

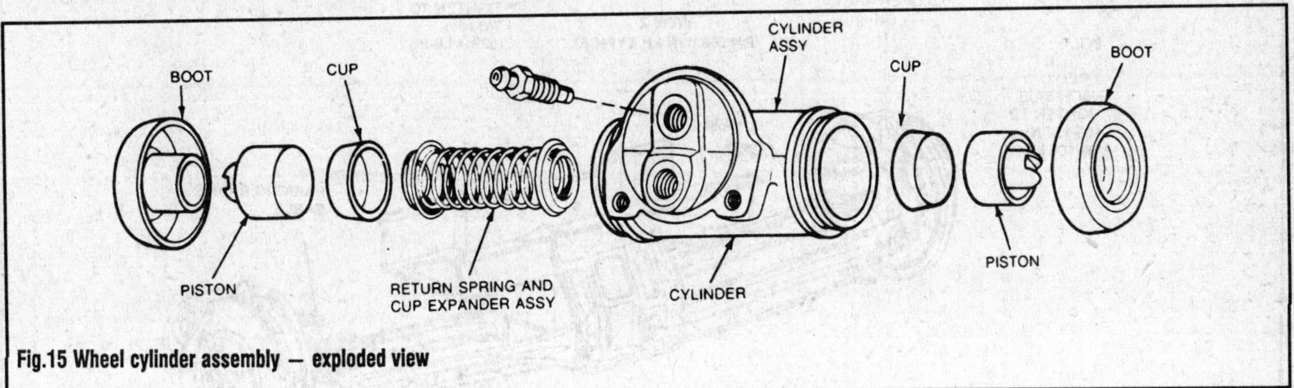

Fig.15 Wheel cylinder assembly — exploded view

REAR DISC BRAKES

✻✻ CAUTION

Brake shoes contain asbestos, which has been determined to be a cancer causing agent. Never clean the brake surfaces with compressed air! Avoid inhaling any dust from and brake surface! When cleaning brake surfaces, use a commercially available brake cleaning fluid.

Brake Pads

REMOVAL & INSTALLATION

➧ SEE FIG. 104–105

1. Remove the master cylinder cap and check the fluid level in the reservoir. Remove the brake fluid until the reservoir is half full. Discard the removed fluid.
2. Raise the vehicle and support it safely.
3. Remove the wheel and tire assembly.
4. Remove the screw retaining the brake hose bracket to the shock absorber bracket. Remove the retaining clip from the parking brake cable at the caliper. Remove the cable end from the parking brake lever.
5. Hold the slider pin hex-heads with an open-end wrench. Remove the upper pinch bolt. Rotate the caliper away from the rotor.
6. Remove the brake pads.

To install:

7. Using a brake piston turning tool, rotate the piston clockwise until it is fully seated. Make sure 1 of the 2 slots in the piston face is positioned so it will engage the nib on the brake pad.
8. Install the brake pads in the anchor plate. Rotate the caliper assembly over the rotor into position on the anchor plate. Make sure the brake pads are installed correctly.
9. Remove the residue from the pinch bolt threads and apply 1 drop of threadlock and sealer. Install and tighten the pinch bolts to 23–26 ft. lbs. (31–35 Nm) while holding the slider pins with an open-end wrench.
10. Attach the cable end to the parking brake lever. Install the cable retaining clip on the caliper assembly. Position the brake flex hose and bracket assembly to the shock absorber bracket and install the retaining screw. Tighten the screw to 8–11 ft. lbs. (11–16 Nm).
11. Install the wheel and tire assembly and lower the vehicle. Pump the brake pedal prior to moving the vehicle to position the brake linings. Refill the master cylinder.

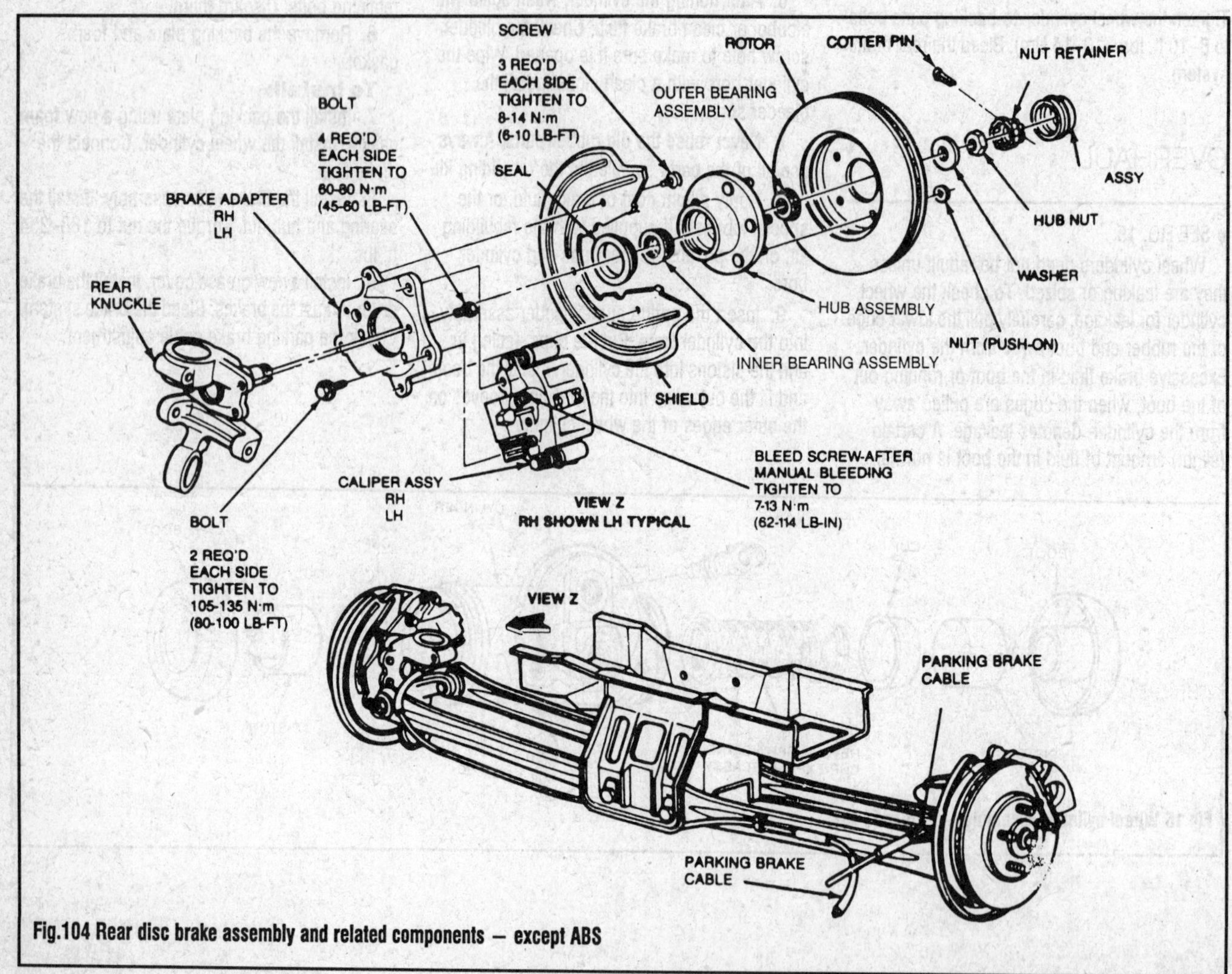

Fig.104 Rear disc brake assembly and related components — except ABS

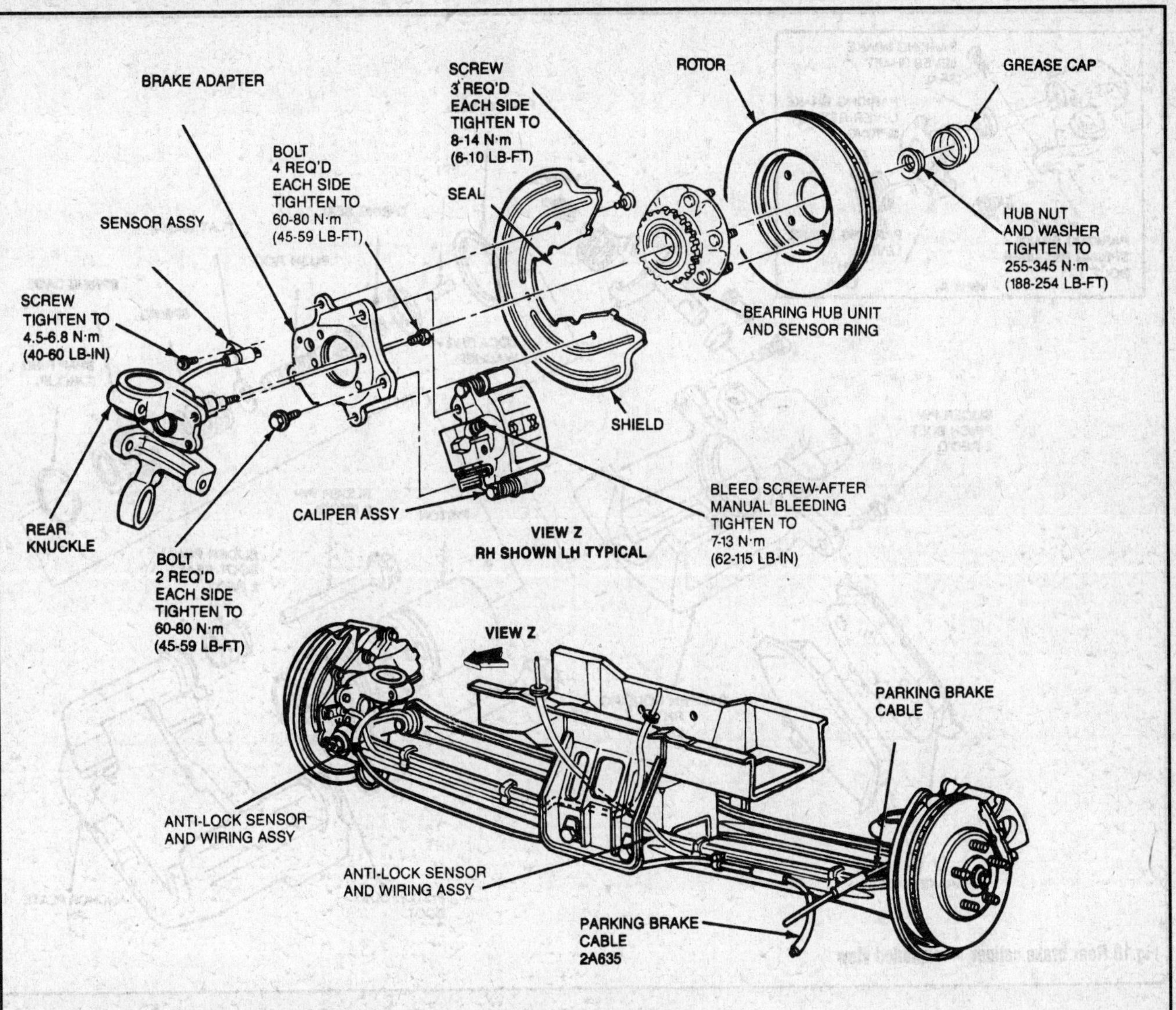

Fig.105 Rear disc brake assembly and related components — ABS except 1992 Wagon

INSPECTION

The rear disc brakes can be inspected through an oval hole in the back of the brake caliper. Raise the rear of the vehicle and remove the wheel and tire assembly to inspect the brake pads. If the brake lining thickness is less than 3mm the brake pads will have to be replaced.

Brake Caliper

REMOVAL & INSTALLATION

➧ SEE FIG. 17–18

1. Raise and support the vehicle safely.
2. Remove the wheel and tire assembly.
3. Remove the brake flex hose from the caliper assembly.
4. Remove the retaining clip from the parking brake at the caliper. Disengage the parking brake cable end from the lever arm.
5. Hold the slider pin hex-heads with an open-end wrench and remove the pinch bolts. Lift the caliper assembly away from the anchor plate. Remove the slider pins and boots from the anchor plate.

To install:

6. Apply silicone dielectric compound to the inside of the slider pin boots and to the slider pins.
7. Position the slider pins and boots in the anchor plate. Position the caliper assembly on the anchor plate. Make sure the brake pads are installed correctly.
8. Remove the residue from the pinch bolt threads and apply 1 drop of threadlock and sealer. Install the pinch bolts and tighten to 23–26 ft. lbs. (31–35 Nm) while holding the slider pins with an open-end wrench.
9. Attach the cable end to the parking brake

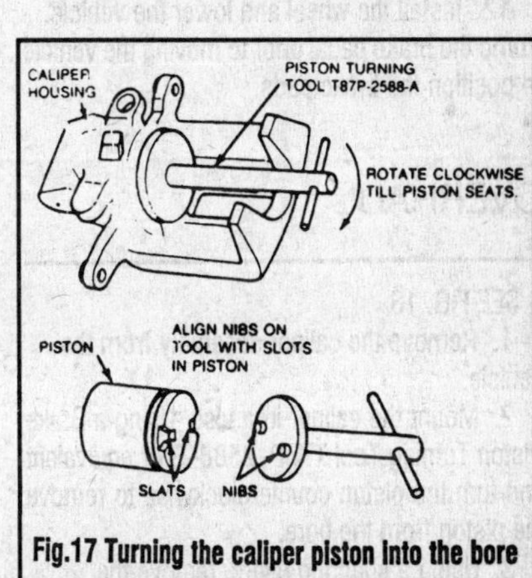

Fig.17 Turning the caliper piston into the bore

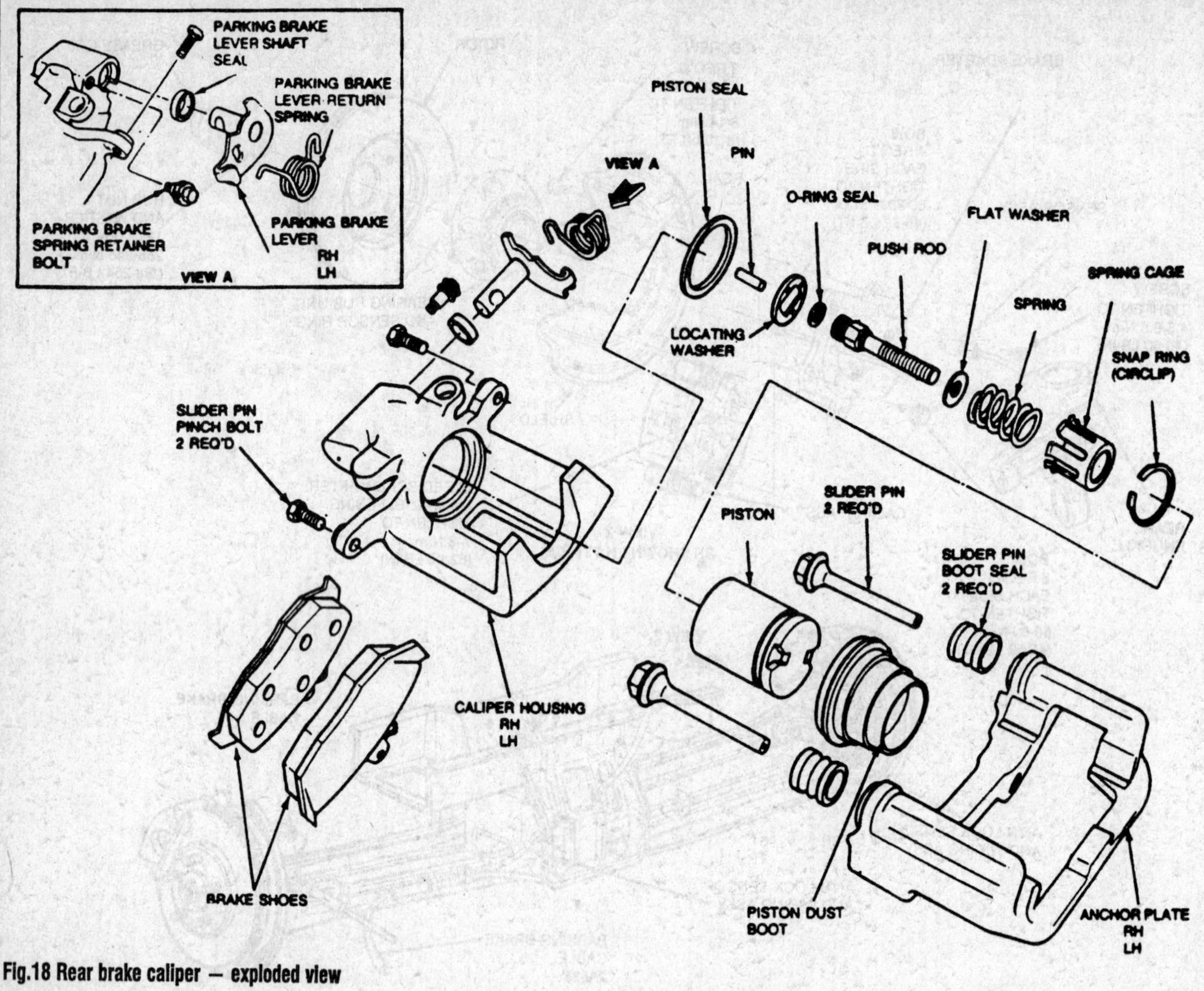

Fig.18 Rear brake caliper — exploded view

lever. Install the cable retaining clip on the caliper assembly.

10. Using new washers, connect the brake flex hose to the caliper. Tighten the retaining bolt to 8–11 ft. lbs. (11–16 Nm).

11. Bleed the brake system, filling the master cylinder as required.

12. Install the wheel and lower the vehicle. Pump the brake pedal prior to moving the vehicle to position the brake pads.

OVERHAUL

➧ SEE FIG. 16

1. Remove the caliper assembly from the vehicle.

2. Mount the caliper in a vise. Using a Brake Piston Turning Tool T75P–2588–B or equivalent and turn the piston counterclockwise to remove the piston from the bore.

3. Using a snapring pliers, remove the snapring retaining the pushrod from the caliper.

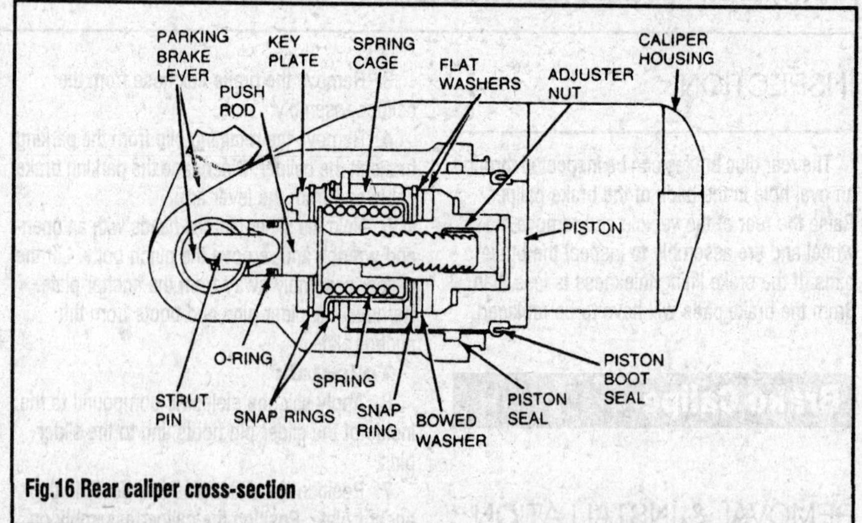

Fig.16 Rear caliper cross-section

✲✲ CAUTION

The snapring and spring cover are under spring load. Be careful when removing the snapring.

4. Remove the spring cover, spring, washer, key plate, and pull out the pushrod strut pin from the piston bore.
5. Remove the parking brake lever return spring, unscrew the parking brake lever stop bolt and pull the parking brake lever out of the caliper housing.
6. Clean all medal parts with isopropyl alcohol. Use clean dry compressed air to clean the grooves and passages. Inspect the caliper bores for damage or excessive wear. If the piston is pitted, scratched, or scored replace the piston.

To assemble:

1. Lightly grease the parking brake lever bore and the lever shaft seal with Silicone Dielectric Compound or equivalent. Press the parking brake lever shaft seal into the caliper bore.
2. Grease the parking brake shaft recess and slightly grease the parking brake lever shaft. Install the shaft into the caliper housing.
3. Install the lever stop bolt into the caliper housing and torque the bolt to 60–84 inch lbs.
4. Attach the parking brake lever return spring to the stop bolt and install the free end into the parking brake lever slot.
5. Install a new O-ring seal in the groove of the pushrod. Grease the pushrod end with Silicone Dielectric Compound or equivalent.
6. Position the strut pin into the caliper housing and in the recess of the parking brake lever shaft. Install the pushrod into the bore. Make sure the pin is positioned correctly between the shaft recess. Install the flat washer, pushrod, spring and spring cover in order.

BRAKE ROTOR

REMOVAL & INSTALLATION

1. Raise the vehicle and support it safely.
2. Remove the wheel and tire assembly.
3. Remove the caliper assembly from the rotor and support it with a length of wire. Do not let the caliper hang from the brake line.
4. Remove the 2 rotor retaining nuts and remove the rotor from the hub.
5. Check the rotor for scoring and/or other wear. Machine or replace, as necessary. If machining, observe the minimum thickness specification.
6. Install the rotor in the reverse order of removal.

INSPECTION

Using a micrometer measure the thickness of the rotor in four different places. If the rotor is not within specification either have it cut, if possible, or replace it.

PARKING BRAKE

Cable

➧ SEE FIG. 19–20

REMOVAL & INSTALLATION

Front Cable

1. Raise the vehicle and support safely.
2. Loosen the adjuster nut at the cable adjuster bracket.
3. Lower the vehicle.
4. Disconnect the cable from the control assembly at the clevis.
5. Raise the vehicle and support safely.
6. At the cable connector, disconnect the front cable from the rear cable.
7. Remove the cable and push-in prong retainer from the cable bracket, using a 13mm box end wrench to depress the retaining prongs. Allow the cable to hang.
8. Push the grommet up through the floor pan and lower the vehicle.
9. Remove the left cowl side panel. Pull the carpet away from the cowl panel.
10. From inside the vehicle, remove the cable end from the clevis and remove the conduit retainer from the control assembly.
11. Pull the cable assembly through the floorpan hole.

To install:

12. Position the cable assembly through the floorpan hole.
13. From inside the vehicle, install the cable end from the clevis and install the conduit retainer to the control assembly.
14. Install the left cowl side panel. Reposition the carpet at the cowl panel.
15. Push the grommet up through the floor pan and raise the vehicle.
16. Install the cable and push-in prong retainer from the cable bracket.
17. At the cable connector, connect the front cable to the rear cable.
18. Lower the vehicle. Connect the cable from the control assembly at the clevis.
19. Raise the vehicle and support it safely. Tighten the adjuster nut at the cable adjuster bracket. Lower the vehicle.

Rear Cable

LEFT SIDE

1. Raise the vehicle and support safely.
2. Remove the parking brake cable adjusting nut.
3. Remove the rear cable end fitting from the front cable connector.
4. Remove the wheel and drum assembly if equipped with drum brakes.
5. Disconnect the brake cable from the parking brake actuating lever. On drum brake vehicles, use a 13mm box end wrench to depress the conduit retaining prongs and remove the cable end pronged fitting from the backing plate. On disc brake vehicles, remove the E-clip from the conduit end of the fitting at the caliper.

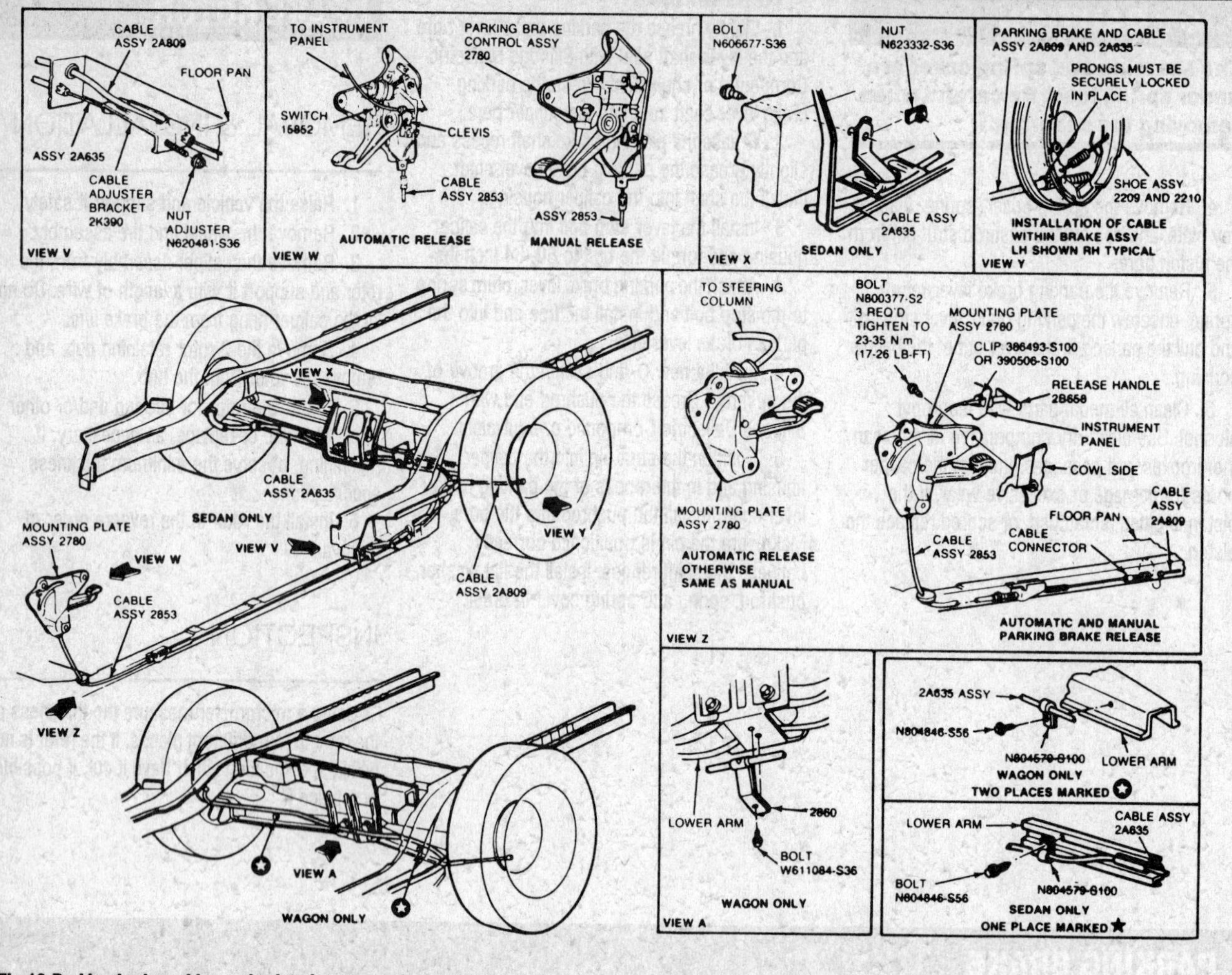

Fig.19 Parking brake cables and related components

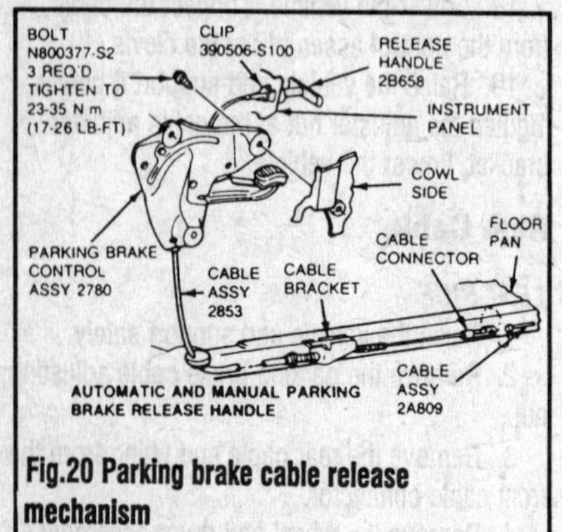

Fig.20 Parking brake cable release mechanism

6. Push the plastic snap-in grommet rearward to disconnect it from the side rail bracket.

7. Remove the pronged connector from the parking park adjuster bracket. Remove the cable assembly.

To Install:

8. Install the pronged connector to the parking park adjuster bracket. Install the cable assembly.

9. Push the plastic snap-in grommet forward to connect it from the side rail bracket.

10. Connect the brake cable to the parking brake actuating lever.

11. Install the wheel and drum assembly if equipped with drum brakes.

12. Install the rear cable end fitting to the front cable connector. Install the parking brake cable adjusting nut. Lower the vehicle.

RIGHT SIDE

1. Raise the vehicle and support it safely.

2. Remove the parking brake cable adjuster nut.

3. Use a 13mm box wrench to remove the conduit retainer prongs and remove the cable from the frame side rail bracket.

4. Remove the rear wheel and drum assembly if equipped with drum brakes.

5. Disconnect the brake cable from the parking brake actuating lever. On drum brake vehicles, use a 13mm box end wrench to depress the conduit retaining prongs and remove the cable end pronged fitting from the backing plate. On disc brake vehicles, remove the E-clip from the conduit end of the fitting at the caliper.

6. On Taurus/Sable sedan vehicles, perform the following:

a. Remove the brake pressure control valve bracket at the control arm.

b. Remove the cable retaining screw and clip from the lower suspension arm.

c. Remove one screw from the cable bracket at the crossmember.

d. Remove the entire right cable assembly.

7. On station wagon, perform the following:

a. Remove the cable retaining clip and screw from each lower suspension arm.

b. Remove the cable clip retaining screw from lower suspension arm inner mounting bracket.

To install:

8. On station wagon, perform the following:

a. Install the cable retaining clip and screw to each lower suspension arm.

b. Install the cable clip retaining screw to the lower suspension arm inner mounting bracket.

9. On Taurus/Sable sedan vehicles, perform the following:

a. Install the brake pressure control valve bracket at the control arm.

b. Install the cable retaining screw and clip to the lower suspension arm.

c. Install one screw to the cable bracket at the crossmember.

d. Install the right cable assembly.

10. Connect the brake cable to the parking brake actuating lever.

11. Install the rear wheel and drum assembly if equipped with drum brakes. Install the parking brake cable adjuster nut.

12. Lower the vehicle and support it safely. Ensure the pronged fitting is securely locked in place. Adjust the parking brake.

ADJUSTMENT

Except Taurus SHO

➧ SEE FIG. 21

1. Make sure the parking brake is fully released. Place the transaxle in the **N** position.

2. Raise the vehicle and support it safely. Working in front of the left rear wheel, tighten the adjusting nut against the cable equalizer causing a rear wheel brake drag. Then loosen the adjusting nut until the rear brakes are fully released. There should be no brake drag.

3. If the brake cables were replaced, stroke the parking brake several times, then release control and repeat Step 2.

4. Check for operation of the parking brake with the vehicle supported and the parking brake fully released. If there is any slack in the cables or if the rear brakes drag when the wheels are turned, adjust as required.

5. Lower the vehicle.

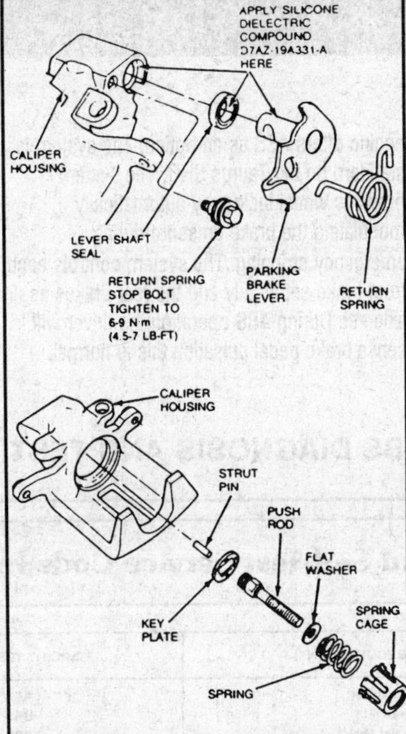

Fig.21 Rear brake caliper and parking brake assembly

Taurus SHO

1. Make sure the parking brake is fully released.

2. Raise and safely support the vehicle.

3. Tighten the adjusting nut against the cable adjuster bracket until there is a slight, less than $\frac{1}{16}$ in. (1.6mm), movement of either rear parking brake lever at the caliper.

4. If the brake cables were replaced, stroke the parking brake several times, then release the control and repeat Step 3.

5. Lower the vehicle.

Brake Pedal

REMOVAL & INSTALLATION

1. Fully release the parking brake. Raise and support the vehicle safely.

2. Remove all tension from the rear cables by backing off the adjusting nut from the equalizer or adjuster.

3. Lower the vehicle. Disconnect the vacuum hose from the vacuum release motor, if equipped.

4. Disconnect the release cable from the parking brake control release arm. Remove the release cable grommet from the parking brake control.

5. Disconnect the wiring connector from the parking brake warning indicator switch. Remove the cable from the clevis at the brake control.

6. Remove the push pin from the cowl side trim panel

7. Remove the conduit retainer from the control assembly by depressing the retaining prongs.

8. Remove the three bolts and one push pin retaining the control assembly to the cowl side panel. Remove the control assembly from the vehicle.

To install:

9. Position the control assembly in the vehicle. Fit the cable through its mounting hole and position it in place.

10. Connect the cable to the control assembly. Install the retaining bolts and push pin. Torque the retaining bolts to 17–26 ft. lbs.

11. If equipped connect the vacuum hose. Connect the release cable to the parking brake control release arm. Install the release cable grommet to the parking brake control.

12. Connect the wiring connector to the warning switch.

13. Raise and support the vehicle safely. Adjust the parking brake assembly.

14. Lower the vehicle. Check the parking brake assembly for proper operation.

ANTI-LOCK BRAKE SYSTEM

Description And Operation

The Taurus and Sable except with the 2.5L engine offers ABS as an option. The system is standard on the Taurus SHO. The system prevents wheel lockup by automatically modulating the brake pressure during emergency stopping. The system controls each front brake separately and the rear brakes as an axle set. During ABS operation the driver will sense brake pedal pulsation this is normal.

Troubleshooting

The following diagnostic charts must be used in conjunction with special tools. These tools are Ford Motor Company breakout box T83–L–50–ECC–IV, adapter T–87P–50–ALA, Star Tester 0007–0000–221 and a digital voltmeter.

➧ SEE FIG. 22–101

FIG. 22 ABS DIAGNOSIS AND TESTING DATA

On-Board Self-Test Service Code Index

SERVICE CODE (COMPONENT)		PINPOINT TEST STEP
11	(Electronic Controller)	AA1
22	(Ref. Voltage of IFL)	BB1
23	(LH Front Outlet Valve)	BB3
24	(RH Front Inlet Valve)	BB4
25	(RH Front Outlet Valve)	BB5
26	(RH Rear Inlet Valve)	BB6
27	(RH Rear Outlet Valve)	BB7
28	(LH Rear Inlet Valve)	BB8
29	(LH Rear Outlet Valve)	BB9
31	(LH Front Sensor)	CC1
32	(RH Front Sensor)	CC6
33	(RH Rear Sensor)	CC11
34	(LH Rear Sensor)	CC16
35	(LH Front Sensor)	CC1
36	(RH Front Sensor)	CC6
37	(RH Rear Sensor)	CC11
38	(LH Rear Sensor)	CC16
41	(LH Front Sensor)	CC1
42	(RH Front Sensor)	CC6
43	(RH Rear Sensor)	CC11
44	(LH Rear Sensor)	CC16
51	(LH Front Outlet Valve)	DD1
52	(RH Front Outlet Valve)	DD3
53	(RH Rear Outlet Valve)	DD5
54	(LH Rear Outlet Valve)	DD7
55	(LH Front Sensor)	CC1
56	(RH Front Sensor)	CC6
57	(RH Rear Sensor)	CC11
58	(LH Rear Sensor)	CC16
61	(FLI Circuits)	EE1
62	(Travel Switch)	EE3
63	(Pump Motor Speed Sensor)	EE5
64	(Pump Motor Pressure)	EE8
71	(LH Front Sensor)	CC1
72	(RH Front Sensor)	CC6
73	(RH Rear Sensor)	CC11
74	(LH Rear Sensor)	CC16
75	(LH Front Sensor)	CC1
76	(RH Front Sensor)	CC6
77	(RH Rear Sensor)	CC11
78	(LH Rear Sensor)	CC16

FIG. 23 ABS DIAGNOSIS AND TESTING DATA

Electronic Controller Diagnosis — Test AA

TEST STEP	RESULT ►	ACTION TO TAKE
AA1 SERVICE CODE 11: ELECTRICAL DISTURBANCE		
• Read all service codes and record. • After all service codes are read and written down, drive vehicle above 40 km/h (25 mph) to clear memory. • Read all service codes again	Service code 11 repeated ►	REPLACE electronic controller.
	Memory erased or other service codes present except code 11 ►	PERFORM test step associated with service code or codes. REFER to On-Board Self-Test service code index, and SERVICE next code.

FIG. 24 ABS DIAGNOSIS AND TESTING DATA

Solenoid Valve Diagnosis — Test BB

TEST STEP	RESULT ►	ACTION TO TAKE
BB1 SERVICE CODE 22: NO REFERENCE VOLTAGE OR LH FRONT INLET VALVE		
• Disconnect 55-pin plug from electronic controller. ELECTRONIC CONTROLLER 55 PIN CONNECTOR • Connect EEC-IV Breakout Box T83L-50-EEC-IV, with Anti-Lock Test Adapter T90P-50-ALA, or equivalent, to the anti-lock 55-pin plug wiring harness. ANTI-LOCK HARNESS ADAPTER T90P-50-ALA 55 PIN CONNECTOR EEC-IV BREAKOUT BOX T83L-50-EEC-IV • With ignition switch ON, measure voltage between breakout box pins 3 and 60.	10 volts minimum ►	GO to Step **BB2**.
	Less than 10 volts ►	REPLACE or SERVICE cable harness Circuit 532, 532C, 532F, or 606 (Taurus/Sable). Circuit 532A, 532B, 532F, 606 or 606A (Taurus SHO).

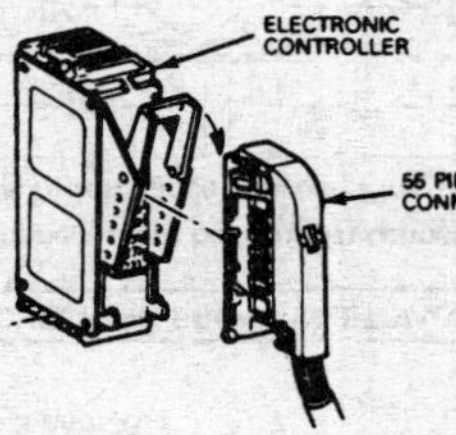

FIG. 25 ABS DIAGNOSIS AND TESTING DATA

Solenoid Valve Diagnosis — Test BB

TEST STEP	RESULT ▶	ACTION TO TAKE
BB2 CHECK LH FRONT INLET VALVE AND CIRCUITRY		
• Measure resistance between breakout box Pins 3 and 20.	5 to 8 ohms ▶	REVERIFY code 22. NOTE: If other codes are output, ignore code 22 and service next code.
	Any other reading ▶	GO to Step **BB2a**.
BB2a CHECK LH FRONT INLET VALVE		
• Disconnect valve body 19-pin connector. • Measure resistance between Pins 17 and 7. 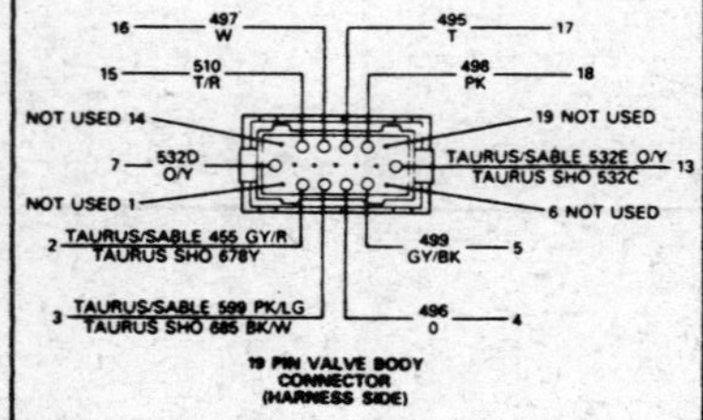 (19 PIN VALVE BODY CONNECTOR (HARNESS SIDE) diagram)	5 to 8 ohms ▶	REPLACE or SERVICE cable harness Circuit 495, 532C, 532D or 532E (Taurus/Sable). Circuit 495, 532C, 532D or 532G (Taurus SHO).
	Any other reading ▶	REPLACE valve body.
BB3 SERVICE CODE 23: CHECK LH FRONT OUTLET VALVE AND CIRCUIT		
• Measure resistance between breakout box Pins 3 and 2.	3 to 6 ohms ▶	GO to Step **BB4**.
	Any other reading ▶	GO to Step **BB3a**.

FIG. 26 ABS DIAGNOSIS AND TESTING DATA

Solenoid Valve Diagnosis — Test BB

TEST STEP	RESULT ▶	ACTION TO TAKE
BB3a CHECK LH FRONT OUTLET VALVE		
• Disconnect valve body 19-pin connector. • Measure resistance between Pins 18 and 7. 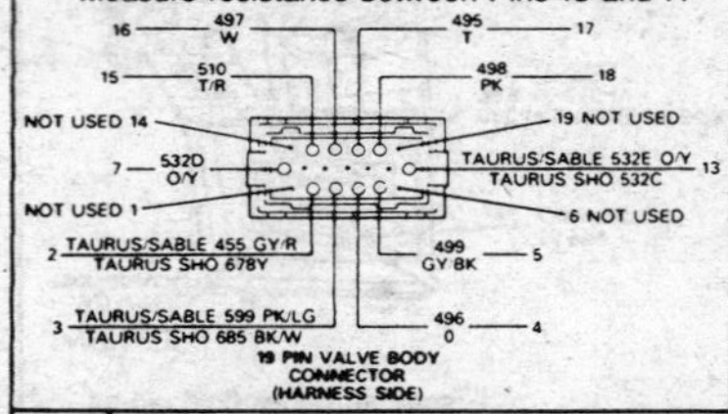 (19 PIN VALVE BODY CONNECTOR (HARNESS SIDE) diagram)	3 to 6 ohms ▶	REPLACE or SERVICE cable harness Circuit 498.
	Any other reading ▶	REPLACE valve body.
BB4 SERVICE CODE 24: CHECK RH FRONT INLET VALVE AND CIRCUIT		
• Measure resistance between breakout box Pins 3 and 38.	5 to 8 ohms ▶	GO to Step **BB5**.
	Any other reading ▶	GO to Step **BB4a**.
BB4a CHECK RH FRONT INLET VALVE		
• Disconnect valve body 19-pin connector. • Measure resistance between Pins 15 and 7. 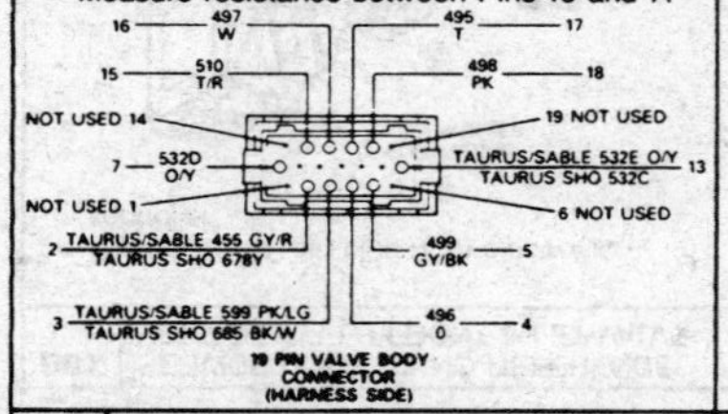 (19 PIN VALVE BODY CONNECTOR (HARNESS SIDE) diagram)	5 to 8 ohms ▶	REPLACE or SERVICE cable harness Circuit 510.
	Any other reading ▶	REPLACE valve body.
BB5 SERVICE CODE 25: CHECK RH FRONT OUTLET VALVE AND CIRCUIT		
• Measure resistance between breakout box Pins 3 and 21.	3 to 6 ohms ▶	GO to Step **BB6**.
	Any other reading ▶	GO to Step **BB5a**.

FIG. 27 ABS DIAGNOSIS AND TESTING DATA

Solenoid Valve Diagnosis — **Test BB**

TEST STEP	RESULT ▶	ACTION TO TAKE
BB5a CHECK RH FRONT OUTLET VALVE		
• Disconnect valve body 19-pin connector. • Measure resistance between Pins 16 and 7.	3 to 6 ohms ▶	REPLACE or SERVICE cable harness Circuit 497.
16 — 497 W; 15 — 510 T/R; NOT USED 14; 7 — 532D O/Y; NOT USED 1; 2 TAURUS/SABLE 455 GY/R TAURUS SHO 678Y; 3 TAURUS/SABLE 599 PK/LG TAURUS SHO 685 BK/W; 495 T — 17; 498 PK — 18; 19 NOT USED; TAURUS/SABLE 532E O/Y TAURUS SHO 532C 13; 6 NOT USED; 499 GY/BK — 5; 496 O — 4 19 PIN VALVE BODY CONNECTOR (HARNESS SIDE)	Any other reading ▶	REPLACE valve body.
BB6 SERVICE CODE 26: CHECK RH REAR INLET VALVE AND CIRCUIT		
• Measure resistance between breakout box Pins 3 and 55.	5 to 8 ohms ▶	GO to Step **BB7**.
	Any other reading ▶	GO to Step **BB6a**.
BB6a CHECK RH REAR INLET VALVE		
• Disconnect valve body 19-pin connector. • Measure resistance between Pins 2 and 7.	5 to 8 ohms ▶	REPLACE or SERVICE cable harness Circuit 455 (Taurus/Sable). Circuit 678 (Taurus SHO).
16 — 497 W; 15 — 510 T/R; NOT USED 14; 7 — 532D O/Y; NOT USED 1; 2 TAURUS/SABLE 455 GY/R TAURUS SHO 678Y; 3 TAURUS/SABLE 599 PK/LG TAURUS SHO 685 BK/W; 495 T — 17; 498 PK — 18; 19 NOT USED; TAURUS/SABLE 532E O/Y TAURUS SHO 532C 13; 6 NOT USED; 499 GY/BK — 5; 496 O — 4 19 PIN VALVE BODY CONNECTOR (HARNESS SIDE)	Any other reading ▶	REPLACE valve body.
BB7 SERVICE CODE 27: CHECK RH REAR OUTLET VALVE AND CIRCUIT		
• Measure resistance between breakout box Pins 3 and 18.	3 to 6 ohms ▶	GO to Step **BB8**.
	Any other reading ▶	GO to Step **BB7a**.

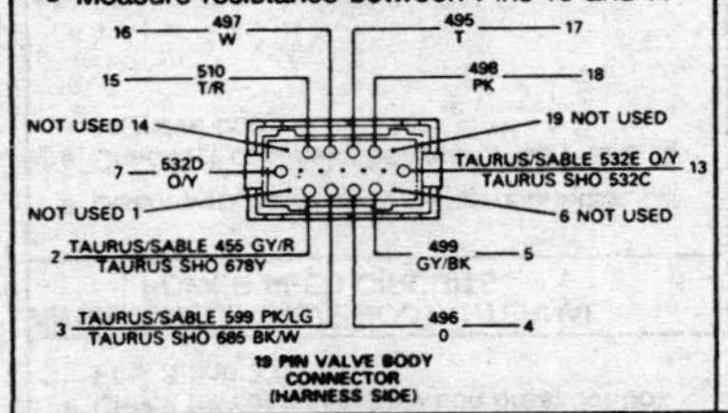

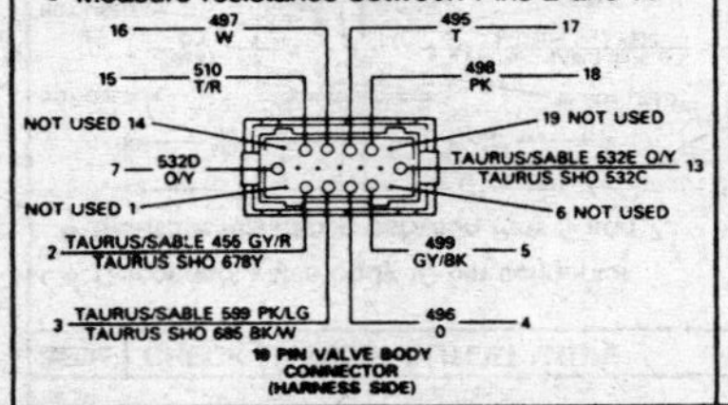

FIG. 28 ABS DIAGNOSIS AND TESTING DATA

Solenoid Valve Diagnosis — **Test BB**

TEST STEP	RESULT ▶	ACTION TO TAKE
BB7a CHECK RH REAR OUTLET VALVE		
• Disconnect valve body 19-pin connector. • Measure resistance between Pins 3 and 7.	3 to 6 ohms ▶	REPLACE or SERVICE cable harness Circuit 599 (Taurus/Sable). Circuit 685 (Taurus SHO).
16 — 497 W; 15 — 510 T/R; NOT USED 14; 7 — 532D O/Y; NOT USED 1; 2 TAURUS/SABLE 455 GY/R TAURUS SHO 678Y; 3 TAURUS/SABLE 599 PK/LG TAURUS SHO 685 BK/W; 495 T — 17; 498 PK — 18; 19 NOT USED; TAURUS/SABLE 532E O/Y TAURUS SHO 532C 13; 6 NOT USED; 499 GY/BK — 5; 496 O — 4 19 PIN VALVE BODY CONNECTOR (HARNESS SIDE)	Any other reading ▶	REPLACE valve body.
BB8 SERVICE CODE 28: CHECK LH REAR INLET VALVE AND CIRCUIT		
• Measure resistance between breakout box Pins 3 and 54.	5 to 8 ohms ▶	GO to Step **BB9**.
	Any other reading ▶	GO to Step **BB8a**.
BB8a CHECK LH REAR INLET VALVE		
• Disconnect valve body 19-pin connector. • Measure resistance between Pins 4 and 7.	5 to 8 ohms ▶	REPLACE or SERVICE cable harness Circuit 496.
16 — 497 W; 15 — 510 T/R; NOT USED 14; 7 — 532D O/Y; NOT USED 1; 2 TAURUS/SABLE 455 GY/R TAURUS SHO 678Y; 3 TAURUS/SABLE 599 PK/LG TAURUS SHO 685 BK/W; 495 T — 17; 498 PK — 18; 19 NOT USED; TAURUS/SABLE 532E O/Y TAURUS SHO 532C 13; 6 NOT USED; 499 GY/BK — 5; 496 O — 4 19 PIN VALVE BODY CONNECTOR (HARNESS SIDE)	Any other reading ▶	REPLACE valve body.
BB9 SERVICE CODE 29: CHECK LH REAR OUTLET VALVE AND CIRCUIT		
• Measure resistance between breakout box Pins 3 and 36.	3 to 6 ohms ▶	GO to Step **BB10**.
	Any other reading ▶	GO to Step **BB9a**.

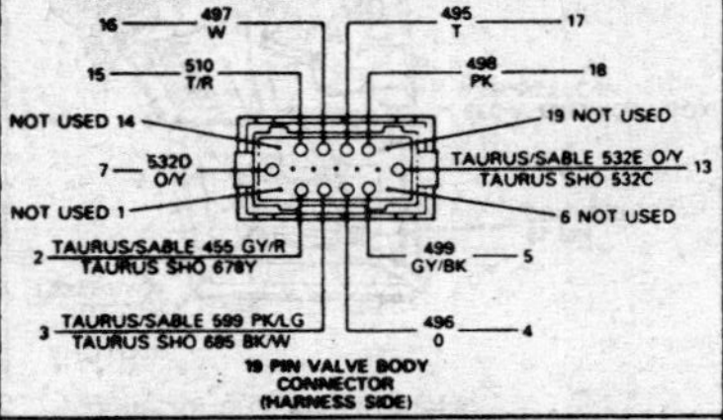

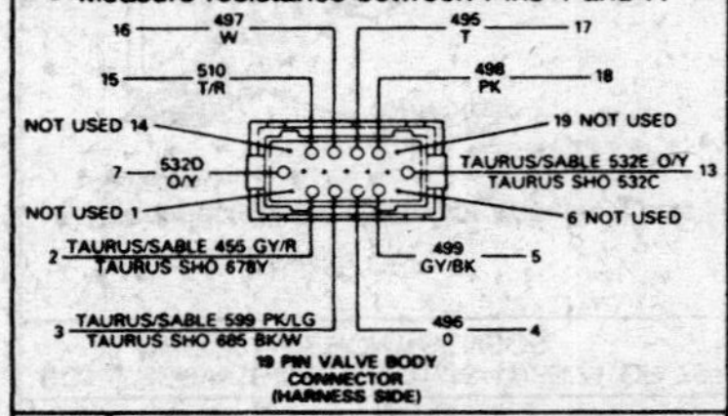

FIG. 29 ABS DIAGNOSIS AND TESTING DATA

Solenoid Valve Diagnosis — Test BB

TEST STEP	RESULT ▶	ACTION TO TAKE
BB9a CHECK LH REAR OUTLET VALVE		
• Disconnect valve body 19-pin connector. • Measure resistance between Pins 5 and 7.	3 to 6 ohms ▶	REPLACE or SERVICE cable harness Circuit 499.
	Any other reading ▶	REPLACE valve body.
BB10 CHECK VALVE BODY POWER FEED AND CIRCUITRY		
• Remove main power relay from harness connector. • Check for continuity between breakout box Pins 3 and 33.	Continuity ▶	REVERIFY symptom
	No continuity ▶	GO to Step **BB10a**.
BB10a CHECK VALVE BODY INTERNAL POWER FEED CIRCUITS		
• Disconnect valve body 19-pin connector. • Check for continuity between Pins 7 and 13 on valve body.	Continuity ▶	REPLACE or SERVICE cable harness Circuit 532B, 532C, or 532F. (Taurus/Sable). Circuit 532E, or 532F (Taurus SHO).
	No Continuity ▶	REPLACE valve body.

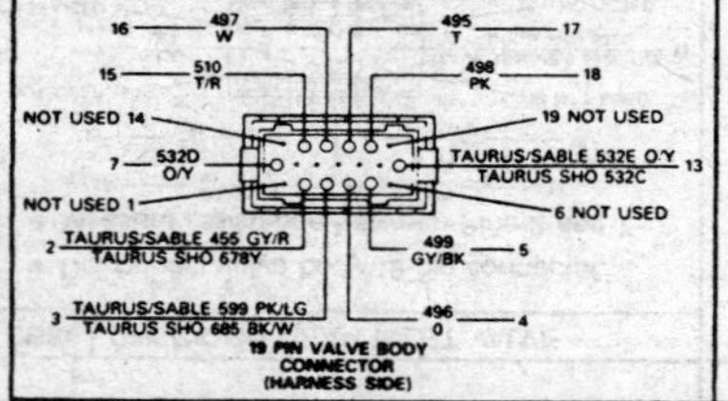

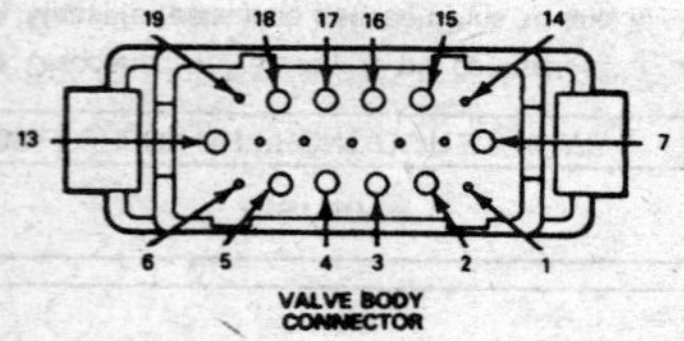

FIG. 30 ABS DIAGNOSIS AND TESTING DATA

Wheel Sensor Diagnosis — Test CC

TEST STEP	RESULT ▶	ACTION TO TAKE
CC1 SERVICE CODES 31/35/41/55/71 OR 75 CHECK LH FRONT SENSOR		
• Turn ignition switch OFF. • Disconnect 55-pin connector from electronic controller. • Connect EEC-IV Breakout Box with Tool T90P-50-ALA or equivalent to the 55-pin connector on wiring harness. • Measure resistance between Pins 30 and 48.	800 to 1400 ohms (0.8 to 1.4K ohms) ▶	GO to Step **CC2**.
	Any other reading ▶	GO to Step **CC1a**.

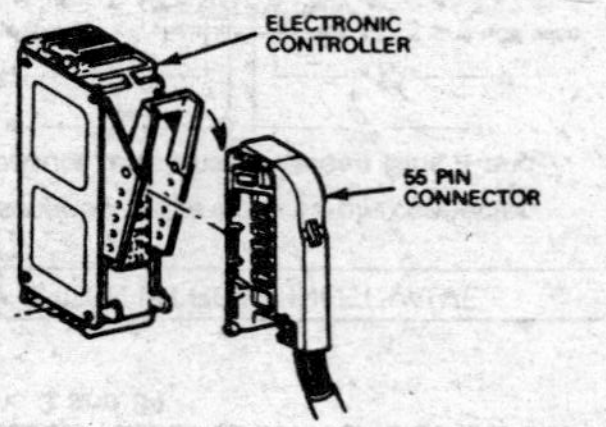

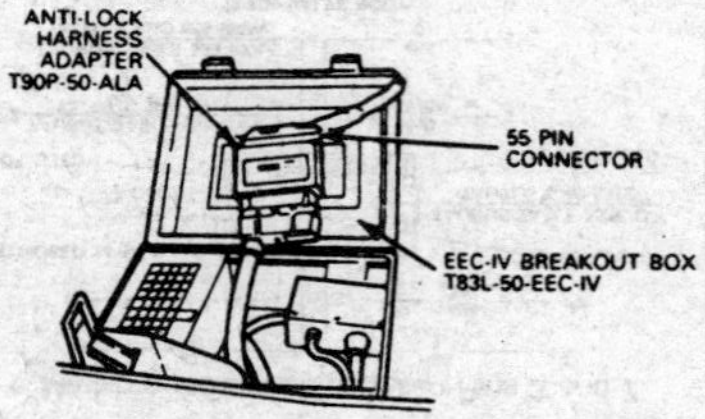

FIG. 31 ABS DIAGNOSIS AND TESTING DATA

Wheel Sensor Diagnosis — Test CC

TEST STEP	RESULT ▶	ACTION TO TAKE
CC1a CHECK LH FRONT SENSOR RESISTANCE		
• Disconnect LH front wheel sensor plug. • Measure resistance of sensor at sensor plug. LH FRONT SENSOR	800 to 1400 ohms (0.8 to 1.4K ohms) ▶	SERVICE or REPLACE cable harness Circuit 521 or 522.
	Any other reading ▶	REPLACE LH front sensor.
CC2 CHECK LH FRONT SENSOR VOLTAGE		
• Turn ignition switch OFF • Turn air suspension switch OFF, if so equipped. • Place vehicle on hoist and raise wheels clear of ground. • Set multi-meter to voltage range (2 volt-AC). • Measure voltage between Pins 30 and 48 at Breakout Box while spinning LH front at approximately 1 revolution per second.	Between 0.10 and 1.40 volts AC ▶	GO to Step **CC3**.
	Less than 0.10 or more than 1.40 volts AC ▶	CHECK sensor mounting, air gap or toothed wheel mounting. CORRECT as required.
CC3 CHECK LH FRONT SENSOR CIRCUIT CONTINUITY TO GROUND		
• Check continuity between Breakout Box Pins 30 and 60.	No Continuity ▶	GO to Step **CC4**.
	Continuity ▶	GO to Step **CC3a**.

FIG. 32 ABS DIAGNOSIS AND TESTING DATA

Wheel Sensor Diagnosis — Test CC

TEST STEP	RESULT ▶	ACTION TO TAKE
CC3a CHECK LH FRONT SENSOR TO GROUND		
• Disconnect LH front wheel sensor plug. • Check for continuity between each sensor plug pin (sensor side) and vehicle ground. LH FRONT SENSOR	Continuity ▶	REPLACE LH front sensor.
	No Continuity ▶	SERVICE or REPLACE cable harness Circuit 521 or 522. RECONNECT sensor plug.
CC4 CHECK ELECTRONIC CONTROLLER TO GROUND WIRE		
• Check continuity between Breakout Box Pin 60 and body ground.	Continuity ▶	GO to Step **CC5**.
	No Continuity ▶	SERVICE or REPLACE cable harness Circuit 530 or 530B (Taurus/Sable). Circuit 530, 57U or 57R (Taurus SHO).
CC5 CHECK LH FRONT WHEEL BEARING		
• Check front wheel bearing end play. • Inspect toothed sensor ring visually for damaged teeth. NOTE: Turn air suspension switch ON when vehicle is off hoist, if so equipped.	Loose or damaged parts ▶	REPLACE faulty parts.
	Not loose or damaged ▶	REVERIFY symptom.

FIG. 33 ABS DIAGNOSIS AND TESTING DATA

Wheel Sensor Diagnosis — Test CC

TEST STEP	RESULT ▶	ACTION TO TAKE
CC6 SERVICE CODES 32/36/42/56/72 OR 76 CHECK RH FRONT SENSOR		
• Turn ignition switch OFF. • Disconnect 55-pin connector from electronic controller.	800 to 1400 ohms (0.8 to 1.4K ohms) ▶	GO to Step **CC7**.
	Any other reading ▶	GO to Step **CC6a**.
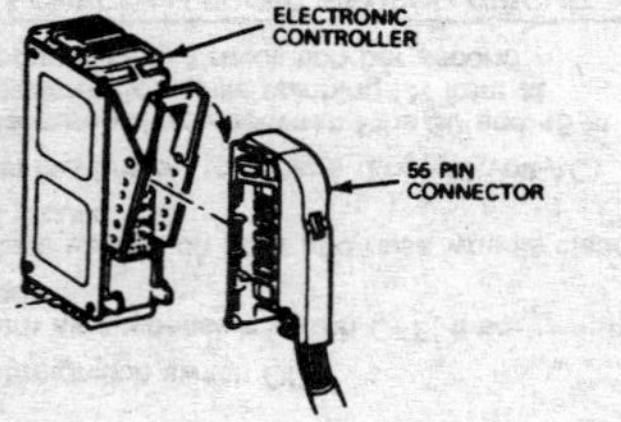 ELECTRONIC CONTROLLER 55 PIN CONNECTOR		
• Connect EEC-IV Breakout Box with Tool T90P-50-ALA or equivalent to the 55-pin connector on wiring harness.		
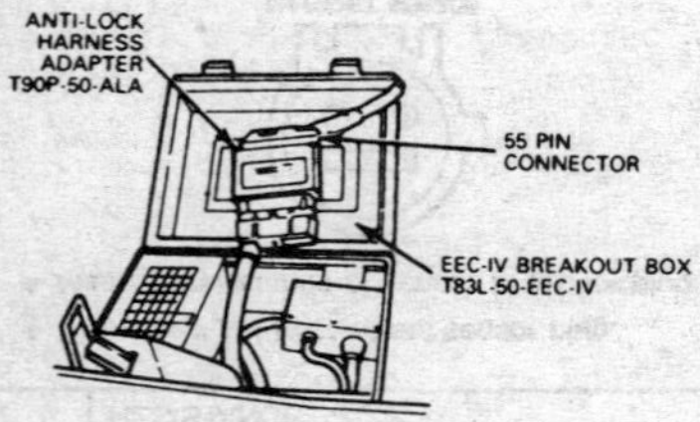 ANTI-LOCK HARNESS ADAPTER T90P-50-ALA 55 PIN CONNECTOR EEC-IV BREAKOUT BOX T83L-50-EEC-IV		
• Measure resistance between Pins 29 and 47.		

FIG. 34 ABS DIAGNOSIS AND TESTING DATA

Wheel Sensor Diagnosis — Test CC

TEST STEP	RESULT ▶	ACTION TO TAKE
CC6a CHECK RH FRONT SENSOR RESISTANCE		
• Disconnect RH front sensor plug. • Measure resistance of sensor at sensor plug.	800 to 1400 ohms (0.8 to 1.4K ohms) ▶	SERVICE or REPLACE cable harness Circuit 514 or 516.
 RH FRONT SENSOR	Any other reading ▶	REPLACE RH front sensor.
CC7 CHECK RH FRONT SENSOR VOLTAGE		
• Turn ignition switch OFF. • Turn air suspension switch OFF, if so equipped. • Place vehicle on hoist and raise wheels clear of ground. • Set multi-meter to voltage range (2 volt-AC). • Measure voltage between Pins 29 and 47 at Breakout Box while spinning RH front at approximately 1 revolution per second.	Between 0.10 and 1.40 volts AC ▶	GO to Step **CC8**.
	Less than 0.10 or more than 1.40 volts AC ▶	CHECK sensor mounting, air gap or toothed wheel mounting. CORRECT as required.
CC8 CHECK RH FRONT SENSOR CIRCUIT CONTINUITY TO GROUND		
• Check continuity between Breakout Box Pins 29 and 60.	No Continuity ▶	GO to Step **CC9**.
	Continuity ▶	GO to Step **CC8a**.

FIG. 35 ABS DIAGNOSIS AND TESTING DATA

Wheel Sensor Diagnosis — Test CC

TEST STEP	RESULT ▶	ACTION TO TAKE
CC8a CHECK RH FRONT SENSOR TO GROUND		
• Disconnect RH front wheel sensor plug. • Check for continuity between each sensor plug pin (sensor side) and vehicle ground. RH FRONT SENSOR	Continuity ▶	REPLACE RH front sensor.
	No Continuity ▶	SERVICE or REPLACE cable harness Circuit 514 or 516. RECONNECT sensor plug.
CC9 CHECK ELECTRONIC CONTROLLER TO GROUND WIRE		
• Check continuity between Breakout Box Pin 60 and body ground.	Continuity ▶	GO to Step **CC10**.
	No Continiuty ▶	SERVICE or REPLACE cable harness Circuit 530 or 530B (Taurus/Sable). Circuit 530, 57U or 57R (Taurus SHO).
CC10 CHECK RH FRONT WHEEL BEARING		
• Check front wheel bearing end play. • Inspect toothed sensor ring visually for damaged teeth. NOTE: Turn air suspension switch ON when vehicle is off hoist, if so equipped.	Loose or damaged parts ▶	REPLACE faulty parts.
	Not loose or damaged ▶	REVERIFY symptom.

FIG. 36 ABS DIAGNOSIS AND TESTING DATA

Wheel Sensor Diagnosis — Test CC

TEST STEP	RESULT ▶	ACTION TO TAKE
CC11 SERVICE CODES 33/37/43/57/73 OR 77 CHECK RH REAR SENSOR		
• Turn ignition switch OFF. • Disconnect 55-pin connector from electronic controller. ELECTRONIC CONTROLLER 55 PIN CONNECTOR	800 to 1400 ohms (0.8 to 1.4K ohms) ▶	GO to Step **CC12**.
	Any other reading ▶	GO to Step **CC11a**.
• Connect EEC-IV Breakout Box with Tool T90P-50-ALA or equivalent to the 55-pin connector on wiring harness. ANTI-LOCK HARNESS ADAPTER T90P-50-ALA 55 PIN CONNECTOR EEC-IV BREAKOUT BOX T83L-50-EEC-IV		
• Measure resistance between Pins 27 and 45.		

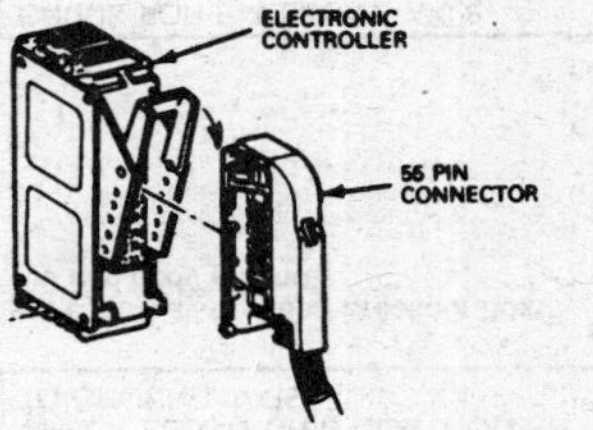

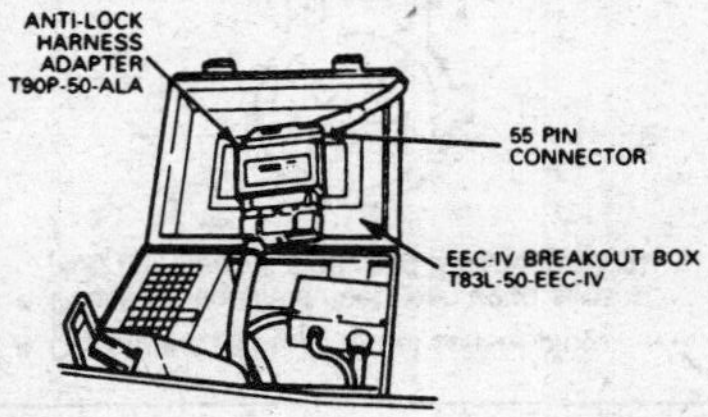

FIG. 37 ABS DIAGNOSIS AND TESTING DATA

Wheel Sensor Diagnosis — Test CC

TEST STEP	RESULT ▶	ACTION TO TAKE
CC11a CHECK RH REAR SENSOR RESISTANCE		
• Disconnect sensor plug (RH REAR). • Measure resistance of sensor at sensor plug.  RH REAR SENSOR	800 to 1400 ohms (0.8 to 1.4K ohms) ▶	SERVICE or REPLACE cable harness Circuit 523 or 524.
	Any other reading ▶	REPLACE RH rear sensor.
CC12 CHECK RH REAR SENSOR VOLTAGE		
• Turn ignition switch OFF. • Turn air suspension switch OFF, if so equipped. • Place vehicle on hoist and raise wheels clear of ground. • Set multi-meter to voltage range (2 volt-AC). • Measure voltage between Pins 27 and 45 at Breakout Box while spinning RH rear at approximately 1 revolution per second.	Between 0.10 and 1.40 volts AC ▶	GO to Step **CC13**.
	Less than 0.10 or more than 1.40 volts AC ▶	CHECK sensor mounting, air gap or toothed wheel mounting. CORRECT as required.
CC13 CHECK RH REAR SENSOR CIRCUIT CONTINUITY TO GROUND		
• Check continuity between Breakout Box Pins 27 and 60.	No Continuity ▶	GO to Step **CC14**.
	Continuity ▶	GO to Step **CC13a**.

FIG. 38 ABS DIAGNOSIS AND TESTING DATA

Wheel Sensor Diagnosis — Test CC

TEST STEP	RESULT ▶	ACTION TO TAKE
CC13a CHECK RH REAR SENSOR TO GROUND		
• Disconnect RH rear wheel sensor plug. • Check for continuity between each sensor plug pin (sensor side) and vehicle ground.  RH REAR SENSOR	Continuity ▶	REPLACE RH rear sensor.
	No Continuity ▶	SERVICE or REPLACE cable harness Circuit 523 or 524. RECONNECT sensor plug.
CC14 CHECK ELECTRONIC CONTROLLER TO GROUND WIRE		
• Check continuity between Breakout Box Pin 60 and body ground.	Continuity ▶	GO to Step **CC15**.
	No Continuity ▶	SERVICE or REPLACE cable harness Circuit 530 or 530B (Taurus/Sable). Circuit 530, 57U or 57R (Taurus SHO).
CC15 CHECK FOR EXCESSIVE AXLE VIBRATION		
• Check rear wheel bearings for excessive play. • Inspect toothed sensor ring for damaged teeth. NOTE: Turn air suspension switch ON when vehicle is off hoist, if so equipped.	Loose or damaged parts ▶	SERVICE or REPLACE damaged parts.
	Not loose or damaged ▶	REVERIFY symptom.

FIG. 39 ABS DIAGNOSIS AND TESTING DATA

Wheel Sensor Diagnosis

Test CC

TEST STEP	RESULT ▶	ACTION TO TAKE
CC16 SERVICE CODES 34/38/44/58/74 OR 78 CHECK LH REAR SENSOR		
• Turn ignition switch OFF. • Disconnect 55-pin connector from electronic controller.	800 to 1400 ohms (0.8 to 1.4K ohms) ▶	GO to Step **CC17**.
	Any other reading ▶	GO to Step **CC16a**.
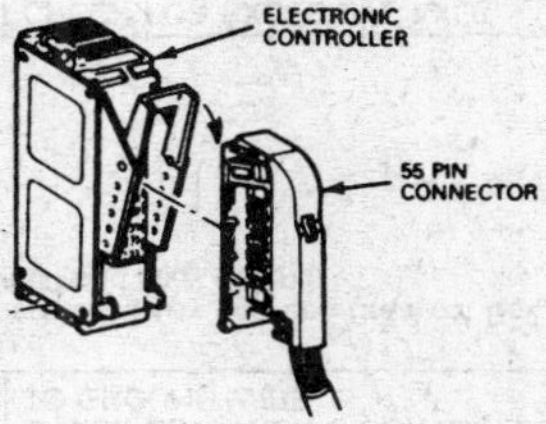 ELECTRONIC CONTROLLER 55 PIN CONNECTOR		
• Connect EEC-IV Breakout Box with Tool T90P-50-ALA or equivalent to the 55-pin connector on wiring harness.		
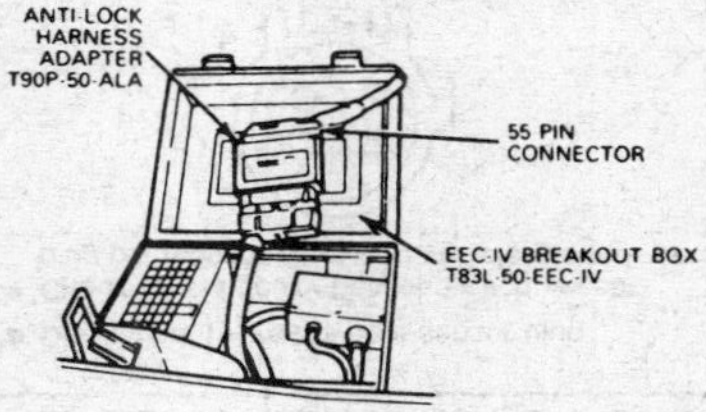 ANTI-LOCK HARNESS ADAPTER T90P-50-ALA 55 PIN CONNECTOR EEC-IV BREAKOUT BOX T83L-50-EEC-IV		
• Measure resistance between Pins 28 and 46.		

FIG. 40 ABS DIAGNOSIS AND TESTING DATA

Wheel Sensor Diagnosis

Test CC

TEST STEP	RESULT ▶	ACTION TO TAKE
CC16a CHECK LH REAR SENSOR RESISTANCE		
• Disconnect LH rear sensor plug. • Measure resistance of sensor at sensor plug.	800 to 1400 ohms (0.8 to 1.4K ohms) ▶	SERVICE or REPLACE cable harness Circuit 518 or 519.
 LH REAR SENSOR	Any other reading ▶	REPLACE LH rear sensor.
CC17 CHECK LH REAR SENSOR VOLTAGE		
• Turn ignition switch OFF. • Turn air suspension switch OFF, if so equipped. • Place vehicle on hoist and raise wheels clear of ground. • Set multi-meter to voltage range (2 volt-AC). • Measure voltage between Pins 28 and 46 at Breakout Box while spinning RH rear at approximately 1 revolution per second.	Between 0.10 and 1.40 volts AC ▶	GO to Step **CC18**.
	Less than 0.10 or more than 1.40 volts AC ▶	CHECK sensor mounting, air gap or toothed wheel mounting. CORRECT as required.
CC18 CHECK LH REAR SENSOR CIRCUIT CONTINUITY TO GROUND		
• Check continuity between Breakout Box Pins 28 and 60.	No Continuity ▶	GO to Step **CC19**.
	Continuity ▶	GO to Step **CC18a**.

FIG. 41 ABS DIAGNOSIS AND TESTING DATA

Wheel Sensor Diagnosis — Test CC

TEST STEP	RESULT ▶	ACTION TO TAKE
CC18a CHECK LH REAR SENSOR TO GROUND		
• Disconnect LH rear wheel sensor plug. • Check for continuity between each sensor plug pin (sensor side) and vehicle ground.  LH REAR SENSOR	Continuity ▶	REPLACE LH rear sensor.
	No Continuity ▶	SERVICE or REPLACE cable harness Circuit 518 or 519. RECONNECT sensor plug.
CC19 CHECK ELECTRONIC CONTROLLER TO GROUND WIRE		
• Check continuity between Breakout Box Pin 60 and body ground.	Continuity ▶	GO to Step **CC20**.
	No Continuity ▶	SERVICE or REPLACE cable harness Circuit 530 or 530B (Taurus/Sable). Circuit 530, 57U or 57R (Taurus SHO).
CC20 CHECK FOR EXCESSIVE AXLE VIBRATION		
• Check rear wheel bearings for excessive play. • Inspect toothed sensor ring for damaged teeth. NOTE: Turn air suspension switch ON when vehicle is off hoist, if so equipped.	Loose or damaged parts ▶	SERVICE or REPLACE damaged parts.
	Not loose or damaged ▶	REVERIFY symptom.

FIG. 42 ABS DIAGNOSIS AND TESTING DATA

Wheel Sensor Diagnosis — Test DD

TEST STEP	RESULT ▶	ACTION TO TAKE
DD1 SERVICE CODE 51 AND/OR 71 CHECK LH FRONT SENSOR CIRCUIT CONTINUITY		
• Turn ignition switch OFF. • Disconnect 55-pin plug from electronic controller. 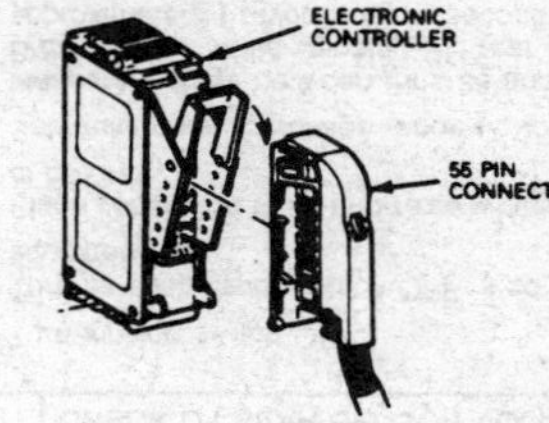 ELECTRONIC CONTROLLER 55 PIN CONNECTOR • Connect EEC-IV Breakout Box, T83L-50-EEC-IV, with Anti-Lock Test Adapter, T90P-50-ALA or equivalent, to the anti-lock 55-pin plug harness.  ANTI-LOCK HARNESS ADAPTER T90P-50-ALA 55 PIN CONNECTOR EEC-IV BREAKOUT BOX T83L-50-EEC-IV • Check for continuity between Breakout Box Pins 60 and 30.	Continuity ▶	GO to Step **DD1a**.
	No Continuity ▶	GO to Step **DD2**.

FIG. 43 ABS DIAGNOSIS AND TESTING DATA

Wheel Sensor Diagnosis — **Test DD**

TEST STEP	RESULT ▶	ACTION TO TAKE
DD1a CHECK LH FRONT SENSOR CONTINUITY		
• Disconnect LH front wheel sensor plug. • Check for continuity between each sensor plug pin (sensor side) and vehicle ground. LH FRONT SENSOR	Continuity ▶	REPLACE LH front sensor.
	No Continuity ▶	SERVICE or REPLACE cable harness Circuit 521 or 522. RECONNECT sensor plug.
DD2 CHECK ELECTRONIC CONTROLLER TO GROUND WIRE		
• Check continuity between Breakout Box Pin 60 and body ground.	Continuity ▶	GO to Step **DD3**.
	No Continuity ▶	SERVICE or REPLACE cable harness Circuit 530 or 530B (Taurus/Sable). Circuit 530, 57U or 57R (Taurus SHO).
DD3 CHECK ANTI-LOCK OPERATION LH FRONT WHEEL		
• Turn air suspension OFF, if so equipped. • Lift vehicle and rotate wheels to ensure they turn freely. • Apply moderate brake pedal effort and check that LH front wheel will not turn. • Short Pins 2, 20 and 60 to each other at Breakout Box. • Check that LH front wheel turns freely with ignition switch ON. **CAUTION: Do not leave ignition on for more than 1 minute, or valve damage may result.** • Turn air suspension ON when vehicle is off hoist, if so equipped.	If wheel turns freely ▶	REVERIFY symptom.
	If wheel does not turn freely or pedal drops ▶	REPLACE solenoid valve body.

FIG. 44 ABS DIAGNOSIS AND TESTING DATA

Wheel Sensor Diagnosis — **Test DD**

TEST STEP	RESULT ▶	ACTION TO TAKE
DD4 SERVICE CODE 52 AND/OR 72 CHECK RH FRONT SENSOR CIRCUIT CONTINUITY		
• Turn ignition switch OFF. • Disconnect 55-pin plug from electronic controller. ELECTRONIC CONTROLLER 55 PIN CONNECTOR • Connect EEC-IV Breakout Box, T83L-50-EEC-IV, with Anti-Lock Test Adapter, T90P-50-ALA, or equivalent, to the anti-lock 55-pin plug wiring harness. ANTI-LOCK HARNESS ADAPTER T90P-50-ALA 55 PIN CONNECTOR EEC-IV BREAKOUT BOX T83L-50-EEC-IV • Check for continuity between Breakout Box Pins 60 and 29.	Continuity ▶	GO to Step **DD4a**.
	No Continuity ▶	GO to Step **DD5**.

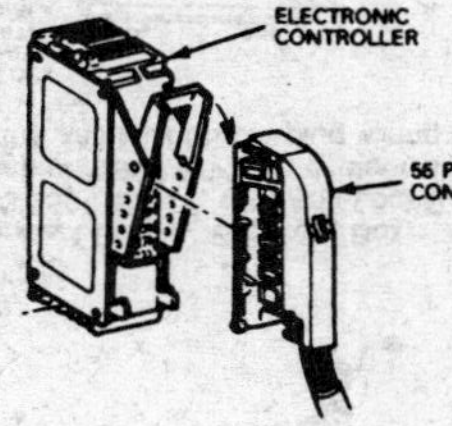

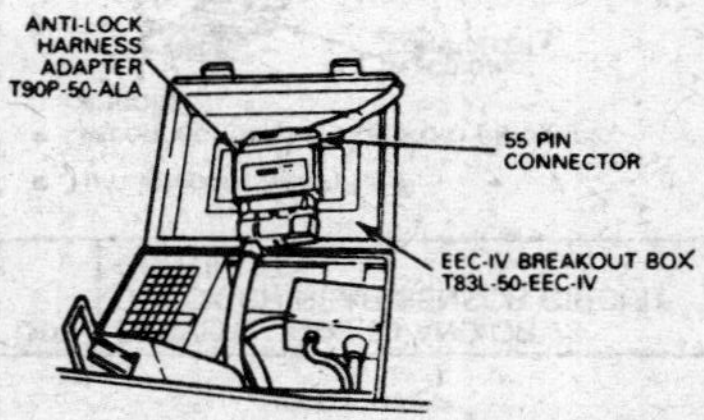

FIG. 45 ABS DIAGNOSIS AND TESTING DATA

Wheel Sensor Diagnosis — **Test DD**

TEST STEP	RESULT ▶	ACTION TO TAKE
DD4a CHECK RH FRONT SENSOR CONTINUITY		
• Disconnect RH front wheel sensor. • Check for continuity between each sensor plug pin (sensor side) and vehicle ground.  RH FRONT SENSOR	Continuity ▶	REPLACE RH front sensor.
	No Continuity ▶	SERVICE or REPLACE cable harness Circuit 514 or 516. RECONNECT sensor plug.
DD5 CHECK ELECTRONIC CONTROLLER TO GROUND WIRE		
• Check continuity between Breakout Box Pin 60 and body ground.	Continuity ▶	GO to Step **DD6**.
	No Continuity ▶	SERVICE or REPLACE cable harness Circuit 530 or 530B (Taurus/Sable). Circuit 530, 57U or 57R (Taurus SHO).
DD6 CHECK ANTI-LOCK OPERATION RH FRONT WHEEL		
• Turn air suspension OFF, if so equipped. • Lift vehicle and rotate wheels to ensure they turn freely. • Apply moderate brake pedal effort and check that RH front wheel will not turn. • Short Pins 21, 38 and 60 to each other at Breakout Box. • Check that RH front wheel turns freely with ignition switch ON. • Turn air suspension ON when vehicle is off hoist, if so equipped.	If wheel turns freely ▶	REVERIFY symptom.
	If wheel does not turn freely or pedal drops ▶	REPLACE solenoid valve body.

FIG. 46 ABS DIAGNOSIS AND TESTING DATA

Wheel Sensor Diagnosis — **Test DD**

TEST STEP	RESULT ▶	ACTION TO TAKE
DD7 SERVICE CODE 53 AND/OR 73 CHECK RH REAR SENSOR CIRCUIT CONTINUITY		
• Turn ignition switch OFF. • Disconnect 55-pin plug from electronic controller. 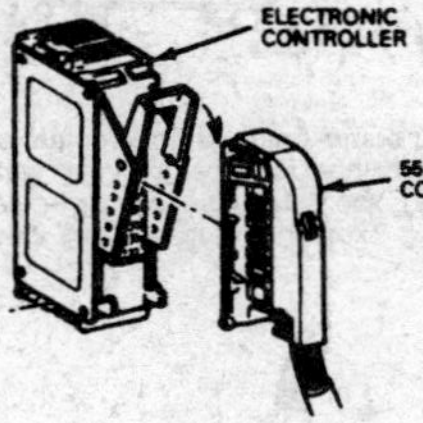 ELECTRONIC CONTROLLER 55 PIN CONNECTOR • Connect EEC-IV Breakout Box, T83L-50-EEC-IV, with Anti-Lock Test Adapter, T90P-50-ALA, or equivalent, to the anti-lock 55-pin plug wiring harness. 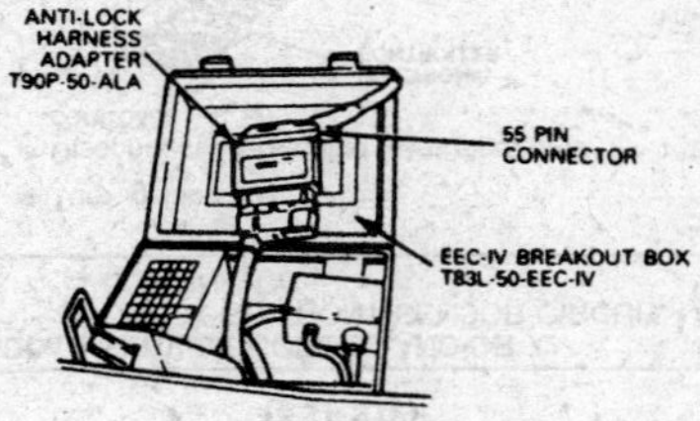 ANTI-LOCK HARNESS ADAPTER T90P-50-ALA 55 PIN CONNECTOR EEC-IV BREAKOUT BOX T83L-50-EEC-IV • Check for continuity between Breakout Box Pins 60 and 27.	Continuity ▶	GO to Step **DD7a**.
	No Continuity ▶	GO to Step **DD8**.

FIG. 47 ABS DIAGNOSIS AND TESTING DATA

Wheel Sensor Diagnosis — Test DD

TEST STEP	RESULT ▶	ACTION TO TAKE
DD7a CHECK RH REAR SENSOR CONTINUITY		
• Disconnect RH rear wheel sensor plug. • Check for continuity between each sensor plug pin (sensor side) and vehicle ground. 	Continuity ▶	REPLACE RH rear sensor.
	No Continuity ▶	SERVICE or REPLACE cable harness Circuit 523 or 524. RECONNECT sensor plug.
RH REAR SENSOR		
DD8 CHECK ELECTRONIC CONTROLLER TO GROUND WIRE		
• Check continuity between Breakout Box Pin 60 and body ground.	Continuity ▶	GO to Step **DD9**.
	No Continuity ▶	SERVICE or REPLACE cable harness Circuit 530 or 530B (Taurus/Sable). Circuit 530, 57U or 57R (Taurus SHO).
DD9 CHECK ANTI-LOCK OPERATION RH REAR WHEEL		
• Turn air suspension OFF, if so equipped. • Lift vehicle and rotate wheels to ensure they turn freely. • Apply moderate brake pedal effort and check that RH rear wheel will not turn. • Short Pins 18, 55 and 60 to each other at Breakout Box. • Check that RH rear wheel turns freely with ignition switch ON. • Turn air suspension ON when vehicle is off hoist, if so equipped.	If wheel turns freely ▶	REVERIFY symptom.
	If wheel does not turn freely or pedal drops ▶	REPLACE solenoid valve body.

FIG. 48 ABS DIAGNOSIS AND TESTING DATA

Wheel Sensor Diagnosis — Test DD

TEST STEP	RESULT ▶	ACTION TO TAKE
DD10 SERVICE CODE 54 AND/OR 74 CHECK LH REAR SENSOR CIRCUIT CONTINUITY		
• Turn ignition switch OFF. • Disconnect 55-pin plug from electronic controller.	Continuity ▶	GO to Step **DD10a**.
	No Continuity ▶	GO to Step **DD11**.
ELECTRONIC CONTROLLER; 55 PIN CONNECTOR		
• Connect EEC-IV Breakout Box, T83L-50-EEC-IV, with Anti-Lock Test Adapter, T90P-50-ALA, or equivalent, to the anti-lock 55-pin plug wiring harness.		
ANTI-LOCK HARNESS ADAPTER T90P-50-ALA; 55 PIN CONNECTOR; EEC-IV BREAKOUT BOX T83L-50-EEC-IV		
• Check for continuity between Breakout Box Pins 60 and 28.		

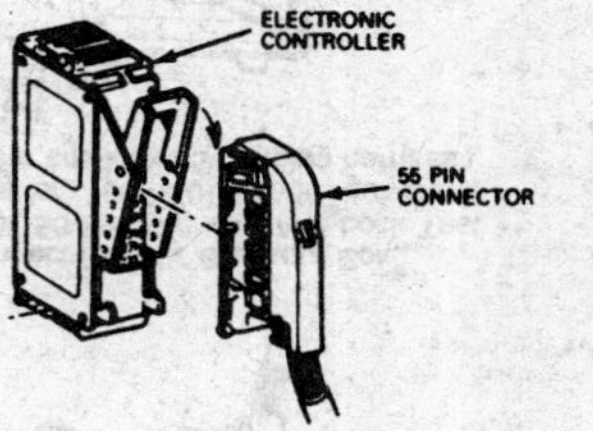

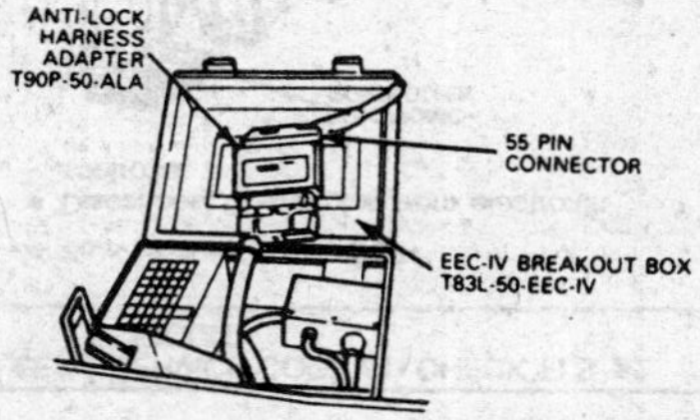

FIG. 49 ABS DIAGNOSIS AND TESTING DATA

Wheel Sensor Diagnosis — Test DD

TEST STEP	RESULT ▶	ACTION TO TAKE
DD10a CHECK LH REAR SENSOR CONTINUITY		
• Disconnect LH rear wheel sensor plug. • Check for continuity between each sensor plug pin (sensor side) and vehicle ground. LH REAR SENSOR	Continuity ▶	REPLACE LH rear sensor.
	No Continuity ▶	SERVICE or REPLACE cable harness Circuit 518 or 519. RECONNECT sensor plug.
DD11 CHECK ELECTRONIC CONTROLLER TO GROUND WIRE		
• Check continuity between Breakout Box Pin 60 and body ground.	Continuity ▶	GO to Step **DD12**.
	No Continuity ▶	SERVICE or REPLACE cable harness Circuit 530 or 530B (Taurus/Sable). Circuit 530, 57U or 57R (Taurus SHO).
DD12 CHECK ANTI-LOCK OPERATION LH REAR WHEEL		
• Turn air suspension OFF, if so equipped. • Lift vehicle and rotate wheels to ensure they turn freely. • Apply moderate brake pedal effort and check that LH rear wheel will not turn. • Short Pins 36, 54 and 60 to each other at Breakout Box. • Check that LH rear wheel turns freely with ignition switch ON. **CAUTION: Do not leave ignition on for more than 1 minute, or valve damage may result.** • Turn air suspension ON when vehicle is off hoist, if so equipped.	If wheel turns freely ▶	REVERIFY symptom.
	If wheel does not turn freely or pedal drops ▶	REPLACE solenoid valve body.

FIG. 50 ABS DIAGNOSIS AND TESTING DATA

Fluid Level Indicator/Pedal Travel Switch/Pump Motor Diagnosis — Test EE

TEST STEP	RESULT ▶	ACTION TO TAKE
EE1 SERVICE CODE 61: CHECK FLS #2 CIRCUIT		
• Turn ignition switch OFF. • Disconnect 55-pin plug from electronic controller. ELECTRONIC CONTROLLER 55 PIN CONNECTOR • Connect EEC-IV Breakout Box, T83L-50-EEC-IV, with Anti-Lock Test Adapter, T90P-50-ALA or equivalent, to the anti-lock 55-pin plug harness. ANTI-LOCK HARNESS ADAPTER T90P-50-ALA 55 PIN CONNECTOR EEC-IV BREAKOUT BOX T83L-50-EEC-IV • Check for continuity between Breakout Box Pins 8 and 60.	No Continuity ▶	GO to Step **EE2**.
	Continuity ▶	GO to Step **EE1a**.

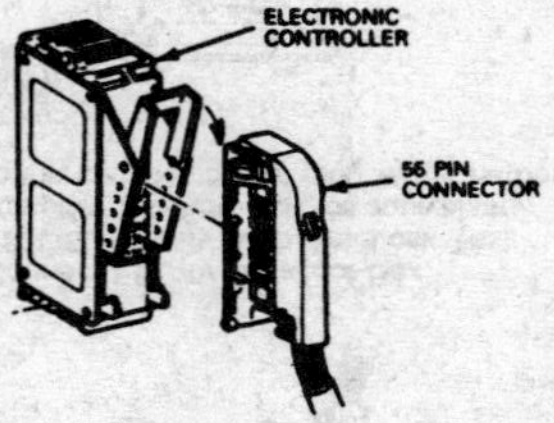

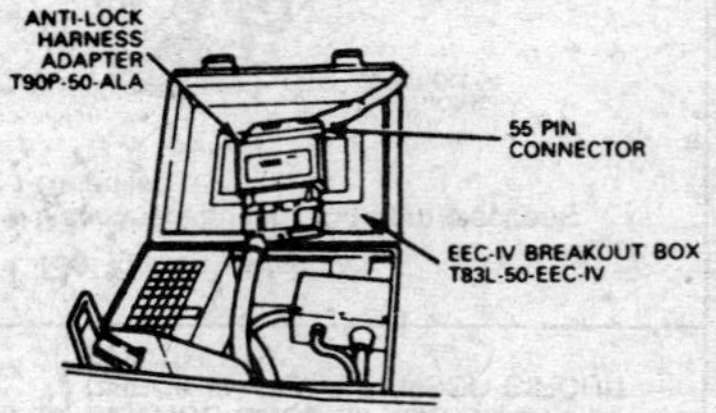

FIG. 51 ABS DIAGNOSIS AND TESTING DATA

Fluid Level Indicator/Pedal Travel Switch/Pump Motor Diagnosis — Test EE

TEST STEP	RESULT ▶	ACTION TO TAKE
EE1a CHECK FLI #2 SWITCH		
• Disconnect 2-pin plug on FLI located on small reservoir on Hydraulic Control Unit.  2 PIN CONNECTOR ON SMALL RESERVOIR ON HCU • Check for continuity between each pin and body ground.	Continuity ▶	REPLACE HCU reservoir.
	No Continuity ▶	SERVICE OR REPLACE cable harness Circuit 542, 535, 535a, 535b or 549 (Taurus/Sable). Circuit 550, 535, 535a, 535b or 549 (Taurus SHO).
EE2 CHECK FOR VOLTAGE ON FLS #2 SWITCH AND CIRCUITRY		
• Turn ignition switch ON. • Measure voltage between Breakout Box Pins 8 and 60.	No voltage ▶	REVERIFY code 61.
	12 volts ▶	GO to Step **EE2a**.
EE2a CHECK FOR VOLTAGE ON FLS #2		
• Disconnect 2-pin plug on FLI located on small reservoir on hydraulic control unit.  2 PIN CONNECTOR ON SMALL RESERVOIR ON HCU • Measure voltage between each pin and body ground.	12 volts ▶	REPLACE HCU reservoir.
	No voltage ▶	SERVICE OR REPLACE cable harness Circuit 542, 535, 535a, 535b or 549 (Taurus/Sable). Circuit 550, 535, 535a, 535b or 549 (Taurus SHO).

FIG. 52 ABS DIAGNOSIS AND TESTING DATA

Fluid Level Indicator/Pedal Travel Switch/Pump Motor Diagnosis — Test EE

TEST STEP	RESULT ▶	ACTION TO TAKE
EE3 SERVICE CODE 62: CHECK PEDAL TRAVEL SWITCH AND CIRCUITRY		
• Turn ignition switch OFF. • Disconnect 55-pin plug from electronic controller. 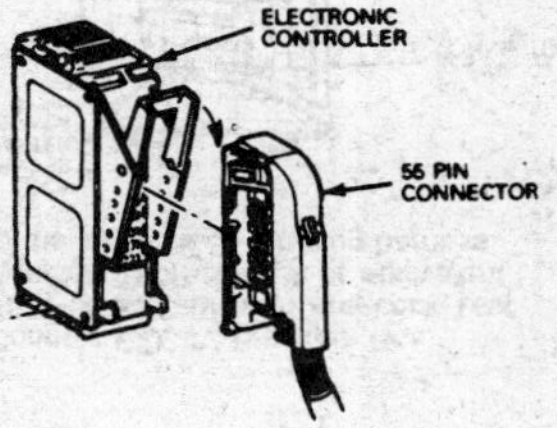 • Connect EEC-IV Breakout Box, T83L-50-EEC-IV, with Anti-Lock Test Adapter, T90P-50-ALA or equivalent, to the anti-lock 55-pin plug harness. 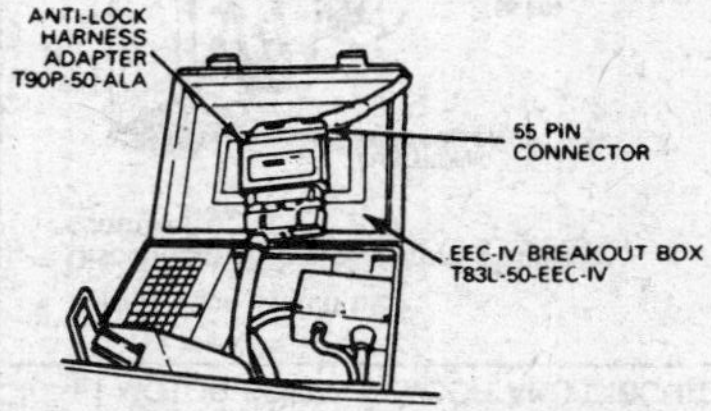 • Check for continuity between Breakout Box Pins 5 and 60.	No Continuity ▶	GO to Step **EE4**.
	Continuity ▶	GO to Step **EE3a**.

FIG. 53 ABS DIAGNOSIS AND TESTING DATA

Fluid Level Indicator/Pedal Travel Switch/Pump Motor Diagnosis — Test EE

TEST STEP	RESULT ▶	ACTION TO TAKE
EE3a CHECK PEDAL TRAVEL SWITCH		
• Disconnect 2-pin plug on pedal travel switch. (2 PIN BRAKE PEDAL POSITION SWITCH) • Check for continuity between each pin and body ground.	Continuity ▶	REPLACE pedal travel switch.
	No Continuity ▶	SERVICE OR REPLACE cable harness (Circuit 535, or 549).
EE4 CHECK FOR VOLTAGE ON PEDAL TRAVEL SWITCH AND CIRCUITRY		
• Turn ignition switch ON. • Measure voltage between Breakout Box Pins 5 and 60.	No voltage ▶	REVERIFY code 62.
	12 volts ▶	GO to Step **EE4a**.
EE4a CHECK FOR VOLTAGE ON PEDAL TRAVEL SWITCH		
• Disconnect 2-pin plug on pedal travel switch. (2 PIN BRAKE PEDAL POSITION SWITCH) • Measure voltage between each pin and body ground.	12 volts ▶	REPLACE pedal travel switch.
	No voltage ▶	SERVICE OR REPLACE cable harness (Circuit 535 or 549).

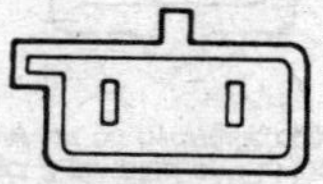

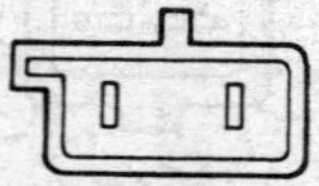

FIG. 54 ABS DIAGNOSIS AND TESTING DATA

Fluid Level Indicator/Pedal Travel Switch/Pump Motor Diagnosis — Test EE

TEST STEP	RESULT ▶	ACTION TO TAKE
EE5 SERVICE CODE 63: CHECK PUMP MOTOR SPEED SENSOR AND CIRCUIT		
• Turn ignition switch OFF. • Disconnect 55-pin plug from electronic controller. (ELECTRONIC CONTROLLER; 55 PIN CONNECTOR) • Connect EEC-IV Breakout Box, T83L-50-EEC-IV, with Anti-Lock Test Adapter, T90P-50-ALA or equivalent, to the anti-lock 55-pin plug harness. (ANTI-LOCK HARNESS ADAPTER T90P-50-ALA; 55 PIN CONNECTOR; EEC-IV BREAKOUT BOX T83L-50-EEC-IV) • Check resistance between Breakout Box Pins 31 and 49.	20 to 40 ohms ▶	GO to Step **EE6**.
	Any other reading ▶	GO to Step **EE5a**.

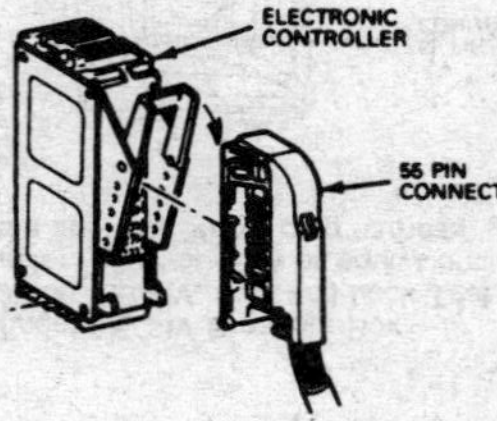

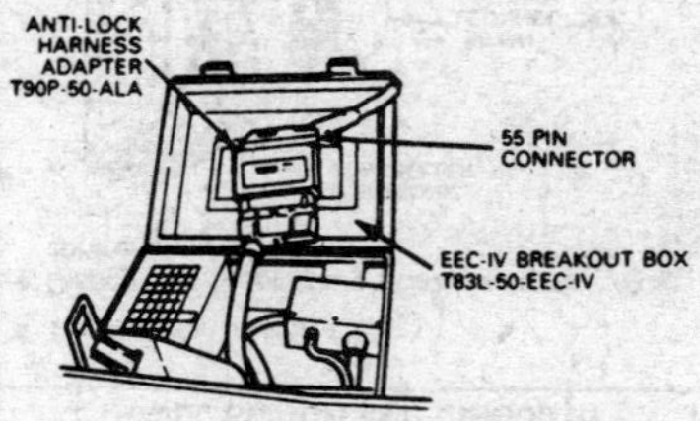

FIG. 55 ABS DIAGNOSIS AND TESTING DATA

Fluid Level Indicator/Pedal Travel Switch/Pump Motor Diagnosis — Test EE

TEST STEP	RESULT ▶	ACTION TO TAKE
EE5a CHECK PUMP MOTOR SPEED SENSOR		
• Disconnect 4-pin plug on pump motor. • Measure resistance between Pins S0 and S1 on pump motor.	20 to 40 ohms ▶	GO to Step **EE5b**.
	Any other reading ▶	REPLACE pump and motor.
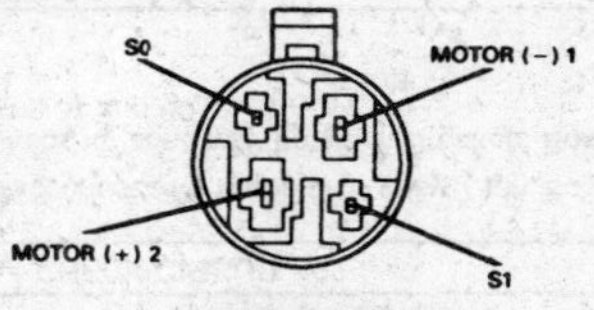 S0 · MOTOR (−) 1 · MOTOR (+) 2 · S1 4 PIN PUMP MOTOR CONNECTOR HARNESS SIDE		
EE5b CHECK PUMP MOTOR RELAY		
• Disconnect 7-pin plug on pump motor relay and remove relay. • Check continuity from Pin S0 on 7-pin side to Pin S0 on 4-pin side of relay.	Continuity ▶	GO to Step **EE5c**.
	No Continuity ▶	REPLACE pump motor relay.
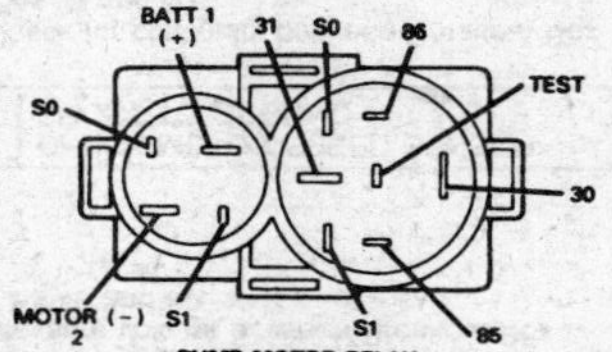 BATT 1 (+) · 31 · S0 · 86 · TEST · S0 · 30 · MOTOR (−) 2 · S1 · S1 · 85 PUMP MOTOR RELAY		
EE5c CHECK PUMP MOTOR RELAY		
• Check continuity from Pin S1 on 7-pin side to Pin S1 on 4-pin side of relay.	Continuity ▶	GO to Step **EE5d**.
	No Continuity ▶	REPLACE pump motor relay.

FIG. 56 ABS DIAGNOSIS AND TESTING DATA

Fluid Level Indicator/Pedal Travel Switch/Pump Motor Diagnosis — Test EE

TEST STEP	RESULT ▶	ACTION TO TAKE
EE5d CHECK CIRCUIT 462		
• Check continuity between Breakout Box Pin 31 and Pin S0 on pump motor connector 7-pin plug (harness side).	Continuity ▶	GO to Step **EE5e**.
	No Continuity ▶	SERVICE or REPLACE cable harness Circuit 462.
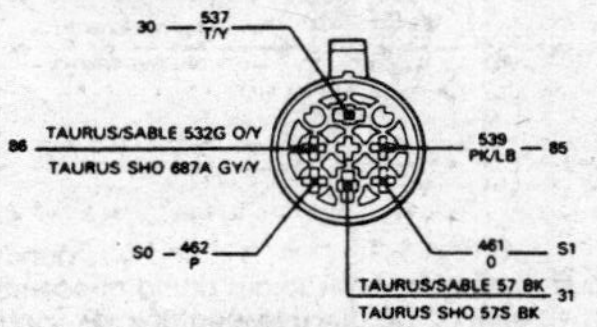 30 — 537 T/Y · 86 — TAURUS/SABLE 532G O/Y, TAURUS SHO 687A GY/Y · 539 PK/LB — 85 · S0 — 462 P · 461 O — S1 · TAURUS/SABLE 57 BK, TAURUS SHO 57S BK — 31 7 PIN PUMP MOTOR RELAY CONNECTOR HARNESS SIDE		
EE5e CHECK CIRCUIT 461		
• Check continuity between Breakout Box Pin 49 and Pin S1 on pump motor connector 7-pin plug (harness side).	Continuity ▶	REVERIFY reading at EE5.
	No Continuity ▶	SERVICE or REPLACE cable harness Circuit 461.
EE6 CHECK MOTOR SPEED SENSOR SHORT TO BATTERY +		
• Turn ignition switch to ON. • Measure voltage between Breakout Box Pins 31 and 60.	No voltage ▶	GO to Step **EE7**.
	12 volts ▶	GO to Step **EE6a**.
EE6a CHECK PUMP MOTOR		
• Disconnect pump motor to relay 4-pin plug connector. • Turn ignition switch to ON. • Measure voltage between Breakout Box Pins 31 and 60.	No voltage ▶	REPLACE pump and motor.
	12 volts ▶	GO to Step **EE6b**.
EE6b CHECK CIRCUIT 462		
• Disconnect wire harness to relay 7-pin plug. • Turn ignition switch to ON. • Measure voltage between Breakout Box Pins 31 and 60.	No voltage ▶	GO to Step **EE6c**.
	12 volts ▶	SERVICE or REPLACE cable harness Circuit 462.

FIG. 57 ABS DIAGNOSIS AND TESTING DATA

Fluid Level Indicator/Pedal Travel Switch/Pump Motor Diagnosis — Test EE

TEST STEP	RESULT ▶	ACTION TO TAKE
EE6c CHECK CIRCUIT 461		
• Turn ignition switch to ON. • Measure voltage between Breakout Box Pins 49 and 60.	No voltage ▶	REPLACE pump motor relay.
	12 volts ▶	SERVICE or REPLACE cable harness Circuit 461.
EE7 CHECK MOTOR SPEED SENSOR SHORT TO GROUND		
• Check for continuity between Breakout Box Pins 31 and 60.	No Continuity ▶	GO to Step **EE8**.
	Continuity ▶	GO to Step **EE7a**.
EE7a CHECK PUMP MOTOR		
• Disconnect pump to motor relay 4-pin plug connector.	Continuity ▶	GO to Step **EE7b**.
• Check for continuity between Breakout Box Pins 31 and 60.	No Continuity ▶	REPLACE pump and motor.
EE7b CHECK CIRCUIT 462		
• Disconnect wire harness to relay 7-pin plug. • Check for continuity between Breakout Box Pins 31 and 60.	Continuity ▶	SERVICE or REPLACE cable harness Circuit 462.
	No Continuity ▶	GO to Step **EE7c**.
EE7c CHECK CIRCUIT 461		
• Check for continuity between Breakout Box Pins 49 and 60.	Continuity ▶	SERVICE or REPLACE cable harness Circuit 461.
	No Continuity ▶	REPLACE pump motor relay.
EE8 CHECK PUMP MOTOR OPERATION		
• Reconnect pump motor relay to pump and wire harness.	Pump motor runs ▶	GO to Step **EE9**.
• Jumper Pins 15, 34 and 60 at Breakout Box. • Turn ignition to ON position.	Pump motor does not run ▶	GO to Step **EE8a**.

FIG. 58 ABS DIAGNOSIS AND TESTING DATA

Fluid Level Indicator/Pedal Travel Switch/Pump Motor Diagnosis — Test EE

TEST STEP	RESULT ▶	ACTION TO TAKE
EE8a CHECK PUMP MOTOR OPERATION		
• Disconnect pump motor relay from pump motor.	Pump motor runs ▶	GO to Step **EE8b**.
• Ground Pin 2 and apply 12 volts to Pin 1 of pump motor connector. S0 · MOTOR (−) 1 · MOTOR (+) 2 · S1 4 PIN PUMP MOTOR CONNECTOR HARNESS SIDE	Pump motor does not run ▶	REPLACE pump motor.
EE8b CHECK POWER TO RELAY		
• Disconnect wire harness from pump motor relay.	Over 10 volts ▶	GO to Step **EE8c**.
• Check voltage between Pin 30 on wire harness to pump motor relay connector and ground. 30 — 537 T/Y · 86 TAURUS/SABLE 532G O/Y · TAURUS SHO 687A GY/Y · 539 PK/LB — 85 · 50 — 462 P · 461 O — S1 · TAURUS/SABLE 57 BK 31 · TAURUS SHO 57S BK 7 PIN PUMP MOTOR RELAY CONNECTOR HARNESS SIDE	Less than 10 volts ▶	SERVICE or REPLACE battery, Circuit 299, 537 or fuse link (Taurus/Sable). Circuit 299B, 537 or fuse link (Taurus SHO).

FIG. 59 ABS DIAGNOSIS AND TESTING DATA

Fluid Level Indicator/Pedal Travel Switch/Pump Motor Diagnosis — Test EE

TEST STEP	RESULT ▶	ACTION TO TAKE
EE8c CHECK POWER TO RELAY COIL		
• Jumper Pins 34 and 60 at Breakout Box. • Turn ignition to ON position. • Measure voltage between Pins 86 and ground.	Over 10 volts ▶	GO to Step **EE8d**.
	Less than 10 volts ▶	SERVICE or REPLACE cable harness Circuit 532A or 532G (Taurus/Sable). Circuit 532, 532B or 532H (Taurus SHO).
EE8d CHECK PUMP MOTOR RELAY COIL		
• Measure resistance between Pins 85 and 86 on pump motor relay.	45 to 105 ohms ▶	GO to Step **EE7e**.
	Any other reading ▶	REPLACE pump motor relay.
EE8e CHECK CIRCUIT 539		
• Check for continuity between Breakout Box Pin 15 and Pin 85 on wire harness to pump motor relay connector.	Continuity ▶	GO to Step **EE8f**.
	No Continuity ▶	SERVICE or REPLACE cable harness Circuit 539.

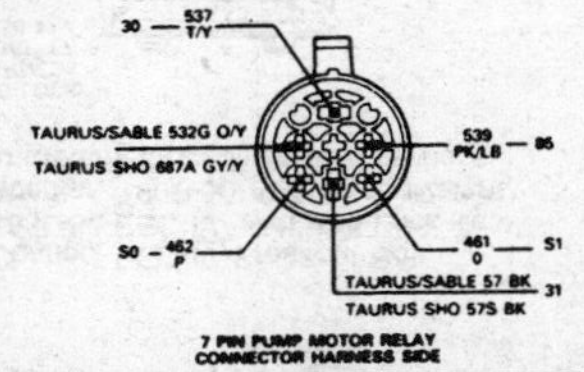

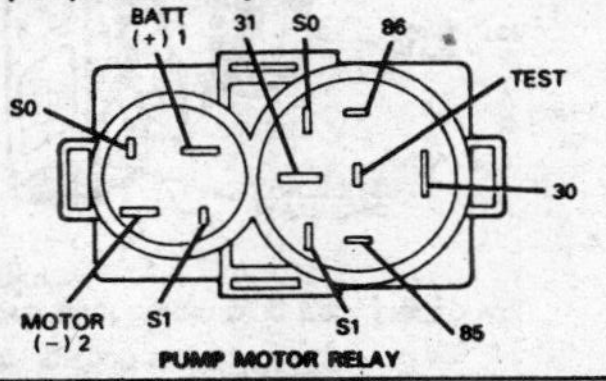

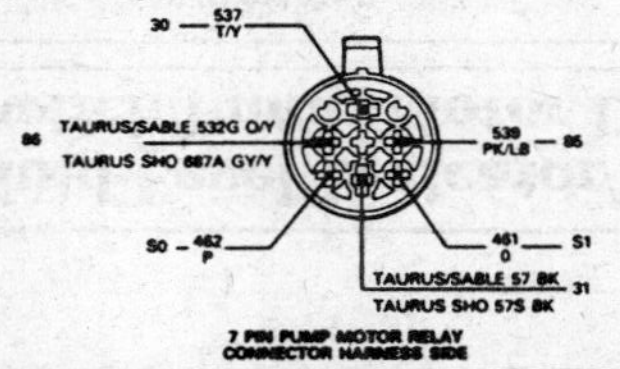

FIG. 60 ABS DIAGNOSIS AND TESTING DATA

Fluid Level Indicator/Pedal Travel Switch/Pump Motor Diagnosis — Test EE

TEST STEP	RESULT ▶	ACTION TO TAKE
EE8f CHECK CIRCUIT 57		
• Check for continuity between wire harness to pump motor relay connector Pin 31 and ground.	Continuity ▶	GO to Step **EE8g**.
	No Continuity ▶	SERVICE or REPLACE cable harness Circuit 57 or 57A (Taurus/Sable). Circuit 57S or 57R (Taurus SHO).
EE8g CHECK PUMP MOTOR RELAY		
• Connect battery positive to Pin 86 and battery negative to Pin 85 of pump motor relay. • Check for continuity between Pin 30 and Pin 1 on relay.	Continuity ▶	GO to Step **EE8h**.
	No Continuity ▶	REPLACE pump motor relay.
EE8h CHECK PUMP MOTOR RELAY		
• Check continuity between Pins 2 and 31 on pump motor relay.	Continuity ▶	REPLACE computer module.
	No Continuity ▶	REPLACE pump motor relay.

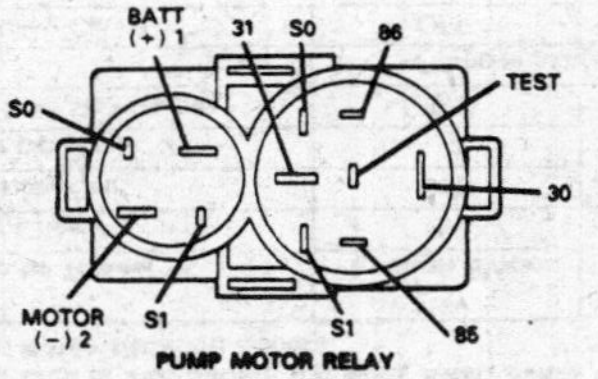

FIG. 61 ABS DIAGNOSIS AND TESTING DATA

Fluid Level Indicator/Pedal Travel Switch/Pump Motor Diagnosis — Test EE

TEST STEP	RESULT ▶	ACTION TO TAKE
EE9 SERVICE CODE 64: CHECK PUMP MOTOR PRESSURE CAPABILITY		
• Turn ignition switch OFF. • Disconnect 55-pin plug from electronic controller. ELECTRONIC CONTROLLER 55 PIN CONNECTOR • Connect EEC-IV Breakout Box, T83L-50-EEC-IV, with Anti-Lock Test Adapter, T90P-50-ALA or equivalent, to the anti-lock 55-pin plug harness. ANTI-LOCK HARNESS ADAPTER T90P-50-ALA 55 PIN CONNECTOR EEC-IV BREAKOUT BOX T83L-50-EEC-IV • Jumper Pins 15, 34 and 60. • Apply and hold brake pedal. • Turn ignition switch to ON.	Brake pedal rises ▶ Brake pedal does not rise ▶	REVERIFY code 64. REPLACE pump and motor.

FIG. 62 ABS DIAGNOSIS AND TESTING DATA

Anti-Lock Quick Check Sheet Using 60-Pin EEC-IV Breakout Box, Tool T83L-50-EEC-IV①

NOTE: Before performing tests below, the Pre-Test Checks must be performed as outlined.

NOTE: If fault is intermittent the tests listed below will NOT find the fault. Use controller service code or call Hot-Line if this situation occurs.

Item to be Tested	Ignition Mode	Measure Between Pin Numbers	Tester Scale/Range	Specification	Test Step
Battery Check	ON	60 + 53	VOLTS	10 minimum	A1
Main Relay Coil	OFF	53 + 34	OHMS	45 to 90 ohms	A3a
Jumper pins 60 + 34					
Power from Main Relay	ON	19 + 33	VOLTS	10 minimum	A2
	Remove jumper from pins 60 + 34				
Main Relay Circuit	OFF	60 + 33	CONTINUITY	continuity	A4
Sensor Resistance (RR)	OFF	27 + 45	K OHMS	0.8-1.4 Kohms	C3
Sensor Resistance (LF)	OFF	30 + 48	K OHMS	0.8-1.4 Kohms	C1
Sensor Resistance (LR)	OFF	28 + 46	K OHMS	0.8-1.4 Kohms	C4
Sensor Resistance (RF)	OFF	29 + 47	K OHMS	0.8-1.4 Kohms	C2
Valve Resistance (IFL)	OFF	3 + 20	OHMS	5-8 ohms	BB2
Valve Resistance (IFR)	OFF	3 + 38	OHMS	5-8 ohms	BB4
Valve Resistance (IRL)	OFF	3 + 54	OHMS	5-8 ohms	BB8
Valve Resistance (IRR)	OFF	3 + 55	OHMS	5-8 ohms	BB6
Valve Resistance (OFL)	OFF	3 + 2	OHMS	3-6 ohms	BB3
Valve Resistance (OFR)	OFF	3 + 21	OHMS	3-6 ohms	BB5
Valve Resistance (ORR)	OFF	3 + 18	OHMS	3-6 ohms	BB7
Valve Resistance (ORL)	OFF	3 + 36	OHMS	3-6 ohms	BB9
Reservoir Warning (FLS #2)	OFF	8 + 26	OHMS	LESS THAN 5 OHMS	A6
Pedal Travel Switch:					
Pedal NOT Applied	OFF	5 + 26	CONTINUITY	continuity	D1
With Minimum 3 Inch Apply	OFF	5 + 26	CONTINUITY	no continuity	D2
Sensor Cable Continuity Wiring to Ground (RR)	OFF	27 + 60	CONTINUITY	no continuity	B2
(LF)	OFF	30 + 60	CONTINUITY	no continuity	B4
(LR)	OFF	28 + 60	CONTINUITY	no continuity	B1
(RF)	OFF	29 + 60	CONTINUITY	no continuity	B3
Sensor Voltage: Rotate wheels @ 1 revolution per second. (RR)	OFF	27 + 45	AC MVOLTS	100-1400 mvolts	C11
(LF)	OFF	30 + 48	AC MVOLTS	100-1400 mvolts	C9
(LR)	OFF	28 + 46	AC MVOLTS	100-1400 mvolts	C12
(RF)	OFF	29 + 47	AC MVOLTS	100-1400 mvolts	C10

① If Quick Test does not isolate symptom, refer to Diagnostic Lamp Symptom Chart.

FIG. 63 ABS DIAGNOSIS AND TESTING DATA

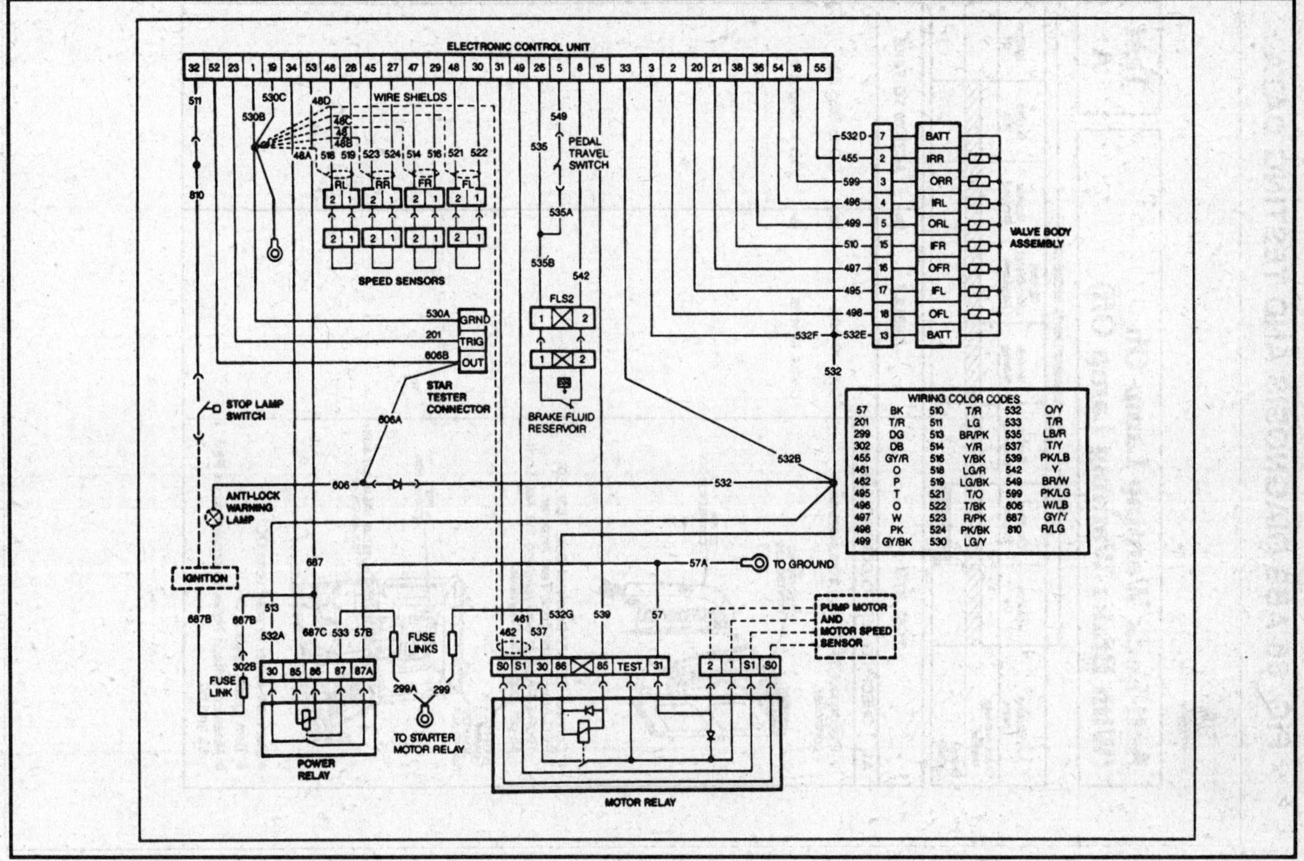

FIG. 64 ABS DIAGNOSIS AND TESTING DATA

Symptom (With Parking Brake Released)	Warning Lamps	Warning Lamp Sequence: Ignition On	Cranking Engine	Engine Running	Vehicle Moving	Braking with/without Anti-Lock	Vehicle Stopped	Engine Idle	Ignition Off	Diagnostic Test To Be Performed
Normal Light Sequence		← 4 Seconds								
Normal Warning Lamps Sequences. (System OK)	Check Anti-lock (Amber)									
	Brake (Red)									
Abnormal Warning Lamps Sequences										
• "Check Anti-Lock Brakes" Warning Lamp On. Normal "Brake" Warning Lamp Sequence.	Check Anti-lock (Amber)									A
	Brake (Red)									
• "Check Anti-Lock Brakes" Warning Lamp On After Starting Engine. Normal "Brake" Warning Lamp Sequence.	Check Anti-lock (Amber)									B
	Brake (Red)									
• "Check Anti-Lock Brakes" Warning Lamp Comes On Again After Vehicle Starts Moving. Normal "Brake" Warning Lamp Sequence.	Check Anti-lock (Amber)									C
	Brake (Red)									
• False Cycling of Anti-Lock System Normal Warning Lamp Sequence.	Check Anti-lock (Amber)									C
	Brake (Red)									
• Normal Warning Lamp Sequence. Brake Pedal Rises or Drops Excessively During ABS Cycling.	Check Anti-lock (Amber)									D
	Brake (Red)									
• Normal Warning Lamp Sequence. ABS Pump Motor Runs Continuously.	Check Anti-lock (Amber)									E
	Brake (Red)									
• Normal "Check Anti-Lock Brakes" Warning Lamp Sequence. "Brake" Warning Lamp On.	Check Anti-lock (Amber)									F
	Brake (Red)									
• No "Check Anti-Lock Brakes" Warning Lamp During Test Cycle. Normal "Brake" Warning Lamp Sequence.	Check Anti-lock (Amber)									G
	Brake (Red)									
• Spongy Brake Pedal. Normal Warning Lamp Sequence.	Check Anti-lock (Amber)									H
	Brake (Red)									
• Rear Vehicle Tracking During Anti-Lock Braking. Normal Warning Lamp Sequence.	Check Anti-lock (Amber)									J
	Brake (Red)									
• Anti-Lock Light Out for Approximately 4 Seconds Then On All The Time	Check Anti-lock (Amber)									Check Diode
	Brake (Red)									

(hatched) "Check Anti-Lock Brakes" Warning Lamp On. (solid) "Brake" Warning Lamp On.

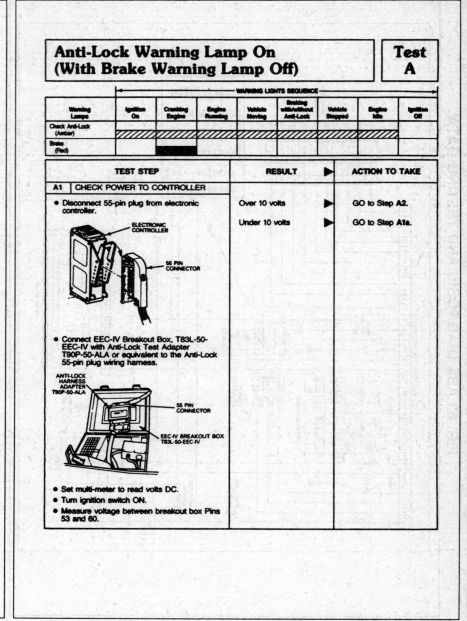

FIG. 65 ABS DIAGNOSIS AND TESTING DATA

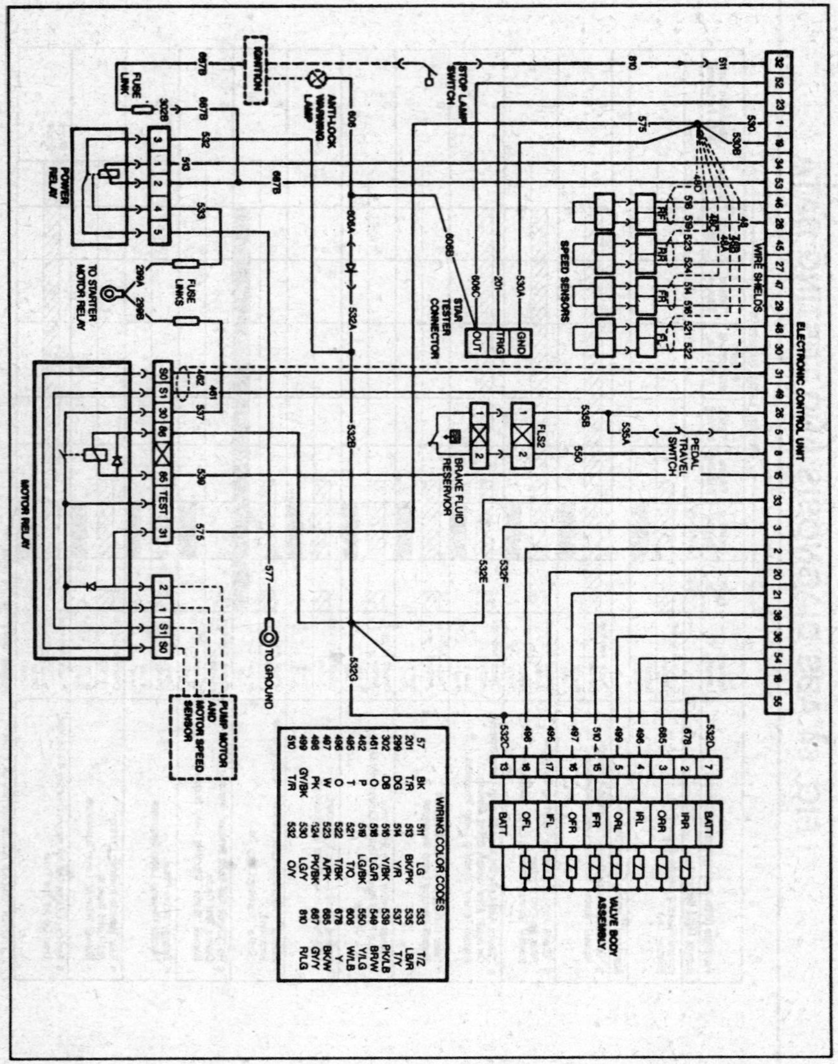

WIRING COLOR CODES

57	BK	511	LG	533	T/Z
201	T/R	513	BK/PK	535	LB/R
299	DG	514	Y/R	537	T/Y
302	DB	516	Y/BK	539	PK/LB
461	O	518	LG/R	549	BR/W
462	P	519	LG/BK	550	Y/LG
495	T	521	T/O	606	W/LB
496	O	522	T/BK	678	Y
497	W	523	A/PK	685	BK/W
498	PK	524	PK/BK	687	GY/Y
499	GY/BK	530	LG/Y	810	R/LG
510	T/R	532	O/Y		

FIG. 66 ABS DIAGNOSIS AND TESTING DATA

Anti-Lock Warning Lamp On (With Brake Warning Lamp Off) — **Test A**

WARNING LIGHTS SEQUENCE

Warning Lamps	Ignition On	Cranking Engine	Engine Running	Vehicle Moving	Braking with/without Anti-Lock	Vehicle Stopped	Engine Idle	Ignition Off
Check Anti-Lock (Amber)								
Brake (Red)								

TEST STEP	RESULT	ACTION TO TAKE
A1 CHECK POWER TO CONTROLLER		
• Disconnect 55-pin plug from electronic controller.	Over 10 volts ▶	GO to Step A2.
	Under 10 volts ▶	GO to Step A1a.
• Connect EEC-IV Breakout Box, T83L-50-EEC-IV with Anti-Lock Test Adapter T90P-50-ALA or equivalent to the Anti-Lock 55-pin plug wiring harness.		
• Set multi-meter to read volts DC.		
• Turn ignition switch ON.		
• Measure voltage between breakout box Pins 53 and 60.		

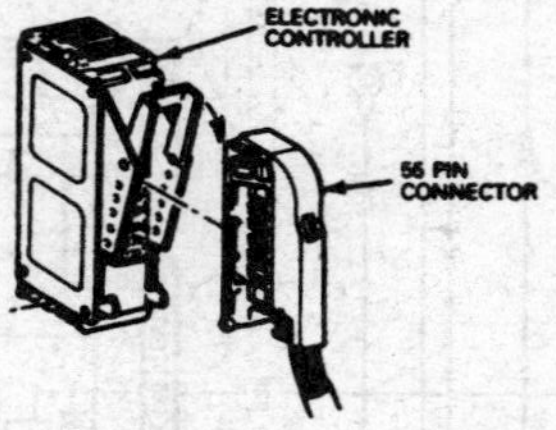

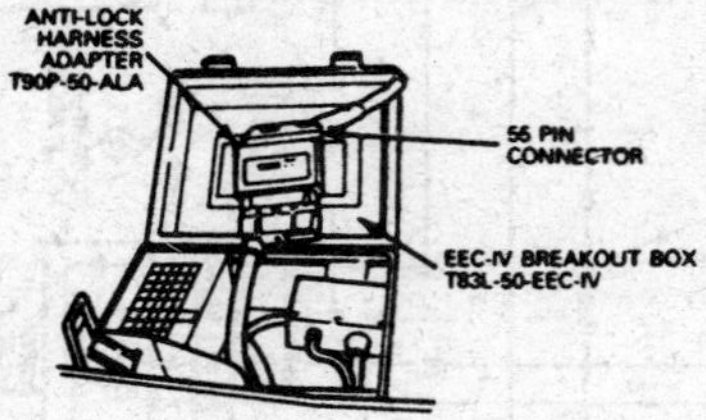

FIG. 67 ABS DIAGNOSIS AND TESTING DATA

Anti-Lock Warning Lamp On (With Brake Warning Lamp Off) — Test A

TEST STEP	RESULT	▶	ACTION TO TAKE
A1a CHECK ELECTRONIC CONTROLLER TO GROUND WIRE			
• Check continuity between breakout box Pin 60 and body ground.	Continuity	▶	GO to Step **A1b**.
	No Continuity	▶	SERVICE or REPLACE cable harness Circuit 530 or 530B (Taurus/Sable). Circuit 530, 57U or 57R (Taurus SHO).
A1b CHECK IGNITION TO ELECTRONIC CONTROLLER WIRE			
• Check for continuity between breakout box Pin 53 and ignition switch wire 687B.	Continuity	▶	CHECK ignition switch.
	No Continuity	▶	SERVICE or REPLACE cable harness circuit 687, 687B, 302B or Fuse Link.
A2 CHECK GROUND			
• Check for continuity between breakout box Pins 19 and 60.	Continuity	▶	GO to Step **A3**.
	No Continuity	▶	SERVICE or REPLACE cable harness circuit 530C (Taurus/Sable). Circuit 530B (Taurus SHO).
A3 CHECK MAIN RELAY OPERATION			
• Jumper pins 34 and 60 at breakout box. • Turn ignition to ON. • Measure voltage between breakout box Pins 33 and 19.	Over 10 volts DC	▶	GO to Step **A4**.
	Under 10 volts DC	▶	GO to Step **A3a**.

FIG. 68 ABS DIAGNOSIS AND TESTING DATA

Anti-Lock Warning Lamp On (With Brake Warning Lamp Off) — Test A

TEST STEP	RESULT	▶	ACTION TO TAKE
A3a CHECK MAIN RELAY COIL			
• Turn ignition to OFF. • Remove jumper from breakout box Pins 34 and 60. • Measure resistance between breakout box Pins 53 and 34.	45 to 90 ohms	▶	GO to Step **A3c**.
	Any other reading	▶	GO to Step **A3b**.
A3b CHECK MAIN RELAY COIL			
• Remove main power relay. 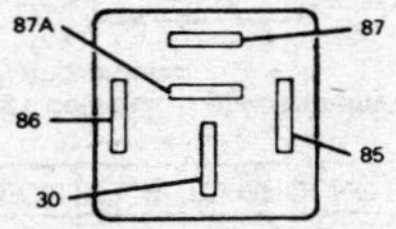 MAIN POWER RELAY CONNECTOR (HARNESS SIDE) • Measure resistance between main relay Pins 85 and 86.	45 to 90 ohms	▶	SERVICE or REPLACE cable harness circuit 513, 687 or 687C (Taurus/Sable). Circuit 513, 687B or 687C (Taurus SHO).
	Any other reading	▶	REPLACE main relay.
A3c CHECK CIRCUIT 687c			
• Turn ignition ON. 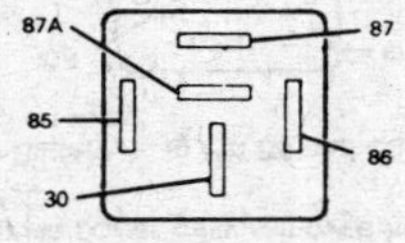 MAIN POWER RELAY CONNECTOR (HARNESS SIDE) • Measure voltage between main relay connector Pin 86 and ground.	Over 10 volts DC	▶	GO to Step **A3d**.
	Under 10 volts DC	▶	SERVICE cable harness circuit 687C.

FIG. 69 ABS DIAGNOSIS AND TESTING DATA

Anti-Lock Warning Lamp On (With Brake Warning Lamp Off) — Test A

TEST STEP	RESULT	▶ ACTION TO TAKE
A3d CHECK POWER TO RELAY		
• Turn ignition ON.	Over 10 volts DC ▶	GO to Step **A3e**.
87A, 87, 85, 86, 30 — MAIN POWER RELAY CONNECTOR (HARNESS SIDE)	Under 10 volts DC ▶	SERVICE cable harness circuit 533, 299A Fuse Link.
• Measure voltage between main relay connector Pin 87 and ground.		
A3e CHECK CIRCUIT 532A & 532B		
• Turn ignition OFF.	Continuity ▶	GO to Step **A3f**.
87A, 87, 85, 86, 30 — MAIN POWER RELAY CONNECTOR (HARNESS SIDE)	No Continuity ▶	SERVICE or REPLACE cable harness circuit 532A or 532B.
• Check for continuity between main relay connector pin 30 and breakout box Pin 33.		

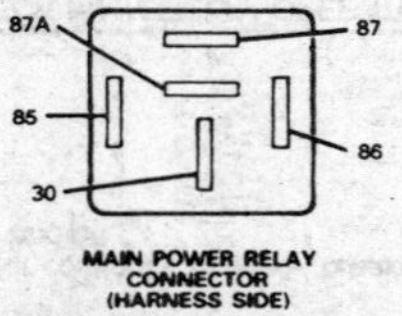

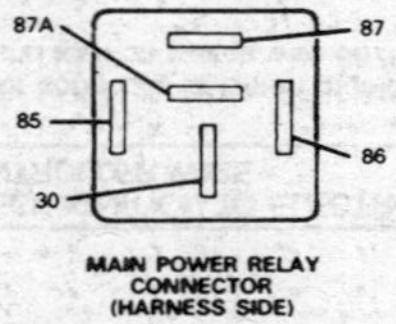

FIG. 70 ABS DIAGNOSIS AND TESTING DATA

Anti-Lock Warning Lamp On (With Brake Warning Lamp Off) — Test A

TEST STEP	RESULT	▶ ACTION TO TAKE
A3f CHECK RELAY OPERATION		
• With main power relay removed from connector.	Continuity ▶	REVERIFY reading at TEST A3.
• Apply Battery + to Pin 86 and Battery − to Pin 85 on relay.	No Continuity ▶	REPLACE main power relay.
87A, 87, 86, 85, 30 — MAIN POWER RELAY CONNECTOR (HARNESS SIDE)		
• Check continuity between relay Pins 30 and 87.		
A4 CHECK RELAY TO GROUND		
• Check for continuity between relay connector Pin 87A and ground.	Continuity ▶	GO to Step **A5**.
87A, 87, 86, 85, 30 — MAIN POWER RELAY CONNECTOR (HARNESS SIDE)	No Continuity ▶	SERVICE or REPLACE cable harness Circuit 57A or 57B (Taurus/Sable). Circuit 57T or 57R (Taurus SHO).
A5 CHECK CIRCUIT 606.		
• Turn ignition ON.	Over 10 volts DC ▶	GO to Step **A6**.
• Check voltage between breakout box Pins 52 and 60.	Under 10 volts DC ▶	SERVICE or REPLACE cable harness Circuits 606, 606A or 606B (Taurus/Sable). Circuit 606, 606B or 606C (Taurus SHO).

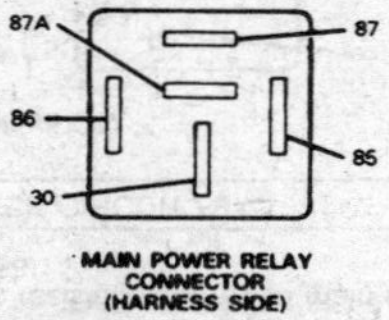

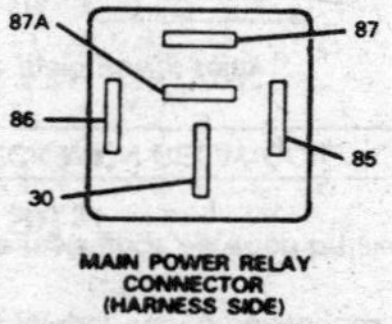

FIG. 71 ABS DIAGNOSIS AND TESTING DATA

Anti-Lock Warning Lamp On (With Brake Warning Lamp Off) — Test A

TEST STEP	RESULT ▶	ACTION TO TAKE
A6 CHECK FLI #2 AND CIRCUITRY		
• Measure resistance between breakout box Pins 8 and 26.	Less than 5 ohms ▶	GO to Step **A7**.
	Any other reading ▶	GO to Step **A6a**.
A6a CHECK FLI #2		
• Disconnect 2-pin plug from FLI #2, located on HCU reservoir. • Measure resistance between Pins 1 and 2 on HCU reservoir.	Less than 5 ohms ▶	SERVICE or REPLACE cable harness Circuit 542, 535 or 535B (Taurus/ Sable). Circuit 550, 535 or 535B (Taurus SHO).
	Any other reading ▶	REPLACE HCU reservoir.
A7 ELECTRONIC CONTROLLER CHECK		
• If Self-Diagnostics, ABS Quick Test and Test A did not find problem. • Replace Electronic Controller with a known good controller.	ABS lamp off ▶	REPLACE Controller.
	ABS lamp still on ▶	REVERIFY that all tests have been performed.

FIG. 72 ABS DIAGNOSIS AND TESTING DATA

Anti-Lock Lamp On After Engine Starts (Brake Warning Lamp Off) — Test B

WARNING LIGHTS SEQUENCE

Warning Lamps	Ignition On	Cranking Engine	Engine Running	Vehicle Moving	Braking with/without Anti-Lock	Vehicle Stopped	Engine Idle	Ignition Off
Check Anti-Lock (Amber)								
Brake (Red)								

TEST STEP	RESULT ▶	ACTION TO TAKE
B1 CHECK CONTINUITY OF CIRCUITS 518 and 519		
• Turn ignition switch Off. • Disconnect 55-pin plug from controller.	Continuity ▶	GO to Step **B1a**.
	No Continuity ▶	GO to Step **B2**.
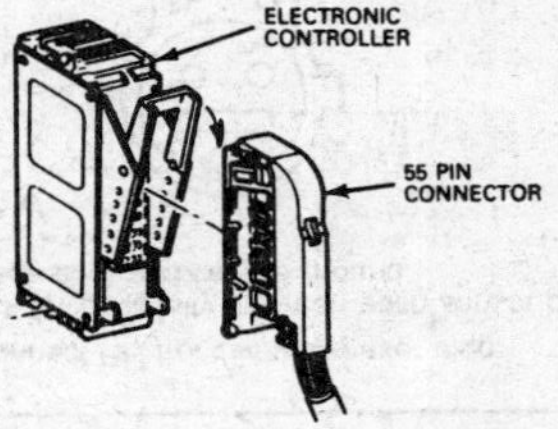 ELECTRONIC CONTROLLER 55 PIN CONNECTOR		
Connect EEC-IV Breakout Box T83L-50-EEC-IV with Anti-Lock Test Adapter T90P-50-ALA or equivalent to the Anti-Lock 55-pin plug on the wiring harness.		
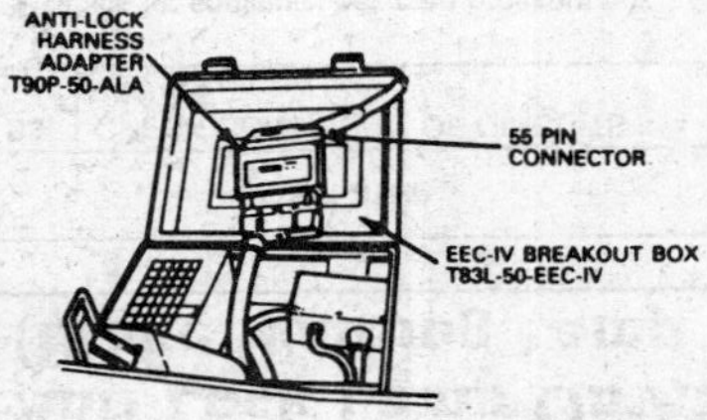 ANTI-LOCK HARNESS ADAPTER T90P-50-ALA 55 PIN CONNECTOR EEC-IV BREAKOUT BOX T83L-50-EEC-IV		
• Check continuity between breakout box Pins 28 and 60.		

FIG. 73 ABS DIAGNOSIS AND TESTING DATA

Anti-Lock Lamp On After Engine Starts (Brake Warning Lamp Off) — Test B

TEST STEP	RESULT ▶	ACTION TO TAKE
B1a CHECK LH REAR SENSOR TO GROUND		
• Disconnect LH rear wheel sensor plug. • Check for continuity between each sensor pin (sensor side) and vehicle ground.  LH REAR SENSOR	Continuity ▶	REPLACE LH rear sensor.
	No Continuity ▶	REPLACE or SERVICE cable harness circuit (518 or 519).
B2 CHECK CONTINUITY OF CIRCUITS 523 and 524		
• Check for continuity between breakout box Pins 27 and 60.	Continuity ▶	GO to Step **B2a**.
	No Continuity ▶	GO to Step **B3**.
B2a CHECK RH REAR SENSOR TO GROUND		
• Disconnect RH rear wheel sensor plug. • Check for continuity between each sensor pin (sensor side) and vehicle ground.  RH REAR SENSOR	Continuity ▶	REPLACE RH rear sensor.
	No Continuity ▶	REPLACE or SERVICE cable harness circuit (523 or 524).

FIG. 74 ABS DIAGNOSIS AND TESTING DATA

Anti-Lock Lamp On After Engine Starts (Brake Warning Lamp Off) — Test B

TEST STEP	RESULT ▶	ACTION TO TAKE
B3 CHECK CONTINUITY OF CIRCUITS 514 and 516		
• Check for continuity between breakout box Pins 29 and 60.	Continuity ▶	GO to Step **B3a**.
	No Continuity ▶	GO to Step **B4**.
B3a CHECK RH FRONT SENSOR TO GROUND		
• Disconnect RH front wheel sensor plug. • Check for continuity between each sensor pin (sensor side) and vehicle ground.  RH FRONT SENSOR	Continuity ▶	REPLACE RH front sensor.
	No Continuity ▶	REPLACE or SERVICE cable harness circuit (514 or 516).
B4 CHECK CONTINUITY OF CIRCUITS 521 and 522		
• Check for continuity between breakout box Pins 30 and 60.	Continuity ▶	GO to Step **B4a**.
	No Continuity ▶	Test complete. If Anti-Lock lamp pattern remains, REPEAT Test B.

FIG. 75 ABS DIAGNOSIS AND TESTING DATA

Anti-Lock Lamp On After Engine Starts (Brake Warning Lamp Off) — Test B

TEST STEP	RESULT ▶	ACTION TO TAKE
B4a CHECK LH FRONT SENSOR TO GROUND		
• Disconnect LH front wheel-sensor plug. • Check for continuity between each sensor pin (sensor side) and vehicle ground.	Continuity ▶	REPLACE LH front sensor.
	No Continuity ▶	REPLACE or SERVICE cable harness circuit (521 or 522).

LH FRONT SENSOR

FIG. 76 ABS DIAGNOSIS AND TESTING DATA

Anti-Lock Warning Lamp On After Vehicle Starts To Move Or False Cycling Of Anti-Lock System — Test C

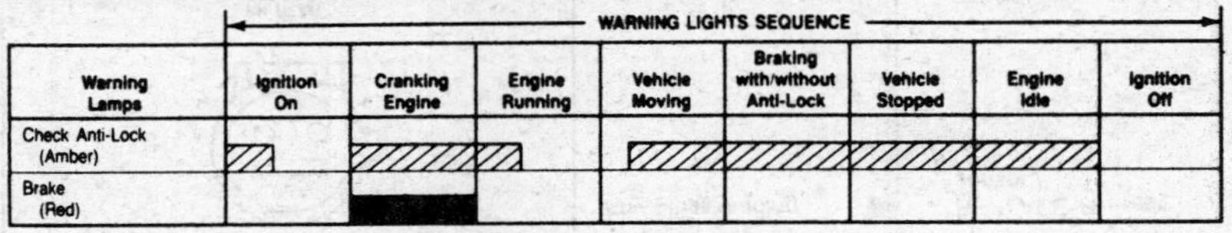

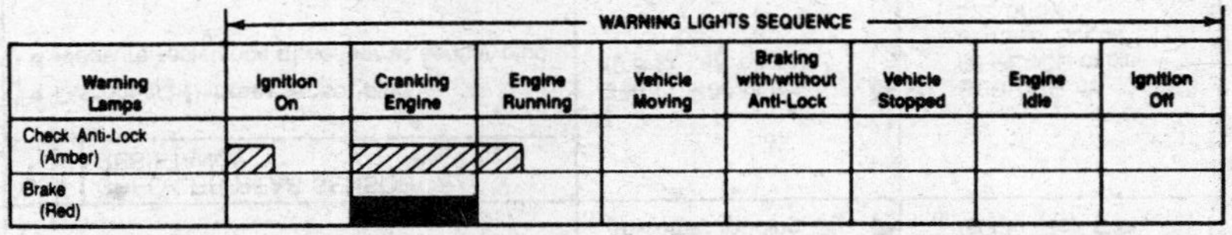

WARNING LIGHTS SEQUENCE

Warning Lamps	Ignition On	Cranking Engine	Engine Running	Vehicle Moving	Braking with/without Anti-Lock	Vehicle Stopped	Engine Idle	Ignition Off
Check Anti-Lock (Amber)								
Brake (Red)								

WARNING LIGHTS SEQUENCE

Warning Lamps	Ignition On	Cranking Engine	Engine Running	Vehicle Moving	Braking with/without Anti-Lock	Vehicle Stopped	Engine Idle	Ignition Off
Check Anti-Lock (Amber)								
Brake (Red)								

TEST STEP	RESULT ▶	ACTION TO TAKE
C1 MEASURE LH FRONT SENSOR CIRCUIT RESISTANCE		
• Turn ignition switch OFF. • Disconnect 55-pin connector from electronic controller.		

ELECTRONIC CONTROLLER

55 PIN CONNECTOR

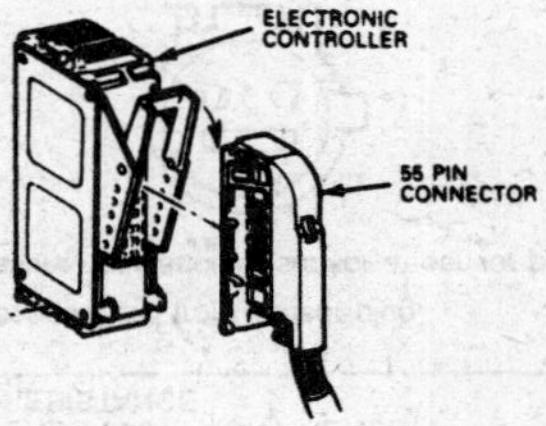

FIG. 77 ABS DIAGNOSIS AND TESTING DATA

Anti-Lock Warning Lamp On After Vehicle Starts To Move Or False Cycling Of Anti-Lock System — **Test C**

TEST STEP	RESULT ▶	ACTION TO TAKE
C1 MEASURE LH FRONT SENSOR CIRCUIT RESISTANCE — Continued		
• Connect EEC-IV Breakout Box with Tool T90P-50-ALA or equivalent to the 55-pin connector on wiring harness.	800 to 1400 ohms (0.8 to 1.4K ohms) ▶	GO to Step **C2**.
ANTI-LOCK HARNESS ADAPTER T90P-50-ALA; 55 PIN CONNECTOR; EEC-IV BREAKOUT BOX T83L-50-EEC-IV	Any other reading ▶	GO to Step **C1a**.
• Set multi-meter to read resistance. • Measure resistance between Pins 30 and 48.		
C1a CHECK LH FRONT SENSOR RESISTANCE		
• Disconnect LH front sensor plug. • Measure resistance of sensor at sensor plug.	800 to 1400 ohms (0.8 to 1.4K ohms) ▶	SERVICE or REPLACE cable harness Circuit 521 or 522.
LH FRONT SENSOR	Any other reading ▶	REPLACE LH front sensor.
C2 MEASURE RH FRONT SENSOR CIRCUIT RESISTANCE		
• Measure resistance between breakout box Pins 29 and 47.	800 to 1400 ohms (0.8 to 1.4K ohms) ▶	GO to Step **C3**.
	Any other reading ▶	GO to Step **C2a**.

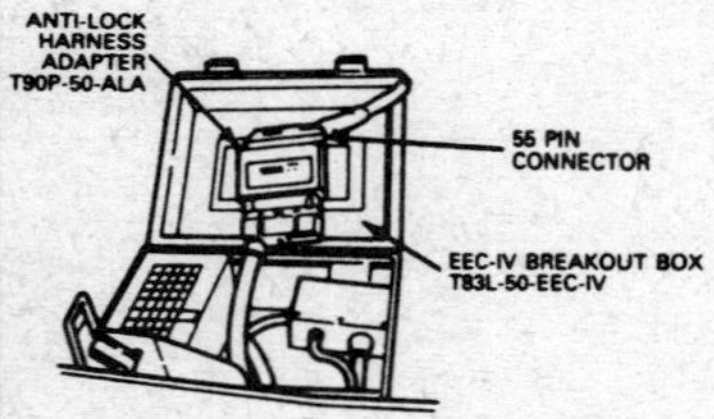

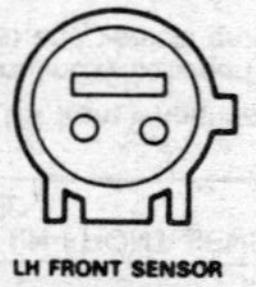

FIG. 78 ABS DIAGNOSIS AND TESTING DATA

Anti-Lock Warning Lamp On After Vehicle Starts To Move Or False Cycling Of Anti-Lock System — **Test C**

TEST STEP	RESULT ▶	ACTION TO TAKE
C2a CHECK RH FRONT SENSOR RESISTANCE		
• Disconnect RH front sensor plug. • Measure resistance of sensor at sensor plug.	800 to 1400 ohms (0.8 to 1.4K ohms) ▶	SERVICE or REPLACE cable harness Circuit 514 or 516.
RH FRONT SENSOR	Any other reading ▶	REPLACE RH front sensor.
C3 MEASURE RH REAR SENSOR CIRCUIT RESISTANCE		
• Measure resistance between Breakout box Pins 27 and 45.	800 to 1400 ohms (0.8 to 1.4K ohms) ▶	GO to Step **C4**.
	Any other reading ▶	GO to Step **C3a**.
C3a CHECK RH REAR SENSOR RESISTANCE		
• Disconnect RH rear sensor plug. • Measure resistance of sensor at sensor plug.	800 to 1400 ohms (0.8 to 1.4K ohms) ▶	SERVICE or REPLACE cable harness Circuit 523 or 524.
RH REAR SENSOR	Any other reading ▶	REPLACE RH rear sensor.

FIG. 79 ABS DIAGNOSIS AND TESTING DATA

Anti-Lock Warning Lamp On After Vehicle Starts To Move Or False Cycling Of Anti-Lock System — **Test C**

TEST STEP	RESULT ▶	ACTION TO TAKE
C4 MEASURE LH REAR SENSOR CIRCUIT RESISTANCE		
• Measure resistance between breakout box Pins 28 and 46.	800 to 1400 ohms (0.8 to 1.4K ohms) ▶	GO to Step **C5**.
	Any other reading ▶	GO to Step **C4a**.
C4a CHECK LH REAR SENSOR RESISTANCE		
• Disconnect LH rear sensor plug. • Measure resistance of sensor at sensor plug.	800 to 1400 ohms (0.8 to 1.4K ohms) ▶	SERVICE or REPLACE cable harness Circuit 518 or 519.
LH REAR SENSOR	Any other reading ▶	REPLACE LH rear sensor.
C5 CHECK LH FRONT SENSOR AND CIRCUITRY TO GROUND		
• Check for continuity between breakout box Pins 30 and 60.	Continuity ▶	GO to Step **C5a**.
	No Continuity ▶	GO to Step **C6**.
C5a CHECK LH FRONT SENSOR TO GROUND		
• Disconnect LH front sensor plug. • Check for continuity between each sensor pin and body ground.	Continuity ▶	REPLACE LH front sensor.
	No Continuity ▶	REPAIR OR REPLACE cable harness Circuit 521 or 522.

FIG. 80 ABS DIAGNOSIS AND TESTING DATA

Anti-Lock Warning Lamp On After Vehicle Starts To Move Or False Cycling Of Anti-Lock System — **Test C**

TEST STEP	RESULT ▶	ACTION TO TAKE
C6 CHECK RH FRONT SENSOR AND CIRCUITRY TO GROUND		
• Check for continuity between breakout box Pins 29 and 60.	Continuity ▶	GO to Step **C6a**.
	No Continuity ▶	GO to Step **C7**.
C6a CHECK RH FRONT SENSOR TO GROUND		
• Disconnect RH front sensor plug. • Check for continuity between each sensor pin and body ground.	Continuity ▶	REPLACE RH front sensor.
	No Continuity ▶	REPAIR OR REPLACE cable harness Circuit 514 or 516.
C7 CHECK RH REAR SENSOR AND CIRCUITRY TO GROUND		
• Check for continuity between breakout box Pins 27 and 60.	Continuity ▶	GO to Step **C7a**.
	No Continuity ▶	GO to Step **C8**.
C7a CHECK RH REAR SENSOR TO GROUND		
• Disconnect RH rear sensor plug. • Check for continuity between each sensor pin and body ground.	Continuity ▶	REPLACE RH rear sensor.
	No Continuity ▶	REPAIR OR REPLACE cable harness Circuit 523 or 524.
C8 CHECK LH REAR SENSOR AND CIRCUITRY TO GROUND		
• Check for continuity between breakout box Pins 28 and 60.	Continuity ▶	GO to Step **C8a**.
	No Continuity ▶	GO to Step **C9**.

FIG. 81 ABS DIAGNOSIS AND TESTING DATA

Anti-Lock Warning Lamp On After Vehicle Starts To Move Or False Cycling Of Anti-Lock System — **Test C**

TEST STEP	RESULT	ACTION TO TAKE
C8a CHECK LH REAR SENSOR TO GROUND		
• Disconnect LH rear sensor plug. • Check for continuity between each sensor pin and body ground.	Continuity ▶	REPLACE LH rear sensor.
	No Continuity ▶	REPAIR OR REPLACE cable harness Circuit 518 or 519.
C9 CHECK LH FRONT SENSOR VOLTAGE OUTPUT		
• Measure voltage between breakout box Pins 30 and 48 while spinning LH front wheel at approximately 1 revolution per second.	Between 0.10 and 1.40 volts AC ▶	GO to Step **C10**.
	Less than 0.10 or more than 1.40 volts AC ▶	CHECK wheel sensor mounting, air gap, or toothed wheel. CORRECT as required.
C10 CHECK RH FRONT SENSOR VOLTAGE OUTPUT		
• Measure voltage between breakout box Pins 29 and 47 while spinning RH front wheel at approximately 1 revolution per second.	Between 0.10 and 1.40 volts AC ▶	GO to Step **C11**.
	Less than 0.10 or more than 1.40 volts AC ▶	CHECK wheel sensor mounting, air gap, or toothed wheel. CORRECT as required.
C11 CHECK RH REAR SENSOR VOLTAGE OUTPUT		
• Measure voltage between breakout box Pins 27 and 45 while spinning RH rear wheel at approximately 1 revolution per second.	Between 0.10 and 1.40 volts AC ▶	GO to Step **C12**.
	Less than 0.10 or more than 1.40 volts AC ▶	CHECK wheel sensor mounting, air gap, or toothed wheel. CORRECT as required.

FIG. 82 ABS DIAGNOSIS AND TESTING DATA

Anti-Lock Warning Lamp On After Vehicle Starts To Move Or False Cycling Of Anti-Lock System — **Test C**

TEST STEP	RESULT	ACTION TO TAKE
C12 CHECK LH REAR SENSOR VOLTAGE OUTPUT		
• Measure voltage between breakout box Pins 28 and 46 while spinning LH rear wheel at approximately 1 revolution per second.	Between 0.10 and 1.40 volts AC ▶	GO to Step **C13**.
	Less than 0.10 or more than 1.40 volts AC ▶	CHECK wheel sensor mounting, air gap, or toothed wheel. CORRECT as required.
C13 CHECK MOTOR SPEED SENSOR AND CIRCUITRY		
• Measure resistance between breakout box Pins 31 and 49.	20 to 40 ohms ▶	GO to Step **C14**.
	Any other reading ▶	GO to Step **C13a**.
C13a CHECK PUMP MOTOR SPEED SENSOR		
• Disconnect 4-Pin plug on pump motor. • Measure resistance between Pins S0 and S1 on pump motor.	20 to 40 ohms ▶	GO to Step **C13b**.
	Any other reading ▶	REPLACE pump and motor.

4 PIN PUMP MOTOR CONNECTOR HARNESS SIDE

FIG. 83 ABS DIAGNOSIS AND TESTING DATA

Anti-Lock Warning Lamp On After Vehicle Starts To Move Or False Cycling Of Anti-Lock System — **Test C**

TEST STEP	RESULT ▶	ACTION TO TAKE
C13b CHECK PUMP MOTOR RELAY		
• Disconnect 7-pin plug on pump motor relay and remove relay. • Check continuity from Pin S0 on 7-pin side to Pin S0 on 4-pin side of relay.	Continuity ▶ No Continuity ▶	GO to Step **C13c**. REPLACE pump motor relay.
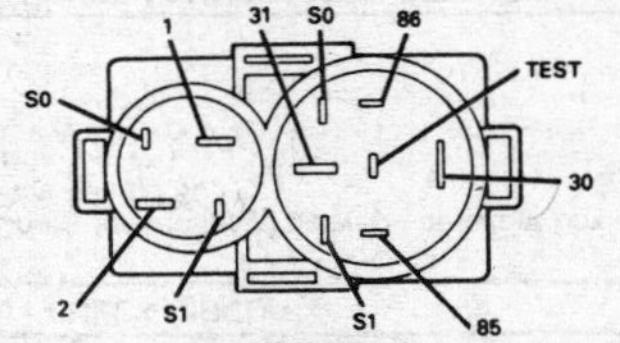 PUMP MOTOR RELAY (diagram labels: 1, 31, S0, 86, TEST, S0, 30, 2, S1, S1, 85)		
C13c CHECK PUMP MOTOR RELAY		
• Check continuity from Pin S1 on 7-pin side to Pin S1 on 4-pin side of relay.	Continuity ▶ No Continuity ▶	GO to Step **C13d**. REPLACE pump motor relay.
C13d CHECK CIRCUIT 462		
• Check continuity between breakout box Pin 31 and Pin S0 on pump motor connector 7-pin plug (harness side).	Continuity ▶ No Continuity ▶	GO to Step **C13e**. SERVICE or REPLACE cable harness Circuit 462.
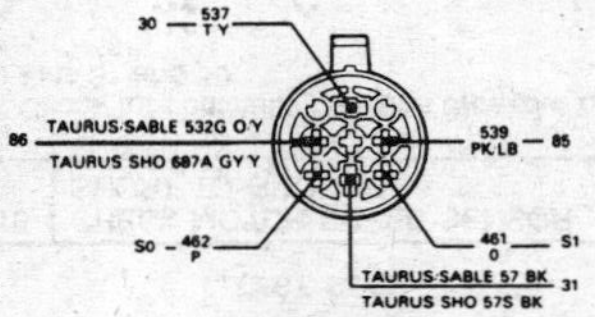 7 PIN PUMP MOTOR RELAY CONNECTOR HARNESS SIDE (diagram labels: 30 — 537 T/Y; 86 TAURUS/SABLE 532G O/Y, TAURUS SHO 687A GY/Y; 539 PK/LB — 85; S0 — 462 P; 461 O — S1; TAURUS/SABLE 57 BK, TAURUS SHO 57S BK — 31)		

FIG. 84 ABS DIAGNOSIS AND TESTING DATA

Anti-Lock Warning Lamp On After Vehicle Starts To Move Or False Cycling Of Anti-Lock System — **Test C**

TEST STEP	RESULT ▶	ACTION TO TAKE
C13e CHECK CIRCUIT 461		
• Check continuity between breakout box Pin 49 and Pin S1 on pump motor connector 7-pin plug (harness side).	Continuity ▶ No Continuity ▶	REVERIFY reading at C13. SERVICE or REPLACE cable harness Circuit 461.
C14 CHECK MOTOR SPEED SENSOR SHORT TO BATTERY +		
• Turn ignition switch to ON. • Measure voltage between breakout box Pins 31 and 60.	No voltage ▶ 12 volts ▶	GO to Step **C15**. GO to Step **C14a**.
C14a CHECK PUMP MOTOR		
• Disconnect pump motor to relay 4-pin plug connector. • Turn ignition switch to ON. • Measure voltage between breakout box Pins 31 and 60.	No voltage ▶ 12 volts ▶	REPLACE pump and motor. GO to Step **C14b**.
C14b CHECK CIRCUIT 462		
• Disconnect wire harness to relay 7-pin plug. • Turn ignition switch to ON. • Measure voltage between breakout box Pins 31 and 60.	No voltage ▶ 12 volts ▶	GO to Step **C14c**. SERVICE or REPLACE cable harness Circuit 462.
C14c CHECK CIRCUIT 461		
• Turn ignition switch to ON. • Measure voltage between breakout box Pins 49 and 60.	No voltage ▶ 12 volts ▶	REPLACE pump motor relay. SERVICE or REPLACE cable harness Circuit 461.

FIG. 85 ABS DIAGNOSIS AND TESTING DATA

Anti-Lock Warning Lamp On After Vehicle Starts To Move Or False Cycling Of Anti-Lock System — **Test C**

TEST STEP	RESULT ▶	ACTION TO TAKE
C15 CHECK MOTOR SPEED SENSOR SHORT TO GROUND		
• Check for continuity between breakout box Pins 31 and 60.	No Continuity ▶	GO to Step **C16**.
	Continuity ▶	GO to Step **C15a**.
C15a CHECK PUMP MOTOR		
• Disconnect pump to motor relay 4-pin plug connector.	Continuity ▶	GO to Step **C15b**.
• Check for continuity between breakout box Pins 31 and 60.	No Continuity ▶	REPLACE pump and motor.
C15b CHECK CIRCUIT 462		
• Disconnect wire harness to relay 7-pin plug. • Check for continuity between breakout box Pins 31 and 60.	Continuity ▶	SERVICE or REPLACE cable harness Circuit 462.
	No Continuity ▶	GO to Step **C15c**.
C15c CHECK CIRCUIT 461		
• Check for continuity between breakout box Pins 49 and 60.	Continuity ▶	SERVICE Or REPLACE cable harness Circuit 461.
	No Continuity ▶	REPLACE pump motor relay.
C16 CHECK PUMP MOTOR OPERATION		
• Reconnect pump motor relay to pump and wire harness.	Pump motor runs ▶	GO to Step **C17**.
• Jumper Pins 15, 34 and 60 at breakout box. • Turn ignition to ON position.	Pump motor does not run ▶	GO to Step **C16a**.

FIG. 86 ABS DIAGNOSIS AND TESTING DATA

Anti-Lock Warning Lamp On After Vehicle Starts To Move Or False Cycling Of Anti-Lock System — **Test C**

TEST STEP	RESULT ▶	ACTION TO TAKE
C16a CHECK PUMP MOTOR OPERATION		
• Disconnect pump motor relay from pump motor.	Pump motor runs ▶	GO to Step **C16b**.
• Ground Pin 2 and apply 12 volts to Pin 1 of pump motor connector. S0 / MOTOR (−) 2 / MOTOR (+) 1 / S1 4 PIN PUMP MOTOR CONNECTOR HARNESS SIDE	Pump motor does not run ▶	REPLACE pump motor.
C16b CHECK POWER TO RELAY		
• Disconnect wire harness from pump motor relay.	Over 10 volts ▶	GO to Step **C16c**.
• Check voltage between Pin 30 on wire harness to pump motor relay connector and ground. 30 — 537 T Y 86 TAURUS SABLE 532G O Y / TAURUS SHO 687A GY Y 539 PK LB — 85 S0 — 462 P 461 O — S1 TAURUS SABLE 57 BK / TAURUS SHO 57S BK 31 7 PIN PUMP MOTOR RELAY CONNECTOR HARNESS SIDE	Less than 10 volts ▶	SERVICE or REPLACE battery Circuit 299, 537 or fuse link (Taurus/Sable). Circuit 299a, 537 or fuse link (Taurus SHO).

FIG. 87 ABS DIAGNOSIS AND TESTING DATA

Anti-Lock Warning Lamp On After Vehicle Starts To Move Or False Cycling Of Anti-Lock System — **Test C**

TEST STEP	RESULT ▶	ACTION TO TAKE
C16c CHECK POWER TO RELAY COIL		
• Jumper Pins 34 and 60 at breakout box. • Turn ignition to ON position. • Measure voltage between pump motor relay connector pin 86 and ground. 30 — 537 T Y; 86 TAURUS SABLE 532G O Y, TAURUS SHO 687A GY Y; 539 PK LB — 85; S0 — 462 P; 461 O — S1; TAURUS SABLE 57 BK, TAURUS SHO 57S BK 31 7 PIN PUMP MOTOR RELAY CONNECTOR HARNESS SIDE	Over 10 volts ▶ Less than 10 volts ▶	GO to Step **C16d**. SERVICE or REPLACE cable harness circuit 532G (Taurus/Sable). Circuit 532H (Taurus SHO).
C16d CHECK PUMP MOTOR RELAY COIL		
• Measure resistance between Pins 85 and 86 on pump motor relay. BATT (+) 1; 31; S0; 86; TEST; S0; 30; MOTOR (−) 2; S1; S1; 85 PUMP MOTOR RELAY	45 to 105 ohms ▶ Any other reading ▶	GO to Step **C16e**. REPLACE pump motor relay.

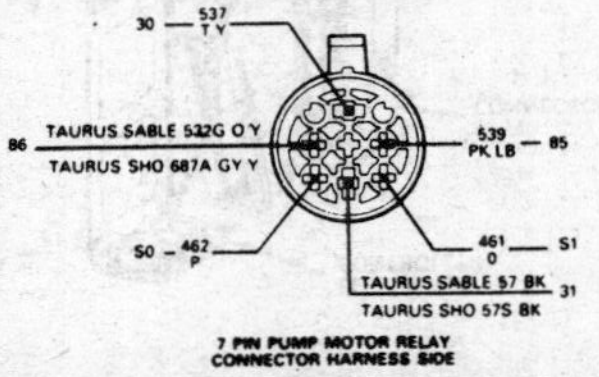

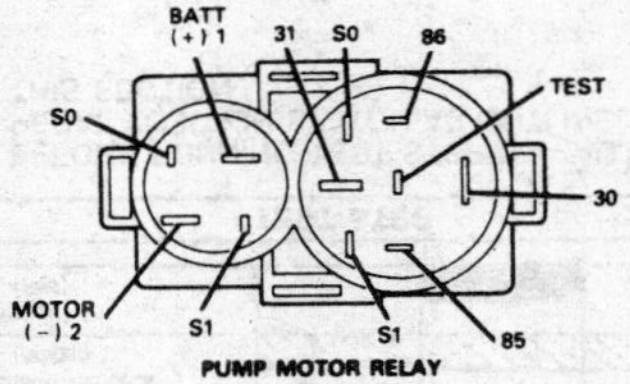

FIG. 88 ABS DIAGNOSIS AND TESTING DATA

Anti-Lock Warning Lamp On After Vehicle Starts To Move Or False Cycling Of Anti-Lock System — **Test C**

TEST STEP	RESULT ▶	ACTION TO TAKE
C16e CHECK CIRCUIT 539		
• Check for continuity between breakout box Pin 15 and Pin 85 on wire harness to pump motor relay connector. 30 — 537 T Y; 86 TAURUS SABLE 532G O Y, TAURUS SHO 687A GY Y; 539 PK LB — 85; S0 — 462 P; 461 O — S1; TAURUS SABLE 57 BK, TAURUS SHO 57S BK 31 7 PIN PUMP MOTOR RELAY CONNECTOR HARNESS SIDE	Continuity ▶ No Continuity ▶	GO to Step **C16f**. SERVICE or REPLACE cable harness Circuit 539.
C16f CHECK CIRCUIT 57		
• Check for continuity between wire harness to pump motor relay connector Pin 31 and ground.	Continuity ▶ No Continuity ▶	GO to Step **C16g**. SERVICE or REPLACE cable harness Circuit 57 or 57A (Taurus/Sable). Circuit 57S or 57R (Taurus SHO).
C16g CHECK PUMP MOTOR RELAY		
• Connect battery + to Pin 86 and battery − to Pin 85 of pump motor relay. • Check for continuity between Pin 30 and Pin 1 on relay.	Continuity ▶ No Continuity ▶	GO to Step **C16h**. REPLACE pump motor relay.
C16h CHECK PUMP MOTOR RELAY		
• Check continuity between Pins 2 and 31 on pump motor relay. BATT (+) 1; 31; S0; 86; TEST; S0; 30; MOTOR (−) 2; S1; S1; 85 PUMP MOTOR RELAY	Continuity ▶ No Continuity ▶	REPLACE computer module. REPLACE pump motor relay.

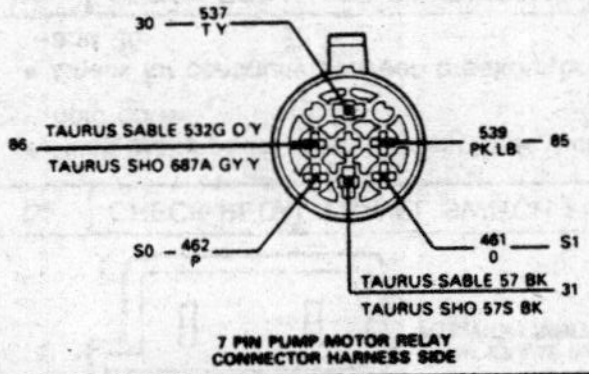

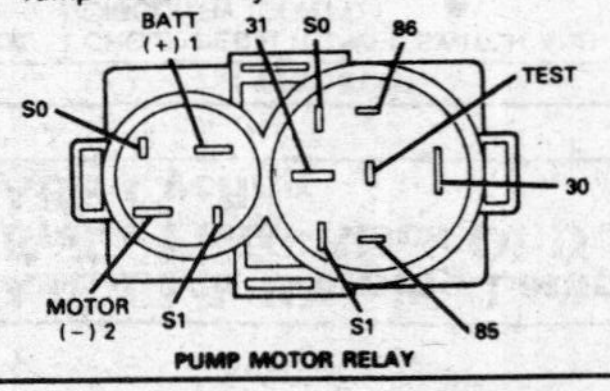

FIG. 89 ABS DIAGNOSIS AND TESTING DATA

Anti-Lock Warning Lamp Sequence Normal — Brake Pedal Rises Or Drops Excessively During ABS Cycling — Test D

WARNING LIGHTS SEQUENCE

Warning Lamps	Ignition On	Cranking Engine	Engine Running	Vehicle Moving	Braking with/without Anti-Lock	Vehicle Stopped	Engine Idle	Ignition Off
Check Anti-Lock (Amber)	▨	▨	▨					
Brake (Red)		■						

TEST STEP	RESULT	ACTION TO TAKE
BEFORE RUNNING TEST STEP D — ADJUST PEDAL POSITION SWITCH AS OUTLINED IN THIS SECTION.	Pedal feel normal during ABS cycling ▶	Condition corrected.
	Pedal feel not normal during ABS ▶	PERFORM Test D.
D1 CHECK PEDAL TRAVEL SWITCH AND CIRCUITRY • Turn ignition switch Off. • Disconnect 55-pin plug from controller. (ELECTRONIC CONTROLLER; 55 PIN CONNECTOR)		

FIG. 90 ABS DIAGNOSIS AND TESTING DATA

Anti-Lock Warning Lamp Sequence Normal — Brake Pedal Rises Or Drops Excessively During ABS Cycling — Test D

TEST STEP	RESULT	ACTION TO TAKE
D1 CHECK PEDAL TRAVEL SWITCH AND CIRCUITRY (CONT'D.)		
• Connect EEC-IV Breakout Box T83L-50-EEC-IV with Anti-Lock Test Adapter T90P-50-ALA to the Anti-Lock 55-pin plug on the wiring harness. (ANTI-LOCK HARNESS ADAPTER T90P-50-ALA; 55 PIN CONNECTOR; EEC-IV BREAKOUT BOX T83L-50-EEC-IV) • Check continuity between breakout box Pins 5 and 26.	Continuity ▶	GO to Step **D2**.
	No Continuity ▶	GO to Step **D1a**.
D1a CHECK PEDAL TRAVEL SWITCH		
• Disconnect pedal travel switch 2-pin plug. • Check for continuity between Pins 1 and 2. (2 PIN BRAKE PEDAL POSITION SWITCH)	Continuity ▶	SERVICE or REPLACE cable harness circuits 535 or 549.
	No Continuity ▶	REPLACE pedal travel switch.
D2 CHECK PEDAL TRAVEL SWITCH FUNCTION		
• Push brake pedal down at least three inches and hold down. • Check for continuity between breakout box Pins 5 and 26.	Continuity ▶	GO to Step **D2a**.
	No Continuity ▶	GO to Step **D3**.
D2a CHECK PEDAL TRAVEL SWITCH		
• Disconnect pedal travel switch 2-pin plug from wire harness. • Check continuity between Pins 1 and 2 (switch side) with brake pedal down at least three inches.	Continuity ▶	REPLACE pedal travel switch.
	No Continuity ▶	SERVICE or REPLACE cable harness circuits 535 or 549.
D3 CHECK PUMP PRESSURE		
• Jumper Pins 15 and 60 at breakout box. • Apply moderate pressure on brake pedal and hold. • Turn ignition switch to On.	Brake pedal rises. ▶	REVERIFY Symptom.
	Brake pedal does not rise. ▶	REPLACE pump and motor.

FIG. 91 ABS DIAGNOSIS AND TESTING DATA

Anti-Lock Warning Lamp Sequence Normal — ABS Pump Motor Runs Continuously (Ignition On/Ignition Off)

Test E

Warning Lamps	WARNING LIGHTS SEQUENCE							
	Ignition On	Cranking Engine	Engine Running	Vehicle Moving	Braking with/without Anti-Lock	Vehicle Stopped	Engine Idle	Ignition Off
Check Anti-Lock (Amber)	▨	▨	▨					
Brake (Red)		■						

TEST STEP	RESULT ▶	ACTION TO TAKE
E1 VERIFY PUMP MOTOR CONDITION		
• With vehicle standing still: • Check if pump motor runs with ignition switch in ON or OFF position.	Pump runs with ignition in OFF. ▶	GO to Step E2.
	Pump runs with ignition in ON. ▶	GO to Step E3.
E2 CHECK PUMP MOTOR RELAY		
• Remove pump motor relay. • Check for continuity between Pin 30 and test pin on the relay.	Continuity ▶	REPLACE pump motor relay.
	No Continuity ▶	REVERIFY that pump motor runs with ignition OFF.

FIG. 92 ABS DIAGNOSIS AND TESTING DATA

Anti-Lock Warning Lamp Sequence Normal — ABS Pump Motor Runs Continuously (Ignition On/Ignition Off)

Test E

TEST STEP	RESULT ▶	ACTION TO TAKE
E3 CHECK CIRCUIT 539 TO GROUND		
• Disconnect 55-pin plug from electronic controller.	Continuity ▶	GO to Step E3a.
	No Continuity ▶	GO to Step E4.
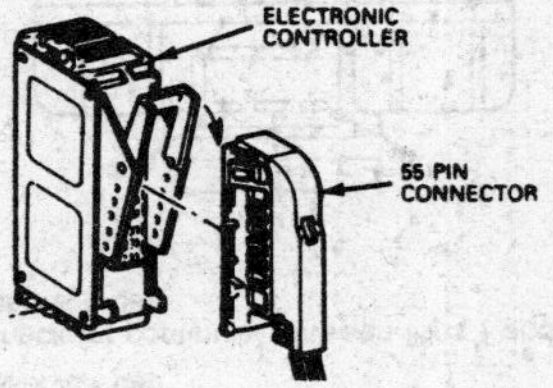 ELECTRONIC CONTROLLER 55 PIN CONNECTOR		
• Connect EEC-IV Breakout Box, T83L-50-EEC-IV with Anti-Lock Test Adapter T90P-50-ALA or equivalent to the Anti-Lock 55-pin plug wiring harness.		
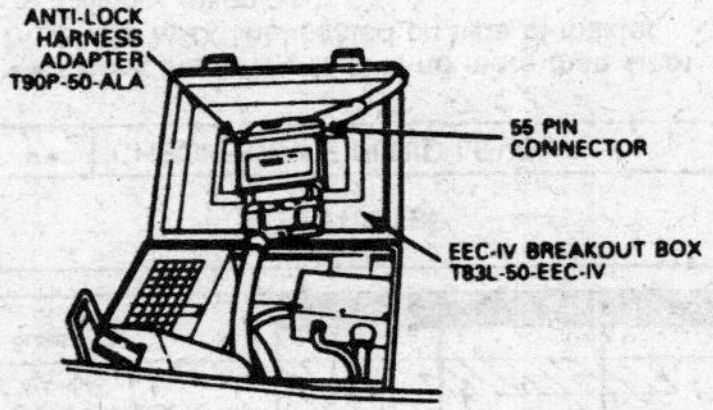 ANTI-LOCK HARNESS ADAPTER T90P-50-ALA 55 PIN CONNECTOR EEC-IV BREAKOUT BOX T83L-50-EEC-IV		
• Check for continuity between breakout box Pins 15 and 60.		

FIG. 93 ABS DIAGNOSIS AND TESTING DATA

Anti-Lock Warning Lamp Sequence Normal — ABS Pump Motor Runs Continuously (Ignition On/Ignition Off)

Test E

TEST STEP	RESULT ▶	ACTION TO TAKE
E3a CHECK CIRCUIT 539		
• Disconnect pump motor relay from wire harness. • Check for continuity between breakout box Pins 15 and 60.	Continuity ▶	SERVICE or REPLACE cable harness circuit 539.
	No Continuity ▶	REPLACE pump motor relay.
E4 CHECK CONTROLLER		
• Reconnect pump motor relay and electronic controller. • Turn ignition to ON.	Pump motor runs ▶	REPLACE electronic controller.
	Pump motor does not run. ▶	REVERIFY symptom.

FIG. 94 ABS DIAGNOSIS AND TESTING DATA

Brake Warning Lamp On (With Anti-Lock Lamp Off, Parking Brake Released And Brake Lining Wear Checked)

Test F

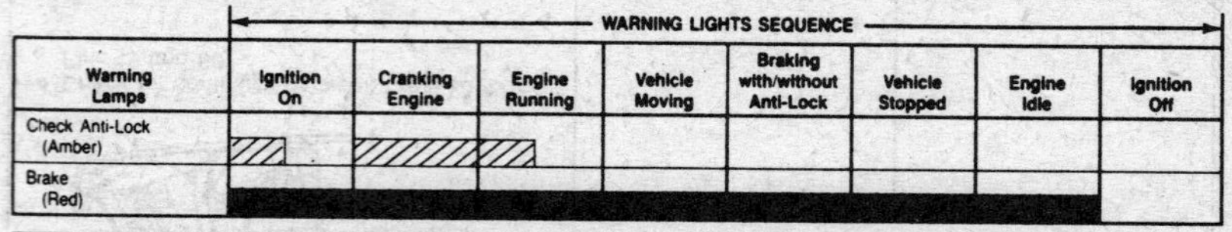

Warning Lamps	WARNING LIGHTS SEQUENCE: Ignition On	Cranking Engine	Engine Running	Vehicle Moving	Braking with/without Anti-Lock	Vehicle Stopped	Engine Idle	Ignition Off
Check Anti-Lock (Amber)	▨	▨	▨					
Brake (Red)	■	■	■	■	■	■	■	

TEST STEP	RESULT ▶	ACTION TO TAKE
F1 CHECK BRAKE FLUID LEVEL		
• Check that brake fluid is no more than 4mm below MAX line located on side of master cylinder reservoir.	Low ▶	CHECK system for external leaks. SERVICE as required.
	Normal ▶	GO to Step F2.
F2 CHECK FLUID LEVEL SWITCH		
• Disconnect 3-pin plug on master cylinder fluid reservoir cap. • Check for continuity between Pins 1 and 3 on reservoir cap.	Continuity ▶	REPLACE reservoir fluid cap.
	No Continuity ▶	GO to Step F3.

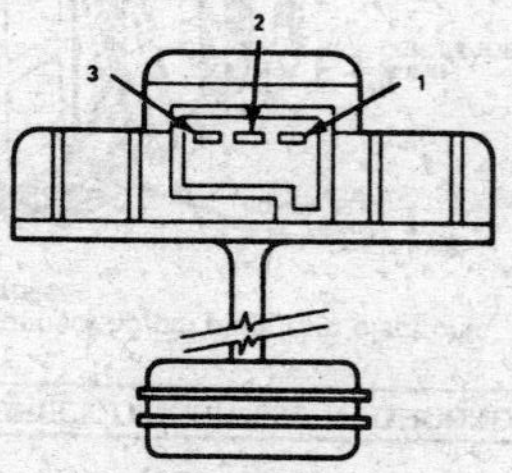

3 2 1

3 PIN FLUID RESERVOIR CAP

FIG. 95 ABS DIAGNOSIS AND TESTING DATA

Brake Warning Lamp On (With Anti-Lock Lamp Off, Parking Brake Released And Brake Lining Wear Checked) — Test F

TEST STEP	RESULT ▶	ACTION TO TAKE
F3 CHECK FOR GROUND PROBLEM		
• Check for grounded wire harness, Circuit 977.	Grounded wire harness ▶	SERVICE or REPLACE cable harness Circuit 977.
	Wire harness not grounded ▶	REVERIFY 'BRAKE' lamp on.

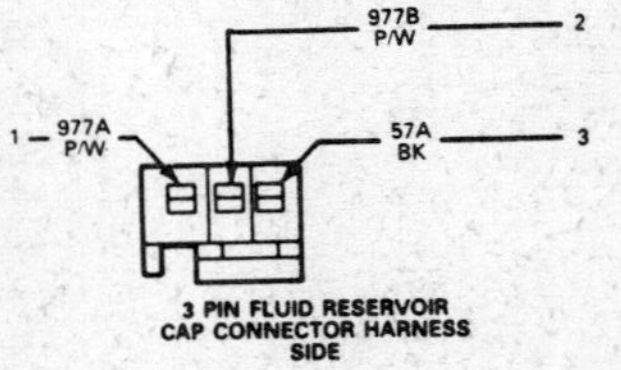

1 — 977A P/W
977B P/W — 2
57A BK — 3
3 PIN FLUID RESERVOIR CAP CONNECTOR HARNESS SIDE

FIG. 96 ABS DIAGNOSIS AND TESTING DATA

No Anti-Lock Warning Lamp On When Ignition Switch Turned On — Test G

WARNING LIGHTS SEQUENCE

Warning Lamps	Ignition On	Cranking Engine	Engine Running	Vehicle Moving	Braking with/without Anti-Lock	Vehicle Stopped	Engine Idle	Ignition Off
Check Anti-Lock (Amber)								
Brake (Red)		■						

TEST STEP	RESULT ▶	ACTION TO TAKE
G1 CHECK IGNITION FEED AND FUSE		
• Check for 12 volts to lamp socket with ignition ON.	12 volts ▶	GO to Step **G2**.
	No voltage ▶	SERVICE ignition feed or fuse as required.
G2 CHECK WARNING LAMP BULB		
• Check warning lamp bulb.	Bulb good ▶	GO to Step **G3**.
	Bulb bad ▶	REPLACE Bulb.
G3 CHECK CIRCUIT 606		
• Check continuity between lamp socket and breakout box Pin 52.	No Continuity ▶	SERVICE or REPLACE cable harness Circuit 606, 606A or 606B (Taurus/Sable). Circuit 606, 606B or 606D (Taurus SHO).
	Continuity ▶	REVERIFY symptom.

FIG. 97 ABS DIAGNOSIS AND TESTING DATA

Spongy Brake Pedal With/Without Anti-Lock Function (No Warning Lamp) — Test H

WARNING LIGHTS SEQUENCE

Warning Lamps	Ignition On	Cranking Engine	Engine Running	Vehicle Moving	Braking with/without Anti-Lock	Vehicle Stopped	Engine Idle	Ignition Off
Check Anti-Lock (Amber)								
Brake (Red)								

TEST STEP	RESULT	ACTION TO TAKE
H1 CHECK COMPONENT MOUNTING		
• Check for proper brake pedal and booster/master cylinder attachment. • Bleed brake system as outlined.	Pedal still spongy ▶	GO to Step **H2**.
	Pedal feels normal ▶	Condition corrected.
H2 BLEED BRAKE SYSTEM		
• Rebleed brake system.	Pedal still spongy ▶	REPLACE master cylinder.
	Pedal feels normal ▶	Condition corrected.

FIG. 98 ABS DIAGNOSIS AND TESTING DATA

Poor Vehicle Tracking During Anti-Lock Function (Warning Lamp Off) — Test J

WARNING LIGHTS SEQUENCE

Warning Lamps	Ignition On	Cranking Engine	Engine Running	Vehicle Moving	Braking with/without Anti-Lock	Vehicle Stopped	Engine Idle	Ignition Off
Check Anti-Lock (Amber)								
Brake (Red)								

TEST STEP	RESULT	ACTION TO TAKE
J1 VERIFY CONDITION		
• Verify condition exists as reported. • Turn air suspension OFF if so equipped. • Bleed brake system as outlined. • Turn air suspension back ON when vehicle is off hoist.	Vehicle tracks properly. ▶	Condition corrected.
	Vehicle still tracks poorly. ▶	GO to Step **J2**.
J2 CHECK ANTI-LOCK VALVE OPERATION		
• Turn air suspension OFF if so equipped. • Turn ignition switch OFF. • Disconnect 55-pin plug from electronic controller.		

ELECTRONIC CONTROLLER
55 PIN CONNECTOR

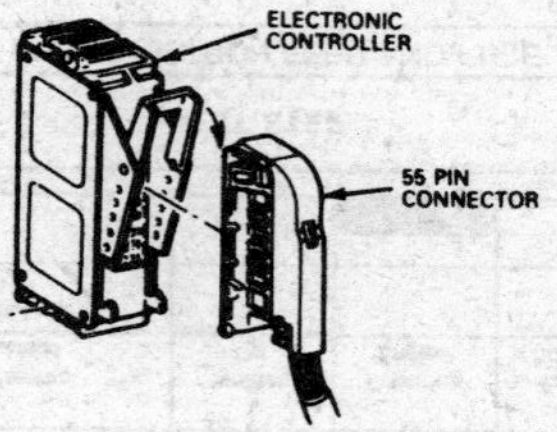

FIG. 99 ABS DIAGNOSIS AND TESTING DATA

Poor Vehicle Tracking During Anti-Lock Function (Warning Lamp Off) — **Test J**

TEST STEP	RESULT ▶	ACTION TO TAKE
J2 CHECK ANTI-LOCK VALVE OPERATION (Cont'd)		
• Connect EEC-IV Breakout Box, Tool T83L-50-EEC-IV with Anti-Lock test adapter, Tool T90P-50-ALA to the Anti-Lock 55-pin connector on wire harness. ANTI-LOCK HARNESS ADAPTER T90P-50-ALA; 55 PIN CONNECTOR; EEC-IV BREAKOUT BOX T83L-50-EEC-IV • Lift vehicle and rotate wheels to assure they turn freely. • Short Pins 20, 2 and 60 to each other at Breakout Box. • Apply moderate brake pedal effort and check that LH front wheel will not turn. • Check to see that LH front wheel turns freely when ignition switch is ON. • Turn air suspension ON when vehicle is off hoist, if so equipped. **CAUTION: DO NOT LEAVE IGNITION ON FOR MORE THAN 1 MINUTE, OR VALVE DAMAGE MAY RESULT.**	Wheel turns freely ▶	TURN ignition switch OFF. DISCONNECT wire leads. GO to Step **J3**.
	Wheel does not turn freely or pedal drops ▶	VERIFY correct wiring between 55-pin connector and 19-pin connector on valve block per wiring diagram. If wiring is correct, REPLACE solenoid valve block.

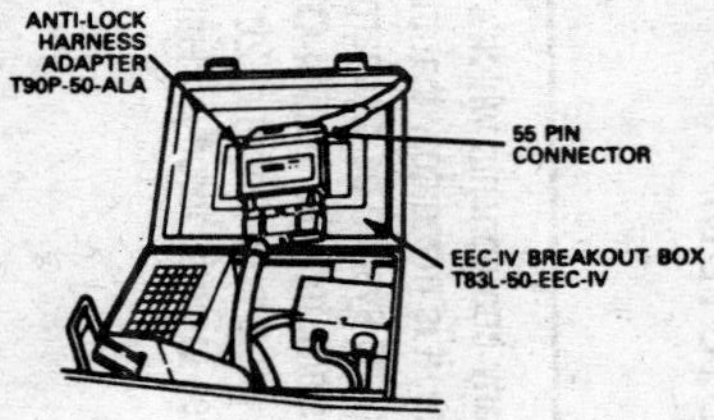

FIG. 100 ABS DIAGNOSIS AND TESTING DATA

Poor Vehicle Tracking During Anti-Lock Function (Warning Lamp Off) — **Test J**

TEST STEP	RESULT ▶	ACTION TO TAKE
J3 CHECK ANTI-LOCK OPERATION RH FRONT WHEEL		
• Short Pins 38, 21 and 60 to each other at breakout box. • Apply moderate brake pedal effort. Check that RH front wheel will not turn with ignition OFF. • Check that RH front wheel turns freely with ignition ON. **CAUTION: DO NOT LEAVE IGNITION ON FOR MORE THAN 1 MINUTE OR VALVE DAMAGE MAY RESULT.**	Wheel turns freely ▶	TURN ignition switch off. DISCONNECT wire leads. GO to Step **J4**.
	Wheel does not turn freely or pedal drops ▶	VERIFY correct wiring between 55-pin connector and 19-pin connector on valve block per wiring diagram. If wiring is correct, REPLACE solenoid valve block.
J4 CHECK ANTI-LOCK OPERATION RH REAR WHEEL		
• Short Pins 55, 18 and 60 to each other at breakout box. • Apply moderate brake pedal effort. Check that RH rear wheel will not turn with ignition OFF. • Check that RH rear wheel turns freely with ignition ON. **CAUTION: DO NOT LEAVE IGNITION ON FOR MORE THAN 1 MINUTE OR VALVE DAMAGE MAY RESULT.**	Wheel turns freely ▶	TURN ignition switch off. DISCONNECT wire leads. GO to Step **J5**.
	Wheel does not turn freely or pedal drops ▶	VERIFY correct wiring between 55-pin connector and 19-pin connector on valve block per wiring diagram. If wiring is correct, REPLACE solenoid valve block.

FIG. 101 ABS DIAGNOSIS AND TESTING DATA

Poor Vehicle Tracking During Anti-Lock Function (Warning Lamp Off) — **Test J**

TEST STEP	RESULT	ACTION TO TAKE
J5 CHECK ANTI-LOCK OPERATION LH REAR WHEEL		
• Short Pins 36, 54 and 60 to each other at breakout box. • Apply moderate brake pedal effort. Check that LH rear wheel will not turn with ignition OFF. • Check that LH rear wheel turns freely with ignition ON. **CAUTION: DO NOT LEAVE IGNITION ON FOR MORE THAN 1 MINUTE OR VALVE DAMAGE MAY RESULT.**	Wheel turns freely ▶	TURN ignition switch off. DISCONNECT wire leads and Breakout Box. LOWER vehicle. REVERIFY symptom.
	Wheel does not turn freely or pedal drops ▶	VERIFY correct wiring between 55-pin connector and 19-pin connector on valve block per wiring diagram. If wiring is correct, REPLACE solenoid valve block.

Anti-Lock Brake System Service

PRECAUTIONS

Failure to observe the following precautions may result in system damage.

• Before servicing any high pressure component, be sure to discharge the hydraulic pressure from the system.

• Do not allow the brake fluid to contact any of the electrical connectors.

• Use care when opening the bleeder screws due to the high pressures available from the accumulator.

RELIEVING SYSTEM PRESSURE

Before servicing any components which contain high pressure, it is mandatory that the hydraulic pressure in the system be discharged. To discharge the system, turn the ignition **OFF** and pump the brake pedal a minimum of 20 times until an increase in pedal force is clearly felt.

Hydraulic Control Unit (HCU)

REMOVAL & INSTALLATION

1. On all vehicles, except Taurus SHO, disconnect the battery cables and remove the battery from the vehicle. Remove the battery tray. Remove the 3 plastic push pins holding the acid shield to the HCU mounting bracket and remove the acid shield. On Taurus SHO, it is only necessary to disconnect the negative battery cable and remove the electronic control unit and it's mounting bracket from the top of the HCU mounting bracket.

2. Disconnect the 19-pin connector from the HCU to the wiring harness and disconnect the 4-pin connector from the HCU to the pump motor relay.

3. Remove the 2 lines from the inlet ports and the 4 lines from the outlet ports of the HCU. Plug each port to prevent brake fluid from spilling onto the paint and wiring.

4. Remove the 3 nuts retaining the HCU assembly to the mounting bracket and remove the assembly from the vehicle. The nut on the front of the HCU also retains the relay mounting bracket.

5. Install in the reverse order of removal. Tighten the 3 retaining nuts to 12–18 ft. lbs. (16–24 Nm) and the brake lines to 10–18 ft. lbs. (14–24 Nm). Bleed the brake system and check for fluid leaks.

Fig.107 Front wheel speed sensor

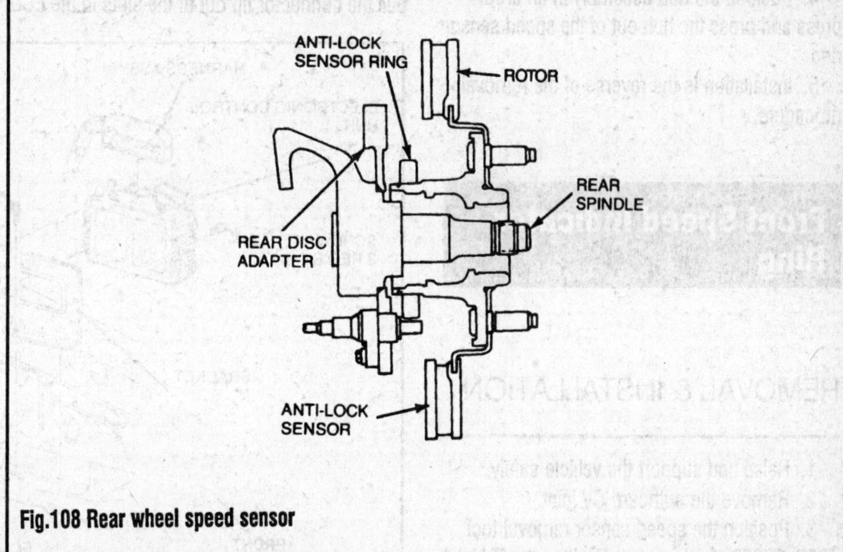

Fig.108 Rear wheel speed sensor

Wheel Sensors

REMOVAL & INSTALLATION

Front

➧ SEE FIG. 107

1. Disconnect the sensor connector located in the engine compartment.

2. For the right front sensor, remove the 2 plastic push studs to loosen the front section of the splash shield in the wheel well. For the left front sensor, remove the 2 plastic push studs to loosen the rear section of the splash shield.

3. Thread the sensor wires through the holes in the fender apron. For the right front sensor, remove the 2 retaining clips behind the splash shield.

4. Raise and support the vehicle safely. Remove the wheel.

5. Disengage the sensor wire grommets at the height sensor bracket and from the retainer clip on the shock strut just above the spindle.

6. Loosen the sensor retaining screw and remove the sensor assembly from the front knuckle.

7. Install in the reverse order of removal. Tighten the sensor retaining screws to 40–60 inch lbs. (4.5–6.8 Nm).

Rear

EXCEPT WAGON

➧ SEE FIG. 108

1. Remove the rear seat and seat back insulation.

2. Disconnect the sensor from the harness and tie the sensor connector to the rear seat sheet metal bracket with wire or string.

3. Push the sensor wire grommet and connector through the floorpan drawing the string or wire with the sensor connector.

4. Disconnect the string or wire from the sensor from underneath the vehicle. Raise and support the vehicle safely.

5. Disconnect the routing clips from the suspension arms and remove the sensor retaining bolts from the rear brake adapters.

6. Install in the reverse order of removal. Use string or wire to pull the new sensor connector through the hole in the floorpan. Tighten the sensor retaining bolt to 40–60 inch lbs. (4.6–6.8 Nm).

STATION WAGON

1. Raise and support the vehicle safely.

2. Remove the sensor wire with the attached grommet from the hole in the floorpan.

3. Disconnect the sensor from the harness.

4. Remove the routing clips. Remove the sensor retaining bolt. Remove the sensor.

5. Installation is the reverse of the removal procedure.

Rear Speed Indicator Ring

REMOVAL & INSTALLATION

➧ SEE FIG. 110

1. Raise and support the vehicle safely. Remove the tire and wheel assembly.

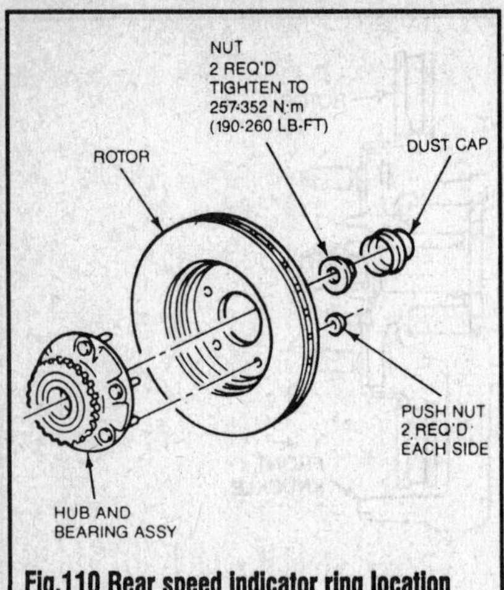

Fig.110 Rear speed indicator ring location

2. Remove the caliper. Remove the rotor.
3. Remove the rear hub assembly.
4. Position the hub assembly in an arbor press and press the hub out of the speed sensor ring.
5. Installation is the reverse of the removal procedure.

Front Speed Indicator Ring

REMOVAL & INSTALLATION

1. Raise and support the vehicle safely.
2. Remove the outboard CV joint.
3. Position the speed sensor removal tool T88P–20202–A in a press. Position the CV joint on the tool.
4. Remove the speed sensor ring from the CV joint.
5. Installation is the reverse of the removal procedure.

Pedal Travel Switch

REMOVAL & INSTALLATION

1. Disconnect the wiring harness lead at the switch.
2. Unsnap the switch hook from the pin on the dump valve adapter bracket.
3. Remove the switch from its mounting.
4. Installation is the reverse of the removal procedure.

Electronic Control Unit (ECU)

REMOVAL & INSTALLATION

➧ SEE FIG. 106

The ECU is located on the front right side of the engine compartment next to the washer bottle, except on Taurus SHO. On Taurus SHO it is mounted on the left side on top of the HCU mounting bracket.

1. Disconnect the negative battery cable.
2. Disconnect the 55-pin connector from the ECU. Unlock the connector by completely pulling up the lever. Move the top of the connector away from the ECU until all terminals are clear, then pull the connector up out of the slots in the ECU.
3. Remove the screws attaching the ECU and remove the ECU.
4. Install in the reverse order of removal. Connect the 55-pin connector by installing the bottom part of the connector into the slots in the ECU and pushing the top portion of the connector into the ECU. Then pull the locking lever completely down to ensure proper installation. Tighten the retaining screws to 15–20 inch lbs. (1.7–2.3 Nm).

Bleeding

PROCEDURE

The anti-lock brake system must be bled in 2 steps.

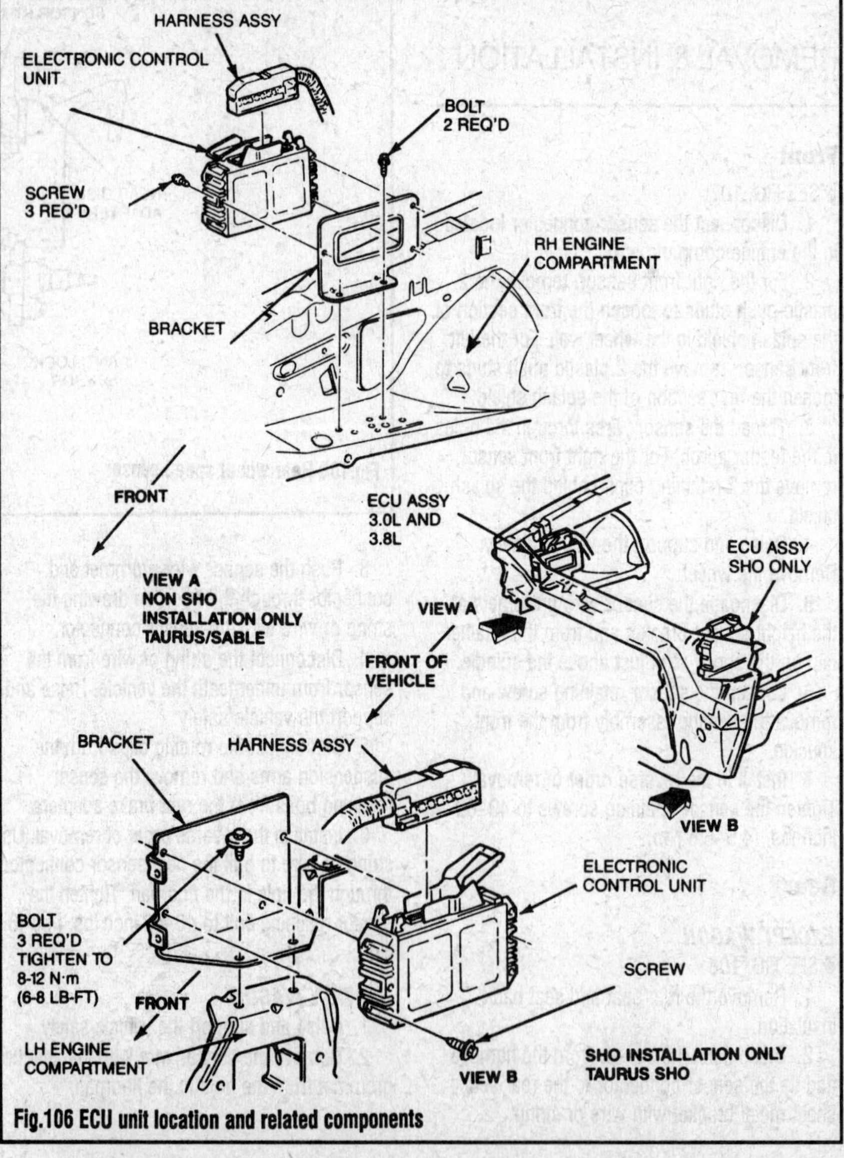

Fig.106 ECU unit location and related components

1. The master cylinder and hydraulic control unit must be bled using the Rotunda Anti-Lock Brake Breakout Box/Bleeding Adapter tool No. T90P–50–ALA or equivalent. If this procedure is not followed, air will be trapped in the hydraulic control unit which will eventually lead to a spongy brake pedal. To bleed the master cylinder and the hydraulic control unit, disconnect the 55-pin plug from the electronic control unit and install the Anti-Lock Brake Breakout Box/Bleeding Adapter to the wire harness 55-pin plug.

a. Place the Bleed/Harness switch in the **BLEED** position.

b. Turn the ignition to the **ON** position. At this point the red off light should come ON.

c. Push the motor button on the adapter down to start the pump motor. The red OFF light will turn OFF and the green ON light will turn ON. The pump motor will run for 60 seconds after the motor button is pushed. If the pump motor is to be turned off for any reason before the 60 seconds has elapsed, push the abort button to turn the pump motor off.

d. After 20 seconds of pump motor operation, push and hold the valve button down. Hold the valve button down for 20 seconds and then release it.

e. The pump motor will continue to run for an additional 20 seconds after the valve button is released.

2. The brake lines can now be bled in the normal fashion. Bleed the brake system by removing the rubber dust cap from the caliper fitting at the right-hand rear of the vehicle. Place a suitable box wrench on the bleeder fitting and attach a rubber drain tube to the fitting. The end of the tube should fit snugly around the bleeder fitting. Submerge the other end of the tube in a container partially filled with clean brake fluid and loosen the fitting 3/4 turn.

3. Have an assistant push the brake pedal down slowly through it's full travel. Close the bleeder fitting and allow the pedal to slowly return to it's full release position. Wait 5 seconds and repeat the procedure until no bubbles appear at the submerged end of the bleeder tube. Secure the bleeder fitting and remove the bleeder tube. Install the rubber dust cap on the bleeder fitting.

4. Repeat the bleeding procedure at the left front, left rear and right front in that order. Refill the master cylinder reservoir after each caliper has been bled and install the master cylinder and gasket. When brake bleeding is completed, the fluid level should be filled to the maximum level indicated on the reservoir.

5. Always make sure the disc brake pistons are returned to their normal positions by depressing the brake pedal several times until normal pedal travel is established. If the pedal feels spongy, repeat the bleeding procedure.

Master Cylinder

REMOVAL & INSTALLATION

1. Disconnect the negative battery cable. Depress the brake pedal several times to exhaust all vacuum in the system.

2. Disconnect the brake lines from the primary and secondary outlet ports of the master cylinder and the pressure control valve.

3. Remove the nuts attaching the master cylinder to the brake booster assembly. Disconnect the brake warning light wire. Disconnect the Hydraulic Control Unit (HCU) supply hose at the master cylinder and secure in a position to prevent loss of brake fluid.

4. Slide the master cylinder forward and upward from the vehicle.

To install:

5. Before installation, bench bleed the new master cylinder as follows:

a. Mount the new master cylinder in a holding fixture. Be careful not to damage the housing.

b. Fill the master cylinder reservoir with brake fluid.

c. Using a suitable tool inserted into the booster pushrod cavity, push the master cylinder piston in slowly. Place a suitable container under the master cylinder to catch the fluid being expelled from the outlet ports.

d. Place a finger tightly over each outlet port and allow the master cylinder piston to return.

e. Repeat the procedure until clear fluid only is expelled from the master cylinder. Plug the outlet ports and remove the master cylinder from the holding fixture.

6. Mount the master cylinder on the booster. Install a new seal in the groove in the master cylinder mounting face. Attach the brake fluid lines to the master cylinder. Install the HCU supply hose to the master cylinder.

7. Install the brake warning light wire.

8. Bleed the system. Operate the brakes several times, then check for external hydraulic leaks.

Master Cylinder Booster

REMOVAL & INSTALLATION

➧ SEE FIG. 109

1. Disconnect the negative battery cable. Pump the brake pedal until all vacuum is removed from the booster. This will prevent the O-ring from being sucked into the booster during disassembly.

2. Disconnect the manifold vacuum hose from the booster check valve and the electrical connector from the master cylinder reservoir cap.

3. Remove the brake lines from the primary and secondary outlet ports of the master cylinder and remove the Hydraulic Control Unit (HCU) supply hose. Plug the ports and reservoir feed to prevent brake fluid from leaking onto paint and wiring.

4. Under the instrument panel, remove the stoplight switch wiring connector from the switch. Disengage the pedal position switch from the stud. Remove the hairpin retainer and outer nylon washer from the pedal pin. Slide the stoplight switch off the brake pedal just far enough for the outer arm to clear the pin. Remove the switch.

5. Remove the booster to dash panel attaching nuts. Slide the bushing and booster pushrod off the brake pedal pin.

6. Move the booster forward until the booster studs clear the dash panel. Remove the booster and master cylinder assembly.

7. Place the booster and master cylinder assembly on a bench. Remove the 2 nuts attaching the master cylinder to the booster and remove the master cylinder.

To install:

8. Slide the master cylinder onto the booster studs. Make sure the O-ring is in place in the groove on the master cylinder and install the 2 attaching nuts. Tighten the nuts to 13–25 ft. lbs. (18–34 Nm).

9. Under the instrument panel, install the booster pushrod and bushing on the brake pedal pin. Fasten the booster to the dash panel with self-locking nuts. Tighten the nuts to 13–25 ft. lbs. (18–34 Nm).

10. Position the stoplight switch so it straddles the booster pushrod with the switch slot towards the pedal blade and hole just clearing the pin. Slide the switch completely onto the pin.

11. Install the outer nylon washer on the pin and secure all parts to the pin with the hairpin

retainer. Make sure the retainer is fully installed and locked over the pedal pin. Install the stoplight switch wiring connector.

12. Install the pedal travel switch. To adjust the switch, push the switch plunger fully into the switch housing. This zeros out the switch adjustment so it can be automatically reset to the correct dimension during the following steps:

a. Slowly pull the arm back out of the switch housing past the detent point. At this point it should be impossible to reattach the arm to the pin unless the brake pedal is forced down.

b. Depress the brake pedal until the switch hook can be snapped onto the pin. Snap the hook onto the pin and pull the brake pedal back up to it's normal at rest position. This automatically sets the switch to the proper adjustment.

13. Connect the brake lines to the master cylinder and tighten to 10–18 ft. lbs. (14–24 Nm). Connect the HCU supply hose to the reservoir.

14. Connect the manifold vacuum hose to the booster check valve and the electrical connector to the master cylinder reservoir cap.

15. Connect the negative battery cable and bleed the brake system.

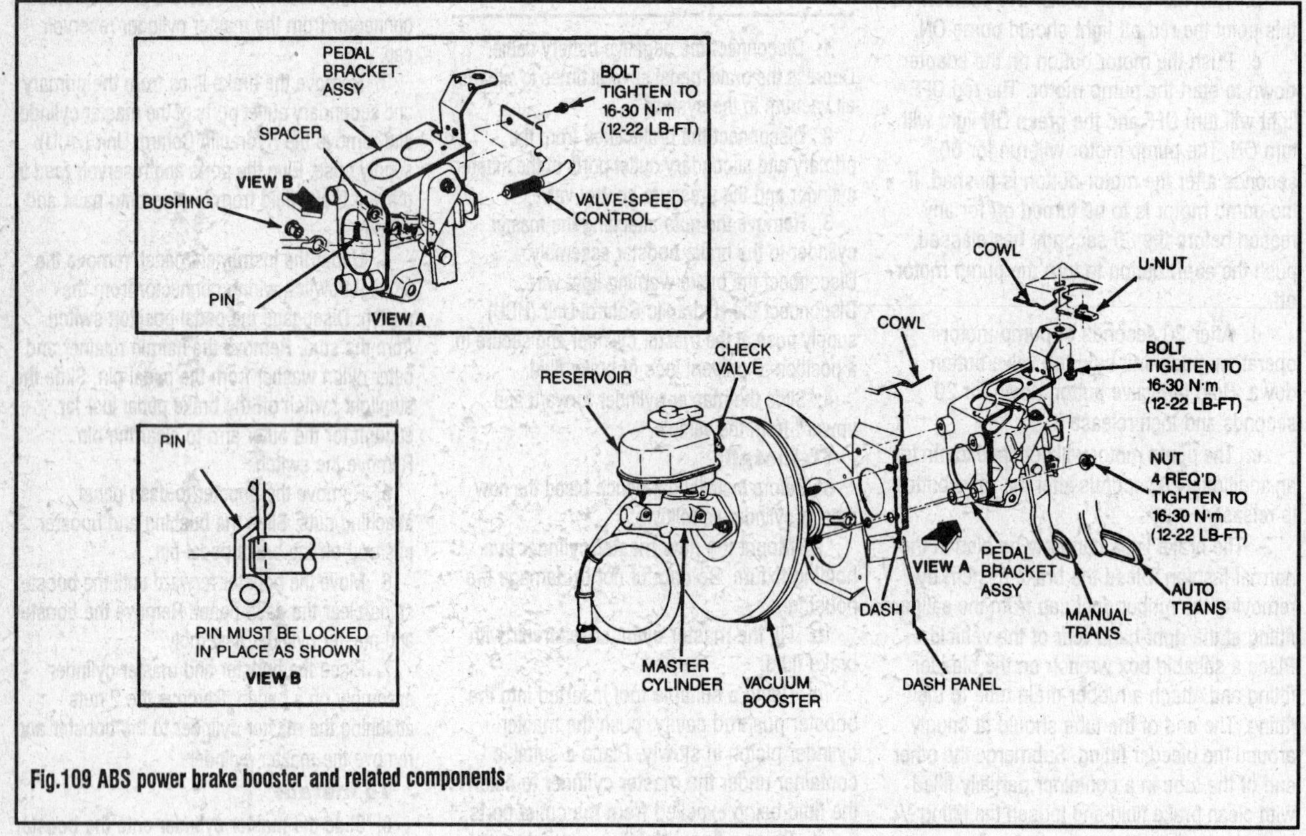

Fig.109 ABS power brake booster and related components

BRAKE SPECIFICATIONS

All measurements in inches unless noted

Year	Model	Master Cylinder Bore	Brake Disc Original Thickness	Brake Disc Minimum Thickness	Brake Disc Maximum Runout	Brake Drum Diameter Original Inside Diameter	Brake Drum Diameter Max. Wear Limit	Brake Drum Diameter Maximum Machine Diameter	Minimum Lining Thickness Front	Minimum Lining Thickness Rear
1986	Taurus	0.875	1.024	0.974	0.003	8.86⑥	0.60	0.059	0.125	0.030
	Sable	0.875	1.024	0.974	0.003	8.86⑥	0.60	0.059	0.125	0.030
1987	Taurus	0.875	1.024	0.974	0.003	8.86⑥	0.60	0.059	0.125	0.030
	Sable	0.875	1.024	0.974	0.003	8.86⑥	0.60	0.059	0.125	0.030
1988	Taurus	0.875	1.024	0.974	0.003	8.86⑥	0.60	0.059	0.125	0.030
	Sable	0.875	1.024	0.974	0.003	8.86⑥	0.60	0.059	0.125	0.030
1989	Taurus	0.875	1.024	0.974	0.003	8.86⑥	0.60	0.059	0.125	0.030
	Taurus SHO	0.875	1.024⑤	0.974①	③	8.86⑥	0.60	0.059	0.125	0.123
	Sable	0.875	1.024	0.974	0.003	8.86⑥	0.60	0.059	0.125	0.030
1990	Taurus	0.875	1.024	0.974	0.003	8.86⑥	0.60	0.059	0.125	0.030
	Taurus SHO	0.875	1.024⑤	0.974①	③	8.86⑥	0.60	0.059	0.125	0.123
	Sable	0.875	1.024	0.974	0.003	8.86⑥	0.60	0.059	0.125	0.030
1991	Taurus	0.875	1.024	0.974	0.003	8.86⑥	0.60	0.059	0.125	0.030
	Taurus SHO	0.875	1.024⑤	0.974①	③	8.86⑥	0.60	0.059	0.125	0.123
	Sable	0.875	1.024	0.974	0.003	8.86⑥	0.60	0.059	0.125	0.030
1992	Taurus	0.875	1.024⑤	0.974②	③	8.86⑥	0.60	0.059	0.125	0.030④
	Taurus SHO	0.875	1.024⑤	0.974②	③	8.86⑥	0.60	0.059	0.125	④
	Sable	0.875	1.024⑤	0.974②	③	8.86⑥	0.60	0.059	0.125	0.030④

① Front and Rear
② Rear—0.900
③ Front—0.003
Rear—0.002
④ Rear disc—0.123
⑤ Rear disc—1.02
⑥ Optional—9.84

Troubleshooting the Brake System

Problem	Cause	Solution
Low brake pedal (excessive pedal travel required for braking action.)	• Excessive clearance between rear linings and drums caused by inoperative automatic adjusters	• Make 10 to 15 alternate forward and reverse brake stops to adjust brakes. If brake pedal does not come up, repair or replace adjuster parts as necessary.
	• Worn rear brakelining	• Inspect and replace lining if worn beyond minimum thickness specification
	• Bent, distorted brakeshoes, front or rear	• Replace brakeshoes in axle sets
	• Air in hydraulic system	• Remove air from system. Refer to Brake Bleeding.
Low brake pedal (pedal may go to floor with steady pressure applied.)	• Fluid leak in hydraulic system	• Fill master cylinder to fill line; have helper apply brakes and check calipers, wheel cylinders, differential valve tubes, hoses and fittings for leaks. Repair or replace as necessary.
	• Air in hydraulic system	• Remove air from system. Refer to Brake Bleeding.
	• Incorrect or non-recommended brake fluid (fluid evaporates at below normal temp).	• Flush hydraulic system with clean brake fluid. Refill with correct-type fluid.
	• Master cylinder piston seals worn, or master cylinder bore is scored, worn or corroded	• Repair or replace master cylinder
Low brake pedal (pedal goes to floor on first application—o.k. on subsequent applications.)	• Disc brake pads sticking on abutment surfaces of anchor plate. Caused by a build-up of dirt, rust, or corrosion on abutment surfaces	• Clean abutment surfaces
Fading brake pedal (pedal height decreases with steady pressure applied.)	• Fluid leak in hydraulic system	• Fill master cylinder reservoirs to fill mark, have helper apply brakes, check calipers, wheel cylinders, differential valve, tubes, hoses, and fittings for fluid leaks. Repair or replace parts as necessary.
	• Master cylinder piston seals worn, or master cylinder bore is scored, worn or corroded	• Repair or replace master cylinder
Spongy brake pedal (pedal has abnormally soft, springy, spongy feel when depressed.)	• Air in hydraulic system	• Remove air from system. Refer to Brake Bleeding.
	• Brakeshoes bent or distorted	• Replace brakeshoes
	• Brakelining not yet seated with drums and rotors	• Burnish brakes
	• Rear drum brakes not properly adjusted	• Adjust brakes

Troubleshooting the Brake System (cont.)

Problem	Cause	Solution
Decreasing brake pedal travel (pedal travel required for braking action decreases and may be accompanied by a hard pedal.)	• Caliper or wheel cylinder pistons sticking or seized	• Repair or replace the calipers, or wheel cylinders
	• Master cylinder compensator ports blocked (preventing fluid return to reservoirs) or pistons sticking or seized in master cylinder bore	• Repair or replace the master cylinder
	• Power brake unit binding internally	• Test unit according to the following procedure: (a) Shift transmission into neutral and start engine (b) Increase engine speed to 1500 rpm, close throttle and fully depress brake pedal (c) Slow release brake pedal and stop engine (d) Have helper remove vacuum check valve and hose from power unit. Observe for backward movement of brake pedal. (e) If the pedal moves backward, the power unit has an internal bind—replace power unit
Grabbing brakes (severe reaction to brake pedal pressure.)	• Brakelining(s) contaminated by grease or brake fluid	• Determine and correct cause of contamination and replace brakeshoes in axle sets
	• Parking brake cables incorrectly adjusted or seized	• Adjust cables. Replace seized cables.
	• Incorrect brakelining or lining loose on brakeshoes	• Replace brakeshoes in axle sets
	• Caliper anchor plate bolts loose	• Tighten bolts
	• Rear brakeshoes binding on support plate ledges	• Clean and lubricate ledges. Replace support plate(s) if ledges are deeply grooved. Do not attempt to smooth ledges by grinding.
	• Incorrect or missing power brake reaction disc	• Install correct disc
	• Rear brake support plates loose	• Tighten mounting bolts
Chatter or shudder when brakes are applied (pedal pulsation and roughness may also occur.)	• Brakeshoes distorted, bent, contaminated, or worn	• Replace brakeshoes in axle sets
	• Caliper anchor plate or support plate loose	• Tighten mounting bolts
	• Excessive thickness variation of rotor(s)	• Refinish or replace rotors in axle sets
Noisy brakes (squealing, clicking, scraping sound when brakes are applied.)	• Bent, broken, distorted brakeshoes	• Replace brakeshoes in axle sets
	• Excessive rust on outer edge of rotor braking surface	• Remove rust

Troubleshooting the Brake System (cont.)

Problem	Cause	Solution
Hard brake pedal (excessive pedal pressure required to stop vehicle. May be accompanied by brake fade.)	• Loose or leaking power brake unit vacuum hose	• Tighten connections or replace leaking hose
	• Incorrect or poor quality brake-lining	• Replace with lining in axle sets
	• Bent, broken, distorted brakeshoes	• Replace brakeshoes
	• Calipers binding or dragging on mounting pins. Rear brakeshoes dragging on support plate.	• Replace mounting pins and bushings. Clean rust or burrs from rear brake support plate ledges and lubricate ledges with molydisulfide grease. **NOTE:** If ledges are deeply grooved or scored, do not attempt to sand or grind them smooth—replace support plate.
	• Caliper, wheel cylinder, or master cylinder pistons sticking or seized	• Repair or replace parts as necessary
	• Power brake unit vacuum check valve malfunction	• Test valve according to the following procedure: (a) Start engine, increase engine speed to 1500 rpm, close throttle and immediately stop engine (b) Wait at least 90 seconds then depress brake pedal (c) If brakes are not vacuum assisted for 2 or more applications, check valve is faulty
	• Power brake unit has internal bind	• Test unit according to the following procedure: (a) With engine stopped, apply brakes several times to exhaust all vacuum in system (b) Shift transmission into neutral, depress brake pedal and start engine (c) If pedal height decreases with foot pressure and less pressure is required to hold pedal in applied position, power unit vacuum system is operating normally. Test power unit. If power unit exhibits a bind condition, replace the power unit.

Troubleshooting the Brake System (cont.)

Problem	Cause	Solution
Hard brake pedal (excessive pedal pressure required to stop vehicle. May be accompanied by brake fade.)	• Master cylinder compensator ports (at bottom of reservoirs) blocked by dirt, scale, rust, or have small burrs (blocked ports prevent fluid return to reservoirs).	• Repair or replace master cylinder **CAUTION:** Do not attempt to clean blocked ports with wire, pencils, or similar implements. Use compressed air only.
	• Brake hoses, tubes, fittings clogged or restricted	• Use compressed air to check or unclog parts. Replace any damaged parts.
	• Brake fluid contaminated with improper fluids (motor oil, transmission fluid, causing rubber components to swell and stick in bores	• Replace all rubber components, combination valve and hoses. Flush entire brake system with DOT 3 brake fluid or equivalent.
	• Low engine vacuum	• Adjust or repair engine
Dragging brakes (slow or incomplete release of brakes)	• Brake pedal binding at pivot	• Loosen and lubricate
	• Power brake unit has internal bind	• Inspect for internal bind. Replace unit if internal bind exists.
	• Parking brake cables incorrrectly adjusted or seized	• Adjust cables. Replace seized cables.
	• Rear brakeshoe return springs weak or broken	• Replace return springs. Replace brakeshoe if necessary in axle sets.
	• Automatic adjusters malfunctioning	• Repair or replace adjuster parts as required
	• Caliper, wheel cylinder or master cylinder pistons sticking or seized	• Repair or replace parts as necessary
	• Master cylinder compensating ports blocked (fluid does not return to reservoirs).	• Use compressed air to clear ports. Do not use wire, pencils, or similar objects to open blocked ports.
Vehicle moves to one side when brakes are applied	• Incorrect front tire pressure	• Inflate to recommended cold (reduced load) inflation pressure
	• Worn or damaged wheel bearings	• Replace worn or damaged bearings
	• Brakelining on one side contaminated	• Determine and correct cause of contamination and replace brakelining in axle sets
	• Brakeshoes on one side bent, distorted, or lining loose on shoe	• Replace brakeshoes in axle sets
	• Support plate bent or loose on one side	• Tighten or replace support plate
	• Brakelining not yet seated with drums or rotors	• Burnish brakelining
	• Caliper anchor plate loose on one side	• Tighten anchor plate bolts
	• Caliper piston sticking or seized	• Repair or replace caliper
	• Brakelinings water soaked	• Drive vehicle with brakes lightly applied to dry linings
	• Loose suspension component attaching or mounting bolts	• Tighten suspension bolts. Replace worn suspension components.
	• Brake combination valve failure	• Replace combination valve

Troubleshooting the Brake System (cont.)

Problem	Cause	Solution
Noisy brakes (squealing, clicking, scraping sound when brakes are applied.) (cont.)	• Brakelining worn out—shoes contacting drum of rotor	• Replace brakeshoes and lining in axle sets. Refinish or replace drums or rotors.
	• Broken or loose holdown or return springs	• Replace parts as necessary
	• Rough or dry drum brake support plate ledges	• Lubricate support plate ledges
	• Cracked, grooved, or scored rotor(s) or drum(s)	• Replace rotor(s) or drum(s). Replace brakeshoes and lining in axle sets if necessary.
	• Incorrect brakelining and/or shoes (front or rear).	• Install specified shoe and lining assemblies
Pulsating brake pedal	• Out of round drums or excessive lateral runout in disc brake rotor(s)	• Refinish or replace drums, re-index rotors or replace

10

BODY

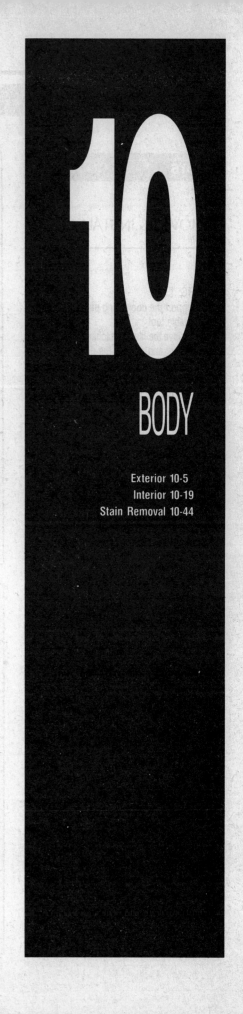

EXTERIOR

Doors

REMOVAL & INSTALLATION

Front

➧ SEE FIG. 1

1. Support the door using padded jack or other suitable tool.
2. Remove the hinge attaching bolts and nuts from the door and remove the door.
3. Disconnect the wiring harness connectors, if so equipped.
4. If the door is to be replaced, transfer the following components to the new door if they are in usable condition: trim panel, watershield, outside moldings, clips, window regulators and the door latch components.

To install:

5. Position the door hinges and partially tighten the bolts.
6. Align the door and tighten the bolts securely to 13–21 ft. lbs.

Rear

➧ SEE FIG. 2

1. Remove the scuff plate.
2. Remove the center pillar trim panel.
3. Remove the seat belt assembly.
4. Open the door and support it with a padded jack or other suitable tool.
5. Scribe the hinge location to the door for a reference point when reinstalling.
6. Remove the upper and lower hinge-to-door hinge attaching washer head bolts.
7. Remove the upper and lower hinge-to-body attaching bolts.
8. Remove the upper and lower hinge-to-body nut and washer assemblies. Remove the hinges.

To install:

9. Install the upper and lower hinge-to-body attaching bolts. Tighten to 13–21 ft. lbs.
10. Install the upper and lower hinge-to-body nuts and washers. Tighten to 13–21 ft. lbs.
11. Position the door to the hinges and install the upper and lower attaching washer head bolts. Tighten to 13–21 ft. lbs.
12. Install the seat belt assembly.
13. Install the center pillar trim panel.
14. Install the scuff plate.

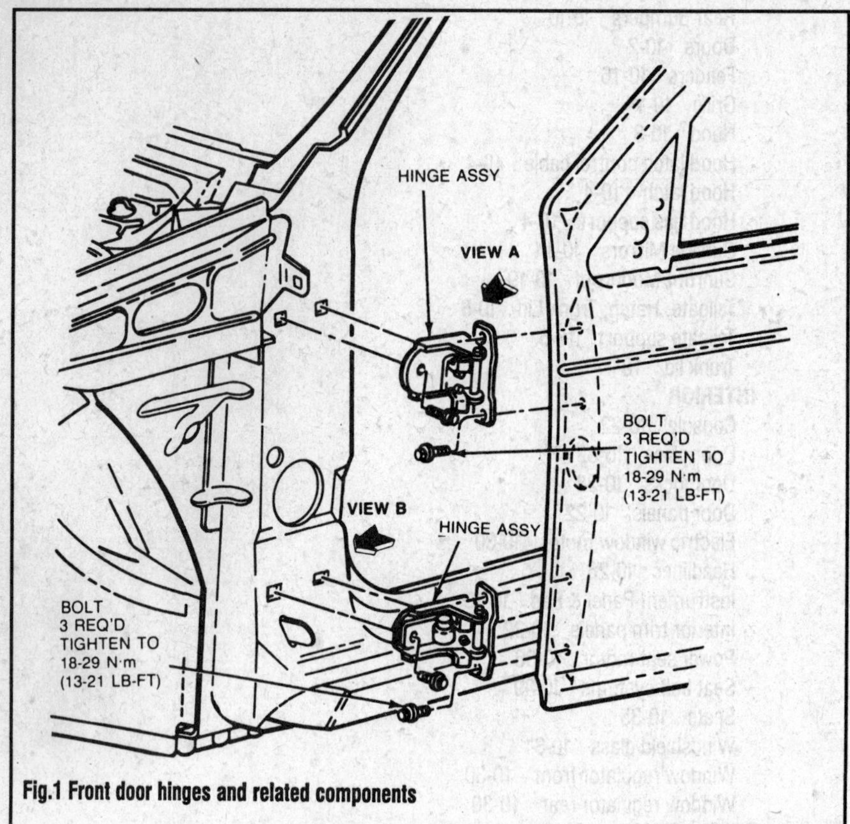

Fig.1 Front door hinges and related components

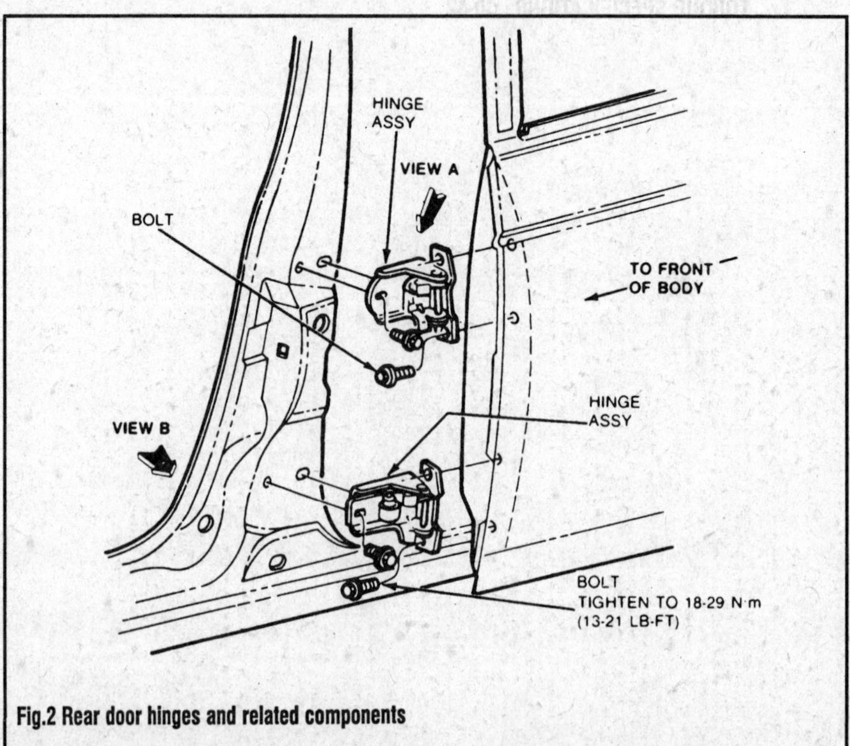

Fig.2 Rear door hinges and related components

ADJUSTMENT

Door Alignment

➧ SEE FIG. 3

1. Determine which hinge bolts and nuts must be loosened to move the door in the desired direction.
2. Loosen the hinge bolts and nuts just enough to permit movement of the door with a padded pry bar.
3. Move the door the distance estimated to be necessary. Tighten the hinge bolts and nuts to 13–21 ft. lbs., and check the door fit to ensure there is no bind or interference with the adjacent panel.
4. Repeat the operation until the desired fit is obtained, and check the striker plate alignment for proper door closing.

Door Latch Striker

The striker pin can be adjusted laterally and vertically as well as fore-and-aft. The latch striker should not be adjusted to correct door sag.

The latch striker should be shimmed to get the clearance shown between the striker and the latch. To check this clearance, clean latch jaws and striker area. Apply a thin layer of dark grease to striker. As door is closed and opened, a measurable pattern will result on the latch striker. Use a maximum of two shims under the striker.

Move the striker assembly in or out to provide a flush fit at the door and pillar or quarter panel. Use the correct Torx® bit to loosen and tighten the latch striker. Tighten the striker to 24–33 ft. lbs.

QUARTER PANEL
0.5mm MIN. (0.02 INCH)
6.3mm MAX. (0.25 INCH)

Fig.3 Front and rear door latches

Hood

REMOVAL & INSTALLATION

1. Open the hood and support it in the open position. Mark the hood hinge locations on the hood.
2. Protect the body with covers to prevent damage to the paint.
3. Disconnect the gas cylinders from hood.
4. Place thick rags under the corners of the hood. Remove the two bolts attaching each hinge to the hood, taking care not to let the hood slip when bolts are removed.
5. Remove the hood from the vehicle.

To install:

6. Position the hood-to-hood hinges. Install the attaching bolts.
7. Adjust the hood for even fit between fenders and for a flush fit with the front of the fenders.
8. Adjust the hood for a flush fit with the top of the cowl and the fenders.
9. Adjust the hood latch, if necessary. Remove the protective fender covers.
10. Attach the gas cylinder to the hood.

ADJUSTMENT

Hood

➧ SEE FIG. 8

The hood can be adjusted fore-and-aft and side-to-side by loosening two hood-to-hinge attaching bolts at each hinge. Then, reposition hood as required and tighten the hood-to-hinge attaching bolts. Always use protective fender covers.

To raise or lower the rear of the hood, loosen the hood hinge pivot nut. The pivot can now move up or down. Raise or lower hood as necessary to obtain a flush condition at the rear of the hood with the fenders. Then, tighten the hood hinge pivot nut to 16–25 ft. lbs.

Hood Latch

Before adjusting hood latch mechanism, make certain that the hood is properly aligned. The hood latch can be moved from side-to-side to align with the opening in the hood inner panel.

Adjust latch up and down to obtain a flush fit with front fenders.

1. Loosen the hood latch attaching bolts in the radiator support until they are just loose enough to move the latch from side-to-side.
2. Move the latch from side-to-side to align it with the opening in the hood.
3. Loosen the locknuts on the two hood bumpers. Lower the bumpers.
4. Move the hood latch up and down as required to obtain a flush fit between the top of hood and the fenders when upward pressure is applied to the front of the hood. Then, tighten the hood latch attaching screw to 7–10 ft. lbs.
5. Raise the two hood bumpers to eliminate any looseness at the front of hood when closed. Then, tighten the hood bumper locknuts.
6. Open and close the hood several times to check its operation.

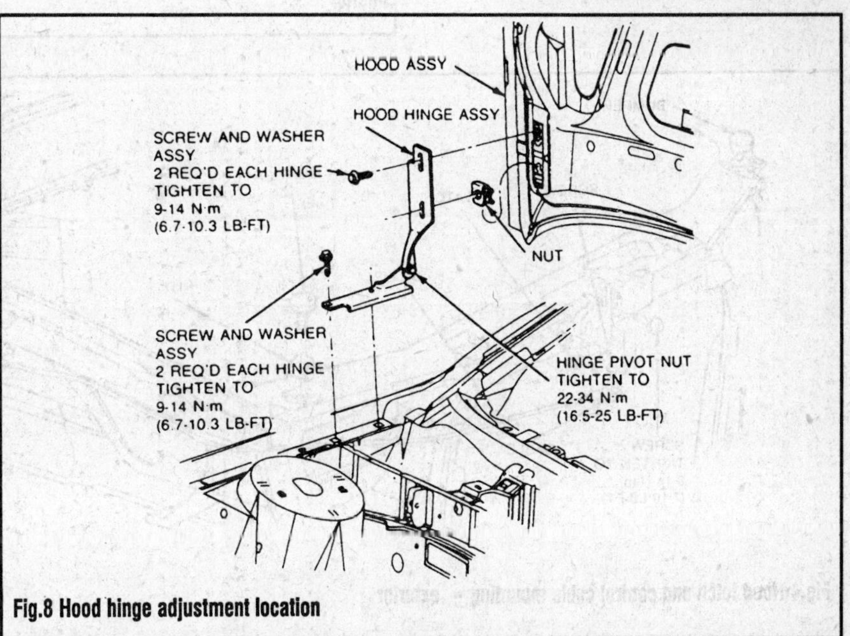

Fig.8 Hood hinge adjustment location

Hood Latch Control Cable

REMOVAL & INSTALLATION

➧ SEE FIG. 4

1. From inside the vehicle, release the hood.
2. Remove the two bolts retaining the latch to the upper radiator support.
3. Remove the screw retaining the cable end retainer to the latch assembly.
4. Disengage the cable by rotating it out of the latch return spring.
5. To facilitate installing the cable, fasten a length of fishing line about 8 ft. long to latch the end of the cable.
6. From the inside vehicle, unseat the sealing grommet from the cowl side, remove the cable mounting bracket attaching screws and carefully pull the cable assembly out. Do not pull the "fish line" out.

To Install:

7. Using the previously installed fish line, pull the new cable assembly through the retaining wall, seat the grommet securely, and install the cable mounting bracket attaching screws.
8. Thread the terminal end of cable into the hood latch return spring.
9. Route the cable through the V-slot on the latch and install the cable end retaining screw.
10. Check the hood latch cable release operation before the closing hood. Adjust if necessary.

Hood Latch

REMOVAL & INSTALLATION

➧ SEE FIG. 5–6

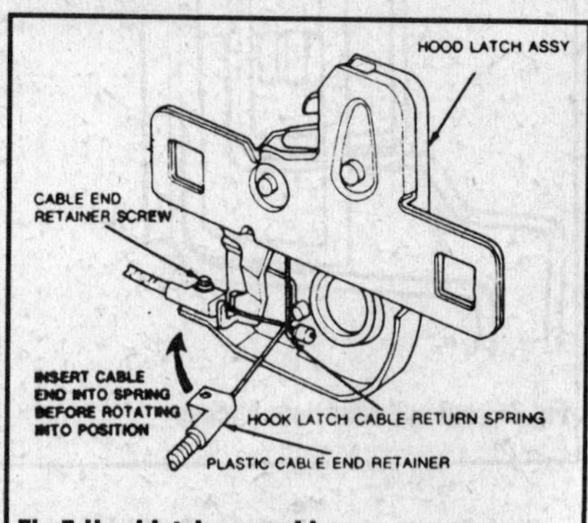

Fig.5 Hood latch assembly

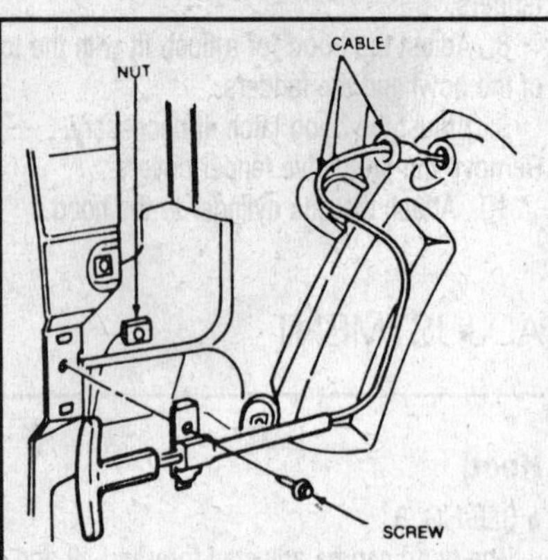

Fig.6 Hood latch and control cable mounting — interior

1. From inside the vehicle release the hood.
2. Remove the two bolts retaining the latch to the upper radiator support.
3. Remove the two bolts retaining the hood latch assembly-to-radiator support and remove the latch.

To Install:

1. Engage the hood latch to the control cable and position the hood latch to the radiator support.
2. Install the two attaching bolts.
3. Adjust the hood latch and torque the attaching bolts to 7–10 ft. lbs.

Hood Gas Support

⁂ CAUTION

Do not heat or try to disassemble the hood gas supports. The supports are gas charged and will explode if heated or disassembled.

REMOVAL & INSTALLATION

➧ SEE FIG. 7

1. Open the hood and temporarily support it.
2. Disengage the gas support from the retainer at the top.
3. Remove the retaining pin at bottom. Remove the gas support.

To Install:

4. Position the gas support. Install the retaining pin at the bottom.

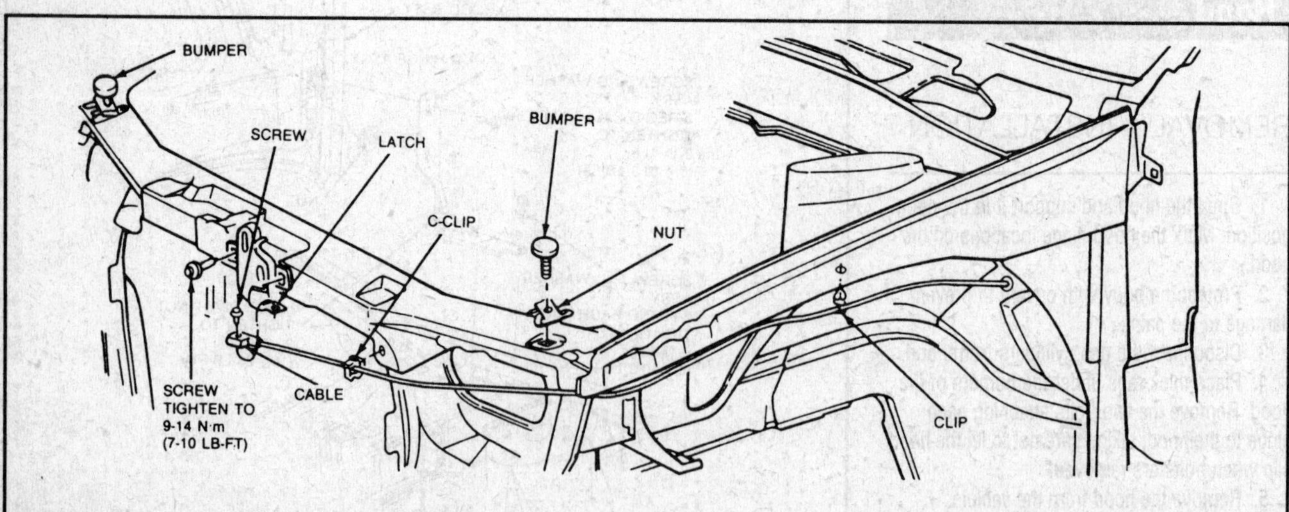

Fig.4 Hood latch and control cable mounting — exterior

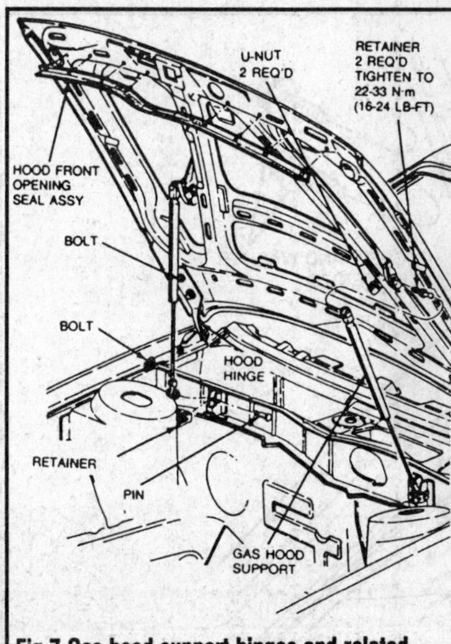

Fig.7 Gas hood support hinges and related components

5. Engage the gas support to the retainer at top.

6. Remove the temporary support and close the hood.

Tailgate

REMOVAL & INSTALLATION

➡ **The liftgate removal and install is a two person operation and should not be attempted alone.**

1. Before removing the hinge-to-roof frame attachments at both hinges, scribe the location of each hinge on roof frame and bolt locations.

2. Remove the hinge-to-roof frame screw and washer assembly at each hinge.

3. Remove the liftgate from the vehicle.

To install:

4. Position the hinges to the scribe marks on the roof frame and reverse the removal procedures. Torque the hinge-to-roof screw and washer assemblies to 16–25 ft. lbs.

ALIGNMENT

The wagon liftgate latch has double-bolt construction, designed to be equivalent in function and load capacity to side door latches. The latch is non-adjustable. All movement for adjustment is accomplished in the striker which has a 5.5mm radial range. This latch system has a two-position latching system. The closing latch cycle consists of a secondary position which latches the liftgate but does not seal the door to the liftgate weatherstrip. The primary position holds the liftgate door firmly into the weatherstrip. Water leaks and rattles may occur because the liftgate appears closed. However, it may only be closed to the secondary (first) position. Be sure that positive primary engagement of the liftgate latch is achieved upon closing. To check it, use the following procedure:

LATCH FUNCTION TEST

1. Close the liftgate to an assumed primary condition.

2. Insert the key into the key cylinder. Place your left hand on the liftgate glass above and left of the key cylinder. Press firmly on the glass with your left hand and slowly turn the key until the latch is released. Return the key and release your left hand pressure. The liftgate should be in the secondary position.

3. If while performing the above test shows that the liftgate will not close to primary the position, adjust the striker rearward (to rear of vehicle) so that a positive primary engagement is obtained upon closing the liftgate.

Liftgate Support Cylinder

REMOVAL & INSTALLATION

➧ SEE FIG. 9

1. Open the liftgate and temporarily support it.

2. The lift cylinder end fitting is a spring-clip design and removal is accomplished by sliding a small screwdriver under it and prying up to remove it from the ball stud.

3. Remove the support cylinder.

To install:

4. Install each cylinder to the C-pillar and the liftgate bracket ball socket by pushing the cylinder's locking wedge onto the socket.

5. Close the liftgate. Check the support cylinder operation.

Trunk Lid

REMOVAL & INSTALLATION

➡ **The trunk lid removal and install is a two person operation and should not be attempted alone.**

1. Remove the four hinge-to-trunk lid screws and remove the trunk lid.

2. To install, position the trunk lid to the hinges and install the four hinge-to-trunk lid retaining bolts.

3. Adjust for fit as outlined below.

4. Torque the retaining bolts to 16–25 ft. lbs.

ALIGNMENT

➧ SEE FIG. 10

The trunk lid door can be shifted fore and aft and from side to side on all models.

The trunk lid door should be adjusted for an even and parallel fit with the door opening. The

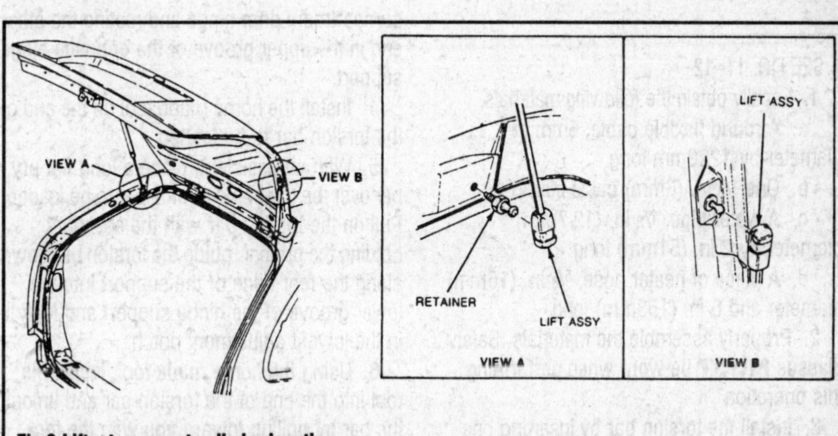

Fig.9 Liftgate support cylinder location

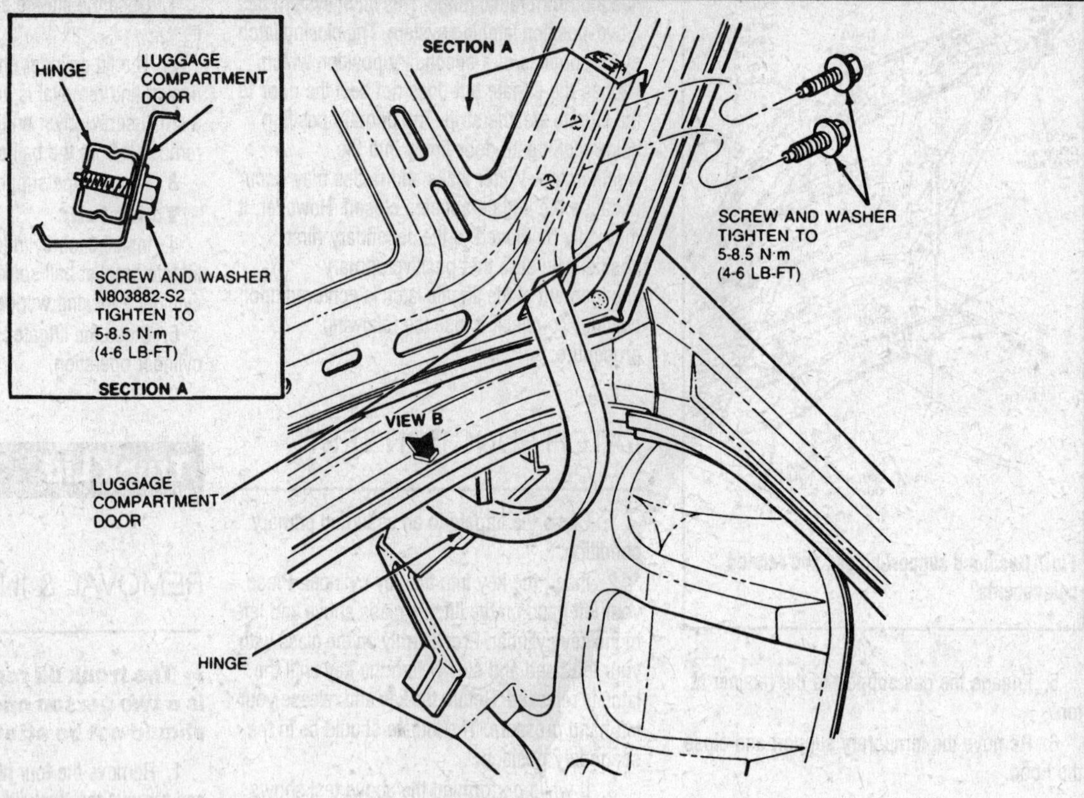

SECTION A

HINGE

LUGGAGE COMPARTMENT DOOR

SCREW AND WASHER N803882-S2 TIGHTEN TO 5-8.5 N·m (4-6 LB-FT)

SECTION A

SCREW AND WASHER TIGHTEN TO 5-8.5 N·m (4-6 LB-FT)

VIEW B

LUGGAGE COMPARTMENT DOOR

HINGE

Fig.10 Trunk lid hinge location

door should also be adjusted up and down for a flush fit with the surrounding panels. Care should be taken not to damage the trunk lid door or surrounding body panel.

Fore-and-aft and up-and-down adjustment of the trunk lid is achieved by loosening the hinge-to-trunk lid attaching screw, shifting the trunk lid to the proper fit and tightening the attaching screw to 7–10 ft. lbs.

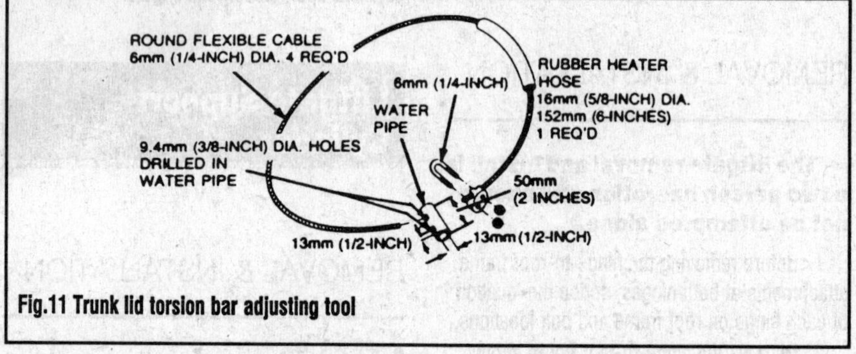

Fig.11 Trunk lid torsion bar adjusting tool

TRUNK LID TORSION BAR LOADING

➧ SEE FIG. 11–12

1. Locally obtain the following materials.
   a. A round flexible cable, 6mm in diameter by 1220mm long.
   b. One 1/4 in. (6mm) cable clamp.
   c. A water pipe, 1/2 in. (12.7mm) diameter by 2 in. (51mm) long.
   d. A piece of heater hose, 5/8 in. (16mm) diameter and 6 in. (153mm) long.
2. Properly assemble the materials. Safety glasses **MUST** be worn when performing this operation
3. Install the torsion bar by inserting one end into the hole provided in the luggage compartment door hinge and resting the other end in the upper groove of the opposite hinge support.
4. Install the home made tool on the end of the torsion bar to be loaded.
5. With an assistant, place a long flat pry bar over the top of the torsion bar to be loaded. Pull on the torsion bar with the assistant holding the pry bar, guide the torsion bar down along the rear edge of the support into the lower groove of the hinge support and lock it in the lowest adjustment notch.
6. Using the home made tool, install the tool into the end of the torsion bar and unlock the bar by pulling toward you with the tool.

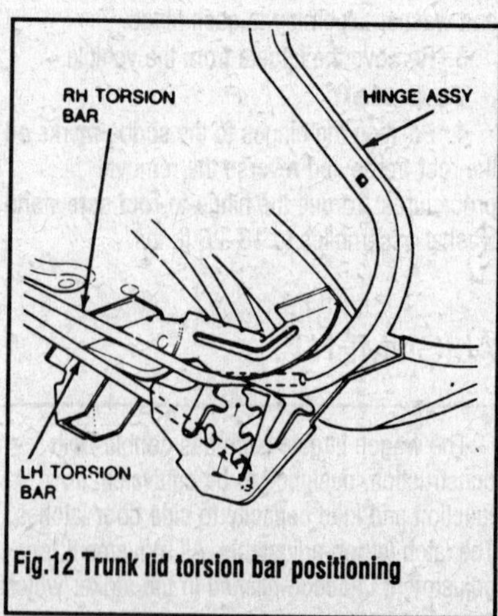

Fig.12 Trunk lid torsion bar positioning

Work the torsion bar into the second notch and release. If further adjustment is needed proceed to step 7.

7. Using a 3/8 in. drive, 1/2 in. deep well socket and a 6 in. (153mm) extension. Position the socket over the end of the torsion bar and unlock the bar. Reposition the torsion bar up the hinge support to the top notch and release.

Trunk Lid Latch And Lock

REMOVAL & INSTALLATION

➧ SEE FIG. 13

1. Open the luggage compartment door.
2. Remove the lever assembly and clip. If the clip breaks, replace with a new lever and clip assembly.
3. Remove the three latch attaching screws and disconnect the electric latch wire, if so equipped.
4. Remove the luggage compartment latch and rod from the vehicle with the retainer and seal.
5. Remove the screw and washer retaining the trunk lid lock cylinder plate-to-support and remove the plate and support.
6. Remove the lock cylinder and rod.

To install:

1. Position the lock cylinder and seal into the hole in the trunk lid. Push the lock cylinder retainer into position until it is locked.
2. Connect the electric latch wire, if so equipped. Install the trunk lid latch and rod assembly. Install the three attaching screws and washers and torque to 7–10 ft. lbs.
3. Install the lever and clip assembly. Close the trunk lid and check for proper alignment and adjust if necessary.

Front Bumper

REMOVAL & INSTALLATION

➧ SEE FIG. 14–16

1. Remove the four screws attaching the front bumper to the fenders. There are two on each side. Disconnect the cornering light electrical connectors, if equipped.
2. Remove the four bolts attaching the front bumper cover-to-radiator grille reinforcement assembly and remove the front bumper cover.

✲✲ CAUTION

Never apply heat to the bumper energy absorbers! The heat may cause the material inside to expand and flow out of the absorbers or crack the metal!

3. Remove the four nut and washer assemblies attaching the isolator to the bumper. With an assistant remove the bumper assembly from the vehicle.

To install:

1. Install the front bumper onto the isolator and torque the six attaching bolt and washer assemblies to 12.5–20 ft. lbs.
2. Install the front bumper cover over the bumper assembly and attach the side bumper cover supports.
3. Install the four front bumper-to-radiator support bolts and torque to 6–10 ft. lbs.
4. Install the four front bumper cover-to-fender attaching bolts and torque to 9–12 inch lbs.

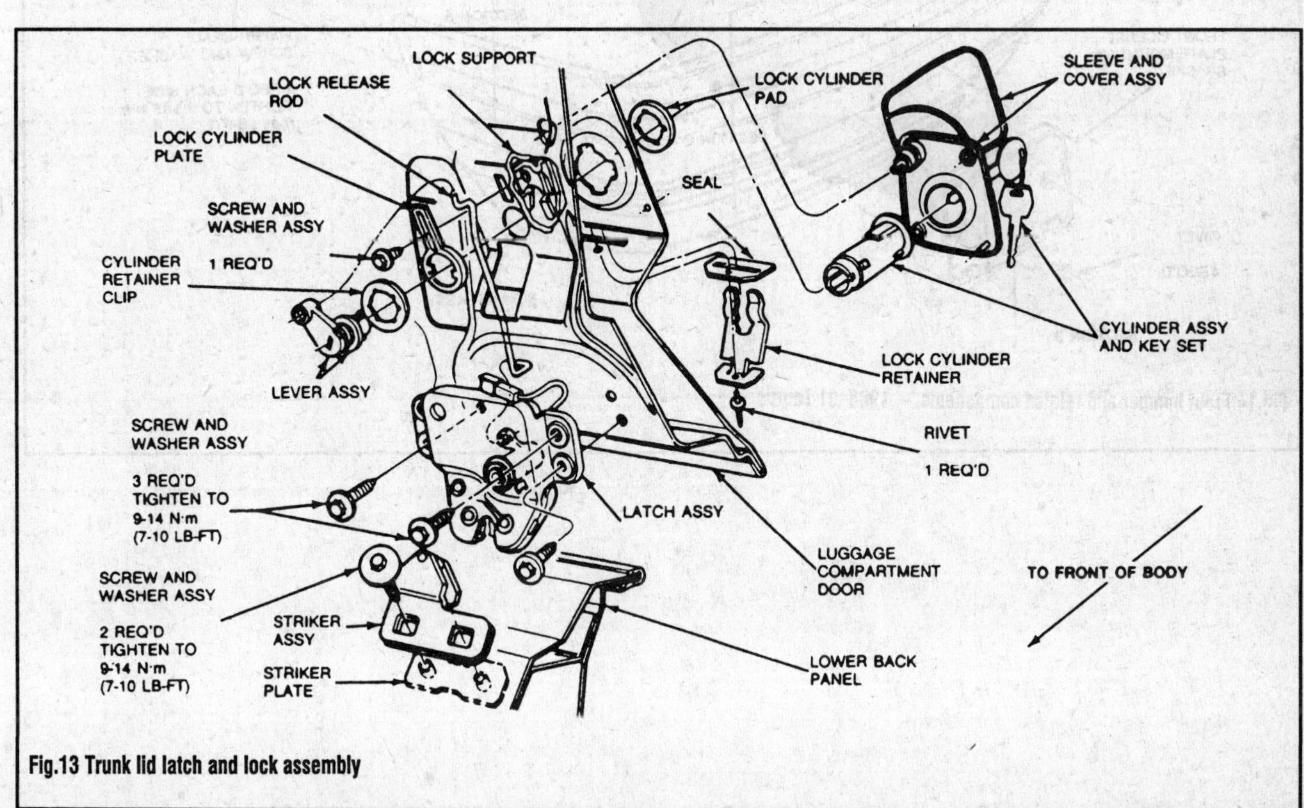

Fig.13 Trunk lid latch and lock assembly

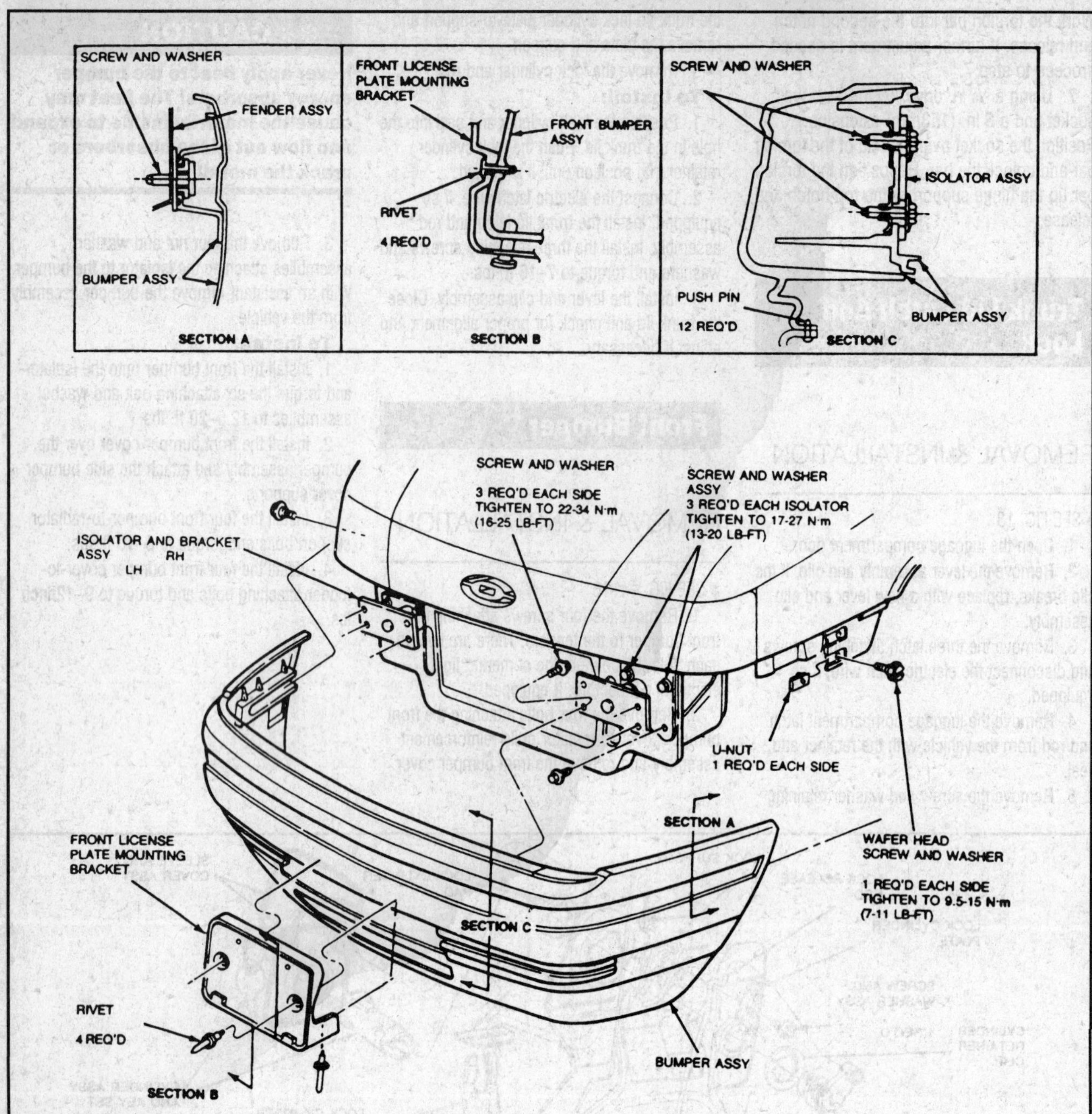
SCREW AND WASHER
FENDER ASSY
BUMPER ASSY
SECTION A
FRONT LICENSE PLATE MOUNTING BRACKET
FRONT BUMPER ASSY
RIVET
4 REQ'D
SECTION B
SCREW AND WASHER
ISOLATOR ASSY
PUSH PIN
12 REQ'D
BUMPER ASSY
SECTION C
SCREW AND WASHER
3 REQ'D EACH SIDE
TIGHTEN TO 22-34 N·m
(16-25 LB-FT)
SCREW AND WASHER ASSY
3 REQ'D EACH ISOLATOR
TIGHTEN TO 17-27 N·m
(13-20 LB-FT)
ISOLATOR AND BRACKET ASSY
LH
RH
U-NUT
1 REQ'D EACH SIDE
SECTION A
WAFER HEAD SCREW AND WASHER
1 REQ'D EACH SIDE
TIGHTEN TO 9.5-15 N·m
(7-11 LB-FT)
FRONT LICENSE PLATE MOUNTING BRACKET
SECTION C
RIVET
4 REQ'D
SECTION B
BUMPER ASSY

Fig.14 Front bumper and related components – 1986–91 Taurus

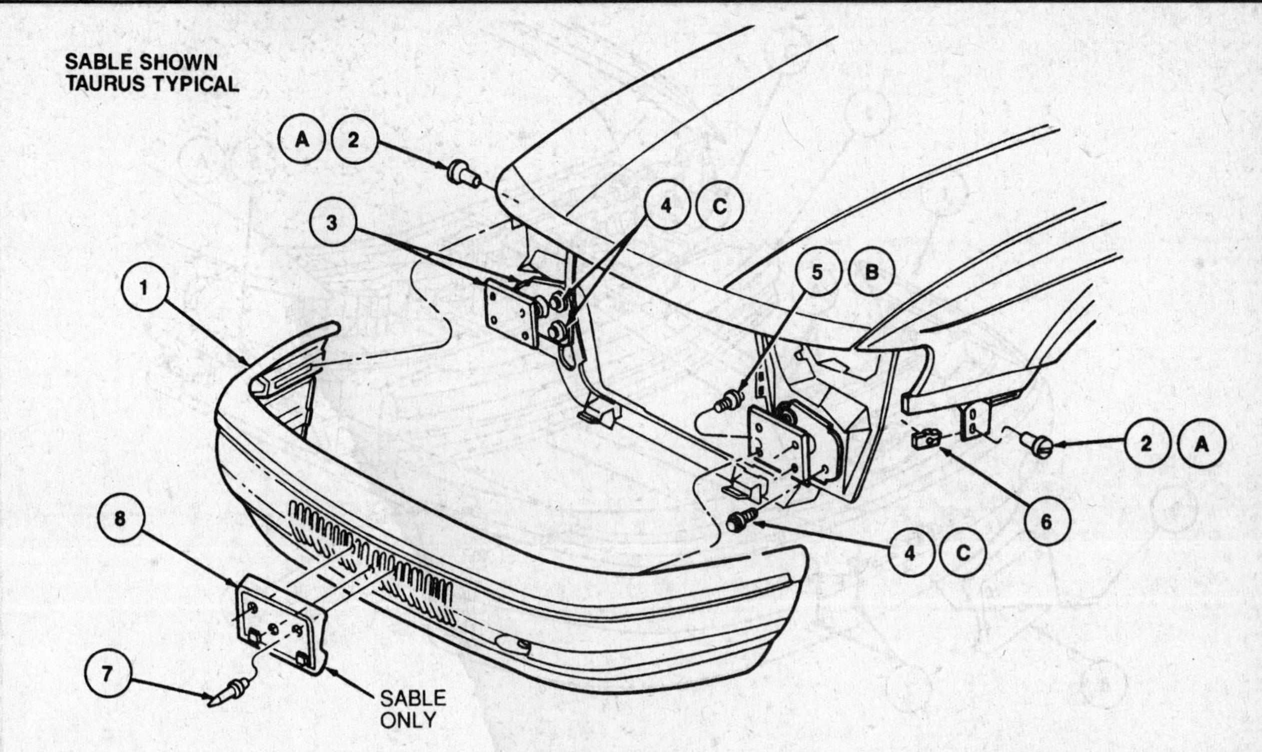

Item	Part Number	Description
1	17750	Front Bumper Assy
2A	N804984-S100	Screw and Washer (1 Req'd Each Side)
3	17D809	Isolator and Bracket Assy
4C	N606689-S2	Screw and Washer Assy (3 Req'd Each Isolator)
5B	N805433-S54	Screw and Washer (3 Req'd Each Side)
6	N800538-S101	U-Nut (1 Req'd Each Side)
7	N805150-S	Rivet (3 Req'd) (Sable Only)
8	17N397	Bracket Assy (Sable Only)
A		Tighten to 9-21 N·m (7-15 Lb-Ft)
B		Tighten to 22-34 N·m (17-25 Lb-Ft)
C		Tighten to 17-27 N·m (13-19 Lb-Ft)

Fig.15 Front bumper and related components — 1992 Taurus except SHO

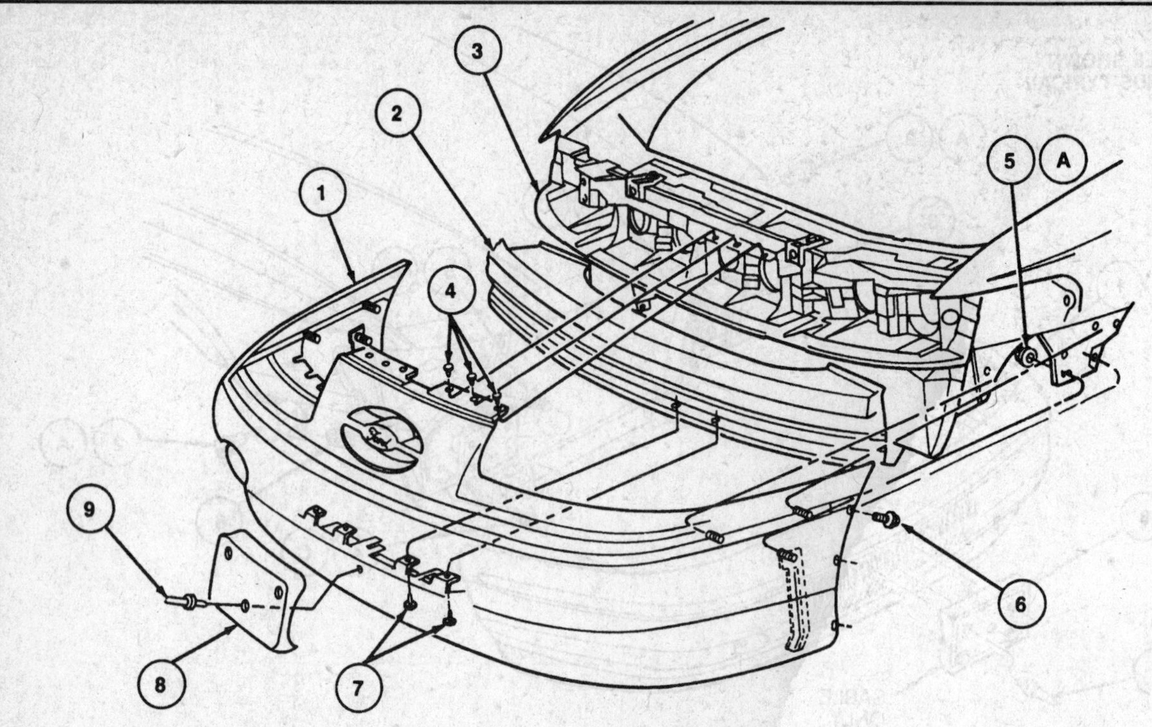

Item	Part Number	Description
1	17D957	Front Bumper Cover
2	—	Front Bumper Assy
3	8A164	Grille Opening Reinforcement
4	388577-S	Push Pin (3 Req'd each side)
5A	N621906-S36	Nut and Washer (2 Req'd each side)
6	388577-S	Push Pin (1 Req'd each side)
7	388577-S	Push Pin (2 Req'd each side)
8	17A385	Front L / Plate Bracket
9	N803043-S	Rivet (3 Req'd)
A		Tighten to 4.5-6.9 N·m (40-61 Lb-In)

Fig.16 Front bumper and related components — 1992 Taurus SHO

Rear Bumper

REMOVAL & INSTALLATION

➧ SEE FIG. 17–20

1. Remove the four screws attaching the rear bumper cover-to-quarter panels.
2. Remove the luggage compartment side cover assemblies and the lower back trim panel.
3. Remove the nuts attaching the rear bumper cover-to-quarter panels and the lower back panel.
4. Remove the bumper cover. Remove the four nut and washer assemblies attaching each isolator to the rear bumper. With an assistant remove the rear bumper.

To install:

➡ Never apply heat to the bumper energy absorbers! The heat may cause the material inside to expand and flow out of the absorbers or crack the metal!

1. With an assistant, install the rear bumper on the vehicle at the isolator and bracket.
2. Install the six bumper-to-isolator nuts and washer assemblies and torque to 33–51 ft. lbs.
3. Install the rear bumper cover over the bumper and install the bumper cover-to-quarter panels and the lower back panel.
4. Install the push pins attaching the rear bumper cover to the rear bumper.
5. Install the luggage compartment side cover and lower trim panels.
6. Install the four screws attaching the rear bumper cover-to-quarter panels and torque the screws to 6–10 ft. lbs.

QUARTER PANEL ASSY
SCREW AND WASHER
BUMPER ASSY
SECTION A
SCREW AND WASHER
N803944-S54
ISOLATOR AND
BRACKET ASSY
BUMPER ASSY
SECTION B
SCREW AND WASHER
ASSY
2 REQ'D EACH SIDE
TIGHTEN TO
35-55 N·m
(25-41 LB-FT)
ISOLATOR AND
BRACKET ASSY
RH
LH
SCREW AND WASHER
3 REQ'D EACH SIDE
TIGHTEN TO 9.5-11 N·m
(7-11 LB-FT)
BUMPER ASSY
SECTION A
SECTION B

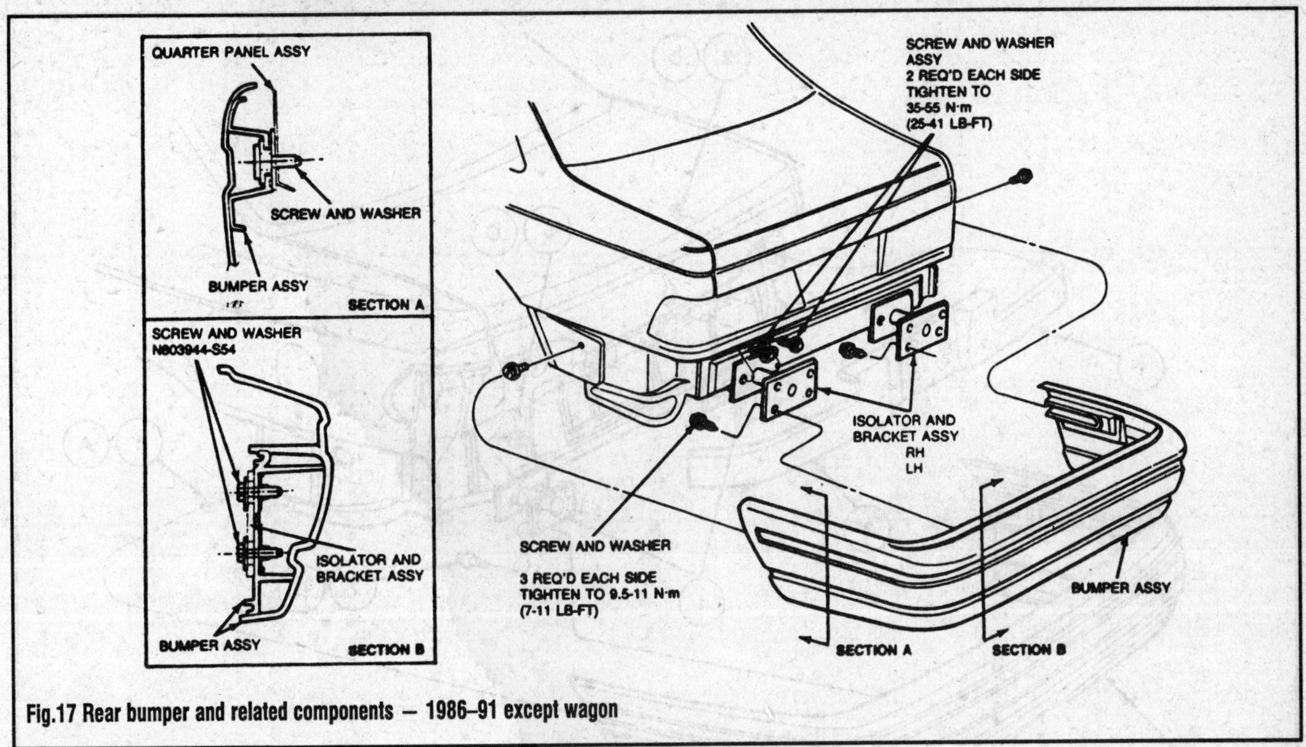

Fig.17 Rear bumper and related components — 1986–91 except wagon

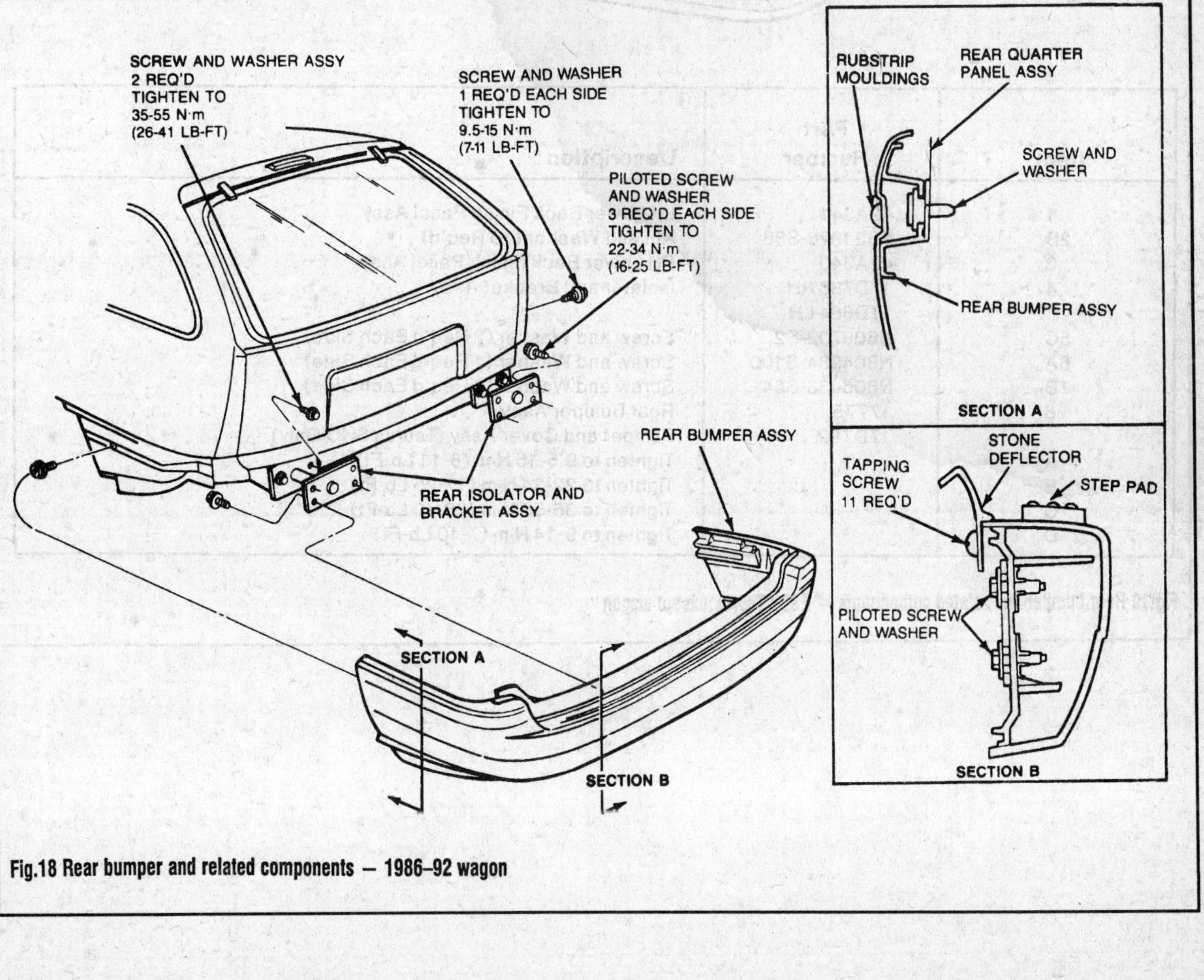

SCREW AND WASHER ASSY
2 REQ'D
TIGHTEN TO
35-55 N·m
(26-41 LB-FT)
SCREW AND WASHER
1 REQ'D EACH SIDE
TIGHTEN TO
9.5-15 N·m
(7-11 LB-FT)
PILOTED SCREW
AND WASHER
3 REQ'D EACH SIDE
TIGHTEN TO
22-34 N·m
(16-25 LB-FT)
REAR BUMPER ASSY
REAR ISOLATOR AND
BRACKET ASSY
SECTION A
SECTION B
RUBSTRIP
MOULDINGS
REAR QUARTER
PANEL ASSY
SCREW AND
WASHER
REAR BUMPER ASSY
SECTION A
STONE
DEFLECTOR
TAPPING
SCREW
11 REQ'D
STEP PAD
PILOTED SCREW
AND WASHER
SECTION B

Fig.18 Rear bumper and related components — 1986–92 wagon

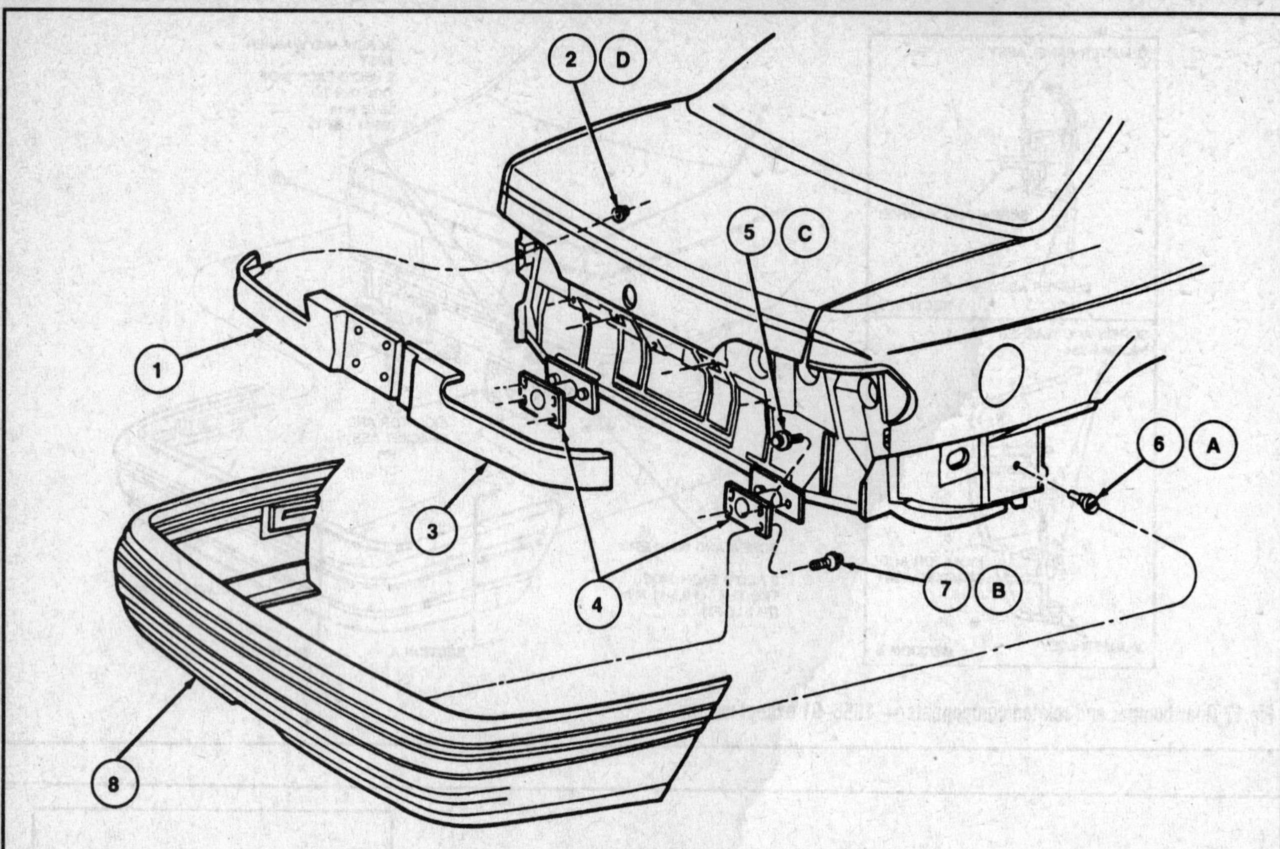

Item	Part Number	Description
1	42A341	LH Lower Back Finish Panel Assy
2D	N621926-S36	Nut and Washer (10 Req'd)
3	42A340	RH Lower Back Finish Panel Assy
4	17D788 RH 17D864 LH	Isolator and Bracket Assy
5C	N606702-S2	Screw and Washer (2 Req'd Each Side)
6A	N804984-S100	Screw and Washer (1 Req'd Each Side)
7B	N805433-S54	Screw and Washer (3 Req'd Each Side)
8	17775 17D780	Rear Bumper Assy Bumper and Cover Assy (Taurus SHO Only)
A		Tighten to 9.5-15 N·m (8-11 Lb-Ft)
B		Tighten to 22-34 N·m (17-25 Lb-Ft)
C		Tighten to 35-55 N·m (26-40 Lb-Ft)
D		Tighten to 9-14 N·m (7-10 Lb-Ft)

Fig.19 Rear bumper and related components — 1992 Taurus except wagon

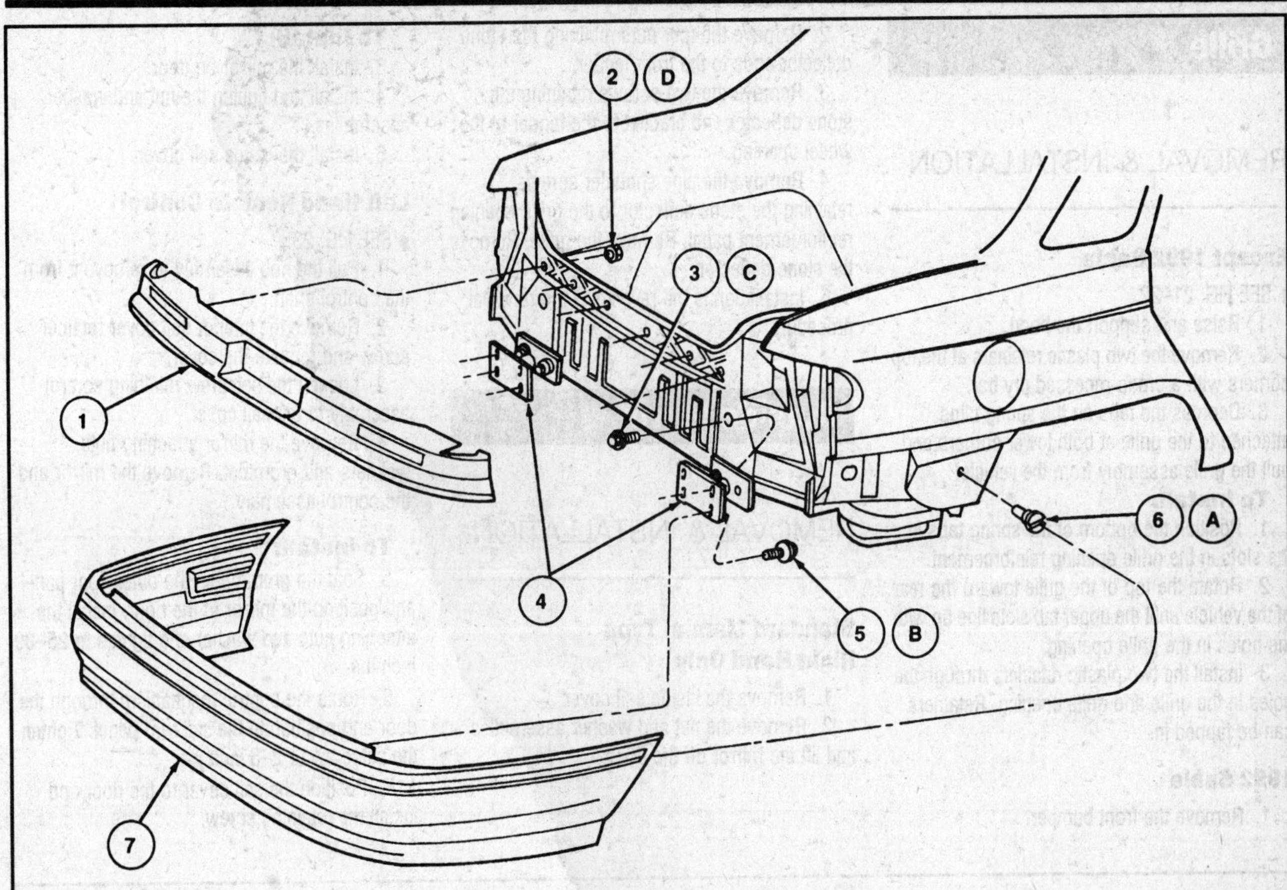

Item	Part Number	Description
1	17805	Deflector Assy
2D	N621927	Nut and Washer Assy (6 Req'd)
3C	N606702-S2	Screw and Washer Assy (2 Req'd)
4	17D788 RH 17D864 LH	Isolator and Bracket Assy
5B	N805433-S54	Screw and Washer (2 Req'd Each Side)
6A	N804984-S100	Screw and Washer (1 Req'd Each Side)
7	17775	Rear Bumper Assy
A		Tighten to 9.5-15 N·m (8-11 Lb-Ft)
B		Tighten to 22-34 N·m (17-25 Lb-Ft)
C		Tighten to 35-55 N·m (26-40 Lb-Ft)
D		Tighten to 9-14 N·m (7-10 Lb-Ft)

Fig.20 Rear bumper and related components — 1992 Sable except wagon

Grille

REMOVAL & INSTALLATION

Except 1992 Sable

➧ SEE FIG. 21–22

1. Raise and support the hood.
2. Remove the two plastic retainers at the top corners with a cross-recessed pry bar.
3. Depress the tabs on the spring clips attached to the grille at both lower corners and pull the grille assembly from the vehicle.

To install:

1. Position the bottom of the spring tabs in the slots in the grille opening reinforcement.
2. Rotate the top of the grille toward the rear of the vehicle until the upper tab slots line up with the holes in the grille opening.
3. Install the two plastic retainers through the holes in the grille and grille opening. Retainers can be tapped in.

1992 Sable

1. Remove the front bumper.
2. Remove the four nuts retaining the stone deflector ends to the front fender.
3. Remove the two screws retaining the stone deflector end bracket to the fender at the wheel opening.
4. Remove the nine shoulder screws retaining the stone deflector to the grille opening reinforcement panel. Remove the grille. Remove the stone deflector.
5. Installation is the reverse of the removal procedure.

Outside Mirror

REMOVAL & INSTALLATION

Standard Manual Type Right Hand Only

1. Remove the inside sail cover.
2. Remove the nut and washer assemblies and lift the mirror off the door.

To install:

3. Install the mirror on door.
4. Install and tighten the nut and washer assemblies.
5. Install the inside sail cover.

Left Hand Remote Control

➧ SEE FIG. 23

1. Pull the nob assembly to remove it from the control shaft.
2. Remove the interior sail cover retainer screw and remove the cover.
3. Loosen the setscrew retaining control assembly to the sail cover.
4. Remove the mirror attaching nuts, washers and grommet. Remove the mirror and the control assembly.

To install:

5. Seat the grommet in the outer door panel and position the mirror to the door. Install the attaching nuts and washer and tighten to 25–39 inch lbs.
6. Route the control mechanism through the door and position to the sail trim panel. Tighten the setscrew to 2–6 inch lbs.
7. Position the sail cover to the door and install the retaining screw.

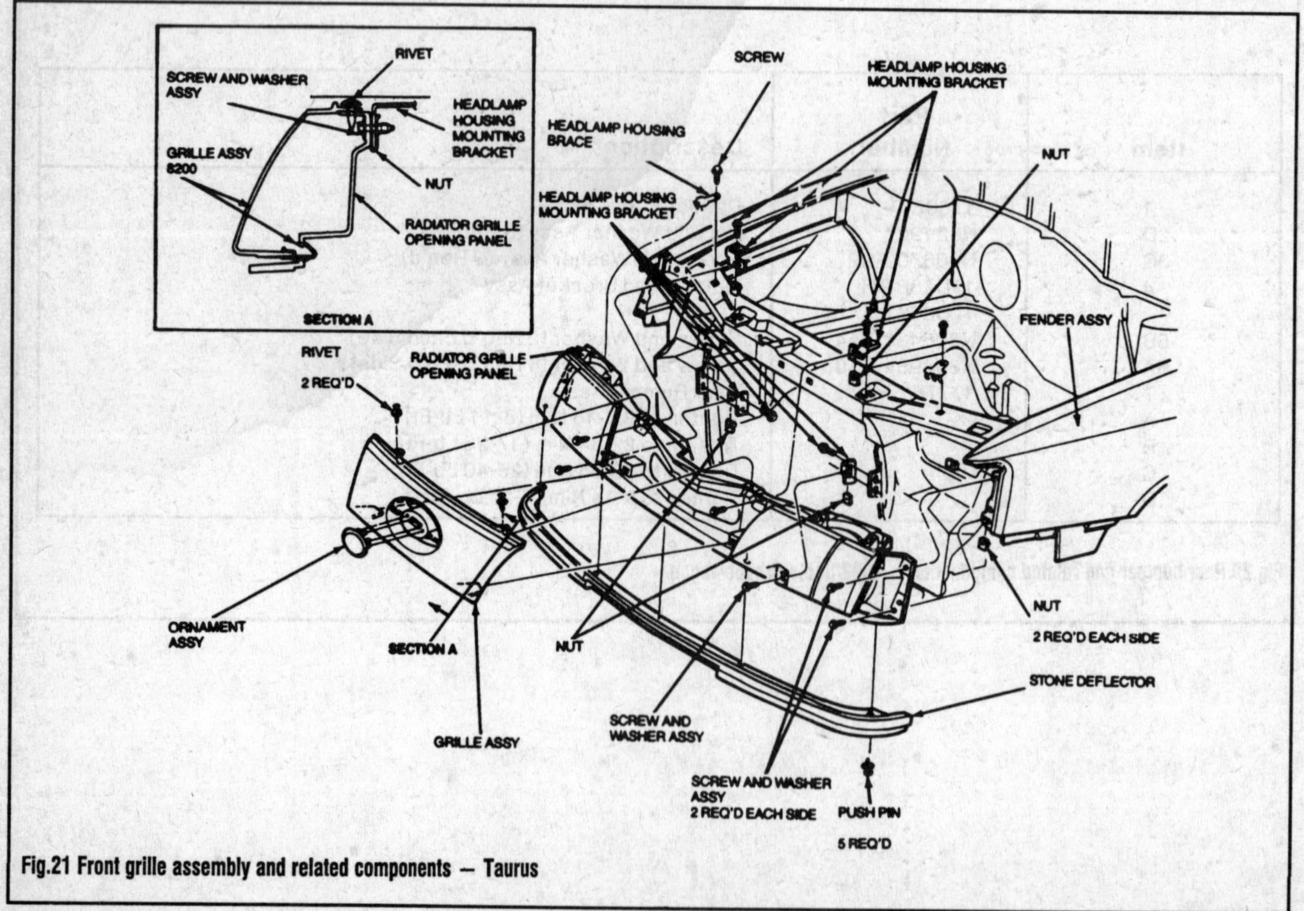

Fig.21 Front grille assembly and related components — Taurus

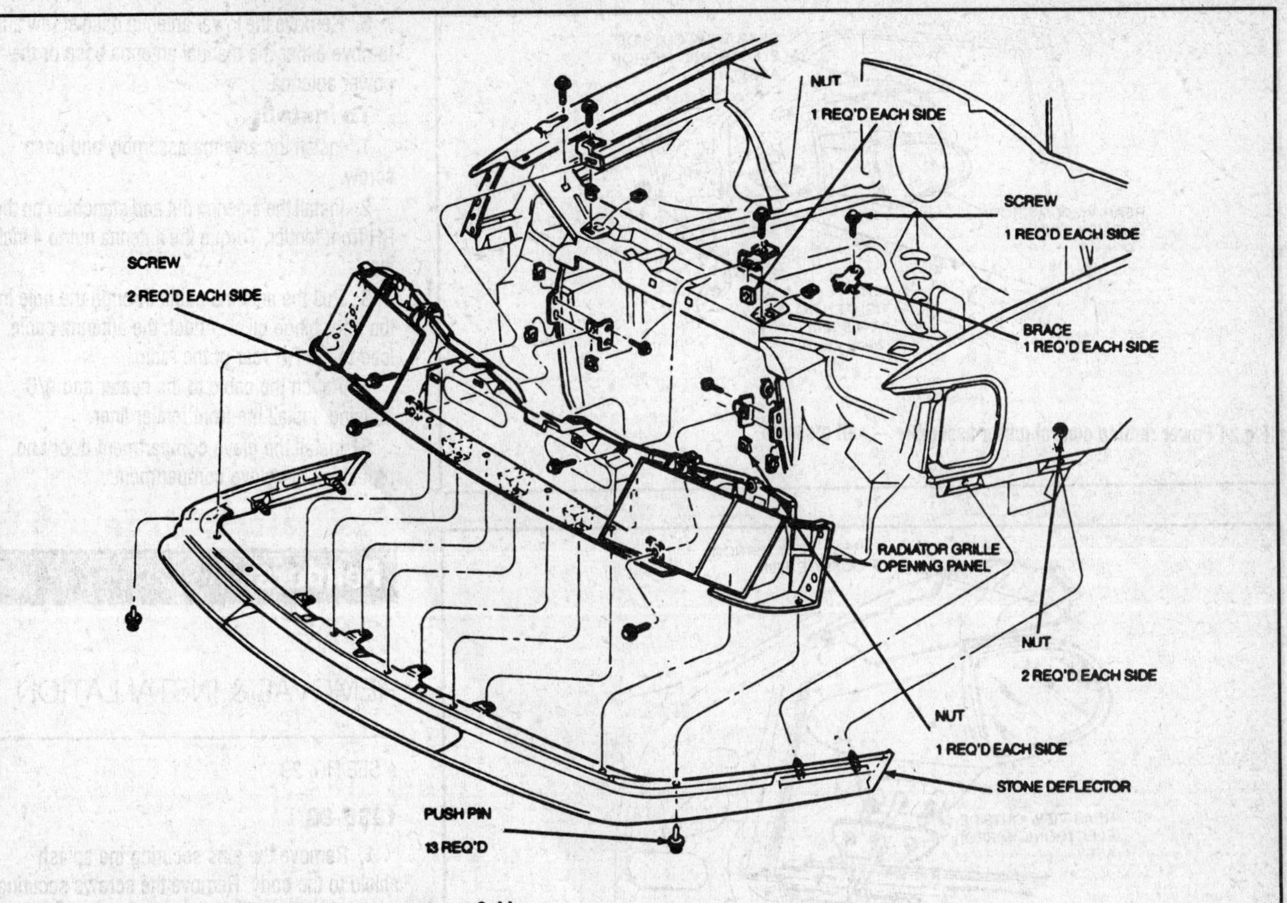

Fig.22 Front grille assembly and related components — Sable

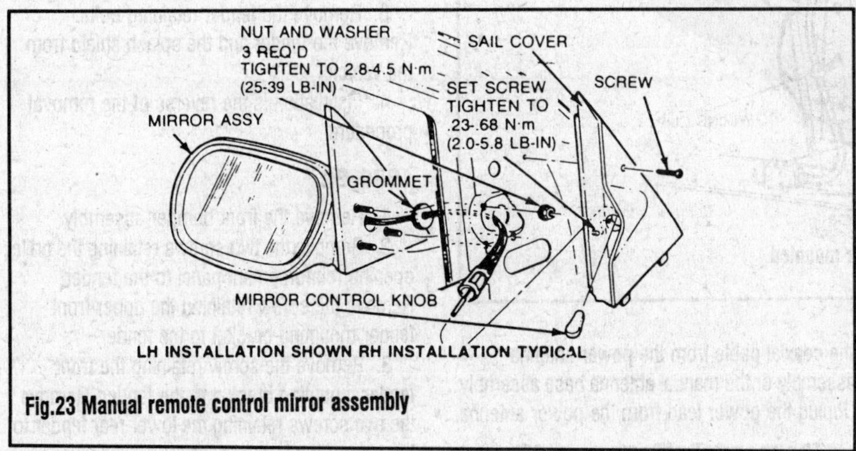

Fig.23 Manual remote control mirror assembly

8. Position the rubber knob onto the control shaft and push to install.

Power Outside Mirrors

➧ SEE FIG. 24–25

➡ Outside mirrors that are frozen must be thawed prior to adjustment. Do not attempt to free-up the mirror by pressing the glass assembly.

1. Disconnect the negative (–) battery cable.
2. Remove the one screw retaining the mirror mounting hole cover and remove the cover.
3. Remove the door trim panel.
4. Disconnect the mirror assembly wiring connector. Remove the necessary wiring guides.
5. Remove the three mirror retaining nuts on the sail mirrors, two on door mirrors. Remove the mirror while guiding the wiring and connector through hole in the door.

To install:

6. Install the mirror assembly by routing the connector and wiring through the hole in the door. Attach with the three retaining nuts on the sail mirrors, two on the door mirrors. Tighten the retaining nuts.
7. Connect the mirror wiring connector and install the wiring guides.
8. Replace the mirror mounting hole cover and install one screw.
9. Replace the door trim panel.
10. Connect the negative (–) battery cable.

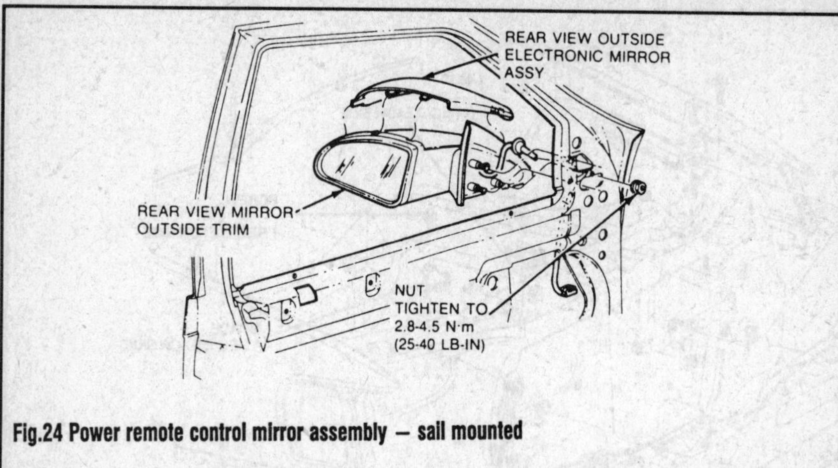

Fig.24 Power remote control mirror assembly — sail mounted

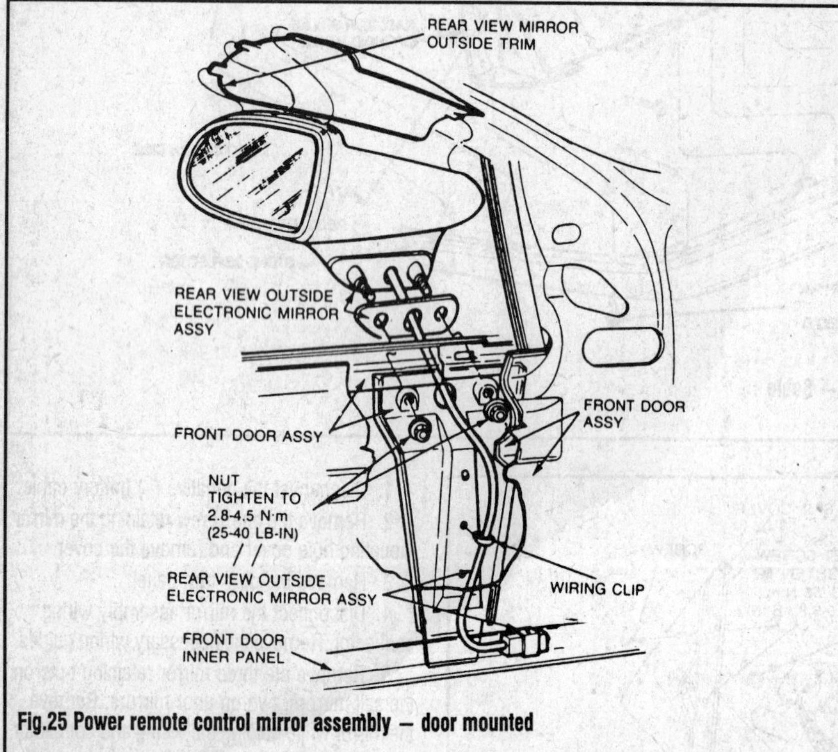

Fig.25 Power remote control mirror assembly — door mounted

Antenna

REMOVAL & INSTALLATION

➧ SEE FIG. 26–28

1. Push in on the sides of glove compartment door and place the door in the hinged downward position.
2. Disconnect the antenna lead from the RH rear of the radio and remove the cable from the heater or the A/C cable retaining clips.
3. Remove the RH front fender liner. Unplug the coaxial cable from the power antenna assembly or the manual antenna base assembly. Unplug the power lead from the power antenna.

➡ **The manual antenna mast is detachable from the base and cable assembly.**

4. Under the RH front fender, pull the antenna cable through the hole in the door hinge pillar and remove the antenna cable assembly from the wheel well area.
5. To remove the manual or power antenna base, remove the antenna nut and stanchion on the RH front fender.
6. Remove the lower antenna base screw and remove either the manual antenna base or the power antenna.

To install:

1. Install the antenna assembly and base screw.
2. Install the antenna nut and stanchion on the RH front fender. Torque the antenna nut to 4 inch lbs.
3. Pull the antenna cable through the hole in the door hinge pillar. Attach the antenna cable lead to the RH rear of the radio.
4. Attach the cable to the heater and A/C housing. Install the front fender liner.
5. Install the glove compartment door and reposition the glove compartment.

Fenders

REMOVAL & INSTALLATION

➧ SEE FIG. 29

1986–88

1. Remove the pins securing the splash shield to the body. Remove the screws securing the fender and splash shield to the body.
2. Remove the insulator assembly from the fender.
3. Remove the fender retaining bolts. Remove the fender and the splash shield from the vehicle.
4. Installation is the reverse of the removal procedure.

1989–92

1. Remove the front bumper assembly.
2. Remove the two screws retaining the grille opening reinforcement panel to the fender. Remove the screw retaining the upper front fender mounting bracket to the fender.
3. Remove the screw retaining the front fender mounting bracket to the fender. Remove the two screws retaining the lower rear fender to the side of the body.
4. Remove the two bolts retaining the upper and lower front fender. Remove the three retaining bolts from the catwalk area of the fender apron. Remove the fender from the vehicle.
5. Installation is the reverse of the removal procedure.

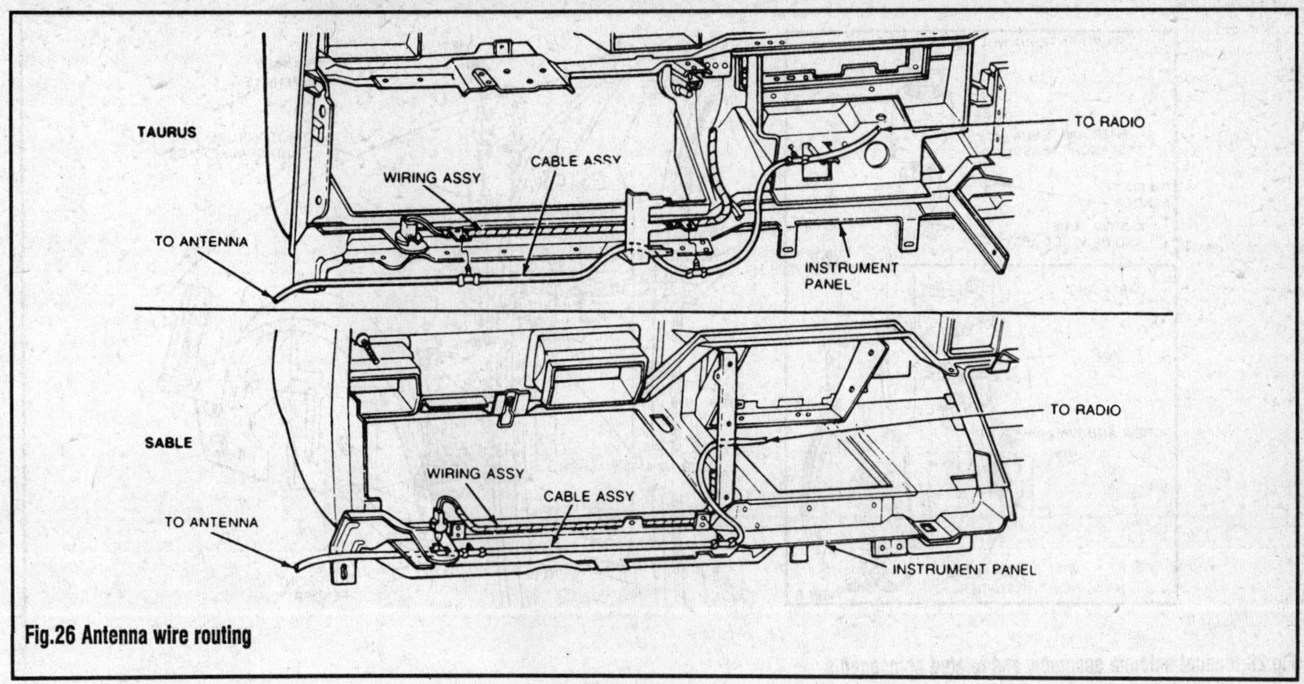

Fig.26 Antenna wire routing

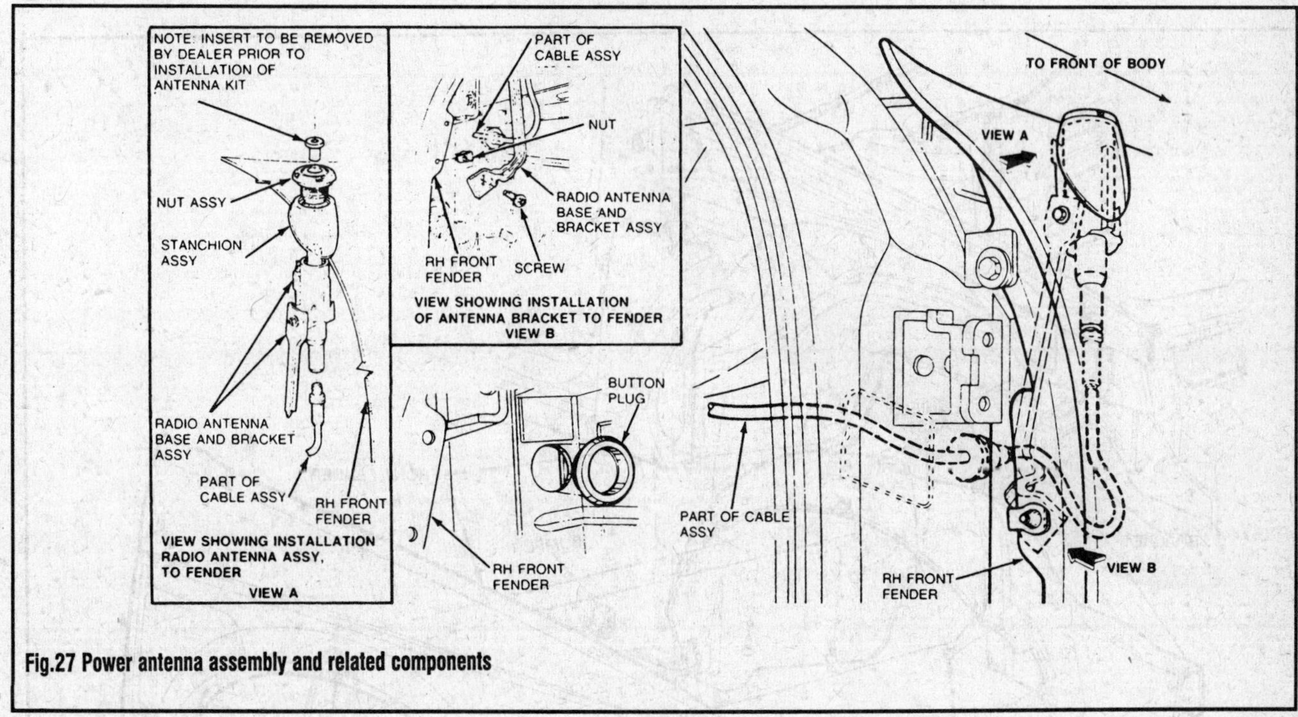

Fig.27 Power antenna assembly and related components

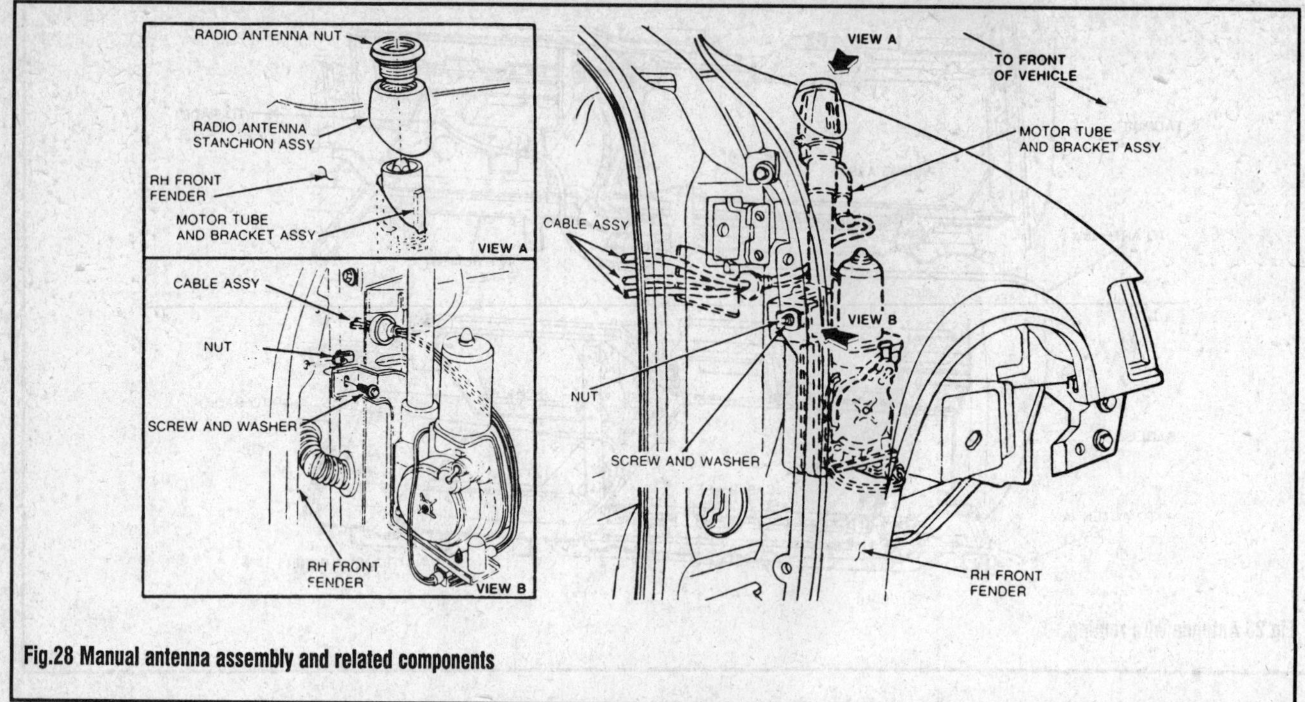

Fig.28 Manual antenna assembly and related components

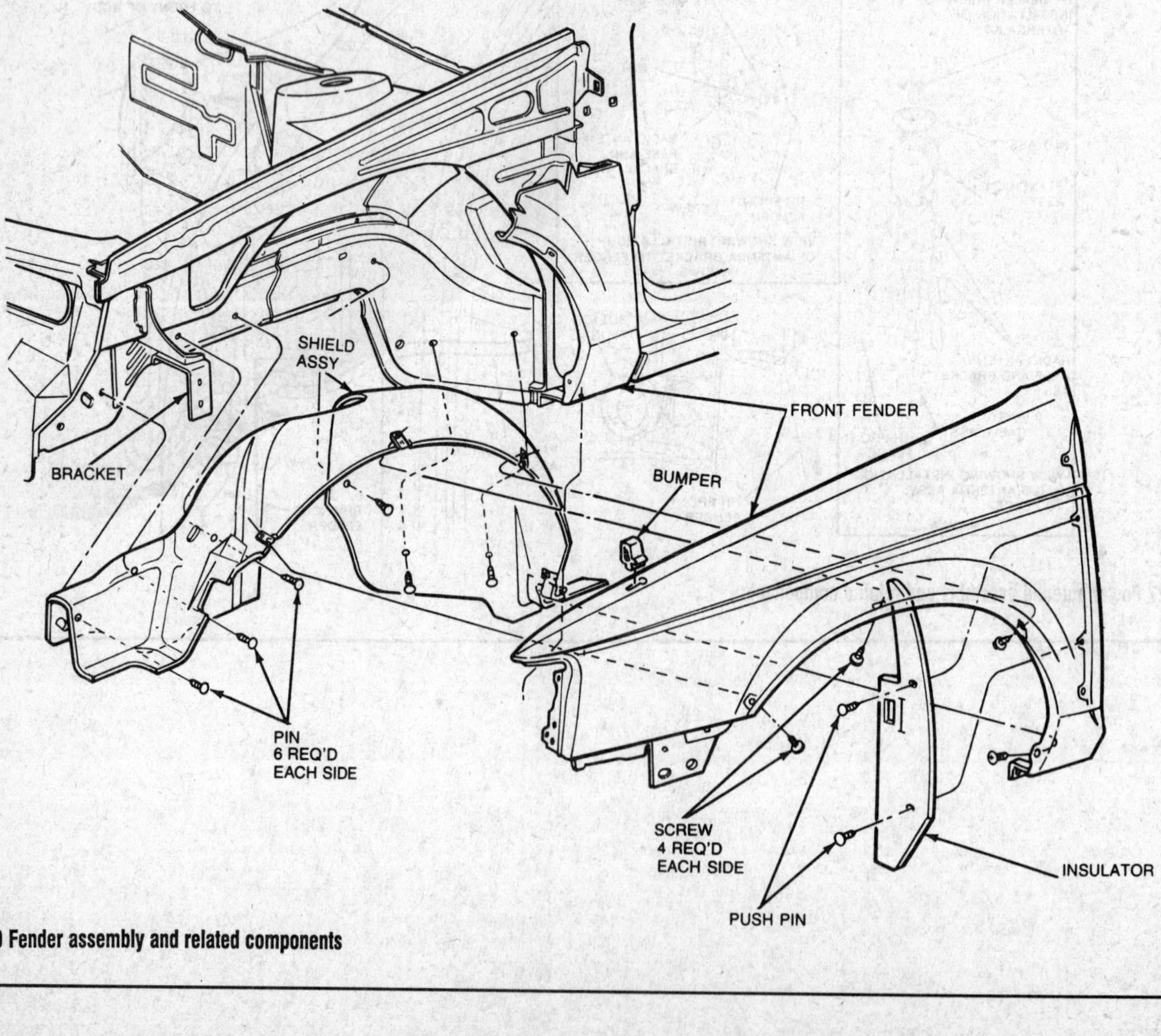

Fig.29 Fender assembly and related components

Power Sunroof

REMOVAL & INSTALLATION

Glass and Sunshade

1. Disconnect the negative battery cable. To remove the glass panel remove the three halo front retaining screws.
2. Slide the halo and the sunshade fully rearward to expose the six glass retaining screws.
3. Remove the glass retaining screws in order to remove the sunshade. Push the glass upward from inside of the vehicle and remove it. Be sure to lift the halo to clear the sunshade.
4. Installation is the reverse of the removal procedure.

INTERIOR

Instrument Panel And Pad

REMOVAL & INSTALLATION

1986–89

➧ SEE FIG. 32

1. Disconnect the negative battery cable. Remove the four screws retaining the steering column opening cover and remove the cover. Remove the sound insulator under the glove compartment.
2. Remove the steering column trim shrouds. Disconnect all electrical connections from the steering column switches.
3. Remove the steering column retaining screws. remove ths steering column.
4. Remove the screws retaining the left hand and lower radio trim panels. Remove the trim panels.
5. Remove the seven cluster trim panel retaining screws, the one jamnut behind the headlight switch and the one screw behind the clock. Remove the trim panel.
6. Disconnect the speedometer cable. The cluster can be removed along with the panel.
7. Release the glove compartment assembly and allow the compartment to hang open.
8. Using all openings remove all the instrument panel electrical connections, air conditioning outlets, air conditioning control cables, antenna wires and anything else that may interfere with panel removal.
9. Disconnect the underhood electrical connectors at the main wire loom. Push the wires and grommets through to the instrument panel area.
10. Remove the right and left speaker covers. Remove the two lower instrument panel to cowl side retaining screws. Remove the instrument panel brace retaining screw.
11. Remove the three upper instrument panel retaining screws. Remove the instrument panel from the vehicle.

To install:

12. Position the instrument panel in place. Connect the underhood electrical connections. Install the instrument panel upper screws. Install the instrument panel lower screws.
13. Install the lower brace and tighten the bolt to 5–8 ft. lbs. Install the radio speaker grilles.
14. Using all openings install all the instrument panel electrical connections, air conditioning outlets, air conditioning control cables, antenna wires and anything else that may have been removed.
15. Connect the speedometer cable. Install the cluster retaining screws and torque them to 18–26 inch lbs. Install the clock or clock cover.
16. Install the lower left and radio trim panels. Install the steering column and torque the retaining bolts to specification.
17. Connect all steering column electrical connectors. Install the lower steering column trim panel. Install the sound deadener under the glove compartment lid.
18. Connect the negative battery cable. Check for proper operation of all components.

1990–91

➧ SEE FIG. 31

➡ Some vehicles are equipped with air bags. Before attempting to service air bag equipped vehicles be sure that the system is properly disarmed and all safety precautions are taken. Serious personal injury and vehicle damage could result if this note is disregarded.

1. Position the wheels in the straight ahead position. Disconnect the negative battery cable.
2. Remove the ignition lock cylinder. Remove the tilt lever, if equipped. Remove the steering column trim shrouds. Disconnect all electrical connectors from the steering column assembly.
3. Remove the two bolts and reinforcement from under the steering column. Disengage the insulator retainer and remove the insulator.
4. Remove the four nuts and the reinforcement from under the steering column. Do not rotate the steering column shaft.
5. Remove the four nuts retaining the steering column to the instrument panel, disconnect the PRNDL cable and lower the steering column on the front seat.
6. Install the ignition lock cylinder to ensure that the steering column shaft does not turn. Remove the one bolt at the steering column opening attaching the instrument panel brace retaining bolt under the radio.
7. Remove the sound insulator from under the glove compartment by removing the two push nuts that secure the insulator to the studs on the climate control case assembly.
8. Disconnect the wires of the main wire loom inside the engine compartment. Push the wires and the grommets inside to the interior of the vehicle.
9. Remove the right and left hand cowl sides. Remove the one screw retaining the instrument panel to the left side and the one screw on the right side.
10. Remove both speaker covers by pulling upward on them. Open the glove compartment door and allow it to hang open.
11. Using all openings remove all the instrument panel electrical connections, air conditioning outlets, air conditioning control cables, antenna wires and anything else that may interfere with panel removal.
12. Close the glove compartment lid.

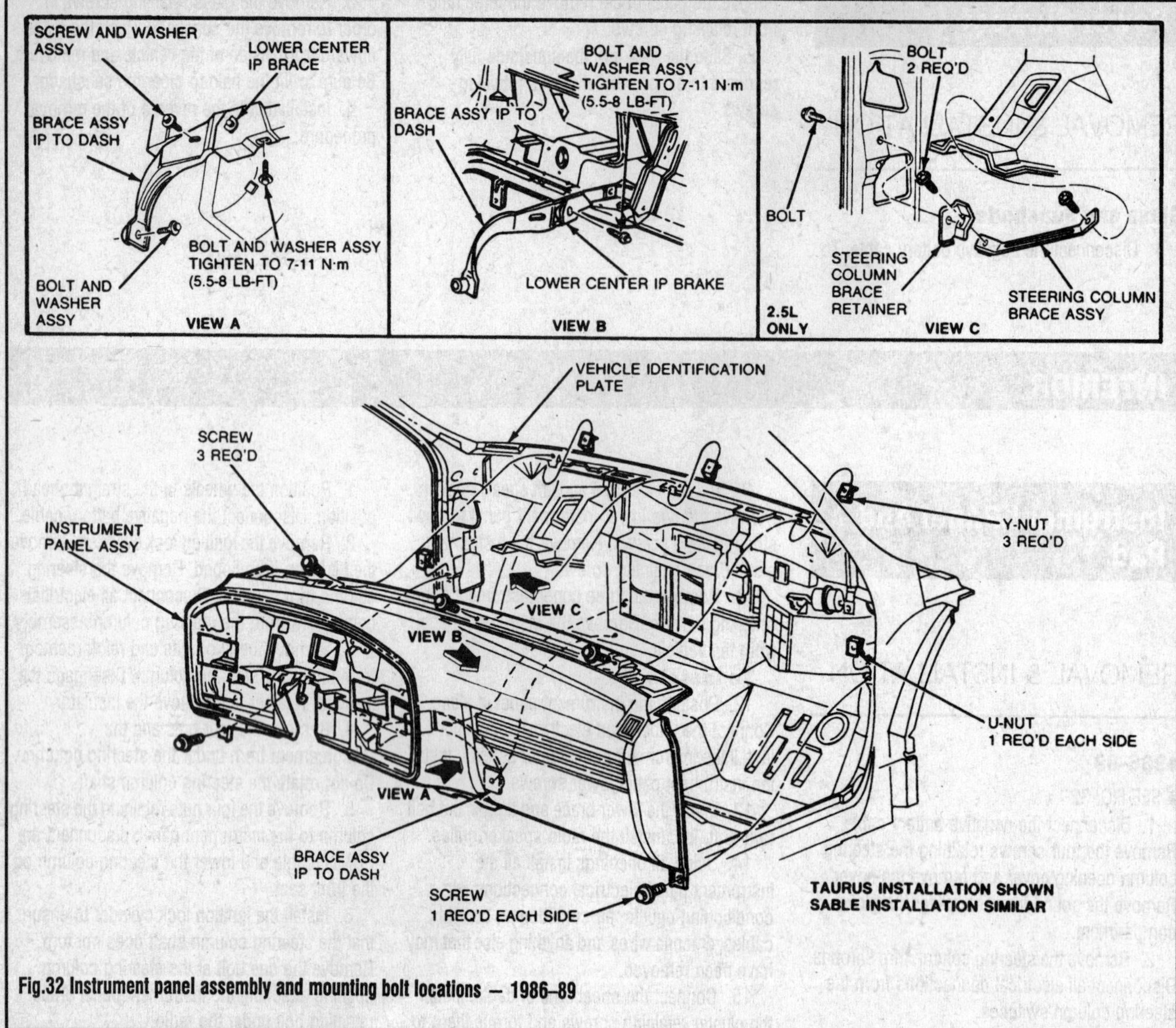

Fig.32 Instrument panel assembly and mounting bolt locations — 1986–89

Remove the three instrument panel screws at the top of the assembly. Disconnect any remaining electrical wires. Remove the instrument panel assembly from the vehicle.

To install:

13. Position the instrument panel in place. Connect the underhood electrical connections. Install the instrument panel upper screws. Install the instrument panel lower screws.

14. Install the lower brace and tighten the bolt to 5–8 ft. lbs. Install the radio speaker grilles.

15. Using all openings install all the instrument panel electrical connections, air conditioning outlets, air conditioning control cables, antenna wires and anything else that may have been removed.

16. Continue the installation in the reverse order of the removal procedure.

17. Check for proper operation of the air bag indicator. Check for proper operation of all components.

1992

SEE FIG. 30

Some vehicles are equipped with air bags. Before attempting to service air bag equipped vehicles be sure that the system is properly disarmed and all safety precautions are taken. Serious personal injury and vehicle damage could result if this note is disregarded.

1. Position the wheels in the straight ahead position. Disconnect the negative battery cable.

2. Remove the ignition lock cylinder. Remove the tilt lever, if equipped. Remove the steering column trim shrouds. Disconnect all electrical connectors from the steering column assembly.

3. Remove the two bolts and reinforcement from under the steering column. Disengage the insulator retainer and remove the insulator.

4. Remove the four nuts and the reinforcement from under the steering column. Do not rotate the steering column shaft.

5. Disconnect the parking brake release cable and wiring connector from the parking brake and ignition switch wiring connector.

6. Remove the four nuts retaining the steering column to the instrument panel, disconnect the PRNDL cable and lower the steering column on the front seat.

7. Install the ignition lock cylinder to ensure that the steering column shaft does not turn. Remove the one bolt at the steering column opening attaching the instrument panel brace retaining bolt under the radio.

8. Remove the sound insulator from under the glove compartment by removing the two push nuts that secure the insulator to the studs on the climate control case assembly.

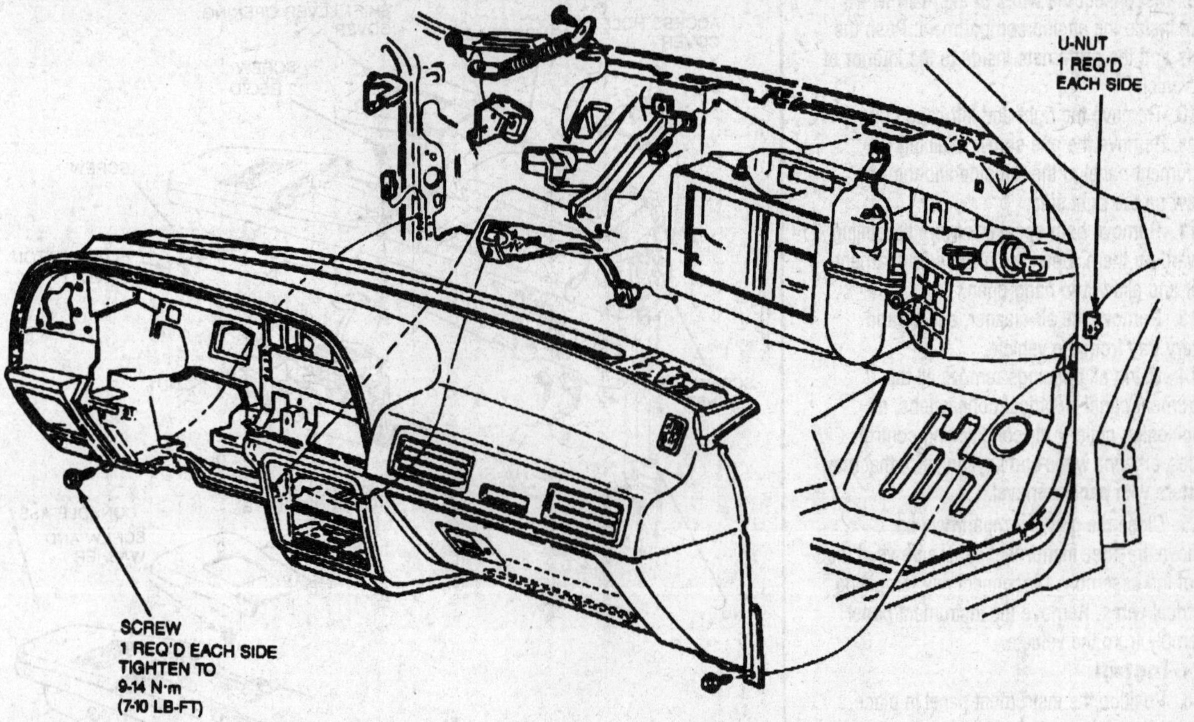

Fig.31 Instrument panel assembly and mounting bolt locations — 1990–91

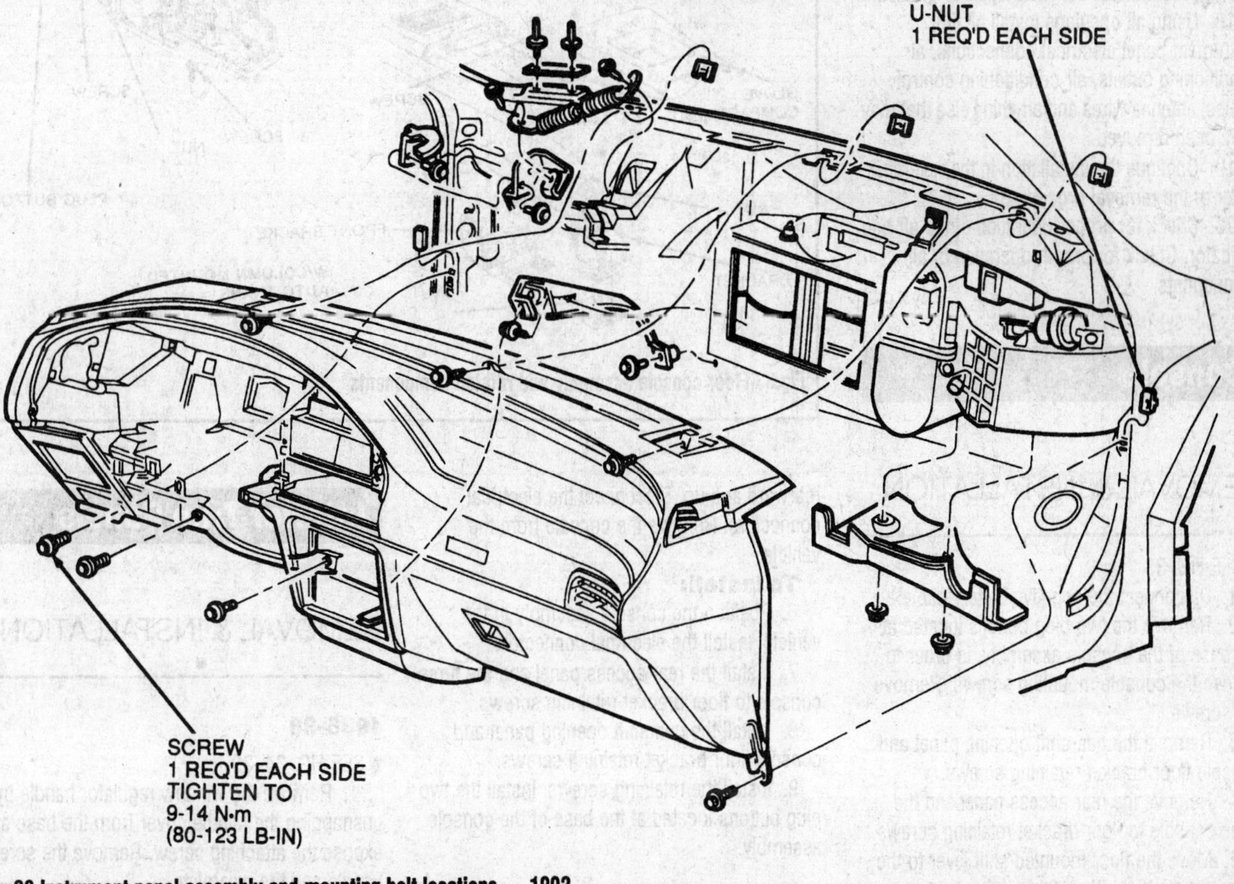

Fig.30 Instrument panel assembly and mounting bolt locations — 1992

9. Disconnect the wires of the main wire loom inside the engine compartment. Push the wires and the grommets inside to the interior of the vehicle.

10. Remove the right and left hand cowl sides. Remove the one screw retaining the instrument panel to the left side and the one screw on the right side.

11. Remove both speaker covers by pulling upward on them. Open the glove compartment door and allow it to hang open.

13. Remove the air cleaner, battery and battery tray from the vehicle.

14. Using all openings remove all the instrument panel electrical connections, air conditioning outlets, air conditioning control cables, antenna wires and anything else that may interfere with panel removal.

15. Close the glove compartment lid. Remove the three instrument panel screws at the top of the assembly. Disconnect any remaining electrical wires. Remove the instrument panel assembly from the vehicle.

To install:

16. Position the instrument panel in place. Connect the underhood electrical connections. Install the instrument panel upper screws. Install the instrument panel lower screws.

17. Install the lower brace and tighten the bolt to 5–8 ft. lbs. Install the radio speaker grilles.

18. Using all openings install all the instrument panel electrical connections, air conditioning outlets, air conditioning control cables, antenna wires and anything else that may have been removed.

19. Continue the installation in the reverse order of the removal procedure.

20. Check for proper operation of the air bag indicator. Check for proper operation of all components.

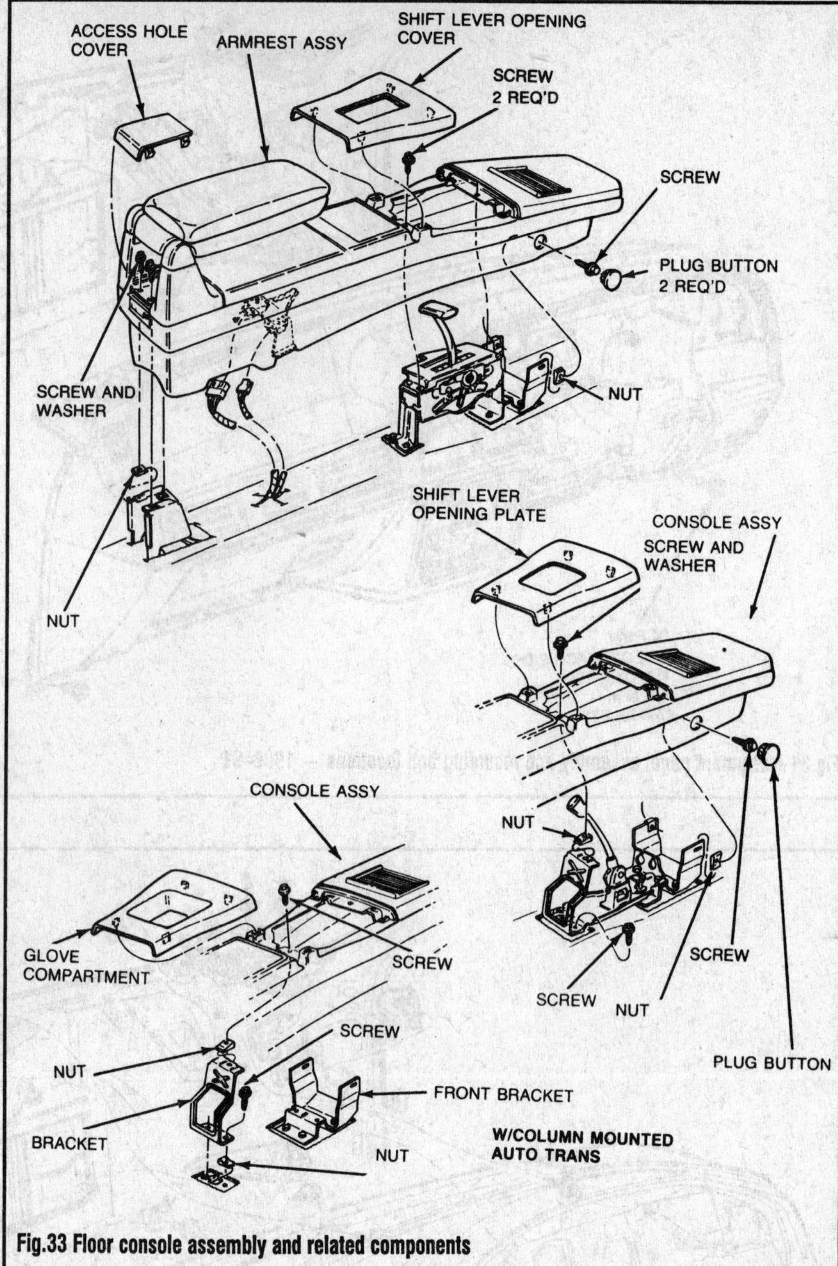

Fig.33 Floor console assembly and related components

Console

REMOVAL & INSTALLATION

➧ SEE FIG. 33

1. Disconnect the negative battery cable.

2. Remove the two plug buttons located at the base of the console assembly, in order to expose the console mounting screws. Remove the screws.

3. Remove the gearshift opening panel and console floor bracket retaining screws.

4. Remove the rear access panel and the three console to floor bracket retaining screws.

5. Move the floor mounted shift lever to the rearward most position. Slide the console rearward and up. Disconnect the electrical connectors. Remove the console from the vehicle.

To install:

6. Position the console assembly in the vehicle. Install the electrical connectors.

7. Install the rear access panel and the three console to floor bracket retaining screws.

8. Install the gearshift opening panel and console floor bracket retaining screws.

9. Install the retaining screws. Install the two plug buttons located at the base of the console assembly.

Interior Trim Panels

REMOVAL & INSTALLATION

1986–88

➧ SEE FIG. 34–39

1. Remove the window regulator handle by unsnapping the handle cover from the base and expose the attaching screw. Remove the screw, handle and the wearplate.

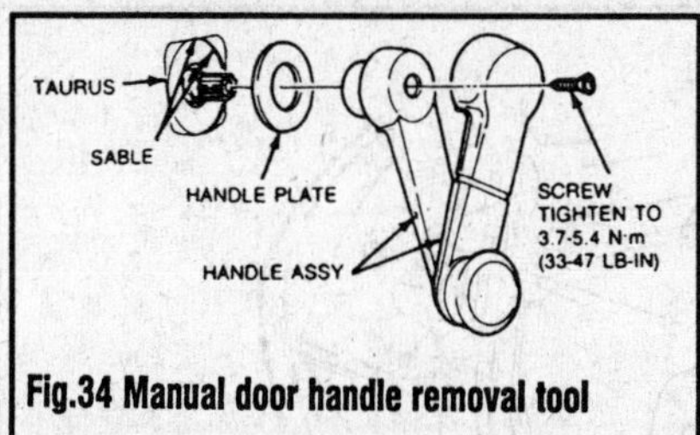

Fig.34 Manual door handle removal tool

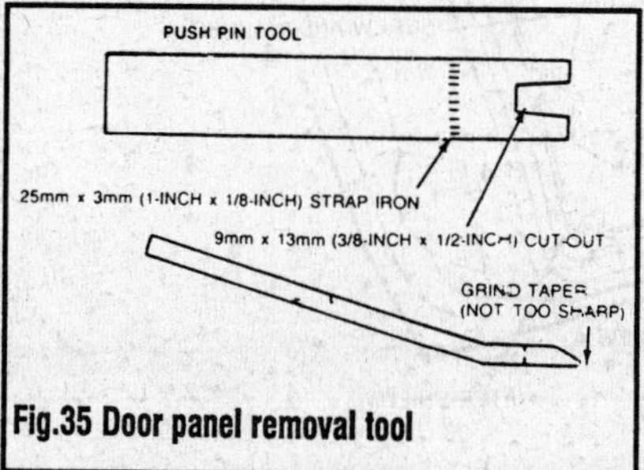

Fig.35 Door panel removal tool

2. Remove the door pull handle retaining screws and cover. Remove the handle.

3. Remove the upper trim panel retaining screws and remove the panel.

4. On Taurus vehicles, remove the trim panel opening panel.

5. Remove the exterior rearview mirror mounting hole cover retaining screw and the cover.

6. Remove all the screws retaining door trim panel to the door, using a door panel removing tool, pry the trim panel retaining push pins from door inner panel.

7. If the trim panel is to be replaced, transfer all the push pins to the new panel. Replace any bend, broken or missing push pins.

To Install:

1. Connect all door wiring and install the trim panel into position ensuring the upper ridge is seated properly in the door channel.

2. Snap the push pins in using your hand. Start at the top and move down the sides and make sure that the push pins align with the holes in the door before applying pressure.

3. Install all the screws retaining the trim panel-to-door.

4. Snap in the door handle retainer cover and install the retaining screws.

5. Snap in the front door lock control knob plate.

6. Install the outside rearview mirror mounting hole cover and retaining screws.

7. Install the window regulator handle (manual only) and snap in the handle cover.

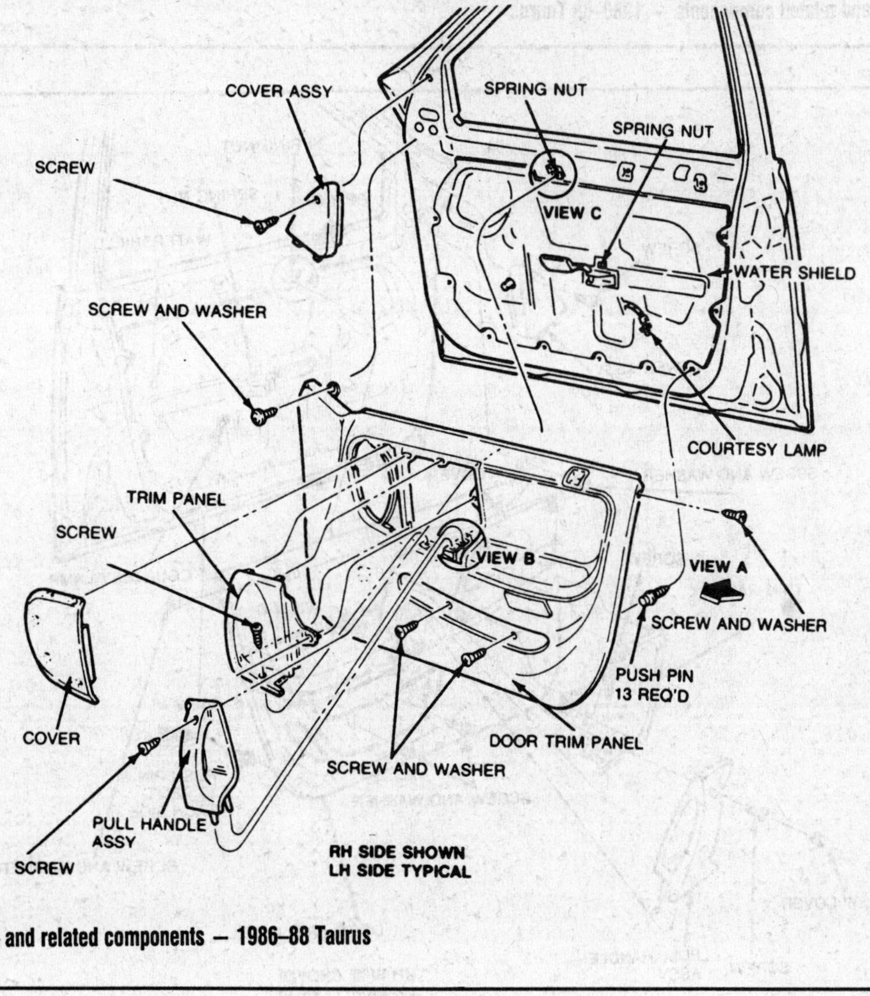

Fig.36 Front door panel and related components — 1986–88 Taurus

TRIM PANEL
DOOR TRIM PANEL ASSY
SCREW AND WASHER
SPRING NUT
SCREW
COVER
SCREW AND WASHER
SCREW
VIEW B
PULL HANDLE
SCREW
VIEW A
RH SHOWN LH TYPICAL
PUSH-PIN 11 REQ'D
WATER SHIELD

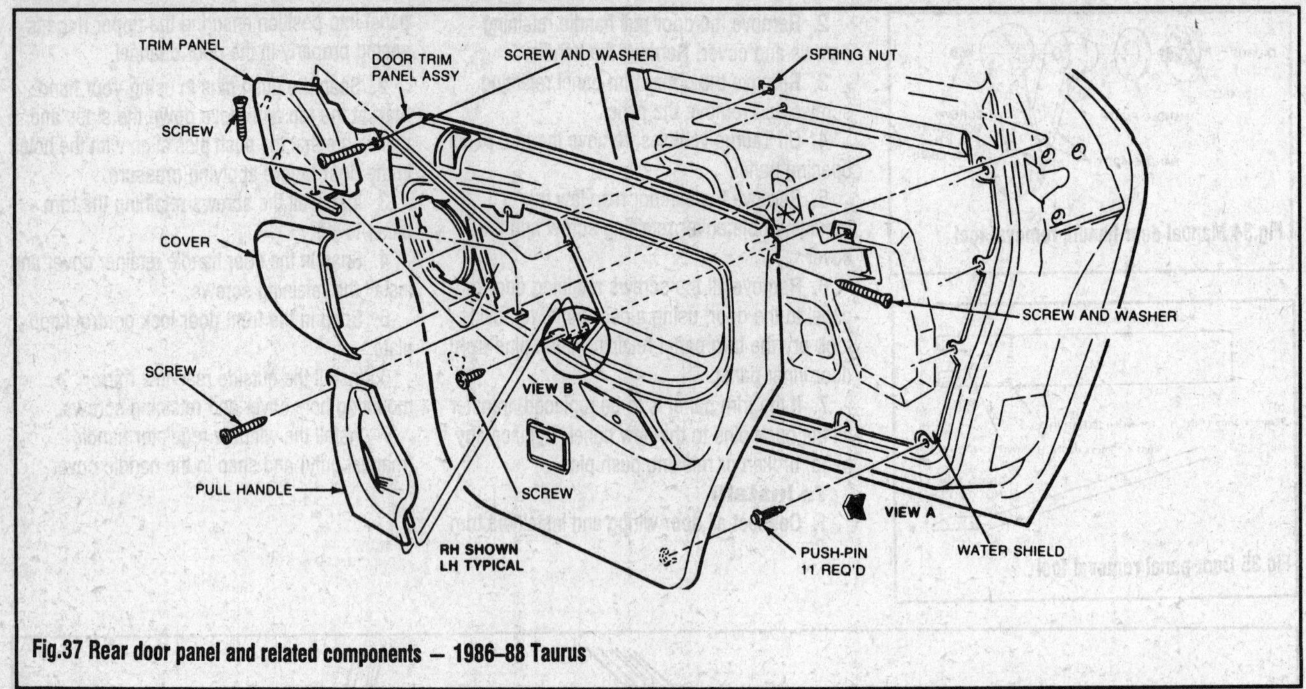

Fig.37 Rear door panel and related components – 1986–88 Taurus

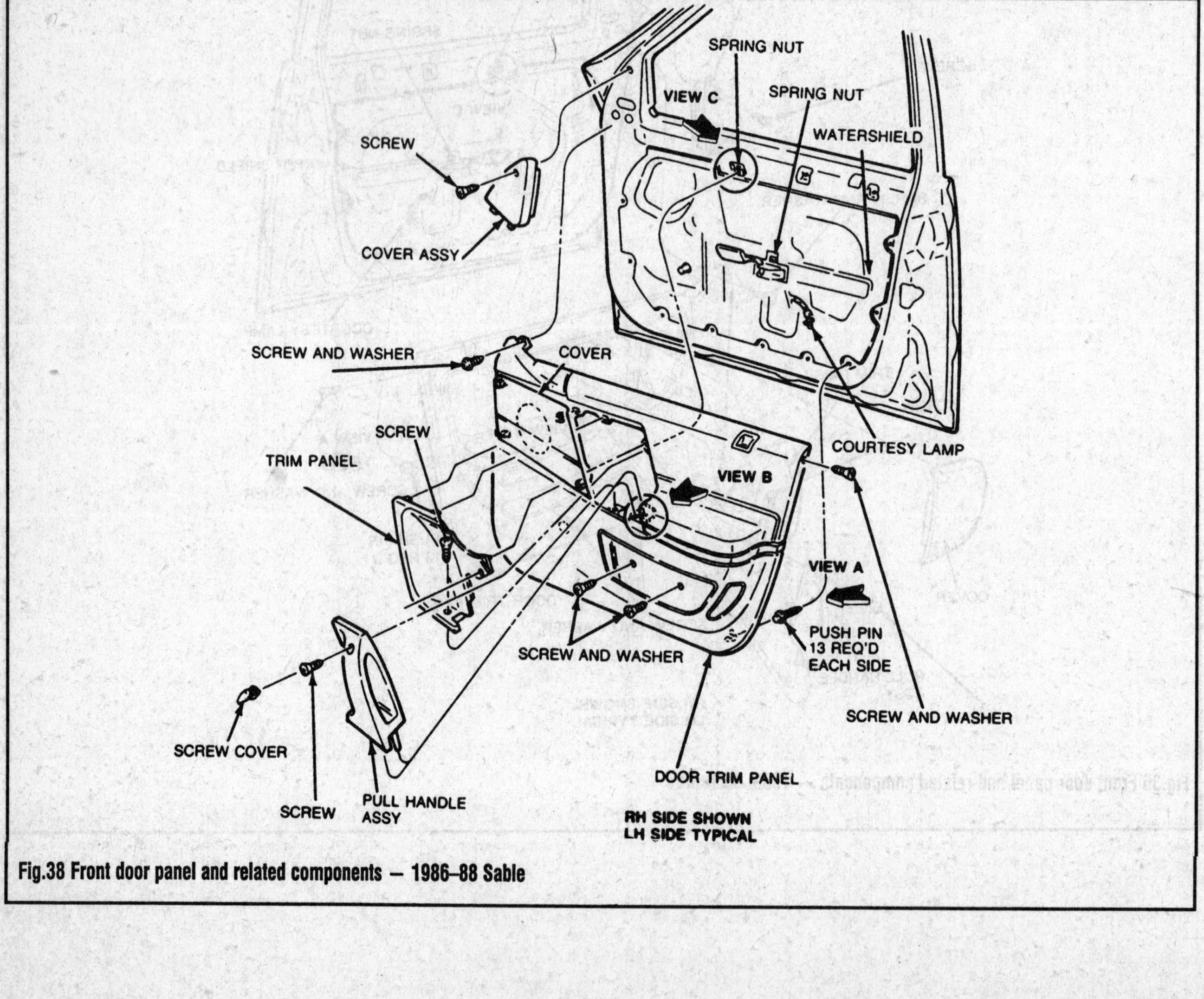

SPRING NUT
VIEW C
SPRING NUT
WATERSHIELD
SCREW
COVER ASSY
SCREW AND WASHER
COVER
SCREW
TRIM PANEL
COURTESY LAMP
VIEW B
VIEW A
PUSH PIN 13 REQ'D EACH SIDE
SCREW AND WASHER
SCREW AND WASHER
SCREW COVER
DOOR TRIM PANEL
SCREW
PULL HANDLE ASSY
RH SIDE SHOWN LH SIDE TYPICAL

Fig.38 Front door panel and related components – 1986–88 Sable

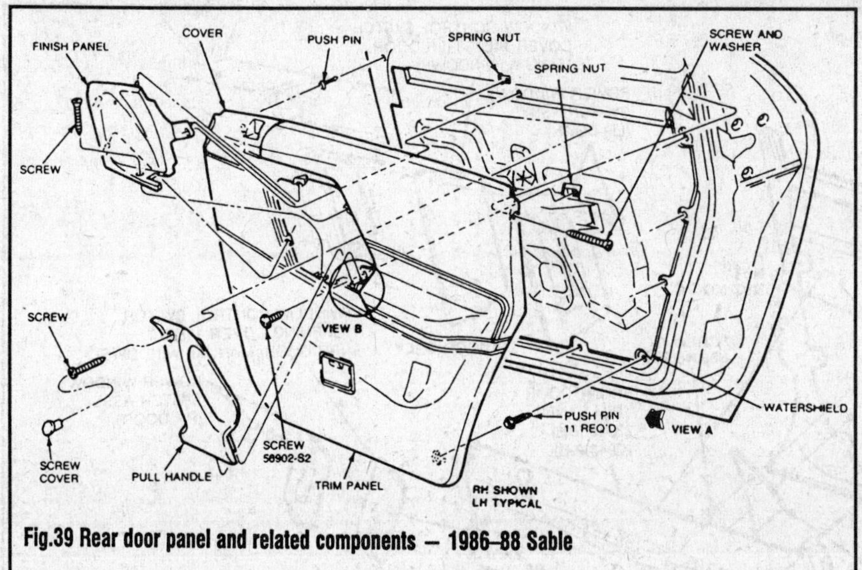

Fig.39 Rear door panel and related components — 1986–88 Sable

1989–92

➧ SEE FIG. 40–43

1. As required, remove the window regulator handle by unsnapping the handle cover from the base and expose the attaching screw. Remove the screw, handle and the wearplate.
2. On the front door panel, remove the outside rear view mirror mounting hole cover retaining screw and cover.
3. If equipped with power window, remove the housing and switch assembly. If equipped with power door locks, remove the housing and switch assembly.
4. Remove the door pull handle opening filler retaining screw. Remove the filler assembly. Snap out the door handle retainer cover.
5. Remove all the screws retaining door trim panel to the door, using a door panel removing tool, pry the trim panel retaining push pins from door inner panel.

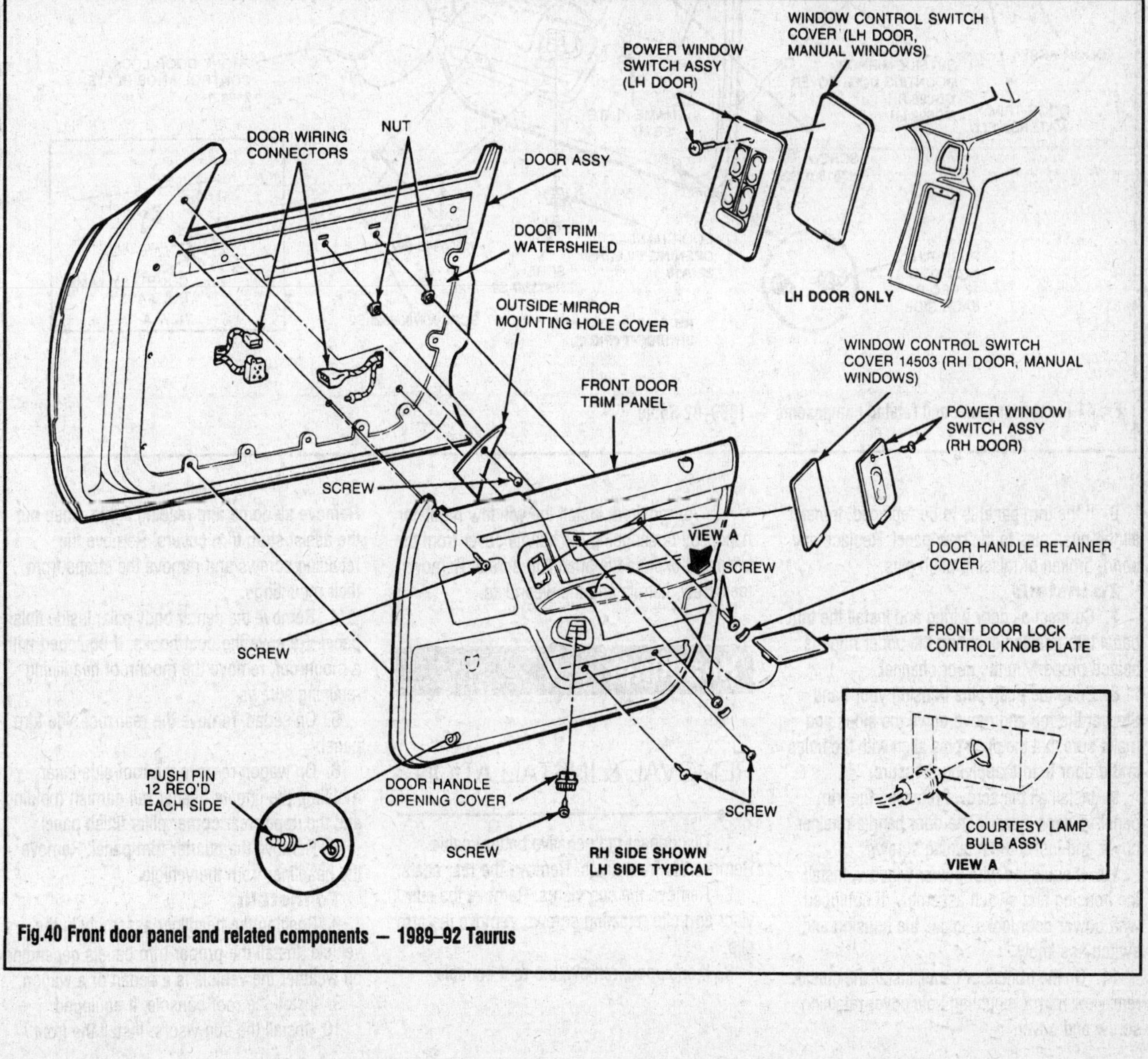

Fig.40 Front door panel and related components — 1989–92 Taurus

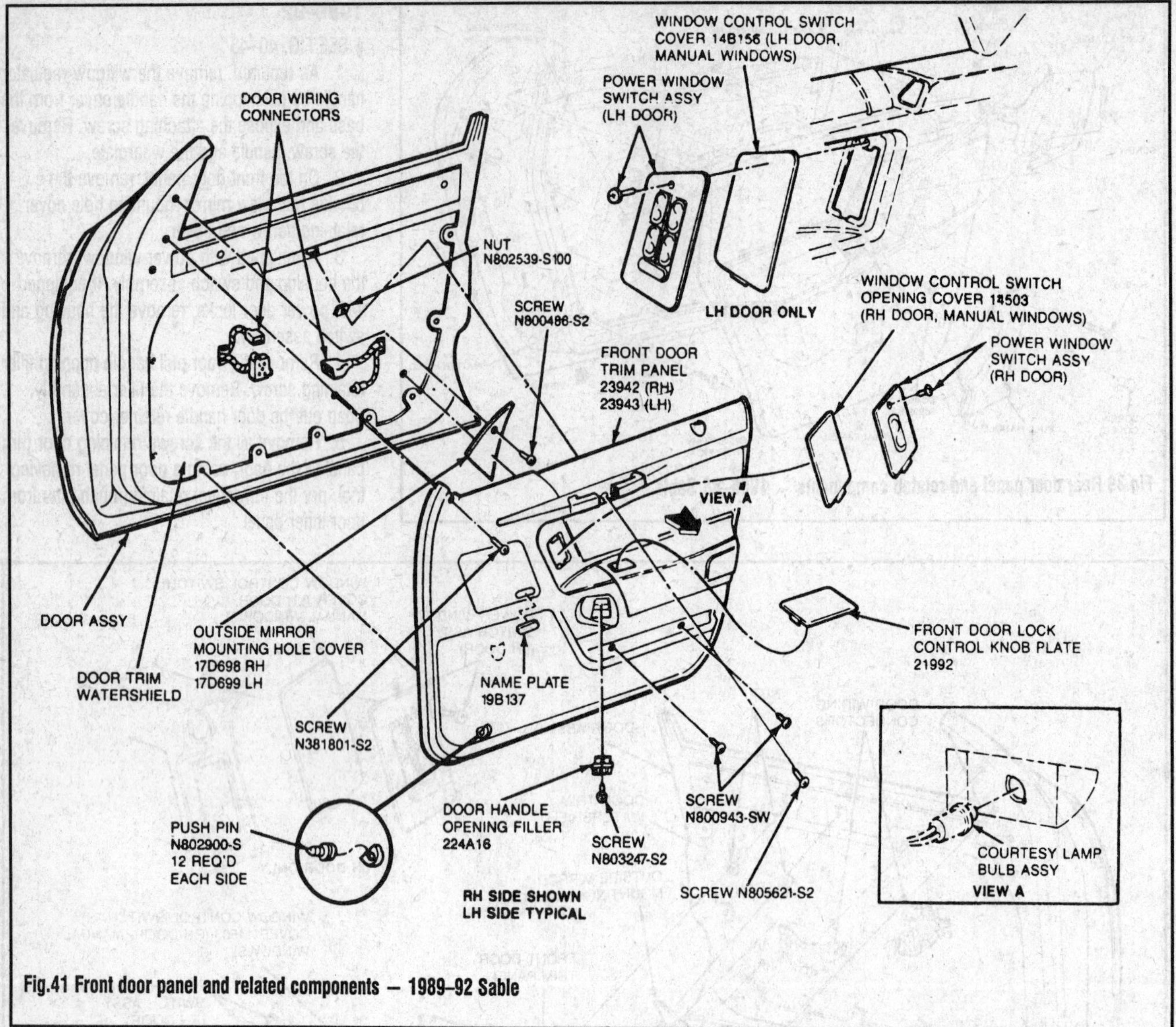

Fig.41 Front door panel and related components — 1989–92 Sable

6. If the trim panel is to be replaced, transfer all the push pins to the new panel. Replace any bend, broken or missing push pins.

To install:

7. Connect all door wiring and install the trim panel into position ensuring the upper ridge is seated properly in the door channel.
8. Snap the push pins in using your hand. Start at the top and move down the sides and make sure that the push pins align with the holes in the door before applying pressure.
9. Install all the screws retaining the trim panel-to-door. Snap in the door handle retainer cover and install the retaining screws.
10. If equipped with power window, install the housing and switch assembly. If equipped with power door locks, install the housing and switch assembly.
11. On the front door panel, install the outside rear view mirror mounting hole cover retaining screw and cover.
12. As required, install the window regulator handle by unsnapping the handle cover from the base and expose the attaching screw. Remove the screw, handle and the wearplate.

Headliner

REMOVAL & INSTALLATION

1. Disconnect the negative battery cable. Remove the front seats. Remove the rear seats.
2. Remove the sun visors. Remove the sun visor arm clip retaining screws, remove the arm clip.
3. If equipped, remove the roof console. Remove all dome and reading lights. Snap out the assist strap trim covers. Remove the retaining screws and remove the straps from their mountings.
4. Remove the center body pillar inside finish panel. Remove the coat hooks. If equipped with a moonroof, remove the moonroof headlining retaining screws.
5. On sedan, remove the rear roof side trim panel.
6. On wagon remove the roof side inner molding, the liftgate header rail garnish molding and the upper rear corner pillar finish panel.
7. Remove the quarter trim panel. Remove the headliner from the vehicle.

To Install:

8. Position the headliner assembly in the vehicle. Install the proper trim panels depending on weather the vehicle is a sedan or a wagon.
9. Install the roof console, if equipped.
10. Install the sun visors. Install the front

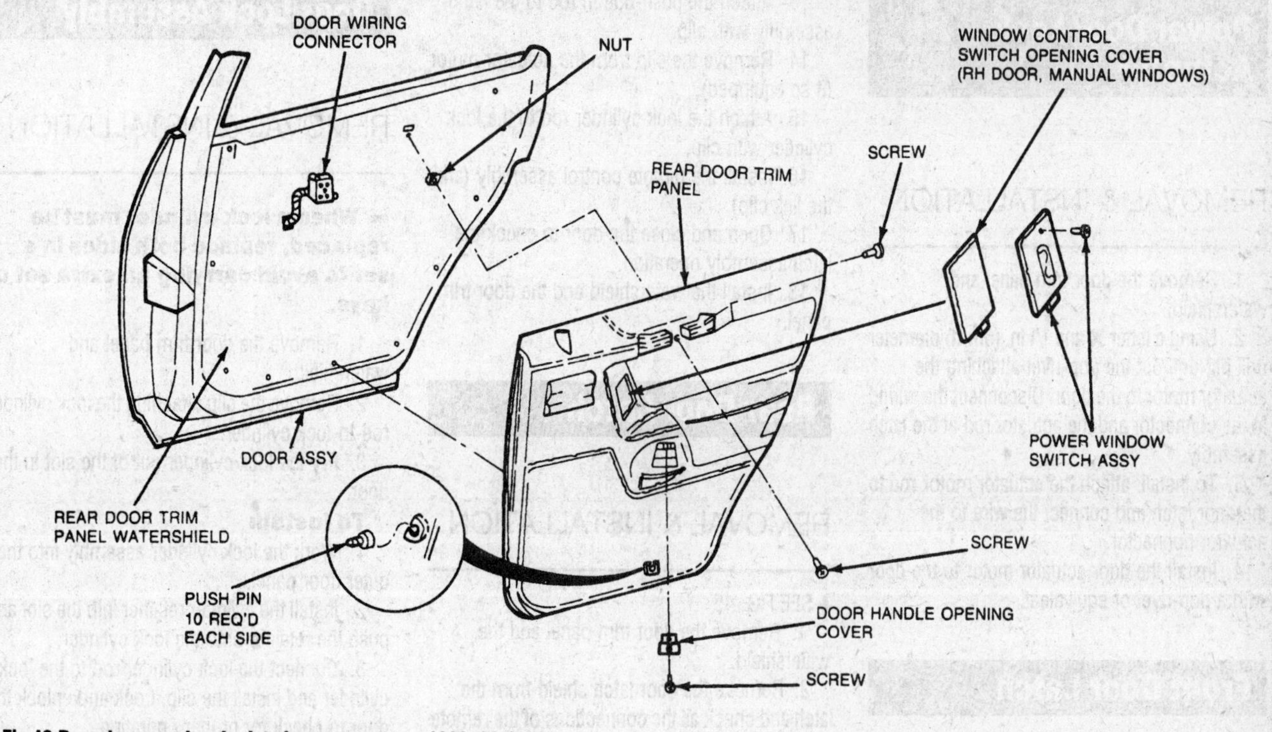

Fig.42 Rear door panel and related components — 1989–92 Sable

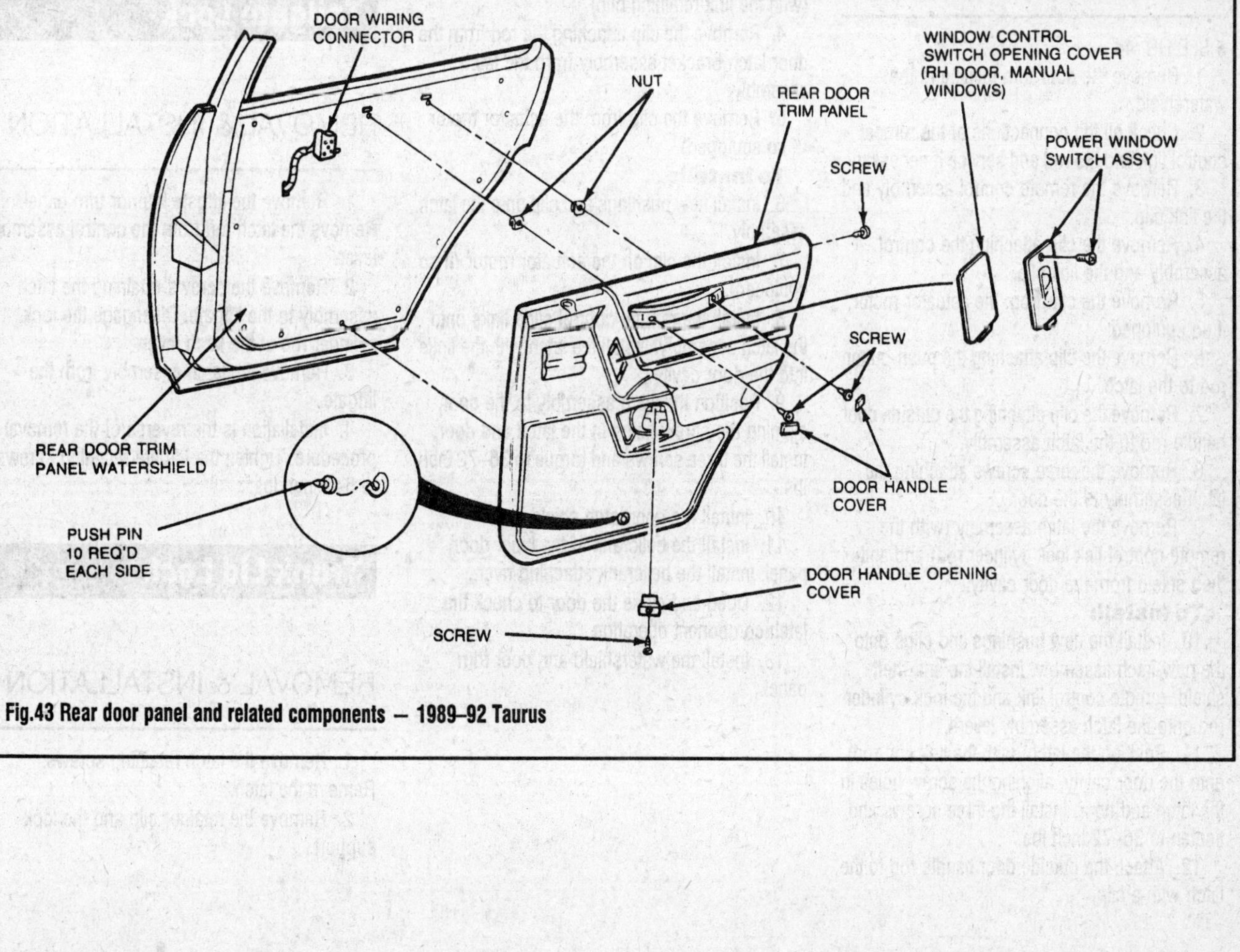

Fig.43 Rear door panel and related components — 1989–92 Taurus

Power Door Lock Actuator

REMOVAL & INSTALLATION

1. Remove the door trim panel and watershield.
2. Using a letter **X** and 1/4 in. (6mm) diameter drill bit, drill out the pop-rivet attaching the actuator motor to the door. Disconnect the wiring at the connector and the actuator rod at the latch assembly.
3. To install, attach the actuator motor rod to the door latch and connect the wire to the actuator connector.
4. Install the door actuator motor to the door with a pop-rivet or equivalent.

Front Door Latch

REMOVAL & INSTALLATION

➧ SEE FIG. 44

1. Remove the door trim panel and the watershield.
2. Check all the connections of the remote control link and the rod and service if necessary.
3. Remove the remote control assembly and the link clip.
4. Remove the clip attaching the control assembly and the link clip.
5. Remove the clip from the actuator motor, if so equipped.
6. Remove the clip attaching the push-button rod to the latch.
7. Remove the clip attaching the outside door handle rod to the latch assembly.
8. Remove the three screws attaching the latch assembly to the door.
9. Remove the latch assembly (with the remote control link lock cylinder rod) and anti-theft shield from the door cavity.

To install:

10. Install the new bushings and clips onto the new latch assembly. Install the anti-theft shield, remote control link and the lock cylinder rod onto the latch assembly levers.
11. Position the latch (with the link and rod) onto the door cavity, aligning the screw holes in the latch and door. Install the three screws and tighten to 36–72 inch lbs.
12. Attach the outside door handle rod to the latch with a clip.
13. Attach the push-button rod to the latch assembly with clip.
14. Remove the clip from the actuator motor (if so equipped).
15. Attach the lock cylinder rod to the lock cylinder with clip.
16. Install the remote control assembly (and the link clip).
17. Open and close the door to check the latch assembly operation.
18. Install the watershield and the door trim panel.

Rear Door Latch

REMOVAL & INSTALLATION

➧ SEE FIG. 45

1. Remove the door trim panel and the watershield.
2. Remove the door latch shield from the latch and check all the connections of the remote control links and rods. Service them as necessary.
3. Remove the remote control assembly (with the link retaining clip).
4. Remove the clip attaching the rod from the door latch bracket assembly from the latch assembly.
5. Remove the clip from the actuator motor (if so equipped).

To install:

6. Install new bushings and clip onto the latch assembly.
7. Install the clip on the actuator motor (if so equipped).
8. Install the remote control slide links onto the latch assembly. Install the latch with the links into the door cavity.
9. Position the latch assembly to the door, aligning the screw holes in the latch and door. Install the three screws and torque to 36–72 inch lbs.
10. Install the door latch shield.
11. Install the bellcrank to the inner door panel. Install the bellcrank attaching rivet.
12. Open and close the door to check the latch component operation.
13. Install the watershield and door trim panel.

Door Lock Assembly

REMOVAL & INSTALLATION

➡ When a lock cylinder must be replaced, replace both sides in a set to avoid carrying an extra set of keys.

1. Remove the door trim panel and watershield.
2. Remove the clip attaching the lock cylinder rod-to-lock cylinder.
3. Pry the lock cylinder out of the slot in the door.

To install:

1. Work the lock cylinder assembly into the outer door panel.
2. Install the cylinder retainer into the slot and push the retainer onto the lock cylinder.
3. Connect the lock cylinder rod to the lock cylinder and install the clip. Lock and unlock the door to check for proper operation.
4. Install the watershield and door trim panel.

Tailgate Lock

REMOVAL & INSTALLATION

1. Remove the liftgate interior trim panel. Remove the latch rod from the control assembly lever.
2. Remove the screws retaining the latch assembly to the liftgate. Disengage the lock cylinder rod at the latch lever.
3. Remove the latch assembly from the liftgate.
4. Installation is the reverse of the removal procedure. Tighten the liftgate retaining screws to 5–8 inch lbs.

Trunk Lid Lock

REMOVAL & INSTALLATION

1. Remove the latch retaining screws. Remove the latch.
2. Remove the retainer clip and the lock support.

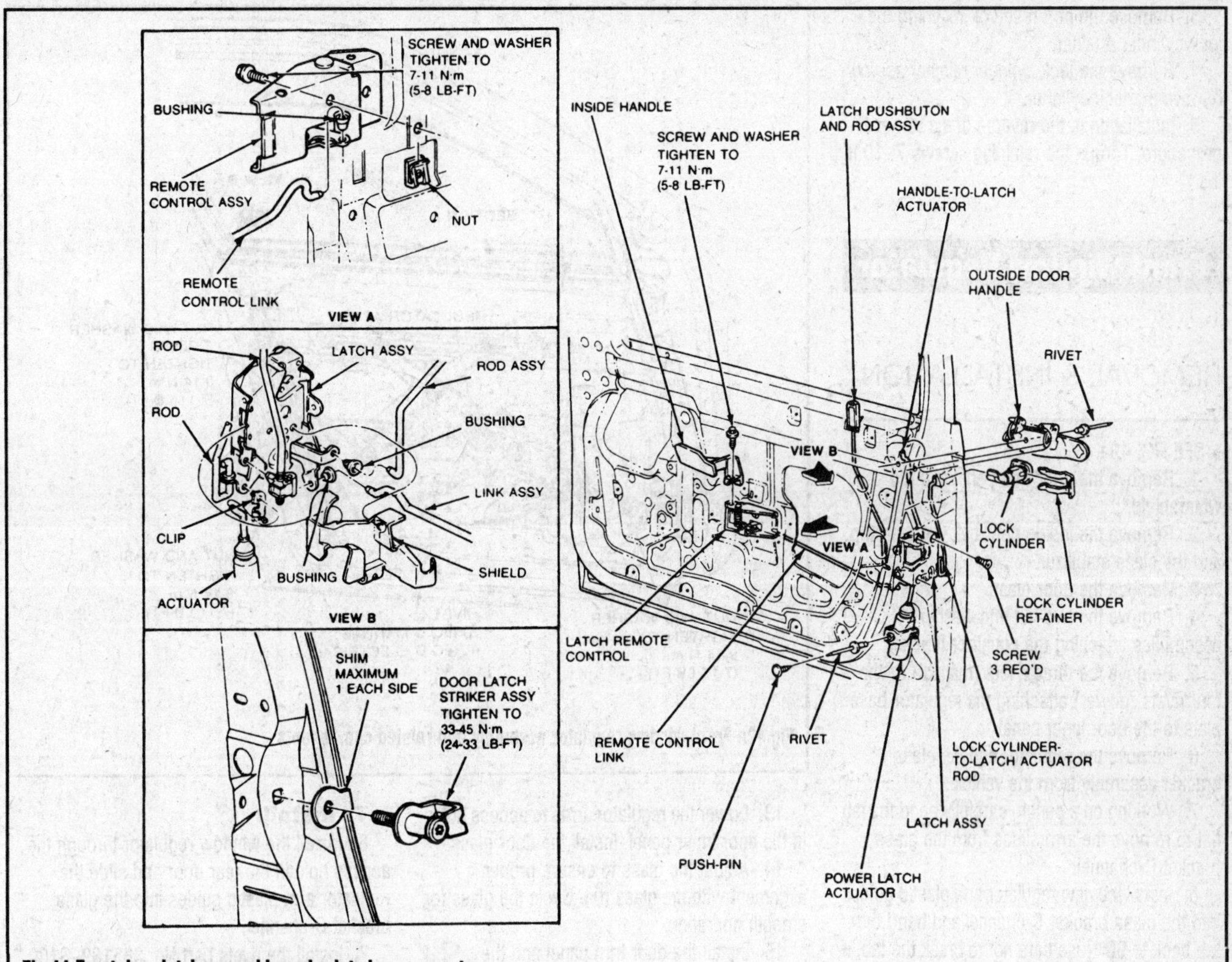

SCREW AND WASHER
TIGHTEN TO
7-11 N·m
(5-8 LB-FT)
BUSHING
REMOTE
CONTROL ASSY
NUT
REMOTE
CONTROL LINK
VIEW A
ROD
LATCH ASSY
ROD ASSY
ROD
BUSHING
LINK ASSY
CLIP
BUSHING
SHIELD
ACTUATOR
VIEW B
SHIM
MAXIMUM
1 EACH SIDE
DOOR LATCH
STRIKER ASSY
TIGHTEN TO
33-45 N·m
(24-33 LB-FT)
INSIDE HANDLE
SCREW AND WASHER
TIGHTEN TO
7-11 N·m
(5-8 LB-FT)
LATCH PUSHBUTON
AND ROD ASSY
HANDLE-TO-LATCH
ACTUATOR
OUTSIDE DOOR
HANDLE
RIVET
VIEW B
VIEW A
LOCK
CYLINDER
LOCK CYLINDER
RETAINER
SCREW
3 REQ'D
LATCH REMOTE
CONTROL
REMOTE CONTROL
LINK
RIVET
LOCK CYLINDER-
TO-LATCH ACTUATOR
ROD
LATCH ASSY
PUSH-PIN
POWER LATCH
ACTUATOR

Fig.44 Front door latch assembly and related components

BUTTON AND LINK
ASSY
SCREW AND WASHER
TIGHTEN TO 7-11 N·m
(5-8 LB-FT)
HANDLE
OUTSIDE HANDLE
LATCH ASSY
RIVET
2 REQ'D
VIEW B
VIEW A
SCREW
3 REQ'D TIGHTEN TO
4-8 N·m (3-5.8 LB-FT)
DOOR LOCK DECAL
ROD ASSY
LINK ASSY
REMOTE CONTROL
ASSY
PUSH-PIN
RIVET
POWER LATCH
ACTUATOR
RIVET
SCREW AND WASHER
TIGHTEN TO 7-11 N·m
(5-8 LB-FT)
HANDLE ASSY
BUSHING
LINK ASSY
NUT
VIEW A
LATCH ASSY
CLIP
BELL CRANK AND
LINK ASSY
HANDLE ASSY
LINK ASSY
SHIELD
CLIP
ACTUATOR ASSY
VIEW B

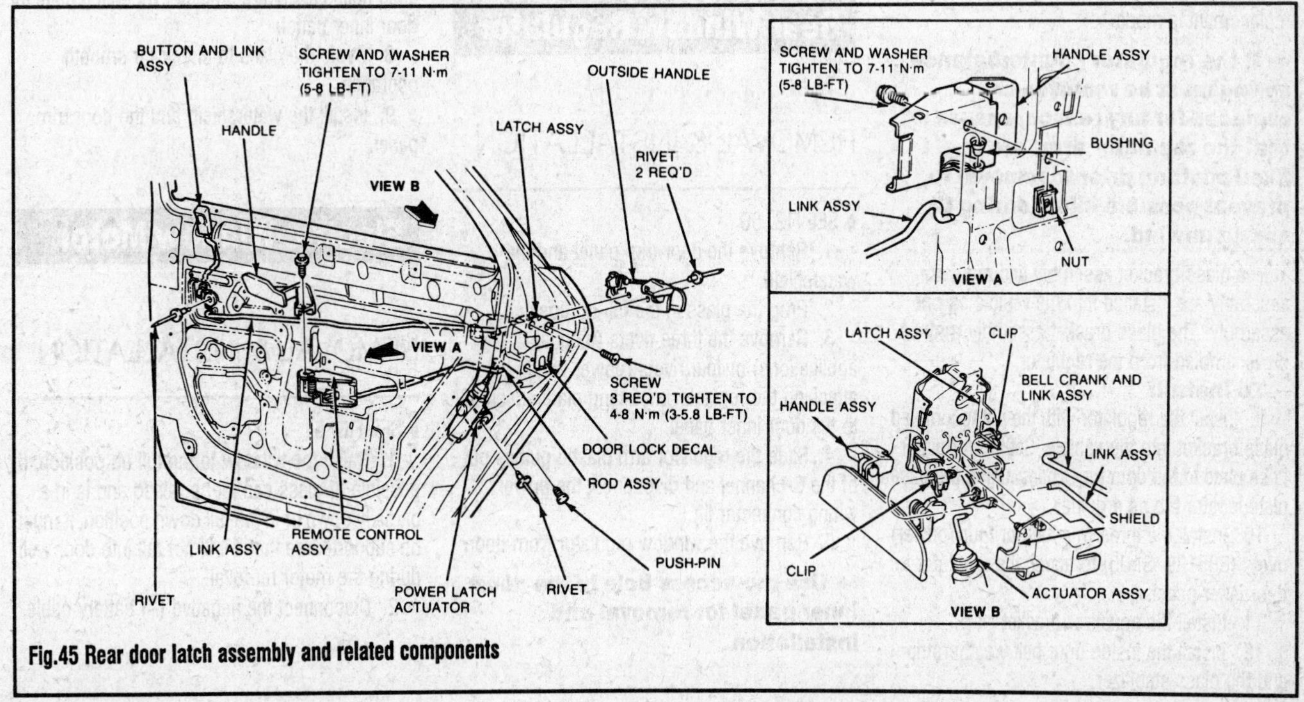

Fig.45 Rear door latch assembly and related components

3. Remove the pop reservoir retaining the lock cylinder retainer.
4. Remove the lock cylinder retainer as you remove the lock cylinder.
5. Installation is the reverse of the removal procedure. Torque the retaining screws 7–10 ft. lbs.

Front Window Regulator

REMOVAL & INSTALLATION

➧ SEE FIG. 49a

1. Remove the door trim panel and the watershield.
2. Remove the inside door belt weatherstrip and the glass stabilizer.
3. Remove the door glass.
4. Remove the two nut and washer assemblies attaching the equalizer bracket.
5. Remove the three rivets (manual) or the four rivets (power) attaching the regulator base plate to the door inner panel.
6. Remove the regulator and the glass bracket assembly from the vehicle.
7. Working on a bench, carefully bend the tab flat to remove the arm slides from the glass bracket C-channel.
8. Install the new regulator arm plastic guides into the glass bracket C-channel and bend the tab back to 90° (use care not to break the tab, if the tab is cracked or broken, replace the glass bracket assembly. Ensure the rubber bumper is installed properly on the new glass bracket, if a replacement is made.

➡ If the regulator counterbalance spring must be removed or replaced for any reason, ensure that the regulator arms are in a fixed position prior to removal to prevent possible injury during C-spring unwind.

The glass bracket assembly and regulator assembly are installed into the vehicle as one assembly. The glass bracket assembly may be disassembled from the regulator.

To install:

9. Install the regulator with the preassembled glass bracket into the vehicle. Set the regulator base plate to the door inner panel using the base plate locator tab as a guide.
10. Install the three (manual) or four (power) rivets (385189–S100) to attach the regulator to door inner panel.
11. Install the equalizer bracket.
12. Install the inside door belt weatherstrip and the glass stabilizer.

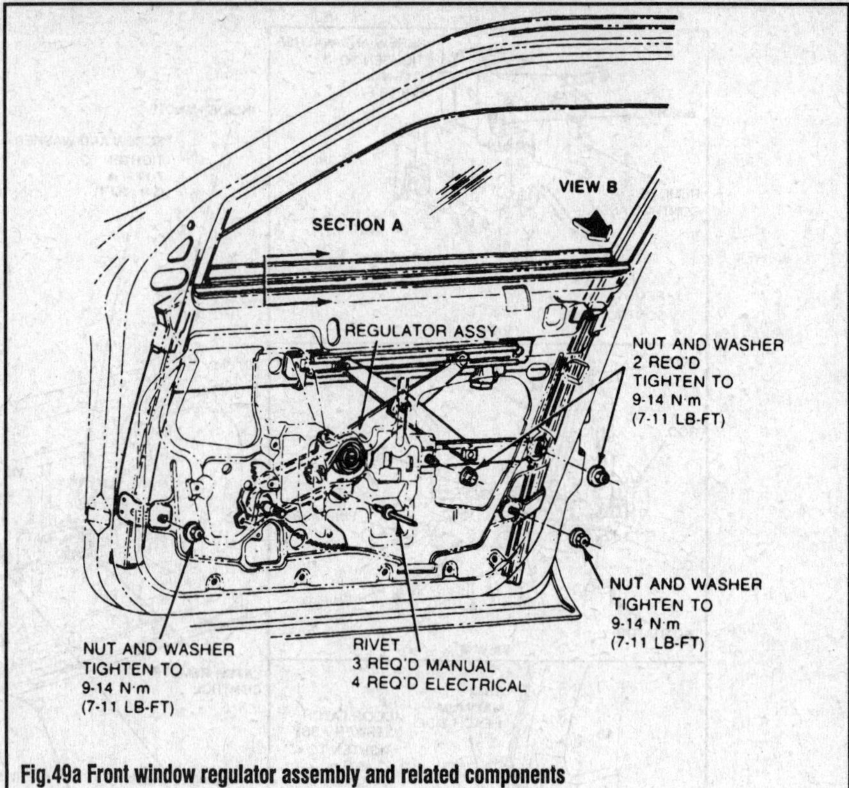

Fig.49a Front window regulator assembly and related components

13. Lower the regulator arms to access holes in the door inner panel. Install the door glass.
14. Adjust the glass to ensure proper alignment with the glass run. Cycle the glass for smooth operation.
15. Install the door trim panel and the watershield.

Rear Window Regulator

REMOVAL & INSTALLATION

➧ SEE FIG. 50

1. Remove the door trim panel and the watershield.
2. Prop the glass in the full-up position.
3. Remove the three rivets (manual applications) or four rivets (power windows) attaching the regulator mounting plate assembly to the door inner panel.
4. Slide the regulator arm plastic guides out of the C-channel and disconnect the power wiring connector lift.
5. Remove the window regulator from door.

➡ Use the access hole in the door inner panel for removal and installation.

To install:

6. Install the window regulator through the access hole in the rear door and slide the regulator arm plastic guides into the glass bracket C-channel.
7. Install the rivets part No. 385189–S100 using Heavy Duty Riveter D80L–23200–A or equivalent, or $^1/_4$–20 x $^1/_2$ in. screw and washer assemblies to secure regulator mounting plate to door inner panel.
8. Cycle the glass to check for smooth operation.
9. Install the watershield and the door trim panel.

Electric Window Motor

REMOVAL & INSTALLATION

➧ SEE FIG. 51

1. Raise the window to the full up position, if possible. If glass cannot be raised and is in a partially down or in the full down position, it must be supported so that it will not fall into door well during the motor removal.
2. Disconnect the negative (–) battery cable.

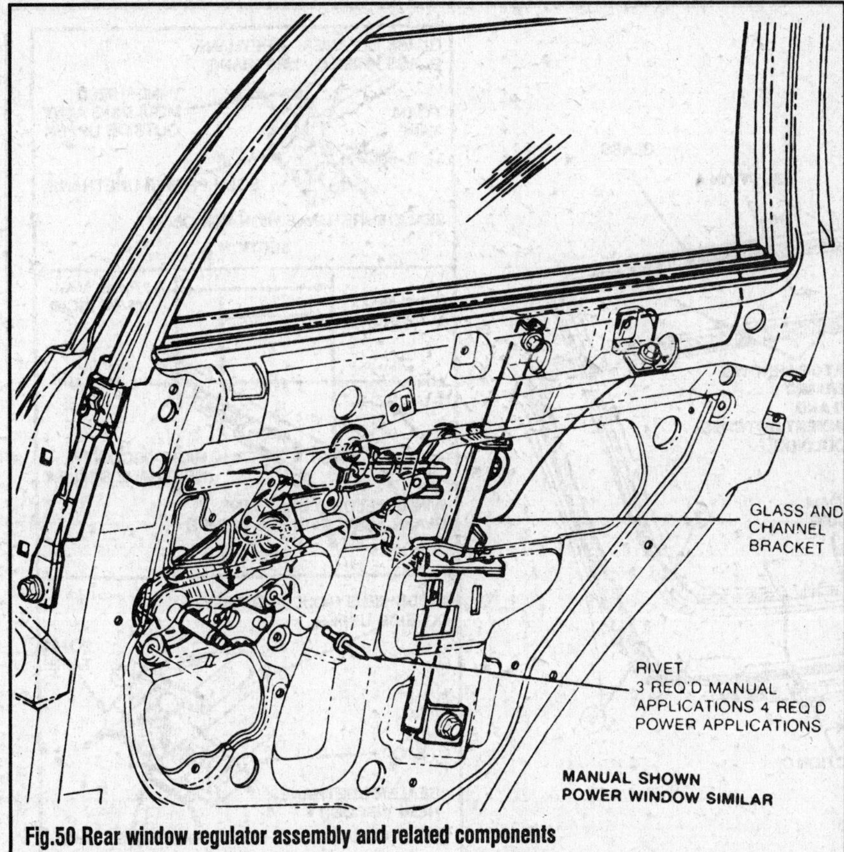

Fig.50 Rear window regulator assembly and related components

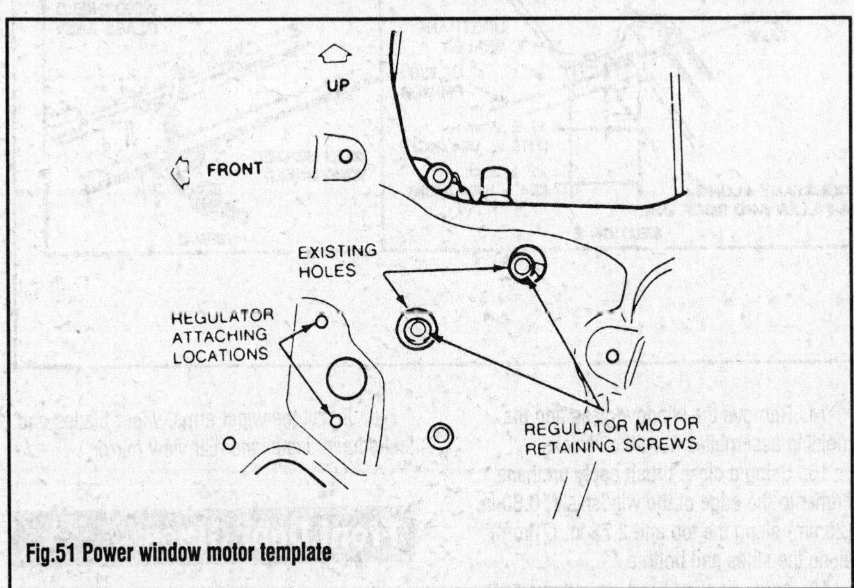

Fig.51 Power window motor template

3. Remove the door trim panel and watershield.

4. Remove the two forward regulator mounting plate attaching rivets. Use a 1/4 in. (6mm) drill bit and drill out the attaching rivets.

➡ **Prior to motor drive assembly removal, ensure that the regulator arm is in a fixed position to prevent dangerous counterbalance spring unwind!**

5. Remove the three window motor mounting screws.

6. Push the regulator mounting plate outboard sufficiently to remove the power window motor.

To install:

7. Install the new motor and drive assembly. Tighten the three motor mounting screws to 50–85 inch lbs.

8. Install the two regulator mounting plate rivets part No. 385189–S100 using a Heavy Duty Riveter No. D80L–23200–A or equivalent. A 1/4–20 × 1/2 in. screw and washer assembly may be used to secure the motor to the drive assembly.

9. Connect the window motor wiring leads.

10. Connect the negative (–) battery cable.

11. Check the power window for proper operation.

12. Install the door trim panel and the watershield.

➡ **Verify that all the drain holes at bottom of doors are open to prevent water accumulation over the motor.**

Windshield Glass

REMOVAL & INSTALLATION

➧ SEE FIG. 52

1. Disconnect the negative battery cable. Remove the windshield wiper arms and blades.

2. Remove all windshield trim moldings. Remove the leaf screen. Remove the interior mirror.

3. Using a three foot length of single strand music wire, smallest diameter available. Cut the urethane seal and rubber seal around the entire edge of the windshield.

4. Be sure that you are wearing safety glasses. Force the music wire through the seal at the bottom of the windshield. With someone holding the wire inside the vehicle and the other person holding the wire outside the vehicle move the wire along the bottom and then along the sides and top of the windshield to cut the seal.

5. Using tool D81T–33610–H or a glass holding tool, remove the windshield from the vehicle.

To install:

6. If the existing urethane remains on the windshield opening flange, the new urethane can be applied over it, but at no time should the thickness of the material be above 0.10 in. (2.5mm).

7. Using a clean brush apply urethane metal primer ESB–M2G234–A or equivalent to any sheet metal that has been exposed along the windshield.

8. Apply vinyl foam tape C6AZ–19627–A or equivalent that meets Ford Motor Company's specification ESB–M3G77–A along the cowl and lower A pillars about 4 in. (102mm).

9. Allow the primer to dry for a minimum of about 30 minutes.

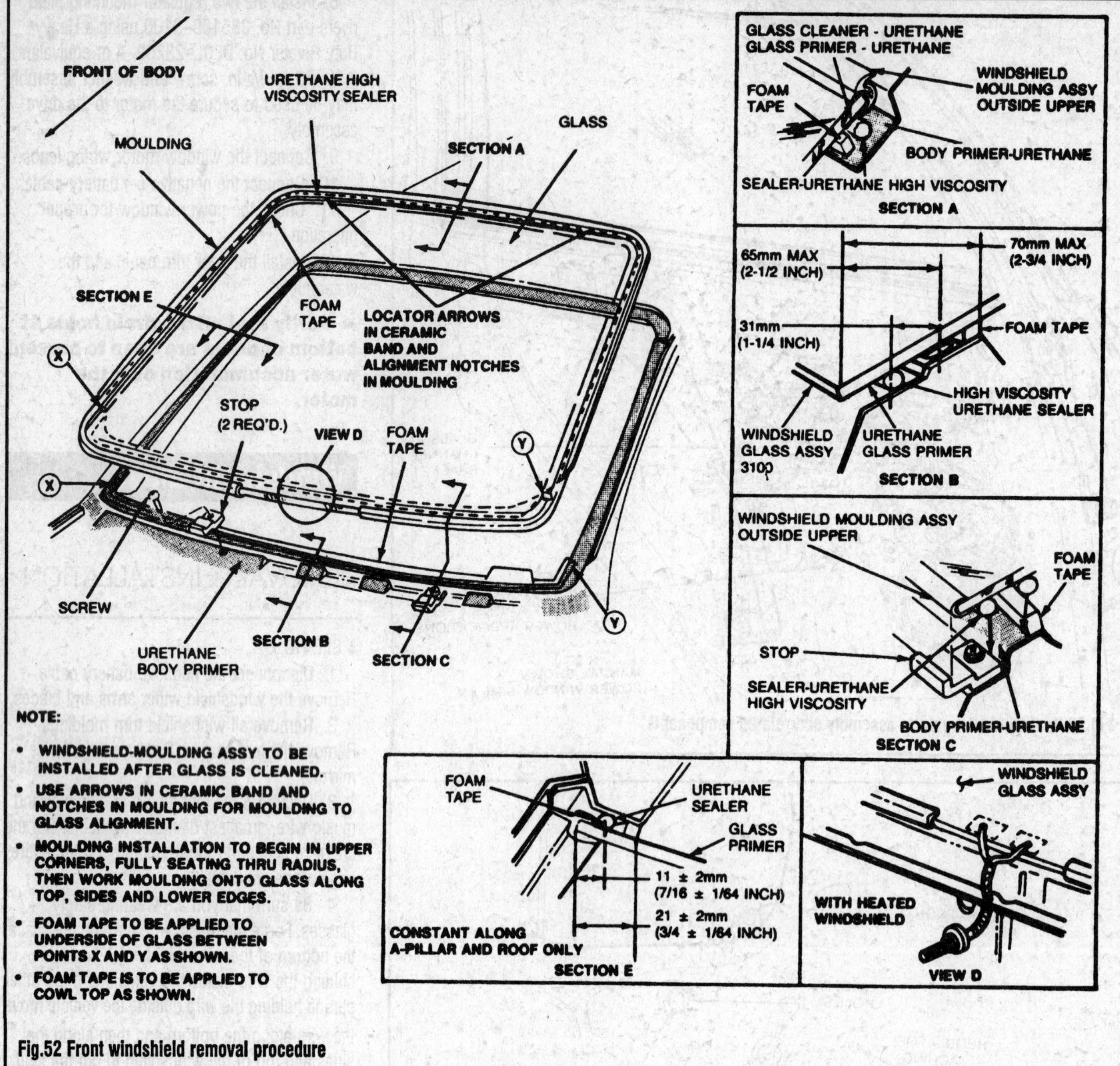

Fig.52 Front windshield removal procedure

10. Be sure that the windshield is clean and free of any dirt or used material. Install the rear view mirror mounting bracket, as required.

11. Using a lint free rag wipe the inside edge of the windshield, 0.80 in. (20mm) along the top and 2.75 in. (70mm) along the sides and bottom with urethane glass wipe ESB–M5B280–A. Wipe off immediately after application because this material will flash dry.

12. Install the windshield molding. Position the glass on top of the lower glass stops. Center it top and bottom and side to side. Adjust the lower glass stops, as required.

13. Using crayon make alignment marks at points on four sides of both the glass and the window opening.

14. Remove the window glass and the molding assemblies from the vehicle.

15. Using a clean brush apply urethane primer to the edge of the windshield, 0.80 in. (20mm) along the top and 2.75 in. (70mm) along the sides and bottom.

16. Apply an even bead of urethane ESB–M2G316–A around the entire sheet metal flange using an air pressure cartridge gun, air pressure should be about 40 psi. The bead should be triangular in shape 0.55 in. (14mm) high, and 0.33 in. (8mm) at the base.

17. Apply a double bead of urethane along the cowl top and bottom of the opening. Install the windshield taking care to align the glass with the alignment marks. This must be done within 15 minutes of applying the urethane.

18. Install the wiper arms, wiper blades and leaf screen. Install the rear view mirror.

Front Door Glass

REMOVAL & INSTALLATION

➧ SEE FIG. 46

1. Remove the door trim panel and the watershield.
2. Remove the inside door belt weatherstrip assembly.
3. Lower the glass to access the holes in the

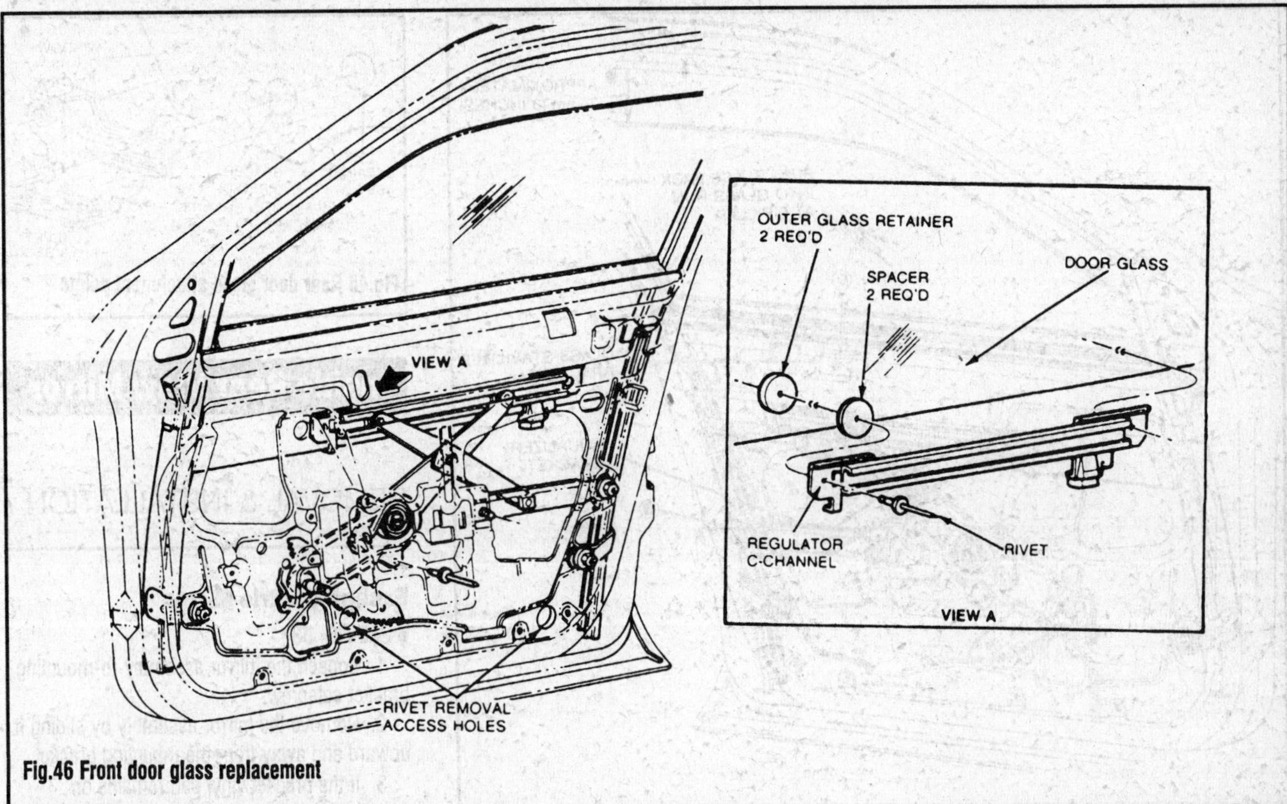

Fig.46 Front door glass replacement

door inner panel. Remove the two rivets retaining the glass to glass bracket.

➡ **Prior to removing the center pins from the rivets, it is recommended that a suitable block support be inserted between the door outer panel and glass bracket to stabilizer glass during rivet removal. Remove the center pin from each rivet using a drift punch. Using a 1/4 in. (6mm) diameter drill, drill out the remaining rivets. Use care when drilling out the rivets to prevent enlarging the bracket and spacer holes and damaging the retainer.**

4. Loosen the nut and washer retaining the door glass stabilizer.
5. Remove the glass by tipping it forward then removing it from between the door belt opening to the outboard side of door.
6. Remove the drilling and pins the from bottom of door.

To install:

1. Snap the plastic retainer and spacer into the two glass retainer holes. Ensure that the metal washer within the retainer assembly is on the outboard side of glass.
2. Install the glass into the door at belt. Ensure that the glass is set within the front and rear glass run retainers.
3. Position the glass to the glass bracket. Install the two rivets to secure the glass to glass bracket.

➡ **Two 1/4-20 x 1 in. bolts and two 1/4-20 nuts and washer assemblies may be used as alternates for glass retention. However, torque must not exceed 36–61 inch lbs. Equivalent metric retainers may be used.**

10. Install the inside door belt weatherstrip assembly.
11. Raise the glass to within 75mm of the full–up position and adjust glass as outlined below.
12. Install the door trim panel and watershield.

ADJUSTMENT

➧ SEE FIG. 47

1. Remove the door trim panel and the watershield.
2. Lower the door glass approximately 75mm from the full-up position.
3. Loosen the nut and washer assemblies **A** and **B** retaining the equalizer bracket to the door inner panel. Refer to the following door glass adjustment illustration.
4. Loosen the nut and washer assembly **C** retaining the door glass stabilizer.
5. With the door open, place your hands on each side of the glass and pull the glass fully into the door glass run assembly at the B-pillar.
6. Tighten the nut and washer **A**, then apply a downward pressure on the equalizer bracket and tighten the nut and washer **B** to 5–8 ft. lbs.
7. Set the door glass stabilizer so that it is slightly touching the glass and tighten the nut and washer assembly to 5–8 ft. lbs.
8. Cycle the door glass to ensure proper function and door fit.

Rear Door Glass

REMOVAL & INSTALLATION

1. Remove the door trim panel and the watershield.
2. Remove the inner door belt weatherstrip by gently pulling the weatherstrip from the door flange.
3. Remove the glass-to-glass bracket attaching rivets.

➡ **Prior to removing rivet center pins, a suitable block support should be inserted between the door outer panel and glass to**

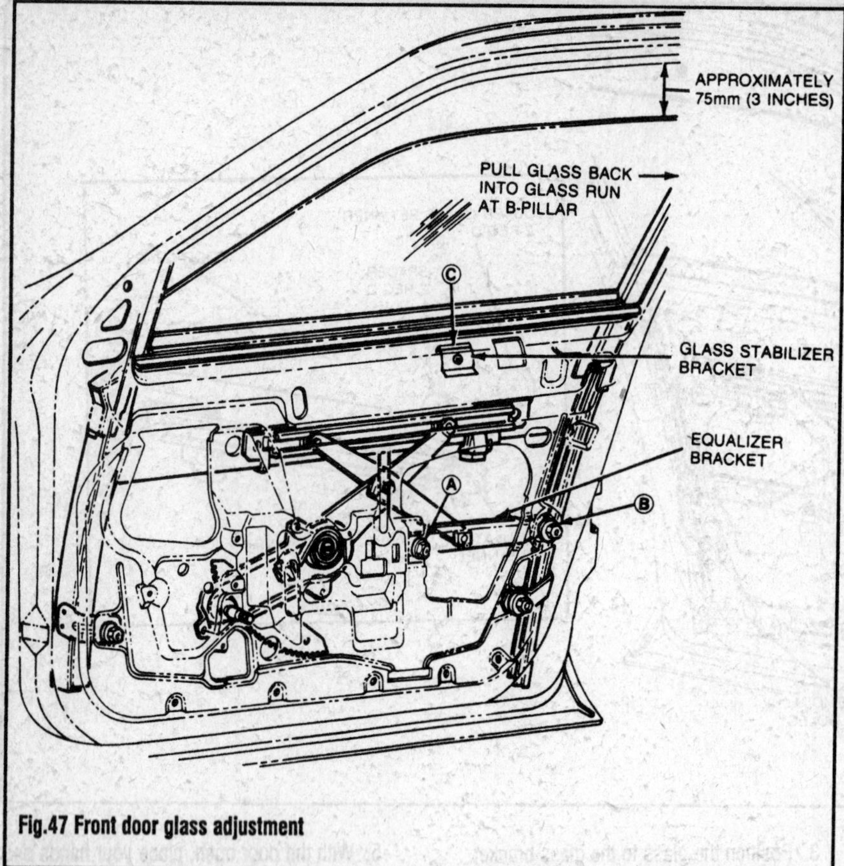

Fig.47 Front door glass adjustment

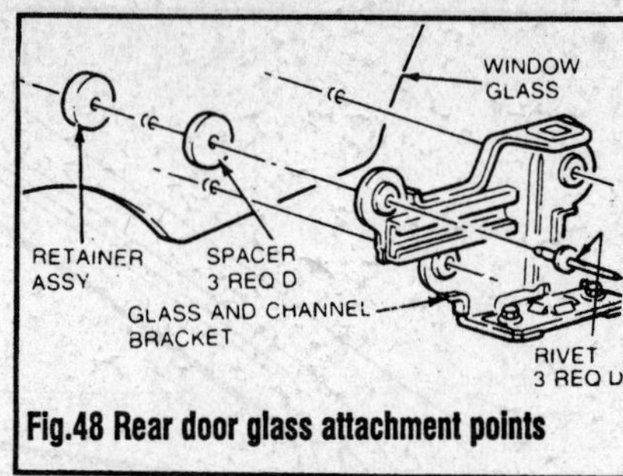

Fig.48 Rear door glass attachment points

stabilizer the glass during rivet pin removal. Use a 1/4 in. (6mm) diameter drill to drill out remainder of rivet, using care not to enlarge sheet metal holes and damage the plastic retainer and spacer.

4. Remove the glass stabilizer bracket retaining screw and the washer and bracket.
5. Lift the glass up between the door belt molding opening and remove it from the door.

To install:

6. Install the plastic spacer and retainers into the main glass. Install the main glass into the door.
7. Secure the glass-to-glass bracket using Heavy Duty Riveter D80L–23200–A or equivalent to install two rivets.

➡ Two 1/4–20 x 1 in. bolts and two 1/4–20 nut and washer assemblies may be used as alternates for glass retention. However, the torque must not exceed 36–61 inch lbs.

8. Install the inner door belt weatherstrip, using hand pressure to push the weatherstrip onto door flange.
9. Install the glass stabilizer bracket and the retaining screw and washer. Tighten to 36–61 inch lbs.
10. Cycle the glass to insure smooth operation.
11. Install the watershield and the door trim panel.

ADJUSTMENT

➧ SEE FIG. 48–49

The rear door glass has in-and-out and fore-and-aft adjustments. The in-and-out adjustment may be accomplished by loosening the two screws in the lower glass bracket assembly and moving the glass in or out as required. The fore-and-aft adjustment is accomplished by loosening the tube run upper screw and washer assembly, and the lower nut and washer assembly attaching the rear door run and bracket assembly to the inner door panel, and adjusting the glass fore or aft as required.

When setting the glass to the window opening, lower the glass approximately 50mm from the full-up position with the four retention points loosely installed. Set the glass forward into the B-pillar and tighten lower run nut and washer number one, then numbers two, three and four.

Inside Rear View Mirror

REMOVAL & INSTALLATION

Except Electric Mirror

➧ SEE FIG. 53

1. Loosen the mirror assembly-to-mounting bracket setscrew.
2. Remove the mirror assembly by sliding it upward and away from the mounting bracket.
3. If the bracket vinyl pad remains on windshield, apply low heat from an electric heat gun until the vinyl softens. Peel the vinyl off the windshield and discard.

To install:

4. Make the sure glass, bracket, and adhesive kit, (Rear view Mirror Repair Kit D9AZ–19554–B or equivalent) are at least at room temperature of 65–75°F (18–24°C).
5. Locate and mark the mirror mounting bracket location on the outside surface of the windshield with a wax pencil.
6. Thoroughly clean the bonding surfaces of the glass and the bracket to remove the old adhesive. Use a mild abrasive cleaner on the glass and fine sandpaper on the bracket to lightly roughen the surface. Wipe it clean with the alcohol-moistened cloth.
7. Crush the accelerator vial (part of Rear view Mirror Repair Kit D9AZ–19554–B or equivalent), and apply the accelerator to the bonding surface of the bracket and windshield. Let it dry for three minutes.
8. Apply two drops of adhesive (Rear view Mirror Repair Kit D9AZ–19554–B or equivalent) to the mounting surface of the bracket. Using a clean toothpick or wooden match, quickly spread the adhesive evenly over the mounting surface of the bracket.
9. Quickly position the mounting bracket on the windshield. The 3/8 in. (10mm) circular depression in the bracket must be toward the inside of the passenger compartment. Press the bracket firmly against the windshield for one minute.

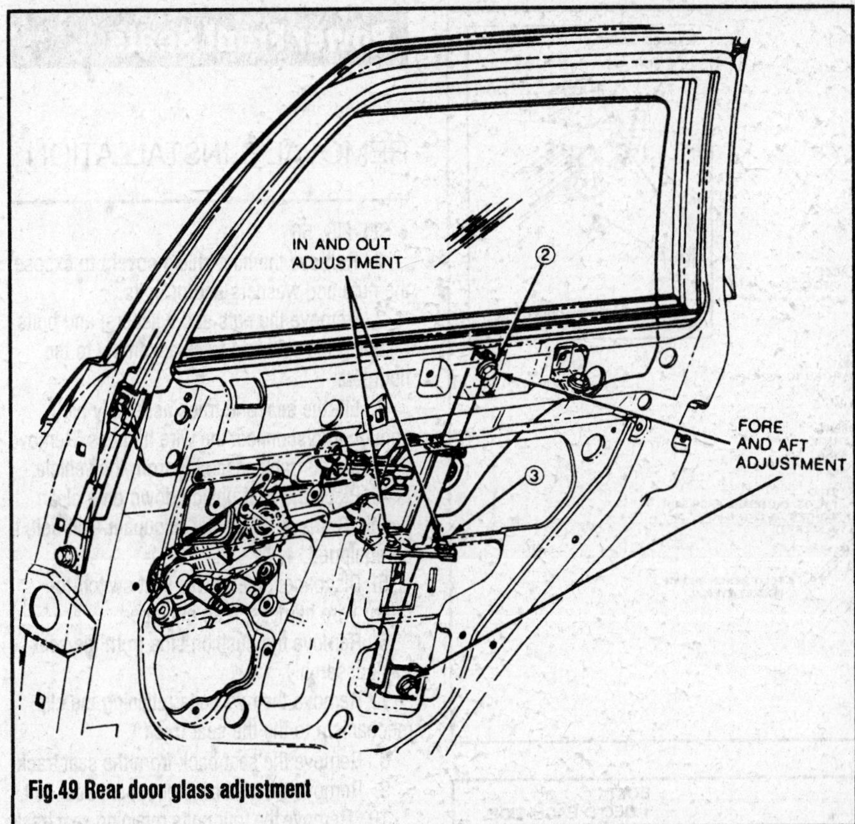

Fig.49 Rear door glass adjustment

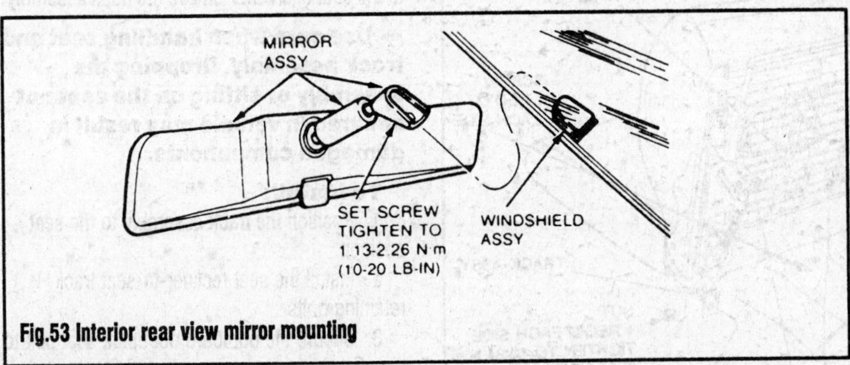

Fig.53 Interior rear view mirror mounting

10. Allow the bond to set for five minutes. Remove any excess bonding material from the windshield with an alcohol dampened cloth.

11. Attach the mirror to the mounting bracket and tighten the setscrew to 10–20 inch lbs.

Electric Mirror

1. Remove the grommet from the garnish molding above the mirror assembly.

2. Pull the wire assembly away from the garnish molding opening until the connector is exposed and disconnect the wire.

3. Loosen the mirror assembly-to-mounting bracket setscrew and remove the mirror by sliding upward away from the bracket.

To install:

1. If the mounting bracket on the windshield has to be serviced, refer to the following procedures.

2. If the bracket vinyl pad remains on windshield, apply low heat from an electric heat gun until the vinyl softens. Peel the vinyl off the windshield and discard.

3. Make the sure glass, bracket, and adhesive kit, (Rear view Mirror Repair Kit D9AZ–19554–B or equivalent) are at least at room temperature of 65–75°F (18–24°C).

4. Locate and mark the mirror mounting bracket location on the outside surface of the windshield with a wax pencil.

5. Thoroughly clean the bonding surfaces of the glass and the bracket to remove the old adhesive. Use a mild abrasive cleaner on the glass and fine sandpaper on the bracket to lightly roughen the surface. Wipe it clean with the alcohol-moistened cloth.

6. Crush the accelerator vial (part of Rear view Mirror Repair Kit D9AZ–19554–B or equivalent), and apply the accelerator to the bonding surface of the bracket and windshield. Let it dry for three minutes.

7. Apply two drops of adhesive (Rear view Mirror Repair Kit D9AZ–19554–B or equivalent) to the mounting surface of the bracket. Using a clean toothpick or wooden match, quickly spread the adhesive evenly over the mounting surface of the bracket.

8. Quickly position the mounting bracket on the windshield. The 3/8 in. (10mm) circular depression in the bracket must be toward the inside of the passenger compartment. Press the bracket firmly against the windshield for one minute.

9. Allow the bond to set for five minutes. Remove any excess bonding material from the windshield with an alcohol dampened cloth.

10. Position the mirror assembly over the mounting bracket after it has dried.

11. Tighten the mounting bracket setscrew to 10–20 inch lbs.

12. Connect the wire connector and push the wire back into the garnish molding. Install the grommet to the garnish molding.

Manual Front Seats

REMOVAL & INSTALLATION

➧ SEE FIG. 54-55

1. Remove the plastic shield retaining screws and remove the shield.

2. Remove the bolts and nut and washer assemblies retaining the seat tracks to the floor.

3. Remove the seat and track assembly from the vehicle and place on a clean working area.

➡ **Use care when handling seat and track assembly. Dropping the assembly or sitting on the seat not secured in the vehicle may result in damaged components.**

4. Remove the seat track-to-seat cushion attaching screws. Remove the seat cushion and assist spring from the tracks.

5. If the seat tracks are being replaced, transfer the assist springs and spacers, if so equipped, to the new track assembly.

To install:

1. Mount the seat tracks to the seat cushion.

2. Install the seat track-to-seat cushion retaining screws.

3. Place the seat assembly into vehicle and ensure proper alignment.

4. Install the screws, studs, plastic shields, and nut and washer assemblies.

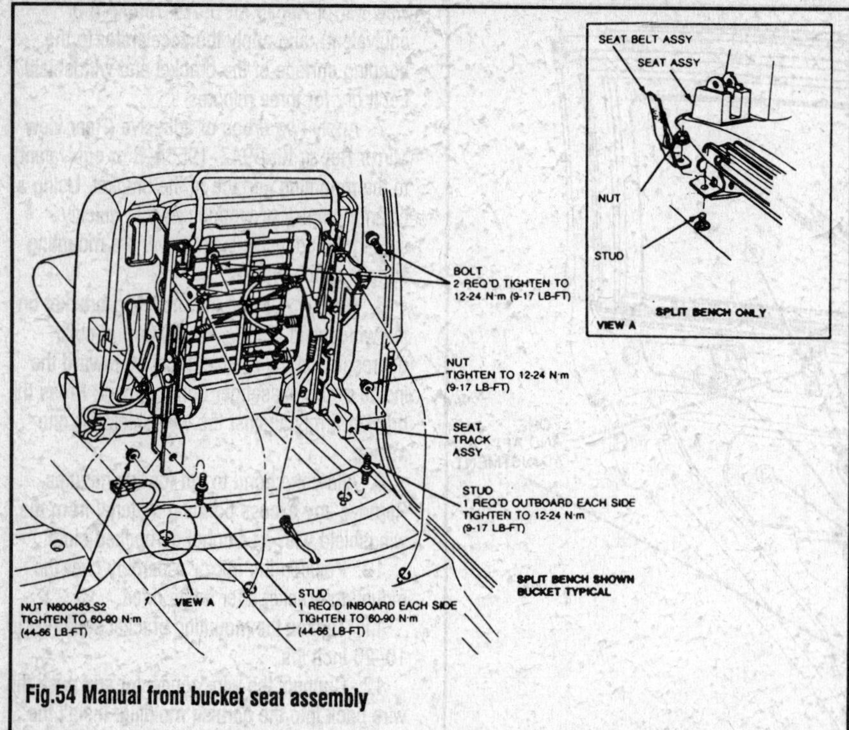

Fig.54 Manual front bucket seat assembly

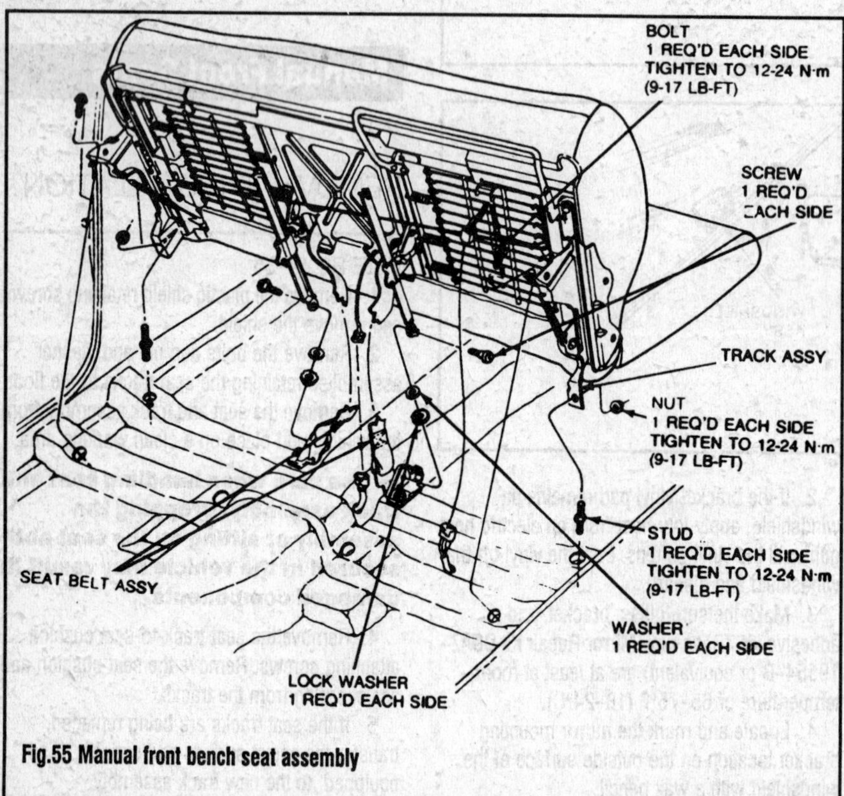

Fig.55 Manual front bench seat assembly

Power Front Seats

REMOVAL & INSTALLATION

➧ SEE FIG. 56

1. Remove the heat shield covers to expose the nuts and washers and/or bolts.
2. Remove the nuts and washers, and bolts retaining the seat and track assembly to the floorpan.
3. Lift the seat and track assembly high enough to disconnect the wire harness. Remove the seat and track assembly from the vehicle.
4. Place the seat upside down on a clean bench. Remove the center occupant seat belt, if so equipped.
5. Disconnect the power seat switch-to-motor wire harness, if so equipped.
6. Remove the cushion side from the seat track assembly.
7. Remove the two bolts retaining the clip mechanism to the the seat track.
8. Remove the seat back from the seat track.
9. Remove the outboard occupant seat belt.
10. Remove the four bolts retaining seat track to the seat cushion. Remove the track assembly.

➡ Use care when handling seat and track assembly. Dropping the assembly or sitting on the seat not secured in vehicle may result in damaged components.

To install:

1. Position the track assembly to the seat cushion.
2. Install the seat recliner-to-seat track retaining bolts.
3. Secure the outboard occupant seat belt to the seat track.
4. Secure the seat track assembly to the seat cushion using the four previously removed attaching bolts. Tighten the bolts.
5. Install the cushion side cover to the seat track assembly.
6. Connect the power seat switch to motor wire harness, if so equipped.
7. Install the center occupant seat belt to seat track.
8. Position the seat and track assembly in vehicle.
9. Lift the seat and track assembly high enough to permit the connection of the wire harness, then, connect wires.
10. Install the seat track-to-floorpan attaching nuts and washer and/or bolts. Tighten the bolts.
11. Install the heat shield covers.

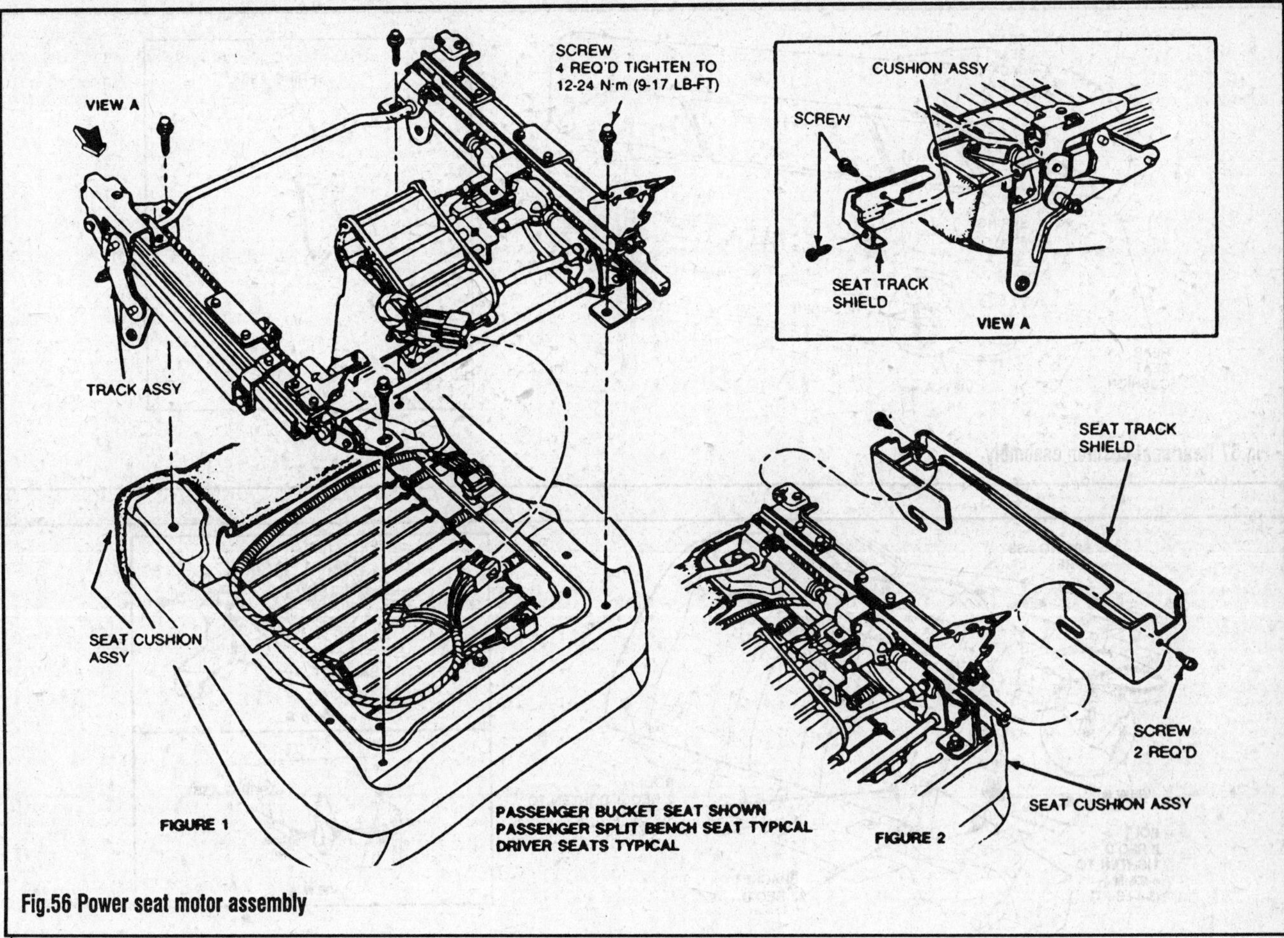

Fig.56 Power seat motor assembly

12. Install the seat belt-to-floorpan attaching bolts.

13. Check the seat tracks for proper operation.

Rear Seats

REMOVAL & INSTALLATION

Seat Cushion

➧ SEE FIG. 57

1. Apply knee pressure to the lower portion of the rear seat cushion. Push rearward to disengage the seat cushion from the retainer brackets.

➡ The armrest is an integral part of the quarter trim panel. Its removal is not required to remove rear seat cushion or back.

To install:

2. Position the seat cushion assembly into the vehicle.

3. Place the seat belts on top of the cushion.

4. Apply knee pressure to the lower portion of the seat cushion assembly. Push rearward and down to lock the seat cushion into position.

5. Pull the rear seat cushion forward to be certain it is secured into its floor retainer.

Seat Back Rest

➧ SEE FIG. 58

1. Remove the rear seat cushion.

2. Remove the seat back bracket attaching bolts.

➡ The seat belt bolts do not secure seat back to the vehicle.

3. Grasp the seat back assembly at the bottom and lift it up to disengage the hanger wire from the retainer brackets.

To install:

4. Position the seat back in the vehicle so that the hanger wires are engaged with the retaining brackets.

5. Install the seat back bolts and tighten to 5–7 ft. lbs.

6. Install the rear seat cushion.

Split Folding Rear Seat Back

➧ SEE FIG. 59

1. Remove the rear seat cushion.

2. Remove the seat back side pads by removing the attaching screws (one each) and sliding the pad upward.

3. Remove the four bolts (two each seat back) retaining the seat back assembly to the floorpan.

4. Remove the seat back from the inboard pivot pin by sliding the seat back toward the outboard side of the vehicle.

To install:

5. Position the seat back onto the inboard pivot pin in the full-up position.

6. Install the seat back-to-floorpan retaining bolts (two each side).

7. Check the seat back latch for proper operation.

➡ A nut and bolt have been provided on the left hand (40 percent) seat back latch only, to align the right hand seat back to the fixed position (± 2° adjustment). To align the right hand seat back, loosen the nut and bolt and reposition the bolt in its slot. Tighten the bolt and nut to 30–40 ft. lbs. Check the seat backs for proper operation after alignment.

8. Install the seat back side pads and the attaching screws.

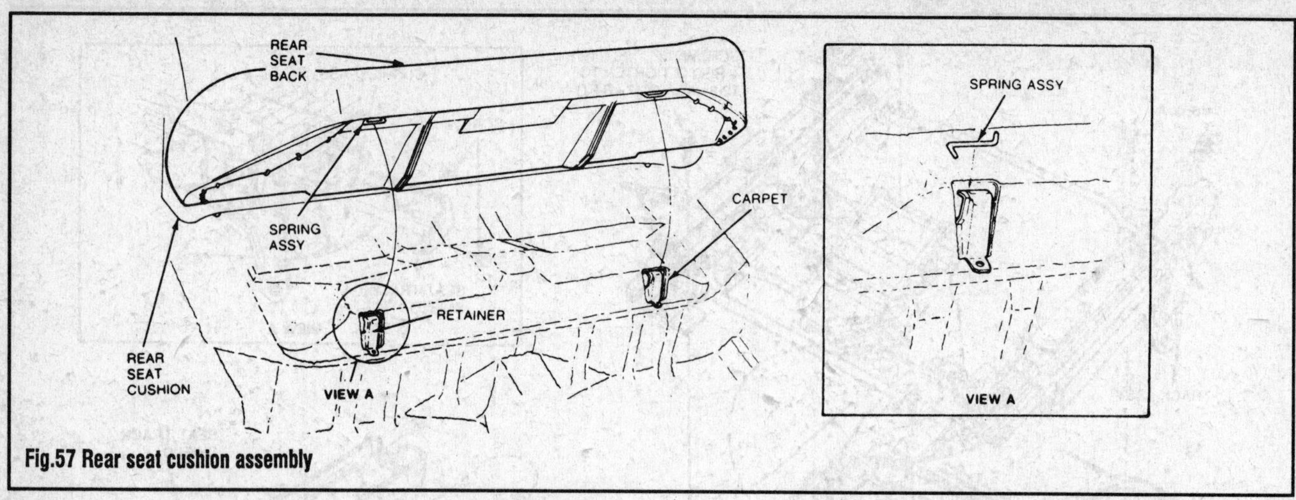

Fig.57 Rear seat cushion assembly

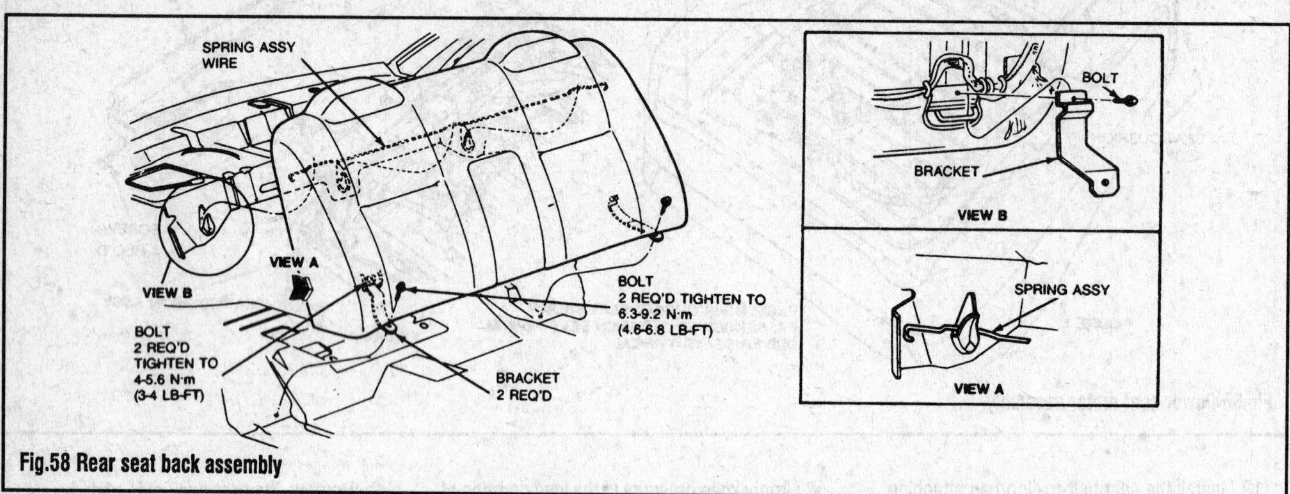

Fig.58 Rear seat back assembly

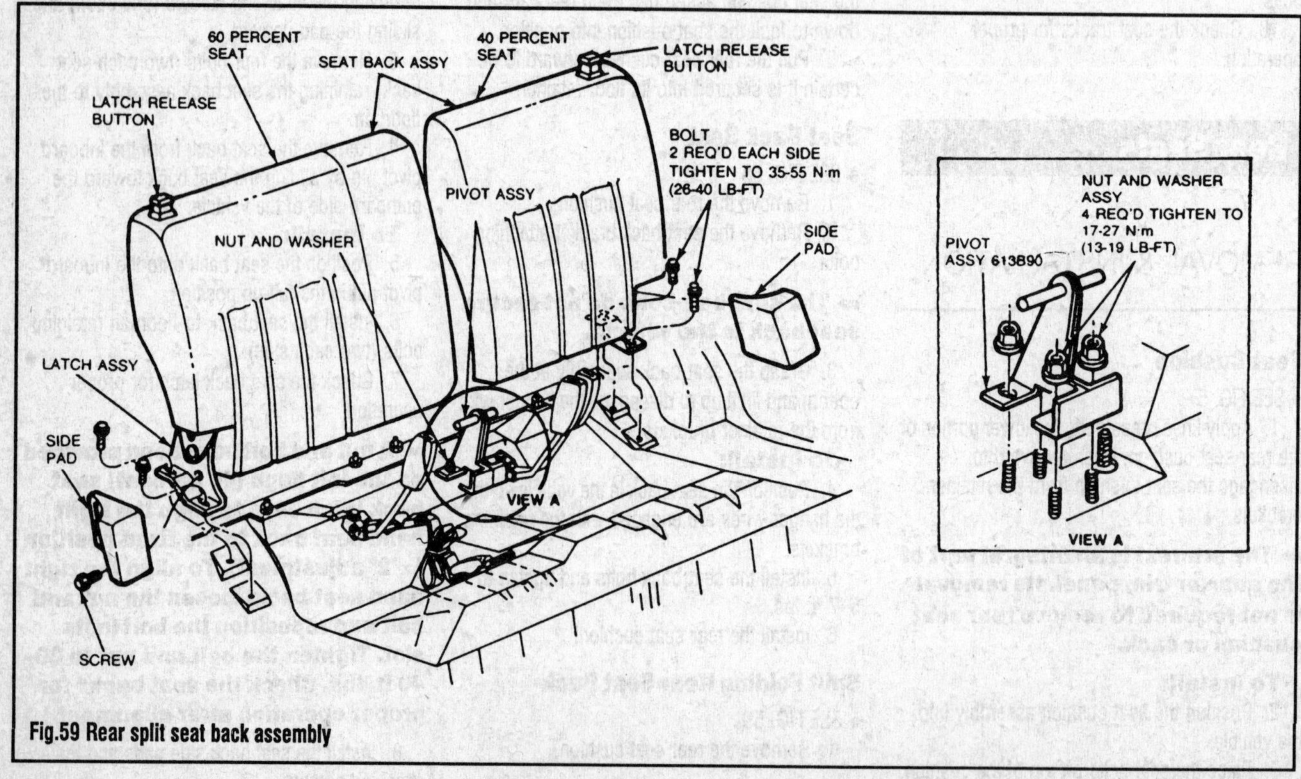

Fig.59 Rear split seat back assembly

Power Seat Motor

REMOVAL & INSTALLATION

1. Remove the seat and track assembly from the vehicle.
2. Remove the seat recliner mechanism and seat back from seat track.
3. Remove the seat belt.
4. Remove the seat track from the seat cushion.
5. Identify the cables and their respective locations.
6. Remove the motor bracket screw.
7. Lift the motor and deflect three left cables toward the left track assembly. Then, remove the three left hand cable assemblies from the motor.
8. Remove the two locknuts retaining the motor to the mounting brackets.

To install:

1. Secure the motor to the mounting bracket using the two previously removed locknuts. Tighten nuts to 8–10 inch lbs.
2. Lower the motor in place.
3. Position the three left hand drive cables to the motor, being sure to fully engage the square ends of cables into the motor armature.
4. Align the right hand drive cable ends with the motor armatures.
5. With the three left hand cables engaged in the motor, lift the motor. Insert the right hand cable into the motor being sure to fully engage the square end of cable into the motor armature. Lower the motor into place.
6. Install the screw used to retain the motor bracket to the seat track. Tighten the screw to 54–70 inch lbs.
7. Install the seat track assembly to the seat cushion.
8. Install the seat recliner and the seat back to the seat track.
9. Install the seat belts.
10. Install the seat and track assembly in the vehicle.

Seat Belt Systems

REMOVAL & INSTALLATION

Front

➧ SEE FIG. 60

1. Remove the D-ring cover. Using the bit, tool T77L–2100–A or equivalent, remove the belt bolt. Remove the B–pillar upper trim panel.
2. Remove the scuff plate retaining screws and panel. Remove the belt through the slot in the upper center trim panel.
3. Remove the belt anchor to sill bolt and rubber washer. Remove the belt retractor bolt. Remove the webb guide retaining screw and slide the guide rearward to remove it from the B-pillar.
4. Remove the outboard safety belt assembly from the vehicle. Remove the nut from the inboard buckle assembly. On the left side disconnect the buzzer wire and pry off the locator.
5. Pull the buckle upward and remove it from the seat.
6. Installation is the reverse of the removal procedure.

Rear

➧ SEE FIG. 61–62

1. Remove the rear seat back and cushion.
2. Remove the angel wing trim and package tray trim.
3. Remove the buckle end anchor nuts. Remove the buckle end belts.
4. Remove the retaining bolt to both rear seat retractors. Remove the retractors.

➡ **When only the outboard or center safety belt assembly is being replaced the brass ring holding the one anchor to the center of the safety belt assembly and the buckle end anchor of the outboard safety belt must be pried open and discarded in order to slide the belt anchor out of the assembly.**

5. Installation is the reverse of the removal procedure.

Safety Belts, Outboard

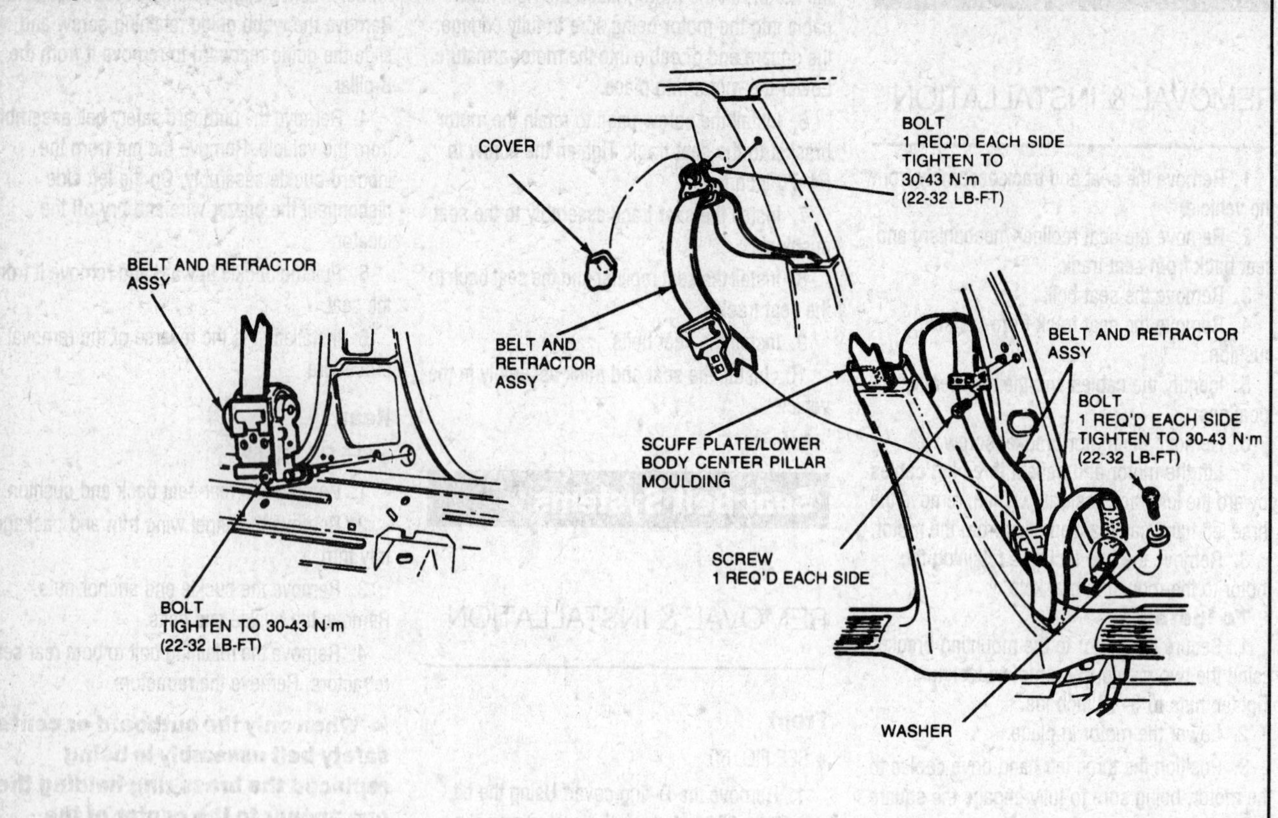

COVER
BOLT
1 REQ'D EACH SIDE
TIGHTEN TO
30-43 N·m
(22-32 LB-FT)
BELT AND RETRACTOR
ASSY
BELT AND
RETRACTOR
ASSY
BELT AND RETRACTOR
ASSY
BOLT
1 REQ'D EACH SIDE
TIGHTEN TO 30-43 N·m
(22-32 LB-FT)
SCUFF PLATE/LOWER
BODY CENTER PILLAR
MOULDING
SCREW
1 REQ'D EACH SIDE
BOLT
TIGHTEN TO 30-43 N·m
(22-32 LB-FT)
WASHER

Safety Belts, Inboard

Split Bench—Power Seat

NUT N800937-S190
TIGHTEN TO
30-43 N·m
(22-32 LB-FT)
CABLE AND
BUCKLE ASSY
VIEW A
VIEW A
CABLE AND
BUCKLE ASSY
CABLE AND BUCKLE
ASSY
CENTER SAFETY
BELT ASSY
CABLE AND
BUCKLE ASSY
VIEW B
NUT
TIGHTEN TO 60-90 N·m
(45-66 LB-FT)
POWER SPLIT BENCH
SHOWN, MANUAL SPLIT
BENCH SIMILAR
NUT
TIGHTEN TO 60-90 N·m
(45-66 LB-FT)
CENTER BELT
ASSY
VIEW B

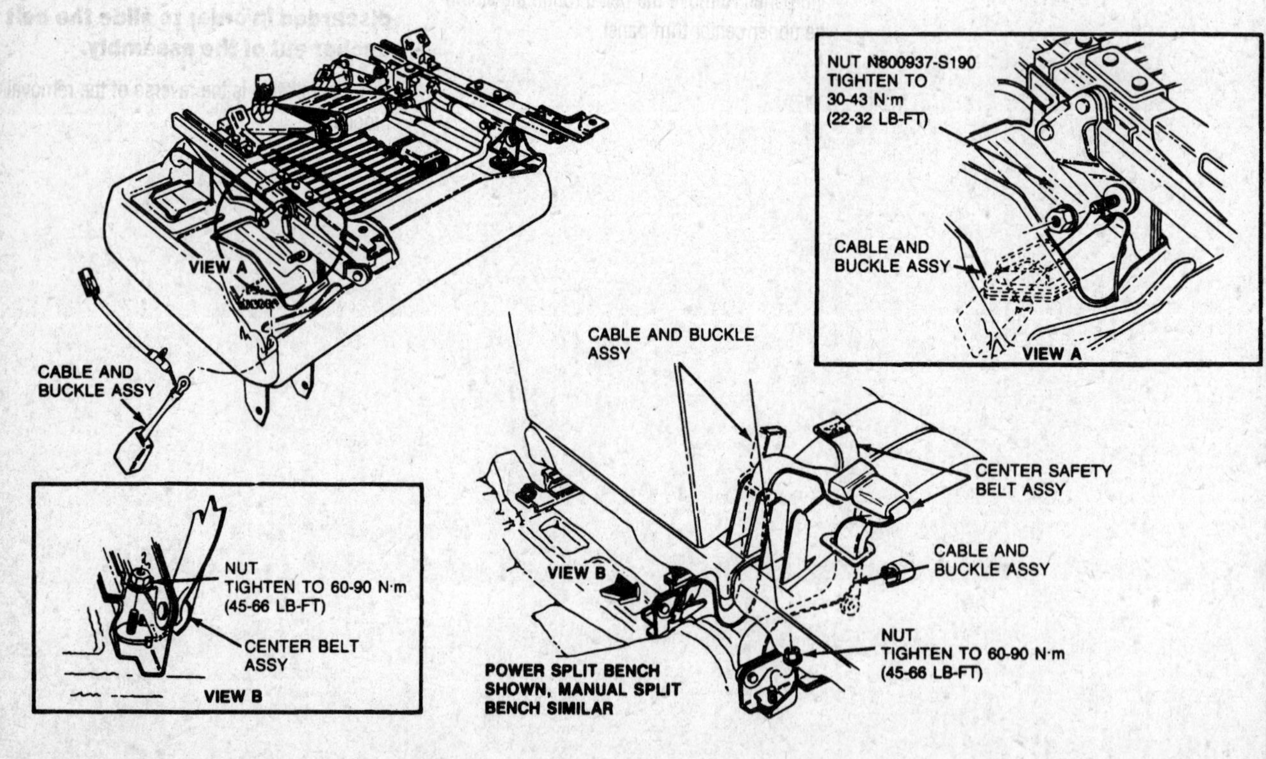

Fig.60 Front safety belt system and related components

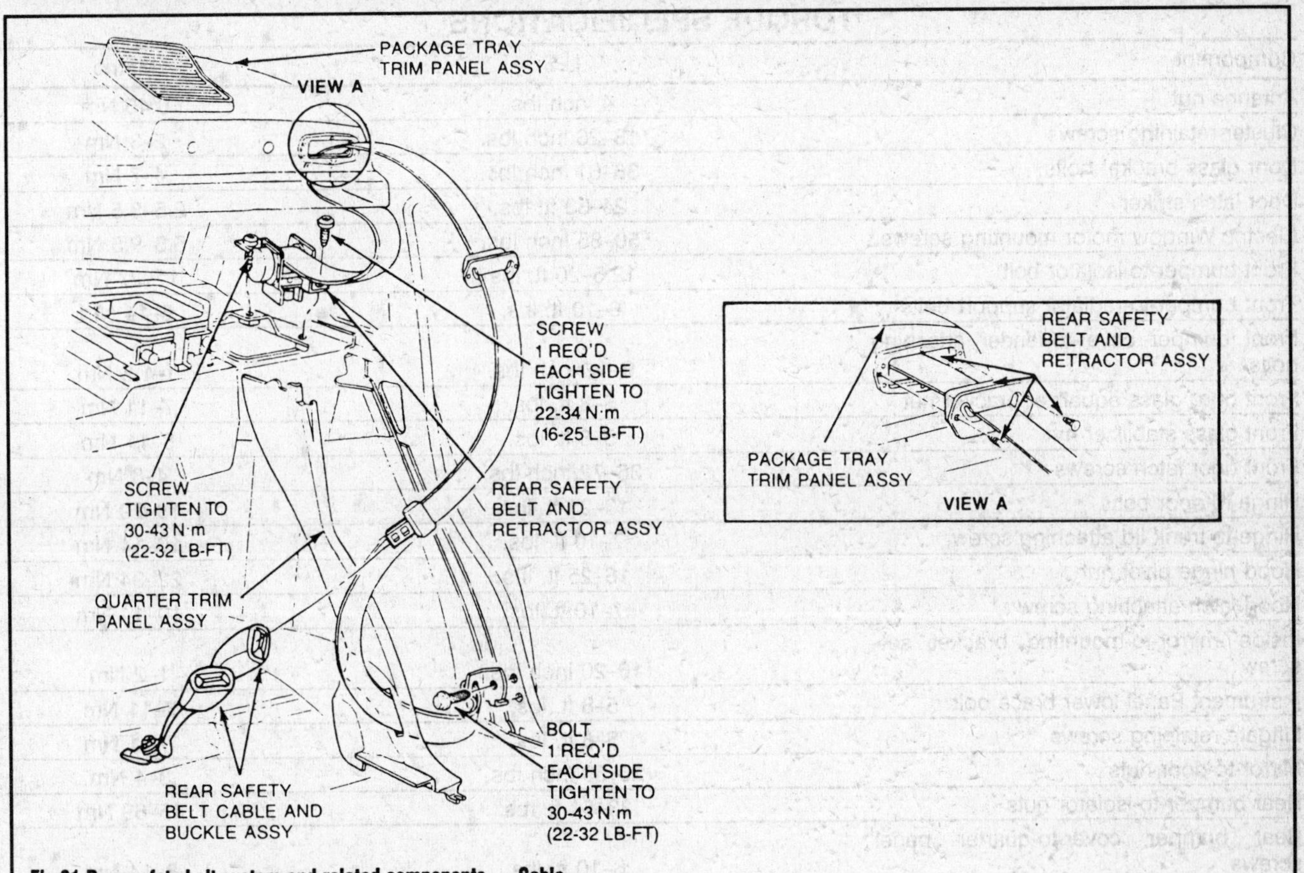

PACKAGE TRAY TRIM PANEL ASSY

VIEW A

SCREW 1 REQ'D EACH SIDE TIGHTEN TO 22-34 N·m (16-25 LB-FT)

REAR SAFETY BELT AND RETRACTOR ASSY

PACKAGE TRAY TRIM PANEL ASSY

VIEW A

SCREW TIGHTEN TO 30-43 N·m (22-32 LB-FT)

REAR SAFETY BELT AND RETRACTOR ASSY

QUARTER TRIM PANEL ASSY

BOLT 1 REQ'D EACH SIDE TIGHTEN TO 30-43 N·m (22-32 LB-FT)

REAR SAFETY BELT CABLE AND BUCKLE ASSY

Fig.61 Rear safety belt system and related components — Sable

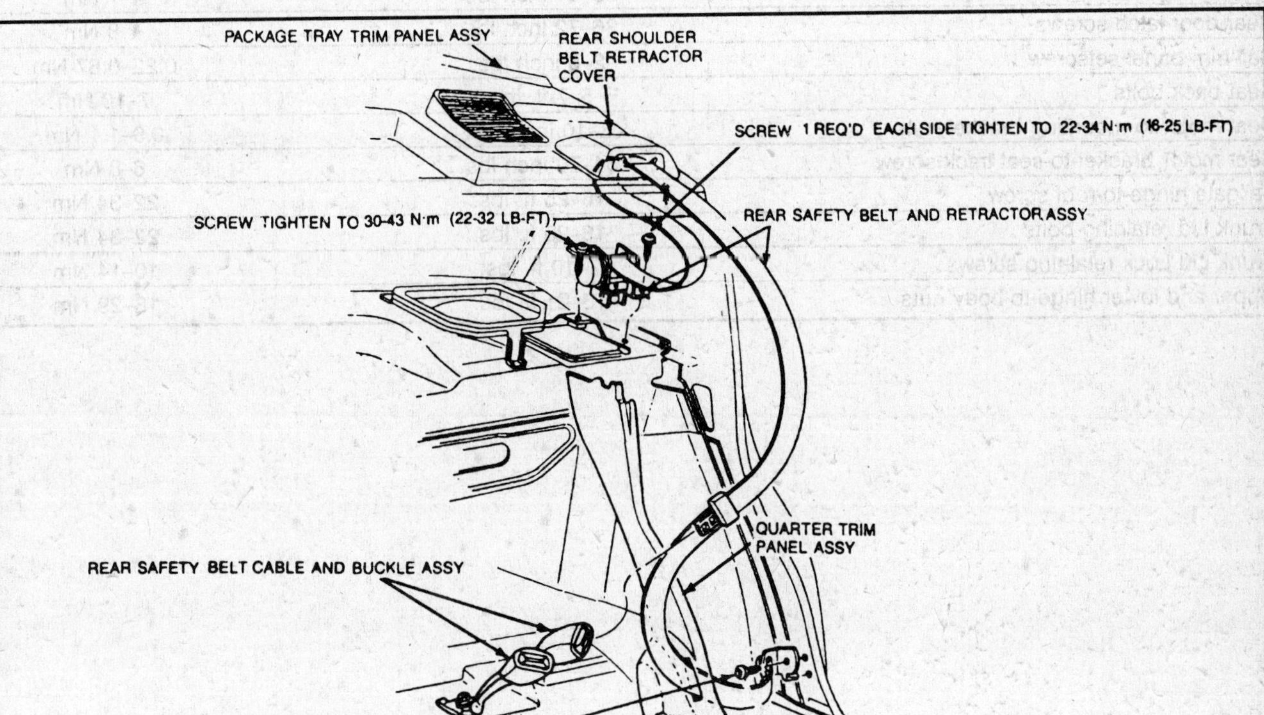

PACKAGE TRAY TRIM PANEL ASSY

REAR SHOULDER BELT RETRACTOR COVER

SCREW 1 REQ'D EACH SIDE TIGHTEN TO 22-34 N·m (16-25 LB-FT)

SCREW TIGHTEN TO 30-43 N·m (22-32 LB-FT)

REAR SAFETY BELT AND RETRACTOR ASSY

QUARTER TRIM PANEL ASSY

REAR SAFETY BELT CABLE AND BUCKLE ASSY

BOLT 1 REQ'D EACH SIDE TIGHTEN TO 30-43 N·m (22-32 LB-FT)

Fig.62 Rear safety belt system and related components — Taurus

TORQUE SPECIFICATIONS

Component	U.S.	Metric
Antenna nut	4 inch lbs.	0.45 Nm
Cluster retaining screws	18–26 inch lbs.	2–3 Nm
Door glass bracket bolts	36–61 inch lbs.	4–7 Nm
Door latch striker	24–33 ft. lbs.	2.5–3.5 Nm
Electric Window motor mounting screws	50–85 inch lbs.	5.5–9.5 Nm
Front bumper-to-isolator bolt	12.5–20 ft. lbs.	17–27 Nm
Front bumper-to-radiator support bolts	6–10 ft. lbs.	8–14 Nm
Front bumper cover-to-fender attaching bolts	9–12 inch lbs.	1–1.5 Nm
Front door glass equalizer bracket nut	5–8 ft. lbs.	7–11 Nm
Front glass stabilizer nut	5–8 ft. lbs.	8–11 Nm
Front door latch screws	36–72 inch lbs.	4–8 Nm
Hinge-to-door bolts	13–21 ft. lbs.	18–29 Nm
Hinge-to-trunk lid attaching screw	7–10 ft. lbs.	10–14 Nm
Hood hinge pivot nut	16–25 ft. lbs.	22–34 Nm
Hood latch attaching screw	7–10 ft. lbs.	10–14 Nm
Inside mirror-to-mounting bracket set-screw	10–20 inch lbs.	1–2 Nm
Instrument Panel lower brace bolt	5–8 ft. lbs.	7–11 Nm
Liftgate retaining screws	5–8 ft. lbs.	7–11 Nm
Mirror-to-door nuts	25–39 inch lbs.	3–4 Nm
Rear bumper-to-isolator nuts	33–51 ft. lbs.	45–69 Nm
Rear bumper cover-to-quarter panel screws	6–10 ft. lbs.	8–14 Nm
Rear glass stabilizer bracket retaining screw	36–61 inch lbs.	4–7 Nm
Rear door latch screws	36–72 inch lbs.	4–8 Nm
Sail trim panel setscrew	2–6 inch lbs.	0.22–0.67 Nm
Seat back bolts	5–7 ft. lbs.	7–10 Nm
Seat motor-to-mounting bracket nuts	8–10 inch lbs.	0.9–1.1 Nm
Seat motor bracket-to-seat track screw	54–70 inch lbs.	6–8 Nm
Tailgate hinge-to-roof screw	16–25 ft. lbs.	22–34 Nm
Trunk Lid retaining bolts	16–25 ft. lbs.	22–34 Nm
Trunk Lid Lock retaining screws	7–10 ft. lbs.	10–14 Nm
Upper and lower hinge-to-body nuts	13–21 ft. lbs.	18–29 Nm

Hood, Trunk Lid, Hatch Lid, Glass and Doors

Problem	Possible Cause	Correction
HOOD/TRUNK/HATCH LID		
Improper closure.	• Striker and latch not properly aligned.	• Adjust the alignment.
Difficulty locking and unlocking.	• Striker and latch not properly aligned.	• Adjust the alignment.
Uneven clearance with body panels.	• Incorrectly installed hood or trunk lid.	• Adjust the alignment.
WINDOW/WINDSHIELD GLASS		
Water leak through windshield	• Defective seal.	• Fill sealant
	• Defective body flange.	• Correct.
Water leak through door window glass.	• Incorrect window glass installation.	• Adjust position.
	• Gap at upper window frame.	• Adjust position.
Water leak through quarter window.	• Defective seal.	• Replace seal.
	• Defective body flange.	• Correct.
Water leak through rear window.	• Defective seal.	• Replace seal.
	• Defective body flange.	• Correct.
FRONT/REAR DOORS		
Door window malfunction.	• Incorrect window glass installation.	• Adjust position.
	• Damaged or faulty regulator.	• Correct or replace.
Water leak through door edge.	• Cracked or faulty weatherstrip.	• Replace.
Water leak from door center.	• Drain hole clogged.	• Remove foreign objects.
	• Inadequate waterproof skeet contact or damage.	• Correct or replace.
Door hard to open.	• Incorrect latch or striker adjustment.	• Adjust.
Door does not open or close completely.	• Incorrect door installation.	• Adjust position.
	• Defective door check strap.	• Correct or replace.
	• Door check strap and hinge require grease.	• Apply grease.
Uneven gap between door and body.	• Incorrect door installation.	• Adjust position.
Wind noise around door.	• Improperly installed weatherstrip.	• Repair or replace.
	• Improper clearance between door glass and door weatherstrip.	• Adjust.
	• Deformed door.	• Repair or replace.

How to Remove Stains from Fabric Interior

For best results, spots and stains should be removed as soon as possible. Never use gasoline, lacquer thinner, acetone, nail polish remover or bleach. Use a 3′ x 3″ piece of cheesecloth. Squeeze most of the liquid from the fabric and wipe the stained fabric from the outside of the stain toward the center with a lifting motion. Turn the cheesecloth as soon as one side becomes soiled. When using water to remove a stain, be sure to wash the entire section after the spot has been removed to avoid water stains. Encrusted spots can be broken up with a dull knife and vacuumed before removing the stain.

Type of Stain	How to Remove It
Surface spots	Brush the spots out with a small hand brush or use a commercial preparation such as K2R to lift the stain.
Mildew	Clean around the mildew with warm suds. Rinse in cold water and soak the mildew area in a solution of 1 part table salt and 2 parts water. Wash with upholstery cleaner.
Water stains	Water stains in fabric materials can be removed with a solution made from 1 cup of table salt dissolved in 1 quart of water. Vigorously scrub the solution into the stain and rinse with clear water. Water stains in nylon or other synthetic fabrics should be removed with a commercial type spot remover.
Chewing gum, tar, crayons, shoe polish (greasy stains)	Do not use a cleaner that will soften gum or tar. Harden the deposit with an ice cube and scrape away as much as possible with a dull knife. Moisten the remainder with cleaning fluid and scrub clean.
Ice cream, candy	Most candy has a sugar base and can be removed with a cloth wrung out in warm water. Oily candy, after cleaning with warm water, should be cleaned with upholstery cleaner. Rinse with warm water and clean the remainder with cleaning fluid.
Wine, alcohol, egg, milk, soft drink (non-greasy stains)	Do not use soap. Scrub the stain with a cloth wrung out in warm water. Remove the remainder with cleaning fluid.
Grease, oil, lipstick, butter and related stains	Use a spot remover to avoid leaving a ring. Work from the outisde of the stain to the center and dry with a clean cloth when the spot is gone.
Headliners (cloth)	Mix a solution of warm water and foam upholstery cleaner to give thick suds. Use only foam—liquid may streak or spot. Clean the entire headliner in one operation using a circular motion with a natural sponge.
Headliner (vinyl)	Use a vinyl cleaner with a sponge and wipe clean with a dry cloth.
Seats and door panels	Mix 1 pint upholstery cleaner in 1 gallon of water. Do not soak the fabric around the buttons.
Leather or vinyl fabric	Use a multi-purpose cleaner full strength and a stiff brush. Let stand 2 minutes and scrub thoroughly. Wipe with a clean, soft rag.
Nylon or synthetic fabrics	For normal stains, use the same procedures you would for washing cloth upholstery. If the fabric is extremely dirty, use a multi-purpose cleaner full strength with a stiff scrub brush. Scrub thoroughly in all directions and wipe with a cotton towel or soft rag.

GLOSSARY

AIR/FUEL RATIO: The ratio of air to gasoline by weight in the fuel mixture drawn into the engine.

AIR INJECTION: One method of reducing harmful exhaust emissions by injecting air into each of the exhaust ports of an engine. The fresh air entering the hot exhaust manifold causes any remaining fuel to be burned before it can exit the tailpipe.

ALTERNATOR: A device used for converting mechanical energy into electrical energy.

AMMETER: An instrument, calibrated in amperes, used to measure the flow of an electrical current in a circuit. Ammeters are always connected in series with the circuit being tested.

AMPERE: The rate of flow of electrical current present when one volt of electrical pressure is applied against one ohm of electrical resistance.

ANALOG COMPUTER: Any microprocessor that uses similar (analogous) electrical signals to make its calculations.

ARMATURE: A laminated, soft iron core wrapped by a wire that converts electrical energy to mechanical energy as in a motor or relay. When rotated in a magnetic field, it changes mechanical energy into electrical energy as in a generator.

ATMOSPHERIC PRESSURE: The pressure on the Earth's surface caused by thc weight of the air in the atmosphere. At sea level, this pressure is 14.7 psi at 32°F (101 kPa at 0°C).

ATOMIZATION: The breaking down of a liquid into a fine mist that can be suspended in air.

AXIAL PLAY: Movement parallel to a shaft or bearing bore.

BACKFIRE: The sudden combustion of gases in the intake or exhaust system that results in a loud explosion.

BACKLASH: The clearance or play between two parts, such as meshed gears.

BACKPRESSURE: Restrictions in the exhaust system that slow the exit of exhaust gases from the combustion chamber.

BAKELITE: A heat resistant, plastic insulator material commonly used in printed circuit boards and transistorized components.

BALL BEARING: A bearing made up of hardened inner and outer races between which hardened steel balls roll.

BALLAST RESISTOR: A resistor in the primary ignition circuit that lowers voltage after the engine is started to reduce wear on ignition components.

BEARING: A friction reducing, supportive device usually located between a stationary part and a moving part.

BIMETAL TEMPERATURE SENSOR: Any sensor or switch made of two dissimilar types of metal that bend when heated or cooled due to the different expansion rates of the alloys. These types of sensors usually function as an on/off switch.

BLOWBY: Combustion gases, composed of water vapor and unburned fuel, that leak past the piston rings into the crankcase during normal engine operation. These gases are removed by the PCV system to prevent the buildup of harmful acids in the crankcase.

BRAKE PAD: A brake shoe and lining assembly used with disc brakes.

BRAKE SHOE: The backing for the brake lining. The term is, however, usually applied to the assembly of the brake backing and lining.

BUSHING: A liner, usually removable, for a bearing; an anti-friction liner used in place of a bearing.

BYPASS: System used to bypass ballast resistor during engine cranking to increase voltage supplied to the coil.

CALIPER: A hydraulically activated device in a disc brake system, which is mounted straddling the brake rotor (disc). The caliper contains at least one piston and two brake pads. Hydraulic pressure on the piston(s) forces the pads against the rotor.

CAMSHAFT: A shaft in the engine on which are the lobes (cams) which operate the valves. The camshaft is driven by the crankshaft, via a belt, chain or gears, at one half the crankshaft speed.

CAPACITOR: A device which stores an electrical charge.

CARBON MONOXIDE (CO): A colorless, odorless gas given off as a normal byproduct of combustion. It is poisonous and extremely dangerous in confined areas, building up slowly to toxic levels without warning if adequate ventilation is not available.

CARBURETOR: A device, usually mounted on the intake manifold of an engine, which mixes the air and fuel in the proper proportion to allow even combustion.

CATALYTIC CONVERTER: A device installed in the exhaust system, like a muffler, that converts harmful byproducts of combustion into carbon dioxide and water vapor by means of a heat-producing chemical reaction.

CENTRIFUGAL ADVANCE: A mechanical method of advancing the spark timing by using fly weights in the distributor that react to centrifugal force generated by the distributor shaft rotation.

CHECK VALVE: Any one-way valve installed to permit the flow of air, fuel or vacuum in one direction only.

CHOKE: A device, usually a movable valve, placed in the intake path of a carburetor to restrict the flow of air.

CIRCUIT: Any unbroken path through which an electrical current can flow. Also used to describe fuel flow in some instances.

CIRCUIT BREAKER: A switch which protects an electrical circuit from overload by opening the circuit when the current flow exceeds a predetermined level. Some circuit breakers must be reset manually, while most reset automatically

COIL (IGNITION): A transformer in the ignition circuit which steps up the voltage provided to the spark plugs.

COMBINATION MANIFOLD: An assembly which includes both the intake and exhaust manifolds in one casting.

COMBINATION VALVE: A device used in some fuel systems that routes fuel vapors to a charcoal storage canister instead of venting them into the atmosphere. The valve relieves fuel tank pressure and allows fresh air into the tank as the fuel level drops to prevent a vapor lock situation.

COMPRESSION RATIO: The comparison of the total volume of the cylinder and combustion chamber with the piston at BDC and the piston at TDC.

CONDENSER: 1. An electrical device which acts to store an electrical charge, preventing voltage surges.

2. A radiator-like device in the air conditioning system in which refrigerant gas condenses into a liquid, giving off heat.

CONDUCTOR: Any material through which an electrical current can be transmitted easily.

CONTINUITY: Continuous or complete circuit. Can be checked with an ohmmeter.

COUNTERSHAFT: An intermediate shaft which is rotated by a mainshaft and transmits, in turn, that rotation to a working part.

CRANKCASE: The lower part of an engine in which the crankshaft and related parts operate.

CRANKSHAFT: The main driving shaft of an engine which receives reciprocating motion from the pistons and converts it to rotary motion.

CYLINDER: In an engine, the round hole in the engine block in which the piston(s) ride.

CYLINDER BLOCK: The main structural member of an engine in which is found the cylinders, crankshaft and other principal parts.

CYLINDER HEAD: The detachable portion of the engine, fastened, usually, to the top of the cylinder block, containing all or most of the combustion chambers. On overhead valve engines, it contains the valves and their operating parts. On overhead cam engines, it contains the camshaft as well.

DEAD CENTER: The extreme top or bottom of the piston stroke.

DETONATION: An unwanted explosion of the air/fuel mixture in the combustion chamber caused by excess heat and compression, advanced timing, or an overly lean mixture. Also referred to as "ping".

DIAPHRAGM: A thin, flexible wall separating two cavities, such as in a vacuum advance unit.

DIESELING: A condition in which hot spots in the combustion chamber cause the engine to run on after the key is turned off.

DIFFERENTIAL: A geared assembly which allows the transmission of motion between drive axles, giving one axle the ability to turn faster than the other.

DIODE: An electrical device that will allow current to flow in one direction only.

DISC BRAKE: A hydraulic braking assembly consisting of a brake disc, or rotor, mounted on an axle, and a caliper assembly containing, usually two brake pads which are activated by hydraulic pressure. The pads are forced against the sides of the disc, creating friction which slows the vehicle.

DISTRIBUTOR: A mechanically driven device on an engine which is responsible for electrically firing the spark plug at a predetermined point of the piston stroke.

DOWEL PIN: A pin, inserted in mating holes in two different parts allowing those parts to maintain a fixed relationship.

DRUM BRAKE: A braking system which consists of two brake shoes and one or two wheel cylinders, mounted on a fixed backing plate, and a brake drum, mounted on an axle, which revolves around the assembly. Hydraulic action applied to the wheel cylinders forces the shoes outward against the drum, creating friction, slowing the vehicle.

DWELL: The rate, measured in degrees of shaft rotation, at which an electrical circuit cycles on and off.

ELECTRONIC CONTROL UNIT (ECU): Ignition module, amplifier or igniter. See Module for definition.

ELECTRONIC IGNITION: A system in which the timing and firing of the spark plugs is controlled by an electronic control unit, usually called a module. These systems have no points or condenser.

ENDPLAY: The measured amount of axial movement in a shaft.

ENGINE: A device that converts heat into mechanical energy.

EXHAUST MANIFOLD: A set of cast passages or pipes which conduct exhaust gases from the engine.

FEELER GAUGE: A blade, usually metal, of precisely predetermined thickness, used to measure the clearance between two parts. These blades usually are available in sets of assorted thicknesses.

F-HEAD: An engine configuration in which the intake valves are in the cylinder head, while the camshaft and exhaust valves are located in the cylinder block. The camshaft operates the intake valves via lifters and pushrods, while it operates the exhaust valves directly.

FIRING ORDER: The order in which combustion occurs in the cylinders of an engine. Also the order in which spark is distributed to the plugs by the distributor.

FLATHEAD: An engine configuration in which the camshaft and all the valves are located in the cylinder block.

FLOODING: The presence of too much fuel in the intake manifold and combustion chamber which prevents the air/fuel mixture from firing, thereby causing a no-start situation.

FLYWHEEL: A disc shaped part bolted to the rear end of the crankshaft. Around the outer perimeter is affixed the ring gear. The starter drive engages the ring gear, turning the flywheel, which rotates the crankshaft, imparting the initial starting motion to the engine.

FOOT POUND (ft.lb. or sometimes, ft. lbs.): The amount of energy or work needed to raise an item weighing one pound, a distance of one foot.

FUSE: A protective device in a circuit which prevents circuit overload by breaking the circuit when a specific amperage is present. The device is constructed around a strip or wire of a lower amperage rating than the circuit it is designed to protect. When an amperage higher than that stamped on the fuse is present in the circuit, the strip or wire melts, opening the circuit.

GEAR RATIO: The ratio between the number of teeth on meshing gears.

GENERATOR: A device which converts mechanical energy into electrical energy.

HEAT RANGE: The measure of a spark plug's ability to dissipate heat from its firing end. The higher the heat range, the hotter the plug fires.
HUB: The center part of a wheel or gear.

HYDROCARBON (HC): Any chemical compound made up of hydrogen and carbon. A major pollutant formed by the engine as a byproduct of combustion.

HYDROMETER: An instrument used to measure the specific gravity of a solution.

INCH POUND (in.lb. or sometimes, in. lbs.): One twelfth of a foot pound.

INDUCTION: A means of transferring electrical energy in the form of a magnetic field. Principle used in the ignition coil to increase voltage.

INJECTION PUMP: A device, usually mechanically operated, which meters and delivers fuel under pressure to the fuel injector.

INJECTOR: A device which receives metered fuel under relatively low pressure and is activated to inject the fuel into the engine under relatively high pressure at a predetermined time.

INPUT SHAFT: The shaft to which torque is applied, usually carrying the driving gear or gears.

INTAKE MANIFOLD: A casting of passages or pipes used to conduct air or a fuel/air mixture to the cylinders.

JOURNAL: The bearing surface within which a shaft operates.

KEY: A small block usually fitted in a notch between a shaft and a hub to prevent slippage of the two parts.

MANIFOLD: A casting of passages or set of pipes which connect the cylinders to an inlet or outlet source.

MANIFOLD VACUUM: Low pressure in an engine intake manifold formed just below the throttle plates. Manifold vacuum is highest at idle and drops under acceleration.

MASTER CYLINDER: The primary fluid pressurizing device in a hydraulic system. In automotive use, it is found in brake and hydraulic clutch systems and is pedal activated, either directly or, in a power brake system, through the power booster.

MODULE: Electronic control unit, amplifier or igniter of solid state or integrated design which controls the current flow in the ignition primary circuit based on input from the pick- up coil. When the module opens the primary circuit, the high secondary voltage is induced in the coil.

NEEDLE BEARING: A bearing which consists of a number (usually a large number) of long, thin rollers.

OHM:(Ω) The unit used to measure the resistance of conductor to electrical flow. One ohm is the amount of resistance that limits current flow to one ampere in a circuit with one volt of pressure.

OHMMETER: An instrument used for measuring the resistance, in ohms, in an electrical circuit.

OUTPUT SHAFT: The shaft which transmits torque from a device, such as a transmission.

OVERDRIVE: A gear assembly which produces more shaft revolutions than that transmitted to it.

OVERHEAD CAMSHAFT (OHC): An engine configuration in which the camshaft is mounted on top of the cylinder head and operates the valves either directly or by means of rocker arms.

OVERHEAD VALVE (OHV): An engine configuration in which all of the valves are located in the cylinder head and the camshaft is located in the cylinder block. The camshaft operates the valves via lifters and pushrods.

OXIDES OF NITROGEN (NOx): Chemical compounds of nitrogen produced as a byproduct of combustion. They combine with hydrocarbons to produce smog.

OXYGEN SENSOR: Used with the feedback system to sense the presence of oxygen in the exhaust gas and signal the computer which can reference the voltage signal to an air/fuel ratio.

PINION: The smaller of two meshing gears.

PISTON RING: An open ended ring which fits into a groove on the outer diameter of the piston. Its chief function is to form a seal between the piston and cylinder wall. Most automotive pistons have three rings: two for compression sealing; one for oil sealing.

PRELOAD: A predetermined load placed on a bearing during assembly or by adjustment.

PRIMARY CIRCUIT: Is the low voltage side of the ignition system which consists of the ignition switch, ballast resistor or resistance wire, bypass, coil, electronic control unit and pick-up coil as well as the connecting wires and harnesses.

PRESS FIT: The mating of two parts under pressure, due to the inner diameter of one being smaller than the outer diameter of the other, or vice versa; an interference fit.

RACE: The surface on the inner or outer ring of a bearing on which the balls, needles or rollers move.

REGULATOR: A device which maintains the amperage and/or voltage levels of a circuit at predetermined values.

RELAY: A switch which automatically opens and/or closes a circuit.

RESISTANCE: The opposition to the flow of current through a circuit or electrical device, and is measured in ohms. Resistance is equal to the voltage divided by the amperage.

RESISTOR: A device, usually made of wire, which offers a preset amount of resistance in an electrical circuit.

RING GEAR: The name given to a ring-shaped gear attached to a differential case,or affixed to a flywheel or as part a planetary gear set.

ROLLER BEARING: A bearing made up of hardened inner and outer races between which hardened steel rollers move.

ROTOR: 1. The disc-shaped part of a disc brake assembly, upon which the brake pads bear; also called, brake disc.
2. The device mounted atop the distributor shaft, which passes current to the distributor cap tower contacts.

SECONDARY CIRCUIT: The high voltage side of the ignition system, usually above 20,000 volts. The secondary includes the ignition coil, coil wire, distributor cap and rotor, spark plug wires and spark plugs.

SENDING UNIT: A mechanical, electrical, hydraulic or electromagnetic device which transmits information to a gauge.

SENSOR: Any device designed to measure engine operating conditions or ambient pressures and temperatures. Usually electronic in nature and designed to send a voltage signal to an on-board computer, some sensors may operate as a simple on/off switch or they may provide a variable voltage signal (like a potentiometer) as conditions or measured parameters change.

SHIM: Spacers of precise, predetermined thickness used between parts to establish a proper working relationship.

SLAVE CYLINDER: In automotive use, a device in the hydraulic clutch system which is activated by hydraulic force, disengaging the clutch.

SOLENOID: A coil used to produce a magnetic field, the effect of which is to produce work.

SPARK PLUG: A device screwed into the combustion chamber of a spark ignition engine. The basic construction is a conductive core inside of a ceramic insulator, mounted in an outer conductive base. An electrical charge from the spark plug wire travels along the conductive core and jumps a preset air gap to a grounding point or points at the end of the conductive base. The resultant spark ignites the fuel/air mixture in the combustion chamber.

SPLINES: Ridges machined or cast onto the outer diameter of a shaft or inner diameter of a bore to enable parts to mate without rotation.

TACHOMETER: A device used to measure the rotary speed of an engine, shaft, gear, etc., usually in rotations per minute.

THERMOSTAT: A valve, located in the cooling system of an engine, which is closed when cold and opens gradually in response to engine heating, controlling the temperature of the coolant and rate of coolant flow.

TOP DEAD CENTER (TDC): The point at which the piston reaches the top of its travel on the compression stroke.

TORQUE: The twisting force applied to an object.

TORQUE CONVERTER: A turbine used to transmit power from a driving member to a driven member via hydraulic action, providing changes in drive ratio and torque. In automotive use, it links the driveplate at the rear of the engine to the automatic transmission.

TRANSDUCER: A device used to change a force into an electrical signal.

TRANSISTOR: A semi-conductor component which can be actuated by a small voltage to perform an electrical switching function.

TUNE-UP: A regular maintenance function, usually associated with the replacement and adjustment of parts and components in the electrical and fuel systems of a vehicle for the purpose of attaining optimum performance.

TURBOCHARGER: An exhaust driven pump which compresses intake air and forces it into the combustion chambers at higher than atmospheric pressures. The increased air pressure allows more fuel to be burned and results in increased horsepower being produced.

VACUUM ADVANCE: A device which advances the ignition timing in response to increased engine vacuum.

VACUUM GAUGE: An instrument used to measure the presence of vacuum in a chamber.

VALVE: A device which control the pressure, direction of flow or rate of flow of a liquid or gas.

VALVE CLEARANCE: The measured gap between the end of the valve stem and the rocker arm, cam lobe or follower that activates the valve.

VISCOSITY: The rating of a liquid's internal resistance to flow.

VOLTMETER: An instrument used for measuring electrical force in units called volts. Voltmeters are always connected parallel with the circuit being tested.

WHEEL CYLINDER: Found in the automotive drum brake assembly, it is a device, actuated by hydraulic pressure, which, through internal pistons, pushes the brake shoes outward against the drums.

MASTER INDEX